Records & Prices

4th Edition

Edited by
Peter Lindblad

Published by

700 East State Street • Iola, WI 54990-0001
715-445-2214 • 888-457-2873
www.krausebooks.com

Our toll-free number to place an order or obtain a free catalog is (800) 258-0929.

Library of Congress Control Number: 2007940511

ISBN-13: 978-0-89689-619-2
ISBN-10: 0-89689-619-6

Designed by Stacy Bloch
Edited by Dan Brownell

Printed in the United States of America

Contents

Note: This book is only a guide to average prices in the marketplace. Actual prices for sales or purchases can vary for many reasons, such as fluctuations in availability and regional demand. Therefore, the publisher and editor cannot be held responsible for any losses incurred from consulting this guide.

Acknowledgments

Many thanks to Wayne Johnson, John Tefteller, and Jim Cooper for their insight on current record collecting trends. Also, thanks to Ian Shirly for his article on the Sex Pistols, and to Tim Neely for his compilation of the database and his sections on Condition, Abbreviations, and How to Use This Book.

Introduction

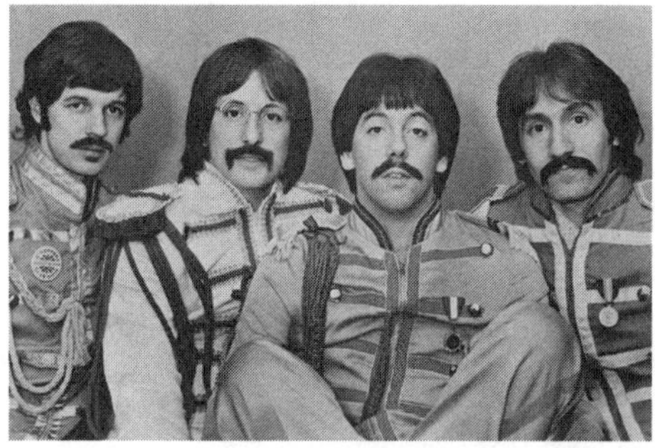
BeatleMagic

Welcome to the fourth edition of *Goldmine Records & Prices.* Besides providing up-to-date prices for all your favorite records, we're including an updated market report, feature articles on Northern Soul, The Sex Pistols, and Beatles butcher covers, advice on buying and selling records, and an overview of record genres in the color section.

While you'll find tens of thousands of listings in *Goldmine Records & Prices,* it is not designed to be exhaustive; the format and size work against that, especially with the literally millions of records that exist. Rather, we cover some of the most popular rock and pop performers of the past 50 years or so, with a focus on artists from the late 1950s to the early 1980s. Some of the artists listed here are among the most collectible in the entire hobby. Some of them are not. Many collectible artists are not included here; many artists with minimal interest also are not included. Even among those artists we chose to include, we've focused our attention on only certain types of records, in order to present a decent cross-section of performers. In general, here's what you will find in *Goldmine Records & Prices*:

- Regularly released singles, in the form of 45 rpm records, and regularly released albums, in the form of LPs.
- In general, we've listed only one label variation for most singles and for albums after 1968. For albums 1968 and earlier, we list two variations—a mono version and a stereo version, if both exist.
- Unless otherwise noted, the prices listed in this book are for original editions. To be the record listed in this book, it must match the listing in EVERY way – label, number, prefix. And it also must have the original label design. Numerous labels put out reissues where the only thing different might be the prefix or even the record label design. A year listed on the record or on the cover may or may not be the year of release for your record!

Market Report

Black Gold Discovered

Boston

An astounding find emerged in late 2006 that set the world of record collecting on its collective ear. Actually, the story begins in 2002, when a Kenny Rogers Roasters employee from Montreal, Canada, named Warren Hill happened to be poring through a box of records at a street sale in Chelsea, N.Y. Along with a Leadbelly 10-inch recording on Folkways and a water-damaged copy of the Modern Lovers first LP, Hill spied a 12-inch piece of acetone-covered aluminum labeled "Velvet Underground. 4-25-66. Att N. Dolph." It was an acetate of the Velvet Underground's debut LP *The Velvet Underground & Nico,* but it was different from the commercial version.

There were different mixes of "Black Angel's Death Song," "All Tomorrow's Parties," "I'll Be Your Mirror," "Femme Fatale" and "Run, Run, Run." The sequencing was not the same, with

The Carpenters

"European Son" leading things off instead of "Sunday Morning." Even more incredible, there were markedly different versions of "European Son," "Heroin," "I'm Waiting For The Man" and "Venus In Furs." Guitar lines and solos were different in some cases. In others, it was the vocals or the drumming that was not the same. Or, there were instances when just the feel of a particular song was different.

The hope of such a discovery is what drives collectors to dig through crate after crate after crate of LPs, searching for that rare recording that nobody knows even exists. It's mostly a fruitless occupation, but Hill's discovery proved it can happen. In the end, the ultrarare Velvet Underground acetate sold for $25,000 in an auction. Initially, a bogus bidder on eBay submitted a bid of $155,000 for it. After much haranguing, it was resold for $25,000. The moral of this story is, no matter how unlikely it is that you'll find something of this value—be it historical or monetary—such finds can happen.

In the meantime, however, you have records to sell, or you're looking to buy. And you want to know the lay of the land. How is the vinyl record collecting market? What's hot and what's not? And more importantly, how much are your records worth? That last question will be answered by the pricing guide included in the book. As for the rest of the queries, we'll try to give you a good sense of what's going on in the marketplace.

How's the Market Doing?

There's no simple answer to that question. However, Wayne Johnson of Rockaway Records in Los Angeles, California, describes it as "very healthy." But that "thumbs up" doesn't apply to everything. While sealed Beatles records, like the *Yesterday and Today* "first state" butcher cover—once owned by former Capitol Records president Alan Livingston and that Johnson sold this year to an unidentified collector for $80,000—still command big dollars, other areas, like the '50s, are soft, he says.

"The problem is, you don't have any new collectors taking the place of those who pass away," says Johnson. "As time goes on, the people of that era are dying away and there are not a lot of kids getting into '50s music."

John Tefteller, a dealer who specializes in rare records, especially blues 78s, doesn't necessarily agree. In talking about the market in general, Tefteller says, "Overall, it's really good, but it's only real, real good if you have real, real good stuff. I talk to a lot of dealers who say it's horrible, that they're having trouble selling, that older stuff doesn't sell." But, says Tefteller, the rarest stuff does, and he has no problem finding buyers. "The rarest of the rare will always be rare," says Tefteller, and he adds that the price will only go up for the stuff. "It's climbing

What's Hot

Northern Soul
Punk/New Wave
Classic Rock
Progressive Rock
Psychedelia
Garage Rock
Early Hip-Hop
Early Blues
Rockabilly 45s
Original Label Beatles Records

What's Not

Easy Listening
Classical Music
Used LPs
Doo-Wop

in value astronomically. It's so expensive that some of the old-time collectors have been priced right out of the market."

On the other hand, used LPs can be had for less than $10, or even $5 in many cases. That's not the case for sealed original LPs, according to Tefteller. "Stuff from the '50s and '60s does very well, but it has to be original seals." Buyer beware: Not all sealed original LPs are legitimate. According to Tefteller, some will try to sell fake sealed Beatles LPs, where they take original Beatles LPs and shrink-wrap them with seal material taken off other LPs.

Eric Clapton

"I tell people constantly to find a dealer who will stand behind what they're selling, who are knowledgeable [about such things] and if not, will make it right if there's a problem," says Tefteller. "Those people are few and far between, especially on the Internet." And while the Internet can be a marketplace to get good prices for fairly common records, those looking to cash in big might want to avoid it.

"People who pay big bucks don't go for eBay," advises Tefteller. "Yes, you will get more than if you go to your local record shop or to a record swap, but the real money doesn't come from eBay. It comes from private sales." With records in their original seal, the question of condition becomes moot. As for the rest of the vinyl world, condition is paramount. "In real estate, it's location, location, location," says Tefteller. "In record collecting, it's condition, condition, condition." Mint is prized.

And then there's the old "supply and demand" issue. Finding a buyer willing to pay what you're asking, if the price is substantial, is the key. "It's condition and you have to have access to customers willing to pay, and you will not get that on eBay," says Tefteller. Johnson feels the collecting landscape has changed over the years, and customers are more sophisticated.

"Collectors are getting more and more picky," he says. "When I started, there was no Internet. The market was local. Now, it's such a global market. You can go online to see what's common and what's not."

What's Hot?

Northern Soul is on fire right now. It's been the flavor of the month—and the next month, and the next month—for a while now. Tefteller knows it sells, but while he's unfamiliar with that market, he is well aware of its skyrocketing value. "It's hot. It sells," says Tefteller. "The only problem with that market is it's up and down and all around. It's really very popular in England. It all depends on what they're playing on the dance floor." Obscurity is the key to a Northern Soul record's value. Other factors enter in, of course, but the rule is the more obscure the artist, the higher the price.

For Jim Cooper of Hip Cat Records, classic rock is where it's at. There is a big market for such acts like Pink Floyd, Led Zeppelin, The Beatles, the Rolling Stones, Jimi Hendrix, Cream, Queen and the Grateful Dead.

"I think it's the enduring quality of the music that keeps them relevant," says Cooper. "With records by a Pink Floyd or Led Zeppelin, with very few exceptions, there is not much filler." Johnson says bands like Pink Floyd and Led Zeppelin are more relevant to kids today, citing that as a reason why they're still collectible when '50s artists aren't.

And yet, not all the big-time acts of the '60s, '70s and '80s are in vogue. Johnson says the market for David Bowie is soft, except for the really rare stuff, and Cooper argues that Bruce Springsteen is a "tough sell." The problem with Springsteen, according to Cooper, is that his records were on one label, Columbia, and that label didn't alter its packaging much during his heyday. "The label didn't change much at all," says Cooper. "The packaging always remained the same." And that wasn't the case with, say, The Beatles, which had different colored vinyl releases and other varieties—issues that might have limited pressings. "The Apple label is highly collectible," says Cooper.

As genres go, punk, prog-rock, garage-rock and psychedelia are all doing well. "Garage music is going strong, and psychedelic has been strong and it's continuing," says Tefteller. "It's not falling off. Also, there's a lot of interest in punk, new wave and early hip-hop." Johnson agrees. "Punk is extremely hot. Anything punk is super hot, including posters and handbills." Punk customers are an interesting breed.

"With punk rock, it's not the general collector [that seeks it]," says Cooper. "When I get a punk collection in, I'll call someone and they'll come in immediately and rifle through the stacks. And it doesn't have to be the famous stuff, like the Clash or the Sex Pistols." In fact, with punk, like Northern Soul, the obscurity of the artist can add value to a record rather than subtract from it.

Digging into the past, Tefteller says early blues, from the '20s to the early '60s, does well, as do rockabilly 45s. Original label Beatles records are always a hot item and surf guitar albums from the '60s do well.

Mono rock albums from the rock era, the '60s and '70s, are more collectible than stereo albums from the same time period, according to Cooper. But, when it comes to the '50s, the opposite is true. Special packages, that aren't missing anything, can also be valuable, according to Cooper. For instance, certain *Dark Side of the Moon* packages from Pink Floyd that have both posters and both stickers that came with the set sell for twice the amount of those that may not have everything included. Same goes for The Who's *Quadrophenia*, once released as package that came with a special booklet. Among newer bands, Nirvana original pressings and colored vinyl releases remain valuable, thanks to limited pressings.

"There are a number of things that came out in the '90s that they didn't press a lot of," says Cooper. "They still pressed 10,000, but it was not a million. Nirvana has appreciated in value." And so has that of a once unknown prog-rock band called Porcupine Tree that has been gaining in popularity in recent years. The group's early recordings had limited pressings.

"They were relatively unknown through '97, and then around '99, they started to appear on the radar," says Cooper. "Their early releases go for hundreds of dollars, because you've now got thousands of people chasing pressings of 500 or 1,000."

Banned covers or ones that were pulled from the market and replaced can fetch good prices. For instance, there's the Rolling Stones' *Some Girls* cover that featured the band members and a selection of female celebrities, including Lucille Ball and Farrah Fawcett, in drag. The threat of lawsuits resulted in it being pulled off the shelves in favor of one that was less offensive. Then there's the Roger Waters' solo album *The Pros and Cons of Hitchhiking*. The original cover had a naked female hitchhiker. Later, a black box was placed over the woman's backside.

Certain promo albums are also prized, including those that came with white timing strips. A copy of Pink Floyd's *The Wall* with such a strip can go for $175 in Mint Minus condition or $100 to $115 in VG Plus. Picture labels are also another sought-after item. The Clash's *Combat Rock* had such a custom label that was replaced after a few months by a standard Epic label. It fetches a good price. So do early Rush albums on Mercury that came with labels showing the skyline of Chicago. All in all, such variations are getting younger kids excited about collecting vinyl, according to Cooper.

"For them, going through crates is like going on an archeological dig," says Cooper. "It's fun for them, because the artwork's bigger and the sound is better."

What's Not?

Taking the temperature of '50s music, as it relates to the collecting field, is tricky. It can be warm or cold depending on whom you talk to. Two genres that are generally considered weak are easy listening and classical music, according to Cooper. "Classical music is almost non-existent," adds Cooper. "I have a bin here where they're priced at a quarter each." As far as groups go, all have their ups and downs, says Johnson. The Beatles are always going to be hot, and the market for acts like Bob Dylan and The Beach Boys is heating up. However, with used LPs, it can be a struggle to not only sell them, but also get the price you're looking for.

"There are thousands of records that are priced $10 to $20 that people can't sell for $2," says Tefteller, unless they're really unique.

The Future

As more and more of today's youth discover vinyl, it seems record collecting has a fairly bright future. And rare records, especially those in exquisite condition, will probably always command high prices, and those prices aren't showing any signs of slowing down. What's more, the vinyl records being issued today are improving in sound quality, as labels produce records that feature half-speed mastering and thicker vinyl. With their deeper grooves, albums that come marked as 180-gram or 200-gram releases are made for hardcore audiophiles. But, when it comes to the records of the past, condition is everything.

"For records in common to mid-range condition, the price is soft, 'cause they're so abundant because of eBay," says Johnson. And the prices those records used to fetch 10 to 15 years ago aren't likely to be available. For rare records, prices are only going up. "In '75, I bought a Robert Johnson record on Vocalion for a couple hundred bucks," says Tefteller. "In '85, it was up to a couple thousand. Today, it's worth $10,000."

Northern Soul: A Hot Trend in Cool Sounds

Soaring Prices

Nothing is hotter in the field of vinyl record collecting than northern soul. A quick look at auction results for 7-inch treasures from this year is evidence that prices are continuing to soar for northern soul rarities. In the spring, Jimmy "Bo" Horne's "I Can't Speak" / "Street Corner," a hard-to-find late-'60s northern soul 45 that appeared on the compilation CD Northern Soul's Classiest Rarities Vol. 2, fetched $3,051. Around the same time, a $3,010 bid was accepted for Joe Jama's "My Life" / Sleep Late My Lady Friend." Then, in the summer, a copy of Sandy Golden's ultra-rare "Your Love Is Everything" / "When We're Alone"—only two or three are known to exist—went for $6,100. All three, however, can't hold a candle to the $30,000 netted several years ago for a copy of Frank Wilson's "Do I Love You."

Obscurity is the Key

Never heard of Jimmy "Bo" Horne or Sandy Golden, or even Frank Wilson? That's not surprising. When it comes to northern soul, as is the case for a lot of collectible records, the more obscure the artist, the bigger the price tag. That doesn't mean you have to pay big money for northern soul records. But what exactly is northern soul and how did it become such a hot commodity? What are its origins, and who are some of the artists whose music is classified as northern soul? The story begins in America, but the U.K. is where this prized music gained popularity.

A Brief History

The term "northern soul" has nothing to do with where the music originated. Ironically, though, much of it did come out of the northern Midwest of the U.S. As with many musical genres, a solid definition of just what northern soul is can be hard to come by. But, to most, northern soul encompasses the soul music of the 1960s and 1970s that was largely ignored in America upon its release but found new life in northern England.

Some of it came from artists that were on obscure soul labels in the U.S. Other northern soul releases were birthed by more well-known labels like Motown Records, Okeh Records and Stax Records—only, for whatever reason, they didn't catch on with American record buyers of the time like works by big-name acts like The Supremes or The Temptations or Marvin Gaye.

Some of that had to do with Motown's dominance of radio playlists. Radio played Motown's most popular acts; the rest received limited, if any, radio airplay. Artists that were left out in the cold include Wilson, The Vows, Bobby Taylor and even more well-known acts like The Isley

Brothers or The Contours. And artists like Edwin Starr and J.J. Barnes, who toiled on smaller labels bought up by Motown but not given much attention by the label, would go on to become stars of the northern soul circuit.

Although there is some debate about its history, it's generally accepted that the term "northern soul" was coined by journalist David Godin in the column he wrote in the 1970s for *Blues and Soul* magazine. Others contend, however, that it was used by denizens of record stores in the south of England to categorize the soul music that was gaining a foothold in the northern part of the country in the '60s and '70s.

The music itself is rooted in black soul music and is often characterized by its muscular beats and driving, mid- to up-tempo pacing. It became popular in the mid-'60s in northern England as the movement inspired dance styles and fashion trends found at ground zero for the genre: the Twisted Wheel club in Manchester. Spearheading northern soul's rise in popularity were the mods who flocked to the Twisted Wheel in their Ben Sherman button-downs and bowling shirts.

Other clubs would spring up. There was The Mojo in Sheffield, Wolverhampton's The Catacombs, the Golden Torch in Stoke, the Room at the Top in Wigan, the Blackpool Mecca, Va Va's in Bolton and, of course, the Wigan Casino, voted the world's No. 1 discotheque by Billboard during northern soul's mid- to late-'70s heyday, beating out New York's Studio 54.

In contrast to places like the Blackpool Mecca, which catered to an audience looking for wide-ranging diversity and obscure playlists, the Wigan Casino, which held 2,000 patrons, stuck to Motown originals and close facsimiles. Though not exactly daring in its choice of music, the Wigan Casino was notorious for its wild all-nighters and, at one time, its card-carrying membership exceeded 100,000 members. City leaders closed the Wigan Casino on Dec. 6, 1981. It later burned to the ground.

Meanwhile, acts like the Velvelettes, The Fascinations and Tami Lynn got a second chance at fame in the U.K. Songs they'd released in the '60s became Top 40 hits in the U.K. in 1971, with Lynn hitting #4 with "I'm Gonna Run Away From You," "Girls Are Out To Get You" by The Fascinations reaching #30 and "These Things Will Keep Me Loving You" by the Velvelettes going all the way to #35.

The party eventually died. Though the Twisted Wheel has survived and still hosts northern soul nights, most of the other clubs have closed. Much of the blame could be placed at the doorstep of commercialism. The genre's rise in the mid-'70s turned off the old guard, who didn't want to be perceived as "top of the poppers."

Still, the new millennium has witnessed a northern soul revival, with a number of acts heading over the pond to England to perform crowd favorites at so-called "all-nighters." And contemporary artists, such as Amy Winehouse, are breathing new life into the genre.

Underground Appeal

Northern soul is not a popularity contest. Obscurity is highly valued in this realm of collecting. In fact, northern soul clubs and DJs used to compete against each other to play the rarest soul and R&B records they could find. And if one venue got its hands on one and started putting it in heavy rotation, others would shun it. The soul music that didn't receive radio play or make a dent in the charts was what northern soul fans were after, and that applied as much to clubbing as it did to record collecting.

However important obscurity is to northern soul collectors, the music that was on those records had to be first-rate as well, and it sometimes exceeded the quality of better-known recordings. Songs had to be danceable, with a strong beat. Many were so-called "stompers," but other segments of the northern soul audience preferred slower shuffles, especially when the amount of rare "stompers" finds began to dry up. One such track was "It Really Hurts Me Girl" by the Carstairs.

Nevertheless, northern soul's fascination with the unknown is legendary. And it started with the unearthing of records released on independent black U.S. labels by DJs like Alan Levine, who sometimes came up with alternate titles, called "cover-ups," in order to keep what they had discovered to themselves. Often, there was a limited pressing of these records and many were solely distributed in one state or one particular region.

Names to Know

The list of artists collected under the northern soul umbrella is long and diverse. Some you may recognize, while others will leave you asking, "Who?" Before embarking on a hunt for collectible northern soul records, do your homework. The Internet is vast sea of resources, and checking eBay can give you a good idea of who and what to look for. Other web sites that can be of assistance include Soulfulkindamusic.net; www.northern-soul.com; NorthernSoul.co.uk; www.soul-source.co.uk/ for rare and northern soul records; www.thesoulgirl.com/; www.allmusic.com, do a search for northern soul; and check out www.bbc.co.uk for the BBC's Northern Soul Show.

In addition to those artists and groups already mentioned here, some names of artists or groups to look for include Edwin Starr, famous for the hit "War," and Earl Van Dyke, keyboardist and band leader for the Motown studio band The Funk Brothers. Others include The Vows, Bobby Taylor, The Hit Pack, The Lewis Sisters, Major Lance, Patti Austin, Al Kent, The Contours, Jerry Butler, The Flamingos, Tony Clarke, The Five Royales, Sam Fletcher, Jimmy Ruffin, Jackie Wilson, and on and on. There are literally hundreds, perhaps even thousands, of names that aren't listed here that made northern soul an undeniable, if underappreciated, musical force.

Labels worth seeking out include the aforementioned Okeh, Abet, Thelma, Volt, Cadet, Delphi, Challenge, Anla, Constellation, Tamla, Solid Hit and Swan, but this is just a small sampling of the labels that put out the rarities that make northern soul such a phenomenon among collectors.

The Hunt

The Internet is where everybody goes to find anything these days. But, to find the undiscovered gem that can bring in hundreds, or even thousands, of dollars, you may need to step away from the computer and actually leave your house. Sometimes availability can hinge on region. Rarities are most often found in the regions that produced them, so do some detective work and find out where a label or an artist originated. If you find yourself in that area, head to the record stores. Visit as many as you can and give yourself time to dig through everything. In addition, try to get to know people from the area who were alive at the time those records were made. They might just be able to clue you in on where to go to find the record you seek. Prices may vary, depending on how knowledgeable the seller is.

One place to go to find northern soul on the cheap is estate sales, especially those being held by people who were in their late teens or early 20s during the '60s and '70s. And, though it may be troubling for your conscience, the best places to go are the older areas or those places where blacks make up a sizable part of the population.

If you're not looking to get rich and just want to have an abundance of northern soul songs in your collection, the search gets easier. You can try to find records that British fans find are too common after all these years. To your American ears, they might just be fresher than for those who've made northern soul a big part of their lives.

Reissues and later pressings can also be a way to get all the northern soul you want. They aren't the originals, mind you, and they probably won't be worth a lot, but at least the songs you want may be available by going this route.

No Slowing Down

The northern soul market shows no signs of leveling off. Prices for rare northern soul recordings continue to rise. Some things to keep in mind when dealing in northern soul, or any area of vinyl record collecting: condition is paramount, and the rarer the recording, the higher the price it'll fetch. When going through a price guide, be sure to remember that you may not get the price that's listed. A number of factors can affect the price people are willing to pay for what you're selling. For example, you may think that you have a record in mint condition, when to someone else, it might just be in very good condition. Then, there is the issue of supply and demand. If there's little or no demand for what you're selling, you may not get what you think the record is worth. That's just the name of the game.

God Save the Sex Pistols: A Guide to Collecting Punk's Snottiest Heroes

By Ian Shirley

It's been 30 years since the Sex Pistols shook up the music business with their image, attitude and music. Since then, there have been reformation tours and the acknowledgment that their debut album, *Never Mind the Bollocks, Here's the Sex Pistols*, is one of the greatest rock albums of all time, influencing bands like Nirvana and Guns 'N' Roses.

The Sex Pistols are also the most collectible punk band, with prices easily outstripping American and British rivals like The Ramones, Television and The Clash. "It's great that we mean a lot to people" says drummer Paul Cook, "and there is good support for us out there amongst collectors." Glen Matlock, the original bass player, is also more than happy to blow the band's trumpet. "I think that we should be the No. 1 collectible band in the world, although I'm not into collecting myself." That may be so, but when Johnny Rotten sang "we're the future, your future" on "God Save the Queen" back in 1977, rather than commenting upon society, was he really calling upon his punk fans to invest in Sex Pistols records as a vinyl pension plan?

Controversy Boosts Prices

Sex Pistols vinyl became collectible from the release of their very first single "Anarchy in the UK" / "I Wanna Be Me" (EMI 2566) in November 1976. By this time, the band was already seen as the leaders of a new "punk rock" in England, with a devoted hard-core following, and with manager Malcolm McLaren, who proved adept at using the music press to attract maximum publicity. The Pistols' appearance, however, on the early evening current affairs TV program *Today*, where they unleashed a torrent of obscenities at presenter Bill Grundy, caused a media outrage beyond his wildest dreams. One consequence was that the Pistols were dropped by their record label EMI, which also withdrew "Anarchy ..." from sale even though it had reached 38 in the U.K. top 40.

Collectors will find that the most common stock copies have a Dave Goodman production credit on the B-side and are worth $50. Those in a black picture sleeve with a Chris Thomas production credit on the B-side are worth $180. Finally, promo copies with "Demo Record Not For Resale" in a black picture sleeve with the Chris Thomas production credit on both sides and an information slip about the release are worth $550. There are also three known copies of a double-sided acetate containing a longer version of "Anarchy ..." timed at 4:01, with a cover version of the Stooges' "No Fun" (EMI 401), which the band originally intended to be the single's B-side. These are worth around $12,000 each, as are one-sided acetates of "Anarchy ..." in its more widely known version timed at 3:36.

Free from EMI—and allowed to keep the $80,000 advance—McLaren negotiated a deal with the U.K. arm of A&M records who, after symbolically signing the contract outside Buckingham Palace, planned to release The Pistols' second single "God Save the Queen" / "No Feelings" in March 1977 to tie in with the Queen's Silver Jubilee celebrations. However, by this time, original bass player Glen Matlock had been replaced by Sid Vicious, and the band's loutish behavior at A&M's head office — guitarist Steve Jones allegedly making love to an employee in the toilet being the least offensive action that day — and the assault of a well-known DJ (by Vicious) saw them being dropped 10 days after the deal was agreed. The single was withdrawn before release, although not before some stock copies escaped captivity. A&M AMS 7284 is now the Holy Grail for Sex Pistols and punk collectors worldwide. Although mint copies are valued at $14,000, a copy sold last year on eBay for a whopping $24,000.

There are also two known double-sided acetates with the same tracks with 'LTS' stamped on the label, which it is believed McLaren had pressed with a view to either obtaining the A&M deal or soliciting gigs for the band as, by this time, the Sex Pistols were so notorious that they had been banned from playing in many U.K venues.

It was only when the Pistols signed to Richard Branson's Virgin records that the band began to release a regular flow of singles. The Virgin issue of "God Save the Queen" (VS 181) was famously kept from the #1 spot in June 1977, not by Rod Stewart's "I Don't Want To Talk About It" but the music industry, which banned airplay of the single and actually inserted a blank in the charts rather than the name of the band and the title of its single. As it was a monster seller, stock copies with the defaced Queen's head sleeve (apparently originally intended for "Anarchy ..." but rejected by EMI) are quite easy to come by and worth $16.

More fascinating—and of course expensive at $3,000—is a one-off, plain blue cover sleeve (with a single inside) that was apparently made up as a sample by Virgin in case any legal action was threatened over the defaced Queen's head sleeve. The following two singles "Pretty Vacant" / "No Fun" (Virgin VS 184) and "Holidays in the Sun" / "Satellite" (VS 191) also charted strongly and are easy to find in picture sleeves, even though the "Holiday ..." artwork was banned, as it used images from a well-known travel brochure without permission. More expensive is the Virgin Records' Christmas card sent out at the end of 1977 containing a Sex Pistols flexi disc which, if you can find one, is worth $3,000. The single on its own usually fetches $800.

When released in November 1977, the Sex Pistols' album *Never Mind the Bollocks, Here's the Sex Pistols* (Virgin V 2086) went to #1. As the album was rush-released, there are some different versions to look for. The most common have a yellow rear sleeve with the tracks listed and are worth $40. Those with a pink back sleeve and no track listing are worth $50. However, the rarest version was a special limited-edition (V 2086/Spots 001), that had a pink rear sleeve with no track listing and was shrink-wrapped with a poster and a one-sided single featuring the track "Submission." These albums came with an orange or green sticker on the front, and unopened copies fetch up to $1,200. If opened and with everything there, prices start at $300.

Novelty Releases

Although the Pistols split at the end of their debut American tour in January 1978, this didn't stop Virgin records from releasing a succession of singles with singers ranging from British train robber Ronnie Biggs, guitarist Steve Jones and even fellow punk Tenpole Tudor taking the lead vocals on "Who Killed Bambi?" These releases are the Sex Pistols in name only and collectible for novelty value at prices between $10 and $30. Sid Vicious' "My Way" is, though, seen as a punk classic and is worth $16, and a one-sided acetate of this track has changed hands for $1,400. After this, Virgin was basically flogging a dead horse, as the double album soundtrack to the film *The Great Rock and Roll Swindle* testifies ($40-$60).

Overseas Pressings

There is great interest in Sex Pistols singles pressed overseas during their existence. Although U.S. copies of "Pretty Vacant" / "Sub-Mission" (Warner Bros 8516) can be picked up at a reasonable $10, New Zealand pressings of "Anarchy in the U.K." and "Pretty Vacant" have been known to change hands for upwards of $1,400. A Belgian "Anarchy ..." with a unique picture sleeve is worth $1,200, although German copies can be had for a more reasonable $350. More fascinating is a Thai EP (SP1011, $5,000+)—with a unique Pistols picture sleeve—which, along with "Holidays in the Sun," contains three tracks by other artists, including Status Quo's "Rockin' All Over the World" and disco classic "Boogie On Up!" There is even a rare Greek pressed "My Way," which, in the past, fetched $1,400. There is other exotica, but collectors must confirm paternity, as there are many bootlegs out there—especially of Thai singles.

After the Split

Finally, Pistols collectors should also pick up some of the material released by band members after the split. Most essential is John Lydon's first Public Image 7-inch "Public Image" / "The Cowboy Song" (Virgin VS 228) with a free newspaper at $20, and an original copy of their second album *Metal Box* (Virgin METAL 1), which came in a tin containing three 12-inch singles ($60). Glen Matlock's first Rich Kids single "Rich Kids" / "Empty Words" (EMI 2738) on red vinyl ($12) is as far as you need to go with him. Steve Jones and Paul Cook's various outings are for the hardcore only.

So, 30 years after leading the U.K. side of the punk rock revolution, the Pistols have become, like the Beatles and the Rolling Stones, one of the blue-chip collectibles. Lydon may have sneered "Ever feel that you have been cheated?" at the finale of the Pistols' last gig, but to collectors buying their rare records, the Pistols are still a great rock and roll.

The Beatles' "Butcher" Covers

Highly prized by collectors, the so-called Beatles "butcher cover" is a Holy Grail that vinyl hounds dream of owning.

Controversial in its day, the Capitol T/ ST 2553 release with the black label and rainbow-colored band, referred to as the "first state" cover, of *Yesterday ... And Today*, featured a photo of the Fab Four in white butcher smocks covered in pieces of raw meat and toy doll parts.

Why is it so revered among collectors? The reason is, hardly any of the "first state" copies were reported to have been sold in stores before Capitol recalled it.

"Ninety-nine percent have another cover pasted over the top," says Wayne Johnson of Rockaway Records.

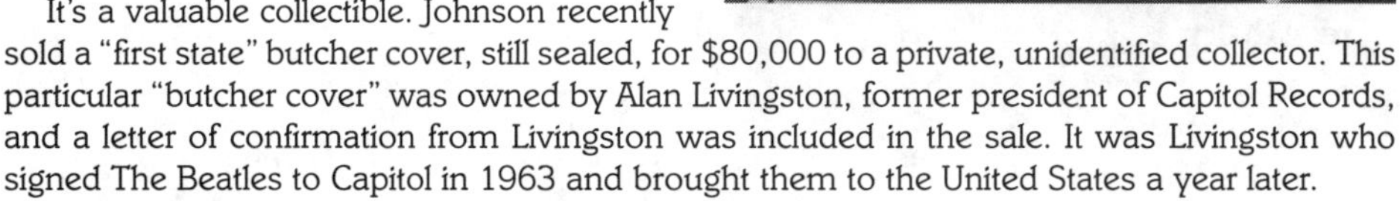

It's a valuable collectible. Johnson recently sold a "first state" butcher cover, still sealed, for $80,000 to a private, unidentified collector. This particular "butcher cover" was owned by Alan Livingston, former president of Capitol Records, and a letter of confirmation from Livingston was included in the sale. It was Livingston who signed The Beatles to Capitol in 1963 and brought them to the United States a year later.

Livingston's part in the butcher cover story has become the stuff of myth and legend. As the story goes, Livingston was not a big Beatles fan, but he was encouraged to take a box of the "butcher cover" albums home in the wake of the recall.

Confirmation of Livingston's stash, and the private sale of 20 "first state" butcher covers, in their original seals, came from Livingston himself in recent years. Noted for being in impeccable, flawless condition, the "Livingston Butchers," as they're called, fetch hefty sums of money these days, starting at $40,000 and going up from there.

The Story Behind the "Butcher" Cover

So, where did the photo come from? And how did it become a part of Beatles lore?

It all started innocently enough with a 1966 photo shoot with photographer Robert Whitaker. The shots were to be part of "A Somnambulant Adventure," a conceptual art project Whitaker had in the works.

For it, the group wore white butcher coats, with plastic baby dolls and pieces of raw meat. Bored with conventional photo sessions, The Beatles, known for their quirky sense of humor, indulged Whitaker.

Originally, the photos were not intended to be considered for album covers; however, The Beatles had other ideas. They turned in photographs from the session for promotional use and, reportedly, John Lennon fought for it to become an album cover.

And that's exactly what happened. One of the photographs of the slaughterhouse scene became the cover for the British "Paperback Writer" single, and eventually it ended up on approximately 750,000 copies of *Yesterday ... And Today*—released June 15, 1966—that Capitol printed in the United States at its U.S. printing plants. To find out which plant printed a particular copy, check the number near the RIAA symbol on the back of the cover.

Yesterday ... And Today was a breaking point for The Beatles. The band had seen all of its U.K. LPs up to that point altered for the U.S. market—this due to business and market differences between the two countries. Also, a few U.S. Beatles LPs were assembled with singles, B-sides and EP tracks that were not released on U.K. 12-inch vinyl.

By 1966, after years of turning a blind eye to the practice, The Beatles grew tired of it, and so, while making *Revolver*, another 11-song U.S. only release was being planned that would nick a clutch of single sides and leftover U.K. album tracks.

Befitting their quirky sense of humor, The Beatles gave the label the "butcher" image to use as the cover. Not only did they find it funny, they were also making a statement about the piecemeal approach of albums like *Yesterday ... And Today* and how they dissected the band's work.

Inexplicably, Capitol went along with it.

After advance copies of the butcher covers were shipped, there was a strong backlash from record store managers and disc jockeys, and Capitol recalled the controversial copies. And although all copies were supposed to be shipped back to Capitol, there are some who maintain that the record, with the butcher cover, was sold in some stores; others say it couldn't have happened since the advance copies were all recalled within a few days of the advances having been sent out and no "first state" copies have surfaced with price stickers.

At first, plant managers were told to destroy all copies. Then Capitol did an about-face. With so many copies printed, Capitol decided to paste a new white cover—with a new, less controversial photo—over the "butcher" image. Ones with the pasted-on cover still intact over the original image are known as "second state" or "pasteovers." "Third-state" covers, the most common variety, have had the white cover steamed or peeled off.

In the end, Capitol apologized for the controversy, while some—but not all—of The Beatles defended the cover. Though the album hit #1 on the U.S. Billboard charts and was certified gold, all the overtime that went into repackaging the LP cost the label so much, it wound up being the only Beatles record to lose money for Capitol.

The Album

Musically, *Yesterday ... And Today* was a hodgepodge that served as a sort of crossroads for the Fab Four.

Along with four songs that didn't make the cut for the British version of 1965's *Rubber Soul*, there were the singles "Yesterday," "We Can Work It Out" and "Day Tripper."

While, in essence, *Yesterday ... And Today* provided a look back at The Beatles of the *Rubber Soul* era, it was also a foreshadowing of what was to come with *Revolver*. A great leap forward for The Beatles, *Revolver* was the stepping-off point where the cute, cuddly Fab Four gave way to the strange, but oddly compelling, experimentation of John Lennon, the maturing pop explorations of Paul McCartney and George Harrison's most assured compositional blends of Indian music and pop. *Yesterday ... And Today* previewed *Revolver's* "Doctor Robert" and "And Your Bird Can Sing," with mixes different from the final ones.

Despite its seemingly incongruent mix, *Yesterday ... And Today* doesn't feel scattered or in any way unfocused. Instead, it's a full portrait of a band equally adept at romantic pop and edgy rockers, and an appetizer for the lyrical and psychedelic musical tour de force that is *Revolver*.

The "Butcher's" Value

As for the "butcher covers," the three variations come with vastly different price tags.

Because of how rare it is, a "first state" version is worth decidedly more than a "second state" or "third state" example. Condition is, again, of utmost importance. If you have a "Livingston Butcher," or one in that's in pristine condition and covered in its original seal, it certainly wouldn't be out of the realm of possibility that such a record would command a price approaching six figures. And it doesn't look like the price will be going down anytime soon.

As Johnson says, "The common stuff will always be common," and therefore, not worth much, but a butcher cover, especially a "first state" copy is one of those rarities that will probably always go for big money.

While not as valuable as "first state" butchers, "second state" covers are rising in value as they become more and more rare, and, even though they are more common, "third state" butchers are still coveted by collectors.

"People like them," says Johnson. "Butcher covers always are at a premium."

Another thing to keep in mind: stereo versions of this much-beloved collectible are, according to Johnson, "three to five times rarer than mono."

Canada's Own "Butcher"

An interesting side note to the butcher cover story is the confirmed existence of the "Canadian Butcher."

Once upon a time, the "Canadian Butcher" was considered a kind of fairy tale, one made up by record collectors with visions of it dancing in their heads. Ultimately, it proved to be true, although in 30 years, only two copies—in VG+ to VG++ condition—have seen the light of day.

The finds were authenticated by Perry Cox, author of the *Beatles Record Guides.*

Much more rare than its American cousin, the "Canadian Butcher" was thought to have been selectively distributed only to Capitol's president and, perhaps, a few label executives. None of them were "pasteovers" and both of the copies that have surfaced are mono versions, though there is an original stereo slick with "Beckett" in the watermark.

Factory laminated similar to the American "Ain't She Sweet," the slick also features "Litho In Canada" in small black print.

"Printed in Canada" is printed on the back, with photos of other Beatles Canadian LP titles.

Also released in the summer of 1966, the record number of this release has the same record number as the U.S. version, (S) T-2553.

According to reports, an American collector took ownership of one from Paul White, once the head of the A&R Department of Capitol of Canada. It was White who brought the famed 6000 series to Canada, which rolled out the three Canadian Beatles albums.

To Learn More ...

Many books and articles have been written about the "butcher covers." One place to find out more is http://www.eskimo.com/~bpentium/butcher.html. To read more, check out Dennis Gaffney's book *The Beatles' "Butcher" Cover*, among other books like *Chronicle Books' The Beatles Anthology* and Nicholas Schaffner's *The Beatles Forever.*

Also check out Bruce Eder's *Yesterday ... and Today Overview* at www.allmusic.com, and go to www.rarebeatles.com/album2/icts2/response.jpg to read the Capitol Customer Response Letter to the controversy.

Selling Records

Determining the best way to sell your records depends on three main factors: 1) how valuable your records are, 2) how eager you are to part with them, and 3) how much (or how little) you are willing to accept for them.

If you have valuable records (those in demand and generally in Mint or Near Mint condition), you should consider selling them directly (not in online auctions) to private collectors, who will probably pay more than any other category of buyer. Record dealers will be easier to find, but will offer lower prices, as they, of course, make their living by reselling at a markup to private collectors. Dealers act as middlemen, who do the legwork of finding the collectors. If you want to hold out for the highest prices, and are willing to do the legwork yourself, find the private collectors on your own. You can do this by attending record shows or advertising in *Goldmine* or *Discoveries*. Most local record stores don't buy common records anymore. It's even difficult to find a used record store of any type. For valuable records, eBay should be your last resort, as it has become a buyer's market, and you won't get the appropriate value.

However, if your records are not valuable, you are eager to dispose of your records, are willing to accept a lower price, and don't want to track down dealers or collectors, eBay is an alternative. Many serious, hardcore collectors now look at eBay as a place to buy. A quarter to half of the serious collectors in the world buy on eBay, far more than a few years ago. Many collectors and dealers often check it, although large numbers of collectors don't want to take the time to sift through all the auctions to find what they want. If you try to sell through eBay or another online auction, your records will probably sell for less than what a dealer would pay, or perhaps not at all. Still, if you would rather sell from home than search for buyers yourself, selling on eBay is better than not selling at all. Better that than leaving unwanted albums to clutter your attic or basement or throwing them in the trash. For those records you can't sell anywhere, at least consider donating them to Goodwill or a similar charity organization.

Tips for Buying and Selling on eBay

If you have never used eBay, log on to eBay (http://www.ebay.com/) and register as a new user. Then visit the eBay Help page to learn the basics. On the Help page, you will find a series of step-by-step tutorials, a search field in which to type key words for any topic on which you want information, answers to FAQs (frequently asked questions), an A-Z index, a list of common eBay acronyms with their meanings, and an eBay glossary.

Also on the Help page, you can click on the Learning Center link to download free courses about eBay. Or you can click on the eBay University link to order a CD-ROM or DVD, or make arrangements to take a course in a classroom setting.

Buying on eBay

- Because of the vast number of records for sale on eBay, you may have to sift through a mountain of listings to find the exact record you want in an acceptable condition. To be efficient, select the option to search both title and description for key words, then choose the most specific, descriptive key words and exclude extraneous words. Click on advanced search tips for special (Boolean) commands to limit your search even more effectively. If the desired record doesn't appear, then progressively select more general terms to broaden the search. Avoid using the words "and," "or," and "the," or extra punctuation in the key word search unless they are actually part of the title or phrase you are searching for.
- Once you find a record you want, check the seller's feedback to ensure you are dealing with someone who is reputable.
- Study descriptions carefully and e-mail or call the seller to clarify any details.
- Read the seller's policies to make sure you understand his or her payment, insurance, shipping, tracking, and return policies. Be aware that some sellers charge an exorbitantly high shipping price to pad their profit margin.
- Pay for your purchase promptly (never in cash) and give appropriate feedback when you receive your package.

Selling on eBay

- Photograph your record, so potential buyers can see it. Including a photo in your auction will cost a little more, but photos are an essential sales tool. After all, a picture really is worth a thousand words.
- Grade your record using the *Goldmine* grading guide that follows.
- Write an accurate description, including the grade, and any flaws in the record and cover, and including label name (record manufacturer such as Columbia, EMI, etc.) and label number.
- Compose a clear set of policies covering payment, insurance, shipping, tracking, and returns. Study a number of other auction listings for examples, if necessary.
- Select a traditional auction, in which bidders compete over a set number of days, or choose a buy-it-now auction or fixed-price sale, both of which are options in which a buyer can purchase an item for a set price without having to wait for an auction to end.
- Once your record sells, and you receive payment (if accepting a check, do not send item until check has cleared), pack it well, and mail it promptly.
- Give appropriate feedback to the buyer once he or she has notified you that the package has been received and he or she is satisfied.

Condition is Everything!

Visual or Play Grading? In an ideal world, every record would be played before it is graded. But the time involved makes it impractical for most dealers, and anyway, it's rare that you get a chance to hear a record before you buy through the mail. Some advertisers play-grade everything and say so. But unless otherwise noted, records are visually graded.

How to Grade. Look at everything about a record — its playing surface, its label, its edges — under a strong light. Then, based on your overall impression, give it a grade based on the following criteria:

Mint (M): Absolutely perfect in every way — certainly never played, possibly even still sealed. (More on still sealed under "Other considerations.") Should be used sparingly as a grade, if at all.

Near Mint (NM or M-): A nearly perfect record. Many dealers won't give a grade higher than this, implying (perhaps correctly) that no record is ever truly perfect.

The record should show no obvious signs of wear. A 45 RPM or EP sleeve should have no more than the most minor defects, such as almost invisible ring wear or other signs of slight handling.

An LP jacket should have no creases, folds, seam splits, or any other noticeable similar defect. No cut-out holes, either. And of course, the same should be true of any other inserts, such as posters, lyric sleeves, and the like.

Basically, an LP in Near Mint condition looks as if you just got it home from a new record store and removed the shrink wrap.

Near Mint is the highest price listed in all *Goldmine* price guides. Anything that exceeds this grade, in the opinion of both buyer and seller, is worth significantly more than the highest *Goldmine* book value.

Very Good Plus (VG+): Generally worth 50 percent of the Near Mint value.

A Very Good Plus record will show some signs that it was played and otherwise handled by a previous owner who took good care of it.

Record surfaces may show some slight signs of wear and may have slight scuffs or very light scratches that don't affect one's listening experience. Slight warps that do not affect the sound are OK.

The label may have some ring wear or discoloration, but it should be barely noticeable. The center hole will not have been misshapen by repeated play.

Picture sleeves and LP inner sleeves will have some slight ring wear, lightly turned-up corners, or a slight seam split. An LP jacket may have slight signs of wear also and may be marred by a cut-out hole, indentation, or corner indicating it was taken out of print and sold at a discount.

In general, if not for a couple minor things wrong with it, this would be Near Mint. All but the most mint-crazy collectors will find a Very Good Plus record highly acceptable.

A synonym used by some collectors and dealers for "Very Good Plus" is "Excellent."

Very Good (VG): Generally worth 25 percent of the Near Mint value.

Many of the defects found in a VG+ record will be more pronounced in a VG disc.

Surface noise will be evident upon playing, especially in soft passages and during a song's intro and fade, but will not overpower the music otherwise. Groove wear will start to be noticeable, as will light scratches (deep enough to feel with a fingernail) that will affect the sound.

Labels may be marred by writing, or have tape or stickers (or their residue) attached. The same will be true of picture sleeves or LP covers. However, it will not have all of these problems at the same time, only two or three of them.

This *Goldmine* price guide lists Very Good as the lowest price. This, not the Near Mint price, should be your guide when determining how much a record is worth, as that is the price a dealer will normally pay you for a Near Mint record.

Good (G), Good Plus (G+): Generally worth 10-15 percent of the Near Mint value.

Good does not mean Bad! A record in Good or Good Plus condition can be put onto a turntable and will play through without skipping. But it will have significant surface noise and scratches and visible groove wear (on a styrene record, the groove will be starting to turn white).

A jacket or sleeve will have seam splits, especially at the bottom or on the spine. Tape, writing, ring wear or other defects will start to overwhelm the object.

If it's a common item, you'll probably find another copy in better shape eventually. Pass it up. But if it's something you have been seeking for years, and the price is right, get it... but keep looking to upgrade.

Poor (P), Fair (F): Generally worth 0-5 percent of the Near Mint value.

The record is cracked, badly warped, and won't play through without skipping or repeating. The picture sleeve is water damaged, split on all three seams and heavily marred by wear and writing. The LP jacket barely keeps the LP inside it. Inner sleeves are fully seam split, crinkled, and written upon.

Except for impossibly rare records otherwise unattainable, records in this condition should be bought or sold for no more than a few cents each.

Other grading considerations. Most dealers give a separate grade to the record and its sleeve or cover. In an ad, a record's grade is listed first, followed by that of the sleeve or jacket.

With **Still Sealed (SS)** records, let the buyer beware, unless it's a U.S. pressing from the last 15-20 years or so. It's too easy to re-seal one. Yes, some legitimately never-opened LPs from the 1960s still exist. But if you're looking for a specific pressing, the only way you can know for sure is to open the record. Also, European imports are not factory-sealed, so if you see them advertised as sealed, someone other than the manufacturer sealed them.

Abbreviations

In addition to the letters used to designate a record's grade, it's not uncommon to see other abbreviations used in dealer advertisements. Knowing the more common ones helps to prevent confusion. Here are some:

boot: bootleg (illegal pressing)
cc: cut corner
co: cutout
coh: cut-out hole
cov, cv, cvr: cover
demo: demonstration record (synonym for promo, this is the more common term overseas)
dh: drill hole
dj: disc jockey (promotional) record
ep: extended play (can be used for both 45s and LPs)
gf: gatefold (cover)
imp: import
ins: insert
lbl: label
m, mo: monaural (mono)
m/s: mono/stereo (usually used to describe a promo single that has the same song on both sides, with the only difference in the type of sound)
nap: (does) not affect play
noc: number on cover
nol: number on label
obi: not actually an abbreviation, "obi" is the Japanese word for "sash" and is used to describe the strip of paper usually wrapped around Japanese (and occasional US) pressings of LPs
orig: original
pr, pro, promo: promotional record
ps: picture sleeve (the cover that appears with some 45s and most 7-inch extended play singles)
q: quadraphonic
re: reissue
rec: record
repro: reproduction
ri: reissue
rw: ring wear
s: stereo
sl: slight
sm: saw mark
soc: sticker on cover
sol: sticker on label
ss: still sealed
s/t: self-titled
st: stereo
sw: shrink wrap
toc: tape on cover
tol: tape on label
ts: taped seam
w/: with
wlp: white label promo
wobc: writing on back cover
woc: writing on cover
wofc: writing on front cover
wol: writing on label
wr: wear
wrp: warp
xol: "x" on label

Using This Book

Artists' names are in bold capital letters. They are alphabetized, for the most part, the way our computer did, so blame anything that seems way out of line on that. We've programmed in some "fudge factors" — artists who have numbers in their names are listed as if they spelled out the name; artists with "Mr." are listed as if their name was "Mister," and the same with "St." and "Saint."

In some cases, you'll see a number after an artist in parentheses. That means we have more than one artist by that name in our database.

Records are listed in two formats. First we list "45s"; then we list "Albums." These are defined for the purposes of this book as follows:

A 45 is a seven-inch record, usually with one song on each side. It need not have a big hole. It need not even play at 45 rpm – for simplicity's sake, we've included Columbia Microgroove 33⅓ rpm singles of the late 1940s and early 1950s in this category. They always have a note attached to them explaining what they are. Sometimes we list a 45 with more than one song on a side; either that's because the record was sold as a 45 or it was part of a record company's regular numbering system for 45s.

An album is defined here as a 10- or 12-inch record (never 7 inches) that has a small hole and isn't a 12-inch single. Defining it any more than that is problematic. Some albums have only one song on a side, others have over a dozen; some play for 15 minutes, others for over an hour; some albums even play at 45 rpm rather than the standard 33⅓ rpm. Unless noted, however, all albums are assumed to be 33⅓s. No 78s are listed under albums.

Under each format listing, the records are sorted alphabetically by label. All the records on each label are listed numerically, ignoring prefixes. The one exception is with RCA Victor 45s, which are arranged with APBO issues first, then PB issues, then 447- series reissues, then other issues in order of prefix.

After many of the numbers is a number or letter in brackets. These designate something special about the listing as follows:

EP: extended play album (only used with album listings for 12-inch releases with 4 to 6 tracks and not as long as a regular album)

M: mono record

P: partially stereo record (rarely are records advertised as such; the determination has been made by careful listening)

Q: quadraphonic record

R: rechanneled stereo record (these will usually be labeled with such terms as "Electronically Re-Channeled for Stereo"; "Enhanced for Stereo"; "Simulated Stereo"; or "Duophonic," but sometimes they aren't labeled as rechanneled)

S: stereo record

10: a 10-inch LP

(x) where x is a number: the number of records in a set (this is in parentheses inside the brackets so that in those rare instances where they exist, 10-record sets won't be confused with 10-inch LPs)

Most albums after 1968 do not have a stereo content designation. After 1968, if no designation is listed, it's probably stereo, though not necessarily. More importantly, it means that there was only one purchasing option available (except for the quadraphonic years of 1972-1977).

In the next, widest, column, we list the titles. For 45s, we list both the A and B side. Albums have one listing with the title as shown on the cover (assuming a title is shown on the cover). Most album listings have a prefix, usually from one to five letters. These prefixes often tell you whether your album is a first pressing and can have a considerable effect on an album's value.

The next column lists the year of release. Please note that the year of release and the year of recording are not necessarily the same! For example, if an album had several singles taken from it, the later singles may not have come out until another year, even though all of the singles have the same year on them. Also note that many archival recordings are reissued many times. Just because an album claims to be "recorded in 1941" doesn't mean that it actually came out in 1941. It's far more likely to be a more modern release.

That said, some of these dates may be off by a year; sometimes a record is released in December of the year before or January of the year after. Other years we can only guess the decade, and the year will have a question mark in it.

The next three columns are the values in Very Good (VG), Very Good Plus (VG+), and Near Mint (NM) condition.

Finally, many items have a descriptive line in italics under the entry. This often conveys important information that plays a role in the above record's value, such as label design, cover design, or color of vinyl. Sometimes, seemingly insignificant differences can make a huge difference in value.

A

ABBA

45s

Number	Title (A Side/B Side)	Yr	VG	VG+	NM
❑ Atlantic 3035	Waterloo/Watch Out	1974	—	2.50	5.00
❑ Atlantic 3209	Honey Honey/Dance (While the Music Still Goes On)	1974	—	2.50	5.00
❑ Atlantic 3240	Hasta Manana/Ring Ring	1975	—	2.50	5.00
❑ Atlantic 3265	SOS/Man in the Middle	1975	—	2.50	5.00
❑ Atlantic 3310	I Do, I Do, I Do, I Do, I Do/Bang-a-Boomerang	1975	—	2.50	5.00
❑ Atlantic 3315	Mamma Mia/Tropical Loveland	1976	—	2.50	5.00
❑ Atlantic 3346	Fernando/Rock Me	1976	—	2.00	4.00
❑ Atlantic 3346	Fernando/Tropical Loveland	1976	—	2.00	4.00
❑ Atlantic 3372	Dancing Queen/That's Me	1976	—	2.00	4.00
❑ Atlantic 3387	Knowing Me, Knowing You/Happy Hawaii	1977	—	2.00	4.00
❑ Atlantic 3434	Money, Money, Money/Crazy World	1977	—	2.00	4.00
❑ Atlantic 3449	The Name of the Game/I Wonder (Departure)	1977	—	2.00	4.00
❑ Atlantic 3457	Take a Chance on Me/I'm a Marionette	1978	—	2.00	4.00
❑ Atlantic 3574	Does Your Mother Know/Kisses of Fire	1979	—	2.00	4.00
❑ Atlantic 3609	Voulez-Vous/Angeleyes	1979	—	2.00	4.00
❑ Atlantic 3629	Chiquitita/Lovelight	1979	—	2.00	4.00
❑ Atlantic 3630	Chiquitita (Spanish Version)/I Have a Dream (Spanish Version)	1979	—	2.50	5.00
❑ Atlantic 3652	Gimme! Gimme! Gimme! (A Man After Midnight)/The Ki .ng Has Lost His Crown	1980	—	2.00	4.00
❑ Atlantic 3776	The Winner Takes It All/Elaine	1980	—	2.00	4.00
❑ Atlantic 3806	Super Trouper/The Piper	1981	—	2.00	4.00
❑ Atlantic 3826	On and On and On/Lay All Your Love on Me	1981	—	2.00	4.00
❑ Atlantic 3889	When All Is Said and Done/Should I Laugh or Cry	1982	—	—	3.00
❑ Atlantic 4031	The Visitors/Head Over Heels	1982	—	—	3.00
❑ Atlantic 89881	One of Us/Should I Laugh or Cry	1983	—	—	3.00
❑ Atlantic 89948	The Day Before You Came/Cassandra	1982	—	—	3.00

Albums

Number	Title (A Side/B Side)	Yr	VG	VG+	NM
❑ Atlantic SD 16000	Voulez-Vous	1979	2.50	5.00	10.00
❑ Atlantic SD 16009	Greatest Hits, Vol. 2	1979	3.00	6.00	12.00
❑ Atlantic SD 16023	Super Trouper	1980	2.50	5.00	10.00
❑ Atlantic SD 18101	Waterloo	1974	3.00	6.00	12.00
❑ Atlantic SD 18146	Abba	1975	3.00	6.00	12.00
❑ Atlantic SD 18189	Greatest Hits	1976	3.00	6.00	12.00
❑ Atlantic SD 18207	Arrival	1977	3.00	6.00	12.00
❑ Atlantic SD 19114	Greatest Hits	1977	2.50	5.00	10.00
❑ Atlantic SD 19115	Arrival	1977	2.50	5.00	10.00
❑ Atlantic SD 19164	The Album	1978	2.50	5.00	10.00
❑ Atlantic SD 19332	The Visitors	1981	2.50	5.00	10.00
❑ Atlantic 80036 [(2)]	The Singles — The First Ten Years	1982	3.75	7.50	15.00
❑ Atlantic 80142	I Love Abba	1984	2.50	5.00	10.00
❑ Atlantic 81675	Abba Live	1986	3.00	6.00	12.00
❑ CBS International DAL 40301	Gracias Por La Musica	1980	10.00	20.00	40.00

—Spanish-language versions of some of their hits, this LP was pressed in the U.S.

AD LIBS, THE

45s

Number	Title (A Side/B Side)	Yr	VG	VG+	NM
❑ AGP 101	New York in the Dark/Human	1968	25.00	50.00	100.00
❑ Blue Cat 102	The Boy from New York City/Kicked Around	1965	3.75	7.50	15.00
❑ Blue Cat 114	Ask Anybody/He Ain't No Angel	1965	2.50	5.00	10.00
❑ Blue Cat 119	On the Corner/Oo-Wee Oh Me Oh My	1965	2.50	5.00	10.00
❑ Blue Cat 123	Just a Down Home Girl/Johnny My Boy	1966	2.50	5.00	10.00
❑ Capitol 2944	Love Me/Know All About You	1970	—	3.00	6.00
❑ Johnnie Boy 01	Santa's On His Way/I Stayed Home (New Year's Eve)	19??	2.00	4.00	8.00
❑ Karen 1527	Think of Me/Every Boy and Girl	1966	5.00	10.00	20.00
❑ Philips 40461	Don't Ever Leave Me/You're in Love	1967	2.00	4.00	8.00
❑ Share 101	You're Just a Rolling Stone/Show a Little Appreciation	1969	2.00	4.00	8.00
❑ Share 104	Giving Up/Appreciation	1969	2.00	4.00	8.00
❑ Share 106	The Boy from New York City/Nothing Worse Than Being Alone	1969	2.00	4.00	8.00

AEROSMITH

45s

Number	Title (A Side/B Side)	Yr	VG	VG+	NM
❑ Columbia 38-08536	Chip Away the Stone/S.O.S.	1989	—	2.00	4.00
❑ Columbia 10034	Train Kept a-Rollin'/Spaced	1974	—	3.00	6.00

Number	Title (A Side/B Side)	Yr	VG	VG+	NM
❑ Columbia 10105	S.O.S. (Too Bad)/Lord of the Thighs	1975	—	3.00	6.00
❑ Columbia 10155	Sweet Emotion/Pandora's Box	1975	—	2.50	5.00
❑ Columbia 10206	Walk This Way/Round and Round	1975	—	3.00	6.00
❑ Columbia 10253	Toys in the Attic/You See Me Crying	1975	—	3.00	6.00
❑ Columbia 10278	Dream On/Somebody	1975	—	2.50	5.00
—Contains the full-length version of A-side					
❑ Columbia 10359	Last Child/Combination	1976	—	2.50	5.00
❑ Columbia 10407	Home Tonight/Pandora's Box	1976	—	2.50	5.00
❑ Columbia 10449	Walk This Way/Uncle Salty	1976	—	2.50	5.00
❑ Columbia 10516	Back in the Saddle/Nobody's Fault	1977	—	2.50	5.00
❑ Columbia 10637	Draw the Line/Bright, Light, Fright	1977	—	2.50	5.00
❑ Columbia 10699	Kings and Queens/Critical Mass	1978	—	2.50	5.00
❑ Columbia 10727	Get It Up/Milk Cow Blues	1978	—	2.50	5.00
❑ Columbia 10802	Come Together/Kings and Queens	1978	—	2.50	5.00
❑ Columbia 10880	Chip Away the Stone (Studio)//S.O.S./Chip Away the Stone (Live)	1979	—	3.00	6.00
❑ Columbia 11181	Remember (Walking in the Sand)/Bone to Bone (Coney Island White Fish Boy)	1980	—	2.50	5.00
❑ Columbia 45894	Dream On/Somebody	1973	—	3.00	6.00
—Contains a remixed, edited version of A-side					
❑ Columbia 46029	Pandora's Box/Same Old Song and Dance	1974	—	3.00	6.00
❑ Geffen 19927	The Other Side/My Girl	1990	—	—	3.00
❑ Geffen 19946	What It Takes/Monkey on My Back	1990	—	—	3.00
❑ Geffen 22845	Love in an Elevator/Young Lust	1989	—	—	3.00
❑ Geffen 27915	Rag Doll/St. John	1988	—	—	3.00
❑ Geffen 28240	Dude (Looks Like a Lady)/Simoriah	1987	—	—	3.00
❑ Geffen 28249	Angel/Girl Keeps Coming Apart	1987	—	—	3.00
❑ Geffen 28814	Shela/Gypsy Boots	1986	—	2.00	4.00
Albums					
❑ Columbia KC 32005	Aerosmith	1973	3.75	7.50	15.00
—Orange cover with correct title "Walking The Dog"					
❑ Columbia KC 32005	Aerosmith	1973	3.00	6.00	12.00
—Light blue cover, most (if not all) of which say "Featuring 'Dream On' " on front					
❑ Columbia KC 32847	Get Your Wings	1974	3.00	6.00	12.00
❑ Columbia PC 33479	Toys in the Attic	1975	3.00	6.00	12.00
—Without bar code					
❑ Columbia PC 34165	Rocks	1976	3.00	6.00	12.00
—Without bar code. Some copies have "Rocks" in quotes on the cover, others don't; no difference in value					
❑ Columbia JC 34856	Draw the Line	1977	3.00	6.00	12.00
❑ Columbia PC2 35564 [(2)]	Live! Bootleg	1978	3.75	7.50	15.00
❑ Columbia FC 36050	Night in the Ruts	1979	2.50	5.00	10.00
❑ Columbia FC 36865	Aerosmith's Greatest Hits	1980	2.50	5.00	10.00
❑ Columbia FC 38061	Rock in a Hard Place	1982	2.50	5.00	10.00
❑ Columbia FC 40329	Classics Live	1986	2.50	5.00	10.00
❑ Columbia FC 40855	Classics Live, Vol. 2	1987	2.50	5.00	10.00
❑ Columbia FC 44487	Gems (1973-1982)	1989	2.50	5.00	10.00
❑ Geffen GHS 24091	Done with Mirrors	1985	2.50	5.00	10.00
❑ Geffen GHS 24162	Permanent Vacation	1987	2.50	5.00	10.00
❑ Geffen GHS 24254	Pump	1989	2.50	5.00	10.00

ALLMAN BROTHERS BAND, THE

Number	Title (A Side/B Side)	Yr	VG	VG+	NM
45s					
❑ Arista 0555	Angeline/So Long	1980	—	2.00	4.00
❑ Arista 0584	Mystery Woman/Hell and High Water	1981	—	2.00	4.00
❑ Arista 0618	Straight from the Heart/Leavin'	1981	—	2.00	4.00
❑ Arista 0643	Two Rights/Never Knew How Much	1981	—	2.00	4.00
❑ Capricorn 0003	Ain't Wastin' Time No More/Melissa	1972	—	2.50	5.00
❑ Capricorn 0007	Melissa/Blue Sky	1972	—	2.50	5.00
❑ Capricorn 0014	One Way Out/Standback	1972	—	2.50	5.00
❑ Capricorn 0027	Ramblin Man/Pony Boy	1973	—	2.50	5.00
❑ Capricorn 0036	Jessica/Come and Go Blues	1973	—	2.50	5.00
❑ Capricorn 0246	Nevertheless/Louisiana Lou and Three Card Monty John	1975	—	2.00	4.00
❑ Capricorn 0320	Crazy Love/Just Ain't Easy	1979	—	2.00	4.00
❑ Capricorn 0326	Can't Take It With You/Sail Away	1979	—	2.00	4.00
❑ Capricorn 8003	Black Hearted Woman/Every Hungry Woman	1970	—	3.00	6.00
❑ Capricorn 8011	Revival (Love Is Everywhere)/Leave My Blues at Home	1971	—	2.50	5.00
❑ Capricorn 8014	Whipping Post/Midnight Rider	1971	—	2.50	5.00
❑ Epic 73504	Good Clean Fun/Seven Turns	1990	—	2.00	4.00
Albums					
❑ Arista AL 9535	Reach for the Sky	1980	2.50	5.00	10.00
❑ Arista AL 9564	Brothers of the Road	1981	2.50	5.00	10.00
❑ Atco SD 33-308	The Allman Brothers Band	1969	3.75	7.50	15.00
❑ Atco SD 33-342	Idlewild South	1970	3.75	7.50	15.00
❑ Atco SD 2-805 [(2)]	Beginnings	1973	5.00	10.00	20.00
❑ Capricorn 2CP 0102 [(2)]	Eat a Peach	1972	3.75	7.50	15.00
❑ Capricorn CPN2 0102 [(2)]	Eat a Peach	198?	3.00	6.00	12.00
❑ Capricorn CX4 0102 [(2)Q]	Eat a Peach	1974	7.50	15.00	30.00
❑ Capricorn CP 0111	Brothers and Sisters	1973	3.00	6.00	12.00
❑ Capricorn CPN 0111	Brothers and Sisters	198?	2.00	4.00	8.00
❑ Capricorn 2CP 0131 [(2)]	The Allman Brothers Band at Fillmore East	1974	3.75	7.50	15.00
❑ Capricorn CPN2 0131 [(2)]	The Allman Brothers Band at Fillmore East	198?	3.00	6.00	12.00
❑ Capricorn 2CX 0132 [(2)]	Beginnings	1974	3.75	7.50	15.00
❑ Capricorn CPN2 0132 [(2)]	Beginnings	198?	3.00	6.00	12.00
❑ Capricorn CP 0156	Win, Lose or Draw	1975	2.50	5.00	10.00
❑ Capricorn CPN 0156	Win, Lose or Draw	198?	2.00	4.00	8.00
❑ Capricorn 2CX 0164 [(2)]	The Road Goes On Forever	1975	3.00	6.00	12.00
❑ Capricorn 2CX 0177 [(2)]	Wipe the Windows, Check the Oil, Dollar Gas	1976	3.00	6.00	12.00
❑ Capricorn CPN 0196	The Allman Brothers Band	1978	2.50	5.00	10.00

Number	Title (A Side/B Side)	Yr	VG	VG+	NM
❑ Capricorn CPN 0197	Idlewild South	1978	2.50	5.00	10.00
❑ Capricorn CPN 0218	Enlightened Rogues	1979	2.50	5.00	10.00
❑ Capricorn 2-802 [(2)M]	The Allman Brothers Band at Fillmore East	1971	20.00	40.00	80.00
—Promo only; sticker on front cover says "Promotional DJ Copy Monaural Not for Sale"					
❑ Capricorn SD 2-802 [(2)S]	The Allman Brothers Band at Fillmore East	1971	5.00	10.00	20.00
❑ Epic E 46144	Seven Turns	1990	3.75	7.50	15.00
❑ Polydor PD-1-6339	The Best of the Allman Brothers Band	1981	2.50	5.00	10.00
❑ Polydor 823273-1 [(2)]	The Allman Brothers Band at Fillmore East	1984	2.50	5.00	10.00
❑ Polydor 823653-1	The Allman Brothers Band	1984	2.00	4.00	8.00
❑ Polydor 823654-1 [(2)]	Eat a Peach	1984	2.50	5.00	10.00
❑ Polydor 823708-1	The Best of the Allman Brothers Band	1984	2.00	4.00	8.00
—Reissue of PD-1-6339					
❑ Polydor 825092-1	Brothers and Sisters	1985	2.00	4.00	8.00
❑ Polydor 839417-1 [(6)]	Dreams	1989	10.00	20.00	40.00

ALPERT, HERB

45s

Number	Title (A Side/B Side)	Yr	VG	VG+	NM
❑ A&M 714	Dina/You're Doin' What You Did with Me with Him	1963	2.50	5.00	10.00
—As "Dore Alpert"					
❑ A&M 729	I'd Do It All Again/Special Kind of Love	1964	2.00	4.00	8.00
—As "Dore Alpert"					
❑ A&M 1231	I Need You/The Lady in My Life	1988	—	—	3.00
❑ A&M 1446	3 O'Clock Jump/Kalimba	1989	—	—	3.00
❑ A&M 2107	Foreign Natives/Mama Way	1979	—	2.00	4.00
—With Hugh Masekela					
❑ A&M 2151	Rise/Aranjuez (Mon Amour)	1979	—	2.00	4.00
❑ A&M 2202	Rotation/Angelina	1979	—	2.00	4.00
❑ A&M 2221	Street Life/1980	1980	—	2.00	4.00
❑ A&M 2246	Beyond/Keep It Goin'	1980	—	2.00	4.00
❑ A&M 2268	Kamali/Interlude (For Erica)	1980	—	2.00	4.00
❑ A&M 2289	Reach for the Stars/Interlude (For Erica)	1980	—	2.00	4.00
❑ A&M 2356	Magic Man/Fantasy Island	1981	—	2.00	4.00
❑ A&M 2375	Manhattan Melody/You Smile, The Song Begins	1981	—	2.00	4.00
❑ A&M 2422	Route 101/Angel	1982	—	2.00	4.00
❑ A&M 2426	Fandango/The Lonely Bull	1982	—	—	—
—Unreleased?					
❑ A&M 2441	Fandango/Coco Loco	1982	—	2.00	4.00
❑ A&M 2515	Love Me the Way I Am (Quiereme Tal Como Say)/California Blues	1982	—	2.00	4.00
❑ A&M 2562	Garden Party/Oriental Eyes	1983	—	2.00	4.00
❑ A&M 2573	Sundown/Garden Party	1983	—	2.00	4.00
❑ A&M 2593	Red Hot/Sundown	1983	—	2.00	4.00
❑ A&M 2621	Oriental Eyes/Sundown	1984	—	2.00	4.00
❑ A&M 2632	We Could Be Flying/Come What May	1984	—	2.00	4.00
—With Lani Hall					
❑ A&M 2757	"8" Ball/Lady Love	1985	—	—	3.00
❑ A&M 2779	You Are the One/Lady Love	1985	—	—	3.00
—With Brenda Russell					
❑ A&M 2802	African Flame/Lady Love	1985	—	—	3.00
❑ A&M 2915	Keep Your Eye on Me/Our Song	1987	—	—	3.00
❑ A&M 2929	Diamonds/African Flame	1987	—	—	3.00
❑ A&M 2949	Making Love in the Rain/Rocket to the Moon	1987	—	—	3.00
❑ A&M 2973	Our Song/African Flame	1987	—	—	3.00
❑ Andex 4036	Summer School/Hully Gully	1959	2.50	5.00	10.00
—As "Herbie Alpert Sextet"					
❑ Carnival 701	Tell It to the Birds/Fallout Shelter	1962	2.50	5.00	10.00
—As "Dore Alpert"					
❑ Carol 700	Sweet Georgia Brown/Vipers Blues	1961	2.50	5.00	10.00
❑ Dot 16396	Fallout Shelter/Tell It to the Birds	1962	2.50	5.00	10.00
—As "Dore Alpert"					
❑ RCA Victor 47-7918	Gotta Get a Girl/Dreamland	1961	3.00	6.00	12.00
—As "Dore Alpert"					
❑ RCA Victor 47-7988	Little Lost Lover/Won't You Be My Valentine	1962	3.00	6.00	12.00
—As "Dore Alpert"					

Albums

Number	Title (A Side/B Side)	Yr	VG	VG+	NM
❑ A&M SP-3717	Beyond	1980	2.00	4.00	8.00
❑ A&M SP-3728	Magic Man	1981	2.00	4.00	8.00
❑ A&M SP-3731	Fandango	1982	2.00	4.00	8.00

Number	Title (A Side/B Side)	Yr	VG	VG+	NM
❑ A&M SP-4591	Just You and Me	1976	2.50	5.00	10.00
❑ A&M SP-4790	Rise	1979	2.50	5.00	10.00
❑ A&M SP-4949	Blow Your Own Horn	1983	2.00	4.00	8.00
❑ A&M SP-5082	Wild Romance	1985	2.00	4.00	8.00
❑ A&M SP-5125	Keep Your Eye on Me	1987	2.00	4.00	8.00
❑ A&M SP-5209	Under a Spanish Moon	1988	2.00	4.00	8.00
❑ A&M SP-5273	My Abstract Heart	1989	2.00	4.00	8.00
❑ A&M 75021 5345 1	North on South Street	1991	3.00	6.00	12.00

ALPERT, HERB, AND THE TIJUANA BRASS

45s

Number	Title (A Side/B Side)	Yr	VG	VG+	NM
❑ A&M 703	The Lonely Bull (El Solo Torro)/Acapulco 1922	1962	2.50	5.00	10.00
—With pale brown label and no horn logo					
❑ A&M 705	Marching Through Madrid/Struttin' with Maria	1963	2.00	4.00	8.00
❑ A&M 711	Mexican Corn/Let It Be Me	1963	2.00	4.00	8.00
❑ A&M 721	Spanish Harlem/A-Mer-I-Ca	1963	2.00	4.00	8.00
❑ A&M 732	Mexican Drummer Man/Great Manolete	1963	2.00	4.00	8.00
❑ A&M 742	The Mexican Shuffle/Numero Cinco	1964	2.00	4.00	8.00
❑ A&M 751	All My Loving/El Presidente	1964	2.00	4.00	8.00
❑ A&M 755	South of the Border/Up Cherry Street	1965	—	3.00	6.00
❑ A&M 760	Whipped Cream/Las Mananitas	1965	—	3.00	6.00
❑ A&M 767	El Garbanzo/Mae	1965	—	3.00	6.00
❑ A&M 775	Taste of Honey/Third Man Theme	1965	—	3.00	6.00
❑ A&M 787	Zorba the Greek/Tijuana Taxi	1965	—	3.00	6.00
❑ A&M 792	What Now My Love/Spanish Flea	1966	—	3.00	6.00
❑ A&M 805	The Work Song/Plucky	1966	—	3.00	6.00
❑ A&M 813	Flamingo/So What's New	1966	—	3.00	6.00
❑ A&M 823	Mame/Our Day Will Come	1966	—	3.00	6.00
❑ A&M 840	Wade in the Water/Mexican Road Race	1967	—	2.50	5.00
❑ A&M 850	Casino Royale/Wall Street Rag	1967	—	2.50	5.00
❑ A&M 860	The Happening/Town Without Pity	1967	—	2.50	5.00
❑ A&M 870	A Banda/Miss Frenchy Brown	1967	—	2.50	5.00
❑ A&M 890	Carmen/A Love So Fine	1967	—	2.50	5.00
❑ A&M 925	Cabaret/Slick	1968	—	2.50	5.00
❑ A&M 929	This Guy's in Love with You/A Quiet Tear	1968	—	2.50	5.00
❑ A&M 960	Yo Doy Ese Amor (This Guy's in Love with You)/A Love So Fine	1968	—	3.00	6.00
❑ A&M 964	To Wait for Love/Bud	1968	—	2.50	5.00
❑ A&M 1001	My Favorite Things/The Christmas Song	1968	—	3.00	6.00
❑ A&M 1015	She Touched Me/My Favorite Things	1969	—	2.50	5.00
❑ A&M 1028	Monday, Monday/Treasure of San Miguel	1969	—	2.50	5.00
❑ A&M 1043	Zazueira/Treasure of San Miguel	1969	—	2.50	5.00
❑ A&M 1065	Without Her/Sandbox	1969	—	2.50	5.00
❑ A&M 1094	Ob-La-Di, Ob-La-Da/Girl Talk	1969	—	2.50	5.00
❑ A&M 1100	Marjorine/Warm	1969	—	2.50	5.00
❑ A&M 1102	Marjorine/Ob-La-Di, Ob-La-Da	1969	—	2.50	5.00
❑ A&M 1143	You Are My Life/Good Morning Mr. Sunshine	1969	—	2.50	5.00
❑ A&M 1159	The Maltese Melody/Country Lake	1969	—	2.50	5.00
❑ A&M 1194	Brasilia/Love Potion #9	1970	—	2.00	4.00
❑ A&M 1225	Jerusalem/Strike Up the Band	1970	—	2.00	4.00
❑ A&M 1237	The Bell That Couldn't Jingle/Las Mananitas	1970	—	2.50	5.00
❑ A&M 1261	Summertime/Hurt So Bad	1971	—	2.00	4.00
❑ A&M 1284	Montezuma's Revenge/Darlin'	1971	—	2.00	4.00
❑ A&M 1337	Without Her/Zazuiera	1972	—	2.00	4.00
❑ A&M 1420	Last Tango in Paris/Fire and Rain	1973	—	2.00	4.00
❑ A&M 1423	The Nicest Things Happen/Last Tango in Paris	1973	—	2.00	4.00
❑ A&M 1526	Fox Hunt/I Can't Go On Living, Baby, Without You	1974	—	2.00	4.00
❑ A&M 1542	You Smile, the Song Begins/Save the Sunlight	1974	—	2.00	4.00
❑ A&M 1688	Coney Island/Ratatouille	1975	—	2.00	4.00
❑ A&M 1714	El Bimbo/Catfish	1975	—	2.00	4.00
❑ A&M 1762	The Whistle Song (Whistlestar)/Carmine	1975	—	2.00	4.00
❑ A&M 1852	Promenade/Musique	1976	—	2.00	4.00
❑ A&M 1962	African Summer/You in Me	1977	—	2.00	4.00
❑ A&M 2655	Bullish/Oriental Eyes	1984	—	2.00	4.00
—As "Herb Alpert Tijuana Brass"					
❑ A&M 2690	Struttin' on Five/Blow Your Own Horn	1984	—	2.00	4.00
—As "Herb Alpert Tijuana Brass"					

Albums

Number	Title (A Side/B Side)	Yr	VG	VG+	NM
❑ A&M LP-101 [M]	The Lonely Bull	1962	5.00	10.00	20.00
—Originals on yellowish label with brown print					
❑ A&M SP-101 [S]	The Lonely Bull	1962	6.25	12.50	25.00
—Original editions had this number					
❑ A&M LP-103 [M]	Herb Alpert's Tijuana Brass, Volume 2	1963	3.75	7.50	15.00
—Brown label with A&M logo at top					
❑ A&M SP-103 [S]	Herb Alpert's Tijuana Brass, Volume 2	1963	5.00	10.00	20.00
—Original issues had this number					
❑ A&M LP-108 [M]	South of the Border	1964	3.00	6.00	12.00
❑ A&M SP-108 [S]	South of the Border	1964	5.00	10.00	20.00
—Original issues had this number					
❑ A&M LP-110 [M]	Whipped Cream & Other Delights	1965	2.50	5.00	10.00
❑ A&M LP-112 [M]	Going Places	1965	2.50	5.00	10.00
❑ A&M LP-114 [M]	What Now My Love	1966	2.50	5.00	10.00
❑ A&M LP-119 [M]	S.R.O.	1966	2.50	5.00	10.00
❑ A&M LP-124 [M]	Sounds Like	1967	2.50	5.00	10.00
❑ A&M SP-3521 [(2)]	Foursider	1973	3.00	6.00	12.00
❑ A&M SP-3620	You Smile — The Song Begins	1974	2.50	5.00	10.00
❑ A&M SP-4110 [S]	Whipped Cream & Other Delights	1965	3.00	6.00	12.00
❑ A&M SP-4112 [S]	Going Places	1965	3.00	6.00	12.00

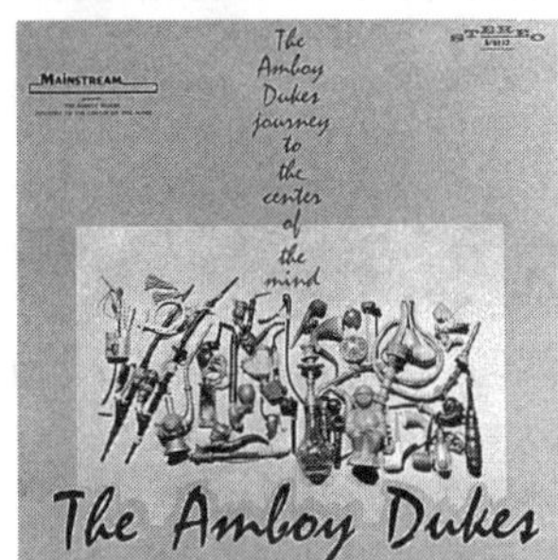

Number	Title (A Side/B Side)	Yr	VG	VG+	NM
❑ A&M SP-4114 [S]	What Now My Love	1966	3.00	6.00	12.00
❑ A&M SP-4119 [S]	S.R.O.	1966	3.00	6.00	12.00
❑ A&M SP-4124 [S]	Sounds Like	1967	3.00	6.00	12.00
❑ A&M SP-4134	Herb Alpert's Ninth	1967	2.50	5.00	10.00
❑ A&M SP-4146	The Beat of the Brass	1968	2.50	5.00	10.00
❑ A&M SP-4166 [S]	Christmas Album	1968	3.00	6.00	12.00
❑ A&M SP-4190	Warm	1969	2.50	5.00	10.00
❑ A&M SP-4228	The Brass Are Comin'	1969	2.50	5.00	10.00
❑ A&M SP-4245	Greatest Hits	1970	2.50	5.00	10.00
❑ A&M SP-4314	Summertime	1971	2.50	5.00	10.00
❑ A&M SP-4341	Solid Brass	1972	2.50	5.00	10.00
❑ A&M SP-4521	Coney Island	1975	2.50	5.00	10.00
❑ A&M SP-4627	Greatest Hits, Vol. 2	1976	2.50	5.00	10.00
❑ A&M SP-5022	Bullish	1984	2.00	4.00	8.00

AMBOY DUKES, THE

45s

Number	Title (A Side/B Side)	Yr	VG	VG+	NM
❑ DiscReet 1199	Sweet Revenge/Ain't It the Truth	1974	—	3.00	6.00
—As "Ted Nugent and the Amboy Dukes"					
❑ Mainstream 676	Baby Please Don't Go/Psalms of Aftermath.	1968	3.00	6.00	12.00
❑ Mainstream 684	Journey to the Center of the Mind/Mississippi Murderer.	1968	3.75	7.50	15.00
❑ Mainstream 693	You Talk Sunshine, I Breathe Fire/Scottish Tea.	1968	3.00	6.00	12.00
❑ Mainstream 700	Prodigal Man/Good Natured Emma.	1969	3.00	6.00	12.00
❑ Mainstream 704	For His Namesake/Loaded for Bear.	1969	3.00	6.00	12.00
❑ Mainstream 711	Flight of the Byrd/Ivory Castles.	1969	3.00	6.00	12.00

Albums

Number	Title (A Side/B Side)	Yr	VG	VG+	NM
❑ DiscReet DS 2181	Call of the Wild	1974	3.75	7.50	15.00
—As "Ted Nugent and the Amboy Dukes"					
❑ DiscReet DS 2203	Tooth, Fang and Claw	1974	3.75	7.50	15.00
—As "Ted Nugent and the Amboy Dukes"					
❑ Mainstream S-414	Dr. Slingshot	1975	3.75	7.50	15.00
❑ Mainstream S-421	Ted Nugent and the Amboy Dukes	1976	7.50	15.00	30.00
—Reissue of early material					
❑ Mainstream S-2-801 [(2)]	Journeys and Migrations	1974	7.50	15.00	30.00
—Reissue of 6112 and 6118					
❑ Mainstream S-6104 [S]	The Amboy Dukes	1967	10.00	20.00	40.00
❑ Mainstream S-6112	Journey to the Center of the Mind	1968	10.00	20.00	40.00
❑ Mainstream S-6118	Migration	1968	10.00	20.00	40.00
❑ Mainstream S-6125	The Best of the Original Amboy Dukes	1969	7.50	15.00	30.00
❑ Mainstream 56104 [M]	The Amboy Dukes	1967	20.00	40.00	80.00
❑ Polydor 24-4012	Marriage on the Rocks/Rock Bottom	1970	6.25	12.50	25.00
❑ Polydor 24-4035	Survival of the Fittest/Live	1971	6.25	12.50	25.00
—As "Ted Nugent and the Amboy Dukes"					

AMERICA

45s

Number	Title (A Side/B Side)	Yr	VG	VG+	NM
❑ American Int'l. 700	California Dreamin'/See It My Way	1979	—	2.50	5.00
—B-side by FDR					
❑ Capitol 4752	Only Game in Town/High in the City	1979	—	2.00	4.00
❑ Capitol 4777	All My Life/One Morning	1979	—	2.00	4.00
❑ Capitol 4817	All Around/1960	1980	—	2.00	4.00
❑ Capitol 4915	You Could've Been the One/Catch That Train	1980	—	2.00	4.00
❑ Capitol 4950	One in a Million/Hangover	1980	—	2.00	4.00
❑ Capitol B-5142	You Can Do Magic/Even the Score	1982	—	2.00	4.00
❑ Capitol B-5177	Right Before Your Eyes/Inspector Mills	1982	—	—	3.00
❑ Capitol B-5236	The Border/Sometimes Lovers	1983	—	—	3.00
❑ Capitol B-5275	Cast the Spirit/My Dear	1983	—	—	3.00
❑ Capitol B-5398	Special Girl/Unconditional Love	1984	—	—	3.00
❑ Capitol B-5430	(Can't Fall Asleep to a) Lullaby/Fallin' Off the World	1984	—	—	3.00
❑ Warner Bros. 7555	A Horse with No Name/Everyone I Meet Is From California	1972	—	3.00	6.00
❑ Warner Bros. 7580	I Need You/Riverside	1972	—	2.50	5.00
❑ Warner Bros. 7641	Ventura Highway/Saturn Nights	1972	—	2.50	5.00
❑ Warner Bros. 7650	A Horse with No Name/I Need You	1973	—	2.00	4.00
—"Back to Back Hits" series					
❑ Warner Bros. 7670	Don't Cross the River/To Each His Own	1972	—	2.50	5.00
❑ Warner Bros. 7694	Only in Your Heart/Moon Song	1973	—	2.50	5.00
❑ Warner Bros. 7725	Muskrat Love/Cornwall Blank	1973	—	2.50	5.00
❑ Warner Bros. 7760	Rainbow Song/Willow Tree Lullaby	1973	—	2.50	5.00

Number	Title (A Side/B Side)	Yr	VG	VG+	NM
❑ Warner Bros. 7785	She's Gonna Let You Down/Green Monkey	1974	—	2.50	5.00
❑ Warner Bros. 7839	Tin Man/In the Country	1974	—	2.50	5.00
❑ Warner Bros. 8014	Tin Man/In the Country	1974	—	2.00	4.00
❑ Warner Bros. 8048	Lonely People/Mad Dog	1974	—	2.50	5.00
❑ Warner Bros. 8086	Sister Golden Hair/Midnight	1975	—	2.50	5.00
❑ Warner Bros. 8118	Daisy Jane/Tomorrow	1975	—	2.50	5.00
❑ Warner Bros. 8157	Woman Tonight/Bell Tree	1975	—	2.50	5.00
❑ Warner Bros. 8212	Today's the Day/Hideaway (Part 2)	1976	—	2.50	5.00
❑ Warner Bros. 8238	Amber Cascades/Who Loves You	1976	—	2.50	5.00
❑ Warner Bros. 8285	She's Beside You/She's a Liar	1976	—	2.50	5.00
❑ Warner Bros. 8373	God of the Sun/Down to the Water	1977	—	2.50	5.00
❑ Warner Bros. 8397	Don't Cry Baby/Monster	1977	—	2.50	5.00
Albums					
❑ Capitol SO-11950	Silent Letter	1979	2.50	5.00	10.00
❑ Capitol SOO-12098	Alibi	1980	2.50	5.00	10.00
❑ Capitol ST-12209	View from the Ground	1982	2.50	5.00	10.00
❑ Capitol ST-12277	Your Move	1983	2.50	5.00	10.00
❑ Capitol ST-12370	Perspective	1984	2.50	5.00	10.00
❑ Capitol ST-12422	In Concert	1985	2.50	5.00	10.00
❑ Capitol SN-16275	Alibi	1982	2.00	4.00	8.00
❑ Capitol SN-16350	View from the Ground	1985	2.00	4.00	8.00
❑ Capitol SN-16361	Your Move	1985	2.00	4.00	8.00
❑ Warner Bros. BS 2576	America	1971	6.25	12.50	25.00
—First pressings omit "A Horse with No Name"					
❑ Warner Bros. BS 2576	America	1972	3.00	6.00	12.00
—With "A Horse with No Name" mentioned on front cover; green label					
❑ Warner Bros. BS 2576	America	1972	3.75	7.50	15.00
—Transitional edition includes "A Horse with No Name" but doesn't mention it on the front cover					
❑ Warner Bros. BS 2655	Homecoming	1972	3.00	6.00	12.00
❑ Warner Bros. BS 2728	Hat Trick	1973	3.00	6.00	12.00
❑ Warner Bros. BS 2808	Holiday	1974	3.00	6.00	12.00
❑ Warner Bros. BS 2852	Hearts	1975	3.00	6.00	12.00
❑ Warner Bros. BS 2894	History/America's Greatest Hits	1975	3.00	6.00	12.00
❑ Warner Bros. BS 2932	Hideaway	1976	3.00	6.00	12.00
❑ Warner Bros. BSK 3017	Harbor	1977	3.00	6.00	12.00
❑ Warner Bros. BSK 3110	History/America's Greatest Hits	1977	2.50	5.00	10.00
—Reissue of BS 2894 with "Burbank" palm trees label (later white labels are $8 NM)					
❑ Warner Bros. BSK 3136	America/Live	1977	3.00	6.00	12.00

AMERICAN BREED, THE

Number	Title (A Side/B Side)	Yr	VG	VG+	NM
45s					
❑ Acta 802	I Don't Think You Know/Give Two Young Lovers a Chance	1967	2.00	4.00	8.00
❑ Acta 804	Step Out of Your Mind/Same Old Thing	1967	2.50	5.00	10.00
❑ Acta 808	Don't Forget About Me/Short Skirts	1967	2.00	4.00	8.00
❑ Acta 811	Bend Me, Shape Me/Mindrocker	1967	3.00	6.00	12.00
❑ Acta 821	Green Light/Don't It Make You Cry	1968	2.00	4.00	8.00
❑ Acta 824	Ready, Willing and Able/Take Me If You Want Me	1968	2.00	4.00	8.00
❑ Acta 827	Anyway You Want Me/Master of My Fate	1968	2.00	4.00	8.00
❑ Acta 830	Private Zoo/Keep the Faith	1968	2.00	4.00	8.00
❑ Acta 833	Hunky Funky/Enter Her Majesty	1969	2.00	4.00	8.00
❑ Acta 836	Room at the Top/Walls	1969	2.00	4.00	8.00
❑ Acta 837	Cool It/The Brain	1969	2.00	4.00	8.00
❑ Paramount 0040	Can't Make It Without You/When I'm With You	1970	—	3.00	6.00
❑ Paramount 100	Bend Me, Shape Me/Step Out of Your Mind	197?	—	3.00	6.00
Albums					
❑ Acta 8002 [M]	The American Breed	1967	5.00	10.00	20.00
❑ Acta 8003 [M]	Bend Me, Shape Me	1968	5.00	10.00	20.00
❑ Acta 8006 [M]	Pumpkin, Powder, Scarlet & Green	1968	12.50	25.00	50.00
—Stock label; the cover is the same as stereo but with a "Monaural" sticker attached					
❑ Acta 8008 [M]	Lonely Side of the City	1969	12.50	25.00	50.00
—In stereo cover with "Monaural" sticker; record is regular yellow label					
❑ Acta 38002 [S]	The American Breed	1967	6.25	12.50	25.00
❑ Acta 38003 [S]	Bend Me, Shape Me	1968	6.25	12.50	25.00
❑ Acta 38006 [S]	Pumpkin, Powder, Scarlet & Green	1968	5.00	10.00	20.00
❑ Acta 38008 [S]	Lonely Side of the City	1969	5.00	10.00	20.00

ANGELS, THE (1)

At least two other groups used this name, on the Cameo, Gee, Grand and Tawny labels; those are outside the scope of this publication.

Number	Title (A Side/B Side)	Yr	VG	VG+	NM
45s					
❑ Ascot 2139	Irresistible/Cotton Fields	1963	3.00	6.00	12.00
❑ Caprice 107	'Til/A Moment Ago	1961	7.50	15.00	30.00
—With horizontal "Caprice" logo; B-side listed as "A Moment Ago" but plays "Cotton Fields"					
❑ Caprice 107	'Til/A Moment Ago	1961	5.00	10.00	20.00
—With semicircular "Caprice" logo					
❑ Caprice 112	Cry Baby Cry/That's All I Ask of You	1962	5.00	10.00	20.00
❑ Caprice 116	Everybody Loves a Lover/Blow Joe	1962	3.75	7.50	15.00
❑ Caprice 118	You Should Have Told Me/I'd Be Good for You	1962	3.75	7.50	15.00
❑ Caprice 121	Cotton Fields/A Moment Ago	1963	3.75	7.50	15.00
❑ Polydor 14222	You're All I Need to Get By/Poppa's Side of the Bed	1974	—	2.50	5.00
❑ RCA Victor 47-9129	I Had a Dream I Lost You/What to Do	1967	2.50	5.00	10.00
❑ RCA Victor 47-9246	Go Out and Play/You'll Never Get to Heaven (If You Break My Heart)	1967	2.50	5.00	10.00
❑ RCA Victor 47-9404	You're the Cause of It/With Love	1967	2.50	5.00	10.00
❑ RCA Victor 47-9541	The Medley: Moments to Remember-Theme from A Summer Place-One Summer Night/If I Didn't Love You	1968	2.50	5.00	10.00
❑ RCA Victor 47-9612	But for Love/The Man with the Green Eyes	1968	2.50	5.00	10.00
❑ RCA Victor 47-9681	Merry Go Round/So Nice (Samba De Verao)	1968	2.50	5.00	10.00

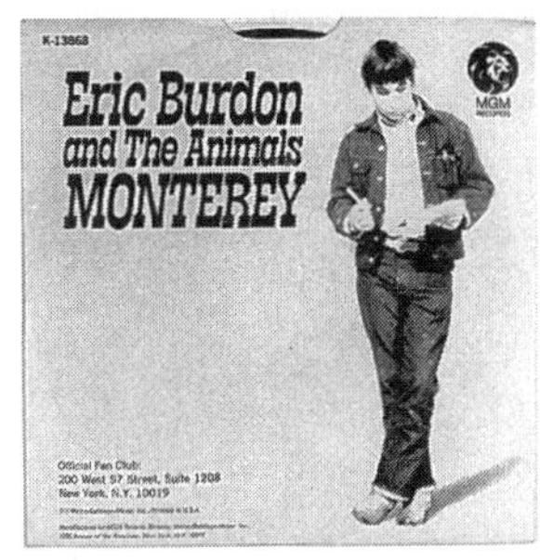

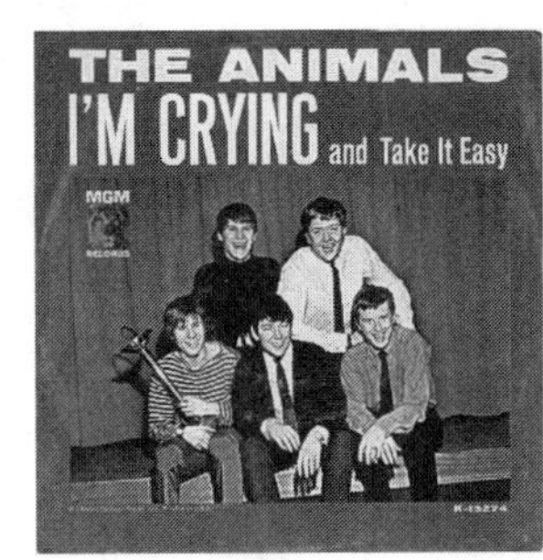

Number	Title (A Side/B Side)	Yr	VG	VG+	NM
❑ Smash 1834	My Boyfriend's Back/(Love Me) Now	1963	4.00	8.00	16.00
❑ Smash 1854	I Adore Him/Thank You and Goodnight	1963	3.75	7.50	15.00
❑ Smash 1870	Wow Wow Wee (He's the Boy for Me)/Snowflakes and Teardrops	1964	3.75	7.50	15.00
❑ Smash 1885	Little Beatle Boy/Java	1964	5.00	10.00	20.00
❑ Smash 1915	Jamaica Joe/Dream Boy	1964	3.75	7.50	15.00
❑ Smash 1931	World Without Love/The Boy from Crosstown	1964	3.75	7.50	15.00
Albums					
❑ Ascot AM 13009 [M]	The Angels Sing — Twelve of Their Greatest Hits	1964	6.25	12.50	25.00
❑ Ascot ALS 16009 [S]	The Angels Sing — Twelve of Their Greatest Hits	1964	7.50	15.00	30.00
❑ Caprice LP 1001 [M]	...And the Angels Sing	1962	30.00	60.00	120.00
❑ Caprice SLP 1001 [S]	...And the Angels Sing	1962	50.00	100.00	200.00
❑ Collectables COL-5085	My Boyfriend's Back: Golden Classics	198?	2.50	5.00	10.00
❑ Smash MGS-27039 [M]	My Boyfriend's Back	1963	10.00	20.00	40.00
❑ Smash MGS-27048 [M]	A Halo to You	1964	10.00	20.00	40.00
❑ Smash SRS-67039 [S]	My Boyfriend's Back	1963	15.00	30.00	60.00
❑ Smash SRS-67048 [S]	A Halo to You	1964	15.00	30.00	60.00
ANIMALS, THE					
45s					
❑ Abkco 4025	House of the Rising Sun/Bring It On Home to Me	1973	2.00	4.00	8.00
—Contains the full-length version of A-side					
❑ Abkco 4026	We Gotta Get Out of This Place/It's My Life	1973	—	2.00	4.00
❑ Abkco 4037	Don't Let Me Be Misunderstood/Talkin' About You	1973	—	2.00	4.00
❑ Abkco 4038	I'm Cryin'/Boom Boom	1973	—	2.00	4.00
❑ I.R.S. 9920	The Night/No John No	1983	—	2.50	5.00
❑ I.R.S. 9923	Love Is For All Time/It's Too Late	1983	—	2.50	5.00
❑ Jet XW-1070	Fire on the Sun/Riverside County	1977	—	3.00	6.00
❑ MGM CS-11-5	Celebrity Scene: The Animals	1967	20.00	40.00	80.00
—Box set of five singles (13791-13795). Price includes box, all 5 singles, jukebox title strips, bio. Records are sometimes found by themselves, so they are also listed separately.					
❑ MGM KGC 178	Gonna Take You Back to Walker/Baby Let Me Take You Home	196?	2.00	4.00	8.00
—Reissue label					
❑ MGM KGC 179	The House of the Rising Sun/I'm Crying	196?	2.50	5.00	10.00
—Reissue label; A-side, despite being labeled 2:58, actually plays 4:29					
❑ MGM KGC 180	Don't Let Me Be Misunderstood/Boom Boom	196?	2.00	4.00	8.00
—Reissue label					
❑ MGM KGC 181	We Gotta Get Out of This Place/Don't Bring Me Down	196?	2.00	4.00	8.00
—Reissue label					
❑ MGM KGC 182	It's My Life/Inside Looking Out	196?	2.00	4.00	8.00
—Reissue label					
❑ MGM 13242	Gonna Send You Back to Walker (Gonna Send You Back to Georgia)/Baby, Let Me Take You Home	1964	3.75	7.50	15.00
❑ MGM 13264	The House of the Rising Sun/Talkin' About You	1964	3.75	7.50	15.00
❑ MGM 13274	I'm Crying/Take It Easy Baby	1964	3.75	7.50	15.00
❑ MGM 13298	Boom Boom/Blue Feeling	1964	3.75	7.50	15.00
❑ MGM 13311	Don't Let Me Be Misunderstood/Club A-Go-Go	1964	3.75	7.50	15.00
❑ MGM 13339	Bring It On Home to Me/For Miss Caulker	1965	3.00	6.00	12.00
❑ MGM 13382	We Gotta Get Out of This Place/I Can't Believe It	1965	3.00	6.00	12.00
❑ MGM 13414	It's My Life/I'm Going to Change the World	1965	3.00	6.00	12.00
❑ MGM 13468	Inside-Looking Out/You're On My Mind	1966	3.00	6.00	12.00
❑ MGM 13514	Don't Bring Me Down/Cheating	1966	3.00	6.00	12.00
❑ MGM 13582	See See Rider/She'll Return It	1966	2.50	5.00	10.00
—Starting here, records are by "Eric Burdon and the Animals"					
❑ MGM 13636	Help Me Girl/That Ain't Where It's At	1966	2.50	5.00	10.00
❑ MGM 13721	When I Was Young/A Girl Called Sandoz	1967	2.50	5.00	10.00
❑ MGM 13769	San Franciscan Nights/Good Times	1967	2.50	5.00	10.00
❑ MGM 13791	Don't Bring Me Down/When I Was Young	1967	3.00	6.00	12.00
❑ MGM 13792	See See Rider/Hey Gyp	1967	3.00	6.00	12.00
❑ MGM 13793	Inside-Looking Out/Help Me Girl	1967	3.00	6.00	12.00
❑ MGM 13794	San Franciscan Nights/Good Times	1967	3.00	6.00	12.00
❑ MGM 13795	It's All Meat/The Other Side of This Life	1967	3.00	6.00	12.00
❑ MGM 13868	Monterey/Ain't That So	1967	2.50	5.00	10.00
❑ MGM 13917	Anything/It's All Meat	1968	2.50	5.00	10.00
❑ MGM 13939	Sky Pilot (Part 1)/Sky Pilot (Part 2)	1968	2.00	4.00	8.00
—Second pressings have blue and gold labels					
❑ MGM 13939	Sky Pilot (Part 1)/Sky Pilot (Part 2)	1968	2.50	5.00	10.00
—First pressings have black labels					

Number	Title (A Side/B Side)	Yr	VG	VG+	NM
❑ MGM 14013	River Deep, Mountain High/White Houses	1968	2.00	4.00	8.00
Albums					
❑ Abkco AB-4226 [(2)]	The Best of the Animals	1973	3.00	6.00	12.00
❑ Abkco AB-4324 [M]	The Best of the Animals	1987	2.50	5.00	10.00
—With alternate version of "We Gotta Get Out of This Place"					
❑ Accord SN-7193	Looking Back	1981	2.00	4.00	8.00
❑ Accord SN-7235	The Animals with Eric Burdon	1982	2.00	4.00	8.00
❑ I.R.S. SP 70037	The Ark	1983	2.50	5.00	10.00
❑ I.R.S. SP 70043	Rip It to Shreds: Their Greatest Hits Live	1984	2.50	5.00	10.00
❑ Jet/UA JT-LA790-H	Before We Were So Rudely Interrupted	1977	2.50	5.00	10.00
—As "The Original Animals"					
❑ MGM E-4264 [M]	The Animals	1964	25.00	50.00	100.00
—Yellow label promo					
❑ MGM E-4264 [M]	The Animals	1964	7.50	15.00	30.00
—"The House of the Rising Sun" is the edited 45 version					
❑ MGM SE-4264 [R]	The Animals	1964	6.25	12.50	25.00
—"The House of the Rising Sun" is the edited 45 version (rechanneled, like the rest of the LP)					
❑ MGM E-4281 [M]	The Animals On Tour	1965	25.00	50.00	100.00
—Yellow label promo					
❑ MGM E-4281 [M]	The Animals On Tour	1965	7.50	15.00	30.00
❑ MGM SE-4281 [R]	The Animals On Tour	1965	6.25	12.50	25.00
❑ MGM E-4305 [M]	Animal Tracks	1965	10.00	20.00	40.00
❑ MGM E-4305 [M]	Animal Tracks	1965	37.50	75.00	150.00
—Yellow label promo					
❑ MGM SE-4305 [R]	Animal Tracks	1965	7.50	15.00	30.00
❑ MGM E-4324 [M]	The Best of the Animals	1966	5.00	10.00	20.00
—This album was the first to contain the full-length version of "House of the Rising Sun."					
❑ MGM E-4324 [M]	The Best of the Animals	1966	20.00	40.00	80.00
—Yellow label promo					
❑ MGM SE-4324 [R]	The Best of the Animals	1966	6.25	12.50	25.00
❑ MGM E-4384 [M]	Animalization	1966	25.00	50.00	100.00
—Yellow label promo					
❑ MGM E-4384 [M]	Animalization	1966	6.25	12.50	25.00
❑ MGM SE-4384 [P]	Animalization	1966	7.50	15.00	30.00
—All stereo except "Inside Looking Out," which is rechanneled.					
❑ MGM E-4414 [M]	Animalism	1966	25.00	50.00	100.00
—Yellow label promo					
❑ MGM E-4414 [M]	Animalism	1966	6.25	12.50	25.00
❑ MGM SE-4414 [S]	Animalism	1966	7.50	15.00	30.00
❑ MGM E-4433 [M]	Eric Is Here	1967	3.75	7.50	15.00
❑ MGM SE-4433 [S]	Eric Is Here	1967	5.00	10.00	20.00
❑ MGM E-4454 [M]	The Best of Eric Burdon and the Animals, Vol. 2	1967	5.00	10.00	20.00
❑ MGM SE-4454 [P]	The Best of Eric Burdon and the Animals, Vol. 2	1967	5.00	10.00	20.00
❑ MGM E-4484 [M]	Winds of Change	1967	5.00	10.00	20.00
❑ MGM SE-4484 [S]	Winds of Change	1967	6.25	12.50	25.00
❑ MGM E-4537 [M]	The Twain Shall Meet	1968	5.00	10.00	20.00
❑ MGM SE-4537 [S]	The Twain Shall Meet	1968	6.25	12.50	25.00
❑ MGM SE-4553 [S]	Every One of Us	1968	6.25	12.50	25.00
❑ MGM SE-4591 [(2)]	Love Is	1968	12.50	25.00	50.00
❑ MGM SE-4602	Greatest Hits of Eric Burdon and the Animals	1969	3.75	7.50	15.00
❑ Pickwick SPC-3330	The Early Animals with Eric Burdon	1971	2.00	4.00	8.00
❑ Polydor 829091-1 [M]	Animalization	1986	2.00	4.00	8.00
❑ Scepter Citation CTN-18026	The Best of the Animals	1972	2.00	4.00	8.00
❑ Springboard SPB-4025	The Best of the Animals	1972	2.00	4.00	8.00
❑ Springboard SPB-4065	The Night Time Is the Right Time	1973	2.00	4.00	8.00
❑ Wand WDS-690	In the Beginning	1970	2.50	5.00	10.00

ANKA, PAUL

45s

Number	Title (A Side/B Side)	Yr	VG	VG+	NM
❑ ABC-Paramount 9831	Diana/Don't Gamble with Love	1957	5.00	10.00	20.00
❑ ABC-Paramount 9855	I Love You, Baby/Tell Me That You Love Me	1957	7.50	15.00	30.00
❑ ABC-Paramount 9880	You Are My Destiny/When I Stop Loving You	1958	5.00	10.00	20.00
❑ ABC-Paramount 9907	Crazy Love/Let the Bells Keep Ringing	1958	5.00	10.00	20.00
❑ ABC-Paramount 9937	Midnight/Verboten!	1958	5.00	10.00	20.00
❑ ABC-Paramount 9956	Just Young/So It's Goodbye	1958	5.00	10.00	20.00
❑ ABC-Paramount 9987 [M]	(All of a Sudden) My Heart Sings/That's Love	1958	5.00	10.00	20.00
❑ ABC-Paramount S-9987 [S]	(All of a Sudden) My Heart Sings/That's Love	1958	12.50	25.00	50.00
❑ ABC-Paramount 10011 [M]	I Miss You So/Late Last Night	1959	3.75	7.50	15.00
❑ ABC-Paramount S-10011 [S]	I Miss You So/Late Last Night	1959	12.50	25.00	50.00
❑ ABC-Paramount 10022 [M]	Lonely Boy/Your Love	1959	3.75	7.50	15.00
❑ ABC-Paramount S-10022 [S]	Lonely Boy/Your Love	1959	12.50	25.00	50.00
❑ ABC-Paramount 10040 [M]	Put Your Head on My Shoulder/Don't Ever Leave Me	1959	3.75	7.50	15.00
❑ ABC-Paramount S-10040 [S]	Put Your Head on My Shoulder/Don't Ever Leave Me	1959	12.50	25.00	50.00
❑ ABC-Paramount 10064 [M]	It's Time to Cry/Something Has Changed Me	1959	3.75	7.50	15.00
❑ ABC-Paramount S-10064 [S]	It's Time to Cry/Something Has Changed Me	1959	12.50	25.00	50.00
❑ ABC-Paramount 10082 [M]	Puppy Love/Adam and Eve	1960	3.75	7.50	15.00
❑ ABC-Paramount S-10082 [S]	Puppy Love/Adam and Eve	1960	12.50	25.00	50.00
❑ ABC-Paramount 10106 [M]	My Home Town/Something Happened	1960	3.75	7.50	15.00
❑ ABC-Paramount S-10106 [S]	My Home Town/Something Happened	1960	12.50	25.00	50.00
❑ ABC-Paramount 10132 [M]	Hello Young Lovers/I Love You in the Same Old Way	1960	3.75	7.50	15.00
❑ ABC-Paramount S-10132 [S]	Hello Young Lovers/I Love You in the Same Old Way	1960	12.50	25.00	50.00
❑ ABC-Paramount 10147 [M]	Summer's Gone/I'd Have to Share	1960	3.75	7.50	15.00
❑ ABC-Paramount S-10147 [S]	Summer's Gone/I'd Have to Share	1960	12.50	25.00	50.00
❑ ABC-Paramount 10163	Rudolph, the Red-Nosed Reindeer/I Saw Mommy Kissing Santa Claus	1960	6.25	12.50	25.00
❑ ABC-Paramount 10168 [M]	The Story of My Love/Don't Say You're Sorry	1960	3.75	7.50	15.00
❑ ABC-Paramount S-10168 [S]	The Story of My Love/Don't Say You're Sorry	1960	12.50	25.00	50.00

Number	Title (A Side/B Side)	Yr	VG	VG+	NM
❑ ABC-Paramount 10169	It's Christmas Everywhere/Rudolph, the Red-Nosed Reindeer	1960	4.00	8.00	16.00
❑ ABC-Paramount 10194	Tonight My Love, Tonight/I'm Just a Fool Anyway	1961	3.00	6.00	12.00
❑ ABC-Paramount 10220	Dance On Little Girl/I Talk to You	1961	3.00	6.00	12.00
❑ ABC-Paramount 10239	Kissin' on the Phone/Cinderella	1961	3.00	6.00	12.00
❑ ABC-Paramount 10279	Loveland/The Bells at My Wedding	1961	3.00	6.00	12.00
❑ ABC-Paramount 10282	The Fools Hall of Fame/Far from the Lights of Town	1961	3.00	6.00	12.00
❑ ABC-Paramount 10311	I'd Never Find Another You/Uh Huh	1962	2.50	5.00	10.00
❑ ABC-Paramount 10338	I'm Coming Home/Cry	1962	2.50	5.00	10.00
❑ Barnaby 2027	You're Some Kind of Friend/Why Are You Leaning on Me, Sir	1971	—	3.00	6.00
❑ Buddah 252	Do I Love You/So Long City	1971	—	2.50	5.00
❑ Buddah 294	Everything's Been Changed/Jubilation	1972	—	2.50	5.00
❑ Buddah 314	Something Good Is Coming/Life Song	1972	—	2.50	5.00
❑ Buddah 337	While We'e Still Young/This Is Your Song	1973	—	2.50	5.00
❑ Buddah 349	Hey Girl/You and Me Today	1973	—	2.50	5.00
❑ Columbia 03897	Hold Me 'Til the Mornin' Comes/This Is the First Time	1983	—	—	3.00
❑ Columbia 04187	Gimme the Word/No Way Out	1983	—	—	3.00
—A-side: With Karla DeVito					
❑ Columbia 04407	Second Chance/Walk a Fine Line	1984	—	—	3.00
❑ Columbia 07358	No Way Out/Just for Once	1987	—	—	3.00
—A-side: Paul Anka and Julia Migenas; B-side: Migenas solo					
❑ Epic 50298	You/Make It Up to Me in Love	1976	—	2.00	4.00
—With Odia Coates					
❑ Eric 197	It's Time to Cry/Crazy Love	197?	—	2.00	4.00
❑ Eric 198	(All of a Sudden) My Heart Sings/My Home Town	197?	—	2.00	4.00
❑ Eric 199	You Are My Destiny/Let the Bells Keep Ringing	197?	—	2.00	4.00
❑ Eric 200	Diana/Don't Gamble with Love	197?	—	2.00	4.00
❑ Eric 201	Lonely Boy/I Miss You So	197?	—	2.00	4.00
❑ Eric 202	Puppy Love/Adam & Eve	197?	—	2.00	4.00
❑ Eric 203	Put Your Head on My Shoulder/Summer's Gone	197?	—	2.00	4.00
❑ Eric 204	Tonight My Love, Tonight/Dance On Little Girl	197?	—	2.00	4.00
❑ Fame XW-345	Flashback/Let Me Get to Know You	1973	—	2.00	4.00
❑ RCA PB-11351	Lovely Lady/Brought Up in New York	1978	—	2.00	4.00
❑ RCA PB-11395	This Is Love/I'm By Myself Again	1978	—	2.00	4.00
❑ RCA PB-11662	As Long As We Keep Believing/Headlines	1979	—	2.00	4.00
❑ RCA PB-11957	Rainbow/After All	1980	—	—	—
—Unreleased					
❑ RCA PB-12184	We Love Each Other/Think I'm in Love Again	1981	—	—	3.00
❑ RCA PB-12225	I've Been Waiting for You All My Life/Think I'm in Love Again	1981	—	—	3.00
❑ RCA PB-12262	Lady Lay Down/You're Still a Part of Me	1981	—	—	3.00
❑ RCA Victor 37-7977	Love Me Warm and Tender/I'd Like to Know	1962	6.25	12.50	25.00
—"Compact Single 33" (small hole, plays at LP speed)					
❑ RCA Victor 47-7977	Love Me Warm and Tender/I'd Like to Know	1962	2.50	5.00	10.00
❑ RCA Victor 47-8030	A Steel Guitar and a Glass of Wine/I Never Knew Your Name	1962	2.50	5.00	10.00
❑ RCA Victor 47-8068	Every Night (Without You)/There You Go	1962	2.50	5.00	10.00
❑ RCA Victor 47-8097	Eso Beso (That Kiss!)/Give Me Back My Heart	1962	2.50	5.00	10.00
❑ RCA Victor 47-8115	Love (Makes the World Go 'Round)/Crying in the Wind	1962	2.50	5.00	10.00
❑ RCA Victor 47-8158	Think About It/At Night	1963	—	—	—
—Unreleased					
❑ RCA Victor 47-8170	Remember Diana/At Night	1963	2.50	5.00	10.00
❑ RCA Victor 47-8195	Hello Jim/You've Got the Nerve to Call This Love	1963	2.50	5.00	10.00
❑ RCA Victor 47-8237	Wondrous Are the Ways of Love/Hurry Up and Tell Me	1963	2.50	5.00	10.00
❑ RCA Victor 47-8272	Did You Have a Happy Birthday/For No Good Reason at All	1963	2.50	5.00	10.00
❑ RCA Victor 47-8311	From Rocking Horse to Rocking Chair/Cheer Up	1964	2.00	4.00	8.00
❑ RCA Victor 47-8349	My Baby's Comin' Home/No, No	1964	2.00	4.00	8.00
❑ RCA Victor 47-8396	In My Imagination/It's Easy to Say	1964	2.00	4.00	8.00
❑ RCA Victor 47-8441	Cindy Go Home/Ogni Volta	1964	2.00	4.00	8.00
❑ RCA Victor 47-8493	Sylvia/Behind My Smile	1965	2.00	4.00	8.00
❑ RCA Victor 47-8595	The Loneliest Boy in the World/Dream Me Happy	1965	2.00	4.00	8.00
❑ RCA Victor 47-8662	Every Day a Heart Is Broken/As If There Were No Tomorrow	1965	2.00	4.00	8.00
❑ RCA Victor 47-8764	Truly Yours/Oh, Such a Stranger	1965	2.00	4.00	8.00
❑ RCA Victor 47-8839	I Wish/I Went to Your Wedding	1966	2.00	4.00	8.00
❑ RCA Victor 47-8893	I Can't Help Loving You/Can't Get Along Very Well Without Her	1966	2.00	4.00	8.00
❑ RCA Victor 47-9032	Poor Old World/I'd Rather Be a Stranger	1966	2.00	4.00	8.00
❑ RCA Victor 47-9128	Until It's Time for You to Go/Would You Still Be My Baby	1967	2.00	4.00	8.00
❑ RCA Victor 47-9228	A Woman Is a Sentimental Thing/That's How Love Goes	1967	2.00	4.00	8.00
❑ RCA Victor 47-9457	Can't Get You Out of My Mind/When We Get There	1968	2.00	4.00	8.00
❑ RCA Victor 47-9648	Goodnight My Love/This Crazy World	1968	2.00	4.00	8.00

Number	Title (A Side/B Side)	Yr	VG	VG+	NM
❑ RCA Victor 47-9767	Happy/Can't Get You Out of My Mind	1969	2.00	4.00	8.00
❑ RCA Victor 47-9846	Midnight Mistress/Before It's Too Late-This Land Is Your Land	1970	2.00	4.00	8.00
❑ RCA Victor 74-0126	In the Still of the Night/Pickin' Up the Pieces	1969	2.00	4.00	8.00
❑ RCA Victor 74-0164	Sincerely/Next Year	1969	2.00	4.00	8.00
❑ RPM 472	I Confess/Blau-Wile Deveest Fontaine	1956	20.00	40.00	80.00
❑ RPM 499	I Confess/Blau-Wile Deveest Fontaine	1957	7.50	15.00	30.00
❑ United Artists XW-454	(You're) Having My Baby/Papa	1974	—	2.00	4.00
❑ United Artists XW-569	One Man Woman/One Woman Man//Let Me Get to Know You	1974	—	2.00	4.00
—A-side: With Odia Coates					
❑ United Artists XW-615	I Don't Like to Sleep Alone/How Can Anything Be Beautiful After You	1975	—	2.00	4.00
❑ United Artists XW-685	(I Believe) There's Nothing Stronger Than Our Love/ Today I Became a Fool	1975	—	2.00	4.00
❑ United Artists XW-737	Times of Your Life/Water Runs Deep	1975	—	2.00	4.00
❑ United Artists XW-789	Anytime (I'll Be There)/Something About You	1976	—	2.00	4.00
❑ United Artists XW-911	Happier/Closing Doors	1976	—	2.00	4.00
❑ United Artists XW-945	I'll Help You/Never Gonna Fall in Love Like I Fell in Love with You	1977	—	2.00	4.00
❑ United Artists XW-972	My Best Friend's Wife/Never Gonna Fall in Love Like I Fell in Love with You	1977	—	2.00	4.00
❑ United Artists XW-1018	Tonight/Everybody Ought to Be in Love	1977	—	2.00	4.00
❑ United Artists XW-1157	(You're) Having My Baby//One Man Woman/One Woman Man	1978	—	—	3.00
—Reissue					
❑ United Artists XW-1158	I Don't Like to Sleep Alone/Times of Your Life	1978	—	—	3.00
—Reissue					
Albums					
❑ ABC-Paramount 240 [M]	Paul Anka	1958	12.50	25.00	50.00
❑ ABC-Paramount 296 [M]	My Heart Sings	1959	7.50	15.00	30.00
❑ ABC-Paramount S-296 [S]	My Heart Sings	1959	12.50	25.00	50.00
❑ ABC-Paramount 323 [M]	Paul Anka Sings His Big 15	1960	12.50	25.00	50.00
❑ ABC-Paramount S-323 [R]	Paul Anka Sings His Big 15	196?	7.50	15.00	30.00
❑ ABC-Paramount 347 [M]	Paul Anka Swings for Young Lovers	1960	7.50	15.00	30.00
❑ ABC-Paramount S-347 [S]	Paul Anka Swings for Young Lovers	1960	10.00	20.00	40.00
❑ ABC-Paramount 353 [M]	Anka at the Copa	1960	7.50	15.00	30.00
❑ ABC-Paramount S-353 [S]	Anka at the Copa	1960	10.00	20.00	40.00
❑ ABC-Paramount ABC 360 [M]	It's Christmas Everywhere	1960	7.50	15.00	30.00
❑ ABC-Paramount ABCS 360 [S]	It's Christmas Everywhere	1960	10.00	20.00	40.00
❑ ABC-Paramount 371 [M]	Strictly Instrumental	1961	7.00	15.00	30.00
❑ ABC-Paramount S-371 [S]	Strictly Instrumental	1961	10.00	20.00	40.00
❑ ABC-Paramount 390 [M]	Paul Anka Sings His Big 15, Vol. 2	1961	7.50	15.00	30.00
❑ ABC-Paramount S-390 [S]	Paul Anka Sings His Big 15, Vol. 2	1961	10.00	20.00	40.00
❑ ABC-Paramount 409 [M]	Paul Anka Sings His Big, Big 15, Volume III	1962	6.25	12.50	25.00
❑ ABC-Paramount S-409 [S]	Paul Anka Sings His Big, Big 15, Volume III	1962	7.50	15.00	30.00
❑ ABC-Paramount 420 [M]	Diana	1962	6.25	12.50	25.00
❑ ABC-Paramount S-420 [S]	Diana	1962	7.50	15.00	30.00
❑ Accord SN-7117	She's a Lady	1981	2.00	4.00	8.00
❑ Buddah BDS 5093	Paul Anka	1971	3.00	6.00	12.00
❑ Buddah BDS 5114	Jubilation	1972	3.00	6.00	12.00
❑ Buddah BDS 5622 [(2)]	This Is Anka	1974	3.75	7.50	15.00
❑ Buddah BDS 5667 [(2)]	The Essential Paul Anka	1974	3.75	7.50	15.00
❑ Columbia FC 38442	Walk a Fine Line	1983	2.00	4.00	8.00
❑ Columbia FC 39323	Paul Anka Live	1984	2.00	4.00	8.00
❑ Liberty LN-10000	Paul Anka: His Best	1980	2.00	4.00	8.00
—Budget-line reissue					
❑ Liberty LN-10001	The Times of Your Life	1980	2.00	4.00	8.00
—Budget-line reissue					
❑ Liberty LN-10149	Feelings	1982	2.00	4.00	8.00
—Budget-line reissue					
❑ Liberty LN-10220	The Painter	1983	2.00	4.00	8.00
—Budget-line reissue					
❑ Pair PDL2-1129 [(2)]	Songs I Write and Sing	1986	3.00	6.00	12.00
❑ Pickwick PTP-2087 [(2)]	Paul Anka Way	197?	2.50	5.00	10.00
❑ Pickwick SPC-3508	Puppy Love	1975	2.00	4.00	8.00
❑ Pickwick SPC-3523	She's a Lady	1975	2.00	4.00	8.00
❑ Ranwood 8203	The Very Best of Paul Anka	1981	2.00	4.00	8.00
❑ RCA Camden ACL1-0616	My Way	1974	2.00	4.00	8.00
❑ RCA Victor ANL1-0896	Remember Diana	1975	2.50	5.00	10.00
❑ RCA Victor ANL1-1054	She's a Lady	1975	2.50	5.00	10.00
❑ RCA Victor ANL1-1584	Paul Anka Sings His Favorites	1976	2.50	5.00	10.00
❑ RCA Victor ANL1-2482	Songs I Wish I'd Written	1977	2.50	5.00	10.00
❑ RCA Victor LPM-2502 [M]	Young, Alive and In Love!	1962	6.25	12.50	25.00
—With portrait of Paul Anka on front cover					
❑ RCA Victor LPM-2502 [M]	Young, Alive and In Love!	1962	3.75	7.50	15.00
—With portrait of Paul Anka on back cover					
❑ RCA Victor LSP-2502 [S]	Young, Alive and In Love!	1962	5.00	10.00	20.00
—With portrait of Paul Anka on back cover					
❑ RCA Victor LSP-2502 [S]	Young, Alive and In Love!	1962	7.50	15.00	30.00
—With portrait of Paul Anka on front cover					
❑ RCA Victor LPM-2575 [M]	Let's Sit This One Out	1962	5.00	10.00	20.00
❑ RCA Victor LSP-2575 [S]	Let's Sit This One Out	1962	6.25	12.50	25.00
❑ RCA Victor LPM-2614 [M]	Our Man Around the World	1963	5.00	10.00	20.00
❑ RCA Victor LSP-2614 [S]	Our Man Around the World	1963	6.25	12.50	25.00
❑ RCA Victor LPM-2691 [M]	Paul Anka's 21 Golden Hits	1963	5.00	10.00	20.00
❑ RCA Victor LSP-2691 [S]	Paul Anka's 21 Golden Hits	1963	6.25	12.50	25.00
—LPM/LSP-2691 has re-recorded versions of ABC-Paramount hits					
❑ RCA Victor LPM-2744 [M]	Songs I Wish I'd Written	1963	3.75	7.50	15.00

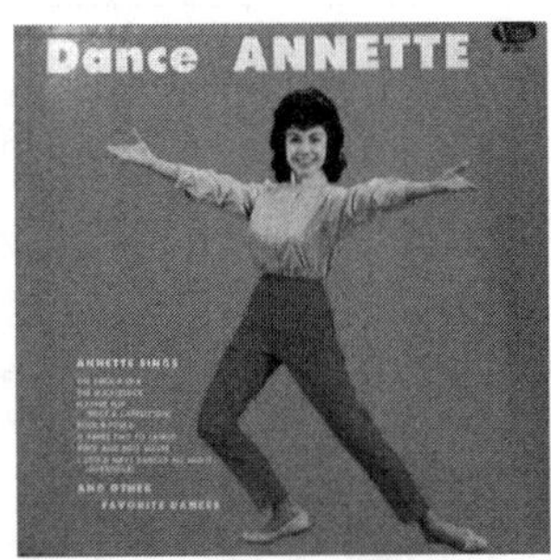

Number	Title (A Side/B Side)	Yr	VG	VG+	NM
❑ RCA Victor LSP-2744 [S]	Songs I Wish I'd Written	1963	5.00	10.00	20.00
❑ RCA Victor AFL1-2892	Listen to Your Heart	1978	2.50	5.00	10.00
❑ RCA Victor LPM-2996 [M]	Excitement on Park Avenue	1964	3.75	7.50	15.00
❑ RCA Victor LSP-2996 [S]	Excitement on Park Avenue	1964	5.00	10.00	20.00
❑ RCA Victor AFL1-3382	Headlines	1979	2.50	5.00	10.00
❑ RCA Victor LPM-3580 [M]	Strictly Nashville	1966	3.75	7.50	15.00
❑ RCA Victor LSP-3580 [S]	Strictly Nashville	1966	5.00	10.00	20.00
❑ RCA Victor AYL1-3808	Paul Anka's 21 Golden Hits	1980	2.00	4.00	8.00
—"Best Buy Series" reissue					
❑ RCA Victor LPM-3875 [M]	Paul Anka Live	1967	3.75	7.50	15.00
❑ RCA Victor LSP-3875 [S]	Paul Anka Live	1967	5.00	10.00	20.00
❑ RCA Victor AFL1-3926	Both Sides of Love	1981	2.50	5.00	10.00
❑ RCA Victor LSP-4142	Goodnight My Love	1969	3.75	7.50	15.00
❑ RCA Victor LSP-4203	Sincerely	1969	3.75	7.50	15.00
❑ RCA Victor LSP-4250	Life Goes On	1969	3.75	7.50	15.00
❑ RCA Victor LSP-4300	Paul Anka 70s	1970	3.75	7.50	15.00
❑ Rhino RNLP-70220	The Best of Paul Anka (14 Original Hits, 1957-1961)	1986	2.50	5.00	10.00
❑ Riviera 0047 [M]	Paul Anka and Others	1959	37.50	75.00	150.00
—With Paul Anka's RPM recordings plus tracks by other artists					
❑ Sire SASH-3704 [(2)]	Paul Anka Gold	1974	3.75	7.50	15.00
❑ Sire SBK 6043 [(2)]	The Vintage Years 1957-1961	1978	3.00	6.00	12.00
❑ United Artists UA-LA314-G	Anka	1974	2.50	5.00	10.00
❑ United Artists UA-LA367-G	Feelings	1975	2.50	5.00	10.00
❑ United Artists UA-LA569-G	Times of Your Life	1975	2.50	5.00	10.00
❑ United Artists UA-LA653-G [Q]	The Painter	1976	3.00	6.00	12.00
—All copies are quadraphonic					
❑ United Artists UA-LA746-H	The Music Man	1977	2.50	5.00	10.00
❑ United Artists UA-LA922-H	Paul Anka: His Best	1978	2.50	5.00	10.00

ANKA, PAUL/GEORGE HAMILTON IV/JOHNNY NASH

45s

Number	Title (A Side/B Side)	Yr	VG	VG+	NM
❑ ABC-Paramount 9974	The Teen Commandments/If You Learn to Pray	1958	6.25	12.50	25.00

ANNETTE

45s

Number	Title (A Side/B Side)	Yr	VG	VG+	NM
❑ Buena Vista 336	Jo Jo the Dog Faced Boy/Love Me Forever	1959	3.75	7.50	15.00
❑ Buena Vista 336	Jo Jo the Dog Faced Boy/Lonely Guitar	1959	5.00	10.00	20.00
❑ Buena Vista 339	Wild Willie/Lonely Guitar	1959	3.75	7.50	15.00
❑ Buena Vista 344	Especially for You/My Heart Became of Age	1959	3.75	7.50	15.00
❑ Buena Vista 349	First Name Initial/My Heart Became of Age	1959	3.75	7.50	15.00
❑ Buena Vista 354	O Dio Mio/It Took Dreams	1960	3.75	7.50	15.00
❑ Buena Vista 359	Train of Love/Tell Me Who's the Girl	1960	3.75	7.50	15.00
❑ Buena Vista 362	Pineapple Princess/Luau Cha Cha Cha	1960	3.75	7.50	15.00
❑ Buena Vista 369	Talk to Me Baby/I Love You Baby	1960	3.75	7.50	15.00
❑ Buena Vista 374	Dream Boy/Please, Please Signore	1961	3.75	7.50	15.00
❑ Buena Vista 375	Indian Giver/Mama, Mama Rosa (Where's the Spumoni)	1961	3.75	7.50	15.00
❑ Buena Vista 384	Hawaiian Love Talk/Blue Muu Muu	1961	3.75	7.50	15.00
❑ Buena Vista 388	Dreamin' About You/Strummin' Song	1961	3.75	7.50	15.00
❑ Buena Vista 392	That Crazy Place From Outer Space/Seven Moons (Of Batalayre)	1962	3.75	7.50	15.00
—B-side by Danny Saval and Tom Tryon					
❑ Buena Vista 394	The Truth About Youth/I Can't Do the Sum	1962	3.75	7.50	15.00
❑ Buena Vista 400	My Little Grass Shack/Hukilau	1962	3.75	7.50	15.00
❑ Buena Vista 405	He's My Ideal/Mr. Piano Man	1962	3.75	7.50	15.00
❑ Buena Vista 407	Bella Bella Florence/Canzone d'Amoure	1962	3.75	7.50	15.00
—With Marcochi					
❑ Buena Vista 414	Teenage Wedding/Walkin' and Talkin'	1962	5.00	10.00	20.00
❑ Buena Vista 427	Treat Him Nicely/Promise Me Anything	1963	3.75	7.50	15.00
❑ Buena Vista 431	Merlin Jones/The Scrambled Egghead	1964	3.00	6.00	12.00
—With Tommy Kirk					
❑ Buena Vista 432	Custom City/Rebel Rider	1964	5.00	10.00	20.00
❑ Buena Vista 433	Muscle Beach Party/I Dream About Frankie	1964	3.75	7.50	15.00
❑ Buena Vista 436	Bikini Beach Party/The Clyde	1964	3.75	7.50	15.00
❑ Buena Vista 437	The Wah-Watusi/The Clyde	1964	3.00	6.00	12.00
❑ Buena Vista 438	Something Borrowed, Something Blue/How Will I Know My Love	1965	3.75	7.50	15.00
❑ Buena Vista 440	The Monkey's Uncle/How Will I Know My Love	1965	3.00	6.00	12.00
—With the Beach Boys backing up					
❑ Buena Vista 442	The Boy to Love/No One Else Could Be Prouder	1965	3.00	6.00	12.00

Number	Title (A Side/B Side)	Yr	VG	VG+	NM
❑ Buena Vista 450	No Way to Go But Up/Crystal Ball	1966	3.00	6.00	12.00
❑ Buena Vista 475	The Computer Wore Tennis Shoes/Merlin Jones	1970	2.00	4.00	8.00
❑ Disneyland 102	How Will I Know My Love/Don't Jump to Conclusions	1958	6.25	15.00	30.00
❑ Disneyland 114	That Crazy Place in Outer Space/Gold Doubloons and Pieces of Eight	1958	10.00	20.00	40.00
—B-side: "Theme from the Hardy Boys"					
❑ Disneyland 118	Tall Paul/Ma, He's Making Eyes at Me	1959	5.00	10.00	20.00
❑ Disneyland 786	That Crazy Place From Outer Space/Happy Glow	196?	2.50	5.00	10.00
—No artist credit on label, but A-side is the same recording as Disneyland 114					
❑ Epic 9829	Baby Needs Me Now/Moment of Silence	1965	6.25	12.50	25.00
—With Cecil Null					
❑ Starview 3001	The Promised Land/In Between and Out of Love	1983	2.50	5.00	10.00
❑ Tower 326	What's a Girl to Do/When You Get What You Want	1967	7.50	15.00	30.00
Albums					
❑ Buena Vista BV-3301 [M]	Annette	1959	30.00	60.00	120.00
❑ Buena Vista BV-3302 [M]	Annette Sings Anka	1960	25.00	50.00	100.00
❑ Buena Vista BV-3303 [M]	Hawaiiannette	1960	18.75	37.50	75.00
❑ Buena Vista BV-3304 [M]	Italiannette	1960	18.75	37.50	75.00
❑ Buena Vista BV-3305 [M]	Dance Annette	1961	18.75	37.50	75.00
❑ Buena Vista BV-3312 [M]	The Story of My Teens	1962	18.75	37.50	75.00
❑ Buena Vista BV-3313 [M]	Teen Street	1962	18.75	37.50	75.00
❑ Buena Vista BV-3314 [M]	Muscle Beach Party	1963	18.75	37.50	75.00
❑ Buena Vista STER-3314 [S]	Muscle Beach Party	1963	37.50	75.00	150.00
❑ Buena Vista BV-3316 [M]	Beach Party	1963	15.00	30.00	60.00
❑ Buena Vista STER-3316 [S]	Beach Party	1963	25.00	50.00	100.00
❑ Buena Vista BV-3320 [M]	Annette on Campus	1964	12.50	25.00	50.00
❑ Buena Vista STER-3320 [S]	Annette on Campus	1964	25.00	50.00	100.00
❑ Buena Vista BV-3324 [M]	Annette at Bikini Beach	1964	12.50	25.00	50.00
❑ Buena Vista STER-3324 [S]	Annette at Bikini Beach	1964	25.00	50.00	100.00
❑ Buena Vista BV-3325 [M]	Annette's Pajama Party	1964	10.00	20.00	40.00
❑ Buena Vista STER-3325 [S]	Annette's Pajama Party	1964	25.00	50.00	100.00
❑ Buena Vista BV-3327 [M]	Annette Sings Golden Surfin' Hits	1964	25.00	50.00	100.00
❑ Buena Vista STER-3327 [S]	Annette Sings Golden Surfin' Hits	1964	37.50	75.00	150.00
❑ Buena Vista BV-3328 [M]	Something Borrowed, Something Blue	1964	15.00	30.00	60.00
❑ Buena Vista STER-3328 [P]	Something Borrowed, Something Blue	1964	25.00	50.00	100.00
❑ Buena Vista BV-4037	Annette Funicello	1972	12.50	25.00	50.00
❑ Rhino RNDF-206	The Best of Annette	1984	3.00	6.00	12.00
ARCHIES, THE					
45s					
❑ Calendar 63-1006	Bang-Shang-a-Lang/Truck Driver	1968	2.00	4.00	8.00
❑ Calendar 63-1007	Feelin' So Good (S.K.O.O.B.Y.-D.O.O.)/Love Light	1968	2.00	4.00	8.00
❑ Calendar 63-1008	Sugar Sugar/Melody Hill	1969	2.50	5.00	10.00
❑ Kirshner 63-1009	Sunshine/Over and Over	1970	2.00	4.00	8.00
❑ Kirshner 63-5002	Jingle Jangle/Justine	1969	2.00	4.00	8.00
❑ Kirshner 63-5003	Who's Your Baby/Senorita Rita	1970	2.00	4.00	8.00
❑ Kirshner 63-5009	Everything's Alright/Together We Two	1970	2.00	4.00	8.00
❑ Kirshner 63-5011	Throw a Little Love My Way/This Is Love	1971	2.00	4.00	8.00
❑ Kirshner 63-5014	A Summer Prayer for Peace/Maybe I'm Wrong	1971	2.00	4.00	8.00
❑ Kirshner 63-5018	Love Is Living in You/Hold On to Lovin'	1972	2.00	4.00	8.00
❑ Kirshner 63-5021	Strangers in the Morning/Plum Crazy	1972	2.00	4.00	8.00
Albums					
❑ Accord SN-7149	Straight A's	1981	2.50	5.00	10.00
❑ Calendar KES-101	The Archies	1968	6.25	12.50	25.00
❑ Calendar KES-103	Everything's Archie	1969	6.25	12.50	25.00
❑ 51 West 16002	The Archies	1979	2.50	5.00	10.00
❑ Kirshner KES-105	Jingle Jangle	1969	6.25	12.50	25.00
❑ Kirshner KES-107	Sunshine	1970	6.25	12.50	25.00
❑ Kirshner KES-109	The Archies Greatest Hits	1970	6.25	12.50	25.00
❑ Kirshner KES-110	This Is Love	1971	7.50	15.00	30.00
ARGENT					
45s					
❑ Date 1659	Liar/Schoolgirl	1970	2.50	5.00	10.00
❑ Epic 10718	Rejoice/Sweet Mary	1971	—	3.00	6.00
❑ Epic 10746	Celebration/Kingdom	1971	—	3.00	6.00
❑ Epic 10852	Hold Your Head Up/Closer to Heaven	1972	2.00	4.00	8.00
❑ Epic 10919	Tragedy/He's a Dynamo	1972	—	2.50	5.00
❑ Epic 10972	God Gave Rock and Roll To You/Christmas for the Free	1973	—	2.50	5.00
❑ Epic 11019	It's Only Money, Part 2/Losing Hold	1973	—	2.50	5.00
❑ Epic 11137	Man for All Seasons/Music from the Spheres	1974	—	2.50	5.00
❑ Epic 50025	The Coming of Kohoutek/Thunder and Lightning	1974	—	2.50	5.00
Albums					
❑ Epic BN 26525	Argent	1970	5.00	10.00	20.00
—Yellow label					
❑ Epic E 30128	A Ring of Hands	1971	5.00	10.00	20.00
—Yellow label					
❑ Epic KE 31556	All Together Now	1972	5.00	10.00	20.00
—Yellow label					
❑ Epic KE 32195	In Deep	1973	6.25	12.50	25.00
—Yellow label					
❑ Epic PE 32573	Nexus	1974	5.00	10.00	20.00
—Orange label					
❑ Epic PEG 33079 [(2)]	Encore — Live in Concert	1975	5.00	10.00	20.00
—Orange labels					
❑ Epic PE 33422	Circus	1975	5.00	10.00	20.00
—Orange label					

Number	Title (A Side/B Side)	Yr	VG	VG+	NM
❑ Epic PE 33955	Anthology	1976	3.75	7.50	15.00
—Orange label					
❑ United Artists UA-LA560-G	Counterpoint	1975	3.00	6.00	12.00

ASSOCIATION, THE

45s

Number	Title (A Side/B Side)	Yr	VG	VG+	NM
❑ Columbia 45602	Indian Wells Woman/Darling Be Home Soon	1972	—	2.50	5.00
❑ Columbia 45654	Come the Fall/Kicking the Gong Around	1972	—	2.50	5.00
❑ Elektra 47094	Dreamer/You Turn the Light On	1980	—	2.00	4.00
❑ Elektra 47146	Small Town Lovers/Across the Persian Gulf	1981	—	2.00	4.00
❑ Jubilee 5505	Babe I'm Gonna Leave You/Baby Can't You Hear Me Call Your Name	1965	6.25	12.50	25.00
❑ Mums 6016	Names, Tags, Numbers & Labels/Rainbows Bent	1973	—	2.00	4.00
❑ RCA Victor PB-10217	One Sunday Morning/Life Is a Carnival	1975	—	2.00	4.00
❑ Valiant 730	Too Many Mornings/Forty Times	1965	3.75	7.50	15.00
❑ Valiant 741	Along Comes Mary/Your Own Love	1966	3.00	6.00	12.00
❑ Valiant 747	Cherish/Don't Blame It On Me	1966	3.00	6.00	12.00
❑ Valiant 755	Pandora's Golden Heebie Jeebies/Standing Still	1966	2.50	5.00	10.00
❑ Valiant 758	No Fair at All/Looking Glass	1967	2.50	5.00	10.00
❑ Warner Bros. 7040	Pandora's Golden Heebie Jeebies/Standing Still	1967	2.00	4.00	8.00
❑ Warner Bros. 7041	Windy/Sometime	1967	2.50	5.00	10.00
❑ Warner Bros. 7074	Never My Love/Requiem for the Masses	1967	2.50	5.00	10.00
—A picture sleeve is rumored to exist					
❑ Warner Bros. 7105	Along Comes Mary/Cherish	1968	2.00	4.00	8.00
—"Back to Back Hits" series on "W7" label					
❑ Warner Bros. 7119	Windy/Never My Love	1968	2.00	4.00	8.00
—"Back to Back Hits" series on "W7" label					
❑ Warner Bros. 7163	Everything That Touches You/We Love Us	1968	2.00	4.00	8.00
—Orange "WB" label					
❑ Warner Bros. 7195	Time for Livin'/Birthday Morning	1968	2.00	4.00	8.00
❑ Warner Bros. 7229	Six Man Band/Like Always	1968	2.00	4.00	8.00
❑ Warner Bros. 7267	Goodbye Columbus/The Time It Is Today	1969	2.00	4.00	8.00
❑ Warner Bros. 7277	Under Branches/Hear in Here	1969	2.00	4.00	8.00
❑ Warner Bros. 7305	Yes, I Will/I Am Up for Europe	1969	2.00	4.00	8.00
❑ Warner Bros. 7349	Are You Ready/Dubuque Blues	1969	2.00	4.00	8.00
❑ Warner Bros. 7372	Just About the Same/Look at Me, Look at You	1970	—	3.00	6.00
❑ Warner Bros. 7429	Along the Way/Traveler's Guide	1970	—	3.00	6.00
❑ Warner Bros. 7471	P.F. Sloan/Traveler's Guide	1971	—	3.00	6.00
❑ Warner Bros. 7515	Bring Yourself Home/It's Gotta Be Real	1971	—	3.00	6.00
❑ Warner Bros. 7524	That's Racin'/Makes Me Cry (Funny Kind of Song)	1971	—	3.00	6.00

7-

Number	Title (A Side/B Side)	Yr	VG	VG+	NM
❑ Warner Bros. S 1767	The Time It Is Today/Everything That Touches You/Along Comes Mary//Enter the Young/No Fair at All/Windy	1968	3.75	7.50	15.00
—Jukebox issue; small hole, plays at 33 1/3 rpm					
❑ Warner Bros. S 1767 [Picture Sleeve]	Greatest Hits	1968	3.75	7.50	15.00

Albums

Number	Title (A Side/B Side)	Yr	VG	VG+	NM
❑ Columbia KC 31348	Waterbeds in Trinidad	1972	2.50	5.00	10.00
❑ Hitbound/Realistic 51-3022	New Memories	1983	3.00	6.00	12.00
❑ Pair PDL2-1061 [(2)]	Songs That Made Them Famous	1986	3.00	6.00	12.00
❑ Valiant VLM-5002 [M]	And Then…Along Comes The Association	1966	5.00	10.00	20.00
❑ Valiant VLM-5004 [M]	Renaissance	1967	3.75	7.50	15.00
—With blurb for "No Fair at All" on cover					
❑ Valiant VLS-25002 [S]	And Then…Along Comes The Association	1966	6.25	12.50	25.00
❑ Valiant VLS-25004 [S]	Renaissance	1967	5.00	10.00	20.00
—With blurb for "No Fair at All" on cover					
❑ Warner Bros. W 1696 [M]	Insight Out	1967	3.75	7.50	15.00
❑ Warner Bros. WS 1696 [S]	Insight Out	1967	5.00	10.00	20.00
—Gold label					
❑ Warner Bros. W 1702 [M]	And Then…Along Comes The Association	1967	5.00	10.00	20.00
❑ Warner Bros. WS 1702 [S]	And Then…Along Comes The Association	1967	5.00	10.00	20.00
—Gold label					
❑ Warner Bros. WS 1704	Renaissance	1967	3.00	6.00	12.00
❑ Warner Bros. WS 1733	Birthday	1968	3.00	6.00	12.00
—With "W7" logo on green label					
❑ Warner Bros. WS 1767	Greatest Hits	1968	3.00	6.00	12.00
—With "W7" logo on green label					

Number	Title (A Side/B Side)	Yr	VG	VG+	NM
❑ Warner Bros. WS 1786	Goodbye Columbus	1969	3.00	6.00	12.00
—With "W7" logo on green label					
❑ Warner Bros. WS 1800	The Association	1969	3.00	6.00	12.00
—With "W7" logo on green label					
❑ Warner Bros. 2WS 1868 [(2)]	The Association "Live"	1970	3.75	7.50	15.00
❑ Warner Bros. WS 1927	Stop Your Motor	1971	3.00	6.00	12.00

ATLANTA RHYTHM SECTION

45s

Number	Title (A Side/B Side)	Yr	VG	VG+	NM
❑ Columbia 18-02471	Alien/Southern Exposure	1981	—	2.00	4.00
❑ Decca 32928	All in Your Mind/Can't Stand It No More	1972	2.00	4.00	8.00
❑ Decca 32948	Earnestine/Another Man's Woman	1972	2.00	4.00	8.00
❑ Decca 33051	Back Up Against the Wall/It Must Be Done	1973	2.00	4.00	8.00
❑ MCA 40059	Cold Turkey, Tennessee/Conversation	1973	—	3.00	6.00
❑ MCA 40719	All in Your Mind/Earnestine	1977	—	2.50	5.00
❑ Polydor 2001	Spooky/It's Only Music	1979	—	2.50	5.00
❑ Polydor 2039	Back Up Against the Wall/Large Time	1980	—	2.50	5.00
❑ Polydor 2079	Conversation/Indigo Passion	1980	—	2.50	5.00
❑ Polydor 2125	Putting My Faith in Love/I Ain't Much	1980	—	2.50	5.00
❑ Polydor 2142	Silver Eagle/Strictly R & R	1981	—	2.50	5.00
❑ Polydor 14248	Doraville/Who Are You Going to Run To	1974	—	2.50	5.00
❑ Polydor 14262	Angel (What in the World's Come Over Us)/Help Yourself	1975	—	2.50	5.00
❑ Polydor 14273	Get Your Head Out of Your Heart/Jesus Hearted People	1975	—	2.50	5.00
❑ Polydor 14289	Bless My Soul/Crazy	1975	—	2.50	5.00
❑ Polydor 14323	Jukin'/Beautiful Dreamer	1976	—	2.50	5.00
❑ Polydor 14339	Free Spirit/Police Police	1976	—	2.50	5.00
❑ Polydor 14373	So In to You/Everybody Gotta Go	1977	—	2.50	5.00
❑ Polydor 14397	Neon Nites/Don't Miss the Message	1977	—	2.50	5.00
❑ Polydor 14411	Dog Days/Cuban Crisis	1977	—	2.50	5.00
❑ Polydor 14459	Imaginary Lover/Silent Treatment	1978	—	2.50	5.00
❑ Polydor 14484	I'm Not Gonna Let It Bother Me Tonight/Ballad of Lois Malone	1978	—	2.50	5.00
❑ Polydor 14504	Champagne Jam/Great Escape	1978	—	2.50	5.00
❑ Polydor 14568	Do It or Die/My Song	1979	—	2.50	5.00
❑ Polydor 14582	Spooky/It's Only Music	1979	—	—	—
—Unreleased?					

Albums

Number	Title (A Side/B Side)	Yr	VG	VG+	NM
❑ Columbia FC 37550	Quinella	1981	2.50	5.00	10.00
❑ Columbia PC 37550	Quinella	1982	2.00	4.00	8.00
—Budget-line reissue					
❑ Decca DL 75265	Atlanta Rhythm Section	1972	6.25	12.50	25.00
❑ Decca DL 75390	Back Up Against the Wall	1973	6.25	12.50	25.00
❑ MCA 2-4114 [(2)]	Atlanta Rhythm Section	1977	3.00	6.00	12.00
—Combines the two Decca LPs into one package					
❑ Polydor PD 6027	Third Annual Pipe Dream	1974	2.50	5.00	10.00
❑ Polydor PD 6041	Dog Days	1975	2.50	5.00	10.00
❑ Polydor PD-1-6060	Red Tape	1976	2.50	5.00	10.00
❑ Polydor PD-1-6080	A Rock and Roll Alternative	1977	2.50	5.00	10.00
❑ Polydor PD-1-6134	Champagne Jam	1978	2.50	5.00	10.00
❑ Polydor PD-1-6200	Underdog	1979	2.50	5.00	10.00
❑ Polydor PD-2-6236 [(2)]	Are You Ready!	1979	3.00	6.00	12.00
❑ Polydor PD-1-6285	The Boys from Doraville	1980	2.50	5.00	10.00

AUSTIN, PATTI

45s

Number	Title (A Side/B Side)	Yr	VG	VG+	NM
❑ ABC 11104	Music to My Heart/Love 'Em and Leave 'Em Kind of Love	1968	3.75	7.50	15.00
❑ Columbia 45337	Are We Ready for Love/Now That I Know What Loneliness Is	1971	—	2.50	5.00
❑ Columbia 45410	Black California/All Good Gifts-Day by Day	1971	—	2.50	5.00
❑ Columbia 45499	God Only Knows/Can't Forget the One I Love	1971	—	2.50	5.00
❑ Columbia 45592	Day by Day/Didn't Say a Word	1972	—	2.50	5.00
❑ Columbia 45785	Come to Him/Turn On the Music	1973	—	2.50	5.00
❑ Columbia 45906	Being with You/Take a Closer Look	1973	—	2.50	5.00
❑ Coral 62455	He's Good Enough for Me/Earl	1965	5.00	10.00	20.00
❑ Coral 62471	I Wanna Be Loved/A Most Unusual Boy	1965	5.00	10.00	20.00
❑ Coral 62478	Someone's Gonna Cry/You'd Better Know What You're Getting	1966	25.00	50.00	100.00
❑ Coral 62491	Take Your Time/Take Away the Pain Stain	1966	5.00	10.00	20.00
❑ Coral 62500	Leave a Little Love/My Lovelight Ain't Gonna Shine	1966	5.00	10.00	20.00
❑ Coral 62511	Got to Check You Out/What a Difference a Day Makes	1967	5.00	10.00	20.00
❑ Coral 62518	Only All the Time/Oh How I Need You Joe	1967	5.00	10.00	20.00
❑ Coral 62541	I'll Keep Loving You/You're Too Much a Part of Me	1967	5.00	10.00	20.00
❑ Coral 62548	(I've Given) All My Love/Why Can't We Try It Again	1968	5.00	10.00	20.00
❑ CTI 7	In My Life (Part 1)/In My Life (Part 2)	1973	—	2.50	5.00
—With Jerry Butler					
❑ CTI 33	Say You Love Me/In My Life	1976	—	2.00	4.00
❑ CTI 41	We're in Love/Golden Oldies	1977	—	2.00	4.00
❑ CTI 51	Love Me by Name/You Fooled Me	1978	—	2.00	4.00
❑ CTI 59	What's at the End of the Rainbow/In My Life	1978	—	2.00	4.00
❑ CTI 9600	Body Language/People in Love	1980	—	2.00	4.00
❑ CTI 9601	I Want You Tonight/Love Me Again	1980	—	2.00	4.00
❑ Qwest 27718	Smoke Gets In Your Eyes/How Long Has This Been Goin' On?	1988	—	—	3.00
❑ Qwest 28573	Only a Breath Away/Summer Is the Coldest Time of Year	1986	—	—	3.00
❑ Qwest 28659	Gettin' Away with Murder/Anything Can Happen Here	1986	—	—	3.00
❑ Qwest 28788	The Heat of Heat/Hot in the Flames of Love	1986	—	—	3.00
❑ Qwest 28935	Honey for the Bees/Hot in the Flames of Love	1985	—	—	3.00
❑ Qwest 29136	All Behind Us Now/Fine Fine Fella (Got to Have You)	1984	—	2.00	4.00
❑ Qwest 29234	Shoot the Moon/Change Your Attitude	1984	—	2.00	4.00
❑ Qwest 29305	Rhythm of the Street/Solero	1984	—	2.00	4.00
❑ Qwest 29373	It's Gonna Be Special/Solero	1984	—	2.00	4.00

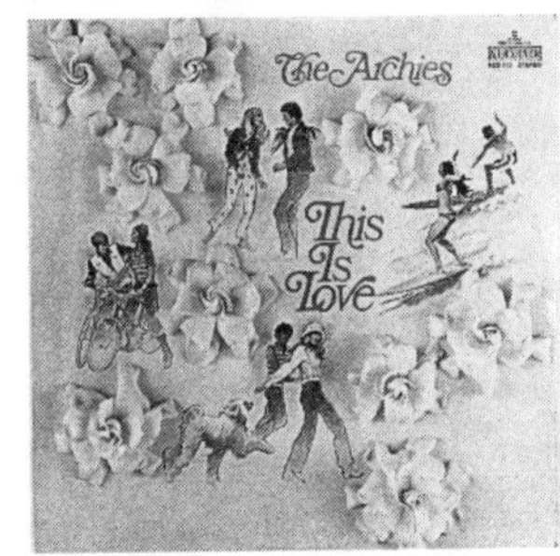

Number	Title (A Side/B Side)	Yr	VG	VG+	NM
❑ Qwest 29618	How Do You Keep the Music Playing/same (Long Version)	1983	—	2.00	4.00
—With James Ingram					
❑ Qwest 29727	Every Home Should Have One/Solero	1983	—	2.00	4.00
❑ Qwest 49754	Do You Love Me/Solero	1981	—	2.00	4.00
❑ Qwest 49854	Every Home Should Have One/Solero	1981	—	2.50	5.00
❑ Qwest 50036	Baby, Come to Me/Solero	1982	—	2.00	4.00
—With James Ingram					
❑ United Artists 50520	The Family Tree/Magical Boy	1969	2.00	4.00	8.00
❑ United Artists 50588	I Will Wait for You/Big Mouth	1969	2.00	4.00	8.00
❑ United Artists 50640	Your Love Made a Difference in Me/It's Easier to Laugh Than Cry	1970	2.00	4.00	8.00
Albums					
❑ CTI 5001	End of a Rainbow	1976	2.50	5.00	10.00
❑ CTI 5006	Havana Candy	1977	2.50	5.00	10.00
❑ CTI 7086	Live at the Bottom Line	1979	2.50	5.00	10.00
❑ CTI JZ 36503	Body Language	1980	2.50	5.00	10.00
❑ CTI PZ 36503	Body Language	198?	2.00	4.00	8.00
—Budget-line reissue					
❑ GRP GR-9603	Love Is Gonna Getcha	1990	2.50	5.00	10.00
❑ Qwest QWS 3591	Every Home Should Have One	1981	2.00	4.00	8.00
❑ Qwest 23974	Patti Austin	1984	2.00	4.00	8.00
❑ Qwest 25276	Gettin' Away with Murder	1985	2.00	4.00	8.00
❑ Qwest 25698	The Real Me	1988	2.00	4.00	8.00
AVALON, FRANKIE					
45s					
❑ Amos 127	The Star/Woman Cryin'	1969	—	2.50	5.00
❑ Bobcat 04103	Such a Miracle/You're the Miracle	1983	—	2.00	4.00
❑ Chancellor 1004	Cupid/Jivin' with the Saints	1957	5.00	10.00	20.00
❑ Chancellor 1006	Shy Guy/Teacher's Pet	1957	5.00	10.00	20.00
❑ Chancellor 1011	Dede Dinah/Ooh La La	1958	3.75	7.50	15.00
❑ Chancellor 1016	You Excite Me/Darlin'	1958	3.75	7.50	15.00
❑ Chancellor 1021	Ginger Bread/Blue Betty	1958	3.75	7.50	15.00
❑ Chancellor 1026	I'll Wait for You/What Little Girl	1958	3.75	7.50	15.00
❑ Chancellor 1031 [M]	Venus/I'm Broke	1959	5.00	10.00	20.00
❑ Chancellor S-1031 [S]	Venus/I'm Broke	1959	10.00	20.00	40.00
❑ Chancellor 1036 [M]	Bobby Sox to Stockings/A Boy Without a Girl	1959	5.00	10.00	20.00
—Originals have pink labels					
❑ Chancellor S-1036 [S]	Bobby Sox to Stockings/A Boy Without a Girl	1959	10.00	20.00	40.00
❑ Chancellor 1040 [M]	Just Ask Your Heart/Two Fools	1959	3.75	7.50	15.00
❑ Chancellor S-1040 [S]	Just Ask Your Heart/Two Fools	1959	10.00	20.00	40.00
❑ Chancellor 1045 [M]	Why/Swingin' on a Rainbow	1959	3.75	7.50	15.00
❑ Chancellor S-1045 [S]	Why/Swingin' on a Rainbow	1959	10.00	20.00	40.00
❑ Chancellor 1048	Don't Throw Away All Those Teardrops/Talk, Talk, Talk	1960	3.75	7.50	15.00
❑ Chancellor 1052	Where Are You/Tuxedo Junction	1960	3.75	7.50	15.00
❑ Chancellor 1056	Togetherness/Don't Let Love Pass You By	1960	3.75	7.50	15.00
❑ Chancellor 1065	A Perfect Love/The Puppet Song	1960	3.75	7.50	15.00
❑ Chancellor 1071	All of Everything/Call Me Anytime	1961	3.00	6.00	12.00
❑ Chancellor 1077	Who Else But You/Gotta Get a Girl	1961	3.00	6.00	12.00
❑ Chancellor 1081	Voyage to the Bottom of the Sea/Summer of '61	1961	3.00	6.00	12.00
❑ Chancellor 1087	True, True Love/Married	1961	2.50	5.00	10.00
❑ Chancellor 1095	Sleeping Beauty/The Lonely Bit	1961	2.50	5.00	10.00
❑ Chancellor 1101	After You've Gone/If You Don't Think I'm Leaving	1962	2.50	5.00	10.00
❑ Chancellor 1107	You Are Mine/Ponchinello	1962	2.50	5.00	10.00
❑ Chancellor 1107	You Are Mine/Italiano	1962	3.00	6.00	12.00
❑ Chancellor 1114	Venus/I'm Broke	1962	2.50	5.00	10.00
❑ Chancellor 1115	A Miracle/Don't Let Me Stand in Your Way	1962	2.50	5.00	10.00
❑ Chancellor 1125	Dance the Bossa Nova/Welcome Home	1962	2.50	5.00	10.00
❑ Chancellor 1131	My Ex-Best Friend/First Love Never Dies	1963	2.50	5.00	10.00
❑ Chancellor 1134	Come Fly with Me/Girl Back Home	1963	2.50	5.00	10.00
❑ Chancellor 1135	Cleopatra/Heartbeats	1963	2.50	5.00	10.00
❑ Chancellor 1139	Beach Party/Don't Stop Now	1963	3.75	7.50	15.00
❑ De-Lite 907	Beauty School Dropout/Midnight Lady	1978	—	2.00	4.00
❑ De-Lite 1578	Venus/Venus (Disco Version)	1976	—	2.00	4.00
❑ De-Lite 1582	Thank You for That Extra Sunrise/It's His Game	1976	—	2.00	4.00
❑ De-Lite 1584	It's Never Too Late/Where ILeave Off (And You Begin)	1976	—	2.00	4.00
❑ De-Lite 1589	Midnight Lady/Does She Wonder Where I Am	1977	—	2.00	4.00
❑ De-Lite 1591	Splish Splash/When I Said I Love You	1977	—	2.00	4.00

Number	Title (A Side/B Side)	Yr	VG	VG+	NM
❑ De-Lite 1595	Roses Grow Beyond the Wall/Midnight Lady	1977	—	2.00	4.00
❑ Metromedia 181	Come On Back to Me Baby/Empty	1970	—	2.50	5.00
❑ Metromedia 192	Heart of Everything/I Want You Near Me	1970	—	2.50	5.00
❑ Regalia 5508	I'm in the Mood for Love/It's the Same Old Dream	1972	—	2.50	5.00
❑ Reprise 0697	Dancing on the Stars/But I Do	1968	2.00	4.00	8.00
❑ Reprise 0796	Don't You Do It/It's Over	1968	2.00	4.00	8.00
❑ Reprise 0826	For Your Love/Why Don't They Understand	1969	2.00	4.00	8.00
❑ United Artists 728	Again/Don't Make Fun of Me	1964	2.50	5.00	10.00
❑ United Artists 748	My Love Is Here to Stay/New-Fangled, Jingle-Jangle, Swimming Suit from Paris	1964	2.50	5.00	10.00
❑ United Artists 800	Moon River/Every Girl Should Get Married	1964	2.50	5.00	10.00
❑ United Artists 895	There'll Be Rainbows Again/I'll Take Sweden	1965	2.50	5.00	10.00
❑ "X" 0006	Trumpet Sorrento/The Rock	1954	12.50	25.00	50.00
❑ "X" 0026	Trumpet Tarantella/Dormi, Dormi	1954	12.50	25.00	50.00
Albums					
❑ ABC ABCX-805 [R]	16 Greatest Hits	1974	3.00	6.00	12.00
❑ Chancellor CHL 5001 [M] *—Pink label*	Frankie Avalon	1958	12.50	25.00	50.00
❑ Chancellor CHL 5002 [M] *—Pink label*	The Young Frankie Avalon	1959	12.50	25.00	50.00
❑ Chancellor CHLS 5002 [S] *—Pink label*	The Young Frankie Avalon	1959	15.00	30.00	60.00
❑ Chancellor CHLX 5004 [M]	Swingin' on a Rainbow	1959	10.00	20.00	40.00
❑ Chancellor CHLXS 5004 [S]	Swingin' on a Rainbow	1959	12.50	25.00	50.00
❑ Chancellor CHL 5011 [M]	Summer Scene	1960	7.50	15.00	30.00
❑ Chancellor CHLS 5011 [S]	Summer Scene	1960	10.00	20.00	40.00
❑ Chancellor CHL 5018 [M]	A Whole Lotta Frankie	1961	7.50	15.00	30.00
❑ Chancellor CHL 5022 [M]	And Now About Mr. Avalon	1961	7.50	15.00	30.00
❑ Chancellor CHLS 5022 [S]	And Now About Mr. Avalon	1961	10.00	20.00	40.00
❑ Chancellor CHL 5025 [M]	Italiano	1962	7.50	15.00	30.00
❑ Chancellor CHLS 5025 [S]	Italiano	1962	10.00	20.00	40.00
❑ Chancellor CHL 5027 [M]	You're Mine	1962	7.50	15.00	30.00
❑ Chancellor CHLS 5027 [S]	You're Mine	1962	10.00	20.00	40.00
❑ Chancellor CHL 5031 [M]	Frankie Avalon's Christmas Album	1962	7.50	15.00	30.00
❑ Chancellor CHLS 5031 [S]	Frankie Avalon's Christmas Album	1962	10.00	20.00	40.00
❑ Chancellor CHL 5032 [M]	Cleopatra Plus 13 Other Great Hits	1963	7.50	15.00	30.00
❑ Chancellor CHLS 5032 [S]	Cleopatra Plus 13 Other Great Hits	1963	10.00	20.00	40.00
❑ Chancellor 69801 [M] *—LP in felt cover and 3-D portrait, all in box*	Young and In Love	1960	20.00	40.00	80.00
❑ De-Lite 2020	Venus	1976	3.75	7.50	15.00
❑ De-Lite 9504	You're My Life	1977	3.75	7.50	15.00
❑ Everest 4187	Greatest Hits	1982	2.50	5.00	10.00
❑ Liberty LN-10193 *—Budget-line reissue*	Songs from Muscle Beach Party	1981	2.00	4.00	8.00
❑ MCA 27096	The Best of Frankie Avalon	1985	2.00	4.00	8.00
❑ Metromedia MD-1034	I Want You Near Me	1970	3.75	7.50	15.00
❑ Sunset SUS-5244	Frankie Avalon	1969	3.75	7.50	15.00
❑ Trip 1621	16 Greatest Hits of Frankie Avalon	1977	2.50	5.00	10.00
❑ United Artists UA-LA450-F	The Very Best of Frankie Avalon	1975	3.00	6.00	12.00
❑ United Artists UAL-3371 [M]	Songs from Muscle Beach Party	1964	6.25	12.50	25.00
❑ United Artists UAL-3382 [M]	Frankie Avalon's 15 Greatest Hits	1964	5.00	10.00	20.00
❑ United Artists UAS-6371 [S]	Songs from Muscle Beach Party	1964	7.50	15.00	30.00
❑ United Artists UAS-6382 [S]	Frankie Avalon's 15 Greatest Hits	1964	6.25	12.50	25.00

AVERAGE WHITE BAND

Number	Title (A Side/B Side)	Yr	VG	VG+	NM
45s					
❑ Arista 0515	Let's Go Round Again/Shine	1980	—	2.00	4.00
❑ Arista 0553	For You, For Love/Whatcha 'Gonna Do for Me	1980	—	2.00	4.00
❑ Arista 0580	Into the Night/(B-side unknown)	1980	—	2.00	4.00
❑ Arista 0679	Easier Said Than Done/(B-side unknown)	1982	—	2.00	4.00
❑ Arista 1022	Cupid's in Fashion/(B-side unknown)	1982	—	2.00	4.00
❑ Atlantic 3044	Nothing You Can Do/I Just Can't Give You Up	1974	—	2.00	4.00
❑ Atlantic 3229	Pick Up the Pieces/Work to Do	1974	—	2.50	5.00
❑ Atlantic 3261	Cut the Cake/Person to Person	1975	—	2.00	4.00
❑ Atlantic 3285	If I Ever Lose This Heaven/High Flyin' Woman	1975	—	2.00	4.00
❑ Atlantic 3304	School Boy Crush/Groovin' the Night Away	1975	—	2.00	4.00
❑ Atlantic 3354	Queen of My Soul/Would You Stay	1976	—	2.00	4.00
❑ Atlantic 3363	Soul Searching/Love of Your Own	1976	—	2.00	4.00
❑ Atlantic 3388	Cloudy/Love Your Life	1977	—	2.00	4.00
❑ Atlantic 3402 *—With Ben E. King*	Get It Up/Keepin' It To Myself	1977	—	2.00	4.00
❑ Atlantic 3427 *—With Ben E. King*	A Star in the Ghetto/What Is Soul?	1977	—	2.00	4.00
❑ Atlantic 3444 *—With Ben E. King*	Fool for You Anyway/The Message	1977	—	2.00	4.00
❑ Atlantic 3481	Your Love Is a Miracle/One Look.	1978	—	2.00	4.00
❑ Atlantic 3500	Big City Lights/She's a Dream.	1978	—	2.00	4.00
❑ Atlantic 3563	Walk On By/Too Late to Cry.	1979	—	2.00	4.00
❑ Atlantic 3581	Feel No Fret/Fire Burning.	1979	—	2.00	4.00
❑ MCA 40168	This World Has Music/The Jugglers.	1973	—	2.50	5.00
❑ MCA 40196	Twilight Zone/How Can You Go Home.	1974	—	2.50	5.00
Albums					
❑ Arista AB 9523	Shine	1980	2.50	5.00	10.00
❑ Arista AB 9594	Cupid's in Fashion	1981	2.50	5.00	10.00
❑ Atlantic SD 2-1002 [(2)]	Person to Person	1977	3.00	6.00	12.00
❑ Atlantic SD 7308	Average White Band	1974	2.50	5.00	10.00
❑ Atlantic SD 18140	Cut the Cake	1975	2.50	5.00	10.00

Number	Title (A Side/B Side)	Yr	VG	VG+	NM
❑ Atlantic SD 18179	Soul Searching	1976	2.50	5.00	10.00
❑ Atlantic SD 19105	Benny and Us	1977	2.50	5.00	10.00
—With Ben E. King					
❑ Atlantic SD 19116	Average White Band	1977	2.00	4.00	8.00
—Reissue					
❑ Atlantic SD 19162	Warmer Communications	1978	2.50	5.00	10.00
❑ Atlantic SD 19207	Feel No Fret	1979	2.50	5.00	10.00
❑ Atlantic SD 19266	Volume VIII	1980	2.50	5.00	10.00
❑ MCA 345	Show Your Hands	1973	6.25	12.50	25.00
❑ MCA 475	Put It Where You Want It	1975	2.50	5.00	10.00
—Reissue of MCA 345					
❑ Track 58830	Aftershock	1988	2.50	5.00	10.00

B

B-52'S, THE

45s

Number	Title (A Side/B Side)	Yr	VG	VG+	NM
❑ DB 52	Rock Lobster/52 Girls	1978	7.50	15.00	30.00
❑ Reprise 18895	Good Stuff/Bad Influence	1992	—	2.00	4.00
❑ Reprise 19430	Love Shack/Roam	199?	—	—	3.00
—Reissue					
❑ Reprise 19938	Deadbeat Club/Planet Claire (Live)	1990	—	—	3.00
❑ Reprise 22667	Roam/Bushfire	1990	—	2.00	4.00
❑ Reprise 22817	Love Shack/Channel Z	1989	—	—	3.00
❑ Warner Bros. GWB 0416	Rock Lobster/Private Idaho	198?	—	—	3.00
—Back to Back Hits reissue					
❑ Warner Bros. 28561	Summer of Love/Housework	1986	—	—	3.00
❑ Warner Bros. 29561	Song for a Future Generation/Trism	1983	—	—	3.00
❑ Warner Bros. 29579	Legal Tender/Moon 83	1983	—	—	3.00
❑ Warner Bros. 29971	Mesopotamia/Throw That Beat in the Garbage Can	1982	—	—	3.00
❑ Warner Bros. 49173	Rock Lobster/6060-842	1980	—	2.00	4.00
❑ Warner Bros. 49212	Planet Claire/There's a Moon in the Sky (Called the Moon)	1980	—	2.00	4.00
❑ Warner Bros. 49537	Private Idaho/Party Out of Bounds	1980	—	2.00	4.00
❑ Warner Bros. 49717	Lava/Quiche Lorraine	1981	2.50	5.00	10.00
❑ Warner Bros. 50064	Deep Sleep/Nip It in the Bud	1982	—	2.00	4.00

Albums

Number	Title	Yr	VG	VG+	NM
❑ Reprise 25854	Cosmic Thing	1989	3.00	6.00	12.00
❑ Warner Bros. BSK 3355	The B-52's	1979	2.50	5.00	10.00
❑ Warner Bros. BSK 3471	Wild Planet	1980	3.00	6.00	12.00
—Originals have red custom labels (deduct 33% for later pressings)					
❑ Warner Bros. MINI 3596 [EP]	Party Mix	1981	3.00	6.00	12.00
❑ Warner Bros. MINI 3641 [EP]	Mesopotamia	1982	2.00	4.00	8.00
❑ Warner Bros. 23819	Whammy!	1983	2.50	5.00	10.00
❑ Warner Bros. 25504	Bouncing Off the Satellites	1986	2.50	5.00	10.00

BACHELORS, THE (1)

Several other groups used this name, on the Aladdin, Epic, Mercury, MGM, National, Poplar, Royal Roost and Smash labels; those are outside the scope of this publication.

45s

Number	Title (A Side/B Side)	Yr	VG	VG+	NM
❑ London 9584	Charmaine/Old Bill	1963	3.00	6.00	12.00
❑ London 9623	Faraway Places/Is There a Chance	1964	3.00	6.00	12.00
❑ London 9632	Whispering/No Light in the Window	1964	3.00	6.00	12.00
❑ London 9639	Diane/Happy Land	1964	3.00	6.00	12.00
❑ London 9639	Diane/I Believe	1964	3.75	7.50	15.00
❑ London 9672	I Believe/Sweet Lullaby	1964	3.00	6.00	12.00
❑ London 9693	I Wouldn't Trade You for the World/Beneath the Willow Tree	1964	3.00	6.00	12.00
❑ London 9724	No Arms Can Ever Hold You/Oh Samuel, Don't Die	1964	3.00	6.00	12.00
❑ London 9762	Marie/You Can Tell	1965	2.50	5.00	10.00
❑ London 9793	Chapel in the Moonlight/The Old Wishing Well	1965	2.50	5.00	10.00
❑ London 9828	Love Me with All of Your Heart/There's No Room in My Heart	1966	2.50	5.00	10.00
❑ London 20010	Can I Trust You/My Girl	1966	2.50	5.00	10.00
❑ London 20018	Walk with Faith in Your Heart/Queen Molly Malone of Ireland	1966	2.50	5.00	10.00
❑ London 20027	Marta/Oh How I Miss You	1967	2.00	4.00	8.00
❑ London 20033	Learn to Live Without You/3 O'Clock Flamingo Street	1967	2.00	4.00	8.00
❑ London 20051	Punky's Dilemma/It's a Beautiful Day	1968	2.00	4.00	8.00
❑ London 20063	Love Is All/The Colours of Love	1970	—	3.00	6.00

Number	Title (A Side/B Side)	Yr	VG	VG+	NM
❑ London 20071	Diamonds Are Forever/Where There's a Heartache	1971	—	3.00	6.00
Albums					
❑ London PS 353 [S]	Presenting the Bachelors	1964	5.00	10.00	20.00
❑ London PS 393 [P]	Back Again	1964	5.00	10.00	20.00
—"I Wouldn't Trade You for the World" is rechanneled.					
❑ London PS 418 [S]	No Arms Can Ever Hold You	1965	5.00	10.00	20.00
❑ London PS 435 [P]	Marie	1965	5.00	10.00	20.00
—"Marie" is rechanneled					
❑ London PS 460 [S]	Hits of the 60's	1966	5.00	10.00	20.00
❑ London PS 491 [P]	The Bachelors' Girls	1966	3.75	7.50	15.00
—"Marie" is rechanneled					
❑ London PS 518 [P]	Golden All Time Hits	1967	3.75	7.50	15.00
❑ London PS 528 [S]	Bachelors '68	1968	3.00	6.00	12.00
❑ London PS 611	Under and Over	1972	2.50	5.00	10.00
❑ London LL 3353 [M]	Presenting the Bachelors	1964	3.75	7.50	15.00
❑ London LL 3393 [M]	Back Again	1964	3.75	7.50	15.00
❑ London LL 3418 [M]	No Arms Can Ever Hold You	1965	3.75	7.50	15.00
❑ London LL 3435 [M]	Marie	1965	3.75	7.50	15.00
❑ London LL 3460 [M]	Hits of the 60's	1966	3.75	7.50	15.00
❑ London LL 3491 [M]	The Bachelors' Girls	1966	3.00	6.00	12.00
❑ London LL 3518 [M]	Golden All Time Hits	1967	3.75	7.50	15.00
❑ London LL 3528 [M]	Bachelors '68	1968	5.00	10.00	20.00

BACHMAN-TURNER OVERDRIVE

Number	Title (A Side/B Side)	Yr	VG	VG+	NM
45s					
❑ Compleat 127	For the Weekend/Just Look at Me Now	1984	—	2.00	4.00
❑ Compleat 133	My Sugaree/Service with a Smile	1984	—	2.00	4.00
❑ Compleat 137	My Sugaree/(B-side unknown)	1985	—	2.00	4.00
❑ Mercury 73383	Gimmie Your Money Please/Little Gandy Dancer	1973	—	2.50	5.00
❑ Mercury 73417	Blue Collar/Hold Back the Water	1973	—	2.50	5.00
❑ Mercury 73457	Let It Ride/Tramp	1974	—	2.00	4.00
❑ Mercury 73487	Takin' Care of Business/Stonegates	1974	—	2.00	4.00
❑ Mercury 73622	You Ain't Seen Nothin' Yet/Free Wheelin'	1974	—	2.00	4.00
❑ Mercury 73656	Roll On Down the Highway/Sledgehammer	1975	—	2.00	4.00
❑ Mercury 73683	Hey You/Flat Broke Love	1975	—	2.00	4.00
❑ Mercury 73724	Down to the Line/She's a Devil	1975	—	2.00	4.00
❑ Mercury 73766	Take It Like a Man/Woncha Take Me for a While	1976	—	2.00	4.00
❑ Mercury 73784	Looking Out for #1/Find Out About Love	1976	—	2.00	4.00
❑ Mercury 73843	Gimme Your Money Please/Four Wheel Drive	1976	—	2.00	4.00
❑ Mercury 73903	Freeways/My Wheels Won't Turn	1977	—	2.00	4.00
❑ Mercury 73926	Shotgun Rider/Down, Down	1977	—	2.00	4.00
❑ Mercury 73951	Life Still Goes On (I'm Lonely)/Just for You	1977	—	2.00	4.00
❑ Mercury 73987	Down the Road/A Long Time for a Little While	1978	—	2.00	4.00
❑ Mercury 74046	Heaven Tonight/Heartaches	1979	—	2.00	4.00
❑ Mercury 74062	End of the Line/Jamaica	1979	—	2.00	4.00
Albums					
❑ Compleat CPL1-1010	Bachman-Turner Overdrive	1984	2.00	4.00	8.00
❑ MCA/Curb 5760	Live! Live! Live!	1986	2.00	4.00	8.00
❑ Mercury SRM-1-673	Bachman-Turner Overdrive	1973	3.00	6.00	12.00
—Red label					
❑ Mercury SRM-1-696	Bachman-Turner Overdrive II	1973	3.00	6.00	12.00
—Red label					
❑ Mercury SRM-1-1004	Not Fragile	1974	2.50	5.00	10.00
❑ Mercury SRM-1-1027	Four Wheel Drive	1975	2.50	5.00	10.00
❑ Mercury SRM-1-1067	Head On	1975	2.50	5.00	10.00
❑ Mercury SRM-1-1101	Best of B.T.O. (So Far)	1976	2.50	5.00	10.00
❑ Mercury SRM-1-3700	Freeways	1977	2.50	5.00	10.00
❑ Mercury SRM-1-3713	Street Action	1978	2.50	5.00	10.00
❑ Mercury SRM-1-3748	Rock N' Roll Nights	1979	2.50	5.00	10.00
❑ Mercury 822786-1	Best of B.T.O. (So Far)	1984	2.00	4.00	8.00
—Reissue of 1101					

BAD COMPANY

Number	Title (A Side/B Side)	Yr	VG	VG+	NM
45s					
❑ Atco 98463	This Could Be the One/How About That	1992	—	2.00	4.00
❑ Atlantic 88939	Shake It Up/Dangerous Age	1989	—	2.00	4.00
❑ Atlantic 89035	No Smoke Without a Fire/Love Attack	1988	—	2.00	4.00
❑ Atlantic 89299	That Girl/If I'm Sleeping	1987	—	2.00	4.00
❑ Atlantic 89355	This Love/Tell It Like It Is	1986	—	2.00	4.00
❑ Swan Song 70015	Can't Get Enough/Little Miss Fortune	1974	—	3.00	6.00
❑ Swan Song 70101	Movin' On/Easy on My Soul	1974	—	2.50	5.00
❑ Swan Song 70103	Good Lovin' Gone Bad/Whiskey Bottle	1975	—	2.50	5.00
❑ Swan Song 70106	Feel Like Makin' Love/Wild Fire Woman	1975	—	3.00	6.00
❑ Swan Song 70108	Young Blood/Do Right by Your Woman	1976	—	2.50	5.00
❑ Swan Song 70109	Honey Child/Fade Away	1976	—	2.00	4.00
❑ Swan Song 70112	Burnin' Sky/Everything I Need	1976	—	2.00	4.00
❑ Swan Song 70119	Rock 'N' Roll Fantasy/Crazy Circles	1979	—	2.50	5.00
❑ Swan Song 71000	Gone, Gone, Gone/Take the Time	1979	—	2.50	5.00
❑ Swan Song 99966	Electricland/Untie the Knot	1982	—	2.50	5.00
Albums					
❑ Atco 91371	Holy Water	1990	3.75	7.50	15.00
❑ Atlantic 81625	10 from 6 (The Best of Bad Company)	1986	2.50	5.00	10.00
❑ Atlantic 81684	Fame and Fortune	1987	2.50	5.00	10.00
❑ Atlantic 81884	Dangerous Age	1988	2.50	5.00	10.00
❑ Swan Song SS 8410	Bad Company	1974	2.50	5.00	10.00
❑ Swan Song SS 8413	Straight Shooter	1975	2.50	5.00	10.00
❑ Swan Song SS 8415	Run with the Pack	1976	2.50	5.00	10.00

Number	Title (A Side/B Side)	Yr	VG	VG+	NM
❑ Swan Song SS 8500	Burnin' Sky	1977	2.50	5.00	10.00
❑ Swan Song SS 8501	Bad Company	1977	2.00	4.00	8.00
❑ Swan Song SS 8502	Straight Shooter	1977	2.00	4.00	8.00
❑ Swan Song SS 8503	Run with the Pack	1977	2.00	4.00	8.00
❑ Swan Song SS 8506	Desolation Angels	1979	2.50	5.00	10.00
❑ Swan Song 90001	Rough Diamonds	1982	2.50	5.00	10.00

BADFINGER

45s

Number	Title (A Side/B Side)	Yr	VG	VG+	NM
❑ Apple 1803	Maybe Tomorrow/And Her Daddy's a Millionaire	1969	5.00	10.00	20.00
—By "The Iveys"; without star on label					
❑ Apple 1815	Come and Get It/Rock of All Ages	1969	—	3.00	6.00
❑ Apple 1822	No Matter What/Carry On Till Tomorrow	1970	—	3.00	6.00
❑ Apple 1841	Day After Day/Money	1971	—	3.00	6.00
❑ Apple 1844	Baby Blue/Flying	1972	—	3.00	6.00
❑ Apple 1864	Apple of My Eye/Blind Owl	1973	—	3.00	6.00
❑ Elektra 46022	Lost Inside Your Love/Come Down Hard	1979	—	2.50	5.00
❑ Elektra 46025	Love Is Gonna Come At Last/Sail Away	1979	—	2.50	5.00
❑ Radio 3793	Hold On/Passin' Time	1981	—	2.50	5.00
❑ Radio 3815	I Got You/Rock and Roll Contract	1981	—	2.50	5.00
❑ Radio 3833	Because I Love You/Too Hung Up on You	1981	—	2.50	5.00
❑ Warner Bros. 7801	I Miss You/Shine On	1974	—	3.00	6.00

Albums

Number	Title (A Side/B Side)	Yr	VG	VG+	NM
❑ Apple ST-3355	Maybe Tomorrow	1969	500.00	1000.	2000.
—As "The Iveys"; album not released in US; price is for an LP slick, which does exist					
❑ Apple ST 3364	Magic Christian Music	1970	5.00	10.00	20.00
❑ Apple SKAO 3367	No Dice	1970	7.50	15.00	30.00
❑ Apple SW 3387	Straight Up	1971	15.00	30.00	60.00
❑ Apple SW 3411	Ass	1973	5.00	10.00	20.00
❑ Elektra 6E-175	Airwaves	1979	3.00	6.00	12.00
❑ Radio RR 16030	Say No More	1981	2.50	5.00	10.00
❑ Ryko Analogue RALP 10189	Day After Day	1990	5.00	10.00	20.00
—Limited edition on clear vinyl with obi					
❑ Warner Bros. BS 2762	Badfinger	1974	3.75	7.50	15.00
❑ Warner Bros. BS 2827	Wish You Were Here	1974	3.75	7.50	15.00

BAEZ, JOAN

45s

Number	Title (A Side/B Side)	Yr	VG	VG+	NM
❑ A&M 1334	Song of Bangladesh/Prison Trilogy (Billy Rose)	1972	—	2.50	5.00
❑ A&M 1362	In the Quiet Morning/To Bobby	1972	—	2.00	4.00
❑ A&M 1393	Love Song to a Stranger/Tumbleweed	1972	—	2.00	4.00
❑ A&M 1454	The Best of Friends/Mary Call	1973	—	2.00	4.00
❑ A&M 1472	Less Than the Song/Windrose	1973	—	2.00	4.00
❑ A&M 1516	Forever Young/Guantanamera	1974	—	2.00	4.00
❑ A&M 1703	Blue Sky/Dida	1975	—	2.00	4.00
❑ A&M 1737	Diamonds and Rust/Winds of the Old Days	1975	—	2.50	5.00
❑ A&M 1802	Please Come to Boston/Love Song to a Stranger	1976	—	2.00	4.00
❑ A&M 1820	Never Dreamed You'd Leave in Summer/Children and All That Jazz	1976	—	2.00	4.00
❑ A&M 1884	Caruso/Time Is Passing Us By	1976	—	2.00	4.00
❑ A&M 1906	O Brother/Still Waters at Night	1977	—	2.00	4.00
❑ Decca 32890	Silent Running/Rejoice in the Sun	1971	—	3.00	6.00
❑ Portrait 70006	I'm Blowing Away/The Altar Boy and the Sheep	1977	—	2.00	4.00
❑ Portrait 70009	Time Rag/Miracles	1977	—	2.00	4.00
❑ Portrait 70032	Light a Light/Michael	1979	—	2.00	4.00
❑ RCA Victor 74-0568	The Ballad of Sacco and Vanzetti/Here's to You	1971	—	3.00	6.00
❑ Vanguard 35012	Banks of the Ohio/Old Blue	1962	2.00	4.00	8.00
❑ Vanguard 35013	Lonesome Road/Pal of Mine	1962	2.00	4.00	8.00
❑ Vanguard 35018	What Have They Done to the Rain/Danger Waters	1963	2.00	4.00	8.00
❑ Vanguard 35023	We Shall Overcome/What Have They Done to the Rain	1963	2.00	4.00	8.00
❑ Vanguard 35026	Medley: With God on Our Side/Railroad Bill//Rambler Gambler	1964	2.00	4.00	8.00
❑ Vanguard 35031	There But for Fortune/Daddy You Been On My Mind	1965	2.00	4.00	8.00
❑ Vanguard 35040	Pack Up Your Sorrows/Swallow Song	1966	2.00	4.00	8.00
❑ Vanguard 35046	Little Drummer Boy/Cantique de Noel	1966	2.50	5.00	10.00
❑ Vanguard 35055	Be Not Too Hard/The North	1967	2.00	4.00	8.00
❑ Vanguard 35088	Love Is Just a Four-Letter Word/Love Minus Zero-No Limit	1969	2.00	4.00	8.00
❑ Vanguard 35092	If I Knew/Rock Salt and Nails	1969	2.00	4.00	8.00
❑ Vanguard 35098	Four Days Gone/Hickory Wind	1969	2.00	4.00	8.00

Number	Title (A Side/B Side)	Yr	VG	VG+	NM
❑ Vanguard 35103	No Expectations/One Day at a Time	1970	—	3.00	6.00
❑ Vanguard 35106	Sweet Sir Galahad/The Ghetto	1970	—	3.00	6.00
❑ Vanguard 35114	Carry It On/Rock Salt and Nails	1970	—	3.00	6.00
❑ Vanguard 35138	The Night They Drove Old Dixie Down/When Time Is Stolen	1971	2.00	4.00	8.00
❑ Vanguard 35145	Let It Be/Poor Wayfaring Stranger	1971	—	3.00	6.00
❑ Vanguard 35148	Will the Circle Be Unbroken/Just a Closer Walk with Thee	1972	—	2.50	5.00
❑ Vanguard 35158	Blessed Are/The Brand New Tennessee Waltz	1972	—	2.50	5.00
Albums					
❑ A&M SP-3103 *—Budget-line reissue*	Come From the Shadows	198?	2.00	4.00	8.00
❑ A&M SP-3233 *—Budget-line reissue*	Diamonds and Rust	198?	2.00	4.00	8.00
❑ A&M SP-3234 *—Budget-line reissue*	The Best of Joan C. Baez	198?	2.00	4.00	8.00
❑ A&M SP-3614	Gracias A La Vida	1974	3.00	6.00	12.00
❑ A&M SP-3704 [(2)]	From Every Stage	1976	3.00	6.00	12.00
❑ A&M SP-4339	Come From the Shadows	1972	2.50	5.00	10.00
❑ A&M SP-4390	Where Are You Now, My Son?	1973	2.50	5.00	10.00
❑ A&M SP-4527	Diamonds and Rust	1975	2.50	5.00	10.00
❑ A&M SP-4603	Gulf Winds	1976	2.50	5.00	10.00
❑ A&M SP-4668	The Best of Joan C. Baez	1977	2.50	5.00	10.00
❑ A&M SP-6506 [(2)] *—Reissue*	From Every Stage	198?	2.50	5.00	10.00
❑ Gold Castle D1-71309 *—Reissue of 171 009*	Recently	1989	3.00	6.00	12.00
❑ Gold Castle D1-71321	Diamonds and Rust in the Bullring	1989	3.00	6.00	12.00
❑ Gold Castle D1-71324	Speaking of Dreams	1989	3.00	6.00	12.00
❑ Gold Castle 171009	Recently	1988	2.50	5.00	10.00
❑ Portrait PR 34697	Blowin' Away	1977	2.50	5.00	10.00
❑ Portrait JR 35766	Honest Lullaby	1979	2.50	5.00	10.00
❑ Squire SQ-33001 [M]	The Best of Joan Baez	1963	5.00	10.00	20.00
❑ Vanguard VSD-41/42 [(2)]	The Joan Baez Ballad Book	1972	3.00	6.00	12.00
❑ Vanguard VSD-49/50 [(2)]	The Contemporary Ballad Book	1974	3.00	6.00	12.00
❑ Vanguard VSD-79/80 [(2)]	The Love Song Album	197?	3.00	6.00	12.00
❑ Vanguard VSD-105/6 [(2)]	The Country Music Album	1979	3.00	6.00	12.00
❑ Vanguard VSD-2077 [S]	Joan Baez	1960	6.25	12.50	25.00
❑ Vanguard VSD-2097 [S]	Joan Baez, Vol. 2	1961	6.25	12.50	25.00
❑ Vanguard VSD-2122 [S]	Joan Baez In Concert	1962	6.25	12.50	25.00
❑ Vanguard VSD-2123 [S]	Joan Baez In Concert, Part 2	1963	6.25	12.50	25.00
❑ Vanguard VSD-6560/1 [(2)]	The First 10 Years	1970	3.75	7.50	15.00
❑ Vanguard VSD-6570/1 [(2)]	Blessed Are...	1971	3.75	7.50	15.00
—Add 50 percent if bonus 7-inch single, "Maria Dolores"/"Plane Wreck at Los Gatos (Deportee)," and its special sleeve are still in the package					
❑ Vanguard VRS-9078 [M]	Joan Baez	1960	5.00	10.00	20.00
❑ Vanguard VRS-9094 [M]	Joan Baez, Vol. 2	1961	5.00	10.00	20.00
❑ Vanguard VRS-9112 [M]	Joan Baez In Concert	1962	5.00	10.00	20.00
❑ Vanguard VRS-9113 [M]	Joan Baez In Concert, Part 2	1963	5.00	10.00	20.00
❑ Vanguard VRS-9160 [M]	Joan Baez/5	1964	3.75	7.50	15.00
❑ Vanguard VRS-9200 [M]	Farewell, Angelina	1965	3.75	7.50	15.00
❑ Vanguard VRS-9230 [M]	Noel	1966	3.75	7.50	15.00
❑ Vanguard VRS-9240 [M]	Joan	1967	3.75	7.50	15.00
❑ Vanguard VMS-73107	The Joan Baez Ballad Book, Vol. 1	1985	2.50	5.00	10.00
❑ Vanguard VMS-73115	The Joan Baez Ballad Book, Vol. 2	1985	2.50	5.00	10.00
❑ Vanguard VMS-73119	The Night They Drove Old Dixie Down	198?	2.50	5.00	10.00
❑ Vanguard VSD-79160 [S]	Joan Baez/5	1964	5.00	10.00	20.00
❑ Vanguard VSD-79200 [S]	Farewell, Angelina	1965	5.00	10.00	20.00
❑ Vanguard VSD-79230 [S]	Noel	1966	5.00	10.00	20.00
❑ Vanguard VSD-79240 [S]	Joan	1967	5.00	10.00	20.00
❑ Vanguard VSD-79275	Baptism	1968	5.00	10.00	20.00
❑ Vanguard VSD-79306/7 [(2)]	Any Day Now	1969	6.25	12.50	25.00
❑ Vanguard VSD-79308	David's Album	1969	3.00	6.00	12.00
❑ Vanguard VSD-79310	One Day at a Time	1970	3.00	6.00	12.00
❑ Vanguard VSD-79313 *—Soundtrack album*	Carry It On	1971	6.25	12.50	25.00
❑ Vanguard VSD-79332	Hits/Greatest & Others	1973	2.50	5.00	10.00
❑ Vanguard VSD-79446/7	Very Early Joan	1981	3.00	6.00	12.00

BALLARD, HANK, AND THE MIDNIGHTERS

Number	Title (A Side/B Side)	Yr	VG	VG+	NM
45s					
❑ Chess 2111	Love, Why Is It Taking You So Long/I'm a Junkie for My Baby's Love	1971	—	3.00	6.00
❑ King S-7 1619 [S] *—Jukebox single; 33 1/3 rpm, small hole*	Let's Go Again (Where We Went Last Night)/These Young Girls	196?	7.50	15.00	30.00
❑ King S-7 1620 [S] *—Jukebox single; 33 1/3 rpm, small hole*	I Must Be Crazy/Move - Move - Move	196?	7.50	15.00	30.00
❑ King S-7 1621 [S] *—Jukebox single; 33 1/3 rpm, small hole*	Hoochi Coochi Coo/Mona Lisa	196?	7.50	15.00	30.00
❑ King S-7 1622 [S] *—Jukebox single; 33 1/3 rpm, small hole*	Summertime/Don't Go I Love You	196?	7.50	15.00	30.00
❑ King S-7 1623 [S] *—Jukebox single; 33 1/3 rpm, small hole*	Finger Poppin' Time/Let's Go, Let's Go, Let's Go	196?	10.00	20.00	40.00
❑ King 5171	Teardrops on Your Letter/The Twist	1959	7.50	15.00	30.00
❑ King 5195 [M]	Kansas City/I'll Keep You Happy	1959	6.25	12.50	25.00
❑ King S-5195 [S]	Kansas City/I'll Keep You Happy	1959	12.50	25.00	50.00
❑ King 5215 [M]	Sugaree/Rain Down Tears	1959	6.25	12.50	25.00
❑ King S-5215 [S]	Sugaree/Rain Down Tears	1959	12.50	25.00	50.00
❑ King 5245	Cute Little Ways/A House with No Windows	1959	6.25	12.50	25.00
❑ King 5275	I Could Love You/Never Knew	1959	6.25	12.50	25.00
❑ King 5289	Look at Little Sister/I Said I Wouldn't Beg You	1959	6.25	12.50	25.00

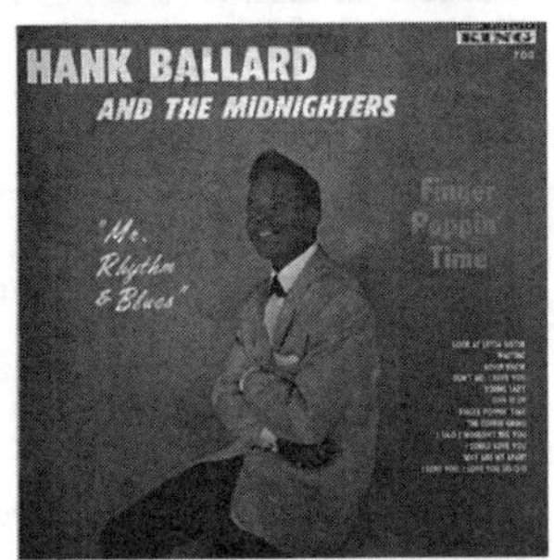

Number	Title (A Side/B Side)	Yr	VG	VG+	NM
❑ King 5312	The Coffee Grind/Waiting	1960	6.25	12.50	25.00
❑ King 5341	Finger Poppin' Time/I Love You, I Love You So-o-o	1960	6.25	12.50	25.00
❑ King 5400	Let's Go, Let's Go, Let's Go/If You'd Forgive Me	1960	6.25	12.50	25.00
❑ King 5430	The Hoochi Coochi Coo/I'm Thinking of You	1960	5.00	10.00	20.00
❑ King 5459	Let's Go Again (Where We Went Last Night)/Deep Blue Sea	1961	5.00	10.00	20.00
❑ King 5491	The Continental Walk/What Is This I See	1961	5.00	10.00	20.00
❑ King 5510	The Switch-A-Roo/The Float	1961	3.75	7.50	15.00
❑ King 5513	The Big Frog/Doin' Everything	1961	3.75	7.50	15.00
—B-side by Henry Moore					
❑ King 5535	Nothing But Good/Keep On Dancing	1961	3.75	7.50	15.00
❑ King 5550	Big Red Sunset/Can't You See — I Need a Friend	1961	3.75	7.50	15.00
❑ King 5578	Do You Remember/I'm Gonna Miss You	1961	3.75	7.50	15.00
❑ King 5593	Do You Know How to Twist/Broadway	1962	3.75	7.50	15.00
❑ King 5601	It's Twistin' Time/Autumn Breeze	1962	3.75	7.50	15.00
❑ King 5635	Good Twistin' Tonight/I'm Young	1962	3.75	7.50	15.00
❑ King 5655	I Want to Thank You/Excuse Me	1962	3.75	7.50	15.00
❑ King 5677	Dream World/When I Need You	1962	3.75	7.50	15.00
❑ King 5693	Shaky Mae/I Love and Care for You	1962	3.75	7.50	15.00
❑ King 5703	Bring Me Your Love/She's the One	1962	3.75	7.50	15.00
❑ King 5713	All the Things in Life That Please You/The Rising Tide	1963	3.75	7.50	15.00
❑ King 5719	The House on the Hill/That Low-Down Move	1963	3.75	7.50	15.00
❑ King 5729	Christmas Time for Everyone But Me/Santa Claus Is Coming	1963	3.75	7.50	15.00
❑ King 5746	How Could You Leave Your Man Alone/Walkin' and Talkin'	1963	3.75	7.50	15.00
❑ King 5798	Those Lonely, Lonely Feelings/It's Love, Baby	1963	3.75	7.50	15.00
❑ King 5821	Buttin' In/I'm Leavin'	1963	3.75	7.50	15.00
❑ King 5835	Don't Let Temptation Turn You Around/Have Mercy, Have a Little Pity	1964	3.75	7.50	15.00
❑ King 5860	Don't Fall in Love with Me/I'm So Mad with You	1964	3.75	7.50	15.00
❑ King 5884	I Don't Know How to Do But One Thing/These Young Girls	1964	3.75	7.50	15.00
❑ King 5901	Stay Away from My Baby/She's Got a Whole Lot of Soul	1964	3.75	7.50	15.00
❑ King 5931	Daddy Rolling Stone/What's Your Name	1964	3.75	7.50	15.00
❑ King 5954	Let's Get the Show on the Road/A Winner Never Quits	1964	3.75	7.50	15.00
❑ King 5963	One Monkey Don't Stop No Show/What Can I Tell You	1964	3.75	7.50	15.00
❑ King 5974	The Handwriting on the Wall/I Done It	1964	3.75	7.50	15.00
❑ King 5996	Poppin' the Whip/You, Just You	1965	3.00	6.00	12.00
❑ King 6001	I'm Just a Fool and Everybody Knows/Do It Zulu Style	1965	3.00	6.00	12.00
❑ King 6018	Sloop and Slide/My Sun Is Going Down	1966	3.00	6.00	12.00
❑ King 6031	I'm Ready/Togetherness	1966	3.00	6.00	12.00
❑ King 6055	I Was Born to Move/He Came Alone	1966	3.00	6.00	12.00
❑ King 6092	Here Comes the Hurt/Dance Till It Hurt Cha	1967	3.00	6.00	12.00
❑ King 6119	You're in Real Good Hands/Unwind Yourself	1967	3.00	6.00	12.00
❑ King 6131	Funky's Soul Train/Which Way Should I Turn	1967	3.00	6.00	12.00
❑ King 6177	I'm Back to Stay/Come On Wit' It	1968	3.00	6.00	12.00
❑ King 6196	How You Gonna Get Respect (When You Haven't Cut Your Process Yet)/Teardrops on Your Letter	1968	2.50	5.00	10.00
—As "Hank Ballard Along With The Dapps"					
❑ King 6215	You're So Sexy/Thrill on the Hill.	1969	2.50	5.00	10.00
—As "Hank Ballard Along With The Dapps"					
❑ King 6228	Are You Lonely for Me Baby/With Our Sweet Lovin' Self.	1969	2.50	5.00	10.00
❑ King 6244	Butter Your Popcorn/Funky Soul Train.	1969	3.75	7.50	15.00
❑ King 6246	Come On with It/Blackenized.	1969	3.75	7.50	15.00
❑ King 6332	Work With Me Annie/Sexy Ways.	1970	2.50	5.00	10.00
❑ People 604	Teardrops on Your Letter/Annie Had a Baby.	1972	—	2.50	5.00
❑ People 606	With Your Sweet Lovin' Self/Finger Poppin' Time	1972	—	2.50	5.00
❑ Polydor 14128	Finger Poppin' Time/From the Love Side	1972	—	2.50	5.00
❑ Polydor 14166	Going to Get a Thrill/(B-side unknown)	1973	—	—	—
—Canceled?					
❑ Silver Fox 23	Sunday Morning Coming Down/Love Made a Fool of Me	1970	—	3.00	6.00
❑ Stang 5053	Let's Go Streaking/Let's Go Streaking (Part 2)	1974	—	2.50	5.00
❑ Stang 5058	Hey There Sexy Lady/(Instrumental)	1975	—	2.50	5.00
❑ Stang 5061	Let's Go Skinny Dipping/Love On Love	1975	—	2.50	5.00
Albums					
❑ King 618 [M]	Singin' and Swingin'	1959	62.50	125.00	250.00
❑ King 674 [M]	The One and Only Hank Ballard	1959	62.50	125.00	250.00
—Brown cover					
❑ King 674 [M]	The One and Only Hank Ballard	1960	37.50	75.00	150.00
—Green cover					
❑ King 700 [M]	Mr. Rhythm and Blues	1960	37.50	75.00	150.00

Number	Title (A Side/B Side)	Yr	VG	VG+	NM
❑ King 740 [M]	Spotlight on Hank Ballard	1961	37.50	75.00	150.00
❑ King KS-740 [S]	Spotlight on Hank Ballard	1961	75.00	150.00	300.00
❑ King 748 [M]	Let's Go Again	1961	30.00	60.00	120.00
❑ King 759 [M]	Dance Along	1961	30.00	60.00	120.00
❑ King 781 [M]	The Twistin' Fools	1962	25.00	50.00	100.00
❑ King 793 [M]	Jumpin' Hank Ballard	1962	25.00	50.00	100.00
❑ King 815 [M]	The 1963 Sound of Hank Ballard	1963	25.00	50.00	100.00
❑ King 867 [M]	Biggest Hits	1963	25.00	50.00	100.00
❑ King 896 [M]	A Star in Your Eyes	1964	25.00	50.00	100.00
❑ King 913 [M]	Those Lazy, Lazy Days	1965	17.50	35.00	70.00
❑ King 927 [M]	Glad Songs, Sad Songs	1965	17.50	35.00	70.00
❑ King 950 [M]	24 Hit Tunes	1966	15.00	30.00	60.00
❑ King 981 [M]	24 Great Songs	1968	10.00	20.00	40.00
❑ King KSD-1052	You Can't Keep a Good Man Down	1969	12.50	25.00	50.00

BARNES, J.J.

45s

Number	Title (A Side/B Side)	Yr	VG	VG+	NM
❑ Buddah 120	Evidence/I'll Keep Coming Back	1969	3.75	7.50	15.00
❑ Contempo 7003	How Long/The Erroll Flynn	1977	—	2.50	5.00
❑ Groovesville 1006	Baby Please Come Back Home/Chains of Love	1967	3.75	7.50	15.00
❑ Groovesville 1008	Now That I Got You Back/Forgive Me	1967	3.75	7.50	15.00
❑ Groovesville 1009	Easy Living/(B-side unknown)	1967	4.00	8.00	16.00
❑ Invasion 1001	My Baby/(You Still) My Baby	1970	2.50	5.00	10.00
❑ Kable 437	Won't You Let Me Know/My Love Came Tumbling Down	1960	12.50	25.00	50.00
❑ Magic Touch 1000	To An Early Grave/Cloudy Days	1970	2.50	5.00	10.00
❑ Mickay's 3004	Just One More Time/Hey Child, I Love You	1963	20.00	40.00	80.00
❑ Mickay's 4472	Get a Hold of Yourself/Lonely No More	1964	20.00	40.00	80.00
❑ Perception 546	Just a Living Doll/Touching You	1974	—	3.00	6.00
❑ Revilot 216	Hold On to It/Now She's Gone	1968	3.75	7.50	15.00
❑ Revilot 218	I'll Keep Coming Back/Sad Day a-Comin'	1968	3.75	7.50	15.00
❑ Revilot 222	Our Love Is in the Pocket/All Your Goodies Are Gone	1968	20.00	40.00	80.00
❑ Revilot 225	So-Called Friends/Now She's Gone	1968	3.75	7.50	15.00
❑ Ric-Tic 106	Please Let Me In/I Think I Found a Love	1965	3.75	7.50	15.00
❑ Ric-Tic 110	Real Humdinger/I Ain't Gonna Do It	1966	3.75	7.50	15.00
❑ Ric-Tic 115	Day Tripper/Don't Bring Me Bad News	1966	3.75	7.50	15.00
❑ Ric-Tic 117	Deeper in Love/Say It	1966	3.75	7.50	15.00
❑ Rich 1005	Won't You Let Me Know/My Love Came Tumbling Down	1960	25.00	50.00	100.00
❑ Rich 1737	Won't You Let Me Know/My Love Came Tumbling Down	1962	6.25	12.50	25.00
❑ Ring 101	She Ain't Ready/Poor-Unfortunate Me	1964	6.25	12.50	25.00
❑ Scepter 1266	Just One More Time/Hey Child, I Love You	1964	7.50	15.00	30.00
❑ Volt 4027	Got to Get Rid of You/Snowflakes	1969	3.75	7.50	15.00

Albums

Number	Title (A Side/B Side)	Yr	VG	VG+	NM
❑ Volt VOS-6001 *—With Steve Mancha*	Rare Stamps	1969	7.50	15.00	30.00

BASS, FONTELLA

45s

Number	Title (A Side/B Side)	Yr	VG	VG+	NM
❑ Bobbin 134	I Don't Hurt Anymore/Brand New Love	1962	3.75	7.50	15.00
❑ Bobbin 140	Honey Bee/Bad Boy	1963	3.75	7.50	15.00
❑ Checker 1097 *—With Bobby McClure*	Don't Mess Up a Good Thing/Baby, What You Want Me to Do	1965	2.50	5.00	10.00
❑ Checker 1111 *—With Bobby McClure*	You'll Miss Me (When I'm Gone)/Don't Jump	1965	2.50	5.00	10.00
❑ Checker 1120 *—Red label with "Checker" vertically on left*	Rescue Me/Soul of the Man	1965	5.00	10.00	20.00
❑ Checker 1131	Recovery/Leave It in the Hands of Love	1965	2.50	5.00	10.00
❑ Checker 1137	I Surrender/I Can't Rest	1966	2.50	5.00	10.00
❑ Checker 1147	Safe and Sound/You'll Never Ever Know	1966	2.50	5.00	10.00
❑ Checker 1183	Lucky in Love/Sweet Lovin' Daddy	1967	2.50	5.00	10.00
❑ Epic 50341	Soon as I Touched Him/You Can Betcha in Love	1977	—	2.00	4.00
❑ Paula 360	Who You Gonna Blame/Hold On This Time	1972	—	2.50	5.00
❑ Paula 367	I Need to Be Loved/I Want Everyone to Know	1972	—	2.50	5.00
❑ Paula 376	It Sure Is Good/I'm Leaving the Choice to You	1973	—	2.50	5.00
❑ Paula 389	Home Wrecker/Now That I've Found a Good Thing	1973	—	2.50	5.00
❑ Paula 393	Talking About Freedom/It's Hard to Get Back In	1974	—	2.50	5.00

Albums

Number	Title (A Side/B Side)	Yr	VG	VG+	NM
❑ Checker LP-2997 [M] *—Blue label with red and black checkers*	The "New" Look	1966	15.00	30.00	60.00
❑ Checker LPS-2997 [S] *—Blue label with red and black checkers*	The "New" Look	1966	20.00	40.00	80.00
❑ Paula LPS-2203	Free	1971	3.00	6.00	12.00

BAY CITY ROLLERS

45s

Number	Title (A Side/B Side)	Yr	VG	VG+	NM
❑ Arista 0120	Bye Bye Baby/It's for You	1975	2.50	5.00	10.00
❑ Arista 0149	Saturday Night/Marlina	1975	—	2.00	4.00
❑ Arista 0170	Money Honey/Maryanne	1976	—	2.00	4.00
❑ Arista 0185	Rock and Roll Love Letter/Shanghai'd in Love	1976	—	2.00	4.00
❑ Arista 0193	Don't Stop the Music (Long)/Don't Stop the Music (Short)	1976	—	3.00	6.00
❑ Arista 0205	I Only Want to Be with You/Write a Letter	1976	—	2.00	4.00
❑ Arista 0216	Yesterday's Hero/My Lisa	1976	—	2.00	4.00
❑ Arista 0233	Dedication/Rock N' Roller	1977	—	2.00	4.00
❑ Arista 0256	You Made Me Believe in Magic/Dance Dance Dance	1977	—	2.00	4.00
❑ Arista 0272	The Way I Feel Tonight/Sweet Virginia	1977	—	2.50	5.00
❑ Arista 0272	The Way I Feel Tonight/Love Power	1977	—	2.50	5.00
❑ Arista 0363	Where Will I Be Now/If You Were My Woman	1978	—	2.00	4.00
❑ Arista 0476 *—As "The Rollers"*	Turn On the Radio/Hello and Welcome Home	1979	—	2.00	4.00

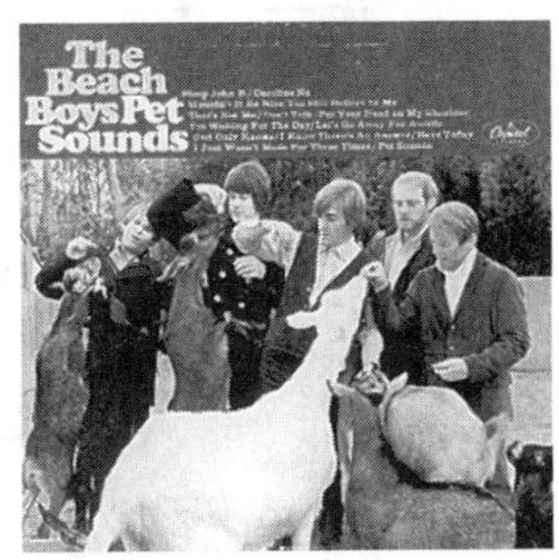

Number	Title (A Side/B Side)	Yr	VG	VG+	NM
❑ Bell 45169	Keep On Dancing/Alright	1972	2.50	5.00	10.00
❑ Bell 45274	Manana/I Heard You Singing Your Song	1972	3.75	7.50	15.00
❑ Bell 45481	Shang-a-Lang/(B-side unknown)	1974	3.75	7.50	15.00
❑ Bell 45607	Summerlove Sensation/(B-side unknown)	1974	3.75	7.50	15.00
❑ Bell 45618	All of Me Loves All of You/The Bump	1974	3.75	7.50	15.00
Albums					
❑ Arista AL 4049	Bay City Rollers	1975	2.50	5.00	10.00
❑ Arista AL 4071	Rock N' Roll Love Letter	1976	2.50	5.00	10.00
❑ Arista AL 4093	Dedication	1976	2.50	5.00	10.00
❑ Arista AB 4158	Greatest Hits	1977	2.50	5.00	10.00
❑ Arista AB 4194	Strangers in the Wind	1978	2.50	5.00	10.00
❑ Arista AB 4241	Elevator	1979	2.50	5.00	10.00
—As "The Rollers"					
❑ Arista AB 7004	It's a Game	1977	2.50	5.00	10.00
BEACH BOYS, THE					
45s					
❑ Brother 1001	Heroes and Villains/You're Welcome	1967	3.00	6.00	12.00
❑ Brother/Reprise 0101	Wouldn't It Be Nice/Sloop John B	1973	—	2.50	5.00
—"Back to Back Hits" series					
❑ Brother/Reprise 0102	God Only Knows/Caroline, No	1973	—	2.50	5.00
—"Back to Back Hits" series					
❑ Brother/Reprise 0103	Good Vibrations/Heroes and Villains	1973	—	2.50	5.00
—"Back to Back Hits" series					
❑ Brother/Reprise 0104	Darlin'/Wild Honey	1973	—	2.50	5.00
—"Back to Back Hits" series					
❑ Brother/Reprise 0105	Friends/Be Here in the Morning	1973	—	2.50	5.00
—"Back to Back Hits" series					
❑ Brother/Reprise 0106	Do It Again/Cottonfields	1973	—	2.50	5.00
—"Back to Back Hits" series					
❑ Brother/Reprise 0107	I Can Hear Music/Bluebirds Over the Mountain	1973	—	2.50	5.00
—"Back to Back Hits" series					
❑ Brother/Reprise 0118	Rock and Roll Music/It's O.K.	1977	—	2.00	4.00
—"Back to Back Hits" series					
❑ Brother/Reprise 0894	Add Some Music to Your Day/Susie Cincinnati	1970	2.00	4.00	8.00
❑ Brother/Reprise 0929	Slip On Through/This Whole World	1970	2.50	5.00	10.00
❑ Brother/Reprise 0957	It's About Time/Tears in the Morning	1970	5.00	10.00	20.00
❑ Brother/Reprise 0998	Cool, Cool Water/Forever	1971	20.00	40.00	80.00
❑ Brother/Reprise 1015	Long Promised Road/Deirdre	1971	5.00	10.00	20.00
❑ Brother/Reprise 1047	Long Promised Road/'Til I Die	1971	5.00	10.00	20.00
❑ Brother/Reprise 1058	Surf's Up/Don't Go Near the Water	1971	12.50	25.00	50.00
❑ Brother/Reprise 1091	You Need a Mess of Help to Stand Alone/Cuddle Up	1972	7.50	15.00	30.00
❑ Brother/Reprise 1101	Marcella/Hold On Dear Brother	1972	7.50	15.00	30.00
❑ Brother/Reprise 1138	Sail On Sailor/Only With You	1972	2.50	5.00	10.00
❑ Brother/Reprise 1156	California Saga (On My Way to Sunny Californ-I-A)/Funky Pretty	1973	2.50	5.00	10.00
❑ Brother/Reprise 1310	I Can Hear Music/Let the Wind Blow	1974	2.50	5.00	10.00
❑ Brother/Reprise 1321	Child of Winter (Christmas Song)/Susie Cincinnati	1974	12.50	25.00	50.00
❑ Brother/Reprise 1325	Sail On Sailor/Only With You	1975	2.00	4.00	8.00
❑ Brother/Reprise 1336	Wouldn't It Be Nice/Caroline, No	1975	3.00	6.00	12.00
❑ Brother/Reprise 1354	Rock and Roll Music/The T M Song	1976	—	2.00	4.00
❑ Brother/Reprise 1368	It's O.K./Had to Phone Ya	1976	—	2.00	4.00
❑ Brother/Reprise 1375	Everyone's In Love with You/Susie Cincinnati	1976	—	2.00	4.00
❑ Brother/Reprise 1389	Honkin' Down the Highway/Solar System	1977	—	2.00	4.00
❑ Brother/Reprise 1394	Peggy Sue/Hey Little Tomboy	1978	—	2.00	4.00
❑ Candix 301	Surfin'/Luau	1961	75.00	150.00	300.00
—No mention of Era Records on label					
❑ Candix 331	Surfin'/Luau	1962	50.00	100.00	200.00
❑ Capitol 2028	Wild Honey/Wind Chimes	1967	3.00	6.00	12.00
❑ Capitol 2068	Darlin'/Here Today	1967	3.00	6.00	12.00
❑ Capitol 2160	Friends/Little Bird	1968	3.00	6.00	12.00
❑ Capitol 2239	Do It Again/Wake the World	1968	3.00	6.00	12.00
❑ Capitol 2360	Bluebirds Over the Mountain/Never Learn Not to Love	1968	3.00	6.00	12.00
❑ Capitol 2432	I Can Hear Music/All I Want to Do	1969	3.00	6.00	12.00
❑ Capitol 2530	Break Away/Celebrate the News	1969	3.00	6.00	12.00
❑ Capitol 2765	Cottonfields/The Nearest Faraway Place	1970	5.00	10.00	20.00
❑ Capitol 3924	Surfin' U.S.A./The Warmth of the Sun	1974	—	2.50	5.00
❑ Capitol 4093	Little Honda/Hawaii	1975	—	2.50	5.00

Number	Title (A Side/B Side)	Yr	VG	VG+	NM
❑ Capitol 4110	Barbara Ann/Little Honda	1975	—	2.50	5.00
❑ Capitol 4334	Be True to Your School/Graduation Day	1976	—	2.50	5.00
❑ Capitol 4777	Surfin' Safari/409	1962	6.25	12.50	25.00
❑ Capitol 4880	Ten Little Indians/County Fair	1962	7.50	15.00	30.00
❑ Capitol 4932	Surfin' U.S.A./Shut Down	1963	6.25	12.50	25.00
—Version 1: Brian Wilson listed as composer of "Surfin' U.S.A."					
❑ Capitol 5009	Surfer Girl/Little Deuce Coupe	1963	6.25	12.50	25.00
❑ Capitol A-5030	The Beach Boys Medley/God Only Knows	1981	—	2.50	5.00
❑ Capitol 5069	Be True to Your School/In My Room	1963	6.25	12.50	25.00
❑ Capitol 5096	Little Saint Nick/The Lord's Prayer	1963	7.50	15.00	30.00
—Orange and yellow swirl label					
❑ Capitol 5118	Fun, Fun, Fun/Why Do Fools Fall in Love	1964	6.25	12.50	25.00
—A-side songwriter listed as "Brian Wilson"					
❑ Capitol 5174	I Get Around/Don't Worry Baby	1964	6.25	12.50	25.00
—Orange and yellow swirl label					
❑ Capitol 5245	When I Grow Up (To Be a Man)/She Knows Me Too Well	1964	6.25	12.50	25.00
❑ Capitol 5306	Dance, Dance, Dance/The Warmth of the Sun	1964	6.25	12.50	25.00
❑ Capitol 5312	The Man with All the Toys/Blue Christmas	1964	7.50	15.00	30.00
❑ Capitol 5372	Do You Wanna Dance/Please Let Me Wonder	1965	5.00	10.00	20.00
❑ Capitol 5395	Help Me, Rhonda/Kiss Me, Baby	1965	6.25	12.50	25.00
❑ Capitol 5464	California Girls/Let Him Run Wild	1965	6.25	12.50	25.00
—Orange and yellow swirl label					
❑ Capitol 5540	The Little Girl I Once Knew/There's No Other (Like My Baby)	1965	5.00	10.00	20.00
❑ Capitol 5561	Barbara Ann/Girl Don't Tell Me	1965	5.00	10.00	20.00
❑ Capitol B-5595	Rock and Roll to the Rescue/Good Vibrations (Live in London)	1986	—	—	3.00
❑ Capitol 5602	Sloop John B/You're So Good to Me	1966	5.00	10.00	20.00
—Orange and yellow swirl label					
❑ Capitol B-5630	California Dreamin'/Lady Liberty	1986	—	—	3.00
❑ Capitol 5676	Good Vibrations/Let's Go Away for Awhile	1966	5.00	10.00	20.00
❑ Capitol 5706	Wouldn't It Be Nice/God Only Knows	1966	5.00	10.00	20.00
—Even though it has a higher number, this single was released before "Good Vibrations."					
❑ Capitol B-44297	Don't Worry Baby/Tequila Dreams	1989	—	2.00	4.00
—A-side: With the Everly Brothers; B-side by Dave Grusin					
❑ Capitol Starline 6059	Be True to Your School/In My Room	1965	3.75	7.50	15.00
—Originals have green swirl labels					
❑ Capitol Starline 6060	Ten Little Indians/She Knows Me Too Well	1965	3.75	7.50	15.00
—Originals have green swirl labels					
❑ Capitol Starline 6081	Help Me, Rhonda/Do You Wanna Dance?	1966	3.75	7.50	15.00
—Originals have green swirl labels					
❑ Capitol Starline 6094	Surfin' U.S.A./Shut Down	1966	3.75	7.50	15.00
—Originals have green swirl labels					
❑ Capitol Starline 6095	Surfin' Safari/409	1966	3.75	7.50	15.00
—Originals have green swirl labels					
❑ Capitol Starline 6105	Dance, Dance, Dance/The Warmth of the Sun	1967	3.00	6.00	12.00
—Originals have red and white "target" labels					
❑ Capitol Starline 6106	Fun, Fun, Fun/Why Do Fools Fall in Love	1967	3.00	6.00	12.00
—Originals have red and white "target" labels					
❑ Capitol Starline 6107	Surfer Girl/Little Deuce Coupe	1967	3.00	6.00	12.00
—Originals have red and white "target" labels					
❑ Capitol Starline 6132	Good Vibrations/Barbara Ann	1968	3.00	6.00	12.00
—Originals have red and white "target" labels					
❑ Capitol Starline 6204	When I Grow Up (To Be a Man)/She Knows Me Too Well	197?	—	2.50	5.00
—Originals have grayish labels					
❑ Capitol Starline 6205	Wendy/Little Honda	197?	—	2.50	5.00
—Originals have grayish labels					
❑ Capitol Starline 6259	Barbara Ann/Little Honda	1978	—	2.00	4.00
—Originals have grayish labels					
❑ Capitol Starline 6277	Little Saint Nick/The Lord's Prayer	1981	—	—	3.00
—Originals have blue labels					
❑ Capitol Starline 6280	I Get Around/Don't Worry Baby	1981	—	—	3.00
—Originals have blue labels					
❑ Capitol Starline 6289	California Girls/Let Him Run Wild	1981	—	—	3.00
—Originals have blue labels					
❑ Capitol Starline 6295	Sloop John B/You're So Good to Me	1981	—	—	3.00
—Originals have blue labels					
❑ Caribou 02633	Come Go with Me/Don't Go Near the Water	1981	—	—	3.00
❑ Caribou 04913	Getcha Back/Male Ego	1985	—	—	3.00
❑ Caribou 05433	It's Gettin' Late/It's OK	1985	—	—	3.00
❑ Caribou 05624	She Believes in Love Again/It's Just a Matter of Time	1985	—	—	3.00
❑ Caribou 9026	Here Comes the Night/Baby Blue	1979	—	2.00	4.00
❑ Caribou 9029	Good Timin'/Love Surrounds Me	1979	—	2.00	4.00
❑ Caribou 9030	Lady Lynda/Full Sail	1979	—	2.00	4.00
❑ Caribou 9031	It's a Beautiful Day/Sumahama	1979	—	2.00	4.00
❑ Caribou 9032	Goin' On/Endless Harmony	1980	—	2.00	4.00
❑ Caribou 9033	Livin' with a Heartache/Santa Ana Winds	1980	—	2.00	4.00
❑ Critique 99392	Happy Endings/California Girls	1987	—	—	3.00
—A-side with Little Richard					
❑ Elektra 69385	Kokomo/Tutti-Frutti	1988	—	—	3.00
—B-side by Little Richard					
❑ Era Back to Back Hits 042	Surfer Girl/The Freeze	197?	2.00	4.00	8.00
—A-side is from the Hite Morgan sessions; B-side by Tony & Jo					
❑ Era Back to Back Hits 043	Surfin'/Surfin' Safari	197?	2.00	4.00	8.00
—Both sides from the Hite Morgan sessions					
❑ FBI 7701	East Meets West/Rhapsody	1986	5.00	10.00	20.00
—With Frankie Valli and the Four Seasons					
❑ Ode 66016	Wouldn't It Be Nice/The Times They Are a-Changing	1971	7.50	15.00	30.00
—B-side by Merry Clayton					

Number	Title (A Side/B Side)	Yr	VG	VG+	NM
❑ X 301	Surfin'/Luau	1961	250.00	500.00	1000.
Albums					
❑ Brother ST 9001 [R]	Smiley Smile	1967	5.00	10.00	20.00
—No mention of Barry Turnbull on cover					
❑ Brother T 9001 [M]	Smiley Smile	1967	10.00	20.00	40.00
—No mention of Barry Turnbull on cover					
❑ Brother/Reprise 2MS 2083 [(2)]	Carl and the Passions "So Tough"/Pet Sounds	1972	7.50	15.00	30.00
❑ Brother/Reprise MS 2118	Holland	1973	3.75	7.50	15.00
—Includes bonus stock-copy EP, "Mount Vernon and Fairway," in picture sleeve, taped to back cover					
❑ Brother/Reprise 2MS 2166 [(2)]	Wild Honey & 20/20	1974	3.75	7.50	15.00
❑ Brother/Reprise 2MS 2167 [(2)]	Friends & Smiley Smile	1974	3.75	7.50	15.00
❑ Brother/Reprise MS 2197 [M]	Pet Sounds	1974	5.00	10.00	20.00
❑ Brother/Reprise MS 2223	Good Vibrations — Best of the Beach Boys	1975	3.00	6.00	12.00
❑ Brother/Reprise MS 2251	15 Big Ones	1976	3.00	6.00	12.00
❑ Brother/Reprise MSK 2258	Love You	1977	3.00	6.00	12.00
❑ Brother/Reprise MSK 2268	M.I.U. Album	1978	3.00	6.00	12.00
❑ Brother/Reprise MSK 2280	Good Vibrations — Best of the Beach Boys	1978	2.50	5.00	10.00
❑ Brother/Reprise RS-6382	Sunflower	1970	6.25	12.50	25.00
❑ Brother/Reprise RS 6453	Surf's Up	1971	5.00	10.00	20.00
❑ Brother/Reprise 2RS 6484 [(2)]	The Beach Boys In Concert	1973	5.00	10.00	20.00
❑ Capitol SKAO-133	20/20	1969	5.00	10.00	20.00
—Black label with colorband					
❑ Capitol SWBB-253 [(2)]	Close-Up	1969	7.50	15.00	30.00
—Reissue of "Surfin"U.S.A." and "All Summer Long" in one package; black labels with colorband					
❑ Capitol ST-442	Good Vibrations	1970	5.00	10.00	20.00
—Lime label (original)					
❑ Capitol STBB-500 [(2)]	All Summer Long/California Girls	1970	5.00	10.00	20.00
—Lime labels; "Special Double Play" pack; two separate LPs (abridged versions of "All Summer Long" and "Summer Days [And Summer Nights!!]") bound together					
❑ Capitol SF-501	All Summer Long	1970	2.50	5.00	10.00
—Individual record from above set					
❑ Capitol SF-502	California Girls	1970	2.50	5.00	10.00
—Individual record from above set					
❑ Capitol STBB-701 [(2)]	Fun, Fun, Fun/Dance, Dance, Dance	1970	5.00	10.00	20.00
—Lime labels; "Special Double Play" pack; two separate LPs (abridged versions of "Shut Down, Volume 2" and "The Beach Boys Today!") bound together					
❑ Capitol SF-702	Fun, Fun, Fun	1971	2.50	5.00	10.00
—Individual record from above set					
❑ Capitol SF-703	Dance, Dance, Dance	1971	2.50	5.00	10.00
—Individual record from above set					
❑ Capitol DT 1808 [R]	Surfin' Safari	1962	6.25	12.50	25.00
—With only the "Duophonic" banner at top					
❑ Capitol T 1808 [M]	Surfin' Safari	1962	10.00	20.00	40.00
❑ Capitol ST 1890 [S]	Surfin' U.S.A.	1963	12.50	25.00	50.00
❑ Capitol T 1890 [M]	Surfin' U.S.A.	1963	10.00	20.00	40.00
❑ Capitol ST 1981 [S]	Surfer Girl	1963	12.50	25.00	50.00
—With reference to The Four Freshmen in liner notes					
❑ Capitol T 1981 [M]	Surfer Girl	1963	10.00	20.00	40.00
—With reference to The Four Freshmen in liner notes					
❑ Capitol ST 1998 [S]	Little Deuce Coupe	1963	10.00	20.00	40.00
❑ Capitol T 1998 [M]	Little Deuce Coupe	1963	10.00	20.00	40.00
❑ Capitol ST 2027 [P]	Shut Down, Volume 2	1964	10.00	20.00	40.00
❑ Capitol T 2027 [M]	Shut Down, Volume 2	1964	10.00	20.00	40.00
❑ Capitol ST 2110 [S]	All Summer Long	1964	7.50	15.00	30.00
—With "Don't Back Down" correctly listed on front cover					
❑ Capitol T 2110 [M]	All Summer Long	1964	7.50	15.00	30.00
—With "Don't Back Down" correctly listed on front cover					
❑ Capitol ST 2164 [S]	The Beach Boys' Christmas Album	1964	12.50	25.00	50.00
❑ Capitol T 2164 [M]	The Beach Boys' Christmas Album	1964	12.50	25.00	50.00
❑ Capitol STAO 2198 [S]	Beach Boys Concert	1964	7.50	15.00	30.00
—With bound-in booklet					

Number	Title (A Side/B Side)	Yr	VG	VG+	NM
❑ Capitol TAO 2198 [M]	Beach Boys Concert	1964	7.50	15.00	30.00
—With bound-in booklet					
❑ Capitol DT 2269 [R]	The Beach Boys Today!	1965	6.25	12.50	25.00
❑ Capitol T 2269 [M]	The Beach Boys Today!	1965	7.50	15.00	30.00
❑ Capitol DT 2354 [R]	Summer Days (And Summer Nights!!)	1965	6.25	12.50	25.00
—With "Duophonic" banner					
❑ Capitol T 2354 [M]	Summer Days (And Summer Nights!!)	1965	7.50	15.00	30.00
❑ Capitol DMAS 2398 [R]	Beach Boys Party!	1965	7.50	15.00	30.00
—With sheet of photos					
❑ Capitol MAS 2398 [M]	Beach Boys Party!	1965	10.00	20.00	40.00
—With sheet of photos					
❑ Capitol DT 2458 [R]	Pet Sounds	1966	7.50	15.00	30.00
❑ Capitol T 2458 [M]	Pet Sounds	1966	10.00	20.00	40.00
❑ Capitol DT 2545 [P]	Best of the Beach Boys	1966	3.75	7.50	15.00
—Black label with colorband					
❑ Capitol T 2545 [M]	Best of the Beach Boys	1966	5.00	10.00	20.00
—Black label with colorband					
❑ Capitol DT 2706 [P]	Best of the Beach Boys, Vol. 2	1967	3.75	7.50	15.00
—Red and while "Starline" label					
❑ Capitol T 2706 [M]	Best of the Beach Boys, Vol. 2	1967	6.25	12.50	25.00
❑ Capitol DTCL 2813 [(3)R]	The Beach Boys Deluxe Set	1967	12.50	25.00	50.00
—Maroon border on box; custom pressings of LPs with "DTCL" prefixes					
❑ Capitol TCL 2813 [(3)M]	The Beach Boys Deluxe Set	1967	62.50	125.00	250.00
—Black border on box; albums have "T" prefixes					
❑ Capitol ST 2859 [S]	Wild Honey	1967	5.00	10.00	20.00
❑ Capitol T 2859 [M]	Wild Honey	1967	10.00	20.00	40.00
❑ Capitol DKAO 2893	Stack-o-Tracks	1968	25.00	50.00	100.00
—With sheet music booklet					
❑ Capitol ST 2895	Friends	1968	6.25	12.50	25.00
❑ Capitol DKAO 2945 [P]	The Best of the Beach Boys, Vol. 3	1968	3.75	7.50	15.00
—Black label with colorband					
❑ Capitol SVBB-11307 [(2)]	Endless Summer	1974	5.00	10.00	20.00
—Orange labels, "Capitol" on bottom; with poster					
❑ Capitol SVBB-11384 [(2)]	Spirit of America	1975	3.75	7.50	15.00
—Orange labels, "Capitol" on bottom					
❑ Capitol ST-11584	Beach Boys '69 (The Beach Boys Live in London)	1976	3.00	6.00	12.00
❑ Capitol SN-12011	Beach Boys '69 (The Beach Boys Live in London)	1979	2.50	5.00	10.00
❑ Capitol SVBB-12220 [(2)]	Sunshine Dream	1982	3.00	6.00	12.00
❑ Capitol ST-12293	Rarities	1983	3.75	7.50	15.00
❑ Capitol STBK-12396 [(2)]	Made in U.S.A.	1986	3.00	6.00	12.00
❑ Capitol N-16012 [M]	Surfin' Safari	1980	2.00	4.00	8.00
❑ Capitol SN-16013 [S]	Little Deuce Coupe	1980	2.00	4.00	8.00
❑ Capitol SN-16014 [S]	Surfer Girl	1980	2.00	4.00	8.00
❑ Capitol SN-16015 [S]	Surfin' U.S.A.	1980	2.00	4.00	8.00
❑ Capitol SN-16016 [S]	All Summer Long	1980	2.00	4.00	8.00
❑ Capitol DN-16017 [R]	California Girls	1980	2.00	4.00	8.00
❑ Capitol SN-16018 [P]	Fun, Fun, Fun	1980	2.00	4.00	8.00
—Reissue of "Shut Down, Vol. 2"					
❑ Capitol DN-16019 [R]	Dance, Dance, Dance	1981	2.00	4.00	8.00
❑ Capitol SN-16134	Beach Boys '69 (The Beach Boys Live in London)	1981	2.00	4.00	8.00
❑ Capitol SN-16156 [M]	Pet Sounds	1981	2.00	4.00	8.00
❑ Capitol SN-16157	Friends	1981	2.00	4.00	8.00
❑ Capitol SN-16158 [M]	Smiley Smile	1981	2.00	4.00	8.00
❑ Capitol SN-16159 [S]	Wild Honey	1981	2.00	4.00	8.00
❑ Capitol DN-16272 [R]	Beach Boys Party!	1982	2.00	4.00	8.00
❑ Capitol N-16273	Be True to Your School	1983	2.00	4.00	8.00
❑ Capitol DN-16318 [R]	Best of the Beach Boys, Vol. 2	1984	2.00	4.00	8.00
❑ Capitol 09463-51370-1-9 [(2)]	Pet Sounds	2006	7.50	15.00	30.00
—Limited two-record edition; one record is on yellow vinyl and contains the original mono mix; the other is on green vinyl and contains the 2003 stereo mix					
❑ Capitol C1-91318 [R]	Best of the Beach Boys	1988	3.00	6.00	12.00
—Purple label, small Capitol logo					
❑ Capitol C1-92639	Still Cruisin'	1989	3.00	6.00	12.00
❑ Caribou JZ 35752	L.A. (Light Album)	1979	2.50	5.00	10.00
❑ Caribou FZ 36283	Keepin' the Summer Alive	1980	2.50	5.00	10.00
❑ Caribou Z2X 37445 [(2)]	Ten Years of Harmony (1970-1980)	1981	3.00	6.00	12.00
❑ Caribou BFZ 39946	The Beach Boys	1985	2.50	5.00	10.00
❑ Era HTE-805 [M]	The Beach Boys' Biggest Beach Hits	1969	3.75	7.50	15.00
—Also contains non-Beach Boys filler					
❑ Everest 4108 [M]	Rare Early Recordings	1981	2.00	4.00	8.00
❑ Orbit OR 688 [M]	The Beach Boys' Greatest Hits 1961-1963	1972	3.00	6.00	12.00
—Also contains non-Beach Boys filler					
❑ Pair PDL2-1068 [(2)]	For All Seasons	1986	3.75	7.50	15.00
❑ Pair PDL2-1084 [(2)]	Golden Harmonies	1986	3.75	7.50	15.00
❑ Pickwick PTP-2059 [(2)]	High Water	1973	3.00	6.00	12.00
❑ Pickwick SPC-3221	Summertime Blues	1970	2.50	5.00	10.00
❑ Pickwick SPC-3269	Good Vibrations	1971	2.50	5.00	10.00
❑ Pickwick SPC-3309	Wow! Great Concert!	1972	2.50	5.00	10.00
❑ Pickwick SPC-3351	Surfer Girl	1973	2.50	5.00	10.00
❑ Pickwick SPC-3562	Little Deuce Coupe	1975	2.50	5.00	10.00
❑ Reader's Digest RBA-178 [(4)]	Their Greatest Hits and Finest Performances	1989	12.50	25.00	50.00
—Box set					
❑ Scepter Citation CTN-18004 [M]	The Best of the Beach Boys (1961-1963)	1972	3.00	6.00	12.00
—Also contains non-Beach Boys filler					
❑ Sears SPS-609	Summertime Blues	1970	12.50	25.00	50.00

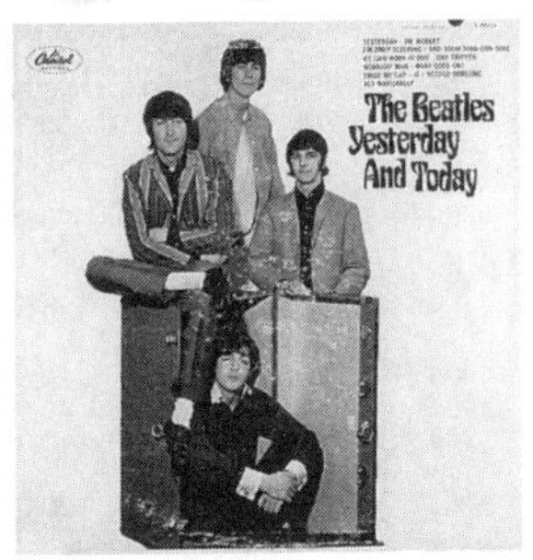

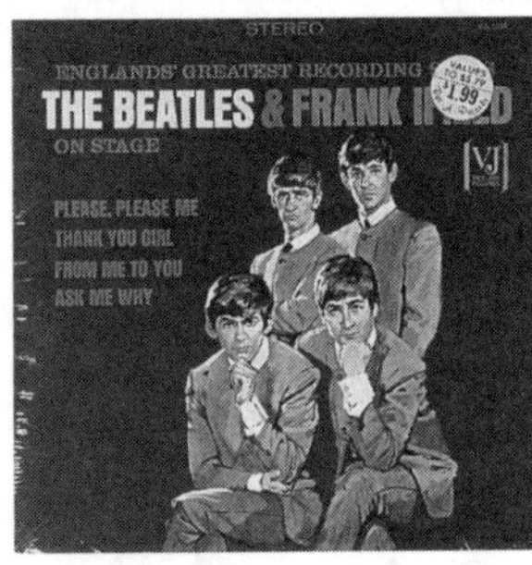

Number	Title (A Side/B Side)	Yr	VG	VG+	NM
❑ Springboard SPB-4021 [M]	The Beach Boys 1961	1977	2.00	4.00	8.00
—Also contains non-Beach Boys filler					
❑ Time-Life SRNR-03 [(2)]	The Beach Boys: 1963-1967	1986	6.25	12.50	25.00
—2 LPs in box with fold-open liner notes; original cover portrays the Beach Boys surfing					
❑ Wand WDS-688 [M]	The Beach Boys' Greatest Hits 1961-1963	1972	3.00	6.00	12.00
—Also contains non-Beach Boys filler					

BEATLES, THE

45s

Number	Title (A Side/B Side)	Yr	VG	VG+	NM
❑ Apple 2276	Hey Jude/Revolution	1968	3.75	7.50	15.00
—Original: With small Capitol logo on bottom of B-side label					
❑ Apple 2490	Get Back/Don't Let Me Down	1969	2.50	5.00	10.00
—Original: With small Capitol logo on bottom of B-side label					
❑ Apple 2531	The Ballad of John and Yoko/Old Brown Shoe	1969	2.50	5.00	10.00
—Original: With small Capitol logo on bottom of B-side label					
❑ Apple 2654	Something/Come Together	1969	2.50	5.00	10.00
—With "Mfd. by Apple" on label					
❑ Apple 2764	Let It Be/You Know My Name (Look Up My Number)	1970	3.00	6.00	12.00
—Original: With small Capitol logo on bottom of B-side label					
❑ Apple 2832	The Long and Winding Road/For You Blue	1970	2.50	5.00	10.00
—With "Mfd. by Apple" on label					
❑ Atco 6302	Sweet Georgia Brown/Take Out Some Insurance On Me Baby	1964	50.00	100.00	200.00
❑ Atco 6308	Ain't She Sweet/Nobody's Child	1964	12.50	25.00	50.00
—With "Vocal by John Lennon" on left of label					
❑ Capitol 2056	Hello Goodbye/I Am the Walrus	1967	7.50	15.00	30.00
—Original: Orange and yellow swirl, without "A Subsidiary Of"... in perimeter label print; publishing credited to "Comet" (we're not sure which came first)					
❑ Capitol 2056	Hello Goodbye/I Am the Walrus	1967	7.50	15.00	30.00
—Original: Orange and yellow swirl, without "A Subsidiary Of"... in perimeter label print; publishing credited to "Maclen" (we're not sure which came first)					
❑ Capitol 2138	Lady Madonna/The Inner Light	1968	7.50	15.00	30.00
—Original: Orange and yellow swirl, without "A Subsidiary Of"... in perimeter label print					
❑ Capitol 4274	Got to Get You Into My Life/Helter Skelter	1976	—	3.00	6.00
—Original: Orange label with "Capitol" at bottom, George Martin's name not on label					
❑ Capitol 4347	Ob-La-Di, Ob-La-Da/Julia	1976	2.00	4.00	8.00
—Original: Orange label with "Capitol" at bottom					
❑ Capitol 4612	Sgt. Pepper's Lonely Hearts Club Band-With a Little Help from My Friends/A Day in the Life	1978	2.00	4.00	8.00
—Original: Purple label; label has reeded edge					
❑ Capitol B-5100	The Beatles' Movie Medley/Fab Four on Film	1982	12.50	25.00	50.00
—Stock copy; not officially released, but some got out by mistake					
❑ Capitol B-5107	The Beatles' Movie Medley/I'm Happy Just to Dance with You	1982	—	2.50	5.00
❑ Capitol 5112	I Want to Hold Your Hand/I Saw Her Standing There	1964	7.50	15.00	30.00
—Third pressings credit "Gil Music" as B-side publisher					
❑ Capitol 5112	I Want to Hold Your Hand/I Saw Her Standing There	1964	8.75	17.50	35.00
—Second pressing credits "George Pincus and Sons" as B-side publisher					
❑ Capitol 5112	I Want to Hold Your Hand/I Saw Her Standing There	1964	10.00	20.00	40.00
—First pressing credits "Walter Hofer" as B-side publisher					
❑ Capitol 5150	Can't Buy Me Love/You Can't Do That	1964	7.50	15.00	30.00
—Original: Orange and yellow swirl, without "A Subsidiary Of"... in perimeter label print					
❑ Capitol B-5189	Love Me Do/P.S. I Love You	1982	—	2.50	5.00
—Original: Orange and yellow swirl label, black print					
❑ Capitol 5222	A Hard Day's Night/I Should Have Known Better	1964	7.50	15.00	30.00
—Original: Orange and yellow swirl, without "A Subsidiary Of". in perimeter label print; first version credited both "Unart" and "Maclen" as publishers					
❑ Capitol 5222	A Hard Day's Night/I Should Have Known Better	1964	7.50	15.00	30.00
—Orange and yellow swirl, without "A Subsidiary Of"... in perimeter label print; second version credited only "Maclen" as publishers					
❑ Capitol 5234	I'll Cry Instead/I'm Happy Just to Dance with You	1964	10.00	20.00	40.00
—Original: Orange and yellow swirl, without "A Subsidiary Of"... in perimeter label print					
❑ Capitol 5235	And I Love Her/If I Fell	1964	7.50	15.00	30.00
—Original: Orange and yellow swirl, without "A Subsidiary Of"... in perimeter label print; publishers listed as "Unart" and "Maclen"					
❑ Capitol 5235	And I Love Her/If I Fell	1964	7.50	15.00	30.00
—Original: Orange and yellow swirl, without "A Subsidiary Of"... in perimeter label print; publishers listed as "Maclen" only					
❑ Capitol 5255	Matchbox/Slow Down	1964	7.50	15.00	30.00
—Original: Orange and yellow swirl, without "A Subsidiary Of"... in perimeter label print					
❑ Capitol 5327	I Feel Fine/She's a Woman	1964	7.50	15.00	30.00
—Original: Orange and yellow swirl, without "A Subsidiary Of"... in perimeter label print					

Number	Title (A Side/B Side)	Yr	VG	VG+	NM
❑ Capitol 5371	Eight Days a Week/I Don't Want to Spoil the Party	1965	7.50	15.00	30.00
—Original: Orange and yellow swirl, without "A Subsidiary Of"... in perimeter label print					
❑ Capitol 5407	Ticket to Ride/Yes It Is	1965	7.50	15.00	30.00
—Original: Orange and yellow swirl, without "A Subsidiary Of"... in perimeter label print					
❑ Capitol 5476	Help!/I'm Down	1965	7.50	15.00	30.00
—Original: Orange and yellow swirl, without "A Subsidiary Of"... in perimeter label print					
❑ Capitol 5498	Yesterday/Act Naturally	1965	7.50	15.00	30.00
—Original: Orange and yellow swirl, without "A Subsidiary Of"... in perimeter label print					
❑ Capitol 5555	We Can Work It Out/Day Tripper	1965	7.50	15.00	30.00
—Original: Orange and yellow swirl, without "A Subsidiary Of"... in perimeter label print					
❑ Capitol 5587	Nowhere Man/What Goes On	1966	6.25	12.50	25.00
—Original: Orange and yellow swirl, without "A Subsidiary Of"... in perimeter label print; composers of B-side listed as "John Lennon-Paul McCartney"					
❑ Capitol B-5624	Twist and Shout/There's a Place	1986	—	2.50	5.00
—Black label with colorband					
❑ Capitol 5651	Paperback Writer/Rain	1966	6.25	12.50	25.00
—Original: Orange and yellow swirl, without "A Subsidiary Of"... in perimeter label print					
❑ Capitol 5715	Yellow Submarine/Eleanor Rigby	1966	6.25	12.50	25.00
—Original: Orange and yellow swirl, without "A Subsidiary Of"... in perimeter label print; print on perimeter is white					
❑ Capitol 5810	Penny Lane/Strawberry Fields Forever	1967	6.25	12.50	25.00
—Original: Orange and yellow swirl, without "A Subsidiary Of"... in perimeter label print; "Penny Lane" time listed as 3:00					
❑ Capitol 5964	All You Need Is Love/Baby, You're a Rich Man	1967	6.25	12.50	25.00
—Original: Orange and yellow swirl, without "A Subsidiary Of"... in perimeter label print					
❑ Capitol Starline 6061	Twist and Shout/There's a Place	1965	30.00	60.00	120.00
—Green swirl label					
❑ Capitol Starline 6062	Love Me Do/P.S. I Love You	1965	30.00	60.00	120.00
—Green swirl label					
❑ Capitol Starline 6063	Please Please Me/From Me to You	1965	30.00	60.00	120.00
—Green swirl label					
❑ Capitol Starline 6064	Do You Want to Know a Secret/Thank You Girl	1965	30.00	60.00	120.00
—Green swirl label					
❑ Capitol Starline 6065	Roll Over Beethoven/Misery	1965	30.00	60.00	120.00
—Green swirl label					
❑ Capitol Starline 6066	Boys/Kansas City	1965	20.00	40.00	80.00
—Green swirl label					
❑ Capitol Starline 6278	I Want to Hold Your Hand/I Saw Her Standing There	1981	5.00	10.00	20.00
—Originals have blue labels					
❑ Capitol Starline 6279	Can't Buy Me Love/You Can't Do That	1981	2.00	4.00	8.00
—Originals have blue labels					
❑ Capitol Starline 6281	A Hard Day's Night/I Should Have Known Better	1981	2.00	4.00	8.00
—Originals have blue labels					
❑ Capitol Starline 6282	I'll Cry Instead/I'm Happy Just to Dance with You	1981	2.00	4.00	8.00
—Originals have blue labels					
❑ Capitol Starline 6283	And I Love Her/If I Fell	1981	2.00	4.00	8.00
—Originals have blue labels					
❑ Capitol Starline 6284	Matchbox/Slow Down	1981	2.00	4.00	8.00
—Originals have blue labels					
❑ Capitol Starline 6286	I Feel Fine/She's a Woman	1981	2.00	4.00	8.00
—Originals have blue labels					
❑ Capitol Starline 6287	Eight Days a Week/I Don't Want to Spoil the Party	1981	2.00	4.00	8.00
—Originals have blue labels					
❑ Capitol Starline 6288	Ticket to Ride/Yes It Is	1981	2.00	4.00	8.00
—Originals have blue labels					
❑ Capitol Starline 6290	Help!/I'm Down	1981	2.00	4.00	8.00
—Originals have blue labels					
❑ Capitol Starline 6291	Yesterday/Act Naturally	1981	2.00	4.00	8.00
—Originals have blue labels					
❑ Capitol Starline 6293	We Can Work It Out/Day Tripper	1981	2.00	4.00	8.00
—Originals have blue labels					
❑ Capitol Starline 6294	Nowhere Man/What Goes On	1981	2.00	4.00	8.00
—Originals have blue labels					
❑ Capitol Starline 6296	Paperback Writer/Rain	1981	2.00	4.00	8.00
—Originals have blue labels					
❑ Capitol Starline 6297	Yellow Submarine/Eleanor Rigby	1981	2.00	4.00	8.00
—Originals have blue labels					
❑ Capitol Starline 6299	Penny Lane/Strawberry Fields Forever	1981	2.00	4.00	8.00
—Originals have blue labels					
❑ Capitol Starline 6300	All You Need Is Love/Baby You're a Rich Man	1981	2.00	4.00	8.00
—Originals have blue labels					
❑ Collectables 1501	I'm Gonna Sit Right Down and Cry Over You/Roll Over Beethoven	1982	—	—	3.00
❑ Collectables 1502	Hippy Hippy Shake/Sweet Little Sixteen	1982	—	—	3.00
❑ Collectables 1503	Lend Me Your Comb/Your Feets Too Big	1982	—	—	3.00
❑ Collectables 1504	Where Have You Been All My Life/Mr. Moonlight	1982	—	—	3.00
❑ Collectables 1505	A Taste of Honey/Besame Mucho	1982	—	—	3.00
❑ Collectables 1506	Till There Was You/Everybody's Trying to Be My Baby	1982	—	—	3.00
❑ Collectables 1507	Kansas City-Hey Hey Hey Hey/Ain't Nothing Shakin Like the Leaves on a Tree	1982	—	—	3.00
❑ Collectables 1508	To Know Her Is To Love Her/Little Queenie	1982	—	—	3.00
❑ Collectables 1509	Falling in Love Again/Sheila	1982	—	—	3.00
❑ Collectables 1510	Be-Bop-a-Lula/Hallelujah I Love Her So	1982	—	—	3.00
❑ Collectables 1511	Red Sails in the Sunset/Matchbox	1982	—	—	3.00
❑ Collectables 1512	Talkin' Bout You/Shimmy Shake	1982	—	—	3.00
❑ Collectables 1513	Long Tall Sally/I Remember You	1982	—	—	3.00
❑ Collectables 1514	Ask Me Why/Twist and Shout	1982	—	—	3.00
❑ Collectables 1515	I Saw Her Standing There/Can't Help It "Blue Angel"	1982	—	—	3.00
—B-side is actually "Reminiscing"					

Number	Title (A Side/B Side)	Yr	VG	VG+	NM
❑ Collectables 1516	I'll Try Anyway/I Don't Know Why I Do (I Just Do)	1987	2.50	5.00	10.00
—Despite label credit to The Beatles, both are Peter Best recordings					
❑ Collectables 1517	She's Not the Only Girl in Town/More Than I Need Myself	1987	2.50	5.00	10.00
—Despite label credit to The Beatles, both are Peter Best recordings					
❑ Collectables 1518	I'll Have Everything Too/I'm Checking Out Now Baby	1987	2.50	5.00	10.00
—Despite label credit to The Beatles, both are Peter Best recordings					
❑ Collectables 1519	How'd You Get to Know Her Name/If You Can't Get Her	1987	2.50	5.00	10.00
—Despite label credit to The Beatles, both are Peter Best recordings					
❑ Collectables 1520	Cry for a Shadow/Rock and Roll Music	1987	—	2.50	5.00
—Despite label credit to The Beatles, B-side is a Peter Best recording					
❑ Collectables 1521	Let's Dance/If You Love Me Baby	1987	—	3.00	6.00
—Despite label credit to The Beatles, A-side is a Tony Sheridan solo recording					
❑ Collectables 1522	What'd I Say/Sweet Georgia Brown	1987	—	3.00	6.00
—Despite label credit to The Beatles, A-side is a Tony Sheridan solo recording					
❑ Collectables 1523	Ruby Baby/Ya Ya	1987	—	3.00	6.00
—Despite label credit to The Beatles, both are by Tony Sheridan without the Fab Four					
❑ Collectables 1524	Why/I'll Try Anyway	1987	—	3.00	6.00
—Despite label credit to The Beatles, B-side is a Peter Best recording					
❑ Decca 31382	My Bonnie/The Saints	1962	7500.	11250.	15000.
—By "Tony Sheridan and the Beat Brothers"; black label with color bars (all-black label with star under "Decca" should be a counterfeit). VG 7500; VG+ 11,250					
❑ MGM 13213	My Bonnie (My Bonnie Lies Over the Ocean)/The Saints (When the Saints Go Marching In)	1964	10.00	20.00	40.00
—The Beatles with Tony Sheridan; no reference to LP on label					
❑ MGM 13227	Why/Cry for a Shadow	1964	37.50	75.00	150.00
—The Beatles with Tony Sheridan					
❑ Oldies 45 149	Do You Want to Know a Secret/Thank You Girl	1964	3.75	7.50	15.00
❑ Oldies 45 150	Please Please Me/From Me to You	1964	3.75	7.50	15.00
❑ Oldies 45 151	Love Me Do/P.S. I Love You	1964	3.75	7.50	15.00
❑ Oldies 45 152	Twist and Shout/There's a Place	1964	3.75	7.50	15.00
❑ Swan 4152	She Loves You/I'll Get You	1963	150.00	300.00	600.00
—Semi-glossy white label/red print; "Don't Drop Out" not on label					
❑ Swan 4152	She Loves You/I'll Get You	1964	7.50	15.00	30.00
—Black label, silver print, "Don't Drop Out" on label					
❑ Swan 4182	Sie Liebt Dich (She Loves You)/I'll Get You	1964	37.50	75.00	150.00
—White label, "(She Loves You)" under "Sie Liebt Dich," narrow print					
❑ Tollie 9001	Twist and Shout/There's a Place	1964	12.50	25.00	50.00
—Yellow label, black print, black "TOLLIE" in thin box					
❑ Tollie 9008	Love Me Do/P.S. I Love You	1964	12.50	25.00	50.00
—Yellow label, black print (any logo or print variation)					
❑ Vee Jay 498	Please Please Me/Ask Me Why	1963	750.00	1125.	1500.
—Misspelled "The Beattles"; number is "VJ 498"					
❑ Vee Jay 498	Please Please Me/Ask Me Why	1963	300.00	600.00	900.00
—Correct spelling; number is "VJ 498"; thick print					
❑ Vee Jay 522	From Me to You/Thank You Girl	1963	150.00	300.00	600.00
—Black rainbow label; "Vee Jay" in oval					
❑ Vee Jay 581	Please Please Me/From Me to You	1964	15.00	30.00	60.00
—Black rainbow label, brackets logo					
❑ Vee Jay 587	Do You Want to Know a Secret/Thank You Girl	1964	10.00	20.00	40.00
—Black rainbow label, brackets logo					
Albums					
❑ Apple SWBO-101 [(2)]	The Beatles	1968	37.50	75.00	200.00
—Numbered copy; includes four individual photos and large poster (included in value); because the white cover shows ring wear so readily, this is an EXTREMELY difficult album to find in near-mint condition; second pressing labels have Side 1, Song 5 correctly listed as "The Continuing Story of Bungalow Bill"; VG value 37.50; VG+ value 75					
❑ Apple SWBO-101 [(2)]	The Beatles	1968	60.00	120.00	400.00
—Numbered copy; includes four individual photos and large poster (included in value); because the white cover shows ring wear so readily, this is an EXTREMELY difficult album to find in near-mint condition; first pressing label has Side 1, Song 5 incorrectly listed as "Bungalow Bill"; VG value 60; VG+ value 120					
❑ Apple SW-153 [P]	Yellow Submarine	1969	12.50	25.00	50.00
—With Capitol logo on Side 2 bottom. "Only a Northern Song" is rechanneled.					
❑ Apple SO-383	Abbey Road	1969	10.00	20.00	40.00
—With Capitol logo on Side 2 bottom; "Her Majesty" IS listed on both the jacket and the label					
❑ Apple SW-385	Hey Jude	1970	5.00	10.00	20.00
—With "Mfd. by Apple" on label; label calls the LP "Hey Jude"					

Number	Title (A Side/B Side)	Yr	VG	VG+	NM
❑ Apple SW-385	Hey Jude	1970	10.00	20.00	40.00
—Label calls the LP "The Beatles Again"; record is "SO-385" (this could be found in retail stores as late as 1973)					
❑ Apple SKBO-3403 [P]	The Beatles 1962-1966	1973	7.50	15.00	30.00
—Custom red Apple labels. "Love Me Do" and "I Want to Hold Your Hand" are rechanneled; "She Loves You," "A Hard Day's Night," "I Feel Fine" and "Ticket to Ride" are mono; "From Me to You," "Can't Buy Me Love" and everything else is stereo.					
❑ Apple SKBO-3404 [B]	The Beatles 1967-1970	1973	7.50	15.00	30.00
—Custom blue Apple labels. "Hello Goodbye" and "Penny Lane" are mono, all others stereo.					
❑ Apple AR-34001	Let It Be	1970	6.25	12.50	25.00
—Red Apple label; originals have "Bell Sound" stamped in trail-off area, counterfeits do not					
❑ Atco 33-169 [M]	Ain't She Sweet	1964	50.00	100.00	200.00
❑ Atco SD 33-169 [P]	Ain't She Sweet	1964	100.00	200.00	400.00
—Tan and purple label; all four Beatles tracks are rechanneled					
❑ Backstage 2-201 [(2)M]	Like Dreamers Do	1982	10.00	20.00	40.00
—Gatefold package, individually numbered (numbers under 100 increase value significantly)					
❑ Backstage BSR-1111 [(3)M]	Like Dreamers Do	1982	15.00	30.00	60.00
—Two picture discs (10 of 15 Decca audition tracks on one, interviews on the other) and one white-vinyl record (same contests as musical picture disc)					
❑ Backstage BSR-1165 [PD]	The Beatles Talk with Jerry G.	1982	6.25	12.50	25.00
—Picture disc					
❑ Backstage BSR-1175 [PD]	The Beatles Talk with Jerry G., Vol. 2	1983	6.25	12.50	25.00
—Picture disc					
❑ Capitol BC-13 [(14)]	The Beatles Collection	1978	62.50	125.00	250.00
—American versions have "EMI" and "BC-13" on box spine; imports go for less					
❑ Capitol ST 2047 [P]	Meet the Beatles!	1964	30.00	60.00	120.00
—Black label with colorband; "Beatles!" on cover in tan to brown print; some labels have "ASCAP" after every title except "I Want to Hold Your Hand"; other labels have "ASCAP" after every title except "I Want to Hold Your Hand," "I Saw Her Standing There" and "I Wanna Be Your Man"; still other labels have "ASCAP" after every title except "I Want to Hold Your Hand" and "I Wanna Be Your Man"; back cover adds "Produced by George Martin" to lower left					
❑ Capitol T 2047 [M]	Meet the Beatles!	1964	37.50	75.00	150.00
—Black label with colorband; "Beatles!" on cover in tan to brown print; some labels have "ASCAP" after every title except "I Want to Hold Your Hand"; other labels have "ASCAP" after every title except "I Want to Hold Your Hand," "I Saw Her Standing There" and "I Wanna Be Your Man"; still other labels have "ASCAP" after every title except "I Want to Hold Your Hand" and "I Wanna Be Your Man"; most of the back covers add "Produced by George Martin" to lower left					
❑ Capitol ST 2080 [P]	The Beatles' Second Album	1964	25.00	50.00	100.00
—Black label with colorband. "She Loves You," "I'll Get You" and "You Can't Do That" are rechanneled					
❑ Capitol ST 2080 [P]	The Beatles' Second Album	1968	12.50	25.00	50.00
—Black colorband label; border print adds "A Subsidiary of Capitol Industries Inc."					
❑ Capitol T 2080 [M]	The Beatles' Second Album	1964	45.00	90.00	180.00
❑ Capitol ST 2108 [S]	Something New	1964	20.00	40.00	80.00
—Black label with colorband					
❑ Capitol ST 2108 [S]	Something New	1968	12.50	25.00	50.00
—Black colorband label; border print adds "A Subsidiary of Capitol Industries Inc."					
❑ Capitol T 2108 [M]	Something New	1964	37.50	75.00	150.00
❑ Capitol STBO 2222 [(2)P]	The Beatles' Story	1964	37.50	75.00	150.00
—Black label with colorband. Some of the musical snippets are rechanneled.					
❑ Capitol STBO 2222 [(2)P]	The Beatles' Story	1968	20.00	40.00	80.00
—Black colorband label; border print adds "A Subsidiary of Capitol Industries Inc."					
❑ Capitol TBO 2222 [(2)M]	The Beatles' Story	1964	50.00	100.00	200.00
❑ Capitol ST 2228 [P]	Beatles '65	1964	20.00	40.00	80.00
—Black label with colorband. "She's a Woman" and "I Feel Fine" are rechanneled.					
❑ Capitol ST 2228 [P]	Beatles '65	1968	12.50	25.00	50.00
—Black colorband label; border print adds "A Subsidiary of Capitol Industries Inc."					
❑ Capitol T 2228 [M]	Beatles '65❑ 196430.0060.00120.00❑ Capitol ST 2309 [P]The Early Beatles	1965	25.00	50.00	100.00
—Black label with colorband. "Love Me Do" and "P.S. I Love You" are rechanneled.					
❑ Capitol ST 2309 [P]	The Early Beatles	1968	12.50	25.00	50.00
—Black colorband label; border print adds "A Subsidiary of Capitol Industries Inc."					
❑ Capitol T 2309 [M]	The Early Beatles❑ 196550.00100.00200.00❑ Capitol ST 2358 [P]Beatles VI	1965	20.00	40.00	80.00
—Black label with colorband; with "See label for correct playing order" on back cover					
❑ Capitol T 2358 [M]	Beatles VI	1965	30.00	60.00	120.00
—With "See label for correct playing order" on back cover					
❑ Capitol MAS 2386 [M]	Help!	1965	37.50	75.00	150.00
❑ Capitol SMAS 2386 [P]	Help!	1965	18.75	37.50	75.00
—Black label with colorband. Has incidental music by George Martin. "Ticket to Ride" is rechanneled.					
❑ Capitol SMAS 2386 [P]	Help!	1968	12.50	25.00	50.00
—Black colorband label; border print adds "A Subsidiary of Capitol Industries Inc."					
❑ Capitol ST 2442 [S]	Rubber Soul	1965	15.00	30.00	60.00
—Black label with colorband					
❑ Capitol ST 2442 [S]	Rubber Soul	1968	12.50	25.00	50.00
—Black colorband label; border print adds "A Subsidiary of Capitol Industries Inc."					
❑ Capitol T 2442 [M]	Rubber Soul	1965	30.00	60.00	120.00
❑ Capitol ST 2553 [P]	Yesterday and Today	1966	20.00	40.00	80.00
—Trunk cover; black label with colorband (all later variations have the trunk cover). "I'm Only Sleeping," "Dr. Robert" and "And Your Bird Can Sing" are rechanneled.					
❑ Capitol ST 2553 [P]	Yesterday and Today	1966	4000.	6000.	8000.
—"First state" butcher cover (never had other cover on top); cover will be the same size as other Capitol Beatles LPs; VG value 4000; VG+ value 6000					
❑ Capitol ST 2553 [P]	Yesterday and Today	1966	500.00	750.00	1000.
—"Second state" butcher cover (trunk cover pasted over original cover)					
❑ Capitol ST 2553 [P]	Yesterday and Today	1966	375.00	750.00	1500.
—"Third state" butcher cover (trunk cover removed, leaving butcher cover intact); cover will be about 3/16-inch narrower than other Capitol Beatles LPs; value is highly negotiable depending upon the success of removing the paste-over					
❑ Capitol ST 2553 [P]	Yesterday and Today	1968	12.50	25.00	50.00
—Black colorband label; border print adds "A Subsidiary of Capitol Industries Inc."					

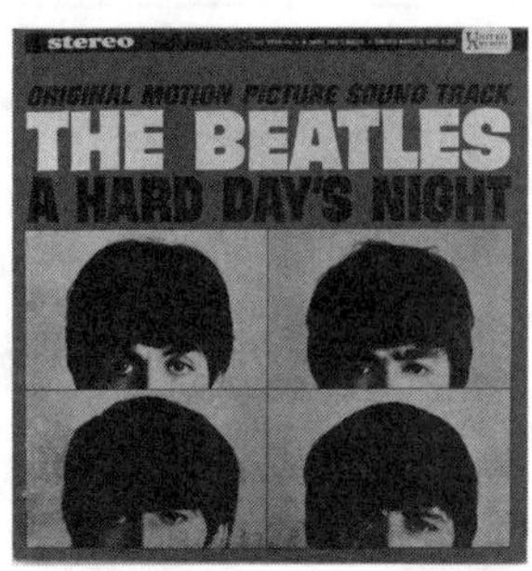

Number	Title (A Side/B Side)	Yr	VG	VG+	NM
❑ Capitol T 2553 [M]	Yesterday and Today	1966	400.00	800.00	1200.
—"Third state" butcher cover (trunk cover removed, leaving butcher cover intact); cover will be about 3/16-inch narrower than other Capitol Beatles LPs; value is highly negotiable depending upon the success of removing the paste-over; VG value 400; VG+ value 800					
❑ Capitol T 2553 [M]	Yesterday and Today	1966	2000.	3000.	4000.
—"First state" butcher cover (never had other cover on top); cover will be the same size as other Capitol Beatles LPs; VG value 2000; VG+ value 3000					
❑ Capitol T 2553 [M]	Yesterday and Today	1966	37.50	75.00	150.00
—Trunk cover					
❑ Capitol T 2553 [M]	Yesterday and Today	1966	250.00	500.00	1000.
—"Second state" butcher cover (trunk cover pasted over original cover)					
❑ Capitol ST 2576 [S]	Revolver	1966	25.00	50.00	100.00
—Black label with colorband					
❑ Capitol ST 2576 [S]	Revolver	1968	12.50	25.00	50.00
—Black colorband label; border print adds "A Subsidiary of Capitol Industries Inc."					
❑ Capitol T 2576 [M]	Revolver	1966	50.00	100.00	200.00
❑ Capitol MAS 2653 [M]	Sgt. Pepper's Lonely Hearts Club Band	1967	75.00	150.00	300.00
❑ Capitol SMAS 2653 [S]	Sgt. Pepper's Lonely Hearts Club Band	1967	25.00	50.00	100.00
—Black label with colorband					
❑ Capitol SMAS 2653 [S]	Sgt. Pepper's Lonely Hearts Club Band	1968	15.00	30.00	60.00
—Black colorband label; border print adds "A Subsidiary of Capitol Industries Inc."					
❑ Capitol MAL 2835 [M]	Magical Mystery Tour	1967	75.00	150.00	300.00
—With 24-page book bound into center of gatefold					
❑ Capitol SMAL 2835 [P]	Magical Mystery Tour	1967	25.00	50.00	100.00
—Black label with colorband; with 24-page booklet. "Penny Lane," "Baby You're a Rich Man" and "All You Need Is Love" is rechanneled, as is the second half of "I Am the Walrus" (every "stereo" version of "Walrus" is this way)					
❑ Capitol SMAL 2835 [P]	Magical Mystery Tour	1968	15.00	30.00	60.00
—Black colorband label; border print adds "A Subsidiary of Capitol Industries Inc."; with 24-page booklet					
❑ Capitol SKBO-11537 [(2)]	Rock 'n' Roll Music	1976	6.25	12.50	25.00
❑ Capitol SMAS-11638	The Beatles at the Hollywood Bowl	1977	5.00	10.00	20.00
—Originals with embossed title and ticket on front cover					
❑ Capitol SKBL-11711 [(2)P]	Love Songs	1977	5.00	10.00	20.00
—With booklet and embossed, leather-like cover. "P.S. I Love You" and "Yes It Is" are rechanneled.					
❑ Capitol SEAX-11840 [PD]	Sgt. Pepper's Lonely Hearts Club Band	1978	5.00	10.00	20.00
—Picture disc; deduct 25% for cut-outs					
❑ Capitol SEBX-11841 [(2)]	The Beatles	1978	12.50	25.00	50.00
—White vinyl; with photos and poster (with number "SEBX-11841" on each)					
❑ Capitol SEBX-11842 [P]	The Beatles 1962-1966	1978	10.00	20.00	40.00
—Red vinyl					
❑ Capitol SEBX-11843 [B]	The Beatles 1967-1970	1978	10.00	20.00	40.00
—Blue vinyl					
❑ Capitol SEAX-11900 [PD]	Abbey Road	1978	10.00	20.00	40.00
—Picture disc; deduct 25% for cut-outs					
❑ Capitol SW-11921 [P]	A Hard Day's Night	1979	3.00	6.00	12.00
—Purple label, large Capitol logo					
❑ Capitol SW-11922	Let It Be	1979	3.75	7.50	15.00
—Purple label, large Capitol logo; with poster and custom innersleeve					
❑ Capitol SHAL-12060 [B]	Rarities	1980	5.00	10.00	20.00
—Black label with colorband. First pressing says that "There's a Place" debuts in stereo (false) and that the screaming at the end of "Helter Skelter" was a "classic Lennon statement" (it's actually Ringo).					
❑ Capitol SV-12199	Reel Music	1982	2.50	5.00	10.00
—Standard issue with 12-page booklet					
❑ Capitol SV-12245 [P]	20 Greatest Hits	1982	5.00	10.00	20.00
—Purple label, large Capitol logo. "Love Me Do" and "She Loves You" are rechanneled, the other 18 tracks are stereo					
❑ Capitol SN-16020	Rock 'n' Roll Music, Volume 1	1980	2.50	5.00	10.00
❑ Capitol SN-16021	Rock 'n' Roll Music, Volume 2	1980	2.50	5.00	10.00
❑ Capitol CLJ-46435 [M]	Please Please Me	1987	5.00	10.00	20.00
—Black label, print in colorband; first Capitol version of original British LP					
❑ Capitol CLJ-46436 [M]	With the Beatles	1987	5.00	10.00	20.00
—Black label, print in colorband; first Capitol version of original British LP					
❑ Capitol CLJ-46437 [M]	A Hard Day's Night	1987	5.00	10.00	20.00
—Black label, print in colorband; first Capitol version of original British LP					
❑ Capitol CLJ-46438 [M]	Beatles for Sale	1987	5.00	10.00	20.00
—Black label, print in colorband; first Capitol version of original British LP					
❑ Capitol CLJ-46439 [S]	Help!	1987	5.00	10.00	20.00
—Black label, print in colorband; first Capitol version of original British LP					
❑ Capitol CLJ-46440 [S]	Rubber Soul	1987	5.00	10.00	20.00
—Black label, print in colorband; first Capitol version of original British LP					

Number	Title (A Side/B Side)	Yr	VG	VG+	NM
❑ Capitol CLJ-46441 [S]	Revolver	1987	5.00	10.00	20.00
—Black label, print in colorband; first Capitol version of original British LP					
❑ Capitol C1-46442 [S]	Sgt. Pepper's Lonely Hearts Club Band	1988	6.25	12.50	25.00
—New number; purple label, small Capitol logo					
❑ Capitol C1-46443 [(2)]	The Beatles	1988	12.50	25.00	50.00
—New number; purple label, small Capitol logo; with photos and poster (some copies have four photos as one perforated sheet)					
❑ Capitol C1-46445 [P]	Yellow Submarine	1988	6.25	12.50	25.00
—New number; purple label, small Capitol logo					
❑ Capitol C1-46446	Abbey Road	1988	6.25	12.50	25.00
—New number; purple label, small Capitol logo					
❑ Capitol C1-46447	Let It Be	1995	3.00	6.00	12.00
—New number (the only 1995 reissue with a completely new number)					
❑ Capitol C1-48062 [P]	Magical Mystery Tour	1988	6.25	12.50	25.00
—New number; purple label, small Capitol logo; no booklet					
❑ Capitol C1-90435 [P]	The Beatles 1962-1966	1988	7.50	15.00	30.00
—New number; purple labels, small Capitol logo					
❑ Capitol C1-90438 [B]	The Beatles 1967-1970	1988	7.50	15.00	30.00
—New number; purple labels, small Capitol logo					
❑ Capitol C1-90441 [P]	Meet the Beatles!	1988	6.25	12.50	25.00
—New number; purple label, small Capitol logo					
❑ Capitol C1-90442	Hey Jude	1988	6.25	12.50	25.00
—New number; purple label, small Capitol logo					
❑ Capitol C1-90443 [S]	Something New	1988	6.25	12.50	25.00
—New number; purple label, small Capitol logo					
❑ Capitol C1-90444 [P]	The Beatles' Second Album	1988	6.25	12.50	25.00
—New number; purple label, small Capitol logo					
❑ Capitol C1-90445 [M]	Beatles VI	1988	6.25	12.50	25.00
—New number; purple label, small Capitol logo; plays in mono despite label designation					
❑ Capitol C1-90446 [P]	Beatles '65	1988	6.25	12.50	25.00
—New number; purple label, small Capitol logo					
❑ Capitol C1-90447 [P]	Yesterday and Today	1988	6.25	12.50	25.00
—New number; purple label, small Capitol logo; stereo content uncertain					
❑ Capitol C1-90452 [S]	Revolver	1988	6.25	12.50	25.00
—New number; purple label, small Capitol logo					
❑ Capitol C1-90453 [S]	Rubber Soul	1988	6.25	12.50	25.00
—New number; purple label, small Capitol logo					
❑ Capitol C1-90454 [P]	Help!	1988	6.25	12.50	25.00
—New number; purple label, small Capitol logo					
❑ Capitol C1-91135 [(2)B]	Past Masters Volume 1 and 2	1988	6.25	12.50	25.00
—Some early tracks are in mono, but "This Boy," "She's a Woman." "Yes It Is," and "The Inner Light" are in stereo.					
❑ Clarion 601 [M]	The Amazing Beatles and Other Great English Group Sounds	1966	25.00	50.00	100.00
❑ Clarion SD 601 [P]	The Amazing Beatles and Other Great English Group Sounds	1966	50.00	100.00	200.00
—All four Beatles tracks are rechanneled					
❑ Great Northwest GNW 4007	Beatle Talk	1978	2.50	5.00	10.00
❑ Hall of Music HM-1-2200 [(2)M]	Live 1962, Hamburg, Germany	1981	12.50	25.00	50.00
—Only American LP with the original Eurpoean contents — "I Saw Her Standing There," "Twist and Shout," "Ask Me Why" and "Reminiscing" replace the four songs listed with the Lingasong issue					
❑ Lingasong LS-2-7001 [(2)R]	Live at the Star Club in Hamburg, Germany, 1962	1977	5.00	10.00	20.00
—American version contains "I'm Gonna Sit Right Down and Cry," "Where Have You Been All My Life," "Till There Was You," and "Sheila," not on imports					
❑ Lloyds ER-MC-LTD	The Great American Tour — 1965 Live Beatlemania Concert	1965	150.00	300.00	600.00
—Another interview album from the Ed Rudy people, with a live Beatles show in the background and the songs poorly overdubbed by the Liverpool Lads					
❑ Metro M-563 [M]	This Is Where It Started	1966	25.00	50.00	100.00
—Reissue of MGM album with two of the "others" tracks deleted					
❑ Metro MS-563 [R]	This Is Where It Started	1966	37.50	75.00	150.00
—In stereo cover					
❑ MGM E-4215 [M]	The Beatles with Tony Sheridan and Their Guests	1964	50.00	100.00	200.00
—Without "And Guests" on cover					
❑ MGM SE-4215 [R]	The Beatles with Tony Sheridan and Their Guests	1964	150.00	300.00	600.00
—With "And Guests" on cover					
❑ PBR International 7005/6 [(2)]	The David Wigg Interviews (The Beatles Tapes)	1980	15.00	30.00	60.00
—Black vinyl					
❑ Pickwick PTP-2098 [(2)M]	The Historic First Live Recordings	1980	4.50	9.00	18.00
—Same contents as Lingasong LP, plus "Hully Gully"					
❑ Pickwick SPC-3661 [M]	The Beatles' First Live Recordings, Volume 1	1979	3.00	6.00	12.00
❑ Pickwick SPC-3662 [M]	The Beatles' First Live Recordings, Volume 2	1979	3.00	6.00	12.00
❑ Pickwick BAN-90051 [M]	Recorded Live in Hamburg, Vol. 1	1978	7.50	15.00	30.00
❑ Pickwick BAN-90061 [M]	Recorded Live in Hamburg, Vol. 2	1978	7.50	15.00	30.00
❑ Pickwick BAN-90071 [M]	Recorded Live in Hamburg, Vol. 3	1978	10.00	20.00	40.00
❑ Polydor 24-4504 [P]	The Beatles — Circa 1960 — In the Beginning Featuring Tony Sheridan	1970	6.25	12.50	25.00
—Originals have gatefold cover					
❑ Polydor 825073-1 [P]	The Beatles — Circa 1960 — In the Beginning Featuring Tony Sheridan	1988	5.00	10.00	20.00
—Reissue with new number					
❑ Radio Pulsebeat News 2	The American Tour with Ed Rudy	1964	25.00	50.00	100.00
—Yellow label; some copies came with a special edition of Teen Talk magazine (add 50%)					
❑ Radio Pulsebeat News 3	1965 Talk Album — Ed Rudy with New U.S. Tour	1965	37.50	75.00	150.00
—"The Beatles" in black print under front cover photo (other versions appear to be bootlegs)					
❑ Raven/PVC 8911	Talk Downunder	1981	2.50	5.00	10.00
❑ Savage BM-69 [M]	The Savage Young Beatles	1964	37.50	75.00	150.00
—Orange label; no legitimate copy says "Stereo" on cover					

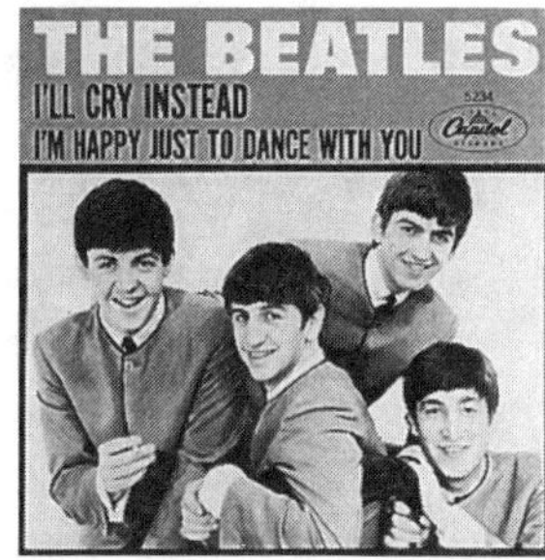

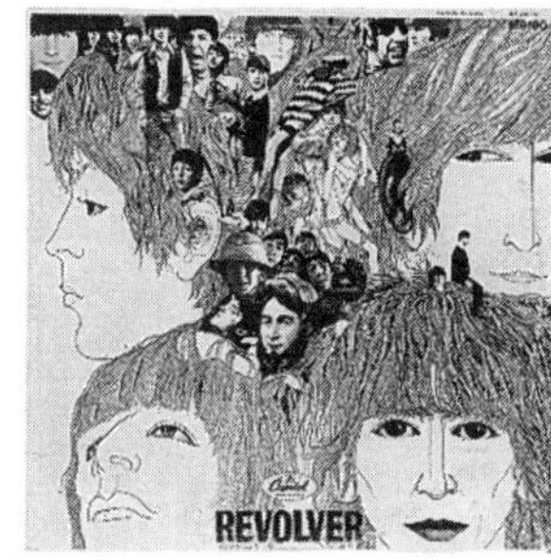

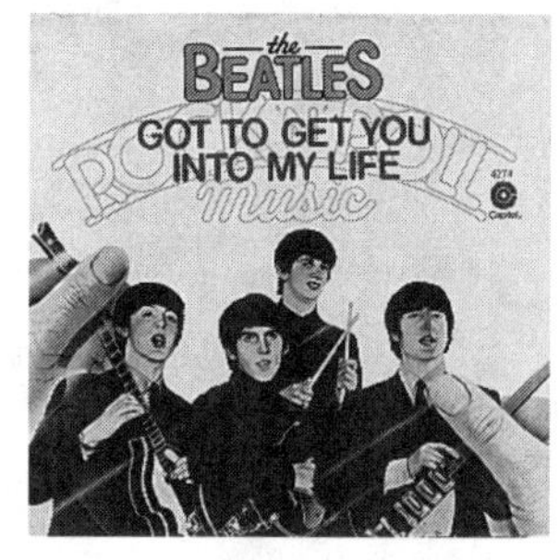

Number	Title (A Side/B Side)	Yr	VG	VG+	NM
❑ United Artists UAL 3366 [M]	A Hard Day's Night	1964	50.00	100.00	200.00
—With "I Cry Instead" listing					
❑ United Artists UAS 6366 [P]	A Hard Day's Night	1964	50.00	100.00	200.00
—With "I Cry Instead" listing					
❑ Vee Jay DX-30 [(2)M]	The Beatles vs. The Four Seasons	1964	200.00	400.00	800.00
—Combines "Introducing the Beatles" with "Golden Hits of the Four Seasons" (Vee Jay 1065)					
❑ Vee Jay DXS-30 [(2)S]	The Beatles vs. The Four Seasons	1964	1500.	2250.	3000.
—Combines "Introducing the Beatles" with "Golden Hits of the Four Seasons" (Vee Jay 1065); VG value 1500; VG+ value 2250					
❑ Vee Jay PRO 202 [M]	Hear the Beatles Tell All	1964	50.00	100.00	200.00
—With "PRO" prefix on label					
❑ Vee Jay PRO 202 [M]	Hear the Beatles Tell All	1979	2.50	5.00	10.00
—Authorized reissue; every copy with the word "Stereo" on the front cover is this edition, though the record still plays in mono (no 1964 copies have "Stereo" on the cover)					
❑ Vee Jay LP 1062 [M]	Introducing the Beatles	1964	62.50	125.00	250.00
—Song titles cover; with "Please Please Me" and "Ask Me Why"; brackets Vee Jay logo with colorband (most common authentic version)					
❑ Vee Jay LP 1062 [M]	Introducing the Beatles	1964	1500.	2750.	4000.
—"Ad back" cover; with "Love Me Do" and "P.S. I Love You"; oval Vee Jay logo with colorband only!; VG value 1500; VG+ value 2750					
❑ Vee Jay SR 1062 [B]	Introducing the Beatles	1964	4000.	8000.	12000.
—"Ad back" cover; with "Love Me Do" and "P.S. I Love You" (both mono); oval Vee Jay logo with colorband only!; VG value 4000; VG+ value 8000					
❑ Vee Jay SR 1062 [S]	Introducing the Beatles	1964	375.00	750.00	1500.
—Song titles cover; with "Please Please Me" and "Ask Me Why"; brackets Vee Jay logo with colorband					
❑ Vee Jay LP 1085 [M]	The Beatles and Frank Ifield on Stage	1964	2000.	3500.	5000.
—Portrait of Beatles cover; counterfeits are poorly reproduced and have no spine print; VG value 2000; VG+ value 3500					
❑ Vee Jay LP 1085 [M]	Jolly What! The Beatles and Frank Ifield on Stage	1964	62.50	125.00	250.00
—Man in Beatle wig cover; originals have printing on spine and a dark blue/purple background (counterfeits have a black background and no spine print)					
❑ Vee Jay SR 1085 [B]	The Beatles and Frank Ifield on Stage	1964	4000.	8000.	12000.
—Portrait of Beatles cover; "Stereo" on both cover and label; VG value 4000; VG+ value 8000					
❑ Vee Jay SR 1085 [B]	Jolly What! The Beatles and Frank Ifield on Stage	1964	125.00	250.00	500.00
—Man in Beatle wig cover; "Stereo" on both cover and label. "From Me to You" is mono.					
❑ Vee Jay LP 1092 [M]	Songs, Pictures and Stories of the Fabulous Beatles	1964	125.00	250.00	500.00
—All copies have gatefold cover with 2/3 width on front; also, all copies have "Introducing the Beatles" records. Oval Vee Jay logo with colorband.					
❑ Vee Jay VJS 1092 [S]	Songs, Pictures and Stories of the Fabulous Beatles	1964	800.00	1600.	2400.
—All copies have gatefold cover with 2/3 width on front; also, all copies have "Introducing the Beatles" records. Oval Vee Jay logo with colorband; VG value 800; VG+ value 1600					

BEAU BRUMMELS, THE

45s

Number	Title (A Side/B Side)	Yr	VG	VG+	NM
❑ Autumn 8	Laugh, Laugh/Still in Love with You Baby	1965	3.75	7.50	15.00
—White label					
❑ Autumn 10	Just a Little/They'll Make You Cry	1965	3.75	7.50	15.00
❑ Autumn 16	You Tell Me Why/I Want You	1965	2.00	4.00	8.00
❑ Autumn 20	Don't Talk to Strangers/In Good Time	1965	2.00	4.00	8.00
❑ Autumn 24	Good Time Music/Sad Little Girl	1965	2.00	4.00	8.00
❑ Rhino RNOR 4506	Laugh, Laugh/Just a Little	1984	—	2.00	4.00
❑ Warner Bros. 5813	One Too Many Mornings/She Reigns	1966	2.00	4.00	8.00
❑ Warner Bros. 5848	Fine with Me/Here We Are Again	1966	2.00	4.00	8.00
❑ Warner Bros. 7014	Don't Make Promises/Two Days 'Til Tomorrow	1967	2.00	4.00	8.00
❑ Warner Bros. 7079	Magic Hollow/Lower Level	1967	2.00	4.00	8.00
❑ Warner Bros. 7204	Are You Happy/Lift Me	1968	—	3.00	6.00
❑ Warner Bros. 7218	I'm a Sleeper/Long Walking Down to Misery	1968	—	3.00	6.00
❑ Warner Bros. 7260	Cherokee Girl/Deep Water	1969	—	3.00	6.00
❑ Warner Bros. 8119	You Tell Me Why/Down to the Bottom	1975	—	2.50	5.00

Albums

Number	Title (A Side/B Side)	Yr	VG	VG+	NM
❑ Accord SN-7175	Just a Little	1982	2.50	5.00	10.00
❑ Autumn LP 103 [M]	Introducing the Beau Brummels	1965	12.50	25.00	50.00
❑ Autumn SLP 103 [S]	Introducing the Beau Brummels	1965	15.00	30.00	60.00
❑ Autumn LP 104 [M]	The Beau Brummels, Volume 2	1965	10.00	20.00	40.00
❑ Autumn SLP 104 [S]	The Beau Brummels, Volume 2	1965	12.50	25.00	50.00
❑ JAS 5000	Original Hits of the Beau Brummels	1976	3.75	7.50	15.00
❑ Post 6000	The Beau Brummels Sing	196?	3.75	7.50	15.00
❑ Rhino RNLP-101	The Best of the Beau Brummels	1981	2.50	5.00	10.00
❑ Rhino RNLP-102	Introducing the Beau Brummels	1981	2.50	5.00	10.00
❑ Rhino RNLP-104	From the Vaults	1981	3.00	6.00	12.00
❑ Rhino RNLP-70171	The Best of the Beau Brummels (Golden Archive Series)	1986	2.50	5.00	10.00
❑ Vault LP-114 [M]	Best of the Beau Brummels	1967	6.25	12.50	25.00

Number	Title (A Side/B Side)	Yr	VG	VG+	NM
❑ Vault SLP-114 [S]	Best of the Beau Brummels	1967	6.25	12.50	25.00
❑ Vault SLP-121	Beau Brummels, Vol. 44	1968	6.25	12.50	25.00
❑ Warner Bros. W 1644 [M]	Beau Brummels '66	1966	5.00	10.00	20.00
❑ Warner Bros. WS 1644 [S]	Beau Brummels '66	1966	6.25	12.50	25.00
❑ Warner Bros. W 1692 [M]	Triangle	1967	5.00	10.00	20.00
❑ Warner Bros. WS 1692 [S]	Triangle	1967	6.25	12.50	25.00
❑ Warner Bros. WS 1760	Bradley's Barn	1968	6.25	12.50	25.00
❑ Warner Bros. BS 2842	The Beau Brummels	1975	5.00	10.00	20.00

BEE GEES

45s

Number	Title (A Side/B Side)	Yr	VG	VG+	NM
❑ Atco 6487	New York Mining Disaster 1941/I Can't See Nobody	1967	3.00	6.00	12.00
❑ Atco 6503	To Love Somebody/Close Another Door	1967	2.50	5.00	10.00
❑ Atco 6521	Holiday/Every Christian Lion Hearted Man Will Show You	1967	2.50	5.00	10.00
❑ Atco 6532	(The Lights Went Out in) Massachusetts/Sir Geoffrey Saved the World	1967	2.50	5.00	10.00
❑ Atco 6548	Words/Sinking Ships	1968	2.50	5.00	10.00
❑ Atco 6570	Jumbo/The Singer Sang His Song	1968	2.00	4.00	8.00
❑ Atco 6603	I've Gotta Get a Message to You/Kitty Can	1968	2.00	4.00	8.00
❑ Atco 6639	I Started a Joke/Kilburn Towers	1969	2.00	4.00	8.00
❑ Atco 6657	First of May/Lamplight	1969	2.00	4.00	8.00
❑ Atco 6682	Tomorrow Tomorrow/Sun in My Morning	1969	2.00	4.00	8.00
❑ Atco 6702	Don't Forget to Remember/The Lord	1969	2.50	5.00	10.00
❑ Atco 6741	If Only I Had My Mind on Something Else/Sweetheart	1970	2.00	4.00	8.00
❑ Atco 6752	I.O.I.O./Then You Left Me	1970	2.00	4.00	8.00
❑ Atco 6795	Lonely Days/Man for All Seasons	1971	—	3.00	6.00
❑ Atco 6824	How Can You Mend a Broken Heart/Country Woman	1971	—	3.00	6.00
❑ Atco 6847	Don't Wanna Live Inside Myself/Walking Back to Waterloo	1971	—	3.00	6.00
❑ Atco 6871	My World/On Time	1972	—	2.50	5.00
❑ Atco 6896	Run to Me/Road to Alaska	1972	—	2.50	5.00
❑ Atco 6909	Alive/Paper Mache, Cabbages and Kings	1972	—	2.50	5.00
❑ RSO 401	Saw a New Morning/My Life Has Been a Song	1973	—	3.00	6.00
❑ RSO 404	Wouldn't I Be Someone/Elisa	1973	—	3.00	6.00
❑ RSO 408	Mr. Natural/It Doesn't Matter Much to Me	1974	—	3.00	6.00
❑ RSO 410	Throw a Penny/I Can't Let Go	1974	—	3.00	6.00
❑ RSO 501	Charade/Heavy Breathing	1974	—	3.00	6.00
❑ RSO 510	Jive Talkin'/Wind of Change	1975	—	2.00	4.00
❑ RSO 515	Nights on Broadway/Edge of the Universe	1975	—	2.00	4.00
❑ RSO 519	Fanny (Be Tender With My Love)/Country Lanes	1975	—	2.00	4.00
❑ RSO 853	You Should Be Dancing/Subway	1976	—	2.00	4.00
❑ RSO 859	Love So Right/You Stepped Into My Life	1976	—	2.00	4.00
❑ RSO 867	Boogie Child/Lovers	1976	—	2.00	4.00
❑ RSO 880	Edge of the Universe/Words	1977	—	2.00	4.00
❑ RSO 882	How Deep Is Your Love/Can't Keep a Good Man Down	1977	—	2.00	4.00
❑ RSO 885	Stayin' Alive/If I Can't Have You	1977	—	2.00	4.00
❑ RSO 889	Night Fever/Down the Road	1978	—	2.00	4.00
❑ RSO 907	She's Leaving Home/Oh! Darling	1978	—	2.00	4.00
—B-side by Robin Gibb solo					
❑ RSO 913	Too Much Heaven/Rest Your Love on Me	1978	—	2.00	4.00
❑ RSO 918	Tragedy/Until	1979	—	2.00	4.00
❑ RSO 925	Love You Inside Out/I'm Satisfied	1979	—	2.00	4.00
❑ RSO 1066	He's a Liar/(Instrumental)	1981	—	—	3.00
❑ RSO 1067	Living Eyes/I Still Love You	1981	—	—	3.00
❑ RSO 8001	Come On Over/Jive Talkin'	1980	—	2.00	4.00
—Reissue series; first time on 45 for A-side					
❑ RSO 8003	You Should Be Dancing/Love So Right	1980	—	—	3.00
—Reissue series					
❑ RSO 8009	Stayin' Alive/How Deep Is Your Love	1980	—	—	3.00
—Reissue series					
❑ RSO 8010	To Love Somebody/How Can You Mend a Broken Heart	1980	—	—	3.00
—Reissue series					
❑ RSO 8011	Lonely Days/Words	1980	—	—	3.00
—Reissue series					
❑ RSO 8012	Nights on Broadway/Boogie Child	1980	—	—	3.00
—Reissue series					
❑ RSO 8019	More Than a Woman/Night Fever	1980	—	2.00	4.00
—Reissue series; first time on 45 for A-side					
❑ RSO 8022	Tragedy/Love You Inside Out	1980	—	—	3.00
—Reissue series					
❑ RSO 8030	Too Much Heaven/Rest Your Love on Me	1980	—	—	3.00
—Reissue series					
❑ RSO 813173-7	The Woman in You/Stayin' Alive	1983	—	—	3.00
❑ RSO 815235-7	Someone Belonging to Someone/I Love You Too Much	1983	—	—	3.00
❑ Warner Bros. 22733	You Win Again/Will You Ever Let Me	1989	—	2.50	5.00
❑ Warner Bros. 22899	One/Wing and a Prayer	1989	—	—	3.00
❑ Warner Bros. 28139	E.S.P./Overnight	1987	—	—	3.00
❑ Warner Bros. 28351	You Win Again/Backtafunk	1987	—	—	3.00

Albums

Number	Title (A Side/B Side)	Yr	VG	VG+	NM
❑ Atco 33-223 [M]	Bee Gees' 1st	1967	7.50	15.00	30.00
❑ Atco SD 33-223 [S]	Bee Gees' 1st	1967	5.00	10.00	20.00
—Brown and purple label original					
❑ Atco 33-233 [M]	Horizontal	1968	7.50	15.00	30.00
❑ Atco SD 33-233 [S]	Horizontal	1968	5.00	10.00	20.00
—Brown and purple label original					
❑ Atco SD 33-253 [S]	Idea	1968	5.00	10.00	20.00
—Brown and purple label original					

Number	Title (A Side/B Side)	Yr	VG	VG+	NM
❑ Atco SD 33-264 [R]	Rare, Precious & Beautiful	1968	3.75	7.50	15.00
—Brown and purple label original					
❑ Atco SD 33-292 [S]	Best of Bee Gees	1969	3.00	6.00	12.00
❑ Atco SD 33-321 [R]	Rare, Precious & Beautiful, Volume 2	1970	3.00	6.00	12.00
❑ Atco SD 33-327	Cucumber Castle	1970	3.00	6.00	12.00
❑ Atco SD 33-353 [S]	2 Years On	1971	3.00	6.00	12.00
❑ Atco SD 2-702 [(2)]	Odessa	1969	10.00	20.00	40.00
—Red felt cover					
❑ Atco SD 7003	Trafalgar	1971	3.00	6.00	12.00
❑ Atco SD 7012	To Whom It May Concern	1972	3.00	6.00	12.00
❑ Pickwick BAN-90011 [R]	Turn Around, Look at Me	1978	2.00	4.00	8.00
—Reissue of Australian recordings					
❑ Pickwick BAN-90021 [R]	Monday's Rain	1978	2.00	4.00	8.00
—Reissue of Australian recordings					
❑ Pickwick BAN-90031 [R]	Take Hold of That Star	1978	2.00	4.00	8.00
—Reissue of Australian recordings					
❑ Pickwick BAN-90041 [R]	Peace of Mind	1978	2.00	4.00	8.00
—Reissue of Australian recordings; tracks on this LP were making their first appearance in the U.S.					
❑ RSO SO 870 [M]	Life in a Tin Can	1973	15.00	30.00	60.00
—Mono is white label promo only; cover has red "d/j copy monaural" sticker on front; Side 1 master number is "SO-14153"; Side 2 master number is "SO-14154"					
❑ RSO SO 870 [S]	Life in a Tin Can	1973	2.50	5.00	10.00
—Side 1 master number is "ST-SO-722677"; Side 2 master number is "ST-SO-722678"					
❑ RSO SO 875	Best of Bee Gees, Vol. 2	1973	2.50	5.00	10.00
❑ RSO RS-1-3003	Children of the World	1976	2.50	5.00	10.00
❑ RSO RS-1-3006	Bee Gees Gold, Volume One	1976	2.50	5.00	10.00
❑ RSO RS-1-3007	Odessa	1976	2.50	5.00	10.00
—Condensed version of Atco original					
❑ RSO RS-1-3024	Main Course	1977	2.00	4.00	8.00
❑ RSO RS-1-3041	Spirits Having Flown	1979	2.50	5.00	10.00
—Some pressings have a cardboard innersleeve, others a paper innersleeve. No difference in value.					
❑ RSO RS-1-3098	Living Eyes	1981	2.50	5.00	10.00
❑ RSO RS-2-3901 [(2)]	Here At Last...Bee Gees...Live	1977	3.00	6.00	12.00
❑ RSO RS-2-4200 [(2)]	Bee Gees' Greatest	1979	3.00	6.00	12.00
❑ RSO SO 4800	Mr. Natural	1974	2.50	5.00	10.00
❑ RSO SO 4807	Main Course	1975	2.50	5.00	10.00
❑ RSO 823274-1 [(2)]	Here At Last...Bee Gees...Live	1984	2.50	5.00	10.00
❑ RSO 823658-1	Children of the World	1984	2.00	4.00	8.00
❑ RSO 823659-1	Bee Gees Gold, Volume One	1984	2.00	4.00	8.00
❑ RSO 825390-1 [(2)]	Bee Gees' Greatest	1984	2.50	5.00	10.00
—Gatefold replaced by single-pocket cover					
❑ Warner Bros. 25541	E.S.P.	1987	2.50	5.00	10.00
❑ Warner Bros. 25887	One	1989	3.00	6.00	12.00

BELL, ARCHIE, AND THE DRELLS

45s

Number	Title (A Side/B Side)	Yr	VG	VG+	NM
❑ Atlantic 2478	Tighten Up/Tighten Up — Part 2	1968	2.00	4.00	8.00
❑ Atlantic 2478	Tighten Up/Dog Eat Dog	1968	3.00	6.00	12.00
❑ Atlantic 2534	I Can't Stop Dancing/You're Such a Beautiful Child	1968	—	3.50	7.00
❑ Atlantic 2559	Do the Choo Choo/Love Will Rain on You	1968	—	3.50	7.00
❑ Atlantic 2583	(There's Gonna Be A) Showdown/Go for What You Know	1968	—	3.50	7.00
❑ Atlantic 2612	I Love My Baby/Just a Little Closer	1969	—	3.50	7.00
❑ Atlantic 2644	Girl You're Too Young/Do the Hand Jive	1969	—	3.50	7.00
❑ Atlantic 2663	My Balloon's Going Up/Giving Up Dancing	1969	—	3.50	7.00
❑ Atlantic 2693	A World Without Music/Here I Go Again	1969	—	3.50	7.00
❑ Atlantic 2721	Don't Let the Music Slip Away/Houston, Texas	1970	—	3.50	7.00
❑ Atlantic 2744	I Wish/Get from the Bottom	1970	—	3.50	7.00
❑ Atlantic 2769	Wrap It Up/Deal with Him	1970	—	3.50	7.00
❑ Atlantic 2793	I Just Want to Fall in Love/Love at First Sight	1971	—	3.00	6.00
❑ Atlantic 2829	Let the World Know/Archie's in Love	1971	—	3.00	6.00
❑ Atlantic 2855	Green Power/I Can't Face You Baby	1972	—	3.00	6.00
❑ Becket 45-4	Any Time Is Right/(B-side unknown)	1981	—	2.00	4.00
❑ East West 2048	She's My Woman/The Yankee Dance	1968	—	3.50	7.00
❑ Glades 1707	Dancing to Your Music/Count the Ways	1973	—	3.00	6.00
❑ Glades 1711	Ain't Nothing for a Man in Love/You Never Know What's On a Woman's Mind	1973	—	3.00	6.00
❑ Glades 1718	Girls Grow Up Faster Than Boys/Love's Gonna Rain on You	1973	—	3.00	6.00

Number	Title (A Side/B Side)	Yr	VG	VG+	NM
❑ Ovide 228	Tighten Up/Dog Eat Dog	1967	15.00	30.00	60.00
❑ Philadelphia Int'l 3605	Nothing Comes Easy/Right Here Is Where I Want to Be	1976	—	2.50	5.00
❑ Philadelphia Int'l 3615	Everybody Have a Good Time/I Bet I Can Do That Dance You're Doin'	1977	—	2.50	5.00
❑ Philadelphia Int'l 3632	Glad You Could Make It/There's No Other Like You	1977	—	2.50	5.00
❑ Philadelphia Int'l 3637	I've Been Missing You/It's Hard Not to Love You	1977	—	2.50	5.00
❑ Philadelphia Int'l 3651	Old People/On the Radio	1978	—	2.50	5.00
❑ Philadelphia Int'l. 3710	Strategy/We Got 'Um Dancin'	1979	—	2.50	5.00
❑ TSOP 4767	I Could Dance All Night/King of the Castle	1975	—	2.50	5.00
❑ TSOP 4774	The Soul City Walk/King of the Castle	1975	—	2.50	5.00
❑ TSOP 4775	Let's Groove (Part 1)/Let's Groove (Part 2)	1976	—	2.50	5.00
❑ WMOT 03057	Touchin' You/(Instrumental)	1982	—	2.50	5.00
Albums					
❑ Atlantic 8181 [M]	Tighten Up	1968	12.50	25.00	50.00
❑ Atlantic SD 8181 [S]	Tighten Up	1968	7.50	15.00	30.00
❑ Atlantic SD 8204	I Can't Stop Dancing	1968	7.50	15.00	30.00
❑ Atlantic SD 8226	There's Gonna Be a Showdown	1969	7.50	15.00	30.00
❑ Philadelphia Int'l. PZ 34323	Where Will You Go When the Party's Over	1976	2.50	5.00	10.00
❑ Philadelphia Int'l. PZ 34855	Hard Not to Like It	1977	2.50	5.00	10.00
❑ Philadelphia Int'l. JZ 36096	Strategy	1979	2.50	5.00	10.00
❑ TSOP PZ 33844	Dance Your Troubles Away	1975	2.50	5.00	10.00

BELMONTS, THE

45s

Number	Title (A Side/B Side)	Yr	VG	VG+	NM
❑ Dot 17173	Reminiscing/She Only Wants to Do Her Thing	1968	3.75	7.50	15.00
❑ Dot 17257	Have You Heard-The Worst That Could Happen/Answer Me My Love	1969	3.75	7.50	15.00
❑ Laurie 3080	We Belong Together/Such a Long Way	1961	7.50	15.00	30.00
❑ Laurie 3631	A Brand New Song/Story Teller	1975	—	2.50	5.00
❑ Laurie 3698	Medley/You're the Only Girl for Me	198?	—	2.50	5.00
—B-side by Ernie Maresca					
❑ Sabina 502	I Need Some One/That American Dance	1961	6.25	12.50	25.00
❑ Sabina 503	Hombre/I Confess	1962	6.25	12.50	25.00
❑ Sabina 505	Come On Little Angel/How About Me	1962	6.25	12.50	25.00
—Black label					
❑ Sabina 507	Diddle-Dee-Dum (What Happens When Your Love Has Gone)/ Farewell	1962	5.00	10.00	20.00
❑ Sabina 509	Ann Marie/Ac-Cent-Tchu-Ate the Positive	1963	5.00	10.00	20.00
❑ Sabina 513	Let's Call It a Day/Walk On Boy	1963	5.00	10.00	20.00
❑ Sabina 517	More Important Things to Do/Walk On Boy	1963	5.00	10.00	20.00
❑ Sabina 519	C'mon Everybody/Why	1964	5.00	10.00	20.00
❑ Sabina 521	Summertime/Nothing in Return	1964	5.00	10.00	20.00
❑ Sabrina 500	Tell Me Why/Smoke from Your Cigarette	1961	6.25	12.50	25.00
❑ Sabrina 501	Searching for a New Love/Don't Get Around Much Anymore	1961	6.25	12.50	25.00
❑ Strawberry 106	Cheek to Cheek/Voyager	1976	—	2.50	5.00
❑ Surprise 1000	Tell Me Why/Smoke from Your Cigarette	1961	25.00	50.00	100.00
❑ United Artists 809	Wintertime/I Don't Know Why, I Just Do	1965	5.00	10.00	20.00
❑ United Artists 904	(Then) I Walked Away/Today My Love Has Gone Away	1965	5.00	10.00	20.00
❑ United Artists 966	I Got a Feeling/To Be with You	1965	5.00	10.00	20.00
❑ United Artists 50007	Come with Me/You're Like a Mystery	1966	6.25	12.50	25.00
Albums					
❑ Buddah BDS-5123	Cigars, Acapella, Candy	1972	12.50	25.00	50.00
❑ Dot DLP-25949	Summer Love	1969	7.50	15.00	30.00
❑ Sabina SALP-5001 [M]	The Belmonts' Carnival of Hits	1962	37.50	75.00	150.00
❑ Strawberry 6001	Cheek to Cheek	1978	3.75	7.50	15.00

BENTON, BROOK

45s

Number	Title (A Side/B Side)	Yr	VG	VG+	NM
❑ All Platinum 2364	Can't Take My Eyes Off You/Weekend with Feathers	1976	—	2.50	5.00
❑ Brut 810	Lay Lady Lay/A Touch of Class	1973	—	2.50	5.00
❑ Brut 816	South Carolina/(B-side unknown)	1973	—	2.50	5.00
❑ Cotillion 13107	Rainy Night in Georgia/Nothing Takes the Place of You	197?	—	2.00	4.00
—Part of "Atlantic Oldies Series"					
❑ Cotillion 44007	I Just Don't Know What to Do with Myself/Do Your Own Thing	1968	2.00	4.00	8.00
❑ Cotillion 44031	She Knows What to Do with 'Em/Touch 'Em with Love	1969	2.00	4.00	8.00
❑ Cotillion 44034	Nothing Can Take the Place of You/Woman Without Love	1969	2.00	4.00	8.00
❑ Cotillion 44057	Rainy Night in Georgia/Where Do You Go from Here	1969	2.50	5.00	10.00
❑ Cotillion 44072	My Way/A Little Bit of Soap	1970	—	3.00	6.00
❑ Cotillion 44078	Don't It Make You Want to Go Home/I've Gotta Be Me	1970	—	3.00	6.00
❑ Cotillion 44093	Shoes/Let Me Fix It	1970	—	3.00	6.00
❑ Cotillion 44110	Whoever Finds This, I Love You/Heaven Help Us All	1971	—	3.00	6.00
❑ Cotillion 44119	Take a Look at Your Hands/If You Think God Is Dead	1971	—	3.00	6.00
❑ Cotillion 44130	Please Send Me Someone to Love/She Even Woke Me Up to Say Goodbye	1971	—	3.00	6.00
❑ Cotillion 44138	A Black Child Can't Smile/If You Think God Is Dead	1971	—	3.00	6.00
❑ Cotillion 44141	Soul Santa/Let Us All Get Together with the Lord	1971	2.00	4.00	8.00
❑ Cotillion 44152	Movin' Day/Poor Make Believer	1972	—	3.00	6.00
❑ Epic 9177	Love Made Me Your Fool/Give Me a Sign	1956	6.25	12.50	25.00
❑ Epic 9199	The Wall/All My Love Belongs to You	1957	6.25	12.50	25.00
❑ Mercury 30101	Merry Christmas, Happy New Year/This Time Of The Year	196?	2.00	4.00	8.00
—Reissue					
❑ Mercury 71394	It's Just a Matter of Time/Hurtin' Inside	1959	3.75	7.50	15.00
❑ Mercury 71443	Endlessly/So Close	1959	3.75	7.50	15.00
❑ Mercury 71478	Thank You Pretty Baby/With All of My Heart	1959	3.75	7.50	15.00
❑ Mercury 71512	So Many Ways/I Want You Forever	1959	3.75	7.50	15.00
❑ Mercury 71554	This Time of the Year/Nothing in the World	1959	3.75	7.50	15.00
❑ Mercury 71558	This Time of the Year/How Many Times	1959	3.75	7.50	15.00

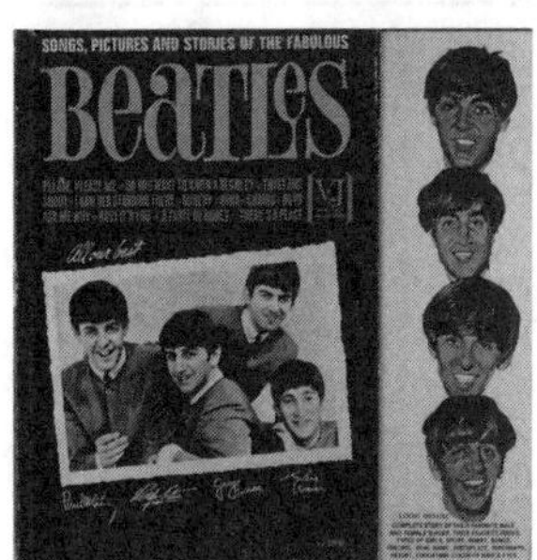

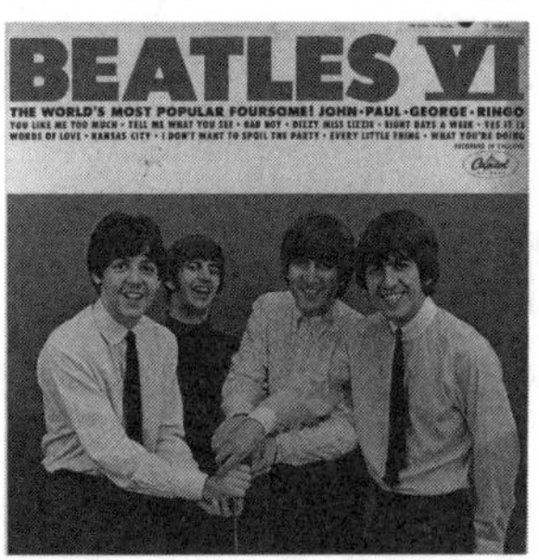

Number	Title (A Side/B Side)	Yr	VG	VG+	NM
❑ Mercury 71566	The Ties That Bind/Hither, Thither and Yon	1960	3.00	6.00	12.00
❑ Mercury 71652	Kiddio/The Same One	1960	3.00	6.00	12.00
❑ Mercury 71722	Fools Rush In (Where Angels Fear to Tread)/Someday You'll Want Me to Want You	1960	3.00	6.00	12.00
❑ Mercury 71730	This Time of the Year/Merry Christmas, Happy New Year	1960	3.00	6.00	12.00
❑ Mercury 71774	Think Twice/For My Baby	1961	3.00	6.00	12.00
❑ Mercury 71820	The Boll Weevil Song/Your Eyes	1961	3.00	6.00	12.00
❑ Mercury 71859	Frankie and Johnny/It's Just a House Without You	1961	3.00	6.00	12.00
❑ Mercury 71903	Revenge/Really Really	1961	3.00	6.00	12.00
❑ Mercury 71912	Shadrack/The Lost Penny	1961	3.00	6.00	12.00
❑ Mercury 71925	Walk on the Wild Side/Somewhere in the Used to Be	1962	2.50	5.00	10.00
❑ Mercury 71962	Hit Record/Thanks to the Fool	1962	2.50	5.00	10.00
❑ Mercury 72009	Two Tickets to Paradise/It's Alright	1962	—	—	—
—Unreleased					
❑ Mercury 72024	Lie to Me/With the Touch of Your Hand	1962	2.50	5.00	10.00
❑ Mercury 72055	Hotel Happiness/Still Waters Run Deep	1962	2.50	5.00	10.00
❑ Mercury 72099	I Got What I Wanted/Dearer Than Life	1963	2.50	5.00	10.00
❑ Mercury 72135	My True Confession/Tender Years	1963	2.50	5.00	10.00
❑ Mercury 72177	Two Tickets to Paradise/Don't Hate Me	1963	2.50	5.00	10.00
❑ Mercury 72214	You're All I Want for Christmas/This Time of the Year	1963	2.50	5.00	10.00
❑ Mercury 72230	Going, Going, Gone/After Midnight	1963	2.50	5.00	10.00
❑ Mercury 72266	Too Late to Turn Back Now/Another Cup of Coffee	1964	2.50	5.00	10.00
❑ Mercury 72303	A House Is Not a Home/Come On Back	1964	2.50	5.00	10.00
❑ Mercury 72333	Lumberjack/Don't Do What I Did (Do What I Say)	1964	2.50	5.00	10.00
❑ Mercury 72365	Do It Right/Please, Please Make It Easy	1964	2.50	5.00	10.00
❑ Mercury 72398	Special Years/Where There's a Will (There's a Way)	1965	2.50	5.00	10.00
❑ Mercury 72446	Love Me Now/A-Sleepin' at the End of the Bed	1965	2.50	5.00	10.00
❑ Mercury 872796-7	It's Just a Matter of Time/Hurtin' Inside	1989	—	2.00	4.00
❑ Mercury 872798-7	Endlessly/So Many Ways	1989	—	2.00	4.00
❑ MGM 14440	If You've Got the Time/You Take Me Home Honey	1972	—	2.50	5.00
❑ Okeh 7058	The Kentuckian Song/Ooh	1955	6.25	12.50	25.00
❑ Okeh 7065	Bring Me Love/Some of My Best Friends	1956	6.25	12.50	25.00
❑ Olde World 1100	Makin' Love Is Good for You/Better Times	1977	—	2.50	5.00
❑ Olde World 1107	Soft/Glow Love	1978	—	2.50	5.00
❑ Polydor 2015	I Cried for You/Love Me a Little	1979	—	2.00	4.00
❑ RCA Victor 47-8693	Mother Nature, Father Time/You're Mine	1965	2.50	5.00	10.00
❑ RCA Victor 47-8768	Where There's Life/Only a Girl Like You	1965	2.50	5.00	10.00
❑ RCA Victor 47-8830	Too Much Good Lovin'/A Sailor Boy's Love Song	1966	2.50	5.00	10.00
❑ RCA Victor 47-8879	Break Her Heart/In the Evening in the Moonlight	1966	2.50	5.00	10.00
❑ RCA Victor 47-8944	Where Does a Man Go to Cry/The Roach Song	1966	2.50	5.00	10.00
❑ RCA Victor 47-8995	So True in Life, So True in Love/If You Only Knew	1966	2.50	5.00	10.00
❑ RCA Victor 47-9031	Our First Christmas Together/Silent Night	1966	3.00	6.00	12.00
❑ RCA Victor 47-9096	Wake Up/All My Love Belongs to You	1967	2.00	4.00	8.00
❑ RCA Victor 47-9105	Keep the Faith Baby/Going to Soulsville	1967	2.00	4.00	8.00
❑ RCA Victor 47-7489	Only Your Love/If Only I Had Known	1959	7.50	15.00	30.00
❑ Reprise 0611	You're the Reason I'm Living/Laura (Tell Me What He's Got That I Ain't Got)	1967	2.00	4.00	8.00
❑ Reprise 0649	Glory of Love/Weakness in a Man	1967	2.00	4.00	8.00
❑ Reprise 0676	Instead (Of Loving You)/Lonely Street	1968	2.00	4.00	8.00
❑ Stax 0231	Winds of Change/I Keep Thinking to Myself	1974	—	2.50	5.00
❑ Vik 0285	I Wanna Do Everything for You/Come On Be Nice	1957	5.00	10.00	20.00
❑ Vik 0311	A Million Miles from Nowhere/Devoted	1957	5.00	10.00	20.00
❑ Vik 0325	Because You Love Me/Crinoline Skirt	1958	5.00	10.00	20.00
❑ Vik 0336	Crazy in Love with You/I'm Coming Back to You	1958	5.00	10.00	20.00
Albums					
❑ All Platinum 3015	This Is Brook Benton	1976	3.00	6.00	12.00
❑ Allegiance AV-5033	Memories Are Made of This	1986	2.50	5.00	10.00
❑ Cotillion SD 9002	Do Your Own Thing	1969	3.00	6.00	12.00
❑ Cotillion SD 9018	Brook Benton Today	1970	3.00	6.00	12.00
❑ Cotillion SD 9028	Home Style	1970	3.00	6.00	12.00
❑ Cotillion SD 9050	Story Teller	1971	3.00	6.00	12.00
❑ Cotillion SD 9058	The Gospel Truth	1972	3.00	6.00	12.00
❑ Epic LN 3573 [M]	Brook Benton At His Best	1959	12.50	25.00	50.00
❑ Harmony HL 7346 [M]	The Soul of Brook Benton	196?	3.00	6.00	12.00
❑ Harmony HS 11146 [R]	The Soul of Brook Benton	196?	3.00	6.00	12.00
❑ HMC 830724	Beautiful Memories of Christmas	1983	3.00	6.00	12.00
❑ Mercury MG-20421 [M]	It's Just a Matter of Time	1959	10.00	20.00	40.00

Number	Title (A Side/B Side)	Yr	VG	VG+	NM
❑ Mercury MG-20464 [M]	Endlessly	1959	7.50	15.00	30.00
❑ Mercury MG-20565 [M]	So Many Ways I Love You	1960	7.50	15.00	30.00
❑ Mercury MG-20602 [M]	Songs I Love to Sing	1960	7.50	15.00	30.00
❑ Mercury MG-20607 [M]	Golden Hits	1961	5.00	10.00	20.00
❑ Mercury MG-20619 [M]	If You Believe	1961	5.00	10.00	20.00
❑ Mercury MG-20641 [M]	The Boll Weevil Song and 11 Other Great Hits	1961	5.00	10.00	20.00
❑ Mercury MG-20673 [M]	There Goes That Song Again	1962	5.00	10.00	20.00
❑ Mercury MG-20740 [M]	Singing the Blues — Lie to Me	1962	5.00	10.00	20.00
❑ Mercury MG-20774 [M]	Golden Hits, Volume 2	1963	5.00	10.00	20.00
❑ Mercury MG-20830 [M]	Best Ballads of Broadway	1963	5.00	10.00	20.00
❑ Mercury MG-20886 [M]	Born to Sing the Blues	1964	5.00	10.00	20.00
❑ Mercury MG-20918 [M]	On the Country Side	1964	3.75	7.50	15.00
❑ Mercury MG-20934 [M]	This Bitter Earth	1964	3.75	7.50	15.00
❑ Mercury SR-60077 [S]	It's Just a Matter of Time	1959	12.50	25.00	50.00
❑ Mercury SR-60146 [S]	Endlessly	1959	10.00	20.00	40.00
❑ Mercury SR-60225 [S]	So Many Ways I Love You	1960	10.00	2.00	40.00
❑ Mercury SR-60602 [S]	Songs I Love to Sing	1960	10.00	20.00	40.00
❑ Mercury SR-60607 [S]	Golden Hits	1961	7.50	15.00	30.00
❑ Mercury SR-60619 [S]	If You Believe	1961	7.50	15.00	30.00
❑ Mercury SR-60641 [S]	The Boll Weevil Song and 11 Other Great Hits	1961	7.50	15.00	30.00
❑ Mercury SR-60673 [S]	There Goes That Song Again	1962	7.50	15.00	30.00
❑ Mercury SR-60740 [S]	Singing the Blues — Lie to Me	1962	7.50	15.00	30.00
❑ Mercury SR-60774 [S]	Golden Hits, Volume 2	1963	7.50	15.00	30.00
❑ Mercury SR-60830 [S]	Best Ballads of Broadway	1963	6.25	12.50	25.00
❑ Mercury SR-60886 [S]	Born to Sing the Blues	1964	6.25	12.50	25.00
❑ Mercury SR-60918 [S]	On the Country Side	1964	5.00	10.00	20.00
❑ Mercury SR-60934 [S]	This Bitter Earth	1964	5.00	10.00	20.00
❑ Mercury 822321-1	It's Just a Matter of Time: His Greatest Hits	1984	2.50	5.00	10.00
❑ MGM SE-4874	Something for Everyone	1973	3.00	6.00	12.00
❑ Musicor 4603 [(2)]	The Best of Brook Benton	1977	3.00	6.00	12.00
❑ Pair PDL2-1100 [(2)]	Brook Benton's Best	1986	3.00	6.00	12.00
❑ RCA Camden CAL-564 [M]	Brook Benton	1960	3.75	7.50	15.00
❑ RCA Camden CAS-2431	I Wanna Be with You	1970	3.00	6.00	12.00
❑ RCA Victor APL1-1044	Book Benton Sings a Love Story	1975	2.50	5.00	10.00
❑ RCA Victor LPM-3514 [M]	That Old Feeling	1966	3.75	7.50	15.00
❑ RCA Victor LSP-3514 [S]	That Old Feeling	1966	5.00	10.00	20.00
❑ RCA Victor LPM-3526 [M]	Mother Nature, Father Time	1965	3.75	7.50	15.00
❑ RCA Victor LSP-3526 [S]	Mother Nature, Father Time	1965	5.00	10.00	20.00
❑ RCA Victor LPM-3590 [M]	My Country	1966	3.75	7.50	15.00
❑ RCA Victor LSP-3590 [S]	My Country	1966	5.00	10.00	20.00
❑ Reprise R-6268 [M]	Laura (What's He Got That I Ain't Got)	1967	5.00	10.00	20.00
❑ Reprise RS-6268 [S]	Laura (What's He Got That I Ain't Got)	1967	3.75	7.50	15.00
❑ Rhino RNFP 71497 [(2)]	The Brook Benton Anthology (1959-1970)	1986	3.00	6.00	12.00
❑ Wing MGW-12314 [M]	Brook Benton	1966	3.00	6.00	12.00
❑ Wing SRW-16314 [S]	Brook Benton	1966	3.00	6.00	12.00

BERRY, CHUCK

45s

Number	Title (A Side/B Side)	Yr	VG	VG+	NM
❑ Atco 7203	Oh What a Thrill/California	1979	—	2.00	4.00
❑ Chess 1604	Maybellene/Wee Wee Hours	1955	12.50	25.00	50.00
❑ Chess 1610	Thirty Days (To Come Back Home)/Together	1955	12.50	25.00	50.00
❑ Chess 1615	No Money Down/Down Bound Train	1956	12.50	25.00	50.00
❑ Chess 1626	Roll Over Beethoven/Drifting Heart	1956	12.50	25.00	50.00
❑ Chess 1635	Too Much Monkey Business/Brown Eyed Handsome Man	1956	12.50	25.00	50.00
❑ Chess 1645	You Can't Catch Me/Havana Moon	1956	12.50	25.00	50.00
❑ Chess 1653	School Day (Ring! Ring! Goes the Bell)/Deep Feeling	1957	12.50	25.00	50.00
❑ Chess 1664	Oh Baby Doll/La Jaunda	1957	12.50	25.00	50.00
❑ Chess 1671	Rock & Roll Music/Blue Feeling	1957	7.50	15.00	30.00
❑ Chess 1683	Sweet Little Sixteen/Reelin' and Rockin'	1958	7.50	15.00	30.00
❑ Chess 1691	Johnny B. Goode/Around and Around	1958	7.50	15.00	30.00
❑ Chess 1697	Beautiful Delilah/Vacation Time	1958	7.50	15.00	30.00
❑ Chess 1700	Carol/Hey Pedro	1958	7.50	15.00	30.00
❑ Chess 1709	Sweet Little Rock and Roll/Joe Joe Gun	1958	7.50	15.00	30.00
❑ Chess 1714	Run Rudolph Run/Merry Christmas Baby	1958	10.00	20.00	40.00
❑ Chess 1716	Anthony Boy/That's My Desire	1959	7.50	15.00	30.00
❑ Chess 1722	Almost Grown/Little Queenie	1959	7.50	15.00	30.00
❑ Chess 1729	Back in the U.S.A./Memphis Tennessee	1959	7.50	15.00	30.00
❑ Chess 1737	Broken Arrow/Childhood Sweetheart	1959	10.00	20.00	40.00
❑ Chess 1747	Too Pooped to Pop ("Casey")/Let It Rock	1960	6.25	12.50	25.00
❑ Chess 1754	Bye Bye Johnny/Worried Life Blues	1960	6.25	12.50	25.00
❑ Chess 1763	I Got to Find My Baby/Mad Lad	1960	6.25	12.50	25.00
❑ Chess 1767	Our Little Rendezvous/Jaguar and Thunderbird	1960	6.25	12.50	25.00
❑ Chess 1779	I'm Talking About You/Little Star	1961	6.25	12.50	25.00
❑ Chess 1799	Come On/Go-Go-Go	1961	5.00	10.00	20.00
❑ Chess 1853	I'm Talking About You/Diploma for Two	1963	5.00	10.00	20.00
❑ Chess 1866	Memphis/Sweet Little Sixteen	1963	5.00	10.00	20.00
❑ Chess 1883	Nadine (Is It You?)/O Rangutang	1964	5.00	10.00	20.00
❑ Chess 1898	No Particular Place to Go/You Two	1964	5.00	10.00	20.00
❑ Chess 1906	You Never Can Tell/Brenda Lee	1964	5.00	10.00	20.00
❑ Chess 1912	Little Marie/Go Bobby Soxer	1964	3.75	7.50	15.00
❑ Chess 1916	Promised Land/Things I Used to Do	1964	3.75	7.50	15.00
❑ Chess 1926	Dear Dad/Lonely School Days	1965	3.75	7.50	15.00
❑ Chess 1943	It Wasn't Me/Welcome Back Pretty Girl	1965	3.75	7.50	15.00
❑ Chess 1963	Ramona Say Yes/Lonely School Days	1966	3.75	7.50	15.00
❑ Chess 1963	Ramona Say Yes/Havana Moon	1966	3.75	7.50	15.00
❑ Chess 2090	Tulane/Have Mercy Judge	1970	—	3.00	6.00
❑ Chess 2131	My Ding-a-Ling/Johnny B. Goode	1972	—	3.00	6.00

—All-blue label

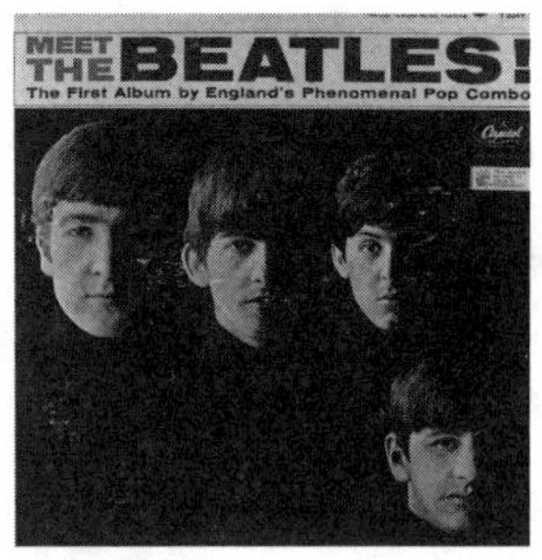

Number	Title (A Side/B Side)	Yr	VG	VG+	NM
❑ Chess 2136	Reelin' & Rockin'/Let's Boogie	1972	—	2.00	4.00
❑ Chess 2140	Roll 'Em Pete/Bio	1973	—	2.00	4.00
❑ Chess 2169	Baby What You Want Me to Do/Shake, Rattle and Roll	1975	—	2.00	4.00
❑ Collectables 3437	Run Rudolph Run/Merry Christmas Baby	199?	—	—	3.00
❑ Mercury 30143	Maybellene/Sweet Little Sixteen	196?	—	3.00	6.00
❑ Mercury 30144	Memphis/School Day (Ring, Ring Goes the Bell)	196?	—	3.00	6.00
❑ Mercury 30145	Back in the U.S.A./Roll Over Beethoven	196?	—	3.00	6.00
❑ Mercury 30146	Johnny B. Goode/Rock and Roll Music	196?	—	3.00	6.00
—The Mercury 30000 series are re-recordings of the Chess hits					
❑ Mercury 72643	Club Nitty Gritty/Laugh and Cry	1966	2.50	5.00	10.00
❑ Mercury 72680	Back to Memphis/I Do Really Love You	1967	2.50	5.00	10.00
❑ Mercury 72748	It Hurts Me Too/Feelin' It	1967	2.50	5.00	10.00
❑ Mercury 72840	Louie to Frisco/Ma Dear	1968	2.50	5.00	10.00
❑ Mercury 72963	It's Too Dark in There/Good Looking Woman	1969	5.00	10.00	20.00
Albums					
❑ Accord SN-7171	Toronto Rock 'N' Roll Revival, Vol. 2	1982	2.50	5.00	10.00
❑ Accord SN-7172	Toronto Rock 'N' Roll Revival, Vol. 3	1982	2.50	5.00	10.00
❑ Atco SD 38-118	Rockit	1979	3.00	6.00	12.00
❑ Chess LP-1426 [M]	After School Session	1958	50.00	100.00	200.00
❑ Chess LPS-1426 [R]	After School Session	196?	3.00	6.00	12.00
❑ Chess LP-1432 [M]	One Dozen Berrys	1958	50.00	100.00	200.00
❑ Chess LPS-1432 [R]	One Dozen Berrys	196?	3.00	6.00	12.00
❑ Chess LP-1435 [M]	Chuck Berry Is On Top	1959	45.00	90.00	180.00
❑ Chess LPS-1435 [R]	Chuck Berry Is On Top	196?	3.00	6.00	12.00
❑ Chess LP-1448 [M]	Rockin' at the Hops	1960	45.00	90.00	180.00
❑ Chess LP-1456 [M]	New Juke Box Hits	1961	45.00	90.00	180.00
❑ Chess LP-1465 [M]	Chuck Berry Twist	1962	25.00	50.00	100.00
❑ Chess LP-1465 [M]	More Chuck Berry	1963	30.00	60.00	120.00
—Retitled version of above					
❑ Chess LPS-1465 [R]	More Chuck Berry	196?	3.00	6.00	12.00
❑ Chess LP-1480 [M]	Chuck Berry On Stage	1963	30.00	60.00	120.00
❑ Chess LPS-1480 [R]	Chuck Berry On Stage	196?	3.00	6.00	12.00
❑ Chess LP-1485 [M]	Chuck Berry's Greatest Hits	1964	30.00	60.00	120.00
❑ Chess LPS-1485 [R]	Chuck Berry's Greatest Hits	196?	3.00	6.00	12.00
❑ Chess LP-1488 [M]	St. Louis to Liverpool	1964	15.00	30.00	60.00
❑ Chess LPS-1488 [S]	St. Louis to Liverpool	1964	20.00	40.00	80.00
❑ Chess LP-1495 [M]	Chuck Berry in London	1965	7.50	15.00	30.00
❑ Chess LPS-1495 [S]	Chuck Berry in London	1965	10.00	20.00	40.00
❑ Chess LP-1498 [M]	Fresh Berry's	1965	7.50	15.00	30.00
❑ Chess LPS-1498 [S]	Fresh Berry's	1965	10.00	20.00	40.00
❑ Chess 2CH-1514 [(2)R]	Chuck Berry's Golden Decade	1972	3.75	7.50	15.00
—New cover has a pink radio					
❑ Chess LP-1514 [(2)M]	Chuck Berry's Golden Decade	1967	10.00	20.00	40.00
❑ Chess LPS-1514 [(2)R]	Chuck Berry's Golden Decade	1967	5.00	10.00	20.00
—Old cover does not have a pink radio					
❑ Chess LPS-1550	Back Home	1970	5.00	10.00	20.00
❑ Chess CH-9171	New Juke Box Hits	1986	2.50	5.00	10.00
—Reissue of 1456					
❑ Chess CH-9186	St. Louis to Liverpool	1988	2.50	5.00	10.00
—Reissue of 1488					
❑ Chess CH-9190	More Rock 'n' Roll Rarities	1986	2.50	5.00	10.00
❑ Chess CH-9256	Chuck Berry Is On Top	1987	2.50	5.00	10.00
—Reissue of 1435					
❑ Chess CH-9259	Rockin' at the Hop	1987	2.50	5.00	10.00
—Reissue of 1448					
❑ Chess CH-9284	After School Session	1989	2.50	5.00	10.00
—Reissue of 1426					
❑ Chess CH-9295	The London Chuck Berry Sessions	1989	2.50	5.00	10.00
—Reissue of 60020					
❑ Chess CH-9318	Missing Berries: Rarities, Volume 3	1990	2.50	5.00	10.00
❑ Chess CH-50008	San Fransisco Dues	1971	5.00	10.00	20.00
❑ Chess CH-50043	Chuck Berry/Bio	1973	5.00	10.00	20.00
❑ Chess CH-60020	The London Chuck Berry Sessions	1972	5.00	10.00	20.00
❑ Chess 2CH-60023 [(2)]	Chuck Berry's Golden Decade, Vol. 2	1973	6.25	12.50	25.00
❑ Chess 2CH-60028 [(2)]	Chuck Berry's Golden Decade, Vol. 3	1974	6.25	12.50	25.00
❑ Chess CH6-80001 [(6)]	The Chess Box	1989	12.50	25.00	50.00
❑ Chess CH2-92500 [(2)]	The Great Twenty-Eight	1983	3.00	6.00	12.00

Number	Title (A Side/B Side)	Yr	VG	VG+	NM
❑ Chess CH2-92521 [(2)]	Rock 'n' Roll Rarities	1986	3.75	7.50	15.00
❑ Everest Archive of Folk & Jazz FS-321	Chuck Berry's Greatest Hits	1976	2.50	5.00	10.00
❑ Gusto 0004	The Best of the Best of Chuck Berry	198?	2.50	5.00	10.00
❑ Mercury SRM-2-6501 [(2)]	St. Louis to Frisco to Memphis	1972	5.00	10.00	20.00
❑ Mercury MG-21103 [M]	Chuck Berry's Golden Hits	1967	3.75	7.50	15.00
❑ Mercury MG-21123 [M]	Chuck Berry in Memphis	1967	3.75	7.50	15.00
❑ Mercury MG-21138 [M]	Love at the Fillmore Auditorium	1967	5.00	10.00	20.00
❑ Mercury SR-61103 [S]	Chuck Berry's Golden Hits	1967	3.75	7.50	15.00
❑ Mercury SR-61123 [S]	Chuck Berry in Memphis	1967	3.75	7.50	15.00
❑ Mercury SR-61138 [S]	Love at the Fillmore Auditorium	1967	5.00	10.00	20.00
❑ Mercury SR-61176	From St. Louie to Frisco	1968	5.00	10.00	20.00
❑ Mercury SR-61223	Concerto in B Goode	1969	5.00	10.00	20.00
❑ Mercury 826256-1	Chuck Berry's Golden Hits	1985	2.00	4.00	8.00
—Reissue					
❑ Pickwick PTP-2061 [(2)]	Flashback	1975	3.00	6.00	12.00
❑ Pickwick SPC-3327	Johnny B. Goode	1973	2.50	5.00	10.00
❑ Pickwick SPC-3345	Sweet Little Rock and Roller	1974	2.50	5.00	10.00
❑ Pickwick SPC-3392	Wild Berrys	1974	2.50	5.00	10.00
❑ Quicksilver QS-1017	Live Hits	198?	2.50	5.00	10.00
❑ SSS International 36	Chuck Berry Live	1981	2.50	5.00	10.00

BIG BOPPER

45s

Number	Title (A Side/B Side)	Yr	VG	VG+	NM
❑ D 1008	Chantilly Lace/The Purple People Eater Meets the Witch Doctor	1958	62.50	125.00	250.00
❑ Mercury 71219	Beggar to a King/Crazy Blue	1957	15.00	30.00	60.00
—As "Jape Richardson"					
❑ Mercury 71312	A Teenage Mom/Monkey Song	1958	15.00	30.00	60.00
—As "Jape Richardson"					
❑ Mercury 71343	Chantilly Lace/The Purple People Eater Meets the Witch Doctor	1958	5.00	10.00	20.00
❑ Mercury 71375	Big Bopper's Wedding/Little Red Riding Hood	1958	3.75	7.50	15.00
❑ Mercury 71416	Someone's Watching Over You/Walking Through My Dreams	1959	3.75	7.50	15.00
❑ Mercury 71451	It's the Truth, Ruth/That's What I'm Talkin' About	1959	3.75	7.50	15.00
❑ Mercury 71482	Pink Petticoats/Time Clock	1959	3.75	7.50	15.00
❑ Wing 17000	Chantilly Lace/Someone Watching Over You	196?	2.50	5.00	10.00
—Reissue					

Albums

Number	Title (A Side/B Side)	Yr	VG	VG+	NM
❑ Mercury MG-20402 [M]	Chantilly Lace	1959	125.00	250.00	500.00
—Black label					
❑ Mercury 832902-1 [M]	Chantilly Lace	1988	3.75	7.50	15.00
—New number, black label					
❑ Pickwick SPC-3365	Chantilly Lace	1973	3.75	7.50	15.00
❑ Rhino R1-70164	Helloooo Baby! The Best of the Big Bopper 1954-1959	1989	3.00	6.00	12.00

BIG BROTHER AND THE HOLDING COMPANY

45s

Number	Title (A Side/B Side)	Yr	VG	VG+	NM
❑ Columbia 44626	Piece of My Heart/Turtle Blues	1968	2.50	5.00	10.00
❑ Columbia 45284	Keep On/Home on the Strange	1970	—	3.00	6.00
❑ Columbia 45502	Black Widow Spider/Nu Boogaloo Jam	1971	—	3.00	6.00
❑ Mainstream 657	All Is Loneliness/Blindman	1967	3.00	6.00	12.00
❑ Mainstream 662	Down on Me/Call On Me	1967	3.00	6.00	12.00
❑ Mainstream 666	Bye Bye Baby/Intruder	1968	3.00	6.00	12.00
❑ Mainstream 675	Women Is Losers/Light Is Faster Than Sound	1968	3.00	6.00	12.00
❑ Mainstream 675	Women Is Losers/Caterpillar	1968	20.00	40.00	80.00
—This is much rarer than the version with the other flip side					
❑ Mainstream 678	Coo Coo/The Last Time	1968	3.00	6.00	12.00

Albums

Number	Title (A Side/B Side)	Yr	VG	VG+	NM
❑ Columbia KCL 2900 [M]	Cheap Thrills	1968	75.00	150.00	300.00
—Red label stock copy has been confirmed					
❑ Columbia KCS 9700 [S]	Cheap Thrills	1968	6.25	12.50	25.00
—Red "360 Sound" label					
❑ Columbia C 30222	Be a Brother	1970	5.00	10.00	20.00
❑ Columbia C 30631	Big Brother and the Holding Company	1971	5.00	10.00	20.00
—Reissue of Mainstream LP with two extra tracks					
❑ Columbia C 30738	How Hard It Is	1971	5.00	10.00	20.00
❑ Mainstream S-6099 [S]	Big Brother and the Holding Company	1967	12.50	25.00	50.00
❑ Mainstream 56099 [M]	Big Brother and the Holding Company	1967	25.00	50.00	100.00

BISHOP, ELVIN

45s

Number	Title (A Side/B Side)	Yr	VG	VG+	NM
❑ Capricorn 0054	Fooled Around and Fell in Love/Struttin' My Stuff	197?	—	2.00	4.00
—Hall of Fame Series					
❑ Capricorn 0202	Travelin' Shoes/Fishin'	1974	—	2.50	5.00
❑ Capricorn 0222	Can't Go Back/Let It Flow	1975	—	2.50	5.00
❑ Capricorn 0237	Sure Feels Good/Arkansas Line	1975	—	2.50	5.00
❑ Capricorn 0243	Calling All Cows/Juke Joint Jump	1975	—	2.50	5.00
❑ Capricorn 0248	Silent Night (Vocal Version)/(Instrumental)	1975	2.00	4.00	8.00
❑ Capricorn 0252	Fooled Around and Fell in Love/Slick Titty Boom	1976	—	2.50	5.00
❑ Capricorn 0252	Fooled Around and Fell in Love/Have a Good Time	1976	—	3.00	6.00
—This is actually the second pressing, bit it's harder to find than the first					
❑ Capricorn 0256	Struttin' My Stuff/Grab All the Love	1976	—	2.50	5.00
❑ Capricorn 0266	Spend Some Time/Sugar Dumplin	1976	—	2.50	5.00
❑ Capricorn 0269	Keep It Cool/Yes Sir	1976	—	2.50	5.00
❑ Capricorn 0285	Rock My Soul/Yes Sir	1978	—	2.00	4.00
❑ Capricorn 0296	Fooled Around and Fell in Love/Travelin' Shoes	1978	—	2.00	4.00
❑ Capricorn 0313	It's a Feeling/Right Now Is the Hour	1979	—	2.00	4.00
❑ Epic 10926	Rock My Soul/Holler and Shout	1973	—	2.50	5.00
❑ Epic 11022	Last Mile/Stealin' Watermelons	1973	—	2.50	5.00
❑ Fillmore 7002	So Fine/(B-side unknown)	1971	—	3.00	6.00

Number	Title (A Side/B Side)	Yr	VG	VG+	NM
❑ Fillmore 7003	Don't Fight It, Feel It/(B-side unknown)	1971	—	3.00	6.00
❑ Fillmore 7004	I Just Can't Go On/(B-side unknown)	1971	—	3.00	6.00
Albums					
❑ Alligator AL-4767	Big Fun	1987	2.50	5.00	10.00
❑ Capricorn CP 0134	Let It Flow	1974	3.00	6.00	12.00
❑ Capricorn CP 0151	Juke Joint Jump	1975	3.00	6.00	12.00
❑ Capricorn CP 0165	Struttin' My Stuff	1975	3.00	6.00	12.00
❑ Capricorn CPN-0165	Struttin' My Stuff	1980	2.50	5.00	10.00
—Reissue with revised prefix and Polygram distribution					
❑ Capricorn CP 0176	Hometown Boy Makes Good!	1976	3.00	6.00	12.00
❑ Capricorn 2CP 0185 [(2)]	Live! Raisin' Hell	1977	3.75	7.50	15.00
❑ Capricorn CPN-0215	Hog Heaven	1978	3.00	6.00	12.00
❑ Epic KE 31563	Rock My Soul	1972	3.75	7.50	15.00
❑ Epic PE 33693	The Best of Elvin Bishop	1975	3.00	6.00	12.00
❑ Fillmore F 30001	Elvin Bishop Group	1969	5.00	10.00	20.00
❑ Fillmore Z 30239	Feel It	1970	5.00	10.00	20.00

BLACKBYRDS, THE

Number	Title (A Side/B Side)	Yr	VG	VG+	NM
45s					
❑ Fantasy 729	Do It, Fluid/Summer Love	1974	—	2.50	5.00
❑ Fantasy 736	Walking in Rhythm/The Baby	1975	—	2.00	4.00
❑ Fantasy 747	Flyin' High/All I Ask	1975	—	2.00	4.00
❑ Fantasy 762	Happy Music/Love So Fine	1976	—	2.00	4.00
❑ Fantasy 771	Rock Creek Park/Thankful 'Bout Yourself	1976	—	2.00	4.00
❑ Fantasy 787	Time Is Movin'/Lady	1977	—	2.00	4.00
❑ Fantasy 794	Party Land/In Life	1977	—	2.00	4.00
❑ Fantasy 809	Soft and Easy/Something Special	1977	—	2.00	4.00
❑ Fantasy 819	Supernatural Feeling/Looking Ahead	1978	—	2.00	4.00
❑ Fantasy 904	What We Have Is Right/What's On Your Mind	1980	—	2.00	4.00
❑ Fantasy 910	Love Don't Strike Twice/Don't Know What to Say	1981	—	2.00	4.00
❑ Fantasy 914	Dancin' Dancin'/Lonelies for Your Love	1981	—	2.00	4.00
Albums					
❑ Fantasy F-9444	The Blackbyrds	1974	3.75	7.50	15.00
❑ Fantasy F-9472	Flying Start	1974	3.75	7.50	15.00
❑ Fantasy F-9490	City Life	1975	3.75	7.50	15.00
❑ Fantasy F-9518	Unfinished Business	1976	3.75	7.50	15.00
❑ Fantasy F-9535	Action	1977	3.00	6.00	12.00
❑ Fantasy F-9570	Night Grooves	1978	3.00	6.00	12.00
❑ Fantasy F-9602	Better Days	1980	3.00	6.00	12.00

BLONDIE

Number	Title (A Side/B Side)	Yr	VG	VG+	NM
45s					
❑ Chrysalis 2220	Denis/I'm On E	1977	—	2.50	5.00
❑ Chrysalis 2251	I'm Gonna Love You Too/Just Go Away	1978	—	2.50	5.00
❑ Chrysalis 2271	Hanging on the Telephone/Fade Away and Radiate	1978	—	2.50	5.00
❑ Chrysalis 2295	Heart of Glass/11:59	1979	—	2.00	4.00
—Standard issue with 3:22 version					
❑ Chrysalis 2336	One Way or Another/Just Go Away	1979	—	2.00	4.00
❑ Chrysalis 2379	Dreaming/Living in the Real World	1979	—	2.00	4.00
❑ Chrysalis 2408	The Hardest Part/Sound Asleep	1980	—	2.00	4.00
❑ Chrysalis 2410	Atomic/Die Young Stay Pretty	1980	—	2.00	4.00
❑ Chrysalis 2414	Call Me/(Instrumental)	1980	—	—	3.00
❑ Chrysalis 2465	The Tide Is High/Suzy and Jeffrey	1980	—	—	3.00
❑ Chrysalis 2485	Rapture/Walk Like Me	1981	—	—	3.00
❑ Chrysalis 2603	Island of Lost Souls/Dragonfly	1982	—	—	3.00
❑ Chrysalis 42944	Heart of Glass/Hanging on the Telephone	1985	—	—	3.00
—Silver label reissue; contains a mysterious 4:33 version of "Heart of Glass"					
❑ Chrysalis 42945	One Way or Another/Dreaming	1985	—	—	3.00
—Silver label reissue					
❑ Chrysalis 42946	Call Me/Atomic	1985	—	—	3.00
—Silver label reissue					
❑ Private Stock 45,097	X Offender/In the Sun	1976	7.50	15.00	30.00
❑ Private Stock 45,141	In the Flesh/Man Overboard	1977	5.00	10.00	20.00
Albums					
❑ Chrysalis CHR 1165	Blondie	1977	3.00	6.00	12.00
—Reissue of Private Stock album					
❑ Chrysalis CHR 1166	Plastic Letters	1977	5.00	10.00	20.00
—Green label					

Number	Title (A Side/B Side)	Yr	VG	VG+	NM
❑ Chrysalis CHR 1192	Parallel Lines	1978	3.75	7.50	15.00
—First pressing, with 3:54 version of "Heart of Glass"					
❑ Chrysalis CHE 1225	Eat to the Beat	1979	2.50	5.00	10.00
❑ Chrysalis CHE 1290	Autoamerican	1980	2.50	5.00	10.00
❑ Chrysalis CHS 1337	The Best of Blondie	1981	2.50	5.00	10.00
❑ Chrysalis CHR 1384	The Hunter	1982	2.00	4.00	8.00
❑ Chrysalis V2X 41658 [(2)]	Once More into the Bleach	1988	3.75	7.50	15.00
—Remixes of Blondie and Debbie Harry tracks					
❑ Private Stock PS-2023	Blondie	1976	6.25	12.50	25.00
BLOOD, SWEAT AND TEARS					
45s					
❑ ABC 12310	Blue Street/Somebody I Trusted	1977	—	2.00	4.00
❑ Columbia 10151	Got to Get You Into My Life/Naked Man	1975	—	2.50	5.00
❑ Columbia 10189	No Show/Yesterday's Music	1975	—	2.50	5.00
❑ Columbia 10400	You're the One/Heavy Blue	1976	—	2.50	5.00
❑ Columbia 44559	I Can't Quit Her/House in the Country	1968	2.00	4.00	8.00
❑ Columbia 44776	You've Made Me So Very Happy/Blues — Part 2	1969	—	3.00	6.00
❑ Columbia 44871	Spinning Wheel/More and More	1969	—	3.00	6.00
❑ Columbia 45008	And When I Die/Sometimes in Winter	1969	—	3.00	6.00
❑ Columbia 45204	Hi-De-Ho/The Battle	1970	—	2.50	5.00
❑ Columbia 45235	Lucretia Mac Evil/Lucretia's Reprise	1970	—	2.50	5.00
❑ Columbia 45427	Go Down Gamblin'/Valentine's Day	1971	—	2.50	5.00
❑ Columbia 45477	Lisa, Listen to Me/Cowboys and Indians	1971	—	2.50	5.00
❑ Columbia 45661	So Long Dixie/Alone	1972	—	2.50	5.00
❑ Columbia 45755	Velvet/I Can't Move No Mountains	1973	—	2.50	5.00
❑ Columbia 45937	Roller Coaster/Inner Crisis	1973	—	2.50	5.00
❑ Columbia 45965	Save Our Ship/Song for John	1973	—	2.50	5.00
❑ Columbia 46059	Tell Me That I'm Wrong/Rock Reprise	1974	—	2.50	5.00
❑ MCA 41198	Nuclear Blues/Agitato	1980	—	2.00	4.00
Albums					
❑ ABC 1015	Brand New Day	1977	2.50	5.00	10.00
❑ CBS Special Products P 16660	Musically Speaking	1982	2.50	5.00	10.00
❑ Columbia CS 9616 [S]	Child Is Father to the Man	1968	3.75	7.50	15.00
—Red "360 Sound" label					
❑ Columbia CS 9720	Blood, Sweat and Tears	1969	3.75	7.50	15.00
—Red "360 Sound" label					
❑ Columbia KC 30090	Blood, Sweat and Tears 3	1970	2.50	5.00	10.00
❑ Columbia KC 30590	BS&T: 4	1971	2.50	5.00	10.00
❑ Columbia KC 31170	Blood, Sweat and Tears' Greatest Hits	1972	2.50	5.00	10.00
—With the single versions of "You've Made Me So Very Happy," "Spinning Wheel," and "And When I Die" (all in mono)					
❑ Columbia KC 31780	New Blood	1972	2.50	5.00	10.00
❑ Columbia KC 32180	No Sweat	1973	2.50	5.00	10.00
❑ Columbia PC 32929	Mirror Image	1974	2.50	5.00	10.00
❑ Columbia PC 33484	New City	1975	2.50	5.00	10.00
❑ Columbia PC 34233	More Than Ever	1976	2.50	5.00	10.00
❑ MCA 3061	Nuclear Blues	1980	2.50	5.00	10.00
BLUE CHEER					
45s					
❑ Philips 40516	Summertime Blues/Out of Focus	1968	3.00	6.00	12.00
❑ Philips 40541	Just a Little Bit/Gypsy Ball	1968	2.50	5.00	10.00
❑ Philips 40561	Feathers from Your Tree/Sun Cycle	1968	2.50	5.00	10.00
❑ Philips 40561	Sun Cycle/Albert's Shuffle	1968	2.50	5.00	10.00
❑ Philips 40602	West Coast Child of Sunshine/When It All Gets Old	1969	2.00	4.00	8.00
❑ Philips 40651	All Night Long/Fortunes	1969	2.00	4.00	8.00
❑ Philips 40664	Hello L.A., Bye-Bye Birmingham/Natural Man	1970	2.00	4.00	8.00
❑ Philips 40682	Ain't That the Way/Fool	1970	2.00	4.00	8.00
❑ Philips 40691	Babji (Twilight Raga)/Fool	1971	2.50	5.00	10.00
❑ Philips 40691	Babji (Twilight Raga)/Pilot	1971	2.00	4.00	8.00
Albums					
❑ Megaforce CAROL-1395-1	The Beast Is Back	198?	3.00	6.00	12.00
❑ Philips PHM 200264 [M]	Vincebus Eruptum	1968	20.00	40.00	80.00
❑ Philips PHS 600264 [S]	Vincebus Eruptum	1968	10.00	20.00	40.00
❑ Philips PHS 600278	Outsideinside	1968	10.00	20.00	40.00
❑ Philips PHS 600305	New! Improved! Blue Cheer	1969	10.00	20.00	40.00
❑ Philips PHS 600333	Blue Cheer	1970	10.00	20.00	40.00
❑ Philips PHS 600347	The Original Human Being	1970	10.00	20.00	40.00
❑ Philips PHS 600350	Oh! Pleasant Hope	1971	10.00	20.00	40.00
❑ Rhino RNLP 70130	Louder Than God (The Best of Blue Cheer, 1968-1969)	1986	2.50	5.00	10.00
BLUE MAGIC					
45s					
❑ Atco 6910	Spell/Guess Who	1972	—	3.00	6.00
❑ Atco 6930	Look Me Up/What's Come Over Me	1973	—	3.00	6.00
❑ Atco 6949	Stop to Start/Where Have You Been	1973	—	3.00	6.00
❑ Atco 6961	Sideshow/Just Don't Want to Be Lonely	1974	—	3.00	6.00
❑ Atco 7004	Three Ring Circus/Welcome to the Club	1974	—	3.00	6.00
❑ Atco 7014	Love Has Found Its Way to Me/When Ya Coming Home	1975	—	3.00	6.00
❑ Atco 7031	Chasing Rainbows/You Won't Have to Tell Me Goodbye	1975	—	2.50	5.00
❑ Atco 7046	Grateful Part 1/Grateful Part 2	1976	—	2.50	5.00
❑ Atco 7052	Freak-N-Stein/Stop and Get a Hold of Yourself	1976	—	2.50	5.00
❑ Atco 7061	Teach Me (It's Something About Love)/Spark of Love	1976	—	2.50	5.00
❑ Atco 7090	I Waited/Can't Get You Out of My Mind	1978	—	2.00	4.00
❑ Capitol 4977	Land of Make Believe/Remember November	1981	—	3.00	6.00
❑ Columbia 38-68900	It's Like Magic/Couldn't Get to Sleep Last Night	1989	—	2.00	4.00
❑ Columbia 38-69017	Secret Lover/There's a Song in My Head	1989	—	2.00	4.00
❑ Def Jam 38-68566	Romeo and Juliet/Couldn't Get to Sleep Last Night	1989	—	2.00	4.00

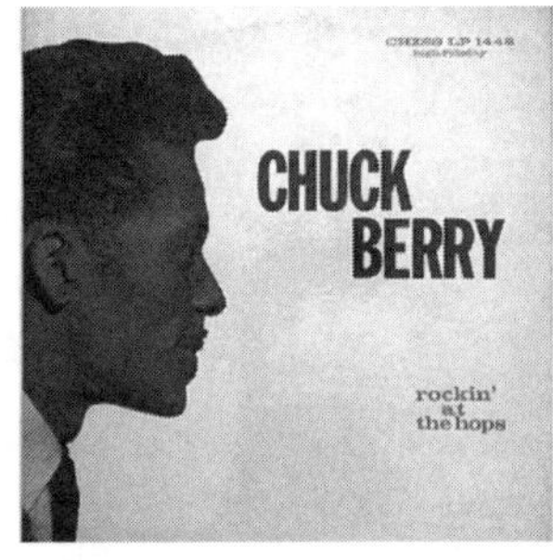

Number	Title (A Side/B Side)	Yr	VG	VG+	NM
❑ Liberty 56146	Can I Say I Love You/One, Two, Three	1969	2.50	5.00	10.00
❑ Mirage 99843	See Through/(B-side unknown)	1983	—	2.00	4.00
❑ Mirage 99869	Since You Been Gone/If You Move You Lose	1983	—	2.00	4.00
❑ Mirage 99914	Magic #/See Through	1983	2.00	4.00	8.00
❑ WMOT 4003	Summer Snow/Spark of Love	1976	—	2.50	5.00
Albums					
❑ Atco SD 36-103	The Magic of the Blue	1974	3.00	6.00	12.00
❑ Atco SD 38-104	The Message	1977	3.00	6.00	12.00
❑ Atco SD 36-120	Thirteen Blue Magic Lane	1975	3.00	6.00	12.00
❑ Atco SD 36-140	Mystic Dragons	1976	3.00	6.00	12.00
❑ Atco SD 7038	Blue Magic	1974	3.00	6.00	12.00
❑ Capitol ST-12143	Welcome Back	1981	2.50	5.00	10.00
❑ Collectables COL-5031	The Magic of the Blue: Greatest Hits	198?	2.50	5.00	10.00
❑ Columbia C 45092	From Out of the Blue	1989	3.00	6.00	12.00
❑ Mirage 90074	Magic #	1983	2.50	5.00	10.00
❑ Omni 90527	Greatest Hits	1986	2.50	5.00	10.00
BLUE OYSTER CULT					
45s					
❑ Columbia 18-02415	Burnin' for You/Vengeance (The Fact)	1981	—	2.00	4.00
❑ Columbia 13-03137	(Don't Fear) The Reaper/Burnin' for You	1982	—	2.00	4.00
—Reissue					
❑ Columbia 38-04298	Shooting Shark/Dragon Lady	1984	—	—	3.00
❑ Columbia 38-04435	Take Me Away/Let Go	1984	—	—	3.00
❑ Columbia 38-05845	Dancin' in the Ruins/Shadow Warrior	1986	—	—	3.00
❑ Columbia 38-06199	Perfect Water/Spy in the House of Knight	1986	—	—	3.00
❑ Columbia 3-10046	Dominance and Submission/Career of Evil	1974	—	3.00	6.00
❑ Columbia 3-10169	Born to Be Wild/(B-side unknown)	1975	—	3.00	6.00
❑ Columbia 3-10384	(Don't Fear) The Reaper/Tattoo Vampire	1976	—	3.00	6.00
❑ Columbia 3-10560	This Ain't the Summer of Love/Debby Denise	1977	—	2.50	5.00
❑ Columbia 3-10659	Goin' Through the Motions/Searchin' for Celine	1977	—	2.50	5.00
❑ Columbia 3-10697	Godzilla/Nosferatu	1978	—	2.50	5.00
❑ Columbia 3-10725	Godzilla (Live Version)/(Studio Version)	1978	—	2.50	5.00
❑ Columbia 3-10841	We Gotta Get Out of This Place/E.T.I. (Extra Terrestrial Intelligence)	1978	—	2.50	5.00
❑ Columbia 11055	In Thee/Lonely Teardrops	1979	—	2.00	4.00
❑ Columbia 1-11145	You're Not the One (I Was Looking For)/Moon Crazy	1979	—	2.00	4.00
❑ Columbia 11-11401	Here's Johnny (The Marshall Plan)/Divine Wind	1980	—	2.00	4.00
❑ Columbia 4-45598	Cities on Flame with Rock and Roll/Before the Kiss, A Redcap	1972	2.50	5.00	10.00
❑ Columbia 4-45879	Hot Rails to Hell/Seven Screaming Diz Busters	1973	—	3.00	6.00
Albums					
❑ Columbia KC 31063	Blue Oyster Cult	1972	3.00	6.00	12.00
❑ Columbia KC 32017	Tyranny and Mutation	1973	3.00	6.00	12.00
❑ Columbia KC 32858	Secret Treaties	1974	3.00	6.00	12.00
❑ Columbia KG 33371 [(2)]	On Your Feet or On Your Knees	1975	3.75	7.50	15.00
❑ Columbia PC 34164	Agents of Fortune	1976	2.50	5.00	10.00
—Original gatefold with no bar code on cover					
❑ Columbia JC 35019	Spectres	1977	2.50	5.00	10.00
❑ Columbia JC 35563	Some Enchanted Evening	1978	2.50	5.00	10.00
❑ Columbia JC 36009	Mirrors	1979	2.50	5.00	10.00
❑ Columbia JC 36550	Cultosaurus Erectus	1980	2.50	5.00	10.00
❑ Columbia FC 37389	Fire of Unknown Origin	1981	2.50	5.00	10.00
❑ Columbia KG 37946 [(2)]	Extraterrestrial Live	1982	3.00	6.00	12.00
❑ Columbia FC 38947	The Revolution by Night	1983	2.50	5.00	10.00
❑ Columbia FC 39979	Club Ninja	1986	2.50	5.00	10.00
❑ Columbia FC 40618	Imaginos	1988	2.50	5.00	10.00
BLUE SWEDE					
45s					
❑ Capitol 3627	Hooked on a Feeling/Gotta Have Your Love	1973	2.00	4.00	8.00
❑ EMI 3627	Hooked on a Feeling/Gotta Have Your Love	1974	—	2.50	5.00
❑ EMI 3893	Silly Milly/Lonely Sunday Afternoon	1974	—	2.00	4.00
❑ EMI 3938	Never My Love/Pinewood Rally	1974	—	2.00	4.00
❑ EMI 4029	Hush-I'm Alive/Lonely Summer Afternoon	1975	—	2.00	4.00
❑ EMI 4065	Dr. Rock and Roll/Gotta Have Your Love	1975	—	2.00	4.00
Albums					
❑ EMI ST-11266	Hooked on a Feeling	1974	2.50	5.00	10.00

Number	Title (A Side/B Side)	Yr	VG	VG+	NM
❑ EMI ST-11346	Out of the Blue	1975	2.50	5.00	10.00

BLUES BROTHERS

45s

Number	Title (A Side/B Side)	Yr	VG	VG+	NM
❑ Atlantic 3545	Soul Man/Excusez Moi Mon Cherie	1978	—	2.00	4.00
❑ Atlantic 3562	Rubber Biscuit/"B" Movie Box Car Blues	1979	—	2.50	5.00
❑ Atlantic 3574	Hey Bartender/(I Got Everything I Need) Almost	1979	—	2.50	5.00
❑ Atlantic 3666	Gimme Some Lovin'/She Caught the Katy	1980	—	2.00	4.00
❑ Atlantic 3758	Jailhouse Rock/Sweet Home Chicago	1980	—	2.50	5.00
❑ Atlantic 3785	Who's Making Love/Perry Mason Theme	1980	—	2.00	4.00
❑ Atlantic 3802	Going Back to Miami/From the Bottom	1981	—	2.50	5.00
❑ Atlantic 3884	Expressway to Your Heart/Rubber Biscuit	1982	—	3.00	6.00

Albums

Number	Title (A Side/B Side)	Yr	VG	VG+	NM
❑ Atlantic SD 16017	The Blues Brothers	1980	2.50	5.00	10.00
—Movie soundtrack; also includes tracks by Aretha Franklin, Ray Charles and James Brown					
❑ Atlantic SD 16025	Made in America	1980	2.50	5.00	10.00
❑ Atlantic SD 19217	Briefcase Full of Blues	1978	2.50	5.00	10.00
❑ Atlantic SD 19331	Best of the Blues Brothers	1981	2.50	5.00	10.00

BLUES IMAGE

45s

Number	Title (A Side/B Side)	Yr	VG	VG+	NM
❑ Atco 6718	Lay Your Sweet Love on Me/Outside Was Night	1969	—	2.00	4.00
❑ Atco 6746	Ride Captain Ride/Pay My Dues	1970	—	2.50	5.00
❑ Atco 6777	Gas Lamps and Clay/Running the Water	1970	—	2.00	4.00
❑ Atco 6798	Rise Up/Take Me Back	1971	—	2.00	4.00
❑ Atco 6814	Behind Every Man/It's the Truth	1971	—	2.00	4.00

Albums

Number	Title (A Side/B Side)	Yr	VG	VG+	NM
❑ Atco SD 33-300	Blues Image	1969	6.25	12.50	25.00
❑ Atco SD 33-317	Open	1970	5.00	10.00	20.00
❑ Atco SD 33-346	Red, White and Blues Image	1971	5.00	10.00	20.00

BLUES MAGOOS

45s

Number	Title (A Side/B Side)	Yr	VG	VG+	NM
❑ ABC 11226	Heartbreak Hotel/I Can Feel It (Feelin' Time)	1969	2.00	4.00	8.00
❑ ABC 11250	Never Goin' Back to Georgia/Feelin' Time	1969	2.00	4.00	8.00
❑ ABC 11283	Gulf Coast Bound/Sea Breeze Express	1970	2.00	4.00	8.00
❑ Ganim 1000	Who Do You Love/Let Your Love Ride	1968	10.00	20.00	40.00
❑ Mercury 72590	Tobacco Road/Sometimes I Think About You	1966	12.50	25.00	50.00
❑ Mercury 72622	(We Ain't Got) Nothin' Yet/Gotta Get Away	1966	5.00	10.00	20.00
❑ Mercury 72660	Pipe Dream/There's a Chance We Can Make It	1967	3.75	7.50	15.00
❑ Mercury 72692	One by One/Dante's Inferno	1967	3.75	7.50	15.00
❑ Mercury 72707	I Wanna Be There/Summer Is the Man	1967	2.50	5.00	10.00
❑ Mercury 72729	Life Is Just a Cher O'Bowlies/There She Goes	1967	2.50	5.00	10.00
❑ Mercury 72762	Jingle Bells/Santa Claus Is Coming to Town	1967	2.50	5.00	10.00
❑ Mercury 72838	I Can Hear the Grass Grow/Yellow Rose	1968	2.50	5.00	10.00
❑ Verve Folkways 5006	People Had No Faces/So I'm Wrong and You Are Right	1966	3.75	7.50	15.00
❑ Verve Folkways 5006	People Had No Faces/So I'm Wrong and You Are Right	1966	5.00	10.00	20.00
—As "The Bloos Magoos"					
❑ Verve Folkways 5044	People Had No Faces/So I'm Wrong and You Are Right	1967	3.75	7.50	15.00

Albums

Number	Title (A Side/B Side)	Yr	VG	VG+	NM
❑ ABC S-697	Never Goin' Back to Georgia	1969	5.00	10.00	20.00
❑ ABC S-710	Gulf Coast Bound	1970	5.00	10.00	20.00
❑ Mercury MG-21096 [M]	Psychedelic Lollipop	1966	10.00	20.00	40.00
—With "21096" in trail-off; this record is mono					
❑ Mercury MG-21096 [S]	Psychedelic Lollipop	1966	10.00	20.00	40.00
—With "2/61096" in trail-off; this record plays stereo, though labeled mono					
❑ Mercury MG-21104 [M]	Electric Comic Book	1967	7.50	15.00	30.00
❑ Mercury SR-61096 [S]	Psychedelic Lollipop	1966	12.50	25.00	50.00
❑ Mercury SR-61104 [S]	Electric Comic Book	1967	10.00	20.00	40.00
❑ Mercury SR-61167	Basic Blues Magoos	1968	7.50	15.00	30.00

BOB B. SOXX AND THE BLUE JEANS

45s

Number	Title (A Side/B Side)	Yr	VG	VG+	NM
❑ Philles 107	Zip-a-Dee-Doo-Dah/Flip and Nitty	1962	5.00	10.00	20.00
❑ Philles 110	Why Do Lovers Break Each Other's Heart?/Dr. Kaplan's Office	1963	5.00	10.00	20.00
❑ Philles 113	Not Too Young to Get Married/Annette	1963	5.00	10.00	20.00

Albums

Number	Title (A Side/B Side)	Yr	VG	VG+	NM
❑ Phillies PHLP-4002 [M]	Zip-a-Dee Doo-Dah	1963	125.00	250.00	500.00

BOBBETTES, THE

45s

Number	Title (A Side/B Side)	Yr	VG	VG+	NM
❑ Atlantic 1144	Mr. Lee/Look at the Stars	1957	6.25	12.50	25.00
❑ Atlantic 1159	Speedy/Come-a Come-a	1957	5.00	10.00	20.00
❑ Atlantic 1181	Zoomy/Rock and Ree-Ah-Zole	1958	5.00	10.00	20.00
❑ Atlantic 1194	The Dream/Um Bow Bow	1958	5.00	10.00	20.00
❑ Atlantic 2027	Don't Say Goodnight/You Are My Sweetheart	1959	5.00	10.00	20.00
❑ Atlantic 2069	I Shot Mr. Lee/Untrue Love	1960	7.50	15.00	30.00
❑ Diamond 133	Row, Row, Row/Teddy	1963	3.00	6.00	12.00
❑ Diamond 142	Close Your Eyes/Somebody Bad Stole De Wedding Bell	1963	3.00	6.00	12.00
❑ Diamond 156	My Mamma Said/Sandman	1964	3.00	6.00	12.00
❑ Diamond 166	I'm Climbing a Mountain/In Paradise	1964	3.00	6.00	12.00
❑ Diamond 181	You Ain't Seen Nothing Yet/I'm Climbing a Mountain	1965	3.00	6.00	12.00
❑ Diamond 189	Love Is Blind/Teddy	1965	3.00	6.00	12.00
❑ End 1093	Mr. Johnny Q/Teach Me Tonight	1961	5.00	10.00	20.00
❑ End 1095	I Don't Like It Like That (Part 1)/I Don't Like It Like That (Part 2)	1961	5.00	10.00	20.00
❑ Gallant 1006	Oh, My Papa/I Cried	1960	5.00	10.00	20.00
❑ Gone 5112	I Don't Like It Like That (Part 1)/Mr. Johnny Q	1961	3.75	7.50	15.00
❑ Jubilee 5427	Over There/Loneliness	1962	3.00	6.00	12.00

Number	Title (A Side/B Side)	Yr	VG	VG+	NM
❑ Jubilee 5442	The Broken Heart/Mama, Papa	1962	3.00	6.00	12.00
❑ King 5490	Oh My Papa/Dance With Me Georgie	1961	3.75	7.50	15.00
❑ King 5551	Are You Satisfied/Looking for a Lover	1961	3.75	7.50	15.00
❑ King 5623	I'm Stepping Out Tonight/My Dearest	1962	3.75	7.50	15.00
❑ RCA Victor 47-8832	I've Gotta Face the World/Having Fun	1966	3.75	7.50	15.00
❑ RCA Victor 47-8983	It's All Over/Happy-Go-Lucky Me	1966	3.75	7.50	15.00
❑ Triple-X 104	I Shot Mr. Lee/Billy	1960	5.00	10.00	20.00
❑ Triple-X 106	Have Mercy Baby/Dance with Me Georgie	1960	5.00	10.00	20.00

BONDS, GARY U.S.

45s

Number	Title (A Side/B Side)	Yr	VG	VG+	NM
❑ Atco 6689	The Star/You Need a Personal Manager	1969	—	3.00	6.00
❑ Bluff City 221	My Love Song/Blue Grass	1974	—	2.50	5.00
❑ Botanic 1002	I'm Glad You're Back/Funky Lies	1968	2.00	4.00	8.00
❑ EMI America 8079	This Little Girl/Way Back When	1981	—	2.00	4.00
❑ EMI America 8089	Jole Blon/Just Like a Child	1981	—	2.00	4.00
❑ EMI America 8099	Your Love/Just Like a Child	1981	—	2.00	4.00
❑ EMI America 8117	Out of Work/Bring Her Back	1982	—	2.00	4.00
❑ EMI America 8133	Love's on the Line/Way Back When	1982	—	2.00	4.00
❑ EMI America 8145	Turn the Music Down/Way Back When	1982	—	2.00	4.00
❑ Legrand 1003	New Orleans/Please Forgive Me	1960	5.00	10.00	20.00
—Original lists artist as "By-U.S. Bonds"; purple label					
❑ Legrand 1005	Not Me/Give Me One More Chance	1961	5.00	10.00	20.00
—Artist listed as "U.S. Bonds"; purple label					
❑ Legrand 1008	Quarter to Three/Time Ole Story	1961	10.00	20.00	40.00
—Artist listed as "U.S. Bonds"; purple label					
❑ Legrand 1009	School Is Out/One Million Years	1961	5.00	10.00	20.00
—Artist listed as "U.S. Bonds"					
❑ Legrand 1012	School Is In/Trip to the Moon	1961	3.75	7.50	15.00
❑ Legrand 1015	Dear Lady/Havin' So Much Fun	1961	5.00	10.00	20.00
—Original title of A-side					
❑ Legrand 1015	Dear Lady Twist/Havin' So Much Fun	1962	3.75	7.50	15.00
❑ Legrand 1018	Twist, Twist Senora/Food of Love	1962	3.75	7.50	15.00
❑ Legrand 1019	Seven Day Weekend/Gettin' a Groove	1962	3.75	7.50	15.00
❑ Legrand 1020	Copy Cat/I'll Change That Too	1962	3.75	7.50	15.00
❑ Legrand 1022	Mixed Up Faculty/I Dig This Station	1962	3.75	7.50	15.00
❑ Legrand 1025	Do the Limbo with Me/Where Did That Naughty Little Girl Go	1962	3.75	7.50	15.00
❑ Legrand 1027	I Don't Wanta Wait/What a Dream	1963	3.00	6.00	12.00
❑ Legrand 1029	No More Homework/She's Alright	1963	3.00	6.00	12.00
❑ Legrand 1030	Perdido Part 1/Perdido Part 2	1963	3.00	6.00	12.00
❑ Legrand 1031	King Kong's Monkey/My Sweet Ruby Rose	1964	3.00	6.00	12.00
❑ Legrand 1032	The Music Goes Round and Round/Ella Is Yella	1964	3.00	6.00	12.00
❑ Legrand 1034	You Little Angel You/My Little Miss America	1964	3.00	6.00	12.00
❑ Legrand 1035	Oh Yeah, Oh Yeah/Let ❑ Oh Yeah, Oh Yeah/Let Me Go Lover	1965	2.50	5.00	10.00
❑ Legrand 1039	Beaches U.S.A./Do the Bumpsie	1965	2.50	5.00	10.00
❑ Legrand 1040	Take Me Back to New Orleans/I'm That Kind of Guy	1966	2.50	5.00	10.00
❑ Legrand 1041	Due to Circumstances Under My Control/Slow Motion	1966	2.50	5.00	10.00
❑ Legrand 1043	Send Her Back to Me/Workin' for My Baby	1967	2.50	5.00	10.00
❑ Legrand 1045	Call Me for Christmas/Mixed Up Faculty	1967	3.00	6.00	12.00
❑ Legrand 1046	Sarah Jane/What a Crazy World	1967	2.50	5.00	10.00
❑ MCA 52335	One More Time Around the Block, Ophelia/Deadline U.S.A.	1984	—	2.00	4.00
—B-side by Shalamar					
❑ MCA 52400	New Orleans/Rhythm of the Rain	1984	—	2.00	4.00
—With Neil Sedaka					
❑ Phoenix 0071	Standing in the Line of Fire/Wild Nights	1984	—	2.50	5.00
❑ Prodigal 0612	Grandma's Washboard/Believing You	1975	—	2.50	5.00
❑ Sue 17	One Broken Heart/Can't Use You in My Business	1970	—	3.00	6.00

Albums

Number	Title	Yr	VG	VG+	NM
❑ EMI America SO-17051	Dedication	1981	2.50	5.00	10.00
❑ EMI America SO-17068	On the Line	1982	2.50	5.00	10.00
❑ Legrand LLP-3001 [M]	Dance 'Til Quarter to Three	1961	25.00	50.00	100.00
❑ Legrand LLP-3002 [M]	Twist Up Calypso	1962	17.50	35.00	70.00
❑ Legrand LLP-3003 [M]	Greatest Hits of Gary U.S. Bonds	1962	17.50	35.00	70.00
❑ MCA 905	The Best of Gary U.S. Bonds	1984	2.50	5.00	10.00
❑ Phoenix PRT 0072	Standing in the Line of Fire	1984	2.50	5.00	10.00
❑ Rhino RNLP-805	Certified Soul	1981	2.50	5.00	10.00

Number	Title (A Side/B Side)	Yr	VG	VG+	NM
BOOKER T. AND THE MG'S					
45s					
❑ A&M 2100	Knockin' on Heaven's Door/Let's Go Dancin'	1978	—	2.00	4.00
—As "Booker T. Jones"					
❑ A&M 2234	The Best of You/Let's Go Dancin'	1980	—	2.00	4.00
—As "Booker T. Jones"					
❑ A&M 2279	Will You Be the One/Cookie	1980	—	2.00	4.00
—As "Booker T. Jones"					
❑ A&M 2374	I Want You/You're the Best	1981	—	2.00	4.00
❑ A&M 2394	Don't Stop Your Love/I Came to Love You	1982	—	2.00	4.00
❑ Asylum 45392	Sticky Stuff/The Stick	1977	—	2.00	4.00
❑ Asylum 45424	Grab Bag/Reincarnation	1977	—	2.00	4.00
❑ Epic 50031	Evergreen/Song for Casey	1974	—	2.00	4.00
❑ Epic 50078	Front Street Rag/Mama Stewart	1975	—	2.00	4.00
❑ Epic 50149	Life Is Funny/Tennessee Voodoo	1975	—	2.00	4.00
❑ Stax 0001	Soul-Limbo/Heads Or Tails	1968	2.00	4.00	8.00
❑ Stax 0013	Hang 'Em High/Over Easy	1968	2.00	4.00	8.00
❑ Stax 0028	Time Is Tight/Johnny I Love You	1969	2.00	4.00	8.00
❑ Stax 0037	Mrs. Robinson/Soul Clap '69	1969	2.00	4.00	8.00
❑ Stax 0049	Slum Baby/Meditation	1969	2.00	4.00	8.00
❑ Stax 0073	Something/Sunday Sermon	1970	—	3.00	6.00
❑ Stax 0082	Melting Pot/Kinda Easy Like	1970	—	3.00	6.00
❑ Stax 127	Green Onions/Behave Yourself	1962	5.00	10.00	20.00
—Gray label					
❑ Stax 131	Jellybread/Aw' Mercy	1963	3.00	6.00	12.00
❑ Stax 134	Big Train/Home Grown	1963	3.00	6.00	12.00
❑ Stax 134	Big Train/Burnt Biscuits	1963	3.00	6.00	12.00
❑ Stax 137	Chinese Checkers/Plum Nellie	1963	3.00	6.00	12.00
❑ Stax 142	Mo' Onions/Fannie Mae	1963	3.00	6.00	12.00
❑ Stax 142	Mo' Onions/Tic Tac Toe	1963	3.00	6.00	12.00
❑ Stax 153	Soul Dressing/MG Party	1964	2.50	5.00	10.00
❑ Stax 161	Can't Be Still/Terrible Thing	1964	2.50	5.00	10.00
❑ Stax 169	Boot-Leg/Outrage	1965	2.50	5.00	10.00
❑ Stax 0169	Sugarcane/Blackride	1973	—	2.50	5.00
—As "The MG's"					
❑ Stax 182	Red Beans and Rice/Be My Lady	1965	2.50	5.00	10.00
❑ Stax 196	Booker-Loo/My Sweet Potato	1966	2.50	5.00	10.00
❑ Stax 0200	Breezy/Neckbone	1974	—	2.50	5.00
—As "The MG's"					
❑ Stax 203	Jingle Bells/Winter Wonderland	1966	3.00	6.00	12.00
❑ Stax 211	Hip-Hug-Her/Summertime	1967	2.50	5.00	10.00
❑ Stax 224	Groovin'/Slim Jenkin's Place	1967	2.50	5.00	10.00
❑ Stax 236	Silver Bells/Winter Snow	1967	3.00	6.00	12.00
❑ Volt 102	Green Onions/Behave Yourself	1962	7.50	15.00	30.00
Albums					
❑ A&M SP-4720	Try and Love Again	1978	2.50	5.00	10.00
—As "Booker T. Jones"					
❑ A&M SP-4798	The Best of You	1979	2.50	5.00	10.00
—As "Booker T. Jones"					
❑ A&M SP-4874	I Want You	1981	2.50	5.00	10.00
—As "Booker T. Jones"					
❑ Asylum 7E-1093	Universal Language	1977	2.50	5.00	10.00
❑ Atlantic SD 8202 [S]	The Best of Booker T. and the MG's	1968	5.00	10.00	20.00
❑ Atlantic 81285	The Best of Booker T. and the MG's	1985	2.00	4.00	8.00
❑ Epic KE 33143	Evergreen	1974	3.00	6.00	12.00
❑ MCA 6282	The Runaway	1989	3.00	6.00	12.00
—As "Booker T. Jones"					
❑ Stax ST-701 [M]	Green Onions	1962	17.50	35.00	70.00
❑ Stax STS-701 [R]	Green Onions	1966	12.50	25.00	50.00
❑ Stax ST-705 [M]	Soul Dressing	1965	17.50	35.00	70.00
❑ Stax STS-705 [R]	Soul Dressing	1966	12.50	25.00	50.00
❑ Stax ST-711 [M]	And Now...Booker T. and the MG's	1966	12.50	25.00	50.00
❑ Stax STS-711 [S]	And Now...Booker T. and the MG's	1966	20.00	40.00	80.00
❑ Stax ST-713 [M]	In the Christmas Spirit	1966	100.00	200.00	400.00
—Fingers and piano keys cover					
❑ Stax ST-713 [M]	In the Christmas Spirit	1967	50.00	100.00	200.00
—Same as above; Santa Claus cover					
❑ Stax STS-713 [S]	In the Christmas Spirit	1966	100.00	200.00	400.00
—Fingers and piano keys cover					
❑ Stax STS-713 [S]	In the Christmas Spirit	1967	50.00	100.00	200.00
—Santa Claus cover					
❑ Stax ST-717 [M]	Hip Hug-Her	1967	10.00	20.00	40.00
❑ Stax STS-717 [S]	Hip Hug-Her	1967	12.50	25.00	50.00
❑ Stax ST-724 [M]	Doin' Our Thing	1968	20.00	40.00	80.00
❑ Stax STS-724 [S]	Doin' Our Thing	1968	12.50	25.00	50.00
❑ Stax STS-2001	Soul Limbo	1968	6.25	12.50	25.00
❑ Stax STS-2006	Uptight	1969	6.25	12.50	25.00
❑ Stax STS-2009	The Booker T. Set	1969	6.25	12.50	25.00
❑ Stax STS-2027	McLemore Avenue	1970	6.25	12.50	25.00
❑ Stax STS-2033	Booker T. and the MG's Greatest Hits	1970	3.75	7.50	15.00
❑ Stax STS-2035 [S]	Melting Pot	1971	3.75	7.50	15.00
❑ Stax STX-4104	Free Ride	1978	2.50	5.00	10.00
❑ Stax STX-4113	Soul Limbo	198?	2.50	5.00	10.00
—Reissue of 2001					
❑ Stax MPS-8505	Booker T. and the MG's Greatest Hits	1981	2.50	5.00	10.00
❑ Stax MPS-8521	Melting Pot	198?	2.50	5.00	10.00
—Reissue of 2035					

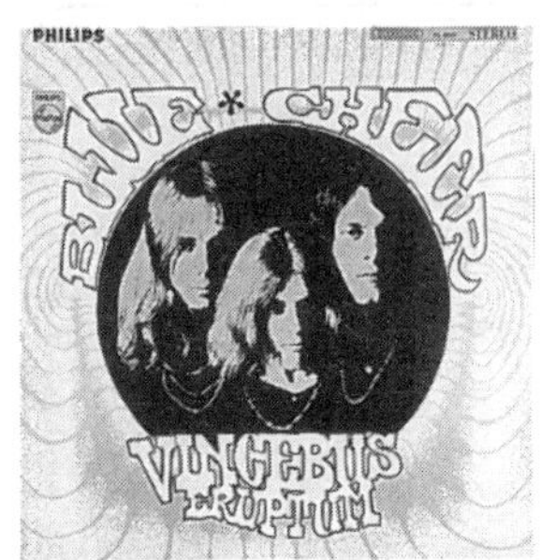

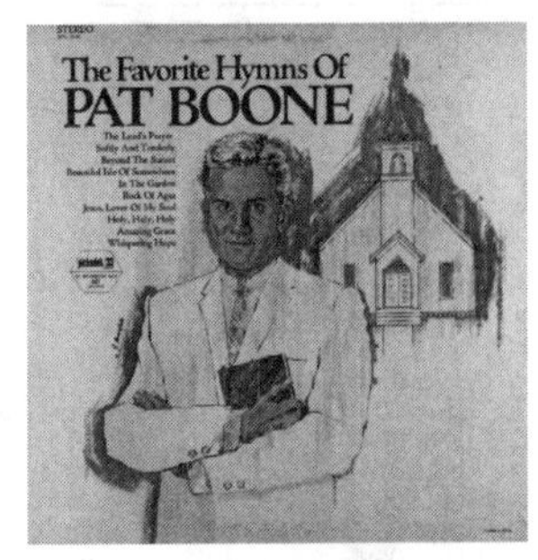

Number	Title (A Side/B Side)	Yr	VG	VG+	NM
❑ Stax MPS-8531	The Booker T. Set	1987	2.50	5.00	10.00
—Reissue of 2009					
❑ Stax MPS-8552	McLemore Avenue	1990	3.00	6.00	12.00
—Reissue of 2027					

BOONE, PAT

45s

Number	Title (A Side/B Side)	Yr	VG	VG+	NM
❑ Buena Vista 487	Little Green Tree/The Sounds of Christmas	1973	—	3.50	7.00
❑ Capitol 2763	What Are You Doing the Rest of Your Life/Now I'm Saved	1970	—	2.50	5.00
❑ Capitol 2860	Picking Up Pebbles/Oh My God	1970	—	2.50	5.00
❑ Dot 15338	Two Hearts/Tra La La	1955	5.00	10.00	20.00
❑ Dot 15377	Ain't That a Shame/Tennessee Saturday Night	1955	5.00	10.00	20.00
❑ Dot 15422	At My Front Door/No Other Arms	1955	5.00	10.00	20.00
❑ Dot 15435	Gee Whittakers!/Take the Time	1955	5.00	10.00	20.00
❑ Dot 15443	Tutti Frutti/I'll Be Home	1956	5.00	10.00	20.00
❑ Dot 15457	Long Tall Sally/Just As Long As I'm with You	1956	5.00	10.00	20.00
❑ Dot 15472	I Almost Lost My Mind/I'm in Love with You	1956	5.00	10.00	20.00
❑ Dot 15490	Friendly Persuasion (Thee I Love)/Chains of Love	1956	5.00	10.00	20.00
—Original on maroon label					
❑ Dot 15521	Don't Forbid Me/Anastasia	1956	3.75	7.50	15.00
❑ Dot 15545	Why Baby Why/I'm Waiting Just for You	1957	3.75	7.50	15.00
❑ Dot 15570	Love Letters in the Sand/Bernardine	1957	3.75	7.50	15.00
❑ Dot 15602	Remember You're Mine/There's a Gold Mine in the Sky	1957	3.75	7.50	15.00
❑ Dot 15660	April Love/When the Swallows Come Back to Capistrano	1957	3.75	7.50	15.00
❑ Dot 15690	It's Too Soon to Know/A Wonderful Time Up There	1958	3.75	7.50	15.00
❑ Dot 15750	Sugar Moon/Cherie, I Love You	1958	3.75	7.50	15.00
❑ Dot 15785	If Dreams Came True/That's How Much I Love You	1958	3.75	7.50	15.00
❑ Dot 15825	Gee, But It's Lonely/For My Good Fortune	1958	3.75	7.50	15.00
❑ Dot 15840	I'll Remember Tonight/The Mardi Gras March	1958	3.75	7.50	15.00
❑ Dot 15888 [M]	With the Wind and the Rain in Your Hair/Good Rockin' Tonight	1959	3.75	7.50	15.00
❑ Dot 15914 [M]	For a Penny/The Wang Dang Taffy Apple Tango	1959	3.75	7.50	15.00
❑ Dot 15955 [M]	Twixt Twlve and Twenty/Rock Boll Weevil	1959	3.75	7.50	15.00
❑ Dot 15982 [M]	Fools Hall of Fame/The Brightest Wishing Star	1959	3.75	7.50	15.00
❑ Dot 16006 [M]	Beyond the Sunset/My Faithful Heart	1959	3.75	7.50	15.00
❑ Dot 16015	To the Center of the Earth Part 1/Part 2	1959	5.00	10.00	20.00
❑ Dot 16028	Ain't That a Shame/I'll Be Home	1960	2.50	5.00	10.00
❑ Dot 16033	I Almost Lost My Mind/Friendly Persuasion	1960	2.50	5.00	10.00
❑ Dot 16034	Don't Forbid Me/April Love	1960	2.50	5.00	10.00
❑ Dot 16035	Love Letters in the Sand/A Wonderful Time Up There	1960	2.50	5.00	10.00
❑ Dot 16048	(Welcome) New Lovers/Words	1960	3.00	6.00	12.00
❑ Dot 16073	Walking the Floor Over You/Spring Rain	1960	3.00	6.00	12.00
❑ Dot 16122	Delia Gone/Candy Street	1960	3.00	6.00	12.00
❑ Dot 16152	Dear John/Alabam	1960	3.00	6.00	12.00
❑ Dot 16176	The Exodus Song (This Land Is Mine)/There's a Moon Out Tonight	1961	3.00	6.00	12.00
❑ Dot 16190	Cherry Pink and Apple Blossom White/On Both Sides	1961	3.00	6.00	12.00
❑ Dot 16209	Moody River/A Thousand Years	1961	3.75	7.50	15.00
❑ Dot 16244	Big Cold Wind/That's My Desire	1961	3.00	6.00	12.00
❑ Dot 16278	Louella (same on both sides)	1961	5.00	10.00	20.00
—Probably a promo only, though it is on the black Dot label with no promo markings					
❑ Dot 16278 [Picture Sleeve]	Louella (same on both sides)	1961	10.00	20.00	40.00
—Title sleeve "Dedicated to Miss Louella Parsons"					
❑ Dot 16284	Johnny Will/Just Let Me Dream	1961	3.00	6.00	12.00
❑ Dot 16312	I'll See You in My Dreams/Pictures in the Fire	1961	3.00	6.00	12.00
❑ Dot 16349	Quando, Quando, Quando (Tell Me When)/Willing and Eager	1962	2.50	5.00	10.00
❑ Dot 16368	Speedy Gonzales/The Locket	1962	3.00	6.00	12.00
❑ Dot 16391	Ten Lonely Guys/Lover's Lane	1962	2.50	5.00	10.00
❑ Dot 16416	In the Room/Mexican Joe	1963	2.50	5.00	10.00
❑ Dot 16439	Days of Wine and Roses/Meditation	1963	2.50	5.00	10.00
❑ Dot 16474	Always You and Me/Main Attraction	1963	2.50	5.00	10.00
❑ Dot 16494	Tie Me Kangaroo Down Sport/I Feel Like Crying	1963	2.50	5.00	10.00
❑ Dot 16498	Main Attraction/Si Si Si	1963	2.50	5.00	10.00
❑ Dot 16498	Amore Baciami/Gondoli Gondola	1963	2.50	5.00	10.00
❑ Dot 16525	Love Me/Mr. Moon	1963	2.50	5.00	10.00
❑ Dot 16547	Santa's Coming in a Whirleybird/Oh Holy Night	1963	2.50	5.00	10.00
❑ Dot 16559	Some Enchanted Evening/That's Me	1963	2.50	5.00	10.00
❑ Dot 16576	I Like What You Do/Never Put It in Writing	1964	2.00	4.00	8.00
❑ Dot 16598	I Understand (Just How You Feel)/Rosemarie	1964	2.00	4.00	8.00

Number	Title (A Side/B Side)	Yr	VG	VG+	NM
❑ Dot 16626	Side by Side/I'll Never Be Free	1964	2.00	4.00	8.00
—By "Pat and Shirley Boone"					
❑ Dot 16641	Sincerely/Don't You Just Know It	1964	2.00	4.00	8.00
❑ Dot 16658	Beach Girl/Little Honda	1964	7.50	15.00	30.00
❑ Dot 16668	Goodbye, Charlie/Love, Who Needs It	1964	2.00	4.00	8.00
❑ Dot 16684	I'd Rather Die Young/I Want It That Way	1964	2.00	4.00	8.00
❑ Dot 16699	Blueberry Hill/Heartaches	1965	2.00	4.00	8.00
❑ Dot 16707	Baby Elephant Walk/Say Goodbye	1965	2.00	4.00	8.00
❑ Dot 16728	Pearly Shells/Crazy Arms	1965	2.00	4.00	8.00
❑ Dot 16738	Mickey Mouse/(Welcome) New Lovers	1965	2.00	4.00	8.00
❑ Dot 16738	Mickey Mouse/Time Marches On	1965	2.00	4.00	8.00
❑ Dot 16754	Rainy Days/With My Eyes Wide Open I'm Dreaming	1965	2.00	4.00	8.00
❑ Dot 16785	I Love You So Much It Hurts/Meet Me Tonight in Dreamland	1965	2.00	4.00	8.00
❑ Dot 16808	A Man Alone/Run to Me, Baby	1966	2.00	4.00	8.00
❑ Dot 16825	As Tears Go By/Judith	1966	2.00	4.00	8.00
❑ Dot 16836	It Seems Like Yesterday/Well Remembered, Highly Thought Of Love Affair	1966	2.00	4.00	8.00
❑ Dot 16871	Five Miles from Home/Don't Put Your Feet in the Lemonade	1966	2.00	4.00	8.00
❑ Dot 16903	Wrath of Grapes/You Don't Need Me Anymore	1966	2.00	4.00	8.00
❑ Dot 16933	Wish You Were Here, Buddy/Love for You	1966	2.00	4.00	8.00
❑ Dot 16998	Hurry Sundown/What If They Gave a War and Nobody Came	1967	—	3.00	6.00
❑ Dot 17018	Have You Heard (It's All Over)/Me	1967	—	3.00	6.00
❑ Dot 17027	In the Mirror of Your Mind/Swanee Is a River	1967	—	3.00	6.00
❑ Dot 17045	By the Time I Get to Phoenix/Ride Ride Ride	1967	—	3.00	6.00
❑ Dot 17056	The Green Kentucky Hills of Home/You Mean All the World to Me	1967	—	3.00	6.00
❑ Dot 17076	It's a Happening World/Emily	1968	—	3.00	6.00
❑ Dot 17098	500 Miles/I Had a Dream	1968	—	3.00	6.00
❑ Dot 17122	Gonna Find Me a Bluebird/Deafening Roar of Silence	1968	—	3.00	6.00
❑ Dot 17156	Beyond One Memory/September Blues	1968	—	3.00	6.00
❑ Hitsville 6037	Texas Woman/It's Gone	1976	—	2.50	5.00
❑ Hitsville 6042	Oklahoma Sunshine/Won't Be Home Tonight	1976	—	2.50	5.00
❑ Hitsville 6047	Country Days and Country Nights/Lovelight Comes a-Shining	1976	—	2.50	5.00
❑ Hitsville 6054	Colorado Country Morning/Don't Want to Fall Away from You	1977	—	2.50	5.00
❑ Lamb & Lion 818	It's OK to Be a Kid at Christmas/Don't Let the Season Pass You By	1979	—	2.50	5.00
❑ Lion 106	Mr. Blue/Song of the Children of Israel (Exodus)	1972	—	2.50	5.00
—With the Boone Girls					
❑ Lion 119	I Believe in Music/Children Learn What They Live	1972	—	2.50	5.00
—With the Boone Family					
❑ Lion 126	Empty Chairs/If You're Gonna Make a Fool of Somebody	1972	—	2.50	5.00
❑ MC 5001	Whatever Happened to the Good Old Honky Tonk/Ain't Going Down in the Ground Before My Time	1977	—	2.50	5.00
❑ Melodyland 6001	Candy Lips/Young Girl	1974	—	2.50	5.00
❑ Melodyland 6005	Indiana Girl/Young Girl	1975	—	2.50	5.00
❑ Melodyland 6018	I'd Do It with You/Yester-Me, Yester-You, Yesterday	1975	—	2.50	5.00
—A-side with Shirley Boone					
❑ Melodyland 6029	Glory Train/U.F.O.	1976	—	2.50	5.00
❑ MGM 14242	All for the Love of Sunshine/M.I.A-P.O.W.	1971	—	2.50	5.00
❑ MGM 14282	C'mon, Give a Hand/Where There's a Heartache	1971	—	2.50	5.00
❑ MGM 14470	I Saw the Light/Great Speckled Bird	1972	—	2.50	5.00
❑ MGM 14521	Tying the Pieces Together/Hayden Carter	1973	—	2.00	4.00
❑ MGM 14601	Everything Begins and Ends with You/Golden Rocket	1973	—	2.00	4.00
❑ Republic 7049	My Heart Belongs to You/Until You Tell Me So	1953	6.25	12.50	25.00
❑ Republic 7062	Remember to Be Mine/Half Way Chance with You	1953	6.25	12.50	25.00
❑ Republic 7084	I Need Someone/Loving You Madly	1954	6.25	12.50	25.00
❑ Republic 7119	My Heart Belongs to You/I Need Someone	1955	5.00	10.00	20.00
❑ Tetragrammaton 1516	July, You're a Woman/Break My Mind	1969	—	2.50	5.00
❑ Tetragrammaton 1529	Never Goin' Back/What's Gnawing at Me	1969	—	2.50	5.00
❑ Tetragrammaton 1540	You Win Again/Good Morning, Dear	1969	—	2.50	5.00
❑ Warner Bros. 49097	Midnight/Can You Feel the Love	1979	—	2.00	4.00
—By "Pat and Shirley Boone"					
❑ Warner Bros. 49255	Hostage Prayer/Love's Got a Way of Hanging On	1980	—	2.00	4.00
❑ Warner Bros. 49596	Colorado Country Morning/Whatever Happened to the Good Old Honky Tonk	1980	—	2.00	4.00
❑ Warner Bros. 49691	Won't Be Home Tonight/Throw It Away	1981	—	2.00	4.00
Albums					
❑ ABC 4006	16 Great Performances	1975	2.50	5.00	10.00
❑ Bible Voice 7076	The Solution to Crisis-America	1970	3.00	6.00	12.00
❑ Dot DLP-3012 [M]	Pat Boone	1956	12.50	25.00	50.00
—Maroon label					
❑ Dot DLP-3030 [M]	Howdy!	1956	12.50	25.00	50.00
—Maroon label					
❑ Dot DLP-3050 [M]	Pat	1957	6.25	12.50	25.00
❑ Dot DLP-3068 [M]	Hymns We Love	1957	6.25	12.50	25.00
❑ Dot DLP-3071 [M]	Pat's Great Hits	1957	6.25	12.50	25.00
❑ Dot DLP-3077 [M]	Pat Boone Sings Irving Berlin	1958	5.00	10.00	20.00
❑ Dot DLP-3118 [M]	Star Dust	1958	5.00	10.00	20.00
❑ Dot DLP-3121 [M]	Yes Indeed!	1958	5.00	10.00	20.00
❑ Dot DLP-3158 [M]	Pat Boone Sings	1959	5.00	10.00	20.00
❑ Dot DLP-3180 [M]	Tenderly	1959	5.00	10.00	20.00
❑ Dot DLP-3199 [M]	Side by Side	1959	5.00	10.00	20.00
❑ Dot DLP-3222 [M]	White Christmas	1959	6.25	12.50	25.00
❑ Dot DLP-3234 [M]	He Leadeth Me	1960	3.75	7.50	15.00
❑ Dot DLP-3261 [M]	Pat's Great Hits Volume 2	1960	3.75	7.50	15.00
❑ Dot DLP-3270 [M]	Moonglow	1960	3.75	7.50	15.00
❑ Dot DLP-3285 [M]	This and That	1960	3.75	7.50	15.00
❑ Dot DLP-3346 [M]	Great! Great! Great!	1961	3.75	7.50	15.00
❑ Dot DLP-3384 [M]	Moody River	1961	3.00	6.00	12.00

Number	Title (A Side/B Side)	Yr	VG	VG+	NM
❑ Dot DLP-3386 [M]	My God and I	1961	3.00	6.00	12.00
❑ Dot DLP-3399 [M]	I'll See You in My Dreams	1961	3.00	6.00	12.00
❑ Dot DLP-3402 [M]	Pat Boone Reads from the Holy Bible	1962	3.75	7.50	15.00
❑ Dot DLP-3455 [M]	Pat Boone's Golden Hits	1962	3.00	6.00	12.00
❑ Dot DLP-3475 [M]	I Love You Truly	1962	3.00	6.00	12.00
❑ Dot DLP-3501 [M]	Pat Boone Sings Guess Who?	1963	12.50	25.00	50.00
❑ Dot DLP-3504 [M]	Pat Boone Sings "Days of Wine and Roses" and Other Great Movie Themes	1963	3.00	6.00	12.00
❑ Dot DLP-3513 [M]	Sing Along Without Pat Boone	1963	3.00	6.00	12.00
❑ Dot DLP-3520 [M]	The Star Spangled Banner	1963	3.00	6.00	12.00
❑ Dot DLP-3534 [M]	Tie Me Kangaroo Down, Sport	1963	3.00	6.00	12.00
❑ Dot DLP-3546 [M]	The Touch of Your Lips	1963	3.00	6.00	12.00
❑ Dot DLP-3582 [M]	The Lord's Prayer And Other Great Hymns	1964	3.00	6.00	12.00
❑ Dot DLP-3594 [M]	Boss Beat	1964	3.00	6.00	12.00
❑ Dot DLP-3601 [M]	Blest Be the Tie That Binds	1965	3.00	6.00	12.00
❑ Dot DLP-3606 [M]	Near You	1965	3.00	6.00	12.00
❑ Dot DLP-3626 [M]	The Golden Era of Country Hits	1965	3.00	6.00	12.00
❑ Dot DLP-3650 [M]	My 10th Anniversary with Dot Records	1965	3.00	6.00	12.00
❑ Dot DLP-3667 [M]	Winner of the Reader's Digest Poll	1965	3.00	6.00	12.00
❑ Dot DLP-3685 [M]	Great Hits of 1965	1965	3.00	6.00	12.00
❑ Dot DLP-3748 [M]	Memories	1966	3.00	6.00	12.00
❑ Dot DLP-3764 [M]	Wish You Were Here, Buddy	1966	3.00	6.00	12.00
❑ Dot DLP-3770 [M]	Christmas Is a-Comin'	1966	3.00	6.00	12.00
❑ Dot DLP-3798 [M]	How Great Thou Art	1967	3.75	7.50	15.00
❑ Dot DLP-3805 [M]	I Was Kaiser Bill's Batman	1967	3.75	7.50	15.00
❑ Dot DLP-3814 [M]	15 Hits of Pat Boone	1967	3.75	7.50	15.00
❑ Dot DLP-3876 [M]	Look Ahead	1968	3.75	7.50	15.00
❑ Dot DLP-25068 [S]	Hymns We Love	1959	7.50	15.00	30.00
❑ Dot DLP-25071 [P]	Pat's Great Hits	1959	7.50	15.00	30.00
❑ Dot DLP-25077 [S]	Pat Boone Sings Irving Berlin	1959	6.25	12.50	25.00
❑ Dot DLP-25118 [S]	Star Dust	1959	6.25	12.50	25.00
❑ Dot DLP-25121 [S]	Yes Indeed!	1959	6.25	12.50	25.00
❑ Dot DLP-25158 [S]	Pat Boone Sings	1959	6.25	12.50	25.00
❑ Dot DLP-25180 [S]	Tenderly	1959	6.25	12.50	25.00
❑ Dot DLP-25199 [S]	Side by Side	1959	6.25	12.50	25.00
❑ Dot DLP-25222 [S]	White Christmas	1959	7.50	15.00	30.00
❑ Dot DLP-25234 [S]	He Leadeth Me	1960	5.00	10.00	20.00
❑ Dot DLP-25261 [S]	Pat's Great Hits Volume 2	1960	5.00	10.00	20.00
❑ Dot DLP-25270 [S]	Moonglow	1960	5.00	10.00	20.00
—Black vinyl					
❑ Dot DLP-25285 [S]	This and That	1960	5.00	10.00	20.00
❑ Dot DLP-25346 [S]	Great! Great! Great!	1961	5.00	10.00	20.00
❑ Dot DLP-25384 [S]	Moody River	1961	3.75	7.50	15.00
❑ Dot DLP-25386 [S]	My God and I	1961	3.75	7.50	15.00
❑ Dot DLP-25399 [S]	I'll See You in My Dreams	1961	3.75	7.50	15.00
❑ Dot DLP-25455 [S]	Pat Boone's Golden Hits	1962	3.75	7.50	15.00
❑ Dot DLP-25475 [S]	I Love You Truly	1962	3.75	7.50	15.00
❑ Dot DLP-25501 [S]	Pat Boone Sings Guess Who?	1963	20.00	40.00	80.00
❑ Dot DLP-25504 [S]	Pat Boone Sings "Days of Wine and Roses" and Other Great Movie Themes	1963	3.75	7.50	15.00
❑ Dot DLP-25513 [S]	Sing Along Without Pat Boone	1963	3.75	7.50	15.00
❑ Dot DLP-25520 [S]	The Star Spangled Banner	1963	3.75	7.50	15.00
❑ Dot DLP-25534 [S]	Tie Me Kangaroo Down, Sport	1963	3.75	7.50	15.00
❑ Dot DLP-25546 [S]	The Touch of Your Lips	1963	3.75	7.50	15.00
❑ Dot DLP-25573 [R]	Pat Boone	1964	3.00	6.00	12.00
❑ Dot DLP-25582 [S]	The Lord's Prayer And Other Great Hymns	1964	3.75	7.50	15.00
❑ Dot DLP-25594 [S]	Boss Beat	1964	3.75	7.50	15.00
❑ Dot DLP-25601 [S]	Blest Be the Tie That Binds	1965	3.75	7.50	15.00
❑ Dot DLP-25606 [S]	Near You	1965	3.75	7.50	15.00
❑ Dot DLP-25626 [S]	The Golden Era of Country Hits	1965	3.75	7.50	15.00
❑ Dot DLP-25650 [S]	My 10th Anniversary with Dot Records	1965	3.75	7.50	15.00
❑ Dot DLP-25667 [S]	Winner of the Reader's Digest Poll	1965	3.75	7.50	15.00
❑ Dot DLP-25685 [S]	Great Hits of 1965	1965	3.75	7.50	15.00
❑ Dot DLP-25748 [S]	Memories	1966	3.75	7.50	15.00
❑ Dot DLP-25764 [S]	Wish You Were Here, Buddy	1966	3.75	7.50	15.00
❑ Dot DLP-25770 [S]	Christmas Is a-Comin'	1966	3.75	7.50	15.00
❑ Dot DLP-25798 [S]	How Great Thou Art	1967	3.00	6.00	12.00

Number	Title (A Side/B Side)	Yr	VG	VG+	NM
❑ Dot DLP-25805 [S]	I Was Kaiser Bill's Batman	1967	3.00	6.00	12.00
❑ Dot DLP-25814 [S]	15 Hits of Pat Boone	1967	3.00	6.00	12.00
❑ Dot DLP-25876 [S]	Look Ahead	1968	3.00	6.00	12.00
❑ Hamilton HLP-118 [M]	12 Great Hits	196?	3.00	6.00	12.00
❑ Hamilton HLP-12118 [S]	12 Great Hits	196?	3.00	6.00	12.00
❑ Hitsville H6-405	Texas Woman	1976	3.00	6.00	12.00
❑ Lamb & Lion 1002	New Songs of the Jesus People	197?	3.00	6.00	12.00
❑ Lamb & Lion 1004	Pat Boone and the First Nashville Jesus Band	197?	3.00	6.00	12.00
❑ Lamb & Lion 1005	Christian People, Vol. 1	197?	2.50	5.00	10.00
❑ Lamb & Lion 1006	The Family Who Prays	197?	2.50	5.00	10.00
❑ Lamb & Lion 1007	Born Again	197?	2.50	5.00	10.00
❑ Lamb & Lion 1008	All in the Boone Family	1972	2.50	5.00	10.00
❑ Lamb & Lion 1013	S-A-V-E-D	197?	2.50	5.00	10.00
❑ Lamb & Lion 1016	Songs from the Inner Court	197?	2.50	5.00	10.00
❑ Lamb & Lion 5000	The Pat Boone Family in the Holy Land	197?	2.50	5.00	10.00
❑ MCA 658	16 Great Performances	1980	2.00	4.00	8.00
❑ MCA 6020 [(2)]	The Best of Pat Boone	1980	3.00	6.00	12.00
❑ MCA 15028 [S]	White Christmas	198?	2.50	5.00	10.00
—Reissue of Dot LP					
❑ Melodyland 6-501	The Country Side of Pat Boone	1975	3.00	6.00	12.00
❑ MGM SE-4899	I Love You More and More Every Day	1973	2.50	5.00	10.00
❑ Paramount 1024 [(2)]	Pat Boone's Greatest Hymns	1974	3.75	7.50	15.00
❑ Paramount 1043 [(2)]	Pat Boone's Greatest Hits	1974	3.75	7.50	15.00
❑ Pickwick SPC-1024	White Christmas	1979	2.50	5.00	10.00
❑ Pickwick SPC-3079	True Love	196?	2.50	5.00	10.00
❑ Pickwick SPC-3107	Love Me Tender	196?	2.50	5.00	10.00
❑ Pickwick SPC-3123	Canadian Sunset	196?	2.50	5.00	10.00
❑ Pickwick SPC-3145	Favorite Hymns	197?	2.50	5.00	10.00
❑ Pickwick SPC-3219	You've Lost That Lovin' Feeling	197?	2.50	5.00	10.00
❑ Pickwick SPC-3568	The Old Rugged Cross	1978	2.00	4.00	8.00
❑ Pickwick SPC-3597	Great Hits	1978	2.00	4.00	8.00
❑ Supreme SS-2060	Rapture	1970	3.00	6.00	12.00
❑ Tetragrammaton T-118	Departure	1969	3.00	6.00	12.00
❑ Word WST-8536	The Pat Boone Family	1970	2.50	5.00	10.00
❑ Word WST-8664	Hymns We Love	197?	2.50	5.00	10.00
❑ Word WST-8711	He Leadeth Me	197?	2.50	5.00	10.00
❑ Word WST-8725	The Star-Spangled Banner	197?	2.50	5.00	10.00
❑ Word WST-8738	I Believe	198?	2.00	4.00	8.00

BOSTON

45s

Number	Title (A Side/B Side)	Yr	VG	VG+	NM
❑ Epic 15-02355	More Than a Feeling/Long Time	1981	—	—	3.00
—"Golden Oldies" reissue					
❑ Epic 15-02365	Peace of Mind/Don't Look Back	1981	—	—	3.00
— "Golden Oldies" reissue					
❑ Epic 8-50266	More Than a Feeling/Smokin'	1976	—	2.00	4.00
❑ Epic 8-50329	Long Time/Let Me Take You Home Tonight	1976	—	2.00	4.00
❑ Epic 8-50381	Peace of Mind/Foreplay	1977	—	2.00	4.00
❑ Epic 8-50590	Don't Look Back/The Journey	1978	—	2.00	4.00
❑ Epic 8-50638	A Man I'll Never Be/Don't Be Afraid	1978	—	2.00	4.00
❑ Epic 8-50677	Feelin' Satisfied/Used to Bad News	1979	—	2.00	4.00
❑ MCA 52756	Amanda/My Destination	1986	—	—	3.00
❑ MCA 52985	We're Ready/The Launch	1986	—	—	3.00
❑ MCA 53029	Can'tcha Say (You Believe in Me)/Still in Love//Cool the Engines	1987	—	—	3.00
❑ MCA 53114	Hollyann/To Be a Man	1987	—	—	3.00
❑ MCA 54803	I Need Your Love/We Can Make It	1994	—	—	3.00
❑ MCA 54917	What's Your Name/Walk On (Short Walk)	1994	—	—	3.00

Albums

Number	Title (A Side/B Side)	Yr	VG	VG+	NM
❑ Epic PE 34188	Boston	1976	2.50	5.00	10.00
—Original edition; orange label					
❑ Epic FE 35050	Don't Look Back	1978	2.50	5.00	10.00
—Original edition; orange label					
❑ MCA 6188	Third Stage	1986	2.00	4.00	8.00
❑ MCA 10973	Walk On	1994	6.25	12.50	25.00

BOWIE, DAVID

45s

Number	Title (A Side/B Side)	Yr	VG	VG+	NM
❑ Backstreet 52024	Cat People (Putting Out Fire)/Paul's Theme (Jogging Chase)	1982	—	—	3.00
—B-side by Georgio Moroder					
❑ Deram 85009	Rubber Band/There Is a Happy Land	1967	25.00	50.00	100.00
❑ Deram 85016	Love You Till Tuesday/Did You Ever Have a Dream	1967	25.00	50.00	100.00
❑ EMI America B-8158	Let's Dance/Cat People (Putting Out Fire)	1983	—	—	3.00
❑ EMI America B-8165	China Girl/Shake It	1983	—	—	3.00
❑ EMI America B-8177	Modern Love/Modern Love (Live)	1983	—	—	3.00
❑ EMI America B-8190	Without You/Criminal World	1984	—	—	3.00
❑ EMI America B-8231	Blue Jean/Dancin' with the Big Boys	1984	—	3.00	6.00
—First pressing on blue vinyl					
❑ EMI America B-8246	Tonight/Tumble and Twirl	1984	—	—	3.00
❑ EMI America B-8251	This Is Not America/(Instrumental)	1984	—	—	3.00
—With the Pat Metheny Group					
❑ EMI America BG-8271	Loving the Alien/Don't Look Down	1985	—	—	3.00
❑ EMI America B-8308	Absolute Beginners/(Dub Mix)	1986	—	—	3.00
❑ EMI America B-8323	Underground/(instrumental)	1986	—	—	3.00
❑ EMI America B-8380	Day In Day Out/Julie	1987	—	—	3.00
❑ EMI America B-43020	Time Will Crawl/Girls	1987	—	—	3.00
❑ EMI America B-43031	Never Let Me Down/'87 and Cry	1987	—	—	3.00
❑ London 20079	The Laughing Gnome/The Gospel According to Tony Day	1973	12.50	25.00	50.00

Number	Title (A Side/B Side)	Yr	VG	VG+	NM
❑ Mercury 72949	Space Oddity/Wild-Eyed Boy from Freecloud	1969	12.50	25.00	50.00
❑ Mercury 73075	Memory of a Free Festival Part 1/Part 2	1970	50.00	100.00	200.00
❑ RCA PB-10664	TVC 15/We Are the Dead	1976	—	3.00	6.00
❑ RCA PB-10736	Stay/Word on a Wing	1976	—	3.00	6.00
❑ RCA PB-10905	Sound and Vision/A New Career in a New Town	1977	—	3.00	6.00
❑ RCA PB-11017	Be My Wife/The Speed of Life	1977	2.00	4.00	8.00
❑ RCA PB-11121	Heroes/V-2 Schneider	1977	2.00	4.00	8.00
❑ RCA PB-11190	Beauty and the Beast/Sense of Doubt	1978	2.00	4.00	8.00
❑ RCA PB-11585	Boys Keep Swinging/Fantastic Voyage	1979	—	3.00	6.00
❑ RCA PB-11661	D.J./Fantastic Voyage	1979	2.00	4.00	8.00
❑ RCA PB-11724	Look Back in Anger/Repetition	1979	—	3.00	6.00
❑ RCA PB-11887	John I'm Only Dancing 1972/Joe the Lion	1980	—	3.00	6.00
❑ RCA PB-12078	Ashes to Ashes/It's No Game	1980	—	2.50	5.00
❑ RCA PB-12134	Fashion/Scream Like a Baby	1980	—	2.50	5.00
❑ RCA PH-13400	Peace on Earth-Little Drummer Boy/Fantastic Voyage	1982	—	2.50	5.00
—A-side with Bing Crosby					
❑ RCA PB-13660	White Light-White Heat/Cracked Actor	1983	—	2.50	5.00
❑ RCA PB-13769	1984/TVC 15	1984	—	2.50	5.00
❑ RCA Victor 74-0605	Changes/Andy Warhol	1971	2.50	5.00	10.00
—Orange label (original)					
❑ RCA Victor 74-0605	Changes/Andy Warhol	1974	—	3.00	6.00
—Tan or gray label					
❑ RCA Victor 74-0719	Starman/Suffragette City	1972	—	3.00	6.00
❑ RCA Victor 74-0838	The Jean Genie/Hang On to Yourself	1972	—	3.00	6.00
❑ RCA Victor 74-0876	Space Oddity/The Man Who Sold the World	1973	—	3.00	6.00
❑ RCA Victor APBO-0001	Time/The Prettiest Star	1973	—	3.00	6.00
❑ RCA Victor APBO-0028	Let's Spend the Night Together/Lady Grinning Soul	1973	—	3.00	6.00
❑ RCA Victor APBO-0160	Sorrow/Amsterdam	1973	—	3.00	6.00
❑ RCA Victor APBO-0287	Rebel Rebel/Lady Grinning Soul	1974	2.50	5.00	10.00
—All copies contain an alternate mix of "Rebel, Rebel"					
❑ RCA Victor APBO-0293	Diamond Dogs/Holy Holy	1974	2.50	5.00	10.00
—Part of U.S. numbering system, but released only outside the U.S.					
❑ RCA Victor PB-10026	1984/Queen Bitch	1974	—	3.00	6.00
❑ RCA Victor PB-10105	Rock and Roll with Me/Panic in Detroit	1974	—	3.00	6.00
❑ RCA Victor PB-10152	Young Americans/Knock on Wood	1975	—	3.00	6.00
—Tan label (Indianapolis pressing)					
❑ RCA Victor PB-10320	Fame/Right	1975	—	3.00	6.00
—Tan label (Indianapolis pressing)					
❑ RCA Victor PB-10441	Golden Years/Can You Hear Me	1975	—	3.00	6.00
❑ Warner Bros. 5815	Can't Stop Thinking About Me/And I Say to Myself	1966	100.00	200.00	400.00
—As "David Bowie and the Lower Third"					
Albums					
❑ Deram DE 16003 [M]	David Bowie	1967	30.00	60.00	120.00
❑ Deram DES 18003 [S]	David Bowie	1967	37.50	75.00	150.00
❑ EMI America SO-17093	Let's Dance	1983	2.50	5.00	10.00
❑ EMI America SJ-17138	Tonight	1984	2.50	5.00	10.00
❑ EMI America PJ-17267	Never Let Me Down	1987	2.50	5.00	10.00
❑ London PS 628/9 [(2)]	Images 1966-1967	1973	12.50	25.00	50.00
—Original pressings have dark blue and silver labels. Later pressings, if any, are worth at least 50% less.					
❑ London LC 50007	Starting Point	1977	3.00	6.00	12.00
❑ Mercury SR 61246	Man of Words, Man of Music	1969	37.50	75.00	150.00
❑ Mercury SR 61325	The Man Who Sold the World	1970	10.00	20.00	40.00
—An often-counterfeited album; originals have matrix numbers stamped in the trail-off area					
❑ RCA Red Seal ARL1-2743	Peter and the Wolf	1978	5.00	10.00	20.00
—With the Philadelphia Orchestra conducted by Eugene Ormandy; green vinyl					
❑ RCA Victor APL1-0291	Pin Ups	1973	5.00	10.00	20.00
❑ RCA Victor CPL1-0576	Diamond Dogs	1974	1000.	2000.	4000.
—Original copies have cover with dog's genitals clearly visible. Almost all were destroyed prior to release.					
❑ RCA Victor CPL1-0576	Diamond Dogs	1974	5.00	10.00	20.00
—Standard issue, with dog's genitals airbrushed					
❑ RCA Victor CPL2-0771 [(2)]	David Live	1974	5.00	10.00	20.00
—At time of release, available with either orange or tan labels					
❑ RCA Victor APL1-0998	Young Americans	1975	3.00	6.00	12.00
—At time of release, available with either orange or tan label					
❑ RCA Victor APL1-1327	Station to Station	1976	3.00	6.00	12.00
—Originals have a brown label					

Number	Title (A Side/B Side)	Yr	VG	VG+	NM
❑ RCA Victor APL1-1732	Changesonebowie	1976	2.50	5.00	10.00
❑ RCA Victor APL1-2030	Low	1977	2.50	5.00	10.00
❑ RCA Victor AFL1-2522	"Heroes"	1977	2.50	5.00	10.00
❑ RCA Victor CPL2-2913 [(2)]	Stage	1978	5.00	10.00	20.00
❑ RCA Victor AQL1-3254	Lodger	1979	2.50	5.00	10.00
❑ RCA Victor AQL1-3647	Scary Monsters	1980	2.50	5.00	10.00
❑ RCA Victor AFL1-4202	Changestwobowie	1981	2.50	5.00	10.00
❑ RCA Victor CPL1-4346 [EP]	David Bowie in Berthold Brecht's Baal	1982	2.50	5.00	10.00
❑ RCA Victor LSP-4623	Hunky Dory	1972	5.00	10.00	20.00
❑ RCA Victor LSP-4702	The Rise and Fall of Ziggy Stardust and the Spiders from Mars	1972	5.00	10.00	20.00
—Orange label					
❑ RCA Victor LSP-4702	The Rise and Fall of Ziggy Stardust and the Spiders from Mars	1975	3.00	6.00	12.00
—Tan label					
❑ RCA Victor LSP-4813	Space Oddity	1973	5.00	10.00	20.00
—Reissue of Mercury SR-61246; add 1/3 if bonus poster is enclosed					
❑ RCA Victor LSP-4816	The Man Who Sold the World	1973	5.00	10.00	20.00
—Reissue of Mercury SR-61325; add 1/3 if bonus poster is enclosed					
❑ RCA Victor LSP-4852	Aladdin Sane	1973	5.00	10.00	20.00
—Orange label is original (deduct 50% for tan labels)					
❑ RCA Victor CPL2-4862 [(2)]	Ziggy Stardust, The Motion Picture	1983	5.00	10.00	20.00
❑ RCA Victor AFL1-4919	Fame and Fashion	1984	2.50	5.00	10.00

BOWIE, DAVID, AND MICK JAGGER

45s

Number	Title (A Side/B Side)	Yr	VG	VG+	NM
❑ EMI America B-8288	Dancing in the Street/(Instrumental)	1985	—	—	3.00

BOX TOPS, THE

45s

Number	Title (A Side/B Side)	Yr	VG	VG+	NM
❑ Arista 9488	Sweet Cream Ladies/Neon Rainbow	1986	—	—	3.00
—"Flashback" oldies series					
❑ Bell 865	Come On Honey/You Keep Tightening Up on Me	1970	2.00	4.00	8.00
❑ Bell 923	Let Me Go/Got to Hold On to You	1970	2.00	4.00	8.00
❑ Bell 981	King's Highway/Since I've Been Gone	1971	2.00	4.00	8.00
❑ Gusto 2112	The Letter/Cry Like a Baby	1981	—	2.00	4.00
—Re-recordings					
❑ Hi 2228	It's All Over/Sugar Creek Woman	1972	—	3.00	6.00
❑ Hi 2242	Hold On Girl/Angel	1973	—	3.00	6.00
❑ Mala 565	The Letter/Happy Times	1967	3.00	6.00	12.00
❑ Mala 580	Neon Rainbow/Everything I Am	1967	2.50	5.00	10.00
❑ Mala 593	Cry Like a Baby/The Door You Closed to Me	1968	3.00	6.00	12.00
❑ Mala 12005	Choo Choo Train/Fields of Clover	1968	2.50	5.00	10.00
❑ Mala 12017	I Met Her in Church/People Gonna Talk	1968	2.50	5.00	10.00
❑ Mala 12035	Sweet Cream Ladies, Forward March/I See Only Sunshine	1968	2.50	5.00	10.00
❑ Mala 12038	I Shall Be Released/I Must Be the Devil	1969	2.50	5.00	10.00
❑ Mala 12040	Soul Deep/The Happy Song	1969	2.50	5.00	10.00
❑ Mala 12042	Turn On a Dream/Together	1969	2.50	5.00	10.00
❑ Sphere Sound 77001	The Letter/Happy Times	1969	2.50	5.00	10.00
—Blue label; reissue					
❑ Sphere Sound 77002	Cry Like a Baby/The Door You Closed to Me	1970	2.00	4.00	8.00
—Silver label; reissue					
❑ Stax 0199	It's Gonna Be O.K./Willobee and Dale	1974	—	3.00	6.00

Albums

Number	Title (A Side/B Side)	Yr	VG	VG+	NM
❑ Bell 6011 [M]	The Letter/Neon Rainbow	1967	6.25	12.50	25.00
❑ Bell S-6011 [S]	The Letter/Neon Rainbow	1967	5.00	10.00	20.00
❑ Bell 6017	Cry Like a Baby	1968	5.00	10.00	20.00
❑ Bell 6023	Non-Stop	1968	5.00	10.00	20.00
❑ Bell 6025	The Box Tops Super Hits	1968	5.00	10.00	20.00
❑ Bell 6032	Dimensions	1969	5.00	10.00	20.00
❑ Rhino RNLP-161	The Greatest Hits	1982	3.00	6.00	12.00

BOYCE, TOMMY, AND BOBBY HART

45s

Number	Title (A Side/B Side)	Yr	VG	VG+	NM
❑ A&M 858	Out and About/My Little Chickadee	1967	2.50	5.00	10.00
❑ A&M 874	Sometimes She's a Little Girl/Love Every Day	1967	2.50	5.00	10.00
❑ A&M 893	I Wonder What She's Doing Tonight/The Ambushers	1967	3.00	6.00	12.00
❑ A&M 919	Goodbye Baby (I Don't Want to See You Cry)/Where Angels Go, Trouble Follows	1968	2.50	5.00	10.00
❑ A&M 948	Alice Long (You're Still My Favorite Girlfriend)/P.O. Box 9847	1968	2.50	5.00	10.00
❑ A&M 993	We're All Going to the Same Place/6 + 6	1968	2.50	5.00	10.00
❑ A&M 1017	Maybe Somebody Heard/It's All Happening on the Inside	1969	2.00	4.00	8.00
❑ A&M 1031	L.U.V. (Let Us Vote)/I Wanna Be Free	1969	2.00	4.00	8.00
❑ Aquarian 380	I'll Blow You a Kiss in the Wind/Smilin'	1970	—	2.00	4.00

Albums

Number	Title (A Side/B Side)	Yr	VG	VG+	NM
❑ A&M LP-126 [M]	Test Patterns	1967	5.00	10.00	20.00
❑ A&M LP-143 [M]	I Wonder What She's Doing Tonite?	1968	7.50	15.00	30.00
❑ A&M SP-4126 [S]	Test Patterns	1967	5.00	10.00	20.00
❑ A&M SP-4143 [S]	I Wonder What She's Doing Tonite?	1968	5.00	10.00	20.00
❑ A&M SP-4162	It's All Happening on the Inside	1968	5.00	10.00	20.00

BREAD

45s

Number	Title (A Side/B Side)	Yr	VG	VG+	NM
❑ Elektra 45365	Lost Without Your Love/Change of Heart	1976	—	2.00	4.00
❑ Elektra 45389	Hooked on You/Our Lady of Sorrow	1977	—	2.00	4.00
❑ Elektra 45666	Dismal Day/Anyway You Want Me	1969	2.00	4.00	8.00
❑ Elektra 45668	Could I/You Can't Measure the Cost	1969	—	3.00	6.00
❑ Elektra 45686	Make It With You/Why Do You Keep Me Waiting	1970	—	2.00	4.00
—Red, black and white label					
❑ Elektra 45701	It Don't Matter to Me/Call on Me	1970	—	2.00	4.00

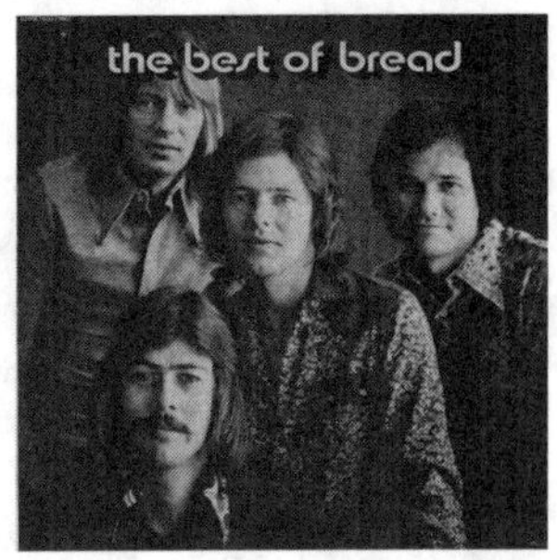

Number	Title (A Side/B Side)	Yr	VG	VG+	NM
❑ Elektra 45711	Let Your Love Go/Too Much Love	1971	—	2.00	4.00
❑ Elektra 45720	If/Take Comfort	1971	—	2.00	4.00
❑ Elektra 45740	Mother Freedom/Life in Your Love	1971	—	2.00	4.00
❑ Elektra 45751	Baby I'm-a Want You/Truckin'	1971	—	2.00	4.00
❑ Elektra 45765	Everything I Own/I Don't Love You	1972	—	2.00	4.00
❑ Elektra 45784	Diary/Down on My Knees	1972	—	2.00	4.00
❑ Elektra 45803	The Guitar Man/Just Like Yesterday	1972	—	2.00	4.00
❑ Elektra 45818	Sweet Surrender/Make It By Yourself	1972	—	2.00	4.00
❑ Elektra 45832	Aubrey/Didn't Even Know Her Name	1973	—	2.00	4.00
Albums					
❑ Elektra 7E-1005	The Best of Bread, Volume 2	1974	3.00	6.00	12.00
❑ Elektra 7E-1094	Lost Without Your Love	1976	2.50	5.00	10.00
❑ Elektra 60414	Anthology of Bread	1985	2.50	5.00	10.00
❑ Elektra EKS-74044	Bread	1969	3.75	7.50	15.00
—Red label with large stylized "E"					
❑ Elektra EKS-74076	On the Waters	1970	3.75	7.50	15.00
—Red label with large stylized "E"					
❑ Elektra EKS-74086	Manna	1971	3.00	6.00	12.00
❑ Elektra EKS-75015	Baby I'm-a Want You	1971	3.75	7.50	15.00
—Gatefold with raised photo on front					
❑ Elektra EKS-75047	Guitar Man	1972	3.00	6.00	12.00
❑ Elektra EKS-75056	The Best of Bread	1973	3.00	6.00	12.00

BREWER AND SHIPLEY

Number	Title (A Side/B Side)	Yr	VG	VG+	NM
45s					
❑ A&M 905	The Keeper of the Keys/I Can't See Her	1968	2.00	4.00	8.00
—Artist reads "Michael Brewer and Tom Shipley"					
❑ A&M 938	Green Bamboo/Truly Right	1968	2.00	4.00	8.00
—Artist reads "Michael Brewer and Tom Shipley"					
❑ A&M 996	Dreamin' in the Shade/Tame and Changes	1968	2.00	4.00	8.00
❑ Buddah 154	Rise Up Easy Rider/Boomerang	1970	—	2.00	4.00
❑ Capitol 3933	Fair Play/How Are You	1974	—	2.00	4.00
❑ Capitol 4105	Brain Damage/Rock and Roll Hostage	1975	—	2.00	4.00
❑ Kama Sutra 512	People Love Each Other/Witchi-Tai-To	1970	—	2.00	4.00
❑ Kama Sutra 516	One Toke Over the Line/Oh Mommy	1970	—	2.50	5.00
❑ Kama Sutra 524	Tarkio Road/Seems Like a Long Time	1971	—	2.00	4.00
❑ Kama Sutra 539	Shake Off the Demon/Indian Summer	1972	—	2.00	4.00
❑ Kama Sutra 547	Natural Child/Yankee Lady	1972	—	2.00	4.00
❑ Kama Sutra 567	Black Sky/Fly, Fly Fly	1972	—	2.00	4.00
Albums					
❑ A&M SP-4154	Down in L.A.	1968	3.75	7.50	15.00
❑ Capitol ST-11261	ST-11261.	1974	2.50	5.00	10.00
❑ Capitol ST-11402	Welcome to Riddle Bridge.	1975	2.50	5.00	10.00
❑ Kama Sutra KSBS-2016	Weeds.	1969	3.00	6.00	12.00
❑ Kama Sutra KSBS-2024	Tarkio.	1970	3.00	6.00	12.00
—LP label calls this "Tarkio Road"					
❑ Kama Sutra KSBS-2039	Shake Off the Demon	1971	3.00	6.00	12.00
❑ Kama Sutra KSBS-2058	Rural Space	1972	3.00	6.00	12.00
❑ Kama Sutra KSBS 2613-2 [(2)]	The Best... Brewer & Shipley	1976	3.75	7.50	15.00

BROOKLYN BRIDGE, THE

Number	Title (A Side/B Side)	Yr	VG	VG+	NM
45s					
❑ Buddah 60	Little Red Boat by the River/From My Window	1968	—	3.00	6.00
❑ Buddah 75	Worst That Could Happen/Your Kite, My Kite	1968	2.00	4.00	8.00
❑ Buddah 95	Welcome Me Love/Blessed Is the Rain	1969	—	3.00	6.00
❑ Buddah 126	Your Husband, My Wife/Upside Down	1969	—	3.00	6.00
❑ Buddah 139	You'll Never Walk Alone/Minstrel Sunday	1969	—	3.00	6.00
❑ Buddah 162	Free as the Wind/He's Not a Happy Man	1970	—	3.00	6.00
❑ Buddah 179	Down by the River/Look Again	1970	—	3.00	6.00
❑ Buddah 193	Day Is Done/Easy Way	1970	—	3.00	6.00
❑ Buddah 193	Day Is Done/Opposites	1970	—	3.00	6.00
❑ Buddah 199	Nights in White Satin/Cynthia	1971	2.00	4.00	8.00
❑ Buddah 230	Wednesday in Your Garden (mono/stereo)	1971	2.00	4.00	8.00
—Stock copy unknown					
❑ Buddah 293	Man in a Band/Bruno's Place	1972	2.00	4.00	8.00
❑ Buddah 317	I Feel Free (mono/stereo)	1972	2.50	5.00	10.00
—As "The Bridge"; stock copy unknown					

Number	Title (A Side/B Side)	Yr	VG	VG+	NM
Albums					
❑ Buddah BDS-5034	Brooklyn Bridge	1969	5.00	10.00	20.00
❑ Buddah BDS-5042	The Second Brooklyn Bridge	1969	5.00	10.00	20.00
❑ Buddah BDS-5065	The Brooklyn Bridge	1970	5.00	10.00	20.00
❑ Buddah BDS-5107	Bridge in Blue	1972	5.00	10.00	20.00
❑ Collectables COL-5015	The Greatest Hits	198?	3.00	6.00	12.00
—As "Johnny Maestro and the Brooklyn Bridge"					
BROOKS, DONNIE					
45s					
❑ Challenge 59331	I Call Your Name/Be Fair	1966	2.00	4.00	8.00
❑ Challenge 59344	Pink Carousel/Mission Man	1966	2.00	4.00	8.00
❑ Era 3004	Lil' Sweetheart/If You're Lookin'	1959	5.00	10.00	20.00
❑ Era 3007	White Orchid/Sway and Move with the Beat	1959	5.00	10.00	20.00
❑ Era 3014	The Devil Ain't a Man/How Long	1960	5.00	10.00	20.00
❑ Era 3018	Mission Bell/Do It for Me	1960	5.00	10.00	20.00
❑ Era 3028	Doll House/Round Robin	1960	3.75	7.50	15.00
❑ Era 3042	Memphis/That's Why	1961	3.75	7.50	15.00
❑ Era 3049	All I Can Give/Wishbone	1961	3.75	7.50	15.00
❑ Era 3052	Boomerang/How Long	1961	3.75	7.50	15.00
❑ Era 3059	Sweet Lorraine/Up to My Ears in Tears	1961	3.75	7.50	15.00
❑ Era 3063	Goodnight Judy/Your Little Boy's Gone Home	1961	3.75	7.50	15.00
❑ Era 3071	My Favorite Kind of Face/He Stole Flo	1962	3.75	7.50	15.00
❑ Era 3077	Oh You Beautiful Doll/Just a Bystander	1962	3.75	7.50	15.00
❑ Era 3095	Cries My Heart/It's Not That Easy	1962	3.75	7.50	15.00
❑ Era 3194	Blue Soldier/Love Is Funny That Way	1968	2.00	4.00	8.00
❑ Happy Tiger 526	Abracadabra/I Know You as a Woman	1970	—	2.50	5.00
❑ Happy Tiger 544	Hush/I Know You as a Woman	1970	—	2.50	5.00
❑ Happy Tiger 551	My God and I/Pink Carousel	1970	—	2.50	5.00
❑ Happy Tiger 566	(I Wanna) Have You for Myself/Rub-a-Dub-Dub	1971	—	2.50	5.00
❑ Happy Tiger 579	I'm Gonna Make You Love Me/Pink Carousel	1971	—	2.50	5.00
❑ Midsong Int'l. 1007	Big John/Get Fame, Son	1978	—	2.00	4.00
❑ Oak 1019	The Song That I Sing Is For You/Country Dude	1971	—	2.50	5.00
❑ Reprise 0261	Gone/Girl Machine	1964	2.50	5.00	10.00
❑ Reprise 0311	Can't Help Lovin' You/Pickin' Up the Pieces	1964	2.50	5.00	10.00
❑ Reprise 0363	Hey, Little Girl/I Never Get to Love You	1965	2.50	5.00	10.00
❑ Yardbird 8006	Sunglasses on the Sand/Sunshine, Summertime and Love	1968	—	3.00	6.00
❑ Yardbird 8008	Hush/Sunshine, Summertime and Love	1968	—	3.00	6.00
❑ Yardbird 8010	Tree Trimming Time/(Instrumental)	1968	—	3.00	6.00
Albums					
❑ Era EL-105 [M]	The Happiest	1961	37.50	75.00	150.00
BROTHERS JOHNSON, THE					
45s					
❑ A&M 1229	Party Avenue/Ball of Fire	1988	—	—	3.00
❑ A&M 1806	I'll Be Good to You/The Devil	1976	—	2.00	4.00
❑ A&M 1851	Get the Funk Out Ma Face/Tomorrow	1976	—	2.00	4.00
❑ A&M 1881	Free and Single/Thunder Thumbs and Lightning Licks	1976	—	2.00	4.00
❑ A&M 1949	Strawberry Letter 23/Dancin' and Prancin'	1977	—	2.00	4.00
❑ A&M 1982	Runnin' for Your Lovin'/Q	1977	—	2.00	4.00
❑ A&M 2015	Love Is/Right On Time	1978	—	2.00	4.00
❑ A&M 2086	Ride-O-Rocket/Dancin' and Prancin'	1978	—	2.00	4.00
❑ A&M 2098	Ain't We Funkin' Now/Dancin' and Prancin'	1978	—	2.00	4.00
❑ A&M 2216	Stomp!/Let's Swing	1980	—	2.00	4.00
❑ A&M 2238	Light Up the Night/Street Wave	1980	—	2.00	4.00
❑ A&M 2254	Treasure/Celebrations	1980	—	2.00	4.00
❑ A&M 2343	The Real Thing/I Want You	1981	—	2.00	4.00
❑ A&M 2368	Dancin' Free/Do It for Love	1981	—	2.00	4.00
❑ A&M 2506	Welcome to the Club/The End of an Era	1982	—	2.00	4.00
❑ A&M 2527	I'm Giving You All My Love/The Real Thing	1983	—	2.00	4.00
❑ A&M 2654	You Keep Me Coming Back/Deceiver	1984	—	2.00	4.00
❑ A&M 2689	Lovers Forever/Hot Mama	1984	—	2.00	4.00
❑ A&M 3013	Kick It to the Curb/P.O. Box 2000 (Instrumental)	1988	—	—	3.00
❑ Qwest 28877	Back Against the Wall Part 1/Part 2	1985	—	—	3.00
Albums					
❑ A&M SP-3716	Light Up the Night	1980	2.50	5.00	10.00
❑ A&M SP-3724	Winners	1981	2.50	5.00	10.00
❑ A&M SP-4567	Look Out for #1	1976	2.50	5.00	10.00
❑ A&M SP-4644	Right on Time	1977	2.50	5.00	10.00
❑ A&M SP-4714	Blam!!	1978	2.50	5.00	10.00
❑ A&M SP-4927	Blast! (The Latest and the Greatest)	1982	2.50	5.00	10.00
❑ A&M SP-4965	Out of Control	1984	2.50	5.00	10.00
❑ A&M SP-5162	Kickin'	1988	2.50	5.00	10.00
BROWN, ARTHUR, THE CRAZY WORLD OF					
45s					
❑ Atlantic 2556	Fire/Rest Cure	1968	2.50	5.00	10.00
❑ Track 2582	I Put a Spell on You/Nightmare	1968	2.00	4.00	8.00
Albums					
❑ Gull GU6-405	Dance	1975	3.00	6.00	12.00
❑ Passport 98003	Journey	1974	3.00	6.00	12.00
❑ Track SD 8198	The Crazy World of Arthur Brown	1968	6.25	12.50	25.00
BROWN, JAMES					
45s					
❑ A&M 3022	I Got You (I Feel Good)/Nowhere to Run	1988	—	2.00	4.00
—B-side by Martha and the Vandellas					
❑ Augusta Sound 94023	Bring It On ... Bring It On/The Night Time Is the Right Time (To Be With the One That You Love)	1983	—	2.00	4.00

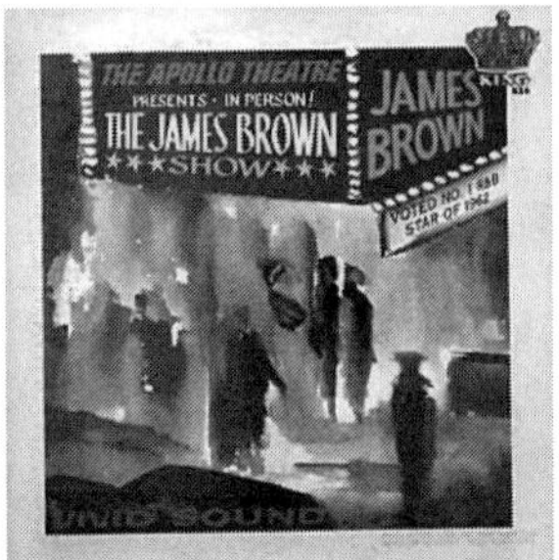

Number	Title (A Side/B Side)	Yr	VG	VG+	NM
❑ Backstreet 52215	King of Soul/Theme from Doctor Detroit	1983	—	—	3.00
—B-side by Devo					
❑ Bethlehem 3089	I Loves You Porgy/Yours and Mine	1969	3.75	7.50	15.00
❑ Bethlehem 3098	A Man Has to Go Back to the Crossroads/The Drunk	1969	3.75	7.50	15.00
❑ Federal 12258	Please, Please, Please/Why Do You Do Me?	1956	10.00	20.00	40.00
❑ Federal 12264	I Don't Know/I Feel That Old Feeling Coming On	1956	6.25	12.50	25.00
❑ Federal 12277	No, No, No, No/Hold My Baby's Hand	1956	6.25	12.50	25.00
❑ Federal 12289	Just Won't Do Right/Let's Make It	1957	6.25	12.50	25.00
❑ Federal 12290	I Won't Plead No More/Chonnie On Chon	1957	6.25	12.50	25.00
❑ Federal 12292	Gonna Try/Can't Be the Same	1957	6.25	12.50	25.00
❑ Federal 12295	Love or a Game/Messing with the Blues	1957	6.25	12.50	25.00
❑ Federal 12300	I Walked Alone/You're Mine, You're Mine	1957	6.25	12.50	25.00
❑ Federal 12311	Baby Cries Over the Ocean/That Dood It	1957	6.25	12.50	25.00
❑ Federal 12316	Begging, Begging/That's When I Lost My Heart	1958	6.25	12.50	25.00
❑ Federal 12337	Try Me/Tell Me What I Did Wrong	1958	7.50	15.00	30.00
❑ Federal 12348	I Want You So Bad/There Must Be a Reason	1959	5.00	10.00	20.00
❑ Federal 12352 [M]	I've Got to Change/It Hurts to Tell You	1959	5.00	10.00	20.00
❑ Federal 12361 [M]	Don't Let It Happen to Me/Good Good Lovin'	1959	5.00	10.00	20.00
❑ Federal 12364	It Was You/Got to Cry	1959	5.00	10.00	20.00
❑ Federal 12369	I'll Go Crazy/I Know It's True	1960	5.00	10.00	20.00
❑ Federal 12370	Think/You've Got the Power	1960	5.00	10.00	20.00
❑ Federal 12378	This Old Heart/I Wonder When You're Coming Home	1960	5.00	10.00	20.00
❑ King 5423	The Bells/And I Do Just What I Want	1960	3.75	7.50	15.00
❑ King 5438	The Scratch/Hold It	1961	3.75	7.50	15.00
❑ King 5442	Bewildered/If You Want Me	1961	3.75	7.50	15.00
❑ King 5466	I Don't Mind/Love Don't Love Nobody	1961	3.75	7.50	15.00
❑ King 5485	Sticky/Suds	1961	3.75	7.50	15.00
❑ King 5519	Night Flying/Cross Firing	1961	3.75	7.50	15.00
❑ King 5524	Baby You're Right/I'll Never, Never Let You Go	1961	3.75	7.50	15.00
❑ King 5547	Just You and Me, Darling/I Love You, Yes I Do	1961	3.75	7.50	15.00
❑ King 5573	Lost Someone/Cross Firing	1961	3.75	7.50	15.00
❑ King 5614	Night Train/Why Does Everything Happen to Me	1962	3.75	7.50	15.00
❑ King 5654	Tell Me Why/Say So Long	1962	3.75	7.50	15.00
—With Yvonne Fair					
❑ King 5657	Shout and Shimmy/Come Over Here	1962	3.75	7.50	15.00
❑ King 5672	Mashed Potatoes U.S.A./You Don't Have to Go	1962	3.75	7.50	15.00
❑ King 5687	It Hurts to Be in Love/You Can Make It If You Try	1962	3.75	7.50	15.00
—With Yvonne Fair					
❑ King 5698	(Can You) Feel It Part 1/(Can You) Feel It Part 2	1962	3.75	7.50	15.00
❑ King 5701	Three Hearts in a Tangle/I've Got Money	1962	3.75	7.50	15.00
❑ King 5710	Like a Baby/Every Beat of My Heart	1963	3.75	7.50	15.00
❑ King 5739	Prisoner of Love/Choo Choo	1963	3.75	7.50	15.00
❑ King 5767	These Foolish Things/Can You Feel It — Part 1	1963	3.75	7.50	15.00
❑ King 5803	Signed, Sealed and Delivered/Waiting in Vain	1963	3.75	7.50	15.00
❑ King 5829	The Bells/I've Got to Change	1963	3.75	7.50	15.00
❑ King 5842	Oh Baby Don't You Weep (Part 1)/Oh Baby Don't You Weep (Part 2)	1964	3.75	7.50	15.00
❑ King 5853	Please, Please, Please/In the Wee Wee Hours	1964	3.75	7.50	15.00
❑ King 5876	How Long Darling/Again	1964	3.75	7.50	15.00
❑ King 5899	So Long/Dancin' Little Thing	1964	3.75	7.50	15.00
❑ King 5922	Tell Me What You're Gonna Do/I Don't Care	1964	3.75	7.50	15.00
❑ King 5952	Think/Try Me	1964	3.75	7.50	15.00
❑ King 5956	Fine Old Foxy Self/Medley	1964	3.75	7.50	15.00
❑ King 5968	Have Mercy Baby/Just Won't Do Right	1964	3.75	7.50	15.00
❑ King 5995	This Old Heart/It Was You	1965	3.00	6.00	12.00
❑ King 5999	Papa's Got a Brand New Bag Part I/Papa's Got a Brand New Bag Part II	1965	3.75	7.50	15.00
❑ King 6015	I Got You (I Feel Good)/I Can't Help It (I Just Do, Do, Do)	1965	3.75	7.50	15.00
❑ King 6020	I'll Go Crazy/Lost Someone	1966	3.00	6.00	12.00
❑ King 6025	Ain't That a Groove Part I/Ain't That a Groove Part II	1966	3.00	6.00	12.00
❑ King 6029	Prisoner of Love/I've Got to Change	1966	3.00	6.00	12.00
❑ King 6033	Come Over Here/Tell Me What You're Gonna Do	1966	3.00	6.00	12.00
❑ King 6035	It's a Man's Man's Man's World/Is It Yes Or Is It No?	1966	3.00	6.00	12.00
❑ King 6037	I've Got Money/Just Won't Do Right	1966	3.00	6.00	12.00
❑ King 6040	I Don't Care/It Was You	1966	3.00	6.00	12.00
❑ King 6044	This Old Heart/How Long Darling	1966	3.00	6.00	12.00
❑ King 6048	Money Won't Change You Part 1/Money Won't Change You Part 2	1966	3.00	6.00	12.00

Number	Title (A Side/B Side)	Yr	VG	VG+	NM
❑ King 6056	Don't Be a Drop-Out/Tell Me That You Love Me	1966	3.00	6.00	12.00
❑ King 6064	The Christmas Song (Version 1)/The Christmas Song (Version 2)	1966	3.75	7.50	15.00
❑ King 6065	Sweet Little Baby Boy (Part 1)/Sweet Little Baby Boy (Part 2)	1966	3.00	6.00	12.00
❑ King 6071	Bring It Up/Nobody Knows	1967	3.00	6.00	12.00
❑ King 6072	Let's Make Christmas Mean Something This Year (Part 1)/ Let's Make Christmas Mean Something This Year (Part 2)	1967	3.00	6.00	12.00
❑ King 6086	Kansas City/Stone Fox	1967	3.00	6.00	12.00
❑ King 6091	Think/Nobody Cares	1967	3.00	6.00	12.00
—A-side: With Vicki Anderson; B-side: Vicki Anderson solo					
❑ King 6100	Let Yourself Go/Good Rockin' Tonight	1967	3.00	6.00	12.00
❑ King 6110	Cold Sweat — Part 1/Cold Sweat — Part 2	1967	3.00	6.00	12.00
❑ King 6111	Mona Lisa/It Won't Be Me	1967	15.00	30.00	60.00
—Evidently not released or pulled shortly after release					
❑ King 6112	America Is My Home — Part 1/America Is My Home — Part 2	1967	3.00	6.00	12.00
❑ King 6122	Get It Together (Part 1)/Get It Together (Part 2)	1967	3.00	6.00	12.00
❑ King 6133	The Soul of J.B./Funky Soul #1	1967	3.00	6.00	12.00
❑ King 6141	I Guess I'll Have to Cry, Cry, Cry/Just Plain Funk	1967	3.00	6.00	12.00
❑ King 6144	I Can't Stand Myself (When You Touch Me)/There Was a Time	1967	3.00	6.00	12.00
❑ King 6151	You've Got to Change Your Mind/I'll Lose My Mind	1968	3.00	6.00	12.00
—A-side: With Bobby Byrd; B-side: Bobby Byrd solo					
❑ King 6152	You've Got the Power/What the World Needs Now Is Love	1968	3.00	6.00	12.00
—A-side: With Vicki Anderson; B-side: Vicki Anderson solo					
❑ King 6155	I Got the Feelin'/If I Ruled the World	1968	3.00	6.00	12.00
❑ King 6164	Here I Go/Shhhh	1968	3.00	6.00	12.00
❑ King 6166	Licking Stick — Licking Stick (Part 1)/Licking Stick — Licking Stick (Part 2)	1968	3.00	6.00	12.00
❑ King 6187	Say It Loud — I'm Black and I'm Proud (Part 1)/Say It Loud — I'm Black and I'm Proud (Part 2)	1968	2.50	5.00	10.00
❑ King 6198	Goodbye My Love/Shades of Brown	1968	2.50	5.00	10.00
❑ King 6203	Santa Claus Go Straight to the Ghetto/You Know It	1968	2.50	5.00	10.00
❑ King 6204	Believers Shall Enjoy/Tit for Tat (Ain't No Turning Back)	1968	2.50	5.00	10.00
❑ King 6205	Let's Unite the World at Christmas/In the Middle (Part 1)	1968	2.50	5.00	10.00
❑ King 6206	In the Middle (Part 2)/Tit for Tat (Ain't No Turning Back)	1969	2.50	5.00	10.00
—A-side: With Marva Whitney					
❑ King 6213	Give It Up or Turnit A Loose/I'll Lose My Mind	1969	2.50	5.00	10.00
❑ King 6216	Shades of Brown (Part 2)/A Talk with the News	1969	2.50	5.00	10.00
—B-side by Steve Soul					
❑ King 6218	You Got to Have a Job/I'm Tired, I'm Tired, I'm Tired	1969	2.50	5.00	10.00
—A-side with Marva Whitney; B-side: Marva Whitney solo					
❑ King 6222	Soul Pride (Part 1)/Soul Pride (Part 2)	1969	2.50	5.00	10.00
❑ King 6223	You've Got to Have a Mother for Me (Part 1)/ You've Got to Have a Mother for Me (Part 2)	1969	2.50	5.00	10.00
❑ King 6224	I Don't Want Nobody to Give Me Nothing (Open Up the Door, I'll Get It Myself) Part 1/Part 2	1969	2.50	5.00	10.00
❑ King 6235	Little Groove Maker (Part 1)/Any Day Now	1969	2.50	5.00	10.00
❑ King 6235	Little Groove Maker (Part 1)/I'm Shook	1969	2.50	5.00	10.00
❑ King 6240	The Popcorn/The Chicken	1969	2.50	5.00	10.00
❑ King 6245	Mother Popcorn (You Got to Have a Mother for Me) Part 1/ Mother Popcorn (You Got to Have a Mother for Me) Part 2	1969	2.50	5.00	10.00
❑ King 6250	Lowdown Popcorn/Top of the Stack	1969	2.50	5.00	10.00
❑ King 6255	Let a Man Come In and Do the Popcorn Part One/Sometime	1969	2.50	5.00	10.00
❑ King 6258	World (Part 1)/World (Part 2)	1969	2.50	5.00	10.00
❑ King 6273	I'm Not Demanding (Part 1)/I'm Not Demanding (Part 2)	1969	2.50	5.00	10.00
❑ King 6275	Part Two (Let a Man Come In and Do the Popcorn)/ Get a Little Hipper	1969	2.50	5.00	10.00
❑ King 6277	It's Christmas Time (Part 1)/It's Christmas Time (Part 2)	1969	2.50	5.00	10.00
❑ King 6280	Ain't It Funky Now (Part 1)/Ain't It Funky Now (Part 2)	1970	2.00	4.00	8.00
❑ King 6290	Funky Drummer (Part 1)/Funky Drummer (Part 2)	1970	2.00	4.00	8.00
❑ King 6292	It's a New Day (Part 1)/It's a New Day (Part 2)	1970	2.00	4.00	8.00
❑ King 6293	Let It Be Me/Baby Don't You Know	1970	2.00	4.00	8.00
—A-side: With Vicki Anderson; B-side: Vicki Anderson solo					
❑ King 6300	Talkin' Loud and Sayin' Nothing (Part 1)/Talkin' Loud and Sayin' Nothing (Part 2)	1970	2.00	4.00	8.00
❑ King 6310	Brother Rapp (Part 1) & (Part 2)/Bewildered	1970	2.00	4.00	8.00
❑ King 6318	Get Up (I Feel Like Being A) Sex Machine (Part 1)/ Get Up (I Feel Like Being A) Sex Machine (Part 2)	1970	2.00	4.00	8.00
❑ King 6322	I'm Not Demanding (Part 1)/I'm Not Demanding (Part 2)	1970	2.00	4.00	8.00
❑ King 6329	Super Bad (Part 1 & Part 2)/Super Bad (Part 3)	1970	2.00	4.00	8.00
❑ King 6329	Call Me Super Bad (Part 1 & Part 2)/Call Me Super Bad (Part 3)	1970	5.00	10.00	20.00
—First pressing: Note longer title					
❑ King 6339	Hey America/(Instrumental)	1970	2.00	4.00	8.00
❑ King 6340	Santa Claus Is Definitely Here to Stay/(Instrumental)	1970	2.00	4.00	8.00
❑ King 6347	Get Up, Get Into It, Get Involved Pt. 1/ Get Up, Get Into It, Get Involved Pt. 2	1971	2.00	4.00	8.00
❑ King 6359	Talking Loud and Saying Nothing — Part 1/ Talking Loud and Saying Nothing — Part 2	1971	2.00	4.00	8.00
❑ King 6363	I Cried/World (Part 2)	1971	2.00	4.00	8.00
❑ King 6366	Spinning Wheel (Part 1)/Spinning Wheel (Part 2)	1971	2.00	4.00	8.00
❑ King 6368	Soul Power Pt. 1/Soul Power Pt 2 & Pt. 3	1971	2.00	4.00	8.00
❑ Mercury 885190-7	Prisoner of Love/Please, Please, Please	1986	—	2.00	4.00
—Reissue					
❑ Mercury 885194-7	Get on the Good Foot/Give It Up or Turnit A Loose	1986	—	2.00	4.00
—Reissue					
❑ People 664	Everybody Wanna Be Funky One More Time Pt. 1/Everybody Wanna Be Funky One More Time Pt. 2	1976	—	2.50	5.00
❑ People 2500	Escape-ism (Part 1)/Escape-ism (Parts 2 & 3)	1971	—	3.00	6.00

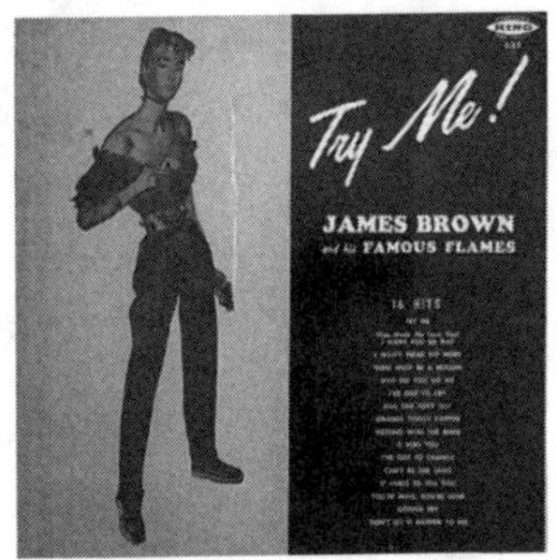

Number	Title (A Side/B Side)	Yr	VG	VG+	NM
❑ People 2501	Hot Pants Pt. 1 (She Got to Use What She Got to Get What She Wants)/Hot Pants Pt. 2	1971	—	3.00	6.00
❑ Polydor 2005	Star Generation/Women Are Something Else	1979	—	2.50	5.00
❑ Polydor 2034	The Original Disco Man/Let the Boogie Do the Rest	1979	—	2.50	5.00
❑ Polydor 2054	Regrets/Stone Cold Drag	1979	—	2.50	5.00
❑ Polydor 2078	Let the Funk Flow/Sometimes That's All There Is	1980	—	2.50	5.00
❑ Polydor 2129	Get Up Offa That Thing/It's Too Funky in Here	1980	—	2.50	5.00
❑ Polydor 2167	Give the Bass Player Some Part 1/Part 2	1981	—	2.50	5.00
❑ Polydor 14088	Make It Funky Part 1/Make It Funky Part 2	1971	—	3.00	6.00
❑ Polydor 14098	My Part/Make It Funky, Part 3//Make It Funky, Part 4	1971	—	3.00	6.00
❑ Polydor 14100	I'm a Greedy Man Part 1/I'm a Greedy Man Part 2	1971	—	3.00	6.00
❑ Polydor 14109	Talking Loud and Saying Nothing Part 1/Part 2	1972	—	3.00	6.00
❑ Polydor 14116	King Heroin/Theme from King Heroin	1972	—	3.00	6.00
❑ Polydor 14125	There It Is Part 1/There It Is Part 2	1972	—	3.00	6.00
❑ Polydor 14129	Honky Tonk Part 1/Honky Tonk Part 2	1972	—	3.00	6.00
—Artist credit: "James Brown Soul Train"					
❑ Polydor 14139	Get On the Good Foot Part 1/Get On the Good Foot Part 2	1972	—	3.00	6.00
❑ Polydor 14153	I Got a Bag of My Own/Public Enemy #1	1972	—	3.00	6.00
❑ Polydor 14155	I Got a Bag of My Own/I Know It's True	1972	7.50	15.00	30.00
—Manufactured in U.S. for export					
❑ Polydor 14157	What My Baby Needs Now Is a Little More Lovin'/ This Guy-This Girl's in Love	1972	—	3.00	6.00
—With Lyn Collins					
❑ Polydor 14161	Santa Claus Goes Straight to the Ghetto/Sweet Little Baby Boy	1972	—	3.00	6.00
❑ Polydor 14162	I Got Ants in My Pants (and I want to dance) Part 1/Part 15 and 16	1973	—	2.50	5.00
❑ Polydor 14168	Down and Out in New York City/Mama's Dead	1973	—	2.50	5.00
❑ Polydor 14169	The Boss/Like It Is, Like It Was	1973	—	2.50	5.00
❑ Polydor 14177	Think/Something	1973	—	2.50	5.00
❑ Polydor 14185	Think/Something	1973	—	2.50	5.00
❑ Polydor 14193	Woman Part 1/Woman Part 2	1973	—	2.50	5.00
❑ Polydor 14194	Sexy, Sexy, Sexy/Slaughter Theme	1973	—	2.50	5.00
❑ Polydor 14210	Stone to the Bone Part 1/Stone to the Bone Part 2	1973	2.50	5.00	10.00
❑ Polydor 14210	Stoned to the Bone Part 1/Stoned to the Bone Part 2	1973	—	2.50	5.00
—Notice corrected title					
❑ Polydor 14223	The Payback Part 1/The Payback Part 2	1974	—	2.50	5.00
❑ Polydor 14244	My Thang/Public Enemy No. 1	1974	—	2.50	5.00
❑ Polydor 14255	Papa Don't Take No Mess Part 1/Part 2	1974	—	2.50	5.00
❑ Polydor 14258	Funky President (People It's Bad)/Coldblooded	1974	—	2.50	5.00
❑ Polydor 14268	Reality/I Need Your Love So Bad	1975	—	2.50	5.00
❑ Polydor 14270	Sex Machine Part 1/Sex Machine Part 2	1975	—	2.50	5.00
❑ Polydor 14274	Thank You For Letting Me Be Myself And... Part 1/Part 2	1975	—	2.50	5.00
❑ Polydor 14281	Hustle (Dead On It) Part 1/Hustle (Dead On It) Part 2	1975	—	2.50	5.00
❑ Polydor 14295	Superbad, Superslick Part 1/Superbad, Superslick Part 2	1975	—	2.50	5.00
❑ Polydor 14301	Hot (I Need to Be Loved, Loved, Loved, Loved)/ Superbad, Superslick	1975	—	2.50	5.00
❑ Polydor 14302	Dooley's Junkyard Dogs Part 1/Part 2	1975	—	2.50	5.00
❑ Polydor 14304	(I Love You) For Sentimental Reasons/Goodnight My Love	1976	—	2.50	5.00
❑ Polydor 14326	Get Up Offa That Thing/Release the Pressure	1976	—	2.50	5.00
❑ Polydor 14354	I Refuse to Lose/Home Again	1976	—	2.50	5.00
❑ Polydor 14360	Bodyheat Part 1/Bodyheat Part 2	1976	—	2.50	5.00
❑ Polydor 14388	Kiss in 77/Woman	1977	—	2.50	5.00
❑ Polydor 14409	Give Me Some Skin/People Wake Up and Live	1977	—	2.50	5.00
—With the J.B.'s					
❑ Polydor 14433	Take Me Higher and Groove Me/Summertime	1977	—	2.50	5.00
—B-side by Martha and James					
❑ Polydor 14438	If You Don't Give a Doggone About It/People Who Criticize	1977	—	2.50	5.00
—With the New J.B.'s					
❑ Polydor 14460	Love Me Tender/Have a Happy Day	1978	—	2.50	5.00
—With the New J.B.'s					
❑ Polydor 14465	Eyesight/I Never Never Never Will Forget	1978	—	2.50	5.00
❑ Polydor 14487	The Spank/Love Me Tender	1978	—	2.50	5.00
❑ Polydor 14512	Nature Part 1/Nature Part 2	1978	—	2.50	5.00
❑ Polydor 14522	For Goodness Sakes, Look at Those Cakes Part 1/Part 2	1979	—	2.50	5.00
❑ Polydor 14540	Someone to Talk To Part 1/Someone to Talk To Part 2	1979	—	2.50	5.00
❑ Polydor 14557	It's Too Funky in Here/Are We Really Dancing	1979	—	2.50	5.00
❑ Polydor 871804-7	Think/Lost Someone	1989	—	—	3.00
—Reissue					

Number	Title (A Side/B Side)	Yr	VG	VG+	NM
❑ Polydor 871808-7	Out of Sight/Maybe the Last Time	1989	—	—	3.00
—Reissue					
❑ Polydor 871810-7	I Got You (I Feel Good)/Papa's Got a Brand New Bag	1989	—	—	3.00
—Reissue					
❑ Polydor 887500-7	(Get Up I Feel Like Being a) Sex Machine/Vincent's Theme	1988	—	—	3.00
—B-side by Ethan James					
❑ Scotti Brothers ZS4-05682	Living in America/Farewell	1985	—	—	3.00
—B-side by Vince Di Cola					
❑ Scotti Brothers ZS4-06275	Gravity/Gravity (Dub Mix)	1986	—	—	3.00
❑ Scotti Brothers ZS4-06568	How Do You Stop/House of Rock	1987	—	—	3.00
❑ Scotti Brothers ZS4-07090	Let's Get Personal/Repeat the Beat	1987	—	—	3.00
❑ Scotti Brothers ZS4-07783	I'm Real/Tribute	1988	—	—	3.00
❑ Scotti Brothers ZS4-07975	Static/Godfather Runnin' the Joint	1988	—	—	3.00
❑ Scotti Brothers ZS4-08088	Time to Get Busy/Busy J.B.	1988	—	—	3.00
❑ Scotti Brothers ZS4-68559	It's Your Money $/You and Me	1989	—	—	3.00
❑ Scotti Brothers 75286	(So Tired of Standing Still We Got to) Move On/ You Are My Everything	1991	—	2.00	4.00
❑ Smash 1898	Caledonia/Evil	1964	3.00	6.00	12.00
❑ Smash 1898	Caldonia/Evil	1964	3.00	6.00	12.00
❑ Smash 1908	The Things That I Used to Do/Out of the Blue	1964	3.00	6.00	12.00
❑ Smash 1919	Out of Sight/Maybe the Last Time	1964	3.00	6.00	12.00
❑ Smash 1975	Devil's Hideaway/Who's Afraid of Virginia Woolf?	1965	2.50	5.00	10.00
❑ Smash 1989	I Got You/Only You	1965	12.50	25.00	50.00
—Withdrawn					
❑ Smash 2008	Try Me/Papa's Got a Brand New Bag	1965	2.50	5.00	10.00
❑ Smash 2028	New Breed Part 1/New Breed Part 2	1966	2.50	5.00	10.00
❑ Smash 2042	James Brown's Boo-Ga-Loo/Lost in the Mood of Changes	1966	2.50	5.00	10.00
❑ Smash 2064	Let's Go Get Stoned/Our Day Will Come	1966	2.50	5.00	10.00
❑ Smash 2093	Jimmy Mack/What Do You Like	1967	2.50	5.00	10.00
❑ T.K. 1039	Rapp Payback (Where Iz Moses) Part 1/Part 2	1980	—	2.00	4.00
❑ T.K. 1042	Stay with Me/Smokin' and Drinkin'	1981	—	2.00	4.00
Albums					
❑ HRB 1004 [(2)]	The Fabulous James Brown	1974	6.25	12.50	25.00
❑ King 610 [M]	Please Please Please	1958	300.00	600.00	1200.
—"Woman's and man's legs" cover; "King" on label is two inches wide					
❑ King 635 [M]	Try Me!	1959	225.00	450.00	900.00
—"Woman with cigarette and gun" cover; "King" on label is two inches wide					
❑ King 683 [M]	Think!	1960	225.00	450.00	900.00
—"Baby" cover; "King" on label is two inches wide					
❑ King 743 [M]	The Amazing James Brown	1961	125.00	250.00	500.00
—"James Brown in suit" cover					
❑ King 771 [M]	Night Train	1961	75.00	150.00	300.00
—Original title					
❑ King 771 [M]	Twist Around	1962	62.50	125.00	250.00
—Second title					
❑ King KS-771 [S]	Jump Around	1963	75.00	150.00	300.00
—Stereo copies of King 771 only exist with this title					
❑ King 780 [M]	Shout and Shimmy	1962	62.50	125.00	250.00
—"Shout and Shimmy" on both cover and label					
❑ King 780 [M]	Good Good Twistin'	1962	50.00	100.00	200.00
—"Good Good Twistin' " on either label or cover, or both					
❑ King 780 [M]	Excitement	1963	37.50	75.00	150.00
—Third title; "crownless" King label					
❑ King 804 [M]	James Brown & His Famous Flames Tour the U.S.A.	1962	37.50	125.00	250.00
—"Crownless" King label					
❑ King 826 [M]	Live at the Apollo	1963	50.00	100.00	200.00
—Custom back cover; "crownless" King label					
❑ King 851 [M]	Prisoner of Love	1963	50.00	100.00	200.00
—Custom back cover; "crownless" King label					
❑ King 883 [M]	Pure Dynamite! Live at the Royal	1964	50.00	100.00	200.00
—"Crownless" King label					
❑ King 909 [M]	Please Please Please	1964	25.00	50.00	100.00
—Reissue of 610; "crownless" King label					
❑ King 919 [M]	The Unbeatable James Brown — 16 Hits	1964	25.00	50.00	100.00
—Reissue of 635; "crownless" King label					
❑ King 938 [M]	Papa's Got a Brand New Bag	1965	20.00	40.00	80.00
—Red cover; "crownless" King label					
❑ King LPS-938 [P]	Papa's Got a Brand New Bag	1965	25.00	50.00	100.00
—Red cover; "crownless" King label					
❑ King 946 [M]	I Got You (I Feel Good)	1966	25.00	50.00	100.00
—"Crownless" King label					
❑ King LPS-946 [S]	I Got You (I Feel Good)	1966	37.50	75.00	150.00
—"Crownless" King label					
❑ King 961 [M]	Mighty Instrumentals	1966	25.00	50.00	100.00
❑ King LPS-961 [S]	Mighty Instrumentals	1966	37.50	75.00	150.00
❑ King 985 [M]	It's a Man's Man's Man's World	1966	12.50	25.00	50.00
❑ King KS-985 [S]	It's a Man's Man's Man's World	1966	17.50	35.00	70.00
❑ King 1010 [M]	Christmas Songs	1966	25.00	50.00	100.00
—Wreath on gray wall, no song titles on back					
❑ King KS-1010 [S]	Christmas Songs	1966	37.50	75.00	150.00
—Wreath on gray wall, no song titles on back					
❑ King 1016 [M]	Raw Soul	1967	12.50	25.00	50.00
❑ King KS-1016 [P]	Raw Soul	1967	17.50	35.00	70.00
❑ King 1018 [M]	Live at the Garden	1967	20.00	40.00	80.00
❑ King KS-1018 [S]	Live at the Garden	1967	25.00	50.00	100.00
❑ King 1020 [M]	Cold Sweat	1967	12.50	25.00	50.00

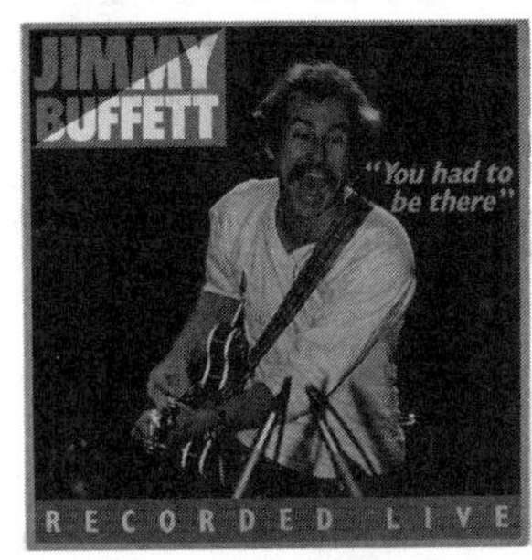

Number	Title (A Side/B Side)	Yr	VG	VG+	NM
❑ King KS-1020 [S]	Cold Sweat	1967	17.50	35.00	70.00
❑ King LPS-1022 [(2)]	Live at the Apollo, Volume II	1968	17.50	35.00	70.00
❑ King LPS-1024	James Brown Presents His Show of Tomorrow	1968	12.50	25.00	50.00
—Various-artists album					
❑ King LPS-1030	I Can't Stand Myself (When You Touch Me)	1968	12.50	25.00	50.00
❑ King LPS-1031	I Got the Feelin'	1968	12.50	25.00	50.00
❑ King LPS-1034	James Brown Plays Nothing But Soul	1968	12.50	25.00	50.00
❑ King LPS-1038	Thinking About Little Willie John and a Few Nice Things	1968	12.50	25.00	50.00
❑ King KS-1040	A Soulful Christmas	1968	20.00	40.00	80.00
❑ King KS-1047	Say It Loud — I'm Black and I'm Proud	1969	12.50	25.00	50.00
❑ King KS-1051	Gettin' Down To It	1969	12.50	25.00	50.00
❑ King KSD-1055	James Brown Plays & Directs The Popcorn	1969	10.00	20.00	40.00
❑ King KSD-1063	It's a Mother	1969	10.00	20.00	40.00
❑ King KSD-1092	Ain't It Funky	1970	10.00	20.00	40.00
❑ King KSD-1095	It's a New Day So Let a Man Come In	1970	10.00	20.00	40.00
❑ King KSD-1100	Soul on Top	1970	10.00	20.00	40.00
❑ King KSD-1110	Sho Is Funky Down Here	1971	10.00	20.00	40.00
❑ King KSD-1115 [(2)]	Sex Machine	1970	12.50	25.00	50.00
❑ King KSD-1124	Hey America!	1970	10.00	20.00	40.00
❑ King KSD-1127	Super Bad	1971	10.00	20.00	40.00
❑ Polydor 25-3003 [(2)]	Revolution of the Mind — Live at the Apollo, Volume III	1971	15.00	30.00	60.00
❑ Polydor PD2-3004 [(2)]	Get On the Good Foot	1972	15.00	30.00	60.00
❑ Polydor PD2-3007 [(2)]	The Payback	1973	12.50	25.00	50.00
❑ Polydor 24-4054	Hot Pants	1971	10.00	20.00	40.00
❑ Polydor PD-5028	There It Is	1972	10.00	20.00	40.00
❑ Polydor SC-5401	James Brown Soul Classics	1972	6.25	12.50	25.00
❑ Polydor SC-5402	Soul Classics, Volume 2	1973	6.25	12.50	25.00
❑ Polydor PD-6014	Black Caesar	1973	12.50	25.00	50.00
❑ Polydor PD-6015	Slaughter's Big Rip-Off	1973	12.50	25.00	50.00
❑ Polydor PD-1-6039	Reality	1975	10.00	20.00	40.00
❑ Polydor PD-1-6042	Sex Machine Today	1975	10.00	20.00	40.00
❑ Polydor PD-1-6054	Everybody's Doin' the Hustle & Dead On the Double Bump	1975	10.00	20.00	40.00
❑ Polydor PD-1-6059	Hot	1976	10.00	20.00	40.00
❑ Polydor PD-1-6071	Get Up Offa That Thing	1976	10.00	20.00	40.00
❑ Polydor PD-1-6093	Bodyheat	1976	10.00	20.00	40.00
❑ Polydor PD-1-6111	Mutha's Nature	1977	10.00	20.00	40.00
❑ Polydor PD-1-6140	Jam/1980s	1978	10.00	20.00	40.00
❑ Polydor PD-1-6181	Take a Look at Those Cakes	1978	7.50	15.00	30.00
❑ Polydor PD-1-6212	The Original Disco Man	1979	7.50	15.00	30.00
❑ Polydor PD-1-6258	People	1980	7.50	15.00	30.00
❑ Polydor PD-2-6290 [(2)]	James Brown...Live/Hot on the One	1980	12.50	25.00	50.00
❑ Polydor PD-1-6318	Nonstop!	1981	7.50	15.00	30.00
❑ Polydor PD-1-6340	The Best of James Brown	1981	5.00	10.00	20.00
❑ Polydor PD-2-9001 [(2)]	Hell	1974	20.00	40.00	80.00
❑ Polydor PD-2-9004 [(2)]	Sex Machine Live	1976	12.50	25.00	50.00
❑ Polydor 821231-1	Ain't That a Groove: The James Brown Story 1966-1969	1984	3.75	7.50	15.00
❑ Polydor 821232-1	Doing It to Death: The James Brown Story 1970-1973	1984	3.75	7.50	15.00
❑ Polydor 823275-1	The Best of James Brown	1984	3.00	6.00	12.00
—Reissue of 6340					
❑ Polydor 827439-1	Dead on the Heavy Funk: The James Brown Story 1974-1978	1985	3.75	7.50	15.00
❑ Polydor 829254-1 [(2)]	Solid Gold: 30 Golden Hits	1985	5.00	10.00	20.00
❑ Polydor 829417-1	James Brown's Funky People	1986	3.75	7.50	15.00
—Various-artists LP					
❑ Polydor 829624-1	In the Jungle Groove	1986	3.75	7.50	15.00
❑ Polydor 835857-1	James Brown's Funky People 2	1988	3.75	7.50	15.00
—Various-artists compilation					
❑ Polydor 837126-1	Motherlode	1988	3.75	7.50	15.00
❑ Rhino RNLP-217	Live at the Apollo, Volume 2, Part 1	1985	3.75	7.50	15.00
❑ Rhino RNLP-218	Live at the Apollo, Volume 2, Part 2	1985	3.75	7.50	15.00
❑ Rhino RNLP-219	Greatest Hits (1964-1968)	1986	3.75	7.50	15.00
❑ Rhino R1 70194	Santa's Got a Brand New Bag	1986	2.50	5.00	10.00
—Reissue of King material					
❑ Rhino R1-70217	Live at the Apollo, Volume 2, Part 1	1988	3.00	6.00	12.00
—Reissue of 217					
❑ Rhino R1-70218	Live at the Apollo, Volume 2, Part 2	1988	3.00	6.00	12.00
—Reissue of 218					

Number	Title (A Side/B Side)	Yr	VG	VG+	NM
❑ Rhino R1-70219	Greatest Hits (1964-1968)	1988	3.00	6.00	12.00
—Reissue of 219					
❑ Scotti Brothers FZ 40380	Gravity	1986	3.00	6.00	12.00
❑ Scotti Brothers FZ 44241	I'm Real	1988	3.00	6.00	12.00
❑ Scotti Brothers FZ 45164	Soul Session Live	1989	3.75	7.50	15.00
❑ Scotti Brothers 75225-1	Love Overdue	1991	5.00	10.00	20.00
❑ Smash MGS-27054 [M]	Showtime	1964	7.50	15.00	30.00
❑ Smash MGS-27057 [M]	Grits & Soul	1965	7.50	15.00	30.00
❑ Smash MGS-27058 [M]	Out of Sight	1965	25.00	50.00	100.00
❑ Smash MGS-27072 [M]	James Brown Plays James Brown — Today & Yesterday	1965	7.50	15.00	30.00
❑ Smash MGS-27080 [M]	James Brown Plays New Breed	1966	7.50	15.00	30.00
❑ Smash MGS-27084 [M]	Handful of Soul	1966	7.50	15.00	30.00
❑ Smash MGS-27087 [M]	The James Brown Show	1967	7.50	15.00	30.00
—Various-artists LP					
❑ Smash MGS-27093 [M]	James Brown Plays the Real Thing	1967	7.50	15.00	30.00
❑ Smash SRS-67054 [S]	Showtime	1964	10.00	2.00	40.00
❑ Smash SRS-67057 [S]	Grits & Soul	1965	10.00	20.00	40.00
❑ Smash SRS-67058 [S]	Out of Sight	1965	37.50	75.00	150.00
❑ Smash SRS-67072 [S]	James Brown Plays James Brown — Today & Yesterday	1965	10.00	20.00	40.00
❑ Smash SRS-67080 [S]	James Brown Plays New Breed	1966	10.00	2.00	40.00
❑ Smash SRS-67084 [S]	Handful of Soul	1966	10.00	20.00	40.00
❑ Smash SRS-67087 [S]	The James Brown Show	1967	10.00	2.00	40.00
—Various-artists LP					
❑ Smash SRS-67093 [S]	James Brown Plays the Real Thing	1967	10.00	20.00	40.00
❑ Smash SRS-67109	James Brown Sings Out of Sight	1968	7.50	15.00	30.00
—Abridged reissue of 67058					
❑ Solid Smoke SS-8006	Live and Lowdown at the Apollo, Vol. 1	1980	3.00	6.00	12.00
❑ Solid Smoke SS-8013	Can Your Heart Stand It	1981	3.00	6.00	12.00
❑ Solid Smoke SS-8023	The Federal Years, Part 1	198?	3.00	6.00	12.00
❑ Solid Smoke SS-8024	The Federal Years, Part 2	198?	3.00	6.00	12.00
❑ T.K. 615	Soul Syndrome	1980	7.50	15.00	30.00

BROWNE, JACKSON

45s

Number	Title (A Side/B Side)	Yr	VG	VG+	NM
❑ Asylum 11004	Doctor My Eyes/Looking Into You	1972	—	2.50	5.00
❑ Asylum 11006	Rock Me on the Water/Something Fine	1972	—	2.00	4.00
❑ Asylum 11023	Redneck Friend/Those Times You've Come	1973	—	2.00	4.00
❑ Asylum 11030	Ready or Not/Take It Easy	1974	—	2.00	4.00
❑ Asylum 45227	Walking Slow/Before the Deluge	1975	—	2.00	4.00
❑ Asylum 45242	Fountains of Sorrow/The Late Show	1975	—	2.00	4.00
❑ Asylum 45379	Here Come Those Tears Again/Linda Paloma	1976	—	2.00	4.00
❑ Asylum 45399	The Pretender/Daddy's Tune	1977	—	2.00	4.00
❑ Asylum 45460	Running on Empty/Nothing But Time	1978	—	2.00	4.00
❑ Asylum 45485-A/B	Stay/Rosie	1978	—	2.50	5.00
❑ Asylum 45485-A/C	Stay/The Load-Out	1978	—	2.00	4.00
❑ Asylum 45543	You Love the Thunder/The Road	1978	—	2.00	4.00
❑ Asylum 47003	Boulevard/Call It a Loan	1980	—	2.00	4.00
❑ Asylum 47036	That Girl Could Sing/Of Missing Persons	1980	—	2.00	4.00
❑ Asylum 69543	In the Shape of a Heart/Voice of America	1986	—	—	3.00
❑ Asylum 69566	For America/Till I Go Down	1986	—	—	3.00
❑ Asylum 69764	For a Rocker/Downtown	1984	—	—	3.00
❑ Asylum 69791	Tender Is the Night/On the Day	1983	—	—	3.00
❑ Asylum 69826	Lawyers in Love/Say It Isn't True	1983	—	—	3.00
❑ Asylum 69982	Somebody's Baby/The Crow on the Cradle [w/Graham Nash & David Lindley]	1982	—	2.00	4.00
❑ Elektra 69292	World in Motion/My Personal Revenge	1989	—	2.00	4.00

Albums

Number	Title (A Side/B Side)	Yr	VG	VG+	NM
❑ Asylum 6E-107	The Pretender	1977	2.50	5.00	10.00
—Reissue of 7E-1079					
❑ Asylum 6E-113	Running on Empty	1977	2.50	5.00	10.00
❑ Asylum 5E-511	Hold Out	1979	2.50	5.00	10.00
❑ Asylum 7E-1017	Late for the Sky	1974	3.00	6.00	12.00
❑ Asylum 7E-1079	The Pretender	1976	3.00	6.00	12.00
❑ Asylum SD 5051	Jackson Browne (Saturate Before Using)	1972	5.00	10.00	20.00
—Burlap cover, opens at top; white label with "Asylum Records" logo in a circle at top					
❑ Asylum SD 5067	For Everyman	1973	3.00	6.00	12.00
❑ Asylum 60268	Lawyers in Love	1983	2.50	5.00	10.00
❑ Asylum 60457	Lives in the Balance	1986	2.50	5.00	10.00
❑ Elektra 60830	World in Motion	1989	2.50	5.00	10.00

BROWNSVILLE STATION

45s

Number	Title (A Side/B Side)	Yr	VG	VG+	NM
❑ Big Tree 144	Rock with the Music/(B-side unknown)	1972	—	2.50	5.00
❑ Big Tree 156	The Red Back Spider/Rock with the Music	1972	—	2.50	5.00
❑ Big Tree 161	Let Your Yeah Be Yeah/Mister Robert	1973	—	2.50	5.00
❑ Big Tree 15005	I'm the Leader of the Gang/Fast Phyllis	1974	—	2.00	4.00
❑ Big Tree 15005	I'm the Leader of the Gang/Meet Me on the Fourth Floor	1974	—	2.00	4.00
❑ Big Tree 16001	Kings of the Party/Ostrich	1974	—	2.00	4.00
❑ Big Tree 16011	Smokin' in the Boy's Room/Barefootin'	1973	—	2.50	5.00
❑ Big Tree 16029	I Got It Bad for You/Mama Don't Allow No Parkin'	1974	—	2.00	4.00
❑ Epic 50695	Love Stealer/Fever	1979	—	2.00	4.00
—As "Brownsville"					
❑ Hideout 1957	Rock and Roll Holiday/Jailhouse Rock	1969	3.00	6.00	12.00
❑ Palladium H-1075	Be-Bop Confidential/City Life	1970	5.00	10.00	20.00
❑ Polydor 14017	Rock and Roll Holiday/Jailhouse Rock	1969	—	2.50	5.00
❑ Private Stock 45,149	Lady (Put the Light on Me)/Rockers and Rollers	1977	—	2.00	4.00
❑ Private Stock 45,167	The Martian Boogie/Mr. Johnson Sez	1977	—	2.00	4.00
❑ Warner Bros. 7441	Be-Bop Confidential/City Life	1970	2.00	4.00	8.00

Number	Title (A Side/B Side)	Yr	VG	VG+	NM
❑ Warner Bros. 7456	Roadrunner/Do the Bosco	1971	2.00	4.00	8.00
❑ Warner Bros. 7501	That's Fine/Tell Me All About It	1971	2.00	4.00	8.00
Albums					
❑ Big Tree BTS-2010	A Night on the Town	1972	3.00	6.00	12.00
❑ Big Tree BTS-2102	Yeah!	1973	3.00	6.00	12.00
❑ Big Tree BT 89500	School Punks	1974	3.00	6.00	12.00
❑ Big Tree BT 89510	Motor City Connection	1975	3.00	6.00	12.00
❑ Epic JE 35606	Air Special	1978	2.50	5.00	10.00
❑ Palladium P-1004	Brownsville Station	1970	7.50	15.00	30.00
❑ Private Stock PS-2026	Brownsville Station	1977	2.50	5.00	10.00
❑ Warner Bros. WS 1888	No B.S.	1970	3.75	7.50	15.00

BUBBLE PUPPY, THE

Number	Title (A Side/B Side)	Yr	VG	VG+	NM
45s					
❑ International Artists 128	Hot Smoke and Sasafrass/Lonely	1969	5.00	10.00	20.00
❑ International Artists 133	Beginning/If I Had a Reason	1969	6.25	12.50	25.00
❑ International Artists 136	Days of Our Time/Thinkin' About Thinkin'	1969	6.25	12.50	25.00
❑ International Artists 138	What Do You See/Hurry Sundown	1970	6.25	12.50	25.00
Albums					
❑ International Artists 10	A Gathering of Promises	1969	25.00	50.00	100.00
—Original does not have "Masterfonics" in the dead wax					

BUCKINGHAMS, THE (1)

Records on Laurie and Seg-Way are by a different Buckinghams who are outside the scope of this book.

Number	Title (A Side/B Side)	Yr	VG	VG+	NM
45s					
❑ Columbia 44053	Don't You Care/Why Don't You Love Me	1967	2.00	4.00	8.00
❑ Columbia 44182	Mercy, Mercy, Mercy/You Are Gone	1967	2.00	4.00	8.00
❑ Columbia 44254	Hey Baby (They're Playing Our Song)/And Our Love	1967	2.00	4.00	8.00
❑ Columbia 44378	Susan/Foreign Policy	1967	2.00	4.00	8.00
❑ Columbia 44533	Back in Love Again/You Misunderstand Me	1968	2.00	4.00	8.00
❑ Columbia 44672	Where Did You Come From/Song of the Breeze	1968	2.00	4.00	8.00
❑ Columbia 44790	This Is How Much I Love You/Can't You Find the Words	1969	2.00	4.00	8.00
❑ Columbia 44923	It's a Beautiful Day/Difference of Opinion	1969	2.00	4.00	8.00
❑ Columbia 45066	It Took Forever/I Got a Feelin'	1970	2.00	4.00	8.00
❑ Red Label 71001	Veronica/Can We Talk About It	1985	—	2.00	4.00
❑ SpectraSound 4618	Sweets for My Sweet/Beginner's Love	1967	5.00	10.00	20.00
❑ U.S.A. 844	I'll Go Crazy/I Don't Wanna Cry	1966	3.00	6.00	12.00
❑ U.S.A. 848	I Call Your Name/Makin' Up and Breakin' Up	1966	3.00	6.00	12.00
❑ U.S.A. 853	I've Been Wrong/Love Ain't Enough	1966	3.00	6.00	12.00
❑ U.S.A. 860	Kind of a Drag/You Make Me Feel So Good	1966	3.75	7.50	15.00
—Light blue label with red, white, blue and black printing					
❑ U.S.A. 869	Lawdy Miss Clawdy/I Call Your Name	1967	3.00	6.00	12.00
❑ U.S.A. 869	Lawdy Miss Clawdy/Making Up and Breaking Up	1967	3.00	6.00	12.00
❑ U.S.A. 873	Summertime/Don't Want to Cry	1967	3.00	6.00	12.00
Albums					
❑ Columbia CL 2669 [M]	Time & Charges	1967	6.25	12.50	25.00
❑ Columbia CL 2798 [M]	Portraits	1968	6.25	12.50	25.00
❑ Columbia CS 9469 [S]	Time & Charges	1967	5.00	10.00	20.00
❑ Columbia CS 9598 [S]	Portraits	1968	5.00	10.00	20.00
❑ Columbia CS 9703	In One Ear and Gone Tomorrow	1968	5.00	10.00	20.00
❑ Columbia CS 9812	The Buckinghams Greatest Hits	1969	5.00	10.00	20.00
—Red "360 Sound" label					
❑ Columbia KG 33333 [(2)]	Made in Chicago	1975	5.00	10.00	20.00
❑ U.S.A. 107 [M]	Kind of a Drag	1967	7.50	15.00	30.00
—Without "I'm a Man"					
❑ U.S.A. 107 [S]	Kind of a Drag	1967	10.00	20.00	40.00
—No known stereo copy has "I'm a Man"					

BUFFALO SPRINGFIELD

Number	Title (A Side/B Side)	Yr	VG	VG+	NM
45s					
❑ Atco 6428	Nowadays Clancy Can't Even Sing/Go And Say Goodbye	1966	5.00	10.00	20.00
❑ Atco 6452	Everybody's Wrong/Burned	1966	5.00	10.00	20.00
❑ Atco 6459	For What It's Worth/Do I Have to Come Right Out and Say It	1967	3.75	7.50	15.00
❑ Atco 6499	Bluebird/Mr. Soul	1967	5.00	10.00	20.00
❑ Atco 6519	Rock 'N' Roll Woman/A Child's Claim to Fame	1967	2.50	5.00	10.00
❑ Atco 6545	Expecting to Fly/Everydays	1968	2.50	5.00	10.00
❑ Atco 6572	Uno Mundo/Merry-Go-Round	1968	2.50	5.00	10.00
❑ Atco 6602	Special Care/Kind Woman	1968	2.50	5.00	10.00

Number	Title (A Side/B Side)	Yr	VG	VG+	NM
❑ Atco 6615	Four Days Gone/On the Way Home	1968	2.50	5.00	10.00
Albums					
❑ Atco SD 38-105 [S]	Retrospective/The Best of Buffalo Springfield	197?	2.00	4.00	8.00
—Reissue of 33-283					
❑ Atco 33-200 [M]	Buffalo Springfield	1967	50.00	100.00	200.00
—With "Baby Don't Scold Me"					
❑ Atco 33-200A [M]	Buffalo Springfield	1967	6.25	12.50	25.00
—With "For What It's Worth" replacing "Baby Don't Scold Me"					
❑ Atco SD 33-200 [S]	Buffalo Springfield	1967	50.00	100.00	200.00
—With "Baby Don't Scold Me"					
❑ Atco SD 33-200A [S]	Buffalo Springfield	1967	6.25	12.50	25.00
—With "For What It's Worth" replacing "Baby Don't Scold Me"; purple and brown label					
❑ Atco 33-226 [M]	Buffalo Springfield Again	1967	20.00	40.00	80.00
❑ Atco SD 33-226 [S]	Buffalo Springfield Again	1967	6.25	12.50	25.00
—Purple and brown label					
❑ Atco SD 33-256 [S]	Last Time Around	1968	7.50	15.00	30.00
—Purple and brown label					
❑ Atco SD 33-283 [S]	Retrospective/The Best of Buffalo Springfield	1969	5.00	10.00	20.00
—Yellow label					
❑ Atco SD 2-806 [(2)]	Buffalo Springfield	1973	5.00	10.00	20.00
—Yellow label					

BUFFETT, JIMMY

Number	Title (A Side/B Side)	Yr	VG	VG+	NM
45s					
❑ ABC 12113	Door Number Three/Dallas	1975	—	2.50	5.00
❑ ABC 12143	Big Red/Havana Daydreamin'	1975	—	2.50	5.00
❑ ABC 12175	The Captain and the Kid/Cliches	1976	—	2.50	5.00
❑ ABC 12200	Something So Feminine About a Mandolin/ Woman Goin' Crazy on Caroline Street	1976	—	2.50	5.00
❑ ABC 12254	Margaritaville/Miss You So Badly	1977	—	2.00	4.00
❑ ABC 12305	Changes in Latitudes, Changes in Attitudes/Landfall	1977	—	2.00	4.00
❑ ABC 12358	Cheeseburger in Paradise/African Friend	1978	—	2.00	4.00
❑ ABC 12391	Livingston Saturday Night/Cowboy in the Jungle	1978	—	2.00	4.00
❑ ABC 12428	Manana/The Coast of Marsailles	1978	—	2.00	4.00
❑ ABC Dunhill 4348	The Great Filling Station Hold Up/Why Don't We Get Drunk	1973	2.00	4.00	8.00
❑ ABC Dunhill 4353	The Great Filling Station Hold Up/They Can't Dance Like Carmen No More	1973	—	2.00	4.00
❑ ABC Dunhill 4359	Grapefruit-Juicy Fruit/I Found Me a Home	1973	—	2.00	4.00
❑ ABC Dunhill 4372	He Went to Paris/Peanut Butter Conspiracy	1973	—	2.00	4.00
❑ ABC Dunhill 4378	Ringling, Ringling/Saxophones	1974	—	2.00	4.00
❑ ABC Dunhill 4385	Come Monday/The Wino and I Know	1974	—	2.50	5.00
❑ ABC Dunhill 15008	Come Monday/The Wino and I Know	1974	—	2.00	4.00
❑ ABC Dunhill 15011	Brand New Country Star/Pencil Thin Moustache	1974	—	2.00	4.00
❑ ABC Dunhill 15029	Presents to Send You/A Pirate Looks at Forty	1975	—	2.00	4.00
❑ Asylum 69890	I Don't Know (Spicoli's Theme)/She's My Baby (And She's Out of Control)	1982	—	2.00	4.00
—B-side by Palmer & Jost					
❑ Barnaby 2013	The Christian/Richard Frost	1970	2.50	5.00	10.00
❑ Barnaby 2019	He Ain't Free/There Ain't Nothing Soft About Hard Times	1970	2.50	5.00	10.00
❑ Barnaby 2023	Captain America/Truckstop Salvation	1970	2.50	5.00	10.00
❑ Full Moon 49659	Survive/Send Me Somebody to Love	1981	—	2.00	4.00
—B-side by Kathy Walker					
❑ Full Moon/Asylum 47073	Hello Texas/Lyin' Eyes [by the Eagles]	1980	—	2.50	5.00
❑ MCA 41109	Fins/Dreamsicle	1979	—	2.00	4.00
❑ MCA 41161	Volcano/Stranded on a Sandbar	1979	—	2.00	4.00
❑ MCA 41199	Boat Drinks/Survive	1980	—	2.00	4.00
❑ MCA 51061	It's My Job/Little Miss Magic	1981	—	2.00	4.00
❑ MCA 51105	Stars Fell on Alabama/Growing Older But Not Up	1981	—	2.00	4.00
❑ MCA 52013	It's Midnight And I'm Not Famous Yet/ When Salome Plays the Drum	1982	—	2.00	4.00
❑ MCA 52050	If I Could Just Get It on Paper/Where's the Party	1982	—	2.00	4.00
❑ MCA 52298	One Particular Harbour/Distantly in Love	1983	—	2.00	4.00
❑ MCA 52333	Brown Eyed Girl/Twelve Volt Man	1984	—	2.00	4.00
❑ MCA 52438	When the Wild Life Betrays Me/Ragtop Day	1984	—	2.00	4.00
❑ MCA 52499	Come to the Moon/Bigger Than the Both of Us	1984	—	2.00	4.00
❑ MCA 52550	Who's the Blond Stranger/She's Going Out of My Mind	1985	—	—	3.00
❑ MCA 52607	Gypies in the Palace/Jolly Mon Sing	1985	—	—	3.00
❑ MCA 52664	If the Phone Doesn't Ring, It's Me/Frank and Lola	1985	—	—	3.00
❑ MCA 52752	Please Bypass This Heart/Beyond the End	1986	—	—	3.00
❑ MCA 52849	I Love the Now/No Plane on Sunday	1986	—	—	3.00
❑ MCA 52932	Creola/You'll Never Work in Dis Bidness Again	1986	—	—	3.00
❑ MCA 53035	Take It Back/Floridays	1987	—	—	3.00
❑ MCA 53360	Homemade Music/L'air de la Louisiane	1988	—	—	3.00
❑ MCA 53396	Bring Back the Magic/That's What Living Is to Me	1988	—	—	3.00
❑ MCA 53675	Take Another Road/Off to See the Lizard	1989	—	—	3.00
❑ MCA 54680	Another Saturday Night/Souvenirs	1993	—	—	3.00
Albums					
❑ ABC D-914	Havana Daydreamin'	1976	3.00	6.00	12.00
❑ ABC AB-990	Changes in Latitudes, Changes in Attitudes	1977	3.00	6.00	12.00
❑ ABC AK-1008 [(2)]	You Had to Be There	1978	3.75	7.50	15.00
❑ ABC AA-1046	Son of a Son of a Sailor	1978	3.00	6.00	12.00
❑ ABC Dunhill DSD-50132	Living and Dying in 3/4 Time	1973	3.75	7.50	15.00
❑ ABC Dunhill DSX-50150	A White Sport Coat and a Pink Crustaceon	1974	3.75	7.50	15.00
❑ ABC Dunhill DSD-50183	A1A	1975	3.75	7.50	15.00
❑ Barnaby BR-6014	High Cumberland Jubilee	1975	10.00	20.00	40.00
❑ Barnaby Z 30093	Down to Earth	1970	25.00	50.00	100.00
❑ MCA 5102	Volcano	1979	2.50	5.00	10.00

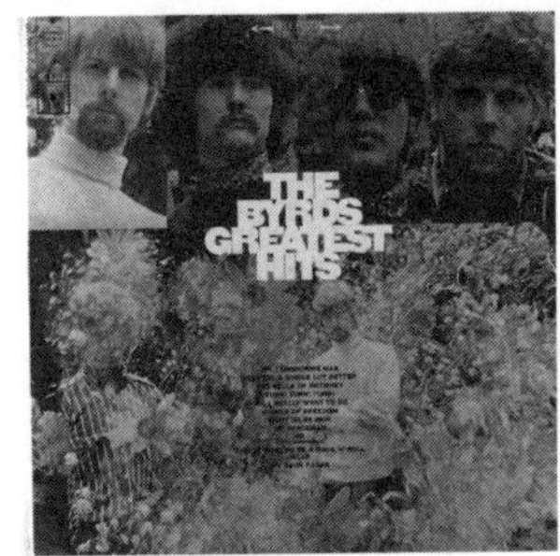

Number	Title (A Side/B Side)	Yr	VG	VG+	NM
❑ MCA 5169	Coconut Telegraph	1981	2.50	5.00	10.00
❑ MCA 5285	Somewhere Over China	1982	2.50	5.00	10.00
❑ MCA 5447	One Particular Harbour	1983	2.50	5.00	10.00
❑ MCA 5512	Riddles in the Sand	1984	2.50	5.00	10.00
❑ MCA 5600	Last Mango in Paris	1985	2.50	5.00	10.00
❑ MCA 5633	Songs You Know By Heart — Jimmy Buffett's Greatest Hit(s)	1985	2.50	5.00	10.00
❑ MCA 5730	Floridays	1986	2.50	5.00	10.00
❑ MCA 2-6005 [(2)]	You Had to Be There	1981	2.50	5.00	10.00
❑ MCA 6314	Off to See the Lizard	1989	2.50	5.00	10.00
❑ MCA 37023	Havana Daydreamin'	1981	2.00	4.00	8.00
❑ MCA 37024	Son of a Son of a Sailor	1981	2.00	4.00	8.00
❑ MCA 37025	Living and Dying in 3/4 Time	1981	2.00	4.00	8.00
❑ MCA 37026	A White Sport Coat and a Pink Crustaceon	1981	2.00	4.00	8.00
❑ MCA 37027	A1A	1981	2.00	4.00	8.00
❑ MCA 37150	Changes in Latitudes, Changes in Attitudes	1982	2.00	4.00	8.00
❑ MCA 37156	Volcano	1982	2.00	4.00	8.00
❑ MCA 37246	Somewhere Over China	1984	2.00	4.00	8.00
❑ MCA 42093	Hot Water	1988	2.50	5.00	10.00

BUOYS, THE

45s

Number	Title (A Side/B Side)	Yr	VG	VG+	NM
❑ Polydor 14201	Liza's Last Ride/Downtown Singer	1973	—	3.00	6.00
❑ Scepter 12254	These Days/Don't You Know It's Over	1969	2.00	4.00	8.00
❑ Scepter 12275	Timothy/It Feels Good	1970	2.50	5.00	10.00
❑ Scepter 12318	Give Up Your Guns/Prince of Thieves	1971	2.00	4.00	8.00
❑ Scepter 12331	Tell Me Heaven Is Here/Bloodknot	1971	2.00	4.00	8.00

Albums

Number	Title (A Side/B Side)	Yr	VG	VG+	NM
❑ Scepter SPS-593	Timothy	1971	6.25	12.50	25.00

BURDON, ERIC, AND WAR

45s

Number	Title (A Side/B Side)	Yr	VG	VG+	NM
❑ ABC 12244	Magic Mountain/Home Dream	1977	—	2.50	5.00
❑ MGM 14118	Spill the Wine/Magic Mountain	1970	—	3.00	6.00
❑ MGM 14196	They Can't Take Away Our Music/Home Cookin'	1970	—	2.50	5.00

Albums

Number	Title (A Side/B Side)	Yr	VG	VG+	NM
❑ ABC D-988	Love Is All Around	1976	3.00	6.00	12.00

—As "War Featuring Eric Burdon"

Number	Title (A Side/B Side)	Yr	VG	VG+	NM
❑ LAX PW 37109	Spill the Wine	1981	2.50	5.00	10.00

—Reissue of MGM 4663 with new title

Number	Title (A Side/B Side)	Yr	VG	VG+	NM
❑ MGM SE-4663	Eric Burdon Declares "War"	1970	3.75	7.50	15.00
❑ MGM SE-4710-2 [(2)]	The Black Man's Burdon	1970	5.00	10.00	20.00

—Add 50% if the package includes an "Official War Bond," entlitling the bearer to $1 off any Eric Burdon and War concert before December 31, 1973

BURNETTE, JOHNNY

45s

Number	Title (A Side/B Side)	Yr	VG	VG+	NM
❑ Capitol 5023	All Week Long/It Isn't There	1963	3.75	7.50	15.00
❑ Capitol 5114	You Taught Me the Way to Love You/The Opposite	1964	3.75	7.50	15.00
❑ Capitol 5176	Walkin' Talkin' Doll/Sweet Suzie	1964	3.75	7.50	15.00
❑ Chancellor 1116	I Wanna Thank Your Folks/The Giant	1962	3.75	7.50	15.00
❑ Chancellor 1123	Party Girl/Tag Along	1962	3.75	7.50	15.00
❑ Chancellor 1129	Remember Me/Time Is Not Enough	1962	3.75	7.50	15.00
❑ Coral 61651	Tear It Up/You're Undecided	1956	75.00	150.00	300.00
❑ Coral 61675	Midnight Train/Oh Baby Babe	1956	75.00	150.00	300.00
❑ Coral 61719	The Train Kept a-Rollin'/Honey Hush	1956	62.50	125.00	250.00
❑ Coral 61758	Lonesome Train/I Just Found Out	1956	75.00	150.00	300.00
❑ Coral 61829	Eager Beaver Baby/Touch Me	1957	75.00	150.00	300.00
❑ Coral 61869	Drinkin' Wine Spo-Dee-O-Dee/Butterfingers	1957	75.00	150.00	300.00
❑ Coral 61918	Rock Billy Boogie/If You Want It Enough	1957	75.00	150.00	300.00
❑ Freedom 44001	I'm Restless/Kiss Me	1958	20.00	40.00	80.00
❑ Freedom 44011	Gumbo/Me and the Bear	1959	20.00	40.00	80.00
❑ Freedom 44017	Sweet Baby Doll/I'll Never Love Again	1959	20.00	40.00	80.00
❑ Liberty 55222	Settin' the Woods on Fire/Kentucky Waltz	1959	5.00	10.00	20.00
❑ Liberty 55243	Don't Do It/Patrick Henry	1959	5.00	10.00	20.00
❑ Liberty 55258	Dreamin'/Cincinnati Fireball	1960	5.00	10.00	20.00
❑ Liberty 55285	You're Sixteen/I Beg Your Pardon	1960	5.00	10.00	20.00
❑ Liberty 55298	Little Boy Sad/(I Go) Down to the River	1961	3.75	7.50	15.00
❑ Liberty 55318	Big Big World/Ballad of the One Eyed Jacks	1961	3.75	7.50	15.00

Number	Title (A Side/B Side)	Yr	VG	VG+	NM
❑ Liberty 55345	Girls/I've Got a Lot of Things to Do	1961	3.75	7.50	15.00
❑ Liberty 55377	Honestly I Do/Fools Like Me	1961	3.75	7.50	15.00
❑ Liberty 55379	God, Country and My Baby/Honestly I Do	1961	3.75	7.50	15.00
❑ Liberty 55416	Clown Shoes/The Way I Am	1962	3.75	7.50	15.00
❑ Liberty 55448	The Fool of the Year/The Poorest Boy in Town	1962	3.75	7.50	15.00
❑ Liberty 55489	Damn the Defiant/Lonesome Waters	1962	3.75	7.50	15.00
❑ Magic Lamp 515	Bigger Man/Less Than a Heartache	1964	12.50	25.00	50.00
❑ Sahara 512	Fountain of Love/What a Summer Day	1964	3.75	7.50	15.00
❑ United Artists 0018	Dreamin'/Little Boy Sad	1973	—	2.00	4.00
—Silver Spotlight Series issue					
❑ United Artists 0019	You're Sixteen/God, Country and My Baby	1973	—	2.00	4.00
—Silver Spotlight Series issue					
❑ Von 1006	You're Undecided/Go, Mule, Go	1954	1500.	2250.	3000.
—VG 1500; VG+ 2250					
Albums					
❑ Coral CRL 57080 [M]	Johnny Burnette & the Rock 'N' Roll Trio	1956	2000.	4000.	6000.
—Originals have maroon labels, machine-stamped (not engraved) numbers in the dead wax, printing on jacket's spine and "Printed in U.S.A." in lower right of back cover; VG value 2000; VG+ value 4000					
❑ Liberty LRP-3179 [M]	Dreamin'	1960	10.00	20.00	40.00
❑ Liberty LRP-3183 [M]	Johnny Burnette	1961	10.00	20.00	40.00
❑ Liberty LRP-3190 [M]	Johnny Burnette Sings	1961	10.00	20.00	40.00
❑ Liberty LRP-3206 [M]	Johnny Burnette's Hits and Other Favorites	1962	10.00	20.00	40.00
❑ Liberty LRP-3255 [M]	Roses Are Red	1962	10.00	20.00	40.00
❑ Liberty LRP-3389 [M]	The Johnny Burnette Story	1964	10.00	20.00	40.00
❑ Liberty LST-7179 [S]	Dreamin'	1960	15.00	30.00	60.00
❑ Liberty LST-7183 [S]	Johnny Burnette	1961	15.00	30.00	60.00
❑ Liberty LST-7190 [S]	Johnny Burnette Sings	1961	15.00	30.00	60.00
❑ Liberty LST-7206 [S]	Johnny Burnette's Hits and Other Favorites	1962	12.50	25.00	50.00
❑ Liberty LST-7255 [S]	Roses Are Red	1962	12.50	25.00	50.00
❑ Liberty LST-7389 [S]	The Johnny Burnette Story	1964	12.50	25.00	50.00
❑ MCA 1513	Listen to Johnny Burnette and the Rock 'N' Roll Trio	1982	2.50	5.00	10.00
❑ Solid Smoke SS-8001	Tear It Up	1978	3.75	7.50	15.00
—Black viinyl					
❑ Solid Smoke SS-8001	Tear It Up	1978	7.50	15.00	30.00
—Blue vinyl					
❑ Sunset SUM-1179 [M]	Dreamin'	1967	3.75	7.50	15.00
❑ Sunset SUS-5179 [S]	Dreamin'	1967	5.00	10.00	20.00
❑ United Artists UA-LA432-G	The Very Best of Johnny Burnette	1975	2.50	5.00	10.00

BUTLER, JERRY

45s

Number	Title (A Side/B Side)	Yr	VG	VG+	NM
❑ Abner 1024	Lost/One by One	1959	7.50	15.00	30.00
❑ Abner 1028	Hold Me Darling/Rainbow Valley	1959	7.50	15.00	30.00
❑ Abner 1030	I Was Wrong/Couldn't Go to Sleep	1959	7.50	15.00	30.00
❑ Abner 1035	A Lonely Soldier/I Found a Love	1960	7.50	15.00	30.00
❑ Fountain 400	No Love Without Changes/All the Way	1982	—	3.00	6.00
❑ Ichiban 269	Angel Flying Too Close to the Ground/You're the Only One	1992	—	—	3.00
❑ Ichiban 290	Need to Belong/Sure Feels Good	1993	—	—	3.00
❑ Lost-Nite 273	A Lonely Soldier/I Found a Love	197?	—	2.50	5.00
—Reissue					
❑ Lost-Nite 279	He Will Break Your Heart/Thanks to You	197?	—	2.50	5.00
—Reissue					
❑ Lost-Nite 284	Moon River/Aware of Love	197?	—	2.50	5.00
—Reissue					
❑ Lost-Nite 291	Make It Easy on Yourself/It's Too Late	197?	—	2.50	5.00
—Reissue					
❑ Lost-Nite 306	Need to Belong/Giving Up on Love	197?	—	2.50	5.00
❑ Lost-Nite 312	I Stand Accused/You Can Run	197?	—	2.50	5.00
❑ MCA 52177	Let's Talk It Over/Especially You	1983	—	2.00	4.00
—With Stix Hooper; B-side by Stix Hooper solo					
❑ Mercury 72592	Love (Oh How Sweet It Is)/Loneliness	1966	2.50	5.00	10.00
❑ Mercury 72625	You Make Me Feel Like Someone/For What You Made of Me	1966	2.50	5.00	10.00
❑ Mercury 72648	I Dig You Baby/Some Kinda Magic	1966	2.50	5.00	10.00
❑ Mercury 72676	Why Do I Lose You/You Walked Into My Life	1967	2.50	5.00	10.00
❑ Mercury 72698	You Don't Know What You've Got Until You Lose It/ The Way I Love You	1967	2.50	5.00	10.00
❑ Mercury 72721	Mr. Dream Merchant/'Cause I Love You So	1967	2.50	5.00	10.00
❑ Mercury 72764	Lost/You Don't Know What You've Got Until You Lose It	1968	2.00	4.00	8.00
❑ Mercury 72798	Never Give You Up/Beside You	1968	2.00	4.00	8.00
❑ Mercury 72850	Hey, Western Union Man/Just Can't Forget About You	1968	2.00	4.00	8.00
❑ Mercury 72876	Are You Happy/I Still Love You	1968	2.00	4.00	8.00
❑ Mercury 72898	Only the Strong Survive/Just Because I Really Love You	1969	2.00	4.00	8.00
❑ Mercury 72929	Moody Woman/Go Away — Find Yourself	1969	2.00	4.00	8.00
❑ Mercury 72960	What's the Use of Breaking Up/Brand New Me	1969	2.00	4.00	8.00
❑ Mercury 72991	Don't Let Love Hang You Up/Walking Around in Teardrops	1969	2.00	4.00	8.00
❑ Mercury 73015	Got to See If I Can't Get Mommy (To Come Back Home)/ I Forgot to Remember	1970	2.00	4.00	8.00
❑ Mercury 73045	I Could Write a Book/Since I Lost You, Baby	1970	2.00	4.00	8.00
❑ Mercury 73101	Where Are You Going/You Can Fly	1970	2.00	4.00	8.00
❑ Mercury 73131	How Does It Feel/Special Memory	1970	2.00	4.00	8.00
❑ Mercury 73169	If It's Real What I Feel/Why Are You Leaving Me	1971	—	3.00	6.00
❑ Mercury 73210	How Did We Lose It baby/Do You Finally Need a Friend	1971	—	3.00	6.00
❑ Mercury 73241	Walk Easy My Son/Let Me Be	1971	—	3.00	6.00
❑ Mercury 73290	I Only Have Eyes for You/A Prayer	1972	—	3.00	6.00
❑ Mercury 73335	One Night Affair/Life's Unfortunate Song	1972	—	3.00	6.00
❑ Mercury 73443	Power of Love/What Do You Do on a Sunday Afternoon	1973	—	3.00	6.00
❑ Mercury 73459	That's How Heartaches Are Made/Too Many Danger Signs	1974	—	3.00	6.00

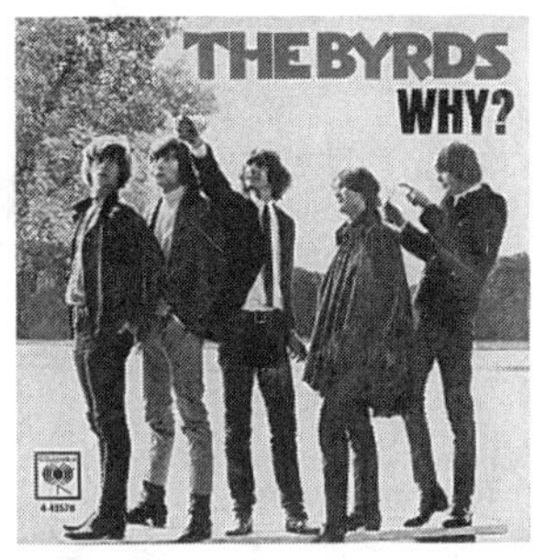

Number	Title (A Side/B Side)	Yr	VG	VG+	NM
❑ Mercury 73495	Take the Time to Tell Her/High Stepper	1974	—	3.00	6.00
❑ Mercury 73629	You and Me Against the World/Playing on You	1974	—	3.00	6.00
❑ Mercury 872914-7	Only the Strong Survive/Lost	1989	—	—	3.00
—Reissue					
❑ Mercury 872916-7	Never Give You Up/Hey, Western Union Man	1989	—	—	3.00
—Reissue					
❑ Mistletoe 803	Silent Night/O Holy Night	1974	—	2.50	5.00
❑ Motown 1403	The Devil in Mrs. Jones/Don't Wanna Be Reminded	1976	—	2.50	5.00
❑ Motown 1414	I Wanna Do It to You/I Don't Wanna Be Reminded	1977	—	2.50	5.00
❑ Motown 1421	Chalk It Up/I Don't Want Nobody to Know	1977	—	2.50	5.00
❑ Motown 1422	It's a Lifetime Thing/Kiss Me Now	1977	—	2.50	5.00
—With Thelma Houston					
❑ Philadelphia Int'l 3113	Don't Be Ashamed/Best Love I Ever Had	1980	—	2.00	4.00
❑ Philadelphia Int'l 3117	Tell Me Girl (Why It Has to End)/We've Got This Feeling Again	1980	—	2.00	4.00
❑ Philadelphia Int'l 3656	(I'm Just Thinking About) Cooling Out/Are You Lonely Tonight	1978	—	2.00	4.00
❑ Philadelphia Int'l 3673	I'm Glad to Be Back/Nothing Says I Love You Like I Love You	1979	—	2.00	4.00
❑ Philadelphia Int'l 3683	Let's Make Love/Dream World	1979	—	2.00	4.00
❑ Vee Jay JB-2 [S]	Butterfly/September Song	196?	12.50	25.00	50.00
—Stereo single, small hole, plays at 33 1/3 rpm					
❑ Vee Jay 354	He Will Break Your Heart/Thanks to You	1960	5.00	10.00	20.00
❑ Vee Jay 371	Silent Night/O Holy Night	1960	5.00	10.00	20.00
❑ Vee Jay 375	Find Another Girl/When Trouble Calls	1961	3.75	7.50	15.00
❑ Vee Jay 390	I See a Fool/I'm a Telling You	1961	3.75	7.50	15.00
❑ Vee Jay 396	For Your Precious Love/Sweet Was the Wine	1961	3.75	7.50	15.00
❑ Vee Jay 405	Moon River/Aware of Love	1961	3.75	7.50	15.00
❑ Vee Jay 426	Isle of Sirens/Chi Town	1962	3.75	7.50	15.00
❑ Vee Jay 451	Make It Easy on Yourself/It's Too Late	1962	3.75	7.50	15.00
❑ Vee Jay 463	You Can Run/I'm the One	1962	3.75	7.50	15.00
❑ Vee Jay 475	Theme from Taras Bulba (Wishing Star)/You Go Right Through Me	1963	3.00	6.00	12.00
❑ Vee Jay 486	You Won't Be Sorry/Whatever You Want	1963	3.00	6.00	12.00
❑ Vee Jay 526	Strawberries/I Almost Lost My Head	1963	3.00	6.00	12.00
❑ Vee Jay 534	Where's the Girl?/How Beautifully You Lie	1963	3.00	6.00	12.00
❑ Vee Jay 556	Just a Little Bit/A Woman with Soul	1963	3.00	6.00	12.00
❑ Vee Jay 567	Need to Belong/Give Me Your Love	1963	3.00	6.00	12.00
❑ Vee Jay 588	Giving Up on Love/I've Been Trying	1964	3.00	6.00	12.00
❑ Vee Jay 598	I Stand Accused/I Don't Want to Hear Anymore	1964	3.00	6.00	12.00
❑ Vee Jay 651	Good Times/I've Grown Accustomed to Her Face	1965	3.00	6.00	12.00
❑ Vee Jay 696	I Can't Stand to See You Cry/Nobody Needs Your Love	1965	3.00	6.00	12.00
❑ Vee Jay 707	Believe in Me/Just for You	1965	3.00	6.00	12.00
❑ Vee Jay 711	Moon River/Make It Easy on Yourself	1966	3.00	6.00	12.00
❑ Vee Jay 715	For Your Precious Love/Give It Up	1966	3.00	6.00	12.00
Albums					
❑ Abner R-2001 [M]	Jerry Butler, Esq.	1959	100.00	200.00	400.00
❑ Buddah BDS-4001	The Very Best of Jerry Butler	1969	3.75	7.50	15.00
❑ Fountain FR 2-82-1	Ice 'n Hot	1982	2.50	5.00	10.00
❑ Mercury SRM-1-689	The Power of Love	1973	3.75	7.50	15.00
❑ Mercury SRM-1-1006	Sweet Sixteen	1974	3.75	7.50	15.00
❑ Mercury SRM-2-7502 [(2)]	The Spice of Life	1972	5.00	10.00	20.00
❑ Mercury MG-21005 [M]	The Soul Artistry of Jerry Butler	1967	5.00	10.00	20.00
❑ Mercury MG-21146 [M]	Mr. Dream Merchant	1967	5.00	10.00	20.00
❑ Mercury SR-61005 [S]	The Soul Artistry of Jerry Butler	1967	3.75	7.50	15.00
❑ Mercury SR-61146 [S]	Mr. Dream Merchant	1967	3.75	7.50	15.00
❑ Mercury SR-61151	Jerry Butler's Golden Hits Live	1968	3.75	7.50	15.00
❑ Mercury SR-61171	The Soul Goes On	1968	3.75	7.50	15.00
❑ Mercury SR-61198	The Ice Man Cometh	1968	3.75	7.50	15.00
❑ Mercury SR-61234	Ice On Ice	1969	3.75	7.50	15.00
❑ Mercury SR-61269	You & Me	1970	3.75	7.50	15.00
❑ Mercury SR-61281	The Best of Jerry Butler	1970	3.75	7.50	15.00
❑ Mercury SR-61320	Jerry Butler Sings Assorted Sounds	1971	3.75	7.50	15.00
❑ Mercury SR-61347	The Sagittarius Movement	1971	3.75	7.50	15.00
❑ Mercury 810369-1	The Best of Jerry Butler	1983	2.50	5.00	10.00
❑ Mercury 822212-1	Only the Strong Survive: The Great Philadelphia Hits	1984	2.50	5.00	10.00
❑ Motown M6-850	Love's on the Menu	1976	3.00	6.00	12.00
❑ Motown M6-878	Suite for the Single Girl	1977	2.50	5.00	10.00
❑ Motown M6-892	It All Comes Out in My Songs	1977	2.50	5.00	10.00
❑ Philadelphia Int'l. JZ 35510	Nothing Says I Love You Like I Love You	1978	2.50	5.00	10.00

Number	Title (A Side/B Side)	Yr	VG	VG+	NM
❑ Philadelphia Int'l. JZ 36413	The Best Love I Ever Had	1979	2.50	5.00	10.00
❑ Rhino RNLP-216	The Best of Jerry Butler (1958-1969)	1984	2.50	5.00	10.00
❑ Tradition TLP-2068	Starring Jerry Butler	1969	3.75	7.50	15.00
❑ Trip 8011 [(2)]	All Time Hits	1972	3.75	7.50	15.00
❑ United Artists UA-LA498-E	The Very Best of Jerry Butler	1975	2.50	5.00	10.00
❑ Vee Jay VJLP2-1003 [(2)]	Jerry Butler Gold	198?	3.75	7.50	15.00
❑ Vee Jay LP-1027 [M]	Jerry Butler, Esquire	1960	37.50	75.00	150.00
—Reissue of Abner 2001					
❑ Vee Jay LP-1029 [M]	He Will Break Your Heart	1960	20.00	40.00	80.00
❑ Vee Jay LP-1034 [M]	Love Me	1961	12.50	25.00	50.00
—Reissue of 1027					
❑ Vee Jay LP-1038 [M]	Aware of Love	1961	10.00	20.00	40.00
❑ Vee Jay SR-1038 [S]	Aware of Love	1961	12.50	25.00	50.00
❑ Vee Jay LP-1046 [M]	Moon River	1962	10.00	20.00	40.00
❑ Vee Jay SR-1046 [S]	Moon River	1962	12.50	25.00	50.00
❑ Vee Jay LP-1048 [M]	The Best of Jerry Butler	1962	6.25	12.50	25.00
❑ Vee Jay SR-1048 [P]	The Best of Jerry Butler	1962	7.50	15.00	30.00
❑ Vee Jay LP-1057 [M]	Folk Songs	1963	6.25	12.50	25.00
❑ Vee Jay SR-1057 [S]	Folk Songs	1963	7.50	15.00	30.00
❑ Vee Jay LP-1075 [M]	For Your Precious Love	1963	6.25	12.50	25.00
❑ Vee Jay SR-1075 [S]	For Your Precious Love	1963	7.50	15.00	30.00
❑ Vee Jay LP-1076 [M]	Giving Up On Love/Need to Belong	1963	6.25	12.50	25.00
❑ Vee Jay VJS-1076 [S]	Giving Up On Love/Need to Belong	1963	7.50	15.00	30.00
❑ Vee Jay LP-1119 [M]	More of the Best of Jerry Butler	1965	6.25	12.50	25.00
❑ Vee Jay VJS-1119 [S]	More of the Best of Jerry Butler	1965	7.50	15.00	30.00
BYRDS, THE					
45s					
❑ Asylum 11016	Full Circle/Long Live the King	1973	—	2.50	5.00
❑ Asylum 11019	Cowgirl in the Sand/Long Live the King	1973	—	2.50	5.00
❑ Columbia 43271	Mr. Tambourine Man/I Knew I'd Want You	1965	3.75	7.50	15.00
❑ Columbia 43332	All I Really Want to Do/I'll Feel a Whole Lot Better	1965	3.75	7.50	15.00
❑ Columbia 43424	Turn! Turn! Turn! (To Everything There Is a Season)/ She Don't Care About Time	1965	3.75	7.50	15.00
❑ Columbia 43501	It Won't Be Wrong/Set You Free This Time	1965	3.00	6.00	12.00
❑ Columbia 43578	Eight Miles High/Why	1966	3.00	6.00	12.00
❑ Columbia 43702	5 D (Fifth Dimension)/Captain Soul	1966	3.00	6.00	12.00
❑ Columbia 43766	Mr. Spaceman/What's Happening	1966	3.00	6.00	12.00
❑ Columbia 43987	So You Want to Be a Rock 'N' Roll Star/Everybody's Been Burned	1967	3.00	6.00	12.00
❑ Columbia 44054	My Back Pages/Renaissance Fair	1967	3.00	6.00	12.00
❑ Columbia 44157	Have You Seen Her Face/Don't Make Waves	1967	2.50	5.00	10.00
❑ Columbia 44230	Lady Friend/Old John Robertson	1967	2.50	5.00	10.00
❑ Columbia 44362	Goin' Back/Change Is Now	1967	2.00	4.00	8.00
❑ Columbia 44499	Artificial Energy/You Ain't Going Nowhere	1968	2.00	4.00	8.00
❑ Columbia 44643	Pretty Boy Floyd/I Am a Pilgrim	1968	2.00	4.00	8.00
❑ Columbia 44746	Drug Store Truck Drivin' Man/Bad Night at the Whiskey	1969	2.00	4.00	8.00
❑ Columbia 44868	Lay Lady Lay/Old Blue	1969	2.00	4.00	8.00
❑ Columbia 44990	Wasn't Born to Follow/Ballad of Easy Rider	1969	2.00	4.00	8.00
❑ Columbia 44990	Ballad of Easy Rider/Oil in My Lamp	1969	2.50	5.00	10.00
❑ Columbia 45071	Jesus Is Just Alright/It's All Over Now, Baby Blue	1970	2.00	4.00	8.00
❑ Columbia 45259	Chestnut Mare/Just a Season	1970	—	3.00	6.00
❑ Columbia 45440	Glory Glory/Citizen Kane	1971	—	3.00	6.00
❑ Columbia 45514	America's Great National Pastime/Farther Along	1971	—	3.00	6.00
❑ Columbia 45761	Jesus Is Just Alright/Mr. Spaceman	1973	2.50	5.00	10.00
Albums					
❑ Asylum SD 5058 [S]	Byrds	1973	3.00	6.00	12.00
❑ Columbia CL 2372 [M]	Mr. Tambourine Man	1965	10.00	20.00	40.00
—"Guaranteed High Fidelity" on label					
❑ Columbia CL 2454 [M]	Turn! Turn! Turn!	1965	7.50	15.00	30.00
❑ Columbia CL 2549 [M]	Fifth Dimension (5D).	1966	7.50	15.00	30.00
❑ Columbia CL 2642 [M]	Younger Than Yesterday.	1967	7.50	15.00	30.00
❑ Columbia CL 2716 [M]	The Byrds' Greatest Hits.	1967	7.50	15.00	30.00
❑ Columbia CL 2775 [M]	The Notorious Byrd Brothers.	1968	12.50	25.00	50.00
❑ Columbia CS 9172 [S]	Mr. Tambourine Man.	1965	10.00	20.00	40.00
—Red label, "360 Sound" in black					
❑ Columbia CS 9254 [S]	Turn! Turn! Turn!	1965	6.25	12.50	25.00
—Red "360 Sound" label					
❑ Columbia CS 9349 [S]	Fifth Dimension (5D)	1966	6.25	12.50	25.00
—Red "360 Sound" label					
❑ Columbia CS 9442 [S]	Younger Than Yesterday	1967	6.25	12.50	25.00
—Red "360 Sound" label					
❑ Columbia CS 9516 [S]	The Byrds' Greatest Hits	1967	5.00	10.00	20.00
—Red "360 Sound" label					
❑ Columbia CS 9575 [S]	The Notorious Byrd Brothers	1968	5.00	10.00	20.00
—Red "360 Sound" label					
❑ Columbia CS 9670 [S]	Sweetheart of the Rodeo	1968	5.00	10.00	20.00
—Red "360 Sound" label					
❑ Columbia CS 9755 [S]	Dr. Byrds and Mr. Hyde	1969	5.00	10.00	20.00
—Red "360 Sound" label					
❑ Columbia CS 9942 [S]	Ballad of Easy Rider	1969	5.00	10.00	20.00
—Red "360 Sound" label					
❑ Columbia G 30127 [(2)]	The Byrds (Untitled)	1970	3.75	7.50	15.00
—Without "Kathleen" listed on back cover					
❑ Columbia KC 30640	Byrdmaniax	1971	3.00	6.00	12.00
❑ Columbia C 31050	Farther Along	1971	3.00	6.00	12.00
❑ Columbia KC 31795	The Best of the Byrds (Greatest Hits, Volume II)	1972	3.00	6.00	12.00
❑ Columbia KC 32183	Preflyte	1973	3.00	6.00	12.00
—Reissue of Together LP					

Number	Title (A Side/B Side)	Yr	VG	VG+	NM
❑ Columbia CG 33645 [(2)]	Mr. Tambourine Man/Turn! Turn! Turn!	1976	3.75	7.50	15.00
❑ Columbia PC 36293	The Byrds Play Dylan	1980	2.50	5.00	10.00
❑ Columbia FC 37335	The Original Singles Volume 1 (1965-1967)	1981	2.50	5.00	10.00
❑ Columbia Limited Edition LE 10215	Farther Along	197?	3.75	7.50	15.00
—Reissue of 31050					
❑ Pair PDL2-1040 [(2)]	The Very Best of the Byrds	1986	3.00	6.00	12.00
❑ Re-Flyte MH-70318	Never Before	1987	3.00	6.00	12.00
—Released by Muuray Hill Records via mail order					
❑ Rhino R1-70244	In the Beginning	1988	2.50	5.00	10.00
❑ Together ST-T-1001	Preflyte	1969	6.25	12.50	25.00

C

CAMPBELL, GLEN

45s

Number	Title (A Side/B Side)	Yr	VG	VG+	NM
❑ Atlantic America 99525	Call Home/Sweet 16	1986	—	—	3.00
❑ Atlantic America 99559	Cowpoke/Rag Doll	1986	—	—	3.00
❑ Atlantic America 99600	It's Just a Matter of Time/Gene Autry, My Hero	1985	—	—	3.00
❑ Atlantic America 99647	(Love Always) Letter to Home/An American Trilogy	1985	—	—	3.00
❑ Atlantic America 99691	A Lady Like You/Tennessee	1984	—	—	3.00
❑ Atlantic America 99768	Faithless Love/Scene of the Crime	1984	—	—	3.00
❑ Atlantic America 99893	On the Wings of My Victory/A Few Good Men	1983	—	—	3.00
❑ Atlantic America 99930	I Love How You Love Me/Hang On Baby (Ease My Mind)	1983	—	—	3.00
❑ Atlantic America 99967	Old Home Town/Heartache #3	1982	—	2.00	4.00
❑ Capehart 5008	Death Valley/Nothin' Better Than a Pretty Woman	1961	6.25	12.50	25.00
❑ Capitol 2015	By the Time I Get to Phoenix/You've Still Got a Place in My Heart	1967	—	3.50	7.00
❑ Capitol 2076	Hey Little One/My Baby's Gone	1968	—	3.50	7.00
❑ Capitol 2146	I Wanna Live/That's All That Matters	1968	—	3.50	7.00
❑ Capitol 2224	Dreams of the Everyday Housewife/Kelli Ho-Down	1968	—	3.50	7.00
❑ Capitol 2302	Wichita Lineman/Fate of Man	1968	—	3.00	6.00
❑ Capitol 2336	Christmas Is for Children/There's No Place Like Home	1968	2.00	4.00	8.00
❑ Capitol 2428	Galveston/How Come Every Time I Itch I Wind Up Scratchin' You	1969	—	3.00	6.00
❑ Capitol 2494	Where's the Playground Susie/Arkansas	1969	—	3.00	6.00
❑ Capitol 2573	True Grit/Hava Nagila	1969	—	3.00	6.00
❑ Capitol 2659	Try a Little Kindness/Lonely My Lonely Friend	1969	—	3.00	6.00
❑ Capitol 2718	Honey Come Back/Where Do You Go	1970	—	3.00	6.00
❑ Capitol 2787	Oh Happy Day/Someone Above	1970	—	3.00	6.00
❑ Capitol 2843	Everything a Man Could Ever Need/Norwood (Me and My Guitar)	1970	—	3.00	6.00
❑ Capitol 2905	It's Only Make Believe/Pave Your Way Into Tomorrow	1970	—	3.00	6.00
❑ Capitol 3062	Dream Baby (How Long Must I Dream)/Here and Now	1971	—	3.00	6.00
❑ Capitol 3123	The Last Time I Saw Her/Bach Talk	1971	—	3.00	6.00
❑ Capitol 3254	Oklahoma Sunday Morning/Everybody's Got to Go There Sometime	1972	—	3.00	6.00
❑ Capitol 3305	Manhattan, Kansas/Wayfaring Stranger	1972	—	3.00	6.00
❑ Capitol 3382	We All Pull the Load/Wherefore and Why	1972	—	3.50	7.00
❑ Capitol 3411	I Will Never Pass This Way Again/We All Pull the Load	1972	—	3.00	6.00
❑ Capitol 3483	One Last Time/All My Tomorrows	1972	—	3.00	6.00
❑ Capitol 3509	I Believe in Christmas/New Snow on the Roof	1972	—	3.00	6.00
❑ Capitol 3548	I Knew Jesus (Before He Was a Star)/On This Road	1973	—	2.50	5.00
❑ Capitol 3669	Bring Back My Yesterday/Beautiful Love Song	1973	—	2.50	5.00
❑ Capitol 3735	Wherefore and Why/Give Me Back That Old Familiar Feeling	1973	—	2.50	5.00
❑ Capitol 3808	Houston (I'm Coming to See You)/Honestly Love	1973	—	2.50	5.00
❑ Capitol 3926	Bonaparte's Retreat/Too Many Mornings	1974	—	2.50	5.00
❑ Capitol 3988	It's a Sin When You Love Somebody/If I Were Loving You	1974	—	2.50	5.00
❑ Capitol 4095	Rhinestone Cowboy/Lovelight	1975	—	2.00	4.00
❑ Capitol 4155	Country Boy (You Got Your Feet in L.A.)/ Record Collector's Dream	1975	—	2.00	4.00
❑ Capitol 4245	Then You Can Tell Me Goodbye-Don't Pull Your Love/ I Miss You Tonight	1976	—	2.00	4.00
❑ Capitol 4288	See You on Sunday/Bloodline	1976	—	2.00	4.00
❑ Capitol 4376	Southern Nights/William Tell Overture	1976	—	2.00	4.00
❑ Capitol 4445	Sunflower/How High Did We Go	1977	—	2.00	4.00
❑ Capitol 4515	God Must Have Blessed America/Amazing Grace	1977	—	2.00	4.00
❑ Capitol 4584	Another Fine Mess/Can You Fool	1978	—	2.00	4.00
❑ Capitol 4638	Can You Fool/Let's All Sing a Song About It	1978	—	2.00	4.00
❑ Capitol 4682	I'm Gonna Love You/Love Takes You Higher	1979	—	2.00	4.00
❑ Capitol 4715	California/Never Tell You No Lies	1979	—	2.00	4.00

Number	Title (A Side/B Side)	Yr	VG	VG+	NM
❑ Capitol 4769	Hound Dog Man/Tennessee Home	1979	—	2.00	4.00
❑ Capitol 4783	Too Late to Worry — Too Blue to Cry/How Do I Tell My Heart Not to Break	1962	3.75	7.50	15.00
❑ Capitol 4799	My Prayer/Don't Lose Me in the Confusion	1979	—	2.00	4.00
❑ Capitol 4856	Long Black Limousine/Here I Am	1962	2.50	5.00	10.00
❑ Capitol 4865	Somethin' 'Bout You Baby I Like/Late Night Confession	1980	—	2.00	4.00
—With Rita Coolidge					
❑ Capitol 4867	Kentucky Means Paradise/Truck Driving Man	1962	3.75	7.50	15.00
—As "The Green River Boys Featuring Glen Campbell"					
❑ Capitol 4909	Hollywood Smiles/Hooked on Love	1980	—	2.00	4.00
❑ Capitol 4925	Oh My Darling/Prima Donna	1963	3.00	6.00	12.00
❑ Capitol 4959	I Don't Want to Know Your Name/Daisy a Day	1981	—	2.00	4.00
❑ Capitol 4986	Why Don't We Just Sleep on It Tonight/It's Your World	1981	—	2.00	4.00
—With Tanya Tucker					
❑ Capitol 4990	Divorce Me C.O.D./Dark As a Dungeon	1963	3.00	6.00	12.00
❑ Capitol 5037	As Far As I'm Concerned/Same Old Places	1963	3.00	6.00	12.00
❑ Capitol 5172	Let Me Tell You About Mary/Through the Eyes of a Child	1964	3.00	6.00	12.00
❑ Capitol 5279	Summer, Winter, Spring and Fall/Heartaches Can Be Fun	1964	3.00	6.00	12.00
❑ Capitol 5360	It's a Woman's World/Tomorrow Never Comes	1965	3.00	6.00	12.00
❑ Capitol 5441	Guess I'm Dumb/That's All Right	1965	30.00	60.00	120.00
—A Brian Wilson "Pet Sounds"-like production					
❑ Capitol 5504	The Universal Soldier/Spanish Shades	1965	2.50	5.00	10.00
❑ Capitol 5545	Less of Me/Private John Q	1965	2.50	5.00	10.00
❑ Capitol 5638	Can't You See I'm Tryin'/Satisfied Mind	1966	2.50	5.00	10.00
❑ Capitol 5773	Burning Bridges/Only the Lonely	1966	2.50	5.00	10.00
❑ Capitol 5854	I Gotta Have My Baby Back/Just to Satisfy You	1967	2.50	5.00	10.00
❑ Capitol 5939	Gentle on My Mind/Just Another Man	1967	2.00	4.00	8.00
—Orange and yellow swirl, without "A Subsidiary Of"... in perimeter label print					
❑ Capitol 5939	Gentle on My Mind/Just Another Man	1968	—	3.00	6.00
—Orange and yellow swirl label with "A Subsidiary Of" in perimeter print					
❑ Ceneco 1324	Dreams for Sale/I've Got to Win	1961	6.25	12.50	25.00
❑ Ceneco 1356	I Wonder/You, You, You	1961	5.00	10.00	20.00
❑ Compleat 113	Letting Go/(Instrumental)	1983	—	2.00	4.00
❑ Crest 1087	Turn Around, Look at Me/Brenda	1961	5.00	10.00	20.00
—With last name spelled correctly					
❑ Crest 1087	Turn Around, Look at Me/Brenda	1961	7.50	15.00	30.00
—With last name spelled incorrectly as "Cambpbell"					
❑ Crest 1096	The Miracle of Love/Once More	1962	3.75	7.50	15.00
❑ Everest 2500	Delight, Arkansas/Walk Right In	1969	—	3.00	6.00
❑ MCA 41323	Dream Lover/Bronco	1980	—	2.00	4.00
—A-side with Tanya Tucker					
❑ MCA 53108	The Hand That Rocks the Cradle/Arkansas	1987	—	—	3.00
—A-side with Steve Wariner					
❑ MCA 53172	Still Within the Sound of My Voice/In My Life	1987	—	—	3.00
❑ MCA 53218	I Have You/I'm a One Woman Man	1987	—	—	3.00
❑ MCA 53245	I Remember You/For Sure, For Certain, Forever, For Always	1988	—	—	3.00
❑ MCA 53426	Heart of the Matter/Light Years	1988	—	—	3.00
❑ MCA 53493	More Than Enough/Our Movie	1989	—	—	3.00
❑ Mirage 3845	I Love My Truck/Melody's Melody	1981	—	2.00	4.00
❑ Starday 853	For the Love of a Woman/Smokey Blue Eyes	1968	2.00	4.00	8.00
❑ Universal UVL-66024	She's Gone, Gone, Gone/William Tell Overture	1989	—	2.00	4.00
❑ Warner Bros. 49609	Any Which Way You Can/Medley from Any Which Way You Can	1980	—	2.00	4.00
—B-side by Texas Opera Company					
Albums					
❑ Atlantic America 90016	Old Home Town	1983	2.00	4.00	8.00
❑ Atlantic America 90164	Letter to Home	1984	2.00	4.00	8.00
❑ Atlantic America 90483	It's Just a Matter of Time	1985	2.00	4.00	8.00
❑ Capitol ST-103	Wichita Lineman	1968	3.75	7.50	15.00
❑ Capitol ST-210	Galveston	1969	3.75	7.50	15.00
❑ Capitol STBO-268	Glen Campbell — "Live"	1969	5.00	10.00	20.00
❑ Capitol SW-389	Try a Little Kindness	1970	3.00	6.00	12.00
❑ Capitol SW-443	Oh Happy Day	1970	3.00	6.00	12.00
❑ Capitol SW-493	The Glen Campbell Goodtime Album	1970	3.00	6.00	12.00
❑ Capitol SW-733	The Last Time I Saw Her	1971	3.00	6.00	12.00
❑ Capitol SW-752	Glen Campbell's Greatest Hits	1971	3.00	6.00	12.00
❑ Capitol ST 1810 [S]	Big Bluegrass Special	1962	25.00	50.00	100.00
—As "The Green River Boys Featuring Glen Campbell"					
❑ Capitol T 1810 [M]	Big Bluegrass Special	1962	20.00	40.00	80.00
—As "The Green River Boys Featuring Glen Campbell"					
❑ Capitol ST 1881 [S]	Too Late to Worry, Too Blue to Cry	1963	6.25	12.50	25.00
❑ Capitol T 1881 [M]	Too Late to Worry, Too Blue to Cry	1963	5.00	10.00	20.00
❑ Capitol ST 2023 [S]	The Astounding 12-String Guitar of Glen Campbell	1964	5.00	10.00	20.00
❑ Capitol T 2023 [M]	The Astounding 12-String Guitar of Glen Campbell	1964	3.75	7.50	15.00
❑ Capitol ST 2392 [S]	The Big Bad Rock Guitar of Glen Campbell	1965	5.00	10.00	20.00
❑ Capitol T 2392 [M]	The Big Bad Rock Guitar of Glen Campbell	1965	3.75	7.50	15.00
❑ Capitol ST 2679 [S]	Burning Bridges	1967	3.75	7.50	15.00
❑ Capitol T 2679 [M]	Burning Bridges	1967	3.75	7.50	15.00
❑ Capitol ST 2809 [S]	Gentle on My Mind	1967	3.75	7.50	15.00
❑ Capitol T 2809 [M]	Gentle on My Mind	1967	3.75	7.50	15.00
❑ Capitol ST 2851 [S]	By the Time I Get to Phoenix	1967	3.75	7.50	15.00
❑ Capitol T 2851 [M]	By the Time I Get to Phoenix	1967	3.75	7.50	15.00
❑ Capitol ST 2878 [S]	Hey, Little One	1968	3.75	7.50	15.00
❑ Capitol T 2878 [M]	Hey, Little One	1968	6.25	12.50	25.00
❑ Capitol ST 2907	A New Place in the Sun	1968	3.75	7.50	15.00
❑ Capitol ST 2978	That Christmas Feeling	1968	3.75	7.50	15.00
❑ Capitol SW-11117	Glen Travis Campbell	1972	2.50	5.00	10.00
❑ Capitol SW-11185	I Knew Jesus (Before He Was a Star)	1973	2.50	5.00	10.00

Number	Title (A Side/B Side)	Yr	VG	VG+	NM
❑ Capitol SW-11253	I Remember Hank Williams	1973	2.50	5.00	10.00
❑ Capitol SW-11293	Hosuton (I'm Comin' to See You)	1974	2.50	5.00	10.00
❑ Capitol SW-11336	Reunion (The Songs of Jimmy Webb)	1974	2.50	5.00	10.00
❑ Capitol SW-11407	Arkansas	1975	2.50	5.00	10.00
❑ Capitol SW-11430	Rhinestone Cowboy	1975	2.50	5.00	10.00
❑ Capitol SW-11516	Bloodline	1976	2.50	5.00	10.00
❑ Capitol ST-11577	The Best of Glen Campbell	1976	2.50	5.00	10.00
❑ Capitol SO-11601	Southern Nights	1977	2.50	5.00	10.00
❑ Capitol SWBC-11707 [(2)]	Live at the Royal Festival Hall	1977	3.00	6.00	12.00
❑ Capitol SW-11722	Basic	1978	2.50	5.00	10.00
❑ Capitol SM-11960	Gentle on My Mind	1979	2.00	4.00	8.00
—Reissue of 2809					
❑ Capitol SOO-12008	Highwayman	1979	2.50	5.00	10.00
❑ Capitol SM-12040	By the Time I Get to Phoenix	1979	2.00	4.00	8.00
—Reissue of 2851					
❑ Capitol SOO-12075	Somethin' 'Bout You Baby I Like	1980	2.50	5.00	10.00
❑ Capitol SOO-12124	It's the World Gone Crazy	1981	2.50	5.00	10.00
❑ Capitol SN-16029	Rhinestone Cowboy	1980	—	3.00	6.00
—Budget-line reissue					
❑ Capitol SN-16030	Southern Nights	1980	—	3.00	6.00
—Budget-line reissue					
❑ Capitol SN-16031	Glen Travis Campbell	1980	—	3.00	6.00
—Budget-line reissue					
❑ Capitol SN-16160	Wichita Lineman	1981	—	3.00	6.00
—Budget-line reissue					
❑ Capitol SN-16258	Hey Little Girl	1982	—	3.00	6.00
—Budget-line reissue					
❑ Capitol SN-16259	Galveston	1982	—	3.00	6.00
—Budget-line reissue					
❑ Capitol SN-16297	Glen Campbell's Greatest Hits	1984	—	3.00	6.00
—Budget-line reissue					
❑ Capitol SN-16335	The Best of Glen Campbell	1984	—	3.00	6.00
—Budget-line reissue					
❑ Longines Symphonette LS-218 [(5)]	Glen Campbell's Golden Favorites	1972	6.25	12.50	25.00
❑ MCA 42009	Still Within the Sound of My Voice	1987	2.00	4.00	8.00
❑ MCA 42210	Light Years	1988	2.00	4.00	8.00
❑ Pair PDL2-1089 [(2)]	All-Time Favorites	1986	3.00	6.00	12.00
❑ Pickwick PTP-2048 [(2)]	Only the Lonely	197?	2.50	5.00	10.00
❑ Pickwick PC-3052 [M]	The 12 String Guitar of Glen Campbell	196?	3.00	6.00	12.00
❑ Pickwick SPC-3052 [S]	The 12 String Guitar of Glen Campbell	196?	2.50	5.00	10.00
❑ Pickwick SPC-3134	A Satisfied Mind	197?	2.00	4.00	8.00
❑ Pickwick SPC-3274	The Glen Campbell Album	197?	2.00	4.00	8.00
❑ Pickwick SPC-3346	I'll Paint You a Song	197?	2.00	4.00	8.00
❑ Starday SLP-424	Country Soul	1968	3.75	7.50	15.00
❑ Starday SLP-437	Country Music Star #1	1969	3.75	7.50	15.00
❑ Surrey S 1007 [M]	Country Shindig	196?	3.00	6.00	12.00
CANNED HEAT					
45s					
❑ Ala 1996	C.C. Shooter/Harley Davidson Blues	1984	—	2.50	5.00
—As "Heat Brothers '84"					
❑ Atlantic 3010	One More River to Cross/Highway 401	1974	—	2.00	4.00
❑ Atlantic 3236	The Harder They Come/Rock 'N' Roll Show	1975	—	2.00	4.00
❑ Liberty 55979	Rolin' and Tumblin'/Bullfrog Blues	1967	2.00	4.00	8.00
❑ Liberty 56005	Evil Woman/The World Is a Jug	1967	2.00	4.00	8.00
❑ Liberty 56038	On the Road Again/Boogie Music	1968	—	3.00	6.00
❑ Liberty 56077	Going Up the Country/One Kind Favor	1968	—	3.00	6.00
❑ Liberty 56079	Christmas Blues/The Chipmunk Song	1968	6.25	12.50	25.00
—B-side with the Chipmunks					
❑ Liberty 56097	Time Was/Low Down	1969	—	3.00	6.00
❑ Liberty 56127	Sic 'Em Pigs/Poor Man	1969	—	3.00	6.00
❑ Liberty 56140	Change My Ways/Get Off My Back	1969	—	3.00	6.00
❑ Liberty 56151	Let's Work Together/I'm Her Man	1970	—	3.00	6.00
❑ Liberty 56180	Future Blues/Going Up the Country	1970	—	3.00	6.00
❑ Liberty 56217	My TIme Ain't Long/Wooly Bully	1970	—	3.00	6.00
❑ United Artists 0058	On the Road Again/This Was	1973	—	2.00	4.00
—"Silver Spotlight Series" reissue					

Number	Title (A Side/B Side)	Yr	VG	VG+	NM
❑ United Artists 0059	Going Up the Country/Let's Work Together	1973	—	2.00	4.00
—"Silver Spotlight Series" reissue					
❑ United Artists XW167	Rock and Roll Music/Lookin' for My Rainbow	1973	—	2.50	5.00
❑ United Artists 50831	Long Way from L.A./Hill's Stomp	1971	—	2.50	5.00
❑ United Artists 50892	Rockin' with the King/I Don't Care What You Tell Me	1972	—	2.50	5.00
❑ United Artists 50927	Sneakin' Around/Cherokee Dance	1972	—	2.50	5.00
Albums					
❑ Accord SN-7144	Captured Live	1981	2.50	5.00	10.00
❑ Atlantic SD 7289	One More River to Cross	1973	3.75	7.50	15.00
❑ Dali DCLP-89022	Reheated	1990	3.75	7.50	15.00
❑ Janus JLS-3009	Vintage — Canned Heat	1969	3.75	7.50	15.00
❑ Liberty LRP-3526 [M]	Canned Heat	1967	6.25	12.50	25.00
❑ Liberty LST-7526 [S]	Canned Heat	1967	5.00	10.00	20.00
❑ Liberty LST-7541 [S]	Boogie with Canned Heat	1968	5.00	10.00	20.00
❑ Liberty LST-7618	Hallelujah	1969	5.00	10.00	20.00
❑ Liberty LN-10105	Boogie with Canned Heat	1981	2.00	4.00	8.00
—Budget-line reissue					
❑ Liberty LN-10106	Canned Heat Cook Book (The Best of Canned Heat)	1981	2.00	4.00	8.00
—Budget-line reissue					
❑ Liberty LST-11000	Canned Heat Cook Book (The Best of Canned Heat)	1969	5.00	10.00	20.00
❑ Liberty LST-11002	Future Blues	1970	3.75	7.50	15.00
❑ Liberty LST-27200 [(2)]	Living the Blues	1968	6.25	12.50	25.00
❑ Pickwick SPC-3364	Live at Topanga Canyon	197?	2.50	5.00	10.00
❑ Pickwick SPC-3614	Boogie	1978	2.50	5.00	10.00
❑ Scepter Citation CTN-18017	The Best of Canned Heat	1972	2.50	5.00	10.00
❑ Sunset SUS-5298	Collage	1971	2.50	5.00	10.00
❑ Takoma 7066	The Human Condition	1980	3.00	6.00	12.00
❑ United Artists UA-LA049-F	The New Age	1973	3.75	7.50	15.00
❑ United Artists LM-1015	Boogie with Canned Heat	1980	3.00	6.00	12.00
—Reissue of Liberty 7541					
❑ United Artists UAS-5509	Canned Heat Concert (Recorded Live in Europe)	1971	3.75	7.50	15.00
❑ United Artists UAS-5557	Historical Figures and Ancient Heads	1972	3.75	7.50	15.00
❑ United Artists UAS-9955 [(2)]	Living the Blues	1971	5.00	10.00	20.00
—Reissue of Liberty 27200					
❑ Wand WDS-693	Live at Topanga Canyon	1970	6.25	12.50	25.00

CANNON, FREDDY

45s

Number	Title (A Side/B Side)	Yr	VG	VG+	NM
❑ Amherst 201	Dance to the Bop/(She's a) Mean Rebel Rouser	1983	—	2.00	4.00
❑ Amherst 327	Rockin' in My Socks/Rockin' in My Socks	1988	—	3.00	6.00
❑ Buddah 242	Rockin' Robin/Red Valley	1971	2.50	5.00	10.00
❑ Claridge 401	Palisades Park/Way Down Yonder in New Orleans	1975	—	3.00	6.00
❑ Claridge 416	Sugar/Sugar (Part 2)	1976	—	3.00	6.00
❑ MCA 40269	Rock and Roll ABC's/Superman	1974	3.75	7.50	15.00
❑ Metromedia 262	If You've Got the Time/Take Me Back	1972	2.50	5.00	10.00
❑ MiaSound 1002	Let's Put the Fun Back in Rock and Roll/ Your Mama Ain't Always Right	1981	—	2.50	5.00
—With the Belmonts					
❑ Radio Active Gold 64	Rockin' Robin/Red Valley	197?	—	2.50	5.00
❑ Royal American 2	Charged-Up, Turned-On Rock-N-Roll Singer/ I Ain't Much, But I'm Yours	1970	2.50	5.00	10.00
❑ Royal American 11	Nite Time Lady/I Ain't Much, But I'm Yours	1970	2.50	5.00	10.00
❑ Royal American 288	Strawberry Wine/Blossom Dear	1969	2.50	5.00	10.00
❑ Sire 4103	Beautiful Downtown Burbank/If You Give Me a Title	1969	2.50	5.00	10.00
❑ Swan 4031	Tallahassee Lassie/You Know	1959	5.00	10.00	20.00
❑ Swan 4038	Okefenokee/Kookie Hat	1959	5.00	10.00	20.00
❑ Swan 4043	Way Down Yonder in New Orleans/Fractured	1959	5.00	10.00	20.00
❑ Swan 4050	Chattanooga Shoe Shine Boy/Boston "My Home Town"	1960	3.75	7.50	15.00
❑ Swan 4053	Jump Over/The Urge	1960	3.75	7.50	15.00
❑ Swan 4057	Happy Shades of Blue/(Kwa-Na-Va-Ka) Cuernavaca Choo Choo	1960	3.75	7.50	15.00
❑ Swan 4061	Humdinger/My Blue Heaven	1960	3.75	7.50	15.00
❑ Swan 4066	Muskrat Ramble/Two Thousand-88	1961	3.75	7.50	15.00
❑ Swan 4071	Buzz Buzz A-Diddle It/Opportunity	1961	3.75	7.50	15.00
❑ Swan 4078	Transistor Sister/Walk to the Moon	1961	3.75	7.50	15.00
❑ Swan 4083	For Me and My Gal/Blue Plate Special	1961	3.75	7.50	15.00
❑ Swan 4096	Teen Queen of the Week/Wild Guy	1962	3.75	7.50	15.00
❑ Swan 4106	Palisades Park/June, July and August	1962	4.00	8.00	16.00
❑ Swan 4117	What's Gonna Happen When Summer's Done/Broadway	1962	3.75	7.50	15.00
❑ Swan 4122	If You Were a Rock and Roll Record/The Truth, Ruth	1962	3.75	7.50	15.00
❑ Swan 4132	Come On and Love Me/Four Letter Man	1963	3.00	6.00	12.00
❑ Swan 4139	Patty Baby/Betty Jean	1963	3.00	6.00	12.00
❑ Swan 4149	Everybody Monkey/Oh Gloria	1963	6.25	12.50	25.00
❑ Swan 4155	Do What the Hippies Do/That's the Way Girls Are	1963	3.00	6.00	12.00
❑ Swan 4168	What a Party/Sweet Georgia Brown	1964	3.00	6.00	12.00
❑ Swan 4178	The Ups and Downs of Love/It's Been Nice	1964	6.25	12.50	25.00
❑ Warner Bros. 5409	Abigail Beecher/All American Girl	1964	3.00	6.00	12.00
❑ Warner Bros. 5434	OK Wheeler, The Used Car Dealer/Odie Cologne	1964	3.00	6.00	12.00
❑ Warner Bros. 5448	Summertime U.S.A./Gotta Good Thing Goin'	1964	3.00	6.00	12.00
❑ Warner Bros. 5487	Little Autograph Seeker/Too Much Monkey Business	1964	3.00	6.00	12.00
❑ Warner Bros. 5615	Little Miss A-Go-Go/In the Night	1965	3.00	6.00	12.00
❑ Warner Bros. 5645	Action/Beachwood City	1965	3.75	7.50	15.00
❑ Warner Bros. 5666	Let Me Show You Where It's At/The Old Rag Man	1965	3.00	6.00	12.00
❑ Warner Bros. 5673	She's Something Else/Little Bitty Corrine	1965	3.00	6.00	12.00
❑ Warner Bros. 5693	The Dedication Song/Come On, Come On	1966	3.00	6.00	12.00
❑ Warner Bros. 5810	The Greatest Show on Earth/Hokie Pokie Girl	1966	3.00	6.00	12.00
❑ Warner Bros. 5832	The Laughing Song/Natalie	1966	3.00	6.00	12.00
❑ Warner Bros. 5859	Run for the Sun/Use Your Imagination	1966	3.00	6.00	12.00

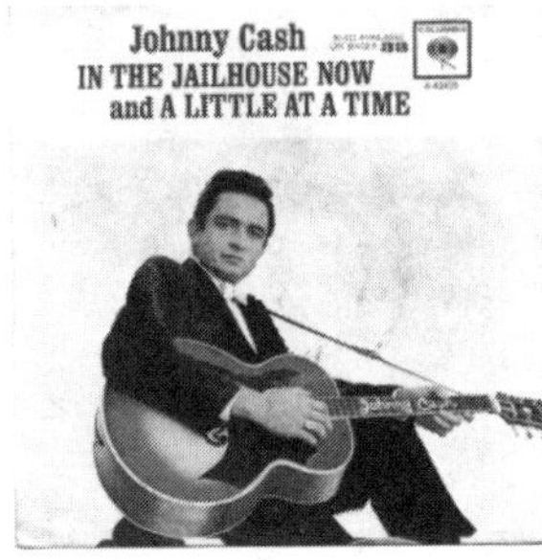

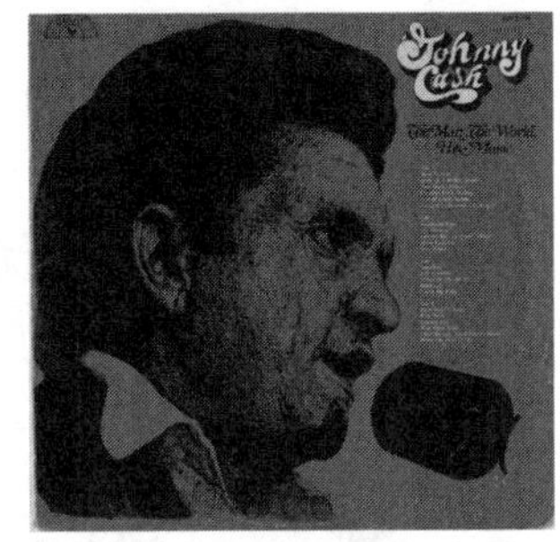

Number	Title (A Side/B Side)	Yr	VG	VG+	NM
❑ Warner Bros. 5876	A Happy Clown/In My Wildest Dreams	1966	6.25	12.50	25.00
❑ Warner Bros. 7019	Maverick's Flat/Run to the Poet Man	1967	6.25	12.50	25.00
❑ Warner Bros. 7075	20th Century Fox/Cincinnati Woman	1967	6.25	12.50	25.00
❑ We Make Rock & Roll 1601	Rock Around the Clock/Sock It to the Judge	1968	—	3.00	6.00
❑ We Make Rock & Roll 1604	Sea Cruise/She's a Friday Night Fox	1968	—	3.00	6.00
Albums					
❑ Rhino RNLP-210	14 Booming Hits	1982	2.50	5.00	10.00
❑ Swan LP-502 [M]	The Explosive! Freddy Cannon	1960	30.00	60.00	120.00
❑ Swan LPS-502 [S]	The Explosive! Freddy Cannon	1960	75.00	150.00	300.00
❑ Swan LP-504 [M]	Happy Shades of Blue	1960	37.50	75.00	150.00
❑ Swan LP-505 [M]	Solid Gold Hits	1961	37.50	75.00	150.00
❑ Swan LP-507 [M]	Freddy Cannon at Palisades Park	1962	37.50	75.00	150.00
❑ Swan LP-511 [M]	Freddy Cannon Steps Out	1963	37.50	75.00	150.00
❑ Warner Bros. W 1544 [M]	Freddie Cannon	1964	7.50	15.00	30.00
❑ Warner Bros. WS 1544 [S]	Freddie Cannon	1964	10.00	20.00	40.00
❑ Warner Bros. W 1612 [M]	Action!	1965	7.50	15.00	30.00
❑ Warner Bros. WS 1612 [S]	Action!	1965	10.00	20.00	40.00
❑ Warner Bros. W 1628 [M]	Freddy Cannon's Greatest Hits	1966	7.50	15.00	30.00
❑ Warner Bros. WS 1628 [S]	Freddy Cannon's Greatest Hits	1966	10.00	20.00	40.00

CAPITOLS, THE (1)

Records on the Carlton, Cindy, Gateway, Pet and Triumph labels appear to be by different groups with the same name; these are outside the scope of this book.

Number	Title (A Side/B Side)	Yr	VG	VG+	NM
45s					
❑ Karen 1524	Cool Jerk/Hello Stranger	1966	3.75	7.50	15.00
❑ Karen 1525	I Got to Handle It/Zig Zagging	1966	2.50	5.00	10.00
❑ Karen 1526	We Got a Thing That's In the Groove/Tired Running from You	1966	2.50	5.00	10.00
❑ Karen 1534	Patty Cake/Take a Chance on Me Baby	1967	2.50	5.00	10.00
❑ Karen 1536	Cool Pearl/Don't Say Maybe Baby	1967	2.50	5.00	10.00
❑ Karen 1537	Cool Jerk '68/Afro Twist	1968	2.50	5.00	10.00
❑ Karen 1543	Soul Brother, Soul Sister/Ain't That Terrible	1968	2.50	5.00	10.00
❑ Karen 1546	Soul Soul/When You're in Trouble	1969	2.50	5.00	10.00
❑ Karen 1549	I Thought She Loved Me/When You're in Trouble	1969	2.50	5.00	10.00
Albums					
❑ Atco 33-190 [M]	Dance the Cool Jerk	1966	10.00	20.00	40.00
❑ Atco SD 33-190 [S]	Dance the Cool Jerk	1966	12.50	25.00	50.00
❑ Atco 33-201 [M]	We Got a Thing That's In the Groove	1966	10.00	20.00	40.00
❑ Atco SD 33-201 [S]	We Got a Thing That's In the Groove	1966	12.50	25.00	50.00
❑ Collectables COL-5105	Golden Classics	1988	2.50	5.00	10.00
❑ Solid Smoke 8019	The Capitols: Their Greatest Hits	1983	3.00	6.00	12.00

CAPTAIN AND TENNILLE

Number	Title (A Side/B Side)	Yr	VG	VG+	NM
45s					
❑ A&M 1624	The Way I Want to Touch You/Disney Girls	1974	—	3.00	6.00
❑ A&M 1672	Love Will Keep Us Together/Gentle Stranger	1975	—	2.00	4.00
❑ A&M 1715	Por Amor Vivremos (Love Will Keep Us Together)/Broddy Bounce	1975	—	2.50	5.00
❑ A&M 1725	The Way I Want to Touch You/Broddy Bounce	1975	—	2.00	4.00
❑ A&M 1774	Como Yo Quiero Sentorte (The Way I Want to Touch You)/ El Rebote de Broddy	1975	2.00	4.00	8.00
❑ A&M 1782	Lonely Night (Angel Face)/Smile for Me One More Time	1976	—	2.00	4.00
❑ A&M 1817	Shop Around/Butterscotch Castle	1976	—	2.00	4.00
❑ A&M 1870	Muskrat Love/Honey Come Love Me	1976	—	2.00	4.00
❑ A&M 1912	Can't Stop Dancin'/Mis Canciones (The Good Songs)	1977	—	2.00	4.00
❑ A&M 1944	Come In from the Rain/We Never Really Said Goodbye	1977	—	2.00	4.00
❑ A&M 1970	Circles/1954 Boogie Blues	1977	—	2.00	4.00
❑ A&M 2027	I'm On My Way/We Never Really Said Goodbye	1978	—	2.00	4.00
❑ A&M 2063	You Never Done It Like That/"D" Keyboard Blues	1978	—	2.00	4.00
❑ A&M 2106	You Need a Woman Tonight/Love Me Like a Baby	1978	—	2.00	4.00
❑ A&M 8600	Lonely Night (Angel Face)/Shop Around	1977	—	2.00	4.00
—"A&M Forget Me Nots" series; green and yellow labels					
❑ A&M 8601	Song of Joy/Wedding Song (There Is Love)	1977	—	2.00	4.00
—"A&M Forget Me Nots" series; green and yellow labels					
❑ Butterscotch Castle 001	The Way I Want to Touch You/Disney Girls	1974	20.00	40.00	80.00
❑ Casablanca 2215	Do That To Me One More Time/Deep in the Dark	1979	—	2.00	4.00
❑ Casablanca 2243	Love on a Shoestring/How Can You Be So Cold	1980	—	2.00	4.00
❑ Casablanca 2247	Amame Una Vez Mas (Do That To Me One More Time)/ Deep in the Dark	1980	2.00	4.00	8.00

Number	Title (A Side/B Side)	Yr	VG	VG+	NM
❑ Casablanca 2264	Happy Together (A Fantasy)/Baby You Still Got It	1980	—	2.00	4.00
❑ Casablanca 2320	This Is Not the First Time/Gentle Stranger	1980	—	2.00	4.00
❑ Casablanca 2328	Don't Forget Me/Keep Our Love Warm	1981	—	2.00	4.00
❑ Joyce 101	The Way I Want to Tocuh You/Disney Girls	1974	10.00	20.00	40.00
❑ Purebred 0001	Tahoe Snow/Here Comes Santa Claus	198?	—	2.50	5.00
Albums					
❑ A&M SP-3105	Captain & Tennille's Greatest Hits	198?	2.00	4.00	8.00
—Reissue of 4667					
❑ A&M SP-3405	Love Will Keep Us Together	1975	3.00	6.00	12.00
❑ A&M SP-4552	Love Will Keep Us Together	1975	2.50	5.00	10.00
—Reissue of 3405					
❑ A&M SP-4561	Por Amor Vivremos	1975	3.00	6.00	12.00
❑ A&M SP-4570	Song of Joy	1976	2.50	5.00	10.00
❑ A&M SP-4667	Captain & Tennille's Greatest Hits	1977	2.50	5.00	10.00
❑ A&M SP-4700	Come In From the Rain	1977	2.50	5.00	10.00
❑ A&M SP-4707	Dream	1978	2.50	5.00	10.00
❑ Casablanca NBLP 7188	Make Your Move	1979	2.50	5.00	10.00
❑ Casablanca NBLP 7250	Keeping Our Love Warm	1980	2.50	5.00	10.00

CARMEN, ERIC

Number	Title (A Side/B Side)	Yr	VG	VG+	NM
45s					
❑ Arista 0165	All By Myself/Everything	1975	—	2.00	4.00
❑ Arista 0184	Never Gonna Fall in Love Again/No Hard Feelings	1976	—	2.00	4.00
❑ Arista 0200	Sunrise/My Girl	1976	—	2.00	4.00
❑ Arista 0266	She Did It/Someday	1977	—	2.00	4.00
❑ Arista 0295	Boats Against the Current/Take It or Leave It	1977	—	2.00	4.00
❑ Arista 0319	Marathon Man/I Think I Found Myself	1978	—	2.00	4.00
❑ Arista 0354	Change of Heart/Hey Deanie	1978	—	2.00	4.00
❑ Arista 0384	Baby I Need Your Lovin'/Heaven Can Wait	1979	—	2.00	4.00
❑ Arista 0435	Haven't We Come a Long Way/End of the World	1979	—	2.00	4.00
❑ Arista 0506	It Hurts Too Much/You Need Some Lovin'	1980	—	2.00	4.00
❑ Arista 0550	All for Love/Tonight You're Mine	1980	—	2.00	4.00
❑ Arista 9686	Make Me Lose Control/That's Rock 'N' Roll	1988	—	—	3.00
❑ Arista 9736	Boats Against the Current/No Hard Feelings	1988	—	—	3.00
❑ Arista 9746	Reason to Try/Sunrise	1988	—	—	3.00
❑ Cool 101	The Rock Stops Here (same on both sides)	1988	—	—	3.00
❑ Geffen 29032	I'm Through with Love/Maybe My Baby	1985	—	—	3.00
❑ Geffen 29118	I Wanna Hear It from Your Lips/Spotlight	1985	—	—	3.00
❑ RCA 5315-7-R	Hungry Eyes/Where Are You Tonight	1987	—	—	3.00
Albums					
❑ Arista AL 4057	Eric Carmen	1975	3.00	6.00	12.00
—Shiny, simulated gold foil cover					
❑ Arista AB 4124	Boats Against the Current	1977	2.00	4.00	8.00
❑ Arista AB 4184	Change of Heart	1978	2.00	4.00	8.00
❑ Arista AL 8547	The Best of Eric Carmen	1988	3.75	7.50	15.00
—Original copies do not contain "Make Me Lose Control"					
❑ Arista AL 9513	Tonight You're Mine	1980	2.00	4.00	8.00
❑ Geffen GHS 24042	Eric Carmen	1985	2.00	4.00	8.00

CARNES, KIM

Number	Title (A Side/B Side)	Yr	VG	VG+	NM
45s					
❑ A&M 1748	Somewhere in the Night/Hang On to Your Airplane (Honeymoon)	1975	—	2.50	5.00
❑ A&M 1767	You're a Part of Me/Hang On to Your Airplane (Honeymoon)	1975	—	2.50	5.00
❑ A&M 1902	The Last Thing You Ever Wanted to Do/Let Your Love Come Easy	1977	—	2.50	5.00
❑ A&M 1943	Sailin'/He'll Come Home	1977	—	2.50	5.00
❑ Amos 165	I Won't Call You Back/To Love	1971	2.00	4.00	8.00
❑ Amos 166	To Love Somebody/Fell in Love with a Poet	1971	2.00	4.00	8.00
❑ Amos 167	It's Love That Keeps It All Together/Long and Lonely Memeories	1971	2.00	4.00	8.00
—With Dave Ellingson					
❑ EMI America 8010	Losing Love/Looking for a Big Night	1979	—	2.50	5.00
❑ EMI America 8011	It Hurts So Bad/Lookin' for a Big Night	1979	—	2.50	5.00
❑ EMI America 8014	What Am I Gonna Do/Goodnight Moon	1979	—	2.50	5.00
❑ EMI America 8045	More Love/Changin'	1980	—	2.00	4.00
❑ EMI America 8058	Cry Like a Baby/In the Chill of the Night	1980	—	2.00	4.00
❑ EMI America 8069	Mas Amor/Changin'	1980	2.00	4.00	8.00
❑ EMI America 8077	Bette Davis Eyes/Miss You Tonight	1981	—	2.00	4.00
❑ EMI America A-8087	Draw of the Cards/Break the Rules Tonite (Out of School)	1981	—	2.00	4.00
❑ EMI America A-8098	Mistaken Identity/Jamaica Sunday Morning	1981	—	2.00	4.00
❑ EMI America B-8127	Voyeur/Thrill of the Grill	1982	—	—	3.00
❑ EMI America B-8147	Does It Make You Remember/Take It on the Chin	1982	—	—	3.00
❑ EMI America B-8154	Say You Don't Know Me/Breakin' Away from Society	1983	—	2.50	5.00
❑ EMI America B-8181	Invisible Hands/I'll Be Here Where the Heart Is	1983	—	—	3.00
❑ EMI America B-8191	You Make My Heart Beat Faster (And That's All That Matters)/ Hangin' On by a Thread	1984	—	—	3.00
❑ EMI America B-8202	I Pretend/Hurricane	1984	—	—	3.00
❑ EMI America B-8250	Invitation to Dance/Breakthrough	1984	—	—	3.00
—B-side by Haven					
❑ EMI America B-8267	Crazy in the Night (Barking at Airplanes)/ Oliver (Voice on the Radio)	1985	—	—	3.00
❑ EMI America B-8281	Abadabadango/He Makes the Sun Rise (Orpheus)	1985	—	—	3.00
❑ EMI America B-8290	Rough Edges/Begging for Favors (Learning How Things Work)	1985	—	2.00	4.00
❑ EMI America B-8322	Divided Hearts/You Say You Love Me (But I Know You Don't)	1986	—	—	3.00
❑ EMI America B-8335	I'd Lie to You for Your Love/Black and White	1986	—	2.00	4.00
❑ MCA 53387	Speed of the Sound of Loneliness/Blood from the Bandit	1988	—	—	3.00
❑ MCA 53433	Crazy in Love/Blood from the Bandit	1988	—	—	3.00
❑ MCA 53494	Fantastic Fire of Love/Brass and Batons	1989	—	—	3.00

Albums

Number	Title (A Side/B Side)	Yr	VG	VG+	NM
❑ A&M SP-3114	Sailin'	198?	2.00	4.00	8.00
—Budget-line reissue					
❑ A&M SP-3204	The Best of Kim Carnes	1982	2.50	5.00	10.00
❑ A&M SP-4548	Kim Carnes	1975	3.00	6.00	12.00
❑ A&M SP-4606	Sailin'	1976	3.00	6.00	12.00
❑ Amos AAS 7016	Rest on Me	1971	5.00	10.00	20.00
❑ EMI America SW-17004	St. Vincent's Court	1978	2.50	5.00	10.00
❑ EMI America SW-17030	Romance Dance	1980	2.50	5.00	10.00
❑ EMI America SO-17052	Mistaken Identity	1981	2.50	5.00	10.00
❑ EMI America SO-17078	Voyeur	1982	2.50	5.00	10.00
❑ EMI America SO-17107	Café Racers	1983	2.50	5.00	10.00
❑ EMI America SO-17159	Barking at Airplanes	1985	2.50	5.00	10.00
❑ EMI America ST-17198	Light House	1986	2.00	4.00	8.00
❑ MCA 914	The Early Years	1984	2.00	4.00	8.00
❑ MCA 42200	View from the House	1988	2.00	4.00	8.00

CARPENTERS

45s

Number	Title (A Side/B Side)	Yr	VG	VG+	NM
❑ A&M 1142	Ticket to Ride/Your Wonderful Parade	1969	2.50	5.00	10.00
❑ A&M 1183	(They Long to Be) Close to You/IKept On Loving You	1970	—	2.50	5.00
❑ A&M 1217	We've Only Just Begun/All of My Life	1970	—	2.50	5.00
❑ A&M 1236	Merry Christmas Darling/Mr. Guder	1970	—	3.00	6.00
—A-side vocal is different than later releases of this song					
❑ A&M 1243	For All We Know/Don't Be Afraid	1971	—	2.00	4.00
❑ A&M 1260	Rainy Days and Mondays/Saturday	1971	—	2.00	4.00
❑ A&M 1289	Superstar/Bless the Beasts and Children	1971	—	2.00	4.00
❑ A&M 1322	Hurting Each Other/Maybe It's You	1972	—	2.00	4.00
❑ A&M 1351	It's Going to Take Some Time/Flat Baroque	1972	—	2.00	4.00
❑ A&M 1367	Goodbye to Love/Crystal Lullaby	1972	—	2.00	4.00
❑ A&M 1413	Sing/Druscilla Penny	1973	—	2.00	4.00
❑ A&M 1446	Yesterday Once More/Road Ode	1973	—	2.00	4.00
❑ A&M 1468	Top of the World/Heather	1973	—	2.00	4.00
—Originals have brown labels					
❑ A&M 1521	I Won't Last a Day Without You/One Love	1974	—	2.00	4.00
❑ A&M 1646	Please Mister Postman/This Masquerade	1974	—	2.00	4.00
❑ A&M 1648	Santa Claus Is Coming to Town/Merry Christmas Darling	1974	—	2.50	5.00
❑ A&M 1677	Only Yesterday/Happy	1975	—	2.00	4.00
❑ A&M 1721	Solitaire/Love Me for What I Am	1975	—	2.00	4.00
❑ A&M 1800	There's a Kind of Hush (All Over the World)/ (I'm Caught Between) Goodbye and I Love You	1976	—	2.00	4.00
❑ A&M 1828	I Need to Be in Love/Sandy	1976	—	2.00	4.00
❑ A&M 1859	Goofus/Boat to Sail	1976	—	2.00	4.00
❑ A&M 1940	All You Get from Love Is a Love Song/I Have You	1977	—	2.00	4.00
❑ A&M 1978	Calling Occupants of Interplanctary Craft/ Can't Smile Without You	1977	—	2.00	4.00
❑ A&M 1991	The Christmas Song/Merry Christmas Darling	1977	—	2.50	5.00
❑ A&M 2008	Sweet, Sweet Smile/I Have You	1978	—	2.00	4.00
❑ A&M 2097	I Believe You/B'wana She No Home	1978	—	2.00	4.00
❑ A&M 2344	Touch Me When We're Dancing/Because We Are in Love (The Wedding Song)	1981	—	2.00	4.00
❑ A&M 2370	(Want You) Back in My Life Again/Somebody's Been Lyin'	1981	—	2.00	4.00
❑ A&M 2386	Those Good Old Dreams/When It's Gone	1981	—	2.00	4.00
❑ A&M 2405	Beechwood 4-5789/Two Sides	1982	—	2.00	4.00
❑ A&M 2585	Make Believe It's Your First Time/Look to Your Dreams	1983	—	2.00	4.00
❑ A&M 2620	Sailing on the Tide/Your Baby Doesn't Love You Anymore	1984	—	2.00	4.00
❑ A&M 2700	Do You Hear What I Hear/Little Altar Boy	1984	2.50	5.00	10.00
❑ A&M 2735	Yesterday Once More/(They Long to Be) Close to You-We've Only Just Begun	1985	5.00	10.00	20.00
❑ A&M 8620	Christmas Song/Merry Christmas Darling	1977	—	2.50	5.00
—"Forget Me Nots" green and gold label					
❑ A&M 8629	Calling Occupants of Interplanetary Craft/ Don't Cry for Me Argentina	1980	—	2.50	5.00
❑ A&M 8667	Honolulu City Lights/I Just Fall in Love Again	1986	—	2.50	5.00
❑ Magic Lamp 704	I'll Be Yours/Looking for Love	1967	500.00	1000.	2000.
—As "Karen Carpenter", but Richard also was on this record					

Number	Title (A Side/B Side)	Yr	VG	VG+	NM
Albums					
❑ A&M SP-3184	Close to You	1982	2.00	4.00	8.00
—Reissue of 4271					
❑ A&M SP-3197	A Kind of Hush	1982	2.00	4.00	8.00
—Reissue of 4581					
❑ A&M SP-3199	Passage	1982	2.00	4.00	8.00
—Reissue of 4703					
❑ A&M SP-3210	Christmas Portrait	198?	2.00	4.00	8.00
—Reissue of SP-4726					
❑ A&M SP-3270	An Old-Fashioned Christmas	1984	2.50	5.00	10.00
❑ A&M SP-3502	Carpenters	1971	3.00	6.00	12.00
❑ A&M SP-3511	A Song for You	1972	3.00	6.00	12.00
❑ A&M SP-3519	Now & Then	1973	3.00	6.00	12.00
❑ A&M SP-3601	The Singles 1969-1973	1973	3.00	6.00	12.00
❑ A&M SP-3723	Made in America	1981	3.00	6.00	12.00
❑ A&M SP-4205	Offering	1969	20.00	40.00	80.00
❑ A&M SP-4205	Ticket to Ride	1970	3.00	6.00	12.00
—Reissue of "Offering" with new title and cover					
❑ A&M SP-4271	Close to You	1970	3.00	6.00	12.00
❑ A&M SP-4530	Horizon	1975	3.00	6.00	12.00
❑ A&M SP-4581	A Kind of Hush	1976	3.00	6.00	12.00
❑ A&M SP-4703	Passage	1977	3.00	6.00	12.00
❑ A&M SP-4726	Christmas Portrait	1978	3.75	7.50	15.00
❑ A&M SP-4954	Voice of the Heart	1983	3.00	6.00	12.00
❑ A&M SP-5172	An Old Fashioned Christmas	1987	2.00	4.00	8.00
—Reissue of 3270 (record still says 3270 but cover is 5172)					
❑ A&M SP-6601 [(2)]	Yesterday Once More	1985	3.75	7.50	15.00
CARTER, CLARENCE					
45s					
❑ ABC 12058	Warning/On Your Way Down	1974	—	2.00	4.00
❑ ABC 12094	Everything Comes Up Roses/A Very Special Love Song	1975	—	2.00	4.00
❑ ABC 12130	I Got Caught/Take It All Off	1975	—	2.00	4.00
❑ ABC 12162	Dear Abby/Love Ain't Here No More	1976	—	2.00	4.00
❑ ABC 12224	Heart Full of Song/All Messed Up	1976	—	2.00	4.00
❑ Atlantic 2461	I Can't See Myself/Looking for a Fox	1967	—	3.00	6.00
❑ Atlantic 2508	Slip Away/Funky Fever	1968	2.00	4.00	8.00
❑ Atlantic 2569	Too Weak to Fight/Let Me Comfort You	1968	—	3.00	6.00
❑ Atlantic 2576	Back Door Santa/That Old Time Feeling	1968	2.00	4.00	8.00
❑ Atlantic 2605	Snatching It Back/Making Love	1969	—	3.00	6.00
❑ Atlantic 2642	The Feeling Is Right/You Can't Miss What You Can't Measure	1969	—	3.00	6.00
❑ Atlantic 2660	Doin' Our Thing/I Smell a Rat	1969	—	3.00	6.00
❑ Atlantic 2702	Take It Off Him and Put It On Me/A Few Troubles I've Had	1970	—	3.00	6.00
❑ Atlantic 2726	I Can't Leave Your Love Alone/Devil Woman	1970	—	3.00	6.00
❑ Atlantic 2748	Patches/Say It One More Time	1970	—	3.00	6.00
❑ Atlantic 2774	It's All in Your Mind/Till I Can't Take It Anymore	1970	—	3.00	6.00
❑ Atlantic 2801	The Court Room/Getting the Bills	1971	—	3.00	6.00
❑ Atlantic 2818	Slipped, Tripped, and Fell in Love/I Hate to Love and Run	1971	—	3.00	6.00
❑ Atlantic 2842	I'm the One/Scratch My Back	1971	—	3.00	6.00
❑ Atlantic 2875	If You Can't Beat 'Em/Lonesomest Lonesome	1972	—	3.00	6.00
—With Candi Carter					
❑ Fame XW179	Put On Your Shoes and Walk/I Found Somebody New	1973	—	2.50	5.00
❑ Fame XW250	Sixty Minute Man/Mother-in-Law	1973	—	2.50	5.00
❑ Fame XW330	I'm the Midnight Special/I Got Another Woman	1973	—	2.50	5.00
❑ Fame XW415	Love's Trying to Come to You/Heartbreak Woman	1974	—	2.50	5.00
❑ Fame 1010	Tell Daddy/I Stayed Away Too Long	1966	3.00	6.00	12.00
❑ Fame 1013	Thread the Needle/Don't Make My Baby Cry	1967	3.00	6.00	12.00
❑ Fame 1016	Road of Love/She Ain't Gonna Do Right	1967	3.00	6.00	12.00
❑ Fame 91006	Back in Your Arms/Holdin' Out	1972	—	2.50	5.00
❑ Ichiban 101	Messin' with My Mind/I Was in the Neighborhood	1986	—	—	3.00
❑ Ichiban 106	If You Let Me Take You Home/So You're Leaving Me	1986	—	—	3.00
❑ Ichiban 108	Strokin'/Love Me with Feelin'	1987	2.00	4.00	8.00
❑ Ichiban 116	Doctor C.C./I Stayed Away Too Long	1987	—	—	3.00
❑ Ichiban 131	Grandpa Can't Find His Kate/What'd I Say	1988	—	—	3.00
❑ Ichiban 135	Trying to Sleep Tonight/(B-side unknown)	1988	—	—	3.00
❑ Ichiban 158	I'm Just Not Good/I'm the Best	1989	—	—	3.00
❑ Ichiban 164	Why Do I Stay Here and Take This Shit fro You/ It's a Man Down There	1989	—	—	3.00
❑ Ichiban 213	In Between a Rock and a Hard Place/Dance to the Blues	1990	—	—	3.00
❑ Ichiban 222	Things Ain't Like They Used to Be/ Pickin' 'Em Up, Layin' 'Em Down	1990	—	—	3.00
❑ Ichiban 238	I Ain't Leaving, Girl/If You See My Lady	1991	—	—	3.00
❑ Ichiban 262	"G" Spot/Hot Dog	1992	—	—	3.00
❑ Ichiban 275	Hand Me Down Love/Let's Get a Quickie	1992	—	—	3.00
❑ Ronn 90	I Couldn't Refuse Your Love/What Was I Supposed to Do?	1977	—	2.50	5.00
❑ Venture 130	Jimmy's Disco/Searching	1980	—	2.00	4.00
❑ Venture 141	Let's Burn/If I Stay	1980	—	2.00	4.00
❑ Venture 145	It's a Monster Thang/If I Were Yours	1981	—	2.00	4.00
❑ Venture 147	Can We Slip Away Again/If I Were Yours	1981	—	2.00	4.00
Albums					
❑ ABC X-833	Real	1974	3.75	7.50	15.00
❑ ABC X-896	Loneliness & Temptation	1975	3.75	7.50	15.00
❑ ABC X-943	A Heart Full of Song	1976	3.75	7.50	15.00
❑ Atlantic SD 8192	This Is Clarence Carter	1968	7.50	15.00	30.00
❑ Atlantic SD 8199	The Dynamic Clarence Carter	1969	7.50	15.00	30.00
❑ Atlantic SD 8238	Testifyin'	1969	7.50	15.00	30.00
❑ Atlantic SD 8267 [S]	Patches	1970	7.50	15.00	30.00

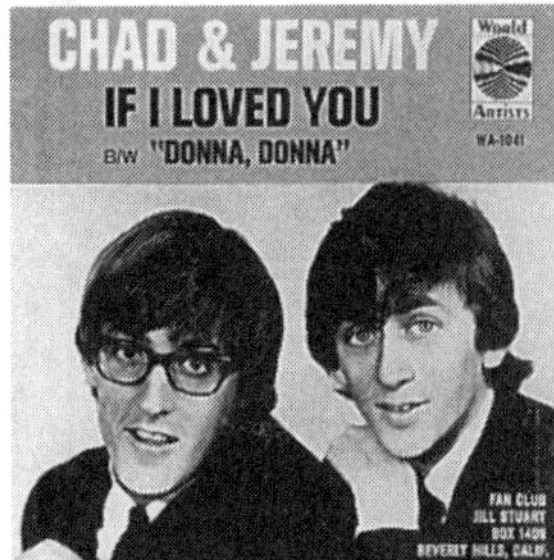

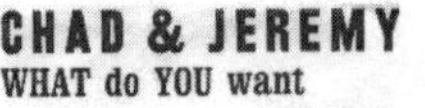

Number	Title (A Side/B Side)	Yr	VG	VG+	NM
❑ Atlantic SD 8282	The Best of Clarence Carter	1971	5.00	10.00	20.00
❑ Fame FM-LA186-F	Sixty Minutes	1973	3.75	7.50	15.00
❑ Ichiban ICH-1001	Messin' with My Mind	1986	3.00	6.00	12.00
❑ Ichiban ICH-1003	Dr. C.C.	1986	3.00	6.00	12.00
❑ Ichiban ICH-1016	Hooked on Love	1987	3.00	6.00	12.00
❑ Ichiban ICH-1032	Touch of Blues	1988	3.00	6.00	12.00
❑ Ichiban ICH-1068	Between a Rock and a Hard Place	1989	3.00	6.00	12.00
❑ Ichiban ICH-1116	The Best of Clarence Carter: The Dr.'s Greatest Presciptions	1991	3.00	6.00	12.00
❑ Venture VL 1005	Let's Burn	1980	2.50	5.00	10.00
❑ Venture VL 1009	Mr. Clarence Carter In Person	1981	2.50	5.00	10.00

CASH, JOHNNY

45s

Number	Title (A Side/B Side)	Yr	VG	VG+	NM
❑ A&M 2291	The Death of Me/One More Shot	1980	—	2.00	4.00
—With Levon Helm					
❑ American 18091	Drive On/Delia's Gone	1994	—	2.00	4.00
❑ Cachet 4504	Wings in the Morning/What on Earth	1980	—	2.50	5.00
❑ Columbia 02189	Mobile Bay/The Hard Way	1981	—	2.00	4.00
❑ Columbia 02669	The Reverend Mr. Black/Chattanooga City Limit Sign	1982	—	2.00	4.00
❑ Columbia 03058	Georgia on a Fast Train/Sing a Song	1982	—	2.00	4.00
❑ Columbia 03317	Fair Weather Friends/Ain't Gonna Hobo No More	1982	—	2.00	4.00
❑ Columbia 03524	I'll Cross Over Jordan Some Day/We Must Believe in Magic	1983	—	2.00	4.00
❑ Columbia 04060	I'm Ragged, But I'm Right/Brand New Dance	1983	—	2.00	4.00
❑ Columbia 04227	Johnny 99/New Cut Road	1983	—	—	3.00
❑ Columbia 04428	That's the Truth/Joshua Gone Barbados	1984	—	—	3.00
❑ Columbia 04513	The Chicken in Black/The Battle of Nashville	1984	—	—	3.00
❑ Columbia 04740	They Killed Him/The Three Bells	1985	—	—	3.00
—With the Carter Family					
❑ Columbia 04860	Crazy Old Soldier/It Ain't Gonna Worry My Mind	1985	—	—	3.00
—A-side: Ray Charles and Johnny Cash; B-side: Ray Charles and Mickey Gilley					
❑ Columbia 04881	Highwayman/The Human Condition	1985	—	—	3.00
—A-side: Willie Nelson/Waylon Jennings/Johnny Cash/Kris Kristofferson; B-side: Nelson, Cash					
❑ Columbia 05594	Desperadoes Waiting for a Train/The Twentieth Century Is Almost Over	1985	—	—	3.00
—A-side: Willie Nelson/Waylon Jennings/Johnny Cash/Kris Kristofferson; B-side: Nelson, Cash					
❑ Columbia 05672	I'm Leaving Now/Easy Street	1985	—	—	3.00
❑ Columbia 08406	Highwayman/Desperadoes Waiting for a Train	1988	—	—	3.00
—Waylon Jennings/Willie Nelson/Johnny Cash/Kris Kristofferson; reissue					
❑ Columbia 10011	The Junkie and the Juicehead/Crystal Chandeliers and Burgundy	1974	—	2.50	5.00
❑ Columbia 10048	Father and Daughter, Father and Son/Don't Take Your Love to Town	1974	—	2.50	5.00
—With Rosey Nix					
❑ Columbia 10066	The Lady Came from Baltimore/Lonesome to the Bone	1974	—	2.50	5.00
❑ Columbia 10116	My Old Kentucky Home (Turpentine and Dandelion Wine)/ Hard Times Comin'	1975	—	2.50	5.00
❑ Columbia 10177	Look at Them Beans/All Around Cowboy	1975	—	2.50	5.00
❑ Columbia 10237	Texas — 1947/I Hardly Ever Sing Beer Drinking Songs	1975	—	2.50	5.00
❑ Columbia 10279	Strawberry Cake/I Got Stripes	1975	—	2.50	5.00
❑ Columbia 10321	One Piece at a Time/Go On Blues	1976	—	2.50	5.00
❑ Columbia 10381	Sold Out of Flagpoles/Mountain Lady	1976	—	2.50	5.00
❑ Columbia 10424	It's All Over/Ridin' on the Cotton Belt	1976	—	2.50	5.00
❑ Columbia 10483	The Last Gunfighter Ballad/City Jail	1977	—	2.50	5.00
❑ Columbia 10587	Lady/Hit the Road and Go	1977	—	2.50	5.00
❑ Columbia 10623	After the Ball/Calilou	1977	—	2.50	5.00
❑ Columbia 10681	I Would Like to See You Again/Lately	1978	—	2.50	5.00
❑ Columbia 10817	Gone Girl/I'm Alright Now	1978	—	2.50	5.00
❑ Columbia 10855	It'll Be Her/It Comes and Goes	1978	—	2.50	5.00
❑ Columbia 10888	I Will Rock and Roll with You/A Song for the Life	1979	—	2.50	5.00
❑ Columbia 10961	(Ghost) Riders in the Sky/I'm Gonna Sit on the Porch and Pick on My Guitar	1979	—	2.50	5.00
❑ Columbia 11103	I'll Say It's True/Cocaine Blues	1979	—	2.50	5.00
❑ Columbia 11237	Bull Rider/Lonesome to the Bone	1980	—	2.00	4.00
❑ Columbia 11283	Song of a Patriot/She's a Go-er	1980	—	2.00	4.00
❑ Columbia 11340	Cold Lonesome Morning/The Cowboy Who Started the Fight	1980	—	2.00	4.00
❑ Columbia 11399	The Last Time/Rockabilly Blues (Texas 1965)	1980	—	2.00	4.00
❑ Columbia 11424	Without Love/It Ain't Nothing New Babe	1981	—	2.00	4.00
❑ Columbia S7 30427 [S]	I Got Stripes/Five Feet High and Rising	1959	7.50	15.00	30.00
—"Stereo Seven" single; small hole, plays at 33 1/3 rpm					

Number	Title (A Side/B Side)	Yr	VG	VG+	NM
❑ Columbia 41251	All Over Again/What Do I Care	1958	3.75	7.50	15.00
❑ Columbia 41313	Don't Take Your Guns to Town/I Still Miss Someone	1959	3.75	7.50	15.00
❑ Columbia 41371	Frankie's Man, Johnny/You, Dreamer, You	1959	3.75	7.50	15.00
❑ Columbia 41427	I Got Stripes/Five Feet High and Rising	1959	3.75	7.50	15.00
❑ Columbia 41481	The Little Drummer Boy/I'll Remember You	1959	3.75	7.50	15.00
❑ Columbia 41618	Seasons of My Heart/Smiling Bill McCall	1960	3.75	7.50	15.00
❑ Columbia 41707	Second Honemoon/Honky Tonk Girl	1960	3.75	7.50	15.00
❑ Columbia 41804	Going to Memphis/Loading Coal	1960	3.75	7.50	15.00
❑ Columbia 41920	Girl in Saskatoon/Locomotive Man	1960	3.75	7.50	15.00
❑ Columbia 41995	The Rebel-Johnny Yuma/Forty Shades of Green	1961	3.00	6.00	12.00
❑ Columbia 42147	Tennessee Flat Top Box/Tall Men	1961	3.00	6.00	12.00
❑ Columbia 42301	The Big Battle/What I've Learned	1962	3.00	6.00	12.00
❑ Columbia 42425	In the Jailhouse Now/A Little at a Time	1962	3.00	6.00	12.00
❑ Columbia 42512	Bonanza!/Pick a Bale o' Cotton	1962	3.00	6.00	12.00
❑ Columbia 42615	Peace in the Valley/Were You There	1962	3.00	6.00	12.00
—With the Carter Family					
❑ Columbia 42665	Busted/Send a Picture of Mother	1963	2.50	5.00	10.00
❑ Columbia 42788	Ring of Fire/I'd Still Be There	1963	2.50	5.00	10.00
❑ Columbia 42880	The Matador/Still in Town	1963	2.50	5.00	10.00
❑ Columbia 4-42964	Understand Your Man/Dark as a Dungeon	1964	2.50	5.00	10.00
❑ Columbia 43058	The Ballad of Ira Hayes/Bad News	1964	2.50	5.00	10.00
❑ Columbia 4-43145	It Ain't Me, Babe/Time and Time Again	1964	2.50	5.00	10.00
❑ Columbia 43206	Orange Blossom Special/All of God's Children Ain't Free	1965	2.00	4.00	8.00
❑ Columbia 43313	Mister Garfield/Streets or Laredo	1965	2.00	4.00	8.00
❑ Columbia 43342	The Sons of Katie Elder/A Certain Kinda Hurtin'	1965	2.00	4.00	8.00
❑ Columbia 43420	Happy to Be with You/Pickin' Time	1965	2.00	4.00	8.00
❑ Columbia 43496	The One on the Right Is On the Left/Cotton Pickin' Hands	1965	2.00	4.00	8.00
❑ Columbia 43673	Everybody Loves a Nut/Austin Prison	1966	—	3.00	6.00
❑ Columbia 43763	Boa Constrictor/Bottom of a Mountain	1966	—	3.00	6.00
❑ Columbia 43921	You Beat All I Ever Saw/Put the Sugar to Bed	1966	—	3.00	6.00
❑ Columbia 44288	The Wind Changes/Red Velvet	1967	—	3.00	6.00
❑ Columbia 44373	Rosanna's Going Wild/Roll Call	1967	—	3.00	6.00
❑ Columbia 44513	Folsom Prison Blues/The Folk Singer	1968	—	3.00	6.00
❑ Columbia 44689	Daddy Sang Bass/He Turned the Water Into Wine	1968	—	3.00	6.00
❑ Columbia 44944	A Boy Named Sue/San Quentin	1969	—	3.00	6.00
❑ Columbia 45020	Blistered/See Ruby Fall	1969	—	3.00	6.00
❑ Columbia 45134	What Is Truth/Sing a Traveling Song	1970	—	2.50	5.00
❑ Columbia 45211	Sonday Morning Coming Down/I'm Gonna Try to Be That Way	1970	—	2.50	5.00
❑ Columbia 45269	Flesh and Blood/This Side of the Law	1970	—	2.50	5.00
❑ Columbia 45339	Man in Black/Little Bit of Yesterday	1971	—	2.50	5.00
❑ Columbia 45393	Singing in Viet Nam Talking Blues/You've Got a New Light Shining	1971	—	2.50	5.00
❑ Columbia 45460	Papa Was a Good Man/I Promise You	1971	—	2.50	5.00
❑ Columbia 45534	A Thing Called Love/Daddy	1972	—	2.50	5.00
❑ Columbia 45590	Kate/Miracle Man	1972	—	2.50	5.00
❑ Columbia 45660	Oney/Country Trash	1972	—	2.50	5.00
❑ Columbia 45740	Any Old Wind That Blows/Kentucky Straight	1972	—	2.50	5.00
❑ Columbia 45786	Children/Last Summer	1973	—	2.50	5.00
❑ Columbia 45938	Pick the Wildwood Flower/Diamonds in the Rough	1973	—	2.50	5.00
—With Mother Maybelle and the Carter Family					
❑ Columbia 45979	Christmas As I Knew It/That Christmasy Feeling	1973	—	2.50	5.00
—With Tommy Cash					
❑ Columbia 45997	Orleans Parish Prison/Jacob Green	1974	—	2.50	5.00
❑ Columbia 46028	Ragged Old Flag/Don't Go Near the Water	1974	—	2.50	5.00
❑ Columbia 60516	The Baron/I Will Dance with You	1981	—	2.00	4.00
❑ Columbia 69067	Ragged Old Flag/I'm Leaving Now	1989	—	—	3.00
❑ Columbia 73233	America Remains/Silver Stallion	1990	—	—	3.00
—Waylon Jennings/Willie Nelson/Johnny Cash/Kris Kristofferson					
❑ Columbia 73381	Born and Raised in Black and White/Texas	1990	—	—	3.00
—The Highwaymen (Waylon Jennings/Willie Nelson/Johnny Cash/Kris Kristofferson)					
❑ Columbia 73572	American Remains/Texas	1990	—	—	3.00
—The Highwaymen (Waylon Jennings/Willie Nelson/Johnny Cash/Kris Kristofferson)					
❑ Epic 50778	There Ain't No Good Chain Gang/I Wish I Was Crazy Again	1979	—	2.50	5.00
—Johnny Cash/Waylon Jennings					
❑ Mercury 870010-7	W. Lee O'Daniel (And the Light Crust Dough Boys)/ Letters from Homes	1987	—	—	3.00
❑ Mercury 870237-7	Cry, Cry, Cry/Get Rhythm	1988	—	—	3.00
❑ Mercury 870688-7	Tennessee Flat Top Box/That Old Wheel	1988	—	—	3.00
—A-side with Hank Williams, Jr.					
❑ Mercury 872420-7	Ballad of a Teenage Queen/Get Rhythm	1988	—	—	3.00
—With Roseanne Cash and the Everly Brothers					
❑ Mercury 874562-7	The Last of the Drifters/Water from the Wells of Home	1989	—	—	3.00
—A-side with Tom T. Hall					
❑ Mercury 875626-7	Cat's in the Cradle/I Love You, Love You	1990	—	—	3.00
❑ Mercury 878292-7	Goin' By the Book/Beans for Breakfast	1990	—	—	3.00
❑ Mercury 878710-7	The Greatest Cowboy of Them All/Hey Porter	1990	—	—	3.00
❑ Mercury 878968-7	The Mystery of Life/I'm an Easy Rider	1990	—	—	3.00
❑ Mercury 888459-7	The Night Hank Williams Came to Town/I'd Rather Have You	1987	—	—	3.00
❑ Mercury 888719-7	Sixteen Tons/The Ballad of Barbara	1987	—	—	3.00
❑ Mercury 888838-7	Let Him Roll/My Ship Will Sail	1987	—	—	3.00
❑ Scotti Bros. 02803	The General Lee/Duelin' Dukes	1982	—	2.00	4.00
—Narration on B-side: Sorrell Booke					
❑ Smash 884934-7	Sixteen Candles/Rock & Roll (Fais-Do-Do)	1986	—	2.00	4.00
—With Jerry Lee Lewis, Roy Orbison and Carl Perkins					
❑ Smash 888142-7	We Remember the King/Class of '55	1987	—	2.00	4.00
—With Jerry Lee Lewis, Roy Orbison and Carl Perkins; B-side by Carl Perkins solo					
❑ Sun 221	Hey Porter/Cry, Cry, Cry	1955	10.00	20.00	40.00
❑ Sun 232	Folsom Prison Blues/So Doggone Lonesome	1956	7.50	15.00	30.00

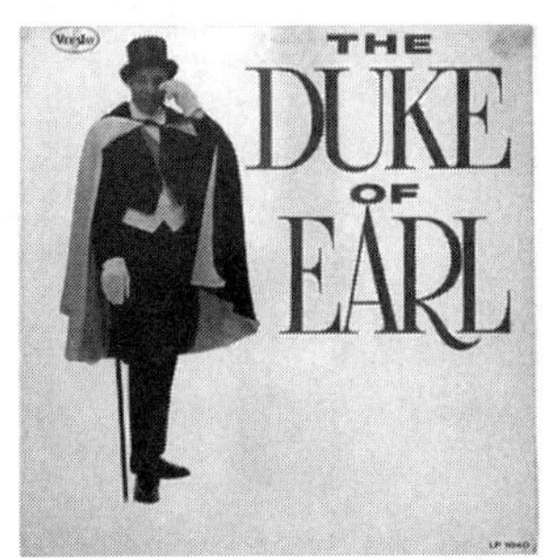

Number	Title (A Side/B Side)	Yr	VG	VG+	NM
❑ Sun 241	I Walk the Line/Get Rhythm	1956	10.00	20.00	40.00
❑ Sun 258	Train of Love/There You Go	1956	7.50	15.00	30.00
❑ Sun 266	Next in Line/Don't Make Me Go	1957	7.50	15.00	30.00
❑ Sun 279	Home of the Blues/Give My Love to Rose	1957	7.50	15.00	30.00
❑ Sun 283	Ballad of a Teenage Queen/Big River	1958	6.25	12.50	25.00
❑ Sun 295	Guess Things Happen That Way/Come In Stranger	1958	6.25	12.50	25.00
❑ Sun 302	The Ways of a Woman in Love/You're the Nearest Thing to Heaven	1958	6.25	12.50	25.00
❑ Sun 309	It's Just About Time/Just Thought You'd Like to Know	1958	6.25	12.50	25.00
❑ Sun 316	Luther Played the Boogie/Thanks a Lot	1959	5.00	10.00	20.00
❑ Sun 321	Katy Too/I Forgot to Remember to Forget	1959	5.00	10.00	20.00
❑ Sun 331	Goodbye Little Darlin'/You Tell Me	1959	5.00	10.00	20.00
❑ Sun 334	Straight A's in Love/I Love You Because	1960	5.00	10.00	20.00
❑ Sun 343	The Story of a Broken Heart/Down the Street to 301	1960	5.00	10.00	20.00
❑ Sun 347	Mean Eyed Cat/Port of Lonely Hearts	1960	5.00	10.00	20.00
❑ Sun 355	Oh Lonesome Me/Life Goes On	1961	5.00	10.00	20.00
❑ Sun 363	Sugartime/My Treasurer	1961	5.00	10.00	20.00
❑ Sun 376	Born to Lose/Blue Train	1962	5.00	10.00	20.00
❑ Sun 392	Wide Open Road/Belshazar	1964	5.00	10.00	20.00
❑ Sun 1103	Get Rhythm/Hey Porter	1969	—	3.00	6.00
❑ Sun 1111	Rock Island Line/Next in Line	1970	—	3.00	6.00
❑ Sun 1121	Big River/Come In Stranger	1971	—	2.50	5.00
Albums					
❑ Accord SN-7134	I Walk the Line	1983	2.50	5.00	10.00
❑ Accord SN-7208	Years Gone By	1983	2.50	5.00	10.00
❑ Allegiance AV-5017	The First Years	1986	2.50	5.00	10.00
❑ American B0002769-01	American V: A Hundred Highways	2006	3.00	6.00	12.00
❑ American 43097	Unchained	1996	30.00	60.00	120.00
❑ American 45520	American Recordings	1994	20.00	40.00	80.00
❑ American C 69691	American III: Solitary Man	2000	12.50	25.00	50.00
❑ Archive of Folk Music 278	Johnny Cash	198?	3.00	6.00	12.00
❑ Cachet 9001	A Believer Sings the Truth	1979	3.75	7.50	15.00
❑ Columbia GP 29 [(2)]	The World of Johnny Cash	1970	3.75	7.50	15.00
❑ Columbia C2L 38 [(2)M]	Ballads of the True West	1965	6.25	12.50	25.00
❑ Columbia C2S 838 [(2)S]	Ballads of the True West	1965	6.25	12.50	25.00
❑ Columbia CL 1253 [M]	The Fabulous Johnny Cash	1958	5.00	10.00	20.00
❑ Columbia CL 1284 [M]	Hymns by Johnny Cash	1959	6.25	12.50	25.00
❑ Columbia CL 1339 [M]	Songs of Our Soil	1959	6.25	12.50	25.00
❑ Columbia CL 1463 [M]	Now, There Was a Song!	1960	6.25	12.50	25.00
❑ Columbia CL 1464 [M]	Ride This Train	1960	6.25	12.50	25.00
❑ Columbia CL 1622 [M]	The Lure of the Grand Canyon	1961	10.00	20.00	40.00
—Cash narrates; with Andre Kostelanetz and His Orchestra					
❑ Columbia CL 1722 [M]	Hymns from the Heart	1962	5.00	10.00	20.00
❑ Columbia CL 1802 [M]	The Sound of Johnny Cash	1962	5.00	10.00	20.00
❑ Columbia CL 1930 [M]	Blood, Sweat & Tears	1963	5.00	10.00	20.00
❑ Columbia STS 2004 [(2)]	The Heart of Johnny Cash	196?	5.00	10.00	20.00
—"Columbia Star Series" release; has "360 Sound" labels					
❑ Columbia CL 2052 [M]	Ring of Fire (The Best of Johnny Cash)	1963	5.00	10.00	20.00
❑ Columbia CL 2117 [M]	The Christmas Spirit	1963	6.25	12.50	25.00
❑ Columbia CL 2190 [M]	I Walk the Line	1964	3.75	7.50	15.00
❑ Columbia CL 2248 [M]	Bitter Tears (Ballads of the American Indian)	1964	3.75	7.50	15.00
❑ Columbia CL 2309 [M]	Orange Blossom Special	1965	3.75	7.50	15.00
❑ Columbia CL 2446 [M]	Mean as Hell	1965	3.75	7.50	15.00
❑ Columbia CL 2492 [M]	Everybody Loves a Nut	1966	3.75	7.50	15.00
❑ Columbia CL 2537 [M]	That's What You Get for Lovin' Me	1966	3.75	7.50	15.00
❑ Columbia CL 2647 [M]	From Sea to Shining Sea	1967	5.00	10.00	20.00
❑ Columbia CL 2678 [M]	Johnny Cash's Greatest Hits, Volume 1	1967	5.00	10.00	20.00
❑ Columbia CS 8122 [S]	The Fabulous Johnny Cash	1959	10.00	20.00	40.00
❑ Columbia CS 8125 [S]	Hymns by Johnny Cash	1959	10.00	20.00	40.00
❑ Columbia CS 8148 [S]	Songs of Our Soil	1959	10.00	20.00	40.00
❑ Columbia CS 8254 [S]	Now, There Was a Song!	1960	10.00	20.00	40.00
❑ Columbia CS 8255 [S]	Ride This Train	1960	10.00	20.00	40.00
❑ Columbia CS 8422 [S]	The Lure of the Grand Canyon	1961	12.50	25.00	50.00
—Cash narrates; with Andre Kostelanetz and His Orchestra					
❑ Columbia CS 8522 [S]	Hymns from the Heart	1962	7.50	15.00	30.00
❑ Columbia CS 8602 [S]	The Sound of Johnny Cash	1962	7.50	15.00	30.00
❑ Columbia CS 8730 [S]	Blood, Sweat & Tears	1963	6.25	12.50	25.00

Number	Title (A Side/B Side)	Yr	VG	VG+	NM
❑ Columbia CS 8852 [S]	Ring of Fire (The Best of Johnny Cash)	1963	6.25	12.50	25.00
❑ Columbia CS 8917 [S]	The Christmas Spirit	1963	7.50	15.00	30.00
❑ Columbia CS 8990 [S]	I Walk the Line	1964	5.00	10.00	20.00
❑ Columbia CS 9048 [S]	Bitter Tears (Ballads of the American Indian)	1964	5.00	10.00	20.00
❑ Columbia CS 9109 [S]	Orange Blossom Special	1965	5.00	10.00	20.00
❑ Columbia CS 9246 [S]	Mean as Hell	1965	5.00	10.00	20.00
❑ Columbia CS 9292 [S]	Everybody Loves a Nut	1966	5.00	10.00	20.00
❑ Columbia CS 9337 [S]	That's What You Get for Lovin' Me	1966	5.00	10.00	20.00
❑ Columbia CS 9447 [S]	From Sea to Shining Sea	1967	5.00	10.00	20.00
❑ Columbia CS 9478 [S]	Johnny Cash's Greatest Hits, Volume 1	1967	5.00	10.00	20.00
❑ Columbia CS 9639 [S]	Johnny Cash at Folsom Prison	1968	5.00	10.00	20.00
—Red label with "360 Sound Stereo" at bottom					
❑ Columbia KCS 9726	The Holy Land	1969	3.75	7.50	15.00
❑ Columbia CS 9827	Johnny Cash at San Quentin	1969	3.00	6.00	12.00
❑ Columbia KCS 9943	Hello, I'm Johnny Cash	1970	3.00	6.00	12.00
❑ Columbia C 30100	The Johnny Cash Show	1970	3.00	6.00	12.00
❑ Columbia S 30397	I Walk the Line	1970	3.00	6.00	12.00
—Soundtrack from movie					
❑ Columbia KC 30550	Man in Black	1971	3.00	6.00	12.00
❑ Columbia KC 30887	The Johnny Cash Collection (His Greatest Hits, Volume II)	1971	3.00	6.00	12.00
❑ Columbia KC 31256	Give My Love to Rose	1972	3.00	6.00	12.00
❑ Columbia KC 31332	A Thing Called Love	1972	3.00	6.00	12.00
❑ Columbia KC 31645	Johnny Cash: America (A 200-Year Salute in Story and Song)	1972	3.00	6.00	12.00
❑ Columbia KC 32091	Any Old Wind That Blows	1973	3.00	6.00	12.00
❑ Columbia C 32240	Sunday Morning Coming Down	1973	3.00	6.00	12.00
❑ Columbia C 32253	The Gospel Road	1973	3.00	6.00	12.00
❑ Columbia CG 32253 [(2)]	The Gospel Road	1973	6.25	12.50	25.00
❑ Columbia KC 32898	Children's Album	1974	3.00	6.00	12.00
❑ Columbia C 32917	The Ragged Old Flag	1974	3.00	6.00	12.00
❑ Columbia C 32951	Five Feet High and Rising	1974	3.00	6.00	12.00
❑ Columbia KC 33086	The Junkie and the Juicehead	1974	3.00	6.00	12.00
❑ Columbia C 33087	Johnny Cash Sings Precious Memories	1974	3.00	6.00	12.00
❑ Columbia KC 33370	John R. Cash	1975	3.00	6.00	12.00
❑ Columbia CG 33639 [(2)]	Johnny Cash at Folsom Prison/Johnny Cash at San Quentin	1974	3.75	7.50	15.00
❑ Columbia KC 33814	Look at Them Beans	1975	3.00	6.00	12.00
❑ Columbia KC 34088	Strawberry Cake	1976	3.00	6.00	12.00
❑ Columbia KC 34193	One Piece at a Time	1976	3.00	6.00	12.00
❑ Columbia JC 34314	The Last Gunfighter Ballad	1977	3.00	6.00	12.00
❑ Columbia JC 34833	The Rambler	1977	3.00	6.00	12.00
❑ Columbia KC 35313	I Would Like to See You Again	1978	2.50	5.00	10.00
❑ Columbia JC 35637	Johnny Cash's Greatest Hits, Volume 3	1978	3.00	6.00	12.00
❑ Columbia JC 36086	Silver	1979	3.00	6.00	12.00
❑ Columbia JC 36779	Rockabilly Blues	1980	2.50	5.00	10.00
❑ Columbia JC 36866	Classic Christmas	1980	3.00	6.00	12.00
❑ Columbia FC 37179	The Baron	1981	2.50	5.00	10.00
❑ Columbia FC 37355	Encore	1981	2.50	5.00	10.00
❑ Columbia PC 38074	A Believer Sings the Truth	1985	2.00	4.00	8.00
—Reissue of Priority 38074					
❑ Columbia FC 38094	The Adventures of Johnny Cash	1982	2.50	5.00	10.00
❑ Columbia FC 38317	Johnny Cash's Biggest Hits	1982	2.50	5.00	10.00
❑ Columbia FC 38696	Johnny 99	1983	2.50	5.00	10.00
❑ Columbia FC 39951	Rainbow	1985	2.50	5.00	10.00
❑ Columbia Limited Edition LE 10063 [S]	The Fabulous Johnny Cash	197?	3.75	7.50	15.00
—Reissue of 8122					
❑ Everest 276	Johnny Cash	19??	3.00	6.00	12.00
❑ Harmony HS 11249	Golden Sounds of Country Music	1968	3.00	6.00	12.00
❑ Harmony HS 11342	Johnny Cash	1969	3.00	6.00	12.00
❑ Harmony KH 30916	Understand Your Man	1971	3.00	6.00	12.00
❑ Harmony KH 31602	The Johnny Cash Songbook	1972	3.00	6.00	12.00
❑ Harmony KH 32388	Ballads of the American Indian	1973	3.00	6.00	12.00
❑ Mercury 832031-1	Johnny Cash Is Coming to Town	1987	2.50	5.00	10.00
❑ Mercury 834778-1	Water from the Wells of Home	1988	2.50	5.00	10.00
❑ Pair PDL2-1107 [(2)]	Classic Cash	1986	3.75	7.50	15.00
❑ Power Pak 246	Country Gold	198?	2.50	5.00	10.00
❑ Priority UG 32253 [(2)]	The Gospel Road	1981	3.75	7.50	15.00
—Reissue of Columbia album of the same name					
❑ Priority PU 33087	Johnny Cash Sings Precious Memories	1982	3.00	6.00	12.00
—Reissue of Columbia album of the same name					
❑ Priority PU 38074	A Believer Sings the Truth	1982	3.00	6.00	12.00
—Reissue of Cachet album					
❑ Rhino RNLP 70229	The Vintage Years	1987	3.00	6.00	12.00
❑ Share 5000	I Walk the Line	197?	3.00	6.00	12.00
❑ Share 5001	Folsom Prison Blues	197?	3.00	6.00	12.00
❑ Share 5002	The Blue Train	197?	3.00	6.00	12.00
❑ Share 5003	Johnny Cash Sings the Greatest Hits	197?	3.00	6.00	12.00
❑ Sun LP-100	Original Golden Hits, Volume I	1969	3.00	6.00	12.00
❑ Sun LP-101	Original Golden Hits, Volume II	1969	3.00	6.00	12.00
❑ Sun LP-104	Story Songs of the Trains and Rivers	1969	3.00	6.00	12.00
❑ Sun LP-105	Get Rhythm	1969	3.00	6.00	12.00
❑ Sun LP-106	Showtime	1969	3.00	6.00	12.00
❑ Sun LP-115	The Singing Story Teller	1970	3.00	6.00	12.00
❑ Sun LP-118 [(2)]	Johnny Cash — The Legend	1970	5.00	10.00	20.00
❑ Sun LP-122	The Rough Cut King of Country Music	1971	3.00	6.00	12.00
❑ Sun LP-126 [(2)]	Johnny Cash: The Man, The World, His Music	1971	5.00	10.00	20.00
❑ Sun LP-127	Original Golden Hits, Volume III	1972	3.00	6.00	12.00
❑ Sun LP-139	I Walk the Line	1979	2.50	5.00	10.00

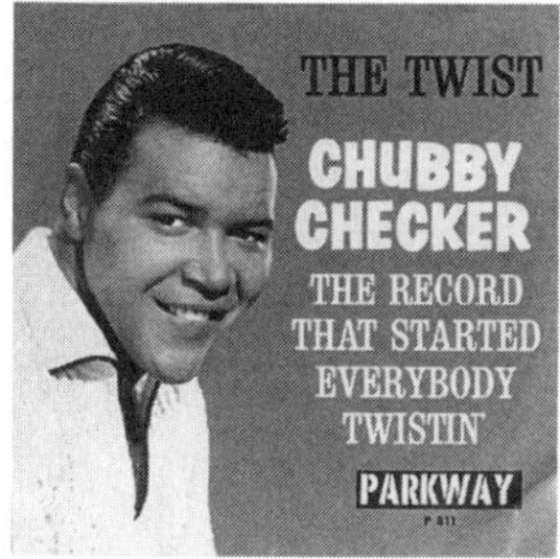

Number	Title (A Side/B Side)	Yr	VG	VG+	NM
❑ Sun LP-140	Folsom Prison Blues	1979	2.50	5.00	10.00
❑ Sun LP-141	The Blue Train	1979	2.50	5.00	10.00
❑ Sun LP-142	Johnny Cash Sings the Greatest Hits	1979	2.50	5.00	10.00
❑ Sun 1002	Superbilly (1955-58)	198?	2.50	5.00	10.00
❑ Sun 1006	The Original Johnny Cash	1980	2.50	5.00	10.00
❑ Sun SLP-1220 [M]	Johnny Cash with His Hot and Blue Guitar	1956	25.00	50.00	100.00
❑ Sun SLP-1220 [R]	Johnny Cash with His Hot and Blue Guitar	196?	5.00	10.00	20.00
—Reissue in rechanneled stereo; front cover says "STEREO"					
❑ Sun SLP-1235 [M]	The Songs That Made Him Famous	1958	25.00	50.00	100.00
❑ Sun SLP-1235 [R]	The Songs That Made Him Famous	196?	5.00	10.00	20.00
—Reissue in rechanneled stereo; front cover says "STEREO"					
❑ Sun SLP-1240 [M]	Johnny Cash's Greatest!	1959	12.50	25.00	50.00
❑ Sun SLP-1245 [M]	Johnny Cash Sings Hank Williams	1960	12.50	25.00	50.00
❑ Sun SLP-1245 [R]	Johnny Cash Sings Hank Williams	196?	5.00	10.00	20.00
—Reissue in rechanneled stereo; front cover says "STEREO"					
❑ Sun SLP-1255 [M]	Now Here's Johnny Cash	1961	12.50	25.00	50.00
❑ Sun SLP-1255 [R]	Now Here's Johnny Cash	196?	5.00	10.00	20.00
—Reissue in rechanneled stereo; front cover says "STEREO"					
❑ Sun SLP-1270 [M]	All Aboard the Blue Train	1963	12.50	25.00	50.00
❑ Sun SLP-1275 [M]	The Original Sun Sound of Johnny Cash	1965	12.50	25.00	50.00
❑ Word WR-8333	Believe in Him	1986	3.00	6.00	12.00

CASINOS, THE (1)

Records by the Casinos on Airtown, Alto, Casino, Certron, Itzy, Name, Olimpic, Sims and Terry may all be by a different group, thus are outside the scope of this book.

45s

Number	Title (A Side/B Side)	Yr	VG	VG+	NM
❑ Buccaneer 3000	Then You Can Tell Me Goodbye/I Still Love You	196?	2.00	4.00	8.00
—Reissue of Fraternity release					
❑ Fraternity 944	She's Out of Sight/The Gallop	1965	2.50	5.00	10.00
❑ Fraternity 949	Right There Beside You/The Gallop	1965	2.50	5.00	10.00
❑ Fraternity 977	Then You Can Tell Me Goodbye/I Still Love You	1967	3.00	6.00	12.00
❑ Fraternity 985	It's All Over Now/Tailor Made	1967	2.50	5.00	10.00
❑ Fraternity 987	Forever and a Night/How Long Has It Been	1967	2.50	5.00	10.00
❑ Fraternity 995	When I Stop Dreaming/Please Love	1967	2.50	5.00	10.00
❑ Fraternity 997	Bye Bye Love/Walk Through This World with Me	1967	2.50	5.00	10.00
❑ Fraternity 1020	These Are the Things We'll Share/Casinos Having Fun	1969	2.50	5.00	10.00
❑ Fraternity 1028	I Wish I Were Anyone But Me/I Just Want to Stay Here	1969	2.50	5.00	10.00
❑ Fraternity 1200	Father John/The Old Saloon	1970	2.50	5.00	10.00
❑ Fraternity 1201	Wisdom of Love/My House	1970	2.50	5.00	10.00
❑ Fraternity 1250	Loving Her Was Easier/A Restless Wind	1971	2.50	5.00	10.00
❑ Million 13	I'm Walking Behind You/Angels Were All Asleep	1972	2.50	5.00	10.00
—As "Gene Hughes and the Casinos"					
❑ United Artists 50255	Here I Am/Peggy	1968	2.50	5.00	10.00
—As "Gene Hughes and the Casinos"					
❑ United Artists 50313	Nobody's Child/Leaving Makes the Rain Come Down	1968	2.50	5.00	10.00
—As "Gene Hughes and the Casinos"					

Albums

Number	Title (A Side/B Side)	Yr	VG	VG+	NM
❑ Fraternity LP-1019 [M]	Then You Can Tell Me Goodbye	1967	10.00	20.00	40.00
❑ Fraternity LPS-1019 [S]	Then You Can Tell Me Goodbye	1967	15.00	30.00	60.00

CASSIDY, DAVID

45s

Number	Title (A Side/B Side)	Yr	VG	VG+	NM
❑ Bell 45150	Cherish/All I Want to Do Is Touch You	1971	—	2.50	5.00
❑ Bell 45187	Could It Be Forever/Blind Hope	1972	—	2.00	4.00
❑ Bell 45220	How Can I Be Sure/Ricky's Tune	1972	—	2.00	4.00
❑ Bell 45260	Rock Me Baby/Two Time Loser	1972	—	2.00	4.00
❑ Bell 45386	Daydream/Can't Go Home Again	1973	—	2.00	4.00
❑ Bell 45413	Daydreamer/The Puppy Song	1973	—	2.00	4.00
❑ Bell 45605	Breaking Up Is Hard to Do/Please Please Me	1974	—	2.00	4.00
❑ MCA 41101	Hurt So Bad/Once a Fool	1979	—	2.00	4.00
❑ RCA PB-10788	I'll Have to Go Away (Saying Goodbye)/Gettin' It in the Streets	1976	2.00	4.00	8.00
❑ RCA PB-10921	Saying Goodbye Ain't Easy (We'll Have to Go Away)/ Rosa's Cantina	1977	2.00	4.00	8.00
❑ RCA Victor PB-10321	Get It Up for Love/Love In Bloom	1975	2.50	5.00	10.00
❑ RCA Victor PB-10405	This Could Be the Night/Darlin'	1975	2.50	5.00	10.00
❑ RCA Victor PB-10585	Tomorrow/Bedtime	1976	2.50	5.00	10.00
❑ RCA Victor PB-10647	Breakin' Down Again/On Fire	1976	2.50	5.00	10.00

Number	Title (A Side/B Side)	Yr	VG	VG+	NM
Albums					
❑ Bell 1109	Rock Me Baby	1972	5.00	10.00	20.00
❑ Bell 1132	Dreams Are Nothing More Than Wishes	1973	5.00	10.00	20.00
❑ Bell 1312	Cassidy Live	1974	6.25	12.50	25.00
❑ Bell 1321	David Cassidy's Greatest Hits	1974	3.75	7.50	15.00
❑ Bell 6070	Cherish	1972	5.00	10.00	20.00
❑ RCA Victor APL1-1066	The Higher They Climb…	1975	3.75	7.50	15.00
—Black vinyl					
❑ RCA Victor APL1-1066	The Higher They Climb…	1975	25.00	50.00	100.00
—Blue vinyl					
❑ RCA Victor APL1-1309	Home Is Where the Heart Is	1976	3.75	7.50	15.00
❑ RCA Victor APL1-1852	Gettin' It in the Street	1976	10.00	20.00	40.00
CASSIDY, SHAUN					
45s					
❑ Warner Bros. 8365	Da Doo Ron Ron/Holiday	1977	—	2.00	4.00
❑ Warner Bros. 8423	That's Rock 'N' Roll/I Wanna Be with You	1977	—	2.00	4.00
❑ Warner Bros. 8488	Hey Deanie/Strange Sensation	1977	—	2.00	4.00
❑ Warner Bros. 8533	Do You Believe in Magic/Teen Dream	1978	—	2.00	4.00
❑ Warner Bros. 8634	Our Night/Right Before Your Eyes	1978	—	2.00	4.00
❑ Warner Bros. 8698	Midnight Sun/She's Right	1978	—	2.50	5.00
❑ Warner Bros. 8859	You're Usin' Me/You Still Surprise Me	1979	—	2.50	5.00
❑ Warner Bros. 49039	Are You Afraid of Me?/You're Usin' Me	1979	—	2.00	4.00
❑ Warner Bros. 49154	Heaven in Your Eyes/Star Trek	1980	—	2.00	4.00
❑ Warner Bros. 49568	Rebel, Rebel/Cool Fire	1980	—	2.50	5.00
❑ Warner Bros. 49640	So Sad About Us/Cool Fire	1980	—	2.50	5.00
—A-side with Todd Rundgren's Utopia					
Albums					
❑ Warner Bros. BS 3067	Shaun Cassidy	1977	2.00	4.00	8.00
❑ Warner Bros. BSK 3126	Born Late	1977	2.00	4.00	8.00
❑ Warner Bros. BSK 3222	Under Wraps	1978	2.00	4.00	8.00
❑ Warner Bros. HS 3265	Live/That's Rock and Roll	1979	2.50	5.00	10.00
❑ Warner Bros. BSK 3351	Room Service	1979	2.50	5.00	10.00
❑ Warner Bros. BSK 3451	Wasp	1980	3.75	7.50	15.00
CHAD AND JEREMY					
45s					
❑ Capitol Starline 6087	A Summer Song/Willow Weep for Me	1966	2.00	4.00	8.00
—Green and white swirl label					
❑ Columbia 43277	Before and After/Fare Thee Well	1965	2.50	5.00	10.00
❑ Columbia 43339	I Don't Wanna Lose You Baby/Pennies	1965	2.00	4.00	8.00
❑ Columbia 43414	I Have Dreamed/Should I?	1966	2.00	4.00	8.00
❑ Columbia 43490	Teenage Failure/Early Morning Rain	1965	2.00	4.00	8.00
❑ Columbia 43682	Distant Shores/Last Night	1966	2.00	4.00	8.00
❑ Columbia 43807	You Are She/I Won't Cry	1966	2.00	4.00	8.00
❑ Columbia 44131	Rest in Peace/Family Way	1967	2.00	4.00	8.00
❑ Columbia 44379	Painted Dayglow Smile/Editorial	1967	2.00	4.00	8.00
❑ Columbia 44525	Sister Marie/Rest in Peace	1968	2.00	4.00	8.00
❑ Columbia 44660	Paxton Quigley's Had the Course/You Need Feet	1968	2.00	4.00	8.00
❑ Lana 145	Yesterday's Gone/Lemon Tree	196?	—	3.00	6.00
—Oldies reissue					
❑ Lana 146	A Summer Song/No Tears for Johnny	196?	—	3.00	6.00
❑ Rocshire 95046	Bite the Bullet/How Many Trains	1983	—	2.00	4.00
❑ Rocshire 95061	Dreams/Zanzibar Sunset	1983	—	2.00	4.00
❑ World Artists 1021	Yesterday's Gone/Lemon Tree	1964	2.50	5.00	10.00
—As "Chad Stuart and Jeremy Clyde"					
❑ World Artists 1027	A Summer Song/No Tears for Johnny	1964	2.50	5.00	10.00
—As "Chad Stuart and Jeremy Clyde"					
❑ World Artists 1034	Willow Weep for Me/If She Was Mine	1964	2.50	5.00	10.00
❑ World Artists 1041	If I Loved You/Donna, Donna	1965	2.50	5.00	10.00
❑ World Artists 1052	What Do You Want with Me/A Very Good Year	1965	2.50	5.00	10.00
—As "Chad Stuart and Jeremy Clyde"					
❑ World Artists 1056	From a Window/My Coloring Book	1965	2.50	5.00	10.00
❑ World Artists 1060	September in the Rain/Only for the Young	1965	2.50	5.00	10.00
Albums					
❑ Capitol ST 2470 [P]	The Best of Chad and Jeremy	1966	3.00	6.00	12.00
—Black label with colorband					
❑ Capitol ST 2470 [P]	The Best of Chad and Jeremy	1967	2.50	5.00	10.00
—"Starline" label					
❑ Capitol T 2470 [M]	The Best of Chad and Jeremy	1966	2.50	5.00	10.00
—Black label with colorband					
❑ Capitol T 2470 [M]	The Best of Chad and Jeremy	1967	2.00	4.00	8.00
—"Starline" label					
❑ Capitol STT 2546 [P]	More Chad and Jeremy	1966	3.00	6.00	12.00
❑ Capitol TT 2546 [M]	More Chad and Jeremy	1966	2.50	5.00	10.00
❑ Capitol SN-16135 [P]	The Best of Chad and Jeremy	1980	2.00	4.00	8.00
—Budget-line reissue					
❑ Columbia CL 2374 [M]	Before and After	1965	5.00	10.00	20.00
❑ Columbia CL 2398 [M]	I Don't Want to Lose You Baby	1966	6.25	12.50	25.00
❑ Columbia CL 2564 [M]	Distant Shores	1966	5.00	10.00	20.00
❑ Columbia CL 2671 [M]	Of Cabbages and Kings	1967	5.00	10.00	20.00
❑ Columbia CL 2899 [M]	The Ark	1968	6.25	12.50	25.00
❑ Columbia CS 9174 [S]	Before and After	1965	7.50	15.00	30.00
❑ Columbia CS 9198 [S]	I Don't Want to Lose You Baby	1966	10.00	20.00	40.00
❑ Columbia CS 9364 [P]	Distant Shores	1966	6.25	12.50	25.00
—"Distant Shores" is rechanneled					
❑ Columbia CS 9471 [S]	Of Cabbages and Kings	1967	6.25	12.50	25.00

Number	Title (A Side/B Side)	Yr	VG	VG+	NM
❑ Columbia CS 9699 [S]	The Ark	1968	6.25	12.50	25.00
—Correct spelling of LP title on cover					
❑ Fidu FM-101 [M]	5 + 10 = 15 Fabulous Hits	1966	2.50	5.00	10.00
❑ Fidu FS-101 [P]	5 + 10 = 15 Fabulous Hits	1966	3.00	6.00	12.00
❑ Harmony HS 11357 [S]	Chad and Jeremy	1973	2.00	4.00	8.00
❑ Rocshire XR-22018	Chad Stuart and Jeremy Clyde	1983	2.50	5.00	10.00
❑ World Artists WAM-2002 [M]	Yesterday's Gone	1964	3.00	6.00	12.00
❑ World Artists WAM-2005 [M]	Chad and Jeremy Sing for You	1965	3.00	6.00	12.00
❑ World Artists WAS-3002 [P]	Yesterday's Gone	1964	3.75	7.50	15.00
—"Yesterday's Gone" is rechanneled.					
❑ World Artists WAS-3005 [S]	Chad and Jeremy Sing for You	1965	3.75	7.50	15.00
CHAIRMEN OF THE BOARD					
45s					
❑ Invictus 1251	Finder's Keepers/Finder's Keepers (Part 2)	1973	—	2.50	5.00
❑ Invictus 1263	Life & Death/Love with Me, Love with Me	1974	—	2.50	5.00
❑ Invictus 1268	Everybody Party All Night/Morning Glory	1974	—	2.50	5.00
❑ Invictus 1271	Let's Have Some Fun/Love at First Sight	1974	—	2.50	5.00
❑ Invictus 1276	The Skin I'm In/Love at First Sight	1975	—	2.50	5.00
❑ Invictus 1278	You've Got Extra Added Power in Your Love/ Someone Just Like You	1975	—	2.50	5.00
❑ Invictus 9074	Give Me Just a Little More Time/Since the Days of Pigtails	1970	—	3.00	6.00
❑ Invictus 9078	(You've Got Me) Dangling on a String/I'll Come Crawling	1970	—	2.50	5.00
❑ Invictus 9079	Everything's Tuesday/Patches	1970	—	2.50	5.00
❑ Invictus 9081	Pay to the Piper/Bless You	1970	—	2.50	5.00
❑ Invictus 9086	Chairman of the Board/When Will She Tell Me She Needs Me	1971	—	2.50	5.00
❑ Invictus 9089	Hanging On (To) A Memory/Tracked and Trapped	1971	—	2.50	5.00
❑ Invictus 9099	Try On My Love for Size/Working on a Building of Love	1971	—	2.50	5.00
❑ Invictus 9103	Men Are Getting Scarce/Bravo! Hurray!	1971	—	2.50	5.00
❑ Invictus 9106	Bittersweet/Elmo James	1972	—	2.50	5.00
❑ Invictus 9122	Everybody's Got a Song to Sing/Working on a Building of Love	1972	—	2.50	5.00
❑ Invictus 9126	Let Me Down Easy/I Can't Find Myself	1972	—	2.50	5.00
Albums					
❑ Invictus ST-7300	Chairmen of the Board (Featuring "Give Me Just a Little More Time")	1970	10.00	20.00	40.00
❑ Invictus SKAO-7304	In Session	1970	10.00	20.00	40.00
❑ Invictus ST-9801	Bittersweet	1972	10.00	20.00	40.00
❑ Invictus KZ 32526	The Skin I'm In	1974	10.00	20.00	40.00
CHAMBERS BROTHERS, THE					
45s					
❑ Avco 4632	Let's Go, Let's Go, Let's Go/Do You Believe in Magic	1974	—	2.00	4.00
❑ Avco 4638	1-2-3/Looking Back	1974	—	2.00	4.00
❑ Avco 4657	Miss Lady Brown/Stealin' Watermelons	1975	—	2.00	4.00
❑ Columbia 4-43816	Time Has Come Today (2:37)/Dinah	1966	3.00	6.00	12.00
—A-side is a different recording than the later hit, both vocally and instrumentally					
❑ Columbia 43957	All Strung Out Over You/Falling in Love	1967	—	3.00	6.00
❑ Columbia 44080	Please Don't Leave Me/I Can't Stand It	1967	—	3.00	6.00
❑ Columbia 44296	Uptown/Love Me Like the Rain	1967	—	3.00	6.00
❑ Columbia 4-44414	Time Has Come Today (4:45)/People Get Ready	1968	2.00	4.00	8.00
—Hit version; label refers to the album "The Time Has Come"					
❑ Columbia 4-44679	I Can't Turn You Loose/Do Your Thing	1968	—	3.00	6.00
❑ Columbia 44779	Are You Ready/You Got the Power to Turn Me On	1969	—	3.00	6.00
❑ Columbia 44890	Wake Up/Everybody Needs Someone	1969	—	3.00	6.00
❑ Columbia 44986	Have a Little Faith/Baby Takes Care of Business	1969	—	2.50	5.00
❑ Columbia 4-45055	Merry Christmas, Happy New Year/ Did You Stop to Pray This Morning	1969	—	3.00	6.00
❑ Columbia 45088	Love, Peace and Happiness/If You Want Me To	1970	—	2.50	5.00
❑ Columbia 45146	To Love Somebody/Let's Do It	1970	—	2.50	5.00
❑ Columbia 45277	Love, Peace and Happiness/Funky	1970	—	2.50	5.00
❑ Columbia 45394	When the Evening Comes/New Generation	1971	—	2.50	5.00
❑ Columbia 45488	Heaven/(By the Hair on) My Chinny Chin Chin	1971	—	3.00	6.00
❑ Columbia 45518	Merry Christmas, Happy New Year/ Did You Stop to Pray This Morning	1971	—	3.00	6.00
❑ Columbia 45837	Boogie Children/You Make the Magic	1973	—	3.00	6.00
❑ Roxbury 2034	Bring It On Down Front Pretty Mama/Midnight Blue	1976	—	2.50	5.00
❑ Vault 920	Call Me/Seventeen	1965	3.75	7.50	15.00
❑ Vault 923	Pretty Girls Everywhere/Love Me Like the Rain	1966	3.00	6.00	12.00

Number	Title (A Side/B Side)	Yr	VG	VG+	NM
❑ Vault 945	Shout Part 1/Shout Part 2	1968	2.00	4.00	8.00
❑ Vault 955	Just a Closer Walk with Thee/Girls We Love You	1969	—	3.00	6.00
❑ Vault 967	House of the Rising Sun/Blues Get Off My Shoulder	1970	—	3.00	6.00

CHAMPS, THE

45s

Number	Title (A Side/B Side)	Yr	VG	VG+	NM
❑ Challenge 1016	Tequila/Train to Nowhere	1958	6.25	12.50	25.00
❑ Challenge 9113	The Shoddy Shoddy/Sombrero	1961	5.00	10.00	20.00
❑ Challenge 9116	Cantina/Panic Button	1961	5.00	10.00	20.00
❑ Challenge 9131	Tequila Twist/Limbo Rock	1961	5.00	10.00	20.00
❑ Challenge 9140	Experiment in Terror/La Cucaracha	1962	3.75	7.50	15.00
❑ Challenge 9143	What a Country/I've Just Seen Her	1962	3.75	7.50	15.00
❑ Challenge 9162	Limbo Dance/Latin Limbo	1962	3.75	7.50	15.00
❑ Challenge 9174	Varsity Rock/That Did It	1962	3.75	7.50	15.00
❑ Challenge 9180	Mr. Cool//3/4 Mash	1963	3.75	7.50	15.00
❑ Challenge 9189	Nik Nak/Shades	1963	3.75	7.50	15.00
❑ Challenge 9199	Cactus Juice/Roots	1963	3.75	7.50	15.00
❑ Challenge 59007	El Rancho Rock/Midnighter	1958	5.00	10.00	20.00
❑ Challenge 59018	Chariot Rock/Subway	1958	5.00	10.00	20.00
❑ Challenge 59026	Turnpike/Rockin' Mary	1958	5.00	10.00	20.00
❑ Challenge 59035	Gone Train/Beatnik	1958	5.00	10.00	20.00
❑ Challenge 59043	Moonlight Bay/Caramba	1959	5.00	10.00	20.00
❑ Challenge 59049	Night Train/The Rattler	1959	5.00	10.00	20.00
❑ Challenge 59053	Sky High/Double Eagle Rock	1959	5.00	10.00	20.00
❑ Challenge 59063	Too Much Tequila/Twenty Thousand Leagues	1960	5.00	10.00	20.00
❑ Challenge 59076	Red Eye/The Little Matador	1960	5.00	10.00	20.00
❑ Challenge 59086	Alley Cat/Coconut Grove	1960	5.00	10.00	20.00
❑ Challenge 59097	The Face/Tough Train	1960	5.00	10.00	20.00
❑ Challenge 59103	Hokey Pokey/Jumping Bean	1961	5.00	10.00	20.00
❑ Challenge 59219	San Juan/Jalisco	1963	3.75	7.50	15.00
❑ Challenge 59236	Switzerland/Only the Young	1964	3.75	7.50	15.00
❑ Challenge 59263	Fraternity Waltz/Kahlua	1964	3.75	7.50	15.00
❑ Challenge 59276	French 75/Bright Lights, Big City	1965	3.75	7.50	15.00
❑ Challenge 59314	The Man from Durango/Red Pepper	1965	3.75	7.50	15.00
❑ Challenge 59322	Anna/Buckaroo	1965	3.75	7.50	15.00
❑ Lana 155	Tequila/Sky High	196?	2.00	4.00	8.00
—Possibly re-recorded version of A-side					
❑ Republic 246	Tequila '76 (Long)/Tequila '76 (Short)	1976	2.00	4.00	8.00
❑ We're Back 1	Tequila '77/From Me to You	1977	2.00	4.00	8.00

Albums

Number	Title (A Side/B Side)	Yr	VG	VG+	NM
❑ Challenge CHL-601 [M]	Go Champs Go	1958	62.50	125.00	250.00
❑ Challenge CHL-605 [M]	Everybody's Rockin' with the Champs	1959	50.00	100.00	200.00
❑ Challenge CHL-613 [M]	Great Dance Hits	1962	30.00	60.00	120.00
❑ Challenge CHL-614 [M]	All American Music from the Champs	1962	30.00	60.00	120.00
❑ Challenge CHS-2500 [S]	Everybody's Rockin' with the Champs	1959	75.00	150.00	300.00
❑ Challenge CHS-2513 [S]	Great Dance Hits	1962	50.00	100.00	200.00
❑ Challenge CHS-2514 [S]	All American Music from the Champs	1962	50.00	100.00	200.00

CHANDLER, GENE

45s

Number	Title (A Side/B Side)	Yr	VG	VG+	NM
❑ Brunswick 55312	Girl Don't Care/My Love	1967	2.00	4.00	8.00
❑ Brunswick 55339	There Goes the Lover/Tell Me What I Can Do	1967	2.00	4.00	8.00
❑ Brunswick 55383	There Was a Time/Those Were the Good Old Days	1968	2.00	4.00	8.00
❑ Brunswick 55394	Teacher, Teacher/Pit of Loneliness	1968	2.00	4.00	8.00
❑ Brunswick 55413	Eleanor Rigby/Familiar Footsteps	1969	2.00	4.00	8.00
❑ Brunswick 55425	This Bitter Earth/Suicide	1969	2.00	4.00	8.00
❑ Checker 1155	I Fooled You This Time/Such a Pretty Thing	1966	2.00	4.00	8.00
❑ Checker 1165	To Be a Lover/After the Laughter	1967	2.00	4.00	8.00
❑ Checker 1190	I Won't Need You/No Peace, No Satisfaction	1967	2.00	4.00	8.00
❑ Checker 1199	River of Tears/It's Time to Settle Down	1968	2.00	4.00	8.00
❑ Checker 1220	Go Back Home/In My Baby's House	1969	2.00	4.00	8.00
❑ Chi-Sound 1001	I'll Make the Living If You Make the Loving Worthwhile/ (B-side unknown)	1982	—	2.50	5.00
❑ Chi-Sound 1168	Give Me the Cue/Tomorrow We May Not Feel the Same	1978	—	2.00	4.00
❑ Chi-Sound 2386	Get Down/I'm the Traveling Kind	1978	—	2.00	4.00
❑ Chi-Sound 2404	Please Sunrise/Greatest Love Ever Known	1979	—	2.00	4.00
❑ Chi-Sound 2411	When You're #1/I'll Remember You	1979	—	2.50	5.00
❑ Chi-Sound 2451	Does She Have a Friend?/Let Me Make Love to You	1980	—	2.00	4.00
❑ Chi-Sound 2468	Lay Me Gently/You've Been So Good to Me	1980	—	2.00	4.00
❑ Chi-Sound 2480	Rainbow '80/I'll Be There	1980	—	2.00	4.00
❑ Chi-Sound 2494	I'm Attracted to You/I've Got to Meet You	1981	—	2.00	4.00
❑ Chi-Sound 2507	Love Is the Answer/Godsend	1981	—	2.00	4.00
❑ Constellation 104	From Day to Day/It's No Good for Me	1963	2.50	5.00	10.00
❑ Constellation 110	Pretty Little Girl/A Little Like Lovin'	1963	2.50	5.00	10.00
❑ Constellation 112	Think Nothing About It/Wish You Were Here	1964	2.50	5.00	10.00
❑ Constellation 114	Soul Hootenanny (Part 1)/Soul Hootenanny (Part 2)	1964	2.50	5.00	10.00
❑ Constellation 124	A Song Called Soul/You Left Me	1964	2.50	5.00	10.00
❑ Constellation 130	Just Be True/A Song Called Soul	1964	2.50	5.00	10.00
❑ Constellation 136	Bless Our Love/London Town	1964	2.50	5.00	10.00
❑ Constellation 141	What Now/If You Can't Be True	1964	2.50	5.00	10.00
❑ Constellation 146	You Can't Hurt Me No More/Everybody Let's Dance	1965	2.00	4.00	8.00
❑ Constellation 149	Nothing Can Stop Me/The Big Lie	1965	2.00	4.00	8.00
❑ Constellation 158	Rainbow '65 (Part 1)/Rainbow '65 (Part 2)	1965	2.00	4.00	8.00
❑ Constellation 160	Good Times/No One Can Love You	1965	2.00	4.00	8.00
❑ Constellation 164	Here Come the Tears/Soul Hootenanny (Part 2)	1965	2.00	4.00	8.00
❑ Constellation 166	Baby That's Love/Bet You Never Thought	1966	2.00	4.00	8.00
❑ Constellation 167	(I'm Just a) Fool for You/Buddy Ain't It a Shame	1966	2.00	4.00	8.00
❑ Constellation 169	I Can Take Care of Myself/If I Can't Save It	1966	2.00	4.00	8.00

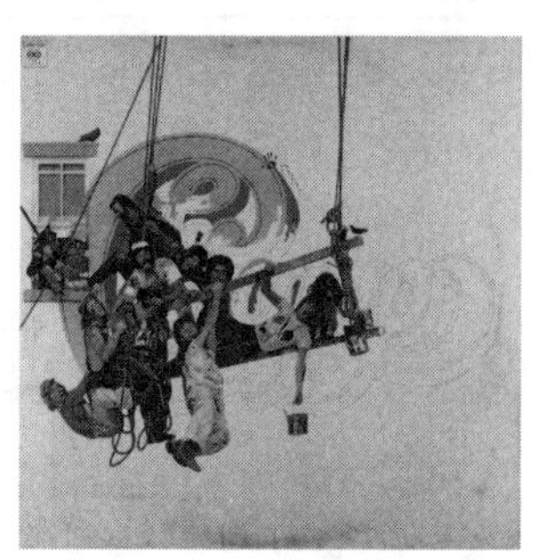

Number	Title (A Side/B Side)	Yr	VG	VG+	NM
❑ Constellation 172	Mr. Big Shot/I Hate to Be the One to Say	1966	2.00	4.00	8.00
❑ Curtom 1979	Don't Have to Be Lyin' Babe (Part 1)/Don't Have to Be Lyin' Babe (Part 2)	1973	—	2.50	5.00
❑ Curtom 1986	Baby I Still Love You/I Understand	1973	—	2.50	5.00
❑ Curtom 1992	Without You Here/Just Be There	1973	—	2.50	5.00
❑ FastFire 7003	Haven't I Heard That Line Before/You'll Never Be Free of Me	1985	—	2.50	5.00
❑ FastFire 7005	Lucy/Please You Tonight	1986	—	2.50	5.00
❑ Lost-Nite 310	Duke of Earl/Rainbow	197?	—	2.50	5.00
❑ Mercury 73083	Groovy Situation/Not the Marrying Kind	1970	—	3.00	6.00
❑ Mercury 73121	Simply Call It Love/Give Me a Chance	1970	—	3.00	6.00
❑ Mercury 73206	You're a Lady/Stone Cold Feeling	1971	—	3.00	6.00
❑ Mercury 73258	Yes I'm Ready (If I Don't Get to Go)/Pillars of Glass	1971	—	3.00	6.00
❑ Salsoul 7051	You're the One/I Keep Comin' Back for More	1983	—	2.00	4.00
—With Jaime Lynn					
❑ 20th Century 2411	When You're #1/I'll Remember You	1979	—	2.00	4.00
❑ 20th Century 2428	Do What Comes So Natural/That Funky Disco Rhythm	1979	—	2.00	4.00
❑ Vee Jay 416	Duke of Earl/Kissin' in the Kitchen	1961	6.25	12.50	25.00
❑ Vee Jay 416	Duke of Earl/Kissin' in the Kitchen	1962	5.00	10.00	20.00
—Some later pressings as "The Duke of Earl"					
❑ Vee Jay 440	Walk On with the Duke/London Town	1962	3.75	7.50	15.00
—As "The Duke of Earl"					
❑ Vee Jay 450	Daddy's Home/The Big Lie	1962	3.75	7.50	15.00
—As "The Duke of Earl"					
❑ Vee Jay 455	I'll Follow You/You Left Me	1962	3.75	7.50	15.00
—As "The Duke of Earl"					
❑ Vee Jay 461	Tear for Tear/Miracle After Miracle	1962	3.75	7.50	15.00
❑ Vee Jay 468	You Threw a Lucky Punch/Rainbow	1962	3.75	7.50	15.00
❑ Vee Jay 511	Check Yourself/Forgive Me	1963	3.75	7.50	15.00
❑ Vee Jay 536	Baby, That's Love/Man's Temptation	1963	3.75	7.50	15.00
Albums					
❑ Brunswick BL 54124 [M]	The Girl Don't Care	1967	6.25	12.50	25.00
❑ Brunswick BL 754124 [S]	The Girl Don't Care	1967	5.00	10.00	20.00
❑ Brunswick BL 754131	There Was a Time	1968	5.00	10.00	20.00
❑ Brunswick BL 754149	The Two Sides of Gene Chandler	1969	5.00	10.00	20.00
❑ Checker LP-3003 [M]	The Duke of Soul	1967	12.50	25.00	50.00
❑ Checker LPS-3003 [R]	The Duke of Soul	1967	7.50	15.00	30.00
❑ Chi-Sound T-578	Get Down	1978	2.50	5.00	10.00
❑ Constellation LP 1421 [M]	Greatest Hits by Gene Chandler	1964	12.50	25.00	50.00
❑ Constellation LP 1423 [M]	Just Be True	1964	12.50	25.00	50.00
❑ Constellation LP 1425 [M]	Gene Chandler — Live On Stage in '65	1965	12.50	25.00	50.00
❑ Mercury SR-61304	The Gene Chandler Situation	1970	3.75	7.50	15.00
❑ Solid Smoke SS-8027	Stroll On with the Duke	198?	2.50	5.00	10.00
❑ 20th Century T-598	When You're #1	1979	2.50	5.00	10.00
❑ 20th Century T-605	Gene Chandler '80	1980	2.50	5.00	10.00
❑ 20th Century T-625	Ear Candy	1980	2.50	5.00	10.00
❑ 20th Century T-629	Here's to Love	1981	2.50	5.00	10.00
❑ Vee Jay LP-1040 [M]	The Duke of Earl	1962	30.00	60.00	120.00
❑ Vee Jay SR-1040 [M]	The Duke of Earl	196?	12.50	25.00	50.00
—"Stereophonic" on front; no "Important Notice..." on back; record plays mono. Most labels are all-black with "VJ" in brackets. This was a semi-authorized reissue after ex-Vee Jay executives bought the company's remnants in bankruptcy court in 1966.					
❑ Vee Jay SR-1040 [S]	The Duke of Earl	1962	62.50	125.00	250.00
—"Stereo" sticker on mono cover; "Stereo" on record labels					
❑ Vee Jay SR-1040 [S]	The Duke of Earl	1962	200.00	400.00	800.00
—"Stereophonic" on front cover; top back cover contains note that begins: "Important Notice...This Is a Stereophonic Record"; "Stereo" on record labels					

CHANDLER, GENE, AND JERRY BUTLER

45s

Number	Title (A Side/B Side)	Yr	VG	VG+	NM
❑ Mercury 73163	You Just Can't Win (By Making the Same Mistake)/ The Show Is Grooving	1971	—	3.00	6.00
❑ Mercury 73195	Two and Two (Take This Woman Off the Corner)/ Everybody Is Waiting	1971	—	3.00	6.00
Albums					
❑ Mercury SR-61330	Gene & Jerry — One & One	1971	3.75	7.50	15.00

CHANTAY'S

45s

Number	Title (A Side/B Side)	Yr	VG	VG+	NM
❑ Dot 145	Pipeline/Move It	1966	2.00	4.00	8.00
—Reissue; black label					

Number	Title (A Side/B Side)	Yr	VG	VG+	NM
❑ Dot 16440	Pipeline/Move It	1963	6.25	12.50	25.00
❑ Dot 16492	Monsoon/Scotch Highs	1963	5.00	10.00	20.00
❑ Downey 104	Pipeline/Move It	1963	15.00	30.00	60.00
❑ Downey 108	Monsoon/Scotch Highs	1963	7.50	15.00	30.00
❑ Downey 116	Space Probe/Continental Missile	1964	5.00	10.00	20.00
❑ Downey 120	Only If You Care/Love Can Be Cruel	1964	5.00	10.00	20.00
❑ Downey 126	Beyond/I'll Be Back Someday	1964	5.00	10.00	20.00
❑ Downey 130	Three Coins in the Fountain/Greens	1965	5.00	10.00	20.00
Albums					
❑ Dot DLP 3516 [M]	Pipeline	1963	12.50	25.00	50.00
❑ Dot DLP 3771 [M]	Two Sides of the Chantays	1966	12.50	25.00	50.00
❑ Dot DLP 25516 [S]	Pipeline	1963	20.00	40.00	80.00
❑ Dot DLP 25771 [S]	Two Sides of the Chantays	1966	20.00	40.00	80.00
❑ Downey DLP-1002 [M]	Pipeline	1963	55.00	110.00	220.00
❑ Downey DLPS-1002 [S]	Pipeline	1963	87.50	175.00	350.00
CHANTELS, THE					
45s					
❑ Carlton 555	Look in My Eyes/Glad to Be Back	1961	5.00	10.00	20.00
❑ Carlton 564	Still/Well, I Told You	1961	5.00	10.00	20.00
❑ Carlton 569	Summertime/Here It Comes Again	1962	5.00	10.00	20.00
❑ End 1001	He's Gone/The Plea	1957	20.00	40.00	80.00
—Black label					
❑ End 1001	He's Gone/The Plea	1959	5.00	10.00	20.00
—Multi-color label					
❑ End 1005	Maybe/Come My Little Baby	1957	20.00	40.00	80.00
—Black label					
❑ End 1005	Maybe/Come My Little Baby	1958	10.00	20.00	40.00
—Gray (white) label					
❑ End 1005	Maybe/Come My Little Baby	1959	5.00	10.00	20.00
—Multi-color label					
❑ End 1015	Every Night/Whoever You Are	1958	7.50	15.00	30.00
—Gray (white) label					
❑ End 1015	Every Night/Whoever You Are	1959	5.00	10.00	20.00
—Multi-color label					
❑ End 1020	I Love You So/How Could You Call It Off	1958	10.00	20.00	40.00
❑ End 1026	Prayer/Sure of Love	1958	6.25	12.50	25.00
❑ End 1030	If You Try/Congratulations	1958	6.25	12.50	25.00
❑ End 1037	Never Let Go/I Can't Take It	1959	6.25	12.50	25.00
❑ End 1048	I'm Confessin'/Goodbye to Love	1959	6.25	12.50	25.00
❑ End 1069	Whoever You Are/How Could You Call It Off	1960	6.25	12.50	25.00
❑ End 1103	Believe Me (My Angel)/I	1961	15.00	30.00	60.00
—Originally released on Princeton 102 as "The Veneers"					
❑ End 1105	There's Our Song Again/I'm the Girl	1961	6.25	12.50	25.00
❑ Ludix 101	Eternally/Swamp Water	1963	5.00	10.00	20.00
❑ Ludix 106	That's Why I'm Happy/Some Tears Fall Dry	1963	5.00	10.00	20.00
❑ RCA Victor 74-0347	I'm Gonna Win Him Back/Love Makes All the Difference in the World	1970	2.50	5.00	10.00
❑ Roulette 7064	Maybe/He's Gone	1969	2.50	5.00	10.00
❑ TCF Hall 123	Take Me As I Am/There's No Forgetting Me	1965	3.75	7.50	15.00
❑ Verve 10387	You're Welcome to My Heart/Soul of a Soldier	1966	3.75	7.50	15.00
❑ Verve 10435	Indian Giver/It's Just Me	1966	3.75	7.50	15.00
Albums					
❑ Carlton LP-144 [M]	The Chantels On Tour/Look in My Eyes	1962	50.00	100.00	200.00
❑ Carlton STLP-144 [P]	The Chantels On Tour/Look in My Eyes	1962	100.00	200.00	400.00
—Eight tracks are true stereo, two are mono, two are rechanneled					
❑ End LP-301 [M]	We Are the Chantels	1958	500.00	1000.	1500.
—Group photo on front cover; gray label with "11-17-58" in trail-off wax; VG value 500; VG+ value 1000					
❑ End LP-301 [M]	We Are the Chantels	1959	100.00	200.00	400.00
—Jukebox on front cover; gray label, "11-17-58" in trail-off wax					
❑ End LP-312 [M]	There's Our Song Again	1962	30.00	60.00	120.00
❑ Forum F-9104 [M]	The Chantels Sing Their Favorites	1964	12.50	25.00	50.00
❑ Forum FS-9104 [R]	The Chantels Sing Their Favorites	1964	6.25	12.50	25.00
CHAPIN, HARRY					
45s					
❑ Boardwalk NB7-11-119	Story of a Love/Salt and Pepper	1981	—	2.00	4.00
❑ Boardwalk 5700	Sequel/I Finally Found It Sandy	1980	—	2.00	4.00
❑ Boardwalk 5705	Remember When the Music/Northwest 222	1981	—	2.00	4.00
❑ Elektra 45203	Cat's in the Cradle/Vacancy	1974	—	2.00	4.00
❑ Elektra 45236	I Wanna Learn a Love Song/She Sings Songs Without Words	1975	—	2.00	4.00
❑ Elektra 45264	Dreams Go By/Sandy	1975	—	2.00	4.00
❑ Elektra 45285	Tangled-Up Puppet/Dirt Get Under the Fingernails	1975	—	2.00	4.00
❑ Elektra 45304	Star Tripper/The Rock	1976	—	2.00	4.00
❑ Elektra 45327	Better Place to Be (Part 1)/Better Place to Be (Part 2)	1976	—	2.00	4.00
❑ Elektra 45368	Corey's Coming/If My Mary Were Here	1976	—	2.00	4.00
❑ Elektra 45426	Dance Band on the Titanic/I Wonder What Happened to Him	1977	—	2.00	4.00
❑ Elektra 45445	My Old Lady/I'd Do It for You, Jane	1977	—	2.00	4.00
❑ Elektra 45497	I Wonder What Would Happen to This World/ If You Want to Feel	1978	—	2.00	4.00
❑ Elektra 45524	Flowers Are Red/Jenny	1978	—	2.00	4.00
❑ Elektra 45770	Taxi/Empty	1972	—	2.50	5.00
❑ Elektra 45792	Could You Put Your Light On, Please?/Any Old Kind of Day	1972	—	2.00	4.00
❑ Elektra 45811	Sunday Morning Sunshine/Burning Herself	1972	—	2.00	4.00
❑ Elektra 45828	Better Place to Be/Winter Song	1973	—	2.00	4.00
❑ Elektra 45874	WOLD/Short Stories	1973	—	2.00	4.00
❑ Elektra 45893	What Made America Famous/Old College Avenue	1974	—	2.00	4.00

Number	Title (A Side/B Side)	Yr	VG	VG+	NM
Albums					
❑ Boardwalk FW 36872	Sequel	1980	2.50	5.00	10.00
❑ Elektra 6E-142	Living Room Suite	1978	2.50	5.00	10.00
❑ Elektra 9E-301 [(2)]	Dance Band on the Titanic	1977	3.00	6.00	12.00
❑ Elektra BB-703 [(2)]	Legends of the Lost and Found — New Greatest Stories Live	1979	3.00	6.00	12.00
❑ Elektra 7E-1012	Verities & Balderdash	1974	2.50	5.00	10.00
❑ Elektra 7E-1041	Portrait Gallery	1975	2.50	5.00	10.00
❑ Elektra 7E-1082	On the Road to Kingdom Come	1976	2.50	5.00	10.00
❑ Elektra 7E-2009 [(2)]	Greatest Stories Live	1976	3.00	6.00	12.00
❑ Elektra 8E-6003 [(2)]	Greatest Stories Live	1978	2.50	5.00	10.00
—Reissue of 7E-2009					
❑ Elektra 60413	Anthology of Harry Chapin	1985	2.50	5.00	10.00
❑ Elektra EKS-75023	Heads and Tales	1972	2.50	5.00	10.00
❑ Elektra EKS-75042	Sniper and Other Love Songs	1972	2.50	5.00	10.00
❑ Elektra EKS-75065	Short Stories	1973	2.50	5.00	10.00
CHARLES, RAY					
45s					
❑ ABC 10808	Let's Go Get Stoned/At the Train	1966	2.00	4.00	8.00
❑ ABC 10840	I Chose to Sing the Blues/Hopelessly	1966	2.00	4.00	8.00
❑ ABC 10865	Please Say You're Fooling/I Don't Need No Doctor	1966	2.00	4.00	8.00
❑ ABC 10901	I Want to Talk About You/Something Inside Me	1967	2.00	4.00	8.00
❑ ABC 10938	Here We Go Again/Somebody Ought to Write a Book About It	1967	2.00	4.00	8.00
❑ ABC 10970	In the Heat of the Night/Somebody's Got to Change	1967	2.00	4.00	8.00
❑ ABC 11009	Yesterday/Never Had Enough of Nothing Yet	1967	2.00	4.00	8.00
❑ ABC 11045	That's a Lie/Go On Home	1968	2.00	4.00	8.00
❑ ABC 11090	Eleanor Rigby/Understanding	1968	2.00	4.00	8.00
❑ ABC 11133	Sweet Young Thing Like You/Listen, They're Playing Our Song	1968	2.00	4.00	8.00
❑ ABC 11170	If It Wasn't for Bad Luck/When I Stop Dreaming	1969	2.00	4.00	8.00
—With Jimmy Lewis					
❑ ABC 11193	I'll Be Your Servant/I Don't Know What Time It Was	1969	2.00	4.00	8.00
❑ ABC 11213	Let Me Love You/I'm Satisfied	1969	2.00	4.00	8.00
❑ ABC 11239	We Can Make It/I Can't Stop Loving You Baby	1969	2.00	4.00	8.00
❑ ABC 11251	Someone to Watch Over Me/Claudie Mae	1969	2.00	4.00	8.00
❑ ABC 11259	Laughin' and Clownin'/That Thing Called Love	1970	2.00	4.00	8.00
❑ ABC 11271	If You Were Mine/Till I Can't Take It Anymore	1970	2.00	4.00	8.00
❑ ABC 11291	Don't Change on Me/Sweet Memories	1971	2.00	4.00	8.00
❑ ABC 11308	Feel So Bad/Your Love Is So Doggone Good	1971	—	3.00	6.00
❑ ABC 11317	What Am I Living For/Tired of My Tears	1971	—	3.00	6.00
❑ ABC 11329	Look What They've Done to My Song, Ma/America the Beautiful	1972	2.50	5.00	10.00
❑ ABC 11337	Hey Mister/There'll Be No Peace Without All Men as One	1972	—	3.00	6.00
❑ ABC 11344	Every Saturday Night/Take Me Home, Country Roads	1973	—	3.00	6.00
❑ ABC 11351	I Can Make It Through the Days (But Oh Those Lonely Nights)/Ring of Fire	1973	—	3.00	6.00
❑ ABC-Paramount 10081	My Baby/Who You Gonna Love	1960	3.75	7.50	15.00
❑ ABC-Paramount 10118	Sticks and Stones/Worried Life Blues	1960	3.00	6.00	12.00
❑ ABC-Paramount 10135	Georgia on My Mind/Carry Me Back to Old Virginny	1960	3.75	7.50	15.00
❑ ABC-Paramount 10141	Them That Got/I Wonder	1960	3.00	6.00	12.00
❑ ABC-Paramount 10164	Ruby/Heard Hearted Woman	1960	3.00	6.00	12.00
❑ ABC-Paramount 10244	Hit the Road Jack/The Danger Zone	1961	3.75	7.50	15.00
❑ ABC-Paramount 10266	Unchain My Heart/But on the Other Hand, Baby	1961	3.75	7.50	15.00
❑ ABC-Paramount 10314	Hide 'Nor Hair/At the Club	1962	3.00	6.00	12.00
❑ ABC-Paramount 10330	I Can't Stop Loving You/Born to Lose	1962	3.75	7.50	15.00
❑ ABC-Paramount 10345	You Don't Know Me/Careless Love	1962	3.75	7.50	15.00
❑ ABC-Paramount 10375	You Are My Sunshine/Your Cheating Heart	1962	3.00	6.00	12.00
❑ ABC-Paramount 10405	Don't Set Me Free/The Brightest Smile in Town	1963	3.00	6.00	12.00
❑ ABC-Paramount 10435	Take These Chains from My Heart/No Letter Today	1963	3.75	7.50	15.00
❑ ABC-Paramount 10453	No One/Without Love (There Is Nothing)	1963	3.00	6.00	12.00
❑ ABC-Paramount 10481	Busted/Making Believe	1963	3.75	7.50	15.00
❑ ABC-Paramount 10509	That Lucky Old Sun/Ol' Man Time	1963	3.00	6.00	12.00
❑ ABC-Paramount 10530	Baby Don't You Cry/My Heart Cries for You	1964	3.00	6.00	12.00
❑ ABC-Paramount 10557	My Baby Don't Dig Me/Something's Wrong	1964	3.00	6.00	12.00
❑ ABC-Paramount 10571	No One to Cry To/A Tear Fell	1964	3.00	6.00	12.00
❑ ABC-Paramount 10588	Smack Dab in the Middle/I Wake Up Crying	1964	3.00	6.00	12.00
❑ ABC-Paramount 10609	Makin' Whoopee/(Instrumental)	1964	3.00	6.00	12.00
❑ ABC-Paramount 10615	Cry/Teardrops from My Eyes	1965	3.00	6.00	12.00
❑ ABC-Paramount 10649	I Gotta Woman (Part 1)/I Gotta Woman (Part 2)	1965	3.00	6.00	12.00

Number	Title (A Side/B Side)	Yr	VG	VG+	NM
❑ ABC-Paramount 10663	Without a Song (Part 1)/Without a Song (Part 2)	1965	3.00	6.00	12.00
❑ ABC-Paramount 10700	I'm a Fool to Care/Love's Gonna Live Here	1965	3.00	6.00	12.00
❑ ABC-Paramount 10720	The Cincinnati Kid/That's All I Am to You	1965	3.00	6.00	12.00
❑ ABC-Paramount 10739	Crying Time/When My Dreamboat Comes Home	1965	3.75	7.50	15.00
❑ ABC-Paramount 10785	Together Again/You're Just About to Lose Your Clown	1966	3.00	6.00	12.00
❑ Atlantic 976	Roll with Me Baby/The Midnight Hour	1952	125.00	250.00	500.00
❑ Atlantic 984	The Sun's Gonna Shine Again/Jumpin' in the Morning	1953	100.00	200.00	400.00
❑ Atlantic 999	Mess Around/Funny (But I Still Love You)	1953	50.00	100.00	200.00
❑ Atlantic 1008	Feelin' Sad/Heartbreaker	1953	25.00	50.00	100.00
❑ Atlantic 1021	It Should've Been Me/Sinner's Prayer	1954	12.50	25.00	50.00
❑ Atlantic 1037	Don't You Know/Losing Hand	1954	7.50	15.00	30.00
❑ Atlantic 1050	I've Got a Woman/Come Back	1954	12.50	25.00	50.00
❑ Atlantic 1063	This Little Girl of Mine/A Fool for You	1955	7.50	15.00	30.00
❑ Atlantic 1076	Blackjack/Greenbacks	1955	7.50	15.00	30.00
❑ Atlantic 1085	Drown in My Own Tears/Mary Ann	1956	6.25	12.50	25.00
❑ Atlantic 1096	Hallelujah, I Love Her So/What Would I Do Without You	1956	5.00	10.00	20.00
❑ Atlantic 1108	Lonely Avenue/Leave My Woman Alone	1956	5.00	10.00	20.00
❑ Atlantic 1124	I Want to Know/Ain't That Love	1957	5.00	10.00	20.00
❑ Atlantic 1143	It's All Right/Get On the Right Track Baby	1957	5.00	10.00	20.00
❑ Atlantic 1154	Swanee River Rock (Talkin' 'Bout That River)/I Want a Little Girl	1957	5.00	10.00	20.00
❑ Atlantic 1172	Talkin' 'Bout You/What Kind of a Man Are You	1958	3.75	7.50	15.00
❑ Atlantic 1180	Yes Indeed/I Had a Dream	1958	3.75	7.50	15.00
—With the Cookies					
❑ Atlantic 1196	My Bonnie/You Be My Baby	1958	3.75	7.50	15.00
❑ Atlantic 2006	Rockhouse (Part 1)/Rockhouse (Part 2)	1958	3.75	7.50	15.00
❑ Atlantic 2010	(Night Time Is) The Right Time/Tell All the World About You	1959	3.75	7.50	15.00
❑ Atlantic 2022	Tell Me How Do You Feel/That's Enough	1959	3.75	7.50	15.00
❑ Atlantic 2031	What'd I Say (Part I)/What'd I Say (Part II)	1959	5.00	10.00	20.00
❑ Atlantic 2043	I'm Movin' On/I Believe to My Soul	1959	3.00	6.00	12.00
❑ Atlantic 2047	Let the Good Times Roll/Don't Let the Sun Catch You Cryin'	1960	3.00	6.00	12.00
❑ Atlantic 2055	Heartbreaker/Just for a Thrill	1960	3.00	6.00	12.00
❑ Atlantic 2068	Tell the Truth/Sweet Sixteen Bars	1960	3.00	6.00	12.00
❑ Atlantic 2084	Come Rain or Come Shine/Tell Me You'll Wait for Me	1960	3.00	6.00	12.00
❑ Atlantic 2094	Early in the Morning/A Bit of Soul	1961	3.00	6.00	12.00
❑ Atlantic 2106	Am I Blue/It Should've Been Me	1961	3.00	6.00	12.00
❑ Atlantic 2118	I Wonder Who/Hard Times (No One Knows Better Than I)	1961	3.00	6.00	12.00
❑ Atlantic 2174	Carryin' That Load/Feelin' Sad	1963	2.50	5.00	10.00
❑ Atlantic 2239	Talkin' 'Bout You/In a Little Spanish Town	1964	2.50	5.00	10.00
❑ Atlantic 2470	Come Rain or Come Shine/Tell Me You'll Wait for Me	1968	2.50	5.00	10.00
❑ Atlantic 3443	I Can See Clearly Now/Anonymous Love	1977	—	2.50	5.00
❑ Atlantic 3473	A Peace That We Never Could Enjoy/Game Number Nine	1978	—	2.50	5.00
❑ Atlantic 3527	Riding Thumb/You Forgot Your Memories	1978	—	2.50	5.00
❑ Atlantic 3611	Some Enchanted Evening/20th Century Fox	1979	—	2.50	5.00
❑ Atlantic 3634	Just Because/Love Me or Set Me Free	1979	—	2.50	5.00
❑ Atlantic 3762	Compared To What/Now That We've Found Each Other	1980	—	2.50	5.00
❑ Atlantic 5005	Doodlin' (Part 1)/Doodlin' (Part 2)	1960	3.75	7.50	15.00
❑ Baronet 7111	See See Rider/I Used to be So Happy	1960	3.00	6.00	12.00
❑ Columbia 38-03429	String Bean/Born to Love Me	1982	—	2.00	4.00
❑ Columbia 38-03810	You Feel Good All Over/ 3/4 Time	1983	—	—	3.00
❑ Columbia 38-04083	Ain't Your Memory Got No Pride at All/I Don't Want No Strangers Sleeping in My Bed	1983	—	—	3.00
❑ Columbia 38-04297	We Didn't See a Thing/I Wish You Were Here Tonight	1983	—	—	3.00
—A-side with George Jones and Chet Atkins					
❑ Columbia 38-04420	Do I Ever Cross Your Mind/They Call It Love	1984	—	—	3.00
❑ Columbia 38-04500	Woman (Sensuous Woman)/I Was On Georgia Time	1984	—	—	3.00
❑ Columbia 38-04531	Rock and Roll Shoes/Then I'll Be Over You	1984	—	—	3.00
—Ray Charles and B.J. Thomas					
❑ Columbia 38-04715	Seven Spanish Angels/Who Cares	1984	—	—	3.00
—A-side with Willie Nelson; B-side with Janie Frickie					
❑ Columbia 38-04860	It Ain't Gonna Worry My Mind/Crazy Old Soldier	1985	—	—	3.00
—A-side with Mickey Gilley; B-side with Johnny Cash					
❑ Columbia 38-05575	Two Old Cats Like Us/Little Hotel Room	1985	—	—	3.00
—A-side with Hank Williams, Jr.; B-side with Merle Haggard					
❑ Columbia 38-06172	Pages of My Mind/Slip Away	1986	—	—	3.00
❑ Columbia 38-06370	Dixie Moon/A Little Bit of Heaven	1986	—	—	3.00
❑ Columbia 38-08393	Seven Spanish Angels/It Ain't Gonna Worry My Mind	1988	—	—	3.00
—Reissue; A-side with Willie Nelson, B-side with Mickey Gilley					
❑ Crossover 973	Come Live with Me/Everybody Sing	1973	—	2.50	5.00
❑ Crossover 974	Louise/Somebody	1974	—	2.50	5.00
❑ Crossover 981	Living for the City/Then We'll Be Home	1975	—	2.50	5.00
❑ Crossover 985	America the Beautiful/Sunshine	1976	—	3.00	6.00
—A-side is a different recording than that on the B-side of ABC 11329					
❑ Impulse! 200	One Mint Julep/Let's Go	1961	2.50	5.00	10.00
❑ Impulse! 202	I've Got News for You/I'm Gonna Move to the Outskirts of Town	1961	2.50	5.00	10.00
❑ RCA PB-10800	Oh Lawd, I'm On My Way/Oh Bess, Where's My Bess	1976	—	2.50	5.00
❑ Rockin' 504	Walkin' and Talkin' (To Myself)/I'm Wonderin' and Wonderin'	1952	75.00	150.00	300.00
❑ Sittin' In With 641	Baby Let Me Hear You Call My Name/Guitar Blues	1952	75.00	150.00	300.00
❑ Swing Time 250	Baby, Let Me Hold Your Hand/Lonely Boy	1951	125.00	250.00	500.00
—Ray Charles records on Swing Time before 250 are unconfirmed on 45 rpm					
❑ Swing Time 274	Kissa Me Baby/I'm Glad for Your Sake	1952	125.00	250.00	500.00
❑ Swing Time 300	Baby Let Me Hear You Call My Name/Guitar Blues	1952	125.00	250.00	500.00
❑ Swing Time 326	The Snow Is Falling/Misery in My Heart	1953	125.00	250.00	500.00
❑ Tangerine 1015	Booty Butt/Sidewinder	1971	—	3.00	6.00
❑ Time 1026	I Found My Baby/Guitar Blues	1960	3.75	7.50	15.00
❑ Time 1054	Why Did You Go/Back Home	1962	3.00	6.00	12.00
❑ Warner Bros. 18611	A Song for You/I Can't Get Enough	1993	—	—	3.00
❑ Warner Bros. 49608	Beers to You/Cotton-Eyed Clint	1980	—	2.50	5.00
—A-side with Clint Eastwood; B-side by Texas Opera Company					

Number	Title (A Side/B Side)	Yr	VG	VG+	NM
Albums					
❑ ABC 590X [(2)M]	A Man and His Soul	1967	3.75	7.50	15.00
❑ ABC S-590X [(2)S]	A Man and His Soul	1967	5.00	10.00	20.00
❑ ABC 595 [M]	Ray Charles Invites You to Listen	1967	5.00	10.00	20.00
❑ ABC S-595 [S]	Ray Charles Invites You to Listen	1967	3.75	7.50	15.00
❑ ABC S-625	A Portrait of Ray	1968	3.00	6.00	12.00
❑ ABC S-675	I'm All Yours — Baby!	1969	3.00	6.00	12.00
❑ ABC S-695	Doing His Thing	1969	3.00	6.00	12.00
❑ ABC S-707	Love Country Style	1971	3.00	6.00	12.00
❑ ABC S-726	Volcanic Action of My Soul	1971	3.00	6.00	12.00
❑ ABC H-731 [(2)]	A 25th Anniversary in Show Business Salute to Ray Charles	1971	3.75	7.50	15.00
❑ ABC X-755	A Message from the People	1972	3.00	6.00	12.00
❑ ABC X-765	Through the Eyes of Love	1972	3.00	6.00	12.00
❑ ABC X-781/2 [(2)]	All-Time Great Country & Western Hits	1973	3.75	7.50	15.00
❑ ABC-Paramount 335 [M]	The Genius Hits the Road	1960	5.00	10.00	20.00
❑ ABC-Paramount S-335 [S]	The Genius Hits the Road	1960	7.50	15.00	30.00
❑ ABC-Paramount 355 [M]	Dedicated to You	1961	5.00	10.00	20.00
❑ ABC-Paramount S-355 [S]	Dedicated to You	1961	7.50	15.00	30.00
❑ ABC-Paramount 410 [M]	Modern Sounds in Country and Western Music	1962	6.25	12.50	25.00
❑ ABC-Paramount S-410 [S]	Modern Sounds in Country and Western Music	1962	7.50	15.00	30.00
❑ ABC-Paramount 415 [M]	Ray Charles' Greatest Hits	1962	5.00	10.00	20.00
❑ ABC-Paramount S-415 [S]	Ray Charles' Greatest Hits	1962	6.25	12.50	25.00
❑ ABC-Paramount 435 [M]	Modern Sounds in Country and Western Music (Volume Two)	1962	5.00	10.00	20.00
❑ ABC-Paramount S-435 [S]	Modern Sounds in Country and Western Music (Volume Two)	1962	6.25	12.50	25.00
❑ ABC-Paramount 465 [M]	Ingredients in a Recipe for Soul	1963	5.00	10.00	20.00
❑ ABC-Paramount S-465 [S]	Ingredients in a Recipe for Soul	1963	6.25	12.50	25.00
❑ ABC-Paramount 480 [M]	Sweet & Sour Tears	1964	5.00	10.00	20.00
❑ ABC-Paramount S-480 [S]	Sweet & Sour Tears	1964	6.25	12.50	25.00
❑ ABC-Paramount 495 [M]	Have a Smile with Me	1964	5.00	10.00	20.00
❑ ABC-Paramount S-495 [S]	Have a Smile with Me	1964	6.25	12.50	25.00
❑ ABC-Paramount 500 [M]	Ray Charles Live in Concert	1965	3.75	7.50	15.00
❑ ABC-Paramount S-500 [S]	Ray Charles Live in Concert	1965	5.00	10.00	20.00
❑ ABC-Paramount 520 [M]	Country & Western Meets Rhythm & Blues	1965	3.75	7.50	15.00
❑ ABC-Paramount S-520 [S]	Country & Western Meets Rhythm & Blues	1965	5.00	10.00	20.00
❑ ABC-Paramount 544 [M]	Crying Time	1966	3.75	7.50	15.00
❑ ABC-Paramount S-544 [S]	Crying Time	1966	5.00	10.00	20.00
❑ ABC-Paramount 550 [M]	Ray's Moods	1966	3.75	7.50	15.00
❑ ABC-Paramount S-550 [S]	Ray's Moods	1966	5.00	10.00	20.00
❑ Atlantic SD 2-503 [(2)]	Ray Charles Live	1973	3.75	7.50	15.00
❑ Atlantic 2-900 [(2)M]	The Ray Charles Story	1962	10.00	20.00	40.00
❑ Atlantic 1259 [M]	The Great Ray Charles	1957	12.50	25.00	50.00
—Black label					
❑ Atlantic SD 1259 [S]	The Great Ray Charles	1959	12.50	25.00	50.00
—Green label					
❑ Atlantic 1289 [M]	Ray Charles at Newport	1958	12.50	25.00	50.00
—Black label					
❑ Atlantic SD 1289 [S]	Ray Charles at Newport	1959	12.50	25.00	50.00
—Green label					
❑ Atlantic 1312 [M]	The Genius of Ray Charles	1960	10.00	20.00	40.00
—Black label					
❑ Atlantic SD 1312 [S]	The Genius of Ray Charles	1960	12.50	25.00	50.00
—Green label					
❑ Atlantic 1369 [M]	The Genius After Hours	1961	6.25	12.50	25.00
—Red and white label, white fan logo on right					
❑ Atlantic SD 1369 [S]	The Genius After Hours	1961	7.50	15.00	30.00
—Blue and green label, white fan logo on right					
❑ Atlantic SD 1543	The Best of Ray Charles	1970	3.00	6.00	12.00
❑ Atlantic 3700 [(6)]	Ray Charles: A Life in Music	198?	12.50	25.00	50.00
❑ Atlantic SD 7101 [S]	The Great Hits of Ray Charles Recorded on 8-Track Stereo	1966	6.25	12.50	25.00
❑ Atlantic 8006 [M]	Ray Charles (Rock and Roll)	1957	22.50	45.00	90.00
—Black label					
❑ Atlantic 8025 [M]	Yes, Indeed!	1958	12.50	25.00	50.00
—Black label; cover has screaming girls					
❑ Atlantic 8029 [M]	What'd I Say	1959	12.50	25.00	50.00
—Black label					
❑ Atlantic 8039 [M]	Ray Charles In Person	1960	10.00	20.00	40.00
—Black label					

Number	Title (A Side/B Side)	Yr	VG	VG+	NM
❑ Atlantic 8052 [M]	The Genius Sings the Blues	1961	6.25	12.50	25.00
—Red and white label, white fan logo on right					
❑ Atlantic 8054 [M]	Do the Twist!	1961	6.25	12.50	25.00
—Red and white label, white fan logo on right					
❑ Atlantic 8063 [M]	The Ray Charles Story, Volume 1	1962	5.00	10.00	20.00
❑ Atlantic 8064 [M]	The Ray Charles Story, Volume 2	1962	5.00	10.00	20.00
❑ Atlantic 8083 [M]	The Ray Charles Story, Volume 3	1963	5.00	10.00	20.00
❑ Atlantic 8094 [M]	The Ray Charles Story, Volume 4	1964	5.00	10.00	20.00
❑ Atlantic SD 8094 [S]	The Ray Charles Story, Volume 4	1964	6.25	12.50	25.00
❑ Atlantic SD 19142	True to Life	1977	3.00	6.00	12.00
❑ Atlantic SD 19199	Love and Peace	1978	3.00	6.00	12.00
❑ Atlantic SD 19251	Ain't It So	1979	3.00	6.00	12.00
❑ Atlantic SD 19281	Brother Ray Is At It Again	1980	3.00	6.00	12.00
❑ Atlantic 90464	The Genius After Hours	1986	2.50	5.00	10.00
—Reissue					
❑ Baronet B-111 [M]	The Artistry of Ray Charles	196?	3.00	6.00	12.00
❑ Baronet BS-111 [R]	The Artistry of Ray Charles	196?	2.50	5.00	10.00
❑ Baronet B-117 [M]	The Great Ray Charles	196?	3.00	6.00	12.00
❑ Baronet BS-117 [R]	The Great Ray Charles	196?	2.50	5.00	10.00
❑ BluesWay 6053	The Genius Live	1973	3.00	6.00	12.00
❑ Columbia FC 38293	Wish You Were Here Tonight	1983	2.50	5.00	10.00
❑ Columbia FC 38990	Do I Ever Cross Your Mind	1984	2.50	5.00	10.00
❑ Columbia FC 39415	Friendship	1985	2.50	5.00	10.00
❑ Columbia FC 40125	The Spirit of Christmas	1985	2.50	5.00	10.00
❑ Columbia FC 40338	From the Pages of My Mind	1986	2.50	5.00	10.00
❑ Columbia FC 45062	Seven Spanish Angels and Other Hits (1982-1986)	1989	3.00	6.00	12.00
❑ Coronet CX-173 [M]	Ray Charles	196?	3.00	6.00	12.00
❑ Coronet CXS-173 [R]	Ray Charles	196?	2.50	5.00	10.00
❑ Crossover 9000	Come Live with Me	1974	3.00	6.00	12.00
❑ Crossover 9005	Renaissance	1975	3.00	6.00	12.00
❑ Crossover 9007	My Kind of Jazz, Part 3	1976	3.00	6.00	12.00
❑ Everest Archive of Folk & Jazz 244	Ray Charles	1970	3.00	6.00	12.00
❑ Everest Archive of Folk & Jazz 292	Ray Charles, Vol. 2	197?	2.50	5.00	10.00
❑ Everest Archive of Folk & Jazz 358	Rockin' with Ray	1979	2.50	5.00	10.00
❑ Hollywood 504 [M]	The Original Ray Charles	1959	37.50	75.00	150.00
❑ Hollywood 505 [M]	The Fabuolus Ray Charles	1959	37.50	75.00	150.00
❑ Impulse! A-2 [M]	Genius + Soul = Jazz	1961	6.25	12.50	25.00
❑ Impulse! AS-2 [S]	Genius + Soul = Jazz	1961	7.50	15.00	30.00
❑ Intermedia QS-5013	Goin' Down Slow	198?	2.50	5.00	10.00
❑ Pair PDL2-1139 [(2)]	The Real Ray Charles	1986	3.00	6.00	12.00
❑ Premier PM 2004 [M]	The Great Ray Charles	196?	3.00	6.00	12.00
❑ Premier PS 2004 [R]	The Great Ray Charles	196?	2.50	5.00	10.00
❑ Premier PS-6001 [R]	Fantastic Ray Charles	196?	2.50	5.00	10.00
❑ Rhino R1-70097	Greatest Hits, Volume 1	1988	2.50	5.00	10.00
❑ Rhino R1-70098	Greatest Hits, Volume 2	1988	2.50	5.00	10.00
❑ Rhino R1-70099	Modern Sounds in Country and Western Music	1988	2.50	5.00	10.00
❑ Tangerine 1512	My Kind of Jazz	1970	3.00	6.00	12.00
❑ Tangerine 1516	My Kind of Jazz No. II	1973	3.00	6.00	12.00
❑ Warner Bros. 26343	Would You Believe?	1990	3.75	7.50	15.00

CHEAP TRICK

45s

Number	Title (A Side/B Side)	Yr	VG	VG+	NM
❑ Asylum 47187	Reach Out/I Must Be Dreamin'	1981	—	2.00	4.00
❑ Columbia 38-06137	Mighty Wings/Dog Fight #3	1986	—	—	3.00
—B-side by Harold Faltermeyer					
❑ Epic 14-02968	If You Want My Love/Four Letter Word	1982	—	2.50	5.00
❑ Epic 34-03233	She's Tight/All I Really Want to Do	1982	—	2.00	4.00
❑ Epic 34-03741	Saturday at Midnight/One on One	1983	—	2.00	4.00
❑ Epic 15-03845	If You Want My Love/She's Tight	1983	—	2.00	4.00
—Reissue					
❑ Epic 34-04078	Dancing the Night Away/Don't Make Our Love a Crime	1983	—	2.00	4.00
❑ Epic 34-04216	I Can't Take It/You Talk Too Much	1983	—	2.00	4.00
❑ Epic 34-05431	Tonight It's You/Wild, Wild Women	1985	—	2.00	4.00
❑ Epic 34-06540	It's Only Love/Name of the Game	1987	—	2.00	4.00
❑ Epic 34-07745	The Flame/Through the Night	1988	—	—	3.00
—Custom label					
❑ Epic 34-07965	Don't Be Cruel/I Know What I Want	1988	—	—	3.00
❑ Epic 34-08097	Ghost Town/Wrong Side of Love	1988	—	—	3.00
❑ Epic 8-50375	Oh, Candy/Daddy Should Have Stayed in High School	1977	2.50	5.00	10.00
❑ Epic 8-50435	I Want You to Want Me/Oh Boy	1977	2.50	5.00	10.00
❑ Epic 8-50485	Southern Girls/You're All Talk	1977	2.50	5.00	10.00
❑ Epic 8-50570	Surrender/Auf Wiedersehn	1978	2.50	5.00	10.00
❑ Epic 8-50625	California Man/I Want You to Want Me	1978	2.50	5.00	10.00
—B-side was first American issue of version that became a hit on Epic 50680					
❑ Epic 8-50680	I Want You to Want Me/Clock Strikes Ten	1979	—	2.00	4.00
❑ Epic 9-50743	Ain't That a Shame/Elo Kiddies	1979	—	2.50	5.00
❑ Epic 9-50774	Dream Police/Heaven Tonight	1979	—	2.50	5.00
❑ Epic 9-50814	Voices/The House Is Rockin' (With Domestic Problems)	1979	—	2.00	4.00
❑ Epic 9-50887	Everything Works If You Let It/Way of the World	1980	—	2.50	5.00
❑ Epic 19-50942	Stop This Game/Who D'King	1980	—	2.50	5.00
❑ Epic 19-50970	The World's Greatest Lover/High Priest of Rhythmic Noise	1981	—	2.50	5.00
❑ Epic 34-68563	Never Had a Lot to Lose/All We Need Is a Dream	1989	—	—	3.00
❑ Epic 34-73444	Can't Stop Fallin' Into Love/You Drive, I'll Steer	1990	—	—	3.00
❑ Epic 34-73580	Wherever Would I Be/Busted	1990	—	—	3.00

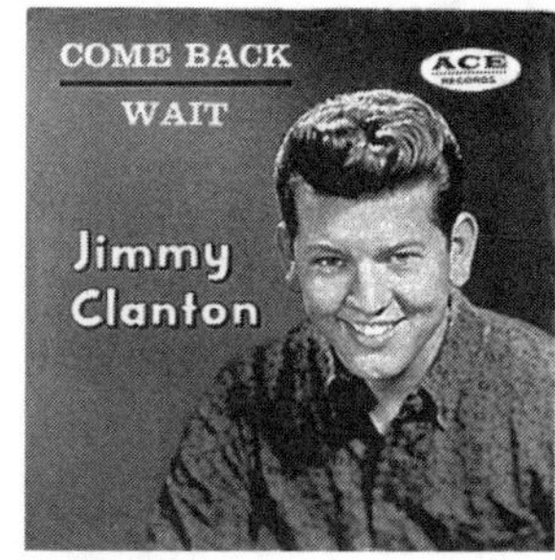

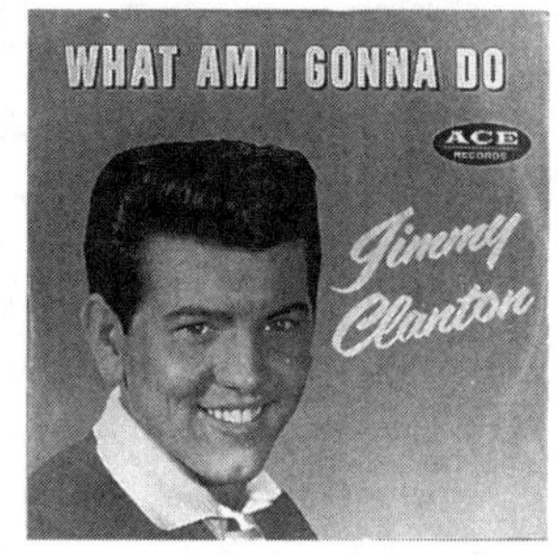

Number	Title (A Side/B Side)	Yr	VG	VG+	NM
❑ Epic 34-73792	The Flame/Through the Night	1991	—	—	3.00
—Reissue					
❑ Pasha ZS4-04392	Up the Creek/Passion in the Dark (One Track Heart)	1984	—	2.00	4.00
—B-side by Danny Spanos					
❑ Warner Bros. 29723	Spring Break/Get Ready	1983	—	3.00	6.00
Albums					
❑ Epic PE 34400	Cheap Trick	1976	3.00	6.00	12.00
—Originals have orange labels					
❑ Epic JE 34884	In Color	1977	3.00	6.00	12.00
—Originals have orange labels					
❑ Epic JE 35312	Heaven Tonight	1978	3.00	6.00	12.00
—Originals have orange labels					
❑ Epic FE 35773	Dream Police	1979	2.50	5.00	10.00
—Despite lower number, this came out after Epic 35795					
❑ Epic FE 35795	Cheap Trick at Budokan	1979	3.00	6.00	12.00
—Orange label; came with gold-colored obi (add 5/6 if there) and booklet (deduct 1/6 if missing)					
❑ Epic FE 36498	All Shook Up	1980	2.50	5.00	10.00
❑ Epic FE 38021	One on One	1982	2.50	5.00	10.00
❑ Epic PE 38541 [EP]	Found All the Parts	1983	2.00	4.00	8.00
—Six-song reissue of Epic/Nu-Disk release on 12-inch LP					
❑ Epic FE 38794	Next Position Please	1983	2.50	5.00	10.00
❑ Epic FE 39592	Standing on the Edge	1985	2.50	5.00	10.00
❑ Epic FE 40405	The Doctor	1986	2.50	5.00	10.00
❑ Epic OE 40922	Lap of Luxury	1988	2.50	5.00	10.00
❑ Epic E 46013	Busted	1990	3.00	6.00	12.00
❑ Epic/Nu-Disk 4E 36453 [10]	Found All the Parts	1980	3.75	7.50	15.00
—10-inch, four-track EP with bonus 45, "Everything Works If You Let It" (AE7 1206)					

CHECKER, CHUBBY

Number	Title (A Side/B Side)	Yr	VG	VG+	NM
45s					
❑ Abkco 4001	The Twist/Loddy Lo	1972	—	2.50	5.00
❑ Abkco 4002	The Hucklebuck/Pony Time	1972	—	2.50	5.00
❑ Abkco 4003	Limbo Rock/Let's Twist Again	1972	—	2.50	5.00
❑ Abkco 4004	Hey Bobba Needle/Hooka Tooka	1972	—	2.50	5.00
❑ Abkco 4027	Slow Twistin'/Birdland	1973	—	2.50	5.00
❑ Amherst 716	The Rub/Move It	1976	—	2.00	4.00
❑ Buddah 100	Back in the U.S.S.R./Windy Cream	1969	3.00	6.00	12.00
❑ MCA 51233	Running/Is Tonight the Night	1982	—	2.50	5.00
❑ MCA 52015	Running/Is Tonight the Night	1982	—	2.00	4.00
❑ MCA 52043	Harder Than Diamond/Your Love	1982	—	2.00	4.00
❑ Parkway 105	You Got the Power/Looking at Tomorrow	1966	3.75	7.50	15.00
❑ Parkway 112	Karate Monkey/Her Heart	1966	3.75	7.50	15.00
❑ Parkway 804	The Class/Schooldays, Oh Schooldays	1959	7.50	15.00	30.00
❑ Parkway 808	Samson and Delilah/Whole Lotta Laughin'	1959	6.25	12.50	25.00
❑ Parkway 810	Dancing Dinosaur/Those Private Eyes (Keep Watchin' Me)	1960	6.25	12.50	25.00
—The existence of both 808 and 810 has been confirmed					
❑ Parkway 811	The Twist/Toot	1960	7.50	15.00	30.00
—First pressings have white label with blue print					
❑ Parkway 811	The Twist/Twistin' U.S.A.	1961	3.75	7.50	15.00
❑ Parkway 813	The Hucklebuck/Whole Lotta Shakin' Goin' On	1960	3.75	7.50	15.00
❑ Parkway 818	Pony Time/Oh, Susannah	1960	3.75	7.50	15.00
❑ Parkway 822	Dance the Mess Around/Good, Good Lovin'	1961	3.75	7.50	15.00
❑ Parkway 824	Let's Twist Again/Everything's Gonna Be Alright	1961	3.75	7.50	15.00
❑ Parkway 830	The Fly/That's the Way It Goes	1961	3.75	7.50	15.00
❑ Parkway 835	Slow Twistin'/La Paloma Twist	1962	3.75	7.50	15.00
—Features female vocal by Dee Dee Sharp					
❑ Parkway 842	Dancin' Party/Gotta Get Myself Together	1962	3.75	7.50	15.00
❑ Parkway 849	Limbo Rock/Popeye The Hitch-Hiker	1962	3.75	7.50	15.00
❑ Parkway 862	Twenty Miles/Let's Limbo Some More	1963	3.75	7.50	15.00
❑ Parkway 873	Birdland/Black Cloud	1963	3.75	7.50	15.00
❑ Parkway 879	Surf Party/Twist It Up	1963	3.75	7.50	15.00
❑ Parkway 890	Loddy Lo/Everything's Gonna Be Alright	1963	4.00	8.00	16.00
❑ Parkway 890	Loddy Lo/Hooka Tooka	1963	3.75	7.50	15.00
❑ Parkway 907	Hey Bobba Needle/Spread Joy	1964	3.75	7.50	15.00
❑ Parkway 920	Lazy Elsie Molly/Rosie	1964	3.75	7.50	15.00
❑ Parkway 922	She Wants T'Swim/You Better Believe It, Baby	1964	3.00	6.00	12.00

Number	Title (A Side/B Side)	Yr	VG	VG+	NM
❑ Parkway 936	Lovely, Lovely (Loverly, Loverly)/The Weekend's Here	1964	3.00	6.00	12.00
❑ Parkway 949	Let's Do the Freddie/(At the) Discotheque	1965	3.00	6.00	12.00
—Original A-side title (number is P-949-A) and probably correct B-side title					
❑ Parkway 959	Everything's Wrong/Cu Me La Be-Stay	1965	12.50	25.00	50.00
❑ Parkway 965	You Just Don't Know/Two Hearts Make One Love	1965	375.00	750.00	1500.
❑ Parkway 989	Hey You! Little Boo-Ga-Loo/Pussy Cat	1966	3.00	6.00	12.00
❑ Sea Bright 5128	Read You Like a Book/(B-side unknown)	1986	—	2.00	4.00
❑ 20th Century 2040	Reggae My Way/Gypsy	1973	—	2.50	5.00
❑ 20th Century 2075	She's a Bad Woman/Happiness Is a Girl Like You	1974	—	2.50	5.00
Albums					
❑ Abkco 4219 [(2)]	Chubby Checker's Greatest Hits	1972	5.00	10.00	20.00
❑ Everest 4111	Chubby Checker's Greatest Hits	1981	3.00	6.00	12.00
❑ MCA 5291	The Change Has Come	1982	2.50	5.00	10.00
❑ Parkway P 7001 [M]	Twist with Chubby Checker	1960	10.00	20.00	40.00
—All-orange label					
❑ Parkway P 7002 [M]	For Twisters Only	1960	10.00	20.00	40.00
—All-orange label					
❑ Parkway P 7003 [M]	It's Pony Time	1961	10.00	20.00	40.00
—All-orange label					
❑ Parkway P 7004 [M]	Let's Twist Again	1961	10.00	20.00	40.00
—All-orange label					
❑ Parkway P 7007 [M]	Your Twist Party	1961	10.00	20.00	40.00
—All-orange label					
❑ Parkway P 7008 [M]	Twistin' Round the World	1962	7.50	15.00	30.00
❑ Parkway SP 7008 [B]	Twistin' Round the World	1962	10.00	20.00	40.00
❑ Parkway P 7009 [M]	For Teen Twisters Only	1962	7.50	15.00	30.00
❑ Parkway SP 7009 [S]	For Teen Twisters Only	1962	10.00	20.00	40.00
❑ Parkway P 7014 [M]	All the Hits (For Your Dancin' Party)	1962	7.50	15.00	30.00
❑ Parkway P 7020 [M]	Limbo Party	1962	7.50	15.00	30.00
❑ Parkway SP 7020 [S]	Limbo Party	1962	10.00	20.00	40.00
❑ Parkway P 7022 [M]	Chubby Checker's Biggest Hits	1962	7.50	15.00	30.00
❑ Parkway SP 7022 [R]	Chubby Checker's Biggest Hits	1962	7.50	15.00	30.00
❑ Parkway P 7026 [M]	Chubby Checker In Person	1963	7.50	15.00	30.00
❑ Parkway SP 7026 [S]	Chubby Checker In Person	1963	10.00	20.00	40.00
—The above record is labeled "Twist It Up"					
❑ Parkway P 7027 [M]	Let's Limbo Some More	1963	7.50	15.00	30.00
❑ Parkway SP 7027 [S]	Let's Limbo Some More	1963	10.00	20.00	40.00
❑ Parkway P 7030 [M]	Beach Party	1963	7.50	15.00	30.00
❑ Parkway SP 7030 [S]	Beach Party	1963	10.00	20.00	40.00
❑ Parkway P 7036 [M]	Chubby Checker With Sy Oliver and His Orchestra	1964	7.50	15.00	30.00
❑ Parkway SP 7036 [S]	Chubby Checker With Sy Oliver and His Orchestra	1964	10.00	20.00	40.00
❑ Parkway P 7040 [M]	Folk Album	1964	7.50	15.00	30.00
❑ Parkway SP 7040 [S]	Folk Album	1964	10.00	20.00	40.00
❑ Parkway P 7045 [M]	Discotheque	1965	7.50	15.00	30.00
❑ Parkway SP 7045 [S]	Discotheque	1965	10.00	20.00	40.00
❑ Parkway P 7048 [M]	Chubby Checker's Eighteen Golden Hits	1966	7.50	15.00	30.00
❑ Parkway SP 7048 [P]	Chubby Checker's Eighteen Golden Hits	1966	10.00	20.00	40.00

CHER

45s

Number	Title (A Side/B Side)	Yr	VG	VG+	NM
❑ Annette 1000	Ringo I Love You/Beatles Blues	1964	175.00	350.00	700.00
—As "Bonnie Jo Mason"; a Phil Spector production					
❑ Atco 6658	Yours Until Tomorrow/Thought of Loving You	1969	—	3.00	6.00
❑ Atco 6684	I Walk on Gilded Splinters/Chastity's Song	1969	—	3.00	6.00
❑ Atco 6704	For What It's Worth/Hangin' On	1969	—	3.00	6.00
❑ Atco 6713	You've Made Me So Very Happy/First Time	1969	—	3.00	6.00
❑ Atco 6793	Superstar/First Time	1971	—	3.00	6.00
❑ Atco 6868	Lay Baby Lay/(Just Enough to Keep Me) Hangin' On	1972	—	2.50	5.00
❑ Casablanca 965	Take Me Home/My Song (Too Far Gone)	1979	—	2.00	4.00
❑ Casablanca 987	Wasn't It Good/It's Too Late to Love Me Now	1979	—	2.00	4.00
❑ Casablanca 2208	Hell on Wheels/Git Down (Guitar Groupie)	1979	—	2.00	4.00
❑ Casablanca 2228	Holdin' Out for Love/Boys and Girls	1979	—	2.00	4.00
❑ Columbia 18-02850	Rudy/Do I Ever Cross Your Mind	1982	—	2.00	4.00
❑ Columbia 18-03150	I Paralyze/Walk With Me	1982	—	2.00	4.00
❑ Geffen 19953	Heart of Stone/All Because of You	1990	—	—	3.00
❑ Geffen 22844	Just Like Jesse James/Starting Over	1989	—	—	3.00
❑ Geffen 22886	If I Could Turn Back Time/Some Guys	1989	—	—	3.00
❑ Geffen 27529	After All (Love Theme from "Chances Are")/Dangerous Times	1989	—	—	3.00
—A-side with Peter Cetera					
❑ Geffen 27742	Main Man/(It's Been Hard Enough) Gettin' Over You	1988	—	—	3.00
❑ Geffen 27894	Skin Deep/Perfection	1988	—	—	3.00
❑ Geffen 27986	We All Sleep Alone/Working Girl	1988	—	—	3.00
❑ Geffen 28191	I Found Someone/Dangerous Times	1987	—	—	3.00
❑ Imperial 66081	Dream Baby/Stan Quetzal	1964	10.00	20.00	40.00
—By "Cherilyn"					
❑ Imperial 66114	All I Really Want to Do/I'm Gonna Love You	1965	3.00	6.00	12.00
❑ Imperial 66136	Where Do You Go/See See Blues	1965	3.00	6.00	12.00
❑ Imperial 66160	Bang Bang (My Baby Shot Me Down)/Needles and Pins	1966	3.00	6.00	12.00
❑ Imperial 66160	Bang Bang (My Baby Shot Me Down)/Our Day Will Come	1966	3.00	6.00	12.00
❑ Imperial 66192	Alfie/She's No Better Than Me	1966	2.50	5.00	10.00
❑ Imperial 66217	Behind the Door/Magic in the Air	1966	2.50	5.00	10.00
❑ Imperial 66223	Dream Baby/Mama (When My Dollies Have Babies)	1966	2.50	5.00	10.00
❑ Imperial 66252	Hey Joe/Our Day Will Come	1967	2.50	5.00	10.00
❑ Imperial 66261	You Better Sit Down Kids/Mama (When My Dollies Have Babies)	1967	2.50	5.00	10.00
❑ Imperial 66261	You Better Sit Down Kids/Elusive Butterfly	1967	3.00	6.00	12.00
❑ Imperial 66282	Click Song Number One/But I Can't Love You More	1968	2.00	4.00	8.00
❑ Imperial 66307	Take Me for a Little While/A Song Called Children	1968	2.00	4.00	8.00

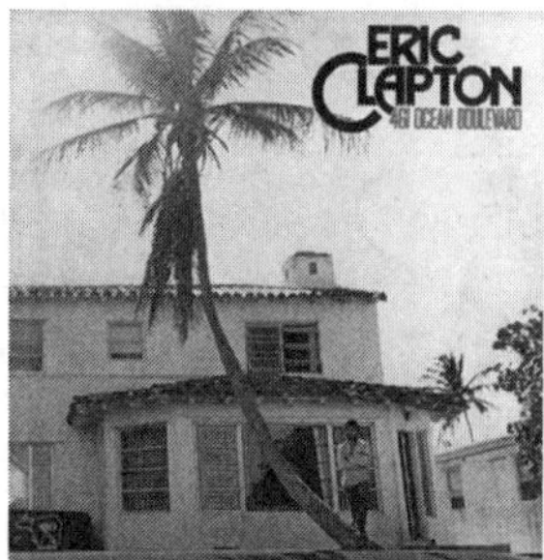

Number	Title (A Side/B Side)	Yr	VG	VG+	NM
❑ Kapp 2134	Classified 1-A/Don't Put It on Me	1971	—	3.00	6.00
❑ Kapp 2146	Gypsys, Tramps and Thieves/He'll Never Know	1971	—	3.00	6.00
—Black label					
❑ Kapp 2158	The Way of Love/Don't Put It on Me	1972	—	2.00	4.00
❑ Kapp 2171	Living in a House Divided/One Honest Man	1972	—	2.00	4.00
❑ Kapp 2184	Don't Hide Your Love/First Time	1972	—	2.00	4.00
❑ MCA 40039	Am I Blue/How Long Has This Been Going On	1973	—	2.00	4.00
❑ MCA 40102	Half-Breed/Melody	1973	—	2.00	4.00
❑ MCA 40161	Dark Lady/Two People Clinging to a Thread	1973	—	2.00	4.00
❑ MCA 40245	Train of Thought/Dixie Girl	1974	—	2.00	4.00
❑ MCA 40273	I Saw a Man and He Danced With His Wife/I Hate to Sleep Alone	1974	—	2.00	4.00
❑ MCA 40324	Carousel Man/When You Find Out Where You're Going Let Me Know	1974	—	2.00	4.00
❑ MCA 40375	Rescue Me/Dixie Girl	1975	—	2.00	4.00
❑ United Artists 0106	All I Really Want to Do/Where Do You Go	1973	—	2.00	4.00
—"Silver Spotlight Series" reissue					
❑ United Artists 0107	Bang Bang (My Baby Shot Me Down)/You Better Sit Down Kids	1973	—	2.00	4.00
—"Silver Spotlight Series" reissue					
❑ United Artists XW511	Sunny/Alfie	1974	—	2.00	4.00
❑ United Artists 50864	Reason to Believe/Will You Still Love Me Tomorrow	1971	—	2.00	4.00
❑ United Artists 50974	Old Man River/Our Day Will Come	1972	—	2.00	4.00
❑ Warner Bros. 8096	Geronimo's Cadillac/These Days	1975	—	2.00	4.00
❑ Warner Bros. 8263	Borrowed Time/Long Distance Love Affair	1976	—	2.00	4.00
❑ Warner Bros. 8311	Pirate/Send the Man Over	1976	—	2.00	4.00
❑ Warner Bros. 8366	War Paint and Soft Feathers/Sand the Man Over	1977	—	2.00	4.00
❑ Warner/Spector 0400	Baby, I Love You/A Woman's Story	1974	2.50	5.00	10.00
❑ Warner/Spector 0402	A Love Like Yours/Just Enough to Keep Me Hangin' On	1975	2.50	5.00	10.00
—With Nilsson					
Albums					
❑ Atco SD 33-298 [S]	3614 Jackson Highway	1969	5.00	10.00	20.00
❑ Casablanca NBLP-7133	Take Me Home	1979	2.50	5.00	10.00
❑ Casablanca NBLP-7184	Prisoner	1980	2.50	5.00	10.00
❑ Columbia FC 38096	I Paralyze	1982	2.50	5.00	10.00
❑ Geffen GHS 24164	Cher	1987	2.50	5.00	10.00
❑ Geffen GHS 24239	Heart of Stone	1989	2.50	5.00	10.00
—Later cover with larger picture of Cher and no rock					
❑ Geffen GHS 24239	Heart of Stone	1989	3.75	7.50	15.00
—Original cover with Cher in heart-shaped pose next to "skeleton rock"					
❑ Imperial LP-9292 [M]	All I Really Want to Do	1965	5.00	10.00	20.00
❑ Imperial LP-9301 [M]	The Sonny Side of Cher	1966	5.00	10.00	20.00
❑ Imperial LP-9320 [M]	Cher	1966	3.75	7.50	15.00
❑ Imperial LP-9358 [M]	With Love — Cher	1967	3.75	7.50	15.00
❑ Imperial LP-12292 [S]	All I Really Want to Do	1965	6.25	12.50	25.00
❑ Imperial LP-12301 [S]	The Sonny Side of Cher	1966	6.25	12.50	25.00
❑ Imperial LP-12320 [S]	Cher	1966	5.00	10.00	20.00
❑ Imperial LP-12358 [S]	With Love — Cher	1967	5.00	10.00	20.00
❑ Imperial LP-12373 [M]	Backstage	1968	10.00	20.00	40.00
—Stereo cover with designate mono sticker attached; label is stock					
❑ Imperial LP-12373 [S]	Backstage	1968	5.00	10.00	20.00
❑ Imperial LP-12406	Cher's Golden Greats	1968	5.00	10.00	20.00
❑ Kapp KS-3649	Cher	1971	5.00	10.00	20.00
—Original title of LP (without "Gypsys, Tramps & Thieves" title on front cover)					
❑ Kapp KS-3649	Gypsys, Tramps & Thieves	1971	3.75	7.50	15.00
—Retitled version of above LP; red and orange swirl label					
❑ Kapp KRS-5514	Foxy Lady	1972	3.75	7.50	15.00
❑ Liberty LN-10110	The Very Best of Cher, Vol. 1	1981	2.00	4.00	8.00
❑ Liberty LN-10111	The Very Best of Cher, Vol. 2	1981	2.00	4.00	8.00
❑ MCA 624	Cher	197?	2.50	5.00	10.00
❑ MCA 2101	Bittersweet White Light	1973	3.00	6.00	12.00
❑ MCA 2104	Half-Breed	1973	3.00	6.00	12.00
❑ MCA 2113	Dark Lady	1974	3.00	6.00	12.00
❑ MCA 2127	Greatest Hits	1974	3.00	6.00	12.00
❑ MCA 37028	Greatest Hits	1981	2.00	4.00	8.00
—Reissue of MCA 2127					
❑ Pickwick SPC-3619	This Is Cher	1978	2.50	5.00	10.00
❑ Springboard SPB-4028	Cher's Greatest Hits	197?	2.50	5.00	10.00

Number	Title (A Side/B Side)	Yr	VG	VG+	NM
❑ Springboard SPB-4029	Cher Sings the Hits	197?	2.50	5.00	10.00
❑ Sunset SUS-5276	This Is Cher	1970	3.75	7.50	15.00
❑ United Artists UXS-88 [(2)]	Cher Superpak	1971	5.00	10.00	20.00
❑ United Artists UXS-89 [(2)]	Cher Superpak, Vol. II	1972	5.00	10.00	20.00
—The above are reissues of Imperial recordings					
❑ United Artists UA-LA237-G	The Very Best of Cher	1974	3.00	6.00	12.00
❑ United Artists UA-LA377-E	The Very Best of Cher	1975	2.50	5.00	10.00
❑ United Artists UA-LA435-E	The Very Best of Cher, Vol. 2	1975	3.00	6.00	12.00
❑ Warner Bros. BS 2850	Stars	1975	3.00	6.00	12.00
❑ Warner Bros. BS 2898	I'd Rather Believe in You	1976	3.00	6.00	12.00
❑ Warner Bros. BS 3046	Cherished	1977	3.00	6.00	12.00

CHI-LITES, THE

45s

Number	Title (A Side/B Side)	Yr	VG	VG+	NM
❑ Blue Rock 4007	I'm So Jealous/The Mix-Mix Song	1965	6.25	12.50	25.00
❑ Blue Rock 4020	Doing the Snatch/Bassology	1965	6.25	12.50	25.00
❑ Blue Rock 4037	Never No More/She's Mine	1965	12.50	25.00	50.00
❑ Brunswick 55398	Give It Away/What Do I Wish For	1969	2.00	4.00	8.00
❑ Brunswick 55414	Let Me Be the Man My Daddy Was/The Twelfth of Never	1969	2.00	4.00	8.00
❑ Brunswick 55422	I'm Gonna Make You Love Me/To Change My Love	1969	2.00	4.00	8.00
❑ Brunswick 55426	24 Hours of Sadness/You're No Longer Part of My Heart	1970	2.00	4.00	8.00
❑ Brunswick 55438	I Like Your Lovin' (Do You Like Mine)/You're No Longer Part of My Heart	1970	2.00	4.00	8.00
❑ Brunswick 55442	Are You My Woman (Tell Me So)/Troubles A-Comin'	1970	2.00	4.00	8.00
❑ Brunswick 55450	(For God's Sake) Give More Power to the People/ Troubles A-Comin'	1971	2.00	4.00	8.00
❑ Brunswick 55455	We Are Neighbors/What Do I Wish For	1971	2.00	4.00	8.00
❑ Brunswick 55458	I Want to Pay You back (For Loving Me)/Love Uprising	1971	2.00	4.00	8.00
❑ Brunswick 55462	Have You Seen Her/Yes I'm Ready	1971	—	3.00	6.00
❑ Brunswick 55471	Oh Girl/Being in Love	1972	—	3.00	6.00
❑ Brunswick 55478	The Coldest Days of My Life (Part 1)/The Coldest Days of My Life (Part 2)	1972	—	3.00	6.00
❑ Brunswick 55483	A Lonely Man/The Man and the Woman (The Boy and the Girl)	1972	—	3.00	6.00
❑ Brunswick 55489	We Need Order/Living in the Footsteps of Another Man	1972	—	3.00	6.00
❑ Brunswick 55491	A Letter to Myself/Sally	1973	—	3.00	6.00
❑ Brunswick 55496	My Heart Just Keeps On Breakin'/Just Two Teenage Kids	1973	—	3.00	6.00
❑ Brunswick 55500	Stoned Out of My Mind/Someone Else's Arms	1973	—	3.00	6.00
❑ Brunswick 55502	I Found Someone/Marriage License	1973	—	3.00	6.00
❑ Brunswick 55505	Homely Girl/Never Had It So Good and Felt So Bad	1974	—	3.00	6.00
❑ Brunswick 55512	There Will Never Be Any Peace (Until God Is Seated at the Conference Table)/Too Good to Be Forgotten	1974	—	3.00	6.00
❑ Brunswick 55514	You Got to Be the One/Happiness Is Your Middle Name	1974	—	3.00	6.00
❑ Brunswick 55515	Toby/That's How Long	1974	—	3.00	6.00
❑ Brunswick 55520	It's Time for Love/Here I Am	1975	—	3.00	6.00
❑ Brunswick 55522	Don't Burn No Bridges/(Instrumental)	1975	—	3.00	6.00
—With Jackie Wilson					
❑ Brunswick 55525	The Devil Is Doing His Work/I'm Not a Gambler	1976	—	3.00	6.00
❑ Brunswick 55528	You Don't Have to Go/(Instrumental)	1976	—	3.00	6.00
❑ Brunswick 55546	First Time/Marriage License	1978	—	2.50	5.00
❑ Chi-Sound 2472	Heavenly Body/Strung Out	1980	—	2.00	4.00
❑ Chi-Sound 2481	Have You Seen Her/Super Mad (About You Baby)	1981	—	2.00	4.00
❑ Chi-Sound 2495	All I Wanna Do Is Make Love to You/Round and Round	1981	—	2.00	4.00
❑ Chi-Sound 2503	Me and You/Tell Me Where It Hurts	1981	—	2.00	4.00
❑ Chi-Sound 2600	Hot on a Thing (Called Love)/Whole Lot of Good Lovin'	1982	—	2.00	4.00
❑ Chi-Sound 2604	Try My Side (Of Love)/Get Down with Me	1982	—	2.00	4.00
❑ Dakar 600	Baby It's Time/Price of Love	1968	3.00	6.00	12.00
—As "Marshall and the Chi-Lites"					
❑ Daran 011	One by One/You Did That to Me	1964	25.00	50.00	100.00
—As "The Hi-Lites"					
❑ Daran 0111	Pretty Girl/Love Bandit	1966	12.50	25.00	50.00
—As "Marshall and the Chi-Lites"					
❑ Daran 222	I'm So Jealous/The Mix-Mix Song	1964	25.00	50.00	100.00
—As "The Hi-Lites"					
❑ Ichiban 90-205	There's a Change/Happy Music	1990	—	2.00	4.00
❑ Inphasion 7205	Higher/Stay a Little Longer	1979	—	2.50	5.00
❑ Inphasion 7208	The Only One for Me (One in a Million)/ You Won't Be Lonely Too Long	1979	—	2.50	5.00
❑ Ja-Wes 0888	You Did That to Me/I Won't Care About You	1966	3.75	7.50	15.00
❑ Larc 81015	Bottom's Up/Bottom's Up Groove	1983	—	2.00	4.00
❑ Larc 81023	Bad Motor Scooter/I Just Wanna Hold You	1983	—	2.00	4.00
❑ Mercury 73844	Happy Being Lonely/Love Can Be Dangerous	1976	—	2.50	5.00
❑ Mercury 73886	Vanishing Love/I Turn Away	1977	—	2.50	5.00
❑ Mercury 73934	My First Mistake/Stop Still	1977	—	2.50	5.00
❑ Mercury 73954	If I Had a Girl/I've Got Love on My Mind	1977	—	2.50	5.00
❑ Nuance 752	Hard Act to Follow/(Instrumental)	1985	—	2.00	4.00
❑ Private I ZS4-04365	Stop What You're Doin'/Little Girl	1984	—	—	3.00
❑ Private I ZS4-04484	Gimme Whatcha Got/Let Today Come Back Tomorrow	1984	—	—	3.00
❑ Revue 11005	Love Is Gone/Love Me	1967	3.00	6.00	12.00
❑ Revue 11018	(Um, Um) My Baby Loves Me/That's My Baby for You	1968	3.00	6.00	12.00

Albums

Number	Title (A Side/B Side)	Yr	VG	VG+	NM
❑ Brunswick BL 754152	Give It Away	1969	6.25	12.50	25.00
❑ Brunswick BL 754165	I Like Your Lovin', Do You Like Mine?	1970	6.25	12.50	25.00
❑ Brunswick BL 754170	(For God's Sake) Give More Power to the People	1971	6.25	12.50	25.00
❑ Brunswick BL 754179	A Lonely Man	1972	6.25	12.50	25.00
❑ Brunswick BL 754184	The Chi-Lites Greatest Hits	1972	6.25	12.50	25.00
❑ Brunswick BL 754188	A Letter to Myself	1973	6.25	12.50	25.00
❑ Brunswick BL 754197	Chi-Lites	1973	6.25	12.50	25.00

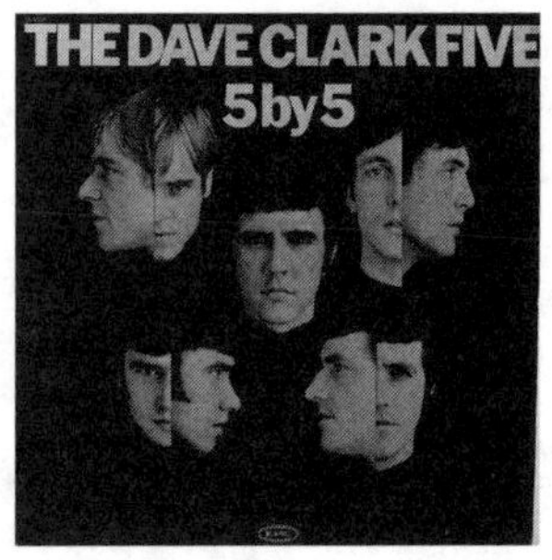

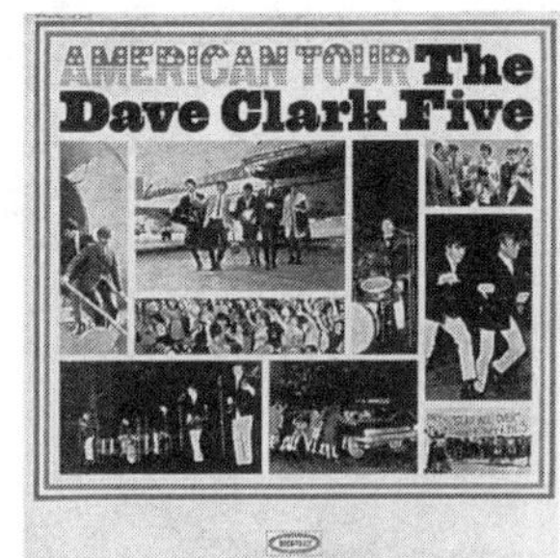

Number	Title (A Side/B Side)	Yr	VG	VG+	NM
❑ Brunswick BL 754200	Toby	1974	6.25	12.50	25.00
❑ Brunswick BL 754204	Half a Love	1975	6.25	12.50	25.00
❑ Brunswick BL 754208	The Chi-Lites Greatest Hits, Volume 2	1976	6.25	12.50	25.00
❑ Chi-Sound T-619	Heavenly Body	1980	3.75	7.50	15.00
❑ Chi-Sound T-635	Me and You	1982	3.75	7.50	15.00
❑ Epic PE 38627	Greatest Hits	1983	2.50	5.00	10.00
❑ Ichiban ICH-1057	Just Say You Love Me	198?	2.50	5.00	10.00
❑ Larc 8103	Bottom's Up	1983	3.00	6.00	12.00
❑ Mercury SRM-1-1118	Happy Being Lonely	1976	3.75	7.50	15.00
❑ Mercury SRM-1-1147	Fantastic	1977	3.75	7.50	15.00
❑ Private I FZ 39316	Steppin' Out	1984	2.50	5.00	10.00
❑ Private I PZ 39316	Steppin' Out	1985	2.00	4.00	8.00
—Budget-line reissue					

CHIC

45s

Number	Title (A Side/B Side)	Yr	VG	VG+	NM
❑ Atlantic 3435	Dance, Dance, Dance (Yowsah, Yowsah, Yowsah)/Sao Paulo	1977	—	2.00	4.00
❑ Atlantic 3469	Everybody Dance/You Can Get By	1978	—	2.00	4.00
❑ Atlantic 3519	Le Freak/Savoir Faire	1978	—	2.00	4.00
❑ Atlantic 3557	I Want Your Love/(Funny) Bone	1979	—	2.00	4.00
❑ Atlantic 3584	Good Times/A Warm Summer Night	1979	—	2.00	4.00
❑ Atlantic 3620	My Forbidden Lover/What About Me	1979	—	2.00	4.00
❑ Atlantic 3638	My Feet Keep Dancing/Will You Cry (When You Hear This Song)	1979	—	2.00	4.00
❑ Atlantic 3665	Rebels Are We/Open Up	1980	—	2.00	4.00
❑ Atlantic 3768	Real People/Chip Off the Old Block	1980	—	2.00	4.00
❑ Atlantic 3887	Stage Fright/So Fine	1982	—	2.00	4.00
❑ Atlantic 89725	Give Me the Lovin'/You Got Some Love for Me	1983	—	—	3.00
❑ Atlantic 89954	Hangin'Chic (Everybody Say)	1982	—	—	3.00
❑ Atlantic Oldies Series OS 13211	Dance, Dance, Dance (Yowsah, Yowsah, Yowsah)/ Everybody Dance	1979	—	—	3.00
—Reissue					
❑ Atlantic Oldies Series OS 13215	Le Freak/I Want Your Love	1980	—	—	3.00
—Reissue					
❑ Atlantic Oldies Series OS 13216	Good Times/My Forbidden Lover	1980	—	—	3.00
—Reissue					
❑ Buddah 583	Dance, Dance, Dance (Yowsah, Yowsah, Yowsah)/Sao Paulo	1977	5.00	10.00	20.00
❑ Mirage 4032	Soup for One/Burn Hard	1982	—	2.00	4.00
❑ Mirage 4051	Why/Why	1982	—	2.00	4.00
—B-side by Carly Simon					

Albums

Number	Title (A Side/B Side)	Yr	VG	VG+	NM
❑ Atlantic SD 16003	Risque	1979	2.00	4.00	8.00
❑ Atlantic SD 16011	Les Plus Grands Succes de Chic — Chic's Greatest Hits	1979	2.00	4.00	8.00
❑ Atlantic SD 16016	Real People	1980	2.00	4.00	8.00
❑ Atlantic SD 19153	Chic	1977	2.00	4.00	8.00
❑ Atlantic SD 19209	C'est Chic	1978	2.00	4.00	8.00
❑ Atlantic SD 19323	Take It Off	1981	2.00	4.00	8.00
❑ Atlantic 80031	Tongue in Chic	1982	2.00	4.00	8.00
❑ Atlantic 80107	Believer	1983	2.00	4.00	8.00

CHICAGO

45s

Number	Title (A Side/B Side)	Yr	VG	VG+	NM
❑ Columbia 10049	Wishing You Were Here/Life Saver	1974	—	2.50	5.00
❑ Columbia 10092	Harry Truman/Till We Meet Again	1975	—	2.50	5.00
❑ Columbia 10131	Old Days/Hideaway	1975	—	2.50	5.00
❑ Columbia 10200	Brand New Love Affair/Hideaway	1975	—	2.50	5.00
❑ Columbia 3-10360	Another Rainy Day in New York City/Hope for Love	1976	—	2.50	5.00
❑ Columbia 3-10390	If You Leave Me Now/Together Again	1976	—	2.50	5.00
❑ Columbia 3-10523	You Are On My Mind/Gently I'll Wake You	1977	—	2.50	5.00
❑ Columbia 3-10620	Baby, What a Big Surprise/Takin' It On Uptown	1977	—	2.50	5.00
❑ Columbia 3-10683	Little One/Till the End of Time	1978	—	2.50	5.00
❑ Columbia 3-10737	Take Me Back to Chicago/Policeman	1978	—	2.50	5.00
❑ Columbia 3-10845	Alive Again/Love Was New	1978	—	2.50	5.00
❑ Columbia 3-10879	No Tell Lover/Take a Chance	1979	—	2.50	5.00
❑ Columbia 3-10935	Gone Long Gone/The Greatest Love on Earth	1979	—	2.00	4.00
❑ Columbia 1-11061	Must Have Been Crazy/Closer to You	1979	—	2.00	4.00

Number	Title (A Side/B Side)	Yr	VG	VG+	NM
❑ Columbia 1-11124	Street Player/Window Dreamin'	1979	—	2.00	4.00
❑ Columbia 1-11341	Song for You/I'd Rather Be Rich	1980	—	—	—
—Canceled?					
❑ Columbia 1-11345	Thunder and Lightning/I'd Rather Be Rich	1980	—	2.00	4.00
❑ Columbia 11-11376	Song for You/The American Dream	1980	—	2.00	4.00
❑ Columbia 4-44909	Questions 67 and 68/Listen	1969	2.00	4.00	8.00
❑ Columbia 45011	Beginnings/Poem 58	1969	—	3.00	6.00
❑ Columbia 45127	Make Me Smile/Colour My World	1970	—	2.50	5.00
❑ Columbia 45194	25 or 6 to 4/Where Do We Go from Here	1970	—	2.50	5.00
❑ Columbia 4-45264	Does Anybody Really Know What Time It Is?/Listen	1970	—	2.50	5.00
❑ Columbia 45331	Free/Free Country	1971	—	2.50	5.00
❑ Columbia 45370	Lowdown/Loneliness Is Just a Word	1971	—	2.50	5.00
❑ Columbia 45417	Beginnings/Colour My World	1971	—	2.50	5.00
❑ Columbia 45467	Questions 67 and 68/I'm a Man	1971	—	2.50	5.00
❑ Columbia 45657	Saturday in the Park/Alma Mater	1972	—	2.50	5.00
❑ Columbia 45717	Dialogue (Parts 1 and 2)/Now That You've Gone	1972	—	2.50	5.00
❑ Columbia 45880	Feelin' Stronger Every Day/Jenny	1973	—	2.50	5.00
❑ Columbia 45933	Just You 'N' Me/Critic's Choice	1973	—	2.50	5.00
❑ Columbia 46020	(I've Been) Searchin' So Long/Byblos	1974	—	2.50	5.00
❑ Columbia 46062	Call On Me/Prelude to Aire	1974	—	2.50	5.00
❑ Full Moon 29798	What You're Missing/Rescue You	1983	—	2.00	4.00
❑ Full Moon 29911	Love Me Tomorrow/Bad Advice	1982	—	2.00	4.00
❑ Full Moon 29979	Hard to Say I'm Sorry/Sonny Think Twice	1982	—	2.00	4.00
❑ Reprise 19466	Chasin' the Wind/Only Time Can Heal the Wounded	1991	—	—	3.00
❑ Reprise 22741	What Kind of Man Would I Be?/25 or 6 to 4	1990	—	—	3.00
❑ Reprise 22985	We Can Last Forever/One More Day	1989	—	—	3.00
❑ Reprise 27757	You're Not Alone/It's Alright	1988	—	—	3.00
❑ Reprise 27766	Look Away/Come In from the Night	1988	—	—	3.00
❑ Reprise 27855	I Don't Wanna Live Without Your Love/I Stand Up	1988	—	—	3.00
❑ Warner Bros. 28283	Niagara Falls/I Believe	1987	—	—	3.00
❑ Warner Bros. 28424	If She Would Have Been Faithful.../Forever	1987	—	—	3.00
❑ Warner Bros. 28512	Will You Still Love Me/25 or 6 to 4	1986	—	—	3.00
❑ Warner Bros. 28628	25 or 6 to 4/One More Day	1986	—	—	3.00
❑ Warner Bros. 29082	Along Comes a Woman/We Can't Stop the Hurtin'	1985	—	—	3.00
❑ Warner Bros. 29126	You're the Inspiration/Once in a Lifetime	1984	—	—	3.00
❑ Warner Bros. 29214	Hard Habit to Break/Remember the Feeling	1984	—	—	3.00
❑ Warner Bros. 29306	Stay the Night/Only You	1984	—	—	3.00
Albums					
❑ Accord SN-7140	Toronto Rock 'n Roll Revival, Part I	1982	3.00	6.00	12.00
—Reissue of Magnum LP					
❑ Columbia GP 8 [(2)]	Chicago Transit Authority	1969	6.25	12.50	25.00
—Red labels with "360 Sound" at bottom					
❑ Columbia KGP 24 [(2)]	Chicago	1970	10.00	20.00	40.00
—Red labels with "360 Sound" at bottom; label and spine call the album "Chicago"					
❑ Columbia C2 30110 [(2)]	Chicago III	1971	3.75	7.50	15.00
❑ Columbia KG 30863 [(2)]	Chicago at Carnegie Hall, Vol. 1 & 2	1971	3.75	7.50	15.00
—First half of the 4-LP box, possibly for Columbia Record Club only					
❑ Columbia KG 30864 [(2)]	Chicago at Carnegie Hall, Vol. 3 & 4	1971	3.75	7.50	15.00
—Second half of the 4-LP box, possibly for Columbia Record Club only					
❑ Columbia C4X 30865 [(4)]	Chicago at Carnegie Hall	1971	7.50	15.00	30.00
—With box, 4 posters and program; deduct for missing items					
❑ Columbia KC 31102	Chicago V	1972	3.75	7.50	15.00
❑ Columbia KC 32400	Chicago VI	1973	3.00	6.00	12.00
❑ Columbia C2 32810 [(2)]	Chicago VII	1974	3.75	7.50	15.00
❑ Columbia PC 33100	Chicago VIII	1975	3.00	6.00	12.00
❑ Columbia PC 33900	Chicago IX — Chicago's Greatest Hits	1975	2.50	5.00	10.00
❑ Columbia PC 34200	Chicago X	1976	2.50	5.00	10.00
❑ Columbia JC 34860	Chicago XI	1977	2.50	5.00	10.00
❑ Columbia FC 35512	Hot Streets	1978	2.50	5.00	10.00
❑ Columbia FC 36105	Chicago 13	1979	3.00	6.00	12.00
❑ Columbia FC 36517	Chicago XIV	1980	3.00	6.00	12.00
❑ Columbia FC 37682	Chicago — Greatest Hits, Volume II	1981	3.00	6.00	12.00
❑ Columbia PC 38590	If You Leave Me Now	1982	3.00	6.00	12.00
❑ Columbia PC 39579	Take Me Back to Chicago	1983	3.00	6.00	12.00
❑ Full Moon 23689	Chicago 16	1982	2.00	4.00	8.00
❑ Magnum MR 604	Chicago Transit Authority Live in Concert	1978	5.00	10.00	20.00
—Taken from their 1969 Toronto Rock 'n Roll Revival performance					
❑ Reprise 25714	Chicago 19	1988	2.00	4.00	8.00
❑ Reprise 26080	Greatest Hits 1982-1989	1989	2.50	5.00	10.00
❑ Warner Bros. 25060	Chicago 17	1984	2.00	4.00	8.00
❑ Warner Bros. 25509	Chicago 18	1986	2.00	4.00	8.00

CHIFFONS, THE

45s

Number	Title (A Side/B Side)	Yr	VG	VG+	NM
❑ B.T. Puppy 558	Secret Love/Strange, Strange Feeling	1970	2.50	5.00	10.00
❑ Big Deal 6003	Tonight's the Night/Do You Know	1960	20.00	40.00	80.00
❑ Buddah 171	So Much in Love/Strange, Strange Feeling	1970	2.50	5.00	10.00
❑ Laurie 3152	He's So Fine/Oh My Love	1963	5.00	10.00	20.00
❑ Laurie 3152	He's So Fine/Oh My Lover	1963	5.00	10.00	20.00
—Both B-side titles have been confirmed; we're not sure which came first					
❑ Laurie 3166	Lucky Me/Why Am I So Shy?	1963	3.75	7.50	15.00
❑ Laurie 3179	One Fine Day/Why Am I So Shy	1963	5.00	10.00	20.00
❑ Laurie 3195	A Love So Fine/Only My Friend	1963	3.00	6.00	12.00
❑ Laurie 3212	I Have a Boyfriend/I'm Gonna Dry My Eyes	1963	3.00	6.00	12.00
❑ Laurie 3224	Tonight I Met an Angel/Easy to Love	1964	3.00	6.00	12.00
❑ Laurie 3262	Sailor Boy/When Summer's Through	1964	3.00	6.00	12.00
❑ Laurie 3275	What Am I Gonna Do with You/Strange, Strange Feeling	1964	3.00	6.00	12.00

Number	Title (A Side/B Side)	Yr	VG	VG+	NM
❑ Laurie 3301	Nobody Knows What's Going On (In My Mind But Me)/ The Real Thing	1965	3.00	6.00	12.00
❑ Laurie 3301	Nobody Knows What's Going On (In My Mind But Me)/ Did You Ever Go Steady	1965	3.00	6.00	12.00
❑ Laurie 3318	Tonight I'm Gonna Dream/Heavenly Place	1965	3.00	6.00	12.00
❑ Laurie 3340	Sweet Talkin' Guy/Did You Ever Go Steady	1966	3.75	7.50	15.00
❑ Laurie 3350	Out of This World/Just a Boy	1966	2.50	5.00	10.00
❑ Laurie 3357	Stop, Look, Listen/March	1966	2.50	5.00	10.00
❑ Laurie 3364	My Boyfriend's Back/I Got Plenty of Nuttin'	1966	2.50	5.00	10.00
❑ Laurie 3377	If I Knew Then/Keep the Boy Happy	1967	2.50	5.00	10.00
❑ Laurie 3423	Just for Tonight/Keep the Boy Happy	1968	2.50	5.00	10.00
❑ Laurie 3423	Just for Tonight/Teach Me How	1968	2.50	5.00	10.00
❑ Laurie 3460	Up on the Bridge/March	1968	2.50	5.00	10.00
❑ Laurie 3497	Love Me Like You're Gonna Lose Me/Three Dips of Ice Cream	1969	2.50	5.00	10.00
❑ Laurie 3630	My Sweet Lord/Main Nerve	1975	2.50	5.00	10.00
❑ Laurie 3648	Dream, Dream, Dream/Oh My Lover	1976	2.50	5.00	10.00
❑ Reprise 20103	After Last Night/Doctor of Hearts	1962	5.00	10.00	20.00
❑ Rust 5070	When the Boy's Happy (The Girl's Happy Too)/Hockaday, Part 1	1963	6.25	12.50	25.00
—As "The Four Pennies"					
❑ Rust 5071	Dry Your Eyes/My Block	1963	6.25	12.50	25.00
—As "The Four Pennies"					
❑ Wildcat 601	Never Never/No More Tomorrows	1961	6.25	12.50	25.00
Albums					
❑ B.T. Puppy S-1011	My Secret Love	1970	100.00	200.00	400.00
❑ Collectables COL-5042	Golden Classics	198?	3.00	6.00	12.00
❑ Laurie LLP-2018 [M]	He's So Fine	1963	30.00	60.00	120.00
❑ Laurie LLP-2020 [M]	One Fine Day	1963	50.00	100.00	200.00
❑ Laurie LLP-2036 [M]	Sweet Talkin' Guy	1966	25.00	50.00	100.00
❑ Laurie SLP-2036 [S]	Sweet Talkin' Guy	1966	37.50	75.00	150.00
❑ Laurie 4001	Everything You Always Wanted to Hear by the Chiffons	1975	5.00	10.00	20.00

CHIPMUNKS, THE, DAVID SEVILLE AND

45s

Number	Title (A Side/B Side)	Yr	VG	VG+	NM
❑ Dot 16997	Apple Picker/Sorry About That, Herb	1967	3.00	6.00	12.00
❑ Liberty 55168	The Chipmunk Song/Almost Good	1958	6.25	12.50	25.00
—Blue-green label					
❑ Liberty 55179	Alvin's Harmonica/Mediocre	1959	5.00	10.00	20.00
❑ Liberty 55200 [M]	Ragtime Cowboy Joe/Flip Side	1959	5.00	10.00	20.00
❑ Liberty 55233	Alvin's Orchestra/Copyright 1960	1960	3.75	7.50	15.00
❑ Liberty 55246	Coming 'Round the Mountain/Sing a Goofy Song	1960	3.75	7.50	15.00
❑ Liberty 55250	The Chipmunk Song/Alvin's Harmonica	1959	3.75	7.50	15.00
—Blue-green label, no horizontal lines					
❑ Liberty 55277	Alvin for President/Sack Time	1960	3.75	7.50	15.00
❑ Liberty 55289	Rudolph, the Red-Nosed Reindeer/Spain	1960	3.75	7.50	15.00
❑ Liberty 55424	The Alvin Twist/I Wish I Could Speak French	1962	3.75	7.50	15.00
❑ Liberty 55452	America the Beautiful/My Wild Irish Rose	1962	3.75	7.50	15.00
❑ Liberty 55544	Alvin's All Star Chipmunk Band/Old MacDonald Cha Cha Cha	1963	3.75	7.50	15.00
❑ Liberty 55632	Eefin' Alvin/Flip Side	1963	3.75	7.50	15.00
❑ Liberty 55635	The Night Before Christmas/Wonderful Day	1963	3.75	7.50	15.00
❑ Liberty 55734	All My Lovin'/Do You Want to Know a Secret	1964	3.75	7.50	15.00
❑ Liberty 55773	Do-Re-Mi/Supercalifragilisticexpialidocious	1965	3.00	6.00	12.00
❑ Liberty 55832	I'm Henry VIII, I Am/What's New Pussycat	1965	3.00	6.00	12.00
❑ Liberty 56079	The Chipmunk Song/Christmas Blues	1968	4.00	8.00	16.00
—With Canned Heat					
❑ Sunset 61002	Talk to the Animals/My Friend the Doctor	1968	2.50	5.00	10.00
❑ Sunset 61003	Chitty Chitty Bang Bang/Hushabye Mountain	1968	2.50	5.00	10.00
❑ United Artists 0056	The Chipmunk Song/Ragtime Cowboy Joe	1973	2.00	4.00	8.00
—"Silver Spotlight Series" reissue					
❑ United Artists 0057	Alvin's Harmonica/Rudolph, the Red-Nosed Reindeer	1973	2.00	4.00	8.00
—"Silver Spotlight Series" reissue					
❑ United Artists XW576	The Chipmunk Song/Rudolph, the Red-Nosed Reindeer	1974	—	3.00	6.00
Albums					
❑ Liberty LM-1070	Christmas with the Chipmunks	1980	2.00	4.00	8.00
—Reissue with two tracks omitted					
❑ Liberty LRP-3132 [M]	Let's All Sing with the Chipmunks	1959	7.50	15.00	30.00
—Black vinyl; original cover features "realistic" chipmunks and no reference to "The Alvin Show"					

Number	Title (A Side/B Side)	Yr	VG	VG+	NM
❑ Liberty LRP-3159 [M]	Sing Again with the Chipmunks	1960	10.00	20.00	40.00
—Original cover features "realistic" chipmunks					
❑ Liberty LRP-3170 [M]	Around the World with the Chipmunks	1960	10.00	20.00	40.00
—Original cover features "realistic" chipmunks on and near a plane					
❑ Liberty LRP-3209 [M]	The Alvin Show	1961	6.25	12.50	25.00
❑ Liberty LRP-3229 [M]	The Chipmunks Songbook	1962	6.25	12.50	25.00
❑ Liberty LRP-3256 [M]	Christmas with the Chipmunks	1962	6.25	12.50	25.00
❑ Liberty LRP-3334 [M]	Christmas with the Chipmunks, Vol. 2	1963	6.25	12.50	25.00
❑ Liberty LRP-3388 [M]	The Chipmunks Sing the Beatles Hits	1964	7.50	15.00	30.00
❑ Liberty LRP-3405 [M]	The Chipmunks Sing with Children	1965	5.00	10.00	20.00
❑ Liberty LRP-3424 [M]	The Chipmunks A-Go-Go	1965	5.00	10.00	20.00
❑ Liberty LST-7132 [S]	Let's All Sing with the Chipmunks	1959	10.00	20.00	40.00
—Black vinyl; original cover features "realistic" chipmunks and no reference to "The Alvin Show"					
❑ Liberty LST-7159 [S]	Sing Again with the Chipmunks	1960	12.50	25.00	50.00
—Original cover features "realistic" chipmunks					
❑ Liberty LST-7170 [S]	Around the World with the Chipmunks	1960	12.50	25.00	50.00
—Original covers have "realistic" chipmunks on and near a plane.					
❑ Liberty LST-7209 [S]	The Alvin Show	1961	7.50	15.00	30.00
❑ Liberty LST-7229 [S]	The Chipmunks Songbook	1962	7.50	15.00	30.00
❑ Liberty LST-7256 [S]	Christmas with the Chipmunks	1962	7.50	15.00	30.00
❑ Liberty LST-7334 [S]	Christmas with the Chipmunks, Vol. 2	1963	7.50	15.00	30.00
❑ Liberty LST-7388 [S]	The Chipmunks Sing the Beatles Hits	1964	10.00	20.00	40.00
❑ Liberty LST-7405 [S]	The Chipmunks Sing with Children	1965	6.25	12.50	25.00
❑ Liberty LST-7424 [S]	The Chipmunks A-Go-Go	1965	6.25	12.50	25.00
❑ Mistletoe MLP-1216	Christmas with the Chipmunks	197?	2.00	4.00	8.00
—Reissue of Liberty LST-7256					
❑ Mistletoe MLP-1217	Christmas with the Chipmunks, Vol. 2	197?	2.00	4.00	8.00
—Reissue of Liberty LST-7334					
❑ Pickwick SPC-1034	Christmas with the Chipmunks	1980	2.50	5.00	10.00
❑ Pickwick SPC-1035	The Twelve Days of Christmas with The Chipmunks	1980	2.50	5.00	10.00
—Reissue of "Christmas with the Chipmunks, Vol. 2"					
❑ Sunset LST-7334 [S]	Christmas with the Chipmunks, Vol. 2	1968	5.00	10.00	20.00
—Budget-line reissue of Liberty LST-7334					
❑ Sunset LST-7424 [S]	The Chipmunks A-Go-Go	196?	3.75	7.50	15.00
—Same cover as Liberty 7424, but with "SUNSET" sticker at upper right					
❑ United Artists UA-LA352-E2 [(2)]	Christmas with the Chipmunks	1974	5.00	10.00	20.00
—Entire contents of both original Liberty LPs					

CHRISTIE, LOU

45s

Number	Title (A Side/B Side)	Yr	VG	VG+	NM
❑ Alcar 207	Close Your Eyes/Funny Thing	1963	6.25	12.50	25.00
❑ Alcar 208	You're With It/Tomorrow Will Come	1963	6.25	12.50	25.00
❑ American Music Makers 006	The Jury/Little Did I Know	1963	7.50	15.00	30.00
❑ Buddah 65	Genesis and the Third Verse/Rake Up the Leaves	1968	2.00	4.00	8.00
❑ Buddah 76	Canterbury Road/Saints of Aquarius	1969	2.00	4.00	8.00
❑ Buddah 116	I'm Gonna Make You Mine/I'm Gonna Get Married	1969	—	3.00	6.00
❑ Buddah 149	Are You Getting Any Sunshine/It'll Take Time	1970	—	2.50	5.00
❑ Buddah 163	Love Is Over/She Sold Me Magic	1970	—	2.50	5.00
❑ Buddah 192	Indian Lady/Glory River	1970	—	2.50	5.00
❑ Buddah 235	Waco/Lighthouse	1971	—	2.50	5.00
❑ Buddah 257	Mickey's Monkey/She Sold Me Magic	1971	6.25	12.50	25.00
❑ Buddah 285	Sing Me, Sing Me/Paper Song	1972	—	2.50	5.00
❑ Buddah 312	Shuffle On Down to Pittsburgh/I'm Gonna Get Married	1972	5.00	10.00	20.00
❑ C&C 102	The Gypsy Cried/Red Sails in the Sunset	1962	50.00	100.00	200.00
❑ Co & Ce 235	Outside the Gates of Heaven/All That Glitters Isn't Gold	1966	2.50	5.00	10.00
❑ Colpix 735	Merry-Go-Round/Guitars and Bongos	1964	3.00	6.00	12.00
❑ Colpix 753	Pot of Gold/Have I Sinned	1964	3.00	6.00	12.00
❑ Colpix 770	Make Summer Last Forever/Why Did You Do It Baby	1965	3.00	6.00	12.00
❑ Colpix 778	A Teenager in Love/Back Track	1965	3.00	6.00	12.00
❑ Colpix 799	Cryin' on My Knees/Big Time	1966	3.00	6.00	12.00
❑ Columbia 44062	Shake Hands and Walk Away Cryin'/Escape	1967	3.75	7.50	15.00
❑ Columbia 44177	Self Expression/Back to the Days of the Romans	1967	3.75	7.50	15.00
❑ Columbia 44240	(I Remember) Gina/Escape	1967	3.75	7.50	15.00
❑ Columbia 44338	Back to the Days of the Romans/Don't Stop Me	1967	3.75	7.50	15.00
❑ Epic 8-50244	Summer in Malibu/Ridin' in My Van	1976	3.75	7.50	15.00
❑ Lifesong 1775	Theme from "People" (Part 1)/Theme from "People" (Part 2)	1978	12.50	25.00	50.00
—As "Sacco"					
❑ MGM 13412	Lightnin' Strikes/Cryin' in the Streets	1965	3.75	7.50	15.00
❑ MGM 13473	Rhapsody in the Rain/Trapeze	1966	5.00	10.00	20.00
—Original version of A-side had racy (by 1966 standards) lyrics: "We were makin' out in the rain/And in this car, our love went much too far." Matrix number in dead wax is "66-XY-308"					
❑ MGM 13473	Rhapsody in the Rain/Trapeze	1966	3.75	7.50	15.00
—Revised A-side has altered lyrics: "We fell in love in the rain/And in this car, love came like a falling star." Matrix number in dead wax is "66-XY-308 D.J."					
❑ MGM 13533	Painter/Du Ronda	1966	2.50	5.00	10.00
❑ MGM 13576	If My Car Could Only Talk/Song of Lita	1966	2.50	5.00	10.00
❑ MGM 13623	Since I Don't Have You/Wild Life's in Season	1966	2.50	5.00	10.00
❑ Midland Int'l. MB-10848	You're Gonna Make Love to Me/Fantasies	1976	3.75	7.50	15.00
❑ Midland Int'l. MB-10959	Spanish Wine/Dancing in the Sand	1977	3.75	7.50	15.00
❑ Midsong Int'l. 72013	Don't Knock My Love (Short)/Don't Knock My Love (Long)	1980	2.50	5.00	10.00
—With Pia Zadora					
❑ Plateau 4551	Guardian Angels/(B-side unknown)	1981	10.00	20.00	40.00
❑ Rhino 90105	O Holy Night (same on both sides)	1991	—	3.00	6.00
—With the University of Pittsburgh Men's Glee Club					
❑ Roulette 4457	The Gypsy Cried/Red Sails in the Sunset	1963	3.75	7.50	15.00
—Pink label					

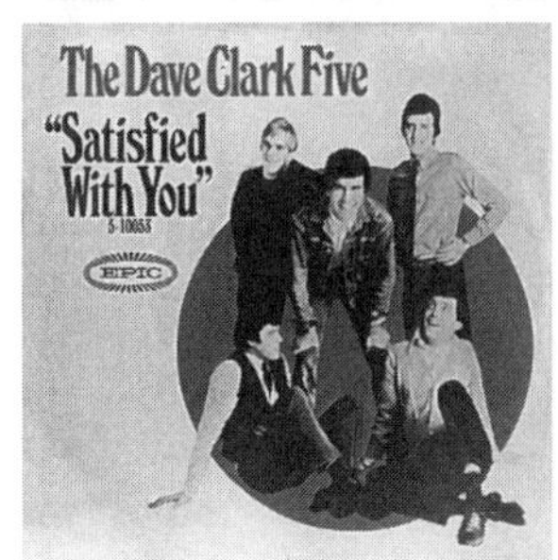

Number	Title (A Side/B Side)	Yr	VG	VG+	NM
❑ Roulette 4481	Two Faces Have I/All That Glitters Isn't Gold	1963	3.75	7.50	15.00
❑ Roulette 4504	How Many Teardrops/You and I (Have a Right to Cry)	1963	3.00	6.00	12.00
❑ Roulette 4527	Shy Boy/It Can Happen	1963	3.00	6.00	12.00
❑ Roulette 4545	Stay/There They Go	1964	3.75	7.50	15.00
❑ Roulette 4554	Maybe You'll Be There/When You Dance	1964	6.25	12.50	25.00
❑ Slipped Disc 45270	Summer Days/The One and Only Original Sunshine Kid	1976	3.75	7.50	15.00
❑ Three Brothers 400	Blue Canadian Rocky Dream/Wilma Lee and Stoney	1973	2.00	4.00	8.00
❑ Three Brothers 402	Beyond the Blue Horizon/Saddle the Wind	1974	—	2.50	5.00
❑ Three Brothers 403	You Were the One/Good Morning	1974	2.00	4.00	8.00
❑ Three Brothers 405	Hey You Cajun/Sunbeam	1974	2.50	5.00	10.00
❑ World 1002	The Jury/Little Did I Know	1963	7.50	15.00	30.00
Albums					
❑ Buddah BDS-5052	I'm Gonna Make You Mine	1969	3.75	7.50	15.00
❑ Buddah BDS-5073	Paint America Love	1971	3.75	7.50	15.00
❑ Co & Ce LP-1231 [M]	Lou Christie Strikes Back	1966	10.00	20.00	40.00
—The front cover and spine use this title, but the back cover and label use "Lou Christie Strikes Again"					
❑ Colpix CP-4001 [M]	Lou Christie Strikes Again	1966	7.50	5.00	30.00
❑ Colpix SCP-4001 [S]	Lou Christie Strikes Again	1966	12.50	25.00	50.00
❑ 51 West P 18260	Lou Christie Does Detroit	1983	3.75	7.50	15.00
❑ MGM E-4360 [M]	Lightnin' Strikes	1966	3.75	7.50	15.00
❑ MGM SE-4360 [S]	Lightnin' Strikes	1966	5.00	10.00	20.00
❑ MGM E-4394 [M]	Painter of Hits	1966	3.75	7.50	15.00
❑ MGM SE-4394 [S]	Painter of Hits	1966	5.00	10.00	20.00
❑ Rhino R1-70246	EnLightnin'Ment: The Best of Lou Christie	1988	3.00	6.00	12.00
❑ Roulette R 25208 [M]	Lou Christie	1963	12.50	25.00	50.00
—Blue background on front cover					
❑ Roulette SR 25208 [S]	Lou Christie	1963	20.00	40.00	80.00
—Blue background on front cover					
❑ Roulette R 25332 [M]	Lou Christie Strikes Again	1966	6.25	12.50	25.00
❑ Roulette SR 25332 [S]	Lou Christie Strikes Again	1966	7.50	15.00	30.00
❑ Spin-O-Rama M-173 [M]	Starring Lou Christie and the Classics	1966	5.00	10.00	20.00
❑ Spin-O-Rama S-173 [R]	Starring Lou Christie and the Classics	1966	3.00	6.00	12.00
—The above LP also includes other artists					
❑ Three Brothers THB-2000	Lou Christie	1973	5.00	10.00	20.00
CLANTON, JIMMY					
45s					
❑ Ace 537	I Trusted You/That's You Baby	1958	5.00	10.00	20.00
❑ Ace 546	Just a Dream/You Aim to Please	1958	5.00	10.00	20.00
❑ Ace 551	A Letter to An Angel/A Part of Me	1958	5.00	10.00	20.00
❑ Ace 560	My Love Is Strong/Ship on a Stormy Sea	1959	3.75	7.50	15.00
❑ Ace 567 [M]	My Own True Love/Little Boy in Love	1959	3.75	7.50	15.00
❑ Ace 575	Go, Jimmy, Go/I Trusted You	1959	5.00	10.00	20.00
—Normal white label					
❑ Ace 585	Another Sleepless Night/I'm Gonna Try	1960	3.75	7.50	15.00
❑ Ace 600	Come Back/Wait	1960	3.75	7.50	15.00
❑ Ace 607	What Am I Gonna Do/If I	1961	3.75	7.50	15.00
❑ Ace 616	Down the Aisle/No Longer Blue	1961	3.75	7.50	15.00
❑ Ace 622	I Just Wanna Make Love/Don't Look at Me	1961	3.75	7.50	15.00
❑ Ace 634	Lucky in Love with You/Not Like a Brother	1961	3.75	7.50	15.00
❑ Ace 641	Twist On Little Girl/Wayward Love	1962	3.75	7.50	15.00
❑ Ace 642	Twist On Little Girl/Wayward Love//Green Light/Happy Times	1962	12.50	25.00	50.00
❑ Ace 655	Just a Moment/Because I Do	1962	3.75	7.50	15.00
❑ Ace 668	Heart Hotel/Many Dreams	1963	3.00	6.00	12.00
❑ Ace 8001	Venus in Blue Jeans/Highway Bound	1962	3.75	7.50	15.00
❑ Ace 8005	Darkest Street in Town/Dreams of a Fool	1962	2.50	5.00	10.00
❑ Ace 8006	Endless Nights/Another Day, Another Heartache	1963	2.50	5.00	10.00
❑ Ace 8007	Cindy/I Care Enough (To Give the Very Best)	1963	2.50	5.00	10.00
❑ Imperial 66242	Absence of Lisa/C'mon Jim	1967	2.00	4.00	8.00
❑ Imperial 66274	Calico Junction/I'll Be Loving You	1968	2.00	4.00	8.00
❑ Laurie 3508	Curly/The Girl Who Cried Love (Once Too Often)	1969	2.00	4.00	8.00
❑ Laurie 3508	Curly/I'll Never Forget Your Love	1969	2.50	5.00	10.00
❑ Laurie 3534	Tell Me/I'll Never Forget Your Love	1969	2.00	4.00	8.00
❑ Mala 500	Hurting Each Other/Don't Keep Your Friends Away	1965	2.50	5.00	10.00
❑ Mala 516	Everything I Touch Turns to Tears/That Special Way	1965	2.50	5.00	10.00
❑ Philips 40161	Red Don't Go with Blue/All the Words in the World	1963	2.50	5.00	10.00
❑ Philips 40181	I'll Step Aside/I Won't Cry Anymore	1964	2.50	5.00	10.00

Number	Title (A Side/B Side)	Yr	VG	VG+	NM
❑ Philips 40208	If I'm a Fool for Loving You/A Million Drums	1964	2.50	5.00	10.00
❑ Philips 40219	Follow the Sun/Lock the Windows	1964	2.50	5.00	10.00
❑ Spiral 3406	The Coolest Hot Pants/(Instrumental)	1971	—	2.50	5.00
❑ Starfire 104	I Wanna Go Home/You Kissed a Fool Goodbye	1976	—	2.50	5.00
❑ Vin 1028	What Am I Living For/Wedding Blues	1962	2.50	5.00	10.00
Albums					
❑ Ace DLP-100 [M]	Jimmy's Happy/Jimmy's Blue	1960	37.50	75.00	150.00
—Black vinyl; also released as two separate albums, 1007 and 1008					
❑ Ace 1001 [M]	Just a Dream	1959	30.00	60.00	120.00
❑ Ace 1007 [M]	Jimmy's Happy	1960	10.00	20.00	40.00
❑ Ace 1008 [M]	Jimmy's Blue	1960	10.00	20.00	40.00
❑ Ace 1011 [M]	My Best to You	1960	25.00	50.00	100.00
❑ Ace 1014 [M]	Teenage Millionaire	1961	25.00	50.00	100.00
❑ Ace 1026 [M]	Venus in Blue Jeans	1962	25.00	50.00	100.00
❑ Philips PHM 200154 [M]	The Best of Jimmy Clanton	1964	6.25	12.50	25.00
❑ Philips PHS 600154 [S]	The Best of Jimmy Clanton	1964	7.50	15.00	30.00

CLAPTON, ERIC

45s

Number	Title (A Side/B Side)	Yr	VG	VG+	NM
❑ Atco 6784	After Midnight/Easy Now	1970	—	3.00	6.00
❑ Duck 28279	Tearing Us Apart/Hold On	1987	—	—	3.00
—A-side with Tina Turner					
❑ Duck 28391	Behind the Sun/Grand Illusion	1987	—	—	3.00
❑ Duck 28514	It's in the Way That You Use It/Grand Illusion	1986	—	—	3.00
❑ Duck 28986	See What Love Can Do/She's Waiting	1985	—	—	3.00
❑ Duck 29081	Forever Man/Too Bad	1985	—	—	3.00
❑ Duck 29647	Pretty Girl/The Shape You're In	1983	—	2.00	4.00
❑ Duck 29780	I've Got a Rock n' Roll Heart/Man in Love	1983	—	2.00	4.00
—Silver label with Duck logo					
❑ Polydor 15049	Let It Rain/Easy Now	1972	—	3.00	6.00
❑ Polydor 15056	Bell Bottom Blues/Little Wing	1973	—	2.50	5.00
—Reissue of Derek and the Dominos recordings, but under Clapton's name					
❑ Polydor 887403-7	After Midnight/I Can't Stand It	1988	—	—	3.00
❑ Reprise 22732	Pretending/Before You Accuse Me	1989	—	—	3.00
❑ RSO 409	I Shot the Sheriff/Give Me Strength	1974	—	2.50	5.00
❑ RSO 500	I Shot the Sheriff/Give Me Strength	1974	—	2.00	4.00
❑ RSO 503	Willie and the Hand Jive/Main Line Florida	1975	—	2.00	4.00
❑ RSO 509	Swing Low Sweet Chariot/Pretty Blue Eyes	1975	—	2.00	4.00
❑ RSO 513	Knockin' on Heaven's Door/Someone Like You	1975	—	2.00	4.00
❑ RSO 861	Hello Old Friend/All Our Pastimes	1976	—	2.00	4.00
❑ RSO 868	Carnival/Hungry	1976	—	2.00	4.00
❑ RSO 886	Lay Down Sally/Next Time You See Her	1978	—	2.00	4.00
❑ RSO 895	Wonderful Tonight/Peaches and Diesel	1978	—	2.00	4.00
❑ RSO 910	Promises/Watch Out for Lucy	1978	—	2.00	4.00
❑ RSO 928	Tulsa Time/Cocaine	1979	—	2.50	5.00
—Studio versions of the two songs					
❑ RSO 1039	Tulsa Time/Cocaine	1980	—	2.00	4.00
—Live versions of the two songs					
❑ RSO 1051	Blues Power/Early in the Morning	1980	—	2.00	4.00
❑ RSO 1060	I Can't Stand It/Black Rose	1981	—	2.00	4.00
❑ RSO 1064	Another Ticket/Rita Mae	1981	—	2.00	4.00
Albums					
❑ Atco SD 33-329	Eric Clapton	1970	5.00	10.00	20.00
❑ Atco SD 2-803 [(2)]	History of Eric Clapton	1972	5.00	10.00	20.00
—Contains tracks from the Yardbirds, John Mayall's Bluesbreakers, Cream, Blind Faith, and solo records					
❑ Duck 23773	Money and Cigarettes	1983	2.50	5.00	10.00
❑ Duck 25166	Behind the Sun	1985	2.50	5.00	10.00
❑ Duck 25476	August	1986	2.50	5.00	10.00
❑ Polydor PD 3503 [(2)]	Eric Clapton at His Best	1972	5.00	10.00	20.00
—Compiles tracks from his first solo album plus Derek and the Dominos					
❑ Polydor 24-5526	Clapton	1973	3.75	7.50	15.00
—Compiles tracks from his first solo album plus Derek and the Dominos					
❑ Polydor 835261-1 [(6)]	Crossroads	1988	12.50	25.00	50.00
—Box set; contains material from all phases of his career					
❑ Reprise 26074	Journeyman	1989	3.00	6.00	12.00
❑ RSO SO 877	Eric Clapton's Rainbow Concert	1973	3.75	7.50	15.00
❑ RSO RS-1-3004	No Reason to Cry	1976	3.00	6.00	12.00
❑ RSO RS-1-3008	Eric Clapton	1977	3.00	6.00	12.00
—Reissue of Atco LP of the same name					
❑ RSO RS-1-3023	461 Ocean Boulevard	1977	3.00	6.00	12.00
—Reissue of RSO 4801					
❑ RSO RS-1-3030	Slowhand	1977	3.00	6.00	12.00
❑ RSO RS-1-3039	Backless	1978	3.00	6.00	12.00
❑ RSO RX-1-3095	Another Ticket	1981	2.50	5.00	10.00
❑ RSO RS-1-3099	Time Pieces/The Best of Eric Clapton	1982	2.50	5.00	10.00
❑ RSO RS-2-4202 [(2)]	Just One Night	1980	3.75	7.50	15.00
❑ RSO SO 4801	461 Ocean Boulevard	1974	3.75	7.50	15.00
—With "Give Me Strength"					
❑ RSO SO 4806	There's One in Every Crowd	1975	3.00	6.00	12.00
❑ RSO SO 4809	E.C. Was Here	1975	3.00	6.00	12.00

CLARK, DAVE, FIVE

45s

Number	Title (A Side/B Side)	Yr	VG	VG+	NM
❑ Congress 212	I Knew It All the Time/That's What I Said	1964	5.00	10.00	20.00
❑ Epic 9656	Glad All Over/I Know You	1964	3.75	7.50	15.00
❑ Epic 9671	Bits and Pieces/All of the Time	1964	3.00	6.00	12.00
❑ Epic 9678	Do You Love Me/Chaquita	1964	3.00	6.00	12.00

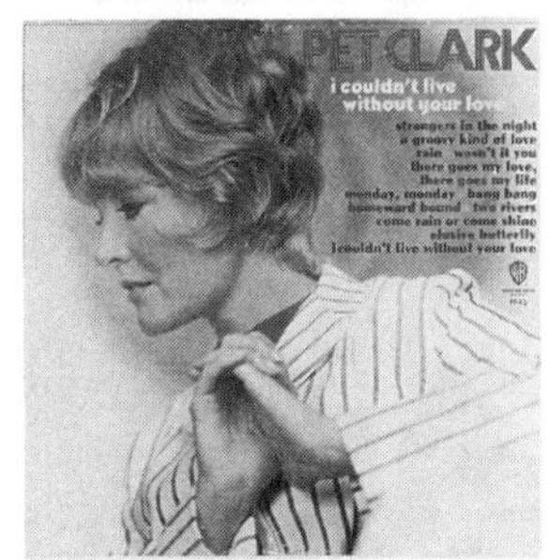

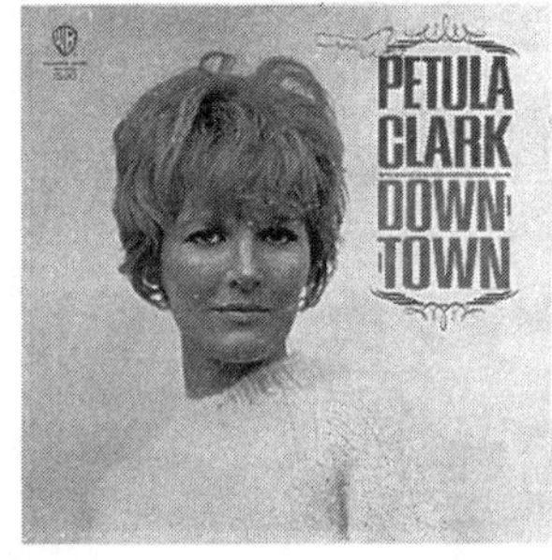

Number	Title (A Side/B Side)	Yr	VG	VG+	NM
❑ Epic 9692	Can't You See That She's Mine/No TIme to Lose	1964	3.00	6.00	12.00
❑ Epic 9704	Because/Theme Without a Name	1964	3.00	6.00	12.00
❑ Epic 9722	Everybody Knows (I Still Love You)/Ol' Sol	1964	3.00	6.00	12.00
❑ Epic 9739	Any Way You Want It/Crying Over You	1964	3.00	6.00	12.00
❑ Epic 9763	Come Home/Your Turn to Cry	1965	3.00	6.00	12.00
❑ Epic 9786	Reelin' and Rockin'/I'm Thinking	1965	3.00	6.00	12.00
❑ Epic 9811	I Like It Like That/Hurting Inside	1965	3.00	6.00	12.00
❑ Epic 9833	Catch Us If You Can/On the Move	1965	3.00	6.00	12.00
❑ Epic 9863	Over and Over/I'll Be Yours (My Love)	1965	3.00	6.00	12.00
❑ Epic 9882	At the Scene/I Miss You	1966	3.00	6.00	12.00
❑ Epic 10004	Try Too Hard/All Night Long	1966	3.00	6.00	12.00
❑ Epic 10031	Please Tell Me Why/Look Before You Leap	1966	3.00	6.00	12.00
❑ Epic 10053	Satisfied with You/Don't Let Me Down	1966	3.00	6.00	12.00
❑ Epic 10076	Nineteen Days/Sitting Here Baby	1966	3.00	6.00	12.00
❑ Epic 10114	I've Got to Have a Reason/Good Time Woman	1966	3.00	6.00	12.00
❑ Epic 10144	You Got What It Takes/Doctor Rhythm	1967	3.00	6.00	12.00
❑ Epic 10179	You Must Have Been a Beautiful Baby/Man in the Pin Stripe Suit	1967	3.00	6.00	12.00
❑ Epic 10209	A Little Bit Now/You Don't Play Me Around	1967	3.75	7.50	15.00
❑ Epic 10244	Red and Blue/Concentration Baby	1967	3.75	7.50	15.00
❑ Epic 10265	Everybody Knows/Inside and Out	1967	3.75	7.50	15.00
❑ Epic 10325	Please Stay/Forget	1968	3.75	7.50	15.00
❑ Epic 10375	Red Balloon/Maze of Love	1968	3.75	7.50	15.00
❑ Epic 10476	Paradise (Is Half As Nice)/34-06	1969	3.75	7.50	15.00
❑ Epic 10509	If Somebody Loves You/Best Day's Work	1969	3.75	7.50	15.00
❑ Epic 10547	Bring It On Home to Me/Darling, I Love You	1969	3.75	7.50	15.00
❑ Epic 10635	Here Comes Summer/Five by Five	1970	3.75	7.50	15.00
❑ Epic 10684	Good Old Rock and Roll (Medley)/One Night	1970	5.00	10.00	20.00
❑ Epic 10704	Southern Man/If You Wanna See Me Cry	1971	10.00	20.00	40.00
❑ Epic 10768	Won't You Be My Lady/Into Your Life	1971	5.00	10.00	20.00
❑ Epic 10894	Rub It In/I'm Sorry Baby	1972	5.00	10.00	20.00
❑ Epic Memory Lane 2225	Glad All Over/Bits and Pieces	1972	—	2.00	4.00
❑ Epic Memory Lane 2230	Because/Do You Love Me	1972	—	2.00	4.00
❑ Epic Memory Lane 2234	Any Way You Want It/Can't You See That She's Mine	1972	—	2.00	4.00
❑ Epic Memory Lane 2239	I Like It Like That/Everybody Knows (I Still Love You)	1972	—	2.00	4.00
❑ Epic Memory Lane 2248	Over and Over/Catch Us If You Can	1972	—	2.00	4.00
❑ Epic Memory Lane 2294	Bring It On Home to Me/If Somebody Loves You	1972	—	2.00	4.00
❑ Epic Memory Lane 2313	I Like It Like That/Can't You See That She's Mine	1972	—	2.00	4.00
❑ Epic Memory Lane 2316	Come Home/You Got What It Takes	1972	—	2.00	4.00
❑ Jubilee 5476	Chaquita/In Your Heart	1964	7.50	15.00	30.00
❑ Laurie 3188	I Walk the Line/First Love	1963	—	—	—
—Not known to exist					
❑ Rust 5078	I Walk the Line/First Love	1964	10.00	20.00	40.00
Albums					
❑ Cortleigh C-1073 [M]	The Dave Clark Five with Ricky Astor	1964	7.50	15.00	30.00
—With two early DC5 tracks and assorted other stuff by other artists					
❑ Cortleigh CS-1073 [R]	The Dave Clark Five with Ricky Astor	1964	3.75	7.50	15.00
—With two early DC5 tracks and assorted other stuff by other artists					
❑ Crown CST-400 [R]	The Dave Clark Five with the Playbacks	1964	3.75	7.50	15.00
—With two early DC5 tracks and assorted other stuff by other artists					
❑ Crown CST-473 [R]	Chaquita/In Your Heart	1964	3.75	7.50	15.00
—With two early DC5 tracks and assorted other stuff by other artists					
❑ Crown CST-644 [R]	The Dave Clark Five with the Playbacks	196?	3.00	6.00	12.00
—Reissue					
❑ Crown CLP-5400 [M]	The Dave Clark Five with the Playbacks	1964	7.50	15.00	30.00
—With two early DC5 tracks and assorted other stuff by other artists					
❑ Crown CLP-5473 [M]	Chaquita/In Your Heart	1964	7.50	15.00	30.00
—With two early DC5 tracks and assorted other stuff by other artists					
❑ Custom CS 1098 [R]	The Dave Clark Five with the Playbacks	196?	3.00	6.00	12.00
—Reissue					
❑ Epic LN 24093 [M]	Glad All Over	1964	10.00	20.00	40.00
—Group photo with instruments					
❑ Epic LN 24104 [M]	The Dave Clark Five Return	1964	10.00	20.00	40.00
❑ Epic LN 24117 [M]	American Tour	1964	10.00	20.00	40.00
❑ Epic LN 24128 [M]	Coast to Coast	1965	10.00	20.00	40.00
❑ Epic LN 24139 [M]	Weekend in London	1965	10.00	20.00	40.00
❑ Epic LN 24162 [M]	Having a Wild Weekend	1965	10.00	20.00	40.00
❑ Epic LN 24178 [M]	I Like It Like That	1965	10.00	20.00	40.00

Number	Title (A Side/B Side)	Yr	VG	VG+	NM
❑ Epic LN 24185 [M]	The Dave Clark Five's Greatest Hits	1966	6.25	12.50	25.00
❑ Epic LN 24198 [M]	Try Too Hard	1966	7.50	15.00	30.00
❑ Epic LN 24212 [M]	Satisfied with You	1966	7.50	15.00	30.00
❑ Epic LN 24221 [M]	More Greatest Hits	1966	6.25	12.50	25.00
❑ Epic LN 24236 [M]	5 by 5	1967	7.50	15.00	30.00
❑ Epic LN 24312 [M]	You Got What It Takes	1967	7.50	15.00	30.00
❑ Epic LN 24354 [M]	Everybody Knows	1968	7.50	15.00	30.00
❑ Epic BN 26093 [R]	Glad All Over	1964	7.50	15.00	30.00
—Group photo with instruments					
❑ Epic BN 26104 [R]	The Dave Clark Five Return	1964	7.50	15.00	30.00
❑ Epic BN 26117 [R]	American Tour	1964	7.50	15.00	30.00
❑ Epic BN 26128 [R]	Coast to Coast	1965	7.50	15.00	30.00
❑ Epic BN 26139 [R]	Weekend in London	1965	7.50	15.00	30.00
❑ Epic BN 26162 [R]	Having a Wild Weekend	1965	7.50	15.00	30.00
❑ Epic BN 26178 [R]	I Like It Like That	1965	7.50	15.00	30.00
❑ Epic BN 26185 [R]	The Dave Clark Five's Greatest Hits	1966	5.00	10.00	20.00
—Yellow label					
❑ Epic BN 26198 [R]	Try Too Hard	1966	6.25	12.50	25.00
❑ Epic BN 26212 [R]	Satisfied with You	1966	6.25	12.50	25.00
❑ Epic BN 26221 [R]	More Greatest Hits	1966	5.00	10.00	20.00
❑ Epic BN 26236 [S]	5 by 5	1967	10.00	20.00	40.00
❑ Epic BN 26312 [S]	You Got What It Takes	1967	10.00	20.00	40.00
❑ Epic BN 26354 [S]	Everybody Knows	1968	10.00	20.00	40.00
❑ Epic EG 30434 [(2)S]	The Dave Clark Five	1971	25.00	50.00	100.00
—Twenty hits and near-hits, all in true stereo! Yellow label.					
❑ Epic KEG 33459 [(2)M]	Glad All Over Again	1975	12.50	25.00	50.00

CLARK, DEE

45s

Number	Title (A Side/B Side)	Yr	VG	VG+	NM
❑ Abner 1019	Nobody But You/When I Call on You	1958	6.25	12.50	25.00
❑ Abner 1026	Just Keep It Up/Whispering Grass	1959	6.25	12.50	25.00
❑ Abner 1029	Hey Little Girl/If It Wasn't for Love	1959	6.25	12.50	25.00
❑ Abner 1032	How About That/Blues Get Off My Shoulder	1959	6.25	12.50	25.00
❑ Abner 1037	At My Front Door/Cling-a-Ling	1960	6.25	12.50	25.00
❑ Chelsea 3025	Ride a Wild Horse/(Instrumental)	1975	—	2.50	5.00
❑ Columbia 44200	In These Very Tender Moments/Lost Girl	1967	2.00	4.00	8.00
❑ Constellation 108	Crossfire Time/I'm Going Home	1963	3.00	6.00	12.00
❑ Constellation 113	It's Raining/That's My Girl	1964	50.00	100.00	200.00
❑ Constellation 120	Come Closer/That's My Girl	1964	37.50	75.00	150.00
❑ Constellation 132	Warm Summer Breeze/Heartbreak	1964	3.00	6.00	12.00
❑ Constellation 142	Ain't Gonna Be Your Fool/In My Apartment	1964	3.00	6.00	12.00
❑ Constellation 147	T.C.B./It's Impossible	1965	3.00	6.00	12.00
❑ Constellation 155	I Can't Run Away/She's My Baby	1965	3.00	6.00	12.00
❑ Constellation 165	I Don't Need (Nobody Like You)/Hot Potatoe	1966	3.00	6.00	12.00
❑ Constellation 173	Old Fashion Love/I'm Goin' Home	1966	3.00	6.00	12.00
❑ Falcon 1002	Gloria/Kangaroo Hop	1957	7.50	15.00	30.00
❑ Falcon 1005	Seven Nights/24 Boy Friends	1957	10.00	20.00	40.00
❑ Falcon 1009	Oh Little Girl/Wondering	1958	10.00	20.00	40.00
❑ Liberty 56152	24 Hours of Loneliness/Where Did All the Good Times Go	1970	—	2.50	5.00
❑ Lost-Nite 303	Raindrops/I Want to Love You	197?	—	2.50	5.00
—Reissue					
❑ United Artists 50759	You Can Make Me Feel So Good/Old Time Religion	1971	—	2.50	5.00
❑ Vee Jay 355	You're Looking Good/Gloria	1960	3.75	7.50	15.00
❑ Vee Jay 372	Your Friends/Because I Love You	1961	3.75	7.50	15.00
❑ Vee Jay 383	Raindrops/I Want to Love You	1961	5.00	10.00	20.00
❑ Vee Jay 394	Gotos Delluvia (Raindrops)/Livin' with Vivian	1961	3.75	7.50	15.00
—B-side by Al Smith					
❑ Vee Jay 409	Don't Walk Away from Me/You're Telling Our Secrets	1961	3.75	7.50	15.00
❑ Vee Jay 428	You Are Like the Wind/Drums in My Heart	1962	3.75	7.50	15.00
❑ Vee Jay 443	Dance On Little Girl/Fever	1962	3.75	7.50	15.00
❑ Vee Jay 462	I'm Going Back to School/Nobody But You	1962	3.75	7.50	15.00
❑ Vee Jay 487	I'm a Soldier Boy/Shook Up Over You	1963	3.75	7.50	15.00
❑ Vee Jay 532	How Is He Treating You/The Jones Boy	1963	3.75	7.50	15.00
❑ Vee Jay 548	Walking My Dog/Nobody But Me	1963	3.75	7.50	15.00
❑ Wand 1177	Nobody But You (Part 1)/Nobody But You (Part 2)	1968	2.00	4.00	8.00
❑ Warner Bros. 7720	Raindrops '73/I'm a Happy Man	1973	—	2.50	5.00

Albums

Number	Title (A Side/B Side)	Yr	VG	VG+	NM
❑ Abner LP-2000 [M]	Dee Clark	1959	30.00	60.00	120.00
❑ Abner SR-2000 [S]	Dee Clark	1959	87.50	175.00	350.00
❑ Abner LP-2002 [M]	How About That	1960	20.00	40.00	80.00
❑ Abner SR-2002 [S]	How About That	1960	30.00	60.00	120.00
❑ Solid Smoke 8026	His Best Recordings	1983	2.50	5.00	10.00
❑ Sunset SUS-5217	Wondering	1968	3.00	6.00	12.00
❑ Vee Jay LP-1019 [M]	You're Looking Good	1960	12.50	25.00	50.00
❑ Vee Jay LP-1037 [M]	Hold On, It's Dee Clark	1961	12.50	25.00	50.00
❑ Vee Jay SR-1037 [S]	Hold On, It's Dee Clark	1961	25.00	50.00	100.00
❑ Vee Jay LP-1047 [M]	The Best of Dee Clark	1964	12.50	25.00	50.00
❑ Vee Jay SR-1047 [S]	The Best of Dee Clark	1964	25.00	50.00	100.00

CLARK, PETULA

45s

Number	Title (A Side/B Side)	Yr	VG	VG+	NM
❑ ABC Dunhill 15007	Never Been a Horse That Couldn't Be Rode/ I'm the Woman You Need	1974	—	2.50	5.00
❑ ABC Dunhill 15019	Loving Arms/I'm the Woman You Need	1974	—	2.50	5.00
❑ Coral 60971	Song of the Mermaid/Tell Me Truly	1953	6.25	12.50	25.00
❑ Coral 61077	Where Did My Snowman Go/Three Little Kittens	1953	6.25	12.50	25.00
❑ Imperial 5582	The Little Blue Man/Baby Lover	1959	5.00	10.00	20.00
❑ Imperial 5600	Where Do I Go from Here/Mama's Talkin' Soft	1959	5.00	10.00	20.00

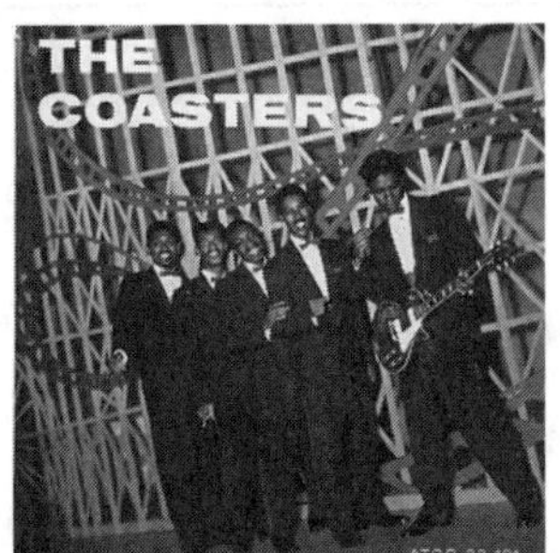

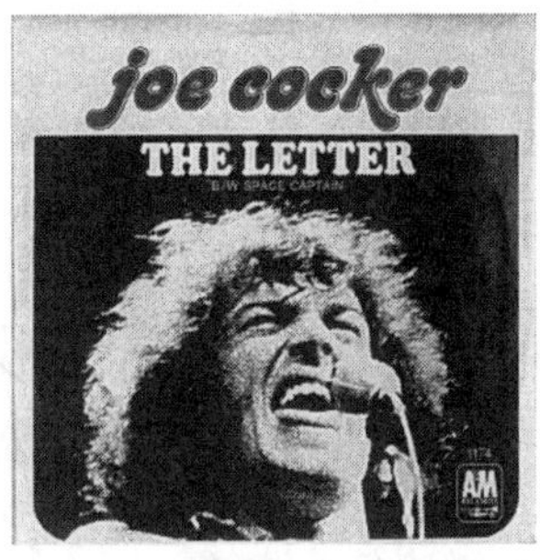

Number	Title (A Side/B Side)	Yr	VG	VG+	NM
❑ Imperial 5655	Now That I Need You/I Love a Violin	1960	5.00	10.00	20.00
❑ King 1371	The Little Shoemaker/Helpless	1954	6.25	12.50	25.00
❑ Laurie 3143	Jumble Sale/The Road	1962	3.75	7.50	15.00
❑ Laurie 3156	I Will Follow Him/Darling Cheri	1963	3.75	7.50	15.00
❑ Laurie 3236	Elle Est Finie/J'ai Tout Oublie	1964	3.75	7.50	15.00
❑ Laurie 3259	In Love/The Road	1964	3.75	7.50	15.00
❑ Laurie 3316	In Love/Darling Cheri	1965	3.00	6.00	12.00
❑ Laurie 3573	Jumble Sale/The Road	1971	—	3.00	6.00
❑ London Int'l. 10504	My Friend the Sea/With All My Love	1962	3.75	7.50	15.00
❑ London Int'l. 10510	I'm Counting on You/Some Other World	1962	3.75	7.50	15.00
❑ London Int'l. 10516	Tender Love/Whistlin' for the Moon	1962	3.75	7.50	15.00
❑ MGM 12049	The Pendulum Song/Romance in Rome	1955	6.25	12.50	25.00
❑ MGM 14392	My Guy/Little Bit of Lovin'	1972	—	2.50	5.00
❑ MGM 14431	Wedding Song (There Is Love)/Song Without End	1972	—	2.50	5.00
❑ MGM 14511	Serenade of Love/I Can't Remember	1973	—	2.50	5.00
❑ MGM 14577	Gratification/I Can't Remember	1973	—	2.50	5.00
❑ MGM 14673	Silver Spoon/Fixing to Live	1973	—	2.50	5.00
❑ MGM 14708	Come On Home/The Old Fashioned Way	1974	—	2.50	5.00
❑ Scotti Bros. 02676	Natural Love/Because I Love Him	1982	—	2.00	4.00
❑ Scotti Bros. 02979	Blue Eyes Crying in the Rain/Love Won't Always Pass You By	1982	—	2.00	4.00
❑ Scotti Bros. 03171	Dreamin' with My Eyes Wide Open/Afterglow	1982	—	2.00	4.00
❑ Warner Bros. 5494	Downtown/You'd Better Love Me	1964	3.75	7.50	15.00
—Originals have red labels with arrows					
❑ Warner Bros. 5612	I Know a Place/Jack and John	1965	2.50	5.00	10.00
❑ Warner Bros. 5643	You'd Better Come Home/Heart	1965	2.50	5.00	10.00
❑ Warner Bros. 5661	Round Every Corner/Two Rivers	1965	2.50	5.00	10.00
❑ Warner Bros. 5684	My Love/Where Am I Going	1965	2.50	5.00	10.00
❑ Warner Bros. 5802	A Sign of the Times/Time for Love	1966	2.50	5.00	10.00
❑ Warner Bros. 5835	I Couldn't Live Without Your Love/Your Way of Life	1966	2.50	5.00	10.00
❑ Warner Bros. 5863	Who Am I/Love Is a Long Journey	1966	2.50	5.00	10.00
❑ Warner Bros. 5882	Color My World/Take Me Home Again	1966	2.50	5.00	10.00
❑ Warner Bros. 7002	This Is My Song/High	1967	2.50	5.00	10.00
❑ Warner Bros. 7049	Don't Sleep in the Subway/Here Comes the Morning	1967	2.50	5.00	10.00
❑ Warner Bros. 7073	The Cat in the Window (The Bird in the Sky)/Fancy Dancin' Man	1967	2.50	5.00	10.00
❑ Warner Bros. 7097	The Other Man's Grass Is Always Greener/At the Crossroads	1967	2.50	5.00	10.00
❑ Warner Bros. 7170	Kiss Me Goodbye/I've Got Love Going for Me	1968	2.50	5.00	10.00
—Originals have orange labels					
❑ Warner Bros. 7216	Don't Give Up/Every Time I See a Rainbow	1968	2.00	4.00	8.00
❑ Warner Bros. 7244	American Boys/Look to the Sky	1968	2.00	4.00	8.00
❑ Warner Bros. 7275	Happy Heart/Love Is the Only Thing	1969	2.00	4.00	8.00
❑ Warner Bros. 7310	Look at Mine/If Somebody Loves You	1969	2.00	4.00	8.00
❑ Warner Bros. 7343	No One Better Than You/Things Bringht and Beautiful	1969	2.00	4.00	8.00
❑ Warner Bros. 7422	Beautiful Sounds/The Song Is Love	1970	2.00	4.00	8.00
❑ Warner Bros. 7467	The Song of My Life/Couldn't Sleep	1971	2.00	4.00	8.00
❑ Warner Bros. 7484	I Don't Know How to Love Him (Superstar)/Maybe	1971	2.00	4.00	8.00
❑ Warwick 652	Romeo/Isn't It a Lovely Day	1961	5.00	10.00	20.00
Albums					
❑ GNP Crescendo 2069	Live at the Royal Albert Hall	1972	2.50	5.00	10.00
❑ GNP Crescendo 2170	The Greatest Hits of Petula Clark	1984	2.00	4.00	8.00
❑ Imperial LP-9079 [M]	Pet Clark	1959	12.50	25.00	50.00
❑ Imperial LP-9281 [M]	Uptown with Petula Clark	1965	5.00	10.00	20.00
—Reissue of Imperial 9079					
❑ Imperial LP-12027 [S]	Pet Clark	1959	20.00	40.00	80.00
❑ Imperial LP-12281 [S]	Uptown with Petula Clark	1965	6.25	12.50	25.00
—Reissue of Imperial 12079					
❑ Jango 779	Give It a Try	1986	2.50	5.00	10.00
❑ Laurie LLP-2032 [M]	In Love!	1965	3.75	7.50	15.00
❑ Laurie SLP-2032 [S]	In Love!	1965	3.75	7.50	15.00
❑ MGM SE-4859	Pet Clark Now	1972	2.50	5.00	10.00
❑ Premier PM-9016 [M]	The English Sound Starring Petula Clark	1965	3.00	6.00	12.00
❑ Premier PS-9016 [S]	The English Sound Starring Petula Clark	1965	3.75	7.50	15.00
❑ Roulette 1 [(3)]	Petula	1975	5.00	10.00	20.00
❑ Sunset SUM-1101 [M]	This Is Petula Clark	1965	3.00	6.00	12.00
❑ Sunset SUS-5101 [S]	This Is Petula Clark	1965	3.75	7.50	15.00
❑ Warner Bros. W 1590 [M]	Downtown	1965	3.75	7.50	15.00
—Originals have gray labels					

Number	Title (A Side/B Side)	Yr	VG	VG+	NM
❑ Warner Bros. WS 1590 [S]	Downtown	1965	5.00	10.00	20.00
—Originals have gold labels					
❑ Warner Bros. W 1598 [M]	I Know a Place	1965	3.75	7.50	15.00
—Originals have gray labels					
❑ Warner Bros. WS 1598 [S]	I Know a Place	1965	5.00	10.00	20.00
—Originals have gold labels					
❑ Warner Bros. W 1608 [M]	The World's Greatest International Hits	1965	3.75	7.50	15.00
—Originals have gray labels					
❑ Warner Bros. WS 1608 [S]	The World's Greatest International Hits	1965	5.00	10.00	20.00
—Originals have gold labels					
❑ Warner Bros. W 1630 [M]	My Love	1966	2.50	5.00	10.00
❑ Warner Bros. WS 1630 [S]	My Love	1966	3.00	6.00	12.00
❑ Warner Bros. W 1645 [M]	I Couldn't Live Without Your Love	1966	2.50	5.00	10.00
❑ Warner Bros. WS 1645 [S]	I Couldn't Live Without Your Love	1966	3.00	6.00	12.00
❑ Warner Bros. W 1673 [M]	Color My World/Who Am I	1967	2.50	5.00	10.00
❑ Warner Bros. WS 1673 [S]	Color My World/Who Am I	1967	3.00	6.00	12.00
❑ Warner Bros. W 1698 [M]	These Are My Songs	1967	2.50	5.00	10.00
❑ Warner Bros. WS 1698 [S]	These Are My Songs	1967	3.00	6.00	12.00
❑ Warner Bros. W 1719 [M]	The Other Man's Grass Is Always Greener	1968	3.00	6.00	12.00
❑ Warner Bros. WS 1719 [P]	The Other Man's Grass Is Always Greener	1968	3.00	6.00	12.00
—"The Other Man's Grass Is Always Greener" is rechanneled.					
❑ Warner Bros. W 1743 [M]	Petula	1968	3.00	6.00	12.00
❑ Warner Bros. WS 1743 [S]	Petula	1968	3.00	6.00	12.00
❑ Warner Bros. WS 1765	Greatest Hits, Volume I	1968	2.50	5.00	10.00
❑ Warner Bros. WS 1789	Portrait of Petula	1969	2.50	5.00	10.00
❑ Warner Bros. WS 1823	Just Pet	1969	2.50	5.00	10.00
❑ Warner Bros. WS 1862	Memphis	1970	2.50	5.00	10.00
❑ Warner Bros. WS 1865	Warm and Tender (The Song of My Life)	1971	2.50	5.00	10.00

CLASH, THE

45s

Number	Title (A Side/B Side)	Yr	VG	VG+	NM
❑ Epic 19-02055	The Magnificent Seven/The Magnificent Dance	1981	2.50	5.00	10.00
❑ Epic 14-03006	Should I Stay or Should I Go/Inoculated City	1982	2.00	4.00	8.00
❑ Epic 14-03034	Should I Stay or Should I Go/First Night Back in London	1982	2.00	4.00	8.00
❑ Epic 14-03061	Should I Stay or Should I Go/First Night Back in London	1982	—	3.00	6.00
❑ Epic 15-03088	Train in Vain (Stand By Me)/London Calling	1982	—	2.00	4.00
—Reissue; originals have "Memory Lane" flower petals label (gray label $3 NM)					
❑ Epic 34-03245	Rock the Casbah/Long Time Jerk	1982	—	2.00	4.00
❑ Epic 34-03547	Should I Stay Or Should I Go?/Cool Confusion	1983	—	2.00	4.00
❑ Epic 15-05540	Rock the Casbah/Long Time Jerk	1984	—	—	3.00
—Gray label reissue					
❑ Epic 15-08470	Rock the Casbah/Should I Stay Or Should I Go	1988	—	—	3.00
—Reissue					
❑ Epic 9-50738	I Fought the Law/White Man in Hammersmith Palais	1979	2.50	5.00	10.00
❑ Epic 9-50851	Train in Vain (Stand By Me)/London Calling	1980	—	2.50	5.00
❑ Epic 19-51013	Hitsville U.K./Police on My Back	1981	2.50	5.00	10.00

Albums

Number	Title (A Side/B Side)	Yr	VG	VG+	NM
❑ Epic JE 35543	Give 'Em Enough Rope	1978	3.75	7.50	15.00
—Block letters on cover; orange label					
❑ Epic JE 35543	Give 'Em Enough Rope	1978	3.75	7.50	15.00
—Script cover; orange label					
❑ Epic JE 36060	The Clash	1979	3.75	7.50	15.00
❑ Epic E2 36329 [(2)]	London Calling	1979	3.75	7.50	15.00
❑ Epic E3X 37037 [(3)]	Sandinista!	1981	5.00	10.00	20.00
❑ Epic FE 37689	Combat Rock	1982	3.75	7.50	15.00
—First pressings (with custom labels) contain a commercial in the middle of the song "Inoculated City"					
❑ Epic PE 38540	Black Market Clash	1982	2.50	5.00	10.00
—12-inch version of 10-inch record					
❑ Epic FE 40017	Cut the Crap	1985	2.50	5.00	10.00
❑ Epic E2 44025 [(2)]	The Story of the Clash, Vol. 1	1988	3.75	7.50	15.00
❑ Epic Nu-Disk 4E 36846 [10]	Black Market Clash	1980	3.75	7.50	15.00

CLASSICS IV

45s

Number	Title (A Side/B Side)	Yr	VG	VG+	NM
❑ Arlen 746	Don't Make Me Wait/It's Too Late	1964	5.00	10.00	20.00
❑ Capitol 5710	Cry Baby/Pollyanna	1966	3.75	7.50	15.00
—As "The Classics"					
❑ Capitol 5816	Little Darlin'/Nothing to Lose	1966	3.75	7.50	15.00
❑ Imperial 66259	Spooky/Poor People	1967	2.00	4.00	8.00
❑ Imperial 66293	Soul Train/Strange Changes	1968	2.00	4.00	8.00
❑ Imperial 66304	Mama's and Papa's/Waves	1968	2.00	4.00	8.00
❑ Imperial 66328	Stormy/24 Hours of Loneliness	1968	2.00	4.00	8.00
❑ Imperial 66328	Stormy/Ladies' Man	1968	5.00	10.00	20.00
❑ Imperial 66352	Traces/Mary, Mary Row Your Boat	1969	2.00	4.00	8.00
❑ Imperial 66378	Everyday With You Girl/Sentimental Lady	1969	2.00	4.00	8.00
❑ Imperial 66393	Change of Heart/Rainy Day	1969	—	3.00	6.00
—Starting here, "Dennis Yost and the Classics IV"					
❑ Imperial 66424	Midnight/The Comic	1969	—	3.00	6.00
❑ Imperial 66439	The Funniest Thing/Nobody Loves You But Me	1970	—	3.00	6.00
❑ Liberty 56182	God Knows I Loved Her/We Miss You	1970	—	3.00	6.00
❑ Liberty 56200	Where Did All the Good Times Go/Ain't It the Truth	1970	—	3.00	6.00
❑ MGM 14785	My First Day Without You/Lovin' Each Other	1975	—	2.00	4.00
❑ MGM South 7002	What Am I Crying For/All in Your Mind	1972	—	2.50	5.00
❑ MGM South 7012	Rosanna/One Man Show	1973	—	2.50	5.00
❑ MGM South 7016	Save the Sunlight/Make Me Believe It	1973	—	2.50	5.00
❑ MGM South 7020	I Knew It Would Happen/Love Me or Leave Me Alone	1973	—	2.50	5.00
❑ MGM South 7027	It's Now Winter's Day/Losing My Mind	1974	—	2.50	5.00

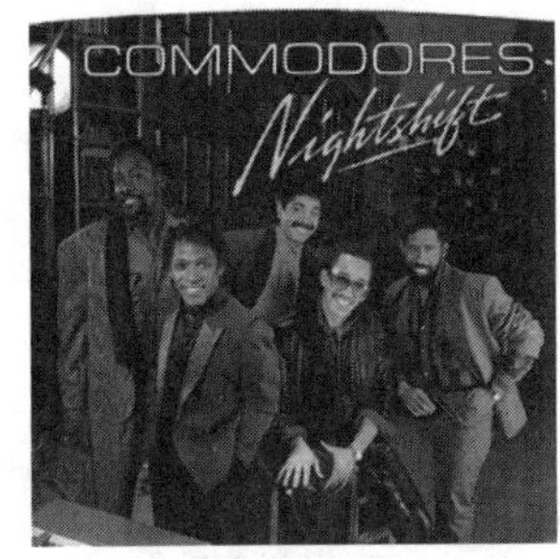

Number	Title (A Side/B Side)	Yr	VG	VG+	NM
❑ United Artists 0125	Stormy/Spooky	1973	—	2.00	4.00
—"Silver Spotlight Series" reissue					
❑ United Artists 0126	Traces/Everyday with You Girl	1973	—	2.00	4.00
—"Silver Spotlight Series" reissue					
❑ United Artists 50777	Most of All/It's Time for Love	1971	—	2.50	5.00
❑ United Artists 50805	Cherry Hill Park/Pick Up the Pieces	1971	—	2.50	5.00
Albums					
❑ Accord SN-7107	Stormy	1981	2.50	5.00	10.00
❑ Imperial LP-9371 [M]	Spooky	1968	10.00	20.00	40.00
—Mono has stock copy label inside stereo cover with white "Monaural" sticker					
❑ Imperial LP-12371 [S]	Spooky	1968	5.00	10.00	20.00
❑ Imperial LP-12407	Mamas and Papas/Soul Train	1969	5.00	10.00	20.00
❑ Imperial LP-12429	Traces	1969	5.00	10.00	20.00
❑ Imperial LP-16000	Dennis Yost & the Classics IV/Golden Greats - Volume I	1969	5.00	10.00	20.00
❑ Liberty LN-10109	The Very Best of the Classics IV	198?	2.00	4.00	8.00
❑ Liberty LST-11003	Song	1970	3.75	7.50	15.00
❑ MGM South 702	Dennis Yost and the Classics IV	1973	3.75	7.50	15.00
❑ United Artists UA-LA446-E	The Very Best of the Classics IV	1975	3.00	6.00	12.00
CLIMAX					
45s					
❑ Carousel 30050	Hard Rock Group/(B-side unknown)	1971	—	2.50	5.00
❑ Carousel 30055	Precious and Few/Park Preserve	1971	—	2.50	5.00
❑ Paramount 0023	You've Gotta Try/Friendship	1970	—	3.00	6.00
❑ Rocky Road 30055	Precious and Few/Park Preserve	1972	—	2.00	4.00
—Reissue of Carousel 30055					
❑ Rocky Road 30061	Life and Breath/If It Feels Good, Do It	1972	—	2.00	4.00
❑ Rocky Road 30064	Caroline This Time/Rainbow Rides Are Free	1972	—	2.00	4.00
❑ Rocky Road 30072	Rock and Roll Heaven/Face the Music	1973	—	2.50	5.00
❑ Rocky Road 30074	Walking in the Georgia Rain/(B-side unknown)	1973	—	2.00	4.00
❑ Rocky Road 30077	It's Gonna Get Better/(B-side unknown)	1974	—	2.00	4.00
Albums					
❑ Rocky Road 3506	Climax	1972	3.75	7.50	15.00
CLIMAX BLUES BAND					
45s					
❑ Sire 351	Reap What I've Sowed/(B-side unknown)	1971	2.00	4.00	8.00
❑ Sire 358	Hey Mama/That's All	1972	2.00	4.00	8.00
❑ Sire 705	Shake Your Love/Mule on the Dole	1973	2.00	4.00	8.00
❑ Sire 712	Goin' to New York/I Am Constant	1974	—	3.00	6.00
❑ Sire 713	Sense of Direction/Losin' the Humbles	1974	—	3.00	6.00
❑ Sire 715	Reaching Out/Milwaukee Truckin' Blues	1974	—	3.00	6.00
❑ Sire 721	Using the Power/Running Out of Time	1975	—	3.00	6.00
❑ Sire 736	Couldn't Get It Right/Sav'ry Gravy	1977	—	2.50	5.00
❑ Sire 747	Together and Free/Berlin Blues	1977	—	2.00	4.00
❑ Sire 1026	Makin' Love/Gospel Singer	1978	—	2.00	4.00
❑ Sire 1031	Mistress Moonshine/Teardrops	1978	—	2.00	4.00
❑ Sire 49012	Children of the Nightime/Long Distance Love	1979	—	2.00	4.00
❑ Sire 49098	Summer Rain/Money in Your Pocket	1979	—	2.00	4.00
❑ Warner Bros. 49605	Gotta Have More Love/One for Me and You	1980	—	2.00	4.00
❑ Warner Bros. 49669	I Love You/Horizontalized	1981	—	2.50	5.00
❑ Warner Bros. 49850	Darlin'/This Time You're the Singer	1981	—	2.00	4.00
❑ Warner Bros. 50018	Breakdown/Shake It Lucy	1982	—	2.00	4.00
Albums					
❑ Sire SRK 3334	Real to Reel	1979	2.50	5.00	10.00
❑ Sire SES-4901	#3	1971	3.75	7.50	15.00
❑ Sire SES-5903	Tightly Knit	1972	3.75	7.50	15.00
❑ Sire SR 6003	The Climax Chicago Blues Band	1978	2.50	5.00	10.00
❑ Sire SR 6004	Lot of Bottle	1977	2.50	5.00	10.00
❑ Sire SR 6008	Tightly Knit	1977	2.50	5.00	10.00
❑ Sire 2XS 6013 [(2)]	FM/Live	1977	3.00	6.00	12.00
❑ Sire SR 6016	Stamp Album	1977	2.50	5.00	10.00
❑ Sire SR 6033	The Climax Chicago Blues Band Plays On	1978	2.50	5.00	10.00
❑ Sire SRK 6056	Shine On	1978	2.50	5.00	10.00
❑ Sire SES-7402	Rich Man	1972	3.75	7.50	15.00
❑ Sire SAS-2-7411 [(2)]	FM/Live	1973	3.75	7.50	15.00
❑ Sire SAS-7501	Sense of Direction	1974	3.00	6.00	12.00

Number	Title (A Side/B Side)	Yr	VG	VG+	NM
❑ Sire SASD-7507	Stamp Album	1975	3.00	6.00	12.00
❑ Sire SASD-7523	Gold Plated	1976	3.00	6.00	12.00
❑ Sire SES-97013	The Climax Chicago Blues Band	1969	3.75	7.50	15.00
❑ Sire SES-97023	The Climax Chicago Blues Band Plays On	1970	3.75	7.50	15.00
❑ Virgin/Epic FE 38631	Sample and Hold	1983	2.50	5.00	10.00
❑ Warner Bros. BSK 3493	Flying the Flag	1981	3.00	6.00	12.00
❑ Warner Bros. BSK 3623	Lucky for Some	1982	2.50	5.00	10.00

COASTERS, THE

45s

Number	Title (A Side/B Side)	Yr	VG	VG+	NM
❑ American Int'l. 1122	If I Had a Hammer/If I Had a Hammer (Disco Version)	1976	—	2.50	5.00
—As "The World Famous Coasters"					
❑ Atco 6064	Down in Mexico/Turtle Dovin'	1956	20.00	40.00	80.00
❑ Atco 6073	One Kiss Led to Another/Brazil	1956	15.00	30.00	60.00
❑ Atco 6087	Searchin'/Young Blood	1957	17.50	35.00	70.00
—Maroon label (first pressing)					
❑ Atco 6098	Idol with the Golden Head/(When She Wants Good Lovin') My Baby Comes to Me	1957	10.00	20.00	40.00
❑ Atco 6104	Sweet Georgia Brown/What Is the Secret of Your Success	1957	10.00	20.00	40.00
❑ Atco 6111	Dance!/Gee, Golly	1958	10.00	20.00	40.00
❑ Atco 6116	Yakety Yak/Zing Went the Strings of My Heart	1958	6.25	12.50	25.00
❑ Atco 6126	The Shadow Knows/Sorry But I'm Gonna Have to Pass	1958	6.25	12.50	25.00
❑ Atco 6132 [M]	Charlie Brown/Three Cool Cats	1959	6.25	12.50	25.00
❑ Atco 6141	Along Came Jones/That Is Rock and Roll	1959	5.00	10.00	20.00
❑ Atco 6146	Poison Ivy/I'm a Hog for You	1959	5.00	10.00	20.00
❑ Atco 6153	Run Red Run/What About Us	1959	5.00	10.00	20.00
❑ Atco 6163	Besame Mucho (Part 1)/Besame Mucho (Part 2)	1960	6.25	12.50	25.00
❑ Atco 6168	Wake Me, Shake Me/Stewball	1960	6.25	12.50	25.00
❑ Atco 6178	Shoppin' for Clothes/The Snake and the Book Worm	1960	6.25	12.50	25.00
❑ Atco 6186	Thumbin' a Ride/Wait a Minute	1961	5.00	10.00	20.00
❑ Atco 6192	Little Egypt (Ying-Yang)/Keep On Rolling	1961	5.00	10.00	20.00
❑ Atco 6204	Girls, Girls, Girls (Part 1)/Girls, Girls, Girls (Part 2)	1961	5.00	10.00	20.00
❑ Atco 6210	Bad Blood/(Ain't That) Just Like Me	1961	5.00	10.00	20.00
❑ Atco 6219	Teach Me How to Shimmy/Ridin' Hood	1962	5.00	10.00	20.00
❑ Atco 6234	The Climb/(Instrumental)	1962	5.00	10.00	20.00
❑ Atco 6251	The P.T.A./Bull Tick Waltz	1962	5.00	10.00	20.00
❑ Atco 6287	Speedo's Back in Town/T'Ain't Nothin' to Me	1964	3.75	7.50	15.00
❑ Atco 6300	Lovey Dovey/Bad Detective	1964	3.75	7.50	15.00
❑ Atco 6321	Wild One/I Must Be Dreaming	1964	3.75	7.50	15.00
❑ Atco 6341	Hungry/Lady Like	1965	3.75	7.50	15.00
❑ Atco 6356	Money Honey/Let's Go Get Stoned	1965	3.75	7.50	15.00
❑ Atco 6379	Bell Bottom Slacks and a Chinese Kimono (She's My Little Spodee-O)/Crazy Baby	1965	6.25	12.50	25.00
❑ Atco 6407	Saturday Night Fish Fry/She's a Yum Yum	1966	3.75	7.50	15.00
❑ Atlantic 89361	Yakety Yak/Stand By Me	1986	—	—	3.00
❑ Chelan 2000	Searchin' '75/Young BLood	1975	—	2.50	5.00
—As "The Coasters 2+2"					
❑ Date 1552	Soul Pad/Down Home Girl	1967	5.00	10.00	20.00
❑ Date 1607	Everybody's Woman/She Can	1968	5.00	10.00	20.00
❑ Date 1617	D.W. Washburn/Everybody's Woman	1968	5.00	10.00	20.00
❑ King 6385	Love Potion #9/D.W. Washburn	1972	—	3.00	6.00
❑ King 6389	Cool Jerk/Talkin' 'Bout a Woman	1972	—	3.00	6.00
❑ King 6404	Soul Pad/D.W. Washburn	1972	—	3.00	6.00
❑ Sal Wa 1001	Take It Easy, Greasy/You Move Me	1975	—	2.50	5.00
❑ Turntable 504	Act Right/The World Is Changing	1969	2.50	5.00	10.00

Albums

Number	Title (A Side/B Side)	Yr	VG	VG+	NM
❑ Atco 33-101 [M]	The Coasters	1958	75.00	150.00	300.00
—Yellow "harp" label					
❑ Atco 33-111 [M]	The Coasters' Greatest Hits	1959	37.50	75.00	150.00
—Yellow "harp" label					
❑ Atco 33-123 [M]	One By One	1960	37.50	75.00	150.00
—Yellow "harp" label					
❑ Atco SD 33-123 [S]	One By One	1960	100.00	200.00	400.00
—Yellow "harp" label					
❑ Atco 33-135 [M]	Coast Along with the Coasters	1962	25.00	50.00	100.00
—Gold and gray label					
❑ Atco SD 33-135 [P]	Coast Along with the Coasters	1962	37.50	75.00	150.00
—Purple and brown label; "Wait a Minute" is rechanneled					
❑ Atco SD 33-371	Their Greatest Recordings/The Early Years	1971	5.00	10.00	20.00
❑ Clarion 605 [M]	That Is Rock and Roll	1965	10.00	20.00	40.00
❑ Clarion SD 605 [S]	That Is Rock and Roll	1965	12.50	25.00	50.00
❑ King KS-1146	The Coasters On Broadway	1971	6.25	12.50	25.00
❑ Power Pak 310	Greatest Hits	198?	2.50	5.00	10.00
❑ Trip 8028	It Ain't Sanitary	197?	3.00	6.00	12.00

COCHRAN, EDDIE

45s

Number	Title (A Side/B Side)	Yr	VG	VG+	NM
❑ Crest 1026	Skinny Jim/Half Loved	1956	75.00	150.00	300.00
❑ Liberty 55056	Sittin' in the Balcony/Dark Lonely Street	1957	7.50	15.00	30.00
❑ Liberty 55070	Mean When I'm Mad/One Kiss	1957	7.50	15.00	30.00
❑ Liberty 55087	Drive In Show/Am I Blue	1957	7.50	15.00	30.00
❑ Liberty 55112	Twenty Flight Rock/Cradle Baby	1957	37.50	75.00	150.00
❑ Liberty 55123	Jeannie, Jeannie, Jeannie/Pocketful of Hearts	1958	7.50	15.00	30.00
❑ Liberty 55138	Pretty Girl/Theresa	1958	8.75	17.50	35.00
❑ Liberty 55144	Summertime Blues/Live Again	1958	7.50	15.00	30.00
❑ Liberty 55166	C'mon Everybody/Don't Ever Let Me Go	1958	7.50	15.00	30.00
❑ Liberty 55177	Teen Age Heaven/I Remember	1959	7.50	15.00	30.00

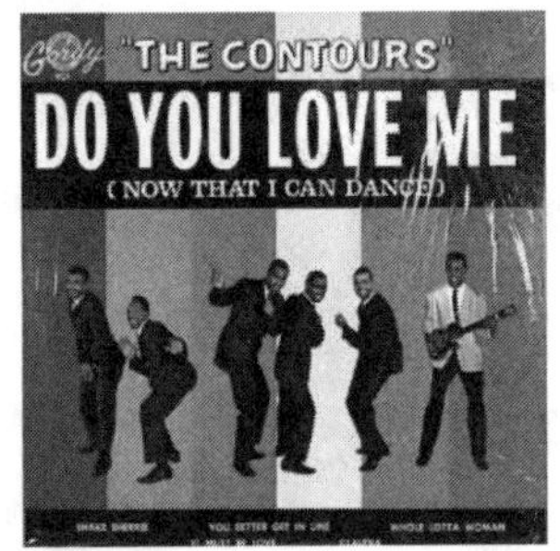

Number	Title (A Side/B Side)	Yr	VG	VG+	NM
❑ Liberty 55177	Teenage Heaven/I Remember	1959	10.00	20.00	40.00
—Note difference in title					
❑ Liberty 55203	The Boll Weevil Song/Somethin' Else	1959	7.50	15.00	30.00
❑ Liberty 55217	Hallelujah I Love Her So/Little Angel	1959	7.50	15.00	30.00
❑ Liberty 55242	Three Steps to Heaven/Cut Across Shorty	1960	10.00	20.00	40.00
❑ Liberty 55278	Lonely/Sweetie Pie	1960	6.25	12.50	25.00
❑ Liberty 55389	Weekend/Lonely	1961	7.50	15.00	30.00
❑ United Artists 0014	Summertime Blues/Cut Across Shorty	1973	—	2.00	4.00
❑ United Artists 0015	C'mon Everybody/Twenty Flight Rock	1973	—	2.00	4.00
❑ United Artists 0016	Sittin' in the Balcony/Somethin' Else	1973	—	2.00	4.00
—0014, 0015, 0016 are "Silver Spotlight Series" reissues					

Albums

Number	Title (A Side/B Side)	Yr	VG	VG+	NM
❑ Liberty LRP-3061 [M]	Singin' to My Baby	1957	200.00	400.00	800.00
—Green label					
❑ Liberty LRP-3172 [M]	Eddie Cochran (12 of His Biggest Hits)	1960	30.00	60.00	120.00
❑ Liberty LRP-3220 [M]	Never to Be Forgotten	1962	25.00	50.00	100.00
❑ Liberty LN-10137	Singin' to My Baby	198?	3.00	6.00	12.00
—Budget-line reissue					
❑ Liberty LN-10204	Great Hits	198?	2.00	4.00	8.00
❑ Sunset SUM-1123 [M]	Summertime Blues	1966	10.00	20.00	40.00
❑ Sunset SUS-5123 [R]	Summertime Blues	1966	6.25	12.50	25.00
❑ United Artists UA-LA428-E	The Very Best of Eddie Cochran	1975	3.00	6.00	12.00
❑ United Artists UAS-9959 [(2)]	Legendary Masters Series #4	1972	6.25	12.50	25.00

COCKER, JOE

45s

Number	Title (A Side/B Side)	Yr	VG	VG+	NM
❑ A&M 928	Marjorine/New Age of the Lily	1968	2.50	5.00	10.00
❑ A&M 991	With a Little Help from My Friends/Something's Coming On	1968	2.50	5.00	10.00
❑ A&M 1063	Feeling Alright/Sandpaper Cadillac	1969	—	3.00	6.00
—Reissued in 1971 with the same number					
❑ A&M 1112	Delta Lady/She's So Good to Me	1969	—	2.50	5.00
❑ A&M 1147	She Came In Through the Bathroom Window/Change in Louise	1969	—	2.50	5.00
❑ A&M 1174	The Letter/Space Captain	1970	—	2.50	5.00
❑ A&M 1200	Cry Me a River/Give Peace a Chance	1970	—	2.50	5.00
❑ A&M 1200	Cry Me a River/Please Give Peace a Chance	1970	—	2.50	5.00
❑ A&M 1258	High Time We Went/Black-Eyed Blues	1971	—	2.00	4.00
❑ A&M 1370	Midnight Rider/Woman to Woman	1972	—	2.00	4.00
❑ A&M 1407	Pardon Me Sir/St. James Infirmary Blues	1973	—	2.00	4.00
❑ A&M 1539	Put Out the Light/If I Love You	1974	—	2.00	4.00
❑ A&M 1626	I Can Stand a Little Rain/I Get Mad	1974	—	2.00	4.00
❑ A&M 1641	You Are So Beautiful/It's a Sin When You Love Somebody	1974	—	2.00	4.00
❑ A&M 1749	I Think It's Going to Rain Today/Oh Mama	1975	—	2.00	4.00
❑ A&M 1758	Jamaica Say You Will/It's All Over But the Shoutin'	1975	—	2.00	4.00
❑ A&M 1805	The Man in Me (Part 1)/The Man in Me (Part 2)	1976	—	2.00	4.00
❑ A&M 1830	Jealous Kind/You Came Along	1976	—	2.00	4.00
❑ A&M 1855	I Broke Down/You Came Along	1976	—	2.00	4.00
❑ A&M 2019	Feeling Alright/Cry Me a River	1978	—	2.00	4.00
❑ Asylum 45540	Fun Time/Watching the River Flow	1978	—	2.00	4.00
❑ Asylum 46001	Lady Put the Light Out/Wasted Years	1978	—	2.00	4.00
❑ Capitol B-5338	Civilized Man/A Girl Like You	1984	—	—	3.00
❑ Capitol B-5390	Crazy in Love/Come On In	1984	—	—	3.00
❑ Capitol B-5412	Edge of a Dream/Tempted	1984	—	—	3.00
❑ Capitol B-5557	Shelter Me/Tell Me There's a Way	1986	—	—	3.00
❑ Capitol B-5589	You Can Leave Your Hat On/Long Drag of the Cigarette	1986	—	2.50	5.00
❑ Capitol B-5626	Don't Drink the Water/Don't You Love Me Anymore	1986	—	—	3.00
❑ Capitol B-44072	Unchain My Heart/Satisfied	1987	—	—	3.00
❑ Capitol B-44101	Two Wrongs (Don't Make a Right)/Isolation	1987	—	—	3.00
❑ Capitol B-44182	A Woman Loves a Man/La Vie En Rose	1988	—	—	3.00
—B-side by Edith Piaf					
❑ Capitol NR-44590	Living in the Promiseland/She Came In Through the Bathroom Window (Live)	1990	—	2.00	4.00
❑ Island 99875	Throw It Away/Easy Rider	1983	—	2.00	4.00
❑ MCA 51177	I'm So Glad I'm Standing Here Today/Standing Tall	1981	—	2.00	4.00
—With the Crusaders					
❑ MCA 51222	This Old World's Too Funky for Me/Standing Tall	1981	—	2.00	4.00
—With the Crusaders					
❑ MCA 53077	Love Lives On/On My Way to You	1987	—	2.00	4.00

Number	Title (A Side/B Side)	Yr	VG	VG+	NM
❑ Philips 40255	I'll Cry Instead/Precious Words	1965	10.00	20.00	40.00
—Originally by "Vance Arnold and the Avengers"					
❑ Philips 40255	I'll Cry Instead/Precious Words	1965	10.00	20.00	40.00
—Artist listed as "Joe Cocker"					

Albums

Number	Title	Yr	VG	VG+	NM
❑ A&M SP-3106	With a Little Help from My Friends	1980	2.00	4.00	8.00
❑ A&M SP-3175	I Can Stand a Little Rain	1980	2.00	4.00	8.00
❑ A&M SP-3257	Joe Cocker's Greatest Hits	1982	2.00	4.00	8.00
❑ A&M SP-3633	I Can Stand a Little Rain	1974	2.50	5.00	10.00
❑ A&M SP-4182	With a Little Help from My Friends	1969	3.00	6.00	12.00
—Brown label					
❑ A&M SP-4224	Joe Cocker!	1969	3.00	6.00	12.00
—Brown label					
❑ A&M SP-4368	Joe Cocker	1972	3.00	6.00	12.00
—Brown label					
❑ A&M SP-4529	Jamaica Say You Will	1975	2.50	5.00	10.00
❑ A&M SP-4574	Stingray	1976	2.50	5.00	10.00
❑ A&M SP-4670	Joe Cocker's Greatest Hits	1977	2.50	5.00	10.00
❑ A&M SP-6002 [(2)]	Mad Dogs and Englishmen	1970	3.75	7.50	15.00
—Brown labels					
❑ Asylum 6E-145	Luxury You Can Afford	1978	2.50	5.00	10.00
❑ Capitol ST-12335	Civilized Man	1984	2.50	5.00	10.00
❑ Capitol ST-12394	Cocker	1986	2.50	5.00	10.00
❑ Capitol CLT-48285	Unchain My Heart	1988	2.50	5.00	10.00
❑ Capitol C1-92861	One Night of Sin	1989	3.00	6.00	12.00
❑ Island IL 9750	Sheffield Steel	1982	2.50	5.00	10.00
❑ Island 90096	One More Time	1983	2.50	5.00	10.00

COCKER, JOE, AND JENNIFER WARNES

45s

Number	Title	Yr	VG	VG+	NM
❑ Island 99996	Up Where We Belong/Sweet Li'l Woman	1982	—	2.00	4.00

COLE, NATALIE

45s

Number	Title	Yr	VG	VG+	NM
❑ Capitol 4109	This Will Be/Joey	1975	—	2.50	5.00
❑ Capitol 4193	Inseparable/How Come You Won't Stay Here	1975	—	2.00	4.00
❑ Capitol 4259	Sophisticated Lady (She's a Different Lady)/ Good Morning Heartache	1976	—	2.00	4.00
❑ Capitol 4328	Mr. Melody/Not Like Mine	1976	—	2.00	4.00
❑ Capitol 4360	I've Got Love on My Mind/Unpredictable You	1976	—	2.00	4.00
❑ Capitol 4439	Party Lights/Peaceful Living	1977	—	2.00	4.00
❑ Capitol 4509	Our Love/La Costa	1977	—	2.00	4.00
❑ Capitol 4572	Annie Mae/Just Can't Stay Away	1978	—	2.00	4.00
❑ Capitol 4623	Lucy in the Sky with Diamonds/Lovers	1978	—	2.00	4.00
❑ Capitol 4690	Stand By/Who Will Carry On	1979	—	2.00	4.00
❑ Capitol 4722	Sorry/You're So Good	1979	—	2.00	4.00
❑ Capitol 4767	Your Lonely Heart/The Winner	1979	—	2.00	4.00
❑ Capitol 4869	Someone That I Used to Love/Don't Look Back	1980	—	2.00	4.00
❑ Capitol 4924	Hold On/Paradise	1980	—	2.00	4.00
❑ Capitol A-5021	You Were Right Girl/Across the Nation	1981	—	2.00	4.00
❑ Capitol A-5045	Nothin' But a Fool/The Joke Is On You	1981	—	2.00	4.00
❑ Elektra 64816	The Christmas Song (Chestnuts Roasting on an Open Fire)/ Nature Boy	1991	—	2.00	4.00
❑ Elektra 64875	Unforgettable/Cottage for Sale	1991	—	2.00	4.00
❑ EMI B-50185	Miss You Like Crazy/Good to Be Back	1989	—	—	3.00
❑ EMI B-50213	I Do/Miss You Like Crazy	1989	—	—	3.00
❑ EMI B-50231	As a Matter of Fact/(B-side unknown)	1989	—	2.50	5.00
❑ EMI Manhattan B-50117	Pink Cadillac/I Wanna Be That Woman	1988	—	—	3.00
❑ EMI Manhattan B-50138	When I Fall in Love/Pink Cadillac	1988	—	—	3.00
❑ Epic 34-04000	Too Much Mister/Where's Your Angel	1983	—	2.00	4.00
❑ Epic 34-04147	Keep 'Em on the Outside/I Won't Deny You	1983	—	2.00	4.00
❑ Geffen 28152	Over You/After Midnite	1987	—	—	3.00
—With Ray Parker Jr.					
❑ Manhattan B-50073	Jump Start/More Than the Stars	1987	—	—	3.00
❑ Manhattan B-50094	I Live for Your Love/More Than the Stars	1987	—	—	3.00
❑ Modern 99589	Secrets/Nobody's Soldier	1985	—	—	3.00
❑ Modern 99630	A Little Bit of Heaven/When I Need It Bad, You Got It Good	1985	—	—	3.00
❑ Modern 99648	Dangerous/Love Is On the Way	1985	—	—	3.00

Albums

Number	Title	Yr	VG	VG+	NM
❑ Capitol ST-11429	Inseparable	1975	2.50	5.00	10.00
❑ Capitol ST-11517	Natalie	1976	2.50	5.00	10.00
❑ Capitol SO-11600	Unpredictable	1977	2.50	5.00	10.00
❑ Capitol SW-11708	Thankful	1978	2.50	5.00	10.00
❑ Capitol SKBL-11709 [(2)]	Natalie..Live!	1978	3.00	6.00	12.00
❑ Capitol SO-11928	I Love You So	1979	2.50	5.00	10.00
❑ Capitol ST-12079	Don't Look Back	1980	2.50	5.00	10.00
❑ Capitol ST-12165	Happy Love	1981	2.50	5.00	10.00
❑ Capitol ST-12242	A Collection	1982	2.50	5.00	10.00
❑ Capitol SN-16038	Inseparable	198?	2.00	4.00	8.00
—Budget-line reissue					
❑ Capitol SN-16310	A Collection	1985	2.00	4.00	8.00
—Budget-line reissue					
❑ Elektra 61049 [(2)]	Unforgettable	1991	5.00	10.00	20.00
❑ EMI E1-48902	Good to Be Back	1989	2.50	5.00	10.00
❑ Epic FE 38280	I'm Ready	1983	2.50	5.00	10.00
❑ Manhattan 53051	Everlasting	1987	2.50	5.00	10.00
❑ Modern 90270	Dangerous	1985	2.50	5.00	10.00

Number	Title (A Side/B Side)	Yr	VG	VG+	NM

COLE, NATALIE, AND PEABO BRYSON

45s

Number	Title (A Side/B Side)	Yr	VG	VG+	NM
❑ Capitol 4804	Gimme Some Time/Love Will Find You	1979	—	2.00	4.00
❑ Capitol 4826	What You Won't Do for Love/Your Lonely Heart	1980	—	2.00	4.00

Albums

Number	Title (A Side/B Side)	Yr	VG	VG+	NM
❑ Capitol SOO-12025	We're the Best of Friends	1979	2.50	5.00	10.00

COLLINS, JUDY

45s

Number	Title (A Side/B Side)	Yr	VG	VG+	NM
❑ Elektra 45008	Turn, Turn, Turn/Farewell	1963	2.50	5.00	10.00
❑ Elektra 45253	Send In the Clowns/Houses	1975	—	2.50	5.00
—Large print label (original)					
❑ Elektra 45289	Angel, Spread Your Wings/The Moon Is a Harsh Mistress	1975	—	2.00	4.00
❑ Elektra 45355	Bread and Roses/Out of Control	1976	—	2.00	4.00
❑ Elektra 45372	Everything Must Change/Special Delivery	1976	—	2.00	4.00
❑ Elektra 45415	Born to the Breed/Special Delivery	1977	—	2.00	4.00
❑ Elektra 45601	I'll Keep It With Mine/Thirsty Boots	1965	2.00	4.00	8.00
❑ Elektra 45610	I Think It's Going to Rain Today/Hard Lovin' Losers	1966	2.00	4.00	8.00
❑ Elektra 45639	Both Sides Now/Who Knows Where the Time Goes	1968	2.00	4.00	8.00
—Red, white and black label					
❑ Elektra 45649	Someday Soon/My Father	1969	—	3.00	6.00
❑ Elektra 45657	Chelsea Morning/Pretty Polly	1969	—	3.00	6.00
❑ Elektra 45680	Pack Up Your Sorrows/Turn, Turn, Turn	1970	—	2.50	5.00
❑ Elektra 45709	Amazing Grace/Nightingale II	1971	—	2.50	5.00
❑ Elektra 45755	Open the Door/Innisfree	1971	—	2.50	5.00
❑ Elektra 45813	In My Life/Sunny Goodge Street	1972	—	2.00	4.00
❑ Elektra 45831	Cook with Honey/So Begins the Task	1973	—	2.00	4.00
❑ Elektra 45849	The Hostage/Secret Gardens	1973	—	2.00	4.00
❑ Elektra 46020	Hard Times for Lovers/Happy End	1979	—	2.00	4.00
❑ Elektra 46050	Where or When/Dorothy	1979	—	2.00	4.00
❑ Elektra 46623	Bright Morning Star/Almost Free	1980	—	2.00	4.00
❑ Elektra 46651	The Rainbow Connection/Running for My Life	1980	—	2.00	4.00
❑ Elektra 47243	Memory/The Life You Dream	1981	—	2.00	4.00
❑ Elektra 47434	It's Gonna Be One of Those Nights/Mama Mama	1982	—	2.00	4.00
❑ Elektra 69662	Only You/Dream On	1985	—	—	3.00
❑ Elektra 69697	Home Again/Dream On	1984	—	2.00	4.00
—A-side with T.G. Sheppard					

Albums

Number	Title (A Side/B Side)	Yr	VG	VG+	NM
❑ Elektra 6E-111	Judith	1977	2.00	4.00	8.00
—Reissue of 7E-1032					
❑ Elektra 6E-171	Hard Times for Lovers	1979	2.50	5.00	10.00
❑ Elektra EKL-209 [M]	Maid of Constant Sorrow	1961	10.00	20.00	40.00
—"Guitar player" label					
❑ Elektra EKL-222 [M]	Golden Apples of the Sun	1962	7.50	15.00	30.00
—"Guitar player" label					
❑ Elektra EKL-243 [M]	Judy Collins #3	1963	7.50	15.00	30.00
—"Guitar player" label					
❑ Elektra EKL-280 [M]	Judy Collins' Concert	1964	7.50	15.00	30.00
—"Guitar player" label					
❑ Elektra EKL-300 [M]	Judy Collins' Fifth Album	1965	7.50	15.00	30.00
—"Guitar player" label					
❑ Elektra EKL-320 [M]	In My Life	1966	5.00	10.00	20.00
❑ Elektra 7E-1032	Judith	1975	3.00	6.00	12.00
❑ Elektra 7E-1076	Bread and Roses	1976	2.50	5.00	10.00
❑ Elektra EKL-4012 [M]	Wildflowers	1967	6.25	12.50	25.00
❑ Elektra 8E-6002 [(2)]	So Early in the Spring: The First 15 Years	1977	3.00	6.00	12.00
❑ Elektra EKS-7209 [R]	Maid of Constant Sorrow	1964	5.00	10.00	20.00
—"Guitar player" label (first edition)					
❑ Elektra EKS-7209 [R]	Maid of Constant Sorrow	1966	3.00	6.00	12.00
—Gold/tan label or red label with large stylized "E"					
❑ Elektra EKS-7222 [R]	Golden Apples of the Sun	196?	3.00	6.00	12.00
—Gold/tan label or red label with large stylized "E"					
❑ Elektra EKS-7243 [S]	Judy Collins #3	1963	10.00	20.00	40.00
—"Guitar player" label					
❑ Elektra EKS-7280 [S]	Judy Collins' Concert	1964	10.00	20.00	40.00
—"Guitar player" label					

Number	Title (A Side/B Side)	Yr	VG	VG+	NM
❑ Elektra EKS-7300 [S]	Judy Collins' Fifth Album	1965	10.00	20.00	40.00
—"Guitar player" label					
❑ Elektra EKS-7320 [S]	In My Life	1966	6.25	12.50	25.00
❑ Elektra 60001	Times of Our Lives	1982	2.50	5.00	10.00
❑ Elektra 60304	Home Again	1985	2.50	5.00	10.00
❑ Elektra EKS-74012 [S]	Wildflowers	1967	5.00	10.00	20.00
—Gold/tan label					
❑ Elektra EKS-74027	In My Life	1968	5.00	10.00	20.00
—Reissue of 7320; gold/tan label					
❑ Elektra EKS-74033	Who Knows Where the Time Goes	1968	5.00	10.00	20.00
—Gold/tan label					
❑ Elektra EKS-74055	Recollections	1969	3.75	7.50	15.00
—Red label with large stylized "E"					
❑ Elektra EKS-75010	Whales & Nightingales	1970	3.00	6.00	12.00
—Butterfly label, no Warner Communications logo					
❑ Elektra EKS-75014	Living	1971	3.00	6.00	12.00
—Butterfly label, no Warner Communications logo					
❑ Elektra EKS-75030	Colors of the Day/The Best of Judy Collins	1972	3.00	6.00	12.00
—Butterfly label, no Warner Communications logo					
❑ Elektra EKS-75053	True Stories and Other Dreams	1973	3.00	6.00	12.00
—Butterfly label					
❑ Gold Castle D1-71302	Trust Your Heart	1989	3.00	6.00	12.00
—Reissue of 171002					
❑ Gold Castle D1-71318	Sanity and Grace	1989	3.00	6.00	12.00
❑ Gold Castle 171002	Trust Your Heart	1988	3.00	6.00	12.00
❑ Pair PDL2-1141 [(2)]	Her Finest Hour	1986	3.00	6.00	12.00

COLLINS, PHIL

45s

Number	Title (A Side/B Side)	Yr	VG	VG+	NM
❑ Atlantic 3790	I Missed Again/I'm Not Moving	1981	—	—	3.00
❑ Atlantic 3824	In the Air Tonight/The Roof Is Leaking	1981	—	—	3.00
❑ Atlantic 87800	Hang In Long Enough/Separate Lives	1990	—	—	3.00
❑ Atlantic 87885	Something Happened on the Way to Heaven/Lionel	1990	—	—	3.00
❑ Atlantic 87955	Do You Remember?/I Wish It Would Rain Down (Live)	1990	—	—	3.00
❑ Atlantic 88738	I Wish It Would Rain Down/You've Been in Love (That Little Bit)	1989	—	—	3.00
❑ Atlantic 88774	Another Day in Paradise/Heat on the Street	1989	—	—	3.00
❑ Atlantic 88980	Two Hearts/The Robbery	1989	—	—	3.00
❑ Atlantic 89017	Groovy Kind of Love/Big Noise	1988	—	—	3.00
❑ Atlantic 89472	Take Me Home/Only You Know and I Know	1985	—	—	3.00
❑ Atlantic 89498	Separate Lives (Love Theme from White Nights)/ I Don't Wanna Know	1985	—	—	3.00
—A-side with Marilyn Martin					
❑ Atlantic 89536	Don't Lose My Number/We Said Hello Goodbye	1985	—	—	3.00
❑ Atlantic 89560	Sussudio/I Like the Way	1985	—	—	3.00
❑ Atlantic 89588	One More Night/The Man with the Horn	1985	—	—	3.00
❑ Atlantic 89700	Against All Odds (Take a Look at Me Now)/The Search	1984	—	—	3.00
—B-side by Larry Carlton					
❑ Atlantic 89864	I Cannot Believe It's True/Thru These Walls	1983	—	—	3.00
❑ Atlantic 89877	I Don't Care Anymore/The West Side	1983	—	—	3.00
❑ Atlantic 89933	You Can't Hurry Love/Do You Know	1982	—	—	3.00
❑ Atlantic Oldies Series OS 13231	In the Air Tonight/I Missed Again	1984	—	—	3.00
—Reissue					

Albums

Number	Title (A Side/B Side)	Yr	VG	VG+	NM
❑ Atlantic SD 16029	Face Value	1981	2.00	4.00	8.00
❑ Atlantic 80035	Hello, I Must Be Going!	1982	2.00	4.00	8.00
❑ Atlantic 81240	No Jacket Required	1985	2.00	4.00	8.00
❑ Atlantic 82050	... But Seriously	1989	3.00	6.00	12.00
❑ Atlantic 82157 [(2)]	Serious Hits... Live!	1990	5.00	10.00	20.00

COMMODORES

45s

Number	Title (A Side/B Side)	Yr	VG	VG+	NM
❑ Motown 1268	Are You Happy/There's a Song in My Heart	1973	—	3.00	6.00
❑ Motown 1307	Machine Gun/There's a Song in My Heart	1974	—	2.50	5.00
❑ Motown 1319	I Feel Sanctified/It Is As Good As You Make It	1974	—	2.50	5.00
❑ Motown 1338	Slippery When Wet/The Bump	1975	—	2.50	5.00
❑ Motown 1361	This Is Your Life/Look What You've Done to Me	1975	—	2.50	5.00
❑ Motown 1381	Sweet Love/Better Never Than Forever	1976	—	2.00	4.00
❑ Motown 1399	High on Sunshine/Thumpin' Music	1976	—	—	—
—Unreleased					
❑ Motown 1402	Just to Be Close to You/Thumpin' Music	1976	—	2.00	4.00
❑ Motown 1408	Fancy Dancer/Cebu	1977	—	2.00	4.00
❑ Motown 1418	Easy/Can't Let You Tease Me	1977	—	2.00	4.00
❑ Motown 1425	Brick House/Captain Quickdraw	1977	—	2.00	4.00
❑ Motown 1432	Too Hot Ta Trot/Funky Situation	1977	—	2.00	4.00
❑ Motown 1443	Three Times a Lady/Look What You've Done to Me	1978	—	2.00	4.00
❑ Motown 1452	Flying High/X-Rated Movie	1978	—	2.00	4.00
❑ Motown 1466	Sail On/Thumpin' Music	1979	—	2.00	4.00
❑ Motown 1474	Still/Such a Woman	1979	—	2.00	4.00
❑ Motown 1479	Wonderland/Lovin' You	1979	—	2.00	4.00
❑ Motown 1489	Old Fashion Love/Sexy Lady	1980	—	2.00	4.00
❑ Motown 1495	Heroes/Funky Situation	1980	—	2.00	4.00
❑ Motown 1502	Jesus Is Love/Mighty Spirit	1980	—	3.00	6.00
❑ Motown 1514	Lady (You Bring Me Up)/Gettin' It	1981	—	2.00	4.00
❑ Motown 1527	Oh No/Lovin' You	1981	—	2.00	4.00
❑ Motown 1604	Why You Wanna Try Me/X-Rated Movie	1982	—	2.00	4.00
❑ Motown 1651	Painted Pictures/Reach High	1982	—	—	3.00

Number	Title (A Side/B Side)	Yr	VG	VG+	NM
❑ Motown 1661	Sexy Lady/Reach High	1983	—	—	3.00
❑ Motown 1694	Only You/Cebu	1983	—	—	3.00
❑ Motown 1719	Been Lovin' You/Turn Off the Lights	1984	—	—	3.00
❑ Motown 1773	Nightshift/I Keep Running	1985	—	—	3.00
❑ Motown 1788	Animal Instinct/Lightin' Up the Sky	1985	—	—	3.00
❑ Motown 1802	Janet/I'm in Love	1985	—	—	3.00
❑ Mowest 5009	I'm Looking for Love/At the Zoo	1972	2.00	4.00	8.00
❑ Mowest 5038	Determination/Don't You Be Worried	1973	2.00	4.00	8.00
❑ Polydor 871370-7	Grrip/Ain't Giving Up	1989	—	—	3.00
❑ Polydor 885358-7	Goin' to the Bank/Serious Love	1986	—	—	3.00
❑ Polydor 885538-7	Take It from Me/I Wanna Rock You	1987	—	—	3.00
❑ Polydor 885760-7	United in Love/Talk to Me	1987	—	—	3.00
❑ Polydor 887939-7	Solitaire/Stretchhh	1988	—	—	3.00
Albums					
❑ Motown M5-121V1	Machine Gun	1981	2.50	5.00	10.00
—Reissue					
❑ Motown M5-179V1	Movin' On	1981	2.00	4.00	8.00
❑ Motown M5-222V1	Commodores	1982	2.00	4.00	8.00
❑ Motown M5-240V1	Caught in the Act	1982	2.00	4.00	8.00
❑ Motown M6-798	Machine Gun	1974	3.75	7.50	15.00
❑ Motown M6-820	Caught in the Act	1975	2.50	5.00	10.00
❑ Motown M6-848	Movin' On	1975	2.50	5.00	10.00
❑ Motown M6-867	Hot on the Tracks	1976	2.50	5.00	10.00
❑ Motown M7-884	Commodores	1977	2.50	5.00	10.00
❑ Motown M9-894 [(2)]	Commodores Live!	1977	3.00	6.00	12.00
❑ Motown M7-902	Natural High	1978	2.50	5.00	10.00
❑ Motown M7-912	Commodores' Greatest Hits	1978	2.50	5.00	10.00
❑ Motown M8-926	Midnight Magic	1979	2.50	5.00	10.00
❑ Motown M8-939	Heroes	1980	2.50	5.00	10.00
❑ Motown M8-955	In the Pocket	1981	2.50	5.00	10.00
❑ Motown 5257 ML	Hot on the Tracks	1983	2.00	4.00	8.00
❑ Motown 5293 ML	Natural High	1983	2.00	4.00	8.00
❑ Motown 6028 ML	All the Great Hits	1982	2.50	5.00	10.00
❑ Motown 6044 ML2 [(2)]	Anthology	1983	3.00	6.00	12.00
❑ Motown 6054 ML	Commodores 13	1983	2.50	5.00	10.00
❑ Motown 6124 ML	Nightshift	1985	2.50	5.00	10.00
❑ Polydor 831194-1	United	1986	2.50	5.00	10.00
❑ Polydor 835369-1	Rock Solid	1988	2.50	5.00	10.00

CONLEY, ARTHUR

Number	Title (A Side/B Side)	Yr	VG	VG+	NM
45s					
❑ Atco 6463	Sweet Soul Music/Let's Go Steady	1967	2.50	5.00	10.00
❑ Atco 6494	Shake, Rattle and Roll/You Don't Have to See Me	1967	2.00	4.00	8.00
❑ Atco 6529	Whole Lot of Woman/Love Comes and Goes	1967	2.00	4.00	8.00
❑ Atco 6563	Funky Street/Put Our Love Together	1968	2.00	4.00	8.00
❑ Atco 6588	People Sure Act Funny/Burning Fire	1968	2.00	4.00	8.00
❑ Atco 6622	Is That You Love/Aunt Dora's Love Soul Shack	1968	2.00	4.00	8.00
❑ Atco 6640	Ob-La-Di, Ob-La-Da/Otis Sleep On	1968	2.00	4.00	8.00
❑ Atco 6661	Speak Her Name/Run On	1969	—	3.00	6.00
❑ Atco 6706	Star Review/Love Sure Is a Powerful Thing	1969	—	3.00	6.00
❑ Atco 6733	Hurt/They Call the Wind Maria	1970	—	3.00	6.00
❑ Atco 6747	God Bless/(Your Love Has Brought Me A) Mighty Long Way	1970	—	3.00	6.00
❑ Atco 6790	Nobody's Fault But Mine/Day-O	1970	—	3.00	6.00
❑ Capricorn 0001	More Sweet Soul Music/Walking on Eggs	1972	2.50	5.00	10.00
❑ Capricorn 0006	Rita/More Sweet Soul Music	1972	2.00	4.00	8.00
❑ Capricorn 0047	Bless You/It's So Nice	1973	2.00	4.00	8.00
❑ Capricorn 8017	I'm Living Good/I'm So Glad You're Here	1971	2.50	5.00	10.00
❑ Fame 1007	I Can't Stop/In the Same Old Way	1966	3.75	7.50	15.00
❑ Fame 1009	Take Me (Just As I Am)/I'm Gonna Forget About You	1966	3.75	7.50	15.00
❑ Jotis 470	I'm a Lonely Stranger/Where Lead Me	1965	5.00	10.00	20.00
❑ Jotis 472	Who's Fooling Who/There's a Place for Us	1966	5.00	10.00	20.00
Albums					
❑ Atco 33-215 [M]	Sweet Soul Music	1967	10.00	20.00	40.00
❑ Atco SD 33-215 [S]	Sweet Soul Music	1967	7.50	15.00	30.00
❑ Atco 33-220 [M]	Shake, Rattle & Roll	1967	10.00	20.00	40.00
❑ Atco SD 33-220 [S]	Shake, Rattle & Roll	1967	7.50	15.00	30.00
❑ Atco SD 33-243 [S]	Soul Directions	1968	7.50	15.00	30.00
❑ Atco SD 33-276 [S]	More Sweet Soul	1969	7.50	15.00	30.00

Number	Title (A Side/B Side)	Yr	VG	VG+	NM
CONTOURS, THE					
45s					
❑ Gordy 7005	Do You Love Me/Move Mr. Man	1962	5.00	10.00	20.00
❑ Gordy 7012	Shake Sherry/You Better Get in Line	1963	3.75	7.50	15.00
❑ Gordy 7016	Don't Let Her Be Your Baby/It Must Be Love	1963	3.00	6.00	12.00
❑ Gordy 7019	Pa I Need a Car/You Get Ugly	1963	3.00	6.00	12.00
❑ Gordy 7029	Can You Do It/I'll Stand By You	1964	3.00	6.00	12.00
❑ Gordy 7037	Can You Jerk Like Me/That Day When She Needed Me	1964	3.00	6.00	12.00
❑ Gordy 7044	First I Look at the Purse/Searching for a Girl	1965	3.00	6.00	12.00
❑ Gordy 7052	Just a Little Misunderstanding/Determination	1966	3.00	6.00	12.00
❑ Gordy 7059	It's So Hard Being a Loser/Your Love Grows More Precious Every Day	1967	3.00	6.00	12.00
❑ Hob 116	I'm So Glad/Yours Is My Heart Alone	1961	30.00	60.00	120.00
❑ Motown 1008	Whole Lotta Woman/Come On and Be Mine	1961	125.00	250.00	500.00
❑ Motown 1012	The Stretch/Funny	1962	200.00	400.00	800.00
❑ Motown Yesteryear 448	Do You Love Me/Shake Sherry	1972	—	2.00	4.00
❑ Rocket 41192	I'm a Winner/Makes Me Wanna Come Back	1980	—	2.00	4.00
❑ Tamla 7012	Shake Sherry/You Better Get in Line	1963	37.50	75.00	150.00
—Tamla label used in error for a Gordy release					
Albums					
❑ Gordy G 901 [M]	Do You Love Me?	1962	125.00	250.00	500.00
❑ Motown M5-188V1	Do You Love Me?	1981	2.50	5.00	10.00
COOKE, SAM					
45s					
❑ Cherie 4501	Darling I Need You Now/Win Your Love for Me	1971	2.00	4.00	8.00
❑ Keen 3-2005	Stealing Kisses/All of My Life	1958	6.25	12.50	25.00
❑ Keen 3-2006 [M]	Win Your Love for Me/Love Song from "Houseboat" (Almost in Your Arms)	1958	6.25	12.50	25.00
❑ Keen 3-2008	Love You Most of All/Blue Moon	1958	6.25	12.50	25.00
❑ Keen 3-2018 [M]	Everybody Likes to Cha Cha Cha/Little Things You Do	1959	6.25	12.50	25.00
❑ Keen 5-2018 [S]	Everybody Likes to Cha Cha Cha/Little Things You Do	1959	10.00	20.00	40.00
❑ Keen 2022 [M]	Only Sixteen/Let's Go Steady Again	1959	6.25	12.50	25.00
❑ Keen 5-2022 [S]	Only Sixteen/Let's Go Steady Again	1959	12.50	25.00	50.00
❑ Keen 2101	Summertime/Summertime (Part 2)	1959	6.25	12.50	25.00
❑ Keen 8-2105	There! I've Said It Again/One Hour Ahead of the Posse	1959	6.25	12.50	25.00
❑ Keen 2118	Steal Away/So Glamorous	1960	5.00	10.00	20.00
❑ Keen 2122	Mary, Mary Lou/Eee-Yi-Ee-Yi-Oh	1960	5.00	10.00	20.00
❑ Keen 4009	You Were Made for Me/Lonely Island	1958	6.25	12.50	25.00
❑ Keen 34002	(I Love You) For Sentimental Reasons/Desire Me	1958	6.25	12.50	25.00
—Black label					
❑ Keen 34013	You Send Me/Summertime	1957	6.25	12.50	25.00
—Black label (original)					
❑ Keen 82111	'T'ain't Nobody's Bizness (If I Do)/No One	1960	6.25	12.50	25.00
❑ Keen 82112	Wonderful World/Along the Navajo Trail	1960	5.00	10.00	20.00
❑ Keen 82117	With You/I Thank God	1960	5.00	10.00	20.00
❑ RCA PB-14146	Bring It On Home to Me/Nothing Can Change This Love	1985	2.00	4.00	8.00
❑ RCA Victor 47-7701	Teenage Sonata/If You Were the Only Girl	1960	5.00	10.00	20.00
❑ RCA Victor 47-7730	You Understand Me/I Belong to Your Heart	1960	3.75	7.50	15.00
❑ RCA Victor 47-7783	Chain Gang/I Fall in Love Every Day	1960	3.75	7.50	15.00
❑ RCA Victor 47-7816	Sad Mood/Love Me	1960	3.75	7.50	15.00
❑ RCA Victor 47-7853	That's It-I Quit-I'm Movin' On/What Do You Say	1961	3.75	7.50	15.00
❑ RCA Victor 47-7883	Cupid/Farewell, My Darling	1961	3.75	7.50	15.00
❑ RCA Victor 47-7927	Feel It/It's All Right	1961	3.75	7.50	15.00
❑ RCA Victor 47-7983	Twistin' the Night Away/One More Time	1962	3.75	7.50	15.00
❑ RCA Victor 47-8036	Bring It On Home to Me/Having a Party	1962	3.75	7.50	15.00
❑ RCA Victor 47-8088	Nothing Can Change This Love/Somebody Have Mercy	1962	3.75	7.50	15.00
❑ RCA Victor 47-8129	Send Me Some Lovin'/Baby, Baby, Baby	1963	3.75	7.50	15.00
❑ RCA Victor 47-8164	Another Saturday Night/Love Will Find a Way	1963	3.75	7.50	15.00
❑ RCA Victor 47-8215	Frankie and Johnny/Cool Train	1963	3.00	6.00	12.00
❑ RCA Victor 47-8247	Little Red Rooster/You Gotta Move	1963	3.00	6.00	12.00
❑ RCA Victor 47-8299	Ain't That Good News/Basin Street Blues	1963	5.00	10.00	20.00
—Original A-side title (or a scarce reissue)					
❑ RCA Victor 47-8299	Good News/Basin Street Blues	1963	3.00	6.00	12.00
❑ RCA Victor 47-8368	Good Times/Tennessee Waltz	1964	3.00	6.00	12.00
❑ RCA Victor 47-8426	Cousin of Mine/That's Where It's At	1964	3.00	6.00	12.00
❑ RCA Victor 47-8486	Shake/A Change Is Gonna Come	1964	3.00	6.00	12.00
❑ RCA Victor 47-8539	It's Got the Whole World Shakin'/Ease My Troublin' Mind	1965	2.50	5.00	10.00
❑ RCA Victor 47-8586	When a Boy Falls in Love/The Piper	1965	2.50	5.00	10.00
❑ RCA Victor 47-8631	Sugar Dumpling/Bridge of Tears	1965	2.50	5.00	10.00
❑ RCA Victor 47-8751	Feel It/That's All	1965	2.50	5.00	10.00
❑ RCA Victor 47-8803	Let's Go Steady Again/Trouble Blues	1966	2.50	5.00	10.00
❑ RCA Victor 47-8934	Meet Me at Mary's Place/If I Had a Hammer	1966	2.50	5.00	10.00
❑ Specialty 596	Forever/Lovable	1957	7.50	15.00	30.00
—As "Dale Cook"					
❑ Specialty 619	I'll Come Running Back to You/Forever	1957	7.50	15.00	30.00
❑ Specialty 627	That's All I Need to Know/I Don't Want to Cry	1958	7.50	15.00	30.00
❑ Specialty 667	Happy in Love/I Need You Now	1959	7.50	15.00	30.00
❑ Specialty 921	Must Jesus Bear the Cross Alone/The Last Mile of the Way	1970	2.50	5.00	10.00
—With the Soul Stirrers					
❑ Specialty 928	Just Another Day/Christ Is All	1973	2.50	5.00	10.00
—With the Soul Stirrers					
❑ Specialty 930	That's Heaven to Me/Lord, Remember Me	1974	2.50	5.00	10.00
—With the Soul Stirrers					
Albums					
❑ Abkco 1124-1	Sam Cooke's Night Beat	1995	3.00	6.00	12.00
—Reissue					

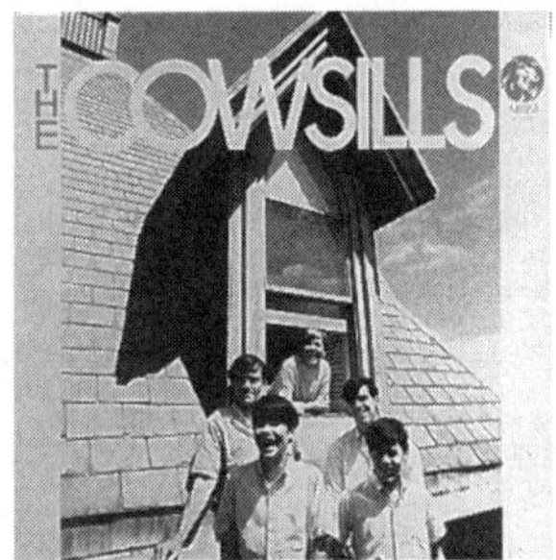

Number	Title (A Side/B Side)	Yr	VG	VG+	NM
❑ Abkco 2970-1	Sam Cooke at the Copa	1988	3.00	6.00	12.00
—Reissue					
❑ Famous 502	Sam's Songs	1969	10.00	20.00	40.00
❑ Famous 505	Only Sixteen	1969	10.00	20.00	40.00
❑ Famous 508	So Wonderful	1969	10.00	20.00	40.00
❑ Famous 509	You Send Me	1969	10.00	20.00	40.00
❑ Famous 512	Cha-Cha-Cha	1969	10.00	20.00	40.00
❑ Keen A-2001 [M]	Sam Cooke	1958	50.00	100.00	200.00
❑ Keen A-2003 [M]	Encore	1958	50.00	100.00	200.00
❑ Keen A-2004 [M]	Tribute to the Lady	1959	37.50	75.00	150.00
❑ Keen AS-2004 [S]	Tribute to the Lady	1959	50.00	100.00	200.00
❑ Keen 86101 [M]	Hit Kit	1959	62.50	125.00	250.00
❑ Keen 86103 [M]	I Thank God	1960	100.00	200.00	400.00
❑ Keen 86106 [M]	The Wonderful World of Sam Cooke	1960	87.50	1175.	350.00
❑ Pair PDL2-1006 [(2)]	You Send Me	1986	3.75	7.50	15.00
❑ RCA Camden ACS1-0445	You Send Me	1974	3.00	6.00	12.00
❑ RCA Camden CAL-2264 [M]	The One and Only Sam Cooke	1967	5.00	10.00	20.00
❑ RCA Camden CAS-2264 [R]	The One and Only Sam Cooke	1967	3.00	6.00	12.00
❑ RCA Camden CAS-2433	Sam Cooke	1970	3.00	6.00	12.00
❑ RCA Camden CAS-2610	The Unforgettable Sam Cooke	1972	3.00	6.00	12.00
❑ RCA Victor LPM-2221 [M]	Cooke's Tour	1960	10.00	20.00	40.00
❑ RCA Victor LSP-2221 [S]	Cooke's Tour	1960	12.50	25.00	50.00
❑ RCA Victor LPM-2236 [M]	Hits of the 50's	1960	10.00	20.00	40.00
❑ RCA Victor LSP-2236 [S]	Hits of the 50's	1960	12.50	25.00	50.00
❑ RCA Victor LPM-2293 [M]	Swing Low	1960	10.00	20.00	40.00
❑ RCA Victor LSP-2293 [S]	Swing Low	1960	12.50	25.00	50.00
❑ RCA Victor LPM-2392 [M]	My Kind of Blues	1961	10.00	20.00	40.00
❑ RCA Victor LSP-2392 [S]	My Kind of Blues	1961	12.50	25.00	50.00
❑ RCA Victor LPM-2555 [M]	Twistin' the Night Away	1962	10.00	20.00	40.00
❑ RCA Victor LSP-2555 [S]	Twistin' the Night Away	1962	12.50	25.00	50.00
❑ RCA Victor LPM-2625 [M]	The Best of Sam Cooke	1962	7.50	15.00	30.00
❑ RCA Victor LSP-2625 [R]	The Best of Sam Cooke	1962	5.00	10.00	20.00
❑ RCA Victor ANL1-2658	Sam Cooke at the Copa	1977	3.00	6.00	12.00
—Reissue of LSP-2970					
❑ RCA Victor LPM-2673 [M]	Mr. Soul	1963	7.50	15.00	30.00
❑ RCA Victor LSP-2673 [S]	Mr. Soul	1963	10.00	20.00	40.00
❑ RCA Victor LPM-2709 [M]	Night Beat	1963	7.50	15.00	30.00
❑ RCA Victor LSP-2709 [S]	Night Beat	1963	10.00	20.00	40.00
❑ RCA Victor LPM-2899 [M]	Ain't That Good News	1964	7.50	15.00	30.00
❑ RCA Victor LSP-2899 [S]	Ain't That Good News	1964	10.00	20.00	40.00
❑ RCA Victor LPM-2970 [M]	Sam Cooke at the Copa	1964	7.50	15.00	30.00
❑ RCA Victor LSP-2970 [S]	Sam Cooke at the Copa	1964	10.00	20.00	40.00
❑ RCA Victor LPM-3367 [M]	Shake	1965	6.25	12.50	25.00
❑ RCA Victor LSP-3367 [S]	Shake	1965	7.50	15.00	30.00
❑ RCA Victor LPM-3373 [M]	The Best of Sam Cooke, Volume 2	1965	6.25	12.50	25.00
❑ RCA Victor LSP-3373 [S]	The Best of Sam Cooke, Volume 2	1965	7.50	15.00	30.00
❑ RCA Victor LPM-3435 [M]	Try a Little Love	1965	6.25	12.50	25.00
❑ RCA Victor LSP-3435 [S]	Try a Little Love	1965	7.50	15.00	30.00
❑ RCA Victor LPM-3517 [M]	The Unforgettable Sam Cooke	1966	5.00	10.00	20.00
❑ RCA Victor LSP-3517 [S]	The Unforgettable Sam Cooke	1966	6.25	12.50	25.00
❑ RCA Victor AYL1-3863	The Best of Sam Cooke	1981	2.00	4.00	8.00
—Budget-line reissue					
❑ RCA Victor LPM-3991 [M]	The Man Who Invented Soul	1968	12.50	25.00	50.00
❑ RCA Victor LSP-3991 [S]	The Man Who Invented Soul	1968	6.25	12.50	25.00
❑ RCA Victor AFL1-5181	Live at the Harlem Square Club, 1963	1985	3.00	6.00	12.00
❑ RCA Victor VPS-6027 [(2)]	This Is Sam Cooke	1970	5.00	10.00	20.00
❑ RCA Victor CPL2-7127 [(2)]	The Man and His Music	1986	3.75	7.50	15.00
❑ Specialty SPS-2106	Sam Cooke and the Soul Stirrers	1970	3.75	7.50	15.00
❑ Specialty SPS-2116	The Gospel Soul of Sam Cooke, Vol. 1	1970	3.75	7.50	15.00
❑ Specialty SPS-2119	Two Sides of Sam Cooke	1970	3.75	7.50	15.00
❑ Specialty SPS-2128	The Gospel Soul of Sam Cooke, Vol. 2	197?	3.75	7.50	15.00
❑ Specialty SPS-2146	That's Heaven to Me	197?	3.75	7.50	15.00
❑ Trip 8030 [(2)]	The Golden Sound of Sam Cooke	1972	3.75	7.50	15.00
❑ Upfront 160	The Billie Holiday Story	1973	3.75	7.50	15.00
COOKIES, THE					
45s					
❑ Atlantic 1061	Precious Love/Later, Later	1955	7.50	15.00	30.00

Number	Title (A Side/B Side)	Yr	VG	VG+	NM
❑ Atlantic 1084	In Paradise/Passing Time	1956	7.50	15.00	30.00
❑ Atlantic 1110	Down By the River/My Lover	1956	6.25	12.50	25.00
❑ Atlantic 2079	Passing Time/In Paradise	1960	5.00	10.00	20.00
❑ Dimension 1002	Chains/Stranger in My Arms	1962	5.00	10.00	20.00
❑ Dimension 1008	Don't Say Nothin' Bad/Softly in the Night	1963	5.00	10.00	20.00
❑ Dimension 1008	Don't Say Nothin' Bad (About My Baby)/Softly in the Night	1963	3.75	7.50	15.00
❑ Dimension 1012	I Want a Boy for My Birthday/Will Power	1963	3.75	7.50	15.00
❑ Dimension 1020	Girls Grow Up Faster Than Boys/Only to Other People	1963	3.75	7.50	15.00
❑ Dimension 1032	I Never Dreamed/The Old Crowd	1964	3.75	7.50	15.00
❑ Josie 822	King of Hearts/Hippy-Dippy-Daddy	1957	7.50	15.00	30.00
❑ Lamp 8008	Don't Let Go/All Night Mambo	1954	10.00	20.00	40.00
❑ Warner Bros. 7025	All My Trials/Wounded	1967	2.50	5.00	10.00
❑ Warner Bros. 7047	Mr. Cupid (Don't You Call on Me)/Hang My Head and Cry	1967	2.50	5.00	10.00
—B-side by the Big Guys					

COOKIES, THE/LITTLE EVA/CAROLE KING

Albums

Number	Title	Yr	VG	VG+	NM
❑ Dimension DLP-6001 [M]	The Dimension Dolls, Vol. 1	1964	62.50	125.00	250.00

COOPER, ALICE

45s

Number	Title	Yr	VG	VG+	NM
❑ Atlantic 3254	Only Women/Cold Ethyl	1975	—	2.50	5.00
❑ Atlantic 3280	Department of Youth/Some Folks	1975	—	2.50	5.00
❑ Atlantic 3298	Welcome to My Nightmare/Cold Ethyl	1975	—	2.50	5.00
❑ Epic 34-08114	I Got a Line on You/Livin' on the Edge	1988	—	—	3.00
—B-side by Britney Fox					
❑ Epic 34-68958	Poison/Trash	1989	—	—	3.00
❑ Epic 34-73085	House of Fire/Ballad of Dwight Fry	1989	—	—	3.00
❑ Epic 34-73845	Hey Stoopid/It Rained All Night	1991	—	—	3.00
❑ Epic 34-73983	Love's a Loaded Gun/Fire	1991	—	—	3.00
❑ MCA 52904	He's Back (The Man Behind the Mask)/Billion Dollar Baby	1986	—	—	3.00
❑ MCA 53212	Freedom/Time to Kill	1987	—	—	3.00
❑ Straight 101	Reflected/Living	1969	75.00	150.00	300.00
—Promos worth about 10% of this value					
❑ Warner Bros. GWB 7141	Eighteen/Caught in a Dream	1972	—	2.00	4.00
—"Back to Back Hits" series; green label					
❑ Warner Bros. 7398	Shoe Salesman/Return of the Spiders	1970	5.00	10.00	20.00
❑ Warner Bros. 7449	Eighteen/Body	1971	—	2.50	5.00
❑ Warner Bros. 7490	Caught in a Dream/Hallowed Be My Name	1971	—	2.50	5.00
❑ Warner Bros. 7529	Under My Wheels/Desperado	1971	—	2.50	5.00
❑ Warner Bros. 7568	Be My Lover/Yeah, Yeah, Yeah	1972	—	2.50	5.00
❑ Warner Bros. 7596	School's Out/Gutter Cat	1972	—	2.50	5.00
❑ Warner Bros. 7631	Elected/Luney Tune	1972	—	2.50	5.00
❑ Warner Bros. 7673	Hello Hurray/Generation Landslide	1972	—	2.50	5.00
❑ Warner Bros. 7691	No More Mr. Nice Guy/Raped and Freezin'	1973	—	2.50	5.00
❑ Warner Bros. 7724	Billion Dollar Babies/Mary Ann	1973	—	2.50	5.00
❑ Warner Bros. 7762	Teenage Lament '74/Hard Hearted Alice	1973	—	2.50	5.00
❑ Warner Bros. 7783	Muscle of Love/Crazy Little Child	1974	—	2.50	5.00
❑ Warner Bros. 8023	I'm Eighteen/Muscle of Love	1974	—	2.50	5.00
❑ Warner Bros. 8228	I Never Cry/Go to Hell	1976	—	2.00	4.00
❑ Warner Bros. 8349	You and Me/It's Hot Tonight	1977	—	2.00	4.00
❑ Warner Bros. 8448	(No More) Love at Your Convenience/I Never Wrote Those Songs	1977	—	2.50	5.00
❑ Warner Bros. 8607	School's Out/Eighteen	1978	2.00	4.00	8.00
❑ Warner Bros. 8695	How You Gonna See Me Now/No Tricks	1978	—	2.50	5.00
❑ Warner Bros. 8760	From the Inside/Nurse Rosetta	1979	—	2.00	4.00
❑ Warner Bros. 29828	I Am the Future/Tag, You're It	1982	—	2.00	4.00
❑ Warner Bros. 29928	I Like Girls/Zorro's Ascent	1982	—	2.00	4.00
❑ Warner Bros. 49204	Clones (We're All)/Model Citizen	1980	—	2.00	4.00
❑ Warner Bros. 49526	Dance Yourself to Death/Talk Talk	1980	—	2.00	4.00
❑ Warner Bros. 49780	You Want It, You Got It/Who Do You Think We Are	1981	—	2.00	4.00
❑ Warner Bros. 49848	Generation Landslide '81/Seven and Seven Is	1981	—	2.00	4.00

Albums

Number	Title	Yr	VG	VG+	NM
❑ Accord SN-7162	Toronto Rock 'n' Roll Revival 1969	1981	3.00	6.00	12.00
❑ Atlantic SD 18130	Welcome to My Nightmare	1975	2.50	5.00	10.00
❑ Atlantic SD 19157	Welcome to My Nightmare	1978	2.00	4.00	8.00
—Reissue of 18130					
❑ Epic OE 45137	Trash	1989	3.00	6.00	12.00
❑ Epic E 46786	Hey Stoopid	1991	3.75	7.50	15.00
❑ MCA 5761	Constrictor	1986	2.00	4.00	8.00
❑ MCA 42091	Raise Your Fist and Yell	1987	2.00	4.00	8.00
❑ Pair PDL2-1163 [(2)]	A Man Called Alice	1987	3.75	7.50	15.00
❑ Straight STS-1051	Pretties for You	1969	37.50	75.00	150.00
—Yellow label stock copy					
❑ Straight WS 1840	Pretties for You	1970	15.00	30.00	60.00
—Pink label stock copy					
❑ Straight WS 1845	Easy Action	1970	12.50	25.00	50.00
—Pink label stock copy; "Alice Cooper" in black on cover					
❑ Straight WS 1883	Love It to Death	1971	12.50	25.00	50.00
—Pink label stock copy					
❑ Warner Bros. WS 1883	Love It to Death	1971	5.00	10.00	20.00
—Version 3: Green "WB" label; cover has large white areas at top and bottom with lower half of the photo cropped out					
❑ Warner Bros. WS 1883	Love It to Death	1971	7.50	15.00	30.00
—Version 1: Green "WB" label; cover has Alice's thumb sticking out in such a way that it appears to be another part of the body					
❑ Warner Bros. WS 1883	Love It to Death	1971	5.00	10.00	20.00
—Version 2: Green "WB" label; same as above, but has a white box reading "Contains the Hit 'I'm Eighteen' "					
❑ Warner Bros. BS 2567	Killer	1971	7.50	15.00	30.00
—Early copies have an attached 1972 calendar/poster					

Number	Title (A Side/B Side)	Yr	VG	VG+	NM
❑ Warner Bros. BS 2623	School's Out	1972	10.00	20.00	40.00
—With paper panties intact; back cover does not list song titles					
❑ Warner Bros. BS 2685	Billion Dollar Babies	1973	3.00	6.00	12.00
—Green "WB" label					
❑ Warner Bros. BS 2748	Muscle of Love	1973	2.50	5.00	10.00
❑ Warner Bros. W 2803	Alice Cooper's Greatest Hits	1974	2.50	5.00	10.00
❑ Warner Bros. BS 2896	Alice Cooper Goes to Hell	1976	2.50	5.00	10.00
❑ Warner Bros. BSK 3027	Lace and Whiskey	1977	2.50	5.00	10.00
❑ Warner Bros. BSK 3107	Alice Cooper's Greatest Hits	1977	2.00	4.00	8.00
—Reissue of BS 2803					
❑ Warner Bros. BSK 3138	The Alice Cooper Show	1977	2.50	5.00	10.00
❑ Warner Bros. BSK 3263	From the Inside	1978	2.50	5.00	10.00
❑ Warner Bros. BSK 3436	Flush the Fashion	1980	2.50	5.00	10.00
❑ Warner Bros. BSK 3581	Special Forces	1981	2.50	5.00	10.00
❑ Warner Bros. 23719	Zipper Catches Skin	1982	2.50	5.00	10.00
❑ Warner Bros. 23969	Da Da	1983	2.50	5.00	10.00

CORNELIUS BROTHERS AND SISTER ROSE

45s

Number	Title (A Side/B Side)	Yr	VG	VG+	NM
❑ Platinum 105/6	Treat Her Like a Lady/Over at My Place	1970	3.00	6.00	12.00
❑ United Artists 0131	Treat Her Like a Lady/Over at My Place	1973	—	2.00	4.00
—"Silver Spotlight Series" reissue					
❑ United Artists XW208	Let Me Down Easy/Gonna Be Sweet for You	1973	—	2.50	5.00
❑ United Artists XW313	I Just Can't Stop Loving You/These Lonely Nights	1973	—	2.50	5.00
❑ United Artists XW377	Big Time Lover/Wonderful Tune	1974	—	2.50	5.00
❑ United Artists XW512	Too Late to Turn Back Now/Don't Ever Be Lonely (A Poor Little Fool Like Me)	1974	—	2.00	4.00
—Reissue					
❑ United Artists XW533	Trouble Child/Got to Testify	1974	—	2.50	5.00
❑ United Artists XW534	Since I Found My Baby/I Love Music	1974	—	2.50	5.00
❑ United Artists 50721	Treat Her Like a Lady/Over at My Place	1970	—	2.50	5.00
❑ United Artists 50910	Too Late to Turn Back Now/Lift Your Love Higher	1972	—	2.50	5.00
❑ United Artists 50954	Don't Ever Be Lonely (A Poor Little Fool Like Me)/ I'm So Glad to Be Loved by You	1972	—	2.50	5.00
❑ United Artists 50996	I'm Never Gonna Be Alone Anymore/Let's Stay Together	1972	—	2.50	5.00

Albums

Number	Title (A Side/B Side)	Yr	VG	VG+	NM
❑ United Artists UA-LA593-G	Greatest Hits	1976	3.00	6.00	12.00
❑ United Artists UAS-5568	Cornelius Brothers and Sister Rose	1972	3.75	7.50	15.00

COSBY, BILL

45s

Number	Title (A Side/B Side)	Yr	VG	VG+	NM
❑ Capitol 4258	Yes, Yes, Yes/Ben	1976	—	2.00	4.00
❑ Capitol 4299	I Luv Myself Better Than I Luv Myself/Do It To Me	1976	—	2.00	4.00
❑ Capitol 4501	Boogie on Your Face/What's in a Slang	1977	—	2.00	4.00
❑ Capitol 4523	Merry Christmas Mama (Vocal)/(Instrumental)	1977	5.00	10.00	20.00
❑ Tetragrammaton 1539	Football/Golf	1969	—	3.00	6.00
❑ Uni 55184	Hikky Burr/Hikky Burr	1969	—	3.00	6.00
—A-side with the Bunions; B-side by the Bradford Band					
❑ Uni 55223	Grover Henson Feels Forgotten/(Instrumental)	1970	—	3.00	6.00
❑ Uni 55247	Hybish Skybish/Martin's Funeral	1970	—	2.50	5.00
—With Bad Foot Brown					
❑ Warner Bros. 5499	Stand Still for My Lovin'/When I Marry	1965	2.50	5.00	10.00
❑ Warner Bros. 7072	Little Ole Man (Uptight-Everything's Alright)/Hush Hush	1967	2.00	4.00	8.00
❑ Warner Bros. 7096	Hooray for the Salvation Army Band/Ursalena	1968	2.00	4.00	8.00
❑ Warner Bros. 7126	Little Ole Man (Uptight-Everything's Alright)/Funky North Philly	1969	—	3.00	6.00
—Hall of Fame Hits (originals have green labels with "W7" logo)					
❑ Warner Bros. 7171	Funky North Philly/Stop, Look and Listen	1968	2.00	4.00	8.00

Albums

Number	Title (A Side/B Side)	Yr	VG	VG+	NM
❑ Capitol ST-11530	Bill Cosby Is Not Himself These Days, Rat Own, Rat Own, Rat Own	1976	2.50	5.00	10.00
❑ Capitol ST-11590	My Father Confused Me...What Must I Do? What Must I Do?	1977	2.50	5.00	10.00
❑ Capitol ST-11683	Let's Boogie (Disco Bill)	1977	2.50	5.00	10.00
❑ Capitol ST-11731	Bill's Best Friend	1978	2.50	5.00	10.00
❑ Geffen GHS 24104	Those of You With or Without Children, You'll Understand	1986	2.50	5.00	10.00
❑ MCA 169	When I Was a Kid	197?	2.00	4.00	8.00
—Reissue of Uni 73100					
❑ MCA 333	Fat Albert	1973	2.50	5.00	10.00

Number	Title (A Side/B Side)	Yr	VG	VG+	NM
❑ MCA 553	For Adults Only	197?	2.00	4.00	8.00
—Reissue of Uni 73112					
❑ MCA 554	Inside the Mind of Bill Cosby	197?	2.00	4.00	8.00
—Reissue of Uni 73139					
❑ MCA 8005 [(2)]	Bill	197?	3.00	6.00	12.00
❑ Motown 5364 ML	Bill Cosby "Himself"	198?	2.50	5.00	10.00
—Reissue of 6026 with new cover					
❑ Motown 6026 ML	Bill Cosby "Himself"	1982	2.50	5.00	10.00
❑ Tetragrammaton TD-5100 [(2)]	8:15 12:15	1969	5.00	10.00	20.00
❑ Uni 73066	Bill Cosby	1969	2.50	5.00	10.00
❑ Uni 73082	"Live" Madison Square Garden Center	1970	2.50	5.00	10.00
❑ Uni 73100	When I Was a Kid	1971	2.50	5.00	10.00
❑ Uni 73101	Bill Cosby Talks to Kids About Drugs	1971	3.75	7.50	15.00
❑ Uni 73112	For Adults Only	1971	2.50	5.00	10.00
❑ Uni 73139	Inside the Mind of Bill Cosby	1972	2.50	5.00	10.00
❑ Warner Bros. W 1518 [M]	Bill Cosby Is a Very Funny Fellow Right!	1964	3.75	7.50	15.00
❑ Warner Bros. W 1567 [M]	I Started Out as a Child	1964	3.75	7.50	15.00
❑ Warner Bros. WS 1567 [S]	I Started Out as a Child	1964	5.00	10.00	20.00
—Gold label					
❑ Warner Bros. W 1606 [M]	Why Is There Air?	1965	3.75	7.50	15.00
❑ Warner Bros. WS 1606 [S]	Why Is There Air?	1965	5.00	10.00	20.00
—Gold label					
❑ Warner Bros. W 1634 [M]	Wonderfulness	1966	3.75	7.50	15.00
❑ Warner Bros. WS 1634 [S]	Wonderfulness	1966	3.75	7.50	15.00
—Gold label					
❑ Warner Bros. W 1691 [M]	Revenge	1967	3.75	7.50	15.00
❑ Warner Bros. W 1709 [M]	Bill Cosby Sings/Silver Throat	1967	3.75	7.50	15.00
❑ Warner Bros. WS 1709 [S]	Bill Cosby Sings/Silver Throat	1967	3.00	6.00	12.00
❑ Warner Bros. W 1728 [M]	Bill Cosby Sings/Hooray for the Salvation Army Band	1968	3.75	7.50	15.00
❑ Warner Bros. WS 1728 [S]	Bill Cosby Sings/Hooray for the Salvation Army Band	1968	3.00	6.00	12.00
❑ Warner Bros. W 1734 [M]	To Russell, My Brother, Whom I Slept With	1968	3.75	7.50	15.00
❑ Warner Bros. WS 1734 [S]	To Russell, My Brother, Whom I Slept With	1968	3.00	6.00	12.00
❑ Warner Bros. WS 1757	200 M.P.H.	1968	3.00	6.00	12.00
❑ Warner Bros. WS 1770	It's True! It's True!	1969	3.00	6.00	12.00
❑ Warner Bros. WS 1798	The Best of Bill Cosby	1969	3.00	6.00	12.00
❑ Warner Bros. WS 1836	More of the Best of Bill Cosby	1970	3.00	6.00	12.00

COSTELLO, ELVIS

45s

Number	Title (A Side/B Side)	Yr	VG	VG+	NM
❑ Columbia 18-02629	A Good Year for the Roses/The Angel Steps Out of Heaven	1981	—	2.50	5.00
❑ Columbia 18-03202	Man Out of Time/Town Cryer	1982	—	2.50	5.00
❑ Columbia CNR-03269	Man Out of Time/(B-side blank)	1982	2.00	4.00	8.00
—One-sided budget release					
❑ Columbia 38-04045	Everyday I Write the Book/Heathen Town	1983	—	2.50	5.00
❑ Columbia 38-04266	Let Them All Talk/Shipbiulding	1983	—	2.50	5.00
❑ Columbia 38-04502	The Only Flame in Town/Turning the Town Red	1984	—	2.50	5.00
❑ Columbia 38-04625	I Wanna Be Loved/Love Field	1984	—	2.50	5.00
❑ Columbia 38-05809	Don't Let Me Be Misunderstood/Brand New Hairdo	1986	—	2.00	4.00
—By "The Costello Show Featuring Elvis Costello"					
❑ Columbia 38-06059	Lovable/Get Yourself Another Fool	1986	—	2.00	4.00
—By "The Costello Show Featuring Elvis Costello"					
❑ Columbia 38-06326	Tokyo Storm Warning (Part 1)/(Part 2)	1986	—	2.50	5.00
❑ Columbia 3-10641	Alison/Miracle Man	1977	2.50	5.00	10.00
—Contains a remix of "Alison" otherwise unavailable on U.S. vinyl					
❑ Columbia 3-10696	Watching the Detectives//Blame It on Cain/Mystery Dance	1978	2.50	5.00	10.00
❑ Columbia 3-10705	Alison/Watching the Detectives	1978	2.50	5.00	10.00
—Contains the same remix of "Alison" as on 10641					
❑ Columbia 3-10762	This Year's Girl/Big Tears	1978	—	3.00	6.00
❑ Columbia 3-10919	Accidents Will Happen/Sunday's Best	1979	2.00	4.00	8.00
❑ Columbia 1-11194	I Can't Stand Up for Falling Down/Girls Talk	1980	—	3.50	7.00
❑ Columbia 1-11284	New Amsterdam/Wednesday Week	1980	—	2.50	5.00
❑ Columbia 1-11389	Getting Mighty Crowded/Radio Sweetheart	1980	—	2.50	5.00
❑ Columbia 3-33401	Accidents Will Happen/Alison	198?	—	—	3.00
—"Hall of Fame" reissue; gray label					
❑ Columbia 3-33401	Accidents Will Happen/Alison	1980	—	2.50	5.00
—"Hall of Fame" reissue; red and black label					
❑ Columbia 11-60519	Watch Your Step/Luxembourg	1981	—	2.50	5.00
❑ Warner Bros. 22981	Veronica/You're No Good	1989	—	—	3.00

Albums

Number	Title (A Side/B Side)	Yr	VG	VG+	NM
❑ Columbia JC 35037	My Aim Is True	1977	3.75	7.50	15.00
—First pressings have yellow back covers					
❑ Columbia JC 35331	This Year's Model	1978	3.00	6.00	12.00
—With "Costello" replacing "Columbia" on labels					
❑ Columbia JC 36347	Get Happy!!	1980	2.50	5.00	10.00
❑ Columbia JC 36839	Taking Liberties	1980	2.50	5.00	10.00
—With custom old-style Columbia label					
❑ Columbia JC 37051	Trust	1981	2.50	5.00	10.00
❑ Columbia FC 37562	Almost Blue	1981	2.50	5.00	10.00
❑ Columbia FC 38157	Imperial Bedroom	1982	2.50	5.00	10.00
❑ Columbia FC 38897	Punch the Clock	1983	2.50	5.00	10.00
❑ Columbia FC 39429	Goodbye Cruel World	1984	2.50	5.00	10.00
❑ Columbia FC 40101	The Best of Elvis Costello	1985	3.00	6.00	12.00
❑ Columbia FC 40173	King of America	1986	2.50	5.00	10.00
—By "The Costello Show Featuring Elvis Costello"					
❑ Columbia FC 40518	Blood & Chocolate	1986	2.50	5.00	10.00
❑ Warner Bros. 25848	Spike	1989	2.50	5.00	10.00

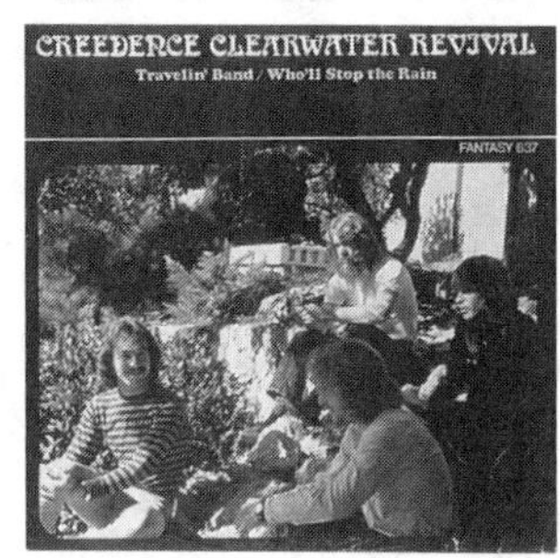

Number	Title (A Side/B Side)	Yr	VG	VG+	NM
COUNT FIVE, THE					
45s					
❑ Double Shot 104	Psychotic Reaction/They're Gonna Get You	1966	3.75	7.50	15.00
—First pressing, with label logo at top					
❑ Double Shot 106	Peace of Mind/The Morning After	1966	3.00	6.00	12.00
❑ Double Shot 110	You Must Believe Me/Teeny Bopper, Teeny Bopper	1967	3.00	6.00	12.00
❑ Double Shot 115	Merry-Go-Round/Contrast	1967	3.00	6.00	12.00
❑ Double Shot 125	Declaration of Independence/Revelation in Slow Motion	1968	3.00	6.00	12.00
❑ Double Shot 141	Mailman/Pretty Big Mouth	1969	3.00	6.00	12.00
Albums					
❑ Double Shot DSM-1001 [M]	Psychotic Reaction	1966	10.00	20.00	40.00
❑ Double Shot DSS-5001 [R]	Psychotic Reaction	1966	6.25	12.50	25.00
COWSILLS, THE					
45s					
❑ Joda 103	All I Really Wanta Be Is Me/And the Next Day, Too	1965	7.50	15.00	30.00
❑ London 149	On My Side/There Is No Child	1971	2.00	4.00	8.00
❑ London 153	You/Crystal Claps	1971	2.00	4.00	8.00
❑ London 170	Blue Road/Covered Wagon	1972	2.00	4.00	8.00
❑ MGM 13810	The Rain, the Park and Other Things/River Blue	1967	2.50	5.00	10.00
❑ MGM 13886	We Can Fly/A Time for Remembrance	1967	2.00	4.00	8.00
❑ MGM 13909	In Need of a Friend/Mister Flynn	1968	2.00	4.00	8.00
❑ MGM 13944	Indian Lake/Newspaper Blanket	1968	2.50	5.00	10.00
—First pressings have black labels					
❑ MGM 13981	Poor Baby/Meet Me at the Wishing Well	1968	2.00	4.00	8.00
❑ MGM 14011	The Impossible Years/Candy Kid	1968	2.00	4.00	8.00
❑ MGM 14026	Hair/What Is Happy	1969	3.00	6.00	12.00
❑ MGM 14063	The Prophecy of Daniel and John the Divine (Six-Six-Six)/ Gotta Get Away from It All	1969	2.00	4.00	8.00
❑ MGM 14084	Silver Threads and Golden Needles/Love, American Style	1969	2.50	5.00	10.00
❑ MGM 14106	Start to Love/Two by Two	1970	2.00	4.00	8.00
❑ Philips 40382	Most of All/Siamese Cat	1966	2.50	5.00	10.00
❑ Philips 40406	Party Girl/What's It Gonna Be Like	1966	2.50	5.00	10.00
❑ Philips 40437	A Most Peculiar Man/Could It Be, Let Me Know	1967	2.50	5.00	10.00
Albums					
❑ London PS 587	On My Side	1971	7.50	15.00	30.00
❑ MGM GAS-103	The Cowsills (Golden Archive Series)	1970	3.75	7.50	15.00
❑ MGM E-4498 [M]	The Cowsills	1967	5.00	10.00	20.00
❑ MGM SE-4498 [S]	The Cowsills	1967	3.75	7.50	15.00
❑ MGM E-4534 [M]	We Can Fly	1968	7.50	15.00	30.00
—Appears to exist only as a yellow label promo					
❑ MGM SE-4534 [S]	We Can Fly	1968	3.75	7.50	15.00
❑ MGM SE-4554 [S]	Captain Sad and His Ship of Fools	1968	3.75	7.50	15.00
❑ MGM SE-4597	The Best of the Cowsills	1968	3.75	7.50	15.00
❑ MGM SE-4619	The Cowsills in Concert	1969	3.75	7.50	15.00
❑ MGM SE-4639	II X II	1969	5.00	10.00	20.00
❑ Wing SRW-16354	The Cowsills Plus the Lincoln Park Zoo	1968	3.00	6.00	12.00
CREAM					
45s					
❑ Atco 6462	I Feel Free/N.S.U.	1967	3.75	7.50	15.00
❑ Atco 6488	Strange Brew/Tales of Brave Ulysses	1967	3.75	7.50	15.00
❑ Atco 6522	Spoonful/Spoonful (Part 2)	1967	3.75	7.50	15.00
❑ Atco 6544	Sunshine of Your Love/SWLABR	1968	2.00	4.00	8.00
❑ Atco 6575	Anyone for Tennis/Pressed Rat and Warthog	1968	2.00	4.00	8.00
❑ Atco 6617	White Room/Those Were the Days	1968	2.00	4.00	8.00
❑ Atco 6646	Crossroads/Passing the Time	1969	2.00	4.00	8.00
❑ Atco 6668	Badge/What a Bringdown	1969	2.00	4.00	8.00
❑ Atco 6708	Sweet Wine/Lawdy Mama	1969	2.50	5.00	10.00
Albums					
❑ Atco 33-206 [M]	Fresh Cream	1967	12.50	25.00	50.00
❑ Atco SD 33-206 [S]	Fresh Cream	1967	7.50	15.00	30.00
—Purple and brown labels					
❑ Atco 33-232 [M]	Disraeli Gears	1967	12.50	25.00	50.00
❑ Atco SD 33-232 [S]	Disraeli Gears	1967	7.50	15.00	30.00
—Purple and brown labels					
❑ Atco SD 33-291	Best of Cream	1969	6.25	12.50	25.00

Number	Title (A Side/B Side)	Yr	VG	VG+	NM
❑ Atco SD 33-328	Live Cream	1970	6.25	12.50	25.00
❑ Atco SD 2-700 [(2)S]	Wheels of Fire	1968	12.50	25.00	50.00
—Purple and brown labels; foil-like cover					
❑ Atco SD 7001	Goodbye	1969	7.50	15.00	30.00
—Purple and brown labels; deduct 33% if poster is missing					
❑ Atco SD 7005	Live Cream — Volume II	1972	6.25	12.50	25.00
❑ Polydor 24-3502 [(2)]	Heavy Cream	1972	3.75	7.50	15.00
❑ Polydor 24-5529	Off the Top	1973	3.75	7.50	15.00
❑ RSO RS-1-3009	Fresh Cream	1977	3.00	6.00	12.00
❑ RSO RS-1-3010	Disraeli Gears	1977	3.00	6.00	12.00
❑ RSO RS-1-3012	Best of Cream	1977	3.00	6.00	12.00
❑ RSO RS-1-3013	Goodbye	1977	3.00	6.00	12.00
❑ RSO RS-1-3014	Live Cream	1977	3.00	6.00	12.00
❑ RSO RS-1-3015	Live Cream — Volume 2	1977	3.00	6.00	12.00
❑ RSO RS-2-3802 [(2)]	Wheels of Fire	1977	3.75	7.50	15.00
❑ Springboard SPB 4037	Early Cream	1972	3.75	7.50	15.00

CREEDENCE CLEARWATER REVIVAL

45s

Number	Title (A Side/B Side)	Yr	VG	VG+	NM
❑ Fantasy 616	Suzie Q (Part One)/Suzie Q (Part Two)	1968	—	3.00	6.00
❑ Fantasy 617	I Put a Spell on You/Walk on the Water	1968	2.00	4.00	8.00
❑ Fantasy 619	Proud Mary/Born on the Bayou	1969	—	3.00	6.00
❑ Fantasy 622	Bad Moon Rising/Lodi	1969	—	3.00	6.00
❑ Fantasy 625	Green River/Commotion	1969	—	3.00	6.00
❑ Fantasy 634	Down on the Corner/Fortunate Son	1969	—	3.00	6.00
❑ Fantasy 637	Travelin' Band/Who'll Stop the Rain	1970	—	3.00	6.00
❑ Fantasy 641	Up Around the Bend/Run Through the Jungle	1970	—	3.00	6.00
❑ Fantasy 645	Lookin' Out My Back Door/Long As I Can See the Light	1970	—	3.00	6.00
❑ Fantasy 655	Have You Ever Seen the Rain/Hey Tonight	1971	—	3.00	6.00
❑ Fantasy 665	Sweet Hitch-Hiker/Door to Door	1971	—	3.00	6.00
❑ Fantasy 676	Someday Never Comes/Tearin' Up the Country	1972	—	3.00	6.00
❑ Fantasy 759	I Heard It Through the Grapevine/Good Golly Miss Molly	1976	—	2.00	4.00
❑ Fantasy 908	Tombstone Shadow/Commotion	1981	—	2.00	4.00
❑ Fantasy 917	Medley U.S.A./Bad Moon Rising	1981	—	2.00	4.00
❑ Fantasy 920	Cotton Fields/Lodi	1981	—	2.00	4.00
❑ Fantasy 957	Medley (from "I Heard It Through the Grapevine" to "Up Around the Bend")/Medley (from "Proud Mary" to "Lodi")	1985	2.50	5.00	10.00
❑ Scorpio 412	Porterville/Call It Pretending	1968	20.00	40.00	80.00

Albums

Number	Title (A Side/B Side)	Yr	VG	VG+	NM
❑ Fantasy CCR-1 [(2)]	Live in Europe	1973	3.00	6.00	12.00
❑ Fantasy CCR-2 [(2)]	Chronicle (The 20 Greatest Hits)	1976	3.75	7.50	15.00
—Brown labels					
❑ Fantasy CCR-2 [(2)]	Chronicle (The 20 Greatest Hits)	1979	3.00	6.00	12.00
—Whitish or light blue labels					
❑ Fantasy CCR-3 [(2)]	Chronicle, Volume 2	1987	3.75	7.50	15.00
❑ Fantasy CCR-68 [(2)]	Creedence Clearwater Revival 1968/69	1981	3.00	6.00	12.00
—Compilation of 8382 and 8387					
❑ Fantasy CCR-69 [(2)]	Creedence Clearwater Revival 1969	1981	3.00	6.00	12.00
—Compilation of 8393 and 8397					
❑ Fantasy CCR-70 [(2)]	Creedence Clearwater Revival 1970	1981	3.00	6.00	12.00
—Compilation of 8402 and 8410					
❑ Fantasy MPF-4501	The Royal Albert Hall Concert	1980	3.75	7.50	15.00
—Album withdrawn and changed when it was discovered this didn't come from the Royal Albert Hall					
❑ Fantasy MPF-4501	The Concert	1981	2.50	5.00	10.00
—Retitled version					
❑ Fantasy MPF-4509	Creedence Country	1981	2.50	5.00	10.00
❑ Fantasy ORC-4512	Creedence Clearwater Revival	1981	2.00	4.00	8.00
—Reissue of 8382					
❑ Fantasy ORC-4513	Bayou Country	1981	2.00	4.00	8.00
—Reissue of 8387					
❑ Fantasy ORC-4514	Green River	1981	2.00	4.00	8.00
—Reissue of 8393					
❑ Fantasy ORC-4515	Willy and the Poor Boys	1981	2.00	4.00	8.00
—Reissue of 8397					
❑ Fantasy ORC-4516	Cosmo's Factory	1981	2.00	4.00	8.00
—Reissue of 8402					
❑ Fantasy ORC-4517	Pendulum	1981	2.00	4.00	8.00
—Reissue of 8410					
❑ Fantasy ORC-4518	Mardi Gras	1981	2.00	4.00	8.00
—Reissue of 9404					
❑ Fantasy MPF-4522	The Movie Album	1985	2.00	4.00	8.00
❑ Fantasy ORC-4526 [(2)]	Live in Europe	1986	2.50	5.00	10.00
❑ Fantasy F-8382	Creedence Clearwater Revival	1968	6.25	12.50	25.00
—With no reference to "Susie Q" on the front cover					
❑ Fantasy F-8387	Bayou Country	1969	3.75	7.50	15.00
—Dark blue label					
❑ Fantasy F-8393	Green River	1969	3.75	7.50	15.00
—Dark blue label					
❑ Fantasy F-8397	Willy and the Poor Boys	1969	3.75	7.50	15.00
—Dark blue label					
❑ Fantasy F-8402	Cosmo's Factory	1970	3.75	7.50	15.00
—Dark blue label					
❑ Fantasy F-8410	Pendulum	1970	3.75	7.50	15.00
—Dark blue label					
❑ Fantasy F-9404	Mardi Gras	1972	3.75	7.50	15.00
—Dark blue label					

Number	Title (A Side/B Side)	Yr	VG	VG+	NM
❑ Fantasy F-9418	Creedence Gold	1972	2.50	5.00	10.00
❑ Fantasy F-9430	More Creedence Gold	1973	2.50	5.00	10.00
❑ Fantasy F-9621	Chooglin'	1982	2.00	4.00	8.00
❑ K-Tel NU 9360	The Best of Creedence Clearwater Revival — 20 Super Hits	1978	3.75	7.50	15.00

CRESTS, THE

45s

Number	Title (A Side/B Side)	Yr	VG	VG+	NM
❑ Coed 501	Pretty Little Angel/I Thank the Moon	1958	37.50	75.00	150.00
—"Coed" in red print					
❑ Coed 506	16 Candles/Beside You	1958	7.50	15.00	30.00
❑ Coed 509	Six Nights a Week/I Do	1959	6.25	12.50	25.00
❑ Coed 511	Flower of Love/Molly Mae	1959	6.25	12.50	25.00
❑ Coed 515	The Angels Listened In/I Thank the Moon	1959	7.50	15.00	30.00
❑ Coed 521	A Year Ago Tonight/Paper Clown	1959	6.25	12.50	25.00
❑ Coed 525	Step by Step/Gee (But I'd Give the World)	1960	6.25	12.50	25.00
❑ Coed 531	Trouble in Paradise/Always You	1960	6.25	12.50	25.00
❑ Coed 535	Journey of Love/If My Heart Could Write a Letter	1960	5.00	10.00	20.00
❑ Coed 537	Isn't It Amazing/Molly Mae	1960	5.00	10.00	20.00
❑ Coed 543	I Remember (In the Still of the Night)/Good Golly Miss Molly	1961	6.25	12.50	25.00
❑ Coed 561	Little Miracles/Baby I Gotta Know	1962	7.50	15.00	30.00
❑ Coral 62403	You Blew Out the Candles/A Love to Last a Lifetime	1964	7.50	15.00	30.00
❑ Harvey 5002	Sixteen Candles/My Juanita	1981	2.50	5.00	10.00
—Red vinyl					
❑ Joyce 103	My Juanita/Sweetest One	1957	75.00	150.00	300.00
—Label name: "JoYce"					
❑ Joyce 105	No One to Love/Wish She Was Mine	1957	75.00	150.00	300.00
❑ King Tut 172	Earth Angel/Tweedlee Dee	197?	2.00	4.00	8.00
❑ Lana 101	16 Candles/Besides You	196?	2.00	4.00	8.00
—Oldies reissue					
❑ Lana 102	Trouble in Paradise/I Thank the Moon	196?	2.00	4.00	8.00
—Oldies reissue					
❑ Lana 103	Step by Step/Gee (But I'd Give the World)	196?	2.00	4.00	8.00
—Oldies reissue					
❑ Lost-Nite 156	No One to Love/Wish She Was Mine	196?	—	3.00	6.00
—Reissue					
❑ Lost-Nite 163	Six Nights a Week/I Do	196?	—	3.00	6.00
—Reissue					
❑ Lost-Nite 166	Step by Step/Gee (But I'd Give the World)	196?	—	3.00	6.00
—Reissue					
❑ Lost-Nite 168	16 Candles/Beside You	196?	—	3.00	6.00
—Reissue					
❑ Lost-Nite 171	The Angels Listened In/I Thank the Moon	196?	—	3.00	6.00
—Reissue					
❑ Lost-Nite 209	My Juanita/Sweetest One	196?	—	3.00	6.00
—Reissue					
❑ Lost-Nite 211	Flower of Love/Molly Mae	196?	—	3.00	6.00
—Reissue					
❑ Lost-Nite 229	Pretty Little Angel/I Thank the Moon	196?	—	2.50	5.00
—Reissue					
❑ Musictone 1106	My Juanita/Sweetest One	1961	5.00	10.00	20.00
❑ Scepter 12112	I'm Stepping Out of the Picture/Afraid of Love	1965	3.75	7.50	15.00
❑ Selma 311	Guilty/Number One with Me	1962	6.25	12.50	25.00
—A-side does not have spoken intro					
❑ Selma 311	Guilty/Number One with Me	1962	18.75	37.50	75.00
—A-side has spoken intro					
❑ Selma 4000	Did I Remember/Tears Will Fall	1963	7.50	15.00	30.00
❑ Times Square 2	No One to Love/Wish She Was Mine	1962	5.00	10.00	20.00
—Red vinyl					
❑ Times Square 6	Baby/I Love You So	1964	3.75	7.50	15.00
❑ Times Square 97	Baby/I Love You So	1964	3.00	6.00	12.00
❑ Trans Atlas 696	The Actor/Three Tears in a Bucket	1962	7.50	15.00	30.00

Albums

Number	Title (A Side/B Side)	Yr	VG	VG+	NM
❑ Coed LPC-901 [M]	The Crests Sing All Biggies	1960	100.00	200.00	400.00
—Yellow label, black print					
❑ Coed LPC-904 [M]	The Best of the Crests/16 Fabulous Hits	1961	100.00	200.00	400.00
—Label simply calls this "16 Fabulous Hits"					
❑ Collectables COL-5009	Greatest Hits	1982	3.00	6.00	12.00

Number	Title (A Side/B Side)	Yr	VG	VG+	NM
❑ Post 3000	The Crests Sing	196?	10.00	20.00	40.00
❑ Rhino R1-70948	The Best of the Crests	1989	3.00	6.00	12.00

CRICKETS, THE (1)

Includes records with and without BUDDY HOLLY. There also was a Crickets black vocal group who made records on Davis, Jay Dee and MGM; these are outside the scope of this book.

45s

Number	Title (A Side/B Side)	Yr	VG	VG+	NM
❑ Barnaby 2061	Rockin' 50's Rock 'N' Roll/True Love Ways	1972	5.00	10.00	20.00
❑ Brunswick 55009	That'll Be the Day/I'm Lookin' for Someone to Love	1957	12.50	25.00	50.00
❑ Brunswick 55035	Oh, Boy!/Not Fade Away	1957	12.50	25.00	50.00
—Note: Picture sleeves for this record are bootlegs					
❑ Brunswick 55053	Maybe Baby/Tell Me How	1958	12.50	25.00	50.00
❑ Brunswick 55072	Think It Over/Fool's Paradise	1958	12.50	25.00	50.00
❑ Brunswick 55094	It's So Easy/Lonesome Tears	1958	12.50	25.00	50.00
❑ Brunswick 55124	Love's Made a Fool of You/Someone, Someone	1959	10.00	20.00	40.00
❑ Brunswick 55153	When You Ask About Love/Deborah	1959	10.00	20.00	40.00
❑ Coral 62198	More Than I Can Say/Baby, My Heart	1960	10.00	20.00	40.00
❑ Coral 62238	Peggy Sue Got Married/Don't Cha Know	1960	10.00	20.00	40.00
❑ Coral 62407	Maybe Baby/Not Fade Away	1964	7.50	15.00	30.00
❑ Epic 34-08028	T-Shirt/Hollywould	1988	—	2.50	5.00
❑ Liberty 55392	He's Old Enough to Know Better/I'm Feeling Better	1961	6.25	12.50	25.00
❑ Liberty 55441	Don't Ever Change/I'm Not a Bad Boy	1962	6.25	12.50	25.00
❑ Liberty 55492	I Believe in You/Parisian Girl	1962	6.25	12.50	25.00
❑ Liberty 55495	Little Hollywood Girl/Parisian Girl	1962	6.25	12.50	25.00
❑ Liberty 55540	My Little Girl/Teardrops Fall Like Rain	1963	6.25	12.50	25.00
❑ Liberty 55603	Don't Say You Love Me/April Avenue	1963	6.25	12.50	25.00
❑ Liberty 55660	Lonely Avenue/You Can't Be In-Between	1964	6.25	12.50	25.00
❑ Liberty 55668	Please, Please Me/From Me to You	1964	12.50	25.00	50.00
❑ Liberty 55696	(They Call Her) La Bomba/All Over You	1964	6.25	12.50	25.00
❑ Liberty 55742	We Gotta Get Together/I Think I've Caught the Blues	1964	6.25	12.50	25.00
❑ Liberty 55767	Everybody's Got a Little Problem/Now Hear This	1965	6.25	12.50	25.00
❑ MGM 14541	Hayride/Wasn't It Nice	1973	3.75	7.50	15.00
❑ Music Factory 415	Million Dollar Movie/A Million Miles Apart	1968	5.00	10.00	20.00

Albums

Number	Title	Yr	VG	VG+	NM
❑ Barnaby Z 30268	Rockin' 50's Rock 'N' Roll	1970	6.25	12.50	25.00
❑ Brunswick BL 54038 [M]	The "Chirping" Crickets	1957	200.00	400.00	800.00
—Textured cover					
❑ Brunswick BL 54038 [M]	The "Chirping" Crickets	1958	150.00	300.00	600.00
—Regular cover					
❑ Coral CRL 57320 [M]	In Style with the Crickets	1960	50.00	100.00	200.00
❑ Coral CRL 757320 [S]	In Style with the Crickets	1960	100.00	200.00	400.00
❑ Epic FE 44446	T-Shirt	1988	3.75	7.50	15.00
❑ Liberty LRP-3272 [M]	Something Old, Something New, Something Blue, Somethin' Else	1962	37.50	75.00	150.00
❑ Liberty LRP-3351 [M]	California Sun/She Loves You	1964	25.00	50.00	100.00
❑ Liberty LST-7272 [S]	Something Old, Something New, Something Blue, Somethin' Else	1962	50.00	100.00	200.00
❑ Liberty LST-7351 [S]	California Sun/She Loves You	1964	37.50	75.00	150.00
❑ Vertigo VEL-1020	Remnants	1973	5.00	10.00	20.00

CROCE, JIM

45s

Number	Title (A Side/B Side)	Yr	VG	VG+	NM
❑ ABC 11328	You Don't Mess Around with Jim/Photographs and Memories	1972	—	2.00	4.00
❑ ABC 11335	Operator (That's Not the Way It Feels)/Rapid Roy (The Stock Car Boy)	1972	—	2.00	4.00
❑ ABC 11346	One Less Set of Footsteps/It Doesn't Have to Be That Way	1973	—	2.00	4.00
❑ ABC 11359	Bad, Bad Leroy Brown/A Good Time Man Like Me Ain't Got No Business (Singin' the Blues)	1973	—	2.50	5.00
—ABC logo in children's building blocks					
❑ ABC 11389	I Got a Name/Alabama Rain	1973	—	2.00	4.00
❑ ABC 11405	Time in a Bottle/Hard Time Losin' Man	1973	—	2.00	4.00
❑ ABC 11413	It Doesn't Have to Be That Way/Roller Derby Queen	1973	—	2.00	4.00
❑ ABC 11424	I'll Have to Say I Love You in a Song/Salon and Saloon	1974	—	2.00	4.00
❑ ABC 11447	Workin' at the Car Wash Blues/Thursday	1974	—	2.00	4.00
❑ ABC 12015	Workin' at the Car Wash Blues/Thursday	1974	—	2.50	5.00
❑ Lifesong 45001	Chain Gang Medley/Stone Walls	1975	—	2.00	4.00
❑ Lifesong 45005	Maybe Tomorrow/Mississippi Lady	1976	—	2.00	4.00
❑ 21 Records 94969	Workin' at the Car Wash Blues/Rapid Roy (The Stock Car Boy)	1987	—	—	3.00
❑ 21 Records 94970	It Doesn't Have to Be That Way/Time in a Bottle	1987	—	—	3.00
❑ 21 Records 94971	I'll Have to Say I Love You in a Song/I Got a Name	1987	—	—	3.00
❑ 21 Records 94972	You Don't Mess Around with Jim/Photographs and Memories	1987	—	—	3.00
❑ 21 Records 94973	Bad, Bad Leroy Brown/Operator (That's Not the Way It Feels)	1987	—	—	3.00

Albums

Number	Title	Yr	VG	VG+	NM
❑ ABC ABCX-756	You Don't Mess Around with Jim	1972	5.00	10.00	20.00
—Original covers have no green box advertising "Time in a Bottle"					
❑ ABC ABCX-756	You Don't Mess Around with Jim	1973	3.75	7.50	15.00
—Posthumous covers have a green box advertising "Time in a Bottle"					
❑ ABC ABCX-769	Life and Times	1973	3.75	7.50	15.00
❑ ABC ABCX-797	I Got a Name	1973	3.75	7.50	15.00
❑ ABC ABCD-835	Photographs & Memories/His Greatest Hits	1974	3.75	7.50	15.00
❑ Capitol SMAS-315	Jim and Ingrid Croce	1970	7.50	15.00	30.00
❑ Croce 101	Facets	1966	75.00	150.00	300.00
❑ Lifesong LS 900 [(2)]	The Faces I've Been	1975	3.75	7.50	15.00
❑ Lifesong LS 6007	Time in a Bottle — Jim Croce's Greatest Love Songs	1976	3.00	6.00	12.00
❑ Lifesong JZ 34993	You Don't Mess Around with Jim	1978	2.50	5.00	10.00
❑ Lifesong JZ 35000	Time in a Bottle — Jim Croce's Greatest Love Songs	1978	2.50	5.00	10.00
❑ Lifesong JZ 35008	Life and Times	1978	2.50	5.00	10.00
❑ Lifesong JZ 35009	I Got a Name	1978	2.50	5.00	10.00
❑ Lifesong JZ 35010	Photographs & Memories/His Greatest Hits	1978	2.50	5.00	10.00

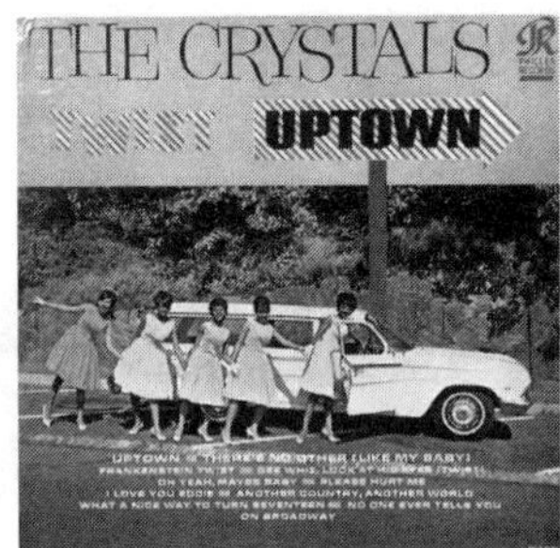

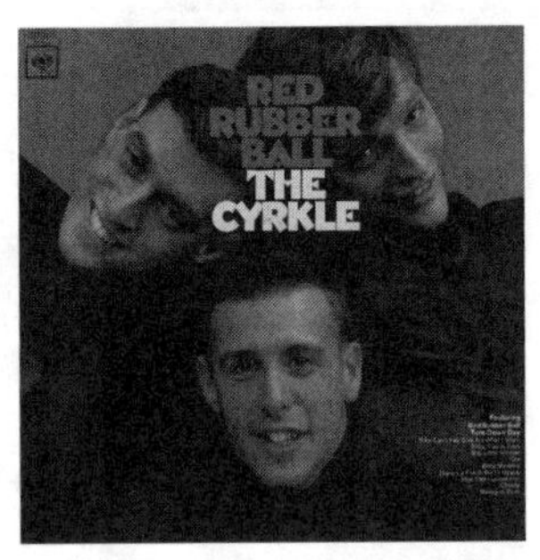

Number	Title (A Side/B Side)	Yr	VG	VG+	NM
❑ Lifesong JZ 35571	Bad, Bad Leroy Brown: Jim Croce's Greatest Character Songs	1978	2.50	5.00	10.00
❑ Pickwick SPC-3332	Another Day, Another Town	1973	2.50	5.00	10.00
—Reissue of Capitol LP					
❑ 21 Records 90467	Photographs & Memories/His Greatest Hits	1985	2.00	4.00	8.00
❑ 21 Records 90468	Time in a Bottle — Jim Croce's Greatest Love Songs	1985	2.00	4.00	8.00
❑ 21 Records 90469	Down the Highway	1985	2.50	5.00	10.00
CROSBY, STILLS AND NASH					
45s					
❑ Atlantic 2652	Marrakesh Express/Helplessly Hoping	1969	—	3.00	6.00
❑ Atlantic 2676	Suite: Judy Blue Eyes/Long Time Gone	1969	—	3.00	6.00
❑ Atlantic 3401	Just a Song Before I Go/Dark Star	1977	—	2.00	4.00
❑ Atlantic 3432	Fair Game/Anything at All	1977	—	2.00	4.00
❑ Atlantic 3453	I Give You Give Blind/Carried Away	1978	—	2.00	4.00
❑ Atlantic 3784	Carry On/Shadow Captain	1980	—	2.50	5.00
❑ Atlantic 4058	Wasted on the Way/Delta	1982	—	—	3.00
❑ Atlantic 87909	Live It Up/Chuck's Lament	1990	—	2.00	4.00
❑ Atlantic 89775	Raise a Voice/For What It's Worth	1983	—	—	3.00
❑ Atlantic 89812	War Games/Shadow Captain	1983	—	—	3.00
❑ Atlantic 89888	Too Much Love to Hide/Song for Susan	1983	—	—	3.00
❑ Atlantic 89969	Southern Cross/Into the Darkness	1982	—	—	3.00
Albums					
❑ Atlantic SD 8229	Crosby, Stills & Nash	1969	5.00	10.00	20.00
❑ Atlantic SD 16026	Replay	1980	3.00	6.00	12.00
—Also has solo cuts by Stephen Stills					
❑ Atlantic SD 19104	CSN	1977	3.00	6.00	12.00
❑ Atlantic SD 19117	Crosby, Stills & Nash	1977	2.50	5.00	10.00
—Reissue of 8229					
❑ Atlantic SD 19360	Daylight Again	1982	3.00	6.00	12.00
❑ Atlantic 80075	Allies	1983	3.00	6.00	12.00
❑ Atlantic 82107	Live It Up	1990	3.75	7.50	15.00
CROSBY, STILLS, NASH & YOUNG					
45s					
❑ Atlantic 2723	Woodstock/Helpless	1970	—	3.00	6.00
❑ Atlantic 2735	Teach Your Children/Carry On	1970	—	3.00	6.00
❑ Atlantic 2740	Ohio/Find the Cost of Freedom	1970	—	3.00	6.00
❑ Atlantic 2760	Our House/Deja Vu	1970	—	3.00	6.00
❑ Atlantic 88966	Got It Made/This Old House	1989	—	—	3.00
❑ Atlantic 89003	American Dream/Compass	1988	—	—	3.00
Albums					
❑ Atlantic SD 2-902 [(2)]	4 Way Street	1971	5.00	10.00	20.00
❑ Atlantic SD 7200	Deja Vu	1970	3.75	7.50	15.00
—Pasted-on front cover photo must still be intact					
❑ Atlantic SD 18100	So Far	1974	3.00	6.00	12.00
❑ Atlantic SD 19118	Deja Vu	1977	2.50	5.00	10.00
—Reissue of 7200, this time with photo as part of the cover rather than as a paste-on					
❑ Atlantic SD 19119	So Far	1977	2.50	5.00	10.00
—Reissue of 18100					
❑ Atlantic 81888	American Dream	1988	2.50	5.00	10.00
CROSS, CHRISTOPHER					
45s					
❑ Arista 9530	Loving Strangers/Seven Summers	1986	—	—	3.00
—B-side by Cruzados					
❑ Columbia 38-04492	A Chance for Heaven/Talking in My Sleep	1984	—	—	3.00
❑ Reprise 7-27673	Swept Away ("Growing Pains" Aloha Show Theme)/ (B-side unknown)	1989	—	—	3.00
❑ Reprise 7-27795	I Will (Take You Forever)/Just One Look	1988	—	—	3.00
—With Frances Ruffelle					
❑ Warner Bros. 28761	Love Is Love (In Any Language)/Love Found a Home	1986	—	—	3.00
❑ Warner Bros. 28804	Every Turn of the World/Open Your Heart	1986	—	—	3.00
❑ Warner Bros. 28864	Charm the Snake/Open Your Heart	1985	—	—	3.00
❑ Warner Bros. 29658	Think of Laura/Words of Wisdom	1983	—	2.00	4.00
❑ Warner Bros. 29662	No Time for Talk/Words of Wisdom	1983	—	2.00	4.00
❑ Warner Bros. 29843	All Right/Long World	1983	—	2.00	4.00
❑ Warner Bros. 49184	Ride Like the Wind/Minstrel Gigolo	1980	—	2.00	4.00
❑ Warner Bros. 49507	Sailing/Poor Shirley	1980	—	2.00	4.00

Number	Title (A Side/B Side)	Yr	VG	VG+	NM
❑ Warner Bros. 49580	Never Be the Same/The Light Is On	1980	—	2.00	4.00
❑ Warner Bros. 49705	Say You'll Be Mine/Spinning	1981	—	2.00	4.00
❑ Warner Bros. 49787	Arthur's Theme (Best That You Can Do)/Minstrel Gigolo	1981	—	2.00	4.00
Albums					
❑ Reprise 25685	Back of My Mind	1988	2.50	5.00	10.00
❑ Warner Bros. BSK 3383	Christopher Cross	1979	2.00	4.00	8.00
❑ Warner Bros. 23757	Another Page	1983	2.00	4.00	8.00
❑ Warner Bros. 25341	Every Turn of the World	1985	2.00	4.00	8.00

CROW

45s

Number	Title (A Side/B Side)	Yr	VG	VG+	NM
❑ Amaret 106	Busy Day/Time to Make a Turn	1969	—	3.00	6.00
❑ Amaret 112	Evil Woman Don't Play Your Games with Me/Gonna Leave a Mark	1969	2.00	4.00	8.00
❑ Amaret 119	Cottage Cheese/Busy Day	1970	—	3.00	6.00
❑ Amaret 119	Cottage Cheese/Slow Down	1970	—	3.00	6.00
❑ Amaret 125	Don't Try to Lay No Boogie-Woogie on the "King of Rock 'n' Roll"/Satisfied	1970	—	3.00	6.00
❑ Amaret 129	Watching Can Waste Up the Time/Yellow Dawg	1971	—	2.50	5.00
❑ Amaret 133	Something in Your Blood/Yellow Dawg	1971	—	2.50	5.00
❑ Amaret 145	Everything Has Got to Be Free/Mobile Blues	1972	—	2.50	5.00
❑ Amaret 148	If It Feels Good, Do It/Cado Queen	1972	—	2.50	5.00
Albums					
❑ Amaret ST-5002	Crow Music	1969	5.00	10.00	20.00
❑ Amaret ST-5006	Crow By Crow	1970	5.00	10.00	20.00
❑ Amaret ST-5009	Mosaic	1971	5.00	10.00	20.00
❑ Amaret AST-5012	Best of Crow	1972	3.75	7.50	15.00
❑ Amaret ST-5013	David Crow d/b/a Crow	1973	3.75	7.50	15.00

CRYSTALS, THE (1)

Records on the Aladdin, Brent, Cub, DeLuxe, Felsted, Indigo, Luna, Mercury, Metro, Regalia, Rockin', and Specialty are by different groups outside the scope of this book.

45s

Number	Title (A Side/B Side)	Yr	VG	VG+	NM
❑ Gusto 2090	Da Doo Ron Ron/Then He Kissed Me	1979	—	2.00	4.00
—Re-recordings					
❑ Michelle 4113	Ring-a-Ting-a-Ling/Should I Keep On Waiting	1967	2.50	5.00	10.00
❑ Pavillion 03333	Rudolph the Red-Nosed Reindeer/I Saw Mommy Kissing Santa Claus	1982	—	2.50	5.00
—B-side by The Ronettes					
❑ Philles 100	There's No Other (Like My Baby)/Oh Yeah, Maybe Baby	1961	10.00	20.00	40.00
❑ Philles 102	Uptown/What a Nice Way to Turn Seventeen	1962	10.00	20.00	40.00
❑ Philles 105	He Hit Me (And It Felt Like a Kiss)/No One Ever Tells You	1962	25.00	50.00	100.00
❑ Philles 106	He's a Rebel/I Love You Eddie	1962	15.00	30.00	60.00
—Orange label					
❑ Philles 109	He's Sure the Boy I Love/Walkin' Along (La-La-La)	1962	7.50	15.00	30.00
❑ Philles 112	Da Doo Ron Ron (When He Walked Me Home)/Git' It	1963	7.50	15.00	30.00
❑ Philles 115	Then He Kissed Me/Brother Julius	1963	10.00	20.00	40.00
—Light blue label					
❑ Philles 119	Little Boy/Harry (From West Virginia) and Milt	1964	6.25	12.50	25.00
❑ Philles 119X	Little Boy/Harry (From West Virginia) and Milt	1964	5.00	10.00	20.00
❑ Philles 122	All Grown Up/Irving (Jaggered Sixteenths)	1964	6.25	12.50	25.00
—Possible Rolling Stones involvement on instrumental B-side; "Jaggered" refers to Mick					
❑ United Artists 994	I Got a Man/Are You Trying to Get Rid of Me, Baby	1966	3.75	7.50	15.00
Albums					
❑ Philles PHLP-4000 [M]	Twist Uptown	1962	150.00	300.00	600.00
❑ Philles PHLP-4001 [M]	He's a Rebel	1963	150.00	300.00	600.00
❑ Philles PHLP-4003 [M]	The Crystals Sing the Greatest Hits, Vol. 1	1963	150.00	300.00	600.00

CUFF LINKS, THE (1)

Records on the Dooto/Dootone label are by a different group outside the scope of this book.

45s

Number	Title (A Side/B Side)	Yr	VG	VG+	NM
❑ Atco 6867	Sandi/The Oke-Fen-Okee Electric Harmonica Band	1972	—	2.50	5.00
❑ Decca 32533	Tracy/Where Do You Go	1969	—	3.00	6.00
❑ Decca 32592	When Julie Comes Around/Sally Ann	1969	—	2.50	5.00
❑ Decca 32639	Run, Sally, Run/I Remember	1970	—	2.50	5.00
❑ Decca 32687	Lay a Little Love on Me/Robin's World	1970	—	2.50	5.00
❑ Decca 32732	Thank You Pretty Baby/Kiss	1970	—	2.50	5.00
❑ Decca 32791	All Because of You/Wake Up Judy	1971	—	2.50	5.00
Albums					
❑ Decca DL 75160	Tracy	1969	5.00	10.00	20.00
❑ Decca DL 75235	The Cuff Links	1970	5.00	10.00	20.00

CUMMINGS, BURTON

Also see THE GUESS WHO.

45s

Number	Title (A Side/B Side)	Yr	VG	VG+	NM
❑ Alfa 7008	You Saved My Soul/Real Good	1981	—	2.00	4.00
❑ Alfa 7014	Mother, Keep Your Daughters In/Someone to Lean On	1982	—	2.50	5.00
❑ Portrait 17-8100	Stand Tall/Takes a Fool to Love a Fool	1981	—	2.00	4.00
—Reissue					
❑ Portrait 6-70001	Stand Tall/Burch Magic	1976	—	2.50	5.00
❑ Portrait 6-70002	I'm Scared/Sugartime Flashback Joys	1977	—	2.50	5.00
❑ Portrait 6-70003	Never Had a Lady Before/Timeless Love	1977	—	2.50	5.00
❑ Portrait 6-70007	My Own Way to Rock/A Song for Him	1977	—	2.50	5.00
❑ Portrait 6-70011	Your Back Yard/Is It Really Right	1978	—	2.50	5.00
❑ Portrait 6-70016	Break It To Them Gently/Roll with the Punches	1978	—	2.50	5.00
❑ Portrait 6-70024	Takes a Fool to Love a Fool/I Will Play a Rhapsody	1978	—	2.50	5.00

Number	Title (A Side/B Side)	Yr	VG	VG+	NM
Albums					
❑ Alfa AAB-11007	Sweet Sweet	1981	2.50	5.00	10.00
❑ Portrait PR 34261	Burton Cummings	1976	2.50	5.00	10.00
❑ Portrait PR 34698	My Own Way to Rock	1977	2.50	5.00	10.00
❑ Portrait JR 35481	Dream of a Child	1978	2.50	5.00	10.00

CYMBAL, JOHNNY

Number	Title (A Side/B Side)	Yr	VG	VG+	NM
45s					
❑ Amaret 110	Big River/Girl from Willow County	1969	2.00	4.00	8.00
❑ Amaret 111	Ode to Bubblegum/Save All Your Lovin' (Hold It for Me)	1969	2.00	4.00	8.00
❑ Bang 558	Cinnamon/This Is My Story	1968	2.00	4.00	8.00
❑ Bang 566	Back Door Man/Tell Your Soul	1969	—	3.00	6.00
❑ Bang 571	Inside Out-Outside In/Sell Your Soul	1969	—	3.00	6.00
❑ Columbia 43842	Good Morning Blues/Jessica	1966	2.00	4.00	8.00
❑ DCP 1135	Go, VW, Go/Sorrow and Pain	1965	7.50	15.00	30.00
❑ DCP 1146	My Last Day/Summertime's Here at Last	1965	3.75	7.50	15.00
❑ Kapp 503	Mr. Bass Man/Sacred Lovers' Vow	1963	5.00	10.00	20.00
❑ Kapp 524	Teenage Heaven/Cinderella Baby	1963	3.75	7.50	15.00
❑ Kapp 539	(Surfin' at) Tia Juana/Dum Dum Dee Dum	1963	3.75	7.50	15.00
❑ Kapp 556	Marshmallow/Hurdy Gurdy Man	1963	3.75	7.50	15.00
❑ Kapp 576	There Goes a Bad Girl/Refreshment Time	1964	3.75	7.50	15.00
❑ Kapp 594	Robinson Crusoe on Mars/Mitsu	1964	3.75	7.50	15.00
❑ Kapp 614	Connie/Little Miss Lonely	1964	3.75	7.50	15.00
❑ Kapp 634	Cheat, Cheat/16 Shades of Blue	1964	3.75	7.50	15.00
❑ Kedlen 2001	Bachelor Man/Growing Up with You	1962	5.00	10.00	20.00
❑ MGM 12935	It'll Be Me/Always, Always	1960	5.00	10.00	20.00
❑ MGM 12978	The Water Was Red/The Bunny	1961	5.00	10.00	20.00
❑ Musicor 1261	It Looks Like Love/May I Get to Know You	1967	3.00	6.00	12.00
❑ Musicor 1272	Breaking Your Balloon/The Marriage of Charlotte Brown	1967	3.00	6.00	12.00
❑ Vee Jay 495	Bachelor Man/Growing Up with You	1963	3.75	7.50	15.00
Albums					
❑ Kapp KL-1324 [M]	Mr. Bass Man	1963	12.50	25.00	50.00
❑ Kapp KS-3324 [S]	Mr. Bass Man	1963	17.50	35.00	70.00

CYRKLE, THE

Number	Title (A Side/B Side)	Yr	VG	VG+	NM
45s					
❑ Columbia 43589	Red Rubber Ball/How Can I Leave Her	1966	3.00	6.00	12.00
❑ Columbia 43729	Turn-Down Day/Big, Little Woman	1966	2.50	5.00	10.00
❑ Columbia 43871	Please Don't Ever Leave Me/Money to Burn	1966	2.00	4.00	8.00
❑ Columbia 43965	I Wish You Could Be Here/The Visit (She Was Here)	1967	2.00	4.00	8.00
❑ Columbia 44108	We Had a Good Thing Goin'/Two Rooms	1967	2.00	4.00	8.00
❑ Columbia 44224	Penny Arcade/The Words	1967	2.00	4.00	8.00
❑ Columbia 44366	Turn of the Century/Don't Cry, No Fears, No Tears Comin'	1967	2.00	4.00	8.00
❑ Columbia 44426	Friends/Reading Her Papers	1968	2.00	4.00	8.00
❑ Columbia 44491	Red Chair Fade Away/Where Are You Going	1968	2.00	4.00	8.00
Albums					
❑ Columbia CL 2544 [M]	Red Rubber Ball	1966	5.00	10.00	20.00
❑ Columbia CL 2632 [M]	Neon	1967	3.75	7.50	15.00
❑ Columbia CS 9344 [S]	Red Rubber Ball	1966	7.50	15.00	30.00
❑ Columbia CS 9432 [S]	Neon	1967	5.00	10.00	20.00

D

DALE AND GRACE

Number	Title (A Side/B Side)	Yr	VG	VG+	NM
45s					
❑ Guyden 6002	What's Happening to Me/Darling It's Wonderful	1972	—	2.50	5.00
❑ Hanna-Barbera 472	Let Them Talk/I'd Rather Be Free	1966	2.00	4.00	8.00
❑ Michelle 921	I'm Leaving It Up to You/That's What I Like	1963	6.25	12.50	25.00
❑ Michelle 923	Stop and Think It Over/Bad Luck	1963	3.75	7.50	15.00
❑ Michelle 928	The Loneliest Night/I'm Not Free	1964	3.75	7.50	15.00
❑ Michelle 930	Darling It's Wonderful/What's Happening to Me	1964	3.75	7.50	15.00
❑ Michelle 936	Cool Water/Rules of Love	1964	3.75	7.50	15.00
❑ Montel 921	I'm Leaving It Up to You/That's What I Like About You	1963	3.00	6.00	12.00
❑ Montel 922	Stop and Think It Over/Bad Luck	1963	3.00	6.00	12.00
❑ Montel 928	The Loneliest Night/I'm Not Free	1964	3.00	6.00	12.00
❑ Montel 930	Darling It's Wonderful/What's Happening to Me	1964	3.00	6.00	12.00
❑ Montel 936	Cool Water/Rules of Love	1964	3.00	6.00	12.00

Number	Title (A Side/B Side)	Yr	VG	VG+	NM
❑ Montel 958	Make the World Go Away/Stranger	1965	3.00	6.00	12.00
❑ Montel 989	It Keeps Right On a-Hurtin'/So Fine	1967	3.00	6.00	12.00
❑ Montel/Michelle 942	Something Special/What Am I Living For	1964	3.00	6.00	12.00
Albums					
❑ Michelle 100 [M]	I'm Leaving It Up to You	1964	37.50	75.00	150.00
❑ Montel 100 [M]	I'm Leaving It Up to You	1964	37.50	75.00	150.00

DALTREY, ROGER

45s

Number	Title (A Side/B Side)	Yr	VG	VG+	NM
❑ A&M 1779	Love's Dream/Orpheus Song	1975	—	2.50	5.00
—With Rick Wakeman					
❑ Atlantic 89419	Under a Raging Moon/The Pride You Hide	1986	—	—	3.00
❑ Atlantic 89457	Quicksilver Lightning/Love Me Like You Do	1986	—	—	3.00
❑ Atlantic 89471	Let Me Down Easy/Fallen Angel	1985	—	—	3.00
❑ Atlantic 89491	After the Fire/Don't Satisfy Me	1985	—	—	3.00
❑ Atlantic 89667	Parting Would Be Painless/Is There Anyone Out There?	1984	—	—	3.00
❑ Atlantic 89704	Walking in My Sleep/Somebody Told Me	1984	—	—	3.00
❑ MCA 40453	Come and Get Your Love/Heart's Right	1975	—	2.50	5.00
❑ MCA 40512	Oceans Away/Feeling	1976	—	2.50	5.00
❑ MCA 40761	One of the Boys/Doing It All Again	1977	—	2.50	5.00
❑ MCA 40765	Satin and Lace/Say It Ain't So, Joe	1977	—	2.00	4.00
❑ MCA 40800	Avenging Annie/The Prisoner	1977	—	2.00	4.00
❑ MCA 40862	Leon/The Prisoner	1978	—	2.00	4.00
❑ MCA 52051	Martyrs and Madmen/Avenging Annie	1982	—	2.00	4.00
❑ Ode 66040	I'm Free/Underture	1973	—	2.50	5.00
❑ Polydor 2105	Free Me/McVicar	1980	—	2.00	4.00
❑ Polydor 2121	Without Your Love/Escape (Part 1)	1980	—	2.00	4.00
❑ Polydor 2153	Waiting for a Friend/Bitter and Twisted	1981	—	2.00	4.00
❑ Polydor 15098	See Me, Feel Me-Listening to You/Overture from Tommy	1975	—	2.50	5.00
—B-side by Pete Townshend					
❑ Track 40053	Giving It All Away/Way of the World	1973	—	3.00	6.00
—B-side by Bryan Daly & the London Festival Orchestra					
❑ Track 40084	Thinking/There Is Love	1973	2.00	4.00	8.00
Albums					
❑ Atlantic 80128	Parting Should Be Painless	1984	2.50	5.00	10.00
❑ Atlantic 81269	Under a Raging Moon	1985	2.50	5.00	10.00
❑ Atlantic 81759	Can't Wait to See the Movie	1987	2.50	5.00	10.00
❑ MCA 2147	Ride a Rock Horse	1975	3.00	6.00	12.00
❑ MCA 2271	One of the Boys	1977	3.00	6.00	12.00
❑ MCA 2349	Daltrey	1977	2.50	5.00	10.00
—Reissue of Track 328					
❑ MCA 5301	Best Bits	1982	2.50	5.00	10.00
❑ MCA 37030	Ride a Rock Horse	1980	2.00	4.00	8.00
—Budget-line reissue					
❑ MCA 37031	One of the Boys	1980	2.00	4.00	8.00
—Budget-line reissue					
❑ MCA 37032	Daltrey	1980	2.00	4.00	8.00
—Budget-line reissue					
❑ Polydor PD-1-6284	McVicar	1980	2.50	5.00	10.00
❑ Track 328	Daltrey	1973	3.00	6.00	12.00

DANLEERS, THE

45s

Number	Title (A Side/B Side)	Yr	VG	VG+	NM
❑ Amp 3 2115	One Summer Night/Wheelin' and Dealin'	1958	10.00	20.00	40.00
—Corrected group name on label					
❑ Amp 3 2115	One Summer Night/Wheelin' and Dealin'	1958	50.00	100.00	200.00
—By "Dandleers"					
❑ Epic 9367	I Live Half a Block from an Angel/If You Don't Care	1960	7.50	15.00	30.00
❑ Epic 9421	I'll Always Be in Love with You/Little Lover	1960	7.50	15.00	30.00
❑ Everest 19412	Foolish/I'm Looking Around	1961	7.50	15.00	30.00
❑ LeMans 004	The Truth Hurts/Baby You've Got It	1963	2.50	5.00	10.00
❑ LeMans 008	I'm Sorry/This Thing Called Love	1963	2.50	5.00	10.00
❑ Mercury 71322	One Summer Night/Wheelin' and a-Dealin'	1958	5.00	10.00	20.00
❑ Mercury 71356	I Really Love You/My Flaming Heart	1958	5.00	10.00	20.00
❑ Mercury 71401	A Picture of You/Prelude to Love	1959	5.00	10.00	20.00
❑ Mercury 71441	I Can't Sleep/Your Love	1959	5.00	10.00	20.00
❑ Smash 1872	Were You There/If	1964	3.00	6.00	12.00
❑ Smash 1895	Where Is Love/The Angels Sent You	1964	3.00	6.00	12.00

DANNY AND THE JUNIORS

45s

Number	Title (A Side/B Side)	Yr	VG	VG+	NM
❑ ABC-Paramount 9871	At the Hop/Sometimes (When I'm All Alone)	1957	7.50	15.00	30.00
❑ ABC-Paramount 9888	Rock and Roll Is Here to Stay/School Boy Romance	1958	7.50	15.00	30.00
❑ ABC-Paramount 9926	Dottie/In the Meantime	1958	6.25	12.50	25.00
❑ ABC-Paramount 9953	A Thief/Crazy Cave	1958	6.25	12.50	25.00
❑ ABC-Paramount 9978	Sassy Fran/I Feel So Lonely	1958	12.50	25.00	50.00
❑ ABC-Paramount 10004	Do You Love Me/Somehow I Can't Forget	1959	6.25	12.50	25.00
❑ ABC-Paramount 10052	Playing Hard to Get/Of Love	1959	6.25	12.50	25.00
❑ Crunch 018001	At the Hop/Let the Good Times Roll	1973	—	2.50	5.00
❑ Guyden 2076	Oo-La-La-Limbo/Now and Then	1962	5.00	10.00	20.00
❑ Luv 252	Rock and Roll Is Here to Stay/Sometimes (When I'm All Alone)	1968	2.50	5.00	10.00
❑ MCA D-2411	At the Hop/Rock and Roll Is Here to Stay	1980	—	2.00	4.00
—Reissue					
❑ Mercury 72240	Sad Girl/Let's Go Ski-ing	1964	5.00	10.00	20.00
❑ Singular 711	At the Hop/Sometimes	1957	250.00	500.00	1000.
—Blue label, machine-stamped in dead wax, no mention of Artie Singer on label					

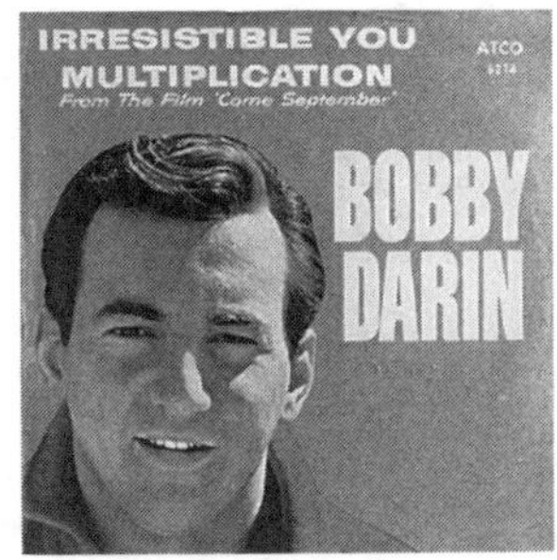

Number	Title (A Side/B Side)	Yr	VG	VG+	NM
❑ Singular 711	At the Hop/Sometimes	1957	250.00	500.00	1000.
—Blue label, machine-stamped in dead wax, with "Orchestra Directed by Artie Singer" credit. Both versions have a "count-in" before the song starts. Singular records on black labels or without the count-in are probably reproductions.					
❑ Swan 4060	Twistin' U.S.A./A Thousand Miles Away	1960	5.00	10.00	20.00
❑ Swan 4064	Candy Cane. Sugary Plum/Oh Holy Night	1960	6.25	12.50	25.00
❑ Swan 4068	Daydreamer/Pony Express	1961	5.00	10.00	20.00
❑ Swan 4072	Cha Cha Go Go (Chicago Cha-Cha)/Mister Whisper	1961	5.00	10.00	20.00
❑ Swan 4082	Back to the Hop/The Charleston Fish	1961	5.00	10.00	20.00
❑ Swan 4084	Just Because/You Hair's Too Long	1961	—	—	—
—Unreleased?					
❑ Swan 4092	Twistin' All Night Long/Some Kind of Nut	1962	5.00	10.00	20.00
❑ Swan 4100	(Do the) Mashed Potatoes/Doin' the Continental Walk	1962	5.00	10.00	20.00
❑ Swan 4113	We Got Soul/Funny	1962	5.00	10.00	20.00

Albums

Number	Title	Yr	VG	VG+	NM
❑ MCA 1555	Rockin' with Danny and the Juniors	1987	2.50	5.00	10.00

DARIN, BOBBY

45s

Number	Title (A Side/B Side)	Yr	VG	VG+	NM
❑ Atco 6092	Million Dollar Baby/Talk to Me	1957	7.50	15.00	30.00
❑ Atco 6103	Don't Call My Name/Pretty Betty	1957	7.50	15.00	30.00
❑ Atco 6109	Just in Case You Change Your Mind/So Mean	1958	7.50	15.00	30.00
❑ Atco 6117	Splish Splash/Judy, Don't Be Moody	1958	5.00	10.00	20.00
❑ Atco 6121	Early in the Morning/Now We're One	1958	5.00	10.00	20.00
❑ Atco 6121	Early in the Morning/Now We're One	1958	10.00	20.00	40.00
—As "The Rinky Dinks"					
❑ Atco 6127	Queen of the Hop/Lost Love	1958	5.00	10.00	20.00
❑ Atco 6128	Mighty Mighty Man/You're Gone	1958	5.00	10.00	20.00
❑ Atco 6128	Mighty Mighty Man/You're Gone	1958	10.00	20.00	40.00
—As "The Rinky Dinks"					
❑ Atco 6133 [M]	Plain Jane/While I'm Gone	1959	5.00	10.00	20.00
❑ Atco SD-45-6133 [S]	Plain Jane/While I'm Gone	1959	10.00	20.00	40.00
❑ Atco 6140	Dream Lover/Bullmoose	1959	5.00	10.00	20.00
❑ Atco 6147	Mack the Knife/Was There a Call for Me	1959	5.00	10.00	20.00
❑ Atco 6158	Beyond the Sea/That's the Way Love Is	1960	5.00	10.00	20.00
❑ Atco 6161	Clementine/Tall Story	1960	5.00	10.00	20.00
❑ Atco 6167	Won't You Come Home Bill Bailey/I'll Be There	1960	5.00	10.00	20.00
❑ Atco 6173	Beachcomber/Autumn Blues	1960	5.00	10.00	20.00
❑ Atco 6179	Artificial Flowers/Somebody to Love	1960	5.00	10.00	20.00
❑ Atco 6183	Christmas Auld Lang Syne/Child of God	1960	6.25	12.50	25.00
❑ Atco 6188	Lazy River/Oo-Ee Train	1961	3.00	6.00	12.00
❑ Atco 6196	Nature Boy/Look for My True Love	1961	3.00	6.00	12.00
❑ Atco 6200	Come September/Walk Back to Me	1961	3.75	7.50	15.00
❑ Atco 6206	You Must Have Been a Beautiful Baby/Sorrow Tomorrow	1961	3.00	6.00	12.00
❑ Atco 6211	Ave Maria/O Come All Ye Faithful	1961	3.00	6.00	12.00
❑ Atco 6214	Irresistible You/Multiplication	1961	3.00	6.00	12.00
❑ Atco 6221	What'd I Say (Part 1)/What'd I Say (Part 2)	1962	3.00	6.00	12.00
❑ Atco 6229	Things/Jalier Bring Me Water	1962	3.00	6.00	12.00
❑ Atco 6236	Baby Face/You Know How	1962	3.00	6.00	12.00
❑ Atco 6244	I Found a New Baby/Keep a-Walkin'	1962	3.00	6.00	12.00
❑ Atco 6297	Milord/Golden Earrings	1964	2.50	5.00	10.00
❑ Atco 6316	Swing Low Sweet Chariot/Similau	1964	2.50	5.00	10.00
❑ Atco 6334	Minnie the Moocher/Hard Hearted Hannah	1965	2.50	5.00	10.00
❑ Atlantic 2305	Funny What Love Can Do/We Didn't Ask to Be Brought Here	1965	2.00	4.00	8.00
❑ Atlantic 2317	Silver Dollar/The Breaking Point	1966	2.00	4.00	8.00
❑ Atlantic 2329	Mame/Walking in the Shadow of Love	1966	2.00	4.00	8.00
❑ Atlantic 2341	Who's Afraid of Virginia Woolf?/Merci, Cheri	1966	2.00	4.00	8.00
❑ Atlantic 2350	If I Were a Carpenter/Rainin'	1966	2.50	5.00	10.00
❑ Atlantic 2367	The Girl That Stood Beside Me/Reason to Believe	1966	2.00	4.00	8.00
❑ Atlantic 2376	Lovin' You/Amy	1967	2.00	4.00	8.00
❑ Atlantic 2395	The Lady Came from Baltimore/I Am	1967	2.00	4.00	8.00
❑ Atlantic 2420	Darlin' Be Home Soon/Hello, Sunshine	1967	2.00	4.00	8.00
❑ Atlantic 2433	Talk to the Animals/After Today	1967	2.00	4.00	8.00
❑ Atlantic 2433	Talk to the Animals/She Knows	1967	2.00	4.00	8.00
❑ Atlantic 89166	Beyond the Sea/Mack the Knife	1987	—	—	3.00
❑ Brunswick 55073	Early in the Morning/Now We're One	1958	20.00	40.00	80.00
—As "The Ding Dongs"; also see Atco 6121					
❑ Capitol 4837	If a Man Answers/True, True Love	1962	2.50	5.00	10.00

Number	Title (A Side/B Side)	Yr	VG	VG+	NM
❑ Capitol 4897	You're the Reason I'm Living/Now You're Gone	1962	2.50	5.00	10.00
❑ Capitol 4970	18 Yellow Roses/Not for Me	1963	2.50	5.00	10.00
❑ Capitol 5019	Treat My Baby Good/Down So Long	1963	2.50	5.00	10.00
❑ Capitol 5079	Be Mad Little Girl/Since You've Been Gone	1963	2.50	5.00	10.00
❑ Capitol 5126	I Wonder Who's Kissing Her Now/As Long As I'm Singing	1964	2.50	5.00	10.00
❑ Capitol 5257	The Things in This House/Wait by the Water	1964	2.50	5.00	10.00
❑ Capitol 5359	Hello, Dolly!/Golden Earrings	1965	2.50	5.00	10.00
❑ Capitol 5399	A World Without You/Venice Blue	1965	2.50	5.00	10.00
❑ Capitol 5443	When I Get Home/Lonely Road	1965	2.50	5.00	10.00
❑ Capitol 5481	Gyp the Cat/That Funny Feeling	1965	2.50	5.00	10.00
❑ Decca 29883	Rock Island Line/Timber	1956	10.00	20.00	40.00
❑ Decca 29922	Silly Willy/Blue Eyed Mermaid	1956	12.50	25.00	50.00
❑ Decca 30031	The Greatest Builder (Of Them All)/Hear Them Bells	1956	10.00	20.00	40.00
❑ Decca 30225	Dealer in Dreams/Help Me	1957	10.00	20.00	40.00
❑ Decca 30737	Silly Willy/Dealer in Dreams	1958	7.50	15.00	30.00
❑ Direction 350	Long Line Rider/Change	1968	2.00	4.00	8.00
❑ Direction 351	Song for a Dollar/Mr. and Mrs. Hohner	1969	2.00	4.00	8.00
❑ Direction 352	Distractions (Part 1)/Jive	1969	2.00	4.00	8.00
❑ Direction 4000	Sugar Man/(9 to 5) Jive's Alive	1970	2.00	4.00	8.00
❑ Direction 4001	Baby May/Sweet Reason	1970	2.00	4.00	8.00
❑ Direction 4002	Maybe We Can Get It Together/Rx Pyro (Prescription: Fire)	1970	2.00	4.00	8.00
❑ Motown 1183	Melodie/Someday We'll Be Together	1971	—	3.00	6.00
❑ Motown 1193	Simple Song of Freedom/I'll Be Your Baby Tonight	1971	—	3.00	6.00
❑ Motown 1203	Sail Away/Something in Her Love	1972	—	3.00	6.00
❑ Motown 1212	Average People/Something in Her Love	1972	—	3.00	6.00
❑ Motown 1217	Happy/Something in Her Love	1973	—	3.00	6.00
Albums					
❑ Atco 33-102 [M]	Bobby Darin	1958	25.00	50.00	100.00
—Yellow "harp" label					
❑ Atco 33-104 [M]	That's All	1959	10.00	20.00	40.00
—Yellow "harp" label					
❑ Atco SD 33-104 [S]	That's All	1959	25.00	50.00	100.00
—Yellow "harp" label					
❑ Atco 33-115 [M]	This Is Darin	1960	10.00	20.00	40.00
—Yellow "harp" label					
❑ Atco SD 33-115 [S]	This Is Darin	1960	20.00	40.00	80.00
—Yellow "harp" label					
❑ Atco 33-122 [M]	Darin at the Copa	1960	10.00	20.00	40.00
—Yellow "harp" label					
❑ Atco SD 33-122 [S]	Darin at the Copa	1960	20.00	40.00	80.00
—Yellow "harp" label					
❑ Atco 33-124 [M]	It's You or No One	1960	10.00	20.00	40.00
—Yellow "harp" label					
❑ Atco SD 33-124 [S]	It's You or No One	1960	20.00	40.00	80.00
—Yellow "harp" label					
❑ Atco 33-125 [M]	The 25th Day of December	1960	12.50	25.00	50.00
—Yellow "harp" label					
❑ Atco SD 33-125 [S]	The 25th Day of December	1960	15.00	30.00	60.00
—Yellow "harp" label					
❑ Atco 33-126 [M]	Two of a Kind	1961	10.00	20.00	40.00
—Yellow "harp" label					
❑ Atco SD 33-126 [S]	Two of a Kind	1961	12.50	25.00	50.00
—Yellow "harp" label					
❑ Atco 33-131 [M]	The Bobby Darin Story	1961	10.00	20.00	40.00
—Yellow "harp" label; white cover					
❑ Atco SD 33-131 [S]	The Bobby Darin Story	1961	12.50	25.00	50.00
—Yellow "harp" label; white cover					
❑ Atco 33-134 [M]	Love Swings	1961	10.00	20.00	40.00
—Yellow "harp" label					
❑ Atco SD 33-134 [S]	Love Swings	1961	12.50	25.00	50.00
—Yellow "harp" label					
❑ Atco 33-138 [M]	Twist with Bobby Darin	1961	10.00	20.00	40.00
—Yellow "harp" label					
❑ Atco SD 33-138 [S]	Twist with Bobby Darin	1961	12.50	25.00	50.00
—Yellow "harp" label					
❑ Atco 33-140 [M]	Bobby Darin Sings Ray Charles	1962	6.25	12.50	25.00
❑ Atco SD 33-140 [S]	Bobby Darin Sings Ray Charles	1962	7.50	15.00	30.00
❑ Atco 33-146 [M]	Things & Other Things	1962	6.25	12.50	25.00
❑ Atco SD 33-146 [S]	Things & Other Things	1962	7.50	15.00	30.00
❑ Atco 33-167 [M]	Winners	1964	6.25	12.50	25.00
❑ Atco SD 33-167 [S]	Winners	1964	7.50	15.00	30.00
❑ Atco SP 1001 [M]	For Teenagers Only	1960	37.50	75.00	150.00
—Gatefold with fold-open poster and paper insert					
❑ Atco 90484	Two of a Kind	1986	2.50	5.00	10.00
❑ Atlantic 8121 [M]	The Shadow of Your Smile	1966	3.75	7.50	15.00
❑ Atlantic SD 8121 [S]	The Shadow of Your Smile	1966	5.00	10.00	20.00
❑ Atlantic 8126 [M]	In a Broadway Bag	1966	3.75	7.50	15.00
❑ Atlantic SD 8126 [S]	In a Broadway Bag	1966	5.00	10.00	20.00
❑ Atlantic 8135 [M]	If I Were a Carpenter	1967	3.75	7.50	15.00
❑ Atlantic SD 8135 [S]	If I Were a Carpenter	1967	12.50	25.00	50.00
—Inexplicably rare in stereo					
❑ Atlantic 8142 [M]	Inside Out	1967	3.75	7.50	15.00
❑ Atlantic SD 8142 [S]	Inside Out	1967	7.50	15.00	30.00
❑ Atlantic 8154 [M]	Bobby Darin Sings Doctor Dolittle	1967	3.75	7.50	15.00
❑ Atlantic SD 8154 [S]	Bobby Darin Sings Doctor Dolittle	1967	3.75	7.50	15.00
❑ Bainbridge 6220	Bobby Darin at the Copa	1981	2.50	5.00	10.00

Number	Title (A Side/B Side)	Yr	VG	VG+	NM
❑ Capitol SW 1791 [S]	Oh! Look at Me Now	1962	6.25	12.50	25.00
❑ Capitol W 1791 [M]	Oh! Look at Me Now	1962	5.00	10.00	20.00
❑ Capitol ST 1826 [S]	Earthy	1963	5.00	10.00	20.00
❑ Capitol T 1826 [M]	Earthy	1963	3.75	7.50	15.00
❑ Capitol ST 1866 [S]	You're the Reason I'm Living	1963	5.00	10.00	20.00
❑ Capitol T 1866 [M]	You're the Reason I'm Living	1963	3.75	7.50	15.00
❑ Capitol ST 1942 [S]	18 Yellow Roses	1963	5.00	10.00	20.00
❑ Capitol T 1942 [M]	18 Yellow Roses	1963	3.75	7.50	15.00
❑ Capitol ST 2007 [S]	Golden Folk Hits	1963	5.00	10.00	20.00
❑ Capitol T 2007 [M]	Golden Folk Hits	1963	3.75	7.50	15.00
❑ Capitol ST 2194 [S]	From Hello Dolly to Goodbye Charlie	1964	5.00	10.00	20.00
❑ Capitol T 2194 [M]	From Hello Dolly to Goodbye Charlie	1964	3.75	7.50	15.00
❑ Capitol ST 2322 [S]	Venice Blue	1965	5.00	10.00	20.00
❑ Capitol T 2322 [M]	Venice Blue	1965	3.75	7.50	15.00
❑ Capitol ST 2571 [S]	The Best of Bobby Darin	1966	3.75	7.50	15.00
❑ Capitol T 2571 [M]	The Best of Bobby Darin	1966	3.75	7.50	15.00
❑ Clarion 603 [M]	Clementine	1966	5.00	10.00	20.00
❑ Clarion SD 603 [S]	Clementine	1966	6.25	12.50	25.00
❑ Direction 1936	Born Walden Robert Cassotto	1968	6.25	12.50	25.00
❑ Direction 1937	Commitment	1969	6.25	12.50	25.00
❑ Motown M5-185V1	Darin 1936-1973	1981	3.00	6.00	12.00
—Reissue					
❑ Motown MS-739	Finally	1972	125.00	250.00	500.00
—Unreleased; value is for RCA test pressing					
❑ Motown M 753L	Bobby Darin	1972	5.00	10.00	20.00
❑ Motown M6-813L	Darin 1936-1973	1974	3.75	7.50	15.00

DARREN, JAMES

45s

Number	Title (A Side/B Side)	Yr	VG	VG+	NM
❑ Buddah 177	That's My World/Wheeling, West Virginia	1970	—	2.50	5.00
❑ Colpix 102	There's No Such Thing/Mighty Pretty Territory	1959	3.75	7.50	15.00
❑ Colpix 113	Gidget/You	1959	3.75	7.50	15.00
❑ Colpix 119 [M]	Angel Face/I Don't Wanna Lose Ya	1959	3.75	7.50	15.00
❑ Colpix SCP-119 [S]	Angel Face/I Don't Wanna Lose Ya	1959	10.00	20.00	40.00
❑ Colpix 128	I Ain't Sharin' Sharon/Love Among the Young	1959	3.75	7.50	15.00
❑ Colpix 130	Teenage Tears/Let There Be Love	1959	3.75	7.50	15.00
❑ Colpix 138	You Are My Dream/Your Smile	1960	3.75	7.50	15.00
❑ Colpix 142	Because They're Young/Tears in My Eyes	1960	3.75	7.50	15.00
❑ Colpix 145	P.S. I Love You/Traveling Down a Lonesome Road	1960	3.75	7.50	15.00
❑ Colpix 155	How Sweet You Are/All the Young Men	1960	3.75	7.50	15.00
❑ Colpix 168	Man About Town/Come On My Love	1960	3.75	7.50	15.00
❑ Colpix 181	Walking My Baby Back Home/Goodbye My Lady	1960	3.75	7.50	15.00
—Colpix 102-181 by "Jimmy Darren"					
❑ Colpix 185	Fool's Paradise/Gotta Have Love	1961	3.75	7.50	15.00
❑ Colpix 189	Gidget Goes Hawaiian/Wild About the Girl	1961	3.75	7.50	15.00
❑ Colpix 194	Hand in Hand/You Are My Dream	1961	3.75	7.50	15.00
❑ Colpix 609	Goodbye Cruel World/Valerie	1961	3.75	7.50	15.00
❑ Colpix 622	Her Royal Majesty/If I Could Only Tell You	1962	3.00	6.00	12.00
❑ Colpix 630	Conscience/Dream Big	1962	3.00	6.00	12.00
❑ Colpix 644	Mary's Little Lamb/The Life of the Party	1962	3.00	6.00	12.00
❑ Colpix 655	Hail to the Conquering Hero/Too Young to Go Steady	1962	3.00	6.00	12.00
❑ Colpix 664	Hear What I Want to Hear/I'll Be Loving You	1962	3.00	6.00	12.00
❑ Colpix 672	Pin a Medal on Joey/Diamond Head	1963	3.00	6.00	12.00
❑ Colpix 685	They Should Have Given You the Oscar/Blame It on My Youth	1963	3.00	6.00	12.00
❑ Colpix 696	Gegetta/Grande Luna, Italiana	1963	3.00	6.00	12.00
❑ Colpix 708	Under the Yum Yum Tree/Backstage	1963	3.00	6.00	12.00
❑ Colpix 758	Punch and Judy/Just Think of Tonight	1964	5.00	10.00	20.00
❑ Colpix 765	A Married Man/Baby, Talk to Me	1964	2.50	5.00	10.00
❑ Kirshner 63-1012	I Think Somebody Loves Me/Ain't Been Home in a Long Time	1970	—	2.50	5.00
❑ Kirshner 63-5013	Bring Me Down Slow/More and More	1971	—	2.50	5.00
❑ Kirshner 63-5015	Mammy Blue/As Long As You Love Me	1971	—	2.50	5.00
❑ Kirshner 63-5025	Brian's Song/Thnak Heaven for Little Girls	1973	—	2.50	5.00
❑ MGM 14558	Let the Heartaches Begin/Sad Song	1973	—	2.00	4.00
❑ MGM 14667	Sad-Eyed Romany Woman/Stay	1973	—	2.00	4.00
❑ Private Stock 45,050	Love on the Screen/Losing You	1975	—	2.00	4.00
❑ Private Stock 45,064	One Has My Name, The Other Has My Heart/ Sleepin' in a Bed of Lies	1975	—	2.00	4.00

Number	Title (A Side/B Side)	Yr	VG	VG+	NM
❑ Private Stock 45,136	You Take My Heart Away/You Take My Heart Away (Disco)	1977	—	2.00	4.00
❑ RCA PB-11316	Let Me Take You in My Arms Again/California	1978	—	2.00	4.00
❑ RCA PB-11419	Next Time/Something Like Nothing Before	1978	—	2.00	4.00
❑ Warner Bros. 5648	Because You're Mine/Millions of Roses	1965	2.00	4.00	8.00
❑ Warner Bros. 5689	I Want to Be Lonely/Tom Hawk	1966	2.00	4.00	8.00
❑ Warner Bros. 5812	Where Did We Go Wrong/Counting the Cracks	1966	2.00	4.00	8.00
❑ Warner Bros. 5838	Crazy Me/They Don't Know	1966	2.00	4.00	8.00
❑ Warner Bros. 5856	Love Is Where You Find It/(Let's Worry About) Tomorrow Tomorrow	1966	2.00	4.00	8.00
❑ Warner Bros. 5874	All/Misty Morning Eyes	1966	2.00	4.00	8.00
❑ Warner Bros. 7013	I Miss You So/Since I Don't Have You	1967	2.00	4.00	8.00
❑ Warner Bros. 7053	Didn't We/Counting the Cracks	1967	2.00	4.00	8.00
❑ Warner Bros. 7071	The House Song/They Don't Know	1967	2.00	4.00	8.00
❑ Warner Bros. 7152	Cherie/Wait Until Dark	1967	2.00	4.00	8.00
❑ Warner Bros. 7206	A Little Bit of Heaven/Each and Every Part of Me	1968	2.00	4.00	8.00
Albums					
❑ Colpix CP-406 [M]	James Darren (Album No. 1)	1960	10.00	20.00	40.00
—Black vinyl					
❑ Colpix CP-418 [M]	Gidget Goes Hawaiian (James Darren Sings the Movies)	1961	7.50	15.00	30.00
❑ Colpix SCP-418 [S]	Gidget Goes Hawaiian (James Darren Sings the Movies)	1961	10.00	20.00	40.00
❑ Colpix CP-424 [M]	James Darren Sings for All Sizes	1962	7.50	15.00	30.00
❑ Colpix SCP-424 [S]	James Darren Sings for All Sizes	1962	10.00	20.00	40.00
❑ Colpix CP-428 [M]	Love Among the Young	1962	7.50	15.00	30.00
❑ Colpix SCP-428 [S]	Love Among the Young	1962	10.00	20.00	40.00
❑ Kirshner KES-115	Mammy Blue	1971	3.75	7.50	15.00
❑ Kirshner KES-116	Love Songs from the Movies	1972	3.75	7.50	15.00
❑ Warner Bros. W 1668 [M]	James Darren/All	1967	3.75	7.50	15.00
❑ Warner Bros. WS 1668 [S]	James Darren/All	1967	5.00	10.00	20.00

DARREN, JAMES/ SHELLEY FABARES/PAUL PETERSEN

Number	Title (A Side/B Side)	Yr	VG	VG+	NM
Albums					
❑ Colpix CP-444 [M]	Teenage Triangle	1963	10.00	20.00	40.00
❑ Colpix SCP-444 [R]	Teenage Triangle	1963	10.00	20.00	40.00
❑ Colpix CP-468 [M]	More Teenage Triangle	1964	10.00	20.00	40.00
❑ Colpix SCP-468 [P]	More Teenage Triangle	1964	15.00	30.00	60.00

DAVIS, SPENCER, GROUP

Number	Title (A Side/B Side)	Yr	VG	VG+	NM
45s					
❑ Atco 6400	Keep On Running/High Time Baby	1966	3.75	7.50	15.00
❑ Atco 6416	Somebody Help Me/Stevie's Blues	1966	3.75	7.50	15.00
❑ Fontana 1960	I Can't Stand It/Midnight Train	1964	3.75	7.50	15.00
❑ United Artists 0115	Gimme Some Lovin'/Keep On Running	1973	—	2.00	4.00
—"Silver Spotlight Series" reissue					
❑ United Artists 0116	I'm a Man/Somebody Help Me	1973	—	2.00	4.00
—"Silver Spotlight Series" reissue					
❑ United Artists 1668	I'm a Man/I Can't Get Enough of It	196?	—	2.50	5.00
—Silver Spotlight Series					
❑ United Artists 50108	Gimme Some Lovin'/Blues in F	1966	3.00	6.00	12.00
❑ United Artists 50144	I'm a Man/Can't Get Enough of It	1967	3.00	6.00	12.00
❑ United Artists 50162	Somebody Help Me/On the Green Light	1967	2.50	5.00	10.00
❑ United Artists 50202	Time Seller/Don't Want You No More	1967	2.50	5.00	10.00
❑ United Artists 50286	Looking Back/After Tea	1968	2.50	5.00	10.00
❑ United Artists 50922	Listen to the Rhythm/Sunday Walk in the Rain	1972	—	3.00	6.00
—Spencer Davis solo					
❑ United Artists 50993	Rainy Season/Tumble-Down Tenement Row	1972	—	3.00	6.00
—Spencer Davis solo					
❑ Vertigo 110	Don't You Let It Bring You Down/ Today Gluggo, Tomorrow the World	1973	—	2.50	5.00
❑ Vertigo 112	Living in a Back Street/Need a Helping Hand	1974	—	2.50	5.00
Albums					
❑ Allegiance AV-442	Crossfire	1983	2.50	5.00	10.00
❑ Date TES-4021	Funky	1971	37.50	75.00	150.00
—Deleted almost immediately upon release					
❑ Mediarts 41-11	It's Been So Long	1971	3.00	6.00	12.00
❑ Rhino RNLP 117	The Best of the Spencer Davis Group	1983	2.00	4.00	8.00
❑ Rhino RNLP 70172	The Best of the Spencer Davis Group (Golden Archive Series)	1987	3.00	6.00	12.00
❑ United Artists UA-LA433-E	The Very Best of the Spencer Davis Group	1975	2.50	5.00	10.00
❑ United Artists UAL 3578 [M]	Gimme Some Lovin'	1967	12.50	25.00	50.00
❑ United Artists UAL 3589 [M]	I'm a Man	1967	10.00	20.00	40.00
❑ United Artists UAS 6578 [R]	Gimme Some Lovin'	1967	10.00	20.00	40.00
❑ United Artists UAS 6589 [P]	I'm a Man	1967	12.50	25.00	50.00
❑ United Artists UAS 6641 [P]	The Spencer Davis Group's Greatest Hits	1968	6.25	12.50	25.00
❑ United Artists UAS 6652	With Their New Face On	1968	5.00	10.00	20.00
❑ United Artists UAS 6691	Heavies	1969	5.00	10.00	20.00
❑ Vertigo VEL-1015	Gluggo	1973	3.00	6.00	12.00
❑ Vertigo VEL-1021	Living in a Back Street	1974	3.00	6.00	12.00

DAWN (1)

Number	Title (A Side/B Side)	Yr	VG	VG+	NM
45s					
❑ Arista 0105	Gimme a Good Old Mammy Song/Little Heads in Bunk Beds	1975	—	2.00	4.00
❑ Arista 0156	Skybird/That's the Way a Wallflower Grows	1975	—	2.00	4.00
❑ Arista 0301	Tie a Yellow Ribbon Round the Ole Oak Tree/Say, Has Anybody Seen My Sweet Gypsy Rose	1978	—	2.00	4.00
❑ Bell 903	Candida/Look At...	1970	—	3.00	6.00
❑ Bell 938	Knock Three Times/Home	1970	—	3.00	6.00
❑ Bell 970	I Play and Sing/Get Out from Where We Are	1971	—	2.50	5.00
❑ Bell 45107	Summer Sand/The Sweet Soft Sounds of Love	1971	—	2.50	5.00
❑ Bell 45141	What Are You Doing Sunday/The Sweet Soft Sounds of Love	1971	—	2.50	5.00

Number	Title (A Side/B Side)	Yr	VG	VG+	NM
❑ Bell 45175	Runaway-Happy Together/Don't Act Like a Baby	1972	—	2.50	5.00
❑ Bell 45225	Vaya Con Dios/I Can't Believe How Much I Love You	1972	—	2.50	5.00
❑ Bell 45285	You're a Lady/In the Park	1972	—	2.00	4.00
❑ Bell 45318	Tie a Yellow Ribbon Round the Ole Oak Tree/ I Can't Believe How Much I Love You	1973	—	2.50	5.00
❑ Bell 45374	Say, Has Anybody Seen My Sweet Gypsy Rose/ The Spark of Love Is Kindlin'	1973	—	2.00	4.00
❑ Bell 45424	Who's in the Strawberry Patch with Sally/Ukulele Man	1973	—	2.00	4.00
❑ Bell 45450	It Only Hurts When I Try to Smile/Sweet Summer Days of My Life	1974	—	2.00	4.00
❑ Bell 45601	Steppin' Out (Gonna Boogie Tonight)/ She Can't Hold a Candle to You	1974	—	2.00	4.00
—As "Tony Orlando and Dawn"					
❑ Bell 45620	Look in My Eyes Pretty Woman/My Love Has No Pride	1974	—	2.00	4.00
❑ Elektra 45240	He Don't Love You (Like I Love You)/Pick It Up	1975	—	2.00	4.00
❑ Elektra 45260	Mornin' Beautiful/Dance, Rosalie, Dance	1975	—	2.00	4.00
❑ Elektra 45275	You're All I Need to Get By/Know You Like a Book	1975	—	2.00	4.00
❑ Elektra 45302	Cupid/You're Growin' on Me	1976	—	2.00	4.00
❑ Elektra 45319	Midnight Love Affair/The Selfish Ones	1976	—	2.00	4.00
❑ Elektra 45387	Sing/Sweet on Candy	1977	—	2.00	4.00
❑ Elektra 45432	Growin' on Me/You're All I Need to Get By	1977	—	2.00	4.00
❑ Elektra 45501	Bring It On Home to Me/Don't Let Go	1978	—	2.00	4.00
❑ Elektra 45542	I Count the Tears/A Lover's Question	1978	—	2.00	4.00
❑ Elektra 45542	I Count the Tears/This Is Rock and Roll	1978	—	2.00	4.00
Albums					
❑ Arista AL 4045	Greatest Hits	1975	2.50	5.00	10.00
❑ Arista AL 4059	Skybird	1975	2.50	5.00	10.00
❑ Arista A2L 9006 [(2)]	The World of Tony Orlando and Dawn	1977	3.00	6.00	12.00
❑ Bell 1112	Tuneweaving	1973	2.50	5.00	10.00
❑ Bell 1130	Dawn's New Ragtime Follies	1973	2.50	5.00	10.00
❑ Bell 1317	Prime Time	1974	2.50	5.00	10.00
❑ Bell 1320	Candida & Knock Three Times	1974	2.50	5.00	10.00
—Reissue of 6052					
❑ Bell 1322	Tony Orlando & Dawn II	1974	2.50	5.00	10.00
—Reissue of 6069					
❑ Bell 6052	Candida	1970	3.00	6.00	12.00
❑ Bell 6069	Dawn Featuring Tony Orlando	1971	3.00	6.00	12.00
❑ Elektra 7E-1034	He Don't Love You (Like I Love You)	1975	2.50	5.00	10.00
❑ Elektra 7E-1049	To Be with You	1976	2.50	5.00	10.00

DAY, BOBBY

45s

Number	Title (A Side/B Side)	Yr	VG	VG+	NM
❑ Cash 1031	The Truth Hurts/Let's Live Together As One	1956	25.00	50.00	100.00
—As "Bobby Byrd and the Birds"					
❑ Class 207	Come Seven/So Long Baby	1957	5.00	10.00	20.00
❑ Class 211	Little Bitty Pretty One/When the Swallows Come Back to Capistrano	1957	6.25	12.50	25.00
❑ Class 215	Beep-Beep-Beep/Darling, If I Had You	1957	5.00	10.00	20.00
❑ Class 225	Little Turtle Dove/Saving My Life for You	1958	5.00	10.00	20.00
❑ Class 229	Rock-N Robin/Over and Over	1958	7.50	15.00	30.00
❑ Class 241	The Bluebird, the Buzzard, and the Oriole/Alone Too Long	1959	5.00	10.00	20.00
❑ Class 245	That's All I Want/Say Yes	1959	3.75	7.50	15.00
❑ Class 252	Mr. and Mrs. Rock & Roll/Gotta New Girl	1959	3.75	7.50	15.00
❑ Class 255	Ain't Gonna Cry No More/Love Is a One-Time Affair	1959	3.75	7.50	15.00
❑ Class 257	Unchained Melody/Three Young Rebs from Georgia	1959	3.75	7.50	15.00
❑ Class 263	My Blue Heaven/I Don't Want To	1960	3.75	7.50	15.00
❑ Class 705	Don't Leave Me Hangin' on a String/When I Started Dancin'	1965	3.00	6.00	12.00
❑ Corvet 1017	Why/Gotta Girl	1958	15.00	30.00	60.00
—As "Bobby Byrd and the Impalas"					
❑ Jamie 1039	Bippin' and Boppin' Over You/Strawberry Stomp	1957	7.50	15.00	30.00
—As "Robert Byrd and His Birdies"					
❑ RCA Victor 47-8133	Another Country, Another World/Know-It-All	1963	2.50	5.00	10.00
❑ RCA Victor 47-8196	Buzz Buzz Buzz/Pretty Little Girl Next Door	1963	2.50	5.00	10.00
❑ RCA Victor 47-8230	Down on My Knees/Jole Blon, Little Darling	1963	2.50	5.00	10.00
❑ RCA Victor 47-8316	When I See My Baby Smile/On the Street Where You Live	1964	2.50	5.00	10.00
❑ Rendezvous 130	Teenage Philosopher/Undecided	1960	3.00	6.00	12.00
❑ Rendezvous 133	Rockin' Robin/Over and Over	1960	3.00	6.00	12.00
❑ Rendezvous 136	Gee Whiz/Over and Over	1960	3.00	6.00	12.00

Number	Title (A Side/B Side)	Yr	VG	VG+	NM
❑ Rendezvous 146	I Need Help/Life Can Be Beautiful	1961	3.00	6.00	12.00
❑ Rendezvous 158	King's Highway/What Fools We Mortals Be	1961	3.00	6.00	12.00
❑ Rendezvous 167	Don't Worry 'Bout Me/Oop-E-Du-Pers Ball	1962	3.00	6.00	12.00
❑ Rendezvous 175	Undecided/Slow Pokey Joe	1962	3.00	6.00	12.00
❑ Sage and Sand 203	Please Don't Hurt Me/Delicious Are Your Kisses	1955	10.00	20.00	40.00
—As "Bobby Byrd"					
❑ Spark 501	Bippin' and Boppin' Over You/Strawberry Stomp	1957	12.50	25.00	50.00
—As "Robert Byrd and His Birdies"					
❑ Sure Shot 5036	So Lonely/Spicks and Specks	1967	2.00	4.00	8.00
❑ Zephyr 70-018	If We Should Meet Again/Looby Loo	1957	7.50	15.00	30.00
—As "Bobby Byrd"					

Albums

Number	Title	Yr	VG	VG+	NM
❑ Class LP-5002 [M]	Rockin' with Robin	1959	100.00	200.00	400.00
❑ Collectables COL-5074	Golden Classics	198?	2.50	5.00	10.00
❑ Rendezvous M-1312 [M]	Rockin' with Robin	196?	20.00	40.00	80.00
❑ Rhino RNDF-208	The Best of Bobby Day	1984	3.00	6.00	12.00

DEE, JOEY, AND THE STARLITERS

45s

Number	Title	Yr	VG	VG+	NM
❑ Bonus 7009	Lorraine/The Girl I Walk to School	1963	12.50	25.00	50.00
❑ Jubilee 5532	Feel Good About It Part 1/Feel Good About It Part 2	1966	3.75	7.50	15.00
❑ Jubilee 5539	Dancing on the Beach/Good Little You	1966	3.75	7.50	15.00
❑ Jubilee 5554	She's So Exceptional/It's Got You	1966	3.75	7.50	15.00
❑ Jubilee 5566	Can't Sit Down/Put Your Heart In It	1967	3.75	7.50	15.00
—Stock copy may not exist					
❑ Little 813/4	Lorraine/The Girl I Walk to School	1958	100.00	200.00	400.00
❑ Roulette 4401	Peppermint Twist — Part 1/Peppermint Twist — Part 2	1961	4.00	8.00	16.00
❑ Roulette 4408	Hey, Let's Twist/Roly Poly	1962	3.75	7.50	15.00
❑ Roulette 4416	Shout — Part 1/Shout — Part 2	1962	3.75	7.50	15.00
❑ Roulette 4431	Every Time (I Think About You) Part 1/ Every Time (I Think About You) Part 2	1962	3.00	6.00	12.00
❑ Roulette 4438	What Kind of Love Is This/Wing Ding	1962	3.00	6.00	12.00
—White label with colored "spokes"					
❑ Roulette 4456	I Lost My Baby/Keep Your Mind on What You're Doing	1962	3.00	6.00	12.00
❑ Roulette 4467	Baby You're Driving Me Crazy/Help Me Pick Up the Pieces	1963	3.00	6.00	12.00
❑ Roulette 4488	Hot Pastrami with Mashed Potatoes — Part 1/ Hot Pastrami with Mashed Potatoes — Part 2	1963	3.00	6.00	12.00
❑ Roulette 4503	Dance, Dance, Dance/Let's Have a Party	1963	3.00	6.00	12.00
❑ Roulette 4523	Ya Ya/Fanny Mae	1963	3.00	6.00	12.00
❑ Roulette 4539	Down by the Riverside/Getting Nearer	1963	5.00	10.00	20.00
❑ Roulette 4617	Cry a Little Sometime/Wing Ding	1965	3.00	6.00	12.00
❑ Scepter 1210	Face of An Angel/Shimmy Baby	1960	7.50	15.00	30.00
—Originals have "Scepter" at top of label and are credited as "Joey Dee and the Starlights"					
❑ Scepter 1210	Face of An Angel/Shimmy Baby	1961	5.00	10.00	20.00
—Reissues have "Scepter Records" at side of label and are credited as listed					
❑ Scepter 1225	Three Memories/(Bad) Bulldog	1961	7.50	15.00	30.00

Albums

Number	Title	Yr	VG	VG+	NM
❑ Forum FC 9099 [M]	Joey Dee and the Starliters	1963	3.00	6.00	12.00
❑ Forum FCS 9099 [S]	Joey Dee and the Starliters	1963	3.00	6.00	12.00
❑ Jubilee JGM-8000 [M]	Hitsville	1966	5.00	10.00	20.00
❑ Jubilee JGS-8000 [S]	Hitsville	1966	6.25	12.50	25.00
❑ Roulette R-25166 [M]	Doin' the Twist at the Peppermint Lounge	1961	10.00	20.00	40.00
❑ Roulette SR-25166 [S]	Doin' the Twist at the Peppermint Lounge	1961	12.50	25.00	50.00
❑ Roulette R-25171 [M]	All the World Is Twistin'	1962	7.50	15.00	30.00
❑ Roulette SR-25171 [S]	All the World Is Twistin'	1962	10.00	20.00	40.00
❑ Roulette R-25173 [M]	Back at the Peppermint Lounge — Twistin'	1962	7.50	15.00	30.00
❑ Roulette SR-25173 [S]	Back at the Peppermint Lounge — Twistin'	1962	10.00	20.00	40.00
❑ Roulette R-25197 [M]	Joey Dee	1963	6.25	12.50	25.00
❑ Roulette SR-25197 [S]	Joey Dee	1963	7.50	15.00	30.00
❑ Roulette R-25221 [M]	Dance, Dance, Dance	1963	6.25	12.50	25.00
❑ Roulette SR-25221 [S]	Dance, Dance, Dance	1963	7.50	15.00	30.00
❑ Scepter S 503 [M]	The Peppermint Twisters	1962	6.25	12.50	25.00
❑ Scepter SS 503 [S]	The Peppermint Twisters	1962	7.50	15.00	30.00

DEEP PURPLE

45s

Number	Title	Yr	VG	VG+	NM
❑ Mercury 880477-7	Knocking at Your Back Door/Wasted Sunset	1984	—	2.00	4.00
❑ Mercury 885617-7	Call of the Wild/Dead or Alive	1987	—	—	3.00
❑ Mercury 885820-7	Bad Attitude/Black and White	1987	—	—	3.00
❑ Tetragrammaton 1503	Hush/One More Rainy Day	1968	3.00	6.00	12.00
❑ Tetragrammaton 1508	Kentucky Woman/Hard Road	1968	3.00	6.00	12.00
❑ Tetragrammaton 1514	River Deep, Mountain High/Listen, Learn, Read On	1969	2.50	5.00	10.00
❑ Tetragrammaton 1519	The Bird Has Flown/Emmaretta	1969	2.50	5.00	10.00
❑ Tetragrammaton 1537	Hallelujah (I Am the Preacher)/April Part 1	1969	2.50	5.00	10.00
❑ Warner Bros. 7405	Black Night/Into the Fire	1970	2.00	4.00	8.00
❑ Warner Bros. 7493	Strange Kind of Woman/I'm Alone	1971	2.00	4.00	8.00
❑ Warner Bros. 7528	Fire Ball/I'm Alone	1971	2.00	4.00	8.00
❑ Warner Bros. 7572	Never Before/When a Blind Man Cries	1972	—	3.00	6.00
❑ Warner Bros. 7595	Lazy/When a Blind Man Cries	1972	—	3.00	6.00
❑ Warner Bros. 7634	Highway Star (Part 1)/Highway Star (Part 2)	1972	—	3.00	6.00
❑ Warner Bros. 7654	Hush/Kentucky Woman	1972	—	3.00	6.00
❑ Warner Bros. 7672	Woman from Tokyo/Super Trouper	1972	—	3.00	6.00
❑ Warner Bros. 7710	Smoke on the Water (Edited Version) Studio/ Smoke on the Water (Edited Version) Live	1973	—	2.50	5.00
❑ Warner Bros. 7737	Woman from Tokyo/Super Trouper	1973	—	2.50	5.00
❑ Warner Bros. 7784	Might Just Take Your Life/Coronorias Regid	1974	—	2.50	5.00
❑ Warner Bros. 7809	Burn/Coronarias Regid	1974	—	2.50	5.00

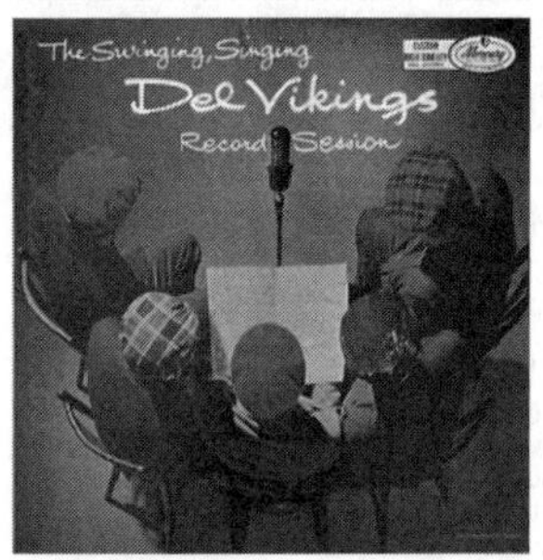

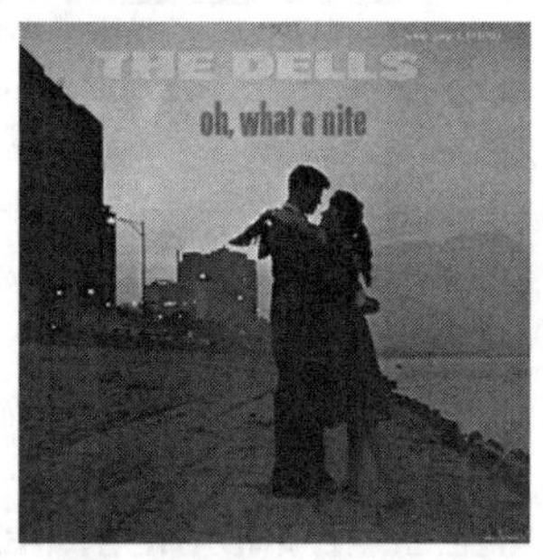

Number	Title (A Side/B Side)	Yr	VG	VG+	NM
❑ Warner Bros. 8049	High Ball Shooter/You Can't Do It Right	1974	—	2.50	5.00
❑ Warner Bros. 8069	Stormbringer/Love Don't Mean a Thing	1975	—	2.50	5.00
❑ Warner Bros. 8182	Gettin' Tighter/Love Child	1976	—	2.50	5.00
Albums					
❑ Eagle Rock ER 20083-1 [(2)]	Rapture of the Deep	2005	5.00	10.00	20.00
❑ Mercury 824003-1	Perfect Strangers	1984	2.50	5.00	10.00
❑ Mercury 831318-1	The House of Blue Light	1987	2.00	4.00	8.00
❑ Mercury 835897-1	Nobody's Perfect	1988	2.50	5.00	10.00
❑ RCA 2421-1-R	Slaves and Masters	1990	3.75	7.50	15.00
❑ Scepter Citation CTN-18010	The Best of Deep Purple	1972	2.50	5.00	10.00
❑ Tetragrammaton T-102	Shades of Deep Purple	1968	7.50	15.00	30.00
❑ Tetragrammaton T-107	The Book of Taliesyn	1968	7.50	15.00	30.00
❑ Tetragrammaton T-119	Deep Purple	1969	7.50	15.00	30.00
❑ Tetragrammaton T-131	Concerto for Group and Orchestra	1970	50.00	100.00	200.00
❑ Warner Bros. WS 1860	Concerto for Group and Orchestra	1970	3.00	6.00	12.00
❑ Warner Bros. WS 1877	Deep Purple in Rock	1970	3.00	6.00	12.00
❑ Warner Bros. BS 2564	Fireball	1971	3.00	6.00	12.00
❑ Warner Bros. BS 2607	Machine Head	1972	3.00	6.00	12.00
—Original copies have green "WB" labels					
❑ Warner Bros. 2LS 2644 [(2)]	(Purple Passages)	1972	3.75	7.50	15.00
❑ Warner Bros. BS 2678	Who Do We Think We Are!	1973	3.00	6.00	12.00
—Original copies have green "WB" labels					
❑ Warner Bros. BS 2678	Who Do We Think We Are!	1973	2.50	5.00	10.00
—"Burbank" labels					
❑ Warner Bros. 2WS 2701 [(2)]	Made in Japan	1973	3.75	7.50	15.00
❑ Warner Bros. W 2766	Burn	1974	2.50	5.00	10.00
❑ Warner Bros. BSK 3100	Machine Head	1976	2.00	4.00	8.00
❑ Warner Bros./ Purple PR 2832	Stormbringer	1974	2.50	5.00	10.00
❑ Warner Bros./ Purple PR 2895	Come Taste the Band	1975	2.50	5.00	10.00
❑ Warner Bros./ Purple PR 2995	Made in Europe	1976	2.50	5.00	10.00
❑ Warner Bros./ Purple PRK 3223	When We Rock, We Rock, and When We Roll, We Roll	1978	2.50	5.00	10.00
❑ Warner Bros./ Purple PRK 3486	Deepest Purple: The Best of Deep Purple	1980	2.50	5.00	10.00

DEFRANCO FAMILY, THE

Number	Title (A Side/B Side)	Yr	VG	VG+	NM
45s					
❑ 20th Century 2030	Heartbeat — It's a Lovebeat/Sweet, Sweet Loretta	1973	—	2.00	4.00
❑ 20th Century 2070	Abra-Ca-Dabra/Some Kind a' Love	1973	—	2.00	4.00
❑ 20th Century 2088	Save the Last Dance for Me/Because We Both Are Young	1974	—	2.00	4.00
❑ 20th Century 2128	Baby Blue/Write Me a Letter	1974	—	2.00	4.00
❑ 20th Century 2214	We Belong Together/Time Enough for Love	1975	2.00	4.00	8.00
Albums					
❑ 20th Century T-422	Heartbeat, It's a Lovebeat	1973	2.50	5.00	10.00
❑ 20th Century T-441	Save the Last Dance for Me	1974	2.50	5.00	10.00

DEKKER, DESMOND, AND THE ACES

Number	Title (A Side/B Side)	Yr	VG	VG+	NM
45s					
❑ Uni 55129	Israelites/My Precious World	1969	—	3.00	6.00
❑ Uni 55150	It Mek/Problems	1969	—	3.00	6.00
❑ Uni 55261	You Can Get It If You Really Want It/Perseverance	1970	—	3.00	6.00
Albums					
❑ Bulldog 1037	The Israelites	198?	2.50	5.00	10.00
❑ Uni 73059	Israelites	1969	7.50	15.00	30.00

DEL VIKINGS, THE

Number	Title (A Side/B Side)	Yr	VG	VG+	NM
45s					
❑ Alpine 66	Pistol Packin' Mama/The Sun	1960	20.00	40.00	80.00
❑ Bim Bam Boom 111	Cold Feet/A Little Man Cried	1972	—	2.50	5.00
❑ Bim Bam Boom 113	Watching the Moon/You Say You Love Me	1972	—	2.50	5.00
❑ Bim Bam Boom 115	I'm Spinning/Girl Girl	1972	—	2.50	5.00
❑ Dot 15538	Come Go with Me/How Can I Find True Love	1957	7.50	15.00	30.00

Number	Title (A Side/B Side)	Yr	VG	VG+	NM
❑ Dot 15571	What Made Maggie Run/Little Billy Boy	1957	7.50	15.00	30.00
❑ Dot 15592	Whispering Bells/Don't Be a Fool	1957	7.50	15.00	30.00
❑ Dot 15636	I'm Spinning/When I Come Home	1957	7.50	15.00	30.00
—As "Kripp Johnson with the Dell-Vikings"					
❑ Dot 16092	Come Go with Me/How Can I Find True Love	1960	5.00	10.00	20.00
❑ Dot 16236	Come Go with Me/Whispering Bells	1961	5.00	10.00	20.00
❑ Dot 16248	I Hear Bells (Wedding Bells)/Don't Get Slick on Me	1961	5.00	10.00	20.00
❑ DRC 101	Can't You See/Oh I	196?	10.00	20.00	40.00
❑ Fee Bee 173	Welfare Blues/Hollywood and Vine	1977	—	2.50	5.00
❑ Fee Bee 205	Come Go with Me/How Can I Find True Love	1957	125.00	250.00	500.00
—Orange label, bee on top					
❑ Fee Bee 205	Come Go with Me/Whispering Bells	1964	5.00	10.00	20.00
❑ Fee Bee 206	Down in Bermuda/Maggie	1964	20.00	40.00	80.00
❑ Fee Bee 210	What Made Maggie Run/When I Come Home	1957	40.00	80.00	120.00
❑ Fee Bee 210	What Made Maggie Run/Uh Uh Baby	1957	20.00	40.00	80.00
❑ Fee Bee 210	What Made Maggie Run/Down by the Stream	1964	7.50	15.00	30.00
❑ Fee Bee 214	Whispering Bells/Don't Be a Fool	1957	100.00	200.00	400.00
❑ Fee Bee 218	I'm Spinning/You Say You Love Me	1957	30.00	60.00	120.00
—Bee on label					
❑ Fee Bee 221	Willette/I Want to Marry You	1958	20.00	40.00	80.00
❑ Fee Bee 221	Willette/Woke Up This Morning	1958	25.00	50.00	100.00
❑ Fee Bee 227	Tell Me/Finger Poppin' Woman	1959	20.00	40.00	80.00
❑ Fee Bee 902	True Love/Baby, Let Me Know	1964	7.50	15.00	30.00
—As "The Original Dell Vikings"					
❑ Gateway 743	We Three/I've Got to Know	1964	7.50	15.00	30.00
❑ Jojo 108	Keep On Walkin'/My Body, Your Shadow	1976	—	2.50	5.00
❑ Luniverse 106	Somewhere Over the Rainbow/Hey, Senorita	1957	25.00	50.00	100.00
❑ Luniverse 110	Yours/Heaven and Paradise	1958	5.00	10.00	20.00
❑ Luniverse 113	In the Still of the Night/The White Cliffs of Dover	1958	5.00	10.00	20.00
❑ Luniverse 114	There I Go/Girl Girl	1958	5.00	10.00	20.00
—The above three Luniverse 45s are bootlegs, but they perversely do have collector's value!					
❑ Mercury 71132	Cool Shake/Jitterbug Mary	1957	7.50	15.00	30.00
❑ Mercury 71180	Come Along with Me/Whatcha Gonna Lose	1957	7.50	15.00	30.00
❑ Mercury 71198	I'm Spinning/When I Come Home	1957	7.50	15.00	30.00
❑ Mercury 71241	Snowbound/Your Book of Life	1957	7.50	15.00	30.00
❑ Mercury 71266	The Voodoo Man/Can't Wait	1958	7.50	15.00	30.00
❑ Mercury 71345	You Cheated/Pretty Little Things Called Girls	1958	7.50	15.00	30.00
—Black label					
❑ Mercury 71390	How Could You/Flat Tire	1958	7.50	15.00	30.00
❑ Scepter 12367	Come Go with Me/When You're Asleep	1973	—	2.50	5.00
❑ Ship 214	Sunday Kind of Love/Over the Rainbow	197?	—	2.00	4.00
Albums					
❑ Collectables COL-5010	The Best of the Dell-Vikings	198?	3.00	6.00	12.00
❑ Dot DLP-3685 [M]	Come Go with Me	1966	50.00	100.00	200.00
❑ Dot DLP-25685 [R]	Come Go with Me	1966	37.50	75.00	150.00
❑ Luniverse LP-1000 [M]	Come Go with the Del Vikings	1957	125.00	250.00	500.00
—Eight tracks, cover is composed of slicks. Counterfeits have more tracks and a preprinted cover (not slicks)					
❑ Mercury MG-20314 [M]	They Sing — They Swing	1957	75.00	150.00	300.00
❑ Mercury MG-20353 [M]	A Swinging, Singing Record Session	1958	50.00	100.00	200.00

DEL VIKINGS, THE / THE SONNETS

Albums

Number	Title (A Side/B Side)	Yr	VG	VG+	NM
❑ Crown CLP-5368 [M]	The Del Vikings and the Sonnets	1963	10.00	20.00	40.00

DELANEY AND BONNIE

45s

Number	Title (A Side/B Side)	Yr	VG	VG+	NM
❑ Atco 6725	Groupie (Superstar)/Comin' Home	1969	2.00	4.00	8.00
❑ Atco 6756	Soul Shake/Free the People	1970	2.00	4.00	8.00
❑ Atco 6788	Miss Ann/They Call It Rock and Roll Music	1970	2.00	4.00	8.00
❑ Atco 6804	Never Ending Song of Love/Don't Deceive Me	1971	2.00	4.00	8.00
❑ Atco 6838	Only You Know and I Know/God Knows I Love You	1971	—	3.00	6.00
❑ Atco 6866	Sing My Way Home/Move 'Em Out	1972	—	2.50	5.00
❑ Atco 6883	Where There's a Will There's a Way/ Lonesome and a Long Way from Home	1972	—	2.50	5.00
❑ Atco 6904	Sing My Way Home/Will the Circle Be Unbroken	1972	—	2.50	5.00
❑ Columbia 45608	Country Life/Walk in the River Jordan	1972	—	2.50	5.00
❑ Elektra 45660	Soldiers of the Cross/Get Ourselves Together	1969	2.50	5.00	10.00
❑ Elektra 45662	When the Battle Is Over/Get Ourselves Together	1969	2.50	5.00	10.00
❑ Garpax 44184	Cherry Pie/Hey Mr. Weatherman	1964	3.75	7.50	15.00
—As "Lani & Boni"					
❑ Independence 78	You've Lost That Lovin' Feelin'/Don't Let It (Be the Last Time)	1967	3.00	6.00	12.00
❑ Stax 0003	It's Been a Long Time Coming/ We've Just Been Feeling Bad	1968	2.50	5.00	10.00
❑ Stax 0057	Hard to Say Goodbye/Just Plain Beautiful	1969	2.50	5.00	10.00
Albums					
❑ Atco SD 33-326	Delaney & Bonnie & Friends On Tour with Eric Clapton	1970	6.25	12.50	25.00
—Yellow label original					
❑ Atco SD 33-341 [S]	To Bonnie from Delaney	1970	6.25	12.50	25.00
❑ Atco SD 33-358	Motel Shot	1971	6.25	12.50	25.00
❑ Atco SD 33-383	Country Life	1972	5.00	10.00	20.00
❑ Atco SD 7014	The Best of Delaney and Bonnie	1972	5.00	10.00	20.00
❑ Columbia KC 31377	D&B Together	1972	5.00	10.00	20.00
❑ Elektra EKS-74039	Accept No Substitute — The Original Delaney & Bonnie & Friends	1969	7.50	15.00	30.00
❑ GNP Crescendo GNPS-2054	Genesis	1970	5.00	10.00	20.00
❑ Stax STS-2026	Home	1969	7.50	15.00	30.00

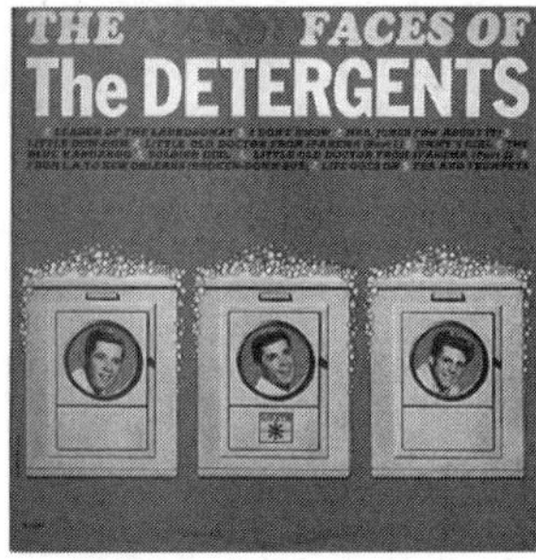

Number	Title (A Side/B Side)	Yr	VG	VG+	NM
DELFONICS, THE					
45s					
❑ Arista 0308	Don't Throw It All Away/I Don't Care What People Say	1978	—	2.00	4.00
❑ Cameo 472	You've Been Untrue/I Was There	1967	3.75	7.50	15.00
❑ Moon Shot 6703	He Don't Really Love You/Without You	1967	3.75	7.50	15.00
❑ Philly Groove 150	La-La Means I Love You/Can't Get Over Losing You	1968	2.50	5.00	10.00
❑ Philly Groove 151	I'm Sorry/You're Gone	1968	2.50	5.00	10.00
❑ Philly Groove 152	Break Your Promise/Alfie	1968	2.50	5.00	10.00
❑ Philly Groove 154	Ready Or Not Here I Come (Can't Hide from Love)/ Somebody Loves You	1968	2.50	5.00	10.00
❑ Philly Groove 156	Funny Feeling/My New Love	1969	2.50	5.00	10.00
❑ Philly Groove 157	You Got Yours and I'll Get Mine/Loving Him	1969	2.50	5.00	10.00
❑ Philly Groove 161	Didn't I (Blow Your Mind This Time)/Down Is Up, Up Is Down	1970	2.50	5.00	10.00
❑ Philly Groove 162	Trying to Make a Fool of Me/Baby I Love You	1970	2.50	5.00	10.00
❑ Philly Groove 163	When You Get Right Down To It/I Gave to You	1970	2.50	5.00	10.00
❑ Philly Groove 166	Over and Over/Hey! Love	1971	2.00	4.00	8.00
❑ Philly Groove 169	Walk Right Up to the Sun/Round and Round	1971	2.00	4.00	8.00
❑ Philly Groove 172	Tell Me This Is a Dream/I'm a Man	1972	2.00	4.00	8.00
❑ Philly Groove 174	Think It Over/I'm a Man	1972	2.00	4.00	8.00
❑ Philly Groove 176	I Don't Want to Make You Wait/Baby I Miss You	1973	2.00	4.00	8.00
❑ Philly Groove 177	Alfie/Start All Over Again	1973	2.00	4.00	8.00
❑ Philly Groove 182	I Told You So/Seventeen and In Love	1973	2.00	4.00	8.00
❑ Philly Groove 184	Lying to Myself/Hey Baby	1974	2.00	4.00	8.00
Albums					
❑ Arista AL 8333	The Best of the Delfonics	198?	2.50	5.00	10.00
❑ Collectables COL-5109	Golden Classics	198?	2.50	5.00	10.00
❑ Kory 1002	The Best of the Delfonics	1977	3.00	6.00	12.00
❑ Philly Groove 1150	La La Means I Love You	1968	20.00	40.00	80.00
❑ Philly Groove 1151	The Sexy Sound of Soul	1969	20.00	40.00	80.00
❑ Philly Groove 1152	The Delfonics Super Hits	1969	12.50	25.00	50.00
❑ Philly Groove 1153	The Delfonics	1970	12.50	25.00	50.00
❑ Philly Groove 1154	Tell Me This Is a Dream	1972	12.50	25.00	50.00
❑ Philly Groove 1501	Alive & Kicking	1974	12.50	25.00	50.00
❑ Poogie 121680	The Delfonics Return	1981	3.00	6.00	12.00
DELLS, THE					
45s					
❑ ABC 12386	Super Woman/My Life Is So Wonderful	1978	—	2.50	5.00
❑ ABC 12422	(I Wanna) Testify/Don't Save Me	1978	—	2.50	5.00
❑ ABC 12422	(I Wanna) Testify/Drowning for Your Love	1978	—	2.50	5.00
❑ ABC 12440	(You Bring Out) The Best in Me/Wrapped Up Tight	1978	—	2.50	5.00
❑ Argo 5415	God Bless the Child/I'm Going Home	1962	3.00	6.00	12.00
❑ Argo 5428	The (Bossa Nova) Bird/Eternally	1962	3.00	6.00	12.00
❑ Argo 5442	Hi Diddle Dee Dum Dum (It's a Good Feelin')/ If It Ain't One Thing, It's Another	1963	3.00	6.00	12.00
❑ Argo 5456	After You/Goodbye Mary Ann	1963	3.00	6.00	12.00
❑ Cadet 5538	Thinkin' About You/The Change We Go Thru (For Love)	1966	—	3.00	6.00
❑ Cadet 5551	Over Again/Run for Cover	1967	—	3.00	6.00
❑ Cadet 5563	You Belong to Someone Else/Inspiration	1967	—	3.00	6.00
❑ Cadet 5574	O-O, I Love You/There Is	1967	—	3.00	6.00
❑ Cadet 5590	There Is/Show Me	1968	2.00	4.00	8.00
❑ Cadet 5599	Wear it On Our Face/Please Don't Change Me Now	1968	—	3.00	6.00
❑ Cadet 5612	Stay in My Corner/Love Is So Simple	1969	—	3.00	6.00
❑ Cadet 5621	Always Together/I Want My Mama	1968	—	3.00	6.00
❑ Cadet 5631	Does Anybody Know I'm Here/ Make Sure (You Have Somebody to Love You)	1968	—	3.00	6.00
❑ Cadet 5636	I Can't Do Enough/Hallways of My Mind	1969	—	3.00	6.00
❑ Cadet 5641	I Can Sing a Rainbow-Love Is Blue/Hallelujah Baby	1969	—	3.00	6.00
❑ Cadet 5649	Oh What a Night/Believe Me	1969	—	3.00	6.00
❑ Cadet 5658	On the Dock of the Bay/When I'm in Your Arms	1969	—	3.00	6.00
❑ Cadet 5663	Oh What a Day/The Change We Go Thru (For Love)	1970	—	3.00	6.00
❑ Cadet 5667	Open Up My Heart/Nadine	1970	—	3.00	6.00
❑ Cadet 5672	Long Lonely Nights/A Little Understanding	1970	—	3.00	6.00
❑ Cadet 5679	The Glory of Love/A Whiter Shade of Pale	1970	—	3.00	6.00
❑ Cadet 5683	The Love We Had (Stays on My Mind)/Freedom Means	1971	—	3.00	6.00
❑ Cadet 5689	It's All Up to You/Oh, My Dear	1972	—	3.00	6.00
❑ Cadet 5691	Walk On By/This Guy's in Love with You	1972	—	3.00	6.00

Number	Title (A Side/B Side)	Yr	VG	VG+	NM
❑ Cadet 5694	Just As Long As We're in Love/I'd Rather Be with You	1972	—	3.00	6.00
❑ Cadet 5696	Give Your Baby a Standing Ovation/Closer	1973	—	3.00	6.00
❑ Cadet 5698	My Pretending Days Are Over/Let's Make It Last	1973	—	3.00	6.00
❑ Cadet 5700	I Miss You/Don't Make Me a Storyteller	1973	—	3.00	6.00
❑ Cadet 5702	I Wish It Was Me You Loved/Two Together Is Better Than One	1974	—	3.00	6.00
❑ Cadet 5703	Sweeter as the Days Go By/Learning to Love You Was Easy (It's So Hard Trying to Get Over You)	1974	—	3.00	6.00
—A-side is the same song with a new title					
❑ Cadet 5703	Bring Back the Love of Yesterday/Learning to Love You Was Easy (It's So Hard Trying to Get Over You)	1974	—	3.00	6.00
❑ Cadet 5707	The Glory of Love/You're the Greatest	1975	—	3.00	6.00
❑ Cadet 5711	We Got to Get Our Thing Together/The Power of Love	1975	2.00	4.00	8.00
❑ Checker 794	Darling I Know/Christine	1954	400.00	800.00	1200.
—As "The El Rays"					
❑ Lost-Nite 272	Dreams of Contentment/Zing, Zing, Zing	197?	—	2.50	5.00
—Reissue					
❑ Lost-Nite 281	Why Do You Have to Go/Dance, Dance, Dance	197?	—	2.50	5.00
—Reissue					
❑ Lost-Nite 290	Stay in My Corner/A Distant Love	197?	—	2.50	5.00
❑ Lost-Nite 297	Pain in My Heart/Time Makes You Change	197?	—	2.50	5.00
—Reissue					
❑ Lost-Nite 305	Oh What a Nite/Jo-Jo	197?	—	2.50	5.00
—Reissue					
❑ MCA 41051	Plastic People/What I Could	1979	—	2.50	5.00
❑ Mercury 73723	We Got to Get Our Thing Together/Reminiscing	1975	—	2.50	5.00
❑ Mercury 73759	The Power of Love/Gotta Get Home to My Baby	1976	—	2.50	5.00
❑ Mercury 73807	Slow Motion/Ain't No Black and White in Music	1976	—	2.50	5.00
❑ Mercury 73842	No Way Back/Too Late for Love	1976	—	2.50	5.00
❑ Mercury 73901	Betcha Never Been Loved (Like This Before)/Get On Down	1977	—	2.50	5.00
❑ Mercury 73909	Our Love/Could It Be	1977	—	2.50	5.00
❑ Mercury 73977	Private Property/Teaser	1977	—	2.50	5.00
❑ Private I 04343	Don't Want Nobody/You Can't Just Walk Away	1984	—	2.00	4.00
❑ Private I 04448	One Step Closer/Come On Back to Me	1984	—	2.00	4.00
❑ Private I 04540	Love On/Don't Want Nobody	1984	—	2.00	4.00
❑ Skylark 558	I Can't Help Myself/She's Just an Angel	198?	—	2.00	4.00
❑ Skylark 581	Someone to Call Me Darling/Now I Pray	198?	—	2.00	4.00
❑ 20th Century 2463	I Touched a Dream/All About the Paper	1980	—	2.00	4.00
❑ 20th Century 2475	Passionate Breezes/Your Song	1980	—	2.00	4.00
❑ 20th Century 2504	Happy Song/Look at Us Now	1981	—	2.00	4.00
❑ 20th Century 2602	Ain't It a Shame/Stay in My Corner	1982	—	2.00	4.00
❑ Vee Jay 134	Tell the World/Blues at Three	1955	500.00	1000.	2000.
❑ Vee Jay 166	Dreams of Contentment/Zing, Zing, Zing	1955	50.00	100.00	200.00
❑ Vee Jay 204	Oh What a Nite/Jo-Jo	1956	30.00	60.00	120.00
❑ Vee Jay 230	Movin' On/I Wanna Go Home	1956	10.00	20.00	40.00
❑ Vee Jay 236	Why Do You Have to Go/Dance, Dance, Dance	1957	10.00	20.00	40.00
❑ Vee Jay 251	A Distant Love/O-Bop She-Bop	1957	10.00	20.00	40.00
❑ Vee Jay 258	Pain in My Heart/Time Makes You Change	1957	10.00	20.00	40.00
❑ Vee Jay 274	The Springer/What You Say Baby	1958	7.50	15.00	30.00
❑ Vee Jay 292	I'm Calling/Jeepers Creepers	1958	7.50	15.00	30.00
❑ Vee Jay 300	Wedding Day/My Best Girl	1958	25.00	50.00	100.00
❑ Vee Jay 324	Dry Your Eyes/Baby Open Up Your Heart	1959	10.00	20.00	40.00
❑ Vee Jay 338	Oh What a Nite/I Wanna Go Home	1960	5.00	10.00	20.00
❑ Vee Jay 376	Hold On to What You've Got/Swingin' Teens	1961	5.00	10.00	20.00
❑ Vee Jay 595	Shy Girl/What Do We Prove	1964	3.00	6.00	12.00
❑ Vee Jay 615	Wait Till Tomorrow/Oh What a Good Night	1964	3.00	6.00	12.00
❑ Vee Jay 674	Stay in My Corner/It's Not Unusual	1965	3.00	6.00	12.00
❑ Vee Jay 712	Poor Little Boy/Hey Sugar (Don't Get Serious)	1966	3.00	6.00	12.00
❑ Veteran 7-101	Thought of You Just a Little Too Much/(B-side unknown)	1989	—	2.50	5.00
Albums					
❑ ABC AA-1100	New Beginnings	1978	3.00	6.00	12.00
❑ ABC AA-1113	Face to Face	1978	3.00	6.00	12.00
❑ Buddah BDS-5053	The Dells	1969	3.75	7.50	15.00
❑ Cadet LPS-804	There Is	1968	12.50	25.00	50.00
❑ Cadet LPS-822	The Dells Musical Menu/Always Together	1969	12.50	25.00	50.00
❑ Cadet LPS-824	The Dells Greatest Hits	1969	12.50	25.00	50.00
❑ Cadet LPS-829	Love Is Blue	1969	12.50	25.00	50.00
❑ Cadet LPS-837	Like It Is, Like It Was	1970	12.50	25.00	50.00
❑ Cadet 50004	Freedom Means	1971	6.25	12.50	25.00
❑ Cadet 50017	The Dells Sing Dionne Warwicke's Greatest Hits	1972	6.25	12.50	25.00
❑ Cadet 50021	Sweet As Funk Can Be	1972	6.25	12.50	25.00
❑ Cadet 50037	Give Your Baby a Standing Ovation	1973	6.25	12.50	25.00
❑ Cadet 50046	The Dells	1973	6.25	12.50	25.00
❑ Cadet 60030	The Mighty Mighty Dells	1974	6.25	12.50	25.00
❑ Cadet 60036	The Dells' Greatest Hits, Vol. 2	1975	5.00	10.00	20.00
❑ Chess CH-9103	The Dells	198?	2.50	5.00	10.00
—Reissue					
❑ Chess CH-9288	There Is	1989	2.50	5.00	10.00
—Reissue of Cadet 804					
❑ Lost-Nite LLP-21 [10]	The Dells	1981	3.75	7.50	15.00
—Red vinyl, generic red cover					
❑ Mercury SRM-1-1059	We Got to Get Our Thing Together	1975	3.75	7.50	15.00
❑ Mercury SRM-1-1084	No Way Back	1976	3.75	7.50	15.00
❑ Mercury SRM-1-1145	They Said It Couldn't Be Done	1977	3.75	7.50	15.00
❑ Mercury SRM-1-3711	Love Connection	1977	3.75	7.50	15.00
❑ Private I BFZ 39309	One Step Closer	1984	2.50	5.00	10.00
❑ Solid Smoke 8029	Breezy Ballads and Tender Tunes: The Best of the Early Years (1955-65)	1984	2.50	5.00	10.00

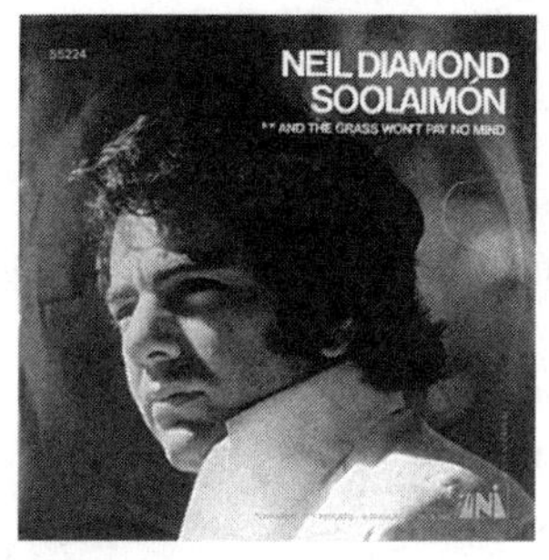

Number	Title (A Side/B Side)	Yr	VG	VG+	NM
❑ 20th Century T-618	I Touched a Dream	1980	3.00	6.00	12.00
❑ 20th Century T-633	Whatever Turns You On	1981	3.00	6.00	12.00
❑ Upfront UPF-105	Stay In My Corner	1968	3.75	7.50	15.00
❑ Urgent URG-4108	The Second Time	1991	3.00	6.00	12.00
❑ Vee Jay LP 1010 [M]	Oh What a Nite	1959	200.00	400.00	800.00
—Maroon label					
❑ Vee Jay LP 1010 [M]	Oh What a Nite	1961	75.00	150.00	300.00
—Black label with colorband					
❑ Vee Jay LP 1141 [M]	It's Not Unusual	1965	25.00	50.00	100.00
❑ Vee Jay LPS 1141 [S]	It's Not Unusual	1965	37.50	75.00	150.00
❑ Zoo 11023	I Salute You	1992	3.75	7.50	15.00

DENVER, JOHN

45s

Number	Title (A Side/B Side)	Yr	VG	VG+	NM
❑ Cherry Mountain 01/02	Let Us Begin (What Are We Making Weapons For)/Flying for Me	1986	—	2.00	4.00
❑ Columbia 02679	Perhaps Love/Annie's Song	1982	—	2.00	4.00
—With Placido Domingo					
❑ Columbia 03148	Perhaps Love/Annie's Song	1982	—	—	3.00
—With Placido Domingo; reissue					
❑ Legacy 77993	For You/Rocky Mountain High (Live)	1995	—	—	2.00
❑ RCA 5086-7-R	Love Again/Let Us Begin (What Are We Making Weapons For)	1987	—	—	3.00
❑ RCA PB-10774	Like a Sad Song/Pegasus	1976	—	2.00	4.00
❑ RCA PB-10854	Baby, You Look Good to Me Tonight/Wrangle Mountain Song	1976	—	2.00	4.00
❑ RCA PB-10911	My Sweet Lady/Welcome to My Morning	1977	—	2.00	4.00
❑ RCA GB-10940	I'm Sorry/Fly Away	1977	—	—	3.00
—Gold Standard Series					
❑ RCA PB-11036	How Can I Leave You Again/To the Wild Country	1977	—	2.00	4.00
❑ RCA PB-11214	It Amazes Me/Druthers	1978	—	2.00	4.00
❑ RCA PB-11267	I Want to Live/Tradewinds	1978	—	2.00	4.00
❑ RCA GB-11327	My Sweet Lady/Like a Sad Song	1978	—	—	3.00
—Gold Standard Series					
❑ RCA PB-11479	Downhill Stuff/Life Is So Good	1979	—	2.00	4.00
❑ RCA PB-11535	Sweet Melinda/What's On Your Mind	1979	—	2.00	4.00
❑ RCA PB-11637	Garden Song/Berkeley Woman	1979	—	2.00	4.00
❑ RCA PB-11915	Autograph/The Mountain Song	1980	—	2.00	4.00
❑ RCA PB-12017	Dancing with the Mountains/American Child	1980	—	2.00	4.00
❑ RCA PB-12246	Some Days Are Diamonds (Some Days Are Stone)/Country Love	1981	—	2.00	4.00
❑ RCA PB-12345	The Cowboy and the Lady/Till You Opened My Eyes	1981	—	2.00	4.00
❑ RCA PB-13071	Shanghai Breezes/What One Man Can Do	1982	—	2.00	4.00
❑ RCA PB-13270	Seasons of the Heart/Islands	1982	—	2.00	4.00
❑ RCA PB-13371	Opposite Tables/Relatively Speaking	1982	—	2.00	4.00
❑ RCA PB-13562	Wild Montana Skies/I Remember Romance	1983	—	2.00	4.00
—A-side with Emmylou Harris					
❑ RCA PB-13642	Flight (The Higher We Fly)/Hold On Tightly	1983	—	2.00	4.00
❑ RCA PB-13740	World Games/It's About Time	1984	—	—	3.00
❑ RCA PB-13782	The Way I Am/The Gold and Beyond	1984	—	—	3.00
❑ RCA PB-13931	Love Again/It's About Time	1984	—	—	3.00
—A-side: With Sylvie Vartan					
❑ RCA GB-14075	Calypso/Some Days Are Diamonds (Some Days Are Stone)	1985	—	—	3.00
—Gold Standard Series					
❑ RCA PB-14115	Don't Close Your Eyes Tonight/A Wild Heart Looking for Home	1985	—	—	3.00
❑ RCA PB-14227	Dreamland Express/African Sunrise	1985	—	—	3.00
❑ RCA PB-14406	Along for the Ride ('56 T-Bird)/Let Us Begin (What Are We Making Weapons For)	1986	—	—	3.00
❑ RCA Victor 74-0275	Daydream/I Wish I Knew How It Would Feel to Be Free	1969	2.50	5.00	10.00
❑ RCA Victor 74-0305	Anthem (Revelation)/Sticky Summer Weather	1970	2.50	5.00	10.00
❑ RCA Victor 74-0332	Follow Me/Isabel	1970	2.50	5.00	10.00
❑ RCA Victor 74-0376	Sail Away Home/I Wish I Could Have Been There	1970	2.50	5.00	10.00
❑ RCA Victor 74-0391	Whose Garden Is This/Mr. Bojangles	1970	2.50	5.00	10.00
❑ RCA Victor 74-0445	Take Me Home, Country Roads/Poems, Prayers and Promises	1971	2.00	4.00	8.00
—With Fat City					
❑ RCA Victor 74-0567	Friends with You/Starwood in Aspen	1971	—	3.00	6.00
❑ RCA Victor 74-0647	Everyday/City of New Orleans	1972	—	3.00	6.00
❑ RCA Victor 74-0737	Goodbye Again/The Eagle and the Hawk	1972	—	3.00	6.00
❑ RCA Victor 74-0801	Late Winter, Early Spring/Hard Life Hard Times	1972	—	3.00	6.00
❑ RCA Victor 74-0829	Rocky Mountain High/Spring	1972	—	2.50	5.00
❑ RCA Victor 74-0955	I'd Rather Be a Cowboy/Sunshine on My Shoulders	1973	—	2.00	4.00

Number	Title (A Side/B Side)	Yr	VG	VG+	NM
❑ RCA Victor APBO-0067	Farewell Andromeda (Welcome to My Morning)/ Whiskey Basin Blues	1973	—	2.00	4.00
❑ RCA Victor APBO-0182	Please, Daddy (Don't Get Drunk This Christmas)/ Rocky Mountain High	1973	—	2.50	5.00
❑ RCA Victor APBO-0213	Sunshine on My Shoulders/Around and Around	1974	—	2.00	4.00
❑ RCA Victor APBO-0295	Annie's Song/Cool An' Green An' Shady	1974	—	2.00	4.00
❑ RCA Victor PB-10065	Back Home Again/It's Up to You	1974	—	2.00	4.00
❑ RCA Victor PB-10148	Sweet Surrender/Summer	1974	—	2.00	4.00
❑ RCA Victor PB-10239	Thank God I'm a Country Boy/My Sweet Lady	1975	—	2.00	4.00
❑ RCA Victor PB-10353	I'm Sorry/Calypso	1975	—	2.00	4.00
❑ RCA Victor PB-10464	Christmas for Cowboys/Silent Night, Holy Night	1975	—	2.00	4.00
❑ RCA Victor GB-10472	Annie's Song/Cool An' Green An' Shady	1975	—	—	3.00
—Gold Standard Series					
❑ RCA Victor GB-10473	Back Home Again/It's Up to You	1975	—	—	3.00
—Gold Standard Series					
❑ RCA Victor GB-10474	Sunshine on My Shoulders/Around and Around	1975	—	—	3.00
—Gold Standard Series					
❑ RCA Victor GB-10475	Farewell Andromeda (Welcome to My Morning)/ Whiskey Basin Blues	1975	—	—	3.00
—Gold Standard Series					
❑ RCA Victor GB-10476	Thank God I'm a Country Boy/My Sweet Lady	1975	—	—	3.00
—Gold Standard Series					
❑ RCA Victor GB-10477	Rocky Mountain High/Spring	1975	—	—	3.00
—Gold Standard Series					
❑ RCA Victor GB-10478	Sweet Surrender/Summer	1975	—	—	3.00
—Gold Standard Series					
❑ RCA Victor PB-10517	Fly Away/Two Shots	1975	—	2.00	4.00
❑ RCA Victor PB-10586	Looking for Space/Windsong	1976	—	2.00	4.00
❑ RCA Victor PB-10687	It Makes Me Giggle/Spirit	1976	—	2.00	4.00
❑ Windstar 75720	Country Girl in Paris/Bread and Roses	1988	—	2.50	5.00
Albums					
❑ HJD 66	John Denver Sings	1966	125.00	250.00	500.00
—Private issue of 300 or so, made by JD as Christmas gifts to friends.					
❑ Mercury SRM-1-704	Beginnings	1972	5.00	10.00	20.00
—With illustration on cover					
❑ RCA 7624-1-R	Back Home Again	1988	2.50	5.00	10.00
—Last vinyl reissue					
❑ RCA 7631-1-R	Poems, Prayers and Promises	1988	2.50	5.00	10.00
—Last vinyl reissue					
❑ RCA 7632-1-R	Rocky Mountain High	1988	2.50	5.00	10.00
—Last vinyl reissue					
❑ RCA Victor APL1-0101	Farewell Andromeda	1973	3.00	6.00	12.00
—Orange label					
❑ RCA Victor CPL1-0374	John Denver's Greatest Hits	1974	2.50	5.00	10.00
—Orange label					
❑ RCA Victor CPL1-0548	Back Home Again	1974	2.50	5.00	10.00
—Orange or tan label					
❑ RCA Victor CPL2-0764 [(2)]	An Evening with John Denver	1975	3.00	6.00	12.00
—Orange or tan labels					
❑ RCA Victor APL1-1183	Windsong	1975	2.50	5.00	10.00
—Tan label					
❑ RCA Victor APL1-1201	Rocky Mountain Christmas	1975	2.50	5.00	10.00
—Tan label					
❑ RCA Victor APL2-1263 [(2)]	The John Denver Gift Pak	1974	7.50	15.00	30.00
—Contains "Rocky Mountain Christmas" and "Windsong" in a special Christmas sleeve.					
❑ RCA Victor APL1-1694	Spirit	1976	2.50	5.00	10.00
—Originals are black label, dog near top					
❑ RCA Victor CPL1-2195	John Denver's Greatest Hits, Volume 2	1977	2.50	5.00	10.00
❑ RCA Victor AFL1-2521	I Want to Live	1977	2.00	4.00	8.00
❑ RCA Victor AQL1-3075	John Denver	1979	2.00	4.00	8.00
❑ RCA Victor AQL1-3449	Autograph	1980	2.00	4.00	8.00
❑ RCA Victor AFL1-4055	Some Days Are Diamonds	1981	2.00	4.00	8.00
❑ RCA Victor LSP-4207	Rhymes & Reasons	1969	3.75	7.50	15.00
—Orange label, non-flexible vinyl					
❑ RCA Victor AFL1-4256	Seasons of the Heart	1982	2.00	4.00	8.00
❑ RCA Victor LSP-4278	Take Me to Tomorrow	1970	3.75	7.50	15.00
—Orange label, non-flexible vinyl					
❑ RCA Victor LSP-4414	Whose Garden Was This?	1970	3.75	7.50	15.00
—Orange label, non-flexible vinyl					
❑ RCA Victor LSP-4499	Poems, Prayers and Promises	1971	3.00	6.00	12.00
—Orange label					
❑ RCA Victor LSP-4607	Aerie	1971	3.00	6.00	12.00
—Orange label					
❑ RCA Victor AFL1-4683	It's About Time	1983	2.00	4.00	8.00
❑ RCA Victor LSP-4731	Rocky Mountain High	1972	3.00	6.00	12.00
—Orange label					
❑ RCA Victor AYL1-5189	Poems, Prayers and Promises	198?	—	3.00	6.00
—"Best Buy Series" reissue					
❑ RCA Victor AYL1-5190	Rocky Mountain High	198?	—	3.00	6.00
—"Best Buy Series" reissue					
❑ RCA Victor AYL1-5191	Windsong	198?	—	3.00	6.00
—"Best Buy Series" reissue					
❑ RCA Victor AYL1-5192	I Want to Live	198?	—	3.00	6.00
—"Best Buy Series" reissue					
❑ RCA Victor AYL1-5193	Back Home Again	198?	—	3.00	6.00
—"Best Buy Series" reissue					

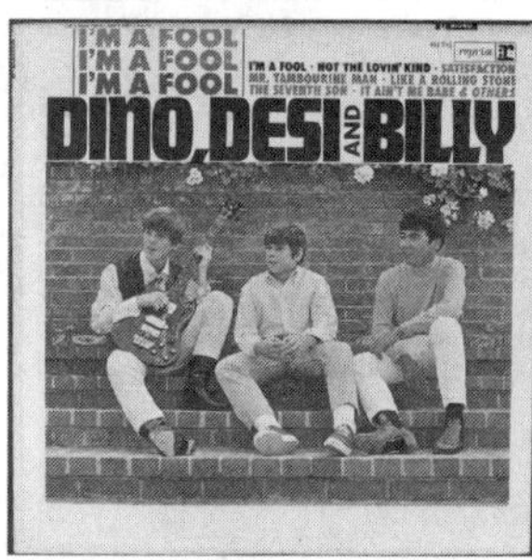

Number	Title (A Side/B Side)	Yr	VG	VG+	NM
❑ RCA Victor AYL1-5194	Spirit	198?	—	3.00	6.00
—"Best Buy Series" reissue					
❑ RCA Victor AYL1-5195	Farewell Andromeda	198?	—	3.00	6.00
—"Best Buy Series" reissue					
❑ RCA Victor AJL1-5313	John Denver's Greatest Hits, Volume 3	1984	2.00	4.00	8.00
❑ RCA Victor AFL1-5458	Dreamland Express	1985	2.00	4.00	8.00
❑ RCA Victor AFL1-5811	One World	1986	2.00	4.00	8.00

DENVER, JOHN, AND THE NITTY GRITTY DIRT BAND

45s

Number	Title (A Side/B Side)	Yr	VG	VG+	NM
❑ Universal UVL-66008	And So It Goes/Amazing Grace	1989	—	2.00	4.00

DEREK AND THE DOMINOS

45s

Number	Title (A Side/B Side)	Yr	VG	VG+	NM
❑ Atco 6780	Tell the Truth/Roll It Over	1970	12.50	25.00	50.00
—Yellow and white label stock copy; withdrawn shortly after release, this is much rarer than promos					
❑ Atco 6803	Bell Bottom Blues/Keep On Growing	1971	2.50	5.00	10.00
❑ Atco 6809	Layla (2:43)/I Am Yours	1971	2.50	5.00	10.00
❑ Atco 6809	Layla (7:10)/I Am Yours	1972	—	3.00	6.00
❑ RSO 400	Presence of the Lord/Why Does Love Got to Be So Sad	1973	—	3.00	6.00

Albums

Number	Title (A Side/B Side)	Yr	VG	VG+	NM
❑ Atco SD 2-704 [(2)S]	Layla and Other Assorted Love Songs	1970	7.50	15.00	30.00
❑ Polydor PD2-3501 [(2)]	Layla and Other Assorted Love Songs	1972	5.00	10.00	20.00
❑ RSO RS-2-3801 [(2)]	Layla and Other Assorted Love Songs	1977	3.75	7.50	15.00
❑ RSO SO 2-8800 [(2)]	Derek and the Dominos in Concert	1973	5.00	10.00	20.00
❑ RSO 823277-1 [(2)]	Layla and Other Assorted Love Songs	1985	3.00	6.00	12.00

DESHANNON, JACKIE

45s

Number	Title (A Side/B Side)	Yr	VG	VG+	NM
❑ Amherst 725	I Don't Think I Can Wait/Don't Let the Flame Burn Out	1978	3.00	6.00	12.00
❑ Amherst 728	To Love Somebody/Just to Feel This Love from You	1978	3.00	6.00	12.00
❑ Amherst 733	You're the Only Dancer/Tonight You're Doin' It Right	1979	3.00	6.00	12.00
❑ Amherst 737	Things We Said Today/Way Above the Angels	1979	3.00	6.00	12.00
❑ Atlantic 2871	Only Love Can Break Your Heart/Vanilla Olay	1972	2.50	5.00	10.00
❑ Atlantic 2895	I Wanna Roo You/Paradise	1972	2.50	5.00	10.00
❑ Atlantic 2919	Sweet Sixteen/Speak Out to Me	1972	2.50	5.00	10.00
❑ Atlantic 2924	Chains on My Soul/Peaceful in My Soul	1972	2.50	5.00	10.00
❑ Atlantic 2994	Your Baby Is a Lady/(If You Never Have a Big Hit Record) You're Still Gonna Be My Star	1973	2.50	5.00	10.00
❑ Atlantic 3041	You've Changed/Jimmie, Just Sing Me One More Song	1974	2.50	5.00	10.00
❑ Capitol 3130	Salinas/Keep Me Warm	1971	2.50	5.00	10.00
❑ Capitol 3185	Stone Cold Soul/West Virginia Mine	1971	2.50	5.00	10.00
❑ Columbia 10221	Boat to Sail/Let the Sailors Dance	1975	3.75	7.50	15.00
—With Brian Wilson on backing vocal					
❑ Columbia 10340	Fire in the City/All Night Desire	1976	2.50	5.00	10.00
❑ Dot 15928	Cajun Blues/Just Another Lie	1959	6.25	12.50	25.00
—As "Jackie Shannon"					
❑ Dot 15980	Trouble/Lies	1959	6.25	12.50	25.00
—As "Jackie Shannon"					
❑ Edison International 416	I Wanna Go Home/So Warm	1960	25.00	50.00	100.00
❑ Edison International 418	Put My Baby Down/The Foolish One	1960	25.00	50.00	100.00
❑ Gone 5008	How Wrong I Was/I'll Be True	1957	7.50	15.00	30.00
—As "Jackie Dee"					
❑ Imperial 66110	What the World Needs Now Is Love/I Remember the Boy	1965	2.00	4.00	8.00
❑ Imperial 66132	A Lifetime of Loneliness/Don't Turn Your Back on Me	1965	—	3.00	6.00
❑ Imperial 66171	Come and Get Me/Splendor in the Grass	1966	—	3.00	6.00
❑ Imperial 66194	Will You Love Me Tomorrow/Are You Ready for This	1966	—	3.00	6.00
❑ Imperial 66196	So Long Johnny/Windows and Doors	1966	—	3.00	6.00
❑ Imperial 66202	I Can Make It with You/To Be Myself	1966	—	3.00	6.00
❑ Imperial 66224	Come On Down/Find Me Love	1967	—	3.00	6.00
❑ Imperial 66236	Where Does the Sun Go/Wishing Doll	1967	—	3.00	6.00
❑ Imperial 66251	It's All in the Game/Changin' My Mind	1967	—	3.00	6.00
❑ Imperial 66281	Me About You/I Keep Wanting You	1968	—	3.00	6.00
❑ Imperial 66301	Nobody's Home to Go Home To/Nicole	1968	—	3.00	6.00
❑ Imperial 66312	Didn't Want to Have to Do It/Splendor in the Grass	1968	—	3.00	6.00
❑ Imperial 66313	The Weight/Splendor in the Grass	1968	—	3.00	6.00
❑ Imperial 66342	Holly Would/My Heart's Been Marching	1968	—	3.00	6.00
❑ Imperial 66370	What Is This/Trust Me	1969	—	2.50	5.00

Number	Title (A Side/B Side)	Yr	VG	VG+	NM
❑ Imperial 66385	Put a Little Love in Your Heart/Always Together	1969	—	3.00	6.00
❑ Imperial 66419	Love Will Find a Way/I Let Go Completely	1969	—	2.50	5.00
❑ Imperial 66430	One Christmas/Do You Know How Christmas Trees Are Grown	1969	—	3.00	6.00
❑ Imperial 66438	Brighton Hill/You Can Come to Me	1970	—	2.50	5.00
❑ Imperial 66452	You Keep Me Hangin' On-Hurt So Bad/What Was Your Day Like	1970	—	2.50	5.00
❑ Liberty 55148	Buddy/Strolypso Dance	1958	6.25	12.50	25.00
—As "Jackie Dee"					
❑ Liberty 55288	Lonely Girl/Teach Me	1960	3.75	7.50	15.00
❑ Liberty 55342	Think About You/Heaven Is Being with You	1961	3.75	7.50	15.00
❑ Liberty 55358	I Won't Turn You Down/Wish I Could Find a Boy	1961	3.75	7.50	15.00
❑ Liberty 55387	Baby (When You Kiss Me)/Ain't That Love	1961	3.75	7.50	15.00
❑ Liberty 55425	The Prince/I'll Drown in My Own Tears	1962	3.75	7.50	15.00
❑ Liberty 55425	The Prince/That's What Boys Are Made Of	1962	3.75	7.50	15.00
❑ Liberty 55484	Guess Who/Just Like in the Movies	1962	3.75	7.50	15.00
❑ Liberty 55497	You Won't Forget Me/I Don't Think So Much of Myself	1962	3.75	7.50	15.00
❑ Liberty 55526	Faded Love/Dancing Silhouettes	1962	3.75	7.50	15.00
❑ Liberty 55563	Needles and Pins/Did He Call Today, Mama?	1963	3.75	7.50	15.00
❑ Liberty 55602	Little Yellow Roses/500 Miles	1963	3.75	7.50	15.00
❑ Liberty 55602	Little Yellow Roses/Oh Sweet Chariot	1963	3.75	7.50	15.00
❑ Liberty 55645	When You Walk in the Room/Til You Say You're Mine	1963	3.75	7.50	15.00
❑ Liberty 55673	I'm Gonna Be Strong/Should I Cry	1964	3.75	7.50	15.00
❑ Liberty 55678	Oh Boy/I'm Looking for Someone to Love	1964	3.75	7.50	15.00
❑ Liberty 55705	Hold Your Head High/She Don't Understand Him Like I Do	1964	3.75	7.50	15.00
❑ Liberty 55730	He's Got the Whole World in His Hands/It's Love Baby	1964	3.75	7.50	15.00
❑ Liberty 55735	When You Walk in the Room/Over You	1964	3.00	6.00	12.00
❑ Liberty 55787	What the World Needs Now Is Love/A Lifetime of Loneliness	1965	—	—	—
—Unreleased					
❑ Liberty 56187	Mediterranean Sky/It's So Nice	1970	—	3.00	6.00
❑ PJ 101	Trouble/Lies	1959	10.00	20.00	40.00
—As "Jackie Shannon"					
❑ RCA PB-11902	I Don't Need You Anymore/Find Love	1980	—	2.50	5.00
❑ Sage and Sand 290	Just Another Lie/Cajun Blues	1960	6.25	12.50	25.00
❑ Sage and Sand 330	Trouble/Lies	1960	6.25	12.50	25.00
❑ United Artists 0033	What the World Needs Now Is Love/Needles and Pins	1973	—	3.00	6.00
—"Silver Spotlight Series" reissue					
❑ United Artists 0034	Put a Little Love in Your Heart/When You Walk in the Room	1973	—	3.00	6.00
—"Silver Spotlight Series" reissue					
Albums					
❑ Amherst AMX 1010	You're the Only Dancer	1977	3.00	6.00	12.00
❑ Amherst AMH 1016	Quick Touches	1978	3.00	6.00	12.00
❑ Atlantic SD 7231	Jackie	1972	3.00	6.00	12.00
❑ Atlantic SD 7303	Your Baby Is a Lady	1974	3.00	6.00	12.00
❑ Capitol ST-772	Songs	1971	3.00	6.00	12.00
❑ Columbia PC 33500	New Arrangement	1975	3.00	6.00	12.00
❑ Imperial LP-9286 [M]	This Is Jackie DeShannon	1965	5.00	10.00	20.00
—Black and pink label					
❑ Imperial LP-9294 [M]	You Won't Forget Me	1965	5.00	10.00	20.00
—Black and pink label					
❑ Imperial LP-9296 [M]	In the Wind	1965	5.00	10.00	20.00
—Black and pink label					
❑ Imperial LP-9328 [M]	Are You Ready for This?	1966	3.75	7.50	15.00
❑ Imperial LP-9344 [M]	New Image	1967	3.75	7.50	15.00
❑ Imperial LP-9352 [M]	For You	1967	3.75	7.50	15.00
❑ Imperial LP-12286 [S]	This Is Jackie DeShannon	1965	6.25	12.50	25.00
—Black and pink label					
❑ Imperial LP-12294 [S]	You Won't Forget Me	1965	6.25	12.50	25.00
—Black and pink label					
❑ Imperial LP-12296 [S]	In the Wind	1965	6.25	12.50	25.00
—Black and pink label					
❑ Imperial LP-12328 [S]	Are You Ready for This?	1966	5.00	10.00	20.00
❑ Imperial LP-12344 [S]	New Image	1967	5.00	10.00	20.00
❑ Imperial LP-12352 [S]	For You	1967	5.00	10.00	20.00
❑ Imperial LP-12386	Me About You	1968	3.75	7.50	15.00
❑ Imperial LP-12404	What the World Needs Now Is Love	1968	3.75	7.50	15.00
❑ Imperial LP-12415	Laurel Canyon	1969	3.75	7.50	15.00
❑ Imperial LP-12442	Put a Little Love in Your Heart	1969	3.75	7.50	15.00
❑ Imperial LP-12453	To Be Free	1970	3.75	7.50	15.00
❑ Liberty LRP-3320 [M]	Jackie DeShannon	1963	10.00	20.00	40.00
❑ Liberty LRP-3390 [M]	Breakin' It Up on the Beatles Tour!	1964	10.00	20.00	40.00
❑ Liberty LST-7320 [S]	Jackie DeShannon	1963	12.50	25.00	50.00
❑ Liberty LST-7390 [S]	Breakin' It Up on the Beatles Tour!	1964	12.50	25.00	50.00
❑ Liberty LN-10179	The Very Best of Jackie DeShannon	1983	2.00	4.00	8.00
—Reissue of United Artists 434					
❑ Liberty LN-10265	Jackie DeShannon	1985	2.00	4.00	8.00
❑ Sunset SUS-5225	Lonely Girl	1968	3.00	6.00	12.00
❑ Sunset SUS-5322	Jackie DeShannon	1970	3.00	6.00	12.00
❑ United Artists UA-LA434-E	The Very Best of Jackie DeShannon	1975	3.00	6.00	12.00

DETERGENTS, THE

45s

Number	Title (A Side/B Side)	Yr	VG	VG+	NM
❑ Kapp 735	I Can Never Eat Home Anymore/Igor's Cellar	1966	3.75	7.50	15.00
❑ Kapp 753	Pushin' the Panic Button/Some Sunday Morning	1966	3.75	7.50	15.00
❑ Roulette 4590	Leader of the Laundromat/Ulcers	1964	5.00	10.00	20.00
❑ Roulette 4603	Double-O-Seven/The Blue Kangaroo	1965	3.75	7.50	15.00
❑ Roulette 4616	Tea and Trumpets/Mrs. Jones (How 'Bout It)	1965	3.75	7.50	15.00
❑ Roulette 4626	Little Dum-Dum/Soldier Girl	1965	3.75	7.50	15.00
❑ Roulette 4642	Bad Girl/Here She Comes	1965	3.75	7.50	15.00

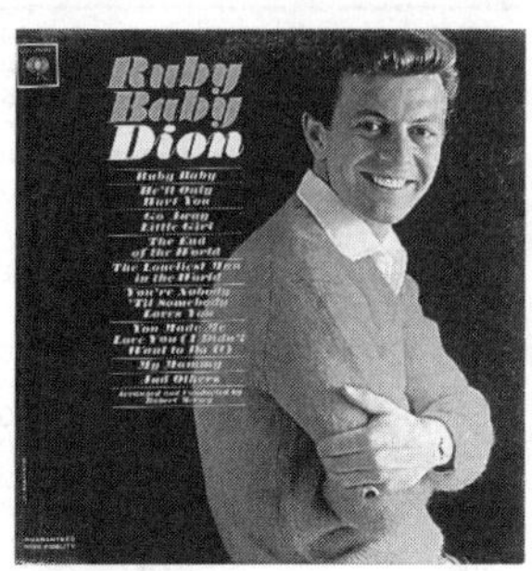

Number	Title (A Side/B Side)	Yr	VG	VG+	NM
Albums					
❑ Roulette R 25308 [M]	The Many Faces of the Detergents	1965	30.00	60.00	120.00
❑ Roulette SR 25308 [R]	The Many Faces of the Detergents	1965	25.00	50.00	100.00
DEVO					
45s					
❑ Backstreet 52215	Theme from Doctor Detroit/King of Soul	1983	—	—	3.00
—B-side by James Brown					
❑ Booji Boy 7033-14	Jocko Homo/Mongoloid	1977	2.00	4.00	8.00
❑ Booji Boy 72843/75677	Satisfaction/Sloppy	1978	—	—	3.00
❑ Enigma 75023	Disco Dancer/Disco Dancer	1989	—	—	3.00
❑ Enigma 75029	Baby Doll (Ivan Ivan Mix)/Baby Doll (Devo Mix)	1988	—	—	3.00
❑ Full Moon/Asylum 47204	Working in the Coal Mine/Planet Earth	1981	—	—	3.00
❑ Warner Bros. GWB 0400	Whip It/Girl U Want	198?	—	—	3.00
—Back to Back Hits series					
❑ Warner Bros. EP 3595	Working in the Coal Mine (same on both sides)	1981	—	—	3.00
—Issued with the New Traditionalists LP					
❑ Warner Bros. 8675	(I Can't Get No) Satisfaction/Uncontrollable Urge	1978	—	—	3.00
❑ Warner Bros. 8745	Come Back Jonee/Praying Hands	1979	—	—	3.00
❑ Warner Bros. 29133	Are You Experienced/Growing Pains	1984	—	—	3.00
❑ Warner Bros. 29811	That's Good/What I Must Do	1983	—	—	3.00
❑ Warner Bros. 29931	Peek-A-Boo/Find Out	1982	—	—	3.00
❑ Warner Bros. 49028	Secret Agent Man/Red Eye	1979	—	—	3.00
❑ Warner Bros. 49524	Girl U Want/Mr. B's Ballroom	1980	—	—	3.00
❑ Warner Bros. 49550	Whip It/Turn Around	1980	—	—	3.00
❑ Warner Bros. 49621	Freedom of Choice/Snowball (Remix)	1980	—	—	3.00
❑ Warner Bros. 49715	Gates of Steel (Live)/Be Still (Live)	1981	—	—	3.00
❑ Warner Bros. 49834	Beautiful World/Enough Said	1981	—	—	3.00
❑ Warner Bros. 50010	Jerkin' Back 'N' Forth/Mecha Mania Boy	1982	—	—	3.00
❑ Warner Bros. 50048	Through Being Cool/Going Under	1982	—	—	3.00
Albums					
❑ Dutch East India DE-112008-1	Smooth Noodle Maps	1991	3.75	7.50	15.00
—Red vinyl, 1,000 copies pressed					
❑ Enigma 73303	Total Devo	1988	2.50	5.00	10.00
❑ Enigma 73514	Now It Can Be Told!	1989	2.50	5.00	10.00
❑ Warner Bros. BSK 3239	Q: Are We Not Men? A: We Are Devo!	1978	2.50	5.00	10.00
❑ Warner Bros. BSK 3337	Duty Now for the Future	1979	2.50	5.00	10.00
❑ Warner Bros. BSK 3435	Freedom of Choice	1980	2.50	5.00	10.00
❑ Warner Bros. MINI 3548 [EP]	Dev-O Live	1981	2.50	5.00	10.00
—All copies came in plastic sleeve					
❑ Warner Bros. BSK 3595	New Traditionalists	1981	3.75	7.50	15.00
—First pressings include bonus 45 (EP 3595) and poster; deduct 1/3 if missing					
❑ Warner Bros. 23741	Oh No! It's Devo	1982	2.50	5.00	10.00
❑ Warner Bros. 25097	Shout	1984	2.50	5.00	10.00
DIAMOND, NEIL					
45s					
❑ Bang 105	Cherry, Cherry/Girl, You'll Be a Woman Soon	1973	—	2.00	4.00
—Reissue					
❑ Bang 108	Solitary Man/I'm a Believer	1973	—	2.00	4.00
—Reissue					
❑ Bang 519	Solitary Man/Do It	1966	3.75	7.50	15.00
❑ Bang 528	Cherry, Cherry/I'll Come Running	1966	3.00	6.00	12.00
❑ Bang 536	I Got the Feelin' (Oh No No)/The Boat That I Row	1966	3.00	6.00	12.00
❑ Bang 540	You Got to Me/Someday Baby	1967	3.00	6.00	12.00
❑ Bang 542	Girl, You'll Be a Woman Soon/You'll Forget	1967	3.00	6.00	12.00
❑ Bang 547	Thank the Lord for the Night Time/The Long Way Home	1967	2.50	5.00	10.00
—Title altered on second pressing					
❑ Bang 547	I Thank the Lord for the Night Time/The Long Way Home	1967	3.75	7.50	15.00
❑ Bang 551	Kentucky Woman/The Time Is Now	1967	2.50	5.00	10.00
❑ Bang 554	New Orleans/Hanky Panky	1968	2.50	5.00	10.00
❑ Bang 556	Red Red Wine/Red Rubber Ball	1968	2.00	4.00	8.00
❑ Bang 561	Shilo/La Bamba	1968	2.00	4.00	8.00
❑ Bang 575	Shilo/La Bamba	1970	—	3.00	6.00
❑ Bang 578	Solitary Man/The Time Is Now	1970	—	3.00	6.00

Number	Title (A Side/B Side)	Yr	VG	VG+	NM
❑ Bang 580	Do It/Hanky Panky	1970	—	3.00	6.00
❑ Bang 586	I'm a Believer/Crooked Street	1971	—	3.00	6.00
❑ Bang 703	The Long Way Home/Monday, Monday	1973	—	2.50	5.00
❑ Capitol 4939	Love on the Rocks/Acapulco	1980	—	2.00	4.00
❑ Capitol 4960	Hello Again/Amazed and Confused	1981	—	2.00	4.00
❑ Capitol 4994	America/Songs of Life	1981	—	2.00	4.00
❑ Columbia 18-02604	Yesterday's Songs/Guitar Heaven	1981	—	—	3.00
❑ Columbia 18-02712	On the Way to the Sky/Save Me	1982	—	—	3.00
❑ Columbia 18-02928	Be Mine Tonight/Right By You	1982	—	—	3.00
❑ Columbia 38-03219	Heartlight/You Don't Know Me	1982	—	—	3.00
❑ Columbia CNR-03345	Heartlight/(B-side blank)	1982	—	3.00	6.00
—One-sided budget release					
❑ Columbia 38-03503	I'm Alive/Lost Among the Stars	1983	—	—	3.00
❑ Columbia CNR-03572	I'm Alive/(B-side blank)	1983	—	3.00	6.00
—One-sided budget release					
❑ Columbia 38-03801	Front Page Story/I'm Guilty	1983	—	—	3.00
❑ Columbia 38-04541	Turn Around/Brooklyn on a Saturday Night	1984	—	—	3.00
❑ Columbia 38-04646	Sleep with Me Tonight/One by One	1984	—	2.00	4.00
❑ Columbia 38-04719	You Make It Feel Like Christmas/Crazy	1984	—	3.00	6.00
❑ Columbia 38-05889	Headed for the Future/Angel	1986	—	—	3.00
❑ Columbia 38-06136	The Story of My Life/Love Doesn't Live Here Anymore	1986	—	—	3.00
❑ Columbia 38-07614	I Dreamed a Dream/Sweet Caroline	1987	—	—	3.00
❑ Columbia 38-07751	Cherry, Cherry/America	1988	—	2.00	4.00
❑ Columbia 38-08514	This Time/If I Couldn't See You Again	1988	—	2.00	4.00
❑ Columbia 10043	Longfellow Serenade/Rosemary's Wine	1974	—	2.50	5.00
❑ Columbia 10084	I've Been This Way Before/Reggae Strut	1975	—	2.50	5.00
❑ Columbia 10138	The Last Picasso/The Gift of Song	1975	—	2.50	5.00
❑ Columbia 3-10366	If You Know What I Mean/Street Life	1976	—	2.50	5.00
❑ Columbia 3-10405	Don't Think...Feel/Home Is a Wounded Heart	1976	—	2.50	5.00
❑ Columbia 3-10452	Beautiful Noise/Signs	1976	—	2.50	5.00
❑ Columbia 3-10657	Desiree/Once in a While	1977	—	2.50	5.00
❑ Columbia 3-10897	Forever in Blue Jeans/Remember Me	1979	—	2.00	4.00
❑ Columbia 3-10945	Say Maybe/Diamond Girls	1979	—	2.00	4.00
❑ Columbia 1-11175	September Morn/I'm a Believer	1980	—	2.00	4.00
❑ Columbia 1-11232	The Good Lord Loves You/Jazz Time	1980	—	2.00	4.00
❑ Columbia 42809	Clown Town/At Night	1963	125.00	250.00	500.00
❑ Columbia 45942	Be/Flight of the Gull	1973	—	2.50	5.00
❑ Columbia 45998	Skybird/Lonely Looking Sky	1974	—	2.50	5.00
❑ Columbia 38-68741	The Best Years of Our Lives/Carmelita's Eyes	1989	—	2.00	4.00
❑ MCA 40017	Cherry, Cherry from Hot August Night/Morningside	1973	—	2.50	5.00
❑ MCA 40092	The Last Thing on My Mind/Canta Libra	1973	—	2.50	5.00
❑ Uni 55065	Brooklyn Roads/Holiday Inn Blues	1968	2.00	4.00	8.00
❑ Uni 55075	Two-Bit Manchild/Broad Old Woman	1968	2.00	4.00	8.00
❑ Uni 55084	Sunday Sun/Honey-Drippin' Times	1968	2.00	4.00	8.00
❑ Uni 55109	Brother Love's Travelling Salvation Show/ A Modern-Day Version of Love	1969	—	3.00	6.00
❑ Uni 55136	Sweet Caroline (Good Times Never Seemed So Good)/Dig In	1969	—	3.00	6.00
❑ Uni 55175	Holly Holy/Hurtin' You Don't Come Easy	1969	—	3.00	6.00
❑ Uni 55204	Until It's Time for You to Go/And the Singer Sings His Song	1970	—	3.00	6.00
❑ Uni 55224	Soolaimon (African Trilogy II)/And the Grass Won't Pay No Mind	1970	—	3.00	6.00
❑ Uni 55250	Cracklin' Rosie/Lordy	1970	—	3.00	6.00
❑ Uni 55264	He Ain't Heavy...He's My Brother/Free Life	1970	—	3.00	6.00
❑ Uni 55278	I Am...I Said/Done Too Soon	1971	—	2.50	5.00
❑ Uni 55310	Stones/Crunchy Granola Suite	1971	—	2.50	5.00
❑ Uni 55326	Song Sung Blue/Gitchy Goomy	1972	—	2.50	5.00
❑ Uni 55346	Play Me/Porcupine Pie	1972	—	2.50	5.00
❑ Uni 55352	Walk on Water/High Rolling Man	1972	—	2.50	5.00
Albums					
❑ Bang BLP 214 [M]	The Feel of Neil Diamond	1966	15.00	30.00	60.00
—All tracks play mono					
❑ Bang BLP 214 [P]	The Feel of Neil Diamond	1966	20.00	40.00	80.00
—Album is labeled mono, but plays in stereo					
❑ Bang BLPS 214 [P]	The Feel of Neil Diamond	1966	25.00	50.00	100.00
—Album is labeled stereo and plays in stereo (except "Solitary Man," "Do It," "I'll Come Running" are rechanneled)					
❑ Bang BLP 217 [M]	Just for You	1967	10.00	20.00	40.00
—With blurb for "Thank the Lord for the Night Time" on cover					
❑ Bang BLPS 217 [P]	Just for You	1967	12.50	25.00	50.00
—With blurb for "Thank the Lord for the Night Time" on cover					
❑ Bang BLPS 219 [P]	Neil Diamond's Greatest Hits	1968	10.00	20.00	40.00
—First editions have the single version of "Solitary Man" in rechanneled stereo					
❑ Bang BLPS 221 [S]	Shilo	1970	10.00	20.00	40.00
❑ Bang BLPS 224 [P]	Do It!	1971	7.50	15.00	30.00
❑ Bang BLPS-227 [(2)S]	Double Gold	1973	10.00	20.00	40.00
❑ Capitol SWAV-12120	The Jazz Singer	1980	2.50	5.00	10.00
❑ Columbia KS 32550	Jonathan Livingston Seagull	1973	3.00	6.00	12.00
—With booklet					
❑ Columbia PC 32919	Serenade	1974	3.00	6.00	12.00
❑ Columbia PC 33965	Beautiful Noise	1976	3.00	6.00	12.00
—Originals have no bar code					
❑ Columbia KC2 34404 [(2)]	Love at the Greek	1977	3.75	7.50	15.00
❑ Columbia JC 34990	I'm Glad You're Here with Me Tonight	1977	3.00	6.00	12.00
❑ Columbia FC 35625	You Don't Bring Me Flowers	1978	3.00	6.00	12.00
❑ Columbia FC 36121	September Morn	1979	3.00	6.00	12.00
❑ Columbia TC 37628	On the Way to the Sky	1981	2.50	5.00	10.00
❑ Columbia TC 38068	12 Greatest Hits, Vol. II	1982	2.50	5.00	10.00
❑ Columbia TC 38359	Heartlight	1982	2.50	5.00	10.00

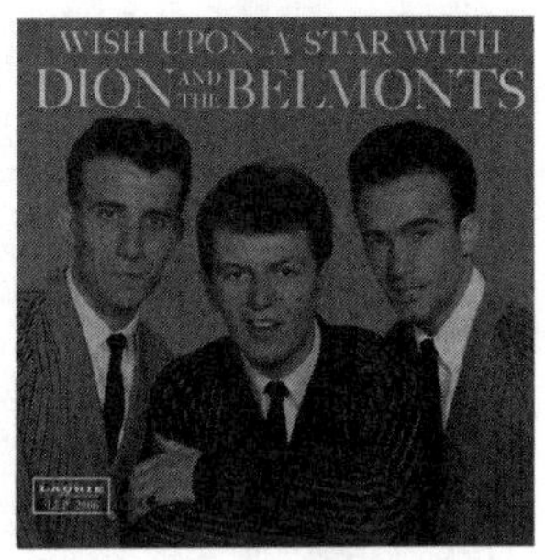

Number	Title (A Side/B Side)	Yr	VG	VG+	NM
❑ Columbia PC 38792	Classics — The Early Years	1983	2.50	5.00	10.00
—Possibly a reissue of Frog King 1					
❑ Columbia QC 39199	Primitive	1984	2.50	5.00	10.00
❑ Columbia OC 40368	Headed for the Future	1986	2.00	4.00	8.00
❑ Columbia CG2 40990 [(2)]	Hot August Night II	1987	3.00	6.00	12.00
❑ Columbia OC 45025	The Best Years of Our Lives	1988	2.00	4.00	8.00
❑ Columbia C 48610	Lovescape	1991	6.25	12.50	25.00
❑ Columbia 8-2876-77507-1 [(2)]	12 Songs	2006	5.00	10.00	20.00
❑ Frog King AAR-1	Early Classics	1972	10.00	20.00	40.00
—Compilation of Bang material for Columbia Record Club; includes songbook (deduct 25% if missing)					
❑ MCA 1489	Neil Diamond/His 12 Greatest Hits	1987	2.00	4.00	8.00
—Reissue of MCA 5219					
❑ MCA 2005	Moods	1973	2.50	5.00	10.00
❑ MCA 2006	Touching You Touching Me	1973	2.50	5.00	10.00
❑ MCA 2007	Neil Diamond/Gold	1973	2.50	5.00	10.00
❑ MCA 2008	Stones	1973	2.50	5.00	10.00
❑ MCA 2011	Sweet Caroline (Brother Love's Travelling Salvation Show)	1973	2.50	5.00	10.00
❑ MCA 2013	Tap Root Manuscript	1973	2.50	5.00	10.00
❑ MCA 2103	Rainbow	1973	3.75	7.50	15.00
—Compilation of Uni tracks					
❑ MCA 2106	Neil Diamond/His 12 Greatest Hits	1974	3.75	7.50	15.00
❑ MCA 2227	And the Singer Sings His Song	1976	3.75	7.50	15.00
❑ MCA 5219	Neil Diamond/His 12 Greatest Hits	1981	2.50	5.00	10.00
—Reissue of MCA 2106					
❑ MCA 5239	Love Songs	1981	2.50	5.00	10.00
❑ MCA 6896 [(2)]	Hot August Night	1980	3.00	6.00	12.00
—Reissue of MCA 2-8000					
❑ MCA 8000 [(2)]	Hot August Night	1972	5.00	10.00	20.00
❑ MCA 37056	Velvet Gloves and Spit	1980	2.00	4.00	8.00
❑ MCA 37057	Sweet Caroline/Brother Love's Travelling Salvation Show	1980	2.00	4.00	8.00
❑ MCA 37058	Touching You Touching Me	1980	2.00	4.00	8.00
❑ MCA 37059	Rainbow	1980	2.00	4.00	8.00
❑ MCA 37060	And the Singer Sings His Song	1980	2.00	4.00	8.00
❑ MCA 37194	Moods	1981	2.00	4.00	8.00
❑ MCA 37195	Stones	1981	2.00	4.00	8.00
❑ MCA 37196	Tap Root Manuscript	1981	2.00	4.00	8.00
❑ MCA 37209	Gold	1981	2.00	4.00	8.00
❑ MCA 37252	Neil Diamond/His 12 Greatest Hits	198?	2.00	4.00	8.00
—Reissue of MCA 5219					
❑ Silver Eagle MSM-35151 [(3)]	The Neil Diamond Collection	1988	6.25	12.50	25.00
—Mail-order offer; contains material from his Uni period					
❑ Uni 73030	Velvet Gloves and Spit	1968	7.50	15.00	30.00
—First editions do not include "Shilo"					
❑ Uni 73047	Brother Love's Travelling Salvation Show	1969	7.50	15.00	30.00
—First editions do not include "Sweet Caroline"					
❑ Uni 73071	Touching You Touching Me	1969	5.00	10.00	20.00
❑ Uni 73084	Neil Diamond/Gold	1970	5.00	10.00	20.00
❑ Uni 73092	Tap Root Manuscript	1970	5.00	10.00	20.00
❑ Uni 93106	Stones	1971	5.00	10.00	20.00
❑ Uni 93136	Moods	1972	5.00	10.00	20.00

DIAMONDS, THE (1)

The group on Atlantic is a different group than those below, and are outside the scope of this book.

45s

Number	Title (A Side/B Side)	Yr	VG	VG+	NM
❑ Coral 61502	Black Denim Trousers and Motorcycle Boots/Nip Sip	1955	5.00	10.00	20.00
❑ Coral 61577	Be My Lovin' Baby/Smooch Me	1956	5.00	10.00	20.00
❑ Gusto 2019	Little Darlin'/The Stroll	1979	—	2.00	4.00
—Re-recordings					
❑ Mercury 70790	Why Do Fools Fall in Love/You Baby You	1956	5.00	10.00	20.00
❑ Mercury 70835	The Church Bells May Ring/Little Girl of Mine	1956	5.00	10.00	20.00
❑ Mercury 70889	Love, Love, Love/Every Night About This Time	1956	5.00	10.00	20.00
❑ Mercury 70934	Ka-Ding-Dong/Soft Summer Breeze	1956	5.00	10.00	20.00
❑ Mercury 70983	My Judge and My Jury/Put Your House in Order	1956	5.00	10.00	20.00
❑ Mercury 71021	A Thousand Miles Away/Ev'ry Minute of the Day	1956	5.00	10.00	20.00
❑ Mercury 71060	Little Darlin'/Faithful and True	1957	6.25	12.50	25.00
—Black label, "Mercury" and logo in double oval at top					

Number	Title (A Side/B Side)	Yr	VG	VG+	NM
❑ Mercury 71060	Little Darlin'/Faithful and True	1957	10.00	20.00	40.00
—Maroon label, "Mercury" and logo by themselves at top					
❑ Mercury 71060	Little Darlin'/Faithful and True	1957	7.50	15.00	30.00
—Maroon Label, "Mercury" and logo in double oval at top					
❑ Mercury 71128	Words of Love/Don't Say Goodbye	1957	5.00	10.00	20.00
❑ Mercury 71165	Zip Zip/Oh How I Wish	1957	5.00	10.00	20.00
❑ Mercury 71197	Silhouettes/Daddy Cool	1957	5.00	10.00	20.00
❑ Mercury 71242	The Stroll/Land of Beauty	1957	7.50	15.00	30.00
❑ Mercury 71291	High Sign/Chick-Lets (Don't Let Me Down)	1958	3.75	7.50	15.00
❑ Mercury 71330	Kathy-O/Happy Years	1958	3.75	7.50	15.00
❑ Mercury 71366	Walking Along/Eternal Lovers	1958	3.75	7.50	15.00
❑ Mercury 71404	She Say (Oom Dooby Doom)/From the Bottom of My Heart	1959	5.00	10.00	20.00
❑ Mercury 71449	A Mother's Love/Gretchen	1959	3.75	7.50	15.00
❑ Mercury 71468	Sneaky Alligator/Holding Your Hand	1959	3.75	7.50	15.00
❑ Mercury 71505	Young in Years/The Twenty-Second Day	1959	3.75	7.50	15.00
❑ Mercury 71534	Walking the Stroll/Batman, Wolfman, Frankenstein or Dracula	1959	5.00	10.00	20.00
❑ Mercury 71586	Real True Love/Tell the Truth	1960	3.75	7.50	15.00
❑ Mercury 71633	The Pencil Song/Slave Girl	1960	3.75	7.50	15.00
❑ Mercury 71734	The Crumble/You'd Be Mine	1960	3.75	7.50	15.00
❑ Mercury 71782	You Sure Changed Me/I Sure Lawd Will	1961	3.75	7.50	15.00
❑ Mercury 71818	The Munch/Woomai Ling	1961	3.75	7.50	15.00
❑ Mercury 71831	One Summer Night/It's a Doggone Shame	1961	3.75	7.50	15.00
❑ Mercury 71956	The Vanishing American/The Horizontal Lieutenant	1962	3.75	7.50	15.00
Albums					
❑ Mercury MG-20213 [M]	Collection of Golden Hits	1956	30.00	60.00	120.00
❑ Mercury MG-20309 [M]	The Diamonds	1957	30.00	60.00	120.00
❑ Mercury MG-20368 [M]	The Diamonds Meet Pete Rugolo	1958	20.00	40.00	80.00
❑ Mercury MG-20480 [M]	Songs from the Old West	1959	20.00	40.00	80.00
❑ Mercury SR-60076 [S]	The Diamonds Meet Pete Rugolo	1959	30.00	60.00	120.00
❑ Mercury SR-60159 [S]	Songs from the Old West	1959	30.00	60.00	120.00
❑ Rhino RNDF-209	The Best of the Diamonds	1984	3.00	6.00	12.00
❑ Wing MGW-12114 [M]	The Diamonds: America's Famous Song Stylists	1959	7.50	15.00	30.00
❑ Wing MGW-12178 [M]	Pop Hits by the Diamonds	1962	7.50	15.00	30.00

DICK AND DEEDEE

45s

Number	Title (A Side/B Side)	Yr	VG	VG+	NM
❑ Dot 17145	Escape Suite/I'm Not Gonna Get Hung-Up About It	1968	3.75	7.50	15.00
❑ Dot 17261	We'll Sing in the Sunshine/In the Season of Our Love	1969	2.50	5.00	10.00
❑ Dot 17305	Do I Love You/You Came Back to Haunt Me	1970	2.50	5.00	10.00
❑ Lama 7778	The Mountain's High/I Want Someone	1961	5.00	10.00	20.00
❑ Lama 7780	Goodbye to Love/Swing Low	1961	4.00	8.00	16.00
❑ Lama 7783	Tell Me/Will You Always Love Me	1961	4.00	8.00	16.00
❑ Liberty 55350	The Mountain's High/I Want Someone	1961	3.75	7.50	15.00
❑ Liberty 55382	Goodbye to Love/Swing Low	1961	3.00	6.00	12.00
❑ Liberty 55412	Tell Me/Will You Always Love Me	1962	3.00	6.00	12.00
❑ Liberty 55478	All I Want/Life's Just a Play	1962	3.00	6.00	12.00
❑ United Artists 0036	The Mountain's High/Tell Me	1973	—	2.50	5.00
—"Silver Spotlight Series" reissue					
❑ Warner Bros. 5320	The River Took My Baby/My Lonely Self	1962	2.50	5.00	10.00
❑ Warner Bros. 5342	Young and In Love/Say to Me	1963	3.00	6.00	12.00
❑ Warner Bros. 5364	Love Is a Once in a Lifetime Thing/Chug-a Chug-a Choo Choo	1963	2.50	5.00	10.00
❑ Warner Bros. 5383	Where Did the Good Times Go/Guess Our Love Must Show	1963	2.50	5.00	10.00
❑ Warner Bros. 5396	Turn Around/Don't Leave Me	1963	2.50	5.00	10.00
❑ Warner Bros. 5411	All My Trials/Don't Think Twice, It's All Right	1964	2.50	5.00	10.00
❑ Warner Bros. 5426	Not Fade Away/The Gift	1964	2.50	5.00	10.00
❑ Warner Bros. 5451	You Were Mine/Remember Then	1964	2.50	5.00	10.00
❑ Warner Bros. 5470	The Riddle Song/Without Your Love	1964	2.50	5.00	10.00
❑ Warner Bros. 5482	Thou Shalt Not Steal/Just 'Round the River Bend	1964	3.75	7.50	15.00
—Red label with arrows					
❑ Warner Bros. 5608	Be My Baby/Room 404	1965	2.50	5.00	10.00
❑ Warner Bros. 5627	Blue Turns to Grey/Some Things Just Stick in Your Mind	1965	5.00	10.00	20.00
—Both sides are Mick Jagger-Keith Richards songs produced by Andrew Loog Oldham					
❑ Warner Bros. 5652	The World Is Waiting/Vini, Vini	1965	2.50	5.00	10.00
❑ Warner Bros. 5671	P.S. 1402 (Your Local Charm School)/Use What You've Got	1965	2.50	5.00	10.00
❑ Warner Bros. 5680	New Orleans/Use What You've Got	1965	2.50	5.00	10.00
❑ Warner Bros. 5699	Till/Sha-Ta	1966	2.50	5.00	10.00
❑ Warner Bros. 5830	She Didn't Even Say Goodbye/So Many Things We Didn't Know	1966	2.50	5.00	10.00
❑ Warner Bros. 5860	Make Up Before We Break Up/Can't Get Enough of Your Love	1966	2.50	5.00	10.00
❑ Warner Bros. 7017	Long Lonely Nights/I'll Always Be Around	1967	2.50	5.00	10.00
❑ Warner Bros. 7069	One in a Million/Baby, I Need You	1967	2.50	5.00	10.00
❑ Warner Bros. 7109	Young and In Love/Thou Shalt Not Steal	1968	2.00	4.00	8.00
—"Back to Back Hits" series; originals have green labels with "W7" logo					
Albums					
❑ Liberty LRP-3236 [M]	Tell Me/The Mountain's High	1962	12.50	25.00	50.00
❑ Liberty LST-7236 [R]	Tell Me/The Mountain's High	1962	10.00	20.00	40.00
❑ Warner Bros. W 1500 [M]	Young and In Love	1963	6.25	12.50	25.00
❑ Warner Bros. WS 1500 [S]	Young and In Love	1963	7.50	15.00	30.00
❑ Warner Bros. W 1538 [M]	Turn Around	1964	6.25	12.50	25.00
❑ Warner Bros. WS 1538 [S]	Turn Around	1964	7.50	15.00	30.00
❑ Warner Bros. W 1586 [M]	Thou Shalt Not Steal	1965	6.25	12.50	25.00
❑ Warner Bros. WS 1586 [S]	Thou Shalt Not Steal	1965	7.50	15.00	30.00
❑ Warner Bros. W 1623 [M]	Song We've Sung on "Shindig"	1966	6.25	12.50	25.00
❑ Warner Bros. WS 1623 [S]	Song We've Sung on "Shindig"	1966	7.50	15.00	30.00

DINO, DESI AND BILLY

45s

Number	Title (A Side/B Side)	Yr	VG	VG+	NM
❑ Columbia 4-44975	Hawley/Let's Talk It Over	1969	3.00	6.00	12.00
❑ Reprise 0324	We Know/Since You Broke My Heart	1964	3.75	7.50	15.00

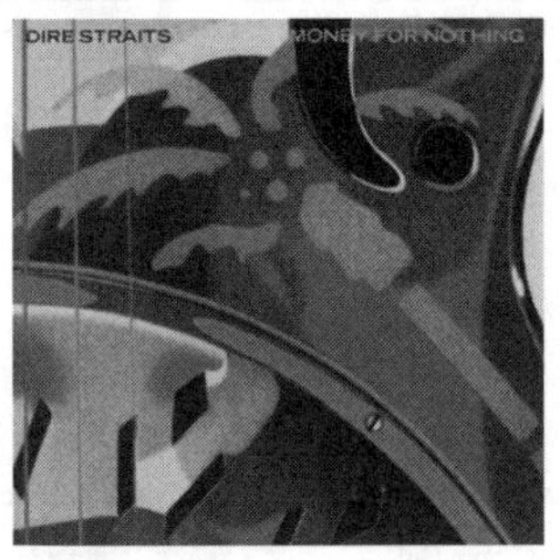

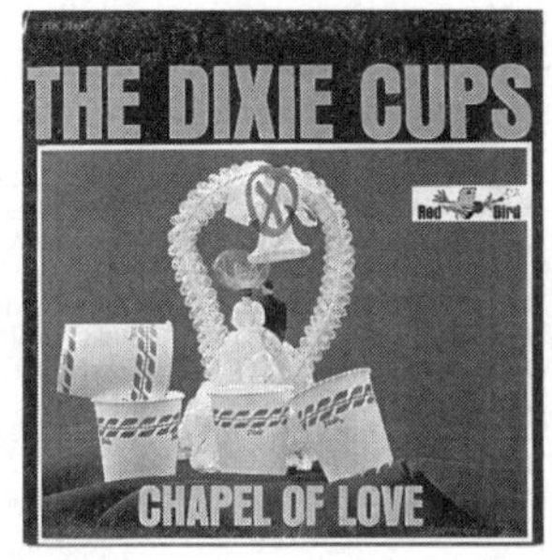

Number	Title (A Side/B Side)	Yr	VG	VG+	NM
❑ Reprise 0367	I'm a Fool/So Many Ways	1965	3.00	6.00	12.00
❑ Reprise 0401	Not the Lovin' Kind/Chimes of Freedom	1965	2.50	5.00	10.00
❑ Reprise 0426	Please Don't Fight It/The Rebel Kind	1965	2.50	5.00	10.00
❑ Reprise 0444	Superman/I Can't Get Her Out of My Mind	1966	2.00	4.00	8.00
❑ Reprise 0462	It's Just the Way You Are/Tie Me Down	1966	2.00	4.00	8.00
❑ Reprise 0496	Look Out Girls/She's So Far Out She's In	1966	2.00	4.00	8.00
❑ Reprise 0529	I Hope She's There Tonight/Josephine	1966	2.00	4.00	8.00
❑ Reprise 0544	If You're Thinkin' What I'm Thinkin'/Pretty Flamingo	1966	2.00	4.00	8.00
❑ Reprise 0579	Two in the Afternoon/Good Luck, Best Wishes to You	1967	2.50	5.00	10.00
❑ Reprise 0619	Kitty Doyle/Without Hurtin' Some	1967	2.50	5.00	10.00
❑ Reprise 0653	My What a Shame/The Inside Outside Caspar Milquetoast Eskimo Flash	1967	3.00	6.00	12.00
❑ Reprise 0698	Tell Someone You Love Them/General Outline	1968	3.00	6.00	12.00
❑ Reprise 0716	I'm a Fool/Not the Lovin' Kind	1968	2.00	4.00	8.00
—"Back to Back Hits" series; originals have both "W7" and "r:" logos					
❑ Reprise 0965	Lady Love/A Certain Sound	1970	7.50	15.00	30.00
—A-side is a Brian Wilson composition					
❑ Uni 55127	Someday/Thru Spray Colored Glasses	1969	3.00	6.00	12.00
Albums					
❑ Reprise R 6176 [M]	I'm a Fool	1965	5.00	10.00	20.00
❑ Reprise RS 6176 [S]	I'm a Fool	1965	6.25	12.50	25.00
❑ Reprise R 6194 [M]	Our Time's Coming	1966	5.00	10.00	20.00
❑ Reprise RS 6194 [S]	Our Time's Coming	1966	6.25	12.50	25.00
❑ Reprise R 6198 [M]	Memories Are Made of This	1966	5.00	10.00	20.00
❑ Reprise RS 6198 [S]	Memories Are Made of This	1966	6.25	12.50	25.00
❑ Reprise R 6224 [M]	Souvenir	1966	5.00	10.00	20.00
❑ Reprise RS 6224 [S]	Souvenir	1966	6.25	12.50	25.00
DION					
45s					
❑ Arista 9797	And the Night Stood Still/Tower of Love	1989	—	2.00	4.00
❑ Big Tree/Spector 16063	Born to Be with You/Running Close Behind You	1976	3.75	7.50	15.00
—Produced by Phil Spector					
❑ Columbia 42662	Ruby Baby/He'll Only Hurt You	1962	5.00	10.00	20.00
❑ Columbia 42776	This Little Girl/The Loneliest Man in the World	1963	3.75	7.50	15.00
❑ Columbia 42810	Be Careful of Stones That You Throw/I Can't Believe (That You Don't Love Me Anymore)	1963	3.75	7.50	15.00
❑ Columbia 42852	Donna the Prima Donna/You're Mine	1963	5.00	10.00	20.00
❑ Columbia 42917	Drip Drop/No One's Waiting for Me	1963	3.75	7.50	15.00
❑ Columbia 42977	I'm the Hoochie Coochie Man/The Road I'm On	1964	3.75	7.50	15.00
❑ Columbia 43096	Johnny B. Goode/Chicago Blues	1964	3.75	7.50	15.00
❑ Columbia 43213	Sweet Sweet Baby/Unloved, Unwanted Me	1965	3.75	7.50	15.00
❑ Columbia 43293	Spoonful/Kickin' Child	1965	3.75	7.50	15.00
❑ Columbia 43423	Tomorrow Won't Bring the Rain/You Move Me Babe	1965	3.75	7.50	15.00
❑ Columbia 43483	Time in My Heart for You/Wake Up Baby	1965	3.75	7.50	15.00
❑ Columbia 43692	So Much Younger/Two-Ton Feather	1966	3.75	7.50	15.00
❑ Columbia 44719	I Can't Help But Wonder Where I'm Bound/Southern Train	1968	2.50	5.00	10.00
❑ Laurie 3070	Lonely Teenager/Little Miss Blue	1960	5.00	10.00	20.00
❑ Laurie 3081	Havin' Fun/Northeast End of the Corner	1961	5.00	10.00	20.00
❑ Laurie 3090	Kissin Game/Heaven Help Me	1961	5.00	10.00	20.00
❑ Laurie 3101	Somebody Nobody Wants/Could Somebody Take My Place Tonight	1961	5.00	10.00	20.00
❑ Laurie 3110 [M]	Runaround Sue/Runaway Girl	1961	6.25	12.50	25.00
❑ Laurie 3110 [S]	Runaround Sue/Runaway Girl	1961	12.50	25.00	50.00
—"Stereo" in white area at right of label					
❑ Laurie 3115 [M]	The Wanderer/The Majestic	1961	6.25	12.50	25.00
❑ Laurie 3115 [M]	The Wanderer/The Majestic	1979	2.50	5.00	10.00
—Reissue on regular Laurie label with "From the Orion Motion Picture 'The Wanderers'" on label					
❑ Laurie 3115 [S]	The Wanderer/The Majestic	1961	12.50	25.00	50.00
—"Stereo" in white area at right of label					
❑ Laurie 3123	Lovers Who Wander/(I Was) Born to Cry	1962	5.00	10.00	20.00
❑ Laurie 3134	Little Diane/Lost for Sure	1962	5.00	10.00	20.00
❑ Laurie 3145	Love Came to Me/Little Girl	1962	5.00	10.00	20.00
❑ Laurie 3153	Sandy/Faith	1963	5.00	10.00	20.00
❑ Laurie 3171	Come Go with Me/King Without a Queen	1963	5.00	10.00	20.00
❑ Laurie 3187	Lonely World/Tag Along	1963	5.00	10.00	20.00
❑ Laurie 3225	After the Dance/Then I'll Be Tired of You	1964	5.00	10.00	20.00

Number	Title (A Side/B Side)	Yr	VG	VG+	NM
❑ Laurie 3240	Shout/Little Girl	1964	5.00	10.00	20.00
❑ Laurie 3303	I Got the Blues/(I Was) Born to Cry	1965	5.00	10.00	20.00
❑ Laurie 3464	Abraham, Martin, and John/Daddy Rollin' (In Your Arms)	1968	3.00	6.00	12.00
❑ Laurie 3478	Purple Haze/The Dolphins	1969	3.00	6.00	12.00
❑ Laurie 3495	From Both Sides Now/Sun Fun Song	1969	3.00	6.00	12.00
❑ Laurie 3504	Loving You Is Sweeter Than Ever/He Looks a Lot Like Me	1969	3.00	6.00	12.00
❑ Laurie Double Gold 100	Runaround Sue/I Wonder Why	197?	—	2.00	4.00
—B-side by Dion and the Belmonts					
❑ Laurie Double Gold 101	The Wanderer/No One Knows	197?	—	2.00	4.00
—B-side by Dion and the Belmonts					
❑ Laurie Double Gold 103	Lonely Teenager/Little Diane	197?	—	2.00	4.00
❑ Laurie Double Gold 104	Lovers Who Wander/Where or When	197?	—	2.00	4.00
—B-side by Dion and the Belmonts					
❑ Laurie Double Gold 105	Love Came to Me/Sandy	197?	—	2.00	4.00
❑ Laurie Double Gold 118	Abraham, Martin and John/From Both Sides Now	197?	—	2.00	4.00
❑ Lifesong 1765	Heart of Saturday Night/You've Awakened Something in Me	1978	—	3.00	6.00
❑ Lifesong 1770	Midtown American Main Street Gang/Guitar Queen	1978	—	3.00	6.00
❑ Lifesong 1785	(I Used to Be a) Brooklyn Dodger/Streetheart Theme	1979	—	3.00	6.00
❑ Lifesong 45082	Fire in the Night/Street Mama	1980	6.25	12.50	25.00
❑ Warner Bros. 7356	Natural Man/If We Only Have Love	1969	2.50	5.00	10.00
❑ Warner Bros. 7401	Your Own Back Yard/Sit Down Old Friend	1970	2.50	5.00	10.00
❑ Warner Bros. 7469	Let It Be/Close to It All	1970	2.50	5.00	10.00
❑ Warner Bros. 7491	Josie/Sunniland	1970	2.50	5.00	10.00
❑ Warner Bros. 7537	Sanctuary/Brand New Morning	1971	2.50	5.00	10.00
❑ Warner Bros. 7663	Seagull/Running Close Behind You	1972	2.50	5.00	10.00
❑ Warner Bros. 7704	Doctor Rock and Roll/Sunshine Lady	1973	2.50	5.00	10.00
❑ Warner Bros. 7793	New York City Song/Richer Than a Rich Man	1974	2.50	5.00	10.00
❑ Warner Bros. 8234	Hey My Love/Lover Boy Supreme	1976	—	3.00	6.00
❑ Warner Bros. 8258	The Way You Do the Things You Do/Lover Boy Supreme	1976	—	3.00	6.00
❑ Warner Bros. 8293	Oh the Night/Queen of '59	1976	—	3.00	6.00
❑ Warner Bros. 8406	Young Virgin Eyes (I'm All Wrapped Up)/Oh the Night	1977	—	3.00	6.00
❑ Warner/Spector 0403	Make the Woman Love Me/Running Close Behind You	1975	3.75	7.50	15.00
—Produced by Phil Spector					
Albums					
❑ Arista AL 8549	Yo Frankie	1989	2.50	5.00	10.00
❑ Collectables 5027	Runaround Sue	198?	2.50	5.00	10.00
❑ Columbia CL 2010 [M]	Ruby Baby	1963	7.50	15.00	30.00
❑ Columbia CL 2107 [M]	Donna the Prima Donna	1963	7.50	15.00	30.00
❑ Columbia CS 8810 [S]	Ruby Baby	1963	10.00	20.00	40.00
❑ Columbia CS 8907 [S]	Donna the Prima Donna	1963	10.00	20.00	40.00
❑ Columbia CS 9773	Wonder Where I'm Bound	1969	5.00	10.00	20.00
❑ Columbia KC 31942	Dion's Greatest Hits	1973	5.00	10.00	20.00
❑ Dayspring DST-4022	Inside Job	1980	3.00	6.00	12.00
❑ Dayspring DST-4027	Only Jesus	198?	3.00	6.00	12.00
❑ Dayspring WR-8111	I Put Away My Idols	198?	3.00	6.00	12.00
❑ Dayspring WR-8112	Seasons (The Best of Dion)	198?	3.00	6.00	12.00
❑ Dayspring 7-01-412901-5	Seasons	1984	3.00	6.00	12.00
❑ Laurie LLP 2004 [M]	Alone with Dion	1960	50.00	100.00	200.00
—With three wallet-size photos on inside strip (deduct 50% if missing)					
❑ Laurie LLP 2009 [M]	Runaround Sue	1961	25.00	50.00	100.00
—Black vinyl					
❑ Laurie LLP 2012 [M]	Lovers Who Wander	1962	17.50	35.00	70.00
❑ Laurie LLP 2013 [M]	Dion Sings His Greatest Hits	1962	17.50	35.00	70.00
❑ Laurie SLP 2013 [R]	Dion Sings His Greatest Hits	196?	12.50	25.00	50.00
❑ Laurie LLP 2015 [M]	Love Came to Me	1963	17.50	35.00	70.00
❑ Laurie LLP 2017 [M]	Dion Sings to Sandy (And All His Other Girls)	1963	12.50	25.00	50.00
❑ Laurie LLP 2019 [M]	Dion Sings the 15 Million Sellers	1963	12.50	25.00	50.00
❑ Laurie SLP 2019 [R]	Dion Sings the 15 Million Sellers	196?	7.50	15.00	30.00
❑ Laurie LLP 2022 [M]	More of Dion's Greatest Hits	1964	12.50	25.00	50.00
❑ Laurie SLP 2022 [R]	More of Dion's Greatest Hits	196?	7.50	15.00	30.00
❑ Laurie SLP 2047	Dion	1968	5.00	10.00	20.00
❑ Laurie LES-4004	Abraham, Martin and John	197?	3.00	6.00	12.00
—Reissue of SLP-2047					
❑ Laurie LES-4013	Dion Sings the Hits of the 50's and 60's	1978	3.00	6.00	12.00
❑ Lifesong JZ 35356	Return of the Wanderer	1978	3.00	6.00	12.00
❑ Warner Bros. WS 1826	Sit Down, Old Friend	1969	5.00	10.00	20.00
❑ Warner Bros. WS 1872	You're Not Alone	1971	3.75	7.50	15.00
❑ Warner Bros. WS 1945	Sanctuary	1971	3.75	7.50	15.00
❑ Warner Bros. BS 2642	Suite for Late Summer	1972	3.75	7.50	15.00
❑ Warner Bros. BS 2954	Streetheart	1976	3.75	7.50	15.00
❑ Word WR-8285	Kingdom in the Streets	1985	3.00	6.00	12.00

DION AND THE BELMONTS

45s

Number	Title (A Side/B Side)	Yr	VG	VG+	NM
❑ ABC 10868	My Girl the Month of May/Berimbau	1966	3.00	6.00	12.00
❑ ABC 10896	For Bobbie/Movin' Man	1967	3.00	6.00	12.00
❑ Laurie 3013	I Wonder Why/Teen Angel	1958	7.50	15.00	30.00
—Light blue label					
❑ Laurie 3015	No One Knows/I Can't Go On (Rosalie)	1958	7.50	15.00	30.00
—Light blue label					
❑ Laurie 3021	Don't Pity Me/Just You	1958	6.25	12.50	25.00
❑ Laurie 3027 [M]	A Teenager in Love/I've Cried Before	1959	6.25	12.50	25.00
❑ Laurie S-3027 [S]	A Teenager in Love/I've Cried Before	1959	12.50	25.00	50.00
❑ Laurie 3035	Every Little Thing I Do/A Lover's Prayer	1959	6.25	12.50	25.00
❑ Laurie 3044	Where or When/That's My Desire	1959	6.25	12.50	25.00
❑ Laurie 3052	When You Wish Upon a Star/Wonderful Girl	1960	6.25	12.50	25.00
❑ Laurie 3059	In the Still of the Night/A Funny Feeling	1960	6.25	12.50	25.00

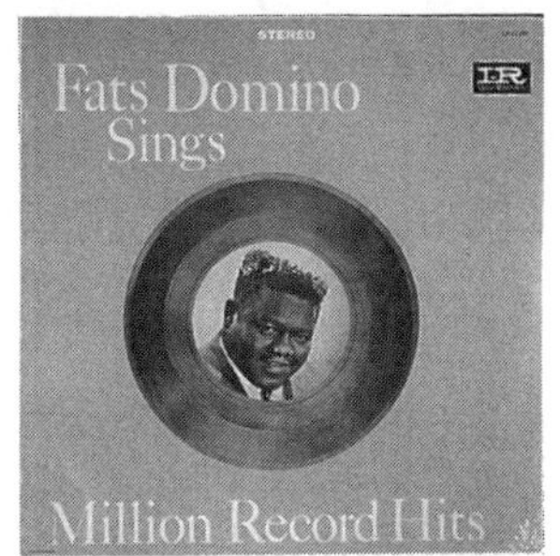

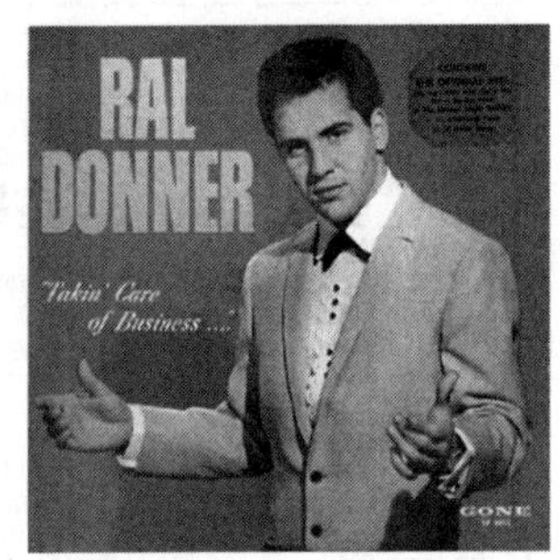

Number	Title (A Side/B Side)	Yr	VG	VG+	NM
❑ Laurie Double Gold 100	I Wonder Why/Runaround Sue	197?	—	2.00	4.00
—B-side by Dion					
❑ Laurie Double Gold 101	No One Knows/The Wanderer	197?	—	2.00	4.00
—B-side by Dion					
❑ Laurie Double Gold 102	A Teenager in Love/A Lover's Prayer	197?	—	2.00	4.00
❑ Laurie Double Gold 104	Where or When/Lovers Who Wander	197?	—	2.00	4.00
—B-side by Dion					
❑ Mohawk 106	Teenage Clementine/Santa Margarita	1957	15.00	30.00	60.00
—May be listed as "The Belmonts"					
❑ Mohawk 107	Tag Along/We Went Away	1957	15.00	30.00	60.00
Albums					
❑ ABC 599 [M]	Together Again	1967	7.50	15.00	30.00
❑ ABC S-599 [S]	Together Again	1967	10.00	20.00	40.00
❑ Arista A2L 8206 [(2)]	24 Original Classics	1984	3.00	6.00	12.00
❑ Collectables 5025	Presenting Dion & The Belmonts	198?	2.50	5.00	10.00
❑ Collectables 5026	Wish Upon a Star	198?	2.50	5.00	10.00
❑ Collectables 5041	20 Golden Classics	198?	2.50	5.00	10.00
❑ Laurie LLP 1002 [M]	Presenting Dion & The Belmonts	1959	62.50	125.00	250.00
❑ Laurie LLP 2002 [M]	Presenting Dion & The Belmonts	1960	37.50	75.00	150.00
❑ Laurie SLP 2002 [R]	Presenting Dion & The Belmonts	196?	300.00	600.00	900.00
—Despite its rechanneled stereo sound, this record is collectible because of its utter rarity					
❑ Laurie LLP 2006 [M]	Wish Upon a Star	1960	37.50	75.00	150.00
❑ Laurie LLP 2016 [M]	"Together" On Records — By Special Request	1963	12.50	25.00	50.00
❑ Laurie LES 4002	Everything You Always Wanted to Hear by Dion and the Belmonts	197?	3.75	7.50	15.00
❑ Laurie SLP 6000 [(3)]	60 Greatest Hits	197?	7.50	15.00	30.00
—In box					
❑ Laurie SLP 6000 [(3)]	60 Greatest Hits	197?	5.00	10.00	20.00
—In regular cover					
❑ Pair PDL2-1142 [(2)]	The Best of Dion and the Belmonts	1986	3.00	6.00	12.00
❑ Pickwick SPC-3521	Doo Wop	1975	2.50	5.00	10.00
—Reissue of ABC tracks					
❑ Rhino RNLP 70228	Reunion — Live at Madison Square Garden — 1972	1987	2.50	5.00	10.00
—Reissue of ABC tracks					
❑ Warner Bros. BS 2664	Reunion — Live at Madison Square Garden — 1972	1973	3.75	7.50	15.00

DIRE STRAITS

Number	Title (A Side/B Side)	Yr	VG	VG+	NM
45s					
❑ Warner Bros. GWB 0385	Sultans of Swing/Down to the Waterline	198?	—	2.00	4.00
—B-side makes its first U.S. 45 appearance here					
❑ Warner Bros. 8736 RE-1	Sultans of Swing/Southbound Again	1979	—	2.00	4.00
—With white label; contains 5:49 LP version (master number on A-side is "WAA 8382 S"); "Produced by Muff Winwood" on A-side label					
❑ Warner Bros. 7-19094	Heavy Fuel/Kingdom Come	1992	—	2.00	4.00
❑ Warner Bros. 7-19199	Calling Elvis/Millionaire Blues	1992	—	2.50	5.00
❑ Warner Bros. 7-21995	Walk of Life/So Far Away	198?	—	—	3.00
—"Back to Back Hits" reissue					
❑ Warner Bros. 7-21996	Money for Nothing/Twisting by the Pool	198?	—	—	3.00
—"Back to Back Hits" reissue					
❑ Warner Bros. 7-28789	So Far Away/If I Had You	1986	—	—	3.00
❑ Warner Bros. 7-28878	Walk of Life/One World	1985	—	—	3.00
❑ Warner Bros. 7-28950	Money for Nothing/Love Over Gold (Live)	1985	—	2.00	4.00
❑ Warner Bros. 7-29013	Walk of Life/One World	1985	2.50	5.00	10.00
❑ Warner Bros. 7-29706	Twisting by the Pool/Badges, Posters, Stickers, T-Shirts	1983	2.00	4.00	8.00
❑ Warner Bros. 7-29880	Industrial Disease/Badges, Posters, Stickers, T-Shirts	1982	2.00	4.00	8.00
❑ Warner Bros. 49006	Lady Writer/Where Do You Think You're Going	1979	—	3.00	6.00
❑ Warner Bros. 49082	Once Upon a Time in the West/News	1979	5.00	10.00	20.00
❑ Warner Bros. 49632	Skateaway/Solid Rock	1980	—	2.50	5.00
❑ Warner Bros. 49688	Romeo and Juliet/Solid Rock	1981	3.00	6.00	12.00
Albums					
❑ Warner Bros. BSK 3266	Dire Straits	1979	2.50	5.00	10.00
❑ Warner Bros. HS 3330	Communique	1979	2.50	5.00	10.00
❑ Warner Bros. BSK 3480	Making Movies	1980	2.50	5.00	10.00
❑ Warner Bros. 23728	Love Over Gold	1982	2.50	5.00	10.00
—On U.S. stock copies, the times of the songs as listed on the labels are rounded to the nearest 0 or 5					
❑ Warner Bros. 25085 [(2)]	Dire Straits Live — Alchemy	1984	3.00	6.00	12.00
❑ Warner Bros. 25264	Brothers in Arms	1985	2.50	5.00	10.00
❑ Warner Bros. 26680	On Every Street	1991	6.25	12.50	25.00

Number	Title (A Side/B Side)	Yr	VG	VG+	NM
❑ Warner Bros. 29800 [EP]	Twisting by the Pool	1983	—	3.00	6.00
—Also known as "ExtendeDancEPlay"					
❑ Warner Bros. 49377-1 [(2)]	Brothers in Arms	2006	7.50	15.00	30.00
—Remastered reissue; contains the full-length version of the album as it appears on the CD version, with longer versions of five songs					

DIXIE CUPS, THE

45s

Number	Title (A Side/B Side)	Yr	VG	VG+	NM
❑ ABC 10855	Love Ain't So Bad (After All)/Daddy Said No	1966	3.00	6.00	12.00
❑ ABC-Paramount 10692	That's Where It's At/Two-Way-Poc-A-Way	1965	3.00	6.00	12.00
❑ ABC-Paramount 10715	I'm Not the Kind of Girl (To Marry)/What Goes Up Must Go Down	1965	3.00	6.00	12.00
❑ ABC-Paramount 10755	A-B-C Song/That's What the Kids Said	1965	3.00	6.00	12.00
❑ Antilles 707	Iko Iko/Hey Hey (Indian's Coming)	1987	—	2.00	4.00
—B-side by The Wild Tchoupitoulas					
❑ Lana 144	Chapel of Love/Ain't That Nice	196?	2.00	4.00	8.00
—Oldies reissue					
❑ Red Bird 10-001	Chapel of Love/Ain't That Nice	1964	7.50	15.00	30.00
❑ Red Bird 10-006	People Say/Girls Can Tell	1964	5.00	10.00	20.00
❑ Red Bird 10-012	You Should Have Seen the Way He Looked at Me/No True Love	1964	5.00	10.00	20.00
❑ Red Bird 10-017	Little Bell/Another Boy Like Me	1964	5.00	10.00	20.00
❑ Red Bird 10-024	Iko Iko/Gee, Baby, Gee	1965	5.00	10.00	20.00
❑ Red Bird 10-024	Iko Iko/I'm Gonna Get You Yet	1965	5.00	10.00	20.00
❑ Red Bird 10-032	Gee, the Moon Is Shining Bright/I'm Gonna Get You Yet	1965	5.00	10.00	20.00

Albums

Number	Title (A Side/B Side)	Yr	VG	VG+	NM
❑ ABC-Paramount 525 [M]	Riding High	1965	15.00	30.00	60.00
❑ ABC-Paramount S-525 [S]	Riding High	1965	20.00	40.00	80.00
❑ Red Bird RB 20-100 [M]	Chapel of Love	1964	15.00	30.00	60.00
❑ Red Bird RBS 20-100 [S]	Chapel of Love	1964	20.00	40.00	80.00
❑ Red Bird RB 20-103 [M]	Iko Iko	1965	37.50	75.00	150.00

DIXIEBELLES, THE

45s

Number	Title (A Side/B Side)	Yr	VG	VG+	NM
❑ Sound Stage 7 2507	(Down at) Papa Joe's/Rock, Rock, Rock	1963	2.50	5.00	10.00
❑ Sound Stage 7 2517	Southtown U.S.A./Why Don't You Set Me Free	1964	2.50	5.00	10.00
❑ Sound Stage 7 2521	New York Town/The Beale Street Dog	1964	2.50	5.00	10.00

Albums

Number	Title (A Side/B Side)	Yr	VG	VG+	NM
❑ Sound Stage 7 SSM-5000 [M]	Down at Papa Joe's	1963	10.00	20.00	40.00
❑ Sound Stage 7 SSS-15000 [R]	Down at Papa Joe's	1963	7.50	15.00	30.00

DR. HOOK

45s

Number	Title (A Side/B Side)	Yr	VG	VG+	NM
❑ Capitol 4081	Levitate/Cooky and Lila	1975	—	2.00	4.00
❑ Capitol 4104	The Millionaire/Cooky and Lila	1975	—	2.00	4.00
❑ Capitol 4171	Only Sixteen/Let Me Be Your Lover	1975	—	2.50	5.00
❑ Capitol 4280	A Little Bit More/A Couple More Years	1976	—	2.50	5.00
❑ Capitol 4364	If Not You/Bad Eye Bill	1976	—	2.00	4.00
❑ Capitol 4423	Walk Right In/Sexy Energy	1977	—	2.00	4.00
❑ Capitol 4534	Making Love and Music/Who Dat	1978	—	2.00	4.00
❑ Capitol 4615	I Don't Want to Be Alone Tonight/ You Make My Pants Want to Get Up and Dance	1978	—	2.00	4.00
❑ Capitol 4621	Sharing the Night Together/ You Make My Pants Want to Get Up and Dance	1978	—	2.00	4.00
❑ Capitol 4677	All the Time in the World/Dooley Jones	1979	—	2.00	4.00
❑ Capitol 4705	When You're in Love with a Beautiful Woman/ Knowing She's There	1979	—	2.00	4.00
❑ Capitol 4785	Better Love Next Time/Mountain Mary	1979	—	2.00	4.00
❑ Capitol 4831	Sexy Eyes/Help Me Mama	1980	—	2.00	4.00
❑ Capitol 4885	Years from Now/I Don't Feel Much Like Smilin'	1980	—	2.00	4.00
❑ Casablanca 2314	Girls Can Get It/Doin' It	1980	—	2.00	4.00
❑ Casablanca 2325	S.O.S. For Love/99 and Me	1981	—	2.00	4.00
❑ Casablanca 2347	Baby Makes Her Blue Jeans Talk/The Turn On	1981	—	2.00	4.00
❑ Casablanca 2351	Loveline/Pity the Fool	1981	—	2.00	4.00
❑ Columbia 3-10032	Make It Easy/Ballad of Lucy Jordan	1974	—	3.00	6.00
—All as "Dr. Hook and the Medicine Show"					
❑ Columbia 4-45392	Last Morning/One More Ride (Lucille and Bunky)	1971	—	3.00	6.00
❑ Columbia 4-45562	Sylvia's Mother/Makin' It Natural	1972	—	3.00	6.00
—Orange label with "Columbia" background print					
❑ Columbia 4-45562	Sylvia's Mother/Makin' It Natural	1972	—	2.50	5.00
—Gray label					
❑ Columbia 4-45667	Carry Me, Carrie/Call That True Love	1972	—	2.50	5.00
❑ Columbia 4-45732	The Cover of "Rolling Stone"/Queen of the Silver Dollar	1972	—	2.50	5.00
—Orange label					
❑ Columbia 4-45732	The Cover of "Rolling Stone"/Queen of the Silver Dollar	1972	—	3.00	6.00
—Gray label					
❑ Columbia 4-45878	Roland the Roadie and Gertrude the Groupie/Put a Little Bit on Me	1973	—	2.50	5.00
❑ Columbia 4-45925	Life Ain't Easy/Wonderful Stone Soup	1973	—	2.50	5.00
❑ Columbia 4-46026	Monterey Jack/Cops and Robbers	1974	—	2.50	5.00

Albums

Number	Title (A Side/B Side)	Yr	VG	VG+	NM
❑ Capitol ST-11397	Bankrupt	1975	2.50	5.00	10.00
❑ Capitol ST-11522	A Little Bit More	1976	2.50	5.00	10.00
❑ Capitol ST-11632	Makin' Love and Music	1977	2.50	5.00	10.00
❑ Capitol SW-11859	Pleasure and Pain	1978	2.50	5.00	10.00
❑ Capitol ST-12018	Sometimes You Win...	1979	2.50	5.00	10.00
❑ Capitol SOO-12023	Sometimes You Win...	1979	2.50	5.00	10.00
—Other than the prefix and the number, we don't know if there are any differences between this and 12018, but both do exist					
❑ Capitol ST-12114	Live	1981	2.50	5.00	10.00

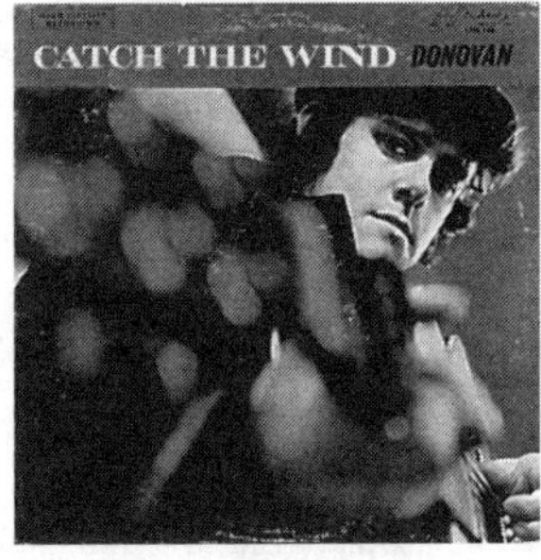

Number	Title (A Side/B Side)	Yr	VG	VG+	NM
❑ Capitol SOO-12122	Dr. Hook/Greatest Hits	1980	2.50	5.00	10.00
❑ Capitol ST-12325	The Rest of Dr. Hook	1984	2.00	4.00	8.00
❑ Capitol SN-16179	Bankrupt	198?	2.00	4.00	8.00
—Budget-line reissue					
❑ Capitol SN-16180	A Little Bit More	198?	2.00	4.00	8.00
—Budget-line reissue					
❑ Capitol SN-16181	Pleasure and Pain	198?	2.00	4.00	8.00
—Budget-line reissue					
❑ Capitol SN-16228	Makin' Love and Music	198?	2.00	4.00	8.00
—Budget-line reissue					
❑ Capitol SN-16229	Sometimes You Win...	198?	2.00	4.00	8.00
—Budget-line reissue					
❑ Capitol SN-16325	Dr. Hook/Greatest Hits	198?	2.00	4.00	8.00
—Budget-line reissue					
❑ Casablanca NBLP-7251	Rising	1980	2.50	5.00	10.00
❑ Casablanca NBLP-7264	Players in the Dark	1982	2.50	5.00	10.00
❑ Columbia KC 30898	Dr. Hook & The Medicine Show	1972	3.75	7.50	15.00
❑ Columbia KC 31622	Sloppy Seconds	1972	3.75	7.50	15.00
❑ Columbia KC 32270	Belly Up!	1973	3.75	7.50	15.00
❑ Columbia C 34147	Dr. Hook and the Medicine Show Revisited	1976	2.50	5.00	10.00
❑ Mercury 800054-1	Players in the Dark	1983	2.00	4.00	8.00
—Reissue of Casablanca 7264					

DR. JOHN

45s

Number	Title (A Side/B Side)	Yr	VG	VG+	NM
❑ A.F.O. 309	The Point/One Naughty Flat	1962	6.25	12.50	25.00
—As "Mac Rebenack"					
❑ Ace 611	Good Times/Sahara	1961	6.25	12.50	25.00
—As "Mac Rebennack"					
❑ Atco 6607	I Walk on Gilded Splinters (Part 1)/ I Walk on Gilded Splinters (Part 2)	1968	3.00	6.00	12.00
❑ Atco 6635	Jump Sturdy/Mama Roox	1968	3.00	6.00	12.00
❑ Atco 6697	Patriotic Flag Waver (Long)/Patriotic Flag Waver (Short)	1969	2.00	4.00	8.00
❑ Atco 6755	Wash, Mama, Wash/Loup Gardo	1970	3.00	6.00	12.00
❑ Atco 6882	Iko Iko/The Huey Smith Medley	1972	2.50	5.00	10.00
❑ Atco 6898	Wang Dang Doodle/Big Chief	1972	—	3.00	6.00
❑ Atco 6900	Let the Good Times Roll/Stack-A-Lee	1972	—	3.00	6.00
❑ Atco 6914	Right Place Wrong Time/I Been Hoodood	1973	—	3.00	6.00
❑ Atco 6937	Such a Night/Cold, Cold, Cold	1973	—	3.00	6.00
❑ Atco 6957	(Everybody Wanna Get Rich) Rite Away/Mos'Scocious	1974	—	3.00	6.00
❑ Atco 6971	Let's Make a Better World/Me Minus You Equals Loneliness	1974	—	3.00	6.00
❑ Horizon 117	Wild Honey/Dance the Night Away with You	1979	—	2.00	4.00
❑ Horizon 125	Keep That Music Simple/I Thought I Heard New Orleans	1979	—	2.00	4.00
❑ RCA PB-11285	Take Me Higher/Sweet Rider	1978	—	2.00	4.00
❑ Rex 1008	Storm Warning/Foolish Little Girl	1959	12.50	25.00	50.00
—As "Mac Rebennack"					
❑ Scepter 12393	One Night Late/She's Just a Square	1974	—	2.50	5.00
❑ Warner Bros. 22976	Makin' Whoopee!/More Than You Know	1989	—	—	3.00
❑ Warner Bros. 49703	The Sailor and the Mermaid/One Good Turn	1981	—	2.00	4.00
—A-side with Libby Titus; B-side by Al Jarreau					

Albums

Number	Title (A Side/B Side)	Yr	VG	VG+	NM
❑ Accord SN-7118	Love Potion	1982	2.50	5.00	10.00
❑ Alligator AL-3901	Dr. John's Gumbo	1986	2.50	5.00	10.00
—Reissue of Atco 7006					
❑ Alligator AL-3904	Gris-Gris	1987	2.50	5.00	10.00
—Reissue of Atco 33-234					
❑ Atco SD 33-234	Gris-Gris	1968	7.50	15.00	30.00
—Purple and brown label					
❑ Atco SD 33-270	Babylon	1969	3.75	7.50	15.00
❑ Atco SD 33-316	Remedies	1970	3.75	7.50	15.00
❑ Atco SD 33-362	Dr. John, The Night Tripper (The Sun, Moon & Herbs)	1971	3.75	7.50	15.00
❑ Atco SD 7006	Dr. John's Gumbo	1972	3.00	6.00	12.00
❑ Atco SD 7018	In the Right Place	1973	3.00	6.00	12.00
❑ Atco SD 7043	Desitively Bonaroo	1974	3.00	6.00	12.00
❑ Clean Cuts 705	Dr. John Plays Mac Rebennack	1982	2.50	5.00	10.00
❑ Clean Cuts 707	The Brightest Smile in Town	1984	2.50	5.00	10.00
❑ Horizon SP-732	City Lights	1978	2.50	5.00	10.00

Number	Title (A Side/B Side)	Yr	VG	VG+	NM
❑ Horizon SP-740	Tango Palace	1979	2.50	5.00	10.00
❑ Karate 5404	One Night Late	1978	2.50	5.00	10.00
❑ Trip TLX-350 [(2)]	Superpak	1975	3.00	6.00	12.00
❑ United Artists UA-LA552-G	Hollywood Be Thy Name	1975	3.00	6.00	12.00
❑ Warner Bros. 25889	In a Sentimental Mood	1989	3.00	6.00	12.00
DOMINO, FATS					
45s					
❑ ABC 10902	I Don't Want to Set the World on Fire/I'm Living Right	1967	2.50	5.00	10.00
❑ ABC-Paramount ABCS 455-1 [S]	I Got a Right to Cry/When I'm Walking (Let Me Walk)	1963	5.00	10.00	20.00
—Small hole, plays at 33 1/3 rpm					
❑ ABC-Paramount 10444	There Goes (My Heart Again)/Can't Go On Without You	1963	2.50	5.00	10.00
❑ ABC-Paramount 10475	When I'm Walking (Let Me Walk)/I've Got a Right to Cry	1963	2.50	5.00	10.00
❑ ABC-Paramount 10484	Red Sails in the Sunset/Song for Rosemary	1963	3.00	6.00	12.00
❑ ABC-Paramount 10512	Who Cares/Just a Lonely Man	1963	2.50	5.00	10.00
❑ ABC-Paramount 10531	Lazy Lady/I Don't Want to Set the World on Fire	1964	2.50	5.00	10.00
❑ ABC-Paramount 10545	If You Don't Know What Love Is/Something You Got, Baby	1964	2.50	5.00	10.00
❑ ABC-Paramount 10567	Mary, Oh Mary/Packin' Up	1964	2.50	5.00	10.00
❑ ABC-Paramount 10584	Sally Was a Good Old Girl/For You	1964	2.50	5.00	10.00
❑ ABC-Paramount 10596	Heartbreak Hill/Kansas City	1964	2.50	5.00	10.00
❑ ABC-Paramount 10631	Why Don't You Do Right/Wigs	1965	2.50	5.00	10.00
❑ ABC-Paramount 10644	Let Me Call You Sweetheart/Goodnight Sweetheart	1965	2.50	5.00	10.00
❑ Broadmoor 104	The Lady in Black/Work My Way Up Steady	1967	3.75	7.50	15.00
❑ Broadmoor 105	Big Mouth/Wait 'Til It Happens to You	1968	5.00	10.00	20.00
❑ Imperial 45-5058	The Fat Man/Detroit City Blues	1950	500.00	1000.	2000.
—Blue-label "script" logo; pressed in 1952 or so; counterfeits exist					
❑ Imperial 45-5099	Korea Blues/Every Night About This Time	1950	200.00	400.00	800.00
—Blue-label "script" logo; pressed in 1952 or so					
❑ Imperial 45-5167	You Know I Miss You/I'll Be Gone	1952	125.00	250.00	500.00
—Fats Domino records on Imperial before 5167 are unconfirmed on 45 rpm, except those listed above.					
❑ Imperial 45-5180	Goin' Home/Reeling and Rocking	1952	75.00	150.00	300.00
❑ Imperial 45-5197	Poor Poor Me/Trust in Me	1952	50.00	100.00	200.00
❑ Imperial 45-5209	How Long/Dreaming	1952	20.00	40.00	80.00
—Black vinyl					
❑ Imperial 45-5220	Nobody Loves Me/Cheatin'	1953	20.00	40.00	80.00
—Black vinyl					
❑ Imperial 45-5231	Going to the River/Mardi Gras in New Orleans	1953	25.00	50.00	100.00
—Black vinyl					
❑ Imperial 45-5240	Please Don't Leave Me/The Girl I Love	1953	15.00	30.00	60.00
—Black vinyl					
❑ Imperial 45-5251	You Said You Loved Me/Rose Mary	1953	15.00	30.00	60.00
❑ Imperial X5262	Something's Wrong/Don't Leave Me This Way	1954	12.50	25.00	50.00
—Black vinyl					
❑ Imperial X5272	Little School Girl/You Done Me Wrong	1954	15.00	30.00	60.00
❑ Imperial X5283	Baby, Please/Where Did You Stay	1954	15.00	30.00	60.00
❑ Imperial X5301	You Can Pack Your Suitcase/I Lived My Life	1954	10.00	20.00	40.00
❑ Imperial X5313	Love Me/Don't You Hear Me Calling You	1954	10.00	20.00	40.00
❑ Imperial X5323	I Know/Thinking of You	1955	12.50	25.00	50.00
—Black vinyl					
❑ Imperial X5357	All By Myself/Troubles of My Own	1955	20.00	40.00	80.00
—Red label, script logo					
❑ Imperial X5369	Poor Me/I Can't Go On	1955	6.25	12.50	25.00
❑ Imperial X5375	Bo Weevil/Don't Blame It on Me	1956	6.25	12.50	25.00
❑ Imperial X5386	I'm in Love Again/My Blue Heaven	1956	6.25	12.50	25.00
❑ Imperial X5396	When My Dreamboat Comes Home/So-Long	1956	6.25	12.50	25.00
❑ Imperial X5407	Blueberry Hill/Honey Chile	1956	6.25	12.50	25.00
—Black vinyl, red label					
❑ Imperial X5417	Blue Monday/What's the Reason I'm Not Pleasing You	1957	6.25	12.50	25.00
❑ Imperial X5428	I'm Walkin'/I'm in the Mood for Love	1957	6.25	12.50	25.00
—Maroon or red label					
❑ Imperial X5442	Valley of Tears/It's You I Love	1957	6.25	12.50	25.00
❑ Imperial X5454	When I See You/What Will I Tell My Heart	1957	6.25	12.50	25.00
❑ Imperial X5467	Wait and See/I Still Love You	1957	6.25	12.50	25.00
❑ Imperial X5477	The Big Beat/I Want You to Know	1957	6.25	12.50	25.00
❑ Imperial X5492	Yes, My Darling/Don't You Know I Love You	1958	6.25	12.50	25.00
—Black vinyl					
❑ Imperial X5515	Sick and Tired/No, No	1958	6.25	12.50	25.00
❑ Imperial X5526	Little Mary/The Prisoner's Song	1958	6.25	12.50	25.00
❑ Imperial X5537	Young School Girl/It Must Be Love	1958	6.25	12.50	25.00
❑ Imperial X5553	Whole Lotta Loving/Coquette	1958	6.25	12.50	25.00
—Black label					
❑ Imperial 5569	Telling Lies/When the Saints Go Marching In	1959	3.75	7.50	15.00
❑ Imperial 5585	I'm Ready/Margie	1959	3.75	7.50	15.00
❑ Imperial 5606	I Want to Walk You Home/I'm Gonna Be a Wheel Some Day	1959	5.00	10.00	20.00
❑ Imperial 5629	Be My Guest/I've Been Around	1959	3.75	7.50	15.00
❑ Imperial 5645	Country Boy/If You Need Me	1960	3.75	7.50	15.00
❑ Imperial 5660	Tell Me That You Love Me/Before I Grow Too Old	1960	3.75	7.50	15.00
❑ Imperial 5675	Walking to New Orleans/Don't Come Knockin'	1960	5.00	10.00	20.00
❑ Imperial 5687	Three Nights a Week/Put Your Arms Around Me Honey	1960	3.75	7.50	15.00
❑ Imperial 5704	My Girl Josephine/Natural Born Lover	1960	5.00	10.00	20.00
❑ Imperial 5723	What a Price/Ain't That Just Like a Woman	1961	3.75	7.50	15.00
❑ Imperial 5734	Shu Rah/Fell in Love on Monday	1961	3.75	7.50	15.00
❑ Imperial 5753	It Keeps Rainin'/I Just Cry	1961	3.75	7.50	15.00
❑ Imperial 5764	Let the Four Winds Blow/Good Hearted Man	1961	3.75	7.50	15.00
❑ Imperial 5779	What a Party/Rockin' Bicycle	1961	3.75	7.50	15.00
❑ Imperial 5796	Jambalaya (On the Bayou)/I Hear You Knocking	1961	3.75	7.50	15.00

Number	Title (A Side/B Side)	Yr	VG	VG+	NM
❑ Imperial 5816	You Win Again/Ida Jane	1962	3.75	7.50	15.00
❑ Imperial 5833	My Real Name/My Heart Is Bleeding	1962	3.75	7.50	15.00
❑ Imperial 5863	Nothing New (Same Old Thing)/Dance with Mr. Domino	1962	3.75	7.50	15.00
❑ Imperial 5875	Did You Ever See a Dream Walking/Stop the Clock	1962	3.75	7.50	15.00
❑ Imperial 5895	Won't You Come On Back/Hands Across the Table	1962	3.75	7.50	15.00
❑ Imperial 5909	Hum Diddy Doo/Those Eyes	1963	3.75	7.50	15.00
❑ Imperial 5937	You Always Hurt the One You Love/Trouble Blues	1963	3.75	7.50	15.00
❑ Imperial 5959	Isle of Capri/True Confession	1963	3.75	7.50	15.00
❑ Imperial 5980	One Night/I Can't Go On This Way	1963	3.75	7.50	15.00
❑ Imperial 5999	Your Cheatin' Heart/Goin' Home	1963	3.75	7.50	15.00
❑ Imperial 66005	I Can't Give You Anything But Love/Goin' Home	1963	3.00	6.00	12.00
❑ Imperial 66016	When I Was Young/Your Cheatin' Heart	1964	3.00	6.00	12.00
❑ Mercury 72463	I Left My Heart in San Francisco/I Done Got Over You	1965	2.50	5.00	10.00
❑ Mercury 72485	It's Never Too Late/What's That You Got	1965	2.50	5.00	10.00
❑ Reprise 0696	One for the Highway/Honest Papas Love Their Mamas Better	1968	3.75	7.50	15.00
❑ Reprise 0763	Lady Madonna/One for the Highway	1968	3.75	7.50	15.00
❑ Reprise 0775	Lovely Rita/Wait Till It Happens to You	1968	3.75	7.50	15.00
❑ Reprise 0810	Everybody's Got Someting to Hide (Except Me and My Monkey)/ So Swell When You're Well	1969	3.75	7.50	15.00
❑ Reprise 0891	Have You Seen My Baby?/Make Me Belong to You	1970	3.75	7.50	15.00
❑ Reprise 0944	New Orleans Ain't the Same/Sweet Patootie	1970	3.75	7.50	15.00
❑ Toot Toot 001	My Toot Toot/My Toot Toot (Rock)	1985	—	2.50	5.00
—With Doug Kershaw					
❑ Toot Toot 002	Don't Mess with My Popeye's/My Toot Toot	1985	—	2.50	5.00
—With Doug Kershaw					
❑ United Artists 0001	Ain't That a Shame/Goin' Home	1973	—	2.00	4.00
❑ United Artists 0002	Blue Monday/I'm Gonna Be a Wheel Someday	1973	—	2.00	4.00
❑ United Artists 0003	I'm in Love Again/Whole Lotta Lovin'	1973	—	2.00	4.00
❑ United Artists 0004	Blueberry Hill/Bo Weevil	1973	—	2.00	4.00
❑ United Artists 0005	I'm Walkin'/One Night	1973	—	2.00	4.00
❑ United Artists 0006	I Hear You Knockin'/My Blue Heaven	1973	—	2.00	4.00
❑ United Artists 0007	Walkin' to New Orleans/Country Boy	1973	—	2.00	4.00
❑ United Artists 0008	I Want to Walk You Home/It's You I Love	1973	—	2.00	4.00
❑ United Artists 0009	I'm Ready/Wait and See	1973	—	2.00	4.00
❑ United Artists 0010	My Girl Josephine/When My Dreamboat Comes Home	1973	—	2.00	4.00
❑ United Artists 0011	Three Nights a Week/Let the Four Winds Blow	1973	—	2.00	4.00
—0001 through 0011 are "Silver Spotlight Series" reissues					
❑ United Artists XW 514	The Fat Man/Valley of Tears	1974	—	2.50	5.00
—Reissue					
❑ Warner Bros. 49610	Whiskey Heaven/Beers to You	1980	—	2.00	4.00
—B-side by Texas Opera Company					
Albums					
❑ ABC-Paramount 455 [M]	Here Comes... Fats Domino	1963	5.00	10.00	20.00
❑ ABC-Paramount S-455 [S]	Here Comes... Fats Domino	1963	6.25	12.50	25.00
❑ ABC-Paramount 479 [M]	Fats on Fire	1964	5.00	10.00	20.00
❑ ABC-Paramount S-479 [S]	Fats on Fire	1964	6.25	12.50	25.00
❑ ABC-Paramount 510 [M]	Get Away with Fats Domino	1965	5.00	10.00	20.00
❑ ABC-Paramount S-510 [S]	Get Away with Fats Domino	1965	6.25	12.50	25.00
❑ Atlantic 81751	Live in Montreux	1987	3.00	6.00	12.00
❑ Columbia C 35996	When I'm Walking	1979	2.50	5.00	10.00
—Reissue of Harmony LP					
❑ Columbia PC 35996	When I'm Walking	1986	2.00	4.00	8.00
—Budget-line reissue					
❑ Everest Archive of Folk & Jazz 280	Fats Domino	1974	2.50	5.00	10.00
❑ Everest Archive of Folk & Jazz 330	Fats Domino, Vol. II	1975	2.50	5.00	10.00
❑ Grand Award 267 [M]	Fats Domino	196?	5.00	10.00	20.00
❑ Grand Award S-267 [R]	Fats Domino	196?	2.50	5.00	10.00
❑ Harlem Hit Parade 5005	Fats' Hits	197?	2.50	5.00	10.00
❑ Harmony HS 11343	When I'm Walking	1969	3.00	6.00	12.00
❑ Imperial LP-9004 [M]	Rock and Rollin' with Fats Domino	1956	37.50	75.00	150.00
—Maroon label					
❑ Imperial LP-9009 [M]	Fats Domino Rock and Rollin'	1956	37.50	75.00	150.00
—Maroon label					
❑ Imperial LP-9028 [M]	This Is Fats Domino!	1957	37.50	75.00	150.00
—Maroon label					

Number	Title (A Side/B Side)	Yr	VG	VG+	NM
❑ Imperial LP-9038 [M]	Here Stands Fats Domino	1957	37.50	75.00	150.00
—Maroon label					
❑ Imperial LP-9040 [M]	This Is Fats	1957	37.50	75.00	150.00
—Maroon label					
❑ Imperial LP-9055 [M]	The Fabulous Mr. D.	1958	25.00	50.00	100.00
—Black label with stars on top					
❑ Imperial LP-9062 [M]	Fats Domino Swings	1959	25.00	50.00	100.00
—Black label with stars on top					
❑ Imperial LP-9065 [M]	Let's Play Fats Domino	1959	25.00	50.00	100.00
—Black label with stars on top					
❑ Imperial LP-9103 [M]	Million Record Hits	1960	25.00	50.00	100.00
—Black label with stars on top					
❑ Imperial LP-9127 [M]	A Lot of Dominos	1960	25.00	50.00	100.00
—Black label with stars on top					
❑ Imperial LP-9138 [M]	I Miss You So	1961	25.00	50.00	100.00
—Black label with stars on top					
❑ Imperial LP-9153 [M]	Let the Four Winds Blow	1961	25.00	50.00	100.00
—Black label with stars on top					
❑ Imperial LP-9164 [M]	What a Party	1962	15.00	30.00	60.00
—Black label with stars on top					
❑ Imperial LP-9170 [M]	Twistin' the Stomp	1962	15.00	30.00	60.00
—Black label with stars on top					
❑ Imperial LP-9195 [M]	Million Sellers by Fats	1962	12.50	25.00	50.00
—Black label with stars on top					
❑ Imperial LP-9208 [M]	Just Domino	1962	12.50	25.00	50.00
—Black label with stars on top					
❑ Imperial LP-9227 [M]	Walking to New Orleans	1963	12.50	25.00	50.00
—Black label with stars on top					
❑ Imperial LP-9239 [M]	Let's Dance with Domino	1963	12.50	25.00	50.00
—Black label with stars on top					
❑ Imperial LP-9248 [M]	Here He Comes Again	1963	12.50	25.00	50.00
—Black label with stars on top					
❑ Imperial LP-12066 [S]	A Lot of Dominos	1961	37.50	75.00	150.00
—Black label with silver top					
❑ Imperial LP-12073 [S]	Let the Four Winds Blow	1961	37.50	75.00	150.00
—Black label with silver top					
❑ Imperial LP-12091 [R]	Fats Domino Swings	1964	5.00	10.00	20.00
—Black and pink label					
❑ Imperial LP-12103 [R]	Million Record Hits	1964	5.00	10.00	20.00
—Black and pink label					
❑ Imperial LP-12195 [R]	Million Sellers by Fats	1964	5.00	10.00	20.00
—Black and pink label					
❑ Imperial LP-12227 [R]	Walking to New Orleans	1964	5.00	10.00	20.00
—Black and pink label					
❑ Imperial LP-12248 [R]	Here He Comes Again	1964	5.00	10.00	20.00
—Black and pink label					
❑ Imperial LP-12387 [R]	Rock and Rollin' with Fats Domino	1968	3.00	6.00	12.00
—Rechanneled reissue of 9004					
❑ Imperial LP-12389 [R]	This Is Fats Domino!	1968	3.00	6.00	12.00
—Rechanneled reissue of 9028					
❑ Imperial LP-12390 [R]	Here Stands Fats Domino	1968	3.00	6.00	12.00
—Rechanneled reissue of 9038					
❑ Imperial LP-12391 [R]	This Is Fats	1968	3.00	6.00	12.00
—Rechanneled reissue of 9040					
❑ Imperial LP-12394 [R]	The Fabulous Mr. D.	1968	3.00	6.00	12.00
—Rechanneled reissue of 9055					
❑ Imperial LP-12395 [R]	Let's Play Fats Domino	1968	3.00	6.00	12.00
—Rechanneled reissue of 9065					
❑ Imperial LP-12398 [R]	I Miss You So	1968	3.00	6.00	12.00
—Rechanneled reissue of 9138					
❑ Liberty LWB-122 [(2)]	Cookin' with Fats (Superpak)	1981	3.00	6.00	12.00
—Budget-line reissue of UA 122					
❑ Liberty LM-1027	Million Sellers by Fats	1981	2.00	4.00	8.00
—Budget-line reissue of UA 1027					
❑ Liberty LWB-9958 [(2)]	Legendary Masters	1981	2.50	5.00	10.00
—Budget-line reissue of UA 9958					
❑ Liberty LN-10135	Let's Play Fats Domino	1981	2.00	4.00	8.00
—Budget-line reissue					
❑ Liberty LN-10136	The Fabulous Mr. D.	1981	2.00	4.00	8.00
—Budget-line reissue					
❑ MCA/Silver Eagle 6170	Greatest Hits	198?	2.50	5.00	10.00
❑ Mercury MG-21039 [M]	Fats Domino '65	1965	6.25	12.50	25.00
❑ Mercury SR-61039 [S]	Fats Domino '65	1965	10.00	20.00	40.00
❑ Pickwick SPC-3111	Blueberry Hill	197?	2.50	5.00	10.00
❑ Pickwick SPC-3165	When My Dreamboat Comes Home	197?	2.50	5.00	10.00
❑ Pickwick SPC-3295	My Blue Heaven	1971	2.50	5.00	10.00
❑ Quicksilver QS-1016	Live Hits	198?	2.50	5.00	10.00
❑ Reprise RS 6304	Fats Is Back	1968	7.50	15.00	30.00
❑ Reprise RS 6439	Fats	1970	125.00	250.00	500.00
—Officially unreleased, test pressings and coverless stock copies are known to exist					
❑ Sears SPS-473	Blueberry Hill!	1970	6.25	12.50	25.00
❑ Sunset SUM-1103 [M]	Fats Domino	1966	3.00	6.00	12.00
❑ Sunset SUM-1158 [M]	Stompin' Fats Domino	1967	3.00	6.00	12.00
❑ Sunset SUS-5103 [R]	Fats Domino	1966	3.00	6.00	12.00
❑ Sunset SUS-5158 [R]	Stompin' Fats Domino	1967	3.00	6.00	12.00
❑ Sunset SUS-5200 [P]	Trouble in Mind	1968	5.00	10.00	20.00

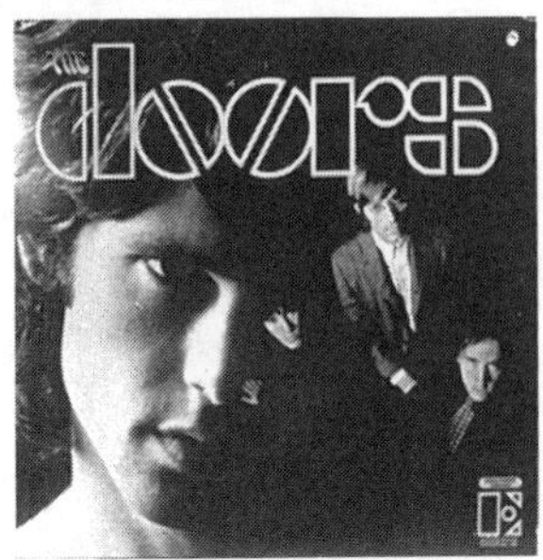

Number	Title (A Side/B Side)	Yr	VG	VG+	NM
❑ Sunset SUS-5299 [R]	Ain't That a Shame	1970	3.00	6.00	12.00
❑ United Artists UA-LA122-F2 [(2)]	Cookin' with Fats (Superpak)	1974	7.50	15.00	30.00
❑ United Artists UA-LA233-G	The Very Best of Fats Domino	1974	3.00	6.00	12.00
❑ United Artists LM-1027	Million Sellers by Fats	1980	2.50	5.00	10.00
❑ United Artists UAS-9958 [(2)]	Legendary Masters	1972	3.75	7.50	15.00

DONALDSON, BO, AND THE HEYWOODS

45s

Number	Title (A Side/B Side)	Yr	VG	VG+	NM
❑ ABC 11402	Deeper and Deeper/Drive Me Crazy	1973	—	2.00	4.00
❑ ABC 11435	Billy, Don't Be a Hero/Don't Ever Look Back	1974	—	2.00	4.00
❑ ABC 12006	Who Do You Think You Are/Fool's Way of Lovin'	1974	—	2.00	4.00
❑ ABC 12011	Billy, Don't Be a Hero/Don't Ever Look Back	1974	—	2.50	5.00
❑ ABC 12039	The Heartbreak Kid/Girl Don't Make Me Wait	1974	—	2.00	4.00
❑ ABC 12072	Make the Most of This World/House on Telegraph Hill	1975	—	2.00	4.00
❑ ABC 12108	Our Last Song Together/Make the Most of This World	1975	—	2.00	4.00
❑ Capitol 4237	Oh Boy/Tie Me Down	1976	—	2.00	4.00
❑ Capitol 4282	Teenage Rampage/Tie Me Down	1976	—	2.00	4.00
❑ Family Productions 0917	Thank You Girl/You Don't Own Me	1972	—	2.50	5.00
❑ Family Productions 0918	All Over the World/Just for You	1972	—	2.50	5.00
❑ Family Productions 0923	Da Doo Ron Ron/Just Because	1973	—	2.50	5.00

Albums

Number	Title (A Side/B Side)	Yr	VG	VG+	NM
❑ ABC D-824	Bo Donaldson and the Heywoods	1974	2.50	5.00	10.00
❑ Capitol ST-11501	Farther On	1976	3.75	7.50	15.00
❑ Family Productions FPS-2711	Special Someone	1972	3.75	7.50	15.00

DONEGAN, LONNIE

45s

Number	Title (A Side/B Side)	Yr	VG	VG+	NM
❑ Apt 25067	Pick a Bale of Cotton/Ramblin' Round	1962	2.50	5.00	10.00
❑ Atlantic 2058	My Old Man's a Dustman/The Golden Vanity	1960	3.00	6.00	12.00
❑ Atlantic 2063	Take This Hammer/Nobody Understands Me	1960	3.00	6.00	12.00
❑ Atlantic 2081	Lorelei/Junco Partner	1960	3.00	6.00	12.00
❑ Atlantic 2108	Have a Drink On Me/Beyond the Sunset	1961	3.00	6.00	12.00
❑ Atlantic 2123	Wreck of the John B/Sorry, But I'm Gonna Have to Pass	1961	3.00	6.00	12.00
❑ Dot 15792	The Grand Coulee Dam/Nobody Loves Like an Irishman	1958	5.00	10.00	20.00
❑ Dot 15873	Sally Don't You Grieve/Times Are Getting Hard, Boys	1958	5.00	10.00	20.00
❑ Dot 15911	Does Your Chewing Gum Lose Its Flavor (On the Bedpost Overnight)/Aunt Rhody	1959	5.00	10.00	20.00
—Reissued in 1961 with the same number					
❑ Dot 15953	Fort Worth Jail/Whoa, Back, Back	1959	5.00	10.00	20.00
❑ Dot 16263	Whoa, Back, Back/Light from the Lighthouse	1961	3.75	7.50	15.00
❑ Felsted 8630	Rock Island Line/John Henry	1961	3.00	6.00	12.00
❑ Hickory 1247	Lemon Tree/A Very Good Year	1964	2.50	5.00	10.00
❑ Hickory 1267	Fisherman's Luck/There's a Big Wheel	1964	2.50	5.00	10.00
❑ Hickory 1274	Bad News/Interstate 40	1964	2.50	5.00	10.00
❑ Hickory 1299	Louisiana Man/Lovey Told Me Goodbye	1965	2.50	5.00	10.00
❑ Hickory 1345	Cajun Jo (Bully of the Bayou)/Nothing to Gain	1965	2.50	5.00	10.00
❑ London 1650	Rock Island Line/John Henry	1956	7.50	15.00	30.00
❑ London 20055	Juanita/Who Knows Where the Time Goes	1969	—	3.00	6.00
❑ Mercury 70872	Lost John/Stewball	1956	6.25	12.50	25.00
❑ Mercury 70949	Bring a Little Water, Sylvie/Dead or Alive	1956	6.25	12.50	25.00
❑ Mercury 71026	Don't You Rock Me Daddy-O/How Long, How Long Blues	1957	6.25	12.50	25.00
❑ Mercury 71094	Cumberland Gap/Wabash Cannonball	1957	6.25	12.50	25.00
❑ Mercury 71181	Puttin' On the Style/Gamblin' Man	1957	6.25	12.50	25.00
❑ Mercury 71248	My Dixie Darling/I'm Just a Rolling Stone	1957	6.25	12.50	25.00

Albums

Number	Title (A Side/B Side)	Yr	VG	VG+	NM
❑ ABC-Paramount 433 [M]	Sing Hallelujah	1963	5.00	10.00	20.00
❑ ABC-Paramount S-433 [S]	Sing Hallelujah	1963	6.25	12.50	25.00
❑ Atlantic 8038 [M]	Skiffle Folk Songs	1960	10.00	20.00	40.00
❑ Atlantic SD 8038 [S]	Skiffle Folk Songs	1960	12.50	25.00	50.00
❑ Dot DLP-3159 [M]	Lonnie Donegan	1959	10.00	20.00	40.00
❑ Mercury MG-20229 [M]	An Englishman Sings American Folk Songs	1957	12.50	25.00	50.00
❑ United Artists UA-LA827-?	Puttin' On the Style	1977	2.50	5.00	10.00

DONNER, RAL

45s

Number	Title (A Side/B Side)	Yr	VG	VG+	NM
❑ Chicago Fire 7402	The Wedding Song/Godfather Per Me	1974	2.00	4.00	8.00

Number	Title (A Side/B Side)	Yr	VG	VG+	NM
❑ End GG-19	You Don't Know What You've Got (Until You Lose It)/ She's Everything (I Wanted You to Be)	1963	7.50	15.00	30.00
—An early, and sought-after, reissue					
❑ Fontana 1502	Poison Ivy League/You Finally Said Something Good	1965	6.25	12.50	25.00
❑ Fontana 1502	Poison Ivy League/A Tear in My Eye	1965	6.25	12.50	25.00
❑ Fontana 1515	Good Lovin'/The Other Side of Me	1965	6.25	12.50	25.00
❑ Gone 5102	Girl of My Best Friend/It's Been a Long, Long Time	1961	6.25	12.50	25.00
—Multi-color label					
❑ Gone 5108	You Don't Know What You've Got (Until You Lose It)/ So Close to Heaven	1961	7.50	15.00	30.00
❑ Gone 5108	To Love/And Then	1961	10.00	20.00	40.00
—Deleted shortly after release					
❑ Gone 5114	Please Don't Go/I Didn't Figure on Him	1961	6.25	12.50	25.00
❑ Gone 5119	School of Heartbreakers/Because We're Young	1961	10.00	20.00	40.00
❑ Gone 5121	She's Everything (I Wanted You to Be)/Because We're Young	1961	6.25	12.50	25.00
❑ Gone 5121	She's Everything (I Wanted You to Be)/ Will You Love Me in Heaven	1961	7.50	15.00	30.00
—B-side sung by a girl group, not Ral Donner.					
❑ Gone 5125	To Love Someone/Will You Love Me in Heaven	1962	6.25	12.50	25.00
—B-side sung by Ral Donner as advertised					
❑ Gone 5129	Loveless Life/Bells of Love	1962	6.25	12.50	25.00
❑ Gone 5133	To Love/Sweetheart	1962	6.25	12.50	25.00
❑ Mid-Eagle 101	(If I Had My) Life to Live Over/Lost	1968	2.50	5.00	10.00
❑ Mid-Eagle 275	The Wedding Song/So Much Lovin'	1976	—	3.00	6.00
❑ MJ 222	(All of a Sudden) My Heart Sings/Lovin' Place	1970	—	3.00	6.00
❑ Red Bird 10-057	Love Isn't Like That/It Will Only Make You Love	1966	37.50	75.00	150.00
❑ Reprise 20135	(These Are the Things That Make Up) Christmas Day/ Second Miracle (Of Christmas)	1962	10.00	20.00	40.00
❑ Reprise 20141	I Got Burned/A Tear in My Eye	1963	10.00	20.00	40.00
❑ Reprise 20176	I Wish This Night Would Never End/ Don't Put Your Heart in His Hand	1963	12.50	25.00	50.00
❑ Reprise 20192	Beyond the Heartbreak/Run Little Linda	1963	15.00	30.00	60.00
❑ Rising Sons 714	Just a Little Sunshine (In the Rain)/If I Promise	1968	2.50	5.00	10.00
❑ Scottie 1310	Tell Me Why/That's All Right with Me	1959	62.50	125.00	250.00
❑ Starfire 100	Don't Let It Slip Away/Wait a Minute Now	1978	2.50	5.00	10.00
—Black vinyl					
❑ Starfire 103	(Things That Make Up) Christmas Day/Second Miracle (Of Christmas)	1978	2.50	5.00	10.00
—Green vinyl					
❑ Starfire 114	Rip It Up/Don't Leave Me Now	1979	2.50	5.00	10.00
❑ Sunlight 1006	Don't Let It Slip Away/Wait a Minute Now	1972	3.00	6.00	12.00
❑ Tau 105	Loneliness of a Star/And Then	1963	7.50	15.00	30.00
—Yellow label					
❑ Thunder 7801	The Day the Beat Stopped/Rock on Me	1978	—	3.00	6.00
Albums					
❑ Gone LP-5012 [M]	Takin' Care of Business	1961	75.00	150.00	300.00
❑ Starfire 1004	An Evening with Ral Donner	1982	3.75	7.50	15.00
—All copies on multi-color vinyl					

DONNO, EDDIE

45s

Number	Title (A Side/B Side)	Yr	VG	VG+	NM
❑ Capehart 5003	Rough Stuff/Our Love	1960	6.25	12.50	25.00

DONOVAN

45s

Number	Title (A Side/B Side)	Yr	VG	VG+	NM
❑ Allegiance 3910	Lady of the Stars/(B-side unknown)	1983	—	2.00	4.00
❑ Arista 0280	Dare to Be Different/International Man	1977	—	2.00	4.00
❑ Epic 10045	Sunshine Superman/The Trip	1966	2.50	5.00	10.00
❑ Epic 10098	Mellow Yellow/Sunny South Kensington	1966	2.50	5.00	10.00
❑ Epic 10127	Epistle to Dippy/Preachin' Love	1967	2.00	4.00	8.00
❑ Epic 10212	There Is a Mountain/Sand and Foam	1967	2.00	4.00	8.00
❑ Epic 10253	Wear Your Love Like Heaven/Oh Gosh	1967	2.00	4.00	8.00
❑ Epic 10300	Jennifer Juniper/Poor Cow	1968	2.00	4.00	8.00
❑ Epic 10345	Hurdy Gurdy Man/Teen Angel	1968	2.00	4.00	8.00
—Features John Paul Jones, Jimmy Page, and possibly John Bonham, all later of Led Zeppelin					
❑ Epic 10393	Lalena/Aye My Love	1968	2.00	4.00	8.00
❑ Epic 10434	Atlantis/To Susan on the West Coast Waiting	1969	2.00	4.00	8.00
❑ Epic 10510	Goo Goo Barabajagal (Love Is Hot)/Trust	1969	2.00	4.00	8.00
❑ Epic 10649	Riki Tiki Tavi/Roots of Oak	1970	2.00	4.00	8.00
❑ Epic 10694	Celia of the Seals/Song of the Wandering Aengus	1971	2.00	4.00	8.00
❑ Epic 10983	I Like You/Earth Sign Man	1973	—	2.50	5.00
❑ Epic 11023	Maria Magenta/Intergalactic Laxative	1973	—	2.50	5.00
❑ Epic 11108	Yellow Star/Sailing Homeward	1974	—	2.50	5.00
❑ Epic 50016	Rock and Roll with Me/Divine Daze of Deathless Delight	1974	—	2.50	5.00
❑ Epic 50077	Rock and Roll Souljer/How Silly	1975	—	2.50	5.00
❑ Epic 50237	Dark Eyed Blue Jean Angel/Well Known Has-Been	1976	—	2.50	5.00
❑ Hickory 1309	Catch the Wind/Why Do You Treat Me Like You Do	1965	3.75	7.50	15.00
❑ Hickory 1324	Colours/Josie	1965	3.00	6.00	12.00
❑ Hickory 1338	Universal Soldier/Do You Hear Me Now	1965	3.00	6.00	12.00
❑ Hickory 1375	You're Gonna Need Somebody on Your Mind/Little Tin Soldier	1966	3.00	6.00	12.00
❑ Hickory 1402	Turquoise/To Try for the Sun	1966	3.00	6.00	12.00
❑ Hickory 1417	Hey Gyp/The War Drags On	1966	3.00	6.00	12.00
❑ Hickory 1470	Sunny Goodge Street/Summer Day Reflection Song	1967	2.50	5.00	10.00
❑ Hickory 1492	Do You Hear Me Now/Why Do You Treat Me Like You Do	1968	2.50	5.00	10.00
❑ Janus 138	Keep On Truckin'/Hey Gyp	1971	2.00	4.00	8.00
Albums					
❑ Allegiance AV-437	Lady of the Stars	1983	2.50	5.00	10.00

Number	Title (A Side/B Side)	Yr	VG	VG+	NM
❑ Arista AB 4143	Donovan	1980	2.50	5.00	10.00
❑ Bell 1135	Early Treasures	1973	2.50	5.00	10.00
❑ Epic B2N 171 [(2)S]	A Gift from a Flower to a Garden	1967	6.25	12.50	25.00
—Boxed set of two LPs with portfolio of lyrics and drawings. The two records also were issued separately as Epic 26349 and 26350.					
❑ Epic L2N 6071 [(2)M]	A Gift from a Flower to a Garden	1967	12.50	25.00	50.00
—Boxed set of two LPs with portfolio of lyrics and drawings. The two records also were issued separately as Epic 24349 and 24350.					
❑ Epic LN 24217 [M]	Sunshine Superman	1966	7.50	15.00	30.00
—Contains the single version of "Sunshine Superman"					
❑ Epic LN 24239 [M]	Mellow Yellow	1967	7.50	15.00	30.00
❑ Epic LN 24349 [M]	Wear Your Love Like Heaven	1967	3.00	6.00	12.00
—Part of Epic 6071, issued simultaneously					
❑ Epic LN 24350 [M]	For Little Ones	1967	3.00	6.00	12.00
—Part of Epic 6071, issued simultaneously					
❑ Epic BN 26217 [R]	Sunshine Superman	1966	3.75	7.50	15.00
—Contains the single version of "Sunshine Superman" (rechanneled)					
❑ Epic BN 26239 [R]	Mellow Yellow	1967	3.75	7.50	15.00
❑ Epic BN 26349 [S]	Wear Your Love Like Heaven	1967	3.75	7.50	15.00
—Part of Epic 171, issued simultaneously					
❑ Epic BN 26350 [S]	For Little Ones	1967	3.75	7.50	15.00
—Part of Epic 171, issued simultaneously					
❑ Epic BN 26386	Donovan in Concert	1968	3.00	6.00	12.00
❑ Epic BN 26420 [S]	Hurdy Gurdy Man	1968	3.00	6.00	12.00
❑ Epic BXN 26439 [P]	Donovan's Greatest Hits	1969	3.00	6.00	12.00
—Yellow label; "Mellow Yellow" is rechanneled; "Sunshine Superman" is the full-length version in stereo; "Catch the Wind" and "Colours" were re-recorded					
❑ Epic BN 26481	Barabajagal	1969	3.00	6.00	12.00
❑ Epic E 30125	Open Road	1970	3.00	6.00	12.00
❑ Epic KEG 31210 [(2)]	The World of Donovan	1972	3.00	6.00	12.00
❑ Epic KE 32156	Cosmic Wheels	1973	3.75	7.50	15.00
—With enclosed poster					
❑ Epic KE 32800	Essence to Essence	1974	3.00	6.00	12.00
❑ Epic PE 33245	7-Tease	1974	3.00	6.00	12.00
❑ Epic EG 33731 [(2)]	Hurdy Gurdy Man/Barabajagal	1975	3.75	7.50	15.00
❑ Epic EG 33734 [(2)]	Donovan in Concert/Sunshine Superman	1975	3.75	7.50	15.00
❑ Epic PE 33945	Slow Down World	1976	3.00	6.00	12.00
❑ Hickory LPM-123 [M]	Catch the Wind	1965	6.25	12.50	25.00
—Most pressings have Donovan facing left, so he is correctly strumming his guitar with his right hand					
❑ Hickory LPS-123 [R]	Catch the Wind	1965	6.25	12.50	25.00
❑ Hickory LPM-127 [M]	Fairy Tale	1965	5.00	10.00	20.00
❑ Hickory LPS-127 [P]	Fairy Tale	1965	6.25	12.50	25.00
—"Colours" is rechanneled					
❑ Hickory LPM-135 [M]	The Real Donovan	1966	5.00	10.00	20.00
❑ Hickory LPS-135 [P]	The Real Donovan	1966	6.25	12.50	25.00
—Half stereo, including "Colours," the rest rechanneled.					
❑ Hickory LPS-143 [P]	Like It Is, Was and Evermore Shall Be	1968	5.00	10.00	20.00
❑ Hickory LPS-149 [P]	The Best of Donovan	1969	5.00	10.00	20.00
❑ Janus 3022	Donovan P. Leitch	1970	2.50	5.00	10.00
❑ Janus 3025	Hear Me Now	1971	2.50	5.00	10.00
❑ Kory 3012	Early Treasures	1977	2.00	4.00	8.00
❑ Pye 502	Donovan	1975	2.50	5.00	10.00

DOOBIE BROTHERS, THE

45s

Number	Title (A Side/B Side)	Yr	VG	VG+	NM
❑ Asylum 46630	Power/Cape Fear River	1980	—	2.50	5.00
—A-side: With John Hall and James Taylor; B-side by Sweet Honey in the Rock					
❑ Capitol B-44376	The Doctor/Too High a Price	1989	—	—	3.00
❑ Sesame Street 49642	Wynken, Blynken and Nod/In Harmony	1980	—	2.50	5.00
—B-side by Kate Taylor and the Simon-Taylor Family					
❑ Warner Bros. 7495	Nobody/Slippery St. Paul	1971	—	3.00	6.00
❑ Warner Bros. 7527	Travelin' Man/Feelin' Down Partner	1971	—	3.00	6.00
❑ Warner Bros. 7544	Beehive State/Closer Every Day	1971	—	3.00	6.00
❑ Warner Bros. 7619	Listen to the Music/Toulouse Street	1972	—	2.50	5.00
❑ Warner Bros. 7661	Jesus Is Just Alright/Rockin' Down the Highway	1972	—	2.50	5.00
❑ Warner Bros. 7698	Long Train Runnin'/Without You	1973	—	2.00	4.00
❑ Warner Bros. 7728	China Grove/Evil Woman	1973	—	2.00	4.00
❑ Warner Bros. 7795	Another Park, Another Sunday/Black Water	1974	—	2.50	5.00
❑ Warner Bros. 7832	Eyes of Silver/You Just Can't Stop It	1974	—	2.50	5.00

Number	Title (A Side/B Side)	Yr	VG	VG+	NM
❑ Warner Bros. 8011	Eyes of Silver/You Just Can't Stop It	1974	—	2.00	4.00
❑ Warner Bros. 8041	Nobody/Flying Cloud	1974	—	2.00	4.00
❑ Warner Bros. 8062	Black Water/Song to See You Through	1974	—	2.00	4.00
❑ Warner Bros. 8092	Take Me in Your Arms (Rock Me)/Slat Key Soquel Rag	1975	—	2.00	4.00
❑ Warner Bros. 8126	Sweet Maxine/Double Dealin' Four Flusher	1975	—	2.00	4.00
❑ Warner Bros. 8161	I Cheat the Hangman/Music Man	1975	—	2.00	4.00
❑ Warner Bros. 8196	Takin' It to the Streets/For Someone Special	1976	—	2.00	4.00
❑ Warner Bros. 8233	Wheels of Fortune/Slat Key Soquel Rag	1976	—	2.00	4.00
❑ Warner Bros. 8282	It Keeps You Runnin'/Turn It Loose	1976	—	2.00	4.00
❑ Warner Bros. 8408	Little Darling (I Need You)/Losin' End	1977	—	2.00	4.00
❑ Warner Bros. 8471	Echoes of Love/There's a Light	1977	—	2.00	4.00
❑ Warner Bros. 8500	Livin' on the Fault Line/Nothin' but a Heartache	1977	—	2.00	4.00
❑ Warner Bros. 8725	What a Fool Believes/Don't Stop to Watch the Wheels	1978	—	2.00	4.00
❑ Warner Bros. 8828	Minute by Minute/Sweet Feelin'	1979	—	2.00	4.00
❑ Warner Bros. 29552	You Belong to Me/South City Midnight Lady	1983	—	2.00	4.00
❑ Warner Bros. 49029	Dependin' on You/How Do the Fools Survive	1979	—	2.00	4.00
❑ Warner Bros. 49503	Real Love/Thank You Love	1980	—	2.00	4.00
❑ Warner Bros. 49622	One Step Closer/South Bay Street	1980	—	2.00	4.00
❑ Warner Bros. 49670	Keep This Train A-Rollin'/Just in Time	1981	—	2.00	4.00
❑ Warner Bros. 50001	Here to Love You/Wynken, Bliinken and Nod	1982	—	2.00	4.00
Albums					
❑ Capitol C1-90371	Cycles	1989	3.00	6.00	12.00
❑ Pickwick SPC-3721	Introducing the Doobie Brothers	1980	10.00	20.00	40.00
—Pre-Warner Bros. recordings; withdrawn shortly after release					
❑ Warner Bros. WS 1919	The Doobie Brothers	1971	3.75	7.50	15.00
—Green label original					
❑ Warner Bros. BS 2634	Toulouse Street	1972	3.75	7.50	15.00
—Green label original					
❑ Warner Bros. BS 2694	The Captain and Me	1973	3.00	6.00	12.00
—"Burbank" label					
❑ Warner Bros. W 2750	What Were Once Vices Are Now Habits	1974	2.50	5.00	10.00
—"Burbank" label					
❑ Warner Bros. BS 2835	Stampede	1975	2.50	5.00	10.00
—"Burbank" label					
❑ Warner Bros. BS 2899	Takin' It to the Streets	1976	2.50	5.00	10.00
—"Burbank" label					
❑ Warner Bros. BS 2978	Best of the Doobies	1976	3.00	6.00	12.00
❑ Warner Bros. BSK 3045	Livin' on the Fault Line	1977	2.50	5.00	10.00
—"Burbank" label					
❑ Warner Bros. BSK 3112	Best of the Doobies	1978	2.50	5.00	10.00
—"Burbank" label					
❑ Warner Bros. BSK 3193	Minute by Minute	1978	2.50	5.00	10.00
❑ Warner Bros. HS 3452	One Step Closer	1980	2.50	5.00	10.00
❑ Warner Bros. BSK 3612	Best of the Doobies, Volume 2	1981	2.50	5.00	10.00
❑ Warner Bros. 23772 [(2)]	Farewell Tour	1983	3.75	7.50	15.00

DOORS, THE

45s

Number	Title (A Side/B Side)	Yr	VG	VG+	NM
❑ Elektra 45051	Light My Fire/Love Me Two Times	1972	—	3.00	6.00
—"Spun Gold" series; originals have a very dark gold label					
❑ Elektra 45052	Touch Me/Hello, I Love You	1972	—	3.00	6.00
—"Spun Gold" series; originals have a very dark gold label					
❑ Elektra 45059	Riders on the Storm/Love Her Madly	1973	—	3.00	6.00
—"Spun Gold" series; originals have a very dark gold label					
❑ Elektra 45122	L.A. Woman/Roadhouse Blues	1983	—	2.00	4.00
—"Spun Gold" series; lighter gold label					
❑ Elektra 45123	People Are Strange/Break On Through	1983	—	2.00	4.00
—"Spun Gold" series; lighter gold label					
❑ Elektra 45611	Break On Through (To the Other Side)/End of the Night	1966	7.50	15.00	30.00
—Originals have a yellow and black label with "ELEKTRA" in all capital letters and a woman's head above a white line at the top of the label					
❑ Elektra 45615	Light My Fire/The Crystal Ship	1967	7.50	15.00	30.00
—Originals have a yellow and black label with "ELEKTRA" in all capital letters and a woman's head above a white line at the top of the label					
❑ Elektra 45621	People Are Strange/Unhappy Girl	1967	3.00	6.00	12.00
❑ Elektra 45624	Love Me Two Times/Moonlight Drive	1967	3.00	6.00	12.00
—Black, red and pink label					
❑ Elektra 45624	Love Me Two Times/Moonlight Drive	1967	3.00	6.00	12.00
—Black, red and white label					
❑ Elektra 45628	The Unknown Soldier/We Could Be So Good Together	1968	3.00	6.00	12.00
—Red, black and white label					
❑ Elektra 45635	Hello, I Love You/Love Street	1968	3.00	6.00	12.00
❑ Elektra 45635	Hello, I Love You, Won't You Tell Me Your Name?/Love Street	1968	5.00	10.00	20.00
—Original pressings have longer title					
❑ Elektra 45646	Touch Me/Wild Child	1968	3.00	6.00	12.00
❑ Elektra 45656	Wishful Sinful/Who Scared You?	1969	2.50	5.00	10.00
❑ Elektra 45663	Tell All the People/Easy Ride	1969	2.50	5.00	10.00
❑ Elektra 45675	Runnin' Blue/Do It	1969	2.50	5.00	10.00
❑ Elektra 45685	You Make Me Real/Roadhouse Blues	1970	2.50	5.00	10.00
❑ Elektra 45726	Love Her Madly/(You Need Meat) Don't Go No Further	1971	2.00	4.00	8.00
❑ Elektra 45738	Riders on the Storm/Changeling	1971	2.00	4.00	8.00
❑ Elektra 45757	Tightrope Ride/Variety Is the Spice of Life	1971	2.00	4.00	8.00
❑ Elektra 45768	Ships w/ Sails/In the Eye of the Sun	1972	2.00	4.00	8.00
❑ Elektra 45793	Get Up and Dance/Treetrunk	1972	2.00	4.00	8.00
❑ Elektra 45807	The Mosquito/It Slipped My Mind	1972	2.00	4.00	8.00
❑ Elektra 45825	The Piano Bird/Good Rockin'	1972	2.00	4.00	8.00
❑ Elektra 46005	Roadhouse Blues (Live)/Albinoni/Adagio	1979	—	2.50	5.00
❑ Elektra 47097	People Are Strange/Not to Touch the Earth	1980	—	2.00	4.00

Number	Title (A Side/B Side)	Yr	VG	VG+	NM
❑ Elektra 69770	Gloria/Moonlight Drive	1983	—	2.00	4.00
—Contrary to prior reports, this was not issued with a picture sleeve					
Albums					
❑ Elektra 5E-502	An American Prayer	1978	3.00	6.00	12.00
—Butterfly labels					
❑ Elektra 5E-515	Greatest Hits	1980	2.50	5.00	10.00
—Red labels with Warner Communications logo in lower right					
❑ Elektra EKL-4007 [M]	The Doors	1967	50.00	100.00	200.00
❑ Elektra EKL-4014 [M]	Strange Days	1967	150.00	300.00	600.00
—Value assumes the record is mono. There are two different covers for this; some copies have mono numbers on the two covers and the stereo number on the spine, and others have the mono number on the spine and stereo number on front and back covers.					
❑ Elektra EKL-4024 [M]	Waiting for the Sun	1968	250.00	500.00	1000.
❑ Elektra 8E-6001 [(2)]	Weird Scenes Inside the Gold Mine	1972	5.00	10.00	20.00
—Butterfly labels					
❑ Elektra EKS-9002 [(2)]	Absolutely Live	1970	6.25	12.50	25.00
—Butterfly labels					
❑ Elektra 60269	Alive, She Cried	1984	3.00	6.00	12.00
❑ Elektra 60345 [(2)]	The Best of the Doors	1985	3.75	7.50	15.00
❑ Elektra 60417	Classics	1986	3.00	6.00	12.00
❑ Elektra 60741 [EP]	Live at the Hollywood Bowl	1988	3.00	6.00	12.00
❑ Elektra E1-61047	The Doors	1991	25.00	50.00	100.00
—Soundtrack from the movie; only available on US vinyl from Columbia House					
❑ Elektra 61812	An American Prayer	1995	3.75	7.50	15.00
—Remastered and lengthened version of 5E-502					
❑ Elektra EKS-74007 [S]	The Doors	1967	12.50	25.00	50.00
—Brown labels					
❑ Elektra EKS-74014 [S]	Strange Days	1967	10.00	20.00	40.00
—Brown labels					
❑ Elektra EKS-74024 [S]	Waiting for the Sun	1968	7.50	15.00	30.00
—Brown labels					
❑ Elektra EKS-74079	13	1970	3.75	7.50	15.00
—Butterfly labels					
❑ Elektra EKS-75005	The Soft Parade	1969	12.50	25.00	50.00
—Brown or tan labels					
❑ Elektra EKS-75007	Morrison Hotel	1970	6.25	12.50	25.00
—Red labels with large stylized "E"					
❑ Elektra EKS-75011	L.A. Woman	1971	12.50	25.00	50.00
—With see-through window on cover and yellow innersleeve with photo of Jim Morrison on a cross					
❑ Elektra EKS-75017	Other Voices	1971	3.75	7.50	15.00
❑ Elektra EKS-75038	Full Circle	1972	3.75	7.50	15.00

DORSEY, LEE

45s					
❑ ABC 12326	Night People/Can I Be the One	1978	—	2.00	4.00
❑ ABC 12361	God Must Have Blessed America/Say It Again	1978	—	2.00	4.00
❑ ABC-Paramount 10192	Lottie Mo/Lover of Love	1961	3.75	7.50	15.00
❑ Ace 640	Lonely Evening/Rock	1961	3.75	7.50	15.00
❑ Amy 927	Ride Your Pony/The Kitty Cat Song	1965	2.00	4.00	8.00
❑ Amy 939	Can You Hear Me/Work, Work, Work	1965	2.00	4.00	8.00
❑ Amy 945	Get Out of My Life, Woman/So Long	1965	2.00	4.00	8.00
❑ Amy 952	Confusion/The Neighbors' Daughter	1966	2.00	4.00	8.00
❑ Amy 958	Working in the Coal Mine/Mexico	1966	2.50	5.00	10.00
❑ Amy 965	Holy Cow/Operation Heartache	1966	2.00	4.00	8.00
❑ Amy 974	Gotta Find a Job/Rain, Rain, Rain, Go Away	1967	—	3.00	6.00
❑ Amy 987	My Old Car/Why Wait Until Tomorrow	1967	—	3.00	6.00
❑ Amy 994	Can't Get Away/Vista Vista	1967	—	3.00	6.00
❑ Amy 998	Go-Go Girl/I Can Hear You Callin'	1967	—	3.00	6.00
❑ Amy 11010	I Can't Get Away/Cynthia	1968	—	3.00	6.00
❑ Amy 11020	Wonder Woman/A Little Dab A Do Ya	1968	—	3.00	6.00
❑ Amy 11031	Four Corners (Part 1)/Four Corners (Part 2)	1968	—	3.00	6.00
❑ Amy 11048	I'm Gonna Sit Right Down/Little Ba-By	1968	—	3.00	6.00
❑ Amy 11052	What Now My Love/A Lover Was Born	1969	—	3.00	6.00
❑ Amy 11055	Everything I Do Gonna be Funky (From Now On)/There Should Be a Book	1969	—	3.00	6.00
❑ Amy 11057	Give It Up/Candy Man	1969	—	3.00	6.00
❑ Bell 908	I Can Hear You Callin'/What You Want	1970	—	2.50	5.00
❑ Constellation 115	Organ Grinder's Swing/I Gotta Find a New Love	1964	5.00	10.00	20.00

Number	Title (A Side/B Side)	Yr	VG	VG+	NM
❑ Constellation 135	You're Breaking Me Up/Messed Around and Fell in Love	1964	5.00	10.00	20.00
❑ Fury 1053	Ya Ya/Give Me You	1961	3.75	7.50	15.00
❑ Fury 1056	Do-Re-Mi/People Gonna' Talk	1961	3.00	6.00	12.00
❑ Fury 1061	Eenie Meenie Miny Moe/Behind the 8-Ball	1962	3.00	6.00	12.00
❑ Fury 1066	You Are My Sunshine/Give Me Your Love	1962	3.00	6.00	12.00
❑ Fury 1074	Hoodlum Joe/When I Met My Baby	1963	3.00	6.00	12.00
❑ Lost-Nite 385	Ya Ya/Give Me You	197?	—	2.50	5.00
—Reissue					
❑ Polydor 14038	Yes We Can — Part 1/O Me O, My O	1970	—	2.50	5.00
❑ Polydor 14055	Sneakin' Sally Through the Alley/Tears, Tears and More Tears	1971	—	2.50	5.00
❑ Polydor 14106	Freedom for the Stallion/If She Won't (Find Someone Who Will)	1971	—	2.50	5.00
❑ Polydor 14147	When Can I Come Home/Gator Tail	1972	—	2.50	5.00
❑ Polydor 14181	On Your Way Down/Freedom for the Stallion	1973	—	2.50	5.00
❑ Rex 1005	Rock/Lonely Evening	1959	6.25	12.50	25.00
❑ Sansu 474	Love Lots of Lovin'/Take Care of Our Love	1967	3.00	6.00	12.00
—With Betty Harris					
❑ Smash 1842	Hello Good Looking/Someday	1963	2.50	5.00	10.00
❑ Spring 114	Occapella/Tears, Tears and More Tears	1971	—	2.50	5.00
❑ Valiant 1001	Lottie Mo/Lover of Love	1958	10.00	20.00	40.00
Albums					
❑ Amy 8010 [M]	Ride Your Pony	1966	7.50	15.00	30.00
❑ Amy 8010-S [S]	Ride Your Pony	1966	10.00	20.00	40.00
❑ Amy 8011 [M]	The New Lee Dorsey/Working in the Coal Mine-Holy Cow	1966	6.25	12.50	25.00
❑ Amy 8011-S [S]	The New Lee Dorsey/Working in the Coal Mine-Holy Cow	1966	7.50	15.00	30.00
❑ Arista AL 8387	Holy Cow! The Best of Lee Dorsey	1985	2.50	5.00	10.00
❑ Fury 1002 [M]	Ya Ya	1962	75.00	150.00	300.00
❑ Polydor 24-4024	Yes We Can	1970	3.00	6.00	12.00
❑ Sphere Sound SR-7003 [M]	Ya Ya	196?	25.00	50.00	100.00
—Reissue of Fury 1002					
❑ Sphere Sound SSR-7003 [R]	Ya Ya	196?	12.50	25.00	50.00
—Rechanneled reissue of Fury 1002					

DOVE, RONNIE

45s

Number	Title (A Side/B Side)	Yr	VG	VG+	NM
❑ Decca 31288	Party Doll/Yes Darling, I'll Be Around	1961	50.00	100.00	200.00
—Price is for stock copy; promos go for 20 to 25 percent of this value					
❑ Decca 32853	Just the Other Side of Nowhere/If I Cried	1971	—	3.00	6.00
❑ Decca 32919	Kiss the Hurt Away/He Cries Like a Baby	1972	—	3.00	6.00
❑ Decca 32997	It's No Sin/My World of Memories	1972	—	3.00	6.00
❑ Decca 33038	Lilacs in Winter/Is It Wrong	1972	—	3.00	6.00
❑ Diamond 163	Sweeter Than Sugar/I Believed in You	1964	2.50	5.00	10.00
❑ Diamond 167	Say You/Let Me Stay Today	1964	2.50	5.00	10.00
❑ Diamond 173	Right or Wrong/Baby Put Your Arms Around Me	1964	2.00	4.00	8.00
❑ Diamond 176	Hello Pretty Girl/Keep It a Secret	1965	2.00	4.00	8.00
❑ Diamond 179	One Kiss for Old Times' Sake/Bluebird	1965	2.00	4.00	8.00
❑ Diamond 179	One Kiss for Old Times' Sake/No Greater Love	1965	2.00	4.00	8.00
❑ Diamond 184	A Little Bit of Heaven/If I Live to Be a Hundred	1965	2.00	4.00	8.00
❑ Diamond 188	I'll Make All Your Dreams Come True/I Had to Lose You	1965	2.00	4.00	8.00
❑ Diamond 191	Kiss Away/Where in the World	1965	2.00	4.00	8.00
❑ Diamond 195	When Liking Turns to Loving/I'm Learning How to Smile Again	1965	2.00	4.00	8.00
❑ Diamond 198	Let's Start All Over Again/That Empty Feeling	1966	2.00	4.00	8.00
❑ Diamond 205	Happy Summer Days/Long After	1966	2.00	4.00	8.00
❑ Diamond 208	I Really Don't Want to Know/Years of Tears	1966	2.00	4.00	8.00
❑ Diamond 214	Cry/Autumn Rhapsody	1966	2.00	4.00	8.00
❑ Diamond 217	One More Mountain to Climb/All	1967	2.00	4.00	8.00
❑ Diamond 221	My Babe/Put My Mind at Ease	1967	2.50	5.00	10.00
—A-side written and produced by Neil Diamond					
❑ Diamond 227	I Want to Love You for What You Are/I Thank You for Your Love	1967	2.00	4.00	8.00
❑ Diamond 233	Dancin' Out of My Heart/Back from Baltimore	1967	5.00	10.00	20.00
—B-side written and produced by Neil Diamond, who also supplies backing vocals					
❑ Diamond 240	In Some Time/Livin' for Your Lovin'	1968	2.00	4.00	8.00
❑ Diamond 244	Mountain of Love/Never Gonna Cry	1968	2.00	4.00	8.00
❑ Diamond 249	Tomboy/Tell Me Tomorrow	1968	2.00	4.00	8.00
❑ Diamond 256	What's Wrong with My World/That Empty Feeling	1969	—	3.00	6.00
❑ Diamond 260	I Need You Now/Bluebird	1969	—	3.00	6.00
❑ Diamond 271	Chains of Love/If I Live to Be a Hundred	1970	3.75	7.50	15.00
—Promos, with "Chains of Love" on both sides, go for about half this amount					
❑ Diamond 379	Rise and Shine/(B-side unknown)	1987	—	2.50	5.00
❑ Dove 1021	Lover Boy/I'll Be Around	1959	1500.	2750.	4000.
—As "Ronnie Dove and the Bell-Tones". VG 1500; VG+ 2750					
❑ Hitsville 6038	Tragedy/Songs We Sang As Children	1976	—	2.50	5.00
❑ Hitsville 6045	The Morning After the Night Before/Why Daddy	1976	—	2.50	5.00
❑ Jalo 1406	No Greater Love/Saddest Hour	1962	6.25	12.50	25.00
❑ M.C. 5013	The Angel in Your Eyes (Brings Out the Devil in Me)/ Songs We Sang As Children	1978	—	3.00	6.00
❑ MCA 40106	So Long Dixie/Take My Love	1973	—	2.50	5.00
❑ Melodyland 6004	Please Come to Nashville/Pictures on Paper	1975	—	2.50	5.00
❑ Melodyland 6011	Things/Here We Go Again	1975	—	2.50	5.00
❑ Melodyland 6021	Drina (Take Your Lady Off for Me)/Your Sweet Love	1975	—	2.50	5.00
❑ Melodyland 6030	Right or Wrong/Guns	1976	—	2.50	5.00
Albums					
❑ Diamond D 5002 [M]	Right or Wrong	1964	5.00	10.00	20.00
❑ Diamond DS 5002 [S]	Right or Wrong	1964	6.25	12.50	25.00
❑ Diamond D 5003 [M]	One Kiss for Old Times' Sake	1965	5.00	10.00	20.00
❑ Diamond DS 5003 [S]	One Kiss for Old Times' Sake	1965	6.25	12.50	25.00
❑ Diamond D 5004 [M]	I'll Make All Your Dreams Come True	1965	5.00	10.00	20.00
❑ Diamond DS 5004 [S]	I'll Make All Your Dreams Come True	1965	6.25	12.50	25.00

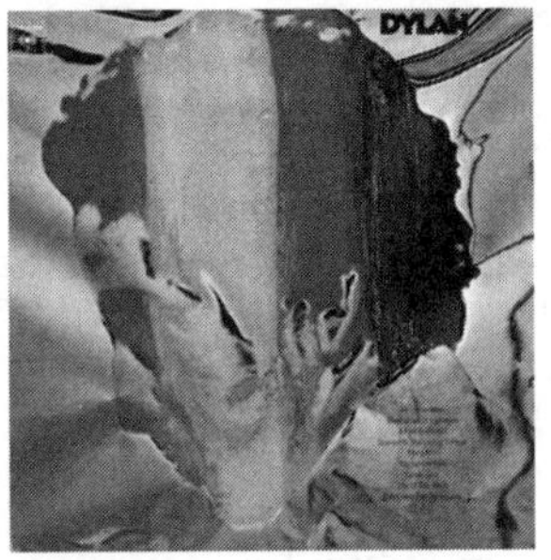

Number	Title (A Side/B Side)	Yr	VG	VG+	NM
❑ Diamond D 5005 [M]	The Best of Ronnie Dove	1966	3.75	7.50	15.00
❑ Diamond DS 5005 [S]	The Best of Ronnie Dove	1966	5.00	10.00	20.00
❑ Diamond D 5006 [M]	Ronnie Dove Sings the Hits for You	1966	3.75	7.50	15.00
❑ Diamond DS 5006 [S]	Ronnie Dove Sings the Hits for You	1966	5.00	10.00	20.00
❑ Diamond D 5007 [M]	Cry	1967	3.75	7.50	15.00
❑ Diamond DS 5007 [S]	Cry	1967	5.00	10.00	20.00
❑ Diamond D-5008 [M]	The Best of Ronnie Dove — Vol. 2	1968	7.50	15.00	30.00
❑ Diamond SD-5008 [S]	The Best of Ronnie Dove — Vol. 2	1968	3.75	7.50	15.00
❑ Power Pak 286	Greatest Hits	1975	3.00	6.00	12.00

DOVELLS, THE

45s

Number	Title (A Side/B Side)	Yr	VG	VG+	NM
❑ Abkco 4011	Bristol Stomp/You Can't Sit Down	1972	—	2.00	4.00
❑ Abkco 4029	Baby Workout/Hully Gully Baby	1973	2.50	5.00	10.00
❑ Abkco 4032	Bristol Twistin' Annie/Betty in Bermudas	1973	—	2.00	4.00
❑ Event 216	Dancing in the Street/Back on the Road Again	1974	—	2.50	5.00
❑ Event 3310	Roll Over Beethoven/Something About You Boy	1970	—	2.50	5.00
❑ Jamie 1369	Our Winter Love/Blue	1969	2.50	5.00	10.00
❑ MGM 13628	There's a Girl/Love Is Everywhere	1966	2.50	5.00	10.00
❑ MGM 14568	Don't Vote for Luke McCabe/Mary's Magic Show	1973	—	2.50	5.00
❑ Paramount 0134	L-O-V-E Love/We're All In This Together	1971	—	2.50	5.00
❑ Parkway 819	No, No, No/Letters of Love	1961	5.00	10.00	20.00
❑ Parkway 827	Bristol Stomp/Letters of Love	1961	3.75	7.50	15.00
❑ Parkway 827	Bristol Stomp/Out in the Cold Again	1961	7.50	15.00	30.00
❑ Parkway 833	Do the New Continental/Mope-Itty Mope Stomp	1962	3.75	7.50	15.00
❑ Parkway 838	Bristol Twistin' Annie/The Actor	1962	3.75	7.50	15.00
❑ Parkway 845	Hully Gully Baby/Your Last Chance	1962	3.75	7.50	15.00
❑ Parkway 855	The Jitterbug/Kissin' in the Kitchen	1962	3.75	7.50	15.00
❑ Parkway 861	Save Me Baby/You Can't Run Away from Yourself	1963	5.00	10.00	20.00
❑ Parkway 867	You Can't Sit Down/Stompin' Everywhere	1963	3.00	6.00	12.00
❑ Parkway 867	You Can't Sit Down/Wildwood Days	1963	3.75	7.50	15.00
❑ Parkway 882	Betty in Bermudas/Dance the Froog	1963	3.00	6.00	12.00
❑ Parkway 889	Stop Monkeyin' Aroun'/No, No, No	1963	3.00	6.00	12.00
❑ Parkway 901	Be My Girl/Dragster on the Prowl	1964	5.00	10.00	20.00
❑ Parkway 911	One Potato/Happy Birthday Just the Same	1964	3.75	7.50	15.00
❑ Parkway 925	Watusi with Lucy/What in the World's Come Over You	1964	3.00	6.00	12.00
❑ Swan 4231	Happy/(Hey, Hey, Hey) Alright	1965	5.00	10.00	20.00
❑ Verve 10701	Far Away/Sometimes	1973	—	2.50	5.00

Albums

Number	Title (A Side/B Side)	Yr	VG	VG+	NM
❑ Cameo C-1082 [M]	Len Barry Sings with the Dovells	1965	7.50	15.00	30.00
❑ Cameo SC-1082 [S]	Len Barry Sings with the Dovells	1965	12.50	25.00	50.00
❑ Parkway P 7006 [M]	The Bristol Stomp	1961	20.00	40.00	80.00
—Light orange label					
❑ Parkway P 7006 [M]	The Bristol Stomp	1962	12.50	25.00	50.00
—Dark orange and yellow label					
❑ Parkway P 7010 [M]	All the Hits of the Teen Groups	1962	12.50	25.00	50.00
❑ Parkway P 7021 [M]	For Your Hully Gully Party	1962	12.50	25.00	50.00
❑ Parkway P 7025 [M]	You Can't Sit Down	1963	12.50	25.00	50.00
❑ Wyncote SW 9052 [R]	Discotheque	1965	3.75	7.50	15.00
❑ Wyncote W 9052 [M]	Discotheque	1965	5.00	10.00	20.00
❑ Wyncote SW 9114 [R]	The Dovells' Biggest Hits	1965	3.75	7.50	15.00
❑ Wyncote W 9114 [M]	The Dovells' Biggest Hits	1965	5.00	10.00	20.00

DRIFTERS, THE

Several different groups with a common heritage, thus we list them together. Records on Capitol, Coral, Rama and Steeltown are unrelated to these Drifters and are oustide the scope of this book. Also see BEN E. KING; CLYDE McPHATTER.

45s

Number	Title (A Side/B Side)	Yr	VG	VG+	NM
❑ Atlantic 1006	Money Honey/The Way I Feel	1953	20.00	40.00	80.00
❑ Atlantic 1019	Such a Night/Lucille	1954	17.50	35.00	70.00
❑ Atlantic 1029	Honey Love/Warm Your Heart	1954	12.50	25.00	50.00
❑ Atlantic 1043	Bip Bam/Someday You'll Want Me to Want You	1954	10.00	20.00	40.00
❑ Atlantic 1048	White Christmas/The Bells of St. Mary's	1954	15.00	30.00	60.00
—Yellow label, no spinner (original)					
❑ Atlantic 1055	What'Cha Gonna Do/Gone	1955	12.50	25.00	50.00
❑ Atlantic 1078	Adorable/Steamboat	1955	10.00	20.00	40.00
❑ Atlantic 1089	Ruby Baby/Your Promise to Be Mine	1956	7.50	15.00	30.00
❑ Atlantic 1101	Soldier of Fortune/I Got to Get Myself a Woman	1956	7.50	15.00	30.00

Number	Title (A Side/B Side)	Yr	VG	VG+	NM
❑ Atlantic 1123	Fools Fall in Love/It Was a Tear	1957	7.50	15.00	30.00
❑ Atlantic 1141	Hypnotized/Drifting Away from You	1957	7.50	15.00	30.00
❑ Atlantic 1161	I Know/Yodee Yakee	1957	7.50	15.00	30.00
❑ Atlantic 1187	Drip Drop/Moonlight Bay	1958	7.50	15.00	30.00
—Last record by the "old" Drifters. The below Atlantic 45s are by a completely different group, although personnel changes resulted in at least one "old" Drifter (Johnny Moore) spending time with the "new" Drifters.					
❑ Atlantic 2025	There Goes My Baby/Oh My Love	1959	6.25	12.50	25.00
❑ Atlantic 2040	Dance with Me/(If You Cry) True Love, True Love	1959	5.00	10.00	20.00
❑ Atlantic 2050	This Magic Moment/Baltimore	1960	5.00	10.00	20.00
❑ Atlantic 2062	Lonely Winds/Hey Senorita	1960	5.00	10.00	20.00
❑ Atlantic 2071	Save the Last Dance for Me/Nobody But Me	1960	5.00	10.00	20.00
❑ Atlantic 2087	I Count the Tears/Suddenly There's a Valley	1960	3.75	7.50	15.00
❑ Atlantic 2096	Some Kind of Wonderful/Honey Bee	1961	3.75	7.50	15.00
❑ Atlantic 2105	Please Stay/No Sweet Lovin'	1961	3.75	7.50	15.00
❑ Atlantic 2117	Sweets for My Sweet/Loneliness or Happiness	1961	3.75	7.50	15.00
❑ Atlantic 2127	Room Full of Tears/Somebody New Dancin' with You	1961	3.75	7.50	15.00
❑ Atlantic 2134	When My Little Girl Is Smiling/Mexican Divorce	1962	3.75	7.50	15.00
❑ Atlantic 2143	Stranger on the Shore/What to Do	1962	3.75	7.50	15.00
❑ Atlantic 2151	Sometimes I Wonder/Jackpot	1962	3.75	7.50	15.00
❑ Atlantic 2162	Up On the Roof/Another Night with the Boys	1962	5.00	10.00	20.00
❑ Atlantic 2182	On Broadway/Let the Music Play	1963	3.75	7.50	15.00
❑ Atlantic 2191	Rat Race/If You Don't Come Back	1963	3.75	7.50	15.00
❑ Atlantic 2201	I'll Take You Home/I Feel Good All Over	1963	3.75	7.50	15.00
❑ Atlantic 2216	Vaya Con Dios/In the Land of Make Believe	1964	3.75	7.50	15.00
❑ Atlantic 2225	One Way Love/Didn't It	1964	3.75	7.50	15.00
❑ Atlantic 2237	Under the Boardwalk/I Don't Want to Go On Without You	1964	3.75	7.50	15.00
❑ Atlantic 2253	I've Got Sand in My Shoes/He's Just a Playboy	1964	3.00	6.00	12.00
❑ Atlantic 2260	Saturday Night at the Movies/Spanish Lace	1964	3.00	6.00	12.00
❑ Atlantic 2261	The Christmas Song/I Remember Christmas	1964	3.00	6.00	12.00
❑ Atlantic 2268	At the Club/Answer the Phone	1965	2.50	5.00	10.00
❑ Atlantic 2285	Come On Over to My Place/Chains of Love	1965	2.50	5.00	10.00
❑ Atlantic 2292	Follow Me/The Outside World	1965	2.50	5.00	10.00
❑ Atlantic 2298	I'll Take You Where the Music's Playing/ Far from the Maddening Crowd	1965	2.50	5.00	10.00
❑ Atlantic 2310	Nylon Stockings/We Gotta Sing	1965	2.50	5.00	10.00
❑ Atlantic 2325	Memories Are Made of This/My Islands in the Sun	1966	2.00	4.00	8.00
❑ Atlantic 2336	Up in the Streets of Harlem/You Can't Love Them All	1966	2.00	4.00	8.00
❑ Atlantic 2366	Aretha/Baby What I Mean	1966	2.00	4.00	8.00
❑ Atlantic 2426	Up Jumped the Devil/Ain't It the Truth	1967	2.00	4.00	8.00
❑ Atlantic 2471	I Need You Now/Still Burning in My Heart	1968	2.00	4.00	8.00
❑ Atlantic 2624	Your Best Friend/Steal Away	1969	2.00	4.00	8.00
❑ Atlantic 2746	You Got to Pay Your Dues/Black Silk	1970	2.50	5.00	10.00
❑ Atlantic 2786	A Rose By Any Other Name/Be My Lady	1971	2.50	5.00	10.00
❑ Atlantic 89189	Ruby Baby/Fever	1987	—	2.00	4.00
—B-side by Little Willie John					
❑ Bell 45320	You've Got Your Troubles/I'm Feelin' Sad	1973	—	2.50	5.00
❑ Bell 45387	The Songs We Used to Sing/Like Sister and Brother	1973	—	2.50	5.00
❑ Bell 45600	Kissin' in the Back Row of the Movies/I'm Feelin' Sad	1974	—	2.50	5.00
❑ Crown 108	The World Is Changing/Sacroiliac Swing	1954	50.00	100.00	200.00
❑ Musicor 1498	Midsummer Night in Harlem/Lonely Drifter, Don't Cry	1974	—	2.50	5.00
—As "Charlie Thomas and the Drifters"					
❑ S&J 800826	(More Than a Number in My) Little Red Book/I Count the Tears	196?	2.50	5.00	10.00
—As "Bill Pinkney and the Original Drifters"					
Albums					
❑ Arista AB 4140	Every Night Is Saturday Night	1976	3.00	6.00	12.00
❑ Atco SD 33-375 [R]	Their Greatest Recordings — The Early Years	1971	3.00	6.00	12.00
❑ Atlantic 8003 [M]	Clyde McPhatter and the Drifters	1956	125.00	250.00	500.00
—Black label					
❑ Atlantic 8022 [M]	Rockin' and Driftin'	1958	150.00	300.00	600.00
—Black label					
❑ Atlantic 8041 [M]	The Drifters' Greatest Hits	1960	150.00	300.00	600.00
—Black label					
❑ Atlantic 8059 [M]	Save the Last Dance for Me	1962	30.00	60.00	120.00
—Red and purple label, white "fan" logo at right					
❑ Atlantic SD 8059 [S]	Save the Last Dance for Me	1962	50.00	100.00	200.00
—Green and blue label, white "fan" logo at right					
❑ Atlantic 8073 [M]	Up on the Roof — The Best of the Drifters	1963	25.00	50.00	100.00
—Red and purple label, black "fan" logo at right					
❑ Atlantic SD 8073 [S]	Up on the Roof — The Best of the Drifters	1963	37.50	75.00	150.00
—Green and blue label, black "fan" logo at right					
❑ Atlantic 8093 [M]	Our Biggest Hits	1964	15.00	30.00	60.00
—Red and purple label, white "fan" logo at right					
❑ Atlantic SD 8093 [S]	Our Biggest Hits	1964	20.00	40.00	80.00
—Mostly red label, black "fan" logo					
❑ Atlantic 8099 [M]	Under the Boardwalk	1964	12.50	25.00	50.00
—Color photo of group on cover					
❑ Atlantic 8099 [M]	Under the Boardwalk	1964	20.00	40.00	80.00
—Black and white photo of group on cover					
❑ Atlantic SD 8099 [S]	Under the Boardwalk	1964	15.00	30.00	60.00
—Color photo of group on cover					
❑ Atlantic SD 8099 [S]	Under the Boardwalk	1964	30.00	60.00	120.00
—Black and white photo of group on cover					
❑ Atlantic 8103 [M]	The Good Life with the Drifters	1965	10.00	20.00	40.00
❑ Atlantic SD 8103 [S]	The Good Life with the Drifters	1965	12.50	25.00	50.00
❑ Atlantic 8113 [M]	I'll Take You Where the Music's Playing	1965	10.00	20.00	40.00
❑ Atlantic SD 8113 [S]	I'll Take You Where the Music's Playing	1965	12.50	25.00	50.00

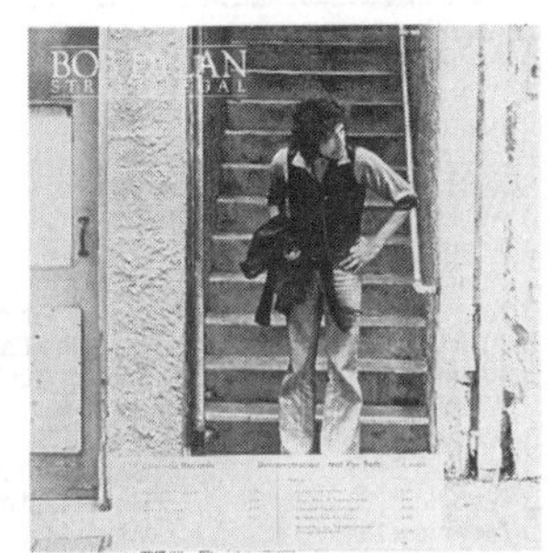

Number	Title (A Side/B Side)	Yr	VG	VG+	NM
❑ Atlantic 8153 [M]	The Drifters' Golden Hits	1968	7.50	15.00	30.00
❑ Atlantic SD 8153 [P]	The Drifters' Golden Hits	1968	7.50	15.00	30.00
—Green and blue label					
❑ Atlantic 81927 [(2)]	Let the Boogie-Woogie Roll: Greatest Hits 1953-1958	1989	3.75	7.50	15.00
❑ Atlantic 81931 [(2)]	All-Time Greatest Hits and More: 1959-1965	1989	3.75	7.50	15.00
❑ Clarion 608 [M]	The Drifters	1964	5.00	10.00	20.00
❑ Clarion SD 608 [P]	The Drifters	1964	7.50	15.00	30.00
❑ Gusto 0063	Greatest Hits — The Drifters	1980	2.50	5.00	10.00
❑ Trip TOP-16-6	16 Greatest Hits — The Drifters	1976	2.50	5.00	10.00

DUPREES, THE

45s

Number	Title (A Side/B Side)	Yr	VG	VG+	NM
❑ Coed 569	You Belong to Me/Take Me As I Am	1962	5.00	10.00	20.00
❑ Coed 571	My Own True Love/Ginny	1962	5.00	10.00	20.00
❑ Coed 574	I'd Rather Be Here in Your Arms/I Wish I Could Believe You	1963	3.75	7.50	15.00
❑ Coed 576	Gone with the Wind/Let's Make Love Again	1963	3.75	7.50	15.00
❑ Coed 580	I Gotta Tell Her Now/Take Me As I Am	1963	3.75	7.50	15.00
❑ Coed 584	Why Don't You Believe Me/The Things I Love	1963	7.50	15.00	30.00
❑ Coed 584	Why Don't You Believe Me/My Dearest One	1963	3.75	7.50	15.00
❑ Coed 585	Have You Heard/Love Eyes	1963	3.75	7.50	15.00
❑ Coed 587	(It's No) Sin/The Sand and the Sea	1964	3.75	7.50	15.00
❑ Coed 591	Please Let Her Know/Where Are You	1964	3.75	7.50	15.00
❑ Coed 593	Unbelievable/So Many Have Told Me	1964	3.75	7.50	15.00
❑ Coed 595	So Little Time/It Isn't Fair	1964	3.75	7.50	15.00
❑ Coed 596	I'm Yours/Wishing Ring	1964	3.75	7.50	15.00
❑ Colossus 110	Check Yourself/The Sky's the Limit	1970	—	3.00	6.00
—As "The Italian Asphalt and Pavement Company" or "The I.A.P. Co." for short					
❑ Columbia 43336	Around the Corner/They Said It Couldn't Be Done	1965	3.00	6.00	12.00
❑ Columbia 43464	Norma Jean/She Waits for Him	1965	3.00	6.00	12.00
❑ Columbia 43577	The Exodus Song/Let Them Talk	1966	3.00	6.00	12.00
❑ Columbia 43802	It's Not Time Now/Don't Want to Have to Do It	1966	2.50	5.00	10.00
❑ Columbia 44078	Be My Love/I Understand	1967	2.50	5.00	10.00
❑ Heritage 804	My Special Angel/Ring of Love	1968	2.50	5.00	10.00
❑ Heritage 805	Goodnight My Love/Ring of Love	1968	2.50	5.00	10.00
❑ Heritage 808	My Love, My Love/The Sky's the Limit	1968	2.50	5.00	10.00
❑ Heritage 811	Two Different Worlds/Hope	1969	2.50	5.00	10.00
❑ Heritage 826	Have You Heard/My Love, My Love	1970	2.50	5.00	10.00
❑ Lost-Nite 165	You Belong to Me/Take Me As I Am	196?	—	3.00	6.00
—Reissue					
❑ Lost-Nite 225	Why Don't You Believe Me/My Dearest One	196?	—	2.50	5.00
—Reissue					
❑ Lost-Nite 228	Have You Heard/It Isn't Fair	196?	—	2.50	5.00
—Reissue					
❑ Lost-Nite 232	Gone with the Wind/Let's Make Love Again	196?	—	2.50	5.00
—Reissue					
❑ Lost-Nite 236	My Own True Love/Ginny	196?	—	2.50	5.00
—Reissue					
❑ RCA Victor PB-10407	The Sky's the Limit/Delicious	1975	2.50	5.00	10.00

Albums

Number	Title (A Side/B Side)	Yr	VG	VG+	NM
❑ Coed LPC-905 [M]	You Belong to Me	1962	75.00	150.00	300.00
❑ Coed LPC-906 [M]	Have You Heard	1963	50.00	100.00	200.00
❑ Collectables COL-5008	The Best of the Duprees	198?	3.00	6.00	12.00
❑ Colossus 5000	Duprees Gold	1970	7.50	15.00	30.00
—As "The Italian Asphalt & Pavement Co."					
❑ Heritage HTS-35002 [S]	Total Recall	1968	7.50	15.00	30.00
❑ Post 1000	The Duprees Sing	196?	7.50	15.00	30.00

DURAN DURAN

45s

Number	Title (A Side/B Side)	Yr	VG	VG+	NM
❑ Capitol B-5215	Rio (3:57)/Hold Back the Rain (6:26)	1983	—	—	3.00
❑ Capitol B-5233	Is There Something I Should Know?/Careless Memories	1983	—	—	3.00
❑ Capitol B-5290	Union of the Snake/Secret Oktober	1983	—	—	3.00
—Custom label					
❑ Capitol B-5309	New Moon on Monday/Tiger Tiger	1984	—	—	3.00
❑ Capitol B-5345	The Reflex/New Religion	1984	—	2.00	4.00
❑ Capitol B-5417	The Wild Boys/(I'm Looking for) Cracks in the Pavement	1984	—	—	3.00
❑ Capitol B-5438	Save a Prayer/Save a Prayer (From the Arena)	1985	—	—	3.00

Number	Title (A Side/B Side)	Yr	VG	VG+	NM
❑ Capitol B-5475	A View to a Kill/A View to a Kill (That Fatal Kiss)	1985	—	—	3.00
—B-side by John Barry					
❑ Capitol B-5648	Notorious/Winter Marches On	1986	—	—	3.00
❑ Capitol B-5670	Skin Trade/We Need You	1987	—	—	3.00
❑ Capitol B-44001	Meet El Presidente/Vertigo (Do the Demolition)	1987	—	—	3.00
❑ Capitol B-44237	I Don't Want Your Love/(LP Version)	1988	—	—	3.00
❑ Capitol B-44287	All She Wants Is//I Believe-All I Need to Know (Medley)	1988	—	—	3.00
❑ Capitol B-44337	Do You Believe in Shame?/The Krush Brothers LSD Edit	1989	—	—	3.00
❑ Harvest A-5017	Planet Earth/To the Shore	1981	7.50	15.00	30.00
❑ Harvest A-5070	Girls on Film/Faster Than Light	1981	6.25	12.50	25.00
❑ Harvest P-A-5070 [DJ]	Girls on Film (same on both sides)	1981	3.00	6.00	12.00
❑ Harvest B-5134	Hungry Like the Wolf (3:23)/Careless Memories	1982	6.25	12.50	25.00
❑ Harvest B-5175	Rio (4:34)/Hold Back the Rain (3:59)	1982	6.25	12.50	25.00
—Custom label; different mixes than on Capitol B-5215					
❑ Harvest B-5195	Hungry Like the Wolf (4:11)/Hungry Like the Wolf (5:14)	1982	—	—	3.00

Albums

Number	Title	Yr	VG	VG+	NM
❑ Capitol ST-12158	Duran Duran	1983	2.50	5.00	10.00
—Reissue of Harvest 12158 with new cover and 9 tracks, adding "Is There Something I Should Know"					
❑ Capitol ST-12211	Rio	1983	2.00	4.00	8.00
—Version 4: Capitol logo replaces Harvest logo on back cover, otherwise it's the same as Harvest Version 3, with the same trail-off markings					
❑ Capitol ST-12310	Seven and the Ragged Tiger	1983	2.00	4.00	8.00
❑ Capitol SWAV-12374	Arena	1984	2.50	5.00	10.00
—With booklet (deduct 25% if cut out or if booklet is missing)					
❑ Capitol PJ-12540	Notorious	1986	2.00	4.00	8.00
❑ Capitol C1-90958	Big Thing	1988	2.50	5.00	10.00
—Deduct 25% for cut-outs					
❑ Capitol C1-93178	Decade	1989	3.00	6.00	12.00
❑ Capitol C1-94292	Liberty	1990	3.75	7.50	15.00
❑ Capitol ST-512211	Rio	1983	2.50	5.00	10.00
—Columbia House edition; otherwise the same as Version 4					
❑ Harvest ST-12158	Duran Duran	1981	3.75	7.50	15.00
—Original US issue with yellow label and 8 songs					
❑ Harvest ST-12211	Rio	1982	3.75	7.50	15.00
—Version 2: Harvest logo on lower back cover, with five songs remixed by David Kershenbaum; Side 1 trail-off wax number is "ST-1-12211-Z13-RE1 #1"					
❑ Harvest ST-12211	Rio	1982	5.00	10.00	20.00
—Version 1: Harvest logo on lower back cover, contains the same versions of the songs as the original UK release; trail-off wax number on Side 1 is "ST-1-12211 Z1"					
❑ Harvest MLP-15006 [EP]	Carnival	1982	5.00	10.00	20.00

DYLAN, BOB

45s

Number	Title (A Side/B Side)	Yr	VG	VG+	NM
❑ Asylum 11033	On a Night Like This/You Angel You	1974	—	3.00	6.00
❑ Asylum 11035	Something There Is About You/Going, Going, Gone	1974	—	3.00	6.00
❑ Asylum 11043	Most Likely You Go Your Way (And I'll Go Mine)/Stage Fright	1974	—	3.00	6.00
—With The Band					
❑ Asylum 45212	All Along the Watchtower/It Ain't Me Babe	1974	3.00	6.00	12.00
❑ Columbia 02510	Heart of Mine/The Groom's Still Waiting at the Altar	1981	—	2.00	4.00
❑ Columbia 04301	Sweetheart Like You/Union Sundown	1983	—	2.00	4.00
❑ Columbia 04425	Jokerman/Isis	1984	—	2.50	5.00
❑ Columbia 04933	Tight Connection to My Heart (Has Anybody Seen My Love)/ We Better Talk This Over	1985	—	2.00	4.00
❑ Columbia 05697	Emotionaly Yours/When the Night Comes Falling from the Sky	1985	—	2.00	4.00
❑ Columbia 07970	Silvio/Too Far from Home	1988	—	2.50	5.00
❑ Columbia 10106	Tangled Up in Blue/If You See Her Say Hello	1975	—	3.00	6.00
❑ Columbia 10217	Million Dollar Bash/Tears of Rage	1975	2.50	5.00	10.00
❑ Columbia 10245	Hurricane (Part 1)/Hurricane (Part 2)	1975	—	3.00	6.00
❑ Columbia 10298	Mozambique/Oh, Sister	1976	—	3.00	6.00
❑ Columbia 10454	Stuck Inside of Mobile with the Memphis Blues Again/Rita Mae	1976	—	2.50	5.00
❑ Columbia 10805	Baby Stop Crying/New Pony	1978	—	2.50	5.00
❑ Columbia 10851	Changing of the Guards/Senor (Tales of Yankee Power)	1978	—	2.00	4.00
❑ Columbia 11072	Gotta Serve Somebody/Trouble in Mind	1979	—	2.00	4.00
❑ Columbia 11168	Man Gave Names to All the Animals/When You Gonna Wake Up	1979	—	2.00	4.00
❑ Columbia 11235	Slow Train/Do Right to Me Baby (Do Unto Others)	1980	—	2.00	4.00
❑ Columbia 11318	Solid Rock/Covenant Woman	1980	—	2.00	4.00
❑ Columbia 11370	Saved/Are You Ready	1980	6.25	12.50	25.00
—Scarce on stock copy (promos worth about 20%)					
❑ Columbia 42656	Mixed-Up Confusion/Corrina, Corrina	1962	500.00	1000.	1500.
—Orange label					
❑ Columbia 42856	Blowin' in the Wind/Don't Think Twice, It's All Right	1963	125.00	250.00	500.00
❑ Columbia 43242	Subterranean Homesick Blues/She Belongs to Me	1965	5.00	10.00	20.00
❑ Columbia 43242	Subterranean Homesick Blues/She Belongs to Me	1972	7.50	15.00	30.00
—Briefly issued on gray label, which was used for about six months in 1972					
❑ Columbia 43346	Like a Rolling Stone/Gates of Eden	1965	5.00	10.00	20.00
❑ Columbia 43389	Positively 4th Street/From a Buick 6	1965	37.50	75.00	150.00
—A-side contains alternate version of "Can You Please Crawl Out Your Window." Evidently must be heard to identify.					
❑ Columbia 43389	Positively 4th Street/From a Buick 6	1965	5.00	10.00	20.00
—Standard version					
❑ Columbia 43477	Can You Please Crawl Out Your Window?/Highway 61 Revisited	1965	5.00	10.00	20.00
❑ Columbia 43541	One of Us Must Know (Sooner or Later)/ Queen Jane Approximately	1966	5.00	10.00	20.00
❑ Columbia 43592	Rainy Day Women #12 and 35/Pledging My Time	1966	3.75	7.50	15.00
❑ Columbia 43683	I Want You/Just Like Tom Thumb's Blues (Live)	1966	3.75	7.50	15.00
❑ Columbia 43792	Just Like a Woman/Obviously 5 Believers	1966	3.75	7.50	15.00
❑ Columbia 44069	Leopard-Skin Pill-Box Hat/Most Likely You'll Go Your Way and I'll Go Mine	1967	5.00	10.00	20.00
❑ Columbia 44826	I Threw It All Away/Drifter's Escape	1969	2.00	4.00	8.00

Number	Title (A Side/B Side)	Yr	VG	VG+	NM
❑ Columbia 44926	Lay Lady Lay/Peggy Day	1969	2.00	4.00	8.00
❑ Columbia 45004	Tonight I'll Be Staying Here with You/Country Pie	1969	2.50	5.00	10.00
❑ Columbia 45199	Wigwam/Copper Kettle (The Pale Moonlight)	1970	—	3.00	6.00
—Red label, black print					
❑ Columbia 45409	Watching the River Flow/Spanish Is the Loving Tongue	1971	—	3.00	6.00
❑ Columbia 45516	George Jackson (Acoustic Version)/George Jackson (Big Band Version)	1971	2.50	5.00	10.00
❑ Columbia 45913	Knockin' on Heaven's Door/Turkey Chase	1973	—	2.50	5.00
❑ Columbia 45982	A Fool Such As I/Lily of the West	1973	—	3.00	6.00
❑ Columbia 73042	Everything Is Broken/Dead Man, Dead Man	1989	2.00	4.00	8.00
❑ MCA 52811	Band of the Hand/Theme from Joe's Death	1986	—	—	3.00
—By "Bob Dylan and the Heartbreakers"					
Albums					
❑ Asylum AB-201 [(2)]	Before the Flood❑ 19745.0010.0020.00❑ Asylum 7E-1003 Planet Waves	1974	5.00	10.00	20.00
—With wraparound (olive green) second cover					
❑ Columbia C2L 41 [(2)M]	Blonde on Blonde	1966	25.00	50.00	100.00
—"Female photos" inner gatefold with two women pictured					
❑ Columbia C2L 41 [(2)M]	Blonde on Blonde	1968	75.00	150.00	300.00
—No photos of women inside gatefold					
❑ Columbia C2S 841 [(2)S]	Blonde on Blonde	1966	15.00	30.00	60.00
—"Female photos" inner gatefold with two women pictured					
❑ Columbia C2S 841 [(2)S]	Blonde on Blonde	1968	7.50	15.00	30.00
—No photos of women inside gatefold; "360 Sound Stereo" on label					
❑ Columbia CL 1779 [M]	Bob Dylan	1962	62.50	125.00	250.00
—Black and red (not orange) label with six white "eye" logos, three at 9 o'clock, three at 3 o'clock; stock copy					
❑ Columbia CL 1986 [M]	The Freewheelin' Bob Dylan	1963	10.00	20.00	40.00
—"Guaranteed High Fidelity" on label; corrected version (record plays what label says)					
❑ Columbia CL 1986 [M]	The Freewheelin' Bob Dylan	1963	4000.	8000.	12000.
—"Guaranteed High Fidelity" on label; plays "Let Me Die in My Footsteps," "Rocks and Gravel," "Talkin' John Birch Blues" and "Gamblin' Willie's Dead Man's Hand." Label does NOT list these. In dead wax, matrix number ends in "--1" followed by a letter; VG value 4000; VG+ value 8000					
❑ Columbia CL 2105 [M]	The Times They Are a-Changin'	1964	10.00	20.00	40.00
—"Guaranteed High Fidelity" on label					
❑ Columbia CL 2193 [M]	Another Side of Bob Dylan	1964	10.00	20.00	40.00
—"Guaranteed High Fidelity" on label					
❑ Columbia CL 2328 [M]	Bringing It All Back Home	1965	12.50	25.00	50.00
—"Guaranteed High Fidelity" on label					
❑ Columbia CL 2389 [M]	Highway 61 Revisited	1965	20.00	40.00	80.00
❑ Columbia KCL 2663 [M]	Bob Dylan's Greatest Hits	1967	12.50	25.00	50.00
❑ Columbia CL 2804 [M]	John Wesley Harding	1968	37.50	75.00	150.00
❑ Columbia CS 8579 [S]	Bob Dylan	1962	100.00	200.00	400.00
—Red and black label with six white "eye" logos, three together at the left, three together at the right, with "Stereo Fidelity" at the top of the label and "Columbia" at the bottom; stock copy					
❑ Columbia CS 8786 [S]	The Freewheelin' Bob Dylan	1963	15000.	22500.	30000.
—"360 Sound Stereo" in black on label (no arrows); record plays, and label lists, "Let Me Die in My Footsteps," "Rocks and Gravel," "Talkin' John Birch Blues" and "Gamblin' Willie's Dead Man's Hand." No known stereo copies play these without listing them, but just in case, check the trail-off for the numbers "XSM-58719-1A" and "XSM-58720-1A." If the number after the dash is "2" or higher, it's the standard version; VG value 15000; VG+ value 22500					
❑ Columbia CS 8786 [S]	The Freewheelin' Bob Dylan	1963	12.50	25.00	50.00
—"360 Sound Stereo" in black on label (no arrows)					
❑ Columbia CS 8905 [S]	The Times They Are a-Changin'	1964	10.00	20.00	40.00
—"360 Sound Stereo" in black on label					
❑ Columbia CS 8993 [S]	Another Side of Bob Dylan	1964	10.00	20.00	40.00
—"360 Sound Stereo" in black on label					
❑ Columbia CS 9128 [S]	Bringing It All Back Home	1965	10.00	20.00	40.00
—"360 Sound Stereo" in black on label					
❑ Columbia CS 9189 [S]	Highway 61 Revisited	1965	7.50	15.00	30.00
—With "regular" take of "From a Buick 6." Matrix number on Side 1 will end in "--2" or higher, plus a letter; "360 Sound Stereo" on label					
❑ Columbia CS 9189 [S]	Highway 61 Revisited	1965	62.50	125.00	250.00
—With alterrnate take of "From a Buick 6." Matrix number on Side 1 will end in "--1" plus a letter					
❑ Columbia KCS 9463 [S]	Bob Dylan's Greatest Hits	1967	3.75	7.50	15.00
—"360 Sound Stereo" label					
❑ Columbia CS 9604 [S]	John Wesley Harding	1968	5.00	10.00	20.00
—"360 Sound Stereo" label					
❑ Columbia KCS 9825	Nashville Skyline	1969	7.50	15.00	30.00
—"360 Sound Stereo" label					

Number	Title (A Side/B Side)	Yr	VG	VG+	NM
❑ Columbia C2X 30050 [(2)]	Self Portrait	1970	37.50	75.00	150.00
—"360 Sound Stereo" labels					
❑ Columbia KC 30290	New Morning	1970	3.75	7.50	15.00
❑ Columbia KG 31120 [(2)]	Bob Dylan's Greatest Hits, Vol. II	1971	3.75	7.50	15.00
❑ Columbia KC 32460	Pat Garrett and Billy the Kid	1973	3.75	7.50	15.00
❑ Columbia PC 32747	Dylan	1973	3.75	7.50	15.00
—No bar code on cover					
❑ Columbia PC 33235	Blood on the Tracks	1975	3.00	6.00	12.00
—First editions have liner notes on the back cover in black print					
❑ Columbia PC 33235	Blood on the Tracks	1975	500.00	1000.	2000.
—First edition cover; with the original rejected version of Side 2, though Side 1 is the standard version; the master number in the trail-off wax on Side 2 is "-1A"; one copy known, but others may exist					
❑ Columbia PC 33235	Blood on the Tracks	1975	2.50	5.00	10.00
—Third editions have liner notes restored (after they won a Grammy), but in white print					
❑ Columbia PC 33235	Blood on the Tracks	1975	3.75	7.50	15.00
—With drawing on back cover and no liner notes. Actually a second pressing, but available only for a short time					
❑ Columbia PC2 33682 [(2)]	The Basement Tapes	1975	5.00	10.00	20.00
❑ Columbia PC 33893	Desire	1976	3.00	6.00	12.00
❑ Columbia PC 34349	Hard Rain	1976	3.00	6.00	12.00
—No bar code on back cover					
❑ Columbia JC 35453	Street Legal	1978	3.00	6.00	12.00
❑ Columbia PC2 36067 [(2)]	Bob Dylan at Budokan	1979	3.75	7.50	15.00
❑ Columbia FC 36120	Slow Train Coming	1979	2.50	5.00	10.00
❑ Columbia FC 36553	Saved	1980	2.50	5.00	10.00
❑ Columbia TC 37496	Shot of Love	1981	2.50	5.00	10.00
❑ Columbia PC 37637	Planet Waves	1981	2.50	5.00	10.00
—Reissue of Asylum 7E-1003					
❑ Columbia CG 37661 [(2)]	Before the Flood	1983	3.00	6.00	12.00
—Reissue of Asylum AB-201					
❑ Columbia QC 38819	Infidels	1983	2.50	5.00	10.00
❑ Columbia C5X 38830 [(5)]	Biograph	1985	7.50	15.00	30.00
❑ Columbia FC 39944	Real Live	1984	2.50	5.00	10.00
❑ Columbia FC 40110	Empire Burlesque	1985	2.50	5.00	10.00
❑ Columbia OC 40439	Knocked Out Loaded	1986	2.50	5.00	10.00
❑ Columbia OC 40957	Down in the Groove	1988	2.50	5.00	10.00
❑ Columbia OC 45056	Dylan and the Dead	1989	3.00	6.00	12.00
—With backing by The Grateful Dead					
❑ Columbia OC 45281	Oh Mercy	1989	3.00	6.00	12.00
❑ Columbia C 46794	Under the Red Sky	1990	3.00	6.00	12.00
❑ Columbia 82876-87606-1 [(2)]	Modern Times	2006	3.75	7.50	15.00

E

EAGLES

45s

Number	Title (A Side/B Side)	Yr	VG	VG+	NM
❑ Asylum 11005	Take It Easy/Get You in the Mood	1972	—	2.50	5.00
❑ Asylum 11008	Witchy Woman/Early Bird	1972	—	2.00	4.00
❑ Asylum 11013	Peaceful Easy Feeling/Trying	1973	—	2.00	4.00
❑ Asylum 11017	Tequila Sunrise/21	1973	—	2.00	4.00
❑ Asylum 11025	Outlaw Man/Certain Kind of Fool	1973	—	2.00	4.00
❑ Asylum 11036	Already Gone/Is It True	1974	—	2.00	4.00
❑ Asylum 45202	James Dean/Good Day in Hell	1974	—	2.00	4.00
❑ Asylum 45218	Best of My Love/Ol' 55	1974	—	2.00	4.00
❑ Asylum 45257	One of These Nights/Visions	1975	—	2.00	4.00
❑ Asylum 45279	Lyin' Eyes/Too Many Hands	1975	—	2.00	4.00
❑ Asylum 45293	Take It to the Limit/After the Thrill Is Gone	1975	—	2.00	4.00
❑ Asylum 45373	New Kid in Town/Victim of Love	1976	—	2.00	4.00
❑ Asylum 45386	Hotel California/Pretty Maids All in a Row	1977	—	2.00	4.00
❑ Asylum 45403	Life in the Fast Lane/The Last Resort	1977	—	2.00	4.00
❑ Asylum 45555	Please Come Home for Christmas/Funky New Year	1978	—	2.00	4.00
—Original with "clouds" label					
❑ Asylum 46545	Heartache Tonight/Teenage Jail	1979	—	2.00	4.00
❑ Asylum 46569	The Long Run/The Disco Strangler	1979	—	2.00	4.00
❑ Asylum 46608	I Can't Tell You Why/The Greeks Don't Want No Freaks	1980	—	2.00	4.00
❑ Asylum 47100	Seven Bridges Road/The Long Run	1980	—	2.00	4.00
❑ Full Moon 49654	I Can't Tell You Why/Outside	1981	—	2.50	5.00
—B-side by Ambrosia					
❑ Full Moon/Asylum 47004	Lyin' Eyes/Looking for Love	1980	—	2.00	4.00
—B-side by Johnny Lee; contains the full-length version of "Lyin' Eyes"					
❑ Full Moon/Asylum 47073	Lyin' Eyes/Hello Texas	1980	—	2.50	5.00
—B-side by Jimmy Buffett					
❑ Geffen 19376	Get Over It/Get Over It (Live)	1994	—	2.50	5.00

Albums

Number	Title (A Side/B Side)	Yr	VG	VG+	NM
❑ Asylum 6E-103	Hotel California	1977	2.00	4.00	8.00
❑ Asylum 6E-105	Eagles — Their Greatest Hits 1971-1975	1977	2.00	4.00	8.00
❑ Asylum 5E-508	The Long Run	1979	2.00	4.00	8.00
❑ Asylum BB-705 [(2)]	Eagles Live	1980	3.00	6.00	12.00
❑ Asylum 7E-1004	On the Border	1974	3.00	6.00	12.00
—Clouds label					
❑ Asylum 7E-1039	One of These Nights	1975	2.50	5.00	10.00
—Clouds label					
❑ Asylum 7E-1052	Eagles — Their Greatest Hits 1971-1975	1976	2.50	5.00	10.00
❑ Asylum 7E-1084	Hotel California	1976	2.50	5.00	10.00
❑ Asylum SD 5054	Eagles	1972	3.75	7.50	15.00
—Gatefold cover; white label with door-in-a-circle logo at top					

Number	Title (A Side/B Side)	Yr	VG	VG+	NM
❑ Asylum SD 5068	Desperado	1973	3.00	6.00	12.00
—Clouds label					
❑ Asylum 60205	Eagles Greatest Hits, Volume 2	1982	2.50	5.00	10.00

EARTH, WIND, AND FIRE

45s

Number	Title (A Side/B Side)	Yr	VG	VG+	NM
❑ ARC 02536	Let's Groove/(Instrumental)	1981	—	2.00	4.00
❑ ARC 02688	Wanna Be with You/Kalimba Tree	1982	—	2.00	4.00
❑ ARC 10854	September/Love's Holiday	1978	—	2.50	5.00
❑ ARC 11033	After the Love Has Gone/Rock That!	1979	—	2.50	5.00
❑ ARC 11093	In the Stone/You and I	1979	—	2.00	4.00
❑ ARC 11165	Star/You and I	1979	—	2.00	4.00
❑ ARC 11366	Let Me Talk/(Instrumental)	1980	—	2.00	4.00
❑ ARC 11407	You/Share Your Love	1980	—	2.00	4.00
❑ ARC 11434	And Love Goes On/Win or Lose	1981	—	2.00	4.00
❑ Columbia 13-03136	Let's Groove/Sing a Song	1982	—	—	3.00
—Reissue					
❑ Columbia 38-03375	Fall in Love with Me/(Instrumental)	1982	—	2.00	4.00
❑ Columbia CNR-03566	Fall in Love with Me	1983	—	3.00	6.00
—One-sided budget release					
❑ Columbia 38-03814	Side by Side/Something Special	1983	—	2.00	4.00
❑ Columbia 38-04002	Spread Your Love/Freedom of Choice	1983	—	2.00	4.00
❑ Columbia 38-04210	Magnetic/Speed of Love	1983	—	2.00	4.00
❑ Columbia 38-04329	Touch/Sweet Sassy Lady	1984	—	2.00	4.00
❑ Columbia 38-04427	Moonwalk/We're Living in Our Own Time	1984	—	2.00	4.00
❑ Columbia 38-07608	System of Survival/Writing on the Wall	1987	—	—	3.00
❑ Columbia 38-07678	You and I/Musical Interlude: New Horizons	1988	—	—	3.00
❑ Columbia 38-07687	Evil Roy/(Instrumental)	1988	—	—	3.00
❑ Columbia 38-07695	Thinking of You/Money Tight	1988	—	—	3.00
❑ Columbia 38-08107	Turn On (The Beat Box)/(Instrumental)	1988	—	—	3.00
❑ Columbia 3-10026	Devotion/Fair But So Uncool	1974	—	3.00	6.00
❑ Columbia 3-10056	Hot Dawgit/R.L. Tambura	1974	—	2.50	5.00
—With Ramsey Lewis					
❑ Columbia 3-10090	Shining Star/Yearnin', Learnin'	1975	—	2.50	5.00
❑ Columbia 3-10103	Sun Goddess/Jungle Strut	1975	—	2.50	5.00
—With Ramsey Lewis					
❑ Columbia 3-10172	That's the Way of the World/Africano	1975	—	2.50	5.00
❑ Columbia 3-10251	Singasong/(Instrumental)	1975	—	3.00	6.00
—Original pressings have title as one word					
❑ Columbia 3-10251	Sing a Song/(Instrumental)	1975	—	2.50	5.00
—Later pressings have title as three words					
❑ Columbia 3-10309	Can't Hide Love/Gratitude	1976	—	2.50	5.00
❑ Columbia 3-10373	Getaway/(Instrumental)	1976	—	2.50	5.00
❑ Columbia 3-10439	Saturday Nite/Departure	1976	—	2.50	5.00
❑ Columbia 3-10492	On Your Face/Biyo	1977	—	2.50	5.00
❑ Columbia 3-10625	Serpentine Fire/(Instrumental)	1977	—	2.50	5.00
❑ Columbia 3-10688	Fantasy/Runnin'	1978	—	2.50	5.00
❑ Columbia 3-10796	Got to Get You Into My Life/I'll Write a Song for You	1978	—	2.50	5.00
❑ Columbia 4-45747	Power/M-O-M	1972	—	3.00	6.00
❑ Columbia 4-45800	Tims Is On Your Side/Where Have All the Flowers Gone	1973	—	3.00	6.00
❑ Columbia 4-45888	Evil/Clover	1973	—	2.50	5.00
❑ Columbia 4-45953	Keep Your Head to the Sky/Build Your Nest	1973	—	2.50	5.00
❑ Columbia 4-46007	Mighty Mighty/Drum Song	1974	—	2.50	5.00
❑ Columbia 4-46070	Kalimba Story/Tee Nine Chee Bit	1974	—	2.50	5.00
❑ Columbia 73205	Heritage/Gotta Find Out	1990	—	2.50	5.00
❑ Warner Bros. 7480	Fan the Fire/This World Today	1971	—	3.00	6.00
❑ Warner Bros. 7492	Love Is Life/This World Today	1971	—	3.00	6.00
❑ Warner Bros. 7549	I Think About Lovin' You/C'mon Children	1972	—	3.00	6.00

Albums

Number	Title (A Side/B Side)	Yr	VG	VG+	NM
❑ ARC FC 35647	The Best of Earth, Wind & Fire, Vol. 1	1978	2.50	5.00	10.00
❑ ARC FC 35730	I Am	1979	2.50	5.00	10.00
❑ ARC PC 35730	I Am	1984	2.00	4.00	8.00
—Budget-line reissue					
❑ ARC KC2 36795 [(2)]	Faces	1980	3.00	6.00	12.00
❑ ARC TC 37548	Raise!	1981	2.50	5.00	10.00
❑ Columbia KC 31702	Last Days and Time	1972	3.75	7.50	15.00
❑ Columbia KC 32194	Head to the Sky	1973	3.00	6.00	12.00

Number	Title (A Side/B Side)	Yr	VG	VG+	NM
❑ Columbia KC 32712	Open Our Eyes	1974	3.00	6.00	12.00
❑ Columbia PC 33280	That's the Way of the World	1975	3.00	6.00	12.00
—No bar code					
❑ Columbia PG 33694 [(2)]	Gratitude	1975	3.75	7.50	15.00
—No bar code					
❑ Columbia PC 34241	Spirit	1976	3.00	6.00	12.00
—No bar code					
❑ Columbia JC 34905	All 'N All	1977	3.00	6.00	12.00
❑ Columbia TC 38367	Powerlight	1983	2.50	5.00	10.00
❑ Columbia QC 38980	Electric Universe	1983	2.50	5.00	10.00
❑ Columbia FC 40596	Touch the World	1987	2.50	5.00	10.00
❑ Columbia OC 45013	The Best of Earth, Wind & Fire, Vol. II	1988	2.50	5.00	10.00
❑ Columbia C 45268	Heritage	1990	3.75	7.50	15.00
❑ Pair PDL2-1064 [(2)]	Beat It to Life	1986	3.00	6.00	12.00
❑ Warner Bros. WS 1905	Earth, Wind, and Fire	1971	5.00	10.00	20.00
—Green label					
❑ Warner Bros. WS 1958	The Need of Love	1971	5.00	10.00	20.00
—Green label					
❑ Warner Bros. 2WS 2798 [(2)]	Another Time	1974	5.00	10.00	20.00
—"Burbank" palm trees labels					

EARTH, WIND, AND FIRE WITH THE EMOTIONS

45s

Number	Title (A Side/B Side)	Yr	VG	VG+	NM
❑ ARC 10956	Boogie Wonderland/(Instrumental)	1979	—	2.50	5.00

EASTON, SHEENA

45s

Number	Title (A Side/B Side)	Yr	VG	VG+	NM
❑ EMI America 8071	Morning Train (Nine to Five)/Calm Before the Storm	1981	—	2.00	4.00
❑ EMI America 8080	Modern Girl/Summer's Over	1981	—	2.00	4.00
❑ EMI America A-8101	You Could Have Been with Me/Savoir Faire	1981	—	2.00	4.00
❑ EMI America B-8113	When He Shines/Family of One	1982	—	2.00	4.00
❑ EMI America B-8131	Machinery/So We Say Goodbye	1982	—	2.00	4.00
❑ EMI America B-8142	I Wouldn't Beg for Water/Some of Us Will	1982	—	2.50	5.00
❑ EMI America B-8150	I Don't Need Your Work/You Do It	1983	2.50	5.00	10.00
❑ EMI America B-8172	Telefone (Long Distance Love Affair)/ Wish You Were Here Tonight	1983	—	2.00	4.00
❑ EMI America B-8186	Almost Over You/I Don't Need Your Word	1983	—	2.00	4.00
❑ EMI America B-8201	Devil in a Fast Car/Sweet Talk	1984	—	—	3.00
❑ EMI America B-8227	Strut/Letters from the Road	1984	—	—	3.00
❑ EMI America B-8253	Sugar Walls/Straight Talking	1984	—	—	3.00
❑ EMI America B-8263	Swear/Double Standard	1985	—	—	3.00
❑ EMI America B-8295	Do It for Love/Can't Wait Till Tomorrow	1985	—	—	3.00
❑ EMI America B-8305	Magic of Love/When the Lightning Strikes	1985	—	—	3.00
❑ EMI America B-8309	Jimmy Mack/Money Back Guarantee	1986	—	—	3.00
❑ EMI America B-8332	So Far So Good/Magic of Love	1986	—	—	3.00
❑ EMI America B-43011	Eternity/Shockwave	1987	—	—	3.00
❑ Liberty A-1418	For Your Eyes Only/(Instrumental)	1981	—	2.50	5.00
—First pressing credited to "Original Motion Picture Soundtrack" with Sheena Easton's name in fine print					
❑ Liberty B-1492	We've Got Tonight/You Are So Beautiful	1983	—	—	3.00
—A-side: With Kenny Rogers; B-side: Kenny Rogers solo					
❑ MCA 53416	The Lover in Me/(Instrumental)	1988	—	—	3.00
❑ MCA 53499	Days Like This/(Instrumental)	1989	—	2.00	4.00
❑ MCA 53629	101/(Instrumental)	1989	—	2.50	5.00
❑ MCA 53691	No Deposit, No Return/(Instrumental)	1989	—	2.50	5.00
❑ Odeon OSK 5058	La Noche Y Tu/Todo Me Recuerda A Ti	1984	5.00	10.00	20.00
—Spanish versions of "We've Got Tonight" and "Almost Over You"; this was indeed pressed in the United States					
❑ Odeon OSK 9027	Me Gustas Tal Como Eres/(B-side unknown)	1984	5.00	10.00	20.00
—With Luis Miguel					

Albums

Number	Title (A Side/B Side)	Yr	VG	VG+	NM
❑ EMI America ST-17049	Sheena Easton	1981	2.00	4.00	8.00
❑ EMI America SW-17061	You Could Have Been with Me	1981	2.00	4.00	8.00
❑ EMI America ST-17080	Madness, Money and Music	1982	2.00	4.00	8.00
❑ EMI America ST-17101	Best Kept Secret	1983	2.00	4.00	8.00
❑ EMI America ST- 17132	A Private Heaven	1984	2.00	4.00	8.00
❑ EMI America SJ-17173	Do You	1985	2.00	4.00	8.00
❑ MCA 10131	What Comes Naturally	1991	3.00	6.00	12.00
❑ MCA 42249	The Lover in Me	1988	2.50	5.00	10.00

EASYBEATS, THE

45s

Number	Title (A Side/B Side)	Yr	VG	VG+	NM
❑ Ascot 2214	In My Book/Make You Feel Alright (Women)	1966	3.75	7.50	15.00
❑ Rare Earth 5009	St. Louis/Can't Find Love	1969	3.75	7.50	15.00
❑ United Artists 0114	Friday on My Mind/Gonna Have a Good Time	1973	—	2.00	4.00
—"Silver Spotlight Series" reissue					
❑ United Artists 50106	Friday on My Mind/Made My Bed; Gonna Lie in It	1966	3.75	7.50	15.00
❑ United Artists 50187	Pretty Girl/Heaven and Hell	1967	2.50	5.00	10.00
❑ United Artists 50206	Falling Off the Edge of the World/Remember Sam	1967	2.50	5.00	10.00
❑ United Artists 50289	Come In, You'll Get Pneumonia/Hello, How Are You	1968	2.50	5.00	10.00
❑ United Artists 50488	Gonna Have a Good Time/Lay Me Down and Die	1969	2.50	5.00	10.00

Albums

Number	Title (A Side/B Side)	Yr	VG	VG+	NM
❑ Rare Earth 517	Easy Ridin'	1970	—	—	—
—Canceled					
❑ Rhino RNLP-124	The Best of the Easybeats	1985	2.00	4.00	8.00
❑ United Artists UAL 3588 [M]	Friday on My Mind	1967	10.00	20.00	40.00
❑ United Artists UAS 6588 [P]	Friday on My Mind	1967	12.50	25.00	50.00
—"Make You Feel Alright" is rechanneled.					

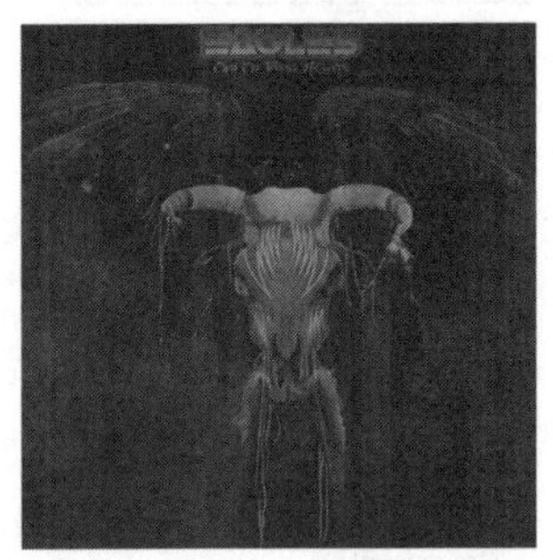

Number	Title (A Side/B Side)	Yr	VG	VG+	NM
❑ United Artists UAS 6667 [P]	Falling Off the Edge of the World	1968	10.00	20.00	40.00
—"Women" is rechanneled.					

ECHOES, THE (1)

45s

Number	Title (A Side/B Side)	Yr	VG	VG+	NM
❑ Seg-Way 103	Baby Blue/Boomerang	1961	6.25	12.50	25.00
❑ Seg-Way 106	Sad Eyes (Don't You Cry)/It's Raining	1961	6.25	12.50	25.00
❑ Seg-Way 1002	Angel of My Heart/Gee Oh Gee	1962	10.00	20.00	40.00
❑ Smash 1766	Bluebirds Over the Mountain/A Chicken Ain't Nothin' But a Bird	1962	3.75	7.50	15.00
❑ Smash 1807	Keep an Eye on Her/A Million Miles from Nowhere	1963	3.75	7.50	15.00
❑ Smash 1850	Annabelle Lee/If Love Is	1963	3.75	7.50	15.00
❑ SRG 101	Baby Blue/Boomerang	1960	50.00	100.00	200.00

EDDY, DUANE

45s

Number	Title (A Side/B Side)	Yr	VG	VG+	NM
❑ Big Tree 157	Renegade/Nightly News	1972	2.00	4.00	8.00
❑ Capitol B-44018	Spies/Rockabilly Holiday	1987	—	2.50	5.00
❑ China 42986	Peter Gunn/Something Always Happens	1986	—	—	3.00
—With Art of Noise; B-side does not feature Eddy					
❑ Colpix 779	Trash/South Phoenix	1965	3.75	7.50	15.00
❑ Colpix 788	Don't Think Twice, It's All Right/House of the Rising Sun	1965	3.75	7.50	15.00
❑ Colpix 795	El Rancho Grande/Poppa's Movin' On	1966	3.75	7.50	15.00
❑ Congress 6010	Freight Train/Put a Little Love in Your Heart	1970	3.75	7.50	15.00
❑ Elektra 45359	You Are My Sunshine/From 8 to 7	1977	—	2.50	5.00
❑ Ford 500	Ramrod/Caravan	1957	500.00	1000.	1500.
—As "Duane Eddy and His Rock-A-Billies"					
❑ Gregmark 5	Caravan (Part 1)/Caravan (Part 2)	1961	3.75	7.50	15.00
—Credited to Duane Eddy, but is actually Al Casey					
❑ Gusto 2047	Rebel Rouser/40 Miles of Bad Road	1979	—	2.00	4.00
—Re-recordings					
❑ Jamie 1101	Moovin N' Groovin'/Up and Down	1958	12.50	25.00	50.00
—Originals have pink labels					
❑ Jamie 1104	Rebel-'Rouser/Stalkin'	1958	6.25	12.50	25.00
❑ Jamie 1109	Ramrod/The Walker	1958	6.25	12.50	25.00
❑ Jamie 1111	Cannonball/Mason Dixon Lion	1958	5.00	10.00	20.00
❑ Jamie 1117 [M]	The Lonely One/Detour	1959	5.00	10.00	20.00
❑ Jamie 1117 [S]	The Lonely One/Detour	1959	12.50	25.00	50.00
❑ Jamie 1122	Yep!/Three-30-Blues	1959	5.00	10.00	20.00
❑ Jamie 1126 [M]	Forty Miles of Bad Road/The Quiet Three	1959	5.00	10.00	20.00
❑ Jamie 1126 [S]	Forty Miles of Bad Road/The Quiet Three	1959	12.50	25.00	50.00
❑ Jamie 1130 [M]	Some Kind-a Earthquake/First Love, First Tears	1959	5.00	10.00	20.00
❑ Jamie 1130 [S]	Some Kind-a Earthquake/First Love, First Tears	1959	12.50	25.00	50.00
❑ Jamie 1144	Bonnie Came Back/Lost Island	1959	5.00	10.00	20.00
❑ Jamie 1151	Shazam!/The Secret Seven	1960	3.75	7.50	15.00
❑ Jamie 1156	Because They're Young/Rebel Walk	1960	3.75	7.50	15.00
❑ Jamie 1163	Kommotion/Theme for Moon Children	1960	3.75	7.50	15.00
❑ Jamie 1168	Peter Gunn/Along the Navaho Trail	1960	3.75	7.50	15.00
❑ Jamie 1175	"Pepe"/Lost Friend	1960	3.75	7.50	15.00
❑ Jamie 1183	Theme from Dixie/Gidget Goes Hawaiian	1961	3.75	7.50	15.00
❑ Jamie 1187	Ring of Fire/Bobbie	1961	3.75	7.50	15.00
❑ Jamie 1195	Drivin' Home/Tammy	1961	3.75	7.50	15.00
❑ Jamie 1200	My Blue Heaven/Along Came Linda	1961	3.75	7.50	15.00
❑ Jamie 1206	The Avenger/Londonderry Air	1961	3.75	7.50	15.00
❑ Jamie 1209	The Battle/Trambone	1962	3.75	7.50	15.00
❑ Jamie 1224	Runaway Pony/Just Because	1962	3.75	7.50	15.00
❑ Jamie 1303	Rebel Rouser/Movin' N' Groovin'	1965	3.00	6.00	12.00
❑ RCA Victor 47-7999	Deep in the Heart of Texas/Saints and Sinners	1962	3.00	6.00	12.00
❑ RCA Victor 47-8047	The Ballad of Paladin/The Wild Westerner	1962	3.00	6.00	12.00
❑ RCA Victor 47-8087	(Dance with the) Guitar Man/Stretchin' Out	1962	3.75	7.50	15.00
❑ RCA Victor 47-8131	Boss Guitar/Desert Rat	1963	3.00	6.00	12.00
❑ RCA Victor 47-8180	Lonely Boy, Lonely Guitar/Joshin'	1963	3.00	6.00	12.00
❑ RCA Victor 47-8214	Your Baby's Gone Surfin'/Shuckin'	1963	3.75	7.50	15.00
❑ RCA Victor 47-8276	The Son of Rebel Rouser/The Story of Three Loves	1963	3.00	6.00	12.00
❑ RCA Victor 47-8335	Guitar Child/Jerky Jalopy	1964	3.00	6.00	12.00
❑ RCA Victor 47-8376	Water Skiing/Theme from A Summer Place	1964	3.00	6.00	12.00
❑ RCA Victor 47-8442	Guitar Star/The Iguana	1964	3.00	6.00	12.00
❑ RCA Victor 47-8507	Moonshot/Roughneck	1965	3.00	6.00	12.00
❑ Reprise 0504	Daydream/This Guitar Was Made for Twangin'	1966	2.50	5.00	10.00

Number	Title (A Side/B Side)	Yr	VG	VG+	NM
❑ Reprise 0557	Roarin'/Monsoon	1967	2.50	5.00	10.00
❑ Reprise 0662	There Is a Mountain/This Town	1968	2.50	5.00	10.00
❑ Reprise 0690	Niki-Hoeky/Velvet Nights	1968	2.50	5.00	10.00
❑ Uni 55237	The Five-Seventeen/Something	1970	3.75	7.50	15.00
Albums					
❑ Capitol ST-12567	Duane Eddy	1987	3.00	6.00	12.00
❑ Colpix CP-490 [M]	Duane A-Go-Go	1965	7.50	15.00	30.00
❑ Colpix CPS-490 [S]	Duane A-Go-Go	1965	10.00	20.00	40.00
❑ Colpix CPL-494 [M]	Duane Eddy Does Bob Dylan	1965	7.50	15.00	30.00
❑ Colpix SCP-494 [S]	Duane Eddy Does Bob Dylan	1965	10.00	20.00	40.00
❑ Jamie JLP-3000 [M]	Have "Twangy" Guitar — Will Travel	1958	30.00	60.00	120.00
—Duane sitting with guitar case, title on cover in white (1st)					
❑ Jamie JLPS-3000 [S]	Have "Twangy" Guitar — Will Travel	1958	100.00	200.00	400.00
—Duane sitting with guitar case, title on cover in white (1st)					
❑ Jamie JLPM-3006 [M]	Especially for You…	1959	10.00	20.00	40.00
❑ Jamie JLPS-3006 [S]	Especially for You…	1959	15.00	30.00	60.00
❑ Jamie JLPM-3009 [M]	The "Twangs" The "Thang"	1959	10.00	20.00	40.00
❑ Jamie JLPS-3009 [S]	The "Twangs" The "Thang"	1959	15.00	30.00	60.00
❑ Jamie JLPM-3011 [M]	Songs of Our Heritage	1960	20.00	40.00	80.00
—Gatefold cover					
❑ Jamie JLPS-3011 [S]	Songs of Our Heritage	1960	25.00	50.00	100.00
—Gatefold cover					
❑ Jamie JLPM-3014 [M]	$1,000,000.00 Worth of Twang	1960	10.00	20.00	40.00
❑ Jamie JLPS-3014 [S]	$1,000,000.00 Worth of Twang	1960	17.50	35.00	70.00
—All but one song — "Up and Down" — is in true stereo					
❑ Jamie JLPM-3019 [M]	Girls! Girls! Girls!	1961	10.00	20.00	40.00
❑ Jamie JLPS-3019 [R]	Girls! Girls! Girls!	1961	7.50	15.00	30.00
❑ Jamie JLPM-3021 [M]	$1,000,000.00 Worth of Twang, Volume 2	1962	10.00	20.00	40.00
❑ Jamie JLPS-3021 [R]	$1,000,000.00 Worth of Twang, Volume 2	1962	7.50	15.00	30.00
❑ Jamie JLPM-3022 [M]	Twistin' with Duane Eddy	1962	10.00	20.00	40.00
❑ Jamie JLPS-3022 [P]	Twistin' with Duane Eddy	1962	10.00	20.00	40.00
❑ Jamie JLPM-3024 [M]	Surfin'	1963	12.50	25.00	50.00
❑ Jamie JLPS-3024 [S]	Surfin'	1963	20.00	40.00	80.00
❑ Jamie JLPM-3025 [M]	Duane Eddy & The Rebels — In Person	1963	7.50	15.00	30.00
❑ Jamie JLPS-3025 [S]	Duane Eddy & The Rebels — In Person	1963	10.00	20.00	40.00
❑ Jamie JLPM-3026 [M]	16 Greatest Hits	1964	10.00	20.00	40.00
❑ Jamie JLPS-3026 [R]	16 Greatest Hits	1964	7.50	15.00	30.00
❑ RCA Victor LPM-2525 [M]	Twistin' 'N' Twangin'	1962	6.25	12.50	25.00
❑ RCA Victor LSP-2525 [S]	Twistin' 'N' Twangin'	1962	10.00	20.00	40.00
❑ RCA Victor LPM-2576 [M]	Twangy Guitar — Silky Strings	1962	6.25	12.50	25.00
❑ RCA Victor LSP-2576 [S]	Twangy Guitar — Silky Strings	1962	10.00	20.00	40.00
❑ RCA Victor LPM-2648 [M]	Dance with the Guitar Man	1962	6.25	12.50	25.00
❑ RCA Victor LSP-2648 [S]	Dance with the Guitar Man	1962	10.00	20.00	40.00
❑ RCA Victor ANL1-2671	Pure Gold	1978	2.50	5.00	10.00
❑ RCA Victor LPM-2681 [M]	Twang a Country Song	1963	6.25	12.50	25.00
❑ RCA Victor LSP-2681 [S]	Twang a Country Song	1963	10.00	20.00	40.00
❑ RCA Victor LPM-2700 [M]	"Twangin'" Up a Storm!	1963	6.25	12.50	25.00
❑ RCA Victor LSP-2700 [S]	"Twangin'" Up a Storm!	1963	10.00	20.00	40.00
❑ RCA Victor LPM-2798 [M]	Lonely Guitar	1964	5.00	10.00	20.00
❑ RCA Victor LSP-2798 [S]	Lonely Guitar	1964	7.50	15.00	30.00
❑ RCA Victor LPM-2918 [M]	Water Skiing	1964	5.00	10.00	20.00
❑ RCA Victor LSP-2918 [S]	Water Skiing	1964	7.50	15.00	30.00
❑ RCA Victor LPM-2993 [M]	Twangin' the Golden Hits	1965	5.00	10.00	20.00
❑ RCA Victor LSP-2993 [S]	Twangin' the Golden Hits	1965	7.50	15.00	30.00
❑ RCA Victor LPM-3432 [M]	Twangsville	1965	5.00	10.00	20.00
❑ RCA Victor LSP-3432 [S]	Twangsville	1965	7.50	15.00	30.00
❑ RCA Victor LPM-3477 [M]	The Best of Duane Eddy	1965	5.00	10.00	20.00
❑ RCA Victor LSP-3477 [P]	The Best of Duane Eddy	1965	6.25	12.50	25.00
—Black "Stereo" label					
❑ Reprise R-6218 [M]	The Biggest Twang of Them All	1966	7.50	15.00	30.00
❑ Reprise RS-6218 [S]	The Biggest Twang of Them All	1966	10.00	20.00	40.00
❑ Reprise R-6240 [M]	The Roaring Twangies	1967	7.50	15.00	30.00
❑ Reprise RS-6240 [S]	The Roaring Twangies	1967	10.00	20.00	40.00
❑ Sire SASH-3707-2 [(2)]	The Vintage Years	1975	6.25	12.50	25.00

EDWARD BEAR

Number	Title (A Side/B Side)	Yr	VG	VG+	NM
45s					
❑ Capitol 2801	You, Me and Mexico/Sinking Ship	1970	—	3.00	6.00
❑ Capitol 2955	You Can't Deny It/Toe Jam	1970	—	3.00	6.00
❑ Capitol 3351	Masquerade/The Pirate King	1972	—	2.00	4.00
❑ Capitol 3452	Last Song/Best Friend	1972	—	2.50	5.00
❑ Capitol 3581	Close Your Eyes/Cachet County	1973	—	2.00	4.00
❑ Capitol 3683	I Love Her (You Love Me)/Walking On Back	1973	—	2.00	4.00
❑ Capitol 3780	Coming Home Christmas/Does Your Mother Know	1973	2.00	4.00	8.00
❑ Capitol 3804	Same Old Feeling/Fool	1973	—	2.00	4.00
❑ Capitol 3869	I Had Dreams/You, Me and Mexico	1974	—	2.00	4.00
❑ Capitol 3978	Freedom for the Stallion/Why Don't You Marry Me	1974	—	2.00	4.00
Albums					
❑ Capitol SKAO-426	Bearings	1970	3.75	7.50	15.00
❑ Capitol ST-580	Eclipse	1971	3.75	7.50	15.00
❑ Capitol ST-11157	Edward Bear	1972	2.50	5.00	10.00
❑ Capitol ST-11192	Close Your Eyes	1973	2.50	5.00	10.00

EGAN, WALTER

Number	Title (A Side/B Side)	Yr	VG	VG+	NM
45s					
❑ Backstreet 52200	Fool Moon Fire/Tammy Ann	1983	—	—	3.00
❑ Backstreet 52249	Star of My Heart/Joyce	1983	—	—	3.00

Number	Title (A Side/B Side)	Yr	VG	VG+	NM
❑ Columbia 10531	Only the Lucky/I'd Rather Have Fun	1977	—	2.50	5.00
❑ Columbia 10591	Waitin'/When I Get My Wheels	1977	—	2.50	5.00
❑ Columbia 10719	Magnet and Steel/Tunnel O' Love	1978	—	2.50	5.00
❑ Columbia 10824	Hot Summer Nights/She's So Tough	1978	—	2.00	4.00
❑ Columbia 10916	Unloved/Make It Alone	1979	—	2.00	4.00
❑ Columbia 11046	You're the One/Like You Do	1979	—	2.00	4.00
❑ Columbia 11116	That's That/Hi-Fi Love	1979	—	2.00	4.00
❑ Columbia 11297	Let's Run Away/Johnny Z (Is a Real Cool Guy)	1980	—	2.00	4.00
Albums					
❑ Backstreet 5400	Wild Exhibitions	1983	2.00	4.00	8.00
❑ Columbia PC 34679	Fundamental Roll	1977	2.50	5.00	10.00
❑ Columbia JC 35077	Not Shy	1978	2.50	5.00	10.00
❑ Columbia JC 35796	Hi Fi	1979	2.50	5.00	10.00
❑ Columbia JC 36513	The Last Stroll	1981	2.50	5.00	10.00

EL DORADOS

Number	Title (A Side/B Side)	Yr	VG	VG+	NM
45s					
❑ Oldies 45 68	Baby, I Need You/Lovers Never Say Goodbye	1964	2.00	4.00	8.00
—B-side by the Flamingos					

ELECTRIC LIGHT ORCHESTRA

Number	Title (A Side/B Side)	Yr	VG	VG+	NM
45s					
❑ CBS Associated 05766	Calling America/Caught in a Trap	1986	—	—	3.00
❑ CBS Associated 05892	So Serious/Endless Lies	1986	—	—	3.00
❑ Jet XW 1099	Turn to Stone/Mister Kingdom	1977	—	2.00	4.00
❑ Jet XW 1145	Sweet Talkin' Woman/Fire on High	1978	—	2.50	5.00
—Purple vinyl					
❑ Jet 02408	Hold On Tight/When Time Stood Still	1981	—	2.00	4.00
❑ Jet 02559	Twilight/Julie Don't Live Here	1981	—	2.00	4.00
❑ Jet 02693	Rain Is Falling/Another Heart Broke	1982	—	2.00	4.00
❑ Jet 03086	Hold On Tight/Mr. Blue Sky	1982	—	—	3.00
—Reissue					
❑ Jet 03964	Rock and Roll Is King/After All	1983	—	2.00	4.00
❑ Jet 04130	Four Little Diamonds/Letter from Spain	1983	—	2.00	4.00
❑ Jet 04208	Stranger/Train of Gold	1983	—	2.00	4.00
❑ Jet 5050	Mr. Blue Sky/One Summer Dream	1978	—	2.00	4.00
❑ Jet 5052	It's Over/The Whale	1978	—	2.00	4.00
❑ Jet 5057	Shine a Little Love/Jungle	1979	—	2.00	4.00
❑ Jet 5060	Don't Bring Me Down/Dreaming of 4000	1979	—	2.00	4.00
❑ Jet 5064	Confusion/Poker	1979	—	2.00	4.00
❑ Jet 5067	Last Train to London/Down Home Town	1979	—	2.00	4.00
❑ MCA 41246	I'm Alive/Drum Dreams	1980	—	2.00	4.00
❑ MCA 41285	Xanadu/Whenever You're Away from Me	1980	—	2.00	4.00
—A-side: Olivia Newton-John/Electric Light Orchestra					
❑ MCA 41289	All Over the World/Drum Dreams	1980	—	2.00	4.00
❑ United Artists XW 173	Roll Over Beethoven/Queen of the Hours	1973	—	3.00	6.00
❑ United Artists XW 337	Showdown/In Old England Town	1973	—	3.00	6.00
❑ United Artists XW 405	Daybreaker/Ma-Ma-Ma-Belle	1974	—	3.00	6.00
❑ United Artists XW 513	Roll Over Beethoven/Showdown	1974	—	2.00	4.00
—Reissue					
❑ United Artists XW 573	Can't Get It Out of My Head/Illusions in G Major	1974	—	2.00	4.00
❑ United Artists XW 634	Boy Blue/Eldorado	1975	—	2.50	5.00
❑ United Artists XW 729	Evil Woman/10538 Overture (Live)	1975	—	2.00	4.00
❑ United Artists XW 770	Strange Magic/New World Rising	1976	—	2.00	4.00
❑ United Artists XW 842	Showdown/Daybreaker (Live)	1976	—	2.50	5.00
❑ United Artists XW 888	Livin' Thing/Ma-Ma-Ma-Belle	1976	—	2.00	4.00
❑ United Artists XW 939	Do Ya/Nightrider	1977	—	2.00	4.00
❑ United Artists XW 1000	Telephone Line/Poorboy (The Greenwood)	1977	—	2.00	4.00
❑ United Artists XW 1176	Can't Get It Out of My Head/Strange Magic	1978	—	2.00	4.00
❑ United Artists XW 1177	Evil Woman/Livin' Thing	1978	—	2.00	4.00
❑ United Artists XW 1178	Do Ya/Nightrider	1978	—	2.00	4.00
❑ United Artists XW 1179	Boy Blue/Telephone Line	1978	—	2.00	4.00
❑ United Artists XW 1180	Ma-Ma-Ma-Belle/10538 Overture	1978	—	2.00	4.00
—1176 through 1180 were available for a very short time just before ELO's rights transfered from UA to CBS.					
❑ United Artists 50914	10538 Overture/(Battle of) Marston Moor	1972	2.00	4.00	8.00
Albums					
❑ CBS Associated FZ 40048	Balance of Power	1986	2.50	5.00	10.00

Number	Title (A Side/B Side)	Yr	VG	VG+	NM
❑ Jet JT-LA823-L2 [(2)]	Out of the Blue	1977	3.75	7.50	15.00
—Originals include poster and die-cut cardboard "spaceship"					
❑ Jet JZ 35524	No Answer	1978	2.50	5.00	10.00
❑ Jet JZ 35525	On the Third Day	1978	2.50	5.00	10.00
❑ Jet JZ 35526	Eldorado	1978	2.50	5.00	10.00
❑ Jet JZ 35527	Face the Music	1978	2.50	5.00	10.00
❑ Jet JZ 35528	Ole Elo	1978	2.50	5.00	10.00
❑ Jet JZ 35529	A New World Record	1978	2.50	5.00	10.00
❑ Jet KZ2 35530 [(2)]	Out of the Blue	1978	3.00	6.00	12.00
❑ Jet JZ 35533	Electric Light Orchestra II	1978	2.50	5.00	10.00
❑ Jet FZ 35769	Discovery	1979	2.50	5.00	10.00
❑ Jet FZ 36310	ELO's Greatest Hits	1979	2.50	5.00	10.00
❑ Jet Z4X 36966 [(4)]	A Box of Their Best	1980	6.25	12.50	25.00
❑ Jet FZ 37371	Time	1981	2.50	5.00	10.00
❑ Jet QZ 38490	Secret Messages	1983	2.50	5.00	10.00
❑ United Artists UA-LA040-F	Electric Light Orchestra II	1973	3.75	7.50	15.00
—Tan label					
❑ United Artists UA-LA188-F	On the Third Day	1973	3.75	7.50	15.00
—Tan label					
❑ United Artists UA-LA339-G	Eldorado	1974	3.00	6.00	12.00
—Tan label					
❑ United Artists UA-LA546-G	Face the Music	1975	3.00	6.00	12.00
—Tan label					
❑ United Artists UA-LA630-G	Ole Elo	1976	3.00	6.00	12.00
—Tan label					
❑ United Artists UA-LA679-G	A New World Record	1976	3.00	6.00	12.00
—All copies have custom labels					
❑ United Artists UAS-5573	No Answer	1972	3.75	7.50	15.00
—Tan label					

ELECTRIC PRUNES, THE

45s

Number	Title (A Side/B Side)	Yr	VG	VG+	NM
❑ Reprise 0473	Ain't It Hard/Little Olive	1966	10.00	20.00	40.00
❑ Reprise 0532	I Had Too Much to Dream (Last Night)/Lovin	1966	5.00	10.00	20.00
❑ Reprise 0564	Get Me to the World on Time/Are You Lovin' Me	1967	6.25	12.50	25.00
❑ Reprise 0594	Hideaway/Dr. Do-Good	1967	6.25	12.50	25.00
❑ Reprise 0607	The Great Banana Hoax/Wind-Up Toys	1967	6.25	12.50	25.00
❑ Reprise 0652	You Never Had It So Good/Everybody Knows You're Not in Love	1967	10.00	20.00	40.00
❑ Reprise 0704	I Had Too Much to Dream (Last Night)/ Get Me to the World On Time	1968	—	2.50	5.00
—"Back to Back Hits" series — originals have "W7" and "r:" logos					
❑ Reprise 0805	Hey, Mr. President/Flowing Smoothly	1969	6.25	12.50	25.00
❑ Reprise 0833	Violent Rose/Sell	1969	10.00	20.00	40.00
❑ Reprise 0858	Love Grows/Finders Keepers, Losers Weepers	1969	6.25	12.50	25.00

Albums

Number	Title (A Side/B Side)	Yr	VG	VG+	NM
❑ Reprise R-6248 [M]	The Electric Prunes	1967	12.50	25.00	50.00
❑ Reprise RS-6248 [S]	The Electric Prunes	1967	10.00	20.00	40.00
❑ Reprise R-6262 [M]	Underground	1967	12.50	25.00	50.00
❑ Reprise RS-6262 [S]	Underground	1967	10.00	20.00	40.00
❑ Reprise R-6275 [M]	Mass in F Minor	1967	10.00	20.00	40.00
❑ Reprise RS-6275 [S]	Mass in F Minor	1967	7.50	15.00	30.00
❑ Reprise RS-6316	Release of an Oath	1968	7.50	15.00	30.00
❑ Reprise RS-6342	Just Good Rock 'n Roll	1969	7.50	15.00	30.00

ELEGANTS, THE

45s

Number	Title (A Side/B Side)	Yr	VG	VG+	NM
❑ ABC-Paramount 10219	I've Seen Everything/Tiny Cloud	1961	10.00	20.00	40.00
❑ Apt 25005	Little Star/Getting Dizzy	1958	10.00	20.00	40.00
—Black label with rainbow					
❑ Apt 25005	Little Star/Getting Dizzy	1958	12.50	25.00	50.00
—All-black label					
❑ Apt 25017	Goodnight/Please Believe Me	1958	7.50	15.00	30.00
❑ Apt 25029	Pay Day/True Love Affair	1959	7.50	15.00	30.00
❑ Bangar 613	Minor Chaos/Lost Souls	1964	7.50	15.00	30.00
❑ Bim Bam Boom 121	It's Just a Matter of Time/Lonesome Weekends	1974	—	2.00	4.00
—Black vinyl					
❑ Crystal Ball 139	Maybe/Woo Woo Train	197?	—	2.50	5.00
❑ Hull 732	Little Boy Blue/Get Well Soon	1960	25.00	50.00	100.00
❑ Laurie 3283	A Letter from Viet Nam/Barbara Beware	1965	7.50	15.00	30.00
❑ Laurie 3298	Wake Up/Bring Back Wendy	1965	12.50	25.00	50.00
❑ Laurie 3324	Belinda/Lazy Love	1965	6.25	12.50	25.00
—As "Vito and the Elegants"					
❑ Photo 2662	Dressin' Up/A Dream Can Come True	1963	12.50	25.00	50.00
❑ United Artists 230	Speak Low/Let My Prayers Be With You	1960	10.00	20.00	40.00
❑ United Artists 295	Happiness/Spiritual	1961	12.50	25.00	50.00

Albums

Number	Title (A Side/B Side)	Yr	VG	VG+	NM
❑ Murray Hill 210	Little Star	1986	2.50	5.00	10.00

ELLIS, SHIRLEY

45s

Number	Title (A Side/B Side)	Yr	VG	VG+	NM
❑ Columbia 43829	Truly, Truly, Truly/Birds, Bees, Cupids and Bows	1966	2.00	4.00	8.00
❑ Columbia 44021	Soul Time/Waitin'	1967	2.00	4.00	8.00
❑ Columbia 44137	Sugar Let's Shing-a-Ling/How Lonely Is Lonely	1967	2.00	4.00	8.00
❑ Congress 202	The Nitty Gritty/Give Me a List	1963	3.75	7.50	15.00
❑ Congress 208	(That's) What the Nitty Gritty Is/Get Out	1964	2.50	5.00	10.00
❑ Congress 210	Shy One/Takin' Care of Business	1964	2.50	5.00	10.00
❑ Congress 221	Such a Night/Bring It On Home to Me	1964	2.50	5.00	10.00

Number	Title (A Side/B Side)	Yr	VG	VG+	NM
❑ Congress 230	The Name Game/Whisper to the Wind	1964	3.00	6.00	12.00
❑ Congress 234	The Clapping Song (Clap Pat Clap Slap)/This Is Beautiful	1965	2.50	5.00	10.00
❑ Congress 238	The Puzzle Song (A Puzzle in Song)/I See It, I Like It, I Want It	1965	2.50	5.00	10.00
❑ Congress 246	I Never Will Forget/I Told You So	1965	2.50	5.00	10.00
❑ Congress 251	One Sour Note/You Better Be Good, World	1965	2.50	5.00	10.00
❑ Congress 260	Ever See a Diver Kiss His Wife While the Bubbles Bounce About Above the Water/Stardust	1965	2.50	5.00	10.00
Albums					
❑ Columbia CL 2679 [M]	Sugar, Let's Shing-a-Ling	1967	5.00	10.00	20.00
❑ Columbia CS 9479 [S]	Sugar, Let's Shing-a-Ling	1967	6.25	12.50	25.00
❑ Congress CGL-3002 [M]	Shirley Ellis In Action	1964	6.25	12.50	25.00
❑ Congress CGS-3002 [S]	Shirley Ellis In Action	1964	7.50	15.00	30.00
❑ Congress CGL-3003 [M]	The Name Game	1965	6.25	12.50	25.00
❑ Congress CGS-3003 [S]	The Name Game	1965	7.50	15.00	30.00

EMOTIONS, THE (1)

These are records by the hit female group. Records on Brainstorm, Calla, Card, Flip, Fury, Kapp, Karate, Laurie 20th Century Fox, and Vardan are not by this Emotions group, thus are outside the scope of this book.

Number	Title (A Side/B Side)	Yr	VG	VG+	NM
45s					
❑ ARC 18-02239	Turn It Out/When You Gonna Wake Up	1981	—	2.00	4.00
❑ ARC 18-02535	Now That I Know/Here You Come Again	1981	—	2.00	4.00
❑ ARC 11134	What's the Name of Your Love?/Layed Back	1979	—	2.50	5.00
❑ ARC 11205	Where Is Your Love?/Layed Back	1980	—	2.50	5.00
❑ Columbia 3-10347	Flowers/I Don't Wanna Lose Your Love	1976	—	2.50	5.00
❑ Columbia 3-10544	Best of My Love/A Feeling Is	1977	—	2.50	5.00
❑ Columbia 3-10622	Don't Ask My Neighbors/Love's What's Happenin'	1977	—	2.50	5.00
❑ Columbia 3-10791	Smile/Changes	1978	—	2.50	5.00
❑ Columbia 3-10828	Whole Lotta Shakin'/Time Is Passing By	1978	—	2.50	5.00
❑ Columbia 3-10874	Walking the Line/Ain't No Doubt About It	1978	—	2.50	5.00
❑ Motown 1784	I Can't Wait to Make You Mine/I'm Gonna Miss Your Love	1985	—	2.00	4.00
❑ Motown 1792	If I Only Knew Then (What I Know Now)/Eternally	1985	—	2.00	4.00
❑ Red Label 001-1	You're the One/I Can Do Anything	1984	—	2.50	5.00
❑ Red Label 001-2	You're the Best/(B-side unknown)	1984	—	2.50	5.00
❑ Red Label 001-3	Are You Through with My Heart/(B-side unknown)	1984	—	2.50	5.00
❑ Stax 1056	What Do The Lonely Do At Christmas?/ Santa Claus Wants Some Lovin'	197?	—	3.00	6.00
—B-side by Albert King; reissue					
❑ Stax 3200	Shouting Out Love/Baby, I'm Through	1977	—	2.50	5.00
❑ Stax 3205	Baby, I'm Through/Any Way You Look at It	1978	—	2.50	5.00
❑ Stax 3215	What Do the Lonely Do at Christmas/(Instrumental)	1978	—	2.50	5.00
❑ Twin Stacks 126	Somebody New/Brushfire	1968	2.50	5.00	10.00
❑ Twin Stacks 130	I Love You But I'll Leave You/Brushfire	1968	2.50	5.00	10.00
❑ Volt 4010	So I Can Love You/Got to Be the Man	1969	2.00	4.00	8.00
❑ Volt 4021	The Best Part of a Love Affair/I Like It	1969	2.00	4.00	8.00
❑ Volt 4031	Stealing Love/When Tomorrow Comes	1970	2.00	4.00	8.00
❑ Volt 4045	Heart Association/The Touch of Your Lips	1970	2.00	4.00	8.00
❑ Volt 4053	Black Christmas/(Instrumental)	1970	2.50	5.00	10.00
❑ Volt 4054	You Make Me Want to Love You/What You See Is What You Get	1971	—	3.50	7.00
❑ Volt 4062	If You Think It/Love Ain't Easy One-Sided	1971	—	3.50	7.00
❑ Volt 4066	Show Me How/Boss Love Maker	1971	—	3.50	7.00
❑ Volt 4077	My Honey and Me/Blind Alley	1972	—	3.50	7.00
❑ Volt 4083	I Could Never Be Happy/I've Fallen in Love	1972	—	3.50	7.00
❑ Volt 4088	From Toys to Boys/I Call This Loving You	1972	—	3.50	7.00
❑ Volt 4095	Runnin' Back (And Forth)/I Wanna Come Back	1973	—	3.50	7.00
❑ Volt 4100	Peace Be Still/Runnin' Back (And Forth)	1973	—	3.50	7.00
❑ Volt 4104	What Do the Lonely Do at Christmas/(Instrumental)	1973	2.00	4.00	8.00
❑ Volt 4106	Put a Little Love Away/I Call This Loving You	1974	—	3.50	7.00
❑ Volt 4110	Baby I'm Through/I Wanna Come Back	1974	—	3.50	7.00
❑ Volt 4113	Any Way You Look At It/There Are More Questions Than Answers	1974	—	3.50	7.00
Albums					
❑ ARC JC 36149	Come Into Our World	1979	2.50	5.00	10.00
❑ ARC FC 37456	New Affair	1981	2.50	5.00	10.00
❑ Columbia PC 34163	Flowers	1976	2.50	5.00	10.00
—No bar code on cover					
❑ Columbia PC 34762	Rejoice	1977	2.50	5.00	10.00
—No bar code on cover					

Number	Title (A Side/B Side)	Yr	VG	VG+	NM
❑ Columbia JC 35385	Sunbeam	1978	2.50	5.00	10.00
❑ Motown 6136 ML	If I Only Knew	1985	2.00	4.00	8.00
❑ Red Label 001	Sincerely	1984	2.50	5.00	10.00
❑ Stax STX-4100	Sunshine	1977	2.50	5.00	10.00
❑ Stax STX-4110	So I Can Love You	1978	2.50	5.00	10.00
—Reissue of Volt 6008					
❑ Stax STX-4112	Untouched	1978	2.50	5.00	10.00
—Reissue of Volt 6015					
❑ Stax STX-4121	Chronicle	1979	2.50	5.00	10.00
❑ Volt VOS-6008	So I Can Love You	1971	6.25	12.50	25.00
❑ Volt VOS-6015	Untouched	1972	6.25	12.50	25.00

ENGLAND DAN AND JOHN FORD COLEY

45s

Number	Title (A Side/B Side)	Yr	VG	VG+	NM
❑ A&M 1278	New Jersey/Tell Her Hello	1971	—	3.00	6.00
❑ A&M 1354	Casey/Simone	1972	—	2.50	5.00
❑ A&M 1369	Carolina/Free the People	1972	—	2.50	5.00
❑ A&M 1465	I Hear the Music/Miss You Song	1973	—	2.50	5.00
❑ A&M 1871	I Hear the Music/Simone	1976	—	2.00	4.00
❑ Big Tree 16069	I'd Really Love to See You Tonight/It's Not the Same	1976	—	2.00	4.00
❑ Big Tree 16079	Nights Are Forever Without You/Showboat Gambler	1976	—	2.00	4.00
❑ Big Tree 16088	It's Sad to Belong/The Time Has Come	1977	—	2.00	4.00
❑ Big Tree 16102	Gone Too Far/Where Do I Go from Here	1977	—	2.00	4.00
❑ Big Tree 16110	We'll Never Have to Say Goodbye Again/Calling for You Again	1978	—	2.00	4.00
❑ Big Tree 16117	You Can't Dance/Wantin' You Desperately	1978	—	2.00	4.00
❑ Big Tree 16125	If the World Ran Out of Love Tonight/ Lovin' Somebody on a Rainy Night	1978	—	2.00	4.00
❑ Big Tree 16130	Westward Wind/Some Things Don't Come Easy	1979	—	2.00	4.00
❑ Big Tree 16131	Love Is the Answer/Running After You	1979	—	2.00	4.00
❑ Big Tree 16135	Hollywood Heckle and Jive/Rolling Fever	1979	—	2.00	4.00
❑ Big Tree 17000	What Can I Do with My Broken Heart/Caught Up in the Middle	1979	—	2.00	4.00
❑ Big Tree 17002	In It for Love/Who's Lonely Now	1980	—	2.00	4.00
❑ MCA 51027	Part of Me, Part of You/Just Tell Me You Love Me	1980	—	2.00	4.00

Albums

Number	Title (A Side/B Side)	Yr	VG	VG+	NM
❑ A&M SP-4305	England Dan and John Ford Coley	1971	3.75	7.50	15.00
❑ A&M SP-4350	Fables	1972	3.75	7.50	15.00
❑ A&M SP-4613	I Hear Music	1976	3.00	6.00	12.00
❑ Big Tree BT 76000	Dowdy Ferry Road	1977	2.50	5.00	10.00
❑ Big Tree BT 76006	Some Things Don't Come Easy	1978	2.50	5.00	10.00
❑ Big Tree BT 76015	Dr. Heckle & Mr. Jive	1979	2.50	5.00	10.00
❑ Big Tree BT 76018	Best of England Dan & John Ford Coley	1980	2.50	5.00	10.00
❑ Big Tree BT 89517	Nights Are Forever	1976	2.50	5.00	10.00

ESQUIRES, THE (1)

Records on Argo, Columbia, Dot, Durco, Epic, Hi-Po and Tower appear to be by other groups with the same name, thus are outside the scope of this book.

45s

Number	Title (A Side/B Side)	Yr	VG	VG+	NM
❑ Bunky 7750	Get On Up/Listen to Me	1967	2.50	5.00	10.00
❑ Bunky 7752	And Get Away/Everybody's Laughin'	1967	2.50	5.00	10.00
❑ Bunky 7753	You Say/State Fair	1968	2.50	5.00	10.00
❑ Bunky 7755	Why Can't I Stop/The Feeling's Gone	1968	2.50	5.00	10.00
❑ Bunky 7756	How Could It Be/I Know I Can	1968	2.50	5.00	10.00
❑ Capitol 2650	Reach Out/Listen to Me	1969	2.00	4.00	8.00
❑ Cigar Man 79880	The Show Ain't Over/What Good Is Music?	1980	—	3.00	6.00
❑ Ju-Par 104	Get On Up '76/Feeling's Gone (Also Known As Disco Dancing)	1976	—	3.00	6.00
❑ Lamarr 1001	Girls in the City/Ain't Gonna Give It Up	1971	2.00	4.00	8.00
❑ Scepter 12232	You've Got the Power/No Doubt About It	1968	—	—	—
—Unreleased? (Possibly reassigned to Wand?)					
❑ Wand 1193	You've Got the Power/No Doubt About It	1968	2.00	4.00	8.00
❑ Wand 1195	I Don't Know/Part Angel	1969	2.00	4.00	8.00
❑ Wand 11201	Whip It On Me/It Was Yesterday	1969	2.00	4.00	8.00

Albums

Number	Title (A Side/B Side)	Yr	VG	VG+	NM
❑ Bunky 300	Get On Up and Get Away	1968	8.75	17.50	35.00

ESSEX, DAVID

45s

Number	Title (A Side/B Side)	Yr	VG	VG+	NM
❑ Columbia 10005	America/Dance Little Girl	1974	—	2.50	5.00
❑ Columbia 10039	Gonna Make You a Star/Window	1974	—	2.50	5.00
❑ Columbia 10183	Rolling Stone/Coconut Ice	1975	—	2.50	5.00
❑ Columbia 10256	Good Ol' Rock 'N' Roll/Hold Me Close	1975	—	2.50	5.00
❑ Columbia 45940	Rock On/On and On	1973	—	2.50	5.00
❑ Columbia 46041	Lamplight/We're All Insane	1974	—	2.50	5.00
❑ RSO 1006	Oh What a Circus (From Evita)/Ships That Pass in the Night	1979	—	2.00	4.00
❑ Uni 55020	She's Leaving Home/He's a Better Man Than Me	1967	2.50	5.00	10.00

Albums

Number	Title (A Side/B Side)	Yr	VG	VG+	NM
❑ Columbia KC 32560	Rock On	1974	5.00	10.00	20.00
❑ Columbia KC 33289	David Essex	1974	3.75	7.50	15.00
❑ Columbia PC 33813	All the Fun of the Fair	1975	3.75	7.50	15.00
❑ Mercury 812936-1	David Essex	1983	3.75	7.50	15.00

ESSEX, THE

45s

Number	Title (A Side/B Side)	Yr	VG	VG+	NM
❑ Bang 537	The Eagle/Moonlight, Music, and You	1966	2.00	4.00	8.00
❑ Roulette 4494	Easier Said Than Done/Are You Going My Way	1963	3.75	7.50	15.00
❑ Roulette 4515	A Walkin' Miracle/What I Don't Know Won't Hurt Me	1963	3.75	7.50	15.00
❑ Roulette 4530	She's Got Everything/Out of Sight, Out of Mind	1964	2.50	5.00	10.00
❑ Roulette 4542	What Did I Do/Curfew Lover	1964	2.50	5.00	10.00

Number	Title (A Side/B Side)	Yr	VG	VG+	NM
Albums					
❑ Roulette R-25234 [M]	Easier Said Than Done	1963	10.00	20.00	40.00
❑ Roulette SR-25234 [S]	Easier Said Than Done	1963	12.50	25.00	50.00
❑ Roulette R-25235 [M]	A Walkin' Miracle	1963	10.00	20.00	40.00
❑ Roulette SR-25235 [S]	A Walkin' Miracle	1963	12.50	25.00	50.00
❑ Roulette R-25246 [M]	Young and Lively	1964	10.00	20.00	40.00
❑ Roulette SR-25246 [S]	Young and Lively	1964	12.50	25.00	50.00
EVANS, PAUL					
45s					
❑ Atco 6138	At My Party/Beat Generation	1959	3.75	7.50	15.00
❑ Atco 6170	Long Gone/Mickey, My Love	1960	3.75	7.50	15.00
❑ Big Tree 16050	Happy Birthday. America/You Made Me Over	1975	—	2.50	5.00
❑ Carlton ST 130-4 [S]	Mister Hangman/British Grenadiers	1961	6.25	12.50	25.00
—Jukebox issue; small hole, plays at 33 1/3 rpm					
❑ Carlton 539	Show Folk/I Love to Make Love to You	1961	3.75	7.50	15.00
❑ Carlton 543	After the Hurricane/Not Me	1961	3.75	7.50	15.00
❑ Carlton 554	Just Because I Love You/This Pullover	1961	3.75	7.50	15.00
❑ Carlton 558	Over the Mountain, Across the Sea/Sisal Twine	1961	3.75	7.50	15.00
❑ Cinnamon 604	One Night Led to Two/Hangin' Out and Hangin' In	1980	—	2.50	5.00
❑ Columbia 44472	One Red Rose/Bound to Silence	1968	—	3.00	6.00
❑ Decca 30680	I Think About You All the Time/Oh No	1958	5.00	10.00	20.00
❑ Dot 17463	That's What Loving You Is All About/Do You Remember	1973	—	2.50	5.00
❑ Epic 9726	Bewitched/I Think I'm Gonna Kill Myself	1964	2.50	5.00	10.00
—By Paul & Mimi Evans					
❑ Epic 9751	Little Miss Tease/Gina Marina Petunia	1964	2.50	5.00	10.00
❑ Epic 9842	I Wonder What to Do/Always Thinking of the Roses	1965	2.50	5.00	10.00
❑ Guaranteed 200	Seven Little Girls Sitting in the Back Seat/Worshipping an Idol	1959	5.00	10.00	20.00
❑ Guaranteed 205	Midnite Special/Since I Met You Baby	1960	3.75	7.50	15.00
❑ Guaranteed 208	Happy-Go-Lucky Me/Fish in the Ocean	1960	3.75	7.50	15.00
❑ Guaranteed 210	The Brigade of Broken Hearts/Twins	1960	3.75	7.50	15.00
❑ Guaranteed 213	Hushabye Little Guitar/Blind Boy	1960	3.75	7.50	15.00
❑ Kapp 473	A Picture of You/Feelin' No Pain	1962	3.00	6.00	12.00
❑ Kapp 486	D-Darling/Gonna Build a Mountain	1962	3.00	6.00	12.00
❑ Kapp 499	The Bell That Couldn't Jingle/Gilding the Lily	1962	3.00	6.00	12.00
❑ Kapp 520	(Mama and Papa) We've Got Something On You/ What Are the Lips of Janet	1963	3.00	6.00	12.00
❑ Kapp 527	Ten Thousand Years/Evan Tan	1963	3.00	6.00	12.00
❑ Laurie 3571	Think Summer/For Old Times Sake	1971	—	3.00	6.00
❑ Laurie 3581	The Man in a Row Boat/Here We Go Around Again	1971	—	3.00	6.00
❑ Mercury 73499	But I Was Born in New York City/Just As Long As You Are There	1974	—	2.50	5.00
❑ Mercury 73650	All My Children/Move In with Me	1975	—	2.50	5.00
❑ Musicor 6305	Roses Are Red Medley/If I Had My Life to Live Over	1977	—	2.00	4.00
❑ Ranwood 928	Try It, You'll Like It/We Liked It	1972	—	3.00	6.00
❑ RCA Victor 47-6806	What Do You Know/Dorothy	1957	5.00	10.00	20.00
❑ RCA Victor 47-6924	Looking for a Sweetie/Any Little Thing	1957	5.00	10.00	20.00
❑ RCA Victor 47-6992	Caught/Poor Broken Heart	1957	5.00	10.00	20.00
❑ Spring 183	Hello, This Is Joanie (The Telephone Answering Machine Song)/ Lullabye Tissue Paper Company	1978	—	2.00	4.00
❑ Spring 187	Down at the Bluebird/I'm Givin' Up My Baby	1978	—	2.00	4.00
❑ Spring 193	Disneyland Daddy/Build An Ark	1979	—	2.00	4.00
Albums					
❑ Carlton STLP-129 [S]	Hear Paul Evans in Your Home Tonight	1961	15.00	30.00	60.00
❑ Carlton TLP-129 [M]	Hear Paul Evans in Your Home Tonight	1961	10.00	20.00	40.00
❑ Carlton STLP-130 [S]	Folk Songs of Many Lands	1961	15.00	30.00	60.00
❑ Carlton TLP-130 [M]	Folk Songs of Many Lands	1961	10.00	20.00	40.00
❑ Guaranteed GUL-1000 [M]	Fabulous Teens	1960	17.50	35.00	70.00
❑ Guaranteed GUS-1000 [S]	Fabulous Teens	1960	20.00	40.00	80.00
❑ Kapp KL-1346 [M]	21 Years in a Tennessee Jail	1964	6.25	12.50	25.00
❑ Kapp KL-1475 [M]	Another Town, Another Jail	1966	6.25	12.50	25.00
❑ Kapp KS-3346 [S]	21 Years in a Tennessee Jail	1964	10.00	20.00	40.00
❑ Kapp KS-3475 [S]	Another Town, Another Jail	1966	7.50	15.00	30.00
EVERETT, BETTY					
45s					
❑ ABC 10829	In Your Arms/Nothing I Wouldn't Do	1966	2.00	4.00	8.00
❑ ABC 10861	Bye, Bye Baby/Your Love Is Important to Me	1966	2.00	4.00	8.00

Number	Title (A Side/B Side)	Yr	VG	VG+	NM
❑ ABC 10919	Love Comes Tumbling Down/People Around Me	1967	2.00	4.00	8.00
❑ ABC 10978	I Can't Say/My Baby Loving My Best Friend	1967	2.00	4.00	8.00
❑ CJ 611	Why Did You Have to Go/Please Come Back	1961	5.00	10.00	20.00
—As "Bettie Everett & Daylighters"					
❑ CJ 619	Your Lovin' Arms/Happy I Long to Be	1961	5.00	10.00	20.00
❑ CJ 674	Days Gone By/Her New Love	1964	3.75	7.50	15.00
❑ Cobra 5019	My Love/My Life Depends on You	1957	7.50	15.00	30.00
❑ Cobra 5024	Ain't Gonna Cry/Killer Diller	1958	6.25	12.50	25.00
❑ Cobra 5031	Weep No More/Tell Me Darling	1959	6.25	12.50	25.00
❑ Fantasy 652	I Got to Tell Somebody/Why Are You Leaving Me	1970	—	2.50	5.00
❑ Fantasy 658	Ain't Nothing Gonna Change Me/What Is It?	1971	—	2.50	5.00
❑ Fantasy 667	I'm a Woman/Prove It	1971	—	2.50	5.00
❑ Fantasy 687	Black Girl/Innocent Bystanders	1972	—	2.50	5.00
❑ Fantasy 687	Black Girl/What Is It?	1972	—	2.50	5.00
❑ Fantasy 696	Danger/Just a Matter of Time Till You're Gone	1973	—	2.50	5.00
❑ Fantasy 714	Sweet Dan/Who Will Your Next Fool Be	1973	—	2.50	5.00
❑ Fantasy 725	Try It, You'll Like It/Wondering	1974	—	2.50	5.00
❑ Fantasy 738	Happy Endings/Keep It Up	1974	—	2.50	5.00
❑ Lost-Nite 313	The Shoop Shoop Song (It's In His Kiss)/Hands Off	197?	—	2.50	5.00
—Reissue					
❑ One-derful 4806	I've Got a Claim on You/Your Love Is Important to Me	1962	3.75	7.50	15.00
❑ One-derful 4823	I'll Be There/Please Love Me	1964	3.00	6.00	12.00
❑ Uni 55100	Take Me/There'll Come a Time	1968	—	3.00	6.00
❑ Uni 55122	I Can't Say No to You/Better Tomorrow Than Today	1969	—	3.00	6.00
❑ Uni 55141	1900 Yesterday/Maybe	1969	—	3.00	6.00
❑ Uni 55174	Just a Man's Way/Been a Long Time	1969	—	3.00	6.00
❑ Uni 55189	Sugar/Just Another Winter	1969	—	3.00	6.00
❑ Uni 55219	Unlucky Girl/Better Tomorrow Than Today	1970	—	3.00	6.00
❑ United Artists XW1200	True Love (You Took My Heart)/You Can Do It	1978	—	2.00	4.00
❑ Vee Jay 513	By My Side/Prince of Players	1963	3.75	7.50	15.00
❑ Vee Jay 566	You're No Good/Chained to Your Love	1963	5.00	10.00	20.00
❑ Vee Jay 585	The Shoop Shoop Song (It's In His Kiss)/Hands Off	1964	5.00	10.00	20.00
❑ Vee Jay 599	I Can't Hear You/Can I Get to Know You	1964	3.75	7.50	15.00
❑ Vee Jay 610	It Hurts to Be in Love/Until You Were Gone	1964	3.75	7.50	15.00
❑ Vee Jay 628	Getting Mighty Crowded/Chained to a Memory	1964	3.75	7.50	15.00
❑ Vee Jay 683	The Real Thing/Gonna Be Ready	1965	3.75	7.50	15.00
❑ Vee Jay 699	I Don't Hurt Anymore/Too Hot to Hold	1965	3.75	7.50	15.00
❑ Vee Jay 716	Trouble Over the Weekend/My Shoe Won't Fly	1966	3.75	7.50	15.00
Albums					
❑ Fantasy 9447	Love Rhymes	1974	3.00	6.00	12.00
❑ Fantasy 9480	Happy Endings	1975	3.00	6.00	12.00
❑ Sunset SUS-5220	I Need You So	1968	3.75	7.50	15.00
❑ Uni 73048	There'll Come a Time	1969	6.25	12.50	25.00
❑ Vee Jay LP 1077 [M]	It's In His Kiss	1964	7.50	15.00	30.00
❑ Vee Jay LP 1077 [M]	You're No Good	1964	10.00	20.00	40.00
❑ Vee Jay SR 1077 [S]	It's In His Kiss	1964	12.50	25.00	50.00
❑ Vee Jay SR 1077 [S]	You're No Good	1964	17.50	35.00	70.00
❑ Vee Jay LP 1122 [M]	The Very Best of Betty Everett	1965	10.00	20.00	40.00
❑ Vee Jay VJS 1122 [S]	The Very Best of Betty Everett	1965	12.50	25.00	50.00

EVERETT, BETTY, AND JERRY BUTLER

Number	Title (A Side/B Side)	Yr	VG	VG+	NM
45s					
❑ Lost-Nite 299	Let It Be Me/Ain't That Loving You Baby	197?	—	2.50	5.00
—Reissue					
❑ Vee Jay 613	Let It Be Me/Ain't That Loving You Baby	1964	3.00	6.00	12.00
❑ Vee Jay 633	Smile/Love Is Strange	1964	3.00	6.00	12.00
❑ Vee Jay 676	Since I Don't Have You/Just Be True	1965	3.00	6.00	12.00
❑ Vee Jay 691	Fever/The Way You Do the Things You Do	1965	3.00	6.00	12.00
Albums					
❑ Buddah BDS-7505	Together	1969	3.75	7.50	15.00
❑ Tradition 2073	Starring Betty Everett with Jerry Butler	197?	3.00	6.00	12.00
❑ Vee Jay LP 1099 [M]	Delicious Together	1964	5.00	10.00	20.00
❑ Vee Jay LP-1099 [M]	Delicious Together	1964	5.00	10.00	20.00
❑ Vee Jay VJS 1099 [S]	Delicious Together	1964	6.25	12.50	25.00
❑ Vee Jay VJS-1099 [S]	Delicious Together	1964	6.25	12.50	25.00

EVERLY BROTHERS, THE

Number	Title (A Side/B Side)	Yr	VG	VG+	NM
45s					
❑ Barnaby 500	('Til) I Kissed You/Oh, What a Feeling	197?	—	2.50	5.00
❑ Barnaby 501	Wake Up Little Susie/Maybe Tomorrow	197?	—	2.50	5.00
❑ Barnaby 502	Bye, Bye Love/I Wonder If I Care As Much	197?	—	2.50	5.00
❑ Barnaby 503	This Little Girl of Mine/Should We Tell Him?	197?	—	2.50	5.00
❑ Barnaby 504	Problems/Love of My Life	197?	—	2.50	5.00
❑ Barnaby 505	Take a Message to Mary/Poor Jenny	197?	—	2.50	5.00
❑ Barnaby 506	Let It Be Me/Since You Broke My Heart	197?	—	2.50	5.00
❑ Barnaby 507	When Will I Be Loved/Be Bop A-Lula	197?	—	2.50	5.00
❑ Barnaby 508	Like Strangers/Brand New Heartache	197?	—	2.50	5.00
❑ Barnaby 509	All I Have to Do Is Dream/Claudette	197?	—	2.50	5.00
❑ Barnaby 510	Bird Dog/Devoted to You	197?	—	2.50	5.00
❑ Barnaby 511	I'm Here to Get My Baby Out of Jail/Lightning Express	197?	—	2.50	5.00
—All Barnaby records are reissues of original Cadence recordings					
❑ Cadence 1315	Bye, Bye Love/I Wonder If I Care As Much	1957	6.25	12.50	25.00
❑ Cadence 1337	Wake Up Little Susie/Maybe Tomorrow	1957	7.50	15.00	30.00
❑ Cadence 1342	This Little Girl of Mine/Should We Tell Him?	1958	6.25	12.50	25.00
❑ Cadence 1348	All I Have to Do Is Dream/Claudette	1958	6.25	12.50	25.00
❑ Cadence 1350	Bird Dog/Devoted to You	1958	6.25	12.50	25.00
❑ Cadence 1355	Problems/Love of My Life	1958	6.25	12.50	25.00

Number	Title (A Side/B Side)	Yr	VG	VG+	NM
❑ Cadence 1364	Take a Message to Mary/Poor Jenny	1959	6.25	12.50	25.00
❑ Cadence 1369	('Til) I Kissed You/Oh, What a Feeling	1959	6.25	12.50	25.00
❑ Cadence 1376	Let It Be Me/Since You Broke My Heart	1959	6.25	12.50	25.00
❑ Cadence 1380	When Will I Be Loved/Be Bop A-Lula	1960	6.25	12.50	25.00
❑ Cadence 1388	Like Strangers/Brand New Heartache	1960	6.25	12.50	25.00
❑ Cadence 1429	I'm Here to Get My Baby Out of Jail/Lightning Express	1962	5.00	10.00	20.00
❑ Capitol B-44297	Don't Worry Baby/Tequila Dreams	1989	—	2.00	4.00
—A-side with the Beach Boys; B-side by Dave Grusin					
❑ Columbia 4-21496	Keep A Lovin' Me/The Sun Keeps Shining	1956	150.00	300.00	600.00
—Maroon label					
❑ Mercury 872098-7	Ride the Wind/Don't Worry Baby	1988	—	—	3.00
❑ Mercury 872420-7	Ballad of a Teenage Queen/Get Rhythm	1988	—	—	3.00
—With Johnny Cash and Roseanne Cash					
❑ Mercury 880213-7	On the Wings of a Nightingale/Asleep	1984	—	2.50	5.00
—A-side written and produced by Paul McCartney					
❑ Mercury 880423-7	The Story of Me/First in Line	1984	—	2.00	4.00
❑ Mercury 884428-7	Don't Say Goodnight/Born Yesterday	1986	—	2.00	4.00
❑ Mercury 884694-7	I Know Love/These Shoes	1986	—	2.00	4.00
❑ RCA Victor 74-0717	Stories We Could Tell/Ridin' High	1972	2.50	5.00	10.00
❑ RCA Victor 74-0849	Lay It Down/Paradise	1972	2.50	5.00	10.00
❑ RCA Victor 74-0901	Not Fade Away/Ladies Love Outlaws	1973	2.50	5.00	10.00
❑ Warner Bros. GWB 0311	That's Old Fashioned/Bowling Green	197?	—	2.00	4.00
—"Back to Back Hits" series; originals have palm-tree labels					
❑ Warner Bros. GWB 0314	Ebony Eyes/Walk Right Back	197?	—	2.00	4.00
—"Back to Back Hits" series; originals have palm-tree labels					
❑ Warner Bros. 5151 [M]	Cathy's Clown/Always It's You	1960	5.00	10.00	20.00
—Original stock copies have pink labels					
❑ Warner Bros. S-5151 [S]	Cathy's Clown/Always It's You	1960	12.50	25.00	50.00
❑ Warner Bros. 5163	So Sad (To Watch Good Love Go Bad)/Lucille	1960	3.75	7.50	15.00
❑ Warner Bros. 5199	Ebony Eyes/Walk Right Back	1961	3.75	7.50	15.00
❑ Warner Bros. 5220	Temptation/Stick With Me, Baby	1961	3.75	7.50	15.00
❑ Warner Bros. 5250	Crying in the Rain/I'm Not Angry	1961	3.75	7.50	15.00
❑ Warner Bros. 5273	That's Old Fashioned (That's the Way Love Should Be)/How Can I Meet Her?	1962	3.75	7.50	15.00
❑ Warner Bros. 5297	Don't Ask Me to Be Friends/No One Can Make My Sunshine Smile	1962	5.00	10.00	20.00
❑ Warner Bros. 5346	(So It Was...So It Is...) So It Always Will Be/Nancy's Minuet	1963	3.75	7.50	15.00
❑ Warner Bros. 5362	I'm Afraid/It's Been Nice	1963	3.75	7.50	15.00
❑ Warner Bros. 5389	Love Her/The Girl Sang the Blues	1963	3.75	7.50	15.00
❑ Warner Bros. 5422	Hello, Amy/Ain't That Loving You, Baby	1964	3.75	7.50	15.00
❑ Warner Bros. 5441	The Ferris Wheel/Don't Forget to Cry	1964	3.75	7.50	15.00
❑ Warner Bros. 5466	You're the One I Love/Ring Around My Rosie	1964	3.75	7.50	15.00
❑ Warner Bros. 5478	Gone, Gone, Gone/Torture	1964	3.75	7.50	15.00
❑ Warner Bros. 5501	Don't Blame Me/Walk Right Back//Muskrat/Lucille	1961	5.00	10.00	20.00
❑ Warner Bros. 5600	You're My Girl/Don't Let the World Know	1965	3.00	6.00	12.00
❑ Warner Bros. 5611	That'll Be the Day/Give Me a Sweetheart	1965	3.00	6.00	12.00
❑ Warner Bros. 5628	The Price of Love/It Only Costs a Dime	1965	3.00	6.00	12.00
❑ Warner Bros. 5639	I'll Never Get Over You/Follow Me	1965	3.00	6.00	12.00
❑ Warner Bros. 5649	Love Is Strange/A Man with Money	1965	3.00	6.00	12.00
❑ Warner Bros. 5682	It's All Over/I Used to Love You	1965	3.00	6.00	12.00
❑ Warner Bros. 5698	The Doll House Is Empty/Lovey Kravezit	1966	3.00	6.00	12.00
❑ Warner Bros. 5808	The Power of Love/Leave My Girl Alone	1966	3.00	6.00	12.00
❑ Warner Bros. 5833	Somebody Help Me/Hard, Hard Year	1966	3.00	6.00	12.00
❑ Warner Bros. 5857	Fifi the Flea/Like Every Time Before	1966	5.00	10.00	20.00
—A-side listed as "Don Everly Brother," B-side as "Phil Everly Brother"					
❑ Warner Bros. 5901	She Never Smiles Anymore/Devil Child	1967	3.00	6.00	12.00
❑ Warner Bros. 7020	Bowling Green/I Don't Want to Love You	1967	3.00	6.00	12.00
❑ Warner Bros. 7062	Mary Jane/Talking to the Flowers	1967	3.00	6.00	12.00
❑ Warner Bros. 7088	Love of the Common People/The Voice Within	1967	3.00	6.00	12.00
❑ Warner Bros. 7110	Cathy's Clown/So Sad	1968	2.00	4.00	8.00
—"Back to Back Hits" series; originals have green "W7" label					
❑ Warner Bros. 7111	Crying in the Rain/Lucille	1968	2.00	4.00	8.00
—"Back to Back Hits" series; originals have green "W7" label					
❑ Warner Bros. 7120	Wake Up Little Susie/Bird Dog	1969	2.00	4.00	8.00
—"Back to Back Hits" series; originals have green "W7" label; re-recordings					
❑ Warner Bros. 7121	Bye Bye Love/All I Have to Do Is Dream	1969	2.00	4.00	8.00
—"Back to Back Hits" series; originals have green "W7" label; re-recordings					
❑ Warner Bros. 7192	Empty Boxes/It's My Time	1968	3.00	6.00	12.00

Number	Title (A Side/B Side)	Yr	VG	VG+	NM
❑ Warner Bros. 7226	Lord of the Manor/Milk Train	1968	3.00	6.00	12.00
❑ Warner Bros. 7262	T for Texas/I Wonder If I Care As Much	1969	3.00	6.00	12.00
❑ Warner Bros. 7290	I'm On My Way Home Again/Cuckoo Bird	1969	3.00	6.00	12.00
❑ Warner Bros. 7326	Carolina on My Mind/My Little Yellow Bird	1969	3.75	7.50	15.00
❑ Warner Bros. 7425	Yves/The Human Race	1970	3.75	7.50	15.00
Albums					
❑ Arista AL9-8207 [(2)]	24 Original Classics	1985	3.75	7.50	15.00
❑ Barnaby BGP-350 [(2)]	The Everly Brothers' Original Golden Hits	1970	5.00	10.00	20.00
❑ Barnaby 4004	Greatest Hits, Vol. 1	1977	2.50	5.00	10.00
❑ Barnaby 4005	Greatest Hits, Vol. 2	1977	2.50	5.00	10.00
❑ Barnaby 4006	Greatest Hits, Vol. 3	1977	2.50	5.00	10.00
❑ Barnaby BR-6006 [(2)]	The Everly Brothers' Greatest Hits	1974	3.75	7.50	15.00
❑ Barnaby BR-15008 [(2)]	History of the Everly Brothers	1973	3.75	7.50	15.00
❑ Barnaby ZG 30260 [(2)]	End of an Era	1971	3.75	7.50	15.00
❑ Cadence CLP-3003 [M]	The Everly Brothers	1958	25.00	50.00	100.00
—Maroon label with metronome logo					
❑ Cadence CLP-3016 [M]	Songs Our Daddy Taught Us	1958	25.00	50.00	100.00
—Maroon label with metronome logo					
❑ Cadence CLP-3025 [M]	The Everly Brothers' Best	1959	22.50	45.00	90.00
—Maroon label with metronome logo					
❑ Cadence CLP-3040 [M]	The Fabulous Style of the Everly Brothers	1960	20.00	40.00	80.00
—Maroon label with metronome logo					
❑ Cadence CLP-3059 [M]	Folk Songs of the Everly Brothers	1963	12.50	25.00	50.00
—Reissue of 3016					
❑ Cadence CLP-3062 [M]	15 Everly Hits 15	1963	10.00	20.00	40.00
❑ Cadence CLP-25040 [P]	The Fabulous Style of the Everly Brothers	1960	30.00	60.00	120.00
—Maroon label with metronome logo					
❑ Cadence CLP-25059 [R]	Folk Songs of the Everly Brothers	1963	10.00	20.00	40.00
❑ Cadence CLP-25062 [P]	15 Everly Hits 15	1963	12.50	25.00	50.00
❑ Harmony HS 11304	Wake Up Little Susie	1969	3.00	6.00	12.00
❑ Harmony HS 11350	Christmas with the Everly Brothers and the Boys Town Choir	1969	5.00	10.00	20.00
❑ Harmony KH 11388	Chained to a Memory	1970	3.00	6.00	12.00
❑ Mercury 822431-1	EB 84	1984	2.50	5.00	10.00
❑ Mercury 826142-1	Born Yesterday	1986	2.50	5.00	10.00
❑ Mercury 832520-1	Some Hearts	1989	3.00	6.00	12.00
❑ Pair PDL1-1063 [(2)]	Living Legends	1986	3.00	6.00	12.00
❑ Passport 11001 [(2)]	The Everly Brothers Reunion Concert	1984	3.75	7.50	15.00
❑ RCA Victor LSP-4620	Stories We Could Tell	1972	3.75	7.50	15.00
❑ RCA Victor LSP-4781	Pass the Chicken and Listen	1972	3.75	7.50	15.00
❑ RCA Victor AFL1-5401	Home Again	1985	2.50	5.00	10.00
❑ Rhino RNLP-211	The Everly Brothers	1985	2.50	5.00	10.00
❑ Rhino RNLP-212	Songs Our Daddy Taught Us	1985	2.50	5.00	10.00
❑ Rhino RNLP-213	The Fabulous Style of the Everly Brothers	1985	2.50	5.00	10.00
❑ Rhino RNLP-214	All They Had to Do Was Dream	1985	2.50	5.00	10.00
❑ Rhino RNLP-70173	The Best of the Everly Brothers (Golden Archive Series)	1987	2.50	5.00	10.00
❑ Time-Life SRNR-09 [(2)]	The Everly Brothers: 1957-1962	1986	5.00	10.00	20.00
—Part of "The Rock 'n' Roll Era" series; box set with insert					
❑ Warner Bros. W 1381 [M]	It's Everly Time!	1960	7.50	15.00	30.00
❑ Warner Bros. WS 1381 [S]	It's Everly Time!	1960	10.00	20.00	40.00
❑ Warner Bros. W 1395 [M]	A Date with the Everly Brothers	1960	12.50	25.00	50.00
—Gatefold edition with poster and wallet-size photos					
❑ Warner Bros. WS 1395 [S]	A Date with the Everly Brothers	1960	18.75	37.50	75.00
—Gatefold edition with poster and wallet-size photos					
❑ Warner Bros. W 1418 [M]	Both Sides of an Evening	1961	7.50	15.00	30.00
❑ Warner Bros. WS 1418 [S]	Both Sides of an Evening	1961	10.00	20.00	40.00
❑ Warner Bros. W 1430 [M]	Instant Party!	1962	7.50	15.00	30.00
❑ Warner Bros. WS 1430 [S]	Instant Party!	1962	10.00	20.00	40.00
❑ Warner Bros. W 1471 [M]	The Golden Hits of the Everly Brothers	1962	7.50	15.00	30.00
❑ Warner Bros. WS 1471 [S]	The Golden Hits of the Everly Brothers	1962	10.00	20.00	40.00
—Gold label					
❑ Warner Bros. W 1483 [M]	Christmas with the Everly Brothers and the Boys Town Choir	1962	10.00	20.00	40.00
❑ Warner Bros. WS 1483 [S]	Christmas with the Everly Brothers and the Boys Town Choir	1962	12.50	25.00	50.00
❑ Warner Bros. W 1513 [M]	Great Country Hits	1963	10.00	20.00	40.00
❑ Warner Bros. WS 1513 [S]	Great Country Hits	1963	12.50	25.00	50.00
❑ Warner Bros. W 1554 [M]	The Very Best of the Everly Brothers	1964	7.50	15.00	30.00
—Originals have yellow covers					
❑ Warner Bros. WS 1554 [S]	The Very Best of the Everly Brothers	1964	10.00	20.00	40.00
—Originals have yellow covers					
❑ Warner Bros. W 1578 [M]	Rock & Soul	1964	10.00	20.00	40.00
❑ Warner Bros. WS 1578 [S]	Rock & Soul	1964	12.50	25.00	50.00
❑ Warner Bros. W 1585 [M]	Gone, Gone, Gone	1965	10.00	20.00	40.00
❑ Warner Bros. WS 1585 [S]	Gone, Gone, Gone	1965	12.50	25.00	50.00
❑ Warner Bros. W 1605 [M]	Beat & Soul	1965	10.00	20.00	40.00
❑ Warner Bros. WS 1605 [S]	Beat & Soul	1965	12.50	25.00	50.00
❑ Warner Bros. W 1620 [M]	In Our Image	1966	10.00	20.00	40.00
❑ Warner Bros. WS 1620 [S]	In Our Image	1966	12.50	25.00	50.00
❑ Warner Bros. W 1646 [M]	Two Yanks in England	1966	10.00	20.00	40.00
❑ Warner Bros. WS 1646 [S]	Two Yanks in England	1966	12.50	25.00	50.00
❑ Warner Bros. W 1676 [M]	The Hit Sound of the Everly Brothers	1967	12.50	25.00	50.00
❑ Warner Bros. WS 1676 [S]	The Hit Sound of the Everly Brothers	1967	10.00	20.00	40.00
❑ Warner Bros. W 1708 [M]	The Everly Brothers Sing	1967	12.50	25.00	50.00
❑ Warner Bros. WS 1708 [S]	The Everly Brothers Sing	1967	10.00	20.00	40.00
❑ Warner Bros. WS 1752	Roots	1968	10.00	20.00	40.00
❑ Warner Bros. WS 1858	The Everly Brothers Show	1970	7.50	15.00	30.00

EVERY MOTHERS' SON

45s

Number	Title (A Side/B Side)	Yr	VG	VG+	NM
❑ MGM 13733	Come On Down to My Boat/I Believe in You	1967	2.50	5.00	10.00

Number	Title (A Side/B Side)	Yr	VG	VG+	NM
❑ MGM 13788	Put Your Mind at Ease/Proper Four Leaf Clover	1967	2.00	4.00	8.00
❑ MGM 13844	Pony with the Golden Mane/Dolls in the Clock	1967	2.00	4.00	8.00
❑ MGM 13887	No One Knows/What Became of Mary	1968	2.00	4.00	8.00
❑ MGM 13987	Rainflowers/For Brandy	1968	2.00	4.00	8.00
Albums					
❑ MGM E-4471 [M]	Every Mothers' Son	1967	5.00	10.00	20.00
❑ MGM SE-4471 [S]	Every Mothers' Son	1967	5.00	10.00	20.00
❑ MGM E-4504 [M]	Every Mothers' Son's Back	1967	5.00	10.00	20.00
❑ MGM SE-4504 [S]	Every Mothers' Son's Back	1967	5.00	10.00	20.00
EXCITERS, THE					
45s					
❑ Bang 515	A Little Bit of Soap/I'm Gonna Get Him Someday	1966	3.00	6.00	12.00
❑ Bang 518	You Better Come Home/Weddings Make Me Cry	1966	7.50	15.00	30.00
❑ Fargo 1400	Alone Again, Naturally/(B-side unknown)	1972	2.00	4.00	8.00
❑ RCA Victor 47-9633	Take One Step (I'll Take Two)/If You Want My Love	1968	7.50	15.00	30.00
❑ RCA Victor 47-9723	You Don't Know What You're Missing ('Til It's Gone!)/ Blowing Up My Mind	1969	7.50	15.00	30.00
❑ RCA Victor 48-1035	You Don't Know What You're Missing ('Til It's Gone!)/ Blowing Up My Mind	1972	3.75	7.50	15.00
❑ Roulette 4591	I Want You to Be My Boy/Tonight, Tonight	1965	3.00	6.00	12.00
❑ Roulette 4594	Are You Satisfied/Just Not Ready	1965	3.00	6.00	12.00
❑ Roulette 4614	My Father/Run Mascara	1965	3.00	6.00	12.00
❑ Roulette 4632	I Knew You Would/There They Go	1965	3.00	6.00	12.00
❑ Shout 205	Number One/You Got Love	1966	2.50	5.00	10.00
❑ Shout 214	Soulmotion/You Know It Ain't Right	1967	2.50	5.00	10.00
❑ Today 1002	Learning How to Fly/Life, Love and Peace	1970	2.00	4.00	8.00
❑ United Artists 0029	Tell Him/Do Wah Diddy	1973	—	2.00	4.00
—"Silver Spotlight Series" reissue					
❑ United Artists 544	Tell Him/Hard Way to Go	1963	3.75	7.50	15.00
❑ United Artists 572	Drama of Love/He's Got the Power	1963	3.00	6.00	12.00
❑ United Artists 604	Get Him/It's So Exciting	1963	3.00	6.00	12.00
❑ United Artists 662	Do-Wah-Diddy/If Love Came Your Way	1963	3.00	6.00	12.00
❑ United Artists 721	Having My Fun/We Were Lovers (When the Party Began)	1964	3.00	6.00	12.00
❑ United Artists 830	Having My Fun/We Were Lovers (When the Party Began)	1965	2.50	5.00	10.00
Albums					
❑ RCA Victor LSP-4211	Caviar and Chitlins	1969	7.50	15.00	30.00
❑ Roulette R 25326 [M]	The Exciters	1966	7.50	15.00	30.00
❑ Roulette SR 25326 [S]	The Exciters	1966	10.00	20.00	40.00
❑ Today 1001	Black Beauty	1971	5.00	10.00	20.00
❑ United Artists UAL-3264 [M]	Tell Him	1963	17.50	35.00	70.00
❑ United Artists UAS-6264 [S]	Tell Him	1963	37.50	75.00	150.00

F

FABARES, SHELLEY

Number	Title (A Side/B Side)	Yr	VG	VG+	NM
45s					
❑ Colpix 621	Johnny Angel/Where's It Gonna Get Me	1962	5.00	10.00	20.00
❑ Colpix 631	What Did They Do Before Rock and Roll/Very Unlikely	1962	5.00	10.00	20.00
—With Paul Petersen					
❑ Colpix 636	Johnny Loves Me/I'm Growing Up	1962	5.00	10.00	20.00
❑ Colpix 654	The Things We Did Last Summer/Breaking Up Is Hard to Do	1962	5.00	10.00	20.00
❑ Colpix 667	Big Star/Telephone (Don't You Ring)	1962	5.00	10.00	20.00
❑ Colpix 682	Ronnie, Call Me When You Get a Chance/I Left a Note to Say Goodbye	1963	5.00	10.00	20.00
❑ Colpix 705	Welcome Home/Billy Boy	1963	5.00	10.00	20.00
❑ Colpix 721	Football Season's Over/He Don't Love Me	1963	25.00	50.00	100.00
—Produced by Jan Berry of Jan and Dean					
❑ Dunhill 4001	My Prayer/Pretty Please	1965	7.50	15.00	30.00
❑ Dunhill 4041	See Ya 'Round on the Rebound/Pretty Please	1966	7.50	15.00	30.00
❑ Vee Jay 632	I Know You'll Be There/Lost Summer Love	1964	10.00	20.00	40.00
Albums					
❑ Colpix CP-426 [M]	Shelley!	1962	37.50	75.00	150.00
❑ Colpix SCP-426 [S]	Shelley!	1962	150.00	300.00	600.00
❑ Colpix CP-431 [M]	The Things We Did Last Summer	1962	25.00	50.00	100.00
❑ Colpix SCP-431 [S]	The Things We Did Last Summer	1962	100.00	200.00	400.00

Number	Title (A Side/B Side)	Yr	VG	VG+	NM
FABIAN					
45s					
❑ Chancellor 1020	I'm in Love/Shivers	1958	6.25	12.50	25.00
❑ Chancellor 1024	Be My Steady Date/Lilly Lou	1958	6.25	12.50	25.00
❑ Chancellor 1029 [M]	I'm a Man/Hypnotized	1959	5.00	10.00	20.00
❑ Chancellor S-1029 [S]	I'm a Man/Hypnotized	1959	12.50	25.00	50.00
❑ Chancellor 1033 [M]	Turn Me Loose/Stop Thief!	1959	5.00	10.00	20.00
❑ Chancellor S-1033 [S]	Turn Me Loose/Stop Thief!	1959	12.50	25.00	50.00
❑ Chancellor 1037 [M]	Tiger/Mighty Cold (To a Warm, Warm Heart)	1959	5.00	10.00	20.00
❑ Chancellor S-1037 [S]	Tiger/Mighty Cold (To a Warm, Warm Heart)	1959	12.50	25.00	50.00
❑ Chancellor 1041 [M]	Come On and Get Me/Got the Feeling	1959	5.00	10.00	20.00
❑ Chancellor S-1041 [S]	Come On and Get Me/Got the Feeling	1959	12.50	25.00	50.00
❑ Chancellor 1044	Hound Dog Man/Friendly World	1959	6.25	12.50	25.00
❑ Chancellor 1044 [M]	Hound Dog Man/This Friendly World	1959	5.00	10.00	20.00
—Note difference in B-side title					
❑ Chancellor S-1044 [S]	Hound Dog Man/This Friendly World	1959	12.50	25.00	50.00
❑ Chancellor 1047 [M]	About This Thing Called Love/String Along	1960	3.00	6.00	12.00
❑ Chancellor S-1047 [S]	About This Thing Called Love/String Along	1960	12.50	25.00	50.00
❑ Chancellor 1051	I'm Gonna Sit Right Down and Write Myself a Letter/ Strollin' in the Springtime	1960	3.00	6.00	12.00
❑ Chancellor 1055	Tomorrow/King of Love	1960	3.00	6.00	12.00
❑ Chancellor 1061	Kissin' and Twistin'/Long Before	1960	3.00	6.00	12.00
❑ Chancellor 1067	You Know You Belong to Someone Else/Hold On	1961	3.00	6.00	12.00
❑ Chancellor 1072	Grapevine/David and Goliath	1961	3.00	6.00	12.00
❑ Chancellor 1079	The Love That I'm Giving to You/You're Only Young Once	1961	3.75	7.50	15.00
❑ Chancellor 1084	A Girl Like You/Dream Factory	1961	3.00	6.00	12.00
❑ Chancellor 1086	Tongue-Tied/Kansas City	1961	5.00	10.00	20.00
❑ Chancellor 1092	Wild Party/Made You	1961	5.00	10.00	20.00
❑ Chancellor 1092	Wild Party/The Gospel Truth	1961	6.25	12.50	25.00
❑ Cream 7717	Ease On (Into My Life)/The American East	1977	—	2.50	5.00
❑ Dot 16413	Break Down and Cry/She's Staying Inside with Me	1963	2.50	5.00	10.00
Albums					
❑ ABC X-806	16 Greatest Hits	1973	3.00	6.00	12.00
❑ Chancellor CHL-5003 [M]	Hold That Tiger!	1959	25.00	50.00	100.00
—Pink label					
❑ Chancellor CHLS-5003 [S]	Hold That Tiger!	1959	37.50	75.00	150.00
—Pink label					
❑ Chancellor CHL-5005 [M]	Fabulous Fabian	1959	12.50	25.00	50.00
❑ Chancellor CHLS-5005 [S]	Fabulous Fabian	1959	18.75	37.50	75.00
❑ Chancellor CHL-5012 [M]	The Good Old Summertime	1960	12.50	25.00	50.00
❑ Chancellor CHLS-5012 [S]	The Good Old Summertime	1960	18.75	37.50	75.00
❑ Chancellor CHL-5019 [M]	Rockin' Hot	1961	18.75	37.50	75.00
❑ Chancellor CHL-5024 [M]	Fabian's 16 Fabulous Hits	1962	18.75	37.50	75.00
❑ Chancellor CHL-69802 [M]	The Fabian Facade: Young and Wonderful	1960	20.00	40.00	80.00
—Felt gatefold cover with die-cut window					
❑ MCA 27095	The Best of Fabian	1985	2.00	4.00	8.00
❑ United Artists UA-LA449-E	The Very Best of Fabian	1975	3.00	6.00	12.00
FABIAN / FRANKIE AVALON					
Albums					
❑ Chancellor CHL-5009 [M]	The Hit Makers	1960	25.00	50.00	100.00
FACES					
45s					
❑ Warner Bros. 7393	Around the Phynth/Wicked Messenger	1970	2.50	5.00	10.00
—As "Small Faces"					
❑ Warner Bros. 7442	Real Good Time/Real Wheel Skid	1970	2.50	5.00	10.00
❑ Warner Bros. 7483	Maybe I'm Amazed/Oh Lord I'm Browned Off	1971	2.00	4.00	8.00
❑ Warner Bros. 7545	Stay with Me/You're So Rude	1971	—	3.00	6.00
❑ Warner Bros. 7681	Cindy Incidentally/Skewiff (Mend the Fuse)	1973	—	2.50	5.00
❑ Warner Bros. 7711	Ooh-La-La/Borstal Boys	1973	—	2.50	5.00
Albums					
❑ Warner Bros. WS 1851	First Step	197?	3.00	6.00	12.00
—Later pressings have "faces." on front cover					
❑ Warner Bros. WS 1851	First Step	1970	5.00	10.00	20.00
—First pressings have "small faces." on front cover					
❑ Warner Bros. WS 1892	Long Player	1971	3.75	7.50	15.00
❑ Warner Bros. BS 2574	A Nod Is As Good As a Wink...To a Blind Horse	1971	3.75	7.50	15.00
—Green label					
❑ Warner Bros. BS 2574	A Nod Is As Good As a Wink...To a Blind Horse	1973	3.00	6.00	12.00
—"Burbank" palm trees label					
❑ Warner Bros. BS 2665	Ooh La La	1973	3.00	6.00	12.00
—"Burbank" palm trees label					
❑ Warner Bros. BS 2665	Ooh La La	1973	3.75	7.50	15.00
—Green label					
❑ Warner Bros. BS 2897	Snakes and Ladders: The Best of Faces	1976	3.00	6.00	12.00
FAME, GEORGIE					
45s					
❑ Epic 10166	Because I Love You/Bidin' My Time ('Cos I Love You)	1967	2.00	4.00	8.00
❑ Epic 10283	The Ballad of Bonnie and Clyde/Beware of the Dog	1968	2.50	5.00	10.00
❑ Epic 10347	Hideaway/Runaway Child	1968	—	3.00	6.00
❑ Epic 10402	Someone to Watch Over Me/For Your Pleasure	1968	—	3.00	6.00
❑ Epic 10477	I'll Be Your Baby Tonight/Down Along the Cove	1969	—	3.00	6.00
❑ Epic 10546	Peaceful/Hideaway	1969	—	3.00	6.00
❑ Epic 10640	Fire and Rain/The Movie Star Song	1970	—	3.00	6.00
❑ Imperial 66086	Yeh, Yeh/Preach and Teach	1965	3.00	6.00	12.00

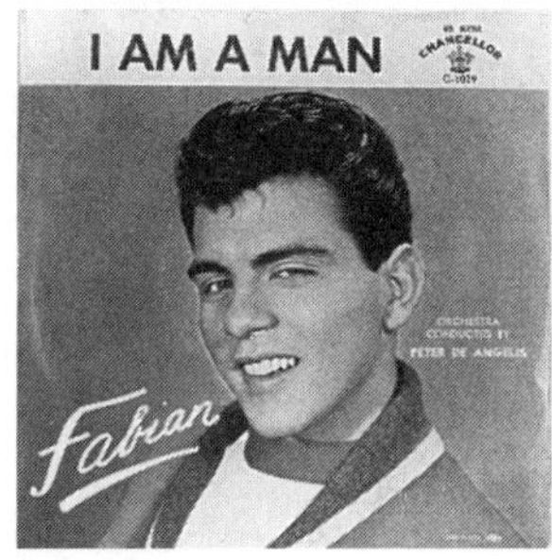

Number	Title (A Side/B Side)	Yr	VG	VG+	NM
❑ Imperial 66104	Let the Sunshine In/In the Meantime	1965	2.50	5.00	10.00
❑ Imperial 66125	Blue Monday/Like We Used to Be	1965	2.50	5.00	10.00
❑ Imperial 66189	El Bandido/Get Away	1966	2.50	5.00	10.00
❑ Imperial 66220	Last Night/Sitting in the Park	1966	2.50	5.00	10.00
❑ Imperial 66299	Funny How Time Slips Away/Last Night	1968	2.00	4.00	8.00
❑ Island 035	Everlovin' Woman/Ozone	1975	—	2.50	5.00
Albums					
❑ Epic BN 26368	The Ballad of Bonnie and Clyde	1968	6.25	12.50	25.00
❑ Imperial LP-9282 [M]	Yeh, Yeh	1965	6.25	12.50	25.00
❑ Imperial LP-9331 [M]	Get Away	1966	6.25	12.50	25.00
❑ Imperial LP-12282 [P]	Yeh, Yeh	1965	7.50	15.00	30.00
—Entire album is stereo except "Yeh, Yeh" (rechanneled)					
❑ Imperial LP-12331 [R]	Get Away	1966	5.00	10.00	20.00
❑ Island ILPS 9293	Georgie Fame	1975	2.50	5.00	10.00

FASCINATIONS, THE (1)

45s

Number	Title (A Side/B Side)	Yr	VG	VG+	NM
❑ ABC-Paramount 10387	Mama Didn't Lie/Someone Like You	1962	5.00	10.00	20.00
—Some of the ABC-Paramount pressings are misspelled "Fasinations"					
❑ ABC-Paramount 10443	Tears In My Eyes/You're Gonna Be Sorry	1963	6.25	12.50	25.00
❑ Mayfield 7711	(Say It Isn't So) Say You'd Never Go/I'm So Lucky	1966	2.50	5.00	10.00
❑ Mayfield 7714	Girls Are Out to Get You/You'll Be Sorry	1966	2.50	5.00	10.00
❑ Mayfield 7716	I Can't Stay Away from You/(B-side unknown)	1967	2.50	5.00	10.00

FIFTH DIMENSION, THE

45s

Number	Title (A Side/B Side)	Yr	VG	VG+	NM
❑ ABC 12136	Magic in My Life/Lean On Me Always	1975	—	2.00	4.00
❑ ABC 12168	Walk Your Feet in the Sunshine/Speaking with My Heart	1976	—	2.00	4.00
❑ ABC 12181	Love Hangover/Will You Be There	1976	—	2.00	4.00
❑ Arista 0101	No Love in the Room/I Don't Know How to Look for Love	1975	—	2.00	4.00
❑ Bell 860	Medley: A Change Is Gonna Come & People Gotta Be Free/ The Declaration	1970	—	2.50	5.00
❑ Bell 880	Puppet Man/A Love Like Ours	1970	—	2.50	5.00
❑ Bell 895	Save the Country/Dimension 5	1970	—	2.50	5.00
❑ Bell 913	On the Beach (In the Summertime)/This Is Your Life	1970	—	2.50	5.00
❑ Bell 940	One Less Bell to Answer/Feelin' Alright?	1970	—	2.50	5.00
❑ Bell 965	Love's Lines, Angles and Rhymes/The Singer	1971	—	2.50	5.00
❑ Bell 999	Light Sings/Viva Tirado	1971	—	2.50	5.00
❑ Bell 45134	Never My Love/A Love Like Ours	1971	—	2.50	5.00
❑ Bell 45170	Together Let's Find Love/I Just Wanta Be Your Friend	1972	—	2.50	5.00
❑ Bell 45195	(Last Night) I Didn't Get to Sleep at All/The River Witch	1972	—	2.50	5.00
❑ Bell 45261	If I Could Reach You/Tomorrow Belongs to the Children	1972	—	2.50	5.00
❑ Bell 45310	Living Together, Growing Together/What Do I Need to Be Me	1973	—	2.00	4.00
❑ Bell 45338	Everything's Been Changed/There Never Was a Day	1973	—	2.00	4.00
❑ Bell 45380	Ashes to Ashes/The Singer	1973	—	2.00	4.00
❑ Bell 45425	Flashback/Diggin' for a Livin'	1973	—	2.00	4.00
❑ Bell 45612	Harlem/My Song	1974	—	2.00	4.00
❑ Motown 1437	You Are the Reason (I Feel Like Dancing)/ Slipping Into Something New	1978	—	2.00	4.00
❑ Motown 1453	Everybody's Got to Give It Up/You're My Star	1978	—	2.00	4.00
❑ Soul City 752	I'll Be Loving You Forever/Train, Keep On Moving	1966	15.00	30.00	60.00
❑ Soul City 753	Go Where You Wanna Go/Too Poor to Die	1967	2.00	4.00	8.00
❑ Soul City 755	Another Day, Another Heartache/Rosecrans Blvd.	1967	2.50	5.00	10.00
❑ Soul City 756	Up-Up and Away/Which Way to Nowhere	1967	2.00	4.00	8.00
❑ Soul City 760	Paper Cup/Poor Side of Town	1967	2.00	4.00	8.00
❑ Soul City 762	Carpet Man/Magic Garden	1968	2.00	4.00	8.00
❑ Soul City 766	Stoned Soul Picnic/The Saliboat Song	1968	2.00	4.00	8.00
❑ Soul City 768	Sweet Blindness/Bobby's Blues	1968	2.00	4.00	8.00
❑ Soul City 770	California Soul/It'll Never Be the Same	1968	2.00	4.00	8.00
❑ Soul City 772	Aquarius/Let the Sunshine In (The Flesh Failures)// Don'tcha Hear Me Callin' To Ya	1969	2.00	4.00	8.00
❑ Soul City 772 [DJ]	Aquarius/Let the Sunshine In (The Flesh Failures) (same on both sides?)	1969	3.75	7.50	15.00
—Promo only on yellow vinyl					
❑ Soul City 776	Workin' on a Groovy Thing/Broken Wing Bird	1969	2.00	4.00	8.00
❑ Soul City 779	Wedding Bell Blues/Lovin' Stew	1969	2.00	4.00	8.00
❑ Soul City 780	Blowing Away/Skinny Man	1970	—	3.00	6.00

Number	Title (A Side/B Side)	Yr	VG	VG+	NM
❑ Soul City 781	The Girls' Song/It'll Never Be the Same Again	1970	—	3.00	6.00
❑ Sutra 122	Surrender/Fantasy	1983	—	2.00	4.00
Albums					
❑ ABC D-897	Earthbound	1975	2.50	5.00	10.00
❑ Arista ABM-1106	Greatest Hits on Earth	1975	2.00	4.00	8.00
—Reissue of Bell 1106					
❑ Arista AL 8335	Greatest Hits on Earth	198?	2.00	4.00	8.00
—Reissue of Arista 1106					
❑ Bell 1106	Greatest Hits on Earth	1972	2.50	5.00	10.00
❑ Bell 1116	Living Together, Growing Together	1973	2.50	5.00	10.00
❑ Bell 1315	Soul and Inspiration	1974	2.50	5.00	10.00
❑ Bell 6045	Portrait	1970	3.00	6.00	12.00
❑ Bell 6060	Love's Lines, Angles and Rhymes	1971	3.00	6.00	12.00
❑ Bell 6065	Reflections	1971	2.50	5.00	10.00
❑ Bell 6073	Individually & Collectively	1972	2.50	5.00	10.00
❑ Bell 9000 [(2)]	The 5th Dimension/Live!!	1971	3.00	6.00	12.00
❑ Motown M7-896	Star	1978	2.50	5.00	10.00
❑ Pair PDL2-1108 [(2)]	The Glory Days	1986	3.00	6.00	12.00
❑ Rhino RNDA-71104 [(2)]	The 5th Dimension Anthology	1986	3.00	6.00	12.00
❑ Soul City SCS-33900	The 5th Dimension/Greatest Hits	1970	3.00	6.00	12.00
❑ Soul City SCS-33901	The July 5th Album	1970	3.00	6.00	12.00
❑ Soul City SCM-91000 [M]	Up, Up and Away	1967	5.00	10.00	20.00
❑ Soul City SCM-91001 [M]	The Magic Garden	1967	5.00	10.00	20.00
❑ Soul City SCS-92000 [S]	Up, Up and Away	1967	3.75	7.50	15.00
❑ Soul City SCS-92001 [S]	The Magic Garden	1967	3.75	7.50	15.00
❑ Soul City SCS-92002	Stoned Soul Picnic	1968	3.75	7.50	15.00
❑ Soul City SCS-92005	The Age of Aquarius	1969	3.75	7.50	15.00
FIFTH ESTATE, THE					
45s					
❑ Jubilee 5573	Ding! Dong! The Witch Is Dead/The Rub-a-Dub	1967	3.00	6.00	12.00
❑ Jubilee 5588	Lost Generation/The Goofin' Song	1967	2.00	4.00	8.00
❑ Jubilee 5595	Heigh-Ho/It's Waiting There for You	1967	2.00	4.00	8.00
❑ Jubilee 5607	Morning, Morning/Tomorrow Is My Turn	1967	2.00	4.00	8.00
❑ Jubilee 5617	Do Drop Inn/That's Love	1968	2.00	4.00	8.00
❑ Jubilee 5627	Coney Island Sally/Tomorrow Is My Turn	1968	2.00	4.00	8.00
❑ Jubilee 5655	Mickey Mouse Club March/I Knew You Before I Met You	1969	2.00	4.00	8.00
❑ Red Bird 10-064	Love Is All a Game/Like I Love You	1966	3.75	7.50	15.00
Albums					
❑ Jubilee JGM-8005 [M]	Ding Dong! The Witch Is Dead	1967	6.25	12.50	25.00
❑ Jubilee JGS-8005 [S]	Ding Dong! The Witch Is Dead	1967	7.50	15.00	30.00
FIREBALLS, THE					
45s					
❑ Astra 1021	Torquay/Sweet Walk	1966	2.50	5.00	10.00
❑ Atco 6491	Bottle of Wine/Can't You See I'm Tryin'	1967	2.50	5.00	10.00
❑ Atco 6569	Goin' Away/Groovy Motions	1968	2.00	4.00	8.00
❑ Atco 6595	Chicken Little/Three Minutes' Time	1968	2.00	4.00	8.00
❑ Atco 6614	Come On, React!/Woman Help Me	1968	2.00	4.00	8.00
❑ Atco 6651	Long Green/Light in the Window	1969	2.00	4.00	8.00
❑ Atco 6678	Watch Her Walk/Good Morning Shame	1969	2.00	4.00	8.00
❑ Dot 16487	Sugar Shack/My Heart Is Free	1963	3.75	7.50	15.00
—Jimmy Gilmer and the Fireballs					
❑ Dot 16493	Torquay Two/Peg Leg	1963	3.75	7.50	15.00
❑ Dot 16539	Daisy Petal Pickin'/When My Tears Have Dried	1963	3.00	6.00	12.00
—Jimmy Gilmer and the Fireballs					
❑ Dot 16583	Ain't Gonna Tell Anybody/Young Am I	1964	3.00	6.00	12.00
—Jimmy Gilmer and the Fireballs					
❑ Dot 16591	Daytona Drag/Gently, Gently	1964	3.75	7.50	15.00
❑ Dot 16609	I'll Send for You/Look at Me	1964	2.50	5.00	10.00
—Jimmy Gilmer and the Fireballs					
❑ Dot 16642	Wishing/What Kinda Love	1964	2.50	5.00	10.00
—Jimmy Gilmer and the Fireballs					
❑ Dot 16661	Dumbo/Mr. Reed	1964	3.75	7.50	15.00
❑ Dot 16666	Cry Baby/Thunder 'N' Lightnin'	1964	2.50	5.00	10.00
—Jimmy Gilmer and the Fireballs					
❑ Dot 16687	Break His Heart for Me/Cinnamon Cindy	1965	2.50	5.00	10.00
—Jimmy Gilmer and the Fireballs					
❑ Dot 16692	Yummie Yama Papa/Baby, What's Wrong	1965	3.75	7.50	15.00
❑ Dot 16714	Born to Be with You/Lonesome Tears	1965	2.50	5.00	10.00
—Jimmy Gilmer and the Fireballs					
❑ Dot 16715	More Than I Can Say/Beating of My Heart	1965	3.75	7.50	15.00
❑ Dot 16743	The Fool/Somebody Stole My Watermelon	1965	2.50	5.00	10.00
—Jimmy Gilmer and the Fireballs					
❑ Dot 16745	Ahhh, Soul/Campusology	1965	3.75	7.50	15.00
❑ Dot 16768	Codine/Come to Me	1965	2.50	5.00	10.00
—Jimmy Gilmer and the Fireballs					
❑ Dot 16786	She Belongs to Me/Rambler's Blues	1965	2.50	5.00	10.00
—Jimmy Gilmer and the Fireballs					
❑ Dot 16833	Hungry, Hungry, Hungry/Wild Roses	1966	2.50	5.00	10.00
—Jimmy Gilmer and the Fireballs					
❑ Dot 16834	Jada/What I Am	1966	3.75	7.50	15.00
❑ Dot 16881	All I Do Is Dream of You/Ain't That Rain	1966	2.50	5.00	10.00
—Jimmy Gilmer and the Fireballs					
❑ Dot 16918	Torquay Two/Say I Am	1966	3.75	7.50	15.00
❑ Dot 16979	Sugar Shack/Daisy Petal Pickin'	1966	2.50	5.00	10.00
—Jimmy Gilmer and the Fireballs					

Number	Title (A Side/B Side)	Yr	VG	VG+	NM
❑ Dot 16992	Shy Girl/I Think I'll Catch a Bus	1967	2.50	5.00	10.00
—Jimmy Gilmer and the Fireballs					
❑ Hamilton 50036	Blacksmith Blues/Tuff-a-Nuff	1960	5.00	10.00	20.00
❑ Jaro 77029	Long, Long Ponytail/Let There Be Love	1960	20.00	40.00	80.00
—Chuck Tharp and the Fireballs					
❑ Kapp 248	Fireball/I Don't Know	1958	25.00	50.00	100.00
—Chuck Tharp and the Fireballs					
❑ 7 Arts 714	Callin' the Sheriff/Don't Stop	1961	—	—	—
—Evidently, record was never released, though its picture sleeve exists					
❑ Top Rank 2008	Torquay/Cry Baby	1959	5.00	10.00	20.00
❑ Top Rank 2026 [M]	Bulldog/Nearly Sunrise	1959	5.00	10.00	20.00
❑ Top Rank 2026ST [S]	Bulldog/Nearly Sunrise	1959	12.50	25.00	50.00
❑ Top Rank 2038 [M]	Foot Patter/Kissin'	1959	5.00	10.00	20.00
❑ Top Rank 2038ST [S]	Foot Patter/Kissin'	1959	12.50	25.00	50.00
❑ Top Rank 2054	Vaquero/Chief Whoopin'-Koff	1960	5.00	10.00	20.00
❑ Top Rank 2081	Almost Paradise/Sweet Talk	1960	5.00	10.00	20.00
❑ Top Rank 3003	Rick-a-Tic/Tacky Doo	1961	5.00	10.00	20.00
❑ Warwick 630	Rik-A-Tik/Yackey-Doo	1961	4.00	8.00	16.00
❑ Warwick 644	Quite a Party/Gunshot	1961	4.00	8.00	16.00
Albums					
❑ Atco 33-239 [M]	Bottle of Wine	1968	10.00	20.00	40.00
❑ Atco SD 33-239 [S]	Bottle of Wine	1968	6.25	12.50	25.00
❑ Atco SD 33-275	Come On, React!	1969	6.25	12.50	25.00
❑ Crown CST-376 [R]	Jimmy Gilmer and the Fireballs & The Sugar Shackers	1963	6.25	12.50	25.00
❑ Crown CST-387 [R]	The Sensational Jimmy Gilmer & The Fireballs	1964	6.25	12.50	25.00
❑ Crown CLP-5376 [M]	Jimmy Gilmer and the Fireballs & The Sugar Shackers	1963	6.25	12.50	25.00
❑ Crown CLP-5387 [M]	The Sensational Jimmy Gilmer & The Fireballs	1964	6.25	12.50	25.00
❑ Dot DLP-3512 [M]	Torquay	1963	12.50	25.00	50.00
❑ Dot DLP-3545 [M]	Sugar Shack	1963	10.00	20.00	40.00
—Jimmy Gilmer and the Fireballs					
❑ Dot DLP-3577 [M]	Buddy's Buddy	1964	12.50	25.00	50.00
—Jimmy Gilmer and the Fireballs					
❑ Dot DLP-3643 [M]	Lucky 'Leven	1965	7.50	15.00	30.00
❑ Dot DLP-3668 [M]	Folkbeat	1965	7.50	15.00	30.00
❑ Dot DLP-3709 [M]	Campusology	1966	7.50	15.00	30.00
❑ Dot DLP-3856 [M]	Firewater	1968	12.50	25.00	50.00
—Stereo cover with "Monaural" and "Promotional Copy Not for Sale" stickers, but the record is stock mono					
❑ Dot DLP-25512 [S]	Torquay	1963	20.00	40.00	80.00
❑ Dot DLP-25545 [S]	Sugar Shack	1963	15.00	30.00	60.00
—Jimmy Gilmer and the Fireballs					
❑ Dot DLP-25577 [S]	Buddy's Buddy	1964	20.00	40.00	80.00
—Jimmy Gilmer and the Fireballs					
❑ Dot DLP-25643 [S]	Lucky 'Leven	1965	10.00	20.00	40.00
❑ Dot DLP-25668 [S]	Folkbeat	1965	10.00	20.00	40.00
❑ Dot DLP-25709 [S]	Campusology	1966	10.00	20.00	40.00
❑ Dot DLP-25856 [S]	Firewater	1968	6.25	12.50	25.00
❑ Sundazed LP-5016	The Fireballs	1995	2.50	5.00	10.00
❑ Sundazed LP-5017	Torquay	1995	2.50	5.00	10.00
❑ Sundazed LP-5018	Gunshot!	1995	2.50	5.00	10.00
❑ Top Rank RM-324 [M]	The Fireballs	1960	37.50	75.00	150.00
❑ Top Rank RM-343 [M]	Vaquero	1960	37.50	75.00	150.00
❑ Top Rank RS-643 [S]	Vaquero	1960	50.00	100.00	200.00
❑ Warwick W-2042 [M]	Here Are the Fireballs	1961	37.50	75.00	150.00
❑ Warwick WST-2042 [S]	Here Are the Fireballs	1961	62.50	125.00	250.00

FIRST EDITION, THE

45s

Number	Title (A Side/B Side)	Yr	VG	VG+	NM
❑ Jolly Rogers 1001	Lady, Play Your Symphony/There's An Old Man in Our Town	1973	—	2.50	5.00
❑ Jolly Rogers 1003	(Do You Remember) The First Time/Indian Joe	1973	—	2.50	5.00
❑ Jolly Rogers 1004	Today I Started Loving You Again/She Thinks I Still Care	1973	—	2.50	5.00
❑ Jolly Rogers 1006	Whatcha Gonna Do/Something About Your Song	1973	—	2.50	5.00
❑ Jolly Rogers 1007	A Stranger in My Place/Makin' Music for Money	1974	—	2.50	5.00
—All of the above as "Kenny Rogers and the First Edition"					
❑ Reprise 0628	Ticket to Nowhere/I Found a Reason	1967	2.00	4.00	8.00
❑ Reprise 0655	Just Dropped In (To See What Condition My Condition Was In)/ Shadow in the Corner of Your Mind	1967	3.00	6.00	12.00
—Original pressing has orange and brown label					

Number	Title (A Side/B Side)	Yr	VG	VG+	NM
❑ Reprise 0683	Dream On/Only Me	1968	—	3.00	6.00
❑ Reprise 0693	Look Around, I'll Be There/Charlie the Fer-De-Lance	1968	—	3.00	6.00
❑ Reprise 0737	Just Dropped In (To See What Condition My Condition Was In)/ But You Know I Love You	1971	—	2.00	4.00
—As "Kenny Rogers and the First Edition"; "Back to Back Hits" series					
❑ Reprise 0738	Ruby, Don't Take Your Love to Town/Reuben James	1971	—	2.00	4.00
—As "Kenny Rogers and the First Edition"; "Back to Back Hits" series					
❑ Reprise 0747	Something's Burning/Someone Who Cares	1972	—	2.00	4.00
—As "Kenny Rogers and the First Edition"; "Back to Back Hits" series					
❑ Reprise 0748	Tell It All Brother/Heed the Call	1972	—	2.00	4.00
—As "Kenny Rogers and the First Edition"; "Back to Back Hits" series					
❑ Reprise 0773	If I Could Only Change Your Mind/Are My Thoughts With You	1968	—	3.00	6.00
❑ Reprise 0799	But You Know I Love You/Homemade Lies	1968	—	3.00	6.00
❑ Reprise 0822	Good Time Liberator/Once Again She's All Alone	1969	—	2.50	5.00
—Starting above, by "Kenny Rogers and the First Edition"					
❑ Reprise 0829	Ruby, Don't Take Your Love to Town/Girl Get a Hold of Yourself	1969	—	2.50	5.00
❑ Reprise 0854	Ruben James/Sunshine	1969	—	2.50	5.00
❑ Reprise 0854	Reuben James/Sunshine	1969	—	2.50	5.00
❑ Reprise 0888	Something's Burning/Mama's Waiting	1970	—	2.50	5.00
❑ Reprise 0923	Tell It All Brother/Just Remember You're My Sunshine	1970	—	2.50	5.00
❑ Reprise 0953	Heed the Call/A Stranger in My Place	1970	—	2.50	5.00
❑ Reprise 0999	Someone Who Cares/Mission of San Mohera	1971	—	2.50	5.00
❑ Reprise 1018	Take My Hand/All God's Lonely Children	1971	—	2.50	5.00
❑ Reprise 1053	Where Does Rosie Go/What Am I Gonna Do	1971	—	2.50	5.00
❑ Reprise 1069	School Teacher/Trigger Happy Kid	1972	—	2.50	5.00
7-					
❑ Reprise PRO 399 [DJ]	Radio Spot for: Something's Burning	1970	3.75	7.50	15.00
—White label; each side has two 60-second radio ads; not issued with cover					
Albums					
❑ Jolly Rogers 5001	Backroads	1973	3.75	7.50	15.00
❑ Jolly Rogers 5003	Rollin'	1974	3.75	7.50	15.00
❑ Jolly Rogers 5004	Monumental	1974	3.75	7.50	15.00
—All the above as "Kenny Rogers and the First Edition"					
❑ MCA 912	Love Songs	1984	2.00	4.00	8.00
❑ MCA 913	Country Songs	1984	2.00	4.00	8.00
❑ MCA 942	Hits and Pieces	1985	2.00	4.00	8.00
❑ MCA 943	The 60's Revisited	1985	2.00	4.00	8.00
❑ MCA 944	Pieces of Calico Silver	1985	2.00	4.00	8.00
❑ MCA 1460	Greatest Hits	1985	2.00	4.00	8.00
—Reissue of Reprise 6437					
❑ Reprise MS 2039	Transition	1971	5.00	10.00	20.00
—As "Kenny Rogers and the First Edition"					
❑ Reprise R-6276 [M]	The First Edition	1967	7.50	15.00	30.00
❑ Reprise RS-6276 [S]	The First Edition	1967	6.25	12.50	25.00
❑ Reprise RS-6302	The First Edition's Second	1968	6.25	12.50	25.00
❑ Reprise RS-6328	The First Edition '69	1969	6.25	12.50	25.00
❑ Reprise RS-6352	Ruby, Don't Take Your Love to Town	1969	5.00	10.00	20.00
—Starting above, as "Kenny Rogers and the First Edition"					
❑ Reprise RS-6385	Something's Burning	1970	5.00	10.00	20.00
❑ Reprise RS-6412	Tell It All Brother	1970	5.00	10.00	20.00
❑ Reprise RS-6437	Greatest Hits	1971	5.00	10.00	20.00
❑ Reprise 2XS 6476 [(2)]	The Ballad of Calico	1972	6.25	12.50	25.00
❑ Reprise ST-92060	Ruby, Don't Take Your Love to Town	1969	6.25	12.50	25.00
—Capitol Record Club edition					

FIVE AMERICANS, THE

Number	Title (A Side/B Side)	Yr	VG	VG+	NM
45s					
❑ ABC-Paramount 10686	Show Me/Love, Love, Love	1965	3.75	7.50	15.00
❑ Abnak 106	Say That You Love Me/Without You	1965	2.50	5.00	10.00
❑ Abnak 109	I See the Light/The Outcast	1965	5.00	10.00	20.00
❑ Abnak 114	Reality/Sympathy	1966	2.50	5.00	10.00
❑ Abnak 116	If I Could/Now That It's Over	1966	2.50	5.00	10.00
❑ Abnak 118	Western Union/Now That It's Over	1967	3.00	6.00	12.00
❑ Abnak 120	Sound of Love/Sympathy	1967	2.00	4.00	8.00
❑ Abnak 123	Zip Code/Sweet Bird of Youth	1967	2.00	4.00	8.00
❑ Abnak 125	Stop Light/Tell Ann I Love Her	1967	2.00	4.00	8.00
❑ Abnak 126	7:30 Guided Tour/See Saw Baby	1967	2.00	4.00	8.00
❑ Abnak 128	The Rain Maker/No Communication	1968	2.00	4.00	8.00
❑ Abnak 131	Con Man/Lovin' Is Lovin'	1968	2.00	4.00	8.00
❑ Abnak 132	Generation Gap/The Source	1968	2.00	4.00	8.00
❑ Abnak 134	Virginia Girl/Call on Me	1969	2.00	4.00	8.00
❑ Abnak 137	Scrooge/Ignert Woman	1969	2.00	4.00	8.00
❑ Abnak 139	I See the Light '69/Red Cape	1969	2.00	4.00	8.00
—As "Michael Rabon and the Five Americans"					
❑ Abnak 142	She's Too Good to Me/Molly Black	1969	2.00	4.00	8.00
❑ Hanna-Barbera 454	I See the Light/The Outcast	1965	3.00	6.00	12.00
❑ Hanna-Barbera 468	Evol-Not Love/Don't Blame Me	1966	3.00	6.00	12.00
❑ Hanna-Barbera 483	Good Times/The Losing Game	1966	3.00	6.00	12.00
❑ Jetstar 104	It's You Girl/I'm Gonna Leave You	1966	6.25	12.50	25.00
❑ Jetstar 105	I'm Feeling OK/Slippin' and Slidin'	1966	7.50	15.00	30.00
Albums					
❑ Abnak AB-1967 [M]	Western Union/Sound of Love	1967	5.00	10.00	20.00
❑ Abnak AB-1969 [M]	Progressions	1967	5.00	10.00	20.00
❑ Abnak ABST-2067 [S]	Western Union/Sound of Love	1967	7.50	15.00	30.00
❑ Abnak ABST-2069 [S]	Progressions	1967	7.50	15.00	30.00
❑ Abnak ABST-2071 [(2)]	Now and Then	1968	6.25	12.50	25.00

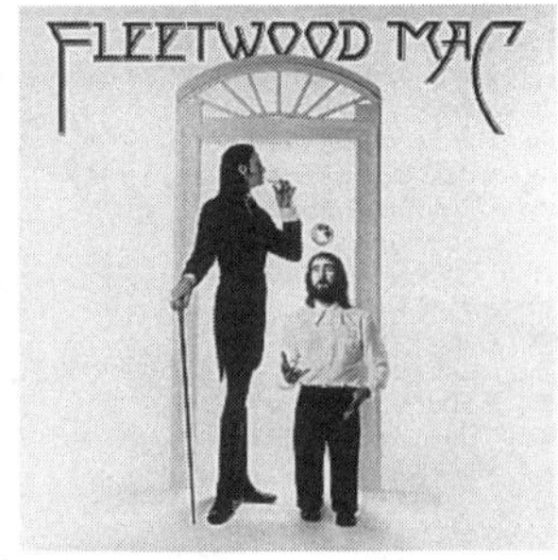

Number	Title (A Side/B Side)	Yr	VG	VG+	NM
❑ Hanna-Barbera HLP-8503 [M]	I See the Light	1966	10.00	20.00	40.00
❑ Hanna-Barbera HST-9503 [S]	I See the Light	1966	15.00	30.00	60.00

FIVE MAN ELECTRICAL BAND

45s

Number	Title (A Side/B Side)	Yr	VG	VG+	NM
❑ Capitol 2562	Sunrise to Sunset/Little Bit of Love	1969	—	3.00	6.00
❑ Capitol 2628	Riverboat/Good	1969	—	3.00	6.00
❑ Lion 112	Coming of Age/The Devil and Miss Lucy	1972	—	2.50	5.00
❑ Lion 127	Money Back Guarantee/Find the One	1972	—	2.50	5.00
❑ Lion 149	I'm a Stranger Here/Doin' The Best We Can Rag	1973	—	2.50	5.00
❑ Lion 160	Sweet Paradise/Baby Wanna Boogie	1973	—	2.50	5.00
❑ Lionel 3213	Signs/Hello Melinda Goodbye	1971	2.00	4.00	8.00
—Lists "Hello Melinda Goodbye" as the A-side and contains the full-length version of "Signs"					
❑ Lionel 3213	Signs/Hello Melinda Goodbye	1971	—	3.00	6.00
—Lists no A and B sides and contains an edited version (3:20) of "Signs"					
❑ Lionel 3220	Absolutely Right/Butterfly	1971	—	2.50	5.00
❑ Lionel 3224	Friends and Family/Julianna	1971	—	2.50	5.00
❑ MGM 14149	Moonshine/Forever Together	1970	—	3.00	6.00
❑ Polydor 14221	Werewolf/Country Angel	1974	—	2.00	4.00
❑ Polydor 14263	Johnnie Get a Gun/And the World Goes Round	1974	—	3.00	6.00

Albums

Number	Title (A Side/B Side)	Yr	VG	VG+	NM
❑ Capitol ST-165	Five Man Electrical Band	1969	5.00	10.00	20.00
❑ Lion LN-1009	Sweet Paradise	1973	5.00	10.00	20.00
❑ Lionel LRS-1100	Good-Byes & Butterflies	1970	7.50	15.00	30.00
❑ Lionel LRS-1101	Coming of Age	1971	5.00	10.00	20.00
❑ MGM SE-4725	Good-Byes & Butterflies	1970	12.50	25.00	50.00
❑ Pickwick SPC-3289	Five Man Electrical Band	1973	2.50	5.00	10.00
—Reissue of Capitol material					

FIVE ROYALES, THE

45s

Number	Title (A Side/B Side)	Yr	VG	VG+	NM
❑ ABC-Paramount 10348	Catch That Teardrop/Goof Ball	1962	2.50	5.00	10.00
❑ ABC-Paramount 10368	What's In Your Heart/I Want It Like That	1962	2.50	5.00	10.00
❑ Apollo 441	Courage to Love/You Know I Know	1952	25.00	50.00	100.00
—Black vinyl					
❑ Apollo 441	Courage to Love/You Know I Know	1952	100.00	200.00	400.00
—Red vinyl					
❑ Apollo 443	Baby Don't Do It/Take All of Me	1952	25.00	50.00	100.00
—Black vinyl					
❑ Apollo 443	Baby Don't Do It/Take All of Me	1952	100.00	200.00	400.00
—Red vinyl					
❑ Apollo 446	Help Me, Somebody/Crazy, Crazy, Crazy	1953	25.00	50.00	100.00
❑ Apollo 448	Too Much Lovin' (Much Too Much)/Laundromat Blues	1953	30.00	60.00	120.00
❑ Apollo 449	I Want to Thank You/All Righty	1953	20.00	40.00	80.00
❑ Apollo 452	I Do/Good Things	1954	20.00	40.00	80.00
❑ Apollo 454	Cry Some More/I Like It Like That	1954	20.00	40.00	80.00
❑ Apollo 458	What's That/Let Me Come Back Home	1954	17.50	35.00	70.00
❑ Apollo 467	With All Your Heart/6 O'Clock in the Morning	1955	17.50	35.00	70.00
❑ Home of the Blues 112	Please, Please, Please/I Got to Know	1960	3.75	7.50	15.00
❑ Home of the Blues 218	If You Don't Need Me/I'm Gonna Tell Them	1961	3.75	7.50	15.00
❑ Home of the Blues 232	Take Me With You Baby/Not Going to Cry	1961	3.75	7.50	15.00
❑ Home of the Blues 234	Nuch in Need/They Don't Know	1962	3.75	7.50	15.00
❑ Home of the Blues 243	Catch That Teardrop/Goof Ball	1962	175.00	350.00	700.00
❑ King 4740	I'm Gonna Run It Down/Behave Yourself	1954	20.00	40.00	80.00
❑ King 4744	Monkey Hips and Rice/Devil with the Rest	1954	20.00	40.00	80.00
❑ King 4762	School Girl/One Mistake	1955	20.00	40.00	80.00
❑ King 4770	Every Dog Has His Day/You Didn't Learn It at Home	1955	20.00	40.00	80.00
❑ King 4785	How I Wonder/Mohawk Squaw	1955	20.00	40.00	80.00
❑ King 4806	I Need Your Lovin'/When I Get Like This	1955	12.50	25.00	50.00
❑ King 4819	Women About to Make Me Go Crazy/Do Unto You	1955	12.50	25.00	50.00
❑ King 4830	I Ain't Gettin' Caught/Someone Made You for Me	1955	12.50	25.00	50.00
❑ King 4869	When You Walked Through the Door/Right Around the Corner	1956	12.50	25.00	50.00
❑ King 4901	I Could Love You/My Wants for Love	1956	12.50	25.00	50.00
❑ King 4952	Get Something Out of It/Come On and Save Me	1956	12.50	25.00	50.00
❑ King 4973	Just As I Am/Mine Forevermore	1956	12.50	25.00	50.00

Number	Title (A Side/B Side)	Yr	VG	VG+	NM
❑ King 5032	Tears of Joy/Thirty Second Lover	1957	10.00	20.00	40.00
❑ King 5053	Think/I'd Better Make a Move	1957	10.00	20.00	40.00
❑ King 5082	Messin' Up/Say It	1957	10.00	20.00	40.00
❑ King 5098	Dedicated to the One I Love/Don't Be Ashamed	1958	10.00	20.00	40.00
❑ King 5131	Do the Cha Cha Cherry/The Feeling Is Real	1958	6.25	12.50	25.00
❑ King 5141	Tell the Truth/Double or Nothing	1958	6.25	12.50	25.00
❑ King 5153	The Slummer the Slum/Don't Let It Be in Vain	1958	6.25	12.50	25.00
❑ King 5162	Your Only Love/The Real Thing	1958	6.25	12.50	25.00
❑ King 5191	Miracle of Love/I Know It's Hard, But It's Fair	1959	6.25	12.50	25.00
❑ King 5237	Tell Me You Care/Wonder Where Your Love Has Gone	1959	6.25	12.50	25.00
❑ King 5266	My Sugar Sugar/It Hurts Inside	1959	6.25	12.50	25.00
❑ King 5329	Don't Give No More Than You Can Take/I'm with You	1960	6.25	12.50	25.00
❑ King 5357	Why/Within My Heart	1960	6.25	12.50	25.00
❑ King 5453	Dedicated to the One I Love/Miracle of Love	1961	3.75	7.50	15.00
❑ King 5756	Dedicated to the One I Love/Tears of Joy	1963	3.75	7.50	15.00
❑ King 5892	I Wonder Where Your Love Has Gone/I Need Your Lovin' Baby	1964	3.75	7.50	15.00
—The Five Royals					
❑ Smash 1936	Baby Don't Do It/I Like It Like That	1964	2.50	5.00	10.00
❑ Smash 1963	Never Turn Your Back/Faith	1965	2.50	5.00	10.00
❑ Todd 1086	I'm Standing in the Shadows/Doin' Everything	1963	2.50	5.00	10.00
❑ Todd 1088	Baby Don't Do It/There's Somebody Over There	1963	2.50	5.00	10.00
❑ Vee Jay 412	Much in Need/They Don't Know	1961	3.75	7.50	15.00
❑ Vee Jay 431	Help Me Somebody/Talk About My Woman	1962	3.75	7.50	15.00
Albums					
❑ Apollo LP-488 [M]	The Rockin' 5 Royales	1956	1000.	1500.	2000.
—Green label; VG value 1000; VG+ value 1500					
❑ Apollo LP-488 [M]	The Rockin' 5 Royales	1956	2000.	3000.	4000.
—Purple label; VG value 2000; VG+ value 3000					
❑ Apollo LP-488 [M]	The Rockin' 5 Royales	1956	250.00	500.00	1000.
—Yellow label					
❑ King 580 [M]	Dedicated to You	1957	125.00	250.00	500.00
❑ King 616 [M]	The 5 Royales Sing for You	1959	100.00	200.00	400.00
❑ King 678 [M]	The Five Royales	1960	62.50	125.00	250.00
❑ King 955 [M]	24 All Time Hits	1966	25.00	50.00	100.00
❑ King 5014	17 Hits	197?	3.00	6.00	12.00

FIVE STAIRSTEPS, THE

Number	Title (A Side/B Side)	Yr	VG	VG+	NM
45s					
❑ Buddah 20	Something's Missing/Tell Me Who	1967	2.00	4.00	8.00
—As "Five Stairsteps and Cubie"					
❑ Buddah 26	A Million to One/You Make Me So Mad	1968	2.00	4.00	8.00
—As "Five Stairsteps and Cubie"					
❑ Buddah 35	The Shadow of Your Love/Bad News	1968	2.00	4.00	8.00
❑ Buddah 165	Dear Prudence/O-o-h Child	1970	2.00	4.00	8.00
❑ Buddah 165	O-o-h Child/Who Do You Belong To	1970	—	3.00	6.00
❑ Buddah 188	Because I Love You/America Standing	1970	—	2.50	5.00
❑ Buddah 213	Didn't It Look So Easy/Peace Is Gonna Come	1971	—	2.50	5.00
—Starting with the above, as "Stairsteps"					
❑ Buddah 222	Snow/Look Out	1971	—	2.50	5.00
❑ Buddah 277	I Love You-Stop/I Feel a Song (In My Heart Again)	1972	—	2.50	5.00
❑ Buddah 291	Hush Child/The Easy Way	1972	—	2.50	5.00
❑ Buddah 320	Every Single Way/Two Weeks' Notice	1972	—	2.50	5.00
❑ Curtom 1931	Don't Change Your Love/New Dance Craze	1968	—	3.00	6.00
—Curtom releases as "Five Stairsteps and Cubie"					
❑ Curtom 1933	I Made a Mistake/Stay Close to Me	1968	—	3.00	6.00
❑ Curtom 1936	Baby Make Me Feel So Good/Little Young Lover	1969	—	3.00	6.00
❑ Curtom 1944	Madame Mary/Little Boy Blue	1969	—	3.00	6.00
❑ Curtom 1945	We Must Be in Love/Little Young Lover	1969	—	3.00	6.00
❑ Dark Horse 10005	From Us to You/Time	1975	—	2.50	5.00
❑ Dark Horse 10009	Tell Me Why/Salaam	1976	—	2.50	5.00
❑ Windy "C" 601	You Waited Too Long/Don't Waste Your Time	1966	2.50	5.00	10.00
❑ Windy "C" 602	World of Fantasy/Playgirl's Love	1966	2.50	5.00	10.00
❑ Windy "C" 603	Come Back/You Don't Love Me	1966	2.50	5.00	10.00
❑ Windy "C" 604	Danger, She's a Stranger/Behind Curtains	1967	2.50	5.00	10.00
❑ Windy "C" 605	Ain't Gonna Rest (Till I Get You)/You Can't See	1967	2.50	5.00	10.00
❑ Windy "C" 607	Oooh, Baby Baby/The Girl I Love	1967	2.50	5.00	10.00
❑ Windy "C" 608	The Touch of You/Change of Face	1967	2.50	5.00	10.00
Albums					
❑ Buddah BDS-5008	Our Family Portrait	1967	5.00	10.00	20.00
❑ Buddah BDS-5061	Stairsteps	1970	3.75	7.50	15.00
—As "Stairsteps"					
❑ Buddah BDS-5068	Step by Step by Step	1970	3.75	7.50	15.00
—As "Stairsteps"					
❑ Collectables COL-5023	Greatest Hits	1985	2.50	5.00	10.00
❑ Curtom 8002	Love's Happening	1969	5.00	10.00	20.00
❑ Windy C 6000 [M]	The Five Stairsteps	1967	6.25	12.50	25.00
❑ Windy C S-6000 [S]	The Five Stairsteps	1967	6.25	12.50	25.00

FLACK, ROBERTA

Number	Title (A Side/B Side)	Yr	VG	VG+	NM
45s					
❑ Atlantic 2665	Compared to What/That's No Way to Say Goodbye	1969	2.00	4.00	8.00
❑ Atlantic 2730	How Many Broken Wings/Baby Baby	1970	—	3.00	6.00
—With Les McCann					
❑ Atlantic 2758	Reverend Lee/Business Goes On As Usual	1970	—	3.00	6.00
❑ Atlantic 2785	Let It Be Me/Do What Cha Gotta Do	1971	—	3.00	6.00
❑ Atlantic 2851	Will You Still Love Me Tomorrow/Go Up Moses	1972	—	2.50	5.00
❑ Atlantic 2864	The First Time Ever I Saw Your Face/Trade Winds	1972	—	2.50	5.00

Number	Title (A Side/B Side)	Yr	VG	VG+	NM
❑ Atlantic 2940	Killing Me Softly with His Song/Just Like a Woman	1973	—	2.50	5.00
❑ Atlantic 2982	Jesse/No Tears	1973	—	2.50	5.00
❑ Atlantic 3025	Feel Like Makin' Love/When You Smile	1974	—	2.50	5.00
❑ Atlantic 3203	Feel Like Makin' Love/When You Smile	1974	—	2.00	4.00
❑ Atlantic 3271	Feelin' That Glow/Some Gospel According to Matthew	1975	—	2.00	4.00
❑ Atlantic 3441	The 25th of Last December/Move In with Me	1977	—	2.00	4.00
❑ Atlantic 3483	If Ever I See You Again/I'd Like to Be a Baby to You	1978	—	2.00	4.00
❑ Atlantic 3521	When It's Over/Come Share My Love	1978	—	2.00	4.00
❑ Atlantic 3560	You Are Everything/Knowing That We're Made for Each Other	1979	—	2.00	4.00
❑ Atlantic 3627	You Are My Heaven/I'll Love You Forever and Ever	1979	—	2.00	4.00
❑ Atlantic 3753	Don't Make Me Wait Too Long/Only Heaven Can Wait (For Love)	1980	—	2.00	4.00
❑ Atlantic 4005	Making Love/Jesse	1982	—	2.00	4.00
❑ Atlantic 4068	I'm the One/'Til the Morning Comes	1982	—	2.00	4.00
❑ Atlantic 87607	Set the Night to Music/Natural Thing	1991	—	2.00	4.00
—A-side: With Maxi Priest					
❑ Atlantic 88898	Shock to My System/You Know What It's Like	1989	—	—	3.00
❑ Atlantic 88941	Uh-Uh Ooh-Ooh Look Out (Here It Comes)/ You Know What It's Like	1989	—	—	3.00
❑ Atlantic 88996	Oasis/You Know What It's Like	1988	—	—	3.00
❑ Atlantic 89295	We Shall Overcome/We Shall Overcome	1987	—	—	3.00
❑ Atlantic 89440	Let Me Be a Light to Shine/We Shall Overcome	1986	—	—	3.00
—With Howard Hewett					
❑ Atlantic 89931	Our Love Will Stop the World/Only Heaven Can Wait (For Love)	1982	—	2.00	4.00
—A-side: With Eric Mercury					
❑ Atlantic 89932	In the Name of Love/Happiness	1982	—	2.00	4.00
❑ Columbia 44050	Si, Si, Senor/This Year	1967	2.50	5.00	10.00
❑ Columbia 44448	Cold, Cold Winter/If You Ever Leave Me Now	1968	2.50	5.00	10.00
❑ MCA 51126	You Stopped Loving Me/Qual E Maundrinio	1981	—	2.00	4.00
❑ MCA 51173	Lovin' You/Hittin' Me Where It Hurts	1981	—	2.00	4.00
❑ Viva 29401	This Side of Forever/Robbery Suspects	1983	—	2.00	4.00
—B-side by The Enforcers					

FLACK, ROBERTA, AND DONNY HATHAWAY

45s

Number	Title (A Side/B Side)	Yr	VG	VG+	NM
❑ Atlantic 2808	You've Got a Friend/Gone Away	1971	—	2.50	5.00
❑ Atlantic 2837	You've Lost That Lovin' Feeling/Be Real Black for Me	1971	—	2.50	5.00
❑ Atlantic 2879	Where Is the Love/Mood	1972	—	2.50	5.00
❑ Atlantic 3463	The Closer I Get to You/Love Is the Healing	1978	—	2.00	4.00
—B-side by Flack alone					
❑ Atlantic 3661	Back Together Again/God Don't Like Ugly	1980	—	2.00	4.00

FLAMINGOS, THE

45s

Number	Title (A Side/B Side)	Yr	VG	VG+	NM
❑ Chance 1133	If I Can't Have You/Someday, Somehow	1953	200.00	400.00	800.00
—Black vinyl					
❑ Chance 1140	That's My Desire/Hurry Home Baby	1953	150.00	300.00	600.00
—Black vinyl					
❑ Chance 1145	Golden Teardrops/Carried Away	1953	250.00	500.00	1000.
—Black vinyl					
❑ Chance 1149	Plan for Love/You Ain't Ready	1953	500.00	1000.	2000.
—Yellow and black label					
❑ Chance 1154	Cross Over the Bridge/Listen to My Plea	1954	250.00	500.00	1000.
❑ Chance 1162	Jump Children/Blues in the Letter	1954	150.00	300.00	600.00
❑ Checker 815	That's My Baby (Chick-a-Boom)/When	1955	20.00	40.00	80.00
❑ Checker 821	I Want to Love You/Please Come Back Home	1955	20.00	40.00	80.00
❑ Checker 830	I'll Be Home/Need Your Love	1956	20.00	40.00	80.00
❑ Checker 837	A Kiss from Your Lips/Get With It	1956	20.00	40.00	80.00
❑ Checker 846	The Vow/Shilly Dilly	1956	20.00	40.00	80.00
❑ Checker 853	Just for a Kick/Would I Be Crying	1957	20.00	40.00	80.00
—Originals of above Checker singles are maroon with a checkerboard at top of label					
❑ Checker 915	Whispering Stars/Dream of a Lifetime	1959	12.50	25.00	50.00
❑ Checker 1084	Lover Come Back to Me/Your Little Guy	1964	3.75	7.50	15.00
❑ Checker 1091	Goodnight Sweetheart/Does It Really Matter	1964	3.75	7.50	15.00
❑ Decca 30335	The Ladder of Love/Let's Make Up	1957	7.50	15.00	30.00
❑ Decca 30454	Helpless/My Faith in You	1957	7.50	15.00	30.00
❑ Decca 30687	Rock and Roll March/Where Mary Go	1958	7.50	15.00	30.00
❑ Decca 30880	Kiss-A Me/Ever Since I Met Lucy	1959	7.50	15.00	30.00

Number	Title (A Side/B Side)	Yr	VG	VG+	NM
❑ Decca 30948	Jerri-Lee/Hey Now	1959	7.50	15.00	30.00
❑ End 1035	Please Wait for Me/That Love Is You	1958	15.00	30.00	60.00
❑ End 1035	Lovers Never Say Goodbye/That Love Is You	1958	10.00	20.00	40.00
—A-sides of End 1035 are the same song, the titles were changed					
❑ End 1040	I Shed a Tear at Your Wedding/But Not for Me	1959	7.50	15.00	30.00
❑ End 1044	At the Prom/Love Walked In	1959	10.00	20.00	40.00
❑ End 1046 [M]	I Only Have Eyes for You/Love Walked In	1959	6.25	12.50	25.00
❑ End 1046 [M]	I Only Have Eyes for You/At the Prom	1959	6.25	12.50	25.00
❑ End 1046 [M]	I Only Have Eyes for You/Goodnight Sweetheart	1959	7.50	15.00	30.00
❑ End 1046 [S]	I Only Have Eyes for You/At the Prom	1959	12.50	25.00	50.00
—This B-side has been confirmed for the stereo version; others are not yet known					
❑ End 1055 [M]	Yours/Love Walked In	1959	6.25	12.50	25.00
❑ End 1055 [S]	Yours/Love Walked In	1959	12.50	25.00	50.00
❑ End 1062	I Was Such a Fool/Heavenly Angel	1959	6.25	12.50	25.00
❑ End 1065	Mio Amore/You, Me and the Sea	1960	6.25	12.50	25.00
❑ End 1068	Nobody Loves Me Like You/Besame Mucho	1960	7.50	15.00	30.00
❑ End 1068	Nobody Loves Me Like You/You, Me and the Sea	1960	6.25	12.50	25.00
❑ End 1070	Besame Mucho/You, Me and the Sea	1960	6.25	12.50	25.00
❑ End 1073	Mio Amore/At Night	1960	5.00	10.00	20.00
❑ End 1079	Beside You/When I Fall in Love	1960	5.00	10.00	20.00
❑ End 1081	Your Other Love/Lovers Gotta Cry	1960	5.00	10.00	20.00
❑ End 1085	Thatr's Why I Love You/Ko Ko Mo	1961	5.00	10.00	20.00
❑ End 1092	Time Was/Dream Girl	1961	5.00	10.00	20.00
❑ End 1099	My Memories of You/I Want to Love You	1961	5.00	10.00	20.00
❑ End 1111	It Must Be Love/I'm No Fool Anymore	1962	5.00	10.00	20.00
❑ End 1116	For All We Know/Near You	1962	5.00	10.00	20.00
❑ End 1121	I Know Better/Flame of Love	1963	5.00	10.00	20.00
❑ End 1124	(Talk About) True Love/Come to My Party	1963	5.00	10.00	20.00
❑ Julmar 506	Dealin' All the Way/Dealin' (Groovin' with Feelin')	1969	2.50	5.00	10.00
❑ Lost-Nite 149	Dream of a Lifetime/On My Merry Way	196?	—	3.00	6.00
—Reissue					
❑ Lost-Nite 154	I'm Yours/Ko Ko Mo	196?	—	3.00	6.00
—Reissue					
❑ Lost-Nite 161	I Really Don't Want to Know/Get With It	196?	—	3.00	6.00
—Reissue					
❑ Lost-Nite 269	If I Can't Have You/Plan for Love	197?	—	2.50	5.00
❑ Lost-Nite 287	That's My Desire/Cross Over the Bridge	197?	—	2.50	5.00
❑ Lost-Nite 316	September Song/Vooit Vooit	197?	—	2.50	5.00
❑ Mercury 72455	Temptation/Call Her on the Phone	1965	—	—	—
—Cancelled					
❑ Oldies 45 35	Golden Teardrops/Carried Away	1963	2.00	4.00	8.00
❑ Oldies 45 43	I Only Have Eyes for You/At the Prom	1963	2.00	4.00	8.00
❑ Oldies 45 68	Lovers Never Say Goodbye/Baby, I Need You	1964	2.00	4.00	8.00
—B-side by the El Dorados					
❑ Parrot 808	Dream of a Lifetime/On My Merry Way	1954	200.00	400.00	800.00
—Black vinyl					
❑ Parrot 811	I Really Don't Want to Know/Get With It	1955	2500.	2750.	5000.
—Black vinyl. VG 2500; VG+ 2750					
❑ Parrot 812	I'm Yours/Ko Ko Mo	1955	200.00	400.00	800.00
—Black vinyl					
❑ Philips 40308	Temptation/Call Her on the Phone	1965	3.75	7.50	15.00
❑ Philips 40347	The Boogaloo Party/The Nearness of You	1965	3.75	7.50	15.00
❑ Philips 40378	Brooklyn Boogaloo/Since My Baby Put Me Down	1966	3.75	7.50	15.00
❑ Philips 40413	Itty Bitty Baby/She Shook My World	1966	3.75	7.50	15.00
❑ Philips 40452	Koo Koo/It Keeps the Doctor Away	1967	3.75	7.50	15.00
❑ Philips 40496	Oh Mary Don't You Worry/Do It, Do It	1967	3.75	7.50	15.00
❑ Polydor 14019	Buffalo Soldier (Long)/Buffalo Soldier (Short)	1970	2.50	5.00	10.00
❑ Polydor 14044	Straighten It Up (Get It Together)/Lover Come Back to Me	1970	2.50	5.00	10.00
❑ Ronze 111	Welcome Home/Gotta Have All Your Lovin'	1971	—	2.50	5.00
❑ Ronze 115	Someone to Watch Over Me/Heavy Hips	1972	—	2.50	5.00
❑ Ronze 116	Love Keeps the Doctor Away (Long)/ Love Keeps the Doctor Away (Short)	1972	—	2.50	5.00
❑ Roulette 4524	Ol' Man River (Part 1)/Ol' Man River (Part 2)	1963	5.00	10.00	20.00
❑ Skylark 541	If I Could Love You/I Found a New Baby	197?	—	2.50	5.00
❑ Times Square 102	A Lovely Way to Spend an Evening/ Walking My Baby Back Home	1964	3.75	7.50	15.00
❑ Vee Jay 384	Golden Teardrops/Carried Away	1961	6.25	12.50	25.00
❑ Worlds 103	Think About Me/(Instrumental)	1974	—	2.50	5.00

FLEETWOOD MAC

45s

Number	Title (A Side/B Side)	Yr	VG	VG+	NM
❑ Blue Horizon 304	Hungry Country Woman/Walkin'	1970	3.00	6.00	12.00
—A-side by Otis Spann with Fleetwood Mac; B-side by Otis Spann					
❑ DJM 1007	Man of the World/Best Girl in the World	1976	2.50	5.00	10.00
—B-side by Danny Kirwan					
❑ Epic 5-10351	Black Magic Woman/Long Grey Mare	1968	3.75	7.50	15.00
❑ Epic 5-10368	Stop Messin' Around/Need Your Love So Bad	1968	3.00	6.00	12.00
❑ Epic 5-10436	Albatross/Jigsaw Puzzle Blues	1969	3.00	6.00	12.00
❑ Epic 5-11029	Albatross/Black Magic Woman	1973	2.00	4.00	8.00
❑ Reprise GRE 0119	Rhiannon (Will You Ever Win)/Over My Head	1978	—	—	3.00
—"Back to Back Hits" series					
❑ Reprise 0860	Rattlesnake Shake/Coming Your Way	1969	6.25	12.50	25.00
❑ Reprise 0883	Oh Well, Part 1/Part 2	1970	5.00	10.00	20.00
❑ Reprise 0925	The Green Manalishi (With the Two-Prong Crown)/ World In Harmony	1970	5.00	10.00	20.00
❑ Reprise 0984	Jewel-Eyed Judy/Station Man	1971	3.75	7.50	15.00
❑ Reprise 1057	Sands of Time/Lay It All Down	1971	2.50	5.00	10.00

Number	Title (A Side/B Side)	Yr	VG	VG+	NM
❑ Reprise 1077	Oh Well, Part 1/The Green Manalishi (With the Two-Prong Crown)	1971	2.00	4.00	8.00
—"Back to Back Hits" reissue					
❑ Reprise 1093	Sentimental Lady/Sunny Side of Heaven	1972	5.00	10.00	20.00
❑ Reprise 1159	Remember Me/Dissatisfied	1973	2.50	5.00	10.00
❑ Reprise 1172	Did You Ever Love Me/Revelation	1973	3.00	6.00	12.00
❑ Reprise 1188	For Your Love/Hypnotized	1973	3.75	7.50	15.00
❑ Reprise 1317	Heroes Are Hard to Find/Born Enchanter	1974	2.00	4.00	8.00
❑ Reprise 1339	Over My Head/I'm So Afraid	1975	—	2.50	5.00
❑ Reprise 1345	Rhiannon (Will You Ever Win)/Sugar Daddy	1976	—	2.50	5.00
❑ Reprise 1356	Say You Love Me (Edited)/Monday Morning	1976	—	2.50	5.00
—The A-sides of Reprise 1339, 1345 and 1356 feature significantly different mixes than those on their parent album, "Fleetwood Mac."					
❑ Warner Bros. GWB 0348	Go Your Own Way/Dreams	1979	—	—	3.00
—"Back to Back Hits" series					
❑ Warner Bros. GWB 0388	Tusk/Sara	1981	—	—	3.00
—"Back to Back Hits" series					
❑ Warner Bros. GWB 0439	Hold Me/Gypsy	1984	—	—	3.00
—"Back to Back Hits" series					
❑ Warner Bros. 8304	Go Your Own Way/Silver Springs	1976	2.00	4.00	8.00
—Sought-after because of its non-LP B-side					
❑ Warner Bros. 8371	Dreams/Songbird	1977	—	2.00	4.00
❑ Warner Bros. 8413	Don't Stop/Never Going Back Again	1977	—	2.00	4.00
❑ Warner Bros. 8483	You Make Loving Fun/Gold Dust Woman	1977	—	2.00	4.00
❑ Warner Bros. 18661	Paper Doll/The Chain	1993	—	2.00	4.00
❑ Warner Bros. 19866	Save Me/Another Woman	1990	—	2.00	4.00
❑ Warner Bros. 19867	Skies the Limit/The Second Time	1990	—	2.00	4.00
❑ Warner Bros. 21888	Little Lies/Everywhere	1989	—	—	3.00
—"Back to Back Hits" series					
❑ Warner Bros. 21943	Big Love/Seven Wonders	1988	—	—	3.00
—"Back to Back Hits" series					
❑ Warner Bros. 21990	Don't Stop/Silver Springs	1988	—	—	3.00
—"Back to Back Hits" series					
❑ Warner Bros. 21991	You Make Loving Fun/Say You Love Me	1988	—	—	3.00
—"Back to Back Hits" series					
❑ Warner Bros. 27644	As Long As You Follow/Oh Well (Live)	1988	—	—	3.00
❑ Warner Bros. 28114	Family Man/Down Endless Street	1988	—	—	3.00
❑ Warner Bros. 28143	Everywhere/When I See You Again	1987	—	—	3.00
❑ Warner Bros. 28291	Little Lies/Ricky	1987	—	—	3.00
❑ Warner Bros. 28317	Seven Wonders/Book of Miracles	1987	—	—	3.00
❑ Warner Bros. 28398	Big Love/You and I, Part 1	1987	—	—	3.00
❑ Warner Bros. 29698	Oh Diane/That's Alright	1983	—	—	3.00
❑ Warner Bros. 29848	Love in Store/Can't Go Back	1983	—	—	3.00
❑ Warner Bros. 29918	Gypsy/Cool Water	1982	—	—	3.00
❑ Warner Bros. 29966	Hold Me/Eyes of the World	1982	—	—	3.00
❑ Warner Bros. 49077	Tusk/Never Make Me Cry	1979	—	2.00	4.00
❑ Warner Bros. 49150	Sara/That's Enough for Me	1979	—	2.00	4.00
❑ Warner Bros. 49196	Think About Me/Save Me a Place	1980	—	2.00	4.00
❑ Warner Bros. 49500	Sisters of the Moon/Walk a Thin Line	1980	2.50	5.00	10.00
—Scarce on stock copy; A-side is a different mix than the LP version					
❑ Warner Bros. 49660	Fireflies/Over My Head (Live)	1981	—	2.00	4.00
❑ Warner Bros. 49700	The Farmer's Daughter/Monday Morning (Live)	1982	—	3.00	6.00
Albums					
❑ Blue Horizon BH-3801 [(2)]	Fleetwood Mac in Chicago	1970	7.50	15.00	30.00
❑ Blue Horizon BH-4802	Blues Jam in Chicago, Vol. 1	1970	3.75	7.50	15.00
❑ Blue Horizon BH-4803	Blues Jam in Chicago, Vol. 2	1970	3.75	7.50	15.00
❑ Epic BN 26402 [S]	Fleetwood Mac	1968	7.50	15.00	30.00
❑ Epic BN 26446 [S]	English Rose	1969	7.50	15.00	30.00
❑ Epic KE 30632 [(2)]	Black Magic Woman	1971	5.00	10.00	20.00
❑ Epic KE 33740 [(2)]	Fleetwood Mac/English Rose	1974	3.75	7.50	15.00
❑ Reprise MS 2080	Bare Trees	1972	3.00	6.00	12.00
—With brown line near all four edges of the front cover					
❑ Reprise MS 2138	Penguin	1973	3.75	7.50	15.00
❑ Reprise MS 2158	Mystery to Me	1973	5.00	10.00	20.00
—With "Good Things (Come to Those Who Wait)" listed on the album cover; it was replaced at the last minute by "For Your Love"					
❑ Reprise MS 2158	Mystery to Me	1973	3.00	6.00	12.00
—With "For Your Love" listed correctly on the back cover					
❑ Reprise MS 2196	Heroes Are Hard to Find	1974	3.00	6.00	12.00

Number	Title (A Side/B Side)	Yr	VG	VG+	NM
❑ Reprise MS 2225	Fleetwood Mac	1975	2.50	5.00	10.00
❑ Reprise MSK 2278	Bare Trees	1977	2.00	4.00	8.00
—Reissue; no brown line on the front cover					
❑ Reprise MSK 2279	Mystery to Me	1977	2.00	4.00	8.00
❑ Reprise MSK 2281	Fleetwood Mac	1977	2.00	4.00	8.00
❑ Reprise RS 6368	Then Play On	1969	6.25	12.50	25.00
—First pressings include "When You Say" and "My Dream"					
❑ Reprise RS 6368	Then Play On	1970	3.75	7.50	15.00
—Later pressings replace above two tracks with "Oh Well (Parts 1 and 2)."					
❑ Reprise RS 6408	Kiln House	1970	3.75	7.50	15.00
❑ Reprise RS 6465	Future Games	1971	6.25	12.50	25.00
—Originals have a pale yellow cover					
❑ Sire SASH-3706 [(2)]	Vintage Years	1975	3.75	7.50	15.00
❑ Sire SASH-3715 [(2)]	Fleetwood Mac in Chicago	1975	3.75	7.50	15.00
—Reissue of Blue Horizon 3801					
❑ Sire 2XS-6006 [(2)]	Vintage Years	1977	3.00	6.00	12.00
❑ Sire 2XS-6009 [(2)]	Fleetwood Mac in Chicago	1977	3.00	6.00	12.00
❑ Sire 2XS-6045 [(2)]	The Original Fleetwood Mac	1977	3.00	6.00	12.00
❑ Varrick VR-020	Jumping at Shadows	1985	3.00	6.00	12.00
❑ Warner Bros. BSK 3010	Rumours	1977	2.50	5.00	10.00
—With short version (2:02) of "Never Going Back Again"; we do not yet know how to identify these without playing them					
❑ Warner Bros. BSK3010	Rumours	1979	—	3.00	6.00
—White label reissue					
❑ Warner Bros. 2HS 3350 [(2)]	Tusk	1979	3.75	7.50	15.00
❑ Warner Bros. 2WB 3500 [(2)]	Fleetwood Mac Live	1980	3.00	6.00	12.00
❑ Warner Bros. 23607	Mirage	1982	2.50	5.00	10.00
❑ Warner Bros. 25471	Tango in the Night	1987	2.50	5.00	10.00
❑ Warner Bros. 25801	Greatest Hits	1989	2.50	5.00	10.00
❑ Warner Bros. 26111	Behind the Mask	1990	3.75	7.50	15.00

FLEETWOODS, THE

45s

Number	Title (A Side/B Side)	Yr	VG	VG+	NM
❑ Dolphin 1	Come Softly to Me/I Care So Much	1959	6.25	12.50	25.00
❑ Dolton 3	Graduation's Here/Oh Lord, Let It Be	1959	5.00	10.00	20.00
❑ Dolton S-3 [S]	Graduation's Here/Oh Lord, Let It Be	1959	12.50	25.00	50.00
❑ Dolton 5	Mr. Blue/You Mean Everything to Me	1959	5.00	10.00	20.00
❑ Dolton 15	Outside My Window/Magic Star	1960	5.00	10.00	20.00
❑ Dolton 22	Runaround/Truly Do	1960	5.00	10.00	20.00
❑ Dolton 27	The Last One to Know/Dormilona	1960	3.75	7.50	15.00
❑ Dolton 30	Confidential/I Love You So	1960	3.75	7.50	15.00
❑ Dolton 40	Tragedy/Little Miss Sad One	1961	3.75	7.50	15.00
❑ Dolton 45	(He's) The Great Impostor/Poor Little Girl	1961	3.75	7.50	15.00
❑ Dolton 49	Billy Old Buddy/Trouble	1962	3.75	7.50	15.00
❑ Dolton 62	They Tell Me It's Summer/Lovers by Night, Strangers by Day	1962	3.75	7.50	15.00
❑ Dolton 74	You Should Have Been There/Sure Is Lonesome Downtown	1963	3.75	7.50	15.00
❑ Dolton 75	Goodnight My Love/Jimmy Beware	1963	3.75	7.50	15.00
❑ Dolton 86	Baby Bye-O/What'll I Do	1963	2.50	5.00	10.00
❑ Dolton 93	Lonesome Town/Ruby Red Baby Blue	1964	2.50	5.00	10.00
❑ Dolton 97	Ten Times Blue/Ska Light Ska Bright	1964	2.50	5.00	10.00
❑ Dolton 98	Mr. Sandman/This Is My Prayer	1964	2.50	5.00	10.00
❑ Dolton 302	Before and After (Losing You)/Lonely Is As Lonely Does	1964	2.50	5.00	10.00
❑ Dolton 307	Come Softly to Me/I'm Not Jimmy	1965	2.50	5.00	10.00
❑ Dolton 310	Rainbow/Just As I Need You	1965	2.50	5.00	10.00
❑ Dolton 315	For Lovin' Me/This Is Where I See Her	1965	2.50	5.00	10.00
❑ Liberty 62	They Tell Me It's Summer/Lovers by Night, Strangers by Day	1970	3.75	7.50	15.00
—Odd reissue keeping the Dolton number					
❑ Liberty 55188 [M]	Come Softly to Me/I Care So Much	1959	6.25	12.50	25.00
❑ Liberty 77188 [S]	Come Softly to Me/I Care So Much	1959	12.50	25.00	50.00
❑ United Artists 0038	Come Softly to Me/Runaround	1973	—	2.00	4.00
❑ United Artists 0039	Mr. Blue/Tragedy	1973	—	2.00	4.00
❑ United Artists 0040	He's the Great Impostor/Goodnight My Love	1973	—	2.00	4.00
—0038, 0039 and 0040 are "Silver Spotlight Series" reissues					
❑ United Artists XW515	(He's) The Great Impostor/Goodnight My Love	1974	—	2.00	4.00
—Reissue					

Albums

Number	Title (A Side/B Side)	Yr	VG	VG+	NM
❑ Dolton BLP-2001 [M]	Mr. Blue	1959	20.00	40.00	80.00
—Pale blue label with dolphins on top					
❑ Dolton BLP-2002 [M]	The Fleetwoods	1960	12.50	25.00	50.00
—Pale blue label with dolphins on top					
❑ Dolton BLP-2005 [M]	Softly	1961	12.50	25.00	50.00
—Pale blue label with dolphins on top					
❑ Dolton BLP-2007 [M]	Deep in a Dream	1961	10.00	20.00	40.00
—Pale blue label with dolphins on top					
❑ Dolton BLP-2011 [M]	The Best of the Oldies	1962	10.00	20.00	40.00
—Pale blue label with dolphins on top					
❑ Dolton BLP-2018 [M]	The Fleetwoods' Greatest Hits	1962	6.25	12.50	25.00
❑ Dolton BLP-2020 [M]	The Fleetwoods Sings for Lovers by Night	1963	7.50	15.00	30.00
❑ Dolton BLP-2025 [M]	Goodnight My Love	1963	7.50	15.00	30.00
❑ Dolton BLP-2030 [M]	Before and After	1965	7.50	15.00	30.00
❑ Dolton BLP-2039 [M]	Folk Rock	1965	7.50	15.00	30.00
❑ Dolton BST-8001 [S]	Mr. Blue	1959	25.00	50.00	100.00
—Pale blue label with dolphins on top					
❑ Dolton BST-8002 [S]	The Fleetwoods	1960	17.50	35.00	70.00
—Pale blue label with dolphins on top					
❑ Dolton BST-8005 [S]	Softly	1961	17.50	35.00	70.00
—Pale blue label with dolphins on top					

Number	Title (A Side/B Side)	Yr	VG	VG+	NM
❑ Dolton BST-8007 [S]	Deep in a Dream	1961	12.50	25.00	50.00
—Pale blue label with dolphins on top					
❑ Dolton BST-8011 [S]	The Best of the Oldies	1962	12.50	25.00	50.00
—Pale blue label with dolphins on top					
❑ Dolton BST-8018 [S]	The Fleetwoods' Greatest Hits	1962	7.50	15.00	30.00
❑ Dolton BST-8020 [S]	The Fleetwoods Sings for Lovers by Night	1963	10.00	20.00	40.00
❑ Dolton BST-8025 [S]	Goodnight My Love	1963	10.00	20.00	40.00
❑ Dolton BST-8030 [S]	Before and After	1965	10.00	20.00	40.00
❑ Dolton BST-8039 [S]	Folk Rock	1965	10.00	20.00	40.00
❑ Liberty LN-10159	The Fleetwoods' Greatest Hits	1982	2.00	4.00	8.00
❑ Liberty LN-10160	The Best Goodies of the Oldies	1982	2.00	4.00	8.00
❑ Liberty LN-10199	Buried Treasure	1983	2.00	4.00	8.00
❑ Sunset SUM-1131 [M]	In a Mellow Mood	1966	3.00	6.00	12.00
❑ Sunset SUS-5131 [S]	In a Mellow Mood	1966	3.75	7.50	15.00
❑ United Artists UA-LA334-E	The Very Best of the Fleetwoods	1975	3.00	6.00	12.00

FLETCHER, SAM

45s

Number	Title (A Side/B Side)	Yr	VG	VG+	NM
❑ Cub 9032	No Such Luck/Time Has a Way	1959	7.50	15.00	30.00
❑ Cub 9048	Only Heaven Knows/Beyond My Wildest Dreams	1959	7.50	15.00	30.00
❑ Metro 20013	Before/Torn Between Two Loves	1959	6.25	12.50	25.00
❑ Metro 20022	Out in the Cold Again/If You Love Me	1959	6.25	12.50	25.00
❑ RCA Victor 47-7676	Take Me in Your Arms/I Just Had to Tell Someone	1960	6.25	12.50	25.00
❑ RCA Victor 47-7817	Tall Hope/Far Away from Home	1960	5.00	10.00	20.00
❑ RCA Victor 47-7872	Hold Me/You Did It	1961	3.75	7.50	15.00
❑ RCA Victor 47-7972	I Believe in You/Sweet Slumber	1961	3.75	7.50	15.00
❑ RCA Victor 47-8027	My Girl/This One Night	1962	5.00	10.00	20.00
❑ RCA Victor 47-8076	The Answer to Everything/Me and the One I Love	1962	5.00	10.00	20.00
❑ Tollie 9012	I'd Think It Over/Friday Night	1964	50.00	100.00	200.00
❑ Vault 502	More Today Than Yesterday/What'll I Do	197?	6.25	12.50	25.00
❑ Vault 934	The Look of Love/You Better Come Home	1967	3.75	7.50	15.00
❑ Vee Jay 623	Guess Who/The Sinner	1964	3.00	6.00	12.00
❑ Warner Bros. 5384	As Time Goes By/My Wish	1963	3.75	7.50	15.00

Albums

Number	Title (A Side/B Side)	Yr	VG	VG+	NM
❑ Vault LP-116 [M]	The Look of Love, the Sound of Soul	1967	7.50	15.00	30.00
❑ Vault VS-116 [S]	The Look of Love, the Sound of Soul	1967	7.50	15.00	30.00
❑ Vee Jay LP-1094 [M]	Sam Fletcher Sings	1964	10.00	20.00	40.00

FLYING MACHINE, THE

45s

Number	Title (A Side/B Side)	Yr	VG	VG+	NM
❑ Congress 6000	Smile a Little Smile for Me/Maybe We've Been Loving Too Long	1969	2.00	4.00	8.00
❑ Congress 6012	There She Goes/Baby Make It Soon	1970	—	3.00	6.00
❑ Janus 121	Hanging on the Edge of Sadness/My Baby's Coming Home	1970	—	3.00	6.00
❑ Janus 137	Hey Little Girl/The Devil Has Possession of My Mind	1971	—	3.00	6.00

Albums

Number	Title (A Side/B Side)	Yr	VG	VG+	NM
❑ Janus JLS-3007	The Flying Machine	1969	5.00	10.00	20.00

FOCUS

45s

Number	Title (A Side/B Side)	Yr	VG	VG+	NM
❑ Atco 7002	Harem Scarem/Birth	1974	—	3.00	6.00
❑ Sire 352	House of the King/Black Beauty	1971	2.00	4.00	8.00
❑ Sire 704	Hocus Pocus/Hocus Pocus II	1973	—	3.00	6.00
❑ Sire 708	Sylvia/Love Remembered	1973	—	2.50	5.00

Albums

Number	Title (A Side/B Side)	Yr	VG	VG+	NM
❑ Atco SD 36-100	Hamburger Concerto	1974	3.00	6.00	12.00
❑ Atco SD 36-117	Mother Focus	1975	3.00	6.00	12.00
❑ Harvest ST-11721	Focus Con Proby	1978	3.00	6.00	12.00
—With P.J. Proby					
❑ Mercury 824524-1	Focus: Jan Akkerman and Thijs Van Leer	1986	3.00	6.00	12.00
❑ Sire SAS-3901 [(2)]	Focus 3	1973	3.75	7.50	15.00
❑ Sire SAS-7401	Moving Waves	1972	3.00	6.00	12.00
❑ Sire SAS-7404	In and Out of Focus	1973	3.00	6.00	12.00
—Reissue of 97027					
❑ Sire SAS-7408	Live at the Rainbow	1973	3.00	6.00	12.00
❑ Sire SASD-7505	Dutch Masters — A Selection of Their Finest Recordings 1969-1973	1975	3.00	6.00	12.00
❑ Sire SASD-7531	Ship of Memories	1977	3.00	6.00	12.00

Number	Title (A Side/B Side)	Yr	VG	VG+	NM
❑ Sire SES-97027	In and Out of Focus	1970	5.00	10.00	20.00
—*Original issue*					

FOGELBERG, DAN

45s

Number	Title (A Side/B Side)	Yr	VG	VG+	NM
❑ Columbia 4-45764	Anyway I Love You/Looking for a Lady	1973	2.00	4.00	8.00
❑ Full Moon/Epic 14-02488	Hard to Say/The Innocent Age	1981	—	2.00	4.00
❑ Full Moon/Epic 14-02647	Leader of the Band/Times Like These	1981	—	2.00	4.00
❑ Full Moon/Epic 14-02821	Run for the Roses/The Sand and the Foam	1982	—	2.00	4.00
❑ Full Moon/Epic 15-03087	Same Old Lang Syne/Hard to Say	1982	—	—	3.00
—*Reissue*					
❑ Full Moon/Epic 34-03289	Missing You/Hearts and Crafts	1982	—	2.00	4.00
❑ Full Moon/Epic ENR-03323	Missing You/(B-side blank)	1982	2.00	4.00	8.00
—*One-sided budget release*					
❑ Full Moon/Epic 34-03525	Make Love Stay/Hearts and Crafts	1983	—	2.00	4.00
❑ Full Moon/Epic ENR-03570	Make Love Stay/(B-side blank)	1983	—	3.00	6.00
—*One-sided budget release*					
❑ Full Moon/Epic 15-03843	Leader of the Band/Run for the Roses	1983	—	—	3.00
—*Reissue*					
❑ Full Moon/Epic 34-04314	The Language of Love/Windows and Walls	1984	—	—	3.00
❑ Full Moon/Epic 34-04447	Believe in Me/Windows and Walls	1984	—	2.00	4.00
❑ Full Moon/Epic 34-04660	Sweet Magnolia and the Traveling Salesman/The Loving Cup	1984	—	2.00	4.00
❑ Full Moon/Epic 34-04835	Go Down Easy/High Country Snows	1985	—	2.00	4.00
❑ Full Moon/Epic 34-05446	Down the Road-Mountain Pass/High Country Snows	1985	—	2.00	4.00
❑ Full Moon/Epic 34-07044	She Don't Look Back/It Doesn't Matter	1987	—	—	3.00
❑ Full Moon/Epic 34-07275	Lonely in Love/Beyond the Edge	1987	—	2.00	4.00
❑ Full Moon/Epic 34-07640	Seeing You Again/Hearts in Decline	1987	—	2.00	4.00
❑ Full Moon/Epic 34-07756	The Way It Must Be/What You're Doing	1988	—	2.00	4.00
❑ Full Moon/Epic 8-50055	Part of the Plan/Song from Half Mountain	1974	—	2.50	5.00
❑ Full Moon/Epic 8-50108	Changing Horses/Morning Sky	1975	—	3.00	6.00
❑ Full Moon/Epic 8-50165	Captured Angel/Next Time	1975	—	3.00	6.00
❑ Full Moon/Epic 8-50189	Below the Surface/Comes and Goes	1976	—	3.00	6.00
❑ Full Moon/Epic 8-50234	Old Tennessee/The Crow	1976	—	3.00	6.00
❑ Full Moon/Epic 8-50412	Love Gone By/Scarecrow's Dream	1977	—	3.00	6.00
❑ Full Moon/Epic 8-50462	Nether Lands/False Faces	1977	—	2.50	5.00
❑ Full Moon/Epic 8-50536	Sketches/Promises Made	1978	—	3.00	6.00
❑ Full Moon/Epic 8-50577	There's a Place in the World for a Gambler/Souvenirs	1978	—	3.00	6.00
❑ Full Moon/Epic 9-50824	Longer/Along the Road	1980	—	2.00	4.00
❑ Full Moon/Epic 9-50862	Heart Hotels/Beggar's Game	1980	—	2.50	5.00
❑ Full Moon/Epic 19-50961	Same Old Lang Syne/Hearts and Crafts	1980	—	2.00	4.00
❑ Full Moon/Epic 34-73513	Rhythm of the Rain-Rain/Ever On	1990	—	2.50	5.00

Albums

Number	Title (A Side/B Side)	Yr	VG	VG+	NM
❑ Columbia KC 31751	Home Free	1972	3.00	6.00	12.00
❑ Full Moon/Epic KE 33137	Souvenirs	1974	3.00	6.00	12.00
—*First pressings have orange Epic label with small Full Moon logo*					
❑ Full Moon/Epic PE 33499	Captured Angel	1975	2.50	5.00	10.00
—*No bar code on cover*					
❑ Full Moon/Epic PE 34185	Nether Lands	1977	2.50	5.00	10.00
—*No bar code on cover*					
❑ Full Moon/Epic FE 35634	Phoenix	1979	2.50	5.00	10.00
❑ Full Moon/ Epic KE2 37393 [(2)]	The Innocent Age	1981	3.00	6.00	12.00
❑ Full Moon/Epic QE 38308	Dan Fogelberg/Greatest Hits	1982	2.50	5.00	10.00
❑ Full Moon/Epic QE 39004	Windows and Walls	1984	2.50	5.00	10.00
❑ Full Moon/Epic FE 39616	High Country Snows	1985	2.50	5.00	10.00
❑ Full Moon/Epic OE 40271	Exiles	1987	2.50	5.00	10.00

FOGERTY, JOHN

45s

Number	Title (A Side/B Side)	Yr	VG	VG+	NM
❑ Asylum 45274	Rockin' All Over the World/The Wall	1975	—	3.00	6.00
❑ Asylum 45293	Almost Saturday Night/Sea Cruise	1975	—	3.00	6.00
❑ Asylum 45309	You Got the Magic/Evil Thing	1976	3.75	7.50	15.00
❑ Fantasy 683	Blue Ridge Mountain Blues/Have Thine Own Way, Lord	1972	—	2.50	5.00
—*As "The Blue Ridge Rangers"*					
❑ Fantasy 689	Jambalaya (On the Bayou)/Workin' on a Building	1972	—	3.00	6.00
—*As "The Blue Ridge Rangers"; green, red and orange label*					
❑ Fantasy 700	Hearts of Stone/Somewhere Listening	1973	—	2.50	5.00
—*As "The Blue Ridge Rangers"*					
❑ Fantasy 710	Back in the Hills/You Don't Own Me	1973	—	2.50	5.00
—*As "The Blue Ridge Rangers"*					
❑ Fantasy 717	Coming Down the Road/Ricochet	1973	—	2.50	5.00
❑ Warner Bros. 28535	Change in the Weather/My Toot Toot	1986	—	2.00	4.00
❑ Warner Bros. 28657	Eye of the Zombie/I Confess	1986	—	2.00	4.00
❑ Warner Bros. 29053	Rock and Roll Girls/Centerfield	1985	—	2.00	4.00
❑ Warner Bros. 29100	The Old Man Down the Road/Big Train (From Memphis)	1985	—	2.00	4.00

Albums

Number	Title (A Side/B Side)	Yr	VG	VG+	NM
❑ Asylum 7E-1046	John Fogerty	1975	3.00	6.00	12.00
❑ Asylum 7E-1081	Hoodoo	1976	—	—	—
—*Canceled; poor quality bootleg cassettes exist*					
❑ Fantasy MPF-4502	John Fogerty: The Blue Ridge Rangers	1981	2.50	5.00	10.00
—*Reissues prominently place John Fogerty's name on the cover*					
❑ Fantasy F-9415	The Blue Ridge Rangers	1973	3.75	7.50	15.00
—*As "The Blue Ridge Rangers"*					
❑ Warner Bros. 25203	Centerfield	1985	3.75	7.50	15.00
—*Originals have the last song on side 2 as "Zanz Kant Danz"*					
❑ Warner Bros. 25203	Centerfield	1986	2.50	5.00	10.00
—*Later editions have the last song on side 2 re-recorded and listed as "Vanz Kant Danz"*					
❑ Warner Bros. 25449	Eye of the Zombie	1986	2.50	5.00	10.00

Number	Title (A Side/B Side)	Yr	VG	VG+	NM

FOGHAT

45s

Number	Title (A Side/B Side)	Yr	VG	VG+	NM
❑ Bearsville 0008	I Just Want to Make Love to You/Hole to Hide In	1973	—	2.50	5.00
❑ Bearsville 0014	What a Shame/Helping Hand	1973	—	2.50	5.00
❑ Bearsville 0019	That'll Be the Day/Wild Cherry	1974	—	2.50	5.00
❑ Bearsville 0021	Maybelline/Step Outside	1974	—	2.50	5.00
❑ Bearsville 0306	Slow Ride/Save Your Loving	1975	—	2.50	5.00
❑ Bearsville 0307	Fool for the City/Take It or Leave It	1976	—	2.50	5.00
❑ Bearsville 0313	Drivin' Wheel/Night Shift	1976	—	2.00	4.00
❑ Bearsville 0315	I'll Be Standing By/Take Me to the River	1977	—	2.00	4.00
❑ Bearsville 0319	I Just Want to Make Love to You (Live)/Fool for the City (Live)	1977	—	2.00	4.00
❑ Bearsville 0325	Stone Blue/Chevrolet	1978	—	2.00	4.00
❑ Bearsville 0329	High on Love/Sweet Home Chicago	1978	—	2.00	4.00
❑ Bearsville 29612	Seven Day Weekend/That's What Love Can Do	1983	—	2.00	4.00
❑ Bearsville 29860	Slipped, Tripped, Fell in Love/And I Do Just What I Want	1982	—	2.00	4.00
❑ Bearsville 49125	Third Time Lucky (First Time I Was a Fool)/Love in Motion	1979	—	2.00	4.00
❑ Bearsville 49510	Stranger in My Home Town/Be My Woman	1980	—	2.00	4.00
❑ Bearsville 49779	Wide Boy/Love Zone	1981	—	2.00	4.00

Albums

Number	Title (A Side/B Side)	Yr	VG	VG+	NM
❑ Bearsville BR 2077	Foghat	1972	3.00	6.00	12.00
❑ Bearsville BR 2136	Foghat	1973	3.00	6.00	12.00
❑ Bearsville BRK 3578	Girls to Chat & Boys to Bounce	1981	2.50	5.00	10.00
❑ Bearsville BR 6950	Energized	1974	2.50	5.00	10.00
❑ Bearsville BR 6956	Rock and Roll Outlaws	1974	2.50	5.00	10.00
❑ Bearsville BR 6959	Fool for the City	1975	2.50	5.00	10.00
❑ Bearsville BR 6962	Night Shift	1976	2.50	5.00	10.00
❑ Bearsville BRK 6971	Foghat Live	1977	2.50	5.00	10.00
❑ Bearsville BRK 6977	Stone Blue	1978	2.50	5.00	10.00
❑ Bearsville BRK 6980	Fool for the City	1978	2.00	4.00	8.00
—Reissue of 6959					
❑ Bearsville BHS 6990	Boogie Motel	1979	2.50	5.00	10.00
❑ Bearsville BHS 6999	Tight Shoes	1980	2.50	5.00	10.00
❑ Bearsville 23747	In the Mood for Something Rude	1982	2.50	5.00	10.00
❑ Bearsville 23888	Zig-Zag Walk	1983	2.50	5.00	10.00
❑ Rhino R1-70088	The Best of Foghat	1989	2.50	5.00	10.00
❑ Rhino RNLP-70881	Stone Blue	1987	2.00	4.00	8.00
—Reissue of Bearsville 6977					
❑ Rhino RNLP-70882	Fool for the City	1987	2.00	4.00	8.00
—Reissue of Bearsville 6980					
❑ Rhino RNLP-70883	Energized	1988	2.00	4.00	8.00
—Reissue of Bearsville 6950					
❑ Rhino RNLP-70884	Foghat Live	1988	2.00	4.00	8.00
—Reissue of Bearsville 6971					
❑ Rhino RNLP-70887	Foghat	1988	2.00	4.00	8.00
—Reissue of Bearsville 2077					
❑ Rhino RNLP-70888	Night Shift	1988	2.00	4.00	8.00
—Reissue of Bearsville 6962					
❑ Rhino R1-70889	Rock and Roll Outlaws	1988	2.00	4.00	8.00
—Reissue of Bearsville 6956					
❑ Rhino R1-70890	Foghat	1988	2.00	4.00	8.00
—Reissue of Bearsville 2136					

FONTANA, WAYNE, AND THE MINDBENDERS

45s

Number	Title (A Side/B Side)	Yr	VG	VG+	NM
❑ A&M 3010	Game of Love/What a Wonderful World	1988	—	2.00	4.00
—B-side by Louis Armstrong					
❑ Fontana 1503	Game of Love/Since You've Been Gone	1965	3.75	7.50	15.00
❑ Fontana 1509	Game of Love/One More Time	1965	3.00	6.00	12.00
❑ Fontana 1514	It's Just a Little Bit Too Late/Long Time Comin'	1965	2.50	5.00	10.00
❑ Fontana 1524	She Needs Love/Like I Do	1965	2.50	5.00	10.00
❑ Fontana 1917	Stop, Look, Listen/Road Runner	1964	3.00	6.00	12.00
❑ Fontana 1945	Um, Um, Um, Um, Um, Um/First Taste of Love	1964	3.00	6.00	12.00

FORD, FRANKIE

45s

Number	Title (A Side/B Side)	Yr	VG	VG+	NM
❑ ABC 11431	All Alone Am I/Blue Monday	1974	—	2.50	5.00
❑ Ace 549	The Last One to Cry/Cheatin' Woman	1958	6.25	12.50	25.00

Number	Title (A Side/B Side)	Yr	VG	VG+	NM
❑ Ace 554	Sea Cruise/Roberta	1959	7.50	15.00	30.00
❑ Ace 566	Alimony/Can't Tell My Heart (What to Do)	1959	6.25	12.50	25.00
❑ Ace 580	Time After Time/Want to Be Your Man	1960	6.25	12.50	25.00
❑ Ace 592	Chinatown/What's Goin' On	1960	6.25	12.50	25.00
❑ Ace 8009	Ocean Full of Tears/Hour of Need	1963	3.75	7.50	15.00
❑ Briarmeade 7600	I've Found Someone of My Own/Battle Hymn of the Republic	1976	—	2.50	5.00
❑ Briarmeade 7701	Desperado/Mardi Gras in New Orleans	1977	—	2.50	5.00
❑ Briarmeade 7901	Halfway to Paradise/I'm Proud of What I Am	1979	—	2.50	5.00
❑ Cinnamon 752	When I Stop Dreamin'/I'm Proud of What I Am	1972	—	2.50	5.00
❑ Cinnamon 767	Talk to a Carpenter/When I Stop Dreamin'	1973	—	2.50	5.00
❑ Constellation 101	Chinatown/Ocean Full of Tears	1963	3.75	7.50	15.00
❑ Doubloon 101	Half a Crown/I Can't Face Tomorrow	1967	2.50	5.00	10.00
❑ Imperial 5686	You Talk Too Much/If You've Got Troubles	1960	3.75	7.50	15.00
❑ Imperial 5706	My Southern Belle/The Groom	1960	3.75	7.50	15.00
❑ Imperial 5735	Seventenn/Doghouse	1961	3.75	7.50	15.00
❑ Imperial 5749	Saturday Night Fish Fry/Love Don't Love Nobody	1961	3.75	7.50	15.00
❑ Imperial 5776	Let 'Em Talk/What Happened to You	1961	3.75	7.50	15.00
❑ Imperial 5819	They Said It Couldn't Be Done/A Man Only Does	1962	3.75	7.50	15.00
❑ Paula 351	Peace of Mind/I'm Proud of What I Am	1971	2.00	4.00	8.00
❑ Starfire 119	Time After Time/Cheatin' Woman	1979	—	2.50	5.00
❑ SYC 1227	Growing Pains/Ups and Downs	1982	—	2.00	4.00
❑ SYC 1228	My Prayer/Gospel Ship	1983	—	2.00	4.00

Albums

Number	Title (A Side/B Side)	Yr	VG	VG+	NM
❑ Ace LP 1005 [M]	Let's Take a Sea Cruise	1959	75.00	150.00	300.00
❑ Briarmeade BR-5002	Frankie Ford	1976	3.00	6.00	12.00

FOREIGNER

45s

Number	Title (A Side/B Side)	Yr	VG	VG+	NM
❑ Atlantic 3394	Feels Like the First Time/Woman, Oh Woman	1977	—	2.00	4.00
❑ Atlantic 3410	Cold As Ice/I Need You	1977	—	2.00	4.00
—Has a different mix (with strings) than the LP version					
❑ Atlantic 3439	Long, Long Way from Home/The Damage Is Done	1977	—	2.00	4.00
—Has a different vocal with slightly altered lyrics from the LP version					
❑ Atlantic 3488	Hot Blooded/Tramontaine	1978	—	2.00	4.00
❑ Atlantic 3514	Double Vision/Lonely Children	1978	—	2.00	4.00
❑ Atlantic 3543	Blue Morning, Blue Day/I Have Waited So Long	1978	—	2.00	4.00
❑ Atlantic 3618	Dirty White Boy/Rev on the Red Line	1979	—	2.00	4.00
❑ Atlantic 3633	Head Games/Do What You Like	1979	—	2.00	4.00
❑ Atlantic 3651	Women/The Modern Day	1980	—	2.00	4.00
❑ Atlantic 3831	Urgent/Girl on the Moon	1981	—	2.00	4.00
❑ Atlantic 3868	Waiting for a Girl Like You/I'm Gonna Win	1981	—	2.00	4.00
❑ Atlantic 4017	Juke Box Hero/Night Life	1982	—	2.00	4.00
❑ Atlantic 4044	Break It Up/Head Games (Live)	1982	—	2.00	4.00
❑ Atlantic 4072	Luanne/Fool For You Anyway	1982	—	2.00	4.00
❑ Atlantic 89046	Heart Turns to Stone/Counting Every Minute	1988	—	—	3.00
❑ Atlantic 89101	I Don't Want to Live Without You/Face to Face	1988	—	—	3.00
❑ Atlantic 89169	Say You Will/A Night to Remember	1987	—	—	3.00
❑ Atlantic 89493	Down on Love/Growing Up the Hard Way	1985	—	—	3.00
❑ Atlantic 89542	Reaction to Action/She's Too Tough	1985	—	—	3.00
❑ Atlantic 89571	That Was Yesterday/Two Different Worlds	1985	—	—	3.00
❑ Atlantic 89596	I Want to Know What Love Is/Street Thunder	1984	—	2.00	4.00
—Generic red and black Atlantic label					
❑ Atlantic Oldies Series OS 13218	Dirty White Boy/Head Games	1981	—	—	3.00
—Reissue					

Albums

Number	Title (A Side/B Side)	Yr	VG	VG+	NM
❑ Atlantic SD 16999	4	1981	2.50	5.00	10.00
—First pressings have a hologram sticker on the upper back cover					
❑ Atlantic SD 18215	Foreigner	1977	2.50	5.00	10.00
❑ Atlantic SD 19109	Foreigner	1977	2.00	4.00	8.00
—Reissue of 18215					
❑ Atlantic SD 19999	Double Vision	1978	3.00	6.00	12.00
—Original cover is mostly brown with the words "Double Vision" barely visible along the bottom edge of front cover					
❑ Atlantic SD 29999	Head Games	1979	2.50	5.00	10.00
❑ Atlantic 80999	Records	1982	2.50	5.00	10.00
❑ Atlantic 81808	Inside Information	1988	2.50	5.00	10.00
❑ Atlantic 81999	Agent Provocateur	1984	2.50	5.00	10.00

FORTUNES, THE (1)

Records on Argo, Checker, Cub, Decca, DRA, Lake, Queen, Top Rank and Yucca are by at least one different group with the same name; they are outside the scope of this book.

45s

Number	Title (A Side/B Side)	Yr	VG	VG+	NM
❑ Capitol 3086	Here Comes That Rainy Day Feeling Again/Bad Side of Town	1971	2.50	5.00	10.00
❑ Capitol 3086	Here Comes That Rainy Day Feeling Again/I Gotta Dream	1971	—	3.00	6.00
❑ Capitol 3179	Freedom Comes, Freedom Goes/There's a Man	1971	—	2.50	5.00
❑ Capitol 3248	Storm in a Teacup/I'm Not Following You	1971	—	2.50	5.00
❑ Capitol 3445	Wait Until September/Don't Sing to Me	1972	—	2.50	5.00
❑ Capitol 3514	I Can't Remember When the Sun Went In/Secret Love	1973	—	2.50	5.00
❑ Capitol 3626	Give Me Some Room/Whenever It's a Sunday	1973	—	2.50	5.00
❑ Press 9773	You've Got Your Troubles/I've Gotta Go	1965	4.00	8.00	16.00
—White label stock copy					
❑ Press 9773	You've Got Your Troubles/I've Gotta Go	1965	3.00	6.00	12.00
—Purple label					
❑ Press 9798	Here It Comes Again/Things I Should Have Known	1965	3.75	7.50	15.00
—White label stock copy					
❑ Press 9798	Here It Comes Again/Things I Should Have Known	1965	2.50	5.00	10.00
—Purple label					

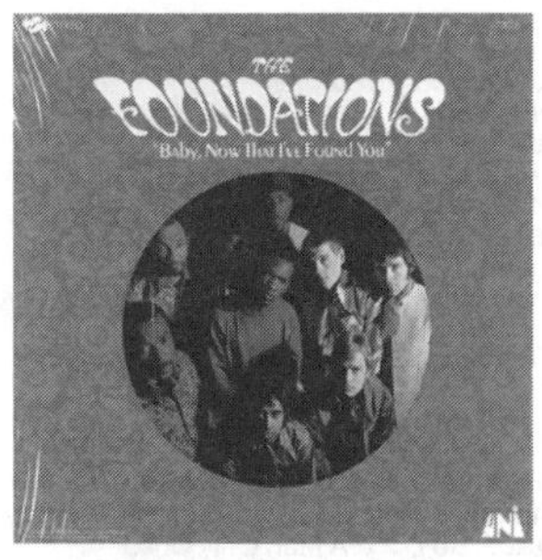

Number	Title (A Side/B Side)	Yr	VG	VG+	NM
❑ Press 9811	This Golden Ring/Someone to Care	1966	2.50	5.00	10.00
❑ Press 60001	Gone from My Mind/Silent Street	1966	2.50	5.00	10.00
❑ United Artists 50211	The Idol/His Smile Was a Lie	1967	2.50	5.00	10.00
❑ United Artists 50280	Painting a Shadow/Fire Brigade	1968	2.50	5.00	10.00
❑ World Pacific 77937	That Same Old Feeling/Lifetime of Love	1970	2.00	4.00	8.00
Albums					
❑ Capitol ST-809	Here Comes That Rainy Day Feeling Again	1971	5.00	10.00	20.00
❑ Capitol ST-11041	Storm in a Teacup	1972	3.75	7.50	15.00
—Contains the canceled "Freedom" LP with one track deleted, plus the title song added					
❑ Press PR 73002 [M]	The Fortunes	1965	8.75	17.50	35.00
❑ Press PRS 83002 [S]	The Fortunes	1965	12.50	25.00	50.00
❑ World Pacific WPS-21904	That Same Old Feeling	1970	3.75	7.50	15.00

FOUNDATIONS, THE

Number	Title (A Side/B Side)	Yr	VG	VG+	NM
45s					
❑ Uni 55038	Baby, Now That I've Found You/Come On Back to Me	1967	2.00	4.00	8.00
❑ Uni 55058	Back on My Feet Again/I Can Take or Leave Your Loving	1968	—	3.00	6.00
❑ Uni 55073	We Are Happy People/Any Old Time	1968	—	3.00	6.00
❑ Uni 55101	Build Me Up Buttercup/New Direction	1968	2.00	4.00	8.00
❑ Uni 55117	In the Bad, Bad Old Days (Before You Loved Me)/Give Me Love	1969	—	3.00	6.00
❑ Uni 55137	My Little Chickadee/Solomon Grundy	1969	—	3.00	6.00
❑ Uni 55162	Why Did You Cry/Born to Live, Born to Die	1969	—	3.00	6.00
❑ Uni 55210	Take a Girl Like You/I'm Gonna Be a Rich Man	1970	—	3.00	6.00
❑ Uni 55315	I'll Give You Love/Stoney Ground	1972	—	3.00	6.00
Albums					
❑ Uni 73016	Baby Now That I've Found You	1968	7.50	15.00	30.00
❑ Uni 73043	Build Me Up Buttercup	1969	7.50	15.00	30.00
❑ Uni 73058	Digging the Foundations	1969	7.50	15.00	30.00

FOUR PREPS, THE

Number	Title (A Side/B Side)	Yr	VG	VG+	NM
45s					
❑ Capitol F3576	Dreamy Eyes/Fools Will Be Fools	1956	5.00	10.00	20.00
❑ Capitol F3621	Moonstruck in Madrid/I Cried a Million Tears	1957	5.00	10.00	20.00
❑ Capitol F3699	Falling Star/Where Wuzz You	1957	5.00	10.00	20.00
❑ Capitol F3761	Promise Me Baby/Again 'N Again 'N Again	1957	5.00	10.00	20.00
❑ Capitol F3775	Band of Angels/How About That	1957	5.00	10.00	20.00
❑ Capitol F3845	26 Miles (Santa Catalina)/It's You	1957	5.00	10.00	20.00
❑ Capitol F3960	Big Man/Stop Baby	1958	5.00	10.00	20.00
❑ Capitol F4023	Lazy Summer Night/Summertime Lies	1958	5.00	10.00	20.00
❑ Capitol F4078	Cinderella/Gidget	1958	5.00	10.00	20.00
❑ Capitol F4126	She Was Five and He Was Ten/Riddle of Love	1959	5.00	10.00	20.00
❑ Capitol F4218	Big Surprise/Try My Arms	1959	5.00	10.00	20.00
❑ Capitol F4256	I Ain't Never/Memories, Memories	1959	5.00	10.00	20.00
❑ Capitol 4312	Down by the Station/Listen Honey	1959	3.00	6.00	12.00
❑ Capitol 4362	Got a Girl/Wait Till You Hear It from Me	1960	3.00	6.00	12.00
❑ Capitol 4400	Sentimental Kid/Madelina	1960	3.00	6.00	12.00
❑ Capitol 4435	The Sand and the Sea/Kaw-Liga	1960	3.00	6.00	12.00
❑ Capitol 4478	Balboa/I've Already Started In	1960	3.00	6.00	12.00
❑ Capitol 4508	Calcutta/Gone Are the Days	1961	3.00	6.00	12.00
❑ Capitol 4568	Dream, Boy, Dream/Grounded	1961	7.50	15.00	30.00
❑ Capitol 4599	More Money for You and Me/Swing Down Chariot	1961	3.75	7.50	15.00
—With full-length version of A-side					
❑ Capitol 4599	More Money for You and Me/Swing Down Chariot	1961	3.00	6.00	12.00
—With edited version of A-side					
❑ Capitol 4641	Smoke Gets In Your Eyes/Swing Down Chariot	1961	3.00	6.00	12.00
❑ Capitol 4659	Once Around the Block/The Seine	1961	3.00	6.00	12.00
❑ Capitol 4716	The Big Draft/Suzy Cockroach	1962	2.50	5.00	10.00
❑ Capitol 4792	Alice/Goodnight Sweetheart	1962	2.50	5.00	10.00
❑ Capitol 4974	Charmaine/Hi-Ho Anybody Home	1963	2.50	5.00	10.00
❑ Capitol 5020	Oh Where, Oh Where/Demons and Witches	1963	2.50	5.00	10.00
❑ Capitol 5074	The Greatest Surfer Couple/I'm Falling in Love with a Girl	1963	2.50	5.00	10.00
❑ Capitol 5143	A Letter to the Beatles/College Cannonball	1964	6.25	12.50	25.00
❑ Capitol 5178	I've Known You All My Life/What Kind of Bird Is That	1964	2.00	4.00	8.00
❑ Capitol 5236	A Girl Without a Top/Two Wrongs Don't Make a Right	1964	2.00	4.00	8.00
❑ Capitol 5274	How to Succeed in Love/My Love, My Love	1964	2.00	4.00	8.00
❑ Capitol 5351	Everlasting/I'll Set My Love to Music	1965	2.00	4.00	8.00
❑ Capitol 5450	Now I'll Never Be the Same/Our First American Dance	1965	2.00	4.00	8.00

Number	Title (A Side/B Side)	Yr	VG	VG+	NM
❑ Capitol 5609	Annie in Her Granny/Something to Remember You By	1966	2.00	4.00	8.00
❑ Capitol 5687	Let's Call It a Day, Girl/The Girl in the Shade of a Striped Umbrella	1966	2.00	4.00	8.00
❑ Capitol 5819	Love of the Common People/What I Don't Know Won't Hurt Me	1967	2.00	4.00	8.00
❑ Capitol 5921	Draft Dodger Rag/The Hitchhiker	1967	2.00	4.00	8.00
Albums					
❑ Capitol T 994 [M]	The Four Preps	1958	7.50	15.00	30.00
❑ Capitol T 1090 [M]	The Things We Did Last Summer	1958	6.25	12.50	25.00
❑ Capitol ST 1216 [S]	Dancing and Dreaming	1959	6.25	12.50	25.00
❑ Capitol T 1216 [M]	Dancing and Dreaming	1959	5.00	10.00	20.00
❑ Capitol DT 1291 [R]	Early in the Morning	1960	3.00	6.00	12.00
❑ Capitol T 1291 [M]	Early in the Morning	1960	6.25	12.50	25.00
❑ Capitol ST 1566 [S]	The Four Preps on Campus	1961	6.25	12.50	25.00
❑ Capitol T 1566 [M]	The Four Preps on Campus	1961	5.00	10.00	20.00
❑ Capitol ST 1647 [S]	Campus Encore	1962	6.25	12.50	25.00
❑ Capitol T 1647 [M]	Campus Encore	1962	5.00	10.00	20.00
❑ Capitol ST 1814 [S]	Campus Confidential	1963	5.00	10.00	20.00
❑ Capitol T 1814 [M]	Campus Confidential	1963	3.75	7.50	15.00
❑ Capitol ST 1976 [S]	Songs for a Campus Party	1963	5.00	10.00	20.00
❑ Capitol T 1976 [M]	Songs for a Campus Party	1963	3.75	7.50	15.00
❑ Capitol ST 2169 [S]	How to Succeed in Love	1964	5.00	10.00	20.00
❑ Capitol T 2169 [M]	How to Succeed in Love	1964	3.75	7.50	15.00
❑ Capitol ST 2708 [S]	The Best of the Four Preps	1967	3.00	6.00	12.00
❑ Capitol T 2708 [M]	The Best of the Four Preps	1967	3.75	7.50	15.00
FOUR SEASONS, THE					
45s					
❑ Crewe 333	And That Reminds Me (My Heart Reminds Me)/The Singles Game	1969	2.00	4.00	8.00
❑ FBI 7701	East Meets West/Rhapsody	1986	5.00	10.00	20.00
—With the Beach Boys					
❑ Four Seasons 0019	I Saw Mommy Kissing Santa Claus/ Santa Claus Is Coming to Town	198?	—	2.00	4.00
❑ Gone 5122	Bermuda/Spanish Lace	1961	20.00	40.00	80.00
❑ MCA/Curb 52618	Streetfighter/Deep Inside Your Love	1985	—	2.00	4.00
❑ MCA/Curb 52724	Moonlight Memories/What About Tomorrow	1985	—	2.00	4.00
❑ MCA/Curb 52871	Book of Love/What About Tomorrow	1986	—	2.00	4.00
❑ MCA/Curb 53440	Big Girls Don't Cry (Enhanced Original Mix)/ Big Girls Don't Cry (Dirty Dancing Rap)	1988	—	2.00	4.00
❑ Motown 1255	How Come/Life and Breath	1973	2.50	5.00	10.00
❑ Motown 1288	Hickory/Charisma	1973	2.50	5.00	10.00
❑ Mowest 5026	Walk On, Don't Look Back/Sun Country	1972	2.50	5.00	10.00
❑ Oldies 45 18	Sherry/I've Cried Before	1964	2.00	4.00	8.00
❑ Oldies 45 47	Big Girls Don't Cry/Connie-O	1964	2.00	4.00	8.00
❑ Oldies 45 60	Walk Like a Man/Lucky Ladybug	1964	2.00	4.00	8.00
❑ Oldies 45 116	Candy Girl/Marlena	1964	2.00	4.00	8.00
❑ Oldies 45 319	Stay/Goodnight My Love	1965	2.00	4.00	8.00
❑ Philips 40166	Dawn (Go Away)/No Surfin' Today	1964	3.75	7.50	15.00
—Black label					
❑ Philips 40185	Ronnie/Born to Wander	1964	3.00	6.00	12.00
❑ Philips 40211	Rag Doll/Silence Is Golden	1964	3.75	7.50	15.00
—Black label					
❑ Philips 40225	Save It for Me/Funny Face	1964	2.50	5.00	10.00
❑ Philips 40238	Big Man in Town/Little Angel	1964	2.50	5.00	10.00
❑ Philips 40260	Bye, Bye Baby (Baby Goodbye)/Searching Wind	1965	2.50	5.00	10.00
❑ Philips 40278	Toy Soldier/Betrayed	1965	2.50	5.00	10.00
❑ Philips 40305	Girl Come Running/Cry Myself to Sleep	1965	2.50	5.00	10.00
❑ Philips 40317	Let's Hang On!/On Broadway Tonight	1965	2.50	5.00	10.00
—Black label					
❑ Philips 40324	Don't Think Twice/Sassy	1965	2.50	5.00	10.00
❑ Philips 40350	Working My Way Back to You/Too Many Memories	1966	2.50	5.00	10.00
❑ Philips 40370	Opus 17 (Don't You Worry 'Bout Me)/Beggar's Paradise	1966	2.50	5.00	10.00
❑ Philips 40380	On the Good Ship Lollipop/ You're Nobody Until Somebody Loves You	1966	2.50	5.00	10.00
❑ Philips 40393	I've Got You Under My Skin/Huggin' My Pillow	1966	2.50	5.00	10.00
❑ Philips 40412	Tell It to the Rain/Show Girl	1966	2.50	5.00	10.00
❑ Philips 40433	Beggin'/Dody	1967	2.00	4.00	8.00
—Light blue label					
❑ Philips 40433	Beggin'/Dody	1967	2.50	5.00	10.00
—Black label					
❑ Philips 40460	C'mon Marianne/Let's Ride Again	1967	2.50	5.00	10.00
—Black label					
❑ Philips 40471	Lonesome Road/Around and Around	1967	2.50	5.00	10.00
❑ Philips 40490	Watch the Flowers Grow/Raven	1967	2.50	5.00	10.00
❑ Philips 40523	Will You Love Me Tomorrow/Around and Around	1968	2.50	5.00	10.00
—Blue label					
❑ Philips 40523	Will You Love Me Tomorrow/Around and Around	1968	3.00	6.00	12.00
—Black label					
❑ Philips 40542	Saturday's Father/Good-Bye Girl	1968	—	3.00	6.00
❑ Philips 40577	Electric Stories/Pity	1968	—	3.00	6.00
❑ Philips 40597	Something's On Her Mind/Idaho	1969	—	3.00	6.00
❑ Philips 40662	Patch of Blue/She Gives Me Light	1970	2.00	4.00	8.00
—As "Frankie Valli & THE 4 SEASONS"					
❑ Philips 40688	Lay Me Down (Wake Me Up)/Heartaches and Rainbows	1970	6.25	12.50	25.00
❑ Philips 40694	Where Are My Dreams?/Any Day Now-Oh Happy Day	1971	6.25	12.50	25.00
❑ Seasons 4-Ever 777	Trance/I Am All Alone	1971	3.75	7.50	15.00
—As "Billy Dixon and the Topics"; blue vinyl					
❑ Topix 6000	Too Young to Start/Red Lips	1960	37.50	75.00	150.00
—As "The Village Voices"; yellow and black label					

Number	Title (A Side/B Side)	Yr	VG	VG+	NM
❑ Topix 6002	I Am All Alone/Trance	1961	37.50	75.00	150.00
—As "Billy Dixon and the Topics"					
❑ Topix 6008	Lost Lullaby/Trance	1961	50.00	100.00	200.00
—As "Billy Dixon and the Topics"					
❑ Vee Jay 456	Sherry/I've Cried Before	1962	6.25	12.50	25.00
—First pressings have black rainbow labels with oval logo					
❑ Vee Jay 465	Big Girls Don't Cry/Connie-O	1962	5.00	10.00	20.00
—First pressings have black rainbow labels with oval logo					
❑ Vee Jay 478	Santa Claus Is Coming to Town/Christmas Tears	1962	6.25	12.50	25.00
❑ Vee Jay 485	Walk Like a Man/Lucky Ladybug	1963	3.75	7.50	15.00
❑ Vee Jay 512	Ain't That a Shame!/Soon (I'll Be Home Again)	1963	5.00	10.00	20.00
❑ Vee Jay 539	Candy Girl/Marlena	1963	3.75	7.50	15.00
❑ Vee Jay 562	New Mexican Rose/That's the Way It Goes	1963	15.00	30.00	60.00
—Wrong title on B-side; stock copy					
❑ Vee Jay 562	New Mexican Rose/That's the Only Way	1963	3.75	7.50	15.00
❑ Vee Jay 576	Peanuts/Stay	1963	25.00	50.00	100.00
❑ Vee Jay 582	Stay/Goodnight My Love	1964	3.75	7.50	15.00
❑ Vee Jay 597	Alone/Long, Lonely Nights	1964	3.75	7.50	15.00
—Black rainbow label					
❑ Vee Jay 608	Sincerely/One Song	1964	5.00	10.00	20.00
❑ Vee Jay 618	Happy, Happy Birthday Baby/You're the Apple of My Eye	1964	5.00	10.00	20.00
❑ Vee Jay 626	I Saw Mommy Kissing Santa Claus/Christmas Tears	1964	5.00	10.00	20.00
❑ Vee Jay 639	Never on Sunday/Connie-O	1965	5.00	10.00	20.00
❑ Vee Jay 664	Since I Don't Have You/Tonite, Tonite	1965	7.50	15.00	30.00
❑ Vee Jay 713	Little Boy (In Grown Up Clothes)/Silver Wings	1965	5.00	10.00	20.00
—Maroon label					
❑ Vee Jay 717	Peanuts/My Sugar	1966	7.50	15.00	30.00
—As "The Wonder Who"					
❑ Vee Jay 719	My Mother's Eyes/Stay	1966	3.75	7.50	15.00
❑ Warner Bros. 8122	Who Loves You/Who Loves You (Disco Version)	1975	—	2.50	5.00
❑ Warner Bros. 8168	December, 1963 (Oh, What a Night)/Slip Away	1975	—	2.50	5.00
❑ Warner Bros. 8203	Silver Star/Mystic Mr. Sam	1976	—	2.50	5.00
❑ Warner Bros. 8407	Down the Hall/I Believe in You	1977	2.00	4.00	8.00
❑ Warner Bros. 49585	Heaven Must Have Sent You (Here in the Night)/Silver Star	1981	2.00	4.00	8.00
❑ Warner Bros. 49597	Spend the Night in Love/Slip Away	1980	2.00	4.00	8.00
Albums					
❑ MCA/Curb 5632	Starfighter	1985	2.50	5.00	10.00
❑ Motown 788	Inside Out	1973	—	—	—
—Canceled					
❑ Mowest MW 108L	Chameleon	1972	3.00	6.00	12.00
❑ Philips PHS-2-6501 [(2)]	Edizione d'Oro	1968	6.25	12.50	25.00
—Number "4" on cover is red on gold foil					
❑ Philips PHM 200124 [M]	Dawn (Go Away) and 11 Other Great Songs	1964	5.00	10.00	20.00
❑ Philips PHM 200129 [M]	Born to Wander	1964	5.00	10.00	20.00
❑ Philips PHM 200146 [M]	Rag Doll	1964	5.00	10.00	20.00
—Without yellow seal noting presence of "Save It For Me"					
❑ Philips PHM 200150 [M]	All the Song Hits of the Four Seasons	1964	5.00	10.00	20.00
❑ Philips PHM 200164 [M]	The 4 Seasons Entertain You	1965	5.00	10.00	20.00
—With orange seal noting presence of "Bye Bye Baby"					
❑ Philips PHM 200193 [M]	Big Hits by Burt Bacharach...Hal David...Bob Dylan	1965	5.00	10.00	20.00
—"Open book" cover					
❑ Philips PHM 200196 [M]	The 4 Seasons' Gold Vault of Hits	1965	5.00	10.00	20.00
—Title in red print with no border					
❑ Philips PHM 200201 [M]	Working My Way Back to You	1966	5.00	10.00	20.00
❑ Philips PHM 200221 [M]	2nd Vault of Golden Hits	1966	3.75	7.50	15.00
❑ Philips PHM 200222 [M]	Lookin' Back	1966	5.00	10.00	20.00
❑ Philips PHM 200223 [M]	The Four Seasons' Christmas Album	1966	6.25	12.50	25.00
—Reissue of Vee Jay album (same contents and order) with new cover					
❑ Philips PHM 200243 [M]	New Gold Hits	1967	5.00	10.00	20.00
❑ Philips PHS 600124 [S]	Dawn (Go Away) and 11 Other Great Songs	1964	6.25	12.50	25.00
❑ Philips PHS 600129 [S]	Born to Wander	1964	6.25	12.50	25.00
❑ Philips PHS 600146 [S]	Rag Doll	1964	6.25	12.50	25.00
—Without yellow seal noting presence of "Save It For Me"					
❑ Philips PHS 600150 [S]	All the Song Hits of the Four Seasons	1964	6.25	12.50	25.00
❑ Philips PHS 600164 [S]	The 4 Seasons Entertain You	1965	6.25	12.50	25.00
—With orange seal noting presence of "Bye Bye Baby"					

Number	Title (A Side/B Side)	Yr	VG	VG+	NM
❑ Philips PHS 600193 [S]	Big Hits by Burt Bacharach...Hal David...Bob Dylan	1965	6.25	12.50	25.00
—"Open book" cover					
❑ Philips PHS 600196 [S]	The 4 Seasons' Gold Vault of Hits	1965	6.25	12.50	25.00
—Title in red print with no border					
❑ Philips PHS 600201 [S]	Working My Way Back to You	1966	6.25	12.50	25.00
❑ Philips PHS 600221 [S]	2nd Vault of Golden Hits	1966	5.00	10.00	20.00
❑ Philips PHS 600222 [S]	Lookin' Back	1966	6.25	12.50	25.00
❑ Philips PHS 600223 [S]	The Four Seasons' Christmas Album	1966	7.50	15.00	30.00
❑ Philips PHS 600243 [S]	New Gold Hits	1967	6.25	12.50	25.00
❑ Philips PHS 600290	The Genuine Imitation Life Gazette	1969	3.75	7.50	15.00
—White newspaper					
❑ Philips PHS 600290	The Genuine Imitation Life Gazette	1969	6.25	12.50	25.00
—Yellow newspaper					
❑ Philips PHS 600341	Half & Half	1970	5.00	10.00	20.00
❑ Pickwick SPC-3223	Brotherhood of Man	1970	3.00	6.00	12.00
—Mass-market version of Sears 609					
❑ Private Stock PS-7000 [(2)]	The Four Seasons Story	1975	3.75	7.50	15.00
❑ Rhino RNLP 70234	The Four Seasons' Christmas Album	1987	3.00	6.00	12.00
—Reissue of Philips album (same contents and order)					
❑ Rhino R1-70247	Working My Way Back to You	1988	2.50	5.00	10.00
—Reissue of Philips 600-201					
❑ Rhino R1-70249	The Genuine Imitation Life Gazette	1988	2.50	5.00	10.00
—Reissue of Philips 600-290					
❑ Rhino R1-71248	Big Hits by Burt Bacharach...Hal David...Bob Dylan	1988	2.50	5.00	10.00
—Reissue of Philips 600-193					
❑ Rhino R1-71490 [(2)]	Anthology	1988	3.00	6.00	12.00
❑ Rhino RNRP-72998 [(4)]	25th Anniversary Collection	1987	6.25	12.50	25.00
❑ Sears SPS-609	Brotherhood of Man	1970	6.25	12.50	25.00
❑ Vee Jay LP-1053 [M]	Sherry & 11 Others	1962	10.00	20.00	40.00
❑ Vee Jay SR-1053 [S]	Sherry & 11 Others	1962	15.00	30.00	60.00
❑ Vee Jay LP 1055 [M]	The Four Seasons Greetings	1962	7.50	15.00	30.00
❑ Vee Jay SR 1055 [S]	The Four Seasons Greetings	1962	10.00	20.00	40.00
❑ Vee Jay LP-1056 [M]	Big Girls Don't Cry and Twelve Others	1963	7.50	15.00	30.00
❑ Vee Jay SR-1056 [S]	Big Girls Don't Cry and Twelve Others	1963	10.00	20.00	40.00
❑ Vee Jay LP-1059 [M]	Ain't That a Shame and 11 Others	1963	7.50	15.00	30.00
❑ Vee Jay SR-1059 [S]	Ain't That a Shame and 11 Others	1963	10.00	20.00	40.00
❑ Vee Jay LP-1065 [M]	Golden Hits of the Four Seasons	1963	7.50	15.00	30.00
❑ Vee Jay SR-1065 [S]	Golden Hits of the Four Seasons	1963	10.00	20.00	40.00
❑ Vee Jay LP-1082 [M]	Stay & Other Great Hits	1964	6.25	12.50	25.00
—Retitled version of Folk-Nanny					
❑ Vee Jay LP-1082 [M]	Folk-Nanny	1964	7.50	15.00	30.00
❑ Vee Jay SR-1082 [S]	Stay & Other Great Hits	1964	7.50	15.00	30.00
—Retitled version of Folk-Nanny					
❑ Vee Jay SR-1082 [S]	Folk-Nanny	1964	10.00	20.00	40.00
❑ Vee Jay LP-1088 [M]	More Golden Hits by the Four Seasons	1964	7.50	15.00	30.00
—With "Long Lonely Nights" on record					
❑ Vee Jay LP-1088 [M]	More Golden Hits by the Four Seasons	1964	5.00	10.00	20.00
—With "Apple of My Eye" on record					
❑ Vee Jay SR-1088 [S]	More Golden Hits by the Four Seasons	1964	10.00	20.00	40.00
—With "Long Lonely Nights" on record					
❑ Vee Jay SR-1088 [S]	More Golden Hits by the Four Seasons	1964	6.25	12.50	25.00
—With "Apple of My Eye" on record					
❑ Vee Jay LP-1121 [M]	We Love Girls	1965	7.50	15.00	30.00
❑ Vee Jay LPS-1121 [S]	We Love Girls	1965	10.00	20.00	40.00
❑ Vee Jay LP-1154 [M]	Recorded Live on Stage	1965	7.50	15.00	30.00
❑ Vee Jay LPS-1154 [S]	Recorded Live on Stage	1965	10.00	20.00	40.00
❑ Warner Bros. BS 2900	Who Loves You	1975	3.00	6.00	12.00
❑ Warner Bros. BS 3016	Helicon	1977	3.00	6.00	12.00
❑ Warner Bros. 2WB 3497 [(2)]	Reunited Live	1980	3.75	7.50	15.00

FOUR TOPS, THE

45s

Number	Title (A Side/B Side)	Yr	VG	VG+	NM
❑ ABC 12096	Seven Lonely Nights/I Can't Hold Out Much Longer	1975	—	2.00	4.00
❑ ABC 12123	We All Gotta Stick Together/(It Would Almost) Drive Me Out of My Mind	1975	—	2.00	4.00
❑ ABC 12155	I'm Glad You Walked Into My Life/Mama, You're All Right with Me	1975	—	2.00	4.00
❑ ABC 12214	Catfish/Look at My Baby	1976	—	2.00	4.00
❑ ABC 12223	Look at My Baby/Catfish	1976	—	2.00	4.00
❑ ABC 12236	Feel Free/I Know You Like It	1976	—	2.00	4.00
❑ ABC 12267	Strung Out for Your Love/You Can't Hold Back on Love	1977	—	2.00	4.00
❑ ABC 12315	Runnin' From Your Love/The Show Must Go On	1977	—	2.00	4.00
❑ ABC 12427	Inside a Brokenhearted Man/H.E.L.P.	1978	—	2.00	4.00
❑ ABC 12457	Just in Time/This House	1978	—	2.00	4.00
❑ ABC Dunhill 4330	Keeper of the Castle/Jubilee with Soul	1972	—	2.50	5.00
❑ ABC Dunhill 4334	Guardian De Tu Castle/Jubilee with Soul	1972	—	2.50	5.00
❑ ABC Dunhill 4339	Ain't No Woman (Like the One I've Got)/The Good Lord Knows	1973	—	2.50	5.00
❑ ABC Dunhill 4354	Are You Man Enough/Peace of Mind	1973	—	2.50	5.00
❑ ABC Dunhill 4366	Sweet Understanding Love/Main Street People	1973	—	2.50	5.00
❑ ABC Dunhill 4377	I Just Can't Get You Out of My Mind/Am I My Brother's Keeper?	1973	—	2.50	5.00
❑ ABC Dunhill 4386	One Chain Don't Make No Prison/Light of Your Love	1974	—	2.50	5.00
❑ ABC Dunhill 15005	Midnight Flower/All My Love	1974	—	2.50	5.00
❑ Arista 9706	Indestructible/Are You With Me	1988	—	—	3.00
❑ Arista 9766	If Ever a Love There Was/Indestructible	1988	—	—	3.00
—A-side with Aretha Franklin					
❑ Arista 9801	Change of Heart/Loco in Acapulco	1989	—	—	3.00
❑ Casablanca 2338	When She Was My Girl/Something to Remember	1981	—	2.00	4.00

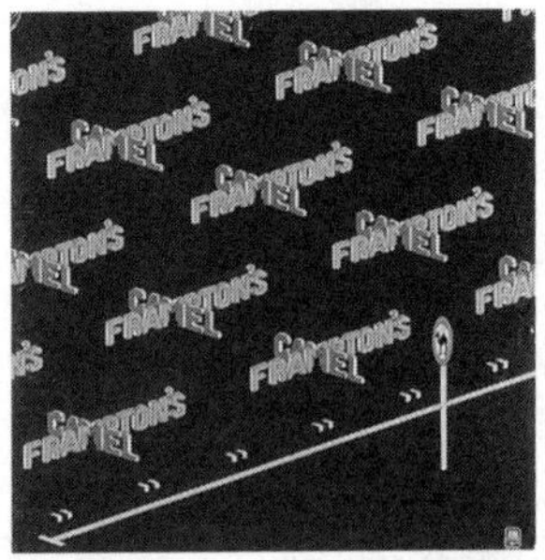

Number	Title (A Side/B Side)	Yr	VG	VG+	NM
❑ Casablanca 2344	Let Me Set You Free/From a Distance	1981	—	2.00	4.00
❑ Casablanca 2345	Tonight I'm Gonna Love You All Over/I'll Never Leave Again	1981	—	2.00	4.00
❑ Casablanca 2353	Sad Hearts/I Believe in You and Me	1982	—	2.00	4.00
❑ Chess 1623	Could It Be You?/Kiss Me, Baby	1956	50.00	100.00	200.00
❑ Columbia 41755	Ain't That Love/Lonely Summer	1960	15.00	30.00	60.00
❑ Columbia 43356	Ain't That Love/Lonely Summer	1965	6.25	12.50	25.00
❑ Grady 012	If Only I Had Known/(B-side unknown)	1956	150.00	300.00	600.00
—As "The Four Aims"					
❑ Motown 1062	Baby I Need Your Loving/Call On Me	1964	3.75	7.50	15.00
❑ Motown 1069	Without the One You Love (Life's Not Worth While)/ Love Has Gone	1964	3.00	6.00	12.00
❑ Motown 1073	Ask the Lonely/Where Did You Go	1965	3.75	7.50	15.00
❑ Motown 1076	I Can't Help Myself/Sad Souvenirs	1965	3.75	7.50	15.00
❑ Motown 1081	It's the Same Old Song/Your Love Is Amazing	1965	3.75	7.50	15.00
❑ Motown 1084	Something About You/Darling, I Hum Our Song	1965	3.75	7.50	15.00
❑ Motown 1090	Shake Me, Wake Me (When It's Over)/ Just As Long As You Need Me	1966	3.75	7.50	15.00
❑ Motown 1096	Loving You Is Sweeter Than Ever/I Like Everything About You	1966	3.75	7.50	15.00
❑ Motown 1098	Reach Out I'll Be There/Until You Love Someone	1966	3.75	7.50	15.00
❑ Motown 1102	Standing in the Shadows of Love/Since You've Been Gone	1966	3.75	7.50	15.00
❑ Motown 1104	Bernadette/I Got a Feeling	1967	3.00	6.00	12.00
❑ Motown 1110	7-Rooms of Gloom/I'll Turn to Stone	1967	3.00	6.00	12.00
❑ Motown 1113	You Keep Running Away/If You Don't Want My Love	1967	3.00	6.00	12.00
❑ Motown 1119	Walk Away Renee/Your Love Is Wonderful	1968	3.00	6.00	12.00
❑ Motown 1124	If I Were a Carpenter/Wonderful Baby	1968	3.00	6.00	12.00
❑ Motown 1127	Yesterday's Dreams/For Once in My Life	1968	2.00	4.00	8.00
❑ Motown 1132	I'm in a Different World/Remember When	1968	2.00	4.00	8.00
❑ Motown 1147	What Is a Man/Don't Bring Back Memories	1969	2.00	4.00	8.00
❑ Motown 1159	Don't Let Him Take Your Love from Me/The Key	1969	2.00	4.00	8.00
❑ Motown 1164	It's All in the Game/Love (Is the Answer)	1970	2.00	4.00	8.00
❑ Motown 1170	Still Water (Love)/Still Water (Peace)	1970	—	3.00	6.00
❑ Motown 1175	Just Seven Numbers (Can Straighten Out My Life)/ I Wish I Were Your Mirror	1971	—	3.00	6.00
❑ Motown 1185	In These Changing Times/Right Before My Eyes	1971	—	3.00	6.00
❑ Motown 1189	MacArthur Park (Part 2)/MacArthur Park (Part 1)	1971	—	3.00	6.00
❑ Motown 1196	A Simple Game/L.A. My Town	1972	—	3.00	6.00
❑ Motown 1198	I Can't Quit Your Love/Happy (Is a Bumpy Road)	1972	—	3.00	6.00
❑ Motown 1210	(It's the Way) Nature Planned It/I'll Never Change	1972	—	3.00	6.00
❑ Motown 1254	Hey Man-We Gotta Get You a Woman/How Can I Forget You	1973	—	—	—
—Unreleased					
❑ Motown 1706	I Just Can't Walk Away/Hang	1983	—	—	3.00
❑ Motown 1718	Make Yourself Right at Home/Sing a Song of Yesterday	1984	—	—	3.00
❑ Motown 1790	Sexy Ways/Body and Soul	1985	—	—	3.00
❑ Motown 1811	Don't Tell Me That It's Over/I'm Ready for Love	1985	—	—	3.00
❑ Motown 1854	Hot Nights/Again	1986	—	—	3.00
❑ Reliant 1691	I'm Here Again/(Instrumental)	1983	—	2.00	4.00
❑ Riverside 4534	Pennies from Heaven/Where Are You?	1962	18.75	37.50	75.00
❑ RSO 1069	Back to School Again/Rock-a-Hula Luau	1982	—	—	3.00
Albums					
❑ ABC D-862	Night Lights Harmony	1975	3.00	6.00	12.00
❑ ABC D-968	Catfish	1976	3.00	6.00	12.00
❑ ABC D-1014	The Show Must Go On	1977	3.00	6.00	12.00
❑ ABC AA-1092	At the Top	1978	3.00	6.00	12.00
❑ ABC Dunhill DSX-50129	Keeper of the Castle	1972	3.00	6.00	12.00
❑ ABC Dunhill DSX-50144	Main Street People	1973	3.00	6.00	12.00
❑ ABC Dunhill DSX-50166	Meeting of the Minds	1974	3.00	6.00	12.00
❑ ABC Dunhill DSX-50188	Live & In Concert	1974	3.00	6.00	12.00
❑ Arista AL-8492	Indestructible	1988	2.00	4.00	8.00
❑ Casablanca NBLP 7258	Tonight!	1981	2.50	5.00	10.00
❑ Casablanca NBLP 7266	One More Mountain	1982	2.50	5.00	10.00
❑ MCA 27019	Greatest Hits	198?	2.50	5.00	10.00
❑ Motown M5-114V1	Superstar Series, Vol. 14	1981	2.50	5.00	10.00
❑ Motown M5-122V1	Four Tops	1981	2.00	4.00	8.00
—Reissue of 622					
❑ Motown M5-149V1	Four Tops Reach Out	1981	2.00	4.00	8.00
—Reissue of 660					

Number	Title (A Side/B Side)	Yr	VG	VG+	NM
❑ Motown M5-209V1	The Four Tops' Greatest Hits	1981	2.00	4.00	8.00
—Reissue of 662					
❑ Motown 622 [M]	Four Tops	1964	7.50	15.00	30.00
❑ Motown MS-622 [S]	Four Tops	1964	10.00	20.00	40.00
❑ Motown 634 [M]	Four Tops Second Album	1965	6.25	12.50	25.00
❑ Motown MS-634 [S]	Four Tops Second Album	1965	7.50	15.00	30.00
❑ Motown 647 [M]	4 Tops On Top	1966	6.25	12.50	25.00
❑ Motown MS-647 [S]	4 Tops On Top	1966	7.50	15.00	30.00
❑ Motown 654 [M]	Four Tops Live!	1966	6.25	12.50	25.00
❑ Motown MS-654 [S]	Four Tops Live!	1966	7.50	15.00	30.00
❑ Motown 657 [M]	4 Tops on Broadway	1967	6.25	12.50	25.00
❑ Motown MS-657 [S]	4 Tops on Broadway	1967	7.50	15.00	30.00
❑ Motown 660 [M]	Four Tops Reach Out	1967	7.50	15.00	30.00
❑ Motown MS-660 [S]	Four Tops Reach Out	1967	6.25	12.50	25.00
❑ Motown 662 [M]	The Four Tops Greatest Hits	1967	7.50	15.00	30.00
❑ Motown MS-662 [S]	The Four Tops Greatest Hits	1967	5.00	10.00	20.00
❑ Motown 669 [M]	Yesterday's Dreams	1968	7.50	15.00	30.00
❑ Motown MS-669 [S]	Yesterday's Dreams	1968	5.00	10.00	20.00
❑ Motown MS-675	Four Tops Now!	1969	5.00	10.00	20.00
❑ Motown MS-695	Soul Spin	1969	5.00	10.00	20.00
❑ Motown MS-704	Still Waters Run Deep	1970	5.00	10.00	20.00
❑ Motown MS-721	Changing Times	1970	5.00	10.00	20.00
❑ Motown M-740L	Four Tops Greatest Hits, Vol. 2	1971	5.00	10.00	20.00
❑ Motown M-748L	Nature Planned It	1972	5.00	10.00	20.00
❑ Motown M-764D [(2)]	The Best of the 4 Tops	1973	3.75	7.50	15.00
❑ Motown M9-809A3 [(3)]	Anthology	1974	5.00	10.00	20.00
❑ Motown 5224 ML	Still Waters Run Deep	1982	2.00	4.00	8.00
—Reissue of 704					
❑ Motown 5258 ML	Four Tops Live!	1983	2.00	4.00	8.00
—Reissue of 654					
❑ Motown 5314 ML	Great Songs	1983	2.50	5.00	10.00
❑ Motown 6066 ML	Back Where I Belong	1983	2.50	5.00	10.00
❑ Motown 6130 ML	Magic	1985	2.50	5.00	10.00
❑ Workshop Jazz 217 [M]	Breakin' Through	1962	—	—	—
—This album is pictured on some early Motown inner sleeves, but is not known to exist					

FRAMPTON, PETER

45s

Number	Title (A Side/B Side)	Yr	VG	VG+	NM
❑ A&M 1379	Jumping Jack Flash/Oh for Another Day	1972	2.50	5.00	10.00
❑ A&M 1456	All Night Long/Don't Fade Away	1973	—	3.00	6.00
—As "Frampton's Camel"					
❑ A&M 1470	I Believe (When I Fall in Love It Will Be Forever)/ Which Way the Wind Blows	1973	2.00	4.00	8.00
—As "Frampton's Camel"					
❑ A&M 1506	Somethin's Happening/I Wanna Go to the Sun	1974	—	3.00	6.00
❑ A&M 1693	Show Me the Way/Crying Clown	1975	2.00	4.00	8.00
❑ A&M 1738	Baby I Love Your Way/(I'll Give You) Money	1975	2.00	4.00	8.00
❑ A&M 1763	(I'll Give You) Money/Nowhere's Too Far (For My Baby)	1975	—	3.00	6.00
❑ A&M 1795	Show Me the Way/Shine On	1976	—	2.00	4.00
❑ A&M 1832	Baby, I Love Your Way/It's a Plain Shame	1976	—	2.00	4.00
❑ A&M 1867	Do You Feel Like We Do/Penny for Your Thoughts	1976	—	2.00	4.00
❑ A&M 1941	I'm in You/St. Thomas (Don't You Know How I Feel)	1977	—	2.00	4.00
❑ A&M 1941	I'm in You/St. Thomas (Know How I Feel)	1977	—	2.50	5.00
❑ A&M 1972	Signed, Sealed, Delivered (I'm Yours)/Rocky's Hot Club	1977	—	2.00	4.00
❑ A&M 1988	Tried to Love/You Don't Have to Worry	1977	—	2.00	4.00
❑ A&M 2070	The Long and Winding Road/Tried to Love	1978	—	3.00	6.00
❑ A&M 2148	I Can't Stand It No More/Where Should I Be	1979	—	2.00	4.00
❑ A&M 2174	She Don't Reply/St. Thomas (Don't You Know How I Feel)	1979	—	2.00	4.00
❑ A&M 2350	Breaking All the Rules/Night Town	1981	—	2.00	4.00
❑ A&M 2362	You Kill Me/Wasting the Night Away	1981	—	3.00	6.00
❑ A&M 2442	Sleepwalk/Theme from Nivram	1982	2.00	4.00	8.00
❑ A&M 8595	Show Me the Way/Baby, I Love Your Way	1977	—	2.00	4.00
—"Forget Me Nots" reissue; green and gold label					
❑ A&M 8604	I'm in You/Do You Feel Like We Do	1978	—	2.00	4.00
—"Forget Me Nots" reissue; green and gold label					
❑ Atlantic 88820	Holding On to You/Give Me a Love That's Real	1990	—	—	3.00
❑ Atlantic 89395	Hiding from a Heartache/Into View	1986	—	—	3.00
❑ Atlantic 89426	All Eyes on You/So Far Away	1986	—	—	3.00
❑ Atlantic 89463	Lying/Into View	1985	—	—	3.00

Albums

Number	Title (A Side/B Side)	Yr	VG	VG+	NM
❑ A&M SP-3133	Wind of Change	198?	2.00	4.00	8.00
—Budget-line reissue					
❑ A&M SP-3619	Somethin's Happening	1974	3.00	6.00	12.00
❑ A&M SP-3703 [(2)]	Frampton Comes Alive!	1976	3.00	6.00	12.00
❑ A&M SP-3710	Where I Should Be	1979	2.50	5.00	10.00
❑ A&M SP-3722	Breaking All the Rules	1981	2.50	5.00	10.00
❑ A&M SP-4348	Wind of Change	1972	3.00	6.00	12.00
—Brown label					
❑ A&M SP-4389	Frampton's Camel	1973	3.00	6.00	12.00
—Brown label					
❑ A&M SP-4512	Frampton	1975	2.50	5.00	10.00
❑ A&M SP-4704	I'm In You	1977	2.50	5.00	10.00
❑ A&M SP-4704 [DJ]	I'm In You	1977	10.00	20.00	40.00
—Promo-only picture disc					
❑ A&M SP-4905	The Art of Control	1982	2.50	5.00	10.00
❑ A&M SP-6505 [(2)]	Frampton Comes Alive!	198?	2.50	5.00	10.00
—Budget-line reissue					

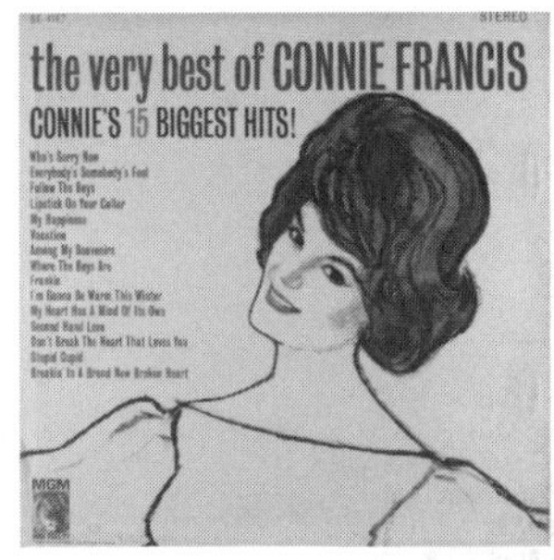

Number	Title (A Side/B Side)	Yr	VG	VG+	NM
❑ Atlantic 81290	Premonition	1986	2.00	4.00	8.00
❑ Atlantic 82030	Where All the Pieces Fit	1989	2.00	4.00	8.00

FRANCIS, CONNIE

45s

Number	Title (A Side/B Side)	Yr	VG	VG+	NM
❑ GSF 6901	The Answer (Should I Tie a Yellow Ribbon Round the Ole Oak Tree?)/Paint the Rain	1973	—	2.50	5.00
❑ Ivanhoe 508	I Don't Wanna Walk Without You/Don't Turn Around	197?	—	2.50	5.00
❑ MGM 126	Stupid Cupid/I'm Sorry I Made You Cry	196?	2.00	4.00	8.00
—Reissue					
❑ MGM 129	Who's Sorry Now/You Were Only Fooling	196?	2.00	4.00	8.00
—Reissue					
❑ MGM 135	Mama/You're Gonna Miss Me	196?	2.00	4.00	8.00
—Reissue					
❑ MGM 136	Among My Souvenirs/God Bless America	196?	2.00	4.00	8.00
—Reissue					
❑ MGM 139	Lipstick on Your Collar/Frankie	196?	2.00	4.00	8.00
—Reissue					
❑ MGM 141	My Happiness/If I Didn't Care	196?	2.00	4.00	8.00
—Reissue					
❑ MGM 148	My Heart Has a Mind of Its Own/Malaguena	196?	2.00	4.00	8.00
—Reissue					
❑ MGM 150	Where the Boys Are/No One	196?	2.00	4.00	8.00
—Reissue					
❑ MGM 153	Breakin' In a Brand New Broken Heart/Somebody Else's Boy	196?	2.00	4.00	8.00
—Reissue					
❑ MGM 155	Together/Too Many Rules	196?	2.00	4.00	8.00
—Reissue					
❑ MGM 156	Many Tears Ago/Senza Mama E Numerata	196?	2.00	4.00	8.00
—Reissue					
❑ MGM 157	Don't Break the Heart That Loves You/Second Hand Love	196?	2.00	4.00	8.00
—Reissue					
❑ MGM 165	Everybody's Somebody's Fool/Al Di La	196?	2.00	4.00	8.00
—Reissue					
❑ MGM 169	Jealous Heart/Forget Domani	196?	2.00	4.00	8.00
—Reissue					
❑ MGM 511	Who's Sorry Now/Stupid Cupid	197?	—	2.50	5.00
—Reissue					
❑ MGM 512	Lipstick on Your Collar/Mama	197?	—	2.50	5.00
—Reissue					
❑ MGM 513	Everybody's Somebody's Fool/Al Di La	197?	—	2.50	5.00
—Reissue					
❑ MGM 524	My Happiness/If I Didn't Care	197?	—	2.50	5.00
—Reissue					
❑ MGM 12015	Freddy/Didn't I Love You Enough	1955	12.50	25.00	50.00
❑ MGM 12056	Oh Please Make Him Jealous/Goody Goodbye	1955	12.50	25.00	50.00
❑ MGM 12122	Are You Satisfied/My Treasure	1956	6.25	12.50	25.00
❑ MGM 12191	My First Real Love/Believe in Me	1956	15.00	30.00	60.00
❑ MGM 12251	Send for My Baby/Forgetting	1956	6.25	12.50	25.00
❑ MGM 12335	My Sailor Boy/Everyone Needs Someone	1956	6.25	12.50	25.00
❑ MGM 12375	I Never Had a Sweetheart/Little Blue Wren	1957	6.25	12.50	25.00
❑ MGM 12440	No Other One/I Leaned on a Man	1957	6.25	12.50	25.00
❑ MGM 12490	Eighteen/Faded Orchid	1957	6.25	12.50	25.00
❑ MGM 12588	Who's Sorry Now?/You Were Only Fooling	1958	5.00	10.00	20.00
❑ MGM 12647	I'm Sorry I Made You Cry/Lock Up Your Heart	1958	5.00	10.00	20.00
❑ MGM 12669	Heartaches/I Miss You So	1958	12.50	25.00	50.00
❑ MGM 12683	Stupid Cupid/Carolina Moon	1958	5.00	10.00	20.00
❑ MGM 12713	Fallin'/Happy Days and Lonely Nights	1958	5.00	10.00	20.00
❑ MGM 12738 [M]	My Happiness/Never Before	1958	5.00	10.00	20.00
❑ MGM 12769	If I Didn't Care/Toward the End of the Day	1959	5.00	10.00	20.00
❑ MGM 12793 [M]	Lipstick on Your Collar/Frankie	1959	5.00	10.00	20.00
❑ MGM 12824 [M]	You're Gonna Miss Me/Plenty Good Lovin'	1959	5.00	10.00	20.00
❑ MGM 12841 [M]	Among My Souvenirs/God Bless America	1959	7.50	15.00	30.00
—First pressing has a yellow label					
❑ MGM 12841 [M]	Among My Souvenirs/God Bless America	1959	5.00	10.00	20.00
—Second pressing has a black label					
❑ MGM 12878	Mama/Teddy	1960	3.75	7.50	15.00

Number	Title (A Side/B Side)	Yr	VG	VG+	NM
❑ MGM 12899	Everybody's Somebody's Fool/Jealous of You	1960	3.75	7.50	15.00
❑ MGM 12923	My Heart Has a Mind of Its Own/Malaguena	1960	3.75	7.50	15.00
❑ MGM 12964	Many Tears Ago/Senza Mama (With No One)	1960	3.75	7.50	15.00
❑ MGM 12971	Where the Boys Are/No One	1961	3.75	7.50	15.00
❑ MGM 12995	Breakin' In a Brand New Broken Heart/Someone Else's Boy	1961	3.75	7.50	15.00
❑ MGM 13005	Atashi-No/Swanee	1961	7.50	15.00	30.00
❑ MGM 13019	Together/Too Many Rules	1961	3.75	7.50	15.00
❑ MGM 13039	(He's My) Dreamboat/Hollywood	1961	3.75	7.50	15.00
❑ MGM 13051	When the Boy in Your Arms (Is the Boy in Your Heart)/ Baby's First Christmas	1961	3.75	7.50	15.00
❑ MGM 13059	Don't Break the Heart That Loves You/Drop It, Joe	1962	3.75	7.50	15.00
❑ MGM 13074	Second Hand Love/Gonna Git That Man	1962	5.00	10.00	20.00
—A-side is said to have been produced by Phil Spector, though Connie Francis disputes this; regardless, Spector did co-write the song					
❑ MGM 13087	Vacation/The Biggest Sin of All	1962	3.75	7.50	15.00
❑ MGM 13096	I Was Such a Fool (To Fall in Love with You)/He Thinks I Still Care	1962	3.00	6.00	12.00
❑ MGM 13116	I'm Gonna' Be Warm This Winter/Al Di La	1962	3.00	6.00	12.00
❑ MGM 13127	Follow the Boys/Waiting for Billy	1962	3.00	6.00	12.00
❑ MGM 13143	If My Pillow Could Talk/You're the Only One Can Hurt Me	1963	3.00	6.00	12.00
❑ MGM 13160	Drownin' My Sorrows/Mala Femmena	1963	3.00	6.00	12.00
❑ MGM 13176	Your Other Love/Whatever Happened to Rosemarie?	1963	3.00	6.00	12.00
❑ MGM 13203	In the Summer of His Years/My Buddy	1963	3.00	6.00	12.00
❑ MGM 13214	Blue Winter/You Know You Don't Want Me (So Why Don't You Leave Me Alone)	1964	3.00	6.00	12.00
❑ MGM 13237	Be Anything (But Be Mine)/Tommy	1964	3.00	6.00	12.00
❑ MGM 13256	Looking for Love/This Is My Happiest Moment	1964	3.00	6.00	12.00
❑ MGM 13287	Don't Ever Leave Me/We Have Something More (Than a Summer Love)	1964	3.00	6.00	12.00
❑ MGM 13303	Whose Heart Are You Breaking Tonight/Come On Jerry	1965	2.50	5.00	10.00
❑ MGM 13325	For Mama (La Mamma)/She'll Be Coming 'Round the Mountain	1965	3.00	6.00	12.00
❑ MGM 13331	Wishing It Was You/You're Mine (Just When You're Lonely)	1965	2.50	5.00	10.00
❑ MGM 13363	Forget Domani/No One Sends Me Roses	1965	2.50	5.00	10.00
❑ MGM 13389	Roundabout/Bossa Nova Hand Dance	1965	2.50	5.00	10.00
❑ MGM 13420	Jealous Heart/Can I Rely on You	1965	2.50	5.00	10.00
❑ MGM 13470	Love Is Me, Love Is You/I'd Let You Break My Heart All Over Again	1966	2.50	5.00	10.00
❑ MGM 13505	It's a Different World/Empty Chapel	1966	2.50	5.00	10.00
❑ MGM 13545	A Letter from a Soldier (Dear Mama)/Somewhere, My Love	1966	2.50	5.00	10.00
❑ MGM 13578	All the Love in the World/So Nice	1966	2.50	5.00	10.00
❑ MGM 13610	Spanish Nights and You/Games That Lovers Play	1966	2.50	5.00	10.00
❑ MGM 13665	Another Page/Souvenir d'Italie	1967	2.50	5.00	10.00
❑ MGM 13708	Mama/Never on Sunday	1967	2.50	5.00	10.00
—Part of Celebrity Series CS-5					
❑ MGM 13709	My Happiness/Al Di La	1967	2.50	5.00	10.00
—Part of Celebrity Series CS-5					
❑ MGM 13710	Malaguena/I Love You Much Too Much	1967	2.50	5.00	10.00
—Part of Celebrity Series CS-5					
❑ MGM 13711	Once in a Lifetime/Oh Lonesome Me	1967	2.50	5.00	10.00
—Part of Celebrity Series CS-5					
❑ MGM 13712	Jealous Heart/Will You Still Be Mine	1967	2.50	5.00	10.00
—Part of Celebrity Series CS-5					
❑ MGM 13718	Time Alone Will Tell/Born Free	1967	2.50	5.00	10.00
❑ MGM 13773	My Heart Cries for You/Someone Took the Sweetness Out of Sweetheart	1967	2.50	5.00	10.00
❑ MGM 13814	Lonely Again/When You Care a Lot for Someone	1967	2.50	5.00	10.00
❑ MGM 13876	My World Is Slipping Away/Till We're Together	1967	2.50	5.00	10.00
❑ MGM 13923	Why Say Goodbye/Adios, Me Amore	1968	2.00	4.00	8.00
❑ MGM 13948	Somebody Else Is Taking My Place/ Brother, Can You Spare a Dime?	1968	2.00	4.00	8.00
❑ MGM 14004	I Don't Wanna Play House/The Welfare Check	1968	2.00	4.00	8.00
❑ MGM 14034	The Wedding Cake/Over Hill, Under Ground	1969	2.00	4.00	8.00
❑ MGM 14058	Gone Like the Wind/Am I Blue?	1969	2.00	4.00	8.00
❑ MGM 14089	Invierno Trieste/Noches Espanolas Y Tu	1969	—	—	—
—Not known to exist					
❑ MGM 14091	Mr. Love/Zingara	1969	2.00	4.00	8.00
❑ MGM 14853	I'm Me Again/Comme Si, Comme Sa	1976	—	3.00	6.00
❑ Polydor 2143	I'm Me Again/Comme Si, Comme Sa	1981	—	2.50	5.00
❑ Polydor 810087-7	There's Still a Few Good Love Songs Left in Me/ Let's Make It Love Tonight	1983	—	2.50	5.00
Albums					
❑ Leo LE-903 [M]	Connie Francis and the Kids Next Door	1967	12.50	25.00	50.00
❑ Leo LES-903 [S]	Connie Francis and the Kids Next Door	1967	15.00	30.00	60.00
❑ Metro M-519 [M]	Connie Francis	1964	5.00	10.00	20.00
❑ Metro MS-519 [S]	Connie Francis	1964	6.25	12.50	25.00
❑ Metro M-538 [M]	Folk Favorites	1965	5.00	10.00	20.00
❑ Metro MS-538 [S]	Folk Favorites	1965	6.25	12.50	25.00
❑ Metro M-571 [M]	Songs of Love	1966	5.00	10.00	20.00
❑ Metro MS-571 [S]	Songs of Love	1966	6.25	12.50	25.00
❑ Metro M-603 [M]	The Incomparable Connie Francis	1967	5.00	10.00	20.00
❑ Metro MS-603 [S]	The Incomparable Connie Francis	1967	6.25	12.50	25.00
❑ MGM GAS-109	Greatest Golden Groovie Goodies (Golden Archive Series)	1970	6.25	12.50	25.00
❑ MGM E-3686 [M]	Who's Sorry Now?	1958	25.00	50.00	100.00
—Yellow label					
❑ MGM E-3761 [M]	The Exciting Connie Francis	1959	20.00	40.00	80.00
—Yellow label					
❑ MGM SE-3761 [S]	The Exciting Connie Francis	1959	25.00	50.00	100.00
—Yellow label					
❑ MGM E-3776 [M]	My Thanks to You	1959	7.50	15.00	30.00
❑ MGM SE-3776 [S]	My Thanks to You	1959	10.00	20.00	40.00

Number	Title (A Side/B Side)	Yr	VG	VG+	NM
❑ MGM E-3791 [M]	Italian Favorites	1959	7.50	15.00	30.00
❑ MGM SE-3791 [S]	Italian Favorites	1959	10.00	20.00	40.00
❑ MGM E-3792 [M]	Christmas in My Heart	1959	7.50	15.00	30.00
❑ MGM SE-3792 [S]	Christmas in My Heart	1959	10.00	20.00	40.00
—Same as above, but in stereo					
❑ MGM E-3793 [M]	Connie's Greatest Hits	1960	7.50	15.00	30.00
❑ MGM E-3794 [M]	Rock 'N' Roll Million Sellers	1960	7.50	15.00	30.00
❑ MGM SE-3794 [S]	Rock 'N' Roll Million Sellers	1960	10.00	20.00	40.00
❑ MGM E-3795 [M]	Country and Western Golden Hits	1960	7.50	15.00	30.00
❑ MGM SE-3795 [S]	Country and Western Golden Hits	1960	10.00	20.00	40.00
❑ MGM E-3853 [M]	Spanish and Latin American Favorites	1960	7.50	15.00	30.00
❑ MGM SE-3853 [S]	Spanish and Latin American Favorites	1960	10.00	20.00	40.00
❑ MGM E-3869 [M]	Jewish Favorites	1961	7.50	15.00	30.00
❑ MGM SE-3869 [S]	Jewish Favorites	1961	10.00	20.00	40.00
❑ MGM E-3871 [M]	More Italian Favorites	1960	7.50	15.00	30.00
❑ MGM SE-3871 [S]	More Italian Favorites	1960	10.00	20.00	40.00
❑ MGM E-3893 [M]	Songs to a Swinging Band	1961	7.50	15.00	30.00
❑ MGM SE-3893 [S]	Songs to a Swinging Band	1961	10.00	20.00	40.00
❑ MGM E-3913 [M]	Connie Francis at the Copa	1961	7.50	15.00	30.00
❑ MGM SE-3913 [S]	Connie Francis at the Copa	1961	10.00	20.00	40.00
❑ MGM E-3942 [M]	More Greatest Hits	1961	7.50	15.00	30.00
❑ MGM SE-3942 [S]	More Greatest Hits	1961	10.00	20.00	40.00
❑ MGM E-3965 [M]	Never on Sunday and Other Title Songs from Motion Pictures	1961	7.50	15.00	30.00
❑ MGM SE-3965 [S]	Never on Sunday and Other Title Songs from Motion Pictures	1961	10.00	20.00	40.00
❑ MGM E-3969 [M]	Folk Song Favorites	1961	7.50	15.00	30.00
❑ MGM SE-3969 [S]	Folk Song Favorites	1961	10.00	20.00	40.00
❑ MGM E-4013 [M]	Irish Favorites	1962	7.50	15.00	30.00
❑ MGM SE-4013 [S]	Irish Favorites	1962	10.00	20.00	40.00
❑ MGM E-4022 [M]	Dance Party	196?	6.25	12.50	25.00
—Retitled version of "Do the Twist"					
❑ MGM E-4022 [M]	Do the Twist	1962	7.50	15.00	30.00
❑ MGM SE-4022 [S]	Dance Party	196?	7.50	15.00	30.00
—Retitled version of "Do the Twist"					
❑ MGM SE-4022 [S]	Do the Twist	1962	10.00	20.00	40.00
❑ MGM E-4023 [M]	Fun Songs for Children	1962	12.50	25.00	50.00
❑ MGM E-4048 [M]	Award Winning Motion Picture Hits	1963	6.25	12.50	25.00
❑ MGM SE-4048 [S]	Award Winning Motion Picture Hits	1963	7.50	15.00	30.00
❑ MGM E-4049 [M]	Connie Francis Sings Second Hand Love and Other Hits	1962	6.25	12.50	25.00
❑ MGM SE-4049 [S]	Connie Francis Sings Second Hand Love and Other Hits	1962	7.50	15.00	30.00
❑ MGM E-4079 [M]	Country Music Connie Style	1962	6.25	12.50	25.00
❑ MGM SE-4079 [S]	Country Music Connie Style	1962	7.50	15.00	30.00
❑ MGM E-4102 [M]	Modern Italian Hits	1963	6.25	12.50	25.00
❑ MGM SE-4102 [S]	Modern Italian Hits	1963	7.50	15.00	30.00
❑ MGM E-4123 [M]	Follow the Boys	1963	6.25	12.50	25.00
❑ MGM SE-4123 [S]	Follow the Boys	1963	7.50	15.00	30.00
❑ MGM E-4124 [M]	German Favorites	1963	6.25	12.50	25.00
❑ MGM SE-4124 [S]	German Favorites	1963	7.50	15.00	30.00
❑ MGM E-4145 [M]	Greatest American Waltzes	1963	6.25	12.50	25.00
❑ MGM SE-4145 [S]	Greatest American Waltzes	1963	7.50	15.00	30.00
❑ MGM E-4161 [M]	Mala Femmena & Connie's Big Hits from Italy	1963	6.25	12.50	25.00
❑ MGM SE-4161 [S]	Mala Femmena & Connie's Big Hits from Italy	1963	7.50	15.00	30.00
❑ MGM E-4167 [M]	The Very Best of Connie Francis	1963	6.25	12.50	25.00
❑ MGM SE-4167 [S]	The Very Best of Connie Francis	1963	7.50	15.00	30.00
❑ MGM E-4210 [M]	In the Summer of His Years	1964	6.25	12.50	25.00
❑ MGM SE-4210 [S]	In the Summer of His Years	1964	7.50	15.00	30.00
❑ MGM E-4229 [M]	Looking for Love	1964	6.25	12.50	25.00
❑ MGM SE-4229 [S]	Looking for Love	1964	7.50	15.00	30.00
❑ MGM E-4253 [M]	A New Kind of Connie	1964	6.25	12.50	25.00
❑ MGM SE-4253 [S]	A New Kind of Connie	1964	7.50	15.00	30.00
❑ MGM E-4294 [M]	Connie Francis Sings For Mama	1965	6.25	12.50	25.00
❑ MGM SE-4294 [S]	Connie Francis Sings For Mama	1965	7.50	15.00	30.00
❑ MGM E-4298 [M]	All Time International Hits	1965	6.25	12.50	25.00
❑ MGM SE-4298 [S]	All Time International Hits	1965	7.50	15.00	30.00
❑ MGM E-4355 [M]	Jealous Heart	1966	6.25	12.50	25.00
❑ MGM SE-4355 [S]	Jealous Heart	1966	7.50	15.00	30.00
❑ MGM E-4382 [M]	Movie Greats of the 60's	1966	6.25	12.50	25.00
❑ MGM SE-4382 [S]	Movie Greats of the 60's	1966	7.50	15.00	30.00

Number	Title (A Side/B Side)	Yr	VG	VG+	NM
❑ MGM E-4399 [M]	Connie's Christmas	1966	6.25	12.50	25.00
❑ MGM SE-4399 [S]	Connie's Christmas	1966	7.50	15.00	30.00
❑ MGM E-4411 [M]	Live at the Sahara in Las Vegas	1967	6.25	12.50	25.00
❑ MGM SE-4411 [S]	Live at the Sahara in Las Vegas	1967	7.50	15.00	30.00
❑ MGM E-4448 [M]	Love, Italian Style	1967	6.25	12.50	25.00
❑ MGM SE-4448 [S]	Love, Italian Style	1967	7.50	15.00	30.00
❑ MGM E-4472 [M]	Connie Francis On Broadway Today	1967	6.25	12.50	25.00
❑ MGM SE-4472 [S]	Connie Francis On Broadway Today	1967	7.50	15.00	30.00
❑ MGM E-4474 [M]	Grandes Exitos del Cine de los Anos 60	1967	6.25	12.50	25.00
❑ MGM SE-4474 [S]	Grandes Exitos del Cine de los Anos 60	1967	7.50	15.00	30.00
❑ MGM E-4487 [M]	My Heart Cries for You	1967	7.50	15.00	30.00
❑ MGM SE-4487 [S]	My Heart Cries for You	1967	6.25	12.50	25.00
❑ MGM E-4522 [M]	Hawaii: Connie	1968	25.00	50.00	100.00
❑ MGM SE-4522 [S]	Hawaii: Connie	1968	6.25	12.50	25.00
❑ MGM SE-4573 [S]	Connie & Clyde	1968	6.25	12.50	25.00
❑ MGM SE-4585	Connie Francis Sings Bacharach & David	1968	6.25	12.50	25.00
❑ MGM SE-4637	The Wedding Cake	1969	6.25	12.50	25.00
❑ MGM SE-4655	The Songs of Les Reed	1969	6.25	12.50	25.00
❑ MGM MG-1-5406	I'm Me Again	198?	3.00	6.00	12.00
❑ MGM MG-1-5410	Greatest Hits	198?	3.00	6.00	12.00
❑ MGM MG-1-5411	Greatest Jewish Hits	198?	3.00	6.00	12.00
❑ MGM ST-90068 [S]	A New Kind of Connie	1964	8.75	17.50	35.00
—Capitol Record Club issue					
❑ MGM T-90068 [M]	A New Kind of Connie	1964	7.50	15.00	30.00
—Capitol Record Club issue					
❑ MGM ST 90510 [S]	The Very Best of Connie Francis	1965	10.00	20.00	40.00
—Capitol Record Club edition					
❑ MGM T 90510 [M]	The Very Best of Connie Francis	1965	10.00	20.00	40.00
—Capitol Record Club edition					
❑ MGM ST-91145	My Best to You	1968	7.50	15.00	30.00
—Capitol Record Club					
❑ Polydor 827569-1	The Very Best of Connie Francis	1985	2.50	5.00	10.00
❑ Polydor 827582-1	Greatest Hits	1985	2.50	5.00	10.00
❑ Polydor 827584-1	Greatest Jewish Hits	1985	2.50	5.00	10.00
❑ Polydor 839922-1	Lo Mejor De Su Repertorio	198?	2.50	5.00	10.00
❑ Polydor 839923-1	12 Exitos De Connie Francis	198?	2.50	5.00	10.00

FRANKLIN, ARETHA

45s

Number	Title (A Side/B Side)	Yr	VG	VG+	NM
❑ Arista 0569	United Together/Take Me With You	1980	—	2.00	4.00
❑ Arista 0591	What a Fool Believes/Love Me Forever	1980	—	2.00	4.00
❑ Arista 0600	Come to Me/School Days	1981	—	2.00	4.00
❑ Arista 0624	Love All the Hurt Away/Whole Lotta Me	1981	—	2.00	4.00
—Aretha Franklin and George Benson					
❑ Arista 0646	It's My Turn/Kind of Man	1981	—	2.00	4.00
❑ Arista 0665	Livin' in the Streets/There's a Star for Everyone	1982	—	2.00	4.00
❑ Arista 0699	Jump To It/Just My Daydream	1982	—	2.00	4.00
❑ Arista 1023	Love Me Right/(It's Just) Your Love	1982	—	2.00	4.00
❑ Arista 1043	This Is for Real/I Just Want to Make It Up to You	1983	—	2.00	4.00
❑ Arista 2239	Everyday People/You Can't Take Me for Granted	1991	—	2.50	5.00
❑ Arista 9034	Get It Right/Giving In	1983	—	2.00	4.00
❑ Arista 9095	Every Girl (Wants My Guy)/I Got Your Love	1983	—	2.00	4.00
❑ Arista 9354	Freeway of Love/Until You Say You Love Me	1985	—	—	3.00
❑ Arista 9410	Who's Zoomin' Who/Sweet Bitter Love	1985	—	—	3.00
❑ Arista 9453	Another Night/Kind of Man	1986	—	—	3.00
❑ Arista 9474	Ain't Nobody Ever Loved You/Push	1986	—	—	3.00
—B-side with Peter Wolf					
❑ Arista 9528	Jumpin' Jack Flash/Integrity	1986	—	—	3.00
—Second pressing on black vinyl					
❑ Arista 9528	Jumpin' Jack Flash/Integrity	1986	—	2.50	5.00
—Original stock pressings on clear vinyl					
❑ Arista 9541	Jumpin' Jack Flash/(Street Mix Radio Edit)	1986	—	2.00	4.00
❑ Arista 9546	Jimmy Lee/If You Need My Love Tonight	1986	—	2.00	4.00
❑ Arista 9557	Jimmy Lee/An Angel Cries	1986	—	—	3.00
❑ Arista 9559	I Knew You Were Waiting (For Me)/(Instrumental)	1987	—	—	3.00
—With George Michael					
❑ Arista 9574	Rock-A-Lott/Look to the Rainbow	1987	—	—	3.00
❑ Arista 9623	If You Need My Love Tonight/He'll Come Along	1987	—	—	3.00
—A-side with Larry Graham					
❑ Arista 9672	Oh Happy Day/The Lord's Prayer	1988	—	2.50	5.00
❑ Arista 9809	Through the Storm/Come to Me	1989	—	—	3.00
—A-side with Elton John					
❑ Arista 9850	It Isn't, It Wasn't, It Ain't Never Gonna Be/If Ever a Love There Was	1989	—	—	3.00
—A-side with Whitney Houston; B-side with the Four Tops					
❑ Arista 9884	Gimme Your Love/Think	1989	—	—	3.00
—With James Brown					
❑ Atlantic 2386	I Never Loved a Man (The Way I Love You)/ Do Right Woman, Do Right Man	1967	2.50	5.00	10.00
❑ Atlantic 2403	Respect/Dr. Feelgood	1967	2.50	5.00	10.00
❑ Atlantic 2427	Baby I Love You/Going Down Now	1967	2.50	5.00	10.00
❑ Atlantic 2441	(You Make Me Feel Like) A Natural Woman/Baby, Baby, Baby	1967	2.50	5.00	10.00
❑ Atlantic 2464	Chain of Fools/Prove It	1967	2.50	5.00	10.00
❑ Atlantic 2486	(Sweet Sweet Baby) Since You've Been Gone/Ain't No Way	1968	2.50	5.00	10.00
❑ Atlantic 2518	Think/You Send Me	1968	2.50	5.00	10.00
❑ Atlantic 2546	I Say a Little Prayer/The House That Jack Built	1968	2.50	5.00	10.00
❑ Atlantic 2574	See Saw/My Song	1968	2.00	4.00	8.00
❑ Atlantic 2603	The Weight/Tracks of My Tears	1969	2.00	4.00	8.00

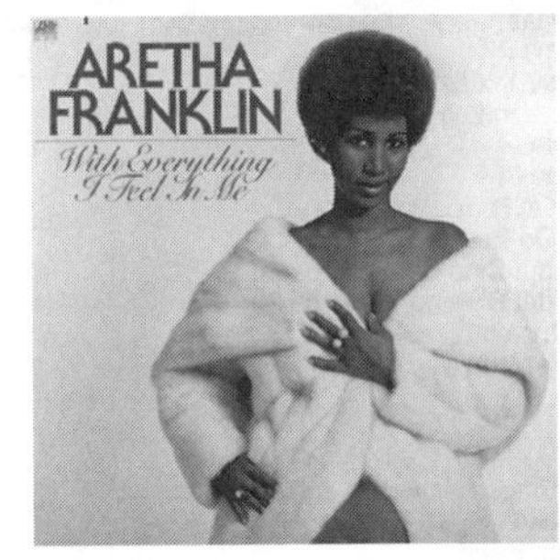

Number	Title (A Side/B Side)	Yr	VG	VG+	NM
❑ Atlantic 2619	I Can't See Myself Leaving You/Gentle On My Mind	1969	2.00	4.00	8.00
❑ Atlantic 2650	Share Your Love with Me/Pledging My Love-The Clock	1969	2.00	4.00	8.00
❑ Atlantic 2683	Eleanor Rigby/It Ain't Fair	1969	2.00	4.00	8.00
❑ Atlantic 2706	Call Me/Son of a Preacher Man	1970	2.00	4.00	8.00
❑ Atlantic 2731	Spirit in the Dark/The Thrill Is Gone	1970	2.00	4.00	8.00
❑ Atlantic 2751	Don't Play That Song/Let It Be	1970	2.00	4.00	8.00
❑ Atlantic 2772	Border Song (Holy Moses)/You and Me	1970	2.00	4.00	8.00
❑ Atlantic 2787	You're All I Need to Get By/Pullin'	1971	—	3.00	6.00
❑ Atlantic 2796	Bridge Over Troubled Water/Brand New Me	1971	—	3.00	6.00
❑ Atlantic 2817	Spanish Harlem/Lean On Me	1971	—	3.00	6.00
❑ Atlantic 2838	Rock Steady/Oh Me Oh My (I'm a Fool for You Baby)	1971	—	3.00	6.00
❑ Atlantic 2866	Day Dreaming/I've Been Loving You Too Long	1972	—	3.00	6.00
❑ Atlantic 2883	All the King's Horses/April Fools	1972	—	3.00	6.00
❑ Atlantic 2901	Wholy Holy/Give Yourself to Jesus	1972	—	3.00	6.00
❑ Atlantic 2941	Master of Eyes (The Deepness of Your Eyes)/ Moody's Mood for You	1973	—	3.00	6.00
❑ Atlantic 2969	Angel/Hey Hey Now (Sister from Texas)	1973	—	3.00	6.00
❑ Atlantic 2995	Until You Come Back to Me (That's What I'm Gonna Do)/ If You Don't Think	1973	—	3.00	6.00
❑ Atlantic 2999	I'm in Love/Oh Baby	1974	—	3.00	6.00
❑ Atlantic 3200	Ain't Nothing Like the Real Thing/Eight Days on the Road	1974	—	3.00	6.00
❑ Atlantic 3224	Without Love/Don't Go Breaking My Heart	1974	—	3.00	6.00
❑ Atlantic 3249	With Everything I Feel in Me/Sing It Again, Say It Again	1975	—	3.00	6.00
❑ Atlantic 3289	Mr. D.J. (5 for the D.J.)/As Long As You Are There	1975	—	3.00	6.00
❑ Atlantic 3311	You/Without You	1975	—	3.00	6.00
❑ Atlantic 3326	Something He Can Feel/Loving You, Baby	1976	—	3.00	6.00
❑ Atlantic 3358	Jump/Hooked on Your Love	1976	—	3.00	6.00
❑ Atlantic 3373	Look Into Your Heart/Rock with Me	1977	—	3.00	6.00
❑ Atlantic 3393	Break It To Me Gently/Meadows of Springtime	1977	—	3.00	6.00
❑ Atlantic 3418	When I Think About You/Touch Me Up	1978	—	3.00	6.00
❑ Atlantic 3468	Almighty Fire (Woman of the Future)/I'm Your Speed	1978	—	3.00	6.00
❑ Atlantic 3495	More Than Just a Joy/This You Can Believe	1979	—	3.00	6.00
❑ Atlantic 3605	Ladies Only/What If I Should Ever Need You	1979	—	2.50	5.00
❑ Atlantic 3632	Half a Love/Only Star	1979	—	2.50	5.00
❑ Checker 861	Never Grow Old/You Grow Closer	1957	5.00	10.00	20.00
❑ Checker 941	Precious Lord, Part 1/Precious Lord, Part 2	1960	3.75	7.50	15.00
❑ Columbia 41793	Today I Sing the Blues/Love Is the Only Thing	1960	3.00	6.00	12.00
❑ Columbia 41923	Won't Be Long/Right Now	1961	3.00	6.00	12.00
❑ Columbia 41965	Are You Sure/Maybe I'm a Fool	1961	3.00	6.00	12.00
❑ Columbia 42157	Rock-A-Bye Your Baby with a Dixie Melody/Operation Heartbreak	1961	3.00	6.00	12.00
❑ Columbia 42266	I Surrender, Dear/Rough Lover	1962	2.50	5.00	10.00
❑ Columbia 42456	Don't Cry, Baby/Without the One You Love	1962	2.50	5.00	10.00
❑ Columbia 42520	Try a Little Tenderness/Just for a Thrill	1962	2.50	5.00	10.00
❑ Columbia 42625	Trouble in Mind/God Bless the Child	1962	2.50	5.00	10.00
❑ Columbia 42796	Here's Where I Came In/Say It Isn't So	1963	2.50	5.00	10.00
❑ Columbia 42874	Skylark/You've Got Her	1963	2.50	5.00	10.00
❑ Columbia 42933	Johnny/Kissin' by the Mistletoe	1963	2.50	5.00	10.00
❑ Columbia 43009	Soulville/Evil Gal Blues	1964	2.50	5.00	10.00
❑ Columbia 43113	Runnin' Out of Fools/It's Just a Matter of Time	1964	2.50	5.00	10.00
❑ Columbia 43177	Winter Wonderland/The Christmas Song (Chestnuts Roasting on an Open Fire)	1964	2.50	5.00	10.00
❑ Columbia 43203	Can't You Just See Me/Little Miss Raggedy Ann	1965	2.50	5.00	10.00
❑ Columbia 43241	One Step Ahead/I Can't Wait Until I See My Baby's Face	1965	2.50	5.00	10.00
❑ Columbia 43333	(No, No) I'm Losing You/Sweet Bitter Love	1965	2.50	5.00	10.00
❑ Columbia 43442	You Made Me Love You/There Is No Greater Love	1966	2.50	5.00	10.00
❑ Columbia 43515	Hands Off/Tighten Up Your Tie, Button Up Your Jacket	1966	2.50	5.00	10.00
❑ Columbia 43637	Until You Were Gone/Swanee	1966	2.50	5.00	10.00
❑ Columbia 43827	Cry Like a Baby/Swanee	1966	2.50	5.00	10.00
❑ Columbia 44181	Until You Were Gone/Lee Cross	1967	2.50	5.00	10.00
❑ Columbia 44270	Take a Look/Follow Your Heart	1967	2.50	5.00	10.00
❑ Columbia 44381	Mockingbird/A Mother's Love	1967	2.00	4.00	8.00
❑ Columbia 44441	Soulville/If Ever I Would Leave You	1968	2.00	4.00	8.00
❑ Columbia 44851	Friendly Persuasion/Jim	1969	2.00	4.00	8.00
❑ Columbia 44951	Today I Sing the Blues/People	1969	2.00	4.00	8.00
❑ JVB 47	Never Grow Old/You Grow Closer	1957	7.50	15.00	30.00
❑ JVB 75	Precious Lord, Part 1/Precious Lord, Part 2	1959	7.50	15.00	30.00

Number	Title (A Side/B Side)	Yr	VG	VG+	NM
Albums					
❑ Arista AL8-8019	Get It Right	1983	2.50	5.00	10.00
❑ Arista AL8-8286	Who's Zoomin' Who	1985	2.50	5.00	10.00
❑ Arista AL-8344	Jump To It	1985	2.00	4.00	8.00
—Budget-line reissue					
❑ Arista AL-8368	Love All the Hurt Away	1985	2.00	4.00	8.00
—Budget-line reissue					
❑ Arista AL-8442	Aretha	1986	2.50	5.00	10.00
—Different album than 9538					
❑ Arista A2L-8497 [(2)]	One Lord, One Faith, One Baptism	1987	5.00	10.00	20.00
❑ Arista AL-8572	Through the Storm	1989	2.50	5.00	10.00
❑ Arista AL-9538	Aretha	1980	2.50	5.00	10.00
❑ Arista AL-9552	Love All the Hurt Away	1981	2.50	5.00	10.00
❑ Arista AL-9602	Jump To It	1982	2.50	5.00	10.00
❑ Atlantic SD 2-906 [(2)]	Amazing Grace	1972	5.00	10.00	20.00
❑ Atlantic SD 7205 [S]	Aretha Live at Fillmore West	1971	3.75	7.50	15.00
❑ Atlantic SD 7213 [S]	Yoing, Gifted & Black	1972	3.75	7.50	15.00
❑ Atlantic SD 7265	Hey Now Hey (The Other Side of the Sky)	1973	3.00	6.00	12.00
❑ Atlantic SD 7292	Let Me in Your Life	1974	3.00	6.00	12.00
❑ Atlantic 8139 [M]	I Never Loved a Man the Way I Love You	1967	6.25	12.50	25.00
❑ Atlantic SD 8139 [S]	I Never Loved a Man the Way I Love You	1967	5.00	10.00	20.00
—Green and blue label					
❑ Atlantic 8150 [M]	Aretha Arrives	1967	6.25	12.50	25.00
❑ Atlantic SD 8150 [S]	Aretha Arrives	1967	5.00	10.00	20.00
—Green and blue label					
❑ Atlantic 8176 [M]	Aretha: Lady Soul	1968	7.50	15.00	30.00
❑ Atlantic SD 8176 [S]	Aretha: Lady Soul	1968	5.00	10.00	20.00
—Green and blue label					
❑ Atlantic SD 8186	Aretha Now	1968	5.00	10.00	20.00
—Green and blue label					
❑ Atlantic SD 8207	Aretha in Paris	1968	3.75	7.50	15.00
❑ Atlantic SD 8212 [S]	Aretha Franklin: Soul '69	1969	3.75	7.50	15.00
❑ Atlantic SD 8227	Aretha's Gold	1969	3.75	7.50	15.00
❑ Atlantic 8248 [M]	This Girl's in Love with You	1970	10.00	20.00	40.00
—Mono is white label promo only; cover has "d/j copy monaural" sticker on front					
❑ Atlantic SD 8248 [S]	This Girl's in Love with You	1970	3.75	7.50	15.00
❑ Atlantic SD 8265 [S]	Spirit in the Dark	1970	3.75	7.50	15.00
❑ Atlantic SD 8295 [S]	Aretha's Greatest Hits	1971	3.75	7.50	15.00
❑ Atlantic SD 18116	With Everything I Feel in Me	1974	3.00	6.00	12.00
❑ Atlantic SD 18151	You	1975	3.00	6.00	12.00
❑ Atlantic SD 18176	Sparkle	1976	3.00	6.00	12.00
❑ Atlantic SD 18204	Ten Years of Gold	1976	3.00	6.00	12.00
❑ Atlantic SD 19102	Sweet Passion	1977	3.00	6.00	12.00
❑ Atlantic SD 19161	Almighty Fire	1978	3.00	6.00	12.00
❑ Atlantic SD 19248	La Diva	1979	3.00	6.00	12.00
❑ Atlantic 81230	Aretha's Jazz	1984	2.50	5.00	10.00
❑ Atlantic 81280	The Best of Aretha Franklin	1985	2.50	5.00	10.00
❑ Atlantic 81668 [(2)]	30 Greatest Hits	1986	3.75	7.50	15.00
❑ Checker 10009 [M]	Songs of Faith	1965	125.00	250.00	500.00
—Original issue of this album; cover has Aretha sitting at a piano					
❑ Checker 10009 [M]	Gospel Soul	1967	5.00	10.00	20.00
—Reissue with new title and cover					
❑ Columbia GP 4 [(2)]	Two All-Time Great Albums in One Great Package	196?	6.25	12.50	25.00
—Contains CS 9081 and CS 9429					
❑ Columbia CL 1612 [M]	Aretha	1961	12.50	25.00	50.00
—Red and black label with six "eye" logos					
❑ Columbia CL 1761 [M]	The Electrifying Aretha Franklin	1962	10.00	20.00	40.00
—Red and black label with six "eye" logos					
❑ Columbia CL 1876 [M]	The Tender, The Moving, The Swinging Aretha Franklin	1962	10.00	20.00	40.00
—Red and black label with six "eye" logos					
❑ Columbia CL 2079 [M]	Laughing on the Outside	1963	5.00	10.00	20.00
—"Guaranteed High Fidelity" on label					
❑ Columbia CL 2163 [M]	Unforgettable	1964	5.00	10.00	20.00
—"Guaranteed High Fidelity" on label					
❑ Columbia CL 2281 [M]	Runnin' Out of Fools	1964	5.00	10.00	20.00
—"Guaranteed High Fidelity" on label					
❑ Columbia CL 2351 [M]	Yeah!!!	1965	5.00	10.00	20.00
—"Guaranteed High Fidelity" on label					
❑ Columbia CL 2521 [M]	Soul Sister	1966	5.00	10.00	20.00
❑ Columbia CL 2629 [M]	Take It Like You Give It	1967	6.25	12.50	25.00
❑ Columbia CL 2673 [M]	Aretha Franklin's Greatest Hits	1967	6.25	12.50	25.00
❑ Columbia CL 2754 [M]	Take a Look	1967	7.50	15.00	30.00
❑ Columbia CS 8412 [S]	Aretha	1961	20.00	40.00	80.00
—Red and black label with six "eye" logos					
❑ Columbia CS 8561 [S]	The Electrifying Aretha Franklin	1962	12.50	25.00	50.00
—Red and black label with six "eye" logos					
❑ Columbia CS 8676 [S]	The Tender, The Moving, The Swinging Aretha Franklin	1962	12.50	25.00	50.00
—Red and black label with six "eye" logos					
❑ Columbia CS 8879 [S]	Laughing on the Outside	1963	6.25	12.50	25.00
—"360 Sound Stereo" on label					
❑ Columbia CS 8963 [S]	Unforgettable	1964	6.25	12.50	25.00
—"360 Sound Stereo" on label					
❑ Columbia CS 9081 [S]	Runnin' Out of Fools	1964	6.25	12.50	25.00
—"360 Sound Stereo" on label					
❑ Columbia CS 9151 [S]	Yeah!!!	1965	6.25	12.50	25.00
—"360 Sound Stereo" on label					

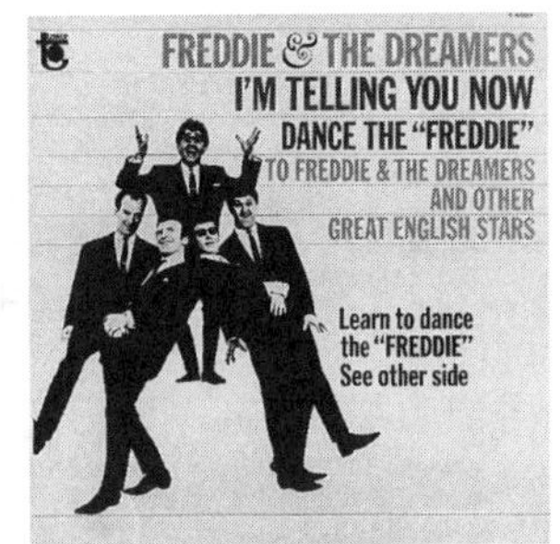

Number	Title (A Side/B Side)	Yr	VG	VG+	NM
❑ Columbia CS 9321 [S]	Soul Sister	1966	6.25	12.50	25.00
—"360 Sound Stereo" on label					
❑ Columbia CS 9429 [S]	Take It Like You Give It	1967	5.00	10.00	20.00
—"360 Sound Stereo" on label					
❑ Columbia CS 9473 [S]	Aretha Franklin's Greatest Hits	1967	5.00	10.00	20.00
—"360 Sound Stereo" on label					
❑ Columbia CS 9554 [S]	Take a Look	1967	5.00	10.00	20.00
—"360 Sound Stereo" on label					
❑ Columbia CS 9601	Aretha Franklin's Greatest Hits, Volume 2	1968	5.00	10.00	20.00
—"360 Sound Stereo" on label					
❑ Columbia CS 9776	Soft and Beautiful	1969	5.00	10.00	20.00
—"360 Sound Stereo" on label					
❑ Columbia CS 9956	Today I Sing the Blues	1970	3.75	7.50	15.00
—"360 Sound Stereo" on label					
❑ Columbia KG 31355 [(2)]	In the Beginning/The World of Aretha Franklin 1960-1967	1972	5.00	10.00	20.00
❑ Columbia KC 31953	The First 12 Sides	1973	3.00	6.00	12.00
❑ Columbia C2 37377 [(2)]	The Legendary Queen of Soul	1981	3.00	6.00	12.00
❑ Columbia PC 38042	Sweet Bitter Love	1982	2.50	5.00	10.00
❑ Columbia FC 40105	Aretha Franklin Sings the Blues	1985	2.50	5.00	10.00
❑ Columbia FC 40708	Aretha After Hours	1987	2.50	5.00	10.00
❑ 4 Men With Beards 4M 101	I Never Loved a Man the Way I Love You	2001	3.75	7.50	15.00
—Reissue on 180-gram vinyl					
❑ 4 Men With Beards 4M 111	Soul '69	2002	3.75	7.50	15.00
—Reissue on 180-gram vinyl					
❑ 4 Men With Beards 4M 114	Spirit in the Dark	2003	3.75	7.50	15.00
—Reissue on 180-gram vinyl					
❑ 4 Men With Beards 4M 115	Aretha Live at Fillmore West	2003	3.75	7.50	15.00
—Reissue on 180-gram vinyl					
❑ 4 Men With Beards 4M 130	Lady Soul	2006	3.75	7.50	15.00
—Reissue on 180-gram vinyl					
❑ 4 Men With Beards 4M 131	Aretha Now	2006	3.75	7.50	15.00
—Reissue on 180-gram vinyl					
❑ Harmony HS 11349	Once in a Lifetime	1969	3.00	6.00	12.00
❑ Harmony HS 11418	Two Sides of Love	1970	3.00	6.00	12.00
❑ Harmony KH 30606	Greatest Hits 1960-1965	1971	3.00	6.00	12.00
❑ Harmony KH 30606	Greatest Hits 1960-1966	1972	3.00	6.00	12.00

FRED, JOHN, AND HIS PLAYBOY BAND

45s

Number	Title (A Side/B Side)	Yr	VG	VG+	NM
❑ Bell 45382	I'm in Love Again/In the Mood	1973	—	2.50	5.00
—As "John Fred and the Creepers"					
❑ Jewel 730	The Fool/There'll Be No Teardrops Tonight	1964	2.50	5.00	10.00
❑ Jewel 736	Lenne/You're Mad at Me	1964	2.50	5.00	10.00
❑ Jewel 737	Boogie Children/My First Love	1964	2.50	5.00	10.00
—As "The Playboys"					
❑ Jewel 743	Wrong to Me/How Can I Prove	1965	2.50	5.00	10.00
❑ Montel 904	Down in New Orleans/I Love You	1959	3.75	7.50	15.00
❑ Montel 1002	Shirley/My Love for You	1959	3.75	7.50	15.00
❑ Montel 1007	Good Lovin'/You Know You Made Me Cry	1961	2.50	5.00	10.00
❑ Montel 2001	Mirror Mirror (On the Wall)/To Have and to Hold	1962	2.50	5.00	10.00
❑ N-Joy 1005	Boogie Children/My First Love	1965	2.50	5.00	10.00
❑ Paula 225	Fortune Teller/Making Love to You	1965	2.00	4.00	8.00
❑ Paula 234	Can't I Get a Word In/Sun City	1966	2.00	4.00	8.00
❑ Paula 244	Doin' the Best I Can/Leave Her Never	1966	2.00	4.00	8.00
❑ Paula 247	Outta My Head/Love Comes in Time	1966	2.00	4.00	8.00
❑ Paula 259	Up and Down/Wind-Up Doll	1967	2.00	4.00	8.00
❑ Paula 273	Agnes English/Sad Story	1967	2.00	4.00	8.00
❑ Paula 282	Judy in Disguise (With Glasses)/When the Lights Go Out	1967	2.00	4.00	8.00
—Pink label					
❑ Paula 294	Hey Hey Bunny/No Letter Today	1968	2.00	4.00	8.00
❑ Paula 303	Lonely Are the Lonely/We Played Games	1968	2.00	4.00	8.00
❑ Paula 310	Tissue Paper/Little Dum Dum	1968	2.00	4.00	8.00
❑ Paula 315	What Is Happiness/Sometimes You Just Can't Win	1968	2.00	4.00	8.00
❑ Sugarcane 1001	Keep It Hid/You Had to Be a Woman	1975	—	2.00	4.00
❑ Sugarcane 1002	Jukebox Shirley/Hey, Good Lookin'	1975	—	2.00	4.00
❑ Uni 55135	Back in the U.S.S.R./Silly Sarah Carter	1969	—	3.00	6.00
❑ Uni 55160	Open Doors/Three Deep Is a Feeling	1969	—	3.00	6.00

Number	Title (A Side/B Side)	Yr	VG	VG+	NM
❑ Uni 55187	Love My Soul/Julia Julia	1969	—	3.00	6.00
❑ Uni 55220	Come with Me/Where's Everybody Going	1970	—	3.00	6.00
Albums					
❑ Jin 9027	The Best of John Fred and His Playboys	198?	2.50	5.00	10.00
❑ Paula LP-2191 [M]	John Fred and His Playboys	1966	5.00	10.00	20.00
❑ Paula LPS-2191 [S]	John Fred and His Playboys	1966	6.25	12.50	25.00
❑ Paula LP-2193 [M]	34:40 of John Fred and His Playboys	1967	5.00	10.00	20.00
❑ Paula LPS-2193 [S]	34:40 of John Fred and His Playboys	1967	6.25	12.50	25.00
❑ Paula LP-2197 [M]	Agnes English	1967	6.25	12.50	25.00
❑ Paula LPS-2197 [S]	Agnes English	1967	5.00	10.00	20.00
❑ Paula LPS-2197 [S]	Judy in Disguise with Glasses	1968	5.00	10.00	20.00
—Retitled version of "Agnes English"					
❑ Paula LPS-2201	Permanently Stated	1969	5.00	10.00	20.00
❑ Uni 73077	Love in My Soul	1970	10.00	20.00	40.00

FREDDIE AND THE DREAMERS

45s

Number	Title (A Side/B Side)	Yr	VG	VG+	NM
❑ Capitol 5053	I'm Telling You Now/What Have I Done to You	1963	5.00	10.00	20.00
❑ Capitol 5137	You Were Made for Me/Send a Letter to Me	1964	5.00	10.00	20.00
❑ Mercury 72285	I Love You Baby/Don't Make Me Cry	1965	2.50	5.00	10.00
❑ Mercury 72327	Don't Do That to Me/Just for You	1965	2.50	5.00	10.00
❑ Mercury 72377	I Understand (Just How You Feel)/I Will	1965	2.50	5.00	10.00
❑ Mercury 72428	Do the Freddie/Tell Me When	1965	2.50	5.00	10.00
❑ Mercury 72428	Do the Freddie/A Love Like You	1965	3.00	6.00	12.00
❑ Mercury 72462	A Little You/Things I'd Like to Say	1965	2.50	5.00	10.00
❑ Mercury 72487	I Don't Know/Windmill in Old Amsterdam	1965	2.50	5.00	10.00
❑ Mercury 72548	When I'm Home with You/If You Got a Minute Baby	1966	2.50	5.00	10.00
❑ Mercury 72604	Some Day/Short Shorts	1966	2.50	5.00	10.00
❑ Super K 146	She Needs Me/Susan's Tuba	1970	2.00	4.00	8.00
❑ Tower 125	I'm Telling You Now/What Have I Done to You	1964	3.75	7.50	15.00
❑ Tower 127	You Were Made for Me/So Fine	1965	3.75	7.50	15.00
—B-side: "Introducing the Beat Merchants"					
❑ Tower 127	You Were Made for Me/Send a Letter to Me	1965	5.00	10.00	20.00
❑ Tower 163	Send a Letter to Me/There's Not One Thing	1965	3.75	7.50	15.00
—B-side by 4 Just Men					
Albums					
❑ Capitol SM-11896 [B]	The Best of Freddie and the Dreamers	1976	2.50	5.00	10.00
—"I'm Telling You Now," "You Were Made for Me," "I Just Don't Understand," "A Little You" and "Over You" are in stereo, the rest are mono.					
❑ Mercury MG-21017 [M]	Freddie and the Dreamers	1965	6.25	12.50	25.00
❑ Mercury MG-21026 [M]	Do the Freddie	1965	5.00	10.00	20.00
❑ Mercury MG-21031 [M]	Seaside Swingers	1965	5.00	10.00	20.00
❑ Mercury MG-21053 [M]	Frantic Freddie	1965	3.75	7.50	15.00
❑ Mercury MG-21061 [M]	Fun Lovin' Freddie	1966	3.75	7.50	15.00
❑ Mercury SR-61017 [R]	Freddie and the Dreamers	1965	5.00	10.00	20.00
❑ Mercury SR-61026 [S]	Do the Freddie	1965	6.25	12.50	25.00
❑ Mercury SR-61031 [S]	Seaside Swingers	1965	6.25	12.50	25.00
❑ Mercury SR-61053 [S]	Frantic Freddie	1965	5.00	10.00	20.00
❑ Mercury SR-61061 [S]	Fun Lovin' Freddie	1966	5.00	10.00	20.00
❑ Tower DT 5003 [R]	I'm Telling You Now	1965	5.00	10.00	20.00
—Contains only two Freddie and the Dreamers songs, but the group's picture is on the cover. Also includes Four Just Men (2), Heinz (2), Linda Laine and the Sinners (2), Mike Rabin and the Demons (2) and The Toggery Five (2)					
❑ Tower T 5003 [M]	I'm Telling You Now	1965	6.25	12.50	25.00
—Contains only two Freddie and the Dreamers songs, but the group's picture is on the cover. Also includes Four Just Men (2), Heinz (2), Linda Laine and the Sinners (2), Mike Rabin and the Demons (2) and The Toggery Five (2)					

FREE

45s

Number	Title (A Side/B Side)	Yr	VG	VG+	NM
❑ A&M 1099	I'm a Mover/Worry	1969	—	2.00	4.00
❑ A&M 1172	I'll Be Creepin'/Mouthful of Grass	1970	—	2.00	4.00
❑ A&M 1206	All Right Now/Mouthful of Grass	1970	—	2.50	5.00
❑ A&M 1230	Stealer/Broad Daylight	1970	—	2.00	4.00
❑ A&M 1248	Highway Song/Love You So	1971	—	2.00	4.00
❑ A&M 1266	Mr. Big/I'll Be Creepin'	1971	—	2.00	4.00
❑ A&M 1276	My Brother Jake/Only My Soul	1971	—	2.00	4.00
❑ A&M 1352	Little Bit of Love/Sail On	1972	—	2.00	4.00
❑ A&M 1720	All Right Now/Stealer	1975	—	2.00	4.00
❑ Island 1212	Wishing Well/Let Me Show You	1972	—	2.00	4.00
Albums					
❑ A&M SP-3126	Fire and Water	198?	2.00	4.00	8.00
—Budget-line reissue					
❑ A&M SP-3663	Best of Free	1975	3.00	6.00	12.00
❑ A&M SP-4198	Tons of Sobs	1969	3.75	7.50	15.00
❑ A&M SP-4204	Free	1969	3.75	7.50	15.00
❑ A&M SP-4268	Fire and Water	1970	3.75	7.50	15.00
❑ A&M SP-4287	Highway	1971	3.75	7.50	15.00
❑ A&M SP-4306	Free Live!	1971	3.75	7.50	15.00
❑ A&M SP-4349	Free at Last	1972	3.75	7.50	15.00
❑ Island ILSD 4 [(2)]	The Free Story	1975	3.75	7.50	15.00
❑ Island ILPS 9217	Heartbreaker	1975	2.50	5.00	10.00
—U.S. reissue with same number as original U.K. issue					
❑ Island SW-9324	Heartbreaker	1973	3.00	6.00	12.00
—Original U.S. number, distributed by Capitol					
❑ Pickwick SPC-3706	Free at Last	197?	2.50	5.00	10.00

FREEMAN, BOBBY

45s

Number	Title (A Side/B Side)	Yr	VG	VG+	NM
❑ Autumn 1	Come to Me/Let's Surf Again	1964	5.00	10.00	20.00

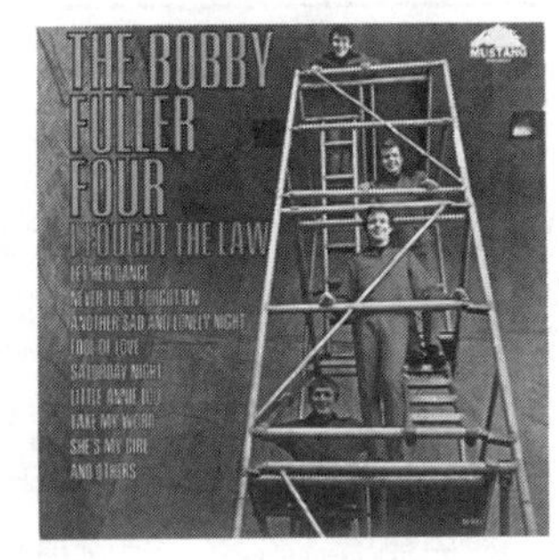

Number	Title (A Side/B Side)	Yr	VG	VG+	NM
❑ Autumn 2	C'mon and Swim/C'mon and Swim — Part 2	1964	3.00	6.00	12.00
—White label, red print					
❑ Autumn 5	S-W-I-M/That Little Old Heartbreaker	1964	2.50	5.00	10.00
❑ Autumn 9	I'll Never Fall in Love Again/Friends	1965	2.50	5.00	10.00
❑ Autumn 25	Cross My Heart/The Duck	1965	2.50	5.00	10.00
❑ Double Shot 139	There Oughta Be a Law/Everybody's Got a Hang-Up	1969	—	3.00	6.00
❑ Double Shot 144	Susie Sunshine/Four Piece Funky Nitty Gritty Junky Band	1969	—	3.00	6.00
❑ Double Shot 148	Can You Stand the Pressure/ Put Another Dime in the Parking Meter	1970	—	3.00	6.00
❑ Double Shot 152	Do You Wanna Dance 1970/ Society for the Prevention of Cruelty to People	1970	—	3.00	6.00
❑ Josie 835	Do You Want to Dance/Big Fat Woman	1958	5.00	10.00	20.00
❑ Josie 841	Betty Lou Got a New Pair of Shoes/Starlight	1958	5.00	10.00	20.00
❑ Josie 844	Need Your Love/Shame On You, Miss Johnson	1958	3.75	7.50	15.00
❑ Josie 855	A Love to Last a Lifetime/When You're Smiling	1959	3.75	7.50	15.00
❑ Josie 863	Love Me/Mary Ann Thomas	1959	3.75	7.50	15.00
❑ Josie 867	My Guardian Angel/Where Did My Baby Go	1959	3.75	7.50	15.00
❑ Josie 872	Ebb Tide/Sinbad	1959	3.75	7.50	15.00
❑ Josie 879	I Need Someone/First Day of Spring	1960	3.00	6.00	12.00
❑ Josie 886	Miss You So/Baby What Would You Do	1961	3.00	6.00	12.00
❑ Josie 887	The Mess Around/So Much to Do	1961	3.00	6.00	12.00
❑ Josie 889	Put You Down/She Said She Wants to Dance	1961	3.00	6.00	12.00
❑ Josie 896	Love Me/Little Girl Don't You Understand	1962	3.00	6.00	12.00
❑ Josie 928	The Mess Around/Little Girl Don't You Understand	1965	2.50	5.00	10.00
❑ King 5373	(I Do the) Shimmy Shimmy/You Don't Understand Me	1960	3.00	6.00	12.00
❑ King 5953	Fever/What Can I Do	1964	2.50	5.00	10.00
❑ King 5962	Somebody, Somewhere/Be My Little Chick-A-Dee	1964	2.50	5.00	10.00
❑ King 5975	Come to Me/There's Gonna Be a Change	1965	2.50	5.00	10.00
❑ Loma 2056	Shadow of Your Love/Soulful Sound of Music	1966	2.00	4.00	8.00
❑ Loma 2080	I Got a Good Thing/Lies	1967	2.00	4.00	8.00
❑ Parkway 875	She's a Hippy/Whip It Up Baby	1963	3.00	6.00	12.00
❑ Rhino 4508	S-W-I-M/C'mon and Swim	198?	—	2.00	4.00
Albums					
❑ Autumn LP 102 [M]	C'mon and S-W-I-M	1964	12.50	25.00	50.00
❑ Josie JM-4007 [M]	Get In the Swim with Bobby Freeman	1965	7.50	15.00	30.00
❑ Josie JS-4007 [R]	Get In the Swim with Bobby Freeman	1965	6.25	12.50	25.00
❑ Jubilee JLP-1086 [M]	Do You Wanna Dance?	1959	35.00	70.00	140.00
❑ Jubilee JLPS-1086 [S]	Do You Wanna Dance?	1959	50.00	100.00	200.00
❑ Jubilee JGM-5010 [M]	Twist with Bobby Freeman	1962	25.00	50.00	100.00
❑ King 930 [M]	The Lovable Style of Bobby Freeman	1965	62.50	125.00	250.00
FREY, GLENN					
45s					
❑ Asylum 47466	I Found Somebody/She Can't Let Go	1982	—	2.00	4.00
❑ Asylum 69857	All Those Lies/That Girl	1982	—	2.00	4.00
❑ Asylum 69974	The One You Love/All Those Lies	1982	—	2.00	4.00
❑ MCA 52413	Sexy Girl/Better in the U.S.A.	1984	—	—	3.00
❑ MCA 52461	The Allnighter/Smuggler's Blues	1984	—	—	3.00
❑ MCA 52512	The Heat Is On/Shoot Out	1984	—	—	3.00
❑ MCA 52546	Smuggler's Blues/New Love	1985	—	—	3.00
❑ MCA 52651	You Belong to the City/Smuggler's Blues	1985	—	—	3.00
❑ MCA 53363	True Love/Working Man	1988	—	—	3.00
❑ MCA 53452	Soul Searchin'/It's Cold in Here	1988	—	—	3.00
❑ MCA 53497	Livin' Right/Soul Searchin'	1989	—	—	3.00
❑ MCA 53684	Two Hearts/Some Kind of Blue	1989	—	—	3.00
❑ MCA 54461	River of Dreams/He Took Advantage (Blues for Ronald Reagan)	1992	—	—	3.00
Albums					
❑ Asylum E1-60129	No Fun Aloud	1982	2.50	5.00	10.00
❑ MCA 5501	The Allnighter	1984	2.50	5.00	10.00
❑ MCA 6239	Soul Searchin'	1988	2.50	5.00	10.00
FRIENDS OF DISTINCTION, THE					
45s					
❑ RCA Victor 74-0107	Grazing in the Grass/I Really Hope You Do	1969	—	3.00	6.00
❑ RCA Victor 74-0204	Going in Circles/Let Yourself Go	1969	—	3.00	6.00
❑ RCA Victor 74-0319	Love Or Let Me Be Lonely/This Generation	1970	—	3.00	6.00
❑ RCA Victor 74-0385	Time Waits for No One/Mother Nature	1970	—	2.50	5.00

Number	Title (A Side/B Side)	Yr	VG	VG+	NM
❑ RCA Victor 74-0416	Check It Out/I Need You	1971	—	2.50	5.00
❑ RCA Victor 74-0516	It Don't Matter to Me/Down I Go	1971	—	2.50	5.00
❑ RCA Victor 74-0562	Let Me Be/Long Time Comin' My Way	1971	—	2.50	5.00
❑ RCA Victor 74-0679	Love Is the Way of Life/Jenny Wants to Know	1972	—	2.50	5.00
❑ RCA Victor 74-0787	Now Is the Time/Thumb Tripping	1972	—	2.50	5.00
❑ RCA Victor 74-0888	Ain't No Woman (Like the One I've Got)/Easy Evil	1973	—	2.50	5.00
❑ RCA Victor 74-0956	Check It Out/Love Can Make It Easier	1973	—	2.50	5.00
❑ RCA Victor PB-10197	Honey Baby Theme Part 1/Honey Baby Theme Part 2	1975	—	2.00	4.00
❑ RCA Victor PB-10220	Love Shack Part 1/Love Shack Part 2	1975	—	2.00	4.00
Albums					
❑ RCA Victor APD1-0276 [Q]	Greatest Hits	1973	5.00	10.00	20.00
❑ RCA Victor LSP-4149	Grazin'	1969	3.75	7.50	15.00
❑ RCA Victor LSP-4212	Highly Distinct	1969	3.75	7.50	15.00
❑ RCA Victor LSP-4313	Real Friends	1970	3.75	7.50	15.00
❑ RCA Victor LSP-4408	Whatever	1970	3.75	7.50	15.00
❑ RCA Victor LSP-4492	Friends & People	1971	3.75	7.50	15.00
❑ RCA Victor LSP-4819	Greatest Hits	1972	3.00	6.00	12.00
❑ RCA Victor LSP-4829	Love Can Make It Easier	1973	3.00	6.00	12.00

FRIJID PINK

45s

Number	Title (A Side/B Side)	Yr	VG	VG+	NM
❑ Lion 115	Earth Omen/Lazy Day	1972	2.00	4.00	8.00
❑ Lion 136	Go Now/Lazy Day	1972	2.00	4.00	8.00
❑ Lion 158	Big Betty/Shady Lady	1973	—	3.00	6.00
❑ Parrot 334	Tell Me Why/Cryin' Shame	1969	—	3.00	6.00
❑ Parrot 340	God Gave Me You/Drivin' Blues	1970	—	3.00	6.00
❑ Parrot 341	House of the Rising Sun/Drivin' Blues	1970	2.00	4.00	8.00
❑ Parrot 349	Sing a Song for Freedom/End of the Line	1970	—	3.00	6.00
❑ Parrot 352	Heartbreak Hotel/Bye Bye Blues	1970	—	3.00	6.00
❑ Parrot 355	Music for the People/Sloony	1971	—	3.00	6.00
❑ Parrot 358	We're Gonna Be There/Shorty Kline	1971	—	3.00	6.00
❑ Parrot 360	Lost Son/I Love Her	1971	—	3.00	6.00
Albums					
❑ Fantasy 9464	All Pink Inside	1974	3.75	7.50	15.00
❑ Lion LN-1004	Earth Omen	1972	5.00	10.00	20.00
❑ Parrot PAS 71033	Frijid Pink	1970	6.25	12.50	25.00
❑ Parrot PAS 71041	Defrosted	1970	6.25	12.50	25.00

FULLER, BOBBY, FOUR

45s

Number	Title (A Side/B Side)	Yr	VG	VG+	NM
❑ Capitol 3038	The Only God I Know/A Name Like Watermelon	1971	5.00	10.00	20.00
❑ Donna 1403	Those Memories of You/Our Favorite Martian	1965	50.00	100.00	200.00
—As "Bobby Fuller and the Fantastics"					
❑ Eastwood 345	Not Fade Away/Nervous Breakdown	1962	25.00	50.00	100.00
❑ Exeter 122	King of the Beach/Wine, Wine, Wine	1964	50.00	100.00	200.00
❑ Exeter 124	I Fought the Law/She's My Girl	1964	87.50	175.00	350.00
❑ Exeter 126	Fool of Love/Shakedown	1964	30.00	60.00	120.00
❑ Liberty 55812	Let Her Dance/Another Sad and Lonely Night	1965	7.50	15.00	30.00
❑ Lost-Nite 257	I Fought the Law/Little Annie Lou	196?	—	2.50	5.00
—Reissue					
❑ Mustang 3004	She's My Girl/Take My Hand	1965	6.25	12.50	25.00
❑ Mustang 3006	Let Her Dance/Another Sad and Lonely Night	1965	3.75	7.50	15.00
❑ Mustang 3011	Never to Be Forgotten/You Kissed Me	1965	6.25	12.50	25.00
❑ Mustang 3012	Let Her Dance/Another Sad and Lonely Night	1965	3.75	7.50	15.00
❑ Mustang 3014	I Fought the Law/Little Annie Lou	1966	3.75	7.50	15.00
❑ Mustang 3016	Love's Made a Fool of You/Don't Ever Let Me Know	1966	3.75	7.50	15.00
❑ Mustang 3018	Magic Touch/My True Love	1966	3.00	6.00	12.00
❑ Todd 1090	Saturday Night/The Stinger	1963	25.00	50.00	100.00
❑ Yucca 140	You're in Love/Guess We'll Fall in Love	1961	20.00	40.00	80.00
—Slow version					
❑ Yucca 140	You're in Love/Guess We'll Fall in Love	1961	10.00	20.00	40.00
—Fast version					
❑ Yucca 144	My Heart Jumped/Gently My Love	1961	20.00	40.00	80.00
Albums					
❑ Mustang M-900 [M]	KRLA King of the Wheels	1965	37.50	75.00	150.00
❑ Mustang MS-900 [S]	KRLA King of the Wheels	1965	50.00	100.00	200.00
❑ Mustang M-901 [M]	I Fought the Law	1966	20.00	40.00	80.00
❑ Mustang MS-901 [S]	I Fought the Law	1966	37.50	75.00	150.00
❑ Rhino RNLP-057	The Bobby Fuller Tapes, Vol. 1	1983	2.50	5.00	10.00
❑ Rhino RNDF-201	The Best of the Bobby Fuller Four	1981	3.00	6.00	12.00
❑ Rhino RNLP 70174	The Best of the Bobby Fuller Four (Golden Archive Series)	1987	2.50	5.00	10.00
❑ Voxx VXS 200028	The Bobby Fuller Tapes, Vol. 2	1984	2.50	5.00	10.00

G

GABRIEL, PETER

45s

Number	Title (A Side/B Side)	Yr	VG	VG+	NM
❑ Atco 7079	Solsbury Hill/Moribund the Burgermeister	1977	2.50	5.00	10.00
❑ Atlantic 3479	D.I.Y. (Do It Yourself)/Mother of Violence	1978	2.50	5.00	10.00
❑ Atlantic 7-89668	Walk Through the Fire/Making a Big Mistake	1984	—	2.00	4.00
❑ Geffen GGEF 0481	Shock the Monkey/Solsbury Hill (Live)	198?	—	—	3.00
—Reissue					
❑ Geffen 19136	Digging in the Dirt/Quiet Steam	1992	—	2.00	4.00
❑ Geffen 19145	Steam/Games Without Frontiers (DB Mix)	1992	—	2.00	4.00
❑ Geffen 28247	Red Rain/I Go Swimming	1987	—	—	3.00
❑ Geffen 28463	Don't Give Up/Curtains	1987	—	—	3.00
—A-side: Peter Gabriel/Kate Bush					

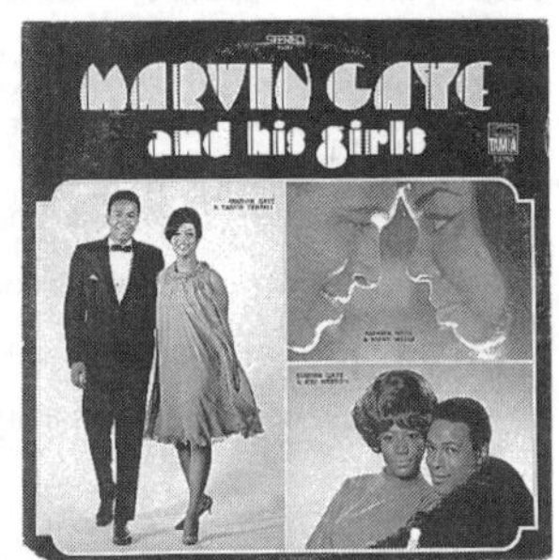

Number	Title (A Side/B Side)	Yr	VG	VG+	NM
❑ Geffen 28503	Big Time/We Do What We're Told (milgram's 37)	1986	—	—	3.00
❑ Geffen 28622	In Your Eyes/In Your Eyes (Special Mix)	1986	—	—	3.00
❑ Geffen 28718	Sledgehammer/Don't Break This Rhythm	1986	—	—	3.00
❑ Geffen 29542	Solsbury Hill (Live)/I Go Swimming	1983	—	2.50	5.00
❑ Geffen 29883	Shock the Monkey/Soft Dog	1982	—	2.50	5.00
❑ Mercury 76063	Games Without Frontiers/Lead a Normal Life	1980	—	2.00	4.00
❑ Mercury 76086	I Don't Remember/Shosholoza	1980	3.75	7.50	15.00
❑ WTG 68936	In Your Eyes/Skankin' to the Beat	1989	—	2.00	4.00
—B-side by Fishbone					
❑ WTG 68977	In Your Eyes/In Your Eyes (Live Version)	1989	—	—	3.00
Albums					
❑ Atco SD 36-147	Peter Gabriel	1977	3.75	7.50	15.00
—(The "Solsbury Hill" album) — Original pressing has yellow labels					
❑ Atlantic SD-19181	Peter Gabriel	1978	3.75	7.50	15.00
—(The "D.I.Y." album)					
❑ Geffen GHS 2011	Peter Gabriel (Security)	1982	2.50	5.00	10.00
❑ Geffen GHSP 2035	Peter Gabriel	1983	2.50	5.00	10.00
—Reissue of Mercury album					
❑ Geffen 2GHS 4012 [(2)]	Plays Live	1983	3.75	7.50	15.00
❑ Geffen GHS 24070	Birdy (Soundtrack)	1985	2.50	5.00	10.00
❑ Geffen GHS 24088	So	1986	2.50	5.00	10.00
❑ Geffen GHS 24206	Passion: Music for "The Last Temptation of Christ"	1989	3.75	7.50	15.00
❑ Mercury SRM-1-3848	Peter Gabriel	1980	3.00	6.00	12.00
—(The "Games Without Frontiers" album)					

GARFUNKEL, ART

45s

Number	Title (A Side/B Side)	Yr	VG	VG+	NM
❑ Columbia 02307	A Heart in New York/Is This Love	1981	—	2.00	4.00
❑ Columbia 02627	Bright Eyes/The Romance	1981	—	2.00	4.00
❑ Columbia 06590	Carol of the Birds/The Decree	1986	—	—	3.00
—With Amy Grant					
❑ Columbia 07711	So Much in Love/King of Tonga	1988	—	—	3.00
❑ Columbia 07949	This Is the Moment/Slow Breakup	1988	—	—	3.00
❑ Columbia 08511	When a Man Loves a Woman/I Have a Love	1988	—	—	3.00
❑ Columbia 10020	Second Avenue/Woyaya	1974	—	2.50	5.00
—As "Garfunkel"					
❑ Columbia 10190	I Only Have Eyes for You/Looking for the Right One	1975	—	2.50	5.00
❑ Columbia 10274	Breakaway/Disney Girls	1975	—	2.50	5.00
❑ Columbia 10608	Crying in My Sleep/Mr. Shuck 'N' Jive	1977	—	2.50	5.00
❑ Columbia 10676	(What a) Wonderful World/Wooden Planes	1978	—	3.00	6.00
—A-side: Art Garfunkel with Paul Simon and James Taylor					
❑ Columbia 10933	In a Little While (I'll Be On My Way)/And I Know	1979	—	2.00	4.00
❑ Columbia 10999	Since I Don't Have You/When Someone Doesn't Want You	1979	—	2.00	4.00
❑ Columbia 11050	Bright Eyes/Sail on a Rainbow	1979	—	2.00	4.00
❑ Columbia 45926	All I Know/Mary Was An Only Child	1973	—	2.50	5.00
—As "Art Garfunkel"					
❑ Columbia 45926	All I Know/Mary Was An Only Child	1973	—	2.50	5.00
—As "Garfunkel"					
❑ Columbia 45926 [DJ]	All I Know (mono/stereo)	1973	2.00	4.00	8.00
—As "Garfunkel"; mono version is about 10 seconds longer than any other version of this song (longer piano fade at the end)					
❑ Columbia 45983	I Shall Sing/Feuilles-Oh: Do Space Men Pass Dead Souls on Their Way to the Moon	1973	—	2.50	5.00
—As "Garfunkel"					
❑ Columbia 46030	Traveling Boy/Old Men	1974	—	2.50	5.00
—As "Garfunkel"					
❑ Octavia 8002	Forgive Me/Private World	1960	10.00	20.00	40.00
—As "Artie Garr"					
❑ Warwick 515	Beat Love/Dream Alone	1959	10.00	20.00	40.00
—As "Artie Garr"					
Albums					
❑ Columbia KC 31474	Angel Clare	1973	3.00	6.00	12.00
❑ Columbia PC 33700	Breakaway	1975	3.00	6.00	12.00
—Originals have no bar code					
❑ Columbia JC 34975	Watermark	1978	3.00	6.00	12.00
—Stock copy with "(What a) Wonderful World" on side 2					
❑ Columbia JC 35780	Fate for Breakfast	1979	3.00	6.00	12.00
—With six different covers, each illustrating Art Garfunkel at a different stage of eating breakfast. No difference in value.					

Number	Title (A Side/B Side)	Yr	VG	VG+	NM
❑ Columbia FC 37392	Scissors Cut	1981	2.50	5.00	10.00
❑ Columbia FC 40212	The Animals' Christmas By Jimmy Webb	1986	2.50	5.00	10.00
—With Amy Grant					
❑ Columbia FC 40942	Lefty	1988	2.00	4.00	8.00
❑ Columbia OC 45008	Garfunkel	1989	2.50	5.00	10.00

GATES, DAVID

45s

Number	Title (A Side/B Side)	Yr	VG	VG+	NM
❑ Arista 0615	Take Me Now/It's What You Say	1981	—	2.00	4.00
❑ Arista 0653	Come Home for Christmas/Lady Valentine	1981	2.00	4.00	8.00
❑ Del-Fi 4206	No One Really Loves a Clown/You Had It Comin' To Ya	1963	6.25	12.50	25.00
❑ EastWest 123	Walkin' and Talkin'/Swingin' Baby Doll	1959	37.50	75.00	150.00
❑ Elektra 45223	Never Let Her Go/Watch Out	1974	—	2.00	4.00
❑ Elektra 45245	Part-Time Love/Chain Me	1975	—	2.00	4.00
❑ Elektra 45450	Goodbye Girl/Sunday Rider	1977	—	2.00	4.00
❑ Elektra 45500	Took the Last Train/Ann	1978	—	2.00	4.00
❑ Elektra 45857	Clouds/I Use the Soap	1973	—	2.00	4.00
❑ Elektra 45868	Sail Around the World/Help Is On the Way	1973	—	2.00	4.00
❑ Elektra 46588	Where Does the Lovin' Go/Starship Ride	1980	—	2.00	4.00
❑ Elektra 46646	Can I Call You/Chingo	1980	—	2.00	4.00
❑ Elektra 47011	Falling in Love Again/Sweet Desire	1980	—	2.00	4.00
❑ Mala 413	You'll Be My Baby/What's This I Hear	1960	12.50	25.00	50.00
❑ Mala 418	The Happiest Man Alive/A Road That Leads to Love	1960	12.50	25.00	50.00
❑ Mala 427	Jo-Baby/Teardrops in My Heart	1961	12.50	25.00	50.00
❑ Manchester 101	There's a Heaven/She Don't Cry	196?	10.00	20.00	40.00
—As "Del Ashley"					
❑ Perspective (no #)	Jo-Baby/Lovin' at Night	1961	37.50	75.00	150.00
❑ Planetary 103	Little Miss Stuck-Up/The Brighter Side	1965	6.25	12.50	25.00
—As "Del Ashley"					
❑ Planetary 108	Let You Go/Once Upon a Time	1965	5.00	10.00	20.00
❑ Robbins 1008	Jo-Baby/Lovin' at Night	1961	25.00	50.00	100.00

Albums

Number	Title (A Side/B Side)	Yr	VG	VG+	NM
❑ Arista AL 9563	Take Me Now	1981	2.50	5.00	10.00
❑ Elektra 6E-148	Goodbye Girl	1978	3.00	6.00	12.00
❑ Elektra 6E-251	Falling in Love Again	1980	2.50	5.00	10.00
❑ Elektra 7E-1028	Never Let Her Go	1975	3.00	6.00	12.00
❑ Elektra EKS-75066	First	1973	3.00	6.00	12.00

GAYE, MARVIN

45s

Number	Title (A Side/B Side)	Yr	VG	VG+	NM
❑ Columbia 38-03302	Sexual Healing/(Instrumental)	1982	—	2.00	4.00
❑ Columbia CNR-03344	Sexual Healing/(B-side blank)	1982	—	3.00	6.00
—One-sided budget release					
❑ Columbia 13-03585	Sexual Healing/(Instrumental)	1983	—	—	3.00
—Reissue					
❑ Columbia 38-03589	'Til Tomorrow/Rockin' After Midnight	1983	—	2.00	4.00
❑ Columbia 38-03860	Joy/(Instrumental)	1983	—	—	—
—Canceled? (Replaced by 38-03935?)					
❑ Columbia 38-03935	Joy/Turn On Some Music	1983	—	2.00	4.00
❑ Columbia 38-04861	Sanctified Lady/(Instrumental)	1985	—	2.00	4.00
❑ Columbia 38-05442	It's Madness/Ain't It Funny (How Things Turn Around)	1985	—	2.00	4.00
❑ Columbia 38-05791	Just Like/More	1986	—	2.00	4.00
❑ Tamla 1836	The World Is Rated X/No Greater Love	1986	—	2.50	5.00
❑ Tamla 54041	Let Your Conscience Be Your Guide/Never Let You Go	1961	100.00	200.00	400.00
❑ Tamla 54055	Sandman/I'm Yours, You're Mine	1962	15.00	30.00	60.00
❑ Tamla 54062	Masquerade (Is Over)/Witchcraft	1962	—	—	—
—Unreleased					
❑ Tamla 54063	Soldier's Plea/Taking My Time	1962	10.00	20.00	40.00
—With label credit "Marvin Gaye Love Tones"					
❑ Tamla 54063	Soldier's Plea/Taking My Time	1962	12.50	25.00	50.00
—With label credit "Marvin Gaye"					
❑ Tamla 54068	Stubborn Kind of Fellow/It Hurts Me Too	1962	7.50	15.00	30.00
❑ Tamla 54075	Hitch Hike/Hello There Angel	1963	5.00	10.00	20.00
❑ Tamla 54079	Pride and Joy/One of These Days	1963	5.00	10.00	20.00
❑ Tamla 54087	Can I Get a Witness/I'm Crazy 'Bout My Baby	1963	5.00	10.00	20.00
❑ Tamla 54093	You're a Wonderful One/When I'm Alone I Cry	1964	3.75	7.50	15.00
❑ Tamla 54095	Try It Baby/If My Heart Could Sing	1964	3.75	7.50	15.00
❑ Tamla 54101	Baby Don't You Do It/Walk on the Wild Side	1964	3.75	7.50	15.00
❑ Tamla 54107	How Sweet It Is To Be Loved By You/Forever	1964	3.75	7.50	15.00
❑ Tamla 54112	I'll Be Doggone/You've Been a Long Time Coming	1965	3.75	7.50	15.00
❑ Tamla 54117	Pretty Little Baby/Now That You've Won Me	1965	3.75	7.50	15.00
❑ Tamla 54122	Ain't That Peculiar/She's Got to Be Real	1965	3.75	7.50	15.00
❑ Tamla 54129	One More Heartache/When I Had Your Love	1966	3.00	6.00	12.00
❑ Tamla 54132	Take This Heart of Mine/Need Your Lovin' (Want You Back)	1966	3.00	6.00	12.00
❑ Tamla 54138	Little Darling, I Need You/Hey Diddle Diddle	1966	3.00	6.00	12.00
❑ Tamla 54153	Your Unchanging Love/I'll Take Care of You	1967	2.50	5.00	10.00
❑ Tamla 54160	You/Change What You Can	1967	2.50	5.00	10.00
❑ Tamla 54170	Chained/At Last I Found a Love	1968	2.50	5.00	10.00
❑ Tamla 54176	I Heard It Through the Grapevine/You're What's Happening (In the World Today)	1968	2.50	5.00	10.00
❑ Tamla 54181	Too Busy Thinking About My Baby/ Wherever I Lay My Hat (That's My Home)	1969	2.00	4.00	8.00
❑ Tamla 54185	That's the Way Love Is/Gonna Keep On Tryin' Till I Win Your Love	1969	2.00	4.00	8.00
❑ Tamla 54190	Gonna Give Her All the Love I've Got/How Can I Forget You	1970	2.00	4.00	8.00
❑ Tamla 54195	The End of Our Road/Me and My Lonely Room	1970	2.00	4.00	8.00
❑ Tamla 54201	What's Going On/God Is Love	1971	—	3.00	6.00
❑ Tamla 54207	Mercy Mercy Me (The Ecology)/Sad Tomorrows	1971	—	3.00	6.00

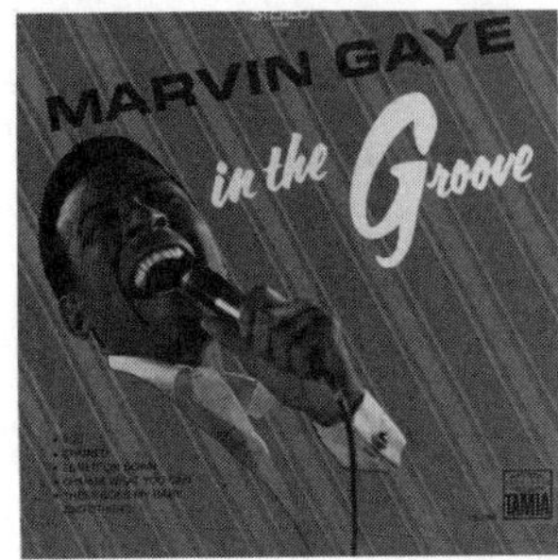

Number	Title (A Side/B Side)	Yr	VG	VG+	NM
❑ Tamla 54209	Inner City Blues (Make Me Wanna Holler)/Wholly Holy	1971	—	3.00	6.00
❑ Tamla 54221	You're the Man (Part 1)/You're the Man (Part 2)	1972	—	3.00	6.00
❑ Tamla 54228	Trouble Man/Don't Mess With Mister "T"	1972	—	3.00	6.00
❑ Tamla 54229	Christmas in the City/I Want to Come Home for Christmas	1972	—	—	—
—Canceled					
❑ Tamla 54234	Let's Get It On/I Wish It Would Rain	1973	—	2.00	4.00
❑ Tamla 54241	Come Get to This/Distant Lover	1973	—	2.00	4.00
❑ Tamla 54244	You Sure Love to Ball/Just to Keep You Satisfied	1974	—	2.00	4.00
❑ Tamla 54253	Distant Lover/Trouble Man	1974	—	2.00	4.00
❑ Tamla 54264	I Want You/I Want You (Instrumental)	1975	—	2.00	4.00
❑ Tamla 54273	After the Dance/Feel All My Love Inside	1976	—	2.00	4.00
❑ Tamla 54280	Got to Give It Up — Pt. 1/Got to Give It Up — Pt. 2	1977	—	2.00	4.00
❑ Tamla 54298	Funky Space Reincarnation — Pt. 1/ Funky Space Reincarnation — Pt. 2	1979	—	2.00	4.00
❑ Tamla 54300	Time to Get It Together/Anger	1979	2.50	5.00	10.00
—Only released in Canada					
❑ Tamla 54305	Ego Tripping Out/(Instrumental)	1979	—	2.00	4.00
❑ Tamla 54322	Funk Me/Praise	1981	—	2.00	4.00
❑ Tamla 54326	Heavy Love Affair/Far Cry	1981	—	2.00	4.00
Albums					
❑ Columbia FC 38197	Midnight Love	1982	2.50	5.00	10.00
❑ Columbia FC 39916	Dream of a Lifetime	1985	2.50	5.00	10.00
❑ Columbia FC 40208	Romantically Yours	1986	2.50	5.00	10.00
❑ Motown M5-115V1	Motown Superstar Series, Vol. 15	1981	2.50	5.00	10.00
❑ Motown M5-125V1	M.P.G.	1981	2.50	5.00	10.00
—Reissue of Tamla 292					
❑ Motown M5-181V1	Marvin Gaye Live!	1981	2.50	5.00	10.00
—Reissue of Tamla 333					
❑ Motown M5-191V1	Marvin Gaye's Greatest Hits	1981	2.50	5.00	10.00
—Reissue of Tamla 348					
❑ Motown M5-192V1	Let's Get It On	1981	2.50	5.00	10.00
—Reissue of Tamla 329					
❑ Motown M5-216V1	A Tribute to the Great Nat King Cole	1981	2.50	5.00	10.00
—Reissue of Tamla 261					
❑ Motown M5-218V1	That Stubborn Kinda' Fellow	1981	2.50	5.00	10.00
—Reissue of Tamla 239					
❑ Motown M9-791A3 [(3)]	Anthology	1974	5.00	10.00	20.00
❑ Motown 5259 ML [(2)]	Marvin Gaye Live at the London Palladium	1983	3.00	6.00	12.00
—Reissue of Tamla 352					
❑ Motown 5306 ML	Super Hits	198?	2.50	5.00	10.00
❑ Motown 5339 ML	What's Going On	198?	2.50	5.00	10.00
—Reissue of Tamla 322					
❑ Motown 6058 ML	Every Great Motown Hit of Marvin Gaye	1983	2.50	5.00	10.00
❑ Motown 6255 ML [(2)]	A Musical Testament 1964-1984	1988	3.00	6.00	12.00
❑ Natural Resources NR 4007T1	The Soulful Moods of Marvin Gaye	1978	3.00	6.00	12.00
—Reissue of Tamla 221					
❑ Tamla TM 221 [M]	The Soulful Moods of Marvin Gaye	1961	250.00	500.00	1000.
❑ Tamla T 239 [M]	That Stubborn Kinda' Fella	1963	150.00	300.00	600.00
❑ Tamla T 242 [M]	Recorded Live — Marvin Gaye on Stage	1963	75.00	150.00	300.00
❑ Tamla T 251 [M]	When I'm Alone I Cry	1964	62.50	125.00	250.00
❑ Tamla T 252 [M]	Marvin Gaye/Greatest Hits	1964	7.50	15.00	30.00
❑ Tamla TS 252 [S]	Marvin Gaye/Greatest Hits	1964	10.00	20.00	40.00
❑ Tamla T 258 [M]	How Sweet It Is to Be Loved by You	1965	10.00	20.00	40.00
❑ Tamla TS 258 [S]	How Sweet It Is to Be Loved by You	1965	12.50	25.00	50.00
❑ Tamla T 259 [M]	Hello Broadway, This Is Marvin	1965	10.00	20.00	40.00
❑ Tamla TS 259 [S]	Hello Broadway, This Is Marvin	1965	12.50	25.00	50.00
❑ Tamla T 261 [M]	A Tribute to the Great Nat King Cole	1965	10.00	20.00	40.00
❑ Tamla TS 261 [S]	A Tribute to the Great Nat King Cole	1965	12.50	25.00	50.00
❑ Tamla T 266 [M]	Moods of Marvin Gaye	1966	10.00	20.00	40.00
❑ Tamla TS 266 [S]	Moods of Marvin Gaye	1966	12.50	25.00	50.00
❑ Tamla T 278 [M]	Marvin Gaye/Greatest Hits, Vol. 2	1967	6.25	12.50	25.00
❑ Tamla TS 278 [S]	Marvin Gaye/Greatest Hits, Vol. 2	1967	5.00	10.00	20.00
❑ Tamla T 285 [M]	In the Groove	1968	12.50	25.00	50.00
❑ Tamla TS 285 [S]	In the Groove	1968	6.25	12.50	25.00
❑ Tamla TS 285 [S]	I Heard It Through the Grapevine	1969	5.00	10.00	20.00
—Retitled version of "In the Groove"					

Number	Title (A Side/B Side)	Yr	VG	VG+	NM
❑ Tamla TS 292	M.P.G.	1969	5.00	10.00	20.00
❑ Tamla TS 293	Marvin Gaye and His Girls	1969	5.00	10.00	20.00
—Includes duets with Tammi Terrell, Mary Wells, Kim Weston					
❑ Tamla TS 299	That's the Way Love Is	1969	5.00	10.00	20.00
❑ Tamla TS 300	Marvin Gaye Super Hits	1970	5.00	10.00	20.00
❑ Tamla T5-310	What's Going On	1971	3.75	7.50	15.00
❑ Tamla T5-322	Trouble Man	1972	3.75	7.50	15.00
❑ Tamla T6-329	Let's Get It On	1973	3.75	7.50	15.00
❑ Tamla T6-333	Marvin Gaye Live!	1974	3.75	7.50	15.00
❑ Tamla T6-342	I Want You	1976	3.75	7.50	15.00
❑ Tamla T6-348	Marvin Gaye's Greatest Hits	1976	3.75	7.50	15.00
❑ Tamla T7-352 [(2)]	Marvin Gaye Live at the London Palladium	1977	3.75	7.50	15.00
❑ Tamla T13-364 [(2)]	Here, My Dear	1978	3.75	7.50	15.00
❑ Tamla T8-374	In Our Lifetime	1981	2.50	5.00	10.00
❑ Tamla 6172 TL	Motown Remembers Marvin Gaye	1986	2.50	5.00	10.00

GAYE, MARVIN, AND TAMMI TERRELL

45s

Number	Title (A Side/B Side)	Yr	VG	VG+	NM
❑ Tamla 54149	Ain't No Mountain High Enough/Give a Little Love	1967	2.00	4.00	8.00
❑ Tamla 54156	Your Precious Love/Hold Me Oh My Darling	1967	2.00	4.00	8.00
❑ Tamla 54161	If I Could Build My Whole World Around You/ If This World Were Mine	1967	2.00	4.00	8.00
❑ Tamla 54163	Ain't Nothing Like the Real Thing/Little Ole Boy, Little Ole Girl	1968	2.00	4.00	8.00
❑ Tamla 54169	You're All I Need to Get By/Two Can Have a Party	1968	2.00	4.00	8.00
❑ Tamla 54173	You Ain't Livin' Till You're Lovin'/Keep On Lovin' Me Honey	1968	—	3.00	6.00
❑ Tamla 54179	Good Lovin' Ain't Easy to Come By/Satisfied Feelin'	1969	—	3.00	6.00
❑ Tamla 54187	What You Gave Me/How You Gonna Keep It	1969	—	3.00	6.00
❑ Tamla 54192	The Onion Song/California Soul	1970	—	3.00	6.00

Albums

Number	Title (A Side/B Side)	Yr	VG	VG+	NM
❑ Motown M5-102V1	Motown Superstar Series, Vol. 2	1981	2.50	5.00	10.00
❑ Motown M5-142V1	You're All I Need	1981	2.50	5.00	10.00
—Reissue of Tamla 284					
❑ Motown M5-200V1	United	1981	2.50	5.00	10.00
—Reissue of Tamla 277					
❑ Tamla T 277 [M]	United	1967	7.50	15.00	30.00
❑ Tamla TS 277 [S]	United	1967	6.25	12.50	25.00
❑ Tamla T 284 [M]	You're All I Need	1968	12.50	25.00	50.00
❑ Tamla TS 284 [S]	You're All I Need	1968	5.00	10.00	20.00
❑ Tamla TS 294	Easy	1969	5.00	10.00	20.00
❑ Tamla TS 302	Marvin Gaye & Tammi Terrell/Greatest Hits	1970	5.00	10.00	20.00

GAYNOR, GLORIA

45s

Number	Title (A Side/B Side)	Yr	VG	VG+	NM
❑ Atlantic 89887	Stop in the Name of Love/For You, My Love	1982	—	2.00	4.00
❑ Atlantic 89947	Tease Me/Mack Side	1982	—	2.00	4.00
❑ Columbia 45909	Honey Bee/All It Took, Boy, Was Losing You	1973	—	3.00	6.00
❑ MGM 14706	Honey Bee/Come Tonight	1974	—	2.50	5.00
❑ MGM 14748	Never Can Say Goodbye/We Can Just Make It	1974	—	2.00	4.00
❑ MGM 14790	Reach Out, I'll Be There/Searchin'	1975	—	2.00	4.00
❑ MGM 14808	Walk On By/Real Good People	1975	—	2.00	4.00
❑ MGM 14823	(If You Want It) Do It Yourself/I'm Still Yours	1975	—	2.00	4.00
❑ MGM 14838	How High the Moon/My Man's Gone	1975	—	2.00	4.00
❑ Polydor 2021	Let Me Know (I Have a Right)/One Plus One	1979	—	2.00	4.00
❑ Polydor 2056	Midnight Rocker/Can't Fight This Feelin'	1980	—	2.00	4.00
❑ Polydor 2089	The Luckiest Girl in the World/Ain't No Bigger Fool	1980	—	2.00	4.00
❑ Polydor 2173	Let's Mend What's Been Broken/I Love You Because	1981	—	2.00	4.00
❑ Polydor 2179	I Kinda Like Me/Fingers in the Rain	1981	—	2.00	4.00
❑ Polydor 14342	Do It Right/Touch of Lightning	1976	—	2.00	4.00
❑ Polydor 14357	Let's Make a Deal/Let's Make Love	1976	—	2.00	4.00
❑ Polydor 14391	Most of All/So Much Love	1977	—	2.00	4.00
❑ Polydor 14443	After the Lovin'/You're All I Need to Get By	1977	—	2.00	4.00
❑ Polydor 14472	This Love Affair/For the First Time in My Life	1978	—	2.00	4.00
❑ Polydor 14508	I Will Survive/Substitute	1978	—	2.00	4.00
❑ Polydor 14558	Anybody Wanna Party?/Please Be There	1979	—	2.00	4.00
❑ Silver Blue 720	I Am What I Am/More Than Enough	1983	—	2.50	5.00
❑ Silver Blue 04294	I Am What I Am/More Than Enough	1983	—	2.00	4.00
❑ Silver Blue 04422	Strive/I've Been Watching You	1984	—	2.00	4.00

Albums

Number	Title (A Side/B Side)	Yr	VG	VG+	NM
❑ Atlantic 80033	Gloria Gaynor	1982	2.50	5.00	10.00
❑ MGM M3G-4982	Never Can Say Goodbye	1975	2.50	5.00	10.00
❑ MGM M3G-4997	Experience Gloria Gaynor	1975	2.50	5.00	10.00
❑ Polydor PD-1-6063	I've Got You	1976	2.50	5.00	10.00
❑ Polydor PD-1-6095	Glorious	1977	2.50	5.00	10.00
❑ Polydor PD-1-6139	Gloria Gaynor's Park Avenue Sound	1978	2.50	5.00	10.00
❑ Polydor PD-1-6184	Love Tracks	1978	2.50	5.00	10.00
❑ Polydor PD-1-6231	I Have a Right	1979	2.50	5.00	10.00
❑ Polydor PD-1-6274	Stories	1980	2.50	5.00	10.00

GEILS, J., BAND

45s

Number	Title (A Side/B Side)	Yr	VG	VG+	NM
❑ Atlantic 2784	First I Look at the Purse/Homework	1971	2.00	4.00	8.00
❑ Atlantic 2802	Cruisin' for a Love/Wait	1971	—	3.00	6.00
❑ Atlantic 2843	Dead Presidents/I Don't Need You No More	1971	—	3.00	6.00
❑ Atlantic 2844	Looking for a Love/What's Your Whammer Jammer	1971	—	3.00	6.00
❑ Atlantic 2929	Hard Drivin' Man/Whammer Jammer	1972	—	3.00	6.00
❑ Atlantic 2953	Give It To Me/Hold Your Loving	1973	—	2.50	5.00
❑ Atlantic 2974	Make Up Your Mind/Southside Shuffle	1973	—	2.50	5.00
❑ Atlantic 3007	Did You No Wrong/That's Why I'm Thinking of You	1974	—	2.50	5.00

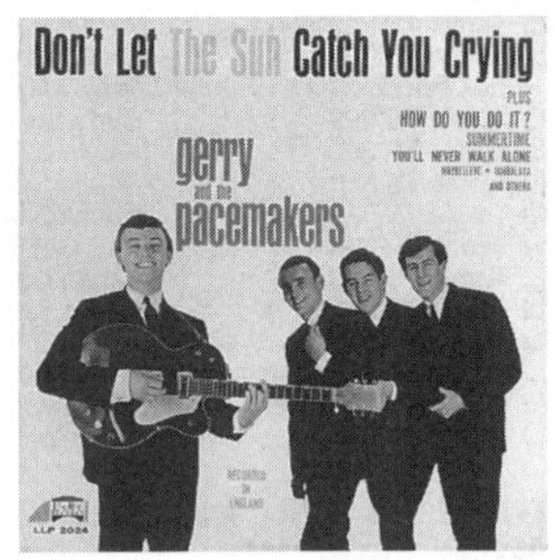

Number	Title (A Side/B Side)	Yr	VG	VG+	NM
❑ Atlantic 3214	Must of Got Lost/Funky Judge	1974	—	2.50	5.00
❑ Atlantic 3251	Givin' It All Up/Gettin' Out	1975	—	2.50	5.00
❑ Atlantic 3301	Think It Over/Love-Itis	1975	—	2.50	5.00
❑ Atlantic 3320	Where Did Our Love Go/What's Your Hurry	1976	—	2.50	5.00
❑ Atlantic 3350	(Ain't Nothing But a) House Party/Give It To Me	1976	—	2.50	5.00
❑ Atlantic 3378	Peanut Buuter/Magic's Mood	1976	—	2.50	5.00
❑ Atlantic 3411	You're the Only One/Wreckage	1977	—	2.50	5.00
—As "Geils"					
❑ Atlantic 3438	Monkey Island (Part 1)/Surrender	1977	—	2.50	5.00
—As "Geils"					
❑ Atlantic 3454	I Do/Trying to Live My Life Without You	1978	—	2.50	5.00
—As "Geils"					
❑ EMI America 8007	One Last Kiss/Revenge	1978	—	2.00	4.00
❑ EMI America 8012	Take It Back/I Can't Believe You	1979	—	2.00	4.00
❑ EMI America 8016	Wild Man/Just Can't Stop Me	1979	—	2.00	4.00
❑ EMI America 8032	Come Back/Takin' You Down	1980	—	2.00	4.00
❑ EMI America 8039	Love Stinks/Till the Walls Come Tumblin' Down	1980	—	2.00	4.00
❑ EMI America 8047	Just Can't Wait/No Anchovies, Please	1980	—	2.00	4.00
❑ EMI America 8100	Angel in Blue/Rage in the Cage	1982	—	—	3.00
❑ EMI America 8102	Centerfold/Rage in the Cage	1981	—	—	3.00
—Custom pink label					
❑ EMI America 8108	Freeze-Frame/Flamethrower	1982	—	—	3.00
❑ EMI America 8148	I Do/Sanctuary	1982	—	—	3.00
❑ EMI America 8156	Land of 1000 Dances/Jus' Can't Stop Me	1983	—	—	3.00
❑ EMI America 8242	Concealed Weapons/Tell 'Em Jonsey	1984	—	—	3.00
❑ EMI America 8260	Eenie Meenie Miney Mo/I Will Carry You Home	1985	—	—	3.00
❑ Private I 05462	Fright Night/Boppin' Tonight	1985	—	—	3.00
—B-side by The Fabulous Fontaines					

Albums

Number	Title (A Side/B Side)	Yr	VG	VG+	NM
❑ Atlantic SD 2-507 [(2)]	Live — Blow Your Face Out	1976	3.75	7.50	15.00
❑ Atlantic SD 7241	"Live" — Full House	1972	3.00	6.00	12.00
❑ Atlantic SD 7260	Bloodshot	1973	3.00	6.00	12.00
—Black vinyl					
❑ Atlantic SD 7286	Ladies Invited	1973	3.00	6.00	12.00
❑ Atlantic SD 8275 [S]	The J. Geils Band	1970	3.75	7.50	15.00
❑ Atlantic SD 8297 [S]	The Morning After	1971	3.00	6.00	12.00
❑ Atlantic SD 18107	Nightmares and Other Tales from the Vinyl Jungle	1974	3.00	6.00	12.00
❑ Atlantic SD 18147	Hotline	1975	3.00	6.00	12.00
❑ Atlantic SD 19103	Monkey Island	1977	3.00	6.00	12.00
—As "Geils"					
❑ Atlantic SD 19234	Best of the J. Geils Band	1979	2.50	5.00	10.00
❑ Atlantic SD 19284	Best of the J. Geils Band — 2	1980	2.50	5.00	10.00
❑ EMI America SN-16316	Sanctuary	1985	2.00	4.00	8.00
—Reissue					
❑ EMI America SN-16373	Showtime!	1986	2.00	4.00	8.00
—Reissue					
❑ EMI America SN-16374	Freeze-Frame	1986	2.00	4.00	8.00
—Reissue					
❑ EMI America SN-16375	Love Stinks	1986	2.00	4.00	8.00
—Reissue					
❑ EMI America SO-17006	Sanctuary	1978	2.50	5.00	10.00
❑ EMI America SOO-17016	Love Stinks	1980	2.50	5.00	10.00
❑ EMI America SOO-17062	Freeze-Frame	1981	2.50	5.00	10.00
❑ EMI America SO-17087	Showtime!	1982	2.50	5.00	10.00
❑ EMI America SJ-17137	You're Gettin' Even While I'm Gettin' Odd	1984	2.00	4.00	8.00
❑ EMI America ST-17174	Flashback — The Best of the J. Geils Band	1985	2.00	4.00	8.00

GENESIS

45s

Number	Title (A Side/B Side)	Yr	VG	VG+	NM
❑ Atco 7013	The Lamb Lies Down on Broadway/Counting Out Time	1975	12.50	25.00	50.00
❑ Atco 7050	Entangled/Ripples	1976	7.50	15.00	30.00
❑ Atco 7076	Your Own Special Way/In That Quiet Earth	1977	6.25	12.50	25.00
❑ Atlantic 3474	Follow You Follow Me/Inside and Out	1978	—	2.50	5.00
—A radically different mix than the LP version of A-side					
❑ Atlantic 3511	Go West Young Man (In the Motherlode)/ Scene from a Night's Dream	1978	5.00	10.00	20.00
❑ Atlantic 3662	Misunderstanding/Behind the Lines	1980	—	2.00	4.00

Number	Title (A Side/B Side)	Yr	VG	VG+	NM
❑ Atlantic 3751	Turn It On Again/Evidence of Autumn	1980	—	2.00	4.00
❑ Atlantic 3858	No Reply At All/Dodo	1981	—	2.00	4.00
❑ Atlantic 3891	Abacab/Who Dunnit?	1982	—	2.00	4.00
❑ Atlantic 4025	Man on the Corner/Submarine	1982	—	2.00	4.00
❑ Atlantic 4053	Paperlate/You Might Recall	1982	—	2.00	4.00
❑ Atlantic 7-89290	Tonight, Tonight, Tonight/In the Glow of the Night	1987	—	—	3.00
❑ Atlantic 7-89316	In Too Deep/I'd Rather Be You	1987	—	—	3.00
❑ Atlantic 7-89336	Land of Confusion/Feeding the Fire	1986	—	—	3.00
—Regular Atlantic red and black label					
❑ Atlantic 7-89372	Throwing It All Away/Do the Neurotic	1986	—	—	3.00
❑ Atlantic 7-89407	Invisible Touch/The Last Domino	1986	—	—	3.00
❑ Atlantic 7-89656	Taking It All Too Hard/Silver Rainbow	1984	—	—	3.00
❑ Atlantic 7-89698	Illegal Alien/Turn It On Again (Live in Philadelphia)	1984	—	2.00	4.00
❑ Atlantic 7-89724	That's All/Second Home by the Sea	1983	—	—	3.00
—With custom labels					
❑ Atlantic 7-89770	Mama/It's Gonna Get Better	1983	—	—	3.00
❑ Charisma 103	Watcher of the Skies/Willow Farm	1973	20.00	40.00	80.00
❑ Charisma 26002	I Know What I Like (In Your Wardrobe)/Twilight Ale House	1973	12.50	25.00	50.00
❑ Parrot 3018	Silent Sun/That's Me	1968	100.00	200.00	400.00
—Stock copy with black label and green and yellow bird					
Albums					
❑ ABC ABCX-816	Trespass	1971	3.75	7.50	15.00
—Reissue of Impulse album; black label					
❑ ABC ABCX-816	Trespass	1974	3.00	6.00	12.00
—Reissue; concentric yellow/orange/purple "target" label					
❑ ABC Impulse! ASD-9205	Trespass	1971	7.50	15.00	30.00
❑ Atco SD 38-100	Wind & Wuthering	1978	2.50	5.00	10.00
—Reissue of SD 36-144					
❑ Atco SD 38-101	A Trick of the Tail	1978	2.50	5.00	10.00
—Reissue of SD 36-129					
❑ Atco SD 36-129	A Trick of the Tail	1976	3.00	6.00	12.00
❑ Atco SD 36-144	Wind & Wuthering	1977	3.00	6.00	12.00
❑ Atco SD 2-401 [(2)]	The Lamb Lies Down on Broadway	1974	3.75	7.50	15.00
—Originals have yellow labels (other labels worth less)					
❑ Atlantic SD 2-2000 [(2)]	Three Sides Live	1982	3.00	6.00	12.00
❑ Atlantic SD 2-9002 [(2)]	Seconds Out	1977	3.00	6.00	12.00
❑ Atlantic SD 16014	Duke	1980	2.50	5.00	10.00
❑ Atlantic SD 19173	...And Then There Were Three	1978	2.50	5.00	10.00
❑ Atlantic SD 19277	Selling England by the Pound	1981	2.00	4.00	8.00
—Reissue of Charisma LP of same name					
❑ Atlantic SD 19313	Abacab	1981	2.50	5.00	10.00
—Released with four different covers, lettered "A" through "D" on the upper part of the spine; no difference in value					
❑ Atlantic 80030	Nursery Cryme	1982	2.00	4.00	8.00
—Reissue of Charisma LP of same name					
❑ Atlantic 80116	Genesis	1983	2.00	4.00	8.00
❑ Atlantic 81641	Invisible Touch	1986	2.00	4.00	8.00
❑ Atlantic 81848	Foxtrot	1988	2.50	5.00	10.00
—Reissue of Charisma LP of the same name					
❑ Atlantic 81855	Genesis Live	1988	2.50	5.00	10.00
—Reissue of Charisma LP of the same name					
❑ Buddah BDS-5659 [(2)]	The Best ... Genesis	1976	5.00	10.00	20.00
—Reissue of "Nursery Cryme" and "Foxtrot" in one set					
❑ Charisma CAS-1052	Nursery Cryme	1971	3.75	7.50	15.00
❑ Charisma CAS-1058	Foxtrot	1972	3.75	7.50	15.00
❑ Charisma CAS-1666	Genesis Live	1974	3.75	7.50	15.00
❑ Charisma CA2-2701 [(2)]	Nursery Cryme/Foxtrot	1976	3.75	7.50	15.00
—Repackage of the individual albums of these names					
❑ Charisma FC-6060	Selling England by the Pound	1973	3.75	7.50	15.00
❑ London PS 643	From Genesis to Revelation	1974	6.25	12.50	25.00
—First US release of debut album					
❑ London LC-50006	In the Beginning	1977	3.00	6.00	12.00
❑ London 820322-1	In the Beginning	198?	2.50	5.00	10.00
—Reissue of London 50006					
❑ MCA ABCX-816	Trespass	1979	2.50	5.00	10.00
—Reissue of ABC ABCX-816					
❑ MCA 37151	Trespass	198?	2.00	4.00	8.00
—Reissue of MCA 816					

GENTRYS, THE

45s

Number	Title (A Side/B Side)	Yr	VG	VG+	NM
❑ Bell 720	You Better Come Home/I Can't Go Back to Denver	1968	—	3.00	6.00
❑ Bell 740	Thinking Like a Child/Silky	1968	—	3.00	6.00
❑ Bell 753	Midnight Train/You Tell Me You Care	1968	—	3.00	6.00
❑ Capitol 3459	Changin'/Let Me Put This Ring Upon Your Finger	1972	—	2.50	5.00
❑ Hit 229	Keep On Dancing/A Lover's Concerto	1965	5.00	10.00	20.00
—B-side by Alpha Zoe					
❑ MGM 13379	Keep On Dancing/Make Up Your Mind	1965	3.75	7.50	15.00
❑ MGM 13432	Spread It On Thick/Brown Paper Sack	1965	3.00	6.00	12.00
❑ MGM 13495	Everyday I Have to Cry/Don't Let It Be (This Time)	1966	3.00	6.00	12.00
❑ MGM 13561	There Are Two Sides to Every Story/Woman of the World	1966	3.00	6.00	12.00
❑ MGM 13690	There's a Love/You Make Me Feel So Good	1967	6.25	12.50	25.00
❑ MGM 13749	I Can See/90 Pound Weakling	1967	2.50	5.00	10.00
❑ Stax 0223	All Hung Up on You/Little Gold Band	1974	—	2.00	4.00
❑ Stax 0242	High Flyer/Little Gold Band	1975	—	2.00	4.00
❑ Sun 1108	I Need Love/Why Should I Cry	1969	—	2.50	5.00
❑ Sun 1114	Cinnamon Girl/I Just Got the News	1970	—	2.50	5.00
❑ Sun 1118	I Hate to See You Go/He'll Never Love Me	1970	—	2.50	5.00

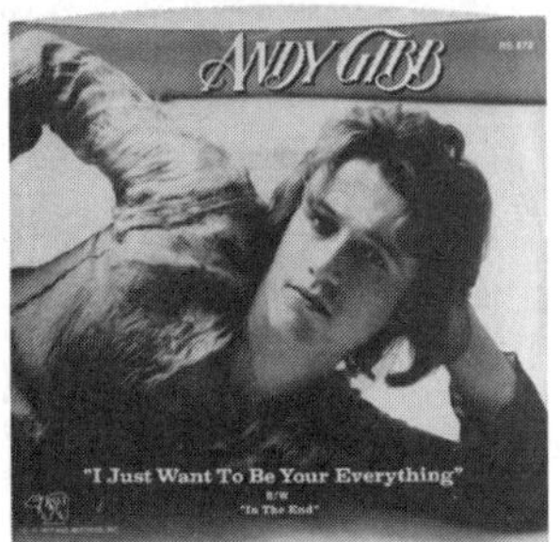

Number	Title (A Side/B Side)	Yr	VG	VG+	NM
❑ Sun 1120	Friends/Goddess of Love	1970	—	2.50	5.00
❑ Sun 1122	Wild World/Sunshine	1971	—	2.50	5.00
❑ Sun 1126	God Save Our Country/Love You All My Life	1971	—	2.50	5.00
❑ Youngstown 600	Sometimes/Little Drops of Water	1965	6.25	12.50	25.00
❑ Youngstown 601	Keep On Dancing/Make Up Your Mind	1965	7.50	15.00	30.00

Albums

Number	Title (A Side/B Side)	Yr	VG	VG+	NM
❑ MGM GAS-127	The Gentrys (Golden Archive Series)	1970	5.00	10.00	20.00
❑ MGM E-4336 [M]	Keep On Dancing	1965	6.25	12.50	25.00
❑ MGM SE-4336 [P]	Keep On Dancing	1965	7.50	15.00	30.00
❑ MGM E-4346 [M]	Gentry Time	1966	5.00	10.00	20.00
❑ MGM SE-4346 [S]	Gentry Time	1966	6.25	12.50	25.00
❑ Sun LP-117	The Gentrys	1970	7.50	15.00	30.00

GERRY AND THE PACEMAKERS

45s

Number	Title (A Side/B Side)	Yr	VG	VG+	NM
❑ Laurie 3162	How Do You Do It/Away From You	1963	5.00	10.00	20.00
❑ Laurie 3196	I Like It/It Happened to Me	1963	5.00	10.00	20.00
❑ Laurie 3218	You'll Never Walk Alone/It's All Right	1964	5.00	10.00	20.00
❑ Laurie 3233	I'm the One/How Do You Do It	1964	3.75	7.50	15.00
❑ Laurie 3233	I'm the One/It's All Right	1964	3.75	7.50	15.00
❑ Laurie 3233	I'm the One/You've Got What I Like	1964	5.00	10.00	20.00
❑ Laurie 3251	Don't Let the Sun Catch You Crying/Away from You	1964	3.75	7.50	15.00
❑ Laurie 3261	How Do You Do It/You'll Never Walk Alone	1964	3.00	6.00	12.00
❑ Laurie 3271	I Like It/Jambalaya	1964	3.00	6.00	12.00
❑ Laurie 3279	I'll Be There/You, You, You	1964	3.00	6.00	12.00
❑ Laurie 3284	Ferry Across the Mersey/Pretend	1965	3.00	6.00	12.00
❑ Laurie 3293	It's Gonna Be Alright/Skinny Minnie	1965	2.50	5.00	10.00
❑ Laurie 3302	You'll Never Walk Alone/Away from You	1965	2.50	5.00	10.00
❑ Laurie 3313	Give All Your Love to Me/You're the Reason	1965	2.50	5.00	10.00
❑ Laurie 3323	Dreams/Walk Hand in Hand	1965	2.50	5.00	10.00
❑ Laurie 3337	La La La/Without You	1966	2.50	5.00	10.00
❑ Laurie 3354	Girl on a Swing/The Way You Look Tonight	1966	2.50	5.00	10.00
❑ Laurie 3370	The Big Bright Green Pleasure Machine/Looking for My Life	1966	3.00	6.00	12.00

Albums

Number	Title (A Side/B Side)	Yr	VG	VG+	NM
❑ Capitol SM-11898 [B]	The Best of Gerry and the Pacemakers	1979	2.00	4.00	8.00
—All stereo except "I Like It," "Away from You" and "I'm the One," which are mono.					
❑ Laurie LLP-2024 [M]	Don't Let the Sun Catch You Crying	1964	7.50	15.00	30.00
❑ Laurie SLP-2024 [R]	Don't Let the Sun Catch You Crying	1964	6.25	12.50	25.00
❑ Laurie LLP-2027 [M]	Gerry and the Pacemakers' Second Album	1964	7.50	15.00	30.00
❑ Laurie SLP-2027 [R]	Gerry and the Pacemakers' Second Album	1964	6.25	12.50	25.00
❑ Laurie LLP-2030 [M]	I'll Be There	1964	7.50	15.00	30.00
❑ Laurie SLP-2030 [R]	I'll Be There	1964	6.25	12.50	25.00
❑ Laurie LLP-2031 [M]	Greatest Hits	1965	6.25	12.50	25.00
❑ Laurie SLP-2031 [R]	Greatest Hits	1965	3.75	7.50	15.00
❑ Laurie LLP-2037 [M]	Girl on a Swing	1966	6.25	12.50	25.00
❑ Laurie SLP-2037 [S]	Girl on a Swing	1966	5.00	10.00	20.00
❑ United Artists UAL 3387 [M]	Ferry Cross the Mersey	1965	6.25	12.50	25.00
—Also contains incidental music by George Martin					
❑ United Artists UAS 6387 [S]	Ferry Cross the Mersey	1965	10.00	20.00	40.00

GIBB, ANDY

45s

Number	Title (A Side/B Side)	Yr	VG	VG+	NM
❑ RSO 872	I Just Want to Be Your Everything/In the End	1977	—	2.00	4.00
❑ RSO 883	(Love Is) Thicker Than Water/Words and Music	1977	—	2.00	4.00
❑ RSO 893	Shadow Dancing/Let It Be Me	1978	—	2.00	4.00
❑ RSO 904	An Everlasting Love/Flowing Rivers	1978	—	2.00	4.00
❑ RSO 911	(Our Love) Don't Throw It All Away/One More Look at the Night	1978	—	2.00	4.00
❑ RSO 1019	Desire/Waiting for You	1980	—	2.00	4.00
—A picture sleeve is rumored to exist, but we haven't seen it					
❑ RSO 1026	I Can't Help It/Someone I Ain't	1980	—	2.00	4.00
—A-side: With Olivia Newton-John					
❑ RSO 1056	Me (Without You)/Melody	1980	—	2.00	4.00
❑ RSO 1059	Time Is Time/I Go for You	1980	—	2.00	4.00
❑ RSO 1065	All I Have to Do Is Dream/Good Feeling	1981	—	2.00	4.00
—With Victoria Principal					

Albums

Number	Title (A Side/B Side)	Yr	VG	VG+	NM
❑ RSO RS-1-3019	Flowing Rivers	1977	2.50	5.00	10.00

Number	Title (A Side/B Side)	Yr	VG	VG+	NM
❑ RSO RS-1-3034	Shadow Dancing	1978	2.50	5.00	10.00
❑ RSO RS-1-3069	After Dark	1980	2.50	5.00	10.00
❑ RSO RS-1-3091	Andy Gibb's Greatest Hits	1980	2.50	5.00	10.00

GLITTER, GARY

45s

Number	Title (A Side/B Side)	Yr	VG	VG+	NM
❑ Arista 0173	I Love You Love Me Love/Hands Up! It's a Stick-Up	1976	—	2.50	5.00
❑ Bell 45237	Rock and Roll, Part 2/Rock and Roll, Part 1	1972	—	3.00	6.00
❑ Bell 45276	I Didn't Know I Loved You (Till I Saw You Rock and Roll)/ Shakey Sue	1972	—	2.50	5.00
❑ Bell 45326	Do You Wanna Touch Me (Oh Yeah)/I Would If I Could But I Can't	1973	—	2.50	5.00
❑ Bell 45345	Baby Please Don't Go/I.O.U.	1973	—	2.50	5.00
❑ Bell 45375	Come On, Come In/Happy Birthday	1973	—	2.50	5.00
❑ Bell 45398	(I'm the) Leader of the Gang (I Am)/(B-side unknown)	1973	—	2.50	5.00
❑ Bell 45438	I Love You Love Me Love/(B-side unknown)	1974	—	2.50	5.00
❑ Decca 32714	Goodbye Seattle/Wait for Me	1970	3.75	7.50	15.00
—As "Paul Raven"					

Albums

Number	Title (A Side/B Side)	Yr	VG	VG+	NM
❑ Bell 1108	Glitter	1972	3.75	7.50	15.00
❑ Bell 6082	Gary Glitter	1973	3.75	7.50	15.00
❑ Epic PE 39299	The Leader	1984	3.75	7.50	15.00
❑ Epic/Nu-Disk 3E 36848 [10]	Glitter & Gold	1981	3.00	6.00	12.00

GO-GO'S

45s

Number	Title (A Side/B Side)	Yr	VG	VG+	NM
❑ I.R.S. 8690	Our Lips Are Sealed/We Got the Beat	198?	—	—	3.00
—Amnesia Series reissue					
❑ I.R.S. 8691	Vacation/Cool Jerk	198?	—	—	3.00
—Reissue					
❑ I.R.S. 9901	Our Lips Are Sealed/Surfing and Spying	1981	—	—	3.00
❑ I.R.S. 9903	We Got the Beat/Can't Stop the World	1982	—	—	3.00
❑ I.R.S. 9907	Vacation/Beatnik Beach	1982	—	—	3.00
❑ I.R.S. 9910	Get Up and Go/Speeding	1982	—	—	3.00
❑ I.R.S. 9911	This Old Feeling/It's Everything But Partytime	1982	—	—	3.00
❑ I.R.S. 9926	Head Over Heels/Good for Gone	1984	—	—	3.00
❑ I.R.S. 9928	Turn to You/I'm With You	1984	—	—	3.00
❑ I.R.S. 9933	Yes or No/Mercenary	1984	—	—	3.00

Albums

Number	Title (A Side/B Side)	Yr	VG	VG+	NM
❑ I.R.S. SP 70021	Beauty and the Beat	1981	2.00	4.00	8.00
—Second pressings with dark blue cover and darker label					
❑ I.R.S. SP 70021	Beauty and the Beat	1981	3.00	6.00	12.00
—First pressings with peach-colored cover and light label					
❑ I.R.S. SP 70031	Vacation	1982	2.00	4.00	8.00
❑ I.R.S. SP 70041	Talk Show	1984	2.00	4.00	8.00

GOLDEN EARRING

45s

Number	Title (A Side/B Side)	Yr	VG	VG+	NM
❑ Atlantic 2710	Eight Miles High/One Huge Road	1970	—	3.00	6.00
❑ Dwarf 2001	Back Home/As Long As the Wind Blows	1969	2.50	5.00	10.00
❑ MCA 40513	Babylon/Sleep Walkin'	1976	—	2.00	4.00
❑ MCA 40802	Radar Love (Live)/Radar Love (Studio)	1977	—	2.00	4.00
❑ Polydor 2004	Weekend Love/Tiger Bay	1979	—	2.00	4.00
❑ Polydor 14001	It's Alright, But I Admit It Could Be Better/Song of a Devil's Servant	1969	2.50	5.00	10.00
❑ Polydor 14581	Weekend Love/Tiger Bay	1979	—	—	—
—Unreleased					
❑ Track 40202	Radar Love/Just Like Vince Taylor	1974	—	3.00	6.00
❑ Track 40309	Candy's Going Bad/She Flies on Strange Wings	1974	—	2.50	5.00
❑ Track 40369	Ce Soir/Lucky Numbers	1975	—	2.50	5.00
❑ Track 40412	The Switch/Lonesome D.J.	1975	—	2.50	5.00
❑ 21 Records 103	Twilight Zone/King Dark	1982	—	2.00	4.00
❑ 21 Records 108	The Devil Made Me Do It/Chargin' Batteries	1983	—	2.00	4.00
❑ 21 Records 112	When the Lady Smiles/Orwell's Ear	1984	—	—	3.00
❑ 21 Records 113	Fist in Glove/One Night Moonlight	1984	—	—	3.00
❑ 21 Records 99515	Love in Motion/Why Do I	1986	—	—	3.00
❑ 21 Records 99533	Quiet Eyes/Love in Motion	1986	—	—	3.00
❑ 21 Records 881415-7	Something Heavy Going Down/Enough Is Enough	1984	—	—	3.00

Albums

Number	Title (A Side/B Side)	Yr	VG	VG+	NM
❑ Atlantic SD 8244	Eight Miles High	1970	6.25	12.50	25.00
❑ Capitol ST-164	Miracle Mirror	1969	10.00	20.00	40.00
❑ Capitol ST 2823 [S]	Winter Harvest	1967	6.25	12.50	25.00
❑ Capitol T 2823 [M]	Winter Harvest	1967	12.50	25.00	50.00
❑ Capitol ST-11315	The Golden Earring	1974	3.00	6.00	12.00
❑ Dwarf 2000	Golden Earring	1971	6.25	12.50	25.00
❑ MCA 703	Grab It For a Second	198?	2.00	4.00	8.00
—Reissue of 3057					
❑ MCA 827	Switch	198?	2.00	4.00	8.00
—Reissue of 2139					
❑ MCA 2139	Switch	197?	2.50	5.00	10.00
—Reissue of Track 2139					
❑ MCA 2183	To the Hilt	1976	3.00	6.00	12.00
❑ MCA 2254	Mad Love	1977	3.00	6.00	12.00
❑ MCA 2352	Moontan	1978	2.50	5.00	10.00
—Reissue of Track 396					
❑ MCA 3057	Grab It For a Second	1978	3.00	6.00	12.00
❑ MCA 6004 [(2)]	Golden Earring Live!	198?	2.50	5.00	10.00
—Reissue of 8009					
❑ MCA 8009 [(2)]	Golden Earring Live!	1977	3.75	7.50	15.00

Number	Title (A Side/B Side)	Yr	VG	VG+	NM
❑ MCA 37172	Moontan	198?	2.00	4.00	8.00
—Reissue of 2352					
❑ Polydor PD-1-6223	No Promises...No Debts	1979	3.00	6.00	12.00
❑ Polydor PD-1-6303	Long Blond Animal	1980	3.00	6.00	12.00
❑ Track 396	Moontan	1974	3.75	7.50	15.00
—Reissue cover with close-up of earring in ear					
❑ Track 396	Moontan	1974	6.25	12.50	25.00
—Original cover with nude dancer					
❑ Track 2139	Switch	1975	3.75	7.50	15.00
❑ 21 Records T1-1-9004	Cut	1982	2.50	5.00	10.00
❑ 21 Records T1-1-9008	N.E.W.S.	1984	2.50	5.00	10.00
❑ 21 Records 90514	The Hole	1986	2.50	5.00	10.00
❑ 21 Records 817585-1	Cut	1985	2.00	4.00	8.00
—Reissue					
❑ 21 Records 823717-1	Something Heavy Going Down — Live from the Twilight Zone	1984	2.50	5.00	10.00

GOLDSBORO, BOBBY

45s

Number	Title (A Side/B Side)	Yr	VG	VG+	NM
❑ Buena Vista 561	These Are the Best Times/(B-side unknown)	1979	—	2.50	5.00
❑ Curb 02117	Love Ain't Never Hurt Nobody/Wings of an Angel	1981	—	2.00	4.00
❑ Curb 02583	The Round-Up Saloon/Green-Eyed Woman, Nashville Blues	1981	—	2.00	4.00
❑ Curb 02726	Lucy and the Stranger/Outrun the Sun	1982	—	2.00	4.00
❑ Curb 5400	Goodbye Marie/Love Has Made a Woman Out of You	1980	—	2.00	4.00
❑ Curb 70052	Alice Doesn't Love Here Anymore/ Green-Eyed Woman, Nashville Blues	1981	—	2.00	4.00
❑ Epic 50342	Me and the Elephants/I Love Music	1977	—	2.00	4.00
❑ Epic 50413	The Cowboy and the Lady/Me and Millie	1977	—	2.00	4.00
❑ Epic 50480	He'll Have to Go/Too Hot to Handle	1977	—	2.00	4.00
❑ Epic 50535	Life Gets Hard on Easy Street/Black Fool's Gold	1978	—	2.00	4.00
❑ Laurie 3130	Lonely Traveler/You Better Go Home	1962	3.75	7.50	15.00
❑ Laurie 3148	Molly/Honey Baby	1962	3.75	7.50	15.00
❑ Laurie 3159	The Letter/The Runaround	1963	3.75	7.50	15.00
❑ Laurie 3168	Light the Candles/That's What Love Will Do	1963	3.75	7.50	15.00
❑ United Artists 0044	See the Funny Little Clown/Little Things	1973	—	2.00	4.00
❑ United Artists 0045	It's Too Late/Voodoo Woman	1973	—	2.00	4.00
❑ United Artists 0046	Honey/Autumn of My Life	1973	—	2.00	4.00
❑ United Artists 0047	Watching Scotty Grow/I'm a Drifter	1973	—	2.00	4.00
—0044 through 0047 are "Silver Spotlight Series" reissues					
❑ United Artists XW251	Summer (The First Time)/Childhood 1949	1973	—	2.50	5.00
❑ United Artists XW371	Marlena/Sing Me a Smile	1973	—	2.50	5.00
❑ United Artists XW422	I Believe the South Is Gonna Rise Again/She	1974	—	2.00	4.00
❑ United Artists XW451	And Then There Was Gina/Quicksand	1974	—	2.00	4.00
❑ United Artists XW517	Summer (The First Time)/Marlena	1974	—	2.00	4.00
—Reissue					
❑ United Artists XW529	Hello Summertime/And Then There Was Gina	1974	—	2.00	4.00
❑ United Artists XW633	And Then There Was Gina/You Pull Me Down (Into Sweet, Sweet Love)	1975	—	2.00	4.00
❑ United Artists 672	See the Funny Little Clown/Hello Loser	1963	2.50	5.00	10.00
❑ United Artists XW681	I Wrote a Song (Sing Along)/You Pull Me Down (Into Sweet, Sweet Love)	1975	—	2.00	4.00
❑ United Artists 710	Whenever He Holds You/If She Was Mine	1964	2.00	4.00	8.00
❑ United Artists 742	Me Japanese Boy, I Love You/Everyone But Me	1964	2.00	4.00	8.00
❑ United Artists 781	I Don't Know You Anymore/Little Drops of Water	1964	2.00	4.00	8.00
❑ United Artists XW793	A Butterfly for Bucky/Another Night Alone	1976	—	2.00	4.00
❑ United Artists 810	Little Things/I Can't Go On Pretending	1965	2.50	5.00	10.00
❑ United Artists 862	Voodoo Woman/It Breaks My Heart	1965	2.00	4.00	8.00
❑ United Artists XW866	She Taught Me How to Live Again/Reunion	1976	—	2.00	4.00
❑ United Artists 908	If You Wait for Love/If You've Got a Heart	1965	2.00	4.00	8.00
❑ United Artists 952	Broomstick Cowboy/Ain't Got Time for Happy	1965	2.00	4.00	8.00
❑ United Artists 980	It's Too Late/I'm Goin' Home	1966	2.00	4.00	8.00
❑ United Artists 50018	I Know You Better Than That/When Your Love Has Gone	1966	2.00	4.00	8.00
❑ United Artists 50044	Longer Than Forever/Take Your Love	1966	2.00	2.00	8.00
❑ United Artists 50056	It Hurts Me/Pity the Fool	1966	2.00	2.00	8.00
❑ United Artists 50087	Blue Autumn/I Just Don't Love You Anymore	1966	2.00	2.00	8.00
❑ United Artists 50138	Love Is/Goodbye to All You Women	1967	2.00	2.00	8.00
❑ United Artists 50186	Three in the Morning/Trusty Little Herbert	1967	2.00	2.00	8.00
❑ United Artists 50224	Pledge of Love/Jo-Jo's Place	1967	2.00	2.00	8.00

Number	Title (A Side/B Side)	Yr	VG	VG+	NM
❑ United Artists 50283	Honey/Danny	1968	2.00	4.00	8.00
—Orange and pink label					
❑ United Artists 50283	Honey/Danny	1968	2.50	5.00	10.00
—Black label					
❑ United Artists 50318	Autumn of My Life/She Chased Me	1968	—	3.00	6.00
❑ United Artists 50321	Autumn of My Life/She Chased Me	1968	—	—	—
—Unreleased; these were edits of the versions on UA 50318					
❑ United Artists 50461	The Straight Life/Tomorrow Is Forgotten	1968	—	3.00	6.00
❑ United Artists 50470	A Christmas Wish/Look Around You (It's Christmas Time)	1968	2.50	5.00	10.00
❑ United Artists 50497	Glad She's a Woman/Letter to Emily	1969	—	3.00	6.00
❑ United Artists 50525	I'm a Drifter/Hobos and Kings	1969	—	3.00	6.00
❑ United Artists 50565	Muddy Mississippi Line/A Richer Man Than I	1969	—	3.00	6.00
❑ United Artists 50614	Mornin' Mornin'/Requiem	1969	—	3.00	6.00
❑ United Artists 50650	Can You Feel It/Time Good, Time Bad	1970	—	2.50	5.00
❑ United Artists 50696	Down on the Bayou/It's Gonna Change	1970	—	2.50	5.00
❑ United Artists 50715	My God and I/The World Beyond	1970	—	2.50	5.00
❑ United Artists 50727	Watching Scotty Grow/Water Color Days	1970	—	2.50	5.00
❑ United Artists 50776	And I Love You So/Gentle of a Man	1971	—	2.50	5.00
❑ United Artists 50807	I'll Remember You/Come Back Home	1971	—	2.50	5.00
❑ United Artists 50846	Poem for the Little Lady/Danny Is a Mirror to Me	1971	—	2.50	5.00
❑ United Artists 50891	California Wine/To Be with You	1972	—	2.50	5.00
❑ United Artists 50938	With Pen in Hand/Southern Fried Singin' Sunday Mornin'	1972	—	2.50	5.00
❑ United Artists 51107	Country Feelin's/Brand New Kind of Love	1973	—	2.50	5.00
Albums					
❑ Curb JZ 36822	Bobby Goldsboro	1980	3.00	6.00	12.00
❑ Curb FZ 37734	Round-Up Saloon	1982	2.50	5.00	10.00
❑ Epic PE 34703	Goldsboro	1977	3.00	6.00	12.00
❑ Liberty LMAS-5502	Bobby Goldsboro's Greatest Hits	1981	2.00	4.00	8.00
—Reissue of United Artists 5502					
❑ Liberty LN-10007	Bobby Goldsboro's 10th Anniversary Album, Volume 1	1981	2.00	4.00	8.00
❑ Liberty LN-10047	Bobby Goldsboro's 10th Anniversary Album, Volume 2	1981	2.00	4.00	8.00
❑ Liberty LN-10114	The Best of Bobby Goldsboro	1981	2.00	4.00	8.00
❑ Sunset SUS-5236	This Is Bobby Goldsboro	1969	3.00	6.00	12.00
❑ Sunset SUS-5284	Pledge of Love	1970	3.00	6.00	12.00
❑ Sunset SUS-5313	Autumn of My Life	1971	3.00	6.00	12.00
❑ United Artists UA-LA019-F	Brand New Kind of Love	1972	3.75	7.50	15.00
❑ United Artists UA-LA124-F	Summer (The First Time)	1973	3.75	7.50	15.00
❑ United Artists UA-LA311-H2 [(2)]	Bobby Goldsboro's 10th Anniversary Album	1974	5.00	10.00	20.00
❑ United Artists UA-LA424-G	Through the Eyes of a Man	1975	3.00	6.00	12.00
❑ United Artists UA-LA639-G	Butterfly for Bucky	1976	3.00	6.00	12.00
❑ United Artists UAL 3358 [M]	The Bobby Goldsbob Album	1964	5.00	10.00	20.00
❑ United Artists UAL 3381 [M]	I Can't Stop Loving You	1964	5.00	10.00	20.00
❑ United Artists UAL 3425 [M]	Little Things	1965	5.00	10.00	20.00
❑ United Artists UAL 3471 [M]	Broomstick Cowboy	1966	5.00	10.00	20.00
❑ United Artists UAL 3486 [M]	It's Too Late	1966	5.00	10.00	20.00
❑ United Artists UAL 3552 [M]	Blue Autumn	1967	5.00	10.00	20.00
❑ United Artists UAL 3561 [M]	Sold Goldsboro/Bobby Goldsboro's Greatest Hits	1967	5.00	10.00	20.00
❑ United Artists UAL 3599 [M]	Romantic, Soulful, Wacky	1967	5.00	10.00	20.00
❑ United Artists UAL 3642 [M]	Honey	1968	10.00	20.00	40.00
—Some, if not all, copies of this have the title "Pledge of Love" on the label					
❑ United Artists UAS 5502	Bobby Goldsboro's Greatest Hits	1970	5.00	10.00	20.00
❑ United Artists UAS 5516	Come Back Home	1971	3.75	7.50	15.00
❑ United Artists UAS-5578	California Wine	1972	3.75	7.50	15.00
❑ United Artists UAS 6358 [S]	I Can't Stop Loving You	1964	6.25	12.50	25.00
❑ United Artists UAS 6358 [S]	The Bobby Goldsbob Album	1964	6.25	12.50	25.00
❑ United Artists UAS 6425 [S]	Little Things	1965	6.25	12.50	25.00
❑ United Artists UAS 6471 [S]	Broomstick Cowboy	1966	6.25	12.50	25.00
❑ United Artists UAS 6486 [S]	It's Too Late	1966	6.25	12.50	25.00
❑ United Artists UAS 6552 [S]	Blue Autumn	1967	6.25	12.50	25.00
❑ United Artists UAS 6561 [S]	Sold Goldsboro/Bobby Goldsboro's Greatest Hits	1967	5.00	10.00	20.00
❑ United Artists UAS 6599 [S]	Romantic, Soulful, Wacky	1967	5.00	10.00	20.00
❑ United Artists UAL 6642 [S]	Honey	1968	7.50	15.00	30.00
—Early copies of this have the title "Pledge of Love" on the label					
❑ United Artists UAS 6642 [S]	Honey	1968	5.00	10.00	20.00
—Later copies have the correct title "Honey" on the label					
❑ United Artists UAS 6657	Word Pictures Featuring Autumn of My Life	1968	5.00	10.00	20.00
❑ United Artists UAS 6704	Today	1969	5.00	10.00	20.00
❑ United Artists UAS 6735	Muddy Mississippi Line	1969	5.00	10.00	20.00
❑ United Artists UAS 6777	We Gotta Start Lovin'	1970	5.00	10.00	20.00
❑ United Artists UAS 6777	Watching Scotty Grow	1971	3.75	7.50	15.00
—Retitled version of above					

GOODMAN, DICKIE

45s

Number	Title (A Side/B Side)	Yr	VG	VG+	NM
❑ ASI 1013	Rocky and the Angel/Pug Rock	1977	—	3.00	6.00
—As "Dickie G. and the Don'ts"					
❑ Audio Spectrum 75	Presidential Interview (Flying Saucer '64)/Paul Revere	1964	10.00	20.00	40.00
❑ Cash 451	Mr. Jaws/Irv's Theme	1975	12.50	25.00	50.00
—Clear purple vinyl, possibly an "after-hours" edition; at least two, and probably more, exist					
❑ Cash 451	Mr. Jaws/Irv's Theme	1975	—	2.50	5.00
❑ Cotique 158	On Campus/Mombo Suzie	1969	—	3.00	6.00
—B-side by Johnny Colo					
❑ Cotique 173	Luna Trip/My Victrola	1969	—	3.00	6.00
—B-side by Joey Pastrana					
❑ Davy Jones 663	White House Happening/President Johnson	1967	6.25	12.50	25.00
❑ Diamond 119	Ben Crazy/Flip Side	1962	3.75	7.50	15.00

Number	Title (A Side/B Side)	Yr	VG	VG+	NM
❑ Extran 601	Hey, E.T./Get a Job	1982	—	2.50	5.00
❑ Goodname 7100	Safe Sex Report/Safety First	1987	3.75	7.50	15.00
—His last record					
❑ Hot Line 1017	Energy Crisis '79/Pain	1979	—	3.00	6.00
—Common version has a light green label and "Hot Line" as two words					
❑ Hot Line 1017	Energy Crisis '79/Pain	1979	2.00	4.00	8.00
—Less common version has a reddish label and the label as "Hotline" (one word)					
❑ J.M.D. 001	Ben Crazy/Flip Side	1962	6.25	12.50	25.00
❑ Janus 271	Star Warts/The Boys Tune	1977	—	2.50	5.00
❑ M.D. 101	Schmonanza/Backwards Theme	1961	5.00	10.00	20.00
❑ Mark-X 8009	The Touchables/Martian Melody	1961	5.00	10.00	20.00
—Black label					
❑ Mark-X 8010	The Touchables in Brooklyn/Mystery	1961	5.00	10.00	20.00
❑ Montage 1220	Hey, E.T./The Ride of Paul Revere	1982	3.75	7.50	15.00
❑ Oron 101	Washington Uptight/The Cat	1967	6.25	12.50	25.00
—As "The Pennsylvania Players"					
❑ Prelude 8018	Election '80 (same on both sides)	1980	—	2.50	5.00
❑ Rainy Wednesday 202	Watergrate/Friends	1973	—	3.00	6.00
❑ Rainy Wednesday 204	Purple People Eater/Ruthie's Theme	1973	—	3.00	6.00
❑ Rainy Wednesday 205	The Constitution/The End	1973	—	3.00	6.00
❑ Rainy Wednesday 206	Energy Crisis '74/The Mistake	1974	—	3.00	6.00
❑ Rainy Wednesday 206	Energy Crisis '74/Ruthie's Theme	1974	2.00	4.00	8.00
❑ Rainy Wednesday 207	Mr. President/Popularity	1974	—	3.00	6.00
❑ Rainy Wednesday 208	Gerry Ford, A Special Report/Robert	1974	—	3.00	6.00
❑ Rainy Wednesday 209	Inflation in the Nation/Jon and Jed's Theme	1975	—	3.00	6.00
❑ Ramgo 501	Speaking of Ecology/Dayton's Theme	1970	6.25	12.50	25.00
❑ Red Bird 10-058	Batman & His Grandmother/Suspense	1966	5.00	10.00	20.00
❑ Rhino 019	Radio Russia/Washington Inside Out	1984	—	2.00	4.00
❑ Rori 601	Horror Movies/Whoa, Mule	1961	6.25	12.50	25.00
❑ Rori 602	The Berlin Top Ten/Little Tiger	1961	6.25	12.50	25.00
❑ Rori 701	Santa and the Touchables/North Pole Rock	1961	6.25	12.50	25.00
❑ Scepter 12339	Speaking of Ecology/Dayton's Theme	1971	3.00	6.00	12.00
❑ Shark 1001	Mrs. Jaws/(B-side unknown)	1979	5.00	10.00	20.00
❑ Shark 1002	Super Superman/Chomp Chomp	1979	3.75	7.50	15.00
❑ Shell 711	Election '84/Herb's Theme	1984	—	2.00	4.00
❑ Shock 6	Kong/Ed's Tune	1977	—	2.50	5.00
❑ 20th Fox 443	Senate Hearing/Lock-Up	1963	3.75	7.50	15.00
❑ Twirl 2015	James Bomb/Seventh Theme	1966	3.75	7.50	15.00
❑ Wacko 1001	Mr. President/Dancin' U.S.A.	1981	—	2.50	5.00
❑ Wacko 1002	Super-Duper Man/Robert's Tune	1981	—	2.50	5.00
❑ Wacko 1381	America '81 (two different versions)	1981	2.00	4.00	8.00

Albums

Number	Title	Yr	VG	VG+	NM
❑ Cash CR 6000	Mr. Jaws and Other Fables	1975	6.25	12.50	25.00
❑ Comet 69	My Son, the Joke	1963	10.00	20.00	40.00
❑ IX Chains NCS 9000	The Original Flying Saucers	1973	10.00	20.00	40.00
❑ Rhino RNLP-811	Dickie Goodman's Greatest Hits	1983	3.75	7.50	15.00
❑ Rori 3301	The Many Heads of Dickie Goodman	1962	20.00	40.00	80.00

GORE, LESLEY

45s

Number	Title (A Side/B Side)	Yr	VG	VG+	NM
❑ A&M 1710	Give It to Me, Sweet Thing/Immortality	1975	—	2.50	5.00
❑ A&M 1830	Sometimes/Give It To Me, Sweet Thing	1976	—	2.50	5.00
❑ Crewe 338	Why Doesn't Love Make Me Happy/Tomorrow's Children	1970	2.50	5.00	10.00
❑ Crewe 344	When Yesterday Was Tomorrow/Why Me, Why You	1970	2.50	5.00	10.00
❑ Crewe 601	Back Together/Quiet Love	1971	2.50	5.00	10.00
❑ Manhattan 50039	Since I Don't Have You-It's Only Make Believe/ Our Love Was Meant to Be	1986	2.00	4.00	8.00
—With Lou Christie					
❑ Mercury 72119	It's My Party/Danny	1963	3.75	7.50	15.00
❑ Mercury 72143	Judy's Turn to Cry/Just Let Me Cry	1963	3.75	7.50	15.00
❑ Mercury 72180	She's a Fool/The Old Crowd	1963	3.75	7.50	15.00
❑ Mercury 72206	You Don't Own Me/Run, Bobby, Run	1963	3.75	7.50	15.00
❑ Mercury 72245	Je Ne Sais Plus/Je N'ose Pas	1964	5.00	10.00	20.00
❑ Mercury 72259	That's the Way Boys Are/That's the Way the Ball Bounces	1964	2.50	5.00	10.00
❑ Mercury 72270	I Don't Wanna Be a Loser/It's Gotta Be You	1964	2.50	5.00	10.00
❑ Mercury 72309	Maybe I Know/Wonder Boy	1964	2.50	5.00	10.00
❑ Mercury 72352	Hey Now/Sometimes I Wish I Were a Boy	1964	2.50	5.00	10.00

Number	Title (A Side/B Side)	Yr	VG	VG+	NM
❑ Mercury 72372	Look of Love/Little Girl Gone Home	1964	2.50	5.00	10.00
❑ Mercury 72412	All of My Life/I Cannot Hope for Anything	1965	2.50	5.00	10.00
❑ Mercury 72433	Sunshine, Lollipops and Rainbows/You've Come Back	1965	2.50	5.00	10.00
❑ Mercury 72475	My Town, My Guy and Me/Girl in Love	1965	2.50	5.00	10.00
❑ Mercury 72513	I Won't Love You Anymore (Sorry)/No Matter What You Do	1966	2.50	5.00	10.00
❑ Mercury 72530	We Know We're in Love/That's What We'll Do	1966	2.50	5.00	10.00
❑ Mercury 72553	Young Love/I Just Don't Know If I Can	1966	2.50	5.00	10.00
❑ Mercury 72580	Off and Running/I Don't Care	1966	2.50	5.00	10.00
❑ Mercury 72611	Maybe Now/Treat Me Like a Lady	1966	2.50	5.00	10.00
❑ Mercury 72649	California Nights/I'm Goin' Out	1967	2.50	5.00	10.00
❑ Mercury 72683	Summer and Sandy/I'm Fallin' Down	1967	2.50	5.00	10.00
❑ Mercury 72726	Brink of Disaster/On a Day Like This	1967	2.50	5.00	10.00
❑ Mercury 72759	It's a Happening/Magic Colors	1967	2.50	5.00	10.00
❑ Mercury 72787	Small Talk/Say What You See	1968	3.00	6.00	12.00
❑ Mercury 72819	He Gives Me Love (La, La, La)/Brand New Me	1968	3.00	6.00	12.00
❑ Mercury 72842	Where Can I Go/I Can't Make It Without You	1968	3.00	6.00	12.00
❑ Mercury 72867	Look the Other Way/I'll Be Standing By	1968	3.00	6.00	12.00
❑ Mercury 72892	Take Good Care (Of My Heart)/I Can't Make It Without You	1969	3.00	6.00	12.00
❑ Mercury 72892	Take Good Care (Of My Heart)/You Sent Me Silver Bells	1969	3.00	6.00	12.00
❑ Mercury 72931	Summer Symphony/98.6-Lazy Day	1969	3.75	7.50	15.00
❑ Mercury 72969	Wedding Bell Blues/One by One	1969	3.75	7.50	15.00
❑ Mowest 5029	The Road I Walk/She Said That	1972	2.50	5.00	10.00
❑ Mowest 5042	Give It to Me, Sweet Thing/Don't Want to Be One	1973	—	—	—
—Unreleased					
Albums					
❑ A&M SP-4564	Love Me by Name	1975	3.75	7.50	15.00
❑ Mercury ML-8016	I'll Cry If I Want To	1980	2.50	5.00	10.00
—Reissue of 60805					
❑ Mercury MG 20805 [M]	I'll Cry If I Want To	1963	7.50	15.00	30.00
—With no blurb for "It's My Party"					
❑ Mercury MG 20849 [M]	Lesley Gore Sings of Mixed-Up Hearts	1963	7.50	15.00	30.00
❑ Mercury MG 20901 [M]	Boys, Boys, Boys	1964	7.50	15.00	30.00
❑ Mercury MG 20943 [M]	Girl Talk	1964	7.50	15.00	30.00
❑ Mercury MG 21024 [M]	The Golden Hits of Lesley Gore	1965	7.50	15.00	30.00
❑ Mercury MG 21042 [M]	My Town, My Guy & Me	1965	7.50	15.00	30.00
❑ Mercury MG 21066 [M]	All About Love	1966	7.50	15.00	30.00
❑ Mercury MG 21120 [M]	California Nights	1967	7.50	15.00	30.00
❑ Mercury SR 60805 [S]	I'll Cry If I Want To	1963	10.00	20.00	40.00
—With no blurb for "It's My Party"					
❑ Mercury SR 60849 [S]	Lesley Gore Sings of Mixed-Up Hearts	1963	10.00	20.00	40.00
❑ Mercury SR 60901 [S]	Boys, Boys, Boys	1964	10.00	20.00	40.00
❑ Mercury SR 60943 [S]	Girl Talk	1964	10.00	20.00	40.00
❑ Mercury SR 61024 [S]	The Golden Hits of Lesley Gore	1965	10.00	20.00	40.00
—Originals have 12 tracks					
❑ Mercury SR 61042 [S]	My Town, My Guy & Me	1965	10.00	20.00	40.00
❑ Mercury SR 61066 [S]	All About Love	1966	10.00	20.00	40.00
—Stereo version has a different cover and liner notes than the mono version					
❑ Mercury SR 61120 [S]	California Nights	1967	10.00	20.00	40.00
❑ Mercury SR 61185	Golden Hits Vol. 2	1968	10.00	20.00	40.00
❑ Mercury 810370-1	The Golden Hits of Lesley Gore	1983	2.50	5.00	10.00
—Reissue of 61024					
❑ Mowest MW 117L	Someplace Else Now	1972	3.75	7.50	15.00
❑ Rhino RNFP-71496 [(2)]	The Lesley Gore Anthology (1963-1968)	1986	3.75	7.50	15.00
❑ Wing PRW-2-119 [(2)]	The Sound of Young Love	1969	5.00	10.00	20.00
❑ Wing SRW-16350	Girl Talk	1968	3.75	7.50	15.00
❑ Wing SRW-16382	Love, Love, Love	1968	3.75	7.50	15.00

GRAND FUNK RAILROAD

Number	Title (A Side/B Side)	Yr	VG	VG+	NM
45s					
❑ Capitol 2567	Time Machine/High on a Horse	1969	—	3.00	6.00
❑ Capitol 2691	Mr. Limousine Driver/High Falootin' Woman	1969	—	3.00	6.00
❑ Capitol 2732	Heartbreaker/Please Don't Worry	1970	—	3.00	6.00
❑ Capitol 2816	Nothing Is the Same/Sin's a Good Man's Brother	1970	—	3.00	6.00
❑ Capitol 2877	Closer to Home/Aimless Lady	1970	—	3.00	6.00
❑ Capitol 2996	Mean Mistreater/Mark Says Alright	1970	—	3.00	6.00
❑ Capitol 3095	Feelin' Alright/I Want Freedom	1971	—	3.00	6.00
❑ Capitol 3160	Gimme Shelter/I Can Feel Him in the Morning	1971	—	3.00	6.00
❑ Capitol 3217	People, Let's Stop the War/Save the Land	1971	—	3.00	6.00
❑ Capitol 3255	Footstompin' Music/I Come Tumblin'	1972	—	3.00	6.00
❑ Capitol 3316	Upsetter/No Lies	1972	—	3.00	6.00
❑ Capitol 3363	Rock 'N Roll Soul/Flight of the Phoenix	1972	—	3.00	6.00
❑ Capitol 3660	We're An American Band/Creepin'	1973	—	3.00	6.00
—Originals on gold vinyl					
❑ Capitol 3760	Walk Like a Man/The Railroad	1973	—	2.00	4.00
❑ Capitol 3840	The Loco-Motion/Destitute and Losin'	1974	—	2.00	4.00
❑ Capitol 3917	Shinin' On/Mr. Pretty Boy	1974	—	2.00	4.00
❑ Capitol 4002	Some Kind of Wonderful/Wild	1974	—	2.00	4.00
❑ Capitol 4046	Bad Time/Good and Evil	1975	—	2.00	4.00
❑ Capitol 4199	Take Me/Genevieve	1975	—	2.00	4.00
❑ Capitol 4235	Sally/Love Is Dyin'	1976	—	2.00	4.00
❑ Full Moon 49823	Y.O.U./Testify	1981	—	2.00	4.00
❑ Full Moon 49866	No Reason Why/Stuck in the Middle	1981	—	2.00	4.00
❑ MCA 40590	Can You Do It/1976	1976	—	2.50	5.00
❑ MCA 40641	Out to Get You/Just Couldn't Wait	1976	—	2.50	5.00
—The MCA sides were produced by Frank Zappa					
Albums					
❑ Capitol ST-307	On Time	1969	3.75	7.50	15.00
❑ Capitol SKAO-406	Grand Funk	1970	3.75	7.50	15.00

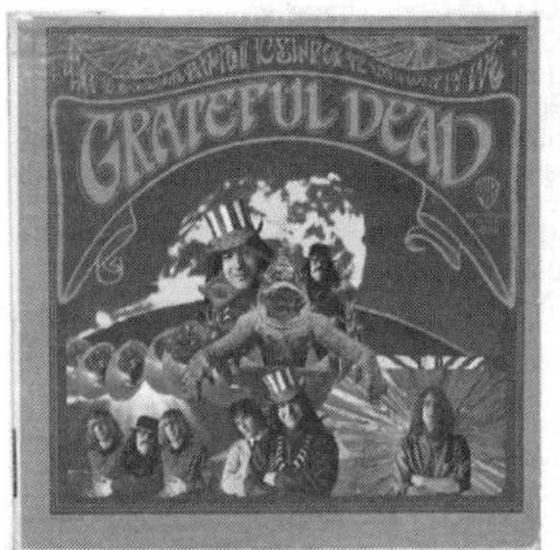

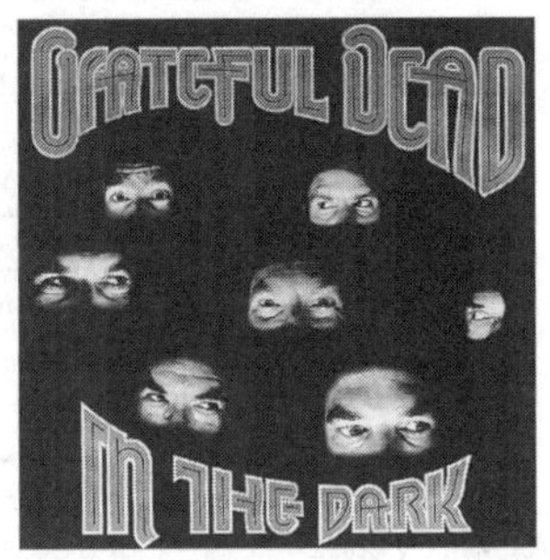

Number	Title (A Side/B Side)	Yr	VG	VG+	NM
❑ Capitol SKAO-471	Closer to Home	1970	3.75	7.50	15.00
❑ Capitol SWBB-633 [(2)]	Live Album	1970	3.75	7.50	15.00
—Includes poster					
❑ Capitol SW-764	Survival	1971	3.00	6.00	12.00
—Red "target" label; add $5 if individual photos of the band members are included					
❑ Capitol SW-764	Survival	1971	3.75	7.50	15.00
—Lime-green label; add $5 if individual photos of the band members are included					
❑ Capitol SW-764	Survival	1973	2.50	5.00	10.00
—Orange label, "Capitol" at bottom					
❑ Capitol SW-853	E Pluribus Funk	1971	3.75	7.50	15.00
—Round cover designed like a coin					
❑ Capitol SABB-11042 [(2)]	Mark, Don and Mel 1969-71	1972	3.75	7.50	15.00
❑ Capitol SMAS-11099	Phoenix	1972	3.00	6.00	12.00
❑ Capitol SMAS-11207	We're An American Band	1973	2.50	5.00	10.00
—Black vinyl					
❑ Capitol SWAE-11278	Shinin' On	1974	3.00	6.00	12.00
—With 3-D glasses attached to cover and with 3-D poster					
❑ Capitol SO-11356	All the Girls in the World Beware!!!	1974	3.75	7.50	15.00
—With poster (deduct 33% if missing)					
❑ Capitol SABB-11445	Caught in the Act	1975	2.50	5.00	10.00
❑ Capitol ST-11482	Born to Die	1976	2.50	5.00	10.00
❑ Capitol ST-11579	Grand Funk Hits	1976	2.50	5.00	10.00
❑ Capitol SN-16138	Grand Funk Hits	1981	2.00	4.00	8.00
❑ Capitol SN-16176	Closer to Home	1981	2.00	4.00	8.00
❑ Capitol SN-16177	Grand Funk	1981	2.00	4.00	8.00
❑ Capitol SN-16178	On Time	1981	2.00	4.00	8.00
❑ Full Moon HS 3625	Grand Funk Lives	1981	2.50	5.00	10.00
❑ Full Moon 23750	What's Funk	1983	2.50	5.00	10.00
❑ MCA 2216	Good Singin' Good Playin'	1976	3.00	6.00	12.00
—Produced by Frank Zappa					

GRASS ROOTS, THE

45s

Number	Title (A Side/B Side)	Yr	VG	VG+	NM
❑ ABC Dunhill 4144	Midnight Confessions/Who Will You Be Tomorrow	1968	2.00	4.00	8.00
❑ ABC Dunhill 4162	Della Linda/Hot Bright Blues	1968	3.00	6.00	12.00
—Some labels have A-side typographical error as shown					
❑ ABC Dunhill 4162	Bella Linda/Hot Bright Blues	1968	2.00	4.00	8.00
❑ ABC Dunhill 4180	Lovin' Things/You and Love Are the Same	1969	2.00	4.00	8.00
❑ ABC Dunhill 4187	The River Is Wide/(You Gotta) Live for Love	1969	2.00	4.00	8.00
❑ ABC Dunhill 4198	I'd Wait a Million Years/Fly Me to Havana	1969	—	3.00	6.00
❑ ABC Dunhill 4217	Heaven Knows/Don't Remind Me	1969	—	3.00	6.00
❑ ABC Dunhill 4227	Walking Through the Country/Truck Drivin' Man	1970	—	3.00	6.00
❑ ABC Dunhill 4237	Baby Hold On/Get It Together	1970	—	3.00	6.00
❑ ABC Dunhill 4249	Come On and Say It/Something's Comin' Over Me	1970	—	3.00	6.00
❑ ABC Dunhill 4263	Temptation Eyes/Keepin' Me Down	1971	—	2.50	5.00
❑ ABC Dunhill 4279	Sooner or Later/I Can Turn Off the Rain	1971	—	2.50	5.00
❑ ABC Dunhill 4289	Two Divided by Love/Let It Go	1971	—	2.50	5.00
❑ ABC Dunhill 4302	Glory Bound/The Only One	1972	—	2.50	5.00
❑ ABC Dunhill 4316	The Runway/Move Along	1972	—	2.50	5.00
❑ ABC Dunhill 4325	Any Way the Wind Blows/Monday Love	1972	—	2.50	5.00
❑ ABC Dunhill 4335	Love Is What You Make It/Someone to Love	1973	—	3.00	6.00
❑ ABC Dunhill 4345	Where There's Smoke There's Fire/Look but Don't Touch	1973	2.50	5.00	10.00
❑ ABC Dunhill 4371	We Can't Dance to Your Music/Look but Don't Touch	1973	2.50	5.00	10.00
❑ ABC Dunhill 15006	Stealin' Love (In the Night)/We Almost Made It Together	1974	3.75	7.50	15.00
❑ Dunhill 4013	Mr. Jones (A Ballad of a Thin Man)/You're a Lonely Girl	1965	5.00	10.00	20.00
❑ Dunhill 4029	Where Were You When I Needed You/(These Are) Bad Times	1966	5.00	10.00	20.00
❑ Dunhill 4043	Only When You're Lonely/This Is What I Was Made For	1966	5.00	10.00	20.00
❑ Dunhill 4053	Tip of My Tongue/Look Out, Girl	1966	6.25	12.50	25.00
❑ Dunhill 4084	Let's Live for Today/Depressed Feeling	1967	3.00	6.00	12.00
❑ Dunhill 4094	Things I Should Have Said/Tip of My Tongue	1967	2.50	5.00	10.00
❑ Dunhill 4105	Wake Up, Wake Up/No Exit	1967	2.50	5.00	10.00
❑ Dunhill 4122	A Melody for You/Hey Friend	1968	2.50	5.00	10.00
❑ Dunhill 4129	Feelings/Here's Where You Belong	1968	2.50	5.00	10.00
❑ Dunhill 4144	Midnight Confessions/Who Will You Be Tomorrow	1968	7.50	15.00	30.00
—Original label has no "ABC" logo next to "Dunhill"					
❑ Haven 802	Out in the Open/Optical Illusion	1976	2.00	4.00	8.00
❑ Haven 7015	Mamacita/Last Time Around	1975	—	2.50	5.00

Number	Title (A Side/B Side)	Yr	VG	VG+	NM
❑ Haven 7021	Naked Man/Nothing Good Comes Easy	1975	—	2.50	5.00
❑ MCA 52058	Here Comes That Feeling Again/Temptation Eyes	1982	2.50	5.00	10.00
❑ MCA 52104	She Don't Know Me/Keep On Burning	1982	2.50	5.00	10.00
Albums					
❑ ABC AC-30003	The ABC Collection	1976	3.75	7.50	15.00
❑ ABC Dunhill DS-50027	Feelings	1968	3.75	7.50	15.00
—Reissue with ABC logo					
❑ ABC Dunhill DS-50047	Golden Grass	1968	5.00	10.00	20.00
❑ ABC Dunhill DS-50052	Lovin' Things	1969	5.00	10.00	20.00
❑ ABC Dunhill DS-50067	Leaving It All Behind	1969	5.00	10.00	20.00
❑ ABC Dunhill DS-50087	More Golden Grass	1970	5.00	10.00	20.00
❑ ABC Dunhill DSX-50107	Their 16 Greatest Hits	1971	5.00	10.00	20.00
❑ ABC Dunhill DSX-50112	Move Along	1972	3.75	7.50	15.00
❑ ABC Dunhill DSX-50137	A Lotta Mileage	1973	3.75	7.50	15.00
❑ Dunhill D-50011 [M]	Where Were You When I Needed You	1966	37.50	75.00	150.00
❑ Dunhill DS-50011 [S]	Where Were You When I Needed You	1966	25.00	50.00	100.00
❑ Dunhill D-50020 [M]	Let's Live for Today	1967	6.25	12.50	25.00
❑ Dunhill DS-50020 [S]	Let's Live for Today	1967	7.50	15.00	30.00
❑ Dunhill D-50027 [M]	Feelings	1968	7.50	15.00	30.00
❑ Dunhill DS-50027 [S]	Feelings	1968	5.00	10.00	20.00
❑ Haven ST-9204	The Grass Roots	1975	3.75	7.50	15.00
❑ MCA 5331	Powers of the Night	1982	3.00	6.00	12.00
❑ MCA 37154	Their 16 Greatest Hits	198?	2.00	4.00	8.00
—Budget-line reissue of ABC Dunhill 50107					

GRATEFUL DEAD, THE

45s

Number	Title (A Side/B Side)	Yr	VG	VG+	NM
❑ Arista 0276	Dancin' in the Streets/Terrapin Station	1977	—	3.00	6.00
❑ Arista 0291	Passenger/Terrapin Station	1977	—	3.00	6.00
❑ Arista 0383	Good Lovin'/Stagger Lee	1978	—	3.00	6.00
❑ Arista 0410	France/Shakedown Street	1979	—	3.00	6.00
❑ Arista 0519	Alabama Getaway/Far from Me	1980	—	2.50	5.00
❑ Arista 0546	Don't Ease Me In/Far from Me	1980	—	2.50	5.00
❑ Arista 9606	Touch of Grey/My Brother Esau	1987	—	—	3.00
—Black vinyl (not issued with picture sleeve)					
❑ Arista 9643	Throwing Stones (Ashes Ashes) Edit/Throwing Stones (Ashes Ashes) LP Version	1987	—	—	3.00
❑ Arista 9899	Foolish Heart/We Can Run	1989	—	2.00	4.00
❑ Grateful Dead 01	Here Comes Sunshine/Let Me Sing Your Blues Away	1973	3.00	6.00	12.00
❑ Grateful Dead 02	Eyes of the World/Weather Report (Part 1)	1974	3.00	6.00	12.00
❑ Grateful Dead 03	U.S. Blues/Loose Lucy	1974	2.50	5.00	10.00
❑ Grateful Dead XW-718	The Music Never Stopped/Help on the Way	1975	3.75	7.50	15.00
❑ Grateful Dead XW-762	Franklin's Tower/Help on the Way	1976	6.25	12.50	25.00
❑ Scorpio 201	Stealin'/Don't Ease Me In	1966	250.00	500.00	1000.
❑ Warner Bros. 7016	The Golden Road (To Unlimited Devotion)/Cream Puff War	1967	6.25	12.50	25.00
❑ Warner Bros. 7186	Dark Star/Born Cross-Eyed	1968	6.25	12.50	25.00
❑ Warner Bros. 7324	Dupree's Diamond Blues/Cosmic Charlie	1969	6.25	12.50	25.00
❑ Warner Bros. 7410	Uncle John's Band/New Speedway Boogie	1970	3.75	7.50	15.00
—A picture sleeve for this is rumored to exist					
❑ Warner Bros. 7464	Truckin'/Ripple	1971	3.75	7.50	15.00
❑ Warner Bros. 7627	Johnny B. Goode/So Fine	1972	5.00	10.00	20.00
—B-side by Elvin Bishop Group					
❑ Warner Bros. 7653	Truckin'/Johnny B. Goode	1973	2.00	4.00	8.00
—"Back to Back Hits" series					
❑ Warner Bros. 7667	Sugar Magnolia/Mr. Charlie	1972	3.75	7.50	15.00
Albums					
❑ Arista AB 4198	Shakedown Street	1978	3.00	6.00	12.00
❑ Arista AL 7001	Terrapin Station	1977	3.75	7.50	15.00
❑ Arista AL 8112 [(2)]	Dead Set	198?	2.50	5.00	10.00
—Budget-line reissue of 8606					
❑ Arista AL 8321	Shakedown Street	198?	2.00	4.00	8.00
—Budget-line reissue of 4198					
❑ Arista AL 8329	Terrapin Station	198?	2.00	4.00	8.00
—Budget-line reissue of 7001					
❑ Arista AL 8332	Go to Heaven	198?	2.00	4.00	8.00
—Budget-line reissue of 9508					
❑ Arista AL 8452	In the Dark	1987	2.50	5.00	10.00
❑ Arista AL 8575	Built to Last	1989	2.50	5.00	10.00
❑ Arista A2L 8604 [(2)]	Reckoning	1981	3.75	7.50	15.00
❑ Arista A2L 8606 [(2)]	Dead Set	1981	3.75	7.50	15.00
❑ Arista AL3 8634 [(3)]	Without a Net	1990	6.25	12.50	25.00
❑ Arista AL 9508	Go to Heaven	1980	3.00	6.00	12.00
❑ Grateful Dead GD-01	Wake of the Flood	1973	5.00	10.00	20.00
—With no contributing artists on back cover					
❑ Grateful Dead GD-102	Grateful Dead from the Mars Hotel	1974	5.00	10.00	20.00
—Without United Artists distribution					
❑ Grateful Dead GD-LA494-G	Blues for Allah	1975	5.00	10.00	20.00
❑ Grateful Dead GD-LA620-J2 [(2)]	Steal Your Face	1976	6.25	12.50	25.00
❑ Pair PDL2-1053 [(2)]	For the Faithful...	1986	3.00	6.00	12.00
❑ Pride PRD 0016	The History of the Grateful Dead	1972	6.25	12.50	25.00
—Reissue of material from Sunflower LPs					
❑ Sunflower SUN-5001	Vintage Dead	1970	10.00	20.00	40.00
—Album has been counterfeited, but bogus covers are 1/4" shorter than normal LP cover					
❑ Sunflower SNF-5004	Historic Dead	1971	10.00	20.00	40.00
❑ Warner Bros. W 1689 [M]	The Grateful Dead	1967	50.00	100.00	200.00

Number	Title (A Side/B Side)	Yr	VG	VG+	NM
❑ Warner Bros. WS 1689 [S]	The Grateful Dead	1967	20.00	40.00	80.00
—Gold label					
❑ Warner Bros. WS 1749	Anthem of the Sun	1968	7.50	15.00	30.00
—Green label with "W7" logo					
❑ Warner Bros. WS 1790	Aoxomoxoa	1969	7.50	15.00	30.00
—Green label with "W7" logo					
❑ Warner Bros. 2WS 1830 [(2)]	Live/Dead	1969	10.00	20.00	40.00
—Green labels with "W7" logo					
❑ Warner Bros. WS 1869	Workingman's Dead	1970	6.25	12.50	25.00
—Green label with "WB" logo; textured cover with back cover slick upside down					
❑ Warner Bros. WS 1893	American Beauty	1970	6.25	12.50	25.00
—Green label with "WB" logo					
❑ Warner Bros. 2WS 1935 [(2)]	Grateful Dead	1971	7.50	15.00	30.00
—Green labels with "WB" logo					
❑ Warner Bros. 3WX 2668 [(3)]	Europe '72	1972	10.00	20.00	40.00
—Green labels with "WB" logo					
❑ Warner Bros. BS 2721	History of the Grateful Dead, Vol. 1 (Bear's Choice)	1973	5.00	10.00	20.00
—"Burbank" palm-trees labels					
❑ Warner Bros. W 2764	The Best of/Skeletons from the Closet	1974	5.00	10.00	20.00
—"Burbank" palm-trees labels					
❑ Warner Bros. 2WS 3091 [(2)]	What a Long Strange Trip It's Been: The Best of the Grateful Dead	1977	5.00	10.00	20.00
—"Burbank" palm-trees labels					

GRAY, DOBIE

45s

Number	Title (A Side/B Side)	Yr	VG	VG+	NM
❑ Anthem 200	Guess Who?/Bits and Pieces	1972	—	2.50	5.00
❑ Arista 1047	One Can Fake It/(B-side unknown)	1983	—	2.00	4.00
❑ Capitol 2241	We the People/Funny and Groovy	1968	2.50	5.00	10.00
❑ Capitol B-5562	Gonna Be a Long Night/That's One to Grown On	1986	—	—	3.00
❑ Capitol B-5596	The Dark Side of Life/A Night in the Life of a Country Boy	1986	—	—	3.00
❑ Capitol B-5647	From Where I Stand/So Far So Good	1986	—	—	3.00
❑ Capitol 5853	River Deep, Mountain High/Tennessee Waltz	1967	3.75	7.50	15.00
❑ Capitol B-44087	Take It Real Easy/You Must Have Been Reading My Heart	1987	—	—	3.00
❑ Capitol B-44126	Love Letters/Steady As She Goes	1988	—	—	3.00
❑ Capricorn 0249	If Love Must Go/Lover's Sweat	1975	—	2.00	4.00
❑ Capricorn 0259	Find 'Em, Fool 'Em and Forget 'Em/Mellow Man	1976	—	2.00	4.00
❑ Capricorn 0267	Let Go/Mellow Man	1976	—	2.00	4.00
❑ Charger 105	The "In" Crowd/Be a Man	1964	3.00	6.00	12.00
❑ Charger 107	See You at the "Go-Go"/Walk with Love	1965	2.50	5.00	10.00
❑ Charger 109	In Hollywood/Mr. Engineer	1965	2.50	5.00	10.00
❑ Charger 113	Monkey Jerk/My Baby	1965	2.50	5.00	10.00
❑ Charger 115	No Room to Cry/Out on the Floor	1966	2.50	5.00	10.00
❑ Cordak 1602	Look at Me/Walkin' and Whistlin'	1962	3.75	7.50	15.00
❑ Decca 33057	Drift Away/City Stars	1973	—	2.50	5.00
❑ Infinity 50003	You Can Do It/Sharing the Night Together	1978	—	2.00	4.00
❑ Infinity 50010	Who's Lovin' You/Thank You for Tonight	1979	—	2.00	4.00
❑ Infinity 50020	Spending Time, Making Love, and Going Crazy/ Let This Man Take Hold of Your Life	1979	—	2.00	4.00
❑ Infinity 50043	The In Crowd/Let This Man Take Hold of Your Life	1979	—	2.00	4.00
❑ Lana 138	The "In" Crowd/Be a Man	196?	—	3.00	6.00
—Oldies reissue					
❑ MCA 40100	Loving Arms/Now That I'm Without You	1973	—	2.00	4.00
❑ MCA 40153	Good Old Song/Reachin' for the Feelin'	1973	—	2.00	4.00
❑ MCA 40188	Rose/Lovin' the Easy Way	1974	—	2.00	4.00
❑ MCA 40201	There's a Honky Tonk Angel (Who'll Take Me Back In)/ Lovin' the Easy Way	1974	—	2.00	4.00
❑ MCA 40268	Watch Out for Lucy/Turning On You	1974	—	2.00	4.00
❑ MCA 40315	The Music's Real/Roll On Sweet Mississippi	1974	—	2.00	4.00
❑ Robox RRS-117	Decorate the Night (same on both sides)	1979	—	2.50	5.00
❑ White Whale 300	Rose Garden/Where's the Girl Gone	1969	2.50	5.00	10.00
❑ White Whale 330	What a Way to Go/Do You Really Have a Heart	1969	50.00	100.00	200.00
❑ White Whale 342	Honey, You Can't Take It Back	1970	15.00	30.00	60.00

Albums

Number	Title (A Side/B Side)	Yr	VG	VG+	NM
❑ Capitol ST-12489	From Where I Stand	1986	2.50	5.00	10.00
❑ Capricorn CP 0163	New Ray of Sunshine	1976	2.50	5.00	10.00
❑ Charger CHR-M-2002 [M]	Dobie Gray Sings for "In" Crowders That Go "Go Go"	1965	10.00	20.00	40.00

Number	Title (A Side/B Side)	Yr	VG	VG+	NM
❑ Charger CHR-S-2002 [S]	Dobie Gray Sings for "In" Crowders That Go "Go Go"	1965	30.00	60.00	120.00
❑ Decca DL 75397	Drift Away	1973	3.00	6.00	12.00
❑ Infinity INF-9001	Midnight Diamond	1979	2.50	5.00	10.00
❑ MCA 371	Loving Arms	1973	2.50	5.00	10.00
❑ MCA 449	Hey Dixie	1974	2.50	5.00	10.00
❑ MCA 515	Drift Away	1974	2.50	5.00	10.00
—Reissue of Decca 75397					
❑ Robox RBX 8102	Welcome Home	1981	2.50	5.00	10.00
❑ Stripe LPM 2001 [M]	Look — Dobie Gray	1963	25.00	50.00	100.00

GREEN, AL

45s

Number	Title (A Side/B Side)	Yr	VG	VG+	NM
❑ A&M 1427	As Long As We're Together/Blessed	1989	—	—	3.00
❑ A&M 2786	Going Away/Building Up	1985	—	2.00	4.00
❑ A&M 2807	True Love/He Is the Light	1986	—	2.00	4.00
❑ A&M 2919	Everything's Gonna Be Alright/So Real to Me	1987	—	—	3.00
❑ A&M 2952	You Know and I Know/True Love	1987	—	—	3.00
❑ A&M 2962	Soul Survivor/Jesus Will Fix It	1987	—	—	3.00
❑ Bell 45258	Guilty/Let Me Help You	1972	—	2.50	5.00
❑ Bell 45305	Hot Wire/Don't Leave Me	1973	—	2.50	5.00
❑ Hi 2159	I Want to Hold Your Hand/What Am I Gonna Do with Myself	1969	2.00	4.00	8.00
❑ Hi 2164	One Woman/Tomorrow's Dream	1969	2.00	4.00	8.00
❑ Hi 2172	You Say It/Gotta Find a New World	1969	—	3.00	6.00
❑ Hi 2177	Right Now, Right Now/All Because I'm a Foolish One	1970	—	3.00	6.00
❑ Hi 2182	I Can't Get Next to You/Ride Sally Ride	1970	—	3.00	6.00
❑ Hi 2188	Driving Wheel/True Love	1971	—	3.00	6.00
❑ Hi 2194	Tired of Being Alone/Get Back Baby	1971	—	2.50	5.00
❑ Hi 2202	Let's Stay Together/Tomorrow's Dream	1971	—	2.50	5.00
❑ Hi 2211	Look What You Done for Me/La La for You	1972	—	2.50	5.00
❑ Hi 2216	I'm Still in Love with You/Old Time Lovin'	1972	—	2.50	5.00
❑ Hi 2227	You Ought to Be with Me/What Is This Feeling	1972	—	2.50	5.00
❑ Hi 2235	Call Me (Come Back Home)/What a Wonderful Thing Love Is	1973	—	2.50	5.00
❑ Hi 2247	Here I Am (Come and Take Me)/I'm Glad You're Mine	1973	—	2.50	5.00
❑ Hi 2257	Livin' for You/It Ain't No Fun to Me	1973	—	2.50	5.00
❑ Hi 2262	Let's Get Married/So Good to Be Here	1974	—	2.50	5.00
❑ Hi 2274	Sha-La-La (Make Me Happy)/School Days	1974	—	2.50	5.00
❑ Hi 2282	L-O-V-E (Love)/I Wish You Were Here	1975	—	2.50	5.00
❑ Hi 2288	Oh Me, Oh My (Dreams in My Arms)/Strong As Death (Sweet As Love)	1975	—	2.50	5.00
❑ Hi 2300	Full of Fire/Could I Be the One	1975	—	2.50	5.00
❑ Hi 2306	Let It Shine/There's No Way	1976	—	2.50	5.00
❑ Hi 2319	Keep Me Cryin'/There Is Love	1976	—	2.50	5.00
❑ Hi 2322	I Tried to Tell Myself/Something	1977	—	2.50	5.00
❑ Hi 2324	Love and Happiness/Glory Glory	1977	—	2.50	5.00
❑ Hi 77505	Belle/Chariots of Fire	1977	—	2.00	4.00
❑ Hi 77680	White Christmas/Winter Wonderland	2001	—	2.50	5.00
—Clear vinyl					
❑ Hi 78511	I Feel Good/Feels Like Summer	1978	—	2.00	4.00
❑ Hi 78522	Wait Here/To Sir with Love	1978	—	2.00	4.00
❑ Hot Line Journal 15000	Back Up Train/Don't Leave Me	1967	6.25	12.50	25.00
❑ Hot Line Journal 15001	Don't Hurt Me No More/Get Yourself Together	1967	7.50	15.00	30.00
❑ Hot Line Journal 15002	I'll Be Good to You/Lover's Hideaway	1967	7.50	15.00	30.00

Albums

Number	Title (A Side/B Side)	Yr	VG	VG+	NM
❑ A&M SP-5150	Soul Survivor	1987	2.50	5.00	10.00
❑ A&M SP-5228	I Get Joy	1989	2.50	5.00	10.00
❑ Bell 6076	Al Green	1972	5.00	10.00	20.00
—Reissue of Hot Line LP					
❑ Blue Note BTE 74584	Everything's OK	2005	3.75	7.50	15.00
❑ Blue Note 93556 [(2)]	I Can't Stop	2003	3.75	7.50	15.00
❑ Hi 6004	The Belle Album	1977	3.00	6.00	12.00
❑ Hi 6009	Truth 'N' Time	1978	3.00	6.00	12.00
❑ Hi 8000	Tired of Being Alone	1977	3.00	6.00	12.00
❑ Hi 8001	Al Green Gets Next to You	1977	3.00	6.00	12.00
❑ Hi 8007	Let's Stay Together	1977	3.00	6.00	12.00
❑ Hi SHL-32055	Green Is Blues	1969	3.75	7.50	15.00
❑ Hi SHL-32062	Al Green Gets Next to You	1971	3.75	7.50	15.00
❑ Hi SHL-32070	Let's Stay Together	1972	3.75	7.50	15.00
❑ Hi SHL-32074	I'm Still in Love with You	1972	3.75	7.50	15.00
❑ Hi SHL-32077	Call Me	1973	3.75	7.50	15.00
❑ Hi SHL-32082	Livin' for You	1973	3.75	7.50	15.00
❑ Hi SHL-32087	Al Green Explores Your Mind	1974	3.75	7.50	15.00
❑ Hi SHL-32089	Al Green/Greatest Hits	1975	3.75	7.50	15.00
❑ Hi SHL-32092	Al Green Is Love	1975	3.75	7.50	15.00
❑ Hi SHL-32097	Full of Fire	1976	3.75	7.50	15.00
❑ Hi SHL-32103	Have a Good Time	1976	3.75	7.50	15.00
❑ Hi SHL-32105	Al Green's Greatest Hits, Volume II	1977	3.75	7.50	15.00
❑ Hot Line 1500 [M]	Back Up Train	1967	12.50	25.00	50.00
—As "Al Greene"					
❑ Hot Line S-1500 [S]	Back Up Train	1967	20.00	40.00	80.00
—As "Al Greene"					
❑ Kory 1005	Al Green	1977	2.50	5.00	10.00
—Reissue of Bell LP					
❑ MCA 42308	Love Ritual	1988	2.50	5.00	10.00
❑ Motown 5283 ML	Al Green/Greatest Hits	198?	2.50	5.00	10.00
—Reissue of Hi 32089					
❑ Motown 5284 ML	I'm Still in Love with You	198?	2.50	5.00	10.00
—Reissue of Hi 32074					

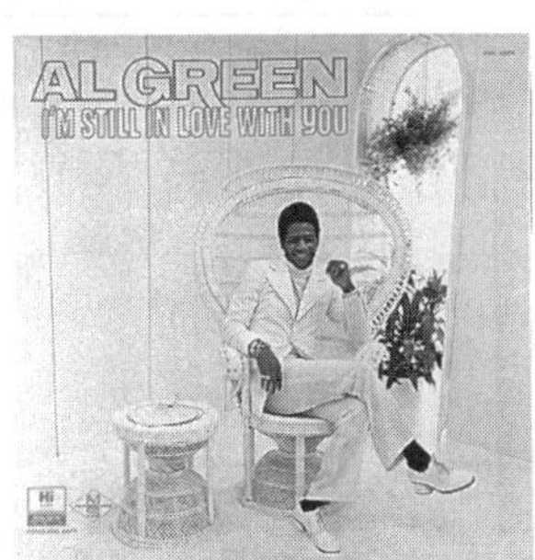

Number	Title (A Side/B Side)	Yr	VG	VG+	NM
❑ Motown 5290 ML	Let's Stay Together	198?	2.50	5.00	10.00
—Reissue of Hi 32070					
❑ Motown 5291 ML	Al Green's Greatest Hits, Volume II	198?	2.50	5.00	10.00
—Reissue of Hi 32105					
❑ Motown 5317 ML	Truth N' Time	198?	2.50	5.00	10.00
❑ Myrrh MSB-6661	The Lord Will Make a Way	1980	2.50	5.00	10.00
❑ Myrrh MSB-6671	Higher Plane	1981	2.50	5.00	10.00
❑ Myrrh MSB-6702	Precious Lord	1981	2.50	5.00	10.00
❑ Myrrh MSB-6747	I'll Rise Again	1982	2.50	5.00	10.00
❑ Myrrh MSB-6774	Al Green and the Full Gospel Tabernacle Choir	1984	2.50	5.00	10.00
❑ Myrrh WR-8113	The Lord Will Make a Way	1985	2.00	4.00	8.00
—Reissue with new number and A&M logo					
❑ Myrrh WR-8114	Higher Plane	1985	2.00	4.00	8.00
—Reissue with new number and A&M logo					
❑ Myrrh WR-8115	Precious Lord	1985	2.00	4.00	8.00
—Reissue with new number and A&M logo					
❑ Myrrh WR-8116	I'll Rise Again	1985	2.00	4.00	8.00
—Reissue with new number and A&M logo					
❑ Myrrh WR-8117	White Christmas	1985	2.50	5.00	10.00
—Reissue with new number and A&M logo					
❑ Myrrh WR-8118	Trust in God	1985	2.00	4.00	8.00
—Reissue with new number and A&M logo					
❑ Myrrh WR-8209	Al Green and the Full Gospel Tabernacle Choir	1986	2.00	4.00	8.00
—Reissue with new number and A&M logo					
❑ Myrrh 7-01-678006-6	White Christmas	1984	3.00	6.00	12.00
❑ Myrrh 7-01-678306-?	Trust in God	1984	2.50	5.00	10.00
❑ Word E 77000	One in a Million	1991	3.00	6.00	12.00

GREENBAUM, NORMAN

45s

Number	Title (A Side/B Side)	Yr	VG	VG+	NM
❑ Gregar 71-0107	Nancy Whiskey/Twentieth Century Fox	1969	2.50	5.00	10.00
❑ Reprise 0739	Spirit in the Sky/Canned Ham	1971	—	2.00	4.00
—"Back to Back Hits" series					
❑ Reprise 0752	Children of Paradise/School for Sweet Talk	1968	2.50	5.00	10.00
❑ Reprise 0818	Marcy/Children of Paradise	1969	2.50	5.00	10.00
❑ Reprise 0846	Jubilee/Skyline	1969	2.50	5.00	10.00
❑ Reprise 0885	Spirit in the Sky/Milk Cow	1969	2.00	4.00	8.00
❑ Reprise 0919	Canned Ham/Junior Cadillac	1970	—	3.00	6.00
❑ Reprise 0956	Rhode Island Red/I.J. Foxx	1970	—	3.00	6.00
❑ Reprise 1008	California Earthquake/Rhode Island Red	1971	—	3.00	6.00
❑ Reprise 1134	Dairy Queen/Petaluma	1972	—	3.00	6.00

Albums

Number	Title (A Side/B Side)	Yr	VG	VG+	NM
❑ Reprise MS 2048	Petaluma	1972	3.75	7.50	15.00
❑ Reprise RS 6365	Spirit in the Sky	1969	5.00	10.00	20.00
❑ Reprise RS 6422	Back Home Again	1970	3.75	7.50	15.00

GUESS WHO, THE

45s

Number	Title (A Side/B Side)	Yr	VG	VG+	NM
❑ Amy 967	And She's Mine/All Right	1966	5.00	10.00	20.00
—The existence of stock copies of this record has been questioned					
❑ Amy 976	His Girl/It's My Pride	1967	7.50	15.00	30.00
—Price is for stock copy; promos go for less					
❑ Fontana 1597	This Time Long Ago/There's No Getting Away from It	1967	7.50	15.00	30.00
❑ Hilltak 7803	C'mon Little Mama/Moon Wave Maker	1979	—	3.00	6.00
❑ Hilltak 7807	Sweet Young Thing/It's Getting Pretty Bad	1979	—	3.00	6.00
❑ RCA Victor 74-0102	These Eyes/Lightfoot	1969	—	3.00	6.00
❑ RCA Victor 74-0195	Laughing/Undun	1969	—	3.00	6.00
❑ RCA Victor 74-0300	No Time/Proper Stranger	1969	—	3.00	6.00
❑ RCA Victor 74-0325	American Woman/No Sugar Tonight	1970	—	2.50	5.00
❑ RCA Victor 74-0367	Hand Me Down World/Runnin' Down the Street	1970	—	2.50	5.00
❑ RCA Victor 74-0388	Share the Land/Bus Rider	1970	—	2.50	5.00
❑ RCA Victor 74-0414	Hang On to Your Life/Do You Miss Me, Darlin'?	1970	—	2.50	5.00
❑ RCA Victor 74-0458	Albert Flasher/Broken	1971	—	2.50	5.00
❑ RCA Victor 74-0522	Rain Dance/One Divided	1971	—	2.50	5.00
❑ RCA Victor 74-0578	Sour Suite/Life in the Bloodstream	1971	—	2.50	5.00
❑ RCA Victor 74-0659	Heartbroken Bopper/Arrividerci Girl	1972	—	2.50	5.00
❑ RCA Victor 74-0708	Guns, Guns, Guns/Heaven Only Moved Once Yesterday	1972	—	2.50	5.00

Number	Title (A Side/B Side)	Yr	VG	VG+	NM
❑ RCA Victor 74-0803	Runnin' Back to Saskatoon/New Mother Nature	1972	—	2.50	5.00
❑ RCA Victor 74-0880	Follow Your Daughter Home/Bye Bye Babe	1973	—	2.50	5.00
❑ RCA Victor 74-0926	The Watcher/Orly	1973	—	2.50	5.00
❑ RCA Victor 74-0977	Lie Down/Glamour Boy	1973	—	2.50	5.00
❑ RCA Victor APBO-0217	Star Baby/Musicione	1974	—	2.50	5.00
❑ RCA Victor APBO-0324	Clap for the Wolfman/Road Food	1974	—	2.50	5.00
❑ RCA Victor PB-10075	Dancin' Fool/Seems Like I Can't Live With You, But I Can't Live Without You	1974	—	2.50	5.00
❑ RCA Victor GB-10161	Clap for the Wolfman/Star Baby	1975	—	2.00	4.00
—Gold Standard Series					
❑ RCA Victor PB-10216	Loves Me Like a Brother/Hoe Down Time	1975	—	2.50	5.00
❑ RCA Victor PB-10360	Dreams/Rosanne	1975	—	2.50	5.00
❑ RCA Victor PB-10410	When the Band Was Singin' (Shakin' All Over)/Women	1975	—	3.00	6.00
❑ RCA Victor PB-10716	Silver Bird/Runnin' Down the Street	1976	3.00	6.00	12.00
❑ Scepter 1295	Shakin' All Over/Till We Kissed	1965	3.75	7.50	15.00
❑ Scepter 1295	Shakin' All Over/Monkey in a Cage	1965	7.50	15.00	30.00
—B-side by the Discotays					
❑ Scepter 12108	Hey Ho What You Do to Me/Goodnight Goodnight	1965	3.75	7.50	15.00
❑ Scepter 12118	Hurting Each Other/Baby's Birthday	1965	5.00	10.00	20.00
❑ Scepter 12131	Believe Me/Baby Feelin'	1966	5.00	10.00	20.00
❑ Scepter 12144	One Day/Clock on the Wall	1966	5.00	10.00	20.00
Albums					
❑ Compleat 672012-1 [(2)]	The Best of the Gues Who, Live	1986	5.00	10.00	20.00
❑ Hilltak HT 19227	All This for a Song	1979	3.00	6.00	12.00
❑ MGM SE-4645	The Guess Who	1969	3.75	7.50	15.00
—Compilation of pre-RCA Victor recordings					
❑ P.I.P. 6806	The Guess Who Play Pure Guess Who	197?	3.00	6.00	12.00
❑ Pickwick SPC-3246	The Guess Who	1970	2.50	5.00	10.00
❑ Pride PRD 0012	The History of the Guess Who	197?	3.00	6.00	12.00
❑ RCA 7622-1-R	The Greatest of the Guess Who	1987	2.50	5.00	10.00
—Late reissue					
❑ RCA Victor APL1-0130	#10	1973	3.75	7.50	15.00
❑ RCA Victor APL1-0269	The Best of the Guess Who, Volume II	1973	3.75	7.50	15.00
❑ RCA Victor APL1-0405	Road Food	1974	3.75	7.50	15.00
❑ RCA Victor CPL1-0636	Flavours	1975	3.75	7.50	15.00
❑ RCA Victor ANL1-0983	Canned Wheat Packed By the Guess Who	1975	2.50	5.00	10.00
—Reissue of LSP-4157					
❑ RCA Victor APL1-0995	Power in the Music	1975	3.75	7.50	15.00
❑ RCA Victor LSPX-1004	The Best of the Guess Who	1971	3.75	7.50	15.00
❑ RCA Victor ANL1-1117	Wheatfield Soul	1975	2.50	5.00	10.00
—Reissue of LSP-4141					
❑ RCA Victor APL1-1778	The Way They Were	1976	3.75	7.50	15.00
❑ RCA Victor APL1-2253	The Greatest of the Guess Who	1977	3.75	7.50	15.00
❑ RCA Victor AFL1-2594	The Best of the Guess Who	1978	2.50	5.00	10.00
—Reissue of LSPX-1004					
❑ RCA Victor AYL1-3662	The Best of the Guess Who	1979	2.00	4.00	8.00
—"Best Buy Series" reissue					
❑ RCA Victor AYL1-3673	American Woman	1979	2.00	4.00	8.00
—"Best Buy Series" reissue					
❑ RCA Victor AYL1-3746	The Greatest of the Guess Who	1980	2.00	4.00	8.00
—"Best Buy Series" reissue					
❑ RCA Victor LSP-4141	Wheatfield Soul	1969	5.00	10.00	20.00
—Orange label, non-flexible vinyl					
❑ RCA Victor LSP-4157	Canned Wheat Packed By the Guess Who	1969	5.00	10.00	20.00
—Orange label, non-flexible vinyl					
❑ RCA Victor LSP-4266	American Woman	1970	5.00	10.00	20.00
—Orange label, non-flexible vinyl					
❑ RCA Victor LSP-4359	Share the Land	1970	5.00	10.00	20.00
—Orange label, non-flexible vinyl					
❑ RCA Victor LSP-4574	So Long, Bannatyne	1971	3.75	7.50	15.00
❑ RCA Victor LSP-4602	Rockin'	1972	3.75	7.50	15.00
❑ RCA Victor LSP-4779	Live at the Paramount (Seattle)	1972	6.25	12.50	25.00
❑ RCA Victor LSP-4830	Artificial Paradise	1973	3.75	7.50	15.00
—Add 1/3 if paper bag is with package					
❑ Scepter SP-533 [M]	Shakin' All Over	1966	10.00	20.00	40.00
❑ Scepter SPS-533 [P]	Shakin' All Over	1966	6.25	12.50	25.00
—The above lists the artist as "The Guess Who's Chad Allan & The Expressions" on the cover					
❑ Springboard SPB-4022	Shakin' All Over	1972	2.50	5.00	10.00
❑ Wand WDS-691 [P]	Born in Canada	1969	3.75	7.50	15.00
—Reissue of Scepter LP; three tracks are rechanneled					

GUTHRIE, ARLO

45s

Number	Title (A Side/B Side)	Yr	VG	VG+	NM
❑ Reprise 0644	Motorcycle Song/Now and Then	1967	3.00	6.00	12.00
❑ Reprise 0793	Motorcycle Song (Part 1)/Motorcycle Song (Part 2)	1968	3.00	6.00	12.00
❑ Reprise 0877	Alice's Rock & Roll Restaurant/Coming Into Los Angeles	1969	3.00	6.00	12.00
❑ Reprise 0951	Gabriel's Mother's Hiway/Ballad #16 Blues	1970	2.00	4.00	8.00
❑ Reprise 0994	The Ballad of Tricky Fred/Shackles and Chains	1971	—	3.00	6.00
❑ Reprise 1103	The City of New Orleans/Days Are Short	1972	—	3.00	6.00
❑ Reprise 1137	Ukulele Lady/Cooper's Lament	1972	—	2.50	5.00
❑ Reprise 1158	A Week on the Rag/Gypsy Dave	1973	—	2.50	5.00
❑ Reprise 1211	Nostalgia Rag/Presidential Rag	1974	—	2.00	4.00
❑ Reprise 1363	Patriot's Dream/Ocean Crossing	1976	—	2.00	4.00
❑ Reprise 1376	Grocery Blues/Guabi, Guabi	1976	—	2.00	4.00
❑ Reprise 1388	Massachusetts/My Love	1977	—	2.00	4.00
❑ Warner Bros. 49037	Wedding Song/Prologue	1979	—	2.00	4.00

Number	Title (A Side/B Side)	Yr	VG	VG+	NM
❑ Warner Bros. 49796	Slow Boat/If I Could Only Touch Your Life	1981	—	2.00	4.00
❑ Warner Bros. 49889	Oklahoma Nights/Power of Love	1981	—	2.00	4.00
Albums					
❑ Reprise MS 2060	Hobo's Lullabye	1972	3.00	6.00	12.00
❑ Reprise MS 2142	Last of the Brooklyn Cowboys	1973	3.00	6.00	12.00
❑ Reprise MS 2183	Arlo Guthrie	1974	3.00	6.00	12.00
❑ Reprise MS 2239	Amigo	1976	3.00	6.00	12.00
❑ Reprise R 6267 [M]	Alice's Restaurant	1967	5.00	10.00	20.00
❑ Reprise RS 6267 [S]	Alice's Restaurant	1967	3.75	7.50	15.00
—Pink, green and gold label					
❑ Reprise RS 6299	Arlo	1968	3.75	7.50	15.00
—With "W7" and "r:" logos on two-tone orange label					
❑ Reprise RS 6346	Running Down the Road	1969	3.75	7.50	15.00
—With "W7" and "r:" logos on two-tone orange label					
❑ Reprise RS 6411	Washington County	1970	3.00	6.00	12.00
❑ Warner Bros. BSK 3117	The Best of Arlo Guthrie	1977	2.50	5.00	10.00
—"Burbank" palm trees label					
❑ Warner Bros. BSK 3117	The Best of Arlo Guthrie	1979	2.00	4.00	8.00
—White or tan label					
❑ Warner Bros. BSK 3232	One Night	1978	2.50	5.00	10.00
❑ Warner Bros. BSK 3336	Outlasting the Blues	1979	2.50	5.00	10.00
❑ Warner Bros. BSK 3558	Power of Love	1981	2.50	5.00	10.00

H

HALEY, BILL, AND HIS COMETS

45s

Number	Title (A Side/B Side)	Yr	VG	VG+	NM
❑ Apt 25087	Haley A-Go-Go/Tongue Tied Tony	1965	6.25	12.50	25.00
❑ Arzee 4677	Yodel Your Blues Away/Within This Broken Heart of Mine	1978	6.25	12.50	25.00
❑ Buddah 169	Rock Around the Clock/Framed	1970	3.75	7.50	15.00
❑ Decca 9-29124	(We're Gonna) Rock Around the Clock/ Thirteen Women (And Only One Man in Town)	1954	15.00	30.00	60.00
—With lines on either side of "Decca"					
❑ Decca 29204	Shake, Rattle and Roll/A.B.C. Boogie	1954	10.00	20.00	40.00
—With lines on either side of "Decca"					
❑ Decca 29317	Dim, Dim the Lights (I Want Some Atmosphere)/Happy Baby	1954	10.00	20.00	40.00
—With lines on either side of "Decca"					
❑ Decca 29418	Mambo Rock/Birth of the Boogie	1955	6.25	12.50	25.00
❑ Decca 29552	Razzle-Dazzle/Two Hound Dogs	1955	6.25	12.50	25.00
❑ Decca 29713	Burn That Candle/Rock-a-Beatin' Boogie	1955	6.25	12.50	25.00
❑ Decca 29791	See You Later, Alligator/The Paper Boy (On Main Street, U.S.A.)	1956	6.25	12.50	25.00
❑ Decca 29870	R-O-C-K/The Saints Rock 'N' Roll	1956	6.25	12.50	25.00
❑ Decca 29948	Hot Dog Buddy Buddy/Rockin' Through the Rye	1956	6.25	12.50	25.00
❑ Decca 30028	Rip It Up/Teenager's Mother (Are You Right?)	1956	6.25	12.50	25.00
❑ Decca 30085	Rudy's Rock/Blue Comet Blues	1956	6.25	12.50	25.00
❑ Decca 30148	Don't Knock the Rock/Choo Choo Ch'Boogie	1956	6.25	12.50	25.00
❑ Decca 30214	Forty Cups of Coffeee/Hook, Line and Sinker	1957	6.25	12.50	25.00
❑ Decca 30314	(You Hit the Wrong Note) Billy Goat/Rockin' Rollin' Rover	1957	6.25	12.50	25.00
❑ Decca 30394	The Dipsy Doodle/Miss You	1957	6.25	12.50	25.00
❑ Decca 30461	Rock the Joint/How Many	1957	6.25	12.50	25.00
❑ Decca 30530	It's a Sin/Mary, Mary Lou	1957	6.25	12.50	25.00
❑ Decca 30592	Skinny Minnie/Sway with Me	1958	7.50	15.00	30.00
❑ Decca 30681	Lean Jean/Don't Nobody Move	1958	6.25	12.50	25.00
❑ Decca 30741	Chiquita Linda/Whoa Mabel	1958	6.25	12.50	25.00
❑ Decca 30781	Corrine, Corrina/B.B. Betty	1958	6.25	12.50	25.00
❑ Decca 30844	Charmaine/I Got a Woman	1959	6.25	12.50	25.00
❑ Decca 30873	(Now and Then, There's) A Fool Such As I/ Where Did You Go Last Night	1959	6.25	12.50	25.00
❑ Decca 30926	Caldonia/Shakey	1959	6.25	12.50	25.00
❑ Decca 30956	Joey's Song/Ooh, Look-a-There, Ain't She Pretty	1959	6.25	12.50	25.00
❑ Decca 31030	Skokiaan (South African Song)/Puerto Rican Peddler	1959	6.25	12.50	25.00
❑ Decca 31080	Music, Music, Music/Strictly Instrumental	1960	6.25	12.50	25.00
❑ Decca 31649	The Green Door/Yeah, She's Evil	1964	3.00	6.00	12.00
❑ Essex 303	Rock the Joint/Icy Heart	1952	25.00	50.00	100.00
—Black vinyl, block logo ("ESSEX" in all caps)					
❑ Essex 305	Rocking Chair on the Moon/Dance with a Dolly (With a Hole in Her Stocking)	1952	25.00	50.00	100.00
—Essex 303 and 305 credit "Bill Haley and the Saddlemen"					

Number	Title (A Side/B Side)	Yr	VG	VG+	NM
❑ Essex 310	Real Rock Drive/Stop Beatin' Round the Mulberry Bush	1952	20.00	40.00	80.00
—Orange label					
❑ Essex 321	Crazy Man, Crazy/Whatcha Gonna Do	1953	15.00	30.00	60.00
❑ Essex 327	Pat-a-Cake/Fractured	1953	10.00	20.00	40.00
❑ Essex 332	Live It Up/Farewell, So Long, Goodbye	1953	10.00	20.00	40.00
❑ Essex 340	Ten Little Indians/I'll Be True	1953	10.00	20.00	40.00
❑ Essex 348	Chattanooga Choo Choo/Straight Jacket	1954	10.00	20.00	40.00
❑ Essex 374	Sundown Boogie/Jukebox Cannonball	1954	18.75	37.50	75.00
❑ Essex 381	Rocket 88/Green Tree Boogie	1955	31.25	62.50	125.00
❑ Essex 399	Rock the Joint/Farewell, So Long, Goodbye	1955	18.75	37.50	75.00
❑ GNP Crescendo 475	I'm Walkin'/Crazy Man, Crazy	1974	3.00	6.00	12.00
❑ Gone 5111	Spanish Twist/My Kind of Woman	1961	6.25	12.50	25.00
❑ Gone 5116	Riviera/War Paint	1961	6.25	12.50	25.00
❑ Holiday 113	Sundown Boogie/Jukebox Cannonball	1951	125.00	250.00	500.00
—As "Bill Haley and the Saddlemen"; the only Holiday single known to exist on a 45. Earlier Holiday singles only exist on 78s.					
❑ Janus 162	Travelin' Band/A Little Piece at a Time	1971	3.00	6.00	12.00
❑ Kama Sutra 508	Rock Around the Clock/Framed	1970	5.00	10.00	20.00
❑ Kasey 7006	A.B.C. Boogie/Rock Around the Clock	1961	5.00	10.00	20.00
—B-side by Phil Flowers					
❑ MCA 60025	(We're Gonna) Rock Around the Clock/ Thirteen Women (And Only One Man in Town)	1973	—	2.50	5.00
—Reissue on black label with rainbow; made the Top 40 in 1974					
❑ Newtown 5013	Tenor Man/Up Goes My Love	1962	5.00	10.00	20.00
❑ Newtown 5024	Dance Around the Clock/What Can I Say After I Say I'm Sorry	1963	5.00	10.00	20.00
❑ Nicetown 5025	You Call Everybody Darling/Tandy	1963	5.00	10.00	20.00
❑ Trans World 718	Real Rock Drive/Yes, Indeed	1954	50.00	100.00	200.00
❑ United Artists 50483	Ain't Love Funny, Ha Ha Ha/That's How I Got to Memphis	1969	3.00	6.00	12.00
❑ Warner Bros. 5145	Candy Kisses/Tamiami	1960	6.25	12.50	25.00
❑ Warner Bros. 5154	Hawk/Chick Safari	1960	6.25	12.50	25.00
❑ Warner Bros. 5171	Let the Good Times Roll, Creole/So Right Tonight	1960	6.25	12.50	25.00
❑ Warner Bros. 5228	Flip, Flop and Fly/Honky Tonk	1961	6.25	12.50	25.00
❑ Warner Bros. 7124	Rock Around the Clock/Shake, Rattle and Roll	1969	3.75	7.50	15.00
Albums					
❑ Accord SN-7125	Rockin' and Rollin'	1981	2.50	5.00	10.00
❑ Decca DL 5560 [10]	Shake, Rattle and Roll	1955	200.00	400.00	800.00
❑ Decca DXSE-7211 [(2)]	Bill Haley's Golden Hits	1972	3.75	7.50	15.00
❑ Decca DL 8225 [M]	Rock Around the Clock	1955	37.50	75.00	150.00
—All-black label with silver print					
❑ Decca DL 8315 [M]	Music for the Boyfriend	1956	37.50	75.00	150.00
❑ Decca DL 8345 [M]	Rock 'n Roll Stage Show	1956	37.50	75.00	150.00
❑ Decca DL 8569 [M]	Rockin' the Oldies	1957	37.50	75.00	150.00
❑ Decca DL 8692 [M]	Rockin' Around the World	1958	37.50	75.00	150.00
❑ Decca DL 8775 [M]	Rockin' the Joint	1958	37.50	75.00	150.00
❑ Decca DL 8821 [M]	Bill Haley's Chicks	1959	25.00	50.00	100.00
❑ Decca DL 8964 [M]	Strictly Instrumental	1960	25.00	50.00	100.00
❑ Decca DL 75027	Bill Haley's Greatest Hits	1968	3.75	7.50	15.00
❑ Decca DL 78225 [R]	Rock Around the Clock	1959	18.75	37.50	75.00
—All-black label with silver print					
❑ Decca DL 78821 [S]	Bill Haley's Chicks	1959	37.50	75.00	150.00
❑ Decca DL 78964 [S]	Strictly Instrumental	1960	37.50	75.00	150.00
❑ Essex LP 202 [M]	Rock with Bill Haley and the Comets	1955	125.00	250.00	500.00
❑ 51 West Q 16120	Live in New York/Greatest Hits	1981	2.50	5.00	10.00
—"All selections under license from Buddah Records"					
❑ GNP Crescendo GNPS-2077	Rock 'N' Roll	1973	3.00	6.00	12.00
❑ GNP Crescendo 108 GNPS-2097	Rock Around the Country	1976	3.00	6.00	12.00
❑ Great Northwest GNW 4015	Interviewed by Red Robinson	1981	3.00	6.00	12.00
❑ Janus 3035	Travelin' Band	1972	6.25	12.50	25.00
❑ Janus 7003 [(2)]	Razzle-Dazzle	1972	3.75	7.50	15.00
❑ Kama Sutra KLPS-2014	Scrapbook	1970	7.50	15.00	30.00
❑ MCA 161	Bill Haley's Greatest Hits	1973	2.50	5.00	10.00
—Reissue of Decca 75027					
❑ MCA 4010 [(2)]	Bill Haley's Golden Hits	1973	3.00	6.00	12.00
—Reissue of Decca 7211					
❑ MCA 5539 [(2)]	From the Original Master Tapes	1987	3.00	6.00	12.00
❑ Pair MSM2-35069 [(2)]	Rock and Roll Giant	1986	3.00	6.00	12.00
❑ Piccadilly PIC-3408	Greatest Hits	1980	2.50	5.00	10.00
❑ Pickwick PTP-2077 [(2)]	Rock 'N' Roll	197?	3.00	6.00	12.00
❑ Pickwick SPC-3256	Bill Haley and the Comets	1970	2.50	5.00	10.00
❑ Pickwick SPC-3280	Rock 'N' Roll Revival	197?	2.50	5.00	10.00
❑ Roulette R 25174 [M]	Twistin' Knights at the Roundtable	1962	20.00	40.00	80.00
❑ Roulette SR 25174 [S]	Twistin' Knights at the Roundtable	1962	25.00	50.00	100.00
❑ Somerset P-4600 [M]	Rock with Bill Haley and the Comets	1958	37.50	75.00	150.00
❑ Trans World LP 202 [M]	Rock with Bill Haley and the Comets	1956	75.00	150.00	300.00
❑ Vocalion VL 3696 [M]	Bill Haley and the Comets	1963	6.25	12.50	25.00
❑ Warner Bros. W 1378 [M]	Bill Haley and His Comets	1959	12.50	25.00	50.00
❑ Warner Bros. WS 1378 [S]	Bill Haley and His Comets	1959	17.50	35.00	70.00
❑ Warner Bros. W 1391 [M]	Bill Haley's Jukebox	1960	12.50	25.00	50.00
❑ Warner Bros. WS 1391 [S]	Bill Haley's Jukebox	1960	17.50	35.00	70.00
❑ Warner Bros. WS 1831	Rock 'N' Roll Revival	1970	3.75	7.50	15.00

HALL, DARYL, AND JOHN OATES

45s

Number	Title (A Side/B Side)	Yr	VG	VG+	NM
❑ Arista 2085	So Close/So Close (Unplugged)	1990	—	—	3.00
❑ Arista 2157	Don't Hold Back Your Love/Change of Season	1990	—	—	3.00

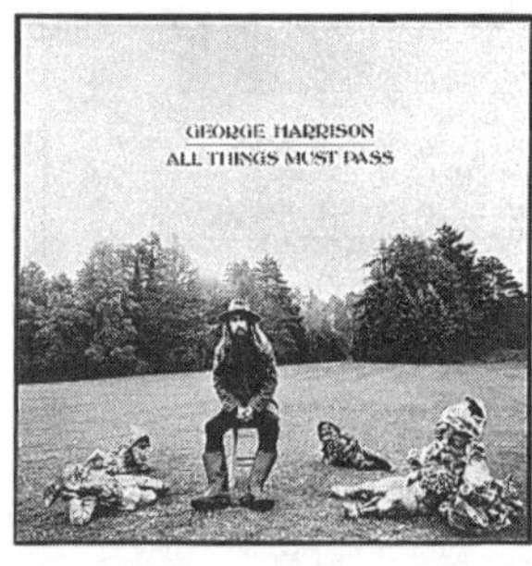

Number	Title (A Side/B Side)	Yr	VG	VG+	NM
❑ Arista 9684	Everything Your Heart Desires/Real Love	1988	—	—	3.00
❑ Arista 9727	Missed Opportunity/Soul Love	1988	—	—	3.00
❑ Arista 9753	Downtown Life (LP Version)/Downtown Life (Urban Mix)	1988	—	—	3.00
❑ Atlantic 2922	Goodnight & Good Morning/All Our Love	1972	2.50	5.00	10.00
—As "Whole Oats"					
❑ Atlantic 2939	Lilly (Are You Happy)/I'm Sorry	1973	2.00	4.00	8.00
❑ Atlantic 2993	She's Gone/I'm Just a Kid (Don't Make Me Feel Like a Man)	1973	2.00	4.00	8.00
❑ Atlantic 3026	Lady Rain/When the Morning Comes	1974	—	2.50	5.00
❑ Atlantic 3239	Can't Stop the Music/70's Scenario	1975	—	2.50	5.00
❑ Atlantic 3332	She's Gone/I'm Just a Kid (Don't Make Me Feel Like a Man)	1976	—	2.00	4.00
❑ Atlantic 3397	It's Uncanny/Lilly (Are You Happy)	1977	—	2.00	4.00
❑ Chelsea 3063	If That's What Makes You Happy/The Reason Why	1977	—	2.50	5.00
—B-side by "Daryl Hall and Gulliver"					
❑ Chelsea 3065	Red River Blues/(B-side unknown)	1977	—	2.50	5.00
❑ Chelsea 3069	Perkiomen/The Provider	1977	—	2.50	5.00
❑ RCA PB-10808	Do What You Want, Be What You Are/You'll Never Learn	1976	—	2.00	4.00
❑ RCA PB-10860	Rich Girl/London Luck, & Love	1976	—	2.00	4.00
❑ RCA GB-10942	Sara Smile/Do What You Want, Be What You Are	1977	—	—	3.00
—Gold Standard Series					
❑ RCA PB-10970	Back Together Again/Room to Breathe	1977	—	2.00	4.00
❑ RCA PB-11132	Why Do Lovers (Break Each Other's Heart?)/ A Girl Who Used to Be	1977	—	2.00	4.00
❑ RCA PB-11181	Don't Change/The Emptiness	1977	—	2.00	4.00
❑ RCA GB-11324	Rich Girl/Back Together Again	1978	—	—	3.00
—Gold Standard Series					
❑ RCA PB-11371	It's a Laugh/Serious Music	1978	—	2.00	4.00
❑ RCA PB-11424	I Don't Wanna Lose You/August Day	1978	—	2.00	4.00
❑ RCA PB-11747	Wait for Me/No Brain No Pain	1979	—	2.00	4.00
❑ RCA PB-11920	All You Want Is Heaven/Who Said the World Was Fair	1980	—	2.00	4.00
❑ RCA GB-11970	It's a Laugh/I Don't Wanna Lose You	1980	—	—	3.00
—Gold Standard Series					
❑ RCA PB-12048	How Does It Feel to Be Back/United State	1980	—	2.00	4.00
❑ RCA PB-12103	You've Lost That Lovin' Feeling/ Diddy Doo Wap (I Hear the Voices)	1980	—	2.00	4.00
❑ RCA PB-12142	Kiss on My List/Africa	1981	—	2.00	4.00
❑ RCA PB-12217	You Make My Dreams/Gotta Lotta Love	1981	—	2.00	4.00
❑ RCA PB-12296	Private Eyes/Tell Me What You Want	1981	—	2.00	4.00
❑ RCA GB-12318	Kiss on My List/You've Lost That Lovin' Feeling	1981	—	—	3.00
—Gold Standard Series					
❑ RCA PB-12357	I Can't Go for That (No Can Do)/Unguarded Minute	1981	—	2.00	4.00
❑ RCA PB-13065	Did It in a Minute/Head Above Water	1982	—	2.00	4.00
❑ RCA PB-13252	Your Imagination/Sara Smile	1982	—	2.00	4.00
❑ RCA PB-13354	Maneater/Delayed Reaction	1982	—	—	3.00
❑ RCA PB-13421	One on One/Art of Heartbreak	1983	—	—	3.00
❑ RCA GB-13480	Private Eyes/I Can't Go for That (No Can Do)	1983	—	—	3.00
—Gold Standard Series					
❑ RCA GB-13481	You Make My Dreams/Did It in a Minute	1983	—	—	3.00
—Gold Standard Series					
❑ RCA PB-13507	Family Man/Open All Night	1983	—	—	3.00
❑ RCA PB-13654	Say It Isn't So/Kiss on My List	1983	—	—	3.00
❑ RCA PB-13714	Adult Education/Maneater	1984	—	—	3.00
❑ RCA GB-13796	Maneater/One on One	1984	—	—	3.00
—Gold Standard Series					
❑ RCA GB-13797	Family Man/Say It Isn't So	1984	—	—	3.00
—Gold Standard Series					
❑ RCA PB-13916	Out of Touch/Cold, Dark, and Yesterday	1984	—	—	3.00
❑ RCA PB-13970	Method of Modern Love (Remix Edit)/Method of Modern Love	1984	—	—	3.00
❑ RCA PB-14035	Some Things Are Better Left Unsaid/All American Girl	1985	—	—	3.00
❑ RCA GB-14064	Out of Touch/Adult Education	1985	—	—	3.00
—Gold Standard Series					
❑ RCA PB-14098	Possession Obsession/Dance on Your Knees	1985	—	—	3.00
❑ RCA PB-14178	A Nite at the Apollo Live! The Way You Do the Things You Do-My Girl/Everytime You Go Away	1985	—	—	3.00
—A-side: With David Ruffin and Eddie Kendrick (sic)					
❑ RCA GB-14340	Method of Modern Love/Possession Obsession	1986	—	—	3.00
—Gold Standard Series					

Number	Title (A Side/B Side)	Yr	VG	VG+	NM
❑ RCA GB-14341	Some Things Are Better Left Unsaid/A Nite at the Apollo Live! The Way You Do the Things You Do-My Girl	1986	—	—	3.00
—Gold Standard Series					
❑ RCA Victor PB-10373	Camellia/Ennui on the Mountain	1975	—	2.50	5.00
❑ RCA Victor PB-10436	Nothing at All/Alone Too Long	1975	—	2.50	5.00
❑ RCA Victor PB-10530	Sara Smile/Soldering	1975	—	2.50	5.00
❑ Sire 22967	Love Train/"Earth Girls Are Easy" Theme	1989	—	—	3.00
Albums					
❑ Allegiance AV-5014	Nucleus	198?	2.00	4.00	8.00
❑ Arista AL-8539	Ooh Yeah!	1988	2.50	5.00	10.00
❑ Arista AL-8614	Change of Season	1989	3.00	6.00	12.00
❑ Atlantic SD 7242	Whole Oats	1972	3.00	6.00	12.00
❑ Atlantic SD 7269	Abandoned Luncheonette	1973	3.00	6.00	12.00
❑ Atlantic SD 18109	War Babies	1974	3.00	6.00	12.00
❑ Atlantic SD 18213	No Goodbyes	1977	2.50	5.00	10.00
❑ Atlantic SD 19139	Abandoned Luncheonette	1977	2.00	4.00	8.00
❑ Chelsea CHL-547	Past Times Behind	1976	3.00	6.00	12.00
❑ Intermedia QS-5040	The Early Years	198?	2.00	4.00	8.00
❑ Jem 55002	Early Years	198?	2.00	4.00	8.00
❑ RCA Victor APL1-1144	Daryl Hall & John Oates	1976	2.50	5.00	10.00
❑ RCA Victor APL1-1467	Bigger Than Both of Us	1976	2.50	5.00	10.00
❑ RCA Victor AFL1-2300	Beauty on a Back Street	1977	2.50	5.00	10.00
❑ RCA Victor AFL1-2802	Livetime!	1978	2.50	5.00	10.00
❑ RCA Victor AFL1-2804	Along the Red Ledge	1978	2.50	5.00	10.00
❑ RCA Victor ANL1-3463	Daryl Hall & John Oates	1979	2.00	4.00	8.00
❑ RCA Victor AFL1-3494	X-Static	1979	2.50	5.00	10.00
❑ RCA Victor AQL1-3646	Voices	1980	3.00	6.00	12.00
—No "RE" of any type on back cover: Embossed lettering and sound waves, Hall's head almost touches the word "Voices" on front					
❑ RCA Victor AYL1-3836	Daryl Hall & John Oates	1980	2.00	4.00	8.00
❑ RCA Victor AYL1-3866	Bigger Than Both of Us	1980	2.00	4.00	8.00
❑ RCA Victor AFL1-4028	Private Eyes	1981	2.50	5.00	10.00
❑ RCA Victor AYL1-4230	Beauty on a Back Street	1981	2.00	4.00	8.00
❑ RCA Victor AYL1-4231	Along the Red Ledge	1981	2.00	4.00	8.00
❑ RCA Victor AYL1-4303	X-Static	1982	2.00	4.00	8.00
❑ RCA Victor AFL1-4383	H2O	1982	2.50	5.00	10.00
❑ RCA Victor AYL1-4722	Livetime!	1983	2.00	4.00	8.00
❑ RCA Victor CPL1-4858	Rock 'n Soul Part 1	1983	3.00	6.00	12.00
—Original cover: back cover says "Plus Two New Songs (Recorded September 1983)" WITHOUT mentioning what the songs are					
❑ RCA Victor AFL1-5309	Big Bam Boom	1984	3.00	6.00	12.00
❑ RCA Victor AJL1-5336	Big Bam Boom	1984	2.50	5.00	10.00
❑ RCA Victor AFL1-7035	Live at the Apollo	1985	2.50	5.00	10.00
HAMILTON, GEORGE, IV					
45s					
❑ ABC 12342	Only the Best/My Ship Will Sail	1978	—	2.50	5.00
❑ ABC 12376	One Day at a Time/Take This Heart	1978	—	2.00	4.00
❑ ABC-Paramount 9765	A Rose and a Baby Ruth/If You Don't Know	1956	7.50	15.00	30.00
❑ ABC-Paramount 9782	Only One Love/If I Possessed a Printing Press	1957	7.50	15.00	30.00
❑ ABC-Paramount 9838	High School Romance/Everybody's Baby	1957	7.50	15.00	30.00
❑ ABC-Paramount 9862	Why Don't They Understand/Even Tho'	1957	7.50	15.00	30.00
❑ ABC-Paramount 9898	Now and For Always/One Heart	1958	6.25	12.50	25.00
❑ ABC-Paramount 9924	I Know Where I'm Goin'/Who's Taking You to the Prom	1958	6.25	12.50	25.00
❑ ABC-Paramount 9946	When Will I Know/Your Cheatin' Heart	1958	6.25	12.50	25.00
❑ ABC-Paramount 9966	Lucy, Lucy/The Two of Us	1958	6.25	12.50	25.00
❑ ABC-Paramount 10009	The Steady Game/Can You Blame Us	1959	5.00	10.00	20.00
❑ ABC-Paramount 10028	Gee/I Know Your Sweetheart	1959	5.00	10.00	20.00
❑ ABC-Paramount 10059	One Little Acre/Little Tom	1959	5.00	10.00	20.00
❑ ABC-Paramount 10090	Why I'm Walkin'/Tremble	1960	5.00	10.00	20.00
❑ ABC-Paramount 10125	Before This Day Ends/Loneliness All Around Me	1960	5.00	10.00	20.00
❑ ABC-Paramount 10167	A Walk on the Wild Side of Life/It's Just the Idea	1960	5.00	10.00	20.00
❑ ABC/Dot 17687	I Wonder Who's Kissing Her Now/In the Palm of Her Hand	1977	—	2.00	4.00
❑ ABC/Dot 17708	Cornbread, Beans and Sweet Potato Pie/ May the Wind Be Always at Your Back	1977	—	2.00	4.00
❑ ABC/Dot 17723	Everlasting (Everlasting Love)/In the Palm of Your Hand	1977	—	2.00	4.00
❑ Colonial 420	A Rose and a Baby Ruth/If You Don't Know	1956	20.00	40.00	80.00
❑ Colonial 451	I've Got a Secret/Sam	1956	10.00	20.00	40.00
❑ GRT 063	Blue Jeans, Ice Cream and Saturday Shoes/Bad Romancer	1976	—	2.50	5.00
❑ MCA 41149	Forever Young/'Rangement Blues	1979	—	2.00	4.00
❑ MCA 41215	I'll Be Here in the Morning/Spin Spin	1980	—	2.00	4.00
❑ MCA 41282	Catfish Bates/Mose Rankin	1980	—	2.00	4.00
❑ RCA 2722-7-R	Abilene/Oh So Many Tears	1990	—	2.00	4.00
❑ RCA Victor 47-7881	Three Steps to the Phone (Millions of Miles)/ The Ballad of Widder Jones	1961	3.75	7.50	15.00
❑ RCA Victor 47-7934	To You and Yours (From Me and Mine)/I Want a Girl	1961	3.75	7.50	15.00
❑ RCA Victor 47-8001	China Doll/Commerce Street and Sixth Avenue North	1962	3.75	7.50	15.00
❑ RCA Victor 47-8062	If You Don't Know, I Ain't Gonna Tell You/ Where Nobody Knows Me	1962	3.75	7.50	15.00
❑ RCA Victor 47-8118	In This Very Same Room/If You Want Me To	1962	3.75	7.50	15.00
❑ RCA Victor 47-8181	Abilene/Oh So Many Years	1963	3.00	6.00	12.00
❑ RCA Victor 47-8250	There's More Pretty Girls Than One/ If You Don't, Somebody Else Will	1963	3.00	6.00	12.00
❑ RCA Victor 47-8304	Linda with the Lonely Eyes/Fair and Tender Ladies	1963	3.00	6.00	12.00
❑ RCA Victor 47-8392	Fort Worth, Dallas or Houston/Life's Railway to Heaven	1964	3.00	6.00	12.00
❑ RCA Victor 47-8462	Truck Driving Man/The Little Grave	1964	3.00	6.00	12.00
❑ RCA Victor 47-8537	The Last Mister Jones/Anymore	1965	2.50	5.00	10.00
❑ RCA Victor 47-8608	Walking the Floor Over You/Driftwood on the River	1965	2.50	5.00	10.00
❑ RCA Victor 47-8690	Write Me a Picture/Twist of the Wrist	1965	2.50	5.00	10.00

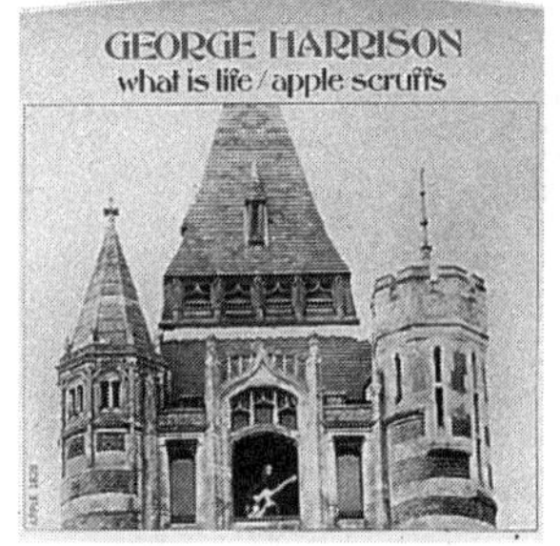

Number	Title (A Side/B Side)	Yr	VG	VG+	NM
❑ RCA Victor 47-8797	Steel Rail Blues/Tobacco	1966	2.50	5.00	10.00
❑ RCA Victor 47-8924	Early Morning Rain/Slightly Used	1966	2.50	5.00	10.00
❑ RCA Victor 47-9059	Urge for Going/Changes	1966	2.50	5.00	10.00
❑ RCA Victor 47-9239	Break My Mind/Something Special to Me	1967	2.00	4.00	8.00
❑ RCA Victor 47-9385	Little World Girl/Song for a Winter's Night	1967	2.00	4.00	8.00
❑ RCA Victor 47-9519	It's My Time/Canadian Railroad Trilogy	1968	2.00	4.00	8.00
❑ RCA Victor 47-9637	Take My Hand for Awhile/Wonderful World of My Dreams	1968	2.00	4.00	8.00
❑ RCA Victor 47-9775	Natividad (The Nativity)/The Little Grave	1969	2.00	4.00	8.00
❑ RCA Victor 47-9829	She's a Little Bit Country/My Nova Scotia Home	1970	—	3.00	6.00
❑ RCA Victor 47-9886	Back Where It's At/Then I Miss You	1970	—	3.00	6.00
❑ RCA Victor 47-9893	Let's Get Together/Everything Is Beautiful	1970	—	3.00	6.00
—With Skeeter Davis					
❑ RCA Victor 47-9937	Natividad (The Nativity)/The Little Grave	1970	—	3.00	6.00
❑ RCA Victor 47-9945	Anyway/The Best That I Can Do	1971	—	3.00	6.00
❑ RCA Victor 74-0100	Back to Denver/Suzanne	1969	2.00	4.00	8.00
❑ RCA Victor 74-0171	Canadian Pacific/Sisters of Mercy	1969	2.00	4.00	8.00
❑ RCA Victor 74-0256	Carolina in My Mind/I'm Gonna Be a Country Boy Again	1969	2.00	4.00	8.00
❑ RCA Victor 74-0469	Countryfied/My North Country Home	1971	—	3.00	6.00
❑ RCA Victor 74-0531	West Texas Highway/There's No Room in This Rat Race	1971	—	3.00	6.00
❑ RCA Victor 74-0622	10 Degrees and Getting Colder/Tumbleweed	1971	—	3.00	6.00
❑ RCA Victor 74-0697	Country Music in My Soul/Child's Song	1972	—	2.50	5.00
❑ RCA Victor 74-0776	Travelin' Light/Alberta Bound	1972	—	2.50	5.00
❑ RCA Victor 74-0854	Blue Train (Of the Heartbreak Line)/Maritime Farewell	1972	—	2.50	5.00
❑ RCA Victor 74-0948	Dirty Old Man/Abilene	1973	—	2.50	5.00
❑ RCA Victor APBO-0084	Second Cup of Coffee/Farmer's Song	1973	—	2.00	4.00
❑ RCA Victor APBO-0203	Claim on Me/Early Mornin' Rain	1973	—	2.00	4.00
❑ RCA Victor APBO-0314	The Ways of a Country Girl/Pictou County Jail	1974	—	2.00	4.00
Albums					
❑ ABC X-750	16 Greatest Hits	1972	2.50	5.00	10.00
❑ ABC AC-30032	The ABC Collection	1975	3.00	6.00	12.00
❑ ABC-Paramount 220 [M]	On Campus	1958	10.00	20.00	40.00
❑ ABC-Paramount S-220 [S]	On Campus	1958	12.50	25.00	50.00
❑ ABC-Paramount 251 [M]	Sing Me a Sad Song (A Tribute to Hank Williams)	1958	10.00	20.00	40.00
❑ ABC-Paramount S-251 [S]	Sing Me a Sad Song (A Tribute to Hank Williams)	1958	12.50	25.00	50.00
❑ ABC-Paramount 461 [M]	George Hamilton IV's Big 15	1963	7.50	15.00	30.00
❑ ABC-Paramount S-461 [P]	George Hamilton IV's Big 15	1963	10.00	20.00	40.00
❑ ABC/Dot DO-2081	Fine Lace	1977	2.50	5.00	10.00
❑ Dot 39033	George Hamilton IV	1985	2.50	5.00	10.00
❑ Harmony HS 11379	Your Cheatin' Heart	1970	2.50	5.00	10.00
❑ Lamb and Lion 1015	Bluegrass Gospel	1974	3.00	6.00	12.00
❑ MCA 705	Forever Young	198?	2.00	4.00	8.00
—Reissue of 3206					
❑ MCA 3206	Forever Young	1980	2.50	5.00	10.00
❑ RCA Camden ACL1-0242	Singin' on the Mountains	1973	2.50	5.00	10.00
❑ RCA Camden CAL-2200 [M]	A Rose and a Baby Ruth	1967	3.75	7.50	15.00
❑ RCA Camden CAS-2200 [S]	A Rose and a Baby Ruth	1967	2.50	5.00	10.00
❑ RCA Camden CAS-2468	Early Morning Rain	1971	2.50	5.00	10.00
❑ RCA Victor APL1-0455	Greatest Hits	1974	3.00	6.00	12.00
❑ RCA Victor LPM-2373 [M]	To You and Yours from Me and Mine	1961	6.25	12.50	25.00
❑ RCA Victor LSP-2373 [S]	To You and Yours from Me and Mine	1961	7.50	15.00	30.00
❑ RCA Victor LPM-2778 [M]	Abilene	1963	6.25	12.50	25.00
❑ RCA Victor LSP-2778 [S]	Abilene	1963	7.50	15.00	30.00
❑ RCA Victor LPM-2972 [M]	Fort Worth, Dallas or Houston	1964	6.25	12.50	25.00
❑ RCA Victor LSP-2972 [S]	Fort Worth, Dallas or Houston	1964	7.50	15.00	30.00
❑ RCA Victor LPM-3371 [M]	Mister Sincerity... A Tribute to Ernest Tubb	1965	6.25	12.50	25.00
❑ RCA Victor LSP-3371 [S]	Mister Sincerity... A Tribute to Ernest Tubb	1965	7.50	15.00	30.00
❑ RCA Victor LPM-3510 [M]	Coast Country	1966	6.25	12.50	25.00
❑ RCA Victor LSP-3510 [S]	Coast Country	1966	7.50	15.00	30.00
❑ RCA Victor LPM-3601 [M]	Steel Rail Blues	1966	5.00	10.00	20.00
❑ RCA Victor LSP-3601 [S]	Steel Rail Blues	1966	5.00	10.00	20.00
❑ RCA Victor LPM-3752 [M]	Folk Country Classics	1967	6.25	12.50	25.00
❑ RCA Victor LSP-3752 [S]	Folk Country Classics	1967	5.00	10.00	20.00
❑ RCA Victor LPM-3854 [M]	Folksy	1967	6.25	12.50	25.00
❑ RCA Victor LSP-3854 [S]	Folksy	1967	5.00	10.00	20.00
❑ RCA Victor LPM-3962 [M]	The Gentle Country Sound of George Hamilton IV	1968	10.00	20.00	40.00

Number	Title (A Side/B Side)	Yr	VG	VG+	NM
❑ RCA Victor LSP-3962 [S]	The Gentle Country Sound of George Hamilton IV	1968	5.00	10.00	20.00
❑ RCA Victor LSP-4066	In the 4th Dimension	1968	5.00	10.00	20.00
❑ RCA Victor LSP-4164	Canadian Pacific	1969	3.75	7.50	15.00
❑ RCA Victor LSP-4265	The Best of George Hamilton IV	1970	3.75	7.50	15.00
❑ RCA Victor LSP-4342	Back Where It's At	1970	3.75	7.50	15.00
❑ RCA Victor LSP-4435	Down Home in the Country	1971	3.75	7.50	15.00
❑ RCA Victor LSP-4517	North Country	1971	3.75	7.50	15.00
❑ RCA Victor LSP-4609	West Texas Highway	1971	3.75	7.50	15.00
❑ RCA Victor LSP-4700	Country Music in My Soul	1972	3.00	6.00	12.00
❑ RCA Victor LSP-4772	Travelin' Light	1972	3.00	6.00	12.00
❑ RCA Victor LSP-4826	International Ambassador	1973	3.00	6.00	12.00
HAMILTON, ROY					
45s					
❑ AGP 113	The Dark End of the Street/100 Years	1969	2.00	4.00	8.00
❑ AGP 116	Angelica/Hang Ups	1969	2.00	4.00	8.00
❑ AGP 125	It's Only Make Believe/100 Years	1969	2.00	4.00	8.00
❑ Capitol 2057	Let This World Be Free/Wait Until Dark	1967	2.00	4.00	8.00
❑ Epic 9015	You'll Never Walk Alone/I'm Gonna Sit Right Down and Cry	1954	6.25	12.50	25.00
❑ Epic 9047	So Let There Be Love/If You Loved Me	1954	6.25	12.50	25.00
❑ Epic 9068	Ebb Tide/Beware	1954	6.25	12.50	25.00
❑ Epic 9086	Hurt/Star of Love	1954	6.25	12.50	25.00
❑ Epic 9092	I Believe/If You Are But a Dream	1955	5.00	10.00	20.00
❑ Epic 9102	Unchained Melody/From Here to Eternity	1955	6.25	12.50	25.00
❑ Epic 9111	Forgive This Fool/You Wanted to Change Me	1955	5.00	10.00	20.00
❑ Epic 9118	A Little Voice/All This Is Mine	1955	5.00	10.00	20.00
❑ Epic 9125	Without a Song/Cuban Love Song	1955	5.00	10.00	20.00
❑ Epic 9132	Everybody's Got a Home/Take Me with You	1955	5.00	10.00	20.00
❑ Epic 9147	There Goes My Heart/Walk Along with Kings	1956	5.00	10.00	20.00
❑ Epic 9160	Somebody, Somewhere/Since I Fell for You	1956	5.00	10.00	20.00
❑ Epic 9180	I Took My Grief to Him/Chained	1956	5.00	10.00	20.00
❑ Epic 9203	The Simple Prayer/A Mother's Love	1957	5.00	10.00	20.00
❑ Epic 9212	My Faith, My Hope, My Love/So Long	1957	5.00	10.00	20.00
❑ Epic 9224	The Aisle/That Old Feeling	1957	5.00	10.00	20.00
❑ Epic 9232	(All of a Sudden) My Heart Sings/I'm Gonna Lock You in My Heart	1957	5.00	10.00	20.00
❑ Epic 9257	Don't Let Go/The Night to Love	1957	5.00	10.00	20.00
❑ Epic 9268	Crazy Feelin'/In a Dream	1958	3.75	7.50	15.00
❑ Epic 9274	Lips/Jungle Fever	1958	3.75	7.50	15.00
❑ Epic 9282	Wait for Me/Everything	1958	3.75	7.50	15.00
❑ Epic 9294	Pledging My Love/My One and Only Love	1958	3.75	7.50	15.00
❑ Epic 9301	It's Never Too Late/Somewhere Along the Way	1959	3.75	7.50	15.00
❑ Epic 9307	I Need Your Lovin'/Blue Prelude	1959	3.75	7.50	15.00
❑ Epic 9323	Time Marches On/Take It Easy, Joe	1959	3.75	7.50	15.00
❑ Epic 9342	Great Romance/On My Way Back Home	1959	3.75	7.50	15.00
❑ Epic 9354	The Ten Commandments/Dowm by the Riverside	1959	3.75	7.50	15.00
❑ Epic 9354	The Ten Commandments/Nobody Knows the Trouble I've Seen	1959	5.00	10.00	20.00
❑ Epic 9372	Down by the Riverside/Nobody Knows the Trouble I've Seen	1960	3.75	7.50	15.00
❑ Epic 9373	I Let a Song Go Out of My Heart/I Get the Blues When It Rains	1960	3.75	7.50	15.00
❑ Epic 9374	My Story/Please Send Me Someone to Love	1960	3.75	7.50	15.00
❑ Epic 9375	Something's Gotta Give/Cheek to Cheek	1960	—	—	—
—Unreleased?					
❑ Epic 9376	Sing You Sinners/Blow, Gabriel, Blow	1960	3.75	7.50	15.00
❑ Epic 9386	Having Myself a Ball/Slowly	1960	3.75	7.50	15.00
—B-side by Bobby Sykes					
❑ Epic 9388	Never Let Me Go/I Get the Blues When It Rains	1960	—	—	—
—Unreleased?					
❑ Epic 9390	The Clock/I Get the Blues When It Rains	1960	3.75	7.50	15.00
❑ Epic 9398	A Lover's Prayer/Never Let Me Go	1960	3.75	7.50	15.00
❑ Epic 9407	Lonely Hands/Your Love	1960	3.75	7.50	15.00
❑ Epic 9434	You Can Have Her/Abide With Me	1961	3.75	7.50	15.00
❑ Epic 9443	You're Gonna Need Magic/To the One I Love	1961	3.75	7.50	15.00
❑ Epic 9449	No Substitute for Love/Please Louise	1961	3.75	7.50	15.00
❑ Epic 9466	There We Were/If	1961	3.00	6.00	12.00
❑ Epic 9492	Don't Come Cryin' to Me/If Only I Had Known	1962	3.00	6.00	12.00
❑ Epic 9520	Climb Ev'ry Mountain/I'll Come Running Back to You	1962	3.00	6.00	12.00
❑ Epic 9538	I Am/Earthquake	1962	3.00	6.00	12.00
❑ Epic 10559	You'll Never Walk Alone/The Golden Boy	1969	2.00	4.00	8.00
❑ MGM 13138	Let Go/You Still Love Him	1963	2.50	5.00	10.00
❑ MGM 13157	Midnight Town-Daybreak City/Intermezzo	1963	2.50	5.00	10.00
❑ MGM 13175	Theme from "The V.I.P.'s" (The Willow)/The Sinner	1963	2.50	5.00	10.00
❑ MGM 13217	The Panic Is On/There She Is	1964	6.25	12.50	25.00
❑ MGM 13247	Answer Me, My Love/Unchained Melody	1964	2.50	5.00	10.00
❑ MGM 13291	You Can Count on Me/She Makes Me Wanna Dance	1964	6.25	12.50	25.00
❑ MGM 13315	Sweet Violets/A Thousand Years Ago	1965	2.50	5.00	10.00
❑ RCA Victor 47-8641	Heartache/Ain't It the Truth	1965	2.50	5.00	10.00
❑ RCA Victor 47-8705	And I Love Her/Tore Up Over You	1965	2.50	5.00	10.00
❑ RCA Victor 47-8813	The Impossible Dream/She's Got a Heart	1966	2.50	5.00	10.00
❑ RCA Victor 47-8960	Walk Hand in Hand/Crackin' Up Over You	1966	6.25	12.50	25.00
❑ RCA Victor 47-9061	I Taught Her Everything She Knows/Lament	1967	2.50	5.00	10.00
❑ RCA Victor 47-9171	So High My Love/You Shook Me Up	1967	12.50	25.00	50.00
❑ RCA Victor 48-1034	Walk Hand in Hand/Crackin' Up Over You	1972	2.50	5.00	10.00
Albums					
❑ Epic BN 518 [S]	With All My Love	1958	10.00	20.00	40.00
❑ Epic BN 525 [S]	Why Fight The Feeling?	1959	7.50	15.00	30.00
❑ Epic BN 530 [S]	Come Out Swingin'	1959	7.50	15.00	30.00
❑ Epic BN 535 [S]	Have Blues, Must Travel	1959	7.50	15.00	30.00
❑ Epic BN 551 [S]	Spirituals	1960	7.50	15.00	30.00

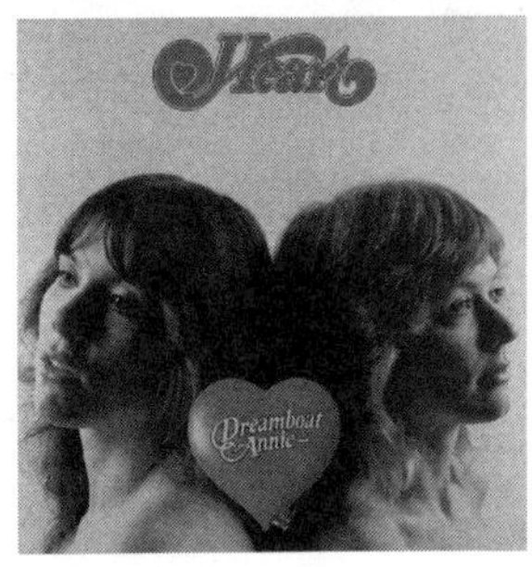

Number	Title (A Side/B Side)	Yr	VG	VG+	NM
❑ Epic BN 578 [S]	Soft 'n Warm	1960	7.50	15.00	30.00
❑ Epic BN 595 [S]	You Can Have Her	1961	10.00	20.00	40.00
❑ Epic BN 610 [S]	Only You	1961	7.50	15.00	30.00
❑ Epic BN 632 [R]	You'll Never Walk Alone	1962	5.00	10.00	20.00
❑ Epic LN 1023 [10]	You'll Never Walk Alone	1954	50.00	100.00	200.00
❑ Epic LN 1103 [10]	The Voice of Roy Hamilton	1954	50.00	100.00	200.00
❑ Epic LN 3176 [M]	Roy Hamilton	1955	15.00	30.00	60.00
❑ Epic LN 3294 [M]	You'll Never Walk Alone	1956	17.50	35.00	70.00
❑ Epic LN 3364 [M]	Golden Boy	1957	12.50	25.00	50.00
❑ Epic LN 3519 [M]	With All My Love	1958	7.50	15.00	30.00
❑ Epic LN 3545 [M]	Why Fight The Feeling?	1959	6.25	12.50	25.00
❑ Epic LN 3561 [M]	Come Out Swingin'	1959	6.25	12.50	25.00
❑ Epic LN 3580 [M]	Have Blues, Must Travel	1959	6.25	12.50	25.00
❑ Epic LN 3628 [M]	Roy Hamilton At His Best	1960	10.00	20.00	40.00
❑ Epic LN 3654 [M]	Spirituals	1960	6.25	12.50	25.00
❑ Epic LN 3717 [M]	Soft 'n Warm	1960	6.25	12.50	25.00
❑ Epic LN 3775 [M]	You Can Have Her	1961	7.50	15.00	30.00
❑ Epic LN 3807 [M]	Only You	1961	6.25	12.50	25.00
❑ Epic LN 24000 [M]	Mr. Rock and Soul	1962	6.25	12.50	25.00
❑ Epic LN 24009 [M]	Roy Hamilton's Greatest Hits	1962	5.00	10.00	20.00
❑ Epic LN 24316 [M]	Roy Hamilton's Greatest Hits, Vol. 2	1967	5.00	10.00	20.00
❑ Epic BN 26000 [S]	Mr. Rock and Soul	1962	7.50	15.00	30.00
❑ Epic BN 26009 [S]	Roy Hamilton's Greatest Hits	1962	6.25	12.50	25.00
❑ Epic BN 26316 [S]	Roy Hamilton's Greatest Hits, Vol. 2	1967	6.25	12.50	25.00
❑ MGM E-4139 [M]	Warm and Soul	1963	3.75	7.50	15.00
❑ MGM SE-4139 [S]	Warm and Soul	1963	5.00	10.00	20.00
❑ MGM E-4233 [M]	Sentimental, Lonely & Blue	1964	3.75	7.50	15.00
❑ MGM SE-4233 [S]	Sentimental, Lonely & Blue	1964	5.00	10.00	20.00
❑ RCA Victor LPM-3552 [M]	The Impossible Dream	1966	3.75	7.50	15.00
❑ RCA Victor LSP-3552 [S]	The Impossible Dream	1966	5.00	10.00	20.00

HAMILTON, JOE FRANK & REYNOLDS

45s

Number	Title (A Side/B Side)	Yr	VG	VG+	NM
❑ ABC Dunhill 4276	Don't Pull Your Love/Funk-In-Wagnall	1971	—	3.00	6.00
❑ ABC Dunhill 4287	Annabelle/Goin' Down	1971	—	2.50	5.00
❑ ABC Dunhill 4296	Daisy Mae/It Takes the Best	1971	—	2.50	5.00
❑ ABC Dunhill 4305	Don't Refuse My Love/One Good Woman	1972	—	2.50	5.00
❑ Playboy 5801	Now That I've Got You/Get On the Bus	1977	—	2.00	4.00
—As "Hamilton, Joe Frank & Dennison"					
❑ Playboy 6024	Fallin' in Love/So Good at Lovin' You	1975	—	2.50	5.00
❑ Playboy 6054	Winners and Losers/Barroom Blues	1975	—	2.00	4.00
❑ Playboy 6068	Everyday Without You/Badman	1976	—	2.00	4.00
❑ Playboy 6077	Light Up the World with Sunshine/Houdini	1976	—	2.00	4.00
—As "Hamilton, Joe Frank & Dennison"					
❑ Playboy 6088	Don't Fight the Hands (That Need You)/Get On the Bus	1976	—	2.00	4.00
—As "Hamilton, Joe Frank & Dennison"					

Albums

Number	Title (A Side/B Side)	Yr	VG	VG+	NM
❑ ABC Dunhill DS-50103	Hamilton, Joe Frank & Reynolds	1971	2.50	5.00	10.00
❑ ABC Dunhill DSX-50113	Hallway Symphony	1972	2.50	5.00	10.00
❑ Playboy PB-407	Fallin' in Love	1975	2.50	5.00	10.00
❑ Playboy PZ 34741	Fallin' in Love	1977	2.00	4.00	8.00
—Reissue of 107					

HAPPENINGS, THE

45s

Number	Title (A Side/B Side)	Yr	VG	VG+	NM
❑ B.T. Puppy 517	Girls on the Go/Go-Go	1966	2.50	5.00	10.00
❑ B.T. Puppy 520	See You in September/He Thinks He's a Hero	1966	2.50	5.00	10.00
❑ B.T. Puppy 522	Go Away Little Girl/Tea Time	1966	2.00	4.00	8.00
❑ B.T. Puppy 523	Goodnight My Love/Lillies By Money	1966	2.00	4.00	8.00
❑ B.T. Puppy 527	I Got Rhythm/You're in a Bad Way	1967	2.00	4.00	8.00
❑ B.T. Puppy 530	My Mammy/I Believe in Nothing	1967	2.00	4.00	8.00
❑ B.T. Puppy 532	Why Do Fools Fall in Love/When the Summer Is Through	1967	2.00	4.00	8.00
❑ B.T. Puppy 538	Music, Music, Music/When I Lock My Door	1968	2.00	4.00	8.00
❑ B.T. Puppy 540	Randy/Love Song of Mommy and Daddy	1968	2.00	4.00	8.00
❑ B.T. Puppy 542	Sealed with a Kiss/Anyway	1968	2.00	4.00	8.00
❑ B.T. Puppy 543	Breaking Up Is Hard to Do/Anyway	1968	2.00	4.00	8.00
❑ B.T. Puppy 545	Crazy Rhythm/Love Song of Mommy and Daddy	1968	2.00	4.00	8.00
❑ B.T. Puppy 549	That's All I Want from You/He Thinks He's a Hero	1968	2.00	4.00	8.00

Number	Title (A Side/B Side)	Yr	VG	VG+	NM
❑ Big Tree 146	Strawberry Morning/Workin' My Way Back to You	1972	—	2.00	4.00
❑ Big Tree 153	Me Without You/God Bless Joanna	1972	—	2.00	4.00
❑ Jubilee 5666	Where Do I Go and Be In/New Day Comin'	1969	—	3.00	6.00
❑ Jubilee 5677	El Paso County Jail/Won't Anybody Listen	1969	—	3.00	6.00
❑ Jubilee 5686	Answer Me, My Love/I Need a Woman	1970	—	3.00	6.00
❑ Jubilee 5698	Tomorrow, Today Will Be Yesterday/Chain of Hands	1970	—	3.00	6.00
❑ Jubilee 5702	Crazy Love/Chain of Hands	1970	—	3.00	6.00
❑ Jubilee 5703	Condition Red/Sweet September	1970	2.50	5.00	10.00
—As "The Honor Society"					
❑ Jubilee 5712	Lullaby in the Rain/I Wish You Could Know Me (Naomi)	1971	—	3.00	6.00
❑ Midland Int'l. MB-10897	That's Why I Love You/Beyond the Hurt	1977	—	2.00	4.00
❑ Midland Int'l. MB-11127	Let Me Stay/Someone Special	1977	—	2.00	4.00
Albums					
❑ B.T. Puppy BTP-1001 [M]	The Happenings (Bye-Bye, So Long, Farewell... See You in September)	1966	6.25	12.50	25.00
❑ B.T. Puppy BTS-1001 [S]	The Happenings (Bye-Bye, So Long, Farewell... See You in September)	1966	7.50	15.00	30.00
❑ B.T. Puppy BTP-1003 [M]	Psycle	1967	6.25	12.50	25.00
❑ B.T. Puppy BTPS-1003 [S]	Psycle	1967	7.50	15.00	30.00
❑ B.T. Puppy BTS-1004	The Happenings Golden Hits!	1968	10.00	20.00	40.00
❑ Jubilee JGS-8028	Piece of Mind	1969	6.25	12.50	25.00
❑ Jubilee JGS-8030	The Happenings' Greatest Hits	1969	6.25	12.50	25.00
HARPERS BIZARRE					
45s					
❑ Warner Bros. 5890	The 59th Street Bridge Song (Feelin' Groovy)/Lost My Love Today	1967	2.50	5.00	10.00
❑ Warner Bros. 7028	Come to the Sunshine/Debutante's Ball	1967	2.00	4.00	8.00
❑ Warner Bros. 7063	Anything Goes/Malibu U.	1967	2.00	4.00	8.00
❑ Warner Bros. 7090	Chattanooga Choo Choo/Hey, You in the Crowd	1967	2.00	4.00	8.00
❑ Warner Bros. 7106	The 59th Street Bridge Song (Feelin' Groovy)/ Come to the Sunshine	1968	—	3.00	6.00
—"Back to Back Hits" series — originals have green labels with "W7" logo					
❑ Warner Bros. 7123	Anything Goes/Chattanooga Choo Choo	1969	—	3.00	6.00
—"Back to Back Hits" series — originals have green labels with "W7" logo					
❑ Warner Bros. 7172	Virginia City/Cotton Candy Sandman	1968	—	3.00	6.00
❑ Warner Bros. 7200	Both Sides Now/Small Talk	1968	—	3.00	6.00
❑ Warner Bros. 7223	Battle of New Orleans/Green Apple Tree	1968	—	3.00	6.00
❑ Warner Bros. 7238	I Love You, Alice B. Toklas/Look to the Rainbow	1968	—	3.00	6.00
❑ Warner Bros. 7296	Knock on Wood/Witchi-Tai-Yo	1969	—	2.50	5.00
❑ Warner Bros. 7377	Poly High/Soft Soundin' Music	1970	—	2.50	5.00
❑ Warner Bros. 7388	Anything Goes/Virginia City	1970	—	2.50	5.00
❑ Warner Bros. 7399	If We Ever Needed the Lord Before/Mad	1970	—	2.50	5.00
❑ Warner Bros. 7647	Knock on Wood/Poly High	1972	—	2.00	4.00
Albums					
❑ Forest Bay 7545	As Time Goes By	1976	3.75	7.50	15.00
❑ Warner Bros. W 1693 [M]	Feelin' Groovy	1967	6.25	12.50	25.00
❑ Warner Bros. WS 1693 [S]	Feelin' Groovy	1967	5.00	10.00	20.00
—Gold label					
❑ Warner Bros. WS 1716	Anything Goes	1967	5.00	10.00	20.00
❑ Warner Bros. WS 1739	The Secret Life of Harpers Bizarre	1968	5.00	10.00	20.00
❑ Warner Bros. WS 1784	Harpers Bizarre Four	1969	5.00	10.00	20.00
HARPTONES, THE					
45s					
❑ Lost-Nite 395	A Sunday Kind of Love/I'll Never Tell	197?	—	2.50	5.00
—Reissue					
HARRISON, GEORGE					
45s					
❑ Apple 1828	What Is Life/Apple Scruffs	1971	2.00	4.00	8.00
—Without star on A-side label					
❑ Apple 1836	Bangla-Desh/Deep Blue	1971	2.00	4.00	8.00
—Without star on A-side label					
❑ Apple 1862	Give Me Love (Give Me Peace on Earth)/Miss O'Dell (2:30)	1973	2.00	4.00	8.00
—With incorrect time for B-side listed					
❑ Apple 1877	Dark Horse/I Don't Care Anymore	1974	2.00	4.00	8.00
—Light blue and white custom photo label					
❑ Apple 1879	Ding Dong, Ding Dong/Hari's on Tour (Express)	1974	5.00	10.00	20.00
—Black and white custom photo label					
❑ Apple 1884	You/World of Stone	1975	—	3.00	6.00
❑ Apple 1885	This Guitar (Can't Keep from Crying)/Maya Love	1975	6.25	12.50	25.00
—The last Apple 45 until 1995					
❑ Apple 2995	My Sweet Lord/Isn't It a Pity	1970	2.00	4.00	8.00
—With "Mfd. by Apple" on label					
❑ Columbia 04887	I Don't Want to Do It/Queen of the Hop	1985	6.25	12.50	25.00
—B-side by Dave Edmunds					
❑ Dark Horse 8294	This Song/Learning How to Love You	1976	2.50	5.00	10.00
—Tan label					
❑ Dark Horse 8313	Crackerbox Palace/Learning How to Love You	1977	—	2.50	5.00
❑ Dark Horse 8763	Blow Away/Soft-Hearted Hana	1979	—	2.50	5.00
—With "RE-1" on label					
❑ Dark Horse 8844	Love Comes to Everyone/Soft Touch	1979	2.50	5.00	10.00
❑ Dark Horse 21891	Got My Mind Set on You/When We Was Fab	198?	—	2.00	4.00
—"Back to Back Hits" series					
❑ Dark Horse 27913	This Is Love/Breath Away from Heaven	1988	—	2.50	5.00
❑ Dark Horse 28131	When We Was Fab/Zig Zag	1988	—	2.50	5.00
❑ Dark Horse 28178	Got My Mind Set on You/Lay His Head	1987	—	2.00	4.00

Number	Title (A Side/B Side)	Yr	VG	VG+	NM
❑ Dark Horse 29744	I Really Love You/Circles	1983	6.25	12.50	25.00
❑ Dark Horse 29864	Wake Up My Love/Greece	1982	2.50	5.00	10.00
❑ Dark Horse 49725	All Those Years Ago/Writing's on the Wall	1981	—	2.50	5.00
❑ Dark Horse 49785	Teardrops/Save the World	1981	2.50	5.00	10.00
❑ Warner Bros. 22807	Cheer Down/That's What It Takes	1989	3.75	7.50	15.00
Albums					
❑ Apple STCH-639 [(3)]	All Things Must Pass	1970	10.00	20.00	40.00
—Apple labels on first two records and "Apple Jam" labels on third; includes poster and lyric innersleeves					
❑ Apple ST-3350	Wonderwall Music	1968	6.25	12.50	25.00
—With "Mfd. by Apple" on label					
❑ Apple SMAS-3410	Living in the Material World	1973	3.75	7.50	15.00
❑ Apple SMAS-3418	Dark Horse	1974	3.75	7.50	15.00
❑ Apple SW-3420	Extra Texture (Read All About It)	1975	3.75	7.50	15.00
❑ Capitol ST-11578	The Best of George Harrison	1976	3.75	7.50	15.00
—Custom label, no bar code on back					
❑ Capitol SN-16055	Dark Horse	1980	3.75	7.50	15.00
—Budget-line reissue; reverses front and back covers					
❑ Capitol SN-16216	Living in the Material World	1980	5.00	10.00	20.00
—Budget-line reissue					
❑ Capitol SN-16217	Extra Texture (Read All About It)	1980	6.25	12.50	25.00
—Budget-line reissue					
❑ Dark Horse DH 3005	Thirty Three and 1/3	1976	2.50	5.00	10.00
—Deduct 30% for cut-outs					
❑ Dark Horse DHK 3255	George Harrison	1979	2.50	5.00	10.00
—Deduct 30% for cut-outs					
❑ Dark Horse DHK 3492	Somewhere in England	1981	2.50	5.00	10.00
—Deduct 30% for cut-outs					
❑ Dark Horse 23724	Gone Troppo	1982	2.50	5.00	10.00
—Deduct 30% for cut-outs					
❑ Dark Horse 25643	Cloud Nine	1987	2.50	5.00	10.00
❑ Dark Horse 25726	Best of Dark Horse 1976-1989	1989	6.25	12.50	25.00
❑ Zapple ST-3358	Electronic Sound	1969	10.00	20.00	40.00

HARRISON, GEORGE, AND FRIENDS

Number	Title (A Side/B Side)	Yr	VG	VG+	NM
Albums					
❑ Apple STCX-3385 [(3)]	The Concert for Bangla Desh	1971	10.00	20.00	40.00
—With 64-page booklet and custom innersleeves					

HAYES, ISAAC

Number	Title (A Side/B Side)	Yr	VG	VG+	NM
45s					
❑ ABC/HBS 12118	Chocolate Chip/(Instrumental)	1975	—	2.00	4.00
❑ ABC/HBS 12138	Come Live with Me/Body Language	1975	—	2.00	4.00
❑ ABC/HBS 12171	Disco Connection/St. Thomas Square	1976	—	2.00	4.00
—By the "Isaac Hayes Movement"					
❑ ABC/HBS 12176	Rock Me Easy Baby (Pt. 1)/Rock Me Easy Baby (Pt. 2)	1976	—	2.00	4.00
❑ ABC/HBS 12206	Juicy Fruit (Disco Freak) (Pt. 1)/Juicy Fruit (Disco Freak) (Pt. 2)	1976	—	2.00	4.00
❑ Brunswick 55258	Sweet Temptation/Laura	1964	2.50	5.00	10.00
❑ Columbia 06363	Ike's Rap/Hey Girl (Edited)	1986	—	—	3.00
❑ Columbia 06655	Thing for You/Thank God for Love	1987	—	—	3.00
❑ Columbia 07104	If You Want My Lovin' (Do Me Right)/(Instrumental)	1987	—	—	3.00
❑ Columbia 07978	Showdown/(Instrumental)	1988	—	—	3.00
❑ Columbia 08116	Let Me Be Your Everything/Curious	1988	—	—	3.00
❑ Enterprise 002	Precious Precious/Going to Chicago Blues	1969	2.00	4.00	8.00
❑ Enterprise 9003	By the Time I Get to Phoenix/Walk On By	1969	—	3.00	6.00
❑ Enterprise 9006	The Mistletoe and Me/Winter Snow	1969	—	3.00	6.00
❑ Enterprise 9017	I Stand Accused/I Just Don't Know What to Do with Myself	1970	—	2.50	5.00
❑ Enterprise 9028	The Look of Love/Ike's Mood	1970	—	2.50	5.00
❑ Enterprise 9031	Never Can Say Goodbye/I Can't Help It If I'm Still in Love with You	1971	—	2.50	5.00
❑ Enterprise 9038	Theme from Shaft/Cafe Regio's	1971	—	2.50	5.00
❑ Enterprise 9042	Do Your Thing/Ellie's Love Theme	1972	—	2.50	5.00
❑ Enterprise 9045	Let's Stay Together/Soulville	1972	—	2.50	5.00
❑ Enterprise 9049	Ain't That Loving You (For More Reasons Than One)/ Baby I'm-a Want You	1972	—	2.50	5.00
—With David Porter					
❑ Enterprise 9058	Theme from The Men/Type Thang	1972	—	2.50	5.00
❑ Enterprise 9065	(If Loving You Is Wrong) I Don't Want to Be Right/ Rolling Down a Mountainside	1973	—	2.50	5.00

Number	Title (A Side/B Side)	Yr	VG	VG+	NM
❑ Enterprise 9085	Joy (Part 1)/Joy (Part 2)	1973	—	2.50	5.00
❑ Enterprise 9095	Wonderful/Someone Made You for Me	1974	—	2.50	5.00
❑ Enterprise 9104	Title Theme/Hung Up on My Baby	1974	—	2.50	5.00
❑ Polydor 2011	Don't Let Go/You Can't Hold Your Woman	1979	—	2.00	4.00
❑ Polydor 2068	A Few More Kisses to Go/What Does It Take	1980	—	2.00	4.00
❑ Polydor 2090	I Ain't Never/Love Has Been Good to Us	1980	—	2.00	4.00
❑ Polydor 2102	It's All in the Game/Wherever You Are	1980	—	2.00	4.00
❑ Polydor 2182	I'm So Proud/I'm Gonna Make Me Love You	1981	—	2.00	4.00
❑ Polydor 2192	Fugitive/Lifetime Thing	1981	—	2.00	4.00
❑ Polydor 14446	Out of the Ghetto/It's Heaven to Me	1977	—	2.00	4.00
❑ Polydor 14464	Moonlight Lovin' (Menage a Trois)/It's Heaven to Me	1978	—	2.00	4.00
❑ Polydor 14521	Zeke the Freak/If We Ever Needed Peace	1978	—	2.00	4.00
❑ Polydor 14534	Just the Way You Are (Part 1)/Just the Way You Are (Part 2)	1979	—	2.00	4.00
❑ Stax 3209	Feel Like Makin' Love (Part 1)/Feel Like Makin' Love (Part 2)	1978	—	2.50	5.00
❑ Virgin 38759	Only If You Were Here/Oh Come All Ye Faithful	2000	—	2.00	4.00
—B-side by Ideal					
Albums					
❑ ABC/HBS D-874	Chocolate Chip	1975	3.75	7.50	15.00
❑ ABC/HBS D-923	Disco Connection	1975	3.00	6.00	12.00
❑ ABC/HBS D-925	Groove-a-Thon	1976	3.00	6.00	12.00
❑ ABC/HBS D-953	Juicy Fruit (Disco Freak)	1976	3.00	6.00	12.00
❑ Atlantic SD 1599	In the Beginning	1972	3.75	7.50	15.00
—Reissue of Enterprise 100					
❑ Columbia FC 40316	U-Turn	1986	2.50	5.00	10.00
❑ Columbia FC 40941	Love Attack	1988	2.50	5.00	10.00
❑ Enterprise E-100 [M]	Presenting Isaac Hayes	1968	10.00	20.00	40.00
❑ Enterprise ES-100 [S]	Presenting Isaac Hayes	1968	7.50	15.00	30.00
❑ Enterprise ENS-1001	Hot Buttered Soul	1969	5.00	10.00	20.00
❑ Enterprise ENS-1010	The Isaac Hayes Movement	1970	5.00	10.00	20.00
❑ Enterprise ENS-1014	To Be Continued	1970	5.00	10.00	20.00
❑ Enterprise ENS-5002 [(2)]	Shaft	1971	5.00	10.00	20.00
❑ Enterprise ENS-5003 [(2)]	Black Moses	1971	5.00	10.00	20.00
❑ Enterprise ENS-5005 [(2)]	Live at the Sahara Tahoe	1973	3.75	7.50	15.00
❑ Enterprise ENS-5007	Joy	1973	3.00	6.00	12.00
❑ Enterprise ENS-7504	Tough Guys	1974	3.00	6.00	12.00
❑ Enterprise ENS-7507 [(2)]	Truck Turner	1974	3.75	7.50	15.00
❑ Enterprise ENS-7510	The Best of Isaac Hayes	1975	3.00	6.00	12.00
❑ Polydor PD-1-6120	New Horizon	1977	2.50	5.00	10.00
❑ Polydor PD-1-6164	For the Sake of Love	1978	2.50	5.00	10.00
❑ Polydor PD-1-6224	Don't Let Go	1979	2.50	5.00	10.00
❑ Polydor PD-1-6269	And Once Again	1980	2.50	5.00	10.00
❑ Stax STX-4102	Hotbed	197?	2.50	5.00	10.00
❑ Stax STX-4114	Hot Buttered Soul	1978	2.50	5.00	10.00
—Reissue of Enterprise 1001					
❑ Stax STX-4129	The Isaac Hayes Movement	197?	2.50	5.00	10.00
—Reissue of Enterprise 1010					
❑ Stax STX-4133	To Be Continued	197?	2.50	5.00	10.00
—Reissue of Enterprise 1014					
❑ Stax MPS-8509	Excerpts from Black Moses	1981	2.50	5.00	10.00
❑ Stax MPS-8515	His Greatest Hit Singles	1982	2.50	5.00	10.00
❑ Stax MPS-8530	Joy	1984	2.50	5.00	10.00
—Reissue of Enterprise 5007					
❑ Stax STX-88002 [(2)]	Shaft	1979	3.00	6.00	12.00
—Reissue of Enterprise 5002					
❑ Stax STX-88003 [(2)]	Enterprise: His Greatest Hits	1980	3.00	6.00	12.00
❑ Stax STX-88004 [(2)]	Live at the Sahara Tahoe	198?	3.00	6.00	12.00
—Reissue of Enterprise 5005					

HAYES, ISAAC, AND DIONNE WARWICK

Albums

Number	Title (A Side/B Side)	Yr	VG	VG+	NM
❑ ABC/HBS D-996 [(2)]	A Man and a Woman	1977	3.75	7.50	15.00

HEART

45s

Number	Title (A Side/B Side)	Yr	VG	VG+	NM
❑ Capitol B-5481	What About Love/Heart of Darkness	1985	—	—	3.00
❑ Capitol B-5512	Never (Remix)/Shell Shock	1985	—	—	3.00
—A-side eventually replaced original mix on "Heart" LP					
❑ Capitol B-5541	These Dreams/Shell Shock	1985	—	—	3.00
❑ Capitol B-5572	Nothin' at All/The Wolf	1986	—	—	3.00
❑ Capitol B-5605	If Looks Could Kill/What He Don't Know	1986	—	—	3.00
❑ Capitol B-44002	Alone/Barracuda (Live)	1987	—	—	3.00
❑ Capitol B-44040	Who Will You Run To/Magic Man (Live)	1987	—	—	3.00
❑ Capitol B-44089	There's the Girl/Bad Animals	1987	—	—	3.00
❑ Capitol B-44116	I Want You So Bad/Easy Target	1988	—	—	3.00
❑ Capitol NR-44507	All I Wanna Do Is Make Love to You/Call of the Wild	1990	—	—	3.00
❑ Capitol NR-44553	I Didn't Want to Need You/The Night	1990	—	—	3.00
❑ Capitol Starline X-6342	What About Love/Never	1986	—	—	3.00
—Reissue					
❑ Epic 14-02925	This Man Is Mine/America	1982	—	—	3.00
❑ Epic 14-03071	Private Audition/Bright Light Girl	1982	—	—	3.00
❑ Epic 34-04047	How Can I Refuse/Johnny Moon	1983	—	—	3.00
❑ Epic 34-04184	Allies/Together Now	1983	—	2.50	5.00
❑ Epic 15-08101	Barracuda/Straight On	1988	—	—	3.00
—Reissue					
❑ Epic 9-50847	Even It Up/Pilot	1980	—	2.00	4.00
❑ Epic 9-50874	Raised on You/Down on Me	1980	—	2.00	4.00
❑ Epic 9-50892	Bebe Le Strange/Silver Wheels	1980	—	2.00	4.00

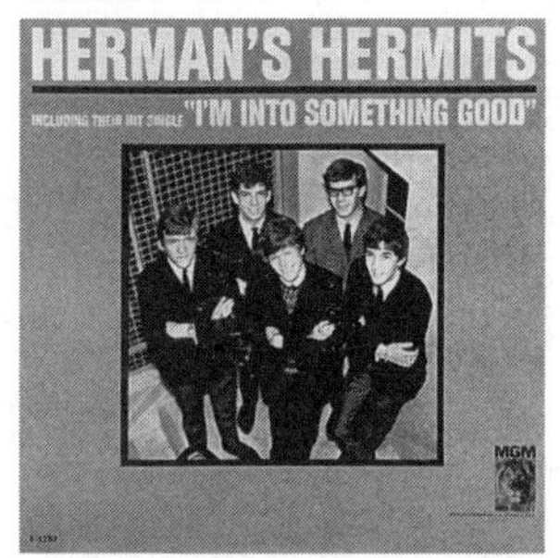

Number	Title (A Side/B Side)	Yr	VG	VG+	NM
❑ Epic 19-50950	Tell It Like It Is/Strange Euphoria	1980	—	2.00	4.00
❑ Epic 19-51010	Unchained Melody/Mistral Wind	1981	—	2.00	4.00
❑ Mushroom 7011	Magic Man/How Deep It Goes	1976	—	2.50	5.00
❑ Mushroom 7021	Crazy on You/Dreamboat Annie	1976	—	3.00	6.00
❑ Mushroom 7023	Dreamboat Annie/Sing Child	1976	—	2.50	5.00
—Bizarre version of A-side with part of the intro to "Crazy on You" grafted on.					
❑ Mushroom 7031	Heartless/Just the Wine	1978	—	2.00	4.00
❑ Mushroom 7035	Without You/Here Song	1978	—	2.00	4.00
❑ Mushroom 7043	Magazine/Devil Delight	1978	—	2.00	4.00
❑ Portrait 17-8101	Barracuda/Straight On	1981	—	2.00	4.00
—Reissue					
❑ Portrait 6-70004	Barracuda/Cry to Me	1977	—	2.00	4.00
❑ Portrait 6-70008	Little Queen/Treat Me Well	1977	—	2.50	5.00
❑ Portrait 6-70010	Kick It Out/Go On, Cry	1977	—	2.50	5.00
❑ Portrait 6-70020	Straight On/Lighter Touch	1978	—	2.00	4.00
—Custom label					
❑ Portrait 6-70025	Dog and Butterfly/Mistral Wind	1979	—	2.50	5.00
Albums					
❑ Capitol ST-12410	Heart	1985	2.50	5.00	10.00
—With remix of "Never." Side one trail-off wax has an "RE-1"					
❑ Capitol SQ-12500	Dreamboat Annie	1986	2.00	4.00	8.00
❑ Capitol SQ-12501	Magazine	1986	2.00	4.00	8.00
❑ Capitol PJ-12546	Bad Animals	1987	2.00	4.00	8.00
❑ Capitol C1-91820	Brigade	1990	3.00	6.00	12.00
❑ Epic FE 36371	Bebe Le Strange	1980	2.50	5.00	10.00
❑ Epic KE2 36888 [(2)]	Greatest Hits/Live	1980	3.00	6.00	12.00
❑ Epic FE 38049	Private Audition	1982	2.50	5.00	10.00
❑ Epic QE 38800	Passionworks	1983	2.50	5.00	10.00
❑ Mushroom MRS-5005	Dreamboat Annie	1976	2.50	5.00	10.00
❑ Mushroom MRS-5008	Magazine	1977	15.00	30.00	60.00
—Original issue, quickly recalled; "Magazine" is the last song on side 1; Side 2, Track 3 is "Blues Medley (Mother Earth) (You Shook Me Babe)"; at the bottom of the back cover is "Mushroom Records regrets that a contractual dispute has made it necessary to complete this record without the cooperation or endorsement of the group Heart, who have expressly disclaimed artistic involvement in completing this record."					
❑ Mushroom MRS-5008	Magazine	1978	2.50	5.00	10.00
—Authorized edition; Side 2, Track 3 is "Mother Earth Blues"					
❑ Portrait JR 34799	Little Queen	1977	2.50	5.00	10.00
❑ Portrait FR 35555	Dog and Butterfly	1978	2.50	5.00	10.00

HELMS, BOBBY

45s

Number	Title (A Side/B Side)	Yr	VG	VG+	NM
❑ Certron 10002	Mary Goes 'Round/Cold Winds Blow on Me	1970	2.00	4.00	8.00
❑ Certron 10021	Jingle Bell Rock/The Old Year Is Gone	1970	2.00	4.00	8.00
❑ Certron 10023	I Wouldn't Take the World for You/Look What You've Done	1970	2.00	4.00	8.00
❑ Columbia 4-42801	Fraulein/My Special Angel	1963	2.50	5.00	10.00
❑ Columbia 4-43031	It's a Girl/Put Your Arms Around Him	1964	2.50	5.00	10.00
❑ Decca 9-29947	Tennessee Rock 'N' Roll/I Don't Owe You Nothing	1956	12.50	25.00	50.00
❑ Decca 9-30194	Fraulein/(Got a) Heartsick Feeling	1957	5.00	10.00	20.00
❑ Decca 9-30423	My Special Angel/Standing at the End of My World	1957	6.25	12.50	25.00
❑ Decca 9-30513	Jingle Bell Rock/Captain Santa Claus	1957	6.25	12.50	25.00
—Black label, star under "Decca"					
❑ Decca 9-30557	Just a Little Lonesome/Love My Baby	1958	5.00	10.00	20.00
❑ Decca 9-30619	Jacqueline/Living in the Shadow of the Past	1958	5.00	10.00	20.00
❑ Decca 9-30682	Schoolboy Crush/Borrowed Dreams	1958	5.00	10.00	20.00
❑ Decca 9-30749	A Hundred Hearts/The Fool and the Angel	1958	5.00	10.00	20.00
❑ Decca 9-30831	New River Train/Miss Memory	1959	3.75	7.50	15.00
❑ Decca 9-30886	Soon It Can Be Told/I Guess I'll Miss the Prom	1959	3.75	7.50	15.00
❑ Decca 9-30928	No Other Baby/You're No Longer Mine	1959	3.75	7.50	15.00
❑ Decca 9-30976	My Lucky Day/Hurry Baby	1959	3.75	7.50	15.00
❑ Decca 9-31041	To My Sorrow/Someone Was Already There	1960	3.75	7.50	15.00
❑ Decca 31103	Let Me Be the One/I Wanna Be with You	1960	3.75	7.50	15.00
❑ Decca 31148	Lonely River Rhine/Guess We Thought the World Would End	1960	3.75	7.50	15.00
❑ Decca 31230	Sad-Eyed Baby/You're the One	1961	3.00	6.00	12.00
❑ Decca 31287	How Can You Divide a Little Child/My Greatest Weakness	1961	3.00	6.00	12.00
❑ Decca 31356	One Deep Love/Once in a Lifetime	1962	3.00	6.00	12.00
❑ Decca 31403	Then Came You/Yesterday's Champagne	1962	3.00	6.00	12.00
❑ Gusto 116	That Heart Belongs to Me/With Jenny on My Mind	1974	—	3.00	6.00
❑ Gusto 119	Work Things Out with Annie/With Jenny on My Mind	1974	—	3.00	6.00

Number	Title (A Side/B Side)	Yr	VG	VG+	NM
❑ Kapp 708	I'm the Man/Have This Love on Me	1965	2.50	5.00	10.00
❑ Kapp 719	Jingle Bell Rock/The Bell That Couldn't Jingle	1965	3.00	6.00	12.00
❑ Kapp 732	Those Snowy Glowy Blowy Days of Winter/Sailor	1965	2.50	5.00	10.00
❑ Kapp 777	The Things I Remember Most/Sorry, My Name Isn't Fred	1966	2.50	5.00	10.00
❑ Kapp 876	I Miss My Fraulein/Where Does a Shadow Go	1967	2.00	4.00	8.00
❑ Little Darlin' 0030	He Thought He'd Die Laughing/You'd Better Make Up Your Mind	1967	2.50	5.00	10.00
❑ Little Darlin' 0034	The Day You Stop Loving Me/You Can Tell the World	1967	2.50	5.00	10.00
❑ Little Darlin' 0038	Jingle Bell Rock/I Wanta Go to Santa Claus Land	1967	3.00	6.00	12.00
❑ Little Darlin' 0041	I Feel You, I Love You/The Day You Stop Loving Me	1968	2.50	5.00	10.00
❑ Little Darlin' 0049	Or Is It Love/Touch My Heart	1968	2.50	5.00	10.00
❑ Little Darlin' 0054	My Special Angel/Expressing My Love	1968	2.50	5.00	10.00
❑ Little Darlin' 0062	So Long/Just Do the Best You Can	1969	2.50	5.00	10.00
❑ Little Darlin' 0073	Echoes and Shadows/Step Into My Soul	1969	2.50	5.00	10.00
❑ Little Darlin' 7801	I'm Gonna Love the Devil Out of You/I Can't Promise You	1978	—	3.00	6.00
❑ Little Darlin' 7807	The Things I Remember Most/I'm Not Sorry	1978	—	3.00	6.00
❑ Little Darlin' 7809	Jingle Bell Rock/I Wanta Go to Santa Claus Land	1978	—	3.00	6.00
❑ Little Darlin' 7916	One More Dollar for the Band/Touch My Heart	1979	—	3.00	6.00
❑ MCA 65026	Jingle Bell Rock/Captain Santa Claus	1973	—	2.50	5.00
—Black label with rainbow					
❑ MCA 65026	Jingle Bell Rock/Captain Santa Claus	1980	—	—	3.00
—Blue label with rainbow					
❑ MCA 65029	Jingle Bell Rock/The Bell That Couldn't Jingle	1973	—	2.50	5.00
—Black label with rainbow; this contains the 1965 Kapp re-recording of the A-side					
❑ MCA 65029	Jingle Bell Rock/The Bell That Couldn't Jingle	1980	—	—	3.00
—Blue label with rainbow					
❑ Million 5	It's the Little Things/Love's Sweet Mystery	1972	—	3.50	7.00
❑ Million 22	It's Starting to Rain Again/Wouldn't Give Up on You	1972	—	3.50	7.00
❑ Mistletoe 802	Jingle Bell Rock/Jingle Bells	197?	—	2.50	5.00
❑ Playback 1305	Lay Me Down Look/Dance with Me	1988	—	3.00	6.00
❑ Playback 1322	Somebody Wrong Is Looking Right/This Song for You	1988	—	3.00	6.00
❑ Playback 1328	Southern Belle/Troubles Wall to Wall	1989	—	3.00	6.00
❑ Playback 75709	Southern Belle/Troubles Wall to Wall	1989	—	2.50	5.00
❑ Speed 45-114	Yesterday's Lovin'/Hanging Around	1957	7.50	15.00	30.00
❑ Speed 45-117	Freedom Lovin' Guy/I've Never Seen Anyone	1957	7.50	15.00	30.00
Albums					
❑ Columbia CL 2060 [M]	The Best of Bobby Helms	1963	6.25	12.50	25.00
❑ Columbia CS 8860 [S]	The Best of Bobby Helms	1963	7.50	15.00	30.00
❑ Decca DL 8638 [M]	Bobby Helms Sings to My Special Angel	1957	30.00	60.00	120.00
❑ Harmony HL 7409 [M]	Fraulein	1967	3.00	6.00	12.00
❑ Harmony HS 11209 [S]	Fraulein	1967	3.00	6.00	12.00
❑ Kapp KL 1463 [M]	I'm the Man	1966	3.75	7.50	15.00
❑ Kapp KL 1505 [M]	Sorry My Name Isn't Fred	1966	3.75	7.50	15.00
❑ Kapp KS 3463 [S]	I'm the Man	1966	5.00	10.00	20.00
❑ Kapp KS 3505 [S]	Sorry My Name Isn't Fred	1966	5.00	10.00	20.00
❑ Little Darlin' 8088	All New Just for You	1968	6.25	12.50	25.00
❑ Mistletoe MLP-1206	Jingle Bell Rock	197?	3.00	6.00	12.00
❑ Power Pak 283	Greatest Hits	197?	2.50	5.00	10.00
❑ Vocalion VL 3743 [M]	Someone Already There	1965	3.75	7.50	15.00
❑ Vocalion VL 73743 [R]	Someone Already There	1965	3.00	6.00	12.00
❑ Vocalion VL 73874	My Special Angel	1969	3.00	6.00	12.00

HENDRIX, JIMI

Number	Title (A Side/B Side)	Yr	VG	VG+	NM
45s					
❑ Audio Fidelity 167	No Such Animal (Part 1)/No Such Animal (Part 2)	1970	3.75	7.50	15.00
❑ Reprise 0572	Hey Joe/51st Anniversary	1967	25.00	50.00	100.00
❑ Reprise 0597	Purple Haze/The Wind Cries Mary	1967	6.25	12.50	25.00
❑ Reprise 0641	Foxey Lady/Hey Joe	1967	6.25	12.50	25.00
❑ Reprise 0665	Up from the Skies/One Rainy Wish	1968	7.50	15.00	30.00
❑ Reprise 0728	Purple Haze/Foxey Lady	1968	3.75	7.50	15.00
—"Back to Back Hits" series —originals have both "r:" and "W7" logos					
❑ Reprise 0742	All Along the Watchtower/Crosstown Traffic	1971	—	3.00	6.00
—"Back to Back Hits" series					
❑ Reprise 0767	All Along the Watchtower/Burning of the Midnight Lamp	1968	7.50	15.00	30.00
❑ Reprise 0792	Crosstown Traffic/Gypsy Eyes	1968	7.50	15.00	30.00
❑ Reprise 0853	If 6 Was 9/Stone Free	1969	10.00	20.00	40.00
❑ Reprise 0905	Stepping Stone/Izabella	1970	25.00	50.00	100.00
—As "Hendrix Band of Gypsys"					
❑ Reprise 1000	Freedom/Angel	1971	3.75	7.50	15.00
❑ Reprise 1044	Dolly Dagger/Star Spangled Banner	1971	3.75	7.50	15.00
❑ Reprise 1082	Johnny B. Goode/Lover Man	1972	3.75	7.50	15.00
❑ Reprise 1118	The Wind Cries Mary/Little Wing	1972	3.75	7.50	15.00
❑ Reprise EP 2239	Gloria (B-side blank)	1979	—	2.50	5.00
❑ Reprise 29845	Fire/Little Wing	1982	—	3.00	6.00
❑ Trip 3002	Hot Trigger/Suspicious	1972	—	2.50	5.00
Albums					
❑ Accord SN-7101	Kaleidoscope	1981	2.50	5.00	10.00
❑ Accord SN-7112	Before London	1981	2.50	5.00	10.00
❑ Accord SN-7139	Cosmic Feeling	1981	2.50	5.00	10.00
❑ Capitol STAO-472	Band of Gypsys	1970	5.00	10.00	20.00
❑ Capitol SWBB-659 [(2)]	Get That Feeling/Flashing	1971	6.25	12.50	25.00
❑ Capitol ST 2856 [S]	Get That Feeling	1967	10.00	20.00	40.00
❑ Capitol T 2856 [M]	Get That Feeling	1967	20.00	40.00	80.00
❑ Capitol ST 2894 [S]	Flashing	1968	10.00	20.00	40.00
❑ Capitol T 2894 [M]	Flashing	1968	25.00	50.00	100.00
❑ Capitol SJ-12416	Band of Gypsys 2	1986	2.50	5.00	10.00
—Side 2 lists, and plays, three songs					
❑ Capitol MLP-15022 [EP]	Johnny B. Goode	1986	2.00	4.00	8.00

Number	Title (A Side/B Side)	Yr	VG	VG+	NM
❑ Capitol SN-16319	Band of Gypsys	1985	2.50	5.00	10.00
—Budget-line reissue					
❑ Nutmeg 1001	High, Live 'N' Dirty	1978	6.25	12.50	25.00
—Black vinyl					
❑ Nutmeg 1002	Cosmic Turnaround	1981	3.00	6.00	12.00
❑ Phoenix 10 PHX 320	Rare Hendrix	1981	2.00	4.00	8.00
❑ Phoenix 10 PHX 324	Roots of Hendrix	1981	2.00	4.00	8.00
❑ Pickwick SPC-3528	Jimi	197?	2.50	5.00	10.00
❑ Reprise MS 2025	Smash Hits	1969	10.00	20.00	40.00
—With "W7" and "r:" logos on two-tone orange label					
❑ Reprise MS 2029	Historic Performances As Recorded at the Monterey International Pop Festival	1970	5.00	10.00	20.00
—Side 1: Jimi Hendrix; Side 2: Otis Redding; with only "r:" logo on all-orange (tan) label					
❑ Reprise MS 2034	The Cry of Love	1971	3.75	7.50	15.00
—With only "r:" logo on all-orange (tan) label					
❑ Reprise MS 2040	Rainbow Bridge	1971	5.00	10.00	20.00
❑ Reprise MS 2049	Hendrix in the West	1972	5.00	10.00	20.00
❑ Reprise MS 2103	War Heroes	1972	5.00	10.00	20.00
❑ Reprise MS 2204	Crash Landing	1975	3.75	7.50	15.00
❑ Reprise MS 2229	Midnight Lightning	1975	3.75	7.50	15.00
❑ Reprise 2RS 2245 [(2)]	The Essential Jimi Hendrix	1978	5.00	10.00	20.00
❑ Reprise MSK 2276	Smash Hits	1977	2.50	5.00	10.00
—Reissue					
❑ Reprise HS 2293	The Essential Jimi Hendrix Volume Two	1979	3.75	7.50	15.00
—Add 100% if bonus single of "Gloria" with picture sleeve is enclosed					
❑ Reprise HS 2299	Nine to the Universe	1980	2.50	5.00	10.00
❑ Reprise R 6261 [M]	Are You Experienced?	1967	50.00	100.00	200.00
❑ Reprise RS 6261 [S]	Are You Experienced?	1967	12.50	25.00	50.00
—Pink, gold and green label					
❑ Reprise R 6281 [M]	Axis: Bold As Love	1968	625.00	1250.	2500.
❑ Reprise RS 6281 [S]	Axis: Bold As Love	1968	20.00	40.00	80.00
—Pink, gold and green label					
❑ Reprise 2RS 6307 [(2)S]	Electric Ladyland	1968	25.00	50.00	100.00
—With "W7" and "r:" logos on two-tone orange label					
❑ Reprise 2RS 6481 [(2)]	Soundtrack Recordings from the Film Jimi Hendrix	1973	6.25	12.50	25.00
❑ Reprise 22306 [(2)]	The Jimi Hendrix Concerts	1982	3.00	6.00	12.00
❑ Reprise 25119	Kiss the Sky	1984	2.50	5.00	10.00
❑ Reprise 25358	Jimi Plays Monterey	1986	2.50	5.00	10.00
❑ Reprise STBO-91568 [(2)]	Electric Ladyland	1968	37.50	75.00	150.00
—Capitol Record Club edition					
❑ Ryko Analogue RALP-0038 [(2)]	Live at Winterland	1988	3.75	7.50	15.00
❑ Ryko Analogue RALP-0078 [(2)]	Radio One	1988	3.75	7.50	15.00
—Clear vinyl					
❑ Springboard SPB-4010	Jimi Hendrix	197?	2.50	5.00	10.00
❑ Trip 3509 [(2)]	Superpak	197?	3.75	7.50	15.00
❑ Trip TLP-9500	Rare Hendrix	1972	3.75	7.50	15.00
❑ Trip TLP-9501	Roots of Hendrix	1972	3.00	6.00	12.00
❑ Trip TLP-9512	Moods	1973	3.00	6.00	12.00
❑ Trip TLP-9523	The Genius of Jimi Hendrix	1973	3.00	6.00	12.00
❑ United Artists UA-LA505-E	The Very Best of Jimi Hendrix	1975	3.00	6.00	12.00

HENDRIX, JIMI, AND LITTLE RICHARD

45s

Number	Title (A Side/B Side)	Yr	VG	VG+	NM
❑ Ala 1175	Goodnight Irene/Why Don't You Love Me	1972	2.00	4.00	8.00

Albums

Number	Title (A Side/B Side)	Yr	VG	VG+	NM
❑ Everest Archive of Folk & Jazz 296	Roots of Rock	1974	3.00	6.00	12.00
❑ Pickwick SPC-3347	Jimi Hendrix and Little Richard Together	1973	3.00	6.00	12.00

HENLEY, DON

45s

Number	Title (A Side/B Side)	Yr	VG	VG+	NM
❑ Asylum 69831	Nobody's Business/Long Way Home	1983	—	2.00	4.00
❑ Asylum 69894	Dirty Laundry/Lilah	1982	—	2.00	4.00
❑ Asylum 69931	I Can't Stand Still/Them and Us	1982	—	2.00	4.00
❑ Asylum 69971	Johnny Can't Read/Long Way Home	1982	—	2.00	4.00

Number	Title (A Side/B Side)	Yr	VG	VG+	NM
❑ Geffen 19660	New York Minute/The Heart of the Matter	1990	—	—	3.00
❑ Geffen 22771	The Last Worthless Evening/Gimme What You Got	1989	—	—	3.00
❑ Geffen 22925	The End of the Innocence/If Dirt Were Dollars	1989	—	—	3.00
❑ Geffen 28906	Sunset Grill/Man with a Mission	1985	—	2.00	4.00
❑ Geffen 29012	Not Enough Love in the World/Man with a Mission	1985	—	—	3.00
❑ Geffen 29065	All She Wants to Do Is Dance/Building the Perfect Beast	1985	—	—	3.00
❑ Geffen 29141	The Boys of Summer/A Month of Sundays	1984	—	—	3.00
Albums					
❑ Asylum E1-60048	I Can't Stand Still	1982	2.50	5.00	10.00
❑ Geffen GHS 24026	Building the Perfect Beast	1984	2.50	5.00	10.00
❑ Geffen GHS 24217	The End of the Innocence	1989	3.00	6.00	12.00

HERMAN'S HERMITS

45s

Number	Title (A Side/B Side)	Yr	VG	VG+	NM
❑ Abkco 4021	Mrs. Brown You've Got a Lovely Daughter/I'm Henry VIII, I Am	1972	—	2.50	5.00
❑ Abkco 4022	I'm Into Something Good/Can't You Hear My Heartbeat	1972	—	2.50	5.00
❑ Abkco 4023	There's a Kind of Hush (All Over the World)/Wonderful World	1972	—	2.50	5.00
❑ Abkco 4024	Listen People/Dandy	1972	—	2.50	5.00
❑ Abkco 4042	Silhouettes/Just a Little Bit Better	1973	—	2.50	5.00
❑ Abkco 4043	A Must to Avoid/Leaning on the Lamp Post	1973	—	2.50	5.00
❑ Buddah 516	Lonely Situation (Love Is All I Need)/Blond Haired Blue Eyed Boy	1976	2.00	4.00	8.00
❑ MGM 13280	I'm Into Something Good/Your Hand in Mine	1964	2.50	5.00	10.00
❑ MGM 13310	Can't You Hear My Heartbeat/I Know Why	1964	2.50	5.00	10.00
❑ MGM 13332	Silhouettes/Walkin' With My Angel	1965	2.50	5.00	10.00
❑ MGM 13341	Mrs. Brown You've Got a Lovely Daughter/I Gotta Dream On	1965	2.50	5.00	10.00
❑ MGM 13354	Wonderful World/Traveling Light	1965	2.50	5.00	10.00
❑ MGM 13367	I'm Henry VIII, I Am/The End of the World	1965	2.50	5.00	10.00
❑ MGM 13398	Just a Little Bit Better/Sea Cruise	1965	2.50	5.00	10.00
❑ MGM 13437	A Must to Avoid/The Man with the Cigar	1966	2.00	4.00	8.00
❑ MGM 13462	Listen People/Got a Feeling	1966	2.00	4.00	8.00
❑ MGM 13500	Leaning on the Lamp Post/Hold On	1966	2.00	4.00	8.00
❑ MGM 13548	This Door Swings Both Ways/For Love	1966	2.00	4.00	8.00
❑ MGM 13603	Dandy/My Reservation's Been Confirmed	1966	2.00	4.00	8.00
❑ MGM 13639	East West/What Is Wrong What Is Right	1966	2.00	4.00	8.00
❑ MGM 13681	There's a Kind of Hush (All Over the World)/No Milk Today	1967	2.50	5.00	10.00
❑ MGM 13681	There's a Kind of Hush/No Milk Today	1967	2.00	4.00	8.00
❑ MGM 13761	Don't Go Out Into the Rain (You're Going to Melt)/Moonshine Man	1967	2.00	4.00	8.00
❑ MGM 13787	Museum/Last Bus Home	1967	2.00	4.00	8.00
❑ MGM 13885	I Can Take or Leave Your Loving/Marcel's	1967	2.00	4.00	8.00
❑ MGM 13934	Sleepy Joe/Just One Girl	1968	2.50	5.00	10.00
—Black label					
❑ MGM 13973	Sunshine Girl/Nobody Needs to Know	1968	2.50	5.00	10.00
❑ MGM 13994	Ooh, She's Done It Again/The Most Beautiful Thing in My Life	1968	2.50	5.00	10.00
❑ MGM 14035	Something's Happening/Little Miss Sorrow, Child of Tomorrow	1969	2.50	5.00	10.00
❑ MGM 14060	My Lady/My Sentimental Friend	1969	2.50	5.00	10.00
❑ MGM 14100	It's Alright Now/(Here Comes) The Star	1969	2.50	5.00	10.00
❑ Private Stock 45,019	Ginny Go Softly/Blond Haired, Blue Eyed Boy	1975	2.00	4.00	8.00
❑ Roulette 7213	Truck Stop Mama/Heart Get Ready for Love	1977	3.75	7.50	15.00
Albums					
❑ Abkco 4227-1	Their Greatest Hits	1988	2.00	4.00	8.00
—Abridged version of AB 4227					
❑ Abkco AB-4227 [(2)]	XX (Greatest Hits)	1973	3.00	6.00	12.00
❑ MGM E-4282 [M]	Introducing Herman's Hermits	1965	6.25	12.50	25.00
—Version 1: With "Including Their Hit Single 'I'm Into Something Good' " on front cover					
❑ MGM SE-4282 [R]	Introducing Herman's Hermits	1965	5.00	10.00	20.00
—Version 1: With "Including Their Hit Single 'I'm Into Something Good' " on front cover					
❑ MGM E-4295 [M]	Herman's Hermits On Tour	1965	3.00	6.00	12.00
❑ MGM SE-4295 [R]	Herman's Hermits On Tour	1965	2.50	5.00	10.00
❑ MGM E-4315 [M]	The Best of Herman's Hermits	1965	3.00	6.00	12.00
❑ MGM SE-4315 [R]	The Best of Herman's Hermits	1965	2.50	5.00	10.00
❑ MGM E-4342 [M]	Hold On!	1966	2.50	5.00	10.00
❑ MGM SE-4342 [P]	Hold On!	1966	3.00	6.00	12.00
❑ MGM E-4386 [M]	Both Sides of Herman's Hermits	1966	2.50	5.00	10.00
❑ MGM SE-4386 [R]	Both Sides of Herman's Hermits	1966	2.00	4.00	8.00
❑ MGM E-4416 [M]	The Best of Herman's Hermits, Volume 2	1966	3.00	6.00	12.00
—Add 50% if bonus photo of Herman is included					
❑ MGM SE-4416 [P]	The Best of Herman's Hermits, Volume 2	1966	2.50	5.00	10.00
—Add 50% if bonus photo of Herman is included. "Hold On" and "Leaning on the Lamp Post" are in true stereo.					
❑ MGM E-4438 [M]	There's a Kind of Hush All Over the World	1967	2.50	5.00	10.00
❑ MGM SE-4438 [R]	There's a Kind of Hush All Over the World	1967	2.00	4.00	8.00
❑ MGM E-4478 [M]	Blaze	1967	2.50	5.00	10.00
❑ MGM SE-4478 [S]	Blaze	1967	2.50	5.00	10.00
❑ MGM E-4505 [M]	The Best of Herman's Hermits, Volume 3	1967	2.50	5.00	10.00
❑ MGM SE-4505 [P]	The Best of Herman's Hermits, Volume 3	1967	2.50	5.00	10.00
—"Don't Go Out Into the Rain," "Museum," "Last Bus Home" and "Mum and Dad" are in true stereo.					
❑ MGM SE-4548 [P]	Mrs. Brown You've Got a Lovely Daughter	1968	2.50	5.00	10.00
—"Mrs. Brown You've Got a Lovely Daughter" and "There's a Kind of Hush" are rechanneled					

HIT PACK, THE

45s

Number	Title (A Side/B Side)	Yr	VG	VG+	NM
❑ Soul 35010	Never Say No to Your Baby/Let's Dance	1965	12.50	25.00	50.00

HOLLIES, THE

45s

Number	Title (A Side/B Side)	Yr	VG	VG+	NM
❑ Atlantic 89784	If the Lights Go Out/Someone Else's Eyes	1983	—	—	3.00
❑ Atlantic 89819	Stop in the Name of Love/Musical Pictures	1983	—	—	3.00
❑ Epic 10180	Carrie-Anne/Signs That Will Never Change	1967	2.00	4.00	8.00
❑ Epic 10234	King Midas in Reverse/Water on the Brain	1967	2.00	4.00	8.00

Number	Title (A Side/B Side)	Yr	VG	VG+	NM
❑ Epic 10251	Dear Eloise/When Your Light's Turned On	1967	2.00	4.00	8.00
❑ Epic 10298	Jennifer Eccles/Try It	1968	2.00	4.00	8.00
❑ Epic 10361	Do the Best You Can/Elevated Observations	1968	2.00	4.00	8.00
❑ Epic 10400	Listen to Me/Everything Is Sunshine	1968	2.00	4.00	8.00
❑ Epic 10454	Sorry Suzanne/Not That Way at All	1969	2.00	4.00	8.00
❑ Epic 10532	He Ain't Heavy, He's My Brother/Cos You Like to Love Me	1969	—	3.00	6.00
—A-side: Elton John on piano					
❑ Epic 10613	I Can't Tell the Bottom from the Top/Mad Professor Blythe	1970	—	3.00	6.00
❑ Epic 10677	Gasoline Alley Bred/Dandelion Wine	1970	2.50	5.00	10.00
❑ Epic 10716	Survival of the Fittest/Man Without a Heart	1971	3.00	6.00	12.00
❑ Epic 10754	Hey Willy/Row the Boat Together	1971	2.50	5.00	10.00
❑ Epic 10842	The Baby/Oh Granny	1972	2.50	5.00	10.00
❑ Epic 10871	Long Cool Woman (In a Black Dress)/Look What We've Got	1972	—	2.50	5.00
❑ Epic 10920	Long Dark Road/Indian Girl	1972	—	2.50	5.00
❑ Epic 10951	Magic Woman Touch/Blue in the Morning	1973	—	2.50	5.00
❑ Epic 10989	Jesus Was a Crossmaker/I Had a Dream	1973	—	2.50	5.00
❑ Epic 11025	Won't We Feel Good/Slow Down	1973	—	2.50	5.00
❑ Epic 11051	The Day That Curley Billy Shot Down Crazy Sam McGee/ Born a Man	1973	—	2.50	5.00
❑ Epic 11100	The Air That I Breathe/No More Riders	1974	—	2.50	5.00
❑ Epic 50029	Don't Let Me Down/Layin' to the Music	1974	—	2.50	5.00
❑ Epic 50086	Sandy/Second Hand Hangups	1975	—	2.50	5.00
❑ Epic 50110	Another Night/Time Machine Jive	1975	—	2.00	4.00
❑ Epic 50144	Look Out Johnny/I'm Down	1975	—	2.00	4.00
❑ Epic 50204	Crocodile Woman (She Bites)/Write On	1976	—	2.00	4.00
❑ Epic 50359	Sandy/Second Hand Hangups	1977	—	2.00	4.00
❑ Epic 50422	Draggin' My Heels/I Won't Move Over	1977	—	2.00	4.00
❑ Epic 50522	Burn Out/Writing on the Wall	1978	—	2.00	4.00
❑ Imperial 54050	Look Through My Window/I'm Alive	196?	3.75	7.50	15.00
—"The Golden Series" gold label reissue with incorrect A-side title					
❑ Imperial 66026	Just One Look/Keep Off That Friend of Mine	1964	5.00	10.00	20.00
❑ Imperial 66044	Here I Go Again/Lucille	1964	3.75	7.50	15.00
❑ Imperial 66070	Come On Back/We're Through	1964	3.75	7.50	15.00
❑ Imperial 66099	Yes I Will/Nobody	1965	10.00	20.00	40.00
❑ Imperial 66119	I'm Alive/You Know He Did	1965	3.75	7.50	15.00
❑ Imperial 66134	Look Through Any Window/So Lonely	1965	3.00	6.00	12.00
❑ Imperial 66158	I Can't Let Go/I've Got a Way of My Own	1966	3.75	7.50	15.00
❑ Imperial 66186	Bus Stop/Don't Run and Hide	1966	3.00	6.00	12.00
❑ Imperial 66214	Stop Stop Stop/It's You	1966	3.00	6.00	12.00
❑ Imperial 66231	On a Carousel/All the World Is Love	1967	3.00	6.00	12.00
❑ Imperial 66240	Pay You Back With Interest/Whatcha Gonna Do 'Bout It	1967	3.00	6.00	12.00
❑ Imperial 66258	Just One Look/Running Through the Night	1967	3.00	6.00	12.00
❑ Imperial 66271	If I Needed Someone/I'll Be True to You (Yes I Will)	1968	10.00	20.00	40.00
❑ Liberty 55674	Stay/Now's the Time	1964	15.00	30.00	60.00
❑ United Artists 50079	After the Fox/The Fox Trot	1966	5.00	10.00	20.00
—With Peter Sellers					
Albums					
❑ Atlantic 80076	What Goes Around	1983	2.50	5.00	10.00
❑ Capitol N-16056	Hollies' Greatest	1980	2.00	4.00	8.00
❑ EMI America SN-16397	More Great Hits (1963-1968)	1986	2.00	4.00	8.00
❑ Epic LN 24315 [M]	Evolution	1967	7.50	15.00	30.00
❑ Epic LN 24344 [M]	Dear Eloise/King Midas in Reverse	1967	7.50	15.00	30.00
❑ Epic BN 26315 [S]	Evolution	1967	6.25	12.50	25.00
❑ Epic BN 26344 [S]	Dear Eloise/King Midas in Reverse	1967	6.25	12.50	25.00
❑ Epic BN 26447	Words and Music by Bob Dylan	1969	3.75	7.50	15.00
—Yellow label					
❑ Epic BN 26447	Words and Music by Bob Dylan	1973	2.50	5.00	10.00
—Orange label					
❑ Epic BN 26538	He Ain't Heavy, He's My Brother	1970	5.00	10.00	20.00
❑ Epic E 30255	Moving Finger	1971	5.00	10.00	20.00
❑ Epic KE 30958	Distant Light	1972	3.75	7.50	15.00
—Yellow label					
❑ Epic KE 30958	Distant Light	1974	2.50	5.00	10.00
—Orange label					
❑ Epic KE 31992	Romany	1972	3.00	6.00	12.00
—Yellow label					

Number	Title (A Side/B Side)	Yr	VG	VG+	NM
❑ Epic KE 32061	The Hollies' Greatest Hits	1973	3.00	6.00	12.00
—Yellow label					
❑ Epic KE 32574	Hollies	1974	2.50	5.00	10.00
❑ Epic PE 33387	Another Night	1975	2.50	5.00	10.00
❑ Epic PE 34714	Clarke, Hicks, Sylvester, Calvert & Elliot	1977	2.50	5.00	10.00
❑ Epic JE 35334	A Crazy Steal	1978	2.50	5.00	10.00
❑ Imperial LP-9265 [M]	Here I Go Again	1964	37.50	75.00	150.00
—Black label with stars					
❑ Imperial LP-9299 [M]	Hear! Here!	1965	12.50	25.00	50.00
❑ Imperial LP-9312 [M]	The Hollies — Beat Group	1966	7.50	15.00	30.00
❑ Imperial LP-9330 [M]	Bus Stop	1966	7.50	15.00	30.00
—Black and pink label					
❑ Imperial LP-9339 [M]	Stop! Stop! Stop!	1966	6.25	12.50	25.00
❑ Imperial LP-9350 [M]	The Hollies' Greatest Hits	1967	5.00	10.00	20.00
❑ Imperial LP-12265 [R]	Here I Go Again	1964	25.00	50.00	100.00
—Black label with silver print					
❑ Imperial LP-12299 [R]	Hear! Here!	1965	7.50	15.00	30.00
❑ Imperial LP-12312 [S]	The Hollies — Beat Group	1966	10.00	20.00	40.00
❑ Imperial LP-12330 [R]	Bus Stop	1966	6.25	12.50	25.00
—Black and pink label					
❑ Imperial LP-12339 [S]	Stop! Stop! Stop!	1966	7.50	15.00	30.00
❑ Imperial LP-12350 [P]	The Hollies' Greatest Hits	1967	6.25	12.50	25.00
❑ Liberty LN-10216	Pay You Back with Interest	1982	2.00	4.00	8.00
❑ Pair PDL2-1041 [(2)]	Hottest Hits	1986	3.75	7.50	15.00
❑ Realm 2V-8026 [(2)]	The Hollies, Volume 1	1976	3.75	7.50	15.00
—Two-record TV package					
❑ Realm 1V-8027	The Hollies, Volume 2	1976	3.00	6.00	12.00
—TV package sold with Realm 8026					
❑ United Artists UA-LA329-E	The Very Best of the Hollies	1975	2.50	5.00	10.00

HOLLOWAY, BRENDA

45s

Number	Title (A Side/B Side)	Yr	VG	VG+	NM
❑ Donna 1358	Echo/Hey Fool	1962	10.00	20.00	40.00
❑ Donna 1366	Game of Love/Echo-Echo-Echo	1962	12.50	25.00	50.00
❑ Donna 1370	I'll Give My Life/More Echo	1962	12.50	25.00	50.00
❑ Tamla 54094	Every Little Bit Hurts/Land of 1,000 Boys	1964	3.00	6.00	12.00
❑ Tamla 54099	I'll Always Love You/Sad Song	1964	3.75	7.50	15.00
❑ Tamla 54111	When I'm Gone/I've Been Good to You	1965	3.75	7.50	15.00
❑ Tamla 54115	Operator/I'll Be Available	1965	3.75	7.50	15.00
❑ Tamla 54121	You Can Cry on My Shoulder/How Many Times Did You Mean It	1965	5.00	10.00	20.00
❑ Tamla 54125	Sad Song/Together 'Til the End of Time	1965	5.00	10.00	20.00
❑ Tamla 54137	Hurt a Little Every Day/Where Were You	1966	7.50	15.00	30.00
❑ Tamla 54144	'Til Johnny Comes/Where Were You	1967	50.00	100.00	200.00
❑ Tamla 54148	Just Look What You've Done/Starting the Hurt All Over Again	1967	6.25	12.50	25.00
❑ Tamla 54155	You've Made Me So Very Happy/I've Got to Find It	1967	5.00	10.00	20.00

Albums

Number	Title (A Side/B Side)	Yr	VG	VG+	NM
❑ Motown 5242 ML	Every Little Bit Hurts	1982	3.00	6.00	12.00
❑ Tamla T 257 [M]	Every Little Bit Hurts	1964	50.00	100.00	200.00
❑ Tamla TS 257 [R]	Every Little Bit Hurts	1964	37.50	75.00	150.00

HOLLY, BUDDY

45s

Number	Title (A Side/B Side)	Yr	VG	VG+	NM
❑ Coral 61852	Words of Love/Mailman, Bring Me No More Blues	1957	150.00	250.00	400.00
—Promos for any Coral title valued at $50 or under Near Mint are worth 2-4 times the stock copy value.					
❑ Coral 61885	Peggy Sue/Everyday	1957	12.50	25.00	50.00
—Orange label					
❑ Coral 61947	I'm Gonna Love You Too/Listen to Me	1958	12.50	25.00	50.00
❑ Coral 61985	Rave On/Take Your Time	1958	12.50	25.00	50.00
❑ Coral 62006	Early in the Morning/Now We're One	1958	12.50	25.00	50.00
❑ Coral 62051	Heartbeat/Well...All Right	1958	12.50	25.00	50.00
❑ Coral 62074	It Doesn't Matter Anymore/Raining in My Heart	1959	10.00	20.00	40.00
❑ Coral 62134	Peggy Sue Got Married/Crying, Waiting, Hoping	1959	15.00	30.00	60.00
❑ Coral 62210	True Love Ways/That Makes It Tough	1960	12.50	25.00	50.00
❑ Coral 62283	You're So Square (Baby I Don't Care)/Valley of Tears	1961	40.00	80.00	160.00
—Evidently only released in Canada					
❑ Coral 62329	Reminiscing/Wait Till the Sun Shines, Nellie	1962	7.50	15.00	30.00
❑ Coral 62352	True Love Ways/Bo Diddley	1963	15.00	30.00	60.00
❑ Coral 62369	Brown Eyed Handsome Man/Wishing	1963	10.00	20.00	40.00
❑ Coral 62390	Rock Around with Ollie Vee/I'm Gonna Love You Too	1963	10.00	20.00	40.00
❑ Coral 62448	Slippin' and Slidin'/What to Do	1965	25.00	50.00	100.00
❑ Coral 62554	Rave On/Early in the Morning	1968	7.50	15.00	30.00
❑ Coral 62558	Love Is Strange/You're the One	1969	5.00	10.00	20.00
❑ Decca 29854	Blue Days, Black Nights/Love Me	1956	75.00	150.00	300.00
—With star under "Decca"					
❑ Decca 30166	Modern Don Juan/You Are My One Desire	1956	62.50	125.00	250.00
—With star under "Decca"					
❑ Decca 30434	That'll Be the Day/Rock Around with Ollie Vee	1957	62.50	125.00	250.00
—With star under "Decca"					
❑ Decca 30543	Love Me/You Are My One Desire	1958	75.00	150.00	300.00
❑ Decca 30650	Ting-a-Ling/Girl on My Mind	1958	75.00	150.00	300.00
❑ MCA 40905	It Doesn't Matter Anymore/Peggy Sue	1978	—	2.50	5.00

Albums

Number	Title (A Side/B Side)	Yr	VG	VG+	NM
❑ Coral CXB 8 [(2)M]	The Best of Buddy Holly	1966	20.00	40.00	80.00
❑ Coral CXSB 8 [(2)R]	The Best of Buddy Holly	1966	12.50	25.00	50.00
❑ Coral CRL 57210 [M]	Buddy Holly	1958	100.00	200.00	400.00
—Maroon label					
❑ Coral CRL 57279 [M]	The Buddy Holly Story	1959	75.00	150.00	300.00
—Maroon label; back color print in black and red					

Number	Title (A Side/B Side)	Yr	VG	VG+	NM
❑ Coral CRL 57326 [M]	The Buddy Holly Story, Vol. 2	1959	50.00	100.00	200.00
—Maroon label					
❑ Coral CRL 57405 [M]	Buddy Holly and the Crickets	1962	37.50	75.00	150.00
—Reissue of the Crickets LP on Brunswick 54038					
❑ Coral CRL 57426 [M]	Reminiscing	1963	50.00	100.00	200.00
—Maroon label					
❑ Coral CRL 57450 [M]	Buddy Holly Showcase	1964	25.00	50.00	100.00
❑ Coral CRL 57463 [M]	Holly in the Hills	1965	30.00	60.00	120.00
❑ Coral CRL 57492 [M]	Buddy Holly's Greatest Hits	1967	20.00	40.00	80.00
❑ Coral CRL 757279 [R]	The Buddy Holly Story	1963	10.00	20.00	40.00
❑ Coral CRL 757326 [R]	The Buddy Holly Story, Vol. 2	1963	10.00	20.00	40.00
❑ Coral CRL 757405 [R]	Buddy Holly and the Crickets	1963	10.00	20.00	40.00
❑ Coral CRL 757426 [R]	Reminiscing	1964	10.00	20.00	40.00
❑ Coral CRL 757450 [R]	Buddy Holly Showcase	1964	20.00	40.00	80.00
❑ Coral CRL 757463 [R]	Holly in the Hills	1965	25.00	50.00	100.00
❑ Coral CRL 757492 [P]	Buddy Holly's Greatest Hits	1967	12.50	25.00	50.00
❑ Coral CRL 757504 [S]	Giant	1969	12.50	25.00	50.00
❑ Cricket C001000	Buddy Holly Live — Volume 1	197?	5.00	10.00	20.00
❑ Cricket C001001	Buddy Holly Live — Volume 1	197?	5.00	10.00	20.00
❑ Decca DXSE 7207 [(2)]	A Rock 'n' Roll Collection	1972	10.00	20.00	40.00
❑ Decca DL 8707 [M]	That'll Be the Day	1958	375.00	750.00	1500.
—Black label with silver print					
❑ Great Northwest GNW-4014	Visions of Buddy	197?	2.50	5.00	10.00
—Interview album					
❑ MCA 737	The Great Buddy Holly	197?	2.50	5.00	10.00
—Reissue of MCA Coral LP					
❑ MCA 1484	Buddy Holly/The Crickets 20 Golden Greats	198?	2.00	4.00	8.00
—Reissue of 3040					
❑ MCA 3040	Buddy Holly/The Crickets 20 Golden Greats	1978	3.75	7.50	15.00
❑ MCA 4009 [(2)]	A Rock 'n' Roll Collection	1973	5.00	10.00	20.00
—Black labels with rainbow					
❑ MCA 4184 [(2)]	Legend	1985	5.00	10.00	20.00
❑ MCA 5540 [(2)]	From the Original Master Tapes	1986	6.25	12.50	25.00
❑ MCA 11161	Buddy Holly	1995	10.00	20.00	40.00
—Audiophile "Heavy Vinyl" reissue with gatefold cover					
❑ MCA 25239	Buddy Holly	1989	3.00	6.00	12.00
—Reissue of Coral 57210					
❑ MCA 27059	For the First Time Anywhere	1983	2.50	5.00	10.00
❑ MCA 80000 [(6)]	The Complete Buddy Holly	1981	20.00	40.00	80.00
—Box set with booklet and custom innersleeves					
❑ MCA Coral CD-20101	The Great Buddy Holly	1973	3.00	6.00	12.00
❑ Vocalion VL 3811 [M]	The Great Buddy Holly	1967	20.00	40.00	80.00
❑ Vocalion VL 73811 [R]	The Great Buddy Holly	1967	12.50	25.00	50.00
❑ Vocalion VL 73923	Good Rockin'	1971	30.00	60.00	120.00

HOLMAN, EDDIE

45s

Number	Title (A Side/B Side)	Yr	VG	VG+	NM
❑ ABC 11149	I Love You/I Surrender	1968	2.50	5.00	10.00
❑ ABC 11240	Hey There Lonely Girl/It's All in the Game	1969	—	3.00	6.00
❑ ABC 11261	Don't Stop Now/Since I Don't Have You	1970	—	3.00	6.00
❑ ABC 11265	I'll Be There/Cause You're Mine Little Girl	1970	—	3.00	6.00
❑ ABC 11276	Cathy Called/I Need Somebody	1970	—	3.00	6.00
❑ ABC 11292	Love Story/Four Walls	1971	—	3.00	6.00
❑ Ascot 2142	Go Get Your Own/Laughing at Me	1963	3.75	7.50	15.00
❑ Bell 712	I'm Not Gonna Give Up/I'll Cry 1,000 Tears	1968	5.00	10.00	20.00
❑ GSF 6873	My Mind Keeps Telling Me (That I Really Love You, Girl)/ Stranded in a Dream	1972	—	3.00	6.00
❑ GSF 6885	Young Girl/I'll Call You Joy	1972	—	3.00	6.00
❑ Leopard 45-5001	What You Don't Know (Won't Hurt You)/I'm Counting Every Tear	196?	7.50	15.00	30.00
❑ Parkway 106	Am I a Loser/You Know That I Will	1966	5.00	10.00	20.00
❑ Parkway 133	Somewhere Waits a Lonely Girl/Stay Mine for Heaven's Sake	1967	5.00	10.00	20.00
❑ Parkway 157	Why Do Fools Fall in Love/Never Let Me Go	1967	5.00	10.00	20.00
❑ Parkway 960	This Can't Be True/A Free Country	1965	5.00	10.00	20.00
❑ Parkway 981	Don't Stop Now/Eddie's My Name	1966	5.00	10.00	20.00
❑ Parkway 994	Return to Me/Stay Mine for Heaven's Sake	1966	5.00	10.00	20.00
❑ Salsoul 2026	This Will Be a Night to Remember/Time Will Tell	1977	—	2.50	5.00
❑ Salsoul 2043	You Make My Life Complete/Somehow You Make Me Feel	1977	—	2.50	5.00

Number	Title (A Side/B Side)	Yr	VG	VG+	NM
❑ Silver Blue 807	You're My Lady (Right Or Wrong)/(Instrumental)	1974	—	2.50	5.00
❑ Silver Blue 815	Just Say I Love Her/Darling Take Me Back	1974	—	2.50	5.00
❑ United Artists 609	Go Get Your Own/Laughing at Me	1963	—	—	—
—Unreleased					
Albums					
❑ ABC S-701	I Love You	1970	7.50	15.00	30.00
❑ Salsoul 5511	A Night to Remember	1977	2.50	5.00	10.00

HOLMES, RUPERT

45s

Number	Title (A Side/B Side)	Yr	VG	VG+	NM
❑ Epic 11014	Philly/Talk	1973	—	3.00	6.00
❑ Epic 11117	Our National Pastime/Phantom of the Opera	1974	—	3.00	6.00
❑ Epic 50013	Terminal/Bagdad	1974	—	3.00	6.00
❑ Epic 50096	I Don't Wanna Hold Your Hand/The Man Behind the Woman	1975	—	3.00	6.00
❑ Epic 50161	Terminal/Deco Lady	1975	—	3.00	6.00
❑ Epic 50223	Weekend Lover/Weekend Lover	1976	—	2.50	5.00
❑ Epic 50295	You Make Me Real/Who, What, When, Where, How	1976	—	2.50	5.00
❑ Infinity 50035	Escape (The Pina Colada Song)/Drop It	1979	—	2.50	5.00
❑ MCA 41173	Him/Get Outta Yourself	1980	—	2.00	4.00
❑ MCA 41235	Answering Machine/Lunch Hour	1980	—	2.00	4.00
❑ MCA 50035	Escape (The Pina Colada Song)/Drop It	1980	—	2.00	4.00
❑ MCA 51019	Morning Man/The Mask	1980	—	2.00	4.00
❑ MCA 51045	Blackjack/Crowd Pleaser	1981	—	2.00	4.00
❑ MCA 51092	I Don't Need You/Cold	1981	—	2.00	4.00
❑ Private Stock 45,183	Bedside Companions/So Beautiful It Hurts	1978	—	2.50	5.00
❑ Private Stock 45,199	Let's Get Crazy Tonight/The Long Way Home	1978	—	2.50	5.00
Albums					
❑ Elektra 5E-560	Full Circle	1982	2.50	5.00	10.00
❑ Epic KE 32864	Widescreen	1974	3.00	6.00	12.00
❑ Epic KE 33443	Rupert Holmes	1975	3.00	6.00	12.00
❑ Epic PE 34288	Singles	1976	3.00	6.00	12.00
❑ Excelsior XMP-6000	Rupert Holmes	1980	2.50	5.00	10.00
❑ Excelsior XMP-6022	She Lets Her Hair Down	1981	2.50	5.00	10.00
❑ Infinity 9020	Partners in Crime	1979	2.50	5.00	10.00
❑ MCA 5129	Adventure	1980	2.50	5.00	10.00
❑ MCA 9020	Partners in Crime	1980	2.00	4.00	8.00
—Reissue of Infinity LP					
❑ MCA 37166	Pursuit of Happiness	198?	2.00	4.00	8.00
—Reissue of Private Stock LP					
❑ Private Stock PS-7006	Pursuit of Happiness	1978	3.00	6.00	12.00

HONDELLS, THE

45s

Number	Title (A Side/B Side)	Yr	VG	VG+	NM
❑ Amos 131	Follow the Bouncing Ball/The Legend of Frankie and Johnny	1969	3.00	6.00	12.00
❑ Amos 150	Shine On Ruby Mountain/The Legend of Frankie and Johnny	1970	3.00	6.00	12.00
❑ Columbia 44361	Just One More Chance/Yes to You	1967	5.00	10.00	20.00
❑ Columbia 44557	Another Woman/Atlanta Georgia Stray	1968	5.00	10.00	20.00
❑ Mercury 72324	Little Honda/Hot Rod High	1964	5.00	10.00	20.00
❑ Mercury 72366	My Buddy Seat/You're Gonna Ride with Me	1964	5.00	10.00	20.00
❑ Mercury 72405	Little Sidewalk Surfer Girl/Come On Baby (Pack It In)	1965	5.00	10.00	20.00
❑ Mercury 72443	Sea of Love/Do As I Say	1965	5.00	10.00	20.00
❑ Mercury 72479	You Meet the Nicest People on a Honda/Sea Cruise	1965	5.00	10.00	20.00
❑ Mercury 72523	Endless Sleep/Follow Your Heart	1966	3.75	7.50	15.00
❑ Mercury 72563	Younger Girl/All American Girl	1966	3.75	7.50	15.00
❑ Mercury 72605	Country Love/Kissin' My Life Away	1966	3.75	7.50	15.00
❑ Mercury 72626	Cheryl's Goin' Home/Show Me	1966	3.75	7.50	15.00
Albums					
❑ Mercury MG-20940 [M]	Go Little Honda	1964	10.00	20.00	40.00
❑ Mercury MG-20982 [M]	The Hondells	1965	12.50	25.00	50.00
❑ Mercury SR-60940 [S]	Go Little Honda	1964	15.00	30.00	60.00
❑ Mercury SR-60982 [S]	The Hondells	1965	20.00	40.00	80.00

HONEY CONE, THE

45s

Number	Title (A Side/B Side)	Yr	VG	VG+	NM
❑ Hot Wax 6901	While You're Out Looking for Sugar?/The Feeling's Gone	1969	—	3.00	6.00
❑ Hot Wax 6903	Girls It Ain't Easy/The Feeling's Gone	1969	—	3.00	6.00
❑ Hot Wax 7001	Take Me With You/Take My Love	1970	—	3.00	6.00
❑ Hot Wax 7005	When Will It End/Take Me With You	1970	—	3.00	6.00
❑ Hot Wax 7011	Want Ads/We Belong Together	1970	—	2.50	5.00
—Mostly orange label					
❑ Hot Wax 7011	Want Ads/We Belong Together	1970	—	3.00	6.00
—Mostly white label					
❑ Hot Wax 7106	Stick-Up/V.I.P.	1971	—	3.00	6.00
❑ Hot Wax 7110	One Monkey Don't Stop No Show Part I/One Monkey Don't Stop No Show Part II	1971	—	3.00	6.00
❑ Hot Wax 7113	The Day I Found Myself/When Will It End	1971	—	3.00	6.00
❑ Hot Wax 7205	Sittin' on a Time Bomb (Waitin' for the Hurt to Come)/It's Better to Have Loved and Lost	1972	—	3.00	6.00
❑ Hot Wax 7208	Innocent Till Proven Guilty/Don't Send Me an Invitation	1972	—	3.00	6.00
❑ Hot Wax 7212	Ace in the Hole/Ooo Baby Baby	1972	—	3.00	6.00
❑ Hot Wax 7301	If I Can't Fly/Woman Can't Live by Bread Alone	1973	—	3.00	6.00
❑ Hot Wax 9255	The Truth Will Come Out/Somebody Is Always Messing Up a Good Thing	1974	—	3.00	6.00
Albums					
❑ Hot Wax HA-701	Take Me With You	1970	3.00	6.00	12.00
❑ Hot Wax HA-706	Sweet Replies	1971	3.00	6.00	12.00
❑ Hot Wax HA-707	Soulful Tapestry	1971	3.00	6.00	12.00
❑ Hot Wax HA-713	Love, Peace & Soul	1972	3.00	6.00	12.00

Number	Title (A Side/B Side)	Yr	VG	VG+	NM
HONEYCOMBS, THE					
45s					
❑ Interphon 7707	Have I the Right?/Please Don't Pretend Again	1964	3.00	6.00	12.00
❑ Interphon 7713	I Can't Stop/I'll Cry Tomorrow	1964	2.50	5.00	10.00
❑ Interphon 7716	Color Slide/That's the Way	1965	2.50	5.00	10.00
❑ Warner Bros. 5634	I'll See You Tomorrow/Something Better Beginning	1965	2.50	5.00	10.00
❑ Warner Bros. 5655	I Can't Get Through to You/That's the Way	1965	2.50	5.00	10.00
❑ Warner Bros. 5803	How Will I Know/Who Is Sylvia	1966	2.50	5.00	10.00
Albums					
❑ Interphon IN-88001 [M]	Here Are the Honeycombs	1964	10.00	20.00	40.00
❑ Interphon IN-88001 [R]	Here Are the Honeycombs	1964	7.50	15.00	30.00
❑ Vee Jay IN-88001 [M]	Here Are the Honeycombs	1964	12.50	25.00	50.00
❑ Vee Jay IN-88001 [R]	Here Are the Honeycombs	1964	10.00	20.00	40.00
HOPKIN, MARY					
45s					
❑ Apple 1801	Those Were the Days/Turn, Turn, Turn	1968	2.50	5.00	10.00
❑ Apple 1806	Goodbye/Sparrow	1969	2.00	4.00	8.00
❑ Apple 1816	Temma Harbour/Lantano Dagli Occhi	1970	2.00	4.00	8.00
❑ Apple 1823	Que Sera, Sera (Whatever Will Be, Will Be)/Fields of St. Etienne	1970	2.00	4.00	8.00
❑ Apple 1825	Think About Your Children/Heritage	1970	2.00	4.00	8.00
❑ Apple 1843	Water, Paper and Clay/Streets of London	1972	2.00	4.00	8.00
❑ Apple 1855	Knock Knock Who's There/International	1972	2.00	4.00	8.00
❑ RCA Victor PB-10694	Tell Me Now/If You Love Me	1976	—	2.00	4.00
Albums					
❑ Apple ST-3351	Post Card	1969	6.25	12.50	25.00
❑ Apple SMAS-3381	Earth Song/Ocean Song	1970	6.25	12.50	25.00
❑ Apple SW-3395	Those Were the Days	1972	10.00	20.00	40.00
HORNE, JIMMY "BO"					
45s					
❑ Alston 3712	Don't Worry About It/Music to Make Love By	1975	2.50	5.00	10.00
❑ Alston 3714	Gimme Some (Part 1)/(Part 2)	1975	—	3.00	6.00
❑ Alston 3724	It's Your Sweet Love/Don't Worry About It	1976	2.50	5.00	10.00
❑ Alston 3729	Get Happy/It's Your Sweet Love	1977	—	3.00	6.00
❑ Alston 4606	Clean Up Man/Down the Road of Love	1972	7.50	15.00	30.00
—Reissue of Dade 2031					
❑ Alston 4612	On the Street Corner/If You Want My Love	1972	7.50	15.00	30.00
❑ Alston 4618	If We Were Still Together/Two People in Love	1973	7.50	15.00	30.00
❑ Dade 2025	I Can't Speak/Street Corners	1969	500.00	1000.	2000.
—Reproductions exist as double A-sides on Dade JBH-001; these usually sell in the $20-$25 range					
❑ Dade 2031	Clean Up Man/Down the Road of Love	1972	25.00	50.00	100.00
—Original issue					
❑ Edge 7011	Show Me How Much (You Want My Love)/(Extended Version).	1987	2.00	4.00	8.00
❑ Sunshine Sound 1003	Dance Across the Floor/It's Your Sweet Love.	1978	2.00	4.00	8.00
❑ Sunshine Sound 1005	Let Me (Let Me Be Your Lover)/Ask the Birds and the Bees.	1978	2.00	4.00	8.00
❑ Sunshine Sound 1007	Spank/I Wanna Go Home with You.	1978	2.00	4.00	8.00
❑ Sunshine Sound 1014	You Get Me Hot/They Long to Be Close to You.	1979	2.00	4.00	8.00
—Light brown label					
❑ Sunshine Sound 1014	You Get Me Hot/They Long to Be Close to You	1979	2.50	5.00	10.00
—Black label					
❑ Sunshine Sound 1015	Without You/Goin' Home for Love	1980	—	3.50	7.00
❑ Sunshine Sound 1016	They Long to Be Close to You/(B-side unknown)	1980	2.00	4.00	8.00
❑ Sunshine Sound 1018	Is It In/I Wanna Go Home with You	1980	—	3.50	7.00
Albums					
❑ Sunshine Sound SSE-7801	Dance Across the Floor	1978	5.00	10.00	20.00
❑ Sunshine Sound SSE-7805	Goin' Home for Love	1979	3.75	7.50	15.00
HOT BUTTER					
45s					
❑ Musicor 1458	Popcorn/At the Movies	1972	—	3.00	6.00
❑ Musicor 1466	Apache/Hot Butter	1972	—	2.50	5.00
❑ Musicor 1468	Tequila/Hot Butter	1972	—	2.50	5.00
❑ Musicor 1473	Percolator/Tristana	1973	—	2.50	5.00
❑ Musicor 1481	Slay Solution/Kappi Maki	1973	—	2.50	5.00
❑ Musicor 1491	Pipeline/Apache	1974	—	2.50	5.00

Number	Title (A Side/B Side)	Yr	VG	VG+	NM
Albums					
❑ Musicor MS-3242 *—Regular cover*	Popcorn	1972	3.00	6.00	12.00
❑ Musicor MS-3242 *—Die-cut cover*	Popcorn	1972	5.00	10.00	20.00
HOT CHOCOLATE					
45s					
❑ Apple 1812 *—As "Hot Chocolate Band"*	Give Peace a Chance/Living Without Tomorrow	1969	2.50	5.00	10.00
❑ Bell 45390	Rumors/(B-side unknown)	1973	—	2.50	5.00
❑ Bell 45466	Emma/(B-side unknown)	1974	—	3.50	7.00
❑ Big Tree 16031	Emma/A Love Like Yours	1975	—	2.50	5.00
❑ Big Tree 16038	Disco Queen/Makin' Music	1975	—	2.50	5.00
❑ Big Tree 16047	You Sexy Thing/Amazing Skin Song	1975	—	2.50	5.00
❑ Big Tree 16060	Don't Stop It Now/Beautiful Lady	1976	—	2.50	5.00
❑ Big Tree 16078	Heaven Is in the Back Seat of My Cadillac/(B-side unknown)	1976	—	2.50	5.00
❑ Big Tree 16096	So You Win Again/Part of Being with You	1977	—	2.50	5.00
❑ Big Tree 16101	Man to Man/Brother Louie	1977	—	2.50	5.00
❑ EMI America 8143	Are You Getting Enough Happiness/One Night's Not Enough	1982	—	2.00	4.00
❑ EMI America 8157	Bed Games/It Started with a Kiss	1983	—	2.00	4.00
❑ Infinity 50002	Every 1's a Winner/Power of Love	1978	—	2.00	4.00
❑ Infinity 50016	Going Through the Motions/Don't Turn It Off	1979	—	2.00	4.00
❑ Infinity 50033	I Just Love What You're Doing/Congas Man	1979	—	2.00	4.00
❑ Infinity 50048	Mindless Boogie/Dance (Get Down To It)	1979	—	2.00	4.00
❑ RAK 4503	You Could Have Been a Lady/Everybody's Laughing	1972	—	3.00	6.00
❑ RAK 4506	I Believe in Love/Caveman Billy	1972	—	3.00	6.00
❑ RAK 4508	Mary Anne/Ruth	1972	—	3.00	6.00
❑ RAK 4515	Brother Louie/I Want to Be Free	1973	—	3.00	6.00
Albums					
❑ Big Tree BT 76002	10 Greatest Hits	1977	2.50	5.00	10.00
❑ Big Tree BT 89503	Cicero Park	1975	2.50	5.00	10.00
❑ Big Tree BT 89512	Hot Chocolate	1975	2.50	5.00	10.00
❑ Big Tree BT 89519	Man to Man	1976	2.50	5.00	10.00
❑ EMI America ST-17077	Mystery	1982	2.50	5.00	10.00
❑ Infinity INF-9002	Every 1's a Winner	1978	2.50	5.00	10.00
❑ Infinity INF-9010	Going Through the Motions	1979	2.50	5.00	10.00
HOUSTON, THELMA					
45s					
❑ ABC Dunhill 4197	Sunshower/If This Was the Last Song	1969	2.50	5.00	10.00
❑ ABC Dunhill 4212	Jumpin' Jack Flash/This Is Your Life	1969	2.50	5.00	10.00
❑ ABC Dunhill 4222	Save the Country/I Just Can't Stay Away	1970	2.00	4.00	8.00
❑ ABC Dunhill 4260	The Good Earth/Ride, Louie, Ride	1970	2.00	4.00	8.00
❑ Capitol 5767	Baby Mine/Woman Behind Her Man	1966	12.50	25.00	50.00
❑ Capitol 5882	Don't Cry, My Soldier Boy/Let's Try to Make It	1967	12.50	25.00	50.00
❑ MCA 52196	Working Girl/Running in Circles	1983	—	—	3.00
❑ MCA 52239	Make It Last/Just Like All the Rest	1983	—	—	3.00
❑ MCA 52489	(I Guess) It Must Be Love/Running in Circles	1984	—	—	3.00
❑ MCA 52491	Love Is a Dangerous Game/You Used to Hold Me So Tight	1984	—	—	3.00
❑ MCA 52574 *—B-side by B.B. King*	Keep It Light/My Lucille	1985	—	—	3.00
❑ MCA 52582	What a Woman Feels Inside/Fantasy and Heartbreak	1985	—	—	3.00
❑ Motown 1245	I'm Just a Part of Yesterday/Piano Man	1973	—	2.50	5.00
❑ Motown 1260	Do You Know Where You're Going/Together	1973	—	2.50	5.00
❑ Motown 1316	You've Been Doing Wrong for So Long/Pick Up the Week	1974	—	2.50	5.00
❑ Motown 1385 *—B-side by William Goldstein*	The Bingo Long Song/Razzle Dazzle	1976	—	2.50	5.00
❑ Mowest 5008	I Want to Go Back There Again/Pick Up the Week	1972	—	3.00	6.00
❑ Mowest 5013	Me and Bobby McGee/No One's Gonna Be a Fool Forever	1972	—	3.00	6.00
❑ Mowest 5023	Piano Man/Me and Bobby McGee	1972	—	3.00	6.00
❑ Mowest 5027	What If/There Is a Fool	1972	—	3.00	6.00
❑ Mowest 5046 *—Unreleased*	If It's the Last Thing I Do/And I Never Did	1973	—	—	—
❑ Mowest 5050	I'm Just a Part of Yesterday/Piano Man	1973	—	3.00	6.00
❑ RCA PB-11913	Suspicious Minds/Gone	1980	—	2.50	5.00
❑ RCA PB-12215	If You Feel It/Hollywood	1981	—	2.00	4.00
❑ RCA PB-12285	96 Tears/There's No Runnin' Away from Love	1981	—	2.00	4.00
❑ Tamla 54275	One Out of Every Six (Censored)/Pick of the Week	1976	2.50	5.00	10.00
❑ Tamla 54278	Don't Leave Me This Way (Short Version)/ Today Will Soon Be Yesterday	1977	—	2.00	4.00
❑ Tamla 54283	If It's the Last Thing I Do/If You Won't Let Me Walk on the Water	1977	—	2.00	4.00
❑ Tamla 54287	I'm Here Again/Sharin' Something Perfect	1977	—	2.00	4.00
❑ Tamla 54292	I Can't Go On Living Without Your Love/Any Way You Like It	1978	—	2.00	4.00
❑ Tamla 54295	I'm Not Strong Enough to Love You/Triplin'	1978	—	2.00	4.00
❑ Tamla 54297	Saturday Night, Sunday Morning/Come to Me	1979	—	2.00	4.00
Albums					
❑ ABC Dunhill DS-50054	Sun Shower	1969	6.25	12.50	25.00
❑ MCA 5395	Thelma Houston	1983	2.50	5.00	10.00
❑ MCA 5527	Qualifying Heat	1984	2.50	5.00	10.00
❑ Motown M5-120V1	Superstar Series, Vol. 20	1981	2.50	5.00	10.00
❑ Motown M5-127V1	Sunshower	1981	2.00	4.00	8.00
❑ Motown M5-226V1	Any Way You Like It	1982	2.50	5.00	10.00
❑ Mowest MW-102	Thelma Houston	1972	5.00	10.00	20.00
❑ RCA Victor AFL1-3500	Breakwater Cat	1980	2.50	5.00	10.00
❑ RCA Victor AFL1-3842	Never Gonna Be Another One	1981	2.50	5.00	10.00
❑ Reprise 26234	Throw You Down	1990	3.75	7.50	15.00

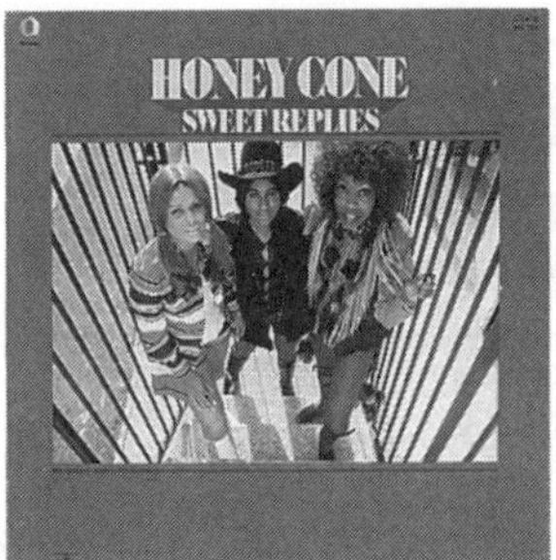

Number	Title (A Side/B Side)	Yr	VG	VG+	NM
❑ Tamla T6-345R1	Any Way You Like It	1976	3.00	6.00	12.00
❑ Tamla T7-358R1	The Devil in Me	1977	2.50	5.00	10.00
❑ Tamla T7-361R1	Ready to Roll	1978	2.50	5.00	10.00

HUES CORPORATION, THE

45s

Number	Title (A Side/B Side)	Yr	VG	VG+	NM
❑ Liberty 56204	Goodfootin'/We're Keepin' Our Business Together	1970	—	3.00	6.00
—As "The Hughes Corporation"					
❑ RCA Victor 74-0813	There He Is Again/Main Chance	1972	—	2.50	5.00
❑ RCA Victor 74-0900	Freedom for the Stallion/Off My Cloud	1973	—	2.50	5.00
❑ RCA Victor APBO-0139	Go to the Poet/Miracle Maker	1973	—	2.50	5.00
❑ RCA Victor APBO-0232	Rock the Boat/All Goin' Down Together	1974	—	2.50	5.00
❑ RCA Victor PB-10066	Rockin' Soul/Go to the Poet	1974	—	2.50	5.00
❑ RCA Victor PB-10200	Love Corporation/He's My Home	1975	—	2.50	5.00
❑ RCA Victor PB-10311	One Good Night Together/When You Look Down the Road	1975	—	2.50	5.00
❑ RCA Victor PB-10390	You Showed Me What Love Is/When You Look Down the Road	1975	—	2.50	5.00
❑ RCA Victor GB-10480	Rockin' Soul/Go to the Poet	1975	—	—	3.00
—Gold Standard Series					
❑ RCA Victor GB-10481	Rock the Boat/All Goin' Down Together	1975	—	—	3.00
—Gold Standard Series					
❑ Warner Bros. 8400	I Caught Your Act/Natural Find	1977	—	2.00	4.00
❑ Warner Bros. 8454	Telegram of Love/Dancing Together Again	1977	—	2.00	4.00
❑ Warner Bros. 8559	Give Me Everything/Needed	1978	—	2.00	4.00
❑ Warner Bros. 8638	Love Dance/With All My Love and Affection	1978	—	2.00	4.00

Albums

Number	Title (A Side/B Side)	Yr	VG	VG+	NM
❑ RCA Victor APL1-0323	Freedom for the Stallion	1973	2.50	5.00	10.00
❑ RCA Victor APL1-0755	Rockin' Soul	1974	2.50	5.00	10.00
❑ RCA Victor APL1-0938	Love Corporation	1975	2.50	5.00	10.00
❑ RCA Victor ANL1-2147	Rock the Boat	1976	2.00	4.00	8.00
❑ RCA Victor APL1-2408	The Best of the Hues Corporation	1977	2.50	5.00	10.00
❑ Warner Bros. BS 3043	I Caught Your Act	1977	2.50	5.00	10.00
❑ Warner Bros. BSK 3196	Your Place or Mine	1978	2.50	5.00	10.00

HUMAN BEINZ, THE

45s

Number	Title (A Side/B Side)	Yr	VG	VG+	NM
❑ Capitol 2119	Turn On Your Love Light/It's Fun to Be Clean	1968	2.50	5.00	10.00
❑ Capitol 2198	Every Time Woman/The Face	1968	2.50	5.00	10.00
❑ Capitol 2431	I've Got to Keep On Pushin'/This Little Girl of Mine	1969	2.50	5.00	10.00
❑ Capitol 5990	Nobody But Me/Sueno	1967	3.75	7.50	15.00
❑ Gateway 828	Gloria/The Times They Are a-Changin'	1967	3.75	7.50	15.00
❑ Gateway 838	You Can't Make Me Cry/The Pied Piper	1967	3.75	7.50	15.00

Albums

Number	Title (A Side/B Side)	Yr	VG	VG+	NM
❑ Capitol ST 2906	Nobody But Me	1968	7.50	15.00	30.00
❑ Capitol ST 2926	Evolutions	1968	10.00	20.00	40.00
❑ Gateway GLP-3012	Nobody But Me	1968	10.00	20.00	40.00
—With added tracks by The Mammals					

HUMAN LEAGUE

45s

Number	Title (A Side/B Side)	Yr	VG	VG+	NM
❑ A&M 2397	Don't You Want Me/Seconds	1982	—	—	3.00
❑ A&M 2425	Love Action (I Believe in Love)/Hard Times	1982	—	2.00	4.00
❑ A&M 2449	Things That Dreams Are Made Of/(Instrumental)	1982	—	3.00	6.00
—B-side by "League Unlimited Orchestra"					
❑ A&M 2508	Don't You Want Me/(Instrumental)	1982	—	3.00	6.00
—B-side by "League Unlimited Orchestra"					
❑ A&M 2547	(Keep Feeling) Fascination/Total Panic	1983	—	—	3.00
❑ A&M 2587	Mirror Man/Non-Stop	1983	—	—	3.00
❑ A&M 2641	The Lebanon/Thirteen	1984	—	—	3.00
❑ A&M 2650	Don't You Know I Want You/Thirteen	1984	—	3.00	6.00
❑ A&M 2657	Louise/The World Tonight	1984	—	2.50	5.00
❑ A&M 2861	Human/(Instrumental)	1986	—	—	3.00
❑ A&M 2893	I Need Your Loving/Are You Ever Coming Back?	1986	—	—	3.00
❑ A&M 2918	Love Is All That Matters/(Instrumental)	1987	—	2.50	5.00
❑ A&M 2934	Are You Ever Coming Back?/Jam	1987	—	3.00	6.00
❑ A&M 8635	(Keep Feeling) Fascination/Mirror Man	198?	—	—	3.00
—"A&M Memories" reissue					
❑ A&M 8647	Don't You Want Me/Love Action (I Believe in Love)	198?	—	—	3.00
—"A&M Memories" reissue					

Number	Title (A Side/B Side)	Yr	VG	VG+	NM
❑ A&M 8670	Human/Love Is All That Matters	198?	—	—	3.00
—"A&M Memories" reissue					
Albums					
❑ A&M SP-3209	Love and Dancing	1982	2.50	5.00	10.00
—As "The League Unlimited Orchestra"; instrumental versions					
❑ A&M SP-6-4892	Dare	1981	2.50	5.00	10.00
❑ A&M SP-4923	Hysteria	1984	2.50	5.00	10.00
❑ A&M SP-5129	Crash	1986	2.50	5.00	10.00
❑ A&M SP-5227	Greatest Hits	1989	3.75	7.50	15.00
❑ A&M SP-12501 [EP]	Fascination!	1983	2.50	5.00	10.00
❑ Virgin 90880	Travelogue	1988	2.50	5.00	10.00
—Reissue of early U.K. album					
❑ Virgin 90881	Reproduction	1988	2.50	5.00	10.00
—First issue of early U.K. album					
❑ Virgin International VI 2160	Travelogue	1980	3.75	7.50	15.00
—U.S. pressings have "VI" prefix; imports, which go for less, have simply a "V" prefix					

HUMPERDINCK, ENGELBERT

45s

Number	Title (A Side/B Side)	Yr	VG	VG+	NM
❑ Epic 02060	Don't You Love Me Anymore/Till I Get It Right	1981	—	—	3.00
❑ Epic 02245	Maybe This Time/When the Night Ends	1981	—	—	3.00
❑ Epic 03817	Till You and Your Lover Are Lovers Again/What Will I Write	1983	—	—	3.00
❑ Epic 50270	After the Lovin'/Let's Remember the Good Times	1976	—	2.50	5.00
❑ Epic 50365	I Believe in Miracles/Goodbye My Friend	1977	—	2.00	4.00
❑ Epic 50447	A Lover's Holiday/Look at Me	1977	—	2.00	4.00
❑ Epic 50488	A Night to Remember/Silent Night	1977	—	2.00	4.00
❑ Epic 50526	The Last of the Romantics/I Have Paid the Toll	1978	—	2.00	4.00
❑ Epic 50566	Love Me Tender/This Time One Year Ago	1978	—	2.00	4.00
❑ Epic 50579	Love's In Need of Love Today/Sweet Marjorene	1978	—	2.00	4.00
❑ Epic 50632	This Moment in Time/And the Day Begins	1978	—	2.00	4.00
❑ Epic 50692	Can't Help Falling in Love/You Know Me	1979	—	2.00	4.00
❑ Epic 50732	Lovin' Too Well/Much, Much Greater Love	1979	—	2.00	4.00
❑ Epic 50844	Love's Only Love/Burning Ember	1980	—	—	3.00
❑ Epic 50899	A Chance to Be a Hero/Any Kind of Love at All	1980	—	—	3.00
❑ Epic 50933	Don't Cry Out Loud/Don't Touch That Dial	1980	—	—	3.00
❑ Epic 50958	It's Not Easy to Live Together/Royal Affair	1980	—	—	3.00
❑ Hickory 1337	Baby Turn Around/If I Could Do the Things I Want to Do	1965	4.00	8.00	16.00
—As "Gerry Dorsey"					
❑ Parrot 40011 [M]	Release Me (And Let Me Love Again)/Ten Guitars	1967	2.00	4.00	8.00
❑ Parrot 40015	There Goes My Everything/You Love	1967	2.00	4.00	8.00
❑ Parrot 40019	The Last Waltz/That Promise	1967	2.00	4.00	8.00
❑ Parrot 40023	Am I That Easy to Forget/Pretty Ribbons	1967	2.00	4.00	8.00
❑ Parrot 40027	A Man Without Love/Call on Me	1968	2.00	4.00	8.00
❑ Parrot 40032	Les Bicyclettes De Belsize/Three Little Words	1968	2.00	4.00	8.00
❑ Parrot 40036	The Way It Used to Be/A Good Thing Going	1969	—	3.00	6.00
❑ Parrot 40040	I'm a Better Man/Cafe	1969	—	3.00	6.00
❑ Parrot 40044	Winter World of Love/Take My Heart	1969	—	3.00	6.00
❑ Parrot 40049	My Marie/Our Song (La Paloma)	1970	—	3.00	6.00
❑ Parrot 40054	Sweetheart/Born to Be Wanted	1970	—	3.00	6.00
❑ Parrot 40059	When There's No You/Stranger, Step In My World	1971	—	3.00	6.00
❑ Parrot 40065	Another Time, Another Place/You're the Window of My World	1971	—	3.00	6.00
❑ Parrot 40069	Too Beautiful to Last/A Hundred Times a Day	1972	—	2.50	5.00
❑ Parrot 40071	In Time/How Does It Feel	1972	—	2.50	5.00
❑ Parrot 40072	I Never Said Goodbye/Time After Time	1972	—	2.50	5.00
❑ Parrot 40073	I'm Leavin' You/My Summer Song	1973	—	2.00	4.00
❑ Parrot 40076	Love Is All/Lady of the Night	1973	—	2.00	4.00
❑ Parrot 40077	Free as the Wind/My Friend the Wind	1974	—	2.00	4.00
❑ Parrot 40079	Catch Me I'm Falling/Love, Oh Precious Love	1974	—	2.00	4.00
❑ Parrot 40082	Forever and Ever/Precious Love	1974	—	2.00	4.00
❑ Parrot 40085	This Is What You Mean to Me/A World Without Music	1975	—	2.00	4.00
Albums					
❑ Epic PE 34381	After the Lovin'	1976	2.50	5.00	10.00
—Orange label					
❑ Epic E 34436	The Ultimate	1977	2.50	5.00	10.00
—Orange label					
❑ Epic E 34719	Golden Love Songs	1977	2.50	5.00	10.00
—Orange label					
❑ Epic PE 34730	Miracles	1977	2.50	5.00	10.00
—Orange label					
❑ Epic JE 35020	Last of the Romantics	1978	2.50	5.00	10.00
—Orange label					
❑ Epic PE 35031	Christmas Tyme	1977	3.00	6.00	12.00
❑ Epic JE 35791	This Moment in Time	1979	2.50	5.00	10.00
❑ Epic JE 36431	Love's Only Love	1980	2.50	5.00	10.00
❑ Epic PE 36765	A Merry Christmas with Engelbert Humperdinck	1980	2.50	5.00	10.00
—Some copies of the record have a "JE" prefix					
❑ Epic E2X 36782 [(2)]	All of Me/Live in Concert	1980	3.00	6.00	12.00
❑ Epic FE 37128	Don't You Love Me Anymore	1981	2.50	5.00	10.00
❑ Epic FE 38087	You and Your Lover	1983	2.50	5.00	10.00
❑ Epic PE 39469	White Christmas	1984	2.50	5.00	10.00
❑ London BP 688/9 [(2)]	Engelbert Humperdinck Sings for You	1977	3.75	7.50	15.00
❑ London PS 709	Love Letters	1978	2.50	5.00	10.00
❑ Parrot PA 61012 [M]	Release Me	1967	5.00	10.00	20.00
❑ Parrot PA 61015 [M]	The Last Waltz	1967	5.00	10.00	20.00
❑ Parrot PAS 71012 [S]	Release Me	1967	3.75	7.50	15.00
❑ Parrot PAS 71015 [S]	The Last Waltz	1967	3.75	7.50	15.00
❑ Parrot PAS 71022	A Man Without Love	1968	3.75	7.50	15.00

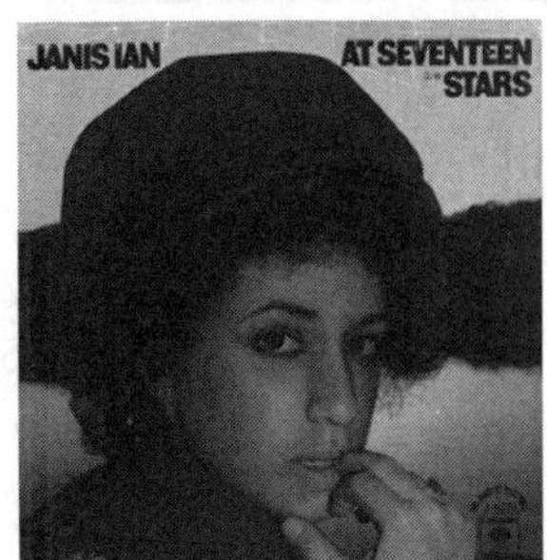

Number	Title (A Side/B Side)	Yr	VG	VG+	NM
❑ Parrot PAS 71026	Engelbert	1969	3.75	7.50	15.00
❑ Parrot XPAS 71030	Engelbert Humperdinck	1969	3.75	7.50	15.00
❑ Parrot XPAS 71038	We Made It Happen	1970	3.75	7.50	15.00
❑ Parrot XPAS 71043	Sweetheart	1971	3.75	7.50	15.00
❑ Parrot XPAS 71048	Another Time, Another Place	1971	3.75	7.50	15.00
❑ Parrot XPAS 71051	Live at the Riviera, Las Vegas	1971	3.75	7.50	15.00
❑ Parrot XPAS 71056	In Time	1972	3.75	7.50	15.00
❑ Parrot XPAS 71061	King of Hearts	1973	3.75	7.50	15.00
❑ Parrot APAS 71065	My Love	1974	3.75	7.50	15.00
❑ Parrot PAS 71067	His Greatest Hits	1974	3.75	7.50	15.00
❑ Silver Eagle SE 1034 [(2)] *—Mail-order offer*	A Lovely Way to Spend an Evening	1985	3.75	7.50	15.00

HYLAND, BRIAN

45s

Number	Title (A Side/B Side)	Yr	VG	VG+	NM
❑ ABC-Paramount 10236	Let Me Belong to You/Let It Die	1961	2.50	5.00	10.00
❑ ABC-Paramount 10262	I'll Never Stop Wanting You/The Night I Cried	1961	2.50	5.00	10.00
❑ ABC-Paramount 10294	Ginny Come Lately/I Should Be Gettin' Better	1962	2.50	5.00	10.00
❑ ABC-Paramount 10336	Sealed with a Kiss/Summer Job	1962	3.00	6.00	12.00
❑ ABC-Paramount 10359	Warmed Over Kisses (Left Over Love)/Walk a Lonely Mile	1962	2.50	5.00	10.00
❑ ABC-Paramount 10374	I May Not Live to See Tomorrow/It Ain't That Way at All	1962	2.50	5.00	10.00
❑ ABC-Paramount 10400	If Mary's There/Remember Me	1963	2.50	5.00	10.00
❑ ABC-Paramount 10427	Somewhere in the Night/I Wish Today Was Yesterday	1963	2.50	5.00	10.00
❑ ABC-Paramount 10452	I'm Afraid to Go Home/Save Your Heart for Me	1963	2.50	5.00	10.00
❑ ABC-Paramount 10494	Nothing Matters But You/Let Us Make Our Own Mistakes	1963	2.50	5.00	10.00
❑ ABC-Paramount 10549	Act Naturally/Out of Sight, Out of Mind	1964	2.50	5.00	10.00
❑ Dot 17050	Apologize/Words on Paper	1967	—	3.00	6.00
❑ Dot 17061	It's Christmas Time Once Again/Words on Paper	1967	3.00	6.00	12.00
❑ Dot 17078	Come with Me/Delilah	1968	—	3.00	6.00
❑ Dot 17109	The Lover/Springfield, Illinois	1968	—	3.00	6.00
❑ Dot 17176	Tragedy/You'd Better Stop and Think It Over	1968	—	3.00	6.00
❑ Dot 17222	A Million to One/It Could All Begin Again	1969	—	3.00	6.00
❑ Dot 17258	Early April Morning/Stay and Love Me All Summer	1969	—	3.00	6.00
❑ Dot 17291	Dreamy Eyes/Gonna Make a Woman Out of You	1970	—	3.00	6.00
❑ Kapp 342	Itsy Bitsy Teeny Weeny Yellow Polka Dot Bikini/ Don't Dilly Dally, Sally	1960	3.75	7.50	15.00
❑ Kapp 352	Four Little Heels (The Clickety Clack Song)/That's How Much	1960	3.00	6.00	12.00
❑ Kapp 363	I Gotta Go/Lopsided, Over Loaded	1960	3.00	6.00	12.00
❑ Kapp 401	Lipstick on Your Lips/When Will I Know	1961	3.00	6.00	12.00
❑ Leader 801	Library Love Affair/Rosemary	1960	5.00	10.00	20.00
❑ Leader 805	Itsy Bitsy Teeny Weeny Yellow Polka Dot Bikini/ Don't Dilly Dally, Sally	1960	7.50	15.00	30.00
❑ Philips 40179	Here's to Our Love/Two Kinds of Girls	1964	2.00	4.00	8.00
❑ Philips 40203	Devoted to You/Pledging My Love	1964	2.00	4.00	8.00
❑ Philips 40221	Now I Belong to You/One Step Forward, Two Steps Back	1964	2.00	4.00	8.00
❑ Philips 40263	He Don't Understand You/Love Will Find a Way	1965	2.00	4.00	8.00
❑ Philips 40306	Stay Away from Her/I Can't Keep a Secret	1965	2.00	4.00	8.00
❑ Philips 40354	3000 Miles/Sometimes They Do, Sometimes They Don't	1966	2.00	4.00	8.00
❑ Philips 40377	The Joker Went Wild/I Can Hear the Rain	1966	2.50	5.00	10.00
❑ Philips 40405	Why Did You Do It/Run, Run, Look and See	1966	2.00	4.00	8.00
❑ Philips 40424	Hung Up in Your Eyes/Why Mine	1967	2.00	4.00	8.00
❑ Philips 40444	Holiday for Clowns/Yesterday I Had a Girl	1967	2.00	4.00	8.00
❑ Philips 40472	Get the Message/Kinda Groovy	1967	—	3.00	6.00
❑ Uni 55193	You and Me/Could You Dig It	1970	—	3.00	6.00
❑ Uni 55240	Gypsy Woman/You and Me (#2)	1970	—	3.00	6.00
❑ Uni 55272	Lonely Teardrops/Lorraine	1971	—	2.50	5.00
❑ Uni 55287	So Long, Marianne/No Place to Run	1971	—	2.50	5.00
❑ Uni 55306	Out of the Blue/If You Came Back	1971	—	2.50	5.00
❑ Uni 55323	I Love Every Little Thing About You/With My Eyes Wide Open	1972	—	2.50	5.00
❑ Uni 55334	Only Wanna Make You Happy/When You're Lovin' Me	1972	—	2.50	5.00

Albums

Number	Title (A Side/B Side)	Yr	VG	VG+	NM
❑ ABC-Paramount 400 [M]	Let Me Belong to You	1961	7.50	15.00	30.00
❑ ABC-Paramount S-400 [S]	Let Me Belong to You	1961	10.00	20.00	40.00
❑ ABC-Paramount 431 [M]	Sealed with a Kiss	1962	7.50	15.00	30.00
❑ ABC-Paramount S-431 [S]	Sealed with a Kiss	1962	10.00	20.00	40.00
❑ ABC-Paramount 463 [M]	Country Meets Folk	1964	7.50	15.00	30.00
❑ ABC-Paramount S-463 [S]	Country Meets Folk	1964	10.00	20.00	40.00

Number	Title (A Side/B Side)	Yr	VG	VG+	NM
❑ Dot DLP 25926	Tragedy/A Million to One	1969	3.75	7.50	15.00
❑ Dot DLP 25954	Stay and Love Me All Summer	1969	3.75	7.50	15.00
❑ Kapp KL 1202 [M]	The Bashful Blonde	1960	12.50	25.00	50.00
❑ Kapp KS 3202 [S]	The Bashful Blonde	1960	20.00	40.00	80.00
❑ Philips PHM 200136 [M]	Here's to Our Love	1964	5.00	10.00	20.00
❑ Philips PHM 200158 [M]	Rockin' Folk	1965	5.00	10.00	20.00
❑ Philips PHM 200217 [M]	Run, Run, Look and See/The Joker Went Wild	1966	5.00	10.00	20.00
—With "200-217" in trail-off; this record plays mono					
❑ Philips PHM 200217 [S]	Run, Run, Look and See/The Joker Went Wild	1966	5.00	10.00	20.00
—With "2/600-217" in trail-off; this record plays stereo, though labeled mono					
❑ Philips PHS 600136 [S]	Here's to Our Love	1964	6.25	12.50	25.00
❑ Philips PHS 600158 [S]	Rockin' Folk	1965	6.25	12.50	25.00
❑ Philips PHS 600217 [S]	Run, Run, Look and See/The Joker Went Wild	1966	6.25	12.50	25.00
❑ Pickwick SPC-3261	Young Years	197?	2.50	5.00	10.00
❑ Private Stock PS-7003	In a State of Bayou	1977	3.00	6.00	12.00
❑ Rhino RNLP-70226	Greatest Hits	1987	2.50	5.00	10.00
❑ Uni 73097	Brian Hyland	1970	3.75	7.50	15.00
—The album is listed as "stereo," but "Gypsy Woman" is rechanneled					
❑ Wing MGW-12341 [M]	Here's to Our Love	1967	3.00	6.00	12.00
❑ Wing SRW-16341 [S]	Here's to Our Love	1967	3.00	6.00	12.00

I

IAN, JANIS

45s

Number	Title (A Side/B Side)	Yr	VG	VG+	NM
❑ Capitol 3107	He's a Rainbow/Here in Spain	1971	2.00	4.00	8.00
❑ Casablanca 2245	Night Rains/Fly Too High	1980	—	2.50	5.00
❑ Columbia 02176	Sugar Mountain/Under the Covers	1981	—	2.00	4.00
❑ Columbia 02546	Restless Eyes/I Remember Yesterday	1981	—	2.00	4.00
❑ Columbia 10119	When the Party's Over/Bright Lights and Promises	1975	—	2.50	5.00
❑ Columbia 10154	At Seventeen/Stars	1975	—	2.50	5.00
❑ Columbia 10228	In the Winter/Thankyouse	1975	—	2.50	5.00
❑ Columbia 10297	Aftertones/Boy, I Really Tied One On	1976	—	2.50	5.00
❑ Columbia 10331	I Would Like to Dance/Goodbye to Morning	1976	—	2.50	5.00
❑ Columbia 10391	Roses/Love Is Blind	1976	—	2.50	5.00
❑ Columbia 10484	Miracle Row/Take It to the Sky	1977	—	2.50	5.00
❑ Columbia 10526	Candlelight/I Want to Make You Love Me	1977	—	2.50	5.00
❑ Columbia 10813	That Grand Illusion/Hopper Paining	1978	—	2.50	5.00
❑ Columbia 10864	The Bridge/Do You Wanna Dance	1978	—	2.50	5.00
❑ Columbia 10979	Here Comes the Night/Tonight Will Last Forever	1979	—	2.00	4.00
❑ Columbia 11111	Night Rains/Fly Too High	1979	—	2.00	4.00
❑ Columbia 11327	The Other Side of the Sun/Memories	1980	—	2.00	4.00
❑ Columbia 46034	Jesse/The Man You Are in Me	1974	—	2.50	5.00
❑ Polydor 14299	Society's Child (Baby I've Been Thinking)/ I'll Give You a Stone If You Throw It	1975	—	3.00	6.00
❑ Verve 5027	Society's Child (Baby I've Been Thinking)/Letter to Jon	1967	2.50	5.00	10.00
❑ Verve Folkways 5027	Society's Child (Baby I've Been Thinking)/Letter to Jon	1966	3.00	6.00	12.00
❑ Verve Forecast 5027	Society's Child (Baby I've Been Thinking)/Letter to Jon	1967	2.00	4.00	8.00
❑ Verve Forecast 5041	I'll Give You a Stone If You'll Throw It/Younger Generation Blues	1967	2.00	4.00	8.00
❑ Verve Forecast 5072	Insanity Comes Quietly to the Structured Mind/ Snowflakes Fall, Snowrays Call	1967	2.00	4.00	8.00
❑ Verve Forecast 5079	Somg for All the Seasons of Your Mind/Lonely One	1968	2.00	4.00	8.00
❑ Verve Forecast 5090	Lady of the Night/Friends Again	1968	2.00	4.00	8.00
❑ Verve Forecast 5099	Everybody Knows/Janey's Blues	1968	2.00	4.00	8.00
❑ Verve Forecast 5113	Month of May/Calling Your Name	1969	2.00	4.00	8.00

Albums

Number	Title (A Side/B Side)	Yr	VG	VG+	NM
❑ Capitol SKAO-683	Present Company	1971	3.75	7.50	15.00
❑ Columbia KC 32857	Stars	1974	2.50	5.00	10.00
❑ Columbia PC 33394	Between the Lines	1975	2.50	5.00	10.00
—No bar code on cover					
❑ Columbia PC 33919	Aftertones	1976	2.50	5.00	10.00
—No bar code on cover					
❑ Columbia JC 34440	Miracle Row	1977	2.50	5.00	10.00
❑ Columbia JC 35325	Janis Ian	1978	2.50	5.00	10.00
❑ Columbia JC 36139	Night Rains	1979	2.50	5.00	10.00
❑ Columbia FC 37360	Restless Eyes	1981	2.50	5.00	10.00
❑ MGM GAS-121	Janis Ian (Golden Archive Series)	1970	6.25	12.50	25.00
❑ Polydor PD-6058	Janis Ian	1976	2.50	5.00	10.00
❑ Verve Folkways FT-3017 [M]	Janis Ian	1967	7.50	15.00	30.00
❑ Verve Folkways FTS-3017 [S]	Janis Ian	1967	7.50	15.00	30.00
❑ Verve Forecast FT-3017 [M]	Janis Ian	1967	5.00	10.00	20.00
❑ Verve Forecast FTS-3017 [S]	Janis Ian	1967	3.75	7.50	15.00
❑ Verve Forecast FT-3024 [M]	For All the Seasons of Your Mind	1967	5.00	10.00	20.00
❑ Verve Forecast FTS-3024 [S]	For All the Seasons of Your Mind	1967	3.75	7.50	15.00
❑ Verve Forecast FTS-3048	The Secret Life of J. Eddy Fink	1968	3.75	7.50	15.00
❑ Verve Forecast FTS-3063	Who Really Cares?	1969	3.75	7.50	15.00

IDES OF MARCH, THE

45s

Number	Title (A Side/B Side)	Yr	VG	VG+	NM
❑ Kapp 992	Nobody Loves Me/Strawberry Sunday	1969	2.50	5.00	10.00
❑ Parrot 304	I'll Keep Searching/You Wouldn't Listen	1966	2.50	5.00	10.00

Number	Title (A Side/B Side)	Yr	VG	VG+	NM
❑ Parrot 310	Roller Coaster/Things Aren't Always What They Seem	1966	2.50	5.00	10.00
❑ Parrot 312	You Need Love/Sha-La-La-La-Lee	1966	2.50	5.00	10.00
❑ Parrot 321	My Foolish Pride/Give Your Mind Wings	1967	2.50	5.00	10.00
❑ Parrot 326	Hole in My Soul/Girls Don't Grow on Trees	1967	2.50	5.00	10.00
❑ RCA Victor 74-0850	Mother America/Ladyland	1972	—	2.50	5.00
❑ RCA Victor APBO-0052	Hot Water/Heavy on the Country	1973	—	2.50	5.00
❑ Warner Bros. 7140	Vehicle/L.A. Goodbye	1972	—	2.00	4.00
—"Back to Back Hits" series — originals have green labels					
❑ Warner Bros. 7334	High on a Hillside/One Woman Man	1969	—	3.00	6.00
❑ Warner Bros. 7378	Vehicle/Lead Me Home, Gently	1970	2.00	4.00	8.00
❑ Warner Bros. 7403	Superman/Home	1970	—	3.00	6.00
❑ Warner Bros. 7426	Melody/The Sky Is Falling	1970	—	3.00	6.00
❑ Warner Bros. 7466	L.A. Goodbye/Mrs. Grayson's Farm	1971	—	3.00	6.00
❑ Warner Bros. 7507	Tie-Dye Princess/Friends of Feeling	1971	—	3.00	6.00
❑ Warner Bros. 7526	Giddy-Up, Ride Me/Freedom Sweet	1971	—	3.00	6.00
Albums					
❑ RCA Victor APL1-0143	Midnight Oil	1973	3.75	7.50	15.00
❑ RCA Victor LSP-4812	World Woven	1972	3.75	7.50	15.00
❑ Warner Bros. WS 1863	Vehicle	1970	3.75	7.50	15.00
—Green "WB" label					
❑ Warner Bros. WS 1863	Vehicle	1970	5.00	10.00	20.00
—Green "W7" label					
❑ Warner Bros. WS 1896	Common Bond	1971	3.75	7.50	15.00

IFIELD, FRANK

45s

Number	Title (A Side/B Side)	Yr	VG	VG+	NM
❑ Capitol 5032	I'm Confessin' (That I Love You)/Waltzing Matilda	1963	2.50	5.00	10.00
❑ Capitol 5089	Please/Mule Train	1963	2.50	5.00	10.00
❑ Capitol 5134	Don't Blame Me/Say It Isn't So	1964	2.50	5.00	10.00
❑ Capitol 5170	Sweet Lorraine/You Came a Long Way from St. Louis	1964	2.50	5.00	10.00
❑ Capitol 5275	True Love Ways/I Should Care	1964	2.50	5.00	10.00
❑ Capitol 5349	Without You/Don't Make Me Laugh	1965	2.50	5.00	10.00
❑ Hickory 1397	No One Will Ever Know/I'm Saving All My Love (For You)	1966	2.00	4.00	8.00
❑ Hickory 1411	Call Her Your Sweetheart/Give Myself a Party	1966	2.00	4.00	8.00
❑ Hickory 1435	I Remember You/Stranger to You	1967	2.00	4.00	8.00
❑ Hickory 1454	Kaw-Liga/Out of Nowhere	1967	2.00	4.00	8.00
❑ Hickory 1473	Just Let Me Make Believe/Fireball Mail	1967	2.00	4.00	8.00
❑ Hickory 1486	Oh, Such a Stranger/Then You Can Tell Me Goodbye	1967	2.00	4.00	8.00
❑ Hickory 1499	Adios Matador/Movin' Lover	1968	2.00	4.00	8.00
❑ Hickory 1507	Don't Forget to Cry/Morning in Your Eyes	1968	2.00	4.00	8.00
❑ Hickory 1514	Good Morning Dear/Innocent Years	1968	2.00	4.00	8.00
❑ Hickory 1525	Maurie/I'm Learning Child	1968	2.00	4.00	8.00
❑ Hickory 1540	Let Me Into Your Life/Mary in the Morning	1969	—	3.00	6.00
❑ Hickory 1550	I Love You Because/It's My Time	1969	—	3.00	6.00
❑ Hickory 1556	Lights of Home/Love Hurts	1969	—	3.00	6.00
❑ Hickory 1574	Sweet Memories/You've Still Got a Place in My Heart	1970	—	3.00	6.00
❑ Hickory 1595	Someone/One More Mile, One More Town (One More Time)	1971	—	3.00	6.00
❑ MAM 3612	Lonesome Jubilee/Teach Me Little Children	1971	—	2.50	5.00
❑ Vee Jay 457	I Remember You/I Listen to My Heart	1962	3.75	7.50	15.00
—With Frank Ifield's name spelled correctly on label					
❑ Vee Jay 457	I Remember You/I Listen to My Heart	1962	5.00	10.00	20.00
—With both labels misspelled "Farnk Ifield"					
❑ Vee Jay 477	Lovesick Blues/Anytime	1962	3.00	6.00	12.00
❑ Vee Jay 499	The Wayward Wind/I'm Smiling Now	1963	3.00	6.00	12.00
❑ Vee Jay 525	Unchained Melody/Nobody's Darlin' But Mine	1963	3.00	6.00	12.00
❑ Vee Jay 553	I'm Confessin' (That I Love You)/Heart and Soul	1963	3.00	6.00	12.00
❑ Warner Bros. 8730	Why Don't We Leave Together/Crawling Back	1979	—	2.00	4.00
❑ Warner Bros. 8853	Crystal/Touch the Morning	1979	—	2.00	4.00
❑ Warner Bros. 49095	Play Born to Lose Again/Yesterday Just Passed My Way Again	1979	—	2.00	4.00
Albums					
❑ Capitol ST 10356 [S]	I'm Confessin'	1963	6.25	12.50	25.00
❑ Capitol T 10356 [M]	I'm Confessin'	1963	5.00	10.00	20.00
❑ Hickory LPM-132 [M]	The Best of Frank Ifield	1966	5.00	10.00	20.00
❑ Hickory LPS-132 [P]	The Best of Frank Ifield	1966	5.00	10.00	20.00
❑ Hickory LPM-136 [M]	Tale of Two Cities	1967	3.75	7.50	15.00
❑ Hickory LPS-136 [S]	Tale of Two Cities	1967	5.00	10.00	20.00

Number	Title (A Side/B Side)	Yr	VG	VG+	NM
❑ Vee Jay LP 1054 [M]	I Remember You	1962	7.50	15.00	30.00
❑ Vee Jay SR 1054 [S]	I Remember You	1962	12.50	25.00	50.00

IMPALAS, THE

45s

Number	Title (A Side/B Side)	Yr	VG	VG+	NM
❑ Bunky 7760	Whay Should He Do/I Still Love You	1969	2.00	4.00	8.00
❑ Bunky 7762	Whip it On Me/I Still Love You	1969	2.00	4.00	8.00
❑ Capitol 2709	Speed Up/Soul	1969	2.00	4.00	8.00
❑ Checker 999	For the Love of Mike/I Need You So Much	1961	3.00	6.00	12.00
❑ Cub 9022	Sorry (I Ran All the Way Home)/Fool, Fool, Fool	1959	5.00	10.00	20.00
❑ Cub 9022	I Ran All the Way Home/Fool, Fool, Fool	1959	15.00	30.00	60.00
—Original A-side title					
❑ Cub 9033	Oh What a Fool/Sandy Went Away	1959	5.00	10.00	20.00
❑ Cub 9053	Peggy Darling/Bye Everybody	1959	5.00	10.00	20.00
❑ Cub 9066	All Alone/When My Heart Does All the Talking	1960	5.00	10.00	20.00
—As "Speedo and the Impalas"					
❑ Hamilton 50026	I Was a Fool/First Date	1960	5.00	10.00	20.00
❑ Red Boy 113	When You Dance/I Can't See Me Without You	1966	6.25	12.50	25.00
❑ Rite-On 101	I Can't See Me Without You/Old Man Mose	196?	5.00	10.00	20.00
❑ Steady 044	When You Dance/I Can't See Me Without You	1967	5.00	10.00	20.00
❑ Sundown 115	The Lonely One/Lost Boogie	1959	3.75	7.50	15.00
❑ 20th Fox 428	Last Night I Saw a Girl/There Is Nothin' Like a Dame	1963	3.00	6.00	12.00

Albums

Number	Title (A Side/B Side)	Yr	VG	VG+	NM
❑ Cub 8003 [M]	Sorry (I Ran All the Way Home)	1959	100.00	200.00	400.00
❑ Cub S-8003 [S]	Sorry (I Ran All the Way Home)	1959	150.00	300.00	600.00

IMPRESSIONS, THE

45s

Number	Title (A Side/B Side)	Yr	VG	VG+	NM
❑ ABC 10831	Can't Satisfy/This Must End	1966	2.00	4.00	8.00
❑ ABC 10869	Love's a-Comin'/Wade in the Water	1966	2.00	4.00	8.00
❑ ABC 10900	You Always Hurt Me/Little Girl	1967	2.00	4.00	8.00
❑ ABC 10932	It's Hard to Believe/You've Got Me Runnin'	1967	2.00	4.00	8.00
❑ ABC 10964	I Can't Stay Away from You/You Ought to Be in Heaven	1967	2.00	4.00	8.00
❑ ABC 11022	We're a Winner/It's All Over	1967	2.00	4.00	8.00
❑ ABC 11071	We're Rolling On (Part 1)/We're Rolling On (Part 2)	1968	2.00	4.00	8.00
❑ ABC 11103	I Loved and I Lost/Up, Up and Away	1968	2.00	4.00	8.00
❑ ABC 11135	Don't Cry My Love/Sometimes I Wonder	1968	2.00	4.00	8.00
❑ ABC 11188	East of Java/Just Before Sunrise	1969	2.00	4.00	8.00
❑ ABC-Paramount 10241	Gypsy Woman/As Long As You Love Me	1961	3.75	7.50	15.00
❑ ABC-Paramount 10289	Grow Closer Together/Can't You See	1962	3.75	7.50	15.00
❑ ABC-Paramount 10328	Little Young Lover/Never Let Me Go	1962	3.75	7.50	15.00
❑ ABC-Paramount 10357	You've Come Home/Minstrel and Queen	1962	3.75	7.50	15.00
❑ ABC-Paramount 10386	I'm the One Who Loves You/I Need Your Love	1962	3.75	7.50	15.00
❑ ABC-Paramount 10431	Sad, Sad Girl and Boy/Twist and Limbo	1963	3.75	7.50	15.00
❑ ABC-Paramount 10487	It's All Right/You'll Want Me Back	1963	3.75	7.50	15.00
❑ ABC-Paramount 10511	Talking About My Baby/Never Too Much Love	1963	3.75	7.50	15.00
❑ ABC-Paramount 10537	Girl You Don't Know Me/A Woman Who Loves Me	1964	3.75	7.50	15.00
❑ ABC-Paramount 10544	I'm So Proud/I Made a Mistake	1964	3.75	7.50	15.00
❑ ABC-Paramount 10554	Keep On Pushing/I Love You (Yeah)	1964	3.75	7.50	15.00
❑ ABC-Paramount 10581	You Must Believe Me/See the Real Me	1964	3.75	7.50	15.00
❑ ABC-Paramount 10602	Amen/Long, Long Winter	1964	3.75	7.50	15.00
❑ ABC-Paramount 10622	People Get Ready/I've Been Trying	1965	3.75	7.50	15.00
❑ ABC-Paramount 10647	Woman's Got Soul/Get Up and Move	1965	3.00	6.00	12.00
❑ ABC-Paramount 10670	Meeting Over Yonder/I've Found That I've Lost	1965	3.00	6.00	12.00
❑ ABC-Paramount 10710	I Need You/Never Could You Be	1965	3.00	6.00	12.00
❑ ABC-Paramount 10725	Just One Kiss from You/Twilight Time	1965	3.00	6.00	12.00
❑ ABC-Paramount 10750	You've Been Cheatin'/Man, Oh Man	1965	3.00	6.00	12.00
❑ ABC-Paramount 10761	Since I Lost the One I Love/Falling in Love with You	1966	2.50	5.00	10.00
❑ ABC-Paramount 10789	Too Slow/No One Else	1966	2.50	5.00	10.00
❑ Abner 1013	For Your Precious Love/Sweet Was the Wine	1958	10.00	20.00	40.00
—As "Jerry Butler and the Impressions"					
❑ Abner 1017	Come Back My Love/Love Me	1958	7.50	15.00	30.00
❑ Abner 1023	The Gift of Love/At the County Fair	1959	7.50	15.00	30.00
❑ Abner 1025	Lonely One/Senorita I Love You	1959	7.50	15.00	30.00
❑ Abner 1034	Say That You Love Me/A New Love	1960	7.50	15.00	30.00
❑ Bandera 2504	Listen/Shorty's Got to Go	1959	12.50	25.00	50.00
❑ Chi-Sound 2418	Sorry/All I Wanna Do Is Make Love to You	1979	—	2.50	5.00
❑ Chi-Sound 2438	Maybe I'm Mistaken/All I Wanna Do Is Make Love to You	1980	—	2.50	5.00
❑ Chi-Sound 2491	For Your Precious Love/You're Mine	1981	—	2.50	5.00
❑ Chi-Sound 2499	Love, Love, Love/Fan the Fire	1981	—	2.50	5.00
❑ Cotillion 44210	This Time/I'm a Fool for Love	1976	—	2.50	5.00
❑ Cotillion 44211	Silent Night/I Saw Mommy Kissing Santa Claus	1976	—	3.00	6.00
❑ Cotillion 44214	You'll Never Find/Stardust	1977	—	2.50	5.00
❑ Cotillion 44222	Can't Get Along/You're So Right for Me	1977	—	2.50	5.00
❑ Curtom 0103	Sooner or Later/Miracle Woman	1975	—	2.50	5.00
❑ Curtom 0106	Same Thing It Took/I'm So Glad	1975	—	2.50	5.00
❑ Curtom 0110	Loving Power/First Impressions	1975	—	2.50	5.00
❑ Curtom 0116	Sunshine/I Wish I'd Stayed in Bed	1976	—	2.50	5.00
❑ Curtom 1932	Fool for You/I'm Loving Nothing	1968	—	3.00	6.00
❑ Curtom 1934	This Is My Country/My Woman's Love	1968	—	3.00	6.00
❑ Curtom 1937	My Deceiving Heart/You Want Somebody Else	1969	—	3.00	6.00
❑ Curtom 1940	Seven Years/The Girl I Find	1969	—	3.00	6.00
❑ Curtom 1943	Choice of Colors/Mighty Mighty Spade and Whitey	1969	—	3.00	6.00
❑ Curtom 1946	Say You Love Me/You'll Be Always Mine	1969	—	3.00	6.00
❑ Curtom 1948	Wherever She Leadeth Me/Amen (1970)	1970	—	3.00	6.00
❑ Curtom 1951	Check Out Your Mind/Can't You See	1970	—	3.00	6.00
❑ Curtom 1954	(Baby) Turn On to Me/Soulful Love	1970	—	3.00	6.00
❑ Curtom 1957	Ain't Got Time/I'm So Proud	1971	—	3.00	6.00

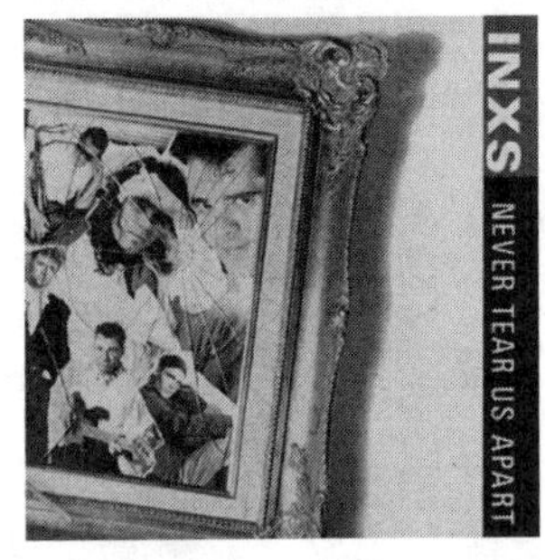

Number	Title (A Side/B Side)	Yr	VG	VG+	NM
❑ Curtom 1959	Love Me/Do You Wanna Win	1971	—	3.00	6.00
❑ Curtom 1966	Inner City Blues/We Must Be in Love	1971	—	3.00	6.00
❑ Curtom 1970	This Loves for Real/Times Have Changed	1972	—	3.00	6.00
❑ Curtom 1973	I Need to Belong to Someone/Love Me	1972	—	3.00	6.00
❑ Curtom 1982	Preacher Man/Times Have Changed	1973	—	3.00	6.00
❑ Curtom 1985	Thin Line/I'm Loving You	1973	—	3.00	6.00
❑ Curtom 1994	If It's In You to Do Wrong/Times Have Changed	1973	—	3.00	6.00
❑ Curtom 1997	Finally Got Myself Together (I'm a Changed Man)/ I'll Always Be Here	1974	—	3.00	6.00
❑ Curtom 2003	Something's Mighty, Mighty Wrong/Three the Hard Way	1974	—	3.00	6.00
❑ Falcon 1013	For Your Precious Love/Sweet Was the Wine	1958	15.00	30.00	60.00
—As "Jerry Butler and the Impressions"					
❑ Lost-Nite 266	For Your Precious Love/Sweet Was the Wine	197?	—	2.50	5.00
—As "Jerry Butler and the Impressions"; reissue					
❑ MCA 52995	Can't Wait 'Til Tomorrow/Love Workin' On Me	1987	—	—	3.00
❑ Port 70031	Listen/Shorty's Got to Go	1962	3.75	7.50	15.00
❑ Swirl 107	I Need Your Love/Don't Leave Me	1962	5.00	10.00	20.00
❑ 20th Fox 172	All Through the Night/Meanwhile, Back in My Heart	1959	10.00	20.00	40.00
❑ Vee Jay 280	For Your Precious Love/Sweet Was the Wine	1958	4000.	6000.	8000.
—As "Jerry Butler and the Impressions." VG 4000; VG+ 6000					
❑ Vee Jay 424	Say That You Love Me/Senorita I Love You	1962	5.00	10.00	20.00
❑ Vee Jay 574	The Gift of Love/At the County Fair	1963	3.75	7.50	15.00
❑ Vee Jay 621	Say That You Love Me/Senorita I Love You	1964	3.75	7.50	15.00
7-					
❑ ABC-Paramount LP-ABCS-505	Woman's Got Soul/Emotions/We're in Love// People Get Ready/See the Real Me/You Must Believe Me	1965	7.50	15.00	30.00
—Stereo jukebox issue; small hole, plays at 33 1/3 rpm					
Albums					
❑ ABC 606 [M]	The Fabulous Impressions	1967	6.25	12.50	25.00
❑ ABC S-606 [S]	The Fabulous Impressions	1967	5.00	10.00	20.00
❑ ABC S-635	We're a Winner	1968	3.75	7.50	15.00
❑ ABC S-654	The Best of the Impressions	1968	3.75	7.50	15.00
❑ ABC S-668	The Versatile Impressions	1969	3.75	7.50	15.00
❑ ABC S-727	16 Greatest Hits	1971	3.00	6.00	12.00
❑ ABC D-780 [(2)]	Curtis Mayfield/His Early Years with the Impressions	1973	5.00	10.00	20.00
❑ ABC-Paramount 450 [M]	The Impressions	1963	7.50	15.00	30.00
❑ ABC-Paramount S-450 [S]	The Impressions	1963	10.00	20.00	40.00
❑ ABC-Paramount 468 [M]	The Never Ending Impressions	1964	7.50	15.00	30.00
❑ ABC-Paramount S-468 [S]	The Never Ending Impressions	1964	10.00	20.00	40.00
❑ ABC-Paramount 493 [M]	Keep On Pushing	1964	7.50	15.00	30.00
❑ ABC-Paramount S-493 [S]	Keep On Pushing	1964	10.00	20.00	40.00
❑ ABC-Paramount 505 [M]	People Get Ready	1965	7.50	15.00	30.00
❑ ABC-Paramount S-505 [S]	People Get Ready	1965	10.00	20.00	40.00
❑ ABC-Paramount 515 [M]	The Impressions' Greatest Hits	1965	5.00	10.00	20.00
❑ ABC-Paramount S-515 [S]	The Impressions' Greatest Hits	1965	6.25	12.50	25.00
❑ ABC-Paramount 523 [M]	One By One	1965	5.00	10.00	20.00
❑ ABC-Paramount S-523 [S]	One By One	1965	6.25	12.50	25.00
❑ ABC-Paramount 545 [M]	Ridin' High	1966	5.00	10.00	20.00
❑ ABC-Paramount S-545 [S]	Ridin' High	1966	6.25	12.50	25.00
❑ Chi-Sound T-596	Come to My Party	1979	2.50	5.00	10.00
❑ Chi-Sound T-624	Fan the Fire	1981	2.50	5.00	10.00
❑ Cotillion SD 9912	It's About Time	1976	3.00	6.00	12.00
❑ Curtom CUR-2006	Lasting Impressions	198?	2.50	5.00	10.00
❑ Curtom CU 5003	First Impressions	1975	3.00	6.00	12.00
❑ Curtom CU 5009	Loving Power	1976	3.00	6.00	12.00
❑ Curtom CRS-8001	This Is My Country	1968	3.75	7.50	15.00
❑ Curtom CRS-8003	The Young Mods' Forgotten Story	1969	3.75	7.50	15.00
❑ Curtom CRS-8004	Best Impressions — Curtis, Sam, Dave	1969	3.75	7.50	15.00
❑ Curtom CRS-8006	Check Out Your Mind	1970	3.75	7.50	15.00
❑ Curtom CRS-8012	Times Have Changed	1972	3.75	7.50	15.00
❑ Curtom CRS-8016	Preacher Man	1973	3.75	7.50	15.00
❑ Curtom CRS-8019	Finally Got Myself Together	1974	3.75	7.50	15.00
❑ Lost-Nite LLP-22 [10]	Jerry Butler and the Impressions	1981	3.75	7.50	15.00
—Red vinyl					
❑ MCA 1500	The Impressions Greatest Hits	1982	2.00	4.00	8.00
❑ MCA 5373	In the Heat of the Night	1982	2.50	5.00	10.00

Number	Title (A Side/B Side)	Yr	VG	VG+	NM
❑ Pickwick SPC-3602	The Impressions	1978	2.00	4.00	8.00
❑ Scepter Citation CTN-18018	The Best of Curtis Mayfield and the Impressions	1972	2.50	5.00	10.00
❑ Sire SASH-3717 [(2)]	The Vintage Years	1977	3.75	7.50	15.00
—Includes solo hits by Jerry Butler and Curtis Mayfield					

INTRUDERS, THE (1)

45s

Number	Title (A Side/B Side)	Yr	VG	VG+	NM
❑ Gamble 201	(We'll Be) United/Up and Down the Ladder	1966	2.50	5.00	10.00
❑ Gamble 203	Devil with an Angel's Smile/A Book for the Broken Hearted	1966	2.50	5.00	10.00
❑ Gamble 204	It Must Be Love/Check Yourself	1966	2.50	5.00	10.00
❑ Gamble 205	Together/Up and Down the Ladder	1967	2.50	5.00	10.00
❑ Gamble 209	Baby I'm Lonely/A Love That's Real	1967	2.50	5.00	10.00
❑ Gamble 214	Cowboys to Girls/Turn the Hands of Time	1968	2.50	5.00	10.00
❑ Gamble 217	(Love Is Like a) Baseball Game/Friends No More	1968	2.50	5.00	10.00
❑ Gamble 221	Slow Drag/So Glad I'm Yours	1968	2.50	5.00	10.00
❑ Gamble 223	Give Her a Transplant/Girls, Girls, Girls	1969	2.50	5.00	10.00
❑ Gamble 225	Me Tarzan You Jane/Favorite Candidate	1969	2.50	5.00	10.00
❑ Gamble 231	Lollipop (I Like You)/Don't Give It Away	1969	2.50	5.00	10.00
❑ Gamble 235	Sad Girl/Let's Go Downtown	1969	2.50	5.00	10.00
❑ Gamble 240	Old Love/Every Day Is a Holiday	1969	2.50	5.00	10.00
❑ Gamble 2501	(Win, Place or Show) She's a Winner/Memories Are Here to Stay	1972	2.00	4.00	8.00
❑ Gamble 2506	I'll Always Love My Mama (Part 1)/ I'll Always Love My Mama (Part 2)	1973	2.00	4.00	8.00
❑ Gamble 2508	I Wanna Know Your Name/Hang On In There	1973	2.00	4.00	8.00
❑ Gamble 4001	Tender (Was the Love We Knew)/By the Time I Get to Phoenix	1970	2.00	4.00	8.00
❑ Gamble 4004	When We Get Married/Doctor Doctor	1970	2.00	4.00	8.00
❑ Gamble 4007	This Is My Love Song/Let Me in Your Mind	1970	2.00	4.00	8.00
❑ Gamble 4009	I'm Girl Scoutin'/Wonder What Kind of Bag She's In	1971	2.00	4.00	8.00
❑ Gamble 4014	Pray for Me/Best Days of My Life	1971	2.00	4.00	8.00
❑ Gamble 4016	I Bet He Don't Love You (Like I Love You)/ Do You Remember Yesterday	1971	2.00	4.00	8.00
❑ Gamble 4019	(Win, Place or Show) She's a Winner/Memories Are Here to Stay	1972	2.50	5.00	10.00
❑ Gowen 1401	I'm Sold on You/Come Home Soon	1961	10.00	20.00	40.00
❑ Lost-Nite 195	I'm Sold on You/Come Home Soon	196?	—	3.00	6.00
—Reissue					
❑ Philadelphia Int'l. 3624	I'll Always Love My Mama (Part 1)/ I'll Always Love My Mama (Part 2)	1977	—	2.50	5.00
❑ Philadelphia Int'l. 3689	I'll Always Love My Mama/Save the Children	1979	—	2.50	5.00
❑ TSOP 4758	A Nice Girl Like You/To Be Happy Is the Real Thing	1974	—	3.00	6.00
❑ TSOP 4766	Rainy Days and Mondays/Be on Time	1975	—	3.00	6.00
❑ TSOP 4771	Plain Old Fashioned Girl/Energy of Love	1975	—	3.00	6.00

Albums

Number	Title (A Side/B Side)	Yr	VG	VG+	NM
❑ Gamble G-5001 [M]	The Intruders Are Together	1967	10.00	20.00	40.00
❑ Gamble GS-5001 [S]	The Intruders Are Together	1967	12.50	25.00	50.00
❑ Gamble GS-5004	Cowboys to Girls	1968	12.50	25.00	50.00
❑ Gamble GS-5005	The Intruders Greatest Hits	1969	10.00	20.00	40.00
❑ Gamble GS-5008	When We Get Married	1970	12.50	25.00	50.00
❑ Gamble KZ 31991	Save the Children	1973	5.00	10.00	20.00
❑ Gamble KZ 32131	Super Hits	1973	5.00	10.00	20.00
❑ Philadelphia Int'l. PZ 32131	Super Hits	198?	2.00	4.00	8.00
—Reissue of Gamble 32131					
❑ TSOP KZ 33149	Energy of Love	1974	3.75	7.50	15.00

INXS

45s

Number	Title (A Side/B Side)	Yr	VG	VG+	NM
❑ Atco 99703	Burn for You/Johnson's Aeroplane	1984	—	2.00	4.00
❑ Atco 99731	I Send a Message/Mechanical	1984	—	2.00	4.00
❑ Atco 99766	Original Sin/Stay Young	1984	—	2.00	4.00
❑ Atco 99833	To Look at You/Sax Thing	1983	—	2.00	4.00
❑ Atco 99874	Don't Change/Long in Tooth	1983	—	2.00	4.00
❑ Atco 99905	The One Thing/Phantim of the Opera	1983	—	2.00	4.00
❑ Atlantic 87784	Disappear/Middle Beast	1990	—	—	3.00
❑ Atlantic 87860	Suicide Blonde/Everyboidy Wants U Tonight	1990	—	—	3.00
—Not issued with picture sleeve in U.S.					
❑ Atlantic 89038	Never Tear Us Apart/Different World	1988	—	—	3.00
❑ Atlantic 89080	New Sensation/Guns in the Sky	1988	—	—	3.00
❑ Atlantic 89144	Devil Inside/On the Rocks	1988	—	—	3.00
❑ Atlantic 89188	Need You Tonight/I'm Comin' Home	1987	—	—	3.00
❑ Atlantic 89237	Good Times/Laying Down the Law	1987	—	—	3.00
—With Jimmy Barnes					
❑ Atlantic 89418	Kiss the Dirt (Falling Down the Mountain)//Six Knots/The One Thing (Live)	1986	—	—	3.00
❑ Atlantic 89429	Listen Like Thieves/Begotten	1986	—	—	3.00
❑ Atlantic 89460	What You Need/Sweet as Sin	1986	—	—	3.00
❑ Atlantic 89497	This Time/I'm Over You	1985	—	—	3.00
❑ Atlantic Oldies Series 84926	New Sensation/Never Tear Us Apart	199?	—	—	3.00
❑ Atlantic Oldies Series 84927	Need You Tonight/Devil Inside	199?	—	—	3.00
❑ Atlantic Oldies Series 84967	What You Need/This Time	198?	—	—	3.00

Albums

Number	Title (A Side/B Side)	Yr	VG	VG+	NM
❑ Atco 90072	Shabooh Shoobah	1983	3.00	6.00	12.00
❑ Atco 90115 [EP]	Dekadance	1983	3.75	7.50	15.00
❑ Atco 90160	The Swing	1984	3.00	6.00	12.00
❑ Atco 90184	INXS	1984	3.00	6.00	12.00
—U.S. issue of 1980 Australian album					

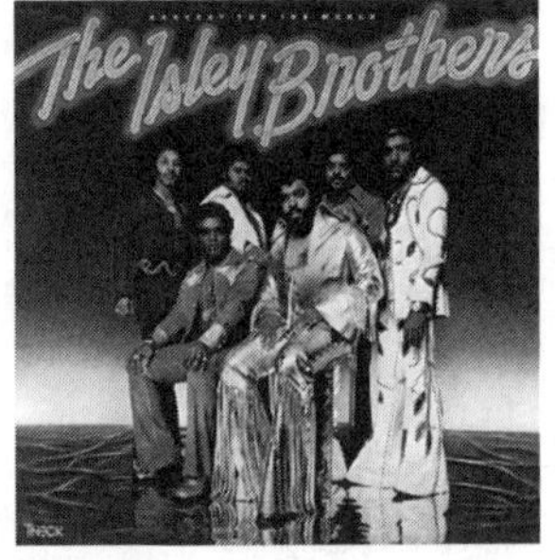

Number	Title (A Side/B Side)	Yr	VG	VG+	NM
❑ Atco 90185	Underneath the Colours	1984	3.00	6.00	12.00
—U.S. issue of 1981 Australian album					
❑ Atlantic 81277	Listen Like Thieves	1985	2.50	5.00	10.00
❑ Atlantic 81796	Kick	1987	2.50	5.00	10.00
❑ Atlantic 82140	X	1990	2.50	5.00	10.00
IRISH ROVERS, THE					
45s					
❑ Decca 32254	The Unicorn/Black Velvet Band	1968	2.50	5.00	10.00
❑ Decca 32333	(The Puppet Song) Whiskey on a Sunday/ The Orange and the Green	1968	2.00	4.00	8.00
❑ Decca 32371	Liverpool Lou/The Bi-Plane, Ever More	1968	2.00	4.00	8.00
❑ Decca 32444	Lily the Pink/Mrs. Crandall's Boardinghouse	1969	2.00	4.00	8.00
❑ Decca 32529	Peter Knight/Did She Mention My Name	1969	2.00	4.00	8.00
❑ Decca 32575	Fifi O'Toole/Winkin', Blinkin', and Nod	1969	2.00	4.00	8.00
❑ Decca 32616	Rhymes and Reasons/Penny Whistler Peddler	1970	—	3.00	6.00
❑ Decca 32723	Two Little Boys/Years May Come, Years May Go	1970	—	3.00	6.00
❑ Decca 32775	The Marvelous Toy/Marika's Lullaby	1970	—	3.00	6.00
Albums					
❑ Decca DL 4835 [M]	First	1967	5.00	10.00	20.00
❑ Decca DL 4951 [M]	The Unicorn	1968	6.25	12.50	25.00
❑ Decca DL 74835 [S]	First	1967	3.75	7.50	15.00
❑ Decca DL 74951 [S]	The Unicorn	1968	3.75	7.50	15.00
❑ Decca DL 75037	All Hung Up	1968	3.75	7.50	15.00
❑ Decca DL 75081	Tales to Warm Your Mind	1969	3.75	7.50	15.00
❑ Decca DL 75157	Life of the Rover	1969	3.75	7.50	15.00
❑ Decca DL 75302	On the Shores of Americay	1971	3.75	7.50	15.00
❑ MCA 15	The Unicorn	1973	2.50	5.00	10.00
—Reissue of Decca 74951					
❑ MCA 175	On the Shores of Americay	1973	2.50	5.00	10.00
—Reissue of Decca 75302					
❑ MCA 249	First	1973	2.50	5.00	10.00
—Reissue of Decca 74835					
❑ MCA 284	Life of the Rover	1973	2.50	5.00	10.00
—Reissue of Decca 75157					
❑ MCA 4066 [(2)]	Greatest Hits	1976	3.75	7.50	15.00
ISLEY BROTHERS, THE					
45s					
❑ Atlantic 2092	Jeepers Creepers/Teach Me How to Shimmy	1961	3.75	7.50	15.00
❑ Atlantic 2100	Shine On Harvest Moon/Standing on the Dance Floor	1961	3.75	7.50	15.00
❑ Atlantic 2110	Your Old Lady/Write to Me	1961	3.75	7.50	15.00
❑ Atlantic 2122	A Fool for You/Just One More Time	1961	3.75	7.50	15.00
❑ Atlantic 2263	Looking for a Love/The Last Girl	1964	2.50	5.00	10.00
❑ Atlantic 2277	Simon Says/Wild As a Tiger	1965	2.50	5.00	10.00
❑ Atlantic 2303	Move Over and Let Me Dance/Have You Ever Been Disappointed	1965	3.75	7.50	15.00
❑ Cindy 3009	Don't Be Jealous/This Is the End	1958	18.75	37.50	75.00
—"Cindy" in regular print					
❑ Cindy 3009	Don't Be Jealous/This Is the End	1958	37.50	75.00	150.00
—"Cindy" in shadow print					
❑ Gone 5022	I Wanna Know/Everybody's Gonna Rock and Roll	1958	20.00	40.00	80.00
❑ Gone 5048	My Love/The Drag	1958	20.00	40.00	80.00
❑ Mark-X 7003	The Drag/Rockin' MacDonald	1957	25.00	50.00	100.00
❑ Mark-X 8000	The Drag/Rockin' MacDonald	1959	7.50	15.00	30.00
❑ RCA 447-0589	Shout (Part 1)/Shout (Part 2)	1976	—	2.00	4.00
—Gold Standard Series; black label, dog near top					
❑ RCA Victor 47-7537	I'm Gonna Knock on Your Door/Turn to Me	1959	6.25	12.50	25.00
❑ RCA Victor 47-7588	Shout (Part 1)/Shout (Part 2)	1959	7.50	15.00	30.00
❑ RCA Victor 47-7657	Respectable/Without a Song	1959	6.25	12.50	25.00
❑ RCA Victor 47-7718	He's Got the Whole World in His Hands/How Deep Is the Ocean	1960	6.25	12.50	25.00
❑ RCA Victor 47-7746	Gypsy Love Song/Open Up Your Heart	1960	6.25	12.50	25.00
❑ RCA Victor 47-7787	Say You Love Me Too/Tell Me Who	1960	6.25	12.50	25.00
❑ RCA Victor 447-0589	Shout (Part 1)/Shout (Part 2)	1962	3.00	6.00	12.00
—Gold Standard Series; black label, dog on top (this charted with this number in 1962)					
❑ RCA Victor 447-0589	Shout (Part 1)/Shout (Part 2)	1965	2.00	4.00	8.00
—Gold Standard Series; black label, dog on side					
❑ RCA Victor 447-0589	Shout (Part 1)/Shout (Part 2)	1969	—	2.50	5.00
—Gold Standard Series; red label					

Number	Title (A Side/B Side)	Yr	VG	VG+	NM
❑ T-Neck 501	Testify (Part 1)/Testify (Part 2)	1964	3.75	7.50	15.00
❑ T-Neck 901	It's Your Thing/Don't Give It Away	1969	—	3.00	6.00
❑ T-Neck 902	I Turned You On/I Know Who You Been Socking It To	1969	—	3.00	6.00
❑ T-Neck 906	Black Berries — Pt. 1/Black Berries — Pt. 2	1969	—	3.00	6.00
❑ T-Neck 908	Was It Good to You/I Got to Get Myself Together	1969	—	3.00	6.00
❑ T-Neck 912	Bless Your Heart/Give the Women What They Want	1969	—	3.00	6.00
❑ T-Neck 914	Keep On Doin'/Save Me	1970	—	3.00	6.00
❑ T-Neck 919	If He Can, You Can/Holdin' On	1970	—	3.00	6.00
❑ T-Neck 921	Girls Will Be Girls, Boys Will Be Boys/Get Down Off of the Train	1970	—	3.00	6.00
❑ T-Neck 924	Get Into Something/Get Into Something (Part 2)	1970	—	3.00	6.00
❑ T-Neck 927	Freedom/I Need You So	1970	—	3.00	6.00
❑ T-Neck 929	Warpath/I Got to Find Me One	1971	—	3.00	6.00
❑ T-Neck 930	Love the One You're With/He's Got Your Love	1971	—	3.00	6.00
❑ T-Neck 932	Spill the Wine/Take Inventory	1971	—	3.00	6.00
❑ T-Neck 933	Lay Lady Lay/Vacuum Cleaner	1971	—	3.00	6.00
❑ T-Neck 934	Lay-Away/Feel Like the World	1972	—	3.00	6.00
❑ T-Neck 935	Pop That Thang/I Got to Find Me One	1972	—	3.00	6.00
❑ T-Neck 936	Work to Do/Beautiful	1972	—	3.00	6.00
❑ T-Neck 937	It's Too Late/Nothing to Do But Today	1973	—	3.00	6.00
❑ T-Neck 02033	Hurry Up and Wait/(Instrumental)	1981	—	2.50	5.00
❑ T-Neck 02151	Don't Say Goodnight (It's Time for Love) (Parts 1 & 2)	1981	—	2.00	4.00
—Reissue					
❑ T-Neck 02179	I Once Had Your Love (And I Can't Let Go)/(Instrumental)	1981	—	2.50	5.00
❑ T-Neck 2251	That Lady (Part 1)/That Lady (Part 2)	1973	—	2.50	5.00
❑ T-Neck 2252	What It Comes Down To/Highways of My Life	1973	—	2.50	5.00
❑ T-Neck 2253	Summer Breeze (Part 1)/Summer Breeze (Part 2)	1974	—	2.50	5.00
❑ T-Neck 2254	Live It Up (Part 1)/Live It Up (Part 2)	1974	—	2.50	5.00
❑ T-Neck 2255	Midnight Sky (Part 1)/Midnight Sky (Part 2)	1974	—	2.50	5.00
❑ T-Neck 2256	Fight the Power Part 1/Fight the Power Part 2	1975	—	2.50	5.00
❑ T-Neck 2259	For the Love of You (Part 1&2)/You Walk Your Way	1975	—	2.50	5.00
❑ T-Neck 2260	Who Loves You Better-Part 1/Who Loves You Better-Part 2	1976	—	2.50	5.00
❑ T-Neck 2261	Harvest for the World/Harvest for the World (Part 2)	1976	—	2.50	5.00
❑ T-Neck 2262	The Pride (Part 1)/The Pride (Part 2)	1977	—	2.50	5.00
❑ T-Neck 2264	Livin' in the Life/Go for Your Guns	1977	—	2.50	5.00
❑ T-Neck 2270	Voyage to Atlantis/Do You Wanna Stay Down	1977	—	2.50	5.00
❑ T-Neck 02270	Voyage to Atlantis/Do You Wanna Stay Down	1981	—	2.00	4.00
—Reissue					
❑ T-Neck 2272	Take Me to the Next Phase (Part 1)/ Take Me to the Next Phase (Part 2)	1978	—	2.50	5.00
❑ T-Neck 2277	Groove with You/Footsteps in the Dark	1978	—	2.50	5.00
❑ T-Neck 2278	Showdown (Part 1)/Showdown (Part 2)	1978	—	2.50	5.00
❑ T-Neck 2279	I Wanna Be with You (Part 1)/I Wanna Be with You (Part 2)	1979	—	2.50	5.00
❑ T-Neck 2284	Winner Takes All/Fun and Games	1979	—	2.50	5.00
❑ T-Neck 2287	It's a Disco Night (Rock Don't Stop)/Ain't Givin' Up on Love	1979	—	2.50	5.00
❑ T-Neck 2290	Don't Say Goodnight (It's Time for Love) (Part 1)/Don't Say Goodnight (It's Time for Love) (Part 2)	1980	—	2.50	5.00
❑ T-Neck 2291	Here We Go Again (Part 1)/Here We Go Again (Part 2)	1980	—	2.50	5.00
❑ T-Neck 2292	Say You Will (Part 1)/Say You Will (Part 2)	1980	—	2.50	5.00
❑ T-Neck 2293	Who Said?/(Can't You See) What You've Done to Me	1980	—	2.50	5.00
❑ T-Neck 02293	Who Said?/(Can't You See) What You Do to Me	1981	—	2.00	4.00
—Reissue					
❑ T-Neck 02531	Inside You (Part 1)/Inside You (Part 2)	1981	—	2.50	5.00
❑ T-Neck 02705	Party Night/Welcome Into My Night	1982	—	2.50	5.00
❑ T-Neck 02985	The Real Deal/(Instrumental)	1982	—	2.50	5.00
❑ T-Neck 03281	It's Alright with Me/(Instrumental)	1982	—	2.50	5.00
❑ T-Neck 03797	Between the Sheets/(Instrumental)	1983	—	2.50	5.00
❑ T-Neck 03994	Choosey Lover/(Instrumental)	1983	—	2.50	5.00
❑ T-Neck 04320	Let's Make Love Tonight/(Instrumental)	1984	—	2.50	5.00
❑ Tamla 54128	This Old Heart of Mine (Is Weak for You)/There's No Love Left	1966	3.75	7.50	15.00
❑ Tamla 54133	Take Some Time Out for Love/Who Could Ever Doubt My Love	1966	3.00	6.00	12.00
❑ Tamla 54135	I Guess I'll Always Love You/I Hear a Symphony	1966	3.00	6.00	12.00
❑ Tamla 54146	Got to Have You Back/Just Ain't Enough Love	1967	3.00	6.00	12.00
❑ Tamla 54154	One Too Many Heartaches/That's the Way Love Is	1967	3.00	6.00	12.00
❑ Tamla 54164	Take Me in Your Arms (Rock Me a Little While)/ Why When Love Is Gone	1968	3.00	6.00	12.00
❑ Tamla 54175	Behind a Painted Smile/All Because I Love You	1968	3.00	6.00	12.00
❑ Tamla 54182	Take Some Time Out for Love/Just Ain't Enough Love	1969	3.00	6.00	12.00
❑ Teenage 1004	Angels Cried/The Cow Jumped Over the Moon	1957	200.00	400.00	800.00
❑ United Artists 605	She's Gone/Tango	1963	5.00	10.00	20.00
❑ United Artists 638	Surf and Shout/Whatcha Gonna Do	1963	5.00	10.00	20.00
❑ United Artists 659	Please, Please, Please/You'll Never Leave Him	1963	5.00	10.00	20.00
❑ United Artists 714	Who's That Lady/My Little Girl	1964	5.00	10.00	20.00
❑ United Artists 798	Love Is a Wonderful Thing/Open Up Her Eyes	1964	—	—	—
—Unreleased					
❑ United Artists 923	Love Is a Wonderful Thing/Open Up Her Eyes	1965	—	—	—
—Unreleased					
❑ V.I.P. 25020	I Hear a Symphony/Who Could Ever Doubt My Love	1965	200.00	400.00	800.00
❑ Veep 1230	Love Is a Wonderful Thing/Open Up Her Eyes	1966	2.50	5.00	10.00
❑ Wand 118	Right Now/The Snake	1962	3.75	7.50	15.00
❑ Wand 124	Twist and Shout/Spanish Twist	1962	5.00	10.00	20.00
❑ Wand 127	Twistin' with Linda/You Better Come Home	1962	3.00	6.00	12.00
❑ Wand 131	Nobody But Me/I'm Laughing to Keep from Crying	1963	3.00	6.00	12.00
❑ Wand 137	I Say Love/Hold On Baby	1963	3.00	6.00	12.00
❑ Warner Bros. 22748	One of a Kind/You'll Never Walk Alone	1989	—	—	3.00
❑ Warner Bros. 22900	Spend the Night (Ce Soir)/(Instrumental)	1989	—	—	3.00
❑ Warner Bros. 27954	It Takes a Good Woman/(Instrumental)	1988	—	2.00	4.00
❑ Warner Bros. 28129	I Wish/(Instrumental)	1988	—	2.00	4.00

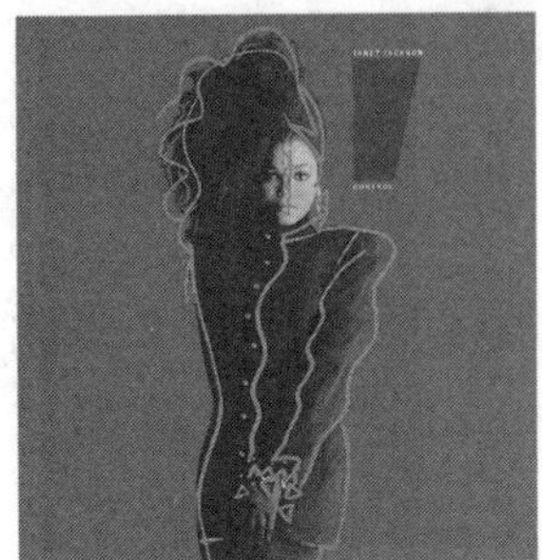

Number	Title (A Side/B Side)	Yr	VG	VG+	NM
❑ Warner Bros. 28241	Come My Way/(Instrumental)	1987	—	2.00	4.00
❑ Warner Bros. 28385	Smooth Sailin' Tonight/(Instrumental)	1987	—	2.00	4.00
❑ Warner Bros. 28764	May I?/(Instrumental)	1986	—	2.00	4.00
❑ Warner Bros. 28860	Colder Are My Nights/(Instrumental)	1985	—	2.00	4.00
Albums					
❑ Buddah BDS-5652 [(2)]	The Best of the Isley Brothers	1976	3.75	7.50	15.00
❑ Collectables COL-5103	Shout!	198?	2.50	5.00	10.00
❑ Def Soul B0004812-01 [(2)]	Baby Makin' Music	2006	3.75	7.50	15.00
❑ Motown M5-106V1	Motown Superstar Series, Volume 6	1981	2.00	4.00	8.00
❑ Motown M5-128V1	This Old Heart of Mine	1981	2.00	4.00	8.00
—Reissue of Tamla 269					
❑ Motown M5-143V1	Doin' Their Thing (Best of the Isley Brothers)	1981	2.00	4.00	8.00
—Reissue of Tamla 287					
❑ Pickwick SPC-3331	Soul Shout!	197?	2.50	5.00	10.00
❑ RCA Camden ACL1-0126	Rock On Brother	1973	3.00	6.00	12.00
❑ RCA Camden ACL1-0861	Rock Around the Clock	1975	3.00	6.00	12.00
❑ RCA Victor LPM-2156 [M]	Shout!	1959	30.00	60.00	120.00
—"Long Play" label					
❑ RCA Victor LSP-2156 [S]	Shout!	1959	50.00	100.00	200.00
—"Living Stereo" label					
❑ Scepter SC-552 [M]	Take Some Time Out for the Isley Brothers	1966	7.50	15.00	30.00
❑ Scepter SCS-552 [S]	Take Some Time Out for the Isley Brothers	1966	10.00	20.00	40.00
❑ Sunset SUS-5257	The Isley Brothers Do Their Thing	1969	3.75	7.50	15.00
❑ T-Neck TNS-3001	It's Our Thing	1969	5.00	10.00	20.00
❑ T-Neck TNS-3002	The Brothers: Isley	1969	5.00	10.00	20.00
❑ T-Neck TNS-3006	Get Into Something	1970	3.75	7.50	15.00
❑ T-Neck TNS-3007	In the Beginning (With Jimi Hendrix)	1970	5.00	10.00	20.00
❑ T-Neck TNS-3008	Givin' It Back	1971	3.75	7.50	15.00
❑ T-Neck TNS-3009	Brother, Brother, Brother	1972	3.75	7.50	15.00
❑ T-Neck TNS-3010 [(2)]	The Isleys Live	1973	5.00	10.00	20.00
❑ T-Neck TNS-3011	Isleys' Greatest Hits	1973	3.75	7.50	15.00
❑ T-Neck KZ 32453	3 + 3	1973	3.00	6.00	12.00
❑ T-Neck PZ 33070	Live It Up	1974	3.00	6.00	12.00
—No bar code on cover					
❑ T-Neck PZ 33536	The Heat Is On	1975	3.00	6.00	12.00
—No bar code on cover					
❑ T-Neck PZ 33809	Harvest for the World	1976	3.00	6.00	12.00
—No bar code on cover					
❑ T-Neck PZ 34432	Go for Your Guns	1977	3.00	6.00	12.00
—No bar code on cover					
❑ T-Neck PZ 34452	Forever Gold	1977	2.50	5.00	10.00
❑ T-Neck JZ 34930	Showdown	1978	2.50	5.00	10.00
❑ T-Neck KZ2 35650 [(2)]	Timeless	1978	3.00	6.00	12.00
❑ T-Neck FZ 36305	Go All the Way	1980	2.50	5.00	10.00
❑ T-Neck FZ 37080	Grand Slam	1981	2.50	5.00	10.00
❑ T-Neck FZ 37533	Inside You	1981	2.50	5.00	10.00
❑ T-Neck FZ 38047	The Real Deal	1982	2.50	5.00	10.00
❑ T-Neck FZ 38674	Between the Sheets	1983	2.50	5.00	10.00
❑ T-Neck FZ 39240	Greatest Hits, Vol. 1	1984	2.50	5.00	10.00
❑ Tamla T-269 [M]	This Old Heart of Mine	1966	6.25	12.50	25.00
❑ Tamla TS-269 [S]	This Old Heart of Mine	1966	7.50	15.00	30.00
❑ Tamla T-275 [M]	Soul on the Rocks	1967	6.25	12.50	25.00
❑ Tamla TS-275 [S]	Soul on the Rocks	1967	7.50	15.00	30.00
❑ Tamla TS-287	Doin' Their Thing (Best of the Isley Brothers)	1969	5.00	10.00	20.00
❑ United Artists UA-LA500-E	The Very Best of the Isley Brothers	1975	2.50	5.00	10.00
❑ United Artists UAL-3313 [M]	The Famous Isley Brothers	1963	12.50	25.00	50.00
❑ United Artists UAS-6313 [S]	The Famous Isley Brothers	1963	15.00	30.00	60.00
❑ Wand WD-653 [M]	Twist & Shout	1962	20.00	40.00	80.00
❑ Wand WDS-653 [S]	Twist & Shout	1962	25.00	50.00	100.00
❑ Warner Bros. 25347	Masterpiece	1985	2.50	5.00	10.00
❑ Warner Bros. 25586	Smooth Sailin'	1987	2.50	5.00	10.00
❑ Warner Bros. 25940	Spend the Night	1989	2.50	5.00	10.00

J

JACKS, TERRY

45s

Number	Title (A Side/B Side)	Yr	VG	VG+	NM
❑ Bell 45432	Seasons in the Sun/Put the Bone In	1974	—	2.50	5.00

Number	Title (A Side/B Side)	Yr	VG	VG+	NM
❑ Bell 45467	If You Go Away/Me and You	1974	—	2.00	4.00
❑ Bell 45606	Love Game/Rock and Roll	1974	—	2.00	4.00
❑ London 181	Concrete Sea/She Even Took the Cat	1972	—	2.50	5.00
❑ London 188	I'm Gonna Love You, Too/Something Good Was Over Before It Ever Got to Start	1972	—	2.50	5.00
❑ Parrot 347	A Good Thing Lost/I'm Gonna Capture You	1970	—	3.00	6.00
❑ Private Stock 45,023	Christina/The Feeling That We've Lost	1975	—	2.00	4.00
❑ Private Stock 45,094	In My Father's Footsteps/Until You're Down	1976	—	2.00	4.00
Albums					
❑ Bell 1307	Seasons in the Sun	1974	2.50	5.00	10.00

JACKSON, JANET

45s

Number	Title (A Side/B Side)	Yr	VG	VG+	NM
❑ A&M AM-1445	Miss You Much/You Need Me	1989	—	3.00	6.00
❑ A&M AM-1455	Rhythm Nation/(Instrumental)	1989	—	2.00	4.00
❑ A&M AM-1475	Come Back to Me/Vuelva A Mi	1990	—	3.00	6.00
—First pressing: Blue label, no bar code					
❑ A&M 75021 1477 7	Black Cat (Video Mix Short Solo)/(Guitar Mix Featuring Vernon Reid)	1990	—	2.50	5.00
—All copies have red labels					
❑ A&M AM-1479	Alright (7" R&B Mix)/(7" Remix)	1990	—	2.50	5.00
—First pressing: Blue label, no bar code					
❑ A&M AM-1490	Escapade/(Instrumental)	1990	—	2.00	4.00
—As this was issued before 1475, 1477, and 1479, it was issued before the "75021" numerical prefix was added to A&M 45s					
❑ A&M 75021 1538 7	Love Will Never Do (Without You)/Work It Out	1990	—	2.00	4.00
❑ A&M 2440	Young Love/The Magic Is Working	1982	—	2.50	5.00
❑ A&M 2522	Come Give Your Love to Me/Forever Yours	1983	—	2.50	5.00
❑ A&M 2537	Say You Do/Don't Mess Up a Good Thing	1983	—	—	—
—Canceled?					
❑ A&M 2545	Say You Do/You'll Never Find (A Love Like Mine)	1983	—	2.50	5.00
❑ A&M 2660	Don't Stand Another Chance/Rock 'N' Roll	1984	—	2.50	5.00
❑ A&M 2682	Dream Street/Love and My Best Friend	1984	—	3.00	6.00
❑ A&M 2693	Fast Girls/Love and My Best Friend	1984	—	2.50	5.00
❑ A&M 2812	What Have You Done for Me Lately/He Doesn't Know I'm Alive	1986	—	—	3.00
❑ A&M 2830	Nasty/You'll Never Find (A Love Like Mine)	1986	—	—	3.00
❑ A&M 2855	When I Think of You/Pretty Boy	1986	—	—	3.00
❑ A&M 2877	Control/Fast Girls	1986	—	—	3.00
❑ A&M 2906	Let's Wait Awhile/Pretty Boy	1987	—	—	3.00
❑ A&M 2927	The Pleasure Principle/Fast Girls	1987	—	—	3.00
Albums					
❑ A&M SP-3905	Control	1986	2.00	4.00	8.00
—Second issue; most have a black label					
❑ A&M SP-3920	Janet Jackson's Rhythm Nation 1814	1989	3.75	7.50	15.00
❑ A&M SP-6-4907	Janet Jackson	1982	3.00	6.00	12.00
❑ A&M SP-4962	Dream Street	1984	3.00	6.00	12.00
❑ A&M SP-5106	Control	1986	2.50	5.00	10.00
—Original issue; silver label with fading A&M logo					

JACKSON, JERMAINE

45s

Number	Title (A Side/B Side)	Yr	VG	VG+	NM
❑ Arista 2029	I'd Like to Get to Know You/Spare the Rod, Love the Child	1990	—	—	3.00
❑ Arista 9190	Dynamite/Tell Me I'm Not Dreaming (Too Good to Be True) (Instrumental)	1984	—	—	3.00
❑ Arista 9275	Take Good Care of My Heart/Tell Me I'm Not Dreaming (Too Good to Be True) (Instrumental)	1984	—	2.50	5.00
—A-side with Whitney Houston					
❑ Arista 9279	Do What You Do/Tell Me I'm Not Dreaming (Too Good to Be True)	1984	—	—	3.00
❑ Arista 9356	(Closest Thing to) Perfect/(Instrumental)	1985	—	—	3.00
❑ Arista 9444	I Think It's Love/Voices in the Dark	1985	—	—	3.00
❑ Arista 9495	Words Into Action/Our Love Story	1986	—	—	3.00
❑ Arista 9502	Do You Remember Me/Whatcha' Doin'	1986	—	—	3.00
❑ Arista 9788	Clean Up Your Act/I'm Gonna Git Ya Sucka	1988	—	—	3.00
—B-side by the Gap Band					
❑ Arista 9875	Don't Take It Personal/Clean Up Your Act	1989	—	—	3.00
❑ Arista 9933	Two Ships (In the Night)/Next to You	1990	—	—	3.00
❑ Motown 1201	That's How Love Goes/I Lost My Love in the Big City	1972	—	2.50	5.00
❑ Motown 1216	Daddy's Home/Take Me in Your Arms (Rock Me for a Little While)	1972	—	2.50	5.00
❑ Motown 1244	You're in Good Hands/Does Your Mama Know About Me	1973	—	2.50	5.00
❑ Motown 1386	She's the Ideal Girl/I'm So Glad You Chose Me	1976	—	—	—
—Unreleased					
❑ Motown 1401	Let's Be Young Tonight/Boss Odyssey	1976	—	2.50	5.00
❑ Motown 1409	You Need to Be Loved/My Touch of Madness	1977	—	2.50	5.00
❑ Motown 1441	Castles of Sand/I Love Every Little Thing About You	1978	—	2.50	5.00
❑ Motown 1469	Let's Get Serious/Je Vous Aime Beaucoups	1980	—	2.00	4.00
❑ Motown 1490	You're Supposed to Keep Your Love for Me/Let It Ride	1980	—	2.00	4.00
❑ Motown 1499	Little Girl Don't You Worry/We Can Put It Back Together	1980	—	2.00	4.00
❑ Motown 1503	You Like Me Don't You/(Instrumental)	1981	—	2.00	4.00
❑ Motown 1525	I'm Just Too Shy/All Because of You	1981	—	2.00	4.00
❑ Motown 1600	Paradise in Your Eyes/I'm My Brother's Keeper	1982	—	2.00	4.00
❑ Motown 1628	Let Me Tickle Your Fancy/Maybe Next Time	1982	—	2.00	4.00
—Devo is the backing group					
❑ Motown 1649	Very Special Part/You're Givin' Me the Runaround	1982	—	2.00	4.00
Albums					
❑ Arista AL8-8203	Jermaine Jackson	1984	2.50	5.00	10.00
❑ Arista AL8-8277	Precious Moments	1986	2.50	5.00	10.00
❑ Arista AL-8421	Jermaine Jackson	1986	2.00	4.00	8.00
—Budget-line reissue					

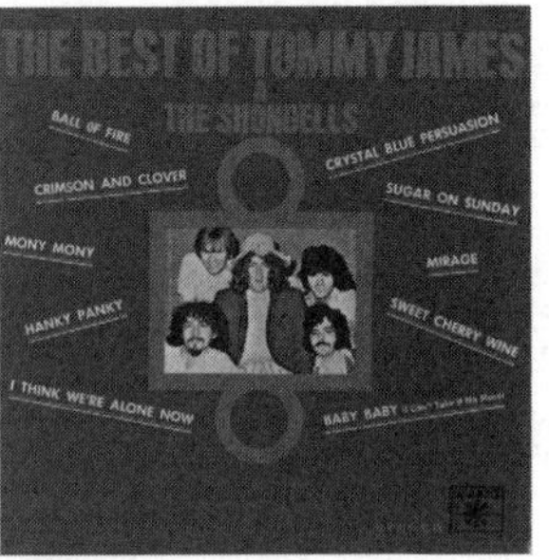

Number	Title (A Side/B Side)	Yr	VG	VG+	NM
❑ Arista AL-8493	Don't Take It Personal	1989	2.50	5.00	10.00
❑ Motown M5-117V1	Motown Superstar Series, Vol. 17	1981	2.50	5.00	10.00
❑ Motown M-752L	Jermaine	1972	2.50	5.00	10.00
❑ Motown M-775L	Come Into My Life	1973	2.50	5.00	10.00
❑ Motown M6-842S1	My Name Is Jermaine	1976	2.50	5.00	10.00
❑ Motown M6-888S1	Feel the Fire	1977	2.50	5.00	10.00
❑ Motown M7-898R1	Frontiers	1978	2.50	5.00	10.00
❑ Motown M7-928R1	Let's Get Serious	1980	2.50	5.00	10.00
❑ Motown M8-948M1	Jermaine	1980	2.50	5.00	10.00
❑ Motown M8-952M1	I Like Your Style	1981	2.50	5.00	10.00
❑ Motown 6017 ML	Let Me Tickle Your Fancy	1982	2.50	5.00	10.00

JACKSON, JOE

45s

Number	Title (A Side/B Side)	Yr	VG	VG+	NM
❑ A&M 1207	Look Sharp (Live)/Memphis (Live)	1988	—	2.50	5.00
❑ A&M 1228	(He's a) Shape in a Drape/Speedway	1988	—	2.00	4.00
❑ A&M 1404	Nineteen Forever/Acropolis Now	1989	—	2.50	5.00
❑ A&M 2132	Is She Really Going Out with Him?/(Do the) Instant Mash	1979	—	2.00	4.00
❑ A&M 2186	It's Different for Girls/Come On	1979	—	2.50	5.00
❑ A&M 2209	I'm the Man/Come On	1979	—	2.50	5.00
❑ A&M 2276	One to One/Enough Is Not Enough	1980	—	2.50	5.00
❑ A&M 2365	Jumpin' Jive/Knock Me a Kiss	1981	2.00	4.00	8.00
❑ A&M 2428	Steppin' Out/Chinatown	1982	—	—	3.00
❑ A&M 2510	Breaking Us in Two/Target	1982	—	—	3.00
❑ A&M 2548	Another World/Otro Mundo	1983	—	2.50	5.00
❑ A&M 2601	Memphis/Breakdown	1983	—	2.00	4.00
❑ A&M 2628	You Can't Get What You Want (Till You Know What You Want)/Cha Cha Loco	1984	—	—	3.00
❑ A&M 2635	Happy Ending/Loisaida	1984	—	2.00	4.00
❑ A&M 2673	Be My Number Two/Heart of Ice	1984	—	2.50	5.00
❑ A&M 2829	Right and Wrong/Breaking Us in Two (Live)	1986	—	2.00	4.00
❑ A&M 2847	Home Town/I'm the Man (Live)	1986	—	2.50	5.00
❑ A&M 2944	Nocturne/Will Power	1987	—	2.50	5.00

Albums

Number	Title (A Side/B Side)	Yr	VG	VG+	NM
❑ A&M SP-3187	Look Sharp!	198?	2.00	4.00	8.00
—Reissue of SP-4743					
❑ A&M SP-3221	I'm the Man	198?	2.00	4.00	8.00
—Reissue of SP-4794					
❑ A&M SP-3241	Beat Crazy	198?	2.00	4.00	8.00
—Reissue of SP-4837					
❑ A&M SP-3271	Joe Jackson's Jumpin' Jive	198?	2.00	4.00	8.00
—Reissue of SP-4871					
❑ A&M SP-3286	Body and Soul	1986	2.00	4.00	8.00
—Reissue of SP-5000					
❑ A&M SP-3666 [(2)]	Look Sharp!	1979	5.00	10.00	20.00
—Two 10-inch records in gatefold sleeve with button					
❑ A&M SP-3908	Will Power	1987	3.00	6.00	12.00
❑ A&M SP-4743	Look Sharp!	1979	3.00	6.00	12.00
❑ A&M SP-4794	I'm the Man	1979	2.50	5.00	10.00
❑ A&M SP-4837	Beat Crazy	1980	2.50	5.00	10.00
❑ A&M SP-4871	Joe Jackson's Jumpin' Jive	1981	2.50	5.00	10.00
❑ A&M SP-4906	Night and Day	1982	2.50	5.00	10.00
❑ A&M SP-4931	Mike's Murder [Soundtrack]	1983	3.00	6.00	12.00
❑ A&M SP-5000	Body and Soul	1984	2.50	5.00	10.00
❑ A&M SP-5249	Blaze of Glory	1989	2.50	5.00	10.00
❑ A&M SP-6021 [(2)]	Big World	1986	3.75	7.50	15.00
❑ A&M SP-6706 [(2)]	Live: 1980-1986	1988	3.75	7.50	15.00

JACKSON, MICHAEL

45s

Number	Title (A Side/B Side)	Yr	VG	VG+	NM
❑ Epic 15-02156	Rock with You/Off the Wall	1981	—	—	3.00
—"Memory Lane" reissue					
❑ Epic 15-02157	She's Out of My Life/Lovely One	1981	—	—	3.00
—"Memory Lane" reissue; B-side by The Jacksons					
❑ Epic 34-03509	Billie Jean/Can't Get Outta the Rain	1983	—	2.00	4.00
❑ Epic ENR-03575	Billie Jean/(B-side blank)	1983	3.75	7.50	15.00
—One-sided budget release					

Number	Title (A Side/B Side)	Yr	VG	VG+	NM
❑ Epic 34-03759	Beat It/Get On the Floor	1983	—	2.00	4.00
❑ Epic 34-03914	Wanna Be Startin' Somethin'/(Instrumental)	1983	—	2.00	4.00
❑ Epic 34-04026	Human Nature/Baby Be Mine	1983	—	2.00	4.00
❑ Epic 34-04165	P.Y.T. (Pretty Young Thing)/Working Day and Night	1983	—	2.00	4.00
❑ Epic 34-04364	Thriller/Can't Get Outta the Rain	1984	—	2.00	4.00
❑ Epic 34-07253	I Just Can't Stop Loving You/Baby Be Mine	1987	—	—	3.00
❑ Epic 34-07418	Bad/I Can't Help It	1987	—	—	3.00
❑ Epic 34-07645	The Way You Make Me Feel/(Instrumental)	1987	—	—	3.00
❑ Epic 34-07668	Man in the Mirror/(Instrumental)	1988	—	—	3.00
❑ Epic 34-07739	Dirty Diana/(Instrumental)	1988	—	—	3.00
❑ Epic 34-07962	Another Part of Me/(Instrumental)	1988	—	—	3.00
❑ Epic 34-08044	Smooth Criminal/(Instrumental)	1988	—	—	3.00
❑ Epic 8-50654	You Can't Win (Part 1)/You Can't Win (Part 2)	1979	—	3.00	6.00
❑ Epic 9-50742	Don't Stop 'Til You Get Enough/I Can't Help It	1979	—	2.00	4.00
❑ Epic 9-50797	Rock with You/Working Day and Night	1979	—	2.00	4.00
❑ Epic 9-50838	Off the Wall/Get On the Floor	1980	—	2.00	4.00
❑ Epic 9-50871	She's Out of My Life/Get On the Floor	1980	—	2.00	4.00
❑ MCA 40947	Ease On Down the Road/Poppy Girls	1978	—	2.50	5.00
—With Diana Ross					
❑ Motown 1191	Got to Be There/Maria (You Were the Only One)	1971	—	2.50	5.00
❑ Motown 1197	Rockin' Robin/Love Is Here and Now You're Gone	1972	—	2.50	5.00
❑ Motown 1202	I Wanna Be Where You Are/We Got a Good Thing Going	1972	—	2.50	5.00
❑ Motown 1207	Ben/You Can Cry on My Shoulder	1972	—	2.50	5.00
❑ Motown 1218	With a Child's Heart/Morning Glow	1973	—	2.50	5.00
❑ Motown 1270	Doggin' Around/Up Again	1974	—	—	—
—Unreleased					
❑ Motown 1341	We're Almost There/Take Me Back	1975	—	2.50	5.00
❑ Motown 1349	Just a Little Bit of You/Dear Michael	1975	—	2.50	5.00
❑ Motown 1512	One Day in Your Life/Take Me Back	1981	—	2.00	4.00
❑ Motown 1739	Farewell My Summer Love/Call On Me	1984	—	2.00	4.00
❑ Motown 1757	Girl You're So Together/Touch the One You Love	1984	—	2.00	4.00
❑ Motown 1914	Twenty-Five Miles/Up on the House Top	1987	2.00	4.00	8.00

Albums

Number	Title	Yr	VG	VG+	NM
❑ Epic FE 35745	Off the Wall	1979	2.00	4.00	8.00
❑ Epic QE 38112	Thriller	1982	2.00	4.00	8.00
❑ Epic OE 40600	Bad	1987	2.00	4.00	8.00
❑ Motown M5-107V1	Motown Superstar Series, Vol. 7	1981	2.00	4.00	8.00
❑ Motown M5-130V1	Got to Be There	1981	2.50	5.00	10.00
—Reissue of Motown 747					
❑ Motown M5-153V1	Ben	1981	2.50	5.00	10.00
—Reissue of Motown 755					
❑ Motown M5-194V1	The Best of Michael Jackson	1981	2.50	5.00	10.00
—Reissue of Motown 851					
❑ Motown M 747	Got to Be There	1972	3.75	7.50	15.00
❑ Motown M 755	Ben	1972	15.00	30.00	60.00
—With Michael Jackson on top half of cover, rats on the bottom half					
❑ Motown M 755	Ben	1972	3.75	7.50	15.00
—With only Michael Jackson on front cover					
❑ Motown M 767	Music and Me	1973	3.75	7.50	15.00
❑ Motown M6-825S	Forever, Michael	1975	3.00	6.00	12.00
❑ Motown M6-851S	The Best of Michael Jackson	1975	3.00	6.00	12.00
❑ Motown M8-956M1	One Day in Your Life	1981	2.50	5.00	10.00
❑ Motown 6099 ML	Michael Jackson and The Jackson 5 — 14 Greatest Hits	1984	2.50	5.00	10.00
—Picture disc packaged with one glove					
❑ Motown 6101 ML	Farewell My Summer Love 1984	1984	2.50	5.00	10.00

JACKSON, MICHAEL, AND PAUL MCCARTNEY

45s

Number	Title	Yr	VG	VG+	NM
❑ Columbia 38-04168	Say, Say, Say/Ode to a Koala Bear	1983	—	2.00	4.00
—As "Paul McCartney and Michael Jackson"; B-side by Paul McCartney					
❑ Epic 34-03288	The Girl Is Mine/Can't Get Outta the Rain	1982	—	2.50	5.00
—B-side by Michael Jackson					
❑ Epic ENR-03372	The Girl Is Mine/(B-side blank)	1982	3.00	6.00	12.00
—One-sided budget release					

JACKSONS, THE

45s

Number	Title	Yr	VG	VG+	NM
❑ Dynamo 146	You Don't Have to Be Over Twenty-One to Fall in Love/Some Girls Want Me for Their Love	1971	10.00	20.00	40.00
❑ Epic 19-01032	Can You Feel It/Everybody	1981	—	2.00	4.00
❑ Epic 19-02132	Walk Right Now/Your Ways	1981	—	2.00	4.00
❑ Epic 15-02157	Lovely One/She's Out of My Life	1981	—	—	3.00
—Reissue; B-side by Michael Jackson					
❑ Epic 14-02720	The Things I Do for You/Working Day and Night	1982	—	2.00	4.00
❑ Epic 34-04503	State of Shock/Your Ways	1984	—	2.00	4.00
—A-side with Mick Jagger					
❑ Epic 34-04575	Torture/(Instrumental)	1984	—	2.00	4.00
❑ Epic 34-04673	Body/(Instrumental)	1984	—	2.00	4.00
❑ Epic 8-50595	Blame It on the Boogie/Do What You Wanna	1978	—	2.00	4.00
❑ Epic 8-50656	Shake Your Body (Down to the Ground)/ That's What You Get (For Being Polite)	1979	—	2.50	5.00
—Original issue has orange label					
❑ Epic 9-50938	Lovely One/Bless His Soul	1980	—	2.00	4.00
❑ Epic 19-50959	Heartbreak Hotel/The Things I Do for You	1980	—	2.00	4.00
❑ Epic 34-68688	Nothin' (That Compares 2 U)/Alright with Me	1989	—	—	3.00
❑ Epic 34-69022	2300 Jackson Street/When I Look at You	1989	—	—	3.00
❑ Epic/Philadelphia Int'l. 8-50289	Enjoy Yourself/Style of Life	1976	—	2.50	5.00

Number	Title (A Side/B Side)	Yr	VG	VG+	NM
❑ Epic/Philadelphia Int'l. 8-50350	Show You the Way to Go/Blues Away	1977	—	2.50	5.00
❑ Epic/Philadelphia Int'l. 8-50454	Goin' Places/Do What You Wanna	1977	—	2.50	5.00
❑ Epic/Philadelphia Int'l. 8-50496	Find Me a Girl/Different Kind of Lady	1977	—	2.50	5.00
❑ MCA 53032	Time Out for the Burglar/News at Eleven	1987	—	—	3.00
—B-side by the Distants					
❑ Motown 1157	I Want You Back/Who's Lovin' You	1969	2.00	4.00	8.00
❑ Motown 1163	ABC/The Young Folks	1970	2.00	4.00	8.00
❑ Motown 1166	The Love You Save/I Found That Girl	1970	2.00	4.00	8.00
❑ Motown 1171	I'll Be There/One More Chance	1970	2.00	4.00	8.00
❑ Motown 1174	Santa Claus Is Coming to Town/ Christmas Won't Be the Same This Year	1970	3.00	6.00	12.00
❑ Motown 1177	Mama's Pearl/Darling Dear	1971	—	3.00	6.00
❑ Motown 1179	Never Can Say Goodbye/She's Good	1971	—	3.00	6.00
❑ Motown 1186	Maybe Tomorrow/I Will Find a Way	1971	—	3.00	6.00
❑ Motown 1194	Sugar Daddy/I'm So Happy	1971	—	3.00	6.00
❑ Motown 1199	Little Bitty Pretty One/If I Had to Move a Mountain	1972	—	3.00	6.00
❑ Motown 1205	Looking Through the Windows/Love Song	1972	—	3.00	6.00
❑ Motown 1214	Corner of the Sky/To Know	1972	—	3.00	6.00
❑ Motown 1224	Hallelujah Day/You Made Me What I Am	1973	—	3.00	6.00
❑ Motown 1230	Boogie Man/Don't Let Your Baby Catch You	1973	—	—	—
—Unreleased					
❑ Motown 1277	Get It Together/Touch	1973	—	3.00	6.00
❑ Motown 1286	Dancing Machine/It's Too Late to Change the Time	1974	—	3.00	6.00
❑ Motown 1308	Whatever You Got, I Want/I Can't Quit Your Love	1974	—	3.00	6.00
❑ Motown 1310	I Am Love (Parts 1 & 2)/I Am Love (Part 2)	1975	—	3.00	6.00
❑ Motown 1310	I Am Love (Part 1)/I Am Love (Part 2)	1975	2.00	4.00	8.00
❑ Motown 1356	Forever Came Today/All I Do Is Think of You	1975	—	3.00	6.00
❑ Motown 1365	Body Language/Call of the Wild	1975	—	—	—
—Unreleased					
❑ Steeltown 681	Big Boy/You've Changed	1968	25.00	50.00	100.00
❑ Steeltown 684	You Don't Have to Be Over Twenty-One to Fall in Love/Some Girls Want Me for Their Love	1968	25.00	50.00	100.00

Albums

Number	Title	Yr	VG	VG+	NM
❑ Epic PE 34229	The Jacksons	1976	2.50	5.00	10.00
—Orange label					
❑ Epic JE 34835	Goin' Places	1977	2.50	5.00	10.00
—Orange label					
❑ Epic JE 35552	Destiny	1978	2.50	5.00	10.00
—Orange label					
❑ Epic FE 36424	Triumph	1980	2.00	4.00	8.00
❑ Epic KE2 37545 [(2)]	Jacksons Live	1981	3.00	6.00	12.00
❑ Epic QE 38946	Victory	1984	2.00	4.00	8.00
❑ Epic OE 40911	2300 Jackson Street	1989	2.00	4.00	8.00
❑ Motown M5-112V1	Motown Superstar Series, Vol. 12	1981	2.50	5.00	10.00
❑ Motown M5-129V1	Diana Ross Presents the Jackson Five	1981	2.00	4.00	8.00
❑ Motown M5-152V1	ABC	1981	2.00	4.00	8.00
❑ Motown M5-157V1	Third Album	1981	2.00	4.00	8.00
❑ Motown M5-201V1	Jackson 5 Greatest Hits	1981	2.00	4.00	8.00
❑ Motown MS 700	Diana Ross Presents the Jackson 5	1969	6.25	12.50	25.00
❑ Motown MS 709	ABC	1970	6.25	12.50	25.00
❑ Motown MS 713	Christmas Album	1970	6.25	12.50	25.00
❑ Motown MS 718	Third Album	1970	3.75	7.50	15.00
❑ Motown M-735	Maybe Tomorrow	1971	3.75	7.50	15.00
❑ Motown M-741	Jackson 5 Greatest Hits	1971	3.75	7.50	15.00
❑ Motown M-742	Goin' Back to Indiana	1971	3.75	7.50	15.00
❑ Motown M-750	Lookin' Through the Windows	1972	3.75	7.50	15.00
❑ Motown M-761	Skywriter	1973	3.00	6.00	12.00
❑ Motown M6-780	Dancing Machine	1974	3.00	6.00	12.00
❑ Motown M6-783	Get It Together	1973	3.00	6.00	12.00
❑ Motown M6-829	Moving Violation	1975	3.00	6.00	12.00
❑ Motown M6-865	Joyful Jukebox Music	1976	3.00	6.00	12.00
❑ Motown M7-868 [(3)]	Anthology	1976	5.00	10.00	20.00
❑ Motown 5228 ML	Maybe Tomorrow	1982	2.00	4.00	8.00

Number	Title (A Side/B Side)	Yr	VG	VG+	NM
❑ Motown 5250 ML	Christmas Album	1982	2.00	4.00	8.00
—Reissue of Motown 713					

JAGGERZ, THE

45s

Number	Title (A Side/B Side)	Yr	VG	VG+	NM
❑ Gamble 218	(That's Why) Baby I Love You/Bring It Back	1968	2.00	4.00	8.00
❑ Gamble 226	Gotta Find My Way Back Home/ Forever Together, Together Forever	1968	2.00	4.00	8.00
❑ Gamble 238	Together/Let Me Be the One	1969	2.00	4.00	8.00
❑ Gamble 4008	Higher and Higher/Ain't No Sun	1970	2.00	4.00	8.00
❑ Gamble 4012	Need Your Love/Here's a Heart	1970	2.00	4.00	8.00
❑ Kama Sutra 502	The Rapper/Born Poor	1970	2.00	4.00	8.00
❑ Kama Sutra 509	I Call My Baby Candy/Will She Believe Me	1970	—	3.00	6.00
❑ Kama Sutra 513	What a Bummer/Memories of the Traveller	1970	—	3.00	6.00
❑ Kama Sutra 517	Let's Talk About Love/I'll Never Forget You	1971	—	2.50	5.00
❑ Kama Sutra 583	Let's Talk About Love/Ain't That Sad	1973	—	2.00	4.00
❑ Wooden Nickel PB-10194	Don't It Make You Want to Dance/2 Plus 2	1975	—	2.00	4.00

Albums

Number	Title (A Side/B Side)	Yr	VG	VG+	NM
❑ Gamble GS-5006	Introducing the Jaggerz	1969	5.00	10.00	20.00
❑ Kama Sutra KSBS-2017	We Went to Different Schools Together	1970	3.75	7.50	15.00
❑ Wooden Nickel BWL1-0772	Come Again	1975	3.00	6.00	12.00

JAMES, RICK

45s

Number	Title (A Side/B Side)	Yr	VG	VG+	NM
❑ A&M 1615	Funkin' Around/My Mama	1974	6.25	12.50	25.00
❑ Gordy 1619	Dance Wit' Me — Part 1/Dance Wit' Me — Part 2	1982	—	2.00	4.00
❑ Gordy 1634	Hard to Get/My Love	1982	—	2.00	4.00
❑ Gordy 1646	She Blew My Mind (69 Times)/(B-side unknown)	1982	—	2.00	4.00
❑ Gordy 1658	Teardrops/Throwdown	1983	—	2.00	4.00
❑ Gordy 1687	Cold Blooded/(Instrumental)	1983	—	2.00	4.00
❑ Gordy 1703	U Bring the Freak Out/He Talks	1983	—	2.00	4.00
❑ Gordy 1714	Ebony Eyes/1,2,3	1983	—	2.00	4.00
—As "Rick James and Smokey Robinson"					
❑ Gordy 1714	Ebony Eyes/1,2,3	1983	—	2.50	5.00
—As "Rick James and Friend"					
❑ Gordy 1730	17/(Instrumental)	1984	—	2.00	4.00
❑ Gordy 1763	You Turn Me On/Fire and Desire	1984	—	2.00	4.00
❑ Gordy 1776	Can't Stop/Oh What a Night	1985	—	2.00	4.00
❑ Gordy 1796	Glow/(Instrumental)	1985	—	2.00	4.00
❑ Gordy 1806	Spend the Night with Me/(Instrumental)	1985	—	2.00	4.00
❑ Gordy 1844	Sweet and Sexy Thing/(Instrumental)	1986	—	—	3.00
❑ Gordy 1862	Forever and a Day/(Instrumental)	1986	—	—	3.00
❑ Gordy 7156	You & I/Hollywood	1978	—	2.50	5.00
❑ Gordy 7162	Mary Jane/Dream Maker	1978	—	2.50	5.00
❑ Gordy 7164	High on Your Love Suite/Stone City Band High	1979	—	2.50	5.00
❑ Gordy 7167	Bustin' Out/Sexy Lady	1979	—	2.50	5.00
❑ Gordy 7171	Fool on the Street/Jefferson Hall	1979	—	2.50	5.00
❑ Gordy 7176	Love Gun/Stormy Love	1979	—	2.50	5.00
❑ Gordy 7177	Come Into My Life (Part 1)/Come Into My Life (Part 2)	1980	—	2.50	5.00
❑ Gordy 7185	Big Time/Island Lady	1980	—	2.50	5.00
❑ Gordy 7191	Gettin' it On (In the Summertime)/Summer Love	1980	—	2.50	5.00
❑ Gordy 7197	Give It to Me Baby/Don't Give Up on Love	1981	—	2.00	4.00
❑ Gordy 7205	Super Freak (Part 1)/Super Freak (Part 2)	1981	—	2.00	4.00
❑ Gordy 7215	Ghetto Life/Below the Funk (Pass the J)	1981	—	2.00	4.00
❑ Reprise 27764	Sexual Love Affair/In the Girls' Room	1988	—	—	3.00
❑ Reprise 27828	Wonderful/(Instrumental)	1988	—	—	3.00
❑ Reprise 27885	Loosey's Rap/(Instrumental)	1988	—	—	3.00
—With Roxanne Shante					
❑ Warner Bros. 27763	This Magic Moment-Dance with Me/(Instrumental)	1989	—	—	3.00

Albums

Number	Title (A Side/B Side)	Yr	VG	VG+	NM
❑ Gordy G7-981	Come Get It!	1978	2.50	5.00	10.00
❑ Gordy G7-984	Bustin' Out of L. Seven	1979	2.50	5.00	10.00
❑ Gordy G8-990	Fire It Up	1979	2.50	5.00	10.00
❑ Gordy G8-995	Garden of Love	1980	2.50	5.00	10.00
❑ Gordy G8-1002	Street Songs	1981	2.00	4.00	8.00
❑ Gordy 6005 GL	Throwin' Down	1982	2.00	4.00	8.00
❑ Gordy 6043 GL	Cold Blooded	1983	2.00	4.00	8.00
❑ Gordy 6095 GL	Reflections	1984	2.00	4.00	8.00
❑ Gordy 6135 GL	Glow	1985	2.00	4.00	8.00
❑ Motown 5263 ML	Come Get It!	198?	2.00	4.00	8.00
❑ Motown 5382 ML	Greatest Hits	1986	2.00	4.00	8.00
❑ Motown MOT-5405	Street Songs	1987	—	3.00	6.00
❑ Reprise 25659	Wonderful	1988	2.50	5.00	10.00

JAMES, TOMMY

45s

Number	Title (A Side/B Side)	Yr	VG	VG+	NM
❑ Fantasy 761	I Love You Love Me Love/Devil Gate Drive	1976	—	2.00	4.00
❑ Fantasy 776	Tighter, Tighter/Comin' Down	1976	—	2.50	5.00
❑ Fantasy 811	Love Is Gonna Find a Way/I Don't Love You Anymore	1977	—	2.50	5.00
❑ Fantasy 886	Tighter, Tighter/Comin' Down	1980	—	2.00	4.00
❑ MCA 40289	Glory, Glory/Comin' Down	1974	—	2.50	5.00
❑ Millennium YB-11785	Three Times in Love/I Just Wanna Play the Music	1980	—	2.00	4.00
❑ Millennium YB-11787	No Hay Dos Sin Tres (Three Times in Love)/ I Just Wanna Play the Music	1980	—	2.50	5.00
❑ Millennium YB-11788	It's Alright (For Now)/You Got Me	1980	—	2.00	4.00
❑ Millennium YB-11802	You're So Easy to Love/Halfway to Heaven	1981	—	2.00	4.00
❑ Millennium YB-11814	The Lady in White/Payin' for My Lover's Mistake	1981	—	2.00	4.00

Number	Title (A Side/B Side)	Yr	VG	VG+	NM
❑ Roulette 7084	Ball and Chain/Candy Maker	1970	—	3.00	6.00
❑ Roulette 7093	Church Street Soul Revival/Draggin' the Line	1970	2.00	4.00	8.00
❑ Roulette 7100	Adrienne/Light of Day	1971	—	3.00	6.00
❑ Roulette 7103	Draggin' the Line/Bits & Pieces	1971	—	3.00	6.00
❑ Roulette 7110	I'm Coming Home/Sing, Sing, Sing	1971	—	2.50	5.00
❑ Roulette 7114	Nothing to Hide/Walk a Country Mile	1971	—	2.50	5.00
❑ Roulette 7119	Tell 'Em Willie Boy's A-Comin'/Forty Days and Dorty Nights	1972	—	2.50	5.00
❑ Roulette 7126	Cat's Eye in the Window/Dark Is the Night	1972	—	2.50	5.00
❑ Roulette 7130	Love Song/Kingston Highway	1972	—	2.50	5.00
❑ Roulette 7135	Celebration/The Last One to Know	1972	—	2.50	5.00
❑ Roulette 7140	Boo, Boo, Don't Cha Be Blue/Rings and Things	1973	—	2.50	5.00
❑ Roulette 7147	Calico/Hey, My Lady	1973	—	2.50	5.00
❑ 21 Records 105	Two-Time Lover/Say Please	1983	—	—	3.00

Albums

Number	Title (A Side/B Side)	Yr	VG	VG+	NM
❑ Fantasy 9509	In Touch	1976	3.00	6.00	12.00
❑ Fantasy 9532	Midnight Rider	1977	3.00	6.00	12.00
❑ Millennium BXL1-7748	Three Times in Love	1980	2.50	5.00	10.00
❑ Millennium BXL1-7758	Easy to Love	1981	2.50	5.00	10.00
❑ Roulette SR-3001	Christian of the World	1971	3.75	7.50	15.00
❑ Roulette SR-3007	My Head, My Bed, My Red Guitar	1972	3.75	7.50	15.00
❑ Roulette SR-42061	Tommy James	1970	3.75	7.50	15.00

JAMES, TOMMY, AND THE SHONDELLS

45s

Number	Title (A Side/B Side)	Yr	VG	VG+	NM
❑ Red Fox 110	Hanky Panky/Thunderbolt	1966	10.00	20.00	40.00
—As "The Shondells"					
❑ Roulette 4686	Hanky Panky/Thunderbolt	1966	2.50	5.00	10.00
❑ Roulette 4695	Say I Am (What I Am)/Lots of Pretty Girls	1966	2.00	4.00	8.00
❑ Roulette 4710	It's Only Love/Ya Ya	1966	3.00	6.00	12.00
❑ Roulette 4710	It's Only Love/Don't Let My Love Pass You By	1966	2.00	4.00	8.00
❑ Roulette 4720	I Think We're Alone Now/Gone, Gone, Gone	1967	2.50	5.00	10.00
❑ Roulette 4736	Mirage/Run, Run, Baby, Run	1967	2.00	4.00	8.00
❑ Roulette 4756	I Like the Way/(Baby) Baby I Can't Take It No More	1967	2.00	4.00	8.00
❑ Roulette 4762	Gettin' Together/Real Girl	1967	2.00	4.00	8.00
❑ Roulette 4775	Out of the Blue/Love's Closin' In on Me	1967	2.00	4.00	8.00
❑ Roulette 7000	Get Out Now/Wish It Were True	1968	2.00	4.00	8.00
❑ Roulette 7008	Mony Mony/One Two Three and I Fell	1968	2.50	5.00	10.00
❑ Roulette 7016	Somebody Cares/Do Unto Me	1968	2.00	4.00	8.00
❑ Roulette 7024	Do Something to Me/Ginger Bread Man	1968	2.00	4.00	8.00
❑ Roulette 7028	Crimson and Clover/(I'm) Taken	1968	3.75	7.50	15.00
❑ Roulette 7028	Crimson and Clover/Some Kind of Love	1968	2.50	5.00	10.00
❑ Roulette 7039	Sweet Cherry Wine/Breakaway	1969	2.00	4.00	8.00
❑ Roulette 7050	Crystal Blue Persuasion/I'm Alive	1969	2.50	5.00	10.00
❑ Roulette 7060	Ball of Fire/Makin' Good Time	1969	2.00	4.00	8.00
❑ Roulette 7066	She/Loved One	1969	2.00	4.00	8.00
❑ Roulette 7071	Gotta Get Back to You/Red Rover	1970	2.00	4.00	8.00
❑ Roulette 7076	Come to Me/Talkin' and Signifyin'	1970	2.00	4.00	8.00
❑ Snap 102	Hanky-Panky/Thunderbolt	1964	37.50	75.00	150.00
—As "The Shondells"; A-side title is hyphenated, which is true only on the 1964 pressings					
❑ Snap 102	Hanky Panky/Thunderbolt	1966	5.00	10.00	20.00
—As "The Shondells"; with "Dist. by Red Fox Records, Pgh, Pa." on label					
❑ Snap 102	Hanky Panky/Thunderbolt	1966	10.00	20.00	40.00
—As "The Shondells"; with A-side title NOT hyphenated; no mention of Red Fox on the label					

Albums

Number	Title (A Side/B Side)	Yr	VG	VG+	NM
❑ Rhino R1-70920 [(2)]	Anthology	1989	3.75	7.50	15.00
❑ Roulette R 25336 [M]	Hanky Panky	1966	5.00	10.00	20.00
❑ Roulette SR 25336 [P]	Hanky Panky	1966	6.25	12.50	25.00
—"Hanky Panky" is rechanneled					
❑ Roulette R 25344 [M]	It's Only Love	1967	7.50	15.00	30.00
❑ Roulette SR 25344 [S]	It's Only Love	1967	6.25	12.50	25.00
❑ Roulette R 25353 [M]	I Think We're Alone Now	1967	7.50	15.00	30.00
❑ Roulette SR 25353 [P]	I Think We're Alone Now	1967	6.25	12.50	25.00
—Footprints cover; "I Think We're Alone Now" is rechanneled					
❑ Roulette R 25355 [M]	Something Special! The Best of Tommy James & The Shondells	1968	12.50	25.00	50.00
❑ Roulette SR 25355 [S]	Something Special! The Best of Tommy James & The Shondells	1968	6.25	12.50	25.00
❑ Roulette R 25357 [M]	Gettin' Together	1968	10.00	20.00	40.00
❑ Roulette SR 25357 [S]	Gettin' Together	1968	6.25	12.50	25.00

Number	Title (A Side/B Side)	Yr	VG	VG+	NM
❑ Roulette SR 42005	Something Special! The Best of Tommy James & The Shondells	1968	3.75	7.50	15.00
❑ Roulette SR 42012	Mony Mony	1968	5.00	10.00	20.00
❑ Roulette SR 42023	Crimson and Clover	1969	5.00	10.00	20.00
❑ Roulette SR 42030	Cellophane Symphony	1969	5.00	10.00	20.00
❑ Roulette SR 42040	The Best of Tommy James & The Shondells	1969	5.00	10.00	20.00
—Original versions are in a Unipak (gatefold must be opened to remove record)					
❑ Roulette SR 42040	The Best of Tommy James & The Shondells	197?	3.75	7.50	15.00
—Later versions have gatefold covers, but record can be removed without opening it					
❑ Roulette SR 42044	Travelin'	1970	3.75	7.50	15.00
❑ Scepter Citation CTN-18025	The Best of Tommy James and the Shondells	1973	2.50	5.00	10.00

JAN AND ARNIE

45s

Number	Title (A Side/B Side)	Yr	VG	VG+	NM
❑ Arwin 108	Jennie Lee/Gotta Getta Date	1958	10.00	20.00	40.00
❑ Arwin 111	Gas Money/Bonnie Lou	1958	10.00	20.00	40.00
❑ Arwin 113	I Love Linda/The Beat That Can't Be Beat	1958	15.00	30.00	60.00
❑ Dore 522	Baby Talk/Jeannette Get Your Hair Done	1959	150.00	300.00	600.00
—Actually by Jan and Dean, but incorrectly credited					
❑ Dot 16116	Gas Money/Gotta Getta Date	1960	12.50	25.00	50.00

JAN AND DEAN

45s

Number	Title (A Side/B Side)	Yr	VG	VG+	NM
❑ Challenge 9111	Heart and Soul/Those Words	1961	10.00	20.00	40.00
❑ Challenge 9111	Heart and Soul/A Midsummer Night's Dream	1961	5.00	10.00	20.00
❑ Challenge 9120	Wanted: One Girl/Something a Little Bit Different	1961	7.50	15.00	30.00
❑ Columbia 44036	Yellow Balloon/Taste of Rain	1967	7.50	15.00	30.00
❑ Dore 522	Baby Talk/Jeannette Get Your Hair Done	1959	7.50	15.00	30.00
❑ Dore 531	There's a Girl/My Heart Sings	1959	6.25	12.50	25.00
❑ Dore 539	Clementine/You're On My Mind	1960	6.25	12.50	25.00
❑ Dore 548	Cindy/Whiter Tennis Sneakers	1960	6.25	12.50	25.00
❑ Dore 555	We Go Together/Rosilane	1960	6.25	12.50	25.00
❑ Dore 555	We Go Together/Rosie Lane	1960	6.25	12.50	25.00
—B-side title was altered after the record no longer was issued with picture sleeve					
❑ Dore 576	Gee/Such a Good Night to Be Together	1960	6.25	12.50	25.00
❑ Dore 583	Baggy Pants/Judy's an Angel	1961	7.50	15.00	30.00
❑ Dore 610	Julie/Don't Fly Away	1961	7.50	15.00	30.00
❑ J&D 001	California Lullabye/Summertime	1966	7.50	15.00	30.00
❑ J&D 402	Like a Summer Rain/Louisiana Man	1966	7.50	15.00	30.00
❑ Jan & Dean 10	Hawaii/Tijuana	1966	18.75	37.50	75.00
❑ Jan & Dean 11	Fan Tan/Love and Hate	1966	30.00	60.00	120.00
❑ Liberty 55397	A Sunday Kind of Love/Poor Little Puppet	1961	6.25	12.50	25.00
❑ Liberty 55454	Tennessee/Your Heart Has Changed Its Mind	1962	6.25	12.50	25.00
❑ Liberty 55496	Who Put the Bomp/My Favorite Dream	1962	12.50	25.00	50.00
❑ Liberty 55522	Frosty (The Snow Man)/(She's Still Talking) Baby Talk	1962	37.50	75.00	150.00
—Promos worth about half this value					
❑ Liberty 55531	Linda/When I Learn How to Cry	1963	6.25	12.50	25.00
❑ Liberty 55580	Surf City/She's My Summer Girl	1963	3.75	7.50	15.00
❑ Liberty 55613	Honolulu Lulu/Someday	1963	3.75	7.50	15.00
❑ Liberty 55641	Drag City/Schlock Rod (Part 1)	1963	3.75	7.50	15.00
❑ Liberty 55672	Dead Man's Curve/The New Girl in School	1964	3.75	7.50	15.00
❑ Liberty 55704	The Little Old Lady (From Pasadena)/My Mighty G.T.O.	1964	3.75	7.50	15.00
❑ Liberty 55724	Ride the Wild Surf/The Anaheim, Azusa and Cucamonga Sewing Circle, Book Review and Timing Association	1964	3.75	7.50	15.00
❑ Liberty 55727	Sidewalk Surfin'/When It's Over	1964	3.75	7.50	15.00
❑ Liberty 55766	(Here They Come) From All Over the World/Freeway Flyer	1965	3.00	6.00	12.00
❑ Liberty 55792	You Really Know How to Hurt a Guy/It's As Easy As 1-2-3	1965	3.00	6.00	12.00
❑ Liberty 55816	It's a Shame to Say Goodbye/The Submarine Races	1965	—	—	—
—Unreleased					
❑ Liberty 55833	I Found a Girl/It's a Shame to Say Goodbye	1965	3.00	6.00	12.00
❑ Liberty 55849	Folk City/A Beginning from an End	1965	3.00	6.00	12.00
❑ Liberty 55860	Batman/Bucket "T"	1966	6.25	12.50	25.00
❑ Liberty 55886	Popsicle/Norwegian Wood	1966	3.00	6.00	12.00
❑ Liberty 55905	Fiddle Around/Surfer's Dream	1966	3.00	6.00	12.00
❑ Liberty 55923	The New Girl in School/School Days	1966	3.00	6.00	12.00
❑ Magic Lamp 401	California Lullabye/Summertime	1966	7.50	15.00	30.00
❑ Ode 66111	Fun City/Totally Wild	1975	6.25	12.50	25.00
❑ United Artists 0089	Jennie Lee/Baby Talk	1973	3.75	7.50	15.00
❑ United Artists 0090	Linda/The New Girl in School	1973	3.75	7.50	15.00
❑ United Artists 0091	Surf City/Ride the Wild Surf	1973	3.75	7.50	15.00
❑ United Artists 0092	Dead Man's Curve/Drag City	1973	3.75	7.50	15.00
❑ United Artists 0093	Honolulu Lulu/Sidewalk Surfin'	1973	3.75	7.50	15.00
❑ United Artists 0094	The Little Old Lady (From Pasadena)/Popsicle	1973	3.75	7.50	15.00
—0089 through 0094 are "Silver Spotlight Series" reissues					
❑ United Artists XW670	Sidewalk Surfin'/Gonna Hustle You	1975	3.75	7.50	15.00
❑ United Artists 50859	Jennie Lee/Vegetables	1971	3.75	7.50	15.00
❑ Warner Bros. 7151	Only a Boy/Love and Hate	1967	10.00	20.00	40.00
❑ Warner Bros. 7219	Laurel and Hardy/I Know My Mind	1968	12.50	25.00	50.00

Albums

Number	Title (A Side/B Side)	Yr	VG	VG+	NM
❑ Columbia CL 2661 [M]	Save for a Rainy Day	1967	—	—	—
—Canceled					
❑ Columbia CS 9461 [S]	Save for a Rainy Day	1967	2000.	3000.	4000.
—LP not known to exist, but an acetate does, and possibly an import on this label and number; VG value 2000; VG+ value 3000					
❑ Dore LP-101 [M]	Jan and Dean	1960	100.00	200.00	400.00
—Original with blue label					
❑ J&D 101 [M]	Save for a Rainy Day	1967	75.00	150.00	300.00
—Private pressing by Dean Torrence of unreleased Columbia album					
❑ Liberty LRP-3248 [M]	Jan and Dean's Golden Hits	1962	7.50	15.00	30.00

Number	Title (A Side/B Side)	Yr	VG	VG+	NM
❑ Liberty LRP-3294 [M]	Jan and Dean Take Linda Surfin'	1963	12.50	25.00	50.00
—With correct title on LP spine					
❑ Liberty LRP-3294 [M]	Jan and Dean Take Linda Surfin'	1963	15.00	30.00	60.00
—With title on spine "Mr. Bass Man Takes Linda Surfin'"					
❑ Liberty LRP-3314 [M]	Surf City and Other Swingin' Cities	1963	10.00	20.00	40.00
❑ Liberty LRP-3339 [M]	Drag City	1963	10.00	20.00	40.00
❑ Liberty LRP-3361 [M]	The New Girl in School/Dead Man's Curve	1964	5.00	10.00	20.00
—Reissue with reversed title					
❑ Liberty LRP-3361 [M]	Dead Man's Curve/The New Girl in School	1964	10.00	20.00	40.00
—Black and white cover with pink tint					
❑ Liberty LRP-3368 [M]	Ride the Wild Surf	1964	7.50	15.00	30.00
❑ Liberty LRP-3377 [M]	The Little Old Lady from Pasadena	1964	7.50	15.00	30.00
❑ Liberty LRP-3403 [M]	Command Performance/Live in Person	1965	7.50	15.00	30.00
❑ Liberty LRP-3417 [M]	Jan and Dean's Golden Hits, Volume 2	1965	6.25	12.50	25.00
❑ Liberty LRP-3431 [M]	Folk 'N' Roll	1965	7.50	15.00	30.00
❑ Liberty LRP-3441 [M]	Filet of Soul	1966	7.50	15.00	30.00
❑ Liberty LRP-3444 [M]	Jan and Dean Meet Batman	1966	12.50	25.00	50.00
❑ Liberty LRP-3458 [M]	Popsicle	1966	7.50	15.00	30.00
❑ Liberty LRP-3460 [M]	Jan and Dean's Golden Hits, Volume 3	1966	6.25	12.50	25.00
❑ Liberty LST-7248 [S]	Jan and Dean's Golden Hits	1962	10.00	20.00	40.00
❑ Liberty LST-7294 [S]	Jan and Dean Take Linda Surfin'	1963	20.00	40.00	80.00
—With correct title on LP spine					
❑ Liberty LST-7294 [S]	Jan and Dean Take Linda Surfin'	1963	25.00	50.00	100.00
—With title on spine "Mr. Bass Man Takes Linda Surfin'"					
❑ Liberty LST-7314 [S]	Surf City and Other Swingin' Cities	1963	12.50	25.00	50.00
❑ Liberty LST-7339 [S]	Drag City	1963	12.50	25.00	50.00
❑ Liberty LST-7361 [S]	The New Girl in School/Dead Man's Curve	1964	7.50	15.00	30.00
—Reissue with reversed title					
❑ Liberty LST-7361 [S]	Dead Man's Curve/The New Girl in School	1964	12.50	25.00	50.00
—Black and white cover with pink tint					
❑ Liberty LST-7368 [S]	Ride the Wild Surf	1964	10.00	20.00	40.00
❑ Liberty LST-7377 [S]	The Little Old Lady from Pasadena	1964	10.00	20.00	40.00
❑ Liberty LST-7403 [S]	Command Performance/Live in Person	1965	10.00	20.00	40.00
❑ Liberty LST-7417 [S]	Jan and Dean's Golden Hits, Volume 2	1965	7.50	15.00	30.00
❑ Liberty LST-7431 [S]	Folk 'N' Roll	1965	10.00	20.00	40.00
❑ Liberty LST-7441 [S]	Filet of Soul	1966	10.00	20.00	40.00
❑ Liberty LST-7444 [S]	Jan and Dean Meet Batman	1966	17.50	35.00	70.00
❑ Liberty LST-7458 [S]	Popsicle	1966	10.00	20.00	40.00
❑ Liberty LST-7460 [S]	Jan and Dean's Golden Hits, Volume 3	1966	7.50	15.00	30.00
❑ Liberty LN-10011	Dead Man's Curve	1980	2.00	4.00	8.00
—Budget-line reissue					
❑ Liberty LN-10115	The Best of Jan and Dean	1981	2.00	4.00	8.00
❑ Liberty LN-10151	The Little Old Lady from Pasadena	1982	2.00	4.00	8.00
—Budget-line reissue					
❑ Pair PDL2-1071 [(2)]	California Gold	1986	3.00	6.00	12.00
❑ Rhino RNDA 1498 [(2)]	One Summer Night — Live	1982	5.00	10.00	20.00
❑ Sunset SUM-1156 [M]	Jan and Dean	1967	3.75	7.50	15.00
❑ Sunset SUS-5156 [S]	Jan and Dean	1967	3.75	7.50	15.00
❑ United Artists UA-LA341-H2 [(2)]	Gotta Take That One Last Ride	1974	3.75	7.50	15.00
❑ United Artists UA-LA443-E	The Very Best of Jan and Dean	1975	2.50	5.00	10.00
❑ United Artists UA-LA515-E	The Very Best of Jan and Dean, Volume 2	1975	2.50	5.00	10.00
❑ United Artists UAS-9961 [(2)]	Anthology (Legendary Masters Series, Vol. 3)	1971	6.25	12.50	25.00

JAY AND THE AMERICANS

45s

Number	Title (A Side/B Side)	Yr	VG	VG+	NM
❑ United Artists 0026	She Cried/Come a Little Bit Closer	1973	—	2.50	5.00
❑ United Artists 0027	Cara Mia/Let's Lock the Door (And Throw Away the Key)	1973	—	2.50	5.00
❑ United Artists 0028	This Magic Moment/Walking in the Rain	1973	—	2.50	5.00
—0026, 0027, 0028 are "Silver Spotlight Series" reissues					
❑ United Artists 353	Tonight/The Other Girls	1961	3.00	6.00	12.00
❑ United Artists 415	She Cried/Dawning	1962	3.75	7.50	15.00
❑ United Artists 479	It's My Turn to Cry/This Is It	1962	3.00	6.00	12.00
❑ United Artists 504	Tomorrow/Yes	1962	3.00	6.00	12.00
❑ United Artists 566	What's the Use/Strangers Tomorrow	1963	2.50	5.00	10.00
❑ United Artists 626	Only in America/My Clair De Lune	1963	2.50	5.00	10.00

Number	Title (A Side/B Side)	Yr	VG	VG+	NM
❑ United Artists 669	Come Dance with Me/Look in My Eyes Maria	1963	2.50	5.00	10.00
❑ United Artists 693	To Wait for Love/Friday	1964	2.50	5.00	10.00
❑ United Artists 759	Come a Little Bit Closer/Goodbye Boys, Goodbye	1964	2.50	5.00	10.00
❑ United Artists 805	Let's Lock the Door (And Throw Away the Key)/I'll Remember You	1965	2.50	5.00	10.00
❑ United Artists 845	Think of the Good Times/If You Were Mine, Girl	1965	2.50	5.00	10.00
❑ United Artists 881	Cara Mia/When It's All Over	1965	2.50	5.00	10.00
❑ United Artists 919	Some Enchanted Evening/Girl	1965	2.50	5.00	10.00
❑ United Artists 948	Sunday and Me/Through This Doorway	1965	2.50	5.00	10.00
❑ United Artists 992	Why Can't You Bring Me Home/Baby Stop Your Cryin'	1966	2.00	4.00	8.00
❑ United Artists 50016	Crying/I Don't Need a Friend	1966	2.00	4.00	8.00
❑ United Artists 50046	Livin' Above Your Head/Look at Me, What Do You See	1966	2.00	4.00	8.00
❑ United Artists 50086	Baby Come Home/Stop the Clock	1966	2.00	4.00	8.00
❑ United Artists 50094	(He's) Raining in My Sunshine/ The Reason for Living (For You My Darling)	1966	2.00	4.00	8.00
❑ United Artists 50139	Nature Boy/You Ain't As Hip As All That, Baby	1967	2.00	4.00	8.00
❑ United Artists 50196	(We'll Meet in the) Yellow Forest/Got Hung Up Along the Way	1967	2.00	4.00	8.00
❑ United Artists 50222	Shanghai Noodle Factory/French Provincial	1967	2.00	4.00	8.00
❑ United Artists 50282	No Other Love/No, I Don't Know Her	1968	2.00	4.00	8.00
❑ United Artists 50448	You Ain't Gonna Wake Up Cryin'/Gemini	1968	2.00	4.00	8.00
❑ United Artists 50475	This Magic Moment/Since I Don't Have You	1969	3.00	6.00	12.00
❑ United Artists 50510	When You Dance/No, I Don't Know Her	1969	—	3.00	6.00
❑ United Artists 50535	Hushabye/Gypsy Woman	1969	—	3.00	6.00
❑ United Artists 50567	(I'd Kill) For the Love of a Lady/Learnin' How to Fly	1969	—	3.00	6.00
❑ United Artists 50605	Walkin' in the Rain/(I'd Kill) For the Love of a Lady	1969	2.00	4.00	8.00
❑ United Artists 50654	Do You Ever Think of Me/Capture the Moment	1970	—	3.00	6.00
❑ United Artists 50683	Do I Love You?/Tricia (Tell Your Daddy)	1970	—	3.00	6.00
❑ United Artists 50858	There Goes My Baby/Solitary Man	1971	—	3.00	6.00
Albums					
❑ Liberty LM-1010	Jay and the Americans Greatest Hits	1981	2.00	4.00	8.00
—Another reissue					
❑ Rhino RNLP 70224	All-Time Greatest Hits	1986	3.00	6.00	12.00
❑ Sunset SUS-5252	Jay and the Americans!!	1968	3.00	6.00	12.00
❑ Sunset SUS-5278	Early American Hits	1969	3.75	7.50	15.00
❑ Unart M-20018 [M]	Jay and the Americans!!	196?	3.00	6.00	12.00
❑ Unart MS-21018 [S]	Jay and the Americans!!	196?	3.00	6.00	12.00
❑ United Artists UA-LA357-E	The Very Best of Jay and the Americans	1975	3.00	6.00	12.00
❑ United Artists LM-1010	Jay and the Americans Greatest Hits	1980	2.50	5.00	10.00
—Reissue					
❑ United Artists UAL-3222 [M]	She Cried	1962	12.50	25.00	50.00
❑ United Artists UAL-3300 [M]	At the Café Wha?	1963	12.50	25.00	50.00
❑ United Artists UAL-3407 [M]	Come a Little Bit Closer	1964	6.25	12.50	25.00
❑ United Artists UAL-3417 [M]	Blockbusters	1965	6.25	12.50	25.00
❑ United Artists UAL-3453 [M]	Jay and the Americans Greatest Hits	1965	5.00	10.00	20.00
❑ United Artists UAL-3474 [M]	Sunday and Me	1966	5.00	10.00	20.00
❑ United Artists UAL-3534 [M]	Livin' Above Your Head	1966	5.00	10.00	20.00
❑ United Artists UAL-3555 [M]	Jay and the Americans Greatest Hits, Volume 2	1966	5.00	10.00	20.00
❑ United Artists UAL-3562 [M]	Try Some of This!	1967	5.00	10.00	20.00
❑ United Artists UAS-6222 [S]	She Cried	1962	25.00	50.00	100.00
❑ United Artists UAS-6300 [S]	At the Café Wha?	1963	25.00	50.00	100.00
❑ United Artists UAS-6407 [S]	Come a Little Bit Closer	1964	7.50	15.00	30.00
❑ United Artists UAS-6417 [S]	Blockbusters	1965	7.50	15.00	30.00
❑ United Artists UAS-6453 [S]	Jay and the Americans Greatest Hits	1965	6.25	12.50	25.00
❑ United Artists UAS-6474 [S]	Sunday and Me	1966	6.25	12.50	25.00
❑ United Artists UAS-6534 [S]	Livin' Above Your Head	1966	6.25	12.50	25.00
❑ United Artists UAS-6555 [S]	Jay and the Americans Greatest Hits, Volume 2	1966	5.00	10.00	20.00
❑ United Artists UAS-6562 [S]	Try Some of This!	1967	5.00	10.00	20.00
❑ United Artists UAS-6671	Sands of Time	1969	5.00	10.00	20.00
❑ United Artists UAS-6719	Wax Museum	1970	5.00	10.00	20.00
❑ United Artists UAS-6751	Wax Museum, Volume 2	1970	5.00	10.00	20.00
❑ United Artists UAS-6762	Capture the Moment	1970	5.00	10.00	20.00

JAY AND THE TECHNIQUES

45s

Number	Title (A Side/B Side)	Yr	VG	VG+	NM
❑ Event 222	I Feel Love Coming On/World of Mine	1975	—	2.50	5.00
❑ Event 228	Number Onederful/Don't Forget to Ask	1975	—	2.50	5.00
❑ Gordy 7123	I'll Be Here/Robot Man	1973	—	3.00	6.00
❑ Smash 2086	Apples, Peaches, Pumpkin Pie/Stronger Than Dirt	1967	2.00	4.00	8.00
❑ Smash 2124	Keep the Ball Rollin'/Here We Go Again	1967	2.00	4.00	8.00
❑ Smash 2142	Strawberry Shortcake/Still (In Love with You)	1967	2.00	4.00	8.00
❑ Smash 2154	Baby Make Your Own Sweet Music/Help Yourself to All My Lovin'	1968	2.00	4.00	8.00
❑ Smash 2171	The Singles Game/Baby How Easy Your Heart Forgets Me	1968	2.00	4.00	8.00
❑ Smash 2185	Hey Diddle Diddle/If I Should Lose You	1968	2.00	4.00	8.00
❑ Smash 2217	Change Your Mind/Are You Ready for This	1969	2.00	4.00	8.00
❑ Smash 2237	Dancin' Mood/If I Should Lose You	1969	2.00	4.00	8.00
Albums					
❑ Smash MGS-27095 [M]	Apples, Peaches, Pumpkin Pie	1967	7.50	15.00	30.00
❑ Smash MGS-27102 [M]	Love Lost and Found	1968	15.00	30.00	60.00
—Mono may be white-label promo only					
❑ Smash SRS-67095 [S]	Apples, Peaches, Pumpkin Pie	1967	7.50	15.00	30.00
—First cover with "live" photo of the band					
❑ Smash SRS-67095 [S]	Apples, Peaches, Pumpkin Pie	1968	5.00	10.00	20.00
—Second cover with "posed" photo of the band					
❑ Smash SRS-67102 [S]	Love Lost and Found	1968	7.50	15.00	30.00

JEFFERSON AIRPLANE

45s

Number	Title (A Side/B Side)	Yr	VG	VG+	NM
❑ Epic 73044	Summer of Love/Panda	1989	—	2.50	5.00

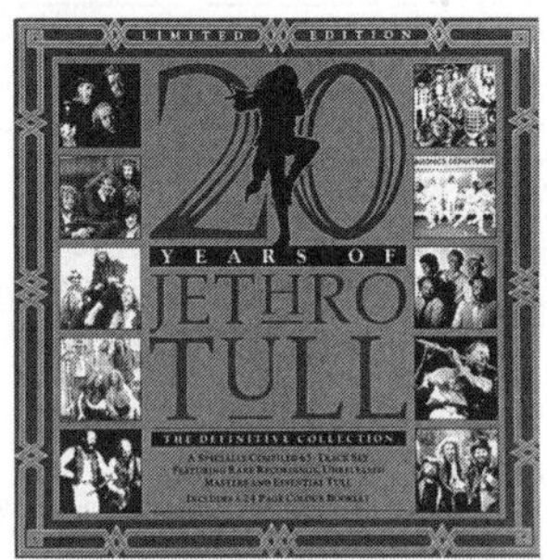

Number	Title (A Side/B Side)	Yr	VG	VG+	NM
❑ Grunt 65-0500	Pretty As You Feel/Wild Turkey	1971	—	2.50	5.00
❑ Grunt 65-0506	Long John Silver/Milk Train	1972	—	2.50	5.00
❑ Grunt 65-0511	Trial by Fire/Twilight Double Leader	1972	—	2.50	5.00
❑ RCA 5156-7-R	White Rabbit/Plastic Fantastic Lover	1987	—	2.50	5.00
—White vinyl					
❑ RCA Victor 47-8769	It's No Secret/Runnin' 'Round This World	1966	3.75	7.50	15.00
❑ RCA Victor 47-8848	Come Up the Years/Blues from an Airplane	1966	3.75	7.50	15.00
❑ RCA Victor 47-8967	Bringing Me Down/Let Me In	1966	3.75	7.50	15.00
❑ RCA Victor 47-9063	My Best Friend/How Do You Feel	1967	3.75	7.50	15.00
❑ RCA Victor 47-9140	Somebody to Love/She Has Funny Cars	1967	3.75	7.50	15.00
❑ RCA Victor 47-9248	White Rabbit/Plastic Fantastic Lover	1967	3.75	7.50	15.00
❑ RCA Victor 47-9297	Ballad of You & Me & Pooneil/Two Heads	1967	2.50	5.00	10.00
❑ RCA Victor 47-9389	Watch Her Ride/Martha	1967	2.50	5.00	10.00
❑ RCA Victor 47-9496	Greasy Heart/Share a Little Joke (With the World)	1968	2.00	4.00	8.00
❑ RCA Victor 47-9644	Crown of Creation/Lather	1968	2.00	4.00	8.00
❑ RCA Victor 74-0150	Plastic Fantastic Lover/Other Side of This Life	1969	—	3.00	6.00
❑ RCA Victor 74-0245	Volunteers/We Can Be Together	1969	—	3.00	6.00
❑ RCA Victor 74-0343	Have You Seen the Saucers/Mexico	1970	—	3.00	6.00
Albums					
❑ Epic OE 45271	Jefferson Airplane	1989	3.75	7.50	15.00
❑ Grunt BFL1-0147	Thirty Seconds Over Winterland	1973	3.00	6.00	12.00
❑ Grunt APL1-0437	Early Flight	1974	3.00	6.00	12.00
❑ Grunt FTR-1001	Bark	1971	3.75	7.50	15.00
—With brown paper bag					
❑ Grunt FTR-1007	Long John Silver	1972	3.00	6.00	12.00
❑ Grunt CYL2-1255 [(2)]	Flight Log 1966-1976	1977	3.00	6.00	12.00
❑ Grunt AYL1-4386	Bark	1981	2.00	4.00	8.00
❑ Grunt AYL1-4391	Thirty Seconds Over Winterland	1981	2.00	4.00	8.00
❑ Pair PDL2-1090 [(2)]	Time Machine	1986	3.00	6.00	12.00
❑ RCA 5724-1-R [(2)]	2400 Fulton Street: An Anthology	1987	3.75	7.50	15.00
❑ RCA Victor LOP-1511 [M]	After Bathing at Baxter's	1967	12.50	25.00	50.00
❑ RCA Victor LSO-1511 [S]	After Bathing at Baxter's	1967	5.00	10.00	20.00
—Black label, dog on top					
❑ RCA Victor LPM-3584 [M]	Jefferson Airplane Takes Off!	1966	6.25	12.50	25.00
—Version 3: No "Runnin' 'Round This World", altered lyrics to "Let Me In" ("Don't tell me it's so funny") and "Run Around ("That sway as you stay here by me"). All later versions confirm to Version 3.					
❑ RCA Victor LPM-3584 [M]	Jefferson Airplane Takes Off!	1966	250.00	500.00	1000.
—Version 2: No "Runnin' 'Round This World", but "questionable" lyrics remain in "Let Me In" ("Don't tell me you want money") and "Run Around" ("That sway as you lay under me"). Until the exact matrix numbers are known, it must be heard to confirm.					
❑ RCA Victor LPM-3584 [M]	Jefferson Airplane Takes Off!	1966	1500.	2250.	3000.
—Version 1: With "Runnin' 'Round This World" as last song on side 1. Count the number of bands on Side 1 of the record; don't rely on the cover listing, as some jackets list the title when it's not on the record; VG value 1500; VG+ value 2250					
❑ RCA Victor LSP-3584 [S]	Jefferson Airplane Takes Off!	1966	2000.	3500.	5000.
—Version 1: See Version 1 note under mono version; VG value 2000; VG+ value 3500					
❑ RCA Victor LSP-3584 [S]	Jefferson Airplane Takes Off!	1966	6.25	12.50	25.00
—Version 3: See Version 3 note under mono version					
❑ RCA Victor LSP-3584 [S]	Jefferson Airplane Takes Off!	1966	450.00	900.00	1800.
—Version 2: See Version 2 note under mono version					
❑ RCA Victor AYL1-3661	The Worst of Jefferson Airplane	1980	2.00	4.00	8.00
❑ RCA Victor AYL1-3738	Surrealistic Pillow	1980	2.00	4.00	8.00
❑ RCA Victor AYL1-3739	Jefferson Airplane Takes Off!	1980	2.00	4.00	8.00
❑ RCA Victor LPM-3766 [M]	Surrealistic Pillow	1967	15.00	30.00	60.00
❑ RCA Victor LSP-3766 [S]	Surrealistic Pillow	1967	7.50	15.00	30.00
—Black label, dog on top					
❑ RCA Victor AYL1-3797	Crown of Creation	1980	2.00	4.00	8.00
❑ RCA Victor AYL1-3798	Bless Its Pointed Little Head	1980	2.00	4.00	8.00
❑ RCA Victor AYL1-3867	Volunteers	1980	2.00	4.00	8.00
❑ RCA Victor LSP-4058	Crown of Creation	1968	7.50	15.00	30.00
—Black label, dog on top					
❑ RCA Victor LSP-4133	Bless Its Pointed Little Head	1969	3.00	6.00	12.00
—Orange label					
❑ RCA Victor LSP-4238	Volunteers	1969	3.00	6.00	12.00
—Orange label					
❑ RCA Victor LSP-4459	The Worst of Jefferson Airplane	1970	3.00	6.00	12.00
❑ RCA Victor AFL1-4545	After Bathing at Baxter's	1981	2.00	4.00	8.00
❑ RCA Victor AYL1-4718	After Bathing at Baxter's	1983	2.00	4.00	8.00

Number	Title (A Side/B Side)	Yr	VG	VG+	NM
❑ Sundazed LP 5186 [M]	Jefferson Airplane Takes Off	2005	3.75	7.50	15.00
—Reissue on 180-gram vinyl					
❑ Sundazed LP 5187 [M]	After Bathing at Baxter's	2005	3.75	7.50	15.00
—Reissue on 180-gram vinyl					

JEFFERSON STARSHIP

45s

Number	Title (A Side/B Side)	Yr	VG	VG+	NM
❑ Grunt FB-10080	Ride the Tiger/Devil's Den	1974	—	2.00	4.00
❑ Grunt FB-10206	Caroline/Be Young You	1975	—	2.00	4.00
❑ Grunt FB-10367	Miracles/Al Garimaso (There Is Love)	1975	—	2.50	5.00
❑ Grunt FB-10456	Play on Love/I Want to See Another World	1975	—	2.00	4.00
❑ Grunt FB-10746	With Your Love/Switchblade	1976	—	2.50	5.00
❑ Grunt FB-10791	St. Charles/Love Lovely Day	1976	—	2.00	4.00
❑ Grunt GB-10941	Miracles/With Your Love	1977	—	—	3.00
—Gold Standard Series					
❑ Grunt FB-11196	Count on Me/Show Yourself	1978	—	2.00	4.00
❑ Grunt FB-11274	Runaway/Hot Water	1978	—	2.00	4.00
❑ Grunt FB-11374	Crazy Feelin'/Love Too Good	1978	—	2.00	4.00
❑ Grunt FB-11426	Light the Sky On Fire/Hyperdrive	1978	—	2.00	4.00
❑ Grunt GB-11506	Count on Me/Runaway	1979	—	—	3.00
—Gold Standard Series					
❑ Grunt FB-11750	Jane/Freedom at Point Zero	1979	—	2.00	4.00
❑ Grunt FB-11921	Girl with the Hungry Eyes/Just the Same	1980	—	2.00	4.00
❑ Grunt FB-11961	Rock Music/Lightning Rose	1980	—	2.00	4.00
❑ Grunt FB-12211	Find Your Way Back/Modern Times	1981	—	2.00	4.00
❑ Grunt FB-12212	Mary/Modern Times	1981	—	—	—
—Unreleased					
❑ Grunt FB-12275	Stranger/Free	1981	—	2.00	4.00
❑ Grunt FB-12332	Save Your Love/Wild Eyes	1981	—	2.00	4.00
❑ Grunt FB-13350	Be My Lady/Out of Control	1982	—	2.00	4.00
❑ Grunt FB-13439	Winds of Change/Black Widow	1983	—	2.00	4.00
❑ Grunt FB-13531	Can't Find Love/I Will Stay	1983	—	2.00	4.00
❑ Grunt FB-13811	No Way Out/Rose Goes to Yale	1984	—	2.00	4.00
❑ Grunt FB-13872	Layin' It on the Line/Showdown	1984	—	2.00	4.00

Albums

Number	Title	Yr	VG	VG+	NM
❑ Grunt BFL1-0717	Dragon Fly	1974	2.50	5.00	10.00
❑ Grunt BFL1-0999	Red Octopus	1975	2.50	5.00	10.00
❑ Grunt BFL1-1557	Spitfire	1976	2.50	5.00	10.00
❑ Grunt BXL1-2515	Earth	1978	2.50	5.00	10.00
❑ Grunt BZL1-3247	Gold	1978	2.50	5.00	10.00
❑ Grunt BZL1-3452	Freedom at Point Zero	1979	2.50	5.00	10.00
❑ Grunt AYL1-3660	Red Octopus	1980	2.00	4.00	8.00
❑ Grunt AYL1-3796	Dragon Fly	1980	2.00	4.00	8.00
❑ Grunt BZL1-3848	Modern Times	1981	2.50	5.00	10.00
❑ Grunt AYL1-3953	Spitfire	1981	2.00	4.00	8.00
❑ Grunt AYL1-4172	Earth	1981	2.00	4.00	8.00
❑ Grunt BXL1-4372	Winds of Change	1982	2.50	5.00	10.00
❑ Grunt BXL1-4921	Nuclear Furniture	1984	2.50	5.00	10.00
❑ Grunt AYL1-5161	Freedom at Point Zero	1984	2.00	4.00	8.00

JETHRO TULL

45s

Number	Title (A Side/B Side)	Yr	VG	VG+	NM
❑ Chrysalis 2006	Living in the Past/Christmas Song	1972	—	3.00	6.00
❑ Chrysalis 2012	A Passion Play (Edit #9)/A Passion Play (Edit #8)	1973	—	3.00	6.00
❑ Chrysalis 2017	A Passion Play (Edit #6)/A Passion Play (Edit #10)	1973	—	2.50	5.00
❑ Chrysalis 2101	Bungle in the Jungle/Back Door Angels	1974	—	2.50	5.00
❑ Chrysalis 2103	Skating Away (On the Thin Ice of a New Day)/Sealion	1975	—	2.50	5.00
❑ Chrysalis 2106	Minstrel in the Gallery/Sumer Day Sand	1975	—	2.50	5.00
❑ Chrysalis 2110	Locomotive Breath/Fat Man	1975	—	2.50	5.00
❑ Chrysalis 2114	Too Old to Rock and Roll, Too Young to Die/ Bad Eyed and Loveless	1976	—	2.50	5.00
❑ Chrysalis 2135	The Whistler/Strip Cartoon	1977	—	2.50	5.00
❑ Chrysalis 2387	Home/Warm Sporran	1979	—	2.50	5.00
❑ Chrysalis 2613	Fallen on Hard Times/Pussy Willow	1982	—	2.00	4.00
❑ Chrysalis 43172	Steel Monkey/Down at the End of Your Road	1987	—	2.00	4.00
❑ Reprise 0886	Reasons for Waiting/Sweet Dream	1970	3.75	7.50	15.00
❑ Reprise 0899	Teacher/Witch's Promise	1970	3.75	7.50	15.00
❑ Reprise 0927	Inside/Time for Everything	1970	—	2.50	5.00
❑ Reprise 1024	Hymn 43/Mother Goose	1971	—	2.50	5.00
❑ Reprise 1054	Locomotive Breath/Wind-Up	1971	—	2.50	5.00
❑ Reprise 1153	Thick as a Brick (Edit)/Hymn 43	1972	—	2.50	5.00
—"Back to Back Hits" series					

Albums

Number	Title	Yr	VG	VG+	NM
❑ Chrysalis CHR 1003	Thick as a Brick	1973	3.00	6.00	12.00
—Green label, "3300 Warner Blvd." address					
❑ Chrysalis 2CH 1035 [(2)]	Living in the Past	1972	5.00	10.00	20.00
—Two-record set with booklet; green labels					
❑ Chrysalis CHR 1040	A Passion Play	1973	3.00	6.00	12.00
—Green label, "3300 Warner Blvd." address					
❑ Chrysalis CHR 1041	This Was	1973	3.00	6.00	12.00
—Green label, "3300 Warner Blvd." address					
❑ Chrysalis CHR 1042	Stand Up	1973	3.00	6.00	12.00
—Green label, "3300 Warner Blvd." address					
❑ Chrysalis CHR 1043	Benefit	1973	3.00	6.00	12.00
—Green label, "3300 Warner Blvd." address					
❑ Chrysalis CHR 1044	Aqualung	1973	3.00	6.00	12.00
—Green label, "3300 Warner Blvd." address					

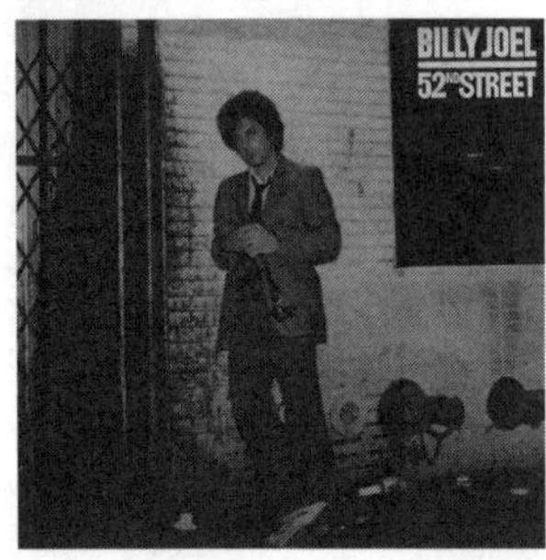

Number	Title (A Side/B Side)	Yr	VG	VG+	NM
❑ Chrysalis CHR 1067	War Child	1974	3.00	6.00	12.00
—Green label, "3300 Warner Blvd." address					
❑ Chrysalis CHR 1078	M.U. — The Best of Jethro Tull	1975	3.00	6.00	12.00
—Green label, "3300 Warner Blvd." address					
❑ Chrysalis CHR 1082	Minstrel in the Gallery	1975	3.00	6.00	12.00
—Green label, "3300 Warner Blvd." address					
❑ Chrysalis CHR 1111	Too Old to Rock 'N' Roll; Too Young to Die!	1976	3.00	6.00	12.00
—Green label, "3300 Warner Blvd." address					
❑ Chrysalis CHR 1132	Songs from the Wood	1977	2.50	5.00	10.00
❑ Chrysalis CHR 1135	Repeat — The Best of Jethro Tull, Vol. II	1977	2.50	5.00	10.00
❑ Chrysalis CHR 1175	Heavy Horses	1978	2.50	5.00	10.00
❑ Chrysalis CHR2 1201 [(2)]	Jethro Tull Live — Bursting Out	1978	3.00	6.00	12.00
❑ Chrysalis CHR 1238	Stormwatch	1979	2.50	5.00	10.00
❑ Chrysalis CHR 1301	"A"	1980	2.50	5.00	10.00
❑ Chrysalis CHR 1380	The Broadsword and the Beast	1982	2.50	5.00	10.00
❑ Chrysalis F1-21708	Rock Island	1989	2.50	5.00	10.00
❑ Chrysalis FV 41003	Thick as a Brick	1983	2.00	4.00	8.00
❑ Chrysalis KV2 41035 [(2)]	Living in the Past	1983	3.00	6.00	12.00
❑ Chrysalis PV 41040	A Passion Play	1983	2.00	4.00	8.00
❑ Chrysalis PV 41041	This Was	1983	2.00	4.00	8.00
❑ Chrysalis PV 41042	Stand Up	1983	2.00	4.00	8.00
❑ Chrysalis PV 41043	Benefit	1983	2.00	4.00	8.00
❑ Chrysalis FV 41044	Aqualung	1983	2.00	4.00	8.00
❑ Chrysalis PV 41067	War Child	1983	2.00	4.00	8.00
❑ Chrysalis FV 41078	M.U. — The Best of Jethro Tull	1983	2.00	4.00	8.00
❑ Chrysalis PV 41082	Minstrel in the Gallery	1983	2.00	4.00	8.00
❑ Chrysalis PV 41111	Too Old to Rock 'N' Roll; Too Young to Die!	1983	2.00	4.00	8.00
❑ Chrysalis PV 41132	Songs from the Wood	1983	2.00	4.00	8.00
❑ Chrysalis FV 41135	Repeat — The Best of Jethro Tull, Vol. II	1983	2.00	4.00	8.00
❑ Chrysalis PV 41135	Repeat — The Best of Jethro Tull, Vol. II	1986	2.00	4.00	8.00
❑ Chrysalis PV 41175	Heavy Horses	1983	2.00	4.00	8.00
❑ Chrysalis V2X 41201 [(2)]	Jethro Tull Live — Bursting Out	1983	3.00	6.00	12.00
❑ Chrysalis PV 41238	Stormwatch	1983	2.00	4.00	8.00
❑ Chrysalis PV 41301	"A"	1983	2.00	4.00	8.00
❑ Chrysalis FV 41380	The Broadsword and the Beast	1983	2.00	4.00	8.00
❑ Chrysalis FV 41461	Under Wraps	1984	2.50	5.00	10.00
❑ Chrysalis FV 41515	Original Masters	1985	2.50	5.00	10.00
❑ Chrysalis FV 41590	Crest of a Knave	1987	2.50	5.00	10.00
❑ Chrysalis V5X 41653 [(5)]	20 Years of Jethro Tull	1988	20.00	40.00	80.00
❑ Chrysalis VX2 41655 [(2)]	20 Years of Jethro Tull	1989	6.25	12.50	25.00
—Abridged version of Chrysalis 41653					
❑ Reprise MS 2035	Aqualung	1971	3.75	7.50	15.00
❑ Reprise MS 2072	Thick as a Brick	1972	3.75	7.50	15.00
❑ Reprise 2MS 2106 [(2)]	Living in the Past	1972	6.25	12.50	25.00
—Two-record set with booklet; original edition, rather than using cardboard outer sleeve for the records, has record sleeves attached to enclosed booklet, and thus is difficult to find intact					
❑ Reprise RS 6336	This Was	1969	5.00	10.00	20.00
—Two-tone orange label with "r:" and "W7" logos on label					
❑ Reprise RS 6360	Stand Up	1969	5.00	10.00	20.00
—Two-tone orange label with "r:" and "W7" logos on label; band "stands up" when gatefold is opened					
❑ Reprise RS 6400	Benefit	1970	5.00	10.00	20.00
—Two-tone orange label with "r:" and "W7" logos on label					

JETT, JOAN, AND THE BLACKHEARTS

45s

Number	Title (A Side/B Side)	Yr	VG	VG+	NM
❑ Blackheart 06336	Good Music/Fantasy	1986	—	—	3.00
❑ Blackheart 06692	Light of Day/Roadrunner (Radio On)	1987	—	—	3.00
—As "The Barbusters"					
❑ Blackheart 07919	I Hate Myself for Loving You/Love Is Pain (Live)	1988	—	—	3.00
❑ Blackheart 08095	Little Liar/What Can I Do for You	1988	—	—	3.00
❑ Blackheart 73267	Dirty Deeds/Let It Bleed	1990	2.00	4.00	8.00
—Credited solely to Joan Jett					
❑ Boardwalk NB7-11-135	I Love Rock 'N Roll/You Don't Know What You've Got	1982	—	—	3.00
❑ Boardwalk NB7-11-144	Crimson and Clover/Oh Woe Is Me	1982	—	—	3.00
❑ Boardwalk NB 11-150-7	Do You Wanna Touch Me (Oh Yeah)/Victim of Circumstance	1982	—	—	3.00
❑ Boardwalk 5706	You Don't Own Me/Jezebel	1981	2.00	4.00	8.00
❑ Def Jam 07630	She's Lost You/Hazy Shade of Winter	1987	—	—	3.00
—B-side by Bangles					

Number	Title (A Side/B Side)	Yr	VG	VG+	NM
❑ MCA 52240	Fake Friends/Nite Time	1983	—	—	3.00
❑ MCA 52254	Fake Friends/Handy Man	1983	—	2.00	4.00
—Evidently a jukebox single with a different flip side so the needle wouldn't get stuck!					
❑ MCA 52272	Everyday People/Why Can't We Be Happy	1983	—	—	3.00
❑ MCA 52472	I Love You Love/Talkin' 'Bout My Baby	1984	—	—	3.00
Albums					
❑ Blackheart JJ 707	Joan Jett	1980	15.00	30.00	60.00
❑ Blackheart BFZ 40544	Good Music	1986	3.00	6.00	12.00
❑ Blackheart FZ 44146	Up Your Alley	1988	2.50	5.00	10.00
❑ Blackheart Z 45473	The Hit List	1990	3.75	7.50	15.00
❑ Boardwalk NB1-33243	I Love Rock-n-Roll	1982	3.00	6.00	12.00
—Second pressing, with "Oh Woe Is Me"					
❑ Boardwalk NB1-33243	I Love Rock-n-Roll	1982	2.50	5.00	10.00
—First pressing contains "Little Drummer Boy," which was replaced on second pressings					
❑ Boardwalk NB1-33251	Bad Reputation	1982	2.50	5.00	10.00
—Reissue of FW 37065					
❑ Boardwalk FW 37065	Bad Reputation	1981	3.00	6.00	12.00
—Essentially a reissue of Blackheart JJ 707					
❑ MCA 5437	Album	1983	3.00	6.00	12.00
❑ MCA 5476	Glorious Results of a Misspent Youth	1984	3.00	6.00	12.00

JIVE FIVE, THE

Number	Title (A Side/B Side)	Yr	VG	VG+	NM
45s					
❑ Ambient Sound 452	Are You Lonesome Tonight/Happier Than Before	1985	—	3.00	6.00
❑ Ambient Sound 02742	Magic Maker, Music Maker/Oh Baby	1982	—	2.50	5.00
❑ Ambient Sound 03053	Hey Sam/Don't Believe Him Donna	1982	—	2.50	5.00
❑ Avco 4568	Come Down in Time/Love Is Pain	1971	—	3.00	6.00
❑ Avco 4589	Follow the Lamb/Lay Lady Lay	1972	—	3.00	6.00
❑ Avco 4589	Follow the Lamb/Let the Feeling Belong	1972	—	3.00	6.00
❑ Beltone 1006	My True Story/When I Was Single	1961	7.50	15.00	30.00
❑ Beltone 1014	Never, Never/People from Another World	1961	5.00	10.00	20.00
❑ Beltone 2019	Hully Gully Calling Time/No, Not Again	1962	5.00	10.00	20.00
❑ Beltone 2024	What Time Is It?/Beggin' You Please	1962	5.00	10.00	20.00
❑ Beltone 2029	These Golden Rings/Do You Hear Wedding Bells	1962	5.00	10.00	20.00
❑ Beltone 2030	Lily Marlene/Johnny Never Knew	1963	5.00	10.00	20.00
❑ Beltone 2034	She's My Girl/Rain	1963	5.00	10.00	20.00
❑ Brut 814	All I Ever Do Is Dream About You/Super Woman (Part 2)	1973	—	3.00	6.00
❑ Decca 32671	(If You Let Me Make Love to You) Why Can't I Touch You/You Showed Me the Light of Love	1970	2.00	4.00	8.00
❑ Decca 32736	I Want You to Be My Baby/Give Me Just a Chance	1970	2.00	4.00	8.00
❑ Lana 105	My True Story/When I Was Single	196?	2.00	4.00	8.00
—Oldies reissue					
❑ Lost-Nite 144	My True Story/When I Was Single	196?	—	3.00	6.00
—Reissue					
❑ Lost-Nite 147	What Time Is It?/Beggin' You Please	196?	—	3.00	6.00
—Reissue					
❑ Musicor 1250	Crying Like a Baby/You'll Fall in Love	1967	3.00	6.00	12.00
❑ Musicor 1270	No More Tears/You'll Fall in Love	1967	3.00	6.00	12.00
❑ Musicor 1305	Sugar (Don't Take Away My Candy)/Blues in the Ghetto	1968	3.00	6.00	12.00
❑ Sketch 219	United/Prove Every Word You Say	1964	3.75	7.50	15.00
❑ United Artists 0100	I'm a Happy Man/It Will Stand	1973	—	2.50	5.00
—"Silver Spotlight Series" reissue; B-side by The Showmen					
❑ United Artists 807	United/Prove Every Word You Say	1965	5.00	10.00	20.00
❑ United Artists 853	I'm a Happy Man/Kiss Kiss Kiss	1965	5.00	10.00	20.00
❑ United Artists 936	Please Baby Please/A Bench in the Park	1965	5.00	10.00	20.00
❑ United Artists 50004	Goin' Wild/Main Street	1966	3.75	7.50	15.00
❑ United Artists 50033	In My Neighborhood/Then Came Heartbreak	1966	3.75	7.50	15.00
❑ United Artists 50069	You're a Puzzle/Ha Ha	1966	3.75	7.50	15.00
❑ United Artists 50107	You/You Promised Me Great Things	1966	3.75	7.50	15.00
Albums					
❑ Ambient Sound FZ 37717	Here We Are	1982	3.75	7.50	15.00
❑ Ambient Sound/ Rounder ASR-801	Way Back	1985	3.00	6.00	12.00
❑ Collectables COL-5022	Greatest Hits	198?	2.50	5.00	10.00
❑ Relic 5020	The Jive Five's Greatest Hits (1961-1963)	198?	2.50	5.00	10.00
❑ United Artists UAL-3455 [M]	The Jive Five	1965	12.50	25.00	50.00
❑ United Artists UAS-6455 [S]	The Jive Five	1965	18.75	37.50	75.00

JOEL, BILLY

Number	Title (A Side/B Side)	Yr	VG	VG+	NM
45s					
❑ Columbia 18-02518	Say Goodbye to Hollywood/Summer, Highland Falls	1981	—	2.00	4.00
❑ Columbia 18-02628	She's Got a Way/The Ballad of Billy the Kid	1981	—	2.00	4.00
❑ Columbia 13-03238	It's Still Rock and Roll to Me/Don't Ask Me Why	1982	—	—	3.00
—Reissue					
❑ Columbia 13-03239	You May Be Right/She's Got a Way	1982	—	—	3.00
—Reissue					
❑ Columbia 13-03241	Honesty/Sometimes a Fantasy	1982	—	—	3.00
—Reissue					
❑ Columbia 38-03244	Pressure/Laura	1982	—	2.00	4.00
❑ Columbia CNR-03321	Pressure/(B-side blank)	1982	2.00	4.00	8.00
—One-sided budget release (large hole)					
❑ Columbia 38-03413	Allentown/Elvis Presley Blvd.	1982	—	2.00	4.00
❑ Columbia CNR-03426	Allentown/(B-side blank)	1982	2.00	4.00	8.00
—One-sided budget release					
❑ Columbia 38-03780	Goodnight Saigon/A Room of Our Own	1983	—	2.00	4.00
❑ Columbia 38-04012	Tell Her About It/Easy Money	1983	—	—	3.00
❑ Columbia 38-04149	Uptown Girl/Careless Talk	1983	—	—	3.00

Number	Title (A Side/B Side)	Yr	VG	VG+	NM
❑ Columbia 53-04149	Uptown Girl/Careless Talk	1984	—	—	3.00
—Gold "Instant Classics" reissue label					
❑ Columbia 38-04259	An Innocent Man/I'll Cry Instead	1983	—	—	3.00
❑ Columbia 38-04400	The Longest Time/Christie Lee	1984	—	—	3.00
❑ Columbia 38-04514	Leave a Tender Moment Alone/This Night	1984	—	—	3.00
❑ Columbia 38-04681	Keeping the Faith (Special Mix)/She's Right On Time	1984	—	—	3.00
❑ Columbia 38-05417	You're Only Human (Second Wind)/Surprises	1985	—	—	3.00
❑ Columbia 38-05657	The Night Is Still Young/Summer, Highland Falls	1985	—	—	3.00
❑ Columbia 38-06108	A Matter of Trust/Getting Closer	1986	—	—	3.00
❑ Columbia 38-06526	This Is the Time/Code of Silence	1986	—	—	3.00
❑ Columbia 38-06994	Baby Grand/Big Man on Mulberry Street	1987	—	—	3.00
—A-side with Ray Charles					
❑ Columbia 38-07626	Back in the U.S.S.R./Big Shot	1987	—	—	3.00
❑ Columbia 38-07664	The Times They Are a-Changin'/Back in the U.S.S.R.	1987	—	2.00	4.00
❑ Columbia 13-08415	Tell Her About It/Easy Money	1988	—	—	3.00
—Reissue					
❑ Columbia 13-08416	An Innocent Man/I'll Cry Instead	1988	—	—	3.00
—Reissue					
❑ Columbia 13-08417	The Longest Time/Christie Lee	1988	—	—	3.00
—Reissue					
❑ Columbia 13-08418	Leave a Tender Moment Alone/This Night	1988	—	—	3.00
—Reissue					
❑ Columbia 13-08419	Keeping the Faith/She's Right on Time	1988	—	—	3.00
—Reissue					
❑ Columbia 13-08420	You're Only Human (Second Wind)/Surprises	1988	—	—	3.00
—Reissue					
❑ Columbia 3-10015	Travelin' Prayer/Ain't No Crime	1974	2.50	5.00	10.00
❑ Columbia 3-10064	The Entertainer/The Mexican Connection	1974	2.00	4.00	8.00
❑ Columbia 3-10412	James/Summer, Highland Falls	1976	2.50	5.00	10.00
❑ Columbia 3-10562	Say Goodbye to Hollywood/I've Loved These Days	1977	2.50	5.00	10.00
❑ Columbia 3-10624	Movin' Out (Anthony's Song)/She's Always a Woman	1977	3.00	6.00	12.00
❑ Columbia 3-10646	Just the Way You Are/Get It Right the First Time	1977	—	2.50	5.00
❑ Columbia 3-10708	Movin' Out (Anthony's Song)/Everybody Has a Dream	1978	—	2.50	5.00
❑ Columbia 3-10750	Only the Good Die Young/Get It Right the First Time	1978	—	2.50	5.00
❑ Columbia 3-10788	She's Always a Woman/Vienna	1978	—	2.50	5.00
❑ Columbia 3-10853	My Life/52nd Street	1978	—	2.50	5.00
❑ Columbia 3-10913	Big Shot/Root Beer Rag	1979	—	2.50	5.00
❑ Columbia 3-10959	Honesty/The Mexican Connection	1979	—	2.50	5.00
❑ Columbia 1-11231	You May Be Right/Close to the Borderline	1980	—	2.00	4.00
❑ Columbia 1-11276	It's Still Rock and Roll to Me/Through the Long Night	1980	—	2.00	4.00
❑ Columbia 1-11331	Don't Ask Me Why/C'etait Toi (You Were the One)	1980	—	2.00	4.00
❑ Columbia 1-11379	Sometimes a Fantasy/All for Leyna	1980	—	2.50	5.00
❑ Columbia 4-45963	Piano Man/You're My Home	1973	2.00	4.00	8.00
❑ Columbia 4-46055	Worse Comes to Worst/Somewhere Along the Line	1974	2.50	5.00	10.00
❑ Columbia 38-73021	We Didn't Start the Fire/House of Blue Light	1989	—	—	3.00
❑ Columbia 38-73091	I Go to Extremes/When in Rome	1989	—	—	3.00
❑ Columbia 38-73442	That's Not Her Style/And So It Goes	1990	—	—	3.00
❑ Epic 34-06118	Modern Woman/Sleeping with the Television On	1986	—	—	3.00
❑ Family Productions 0900	She's Got a Way/Everybody Loves You Now	1971	7.50	15.00	30.00
❑ Family Productions 0906	Tomorrow Is Today/Everybody Loves You Now	1971	7.50	15.00	30.00
Albums					
❑ Columbia KC 32544	Piano Man	1973	3.00	6.00	12.00
—Some copies have the first song spelled "Travelin' Prayer," others have it "Travellin' Prayer." No difference in value.					
❑ Columbia PC 33146	Streetlife Serenade	1975	2.50	5.00	10.00
—No bar code on back cover					
❑ Columbia PC 33848	Turnstiles	1976	2.50	5.00	10.00
—No bar code on back cover					
❑ Columbia JC 34987	The Stranger	1977	2.50	5.00	10.00
❑ Columbia FC 35609	52nd Street	1978	2.50	5.00	10.00
❑ Columbia FC 36384	Glass Houses	1980	2.50	5.00	10.00
❑ Columbia TC 37461	Songs in the Attic	1981	2.50	5.00	10.00
❑ Columbia QC 38200	The Nylon Curtain	1982	2.50	5.00	10.00
❑ Columbia QC 38837	An Innocent Man	1983	2.50	5.00	10.00
❑ Columbia PC 38984	Cold Spring Harbor	1983	2.00	4.00	8.00
—Remixed, remastered version of Family Productions album					
❑ Columbia C2 40121 [(2)]	Greatest Hits, Volumes 1 and 2	1985	3.00	6.00	12.00

Number	Title (A Side/B Side)	Yr	VG	VG+	NM
❑ Columbia OC 40402	The Bridge	1986	2.50	5.00	10.00
❑ Columbia C2 40996 [(2)]	KOHUEPT	1987	3.75	7.50	15.00
❑ Columbia OC 44366	Storm Front	1989	3.00	6.00	12.00
❑ Family Productions FPS-2700	Cold Spring Harbor	1971	10.00	20.00	40.00

—Authentic copies have mostly dark blue labels; when reissued on Columbia, the entire LP was remixed and remastered, and "You Can Make Me Free" was shortened by three minutes

JOHN, ELTON

45s

Number	Title (A Side/B Side)	Yr	VG	VG+	NM
❑ Congress 6017	Lady Samantha/It's Me That You Need	1970	12.50	25.00	50.00
❑ Congress 6022	Border Song/Bad Side of the Moon	1970	12.50	25.00	50.00
❑ DJM 70008	Lady Samantha/All Across the Havens	1969	75.00	150.00	300.00
❑ Geffen 28578	Heartache All Over the World/Highlander	1986	—	—	3.00
❑ Geffen 28800	Nikita/Restless	1985	—	—	3.00
❑ Geffen 28873	Wrap Her Up/The Man Who Never Died	1985	—	—	3.00
❑ Geffen 29111	In Neon/Tactics	1984	—	—	3.00
❑ Geffen 29189	Who Wears These Shoes?/Lonely Boy	1984	—	—	3.00
❑ Geffen 29292	Sad Songs (Say So Much)/A Simple Man	1984	—	—	3.00
❑ Geffen 29460	I Guess That's Why They Call It the Blues/The Retreat	1983	—	—	3.00
❑ Geffen 29568	Kiss the Bride/Choc Ice Goes Mental	1983	—	—	3.00
❑ Geffen 29639	I'm Still Standing/Love So Cold	1983	—	—	3.00
❑ Geffen 29846	Ball & Chain/Where Have All the Good Times Gone?	1982	—	2.00	4.00
❑ Geffen 29954	Blue Eyes/Hey Papa Legba	1982	—	2.00	4.00
❑ Geffen 49722	Nobody Wins/Fools in Fashion	1981	—	2.00	4.00
❑ Geffen 49788	Chloe/Tortured	1981	—	2.00	4.00
❑ Geffen 50049	Empty Garden (Hey Hey Johnny)/Take Me Down to the Ocean	1982	—	2.00	4.00
❑ MCA 40000	Crocodile Rock/Elderberry Wine	1972	—	3.00	6.00

—Original pressings have a solid black label

Number	Title (A Side/B Side)	Yr	VG	VG+	NM
❑ MCA 40046	Daniel/Skyline Pigeon	1973	—	2.50	5.00
❑ MCA 40105	Saturday Night's Alright for Fighting//Jack Rabbit/Whenever You're Ready	1973	—	2.50	5.00
❑ MCA 40148	Goodbye Yellow Brick Road/Young Man's Blues	1973	—	2.50	5.00
❑ MCA 40198	Bennie and the Jets/Harmony	1974	—	2.50	5.00
❑ MCA 40259	Don't Let the Sun Go Down on Me/Sick City	1974	—	2.50	5.00
❑ MCA 40297	The Bitch Is Back/Cold Highway	1974	—	2.50	5.00
❑ MCA 40344	Lucy in the Sky with Diamonds/One Day at a Time	1974	—	2.50	5.00

—Both sides feature "Dr. Winston O'Boogie" (John Lennon)

Number	Title (A Side/B Side)	Yr	VG	VG+	NM
❑ MCA 40364	Philadelphia Freedom/I Saw Her Standing There	1975	—	2.50	5.00

—B-side features John Lennon

Number	Title (A Side/B Side)	Yr	VG	VG+	NM
❑ MCA 40421	Someone Saved My Life Tonight/House of Cards	1975	—	2.50	5.00

—Original copies have "Captain Fantastic" label

Number	Title (A Side/B Side)	Yr	VG	VG+	NM
❑ MCA 40461	Island Girl/Sugar on the Floor	1975	—	2.00	4.00
❑ MCA 40505	Grow Some Funk of Your Own/I Feel Like a Bullet (in the Gun of Robert Ford)	1976	—	2.00	4.00
❑ MCA 40892	Ego/Flinstone Boy	1978	—	2.00	4.00
❑ MCA 40973	Part-Time Love/I Cry at Night	1978	—	2.00	4.00
❑ MCA 40993	Song for Guy/Lovesick	1979	2.50	5.00	10.00

—The stock copy is much scarcer than the promo, the only Elton John MCA single where this is the case.

Number	Title (A Side/B Side)	Yr	VG	VG+	NM
❑ MCA 41042	Mama Can't Buy You Love/Three Way Love Affair	1979	—	2.00	4.00
❑ MCA 41126	Victim of Love/Strangers	1979	—	2.00	4.00

—Label correctly says "From the MCA LP... 'Victim of Love'"

Number	Title (A Side/B Side)	Yr	VG	VG+	NM
❑ MCA 41159	Johnny B. Goode/Georgia	1980	—	2.50	5.00
❑ MCA 41236	Little Jeannie/Conquer the Sun	1980	—	2.00	4.00

—Originals have a colorful custom label

Number	Title (A Side/B Side)	Yr	VG	VG+	NM
❑ MCA 41293	(Sartorial Eloquence) Don't Ya Wanna Play This Game No More?//Cartier/White Man Danger	1980	—	2.00	4.00
❑ MCA 53196	Candle in the Wind/Sorry Seems to Be the Hardest Word	1987	—	—	3.00
❑ MCA 53260	Take Me to the Pilot/Tonight	1988	—	2.00	4.00
❑ MCA 53345	I Don't Wanna Go On with You Like That/Rope Around a Fool	1988	—	—	3.00
❑ MCA 53408	A Word in Spanish/Heavy Traffic	1988	—	—	3.00
❑ MCA 53692	Healing Hands/Dancing in the End Zone	1989	—	—	3.00
❑ MCA 53750	Sacrifice/Love Is a Cannibal	1989	—	—	3.00
❑ MCA 65018	Step Into Christmas/Ho! Ho! Ho! (Who'd Be a Turkey at Christmas)	1973	—	2.50	5.00

—Originals have black labels with rainbow

Number	Title (A Side/B Side)	Yr	VG	VG+	NM
❑ MCA 79026	Club at the End of the Street/Sacrifice	1990	—	—	3.00
❑ Rocket 40645	Sorry Seems to Be the Hardest Word/Shoulder Holster	1976	—	2.00	4.00
❑ Rocket 40677	Bite Your Lip (Get up and dance!)/Chameleon	1977	—	2.00	4.00
❑ Uni 55246	Border Song/Bad Side of the Moon	1970	—	3.00	6.00
❑ Uni 55265	Your Song/Take Me to the Pilot	1970	—	3.00	6.00
❑ Uni 55277	Friends/Honey Roll	1971	—	3.00	6.00
❑ Uni 55314	Levon/Goodbye	1971	—	3.00	6.00
❑ Uni 55318	Tiny Dancer/Razor Face	1971	—	3.00	6.00

—Stock copies have full-length version of A-side

Number	Title (A Side/B Side)	Yr	VG	VG+	NM
❑ Uni 55328	Rocket Man/Suzie (Dramas)	1972	—	3.00	6.00
❑ Uni 55343	Honky Cat/Slave	1972	—	3.00	6.00
❑ Viking 1010	From Denver to L.A./Warm Summer Rain	1970	15.00	30.00	60.00

—Credited to "Elton Johns"; B-side by The Barbara Moore Singers

Albums

Number	Title (A Side/B Side)	Yr	VG	VG+	NM
❑ Geffen GHS 2002	The Fox	1981	2.50	5.00	10.00
❑ Geffen GHS 2013	Jump Up!	1982	2.50	5.00	10.00
❑ Geffen GHS 4006	Too Low for Zero	1983	2.50	5.00	10.00
❑ Geffen GHS 24031	Breaking Hearts	1984	2.50	5.00	10.00
❑ Geffen GHS 24077	Ice on Fire	1985	2.50	5.00	10.00
❑ Geffen GHS 24114	Leather Jackets	1986	2.50	5.00	10.00
❑ Geffen GHS 24153	Elton John's Greatest Hits, Vol. 3, 1979-1987	1987	2.50	5.00	10.00
❑ MCA 619	11-17-70	1979	2.00	4.00	8.00

Number	Title (A Side/B Side)	Yr	VG	VG+	NM
❑ MCA 620	Empty Sky	1979	2.00	4.00	8.00
❑ MCA 621	Rock of the Westies	1979	2.00	4.00	8.00
❑ MCA 622	Here and There	1979	2.00	4.00	8.00
❑ MCA 771	Victim of Love	1981	2.00	4.00	8.00
❑ MCA 772	21 at 33	1981	2.00	4.00	8.00
❑ MCA 1689	Elton John's Greatest Hits	198?	2.00	4.00	8.00
❑ MCA 2012	Elton John	1973	2.50	5.00	10.00
❑ MCA 2014	Tumbleweed Connection	1973	2.50	5.00	10.00
—With booklet					
❑ MCA 2015	11-17-70	1973	2.50	5.00	10.00
❑ MCA 2016	Madman Across the Water	1973	2.50	5.00	10.00
—With booklet					
❑ MCA 2017	Honky Chateau	1973	2.50	5.00	10.00
❑ MCA 2100	Don't Shoot Me, I'm Only the Piano Player	1973	5.00	10.00	20.00
—With all-black label (no rainbow) and booklet					
❑ MCA 2116	Caribou	1974	2.50	5.00	10.00
❑ MCA 2128	Elton John's Greatest Hits	1974	2.50	5.00	10.00
❑ MCA 2130	Empty Sky	1975	2.50	5.00	10.00
—First American issue of his 1969 debut					
❑ MCA 2142	Captain Fantastic and the Brown Dirt Cowboy	1975	3.00	6.00	12.00
—With custom label, two booklets and poster					
❑ MCA 2163	Rock of the Westies	1975	2.50	5.00	10.00
❑ MCA 2197	Here and There	1976	2.50	5.00	10.00
❑ MCA 3001	Tumbleweed Connection	1977	2.00	4.00	8.00
❑ MCA 3003	Madman Across the Water	1977	2.00	4.00	8.00
❑ MCA 3027	Elton John's Greatest Hits, Volume 2	1977	2.50	5.00	10.00
❑ MCA 3065	A Single Man	1978	2.50	5.00	10.00
❑ MCA 5104	Victim of Love	1979	2.50	5.00	10.00
❑ MCA 5121	21 at 33	1980	2.50	5.00	10.00
—Originals have custom labels					
❑ MCA 5224	Elton John's Greatest Hits	1981	2.00	4.00	8.00
❑ MCA 5225	Elton John's Greatest Hits, Volume 2	1981	2.00	4.00	8.00
❑ MCA 6011 [(2)]	Blue Moves	1979	2.50	5.00	10.00
❑ MCA 6240	Reg Strikes Back	1988	2.50	5.00	10.00
❑ MCA 6321	Sleeping with the Past	1989	2.50	5.00	10.00
❑ MCA 6894 [(2)]	Goodbye Yellow Brick Road	1980	2.50	5.00	10.00
❑ MCA 8022 [(2)]	Live in Australia with the Melbourne Symphony Orchestra	1987	3.75	7.50	15.00
❑ MCA 2-10003 [(2)]	Goodbye Yellow Brick Road	1973	3.75	7.50	15.00
❑ MCA 13921 [EP]	The Thom Bell Sessions	1979	2.00	4.00	8.00
❑ MCA 37064	Honky Chateau	1979	2.00	4.00	8.00
❑ MCA 37065	Caribou	1979	2.00	4.00	8.00
❑ MCA 37066	Captain Fantastic and the Brown Dirt Cowboy	1979	2.00	4.00	8.00
❑ MCA 37067	Elton John	1979	2.00	4.00	8.00
❑ MCA 37068	A Single Man	1979	2.00	4.00	8.00
❑ MCA 37113	Don't Shoot Me, I'm Only the Piano Player	1979	2.00	4.00	8.00
❑ MCA 37199	Tumbleweed Connection	1982	2.00	4.00	8.00
❑ MCA 37200	Madman Across the Water	1982	2.00	4.00	8.00
❑ MCA 37215	Elton John's Greatest Hits	1983	2.00	4.00	8.00
❑ MCA 37216	Elton John's Greatest Hits	1983	2.00	4.00	8.00
❑ MCA 37266	Your Songs	1986	2.50	5.00	10.00
❑ MCA 39115	The Complete Thom Bell Sessions	1989	7.50	15.00	30.00
❑ MCA R231711 [(2)]	Greatest Hits Volumes One and Two	198?	3.75	7.50	15.00
—RCA Music Service exclusive; combines both MCA greatest-hits sets					
❑ Paramount PAS 6004	Friends (Soundtrack)	1971	5.00	10.00	20.00
—Whitish gray label original					
❑ Rocket 2-11004 [(2)]	Blue Moves	1976	3.75	7.50	15.00
—Originals have light blue labels with a train at the top of the label					
❑ Uni 73090	Elton John	1970	3.75	7.50	15.00
❑ Uni 73096	Tumbleweed Connection	1971	3.75	7.50	15.00
—With booklet					
❑ Uni 93090	Elton John	1971	3.00	6.00	12.00
❑ Uni 93096	Tumbleweed Connection	1971	3.00	6.00	12.00
—With booklet					
❑ Uni 93105	11-17-70	1971	3.75	7.50	15.00
❑ Uni 93120	Madman Across the Water	1971	3.75	7.50	15.00
—With booklet					

Number	Title (A Side/B Side)	Yr	VG	VG+	NM
❑ Uni 93135	Honky Chateau	1972	5.00	10.00	20.00
—With "(P) 1972 MCA Records, Inc." on label					
❑ Uni 93135	Honky Chateau	1972	3.75	7.50	15.00
—With "(P) 1972 This Record Co., Ltd." on label					

JOHN, ELTON, AND KIKI DEE

45s

Number	Title (A Side/B Side)	Yr	VG	VG+	NM
❑ Rocket 40585	Don't Go Breakin' My Heart/Snow Queen	1976	—	2.00	4.00

JOHNNY AND THE HURRICANES

45s

Number	Title (A Side/B Side)	Yr	VG	VG+	NM
❑ Atila 214	Judy's Moody/I Love You	1967	2.50	5.00	10.00
❑ Atila 215	Because I Love You/Wisdom's 5th Take	1967	2.50	5.00	10.00
❑ Atila 216	Red River Rock '67/The Psychedlic Woman	1967	2.50	5.00	10.00
❑ Big Top 3036	Down Yonder/Sheba	1960	5.00	10.00	20.00
❑ Big Top 3051	Revival/Rocking Goose	1960	5.00	10.00	20.00
❑ Big Top 3056	You Are My Sunshine/Molly-O	1960	5.00	10.00	20.00
❑ Big Top 3063	Ja-Da/Mr. Lonely	1961	5.00	10.00	20.00
❑ Big Top 3076	Old Smokie/High Voltage	1961	5.00	10.00	20.00
❑ Big Top 3090	Traffic Jam/Farewell, Farewell	1961	5.00	10.00	20.00
❑ Big Top 3103	Misirlou/Salvation	1962	5.00	10.00	20.00
❑ Big Top 3113	San Antonio Rose/Come On Train	1962	5.00	10.00	20.00
❑ Big Top 3125	Shiek of Araby/Minnesota Fats	1962	5.00	10.00	20.00
❑ Big Top 3132	Whatever Happened to Baby Jane/Greens and Beans	1963	5.00	10.00	20.00
❑ Big Top 3146	James Bond Theme/Hungry Eye	1963	5.00	10.00	20.00
❑ Big Top 3159	Rough Road/Kaw-Liga	1963	5.00	10.00	20.00
❑ Jeff 211	Saga of the Beatles/Rene	1964	3.75	7.50	15.00
❑ Lost-Nite 221	Reveille Rock/Sheba	196?	—	2.50	5.00
—Reissue					
❑ Mala 470	It's a Mad, Mad, Mad, Mad World/Shadows	1963	2.50	5.00	10.00
❑ Mala 483	That's All/Honey, Honey	1964	2.50	5.00	10.00
❑ Twirl 1001	Crossfire/Lazy	1958	12.50	25.00	50.00
❑ Warwick 502	Crossfire/Lazy	1959	6.25	12.50	25.00
❑ Warwick 509 [M]	Red River Rock/Buckeye	1959	6.25	12.50	25.00
❑ Warwick 509 ST [S]	Red River Rock/Buckeye	1959	12.50	25.00	50.00
❑ Warwick 513 [M]	Reveille Rock/Time Bomb	1959	6.25	12.50	25.00
❑ Warwick 513 ST [S]	Reveille Rock/Time Bomb	1959	12.50	25.00	50.00
❑ Warwick 520	Beatnik Fly/Sand Storm	1960	5.00	10.00	20.00

Albums

Number	Title (A Side/B Side)	Yr	VG	VG+	NM
❑ Atila 1030 [M]	Live at the Star-Club	1964	75.00	150.00	300.00
❑ Big Top 12-1302 [M]	The Big Sound of Johnny and the Hurricanes	1960	62.50	125.00	250.00
❑ Big Top ST 12-1302 [S]	The Big Sound of Johnny and the Hurricanes	1960	75.00	150.00	300.00
❑ Warwick W-2007 [M]	Johnny and the Hurricanes	1959	37.50	75.00	150.00
❑ Warwick W-2007ST [S]	Johnny and the Hurricanes	1959	75.00	150.00	300.00
❑ Warwick W-2010 [M]	Stormsville	1960	37.50	75.00	150.00
❑ Warwick W-2010ST [S]	Stormsville	1960	62.50	125.00	250.00

JONES, JIMMY

45s

Number	Title (A Side/B Side)	Yr	VG	VG+	NM
❑ ABC-Paramount 10094	Blue and Lonely/Daddy Needs Baby	1960	37.50	75.00	150.00
—As "Jimmy Jones and the Pretenders"					
❑ Arrow 717	Heaven in Your Eyes/The Whistlin' Man	1957	45.00	90.00	180.00
—As "Jimmy Jones and the Jones Boys"					
❑ Bell 682	Personal Property/39-21-40	1967	2.00	4.00	8.00
❑ Bell 689	True Love Ways/Snap My Fingers	1967	2.00	4.00	8.00
❑ Capitol 3849	If I Knew Then (What I Know Now)/ Everything's Gonna Be All Right	1974	—	2.50	5.00
❑ Conchillo 1	Ain't Nothing Wrong Makin' Love the First Night/ Time and Changes	1976	—	3.00	6.00
❑ Cub 9049	Handy Man/The Search Is Over	1959	6.25	12.50	25.00
❑ Cub 9067	Good Timin'/My Precious Angel	1960	6.25	12.50	25.00
❑ Cub 9072	That's When I Cried/I Just Go for You	1960	5.00	10.00	20.00
❑ Cub 9076	Itchin'/Ee-I-Ee-I-Oh	1960	5.00	10.00	20.00
❑ Cub 9082	Ready for Love/For You	1960	5.00	10.00	20.00
❑ Cub 9085	I Told You So/You Got It	1961	3.75	7.50	15.00
❑ Cub 9093	Dear One/I Say Love	1961	3.75	7.50	15.00
❑ Cub 9102	Mr. Music Man/Holler Hey	1961	3.75	7.50	15.00
❑ Cub 9110	You're Much Too Young/Nights of Mexico	1962	3.75	7.50	15.00
❑ Epic 9339	Whenever You Need Me/You for Me to Love	1959	30.00	60.00	120.00
❑ Parkway 988	Don't You Just Know It/Dynamite	1966	2.50	5.00	10.00
❑ Rama 210	Lover/Plain Old Love	1956	30.00	60.00	120.00
—As "Jimmy Jones and the Pretenders"					
❑ Roulette 4232	Lover/Plain Old Love	1960	7.50	15.00	30.00
—As "Jimmy 'Handyman' Jones"					
❑ Vee Jay 505	No Insurance (For a Broken Heart)/Mr. Fix-It	1963	3.75	7.50	15.00

Albums

Number	Title (A Side/B Side)	Yr	VG	VG+	NM
❑ Jen Jillus 1001	The Handy Man's Back in Town	1977	3.00	6.00	12.00
❑ MGM E-3847 [M]	Good Timin'	1960	30.00	60.00	120.00
❑ MGM SE-3847 [S]	Good Timin'	1960	40.00	80.00	160.00

JONES, TOM

45s

Number	Title (A Side/B Side)	Yr	VG	VG+	NM
❑ China 871038-7	Kiss/E.F.L.	1989	—	—	3.00
—A-side: The Art of Noise with Tom Jones; B-side by Art of Noise					
❑ Epic 50308	Say You'll Stay Until Tomorrow/Lady Lay	1976	—	2.00	4.00
❑ Epic 50382	Take Me Tonight/I Hope You'll Understand	1977	—	2.00	4.00
❑ Epic 50468	What a Night/That's Where I Belong	1977	—	2.00	4.00
❑ Epic 50506	There's Nothing Stronger Than Our Love/No One Gave Me Love	1978	—	2.00	4.00

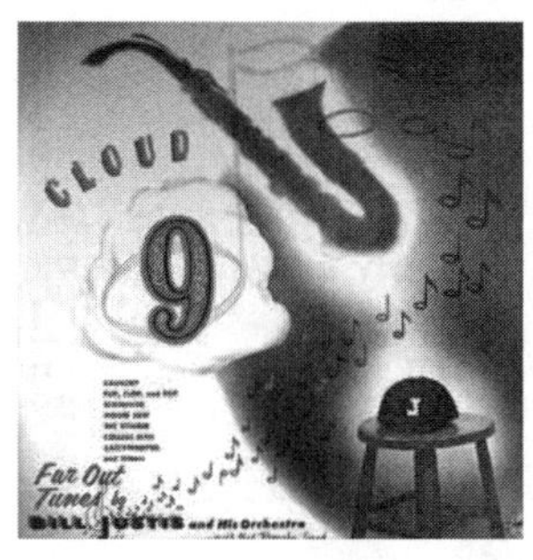

Number	Title (A Side/B Side)	Yr	VG	VG+	NM
❑ Epic 50636	Hey Love/Baby, As You Turn Away	1978	—	2.00	4.00
❑ MCA 41127	Dancing Endlessly/Never Had a Lady Before	1979	—	2.00	4.00
❑ Mercury 76100	Darlin'/I Don't Want to Know You That Way	1981	—	2.00	4.00
❑ Mercury 76115	What in the World's Come Over You/ The Things That Matter Most to Me	1981	—	2.00	4.00
❑ Mercury 76125	Lady Lay Down/A Daughter's Question	1981	—	2.00	4.00
❑ Mercury 76172	A Woman's Touch/I'll Never Get Over You	1982	—	2.00	4.00
❑ Mercury 810445-7	Touch Me (I'll Be Your Fool Once More)/We're Wasting Our Time	1983	—	—	3.00
❑ Mercury 812631-7	It'll Be Me/If I Ever Had to Say Goodbye to You	1983	—	—	3.00
❑ Mercury 814820-7	I've Been Rained On Too/That Old Piano	1983	—	—	3.00
❑ Mercury 818801-7	This Time/Memphis, Tennessee	1984	—	—	3.00
❑ Mercury 870233-7	Things That Matter Most to Me/Green, Green Grass of Home	1988	—	—	3.00
❑ Mercury 880173-7	All the Love Is On the Radio/(B-side unknown)	1984	—	—	3.00
❑ Mercury 880402-7	I'm an Old Rock and Roller (Dancin' to a Different Beat)/ My Kind of Girl	1984	—	—	3.00
❑ Mercury 880569-7	Give Her All the Roses (Don't Wait Until Tomorrow)/ A Picture of You	1985	—	—	3.00
❑ Mercury 884039-7	Not Another Heart Song/Only My Heart Knows	1985	—	—	3.00
❑ Mercury 884252-7	It's Four in the Morning/I'll Never Get Over You	1985	—	—	3.00
❑ Mercury 888911-7	Lover to Lover/A Daughter's Question	1987	—	—	3.00
❑ Parrot 9737	It's Not Unusual/To Wait for Love (Is to Waste Your Life Away)	1965	2.50	5.00	10.00
❑ Parrot 9765	What's New Pussycat/Once Upon a Time	1965	2.50	5.00	10.00
❑ Parrot 9787	With These Hands/Some Other Guy	1965	2.00	4.00	8.00
❑ Parrot 9801	Thunderball/Key to My Heart	1965	2.00	4.00	8.00
❑ Parrot 9809	Promise Her Anything/Little You	1966	2.00	4.00	8.00
❑ Parrot 40006	Not Responsible/Once There Was a Time	1966	2.00	4.00	8.00
❑ Parrot 40008	City Girl/What a Party	1966	2.00	4.00	8.00
❑ Parrot 40009	Green, Green Grass of Home/If I Had You	1966	2.00	4.00	8.00
❑ Parrot 40012	Detroit City/Ten Guitars	1967	2.00	4.00	8.00
❑ Parrot 40014	Funny Familiar Forgotten Feelings/I'll Never Let You Go	1967	2.00	4.00	8.00
❑ Parrot 40016	Sixteen Tons/Things I Wanna Do	1967	2.00	4.00	8.00
❑ Parrot 40018	I'll Never Fall in Love Again/Once Upon a Time	1967	3.00	6.00	12.00
—First pressings contain the full-length version of the A-side; time is listed at over four minutes					
❑ Parrot 40018	I'll Never Fall in Love Again/Once Upon a Time	1967	2.00	4.00	8.00
—Later pressings delete a verse from the A-side; time is listed at 2:55					
❑ Parrot 40020	Land of a Thousand Dances/I Can't Stop Loving You	1967	5.00	10.00	20.00
—May be promo only					
❑ Parrot 40024	I'm Coming Home/Lonely One	1967	2.00	4.00	8.00
❑ Parrot 40025	Delilah/Smile Away Your Blues	1968	2.00	4.00	8.00
❑ Parrot 40029	Help Yourself/Day by Day	1968	2.00	4.00	8.00
❑ Parrot 40035	A Minute of Your Time/Looking Out My Window	1968	2.00	4.00	8.00
❑ Parrot 40038	Love Me Tonight/Hide and Seek	1969	—	3.00	6.00
❑ Parrot 40045	Without Love (There Is Nothing)/The Man Who Knows Too Much	1969	—	3.00	6.00
❑ Parrot 40048	Daughter of Darkness/Tupelo Mississippi Flash	1970	—	3.00	6.00
❑ Parrot 40051	I (Who Have Nothing)/Stop Breaking My Heart	1970	—	3.00	6.00
❑ Parrot 40056	Can't Stop Loving You/Never Give Away Love	1970	—	3.00	6.00
❑ Parrot 40058	She's a Lady/My Way	1971	—	3.00	6.00
❑ Parrot 40062	Puppet Man/Every Mile	1971	—	3.00	6.00
❑ Parrot 40064	Puppet Man/Resurrection Shuffle	1971	—	2.50	5.00
❑ Parrot 40067	Till/One Day Soon	1971	—	2.50	5.00
❑ Parrot 40070	The Young New Mexican Puppeteer/All That I Need Is Time	1972	—	2.50	5.00
❑ Parrot 40074	Letter to Lucille/Thank the Lord	1973	—	2.50	5.00
❑ Parrot 40078	La, La, La (Just Having You Here)/Love, Love, Love	1973	—	2.50	5.00
❑ Parrot 40080	Somethin' 'Bout You Baby I Like/Keep a-Talkin' 'Bout Love	1973	—	2.50	5.00
❑ Parrot 40081	Pledging My Love/I'm Too Far Gone	1974	—	2.50	5.00
❑ Parrot 40083	Ain't No Love/When the Band Goes Home	1974	—	2.50	5.00
❑ Parrot 40084	I Got Your Number/The Pain of Love	1974	—	2.50	5.00
❑ Parrot 40086	Memories Don't Leave Like People Do/Helping Hand	1975	—	2.50	5.00
❑ Tower 126	Little Lonely One/That's What We'll All Do	1965	3.00	6.00	12.00
❑ Tower 176	Lonely One/I Was a Fool	1965	3.00	6.00	12.00
❑ Tower 190	Baby I'm in Love/Chills and Fever	1966	2.50	5.00	10.00
Albums					
❑ Epic PE 34383	Classic Tom Jones	1976	3.00	6.00	12.00
❑ Epic PE 34468	Say You'll Stay Until Tomorrow	1977	3.00	6.00	12.00
❑ Epic PE 34720	Tom Is Love	1977	2.50	5.00	10.00
❑ Epic JE 35023	What a Night	1978	2.50	5.00	10.00
❑ Jive 1214-1-J	Move Closer	1989	3.00	6.00	12.00

Number	Title (A Side/B Side)	Yr	VG	VG+	NM
❑ London PS 717	The Country Side of Tom Jones	1978	2.50	5.00	10.00
❑ London LC-50002	Tom Jones' Greatest Hits	1977	3.00	6.00	12.00
❑ London 820234-1	This Is Tom Jones	1985	2.00	4.00	8.00
❑ London 820319-1	Tom Jones' Greatest Hits	1985	2.50	5.00	10.00
❑ MCA 3182	Tom Jones	1979	2.50	5.00	10.00
❑ MCA 37114	Rescue Me	1980	2.00	4.00	8.00
❑ Mercury SRM-1-4010	Darlin'	1981	2.50	5.00	10.00
❑ Mercury SRM-1-4062	Tom Jones Country	1982	2.50	5.00	10.00
❑ Mercury 814448-1	Don't Let Our Dreams Die Young	1983	2.50	5.00	10.00
❑ Mercury 822701-1	Love Is on the Radio	1984	2.50	5.00	10.00
❑ Mercury 826140-1	Tender Loving Care	1985	2.50	5.00	10.00
❑ Mercury 830409-1	Things That Matter Most to Me	1987	2.50	5.00	10.00
❑ Parrot PA 61004 [M]	It's Not Unusual	1965	3.75	7.50	15.00
❑ Parrot PA 61006 [M]	What's New Pussycat?	1965	3.75	7.50	15.00
❑ Parrot PA 61007 [M]	A-Tom-Ic Jones	1966	3.75	7.50	15.00
❑ Parrot PA 61009 [M]	Green, Green Grass of Home	1967	3.75	7.50	15.00
❑ Parrot PA 61011 [M]	Funny Familiar Forgotten Feelings	1967	3.75	7.50	15.00
❑ Parrot PA 61014 [M]	Tom Jones Live	1967	3.75	7.50	15.00
❑ Parrot PAS 71004 [S]	It's Not Unusual	1965	3.75	7.50	15.00
❑ Parrot PAS 71006 [S]	What's New Pussycat?	1965	3.75	7.50	15.00
❑ Parrot PAS 71007 [S]	A-Tom-Ic Jones	1966	3.75	7.50	15.00
❑ Parrot PAS 71009 [S]	Green, Green Grass of Home	1967	3.75	7.50	15.00
❑ Parrot PAS 71011 [S]	Funny Familiar Forgotten Feelings	1967	3.75	7.50	15.00
❑ Parrot PAS 71014 [S]	Tom Jones Live	1967	3.75	7.50	15.00
❑ Parrot PAS 71019	The Tom Jones Fever Zone	1968	3.00	6.00	12.00
❑ Parrot PAS 71025	Help Yourself	1969	3.00	6.00	12.00
❑ Parrot PAS 71028	This Is Tom Jones	1969	3.00	6.00	12.00
❑ Parrot PAS 71031	Live in Las Vegas	1969	3.00	6.00	12.00
❑ Parrot PAS 71037	Tom	1970	3.00	6.00	12.00
❑ Parrot PAS 71039	I (Who Have Nothing)	1970	3.00	6.00	12.00
❑ Parrot PAS 71046	She's a Lady	1971	3.00	6.00	12.00
❑ Parrot 2XPAS 71049/50 [(2)]	Live at Caesar's Palace	1971	3.00	6.00	12.00
❑ Parrot XPAS 71055	Close Up	1972	3.00	6.00	12.00
❑ Parrot XPAS 71060	The Body and Soul of Tom Jones	197?	3.00	6.00	12.00
❑ Parrot XPAS 71062	Tom Jones' Greatest Hits	1973	3.00	6.00	12.00
❑ Parrot PAS 71066	Somethin' 'Bout You Baby I Like	1974	3.00	6.00	12.00
❑ Parrot PAS 71068	Memories Don't Leave Like People Do	197?	3.00	6.00	12.00
JOPLIN, JANIS					
45s					
❑ Columbia 45023	Kozmik Blues/Little Girl Blue	1969	—	3.00	6.00
❑ Columbia 45080	One Good Man/Try (Just a Little Bit Harder)	1970	—	3.00	6.00
❑ Columbia 45128	Wake Me, Lord/Maybe	1970	—	3.00	6.00
❑ Columbia 45314	Me and Bobby McGee/Half Moon	1971	—	2.50	5.00
❑ Columbia 45379	Mercedez Benz/Cry Baby	1971	—	2.50	5.00
❑ Columbia 45433	Get It While You Can/Move Over	1971	—	2.50	5.00
❑ Columbia 45630	Bye Bye Baby/Down on Me	1972	—	2.50	5.00
Albums					
❑ Columbia KCS 9913	I Got Dem Ol' Kozmik Blues Again Mama!	1969	5.00	10.00	20.00
—"360 Sound Stereo" on label					
❑ Columbia KC 30322	Pearl	1971	3.75	7.50	15.00
❑ Columbia PC 30322	Pearl	198?	2.00	4.00	8.00
—Reissue with bar code					
❑ Columbia C2X 31160 [(2)]	Joplin in Concert	1972	5.00	10.00	20.00
❑ Columbia KC 32168	Janis Joplin's Greatest Hits	1973	3.75	7.50	15.00
❑ Columbia PG 33345 [(2)]	Janis	1975	3.75	7.50	15.00
❑ Columbia PC 37569	Farewell Song	1982	2.50	5.00	10.00
JOURNEY					
45s					
❑ Columbia 18-02241	Who's Crying Now/Mother, Father	1981	—	—	3.00
❑ Columbia 18-02567	Don't Stop Believin'/Natural Thing	1981	—	—	3.00
❑ Columbia 18-02687	Open Arms/Little Girl	1982	—	—	3.00
❑ Columbia 18-02883	Still They Ride/La Raza Del Sol	1982	—	—	3.00
❑ Columbia 13-03133	Open Arms/The Party's Over	1982	—	—	3.00
—Reissue					
❑ Columbia 13-03134	Who's Crying Now/Don't Stop Believin'	1982	—	—	3.00
—Reissue					
❑ Columbia 38-03513	Separate Ways (Worlds Apart)/Frontiers	1983	—	—	3.00
❑ Columbia CNR-03568	Separate Ways (Worlds Apart)/(B-side blank)	1983	—	2.50	5.00
—One-sided budget release					
❑ Columbia 38-03840	Faithfully/Frontiers	1983	—	—	3.00
❑ Columbia 38-04004	After the Fall/Only Solutions	1983	—	—	3.00
❑ Columbia 38-04151	Send Her My Love/Chain Reaction	1983	—	—	3.00
❑ Columbia 38-05869	Be Good to Yourself/Only the Young	1986	—	—	3.00
❑ Columbia 38-06134	Suzanne/Ask the Lonely	1986	—	—	3.00
❑ Columbia 38-06301	I'll Be Alright Without You/The Eyes of a Woman	1986	—	—	3.00
❑ Columbia 38-06302	Girl Can't Help It/It Could Have Been You	1986	—	—	3.00
❑ Columbia 38-07043	Why Can't This Night Go On Forever/Positive Touch	1987	—	—	3.00
❑ Columbia 3-10137	To Play Some Music/Topaz	1975	—	3.00	6.00
❑ Columbia 3-10324	On a Saturday Night/To Play Some Music	1976	—	3.00	6.00
❑ Columbia 3-10370	She Makes Me (Feel Alright)/It's All Too Much	1976	—	3.00	6.00
❑ Columbia 3-10522	Spaceman/Nickel and Dime	1977	—	3.00	6.00
❑ Columbia 3-10700	Wheel in the Sky/Can Do	1978	—	2.50	5.00
❑ Columbia 3-10757	Anytime/Can Do	1978	—	2.50	5.00
❑ Columbia 3-10800	Lights/Somethin' to Hide	1978	—	2.50	5.00

Number	Title (A Side/B Side)	Yr	VG	VG+	NM
❑ Columbia 3-10928	Just the Same Way/Somethin' to Hide	1979	—	2.00	4.00
❑ Columbia 3-11036	Lovin', Touchin', Squeezin'/Daydream	1979	—	2.00	4.00
❑ Columbia 1-11143	Too Late/Do You Recall	1979	—	2.00	4.00
❑ Columbia 1-11213	Any Way You Want It/When You're Alone (It Ain't Easy)	1980	—	2.00	4.00
❑ Columbia 1-11275	Walks Like a Lady/People and Places	1980	—	2.00	4.00
❑ Columbia 1-11339	Good Morning Girl//Stay Awhile/Line of Fire	1980	—	2.00	4.00
❑ Columbia 11-60505	The Party's Over (Hopelessly in Love)/Just the Same Way	1981	—	2.00	4.00
❑ Geffen 7-29090	Only the Young/I'll Only Fall in Love Again	1985	—	2.00	4.00
—B-side by Sammy Hagar					
Albums					
❑ Columbia PC 33388	Journey	1975	2.50	5.00	10.00
—No bar code on cover					
❑ Columbia PC 33904	Look Into the Future	1976	2.50	5.00	10.00
—No bar code on cover					
❑ Columbia PC 34311	Next	1977	2.50	5.00	10.00
—No bar code on cover					
❑ Columbia JC 34912	Infinity	1978	2.50	5.00	10.00
—No bar code on cover					
❑ Columbia FC 35797	Evolution	1979	2.00	4.00	8.00
❑ Columbia C2 36324 [(2)]	In the Beginning	1979	2.50	5.00	10.00
❑ Columbia FC 36339	Departure	1980	2.00	4.00	8.00
❑ Columbia KC2 37016 [(2)]	Captured	1981	2.50	5.00	10.00
❑ Columbia TC 37408	Escape	1981	2.00	4.00	8.00
❑ Columbia FC 37998	Dream After Dream	1982	3.00	6.00	12.00
❑ Columbia OC 39936	Raised on Radio	1986	2.00	4.00	8.00
❑ Columbia OC 44493	Greatest Hits	1988	2.50	5.00	10.00
JUSTIS, BILL					
45s					
❑ Bell 921	Electric Dreams/Dark Continent Contribution	1970	—	2.50	5.00
❑ MCA 40810	Foxy Lady/Orange Blossom Special	1977	—	2.00	4.00
❑ Monument 956	Yellow Summer/So Until I See You	1966	2.50	5.00	10.00
❑ Monument 8699	Sea Dream/Touching, Feeling, Dreaming	1976	—	2.50	5.00
❑ NRC 1119	Boogie Woogie Rock/Blowing Rock	1959	5.00	10.00	20.00
❑ Phillips International 3519	Raunchy/The Midnite Man	1957	5.00	10.00	20.00
❑ Phillips International 3522	College Man/The Stranger	1958	5.00	10.00	20.00
❑ Phillips International 3525	Wild Rice/Scroungie	1958	5.00	10.00	20.00
❑ Phillips International 3529	Cattywampus/Summer Holiday	1958	5.00	10.00	20.00
❑ Phillips International 3535	Bop Train/String of Pearls	1958	5.00	10.00	20.00
❑ Phillips International 3544	Flea Circus/Cloud Nine	1959	5.00	10.00	20.00
❑ Smash 1812	I'm Gonna Learn to Dance/Tamoure	1963	2.50	5.00	10.00
❑ Smash 1851	Sunday in Madrid/Satin and Velvet	1963	2.50	5.00	10.00
❑ Smash 1902	Lavender Sax/Fia, Fia	1964	2.50	5.00	10.00
❑ Smash 1955	How Soon/Ska-Ha	1964	2.50	5.00	10.00
❑ Smash 1977	Late Game/Last Farewell	1965	2.50	5.00	10.00
Albums					
❑ Harmony KH 31189	Enchanted Sea	1972	3.00	6.00	12.00
❑ Monument MLP 8078 [M]	The Eternal Sea	1967	3.75	7.50	15.00
❑ Monument SLP 18078 [S]	The Eternal Sea	1967	3.75	7.50	15.00
❑ Phillips International PLP-1950 [M]	Cloud Nine	1959	100.00	200.00	400.00
❑ Smash MGS-27021 [M]	Bill Justis Plays 12 Big Instrumental Hits (Alley Cat/Green Onions)	1962	3.75	7.50	15.00
❑ Smash MGS-27030 [M]	Bill Justis Plays 12 More Big Instrumental Hits (Telstar/The Lonely Bull)	1963	3.75	7.50	15.00
❑ Smash MGS-27031 [M]	Bill Justis Plays 12 Smash Instrumental Hits	1963	3.75	7.50	15.00
❑ Smash MGS-27036 [M]	Bill Justis Plays 12 Top Tunes	1963	3.75	7.50	15.00
❑ Smash MGS-27043 [M]	Bill Justis Plays 12 Other Instrumental Hits	1964	3.75	7.50	15.00
❑ Smash MGS-27047 [M]	Dixieland Folk Style	1964	3.75	7.50	15.00
❑ Smash MGS-27065 [M]	More Instrumental Hits	1965	3.75	7.50	15.00
❑ Smash MGS-27077 [M]	Taste of Honey/The "In" Crowd	1966	3.75	7.50	15.00
❑ Smash SRS-67021 [S]	Bill Justis Plays 12 Big Instrumental Hits (Alley Cat/Green Onions)	1962	5.00	10.00	20.00
❑ Smash SRS-67030 [S]	Bill Justis Plays 12 More Big Instrumental Hits (Telstar/The Lonely Bull)	1963	5.00	10.00	20.00
❑ Smash SRS-67031 [S]	Bill Justis Plays 12 Smash Instrumental Hits	1963	5.00	10.00	20.00
❑ Smash SRS-67036 [S]	Bill Justis Plays 12 Top Tunes	1963	5.00	10.00	20.00
❑ Smash SRS-67043 [S]	Bill Justis Plays 12 Other Instrumental Hits	1964	5.00	10.00	20.00
❑ Smash SRS-67047 [S]	Dixieland Folk Style	1964	5.00	10.00	20.00

Number	Title (A Side/B Side)	Yr	VG	VG+	NM
❑ Smash SRS-67065 [S]	More Instrumental Hits	1965	5.00	10.00	20.00
❑ Smash SRS-67077 [S]	Taste of Honey/The "In" Crowd	1966	5.00	10.00	20.00
❑ Smash 830898-1	Raunchy	1987	2.50	5.00	10.00
❑ Sun LP-109	Raunchy	1969	3.00	6.00	12.00

K

K.C. AND THE SUNSHINE BAND

45s

Number	Title (A Side/B Side)	Yr	VG	VG+	NM
❑ Casablanca 2227	Yes I'm Ready/With Your Love	1979	—	2.00	4.00
—As "Teri DeSario with K.C."					
❑ Casablanca 2278	Dancin' in the Streets/Moonlight Madness	1980	—	2.00	4.00
—As "Teri DeSario with K.C."					
❑ Casablanca 812991-7	Yes I'm Ready/Dancin' in the Streets	1983	—	2.00	4.00
—As "Teri DeSario with K.C."; reissue					
❑ Epic 14-02545	Love Me/Don't Say No	1981	—	2.00	4.00
❑ Epic 14-02652	It Happens Every Night/Stand Up	1981	—	2.00	4.00
❑ Epic 34-03286	(You Said) You'd Gimme Some More/ When You Dance to the Music	1982	—	2.00	4.00
❑ Epic 34-03556	Don't Run (Come Back to Me)/On the One	1983	—	2.00	4.00
❑ Meca 1001	Give It Up/Uptight	1983	—	2.00	4.00
—K.C. solo					
❑ Meca 1003	On the Top/(B-side unknown)	1984	—	3.00	6.00
❑ T.K. 1001	Blow Your Whistle/I'm Going to Do Something Good to You	1973	—	2.50	5.00
—As "K.C. and the Sunshine Junkanoo Band"					
❑ T.K. 1003	Sound Your Funky Horn/Why Don't We Get Together	1974	—	2.50	5.00
❑ T.K. 1005	Queen of Clubs/Do It Good	1974	—	2.50	5.00
❑ T.K. 1008	I'm a Pushover/You Don't Know	1974	—	2.50	5.00
❑ T.K. 1009	Get Down Tonight/You Don't Know	1975	—	2.00	4.00
❑ T.K. 1010	Shotgun Shuffle/Hey J	1975	—	2.00	4.00
—As "The Sunshine Band"					
❑ T.K. 1015	That's the Way (I Like It)/What Makes You Happy	1975	—	2.00	4.00
❑ T.K. 1018	Rock Your Baby/S.O.S.	1976	—	2.00	4.00
—As "The Sunshine Band"					
❑ T.K. 1019	(Shake, Shake, Shake) Shake Your Booty/Boogie Shoes	1976	—	2.00	4.00
❑ T.K. 1020	I Like to Do It/Come On In	1976	—	2.00	4.00
❑ T.K. 1022	I'm Your Boogie Man/Wrap Your Arms Around Me	1977	—	2.00	4.00
❑ T.K. 1023	Keep It Comin' Love/Baby I Love You	1977	—	2.00	4.00
❑ T.K. 1025	Boogie Shoes/I Get Lifted	1978	—	2.00	4.00
❑ T.K. 1026	Black Water Gold (Part 1)/Black Water Gold (Part 2)	1978	—	2.00	4.00
—As "The Sunshine Band"					
❑ T.K. 1028	It's the Same Old Song/Let's Go Party	1978	—	2.00	4.00
❑ T.K. 1030	Do You Feel All Right/I Will Love You Tomorrow	1978	—	2.00	4.00
❑ T.K. 1031	Who Do Ya Love/Sho-Nuff	1978	—	2.00	4.00
❑ T.K. 1033	Do You Wanna Go Party/Come to My Island	1979	—	2.00	4.00
❑ T.K. 1035	Please Don't Go/I Betcha Didn't Know That	1979	—	2.00	4.00
❑ T.K. 1036	Let's Go Rock and Roll/I've Got the Feeling	1980	—	2.00	4.00
❑ T.K. 1037	Que Pasa?/Por Favor No Te Vayas	1980	—	2.00	4.00
❑ T.K. 1038	Make Me a Star/Do Me	1980	—	2.00	4.00
—K.C. solo					
❑ T.K. 1044	Space Cadet/Do Me	1981	—	2.00	4.00
—K.C. solo					
❑ T.K. 1048	Redlight/I Don't Wanna Make Love	1982	—	2.00	4.00
—K.C. solo					

Albums

Number	Title (A Side/B Side)	Yr	VG	VG+	NM
❑ Epic FE 37490	The Painter	1981	2.50	5.00	10.00
❑ Epic FE 38073	All in a Night's Work	1982	2.50	5.00	10.00
❑ Meca 8301	KC Ten	1984	2.50	5.00	10.00
❑ Sunshine Sound 614	Space Cadet/Solo Flight	1981	2.50	5.00	10.00
❑ T.K. 500	Do It Good	1974	3.00	6.00	12.00
❑ T.K. 603	K.C. and the Sunshine Band	1975	2.50	5.00	10.00
❑ T.K. 604	The Sound of Sunshine	1975	2.50	5.00	10.00
—By "The Sunshine Band" (all instrumental)					
❑ T.K. 605	Part 3	1976	2.50	5.00	10.00
❑ T.K. 607	Who Do Ya (Love)	1978	2.50	5.00	10.00
❑ T.K. 611	Do You Wanna Go Party	1979	2.50	5.00	10.00
❑ T.K. 612	Greatest Hits	1980	2.50	5.00	10.00

KANSAS

45s

Number	Title (A Side/B Side)	Yr	VG	VG+	NM
❑ CBS Associated ZS4-04057	Fight Fire with Fire/Incident on a Bridge	1983	—	—	3.00
❑ CBS Associated ZS4-04213	Everybody's My Friend/End of the Age	1983	—	—	3.00
❑ Kirshner ZS5-02903	Play the Game Tonight/Play On	1982	—	2.00	4.00
❑ Kirshner ZS5-03084	Right Away/Windows	1982	—	2.00	4.00
❑ Kirshner ZS7 4253	Can I Tell You/The Pilgrimage	1974	—	3.00	6.00
❑ Kirshner ZS8 4256	Lonely Wind/Bringing It Back	1974	—	3.00	6.00
❑ Kirshner ZS8 4258	Song for America (Part 1)/(Part 2)	1975	—	3.00	6.00
❑ Kirshner ZS8 4259	It's You/It Takes a Woman's Love to Make a Man	1975	—	3.00	6.00
❑ Kirshner ZS8 4267	Carry On Wayward Son/Questions of My Childhood	1976	—	2.50	5.00
❑ Kirshner ZS8 4270	What's On My Mind/Lonely Street	1977	—	2.00	4.00
❑ Kirshner ZS8 4273	Point of Know Return/Closet Chronicles	1977	—	2.00	4.00
❑ Kirshner ZS8 4274	Dust in the Wind/Paradox	1978	—	2.50	5.00
❑ Kirshner ZS8 4276	Portrait (He Knew)/Lightning's Hand	1978	—	2.00	4.00
❑ Kirshner ZS8 4280	Lonely Wind/Song for America	1979	—	2.00	4.00

Number	Title (A Side/B Side)	Yr	VG	VG+	NM
❑ Kirshner ZS8 4284	People of the South Wind/Stay Out of Trouble	1979	—	2.00	4.00
❑ Kirshner ZS9 4285	Reason to Be/How My Soul Cries Out for You	1979	—	2.00	4.00
❑ Kirshner ZS9 4291	Hold On/Don't Open Your Eyes	1980	—	2.00	4.00
❑ Kirshner ZS6 4292	Got to Rock On/No Room for a Stranger	1980	—	2.00	4.00
❑ MCA 52958	All I Wanted/We're Not Alone Anymore	1986	—	—	3.00
❑ MCA 53027	Power/Tomb 19	1987	—	—	3.00
❑ MCA 53070	Can't Cry Anymore/Three Pretenders	1987	—	—	3.00
❑ MCA 53425	Stand Beside Me/House on Fire	1988	—	—	3.00
Albums					
❑ CBS Associated QZ 38733	Drastic Measures	1983	2.00	4.00	8.00
❑ CBS Associated QZ 39283	The Best of Kansas	1984	2.00	4.00	8.00
❑ Kirshner KZ 32817	Kansas	1974	3.00	6.00	12.00
❑ Kirshner PZ 33385	Song for America	1975	3.00	6.00	12.00
—Without bar code on cover					
❑ Kirshner PZ 33806	Masque	1975	3.00	6.00	12.00
—Without bar code on cover					
❑ Kirshner JZ 34224	Leftoverture	1976	2.50	5.00	10.00
❑ Kirshner JZ 34929	Point of Know Return	1977	2.50	5.00	10.00
❑ Kirshner PZ2 35660 [(2)]	Two for the Show	1978	3.75	7.50	15.00
❑ Kirshner FZ 36008	Monolith	1979	2.50	5.00	10.00
❑ Kirshner FZ 36588	Audio-Visions	1980	2.50	5.00	10.00
❑ Kirshner PZ 38002	Vinyl Confessions	198?	2.00	4.00	8.00
—Budget-line reissue					
❑ MCA 5838	Power	1986	2.00	4.00	8.00
❑ MCA 6254	In the Spirit of Things	1988	2.00	4.00	8.00

KEITH

45s

Number	Title (A Side/B Side)	Yr	VG	VG+	NM
❑ Columbia 43268	Dream/Caravan of Lonely Men	1965	3.75	7.50	15.00
—As "Keith and the Admirations"					
❑ DiscReet 1193	What Did You Do in the Revolution, Dad/In and Out of Love	1974	—	2.50	5.00
❑ Mercury 72596	Ain't Gonna Lie/Our Love Started All Over Again	1966	2.00	4.00	8.00
❑ Mercury 72639	98.6/The Teenie Bopper Song	1966	2.50	5.00	10.00
❑ Mercury 72652	Tell Me To My Face/Pretty Little Shy One	1967	2.00	4.00	8.00
❑ Mercury 72695	Daylight Savin' Time/Happy Walking Around	1967	2.00	4.00	8.00
❑ Mercury 72715	Easy-As-Pie/Sugar Man	1967	2.00	4.00	8.00
❑ Mercury 72746	I'm So Proud/Candy Candy	1967	2.00	4.00	8.00
❑ Mercury 72794	Hurry/Pleasure of Your Company	1968	2.00	4.00	8.00
❑ Mercury 72824	Always Tomorrow/I Can't Go Wrong	1968	2.00	4.00	8.00
❑ RCA Victor 74-0140	Marstrand/The Problem	1969	—	3.00	6.00
❑ RCA Victor 74-0222	Trixin's Election/A Fairy Tale or Two	1969	—	3.00	6.00
Albums					
❑ Mercury MG-21102 [M]	98.6/Ain't Gonna Lie	1967	3.75	7.50	15.00
❑ Mercury MG-21129 [M]	Out of Crank	1967	3.75	7.50	15.00
❑ Mercury SR-61102 [S]	98.6/Ain't Gonna Lie	1967	5.00	10.00	20.00
❑ Mercury SR-61129 [S]	Out of Crank	1967	5.00	10.00	20.00
❑ RCA Victor LSP-4143	The Adventures of Keith	1969	5.00	10.00	20.00

KENDRICKS, EDDIE

45s

Number	Title (A Side/B Side)	Yr	VG	VG+	NM
❑ Arista 0325	Ain't No Smoke Without Fire/Love, Love, Love	1978	—	2.00	4.00
❑ Arista 0346	The Best of Strangers Now/ Don't Underestimate the Power of Love	1978	—	2.00	4.00
❑ Arista 0466	I Just Want to Be the One in Your Life/I Can't Let You Walk Away	1979	—	2.00	4.00
❑ Arista 0500	Your Love Has Been So Good/I Never Used to Dance	1980	—	2.00	4.00
❑ Atlantic 3796	Looking for Love/Need Your Lovin'	1981	—	2.00	4.00
❑ Corner Stone 1001	Surprise Attack/(B-side unknown)	1984	—	2.00	4.00
❑ Tamla 54203	It's So Hard for Me to Say Good-Bye/ This Used to Be the Home of Johnnie Mae	1971	—	2.50	5.00
❑ Tamla 54210	Can I/I Did It All for You	1971	—	2.50	5.00
❑ Tamla 54218	Eddie's Love/Let Me Run Into Your Lonely Heart	1972	—	2.50	5.00
❑ Tamla 54222	If You Let Me/Just Memories	1972	—	2.50	5.00
❑ Tamla 54230	Girl You Need a Change of Mind (Part 1)/ Girl You Need a Change of Mind (Part 2)	1973	—	2.50	5.00
❑ Tamla 54236	Darling Come Back Home/Loving You the Second Time Around	1973	—	2.50	5.00
❑ Tamla 54238	Keep On Truckin' (Part 1)/Keep On Truckin' (Part 2)	1973	—	2.50	5.00
❑ Tamla 54243	Boogie Down/Can't Help What I Am	1974	—	2.50	5.00

Number	Title (A Side/B Side)	Yr	VG	VG+	NM
❑ Tamla 54247	Son of Sagittarius/Trust Your Heart	1974	—	2.50	5.00
❑ Tamla 54249	Tell Her Love Has Felt the Need/ Loving You the Second Time Around	1974	—	2.50	5.00
❑ Tamla 54255	One Tear/The Thin Man	1974	—	2.50	5.00
❑ Tamla 54257	Shoeshine Boy/Hooked on Your Love	1975	—	2.50	5.00
❑ Tamla 54260	Get the Cream Off the Top/Honey Brown	1975	—	2.50	5.00
❑ Tamla 54263	Happy/Deep and Quiet Love	1975	—	2.50	5.00
❑ Tamla 54266	He's a Friend/All of My Life	1976	—	2.50	5.00
❑ Tamla 54270	Get It While It's Hot/Never Gonna Leave You	1976	—	2.50	5.00
❑ Tamla 54277	Goin' Up in Smoke/Thanks for the Memories	1976	5.00	10.00	20.00
❑ Tamla 54285	Date with the Rain/Born Again	1977	—	2.50	5.00
❑ Tamla 54289	Baby/I Want to Live (My Life with You)	1977	—	—	—
—Unreleased					
❑ Tamla 54290	Baby/Intimate Friends	1977	—	2.50	5.00
Albums					
❑ Arista AB 4170	Vintage '78	1978	2.50	5.00	10.00
❑ Arista AB 4250	Something More	1979	2.50	5.00	10.00
❑ Atlantic SD 19294	Love Keys	1981	2.50	5.00	10.00
❑ Motown M5-151V1	Eddie Kendricks	1981	2.00	4.00	8.00
—Reissue of Tamla 327					
❑ Motown M5-196V1	He's a Friend	1981	2.00	4.00	8.00
—Reissue of Tamla 343					
❑ Tamla T-309	All By Myself	1971	2.50	5.00	10.00
❑ Tamla T 315L	People...Hold On	1972	2.50	5.00	10.00
❑ Tamla T 327L	Eddie Kendricks	1973	2.50	5.00	10.00
❑ Tamla T 330V1	Boogie Down!	1974	2.50	5.00	10.00
❑ Tamla T6-335	For You	1974	2.50	5.00	10.00
❑ Tamla T6-338	The Hit Man	1975	2.50	5.00	10.00
❑ Tamla T6-343	He's a Friend	1976	2.50	5.00	10.00
❑ Tamla T6-346	Goin' Up in Smoke	1976	2.50	5.00	10.00
❑ Tamla T7-354	Eddie Kendricks at His Best	1977	2.50	5.00	10.00
❑ Tamla T8-356	Slick	1978	2.50	5.00	10.00

KENNER, CHRIS

45s

Number	Title (A Side/B Side)	Yr	VG	VG+	NM
❑ Baton 220	Grandma's House/Don't Let Her Pin That Charge	1956	10.00	20.00	40.00
❑ Imperial 5448	Sick and Tired/Nothing Will Keep Me from You	1957	6.25	12.50	25.00
❑ Imperial 5488	Will You Be Mine/I Have News for You	1958	6.25	12.50	25.00
❑ Imperial 5767	Sick and Tired/Nothing Will Keep Me from You	1961	3.00	6.00	12.00
❑ Instant 3229	I Like It Like That, Part 1/I Like It Like That, Part 2	1961	3.75	7.50	15.00
❑ Instant 3234	A Very True Story/Packin' Up	1961	3.00	6.00	12.00
❑ Instant 3237	Something You Got/Come See About Me	1961	3.00	6.00	12.00
❑ Instant 3244	How Far/Time	1962	3.00	6.00	12.00
❑ Instant 3247	Let Me Show You How (To Twist)/Johnny Little	1962	3.00	6.00	12.00
❑ Instant 3252	Land of 1000 Dances/That's My Girl	1962	3.00	6.00	12.00
❑ Instant 3257	Come Back and See/Go Thru Life	1963	3.00	6.00	12.00
❑ Instant 3263	What's Wrong with Life/Never Reach Perfection	1963	3.00	6.00	12.00
❑ Instant 3265	She Can Dance/Anybody Here See My Baby	1964	3.00	6.00	12.00
❑ Instant 3277	I'm Lonely, Take Me/Cinderella	1966	2.50	5.00	10.00
❑ Instant 3280	All Night Rambler, Part 1/All Night Rambler, Part 2	1966	2.50	5.00	10.00
❑ Instant 3283	Shoo Rah/Stretch My Hands to You	1967	2.50	5.00	10.00
❑ Instant 3286	Fumigate Funky Broadway/Wind the Clock	1967	2.50	5.00	10.00
❑ Instant 3290	Memories of a King (Let Freedom Ring), Part 1/ Memories of a King (Let Freedom Ring), Part 2	1968	3.00	6.00	12.00
❑ Instant 3293	Mini-Skirts and Soul/Sad Mistake	1968	2.50	5.00	10.00
❑ Ron 335	Rocket to the Moon/Life's Just a Struggle	1961	3.00	6.00	12.00
❑ Uptown 708	Life of My Baby/They Took My Money	1965	2.50	5.00	10.00
❑ Uptown 716	I'm the Greatest/Get On This Train	1965	2.50	5.00	10.00
❑ Valiant 3229	I Like It Like That, Part 1/I Like It Like That, Part 2	1960	10.00	20.00	40.00
Albums					
❑ Atlantic 8117 [M]	Land of 1,000 Dances	1965	20.00	40.00	80.00
❑ Collectables COL-5116	Golden Classics: I Like It Like That	198?	3.00	6.00	12.00

KENT, AL

45s

Number	Title (A Side/B Side)	Yr	VG	VG+	NM
❑ Baritone 942	Hold Me/Tell Me Why	1960	37.50	75.00	150.00
❑ Checker 881	Dat's Why (I Love You So)/Am I the Man	1958	15.00	30.00	60.00
❑ Ric-Tic 123	The Way You Been Acting Lately/(Instrumental)	1967	5.00	10.00	20.00
❑ Ric-Tic 127	You've Got to Pay the Price/Where Do I Go from Here	1967	5.00	10.00	20.00
❑ Ric-Tic 133	Finders Keepers/Ooh! Pretty Lady	1967	5.00	10.00	20.00
❑ Ric-Tic 140	Bless You (My Love)/(Instrumental)	1968	3.75	7.50	15.00
❑ Wingate 004	You Know I Love You/Country Boy	1965	6.25	12.50	25.00
❑ Wizard 100	Hold Me/You Know Me	1959	25.00	50.00	100.00

KHAN, CHAKA

45s

Number	Title (A Side/B Side)	Yr	VG	VG+	NM
❑ Atlantic 89449	The Other Side of the World/(Instrumental)	1986	—	—	3.00
❑ Warner Bros. 8683	I'm Every Woman/Woman in a Man's World	1978	—	2.50	5.00
—Tan label					
❑ Warner Bros. 8740	Life Is a Dance/Some Love	1979	—	2.00	4.00
❑ Warner Bros. 22913	Soul Talkin'/I'm Every Woman	1989	—	—	3.00
❑ Warner Bros. 27541	Baby Me/Everybody Needs Some Love	1989	—	—	3.00
❑ Warner Bros. 27678	It's My Party/Where Are You Tonite	1988	—	—	3.00
❑ Warner Bros. 28459	Earth to Mickey/My Destiny	1987	—	—	3.00
❑ Warner Bros. 28576	Tight Fit/Who's It Gonna Be	1986	—	—	3.00
❑ Warner Bros. 28671	Love of a Lifetime/Coltrane Dreams	1986	—	—	3.00
❑ Warner Bros. 28923	(Krush Groove) Can't Stop the Street/(Instrumental)	1985	—	—	3.00
❑ Warner Bros. 29025	Through the Fire/La Flamme	1985	—	—	3.00

Number	Title (A Side/B Side)	Yr	VG	VG+	NM
❑ Warner Bros. 29097	This Is My Night/Caught in the Act	1985	—	—	3.00
❑ Warner Bros. 29195	I Feel for You/Chinatown	1984	—	2.00	4.00
❑ Warner Bros. 29745	Tearin' It Up/So Not to Worry	1983	—	2.00	4.00
❑ Warner Bros. 29881	Got to Be There/Pass It On, A Sure Thing	1982	—	2.00	4.00
❑ Warner Bros. 49216	Clouds/What You Did	1980	—	2.00	4.00
❑ Warner Bros. 49256	Papillon (AKA Hot Butterfly)/Too Much Love	1980	—	2.00	4.00
❑ Warner Bros. 49571	Get Ready, Get Set/So Naughty	1980	—	2.00	4.00
❑ Warner Bros. 49692	What Cha' Gonna Do for Me/Lover's Touch	1981	—	2.00	4.00
❑ Warner Bros. 49759	We Can Work It Out/Only Once	1981	—	2.00	4.00
❑ Warner Bros. 49804	Any Old Sunday/Heed the Warning	1981	—	2.00	4.00
❑ Warner Bros. 49847	And the Melody Still Lingers On/I Know You, I Live You	1981	—	2.00	4.00
Albums					
❑ Warner Bros. BSK 3245	Chaka	1978	2.50	5.00	10.00
❑ Warner Bros. BSK 3385	Naughty	1980	2.50	5.00	10.00
❑ Warner Bros. HS 3526	What Cha' Gonna Do for Me	1981	2.50	5.00	10.00
❑ Warner Bros. 23729	Chaka Khan	1982	2.50	5.00	10.00
❑ Warner Bros. 25162	I Feel for You	1984	2.50	5.00	10.00
❑ Warner Bros. 25425	Destiny	1986	2.50	5.00	10.00
❑ Warner Bros. 25707	C.K.	1988	2.50	5.00	10.00
❑ Warner Bros. 25946 [(2)]	Life Is a Dance: The Remix Project	1989	3.75	7.50	15.00

KIM, ANDY

Number	Title (A Side/B Side)	Yr	VG	VG+	NM
45s					
❑ Capitol 3895	Rock Me Gently/Rock Me Gently (Part 2)	1974	—	2.50	5.00
❑ Capitol 3962	Fire, Baby, I'm on Fire/Here Comes the Mornin'	1974	—	2.00	4.00
❑ Capitol 4032	Hang Up Those Rock 'N' Roll Shoes/Essence of Joan	1975	—	2.00	4.00
❑ Capitol 4086	Mary Ann/You Are My Everything	1975	—	2.00	4.00
❑ Capitol 4130	(She Got Me) Dancin'/Baby, You're All I Got	1975	—	2.00	4.00
❑ Capitol 4234	Oh, Pretty Woman/Baby You're All I Got	1976	—	2.00	4.00
❑ Red Bird 10-040	I Hear You Say (I Love You Baby)/Falling in Love	1965	3.75	7.50	15.00
❑ Steed 707	How'd We Ever Get This Way/Are You Ever Coming Home	1968	2.00	4.00	8.00
❑ Steed 710	Shoot 'Em Up Baby/Ordinary Kind of Girl	1968	2.00	4.00	8.00
❑ Steed 711	Rainbow Ride/Resurrection	1968	2.00	4.00	8.00
❑ Steed 715	Foundation of My Soul/Tricia Tell Your Daddy	1969	2.00	4.00	8.00
❑ Steed 716	Baby I Love You/Gee Girl	1969	2.00	4.00	8.00
❑ Steed 720	So Good Together/I Got to Know	1969	—	3.00	6.00
❑ Steed 723	A Friend in the City/You	1970	—	3.00	6.00
❑ Steed 727	It's Your Life/To Be Continued	1970	—	3.00	6.00
❑ Steed 729	Be My Baby/Love That Little Woman	1970	—	3.00	6.00
❑ Steed 731	I Wish I Were/Walking My La De La	1971	—	3.00	6.00
❑ Steed 734	I Been Moved/If I Had You Here	1971	—	3.00	6.00
❑ TCF 5	Give Me Your Love/Li'l Liz (I Love You)	1964	3.75	7.50	15.00
❑ 20th Century Fox 6709	Give Me Your Love/That Girl	1968	2.00	4.00	8.00
❑ Uni 55332	Who Has the Answers?/Shady Hollow Dreamers	1972	—	2.50	5.00
❑ Uni 55353	Love Song/Love the Poor Boy	1972	—	2.50	5.00
❑ Uni 55356	Oh What a Day/Sunshine	1972	—	2.50	5.00
❑ United Artists 591	Love Me, Love Me/I Loved You Once	1963	3.75	7.50	15.00
Albums					
❑ ABC Dunhill DSDP-50193	Andy Kim's Greatest Hits	1974	3.00	6.00	12.00
—Reissue of Steed 37008					
❑ Capitol ST-11318	Andy Kim	1974	3.00	6.00	12.00
❑ Capitol ST-11368	The Pilot	1975	3.00	6.00	12.00
❑ Steed ST-7001 [M]	How Did We Ever Get This Way?	1968	10.00	20.00	40.00
—In stereo cover with "Monaural" sticker					
❑ Steed STS-37001 [S]	How Did We Ever Get This Way?	1968	3.75	7.50	15.00
❑ Steed STS-37002	Rainbow Ride	1969	3.75	7.50	15.00
❑ Steed ST 37004	Baby I Love You	1969	3.75	7.50	15.00
❑ Steed ST 37008	Andy Kim's Greatest Hits	1970	3.75	7.50	15.00
❑ Uni 73137	Andy Kim	1972	3.00	6.00	12.00

KING, BEN E.

Number	Title (A Side/B Side)	Yr	VG	VG+	NM
45s					
❑ Atco 6166	Show Me the Way/Brace Yourself	1960	4.00	8.00	16.00
❑ Atco 6185	Spanish Harlem/First Taste of Love	1960	5.00	10.00	20.00
❑ Atco 6194	Stand By Me/On the Horizon	1961	5.00	10.00	20.00
❑ Atco 6203	Amor/Souvenir of Mexico	1961	4.00	8.00	16.00
❑ Atco 6207	Young Boy Blues/Here Comes the Night	1961	4.00	8.00	16.00

Number	Title (A Side/B Side)	Yr	VG	VG+	NM
❑ Atco 6215	Ecstasy/Yes	1962	4.00	8.00	16.00
❑ Atco 6222	Don't Play That Song (You Lied)/Hermit of Misty Mountain	1962	4.00	8.00	16.00
❑ Atco 6231	Too Bad/My Heart Cries for You	1962	3.00	6.00	12.00
❑ Atco 6237	I'm Standing By/Walking in the Footsteps of a Fool	1962	3.00	6.00	12.00
❑ Atco 6246	Tell Daddy/Auf Weidersehn, My Dear	1962	3.00	6.00	12.00
❑ Atco 6256	How Can I Forget/Gloria Gloria	1963	3.00	6.00	12.00
❑ Atco 6267	I (Who Have Nothing)/The Beginning of Time	1963	3.00	6.00	12.00
❑ Atco 6275	I Could Have Danced All Night/Gypsy	1963	3.00	6.00	12.00
❑ Atco 6284	What Now My Love/Groovin'	1964	2.50	5.00	10.00
❑ Atco 6288	That's When It Hurts/Around the Corner	1964	2.50	5.00	10.00
❑ Atco 6303	What Can a Man Do/Si, Senor	1964	2.50	5.00	10.00
❑ Atco 6315	It's All Over/Let the Water Run Down	1964	2.50	5.00	10.00
❑ Atco 6328	Seven Letters/River of Tears	1964	2.50	5.00	10.00
❑ Atco 6343	The Record (Baby I Love You)/The Way You Shake It	1965	2.50	5.00	10.00
❑ Atco 6357	She's Gone Again/Not Now (I'll Tell You When)	1965	2.50	5.00	10.00
❑ Atco 6371	Cry No More/There's No Place to Hide	1965	2.50	5.00	10.00
❑ Atco 6390	Goodnight My Love/I Can't Break the News to Myself	1965	2.50	5.00	10.00
❑ Atco 6413	So Much Love/Don't Drive Me Away	1966	2.00	4.00	8.00
❑ Atco 6431	Get in a Hurry/I Swear by Stars Above	1966	2.00	4.00	8.00
❑ Atco 6454	They Don't Give Medals to Yesterday's Heroes/What Is Soul	1966	2.00	4.00	8.00
❑ Atco 6472	A Man Without a Dream/Tears, Tears, Tears	1967	2.00	4.00	8.00
❑ Atco 6493	Katherine/Teeny Weeny Little Bit	1967	2.00	4.00	8.00
❑ Atco 6527	Don't Take Your Sweet Love Away/She Knows What to Do for Me	1967	2.50	5.00	10.00
❑ Atco 6557	We Got a Thing Goin' On/What 'Cha Gonna Do About It	1968	2.00	4.00	8.00
—With Dee Dee Sharp					
❑ Atco 6571	Don't Take Your Love from Me/Forgive This Soul	1968	2.00	4.00	8.00
❑ Atco 6596	Where's the Girl/It's Amazing	1968	2.00	4.00	8.00
❑ Atco 6637	It Ain't Fair/Till I Can't Take It Anymore	1968	2.00	4.00	8.00
❑ Atco 6666	Hey Little One/When You Love Someone	1969	2.50	5.00	10.00
❑ Atlantic 3241	Supernatural Thing — Part 1/Supernatural Thing — Part 2	1975	—	2.50	5.00
❑ Atlantic 3274	Do It in the Name of Love/Imagination	1975	—	2.50	5.00
❑ Atlantic 3308	We Got Love/I Had a Love	1975	—	2.50	5.00
❑ Atlantic 3337	I Betch'a You Didn't Know/Smooth Sailing	1976	—	2.50	5.00
❑ Atlantic 3359	One More Time/Somebody's Knocking	1976	—	2.50	5.00
❑ Atlantic 3402	Get It Up/Keepin' It To Myself	1977	—	2.50	5.00
—With the Average White Band					
❑ Atlantic 3427	A Star in the Ghetto/What Is Soul?	1977	—	2.50	5.00
—With the Average White Band					
❑ Atlantic 3444	Fool for You Anyway/The Message	1977	—	2.50	5.00
—With the Average White Band					
❑ Atlantic 3494	I See the Light/Tippin'	1978	—	2.50	5.00
❑ Atlantic 3535	Fly Away to My Wonderland/Spoiled	1978	—	2.50	5.00
❑ Atlantic 3635	Music Trance/And This Is Love	1979	—	2.00	4.00
❑ Atlantic 3808	Street Tough/Why Is the Question	1981	—	2.00	4.00
❑ Atlantic 3839	You Made the Difference in My Life/Souvenirs of Love	1981	—	2.00	4.00
❑ Atlantic 89234	Spanish Harlem/First Taste of Love	1987	—	—	3.00
❑ Atlantic 89361	Stand By Me/Yakety Yak	1986	—	—	3.00
—B-side by the Coasters					
❑ Ichiban 254	You've Got All of Me/It's All Right	1992	—	—	3.00
❑ Ichiban 257	You Still Move Me/I'm Gonna Be Somebody	1992	—	—	3.00
❑ Mandala 2512	Take Me to the Pilot/I Guess It's Goodbye	1972	—	2.50	5.00
❑ Mandala 2513	Into the Mystic/White Moon	1972	—	2.50	5.00
❑ Mandala 2518	Spread Myself Around/Travellin' Woman	1973	—	2.50	5.00
❑ Manhattan 50078	Save the Last Dance for Me/Wheel of Love	1987	—	—	3.00
❑ Maxwell 800	I Can't Take It Like a Man/(B-side unknown)	1969	2.00	4.00	8.00
Albums					
❑ Atco 33-133 [M]	Spanish Harlem	1961	25.00	50.00	100.00
—Yellow label with harp					
❑ Atco SD 33-133 [S]	Spanish Harlem	1961	37.50	75.00	150.00
—Yellow label with harp					
❑ Atco 33-137 [M]	Ben E. King Sings for Soulful Lovers	1962	10.00	20.00	40.00
❑ Atco SD 33-137 [S]	Ben E. King Sings for Soulful Lovers	1962	15.00	30.00	60.00
❑ Atco 33-142 [M]	Don't Play That Song	1962	10.00	20.00	40.00
❑ Atco SD 33-142 [S]	Don't Play That Song	1962	15.00	30.00	60.00
❑ Atco 33-165 [M]	Ben E. King's Greatest Hits	1964	7.50	15.00	30.00
❑ Atco SD 33-165 [S]	Ben E. King's Greatest Hits	1964	10.00	20.00	40.00
—Purple and brown label					
❑ Atco 33-174 [M]	Seven Letters	1965	10.00	20.00	40.00
❑ Atco SD 33-174 [S]	Seven Letters	1965	12.50	25.00	50.00
❑ Atlantic SD 18132	Supernatural	1975	3.00	6.00	12.00
❑ Atlantic SD 18169	I Have a Love	1976	3.00	6.00	12.00
❑ Atlantic SD 18191	Rhapsody	1976	3.00	6.00	12.00
❑ Atlantic SD 19200	Let Me Live in Your Life	1978	3.00	6.00	12.00
❑ Atlantic SD 19269	Music Trance	1980	2.50	5.00	10.00
❑ Atlantic SD 19300	Street Tough	1981	2.50	5.00	10.00
❑ Atlantic 81716	Stand By Me: The Best of Ben E. King	1987	2.00	4.00	8.00
—Includes seven Ben E. King tracks and three by the Drifters					
❑ Clarion 606 [M]	Young Boy Blues	1966	6.25	12.50	25.00
❑ Clarion SD 606 [S]	Young Boy Blues	1966	7.50	15.00	30.00
❑ Mandala MLP 3007	The Beginning of It All for Ben E. King	1972	5.00	10.00	20.00
❑ Maxwell ML-88001	Rough Edges	1969	5.00	10.00	20.00

KING, CAROLE

45s

Number	Title (A Side/B Side)	Yr	VG	VG+	NM
❑ ABC-Paramount 9921	Goin' Wild/The Right Girl	1958	37.50	75.00	150.00
❑ ABC-Paramount 9986	Baby Sittin'/Under the Stars	1958	37.50	75.00	150.00
❑ Alpine 57	Oh, Neil/A Very Special Boy	1959	175.00	350.00	700.00

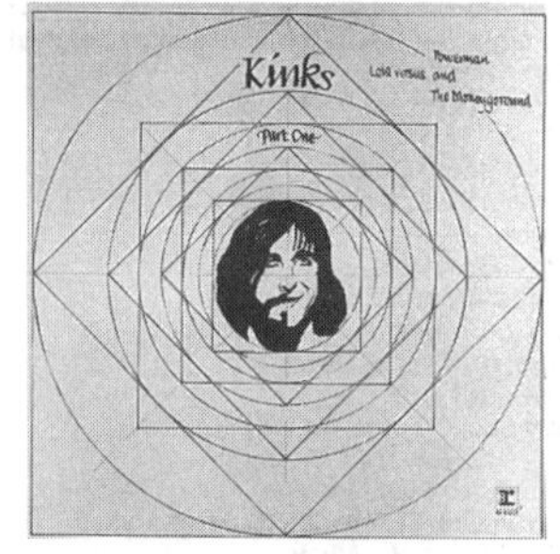

Number	Title (A Side/B Side)	Yr	VG	VG+	NM
❑ Atlantic 4026	One to One/Goat Annie	1982	—	2.00	4.00
❑ Atlantic 4062	Read Between the Lines/Life Without Love	1982	—	2.00	4.00
❑ Atlantic 89756	Crying in the Rain/Sacred Heart of Stone	1983	—	2.00	4.00
❑ Capitol 4455	Hard Rock Cafe/To Know That I Love You	1977	—	2.00	4.00
❑ Capitol 4497	Simple Things/Hold On	1977	—	2.00	4.00
❑ Capitol 4593	Main Street Saturday Night/Changes	1978	—	2.00	4.00
❑ Capitol 4649	Sunbird/Morning Sun	1978	—	2.00	4.00
❑ Capitol 4718	Move Lightly/Whiskey	1979	—	2.00	4.00
❑ Capitol 4766	Time Gone By/Dreamlike I Wander	1979	—	2.00	4.00
❑ Capitol 4864	One Fine Day/Rulers of This World	1980	—	2.00	4.00
❑ Capitol 4911	The Locomotion/Oh No Not My Baby	1980	—	2.00	4.00
❑ Capitol 4941	Chains/Bad Girl	1980	—	2.00	4.00
❑ Capitol B-44336	City Streets/Time Heals All Wounds	1989	—	—	3.00
❑ Companion 2000	It Might As Well Rain Until September/Nobody's Perfect	1962	75.00	150.00	300.00
❑ Dimension 1004	School Bells Are Ringing/I Didn't Have Any Summer Romance	1962	5.00	10.00	20.00
❑ Dimension 1009	He's a Bad Boy/We Grew Up Together	1963	5.00	10.00	20.00
❑ Dimension 2000	It Might As Well Rain Until September/Nobody's Perfect	1962	3.75	7.50	15.00
—Purple label					
❑ Ode 66006	Eventually/Up On the Roof	1970	2.00	4.00	8.00
❑ Ode 66015	It's Too Late/I Feel the Earth Move	1971	—	2.00	4.00
❑ Ode 66019	So Far Away/Smackwater Jack	1971	—	2.00	4.00
❑ Ode 66022	Sweet Seasons/Pocket Money	1971	—	2.00	4.00
❑ Ode 66026	It's Going to Take Some Time/Brother Brother	1972	—	3.00	6.00
❑ Ode 66031	Been to Canaan/Bitter with the Sweet	1972	—	2.00	4.00
❑ Ode 66035	Believe in Humanity/You Light Up My Life	1973	—	2.00	4.00
❑ Ode 66039	Corazon/That's How Things Go Down	1973	—	2.00	4.00
❑ Ode 66047	Jazzman/You Go Your Way, I'll Go Mine	1974	—	2.50	5.00
❑ Ode 66101	Jazzman/You Go Your Way, I'll Go Mine	1974	—	2.00	4.00
❑ Ode 66106	Nightingale/You're Something New	1975	—	2.00	4.00
❑ Ode 66119	Only Love Is Real/Still Here Thinking of You	1976	—	2.00	4.00
❑ Ode 66123	High Out of Time/I'd Like to Know You Better	1976	—	2.00	4.00
❑ RCA Victor 47-7560	Short Mort/Queen of the Beach	1959	25.00	50.00	100.00
❑ Tomorrow 7502	A Road to Nowhere/Some of Your Lovin'	1966	10.00	20.00	40.00
Albums					
❑ Atlantic SD 19344	One to One	1982	2.50	5.00	10.00
❑ Atlantic 80118	Speeding Time	1983	2.50	5.00	10.00
❑ Capitol SMAS-11667	Simple Things	1977	2.50	5.00	10.00
❑ Capitol SW-11785	Welcome Home	1978	2.50	5.00	10.00
❑ Capitol ST-11953	Touch the Sky	1979	2.50	5.00	10.00
❑ Capitol SWAK-11963	Touch the Sky	1979	2.50	5.00	10.00
❑ Capitol SOO-12073	Pearls — Songs of Goffin and King	1980	2.50	5.00	10.00
❑ Capitol SN-16057	Simple Things	1980	2.00	4.00	8.00
—Budget-line reissue					
❑ Capitol SN-16058	Welcome Home	1980	2.00	4.00	8.00
—Budget-line reissue					
❑ Capitol SN-16059	Touch the Sky	1980	2.00	4.00	8.00
—Budget-line reissue					
❑ Capitol C1-90885	City Streets	1989	3.00	6.00	12.00
❑ Ode PE 34944	Carole King: Writer	1977	2.50	5.00	10.00
—Reissue of 77006					
❑ Ode PE 34946	Tapestry	1977	2.50	5.00	10.00
—Reissue of 77009					
❑ Ode PE 34949	Music	1977	2.50	5.00	10.00
—Reissue of 77013					
❑ Ode PE 34950	Rhymes and Reasons	1977	2.50	5.00	10.00
—Reissue of 77016					
❑ Ode PE 34953	Wrap Around Joy	1977	2.50	5.00	10.00
—Reissue of 77024					
❑ Ode PE 34955	Really Rosie	1977	2.50	5.00	10.00
—Reissue of 77027					
❑ Ode PE 34962	Fantasy	1977	2.50	5.00	10.00
—Reissue of 77018					
❑ Ode PE 34963	Thoroughbred	1977	2.50	5.00	10.00
—Reissue of 77034					
❑ Ode JE 34967	Her Greatest Hits	1978	2.50	5.00	10.00
❑ Ode SP-77006	Writer: Carole King	1970	3.00	6.00	12.00

Number	Title (A Side/B Side)	Yr	VG	VG+	NM
❑ Ode SP-77009	Tapestry	1971	3.00	6.00	12.00
❑ Ode SP-77013	Music	1971	3.00	6.00	12.00
❑ Ode SP-77016	Rhymes and Reasons	1972	3.00	6.00	12.00
❑ Ode SP-77018	Fantasy	1973	3.00	6.00	12.00
❑ Ode SP-77024	Wrap Around Joy	1974	3.00	6.00	12.00
❑ Ode SP-77027	Really Rosie	1975	3.00	6.00	12.00
❑ Ode SP-77034	Thoroughbred	1976	3.00	6.00	12.00

KING, JONATHAN

45s

Number	Title (A Side/B Side)	Yr	VG	VG+	NM
❑ Parrot 3005	Just Like a Woman/Land of the Golden Tree	1966	2.00	4.00	8.00
❑ Parrot 3008	Icicles (Fell from the Heart of a Bluebird)/ In a Hundred Years from Now	1966	2.00	4.00	8.00
❑ Parrot 3011	Round, Round/Time and Motion	1967	2.00	4.00	8.00
❑ Parrot 3021	1968 (Message to the Presidential Candidates)/Colloquial Sex	1968	2.00	4.00	8.00
❑ Parrot 3027	Lazy Bones/Just Want to Say Thank You	1968	2.00	4.00	8.00
❑ Parrot 3029	Hooked on a Feeling/I Don't Want to Be Gay	1969	—	3.00	6.00
❑ Parrot 3030	Flirt/Hey Jim	1969	—	3.00	6.00
❑ Parrot 9774	Everyone's Gone to the Moon/Summer's Coming	1965	2.50	5.00	10.00
❑ Parrot 9804	Green Is the Grass/Where the Sun Has Never Shown	1965	2.00	4.00	8.00
❑ Parrot 40047	Let It All Hang Out/Colloquial Sex	1970	—	3.00	6.00
❑ Parrot 40055	Cherry Cherry/Gay Girl	1970	—	3.00	6.00
❑ UK 49002	It's a Tall Order for a Short Guy/Learned Tax Counsel	1972	—	2.50	5.00
❑ UK 49014	Mary, My Love/A Little Bit Left of Right	1973	—	2.50	5.00
❑ UK 49018	The Kung Fu Anthem/A Little Bit Left of Right	1973	—	2.50	5.00
❑ UK 49034	The Way You Look Tonight/The True Story of Molly Malone	1974	—	2.50	5.00

Albums

Number	Title (A Side/B Side)	Yr	VG	VG+	NM
❑ Parrot PA 61013 [M]	Jonathan King Or Then Again....	1967	10.00	20.00	40.00
❑ Parrot PAS 71013 [P]	Jonathan King Or Then Again....	1967	12.50	25.00	50.00
—Only "Where the Sun Has Never Shown" is rechanneled.					
❑ U.K. 53101	Bubble Rock Is Here to Stay	1972	6.25	12.50	25.00
❑ U.K. 53104	Pandora's Box	1973	6.25	12.50	25.00

KINGSMEN, THE (1)

Northwest garage band.

45s

Number	Title (A Side/B Side)	Yr	VG	VG+	NM
❑ Forever Oldies 21011	Louie Louie/Haunted Castle	197?	—	2.00	4.00
—Later issue of Scepter-Wand Forever 21011, "a product of Springboard International" at bottom					
❑ Jerden 712	Louie Louie/Haunted Castle	1963	15.00	30.00	60.00
❑ Scepter-Wand Forever 21011	Louie Louie/Haunted Castle	197?	—	2.50	5.00
—Reissue					
❑ Wand 143	Louie Louie/Little Green Thing	196?	3.75	7.50	15.00
❑ Wand 143	Louie, Louie/Haunted Castle	1963	5.00	10.00	20.00
❑ Wand 143	Louie Louie 64-65-66.../Haunted Castle	1966	3.75	7.50	15.00
❑ Wand 150	Money/Bent Scepter	1964	3.00	6.00	12.00
❑ Wand 157	Little Latin Lupe Lu/David's Mood	1964	2.50	5.00	10.00
❑ Wand 164	Death of an Angel/Searching for Love	1964	2.50	5.00	10.00
❑ Wand 172	The Jolly Green Giant/Long Green	1965	3.00	6.00	12.00
❑ Wand 183	The Climb/I'm Waiting	1965	2.50	5.00	10.00
❑ Wand 189	Annie Fanny/Give Her Lovin'	1965	2.50	5.00	10.00
❑ Wand 1107	(You Got) Gamma Goochie/It's Only the Dog	1965	3.75	7.50	15.00
❑ Wand 1115	Killer Joe/Little Green Thing	1966	3.75	7.50	15.00
❑ Wand 1118	The Krunch/The Climb	1966	3.75	7.50	15.00
❑ Wand 1127	My Wife Can't Dance/Little Sally Tease	1966	2.50	5.00	10.00
❑ Wand 1137	If I Need Someone/The Grass Is Green	1966	2.50	5.00	10.00
❑ Wand 1147	Trouble/Daytime Shadows	1967	2.00	4.00	8.00
❑ Wand 1154	The Wolf of Manhattan/Children's Caretaker	1967	2.00	4.00	8.00
❑ Wand 1157	(I Have Found) Another Girl/Don't Say No	1967	2.00	4.00	8.00
❑ Wand 1164	Bo Diddley Bach/Just Before the Break of Day	1968	2.00	4.00	8.00
❑ Wand 1174	Get Out of My Life Woman/Since You've Been Gone	1968	2.00	4.00	8.00
❑ Wand 1180	I Guess I Was Dreamin'/Oh Love	1968	2.00	4.00	8.00

Albums

Number	Title (A Side/B Side)	Yr	VG	VG+	NM
❑ Rhino RNLP-126	The Best of the Kingsmen	1985	2.50	5.00	10.00
❑ Scepter CTN-18002	The Best of the Kingsmen	1972	2.50	5.00	10.00
❑ Wand WDM-657 [M]	The Kingsmen In Person	1964	7.50	15.00	30.00
❑ Wand WDS-657 [P]	The Kingsmen In Person	1964	10.00	20.00	40.00
❑ Wand WDM-659 [M]	The Kingsmen, Volume II	1964	7.50	15.00	30.00
—With "Death of an Angel"					
❑ Wand WDM-659 [M]	The Kingsmen, Volume II	1964	10.00	20.00	40.00
—Without "Death of an Angel" (replaced by untitled instrumental)					
❑ Wand WDS-659 [S]	The Kingsmen, Volume II	1964	10.00	20.00	40.00
—With "Death of an Angel"					
❑ Wand WDS-659 [S]	The Kingsmen, Volume II	1964	12.50	25.00	50.00
—Without "Death of an Angel" (replaced by untitled instrumental)					
❑ Wand WDM-662 [M]	The Kingsmen, Volume 3	1965	6.25	12.50	25.00
❑ Wand WDS-662 [S]	The Kingsmen, Volume 3	1965	7.50	15.00	30.00
❑ Wand WDM-670 [M]	The Kingsmen On Campus	1965	6.25	12.50	25.00
❑ Wand WDS-670 [S]	The Kingsmen On Campus	1965	7.50	15.00	30.00
❑ Wand WDM-674 [M]	15 Great Hits	1966	5.00	10.00	20.00
❑ Wand WDS-674 [P]	15 Great Hits	1966	6.25	12.50	25.00
❑ Wand WDM-675 [M]	Up and Away	1966	5.00	10.00	20.00
❑ Wand WDS-675 [S]	Up and Away	1966	6.25	12.50	25.00
❑ Wand WDM-681 [M]	The Kingsmen's Greatest Hits	1967	3.75	7.50	15.00
❑ Wand WDS-681 [S]	The Kingsmen's Greatest Hits	1967	5.00	10.00	20.00

KINKS, THE

45s

Number	Title (A Side/B Side)	Yr	VG	VG+	NM
❑ Arista 0247	Life Goes On/Juke Box Music	1977	—	2.00	4.00

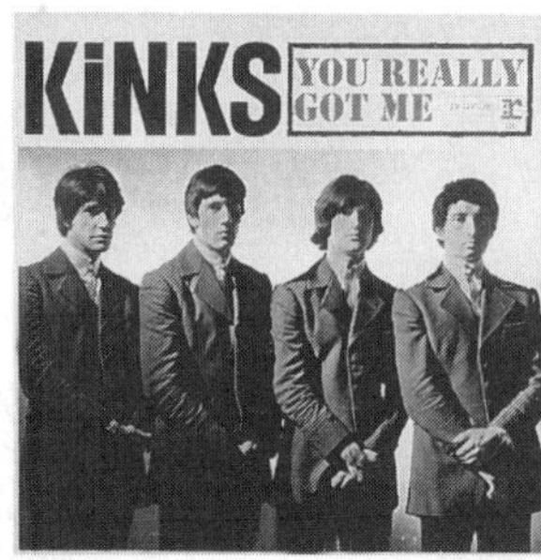

Number	Title (A Side/B Side)	Yr	VG	VG+	NM
❑ Arista 0296	Father Christmas/Prince of the Punks	1977	—	2.50	5.00
❑ Arista 0342	A Rock and Roll Fantasy/Live Life	1978	—	2.00	4.00
❑ Arista 0372	Black Messiah/Live Life	1978	—	2.00	4.00
❑ Arista 0409	(Wish I Could Fly Like) Superman/Party Line	1979	—	2.00	4.00
❑ Arista 0409	Superman/Low Budget	1979	—	2.50	5.00
❑ Arista 0448	Low Budget/A Gallon of Gas	1979	—	2.00	4.00
❑ Arista 0458	Catch Me Now I'm Falling/Low Budget	1979	—	2.00	4.00
❑ Arista 0541	Lola/Celluloid Heroes	1980	—	2.00	4.00
❑ Arista 0577	You Really Got Me/Attitude	1980	—	2.00	4.00
❑ Arista 0619	Destroyer/Back to Back	1981	—	2.00	4.00
❑ Arista 0649	Better Things/Yo-Yo	1981	—	2.00	4.00
❑ Arista 1054	Come Dancing/Noise	1983	—	2.00	4.00
❑ Arista 9016	Come Dancing/Noise	1983	—	—	3.00
❑ Arista 9075	Don't Forget to Dance/Young Conservatives	1983	—	—	3.00
❑ Arista 9309	Do It Again/Guilty	1984	—	—	3.00
❑ Arista 9334	Summer's Gone/Going Solo	1985	—	—	3.00
❑ Cameo 308	Long Tall Sally/I Took My Baby Home	1964	150.00	300.00	600.00
❑ Cameo 345	Long Tall Sally/I Took My Baby Home	1965	75.00	150.00	300.00
❑ MCA 52960	Rock 'N' Roll Cities/Sleazy Town	1986	—	—	3.00
❑ MCA 53015	Lost and Found/Killing Time	1987	—	—	3.00
❑ MCA 53093	Working at the Factory/How Are You	1987	2.50	5.00	10.00
❑ MCA 53699	How Do I Get Close/War Is Over	1989	2.50	5.00	10.00
❑ RCA Victor 74-0620	20th Century Man/Skin and Bones	1971	2.00	4.00	8.00
❑ RCA Victor 74-0807	Supersonic Rocket Ship/You Don't Know My Name	1972	2.00	4.00	8.00
❑ RCA Victor 74-0852	Celluloid Heroes/Hot Potatoes	1972	2.00	4.00	8.00
❑ RCA Victor 74-0940	One of the Survivors/Scrap Heap City	1973	50.00	100.00	200.00
—Released with acoustic versions of the two songs rather than the LP versions and quickly deleted					
❑ RCA Victor APBO-0275	Money Talks/Here Comes Flash	1974	2.50	5.00	10.00
❑ RCA Victor LPBO-5001	Sitting in the Midday Sun/Sweet Lady Genevieve	1973	2.50	5.00	10.00
❑ RCA Victor PB-10019	Mirror of Love/It's Evil	1974	—	3.00	6.00
❑ RCA Victor PB-10121	Preservation/Salvation Road	1974	—	3.00	6.00
❑ RCA Victor PB-10251	Everybody's a Star (Starmaker)/Ordinary People	1975	—	3.00	6.00
❑ RCA Victor PB-10551	I'm in Disgrace/The Hard Way	1976	—	3.00	6.00
❑ Reprise 0306	You Really Got Me/It's All Right	1964	3.75	7.50	15.00
—Second pressings have orange and brown labels					
❑ Reprise 0306	You Really Got Me/It's All Right	1964	6.25	12.50	25.00
—Originals have peach labels					
❑ Reprise 0334	All Day and All of the Night/I Gotta Move	1964	5.00	10.00	20.00
❑ Reprise 0347	Tired of Waiting for You/Come On Now	1965	5.00	10.00	20.00
❑ Reprise 0366	Who'll Be the Next in Line/Everybody's Gonna Be Happy	1965	5.00	10.00	20.00
❑ Reprise 0379	Set Me Free/I Need You	1965	5.00	10.00	20.00
❑ Reprise 0409	See My Friends/Never Met a Girl Like You Before	1965	3.75	7.50	15.00
❑ Reprise 0420	A Well Repected Man/Such a Shame	1965	3.75	7.50	15.00
❑ Reprise 0454	Till the End of the Day/Where Have All the Good Times Gone	1966	3.75	7.50	15.00
❑ Reprise 0471	Dedicated Follower of Fashion/Sittin' on My Sofa	1966	3.75	7.50	15.00
❑ Reprise 0497	Sunny Afternoon/I'm Not Like Everybody Else	1966	3.75	7.50	15.00
❑ Reprise 0540	Dead End Street/Big Black Smoke	1966	10.00	20.00	40.00
❑ Reprise 0587	Mr. Pleasant/Harry Rag	1967	10.00	20.00	40.00
❑ Reprise 0612	Waterloo Sunset/Two Sisters	1967	10.00	20.00	40.00
❑ Reprise 0647	Autumn Almanac/David Watts	1967	10.00	20.00	40.00
❑ Reprise 0691	Wonderboy/Polly	1968	10.00	20.00	40.00
❑ Reprise 0708	Sunny Afternoon/Dead End Street	1968	2.50	5.00	10.00
❑ Reprise 0712	Dedicated Follower of Fashion/Who'll Be the Next in Line	1968	2.50	5.00	10.00
❑ Reprise 0715	A Well Respected Man/Set Me Free	1968	2.50	5.00	10.00
❑ Reprise 0719	Tired of Waiting for You/All Day and All of the Night	1968	2.50	5.00	10.00
❑ Reprise 0722	You Really Got Me/It's All Right	1968	2.50	5.00	10.00
—0708 through 0722 are "Back to Back Hits" series -- originals have both "r:" and "W7" on label					
❑ Reprise 0743	Lola/Apeman	1972	—	2.50	5.00
—"Back to Back Hits" series					
❑ Reprise 0762	Days/She's Got Everything	1968	10.00	20.00	40.00
❑ Reprise 0806	Starstruck/Picture Book	1969	10.00	20.00	40.00
❑ Reprise 0847	The Village Green Preservation Society/Do You Remember Walter	1969	10.00	20.00	40.00
❑ Reprise 0863	Victoria/Brainwashed	1969	3.75	7.50	15.00
❑ Reprise 0930	Lola/Mindless Child of Motherhood	1970	2.50	5.00	10.00
❑ Reprise 0979	Apeman/Rats	1970	2.50	5.00	10.00
❑ Reprise 1017	God's Children/The Way Love Used to Be	1971	5.00	10.00	20.00

Number	Title (A Side/B Side)	Yr	VG	VG+	NM
❑ Reprise 1094	King Kong/Waterloo Sunset	1972	3.75	7.50	15.00
Albums					
❑ Arista AL 4106	Sleepwalker	1977	2.50	5.00	10.00
❑ Arista AL 4167	Misfits	1978	2.50	5.00	10.00
❑ Arista AB 4240	Low Budget	1979	2.50	5.00	10.00
❑ Arista AL 8-8018	State of Confusion	1983	2.50	5.00	10.00
❑ Arista AL13 8041 [(2)]	One for the Road	1983	2.50	5.00	10.00
—Reissue of 8609					
❑ Arista AL 8264	Word of Mouth	1984	2.50	5.00	10.00
❑ Arista ALB6 8300	Low Budget	1985	2.00	4.00	8.00
—Budget-line reissue					
❑ Arista ALB6 8328	Give the People What They Want	1985	2.00	4.00	8.00
—Budget-line reissue					
❑ Arista ALB6 8375	Sleepwalker	1985	2.00	4.00	8.00
—Budget-line reissue					
❑ Arista ALB6 8377	Misfits	1985	2.00	4.00	8.00
—Budget-line reissue					
❑ Arista A2L 8401 [(2)]	One for the Road	1980	3.75	7.50	15.00
—Original edition has this number					
❑ Arista AL11 8428 [(2)]	Come Dancing with the Kinks	1986	3.00	6.00	12.00
❑ Arista A2L 8609 [(2)]	One for the Road	198?	3.00	6.00	12.00
—Second edition of 8401					
❑ Arista AL 9567	Give the People What They Want	1981	2.50	5.00	10.00
❑ Compleat CPL2-2001 [(2)]	A Compleat Collection	1984	3.00	6.00	12.00
❑ Compleat CPL2-2003 [(2)]	20th Anniversary Edition	1984	3.00	6.00	12.00
❑ MCA 5822	Think Visual	1987	2.50	5.00	10.00
❑ MCA 6337	UK Jive	1989	3.00	6.00	12.00
❑ MCA 42107	Live: The Road	1988	2.50	5.00	10.00
❑ Pickwick ACL-7072	Preservation Act 1	197?	3.00	6.00	12.00
—Reissue of RCA Victor LPL1-5002					
❑ Pye 505	The Kinks	1975	3.00	6.00	12.00
❑ Pye 509	The Kinks, Vol. 2	1976	3.00	6.00	12.00
❑ RCA Victor APL1-1743	Celluloid Heroes (The Kinks' Greatest)	1976	2.50	5.00	10.00
❑ RCA Victor APL1-3520	Second Time Around	1980	2.50	5.00	10.00
❑ RCA Victor AYL1-3749	Schoolboys in Disgrace	1980	2.00	4.00	8.00
—Budget-line reissue					
❑ RCA Victor AYL1-3750	Soap Opera	1980	2.00	4.00	8.00
—Budget-line reissue					
❑ RCA Victor AYL1-3869	Celluloid Heroes (The Kinks' Greatest)	1981	2.00	4.00	8.00
—Budget-line reissue					
❑ RCA Victor AYL1-4558	Muswell Hillbillies	1982	2.00	4.00	8.00
—Budget-line reissue					
❑ RCA Victor LSP-4644	Muswell Hillbillies	1971	7.50	15.00	30.00
❑ RCA Victor AYL1-4719	Second Time Around	1983	2.00	4.00	8.00
—Budget-line reissue					
❑ RCA Victor LPL1-5002	Preservation Act 1	1973	3.75	7.50	15.00
❑ RCA Victor CPL2-5040 [(2)]	Preservation Act 2	1974	5.00	10.00	20.00
❑ RCA Victor LPL1-5081	Soap Opera	1975	3.75	7.50	15.00
—Orange label					
❑ RCA Victor LPL1-5081	Soap Opera	1975	2.50	5.00	10.00
—Brown label					
❑ RCA Victor LPL1-5102	Schoolboys in Disgrace	1975	2.50	5.00	10.00
❑ RCA Victor VPS-6065 [(2)]	Everybody's in Showbiz	1972	5.00	10.00	20.00
—Orange label					
❑ Reprise MS-2127	The Great Lost Kinks Album	1973	12.50	25.00	50.00
❑ Reprise R-6143 [M]	You Really Got Me	1965	15.00	30.00	60.00
❑ Reprise RS-6143 [P]	You Really Got Me	1965	20.00	40.00	80.00
—Pink, gold and green label					
❑ Reprise R-6158 [M]	Kinks-Size	1965	12.50	25.00	50.00
❑ Reprise RS-6158 [R]	Kinks-Size	1965	7.50	15.00	30.00
❑ Reprise R-6173 [M]	Kinda Kinks	1965	12.50	25.00	50.00
❑ Reprise RS-6173 [R]	Kinda Kinks	1965	7.50	15.00	30.00
❑ Reprise R-6184 [M]	Kinks Kinkdom	1965	12.50	25.00	50.00
❑ Reprise RS-6184 [R]	Kinks Kinkdom	1965	7.50	15.00	30.00
❑ Reprise R-6197 [M]	The Kink Kontroversy	1966	12.50	25.00	50.00
❑ Reprise RS-6197 [R]	The Kink Kontroversy	1966	7.50	15.00	30.00
❑ Reprise R-6217 [M]	The Kinks Greatest Hits!	1966	10.00	20.00	40.00
❑ Reprise RS-6217 [R]	The Kinks Greatest Hits!	1966	6.25	12.50	25.00
—Pink, gold and green label					
❑ Reprise R-6228 [M]	Face to Face	1967	10.00	20.00	40.00
❑ Reprise RS-6228 [P]	Face to Face	1967	7.50	15.00	30.00
—Pink, gold and green label					
❑ Reprise R-6260 [M]	The Live Kinks	1967	8.75	17.50	35.00
❑ Reprise RS-6260 [S]	The Live Kinks	1967	6.25	12.50	25.00
—Pink, gold and green label					
❑ Reprise R-6279 [M]	Something Else by the Kinks	1968	75.00	150.00	300.00
—White label promo; no stock copies were issued in mono					
❑ Reprise RS-6279 [S]	Something Else by the Kinks	1968	7.50	15.00	30.00
—Pink, gold and green label					
❑ Reprise RS-6327	The Kinks Are the Village Green Preservation Society	1969	7.50	15.00	30.00
—Two-tone orange label with "r: and "W7" logos with steamboat					
❑ Reprise RS-6366	Arthur (Or The Decline and Fall of the British Empire)	1969	6.25	12.50	25.00
—Two-tone orange label with "r: and "W7" logos with steamboat					
❑ Reprise RS-6423	Lola Versus Powerman and the Moneygoround, Part One	1970	3.75	7.50	15.00
—Original pressings have blue printing on a white cover					

Number	Title (A Side/B Side)	Yr	VG	VG+	NM
❑ Reprise 2XS-6454 [(2)]	The Kink Kronicles	1972	3.75	7.50	15.00
❑ Rhino R1 70086	The Kinks Greatest Hits! Vol. 1	1989	3.00	6.00	12.00
❑ Rhino R1 70315	You Really Got Me	1988	3.00	6.00	12.00
❑ Rhino R1 70316	Kinda Kinks	1988	3.00	6.00	12.00
❑ Rhino R1 70317	Kinks-Size	1988	3.00	6.00	12.00
❑ Rhino R1 70318	Kinks Kinkdom	1988	3.00	6.00	12.00
KISS					
45s					
❑ Casablanca 0004	Love Theme from Kiss/Nothin' to Lose	1974	3.75	7.50	15.00
❑ Casablanca 0011	Kissin' Time/Nothin' to Lose	1974	3.75	7.50	15.00
❑ Casablanca 0015	Strutter/100,000 Years	1974	3.75	7.50	15.00
❑ Casablanca 823	Let Me Go, Rock and Roll/Hotter Than Hell	1975	5.00	10.00	20.00
—Blue label					
❑ Casablanca 829	Rock and Roll All Nite/Getaway	1975	5.00	10.00	20.00
❑ Casablanca 841	C'mon and Love Me/Getaway	1975	5.00	10.00	20.00
—Blue label					
❑ Casablanca 850	Rock and Roll All Nite (Live)/Rock and Roll All Nite (Studio)	1975	2.50	5.00	10.00
—Blue label					
❑ Casablanca 854	Shout It Out Loud/Sweet Pain	1976	2.50	5.00	10.00
—Blue label					
❑ Casablanca 858	Flaming Youth/God of Thunder	1976	2.50	5.00	10.00
❑ Casablanca 863	Beth/Detroit Rock City	1976	—	3.00	6.00
—With "Beth" listed as "Side A"; brown label with camel					
❑ Casablanca 863	Detroit Rock City/Beth	1976	2.50	5.00	10.00
—With "Detroit Rock City" listed as "Side A"					
❑ Casablanca 873	Hard Luck Woman/Mr. Speed	1976	—	3.00	6.00
❑ Casablanca 880	Calling Dr. Love/Take Me	1977	—	3.00	6.00
—Brown label with camel					
❑ Casablanca 889	Christine Sixteen/Shock Me	1977	—	3.00	6.00
—A-side time listed as 3:10, B-side time listed as 3:45; brown label with camel					
❑ Casablanca 889	Christine Sixteen/Shock Me	1977	—	3.00	6.00
—A-side time listed as 2:52, B-side time listed as 4:17; brown label with camel					
❑ Casablanca 895	Love Gun/Hooligan	1977	—	3.00	6.00
❑ Casablanca 906	Shout It Out Loud (Live)/Nothin' to Lose	1977	—	3.00	6.00
❑ Casablanca 915	Rocket Ride/Tomorrow and Tonight	1978	—	3.00	6.00
❑ Casablanca 928	Strutter '78/Shock Me	1978	—	3.00	6.00
❑ Casablanca 983	I Was Made for Lovin' You/Hard Times	1979	—	2.50	5.00
❑ Casablanca 2205	Sure Know Something/Dirty Livin'	1979	—	2.50	5.00
❑ Casablanca 2282	Shandi/She's So European	1980	—	2.50	5.00
❑ Casablanca 2299	Tomorrow/Naked City	1980	—	2.50	5.00
❑ Casablanca 2343	A World Without Heroes/Dark Light	1981	—	2.50	5.00
❑ Casablanca 2365	I Love It Loud/Danger	1982	—	2.50	5.00
❑ Mercury 814671-7	Lick It Up/Dance All Over Your Face	1983	—	2.00	4.00
❑ Mercury 818216-7	All Hell's Breaking Loose/Young and Wasted	1984	—	2.00	4.00
❑ Mercury 858894-7	Detroit Rock City/Detroit Rock City	1994	—	2.00	4.00
—B-side by Mighty Mighty Bosstones; small center hole; green vinyl					
❑ Mercury 870022-7	Reason to Live/Thief in the Night	1987	—	2.00	4.00
❑ Mercury 870215-7	Turn On the Night/Hell or High Water	1988	—	2.00	4.00
❑ Mercury 872244-7	Let's Put the X in Sex/Calling Dr. Love	1989	—	2.50	5.00
❑ Mercury 876146-7	Hide Your Heart/Betrayed	1989	—	2.50	5.00
❑ Mercury 876716-7	Forever/The Street Giveth and the Street Taketh Away	1990	—	2.50	5.00
❑ Mercury 880205-7	Heaven's on Fire/Lonely Is the Hunter	1984	—	2.00	4.00
❑ Mercury 880535-7	Thrills in the Night/Burn Bitch Burn	1985	—	2.00	4.00
❑ Mercury 884141-7	Tears Are Falling/Any Way You Slice It	1985	—	2.00	4.00
❑ Mercury 888796-7	Crazy Crazy Nights/No, No, No	1987	—	2.00	4.00
Albums					
❑ Casablanca NBLP 7001	Kiss	1974	7.50	15.00	30.00
—All renumbered versions have "Kissin' Time"; dark blue label					
❑ Casablanca NBLP 7006	Hotter Than Hell	1974	7.50	15.00	30.00
—Dark blue label					
❑ Casablanca NBLP 7016	Dressed to Kill	1975	7.50	15.00	30.00
—Dark blue label					
❑ Casablanca NBLP 7020 [(2)]	Alive!	1975	10.00	20.00	40.00
—Dark blue labels; with booklet					

Number	Title (A Side/B Side)	Yr	VG	VG+	NM
❑ Casablanca NBLP 7025	Destroyer	1976	7.50	15.00	30.00
—*Dark blue label*					
❑ Casablanca NBLP 7032 [(3)]	The Originals	1976	37.50	75.00	150.00
—*Tan label with desert scene, "Casablanca" label; with booklet, six Kiss cards, a Kiss Army sticker*					
❑ Casablanca NBLP 7037	Rock and Roll Over	1976	5.00	10.00	20.00
—*Tan label with desert scene, "Casablanca" label; comes with sticker and Kiss Army paraphenalia order form*					
❑ Casablanca NBLP 7057	Love Gun	1977	10.00	20.00	40.00
—*with "Hot Goods from the Supply Depot" order form, unpunched-out cardboard gun and "Bang!" sticker. All items must be intact to get top dollar for this.*					
❑ Casablanca NBLP 7076 [(2)]	Alive II	1977	10.00	20.00	40.00
—*With 8-page booklet, tattoo insert and "Combat Gear" order form; back cover contents are correct*					
❑ Casablanca NBLP 7100 [(2)]	Double Platinum	1978	10.00	20.00	40.00
—*With "platinum award" cardboard insert and "Double Platinum Kiss Gear" order form*					
❑ Casablanca NBLP 7152	Dynasty	1979	3.75	7.50	15.00
—*With poster and merchandise order form*					
❑ Casablanca NBLP 7225	Kiss Unmasked	1980	3.75	7.50	15.00
—*With poster and "Kiss Essential Gear" order form*					
❑ Casablanca NBLP 7261	Music from The Elder	1981	7.50	15.00	30.00
—*Various editions have paper or plastic innersleeves, lyric sheets, even incorrect track listings on the back cover; no difference in value is noted between variations*					
❑ Casablanca NBLP 7270	Creatures of the Night	1982	10.00	20.00	40.00
—*Original version has band with makeup*					
❑ Casablanca NB 9001	Kiss	1974	20.00	40.00	80.00
—*First Warner Bros.-distributed version does NOT have "Kissin' Time"*					
❑ Casablanca 812770-1	Dynasty	1983	2.00	4.00	8.00
—*Reissue*					
❑ Casablanca 822780-1 [(2)]	Alive!	1984	2.50	5.00	10.00
—*Reissue*					
❑ Casablanca 822781-1 [(2)]	Alive II	1984	2.50	5.00	10.00
—*Reissue*					
❑ Casablanca 824146-1	Kiss	1984	2.00	4.00	8.00
—*Reissue*					
❑ Casablanca 824147-1	Hotter Than Hell	1984	2.00	4.00	8.00
—*Reissue*					
❑ Casablanca 824148-1	Dressed to Kill	1984	2.00	4.00	8.00
—*Reissue*					
❑ Casablanca 824149-1	Destroyer	1984	2.00	4.00	8.00
—*Reissue*					
❑ Casablanca 824150-1	Rock and Roll Over	1984	2.00	4.00	8.00
—*Reissue*					
❑ Casablanca 824151-1	Love Gun	1984	2.00	4.00	8.00
—*Reissue*					
❑ Casablanca 824153-1	Music from The Elder	1984	2.00	4.00	8.00
—*Reissue*					
❑ Casablanca 824154-1	Creatures of the Night	1984	2.00	4.00	8.00
—*Reissue; features band without its makeup on cover*					
❑ Casablanca 824155-1 [(2)]	Double Platinum	1984	2.50	5.00	10.00
—*Reissue*					
❑ Casablanca 826242-1	Unmasked	1985	2.00	4.00	8.00
—*Reissue*					
❑ Mercury 528674-1 [PD]	Creatures of the Night	1995	6.25	12.50	25.00
—*Reissue; picture disc of makeup cover*					
❑ Mercury 814297-1	Lick It Up	1983	3.00	6.00	12.00
❑ Mercury 822495-1	Animalize	1984	3.00	6.00	12.00
❑ Mercury 826099-1	Asylum	1985	2.50	5.00	10.00
❑ Mercury 832632-1	Crazy Nights	1987	2.50	5.00	10.00
❑ Mercury 836427-1	Smashes, Thrashes and Hits	1988	2.50	5.00	10.00
❑ Mercury 838913-1	Hot in the Shade	1989	2.50	5.00	10.00

KNACK, THE

45s

Number	Title (A Side/B Side)	Yr	VG	VG+	NM
❑ Capitol 4731	My Sharona/Let Me Out	1979	—	2.00	4.00
❑ Capitol 4771	Good Girls Don't/Frustrated	1979	—	2.00	4.00
—*A-side contains different lyrics from LP version in three places*					
❑ Capitol 4822	Baby Talks Dirty/End of the Game	1980	—	2.00	4.00
❑ Capitol 4853	Can't Put a Price on Love/Rave Up	1980	—	2.00	4.00
❑ Capitol A-5054	Pay the Devil (Ooo, Baby, Ooo)/Lil' Cal's Big Mistake	1981	—	2.00	4.00
❑ Capitol A-5078	Boys Go Crazy/We Are Waiting	1981	—	3.00	6.00

Albums

Number	Title (A Side/B Side)	Yr	VG	VG+	NM
❑ Capitol SO-11948	Get the Knack	1979	2.00	4.00	8.00
❑ Capitol SOO-12045	...But the Little Girls Understand	1980	2.00	4.00	8.00
❑ Capitol ST-12168	Round Trip	1981	2.50	5.00	10.00

KNIGHT, GLADYS, AND THE PIPS

45s

Number	Title (A Side/B Side)	Yr	VG	VG+	NM
❑ Brunswick 55048	Whistle My Love/Ching Ching	1958	30.00	60.00	120.00
❑ Buddah 363	Where Peaceful Waters Flow/Perfect Love	1973	—	2.50	5.00
❑ Buddah 383	Midnight Train to Georgia/(Instrumental)	1973	—	3.00	6.00
❑ Buddah 383	Midnight Train to Georgia/Window Raising Granny	1973	—	2.50	5.00
❑ Buddah 393	I've Got to Use My Imagination/I Can See Clearly Now	1973	—	2.50	5.00
❑ Buddah 403	Best Thing That Ever Happened to Me/Once in a Lifetime	1974	—	2.50	5.00
❑ Buddah 423	On and On/The Makings of You	1974	—	2.50	5.00
❑ Buddah 433	I Feel a Song (In My Heart)/Don't Burn Down the Bridge	1974	—	2.50	5.00

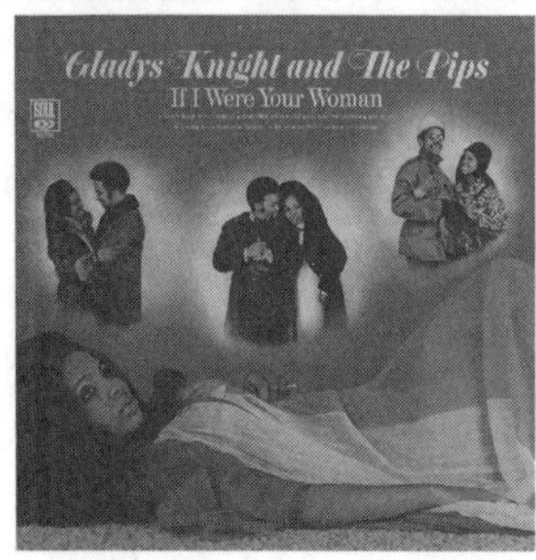

Number	Title (A Side/B Side)	Yr	VG	VG+	NM
❑ Buddah 453	Love FInds It's Own Way/Better You Go Your Way	1975	—	2.50	5.00
—Some copies have a grammatically incorrect A-side title as above					
❑ Buddah 453-N	Love FInds Its Own Way/Better You Go Your Way	1975	—	3.00	6.00
—Some copies have the grammatically correct A-side title as above					
❑ Buddah 463	The Way We Were-Try to Remember/The Need to Be	1975	—	2.50	5.00
❑ Buddah 487	Money/Street Brothers	1975	—	2.50	5.00
❑ Buddah 513	Part Time Love/Where Did I Put His Memory	1975	—	2.50	5.00
❑ Buddah 523	Make Yours a Happy Home/The Going Up and the Coming Down	1976	—	2.50	5.00
❑ Buddah 544	So Sad the Song/(Instrumental)	1976	—	2.50	5.00
❑ Buddah 569	Baby Don't Change Your Mind/I Love to Feel That Feeling	1977	—	2.50	5.00
❑ Buddah 584	Sorry Doesn't Always Make It Right/You Put a New Life in My Body	1977	—	2.50	5.00
❑ Buddah 592	The One and Only/Pipe Dreams	1978	—	2.50	5.00
❑ Buddah 598	It's a Better Than Good Time/Everybody's Got to Find a Way	1978	—	2.50	5.00
❑ Buddah 601	I'm Coming Home Again/Love Gives You the Power	1978	—	2.50	5.00
❑ Buddah 605	Sail Away/I'm Still Caught Up with You	1979	—	2.50	5.00
❑ Casablanca 912	If I Could Bring Back Yesterday/Since I Found Love	1978	—	2.00	4.00
—As "The Pips"					
❑ Casablanca 949	Baby I'm Your Fool/Lights of the City	1978	—	2.00	4.00
—As "The Pips"					
❑ Columbia 11-02113	Forever Yesterday (For the Children)/(Instrumental)	1981	—	2.00	4.00
❑ Columbia 18-02413	If That'll Make You Happy/Love Was Made for Two	1981	—	2.00	4.00
❑ Columbia 18-02549	I Will Fight/God Is	1981	—	2.00	4.00
❑ Columbia 18-02706	Friend of Mine/Reach High	1982	—	2.00	4.00
❑ Columbia 38-03418	That Special Time of Year/Santa Claus Is Comin' to Town	1982	—	2.50	5.00
❑ Columbia 38-03761	Save the Overtime (For Me)/Ain't No Greater Love	1983	—	2.00	4.00
❑ Columbia 38-04033	You're Number 1 in My Book/Oh La De Dah	1983	—	2.00	4.00
❑ Columbia 38-04219	Hero (The Wind Beneath My Wings)/Seconds	1983	—	2.50	5.00
❑ Columbia 38-04333	Here's That Sunny Day/Oh La De Da	1984	—	2.00	4.00
❑ Columbia 38-04369	When You're Far Away/Seconds	1984	—	2.00	4.00
❑ Columbia 38-04761	My Time/(Instrumental)	1985	—	2.00	4.00
❑ Columbia 38-04873	Keep Givin' Me Love/Do You Wanna Have Some Fun	1985	—	2.00	4.00
❑ Columbia 38-05679	Till I See You Again/Strivin'	1985	—	2.00	4.00
❑ Columbia 3-10922	Am I Too Late/It's the Same Old Song	1979	—	2.00	4.00
❑ Columbia 3-10997	You Bring Out the Best in Me/You Loved Away the Pain	1979	—	2.00	4.00
❑ Columbia 3-11088	The Best Thing We Can Do Is Say Goodbye/ You Don't Have to Say I Love You	1979	—	2.00	4.00
❑ Columbia 1-11239	Landlord/We Need Hearts	1980	—	2.00	4.00
❑ Columbia 1-11330	Taste of Bitter Love/Add It Up	1980	—	2.00	4.00
❑ Columbia 1-11375	Bourgie', Bourgie'/Get the Love	1980	—	2.00	4.00
❑ Columbia 11-11409	When a Child Is Born/The Lord's Prayer	1980	—	2.50	5.00
—With Johnny Mathis					
❑ Enjoy 2012	What Shall I Do/Love Call	1964	3.75	7.50	15.00
❑ Everlast 5025	Happiness/I Had a Dream Last Night	1963	6.25	12.50	25.00
—As "The Pips"					
❑ Fury 1050	Every Beat of My Heart/Room in Your Heart	1961	6.25	12.50	25.00
—Re-recordings of the same songs on Huntom and Vee Jay					
❑ Fury 1052	Guess Who/Stop Running Around	1961	3.75	7.50	15.00
❑ Fury 1054	Letter Full of Tears/You Broke Your Promise	1961	3.75	7.50	15.00
❑ Fury 1064	Operator/I'll Trust in You	1962	3.75	7.50	15.00
❑ Fury 1067	Darling/Linda	1962	5.00	10.00	20.00
—As "The Pips"					
❑ Fury 1073	Come See About Me/I Want That Kind of Love	1963	7.50	15.00	30.00
❑ Huntom 2510	Every Beat of My Heart/Room in Your Heart	1961	125.00	250.00	500.00
—As "The Pips"					
❑ Lost-Nite 261	Giving Up/Lovers Always Forgive	196?	—	2.50	5.00
—Reissue					
❑ Lost-Nite 382	Every Beat of My Heart/Room in Your Heart	197?	—	3.00	6.00
—Reissue of Fury versions					
❑ Lost-Nite 386	Letter Full of Tears/You Broke Your Promise	197?	—	2.50	5.00
—Reissue					
❑ Lost-Nite 389	Darling/Linda	197?	—	2.50	5.00
—As "The Pips"; reissue					
❑ Maxx 326	Giving Up/Maybe, Maybe Baby	1964	3.75	7.50	15.00
❑ Maxx 329	Lovers Always Forget/Another Love	1964	3.75	7.50	15.00
❑ Maxx 331	Either Way I Lose/Go Away, Stay Away	1964	3.75	7.50	15.00
❑ Maxx 334	Who Knows/Stop and Get a Hold of Myself	1965	3.75	7.50	15.00
❑ Maxx 335	Tell Her You're Mine/If I Should Ever Be in Love	1965	3.75	7.50	15.00

Number	Title (A Side/B Side)	Yr	VG	VG+	NM
❑ MCA 53002	Send It to Me/When You Love Somebody (It's Christmas Every Day)	1987	—	—	3.00
❑ MCA 53210	Love Overboard/(Instrumental)	1987	—	—	3.00
❑ MCA 53211	Lovin' on Next to Nothin'/(Instrumental)	1988	—	—	3.00
❑ MCA 53351	It's Gonna Take All Our Love/(Instrumental)	1988	—	—	3.00
❑ MCA 53657	Licence to Kill/You	1989	—	—	3.00
❑ MCA 53676	Licence to Kill/Pam	1989	—	—	3.00
—B-side by National Philharmonic Orchestra					
❑ MCA 54117	Men/(Instrumental)	1991	—	—	3.00
❑ Scotti Bros. ZS4-06267	Loving on Borrowed Time (Love Theme from Cobra)/ Angel of the City	1986	—	—	3.00
—A-side: Gladys Knight and Bill Medley; B-side: Robert Tepper					
❑ Soul 35023	Just Walk in My Shoes/Stepping Closer to Your Heart	1966	2.00	4.00	8.00
❑ Soul 35033	Take Me in Your Arms and Love Me/ Do You Love Me Just a Little More?	1967	2.00	4.00	8.00
❑ Soul 35034	Everybody Needs Love/Since I've Lost You	1967	2.00	4.00	8.00
❑ Soul 35039	I Heard It Through the Grapevine/It's Time to Go Now	1967	2.50	5.00	10.00
❑ Soul 35042	The End of Our Road/Don't Let Her Take Your Love from Me	1968	2.00	4.00	8.00
❑ Soul 35045	It Should Have Been Me/You Don't Love Me No More	1968	2.00	4.00	8.00
❑ Soul 35047	I Wish It Would Rain/It's Summer	1968	2.00	4.00	8.00
❑ Soul 35057	Didn't You Know (You'd Have to Cry Sometime)/Keep an Eye	1969	2.00	4.00	8.00
❑ Soul 35063	The Nitty Gritty/Got Myself a Good Man	1969	2.00	4.00	8.00
❑ Soul 35068	Friendship Train/Cloud Nine	1969	2.00	4.00	8.00
❑ Soul 35071	You Need Love Like I Do (Don't You)/You're My Everything	1970	2.00	4.00	8.00
❑ Soul 35078	If I Were Your Woman/The Tracks of My Tears	1970	—	3.50	7.00
❑ Soul 35083	I Don't Want to Do Wrong/Is There a Place In His Heart for Me	1971	—	3.00	6.00
❑ Soul 35091	Make Me the Woman You Come Home To/ If You're Gonna Leave (Just Leave)	1972	—	3.00	6.00
❑ Soul 35094	Help Me Make It Through the Night/ If You're Gonna Leave (Just Leave)	1972	—	3.00	6.00
❑ Soul 35098	Neither One of Us (Wants to Be the First to Say Goodbye)/ Can't Give It Up No More	1972	—	3.00	6.00
❑ Soul 35105	Daddy Could Swear I Declare/For Once in My Life	1973	—	3.00	6.00
❑ Soul 35107	All I Need Is Time/The Only Time You Love Me (Is When You're Losing Me)	1973	—	3.00	6.00
❑ Soul 35111	Betwen Her Goodbye and My Hello/This Child Needs Its Father	1974	—	3.00	6.00
❑ Trip 3004	It Hurt Me So Bad/What Will Become of Me	1973	—	3.00	6.00
❑ Vee Jay 386	Every Beat of My Heart/Ain'tcha Got Some Room (In Your Heart for Me)	1961	5.00	10.00	20.00
—By "The Pips"; same B-side, different title					
❑ Vee Jay 386	Every Beat of My Heart/Room in Your Heart	1961	5.00	10.00	20.00
—By "The Pips"					
❑ Vee Jay 545	A Love Like Mine/Queen of Tears	1963	5.00	10.00	20.00
Albums					
❑ Accord SN-7103	Every Beat of My Heart	1981	2.50	5.00	10.00
❑ Accord SN-7105	Letter Full of Tears	1981	2.50	5.00	10.00
❑ Accord SN-7131	I Feel a Song	1981	2.50	5.00	10.00
❑ Accord SN-7188	It's Showtime	1982	2.50	5.00	10.00
❑ Allegiance AV-5002	Glad to Be...	198?	2.50	5.00	10.00
❑ Bell 1323	In the Beginning	1975	3.00	6.00	12.00
❑ Bell 6013	Tastiest Hits	1968	5.00	10.00	20.00
❑ Buddah BDS-5141	Imagination	1973	3.00	6.00	12.00
❑ Buddah BDS-5602	Claudine	1974	7.50	15.00	30.00
❑ Buddah BDS-5612	I Feel a Song	1974	3.00	6.00	12.00
❑ Buddah BDS-5639	2nd Anniversary	1975	3.00	6.00	12.00
❑ Buddah BDS-5653	The Best of Gladys Knight & The Pips	1976	3.00	6.00	12.00
❑ Buddah BDS-5676	Pipe Dreams	1976	3.00	6.00	12.00
❑ Buddah BDS-5689	Still Together	1977	3.00	6.00	12.00
❑ Buddah BDS-5701	The One and Only	1978	3.00	6.00	12.00
❑ Buddah BDS-5714	Miss Gladys Knight	1978	3.00	6.00	12.00
❑ Casablanca NBLP 7081	At Last...The Pips	1977	2.50	5.00	10.00
—As "The Pips"					
❑ Casablanca NBLP 7113	Callin'	1978	2.50	5.00	10.00
—As "The Pips"					
❑ Collectables COL-5154	Golden Classics: Letter Full of Tears	198?	2.50	5.00	10.00
❑ Columbia JC 35704	Gladys Knight	1979	2.50	5.00	10.00
❑ Columbia JC 36387	About Love	1980	2.50	5.00	10.00
❑ Columbia FC 37086	Touch	1981	2.50	5.00	10.00
❑ Columbia FC 38114	That Special Time of Year	1982	2.50	5.00	10.00
❑ Columbia FC 38205	Visions	1983	2.50	5.00	10.00
❑ Columbia FC 39423	Life	1985	2.50	5.00	10.00
❑ Columbia FC 40376	Greatest Hits	1986	2.50	5.00	10.00
❑ Columbia FC 40878	The Best of Gladys Knight and the Pips/The Columbia Years	1988	2.50	5.00	10.00
❑ Fury 1003 [M]	Letter Full of Tears	1962	125.00	250.00	500.00
❑ Lost-Nite LLP-17 [10]	The Best of Gladys Knight and the Pips	1981	3.00	6.00	12.00
—Red vinyl					
❑ Maxx 3000 [M]	Gladys Knight and the Pips	1964	37.50	75.00	150.00
❑ MCA 10329	Good Woman	1991	3.75	7.50	15.00
❑ MCA 42004	All Our Love	1987	2.50	5.00	10.00
❑ Motown M5-113V	Motown Superstar Series, Vol. 13	1981	2.50	5.00	10.00
❑ Motown M5-126V1	Everybody Needs Love	1981	3.00	6.00	12.00
—Reissue of Soul 706					
❑ Motown M5-148V1	Nitty Gritty	1981	3.00	6.00	12.00
—Reissue of Soul 713					
❑ Motown M5-193V1	Neither One of Us	1981	3.00	6.00	12.00
—Reissue of Soul 737					
❑ Motown M 792S2 [(2)]	Anthology	1974	3.75	7.50	15.00

Number	Title (A Side/B Side)	Yr	VG	VG+	NM
❑ Motown MOT 5303	All the Great Hits of Gladys Knight and the Pips	198?	2.00	4.00	8.00
❑ Natural Resources NR 4004T1	Silk N' Soul	1978	2.50	5.00	10.00
—Reissue of Soul 711					
❑ Pair PDL2-1198	The Best of Gladys Knight and the Pips	1987	3.00	6.00	12.00
❑ Pickwick SPC-3349	Every Beat of My Heart	197?	2.50	5.00	10.00
❑ Soul S 706 [M]	Everybody Needs Love	1967	5.00	10.00	20.00
❑ Soul SS 706 [S]	Everybody Needs Love	1967	6.25	12.50	25.00
❑ Soul S 707 [M]	Feelin' Bluesy	1968	10.00	20.00	40.00
—Mono copies are white label promo only; cover has "Monaural Record DJ Copy" sticker					
❑ Soul SS 707 [S]	Feelin' Bluesy	1968	6.25	12.50	25.00
❑ Soul SS 711	Silk N' Soul	1968	6.25	12.50	25.00
❑ Soul SS 713	Nitty Gritty	1969	6.25	12.50	25.00
❑ Soul SS 723	Gladys Knight and the Pips Greatest Hits	1970	3.75	7.50	15.00
❑ Soul SS 730	All in a Knight's Work	1970	3.75	7.50	15.00
❑ Soul SS 731	If I Were Your Woman	1971	3.75	7.50	15.00
❑ Soul S 736L	Standing Ovation	1971	3.75	7.50	15.00
❑ Soul S 737L	Neither One of Us	1973	3.75	7.50	15.00
❑ Soul S 739L	All I Need Is Time	1973	3.75	7.50	15.00
❑ Soul S 741	Knight Time	1974	3.00	6.00	12.00
❑ Soul S 744	A Little Knight Music	1975	3.00	6.00	12.00
❑ Sphere Sound SR-7006 [M]	Gladys Knight and the Pips	196?	50.00	100.00	200.00
❑ Sphere Sound SSR-7006 [R]	Gladys Knight and the Pips	196?	30.00	60.00	120.00
❑ Springboard SPB-4035	Early Hits	1972	2.50	5.00	10.00
❑ Springboard SPB-4050	How Do You Say Goodbye	1973	2.50	5.00	10.00
❑ Trip TLP-9509	It Hurt Me So Bad	1973	2.50	5.00	10.00
❑ United Artists UA-LA503-E	The Very Best of Gladys Knight and the Pips	1975	3.00	6.00	12.00
❑ Upfront UPF 130	Gladys Knight and the Pips	197?	2.50	5.00	10.00
❑ Upfront UPF 185	Gladys Knight and the Pips	197?	2.50	5.00	10.00

KNOX, BUDDY

45s

Number	Title (A Side/B Side)	Yr	VG	VG+	NM
❑ Liberty 55290	Lovey Dovey/I Got You	1960	3.00	6.00	12.00
❑ Liberty 55305	Ling, Ting, Tong/The Kisses	1961	3.00	6.00	12.00
❑ Liberty 55366	All By Myself/Three Eyed Man	1961	3.00	6.00	12.00
❑ Liberty 55411	Cha-Hua-Hua/Open	1962	3.00	6.00	12.00
❑ Liberty 55473	She's Gone/There's Only Me	1962	3.00	6.00	12.00
❑ Liberty 55503	Dear Abby/Three Way Love Affair	1962	3.00	6.00	12.00
❑ Liberty 55592	Shadaroom/Tomorrow Is a-Comin'	1963	2.50	5.00	10.00
❑ Liberty 55650	Thanks a Lot/Hitchhike Back to Georgia	1963	2.50	5.00	10.00
❑ Liberty 55694	Good Lovin'/All Time Loser	1964	2.50	5.00	10.00
❑ Reprise 0395	Livin' in a House Full of Love/Good Time Girl	1965	2.50	5.00	10.00
❑ Reprise 0431	A Lover's Question/You Said Goodbye	1965	2.50	5.00	10.00
❑ Reprise 0463	A White Sport Coat/That Don't Do Me No Good	1966	2.50	5.00	10.00
❑ Reprise 0501	Love Has Many Ways/Sixteen Feet of Patio	1966	2.50	5.00	10.00
❑ Roulette 4002	Party Doll/My Baby's Gone	1957	12.50	25.00	50.00
—Maroon label, silver print, with roulette wheel around outside					
❑ Roulette 4009	Rock Your Little Baby to Sleep/Don't Make Me Cry	1957	10.00	20.00	40.00
—Red label with roulette wheel around outside					
❑ Roulette 4018	Hula Love/Devil Woman	1957	6.25	12.50	25.00
❑ Roulette 4042	Swingin' Daddy/Whenever I'm Lonely	1958	6.25	12.50	25.00
❑ Roulette 4082	Somebody Touched Me/C'mon Baby	1958	6.25	12.50	25.00
❑ Roulette 4120	That's Why I Cry/Teaseable, Pleaseable You	1958	6.25	12.50	25.00
❑ Roulette 4140	I Think I'm Gonna Kill Myself/To Be with You	1959	6.25	12.50	25.00
❑ Roulette 4179	Taste of the Blues/I Ain't Sharin' Sharon	1959	6.25	12.50	25.00
❑ Roulette 4262	Long Lonely Nights/Storm Clouds	1960	6.25	12.50	25.00
❑ Ruff 1001	Jo-Ann/Don't Make a Ripple	1965	2.50	5.00	10.00
❑ Triple D 798	Party Doll/I'm Stickin' With You	1956	250.00	500.00	1000.
—B-side by Jimmy Bowen					
❑ United Artists 50301	This Time Tomorrow/Gypsy Man	1968	2.00	4.00	8.00
❑ United Artists 50463	Today My Sleepless Nights Came Back to Town/ A Million Years or So	1968	2.00	4.00	8.00
❑ United Artists 50526	God Knows I Love You/Night Runners	1969	2.00	4.00	8.00
❑ United Artists 50596	Salt Lake City/I'm Only Rockin'	1969	2.00	4.00	8.00
❑ United Artists 50644	Yesterday Is Gone/Back to New Orleans	1970	—	3.00	6.00
❑ United Artists 50722	White Dove/Glory Train	1970	—	3.00	6.00

Number	Title (A Side/B Side)	Yr	VG	VG+	NM
❑ United Artists 50789	Come Softly to Me/Travelin' Light	1971	—	3.00	6.00
Albums					
❑ Accord SN-7218	Party Doll and Other Hits	1981	2.50	5.00	10.00
❑ Liberty LRP-3251 [M]	Buddy Knox's Golden Hits	1962	7.50	15.00	30.00
❑ Liberty LST-7251 [S]	Buddy Knox's Golden Hits	1962	10.00	20.00	40.00
❑ Roulette R 25003 [M]	Buddy Knox	1957	50.00	100.00	200.00
—Black label, all silver print (original)					
❑ Roulette R 25048 [M]	Buddy Knox and Jimmy Bowen	1959	50.00	100.00	200.00
—Black label, red and silver print					

KOOL AND THE GANG

Number	Title (A Side/B Side)	Yr	VG	VG+	NM
45s					
❑ De-Lite 519	Kool and the Gang/Raw Hamburger	1969	—	3.00	6.00
❑ De-Lite 523	The Gangs Back Again/Kools Back Again	1969	—	3.00	6.00
❑ De-Lite 525	Kool It (Here Comes the Fuzz)/Can't Stop	1970	—	3.00	6.00
❑ De-Lite 529	Let the Music Take Your Mind/Chocolate Buttermilk	1970	—	3.00	6.00
❑ De-Lite 534	Funky Man/1,2,3,4,5,6,7,8	1970	—	3.00	6.00
❑ De-Lite 538	Who's Gonna Take the Weight (Part One)/ Who's Gonna Take the Weight (Part Two)	1970	—	3.00	6.00
❑ De-Lite 540	I Want to Take You Higher/Pneumonia	1971	—	3.00	6.00
❑ De-Lite 543	The Penguin/Lucky for Me	1971	—	3.00	6.00
❑ De-Lite 544	N.T. (Part One)/N.T. (Part Two)	1971	—	3.00	6.00
❑ De-Lite 546	Love the Life You Live, Part I/Love the Life You Live, Part II	1972	—	3.00	6.00
❑ De-Lite 547	You've Lost That Lovin' Feeling/Ike's Mood	1972	—	3.00	6.00
❑ De-Lite 550	Music Is the Messenger, Part I/Music Is the Messenger, Part II	1972	—	3.00	6.00
❑ De-Lite 552	Good Times/The Frog	1972	—	3.00	6.00
❑ De-Lite 553	Funky Granny/Blowing with the Wind	1973	—	3.00	6.00
❑ De-Lite 555	Country Junkie/I Remember John W. Coltrane	1973	—	3.00	6.00
❑ De-Lite 557	Funky Stuff/More Funky Stuff	1973	—	3.00	6.00
❑ De-Lite 559	Jungle Boogie/North, East, South, West	1973	—	2.50	5.00
❑ De-Lite 561	Hollywood Swinging/Dujii	1974	—	2.50	5.00
❑ De-Lite 801	Ladies Night/If You Feel Like Dancin'	1979	—	2.00	4.00
❑ De-Lite 802	Too Hot/Tonight's the Night	1979	—	2.00	4.00
❑ De-Lite 804	Hangin' Out/Got You Into My Life	1980	—	2.00	4.00
❑ De-Lite 807	Celebration/Morning Star	1980	—	2.00	4.00
❑ De-Lite 810	Take It to the Top/Love Affair	1981	—	2.00	4.00
❑ De-Lite 813	Jones Vs. Jones/Night People	1981	—	2.00	4.00
❑ De-Lite 815	Take My Heart/Just Friends	1981	—	2.50	5.00
—First pressings have no subtitle					
❑ De-Lite 815	Take My Heart (You Can Have It If You Want It)/Just Friends	1981	—	2.00	4.00
❑ De-Lite 816	Steppin' Out/Love Festival	1982	—	2.00	4.00
❑ De-Lite 818	Get Down On It/Steppin' Out	1982	—	2.00	4.00
❑ De-Lite 822	Big Fun/No Show	1982	—	2.00	4.00
❑ De-Lite 824	Let's Go Dancin' (Ooh, La, La, La)/Be My Lady	1982	—	2.00	4.00
❑ De-Lite 825	Street Kids/As One	1983	—	2.00	4.00
❑ De-Lite 829	Joanna/A Place for Us	1983	—	—	3.00
❑ De-Lite 830	Tonight/Home Is Where the Heart Is	1984	—	—	3.00
❑ De-Lite 831	Straight Ahead/September Love	1984	—	—	3.00
❑ De-Lite 901	Slick Superchick/Life's a Song	1978	—	2.50	5.00
❑ De-Lite 905	A Place in Space/The Force	1978	—	2.50	5.00
❑ De-Lite 909	I Like Music/It's All You Need	1978	—	2.50	5.00
❑ De-Lite 910	Everybody's Dancin'/Stay Awhile	1978	—	2.50	5.00
❑ De-Lite 1562	Higher Plane/Wild Is Love	1974	—	2.50	5.00
❑ De-Lite 1563	Rhyme Tyme People/Father, Father	1974	—	2.50	5.00
❑ De-Lite 1567	Spirit of the Boogie/Summer Madness	1975	—	2.50	5.00
❑ De-Lite 1573	Caribbean Festival/Caribbean Festival (Disco Version)	1975	—	2.50	5.00
❑ De-Lite 1577	Winter Sadness/Father, Father	1975	—	2.50	5.00
❑ De-Lite 1579	Love and Understanding (Come Together)/Sunshine and Love	1976	—	2.50	5.00
❑ De-Lite 1583	Universal Sound/Ancestral Ceremony	1976	—	2.50	5.00
❑ De-Lite 1586	Open Sesame — Part 1/Open Sesame — Part 2	1976	—	2.50	5.00
❑ De-Lite 1590	Super Band/Sunshine	1977	—	2.50	5.00
❑ De-Lite 880431-7	Misled/Rollin'	1984	—	—	3.00
❑ De-Lite 880623-7	Fresh/In the Heart	1985	—	—	3.00
❑ De-Lite 880869-7	Cherish/(Instrumental)	1985	—	—	3.00
❑ De-Lite 884199-7	Emergency/You Are the One	1985	—	—	3.00
❑ Mercury 870513-7	Rags to Riches/Rags to Riches (Remix)	1988	—	—	3.00
❑ Mercury 872038-7	Strong/Funky Stuff	1988	—	—	3.00
❑ Mercury 874402-7	Raindrops/Amor Amore	1989	—	—	3.00
❑ Mercury 876072-7	Never Give Up/Amor Amore	1989	—	—	3.00
❑ Mercury 888074-7	Victory/Bad Woman	1986	—	—	3.00
❑ Mercury 888292-7	Stone Love/Dance Champion	1987	—	—	3.00
❑ Mercury 888712-7	Holiday/(Jam Mix)	1987	—	—	3.00
❑ Mercury 888867-7	In a Special Way/God's Country	1987	—	—	3.00
Albums					
❑ De-Lite 2003	Kool and the Gang	1969	6.25	12.50	25.00
❑ De-Lite 2008	Live at the Sex Machine	1971	3.00	6.00	12.00
❑ De-Lite 2009	The Best of Kool and the Gang	1971	3.00	6.00	12.00
❑ De-Lite 2010	Live at PJ's	1971	3.00	6.00	12.00
❑ De-Lite 2011	Music Is the Message	1972	3.00	6.00	12.00
❑ De-Lite 2012	Good Times	1973	3.00	6.00	12.00
❑ De-Lite 2013	Wild and Peaceful	1973	2.50	5.00	10.00
❑ De-Lite 2014	Light of Worlds	1974	2.50	5.00	10.00
❑ De-Lite 2015	Kool & The Gang Greatest Hits!	1975	2.50	5.00	10.00
❑ De-Lite 2016	Spirit of the Boogie	1975	2.50	5.00	10.00
❑ De-Lite 2018	Love and Understanding	1976	2.50	5.00	10.00
❑ De-Lite 2023	Open Sesame	1976	2.50	5.00	10.00
❑ De-Lite 4001	Kool Jazz	1973	2.50	5.00	10.00

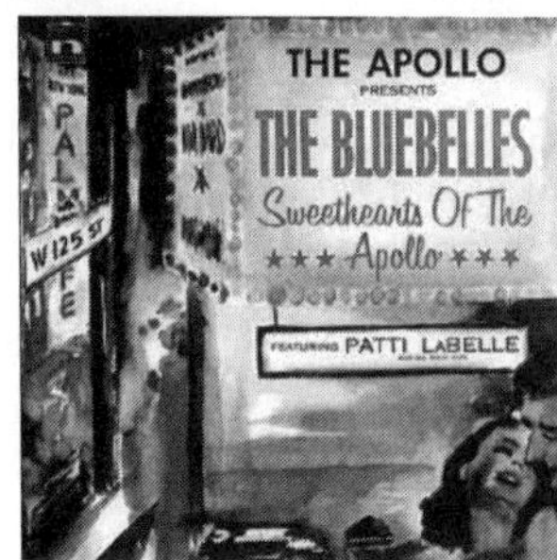

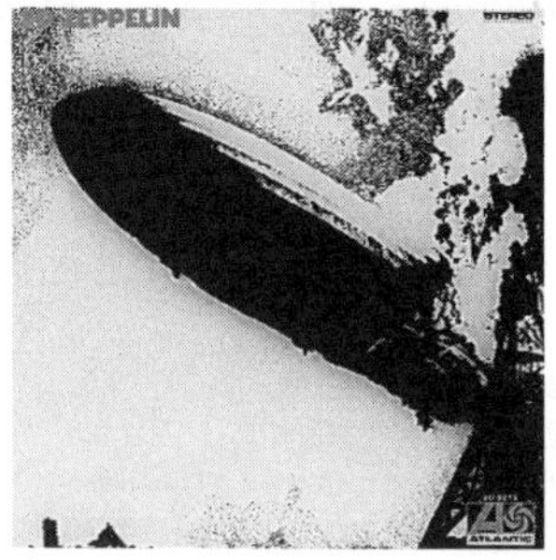

Number	Title (A Side/B Side)	Yr	VG	VG+	NM
❑ De-Lite 8502	Something Special	1981	2.50	5.00	10.00
❑ De-Lite 8505	As One	1982	2.50	5.00	10.00
❑ De-Lite 8508	In the Heart	1983	2.50	5.00	10.00
❑ De-Lite 9501	The Force	1978	2.50	5.00	10.00
❑ De-Lite 9507	Kool & The Gang Spin Their Top Ten Hits	1978	2.50	5.00	10.00
❑ De-Lite 9509	Everybody's Dancin'	1979	2.50	5.00	10.00
❑ De-Lite 9513	Ladies Night	1979	2.50	5.00	10.00
❑ De-Lite 9518	Celebrate!	1980	2.50	5.00	10.00
❑ De-Lite 814351-1 *—Reissue*	In the Heart	1984	2.00	4.00	8.00
❑ De-Lite 822534-1 *—Reissue*	Something Special	1984	2.00	4.00	8.00
❑ De-Lite 822535-1 *—Reissue*	As One	1984	2.00	4.00	8.00
❑ De-Lite 822536-1 *—Reissue*	Kool & The Gang Spin Their Top Ten Hits	1984	2.00	4.00	8.00
❑ De-Lite 822537-1 *—Reissue*	Ladies Night	1984	2.00	4.00	8.00
❑ De-Lite 822538-1 *—Reissue*	Celebrate!	1984	2.00	4.00	8.00
❑ De-Lite 822943-1	Emergency	1984	2.00	4.00	8.00
❑ Mercury 830398-1	Forever	1986	2.00	4.00	8.00
❑ Mercury 834780-1	Everything's Kool & the Gang: Greatest Hits & More	1988	2.00	4.00	8.00
❑ Mercury 838233-1	Sweat	1989	2.00	4.00	8.00

KRAMER, BILLY J., AND THE DAKOTAS

45s

Number	Title (A Side/B Side)	Yr	VG	VG+	NM
❑ Epic 10331	1941/His Love Is Just a Lie	1968	2.50	5.00	10.00
❑ Imperial 66027	Little Children/Bad to Me	1964	3.00	6.00	12.00
❑ Imperial 66048	I'll Keep You Satisfied/I Know	1964	3.00	6.00	12.00
❑ Imperial 66051	From a Window/I'll Be On My Way	1964	3.00	6.00	12.00
❑ Imperial 66085	It's Gotta Last Forever/They Remind Me of You	1965	3.00	6.00	12.00
❑ Imperial 66115	Trains and Boats and Planes/That's the Way I Feel	1965	2.50	5.00	10.00
❑ Imperial 66115	Trains and Boats and Planes/I'll Be On My Way	1965	3.00	6.00	12.00
❑ Imperial 66135	Irresistible You/Twilight Time	1965	2.50	5.00	10.00
❑ Imperial 66143	I'll Be Doggone/Neon City	1965	2.50	5.00	10.00
❑ Imperial 66210	You Make Me Feel Like Someone/Take My Hand	1966	2.50	5.00	10.00
❑ Liberty 55586	Do You Want to Know a Secret/I'll Be On My Way	1963	7.50	15.00	30.00
❑ Liberty 55618	The Cruel Surf/The Millionaire	1963	10.00	20.00	40.00
❑ Liberty 55626	Bad to Me/I Call Your Name	1963	7.50	15.00	30.00
❑ Liberty 55643	I'll Keep You Satisfied/I Know	1963	7.50	15.00	30.00
❑ Liberty 55667	Bad to Me/Do You Want to Know a Secret	1964	6.25	12.50	25.00
❑ Liberty 55687 *—Unreleased*	Little Children/They Remind Me of You	1964	—	—	—

Albums

Number	Title (A Side/B Side)	Yr	VG	VG+	NM
❑ Capitol SM-11897 [P]	The Best of Billy J. Kramer and the Dakotas	1979	2.50	5.00	10.00
❑ Imperial LP 9267 [M] *—Black label with stars*	Little Children	1964	12.50	25.00	50.00
❑ Imperial LP 9273 [M]	I'll Keep You Satisfied/From a Window	1964	7.50	15.00	30.00
❑ Imperial LP 9291 [M]	Trains and Boats and Planes	1965	7.50	15.00	30.00
❑ Imperial LP 12267 [P] *—Black label with silver print*	Little Children	1964	20.00	40.00	80.00
❑ Imperial LP 12273 [P]	I'll Keep You Satisfied/From a Window	1964	10.00	20.00	40.00
❑ Imperial LP 12921 [R]	Trains and Boats and Planes	1965	6.25	12.50	25.00

L

L.T.D.

45s

Number	Title (A Side/B Side)	Yr	VG	VG+	NM
❑ A&M 1514	Elegant Love/Success	1974	—	2.50	5.00
❑ A&M 1537	What Goes Around/To the Bone	1974	—	2.50	5.00
❑ A&M 1665	Don't Lose Your Cool/Thank You Mother	1975	—	2.50	5.00
❑ A&M 1681	Trying to Find a Way/I Told You I'd Be Back	1975	—	2.50	5.00
❑ A&M 1731	Rated X/Ain't No Way	1975	—	2.50	5.00
❑ A&M 1847	Love Ballad/Let the Music Keep Playing	1976	—	2.50	5.00
❑ A&M 1897	Love to the World/Get Your It Together	1976	—	2.50	5.00
❑ A&M 1974	(Every Time I Turn Around) Back in Love Again/Material Things	1977	—	2.50	5.00

Number	Title (A Side/B Side)	Yr	VG	VG+	NM
❑ A&M 2005	Never Get Enough of Your Love/Make Someone Smile Today	1978	—	2.50	5.00
❑ A&M 2057	Holding On (When Love Is Gone)/Together Forever	1978	—	2.50	5.00
❑ A&M 2095	We Both Deserve Each Other's Love/It's Time to Be Real	1978	—	2.50	5.00
❑ A&M 2142	Dance "N" Sing "N"/Give It All	1979	—	2.50	5.00
❑ A&M 2176	Share My Love/Sometimes	1979	—	2.50	5.00
❑ A&M 2192	Stranger/Sometimes	1979	—	2.50	5.00
❑ A&M 2250	Where Did We Go Wrong/Stand Up L.T.D.	1980	—	2.50	5.00
❑ A&M 2283	Shine On/Love Is What You Need	1980	—	2.50	5.00
❑ A&M 2346	Shine On (Spanish Version)/Where Did We Go Wrong	1981	—	2.50	5.00
❑ A&M 2382	Kickin' Back/Now	1981	—	2.50	5.00
❑ A&M 2395	April Love/Stay on the One	1982	—	2.50	5.00
❑ A&M 2414	Cuttin' It Up/Love Magic	1982	—	2.00	4.00
❑ Montage 908	For You/Party with You (All Night)	1983	—	2.00	4.00
Albums					
❑ A&M SP-3119	L.T.D.	198?	2.00	4.00	8.00
—Budget-line reissue					
❑ A&M SP-3146	Love to the World	198?	2.00	4.00	8.00
—Budget-line reissue					
❑ A&M SP-3148	Something to Love	198?	2.00	4.00	8.00
—Budget-line reissue					
❑ A&M SP-3602	L.T.D.	1974	3.00	6.00	12.00
❑ A&M SP-3660	Gittin' Down	1975	3.00	6.00	12.00
❑ A&M SP-4589	Love to the World	1976	2.50	5.00	10.00
❑ A&M SP-4646	Something to Love	1977	2.50	5.00	10.00
❑ A&M SP-4705	Togetherness	1978	2.50	5.00	10.00
❑ A&M SP-4771	Devotion	1979	2.50	5.00	10.00
❑ A&M SP-4819	Shine On	1980	2.50	5.00	10.00
❑ A&M SP-4881	Love Magic	1981	2.50	5.00	10.00
LABELLE					
45s					
❑ Epic 50048	Lady Marmalade/Space Children	1974	—	3.00	6.00
❑ Epic 50097	Night Bird/What Can I Do for You	1975	—	3.00	6.00
❑ Epic 50140	Messin' My Mind/Take the Night Off	1975	—	3.00	6.00
❑ Epic 50168	Slow Burn/Far As We Felt Like Going	1975	—	3.00	6.00
❑ Epic 8-50262	Get You Somebody New/Who's Watching the Watcher	1976	2.00	4.00	8.00
❑ Epic 50315	Isn't It a Shame/Gypsy Moths	1976	—	3.00	6.00
❑ RCA Victor 74-0965	Open Up Your Heart/Going Up a Holiday	1973	2.00	4.00	8.00
❑ RCA Victor APBO-0157	Mr. Sunshine Man/Sunshine	1973	2.00	4.00	8.00
❑ Warner Bros. 7512	Morning Much Better/Shades of Difference	1971	2.00	4.00	8.00
❑ Warner Bros. 7579	Moonshadow/If I Can't Have You	1972	2.00	4.00	8.00
❑ Warner Bros. 7624	Touch Me All Over/Ain't It Sad It's All Over	1972	2.00	4.00	8.00
Albums					
❑ Epic KE 33075	Nightbirds	1974	3.00	6.00	12.00
❑ Epic PE 33579	Phoenix	1975	2.50	5.00	10.00
❑ Epic PE 34189	Chameleon	1976	2.50	5.00	10.00
—Original with no bar code and orange label					
❑ RCA Victor APL1-0205	Pressure Cookin'	1973	3.00	6.00	12.00
❑ RCA Victor AYL1-4176	Pressure Cookin'	1982	2.00	4.00	8.00
—"Best Buy Series" reissue					
❑ Warner Bros. WS 1943	LaBelle	1971	3.75	7.50	15.00
❑ Warner Bros. BS 2618	Moonshadow	1972	3.75	7.50	15.00
LABELLE, PATTI, AND THE BLUE BELLES					
45s					
❑ Atlantic 2311	All or Nothing/You Forgot How to Love	1965	3.00	6.00	12.00
❑ Atlantic 2318	A Groovy Kind of Love/Over the Rainbow	1966	2.50	5.00	10.00
❑ Atlantic 2333	Ebb Tide/Patti's Prayer	1966	2.50	5.00	10.00
❑ Atlantic 2347	I'm Still Waiting/Family Man	1966	2.50	5.00	10.00
❑ Atlantic 2373	Take Me for a Little While/I Don't Want to Go On Without You	1967	2.50	5.00	10.00
❑ Atlantic 2390	(There's) Always Something There to Remind Me/Tender Words	1967	2.50	5.00	10.00
❑ Atlantic 2408	Unchained Melody/Dreamer	1967	2.50	5.00	10.00
❑ Atlantic 2446	Oh My Love/I Need Your Love	1967	2.50	5.00	10.00
❑ Atlantic 2548	He's My Man/Wonderful	1968	2.50	5.00	10.00
❑ Atlantic 2610	Dance to the Rhythm of Love/He's Gone	1969	2.50	5.00	10.00
❑ Atlantic 2629	Loving Blues/Pride's No Match for Love	1969	2.50	5.00	10.00
❑ Atlantic 2712	Suffer/Trustin' in You	1970	2.50	5.00	10.00
❑ King 5777	Down the Aisle (Wedding Song)/C'est La Vie	1963	3.75	7.50	15.00
❑ Lost-Nite 250	You'll Never Walk Alone/Decatur Street	196?	—	2.50	5.00
—Reissue					
❑ Lost-Nite 251	Down the Aisle (Wedding Song)/C'est La Vie	196?	—	2.50	5.00
—Reissue					
❑ Lost-Nite 252	I Sold My Heart to the Junkman/Itty Bitty Twist	196?	—	2.50	5.00
—Reissue					
❑ Newtime 510	Love Me Just a Little/The Joke's On You	1962	5.00	10.00	20.00
❑ Newtown 5000	I Sold My Heart to the Junkman/Itty Bitty Twist	1962	5.00	10.00	20.00
—Credited to "The Blue-Belles" but actually recorded by The Starlets					
❑ Newtown 5006	I Found a New Love/Pitter Patter	1962	5.00	10.00	20.00
—Most of the Newtown sides credit "The Blue-Belles"					
❑ Newtown 5007	Tear After Tear/Go On, This Is Goodbye	1962	5.00	10.00	20.00
❑ Newtown 5009	Cool Water/When Johnny Comes Marching Home	1962	5.00	10.00	20.00
❑ Newtown 5019	Academy Award/Decatur Street	1963	5.00	10.00	20.00
❑ Newtown 5777	Down the Aisle (Wedding Song)/C'est La Vie	1963	3.75	7.50	15.00
❑ Nicetown 5020	You'll Never Walk Alone/Where Are You	1963	3.75	7.50	15.00
❑ Parkway 896	You'll Never Walk Alone/Decatur Street	1964	3.00	6.00	12.00
❑ Parkway 913	One Phone Call/You Will Fill My Eyes No More	1964	3.00	6.00	12.00
❑ Parkway 935	Danny Boy/I Believe	1964	3.00	6.00	12.00

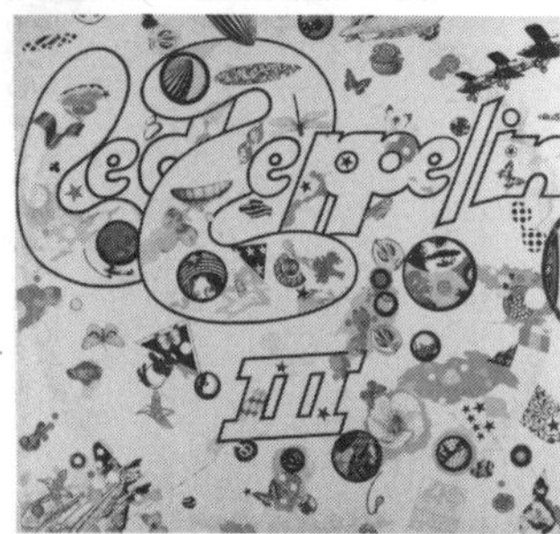

Number	Title (A Side/B Side)	Yr	VG	VG+	NM
❑ Peak 7042	I've Got to Let Him Know/I Sold My Heart to the Junkman	1962	6.25	12.50	25.00
—Credited to "The Blue-Belles" but actually recorded by The Starlets					
Albums					
❑ Atlantic 8119 [M]	Over the Rainbow	1966	7.50	15.00	30.00
❑ Atlantic SD 8119 [S]	Over the Rainbow	1966	10.00	20.00	40.00
❑ Atlantic 8147 [M]	Dreamer	1967	7.50	15.00	30.00
❑ Atlantic SD 8147 [S]	Dreamer	1967	10.00	20.00	40.00
❑ Mistletoe MLP-1204	Merry Christmas from LaBelle	1976	5.00	10.00	20.00
❑ Newtown 631 [M]	Sweethearts of the Apollo	1963	100.00	200.00	400.00
❑ Newtown 632 [M]	Sleigh Bells, Jingle Bells and Blue Bells	1963	75.00	150.00	300.00
❑ Parkway P-7043 [M]	The Bluebelles On Stage	1965	30.00	60.00	120.00
—Without bonus single					
❑ Parkway P-7043 [M]	The Bluebelles On Stage	1965	37.50	75.00	150.00
—With bonus single					
❑ Trip 3508	Patti LaBelle and the Bluebelles	197?	2.50	5.00	10.00
❑ Trip 8000	Patti LaBelle and the Bluebelles' Greatest Hits	1971	2.50	5.00	10.00
❑ Trip 9525	Early Hits	197?	2.50	5.00	10.00
❑ United Artists UA-LA504-E	The Very Best of Patti LaBelle and the Bluebelles	1975	2.50	5.00	10.00
LANCE, MAJOR					
45s					
❑ Curtom 1953	Stay Away from Me (I Love You Too Much)/Gypsy Woman	1970	—	3.00	6.00
❑ Curtom 1956	Must Be Love Coming Down/Little Young Lover	1970	—	3.00	6.00
❑ Dakar 608	Follow the Leader/Since You've Been Gone	1969	2.00	4.00	8.00
❑ Dakar 612	Shadows of a Memory/Sweeter As the Days Go By	1969	2.00	4.00	8.00
❑ Kat Family 03024	I Wanna Go Home/(Instrumental)	1982	—	2.00	4.00
❑ Kat Family 04185	Are You Leaving Me/I Wanna Go Home	1983	—	2.00	4.00
❑ Mercury 71582	I've Got a Girl/Phyllis	1960	7.50	15.00	30.00
❑ Okeh 7175	The Monkey Time/Mama Didn't Know	1963	3.75	7.50	15.00
❑ Okeh 7181	Hey Little Girl/Crying in the Rain	1963	3.00	6.00	12.00
❑ Okeh 7187	Um, Um, Um, Um, Um, Um/Sweet Music	1964	3.75	7.50	15.00
❑ Okeh 7191	The Matador/Gonna Get Married	1964	2.50	5.00	10.00
❑ Okeh 7197	It Ain't No Use/Girls	1964	2.50	5.00	10.00
❑ Okeh 7200	Think Nothing About It/It's Alright	1964	12.50	25.00	50.00
❑ Okeh 7203	Rhythm/Please Don't Say No More	1964	2.50	5.00	10.00
❑ Okeh 7209	Sometimes I Wonder/I'm So Lost	1965	2.50	5.00	10.00
❑ Okeh 7216	Come See/You Belong to Me My Love	1965	2.50	5.00	10.00
❑ Okeh 7223	Ain't It a Shame/Gotta Get Away	1965	2.50	5.00	10.00
❑ Okeh 7226	Too Hot to Hold/Dark and Lovely	1965	2.50	5.00	10.00
❑ Okeh 7233	Everybody Loves a Good Time/I Just Can't Help It	1965	3.75	7.50	15.00
❑ Okeh 7250	Little Young Lover/Investigate	1966	3.75	7.50	15.00
❑ Okeh 7255	It's the Beat/You'll Want Me Back	1966	2.50	5.00	10.00
❑ Okeh 7266	Ain't No Soul (In These Shoes)/I	1966	3.75	7.50	15.00
❑ Okeh 7284	You Don't Want Me No More/Wait Till I Get You in Your Arms	1967	12.50	25.00	50.00
❑ Okeh 7298	Without a Doubt/Forever	1967	2.50	5.00	10.00
❑ Osiris 001	You're Everything I Need/(Instrumental)	1975	—	2.50	5.00
❑ Playboy 6017	Um, Um, Um, Um, Um, Um/Last of the Red Hot Lovers	1974	—	2.50	5.00
❑ Playboy 6020	Sweeter/Wild and Free	1975	—	2.50	5.00
❑ Soul 35123	I Never Thought I'd Be Losing You/Chicago Disco	1977	—	2.50	5.00
❑ Volt 4079	I Wanna Make Up/That's the Story of My Life	1972	—	3.00	6.00
❑ Volt 4085	Ain't No Sweat/Since I Lost My Baby's Love	1972	—	3.00	6.00
Albums					
❑ Okeh OKM-12105 [M]	The Monkey Time	1963	10.00	20.00	40.00
❑ Okeh OKM-12106 [M]	Um, Um, Um, Um, Um, Um	1964	10.00	20.00	40.00
❑ Okeh OKM-12110 [M]	Major's Greatest Hits	1965	7.50	15.00	30.00
❑ Okeh OKS-14105 [S]	The Monkey Time	1963	12.50	25.00	50.00
❑ Okeh OKS-14106 [S]	Um, Um, Um, Um, Um, Um	1964	12.50	25.00	50.00
❑ Okeh OKS-14110 [S]	Major's Greatest Hits	1965	10.00	20.00	40.00
❑ Soul S7-751	Now Arriving	1978	3.00	6.00	12.00
LARKS, THE (1)					
45s					
❑ Money 106	The Jerk/Forget Me	1964	5.00	10.00	20.00
❑ Money 109	Mickey's East Coast Jerk/Soul Jerk	1965	3.00	6.00	12.00
❑ Money 110	The Slauson Shuffle/Soul Jerk	1965	3.00	6.00	12.00
❑ Money 112	The Roman/Heavenly Father	1965	3.00	6.00	12.00
❑ Money 115	Can You Do the Duck/Sad Sad Boy	1965	3.00	6.00	12.00

Number	Title (A Side/B Side)	Yr	VG	VG+	NM
❑ Money 119	Lost My Love Yesterday/The Answer Came Too Late	1966	3.00	6.00	12.00
❑ Money 122	Philly Dog/Heaven Only Knows	1966	3.00	6.00	12.00
❑ Money 127	The Skate/Come Back Baby	1967	3.00	6.00	12.00
❑ Money 601	I Love You/I Want You Back	1973	—	3.00	6.00
❑ Money 604	My Favorite Beer Joint/(Instrumental)	1973	—	3.00	6.00
❑ Money 607	Shorty the Pimp (Part 1)/Shorty the Pimp (Part 2)	1974	—	3.00	6.00
—Money 604 and 607 as "Don Julian and the Larks"					
Albums					
❑ Collectables COL-5176	Golden Classics: The Jerk	198?	2.50	5.00	10.00
❑ Money LP-1102 [M]	The Jerk	1965	10.00	20.00	40.00
❑ Money ST-1102 [S]	The Jerk	1965	12.50	25.00	50.00
❑ Money LP-1107 [M]	Soul Kaleidoscope	1966	10.00	20.00	40.00
❑ Money ST-1107 [S]	Soul Kaleidoscope	1966	12.50	25.00	50.00
❑ Money LP-1110 [M]	Superslick	1967	10.00	20.00	40.00
❑ Money ST-1110 [S]	Superslick	1967	12.50	25.00	50.00

LED ZEPPELIN

Number	Title (A Side/B Side)	Yr	VG	VG+	NM
45s					
❑ Atlantic 2613	Communication Breakdown/Good Times Bad Times	1969	6.25	12.50	25.00
❑ Atlantic 2613	Communication Breakdown/Good Times Bad Times	198?	2.00	4.00	8.00
—Later edition with Warner Communcations logo in perimeter print and a reference to "From Atlantic LP 19126 — 'Led Zeppelin'" at bottom, plus a "(P) 1969 Atlantic Recording Corp." underneath					
❑ Atlantic 2690	Whole Lotta Love/Living Loving Maid (She's Just a Woman)	1969	3.75	7.50	15.00
—With A-side time of 3:12					
❑ Atlantic 2690	Whole Lotta Love/Living Loving Maid (She's Just a Woman)	1969	5.00	10.00	20.00
—With A-side time of 5:33; no Warner Communications logo in perimeter print					
❑ Atlantic 2690	Whole Lotta Love/Living Loving Maid (She's Just a Woman)	198?	2.00	4.00	8.00
—Later edition with Warner Communcations logo in perimeter print, "(P) 1969 Atlantic Recording Corp." at right and a reference to "From Atlantic LP 19127 — 'Led Zeppelin II'" at bottom					
❑ Atlantic 2777	Immigrant Song/Hey, Hey, What Can I Do	1971	3.75	7.50	15.00
—Second pressings without "Do What Thou Wilt Shalt Be the Whole of the Law" in trail-off; no Warner Commuications logo in perimeter print					
❑ Atlantic 2849	Black Dog/Misty Mountain Hop	1971	2.50	5.00	10.00
❑ Atlantic 2865	Rock and Roll/Four Sticks	1972	2.50	5.00	10.00
—Label has "From Atlantc LP 7208" on label; no Warner Commuications logo in perimeter print					
❑ Atlantic 2970	Over the Hills & Far Away/Dancing Days	1973	2.50	5.00	10.00
❑ Atlantic 2986	D'yer Mak'er/The Crunge	1973	2.50	5.00	10.00
—Normal pressing in true stereo throughout					
❑ Atlantic Oldies Series 13116	Whole Lotta Love/Living Loving Maid (She's Just a Woman)	197?	2.00	4.00	8.00
—Gold label; at least some of these, if not all, contain the single edit ot "Whole Lotta Love"					
❑ Atlantic Oldies Series 13129	Black Dog/Misty Mountain Hop	197?	—	2.00	4.00
❑ Atlantic Oldies Series 13130	Rock and Roll/Four Sticks	197?	—	2.00	4.00
❑ Atlantic Oldies Series 13131	Immigrant Song/Hey, Hey, What Can I Do	197?	—	2.00	4.00
❑ Swan Song 70102	Trampled Under Foot/Black Country Woman	1975	—	3.00	6.00
❑ Swan Song 70110	Candy Store Rock/Royal Orleans	1976	—	3.00	6.00
Albums					
❑ Atlantic SD 7201 [S]	Led Zeppelin III	1970	3.75	7.50	15.00
—Die-cut cover with movable wheel; "1841 Broadway" address on label					
❑ Atlantic SD 7208 [S]	Led Zeppelin (IV) (Runes)	1971	3.00	6.00	12.00
—"1841 Broadway" address on label					
❑ Atlantic SD 7255 [S]	Houses of the Holy	1973	3.00	6.00	12.00
—"1841 Broadway" address on label					
❑ Atlantic SD 8216 [S]	Led Zeppelin	1969	5.00	10.00	20.00
—"1841 Broadway" address on label					
❑ Atlantic SD 8236 [S]	Led Zeppelin II	1969	5.00	10.00	20.00
—"1841 Broadway" address on label					
❑ Atlantic SD 19126	Led Zeppelin	1977	2.00	4.00	8.00
❑ Atlantic SD 19127	Led Zeppelin II	1977	2.00	4.00	8.00
❑ Atlantic SD 19128	Led Zeppelin III	1977	2.00	4.00	8.00
❑ Atlantic SD 19129	Led Zeppelin (IV) (Runes)	1977	2.00	4.00	8.00
❑ Atlantic SD 19130	Houses of the Holy	1977	2.00	4.00	8.00
❑ Atlantic 82144 [(6)]	Led Zeppelin (Box Set)	1990	25.00	50.00	100.00
❑ Swan Song SS 2-200 [(2)]	Physical Graffiti	1975	3.75	7.50	15.00
❑ Swan Song SS 2-201 [(2)]	The Song Remains the Same	1976	3.75	7.50	15.00
❑ Swan Song SS 8416	Presence	1976	2.50	5.00	10.00
❑ Swan Song SS 16002	In Through the Out Door	1979	2.50	5.00	10.00
—Letter "A" on spine; add 50% if brown paper bag is still with jacket					
❑ Swan Song 90051	Coda	1982	2.50	5.00	10.00

LEE, BRENDA

Number	Title (A Side/B Side)	Yr	VG	VG+	NM
45s					
❑ Decca 30050	Jambalaya (On the Bayou)/Bigelow 6-2000	1956	7.50	15.00	30.00
❑ Decca 30107	Christy Christmas/I'm Gonna Lasso Santa Claus	1956	6.25	12.50	25.00
❑ Decca 30198	One Step at a Time/Fairyland	1957	6.25	12.50	25.00
❑ Decca 30333	Dynamite/Love You 'Til I Die	1957	6.25	12.50	25.00
❑ Decca 30411	Ain't That Love/One Teenager to Another	1957	6.25	12.50	25.00
❑ Decca 30535	Rock-a-Bye Baby Blues/Rock the Bop	1958	6.25	12.50	25.00
❑ Decca 30673	Ring-a My Phone/Little Jonah	1958	7.50	15.00	30.00
❑ Decca 30776	Rockin' Around the Christmas Tree/Papa Noel	1958	6.25	12.50	25.00
—Originals have black labels with star under "Decca"					
❑ Decca 30776	Rockin' Around the Christmas Tree/Papa Noel	1960	3.75	7.50	15.00
—Reissues have black labels with color bars					
❑ Decca 30806	Bill Bailey Won't You Please Come Home/Hummin' the Blues	1959	6.25	12.50	25.00
❑ Decca 30885	Let's Jump the Broomstick/One of These Days	1959	7.50	15.00	30.00

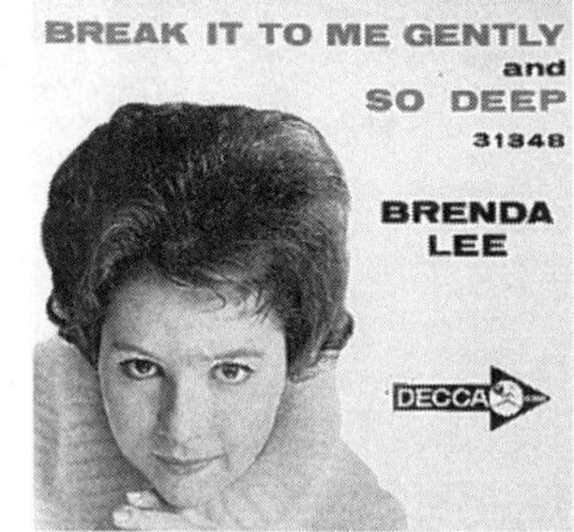

Number	Title (A Side/B Side)	Yr	VG	VG+	NM
❑ Decca 30967	Sweet Nothin's/Weep No More My Baby	1959	5.00	10.00	20.00
❑ Decca 31093	I'm Sorry/That's All You Gotta Do	1960	5.00	10.00	20.00
❑ Decca 31149	I Want to Be Wanted/Just a Little	1960	3.75	7.50	15.00
❑ Decca 31195	Emotions/I'm Learning About Love	1961	3.75	7.50	15.00
❑ Decca 31231	You Can Depend on Me/It's Never Too Late	1961	3.75	7.50	15.00
❑ Decca 31272	Dum Dum/Eventually	1961	3.75	7.50	15.00
❑ Decca 31309	Fool #1/Anybody But Me	1961	3.75	7.50	15.00
❑ Decca 31348	Break It To Me Gently/So Deep	1962	3.75	7.50	15.00
❑ Decca 31379	Everybody Loves Me But You/Here Comes That Feelin'	1962	3.75	7.50	15.00
❑ Decca 31407	Heart in Hand/It Started All Over Again	1962	3.75	7.50	15.00
❑ Decca 31424	All Alone Am I/Save All Your Lovin' for Me	1962	3.75	7.50	15.00
❑ Decca 31454	Your Used to Be/She'll Never Know	1963	3.75	7.50	15.00
❑ Decca 31478	Losing You/He's So Heavenly	1963	3.75	7.50	15.00
❑ Decca 31510	My Whole World Is Falling Down/I Wonder	1963	3.75	7.50	15.00
❑ Decca 31539	The Grass Is Greener/Sweet Impossible You	1963	3.75	7.50	15.00
❑ Decca 31570	As Usual/Lonely Lonely Lonely Me	1963	3.75	7.50	15.00
❑ Decca 31599	Think/The Waiting Game	1964	2.50	5.00	10.00
❑ Decca 31628	Alone with You/My Dreams	1964	2.50	5.00	10.00
❑ Decca 31654	When You Loved Me/He's Sure to Remember Me	1964	2.50	5.00	10.00
❑ Decca 31687	Jingle Bell Rock/Winter Wonderland	1964	3.00	6.00	12.00
❑ Decca 31688	This Time of the Year/Christmas Will Be Just Another Lonely Day	1964	3.00	6.00	12.00
❑ Decca 31690	Is It True/Just Behind the Rainbow	1964	2.50	5.00	10.00
❑ Decca 31728	Thanks a Lot/The Crying Game	1965	2.50	5.00	10.00
❑ Decca 31762	Truly, Truly, True/I Still Miss Someone	1965	2.50	5.00	10.00
❑ Decca 31792	Too Many Rivers/No One	1965	2.50	5.00	10.00
❑ Decca 31849	Rusty Bells/If You Don't (Not Like You)	1965	2.50	5.00	10.00
❑ Decca 31917	Too Little Time/Time and Time Again	1966	2.00	4.00	8.00
❑ Decca 31970	Ain't Gonna Cry No More/It Takes One to Know One	1966	2.00	4.00	8.00
❑ Decca 32018	Coming On Strong/You Keep Coming Back to Me	1966	2.00	4.00	8.00
❑ Decca 32079	Ride, Ride, Ride/Lonely People Do Foolish Things	1967	2.00	4.00	8.00
❑ Decca 32119	Born to Be By Your Side/Take Me	1967	2.00	4.00	8.00
❑ Decca 32161	My Heart Keeps Hangin' On/Where Love Is	1967	2.00	4.00	8.00
❑ Decca 32213	Where's the Melody/Save Me for a Rainy Day	1967	2.00	4.00	8.00
❑ Decca 32248	That's All Right/Fantasy	1967	2.00	4.00	8.00
❑ Decca 32299	Cabaret/Mood Indigo	1968	2.00	4.00	8.00
—With Pete Fountain					
❑ Decca 32330	Kansas City/Each Day Is a Rainbow	1968	2.00	4.00	8.00
❑ Decca 32428	Johnny One Time/I Must Have Been Out of My Mind	1968	2.00	4.00	8.00
❑ Decca 32491	You Don't Need Me for Anything Anymore/Bring Me Sunshine	1969	—	3.00	6.00
❑ Decca 32560	Let It Be Me/You Better Move On	1969	—	3.00	6.00
❑ Decca 32675	I Think I Love You Again/Hello Love	1970	—	3.00	6.00
❑ Decca 32734	Do Right Woman, Do Right Man/Sisters in Sorrow	1970	—	3.00	6.00
❑ Decca 32848	If This Is Our Last Time/Everybody's Reaching Out for Someone	1971	—	3.00	6.00
❑ Decca 32918	I'm a Memory/Misty Memories	1972	—	3.00	6.00
❑ Decca 32975	Always on My Mind/That Ain't Right	1972	—	3.00	6.00
❑ Decca 88215	Christy Christmas/I'm Gonna Lasso Santa Claus	1956	12.50	25.00	50.00
—As "Little Brenda Lee" on Decca's Children's Series					
❑ Elektra 45492	Left-Over Love/Could It Be I Found Love Tonight	1978	—	2.50	5.00
❑ MCA 40003	Nobody Wins/We Had a Good Thing Goin'	1973	—	2.50	5.00
❑ MCA 40107	Sunday Sunrise/Must I Believe	1973	—	2.50	5.00
❑ MCA 40171	Wrong Ideas/Something For A Rainy Day	1973	—	2.50	5.00
❑ MCA 40262	Big Four Poster Bed/Castles In The Sand	1974	—	2.50	5.00
❑ MCA 40318	Rock On Baby/More Than A Memory	1974	—	2.50	5.00
❑ MCA 40385	He's My Rock/Feel Free	1975	—	2.50	5.00
❑ MCA 40442	Bringing It Back/Papa's Knee	1975	—	2.50	5.00
❑ MCA 40511	Find Yourself Another Puppet/What I Had With You	1976	—	2.50	5.00
❑ MCA 40584	Brother Shelton/Now He's Coming Home	1976	—	2.50	5.00
❑ MCA 40640	Takin' What I Can Get/Your Favorite Wornout Nightmare's Coming Home	1976	—	2.50	5.00
❑ MCA 40683	Ruby's Lounge/Oklahoma Superstar	1977	—	2.50	5.00
❑ MCA 41130	Tell Me What It's Like/Let Your Love Fall Back On Me	1979	—	2.50	5.00
❑ MCA 41187	The Cowgirl And The Dandy/Do You Wanna Spend The Night	1980	—	2.50	5.00
❑ MCA 41262	Keeping Me Warm For You/At The Moonlight	1980	—	2.50	5.00
❑ MCA 41270	Don't Promise Me Anything (Do It)/You Only Broke My Heart	1980	—	2.50	5.00
❑ MCA 41322	Broken Trust/Right Behind The Rain	1980	—	2.50	5.00
—With the Oak Ridge Boys					
❑ MCA 51047	Every Now And Then/He'll Play The Music	1981	—	2.00	4.00

Number	Title (A Side/B Side)	Yr	VG	VG+	NM
❑ MCA 51113	Fool, Fool/Right Behind The Rain	1981	—	2.00	4.00
❑ MCA 51154	Enough For You/What Am I Gonna Do	1981	—	2.00	4.00
❑ MCA 51195	Only When I Laugh/Too Many Nights Alone	1981	—	2.00	4.00
❑ MCA 51230	From Levis To Calvin Klein Jeans/I Know A Lot About Love	1982	—	2.00	4.00
❑ MCA 52060	Keeping Me Warm For You/ There's More To Me Than You Can See	1982	—	2.00	4.00
❑ MCA 52124	Just For The Moment/Love Letters	1982	—	2.00	4.00
—With the Oak Ridge Boys					
❑ MCA 52268	Didn't We Do It Good/We're So Close	1983	—	2.00	4.00
❑ MCA 52394	A Sweeter Love (I'll Never Know)/A Woman's Mind	1984	—	2.00	4.00
❑ MCA 52654	I'm Takin' My Time/That's The Way It Was Then	1985	—	2.00	4.00
❑ MCA 52720	Why You Been Gone So Long/He Can't Make Your Kind of Love	1985	—	2.00	4.00
❑ MCA 52720 [DJ]	Why You Been Gone So Long (same on both sides)	1985	2.50	5.00	10.00
—Promo only on gold vinyl					
❑ MCA 52804	Two Hearts/Loving Arms	1986	—	2.00	4.00
❑ MCA 60069	Sweet Nothin's/I Want to Be Wanted	197?	—	2.00	4.00
—Reissue; originals have black rainbow label					
❑ MCA 60070	I'm Sorry/All Alone Am I	197?	—	2.00	4.00
—Reissue; originals have black rainbow label					
❑ MCA 65027	Rockin' Around the Christmas Tree/Papa Noel	1973	—	2.00	4.00
—Black label with rainbow					
❑ MCA 65027	Rockin' Around the Christmas Tree/Papa Noel	1980	—	—	3.00
—Blue label with rainbow					
❑ MCA 65028	Jingle Bell Rock/Winter Wonderland	1973	—	2.00	4.00
—Black label with rainbow					
❑ Monument 03781	You're Gonna Love Yourself (In the Morning)/ What Do You Think About Lovin'	1983	—	2.00	4.00
—A-side: With Willie Nelson; B-side: With Dolly Parton					
❑ Warner Bros. 19303	A Little Unfair/Some of These Days	1991	—	—	3.00
❑ Warner Bros. 19397	Your One and Only/You Better Do Better	1991	—	—	3.00
Albums					
❑ Decca DL 4039 [M]	Brenda Lee	1960	6.25	12.50	25.00
❑ Decca DL 4082 [M]	This Is...Brenda	1960	6.25	12.50	25.00
❑ Decca DL 4104 [M]	Emotions	1961	6.25	12.50	25.00
❑ Decca DL 4176 [M]	All the Way	1961	6.25	12.50	25.00
❑ Decca DL 4216 [M]	Sincerely	1962	6.25	12.50	25.00
❑ Decca DL 4326 [M]	Brenda, That's All	1962	6.25	12.50	25.00
❑ Decca DL 4370 [M]	All Alone Am I	1963	6.25	12.50	25.00
❑ Decca DL 4439 [M]	Let Me Sing	1963	6.25	12.50	25.00
❑ Decca DL 4509 [M]	By Request	1964	5.00	10.00	20.00
❑ Decca DL 4583 [M]	Merry Christmas from Brenda Lee	1964	5.00	10.00	20.00
❑ Decca DL 4626 [M]	Top Teen Hits	1965	5.00	10.00	20.00
❑ Decca DL 4661 [M]	The Versatile Brenda Lee	1965	5.00	10.00	20.00
❑ Decca DL 4684 [M]	Too Many Rivers	1965	5.00	10.00	20.00
❑ Decca DL 4755 [M]	Bye Bye Blues	1966	5.00	10.00	20.00
❑ Decca DL 4757 [M]	10 Golden Years	1966	6.25	12.50	25.00
—With gatefold cover					
❑ Decca DL 4825 [M]	Coming On Strong	1966	3.75	7.50	15.00
❑ Decca DL 4941 [M]	Reflections in Blue	1967	5.00	10.00	20.00
❑ Decca DL 8873 [M]	Grandma, What Great Songs You Sang	1960	10.00	20.00	40.00
❑ Decca DL 74039 [S]	Brenda Lee	1960	7.50	15.00	30.00
❑ Decca DL 74082 [S]	This Is...Brenda	1960	7.50	15.00	30.00
❑ Decca DL 74104 [S]	Emotions	1961	7.50	15.00	30.00
❑ Decca DL 74176 [S]	All the Way	1961	7.50	15.00	30.00
❑ Decca DL 74216 [S]	Sincerely	1962	7.50	15.00	30.00
❑ Decca DL 74326 [S]	Brenda, That's All	1962	7.50	15.00	30.00
❑ Decca DL 74370 [S]	All Alone Am I	1963	7.50	15.00	30.00
❑ Decca DL 74439 [S]	Let Me Sing	1963	7.50	15.00	30.00
❑ Decca DL 74509 [S]	By Request	1964	6.25	12.50	25.00
❑ Decca DL 74583 [S]	Merry Christmas from Brenda Lee	1964	6.25	12.50	25.00
❑ Decca DL 74626 [S]	Top Teen Hits	1965	6.25	12.50	25.00
❑ Decca DL 74661 [S]	The Versatile Brenda Lee	1965	6.25	12.50	25.00
❑ Decca DL 74684 [S]	Too Many Rivers	1965	6.25	12.50	25.00
❑ Decca DL 74755 [S]	Bye Bye Blues	1966	6.25	12.50	25.00
❑ Decca DL 74757 [S]	10 Golden Years	1966	7.50	15.00	30.00
—With gatefold cover					
❑ Decca DL 74825 [S]	Coming On Strong	1966	5.00	10.00	20.00
❑ Decca DL 74941 [S]	Reflections in Blue	1967	3.75	7.50	15.00
❑ Decca DL 74955	For the First Time	1968	3.75	7.50	15.00
—With Pete Fountain					
❑ Decca DL 75111	Johnny One Time	1969	3.75	7.50	15.00
❑ Decca DL 75232	Memphis Portrait	1970	3.75	7.50	15.00
❑ Decca DL 78873 [S]	Grandma, What Great Songs You Sang	1960	12.50	25.00	50.00
❑ MCA 232 [S]	Merry Christmas from Brenda Lee	1973	3.00	6.00	12.00
❑ MCA 305	Brenda	1973	3.75	7.50	15.00
❑ MCA 373	New Sunrise	1973	3.00	6.00	12.00
❑ MCA 433	Brenda Lee Now	1974	3.00	6.00	12.00
❑ MCA 477	Sincerely, Brenda Lee	1975	2.50	5.00	10.00
❑ MCA 758	Even Better	198?	2.00	4.00	8.00
—Reissue of 3211					
❑ MCA 824	Only When I Laugh	1982	2.00	4.00	8.00
—Reissue of 5278					
❑ MCA 2233	L.A. Sessions	1976	2.50	5.00	10.00
❑ MCA 3211	Even Better	1979	2.50	5.00	10.00
❑ MCA 2-4012 [(2)]	The Brenda Lee Story — Her Greatest Hits	1973	5.00	10.00	20.00
❑ MCA 5143	Take Me Back	1980	2.50	5.00	10.00
❑ MCA 5278	Only When I Laugh	1981	2.50	5.00	10.00

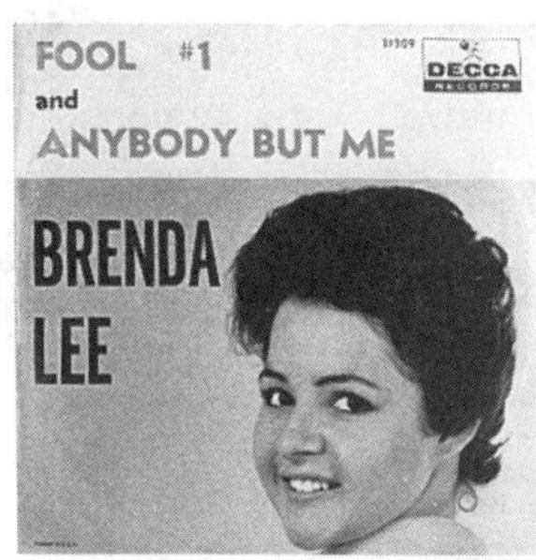

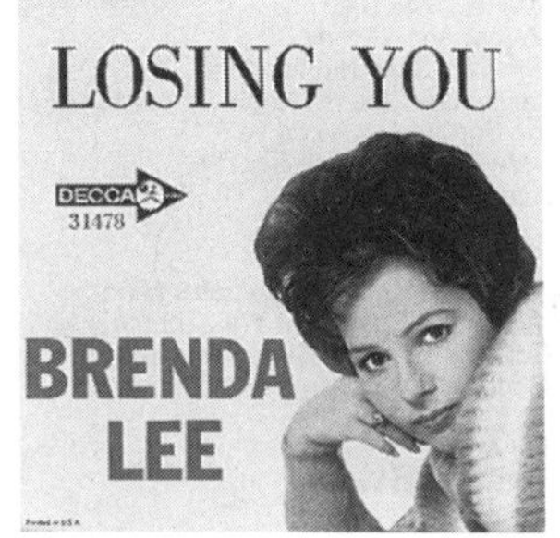

Number	Title (A Side/B Side)	Yr	VG	VG+	NM
❑ MCA 5342	Greatest Country Hits	1982	2.50	5.00	10.00
❑ MCA 5626	Feels So Right	1985	2.50	5.00	10.00
❑ MCA 15021 [S]	Merry Christmas from Brenda Lee	197?	2.50	5.00	10.00
❑ MCA 15038	Rockin' Around the Christmas Tree	198?	2.50	5.00	10.00
❑ MCA Coral CB-20044	Let It Be Me	197?	2.50	5.00	10.00
❑ Vocalion VL 3795 [M]	Here's Brenda Lee	1967	3.00	6.00	12.00
❑ Vocalion VL 73795 [S]	Here's Brenda Lee	1967	3.00	6.00	12.00
❑ Vocalion VL 73890	Let It Be Me	1970	3.00	6.00	12.00

LEE, DICKEY

45s

Number	Title (A Side/B Side)	Yr	VG	VG+	NM
❑ Atco 6546	Run Right Back/Red, Green, Yellow, Blue	1968	2.00	4.00	8.00
❑ Atco 6580	All My Life/Hang-Ups	1968	2.00	4.00	8.00
❑ Atco 6609	You're Young and You'll Forget/Waitin' for Love to Come My Way	1968	2.00	4.00	8.00
❑ Diamond 266	Ruby Baby/I Remember Barbara	1969	2.00	4.00	8.00
❑ Dot 16087	Life in a Teenage World/Why Don't You Write On	1960	3.75	7.50	15.00
❑ Hallway 1924	Big Brother/She's Walking Away	1964	2.50	5.00	10.00
❑ Mercury 55068	I'm Just a Heartache Away/Midnight Flyer	1979	—	2.00	4.00
❑ Mercury 57005	He's an Old Rock 'N' Roller/It Hurts to Be in Love	1979	—	2.00	4.00
❑ Mercury 57017	Don't Look Back/I'm Trustin' a Feelin'	1980	—	2.00	4.00
❑ Mercury 57027	Workin' My Way to Your Heart/If You Want Me	1980	—	2.00	4.00
❑ Mercury 57036	Lost in Love/Again	1980	—	2.00	4.00
—A-side with Kathy Burdick					
❑ Mercury 57052	Honky Tonk Hearts/Best I Hit the Road	1981	—	2.00	4.00
❑ Mercury 57056	I Wonder If I Care As Much/Further Than a Country Mile	1981	—	2.00	4.00
❑ Mercury 76129	Everybody Loves a Winner/You Won't Be Here Tonight	1982	—	2.00	4.00
❑ RCA PB-10764	9,999,999 Tears/I Never Will Get Over You	1976	—	2.00	4.00
❑ RCA PB-10914	If You Gotta Make a Fool of Somebody/My Love Shows Thru	1977	—	2.00	4.00
❑ RCA GB-10929	Rocky/9,999,999 Tears	1977	—	—	3.00
—Gold Standard Series					
❑ RCA PB-11009	Virginia, How Far Will You Go/My Love Shows Thru	1977	—	2.00	4.00
❑ RCA PB-11125	Peanut Butter/Breezy Was Her Name	1977	—	2.00	4.00
❑ RCA PB-11191	Love Is a Word/I'll Be Leaving Alone	1978	—	2.00	4.00
❑ RCA PB-11294	My Heart Won't Cry Anymore/Danna	1978	—	2.00	4.00
❑ RCA PB-11389	It's Not Easy/I've Been Honky-Tonkin' Too Long	1978	—	2.00	4.00
❑ RCA Victor 47-9862	All Too Soon/Charlie	1970	—	3.00	6.00
❑ RCA Victor 47-9941	Home To/Special	1971	—	3.00	6.00
❑ RCA Victor 47-9988	The Mahogany Pulpit/Everybody's Reaching Out for Someone	1971	—	3.00	6.00
❑ RCA Victor 48-1013	Never Ending Song of Love/On the Southbound	1971	—	3.00	6.00
❑ RCA Victor 74-0623	I Saw My Lady/What We Used to Hang On To	1971	—	3.00	6.00
❑ RCA Victor 74-0710	Ashes of Love/The Kingdom I Call Home	1972	—	2.50	5.00
❑ RCA Victor 74-0798	Baby, Bye Bye/She Thinks I Still Care	1972	—	2.50	5.00
❑ RCA Victor 74-0892	Crying Over You/My World Around You	1973	—	2.50	5.00
❑ RCA Victor 74-0980	Put Me Down Softly/If She Turns Up in Atlanta	1973	—	2.50	5.00
❑ RCA Victor APBO-0082	Sparklin' Brown Eyes/Country Song	1973	—	2.50	5.00
❑ RCA Victor APBO-0227	I Use the Soap/Strawberry Women	1974	—	2.50	5.00
❑ RCA Victor PB-10014	Give Me One Good Reason/Sweet Fever	1974	—	2.50	5.00
❑ RCA Victor PB-10091	The Busiest Memory in Town/Way to Go On	1974	—	2.50	5.00
❑ RCA Victor PB-10289	You Make It Look So Easy/The Door's Always Open	1975	—	2.00	4.00
❑ RCA Victor PB-10361	Rocky/The Closest Thing to You	1975	—	2.00	4.00
❑ RCA Victor PB-10543	Angels, Roses and Rain/Danna	1976	—	2.00	4.00
❑ RCA Victor PB-10684	Makin' Love Don't Always Make Love Grow/ I Never Will Get Over You	1976	—	2.00	4.00
❑ Rendezvous 188	Dream Boy/Stay True Baby	1962	6.25	12.50	25.00
❑ Smash 1758	Patches/More or Less	1962	3.75	7.50	15.00
❑ Smash 1791	I Saw Linda Yesterday/The Girl I Can't Forget	1962	3.00	6.00	12.00
❑ Smash 1808	Don't Wanna Talk About Paula/Just a Friend	1963	3.00	6.00	12.00
❑ Smash 1822	I Go Lonely/Ten Million Faces	1963	3.00	6.00	12.00
❑ Smash 1844	She Wants to Be Bobby's Girl/The Day the Sawmill Closed Down	1963	3.00	6.00	12.00
❑ Smash 1871	To the Aisle/Mother Nature	1964	3.00	6.00	12.00
❑ Smash 1913	Me and My Teardrops/Only Trust in Me	1964	3.00	6.00	12.00
❑ Sun 280	Good Lovin'/Memories Never Grow Old	1957	7.50	15.00	30.00
❑ Sun 297	Dreamy Nights/Fool, Fool, Fool	1958	20.00	40.00	80.00
❑ Tampa 131	Dream Boy/Stay True Baby	1957	7.50	15.00	30.00
❑ TCF Hall 102	Laurie (Strange Things Happen)/Party Doll	1965	2.50	5.00	10.00
❑ TCF Hall 111	The Girl from Peyton Place/The Girl I Used to Know	1965	2.50	5.00	10.00
❑ TCF Hall 118	Good Girl Goin' Bad/Pretty White Dress	1965	2.50	5.00	10.00
❑ TCF Hall 128	Good Guy/Annie	1966	2.50	5.00	10.00

Number	Title (A Side/B Side)	Yr	VG	VG+	NM
Albums					
❑ Mercury SRM-1-5020	Dickey Lee	1979	2.50	5.00	10.00
❑ Mercury SRM-1-5026	Dickey Lee Again	1980	2.50	5.00	10.00
❑ RCA Victor APL1-0311	Sparklin' Brown Eyes	1974	3.00	6.00	12.00
❑ RCA Victor APL1-1243	Rocky	1975	3.00	6.00	12.00
❑ RCA Victor APL1-1725	Angels, Roses and Rain	1976	3.00	6.00	12.00
❑ RCA Victor LSP-4637	Never Ending Song of Love	1971	3.00	6.00	12.00
❑ RCA Victor LSP-4715	Ashes of Love	1972	3.00	6.00	12.00
❑ RCA Victor LSP-4791	Baby, Bye Bye	1972	3.00	6.00	12.00
❑ RCA Victor LSP-4857	Crying Over You	1973	3.00	6.00	12.00
❑ Smash MGS-27020 [M]	The Tale of Patches	1962	7.50	15.00	30.00
❑ Smash SRS-67020 [S]	The Tale of Patches	1962	10.00	20.00	40.00
❑ TCF Hall TCF-8001 [M]	Dickey Lee Sings "Laurie" and "The Girl from Peyton Place"	1965	5.00	10.00	20.00
❑ TCF Hall TCF-9001 [S]	Dickey Lee Sings "Laurie" and "The Girl from Peyton Place"	1965	6.25	12.50	25.00
LEFT BANKE, THE					
45s					
❑ Camerica 005	Queen of Paradise/And One Day	1978	—	2.50	5.00
❑ Smash 2041	Walk Away Renee/I Haven't Got the Nerve	1966	3.75	7.50	15.00
❑ Smash 2074	Pretty Ballerina/Lazy Day	1966	3.75	7.50	15.00
❑ Smash 2089	Ivy, Ivy/And Suddenly	1967	3.00	6.00	12.00
❑ Smash 2097	She May Call You Up Tonight/Barterers and Their Wives	1967	3.00	6.00	12.00
❑ Smash 2119	Desiree/I've Got Something on My Mind	1967	3.00	6.00	12.00
❑ Smash 2165	Dark Is the Bark/My Friend Today	1968	3.00	6.00	12.00
❑ Smash 2198	Goodbye Holly/Sing, Little Bird, Sing	1968	3.00	6.00	12.00
❑ Smash 2209	Bryant Hotel/Give the Man a Hand	1969	3.00	6.00	12.00
❑ Smash 2243	Myrah/Pedestal	1969	10.00	20.00	40.00
—Picture sleeves are bootlegs					
Albums					
❑ Rhino RNLP-123	History of the Left Banke	1985	2.50	5.00	10.00
❑ Smash MGS-27088 [M]	Walk Away Renee/Pretty Ballerina	1967	10.00	20.00	40.00
❑ Smash SRS-67088	Walk Away Renee/Pretty Ballerina	198?	2.50	5.00	10.00
—Reissue with thinner vinyl					
❑ Smash SRS-67088 [S]	Walk Away Renee/Pretty Ballerina	1967	10.00	20.00	40.00
❑ Smash SRS-67113	The Left Banke, Too	1968	12.50	25.00	50.00
LEMON PIPERS, THE					
45s					
❑ Buddah 11	Turn Around and Take a Look/Danger	1967	2.50	5.00	10.00
❑ Buddah 23	Green Tambourine/No Help from Me	1967	3.00	6.00	12.00
❑ Buddah 31	Rice Is Nice/Blueberry Blue	1968	2.50	5.00	10.00
❑ Buddah 41	Jelly Jungle (Of Orange Marmalade)/Shoe Shine Boy	1968	2.50	5.00	10.00
❑ Buddah 63	Wine and Violet/Lonely Atmosphere	1968	2.50	5.00	10.00
❑ Buddah 136	I Was Not Born to Follow/Rainbow Tree	1969	2.00	4.00	8.00
❑ Carol 107	Quiet Please/Monaural 78	1966	3.75	7.50	15.00
Albums					
❑ Buddah BDM-1009 [M]	Green Tambourine	1968	6.25	12.50	25.00
❑ Buddah BDS-5009 [S]	Green Tambourine	1968	6.25	12.50	25.00
❑ Buddah BDS-5016 [S]	Jungle Marmalade	1968	6.25	12.50	25.00
LENNON, JOHN					
45s					
❑ Apple 1809	Give Peace a Chance/Remember Love	1969	—	2.50	5.00
—As "Plastic Ono Band"					
❑ Apple 1813	Cold Turkey/Don't Worry Kyoko (Mummy's Only Looking for a Hand in the Snow)	1969	—	2.50	5.00
—As "Plastic Ono Band"; most copies skip on A-side on the third chorus because of a pressing defect					
❑ Apple 1818	Instant Karma! (We All Shine On)/Who Has Seen the Wind?	1970	—	2.00	4.00
—As "John Ono Lennon"; B-side by "Yoko Ono Lennon"					
❑ Apple 1827	Mother/Why	1970	2.00	4.00	8.00
—As "John Lennon/Plastic Ono Band"; B-side by "Yoko Ono/Plastic Ono Band"					
❑ Apple 1830	Power to the People/Touch Me	1971	2.00	4.00	8.00
—As "John Lennon/Plastic Ono Band"; B-side by "Yoko Ono/Plastic Ono Band"					
❑ Apple 1840	Imagine/It's So Hard	1971	2.00	4.00	8.00
—As "John Lennon Plastic Ono Band"; tan label					
❑ Apple 1842	Happy Xmas (War Is Over)/Listen, the Snow Is Falling	1971	3.75	7.50	15.00
—As "John & Yoko/Plastic Ono Band with the Harlem Community Choir"; green vinyl, faces label					
❑ Apple 1848	Woman Is the Nigger of the World/Sisters O Sisters	1972	2.00	4.00	8.00
—As "John Lennon/Plastic Ono Band..."; B-side by "Yoko Ono/Plastic Ono Band..."					
❑ Apple 1868	Mind Games/Meat City	1973	—	3.00	6.00
❑ Apple 1874	Whatever Gets You Thru the Night/Beef Jerky	1974	—	3.00	6.00
—As "John Lennon and the Plastic Ono Nuclear Band"					
❑ Apple 1878	#9 Dream/What You Got	1974	2.00	4.00	8.00
❑ Apple 1881	Stand By Me/Move Over Ms. L.	1975	2.00	4.00	8.00
❑ Capitol B-44230	Jealous Guy/Give Peace a Chance	1988	—	2.50	5.00
❑ Geffen 29855	Happy Xmas (War Is Over)/Beautiful Boy (Darling Boy)	1982	—	2.50	5.00
❑ Geffen 49604	(Just Like) Starting Over/Kiss Kiss Kiss	1980	—	2.00	4.00
—B-side by Yoko Ono					
❑ Geffen 49644	Woman/Beautiful Boys	1980	—	2.00	4.00
—B-side by Yoko Ono					
❑ Geffen 49695	Watching the Wheels/Yes, I'm Your Angel	1981	—	2.00	4.00
—B-side by Yoko Ono					
❑ Polydor 817254-7	Nobody Told Me/O' Sanity	1983	—	2.50	5.00
—With "Manufactured and Marketed by Polygram..." on label; B-side by Yoko Ono					
❑ Polydor 821107-7	I'm Stepping Out/Sleepless Night	1984	—	2.00	4.00
—B-side by Yoko Ono					
❑ Polydor 821204-7	Borrowed Time/Your Hands	1984	—	2.50	5.00
—B-side by Yoko Ono					

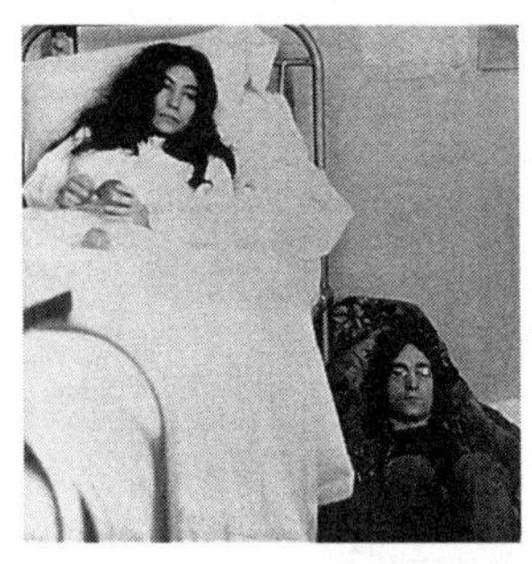

Number	Title (A Side/B Side)	Yr	VG	VG+	NM
❑ Polydor 881378-7	Every Man Has a Woman Who Loves Him/It's Alright	1984	2.00	4.00	8.00
—B-side by Sean Ono Lennon					
Albums					
❑ Adam VIII A-8018	John Lennon Sings the Great Rock & Roll Hits (Roots)	1975	250.00	500.00	1000.
—Counterfeits abound. On authentic copies, cover is posterboard (not slicks); labels are normal size (not overly large); printing on cover is sharp, not blurry; the word "Greatest" does NOT appear on the spine. Authentic copies usually have ad sleeve also.					
❑ Apple SMAX-3361	Wedding Album	1969	37.50	75.00	150.00
—With photo strip, postcard, poster of wedding photos, poster of lithographs, "Bagism" bag, booklet, photo of slice of wedding cake. Missing inserts reduce the value.					
❑ Apple SW-3362	Live Peace in Toronto 1969	1970	3.75	7.50	15.00
—By "The Plastic Ono Band" — without calendar					
❑ Apple SW-3372	John Lennon Plastic Ono Band	1970	5.00	10.00	20.00
❑ Apple SW-3379	Imagine	1971	5.00	10.00	20.00
—With either of two postcard inserts, lyric sleeve, poster					
❑ Apple SVBB-3392 [(2)]	Some Time in New York City	1972	7.50	15.00	30.00
—By John and Yoko; with photo card and petition					
❑ Apple SW-3414	Mind Games	1973	5.00	10.00	20.00
❑ Apple SW-3416	Walls and Bridges	1974	5.00	10.00	20.00
—With fold-open segmented front cover					
❑ Apple SK-3419	Rock 'N' Roll	1975	5.00	10.00	20.00
❑ Apple SW-3421	Shaved Fish	1975	5.00	10.00	20.00
❑ Apple T-5001	Two Virgins — Unfinished Music No. 1	1968	37.50	75.00	150.00
—With Yoko Ono; price with brown bag					
❑ Capitol ST-12239	Live Peace in Toronto 1969	1982	2.50	5.00	10.00
—By "The Plastic Ono Band"; reissue, purple Capitol label					
❑ Capitol SV-12451	Live in New York City	1986	3.00	6.00	12.00
❑ Capitol SJ-12533	Menlove Ave.	1986	3.75	7.50	15.00
❑ Capitol SN-16068	Mind Games	1980	3.00	6.00	12.00
—Budget-line reissue					
❑ Capitol SN-16069	Rock 'N' Roll	1980	3.00	6.00	12.00
—Budget-line reissue					
❑ Capitol C1-90803 [(2)]	Imagine: Music from the Motion Picture	1988	5.00	10.00	20.00
❑ Capitol C1-91425	Double Fantasy	1989	5.00	10.00	20.00
—Very briefly available reissue					
❑ Geffen GHS 2001	Double Fantasy	1980	2.50	5.00	10.00
—Seven tracks by John, seven by Yoko; off-white label; titles on back cover out of order					
❑ Geffen GHSP 2023	The John Lennon Collection	1982	5.00	10.00	20.00
❑ Polydor 817160-1	Milk and Honey	1983	2.50	5.00	10.00
—Six tracks by John, six by Yoko					
❑ Polydor 817238-1	Heart Play (Unfinished Dialogue)	1983	3.00	6.00	12.00
—Interviews with John Lennon and Yoko Ono					
❑ Silhouette SM-10012 [(2)]	Reflections and Poetry	1984	6.25	12.50	25.00
❑ Zapple ST-3357	Life with the Lions — Unfinished Music No. 2	1969	5.00	10.00	20.00
—With Yoko Ono					

LEWIS, BARBARA

45s

Number	Title (A Side/B Side)	Yr	VG	VG+	NM
❑ Atlantic 2141	My Heart Went Do Dat Da/The Longest Night of the Year	1962	3.00	6.00	12.00
❑ Atlantic 2159	My Mama Told Me/Gonna Love You Till the Day I Die	1962	3.00	6.00	12.00
❑ Atlantic 2184	Hello Stranger/Think a Little Sugar	1963	5.00	10.00	20.00
❑ Atlantic 2200	Straighten Up Your Heart/If You Love Her	1963	3.00	6.00	12.00
❑ Atlantic 2214	Puppy Love/Snap Your Fingers	1963	3.00	6.00	12.00
❑ Atlantic 2227	Someday We're Gonna Love Again/Spend a Little Time	1964	2.50	5.00	10.00
❑ Atlantic 2255	Come Home/Pushin' a Good Thing Too Far	1964	2.50	5.00	10.00
❑ Atlantic 2283	Baby, I'm Yours/I Say Love	1965	3.75	7.50	15.00
❑ Atlantic 2300	Make Me Your Baby/Love to Be Loved	1965	3.75	7.50	15.00
❑ Atlantic 2316	Don't Forget About Me/It's Magic	1965	2.50	5.00	10.00
❑ Atlantic 2346	Make Me Belong to You/Girls Need Loving Care	1966	2.00	4.00	8.00
❑ Atlantic 2361	I Remember the Feeling/Baby What You Want Me to Do	1966	2.00	4.00	8.00
❑ Atlantic 2400	Love Makes the World Go Round/I'll Make Him Love Me	1967	2.00	4.00	8.00
❑ Atlantic 2413	Fool, Fool, Fool/Only All the Time	1967	2.00	4.00	8.00
❑ Atlantic 2482	Thankful for What I Got/Sho Nuff	1968	2.00	4.00	8.00
❑ Atlantic 2514	On Bended Knees/I'll Keep Believing	1968	2.00	4.00	8.00
❑ Atlantic 2550	I'm All You've Got/You're a Dream Maker	1968	2.00	4.00	8.00
❑ Enterprise 9012	You Made Me a Woman/Just the Way You Are Today	1970	—	3.00	6.00
❑ Enterprise 9027	Ask the Lonely/Why Did It Take You So Long	1970	—	3.00	6.00
❑ Enterprise 9029	Anyway/That's the Way I Like It	1970	—	3.00	6.00

Number	Title (A Side/B Side)	Yr	VG	VG+	NM
❑ Karen 313	My Heart Went Do Dat Da/The Longest Night of the Year	1961	7.50	15.00	30.00
❑ Reprise 1146	Rock and Roll Lullaby/I'm So Thankful	1972	—	2.50	5.00
Albums					
❑ Atlantic 8086 [M]	Hello Stranger	1963	10.00	20.00	40.00
❑ Atlantic SD 8086 [S]	Hello Stranger	1963	12.50	25.00	50.00
❑ Atlantic 8090 [M]	Snap Your Fingers	1964	10.00	20.00	40.00
❑ Atlantic SD 8090 [S]	Snap Your Fingers	1964	12.50	25.00	50.00
❑ Atlantic 8110 [M]	Baby, I'm Yours	1965	10.00	20.00	40.00
❑ Atlantic SD 8110 [S]	Baby, I'm Yours	1965	12.50	25.00	50.00
❑ Atlantic 8118 [M]	It's Magic	1966	7.50	15.00	30.00
❑ Atlantic SD 8118 [S]	It's Magic	1966	10.00	20.00	40.00
❑ Atlantic SD 8173	Workin' on a Groovy Thing	1968	6.25	12.50	25.00
❑ Atlantic SD 8286 [S]	The Best of Barbara Lewis	1971	5.00	10.00	20.00
❑ Collectables COL-5104	Golden Classics	198?	2.50	5.00	10.00
❑ Enterprise ENS-1006	The Many Grooves of Barbara Lewis	1970	6.25	12.50	25.00

LEWIS, BOBBY (1)

R&B singer; not to be confused with the country singer of the same name, who recorded for Ace of Hearts, Capricorn, GRT, HME, RPA and United Artists.

Number	Title (A Side/B Side)	Yr	VG	VG+	NM
45s					
❑ ABC-Paramount 10565	That's Right/Fannie Lewis	1964	3.00	6.00	12.00
❑ ABC-Paramount 10592	Jealous Love/Stark Raving Wild	1964	3.00	6.00	12.00
❑ Beltone 1002	Tossin' and Turnin'/Oh Yes I Love You	1961	6.25	12.50	25.00
❑ Beltone 1012	One Track Mind/Are You Ready	1961	6.25	12.50	25.00
❑ Beltone 1015	What a Walk/Cry No More	1961	3.75	7.50	15.00
❑ Beltone 1016	Yes, Oh Yes, It Did/Mamie in the Afternoon	1962	3.75	7.50	15.00
❑ Beltone 2018	A Man's Gotta Be a Man/Day by Day I Need Your Love	1962	3.75	7.50	15.00
❑ Beltone 2023	I'm Tossin' and Turnin' Again/Nothin' But the Blues	1962	3.75	7.50	15.00
❑ Beltone 2026	Lonely Teardrops/Boom-a-Chick-Chick	1962	3.75	7.50	15.00
❑ Beltone 2035	Nothin' But the Blues/Intermission	1963	3.75	7.50	15.00
❑ Lana 104	Tossin' and Turnin'/Oh Yes I Love You	196?	2.00	4.00	8.00
—Oldies reissue					
❑ Lost-Nite 146	Tossin' An' Turnin'/Oh Yes I Love You	196?	—	3.00	6.00
—Reissue; note slightly different spelling of A-side					
❑ Mercury 71245	Mumbles Blues/Oh Baby	1957	6.25	12.50	25.00
❑ Philips 40519	Soul Seekin'/Give Me Your Yesterdays	1968	5.00	10.00	20.00
❑ Roulette 4182	You Better Stop/Fire of Love	1959	3.75	7.50	15.00
❑ Roulette 4382	Solid as a Rock/Oh Mr. Somebody	1961	3.75	7.50	15.00
❑ Spotlight 394	Mumbles Blues/Oh Baby	1957	7.50	15.00	30.00
❑ Spotlight 397	Solid as a Rock/You Even Forgot My Name	1957	7.50	15.00	30.00
Albums					
❑ Beltone 4000 [M]	Tossin' and Turnin'	1961	50.00	100.00	200.00

LEWIS, GARY, AND THE PLAYBOYS

Number	Title (A Side/B Side)	Yr	VG	VG+	NM
45s					
❑ Epic 50068	One Good Woman/Ooh Baby	1975	2.00	4.00	8.00
—Gary Lewis solo					
❑ Liberty 55756	This Diamond Ring/Tijuana Wedding	1964	2.50	5.00	10.00
❑ Liberty 55756	This Diamond Ring/Hard to Find	1964	3.00	6.00	12.00
❑ Liberty 55778	Count Me In/Little Miss Go-Go	1965	2.50	5.00	10.00
❑ Liberty 55809	Save Your Heart for Me/Without a Word of Warning	1965	2.50	5.00	10.00
❑ Liberty 55818	Everybody Loves a Clown/Time Stands Still	1965	2.50	5.00	10.00
❑ Liberty 55846	She's Just My Style/I Won't Make That Mistake Again	1965	2.50	5.00	10.00
❑ Liberty 55865	Sure Gonna Miss Her/I Don't Wanna Say Goodnight	1966	2.50	5.00	10.00
❑ Liberty 55880	Green Grass/I Can Read Between the Lines	1966	2.50	5.00	10.00
❑ Liberty 55898	My Heart's Symphony/Tina	1966	2.50	5.00	10.00
❑ Liberty 55914	(You Don't Have to) Paint Me a Picture/Looking for the Stars	1966	2.50	5.00	10.00
❑ Liberty 55932	Down on the Sloop John B/Ice Melts in the Sun	1966	—	—	—
—Unreleased					
❑ Liberty 55933	Where Will the Words Come From/May the Best Man Win	1966	2.50	5.00	10.00
❑ Liberty 55949	The Loser (With a Broken Heart)/Ice Melts in the Sun	1967	2.50	5.00	10.00
❑ Liberty 55971	Girls in Love/Let's Be More Than Friends	1967	2.00	4.00	8.00
❑ Liberty 55985	Jill/New in Town	1967	2.00	4.00	8.00
❑ Liberty 56011	Has She Got the Nicest Eyes/Happiness	1967	2.00	4.00	8.00
❑ Liberty 56037	Sealed with a Kiss/Sara Jane	1968	2.00	4.00	8.00
❑ Liberty 56075	C.C. Rider/Main Street	1968	—	3.00	6.00
❑ Liberty 56093	Rhythm of the Rain/Mister Memory	1969	—	3.00	6.00
❑ Liberty 56093	Every Day I Have to Cry Some/Mister Memory	1969	—	3.00	6.00
❑ Liberty 56121	Hayride/Gary's Groove	1969	—	3.00	6.00
❑ Liberty 56144	I Saw Elvis Presley Last Night/Something Is Wrong	1969	3.00	6.00	12.00
❑ Liberty 56158	Great Balls of Fire/I'm On the Road Right Now	1970	—	3.00	6.00
❑ Scepter 12359	Peace of Mind/Then Again Maybe	1972	2.00	4.00	8.00
—Gary Lewis solo					
❑ United Artists 0064	This Diamond Ring/My Heart's Symphony	1973	—	2.00	4.00
❑ United Artists 0065	Count Me In/Save Your Heart for Me	1973	—	2.00	4.00
❑ United Artists 0066	Everybody Loves a Clown/Sure Gonna Miss Her	1973	—	2.00	4.00
❑ United Artists 0067	She's Just My Style/Green Grass	1973	—	2.00	4.00
—0064 through 0067 are "Silver Spotlight Series" reissues					
Albums					
❑ Liberty LM-1003	This Diamond Ring	1981	2.00	4.00	8.00
—Reissue of United Artists 1008					
❑ Liberty LRP-3408 [M]	This Diamond Ring	1965	5.00	10.00	20.00
❑ Liberty LRP-3419 [M]	A Session with Gary Lewis and the Playboys	1965	5.00	10.00	20.00
❑ Liberty LRP-3428 [M]	Everybody Loves a Clown	1965	5.00	10.00	20.00
❑ Liberty LRP-3435 [M]	She's Just My Style	1966	3.75	7.50	15.00
❑ Liberty LRP-3452 [M]	Hits Again!	1966	3.75	7.50	15.00

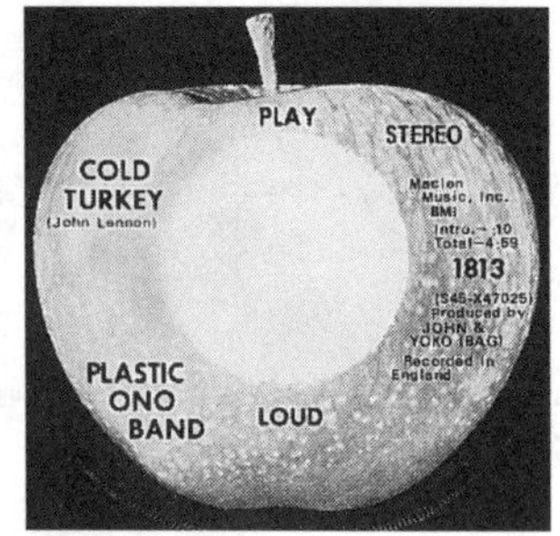

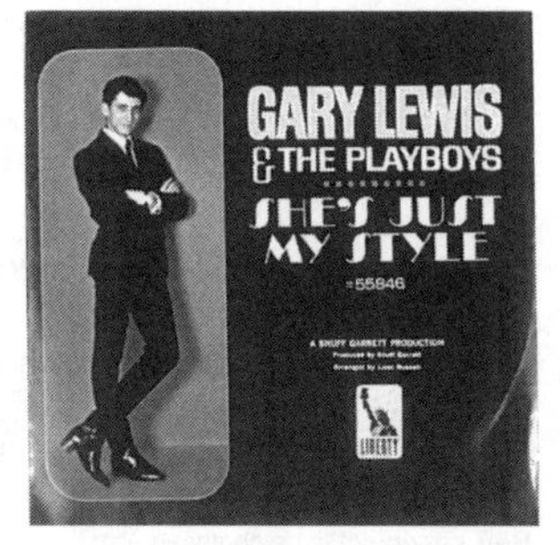

Number	Title (A Side/B Side)	Yr	VG	VG+	NM
❑ Liberty LRP-3468 [M]	Golden Greats	1966	3.75	7.50	15.00
❑ Liberty LRP-3487 [M]	(You Don't Have to) Paint Me a Picture	1967	3.75	7.50	15.00
—Side 1 plays as listed					
❑ Liberty LRP-3519 [M]	New Directions	1967	3.75	7.50	15.00
❑ Liberty LRP-3524 [M]	Listen	1967	3.75	7.50	15.00
❑ Liberty LST-7408 [S]	This Diamond Ring	1965	6.25	12.50	25.00
❑ Liberty LST-7419 [S]	A Session with Gary Lewis and the Playboys	1965	6.25	12.50	25.00
❑ Liberty LST-7428 [S]	Everybody Loves a Clown	1965	6.25	12.50	25.00
❑ Liberty LST-7435 [S]	She's Just My Style	1966	5.00	10.00	20.00
❑ Liberty LST-7452 [S]	Hits Again!	1966	5.00	10.00	20.00
❑ Liberty LST-7468 [S]	Golden Greats	1966	5.00	10.00	20.00
—Side 2 plays as listed					
❑ Liberty LST-7487 [S]	(You Don't Have to) Paint Me a Picture	1967	6.25	12.50	25.00
—Side 1, Song 4 claims to be "Tina" but plays "Ice Melts in the Sun"					
❑ Liberty LST-7519 [S]	New Directions	1967	3.75	7.50	15.00
❑ Liberty LST-7524 [S]	Listen	1967	3.75	7.50	15.00
❑ Liberty LST-7568	Gary Lewis Now!	1968	3.75	7.50	15.00
❑ Liberty LST-7589	More Golden Greats	1968	3.75	7.50	15.00
❑ Liberty LST-7606	Close Cover Before Playing	1969	3.75	7.50	15.00
❑ Liberty LST-7623	Rhythm of the Rain	1969	3.75	7.50	15.00
❑ Liberty LST-7633	I'm On the Right Road Now	1970	3.75	7.50	15.00
❑ Liberty LN-10241	Golden Greats	198?	2.00	4.00	8.00
—Budget-line reissue					
❑ Rhino RNLP-163	Greatest Hits (1965-1968)	1985	2.50	5.00	10.00
❑ Sunset SUM-1168 [M]	Gary Lewis and the Playboys	1967	3.00	6.00	12.00
❑ Sunset SUS-5168 [S]	Gary Lewis and the Playboys	1967	3.00	6.00	12.00
❑ Sunset SUS-5262	Rhythm!	1969	3.00	6.00	12.00
❑ United Artists UA-LA430-E	The Very Best of Gary Lewis and the Playboys	1975	2.50	5.00	10.00
❑ United Artists LM-1003	This Diamond Ring	1980	2.50	5.00	10.00
—Edited reissue of Liberty 7408					

LEWIS, HUEY, AND THE NEWS

45s

Number	Title (A Side/B Side)	Yr	VG	VG+	NM
❑ Chrysalis 2446	Some of My Lies Are True/Hearts	1980	2.50	5.00	10.00
❑ Chrysalis 2458	Now Here's You/Hearts	1980	2.50	5.00	10.00
❑ Chrysalis 2589	Do You Believe in Love/Is It Me	1981	—	2.50	5.00
❑ Chrysalis 2604	Hope You Love Me Like You Say You Do/ Whatever Happened to True Love	1982	—	2.50	5.00
❑ Chrysalis 2630	Workin' for a Livin'/(Live)	1982	—	2.50	5.00
❑ Chrysalis VS4 42726	Heart and Soul/You Crack Me Up	1983	—	—	3.00
❑ Chrysalis VS4 42766	I Want a New Drug/Finally Found a Home	1983	—	—	3.00
❑ Chrysalis VS4 42782	The Heart of Rock and Roll/Workin' for a Livin' (Live)	1984	—	—	3.00
❑ Chrysalis VS4 42803	If This Is It/Change of Heart	1984	—	—	3.00
❑ Chrysalis VS4 42825	Walking on a Thin Line/The Only One	1984	—	—	3.00
❑ Chrysalis VS4 42876	Power of Love/Bad Is Bad	1985	—	2.50	5.00
—Original edition					
❑ Chrysalis VS4 42876	The Power of Love/Bad Is Bad	1985	—	—	3.00
—Later edition, with "The" added to A-side title					
❑ Chrysalis VS8 42947	Do You Believe in Love/Working for a Living	1986	—	2.00	4.00
—Silver label reissue					
❑ Chrysalis VS8 42948	Heart and Soul/I Want a New Drug	1986	—	2.00	4.00
—Silver label reissue					
❑ Chrysalis VS8 42949	The Heart of Rock and Roll/If This Is It	1986	—	2.00	4.00
—Silver label reissue					
❑ Chrysalis VS4 43019	Stuck with You/Don't Ever Tell Me That You Love Me	1986	—	—	3.00
❑ Chrysalis VS4 43065	Hip to Be Square/Some of My Lies Are True	1986	—	—	3.00
❑ Chrysalis VS4 43097	Jacob's Ladder/The Heart of Rock and Roll	1987	—	—	3.00
❑ Chrysalis VS4 43108	I Know What I Like/Forest for the Trees	1987	—	—	3.00
❑ Chrysalis VS4 43143	Doing It All for My Baby/Naturally	1987	—	—	3.00
❑ Chrysalis VS4 43265	Perfect World/Slammin'	1988	—	—	3.00
❑ Chrysalis VS4 43306	Small World/(Instrumental)	1988	—	—	3.00
❑ Chrysalis VS4 43335	Give Me the Keys (And I'll Drive You Crazy)/It's All Right (Live)	1989	—	2.00	4.00
❑ Collectables 6316	Do You Believe in Love/It Hit Me Like a Hammer	199?	—	2.00	4.00
—B-side's only appearance on a U.S. 45					
❑ Collectables 6317	Hip to Be Square/Heart and Soul	199?	—	—	3.00
❑ Collectables 6318	I Want a New Drug/Couple Days Off	199?	—	2.00	4.00
—B-side's only appearance on a U.S. 45					

Number	Title (A Side/B Side)	Yr	VG	VG+	NM
❑ Collectables 6319	Jacob's Ladder/The Heart of Rock and Roll	199?	—	—	3.00
❑ Collectables 6320	The Power of Love/If This Is It	199?	—	—	3.00
❑ Collectables 6321	Stuck with You/Doing It All for My Baby	199?	—	—	3.00
Albums					
❑ Chrysalis CHR 1292	Huey Lewis and the News	1980	3.00	6.00	12.00
❑ Chrysalis CHR 1340	Picture This	1982	2.50	5.00	10.00
❑ Chrysalis FV 41292	Huey Lewis and the News	1983	2.00	4.00	8.00
—Reissue of 1292					
❑ Chrysalis FV 41340	Picture This	1983	2.00	4.00	8.00
—Reissue of 1340					
❑ Chrysalis FV 41412	Sports	1983	2.00	4.00	8.00
❑ Chrysalis OV 41534	Fore!	1986	2.00	4.00	8.00
❑ Chrysalis OV 41622	Small World	1988	2.00	4.00	8.00
❑ Chrysalis 8V8 42795 [EP]	84 Sports Tour	1984	3.75	7.50	15.00
—Three-song picture disc numbered as if it were a single					

LEWIS, JERRY LEE

45s

Number	Title (A Side/B Side)	Yr	VG	VG+	NM
❑ Elektra 46030	Rockin' My Life Away/I Wish I Was Eighteen Again	1979	—	2.00	4.00
❑ Elektra 46067	Who Will the Next Fool Be/Rita May	1979	—	2.00	4.00
❑ Elektra 46591	When Two Worlds Collide/Good News Travels Fast	1980	—	2.00	4.00
❑ Elektra 46642	Honky Tonk Stuff/Rockin' Jerry Lee	1980	—	2.00	4.00
❑ Elektra 47026	Over the Rainbow/Folsom Prison Blues	1980	—	2.00	4.00
❑ Elektra 47095	Thirty-Nine and Holding/Change Places with Me	1980	—	2.00	4.00
❑ Elektra 69962	I'd Do It All Again/Who Will Buy the Wine	1982	—	2.00	4.00
❑ MCA 52151	My Fingers Do the Talkin'/Forever Forgiving	1983	—	—	3.00
❑ MCA 52188	Come As You Were/Circumstantial Evidence	1983	—	—	3.00
❑ MCA 52233	She Sings Amazing Grace/Why You Been Gone So Long	1983	—	—	3.00
❑ MCA 52369	I Am What I Am/That Was the Way It Was Then	1984	—	—	3.00
❑ Mercury 55011	Middle Age Crazy/Georgia on My Mind	1977	—	3.00	6.00
❑ Mercury 55021	Come On In/Who's Sorry Now	1977	—	3.00	6.00
❑ Mercury 55028	I'll Find It Where I Can/Don't Let the Stars Get In Your Eyes	1977	—	3.00	6.00
❑ Mercury 73099	There Must Be More to Love Than This/Home Away from Home	1970	2.00	4.00	8.00
❑ Mercury 73155	I Can't Have a Merry Christmas, Mary (Without You)/ In Loving Memories	1970	2.50	5.00	10.00
❑ Mercury 73192	Touching Home/Woman, Woman	1971	2.00	4.00	8.00
❑ Mercury 73227	When He Walks on You (Like You Have Walked on Me)/ Foolish Kind of Man	1971	2.00	4.00	8.00
❑ Mercury 73248	Would You Take Another Chance on Me/Me and Bobby McGee	1971	2.00	4.00	8.00
❑ Mercury 73273	Chantilly Lace/Think About It Darlin'	1972	2.00	4.00	8.00
❑ Mercury 73296	Lonely Weekends/Turn On Your Love Light	1972	2.00	4.00	8.00
❑ Mercury 73328	Who's Gonna PlayThis Old Piano/No Honky Tonks in Heaven	1972	2.00	4.00	8.00
❑ Mercury 73361	No More Hanging On/Mercy of a Letter	1973	2.00	4.00	8.00
❑ Mercury 73374	Drinking Wine Spo-Dee O'Dee/Rock and Roll Medley	1973	2.00	4.00	8.00
❑ Mercury 73402	No Headstone on My Grave/Jack Daniels	1973	2.00	4.00	8.00
❑ Mercury 73423	Sometimes a Memory Ain't Enough/I Think I Need to Pray	1973	2.00	4.00	8.00
❑ Mercury 73452	I'm Left, You're Right, She's Gone/I've Fallen to the Bottom	1974	2.00	4.00	8.00
❑ Mercury 73462	Meat Man/Just a Little Bit	1974	2.00	4.00	8.00
❑ Mercury 73491	Tell Tale Signs/Cold, Cold Morning Light	1974	2.00	4.00	8.00
❑ Mercury 73618	He Can't Fill My Shoes/Tomorrow's Taking Baby Away	1974	—	3.00	6.00
❑ Mercury 73661	I Can Still Hear the Music in the Restroom/Remember Me	1975	—	3.00	6.00
❑ Mercury 73685	Boogie Woogie Country Man/I'm Still Jealous of You	1975	—	3.00	6.00
❑ Mercury 73729	A Damn Good Country Song/When I Take My Vacation in Heaven	1975	—	3.00	6.00
❑ Mercury 73763	Don't Boogie Woogie/That Kind of Fool	1976	—	3.00	6.00
❑ Mercury 73822	Let's Put It Back Together Again/ Jerry Lee's Rock and Roll Revival Show	1976	—	3.00	6.00
❑ Mercury 73872	The Closest Thing to You/You Belong to Me	1976	—	3.00	6.00
❑ Mercury 76148	I'm So Lonesome I Could Cry/Pick Me Up on Your Way Down	1982	—	2.50	5.00
❑ Phillips Int'l. 3559	In the Mood/I Get the Blues When It Rains	1960	12.50	25.00	50.00
—As "The Hawk"					
❑ Polydor 889312-7	Breathless/Great Balls of Fire	1989	—	2.00	4.00
❑ Polydor 889798-7	Crazy Arms/Great Balls of Fire	1989	—	2.00	4.00
❑ SCR 386	Get Out Your Big Roll, Daddy/ Honky Tonkin' Rock 'N' Roll Piano Man	1985	—	2.50	5.00
❑ Sire 19809	It Was the Whiskey Talkin' (Not Me)/same (Rock and Roll Version)	1990	—	—	3.00
❑ Sire 64423	Goose Bumps/Crown Victoria 51	1995	—	2.50	5.00
❑ Smash 1857	Pen and Paper/Hit the Road Jack	1963	3.75	7.50	15.00
❑ Smash 1886	I'm on Fire/Bread and Butter Man	1964	10.00	20.00	40.00
❑ Smash 1906	She Was My Baby (He Was My Friend)/ The Hole He Said He'd Dig for Me	1964	3.75	7.50	15.00
❑ Smash 1930	High Heel Sneakers/You Went Back on Your Word	1964	3.75	7.50	15.00
❑ Smash 1969	Baby Hold Me Close/I Believe in You	1965	3.75	7.50	15.00
❑ Smash 1992	This Must Be the Place/Rocking Pneumonia and the Boogie Woogie Flu	1965	3.75	7.50	15.00
❑ Smash 2006	Green, Green Grass of Home/You've Got What It Takes	1965	3.75	7.50	15.00
❑ Smash 2027	Sticks and Stones/What a Heck of a Mess	1966	3.00	6.00	12.00
❑ Smash 2053	If I Had It All to Do Over/Memphis Beat	1966	3.00	6.00	12.00
❑ Smash 2103	Holding On/It's a Hang-Up, Baby	1967	3.00	6.00	12.00
❑ Smash 2122	Turn On Your Love Light/Shotgun Man	1967	3.00	6.00	12.00
❑ Smash 2146	Another Place, Another Time/Walking the Floor Over You	1968	2.50	5.00	10.00
❑ Smash 2164	What's Made Milwaukee Famous (Has Made a Loser Out of Me)/ All the Good Is Gone	1968	2.50	5.00	10.00
❑ Smash 2186	She Still Comes Around (To Love What's Left of Me)/ Slipping Around	1968	2.50	5.00	10.00
❑ Smash 2202	To Make Love Sweeter for You/Let's Talk About Us	1968	2.50	5.00	10.00
❑ Smash 2224	One Has My Name (The Other Has My Heart)/ I Can't Stop Loving You	1969	2.50	5.00	10.00

Number	Title (A Side/B Side)	Yr	VG	VG+	NM
❑ Smash 2244	She Even Woke Me Up to Say Goodbye/Echoes	1969	2.50	5.00	10.00
❑ Smash 2257	Once More with Feeling/You Went Out of Your Way (To Walk on Me)	1970	2.50	5.00	10.00
❑ Smash 884934-7	Sixteen Candles/Rock and Roll (Fais-Do-Do)	1986	—	2.00	4.00
—B-side with Roy Orbison, Carl Perkins and Johnny Cash					
❑ Smash 888142-7	We Remember the King/Class of '55	1987	—	2.00	4.00
—With Johnny Cash, Roy Orbison and Carl Perkins; B-side by Carl Perkins solo					
❑ Sun 259	Crazy Arms/End of the Road	1957	25.00	50.00	100.00
—As "Jerry Lee Lewis"					
❑ Sun 259	Crazy Arms/End of the Road	1957	12.50	25.00	50.00
—As "Jerry Lee Lewis and His Pumping Piano"					
❑ Sun 267	Whole Lot of Shakin' Going On/It'll Be Me	1957	10.00	20.00	40.00
❑ Sun 281	Great Balls of Fire/You Win Again	1957	10.00	20.00	40.00
❑ Sun 288	Breathless/Down the Line	1958	10.00	20.00	40.00
❑ Sun 296	High School Confidential/Fools Like Me	1958	7.50	15.00	30.00
❑ Sun 301	Lewis Boogie/The Return of Jerry Lee	1958	7.50	15.00	30.00
—B-side by George and Louis					
❑ Sun 303	I'll Make It All Up to You/Break-Up	1958	6.25	12.50	30.00
❑ Sun 312	I'll Sail My Ship Alone/It Hurt Me So	1958	6.25	12.50	25.00
❑ Sun 317	Lovin' Up a Storm/Big Blon' Baby	1959	6.25	12.50	25.00
❑ Sun 324	Let's Talk About Us/Ballad of Billy Joe	1959	6.25	12.50	25.00
❑ Sun 330	Little Queenie/I Could Never Be Ashamed of You	1959	6.25	12.50	25.00
❑ Sun 337	Old Black Joe/Baby Baby, Bye Bye	1960	5.00	10.00	20.00
❑ Sun 344	Hang Up My Rock and Roll Shoes/John Henry	1960	5.00	10.00	20.00
❑ Sun 352	Love Made a Fool of Me/When I Get Paid	1960	5.00	10.00	20.00
❑ Sun 356	What'd I Say/Livin' Lovin' Wreck	1961	5.00	10.00	20.00
❑ Sun 364	Cold, Cold Heart/It Won't Happen with Me	1961	5.00	10.00	20.00
❑ Sun 367	Save the Last Dance for Me/As Long As I Live	1961	5.00	10.00	20.00
❑ Sun 371	Money/Bonnie B	1961	5.00	10.00	20.00
❑ Sun 374	I've Been Twistin'/Ramblin' Rose	1962	5.00	10.00	20.00
❑ Sun 379	Sweet Little Sixteen/How's My Ex Treating You	1962	5.00	10.00	20.00
❑ Sun 382	Good Golly Miss Molly/I Can't Trust Me	1962	5.00	10.00	20.00
❑ Sun 384	Teenage Letter/Seasons of My Heart	1963	5.00	10.00	20.00
❑ Sun 396	Carry Me Back to Old Virginny/I Know What It Means	1965	5.00	10.00	20.00
❑ Sun 1101	Invitation to Your Party/I Could Never Be Ashamed of You	1969	—	3.00	6.00
❑ Sun 1107	One Minute Past Eternity/Frankie and Johnny	1969	—	3.00	6.00
❑ Sun 1115	I Can't Seem to Say Goodbye/Goodnight Irene	1970	—	2.50	5.00
❑ Sun 1119	Waiting for the Train (All Around the Watertank)/ Big Legged Woman	1970	—	2.50	5.00
❑ Sun 1125	Love on Broadway/Matchbox	1971	—	2.50	5.00
❑ Sun 1128	Your Loving Ways/I Can't Trust Me in Your Arms Anymore	1972	—	2.50	5.00
❑ Sun 1130	Good Rockin' Tonight/I Can't Trust Me in Your Arms Anymore	1973	—	2.50	5.00
❑ Sun 1138	Matchbox/Am I to Be the One	1978	—	2.00	4.00
❑ Sun 1139	Save the Last Dance for Me/Am I to Be the One	1978	—	2.00	4.00
—With uncredited "duet" partner, actually Orion (Jimmy Ellis); a shameless attempt to concoct a "lost Elvis Presley duet"					
❑ Sun 1141	Cold, Cold Heart/Hello Josephine	1979	—	2.00	4.00
❑ Sun 1151	Be-Bop-a-Lula/The Breakup	1980	—	2.00	4.00
—B-side by Charlie Rich; both sides are duets with Orion					
Albums					
❑ Accord SN-7133	I Walk the Line	1981	2.50	5.00	10.00
❑ Design DLP-165 [M]	Rockin' with Jerry Lee Lewis	1963	6.25	12.50	25.00
❑ Design DST-165 [R]	Rockin' with Jerry Lee Lewis	1963	5.00	10.00	20.00
❑ Elektra 6E-184	Jerry Lee Lewis	1979	3.00	6.00	12.00
❑ Elektra 6E-254	When Two Worlds Collide	1980	3.00	6.00	12.00
❑ Elektra 6E-291	Killer Country	1980	3.00	6.00	12.00
❑ Elektra 60191	The Best of Jerry Lee Lewis Featuring 39 and Holding	1982	2.50	5.00	10.00
❑ Hilltop 6102	Sunday After Church	1971	2.50	5.00	10.00
❑ Hilltop 6110	Roll Over Beethoven	1972	2.50	5.00	10.00
❑ Hilltop 6120	Rural Route #1	1972	2.50	5.00	10.00
❑ MCA 5387	My Fingers Do the Talkin'	1983	2.50	5.00	10.00
❑ MCA 5478	I Am What I Am	1984	2.50	5.00	10.00
❑ Mercury SRM-1-637	The "Killer" Rocks On	1972	3.75	7.50	15.00
❑ Mercury SRM-1-677	Sometimes a Memory Ain't Enough	1973	3.75	7.50	15.00
❑ Mercury SRM-1-690	Southern Roots — Back Home to Memphis	1973	3.75	7.50	15.00
❑ Mercury SRM-1-710	I-40 Country	1974	3.75	7.50	15.00
❑ Mercury SRM-2-803 [(2)]	The Session	1973	5.00	10.00	20.00
❑ Mercury SRM-1-1030	Boogie Woogie Country Man	1975	3.75	7.50	15.00

Number	Title (A Side/B Side)	Yr	VG	VG+	NM
❑ Mercury SRM-1-1064	Odd Man In	1975	3.75	7.50	15.00
❑ Mercury SRM-1-1109	Country Class	1976	3.75	7.50	15.00
❑ Mercury SRM-1-5004	Country Memories	1977	3.75	7.50	15.00
❑ Mercury SRM-1-5006	The Best of Jerry Lee Lewis Volume II	1978	3.75	7.50	15.00
❑ Mercury SRM-1-5010	Jerry Lee Lewis Keeps Rockin'	1978	3.75	7.50	15.00
❑ Mercury SR-61278	Live at the International, Las Vegas	1970	3.75	7.50	15.00
❑ Mercury SR-61318	In Loving Memories	1970	7.50	15.00	30.00
❑ Mercury SR-61323	There Must Be More to Love Than This	1971	3.75	7.50	15.00
❑ Mercury SR-61343	Touching Home	1971	3.75	7.50	15.00
—With photo of Jerry Lee in front of a brick wall					
❑ Mercury SR-61346	Would You Take Another Chance on Me?	1971	3.75	7.50	15.00
❑ Mercury SR-61366	Who's Gonna PlayThis Old Piano... (Think About It Darlin')	1972	3.75	7.50	15.00
❑ Mercury 822789-1	The Best of Jerry Lee Lewis Volume II	198?	2.50	5.00	10.00
❑ Mercury 826251-1	Greatest Hits	198?	2.50	5.00	10.00
❑ Mercury 830399-1	Would You Take Another Chance on Me	1987	2.50	5.00	10.00
—Reissue of 61346					
❑ Mercury 836935-1	Killer: The Mercury Years Volume One, 1963-1968	1989	3.00	6.00	12.00
❑ Mercury 836938-1	Killer: The Mercury Years Volume Two, 1969-1972	1989	3.00	6.00	12.00
❑ Mercury 836941-1	Killer: The Mercury Years Volume Three, 1973-1977	1989	3.00	6.00	12.00
❑ Pair PDL2-1132 [(2)]	Solid Gold	1986	3.00	6.00	12.00
❑ Pickwick PTP-2055 [(2)]	Jerry Lee Lewis	1973	3.00	6.00	12.00
❑ Pickwick SPC-3224	High Heel Sneakers	1970	2.50	5.00	10.00
❑ Pickwick SPC-3344	Drinking Wine Spo-Dee-O-Dee	1973	2.50	5.00	10.00
❑ Polydor 826139-1	I'm on Fire	1985	2.50	5.00	10.00
❑ Polydor 839516-1	Great Balls of Fire!	1989	3.00	6.00	12.00
❑ Power Pak 247	From the Vaults of Sun	1974	2.50	5.00	10.00
❑ Rhino RNDA-1499 [(2)]	Milestones	1985	3.75	7.50	15.00
❑ Rhino R1-70255	Original Sun Greatest Hits	1989	2.50	5.00	10.00
—Reissue of 255 on black vinyl					
❑ Rhino R1-70656	Jerry Lee Lewis	1989	3.00	6.00	12.00
—Reissue of Sun 1230					
❑ Rhino R1-70657	Jerry Lee's Greatest	1989	3.00	6.00	12.00
—Reissue of Sun 1265					
❑ Rhino R1-70899	Wild One: Rare Tracks from Jerry Lee Lewis	1989	3.00	6.00	12.00
❑ Rhino R1-71499 [(2)]	Milestones	1989	3.00	6.00	12.00
—Reissue of 1499					
❑ Sears SPS-610	Hound Dog	1970	6.25	12.50	25.00
❑ Smash SL-7001	Golden Hits	1980	3.00	6.00	12.00
❑ Smash MGS-27040 [M]	The Golden Hits of Jerry Lee Lewis	1964	6.25	12.50	25.00
❑ Smash MGS-27056 [M]	The Greatest Live Show on Earth	1964	25.00	50.00	100.00
❑ Smash MGS-27063 [M]	The Return of Rock	1965	7.50	15.00	30.00
❑ Smash MGS-27071 [M]	Country Songs for City Folks	1965	6.25	12.50	25.00
❑ Smash MGS-27079 [M]	Memphis Beat	1966	6.25	12.50	25.00
❑ Smash MGS-27086 [M]	By Request — More of the Greatest Live Show on Earth	1966	7.50	15.00	30.00
❑ Smash MGS-27097 [M]	Soul My Way	1967	7.50	15.00	30.00
❑ Smash SRS-67040 [S]	The Golden Hits of Jerry Lee Lewis	1964	7.50	15.00	30.00
❑ Smash SRS-67056 [S]	The Greatest Live Show on Earth	1964	37.50	75.00	150.00
❑ Smash SRS-67063 [S]	The Return of Rock	1965	10.00	20.00	40.00
❑ Smash SRS-67071 [S]	Country Songs for City Folks	1965	7.50	15.00	30.00
❑ Smash SRS-67079 [S]	Memphis Beat	1966	7.50	15.00	30.00
❑ Smash SRS-67086 [S]	By Request — More of the Greatest Live Show on Earth	1966	10.00	20.00	40.00
❑ Smash SRS-67097 [S]	Soul My Way	1967	10.00	20.00	40.00
❑ Smash SRS-67104	Another Place Another Time	1968	5.00	10.00	20.00
❑ Smash SRS-67112	She Still Comes Around (To Love What's Left of Me)	1969	5.00	10.00	20.00
❑ Smash SRS-67117	Jerry Lee Lewis Sings the Country Music Hall of Fame Hits, Vol. 1	1969	5.00	10.00	20.00
❑ Smash SRS-67118	Jerry Lee Lewis Sings the Country Music Hall of Fame Hits, Vol. 2	1969	5.00	10.00	20.00
❑ Smash SRS-67128	She Even Woke Me Up to Say Goodbye	1970	5.00	10.00	20.00
❑ Smash SRS-67131	The Best of Jerry Lee Lewis	1970	5.00	10.00	20.00
❑ Sun LP-102	Original Golden Hits — Volume 1	1969	3.75	7.50	15.00
❑ Sun LP-103	Original Golden Hits — Volume 2	1969	3.75	7.50	15.00
❑ Sun LP-107	Rockin' Rhythm and Blues	1969	3.75	7.50	15.00
❑ Sun SUN-108	The Golden Cream of the Country	1969	3.75	7.50	15.00
❑ Sun SUN-108 [M]	The Golden Cream of the Country	1969	10.00	20.00	40.00
—Mono version is white label promo only; the word "MONO" appears at 9 o'clock on the label					
❑ Sun LP-114	A Taste of Country	1970	3.75	7.50	15.00
❑ Sun LP-121	Ole Tyme Country Music	1971	3.75	7.50	15.00
❑ Sun LP-124	Monsters	1971	3.75	7.50	15.00
❑ Sun LP-128	Original Golden Hits — Volume 3	1972	3.75	7.50	15.00
❑ Sun SUN-145	Roots	1982	3.00	6.00	12.00
❑ Sun 1005	The Original	1978	3.00	6.00	12.00
❑ Sun SUN-1011	Duets	1978	3.75	7.50	15.00
—As "Jerry Lee Lewis and Friends"; gold vinyl					
❑ Sun 1018	Trio +	1979	3.00	6.00	12.00
—With Carl Perkins, Charlie Rich and (uncredited) Orion					
❑ Sun SLP-1230 [M]	Jerry Lee Lewis	1958	50.00	100.00	200.00
❑ Sun SLP-1265 [M]	Jerry Lee's Greatest	1961	62.50	125.00	250.00
❑ Sun SLP-1265 [M]	Jerry Lee's Greatest	1961	200.00	400.00	800.00
—White label promo					
❑ Sunnyvale 905	The Sun Story, Vol. 5	1977	2.50	5.00	10.00
❑ Wing PKW2-125 [(2)]	The Legend of Jerry Lee Lewis	1969	6.25	12.50	25.00
❑ Wing MGW-12340 [M]	The Return of Rock	1967	3.00	6.00	12.00
❑ Wing SRW-16340	In Demand	1968	2.50	5.00	10.00
❑ Wing SRW-16340 [S]	The Return of Rock	1967	3.00	6.00	12.00
❑ Wing SRW-16406	Unlimited	1968	3.00	6.00	12.00

LIGHTFOOT, GORDON

45s

Number	Title (A Side/B Side)	Yr	VG	VG+	NM
❑ ABC-Paramount 10352	Daisy-Doo/I'm the One (Remember Me)	1962	6.25	12.50	25.00
—As "Gord Lightfoot"					

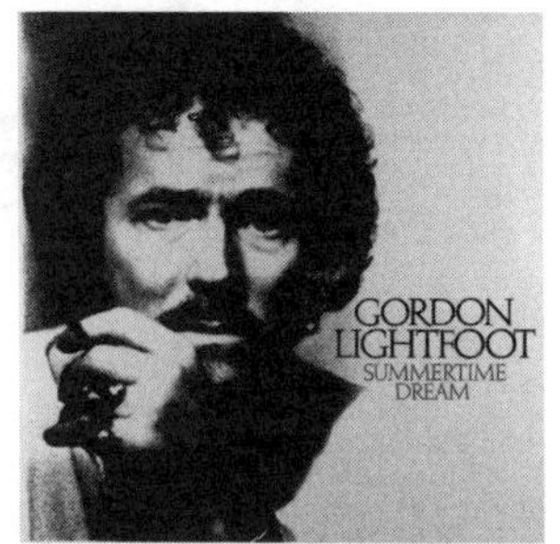

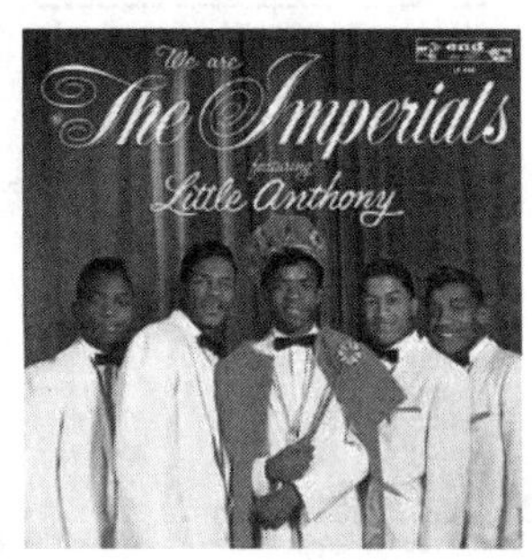

Number	Title (A Side/B Side)	Yr	VG	VG+	NM
❑ ABC-Paramount 10373	It's Too Late, He Wins/Negotiations	1962	6.25	12.50	25.00
❑ Chateau 142	Daisy-Doo/I'm the One (Remember Me)	1962	12.50	25.00	50.00
❑ Chateau 148	It's Too Late, He Wins/Negotiations	1962	12.50	25.00	50.00
❑ Chateau 152	I'll Meet You in Michigan/Is My Baby Blue Tonight	1962	10.00	20.00	40.00
❑ Reprise 0744	If You Could Read My Mind/Me and Bobby McGee	1972	—	2.00	4.00
—"Back to Back Hits" series					
❑ Reprise 0745	Talking in Your Sleep/Summer Side of Life	1972	—	2.00	4.00
—"Back to Back Hits" series					
❑ Reprise 0926	Me and Bobby McGee/Pony Man	1970	—	2.50	5.00
❑ Reprise 0974	If You Could Read My Mind/Poor Little Allison	1970	—	3.00	6.00
❑ Reprise 1020	Talking in Your Sleep/Nous Vivons Ensemble	1971	—	2.50	5.00
❑ Reprise 1035	Summer Side of Life/Love and Maple Syrup	1971	—	2.50	5.00
❑ Reprise 1088	Beautiful/Don Quixote	1972	—	2.50	5.00
❑ Reprise 1128	You Are What I Am/The Same Old Obsession	1972	—	2.50	5.00
❑ Reprise 1145	Can't Depend on You/It's Worth Believin'	1972	—	2.50	5.00
❑ Reprise 1194	Sundown/Too Late for Prayin'	1974	—	2.00	4.00
❑ Reprise 1309	Carefree Highway/Seven Island Suite	1974	—	2.00	4.00
❑ Reprise 1328	Rainy Day People/Cherokee Bend	1975	—	2.00	4.00
❑ Reprise 1369	The Wreck of the Edmund Fitzgerald/The House You Live In	1976	—	2.00	4.00
❑ Reprise 1380	Race Among the Ruins/Protocol	1976	—	2.00	4.00
❑ United Artists 929	Just Like Tom Thumb's Blues/Ribbon of Darkness	1965	2.50	5.00	10.00
❑ United Artists 50055	For Lovin' Me/Spin, Spin	1966	2.00	4.00	8.00
❑ United Artists 50114	I'll Be Alright/Go Go Round	1967	2.00	4.00	8.00
❑ United Artists 50152	The Way I Feel/Peaceful Waters	1967	2.00	4.00	8.00
❑ United Artists 50281	Pussywillows, Cat-Tails/Black Day in July	1968	2.00	4.00	8.00
❑ United Artists 50447	Does Your Mother Know/Bitter Green	1968	2.00	4.00	8.00
❑ United Artists 50765	If I Could/Softly	1971	—	2.50	5.00
❑ Warner Bros. 5621	For Lovin' Me/I'm Not Sayin'	1965	3.75	7.50	15.00
❑ Warner Bros. 8518	The Circle Is Small (I Can See It In Your Eyes)/Sweet Guinevere	1978	—	2.00	4.00
—Subtitle added to later pressings					
❑ Warner Bros. 8518	The Circle Is Small/Sweet Guinevere	1978	—	2.50	5.00
—Without A-side subtitle					
❑ Warner Bros. 8579	Daylight Katy/Hangdog Hotel Room	1978	—	2.00	4.00
❑ Warner Bros. 8644	Dreamland/Songs the Minstrel Sang	1978	—	2.00	4.00
❑ Warner Bros. 28222	Ecstasy Made Easy/Morning Glory	1987	—	—	3.00
❑ Warner Bros. 28422	East of Midnight/I'll Tag Along	1987	—	—	3.00
❑ Warner Bros. 28553	Stay Loose/Morning Glory	1986	—	—	3.00
❑ Warner Bros. 28655	Anything for Love/Let It Ride	1986	—	—	3.00
❑ Warner Bros. 29466	Someone to Believe In/Without You	1983	—	2.00	4.00
❑ Warner Bros. 29511	Knotty Pine/Salute	1983	—	2.00	4.00
❑ Warner Bros. 29859	Shadows/In My Fashion	1982	—	2.00	4.00
❑ Warner Bros. 29963	Blackberry Wine/(B-side unknown)	1982	—	2.00	4.00
❑ Warner Bros. 49230	Dream Street Rose/Make Way for the Lady	1980	—	2.00	4.00
❑ Warner Bros. 49516	If You Need Me/Mister Rock of Ages	1980	—	2.00	4.00
❑ Warner Bros. 50012	Baby Step Back/Thank You for the Promises	1982	—	2.00	4.00
Albums					
❑ Liberty LN-10038	The Best of Lightfoot	198?	2.00	4.00	8.00
—Budget-line reissue					
❑ Liberty LN-10039	Sunday Concert	198?	2.00	4.00	8.00
—Budget-line reissue					
❑ Liberty LN-10040	Back Here on Earth	198?	2.00	4.00	8.00
—Budget-line reissue					
❑ Liberty LN-10041	Did She Mention My Name	198?	2.00	4.00	8.00
—Budget-line reissue					
❑ Liberty LN-10043	The Way I Feel	198?	2.00	4.00	8.00
—Budget-line reissue					
❑ Liberty LN-10044	Lightfoot	198?	2.00	4.00	8.00
—Budget-line reissue					
❑ Pair PDL2-1081 [(2)]	Songbook	1986	3.00	6.00	12.00
❑ Reprise MS 2037	Summer Side of Life	1971	3.00	6.00	12.00
❑ Reprise MS 2056	Don Quixote	1972	3.00	6.00	12.00
❑ Reprise MS 2116	Old Dan's Records	1972	3.00	6.00	12.00
❑ Reprise MS 2177	Sundown	1974	3.00	6.00	12.00
❑ Reprise MS 2206	Cold on the Shoulder	1975	3.00	6.00	12.00
❑ Reprise 2RS 2237 [(2)]	Gord's Gold	1975	3.75	7.50	15.00
❑ Reprise MS 2246	Summertime Dream	1976	3.00	6.00	12.00

Number	Title (A Side/B Side)	Yr	VG	VG+	NM
❑ Reprise RS 6392	Sit Down Young Stranger	1970	3.75	7.50	15.00
❑ Reprise RS 6392	If You Could Read My Mind	1971	2.50	5.00	10.00
—Retitled version					
❑ Reprise ST-93228	Sit Down Young Stranger	1970	5.00	10.00	20.00
—Capitol Record Club edition					
❑ United Artists UA-LA243-G	The Very Best of Gordon Lightfoot	1974	3.00	6.00	12.00
❑ United Artists UAL-3487 [M]	Lightfoot	1966	5.00	10.00	20.00
❑ United Artists UAL-3587 [M]	The Way I Feel	1967	5.00	10.00	20.00
❑ United Artists UAS-5510	Classic Lightfoot (The Best of Lightfoot/Volume 2)	1971	3.75	7.50	15.00
❑ United Artists UAS-6487 [S]	Lightfoot	1966	6.25	12.50	25.00
❑ United Artists UAS-6587 [S]	The Way I Feel	1967	6.25	12.50	25.00
❑ United Artists UAS-6649	Did She Mention My Name	1968	5.00	10.00	20.00
❑ United Artists UAS-6672	Back Here on Earth	1969	5.00	10.00	20.00
❑ United Artists UAS-6714	Sunday Concert	1969	3.75	7.50	15.00
❑ United Artists UAS-6754	The Best of Gordon Lightfoot	1970	3.75	7.50	15.00
❑ Warner Bros. BSK 3149	Endless Wire	1978	2.50	5.00	10.00
❑ Warner Bros. HS 3426	Dream Street Rose	1980	2.50	5.00	10.00
❑ Warner Bros. BSK 3633	Shadows	1982	2.50	5.00	10.00
❑ Warner Bros. 23901	Salute	1983	2.50	5.00	10.00
❑ Warner Bros. 25482	East of Midnight	1986	2.50	5.00	10.00
❑ Warner Bros. 25784	Gord's Gold, Volume II	1989	3.00	6.00	12.00

LINDSAY, MARK

45s

Number	Title (A Side/B Side)	Yr	VG	VG+	NM
❑ Columbia 10081	Mamacita/Song for a Friend	1974	—	2.50	5.00
❑ Columbia 10114	Photograph/Song for a Friend	1975	—	2.50	5.00
❑ Columbia 44875	First Hymn from Grand Terrace/The Old Man at the Fair	1969	—	3.00	6.00
❑ Columbia 45037	Arizona/Man from Houston	1969	—	3.00	6.00
❑ Columbia 45125	Miss America/Small Town Woman	1970	—	3.00	6.00
❑ Columbia 45180	Silver Bird/So Hard to Leave You	1970	—	3.00	6.00
❑ Columbia 45229	And the Grass Won't Pay No Mind/Funny How Little Men Care	1970	—	3.00	6.00
❑ Columbia 45286	Problem Child/Bookends	1970	—	3.00	6.00
❑ Columbia 45385	Been Too Long on the Road/All I Really See Is You	1971	—	2.50	5.00
❑ Columbia 45462	Are You Old Enough/Don't You Know	1971	—	2.50	5.00
❑ Columbia 45506	Pretty Pretty/Something Big	1971	—	2.50	5.00
❑ Columbia 45895	California/Someone's Been Hiding	1973	—	2.50	5.00
❑ Elka 310	Sing Your Own Song/Sing Your Own Song (Theme)	1976	2.50	5.00	10.00
❑ Greedy 106	Sing Your Own Song/Sing Your Own Song (Theme)	1976	—	3.00	6.00
❑ Warner Bros. 8359	Sing Me High, Sing Me Low/Flips-Eyed	1977	—	2.00	4.00
❑ Warner Bros. 8479	Little Ladies of the Night/Flips-Eyed	1977	—	2.00	4.00

Albums

Number	Title (A Side/B Side)	Yr	VG	VG+	NM
❑ Columbia CS 9986	Arizona	1970	3.00	6.00	12.00
—Orange label					
❑ Columbia CS 9986	Arizona	1970	3.75	7.50	15.00
—Red "360 Sound" label					
❑ Columbia C 30111	Silver Bird	1970	3.00	6.00	12.00
❑ Columbia C 30735	You've Got a Friend	1971	3.00	6.00	12.00

LITTLE ANTHONY AND THE IMPERIALS

45s

Number	Title (A Side/B Side)	Yr	VG	VG+	NM
❑ Apollo 521	The Fires Burn No More/Lift Up Your Hands	1957	15.00	30.00	60.00
—As "The Chesters"					
❑ Avco 4635	I'm Falling in Love with You/What Good Am I Without You	1974	—	2.50	5.00
❑ Avco 4645	I Don't Have to Worry/Loneliest House on the Block	1974	—	2.50	5.00
❑ Avco 4651	Hold On (Just a Little Bit Longer)/I've Got to Let You Go (Part 1)	1975	—	2.50	5.00
❑ Avco 4655	I'll Be Loving You Sooner or Later/Young Girl	1975	—	2.50	5.00
❑ DCP 1104	I'm On the Outside (Looking In)/Please Go	1964	2.50	5.00	10.00
❑ DCP 1119	Goin' Out of My Head/Make It Easy on Yourself	1964	2.50	5.00	10.00
❑ DCP 1128	Hurt So Bad/Reputation	1965	2.50	5.00	10.00
❑ DCP 1136	Take Me Back/Our Song	1965	2.00	4.00	8.00
❑ DCP 1149	I Miss You So/Get Out of My Life	1965	2.00	4.00	8.00
❑ DCP 1154	Hurt/Never Again	1966	2.00	4.00	8.00
❑ End 1027	Tears on My Pillow/Two People in the World	1958	10.00	20.00	40.00
—As "The Imperials"					
❑ End 1027	Tears on My Pillow/Two People in the World	1958	6.25	12.50	25.00
—As "Little Anthony and the Imperials"					
❑ End 1036	So Much/Oh Yeah	1958	6.25	12.50	25.00
❑ End 1038	The Diary/Cha Cha Henry	1959	6.25	12.50	25.00
❑ End 1039	When You Wish Upon a Star/Wishful Thinking	1959	6.25	12.50	25.00
❑ End 1047	A Prayer and a Juke Box/River Path	1959	6.25	12.50	25.00
❑ End 1053	So Near and Yet So Far/I'm Alright	1959	6.25	12.50	25.00
❑ End 1060	Shimmy, Shimmy, Ko-Ko Bop/I'm Still in Love with You	1959	7.50	15.00	30.00
❑ End 1067	My Empty Room/Bayou, Bayou, Baby	1960	3.75	7.50	15.00
❑ End 1074	I'm Taking a Vacation from Love/Only Sympathy	1960	3.75	7.50	15.00
❑ End 1080	Limbo (Part 1)/Limbo (Part 2)	1960	3.75	7.50	15.00
❑ End 1083	Formula of Love/Dream	1961	3.75	7.50	15.00
❑ End 1086	Please Say You Want Me/So Near Yet So Far	1961	3.75	7.50	15.00
❑ End 1091	Traveling Stranger/Say Yea	1961	3.75	7.50	15.00
❑ End 1104	Dream/A Lovely Way to Spend an Evening	1961	3.75	7.50	15.00
❑ Janus 160	Father, Father/Each One, Teach One	1971	—	3.00	6.00
❑ Janus 166	Madeline/Universe	1971	—	3.00	6.00
❑ Janus 178	(Where Do I Begin) Love Story/There's an Island	1972	—	3.00	6.00
❑ Liberty 55119	The Glory of Love/C'mon Tiger (Gimme a Growl)	1958	7.50	15.00	30.00
—As "The Imperials"					

Number	Title (A Side/B Side)	Yr	VG	VG+	NM
❑ MCA 41258	Daylight/Your Love	1980	—	2.00	4.00
—Little Anthony solo					
❑ Newtime 503	A Short Prayer/Where Will You Be	196?	3.00	6.00	12.00
—As "Anthony and the Imperials"					
❑ PCM 202	This Time We're Winning/Your Love	1983	—	2.00	4.00
❑ Pure Gold 101	Nothing from Nothing/Running with the Wrong Crowd	1976	—	2.50	5.00
❑ Roulette 4379	That Lil' Ole Lovemaker Me/It Just Ain't Fair	1961	3.00	6.00	12.00
—Little Anthony solo					
❑ Roulette 4477	Lonesome Romeo/I've Got a Lot to Offer Darling	1963	3.00	6.00	12.00
—Little Anthony solo					
❑ United Artists 0117	Goin' Out of My Head/I'm On the Outside (Looking In)	1973	—	2.00	4.00
—"Silver Spotlight Series" reissue					
❑ United Artists 0118	Hurt So Bad/Take Me Back	1973	—	2.00	4.00
—"Silver Spotlight Series" reissue					
❑ United Artists 50552	Out of Sight, Out of MInd/Summer's Comin'	1969	—	3.00	6.00
❑ United Artists 50598	The Ten Commandments of Love/Let the Sunshine In	1969	—	3.00	6.00
❑ United Artists 50625	It'll Never Be the Same Again/Don't Get Close	1970	—	3.00	6.00
❑ United Artists 50677	World of Darkness/The Change	1970	—	3.00	6.00
❑ United Artists 50720	Help Me Find a Way (To Say I Love You)/If I Love You	1970	—	3.00	6.00
❑ Veep 1228	Better Use Your Head/The Wonder of It All	1966	2.00	4.00	8.00
❑ Veep 1233	You Better Take It Easy Baby/Gonna Fix You Good (Every Time You're Bad)	1966	2.00	4.00	8.00
❑ Veep 1239	Tears on My Pillow/Who's Sorry Now	1966	—	3.00	6.00
❑ Veep 1240	I'm On the Outside (Looking In)/Please Go	1966	—	3.00	6.00
❑ Veep 1241	Goin' Out of My Head/Shing-a-Ling	1966	—	3.00	6.00
❑ Veep 1242	Hurt So Bad/Reputation	1966	—	3.00	6.00
❑ Veep 1243	Take Me Back/Our Song	1966	—	3.00	6.00
❑ Veep 1244	I Miss You So/Get Out of My Life	1966	—	3.00	6.00
❑ Veep 1245	Hurt/Never Again	1966	—	3.00	6.00
❑ Veep 1248	It's Not the Same/Down on Love	1966	2.00	4.00	8.00
❑ Veep 1255	Don't Tie Me Down/Where There's a Will There's a Way	1967	2.00	4.00	8.00
❑ Veep 1262	Hold On to Someone/Lost in Love	1967	2.00	4.00	8.00
❑ Veep 1269	You Only Live Twice/Hungry Heart	1967	2.00	4.00	8.00
❑ Veep 1275	Beautiful People/If I Remember to Forget	1967	2.00	4.00	8.00
❑ Veep 1278	I'm Hypnotized/Hungry Heart	1968	2.00	4.00	8.00
❑ Veep 1283	What Greater Love/In the Back of My Heart	1968	2.00	4.00	8.00
❑ Veep 1285	Yesterday Has Gone/My Love Is a Rainbow	1968	2.00	4.00	8.00
❑ Veep 1293	The Flesh Failures (Let the Sunshine In)/Gentle Rain	1969	2.00	4.00	8.00
❑ Veep 1303	Anthem (Revelation)/Goodbye Good Times	1969	2.00	4.00	8.00
Albums					
❑ Accord SN-7216	Tears on My Pillow	1983	2.50	5.00	10.00
❑ Avco AV-11012	On a New Street	1973	5.00	10.00	20.00
❑ DCP DCL-3801 [M]	I'm On the Outside Looking In	1964	6.25	12.50	25.00
❑ DCP DCL-3808 [M]	Goin' Out of My Head	1965	6.25	12.50	25.00
❑ DCP DCL-3809 [M]	The Best of Little Anthony and the Imperials	1965	5.00	10.00	20.00
❑ DCP DCS-6801 [S]	I'm On the Outside Looking In	1964	7.50	15.00	30.00
❑ DCP DCS-6808 [S]	Goin' Out of My Head	1965	7.50	15.00	30.00
❑ DCP DCS-6809 [S]	The Best of Little Anthony and the Imperials	1965	6.25	12.50	25.00
❑ End LP 303 [M]	We Are The Imperials Featuring Little Anthony	1959	62.50	125.00	250.00
❑ End LP 311 [M]	Shades of the 40's	1960	50.00	100.00	200.00
❑ Forum F-9107 [M]	Little Anthony and the Imperials' Greatest Hits	196?	3.75	7.50	15.00
❑ Forum FS-9107 [R]	Little Anthony and the Imperials' Greatest Hits	196?	3.00	6.00	12.00
❑ Liberty LM-1017	Out of Sight, Out of Mind	1981	2.00	4.00	8.00
—Reissue of United Artists 1017					
❑ Liberty LN-10133	The Best of Little Anthony and the Imperials	1981	2.00	4.00	8.00
—Budget-line reissue					
❑ Pickwick SPC-3029	The Hits of Little Anthony and the Imperials	196?	3.00	6.00	12.00
❑ Rhino R1-70919	The Best of Little Anthony and the Imperials	1989	3.00	6.00	12.00
❑ Roulette R-25294 [M]	Little Anthony and the Imperials' Greatest Hits	1965	6.25	12.50	25.00
❑ Roulette SR-25294 [R]	Little Anthony and the Imperials' Greatest Hits	1965	5.00	10.00	20.00
❑ Roulette SR-42007	Forever Yours	1968	3.75	7.50	15.00
❑ Songbird 3245	Daylight	1980	2.50	5.00	10.00
❑ Sunset SUS-5287	Little Anthony and the Imperials	1970	3.75	7.50	15.00
❑ United Artists UA-LA026-G [(2)]	Legendary Masters Series	1972	6.25	12.50	25.00
❑ United Artists UA-LA255-G	The Very Best of Little Anthony and the Imperials	1974	2.50	5.00	10.00

Number	Title (A Side/B Side)	Yr	VG	VG+	NM
❑ United Artists LM-1017	Out of Sight, Out of Mind	1980	2.50	5.00	10.00
—Reissue of United Artists 6720					
❑ United Artists UAS 6720	Out of Sight, Out of Mind	1969	5.00	10.00	20.00
❑ Veep VP 13510 [M]	I'm On the Outside Looking In	1966	3.75	7.50	15.00
❑ Veep VP 13511 [M]	Goin' Out of My Head	1966	3.75	7.50	15.00
❑ Veep VP 13512 [M]	The Best of Little Anthony and the Imperials	1966	3.75	7.50	15.00
❑ Veep VP 13513 [M]	Payin' Our Dues	1966	3.75	7.50	15.00
❑ Veep VP 13514 [M]	Reflections	1967	3.75	7.50	15.00
❑ Veep VP 13516 [M]	Movie Grabbers	1967	3.75	7.50	15.00
❑ Veep VPS 16510 [S]	I'm On the Outside Looking In	1966	5.00	10.00	20.00
❑ Veep VPS 16511 [S]	Goin' Out of My Head	1966	5.00	10.00	20.00
❑ Veep VPS 16512 [S]	The Best of Little Anthony and the Imperials	1966	5.00	10.00	20.00
❑ Veep VPS 16513 [S]	Payin' Our Dues	1966	5.00	10.00	20.00
❑ Veep VPS 16514 [S]	Reflections	1967	5.00	10.00	20.00
❑ Veep VPS 16516 [S]	Movie Grabbers	1967	5.00	10.00	20.00
❑ Veep VPS 16519	The Best of Little Anthony, Volume 2	1968	3.75	7.50	15.00

LITTLE EVA

45s

Number	Title (A Side/B Side)	Yr	VG	VG+	NM
❑ Amy 943	Stand By Me/That's My Man	1965	2.00	4.00	8.00
❑ Bell 45264	The Loco-Motion/Will You Love Me Tomorrow	1972	—	2.50	5.00
❑ Dimension 1000	The Loco-Motion/He Is the Boy	1962	5.00	10.00	20.00
❑ Dimension 1003	Keep Your Hands Off My Baby/Where Do I Go	1962	3.00	6.00	12.00
—Most copies have longer, and correct, title					
❑ Dimension 1003	Keep Your Hands Off/Where Do I Go	1962	3.75	7.50	15.00
—Some copies have this shortened title					
❑ Dimension 1006	Let's Turkey Trot/Down Home	1963	3.00	6.00	12.00
❑ Dimension 1011	Old Smokey Locomotion/Just a Little Girl	1963	3.00	6.00	12.00
❑ Dimension 1013	The Trouble with Boys/What I Gotta Do	1963	3.00	6.00	12.00
❑ Dimension 1019	Let's Start the Party Again/Please Hurt Me	1963	3.00	6.00	12.00
❑ Dimension 1021	The Christmas Song/I Wish You a Merry Christmas	1963	3.75	7.50	15.00
—With Big Dee Irwin					
❑ Dimension 1035	Makin' with the Magilla/Run to Her	1964	2.50	5.00	10.00
❑ Dimension 1035	Makin' with the Magilla/Conga	1964	2.50	5.00	10.00
❑ Dimension 1042	Wake Up John/Takin' Back What I Said	1964	2.50	5.00	10.00
❑ Spring 101	Mama Said/Something About You Boy	1970	—	3.00	6.00
❑ Spring 107	Night After Night/Something About You Boy	1970	—	3.00	6.00
❑ Verve 10459	Bend It/Just One Word Isn't Enough	1966	2.00	4.00	8.00
❑ Verve 10529	Everything Is Beautiful About You Boy/Take a Step in My Direction	1967	2.00	4.00	8.00

Albums

Number	Title (A Side/B Side)	Yr	VG	VG+	NM
❑ Dimension DLP-6000 [M]	LLLLLoco-Motion	1962	37.50	75.00	150.00
—Without "Keep Your Hands Off My Baby"					
❑ Dimension DLPS-6000 [R]	LLLLLoco-Motion	1962	37.50	75.00	150.00
—Without "Keep Your Hands Off My Baby"					

LITTLE RICHARD

45s

Number	Title (A Side/B Side)	Yr	VG	VG+	NM
❑ Atlantic 2181	Crying in the Chapel/Hole in the Wall	1963	3.00	6.00	12.00
❑ Atlantic 2192	It Is No Secret (What God Can Do)/Travelin' Shoes	1963	3.00	6.00	12.00
❑ Bell 45385	Good Golly Miss Molly/Good Golly Miss Molly (Part 2)	1973	—	2.50	5.00
❑ Brunswick 55362	She's Together/Try Some of Mine	1968	2.00	4.00	8.00
❑ Brunswick 55377	Stingy Jenny/Baby Don't You Tear My Clothes	1968	2.00	4.00	8.00
❑ Brunswick 55386	Soul Train/Can I Count on You	1968	2.00	4.00	8.00
❑ Coral 62366	Milky White Way/Need Him	1963	2.50	5.00	10.00
❑ Critique 99392	Happy Endings/California Girls	1987	—	2.00	4.00
—A-side with the Beach Boys; B-side is The Beach Boys without Little Richard					
❑ Elektra 69370	Tutti Frutti/Rave On	1988	—	—	3.00
—B-side by John Cougar Mellencamp					
❑ Elektra 69384	Tutti Frutti/Powerful Stuff	1988	—	—	3.00
—B-side by the Fabulous Thunderbirds					
❑ Elektra 69385	Tutti Frutti/Kokomo	1988	—	—	3.00
—B-side by the Beach Boys					
❑ End 1057	Troubles of the World/Save Me Lord	1959	3.75	7.50	15.00
❑ End 1058	Milky White Way/I've Just Come From the Fountain	1959	3.75	7.50	15.00
❑ Green Mountain 413	In the Middle of the Night/Where Will I Find a Place to Sleep This Evening	1973	—	2.50	5.00
❑ Kent 4567	Mississippi/In the Name	1972	—	—	—
—Unreleased					
❑ Kent 4568	Don't You Know I/In the Name	1972	—	2.50	5.00
❑ Lost-Nite 296	Keep a-Knockin'/She's Got It	197?	—	3.00	6.00
—Reissue from Vee-Jay masters (not the original versions)					
❑ Lost-Nite 302	Lucille/Good Golly Miss Molly	197?	—	3.00	6.00
—Reissue from Vee-Jay masters (not the original versions)					
❑ Lost-Nite 309	Tutti Frutti/Long Tall Sally	197?	—	3.00	6.00
—Reissue from Vee-Jay masters (not the original versions)					
❑ Lost-Nite 315	The Girl Can't Help It/Rip It Up	197?	—	3.00	6.00
—Reissue from Vee-Jay masters (not the original versions)					
❑ Mainstream 5572	Try to Help Your Brother/Funk Proof	1975	—	2.50	5.00
❑ Manticore 7007	Call My Name/Steal Miss Liza (Miss Liza Jane)	1975	—	2.00	4.00
❑ MCA 52780	Great Gosh A-Mighty! (It's a Matter of Time)/The Ride	1986	—	—	3.00
—B-side by Charlie Midnight					
❑ Mercury 71884	He's Not Just a Soldier/Joy, Joy, Joy	1962	3.75	7.50	15.00
❑ Mercury 71911	Do You Care/Ride On King Jesus	1962	3.75	7.50	15.00
❑ Mercury 71965	Why Don't You Change Your Ways/He Got What He Wanted	1962	3.75	7.50	15.00
❑ Modern 1018	Holy Mackeral/Baby, Don't You Want a Man Like Me	1966	3.00	6.00	12.00
❑ Modern 1019	Do You Feel It (Part 1)/Do You Feel It (Part 2)	1966	3.00	6.00	12.00
❑ Modern 1022	Directly from My Heart to You/I'm Back	1966	3.00	6.00	12.00

Number	Title (A Side/B Side)	Yr	VG	VG+	NM
❑ Modern 1030	Slippin' and Slidin'/Bring It Back Home to Me	1967	3.00	6.00	12.00
❑ Modern 1043	Baby What You Want Me to Do (Part 1)/ Baby What You Want Me to Do (Part 2)	1967	3.00	6.00	12.00
❑ Okeh 7251	Poor Dog (Who Can't Wag His Own Tail)/Well	1966	3.75	7.50	15.00
❑ Okeh 7262	I Need Love/Commandments of Love	1966	3.00	6.00	12.00
❑ Okeh 7271	Hurry Sundown/I Don't Want to Discuss It	1967	3.00	6.00	12.00
❑ Okeh 7278	Don't Deceive Me (Please Don't Go)/Never Gonna Let You Go	1967	3.00	6.00	12.00
❑ Okeh 7286	Money/Little Bit of Something	1967	3.00	6.00	12.00
❑ Okeh 7325	Lucille/Whole Lotta Shakin' Goin' On	1969	2.50	5.00	10.00
❑ Peacock 1658	Little Richard's Boogie/Directly from My Heart to You	1956	37.50	75.00	150.00
❑ Peacock 1673	Maybe I'm Right/I Love My Baby	1957	20.00	40.00	80.00
❑ RCA Victor 47-4392	Taxi Blues/Every Hour	1951	225.00	450.00	900.00
❑ RCA Victor 47-4582	Get Rich Quick/Thinkin' 'Bout My Mother	1952	200.00	400.00	800.00
❑ RCA Victor 47-4772	Why Did You Leave Me?/Ain't Nothin' Happenin'	1952	200.00	400.00	800.00
❑ RCA Victor 47-5025	Please Have Mercy on Me/I Brought It All on Myself	1952	150.00	300.00	600.00
❑ Reprise 0907	Freedom Blues/Dew Drop Inn	1970	2.50	5.00	10.00
❑ Reprise 0942	Greenwood Mississippi/I Saw Her Standing There	1970	2.50	5.00	10.00
❑ Reprise 1005	Shake a Hand (If You Can)/Somebody Saw You	1971	2.00	4.00	8.00
❑ Reprise 1043	Green Power/Dancing in the Street	1971	2.00	4.00	8.00
❑ Reprise 1062	Money Is/Money Runner	1972	2.00	4.00	8.00
—B-side by Quincy Jones					
❑ Reprise 1130	Mockingbird Sally/Nuki Suki	1972	2.00	4.00	8.00
❑ Specialty 561	Tutti-Frutti/I'm Just a Lonely Guy	1955	12.50	25.00	50.00
❑ Specialty 572	Long Tall Sally/Slippin' and Slidin' (Peepin' and Hidin')	1956	10.00	20.00	40.00
❑ Specialty 579	Rip It Up/Ready Teddy	1956	10.00	20.00	40.00
❑ Specialty 584	Heebie-Jeebies/She's Got it	1956	10.00	20.00	40.00
❑ Specialty 591	The Girl Can't Help It/All Around the World	1956	10.00	20.00	40.00
❑ Specialty 598	Lucille/Send Me Some Lovin'	1957	10.00	20.00	40.00
❑ Specialty 606	Jenny, Jenny/Miss Ann	1957	10.00	20.00	40.00
❑ Specialty 611	Keep a Knockin'/Can't Believe You Wanna Leave	1957	7.50	15.00	30.00
❑ Specialty 624	Good Golly, Miss Molly/Hey-Hey-Hey-Hey!	1958	7.50	15.00	30.00
❑ Specialty 633	Ooh! My Soul/True, Fine Mama	1958	6.25	12.50	25.00
❑ Specialty 645	Baby Face/I'll Never Let You Go	1958	6.25	12.50	25.00
❑ Specialty 652	She Knows How to Rock/Early One Morning	1958	6.25	12.50	25.00
❑ Specialty 660	By the Light of the Silvery Moon/Wonderin'	1959	6.25	12.50	25.00
❑ Specialty 664	Kansas City/Lonesome and Blue	1959	6.25	12.50	25.00
❑ Specialty 670	Shake a Hand/All Night Long	1959	6.25	12.50	25.00
❑ Specialty 680	Whole Lotta Shakin' Goin' On/Maybe I'm Right	1959	6.25	12.50	25.00
❑ Specialty 681	I Got It/Baby	1960	6.25	12.50	25.00
❑ Specialty 686	The Most I Can Offer/Directly from My Heart	1964	3.75	7.50	15.00
❑ Specialty 692	Bama Lama Bama Loo/Annie Is Back	1964	3.75	7.50	15.00
❑ Specialty 697	Keep a Knockin'/Bama Lama Bama Loo	1964	3.75	7.50	15.00
❑ Specialty 699	Poor Boy Paul/Wonderin'	1964	3.75	7.50	15.00
❑ Specialty 734	Chicken Little Baby/Oh Why	1974	—	3.00	6.00
❑ Vee Jay 612	Whole Lotta Shakin' Goin' On/Goodnight Irene	1964	2.50	5.00	10.00
❑ Vee Jay 625	Blueberry Hill/Cherry Red	1964	2.50	5.00	10.00
❑ Vee Jay 652	It Ain't Whatcha Do/Cross Over	1965	2.50	5.00	10.00
❑ Vee Jay 665	Without Love/Dance What You Wanna	1965	2.50	5.00	10.00
❑ Vee Jay 698	I Don't Know What You've Got But It's Got Me — Part I/ I Don't Know What You've Got But It's Got Me — Part II	1965	2.50	5.00	10.00
❑ Warner Bros. 28491	Big House Reunion/Somebody's Comin'	1987	—	2.00	4.00
❑ WTG 08492	Twins (Long)/Twins (Short)	1988	—	2.00	4.00
—With Philip Bailey					

Albums

Number	Title	Yr	VG	VG+	NM
❑ Accord SN-7123	Tutti Frutti	1981	2.50	5.00	10.00
❑ Audio Encores 1002	Little Richard	1980	6.25	12.50	25.00
❑ Buddah BDS-7501	Little Richard	1969	7.50	15.00	30.00
❑ Coral CRL 57446 [M]	Coming Home	1963	10.00	20.00	40.00
❑ Coral CRL 757446 [S]	Coming Home	1963	12.50	25.00	50.00
❑ Crown CLP-5362 [M]	Little Richard Sings Freedom Songs	1963	5.00	10.00	20.00
❑ Custom 2061 [M]	Little Richard Sings Spirituals	196?	3.00	6.00	12.00
❑ Epic EG 30428 [(2)]	Cast a Long Shadow	1971	5.00	10.00	20.00
❑ Epic PE 40389	Little Richard's Greatest Hits	1986	2.50	5.00	10.00
❑ Epic PE 40390	The Explosive Little Richard	1986	2.50	5.00	10.00
❑ Exact 206	The Best of Little Richard	1980	2.50	5.00	10.00
❑ GNP Crescendo GNP-9033	The Big Hits	1974	3.00	6.00	12.00

Number	Title (A Side/B Side)	Yr	VG	VG+	NM
❑ GRT 2103	The Original Little Richard	1977	2.50	5.00	10.00
❑ Guest Star GS-1429 [M]	Little Richard with Sister Rosetta Tharpe	196?	3.00	6.00	12.00
❑ Guest Star GSS-1429 [R]	Little Richard with Sister Rosetta Tharpe	196?	3.00	6.00	12.00
❑ Kama Sutra KSBS-2023	Little Richard	1970	6.25	12.50	25.00
❑ Mercury MG-20656 [M]	It's Real	1961	12.50	25.00	50.00
❑ Mercury SR-60656 [S]	It's Real	1961	15.00	30.00	60.00
❑ Modern 100 [M]	His Greatest Hits/Recorded Live	1966	5.00	10.00	20.00
❑ Modern 103 [M]	The Explosive Little Richard	1966	5.00	10.00	20.00
❑ Modern 1000 [S]	His Greatest Hits/Recorded Live	1966	6.25	12.50	25.00
❑ Modern 1003 [S]	The Explosive Little Richard	1966	6.25	12.50	25.00
❑ Okeh OKM 12117 [M]	The Explosive Little Richard	1967	6.25	12.50	25.00
❑ Okeh OKM 12121 [M]	Little Richard's Greatest Hits	1967	6.25	12.50	25.00
❑ Okeh OKS 14117 [S]	The Explosive Little Richard	1967	5.00	10.00	20.00
❑ Okeh OKS 14121 [S]	Little Richard's Greatest Hits	1967	5.00	10.00	20.00
❑ Pickwick SPC-3258	King of the Gospel Singers	197?	2.50	5.00	10.00
❑ RCA Camden CAL-420 [M]	Little Richard	1956	50.00	100.00	200.00
❑ RCA Camden CAS-2430(e)	Every Hour with Little Richard	1970	3.00	6.00	12.00
❑ Reprise MS 2107	The Second Coming	1973	5.00	10.00	20.00
❑ Reprise RS 6406	The Rill Thing	1971	5.00	10.00	20.00
❑ Reprise RS 6462	King of Rock and Roll	1972	5.00	10.00	20.00
❑ Rhino R1-70236	Shut Up! A Collection of Rare Tracks, 1951-1964	1988	3.00	6.00	12.00
❑ Scepter Citation CTN-18020	The Best of Little Richard	1972	3.00	6.00	12.00
❑ Specialty 100 [M]	Here's Little Richard	1957	175.00	350.00	700.00
❑ Specialty SP-2100 [M]	Here's Little Richard	1957	50.00	100.00	200.00
—Thick vinyl					
❑ Specialty SP-2103 [M]	Little Richard	1958	37.50	75.00	150.00
—Front cover photo occupies the entire cover					
❑ Specialty SP-2104 [M]	The Fabulous Little Richard	1958	37.50	75.00	150.00
—Thick vinyl					
❑ Specialty SP-2111	Little Richard — His Biggest Hits	1963	12.50	25.00	50.00
—Thick vinyl					
❑ Specialty SP-2113	Little Richard's Grooviest 17 Original Hits	1968	6.25	12.50	25.00
—Thick vinyl					
❑ Specialty SP-2136	Well Alright!	1970	5.00	10.00	20.00
❑ Specialty SP-8508 [(5)]	The Specialty Sessions	1989	10.00	20.00	40.00
❑ Spin-O-Rama 119 [M]	Clap Your Hands	196?	3.00	6.00	12.00
❑ Trip 8013 [(2)]	Greatest Hits	1972	3.00	6.00	12.00
❑ 20th Fox FXG-5010 [M]	Little Richard Sings Gospel	1959	25.00	50.00	100.00
❑ 20th Fox SGM-5010 [S]	Little Richard Sings Gospel	1959	37.50	75.00	150.00
❑ United US-7775	His Greatest Hits/Recorded Live	197?	2.50	5.00	10.00
❑ United US-7777	The Wild and Frantic Little Richard	197?	2.50	5.00	10.00
❑ United Artists UA-LA497-E	The Very Best of Little Richard	1975	2.50	5.00	10.00
❑ Upfront UPF-123	The Best of Little Richard	197?	2.50	5.00	10.00
❑ Upfront UPF-197	Little Richard Sings Gospel	197?	2.50	5.00	10.00
❑ Vee Jay LP-1107 [M]	Little Richard Is Back!	1964	12.50	25.00	50.00
❑ Vee Jay LPS-1107 [S]	Little Richard Is Back!	1964	17.50	35.00	70.00
❑ Vee Jay LP-1124 [M]	Little Richard's Greatest Hits	1965	6.25	12.50	25.00
❑ Vee Jay LPS-1124 [S]	Little Richard's Greatest Hits	1965	10.00	20.00	40.00
❑ Wing MGW-12288 [M]	King of the Gospel Singers	1964	3.75	7.50	15.00
❑ Wing SRW-16288 [S]	King of the Gospel Singers	1964	5.00	10.00	20.00

LITTLE RIVER BAND

45s

Number	Title (A Side/B Side)	Yr	VG	VG+	NM
❑ Capitol 4748	Lonesome Loser/Shut Down Turn Off	1979	—	2.00	4.00
❑ Capitol 4789	Cool Change/Middle Man	1979	—	2.00	4.00
❑ Capitol 4862	It's Not a Wonder/Man on the Run	1980	—	2.00	4.00
❑ Capitol A-5033	The Night Owls/Suicide Blvd.	1981	—	2.00	4.00
❑ Capitol A-5057	Take It Easy on Me/Orbit Zero	1981	—	2.00	4.00
❑ Capitol A-5061	Man on Your Mind/Orbit Zero	1982	—	2.00	4.00
❑ Capitol B-5185	The Other Guy/No More Tears	1982	—	2.00	4.00
❑ Capitol B-5231	We Two/Falling	1983	—	—	3.00
❑ Capitol B-5256	You're Driving Me Out of My Mind/Mr. Socialite	1983	—	—	3.00
❑ Capitol B-5411	Playing to Win/Through Her Eyes	1984	—	—	3.00
—As "LRB"					
❑ Capitol B-5469	Blind Eyes/Butterfly	1985	—	—	3.00
❑ Capitol B-5579	It Was the Night/Time for Love	1986	—	—	3.00
❑ Capitol B-5609	Paper Paradise/Face in a Crowd	1986	—	—	3.00
❑ Harvest 4318	It's a Long Way There/Meanwhile	1976	—	2.00	4.00
❑ Harvest 4380	I'll Always Call Your Name/Man in Black	1976	—	2.00	4.00
❑ Harvest 4428	Help is On Its Way/Inner Light	1977	—	2.00	4.00
❑ Harvest 4524	Happy Anniversary/Changed and Different	1978	—	2.00	4.00
❑ Harvest 4605	Reminiscing/So Many Paths	1978	—	2.00	4.00
❑ Harvest 4667	Lady/Take Me Home	1978	—	2.00	4.00
❑ MCA 53201	Love Is a Bridge/Inside Story	1988	—	—	3.00
❑ MCA 53424	It's Cold Out Tonight/The Great Unknown	1988	—	—	3.00
❑ MCA 53677	Listen to Your Heart/High Wire	1989	—	—	3.00
—B-side by Glenn Medeiros					
❑ MCA 53767	If I Get Lucky/Piece of My Heart	1989	—	—	3.00

Albums

Number	Title (A Side/B Side)	Yr	VG	VG+	NM
❑ Capitol SOO-11954	First Under the Wire	1979	2.00	4.00	8.00
❑ Capitol SWBK-12061 [(2)]	Backstage Pass	1980	2.50	5.00	10.00
❑ Capitol ST-12163	Time Exposure	1981	2.00	4.00	8.00
❑ Capitol ST-12247	Greatest Hits	1982	2.00	4.00	8.00
❑ Capitol ST-12273	The Net	1983	2.00	4.00	8.00
❑ Capitol SJ-12365	Playing to Win	1985	2.00	4.00	8.00
—As "LRB"					

Number	Title (A Side/B Side)	Yr	VG	VG+	NM
❑ Capitol ST-12480	No Reins	1986	2.00	4.00	8.00
❑ Capitol SN-16072	After Hours	1979	2.50	5.00	10.00
—First U.S. issue of their second Australian LP					
❑ Capitol SN-16141	Beginnings	1980	2.50	5.00	10.00
❑ Capitol SN-16142	Beginnings, Vol. 2	1980	2.50	5.00	10.00
❑ Capitol SN-16345	First Under the Wire	198?	—	3.00	6.00
—Budget-line reissue					
❑ Capitol SN-16346	Time Exposure	198?	—	3.00	6.00
—Budget-line reissue					
❑ Capitol SN-16454	Little River Band	1987	—	3.00	6.00
—Budget-line reissue					
❑ Capitol SN-16455	Diamantina Cocktail	1987	—	3.00	6.00
—Budget-line reissue					
❑ Capitol SN-16456	Sleeper Catcher	1987	—	3.00	6.00
—Budget-line reissue					
❑ Capitol SN-16457	Greatest Hits	1987	—	3.00	6.00
—Budget-line reissue					
❑ Harvest ST-11512	Little River Band	1976	2.50	5.00	10.00
❑ Harvest SW-11645	Diamantina Cocktail	1977	2.50	5.00	10.00
❑ Harvest SW-11783	Sleeper Catcher	1978	2.50	5.00	10.00
❑ MCA 6269	Get Lucky	1990	3.00	6.00	12.00
❑ MCA 42193	Monsoon	1989	2.50	5.00	10.00

LOBO

45s

Number	Title (A Side/B Side)	Yr	VG	VG+	NM
❑ Big Tree 112	Me and You and a Dog Named Boo/Walk Away from It All	1971	—	3.00	6.00
❑ Big Tree 116	She Didn't Do Magic/I'm the Only One	1971	—	2.50	5.00
❑ Big Tree 119	California Kid and Reemo/A Little Different	1971	—	2.50	5.00
❑ Big Tree 134	The Albatross/We'll Make It, I Know We Will	1972	—	2.50	5.00
❑ Big Tree 141	A Simple Man/Don't Expect Me to Be Your Friend	1972	—	2.50	5.00
❑ Big Tree 147	I'd Love You to Want Me/Am I True to Myself	1972	—	2.50	5.00
❑ Big Tree 158	Don't Expect Me to Be Your Friend/A Big Red Kite	1973	—	2.00	4.00
❑ Big Tree 15001	Standing at the End of the Line/Stoney	1974	—	2.00	4.00
❑ Big Tree 15008	Rings/I'm Only Sleeping	1974	—	2.00	4.00
❑ Big Tree 16001	It Sure Took a Long, Long Time/Running Deer	1973	—	2.00	4.00
❑ Big Tree 16004	How Can I Tell Her/Hope You're Proud of Me Girl	1973	—	2.00	4.00
❑ Big Tree 16012	There Ain't No Way/Love Me for What I Am	1973	—	2.00	4.00
❑ Big Tree 16033	Don't Tell Me Goodnight/My Mama Had Soul	1975	—	2.00	4.00
❑ Big Tree 16040	Would I Still Have You/Morning Sun	1975	—	2.00	4.00
❑ Elektra 47099	I Can't Believe You Anymore/Fight Fire with Fire	1980	—	2.00	4.00
❑ Evergreen 1028	Am I Going Crazy (Or Just Out of My Mind)/ I Don't Want to Want You	1985	—	2.50	5.00
—Stock copies have corrected title					
❑ Laurie 3526	Happy Days in New York City/My Friend Is Here	1969	3.75	7.50	15.00
—As "Kent LaVoie"					
❑ Lobo I	I Don't Want to Want You/No One Will Ever Know	1981	—	2.50	5.00
❑ Lobo IV	Come Looking for Me/I Don't Want to Want You	1982	—	2.50	5.00
❑ Lobo X	Living My Life Without You/A Simple Man	1982	—	2.50	5.00
❑ MCA 41065	Where Were You When I Was Falling in Love/ I Don't Wanna Make Love Anymore	1979	—	2.00	4.00
❑ MCA 41152	Holdin' On for Dear Love/Gus, the Dancing Dog	1979	—	2.00	4.00
❑ Warner Bros. 8493	Afterglow/Our Best Time	1977	—	2.00	4.00
❑ Warner Bros. 8537	You Are All I'll Ever Need/Our Best Time	1978	—	2.00	4.00

Albums

Number	Title (A Side/B Side)	Yr	VG	VG+	NM
❑ Big Tree 2003	Introducing Lobo	1971	3.75	7.50	15.00
❑ Big Tree 2013	Of a Simple Man	1972	3.75	7.50	15.00
❑ Big Tree 2100	Introducing Lobo	1973	3.00	6.00	12.00
—Reissue of 2003 with new cover					
❑ Big Tree 2101	Calumet	1973	3.75	7.50	15.00
❑ Big Tree BT 89501	Just a Singer	1974	3.00	6.00	12.00
❑ Big Tree BT 89505	A Cowboy Afraid of Horses	1975	3.00	6.00	12.00
❑ Big Tree BT 89513	The Best of Lobo	1976	3.00	6.00	12.00
❑ MCA 3194	Lobo	1979	2.50	5.00	10.00

LOGGINS, KENNY

45s

Number	Title (A Side/B Side)	Yr	VG	VG+	NM
❑ Columbia 13-02167	I'm Alright (Theme from "Caddyshack")/This Is It	1981	—	—	3.00
—Reissue					

Number	Title (A Side/B Side)	Yr	VG	VG+	NM
❑ Columbia 18-03192	Don't Fight It/The More We Try	1982	—	—	3.00
—A-side with Steve Perry					
❑ Columbia CNR-03270	Don't Fight It/(B-side blank)	1982	—	3.00	6.00
—Kenny Loggins with Steve Perry; one-sided budget release					
❑ Columbia 38-03377	Heart to Heart/The More We Try	1982	—	—	3.00
❑ Columbia CNR-03427	Heart to Heart/(B-side blank)	1982	2.00	4.00	8.00
—One-sided budget release					
❑ Columbia 38-03555	Welcome to Heartlight/Only a Miracle	1983	—	—	3.00
❑ Columbia 38-04310	Footloose/Swear Your Love	1984	—	—	3.00
❑ Columbia 38-04452	I'm Free (Heaven Helps the Man)/Welcome to Heartlight (Live)	1984	—	—	3.00
❑ Columbia 38-04849	Vox Humana/Love Will Follow	1985	—	—	3.00
❑ Columbia 38-04931	Forever/At Last	1985	—	—	3.00
❑ Columbia 38-05625	I'll Be There/No Lookin' Back	1985	—	2.00	4.00
❑ Columbia 38-05893	Danger Zone/I'm Gonna Do It Right	1986	—	—	3.00
❑ Columbia 38-05902	Playing with the Boys/Love Will Follow	1986	—	—	3.00
❑ Columbia 38-06690	Meet Me Half Way/Semifinal	1987	—	—	3.00
—B-side by Giorgio Moroder					
❑ Columbia 38-07971	Nobody's Fool (Theme from Caddyshack II)/I'm Gonna Do It Right	1988	—	—	3.00
❑ Columbia 38-08091	I'm Gonna Miss You/Isabella's Eyes	1988	—	—	3.00
❑ Columbia 3-10569	I Believe in Love/Enter My Dream	1977	—	2.50	5.00
❑ Columbia 3-10652	Celebrate Me Home/Why Do People Lie	1977	—	2.50	5.00
❑ Columbia 3-10794	Whenever I Call You "Friend"/Angelique	1978	—	2.50	5.00
—With Stevie Nicks on A-side (uncredited)					
❑ Columbia 3-10866	Easy Driver/Somebody Knows	1978	—	2.50	5.00
❑ Columbia 1-11109	This Is It/Will It Last	1979	—	2.50	5.00
❑ Columbia 1-11215	Keep the Fire/Now and Then	1980	—	2.00	4.00
❑ Columbia 1-11290	Love Has Come of Age/Junkanoo Holiday (Fallin', Flyin')	1980	—	3.00	6.00
❑ Columbia 1-11317	I'm Alright (Theme from "Caddyshack")/Lead the Way	1980	—	2.00	4.00
❑ Columbia 11-11417	Celebrate Me Home (Live)/Celebrate Me Home (Studio)	1980	—	2.50	5.00
❑ Columbia 38-68531	Tell Her/Hope for the Runaway	1989	—	2.00	4.00
❑ Columbia 38-74029	Conviction of the Heart/My Father's House	1991	—	2.00	4.00
Albums					
❑ Columbia PC 34655	Celebrate Me Home	1977	2.50	5.00	10.00
—Originals have no bar code					
❑ Columbia JC 35387	Nightwatch	1978	2.50	5.00	10.00
—Originals have no bar code					
❑ Columbia PC 35387	Nightwatch	198?	2.00	4.00	8.00
—Reissue with new prefix					
❑ Columbia JC 36172	Keep the Fire	1979	2.50	5.00	10.00
❑ Columbia C2X 36738 [(2)]	Kenny Loggins Alive	1980	3.00	6.00	12.00
❑ Columbia TC 38127	High Adventure	1982	2.50	5.00	10.00
❑ Columbia FC 39174	Vox Humana	1985	2.00	4.00	8.00
❑ Columbia OC 40535	Back to Avalon	1988	2.50	5.00	10.00

LOGGINS AND MESSINA

Number	Title (A Side/B Side)	Yr	VG	VG+	NM
45s					
❑ Columbia 10077	Changes/Get a Hold	1974	—	2.50	5.00
❑ Columbia 10118	Growin'/Keep Me in Mind	1975	—	2.50	5.00
❑ Columbia 10188	I Like It Like That/Angry Eyes	1975	—	2.50	5.00
❑ Columbia 10222	A Lover's Question/Oh, Lonesome Me	1975	—	2.50	5.00
❑ Columbia 10311	When I Was a Child/Peacemaker	1976	—	2.50	5.00
❑ Columbia 10376	Native Son/Pretty Princess	1976	—	2.50	5.00
❑ Columbia 10444	Angry Eyes/Watching the River Run	1976	—	2.50	5.00
❑ Columbia 45550	Same Old Wine/Vahevelia	1972	—	3.00	6.00
—As "Kenny Loggins and Jim Messina"					
❑ Columbia 45617	Nobody But You/Danny's Song	1972	—	3.00	6.00
—As "Kenny Loggins and Jim Messina"					
❑ Columbia 45664	Peace of Mind/House at Pooh Corner	1972	—	3.00	6.00
—As "Kenny Loggins and Jim Messina"					
❑ Columbia 45719	Your Mama Don't Dance/Golden Ribbons	1972	—	2.50	5.00
—As "Kenny Loggins and Jim Messina"; orange label					
❑ Columbia 45719	Your Mama Don't Dance/Golden Ribbons	1972	—	3.00	6.00
—As "Kenny Loggins and Jim Messina"; gray label					
❑ Columbia 45815	Thinking of You/Till the Ends Meet	1973	—	2.50	5.00
—A-side is a different version than on most LPs					
❑ Columbia 45952	My Music/A Love Song	1973	—	2.50	5.00
❑ Columbia 46010	Watching the River Run/Travelin' Blues	1974	—	2.50	5.00
Albums					
❑ Columbia C 31044	Kenny Loggins with Jim Messina Sittin' In	1972	2.50	5.00	10.00
❑ Columbia KC 31748	Loggins and Messina	1972	2.50	5.00	10.00
❑ Columbia KC 32540	Full Sail	1973	2.50	5.00	10.00
❑ Columbia PG 32848 [(2)]	On Stage	1974	3.00	6.00	12.00
—Original with no bar code					
❑ Columbia PC 33175	Mother Lode	1974	2.50	5.00	10.00
—Original with no bar code					
❑ Columbia PC 33578	Native Sons	1976	2.50	5.00	10.00
—Original with no bar code					
❑ Columbia PC 33810	So Fine	1975	2.50	5.00	10.00
—Original with no bar code					
❑ Columbia JG 34167 [(2)]	Finale	1977	3.00	6.00	12.00
❑ Columbia PC 34388	The Best of Friends	1976	2.50	5.00	10.00
—Original with no bar code					

LOOKING GLASS

Number	Title (A Side/B Side)	Yr	VG	VG+	NM
45s					
❑ Epic 10834	Don't It Make You Feel Good/Catherine Street	1972	—	2.50	5.00
❑ Epic 10874	Brandy (You're a Fine Girl)/One by One	1972	—	3.00	6.00

Number	Title (A Side/B Side)	Yr	VG	VG+	NM
❑ Epic 10900	Jenn-Lyne/Golden Rainbow	1972	—	2.50	5.00
❑ Epic 10953	Sweet Somethin'/Rainbow Man	1973	—	2.50	5.00
❑ Epic 11001	Jimmy Loves Mary-Anne/Wooly Eyes	1973	—	2.50	5.00
❑ Epic 11061	City Lady/Who's Gonna Sing My Rock 'N' Roll Song	1973	—	2.50	5.00
❑ Epic 11085	Sweet Somethin'/Who's Gonna Sing My Rock 'N' Roll Song	1974	—	2.50	5.00
❑ Epic 20001	Rock This Town/Highway to Hollywood	1974	—	2.50	5.00
Albums					
❑ Epic KE 31320	Looking Glass	1972	3.75	7.50	15.00
❑ Epic KE 32167	Subway Serenade	1973	3.75	7.50	15.00

LOS BRAVOS

45s

Number	Title (A Side/B Side)	Yr	VG	VG+	NM
❑ Parrot 3020	Bring a Little Lovin'/Make It Last	1968	3.00	6.00	12.00
❑ Parrot 3023	Dirty Street/Two People in Me	1968	2.50	5.00	10.00
❑ Press 60002	Black Is Black/I Want a Name	1966	3.75	7.50	15.00
❑ Press 60003	Going Nowhere/Brand New Baby	1966	2.50	5.00	10.00
❑ Press 60004	You'll Never Get the Chance Again/I'm All Ears	1967	2.50	5.00	10.00
Albums					
❑ Parrot PAS 71021	Bring a Little Lovin'	1968	20.00	40.00	80.00
—Among the other tracks, "Black Is Black" in in true stereo.					
❑ Press PR 73003 [M]	Black Is Black	1966	12.50	25.00	50.00
❑ Press PRS 83003 [R]	Black Is Black	1966	7.50	15.00	30.00

LOVERBOY

45s

Number	Title (A Side/B Side)	Yr	VG	VG+	NM
❑ Columbia 02068	The Kid Is Hot Tonite/Teenage Overdose	1981	—	2.00	4.00
❑ Columbia 02589	Working for the Weekend/Emotional	1981	—	2.00	4.00
❑ Columbia 02814	When It's Over/It's Your Life	1982	—	2.00	4.00
❑ Columbia 03054	Lucky Ones/Gangs in the Streets	1982	—	2.00	4.00
❑ Columbia 03108	Turn Me Loose/The Kid Is Hot Tonite	1982	—	—	3.00
—Reissue					
❑ Columbia 38-03346	Jump/Take Me to the Top	1982	—	2.00	4.00
❑ Columbia 03866	Working for the Weekend/When It's Over	1983	—	—	3.00
—Reissue					
❑ Columbia 38-03941	Hot Girls in Love/Meltdown	1983	—	—	3.00
❑ Columbia 38-04096	Queen of the Broken Hearts/Chance of a Lifetime	1983	—	—	3.00
❑ Columbia 05569	Lovin' Every Minute of It/Bullet in the Chamber	1985	—	—	3.00
❑ Columbia 05711	Dangerous/Too Much Too Soon	1985	—	—	3.00
❑ Columbia 05765	This Could Be the Night/It's Your Life	1986	—	—	3.00
❑ Columbia 05867	Lead a Double Life/Steal the Thunder	1986	—	—	3.00
❑ Columbia 06178	Heaven in Your Eyes/Friday Night	1986	—	—	3.00
❑ Columbia 07324	Notorious/Wildside	1987	—	—	3.00
❑ Columbia 07652	Love Will Rise Again/Read My Lips	1987	—	—	3.00
❑ Columbia 11421	Turn Me Loose/Prissy Prissy	1981	—	2.50	5.00
Albums					
❑ Columbia JC 36762	Loverboy	1980	2.00	4.00	8.00
❑ Columbia FC 37638	Get Lucky	1981	2.00	4.00	8.00
❑ Columbia QC 38703	Keep It Up	1983	2.00	4.00	8.00
❑ Columbia FC 39953	Lovin' Every Minute of It	1985	2.00	4.00	8.00
❑ Columbia OC 40893	Wildside	1987	2.00	4.00	8.00
❑ Columbia OC 45411	Big Ones	1989	3.00	6.00	12.00

LOVIN' SPOONFUL, THE

45s

Number	Title (A Side/B Side)	Yr	VG	VG+	NM
❑ Kama Sutra 201	Do You Believe in Magic/On the Road Again	1965	3.75	7.50	15.00
—Mostly red-orange label					
❑ Kama Sutra 205	You Didn't Have to Be So Nice/My Gal	1965	3.00	6.00	12.00
—Mostly red-orange label					
❑ Kama Sutra 208	Daydream/Night Owl Blues	1966	3.75	7.50	15.00
—Mostly red-orange label					
❑ Kama Sutra 209	Did You Ever Have to Make Up Your Mind/ Didn't Want to Have to Do It	1966	2.50	5.00	10.00
❑ Kama Sutra 211	Summer in the City/Butchie's Tune	1966	2.50	5.00	10.00
❑ Kama Sutra 216	Rain on the Roof/Pow	1966	2.50	5.00	10.00
❑ Kama Sutra 219	Nashville Cats/Full Measure	1966	2.50	5.00	10.00
❑ Kama Sutra 220	Darling Be Home Soon/Darlin' Companion	1967	2.50	5.00	10.00
❑ Kama Sutra 225	Six O'Clock/The Finale	1967	2.50	5.00	10.00

Number	Title (A Side/B Side)	Yr	VG	VG+	NM
❑ Kama Sutra 231	Lonely (Amy's Theme)/You're a Big Boy Now	1967	3.75	7.50	15.00
❑ Kama Sutra 239	She Is Still a Mystery/Only Pretty, What a Pity	1967	2.50	5.00	10.00
❑ Kama Sutra 241	Money/Close Your Eyes	1967	2.00	4.00	8.00
❑ Kama Sutra 250	Never Going Back/Forever	1968	2.00	4.00	8.00
❑ Kama Sutra 251	Revelation Revolution '69/Run with You	1968	2.00	4.00	8.00
❑ Kama Sutra 255	Me About You/Amazing Air	1968	2.00	4.00	8.00
❑ Kama Sutra 551	Summer in the City/You and Me and Rain on the Roof	1972	—	3.00	6.00
Albums					
❑ Accord SN-7196	Distant Echoes	1981	2.50	5.00	10.00
❑ Buddah BDM-5706	The Best of the Lovin' Spoonful	197?	3.00	6.00	12.00
❑ Buddah BLB6-8339	The Best of the Lovin' Spoonful	198?	2.50	5.00	10.00
—Reissue of 5706					
❑ 51 West Q 16023	... So Nice	1979	2.50	5.00	10.00
❑ Kama Sutra KLPS-750-2 [(2)]	24 Karat Hits	1968	5.00	10.00	20.00
❑ Kama Sutra KSBS-2011	The John Sebastian Song Book	1970	3.75	7.50	15.00
❑ Kama Sutra KSBS-2013	The Very Best of the Lovin' Spoonful	1970	3.75	7.50	15.00
❑ Kama Sutra KSBS-2029	Once Upon a Time	1971	3.75	7.50	15.00
❑ Kama Sutra KSBS-2608 [(2)]	The Best...Lovin' Spoonful	1976	5.00	10.00	20.00
❑ Kama Sutra KLP-8050 [M]	Do You Believe in Magic	1965	5.00	10.00	20.00
❑ Kama Sutra KLPS-8050 [S]	Do You Believe in Magic	1965	7.50	15.00	30.00
❑ Kama Sutra KLP-8051 [M]	Daydream	1966	5.00	10.00	20.00
❑ Kama Sutra KLPS-8051 [S]	Daydream	1966	7.50	15.00	30.00
❑ Kama Sutra KLP-8053 [M]	What's Up, Tiger Lily?	1966	5.00	10.00	20.00
❑ Kama Sutra KLPS-8053 [S]	What's Up, Tiger Lily?	1966	7.50	15.00	30.00
❑ Kama Sutra KLP-8054 [M]	Hums of the Lovin' Spoonful	1966	5.00	10.00	20.00
❑ Kama Sutra KLPS-8054 [S]	Hums of the Lovin' Spoonful	1966	7.50	15.00	30.00
❑ Kama Sutra KLP-8056 [M]	The Best of the Lovin' Spoonful	1967	3.75	7.50	15.00
—Came with four bonus photos of the band, which are priced separately					
❑ Kama Sutra KLPS-8056 [S]	The Best of the Lovin' Spoonful	1967	3.75	7.50	15.00
—Came with four bonus photos of the band, which are priced separately					
❑ Kama Sutra KLP-8058 [M]	You're a Big Boy Now	1967	5.00	10.00	20.00
❑ Kama Sutra KLPS-8058 [S]	You're a Big Boy Now	1967	5.00	10.00	20.00
❑ Kama Sutra KLP-8061 [M]	Everything Playing	1968	7.50	15.00	30.00
❑ Kama Sutra KLPS-8061 [S]	Everything Playing	1968	5.00	10.00	20.00
❑ Kama Sutra KLP-8064 [M]	The Best of the Lovin' Spoonful, Volume 2	1968	12.50	25.00	50.00
❑ Kama Sutra KLPS-8064 [S]	The Best of the Lovin' Spoonful, Volume 2	1968	5.00	10.00	20.00
❑ Kama Sutra KLPS-8073	Revelation: Revolution '69	1969	6.25	12.50	25.00
❑ Koala KO 14221	Day Dream	1979	2.50	5.00	10.00
❑ Pair PDL2-1200 [(2)]	The Best of the Lovin' Spoonful	1986	3.00	6.00	12.00
❑ Rhino RNLP-114	The Best of the Lovin' Spoonful, Vol. 2	1985	2.50	5.00	10.00

LULU

45s

Number	Title (A Side/B Side)	Yr	VG	VG+	NM
❑ Alfa 7006	I Could Never Miss You (More Than I Do)/Dance to the Feeling	1981	—	2.00	4.00
❑ Alfa 7011	If I Were You/You Win, I Lose	1981	—	2.00	4.00
❑ Alfa 7021	Who's Foolin' Who/You Win, I Lose	1982	—	2.00	4.00
❑ Atco 6722	Oh Me Oh My (I'm a Fool for You Baby)/ Sweep Around Your Own Back Door	1969	2.00	4.00	8.00
❑ Atco 6749	Hum a Song (From Your Heart)/Where's Eddie	1970	—	3.00	6.00
❑ Atco 6761	Good Day Sunshine/After the Feeling Is Gone	1970	—	3.00	6.00
❑ Atco 6774	Melody Fair/To the Other Woman	1970	—	3.00	6.00
❑ Atco 6819	Goodbye My Love, Goodbye/Everybody's Got to Clap	1971	—	3.00	6.00
❑ Atco 6885	It Takes a Real Man/You Ain't Wrong, You Just Ain't Right	1972	—	3.00	6.00
❑ Chelsea 78-0121	Make Believe World/Help Me Help You	1973	2.00	4.00	8.00
❑ Chelsea 3001	The Man Who Sold the World/Watch That Man	1974	7.50	15.00	30.00
—A David Bowie song on the A-side...and produced by Bowie, too					
❑ Chelsea 3009	The Man with a Golden Gun/Baby I Don't Care	1974	5.00	10.00	20.00
❑ Chelsea 3011	Take Your Mama for a Ride (Long)/ Take Your Mama for a Ride (Short)	1975	2.50	5.00	10.00
❑ Chelsea 3019	Boy Meets Girl/(B-side unknown)	1975	2.50	5.00	10.00
❑ Chelsea 3038	Heaven and Earth and the Stars/(B-side unknown)	1976	5.00	10.00	20.00
❑ Epic 10187	To Sir with Love/The Boat That I Row	1967	2.50	5.00	10.00
❑ Epic 10210	Dreamy Nights and Days/Let's Pretend	1967	2.00	4.00	8.00
❑ Epic 10260	Best of Both Worlds/Love Loves to Love Love	1967	2.00	4.00	8.00
❑ Epic 10302	Me, the Peaceful Heart/Look Out	1968	2.00	4.00	8.00
❑ Epic 10346	Sad Memories/Boy	1968	2.00	4.00	8.00
❑ Epic 10367	Morning Dew/You and I	1968	2.00	4.00	8.00
❑ Epic 10403	Without Him/This Time	1968	2.00	4.00	8.00
❑ Epic 10420	Rattler/I'm a Tiger	1968	2.00	4.00	8.00
❑ Parrot 9678	Shout/Forget Me Baby	1964	5.00	10.00	20.00
❑ Parrot 9714	Here Comes the Night/I'll Come Running	1964	5.00	10.00	20.00
❑ Parrot 9778	Leave a Little Love/He Don't Want Your Love Anymore	1965	5.00	10.00	20.00
❑ Parrot 9791	Try to Understand/Not in This Whole World	1965	5.00	10.00	20.00
❑ Parrot 40021	Shout/When He Touches Me	1967	2.50	5.00	10.00
❑ Rocket YB-11355	Don't Take Love for Granted/Love Is the Sweetest Mistake	1978	—	2.50	5.00
Albums					
❑ Alfa 10006	Lulu	1981	3.00	6.00	12.00
❑ Atco SD 33-310 [S]	New Routes	1970	3.00	6.00	12.00
❑ Atco SD 33-330 [S]	Melody Fair	1970	3.00	6.00	12.00
❑ Chelsea BCL1-0144	Lulu	1973	3.00	6.00	12.00
❑ Chelsea CHL-518	Heaven and Earth and the Stars	1976	5.00	10.00	20.00
❑ Epic LN 24339 [M]	To Sir with Love	1967	6.25	12.50	25.00
❑ Epic BN 26339 [P]	To Sir with Love	1967	7.50	15.00	30.00
❑ Epic BN 26536	It's Lulu	1970	3.00	6.00	12.00
❑ Harmony H 30249	To Love Somebody	1970	5.00	10.00	20.00

Number	Title (A Side/B Side)	Yr	VG	VG+	NM
❑ Parrot PA 61016 [M]	From Lulu with Love	1967	15.00	30.00	60.00
❑ Parrot PAS 71016 [S]	From Lulu with Love	1967	20.00	40.00	80.00
❑ Pickwick SPC-3237	Lulu	1973	2.00	4.00	8.00
❑ Rocket BXL1-3073	Don't Take Love for Granted	1978	3.00	6.00	12.00

LYMON, FRANKIE, AND THE TEENAGERS

45s

Number	Title (A Side/B Side)	Yr	VG	VG+	NM
❑ Gee 1002	Why Do Fools Fall in Love/Please Be Mine	1956	20.00	40.00	80.00
—Red and gold label					
❑ Gee 1012	I Want You to Be My Girl/I'm Not a Know-It-All	1956	12.50	25.00	50.00
—As "The Teenagers featuring Frankie Lymon"					
❑ Gee 1018	I Promise to Remember/Who Can Explain	1956	7.50	15.00	30.00
❑ Gee 1022	The ABC's of Love/Share	1956	7.50	15.00	30.00
❑ Gee 1026	I'm Not a Juvenile Delinquent/Baby Baby	1957	7.50	15.00	30.00
❑ Gee 1032	Teenage Love/Paper Castles	1957	7.50	15.00	30.00
❑ Gee 1035	Am I Fooling Myself Again/Love Is a Clown	197?	—	—	—
—Evidently a 1970s bootleg to fill in a gap in the Gee Records discography					
❑ Gee 1036	Miracle of Love/Out in the Cold Again	1957	7.50	15.00	30.00
❑ Gee 1039	Goody Goody/Creation of Love	1957	10.00	20.00	40.00
—Actually a Frankie Lymon solo recording; the first pressing credited the entire group					

Albums

Number	Title (A Side/B Side)	Yr	VG	VG+	NM
❑ Accord SN-7203	Why Do Fools Fall in Love	1982	2.50	5.00	10.00
❑ Gee GLP-701 [M]	The Teenagers Featuring Frankie Lymon	1956	125.00	250.00	500.00
—Red label					
❑ Murray Hill 148 [(5)]	Frankie Lymon and the Teenagers	198?	17.50	35.00	70.00
❑ Rhino R1-70918	The Best of Frankie Lymon and the Teenagers	1989	3.00	6.00	12.00

LYNYRD SKYNYRD

45s

Number	Title (A Side/B Side)	Yr	VG	VG+	NM
❑ Atina 129	Need All My Friends/Michelle	1978	3.75	7.50	15.00
❑ MCA 40258	Sweet Home Alabama/Take Your Time	1974	—	2.50	5.00
❑ MCA 40328	Free Bird/Down South Jukin'	1974	—	2.50	5.00
❑ MCA 40416	Saturday Night Special/Made in the Shade	1975	—	2.50	5.00
❑ MCA 40532	Double Trouble/Roll Gypsy Roll	1975	—	2.50	5.00
❑ MCA 40565	Gimme Back My Bullets/All I Can Do Is Write About It	1976	—	2.50	5.00
❑ MCA 40647	Gimme Three Steps/Travelin' Man	1976	—	2.50	5.00
❑ MCA 40665	Free Bird/Searching	1976	—	2.50	5.00
❑ MCA 40819	What's Your Name/I Know a Little	1977	—	2.50	5.00
—"What's Your Name" is a different mix than that on the Street Survivors LP.					
❑ MCA 40888	You Got That Right/Ain't No Good Life	1978	—	2.50	5.00
❑ MCA 40957	Down South Jukin'/Wino	1978	—	2.50	5.00
❑ MCA 53206	When You Got Good Friends/Truck Drivin' Man	1987	—	2.00	4.00
❑ MCA 60191	Sweet Home Alabama/Saturday Night Special	1976	—	2.00	4.00
—Reissue					
❑ Shade Tree 101	Need All My Friends/Michelle	1971	375.00	750.00	1500.
—As "Lynard Skynard"; approximately 300 copies pressed					
❑ Sounds of the South 40158	Gimme Three Steps/Mr. Banker	1973	2.00	4.00	8.00
❑ Sounds of the South 40231	Don't Ask Me No Questions/Take Your Time	1974	2.00	4.00	8.00
❑ Sounds of the South 40258	Sweet Home Alabama/Take Your Time	1974	2.00	4.00	8.00

Albums

Number	Title (A Side/B Side)	Yr	VG	VG+	NM
❑ MCA 363	(pronounced leh-nerd skin-nerd)	1975	3.00	6.00	12.00
—Reissue on black rainbow label					
❑ MCA 413	Second Helping	1975	3.00	6.00	12.00
—Reissue on black rainbow label					
❑ MCA 1448	Best of the Rest	1985	2.00	4.00	8.00
❑ MCA 2137	Nuthin' Fancy	1975	3.00	6.00	12.00
❑ MCA 2170	Gimme Back My Bullets	1976	3.00	6.00	12.00
❑ MCA 3019	(pronounced leh-nerd skin-nerd)	1976	2.50	5.00	10.00
—Second reissue with new number on black rainbow label					
❑ MCA 3020	Second Helping	1976	2.50	5.00	10.00
—Second reissue with new number on black rainbow label					
❑ MCA 3021	Nuthin' Fancy	1976	2.50	5.00	10.00
—Reissue with new number on black rainbow label					
❑ MCA 3022	Gimme Back My Bullets	1977	2.50	5.00	10.00
—Reissue with new number on black rainbow label					
❑ MCA 3029	Street Survivors	1977	6.25	12.50	25.00
—Originals with the band in flames on the front cover and a smaller band photo on the back cover					

Number	Title (A Side/B Side)	Yr	VG	VG+	NM
❑ MCA 3029	Street Survivors	1977	2.50	5.00	10.00
—After the band's plane crash, the "flames" photo was replaced with the back cover photo; the back cover is black with only the song titles					
❑ MCA 3047	Skynyrd's First and...Last	1978	3.00	6.00	12.00
—Originals with tan labels and gatefold cover					
❑ MCA 5221	(pronounced leh-nerd skin-nerd)	1980	2.00	4.00	8.00
❑ MCA 5222	Second Helping	1980	2.00	4.00	8.00
❑ MCA 5223	Street Survivors	1980	2.00	4.00	8.00
❑ MCA 5370	Best of the Rest	1982	2.50	5.00	10.00
—Original version					
❑ MCA 6001 [(2)]	One More From the Road	1976	3.75	7.50	15.00
—Originals with black rainbow label and gatefold cover					
❑ MCA 6897 [(2)]	One More From the Road	1985	2.50	5.00	10.00
—Most, if not all, of these pressings have no gatefold					
❑ MCA 6898 [(2)]	Gold & Platinum	1985	2.50	5.00	10.00
—Most, if not all, of these pressings have no gatefold					
❑ MCA 8011 [(2)]	One More From the Road	1977	3.00	6.00	12.00
—First reissue with new number					
❑ MCA 8027 [(2)]	Southern by the Grace of God	1988	3.00	6.00	12.00
❑ MCA 10014 [(2)]	One More From the Road	1980	2.50	5.00	10.00
—Second reissue					
❑ MCA 11008 [(2)]	Gold & Platinum	1979	3.00	6.00	12.00
—Originals with embossed gatefold cover					
❑ MCA 37069	Gimme Back My Bullets	1980	2.00	4.00	8.00
❑ MCA 37070	Nuthin' Fancy	1980	2.00	4.00	8.00
❑ MCA 37071	Skynyrd's First and...Last	1980	2.00	4.00	8.00
❑ MCA 37211	(pronounced leh-nerd skin-nerd)	1985	2.00	4.00	8.00
❑ MCA 37212	Second Helping	1985	2.00	4.00	8.00
❑ MCA 37213	Street Survivors	1985	2.00	4.00	8.00
❑ MCA 42084	Legend	1987	2.50	5.00	10.00
❑ MCA 42293	Skynyrd's Innyrds	1989	3.00	6.00	12.00
❑ Sounds of the South 363	(pronounced leh-nerd skin-nerd)	1973	5.00	10.00	20.00
❑ Sounds of the South 413	Second Helping	1974	5.00	10.00	20.00
—Both of the above are original pressings with yellow labels					

M

MACK, LONNIE

45s

Number	Title (A Side/B Side)	Yr	VG	VG+	NM
❑ Buccaneer 3001	Memphis/Lonnie on the Move	196?	2.00	4.00	8.00
—Reissue of Fraternity material					
❑ Capitol 4441	Running Wild/Funky Country Living	1977	—	2.50	5.00
❑ Elektra 45638	Memphis/Why	1968	2.50	5.00	10.00
❑ Elektra 45652	Save Your Money/In the Band	1969	2.50	5.00	10.00
❑ Elektra 45715	Lay It Down/She Even Woke Me Up to Say Goodbye	1971	2.00	4.00	8.00
❑ Elektra 45761	Rings/Florida	1972	2.00	4.00	8.00
❑ Epic 07973	Too Rock for Country, Too Country for Rock and Roll/Lucille	1988	—	2.00	4.00
❑ Epic 08117	Hard Life/50's-60's Man	1988	—	2.00	4.00
❑ Fraternity 906	Memphis/Down in the Dumps	1963	3.75	7.50	15.00
❑ Fraternity 912	Wham!/Susie-Q	1963	3.75	7.50	15.00
❑ Fraternity 918	Baby, What's Wrong/Where There's a Will	1963	3.00	6.00	12.00
❑ Fraternity 920	Say Something Nice to Me/Lonnie on the Move	1964	3.00	6.00	12.00
❑ Fraternity 925	I've Had It/Nashville	1964	3.00	6.00	12.00
❑ Fraternity 932	Chicken Pickin'/Sa-Ba-Hoola	1964	3.00	6.00	12.00
❑ Fraternity 938	Don't Make My Baby Blue/Oh Boy	1964	3.00	6.00	12.00
❑ Fraternity 942	Crying Over You/Coastin'	1965	3.00	6.00	12.00
❑ Fraternity 946	Tonky Go Go/When I'm Alone	1965	3.00	6.00	12.00
❑ Fraternity 951	Honky Tonk '65/Chicken Pickin'	1965	3.00	6.00	12.00
❑ Fraternity 957	Crying Over You/Are You Guilty	1966	3.00	6.00	12.00
❑ Fraternity 959	The Circus/Bucaroo	1966	3.00	6.00	12.00
❑ Fraternity 967	Tension (Part 1)/Tension (Part 2)	1966	3.00	6.00	12.00
❑ Fraternity 969	Wildwood Flower/Snow on the Mountain	1966	3.00	6.00	12.00
❑ Fraternity 981	I Left My Heart in San Francisco/Omaha	1967	2.50	5.00	10.00
❑ Fraternity 986	Save Your Money/Snow on the Mountain	1967	2.50	5.00	10.00
❑ Fraternity 1004	Soul Express/Down and Out	1968	2.50	5.00	10.00
❑ Fraternity 1278	Soul Express/I Found a Love	197?	—	3.00	6.00
❑ Roulette 7175	All We Need Is Love, You and Me/Highway 56	1975	—	3.00	6.00

Albums

Number	Title (A Side/B Side)	Yr	VG	VG+	NM
❑ Alligator AL-3903	The Wham of That Memphis Man	1987	2.50	5.00	10.00
—Reissue of Fraternity LP					
❑ Alligator AL-4739	Strike Like Lightning	1985	2.50	5.00	10.00
❑ Alligator AL-4750	Second Sight	1987	2.50	5.00	10.00
❑ Alligator AL-4786	Live!: Attack of the Killer V	1990	3.00	6.00	12.00
❑ Capitol ST-11619	Home at Last	1976	3.00	6.00	12.00
❑ Capitol ST-11703	Lonnie Mack and Pismo	1977	3.00	6.00	12.00
❑ Elektra EKS-74040	Glad I'm In the Band	1969	6.25	12.50	25.00
❑ Elektra EKS-74050	Whatever's Right	1969	6.25	12.50	25.00
❑ Elektra EKS-74077	For Collectors Only	1970	6.25	12.50	25.00
❑ Elektra EKS-74102	The Hills of Indiana	1971	6.25	12.50	25.00
❑ Epic FE 44075	Roadhouses and Dance Halls	1989	3.00	6.00	12.00
❑ Fraternity SF-1014 [M]	The Wham of That Memphis Man	1963	30.00	60.00	120.00
❑ Fraternity SSF-1014 [S]	The Wham of That Memphis Man	1963	75.00	150.00	300.00
❑ Trip TLX-9522 [(2)]	The Memphis Sounds of Lonnie Mack	1975	3.00	6.00	12.00

MADONNA

45s

Number	Title (A Side/B Side)	Yr	VG	VG+	NM
❑ Geffen GGEF 0540	Gambler/Crazy for You	198?	—	—	3.00
—"Back to Back Hits" series; first issue of A-side on U.S. 45					

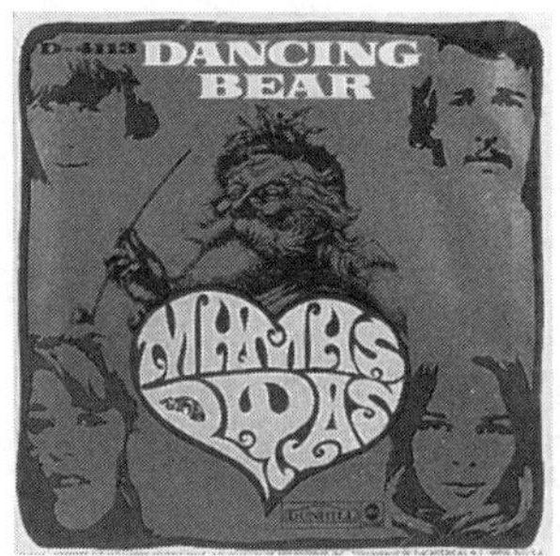

Number	Title (A Side/B Side)	Yr	VG	VG+	NM
❑ Geffen 29051	Crazy for You/No More Words	1985	—	—	3.00
—B-side by Berlin					
❑ Sire 19986	Keep It Together/(Instrumental)	1990	—	—	3.00
❑ Sire 21860	Express Yourself/Cherish	199?	—	—	3.00
—"Back to Back Hits" reissue					
❑ Sire 21861	Like a Prayer/Oh Father	199?	—	—	3.00
—"Back to Back Hits" reissue					
❑ Sire 21940	Who's That Girl/Causing a Commotion	198?	—	—	3.00
—"Back to Back Hits" reissue					
❑ Sire 21941	La Isla Bonita/Open Your Heart	198?	—	—	3.00
—"Back to Back Hits" reissue					
❑ Sire 21985	Live to Tell/True Blue	198?	—	—	3.00
—"Back to Back Hits" reissue					
❑ Sire 21986	Papa Don't Preach/Everybody	198?	—	—	3.00
—"Back to Back Hits" reissue					
❑ Sire 22723	Oh Father/Pray for Spanish Eyes	1989	—	—	3.00
❑ Sire 22883	Cherish/Supernatural	1989	—	—	3.00
❑ Sire 22948	Express Yourself/The Look of Love	1989	—	—	3.00
❑ Sire 27539	Like a Prayer/Act of Contrition	1989	—	—	3.00
❑ Sire 28224	Causing a Commotion/Jimmy, Jimmy	1987	—	—	3.00
❑ Sire 28341	Who's That Girl?/White Heat	1987	—	—	3.00
❑ Sire 28425	La Isla Bonita/(Instrumental)	1987	—	—	3.00
❑ Sire 28508	Open Your Heart/White Heat	1986	—	—	3.00
❑ Sire 28591	True Blue/Ain't No Big Deal	1986	—	—	3.00
❑ Sire 28591	True Blue/Ain't No Big Deal	1986	—	2.50	5.00
—Blue vinyl					
❑ Sire 28660	Papa Don't Preach/Pretender	1986	—	—	3.00
❑ Sire 28717	Live to Tell/(Instrumental)	1986	—	—	3.00
❑ Sire 28919	Dress You Up/Shoo-Be-Doo	1985	—	—	3.00
❑ Sire 29008	Angel/(12" Remix Edit)	1985	—	—	3.00
❑ Sire 29083	Material Girl/Pretender	1985	—	—	3.00
❑ Sire 29177	Lucky Star/I Know It	1984	—	2.00	4.00
❑ Sire 29210	Like a Virgin/Stay	1984	—	—	3.00
❑ Sire 29354	Borderline/Think of Me	1984	—	2.00	4.00
❑ Sire 29478	Holiday/I Know It	1983	—	2.00	4.00
❑ Sire 29841	Everybody/(Instrumental)	1982	5.00	10.00	20.00
Albums					
❑ Sire 23867	Madonna	1983	2.50	5.00	10.00
—Second pressing with 3:49 version of "Burning Up"					
❑ Sire 25157	Like a Virgin	1984	2.50	5.00	10.00
❑ Sire 25442	True Blue	1986	3.00	6.00	12.00
—With poster					
❑ Sire 25535	You Can Dance	1987	3.00	6.00	12.00
—With gold obi "Madonna and Dancing"					
❑ Sire 25844	Like a Prayer	1989	2.50	5.00	10.00
MAIN INGREDIENT, THE					
45s					
❑ Mercury 73831	Magic Touch/Very White	1976	—	2.50	5.00
—As "Tony Sylvester and the New Ingredient"					
❑ Mercury 73871	Puzuzu/Soca	1977	—	2.50	5.00
—As "Tony Sylvester and the New Ingredient"					
❑ Polydor 889910-7	I Just Wanna Love You/When We Need It Bad	1989	—	—	3.00
❑ RCA PB-12060	Think Positive/Spoiled	1980	—	2.00	4.00
—RCA 1980s titles as "Cuba Gooding and the Main Ingredient"					
❑ RCA PB-12107	What Can a Miracle Do/Makes No Diff'rence to Me	1980	—	2.00	4.00
❑ RCA PB-12320	Evening of Love/(Instrumental)	1981	—	—	—
—Unreleased					
❑ RCA PB-12340	I Only Have Eyes for You/Only	1981	—	2.00	4.00
❑ RCA PB-13045	Party People/Save Me	1982	—	2.00	4.00
❑ RCA Victor 47-9748	I Was Born to Lose You/Psychedelic Ride	1969	—	3.00	6.00
❑ RCA Victor 74-0252	Get Back/Brotherly Love	1969	—	3.00	6.00
❑ RCA Victor 74-0313	The Girl I Left Behind/Can't Stand Your Love	1970	—	2.50	5.00
❑ RCA Victor 74-0340	You've Been My Inspiration/Life Won't Be the Same (Without You)	1970	—	2.50	5.00
❑ RCA Victor 74-0385	Need Your Love/I'm Better Off Without You	1970	—	2.50	5.00
❑ RCA Victor 74-0401	I'm So Proud/Brother Love	1970	—	2.50	5.00
❑ RCA Victor 74-0456	Spinning Around (I Must Be Falling in Love)/Magic Shoes	1971	—	2.50	5.00

Number	Title (A Side/B Side)	Yr	VG	VG+	NM
❑ RCA Victor 74-0517	Black Seeds Keep On Growing/Baby Change Your Mind	1971	—	2.50	5.00
❑ RCA Victor 74-0603	I'm Leaving This Time/Another Day Has Come	1971	—	2.50	5.00
❑ RCA Victor 74-0731	Everybody Plays the Fool/Who Can I Turn To	1972	—	3.00	6.00
❑ RCA Victor 74-0856	You've Got to Take It (If You Want It)/Travelling	1973	—	2.50	5.00
❑ RCA Victor 74-0939	You Can Call Me Rover/I'm Better Off Without You	1973	—	2.50	5.00
❑ RCA Victor APBO-0046	Girl Blue/Movin' On	1973	—	2.50	5.00
❑ RCA Victor AMBO-0124	Everybody Plays the Fool/I'm So Proud	1973	—	2.00	4.00
—Gold Standard Series					
❑ RCA Victor APBO-0205	Just Don't Want to Be Lonely/Goodbye My Love	1974	—	2.50	5.00
❑ RCA Victor APBO-0305	Happiness Is Just Around the Bend/Why Can't We All Unite	1974	—	2.50	5.00
❑ RCA Victor PB-10095	California My Way/Looks Like Rain	1974	—	2.50	5.00
❑ RCA Victor PB-10224	Rolling Down a Mountainside/Family Man	1975	—	2.50	5.00
❑ RCA Victor PB-10334	The Good Old Days/I Want to Make You Glad	1975	—	2.50	5.00
❑ RCA Victor PB-10431	Shame on the World/Lillian	1975	—	2.50	5.00
❑ RCA Victor GB-10482	Why Can't We All Unite/Happiness Is Just Around the Corner	1975	—	2.00	4.00
—Gold Standard Series					
❑ RCA Victor GB-10483	Just Don't Want to Be Lonely/Goodbye My Love	1975	—	2.00	4.00
—Gold Standard Series					
❑ Zakia 015	Do Me Right/(B-side unknown)	1986	—	2.00	4.00
Albums					
❑ Collectables COL-5101	Golden Classics	198?	2.50	5.00	10.00
❑ Polydor 841249-1	I Just Wanna Love You	1989	3.00	6.00	12.00
❑ RCA Victor APL1-0314	Greatest Hits	1974	3.00	6.00	12.00
❑ RCA Victor APL1-0335	Euphrates River	1974	3.00	6.00	12.00
❑ RCA Victor APL1-0644	Rolling Down a Mountainside	1975	3.00	6.00	12.00
❑ RCA Victor APL1-1003	Shame On the World	1975	3.00	6.00	12.00
❑ RCA Victor APL1-1558	Music Maximus	1977	3.00	6.00	12.00
❑ RCA Victor APL1-1858	Super Hits	1977	3.00	6.00	12.00
❑ RCA Victor ANL1-2667	Rolling Down a Mountainside	1978	2.50	5.00	10.00
—Reissue of APL1-0644					
❑ RCA Victor AFL1-3641	Ready for Love	1980	2.50	5.00	10.00
❑ RCA Victor AFL1-3963	I Only Have Eyes for You	1981	2.50	5.00	10.00
❑ RCA Victor LSP-4253	The Main Ingredient L.T.D.	1970	3.00	6.00	12.00
❑ RCA Victor LSP-4412	Tasteful Soul	1971	3.00	6.00	12.00
❑ RCA Victor LSP-4483	Black Seeds	1971	3.00	6.00	12.00
❑ RCA Victor LSP-4677	Bitter Sweet	1972	3.00	6.00	12.00
❑ RCA Victor LSP-4834	Afrodisiac	1973	3.00	6.00	12.00

MAMAS AND THE PAPAS, THE

45s

Number	Title (A Side/B Side)	Yr	VG	VG+	NM
❑ ABC Dunhill 4125	Safe in My Garden/Too Late	1968	2.00	4.00	8.00
❑ ABC Dunhill 4150	For the Love of Ivy/Strange Young Girls	1968	2.00	4.00	8.00
❑ ABC Dunhill 4171	Do You Wanna Dance/My Girl	1968	2.00	4.00	8.00
❑ ABC Dunhill 4301	Step Out/Shooting Star	1972	—	3.00	6.00
❑ Dunhill 4020	California Dreamin'/Somebody Groovy	1966	2.50	5.00	10.00
—Most of the 1966 Dunhill singles credited "The Mama's and the Papa's"					
❑ Dunhill 4026	Monday, Monday/Got a Feeling	1966	2.50	5.00	10.00
❑ Dunhill 4031	I Saw Her Again/Even If I Could	1966	2.50	5.00	10.00
❑ Dunhill 4050	Look Through My Window/Once Was a Time I Thought	1966	2.50	5.00	10.00
❑ Dunhill 4057	Words of Love/Dancing in the Street	1966	2.50	5.00	10.00
❑ Dunhill 4077	Dedicated to the One I Love/Free Advice	1967	2.50	5.00	10.00
❑ Dunhill 4083	Creeque Alley/Did You Ever Want to Cry	1967	2.50	5.00	10.00
❑ Dunhill 4099	Twelve Thirty (Young Girls Are Coming to the Canyon)/Straight Shooter	1967	2.50	5.00	10.00
❑ Dunhill 4107	Glad to Be Unhappy/Hey Girl	1967	2.50	5.00	10.00
❑ Dunhill 4113	Dancing Bear/John's Music Box	1967	2.50	5.00	10.00
❑ Dunhill 4125	Safe in My Garden/Too Late	1968	6.25	12.50	25.00
—Without the "ABC" logo at top of label					
Albums					
❑ ABC AC-30005	The ABC Collection	1976	3.75	7.50	15.00
❑ ABC Dunhill DS-50031	The Papas and the Mamas	1968	3.75	7.50	15.00
—The five LPs above are reissues of records originally without the ABC logo					
❑ ABC Dunhill DS-50038	Golden Era, Volume 2	1968	5.00	10.00	20.00
❑ ABC Dunhill DS-50064	16 of Their Greatest Hits	1969	3.75	7.50	15.00
❑ ABC Dunhill DS-50073 [(2)]	A Gathering of Flowers	1970	6.25	12.50	25.00
❑ ABC Dunhill DSX-50100	Monterey International Pop Festival	1970	3.75	7.50	15.00
❑ ABC Dunhill DSX-50106	People Like Us	1971	3.00	6.00	12.00
❑ ABC Dunhill DSX-50145 [(2)]	20 Golden Hits	1973	5.00	10.00	20.00
❑ Dunhill D-50006 [M]	If You Can Believe Your Eyes and Ears	1966	5.00	10.00	20.00
—With scroll over toilet					
❑ Dunhill DS-50006 [S]	If You Can Believe Your Eyes and Ears	1966	6.25	12.50	25.00
—With scroll over toilet proclaiming "Includes California Dreamin'... Monday Monday... I Call Your Name"					
❑ Dunhill D-50010 [M]	The Mamas and the Papas	1966	5.00	10.00	20.00
❑ Dunhill DS-50010 [S]	The Mamas and the Papas	1966	6.25	12.50	25.00
❑ Dunhill D-50014 [M]	The Mamas and the Papas Deliver	1967	5.00	10.00	20.00
❑ Dunhill DS-50014 [S]	The Mamas and the Papas Deliver	1967	6.25	12.50	25.00
❑ Dunhill D-50025 [M]	Farewell to the First Golden Era	1967	5.00	10.00	20.00
❑ Dunhill DS-50025 [S]	Farewell to the First Golden Era	1967	5.00	10.00	20.00
❑ Dunhill DS-50031	The Papas and the Mamas	1968	6.25	12.50	25.00
❑ MCA 709	Farewell to the First Golden Era	1980	2.00	4.00	8.00
❑ MCA 710	The Papas and the Mamas	1980	2.00	4.00	8.00
❑ MCA 6019 [(2)]	The Best of the Mamas and the Papas	1986	3.00	6.00	12.00
❑ MCA 37145	16 of Their Greatest Hits	1980	2.00	4.00	8.00
❑ Pickwick SPC-3352	California Dreaming	1972	3.00	6.00	12.00

Number	Title (A Side/B Side)	Yr	VG	VG+	NM
MANCHESTER, MELISSA					
45s					
❑ Arista 0116	Midnight Blue/I Got Eyes	1975	—	2.00	4.00
❑ Arista 0146	Just Too Many People/This Lady's Not Home	1975	—	2.00	4.00
❑ Arista 0168	Just You and I/My Sweet Thing	1976	—	2.00	4.00
❑ Arista 0183	Better Days/Sing, Sing, Sing	1976	—	2.00	4.00
❑ Arista 0196	Happy Endings/Rescue Me	1976	—	2.00	4.00
❑ Arista 0218	Monkey See, Monkey Do/So's My Old Man	1976	—	2.00	4.00
❑ Arista 0237	Dirty Work/Be Somebody	1977	—	2.00	4.00
❑ Arista 0267	I Wanna Be Where You Are/No One's Ever Seen This Side of Me	1977	—	2.00	4.00
❑ Arista 0373	Don't Cry Out Loud/We Had This Time	1978	—	2.00	4.00
—Originals have black labels					
❑ Arista 0405	Theme from "Ice Castles"/Such a Night	1979	—	2.00	4.00
❑ Arista 0456	Pretty Girls/It's All in the Sky Above	1979	—	2.00	4.00
❑ Arista 0485	Fire in the Morning/Lights of Dawn	1980	—	2.00	4.00
❑ Arista 0551	If This Is Love/Talk	1980	—	2.00	4.00
❑ Arista 0579	Without You/Boys in the Back Room	1980	—	2.00	4.00
❑ Arista 0587	Lovers After All/Happier Than I've Ever Been	1981	—	2.00	4.00
—With Peabo Bryson					
❑ Arista 0657	Race to the End/Long Goodbyes	1982	—	2.00	4.00
❑ Arista 0676	You Should Hear How She Talks About You/Long Goodbyes	1982	—	2.00	4.00
❑ Arista 1028	Come In from the Rain/Hey Ricky (You're a Low Down Heel)	1982	—	2.00	4.00
❑ Arista 1045	Nice Girls/Hey Ricky (You're a Low Down Heel)	1983	—	2.00	4.00
❑ Arista 1057	My Boyfriend's Back/Looking for the Perfect Aah	1983	—	2.00	4.00
❑ Arista 9014	My Boyfriend's Back/Looking for the Perfect Aah	1983	—	—	3.00
❑ Arista 9087	No One Can Love You More Than Me/White Rose	1983	—	—	3.00
❑ Arista 9162	I Don't Care What the People Say/Emergency	1984	—	—	3.00
❑ Bell 45399	Never Never Land/Be Happy Now	1973	—	2.50	5.00
❑ Bell 45465	Heaven/Inclined	1974	—	2.50	5.00
❑ Casablanca 880308-7	Thief of Hearts/(B-side unknown)	1984	—	—	3.00
❑ MB 1005	Beautiful People/A Song for You	1967	3.75	7.50	15.00
❑ MCA 52575	Mathematics/So Full of Yourself	1985	—	—	3.00
❑ MCA 52616	Energy/So Full of Yourself	1985	—	—	3.00
❑ MCA 52688	Just One Lifetime/So Full of Yourself	1985	—	—	3.00
❑ MCA 52784	Music of Goodbye (Love Theme from Out of Africa)/Have You Got a Story for Me	1986	—	—	3.00
—With Al Jarreau					
❑ RCA Victor 74-0366	Tellin' the World/(B-side unknown)	1970	3.00	6.00	12.00
—With Grover Kimball					
Albums					
❑ Arista AL 4006	Home to Myself	1975	2.50	5.00	10.00
—Reissue of Bell 1123					
❑ Arista AL 4011	Bright Eyes	1975	2.50	5.00	10.00
—Reissue of Bell 1303					
❑ Arista AL 4031	Melissa	1975	2.50	5.00	10.00
❑ Arista AL 4067	Better Days & Happy Endings	1976	2.50	5.00	10.00
❑ Arista AL 4095	Help Is On the Way	1976	2.50	5.00	10.00
❑ Arista AL 4136	Singin'	1977	2.50	5.00	10.00
❑ Arista AB 4186	Don't Cry Out Loud	1978	2.50	5.00	10.00
❑ Arista AL 8055	Melissa	1983	2.00	4.00	8.00
—Budget-line reissue of 4031					
❑ Arista AL 8094	Emergency	1983	2.50	5.00	10.00
❑ Arista AL 8293	Greatest Hits	198?	2.00	4.00	8.00
—Budget-line reissue of 9611					
❑ Arista AL 8350	Hey Ricky	198?	2.00	4.00	8.00
—Budget-line reissue of 9574					
❑ Arista AL 8373	Don't Cry Out Loud	198?	2.00	4.00	8.00
—Budget-line reissue of 4186					
❑ Arista AL 9506	Melissa Manchester	1979	2.50	5.00	10.00
❑ Arista AL 9533	For the Working Girl	1980	2.50	5.00	10.00
❑ Arista AL 9574	Hey Ricky	1982	2.50	5.00	10.00
❑ Arista AL 9611	Greatest Hits	1983	2.50	5.00	10.00
❑ Bell 1123	Home to Myself	1973	3.00	6.00	12.00
❑ Bell 1303	Bright Eyes	1974	3.00	6.00	12.00
❑ MCA 5587	Mathematics	1985	2.50	5.00	10.00
❑ Mika 841273-1	Tribute	1989	3.00	6.00	12.00
❑ Pair PDL2-1086 [(2)]	The Many Moods of Melissa Manchester	1986	3.00	6.00	12.00

From '50s to New Wave: An Overview of Music Genres

"To each his own" is an adage that applies to music just as much, if not more, than every other area of life. We all have our own tastes, formed partly from our experience, our environment, our heritage, our friends, our individual temperament and tastes, and the time period in which we live. Needless to say, music encompasses a vastly diverse range of styles.

The following pages contain just a sampling of some of the genres that have developed over the last century and that have both shaped and mirrored our culture.

Not all the albums in this section are listed in the price guide part of this book. They are presented here to illustrate some of the major influences in each genre rather than to list their value. Often, some of the most well known albums were produced in such large numbers that their commonness makes them of relatively little monetary value to collectors. Still, they are priceless to those who love the music.

’50s/Rockabilly

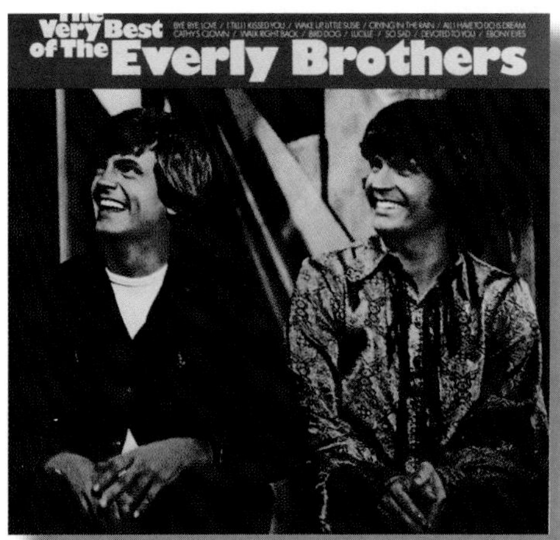

The Everly Brothers

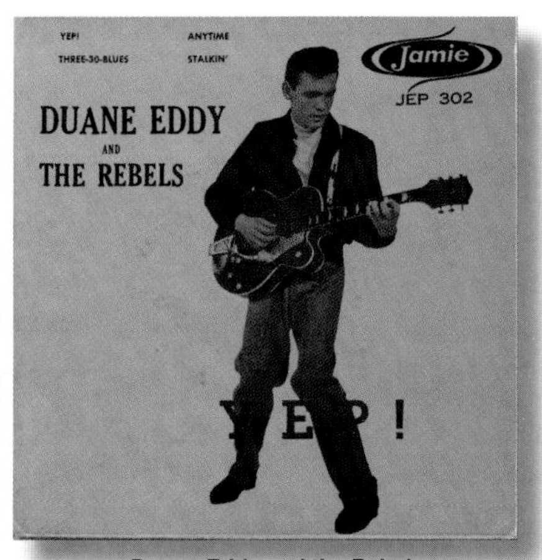

Duane Eddy and the Rebels

Del Shannon

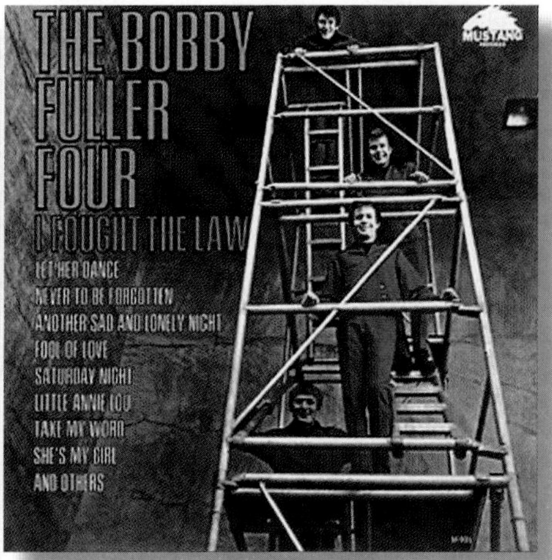

The Bobby Fuller Four

Early rock ‘n’ roll grew out of an amalgam of influences. A swaggering hybrid of blues (the kind emerging from Louisiana, Texas, California and Chicago) and jump blues — otherwise known as R&B — that featured boogie-woogie rhythms and a strong backbeat, rock ‘n’ roll also embraced country and western music, Appalachian folk, jazz and gospel.

Rock ‘n’ roll rose to popularity in the late 1940s and early ’50s with a basic format of one or two electric guitars, a string bass or an electric bass (which came into vogue after the mid ’50s), and a drum kit, augmented by piano or saxophone. Its social impact would be felt for generations, infiltrating all aspects of entertainment, including movies, TV and radio.

An offshoot of rock ‘n’ roll, rockabilly was a rowdy mix of hillbilly country, Western swing, blues (and jump blues) and boogie woogie in a musical style that leapt out of speakers and got joints jumping. Among its evangelists were Carl Perkins, Elvis Presley, Bill Haley and Johnny Cash.

Blues

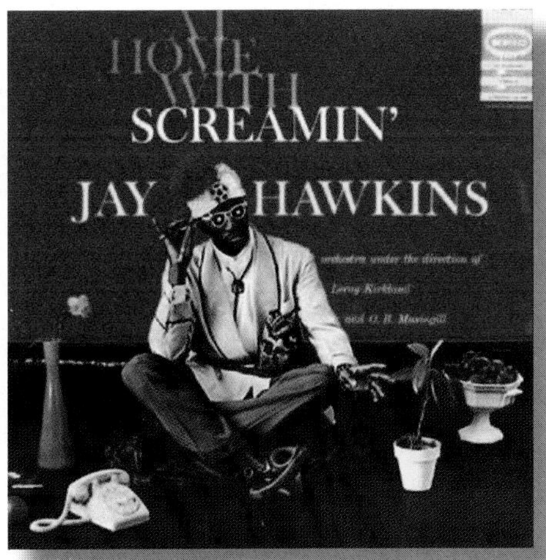

Jay Hawkins

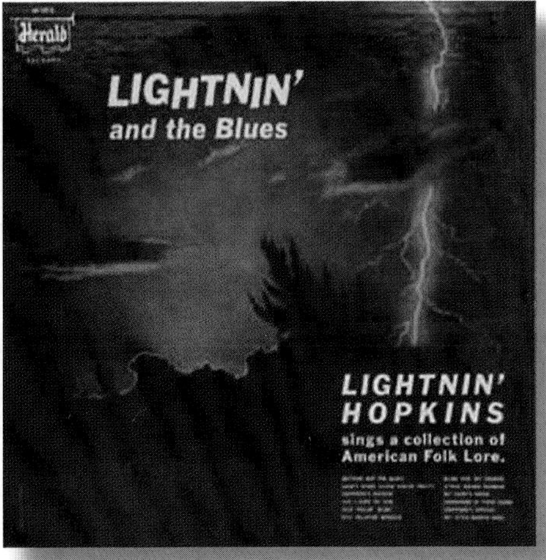

Lightnin' Hopkins

John Lee Hooker

Leadbelly

The Blues hasn't changed much over the years. One of the most traditional and expressive forms of music, it is structured simply, mostly employing basic, three-chord progressions. But, over the years, many innovators have taken that template and experimented with it, often altering it beyond recognition.

A direct descendant of African spirituals and worksongs, the blues has its foundations in the late 1800s and the oral tradition of southern African-Americans, who passed the songs down to generations that followed. Blending with American folk and Appalachian country, the blues mutated into new, regional strains, but during the 1900s, it retained its rustic character, thanks to the bucolic acoustic guitars and pianos that produced it. That changed with World War II, as traditionalists hung onto its acoustic origins, while others brought jazz into the mix. Eventually, spurred on by Muddy Waters, the majority of bluesmen began playing on electric instruments, and the blues continued to evolve, though many have preserved its acoustic traditions.

British Invasion

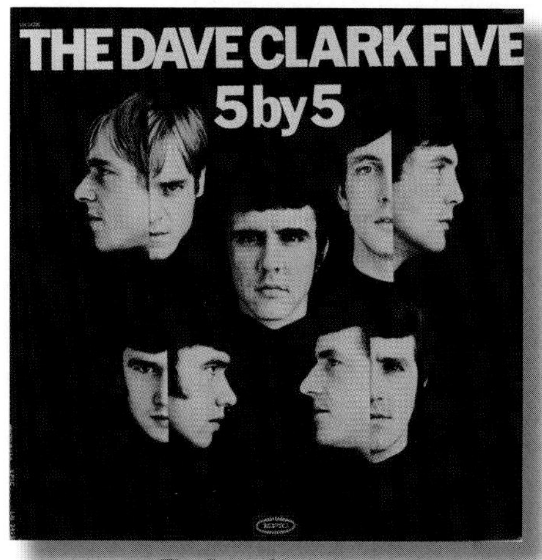

The Dave Clark Five

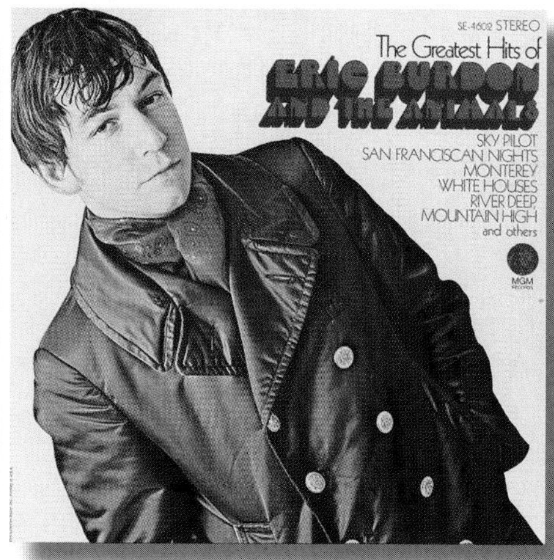

Eric Burdon and the Animals

The Dave Clark Five

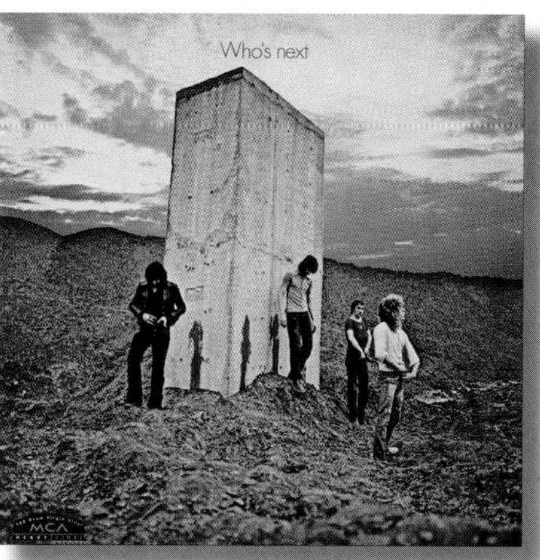

The Who

Between 1964 and 1967, America was overrun with rock 'n' roll, beat, and pop imports from England, but the story goes back further than that. American rock 'n' roll gained a foothold in U.K., just as did in the States, and that, in part, fueled the movement. But, so did skiffle, an English reworking of traditional American folk.

Liverpool was ground zero for the British Invasion, as bands like The Beatles, The Searchers, the Fourmost and Gerry and the Pacemakers cut their teeth, becoming tight units that developed a strong R&B-influenced sound rooted in early rock 'n' roll. And that Merseybeat scene birthed still more acts.

It was The Beatles who paved the way with their hit, "I Wanna Hold Your Hand." In their wake came the Dave Clark Five, The Rolling Stones, The Who, The Kinks and The Yardbirds, among others. Hits from across the pond scaled U.S. charts, with acts like Herman's Hermits, the Animals, Manfred Mann and others scoring big with American audiences.

Classic Rock

Grateful Dead

Jimi Hendrix

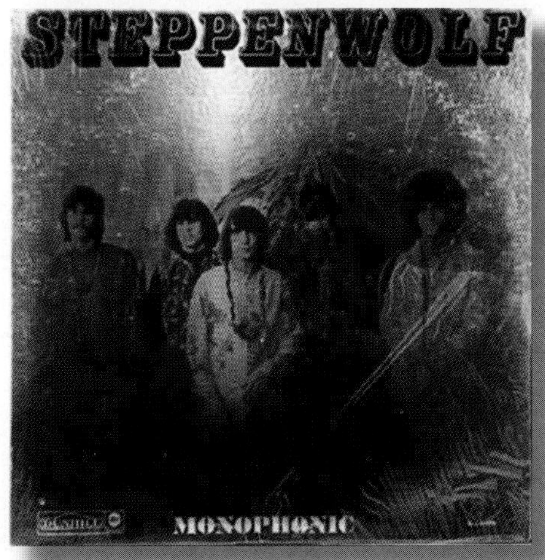

Steppenwolf

Aerosmith

Not so much a genre as a radio programming format, classic rock emerged from the album oriented rock format of the early '80s, becoming an umbrella term for the rock music played on FM stations produced by a diverse list of artists popular during the late '60s, the '70s and early '80s.

It all started with The Beatles' trailblazing "Sgt. Pepper's Lonely Hearts Club Band" album and the rise of FM radio. The progressive rock direction of many FM stations in the '60s and '70s grew into more commercially viable AOR programming. British hard rock acts like Black Sabbath and Cream and progressive-rock bands such as Supertramp, Jethro Tull, and Yes formed the core of classic rock, which came to include American acts like Jimi Hendrix, Aerosmith, The Doors, Boston, Fleetwood Mac, Crosby, Stills & Nash, Creedence Clearwater Revival, Reo Speedwagon, Steve Miller Band, Grand Funk Railroad and Lynyrd Skynyrd.

Country

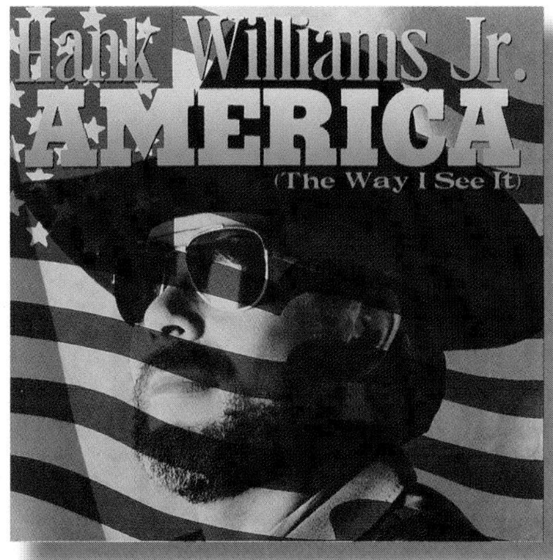

Hank Williams Jr.

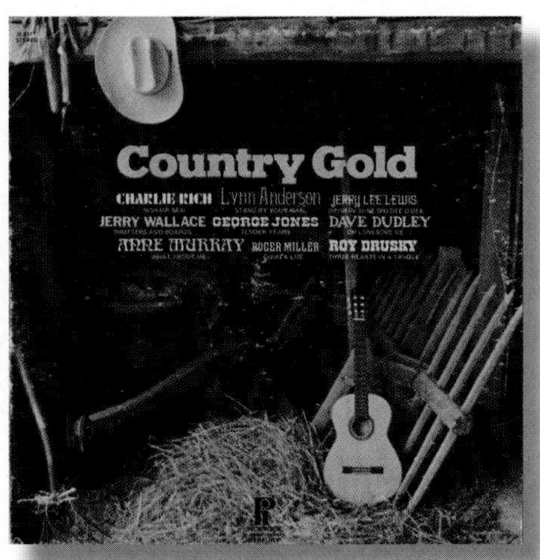

Charlie Rich, Jerry Lee Lewis, George Jones and Others

Merle Haggard

Dolly Parton

Originating in the Southern United States, country was once known as hillbilly music, and then, country and western, as those associated with the genre took exception to term "hillbilly music." The term country took hold in the '70s.

A mix of traditional folk music, blues, gospel music, Celtic music, hokum, and old-time music, country music evolved in the 1920s. Regional differences grew, as artists from the Southwestern U.S. developed more of a country and western sound that arose from the different ethnic groups of the region.

Other sub-genres appeared, including the electrified, honky-tonkin' "Bakersfield Sound," the bluegrass sounds of fiddle, banjo and mandolin, Bob Willis' Western Swing, and the outlaw country of the '70s that propelled Willie Nelson, Waylon Jennings and Kris Kristofferson into the national spotlight. Each one was distinguished from the rest by its use of rhythms and chord structures.

Country was the tradition that Elvis grew out of, and the musical form remains popular today, with artists like Garth Brooks ruling the charts.

Doo-Wop

The Flamingos

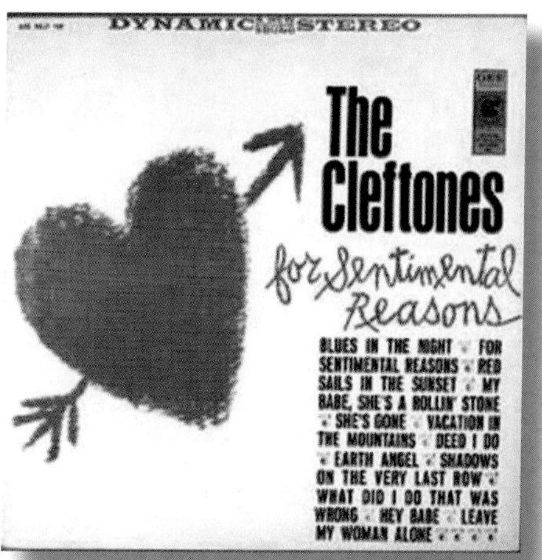

The Cleftones

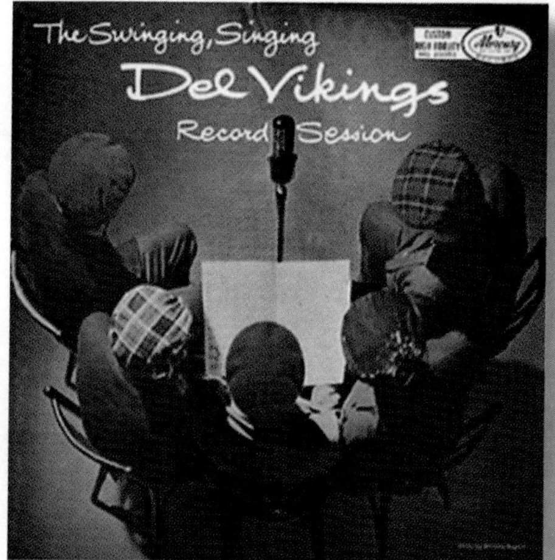

The Del Vikings

The Five Satins

A vocal-based style of rhythm and blues, doo-wop originated in the black community and rose up from the streets of New York City and Philadelphia to become one of the most popular music styles of the '50s and early '60s.

Characterized by smooth harmonies, the term "doo-wop" (sometimes referred to as "group vocal harmony") came from the ad-lib syllables sung in harmony doo-wop songs.

As a genre, doo-wop came of age around 1951, with hit songs such as "My Reverie" by The Larks, "I Couldn't Sleep a Wink Last Night" by The Mello-Moods, "Glory of Love" by The Five Keys, "Shouldn't I Know" by The Cardinals, and "It Ain't the Meat" by The Swallows climbing the charts.

Two years later, radio legend Alan Freed began introducing white audiences to doo-wop, and groups like the Coasters, the Drifters, the Moonglows, and the Platters took off, along with The Spaniels and The Flamingos. Many consider 1961 the apex for doo-wop. Then came the British Invasion and doo-wop's popularity fell.

Folk

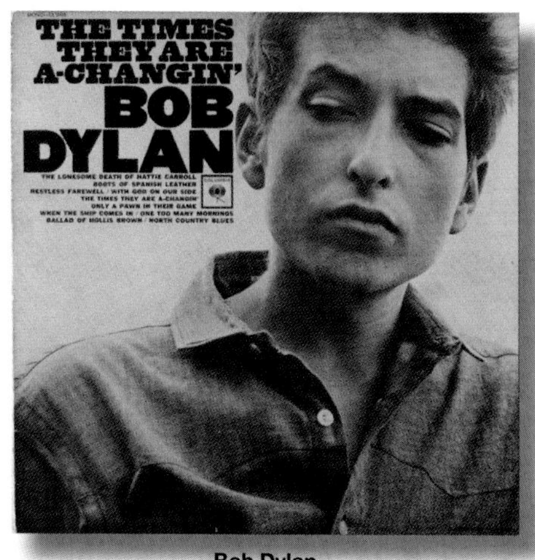

Bob Dylan

Bob Dylan

Arlo Guthrie

The Kingston Trio

In essence, folk music is traditional music. But, one culture's definition of what is "traditional music" usually differs from that of other cultures. As far as America goes, folk music refers to the American folk music revival of the 1950s and the '60s brought to bear by artists like Joan Baez, Bob Dylan, Pete Seeger and Woody Guthrie.

Characterized by acoustic instrumentation, including guitars and banjos, the folk movement's revival is said to have started with Seeger and his group, the Weavers. In 1949, they scored a hit with Leadbelly's "Goodnight, Irene." Folk music became a cult phenomenon in the '50s, its acoustic stirrings lighting up coffeehouses and college campuses in major cities. A watershed moment for folk came when the Kingston Trio was signed to Capitol Records after being discovered at a college club. In 1958, they had a gold record with the old-time folk song "Tom Dooley."

As the social issues of the '60s began to take on more importance, artists like Baez and Dylan became prominent. Folk rock, as a genre, later evolved, with Dylan embracing electric instrumentation.

Garage/Pyschedelia

The Fugs

The Chocolate Watch Band

Question Mark & The Mysterians

The Kingsmen

As the drug culture of the '60s expanded, the music of the times reflected this trend by growing more and more hallucinogenic, trying to replicate the effects of mind-altering substances through trippy electronic effects such as distortion, delays, phase shifting, loops, and echo.

Heightened production values, lyrics that probed the sub-conscious, and modal melodies took early, blues-based rock to strange new worlds. Artists began to view the studio as another instrument. Sitars and other exotic instruments were incorporated into the mix, along with a variety of keyboards, including the harpsichord and the mellotron. The Beatles were at the forefront of this revolution, taking baby steps with the album Revolver and then blossoming fully with Sgt. Pepper's Lonely Hearts Club Band.

Unlike the mellow, dream-like qualities of psychedelia, garage-rock was a gritty, gutteral howl that seemed almost tribal in its execution, with bands like The Sonics and Iggy Pop and The Stooges roughing up early rock 'n' roll. The two seemingly disparate genres would, however, form an unlikely bond in later years.

Heavy Metal

Black Sabbath

Def Leppard

AC/DC

Kiss

Ear-splittingly loud and powered by guitar and drums, heavy metal is rooted in blues-rock and psychedelia. Early progenitors like Black Sabbath, Deep Purple and Led Zeppelin developed a thick, weighty sound made all the more voluminous by highly amplified distortion and fast guitar solos. And it is, and always has been, dripping with machismo and theatricality.

Often trashed by critics, heavy metal, nonetheless, has attracted legions of fans, referred to as "metalheads" or "headbangers." And its fanbase has only grown over the years as new sub-genres like death metal, thrash metal, and the hair metal of the '80s emerged. By the mid-'70s, heavy metal had lost much of its blues influence, thanks to the rise of bands like Judas Priest and The New Wave of British Heavy Metal that followed, which took inspiration from punk rock and made speed more of a factor.

A more commercially viable strain emerged in the '80s with glam metal, which put as much emphasis on looks as it did the music. Below the surface, other mutated forms of metal welcomed funk and hip-hop, while others took on a more extreme character.

Jazz

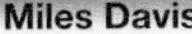
Miles Davis

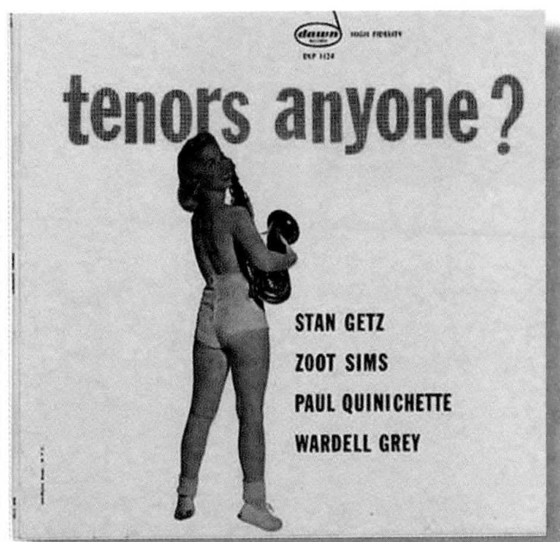

Stan Getz, Zoot Sims, Paul Quinichette, Wardell Grey

Chet Baker Quartet

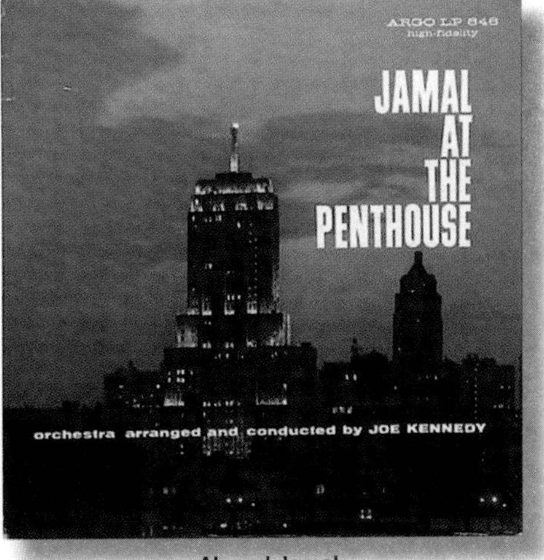

Ahmad Jamal

A truly American art form, jazz, along with the blues, is one of the only musical genres indigenous to the United States. It gained critical acceptance among music scholars by taking chances with its spirit of exploration and wild improvisation.

Originally, jazz was performed by swinging big bands that made music people could dance to. That changed as improvisation took over, pushing jazz into new, unchartered territory and taking dance out of the equation.

Over the years, as jazz evolved, it splintered into different styles. Competing against the relaxed, yet sophisticated, cool jazz was a new form known as be-bop, practiced by such luminaries as Charlier Parker, John Coltrane and Miles Davis, that relied on fast playing and colliding, careening rhythms. Free jazz adopted an atonal, almost nervous, quality, while soul jazz tilled earthy grooves.

At its heart, though, jazz was based in the blues, but what set it apart from other genres was the preternatural interplay of its groups and the chances it took with improvisation.

Punk/New Wave

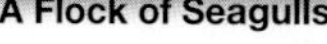
A Flock of Seagulls

Blondie

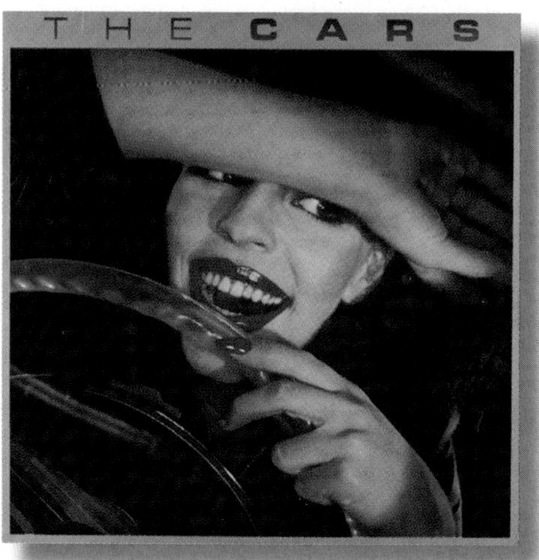

The Cars

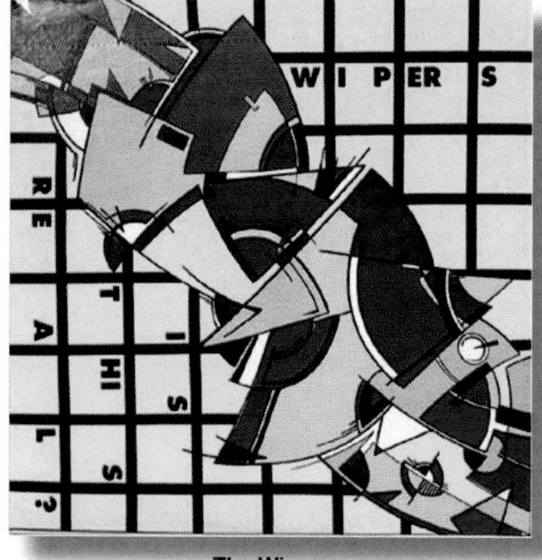
The Wipers

In response to the excesses of '70s rock, especially progressive rock, punk emerged both in the States and in Britain in the latter part of the decade, though proto-punks like Iggy Pop and The Stooges and the Velvet Underground had prophesied its emergence years earlier.

Centered around a primal makeup of guitars, drums and bass, punk sought a return to the no-nonsense rock 'n' roll of the '50s, while giving it a decidedly edgier, angrier, more political tone. Bands like The Ramones in America and The Sex Pistols in England, with their monumental album Never Mind The Bollocks, Here's the Sex Pistols, played short, three-minute bursts of gutteral, focused rage, though the Ramones spiked their snotty sound with a healthy dose of humor. Later, acts like The Clash and the Talking Heads expanded the template, incorporating reggae and funk elements to break punk out of its myopic mold. Out of punk came new wave in the '80s. Commercially more acceptable, new wave adopted the use of synthesizers for a more stylized sound that welcomed increased production values. Many punks denounced it, however.

Pop

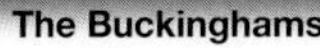
The Buckinghams

The Cowsills

Leslely Gore

Nat King Cole

Pop music encompasses a broad range of genres, as it is basically a catch-all term for the popular music of the day. But, dig a little deeper and you find that pop music is actually a sub-genre of contemporary popular music that typically features simple, hummable melodies, lighthearted rhythms and beats, and repeating structures—with verse, chorus, and bridge being elements used to construct songs. Lyrically, pop songs focus on love and loss, and are imbued with emotion.

Welcoming rock 'n' roll and other forms of music into the mix, including disco, reggae and even country, pop artists sought to write songs that get stuck in your memory. The pop artist began to emerge in the '30s and '40s, but it was the '50s and the birth of rock 'n' roll that fueled an explosion of pop idols. Big-name entertainers like Frank Sinatra, Dean Martin, Peggy Lee, and Bing Crosby butted up against rock 'n' roll and R&B heroes such as Elvis, Bill Haley and the Comets, and Ray Charles. The '60s saw the emergence of pop groups, with The Beatles, The Who, The Rolling Stones, and The Beach Boys scaling the charts, while acts like ABBA and the Bee Gees sold big in the '70s.

Progressive Rock

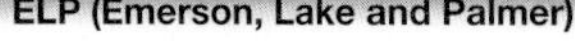

ELP (Emerson, Lake and Palmer)

Genesis

ELP (Emerson, Lake and Palmer)

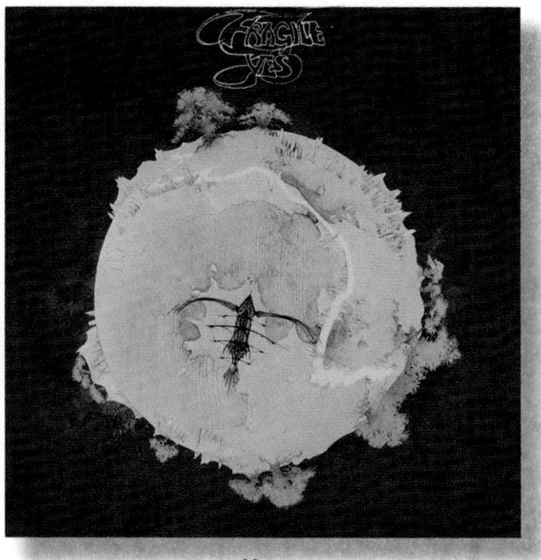

Yes

Emerging in the late '60s and early '70s, progressive rock, often called "prog rock" or "prog," was an experimental wing of rock that produced complex compositions with classical, jazz, and avant-garde elements. Using guitar, bass, keyboards, drums, and other instrumentation, prog acts sought to alter and experiment with the standard verse-chorus-bridge song structures, and extended soloing was embraced as technically proficient musicians showed off their virtuosity.

Starting with a base of blues rock, psychedelic rock, folk, and hard rock, prog acts such as Yes, King Crimson, Genesis, Pink Floyd, Emerson, Lake and Palmer, and Jethro Tull were also influenced by classical music and jazz fusion and introduced conceptual, abstract lyrics that often approached fantasy literature.

Progressive rock's heyday was in the 1970s, but its popularity has continued, with bands like Rush and Porcupine Tree carrying the flag for the genre.

Soul/Rhythm & Blues

Aretha Franklin

The Brothers Johnson

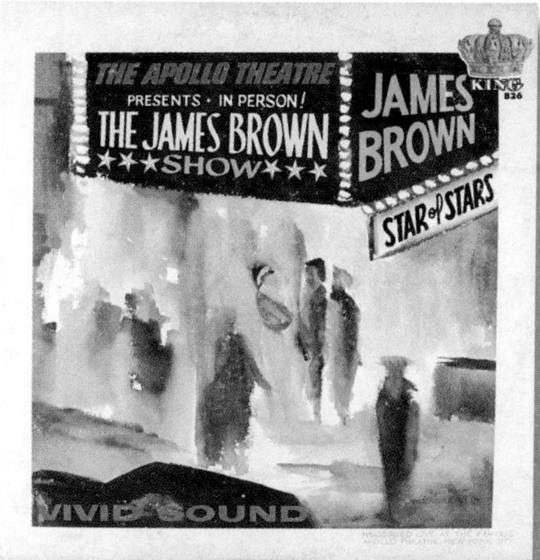

James Brown

The Vibrations

Without R&B, the rock 'n' roll revolution never would have happened. A form of music that grew out of the jump blues of the late '40s, maintaining its high-energy drive and hard-hitting rhythms, R&B employed sparser instrumentation and favored song structure over improvisation, pairing blues chord changes with an insistent backbeat.

In the '50s, vocalists like Ray Charles and Ruth Brown held dominion over R&B, with vocal groups like the Drifters and the Coasters also scoring hits. Then came soul, a variety of R&B that was funkier and looser that became an umbrella term for a number of R&B-based music styles. Within soul was a great diversity. Two of the main varieties were Motown's catchy, buoyant, pop-infused R&B and Stax/Volt's tougher, horn-swaddled sound. At first, during the early '60s, soul didn't stray far from its R&B roots, but in time, different regions of America produced new strains of soul—with smooth vocals dominating urban centers, while the South embraced a louder, more rugged sound. Whatever the type, soul ruled Black music charts throughout the '60s.

Surf

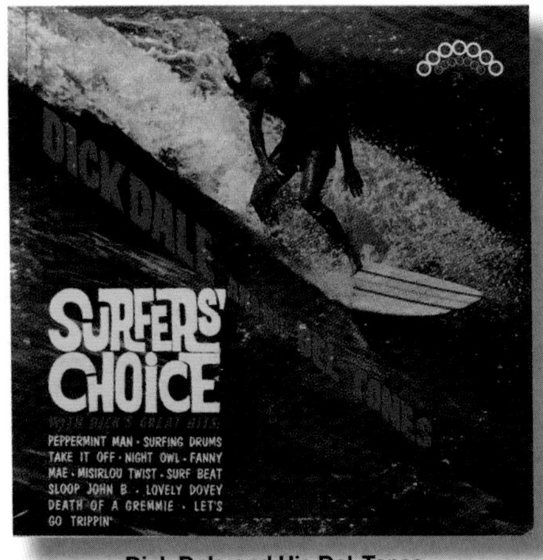

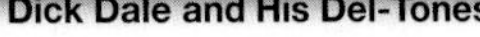
Dick Dale and His Del-Tones

The Beach Boys

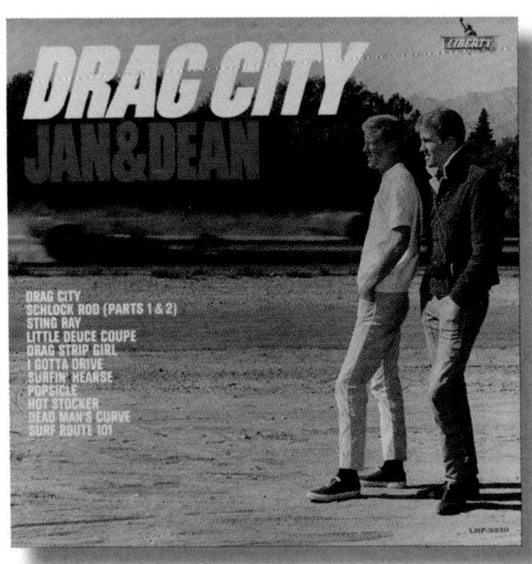

Jan & Dean

The Trashmen

Surf music originated in California surf culture and peaked in the '50s and '60s.

There are three varieties of surf music. One is the instrumental dance music of acts like Dick Dale and The Ventures that features stinging electric guitars featuring undistorted, almost Hawaiian, tone and sustained riffs produced using bridge pickup, treble boost, and tremolo arm, with double picking and spring reverb producing sustain.

On the opposite end of the spectrum is surf pop music, which includes distinctive male vocal harmonies. Made popular by The Beach Boys and Jan and Dean, surf pop music includes surf ballads and dance music.

Combining elements of both is surf rock, with such dances as the Watusi and the Stomp. Basically, it is surf music made by rock bands. Many surf bands have been noted for both surf instrumental and surf pop music, so surf music is considered a single genre.

Recordings in all three subgenres are normally attributed to the bands that performed them, rather than to individual artists.

Number	Title (A Side/B Side)	Yr	VG	VG+	NM

MANHATTANS, THE (1)

45s

Number	Title (A Side/B Side)	Yr	VG	VG+	NM
❑ Carnival 504	I've Got Everything But You/For the Very First Time	1964	5.00	10.00	20.00
❑ Carnival 506	There Goes a Fool/Call Somebody Please	1964	10.00	20.00	40.00
❑ Carnival 507	I Wanna Be (Your Everything)/What's It Gonna Be	1965	3.75	7.50	15.00
❑ Carnival 509	Searchin' for My Baby/I'm the One That Love Forgot	1965	3.75	7.50	15.00
❑ Carnival 512	Follow Your Heart/The Boston Money	1965	3.75	7.50	15.00
❑ Carnival 514	Baby I Need You/Teach Me the Philly Dog	1966	3.75	7.50	15.00
❑ Carnival 517	Can I/That New Girl	1966	3.75	7.50	15.00
❑ Carnival 522	I Betcha (Couldn't Love Me)/Sweet Little Girl	1966	3.75	7.50	15.00
❑ Carnival 524	It's That Time of the Year/Alone on New Year's Eve	1966	5.00	10.00	20.00
❑ Carnival 526	All I Need Is Your Love/Our Love Will Never Die	1967	3.75	7.50	15.00
❑ Carnival 529	When We're Made As One/Baby I'm Sorry	1967	3.75	7.50	15.00
❑ Carnival 533	I Call It Love/Manhattan Stomp	1967	3.75	7.50	15.00
❑ Carnival 542	I Don't Wanna Go/Love Is Breaking Out	1968	3.75	7.50	15.00
❑ Carnival 545	Til You Come Back to Me/Call Somebody Please	1968	3.75	7.50	15.00
❑ Columbia 02164	Shining Star/Summertime in the City	1981	—	—	3.00
—Reissue					
❑ Columbia 02191	Just One Moment Away/When I Leave Tomorrow	1981	—	2.00	4.00
❑ Columbia 02548	Let Your Love Come Down/I Gotta Thank You	1981	—	2.00	4.00
❑ Columbia 02666	Money, Money/I Wanta Thank You	1982	—	2.00	4.00
❑ Columbia 03939	Crazy/Gonna Find You	1983	—	2.00	4.00
❑ Columbia 04110	Forever By Your Side/Locked Up in Your Love	1983	—	2.00	4.00
❑ Columbia 04754	You Send Me/You're Gonna Love Being Loved By Me	1985	—	2.00	4.00
❑ Columbia 04930	Don't Say No/Dreamin'	1985	—	2.00	4.00
❑ Columbia 06376	Where Did We Go Wrong/Maybe Tomorrow	1986	—	2.00	4.00
—With Regina Belle					
❑ Columbia 07010	Mr. D.J./All I Need	1987	—	2.00	4.00
❑ Columbia 10045	Don't Take Your Love/The Day the Robins Sang to Me	1974	—	2.50	5.00
❑ Columbia 10140	Hurt/Nursery Rhymes	1975	—	2.50	5.00
❑ Columbia 10310	Kiss and Say Goodbye/Wonderful World of Love	1976	—	2.50	5.00
❑ Columbia 10430	I Kinda Miss You/Gypsy Man	1976	—	2.50	5.00
❑ Columbia 10495	It Feels So Good to Be Loved By You/On the Street (Where I Live)	1977	—	2.50	5.00
❑ Columbia 10586	We Never Danced to a Love Song/Let's Start It All Over Again	1977	—	2.50	5.00
❑ Columbia 10674	Am I Losing You/Movin'	1978	—	2.50	5.00
❑ Columbia 10766	Everybody Has a Dream/Happiness	1978	—	2.50	5.00
❑ Columbia 10921	Here Comes the Hurt Again/Don't Say Goodbye	1979	—	2.50	5.00
❑ Columbia 11024	The Way We Were-Memories/New York City	1979	—	2.50	5.00
❑ Columbia 11222	Shining Star/I'll Never Run Away from Love Again	1980	—	2.00	4.00
❑ Columbia 11321	Girl of My Dreams/The Closer You Are	1980	—	2.00	4.00
❑ Columbia 11398	I'll Never Find Another (Another Just Like You)/Rendezvous	1980	—	2.00	4.00
❑ Columbia 45838	There's No Me Without You/I'm Not a Run-Around	1973	—	3.00	6.00
❑ Columbia 45927	You'd Better Believe It/Soul Train	1973	—	3.00	6.00
❑ Columbia 45971	Wish That You Were Mine/It's So Hard Loving You	1973	—	3.00	6.00
❑ Columbia 46081	Summertime in the City/The Other Side of Me	1974	—	3.00	6.00
❑ Columbia 60511	Do You Really Mean Goodbye/Rendezvous	1981	—	2.00	4.00
❑ DeLuxe 109	The Picture Became Quite Clear/ Oh Lord, How I Wish I Could Sleep	1969	2.50	5.00	10.00
❑ DeLuxe 115	It's Gonna Take a Lot to Bring Me Back/Give Him Up	1970	2.50	5.00	10.00
❑ DeLuxe 122	If My Heart Could Speak/Loneliness	1970	2.50	5.00	10.00
❑ DeLuxe 129	From Atlanta to Goodbye/Fantastic Journey	1970	2.50	5.00	10.00
❑ DeLuxe 132	Let Them Talk/Straight to My Heart	1970	2.50	5.00	10.00
❑ DeLuxe 136	Do You Ever/I Can't Stand for You to Leave Me	1971	2.50	5.00	10.00
❑ DeLuxe 137	A Million to One/Cry If You Wanna Cry	1971	2.50	5.00	10.00
❑ DeLuxe 139	One Life to Live/It's the Only Way	1972	2.50	5.00	10.00
❑ DeLuxe 144	Back Up/Fever	1972	2.50	5.00	10.00
❑ DeLuxe 146	Rainbow Week/Loneliness	1973	2.50	5.00	10.00
❑ DeLuxe 152	Do You Ever/If My Heart Could Speak	1973	2.50	5.00	10.00
❑ Starfire 121	Alone on New Year's Eve/It's That Time of the Year	1979	—	2.50	5.00
❑ Valley Vue 75723	Sweet Talk/(B-side unknown)	1989	—	3.00	6.00
❑ Valley Vue 75749	Why You Wanna Love Me Like That/(B-side unknown)	1989	—	3.00	6.00

Albums

Number	Title (A Side/B Side)	Yr	VG	VG+	NM
❑ Carnival CMLP-201 [M]	Dedicated to You	1966	62.50	125.00	250.00
❑ Carnival CSLP-201 [S]	Dedicated to You	1966	125.00	250.00	500.00
❑ Carnival CMLP-202 [M]	For You and Yours	1967	37.50	75.00	150.00
❑ Carnival CSLP-202 [S]	For You and Yours	1967	75.00	150.00	300.00
❑ Collectables COL-5135	Dedicated to You: Golden Carnival Classics, Part One	198?	2.50	5.00	10.00
❑ Collectables COL-5136	For You and Yours: Golden Carnival Classics, Part Two	198?	2.50	5.00	10.00
❑ Columbia KC 32444	There's No Me Without You	1973	3.75	7.50	15.00
❑ Columbia KC 33064	That's How Much I Love You	1975	3.75	7.50	15.00
❑ Columbia PC 33820	The Manhattans	1976	3.00	6.00	12.00
—No bar code on back cover					
❑ Columbia PC 34450	It Feels So Good	1977	3.00	6.00	12.00
—No bar code on back cover					
❑ Columbia JC 35252	There's No Good in Goodbye	1978	3.00	6.00	12.00
❑ Columbia JC 35693	Love Talk	1979	3.00	6.00	12.00
❑ Columbia JC 36411	After Midnight	1980	3.00	6.00	12.00
❑ Columbia JC 36861	Manhattans Greatest Hits	1980	3.00	6.00	12.00
❑ Columbia FC 37156	Black Tie	1981	2.50	5.00	10.00
❑ Columbia FC 38600	Forever By Your Side	1983	2.50	5.00	10.00
❑ Columbia FC 39277	Too Hot to Stop It	1985	2.50	5.00	10.00
❑ DeLuxe 12000	With These Hands	1971	6.25	12.50	25.00
❑ DeLuxe 12004	A Million to One	1972	6.25	12.50	25.00
❑ Solid Smoke 8007	Follow Your Heart	1981	2.50	5.00	10.00
❑ Valley Vue D1-72946	Sweet Talk	1989	3.00	6.00	12.00

Number	Title (A Side/B Side)	Yr	VG	VG+	NM
MANILOW, BARRY					
45s					
❑ Arista 0108	It's a Miracle/One of These Days	1975	—	2.00	4.00
❑ Arista 0126	Could It Be Magic/I Am Your Child	1975	—	2.00	4.00
❑ Arista 0157	I Write the Songs/A Nice Boy Like Me	1975	—	2.00	4.00
❑ Arista 0172	Tryin' to Get the Feeling Again/Beautiful Music	1976	—	2.00	4.00
❑ Arista 0206	This One's for You/Riders to the Stars	1976	—	2.00	4.00
❑ Arista 0212	Weekend in New England/Say the Words	1976	—	2.00	4.00
❑ Arista 0244	Looks Like We Made It/New York City Rhythm	1977	—	2.00	4.00
❑ Arista 0273	Daybreak/Jump Shout Boogie	1977	—	2.00	4.00
❑ Arista 0305	Can't Smile Without You/Sunrise	1978	—	2.00	4.00
❑ Arista 0330	Even Now/I Was a Fool (To Let You Go)	1978	—	2.00	4.00
❑ Arista 0339	Copacabana (Short Version)/Copacabana (Long Version)	1978	—	2.00	4.00
❑ Arista 0357	Ready to Take a Chance Again/Sweet Life	1978	—	2.00	4.00
❑ Arista 0382	Somewhere in the Night/Leavin' in the Morning	1978	—	2.00	4.00
❑ Arista 0464	Ships/They Gave In to the Blues	1979	—	2.00	4.00
❑ Arista 0481	When I Wanted You/Bobbie Lee (What's the Difference I Gotta Live)	1979	—	2.00	4.00
❑ Arista 0501	I Don't Want to Walk Without You/One Voice	1980	—	2.00	4.00
❑ Arista 0566	I Made It Through the Rain/Only in Chicago	1980	—	2.00	4.00
❑ Arista 0596	Lonely Together/The Last Duet	1981	—	2.00	4.00
—B-side with Lily Tomlin					
❑ Arista 0633	The Old Songs/Don't Fall in Love with Me	1981	—	2.00	4.00
❑ Arista 0658	Somewhere Down the Road/Let's Take All Night to Say Goodbye	1982	—	2.00	4.00
❑ Arista 0675	Let's Hang On/No Other Love	1982	—	2.00	4.00
❑ Arista 0698	Oh Julie/Break Down the Door	1982	—	2.00	4.00
❑ Arista 1025	Memory/Heart of Steel	1982	—	2.00	4.00
❑ Arista 1046	Some Kind of Friend/Heaven	1983	—	2.00	4.00
❑ Arista 2094	Jingle Bells/Because It's Christmas (For All the Children)	1990	—	—	3.00
—A-side with Expose					
❑ Arista 9003	Some Kind of Friend/Heaven	1983	—	—	3.00
❑ Arista 9101	Read 'Em and Weep/One Voice	1983	—	—	3.00
❑ Arista 9185	You're Lookin' Hot Tonight/Put a Quarter in the Jukebox	1984	—	—	3.00
—B-side with Ronnie Milsap					
❑ Arista 9666	Hey Mambo/When October Goes	1988	—	—	3.00
—With Kid Creole and the Coconuts					
❑ Arista 9811	Please Don't Be Scared/A Little Traveling Music, Please	1989	—	—	3.00
❑ Arista 9838	Keep Each Other Warm/A Little Traveling Music, Please	1989	—	2.50	5.00
❑ Bell 45357	Sweetwater Jones/One of These Days	1973	—	3.00	6.00
❑ Bell 45422	Cloudburst/Could It Be Magic	1973	—	3.00	6.00
❑ Bell 45443	Let's Take Some Time to Say Goodbye/Seven More Years	1974	—	3.00	6.00
❑ Bell 45613	Mandy/Something's Comin' Up	1974	—	2.50	5.00
❑ RCA PB-14223	In Search of Love/At the Dance	1985	—	—	3.00
❑ RCA PB-14302	He Doesn't Care (But I Do)/It's All Behind Us Now	1986	—	—	3.00
❑ RCA PB-14397	I'm Your Man/I'm Your Man (Dub)	1986	—	—	3.00
Albums					
❑ Arista AB 2500 [EP]	Oh, Julie!	1982	5.00	10.00	20.00
❑ Arista AL 4007	Barry Manilow I	1975	2.50	5.00	10.00
—Revised version of Bell 1129 with new cover; "Could It Be Magic" especially is noticeably different between the Bell and Arista versions					
❑ Arista AL 4016	Barry Manilow II	1975	2.50	5.00	10.00
—Reissue of Bell 1314					
❑ Arista AL 4060	Tryin' to Get the Feeling	1975	2.50	5.00	10.00
❑ Arista AL 4090	This One's for You	1976	2.50	5.00	10.00
❑ Arista AB 4164	Even Now	1978	2.00	4.00	8.00
❑ Arista AL8-8003	Here Comes the Night	198?	—	3.00	6.00
—Reissue of 9610					
❑ Arista AL13-8039 [(2)]	Greatest Hits	1983	2.50	5.00	10.00
❑ Arista AL5-8046	One Voice	198?	—	3.00	6.00
—Reissue of 9505					
❑ Arista AL13-8049 [(2)]	Barry Manilow/Live	1983	2.50	5.00	10.00
❑ Arista AL5-8052	Even Now	198?	—	3.00	6.00
—Reissue of 8322					
❑ Arista AL5-8070	Tryin' to Get the Feeling	198?	—	3.00	6.00
—Reissue of 8336					
❑ Arista AL5-8085	Barry Manilow II	198?	—	3.00	6.00
—Reissue of 8370					

Number	Title (A Side/B Side)	Yr	VG	VG+	NM
❑ Arista AL8-8102	Barry Manilow/Greatest Hits, Vol. II	1983	2.00	4.00	8.00
❑ Arista AL8-8117	Barry	198?	—	3.00	6.00
—Reissue of 9537					
❑ Arista AL8-8123	If I Should Love Again	198?	—	3.00	6.00
—Reissue of 9573					
❑ Arista AL5-8153	Barry Manilow I	198?	—	3.00	6.00
—Reissue of 8372					
❑ Arista AL5-8160	This One's for You	198?	—	3.00	6.00
—Reissue of 8331					
❑ Arista AL8-8254	2:00 A.M. Paradise Café	1984	2.00	4.00	8.00
❑ Arista AL9-8274	The Manilow Collection — 20 Classic Hits	1985	2.00	4.00	8.00
❑ Arista AL8-8291	Barry Manilow/Greatest Hits, Vol. II	1985	—	3.00	6.00
❑ Arista AL8-8322	Even Now	1985	—	3.00	6.00
❑ Arista AL8-8331	This One's for You	1985	—	3.00	6.00
❑ Arista AL8-8336	Tryin' to Get the Feeling	1985	—	3.00	6.00
❑ Arista AL8-8370	Barry Manilow II	1985	—	3.00	6.00
❑ Arista AL8-8372	Barry Manilow I	1985	—	3.00	6.00
❑ Arista AL 8500 [(2)]	Barry Manilow/Live	1977	3.00	6.00	12.00
❑ Arista AL-8527	Swing Street	1987	2.00	4.00	8.00
❑ Arista AL-8570	Barry Manilow	1989	2.00	4.00	8.00
❑ Arista AL-8598	Greatest Hits, Vol. 1	1989	2.50	5.00	10.00
❑ Arista AL-8599	Greatest Hits, Vol. 2	1989	2.50	5.00	10.00
❑ Arista AL-8600	Greatest Hits, Vol. 3	1989	2.50	5.00	10.00
❑ Arista A2L 8601 [(2)]	Greatest Hits	1978	3.00	6.00	12.00
❑ Arista AL-8638 [(2)]	Live on Broadway	1990	5.00	10.00	20.00
❑ Arista AL-8644	Because It's Christmas	1990	3.75	7.50	15.00
❑ Arista AL 9505	One Voice	1979	2.00	4.00	8.00
❑ Arista AL 9537	Barry	1980	2.00	4.00	8.00
❑ Arista AL 9573	If I Should Love Again	1981	2.00	4.00	8.00
❑ Arista AL-9610	Here Comes the Night	1982	2.00	4.00	8.00
❑ Arista NU 9740	Manilow Magic	1982	3.00	6.00	12.00
—Manufactured by K-Tel					
❑ Bell 1129	Barry Manilow	1973	6.25	12.50	25.00
❑ Bell 1314	Barry Manilow II	1974	3.75	7.50	15.00
❑ RCA Victor AFL1-7044	Manilow	1985	2.00	4.00	8.00

MANN, BARRY

45s

Number	Title (A Side/B Side)	Yr	VG	VG+	NM
❑ ABC-Paramount 10143	War Paint/Counting Teardrops	1960	5.00	10.00	20.00
❑ ABC-Paramount 10180	Happy Birthday, Broken Heart/Millionaire	1961	5.00	10.00	20.00
❑ ABC-Paramount 10237	Who Put the Bomp (In the Bomp, Bomp, Bomp)/Love, True Love	1961	6.25	12.50	25.00
❑ ABC-Paramount 10263	Little Miss U.S.A./Find Another Fool	1961	5.00	10.00	20.00
❑ ABC-Paramount 10356	Hey Baby I'm Dancin'/Like I Don't Love You	1962	5.00	10.00	20.00
❑ ABC-Paramount 10380	Teenage Has-Been/Bless You	1962	5.00	10.00	20.00
❑ Arista 0194	The Princess and the Punk/Jennifer	1976	—	2.00	4.00
❑ Capitol 2082	Young Electric Psychedelic Hippy Flippy Folk & Funky Philosophic Turned On Groovy Twelve-String Band/ Take Your Love	1968	3.75	7.50	15.00
❑ Capitol 2217	I Just Can't Help Believin'/Where Do I Go from Here	1968	2.50	5.00	10.00
❑ Capitol 5695	Looking at Tomorrow/Angelica	1966	2.50	5.00	10.00
❑ Capitol 5894	Where Do I Go from Here/She Is Today	1967	2.50	5.00	10.00
❑ Casablanca 2287	Brown-Eyed Woman/In My Own Way	1980	—	2.00	4.00
❑ Colpix 691	Graduation Time/Johnny Surfboard	1963	5.00	10.00	20.00
❑ JDS 5002	I Love to Last a Lifetime/All the Things You Are	1959	7.50	15.00	30.00
❑ New Design 1000	Carry Me Home/Sundown	1971	—	2.50	5.00
❑ New Design 1005	When You Get Right Down to It/Don't Give Up on Me	1972	—	2.50	5.00
❑ New Design 1006	Too Many Mornings/On Broadway	1972	—	2.50	5.00
❑ New Design 1006	Too Many Mornings/Lay It All Out	1972	—	2.50	5.00
❑ RCA Victor PB-10104	Nobody But You/Woman, Woman, Woman	1974	—	2.50	5.00
❑ RCA Victor PB-10230	Nothing Good Comes Easy/Woman, Woman, Woman	1975	—	2.50	5.00
❑ RCA Victor PB-10319	Don't Seem Right/I'm a Survivor	1975	—	2.50	5.00
❑ Red Bird 10-015	Talk to Me Baby/Amy	1964	3.75	7.50	15.00
❑ Scepter 12281	Feelings/Let Me Stay with You	1970	—	3.00	6.00
❑ United Artists XW1021	Best That I Know How/Lettin' Good Times Get Away	1977	—	2.00	4.00
❑ Warner Bros. 8752	For No Reason at All/Almost Gone	1979	—	2.00	4.00

Albums

Number	Title (A Side/B Side)	Yr	VG	VG+	NM
❑ ABC-Paramount 399 [M]	Who Put the Bomp	1963	30.00	60.00	120.00
❑ ABC-Paramount S-399 [S]	Who Put the Bomp	1963	75.00	150.00	300.00
❑ Casablanca NBLP 7226	Barry Mann	1980	2.50	5.00	10.00
❑ New Design Z 30876	Lay It All Out	1971	3.00	6.00	12.00
❑ RCA Victor APL1-0860	Survivor	1975	3.00	6.00	12.00

MANN, MANFRED

45s

Number	Title (A Side/B Side)	Yr	VG	VG+	NM
❑ Ascot 2151	Hubble Bubble (Toil and Trouble)/I'm Your Kingpin	1964	50.00	100.00	200.00
❑ Ascot 2157	Do Wah Diddy Diddy/What You Gonna Do?	1964	3.75	7.50	15.00
❑ Ascot 2165	Sha La La/John Hardy	1964	2.50	5.00	10.00
❑ Ascot 2170	Come Tomorrow/What Did I Do Wrong	1965	2.50	5.00	10.00
❑ Ascot 2181	Poison Ivy/I Can't Believe What You Say	1965	—	—	—
—Unreleased?					
❑ Ascot 2184	My Little Red Book/What Am I Doing Wrong	1965	2.50	5.00	10.00
❑ Ascot 2194	If You Gotta Go, Go Now/The One in the Middle	1965	2.50	5.00	10.00
❑ Ascot 2210	She Needs Company/Hi Lili, Hi Lo	1966	2.50	5.00	10.00
❑ Ascot 2241	My Little Red Book/I Can't Believe What You Say	1967	2.50	5.00	10.00
❑ Mercury 72607	Just Like a Woman/I Wanna Be Rich	1966	2.50	5.00	10.00
❑ Mercury 72629	Semi-Detached Suburban Mr. Jones/Each and Every Day	1966	2.50	5.00	10.00
❑ Mercury 72675	Ha, Ha, Said the Clown/Feeling So Good	1967	2.50	5.00	10.00

Number	Title (A Side/B Side)	Yr	VG	VG+	NM
❑ Mercury 72770	The Mighty Quinn (Quinn the Eskimo)/By Request — Edwin Garvey	1968	2.00	4.00	8.00
—Red label with white "Mercury" in a circle					
❑ Mercury 72770	The Mighty Quinn (Quinn the Eskimo)/By Request — Edwin Garvey	1968	3.00	6.00	12.00
—Red label with "Mercury" in all capital letters					
❑ Mercury 72770	Quinn the Eskimo/By Request — Edwin Garvey	1968	2.50	5.00	10.00
—Red label with white "Mercury" in a circle					
❑ Mercury 72770	Quinn the Eskimo/By Request — Edwin Garvey	1968	3.00	6.00	12.00
—Orange and red swirl label					
❑ Mercury 72770	The Mighty Quinn (Quinn the Eskimo)/By Request — Edwin Garvey	1968	3.75	7.50	15.00
—Black label, silver print, "Mercury Records" in double oval at top; as this label was last used in 1964, this shouldn't exist, but it does					
❑ Mercury 72770	The Mighty Quinn (Quinn the Eskimo)/By Request — Edwin Garvey	1968	2.50	5.00	10.00
—Orange and red swirl label					
❑ Mercury 72822	My Name Is Jack/There Is a Man	1968	2.00	4.00	8.00
❑ Mercury 72879	Fox on the Run/Too Many People	1968	2.00	4.00	8.00
❑ Mercury 72921	Ragamuffin Man/A B-Side	1969	2.00	4.00	8.00
❑ Polydor 14026	Sometimes/Snakeskin Garter	1970	—	3.00	6.00
❑ Polydor 14074	California Coastline/Part Time	1971	—	—	—
—Unreleased					
❑ Polydor 14097	Please Mrs. Henry/Prayers	1971	—	2.50	5.00
❑ Prestige 312	5-4-3-2-1/Without You	1964	10.00	20.00	40.00
❑ Prestige 314	Blue Brave/Brother Jack	1964	25.00	50.00	100.00
❑ United Artists 0048	Do Wah Diddy Diddy/Sha La La	1973	—	2.50	5.00
—"Silver Spotlight Series" reissue					
❑ United Artists 0049	Pretty Flamingo/Come Tomorrow	1973	—	2.50	5.00
—"Silver Spotlight Series" reissue					
❑ United Artists 50040	Pretty Flamingo/You're Standing By	1966	2.50	5.00	10.00
❑ United Artists 50066	When Will I Be Loved/Do You Have to Do That	1966	2.50	5.00	10.00

Albums

Number	Title (A Side/B Side)	Yr	VG	VG+	NM
❑ Ascot AM-13015 [M]	The Manfred Mann Album	1964	10.00	20.00	40.00
❑ Ascot AM-13018 [M]	The Five Faces of Manfred Mann	1965	10.00	20.00	40.00
❑ Ascot AM-13021 [M]	My Little Red Book of Winners	1965	10.00	20.00	40.00
❑ Ascot AM-13024 [M]	Mann Made	1966	10.00	20.00	40.00
❑ Ascot AS-16015 [P]	The Manfred Mann Album	1964	12.50	25.00	50.00
❑ Ascot AS-16018 [P]	The Five Faces of Manfred Mann	1965	12.50	25.00	50.00
❑ Ascot AS-16021 [S]	My Little Red Book of Winners	1965	12.50	25.00	50.00
❑ Ascot AS-16024 [S]	Mann Made	1966	12.50	25.00	50.00
❑ Capitol SM-11688	The Best of Manfred Mann	1977	2.50	5.00	10.00
❑ Capitol SN-16073	The Best of Manfred Mann	1980	2.00	4.00	8.00
❑ Janus JXS-3064	The Best of Manfred Mann	1974	3.00	6.00	12.00
❑ Mercury SR-61168	The Mighty Quinn	1968	6.25	12.50	25.00
❑ Polydor 24-4013	Chapter Three	1970	3.75	7.50	15.00
❑ United Artists UAL 3549 [M]	Pretty Flamingo	1966	7.50	15.00	30.00
❑ United Artists UAL 3551 [M]	Manfred Mann's Greatest Hits	1966	7.50	15.00	30.00
❑ United Artists UAS 6549 [S]	Pretty Flamingo	1966	10.00	20.00	40.00
❑ United Artists UAS 6551 [P]	Manfred Mann's Greatest Hits	1966	10.00	20.00	40.00
—"Do Wah Diddy Diddy," "Sha La La," "I Got You Babe" and "Satisfaction" are rechanneled.					

MANN, MANFRED'S, EARTH BAND

45s

Number	Title (A Side/B Side)	Yr	VG	VG+	NM
❑ Arista 9143	Runner/Where Do They Send Them	1984	—	2.00	4.00
—First pressing has whitish label					
❑ Arista 9203	Rebel/Figures on a Rock	1984	—	—	3.00
❑ Polydor 14113	Living Without You/Tribute	1972	—	2.50	5.00
❑ Polydor 14130	I'm Up and Leaving/Part Time Man	1972	—	2.50	5.00
❑ Polydor 14160	It's All Over Now, Baby Blue/Ashes	1973	—	2.50	5.00
❑ Polydor 14173	Mardi Gras Day/Sad Joy	1973	—	2.50	5.00
❑ Polydor 14191	Get Your Rocks Off/Wind	1973	—	2.50	5.00
❑ Polydor 14205	Joybringer/Cloudy Eyes	1973	—	2.50	5.00
❑ Polydor 14225	Father of Night/Solar Fire Two	1974	—	2.50	5.00
❑ Warner Bros. 8152	Spirit in the Night/As Above So Below	1975	2.00	4.00	8.00
❑ Warner Bros. 8176	Spirit in the Night/As Above So Below	1976	—	3.00	6.00
❑ Warner Bros. 8252	Blinded by the Light/Starbird No. 2	1976	—	2.50	5.00

Number	Title (A Side/B Side)	Yr	VG	VG+	NM
❑ Warner Bros. 8355	Spirit in the Night/Questions	1977	—	2.50	5.00
—This has newly-recorded vocal tracks by Chris Thompson					
❑ Warner Bros. 8355 [DJ]	Spirit (same on both sides)	1977	2.50	5.00	10.00
—Newly-recorded vocal tracks by Chris Thompson; some early promos use this title in error and include a card that says "The correct title should be 'Spirit in the Night' WBS 8355"					
❑ Warner Bros. 8574	California/Bouillabaise	1978	—	2.50	5.00
❑ Warner Bros. 8620	Davy's on the Road Again/Bouillabaise	1978	—	2.50	5.00
❑ Warner Bros. 8850	You Angel You/"Belle" of the Earth	1979	—	2.00	4.00
❑ Warner Bros. 49678	For You/Fool I Am	1981	—	2.50	5.00
❑ Warner Bros. 49762	Adolescent Dream/Lies (Through the 80's)	1981	—	2.00	4.00
Albums					
❑ Arista AL 8194	Somewhere in Afrika	1983	2.50	5.00	10.00
❑ Polydor PD-5015	Manfred Mann's Earth Band	1971	3.75	7.50	15.00
❑ Polydor PD-5031	Glorified, Magnified	1972	3.75	7.50	15.00
❑ Polydor PD-5050	Get Your Rocks Off	1973	3.75	7.50	15.00
❑ Polydor PD-1-6019	Solar Fire	1974	3.75	7.50	15.00
❑ Warner Bros. BS 2826	The Good Earth	1974	3.00	6.00	12.00
❑ Warner Bros. BS 2877	Nightingales and Bombers	1975	3.00	6.00	12.00
❑ Warner Bros. BS 2965	The Roaring Silence	1976	3.00	6.00	12.00
—Orange cover					
❑ Warner Bros. BSK 3055	The Roaring Silence	1977	2.50	5.00	10.00
—Blue cover; re-recording of "Spirit in the Night" is added					
❑ Warner Bros. BSK 3157	Watch	1978	2.50	5.00	10.00
❑ Warner Bros. BSK 3302	Angel Station	1979	2.50	5.00	10.00
❑ Warner Bros. BSK 3498	Chance	1980	2.50	5.00	10.00

MAR-KEYS

Number	Title (A Side/B Side)	Yr	VG	VG+	NM
45s					
❑ Satellite 107	Last Night/Night Before	1960	7.50	15.00	30.00
❑ Stax 112	Morning After/Diana	1961	3.00	6.00	12.00
❑ Stax 114	About Noon/Sack-O-Woe	1961	3.00	6.00	12.00
❑ Stax 115	Foxy/One Degree North	1961	3.00	6.00	12.00
❑ Stax 121	Pop-Eye Stroll/Po-Dunk	1962	3.00	6.00	12.00
❑ Stax 124	What's Happening/You Got It	1962	3.00	6.00	12.00
❑ Stax 129	Sailor Man Waltz/Sack-O-Woe	1963	3.00	6.00	12.00
❑ Stax 133	The Dribble/Bo Time	1963	3.00	6.00	12.00
❑ Stax 156	Beach Bash/Bush Bash	1964	2.50	5.00	10.00
❑ Stax 166	The Shovel/Banana Juice	1965	2.50	5.00	10.00
❑ Stax 181	Grab This Thing (Part 1)/Grab This Thing (Part 2)	1965	2.50	5.00	10.00
❑ Stax 185	Philly Dog/Honey Pot	1966	2.50	5.00	10.00
Albums					
❑ Atlantic 8055 [M]	Last Night	1961	25.00	50.00	100.00
—White "fan" logo on right					
❑ Atlantic SD 8055 [R]	Last Night	1966	10.00	20.00	40.00
❑ Atlantic 8062 [M]	Do the Pop-Eye with the Mar-Keys	1962	12.50	25.00	50.00
❑ Atlantic SD 8062 [R]	Do the Pop-Eye with the Mar-Keys	1966	10.00	20.00	40.00
❑ Stax ST-707 [M]	The Great Memphis Sound	1966	12.50	25.00	50.00
❑ Stax STS-707 [R]	The Great Memphis Sound	1966	10.00	20.00	40.00
❑ Stax STS-2025	Damifiknew	1969	5.00	10.00	20.00
❑ Stax STS-2036	Memphis Experience	1971	5.00	10.00	20.00

MAR-KEYS/BOOKER T. AND THE MG'S

Number	Title (A Side/B Side)	Yr	VG	VG+	NM
Albums					
❑ Stax ST-720 [M]	Back to Back	1967	5.00	10.00	20.00
❑ Stax STS-720 [S]	Back to Back	1967	6.25	12.50	25.00

MARCELS, THE

Number	Title (A Side/B Side)	Yr	VG	VG+	NM
45s					
❑ All Ears 810085	Blue Moon/Clap Your Hands (When I Clap My Hands)	1981	—	3.00	6.00
❑ Baron 109	Betty Lou/Take Me Back	197?	2.00	4.00	8.00
❑ Chartbound 009	Letter Full of Tears/Tell Me	197?	2.00	4.00	8.00
❑ Colpix TL-147	Blue Moon/Friendly Loans	196?	3.75	7.50	15.00
—"Torchlite Series" reissue on red label					
❑ Colpix 186	Blue Moon/Goodbye to Love	1961	7.50	15.00	30.00
❑ Colpix 196	Summertime/Teeter-Totter Love	1961	6.25	12.50	25.00
❑ Colpix 606	You Are My Sunshine/Find Another Fool	1961	6.25	12.50	25.00
❑ Colpix 612	Heartaches/My Love for You	1961	6.25	12.50	25.00
❑ Colpix 617	Merry Twist-Mas/Don't Cry for Me This Christmas	1961	6.25	12.50	25.00
❑ Colpix 624	My Melancholy Baby/Really Need Your Love	1962	5.00	10.00	20.00
❑ Colpix 629	Footprints in the Sand/Twistin' Fever	1962	12.50	25.00	50.00
❑ Colpix 640	Flowerpot/Hold On	1962	7.50	15.00	30.00
❑ Colpix 651	Loved Her the Whole Week Through/Friendly Loans	1962	6.25	12.50	25.00
❑ Colpix 665	Alright, Okay, You Win/Lollipop Baby	1962	6.25	12.50	25.00
❑ Colpix 683	That Old Black Magic/Don't Turn Your Back on Me	1963	6.25	12.50	25.00
❑ Colpix 687	Give Me Back Your Love/I Wanna Be the Leader	1963	7.50	15.00	30.00
❑ Colpix 694	One Last Kiss/You Got to Be Sincere	1963	50.00	100.00	200.00
❑ Colpix 694	One Last Kiss/Teeter-Totter Love	1963	25.00	50.00	100.00
❑ 888 101	How Deep Is the Ocean/Lonely Boy	1964	3.75	7.50	15.00
❑ Kyra 100	Comes Love/Your Red Wagon	1964	12.50	25.00	50.00
❑ Monogram 112	I'll Be Forever Loving You/A Fallen Tear	1974	3.00	6.00	12.00
❑ Monogram 113	Sweet Was the Wine/Over the Rainbow	1974	3.00	6.00	12.00
❑ Monogram 115	Two People in the World/Most of All	1974	3.00	6.00	12.00
❑ Owl 324	(You Gave Me) Peace of Mind/Crazy Bells	197?	2.00	4.00	8.00
❑ Queen Bee 47001	In the Still of the Night/High on a Hill	1973	3.75	7.50	15.00
❑ Rocky 13711	(You Gave Me) Peace of Mind/That Lucky Old Sun	1975	2.00	4.00	8.00
—As "The Fabulous Marcels"					
❑ St. Clair 13711	(You Gave Me) Peace of Mind/That Lucky Old Sun	1975	2.50	5.00	10.00
—As "The Fabulous Marcels"					

Number	Title (A Side/B Side)	Yr	VG	VG+	NM
Albums					
❑ Colpix CP-416 [M]	Blue Moon	1961	87.50	175.00	350.00
—Gold label					

MARCH, LITTLE PEGGY

Number	Title (A Side/B Side)	Yr	VG	VG+	NM
45s					
❑ Olde World 1105	Average People/Isn't This the Way We Are	1975	2.00	4.00	8.00
❑ RCA Victor 47-8107	Little Me/Pagan Love Song	1962	3.75	7.50	15.00
❑ RCA Victor 47-8139	I Will Follow Him/Wind-Up Doll	1963	5.00	10.00	20.00
❑ RCA Victor 47-8189	I Wish I Were a Princess/My Teenage Castle	1963	3.75	7.50	15.00
❑ RCA Victor 47-8221	Hello Heartache, Goodbye Love/Boy Crazy	1963	3.75	7.50	15.00
❑ RCA Victor 47-8267	The Impossible Happened/Waterfall	1963	3.00	6.00	12.00
❑ RCA Victor 47-8291	My Heart Keeps Telling Me/His	1963	—	—	—
—Unreleased					
❑ RCA Victor 47-8302	(I'm Watching) Every Little Move You Make/After You	1963	3.00	6.00	12.00
❑ RCA Victor 47-8357	Takin' the Long Way Home/Leave Me Alone	1964	2.50	5.00	10.00
—All records from 1964 on are as "Peggy March"					
❑ RCA Victor 47-8418	Oh My, What a Guy/Only You Could Do That to My Heart	1964	2.50	5.00	10.00
❑ RCA Victor 47-8460	Watch What You Do With My Baby/Can't Stop Thinking About Him	1964	2.50	5.00	10.00
❑ RCA Victor 47-8534	Why Can't He Be You/Losin' My Touch	1965	2.50	5.00	10.00
❑ RCA Victor 47-8605	Let Her Go/Your Girl	1965	2.50	5.00	10.00
❑ RCA Victor 47-8710	He Couldn't Care Less/Heaven for Lovers	1965	2.50	5.00	10.00
❑ RCA Victor 47-8840	Ein Boy Wie Du (A Boy Like You)/ Sechs Tage Lang (Six Long Days)	1966	5.00	10.00	20.00
❑ RCA Victor 47-8877	Play a Simple Melody/Old Fashioned Wedding	1966	2.50	5.00	10.00
—With Gary Marshall					
❑ RCA Victor 47-8903	He's Back Again/Running Scared	1966	2.50	5.00	10.00
❑ RCA Victor 47-9033	Fool, Fool, Fool (Look in the Mirror)/Try to See It My Way	1966	2.50	5.00	10.00
❑ RCA Victor 47-9143	January First/How Can I Tell Him	1967	2.50	5.00	10.00
❑ RCA Victor 47-9223	Mama Dear, Papa Dear/Your Good Girl's Gonna Go Bad	1967	2.50	5.00	10.00
❑ RCA Victor 47-9283	This Heart Wasn't Made to Kick Around/Foolin' Around	1967	2.50	5.00	10.00
❑ RCA Victor 47-9359	Have a Good Time/Let Me Down Hard	1967	2.50	5.00	10.00
❑ RCA Victor 47-9494	If You Would Love Me/Thinking Through My Tears	1968	2.50	5.00	10.00
❑ RCA Victor 47-9566	Roses on the Sea/Time and Time Again	1968	2.50	5.00	10.00
❑ RCA Victor 47-9627	I've Been Here Before/Aren't You Glad	1968	2.50	5.00	10.00
❑ RCA Victor 47-9718	Purple Hat/Try to See It My Way	1969	2.50	5.00	10.00
❑ RCA Victor 74-0136	Boom Bang-a Bang/Lilac Skies	1969	2.50	5.00	10.00
Albums					
❑ RCA Victor LPM-2732 [M]	I Will Follow Him	1963	15.00	30.00	60.00
❑ RCA Victor LSP-2732 [S]	I Will Follow Him	1963	20.00	40.00	80.00
❑ RCA Victor LPM-3883 [M]	No Foolin'	1968	10.00	20.00	40.00
❑ RCA Victor LSP-3883 [S]	No Foolin'	1968	6.25	12.50	25.00

MARKETTS, THE

Number	Title (A Side/B Side)	Yr	VG	VG+	NM
45s					
❑ Arvee 5063	Beach Bum/Sweet Potatoes	1962	5.00	10.00	20.00
❑ Calliope 8003	Mary Hartman, Mary Hartman/(B-side unknown)	1977	—	2.50	5.00
—As "The New Marketts"					
❑ Calliope 8009	City Nights/Soul Coaxing	1977	—	2.50	5.00
—As "The New Marketts"					
❑ Farr 007	Song from M.A.S.H./Song from M.A.S.H. (Disco Version)	1976	—	2.50	5.00
—As "The New Marketts"					
❑ Farr 019	The Hustle/Song from M.A.S.H.	1977	—	2.50	5.00
—As "The New Marketts"					
❑ Farr 021	Looking for Mr. Goodbar (Terry's Theme)/Black	1977	—	2.50	5.00
—As "Danny Welton and the New Marketts"					
❑ Liberty 55401	Surfer's Stomp/Start	1962	5.00	10.00	20.00
—As "The Mar-Kets"					
❑ Liberty 55443	Balboa Blue/Stompede	1962	5.00	10.00	20.00
—As "The Mar-Kets"					
❑ Liberty 55506	Stomping Room Only/Canadian Sunset	1962	5.00	10.00	20.00
—As "The Mar-Kets"					
❑ Mercury 73433	Mystery Movie Theme/Sister Candy	1973	2.00	4.00	8.00
❑ Seminole 501	Song from M.A.S.H./Song from M.A.S.H. (Disco Version)	1976	2.00	4.00	8.00
—As "The New Marketts"					
❑ Uni 55173	The Undefeated/They Call the Wind Maria	1969	2.00	4.00	8.00
❑ Union 501	Surfer's Stomp/Start	1961	7.50	15.00	30.00

Number	Title (A Side/B Side)	Yr	VG	VG+	NM
❑ Union 504	Balboa Blue/Stompede	1962	7.50	15.00	30.00
❑ Union 507	Stomping Room Only/Canadian Sunset	1962	7.50	15.00	30.00
❑ United Artists 0043	Surfer's Stomp/Balboa Blue	1973	—	2.50	5.00
—"Silver Spotlight Series" reissue					
❑ Warner Bros. 5365	Woody Wagon/Cobra	1963	3.75	7.50	15.00
❑ Warner Bros. 5391	Out of Limits/Bella Dalena	1963	5.00	10.00	20.00
❑ Warner Bros. 5391	Outer Limits/Bella Dalena	1963	7.50	15.00	30.00
—Original title of A-side					
❑ Warner Bros. 5423	Vanishing Point/Borealis	1964	3.00	6.00	12.00
❑ Warner Bros. 5468	Come See, Come Ska/Look for a Star	1964	3.00	6.00	12.00
❑ Warner Bros. 5641	Miami's Blue/Napoleon's Solo	1965	2.50	5.00	10.00
❑ Warner Bros. 5670	Ready Steady Go/Lady in the Cage	1965	2.50	5.00	10.00
❑ Warner Bros. 5696	Batman Theme/Richie's Theme	1966	3.00	6.00	12.00
❑ Warner Bros. 5814	Theme from "The Avengers"/A Touch of Velvet, a Sting of Brass	1966	5.00	10.00	20.00
❑ Warner Bros. 5847	Tarzan/Stirrin' Up Some Soul	1966	2.50	5.00	10.00
❑ Warner Bros. 7116	Out of Limits/Batman Theme	1968	—	3.00	6.00
—"Back to Back Hits" series -- originals have green labels with "W7" logo					
❑ World Pacific 77874	Sunshine Girl/Sun Power	1967	2.50	5.00	10.00
❑ World Pacific 77899	California Summer (People Moving West)/Groovin' Time	1968	2.50	5.00	10.00
Albums					
❑ Liberty LRP-3226 [M]	The Surfing Scene	196?	7.50	15.00	30.00
—Retitled version of above					
❑ Liberty LRP-3226 [M]	Surfer's Stomp	1962	10.00	20.00	40.00
—Add 20% if "Surfer's Stomp" instruction sheet is enclosed					
❑ Liberty LST-7226 [S]	The Surfing Scene	196?	10.00	20.00	40.00
—Retitled version of above					
❑ Liberty LST-7226 [S]	Surfer's Stomp	1962	12.50	25.00	50.00
—Add 20% if "Surfer's Stomp" instruction sheet is enclosed					
❑ Mercury SRM-1-679	AM, FM, Etc.	1973	3.75	7.50	15.00
❑ Warner Bros. W 1509 [M]	The Marketts Take to Wheels	1963	10.00	20.00	40.00
❑ Warner Bros. WS 1509 [S]	The Marketts Take to Wheels	1963	12.50	25.00	50.00
❑ Warner Bros. W 1537 [M]	Out of Limits!	1964	7.50	15.00	30.00
❑ Warner Bros. WS 1537 [S]	Out of Limits!	1964	10.00	20.00	40.00
❑ Warner Bros. W 1642 [M]	The Batman Theme	1966	10.00	20.00	40.00
❑ Warner Bros. WS 1642 [S]	The Batman Theme	1966	12.50	25.00	50.00
❑ World Pacific WP-1870 [M]	Sun Power	1967	6.25	12.50	25.00
❑ World Pacific WPS-21870 [S]	Sun Power	1967	5.00	10.00	20.00

MARMALADE, THE

Number	Title (A Side/B Side)	Yr	VG	VG+	NM
45s					
❑ Ariola America 7619	Falling Apart at the Seams/Fly, Fly, Fly	1976	—	2.00	4.00
❑ Ariola America 7631	My Everything/Walking a Tightrope	1976	—	2.00	4.00
❑ EMI 3676	Engine Driver/Wishing Well	1973	—	2.00	4.00
❑ Epic 10162	Can't Stop Now/There Ain't No Use in Hanging On	1967	2.50	5.00	10.00
❑ Epic 10236	Otherwise It's Been a Perfect Day/I See the Rain	1967	2.50	5.00	10.00
❑ Epic 10284	Cry/Man in a Shop	1968	2.00	4.00	8.00
❑ Epic 10340	Hey Joe/Lovin' Things	1968	2.00	4.00	8.00
❑ Epic 10404	Wait for Me Mary-Ann/Mess Around	1968	2.00	4.00	8.00
❑ Epic 10428	Ob-La-Di, Ob-La-Da/Chains	1969	2.50	5.00	10.00
❑ Epic 10493	Time Is On My Side/Baby Make It Soon	1969	2.00	4.00	8.00
❑ London 20058	Reflections of My Life/Rollin' My Thing	1970	—	3.00	6.00
❑ London 20059	Rainbow/The Ballad of Cherry Flavar	1970	—	2.50	5.00
❑ London 20066	My Little One/Is Your Life Your Own	1971	—	2.50	5.00
❑ London 20068	Lonely Man/Cousin Norman	1971	—	2.50	5.00
❑ London 20072	Just One Woman/Radancer	1971	—	2.50	5.00
Albums					
❑ Epic BN 26553	The Best of the Marmalade	1970	5.00	10.00	20.00
❑ London PS 575	Reflections of My Life	1970	5.00	10.00	20.00

MARSHALL TUCKER BAND, THE

Number	Title (A Side/B Side)	Yr	VG	VG+	NM
45s					
❑ Capricorn 0021	Can't You See/See You Later, I'm Gone	1973	—	3.00	6.00
❑ Capricorn 0030	Take the Highway/Jesus Told Me So	1973	—	3.00	6.00
❑ Capricorn 0049	Another Cruel Love/Blue Ridge Mountain Sky	1974	—	2.50	5.00
❑ Capricorn 0228	This Ol' Cowboy/Try One More Time	1975	—	2.50	5.00
❑ Capricorn 0244	Fire on the Mountain/Bop Away My Blues	1975	—	2.50	5.00
❑ Capricorn 0251	Searchin' for a Rainbow/Walkin' and Talkin'	1976	—	2.50	5.00
❑ Capricorn 0258	Long Hard Ride/Windy City Blues	1976	—	2.50	5.00
❑ Capricorn 0270	Heard It in a Love Song/Life in a Song	1977	—	2.50	5.00
❑ Capricorn 0278	Can't You See/Fly Like an Eagle	1977	—	2.50	5.00
❑ Capricorn 0300	Dream Lover/A Change Is Gonna Come	1978	—	2.50	5.00
❑ Capricorn 0307	I'll Be Seeing You/Everybody Needs Somebody	1978	—	2.50	5.00
❑ Mercury 870050-7	Once You Get the Feel of It/Slow Down	1987	—	—	3.00
❑ Mercury 870505-7	Dancin' Shoes/I'm Glad It's Gone	1988	—	—	3.00
❑ Mercury 872096-7	Still Holdin' On/Same Old Moon	1989	—	—	3.00
❑ Mercury 888774-7	Hangin' Out in Smokey Places/He Don't Know	1987	—	—	3.00
❑ Warner Bros. 8841	Last of the Singing Cowboys/Pass It On	1979	—	2.50	5.00
❑ Warner Bros. 29355	I May Be Easy But You Make It Hard/Shot Down Where You Stand	1984	—	2.00	4.00
❑ Warner Bros. 29619	A Place I've Never Been/8:05	1983	—	2.00	4.00
❑ Warner Bros. 29939	Reachin' for a Little Bit More/Sweet Elaine	1982	—	2.00	4.00
❑ Warner Bros. 29995	Mr. President/The Sea, Dreams and Fairy Tales	1982	—	2.00	4.00
❑ Warner Bros. 49068	Running Like the Wind/(B-side unknown)	1979	—	2.50	5.00
❑ Warner Bros. 49215	It Takes Time/Jimi	1980	—	2.50	5.00
❑ Warner Bros. 49259	Disillusioned/Without You	1980	—	2.00	4.00
❑ Warner Bros. 49724	This Time I Believe/Tell the Blues to Take Off the Night	1981	—	2.00	4.00
❑ Warner Bros. 49764	Time Has Come/Love Some	1981	—	2.00	4.00

Number	Title (A Side/B Side)	Yr	VG	VG+	NM
Albums					
❑ Capricorn CP 0112	The Marshall Tucker Band	1973	3.00	6.00	12.00
❑ Capricorn CP 0124	A New Life	1974	3.00	6.00	12.00
❑ Capricorn 2CP 0145 [(2)]	Where We All Belong	1974	3.75	7.50	15.00
❑ Capricorn CP 0161	Searchin' for a Rainbow	1975	3.00	6.00	12.00
❑ Capricorn CP 0170	Long Hard Ride	1976	3.00	6.00	12.00
❑ Capricorn CPK 0180	Carolina Dreams	1977	3.00	6.00	12.00
❑ Capricorn CP 0205	Together Forever	1978	3.00	6.00	12.00
❑ Capricorn CPN-0214	Greatest Hits	1978	3.00	6.00	12.00
❑ Mercury 832794-1	Still Holdin' On	1988	2.50	5.00	10.00
❑ Warner Bros. BSK 3317	Running Like the Wind	1979	2.50	5.00	10.00
❑ Warner Bros. HS 3410	Tenth	1980	2.50	5.00	10.00
❑ Warner Bros. HS 3525	Dedicated	1981	2.50	5.00	10.00
❑ Warner Bros. BSK 3606	The Marshall Tucker Band	1982	2.50	5.00	10.00
—Reissue of Capricorn 0112					
❑ Warner Bros. 2WS 3608 [(2)]	Where We All Belong	1982	3.00	6.00	12.00
—Reissue of Capricorn 0145					
❑ Warner Bros. BSK 3609	Searchin' for a Rainbow	1982	2.50	5.00	10.00
—Reissue of Capricorn 0161					
❑ Warner Bros. BSK 3610	Carolina Dreams	1982	2.50	5.00	10.00
—Reissue of Capricorn 0180					
❑ Warner Bros. BSK 3611	Greatest Hits	1982	2.50	5.00	10.00
—Reissue of Capricorn 0214					
❑ Warner Bros. BSK 3662	A New Life	1982	2.50	5.00	10.00
—Reissue of Capricorn 0124					
❑ Warner Bros. BSK 3663	Long Hard Ride	1982	2.50	5.00	10.00
—Reissue of Capricorn 0170					
❑ Warner Bros. BSK 3664	Together Forever	1982	2.50	5.00	10.00
—Reissue of Capricorn 0205					
❑ Warner Bros. BSK 3684	Tuckerized	1982	2.50	5.00	10.00
❑ Warner Bros. 23803	Just Us	1983	2.50	5.00	10.00

MARTHA AND THE VANDELLAS

Number	Title (A Side/B Side)	Yr	VG	VG+	NM
45s					
❑ A&M 3022	Nowhere to Run/I Got You (I Feel Good)	1988	—	2.00	4.00
—B-side by James Brown					
❑ Gordy 7011	I'll Have to Let Him Go/My Baby Won't Come Back	1962	6.25	12.50	25.00
❑ Gordy 7014	Come and Get These Memories/Jealous Love	1963	7.50	15.00	30.00
❑ Gordy 7022	Heat Wave/A Love Like Yours	1963	5.00	10.00	20.00
❑ Gordy 7025	Quicksand/Darling, I Hum Our Song	1963	3.75	7.50	15.00
❑ Gordy 7027	Live Wire/Old Love	1964	3.75	7.50	15.00
❑ Gordy 7031	In My Lonely Room/A Tear for the Girl	1964	3.75	7.50	15.00
❑ Gordy 7033	Dancing in the Street/There He Is (At My Door)	1964	3.75	7.50	15.00
❑ Gordy 7036	Wild One/Dancing Slow	1964	3.00	6.00	12.00
❑ Gordy 7039	Nowhere to Run/Motoring	1965	3.00	6.00	12.00
❑ Gordy 7045	You've Been in Love Too Long/Love (Makes You Do Foolish Things)	1965	3.00	6.00	12.00
❑ Gordy 7048	My Baby Loves Me/Never Leave Your Baby's Side	1965	3.00	6.00	12.00
❑ Gordy 7053	What Am I Gonna Do Without Your Love/Go Ahead and Laugh	1966	3.00	6.00	12.00
❑ Gordy 7056	I'm Ready for Love/He Doesn't Love Her Anymore	1966	3.75	7.50	15.00
—"Gordy" logo at top					
❑ Gordy 7056	I'm Ready for Love/He Doesn't Love Her Anymore	1966	3.00	6.00	12.00
—"Gordy" logo at left					
❑ Gordy 7058	Jimmy Mack/Third Finger, Left Hand	1967	2.50	5.00	10.00
❑ Gordy 7062	Love Bug Leave My Heart Alone/One Way Out	1967	2.50	5.00	10.00
❑ Gordy 7067	Honey Chile/Show Me the Way	1967	2.50	5.00	10.00
—Starting here, as "Martha Reeves and the Vandellas"					
❑ Gordy 7070	I Promise to Wait My Love/Forget Me Not	1968	2.50	5.00	10.00
❑ Gordy 7075	I Can't Dance to That Music You're Playin'/I Tried	1968	2.50	5.00	10.00
❑ Gordy 7080	Sweet Darlin'/Without You	1968	2.50	5.00	10.00
❑ Gordy 7085	(We've Got) Honey Love/I'm In Love (And I Know It)	1969	2.00	4.00	8.00
❑ Gordy 7094	Taking My Love (And Leaving Me)/Heartless	1969	2.00	4.00	8.00
❑ Gordy 7098	I Should Be Pround/Love, Guess Who	1970	2.00	4.00	8.00
❑ Gordy 7103	I Gotta Let You Go/You're the Loser Now	1970	2.00	4.00	8.00
❑ Gordy 7110	Bless You/Hope I Don't Get My Heart Broke	1971	2.00	4.00	8.00
❑ Gordy 7113	In and Out of My Life/Your Love Makes It All Worthwhile	1972	2.00	4.00	8.00

Number	Title (A Side/B Side)	Yr	VG	VG+	NM
❑ Gordy 7118	Tear It On Down/I Want You Back	1972	2.00	4.00	8.00
❑ Gordy 7127	Baby Don't Leave Me/I Won't Be the Fool I've Been Again	1973	2.00	4.00	8.00

7-

Number	Title (A Side/B Side)	Yr	VG	VG+	NM
❑ Gordy G-60917	Come and Get These Memories/Love Is Like a Heat Wave/ Dancing in the Street//Love (Makes Me Do Foolish Things)/A Love Like Yours (Don't Come Knocking Everyday)/Nowhere to Run	1966	12.50	25.00	50.00
—Jukebox issue; small hole, plays at 33 1/3 rpm					
❑ Gordy G-60917 [Picture Sleeve]	Greatest Hits	1966	12.50	25.00	50.00
❑ Gordy G-60920	I'm Ready for Love/One Way Out/Jimmy Mack//I'll Follow You/ No More Tearstained Makeup/Tell Me I'll Never Be Alone	1966	10.00	20.00	40.00
—Jukebox issue; small hole, plays at 33 1/3 rpm					
❑ Gordy G-60920 [Picture Sleeve]	Watchout!	1966	10.00	20.00	40.00

Albums

Number	Title (A Side/B Side)	Yr	VG	VG+	NM
❑ Gordy G-902 [M]	Come and Get These Memories	1963	100.00	200.00	400.00
❑ Gordy GS-902 [S]	Come and Get These Memories	1963	200.00	400.00	800.00
❑ Gordy G-907 [M]	Heat Wave	1963	37.50	75.00	150.00
❑ Gordy GS-907 [R]	Heat Wave	1963	37.50	75.00	150.00
—"Stereo" banner pre-printed on cover					
❑ Gordy G-915 [M]	Dance Party	1965	10.00	20.00	40.00
❑ Gordy GS-915 [S]	Dance Party	1965	15.00	30.00	60.00
❑ Gordy G-917 [M]	Greatest Hits	1966	6.25	12.50	25.00
❑ Gordy GS-917 [S]	Greatest Hits	1966	7.50	15.00	30.00
❑ Gordy G-920 [M]	Watchout!	1966	6.25	12.50	25.00
❑ Gordy GS-920 [S]	Watchout!	1966	7.50	15.00	30.00
❑ Gordy G-925 [M]	Martha and the Vandellas Live!	1967	7.50	15.00	30.00
❑ Gordy GS-925 [S]	Martha and the Vandellas Live!	1967	6.25	12.50	25.00
❑ Gordy G-926 [M]	Ridin' High	1968	10.00	20.00	40.00
—Mono is promo only					
❑ Gordy GS-926 [S]	Ridin' High	1968	5.00	10.00	20.00
❑ Gordy GS-944	Sugar 'N Spice	1969	5.00	10.00	20.00
❑ Gordy GS-952	Natural Resources	1970	5.00	10.00	20.00
❑ Gordy GS-958	Black Magic	1972	5.00	10.00	20.00
❑ Motown M5-111V1	Motown Superstar Series, Vol. 11	1981	2.50	5.00	10.00
❑ Motown M5-145V1	Heat Wave	1981	2.50	5.00	10.00
—Reissue of Gordy 907					
❑ Motown M5-204V1	Greatest Hits	1981	2.50	5.00	10.00
—Reissue of Gordy 917					
❑ Motown M7-778 [(2)]	Anthology	1974	3.75	7.50	15.00

MARVELETTES, THE

45s

Number	Title (A Side/B Side)	Yr	VG	VG+	NM
❑ A&M 1201	Danger Heartbreak Dead Ahead/Baby Please Don't Go	1988	—	2.00	4.00
—B-side by Them					
❑ Gordy 7024	Too Hurt to Cry, Too Much in Love to Say Goodbye/ Come On Home	1963	20.00	40.00	80.00
—As "The Darnells"					
❑ Tamla 54046	Please Mr. Postman/So Long Baby	1961	6.25	12.50	25.00
❑ Tamla 54054	Twistin' Postman/I Want a Guy	1962	5.00	10.00	20.00
❑ Tamla 54060	Playboy/All the Love I've Got	1962	5.00	10.00	20.00
❑ Tamla 54065	Beechwood 4-5789/Someday, Someway	1962	5.00	10.00	20.00
❑ Tamla 54072	Strange I Know/Too Strong to Be Strung Along	1962	3.75	7.50	15.00
❑ Tamla 54077	Forever/Locking Up My Heart	1963	3.75	7.50	15.00
❑ Tamla 54082	Tie a String Around My Finger/My Daddy Knows Best	1963	5.00	10.00	20.00
❑ Tamla 54088	As Long As I Know He's Mine/Little Girl Blue	1963	3.00	6.00	12.00
❑ Tamla 54091	He's a Good Guy (Yes He Is)/Goddess of Love	1964	3.00	6.00	12.00
❑ Tamla 54097	You're My Remedy/A Little Bit of Sympathy, A Little Bit of Love	1964	2.50	5.00	10.00
❑ Tamla 54105	Too Many Fish in the Sea/A Need for Love	1964	2.50	5.00	10.00
❑ Tamla 54116	I'll Keep Holding On/No Time for Tears	1965	2.50	5.00	10.00
❑ Tamla 54120	Danger, Heartbreak Dead Ahead/Your Cheating Ways	1965	2.50	5.00	10.00
❑ Tamla 54126	Don't Mess with Bill/Anything You Wanna Do	1965	2.50	5.00	10.00
❑ Tamla 54131	You're the One/Paper Boy	1966	2.50	5.00	10.00
❑ Tamla 54143	The Hunter Gets Captured by the Game/I Think I Can Change You	1967	2.50	5.00	10.00
❑ Tamla 54150	When You're Young and In Love/The Day You Take One, You Have to Take the Other	1967	2.50	5.00	10.00
❑ Tamla 54158	My Baby Must Be a Magician/I Need Someone	1967	2.50	5.00	10.00
❑ Tamla 54166	Here I Am Baby/Keep Off, No Trespassing	1968	2.50	5.00	10.00
❑ Tamla 54171	Destination: Anywhere/What's So Easy for Two Is So Hard for One	1968	2.50	5.00	10.00
❑ Tamla 54177	I'm Gonna Hold On Long As I Can/Don't Make Hurting Me a Habit	1968	2.50	5.00	10.00
❑ Tamla 54186	That's How Heartaches Are Made/Rainy Mourning	1969	2.50	5.00	10.00
❑ Tamla 54198	Marionette/After All	1970	2.00	4.00	8.00
❑ Tamla 54213	A Breath Taking Guy/You're the One for Me Baby	1972	2.00	4.00	8.00

Albums

Number	Title (A Side/B Side)	Yr	VG	VG+	NM
❑ Motown M5-180V1	Greatest Hits	1981	2.50	5.00	10.00
—Reissue of Tamla 253					
❑ Motown M7-827 [(2)]	Anthology	1975	3.75	7.50	15.00
❑ Motown 5266 ML	Please Mr. Postman	1982	2.50	5.00	10.00
—Reissue of Tamla 228					
❑ Tamla T-228 [M]	Please Mr. Postman	1961	150.00	300.00	600.00
—White label					
❑ Tamla T-229 [M]	Smash Hits of 62'	1962	600.00	900.00	1200.
—Title as listed on front cover; large black "M" with song titles in circles; VG value 600; VG+ value 900					
❑ Tamla T-231 [M]	Playboy	1962	125.00	250.00	500.00
—Yellow label with overlapping record and globe logo					
❑ Tamla T-237 [M]	The Marvelous Marvelettes	1963	37.50	75.00	150.00
❑ Tamla T-243 [M]	Recorded Live on Stage	1963	20.00	40.00	80.00
❑ Tamla T-253 [M]	Greatest Hits	1966	7.50	15.00	30.00
—Yellow cover					

Number	Title (A Side/B Side)	Yr	VG	VG+	NM
❑ Tamla TS-253 [S]	Greatest Hits	1966	10.00	20.00	40.00
—Yellow cover					
❑ Tamla T-274 [M]	The Marveletttes	1967	7.50	15.00	30.00
❑ Tamla TS-274 [S]	The Marveletttes	1967	5.00	10.00	20.00
❑ Tamla T-286 [M]	Sophisticated Soul	1968	10.00	20.00	40.00
❑ Tamla TS-286 [S]	Sophisticated Soul	1968	5.00	10.00	20.00
❑ Tamla TS-288	In Full Bloom	1969	3.75	7.50	15.00
❑ Tamla TS-305	Return of the Marvelettes	1970	3.75	7.50	15.00
MAYFIELD, CURTIS					
45s					
❑ Arista 9806	He's a Flyguy/(Instrumental)	1989	—	—	2.00
❑ Boardwalk NB7-11-122	She Don't Let Nobody (But Me)/You Get All My Love	1981	—	2.00	4.00
❑ Boardwalk NB7-11-132	Toot An'Toot An'Toot/Come Free Your People	1981	—	2.00	4.00
❑ Boardwalk NB7-11-155	Hey Baby (Give It All to Me)/Summer Hot	1982	—	2.00	4.00
❑ Boardwalk NB7-11-169	Dirty Laundry/Nobody But You	1982	—	2.00	4.00
❑ Columbia 10147	Stash That Butt, Sucker/Zanzibar	1975	—	2.50	5.00
❑ CRC 001	Baby It's You/Breakin' in the Streets	1985	—	3.00	6.00
❑ Curtom 0105	So in Love/Hard Times	1975	—	2.50	5.00
❑ Curtom 0118	Only You Babe/Love to the People	1976	—	2.50	5.00
❑ Curtom 0122	Party Night/P.S. I Love You	1976	—	2.50	5.00
❑ Curtom 0125	Show Me Love/Just Want to Be with You	1977	—	2.50	5.00
❑ Curtom 0131	Do Do Wap Is Strong in Here/Need Someone to Love	1977	—	2.50	5.00
❑ Curtom 0135	You Are, You Are/Get a Little Bit (Give, Get, Take and Have)	1978	—	2.50	5.00
❑ Curtom 0141	Do It All Night/Party Party	1978	—	2.50	5.00
❑ Curtom 0142	In Love, In Love, In Love/Keeps Me Loving You	1978	—	2.50	5.00
❑ Curtom 1955	(Don't Worry) If There's a Hell Below We're All Going to Go/ The Makings of You	1970	—	3.00	6.00
❑ Curtom 1960	Beautiful Brother of Mine/Give It Up	1971	—	3.00	6.00
❑ Curtom 1963	Mighty Mighty (Spade and Whitey)/(B-side unknown)	1971	—	3.00	6.00
❑ Curtom 1966	Get Down/We're a Winner	1971	—	3.00	6.00
❑ Curtom 1968	We Got to Have Peace/We're a Winner	1972	—	3.00	6.00
❑ Curtom 1972	Beautiful Brother of Mine/Love to Keep You In My Mind	1972	—	3.00	6.00
❑ Curtom 1974	Move On Up/Underground	1972	—	3.00	6.00
❑ Curtom 1975	Freddie's Dead (Theme from "Superfly")/Underground	1972	—	3.00	6.00
❑ Curtom 1978	Superfly/Underground	1972	—	3.00	6.00
❑ Curtom 1987	Future Shock/The Other Side of Town	1973	—	3.00	6.00
❑ Curtom 1991	If I Were Only a Child Again/Think	1973	—	3.00	6.00
❑ Curtom 1993	Can't Say Nothin'/Future Song	1973	—	3.00	6.00
❑ Curtom 1999	Kung Fu/Right On for the Darkness	1974	—	3.00	6.00
❑ Curtom 2005	Sweet Exorcist/Suffer	1974	—	3.00	6.00
❑ Curtom 2006	Mother's Son/Love Me	1974	—	3.00	6.00
❑ RSO/Curtom 919	This Year/(Instrumental)	1979	—	2.50	5.00
❑ RSO/Curtom 941	You're So Good to Me/Between You, Babe, and Me	1979	—	2.50	5.00
—With Linda Clifford					
❑ RSO/Curtom 1029	Love's Sweet Sensation/(Instrumental)	1980	—	2.50	5.00
—With Linda Clifford					
❑ RSO/Curtom 1036	Love Me, Love Me Now/It's Alright	1980	—	2.50	5.00
❑ RSO/Curtom 1046	Tripping Out/Never Stop Loving	1980	—	2.50	5.00
7-					
❑ Curtom CRS-8014-EP	Pusherman/Think (Instrumental)//Give Me Your Love/ Eddie You Should Know Better/Junkie Chase (Instrumental)	1972	3.75	7.50	15.00
—Jukebox issue; small hole, plays at 33 1/3 rpm					
❑ Curtom CRS-8014-EP [Picture Sleeve]	Super Fly	1972	3.75	7.50	15.00
Albums					
❑ Boardwalk NB1-33239	Love Is the Place	1981	2.50	5.00	10.00
❑ Boardwalk NB1-33256	Honesty	1982	2.50	5.00	10.00
❑ CRC 2001	We Come in Peace with a Message of Love	1985	3.00	6.00	12.00
❑ Curtom CUR-2003	There's No Place Like America Today	198?	2.00	4.00	8.00
—Reissue of 5001					
❑ Curtom CUR-2005	Something to Believe In	198?	2.00	4.00	8.00
—Reissue of RSO 3077					
❑ Curtom CUR-2008	Take It to the Street	198?	2.50	5.00	10.00
❑ Curtom CUR-2901 [(2)]	Live in Europe	198?	3.00	6.00	12.00
❑ Curtom CUR-2902 [(2)]	Greatest Hits of All Time (Classic Collection)	198?	3.00	6.00	12.00
❑ Curtom CU 5001	There's No Place Like America Today	1975	3.00	6.00	12.00

Number	Title (A Side/B Side)	Yr	VG	VG+	NM
❑ Curtom CU 5007	Give, Get, Take and Have	1976	3.00	6.00	12.00
❑ Curtom CU 5013	Never Say You Can't Survive	1977	3.00	6.00	12.00
❑ Curtom CUK 5022	Do It All Night	1978	3.00	6.00	12.00
❑ Curtom CRS-8005	Curtis	1970	3.75	7.50	15.00
❑ Curtom CRS-8008 [(2)]	Curtis/Live!	1971	5.00	10.00	20.00
❑ Curtom CRS-8009	Roots	1971	3.75	7.50	15.00
❑ Curtom CRS-8014	Superfly	1972	5.00	10.00	20.00
❑ Curtom CRS-8015	Back to the World	1973	3.75	7.50	15.00
❑ Curtom CRS-8018	Curtis in Chicago	1973	3.75	7.50	15.00
❑ Curtom CRS-8601	Sweet Exorcist	1974	3.00	6.00	12.00
❑ Curtom CRS-8604	Got to Find a Way	1974	3.00	6.00	12.00
❑ RSO RS-1-3053	Heartbeat	1979	2.50	5.00	10.00
❑ RSO RS-1-3077	Something to Believe In	1980	2.50	5.00	10.00

MCCARTNEY, PAUL

45s

Number	Title (A Side/B Side)	Yr	VG	VG+	NM
❑ Apple 1829	Another Day/Oh Woman, Oh Why	1971	2.00	4.00	8.00
❑ Apple 1837	Uncle Albert/Admiral Halsey//Too Many People	1971	2.00	4.00	8.00
—Paul and Linda McCartney; with no misspelling					
❑ Apple 1847	Give Ireland Back to the Irish/Give Ireland Back to the Irish (Version)	1972	2.50	5.00	10.00
—Wings					
❑ Apple 1851	Mary Had a Little Lamb/Little Woman Love	1972	2.50	5.00	10.00
—Wings					
❑ Apple 1857	Hi Hi Hi/C Moon	1972	2.50	5.00	10.00
—Wings; red label					
❑ Apple 1861	My Love/The Mess	1973	2.00	4.00	8.00
—Paul McCartney and Wings; custom "Red Rose Speedway" label					
❑ Apple 1863	Live and Let Die/I Lie Around	1973	2.00	4.00	8.00
—Wings					
❑ Apple 1869	Helen Wheels/Country Dreamer	1973	2.00	4.00	8.00
—Paul McCartney and Wings					
❑ Apple 1871	Jet/Let Me Roll It	1974	2.00	4.00	8.00
—Paul McCartney and Wings					
❑ Apple 1871	Jet/Mamunia	1974	2.50	5.00	10.00
—Paul McCartney and Wings					
❑ Apple 1873	Band on the Run/Nineteen Hundred and Eighty-Five	1974	2.00	4.00	8.00
—Paul McCartney and Wings					
❑ Apple 1875	Junior's Farm/Sally G	1974	2.00	4.00	8.00
—Paul McCartney and Wings					
❑ Capitol 4091	Listen to What the Man Said/Love in Song	1975	—	2.50	5.00
—Credited to "Wings"					
❑ Capitol 4145	Letting Go/You Gave Me the Answer	1975	—	2.50	5.00
—Credited to "Wings"					
❑ Capitol 4175	Venus and Mars Rock Show/Magneto and Titanium Man	1975	—	2.50	5.00
—Credited to "Wings"					
❑ Capitol 4256	Silly Love Songs/Cook of the House	1976	—	2.00	4.00
—Credited to "Wings"; "Speed of Sound" label (more common version)					
❑ Capitol 4293	Let 'Em In/Beware My Love	1976	—	3.00	6.00
—Credited to "Wings"; black label (more common version)					
❑ Capitol 4385	Maybe I'm Amazed/Soily	1976	—	2.00	4.00
—Credited to "Wings"; custom label (more common version)					
❑ Capitol 4504	Girls' School/Mull of Kintyre	1977	—	2.50	5.00
—Credited to "Wings"; black label (more common version)					
❑ Capitol 4559	With a Little Luck/Backwards Traveller-Cuff Link	1978	—	2.00	4.00
—Credited to "Wings"					
❑ Capitol 4594	I've Had Enough/Deliver Your Children	1978	—	2.00	4.00
—Credited to "Wings"					
❑ Capitol 4625	London Town/I'm Carrying	1978	—	2.00	4.00
—Credited to "Wings"					
❑ Capitol B-5537	Spies Like Us/My Carnival	1985	—	—	3.00
❑ Capitol B-5597	Press/It's Not True	1986	—	2.50	5.00
❑ Capitol B-5636	Stranglehold/Angry	1986	—	2.50	5.00
❑ Capitol B-5672	Only Love Remains/Tough on a Tightrope	1987	—	2.50	5.00
❑ Capitol B-44367	My Brave Face/Flying to My Home	1989	2.50	5.00	10.00
—Version 1: Both title and artist in block print, time of A-side is "3:17"					
❑ Columbia 18-02171	Silly Love Songs/Cook of the House	1981	6.25	12.50	25.00
—Credited to "Wings"; despite label information, this has an edited version of A-side					
❑ Columbia 18-03018	Take It Away/I'll Give You a Ring	1982	—	—	3.00
❑ Columbia 38-03235	Tug of War/Get It	1982	3.00	6.00	12.00
❑ Columbia 38-04127	Wonderful Christmastime/Rudolph the Red-Nosed Reggae	1983	7.50	15.00	30.00
—Scarce reissue with B-side in stereo					
❑ Columbia 38-04296	So Bad/Pipes of Peace	1983	—	2.50	5.00
❑ Columbia 38-04581	No More Lonely Nights/(playout version)	1984	—	2.00	4.00
❑ Columbia 3-10939	Goodnight Tonight/Daytime Nighttime Suffering	1979	—	3.00	6.00
—Credited to "Wings"					
❑ Columbia 3-11020	Getting Closer/Spin It On	1979	—	3.00	6.00
—Credited to "Wings"					
❑ Columbia 1-11070	Arrow Through Me/Old Siam, Sir	1979	—	3.00	6.00
—Credited to "Wings"					
❑ Columbia 1-11162	Wonderful Christmastime/Rudolph the Red-Nosed Reggae	1979	2.50	5.00	10.00
❑ Columbia 1-11263	Coming Up//Coming Up (Live at Glasgow)/Lunch Box-Odd Sox	1980	—	2.00	4.00
—The first song on side 2 is credited to "Paul McCartney & Wings"					
❑ Columbia 1-11335	Waterfalls/Check My Machine	1980	—	3.00	6.00
❑ Columbia 13-33405	Goodnight Tonight/Getting Closer	1980	2.50	5.00	10.00
—Credited to "Wings"; red label "Hall of Fame" series					

Number	Title (A Side/B Side)	Yr	VG	VG+	NM
❑ Columbia 13-33407	My Love/Maybe I'm Amazed	1980	2.50	5.00	10.00
—Credited to "Paul McCartney and Wings"; red label "Hall of Fame" series; B-side is the studio version, making its first appearance on U.S. 45 here					
❑ Columbia 13-33408	Jet//Uncle Albert/Admiral Halsey	1980	2.50	5.00	10.00
—Credited to "Paul McCartney and Wings"; red label "Hall of Fame" series					
❑ Columbia 13-33409	Band on the Run/Helen Wheels	1980	2.50	5.00	10.00
—Credited to "Paul McCartney and Wings"; red label "Hall of Fame" series					
❑ EMI 3977	Walking in the Park with Eloise/Bridge on the River Suite	1974	15.00	30.00	60.00
Albums					
❑ Apple STAO-3363	McCartney	1970	5.00	10.00	20.00
—Only "McCartney" on label; back cover does NOT say "An Abkco managed company"					
❑ Apple SMAS-3375	Ram	1971	3.75	7.50	15.00
—Credited to "Paul and Linda McCartney"; unsliced apple on one label, sliced apple on other					
❑ Apple SW-3386	Wild Life	1971	3.75	7.50	15.00
—Credited to "Wings"					
❑ Apple SMAL-3409	Red Rose Speedway	1973	5.00	10.00	20.00
—Credited to "Paul McCartney and Wings"; with bound-in booklet					
❑ Apple SO-3415	Band on the Run	1973	5.00	10.00	20.00
—Credited to "Paul McCartney and Wings"; with photo innersleeve and poster					
❑ Capitol SMAS-11419	Venus and Mars	1975	3.75	7.50	15.00
—Credited to "Wings"; with two posters and two stickers					
❑ Capitol SW-11525	Wings at the Speed of Sound	1976	2.50	5.00	10.00
—Credited to "Wings"; custom label					
❑ Capitol SWCO-11593 [(3)]	Wings Over America	1976	6.25	12.50	25.00
—Credited to "Wings"; custom labels with poster					
❑ Capitol ST-11642	Thrillington	1977	25.00	50.00	100.00
—Credited to "Percy 'Thrills' Thrillington"; instrumental versions of songs from Ram LP					
❑ Capitol SW-11777	London Town	1978	3.75	7.50	15.00
—Credited to "Wings"; custom label with poster					
❑ Capitol SOO-11905	Wings Greatest	1978	3.75	7.50	15.00
—Credited to "Wings"; custom label with poster					
❑ Capitol PJAS-12475	Press to Play	1986	3.00	6.00	12.00
❑ Capitol CLW-48287 [(2)]	All the Best!	1987	5.00	10.00	20.00
❑ Capitol C1-91653	Flowers in the Dirt	1989	5.00	10.00	20.00
❑ Columbia FC 36057	Back to the Egg	1979	2.50	5.00	10.00
—Credited to "Wings"; custom label					
❑ Columbia JC 36478	McCartney	1979	3.75	7.50	15.00
❑ Columbia JC 36479	Ram	1980	3.75	7.50	15.00
—Credited to "Paul and Linda McCartney"					
❑ Columbia JC 36480	Wild Life	1980	3.75	7.50	15.00
—Credited to "Wings"					
❑ Columbia JC 36481	Red Rose Speedway	1980	3.75	7.50	15.00
—Credited to "Paul McCartney and Wings"; flat or glossy cover					
❑ Columbia JC 36482	Band on the Run	1980	3.75	7.50	15.00
—Credited to "Paul McCartney and Wings"; custom label					
❑ Columbia FC 36511	McCartney II	1980	2.50	5.00	10.00
—Add 80% if bonus single of "Coming Up (Live at Glasgow)" (AE7 1204) is with package					
❑ Columbia JC 36801	Venus and Mars	1980	3.75	7.50	15.00
—Credited to "Wings"; with one poster and two stickers					
❑ Columbia PC 36987	The McCartney Interview	1980	3.00	6.00	12.00
—Stock release of interview originally intended for promotional use only					
❑ Columbia FC 37409	Wings at the Speed of Sound	1981	3.75	7.50	15.00
—Credited to "Wings"; custom label					
❑ Columbia TC 37462	Tug of War	1982	2.50	5.00	10.00
❑ Columbia C3X 37990 [(3)]	Wings Over America	1982	12.50	25.00	50.00
—Credited to "Wings"; custom labels, no poster					
❑ Columbia QC 39149	Pipes of Peace	1983	3.00	6.00	12.00
❑ Columbia SC 39613	Give My Regards to Broad Street	1984	3.75	7.50	15.00
MCCARTNEY, PAUL, AND STEVIE WONDER					
45s					
❑ Columbia 18-02860	Ebony and Ivory/Rainclouds	1982	—	2.00	4.00
—B-side by McCartney solo					
MCCOYS, THE					
45s					
❑ Bang 506	Hang On Sloopy/I Can't Explain It	1965	3.75	7.50	15.00

Number	Title (A Side/B Side)	Yr	VG	VG+	NM
❑ Bang 511	Fever/Sorrow	1965	2.50	5.00	10.00
❑ Bang 516	Up and Down/If You Tell a Lie	1966	2.50	5.00	10.00
❑ Bang 522	Come On Let's Go/Little People	1966	2.50	5.00	10.00
❑ Bang 527	(You Make Me Feel) So Good/Runaway	1966	2.50	5.00	10.00
❑ Bang 532	Don't Worry Mother, Your Son's Heart Is Pure/Ko-Ko	1966	2.50	5.00	10.00
❑ Bang 538	I Got to Go Back (And Watch That Little Girl Dance)/Dynamite	1966	2.50	5.00	10.00
❑ Bang 543	Beat the Clock/Like You Do to Me	1967	2.50	5.00	10.00
❑ Bang 549	I Wonder If She Remembers Me/Say Those Magic Words	1967	2.50	5.00	10.00
❑ Mercury 72843	Jesse Brady/Resurrection	1968	2.00	4.00	8.00
❑ Mercury 72897	Daybreak/Epilogue	1969	2.00	4.00	8.00
❑ Mercury 72967	Don't Fight It/Rosa Rodriguez	1969	3.75	7.50	15.00
❑ RCA Victor 47-7204	Daddy's Geisha Girl/Our Love Goes On and On	1958	5.00	10.00	20.00
❑ RCA Victor 47-7354	Full Grown Cat/Throwing Kisses	1958	6.25	12.50	25.00
Albums					
❑ Bang BLP-212 [M]	Hang On Sloopy	1965	7.50	15.00	30.00
❑ Bang BLPS-212 [S]	Hang On Sloopy	1965	10.00	20.00	40.00
❑ Bang BLP-213 [M]	You Make Me Feel So Good	1966	7.50	15.00	30.00
❑ Bang BLPS-213 [S]	You Make Me Feel So Good	1966	10.00	20.00	40.00
❑ Mercury SR-61163	Infinite McCoys	1968	6.25	12.50	25.00
❑ Mercury SR-61207	Human Ball	1969	6.25	12.50	25.00

MCDANIELS, GENE

45s

Number	Title (A Side/B Side)	Yr	VG	VG+	NM
❑ Atlantic 2805	The Lord Is Back/Tell Me Mr. President	1971	—	3.00	6.00
—As "Eugene McDaniels"					
❑ Columbia 43800	Something Blue/Cause I Love You So	1966	2.50	5.00	10.00
❑ Columbia 44010	Touch of Your Lips/Sweet Lover No More	1967	2.50	5.00	10.00
❑ Liberty 55231	In Times Like These/Once Before	1959	3.75	7.50	15.00
❑ Liberty 55265	The Green Door/Facts of Life	1960	3.75	7.50	15.00
❑ Liberty 55308	A Hundred Pounds of Clay/Take a Chance on Love	1961	4.00	8.00	16.00
❑ Liberty 55344	A Tear/She's Come Back	1961	3.75	7.50	15.00
❑ Liberty 55371	Tower of Strength/The Secret	1961	4.00	8.00	16.00
❑ Liberty 55405	Chip Chip/Another Tear Falls	1962	3.75	7.50	15.00
❑ Liberty 55444	Funny/Chapel of Tears	1962	3.75	7.50	15.00
❑ Liberty 55480	Point of No Return/Warmer Than a Whisper	1962	3.75	7.50	15.00
❑ Liberty 55510	Spanish Lace/Somebody's Waiting	1962	3.75	7.50	15.00
❑ Liberty 55541	The Puzzle/Cry Baby Cry	1963	3.00	6.00	12.00
❑ Liberty 55597	It's a Lonely Town/False Friends	1963	3.00	6.00	12.00
❑ Liberty 55637	Old Country/Anyone Else	1963	3.00	6.00	12.00
❑ Liberty 55723	Make Me a Present of You/In Times Like These	1964	3.00	6.00	12.00
❑ Liberty 55752	Emily/Forgotten Man	1964	3.00	6.00	12.00
❑ Liberty 55805	A Miracle/Walk with a Winner	1965	2.50	5.00	10.00
❑ Liberty 55834	Hang On/Will It Last Forever	1965	2.50	5.00	10.00
❑ MGM 14613	Ol' Heartbreak Top Ten/River	1973	—	2.50	5.00
❑ Ode 66107	Lady Fair/Natural Juices	1975	—	2.00	4.00
❑ United Artists 0053	A Hundred Pounds of Clay/Tower of Strength	1973	—	2.00	4.00
—"Silver Spotlight Series" reissue					
❑ United Artists 0054	Chip Chip/Point of No Return	1973	—	2.00	4.00
—"Silver Spotlight Series" reissue					
Albums					
❑ Atlantic SD 8259	Outlaw	1970	3.75	7.50	15.00
❑ Atlantic SD 8281	Headless Heroes	1971	3.75	7.50	15.00
❑ Liberty LRP-3146 [M]	In Times Like These	1960	7.50	15.00	30.00
❑ Liberty LRP-3175 [M]	Sometimes I'm Happy, Sometimes I'm Blue	1960	7.50	15.00	30.00
❑ Liberty LRP-3191 [M]	100 Lbs. of Clay!	1961	7.50	15.00	30.00
❑ Liberty LRP-3204 [M]	Gene McDaniels Sings Movie Memories	1962	7.50	15.00	30.00
❑ Liberty LRP-3215 [M]	Tower of Strength	1962	7.50	15.00	30.00
❑ Liberty LRP-3258 [M]	Hit After Hit	1962	7.50	15.00	30.00
❑ Liberty LRP-3275 [M]	Spanish Lace	1963	6.25	12.50	25.00
❑ Liberty LRP-3311 [M]	The Wonderful World of Gene McDaniels	1963	6.25	12.50	25.00
❑ Liberty LST-7146 [S]	In Times Like These	1960	10.00	20.00	40.00
—Black vinyl					
❑ Liberty LST-7146 [S]	In Times Like These	1960	50.00	100.00	200.00
—Blue vinyl					
❑ Liberty LST-7175 [S]	Sometimes I'm Happy, Sometimes I'm Blue	1960	10.00	20.00	40.00
❑ Liberty LST-7191 [S]	100 Lbs. of Clay!	1961	10.00	20.00	40.00
❑ Liberty LST-7204 [S]	Gene McDaniels Sings Movie Memories	1962	10.00	20.00	40.00
❑ Liberty LST-7215 [S]	Tower of Strength	1962	10.00	20.00	40.00
❑ Liberty LST-7258 [S]	Hit After Hit	1962	10.00	20.00	40.00
❑ Liberty LST-7275 [S]	Spanish Lace	1963	7.50	15.00	30.00
❑ Liberty LST-7311 [S]	The Wonderful World of Gene McDaniels	1963	7.50	15.00	30.00
❑ Ode SP-77028	Natural Juices	1975	3.00	6.00	12.00
❑ Sunset SUM-1122 [M]	Facts of Life	1967	3.00	6.00	12.00
❑ Sunset SUS-5122 [S]	Facts of Life	1967	3.75	7.50	15.00
❑ United Artists UA-LA447-E	The Very Best of Gene McDaniels	1975	2.50	5.00	10.00

MCGUIRE, BARRY

45s

Number	Title (A Side/B Side)	Yr	VG	VG+	NM
❑ Dunhill 4009	Eve of Destruction/What Exactly's the Matter with Me	1965	3.00	6.00	12.00
❑ Dunhill 4014	Child of Our Times/Upon a Painted Ocean	1965	2.50	5.00	10.00
❑ Dunhill 4019	This Precious Time/Don't You Wonder Where It's At	1966	3.00	6.00	12.00
—A-side backing group: The Mamas and The Papas					
❑ Dunhill 4028	Cloudy Summer Afternoon (Raindrops)/ I'd Have to Be Outta My Mind	1966	2.50	5.00	10.00
❑ Dunhill 4048	There's Nothing Else on My Mind/Why Not Stop and Dig It	1966	2.50	5.00	10.00
❑ Dunhill 4098	Masters of War/Stop Now and Dig It While You Can	1967	2.00	4.00	8.00
❑ Dunhill 4116	Lollipop Train/Inner-Manipulations	1968	2.00	4.00	8.00

Number	Title (A Side/B Side)	Yr	VG	VG+	NM
❑ Dunhill 4124	Grasshopper Song/Top o' the Hill	1968	2.50	5.00	10.00
❑ Horizon 4	One by One/Town and Country	1963	3.00	6.00	12.00
❑ Horizon 8	Oh, Miss Mary/So Long, Stay Well	1963	3.00	6.00	12.00
❑ Mira 205	Greenback Dollar/Oh, Miss Mary	1965	2.50	5.00	10.00
❑ Mosaic 1001	The Three/Theme from The Tree	1961	3.00	6.00	12.00
❑ Mosaic 1004	I've Got a Secret/Cindy and Johnny	1962	3.00	6.00	12.00
❑ Myrrh 119	Love Is/David and Goliath	1973	—	2.50	5.00
❑ Ode 66010	Old Farm/South of the Border	1970	—	3.00	6.00
❑ Sparrow 1023	Cosmic Cowboy/What Good Would It Do	197?	—	3.00	6.00
Albums					
❑ ABC Dunhill DS-50033	The World's Last Private Citizen	1968	6.25	12.50	25.00
❑ Dunhill D-50003 [M]	Eve of Destruction	1965	7.50	15.00	30.00
❑ Dunhill DS-50003 [S]	Eve of Destruction	1965	10.00	20.00	40.00
❑ Dunhill D-50005 [M]	This Precious Time	1966	6.25	12.50	25.00
❑ Dunhill DS-50005 [S]	This Precious Time	1966	7.50	15.00	30.00
❑ Horizon ST-1636 [S]	The Barry McGuire Album	1963	10.00	20.00	40.00
❑ Horizon WP-1636 [M]	The Barry McGuire Album	1963	7.50	15.00	30.00
❑ Mira LP-3000 [M]	The Barry McGuire Album	1965	5.00	10.00	20.00
—Reissue of Horizon LP					
❑ Mira LPS-3000 [S]	The Barry McGuire Album	1965	6.25	12.50	25.00
—Reissue of Horizon LP					
❑ Myrrh MSA-6519	Seeds	1974	3.00	6.00	12.00
❑ Myrrh MSA-6531	Lighten Up	1975	3.00	6.00	12.00
❑ Ode SP-77004	Barry McGuire with the Doctor	1970	3.75	7.50	15.00

MCKENZIE, SCOTT

Number	Title (A Side/B Side)	Yr	VG	VG+	NM
45s					
❑ Capitol 5348	All I Want Is You/Look in Your Eyes	1965	2.50	5.00	10.00
❑ Capitol 5500	There Stands the Glass/Wipe the Tears (From Your Face)	1965	2.50	5.00	10.00
❑ Capitol 5961	All I Want Is You/Look in Your Eyes	1967	—	3.00	6.00
❑ Epic 10124	No, No, No, No, No/I Want to Be Alone	1967	2.00	4.00	8.00
—B-side by McKenzie's Musicians					
❑ Ode 103	San Francisco (Be Sure to Wear Flowers in Your Hair)/ What's the Difference	1967	2.00	4.00	8.00
—Revised title and revised mix					
❑ Ode 103	San Francisco "Wear Some Flowers in Your Hair"/ What's the Difference	1967	3.75	7.50	15.00
—Original title; also has a different mix (echoey bass drum in bridge) than the later, more common version					
❑ Ode 105	Like and Old Time Movie/What's the Difference, Chapter II	1967	—	3.00	6.00
❑ Ode 107	Holy Man/What's the Difference, Chapter III	1968	—	3.00	6.00
❑ Ode 66012	Going Home Again/Take a Moment	1970	—	2.50	5.00
Albums					
❑ Ode Z12 44001 [M]	The Voice of Scott McKenzie	1967	10.00	20.00	40.00
❑ Ode Z12 44002 [S]	The Voice of Scott McKenzie	1967	6.25	12.50	25.00
❑ Ode SP-77007	Stained Glass Morning	1970	3.75	7.50	15.00

MCLEAN, DON

Number	Title (A Side/B Side)	Yr	VG	VG+	NM
45s					
❑ Arista 0284	Prime Time/The Statue	1977	—	2.00	4.00
❑ Arista 0379	It Doesn't Matter Anymore/If We Try	1978	—	2.00	4.00
❑ Capitol B-44098	Perfect Love/Can't Blame the Train	1987	—	—	3.00
❑ Capitol B-44186	Love in the Heart/Every Day's a Miracle	1988	—	—	3.00
❑ Capitol B-44258	Eventually/It's Not Your Fault	1988	—	—	3.00
❑ EMI 9100	American Pie/Vincent	1992	2.00	4.00	8.00
—Scarce reissue with entire 8:30 version of "American Pie" on one side					
❑ EMI America 8375	He's Got You/To Have and To Hold	1987	—	—	3.00
❑ EMI America 43025	Superman's Ghost/(B-side unknown)	1987	—	—	3.00
❑ Mediarts 108	And I Love You So/Castles in the Air	1970	2.50	5.00	10.00
❑ Millennium YB-11799	Crying/Genesis (In the Beginning)	1980	—	2.00	4.00
❑ Millennium YB-11803	Lloras "Crying"/Genesis (In the Beginning)	1981	—	—	—
—Unreleased					
❑ Millennium YB-11804	Since I Don't Have You/Your Cheating Heart	1981	—	2.00	4.00
❑ Millennium YB-11809	It's Just the Sun/Words and Music	1981	—	2.00	4.00
❑ Millennium YB-11819	Castles in the Air/Crazy Eyes	1981	—	2.00	4.00
❑ Millennium YB-13106	Jerusalem/Left for Dead on the Road of Love	1982	—	2.00	4.00
❑ Millennium GB-13477	Crying/Since I Don't Have You	1983	—	—	3.00
—Gold Standard Series					

Number	Title (A Side/B Side)	Yr	VG	VG+	NM
❑ United Artists XW206	If We Try/The More You Pay	1973	—	2.00	4.00
❑ United Artists XW363	Fool's Paradise/Happy Trails	1973	—	2.00	4.00
❑ United Artists XW519	Vincent/Dreidel	1974	—	2.00	4.00
—Reissue					
❑ United Artists XW520	American Pie (Part 1)/American Pie (Part 2)	1974	—	2.00	4.00
—Reissue					
❑ United Artists XW541	Sitting on Top of the World/Mule Skinner Blues	1974	—	2.00	4.00
❑ United Artists XW579	Homeless Brothers/La La Love You	1974	—	2.00	4.00
❑ United Artists XW614	Wonderful Baby/Birthday Song	1975	—	2.00	4.00
❑ United Artists 50796	And I Love You So/Castles in the Air	1971	—	3.00	6.00
❑ United Artists 50856	American Pie/Empty Chairs	1971	—	—	—
—Unreleased?					
❑ United Artists 50856	American Pie — Part 1/American Pie — Part 2	1971	—	2.50	5.00
❑ United Artists 50887	Vincent/Castles in the Air	1972	—	2.50	5.00
❑ United Artists 51100	Dreidel/Bronco Bill's Lament	1973	—	2.00	4.00
Albums					
❑ Arista AL 4149	Prime Time	1978	2.50	5.00	10.00
❑ Capitol C1-48080	Love Tracks	1988	2.50	5.00	10.00
❑ Casablanca NBLP 7173	Chain Lightning	1979	—	—	—
—Canceled					
❑ EMI America ST-17255	Don McLean's Greatest Hits, Then and Now	1987	2.50	5.00	10.00
❑ Liberty LN-10037	American Pie	1980	2.00	4.00	8.00
—Reissue of United Artists 5535					
❑ Liberty LN-10157	Tapestry	1982	2.00	4.00	8.00
—Reissue of United Artists 5522					
❑ Liberty LN-10211	Homeless Brother	198?	2.00	4.00	8.00
—Reissue of United Artists 315					
❑ Mediarts 41-4	Tapestry	1970	5.00	10.00	20.00
❑ Millennium BXL1-7756	Chain Lightning	1981	2.50	5.00	10.00
❑ Millennium BXL1-7762	Believers	1981	2.50	5.00	10.00
❑ United Artists UA-LA161-F	Playin' Favorites	1973	3.00	6.00	12.00
❑ United Artists UA-LA315-G	Homeless Brother	1974	3.00	6.00	12.00
❑ United Artists UA-LA652-H2 [(2)]	Solo	1976	3.75	7.50	15.00
❑ United Artists UAS-5522	Tapestry	1971	3.00	6.00	12.00
—Reissue of Mediarts LP					
❑ United Artists UAS-5535	American Pie	1971	3.00	6.00	12.00
❑ United Artists UAS-5651	Don McLean	1972	3.00	6.00	12.00

MCPHATTER, CLYDE

45s

Number	Title (A Side/B Side)	Yr	VG	VG+	NM
❑ Amy 941	Everybody's Somebody's Fool/I Belong to You	1965	3.75	7.50	15.00
❑ Amy 950	Little Bit of Sunshine/Everybody Loves a Good Time	1966	3.00	6.00	12.00
❑ Amy 968	A Shot of Rhythm and Blues/I'm Not Going to Work Today	1966	3.00	6.00	12.00
❑ Amy 975	Sweet and Innocent/Lavender Lace	1967	3.00	6.00	12.00
❑ Amy 993	I Dreamt I Died/Lonely People Can't Afford to Cry	1967	3.00	6.00	12.00
❑ Atlantic 1070	Everybody's Laughing/Hot Ziggity	1955	7.50	15.00	30.00
❑ Atlantic 1077	Love Has Joined Us Together/I Gotta Have You	1955	7.50	15.00	30.00
—With Ruth Brown					
❑ Atlantic 1081	Seven Days/I'm Not Worthy	1956	7.50	15.00	30.00
❑ Atlantic 1092	Treasure of Love/When You're Sincere	1956	10.00	20.00	40.00
❑ Atlantic 1106	Thirty Days/I'm Lonely Tonight	1956	7.50	15.00	30.00
❑ Atlantic 1117	Without Love (There Is Nothing)/I Make Believe	1956	7.50	15.00	30.00
❑ Atlantic 1133	No Matter What/Just to Hold My Hand	1957	6.25	12.50	25.00
❑ Atlantic 1149	Long Lonely Nights/Heartaches	1957	6.25	12.50	25.00
❑ Atlantic 1158	You'll Be There/Rock and Cry	1957	6.25	12.50	25.00
❑ Atlantic 1170	That's Enough for Me/No Love Like Her Love	1958	6.25	12.50	25.00
❑ Atlantic 1185	Come What May/Let Me Know	1958	6.25	12.50	25.00
❑ Atlantic 1199	A Lover's Question/I Can't Stand Up Long	1958	6.25	12.50	25.00
❑ Atlantic 2018	Lovey Dovey/My Island of Dreams	1959	5.00	10.00	20.00
❑ Atlantic 2028	Since You've Been Gone/Try, Try Baby	1959	5.00	10.00	20.00
—B-side actually the "old" Drifters (uncredited)					
❑ Atlantic 2038	You Went Back on Your Word/There You Go	1959	5.00	10.00	20.00
—B-side actually the "old" Drifters (uncredited)					
❑ Atlantic 2049	Just Give Me a Ring/Don't Dog Me	1960	5.00	10.00	20.00
—B-side actually the "old" Drifters (uncredited)					
❑ Atlantic 2060	Deep Sea Ball/Let the Boogie-Woogie Roll	1960	5.00	10.00	20.00
—B-side actually the "old" Drifters (uncredited)					
❑ Atlantic 2082	If I Didn't Love You Like I Do/Go! Yes Go!	1960	5.00	10.00	20.00
—B-side actually the "old" Drifters (uncredited)					
❑ Decca 32719	Book of Memories/I'll Belong to You	1970	2.00	4.00	8.00
❑ Decca 32753	Why Can't We Get Together/Mixed-Up Cup	1970	2.00	4.00	8.00
❑ Deram 85032	Thank You Love/Only a Fool	1968	2.50	5.00	10.00
❑ Deram 85039	Baby You've Got It/Baby I Could Be So Good at Loving You	1969	2.50	5.00	10.00
❑ Mercury 71660	Ta Ta/I Ain't Givin' Up Nothin'	1960	3.75	7.50	15.00
❑ Mercury 71692	I Just Want to Love You/You're for Me	1960	3.75	7.50	15.00
❑ Mercury 71740	One More Chance/Before I Fall in Love Again	1960	3.75	7.50	15.00
❑ Mercury 71783	Tomorrow Is a-Comin'/I'll Love You Till the Cows Come Home	1961	3.75	7.50	15.00
❑ Mercury 71809	A Whole Heap o'Love/You're Movin' Me	1961	3.75	7.50	15.00
❑ Mercury 71841	I Never Knew/Happiness	1961	3.75	7.50	15.00
❑ Mercury 71868	Same Time, Same Place/Your Second Choice	1961	3.75	7.50	15.00
❑ Mercury 71941	Lover Please/Let's Forget About the Past	1962	5.00	10.00	20.00
❑ Mercury 71987	Little Bitty Pretty One/Next to Me	1962	3.75	7.50	15.00
❑ Mercury 72025	Maybe/I Do Believe	1962	3.75	7.50	15.00
❑ Mercury 72051	The Best Man Cried/Stop	1962	3.75	7.50	15.00
❑ Mercury 72166	So Close to Being in Love/From One to One	1963	3.75	7.50	15.00
❑ Mercury 72220	Deep in the Heart of Harlem/Happy Good Times	1963	3.75	7.50	15.00

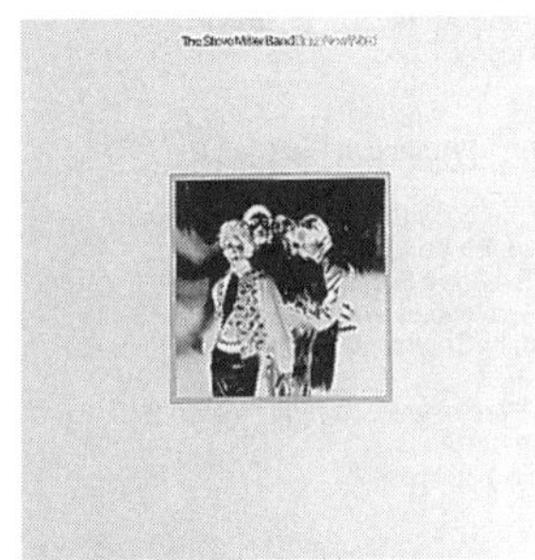

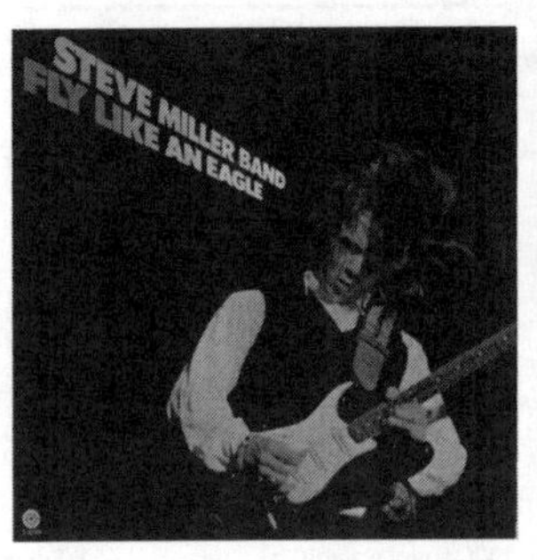

Number	Title (A Side/B Side)	Yr	VG	VG+	NM
❑ Mercury 72253	Second Window, Second Floor/In My Tenement	1964	3.75	7.50	15.00
❑ Mercury 72317	Lucille/Baby, Baby	1964	3.75	7.50	15.00
❑ Mercury 72407	Crying Won't Help You Now/I Found My Love	1965	3.75	7.50	15.00
❑ MGM 12780	I Told Myself a Lie/The Masquerade Is Over	1959	5.00	10.00	20.00
❑ MGM 12816	Twice As Nice/Where Did I Make My Mistake	1959	5.00	10.00	20.00
❑ MGM 12843 [M]	Let's Try Again/Bless You	1959	5.00	10.00	20.00
❑ MGM 12877	Think Me a Kiss/When the Right Time Comes Along	1960	5.00	10.00	20.00
❑ MGM 12949	One Right After Another/This Is Not Goodbye	1960	5.00	10.00	20.00
❑ MGM 12988	The Glory of Love/Take a Step	1961	5.00	10.00	20.00

7-

Number	Title (A Side/B Side)	Yr	VG	VG+	NM
❑ Mercury SR-619-C	Lover Please/Money Honey/Don't Let Go//Little Bitty Pretty One/ Sixty Minute Man/I'm Movin' On	196?	7.50	15.00	30.00

—Jukebox issue; small hole, plays at 33 1/3 rpm

Number	Title (A Side/B Side)	Yr	VG	VG+	NM
❑ Mercury SR-619-C [Picture Sleeve]	Lover Please!	196?	7.50	15.00	30.00

Albums

Number	Title (A Side/B Side)	Yr	VG	VG+	NM
❑ Allegiance AV-5029	The Pretty One	198?	2.50	5.00	10.00
❑ Atlantic 8024 [M]	Love Ballads	1958	125.00	250.00	500.00

—Black label

Number	Title (A Side/B Side)	Yr	VG	VG+	NM
❑ Atlantic 8031 [M]	Clyde	1959	125.00	250.00	500.00

—Black label

Number	Title (A Side/B Side)	Yr	VG	VG+	NM
❑ Atlantic 8077 [M]	The Best of Clyde McPhatter	1963	50.00	100.00	200.00
❑ Decca DL 75231	Welcome Home	1970	6.25	12.50	25.00
❑ Mercury MG-20597 [M]	Ta Ta	1960	12.50	25.00	50.00
❑ Mercury MG-20655 [M]	Golden Blues Hits	1961	12.50	25.00	50.00
❑ Mercury MG-20711 [M]	Lover Please	1962	12.50	25.00	50.00
❑ Mercury MG-20750 [M]	Rhythm and Soul	1962	12.50	25.00	50.00
❑ Mercury MG-20783 [M]	Clyde McPhatter's Greatest Hits	1963	7.50	15.00	30.00
❑ Mercury MG-20902 [M]	Songs of the Big City	1964	7.50	15.00	30.00
❑ Mercury MG-20915 [M]	Live at the Apollo	1964	7.50	15.00	30.00
❑ Mercury SR-60262 [S]	Ta Ta	1960	17.50	35.00	70.00
❑ Mercury SR-60655 [S]	Golden Blues Hits	1961	17.50	35.00	70.00
❑ Mercury SR-60711 [S]	Lover Please	1962	17.50	35.00	70.00
❑ Mercury SR-60750 [S]	Rhythm and Soul	1962	17.50	35.00	70.00
❑ Mercury SR-60783 [S]	Clyde McPhatter's Greatest Hits	1963	10.00	20.00	40.00
❑ Mercury SR-60902 [S]	Songs of the Big City	1964	10.00	20.00	40.00
❑ Mercury SR-60915 [S]	Live at the Apollo	1964	10.00	20.00	40.00
❑ MGM E-3775 [M]	Let's Start Over Again	1959	37.50	75.00	150.00
❑ MGM SE-3775 [S]	Let's Start Over Again	1959	50.00	100.00	200.00
❑ MGM E-3866 [M]	Clyde McPhatter's Greatest Hits	1960	17.50	35.00	70.00
❑ MGM SE-3866 [S]	Clyde McPhatter's Greatest Hits	1960	20.00	40.00	80.00
❑ Wing MGW-12224 [M]	May I Sing for You?	1962	6.25	12.50	25.00
❑ Wing SRW-16224 [S]	May I Sing for You?	1962	7.50	15.00	30.00

MEAT LOAF

45s

Number	Title (A Side/B Side)	Yr	VG	VG+	NM
❑ Atlantic 89303	Rock 'N' Roll Mercenaries/Execution Day	1987	—	—	3.00

—A-side with John Parr

Number	Title (A Side/B Side)	Yr	VG	VG+	NM
❑ Atlantic 89340	Getting Away with Murder/Rock 'N' Roll Hero	1986	—	—	3.00
❑ Cleveland Int'l. 02490	I'm Gonna Love Her for Both of Us/Peel Out	1981	—	2.00	4.00
❑ Cleveland Int'l. 02607	Read 'Em and Weep/Peel Out	1981	—	2.00	4.00
❑ Cleveland Int'l. 04028	The Razor's Edge/You Never Can Be Too Sure About the Girl	1983	—	2.00	4.00
❑ Epic 50467	You Took the Words Right Out of My Mouth/For Crying Out Loud	1977	2.00	4.00	8.00
❑ Epic 50513	Two Out of Three Ain't Bad (3:50)/For Crying Out Loud	1978	—	2.50	5.00
❑ Epic 50513	Two Out of Three Ain't Bad (5:12)/For Crying Out Loud	1978	—	3.00	6.00
❑ Epic 50588	Paradise by the Dashboard Light/"Bat" Overture	1978	—	2.50	5.00
❑ Epic 50634	You Took the Words Right Out of My Mouth/ Paradise by the Dashboard Light	1978	—	2.50	5.00
❑ RCA PB-14101	(Give Me the Future with a) Modern Girl/Sailor to a Siren	1985	—	—	3.00
❑ RCA PB-14149	Surf's Up/Jumpin' the Sun	1985	—	—	3.00
❑ RSO 407	More Than You Deserve/Presence of the Lord	1974	3.00	6.00	12.00

Albums

Number	Title (A Side/B Side)	Yr	VG	VG+	NM
❑ Atlantic 81698	Blind Before I Stop	1986	2.00	4.00	8.00
❑ Cleveland Int'l. FE 36007	Dead Ringer	1981	2.00	4.00	8.00
❑ Epic PE 34974	Bat Out of Hell	1977	2.50	5.00	10.00

—Orange label; originals do not have bar code on back cover

Number	Title (A Side/B Side)	Yr	VG	VG+	NM
❑ Epic FE 38444	Midnight at the Lost and Found	1983	2.00	4.00	8.00
❑ RCA Victor AFL1-5451	Bad Attitude	1985	2.00	4.00	8.00

Number	Title (A Side/B Side)	Yr	VG	VG+	NM
MELANIE					
45s					
❑ Amherst 300	Who's Been Sleeping in My Bed (Edited)/ Who's Been Sleeping in My Bed	1985	—	2.00	4.00
❑ Atlantic 3380	If I Needed You/Cyclone	1977	—	2.50	5.00
❑ Blanche 1	Imaginary Heroes/Detroit or Buffalo	1982	—	2.00	4.00
❑ Blanche 110	When You're Dead and Gone/Detroit or Buffalo	1982	—	2.00	4.00
❑ Buddah 113	Bo Bo's Party/I'm Back in Town	1969	—	3.00	6.00
❑ Buddah 135	Beautiful People/Any Guy	1969	—	3.00	6.00
❑ Buddah 167	Lay Down (Candles in the Rain)/Candles in the Rain	1970	—	3.00	6.00
❑ Buddah 186	Peace Will Come (According to Plan)/Close to It All	1970	—	2.50	5.00
❑ Buddah 186	Peace Will Come (According to Plan)/ Stop (I Don't Want to Hear It Anymore)	1970	—	2.50	5.00
❑ Buddah 202	Ruby Tuesday/Merry Christmas	1970	—	2.50	5.00
❑ Buddah 202	Ruby Tuesday/Lovin Baby Girl	1971	—	3.00	6.00
—Scarcer than the original B-side					
❑ Buddah 224	We Don't Know Where We're Going/The Good Book	1971	—	2.50	5.00
❑ Buddah 268	The Nickel Song/What Have They Done to My Song Ma	1971	—	2.50	5.00
❑ Buddah 304	I'm Back in Town/Johnny Boy	1972	—	2.50	5.00
❑ Columbia 44349	My Beautiful People/God's Only Daughter	1967	2.50	5.00	10.00
❑ Columbia 44524	Garden in the City/Why Didn't My Mother Tell Me	1968	2.50	5.00	10.00
❑ Gordian 1947	Rag Doll/(B-side unknown)	1985	—	2.00	4.00
❑ Midsong Int'l. 40858	I'd Rather Leave While I'm in Love/Record People	1978	—	2.50	5.00
❑ Midsong Int'l. 40903	Knock on Wood/Record People	1978	—	2.50	5.00
❑ Neighborhood 4201	Brand New Key/Some Say (I Got Devil)	1971	—	3.00	6.00
—White label (not a promo)					
❑ Neighborhood 4201	Brand New Key/Some Say (I Got Devil)	1971	—	2.50	5.00
—Multicolor label					
❑ Neighborhood 4202	Ring the Living Bell/Railroad	1972	—	2.00	4.00
❑ Neighborhood 4204	Steppin'/Someday I'll Be a Farmer	1972	—	2.00	4.00
❑ Neighborhood 4207	Together Alone/Center of the Circle	1972	—	2.00	4.00
❑ Neighborhood 4209	Stoneground Woman/Do You Believe	1972	—	2.00	4.00
❑ Neighborhood 4210	Bitter Bad/Do You Believe	1973	—	2.00	4.00
❑ Neighborhood 4212	Seeds/Some Say (I Got Devil)	1973	—	2.00	4.00
❑ Neighborhood 4213	Will You Love Me Tomorrow/Here I Am	1973	—	2.00	4.00
❑ Neighborhood 4214	Love to Love Again/Fine and Feather	1974	—	2.00	4.00
❑ Neighborhood 4215	Lover's Cross/Holding Out	1974	—	2.00	4.00
❑ Neighborhood 10000	You're Not a Bad Ghost, Just an Old Song/Eyes of Man	1975	—	2.00	4.00
❑ Neighborhood 10001	Sweet Misery/Record Machine	1975	—	2.00	4.00
❑ Portrait 51001	One More Try/Apathy	1981	—	2.00	4.00
❑ Tomato 10007	Running After Love/Holding Out	1979	—	2.50	5.00
❑ World United 1947	Oh Boy/Brand New Key	1978	—	2.50	5.00
Albums					
❑ ABC ABND-879	From the Beginning/Twelve Great Performances	1975	2.50	5.00	10.00
❑ Accord SN-7109	What Have They Done to My Song Ma	1981	2.50	5.00	10.00
❑ Accord SN-7191	Beautiful People	1982	2.50	5.00	10.00
❑ Amherst AMH-3302	Am I Real or What	1985	2.50	5.00	10.00
❑ Atlantic SD 18190	Photograph	1976	2.50	5.00	10.00
❑ Blanche BL 6177	Arabesque	1982	2.50	5.00	10.00
❑ Buddah BDS-5024	Born to Be	1969	3.75	7.50	15.00
❑ Buddah BDS-5041	Melanie	1969	3.75	7.50	15.00
❑ Buddah BDS-5060	Candles in the Rain	1970	3.75	7.50	15.00
❑ Buddah BDS-5066	Leftover Wine	1970	3.75	7.50	15.00
❑ Buddah BDS-5074	My First Album	1971	3.00	6.00	12.00
❑ Buddah BDS-5095	Garden in the City	1971	3.00	6.00	12.00
❑ Buddah BDS-5132	Please Love Me	1973	3.00	6.00	12.00
❑ Buddah B2D-5664 [(2)]	The Best...Melanie	197?	3.75	7.50	15.00
❑ Buddah BDS-95000	The Good Book	1971	3.75	7.50	15.00
❑ Buddah BDS-95005 [(2)]	Four Sides of Melanie	1972	3.75	7.50	15.00
❑ Midsong MCA-3033	Phonogenic: Not Just Another Pretty Face	1978	2.50	5.00	10.00
❑ Neighborhood 3000	As I See It Now	1974	3.00	6.00	12.00
❑ Neighborhood 3001	Sunsets and Other Beginnings	1975	3.00	6.00	12.00
❑ Neighborhood 47001	Gather Me	1971	3.00	6.00	12.00
❑ Neighborhood 47005	Stoneground Words	1972	3.00	6.00	12.00
❑ Neighborhood 48001	Madrugada	1974	3.00	6.00	12.00
❑ Neighborhood 49001 [(2)]	Melanie at Carnegie Hall	1973	3.75	7.50	15.00
❑ Pickwick SPC-3317	Try the Real Thing	197?	2.50	5.00	10.00
❑ Tomato TOM-2-9003 [(2)]	Ballroom Streets	1979	3.00	6.00	12.00
MELLENCAMP, JOHN					
45s					
❑ Elektra 69370	Rave On/Tutti Frutti	1988	—	—	3.00
—B-side by Little Richard					
❑ MCA 40634	American Dream/Oh, Pretty Woman	1976	2.50	5.00	10.00
—As "Johnny Cougar"					
❑ Mercury 574244-7	Key West Intermezzo (I Saw You First)/Just Another Day	1997	—	—	3.00
❑ Mercury 856258-7	Dance Naked/R.O.C.K. in the U.S.A.	1994	—	2.00	4.00
❑ Mercury 858738-7	Wild Night/Brothers	1994	—	2.00	4.00
—With Me'Shell NgedeOcelo					
❑ Mercury 862702-7	Human Wheels/Human Wheels (Edit)	1993	—	2.00	4.00
❑ Mercury 866414-7	Again Tonight/Get a Leg Up (Live)	1992	—	2.00	4.00
❑ Mercury 867890-7	Get a Leg Up (Family Version)/Whenever We Wanted	1991	—	2.00	4.00
❑ Mercury 870126-7	Check It Out/We Are the People	1988	—	—	3.00
—Mercury releases starting with "870" and "888" are by "John Cougar Mellecamp"					
❑ Mercury 870327-7	Rooty Toot Toot/Check It Out	1988	—	—	3.00
❑ Mercury 874012-7	Pop Singer/J.M.'s Question	1989	—	—	3.00
❑ Mercury 874644-7	Jackie Brown/Jackie Brown (Acoustic Version)	1989	—	—	3.00

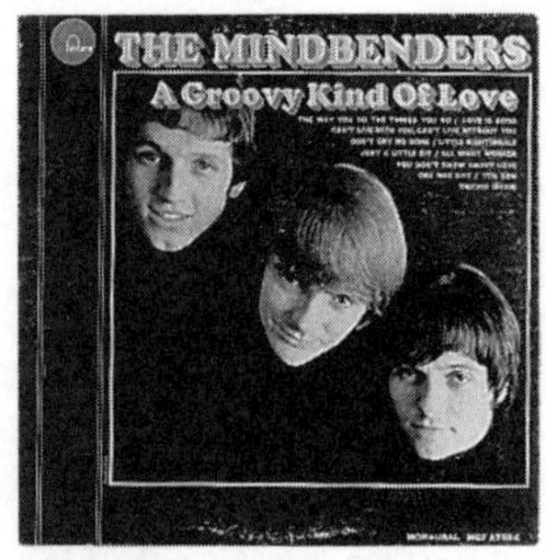

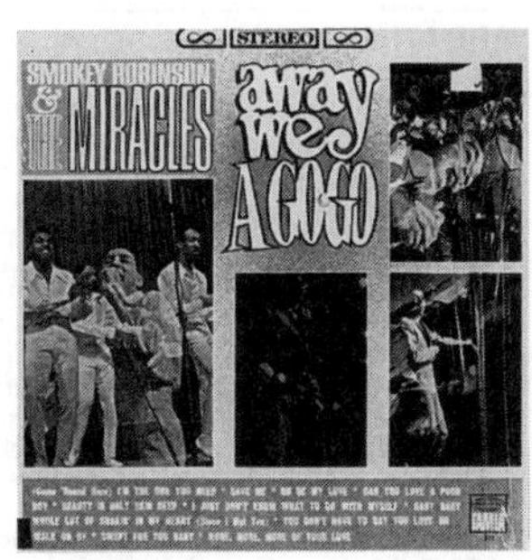

Number	Title (A Side/B Side)	Yr	VG	VG+	NM
❑ Mercury 874932-7	Let It All Hang Out/Country Gentleman	1989	—	2.00	4.00
❑ Mercury 888763-7	Paper in Fire/Never Too Old	1987	—	—	3.00
❑ Mercury 888934-7	Cherry Bomb/Shama Lama Ding Dong	1987	—	—	3.00
❑ Riva 202	I Need a Lover/Welcome to Chinatown	1979	—	2.00	4.00
—Riva 202-211 as "John Cougar"					
❑ Riva 203	Small Paradise/Sugar Marie	1980	—	2.00	4.00
❑ Riva 204	A Little Night Dancin'/Pray for Me	1980	—	2.50	5.00
❑ Riva 205	This Time/Don't Misunderstand Me	1980	—	2.00	4.00
❑ Riva 207	Ain't Even Done with the Night/Make Me Feel	1981	—	2.00	4.00
❑ Riva 209	Hurts So Good/Close Enough	1982	—	2.00	4.00
❑ Riva 210	Jack and Diane/Can You Take It	1982	—	2.00	4.00
❑ Riva 211	Hand to Hold On To/Small Paradise	1982	—	2.00	4.00
❑ Riva 214	Crumblin' Down/Golden Gates	1983	—	2.00	4.00
—Riva 214 on as "John Cougar Mellencamp"					
❑ Riva 215 [DJ]	Pink Houses (Long Version 4:43)/(Short Version 3:59)	1983	5.00	10.00	20.00
❑ Riva 215 [DJ]	Pink Houses (Long Version 4:43)/(Short Version 3:59)	1983	5.00	10.00	20.00
—Promo only on pink vinyl					
❑ Riva 216	Authority Song/Pink Houses (Acoustic Version)	1984	—	2.00	4.00
❑ Riva 880984-7	Lonely Ol' Night/The Kind of Fella I Am	1985	—	—	3.00
❑ Riva 884202-7	Small Town/(Acoustic Version)	1985	—	—	3.00
❑ Riva 884455-7	R.O.C.K. in the U.S.A. (A Salute to 60's Rock)/Under the Boardwalk	1986	—	—	3.00
❑ Riva 884635-7	Rain on the Scarecrow/Pretty Ballerina	1986	—	—	3.00
❑ Riva 884856-7	Rumbleseat/Cold Sweat	1986	—	—	3.00
Albums					
❑ MCA 2225	Chestnut Street Incident	1977	6.25	12.50	25.00
—As "Johnny Cougar"					
❑ Mercury 832465-1	The Lonesome Jubilee	1987	2.00	4.00	8.00
❑ Mercury 838220-1	Big Daddy	1989	2.50	5.00	10.00
❑ Riva RVL 7401	John Cougar	1979	2.50	5.00	10.00
—As "John Cougar"					
❑ Riva RVL 7403	Nothin' Matters and What If It Did	1980	2.50	5.00	10.00
—As "John Cougar"					
❑ Riva RVL 7501	American Fool	1982	2.00	4.00	8.00
—As "John Cougar"					
❑ Riva RVL 7504	Uh-Huh	1983	2.00	4.00	8.00
—As "John Cougar Mellencamp"					
❑ Riva 824865-1	Scarecrow	1985	2.00	4.00	8.00
—As "John Cougar Mellencamp"					

MELVIN, HAROLD, AND THE BLUE NOTES

45s

Number	Title (A Side/B Side)	Yr	VG	VG+	NM
❑ ABC 12240	Reaching for the World/Stay Together	1976	—	2.50	5.00
❑ ABC 12268	After You Love Me, Why Do You Leave Me/Big Singing Star	1977	—	2.50	5.00
—With Sharon Paige					
❑ ABC 12327	Baby, You Got My Nose Open/Try to Live a Day	1978	—	2.50	5.00
❑ ABC 12368	Power of Love/Now Is the Time	1978	—	2.50	5.00
❑ Arctic 135	Go Away/What Can a Man Do	1967	2.50	5.00	10.00
❑ Landa 703	Get Out (And Let Me Cry)/You May Not Love Me	1964	4.00	8.00	16.00
—As "The Blue Notes"					
❑ MCA 41291	Tonight's the Night/If You're Looking for Someone to Love	1980	—	2.00	4.00
—With Sharon Paige					
❑ MCA 51190	Hang On In There/If You Love Me, Really Love Me	1982	—	2.00	4.00
❑ Philadelphia Int'l. 3516	I Miss You (Part I)/I Miss You (Part II)	1972	—	2.50	5.00
❑ Philadelphia Int'l. 3520	If You Don't Know Me By Now/Let Me Into Your World	1972	—	2.50	5.00
❑ Philadelphia Int'l. 3525	Yesterday I Had the Blues/Ebony Woman	1973	—	2.50	5.00
❑ Philadelphia Int'l. 3533	The Love I Lost (Part 1)/The Love I Lost (Part 2)	1973	—	2.50	5.00
❑ Philadelphia Int'l. 3543	Satisfaction Guaranteed (Or Take Your Love Back)/ I'm Weak for You	1974	—	2.50	5.00
❑ Philadelphia Int'l. 3552	Where Are All My Friends/Let It Be You	1974	—	2.50	5.00
❑ Philadelphia Int'l. 3562	Bad Luck (Part 1)/Bad Luck (Part 2)	1975	—	2.50	5.00
❑ Philadelphia Int'l. 3569	Hope That We Can Be Together Soon/Be for Real	1975	—	2.50	5.00
—With Sharon Paige					
❑ Philadelphia Int'l. 3579	Wake Up Everybody (Part 1)/Wake Up Everybody (Part 2)	1975	—	2.50	5.00
❑ Philadelphia Int'l. 3588	Tell the World How I Feel About 'Cha Baby/You Know How to Make Me Feel So Good	1976	—	2.50	5.00
❑ Philly World 99709	I Really Love You/I Can't Let Go	1984	—	2.00	4.00

Number	Title (A Side/B Side)	Yr	VG	VG+	NM
❑ Philly World 99735	Today's Your Lucky Day (Long)/Today's Your Lucky Day (Short)	1984	—	2.00	4.00
❑ Philly World 99761	Don't Give Me Up/(Instrumental)	1984	—	2.00	4.00
❑ Source 41156	Prayin'/(Instrumental)	1979	7.50	15.00	30.00
❑ Source 41157	Tonight's the Night/Your Love Is Taking Me on a Journey	1979	—	2.00	4.00
—As "Sharon Paige with Harold Melvin and the Blue Notes"					
❑ Source 41231	I Should Be Your Lover (Part 1)/I Should Be Your Lover (Part 2)	1980	—	2.00	4.00
Albums					
❑ ABC AB-969	Reaching for the World	1977	2.50	5.00	10.00
❑ ABC AB-1041	Now Is the Time	1978	2.50	5.00	10.00
❑ MCA 5261	All Things Happen in Time	1981	2.50	5.00	10.00
❑ Philadelphia Int'l. KZ 31648	Harold Melvin and the Blue Notes	1972	3.00	6.00	12.00
❑ Philadelphia Int'l. KZ 32407	Black & Blue	1973	3.00	6.00	12.00
❑ Philadelphia Int'l. PZ 33148	To Be True	1975	3.00	6.00	12.00
❑ Philadelphia Int'l. PZ 33808	Wake Up Everybody	1975	3.00	6.00	12.00
❑ Philadelphia Int'l. PZ 34232	Collector's Item — All Their Greatest Hits!	1976	3.00	6.00	12.00
❑ Philly World 90187	Talk It Up (Tell Everybody)	1985	2.50	5.00	10.00
❑ Source 3197	The Blue Album	1980	2.50	5.00	10.00
MEN AT WORK					
45s					
❑ Columbia 18-02888	Who Can It Be Now?/Anyone for Tennis	1982	—	2.00	4.00
❑ Columbia 38-03303	Down Under/Crazy	1982	—	2.00	4.00
❑ Columbia CNR-03373	Down Under/(B-side blank)	1982	—	2.50	5.00
—One-sided budget release					
❑ Columbia 38-03795	Overkill/Till the Money Runs Out	1983	—	—	3.00
❑ Columbia 38-03959	It's a Mistake/Shintano	1983	—	—	3.00
❑ Columbia 38-04111	Dr. Heckyll & Mr. Jive/I Like To (Live)	1983	—	—	3.00
❑ Columbia 38-04929	Everything I Need/Sail to You	1985	—	—	3.00
❑ Columbia 38-05454	Maria/Snakes and Ladders	1985	—	—	3.00
❑ Columbia 38-05649	Hard Luck Story/Snakes and Ladders	1985	—	—	3.00
Albums					
❑ Columbia ARC 37978	Business as Usual	1982	2.50	5.00	10.00
❑ Columbia QC 38660	Cargo	1983	2.50	5.00	10.00
❑ Columbia FC 40078	Two Hearts	1985	2.00	4.00	8.00
MERCY					
45s					
❑ Sundi 6811	Love (Can Make You Happy)/Fire Ball	1969	2.00	4.00	8.00
❑ Warner Bros. 7297	Forever/The Morning's Come	1969	—	3.00	6.00
❑ Warner Bros. 7331	Hello Baby/Heard You Went Away	1969	—	3.00	6.00
Albums					
❑ Sundi SRLP-803	The Mercy & Love (Can Make You Happy)	1969	5.00	10.00	20.00
—Has the original version of the title song plus filler instrumentals					
❑ Warner Bros. WS 1799	Love (Can Make You Happy)	1969	3.75	7.50	15.00
—"Love (Can Make You Happy)" was re-recorded for this LP					
MICKEY AND SYLVIA					
45s					
❑ All Platinum 2307	Lovedrops/Because You Do It to Me	1969	—	3.00	6.00
❑ All Platinum 2310	Anytime/Souling with Mickey and Sylvia	1969	—	3.00	6.00
❑ Cat 102	Fine Love/Speedy Life	1954	10.00	20.00	40.00
—As "Little" Sylvia Vanderpool and Mickey Baker					
❑ Groove 0164	No Good Lover/Walkin' in the Rain	1956	7.50	15.00	30.00
❑ Groove 0175	Love Is Strange/I'm Going Home	1956	7.50	15.00	30.00
❑ King 5737	Baby, Let's Dance/Oh Yea, Ah Ah	1963	3.00	6.00	12.00
❑ King 6006	Love Is Strange/Darling	1965	2.50	5.00	10.00
❑ Rainbow 316	I'm So Glad/Se De Boom Run Dun	1955	7.50	15.00	30.00
❑ Rainbow 318	Forever and a Day/Ride, Sally, Ride	1955	7.50	15.00	30.00
❑ RCA 5224-7-RX	Love Is Strange/(I've Had) The Time of My Life	1987	—	—	3.00
—B-side by Bill Medley and Jennifer Warnes					
❑ RCA Victor 37-7877	Love Is the Only Thing/Love Lesson	1961	12.50	25.00	50.00
—"Compact Single 33" (small hole, plays at LP speed)					
❑ RCA Victor 47-7403	To the Valley/Oh Yeah! Uh-Huh	1958	5.00	10.00	20.00
❑ RCA Victor 47-7774 [M]	Sweeter As the Days Go By/Mommy Out De Light	1960	3.75	7.50	15.00
❑ RCA Victor 47-7811 [M]	What Would I Do/This Is My Story	1960	5.00	10.00	20.00
❑ RCA Victor 47-7877	Love Is the Only Thing/Love Lesson	1961	3.75	7.50	15.00
❑ RCA Victor 47-8517	Let's Shake Some More/Gypsy	1965	3.00	6.00	12.00
❑ RCA Victor 47-8582	Fallin' in Love/From the Beginning of Time	1965	3.00	6.00	12.00
❑ RCA Victor APAO-0080	Love Is Strange/Dearest	1973	—	3.00	6.00
❑ Stang 5004	Rocky Raccoon/Souling with Mickey and Sylvia	1969	2.00	4.00	8.00
❑ Stang 5047	Baby You're So Fine/Anytime You Want To	1973	—	3.00	6.00
❑ Vik 0252	Love Is Strange/I'm Going Home	1957	7.50	15.00	30.00
❑ Vik 0267	There Oughta Be a Law/Dearest	1957	6.25	12.50	25.00
❑ Vik 0280	Two Shadows on Your Window/Love Will Make You Fail in School	1957	6.25	12.50	25.00
❑ Vik 0290	Love Is a Treasure/Let's Have a Picnic	1957	6.25	12.50	25.00
❑ Vik 0297	There'll Be No Backin' Out/Where Is My Honey	1957	6.25	12.50	25.00
❑ Vik 0324	Rock and Stroll Room/Bewildered	1958	5.00	10.00	20.00
❑ Vik 0334	It's You I Love/True, True Love	1958	5.00	10.00	20.00
❑ Willow 23000	Baby, You're So Fine/Lovedrops	1961	3.75	7.50	15.00
❑ Willow 23002	Darling (I Miss You So)/I'm Guilty	1961	3.75	7.50	15.00
❑ Willow 23004	Since I Fell for You/He Gave Me Everything	1962	3.75	7.50	15.00
❑ Willow 23006	Love Is Strange/Walking in the Rain	1962	3.75	7.50	15.00
Albums					
❑ RCA Camden CAL-863 [M]	Love Is Strange	1965	12.50	25.00	50.00
❑ RCA Camden CAS-863(e) [R]	Love Is Strange	1965	7.50	15.00	30.00
❑ RCA Victor APM1-0327	Do It Again	1973	3.00	6.00	12.00

Number	Title (A Side/B Side)	Yr	VG	VG+	NM
❑ Vik LX-1102 [M]	New Sounds	1957	100.00	200.00	400.00

MIDLER, BETTE

45s

Number	Title (A Side/B Side)	Yr	VG	VG+	NM
❑ Atlantic 2928	Do You Want to Dance/Superstar	1972	—	2.50	5.00
❑ Atlantic 2964	Boogie Woogie Bugle Boy/Delta Dawn	1973	—	2.50	5.00
❑ Atlantic 2980	Friends/Chapel of Love	1973	—	3.00	6.00
❑ Atlantic 3004	In the Mood/Drinking Again	1974	—	3.00	6.00
❑ Atlantic 3319	Stranger in the Night/Samedi Et Vendredi	1976	—	3.00	6.00
❑ Atlantic 3325	Old Cape Cod/Tragedy	1976	—	3.00	6.00
❑ Atlantic 3379	You're Movin' Out Today/Let Me Just Follow Behind	1976	—	2.50	5.00
❑ Atlantic 3431	Storybook Children (Daybreak)/Empty Bed Blues	1977	—	2.50	5.00
❑ Atlantic 3475	Paradise/Red	1978	—	3.00	6.00
❑ Atlantic 3582	Married Men/Bang, You're Dead	1979	—	2.50	5.00
❑ Atlantic 3616	Hang On In There Baby/Cradle Days	1979	—	3.00	6.00
❑ Atlantic 3628	Big Noise from Winnetka/Rain	1979	—	3.00	6.00
❑ Atlantic 3643	When a Man Loves a Woman/Love Me with a Feeling	1980	—	2.00	4.00
❑ Atlantic 3656	The Rose/Stay with Me	1980	—	2.00	4.00
❑ Atlantic 3771	My Mother's Eyes/Chapel of Love	1980	—	2.50	5.00
❑ Atlantic 7-87572	Every Road Leads Back to You/I Remember You-Dixie's Dream	1991	—	2.00	4.00
❑ Atlantic 7-87820	From a Distance/One More Round	1990	—	2.00	4.00
❑ Atlantic 7-87825	Night and Day/The Girl Is On to You	1990	—	2.00	4.00
❑ Atlantic 7-88972	Wind Beneath My Wings/Oh Industry	1989	—	—	3.00
❑ Atlantic 7-88976	Under the Boardwalk/Otto Titsling	1989	—	2.50	5.00
❑ Atlantic 7-88976	Under the Boardwalk/The Friendship Theme	1989	—	—	3.00
❑ Atlantic 7-89712	Beast of Burden/Come Back Jimmy Dean	1984	—	2.50	5.00
❑ Atlantic 7-89761	Favorite Waste of Time/My Eye on You	1983	—	2.50	5.00
❑ Atlantic 7-89789	All I Need to Know/My Eye on You	1983	—	2.50	5.00
❑ Atlantic Oldies Series OS-13155	Boogie Woogie Bugle Boy/Do You Want to Dance?	197?	—	2.00	4.00
—Gold label with "Oldies Series" at 3 o'clock					
❑ Atlantic Oldies Series OS-13169	Friends/In the Mood	197?	—	2.00	4.00
—Gold label; "Oldies Series" at 3 o'clock					
❑ Atlantic Oldies Series OS-13198	Old Cape Cod/Strangers in the Night	197?	—	2.00	4.00
❑ Atlantic Oldies Series OS-13222	The Rose/When a Man Loves a Woman	198?	—	—	3.00
—Reissue					
❑ Atlantic Oldies Series 7-84896	Wind Beneath My Wings/Under the Boardwalk	199?	—	—	3.00
—Reissue					

Albums

Number	Title (A Side/B Side)	Yr	VG	VG+	NM
❑ Atlantic SD 7238 [S]	The Divine Miss M	1972	2.50	5.00	10.00
—"1841 Broadway" address on label					
❑ Atlantic SD 7270	Bette Midler	1973	3.00	6.00	12.00
—"1841 Broadway" address on label; with poster					
❑ Atlantic SD 2-9000 [(2)]	Live! At Last	1977	3.00	6.00	12.00
❑ Atlantic SD 16004	Thighs and Whispers	1979	2.50	5.00	10.00
❑ Atlantic SD 16010	The Rose	1979	2.50	5.00	10.00
❑ Atlantic SD 16022	Divine Madness	1980	2.50	5.00	10.00
❑ Atlantic SD 18155	Songs for the New Depression	1976	2.50	5.00	10.00
❑ Atlantic SD 19151	Broken Blossom	1977	2.50	5.00	10.00
❑ Atlantic 80070	No Frills	1983	2.50	5.00	10.00
❑ Atlantic 81291	Mud Will Be Flung Tonight!	1985	2.50	5.00	10.00
❑ Atlantic 81933	Beaches	1988	2.50	5.00	10.00
❑ Atlantic 82129	Some People's Lives	1990	3.00	6.00	12.00

MILLER, ROGER

45s

Number	Title (A Side/B Side)	Yr	VG	VG+	NM
❑ Buena Vista 493	Whistle Stop/Not in Nottingham	1973	—	2.50	5.00
❑ Columbia 02681	Old Friends/When a House Is Not a Home	1982	—	2.00	4.00
—Roger Miller/Willie Nelson/Ray Price					
❑ Columbia 10052	Our Love/Yester Waltz	1974	—	2.50	5.00
❑ Columbia 10107	I Love a Rodeo/Lovin' You Is Always on My Mind	1975	—	2.50	5.00
❑ Columbia 45873	Open Up Your Heart/Qua La Linta	1973	—	2.50	5.00
❑ Columbia 45948	I Believe in the Sunrise/Shannon's Song	1973	—	2.50	5.00

Number	Title (A Side/B Side)	Yr	VG	VG+	NM
❑ Columbia 46000	Whistle Stop/The 4th of July	1974	—	2.50	5.00
❑ Decca 30838	Wrong Kind of Girl/A Man Like Me	1959	3.75	7.50	15.00
❑ Decca 30953	Sweet Ramona/Jason Fleming	1959	3.75	7.50	15.00
❑ Elektra 47192	Everyone Gets Crazy Now and Then/Aladam Bama	1981	—	2.00	4.00
❑ MCA 52663	River in the Rain/Hand for the Hog	1985	—	—	3.00
❑ MCA 52855	Some Hearts Get All the Breaks/Arkansas	1986	—	—	3.00
❑ Mercury 71212	Poor Little John/My Fellow	1957	6.25	12.50	25.00
❑ Mercury 73102	South/Don't We All Have the Right	1970	—	2.50	5.00
❑ Mercury 73190	Tomorrow Night in Baltimore/A Million Years or So	1971	—	2.50	5.00
❑ Mercury 73230	Loving Her Was Easier (Than Anything I'll Ever Do Again)/ Que La Linta	1971	—	2.50	5.00
❑ Mercury 73268	We Found It in Each Other's Arms/Sunny Side of My Life	1972	—	2.50	5.00
❑ Mercury 73321	Rings for Sale/Conversations	1972	—	2.50	5.00
❑ Mercury 73354	Hoppy's Gone/I Jumped from Uncle Harvey's Plane	1972	—	2.50	5.00
❑ Musicor 1102	Can't Stop Loving You/You're Forgetting Me	1965	2.50	5.00	10.00
❑ RCA Victor 47-7776	Footprints in the Snow/You Don't Want My Love	1960	3.75	7.50	15.00
❑ RCA Victor 47-7878	When Two Worlds Collide/Every Which-A-Way	1961	3.75	7.50	15.00
❑ RCA Victor 47-7958	Burma Shave/Fair Swiss Maiden	1961	3.75	7.50	15.00
❑ RCA Victor 47-8028	Sorry, Willie/Hitch-Hiker	1962	3.00	6.00	12.00
❑ RCA Victor 47-8091	Trouble on the Turnpike/Hey Little Star	1962	3.00	6.00	12.00
❑ RCA Victor 47-8175	Lock, Stock and Teardrops/I Know Who It Is	1963	3.00	6.00	12.00
❑ RCA Victor 47-8651	If You Want Me To/Hey Little Star	1965	2.50	5.00	10.00
❑ Smash 1876	Less and Less/Got Two Again	1964	—	—	—
—Canceled?					
❑ Smash 1881	Dang Me/Got Two Again	1964	2.50	5.00	10.00
❑ Smash 1926	Chug-a-Lug/Reincarnation	1964	2.50	5.00	10.00
❑ Smash 1947	Do-Wacka-Do/Love Is Not for Me	1964	2.50	5.00	10.00
❑ Smash 1965	King of the Road/Atta Boy Girl	1965	3.00	6.00	12.00
❑ Smash 1983	Engine, Engine #9/The Last Word in Lonesome Is Me	1965	2.00	4.00	8.00
❑ Smash 1994	One Dyin' and a-Buryin'/It Happened Just That Way	1965	2.00	4.00	8.00
❑ Smash 1998	Kansas City Star/Guess I'll Pack Up My Heart (And Go Home)	1965	2.00	4.00	8.00
❑ Smash 2010	England Swings/Good Old Days	1965	2.00	4.00	8.00
❑ Smash 2024	Husbands and Wives/I've Been a Long Time Leavin'	1966	2.00	4.00	8.00
❑ Smash 2043	You Can't Roller Skate in a Buffalo Herd/Train of Life	1966	2.00	4.00	8.00
❑ Smash 2055	My Uncle Used to Love Me But She Died/You're My Kingdom	1966	2.00	4.00	8.00
❑ Smash 2066	Heartbreak Hotel/Less and Less	1966	2.00	4.00	8.00
❑ Smash 2081	Walkin' in the Sunshine/Home	1967	2.00	4.00	8.00
❑ Smash 2121	The Ballad of Waterhole #3 (Code of the West)/Rainbow Valley	1967	2.00	4.00	8.00
❑ Smash 2130	Old Toy Trains/Silent Night	1967	2.50	5.00	10.00
❑ Smash 2148	Little Green Apples/Our Little Love	1968	2.00	4.00	8.00
❑ Smash 2183	What I'd Give (To Be the Wind)/Toliver	1968	2.00	4.00	8.00
❑ Smash 2197	Vance/Little Children Run and Play	1968	2.00	4.00	8.00
❑ Smash 2230	Me and Bobby McGee/I'm Gonna Teach My Heart to Bend (Instead of Break)	1969	—	3.00	6.00
❑ Smash 2246	Where Have All the Average People Gone/Boeing Boeing 707	1969	—	3.00	6.00
❑ Smash 2258	The Tom Green County Fair/I Know Who It Is	1970	—	3.00	6.00
❑ Starday 356	Can't Stop Loving You/You're Forgetting Me	1958	5.00	10.00	20.00
❑ Starday 718	Playboy/Poor Little John	1965	2.50	5.00	10.00
❑ Starday 7029	Under Your Spell Again/I Ain't Never	197?	—	2.50	5.00
❑ Starday 7032	Country Girl/Jimmy Brown, The Newsboy	197?	—	2.50	5.00
❑ Starday 7038	Tip of My Fingers/I Wish I Could Fall in Love Today	197?	—	2.50	5.00
❑ 20th Century 2421	The Hat/Pleasing the Crowd	1979	—	2.00	4.00
❑ Windsong CB-11072	Baby Me Baby/Dark Side of the Moon	1977	—	2.00	4.00
❑ Windsong CB-11166	Oklahoma Woman/There's Nobody Like You	1977	—	2.00	4.00
7-					
❑ Smash SRS-702-C	Dang Me/I Ain't Comin' Home Tonight/If You Want Me To//Chug-a-Lug/The Moon Is High/Squares Make the World Go Round	1964	3.00	6.00	12.00
—Jukebox issue; small hole, plays at 33 1/3 rpm; label has title "Roger and Out (Dang Me)"					
❑ Smash SRS-702-C [Picture Sleeve]	Dang Me	1964	3.00	6.00	12.00
—This is the title on the cover					
❑ Smash SRS-705-C	Love Is Not for Me/You Can't Roller Skate in a Buffalo Herd/Do-Wacka-Do//There I Go Dreamin'/ Ain't That Fine/King of the Road	1965	3.00	6.00	12.00
—Jukebox issue; small hole, plays at 33 1/3 rpm					
❑ Smash SRS-705-C [Picture Sleeve]	The Return of Roger Miller	1965	3.00	6.00	12.00
❑ Smash SRS-706-C	King of the Road/Dang Me/Chug-a-Lug//Engine, Engine No. 9/ (And You Had a) Do-Wacka-Do/You Can't Roller Skate in a Buffalo Herd	1965	3.00	6.00	12.00
—Jukebox issue; small hole, plays at 33 1/3 rpm					
❑ Smash SRS-706-C [Picture Sleeve]	Golden Hits	1965	3.00	6.00	12.00
Albums					
❑ Columbia KC 32449	Dear Folks Sorry I Haven't Written Lately	1973	3.75	7.50	15.00
❑ Columbia KC 33472	Supersongs	1975	3.75	7.50	15.00
❑ Hilltop 6109	King of the Road	197?	2.50	5.00	10.00
❑ Hilltop 6131	Little Green Apples	197?	2.50	5.00	10.00
❑ MCA 5722	Roger Miller	1986	2.50	5.00	10.00
❑ Mercury SR-61297	A Trip in the Country	1970	3.75	7.50	15.00
❑ Mercury SR-61361	The Best of Roger Miller	1971	3.75	7.50	15.00
❑ Mercury 826261-1	Golden Hits	198?	2.00	4.00	8.00
—Reissue of Smash 67073					
❑ Nashville 2046	The Amazing Roger Miller	196?	3.00	6.00	12.00
❑ Pickwick PTP-2057 [(2)]	King High	1973	3.00	6.00	12.00
❑ Pickwick SPC-3226	Engine #9	197?	2.50	5.00	10.00
❑ RCA Camden CAL-851 [M]	Roger Miller	1964	3.00	6.00	12.00

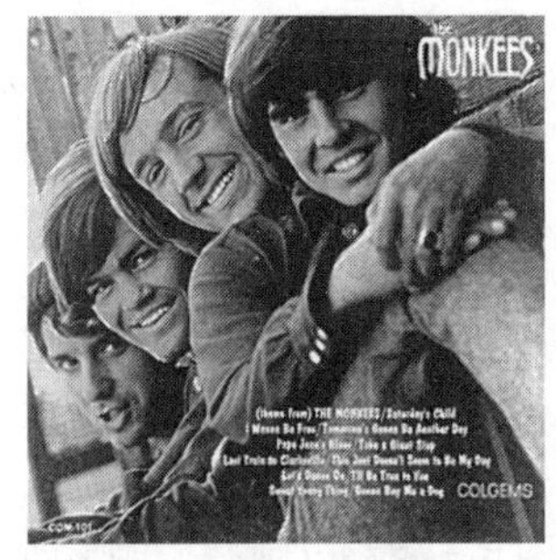

Number	Title (A Side/B Side)	Yr	VG	VG+	NM
❑ RCA Camden CAS-851 [S]	Roger Miller	1964	3.75	7.50	15.00
❑ RCA Camden CAL-903 [M]	The One and Only Roger Miller	1965	3.00	6.00	12.00
❑ RCA Camden CAS-903 [S]	The One and Only Roger Miller	1965	3.75	7.50	15.00
❑ Smash MGS-27049 [M]	Dang Me	196?	3.00	6.00	12.00
—Yet another retitled version of "Roger and Out"					
❑ Smash MGS-27049 [M]	Dang Me/Chug-a-Lug	196?	3.00	6.00	12.00
—Retitled version of "Roger and Out"					
❑ Smash MGS-27049 [M]	Roger and Out	1964	3.75	7.50	15.00
❑ Smash MGS-27061 [M]	The Return of Roger Miller	1965	3.75	7.50	15.00
❑ Smash MGS-27068 [M]	The 3rd Time Around	1965	3.75	7.50	15.00
❑ Smash MGS-27073 [M]	Golden Hits	1965	3.75	7.50	15.00
❑ Smash MGS-27075 [M]	Words and Music	1966	3.75	7.50	15.00
❑ Smash MGS-27092 [M]	Walkin' in the Sunshine	1967	5.00	10.00	20.00
❑ Smash MGS-27096 [M]	Waterhole #3	1967	6.25	12.50	25.00
❑ Smash SRS-67049 [S]	Dang Me/Chug-a-Lug	196?	3.75	7.50	15.00
—Retitled version of "Roger and Out"					
❑ Smash SRS-67049 [S]	Dang Me	196?	3.75	7.50	15.00
—Yet another retitled version of "Roger and Out"					
❑ Smash SRS-67049 [S]	Roger and Out	1964	5.00	10.00	20.00
❑ Smash SRS-67061 [S]	The Return of Roger Miller	1965	5.00	10.00	20.00
❑ Smash SRS-67068 [S]	The 3rd Time Around	1965	5.00	10.00	20.00
❑ Smash SRS-67073 [S]	Golden Hits	1965	5.00	10.00	20.00
❑ Smash SRS-67075 [S]	Words and Music	1966	5.00	10.00	20.00
❑ Smash SRS-67092 [S]	Walkin' in the Sunshine	1967	5.00	10.00	20.00
❑ Smash SRS-67096 [S]	Waterhole #3	1967	5.00	10.00	20.00
❑ Smash SRS-67103	A Tender Look at Love	1968	5.00	10.00	20.00
❑ Smash SRS-67123	Roger Miller	1969	5.00	10.00	20.00
❑ Smash SRS-67129	Roger Miller 1970	1970	5.00	10.00	20.00
❑ Starday SLP-318 [M]	The Country Side of Roger Miller	196?	6.25	12.50	25.00
—Retitled version of "Wild Child"					
❑ Starday SLP-318 [M]	Wild Child Roger Miller	1965	7.50	15.00	30.00
❑ Starday 3011	Painted Poetry	1978	2.50	5.00	10.00
❑ 20th Century T-592	Making a Name for Myself	1979	3.00	6.00	12.00
❑ Windsong BHL1-2337	Off the Wall	1977	3.00	6.00	12.00

MILLER, STEVE, BAND

45s

Number	Title (A Side/B Side)	Yr	VG	VG+	NM
❑ Capitol 2156	Roll With It/Sittin' in Circles	1968	3.00	6.00	12.00
❑ Capitol 2287	Living in the U.S.A./Quicksilver Girl	1968	3.00	6.00	12.00
❑ Capitol 2447	Rock Love/(B-side unknown)	1969	2.50	5.00	10.00
❑ Capitol 2520	My Dark Hour/Song for Our Ancestors	1969	2.00	4.00	8.00
❑ Capitol 2638	Don't Let Nobody Turn You Around/Little Girl	1969	2.00	4.00	8.00
❑ Capitol 2878	Going to the Country/Never Kill Another Man	1970	—	3.00	6.00
❑ Capitol 2945	Going to Mexico/Steve Miller's Midnight Tango	1970	—	3.00	6.00
❑ Capitol 3228	Rock Love/Let Me Serve You	1971	—	3.00	6.00
❑ Capitol 3344	Fandango/Love's Riddle	1972	—	3.00	6.00
❑ Capitol 3732	The Joker/Something to Believe In	1973	—	2.50	5.00
❑ Capitol 3837	Your Cash Ain't Nothin' But Trash/Evil	1974	—	2.50	5.00
❑ Capitol 3884	Living in the U.S.A./Kow Kow Calqulator	1974	—	2.50	5.00
❑ Capitol 4260	Take the Money and Run/Sweet Maree	1976	—	2.00	4.00
❑ Capitol 4323	Rock'n Me/Shu Ba Du Da Ma Ma Ma Ma	1976	—	2.00	4.00
❑ Capitol 4323	Rockin' Me/Living in the U.S.A.	1976	—	2.50	5.00
❑ Capitol 4372	Fly Like an Eagle/Lovin' Cup	1976	—	2.00	4.00
❑ Capitol 4424	Jet Airliner/Babes in the Wood	1977	—	2.00	4.00
❑ Capitol 4466	Jungle Love/Wish Upon a Star	1977	—	2.00	4.00
❑ Capitol 4496	Swingtown/Winter Time	1977	—	2.00	4.00
❑ Capitol A-5068	Heart Like a Wheel/True Fine Love	1981	—	—	3.00
❑ Capitol A-5086	Circle of Love/(Instrumental)	1982	—	—	3.00
❑ Capitol B-5126	Abracadabra/Give It Up	1982	—	2.00	4.00
❑ Capitol B-5126	Abracadabra/Baby Wanna Dance	1982	—	—	3.00
❑ Capitol B-5162	Cool Magic/Young Girl's Heart	1982	—	—	3.00
❑ Capitol B-5194	Give It Up/Heart Like a Wheel	1982	—	—	3.00
❑ Capitol B-5223	Buffalo's Serenade/Living in the U.S.A.	1983	—	—	3.00
❑ Capitol B-5407	Shangri-La/Circle of Love	1984	—	—	3.00
❑ Capitol B-5442	Bongo Bongo/Get On Home	1985	—	—	3.00
❑ Capitol B-5476	Italian X-Rays/Who Do You Love	1985	—	—	3.00
❑ Capitol B-5646	I Want to Make the World Turn Around/Slinky	1986	—	—	3.00

Number	Title (A Side/B Side)	Yr	VG	VG+	NM
❑ Capitol B-5671	Nobody But You Baby/Maelstrom	1987	—	—	3.00
❑ Capitol B-5704	I Wanna Be Loved/I Wanna Be Loved	1987	—	—	3.00
❑ Capitol B-44222	Ya Ya/Filthy McNasty	1988	—	—	3.00
Albums					
❑ Capitol SKAO-184	Brave New World	1969	5.00	10.00	20.00
—Black label with colorband					
❑ Capitol ST-331	Your Saving Grace	1969	3.75	7.50	15.00
❑ Capitol SKAO-436	Number 5	1970	3.75	7.50	15.00
❑ Capitol STBB-717 [(2)]	Children of the Future/Living in the U.S.A.	1971	3.75	7.50	15.00
—Repackage of 2920 and 2984 (with new title for the latter)					
❑ Capitol SW-748	Rock Love	1971	3.75	7.50	15.00
❑ Capitol SKAO 2920	Children of the Future	1968	6.25	12.50	25.00
—Black label with colorband					
❑ Capitol ST 2984	Sailor	1968	6.25	12.50	25.00
—Black label with colorband					
❑ Capitol SMAS-11022	Recall the Beginning...A Journey from Eden	1972	3.75	7.50	15.00
❑ Capitol SVBB-11114 [(2)]	Anthology	1972	3.75	7.50	15.00
❑ Capitol SMAS-11235	The Joker	1973	2.50	5.00	10.00
❑ Capitol ST-11497	Fly Like an Eagle	1976	2.50	5.00	10.00
❑ Capitol SO-11630	Book of Dreams	1977	2.50	5.00	10.00
❑ Capitol SOO-11872	Greatest Hits 1974-1978	1978	2.50	5.00	10.00
❑ Capitol ST-12121	Circle of Love	1981	2.50	5.00	10.00
❑ Capitol ST-12216	Abracadabra	1982	2.50	5.00	10.00
❑ Capitol ST-12263	Steve Miller Live	1983	2.50	5.00	10.00
❑ Capitol SJ-12339	Italian X-Rays	1985	2.50	5.00	10.00
❑ Capitol PJ-12445	Living in the 20th Century	1987	2.50	5.00	10.00
❑ Capitol SN-16078	Brave New World	1980	2.00	4.00	8.00
❑ Capitol SN-16079	Your Saving Grace	1980	2.00	4.00	8.00
❑ Capitol SN-16262	Children of the Future	1982	2.00	4.00	8.00
❑ Capitol SN-16263	Sailor	1982	2.00	4.00	8.00
❑ Capitol SN-16321	Greatest Hits 1974-1978	1984	2.00	4.00	8.00
❑ Capitol SN-16323	Book of Dreams	1984	2.00	4.00	8.00
❑ Capitol SN-16339	Fly Like an Eagle	1984	2.00	4.00	8.00
❑ Capitol SN-16357	Circle of Love	1985	2.00	4.00	8.00
❑ Capitol C1-48303	Born 2 B Blue	1988	2.50	5.00	10.00
MINDBENDERS, THE					
45s					
❑ Fontana 1541	A Groovy Kind of Love/Love Is Good	1966	3.00	6.00	12.00
❑ Fontana 1555	Ashes to Ashes/Don't Know About Love	1966	2.00	4.00	8.00
❑ Fontana 1571	I Want Her, She Wants Me/Morning After	1967	2.00	4.00	8.00
❑ Fontana 1595	It's Getting Harder All the Time/Off and Running	1967	2.00	4.00	8.00
❑ Fontana 1620	Yellow Brick Road/Blessed Are the Lonely	1968	2.00	4.00	8.00
❑ Fontana 1628	Uncle Joe the Ice Cream Man/The Man Who Loved Trees	1968	2.00	4.00	8.00
Albums					
❑ Fontana MGF-27554 [M]	A Groovy Kind of Love	1966	6.25	12.50	25.00
—With "Ashes to Ashes"					
❑ Fontana MGF-27554 [M]	A Groovy Kind of Love	1966	7.50	15.00	30.00
—With "Don't Cry No More"					
❑ Fontana SRF-67554 [R]	A Groovy Kind of Love	1966	5.00	10.00	20.00
—With "Ashes to Ashes"					
❑ Fontana SRF-67554 [R]	A Groovy Kind of Love	1966	6.25	12.50	25.00
—With "Don't Cry No More"					
MIRACLES, THE					
45s					
❑ Chess 1734	Bad Girl/I Love Your Baby	1959	15.00	30.00	60.00
—Blue label with vertical Chess logo (original)					
❑ Chess 1768	I Need a Change/All I Want (Is You)	1960	10.00	20.00	40.00
❑ Columbia 3-10464	Spy for Brotherhood/The Bird Must Fly Away	1976	—	2.50	5.00
❑ Columbia 3-10517	Women (Make the World Go 'Round)/I Can Touch the Sky	1977	—	2.50	5.00
❑ Columbia 3-10706	Mean Machine/The Magic of Your Eyes (Laura's Eyes)	1978	—	2.50	5.00
❑ End 1016	Got a Job/My Mama Done Told Me	1958	15.00	30.00	60.00
❑ End 1029	Money/I Cry	1958	12.50	25.00	50.00
—Mostly gray-white label, no mention of Roulette Records					
❑ End 1084	Money/I Cry	1961	6.25	12.50	25.00
❑ Motown G 1/G 2	Bad Girl/I Love Your Baby	1959	1250.	1875.	2500.
—VG 1250; VG+ 1875					
❑ Motown TLX-2207	Bad Girl/I Love Your Baby	1959	1250.	1875.	2500.
—VG 1250; VG+ 1875					
❑ Tamla 54028	The Feeling Is So Fine/You Can Depend On Me	1960	100.00	200.00	400.00
❑ Tamla 54028	Way Over There/Depend On Me	1960	15.00	30.00	60.00
—With overdubbed strings on A-side					
❑ Tamla 54034	Shop Around/Who's Lovin' You	1960	7.50	15.00	30.00
—Hit take; "L-1" in trail-off wax; horizontal lines label					
❑ Tamla 54034	Shop Around/Who's Lovin' You	1960	10.00	20.00	40.00
—Hit take; "ZTSC-67018" on label and in trail-off wax of Side 1 and "ZTSC-67019" on label and in trail-off wax of Side 2; horizontal lines label					
❑ Tamla 54034	Shop Around/Who's Lovin' You	1960	45.00	90.00	180.00
—Original take, withdrawn shortly after release; "H55518A" in trail-off wax					
❑ Tamla 54036	Ain't It Baby/The Only One I Love	1961	37.50	75.00	150.00
❑ Tamla 54044	Mighty Good Lovin'/Broken Hearted	1961	12.50	25.00	50.00
❑ Tamla 54048	Everybody's Gotta Pay Some Dues/I Can't Believe	1961	12.50	25.00	50.00
❑ Tamla 54048	You Gotta Pay Some Dues/I Can't Believe	1961	25.00	50.00	100.00
—Alternate A-side title					
❑ Tamla 54053	What's So Good About Good-By/I've Been Good to You	1962	7.50	15.00	30.00
❑ Tamla 54059	I'll Try Something New/You Never Miss a Good Thing	1962	5.00	10.00	20.00
❑ Tamla 54069	Way Over There/If Your Mother Only Knew	1962	5.00	10.00	20.00

Number	Title (A Side/B Side)	Yr	VG	VG+	NM
❑ Tamla 54073	You've Really Got a Hold on Me/Happy Landing	1962	5.00	10.00	20.00
❑ Tamla 54078	A Love She Can Count On/I Can Take a Hint	1963	5.00	10.00	20.00
❑ Tamla 54083	Mickey's Monkey/Whatever Makes You Happy	1963	5.00	10.00	20.00
❑ Tamla 54089	I Gotta Dance to Keep from Crying/Such Is Love, Such Is Life	1963	3.75	7.50	15.00
❑ Tamla 54092	(You Can't Let the Boy Overpower) The Man in You/ Heartbreak Road	1964	3.75	7.50	15.00
❑ Tamla 54098	I Like It Like That/You're So Fine and Sweet	1964	3.75	7.50	15.00
❑ Tamla 54102	That's What Love Is Made Of/Would I Love You	1964	3.75	7.50	15.00
❑ Tamla 54109	Come On Do the Jerk/Baby Don't You Go	1964	3.75	7.50	15.00
❑ Tamla 54113	Ooo Baby Baby/All That's Good	1965	3.75	7.50	15.00
❑ Tamla 54118	The Tracks of My Tears/A Fork in the Road	1965	3.75	7.50	15.00
❑ Tamla 54123	My Girl Has Gone/Since You Won My Heart	1965	3.75	7.50	15.00
❑ Tamla 54127	Going to A-Go-Go/Choosey Beggar	1965	3.75	7.50	15.00
❑ Tamla 54134	Whole Lot of Shakin' in My Heart (Since I Met You)/ Oh Be My Lover	1966	2.50	5.00	10.00
❑ Tamla 54140	Come 'Round Here — I'm the One You Need/Save Me	1966	2.50	5.00	10.00
❑ Tamla 54145	The Love I Saw in You Was Just a Mirage/Come Spy with Me	1967	2.00	4.00	8.00
—Starting here, through Tamla 54225, as "Smokey Robinson and the Miracles"					
❑ Tamla 54152	More Love/Swept for You Baby	1967	2.00	4.00	8.00
❑ Tamla 54159	I Second That Emotion/You Must Be Love	1967	2.00	4.00	8.00
❑ Tamla 54162	If You Can Want/When the Words from Your Heart Get Caught Up in Your Throat	1968	2.00	4.00	8.00
—"Tamla" in box on label					
❑ Tamla 54167	Yester Love/Much Better Off	1968	2.00	4.00	8.00
❑ Tamla 54172	Special Occasion/Give Her Up	1968	2.00	4.00	8.00
❑ Tamla 54178	Baby, Baby Don't Cry/Your Mother's Only Daughter	1968	2.00	4.00	8.00
❑ Tamla 54183	Here I Go Again/Doggone Right	1969	2.00	4.00	8.00
❑ Tamla 54184	Abraham, Martin, and John/Much Better Off	1969	2.00	4.00	8.00
❑ Tamla 54189	Point It Out/Darling Dear	1969	2.00	4.00	8.00
❑ Tamla 54194	Who's Gonna Take the Blame/I Gotta Thing For You	1970	2.00	4.00	8.00
❑ Tamla 54199	The Tears of a Clown/Promise Me	1970	—	3.00	6.00
❑ Tamla 54205	I Don't Blame You at All/That Girl	1971	—	3.00	6.00
❑ Tamla 54206	Crazy About the La La La/Oh Baby Baby I Love You	1971	—	3.00	6.00
❑ Tamla 54211	Satisfaction/Flower Girl	1971	—	3.00	6.00
❑ Tamla 54220	We've Come Too Far to End It Now/When Sundown Comes	1972	—	3.00	6.00
❑ Tamla 54225	I Can't Stand to See You Cry/With Your Love Came	1972	—	3.00	6.00
❑ Tamla 54237	Don't Let It End (Til You Let It Begin)/Wigs and Lashes	1973	—	2.50	5.00
—Starting here, name reverts to The Miracles					
❑ Tamla 54240	Give Me Just Another Day/I Wanna Be with You	1973	—	2.50	5.00
❑ Tamla 54248	Do It Baby/I Wanna Be with You	1974	—	2.50	5.00
❑ Tamla 54256	Don't Cha Love It/Up Again	1974	—	2.50	5.00
❑ Tamla 54259	You Are Love/Gemini	1975	—	2.50	5.00
❑ Tamla 54262	Love Machine (Part 1)/Love Machine (Part 2)	1975	—	2.50	5.00
❑ Tamla 54268	Night Life/Smog	1976	—	2.50	5.00
7-					
❑ Tamla TM-60254	Mickey's Monkey/You've Really Got a Hold on Me/ I Like It Like That//Shop Around/I've Been Good to You/ What's So Good About Good-Bye	196?	12.50	25.00	50.00
—Jukebox issue; small hole, plays at 33 1/3 rpm					
❑ Tamla TM-60254 [Picture Sleeve]	Greatest Hits from the Beginning	196?	12.50	25.00	50.00
❑ Tamla TM-60267	The Tracks of My Tears/Going To a Go-Go/Ooo Baby Baby// My Girl Has Gone/Choosey Beggar/In Case You Need Love	1966	12.50	25.00	50.00
—Jukebox issue; small hole, plays at 33 1/3 rpm					
❑ Tamla TM-60267 [Picture Sleeve]	Going to a Go-Go	1966	12.50	25.00	50.00
Albums					
❑ Columbia PC 34460	Love Crazy	1977	3.00	6.00	12.00
❑ Columbia JC 34910	The Miracles	1978	3.00	6.00	12.00
❑ Motown M5-133V1	Do It Baby	1981	2.00	4.00	8.00
—Reissue of Tamla 334					
❑ Motown M5-136V1	Away We a Go-Go	1981	2.00	4.00	8.00
—Reissue of Tamla 271					
❑ Motown M5-156V1	The Tears of a Clown	1981	2.00	4.00	8.00
—Reissue of Tamla 276					
❑ Motown M5-160V1	Hi, We're the Miracles	1981	2.00	4.00	8.00
—Reissue of Tamla 220					

Number	Title (A Side/B Side)	Yr	VG	VG+	NM
❑ Motown M5-210V1	Greatest Hits, Vol. 2	1981	2.00	4.00	8.00
—Reissue of Tamla 280					
❑ Motown M5-217V1	Doin' Mickey's Monkey	1981	2.00	4.00	8.00
—Reissue of Tamla 245					
❑ Motown M5-220V1	Recorded Live on Stage	1981	2.00	4.00	8.00
—Reissue of Tamla 241					
❑ Motown M8-238M2 [(2)]	Greatest Hits from the Beginning	1982	3.00	6.00	12.00
—Reissue of Tamla 254					
❑ Motown M 793R3 [(3)]	Smokey Robinson and the Miracles Anthology	1974	5.00	10.00	20.00
❑ Motown 5253 ML	The Season for Miracles	1982	2.00	4.00	8.00
—Reissue of Tamla 307					
❑ Motown 5254 ML	Christmas with the Miracles	1982	2.00	4.00	8.00
—Reissue of Tamla 236					
❑ Tamla T 220 [M]	Hi We're the Miracles	1961	150.00	300.00	600.00
—White label					
❑ Tamla T 223 [M]	Cookin' with the Miracles	1962	200.00	400.00	800.00
—White label					
❑ Tamla T 230 [M]	I'll Try Something New	1962	150.00	300.00	600.00
—White label					
❑ Tamla T 236 [M]	Christmas with the Miracles	1963	75.00	150.00	300.00
—Originals have two globes on the top of the label					
❑ Tamla T 238 [M]	The Fabulous Miracles	1963	75.00	150.00	300.00
❑ Tamla T 238 [M]	You've Really Got a Hold on Me	1963	50.00	100.00	200.00
—Retitled version of "The Fabulous Miracles"					
❑ Tamla T 241 [M]	The Miracles On Stage	1963	50.00	100.00	200.00
❑ Tamla T 245 [M]	Doin' Mickey's Monkey	1963	50.00	100.00	200.00
❑ Tamla TS 245 [S]	Doin' Mickey's Monkey	1963	75.00	150.00	300.00
❑ Tamla T 254 [(2)M]	Greatest Hits from the Beginning	1965	12.50	25.00	50.00
❑ Tamla TS 254 [(2)P]	Greatest Hits from the Beginning	1965	10.00	20.00	40.00
❑ Tamla T 267 [M]	Going to a Go-Go	1966	7.50	15.00	30.00
❑ Tamla TS 267 [S]	Going to a Go-Go	1966	10.00	20.00	40.00
❑ Tamla T 271 [M]	Away We a Go-Go	1966	6.25	12.50	25.00
❑ Tamla TS 271 [S]	Away We a Go-Go	1966	7.50	15.00	30.00
❑ Tamla T 276 [M]	Make It Happen	1967	6.25	12.50	25.00
❑ Tamla TS 276 [S]	Make It Happen	1967	7.50	15.00	30.00
❑ Tamla TS 276 [S]	The Tears of a Clown	1970	3.75	7.50	15.00
—Retitled version of "Make It Happen"					
❑ Tamla TS 280	Greatest Hits, Vol. 2	1968	6.25	12.50	25.00
❑ Tamla TS 289	Live!	1969	5.00	10.00	20.00
❑ Tamla T 290 [M]	Special Occasion	1968	12.50	25.00	50.00
❑ Tamla TS 290 [S]	Special Occasion	1968	5.00	10.00	20.00
❑ Tamla TS 295	Time Out for Smokey Robinson & the Miracles	1969	5.00	10.00	20.00
❑ Tamla TS 297	Four in Blue	1969	5.00	10.00	20.00
❑ Tamla TS 301	What Love Has...Joined Together	1970	3.75	7.50	15.00
❑ Tamla TS 306	A Pocket Full of Miracles	1970	3.75	7.50	15.00
❑ Tamla TS 307	The Season for Miracles	1970	3.75	7.50	15.00
❑ Tamla TS 312	One Dozen Roses	1971	3.75	7.50	15.00
❑ Tamla TS 318	Flying High Together	1972	3.75	7.50	15.00
❑ Tamla TS 320 [(2)]	1957-1972	1972	5.00	10.00	20.00
❑ Tamla T 325F	Renaissance	1973	3.00	6.00	12.00
❑ Tamla T6-334	Do It Baby	1974	3.00	6.00	12.00
❑ Tamla T6-336	Don't Cha Love It	1975	3.00	6.00	12.00
❑ Tamla T6-339	City of Angels	1975	3.00	6.00	12.00
❑ Tamla T6-344	The Power of Music	1976	3.00	6.00	12.00
❑ Tamla T7-357	Greatest Hits	1977	3.00	6.00	12.00

MITCHELL, JONI

45s

Number	Title (A Side/B Side)	Yr	VG	VG+	NM
❑ Asylum 11010	You Turn Me On, I'm a Radio/Urge for Going	1972	—	2.50	5.00
❑ Asylum 11029	Raised on Robbery/Court and Spark	1973	—	2.50	5.00
❑ Asylum 11034	Help Me/Just Like This Train	1974	—	2.50	5.00
❑ Asylum 11041	Free Man in Paris/People's Parties	1974	—	2.50	5.00
❑ Asylum 45221	Big Yellow Taxi/Rainy Night House	1974	—	2.00	4.00
❑ Asylum 45244	Jericho/Carey	1975	—	2.00	4.00
❑ Asylum 45298	In France They Kiss on Main Street/Boho Dance	1976	—	2.00	4.00
❑ Asylum 45377	Coyote/Blue Motel Room	1976	—	2.00	4.00
❑ Asylum 45467	Dreamland/Jericho	1978	—	2.00	4.00
❑ Asylum 46506	The Dry Cleaner from Des Moines/God Must Be a Boogie Man	1979	—	2.00	4.00
❑ Asylum 47038	Why Do Fools Fall in Love/Black Crow	1980	—	2.00	4.00
❑ Geffen 27887	My Secret Place/Lakota	1988	—	2.00	4.00
❑ Geffen 28675	Shiny Toys/Three Great Stimulants	1986	—	2.00	4.00
❑ Geffen 28840	Good Friends/Smokin' Empty (Try Another)	1985	—	2.00	4.00
❑ Geffen 29757	Underneath the Streetlight/Be Cool	1983	—	2.00	4.00
❑ Geffen 29849	(You're So Square) Baby I Don't Care/Love	1982	—	2.00	4.00
❑ Reprise 0694	I Had a King/Night in the City	1968	2.00	4.00	8.00
❑ Reprise 0906	Big Yellow Taxi/Woodstock	1970	2.00	4.00	8.00
❑ Reprise 1029	Carey/This Flight Tonight	1971	2.00	4.00	8.00
❑ Reprise 1049	Case of You/California	1971	—	3.00	6.00
❑ Reprise 1154	Both Sides Now/Chelsea Morning	1972	—	2.50	5.00
—"Back to Back Hits" series					
❑ Reprise 1155	Big Yellow Taxi/Carey	1972	—	2.50	5.00
—"Back to Back Hits" series					

Albums

Number	Title (A Side/B Side)	Yr	VG	VG+	NM
❑ Asylum AB-202	Miles of Aisles	1974	2.50	5.00	10.00
❑ Asylum 5E-505	Mingus	1979	2.50	5.00	10.00
❑ Asylum BB-701 [(2)]	Don Juan's Reckless Daughter	1977	3.00	6.00	12.00
❑ Asylum BB-704 [(2)]	Shadows and Light	1980	3.00	6.00	12.00

Number	Title (A Side/B Side)	Yr	VG	VG+	NM
❑ Asylum 7E-1001	Court and Spark	1974	2.50	5.00	10.00
❑ Asylum 7E-1051	The Hissing of Summer Lawns	1975	2.50	5.00	10.00
❑ Asylum 7E-1087	Hejira	1976	2.50	5.00	10.00
❑ Asylum SD 5057	For the Roses	1972	2.50	5.00	10.00
❑ Geffen GHS 2019	Wild Things Run Fast	1982	2.00	4.00	8.00
❑ Geffen GHS 24074	Dog Eat Dog	1985	2.00	4.00	8.00
❑ Geffen GHS 24172	Chalk Mark in a Rain Storm	1988	2.00	4.00	8.00
❑ Geffen GEF 24302	Night Ride Home	1991	3.75	7.50	15.00
❑ Reprise MS 2038	Blue	1970	3.75	7.50	15.00
❑ Reprise RS 6293 [S]	Joni Mitchell	1968	5.00	10.00	20.00
—With "W7" and "r:" logos on two-tone orange label					
❑ Reprise RS 6341	Clouds	1969	5.00	10.00	20.00
—With "W7" and "r:" logos on two-tone orange label					
❑ Reprise RS 6376	Ladies of the Canyon	1970	5.00	10.00	20.00
—With "W7" and "r:" logos on two-tone orange label					
❑ Rhino Vinyl 74842	Blue	2007	6.25	12.50	25.00
—Reissue on 180-gram vinyl; has replica Reprise label					

MOMENTS, THE

Includes records as "Ray, Goodman and Brown." Records on Era and World Artists are by different groups and are outside the scope of this book.

45s

Number	Title (A Side/B Side)	Yr	VG	VG+	NM
❑ All Platinum 2350	Sho Nuff Boogie (Part 1)/Sho Nuff Boogie (Part 2)	1974	—	2.50	5.00
—With Sylvia					
❑ EMI America 8365	Take It to the Limit/(Instrumental)	1986	—	—	3.00
❑ EMI America 8378	Celebrate Our Love/(Instrumental)	1987	—	—	3.00
❑ EMI America 43022	Tonight (Baby)/Good Love	1987	—	—	3.00
❑ EMI Manhattan 50155	Where Did You Get That Body, (Baby)?/Where Are You Now	1988	—	—	3.00
❑ Hog 1000	Baby I Want You/Pray for Me	196?	500.00	1000.	2000.
❑ Panoramic 201	Who's Gonna Make the First Move/Look Like Lovers	1984	—	2.00	4.00
❑ Polydor 2033	Special Lady/Deja Vu	1979	—	2.50	5.00
❑ Polydor 2077	Inside of You/Treat Her Right	1980	—	2.00	4.00
❑ Polydor 2116	My Prayer/The Way It Should Be	1980	—	2.00	4.00
❑ Polydor 2135	Happy Anniversary/You	1980	—	2.00	4.00
❑ Polydor 2159	Shoestrings/Me	1981	—	2.00	4.00
❑ Polydor 2191	How Can Love Be So Right (Yet So Wrong)/Each Time Is Like the First Time	1981	—	2.00	4.00
❑ Polydor 2203	Stay/Good Ole Days	1982	—	2.00	4.00
❑ Polydor 2208	Till the Right One Comes Along/Heaven in the Rain	1982	—	2.00	4.00
❑ Polydor 2222	Gambled on Your Love/Pool of Love	1982	—	2.00	4.00
❑ Polydor 2227	After All/Love Minus One	1982	—	2.00	4.00
❑ Polydor 810056-7	Special Lady/My Prayer	1983	—	—	3.00
—Reissue					
❑ Stang 5000	Not on the Outside/Understanding	1968	2.00	4.00	8.00
❑ Stang 5003	Sunday/Everybody Loves My Baby	1969	—	3.00	6.00
❑ Stang 5005	I Do/Pocketful of Heartbreaks	1969	—	3.00	6.00
❑ Stang 5008	I'm So Lost/Where	1969	—	3.00	6.00
❑ Stang 5009	Lovely Way She Loves/I've Got to Keep On Loving, Love	1969	—	3.00	6.00
❑ Stang 5012	Love on a Two-Way Street/I Won't Do Anything	1970	2.00	4.00	8.00
❑ Stang 5016	If I Didn't Care/You Make Me Feel Good	1970	—	3.00	6.00
❑ Stang 5017	All I Have/The Hurt's On Me	1970	—	3.00	6.00
❑ Stang 5020	I Can't Help It/To You with Love	1971	—	3.00	6.00
❑ Stang 5024	That's How It Feels/That's How It Feels (Long)	1971	—	3.00	6.00
❑ Stang 5031	Lucky Me/I Lost One Bird in the Hand (Reaching Out for Two in the Bush)	1971	—	3.00	6.00
❑ Stang 5033	To You with Love/Key to My Happiness	1971	—	3.00	6.00
❑ Stang 5036	Thanks a Lot/I Lost One Bird in the Hand (Reaching Out for Two in the Bush)	1972	—	3.00	6.00
❑ Stang 5041	Just Because He Wants to Make Love (Doesn't Mean He Loves You)/So This Is Our Good-Bye	1972	—	3.00	6.00
❑ Stang 5045	My Thing/Thanks a Lot	1972	—	3.00	6.00
❑ Stang 5048	Girl I'm Gonna Miss You/I Think So	1973	—	2.50	5.00
❑ Stang 5050	Gotta Find a Way/Sweeter As the Days Go By	1973	—	2.50	5.00
❑ Stang 5052	Sexy Mama/Where Can I Find Her	1973	—	3.00	6.00
❑ Stang 5054	Sweet Sweet Lady/Next Time I See You	1974	—	2.50	5.00
❑ Stang 5056	What's Your Name/Mama I Miss You	1974	—	2.50	5.00

Number	Title (A Side/B Side)	Yr	VG	VG+	NM
❑ Stang 5057	Girls (Part 1)/Girls (Part 2)	1974	—	2.50	5.00
—With the Whatnauts					
❑ Stang 5060	Look at Me (I'm in Love)/You've Come a Long Way	1975	—	2.50	5.00
❑ Stang 5064	Got to Get to Know You/I Feel So Bad	1975	—	2.50	5.00
❑ Stang 5066	Nine Times/When the Morning Comes	1976	—	2.50	5.00
❑ Stang 5068	With You/The Next Time I See You	1976	—	2.50	5.00
❑ Stang 5071	We Don't Cry Out Loud/Come In Girl	1977	—	2.50	5.00
❑ Stang 5073	I Don't Wanna Go/Oh I Could Have Loved You	1977	—	2.50	5.00
❑ Stang 5075	I Could Have Loved You/Jack in the Box	1978	—	2.50	5.00
❑ Stang 5076	Rain in My Backyard/Disco Man	1978	7.50	15.00	30.00
❑ Sugar Hill 758	Baby Let's Rap Now (Part 1)/Baby Let's Rap Now (Part 2)	1980	—	2.50	5.00
❑ Sugar Hill 769	Record Breakin' Love Affair/(B-side unknown)	1981	—	2.50	5.00
Albums					
❑ Chess CH2-92517 [(2)]	Greatest Hits	198?	3.00	6.00	12.00
❑ Polydor PD-1-6240	Ray, Goodman & Brown	1979	2.50	5.00	10.00
❑ Polydor PD-1-6299	Ray, Goodman & Brown II	1980	2.50	5.00	10.00
❑ Polydor PD-1-6341	Stay	1981	2.50	5.00	10.00
❑ Stang ST-1000	Not On the Outside, But On the Inside Strong	1969	7.50	15.00	30.00
❑ Stang ST-1002	The Moments On Top	1970	7.50	15.00	30.00
❑ Stang ST-1003	A Moment with the Moments	1970	7.50	15.00	30.00
❑ Stang ST-1004	Moments Greatest Hits	1971	5.00	10.00	20.00
❑ Stang ST-1006	The Moments Live at the New York State Womans Prison	1971	6.25	12.50	25.00
❑ Stang ST-1009	The Other Side of the Moments	1972	6.25	12.50	25.00
❑ Stang ST-1015	Live at the Miss Black America Pageant	1972	5.00	10.00	20.00
❑ Stang ST-1019	The Best of the Moments	1975	3.75	7.50	15.00
❑ Stang ST-1022	My Thing	1973	3.75	7.50	15.00
❑ Stang ST-1023	The Sexy Moments	1974	3.75	7.50	15.00
❑ Stang ST-1026	Look at Me	1975	3.75	7.50	15.00
❑ Stang ST-1030	Moments With You	1976	3.75	7.50	15.00
❑ Stang 2ST-1033 [(2)]	Greatest Hits	1977	5.00	10.00	20.00
❑ Stang ST-1034	Sharp	1978	3.75	7.50	15.00
MONKEES, THE					
45s					
❑ Arista 0201	Daydream Believer/Monkee's Theme	1976	2.50	5.00	10.00
❑ Arista 9505	That Was Then, This Is Now/(Theme from) The Monkees	1986	—	—	3.00
—With A-side artist listed as " Mickey Dolenz and Peter Tork (of the Monkees)"					
❑ Arista 9532	Daydream Believer/Randy Scouse Git	1986	—	2.00	4.00
❑ Colgems 66-1001	Last Train to Clarksville/Take a Giant Step	1966	3.75	7.50	15.00
❑ Colgems 66-1002	I'm a Believer/(I'm Not Your) Steppin' Stone	1966	3.75	7.50	15.00
❑ Colgems 66-1004	A Little Bit Me, A Little Bit You/The Girl I Knew Somewhere	1967	3.75	7.50	15.00
❑ Colgems 66-1007	Pleasant Valley Sunday/Words	1967	3.75	7.50	15.00
❑ Colgems 66-1012	Daydream Believer/Goin' Down	1967	3.75	7.50	15.00
❑ Colgems 66-1019	Valleri/Tapioca Tundra	1968	2.50	5.00	10.00
❑ Colgems 66-1023	D.W. Washburn/It's Nice to Be with You	1968	2.50	5.00	10.00
❑ Colgems 66-1031	Porpoise Song/As We Go Along	1968	2.50	5.00	10.00
❑ Colgems 66-5000	Tear Drop City/A Man Without a Dream	1969	2.50	5.00	10.00
❑ Colgems 66-5004	Listen to the Band/Someday Man	1969	2.50	5.00	10.00
❑ Colgems 66-5005	Good Clean Fun/Mommy and Daddy	1969	3.75	7.50	15.00
❑ Colgems 66-5011	Oh My My/I Love You Better	1970	3.75	7.50	15.00
❑ Rhino 74408	Heart and Soul/M.G.B.G.T.	1987	—	—	3.00
—Black vinyl					
❑ Rhino 74410	Every Step of the Way/(I'll) Love You Forever	1987	—	—	3.00
Albums					
❑ Arista AL 4089	The Monkees' Greatest Hits	1976	3.00	6.00	12.00
—Reissue of Bell LP					
❑ Arista AL8-8313	The Monkees' Greatest Hits	198?	2.00	4.00	8.00
—Reissue of Arista 4089					
❑ Arista AL9-8432	Then & Now...The Best of the Monkees	1986	3.00	6.00	12.00
❑ Arista AL-8524	The Monkees	1988	3.00	6.00	12.00
❑ Arista AL-8525	More of the Monkees	1988	3.00	6.00	12.00
❑ Bell 6081	Re-Focus	1972	7.50	15.00	30.00
❑ Colgems COM-101 [M]	The Monkees	1966	5.00	10.00	20.00
—Second pressing: Side 1, Song 5 listed as "Papa Gene's Blues" (RE after number on upper right back cover)					
❑ Colgems COS-101 [S]	The Monkees	1966	5.00	10.00	20.00
—Second pressing: Side 1, Song 5 listed as "Papa Gene's Blues" (RE after number on upper right back cover)					
❑ Colgems COM-102 [M]	More of the Monkees	1966	5.00	10.00	20.00
❑ Colgems COS-102 [S]	More of the Monkees	1966	5.00	10.00	20.00
❑ Colgems COM-103 [M]	The Monkees' Headquarters	1967	5.00	10.00	20.00
—First pressing: Back cover, center bottom photo is of two of the LP's producers					
❑ Colgems COS-103 [S]	The Monkees' Headquarters	1967	5.00	10.00	20.00
—First pressing: Back cover, center bottom photo is of two of the LP's producers					
❑ Colgems COM-104 [M]	Pisces, Aquarius, Capricorn & Jones Ltd.	1967	10.00	20.00	40.00
❑ Colgems COS-104 [S]	Pisces, Aquarius, Capricorn & Jones Ltd.	1967	5.00	10.00	20.00
❑ Colgems COM-109 [M]	The Birds, the Bees & the Monkees	1968	25.00	50.00	100.00
❑ Colgems COS-109 [S]	The Birds, the Bees & the Monkees	1968	5.00	10.00	20.00
❑ Colgems COS-113	Instant Replay	1969	10.00	20.00	40.00
❑ Colgems COS-115	The Monkees Greatest Hits	1969	10.00	20.00	40.00
❑ Colgems COS-117	The Monkees Present	1969	12.50	25.00	50.00
❑ Colgems COS-119	Changes	1970	20.00	40.00	80.00
❑ Colgems SCOS-1001 [(2)]	A Barrel Full of Monkees	1971	18.75	37.50	75.00
❑ Colgems COSO-5008	Head	1968	12.50	25.00	50.00
❑ FSH 71110	Live, 20th Anniversary Tour	1987	5.00	10.00	20.00
—Live album sold at tour stops					
❑ Laurie House LH-8009	The Monkees	1974	5.00	10.00	20.00
—TV mail-order offer					
❑ Pair ARPDL2-1109 [(2)]	Hit Factory	1986	5.00	10.00	20.00

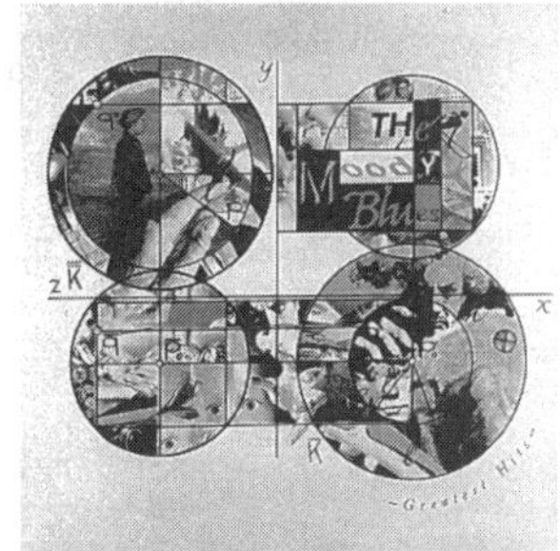

Number	Title (A Side/B Side)	Yr	VG	VG+	NM
❑ Rhino RNLP-113	Monkee Flips	1984	3.00	6.00	12.00
❑ Rhino RNLP-144	The Birds, the Bees and the Monkees	1985	3.00	6.00	12.00
❑ Rhino RNLP-145	Head	1985	3.00	6.00	12.00
❑ Rhino RNLP-146	Instant Replay	1985	3.00	6.00	12.00
❑ Rhino RNLP-147	The Monkees Present	1985	3.00	6.00	12.00
❑ Rhino RNLP-70139	Live 1967	1987	3.00	6.00	12.00
❑ Rhino RNLP-70140	The Monkees	1986	3.00	6.00	12.00
❑ Rhino RNLP-70141	Pisces, Aquarius, Capricorn & Jones Ltd.	1986	3.00	6.00	12.00
❑ Rhino RNLP-70142	More of the Monkees	1986	3.00	6.00	12.00
❑ Rhino RNLP-70143	The Monkees' Headquarters	1986	3.00	6.00	12.00
❑ Rhino RNLP-70148	Changes	1986	3.00	6.00	12.00
❑ Rhino RNLP-70150	Missing Links	1987	3.00	6.00	12.00
❑ Rhino RNIN-70706	Pool It!	1987	2.50	5.00	10.00
❑ Silver Eagle SE-1048 [(2)]	The Best of the Monkees	1986	3.75	7.50	15.00
—TV mail-order offer					

MONOTONES, THE (1)

45s

Number	Title (A Side/B Side)	Yr	VG	VG+	NM
❑ Argo 5290	Book of Love/You Never Loved Me	1958	7.50	15.00	30.00
❑ Argo 5301	Tom Foolery/Zombi	1958	7.50	15.00	30.00
❑ Argo 5321	The Legend of Sleepy Hollow/Soft Shadows	1958	7.50	15.00	30.00
❑ Argo 5339	Tell It to the Judge/Fools Will Be Fools	1959	12.50	25.00	50.00
❑ Hull 735	Reading the Book of Love/Dream	1960	12.50	25.00	50.00
❑ Hull 743	Daddy's Home, But Momma's Gone/Tattle Tale	1961	12.50	25.00	50.00
❑ Mascot 124	Book of Love/You Never Loved Me	1957	200.00	400.00	800.00

MONTEZ, CHRIS

45s

Number	Title (A Side/B Side)	Yr	VG	VG+	NM
❑ A&M 780	Call Me/Go Head On	1965	2.00	4.00	8.00
❑ A&M 796	The More I See You/You, I Love You	1966	2.50	5.00	10.00
❑ A&M 810	There Will Never Be Another You/You Can Hurt the One You Love	1966	2.00	4.00	8.00
❑ A&M 822	Keep Talkin'/Time After Time	1966	2.00	4.00	8.00
❑ A&M 839	Because of You/Elena	1967	2.00	4.00	8.00
❑ A&M 852	Just Friends/Twiggy	1967	—	3.00	6.00
❑ A&M 855	Foollin' Around/Dindi (Jin-Jee)	1967	—	3.00	6.00
❑ A&M 906	Once in a While/The Face I Love	1968	—	3.00	6.00
❑ A&M 958	Love Is Here to Stay/Nothing to Hide	1968	—	3.00	6.00
❑ A&M 985	Where Are You Now/Watch What Happens	1968	—	3.00	6.00
❑ Jamie 1410	Let's Dance/Somebody Loves You	1973	—	2.50	5.00
❑ Monogram 500	All You Had to Do (Was Tell Me)/Love Me	1962	3.00	6.00	12.00
❑ Monogram 505	Let's Dance/You're the One	1962	5.00	10.00	20.00
❑ Monogram 507	Some Kinda Fun/Tell Me	1962	3.00	6.00	12.00
❑ Monogram 508	Rockin' Blues/(Let's Do the) Limbo	1963	3.75	7.50	15.00
❑ Monogram 513	In An English Towne/My Baby Loves to Dance	1963	3.00	6.00	12.00
❑ Monogram 516	No, No, No/Monkey Fever	1963	3.00	6.00	12.00
❑ Monogram 517	You're the One/All You Had to Do Was Tell Me	1964	3.00	6.00	12.00
—With Kathy Young					
❑ Monogram 520	It Takes Two/To Shoot the Curl	1964	3.00	6.00	12.00
—With Kathy Young					
❑ Monogram 522	(It's Not) Puppy Love/He's Been Leading You On	1964	3.00	6.00	12.00
❑ Paramount 0109	We Can Make the World a Whole Lot Brighter/The End of the Line	1971	—	2.50	5.00

Albums

Number	Title (A Side/B Side)	Yr	VG	VG+	NM
❑ A&M LP-115 [M]	The More I See You/Call Me	1966	5.00	10.00	20.00
❑ A&M LP-120 [M]	Time After Time	1966	3.75	7.50	15.00
❑ A&M LP-128 [M]	Foolin' Around	1967	3.75	7.50	15.00
❑ A&M LP-157 [M]	Watch What Happens	1967	3.75	7.50	15.00
❑ A&M ST-4115 [S]	The More I See You/Call Me	1966	6.25	12.50	25.00
❑ A&M SP-4120 [S]	Time After Time	1966	5.00	10.00	20.00
❑ A&M SP-4128 [S]	Foolin' Around	1967	5.00	10.00	20.00
❑ A&M SP-4157 [S]	Watch What Happens	1967	5.00	10.00	20.00
❑ Monogram M-100 [M]	Let's Dance and Have Some Kinda' Fun!!!	1963	100.00	200.00	400.00

MOODY BLUES, THE

45s

Number	Title (A Side/B Side)	Yr	VG	VG+	NM
❑ Deram 85023	Nights in White Satin/Cities	1968	2.50	5.00	10.00
—Composer of "Nights in White Satin" listed as "Redwave"					
❑ Deram 85028	Tuesday Afternoon (Forever Afternoon)/Another Morning	1968	2.00	4.00	8.00
❑ Deram 85033	Ride My See-Saw/Voices in the Sky	1968	2.00	4.00	8.00

Number	Title (A Side/B Side)	Yr	VG	VG+	NM
❑ Deram 85044	Never Comes the Day/So Deep Within You	1969	2.00	4.00	8.00
❑ London 270	Steppin' in a Slide Zone/I'll Be Level with You	1978	—	2.00	4.00
❑ London 273	Driftwood/I'm Your Man	1978	—	2.50	5.00
❑ London 1005	This Is My House (But Nobody Calls)/Boulevard de la Madelaine	1967	3.00	6.00	12.00
❑ London 9726	Go Now!/Lose Your Money	1965	5.00	10.00	20.00
—White, purple and blue label					
❑ London 9764	From the Bottom of My Heart (I Love You)/And My Baby's Gone	1965	3.75	7.50	15.00
❑ London 9799	Ev'ry Day/You Don't	1965	3.75	7.50	15.00
❑ London 9810	Stop!/Bye Bye Bird	1966	3.75	7.50	15.00
❑ London 20030	Fly Me High/I Really Haven't Got the Time	1967	3.00	6.00	12.00
❑ Polydor 870990-7	No More Lies/River of Endless Love	1988	—	—	3.00
❑ Polydor 871270-7	Al Fin Voy a Encontrarte (I Know You're Out There Somewhere — Spanish Version)/I Know You're Out There Somewhere	1989	—	2.50	5.00
❑ Polydor 883906-7	Your Wildest Dreams/Talkin' Talkin'	1986	—	—	3.00
❑ Polydor 885201-7	The Other Side of Life/The Spirit	1986	—	2.50	5.00
—Blue vinyl					
❑ Polydor 885212-7	The Other Side of Life/The Spirit	1986	—	—	3.00
❑ Polydor 887600-7	I Know You're Out There Somewhere/Miracle	1988	—	—	3.00
❑ Polydor 887815-7	Here Comes the Weekend/River of Endless Love	1988	—	—	3.00
❑ Threshold 601	Gemini Dream/Painted Smile	1981	—	2.00	4.00
❑ Threshold 602	The Voice/22,000 Days	1981	—	2.00	4.00
❑ Threshold 603	Talking Out of Turn/Veteran Cosmic Rocker	1981	—	2.00	4.00
❑ Threshold 604	Sitting at the Wheel/Going Nowhere	1983	—	2.00	4.00
❑ Threshold 605	Blue World/Sorry	1983	—	2.00	4.00
❑ Threshold 606	Running Water/Under My Feet	1983	—	2.00	4.00
❑ Threshold 67004	Question/Candle of Life	1970	—	3.00	6.00
❑ Threshold 67006	The Story in Your Eyes/Melancholy Man	1971	—	3.00	6.00
❑ Threshold 67009	Isn't Life Strange/After You Came	1972	—	2.50	5.00
❑ Threshold 67012	I'm Just a Singer (In a Rock and Roll Band)/For My Lady	1973	—	2.50	5.00
Albums					
❑ Compleat 672008 [(2)]	Early Blues	1985	3.75	7.50	15.00
—Reissue of London 1964-66 material					
❑ Deram DE 16012 [M]	Days of Future Passed	1968	62.50	125.00	250.00
❑ Deram DES 18012 [S]	Days of Future Passed	1968	5.00	10.00	20.00
—With large "DERAM" on top half of label					
❑ Deram DES 18017	In Search of the Lost Chord	1968	5.00	10.00	20.00
—Originals have gatefold covers					
❑ Deram DES 18025	On the Threshold of a Dream	1969	5.00	10.00	20.00
—Originals have gatefold covers and lyric booklet					
❑ Deram DES 18051 [R]	In the Beginning	1971	5.00	10.00	20.00
❑ Deram 820006-1 [S]	Days of Future Passed	1985	2.00	4.00	8.00
❑ Deram 820168-1	In Search of the Lost Chord	1985	2.00	4.00	8.00
❑ Deram 820170-1	On the Threshold of a Dream	1985	2.00	4.00	8.00
❑ London PS 428 [R]	Go Now — The Moody Blues #1	1965	10.00	20.00	40.00
❑ London PS 690/1 [(2)]	Caught Live + 5	1977	3.00	6.00	12.00
❑ London PS 708	Octave	1978	2.50	5.00	10.00
❑ London LL 3428 [M]	Go Now — The Moody Blues #1	1965	12.50	25.00	50.00
❑ London 820161-1 [(2)]	Caught Live + 5	1985	2.00	4.00	8.00
❑ London 820329-1	Octave	1986	2.00	4.00	8.00
❑ Polydor 829 179-1	The Other Side of Life	1986	2.50	5.00	10.00
❑ Polydor 835 756-1	Sur La Mer	1988	3.00	6.00	12.00
❑ Polydor 840 659-1	Greatest Hits (1967-1988)	1989	3.75	7.50	15.00
❑ Threshold THS 1	To Our Children's Children's Children	1969	3.75	7.50	15.00
—White label with purple logo; gatefold cover					
❑ Threshold THS 3	A Question of Balance	1970	3.75	7.50	15.00
—White label with purple logo; gatefold cover					
❑ Threshold THS 5	Every Good Boy Deserves Favour	1971	3.75	7.50	15.00
—White label with purple logo; gatefold cover					
❑ Threshold THS 7	Seventh Sojourn	1972	3.75	7.50	15.00
—White label with purple logo; gatefold cover					
❑ Threshold THS 12/13 [(2)]	This Is the Moody Blues	1974	3.75	7.50	15.00
❑ Threshold TR-1-2901	Long Distance Voyager	1981	2.50	5.00	10.00
❑ Threshold TR-1-2902	The Present	1982	2.50	5.00	10.00
❑ Threshold 810119-1	The Present	1983	2.00	4.00	8.00
❑ Threshold 820007-1 [(2)]	This Is the Moody Blues	1985	2.00	4.00	8.00
❑ Threshold 820105-1	Long Distance Voyager	1985	2.00	4.00	8.00
❑ Threshold 820155-1	Voices in the Sky/The Best of the Moody Blues	1985	2.50	5.00	10.00
❑ Threshold 820159-1	Seventh Sojourn	1985	2.00	4.00	8.00
❑ Threshold 820160-1	Every Good Boy Deserves Favour	1985	2.00	4.00	8.00
❑ Threshold 820211-1	A Question of Balance	1985	2.00	4.00	8.00

MORRISON, VAN

45s

Number	Title (A Side/B Side)	Yr	VG	VG+	NM
❑ Bang 545	Brown Eyed Girl/Goodbye, Baby	1967	3.00	6.00	12.00
❑ Bang 552	Chick-a-Boom/Ro Ro Rosey	1967	2.50	5.00	10.00
❑ Bang 585	Spanish Rose/Midnight Special	1971	2.00	4.00	8.00
❑ Mercury 880669-7	Haunts of Ancient Peace/Tore Down A La Rimbaud	1985	—	2.00	4.00
❑ Mercury 884841-7	Ivory Tower/New Kind of Man	1986	—	2.00	4.00
❑ Warner Bros. 7383	Come Running/Crazy Love	1970	—	3.00	6.00
❑ Warner Bros. 7434	Domino/Sweet Janine	1970	—	3.00	6.00
❑ Warner Bros. 7462	Blue Money/Sweet Thing	1971	—	3.00	6.00
❑ Warner Bros. 7488	Call Me Up in Dreamland/Street Choir	1971	—	3.00	6.00
❑ Warner Bros. 7518	Wild Night/When That Evening Sun Goes Down	1971	—	3.00	6.00
❑ Warner Bros. 7543	Tupelo Honey/Starting a New Life	1971	—	3.00	6.00
❑ Warner Bros. 7573	Straight to My Heart Like a Cannonball/Old Old Woodstock	1972	—	2.50	5.00
❑ Warner Bros. 7616	Jackie Wilson Said (I'm in Heaven When You Smile)/You've Got the Power	1972	—	2.50	5.00

Number	Title (A Side/B Side)	Yr	VG	VG+	NM
❑ Warner Bros. 7638	Redwood Tree/Saint Dominic's Preview	1972	—	2.50	5.00
❑ Warner Bros. 7665	Gypsy/Saint Dominic's Preview	1972	—	2.50	5.00
❑ Warner Bros. 7706	Warm Love/I Will Be There	1973	—	2.50	5.00
❑ Warner Bros. 7744	Green/Wild Children	1973	—	2.50	5.00
❑ Warner Bros. 7786	Gloria/(B-side unknown)	1973	—	2.50	5.00
❑ Warner Bros. 7797	Ain't Nothin' You Can Do/Wild Children	1974	—	2.50	5.00
❑ Warner Bros. 8029	Bulbs/Cul-De-Sac	1974	—	2.50	5.00
❑ Warner Bros. 8411	Joyous Sound/Mechanical Bliss	1977	—	2.50	5.00
❑ Warner Bros. 8450	Moondance/Cold Wind in August	1977	—	2.50	5.00
❑ Warner Bros. 8661	Wavelength/Checkin' It Out	1978	—	2.50	5.00
❑ Warner Bros. 8743	Lifetimes/Natalia	1979	—	2.00	4.00
❑ Warner Bros. 8805	Checkin' It Out/Kingdom Hall	1979	—	2.00	4.00
❑ Warner Bros. 49086	Rolling Hills/Bright Side of the Road	1979	—	2.00	4.00
❑ Warner Bros. 49162	Full Force Gale/You Make Me Feel So Free	1980	—	2.00	4.00
❑ Warner Bros. 50031	Scandinavia/Cleaning Windows	1982	—	2.00	4.00
Albums					
❑ Bang BLB-218 [M]	Blowin' Your Mind	1968	12.50	25.00	50.00
—With the censored "Brown Eyed Girl" lyric, "Laughin' and a-runnin', hey hey, behind the stadium with you," part of which was spliced in from another part of the song. This has been confirmed to exist in mono.					
❑ Bang BLBS-218 [S]	Blowin' Your Mind	1968	5.00	10.00	20.00
—With the censored "Brown Eyed Girl" lyric, "Laughin' and a-runnin', hey hey, behind the stadium with you," part of which was spliced in from another part of the song!					
❑ Bang BLP-218 [M]	Blowin' Your Mind	1967	7.50	15.00	30.00
—With the true "Brown Eyed Girl" lyric, "Makin' love in the green grass behind the stadium with you."					
❑ Bang BLPS-218 [S]	Blowin' Your Mind	1967	10.00	20.00	40.00
—With the true "Brown Eyed Girl" lyric, "Makin' love in the green grass behind the stadium with you."					
❑ Bang BLPS-222	The Best of Van Morrison	1970	3.75	7.50	15.00
❑ Bang BLPS-400	T.B. Sheets	1973	5.00	10.00	20.00
❑ Lost Highway B0005968-01	Pay the Devil	2006	3.00	6.00	12.00
❑ Mercury 818336-1	Live at the Grand Opera House, Belfast	1985	2.50	5.00	10.00
❑ Mercury 822895-1	A Sense of Wonder	1985	2.00	4.00	8.00
❑ Mercury 830077-1	No Guru, No Method, No Teacher	1986	2.00	4.00	8.00
❑ Mercury 832585-1	Poetic Champions Compose	1987	2.00	4.00	8.00
❑ Mercury 834496-1	Irish Heartbeat	1988	2.00	4.00	8.00
—With the Chieftains					
❑ Mercury 839262-1	Avalon Sunset	1989	2.50	5.00	10.00
❑ Mercury 841970-1	The Best of Van Morrison	1990	3.75	7.50	15.00
❑ Mercury 847100-1	Enlightenment	1990	3.75	7.50	15.00
❑ Warner Bros. WS 1768	Astral Weeks	1968	6.25	12.50	25.00
—With "W7" logo on green label					
❑ Warner Bros. WS 1835	Moondance	1969	5.00	10.00	20.00
—With "W7" logo on green label					
❑ Warner Bros. WS 1884	His Band and the Street Choir	1970	3.75	7.50	15.00
—With "WB" logo on green label					
❑ Warner Bros. WS 1950	Tupelo Honey	1971	3.75	7.50	15.00
—With "WB" logo on green label, plus poster					
❑ Warner Bros. WS 2633	Saint Dominic's Preview	1972	3.75	7.50	15.00
—With "WB" logo on green label					
❑ Warner Bros. BS 2712	Hard Nose the Highway	1973	3.00	6.00	12.00
—"Burbank" palm-tree label					
❑ Warner Bros. 2BS 2760 [(2)]	It's Too Late to Stop Now	1974	3.75	7.50	15.00
—"Burbank" palm-tree labels					
❑ Warner Bros. BS 2805	Veedon Fleece	1974	3.00	6.00	12.00
—"Burbank" palm-tree labels					
❑ Warner Bros. BS 2987	A Period of Transition	1977	3.00	6.00	12.00
—"Burbank" palm-tree labels					
❑ Warner Bros. BSK 3103	Moondance	1977	2.50	5.00	10.00
—Reissue with new number; "Burbank" palm-tree label					
❑ Warner Bros. BSK 3212	Wavelength	1978	3.00	6.00	12.00
❑ Warner Bros. HS 3390	Into the Music	1979	3.00	6.00	12.00
❑ Warner Bros. BSK 3462	Common One	1980	3.00	6.00	12.00
❑ Warner Bros. BSK 3652	Beautiful Vision	1981	3.00	6.00	12.00
❑ Warner Bros. 23802	Inarticulate Speech of the Heart	1983	3.00	6.00	12.00

MULDAUR, MARIA

45s

Number	Title (A Side/B Side)	Yr	VG	VG+	NM
❑ Reprise 1183	Midnight at the Oasis/Any Old Time	1973	—	2.50	5.00

Number	Title (A Side/B Side)	Yr	VG	VG+	NM
❑ Reprise 1319	I'm a Woman/Cool River	1974	—	2.00	4.00
❑ Reprise 1331	Oh Papa/Gringo de Mexico	1975	—	2.00	4.00
❑ Reprise 1352	Sad Eyes/Wild Bird	1976	—	2.00	4.00
❑ Reprise 1362	Sweet Harmony/Jon the Generator	1976	—	2.00	4.00
❑ Warner Bros. 8580	Make Love to the Music/I'll Keep My Light in My Window	1978	—	2.00	4.00
❑ Warner Bros. 49058	Dancin' in the Street/Birds Fly South (When Winter Comes)	1979	—	2.00	4.00
❑ Warner Bros. 49131	Fall in Love Again/Love Is Everything	1979	—	2.00	4.00
Albums					
❑ Myrrh MSB-6685	There Is a Love	1984	2.50	5.00	10.00
❑ Reprise MS 2148	Maria Muldaur	1973	3.00	6.00	12.00
❑ Reprise MS 2194	Waitress in a Donut Shop	1974	3.00	6.00	12.00
❑ Reprise MS 2235	Sweet Harmony	1976	3.00	6.00	12.00
❑ Takoma 7084	Gospel Nights	1980	2.50	5.00	10.00
❑ Tudor 109902	Sweet & Sour	1983	2.50	5.00	10.00
❑ Warner Bros. BSK 3162	Southern Winds	1978	2.50	5.00	10.00
❑ Warner Bros. BSK 3305	Open Your Eyes	1979	2.50	5.00	10.00
MUNGO JERRY					
45s					
❑ Bell 45123	Lady Rose/Little Louis	1971	—	2.00	4.00
❑ Bell 45383	Alright, Alright, Alright/Little Miss Hipshake	1973	—	2.00	4.00
❑ Bell 45427	Wild Love/Glad I'm a Rocker	1973	—	2.00	4.00
❑ Bell 45451	Long Legged Woman Dressed in Black/Gonna Bop Till I Drop	1974	—	2.00	4.00
❑ Janus 125	In the Summertime/Mighty Man	1970	—	3.00	6.00
❑ Janus 128	Johnny B. Badde/My Friend	1970	—	2.50	5.00
❑ Janus 148	Baby Jump/The Man Beside the Piano	1971	—	2.50	5.00
❑ Pye 65003	You Don't Have to Be in the Army/O'Reilly	1972	—	2.00	4.00
❑ Pye 65009	Going Back Home/Open Up	1972	—	2.00	4.00
❑ Pye 71032	In the Summertime/(B-side unknown)	1975	—	2.00	4.00
Albums					
❑ Janus JLS-3027	Memoirs of a Stockbroker	1972	3.75	7.50	15.00
❑ Janus JXS-7000	Mungo Jerry	1970	3.75	7.50	15.00
MURRAY, ANNE					
45s					
❑ Capitol 2738	Snowbird/Just Bidin' My Time	1970	—	3.00	6.00
❑ Capitol 2988	Sing High — Sing Low/Days of the Looking Glass	1970	—	2.50	5.00
❑ Capitol 3059	A Stranger in My Place/Sycamore Slick	1971	—	2.50	5.00
❑ Capitol 3082	Put Your Hand in the Hand/It Takes Time	1971	—	2.50	5.00
❑ Capitol 3159	Talk It Over in the Morning/Head Above the Water	1971	—	2.50	5.00
❑ Capitol 3260	Cotton Jenny/Destiny	1972	—	2.50	5.00
❑ Capitol 3352	Bobbie's Song for Jesus/You Can't Have a Hand on Me	1972	—	2.50	5.00
❑ Capitol 3481	Danny's Song/Drown Me	1972	—	2.00	4.00
❑ Capitol 3600	What About Me/Let Sunshine Have Its Day	1973	—	2.00	4.00
❑ Capitol 3648	Send a Little Love My Way/Head Above the Water	1973	—	2.00	4.00
❑ Capitol 3776	Love Song/You Can't Go Back	1973	—	2.00	4.00
❑ Capitol 3867	You Won't See Me/He Thinks I Still Care	1974	—	2.50	5.00
❑ Capitol 3955	Just One Look/Son of a Rotten Gambler	1974	—	2.00	4.00
❑ Capitol 4000	Day Tripper/Lullaby	1974	—	2.00	4.00
❑ Capitol 4025	Uproar/Lift Your Hearts to the Sun	1975	—	2.00	4.00
❑ Capitol 4072	A Stranger in My Place/Dream Lover	1975	—	2.00	4.00
❑ Capitol 4142	Sunday Sunrise/Out on the Road Again	1975	—	2.00	4.00
❑ Capitol 4207	The Call/Lady Bug	1976	—	2.00	4.00
❑ Capitol 4265	Golden Oldie/Together	1976	—	2.00	4.00
❑ Capitol 4329	Things/Caress Me Pretty Music	1976	—	2.00	4.00
❑ Capitol 4375	Sunday School to Broadway/Dancin' All Night Long	1976	—	2.00	4.00
❑ Capitol 4402	Canterbury Song/Shilo Song	1977	—	2.00	4.00
—With Gene MacLellan					
❑ Capitol 4527	Walk Right Back/A Million More	1978	—	2.00	4.00
❑ Capitol 4574	You Needed Me/I Still Wish the Very Best for You	1978	—	2.00	4.00
❑ Capitol 4675	I Just Fall in Love Again/Just to Feel This Love from You	1979	—	2.00	4.00
❑ Capitol 4716	Shadows in the Moonlight/Yucatan Cafe	1979	—	2.00	4.00
❑ Capitol 4773	Broken Hearted Me/Why Don't You Stick Around	1979	—	2.00	4.00
❑ Capitol 4813	Daydream Believer/Do You Think of Me	1979	—	2.00	4.00
❑ Capitol 4848	Lucky Me/Somebody's Waiting	1980	—	2.00	4.00
❑ Capitol 4878	I'm Happy Just to Dance with You/What's Forever For	1980	—	2.00	4.00
❑ Capitol 4920	Could I Have This Dance/Somebody's Waiting	1980	—	2.00	4.00
❑ Capitol 4987	Blessed Are the Believers/Only Love	1981	—	2.00	4.00
❑ Capitol A-5013	We Don't Have to Hold Out/Call Me with the News	1981	—	2.00	4.00
❑ Capitol A-5023	It's All I Can Do/If a Heart Must Be Broken	1981	—	2.00	4.00
❑ Capitol A-5083	Another Sleepless Night/It Should Have Been Easy	1982	—	2.00	4.00
❑ Capitol B-5145	Hey! Baby!/Song for the Mira	1982	—	—	3.00
❑ Capitol B-5183	Somebody's Always Saying Goodbye/That'll Keep Me Dreamin'	1982	—	—	3.00
❑ Capitol B-5264	A Little Good News/I'm Not Afraid Anymore	1983	—	—	3.00
❑ Capitol B-5305	That's Not the Way (It's S'posed to Be)/The More We Try	1983	—	—	3.00
❑ Capitol B-5344	Just Another Woman in Love/Heart Stealer	1984	—	—	3.00
❑ Capitol B-5384	Let Your Heart Do the Talking/I Don't Think I'm Ready for You	1984	—	—	3.00
❑ Capitol B-5401	Nobody Loves Me Like You Do/Love You Out of Your Mind	1984	—	—	3.00
—A-side with Dave Loggins					
❑ Capitol B-5436	Time Don't Run Out on Me/Let Your Heart Do the Talking	1985	—	—	3.00
❑ Capitol B-5472	I Don't Think I'm Ready for You/Take Good Care of My Baby	1985	—	—	3.00
❑ Capitol B-5536	Go Tell It On the Mountain/O Holy Night	1985	—	2.00	4.00
❑ Capitol B-5547	Now and Forever (You and Me)/I Don't Wanna Spend Another Night Without You	1986	—	—	3.00
❑ Capitol B-5576	Who's Leaving Who/Reach for Me	1986	—	—	3.00
❑ Capitol B-5610	My Life's a Dance/Call Us Fools	1986	—	—	3.00
❑ Capitol B-5655	On and On/Gotcha	1986	—	—	3.00
❑ Capitol B-44005	Are You Still in Love with Me/Give Me Your Love	1987	—	—	3.00

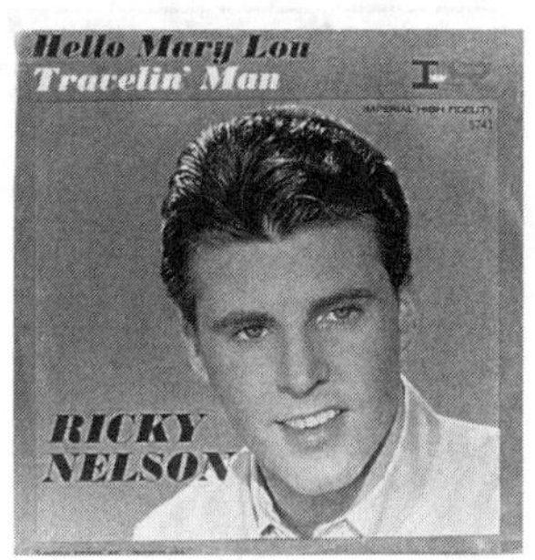

Number	Title (A Side/B Side)	Yr	VG	VG+	NM
❑ Capitol B-44053	Anyone Can Do the Heartbreak/Without You	1987	—	—	3.00
❑ Capitol B-44134	Perfect Strangers/It Happens All the Time	1988	—	—	3.00
—With Doug Mallory					
❑ Capitol B-44219	Flying On Your Own/Slow All Night	1988	—	—	3.00
❑ Capitol B-44272	Slow Passin' Time/Flying on Your Own	1989	—	—	3.00
❑ Capitol B-44341	Who But You/You Make Me Curious	1989	—	—	3.00
❑ Capitol B-44432	If I Ever Fall in Love Again/Just Another Woman in Love	1989	—	—	3.00
—A-side: With Kenny Rogers					
❑ Capitol B-44495	I'd Fall in Love Tonight/Now and Forever (You and Me)	1989	—	—	3.00
Albums					
❑ Capitol ST-579	Snowbird	1970	3.00	6.00	12.00
❑ Capitol ST-667	Anne Murray	1971	3.00	6.00	12.00
❑ Capitol ST-821	Talk It Over in the Morning	1971	3.00	6.00	12.00
❑ Capitol ST-11024	Annie	1972	2.50	5.00	10.00
❑ Capitol ST-11172	Danny's Song	1973	2.50	5.00	10.00
❑ Capitol ST-11266	Love Song	1974	2.50	5.00	10.00
❑ Capitol ST-11324	Country	1974	2.50	5.00	10.00
❑ Capitol ST-11354	Highly Prized Possession	1974	2.50	5.00	10.00
❑ Capitol ST-11433	Together	1975	2.50	5.00	10.00
❑ Capitol ST-11559	Keeping in Touch	1976	2.50	5.00	10.00
❑ Capitol ST-11743	Let's Keep It That Way	1978	2.50	5.00	10.00
❑ Capitol SW-11849	New Kind of Feeling	1979	2.50	5.00	10.00
❑ Capitol SOO-12012	I'll Always Love You	1979	2.50	5.00	10.00
❑ Capitol ST-12039	A Country Collection	1980	2.50	5.00	10.00
❑ Capitol SOO-12064	Somebody's Waiting	1980	2.50	5.00	10.00
❑ Capitol SOO-12110	Anne Murray's Greatest Hits	1980	2.50	5.00	10.00
❑ Capitol SOO-12144	Where Do You Go When You Dream	1981	2.50	5.00	10.00
❑ Capitol ST-12225	The Hottest Night of the Year	1982	2.50	5.00	10.00
❑ Capitol ST-12301	A Little Good News	1983	2.50	5.00	10.00
❑ Capitol SJ-12363	Heart Over Mind	1984	2.50	5.00	10.00
❑ Capitol SJ-12466	Something to Talk About	1986	2.50	5.00	10.00
❑ Capitol PJ-12562	Harmony	1987	2.50	5.00	10.00
❑ Capitol SN-16080	Talk It Over in the Morning	1980	2.00	4.00	8.00
—Budget-line reissue					
❑ Capitol SN-16081	Highly Prized Possession	1980	2.00	4.00	8.00
—Budget-line reissue					
❑ Capitol SN-16082	Keeping in Touch	1980	2.00	4.00	8.00
—Budget-line reissue					
❑ Capitol SN-16211	Danny's Song	1981	2.00	4.00	8.00
—Budget-line reissue					
❑ Capitol SN-16212	Love Song	1981	2.00	4.00	8.00
—Budget-line reissue					
❑ Capitol SN-16213	Country	1981	2.00	4.00	8.00
—Budget-line reissue					
❑ Capitol SN-16232	Christmas Wishes	1981	2.50	5.00	10.00
—Original issue was on the budget-line series					
❑ Capitol SN-16233	There's a Hippo in My Tub	1981	2.50	5.00	10.00
—Original issue was on the budget-line series					
❑ Capitol SN-16282	Together	1982	2.00	4.00	8.00
—Budget-line reissue					
❑ Capitol SN-16283	New Kind of Feeling	1982	2.00	4.00	8.00
—Budget-line reissue					
❑ Capitol SN-16338	A Country Collection	198?	2.00	4.00	8.00
—Budget-line reissue					
❑ Capitol SN-16341	Let's Keep It That Way	198?	2.00	4.00	8.00
—Budget-line reissue					
❑ Capitol C1-48764	As I Am	1988	2.50	5.00	10.00
❑ Capitol C1-90886	Christmas	1987	2.00	4.00	8.00
❑ Capitol C1-92072	Greatest Hits Volume II	1989	3.00	6.00	12.00
❑ Pickwick SPC-3350	What About Me	197?	2.00	4.00	8.00

MUSIC EXPLOSION, THE

45s

Number	Title (A Side/B Side)	Yr	VG	VG+	NM
❑ Attack 1404	The Little Black Egg/Stay By My Side	1966	6.25	12.50	25.00
❑ Laurie 3380	Little Bit O'Soul/I See the Light	1967	3.00	6.00	12.00
❑ Laurie 3400	Can't Stop Now/Sunshine Games	1967	2.00	4.00	8.00
❑ Laurie 3414	We Gotta Go Home/Hearts and Flowers	1967	2.00	4.00	8.00

Number	Title (A Side/B Side)	Yr	VG	VG+	NM
❑ Laurie 3429	What You Want/Road Runner	1968	2.00	4.00	8.00
❑ Laurie 3440	Where Are We Going/Flash	1968	2.00	4.00	8.00
❑ Laurie 3454	Yes Sir/Dazzling	1968	2.00	4.00	8.00
❑ Laurie 3466	Jack in the Box/Rewind	1968	2.00	4.00	8.00
❑ Laurie 3479	What's Your Name/Call Me Anything	1969	2.00	4.00	8.00
❑ Laurie 3500	The Little Black Egg/Stay By My Side	1969	2.00	4.00	8.00
Albums					
❑ Laurie LLP-2040 [M]	Little Bit O'Soul	1967	5.00	10.00	20.00
❑ Laurie SLLP-2040 [S]	Little Bit O'Soul	1967	6.25	12.50	25.00
MUSIC MACHINE, THE					
45s					
❑ Bell 764	Mother Nature—Father Earth/Advise and Consent	1969	2.00	4.00	8.00
❑ Original Sound 61	Talk Talk/Come On In	1966	3.00	6.00	12.00
❑ Original Sound 67	The People in Me/Masculine Institution	1967	2.50	5.00	10.00
❑ Original Sound 71	Double Yellow Line/Absolutely Positive	1967	2.50	5.00	10.00
❑ Original Sound 75	I've Loved You/The Eagle Never Hunts the Fly	1967	2.50	5.00	10.00
❑ Original Sound 82	Hey Joe/Wrong	1968	2.50	5.00	10.00
❑ Warner Bros. 7093	Bottom of the Soul/Astrologically Incompatible	1968	2.00	4.00	8.00
❑ Warner Bros. 7199	To the Light/You'll Love Me Again	1968	2.00	4.00	8.00
Albums					
❑ Original Sound 5015 [M]	(Turn On) The Music Machine	1966	10.00	20.00	40.00
❑ Original Sound 8875 [S]	(Turn On) The Music Machine	1966	12.50	25.00	50.00
❑ Warner Bros. W 1732 [M]	Bonniwell's Music Machine	1967	6.25	12.50	25.00
❑ Warner Bros. WS 1732 [S]	Bonniwell's Music Machine	1967	10.00	20.00	40.00
MYSTICS, THE					
45s					
❑ Ambient Sound 02871	Now That Summer Is Here/Prayer to An Angel	1982	—	2.50	5.00
❑ Black Cat 101	Snoopy/Ooh Poo Pah Doo	1966	10.00	20.00	40.00
❑ Constellation 138	She's Got Everything/Just a Loser	1964	3.00	6.00	12.00
❑ Dot 16862	Now and For Always/Didn't We Have a Good Time	1966	2.50	5.00	10.00
❑ King 5678	Mashed Potatoes With Me/The Hoppy Hop	1962	3.75	7.50	15.00
❑ King 5735	The Jumpin' Bean/Just For Your Love	1963	3.75	7.50	15.00
❑ Laurie 3028 [M]	Hushabye/Adam and Eve	1959	7.50	15.00	30.00
❑ Laurie S-3028 [S]	Hushabye/Adam and Eve	1959	30.00	60.00	120.00
❑ Laurie 3038	Don't Take the Stars/So Tenderly	1959	6.25	12.50	25.00
❑ Laurie 3047	All Through the Night/To Think of You Again	1960	6.25	12.50	25.00
❑ Laurie 3058	White Cliffs of Dover/Blue Star	1960	6.25	12.50	25.00
❑ Laurie 3086	Star Crossed Lovers/Goodbye Mr. Blue	1961	6.25	12.50	25.00
❑ Laurie 3104	Sunday Kind of Love/Darling I Know How	1961	7.50	15.00	30.00
❑ Nolta 353	The Fox/Dan	1963	3.75	7.50	15.00
Albums					
❑ Ambient Sound FZ 37716	Crazy for You	1982	2.50	5.00	10.00
❑ Collectables COL-5043	16 Golden Classics	198?	2.50	5.00	10.00

N

Number	Title (A Side/B Side)	Yr	VG	VG+	NM
NAPOLEON XIV					
45s					
❑ Warner Bros. 5831	They're Coming to Take Me Away, Ha-Haaa!/Yawa Em Ekat ot Gnimoc Er'yeht, !Aaah-Ah	1966	3.00	6.00	12.00
❑ Warner Bros. 5853	I'm in Love with My Little Red Tricycle/Doin' the Napoleon	1966	2.50	5.00	10.00
❑ Warner Bros. 7726	They're Coming to Take Me Away, Ha-Haaa!/!Aaah-Ah, Yawa Em Ekat ot Gnimoc Er'yeht	1973	2.00	4.00	8.00
Albums					
❑ Rhino RNLP 816	They're Coming to Take Me Away, Ha-Haaa!	1985	3.00	6.00	12.00
❑ Warner Bros. W 1661 [M]	They're Coming to Take Me Away, Ha-Haaa!	1966	15.00	30.00	60.00
❑ Warner Bros. WS 1661 [S]	They're Coming to Take Me Away, Ha-Haaa!	1966	25.00	50.00	100.00
NASH, JOHNNY					
45s					
❑ ABC-Paramount 9743	Out of Town/A Teenager Sings the Blues	1956	5.00	10.00	20.00
❑ ABC-Paramount 9844	The Ladder of Love/I'll Walk Alone	1957	5.00	10.00	20.00
❑ ABC-Paramount 9874	A Very Special Love/Won't You Let Me Share My Love with You	1957	5.00	10.00	20.00
❑ ABC-Paramount 9894	My Pledge to You/It's So Easy to Say	1958	5.00	10.00	20.00
❑ ABC-Paramount 9927	Please Don't Go/I Lost My Love Last Night	1958	5.00	10.00	20.00
❑ ABC-Paramount 9942	Truly Love/You're Looking at Me	1958	5.00	10.00	20.00
❑ ABC-Paramount 9960	Almost in Your Arms/Midnight Moonlight	1958	5.00	10.00	20.00
❑ ABC-Paramount 9989	Roots of Heaven/Walk with Faith in Your Heart	1958	5.00	10.00	20.00
❑ ABC-Paramount 9996	As Time Goes By/The Voice of Love	1959	5.00	10.00	20.00
❑ ABC-Paramount 10026	And the Angels Sing/Baby, Baby, Baby	1959	5.00	10.00	20.00
❑ ABC-Paramount 10046	Take a Giant Step/But Not for Me	1959	5.00	10.00	20.00
❑ ABC-Paramount 10060	The Wish/Too Proud	1959	5.00	10.00	20.00
❑ ABC-Paramount 10076	A Place in the Sun/Goodbye	1960	3.75	7.50	15.00
❑ ABC-Paramount 10095	Never My Love/(You've Got the) Love I Love	1960	3.75	7.50	15.00
❑ ABC-Paramount 10112	Let the Rest of the World Go By/Music of Love	1960	3.75	7.50	15.00
❑ ABC-Paramount 10137	(Looks Like) The End of the World/We Kissed	1960	3.75	7.50	15.00
❑ ABC-Paramount 10160	Kisses/Somebody	1960	3.75	7.50	15.00
❑ ABC-Paramount 10181	World of Tears/Some of Your Lovin'	1961	3.00	6.00	12.00
❑ ABC-Paramount 10205	I Need Someone to Stand By/A House on the Hill	1961	3.00	6.00	12.00
❑ ABC-Paramount 10212	A Thousand Miles Away/I Need Someone to Stand By Me	1961	3.00	6.00	12.00
❑ ABC-Paramount 10230	I'm Counting on You/I Lost My Baby	1961	3.00	6.00	12.00
❑ ABC-Paramount 10251	Too Much Love/Love's Young Dream	1961	3.00	6.00	12.00
❑ Argo 5471	Talk to Me/Love Ain't Nothin'	1964	2.00	4.00	8.00
❑ Argo 5479	Then You Can Tell Me Goodbye/Always	1964	2.00	4.00	8.00
❑ Argo 5492	Spring Is Here/Strange Feeling	1965	2.00	4.00	8.00

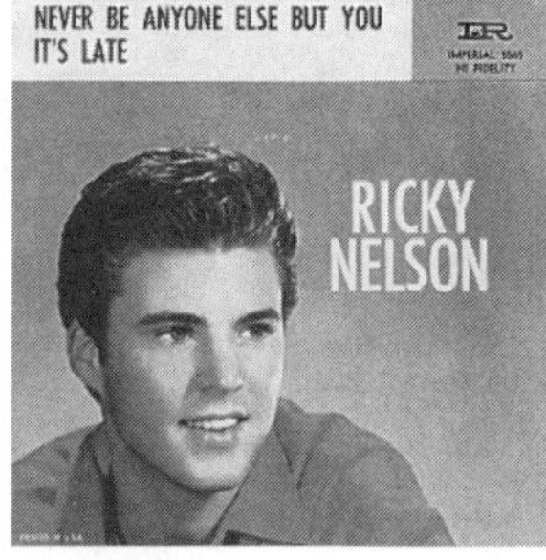

Number	Title (A Side/B Side)	Yr	VG	VG+	NM
❑ Argo 5501	Teardrops in the Rain/I Know What I Want	1965	2.00	4.00	8.00
❑ Atlantic 2344	Big City/Somewhere	1966	2.00	4.00	8.00
❑ Cadet 5528	Teardrops in the Rain/Get Myself Together	1966	5.00	10.00	20.00
❑ Epic 10873	Stir It Up/Cream Puff	1972	—	3.50	7.00
❑ Epic 10902	I Can See Clearly Now/How Good It Is	1972	—	3.00	6.00
❑ Epic 10949	Stir It Up/Ooh Baby You've Been Good to Me	1973	—	3.00	6.00
❑ Epic 11003	My Merry-Go-Round/We're Trying to Get Back to You	1973	—	2.50	5.00
❑ Epic 11034	Ooh What a Feeling/Yellow House	1973	—	2.50	5.00
❑ Epic 11070	Loving You/Gonna Open Up My Heart Again	1973	—	2.50	5.00
❑ Epic 50021	You Can't Go Halfway/The Very First Time	1974	—	2.50	5.00
❑ Epic 50051	Beautiful Baby/Celebrate Life	1974	—	2.50	5.00
❑ Epic 50091	Good Vibrations/The Very First Time	1975	—	2.50	5.00
❑ Epic 50138	Tears on My Pillow (I Can't Take It)/Beautiful Baby	1975	—	2.50	5.00
❑ Epic 50219	(What a) Wonderful World/Rock It Baby (We've Got a Date)	1976	—	2.50	5.00
❑ Epic 50386	Back in Time/That Woman	1977	—	2.00	4.00
❑ Epic 50737	Closer/Mr. Sea	1979	—	2.00	4.00
❑ Epic 50821	You're the One/Don't Forget	1980	—	2.00	4.00
❑ Groove 58-0018	Helpless/I've Got a Lot to Offer, Darling	1963	2.50	5.00	10.00
❑ Groove 58-0021	Deep in the Heart of Harlem/What Kind of Love Is This	1963	10.00	20.00	40.00
❑ Groove 58-0026	It's No Good for Me/Town of Lonely Hearts	1963	2.50	5.00	10.00
❑ Groove 58-0030	I'm Leaving/Oh Mary Don't You Weep	1964	2.50	5.00	10.00
❑ Jad 207	Hold Me Tight/Cupid	1968	2.00	4.00	8.00
—Mostly light green label with purple trim					
❑ Jad 209	You Got Soul/Don't Cry	1968	2.00	4.00	8.00
❑ Jad 214	Lovey Dovey/You Got Soul	1969	—	3.00	6.00
❑ Jad 215	Sweet Charity/People in Love	1969	—	3.00	6.00
❑ Jad 218	Love and Peace/People in Love	1969	—	3.00	6.00
❑ Jad 220	Cupid/Hold Me Tight	1969	—	3.00	6.00
❑ Jad 223	What a Groovy Feeling/You Got Soul (Part 1)	1970	—	3.00	6.00
❑ Janus 136	Falling In and Out of Love/You've Got to Change Your Ways	1970	—	3.00	6.00
❑ Joda 102	Let's Move and Groove (Together)/Understanding	1965	2.50	5.00	10.00
❑ Joda 105	One More Time/Got to Find Her	1965	2.50	5.00	10.00
❑ Joda 106	Somewhere/Big City	1966	2.50	5.00	10.00
❑ MGM 13637	Amen/Perfumed Flower	1966	2.00	4.00	8.00
❑ MGM 13683	Good Goodness/You Never Know	1967	2.00	4.00	8.00
❑ MGM 13805	Stormy/(I'm So) Glad You're My Baby	1967	2.00	4.00	8.00
❑ Warner Bros. 5270	Don't Take Your Love Away/Moment of Weakness	1962	3.00	6.00	12.00
❑ Warner Bros. 5301	Ol' Man River/My Dear Little Sweetheart	1962	3.00	6.00	12.00
❑ Warner Bros. 5336	Cigarettes, Whiskey and Wild, Wild Women/I'm Movin' On	1963	3.00	6.00	12.00
Albums					
❑ ABC-Paramount 244 [M]	Johnny Nash	1958	7.50	15.00	30.00
❑ ABC-Paramount S-244 [S]	Johnny Nash	1959	10.00	20.00	40.00
❑ ABC-Paramount 276 [M]	Quiet Hour	1959	7.50	15.00	30.00
❑ ABC-Paramount S-276 [S]	Quiet Hour	1959	10.00	20.00	40.00
❑ ABC-Paramount 299 [M]	I Got Rhythm	1959	7.50	15.00	30.00
❑ ABC-Paramount S-299 [S]	I Got Rhythm	1959	10.00	20.00	40.00
❑ ABC-Paramount 344 [M]	Let's Get Lost	1960	7.50	15.00	30.00
❑ ABC-Paramount S-344 [S]	Let's Get Lost	1960	10.00	20.00	40.00
❑ ABC-Paramount 383 [M]	Studio Time	1961	7.50	15.00	30.00
❑ ABC-Paramount S-383 [S]	Studio Time	1961	10.00	20.00	40.00
❑ Argo LP-4038 [M]	Composer's Choice	1964	5.00	10.00	20.00
❑ Argo LPS-4038 [S]	Composer's Choice	1964	6.25	12.50	25.00
❑ Epic KE 31607	I Can See Clearly Now	1972	3.75	7.50	15.00
—Yellow label					
❑ Epic KE 32158	My Merry-Go-Round	1973	3.75	7.50	15.00
❑ Epic PE 32828	Celebrate Life	1974	3.75	7.50	15.00
❑ Jad JS-1001	Prince of Peace	1969	6.25	12.50	25.00
❑ Jad JS-1006	Folk Soul	1970	6.25	12.50	25.00
❑ Jad JS-1207	Hold Me Tight	1968	7.50	15.00	30.00

NASHVILLE TEENS, THE

45s

Number	Title (A Side/B Side)	Yr	VG	VG+	NM
❑ London 9689	Tobacco Road/I Like It Like That	1964	3.75	7.50	15.00
❑ London 9712	T.N.T./Google Eyes	1964	3.00	6.00	12.00
❑ London 9736	Devil-in-Law/Find My Way Back Home	1965	3.00	6.00	12.00
❑ MGM 13357	Little Bird/Whatcha Gonna Do	1965	2.50	5.00	10.00
❑ MGM 13406	I Know How It Feels to Be Loved/Soon Forgotten	1965	2.50	5.00	10.00

Number	Title (A Side/B Side)	Yr	VG	VG+	NM
❑ MGM 13483	The Hard Way/Upside Down	1966	2.50	5.00	10.00
❑ MGM 13678	That's My Woman/Words	1967	2.50	5.00	10.00
❑ United Artists 50880	Tennessee Woman/Ella James	1972	5.00	10.00	20.00
Albums					
❑ London PS 407 [R]	Tobacco Road	1964	20.00	40.00	80.00
❑ London LL 3407 [M]	Tobacco Road	1964	25.00	50.00	100.00
NAZARETH					
45s					
❑ A&M 1453	Broken Down Angel/Hard Living	1973	—	2.50	5.00
❑ A&M 1469	Bad Bad Boy/Razamanaz	1973	—	2.50	5.00
❑ A&M 1511	Go Down Fighting/This Flight Tonight	1974	—	2.50	5.00
❑ A&M 1548	Sunshine/This Flight Tonight	1974	—	2.50	5.00
❑ A&M 1671	Love Hurts/Hair of the Dog	1975	—	2.00	4.00
❑ A&M 1854	Loretta/Lift the Lid	1976	—	2.00	4.00
❑ A&M 1895	I Want To (Do Everything for You)/ I Don't Want to Go On Without You	1976	—	2.00	4.00
❑ A&M 1936	Somebody to Roll/This Flight Tonight	1976	—	2.00	4.00
❑ A&M 2009	Kentucky Fried Blues/Shot Me Down	1978	—	2.00	4.00
❑ A&M 2029	Gone Dead Train/Kentucky Fried Blues	1978	—	2.00	4.00
❑ A&M 2116	Expect No Mercy/May the Sunshine	1979	—	2.00	4.00
❑ A&M 2130	Whatever You Want Babe/Expect No Mercy	1979	—	2.00	4.00
❑ A&M 2158	Star/Expect No Mercy	1979	—	2.00	4.00
❑ A&M 2219	Holiday/Ship of Dreams	1980	—	2.00	4.00
❑ A&M 2237	Hearts Grown Cold/Ship of Dreams	1980	—	2.00	4.00
❑ A&M 2324	Dressed to Kill/Pop the Silo	1981	—	2.00	4.00
❑ A&M 2378	Juicy Lucy/Morning Dew	1981	—	2.00	4.00
❑ A&M 2389	Hair of the Dog/Holiday	1982	—	2.00	4.00
❑ A&M 2421	Love Leads to Madness/Take the Rap	1982	—	2.00	4.00
❑ A&M 2444	Dream On/Take the Rap	1982	—	2.00	4.00
❑ Warner Bros. 7599	Morning Dew (Take Me for a Walk)/Dear John	1972	2.00	4.00	8.00
Albums					
❑ A&M SP-3109	Close Enough for Rock 'N' Roll	1981	2.00	4.00	8.00
—Budget-line reissue					
❑ A&M SP-3168	Exercises	1982	2.00	4.00	8.00
—Reissue of Warner Bros. 2639					
❑ A&M SP-3169	Nazareth	1982	2.00	4.00	8.00
—Reissue of Warner Bros. 2615					
❑ A&M SP-3225	Hair of the Dog	1984	2.00	4.00	8.00
—Budget-line reissue					
❑ A&M SP-3226	Hot Tracks	1984	2.00	4.00	8.00
—Budget-line reissue					
❑ A&M SP-3609	Loud 'N' Proud	1974	2.50	5.00	10.00
❑ A&M SP-3641	Rampant	1974	2.50	5.00	10.00
❑ A&M SP-4396	Razamanaz	1973	3.75	7.50	15.00
—First edition with brown label					
❑ A&M SP-4511	Hair of the Dog	1975	2.50	5.00	10.00
❑ A&M SP-4562	Close Enough for Rock 'N' Roll	1976	2.50	5.00	10.00
❑ A&M SP-4610	Play 'N' the Game	1976	2.50	5.00	10.00
❑ A&M SP-4643	Hot Tracks	1977	2.50	5.00	10.00
❑ A&M SP-4666	Expect No Mercy	1977	2.50	5.00	10.00
❑ A&M SP-4741	No Mean City	1979	2.50	5.00	10.00
❑ A&M SP-4799	Malice in Wonderland	1980	2.50	5.00	10.00
❑ A&M SP-4844	The Fool Circle	1981	2.50	5.00	10.00
❑ A&M SP-4901	2XS	1982	2.50	5.00	10.00
❑ A&M SP-6703 [(2)]	'Snaz	1981	3.00	6.00	12.00
❑ MCA 5458	Sound Elixir	1983	2.50	5.00	10.00
❑ Warner Bros. BS 2615	Nazareth	1972	5.00	10.00	20.00
❑ Warner Bros. BS 2639	Exercises	1972	5.00	10.00	20.00
NELSON, RICKY					
45s					
❑ Capitol 4962	Almost Saturday Night/The Loser Babe Is You	1981	—	2.50	5.00
❑ Capitol 4974	Call It What You Want/It Hasn't Happened Yet	1981	—	2.50	5.00
❑ Capitol 4988	Believe What You Say/The Loser Babe Is You	1981	—	2.50	5.00
❑ Decca 31475	You Don't Love Me Anymore (And I Can Tell)/I Got a Woman	1963	3.75	7.50	15.00
❑ Decca 31495	String Along/Gypsy Woman	1963	3.75	7.50	15.00
❑ Decca 31533	Fools Rush In/Down Home	1963	3.75	7.50	15.00
❑ Decca 31574	For You/That's All She Wrote	1963	3.75	7.50	15.00
❑ Decca 31612	The Very Thought of You/I Wonder (If Your Love Will Ever Belong to Me)	1964	3.00	6.00	12.00
❑ Decca 31656	There's Nothing I Can Say/Lonely Corner	1964	3.00	6.00	12.00
❑ Decca 31703	A Happy Guy/Don't Breathe a Word	1964	3.00	6.00	12.00
❑ Decca 31756	Mean Old World/When the Chips Are Down	1965	3.00	6.00	12.00
❑ Decca 31800	Yesterday's Love/Come Out Dancin'	1965	3.00	6.00	12.00
❑ Decca 31845	Love and Kisses/Say You Love Me	1965	3.00	6.00	12.00
❑ Decca 31900	Your Kind of Lovin'/Fire Breathin' Dragon	1966	3.00	6.00	12.00
❑ Decca 31956	Louisiana Man/You Just Can't Quit	1966	3.00	6.00	12.00
❑ Decca 32026	Alone/Things You Gave Me	1966	3.00	6.00	12.00
❑ Decca 32055	They Don't Give Medals (To Yesterday's Heroes)/ Take a Broken Heart	1966	3.00	6.00	12.00
❑ Decca 32120	Take a City Bride/I'm Called Lonely	1967	2.50	5.00	10.00
❑ Decca 32176	Moonshine/Suzanne on a Sunday Morning	1967	2.50	5.00	10.00
❑ Decca 32222	Dream Weaver/Baby Close Your Eyes	1967	2.50	5.00	10.00
❑ Decca 32284	Don't Blame It on Your Wife/Promenade in Green	1968	2.50	5.00	10.00
❑ Decca 32298	Barefoot Boy/Don't Make Promises	1968	2.50	5.00	10.00
❑ Decca 32550	She Belongs to Me/Promises	1969	2.00	4.00	8.00

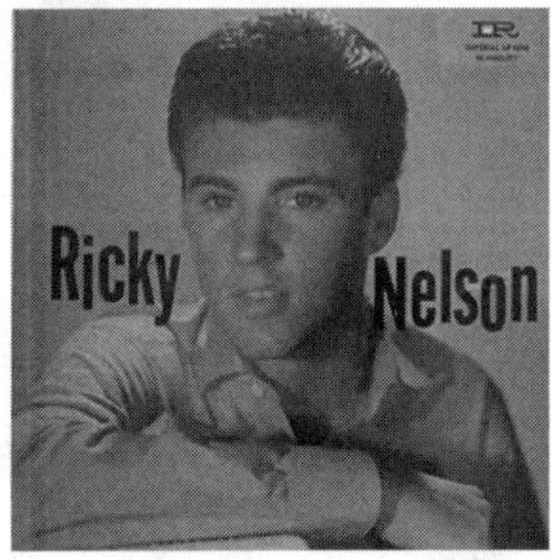

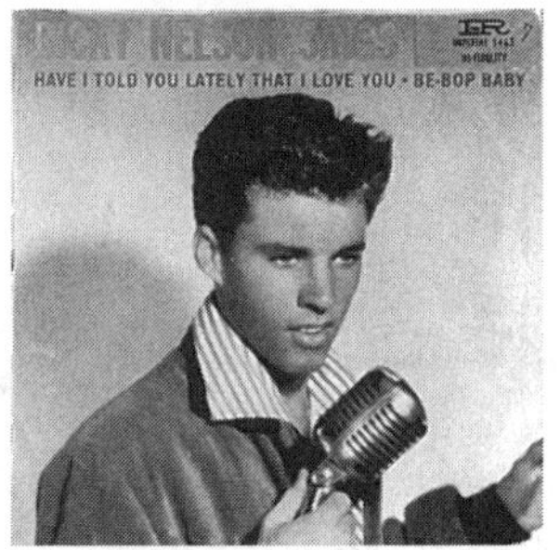

Number	Title (A Side/B Side)	Yr	VG	VG+	NM
❑ Decca 32635	Easy to Be Free/Come On In	1970	2.00	4.00	8.00
❑ Decca 32676	I Shall Be Released/If You Gotta Go, Go Now	1970	2.00	4.00	8.00
❑ Decca 32711	Look at Mary/We Got Such a Long Way to Go	1970	2.00	4.00	8.00
❑ Decca 32739	How Long/Down Along the Bayou Country	1970	2.00	4.00	8.00
❑ Decca 32779	Life/California	1971	2.00	4.00	8.00
❑ Decca 32860	Thank You Lord/Sing Me a Song	1971	2.00	4.00	8.00
❑ Decca 32906	Love Minus Zero-No Limit/Gypsy Pilot	1971	2.00	4.00	8.00
❑ Decca 32980	Garden Party/So Long Mama	1972	2.50	5.00	10.00
❑ Epic 34-06066	Dream Lover/Rave On	1986	—	2.00	4.00
❑ Epic 50458	It's Another Day/You Can't Dance	1977	—	2.50	5.00
❑ Epic 50501	Gimme A Little Sign/Something You Can't Buy	1978	—	2.50	5.00
❑ Epic 50674	Dream Lover/That Ain't the Way Love's Supposed to Be	1979	—	2.50	5.00
❑ Imperial 5463	Be-Bop Baby/Have I Told You Lately That I Love You	1957	6.25	12.50	25.00
—Black label					
❑ Imperial 5483	Stood Up/Waitin' in School	1957	6.25	12.50	25.00
—Black label					
❑ Imperial 5503	Believe What You Say/My Bucket's Got a Hole in It	1958	7.50	15.00	30.00
—Black label					
❑ Imperial 5528	Poor Little Fool/Don't Leave Me This Way	1958	7.50	15.00	30.00
❑ Imperial 5545	Lonesome Town/I Got a Feeling	1958	7.50	15.00	30.00
❑ Imperial 5565	Never Be Anyone Else But You/It's Late	1959	6.25	12.50	25.00
—Black label					
❑ Imperial 5595	Just a Little Too Much/Sweeter Than You	1959	6.25	12.50	25.00
❑ Imperial 5614	I Wanna Be Loved/Mighty Good	1959	6.25	12.50	25.00
❑ Imperial 5663	Young Emotions/Right By My Side	1960	6.25	12.50	25.00
❑ Imperial 5685	I'm Not Afraid/Yes Sir, That's My Baby	1960	6.25	12.50	25.00
❑ Imperial 5707	You Are the Only One/Milk Cow Blues	1960	6.25	12.50	25.00
❑ Imperial 5741	Travelin' Man/Hello Mary Lou	1961	6.25	12.50	25.00
—Black vinyl					
❑ Imperial 5770	A Wonder Like You/Everlovin'	1961	5.00	10.00	20.00
—Starting here, Imperial singles by "Rick Nelson"					
❑ Imperial 5805	Young World/Summertime	1962	5.00	10.00	20.00
❑ Imperial 5864	Teen Age Idol/I've Got My Eyes on You	1962	5.00	10.00	20.00
❑ Imperial 5901	It's Up to You/I Need You	1962	5.00	10.00	20.00
❑ Imperial 5910	That's All/I'm in Love Again	1963	6.25	12.50	25.00
❑ Imperial 5935	Old Enough to Love/If You Can't Rock Me	1963	5.00	10.00	20.00
❑ Imperial 5958	A Long Vacation/Mad Mad World	1963	5.00	10.00	20.00
❑ Imperial 5985	Time After Time/There's Not a Minute	1963	5.00	10.00	20.00
❑ Imperial 66004	Today's Teardrops/Thank You Darlin'	1963	3.75	7.50	15.00
❑ Imperial 66017	Congratulations/One Minute to One	1964	3.75	7.50	15.00
❑ Imperial 66039	Everybody But Me/Lucky Star	1964	3.75	7.50	15.00
❑ MCA 40001	Palace Guard/A Flower Opens Gently By	1973	—	3.00	6.00
❑ MCA 40130	Evil Woman Child/Lifestream	1973	—	3.00	6.00
❑ MCA 40187	Windfall/Legacy	1974	—	3.00	6.00
❑ MCA 40214	One Night Stand/Lifestream	1974	—	3.00	6.00
❑ MCA 40392	Louisiana Belle/Try (Try to Fall in Love)	1975	—	3.00	6.00
❑ MCA 40458	Rock and Roll Lady/Fadeaway	1975	—	3.00	6.00
❑ MCA 52781	You Know What I Mean/Don't Leave Me This Way	1986	—	2.50	5.00
❑ United Artists 0071	Be-Bop Baby/Stood Up	1973	—	2.50	5.00
❑ United Artists 0072	Lonesome Town/It's Up to You	1973	—	2.50	5.00
❑ United Artists 0073	Poor Little Fool/My Bucket's Got a Hole in It	1973	—	2.50	5.00
❑ United Artists 0074	Travelin' Man/Believe What You Say	1973	—	2.50	5.00
❑ United Artists 0075	Teen Age Idol/Young Emotions	1973	—	2.50	5.00
❑ United Artists 0076	Never Be Anyone Else But You/That's All	1973	—	2.50	5.00
❑ United Artists 0077	Young World/It's Late	1973	—	2.50	5.00
❑ United Artists 0078	Just a Little Too Much/Waitin' in School	1973	—	2.50	5.00
❑ United Artists 0079	Hello Mary Lou/Sweeter Than You	1973	—	2.50	5.00
❑ United Artists 0080	A Wonder Like You/Everlovin'	1973	—	2.50	5.00
—0071 through 0080 are "Silver Spotlight Series" reissues					
❑ Universal Pictures CPM 7-112/3 [DJ]	Love and Kisses Radio Spots	1965	75.00	150.00	300.00
—Red vinyl; three segments on one side, three on the other; double the value if a six-page transcription is with the record					
❑ Verve 10047	I'm Walkin'/A Teenager's Romance	1957	10.00	20.00	40.00
—Black and white label					
❑ Verve 10070	You're My One and Only Love/Honey Rock	1957	10.00	20.00	40.00
—B-side by Barney Kessel					
Albums					
❑ Capitol SOO-12109	Playing to Win	1981	2.50	5.00	10.00

Number	Title (A Side/B Side)	Yr	VG	VG+	NM
❑ Decca DL 4419 [M]	For Your Sweet Love	1963	7.50	15.00	30.00
❑ Decca DL 4479 [M]	Rick Nelson Sings "For You"	1963	7.50	15.00	30.00
❑ Decca DL 4559 [M]	The Very Thought of You	1964	7.50	15.00	30.00
❑ Decca DL 4608 [M]	Spotlight on Rick	1964	7.50	15.00	30.00
❑ Decca DL 4660 [M]	Best Always	1965	7.50	15.00	30.00
❑ Decca DL 4678 [M]	Love and Kisses	1965	7.50	15.00	30.00
❑ Decca DL 4779 [M]	Bright Lights and Country Music	1966	6.25	12.50	25.00
❑ Decca DL 4827 [M]	Country Fever	1967	6.25	12.50	25.00
❑ Decca DL 4944 [M]	Another Side of Rick	1967	6.25	12.50	25.00
❑ Decca DL 5014 [M]	Perspective	1968	12.50	25.00	50.00
—Mono copies are promo only					
❑ Decca DL 74419 [S]	For Your Sweet Love	1963	10.00	2.00	40.00
❑ Decca DL 74479 [S]	Rick Nelson Sings "For You"	1963	10.00	20.00	40.00
❑ Decca DL 74559 [S]	The Very Thought of You	1964	10.00	20.00	40.00
❑ Decca DL 74608 [S]	Spotlight on Rick	1964	10.00	20.00	40.00
❑ Decca DL 74660 [S]	Best Always	1965	10.00	20.00	40.00
❑ Decca DL 74678 [S]	Love and Kisses	1965	10.00	20.00	40.00
❑ Decca DL 74779 [S]	Bright Lights and Country Music	1966	7.50	15.00	30.00
❑ Decca DL 74827 [S]	Country Fever	1967	7.50	15.00	30.00
❑ Decca DL 74944 [S]	Another Side of Rick	1967	7.50	15.00	30.00
❑ Decca DL 75014 [S]	Perspective	1968	7.50	15.00	30.00
❑ Decca DL 75162	Rick Nelson In Concert	1970	6.25	12.50	25.00
❑ Decca DL 75236	Rick Sings Nelson	1970	6.25	12.50	25.00
—Deduct 20 percent if poster is missing					
❑ Decca DL 75297	Rudy the Fifth	1971	6.25	12.50	25.00
❑ Decca DL 75391	Garden Party	1972	6.25	12.50	25.00
❑ EMI America SQ-17192	The Very Best of Rick Nelson	1986	2.50	5.00	10.00
—Reissue of United Artists UA-LA330					
❑ Epic JE 34420	Intakes	1977	3.00	6.00	12.00
❑ Epic FE 40388	The Memphis Sessions	1986	2.50	5.00	10.00
❑ Epic/Nu-Disk 3E 36868 [10]	Four You	1981	3.00	6.00	12.00
❑ Imperial LP 9048 [M]	Ricky	1957	25.00	50.00	100.00
—Black label with stars					
❑ Imperial LP 9050 [M]	Ricky Nelson	1958	25.00	50.00	100.00
—Black label with stars					
❑ Imperial LP 9061 [M]	Ricky Sings Again	1959	25.00	50.00	100.00
—Black label with stars					
❑ Imperial LP 9082 [M]	Songs by Ricky	1959	18.75	37.50	75.00
—Black label with stars					
❑ Imperial LP 9122 [M]	More Songs by Ricky	1960	18.75	37.50	75.00
—Black label with stars					
❑ Imperial LP 9152 [M]	Rick Is 21	1961	10.00	20.00	40.00
—Black label with stars					
❑ Imperial LP 9167 [M]	Album Seven by Rick	1962	10.00	20.00	40.00
—Black label with stars					
❑ Imperial LP 9218 [M]	Best Sellers by Rick Nelson	1963	10.00	20.00	40.00
—Black label with stars					
❑ Imperial LP 9223 [M]	It's Up to You	1963	10.00	20.00	40.00
—Black label with stars					
❑ Imperial LP 9232 [M]	Million Sellers	1963	10.00	20.00	40.00
—Black label with stars					
❑ Imperial LP 9244 [M]	A Long Vacation	1963	10.00	20.00	40.00
—Black label with stars					
❑ Imperial LP 9251 [M]	Rick Nelson Sings for You	1964	10.00	20.00	40.00
—Black label with stars					
❑ Imperial LP 12030 [S]	Songs by Ricky	1959	50.00	100.00	200.00
—Black label with silver print					
❑ Imperial LP 12059 [S]	More Songs by Ricky	1960	25.00	50.00	100.00
—Black label with silver print					
❑ Imperial LP 12071 [S]	Rick Is 21	1961	25.00	50.00	100.00
—Black label with silver print					
❑ Imperial LP 12082 [S]	Album Seven by Rick	1962	25.00	50.00	100.00
—Black label with silver print					
❑ Imperial LP 12090 [S]	Ricky Sings Again	1962	37.50	75.00	150.00
—Black label with silver print					
❑ Imperial LP 12218 [R]	Best Sellers	1964	5.00	10.00	20.00
—Black label with pink and white at left					
❑ Imperial LP 12232 [R]	Million Sellers	1964	5.00	10.00	20.00
—Black label with pink and white at left					
❑ Imperial LP 12244 [R]	A Long Vacation	1964	5.00	10.00	20.00
—Black label with pink and white at left					
❑ Imperial LP 12251 [R]	Rick Nelson Sings for You	1964	6.25	12.50	25.00
—Black label with silver print					
❑ Imperial LP 12392 [R]	Ricky	1968	3.75	7.50	15.00
—Rechanneled reissue of 9048					
❑ Imperial LP 12393 [R]	Ricky Nelson	1968	3.75	7.50	15.00
—Rechanneled reissue of 9050					
❑ Liberty LM-1004	Ricky	1981	2.00	4.00	8.00
—Reissue of United Artists 1004					
❑ Liberty LXB-9960 [(2)]	Legendary Masters	198?	3.00	6.00	12.00
—Reissue of United Artists 9960					
❑ Liberty LN-10134	Ricky Sings Again	1982	2.50	5.00	10.00
—Reissue of Imperial 12090					
❑ Liberty LN-10205	Souvenirs	1983	2.00	4.00	8.00
❑ Liberty LN-10253	Teen Age Idol	1984	2.00	4.00	8.00
❑ Liberty LN-10304	I Need You	1986	2.00	4.00	8.00
—Reissue of Sunset 5205					

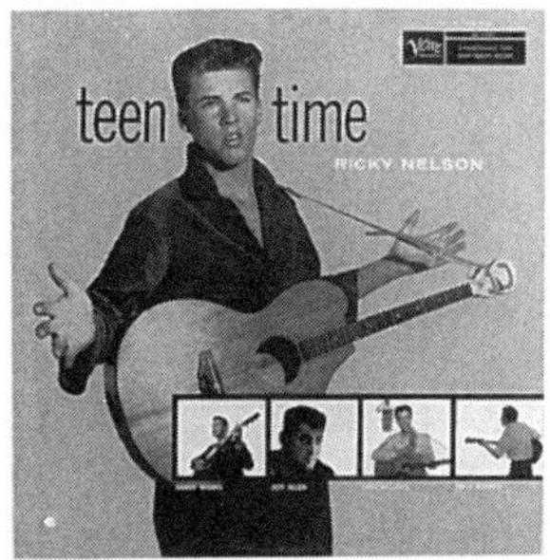

Number	Title (A Side/B Side)	Yr	VG	VG+	NM
❑ Liberty LN-10305	Ricky Nelson	1986	2.00	4.00	8.00
—Another reissue					
❑ Liberty LM-51004	Ricky	1983	2.00	4.00	8.00
—Reissue of Liberty 1004					
❑ MCA 3	Rick Nelson In Concert	1973	3.00	6.00	12.00
—Reissue of Decca 75162					
❑ MCA 20	Rick Sings Nelson	1973	3.00	6.00	12.00
—Reissue of Decca 75236					
❑ MCA 37	Rudy the Fifth	1973	3.00	6.00	12.00
—Reissue of Decca 75297					
❑ MCA 62	Garden Party	1973	3.00	6.00	12.00
—Reissue of Decca 75391					
❑ MCA 383	Windfall	1974	3.75	7.50	15.00
❑ MCA 1517	The Decca Years	1982	2.00	4.00	8.00
❑ MCA 2-4004 [(2)]	Rick Nelson Country	1973	3.75	7.50	15.00
❑ MCA 6163	All My Best	1986	2.50	5.00	10.00
❑ MCA 25983	Rick Nelson In Concert The Troubadour, 1969	1987	2.50	5.00	10.00
—Reissue of MCA 3 with revised title					
❑ Rhino RNLP 215	Greatest Hits	1985	3.00	6.00	12.00
❑ Rhino R1-70215	Greatest Hits	1987	2.50	5.00	10.00
❑ Rhino R1-71114	Live 1983-1985	1989	3.00	6.00	12.00
❑ Sunset SUM-1118 [M]	Ricky Nelson	1966	3.75	7.50	15.00
❑ Sunset SUS-5118 [P]	Ricky Nelson	1966	5.00	10.00	20.00
❑ Sunset SUS-5205	I Need You	1968	3.75	7.50	15.00
❑ Time-Life SRNR 31 [(2)]	Rick Nelson: 1957-1972	1989	3.75	7.50	15.00
❑ United Artists UA-LA330-E	The Very Best of Rick Nelson	1974	3.00	6.00	12.00
❑ United Artists LM-1004	Ricky	1980	2.50	5.00	10.00
—Reissue of Imperial 9048					
❑ United Artists UAS-9960 [(2)]	Legendary Masters	1971	6.25	12.50	25.00
❑ Verve V 2083 [M]	Teen Time	1957	125.00	250.00	500.00
—Has three Ricky Nelson songs plus tracks by four others; usually treated as Rick's LP because of his prominence on the cover					

NEON PHILHARMONIC, THE

45s

Number	Title (A Side/B Side)	Yr	VG	VG+	NM
❑ MCA 40518	So Glad You're a Woman/Making Out the Best You Can	1976	—	2.50	5.00
❑ TRX 5039	Annie Poor/Love Will Find a Way	1972	—	2.50	5.00
❑ Warner Bros. 7261	Morning Girl/Brilliant Colors	1969	2.00	4.00	8.00
❑ Warner Bros. 7311	No One Is Going to Hurt You/You Lied	1969	—	3.00	6.00
❑ Warner Bros. 7355	Clouds/Snow	1969	—	3.00	6.00
❑ Warner Bros. 7380	Heighdy-Ho Princess/Don't Know My Way Around My Soul	1970	—	3.00	6.00
❑ Warner Bros. 7419	Flowers for Your Pillow/To Be Continued	1970	—	3.00	6.00
❑ Warner Bros. 7457	Something to Believe In/A Little Love	1971	—	3.00	6.00
❑ Warner Bros. 7497	Gotta Feeling in My Bones/Keep the Faith in Me	1971	—	3.00	6.00

Albums

Number	Title (A Side/B Side)	Yr	VG	VG+	NM
❑ Warner Bros. WS 1769	The Moth Confesses	1968	6.25	12.50	25.00
❑ Warner Bros. WS 1804	The Neon Philharmonic	1969	3.75	7.50	15.00

NEVILLE, AARON

45s

Number	Title (A Side/B Side)	Yr	VG	VG+	NM
❑ Bell 746	You Can Give, But You Can't Take/Where Is My Baby	1968	2.00	4.00	8.00
❑ Bell 781	Speak to Me/You Don't Love Me Anymore	1969	2.00	4.00	8.00
❑ Bell 834	All These Things/She's On My Mind	1969	2.00	4.00	8.00
❑ Mercury 73310	Baby I'm-a Want You/Mojo Hannah	1972	—	3.00	6.00
❑ Mercury 73387	Hercules/Going Home	1973	—	3.00	6.00
❑ Minit 612	Over You/Every Day	1960	3.75	7.50	15.00
—As "Arron Neville"					
❑ Minit 618	Show Me the Way/Get Out of My Life	1960	3.00	6.00	12.00
❑ Minit 624	Don't Cry/Reality	1961	3.00	6.00	12.00
❑ Minit 631	Let's Live/I Found Another Love	1961	3.00	6.00	12.00
❑ Minit 639	How Many Times/I'm Waitin' at the Station	1962	3.00	6.00	12.00
❑ Minit 650	Humdinger/Sweet Little Mama	1962	3.00	6.00	12.00
❑ Minit 657	Wrong Number/How Could I Help But Love You	1963	3.00	6.00	12.00
❑ Par-Lo 101	Tell It Like It Is/Why Worry	1966	5.00	10.00	20.00
—Black and white label					
❑ Par-Lo 103	She Took You for a Ride/Space Man	1967	2.00	4.00	8.00
❑ Polydor 14426	Greatest Love/Performance	1977	—	2.00	4.00

Number	Title (A Side/B Side)	Yr	VG	VG+	NM
❑ Safari 201	Forever More/Ape Man	1967	2.50	5.00	10.00
❑ Who Dat? VPAG-4476/7	Who Dat? (The History of the Saints)/(Extended Version)	1987	2.00	4.00	8.00
Albums					
❑ Minit LP 24007 [R]	Like It 'Tis	1967	7.50	15.00	30.00
❑ Minit LP 40007 [M]	Like It 'Tis	1967	10.00	20.00	40.00
❑ Par-Lo 1 [M]	Tell It Like It Is	1967	20.00	40.00	80.00
❑ Par-Lo 1 [S]	Tell It Like It Is	1967	50.00	100.00	200.00
NEW COLONY SIX, THE					
45s					
❑ Centaur 1201	I Confess/Dawn Is Breaking	1966	3.75	7.50	15.00
❑ Centaur 1202	I Like Awake/At the River's Edge	1966	3.75	7.50	15.00
❑ MCA 40215	Never Be Lonely/Long Time to Be Alone	1974	6.25	12.50	25.00
❑ MCA 40288	I Really Don't Want to Go/Run	1974	7.50	15.00	30.00
❑ Mercury 72737	Treat Her Groovy/Rap-a-Tap	1967	2.50	5.00	10.00
—Orange and red swirl label					
❑ Mercury 72775	I Will Always Think About You/Hold Me with Your Eyes	1968	2.50	5.00	10.00
—Orange and red swirl label					
❑ Mercury 72817	Can't You See Me Cry/Summertime's Another Name for Love	1968	2.00	4.00	8.00
❑ Mercury 72858	Things I'd Like to Say/Come and Give Your Love to Me	1968	2.50	5.00	10.00
—Red label with "Mercury" logo in an oval					
❑ Mercury 72920	I Could Never Lie to You/Just Feel Worse	1969	2.00	4.00	8.00
❑ Mercury 72961	I Want You to Know/Free	1969	2.00	4.00	8.00
❑ Mercury 73004	Barbara, I Love You/Prairie Grey	1970	2.00	4.00	8.00
❑ Mercury 73063	People and Me/Ride the Wicked Wind	1970	3.75	7.50	15.00
❑ Mercury 73093	Close Your Eyes Little Girl/Love, That's the Best I Can Do	1970	5.00	10.00	20.00
—Promo copies go for less					
❑ Sentar 1203	Cadillac/Sunshine	1966	3.75	7.50	15.00
❑ Sentar 1204	(Ballad of the) Wingbat Marmaduke/Power of Love	1966	3.75	7.50	15.00
❑ Sentar 1205	Love You So Much/Let Me Love You	1967	3.75	7.50	15.00
❑ Sentar 1206	You're Gonna Be Mine/Woman	1967	3.75	7.50	15.00
❑ Sentar 1207	I'm Just Waiting Anticipating for Her to Show Up/Hello Lonely	1967	3.75	7.50	15.00
❑ Sentaur 1202	I Like Awake/At the River's Edge	1966	5.00	10.00	20.00
—Reissue of Centaur 1202, but harder to find					
❑ Sunlight 1001	Roll On/If You Could See	1971	—	3.00	6.00
❑ Sunlight 1004	Long Time to Be Alone/Never Be Lonely	1971	—	3.00	6.00
❑ Sunlight 1005	Someone, Sometime/Come On Down	1972	2.00	4.00	8.00
Albums					
❑ Mercury SR-61165	Revelations	1968	7.50	15.00	30.00
❑ Mercury SR-61228	Attacking a Straw Man	1969	7.50	15.00	30.00
❑ Sentar LP-101 [M]	Breakthrough	1966	125.00	250.00	500.00
❑ Sentar SST-3001 [S]	Colonization	1967	15.00	30.00	60.00
❑ Sentar ST-3001 [M]	Colonization	1967	12.50	25.00	50.00
NEW EDITION					
45s					
❑ MCA 52455	Cool It Now/(Instrumental)	1984	—	2.00	4.00
❑ MCA 52484	Mr. Telephone Man/(Instrumental)	1984	—	2.00	4.00
❑ MCA 52553	Lost in Love/Gold Mine	1985	—	2.00	4.00
❑ MCA 52627	My Secret (Didja Gitit Yet?)/I'm Leaving You Again	1985	—	2.00	4.00
❑ MCA 52703	Count Me Out/Good Boys	1985	—	—	3.00
❑ MCA 52745	It's Christmas (All Over the World)/ All I Want for Christmas Is My Girl	1985	—	2.00	4.00
—Red vinyl stock copy					
❑ MCA 52768	A Little Bit of Love (Is All It Takes)/Sneakin' Around	1986	—	—	3.00
❑ MCA 52829	With You All the Way/All for Love	1986	—	—	3.00
❑ MCA 52905	Earth Angel/With You All the Way	1986	—	—	3.00
❑ MCA 52959	Once in a Lifetime Groove/Once in a Lifetime Groove (Acapella)	1986	—	—	3.00
❑ MCA 53019	Tears on My Pillow/Bring Back the Memories	1987	—	2.50	5.00
—Little Anthony appears on this record					
❑ MCA 53079	Duke of Earl/What's Your Name	1987	—	—	3.00
❑ MCA 53164	Helplessly in Love/(Instrumental)	1987	—	—	3.00
❑ MCA 53264	If It Isn't Love/(Instrumental)	1988	—	—	3.00
❑ MCA 53391	N.E. Heart Break/(Instrumental)	1988	—	—	3.00
❑ MCA 53405	You're Not My Kind of Girl/(Instrumental)	1988	—	—	3.00
❑ MCA 53464	Can You Stand the Rain/(Instrumental)	1988	—	—	3.00
❑ MCA 53500	Crucial (Dance Remix)/Crucial (Uptown Mix Instrumental)	1989	—	—	3.00
❑ Streetwise 1108	Candy Girl/(Instrumental)	1983	2.00	4.00	8.00
❑ Streetwise 1111	Is This the End/(Instrumental)	1983	2.00	4.00	8.00
❑ Streetwise 1116	Popcorn Love/Jealous Girl	1983	2.00	4.00	8.00
Albums					
❑ MCA 5515	New Edition	1984	2.00	4.00	8.00
❑ MCA 5679	All for Love	1985	2.00	4.00	8.00
❑ MCA 5912	Under the Blue Moon	1986	2.00	4.00	8.00
❑ MCA 39040 [EP]	Christmas All Over the World	1985	2.00	4.00	8.00
❑ MCA 42207	Heart Break	1988	2.00	4.00	8.00
❑ Streetwise 3301	Candy Girl	1983	3.00	6.00	12.00
NEW SEEKERS, THE					
45s					
❑ Columbia 10559	You Never Can Tell/Give Me Love Your Way	1977	—	2.50	5.00
❑ Elektra 45699	Look What They've Done to My Song, Ma/It's a Beautiful Day	1970	—	3.00	6.00
❑ Elektra 45710	Beautiful People/When There's No Love Left	1970	—	2.50	5.00
❑ Elektra 45719	The Nickel Song/Cincinnati	1971	—	2.50	5.00
❑ Elektra 45734	Never Ending Song of Love/All Right My Love	1971	—	—	—
—Unreleased					
❑ Elektra 45747	Tonight/Sweet Louise	1971	—	2.50	5.00

Number	Title (A Side/B Side)	Yr	VG	VG+	NM
❑ Elektra 45762	I'd Like to Teach the World to Sing/Boom Town	1971	—	3.00	6.00
❑ Elektra 45780	Beg, Steal or Borrow/Mystic Queen	1972	—	2.50	5.00
❑ Elektra 45787	Circles/I Can Say You're Beautiful	1972	—	2.50	5.00
❑ Elektra 45805	Dance, Dance, Dance/I Can Say You're Beautiful	1972	—	2.50	5.00
❑ MGM 14586	The Greatest Song I've Ever Heard/Woman Grows	1973	—	2.50	5.00
❑ MGM 14683	Reach Out I'll Be There/You Won't Find Another Fool Like Me	1973	—	2.50	5.00
❑ MGM 14691	Song for You and Me/You Won't Find Another Fool Like Me	1974	—	2.50	5.00
❑ MGM Verve 10698	Come Softly to Me/Unwithered Rose	1972	—	2.50	5.00
❑ MGM Verve 10709	Pinball Wizard-See Me, Feel Me/Come Softly to Me	1973	—	2.50	5.00
Albums					
❑ Elektra EKS-74088	Beautiful People	1971	3.00	6.00	12.00
❑ Elektra EKS-74108	New Colours	1971	3.00	6.00	12.00
❑ Elektra EKS-74115	We'd Like to Teach the World to Sing	1971	3.00	6.00	12.00
❑ Elektra EKS-75034	Circles	1972	3.00	6.00	12.00
❑ Elektra EKS-75051	The Best of the New Seekers	1973	3.00	6.00	12.00
❑ MGM Verve V 5090	Come Softly to Me	1972	2.50	5.00	10.00
❑ MGM Verve V 5095	The History of the New Seekers	1973	2.50	5.00	10.00
❑ MGM Verve V 5098	Pinball Wizards	1973	2.50	5.00	10.00

NEW VAUDEVILLE BAND, THE

Number	Title (A Side/B Side)	Yr	VG	VG+	NM
45s					
❑ Fontana 1562	Winchester Cathedral/Wait for Me Baby	1966	2.00	4.00	8.00
❑ Fontana 1573	Peek-A-Boo/Amy	1967	—	3.00	6.00
❑ Fontana 1589	Finchley Central/Sadie Moonshine	1967	—	3.00	6.00
❑ Fontana 1598	Green Street Green/Fourteen Lovely Women	1967	—	3.00	6.00
❑ Fontana 1612	Bonnie and Clyde/Anniversary Song	1968	—	3.00	6.00
Albums					
❑ Fontana MGF-27560 [M]	Winchester Cathedral	1966	3.75	7.50	15.00
—With "Oh, Donna Clara"; record has mono number and actually plays in mono; the number "27560" is in the trail-off					
❑ Fontana MGF-27560 [M]	Winchester Cathedral	1966	3.75	7.50	15.00
—With "Whatever Happened to Phyllis Puke" and "Diana Goodbye"					
❑ Fontana MGF-27560 [P]	Winchester Cathedral	1966	3.00	6.00	12.00
—With "Oh, Donna Clara"; record has mono number, but plays stereo; the number "2/67560" is in trail-off area					
❑ Fontana MGF-27688 [M]	The New Vaudeville Band on Tour	1967	3.00	6.00	12.00
❑ Fontana SRF-67560 [P]	Winchester Cathedral	1966	3.00	6.00	12.00
—With "Oh, Donna Clara"					
❑ Fontana SRF-67560 [P]	Winchester Cathedral	1966	3.75	7.50	15.00
—With "Whatever Happened to Phyllis Puke" and "Diana Goodbye"					
❑ Fontana SRF-67688 [P]	The New Vaudeville Band on Tour	1967	3.00	6.00	12.00

NEWBEATS, THE

Number	Title (A Side/B Side)	Yr	VG	VG+	NM
45s					
❑ Buddah 390	The Way You Do the Things You Do/Does Your Body Need Lovin'	1973	2.00	4.00	8.00
❑ Hickory 326	Bread and Butter/Tough Little Buggy	1974	—	3.00	6.00
❑ Hickory 1269	Bread and Butter/Tough Little Buggy	1964	3.75	7.50	15.00
❑ Hickory 1282	Everything's All Right/Pink Dally Rue	1964	3.00	6.00	12.00
❑ Hickory 1290	Break Away (From That Boy)/Hey-O Daddy-O	1965	2.50	5.00	10.00
❑ Hickory 1305	(The Bees Are For the Birds) The Birds Are For the Bees/ Better Watch Your Step	1965	2.50	5.00	10.00
❑ Hickory 1320	Little Child/I Can't Hear You No More	1965	2.50	5.00	10.00
❑ Hickory 1332	Run, Baby, Run (Back Into My Arms)/Mean Wooly Willie	1965	3.00	6.00	12.00
❑ Hickory 1366	Shake Hands (And Come Out Crying)/Too Sweet to Be Forgotten	1966	2.50	5.00	10.00
❑ Hickory 1387	Short on Love/Crying My Heart Out	1966	2.00	4.00	8.00
❑ Hickory 1408	Bird Dog/Evil Eva	1966	2.00	4.00	8.00
❑ Hickory 1422	My Yesterday Love/Patent on Love	1966	2.00	4.00	8.00
❑ Hickory 1436	So Fine/Top Secret	1967	2.00	4.00	8.00
❑ Hickory 1467	Hide the Moon/It's Really Goodbye	1967	2.00	4.00	8.00
❑ Hickory 1485	Don't Turn Me Loose/You and Me and Happiness	1967	2.00	4.00	8.00
❑ Hickory 1496	Bad Dreams/Swinger	1968	2.00	4.00	8.00
❑ Hickory 1510	I've Been a Long Time Loving You/Michelle de Ann	1968	2.00	4.00	8.00
❑ Hickory 1522	Ain't That Lovin' You/The Girls and the Boys	1968	2.00	4.00	8.00
❑ Hickory 1539	Great Balls of Fire/Thou Shalt Not Steal	1969	2.00	4.00	8.00
❑ Hickory 1552	Groovin' (Out on Life)/Bread and Butter	1969	2.50	5.00	10.00
❑ Hickory 1562	Laura (What's He Got That I Ain't Got)/ Break Away (From That Boy)	1970	—	3.00	6.00
❑ Hickory 1569	I'm a Teardrop/She Won't Hang Her Love (Out on the Line)	1970	—	3.00	6.00
❑ Hickory 1600	Am I Not My Brother's Keeper/Run, Baby, Run (Back Into My Arms)	1971	2.50	5.00	10.00

Number	Title (A Side/B Side)	Yr	VG	VG+	NM
❑ Hickory 1624	Oh, Pretty Woman/Remember Love	1972	2.50	5.00	10.00
❑ Hickory 1637	Love Gets Sweeter/Eveything's All Right	1972	2.50	5.00	10.00
❑ Playboy 6013	I Believe I'm in Love with You/I Know (You Don't Want Me No More)	1974	—	3.00	6.00
Albums					
❑ Hickory LPM 120 [M]	Bread and Butter	1964	12.50	25.00	50.00
❑ Hickory LPS 120 [S]	Bread and Butter	1964	37.50	75.00	150.00
❑ Hickory LPM 122 [M]	Big Beat Sounds by the Newbeats	1965	12.50	25.00	50.00
❑ Hickory LPS 122 [S]	Big Beat Sounds by the Newbeats	1965	25.00	50.00	100.00
❑ Hickory LPM 128 [M]	Run Baby Run	1965	12.50	25.00	50.00
❑ Hickory LPS 128 [S]	Run Baby Run	1965	25.00	50.00	100.00

NEWMAN, RANDY

Number	Title (A Side/B Side)	Yr	VG	VG+	NM
45s					
❑ Dot 16411	Golden Gridiron Boy/Country Boy	1962	12.50	25.00	50.00
—May be promo only					
❑ Reprise 0692	I Think It's Going to Rain Today/The Beehive State	1968	3.75	7.50	15.00
❑ Reprise 0771	Last Night I Had a Dream/I Think He's Hiding	1968	6.25	12.50	25.00
—May be promo only					
❑ Reprise 0917	Have You Seen My Baby/Hold On	1970	3.75	7.50	15.00
❑ Reprise 0945	Gone Dead Train/Harry Flowers	1970	3.75	7.50	15.00
❑ Reprise 1102	Sail Away/Political Science	1972	—	3.00	6.00
❑ Reprise 1123	You Can Leave Your Hat On/Memo to My Son	1972	—	3.00	6.00
❑ Reprise 1324	Guilty/Naked Man	1975	—	2.50	5.00
❑ Reprise 1387	Louisiana 1927/Marie	1977	—	2.50	5.00
❑ Reprise 22798	I'd Love to See You Smile/End Title (I'd Love to See You Smile)	1989	—	—	3.00
❑ Reprise 27709	It's Money That Matters/Roll with the Punches	1988	—	—	3.00
❑ Reprise 27856	Falling in Love/Bad News from Home	1989	—	—	3.00
❑ Warner Bros. 8492	Short People/Old Man on the Farm	1977	—	2.50	5.00
❑ Warner Bros. 8550	Baltimore/You Can't Fool the Fat Man	1978	—	2.00	4.00
❑ Warner Bros. 8630	Rider in the Rain/Sigmund Freud's Impersonation of Albert Einstein in America	1978	—	2.00	4.00
❑ Warner Bros. 29241	The Natural/The Natural (Final Game)	1984	—	2.00	4.00
❑ Warner Bros. 29687	I Love L.A./Song for the Dead	1983	—	2.00	4.00
❑ Warner Bros. 29803	The Blues/The Same Girl	1983	—	2.00	4.00
—A-side: With Paul Simon					
❑ Warner Bros. 49088	It's Money That I Love/Ghosts	1979	—	2.00	4.00
❑ Warner Bros. 49149	Half a Man/The Story of a Rock and Roll Band	1979	—	2.00	4.00
❑ Warner Bros. 49223	Spies/Political Science (Let's Drop the Big One)	1980	—	2.00	4.00
7-					
❑ Reprise PRO 374	Radio Spots for: 12 Songs	1970	5.00	10.00	20.00
—White label; three 60-second ads on each side; not issued with cover					
Albums					
❑ Reprise MS 2064	Sail Away	1972	3.75	7.50	15.00
—With no song titles listed on back					
❑ Reprise MS 2193	Good Old Boys	1974	2.50	5.00	10.00
❑ Reprise RS 6286	Randy Newman	1968	5.00	10.00	20.00
—Cover with Randy standing in the clouds					
❑ Reprise RS 6373	12 Songs	1970	3.75	7.50	15.00
—With "W7" and "r:" logos on two-tone orange label					
❑ Reprise RS 6459	Randy Newman/Live	1971	2.50	5.00	10.00
❑ Reprise 25773	Land of Dreams	1988	2.50	5.00	10.00
❑ Warner Bros. BSK 3079	Little Criminals	1977	2.50	5.00	10.00
❑ Warner Bros. HS 3346	Born Again	1979	2.50	5.00	10.00
❑ Warner Bros. 23755	Trouble in Paradise	1983	2.50	5.00	10.00

NEWTON-JOHN, OLIVIA

Number	Title (A Side/B Side)	Yr	VG	VG+	NM
45s					
❑ Atlantic 89420	The Best of Me/Sage	1986	—	—	3.00
—With David Foster					
❑ MCA 40043	Take Me Home, Country Roads/Sail Into Tomorrow	1973	7.50	15.00	30.00
—This has (finally) been proven to exist					
❑ MCA 40101	Let Me Be There/Maybe Then I'll Think of You	1973	—	2.50	5.00
❑ MCA 40209	If You Love Me (Let Me Know)/Brotherly Love	1974	—	2.50	5.00
❑ MCA 40280	I Honestly Love You/Home Ain't Home Anymore	1974	—	2.50	5.00
❑ MCA 40349	Have You Never Been Mellow/Water Under the Bridge	1974	—	2.50	5.00
❑ MCA 40418	Please Mr. Please/And In the Morning	1975	—	2.50	5.00
❑ MCA 40459	Something Better to Do/He's My Rock	1975	—	2.50	5.00
❑ MCA 40495	Let It Shine/He Ain't Heavy, He's My Brother	1975	—	2.50	5.00
❑ MCA 40525	Come On Over/Small Talk and Pride	1976	—	2.00	4.00
❑ MCA 40600	Don't Stop Believin'/Greensleeves	1976	—	2.00	4.00
❑ MCA 40642	Every Face Tells a Story/Love You Hold the Key	1976	—	2.00	4.00
❑ MCA 40670	Sam/I'll Bet You a Kangaroo	1976	—	2.00	4.00
❑ MCA 40737	Making a Good Thing Better/I Think I'll Say Goodbye	1977	—	2.00	4.00
❑ MCA 40811	I Honestly Love You/Don't Cry for Me Argentina	1977	—	2.50	5.00
❑ MCA 40975	A Little More Love/Borrowed Time	1978	—	2.00	4.00
❑ MCA 41009	Deeper Than the Night/Please Don't Keep Me Waiting	1979	—	2.00	4.00
❑ MCA 41074	Totally Hot/Dancing Round and Round	1979	—	2.00	4.00
❑ MCA 41247	Magic/Fool Country	1980	—	2.50	5.00
—Custom pink "Xanadu" label					
❑ MCA 41285	Xanadu/Whenever You're Away from Me	1980	—	2.00	4.00
—A-side with Electric Light Orchestra; B-side with Gene Kelly. Persistent rumors claim existence of a U.S. picture sleeve for this record, but we've never seen one.					
❑ MCA 41286	Suddenly/You Made Me Love You	1980	—	2.50	5.00
—A-side with Cliff Richard					
❑ MCA 51007	Suddenly/You Made Me Love You	1980	—	2.00	4.00
—A-side with Cliff Richard					

Number	Title (A Side/B Side)	Yr	VG	VG+	NM
❑ MCA 51182	Physical/The Promise (The Dolphin Song)	1981	—	—	3.00
❑ MCA 52000	Make a Move on Me/Falling	1982	—	—	3.00
❑ MCA 52069	Landslide/Recovery	1982	—	—	3.00
❑ MCA 52100	Heart Attack/Strangers Touch	1982	—	—	3.00
❑ MCA 52155	Tied Up/Silvery Rain	1983	—	—	3.00
❑ MCA 52284	Twist of Fate/Take a Chance	1983	—	—	3.00
❑ MCA 52341	Livin' in Desperate Times/Landslide	1984	—	—	3.00
❑ MCA 52686	Soul Kiss/Electric	1985	—	—	3.00
❑ MCA 52757	Toughen Up/Driving Music	1986	—	—	3.00
❑ MCA 53294	The Rumour/Winter Angel	1988	—	—	3.00
❑ MCA 53438	Can't We Talk It Over in Bed/Get Out	1988	—	—	3.00
❑ RSO 903	Hopelessly Devoted to You/Love Is a Many-Splendored Thing	1978	—	2.00	4.00
❑ Uni 55281	If Not for You/The Biggest Clown	1971	2.50	5.00	10.00
❑ Uni 55304	Banks of the Ohio/It's So Hard to Say Goodbye	1971	2.00	4.00	8.00
❑ Uni 55317	What Is Life/I'm a Small and Lonely Light	1972	2.00	4.00	8.00
❑ Uni 55348	Just a Little Too Much/My Old Man's Gotta Gun	1972	3.00	6.00	12.00

Albums

Number	Title	Yr	VG	VG+	NM
❑ Geffen GHS 24257	Warm and Tender	1989	3.00	6.00	12.00
❑ MCA 389	Let Me Be There	1973	3.75	7.50	15.00
❑ MCA 411	If You Love Me Let Me Know	1974	2.50	5.00	10.00
—With corrected song title: "I Honestly Love You"					
❑ MCA 2133	Have You Never Been Mellow	1975	2.50	5.00	10.00
❑ MCA 2148	Clearly Love	1975	2.50	5.00	10.00
❑ MCA 2186	Come On Over	1976	2.50	5.00	10.00
❑ MCA 2223	Don't Stop Believin'	1976	2.50	5.00	10.00
❑ MCA 2280	Making a Good Thing Better	1977	2.50	5.00	10.00
❑ MCA 3012	Let Me Be There	1977	2.00	4.00	8.00
—Reissue					
❑ MCA 3013	If You Love Me Let Me Know	1977	2.00	4.00	8.00
—Reissue					
❑ MCA 3014	Have You Never Been Mellow	1977	2.00	4.00	8.00
—Reissue					
❑ MCA 3015	Clearly Love	1977	2.00	4.00	8.00
—Reissue					
❑ MCA 3016	Come On Over	1977	2.00	4.00	8.00
—Reissue					
❑ MCA 3017	Don't Stop Believin'	1977	2.00	4.00	8.00
—Reissue					
❑ MCA 3018	Making a Good Thing Better	1977	2.00	4.00	8.00
—Reissue					
❑ MCA 3028	Olivia Newton-John's Greatest Hits	1977	2.50	5.00	10.00
❑ MCA 3067	Totally Hot	1978	2.50	5.00	10.00
❑ MCA 5229	Physical	1981	2.00	4.00	8.00
❑ MCA 5347	Olivia's Greatest Hits, Vol. 2	1982	2.00	4.00	8.00
❑ MCA 6151	Soul Kiss	1985	2.00	4.00	8.00
❑ MCA 6245	The Rumour	1988	2.00	4.00	8.00
❑ MCA 16011	Physical	1982	6.25	12.50	25.00
—Audiophile edition					
❑ MCA 37061	Clearly Love	1980	2.00	4.00	8.00
—Reissue					
❑ MCA 37062	Come On Over	1980	2.00	4.00	8.00
—Reissue					
❑ MCA 37063	Don't Stop Believin'	1980	2.00	4.00	8.00
—Reissue					
❑ MCA 37123	Totally Hot	1981	2.00	4.00	8.00
—Reissue					
❑ Uni 73117	If Not for You	1971	20.00	40.00	80.00

NICKS, STEVIE

45s

Number	Title	Yr	VG	VG+	NM
❑ Atlantic Oldies Series OS 13236	Stop Draggin' My Heart Around/Leather and Lace	1983	—	—	3.00
❑ Atlantic Oldies Series OS 13258	Edge of Seventeen/Stand Back	1985	—	—	3.00
❑ Atlantic Oldies Series 84964	Talk to Me/I Can't Wait	1987	—	—	3.00

Number	Title (A Side/B Side)	Yr	VG	VG+	NM
❑ Atlantic Oldies Series 84998	If Anyone Falls/Nightbird	1986	—	—	3.00
❑ Modern 7336	Stop Draggin' My Heart Around/Kind of Woman	1981	—	2.00	4.00
—With Tom Petty and the Heartbreakers					
❑ Modern 7341	Leather and Lace/Bella Donna	1981	—	2.00	4.00
—With Don Henley; with no reference to Waylon Jennings and Jessi Colter on label					
❑ Modern 7341	Leather and Lace/Bella Donna	1981	—	2.50	5.00
—With Don Henley; first pressing states "Written for Waylon Jennings and Jessi Colter"					
❑ Modern 7401	Edge of Seventeen (Just Like the White Winged Dove)/Edge of Seventeen (Live)	1982	—	2.00	4.00
❑ Modern 7405	After the Glitter Fades/Think About It	1982	—	3.00	6.00
❑ Modern 99150	Whole Lotta Trouble/Ghosts	1989	—	—	3.00
❑ Modern 99179	Two Kinds of Love/Real Tears	1989	—	—	3.00
❑ Modern 99216	Rooms on Fire/Alice	1989	—	—	3.00
❑ Modern 99532	Has Anyone Ever Written Anything for You/Imperial Hotel	1986	—	—	3.00
❑ Modern 99565	I Can't Wait/The Nightmare	1986	—	—	3.00
❑ Modern 99582	Talk to Me/One More Big Time Rock and Roll Star	1985	—	—	3.00
❑ Modern 99799	Nightbird/Gate and Garden	1984	—	—	3.00
❑ Modern 99832	If Anyone Falls/Wild Heart	1983	—	2.00	4.00
❑ Modern 99863	Stand Back/Garbo	1983	—	—	3.00
Albums					
❑ Modern MR 38-139	Bella Donna	1981	2.50	5.00	10.00
❑ Modern 90084	The Wild Heart	1983	2.50	5.00	10.00
❑ Modern 90479	Rock a Little	1985	2.50	5.00	10.00
❑ Modern 91245	The Other Side of the Mirror	1989	2.50	5.00	10.00

NILSSON

45s

Number	Title (A Side/B Side)	Yr	VG	VG+	NM
❑ Crusader 103	Baa Baa Black Sheep/Baa Baa Black Sheep (Part 2)	1964	7.50	15.00	30.00
—As "Bo Pete"					
❑ Musicor 6308	Please Mr. Music Man/Foolish Clock	1977	—	2.00	4.00
❑ Polydor 881177-7	Silver Horse/Loneliness	1984	—	2.00	4.00
❑ RCA PB-10759	Just One Look-Baby I'm Yours/That Is All	1976	—	2.00	4.00
—With Lynda Lawrence					
❑ RCA PB-11059	Perfect Day/Who Done It	1977	—	2.00	4.00
❑ RCA PB-11144	All I Think About Is You/I Never Thought I'd Get This Lonely	1977	—	2.00	4.00
❑ RCA PB-11193	Ain't It Kinda Wonderful/I'm Bringing a Red, Red Rose	1978	—	2.00	4.00
❑ RCA PB-11318	Spaceman/Me and My Arrow	1978	—	2.00	4.00
❑ RCA Victor 47-9206	Without Her/Freckles	1967	2.00	4.00	8.00
❑ RCA Victor 47-9298	You Can't Do That/Ten Little Indians	1967	2.50	5.00	10.00
❑ RCA Victor 47-9383	River Deep Mountain High/She Sang Hymns Out of Tune	1967	2.00	4.00	8.00
❑ RCA Victor 47-9442	One/Sister Marie	1968	2.00	4.00	8.00
❑ RCA Victor 47-9544	Everybody's Talkin'/Don't Leave Me	1968	3.00	6.00	12.00
❑ RCA Victor 47-9675	Rainmaker/I Will Take You There	1968	2.00	4.00	8.00
❑ RCA Victor 74-0161	Everybody's Talkin'/Rainmaker	1969	2.50	5.00	10.00
❑ RCA Victor 74-0207	Maybe/Marchin' Down Broadway	1969	2.00	4.00	8.00
❑ RCA Victor 74-0261	I Guess the Lord Must Be in New York City/Maybe	1969	2.00	4.00	8.00
❑ RCA Victor 74-0310	I'll Be Home/Waiting	1970	—	3.00	6.00
❑ RCA Victor 74-0336	Caroline/Yellow Man	1970	—	3.00	6.00
❑ RCA Victor 74-0362	Down to the Valley/Buy My Album	1970	—	3.00	6.00
❑ RCA Victor 74-0443	Me and My Arrow/Are You Sleeping	1971	—	3.00	6.00
❑ RCA Victor 74-0524	Without Her/Good Old Desk	1971	—	3.00	6.00
❑ RCA Victor 74-0604	Without You/Gotta Get Up	1971	—	2.50	5.00
❑ RCA Victor 74-0673	Jump Into the Fire/The Moonbeam Song	1972	—	2.50	5.00
❑ RCA Victor 74-0718	Coconut/Down	1972	—	2.50	5.00
❑ RCA Victor 74-0788	Spaceman/Turn On Your Radio	1972	—	2.50	5.00
❑ RCA Victor 74-0855	Remember (Christmas)/The Lottery Song	1972	—	2.50	5.00
❑ RCA Victor APBO-0039	As Time Goes By/Lullabye in Ragtime	1973	—	3.00	6.00
❑ RCA Victor APBO-0246	Daybreak/Down	1974	—	2.00	4.00
❑ RCA Victor PB-10001	Many Rivers to Cross/Don't Forget Me	1974	2.00	4.00	8.00
❑ RCA Victor PB-10078	Subterranean Homesick Blues/Mucho Mungo	1974	2.00	4.00	8.00
❑ RCA Victor PB-10130	Remember (Christmas)/The Lottery Song	1974	—	2.00	4.00
❑ RCA Victor PB-10139	Loop De Loop/Don't Forget Me	1974	—	2.00	4.00
❑ RCA Victor PB-10183	Kojak Columbo/Turn Out the Light	1975	—	2.00	4.00
❑ RCA Victor PB-10634	Sail Away/Moonshine Bandit	1976	—	2.00	4.00
❑ Tower 103	Sixteen Tons/I'm Gonna Lose My Mind	1964	3.75	7.50	15.00
❑ Tower 136	You Can't Take Your Love Away from Me/Born in Grenada	1965	3.75	7.50	15.00
❑ Tower 244	She's Yours/Growing Up	1966	3.75	7.50	15.00
❑ Tower 518	Good Time/Growin' Up	1969	3.75	7.50	15.00
❑ Try 501	Do You Wanna/Groovy Little Suzie	1964	10.00	20.00	40.00
—As "Bo Pete"					
Albums					
❑ Musicor MUS-2505 [S]	Early Tymes	1977	3.75	7.50	15.00
❑ Pickwick SPC-3321	Rock 'N' Roll	1977	2.50	5.00	10.00
❑ Rapple ABL1-0220	Son of Dracula	1974	3.00	6.00	12.00
❑ RCA Victor (no #) [M]	The True One	1967	50.00	100.00	200.00
—Boxed set with mono copy of RCA Victor 3874, two photos, button, poster, sticker, bios					
❑ RCA Victor APL1-0097	A Little Touch of Schmilsson in the Night	1973	3.00	6.00	12.00
❑ RCA Victor APL1-0203	Nilsson Sings Newman	1974	2.50	5.00	10.00
—Reissue of LSP-4289					
❑ RCA Victor CPL1-0570	Pussy Cats	1974	5.00	10.00	20.00
❑ RCA Victor APL1-0817	Duit On Mon Dei	1975	3.00	6.00	12.00
❑ RCA Victor LSPX-1003	The Point!	1971	3.00	6.00	12.00
❑ RCA Victor APL1-1031	Sandman	1976	3.00	6.00	12.00
❑ RCA Victor APL1-1119	That's the Way It Is	1976	3.00	6.00	12.00
❑ RCA Victor AFL1-2276	Knnillssonn	1977	3.00	6.00	12.00
❑ RCA Victor AFL1-2798	Greatest Hits	1978	3.00	6.00	12.00

Number	Title (A Side/B Side)	Yr	VG	VG+	NM
❑ RCA Victor ANL1-3464	Nilsson Schmilsson	1979	2.00	4.00	8.00
❑ RCA Victor AYL1-3761	A Little Touch of Schmilsson in the Night	1980	2.00	4.00	8.00
—"Best Buy Series" reissue					
❑ RCA Victor AYL1-3811	The Point!	1980	2.00	4.00	8.00
—"Best Buy Series" reissue					
❑ RCA Victor AYL1-3812	Son of Schmilsson	1980	2.00	4.00	8.00
—"Best Buy Series" reissue					
❑ RCA Victor LPM-3874 [M]	Pandemonium Shadow Show	1967	10.00	20.00	40.00
❑ RCA Victor LSP-3874 [S]	Pandemonium Shadow Show	1967	5.00	10.00	20.00
—"Stereo" on black label					
❑ RCA Victor LPM-3956 [M]	Aerial Ballet	1968	12.50	25.00	50.00
❑ RCA Victor LSP-3956 [S]	Aerial Ballet	1968	5.00	10.00	20.00
—"Stereo" on black label					
❑ RCA Victor LSP-4197	Harry	1969	3.75	7.50	15.00
—Orange label, non-flexible vinyl					
❑ RCA Victor LSP-4289	Nilsson Sings Newman	1970	3.00	6.00	12.00
—Orange label, non-flexible vinyl					
❑ RCA Victor LSP-4417	The Point!	1971	2.50	5.00	10.00
—Reissue of LSPX-1003					
❑ RCA Victor LSP-4515	Nilsson Schmilsson	1971	3.00	6.00	12.00
❑ RCA Victor LSP-4543	Aerial Pandemonium Ballet	1971	3.00	6.00	12.00
—Collection of tracks from 3874 and 3956, remixed with, in some cases, new vocals					
❑ RCA Victor LSP-4717	Son of Schmilsson	1972	3.00	6.00	12.00
—With custom black "Victor" label					
❑ Tower ST 5095 [S]	Spotlight on Nilsson	1967	5.00	10.00	20.00
❑ Tower T 5095 [M]	Spotlight on Nilsson	1967	5.00	10.00	20.00
❑ Tower DT 5165 [R]	Spotlight on Nilsson	1969	3.75	7.50	15.00

1910 FRUITGUM COMPANY

45s

Number	Title (A Side/B Side)	Yr	VG	VG+	NM
❑ Attack 10293	Lawdy, Lawdy/The Clock	1970	3.00	6.00	12.00
❑ Buddah 24	Simon Says/Reflections from the Looking Glass	1968	2.50	5.00	10.00
❑ Buddah 39	May I Take a Giant Step (Into Your Heart)/(Poor Old) Mr. Jensen	1968	2.00	4.00	8.00
❑ Buddah 54	1,2,3, Red Light/Sticky, Sticky	1968	2.50	5.00	10.00
❑ Buddah 71	Goody Goody Gumdrops/Candy Kisses	1968	2.00	4.00	8.00
❑ Buddah 91	Indian Giver/Pow Wow	1969	2.50	5.00	10.00
❑ Buddah 114	Special Delivery/No Good Annie	1969	2.00	4.00	8.00
❑ Buddah 130	The Train/Eternal Light	1969	2.00	4.00	8.00
❑ Buddah 146	When We Get Married/Baby Sweet	1969	2.00	4.00	8.00
❑ Super K 115	Go Away/The Track	1970	3.00	6.00	12.00

Albums

Number	Title (A Side/B Side)	Yr	VG	VG+	NM
❑ Buddah BDS-5010 [S]	Simon Says	1968	6.25	12.50	25.00
❑ Buddah BDS-5022	1,2,3 Red Light	1968	6.25	12.50	25.00
❑ Buddah BDS-5027	Goody, Goody Gumdrops	1969	6.25	12.50	25.00
❑ Buddah BDS-5036	Indian Giver	1969	6.25	12.50	25.00
❑ Buddah BDS-5043	Hard Ride	1969	6.25	12.50	25.00
❑ Buddah BDS-5057	Juiciest Fruitgum	1970	6.25	12.50	25.00

NITTY GRITTY DIRT BAND

45s

Number	Title (A Side/B Side)	Yr	VG	VG+	NM
❑ Decca 55206	Maybe Baby/Crying, Waiting, Hoping	1996	—	—	3.00
—B-side by Marty Stuart and Steve Earle					
❑ Liberty 1389	High School Yearbook/Too Good to Be True	1980	—	2.00	4.00
—As "The Dirt Band"					
❑ Liberty 1398	Nazamas Nuestra Magic (Make a Little Magic)/Jas' Moon	1981	—	2.00	4.00
—As "The Dirt Band"					
❑ Liberty 1429	Fire in the Sky/EZ Slow	1981	—	2.00	4.00
—As "The Dirt Band"					
❑ Liberty 1449	Badlands/Jealousy	1982	—	2.00	4.00
—As "The Dirt Band"					
❑ Liberty 1467	Too Close for Comfort/Circular Man	1982	—	2.00	4.00
—As "The Dirt Band"					
❑ Liberty 1499	Let's Go/Shot Full of Love	1983	—	2.00	4.00
❑ Liberty 1507	Mary Anne/Dance Little Jean	1983	—	2.00	4.00
❑ Liberty 1513	Colorado Christmas/Mr. Bojangles	1983	—	3.00	6.00
❑ Liberty 55948	Buy for Me the Rain/Candy Man	1967	2.50	5.00	10.00
❑ Liberty 56159	Rave On/The Cure	1970	—	3.00	6.00

Number	Title (A Side/B Side)	Yr	VG	VG+	NM
❑ Liberty 56197	Mr. Bojangles/Mr. Bojangles (Prelude: Uncle Charlie and His Dog Teddy)	1970	—	3.00	6.00
❑ Liberty 56197	Mr. Bojangles (Prelude: Uncle Charlie and His Dog Teddy)/ Spanish Fandango	1970	2.00	4.00	8.00
❑ MCA 53795	One Step Over the Line/Riding Along	1990	—	—	3.00
—A-side: With Roseanne Cash; B-side: With Emmylou Harris					
❑ MCA 53964	The Rest of the Dream/Snowballs	1990	—	—	3.00
❑ MCA 55182	You Believed in Me/Atlanta Reel '96	1996	—	—	3.00
—A-side by Karla Bonoff and the Nitty Gritty Dirt Band; B-side by Michael Omartian					
❑ MCA 79013	From Small Things (Big Things One Day Come)/Blues Berry Hill	1990	—	—	3.00
❑ MCA 79075	You Make Life Good Again/Snowballs	1990	—	—	3.00
❑ United Artists 0061	Mr. Bojangles/Buy for Me the Rain	1973	—	2.00	4.00
—"Silver Spotlight Series" reissue					
❑ United Artists XW177	Will the Circle Be Unbroken/Honky Tonkin'	1973	—	2.50	5.00
❑ United Artists XW247	Grand Ole Opry Song/Orange Blossom Special	1973	—	2.50	5.00
❑ United Artists XW263	Cosmic Cowboy (Part 1)/Cosmic Cowboy (Part 2)	1973	—	2.50	5.00
❑ United Artists XW321	Tennessee Stud/Way Down Town	1973	—	2.50	5.00
—With Doc Watson					
❑ United Artists XW544	The Battle of New Orleans/Mountain Whipporwill	1974	—	2.50	5.00
❑ United Artists XW655	(All I Have to Do Is) Dream/Raleigh-Durham Reel	1975	—	2.50	5.00
❑ United Artists XW741	Mother of Love/The Moon Just Turned Blue	1975	—	2.50	5.00
❑ United Artists XW830	Cosmic Cowboy/Stars and Stripes Forever	1976	—	2.00	4.00
—As "The Dirt Band"					
❑ United Artists XW889	Jamaica Lady/Bayou Jubilee-Sally Was a Goodun	1976	—	2.00	4.00
—As "The Dirt Band"					
❑ United Artists XW936	Buy for Me the Rain/Mother Earth (Provides for Me)	1976	—	2.00	4.00
—As "The Dirt Band"					
❑ United Artists XW1164	Orange Blossom Special/Will the Circle Be Unbroken	1978	—	2.00	4.00
❑ United Artists XW1228	Wild Nights/In for the Night	1978	—	2.00	4.00
—As "The Dirt Band"					
❑ United Artists XW1268	For a Little While/On the Loose	1978	—	2.00	4.00
—As "The Dirt Band"					
❑ United Artists 1312	In Her Eyes/Jas' Moon	1979	—	2.00	4.00
—As "The Dirt Band"					
❑ United Artists 1330	An American Dream/Take Me Back	1979	—	2.50	5.00
—As "The Dirt Band"					
❑ United Artists 1356	Make a Little Magic/Jas' Moon	1980	—	2.00	4.00
—As "The Dirt Band"					
❑ United Artists 1378	Badlands/Too Good to Be True	1980	—	2.00	4.00
—As "The Dirt Band"					
❑ United Artists 50769	House at Pooh Corner/Travelin' Mood	1971	—	3.00	6.00
❑ United Artists 50817	The Cure/Some of Shelly's Blues	1971	—	3.00	6.00
❑ United Artists 50849	Precious Jewel/I Saw the Light	1971	—	3.00	6.00
—With Roy Acuff					
❑ United Artists 50861	I Saw the Light/Sixteen Tracks	1971	—	3.00	6.00
❑ United Artists 50890	Jambalaya (On the Bayou)/Hoping to Say	1972	—	3.00	6.00
❑ United Artists 50921	Baltimore/Fish Song	1972	—	3.00	6.00
❑ United Artists 50965	Honky Tonkin'/Jamaica	1972	—	3.00	6.00
❑ Universal UVL-66009	Turn of the Century/Blueberry Hill	1989	—	—	3.00
❑ Universal UVL-66023	When It's Gone/I'm Sittin' on Top of the World	1989	—	2.00	4.00
❑ Warner Bros. 27679	Down That Road Tonight/A Lot Like Me	1989	—	—	3.00
❑ Warner Bros. 27750	I've Been Lookin'/Must Be Love	1988	—	—	3.00
❑ Warner Bros. 27940	Workin' Man/Brass Sky	1988	—	—	3.00
❑ Warner Bros. 28173	Oh What a Love/America, My Sweetheart	1987	—	—	3.00
❑ Warner Bros. 28311	Fishin' in the Dark/Keepin' the Road Hot	1987	—	—	3.00
❑ Warner Bros. 28443	Baby's Got a Hold on Me/Oleanna	1987	—	—	3.00
❑ Warner Bros. 28547	Cadillac Ranch/Fire in the Sky	1986	—	—	3.00
❑ Warner Bros. 28690	Stand a Little Rain/Miner's Night Out	1986	—	—	3.00
❑ Warner Bros. 28780	Partners, Brothers and Friends/Redneck Riviera	1986	—	—	3.00
❑ Warner Bros. 28897	Home Again in My Heart/Telluride	1985	—	2.00	4.00
❑ Warner Bros. 29027	Modern Day Romance/Queen of the Road	1985	—	2.00	4.00
❑ Warner Bros. 29099	High Horse/Must Be Love	1985	—	2.00	4.00
❑ Warner Bros. 29203	I Love Only You/Face on the Cutting Room Floor	1984	—	2.00	4.00
❑ Warner Bros. 29282	Long Hard Road (The Sharecropper's Dream)/Video Tape	1984	—	2.00	4.00
Albums					
❑ Liberty LWB-184 [(2)]	Stars and Stripes Forever	1981	2.50	5.00	10.00
❑ Liberty LKCL-670 [(3)]	Dirt, Silver and Gold	1981	3.00	6.00	12.00
❑ Liberty LO-974	An American Dream	1981	2.00	4.00	8.00
❑ Liberty LT-1042	Make a Little Magic	1981	2.00	4.00	8.00
❑ Liberty LRP-3501 [M]	The Nitty Gritty Dirt Band	1967	6.25	12.50	25.00
❑ Liberty LRP-3516 [M]	Ricochet	1967	6.25	12.50	25.00
❑ Liberty LMAS-5553	All the Good Times	1981	2.00	4.00	8.00
❑ Liberty LST-7501 [S]	The Nitty Gritty Dirt Band	1967	7.50	15.00	30.00
❑ Liberty LST-7516 [S]	Ricochet	1967	7.50	15.00	30.00
❑ Liberty LST-7540	Rare Junk	1968	6.25	12.50	25.00
❑ Liberty LST-7611	Alive	1969	6.25	12.50	25.00
❑ Liberty LST-7642	Uncle Charlie and His Dog Teddy	1970	6.25	12.50	25.00
—Standard issue of LP					
❑ Liberty LTAO-7642	Uncle Charlie and His Dog Teddy	1981	2.00	4.00	8.00
❑ Liberty LT-51146	Let's Go	1982	2.50	5.00	10.00
❑ Liberty LWCL-51158 [(3)]	Will the Circle Be Unbroken	1986	3.75	7.50	15.00
❑ MCA 6407	The Rest of the Dream	1990	3.00	6.00	12.00
❑ United Artists UA-LA184-J2 [(2)]	Stars and Stripes Forever	1974	3.75	7.50	15.00
❑ United Artists UA-LA469-G	Dream	1975	3.00	6.00	12.00

Number	Title (A Side/B Side)	Yr	VG	VG+	NM
❑ United Artists UA-LA670-L3 [(3)]	Dirt, Silver and Gold	1976	5.00	10.00	20.00
❑ United Artists UA-LA830-H	The Chicken Chronicles	1978	2.50	5.00	10.00
❑ United Artists UA-LA854-H	The Dirt Band	1978	2.50	5.00	10.00
❑ United Artists UA-LA974-H	An American Dream	1979	2.50	5.00	10.00
❑ United Artists LT-1042	Make a Little Magic	1980	2.50	5.00	10.00
❑ United Artists LW-1106	Jealousy	1981	2.50	5.00	10.00
❑ United Artists UAS-5553	All the Good Times	1972	3.75	7.50	15.00
❑ United Artists UAS-9801 [(3)]	Will the Circle Be Unbroken	1972	7.50	15.00	30.00
❑ Universal UVL2-12500 [(2)]	Will the Circle Be Unbroken, Volume Two	1989	5.00	10.00	20.00
❑ Warner Bros. 25113	Plain Dirt Fashion	1984	2.00	4.00	8.00
❑ Warner Bros. 25304	Partners, Brothers and Friends	1985	2.00	4.00	8.00
❑ Warner Bros. 25382	Twenty Years of Dirt: The Best of the Nitty Gritty Dirt Band	1986	2.00	4.00	8.00
❑ Warner Bros. 25573	Hold On	1987	2.00	4.00	8.00
❑ Warner Bros. 25722	Workin' Band	1988	2.00	4.00	8.00
❑ Warner Bros. 25830	More Great Dirt: The Best of the Nitty Gritty Dirt Band, Vol. 2	1989	2.50	5.00	10.00
NOBLES, CLIFF					
45s					
❑ Atlantic 2352	My Love Is Getting Stronger/Too Fond of You	1966	2.00	4.00	8.00
❑ Atlantic 2380	Your Love Is All I Need/Everybody Is Weak for Somebody	1967	2.00	4.00	8.00
❑ Jamie 1406	The Horse/If You Don't	1972	—	3.00	6.00
❑ Moon Shot 6710	Pony the Horse/Little Claudie	1969	2.00	4.00	8.00
❑ Phil-L.A. of Soul 310	The More I Do for You Baby/This Love Will Last	1968	2.00	4.00	8.00
❑ Phil-L.A. of Soul 313	The Horse/Love Is All Right	1968	2.50	5.00	10.00
❑ Phil-L.A. of Soul 318	Horse Fever/Judge Baby, I'm Back	1968	2.00	4.00	8.00
❑ Phil-L.A. of Soul 324	Switch It On/Burning Desire	1969	2.00	4.00	8.00
❑ Phil-L.A. of Soul 329	The Camel/Goin' Away	1969	2.00	4.00	8.00
❑ Roulette 7142	This Feeling of Loneliness/We Got Our Thing Together	1973	—	3.00	6.00
Albums					
❑ Moon Shot 601	Pony the Horse	1969	10.00	20.00	40.00
❑ Phil-L.A. of Soul 4001	The Horse	1968	15.00	30.00	60.00
NUTTY SQUIRRELS, THE					
45s					
❑ Columbia 41818	Please Don't Take Our Tree for Christmas/Nutty Noel	1960	5.00	10.00	20.00
❑ Hanover 4540	Uh! Oh! (Part 1)/Uh! Oh! (Part 2)	1959	6.25	12.50	25.00
❑ Hanover 4551	Eager Beaver/Zowee	1960	5.00	10.00	20.00
❑ RCA Victor 47-8287	Hello Again/Bluesette	1963	3.75	7.50	15.00
Albums					
❑ Columbia CL 1589 [M]	Bird Watching	1961	7.50	15.00	30.00
❑ Columbia CS 8389 [S]	Bird Watching	1961	10.00	20.00	40.00
❑ Hanover HML-8014 [M]	The Nutty Squirrels	1960	12.50	25.00	50.00
❑ MGM E-4272 [M]	A Hard Day's Night	1964	6.25	12.50	25.00
❑ MGM SE-4272 [S]	A Hard Day's Night	1964	7.50	15.00	30.00

O

O'JAYS, THE

45s

Number	Title (A Side/B Side)	Yr	VG	VG+	NM
❑ Apollo 759	Miracles/Can't Take It	1961	7.50	15.00	30.00
❑ Astroscope 106	Wisdom of a Child/Peace	1974	2.00	4.00	8.00
❑ Astroscope 110	Peace/Don't You Know a True Love (When You See Her)	1974	2.00	4.00	8.00
❑ Bell 691	I'll Be Sweeter Tomorrow (Than I Was Today)/I Dig Your Act	1967	2.50	5.00	10.00
❑ Bell 704	Look Over Your Shoulder/I'm So Glad I Found You	1968	2.50	5.00	10.00
❑ Bell 737	The Choice/Going, Going, Gone	1968	2.50	5.00	10.00
❑ Bell 749	I Miss You/Now That I Found You	1968	2.50	5.00	10.00
❑ Bell 770	Don't You Know a True Love/That's All Right	1969	2.00	4.00	8.00
❑ Bell 45378	Look Over Your Shoulder/Four for the Price of One	1973	—	2.50	5.00
❑ EMI B-50180	Have You Had Your Love Today/Pot Can't Call the Kettle Black	1989	—	—	3.00
❑ EMI B-50212	Out of My Mind (Radio Mix)/(Soul 2 Mix)	1989	—	—	3.00
❑ EMI B-50230	Serious Hold on Me/(Instrumental)	1989	—	2.00	4.00
❑ Imperial 5942	How Does It Feel/Crack Up Laughing	1963	3.75	7.50	15.00
❑ Imperial 5976	Lonely Drifter/That's Enough	1963	2.50	5.00	10.00
❑ Imperial 66007	Stand Tall/The Storm Is Over	1963	2.50	5.00	10.00
❑ Imperial 66025	I'll Never Stop Loving You/My Dearest Beloved	1964	2.50	5.00	10.00

Number	Title (A Side/B Side)	Yr	VG	VG+	NM
❑ Imperial 66037	You're on Top/Lovely Dee	1964	2.50	5.00	10.00
❑ Imperial 66076	Girl Machine/Oh How You Hurt Me	1964	2.50	5.00	10.00
❑ Imperial 66102	Lipstick Traces/Think It Over, Baby	1965	2.50	5.00	10.00
❑ Imperial 66121	Whip It On Me Baby/I've Cried My Last Tear	1965	2.50	5.00	10.00
❑ Imperial 66131	You're the One (You're the Only One)/Let It All Come Out	1965	2.50	5.00	10.00
❑ Imperial 66145	I'll Never Let You Go/It Won't Hurt	1965	2.50	5.00	10.00
❑ Imperial 66162	I'll Never Forget You/Pretty Words	1966	20.00	40.00	80.00
❑ Imperial 66177	No Time for You/It's a Blowin' Wind	1966	2.50	5.00	10.00
❑ Imperial 66197	Friday Night/Stand In for Love	1966	2.50	5.00	10.00
❑ Imperial 66200	Lonely Drifter/That's Enough	1966	2.50	5.00	10.00
❑ Little Star 124	How Does It Feel/Crack Up Laughing	1963	6.25	12.50	25.00
❑ Little Star 125	Dream Girl/Joey St. Vincent	1963	6.25	12.50	25.00
❑ Little Star 1401	Now He's Home/Just to Be with You	1962	6.25	12.50	25.00
❑ Minit 32015	Hold On/Working on Your Case	1967	2.50	5.00	10.00
❑ Neptune 12	One Night Affair/There's Someone (Waiting Back Home)	1969	2.00	4.00	8.00
❑ Neptune 18	Branded Bad/You're the Best Thing Since Candy	1969	2.00	4.00	8.00
❑ Neptune 20	Christmas Ain't Christmas New Year's Ain't New Year's Without the One You Love/There's Someone Waiting	1969	2.50	5.00	10.00
❑ Neptune 22	Deeper (In Love with You)/I've Got the Groove	1970	2.00	4.00	8.00
❑ Neptune 31	Looky Looky (Look at Me Girl)/Let Me in Your World	1970	2.00	4.00	8.00
❑ Neptune 33	Christmas Ain't Christmas New Year's Ain't New Year's Without the One You Love/Just Can't Get Enough	1970	2.00	4.00	8.00
❑ Philadelphia Int'l. ZS8-02096 —*Reissue*	Forever Mine/Girl, Don't Let It Get You Down	1981	—	—	3.00
❑ Philadelphia Int'l. ZS5-02834	I Just Want to Satisfy/Don't Walk Away Mad	1982	—	2.00	4.00
❑ Philadelphia Int'l. ZS4-02982	My Favorite Person/One by One	1982	—	2.00	4.00
❑ Philadelphia Int'l. ZS5-03009	Your Body's Here with Me (But Your Mind's on the Other Side of Town)/Out in the Real World	1982	—	2.00	4.00
❑ Philadelphia Int'l. 3101	Hurry Up and Come Back/Identify	1979	—	2.50	5.00
❑ Philadelphia Int'l. 3517	Back Stabbers/Sunshine	1972	—	2.50	5.00
❑ Philadelphia Int'l. 3522	992 Arguments/Listen to the Clock on the Wall	1972	—	2.50	5.00
❑ Philadelphia Int'l. 3524	Love Train/Who Am I	1973	—	2.50	5.00
❑ Philadelphia Int'l. 3531	Time to Get Down/Shiftless, Shady, Jealous Kind of People	1973	—	2.50	5.00
❑ Philadelphia Int'l. 3535	Put Your Hands Together/You Got Your Hooks in Me	1973	—	2.50	5.00
❑ Philadelphia Int'l. 3537	Christmas Ain't Christmas New Year's Ain't New Year's Without the One You Love/Just Can't Get Enough	1973	—	3.00	6.00
❑ Philadelphia Int'l. 3544	For the Love of Money/People Keep Tellin' Me	1974	—	2.50	5.00
❑ Philadelphia Int'l. 3558	Sunshine (Part 1)/Sunshine (Part 2)	1974	—	2.50	5.00
❑ Philadelphia Int'l. 3565	Give the People What They Want/What Am I Waiting For	1975	—	2.50	5.00
❑ Philadelphia Int'l. 3573	Let Me Make Love to You/Survival	1975	—	2.50	5.00
❑ Philadelphia Int'l. 3577	I Love Music (Part 1)/I Love Music (Part 2)	1975	—	2.50	5.00
❑ Philadelphia Int'l. 3581	Christmas Ain't Christmas New Year's Ain't New Year's Without the One You Love/Just Can't Get Enough	1975	—	2.50	5.00
❑ Philadelphia Int'l. 3587	Livin' for the Weekend/Stairway to Heaven	1976	—	2.50	5.00
❑ Philadelphia Int'l. 3596	Family Reunion/Unity	1976	—	2.50	5.00
❑ Philadelphia Int'l. 3601	Message in Our Music/She's Only a Woman	1976	—	2.50	5.00
❑ Philadelphia Int'l. 3610	Darlin' Darlin' Baby (Sweet, Tender, Love)/A Prayer	1976	—	2.50	5.00
❑ Philadelphia Int'l. 3631	Work On Me/Let's Spend Some Time Together	1977	—	2.50	5.00
❑ Philadelphia Int'l. 3642	Use Ta Be My Girl/This Time Baby	1978	—	2.50	5.00
❑ Philadelphia Int'l. 3652	Brandy/Take Me to the Stars	1978	—	2.50	5.00
❑ Philadelphia Int'l. 3666	Cry Together/Strokety Stroke	1978	—	2.50	5.00
❑ Philadelphia Int'l. 3707	Sing a Happy Song/One in a Million (Girl)	1979	—	2.50	5.00
❑ Philadelphia Int'l. 3726	I Want You Here with Me/Get On Out and Party	1979	—	2.50	5.00
❑ Philadelphia Int'l. 3727	Forever Mine/Get On Out and Party	1979	—	2.50	5.00
❑ Philadelphia Int'l. ZS4-03892	I Can't Stand the Pain/A Letter to My Friends	1983	—	2.00	4.00
❑ Philadelphia Int'l. ZS4-04069	Put Our Heads Together/Nice and Easy	1983	—	2.00	4.00
❑ Philadelphia Int'l. ZS4-04437	Extraordinary Girl/I Really Need You Now	1984	—	2.00	4.00
❑ Philadelphia Int'l. ZS4-04535	Let Me Show You (How Much I Really Love You)/Love You Direct	1984	—	2.00	4.00
❑ Philadelphia Int'l. B-50013	Just Another Lonely Night/What Good Are These Arms of Mine	1985	—	—	3.00
❑ Philadelphia Int'l. B-50021	What a Woman/I Love America	1985	—	—	3.00
❑ Philadelphia Int'l. B-50067	Don't Take Your Love Away/I Just Want Somebody to Love Me	1987	—	—	3.00
❑ Philadelphia Int'l. B-50084	Lovin' You/Don't Let the Dream Get Away	1987	—	—	3.00
❑ Philadelphia Int'l. B-50104	Let Me Touch You/Undercover Lover	1987	—	—	3.00
❑ Philadelphia Int'l. B-50122	I Just Want Someone to Love Me/Lovin' You	1988	—	—	3.00
❑ Saru 1220	Shattered Man/La De Da (Means I'm Out to Get You)	1971	—	3.00	6.00
❑ TSOP 3771	Christmas Ain't Christmas New Year's Ain't New Year's Without the One You Love/Just Can't Get Enough	1980	—	2.50	5.00
❑ TSOP 4790	Girl, Don't Let It Get You Down/You're the Girl of My Dreams	1980	—	2.00	4.00
❑ TSOP 4791	Once Is Not Enough/To Prove I Love You	1980	—	2.00	4.00
❑ TSOP 70050	You Won't Fall/You'll Never Know (All There Is to Know 'Bout Love)	1981	—	2.00	4.00
Albums					
❑ Bell 6014	Back on Top	1968	5.00	10.00	20.00
❑ Bell 6082	The O'Jays	1973	3.00	6.00	12.00
❑ EMI E1-90921	Serious	1989	2.50	5.00	10.00
❑ EMI E1-93390	Emotionally Yours	1991	3.75	7.50	15.00
❑ EMI E1-96420	Home for Christmas	1991	3.75	7.50	15.00
❑ Imperial LP 9290 [M]	Comin' Through	1965	10.00	20.00	40.00
❑ Imperial LP 12290 [S]	Comin' Through	1965	12.50	25.00	50.00

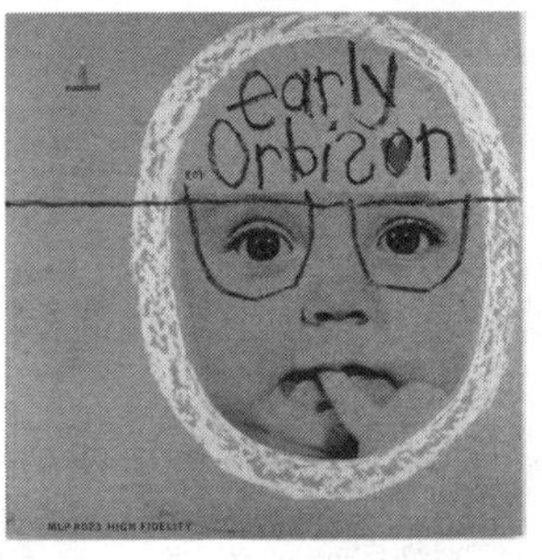

Number	Title (A Side/B Side)	Yr	VG	VG+	NM
❑ Kory 1006	The O'Jays	1977	2.50	5.00	10.00
❑ Liberty LN-10119	Greatest Hits	1980	2.00	4.00	8.00
—Budget-line reissue of Imperial material					
❑ Minit LP-24008 [S]	Soul Sounds	1967	12.50	25.00	50.00
❑ Minit LP-40008 [M]	Soul Sounds	1967	10.00	20.00	40.00
❑ Neptune 202	The O'Jays in Philadelphia	1969	7.50	15.00	30.00
❑ Philadelphia Int'l. KZ 31712	Back Stabbers	1972	3.00	6.00	12.00
❑ Philadelphia Int'l. KZ 32120	The O'Jays in Philadelphia	1973	3.00	6.00	12.00
—Reissue of Neptune LP					
❑ Philadelphia Int'l. KZ 32408	Ship Ahoy	1973	2.50	5.00	10.00
❑ Philadelphia Int'l. PZ 32408	Ship Ahoy	198?	2.00	4.00	8.00
—Budget-line reissue					
❑ Philadelphia Int'l. KZ 32953	The O'Jays Live in London	1974	2.50	5.00	10.00
❑ Philadelphia Int'l. PZ 33150	Survival	1975	2.50	5.00	10.00
❑ Philadelphia Int'l. PZ 33807	Family Reunion	1975	2.50	5.00	10.00
—No bar code on back cover					
❑ Philadelphia Int'l. PZ 34245	Message in the Music	1976	2.50	5.00	10.00
❑ Philadelphia Int'l. PZ 34684	Travelin' at the Speed of Thought	1977	2.50	5.00	10.00
❑ Philadelphia Int'l. Z2 35024 [(2)]	The O'Jays: Collector's Items	198?	2.50	5.00	10.00
—Reissue					
❑ Philadelphia Int'l. JZ 35355	So Full of Love	1978	2.50	5.00	10.00
❑ Philadelphia Int'l. FZ 36027	Identify Yourself	1979	2.50	5.00	10.00
❑ Philadelphia Int'l. FZ 37999	My Favorite Person	1982	2.50	5.00	10.00
❑ Philadelphia Int'l. FZ 38518	When Will I See You Again	1983	2.50	5.00	10.00
❑ Philadelphia Int'l. FZ 39251	Greatest Hits	1984	2.50	5.00	10.00
❑ Philadelphia Int'l. 53015	Love Fever	1985	2.50	5.00	10.00
❑ Philadelphia Int'l. 53036	Let Me Touch You	1987	2.50	5.00	10.00
❑ Sunset SUS-5222	Full of Soul	1968	3.75	7.50	15.00
—Reissue of Imperial LP					
❑ TSOP FZ 36416	The Year 2000	1980	2.50	5.00	10.00
❑ United Artists UAS-5655	The O'Jays Greatest Hits	1972	3.00	6.00	12.00
❑ Volcano 31149	Love You to Tears	1997	3.75	7.50	15.00

O'KAYSIONS, THE

45s

Number	Title (A Side/B Side)	Yr	VG	VG+	NM
❑ ABC 11094	Girl Watcher/Deal Me In	1968	2.00	4.00	8.00
❑ ABC 11153	Love Machine/Dedicated to the One I Love	1968	—	3.00	6.00
❑ ABC 11207	Twenty-Four Hours from Tulsa/Colors	1969	—	3.00	6.00
❑ Cotillion 44089	Happiness/Watch Out Girl	1970	—	2.50	5.00
❑ Cotillion 44134	Life and Things/Travelin' Life	1971	—	2.50	5.00
❑ North State 1001	Girl Watcher/Deal Me In	1968	25.00	50.00	100.00

Albums

Number	Title (A Side/B Side)	Yr	VG	VG+	NM
❑ ABC S-664	Girl Watcher	1968	10.00	20.00	40.00

O'SULLIVAN, GILBERT

45s

Number	Title (A Side/B Side)	Yr	VG	VG+	NM
❑ Epic 50415	You Got Me Going/Call On Me	1977	—	2.00	4.00
❑ Epic 50967	What's in a Kiss/Down, Down, Down	1981	—	2.00	4.00
❑ MAM 3602	Nothing Rhymed/Everybody Knows	1971	—	3.00	6.00
❑ MAM 3607	Underneath the Blanket Go/(B-side unknown)	1971	—	3.00	6.00
❑ MAM 3613	We Will/I Didn't Know What to Do	1971	—	3.00	6.00
❑ MAM 3617	No Matter How I Try/If I Don't Get You Back	1972	—	2.50	5.00
❑ MAM 3619	Alone Again (Naturally)/Save It	1972	—	3.00	6.00
❑ MAM 3626	Clair/Ooh Wakka Doo Wakka Day	1972	—	2.50	5.00
❑ MAM 3628	Out of the Question/Everybody Knows	1973	—	2.50	5.00
❑ MAM 3629	Get Down/A Very Extraordinary Sort of Girl	1973	—	2.50	5.00
❑ MAM 3633	Ooh Baby/Good Company	1973	—	2.00	4.00
❑ MAM 3636	Happiness Is Me and You/Breakfast, Dinner and Tea	1974	—	2.00	4.00
❑ MAM 3641	A Woman's Place/Too Bad	1974	—	2.00	4.00
❑ MAM 3642	You Are You/To Cut a Long Story Short	1974	—	2.00	4.00
❑ MAM 3643	Marriage Machine/Tell Me Why	1975	—	2.00	4.00
❑ MAM 3644	I Don't Love You But I Think I Like You/That's a Fact	1975	—	2.00	4.00
❑ MAM 3645	Christmas Song/Just As You Are	1975	—	2.50	5.00

Albums

Number	Title (A Side/B Side)	Yr	VG	VG+	NM
❑ Epic JE 37013	Off Centre	1981	2.50	5.00	10.00
❑ MAM 4	Gilbert O'Sullivan — Himself	1972	3.75	7.50	15.00

Number	Title (A Side/B Side)	Yr	VG	VG+	NM
❑ MAM 5	Back to Front	1972	3.75	7.50	15.00
❑ MAM 7	I'm a Writer, Not a Fighter	1973	3.75	7.50	15.00
❑ MAM 10	Stranger in My Own Backyard	1974	3.75	7.50	15.00

OCEAN, BILLY

45s

Number	Title (A Side/B Side)	Yr	VG	VG+	NM
❑ Ariola America 7621	Love Really Hurts Without You/You're Running Out of Fools	1976	—	3.00	6.00
❑ Ariola America 7630	L.O.D. (Love On Delivery)/Mr. Business Man	1976	—	3.00	6.00
❑ Epic 19-02053	Night (Feel Like Gettin' Down)/Stay the Night	1981	—	2.00	4.00
❑ Epic 14-02464	Are You Ready/Taking Chances	1981	—	2.00	4.00
❑ Epic 14-02485	Another Day Won't Matter/Whatever Turns You On	1981	—	2.00	4.00
❑ Epic 14-02942	Calypso Funkin'/City Limits	1982	—	2.00	4.00
❑ Epic 14-03174	Inner Feelings/Tryin' to Get Through to You	1982	—	2.00	4.00
❑ Epic 8-50810	American Hearts/My Love	1979	—	2.50	5.00
❑ Jive 1283-7-J	Licence to Chill/Pleasure	1989	—	—	3.00
❑ Jive/Arista 9199	Caribbean Queen (No More Love on the Run)/(Instrumental)	1984	—	—	3.00
❑ Jive/Arista 9284	Loverboy/(Dub)	1984	—	—	3.00
❑ Jive/Arista 9323	Suddenly/Lucky Man	1985	—	—	3.00
❑ Jive/Arista 9374	Mystery Lady/African Queen (No More Love on the Run)	1985	—	—	3.00
❑ Jive/Arista 9432	When the Going Gets Tough, the Tough Get Going/(Instrumental)	1985	—	—	3.00
❑ Jive/Arista 9465	There'll Be Sad Songs (To Make You Cry)/If I Should Lose You	1986	—	—	3.00
❑ Jive/Arista 9510	Love Zone/(Instrumental)	1986	—	—	3.00
❑ Jive/Arista 9540	Love Is Forever/Dance Floor	1986	—	—	3.00
❑ Jive/Arista 9678	Get Outta My Dreams, Get Into My Car/Showdown	1988	—	—	3.00
❑ Jive/Arista 9707	The Colour of Love/It's Never Too Late to Try	1988	—	—	3.00
❑ Jive/Arista 9740	Tear Down These Walls/Without You	1988	—	—	3.00

Albums

Number	Title (A Side/B Side)	Yr	VG	VG+	NM
❑ Epic FE 37406	Nights (Feel Like Gettin' Down)	1981	3.75	7.50	15.00
❑ Epic FE 38129	Inner Feelings	1982	3.75	7.50	15.00
❑ Jive 1271-1-J	Greatest Hits	1989	2.50	5.00	10.00
❑ Jive/Arista JL8-8213	Suddenly	1984	3.75	7.50	15.00
—Original cover: Photo of Billy Ocean on blue background					
❑ Jive/Arista JL8-8213	Suddenly	1984	2.00	4.00	8.00
—Second cover: Drawing of Billy Ocean on white background					
❑ Jive/Arista JL8-8409	Love Zone	1986	2.00	4.00	8.00
❑ Jive/Arista JL8-8495	Tear Down These Walls	1988	2.00	4.00	8.00

OHIO EXPRESS, THE

45s

Number	Title (A Side/B Side)	Yr	VG	VG+	NM
❑ Buddah 38	Yummy Yummy Yummy/Zig Zag	1968	2.50	5.00	10.00
❑ Buddah 56	Down at Lulu's/She's Not Coming Home	1968	2.00	4.00	8.00
❑ Buddah 70	Chewy Chewy/Firebird	1968	2.50	5.00	10.00
❑ Buddah 92	Sweeter Than Sugar/Bitter Than Lemon	1969	2.00	4.00	8.00
❑ Buddah 102	Mercy/Roll It Up	1969	2.00	4.00	8.00
❑ Buddah 117	Pinch Me (Baby, Convince Me)/Peanuts	1969	2.00	4.00	8.00
❑ Buddah 129	Sausalito (Is the Place to Go)/Make Love Not War	1969	2.00	4.00	8.00
—With Graham Gouldman, later of 10CC, on lead vocal					
❑ Buddah 147	Cowboy Convention/The Race (That Took Place)	1970	2.00	4.00	8.00
❑ Buddah 160	Love Equals Love/Peanuts	1970	2.00	4.00	8.00
❑ Buddah 386	Wham Bam/Slow and Steady	1973	3.75	7.50	15.00
—As "Ohio Ltd."					
❑ Cameo 483	Beg, Borrow and Steal/Maybe	1967	3.00	6.00	12.00
❑ Cameo 2001	Try It/Soul Struttin'	1967	3.00	6.00	12.00
❑ Super K 114	Hot Dog/Ooh La La	1970	2.50	5.00	10.00

Albums

Number	Title (A Side/B Side)	Yr	VG	VG+	NM
❑ Buddah BDM 1018 [M]	The Ohio Express	1968	10.00	20.00	40.00
—Stereo cover with "mono" sticker attached; white label promo					
❑ Buddah BDS 5018 [S]	The Ohio Express	1968	5.00	10.00	20.00
❑ Buddah BDS 5026	Chewy, Chewy	1969	5.00	10.00	20.00
❑ Buddah BDS 5037	Mercy	1969	5.00	10.00	20.00
❑ Buddah BDS 5058	The Very Best of the Ohio Express	1970	5.00	10.00	20.00
❑ Cameo C 20000 [M]	Beg, Borrow and Steal	1967	7.50	15.00	30.00
❑ Cameo CS 20000 [S]	Beg, Borrow and Steal	1967	10.00	20.00	40.00

OHIO PLAYERS, THE

45s

Number	Title (A Side/B Side)	Yr	VG	VG+	NM
❑ Air City 402	Sight for Sore Eyes/(Instrumental)	1984	—	2.00	4.00
❑ Air City 1007	Follow Me/(B-side unknown)	1984	—	2.50	5.00
❑ Arista 0408	Everybody Up/Take De Funk Off, Fly	1979	—	2.00	4.00
❑ Arista 0440	Don't Say Goodbye/Say It	1979	—	2.00	4.00
❑ Boardwalk NB7-11-133	Star of the Party/I Better Take a Coffee Break	1981	—	2.00	4.00
❑ Boardwalk WS8-02063	Skinny/Call Me	1981	—	2.00	4.00
❑ Boardwalk 5708	Try a Little Tenderness/Try to Be a Man	1981	—	2.00	4.00
❑ Capitol 2385	Bad Bargain/Here Today and Gone Tomorrow	1969	2.50	5.00	10.00
❑ Capitol 2523	Find Someone to Love/Over the Rainbow	1969	2.50	5.00	10.00
❑ Compass 7015	Tresspassin'/You Don't Mean It	1967	3.00	6.00	12.00
❑ Compass 7018	It's a Crying Shame/I've Got to Hold On	1968	3.00	6.00	12.00
❑ Mercury 73480	Jive Turkey (Part 1)/Streakin' Cheek to Cheek	1974	—	2.50	5.00
❑ Mercury 73609	Skin Tight/Heaven Must Be Like This	1974	—	2.50	5.00
❑ Mercury 73643	Fire/Together	1974	—	2.50	5.00
❑ Mercury 73675	I Want to Be Free/Smoke	1975	—	2.50	5.00
❑ Mercury 73713	Sweet Sticky Thing/Alone	1975	—	2.50	5.00
❑ Mercury 73734	Love Rollercoaster/It's All Over	1975	—	2.50	5.00
❑ Mercury 73753	Happy Holidays (Part 1)/Happy Holidays (Part 2)	1975	—	3.00	6.00
❑ Mercury 73775	Fopp/Let's Love	1976	—	2.50	5.00
❑ Mercury 73814	Who'd She Coo?/Bi-Centennial	1976	—	2.50	5.00
❑ Mercury 73860	Far East Mississippi/Only a Child Can Love	1976	—	2.50	5.00
❑ Mercury 73881	Feel the Beat (Everybody Disco)/Contradiction	1976	—	2.50	5.00

Number	Title (A Side/B Side)	Yr	VG	VG+	NM
❑ Mercury 73913	Body Vibes/Don't Fight My Love	1977	—	2.50	5.00
❑ Mercury 73932	O-H-I-O/Can You Still Love Me	1977	—	2.50	5.00
❑ Mercury 73956	Merry Go Round/Angel	1977	—	2.50	5.00
❑ Mercury 73974	Good Luck Charm (Part 1)/Good Luck Charm (Part 2)	1977	—	2.50	5.00
❑ Mercury 73983	Magic Trick/Mr. Mean	1978	—	2.50	5.00
❑ Mercury 74014	Funk-O-Nots/Sleepwalkin'	1978	—	2.50	5.00
❑ Mercury 74031	Time Slips Away/Nott Enuff	1978	—	2.50	5.00
❑ Tangerine 978	Neighbors/A Thing Called Love	1967	3.00	6.00	12.00
❑ Track 58812	Let's Play (From Now On)/Show Off	1988	—	—	3.00
❑ Track 58815	Sweat/Rock the House	1988	—	—	3.00
❑ Westbound 188	Pain (Part 1)/Pain (Part 2)	1971	—	3.00	6.00
❑ Westbound 204	Pleasure/I Wanna Hear from You	1972	—	3.00	6.00
❑ Westbound 208	Walt's First Trip/Varce Is Love	1972	—	3.00	6.00
❑ Westbound 214	Funky Worm/Paint Me	1973	—	3.00	6.00
❑ Westbound 216	Ecstasy/Not So Sad and Lonely	1973	—	3.00	6.00
❑ Westbound 228	Sleep Talk/Food Stamps Y'All	1974	—	3.00	6.00
❑ Westbound 5018	Rattlesnake/Gone Forever	1976	—	3.00	6.00
Albums					
❑ Accord SN-7102	Young and Ready	1981	2.00	4.00	8.00
❑ Arista AB 4226	Everybody Up	1979	2.00	4.00	8.00
❑ Boardwalk FW 37090	Tenderness	1981	2.00	4.00	8.00
❑ Capitol ST-192	Observations in Time	1969	12.50	25.00	50.00
❑ Capitol ST-11291	The Ohio Players	1974	3.00	6.00	12.00
—Reissue of 192					
❑ Mercury SRM-1-705	Skin Tight	1974	3.00	6.00	12.00
—Red label					
❑ Mercury SRM-1-1013	Fire	1974	2.50	5.00	10.00
❑ Mercury SRM-1-1038	Honey	1975	2.50	5.00	10.00
❑ Mercury SRM-1-1088	Contradiction	1976	2.50	5.00	10.00
❑ Mercury SRM-1-1122	Ohio Players Gold	1976	2.50	5.00	10.00
❑ Mercury SRM-1-3701	Angel	1977	2.50	5.00	10.00
❑ Mercury SRM-1-3707	Mr. Mean	1977	2.50	5.00	10.00
❑ Mercury SRM-1-3730	Jass-Ay-Lay-Dee	1978	2.50	5.00	10.00
❑ Mercury 824461-1	Ohio Players Gold	198?	2.00	4.00	8.00
—Reissue of 1122					
❑ Track TRK 58810	Back	1988	2.50	5.00	10.00
❑ Trip 8029	First Impression	1972	3.00	6.00	12.00
❑ United Artists UA-LA502-E	The Very Best of The Ohio Players	1975	3.00	6.00	12.00
❑ Westbound 211	Rattlesnake	1975	3.00	6.00	12.00
❑ Westbound 219	Pain	1976	3.00	6.00	12.00
—Reissue of 2015					
❑ Westbound 220	Pleasure	1976	3.00	6.00	12.00
—Reissue of 2017					
❑ Westbound 222	Ecstasy	1976	3.00	6.00	12.00
—Reissue of 2021					
❑ Westbound 304	The Best of the Early Years	1977	3.75	7.50	15.00
❑ Westbound 1003	Climax	1974	3.75	7.50	15.00
❑ Westbound 1005	Ohio Players Greatest Hits	1975	3.75	7.50	15.00
❑ Westbound 2015	Pain	1972	5.00	10.00	20.00
❑ Westbound 2017	Pleasure	1973	5.00	10.00	20.00
❑ Westbound 2021	Ecstasy	1973	5.00	10.00	20.00

OLIVER

45s

Number	Title (A Side/B Side)	Yr	VG	VG+	NM
❑ Crewe 334	Jean/The Arrangement	1969	2.00	4.00	8.00
❑ Crewe 337	Sunday Mornin'/Let Me Kiss You with a Dream	1969	—	3.00	6.00
❑ Crewe 341	Angelica/Anna	1970	—	3.00	6.00
❑ Crewe 346	I Can Remember/Where There's a Heartache There Must Be a Heart	1970	—	3.00	6.00
❑ Jubilee 5659	Good Morning Starshine/Can't You See	1969	2.00	4.00	8.00
❑ MCA 52063	Don't Take Your Love Away/Everybody Wants to Be the Boss	1982	—	—	3.00
❑ MCA 52113	I Want Your Love, I Need Your Love/Make Up Your Mind	1982	—	—	3.00
❑ Paramount 0198	Everybody I Love You/I Am Reaching	1973	—	2.00	4.00
❑ United Artists 0130	Good Morning Starshine/Jean	1973	—	2.00	4.00
—"Silver Spotlight Series" reissue					
❑ United Artists 50735	Sweet Kindness/Light the Way	1970	—	2.50	5.00
❑ United Artists 50750	Dedicated to the One I Love/Light the Way	1971	—	—	—
—Unreleased					

Number	Title (A Side/B Side)	Yr	VG	VG+	NM
❑ United Artists 50762	Early Morning Rain/Catch Me If You Can	1971	—	2.50	5.00
❑ United Artists 50814	Walkin' Down the Line/Firelight	1971	—	2.50	5.00
❑ United Artists 50862	Why You Been Gone So Long/Please	1971	—	2.50	5.00
Albums					
❑ Crewe CR-1333	Good Morning Starshine	1969	3.75	7.50	15.00
❑ Crewe CR-1344	Oliver Again	1970	3.75	7.50	15.00
❑ United Artists UAS-5511	Prisms	1971	3.75	7.50	15.00
OLYMPICS, THE					
45s					
❑ Arvee 562	(Baby) Hully Gully/Private Eye	1959	6.25	12.50	25.00
❑ Arvee 595	Big Boy Pete/The Slop	1960	6.25	12.50	25.00
❑ Arvee 5006	Shimmy Like Kate/Workin' Hard	1960	5.00	10.00	20.00
❑ Arvee 5020	Dance by the Light of the Moon/Dodge City	1960	5.00	10.00	20.00
❑ Arvee 5023	Little Pedro/The Bullfight	1961	5.00	10.00	20.00
❑ Arvee 5031	Stay Where You Are/Dooley	1961	10.00	20.00	40.00
❑ Arvee 5044	Mash Them 'Taters/The Stomp	1961	5.00	10.00	20.00
❑ Arvee 5051	Everybody Likes to Cha Cha Cha/The Twist	1962	3.75	7.50	15.00
❑ Arvee 5056	Baby It's Hot/The Scotch	1962	3.75	7.50	15.00
❑ Arvee 5073	What'd I Say (Part 1)/What'd I Say (Part 2)	1963	3.75	7.50	15.00
❑ Arvee 6501	Big Boy Pete '65/Stay Where You Are	1965	3.00	6.00	12.00
❑ Demon 1508	Western Movies/Well!	1958	7.50	15.00	30.00
❑ Demon 1512	Dance with the Teacher/Everybody Needs Love	1958	6.25	12.50	25.00
❑ Demon 1514	Your Love/The Chicken	1959	6.25	12.50	25.00
❑ Duo Disc 104	The Boogler (Part 1)/The Boogler (Part 2)	1964	3.00	6.00	12.00
❑ Duo Disc 105	Return of Big Boy Pete/Return of the Watusi	1964	3.00	6.00	12.00
❑ Jubilee 5674	The Cartoon Song/Things That Make Me Laugh	1969	2.00	4.00	8.00
❑ Loma 2010	I'm Comin' Home/Rainin' in My Heart	1965	2.50	5.00	10.00
❑ Loma 2013	Good Lovin'/Olympic Shuffle	1965	2.50	5.00	10.00
❑ Loma 2017	Baby I'm Yours/No More Will I Cry	1965	2.50	5.00	10.00
❑ Lost-Nite 311	Big Boy Pete/Mine Exclusively	197?	—	2.50	5.00
❑ MGM 14505	Worm in Your Wheatgerm/The Apartment	1973	—	2.50	5.00
❑ Mirwood 5504	We Go Together (Pretty Baby)/Secret Agents	1966	2.00	4.00	8.00
❑ Mirwood 5513	Mine Exclusively/Secret Agents	1966	2.00	4.00	8.00
❑ Mirwood 5523	Baby Do the Philly Dog/Western Movies	1966	2.00	4.00	8.00
❑ Mirwood 5525	The Bounce/The Duck	1966	2.00	4.00	8.00
❑ Mirwood 5529	The Same Old Thing/I'll Do a Little Bit More	1967	2.00	4.00	8.00
❑ Mirwood 5533	Big Boy Pete/(Baby) Hully Gully	1967	2.00	4.00	8.00
❑ Parkway 6003	Lookin' for a Love/Good Things	1968	2.00	4.00	8.00
❑ Titan 1718	The Chicken/Cool Short	1961	6.25	12.50	25.00
❑ Tri Disc 105	Return of Big Boy Pete/Return of the Watusi	1962	3.75	7.50	15.00
❑ Tri Disc 106	The Bounce/Fireworks	1963	3.75	7.50	15.00
❑ Tri Disc 107	Dancin' Holiday/Do the Slauson Shuffle	1963	3.75	7.50	15.00
❑ Tri Disc 110	Bounce Again/A New Dancin' Partner	1963	3.75	7.50	15.00
❑ Tri Disc 112	The Broken Hip/So Goodbye	1963	3.75	7.50	15.00
❑ Warner Bros. 7369	Girl, You're My Kind of People/Please, Please, Please	1970	—	3.00	6.00
Albums					
❑ Arvee A-423 [M]	Doin' the Hully Gully	1960	40.00	80.00	160.00
❑ Arvee A-424 [M]	Dance by the Light of the Moon	1961	30.00	60.00	120.00
❑ Arvee A-429 [M]	Party Time	1961	30.00	60.00	120.00
❑ Everest 4109	The Olympics	1981	2.50	5.00	10.00
❑ Mirwood MS-7003 [S]	Something Old, Something New	1966	12.50	25.00	50.00
❑ Mirwood MW-7003 [M]	Something Old, Something New	1966	10.00	20.00	40.00
❑ Post 8000	The Olympics Sing	196?	6.25	12.50	25.00
❑ Rhino RNDF-207	The Official Record Album of the Olympics	1983	3.00	6.00	12.00
❑ Tri-Disc 1001 [M]	Do the Bounce	1963	20.00	40.00	80.00
ORBISON, ROY					
45s					
❑ Asylum 46048	Tears/Easy Way Out	1979	—	2.50	5.00
❑ Asylum 46541	Poor Baby/Lay It Down	1979	—	2.50	5.00
❑ Eric 7101	Pretty Paper/Oh Pretty Woman	197?	—	2.00	4.00
❑ Je-Wel 101	Ooby Dooby/Tryin' to Get to You	1956	1500.	2750.	4000.
—As "The Teen Kings"; with "Vocal: Roy Orbison" credit (spelled correctly). VG 1500; VG+ 2750					
❑ Mercury 73610	Sweet Mama Blue/Heartache	1974	2.00	4.00	8.00
❑ Mercury 73652	Hung Up onYou/Spanish Nights	1975	—	3.00	6.00
❑ Mercury 73705	It's Lonely/Still	1975	—	3.00	6.00
❑ MGM 13386	Ride Away/Wonderin'	1965	2.50	5.00	10.00
❑ MGM 13410	Crawling Back/If You Can't Say Something Nice	1965	2.50	5.00	10.00
❑ MGM 13446	Breakin' Up Is Breakin' My Heart/Wait	1966	2.50	5.00	10.00
❑ MGM 13498	Twinkle Toes/Where Is Tomorrow	1966	2.50	5.00	10.00
❑ MGM 13549	Too Soon to Know/You'll Never Be Sixteen Again	1966	2.50	5.00	10.00
❑ MGM 13634	Communication Breakdown/Going Back to Gloria	1966	2.50	5.00	10.00
❑ MGM 13685	So Good/Memories	1967	2.50	5.00	10.00
❑ MGM 13756	Ride Away/Crawlin' Back	1967	3.75	7.50	15.00
—Part of Celebrity Scene CS9-5					
❑ MGM 13757	Breakin' Up Is Breakin' My Heart/Too Soon to Know	1967	3.75	7.50	15.00
—Part of Celebrity Scene CS9-5					
❑ MGM 13758	Twinkle Toes/Where Is Tomorrow?	1967	3.75	7.50	15.00
—Part of Celebrity Scene CS9-5					
❑ MGM 13759	Sweet Dreams/Going Back to Gloria	1967	3.75	7.50	15.00
—Part of Celebrity Scene CS9-5					
❑ MGM 13760	You'll Never Be Sixteen Again/There Won't Be Many Coming Home	1967	3.75	7.50	15.00
—Part of Celebrity Scene CS9-5					
❑ MGM 13764	Cry Softly Lonely One/Pistolero	1967	2.50	5.00	10.00
❑ MGM 13817	She/Here Comes the Rain Baby	1967	2.50	5.00	10.00

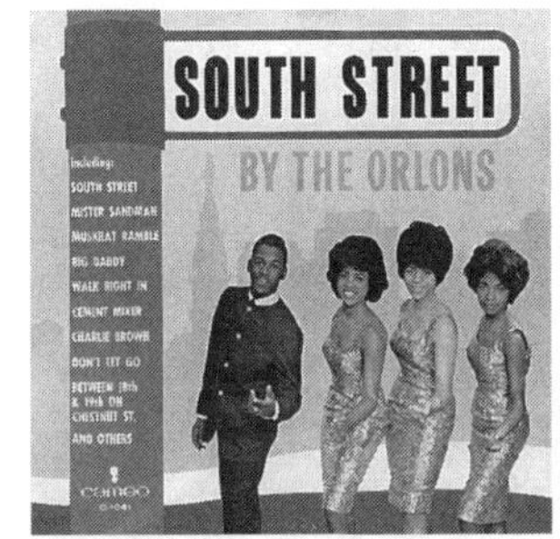

Number	Title (A Side/B Side)	Yr	VG	VG+	NM
❑ MGM 13889	Shy Away/Born to Be Loved by You	1968	2.50	5.00	10.00
❑ MGM 13950	Flowers/Walk On	1968	2.50	5.00	10.00
❑ MGM 13991	Heartache/Sugar Man	1968	2.50	5.00	10.00
❑ MGM 14039	Southbound Jericho Parkway/My Friend	1969	2.50	5.00	10.00
❑ MGM 14079	Penny Arcade/Tennessee Own My Soul	1969	2.50	5.00	10.00
❑ MGM 14105	How Do You Start Over/She Cheats on Me	1970	2.50	5.00	10.00
❑ MGM 14121	So Young/If I Had a Woman Like You	1970	2.50	5.00	10.00
❑ MGM 14293	Close Again/Last Night	1971	2.50	5.00	10.00
❑ MGM 14358	Changes/God Loves You	1972	2.50	5.00	10.00
❑ MGM 14413	Remember the Good/Harlem Woman	1972	2.50	5.00	10.00
❑ MGM 14413	Remember the Good/If Only for a While	1972	2.50	5.00	10.00
❑ MGM 14441	I Can Read Between the Lines/Memphis, Tennessee	1972	2.50	5.00	10.00
❑ MGM 14552	Rain Rain (Coming Down)/Sooner or Later	1973	2.50	5.00	10.00
❑ MGM 14626	I Wanna Live/You Lay So Easy on My Mind	1973	2.50	5.00	10.00
❑ Monument 45-200	(I'm a) Southern Man/Born to Love Me	1976	—	2.50	5.00
❑ Monument 45-215	Drifting Away/Under Suspicion	1977	—	2.50	5.00
❑ Monument 409	Paper Boy/With the Bug	1959	20.00	40.00	80.00
—White label with vertical lines					
❑ Monument 412	Uptown/Pretty One	1959	7.50	15.00	30.00
❑ Monument 421	Only the Lonely (Know the Way I Feel)/ Here Comes That Song Again	1960	6.25	12.50	25.00
❑ Monument 425	Blue Angel/Today's Teardrops	1960	5.00	10.00	20.00
❑ Monument 433	I'm Hurtin'/I Can't Stop Loving You	1960	5.00	10.00	20.00
❑ Monument 438	Running Scared/Love Hurts	1961	5.00	10.00	20.00
❑ Monument 447	Crying/Candy Man	1961	5.00	10.00	20.00
❑ Monument 456	Dream Baby (How Long Must I Dream)/The Actress	1962	5.00	10.00	20.00
❑ Monument 461	The Crowd/Mama	1962	5.00	10.00	20.00
❑ Monument 467	Leah/Workin' for the Man	1962	5.00	10.00	20.00
❑ Monument 503	Paper Boy/With the Bug	196?	3.00	6.00	12.00
—Reissue of 409					
❑ Monument 505	Uptown/Pretty One	196?	3.00	6.00	12.00
—Reissue of 412					
❑ Monument 508	Only the Lonely (Know the Way I Feel)/ Here Comes That Song Again	196?	3.00	6.00	12.00
—Reissue of 421					
❑ Monument 509	Blue Angel/Today's Teardrops	196?	3.00	6.00	12.00
—Reissue of 425					
❑ Monument 510	I'm Hurtin'/I Can't Stop Loving You	196?	3.00	6.00	12.00
—Reissue of 433					
❑ Monument 514	Running Scared/Love Hurts	196?	3.00	6.00	12.00
—Reissue of 438					
❑ Monument 517	Crying/Candy Man	196?	3.00	6.00	12.00
—Reissue of 447					
❑ Monument 519	Dream Baby (How Long Must I Dream)/The Actress	196?	3.00	6.00	12.00
—Reissue of 456					
❑ Monument 520	The Crowd/Mama	196?	3.00	6.00	12.00
—Reissue of 461					
❑ Monument 521	Leah/Working for the Man	196?	3.00	6.00	12.00
—Reissue of 467; note that the B-side title is slightly different here than on 467					
❑ Monument 526	In Dreams/Shahdaroba	196?	3.00	6.00	12.00
—Reissue of 806					
❑ Monument 527	Falling/Distant Drums	196?	3.00	6.00	12.00
—Reissue of 815					
❑ Monument 530	Mean Woman Blues/Blue Bayou	196?	3.00	6.00	12.00
—Reissue of 824					
❑ Monument 531	Pretty Paper/Beautiful Dreamer	196?	3.00	6.00	12.00
—Reissue of 830					
❑ Monument 533	It's Over/Indian Wedding	196?	3.00	6.00	12.00
—Reissue of 837					
❑ Monument 806	In Dreams/Shahdaroba	1963	5.00	10.00	20.00
❑ Monument 815	Falling/Distant Drums	1963	5.00	10.00	20.00
❑ Monument 824	Mean Woman Blues/Blue Bayou	1963	5.00	10.00	20.00
❑ Monument 830	Pretty Paper/Beautiful Dreamer	1963	5.00	10.00	20.00
❑ Monument 837	It's Over/Indian Wedding	1964	5.00	10.00	20.00
❑ Monument 851	Pretty Woman/Yo Te Amo Maria	1964	7.50	15.00	30.00
—Original title					

Number	Title (A Side/B Side)	Yr	VG	VG+	NM
❑ Monument 851 *—Revised title*	Oh Pretty Woman/Yo Te Amo Maria	1964	5.00	10.00	20.00
❑ Monument 873	Goodnight/Only with You	1965	3.75	7.50	15.00
❑ Monument 891	(Say) You're My Girl/Sleepy Hollow	1965	3.75	7.50	15.00
❑ Monument 906	Let the Good Times Roll/Distant Drums	1965	3.75	7.50	15.00
❑ Monument 939	Lana/Our Summer Song	1966	3.75	7.50	15.00
❑ Monument 1900 *—"Golden Series" reissue*	Running Scared/Love Hurts	197?	—	2.00	4.00
❑ Monument 1901 *—"Golden Series" reissue*	Crying/Candy Man	197?	—	2.00	4.00
❑ Monument 1902 *—"Golden Series" reissue*	Leah/Workin' for the Man	197?	—	2.00	4.00
❑ Monument 1903 *—"Golden Series" reissue*	Mean Woman Blues/Blue Bayou	197?	—	2.00	4.00
❑ Monument 1904 *—"Golden Series" reissue*	Falling/Distant Drums	197?	—	2.00	4.00
❑ Monument 1906 *—"Golden Series" reissue*	Only the Lonely (Know the Way I Feel)/Uptown	197?	—	2.00	4.00
❑ Monument 1907 *—"Golden Series" reissue*	Dream Baby (How Long Must I Dream)/I'm Hurtin'	197?	—	2.00	4.00
❑ Monument 1908 *—"Golden Series" reissue*	In Dreams/The Crowd	197?	—	2.00	4.00
❑ Monument 1910 *—"Golden Series" reissue*	Oh Pretty Woman/It's Over	197?	—	2.00	4.00
❑ Monument 1915 *—"Golden Series" reissue*	Blue Angel/Paper Boy	197?	—	2.00	4.00
❑ Monument 1936 *—"Golden Series" reissue*	Pretty Paper/Beautiful Dreamer	1976	—	2.00	4.00
❑ Monument 8690	Belinda/All These Chains	1976	—	2.50	5.00
❑ RCA Victor 47-7381	Sweet and Innocent/Seems to Me	1958	10.00	20.00	40.00
❑ RCA Victor 47-7447	Almost Eighteen/Julie	1959	10.00	20.00	40.00
❑ Sun 242	Ooby Dooby/Go! Go! Go!	1956	25.00	50.00	100.00
❑ Sun 251	Rockhouse/You're My Baby	1956	15.00	30.00	60.00
❑ Sun 265	Devil Doll/Sweet and Easy to Love	1957	20.00	40.00	80.00
❑ Sun 284	Chicken Hearted/I Like Love	1958	12.50	25.00	50.00
❑ Sun 353	Devil Doll/Sweet and Easy to Love	1960	62.50	125.00	250.00
❑ Virgin 99159	Oh Pretty Woman/Claudette	1989	—	—	3.00
❑ Virgin 99202	California Blue/In Dreams	1989	—	—	3.00
❑ Virgin 99227	She's a Mystery to Me/Dream Baby	1989	—	—	3.00
❑ Virgin 99245	You Got It/The Only One	1989	—	—	3.00
❑ Virgin 99245 *—B-side with k.d. lang*	You Got It/Crying	1989	—	2.00	4.00
❑ Virgin 99388 *—A-side with k.d. lang*	Crying/Falling	1988	—	—	3.00
❑ Virgin 99434	In Dreams/Leah	1987	—	—	3.00
❑ Warner Bros. 49262 *—A-side with Emmylou Harris; B-side by Craig Hundley*	That Lovin' You Feeling Again/Lola	1980	—	2.50	5.00
Albums					
❑ Accord SN-7150	Ooby Dooby	1981	2.00	4.00	8.00
❑ Asylum 6E-198	Laminar Flow	1979	3.00	6.00	12.00
❑ Buckboard BBS-1015	Roy Orbison's Golden Hits	197?	2.50	5.00	10.00
❑ Candelite P2 12946 [(2)]	The Living Legend of Roy Orbison	1976	3.75	7.50	15.00
❑ Design DLP-164 [M]	Orbiting with Roy Orbison	196?	3.75	7.50	15.00
❑ Design DLPS-164 [R]	Orbiting with Roy Orbison	196?	2.50	5.00	10.00
❑ Hallmark SHM-824	The Exciting Roy Orbison	197?	2.00	4.00	8.00
❑ Hits Unlimited 233-0	My Spell on You	1982	2.00	4.00	8.00
❑ Mercury SRM-1-1045	I'm Still in Love with You	1975	3.00	6.00	12.00
❑ MGM E-4308 [M]	There Is Only One Roy Orbison	1965	6.25	12.50	25.00
❑ MGM SE-4308 [S]	There Is Only One Roy Orbison	1965	8.75	17.50	35.00
❑ MGM E-4322 [M]	The Orbison Way	1965	6.25	12.50	25.00
❑ MGM SE-4322 [S]	The Orbison Way	1965	8.75	17.50	35.00
❑ MGM E-4379 [M]	The Classic Roy Orbison	1966	6.25	12.50	25.00
❑ MGM SE-4379 [S]	The Classic Roy Orbison	1966	8.75	17.50	35.00
❑ MGM E-4424 [M]	Roy Orbison Sings Don Gibson	1967	6.25	12.50	25.00
❑ MGM SE-4424 [S]	Roy Orbison Sings Don Gibson	1967	8.75	17.50	35.00
❑ MGM E-4514 [M]	Cry Softly, Lonely One	1967	6.25	12.50	25.00
❑ MGM SE-4514 [S]	Cry Softly, Lonely One	1967	8.75	17.50	35.00
❑ MGM SE-4636	The Many Moods of Roy Orbison	1969	6.25	12.50	25.00
❑ MGM SE-4659	The Great Songs of Roy Orbison	1970	6.25	12.50	25.00
❑ MGM SE-4683	Hank Williams the Roy Orbison Way	1970	6.25	12.50	25.00
❑ MGM SE-4835	Roy Orbison Sings	1972	3.75	7.50	15.00
❑ MGM SE-4867	Memphis	1972	3.75	7.50	15.00
❑ MGM SE-4934	Milestones	1973	3.75	7.50	15.00
❑ Monument M-4002 [M]	Lonely and Blue	1961	37.50	75.00	150.00
❑ Monument M-4007 [M]	Crying	1962	30.00	60.00	120.00
❑ Monument M-4009 [M]	Roy Orbison's Greatest Hits	1962	12.50	25.00	50.00
❑ Monument MC-6619	Roy Orbison's Greatest Hits	1977	3.00	6.00	12.00
❑ Monument MC-6620	In Dreams	1977	3.00	6.00	12.00
❑ Monument MC-6621	More of Roy Orbison's Greatest Hits	1977	3.00	6.00	12.00
❑ Monument MC-6622	The Very Best of Roy Orbison	1977	3.00	6.00	12.00
❑ Monument MG-7600	Regeneration	1976	3.75	7.50	15.00
❑ Monument MLP-8000 [M]	Roy Orbison's Greatest Hits	1963	7.50	15.00	30.00
❑ Monument MLP-8003 [M] *—White and rainbow label*	In Dreams	1963	12.50	25.00	50.00
❑ Monument MLP-8003 [M] *—Green and gold label*	In Dreams	1964	7.50	15.00	30.00

Number	Title (A Side/B Side)	Yr	VG	VG+	NM
❑ Monument MLP-8023 [M]	Early Orbison	1964	7.50	15.00	30.00
❑ Monument MLP-8024 [M]	More of Roy Orbison's Greatest Hits	1964	7.50	15.00	30.00
❑ Monument MLP-8035 [M]	Orbisongs	1965	6.25	12.50	25.00
❑ Monument MLP-8045 [M]	The Very Best of Roy Orbison	1966	6.25	12.50	25.00
❑ Monument MP-8600 [(2)]	The All-Time Greatest Hits of Roy Orbison	1977	4.00	8.00	16.00
❑ Monument SM-14002 [S]	Lonely and Blue	1961	150.00	300.00	600.00
❑ Monument SM-14007 [S]	Crying	1962	150.00	300.00	600.00
❑ Monument SM-14009 [S]	Roy Orbison's Greatest Hits	1962	20.00	40.00	80.00
❑ Monument SLP-18000 [S]	Roy Orbison's Greatest Hits	1963	10.00	20.00	40.00
❑ Monument SLP-18003 [S]	In Dreams	1963	25.00	50.00	100.00
—White and rainbow label					
❑ Monument SLP-18003 [S]	In Dreams	1964	12.50	25.00	50.00
—Green and gold label					
❑ Monument SLP-18023 [S]	Early Orbison	1964	12.50	25.00	50.00
❑ Monument SLP-18024 [S]	More of Roy Orbison's Greatest Hits	1964	10.00	20.00	40.00
❑ Monument SLP-18035 [S]	Orbisongs	1965	8.75	17.50	35.00
❑ Monument SLP-18045 [P]	The Very Best of Roy Orbison	1966	8.75	17.50	35.00
—"It's Over" is rechanneled					
❑ Monument KZG 31484 [(2)]	The All-Time Greatest Hits of Roy Orbison	1972	6.25	12.50	25.00
❑ Monument KWG 38384 [(2)]	The All-Time Greatest Hits of Roy Orbison	1982	2.50	5.00	10.00
❑ Rhino R1 70711	The Classic Roy Orbison	1989	3.00	6.00	12.00
❑ Rhino R1 70916	The Sun Years	1989	3.75	7.50	15.00
❑ Rhino R1 71493 [(2)]	For the Lonely: A Roy Orbison Anthology	1988	3.00	6.00	12.00
❑ S&P 507 [(2)]	The All-Time Greatest Hits of Roy Orbison	2004	10.00	20.00	40.00
—Reissue on 180-gram vinyl					
❑ Sun 113	The Original Sound	1969	3.00	6.00	12.00
❑ Sun LP-1260 [M]	Roy Orbison at the Rock House	1961	150.00	300.00	600.00
❑ Time-Life SRNR 34 [(2)]	Roy Orbison 1960-1965	1990	5.00	10.00	20.00
—Box set in "The Rock 'n' Roll Era" series					
❑ Trip TLX-8505	The Best of Roy Orbison	197?	2.00	4.00	8.00
❑ Virgin 90604 [(2)]	In Dreams: The Greatest Hits	1987	3.00	6.00	12.00
—Re-recordings of his original hits					
❑ Virgin 91058	Mystery Girl	1989	2.50	5.00	10.00
❑ Virgin 91295	A Black and White Night	1990	3.75	7.50	15.00

ORIGINALS, THE (1)

45s

Number	Title (A Side/B Side)	Yr	VG	VG+	NM
❑ Fantasy 820	Take This Love/Ladies (We Need You)	1978	—	2.50	5.00
❑ Fantasy 847	Blue Moon/Ladies (We Need You)	1979	—	2.50	5.00
❑ Fantasy 856	J-E-A-L-O-U-S (Means I Love You)/Jezebel (You've Got Me Under Your Spell)	1979	—	2.50	5.00
❑ Motown 1355	Good Lovin' Is Just a Dime Away/Nothing Can Take the Place (Of Your Love)	1975	—	3.00	6.00
❑ Motown 1370	50 Years/Financial Affair	1975	—	3.00	6.00
❑ Motown 1379	Everybody's Got to Do Something/(Instrumental)	1975	—	3.00	6.00
❑ Phase II WS8-02061	Baby I'm for Real/Share Your Love with Me	1981	—	2.00	4.00
❑ Phase II WS8-02147	The Magic Is You/Let Me Dance	1981	—	2.00	4.00
❑ Phase II ZS5-02724	Baby I'm for Real/The Magic Is You	1982	—	2.00	4.00
—As "Hank Dixon and the Originals"					
❑ Phase II 5653	Waitin' on a Letter/Mr. Postman//(B-side unknown)	1981	—	2.50	5.00
❑ Soul 35029	Goodnight Irene/Need Your Loving (Want It Back)	1967	3.00	6.00	12.00
❑ Soul 35056	We've Got a Way Out Love/You're the One	1969	3.00	6.00	12.00
❑ Soul 35061	Green Grow the Lilacs/You're the One	1969	3.00	6.00	12.00
❑ Soul 35066	Baby I'm for Real/The Moment of Truth	1969	2.00	4.00	8.00
❑ Soul 35069	The Bells/I'll Wait for You	1970	2.00	4.00	8.00
❑ Soul 35074	We Can Make It/I Like Your Style	1970	3.00	6.00	12.00
❑ Soul 35074	We Can Make It Baby/I Like Your Style	1970	2.00	4.00	8.00
❑ Soul 35079	God Bless Whoever Sent You/Desperate Young Man	1970	2.00	4.00	8.00
❑ Soul 35085	Keep Me/A Man Without Love	1971	—	3.00	6.00
❑ Soul 35093	I'm Someone Who Cares/Once I Have You	1972	—	3.00	6.00
❑ Soul 35102	Be My Love/Endlessly Love	1973	—	3.00	6.00
❑ Soul 35109	First Lady (Sweet Mother's Love)/There's a Chance When You Love, You Love	1973	—	3.00	6.00
❑ Soul 35112	Supernatural Voodoo Woman (Part 1)/Supernatural Voodoo Woman (Part 2)	1974	—	3.00	6.00
❑ Soul 35113	Game Called Love/Ooh You Put a Spell on Me	1974	—	3.00	6.00
❑ Soul 35115	You're My Only World/So Near (And Yet So Far)	1974	—	3.00	6.00

Number	Title (A Side/B Side)	Yr	VG	VG+	NM
❑ Soul 35117	Touch/Ooh You Put a Spell on Me	1975	—	3.00	6.00
❑ Soul 35119	Down to Love Town/Just to Be Closer to You	1976	—	3.00	6.00
Albums					
❑ Fantasy F-9546	Another Time, Another Place	1978	2.50	5.00	10.00
❑ Fantasy F-9577	Come Away with Me	1979	2.50	5.00	10.00
❑ Motown M5-110V	Motown Superstar Series, Vol. 10	1982	2.50	5.00	10.00
❑ Motown M7-826	California Sunset	1975	3.75	7.50	15.00
❑ Phase II JW 37075	Yesterday and Today	1981	3.00	6.00	12.00
❑ Soul SS-716	Baby I'm for Real	1969	10.00	20.00	40.00
❑ Soul SS-724	Portrait of the Originals	1970	6.25	12.50	25.00
❑ Soul SS-729	Naturally Together	1971	6.25	12.50	25.00
❑ Soul SS-734	Definitions	1971	5.00	10.00	20.00
❑ Soul SS-740	The Game Called…	1973	3.75	7.50	15.00
❑ Soul SS-743	California Sunset	1974	—	—	—
—Unreleased					
❑ Soul S7-746	Communique	1976	3.75	7.50	15.00
❑ Soul S7-749	Down to Love Town	1977	3.75	7.50	15.00
ORLANDO, TONY					
45s					
❑ Atco 6376	Think Before You Act/She Loves Me (For What I Am)	1965	2.50	5.00	10.00
❑ Cameo 471	Sweet Sweet/Manuelito (Little Manuel	1967	2.50	5.00	10.00
❑ Casablanca 967	They're Playing Our Song (Medley)/Moonlight	1979	—	2.00	4.00
❑ Casablanca 991	Sweets for My Sweet/High Steppin'	1979	—	2.00	4.00
❑ Casablanca 2229	San Pedros Children/High Steppin'	1979	—	2.00	4.00
❑ Casablanca 2249	Pullin' Together/She Always Knew	1980	—	2.00	4.00
❑ Epic 9441	Halfway to Paradise/Lonely Tomorrows	1961	3.75	7.50	15.00
❑ Epic 9452	Bless You/Am I the Guy	1961	3.75	7.50	15.00
❑ Epic 9476	Hapy Times (Are Here to Stay)/Lonely Am I	1961	3.00	6.00	12.00
❑ Epic 9491	My Baby's a Starnger/Talkin' About You	1962	3.00	6.00	12.00
❑ Epic 9502	I'd Never Find Another You/Love on Your Lips	1962	3.00	6.00	12.00
❑ Epic 9519	At the Edge of Tears/Chills	1962	3.00	6.00	12.00
❑ Epic 9562	Beautiful Dreamer/The Loneliest	1962	2.50	5.00	10.00
❑ Epic 9570	Joanie/Shirley	1963	2.50	5.00	10.00
❑ Epic 9622	I'll Be There/What Am I Gonna Do	1963	2.50	5.00	10.00
❑ Epic 9668	She Doesn't Know It/Tell Me What I Can Do	1964	2.50	5.00	10.00
❑ Epic 9715	To Wait for Love/Accept It	1964	2.50	5.00	10.00
Albums					
❑ Casablanca NBLP 7153	I Got Rhythm	1979	2.50	5.00	10.00
❑ Casablanca NBLP 7209	Living for the Music	1980	2.50	5.00	10.00
❑ Epic BN 611 [S]	Bless You and 11 Other Great Hits	1961	10.00	20.00	40.00
❑ Epic LN 3808 [M]	Bless You and 11 Other Great Hits	1961	7.50	15.00	30.00
❑ Epic BG 33785 [(2)]	Before Dawn	1975	3.75	7.50	15.00
ORLEANS					
45s					
❑ ABC 11408	Please Be There/Mountains	1973	—	2.50	5.00
❑ ABC 11420	If/Stoned	1974	—	2.50	5.00
❑ Asylum 45243	Let There Be Music/Give One Heart	1975	—	2.00	4.00
❑ Asylum 45261	Dance with Me/Ending of a Song	1975	—	2.50	5.00
❑ Asylum 45336	Still the One/Siam Sam	1976	—	2.50	5.00
—Clouds label					
❑ Asylum 45375	Reach/Sweet Destiny	1976	—	2.00	4.00
❑ Asylum 45391	The Bum/Spring Fever	1977	—	2.00	4.00
❑ Asylum 45447	Business As Usual/Time Passes On	1977	—	2.00	4.00
❑ Atlantic America 99981	One of a Kind/Beatin' Around the Bush	1982	—	2.00	4.00
❑ Infinity 50006	Love Takes Time/Isn't It Easy	1979	—	2.00	4.00
❑ Infinity 50017	Don't Throw Our Love Away/The Flame and the Moth	1979	—	2.00	4.00
❑ Infinity 50036	Forever/Keep On Rollin'	1979	—	2.00	4.00
❑ MCA 41228	Change Your Mind/When Are You Coming Home	1980	—	2.00	4.00
❑ MCA 41283	No Ordinary Lady/Dukie's Tune	1980	—	2.00	4.00
❑ MCA 52862	Lady Liberty/On Hold	1986	—	—	3.00
❑ MCA 52909	Grown-Up Children/On Hold	1986	—	—	3.00
❑ MCA 52963	You're Mine/Language of Love	1986	—	—	3.00
Albums					
❑ ABC ABCX-795	Orleans	1973	3.75	7.50	15.00
❑ ABC AA-1058-2 [(2)]	Before the Dance	1977	3.00	6.00	12.00
❑ ABC AC-30011	The ABC Collection	1976	2.50	5.00	10.00
❑ Asylum 7E-1029	Let There Be Music	1975	2.50	5.00	10.00
❑ Asylum 7E-1070	Waking and Dreaming	1976	2.50	5.00	10.00
❑ Infinity INF-9006	Forever	1979	2.50	5.00	10.00
❑ MCA 5110	Orleans	1980	2.50	5.00	10.00
❑ MCA 5767	Grown Up Children	1986	2.00	4.00	8.00
❑ Radio 90012	One of a Kind	1982	2.50	5.00	10.00
ORLONS, THE					
45s					
❑ ABC 10894	Everything/Keep Your Hands Off My Baby	1967	2.50	5.00	10.00
❑ ABC 10948	Kissin' Time/Once Upon a Time	1967	2.50	5.00	10.00
❑ Calla 113	Spinnin' Top/Anyone Who Had a Heart	1966	2.50	5.00	10.00
❑ Cameo 198	I'll Be True/Heart Darling Angel	1961	12.50	25.00	50.00
❑ Cameo 211	Mr. 21/Please Let It Be Me	1961	12.50	25.00	50.00
❑ Cameo 218	The Wah-Watusi/Holiday Hill	1962	5.00	10.00	20.00
❑ Cameo 231	Don't Hang Up/The Conservative	1962	5.00	10.00	20.00
❑ Cameo 243	South Street/Them Terrible Boots	1963	5.00	10.00	20.00
❑ Cameo 257	Not Me/My Best Friend	1963	5.00	10.00	20.00
❑ Cameo 273	Cross Fire!/It's No Big Thing	1963	5.00	10.00	20.00

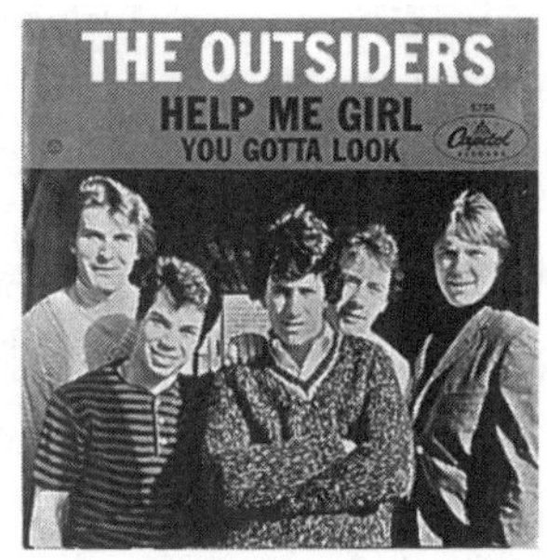

Number	Title (A Side/B Side)	Yr	VG	VG+	NM
❑ Cameo 287	Bon-Doo-Wah/Don't Throw Your Love Away	1963	3.75	7.50	15.00
❑ Cameo 295	Shimmy Shimmy/Everything Nice	1964	3.75	7.50	15.00
❑ Cameo 319	Rules of Love/Heartbreak Hotel	1964	3.75	7.50	15.00
❑ Cameo 332	Knock! Knock! (Who's There)/Goin' Places	1964	3.75	7.50	15.00
❑ Cameo 346	I Ain't Coming Back/Envy (In My Eyes)	1965	3.00	6.00	12.00
❑ Cameo 352	Come On Down Baby/I Ain't Coming Back	1965	3.00	6.00	12.00
❑ Cameo 372	Don't You Want My Lovin'/I Can't Take It	1965	3.00	6.00	12.00
❑ Cameo 384	No Love But Your Love/Envy (In My Eyes)	1965	10.00	20.00	40.00
Albums					
❑ Cameo C 1020 [M]	The Wah-Watusi	1962	15.00	30.00	60.00
❑ Cameo C 1033 [M]	All the Hits by the Orlons	1962	15.00	30.00	60.00
❑ Cameo C 1041 [M]	South Street	1963	15.00	30.00	60.00
❑ Cameo C 1054 [M]	Not Me	1963	12.50	25.00	50.00
❑ Cameo C 1061 [M]	The Orlons' Biggest Hits	1964	12.50	25.00	50.00
❑ Cameo C 1073 [M]	Down Memory Lane with the Orlons	1964	12.50	25.00	50.00
ORLONS, THE / THE DOVELLS					
Albums					
❑ Cameo C 1067 [M]	Golden Hits of the Orlons and the Dovells	1964	12.50	25.00	50.00
OSMOND, DONNY					
45s					
❑ Capitol B-44369	Soldier of Love/My Secret Touch	1989	—	—	3.00
❑ Capitol B-44379	Sacred Emotion/Groove	1989	—	—	3.00
❑ MGM 14227	Sweet and Innocent/Flirtin'	1971	—	3.00	6.00
❑ MGM 14285	Go Away Little Girl/The Wild Rover (Time to Ride)	1971	—	2.50	5.00
—Altered B-side title					
❑ MGM 14285	Go Away Little Girl/Time to Ride	1971	—	3.00	6.00
❑ MGM 14322	Hey Girl/I Knew You When	1971	—	3.00	6.00
❑ MGM 14367	Puppy Love/Let My People Go	1972	—	3.00	6.00
❑ MGM 14407	Too Young/Love Me	1972	—	3.00	6.00
❑ MGM 14424	Lonely Boy/Why	1972	—	3.00	6.00
❑ MGM 14503	The Twelfth of Never/Life Is Just What You Make It	1973	—	2.50	5.00
❑ MGM 14583	A Million to One/Young Love	1973	—	2.50	5.00
❑ MGM 14677	Are You Lonesome Tonight/When I Fall in Love	1973	—	2.50	5.00
❑ MGM 14781	I Have a Dream/I'm Dyin'	1975	—	2.00	4.00
❑ Polydor 14320	C'mon Marianne/Ol' Man Auctioneer	1976	—	2.00	4.00
❑ Polydor 14417	You Got Me Dangling on a String/I'm Sorry	1977	—	2.00	4.00
Albums					
❑ Capitol C1-92354	Donny Osmond	1989	3.00	6.00	12.00
❑ Capitol C1-94051	Eyes Don't Lie	1990	3.75	7.50	15.00
❑ MGM SE-4782	The Donny Osmond Album	1971	3.00	6.00	12.00
❑ MGM SE-4797	To You with Love, Donny	1971	2.50	5.00	10.00
❑ MGM SE-4820	Portrait of Donny	1972	2.50	5.00	10.00
❑ MGM SE-4854	Too Young	1972	2.50	5.00	10.00
❑ MGM SE-4872	My Best to You	1972	2.50	5.00	10.00
❑ MGM SE-4886	Alone Together	1973	6.25	12.50	25.00
—With tear-off 10x10 photo intact; deduct 60 percent if missing					
❑ MGM M3G-4930	A Time for Us	1973	2.50	5.00	10.00
❑ MGM M3G-4978	Donny	1974	2.50	5.00	10.00
❑ Polydor PD-1-6067	Disco Train	1976	2.00	4.00	8.00
❑ Polydor PD-1-6109	Donald Clark Osmond	1977	2.00	4.00	8.00
OSMOND, DONNY AND MARIE					
45s					
❑ MGM 14735	I'm Leaving It (All) Up to You/The Umbrella Song	1974	—	2.50	5.00
❑ MGM 14765	Morning Side of the Mountain/One of These Days	1974	—	2.00	4.00
❑ MGM 14807	Make the World Go Away/Living on My Suspicion	1975	—	2.00	4.00
❑ MGM 14840	Deep Purple/Take Me Back Again	1975	—	2.00	4.00
❑ Polydor 14363	Ain't Nothin' Like the Real Thing/Sing	1976	—	2.00	4.00
❑ Polydor 14439	(You're My) Soul and Inspiration/Now We're Together	1977	—	2.00	4.00
❑ Polydor 14456	Baby, I'm Sold on You/Sure Would Be Nice	1978	—	2.00	4.00
❑ Polydor 14474	May Tomorrow Be a Perfect Day/I Want to Give You My Everything	1978	—	2.00	4.00
❑ Polydor 14510	On the Shelf/Certified Honey	1978	—	2.00	4.00
Albums					
❑ MGM M3G-4968	I'm Leaving It All Up to You	1974	2.50	5.00	10.00

Number	Title (A Side/B Side)	Yr	VG	VG+	NM
❑ MGM M3G-4996	Make the World Go Away	1975	2.50	5.00	10.00
❑ Polydor PD-1-6068	Donny & Marie — Featuring Songs from Their Television Show	1976	2.00	4.00	8.00
❑ Polydor PD-1-6083	Donny & Marie — New Season	1976	2.00	4.00	8.00
❑ Polydor PD-1-6127	Winning Combination	1978	2.00	4.00	8.00
❑ Polydor PD-1-6169	Goin' Coconuts	1978	2.00	4.00	8.00

OSMOND, MARIE

45s

Number	Title (A Side/B Side)	Yr	VG	VG+	NM
❑ Capitol B-5445	Until I Fall in Love Again/I Don't Want to Go Too Far	1985	—	—	3.00
❑ Capitol B-5478	Meet Me in Montana/What Do Lonely People Do	1985	—	—	3.00
—With Dan Seals					
❑ Capitol B-5521	There's No Stopping Your Heart/Blue Sky Shinin'	1985	—	—	3.00
❑ Capitol B-5521 [Picture Sleeve]	There's No Stopping Your Heart/Blue Sky Shinin'	1985	—	2.50	5.00
❑ Capitol B-5563	Read My Lips/That Old Devil Moon	1986	—	—	3.00
❑ Capitol B-5613	You're Still New to Me/New Love	1986	—	—	3.00
—With Paul Davis					
❑ Capitol B-5663	I Only Wanted You/We're Gonna Need a Love Song	1986	—	—	3.00
❑ Capitol B-5703	Everybody's Crazy 'Bout My Baby/Making Music	1987	—	—	3.00
❑ Capitol B-44044	Cry Just a Little/More Than Dancing	1987	—	—	3.00
❑ Capitol B-44176	Without a Trace/Baby's Blue Eyes	1988	—	—	3.00
❑ Capitol B-44215	Sweet Life/My Home Town Boy	1988	—	—	3.00
—A-side: With Paul Davis					
❑ Capitol B-44269	I'm in Love and He's in Dallas/My Home Town Boy	1989	—	—	3.00
❑ Capitol B-44412	Steppin' Stone/What Would You Do About Me If You Were Me	1989	—	—	3.00
❑ Capitol B-44468	Slowly But Surely/What Would You Do About You	1989	—	2.00	4.00
❑ Capitol NR-44505	Let Me Be the First/What's a Little Lovin' Between Friends	1990	—	2.50	5.00
❑ Curb 76840	Like a Hurricane/I'll Be Faithful to You	1990	—	2.00	4.00
❑ Curb 76851	Paper Roses/Think with Your Heart	1990	—	2.00	4.00
❑ Elektra 69882	I'm Learning/Look Who's Getting Over Who	1982	—	2.00	4.00
❑ Elektra 69995	Back to Believing Again/Look Who's Getting Over Who	1982	—	2.00	4.00
❑ MGM 14609	Paper Roses/Least of All You	1973	—	2.50	5.00
❑ MGM 14694	My Little Corner of the World/It's Just the Other Way Around	1974	—	2.00	4.00
❑ MGM 14786	Who's Sorry Now/This I Promise You	1975	—	2.00	4.00
❑ Polydor 14333	"A" My Name Is Alice/Weeping Willow	1976	—	2.00	4.00
❑ Polydor 14385	This Is the Way That I Feel/Play the Music Loud	1977	—	2.00	4.00
❑ Polydor 14405	Cry, Baby, Cry/Please Tell Him I Said Hello	1977	—	2.00	4.00
❑ RCA PB-13680	Who's Counting/'Til the Best Comes Along	1983	—	2.00	4.00

Albums

Number	Title (A Side/B Side)	Yr	VG	VG+	NM
❑ Capitol ST-12414	There's No Stopping Your Heart	1985	2.00	4.00	8.00
❑ Capitol ST-12516	I Only Wanted You	1986	2.00	4.00	8.00
❑ Capitol C1-48968	All in Love	1988	2.00	4.00	8.00
❑ Capitol C1-91781	Steppin' Stone	1989	2.50	5.00	10.00
❑ MGM SE-4910	Paper Roses	1973	3.00	6.00	12.00
❑ MGM M3G-4944	In My Little Corner of the World	1974	3.00	6.00	12.00
❑ MGM M3G-4979	Who's Sorry Now	1975	3.00	6.00	12.00
❑ Polydor PD-1-6099	This Is the Way That I Feel	1977	2.00	4.00	8.00

OSMONDS, THE

45s

Number	Title (A Side/B Side)	Yr	VG	VG+	NM
❑ Barnaby 2002	Mary Elizabeth/Speak Like a Child	1968	2.50	5.00	10.00
❑ Barnaby 2004	I've Got Loving on My Mind/Mollie- "A"	1968	2.50	5.00	10.00
❑ Barnaby 2005	Taking a Chance on Love/Groove With What You Got	1969	2.50	5.00	10.00
❑ Elektra 47438	I Think About Your Lovin'/Working Man's Blues	1982	—	2.00	4.00
❑ Elektra 69883	Never Ending Song of Love/You'll Be Seeing Me	1982	—	2.00	4.00
❑ Elektra 69969	It's Like Falling in Love/Your Leaving Was the Last Thing on My Mind	1982	—	2.00	4.00
❑ EMI America 8298	Baby When Your Heart Breaks Down/Love Burning Down	1985	—	—	3.00
❑ EMI America 8313	Baby Wants/Lovin' Proof	1986	—	—	3.00
❑ EMI America 8325	You Look Like the One I Love/It's Only a Heartache	1986	—	—	3.00
❑ EMI America 8360	Looking for Suzanne/Back in Your Arms	1986	—	—	3.00
❑ EMI America 43033	Slow Ride/Heartbreak Radio	1987	—	—	3.00
❑ Mercury 74056	Love on the Line/You're Mine	1979	—	2.00	4.00
❑ Mercury 74079	Emily/Rainin'	1979	—	2.00	4.00
❑ MGM 13162	Be My Little Baby Bumble Bee/I Wouldn't Trade the Silver in My Mother's Hair	1963	3.75	7.50	15.00
❑ MGM 13174	Theme from "The Travels of Jamie McPheeters"/Aura Lee	1963	3.75	7.50	15.00
❑ MGM 13281	Mr. Sandman/My Mom	1964	5.00	10.00	20.00
❑ MGM 14159	Movin' Along/Open Up Your Heart	1970	2.00	4.00	8.00
❑ MGM 14193	One Bad Apple/He Ain't Heavy, He's My Brother	1970	—	3.00	6.00
❑ MGM 14259	Double Lovin'/Chilly Winds	1971	—	3.00	6.00
❑ MGM 14295	Yo-Yo/Keep on My Side	1971	—	3.00	6.00
❑ MGM 14324	Down by the Lazy River/He's the Light of the World	1971	—	3.00	6.00
❑ MGM 14405	Hold Her Tight/Love Is	1972	—	2.50	5.00
❑ MGM 14450	Crazy Horses/That's My Girl	1972	—	2.50	5.00
❑ MGM 14562	Goin' Home/Are You Up There	1973	—	2.50	5.00
❑ MGM 14617	Let Me In/One Way Ticket to Anywhere	1973	—	2.50	5.00
❑ MGM 14746	Love Me for a Reason/Fever	1974	—	2.50	5.00
❑ MGM 14791	The Proud One/The Last Day Is Coming	1975	—	2.50	5.00
❑ MGM 14831	Thank You/I'm Still Gonna Need You	1975	—	2.50	5.00
❑ Polydor 14348	Check It Out/I Can't Live a Dream	1976	—	2.00	4.00
❑ Uni 55015	I Can't Stop/Flower Music	1967	2.50	5.00	10.00
❑ Uni 55276	I Can't Stop/Flower Music	1971	—	3.00	6.00
❑ Warner Bros. 28982	Any Time/Desperately	1985	—	—	3.00
❑ Warner Bros. 29312	If Every Man Had a Woman Like You/Come Back to Me	1984	—	2.00	4.00
❑ Warner Bros. 29387	Where Does An Angel Go When She Cries/One More for Lovers	1984	—	2.00	4.00
❑ Warner Bros. 29594	She's Ready for Someone to Love Her/You Make the Long Road Shorter with Your Love	1983	—	2.00	4.00

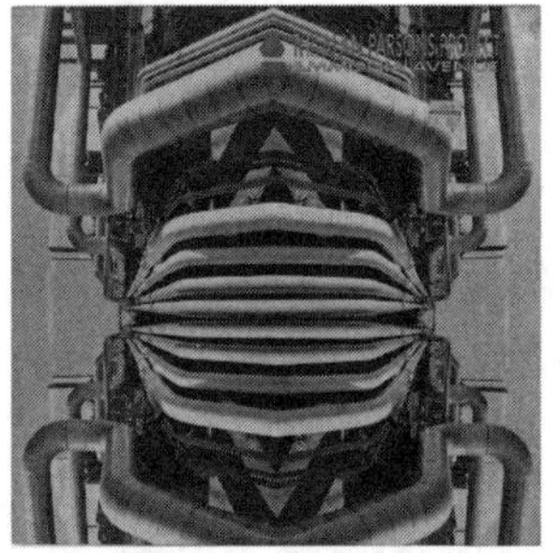

Number	Title (A Side/B Side)	Yr	VG	VG+	NM
Albums					
❑ Elektra 60180	The Osmond Brothers	1982	2.50	5.00	10.00
❑ Mercury SRM-1-3766	Steppin' Out	1979	2.50	5.00	10.00
❑ Metro M 543 [M]	We Sing You a Merry Christmas	1965	3.75	7.50	15.00
—Reissue of 4187 with one track missing and remaining contents rearranged					
❑ Metro MS 543 [S]	We Sing You a Merry Christmas	1965	5.00	10.00	20.00
❑ MGM E-4146 [M]	Songs We Sang on the Andy Williams Show	1963	6.25	12.50	25.00
❑ MGM SE-4146 [S]	Songs We Sang on the Andy Williams Show	1963	7.50	15.00	30.00
—As "The Osmond Brothers"					
❑ MGM E-4187 [M]	We Sing You a Merry Christmas	1963	6.25	12.50	25.00
—As "The Osmond Brothers"					
❑ MGM SE-4187 [S]	We Sing You a Merry Christmas	1963	7.50	15.00	30.00
❑ MGM E-4235 [M]	The Osmond Brothers Sing the All-Time Hymn Favorites	1964	5.00	10.00	20.00
❑ MGM SE-4235 [S]	The Osmond Brothers Sing the All-Time Hymn Favorites	1964	6.25	12.50	25.00
❑ MGM E-4291 [M]	The New Sound of the Osmond Brothers	1965	5.00	10.00	20.00
❑ MGM SE-4291 [S]	The New Sound of the Osmond Brothers	1965	6.25	12.50	25.00
❑ MGM SE-4724	Osmonds	1971	3.00	6.00	12.00
❑ MGM SE-4770	Homemade	1971	7.50	15.00	30.00
—With tear-off poster intact; deduct 60 percent if poster is not attached					
❑ MGM SE-4796	Phase-III	1972	3.00	6.00	12.00
❑ MGM SE-4826 [(2)]	The Osmonds "Live"	1972	3.75	7.50	15.00
❑ MGM SE-4851	Crazy Horses	1972	3.00	6.00	12.00
❑ MGM SE-4902	The Plan	1973	2.50	5.00	10.00
❑ MGM M3G-4939	Love Me for a Reason	1974	2.50	5.00	10.00
❑ MGM M3G-4993	The Proud One	1975	2.50	5.00	10.00
❑ MGM MG-2-5012 [(2)]	Around the World — Live in Concert	1975	3.00	6.00	12.00
❑ Polydor PD-1-6077	Brainstorm	1976	2.50	5.00	10.00
❑ Polydor PD-2-8001 [(2)]	The Osmond Christmas Album	1976	3.75	7.50	15.00
—Includes group, solo and duet recordings					
❑ Polydor PD-2-9005	The Osmonds Greatest Hits	1977	3.00	6.00	12.00
❑ Warner Bros. 25070	One Way Rider	1984	2.00	4.00	8.00
OTIS, JOHNNY					
45s					
❑ Atlantic 2409	Keep the Faith — Part I/Keep the Faith — Part II	1967	3.00	6.00	12.00
❑ Capitol F3799	Can't You Hear Me Callin'/My Ding-a-Ling	1957	12.50	25.00	50.00
❑ Capitol F3800	Ma, He's Makin' Eyes at Me/In the Dark	1957	12.50	25.00	50.00
❑ Capitol F3801	Stay with Me/Tell Me So	1957	12.50	25.00	50.00
❑ Capitol F3802	It's Too Soon to Know/Star of Love	1957	12.50	25.00	50.00
❑ Capitol F3852	Bye Bye Baby/Good Golly	1957	6.25	12.50	25.00
❑ Capitol F3889	Well, Well, Well/You Just Kissed Me Goodbye	1958	6.25	12.50	25.00
❑ Capitol F3966	Willie and the Hand Jive/Ring-a-Ling	1958	7.50	15.00	30.00
❑ Capitol F4060	Willie Did the Cha Cha/Crazy Country Hop	1958	6.25	12.50	25.00
❑ Capitol F4156	My Dear/You	1959	5.00	10.00	20.00
❑ Capitol F4168 [M]	Castin' My Spell/Telephone Baby	1959	5.00	10.00	20.00
❑ Capitol F4168 [S]	Castin' My Spell/Telephone Baby	1959	12.50	25.00	50.00
❑ Capitol F4226	Three Girls Named Molly (Doin' the Hully Gully)/I'll Do the Same for You	1959	5.00	10.00	20.00
❑ Capitol F4260	Let the Sun Shine in My Life/Baby, Just You	1959	5.00	10.00	20.00
❑ Capitol 4326	Mumblin' Mosie/Hey Baby, Don't You Know	1960	3.75	7.50	15.00
❑ Dig 119	Hey! Hey! Hey! Hey!/Let the Sunshine in My Heart	1956	7.50	15.00	30.00
❑ Dig 122	The Midnite Creeper (Part 1)/The Midnite Creeper (Part 2)	1956	7.50	15.00	30.00
❑ Dig 132	My Eyes Are Full of Tears/Turtle Dove	1957	7.50	15.00	30.00
❑ Dig 134	Wa Wa (Part 1)/Wa Wa (Part 2)	1957	7.50	15.00	30.00
❑ Dig 139	Stop, Look and Love Me/The Night Is Young	1957	7.50	15.00	30.00
❑ Eldo 106	The New Bo Diddley/The Jelly Roll	1960	3.75	7.50	15.00
❑ Eldo 152	Keep the Faith (Part 1)/Keep the Faith (Part 2)	1968	2.00	4.00	8.00
❑ Eldo 153	Long Distance/Banana Peels	1968	2.00	4.00	8.00
❑ Epic 5-10606	You Can Depend on Me/The Watts Breakaway	1970	—	3.00	6.00
❑ Epic 5-10757	Willie and the Hand Jive/Goin' Back to L.A.	1971	—	3.00	6.00
—B-side with Delmar Evans					
❑ Hawk Sound 1003	Jaws/Good to the Last Drop	1975	—	2.50	5.00
❑ Kent 506	Country Girl/Bye Bye Baby	1969	2.00	4.00	8.00
❑ Kent 4521	Shuggie's Blues/Cool Ade	1969	2.00	4.00	8.00
❑ King 5581	Hand Jive One More Time/Baby I Got News for You	1961	3.75	7.50	15.00
❑ King 5606	She's All Right/It Must Be Love	1962	3.75	7.50	15.00
❑ King 5634	Queen of the Twist/I Know My Love Is True	1962	3.75	7.50	15.00

Number	Title (A Side/B Side)	Yr	VG	VG+	NM
❑ King 5690	The Hey Hey Hey Song/Early in the Morning Blues	1962	3.75	7.50	15.00
❑ King 5707	Somebody Call the Station/Yes	1963	3.00	6.00	12.00
❑ King 5790	Bye, Bye Baby/The Hash	1963	3.00	6.00	12.00
❑ Mercury 8263	Oopy Doo/Stardust	1952	12.50	25.00	50.00
❑ Mercury 8273	One-Nighter Blues/Goomp Blues	1952	12.50	25.00	50.00
❑ Mercury 8289	Call Operator 210/Baby Baby Blues	1952	12.50	25.00	50.00
❑ Mercury 8295	Gypsy Blues/The Candle's Burning Low	1952	12.50	25.00	50.00
❑ Mercury 70038	Why Don't You Believe Me/Wishing Well	1953	12.50	25.00	50.00
❑ Mercury 70050	Love Bug Boogie/Brown Skin Butterball	1953	12.50	25.00	50.00
❑ Okeh 7332	Watts Breakaway/You Can Depend On Me	1969	—	3.00	6.00
❑ Peacock 1625	Young Girl/Rock Me Baby	1953	20.00	40.00	80.00
❑ Peacock 1636	Shake It/I Won't Be Your Fool No More	1954	12.50	25.00	50.00
❑ Peacock 1648	Sittin' Here Drinkin'/You Got Me Crying	1955	12.50	25.00	50.00
❑ Peacock 1675	Butter Ball/Dandy's Boogie	1957	12.50	25.00	50.00
❑ Savoy 731	Double Crossing Blues/Back Alley Blues	1950	25.00	50.00	100.00
—B-side by the Beale Street Gang					
❑ Savoy 731	Double Crossing Blues/Ain't Nothin' Shakin'	1950	30.00	60.00	120.00
❑ Savoy 750	Cupid Boogie/Just Can't Get Free	1950	15.00	30.00	60.00
❑ Savoy 764	Wedding Blues/Far Away Blues (Xmas Blues)	1950	15.00	30.00	60.00
❑ Savoy 766	Rockin' Blues/My Heart Tells Me	1950	15.00	30.00	60.00
❑ Savoy 777	Gee Baby/Mambo Boogie	1951	12.50	25.00	50.00
❑ Savoy 780	Doggin' Blues/Living and Loving You	1951	12.50	25.00	50.00
❑ Savoy 787	I Dream/Hangover Blues	1951	12.50	25.00	50.00
❑ Savoy 788	All Nite Long/New Love	1951	12.50	25.00	50.00
❑ Savoy 812	Warning Blues/I'll Ask My Heart	1951	12.50	25.00	50.00
❑ Savoy 815	Harlem Nocturne/Midnight in the Barrelhouse	1951	12.50	25.00	50.00
❑ Savoy 824	Get Together Blues/Chittlin' Switch	1951	12.50	25.00	50.00
❑ Savoy 855	It Ain't the Beauty/Gonna Take a Train	1952	12.50	25.00	50.00
Albums					
❑ Alligator AL-4726	The New Johnny Otis Show	1982	2.50	5.00	10.00
❑ Capitol T 940 [M]	The Johnny Otis Show	1958	62.50	125.00	250.00
❑ Capitol C1-92858 [(2)]	The Capitol Years	1989	3.75	7.50	15.00
❑ Epic BN 26524	Cuttin' Up	1970	6.25	12.50	25.00
❑ Epic EG 30473 [(2)]	The Johnny Otis Show Live at Monterey	1971	7.50	15.00	30.00
❑ Kent KST-534	Cold Shot	1968	6.25	12.50	25.00
❑ Savoy SJL-2230 [(2)]	The Original Johnny Otis Show	1978	3.75	7.50	15.00
❑ Savoy SJL-2252 [(2)]	The Original Johnny Otis Show, Vol. 2	1980	3.75	7.50	15.00

OUTSIDERS, THE

Number	Title (A Side/B Side)	Yr	VG	VG+	NM
45s					
❑ Bell 904	Changes/Lost in My World	1970	—	3.00	6.00
❑ Capitol 2055	Little Bit of Lovin'/I Will Love You	1967	2.00	4.00	8.00
❑ Capitol 2216	Oh How It Hurts/We Ain't Gonna Make It	1968	2.00	4.00	8.00
❑ Capitol 5573	Time Won't Let Me/Was It Really Real	1966	3.00	6.00	12.00
❑ Capitol 5646	Girl in Love/What Makes You So Bad	1966	2.50	5.00	10.00
❑ Capitol 5701	Respectable/Lost in My World	1966	2.50	5.00	10.00
❑ Capitol 5759	Help Me Girl/You Gotta Look	1966	2.50	5.00	10.00
❑ Capitol 5843	I'll Give You Time/I'm Not Trying to Hurt You	1967	2.00	4.00	8.00
❑ Capitol 5892	I Just Can't See You Anymore/Gotta Leave Us Alone	1967	2.00	4.00	8.00
❑ Capitol 5955	I'll See You in the Summertime/And Now You Want My Sympathy	1967	2.00	4.00	8.00
❑ Ellen 503	Rickity-Boom-Bal-Aye/The Bird Rattle	196?	3.75	7.50	15.00
❑ Kapp 2104	Tinker, Tailor/Oh You're Not So Pretty	1970	—	3.00	6.00
Albums					
❑ Capitol ST 2501 [S]	Time Won't Let Me	1966	7.50	15.00	30.00
❑ Capitol T 2501 [M]	Time Won't Let Me	1966	6.25	12.50	25.00
❑ Capitol ST 2558 [S]	The Outsiders Album #2	1966	7.50	15.00	30.00
❑ Capitol T 2568 [M]	The Outsiders Album #2	1966	6.25	12.50	25.00
❑ Capitol ST 2636 [S]	In	1967	6.25	12.50	25.00
❑ Capitol T 2636 [M]	In	1967	7.50	15.00	30.00
❑ Capitol ST 2745 [S]	Happening "Live!"	1967	6.25	12.50	25.00
❑ Capitol T 2745 [M]	Happening "Live!"	1967	7.50	15.00	30.00
❑ Rhino RNLP-70132	The Best of the Outsiders (1965-1968)	1986	2.50	5.00	10.00

OZARK MOUNTAIN DAREDEVILS

Number	Title (A Side/B Side)	Yr	VG	VG+	NM
45s					
❑ A&M 1477	Country Girl/Within Without	1973	—	2.50	5.00
❑ A&M 1515	If You Wanna Get to Heaven/Spaceship Orion	1974	—	2.50	5.00
❑ A&M 1623	Look Away/It Probably Always Will	1974	—	2.00	4.00
❑ A&M 1654	Jackie Blue/Better Days	1974	—	2.00	4.00
❑ A&M 1709	Colorado Song/Thin Ice	1975	—	2.00	4.00
❑ A&M 1772	If I Only Knew/Dreams	1975	—	2.00	4.00
❑ A&M 1808	Keep On Churnin'/Time Warp	1976	—	2.00	4.00
❑ A&M 1809	You Make It Right/Dreams	1976	—	2.00	4.00
❑ A&M 1842	Chicken Train Stomp/Journey to the Center of Your Heart	1976	—	2.00	4.00
❑ A&M 1880	Noah (Let It Rain)/Red Plum	1976	—	2.00	4.00
❑ A&M 1888	You Know Like I Know/Arroyo	1976	—	2.00	4.00
❑ A&M 1989	Crazy Lovin'/Stinghead	1977	—	2.00	4.00
❑ A&M 2016	Following (The Way That I Feel)/Snowbound	1978	—	2.00	4.00
❑ Columbia 1-11247	Take You Tonight/Runnin' Out	1980	—	2.00	4.00
❑ Columbia 1-11357	Oh Darlin'/Sailin' Around the World	1980	—	2.00	4.00
Albums					
❑ A&M SP-3110	The Ozark Mountain Daredevils	198?	2.00	4.00	8.00
—Budget-line reissue					
❑ A&M SP-3192	It'll Shine When It Shines	198?	2.00	4.00	8.00
—Budget-line reissue					
❑ A&M SP-3202	The Best of Ozark Mountain Daredevils	1982	2.50	5.00	10.00
❑ A&M SP-3654	It'll Shine When It Shines	1974	3.00	6.00	12.00

Number	Title (A Side/B Side)	Yr	VG	VG+	NM
❑ A&M SP-4411	The Ozark Mountain Daredevils	1973	3.00	6.00	12.00
❑ A&M SP-4549	The Car Over the Lake Album	1975	3.00	6.00	12.00
❑ A&M SP-4601	Men from Earth	1976	3.00	6.00	12.00
❑ A&M SP-4662	Don't Look Down	1977	3.00	6.00	12.00
❑ A&M SP-6006 [(2)]	It's Alive	1978	3.75	7.50	15.00
❑ Columbia JC 36375	Ozark Mountain Daredevils	1980	2.50	5.00	10.00
❑ Sounds Great SG-5004	The Lost Cabin Sessions	1985	2.50	5.00	10.00

P

PABLO CRUISE

45s

Number	Title (A Side/B Side)	Yr	VG	VG+	NM
❑ A&M 1695	Island Woman/Denny	1975	—	2.50	5.00
❑ A&M 1742	What Does It Take/In My Own Quiet Way	1975	—	2.50	5.00
❑ A&M 1815	(I Think) It's Finally Over/Look to the Sky	1976	—	2.50	5.00
❑ A&M 1834	Don't Believe It/Look to the Sky	1976	—	2.50	5.00
❑ A&M 1876	Crystal/Look to the Sky	1976	—	2.50	5.00
❑ A&M 1910	A Place in the Sun/El Verano	1977	—	2.50	5.00
❑ A&M 1920	Whatcha Gonna Do?/Atlanta June	1977	—	2.00	4.00
❑ A&M 1976	A Place in the Sun/El Verano	1977	—	2.00	4.00
❑ A&M 1999	Atlanta June/Never Had a Love	1977	—	2.00	4.00
❑ A&M 2048	Love Will Find a Way/Always Be Together	1978	—	2.00	4.00
❑ A&M 2076	Don't Want to Live Without It/Raging Fire	1978	—	2.00	4.00
❑ A&M 2112	I Go to Rio/Raging Fire	1979	—	2.00	4.00
❑ A&M 2195	I Want You Tonight/Family Man	1979	—	2.00	4.00
❑ A&M 2349	Cool Love/Jenny	1981	—	2.00	4.00
❑ A&M 2373	Slip Away/That's When	1981	—	2.00	4.00
❑ A&M 2570	Another World/Will You, Won't You	1983	—	—	3.00

Albums

Number	Title (A Side/B Side)	Yr	VG	VG+	NM
❑ A&M SP-3111	Pablo Cruise	198?	2.00	4.00	8.00
—Budget-line reissue of 4528					
❑ A&M SP-3198	Worlds Away	198?	2.00	4.00	8.00
—Budget-line reissue of 4697					
❑ A&M SP-3236	A Place in the Sun	198?	2.00	4.00	8.00
—Budget-line reissue of 4625					
❑ A&M SP-3712	Part of the Game	1979	2.50	5.00	10.00
❑ A&M SP-3726	Reflector	1981	2.50	5.00	10.00
❑ A&M SP-4528	Pablo Cruise	1975	2.50	5.00	10.00
❑ A&M SP-4575	Lifeline	1976	2.50	5.00	10.00
❑ A&M SP-4625	A Place in the Sun	1977	2.50	5.00	10.00
❑ A&M SP-4697	Worlds Away	1978	2.50	5.00	10.00
❑ A&M SP-4909	Out of Our Hands	1983	2.50	5.00	10.00

PACIFIC GAS & ELECTRIC

45s

Number	Title (A Side/B Side)	Yr	VG	VG+	NM
❑ Columbia 45009	Redneck/Bluebuster	1969	—	3.00	6.00
❑ Columbia 45158	Are You Ready?/Staggolee	1970	—	3.00	6.00
—Available with at least three different label variations, all equal in value					
❑ Columbia 45221	Elvira/Father Come On Home	1970	—	2.50	5.00
❑ Columbia 45304	The Time Has Come/Death Row No. 172	1971	—	2.50	5.00
❑ Columbia 45444	One More River to Cross/Rocky Roller's Lament	1971	—	2.50	5.00
❑ Columbia 45519	Thank God for You Baby/See the Monkey Run	1971	—	2.50	5.00
❑ Columbia 45621	Heat Wave/We Did What We Could	1972	—	2.50	5.00
❑ Kent 4538	The Hunter/Long Handled Shovel	1971	3.00	6.00	12.00
❑ Power 1701	Wade in the Water/Live Love	1969	2.50	5.00	10.00

Albums

Number	Title (A Side/B Side)	Yr	VG	VG+	NM
❑ ABC Dunhill DSX-50157	Pacific Gas and Electric Starring Charlie Allen	1974	3.00	6.00	12.00
❑ Bright Orange 701	Get It On	1968	10.00	20.00	40.00
❑ Columbia CS 1017	Are You Ready	1970	3.75	7.50	15.00
—"360 Sound" label					
❑ Columbia CS 9900	Pacific Gas and Electric	1969	3.75	7.50	15.00
—"360 Sound" label					
❑ Columbia C 30362	PG&E	1971	3.00	6.00	12.00
❑ Columbia C 32019	The Best of Pacific Gas & Electric	1972	3.00	6.00	12.00
❑ Power 701	Get It On	1969	6.25	12.50	25.00

Number	Title (A Side/B Side)	Yr	VG	VG+	NM
PALMER, ROBERT					
45s					
❑ EMI 50183	She Makes My Day/Casting a Spell	1989	—	—	3.00
❑ EMI Manhattan 50133	Simply Irresistible/Nova	1988	—	—	3.00
❑ EMI Manhattan 50157	Early in the Morning/Disturbing Behavior	1988	—	—	3.00
❑ Island 006	Sneakin' Sally Through the Alley/Epidemic	1974	—	2.50	5.00
❑ Island 015	Get Ta Steppin'/Get Right On Down	1975	—	2.50	5.00
❑ Island 042	Which One of Us Is the Fool/Get Outside	1975	—	2.50	5.00
❑ Island 049	Pressure Drop/Give Me an Inch Girl	1976	—	2.50	5.00
❑ Island 075	Man Smart, Woman Smarter/Keep in Touch	1976	—	2.50	5.00
❑ Island 081	One Last Look/Some People Can Do What They Want	1977	—	2.50	5.00
❑ Island 100	Every Kinda People/How Much Fun	1978	—	2.00	4.00
❑ Island 105	You Overwhelm Me/Come Over	1978	—	2.00	4.00
❑ Island 8697	Where Can It Go/You're Gonna Get What's Coming	1978	—	2.00	4.00
❑ Island 49016	Bad Case of Loving You (Doctor, Doctor)/Love Can Run Faster	1979	—	2.00	4.00
❑ Island 49094	In Walks Love Again/Jealous	1979	—	2.00	4.00
❑ Island 49137	Can We Still Be Friends/Remember to Remember	1979	—	2.00	4.00
❑ Island 49554	Style Kills/Johnny and Mary	1980	—	2.00	4.00
❑ Island 49620	Looking for Clues/Woke Up Laughing	1980	—	2.00	4.00
❑ Island 50042	Some Guys Have All the Luck/Too Good to Be True	1982	—	2.00	4.00
❑ Island 99139	Bad Case of Loving You/Sweet Lies	1989	—	—	3.00
❑ Island 99377	Sweet Lies/Want You More	1988	—	—	3.00
❑ Island 99537	I Didn't Mean to Turn You On/Get It Through Your Heart	1986	—	—	3.00
❑ Island 99545	Hyperactive/Woke Up Laughing	1986	—	—	3.00
❑ Island 99570	Addicted to Love/Let's Fall in Love Tonight	1986	—	—	3.00
❑ Island 99597	Discipline of Love (Why Did You Do It)/Dance for Me	1985	—	—	3.00
❑ Island 99835	Pride/(B-side unknown)	1983	—	—	3.00
❑ Island 99866	You Are In My System/Deadline	1983	—	—	3.00
❑ MCA 52643	All Around the World/It's Not Difficult	1985	—	—	3.00
Albums					
❑ EMI Manhattan E1-48057	Heavy Nova	1988	2.50	5.00	10.00
❑ Island ILPS 9294	Sneakin' Sally Through the Alley	1975	3.00	6.00	12.00
❑ Island ILPS 9372	Pressure Drop	1976	3.00	6.00	12.00
❑ Island ILPS 9420	Some People Can Do What They Like	1977	3.00	6.00	12.00
❑ Island ILPS 9476	Double Fun	1978	3.00	6.00	12.00
—Original copies of the above four albums were NOT distributed by Warner Bros.					
❑ Island ILPS 9544	Secrets	1979	2.50	5.00	10.00
❑ Island ILPS 9595	Clues	1980	2.50	5.00	10.00
❑ Island ILPS 9665	Maybe It's Live	1982	2.50	5.00	10.00
❑ Island 90065	Pride	1983	2.50	5.00	10.00
❑ Island 90086	Sneakin' Sally Through the Alley	1984	2.00	4.00	8.00
❑ Island 90087	Pressure Drop	1984	2.00	4.00	8.00
❑ Island 90089	Secrets	1984	2.00	4.00	8.00
❑ Island 90471	Riptide	1985	2.50	5.00	10.00
❑ Island 90493	Clues	1986	2.00	4.00	8.00
❑ Island 90494	Double Fun	1986	2.00	4.00	8.00
❑ Island 91318	Addictions Volume I	1989	3.00	6.00	12.00
—Original pressing available only for a short time					
PARIS SISTERS, THE					
45s					
❑ Capitol 2081	Golden Days/Greener Days	1968	2.00	4.00	8.00
❑ Cavalier 828	Christmas in My Home Town/Man with the Mistletoe Moustache	197?	—	3.00	6.00
❑ Decca 29372	Ooh La La/Whose Arms Are You Missing	1954	6.25	12.50	25.00
❑ Decca 29488	Baby, Honey, Baby/Huckleberry Pie	1955	6.25	12.50	25.00
❑ Decca 29527	His and Hers/Truly Do	1955	6.25	12.50	25.00
—With Gary Crosby					
❑ Decca 29574	The Know How/I Wanna	1955	6.25	12.50	25.00
❑ Decca 29744	Lover Boy/Oh Yes You Do	1955	6.25	12.50	25.00
❑ Decca 29891	I Love You Dear/Mistaken	1956	6.25	12.50	25.00
❑ Decca 29970	Daughter! Daughter!/So Much — So Very Much	1956	6.25	12.50	25.00
❑ Decca 30554	Don't Tell Anybody/Mind Reader	1958	5.00	10.00	20.00
❑ GNP Crescendo 410	Stand Naked Clown/Ugliest Girl in Town	1968	2.00	4.00	8.00
❑ Gregmark 2	Be My Boy/I'll Be Crying Tomorrow	1961	5.00	10.00	20.00
❑ Gregmark 6	I Love How You Love Me/All Through the Night	1961	6.25	12.50	25.00
❑ Gregmark 10	He Knows I Love Him Too Much/Lonely Girl's Prayer	1962	5.00	10.00	20.00
❑ Gregmark 12	Let Me Be the One/What Am I to Do	1962	5.00	10.00	20.00
❑ Gregmark 13	Yes I Love You/Once Upon a While Ago	1962	5.00	10.00	20.00
—All the Gregmark records were Phil Spector productions					
❑ Imperial 5465	Old Enough to Cry/Tell Me More	1957	5.00	10.00	20.00
❑ Imperial 5487	Some Day/My Original Love	1958	5.00	10.00	20.00
❑ Mercury 72320	Once Upon a Time/When I Fall in Love	1964	2.50	5.00	10.00
❑ Mercury 72468	Always Waitin'/Why Do I Take It from You	1965	2.50	5.00	10.00
❑ MGM 13236	Dream Lover/Lonely Girl	1964	3.75	7.50	15.00
❑ Reprise 0440	Sincerely/Too Good to Be True	1965	2.50	5.00	10.00
❑ Reprise 0472	I'm Me/You	1966	2.50	5.00	10.00
❑ Reprise 0511	It's My Party/My Good Friend	1966	2.50	5.00	10.00
❑ Reprise 0548	Some of Your Lovin'/Long After Tonight Is All Over	1967	2.50	5.00	10.00
Albums					
❑ Reprise R-6259 [M]	Everything Under the Sun	1967	10.00	20.00	40.00
❑ Reprise RS-6359 [S]	Everything Under the Sun	1967	15.00	30.00	60.00
❑ Sidewalk DT 5906 [R]	Golden Hits of the Paris Sisters	1967	7.50	15.00	30.00
❑ Sidewalk T 5906 [M]	Golden Hits of the Paris Sisters	1967	12.50	25.00	50.00
❑ Unifilms 505 [M]	The Paris Sisters Sing Songs from Glass House	1966	10.00	20.00	40.00
❑ Unifilms S-505 [S]	The Paris Sisters Sing Songs from Glass House	1966	12.50	25.00	50.00

Number	Title (A Side/B Side)	Yr	VG	VG+	NM
PARLIAMENT					
45s					
❑ Casablanca 0003	The Goose (Part 1)/The Goose (Part 2)	1974	—	3.00	6.00
❑ Casablanca 0013	Up for the Down Stroke/Presence of a Brain	1974	—	3.00	6.00
❑ Casablanca 0104	Up for the Down Stroke/Presence of a Brain	1974	—	2.50	5.00
❑ Casablanca 803	Up for the Down Stroke/Presence of a Brain	1974	—	2.50	5.00
❑ Casablanca 811	Testify/I Can Move You	1974	—	2.50	5.00
❑ Casablanca 831	Chocolate City/Chocolate City (Part 2)	1975	—	2.50	5.00
❑ Casablanca 843	Ride On/Big Footin'	1975	—	2.50	5.00
❑ Casablanca 852	P. Funk (Wants to Get Funked Up)/Night of the Tempasaurus Peoples	1976	—	2.50	5.00
❑ Casablanca 856	Tear the Roof Off the Sucker (Give Up the Funk)/P-Funk	1976	—	2.50	5.00
—Blue label					
❑ Casablanca 864	Star Child (Mothership Connection)/Supergroovealistic	1976	—	2.50	5.00
❑ Casablanca 871	Do That Stuff/Handcuffs	1976	—	2.50	5.00
❑ Casablanca 875	Dr. Funkenstein/Children of Production	1977	—	2.50	5.00
❑ Casablanca 892	Fantasy Is Reality/The Landing (Of the Mothership)	1977	—	2.50	5.00
❑ Casablanca 900	Bop Gun (Endangered Species)/I've Been Watchin' You	1977	—	2.50	5.00
❑ Casablanca 909	Flash Light/Swing Down, Sweet Chariot	1978	—	2.50	5.00
❑ Casablanca 921	Funkentelechy/Funkentelechy (Part 2)	1978	—	2.50	5.00
❑ Casablanca 950	Aqua Boogie (A Psychoalphadiscobetabioaquadoloop)/ (You're a Fish and I'm a) Water Sign	1978	—	2.50	5.00
❑ Casablanca 976	Rumpofsteelskin/Liquid Sunshine	1979	—	2.50	5.00
❑ Casablanca 2222	Party People/Party People (Part 2)	1979	—	2.50	5.00
❑ Casablanca 2235	Theme from The Black Hole/(You're a Fish and I'm a) Water Sign	1980	—	2.50	5.00
❑ Casablanca 2250	The Big Bang Theory/The Big Bang Theory (Part 2)	1980	—	2.50	5.00
❑ Casablanca 2317	Agony of DeFeet/The Freeze	1980	—	2.50	5.00
❑ Casablanca 2330	Crush It/Body Language	1981	—	2.50	5.00
❑ Invictus 9077	I Call My Baby Pussy Cat/Little Ole Country Boy	1970	2.50	5.00	10.00
❑ Invictus 9091	Red Hot Mama/Little Ole Country Boy	1971	2.50	5.00	10.00
❑ Invictus 9095	Breakdown/Little Ole Country Boy	1971	2.50	5.00	10.00
❑ Invictus 9123	Come In Out of the Rain/Little Ole Country Boy	1972	2.00	4.00	8.00
Albums					
❑ Casablanca NBLP 7002	Up for the Down Stroke	1974	10.00	20.00	40.00
❑ Casablanca NBLP 7014	Chocolate City	1975	10.00	20.00	40.00
❑ Casablanca NBLP 7022	Mothership Connection	1976	7.50	15.00	30.00
❑ Casablanca NBLP 7034	The Clones of Dr. Funkenstein	1976	7.50	15.00	30.00
❑ Casablanca NBLP 7053 [(2)]	Parliament Live/P. Funk Earth Tour	1977	10.00	20.00	40.00
❑ Casablanca NBLP 7084	Funkentelechy vs. the Placebo Syndrome	1977	7.50	15.00	30.00
❑ Casablanca NBLP 7125	Motor-Booty Affair	1978	7.50	15.00	30.00
❑ Casablanca NBLP 7195	Gloryhallastoopid (Or Pin the Tale on the Funky)	1979	7.50	15.00	30.00
❑ Casablanca NBLP 7249	Trombipulation	1980	7.50	15.00	30.00
❑ Casablanca NBLP 9003	Up for the Down Stroke	1974	12.50	25.00	50.00
—Original pressing, distributed by Warner Bros.					
❑ Casablanca 822637-1	Greatest Hits	1984	3.75	7.50	15.00
❑ Casablanca 824501-1	Funkentelechy vs. the Placebo Syndrome	1985	3.75	7.50	15.00
❑ Casablanca 824502-1	Mothership Connection	1985	3.75	7.50	15.00
❑ Invictus ST-7302	Osmium	1970	25.00	50.00	100.00
PARLIAMENTS, THE					
45s					
❑ Apt 25036	Poor Willie/Party Boys	1959	10.00	20.00	40.00
❑ Atco 6675	A New Day Begins/I'll Wait	1969	5.00	10.00	20.00
❑ Flipp 100/1	Lonely Island/You Make Me Wanna Cry	1960	7.50	15.00	30.00
—Yellow label					
❑ Golden World 46	Heart Trouble/That Was My Girl	1966	37.50	75.00	150.00
❑ Len 101	Don't Need You Anymore/Honey, Take Me Home with You	1958	20.00	40.00	80.00
❑ Revilot 207	(I Wanna) Testify/I Can Feel the Ice Melting	1967	3.75	7.50	15.00
❑ Revilot 211	All Your Goodies Are Gone (The Loser's Seat)/ Don't Be Sore at Me	1967	3.75	7.50	15.00
❑ Revilot 214	Little Man/The Goose (That Laid the Golden Egg)	1968	3.75	7.50	15.00
❑ Revilot 217	Look at What I Almost Missed/What You Been Growing	1968	3.75	7.50	15.00
❑ Revilot 223	Good Old Music/Time	1968	3.75	7.50	15.00
❑ Revilot 228	A New Day Begins/I'll Wait	1968	50.00	100.00	200.00
❑ Symbol 917	You're Cute/I'll Get You Yet	1962	6.25	12.50	25.00
❑ U.S.A. 719	My Only Love/To Be Alone	1961	5.00	10.00	20.00

Number	Title (A Side/B Side)	Yr	VG	VG+	NM
PARSONS, ALAN, PROJECT					
45s					
❑ Arista 0260	I Wouldn't Want to Be Like You/Nucleus	1977	—	2.00	4.00
❑ Arista 0288	I Robot/Don't Let It Show	1977	—	2.00	4.00
❑ Arista 0310	Day After Day/Breakdown	1978	—	2.00	4.00
❑ Arista 0352	What Goes Up/In the Lap of the Gods	1978	—	2.00	4.00
❑ Arista 0454	Damned If I Do/If I Could Change Your Mind	1979	—	2.00	4.00
❑ Arista 0491	You Won't Be There/Secret Garden	1980	—	2.00	4.00
❑ Arista 0502	You Lie Down with Dogs/Lucifer	1980	—	2.00	4.00
❑ Arista 0573	Games People Play/Ace of Swords	1980	—	2.00	4.00
❑ Arista 0598	Time/The Gold Bug	1981	—	2.00	4.00
❑ Arista 0635	Snake Eyes/I Don't Wanna Go Home	1981	—	2.00	4.00
❑ Arista 0696	Eye in the Sky/Gemini	1982	—	2.00	4.00
❑ Arista 1029	Psychobabble/Children of the Moon	1982	—	2.00	4.00
❑ Arista 1048	Old and Wise/You're Gonna Get Your Fingers Burned	1983	—	2.00	4.00
❑ Arista 9108	You Don't Believe/Lucifer	1983	—	2.00	4.00
❑ Arista 9160	Don't Answer Me/Don't Let It Show	1984	—	—	3.00
❑ Arista 9208	Prime Time/Gold Bug	1984	—	—	3.00
❑ Arista 9282	Let's Talk About Me/Hawkeye	1984	—	—	3.00
❑ Arista 9349	Days Are Numbers (The Traveller)/Somebody Out There	1985	—	—	3.00
❑ Arista 9443	Stereotomy/Urbania	1985	—	—	3.00
❑ Arista 9576	Standing on Higher Ground/Inside Looking Out	1987	—	—	3.00
❑ 20th Century 2297	(The System of) Doctor Tarr and Professor Fether/ Dream Within a Dream	1976	—	2.50	5.00
❑ 20th Century 2308	The Raven/Prelude to Fall of the House of Usher	1976	—	2.50	5.00
❑ 20th Century 2333	To One in Paradise/The Cask of Amontillado	1977	—	3.00	6.00
Albums					
❑ Arista AB 4180	Pyramid	1978	2.50	5.00	10.00
❑ Arista AL 7002	I Robot	1977	2.50	5.00	10.00
❑ Arista AL 8040	I Robot	1983	2.00	4.00	8.00
—Reissue					
❑ Arista AL 8193	The Best of the Alan Parsons Project	1983	2.00	4.00	8.00
❑ Arista AL 8204	Ammonia Avenue	1984	2.50	5.00	10.00
❑ Arista AL 8263	Vulture Culture	1985	2.00	4.00	8.00
❑ Arista AL 8289	Ammonia Avenue	1985	2.00	4.00	8.00
—Reissue					
❑ Arista AL 8290	Eye in the Sky	1985	2.00	4.00	8.00
—Reissue					
❑ Arista AL 8315	The Turn of a Friendly Card	1985	2.00	4.00	8.00
—Reissue					
❑ Arista AL 8318	Eve	1985	2.00	4.00	8.00
—Reissue					
❑ Arista AL 8320	Pyramid	1985	2.00	4.00	8.00
—Reissue					
❑ Arista AL 8384	Stereotomy	1986	2.00	4.00	8.00
—With regular LP jacket					
❑ Arista AL 8384	Stereotomy	1986	3.75	7.50	15.00
—First editions came in an oversize vinyl jacket					
❑ Arista AL 8448	Gaudi	1987	2.00	4.00	8.00
❑ Arista AL 8486	The Best of the Alan Parsons Project, Vol. 2	1987	2.00	4.00	8.00
❑ Arista AL 8487	The Instrumental Works of the Alan Parsons Project	1988	2.50	5.00	10.00
❑ Arista AB 9504	Eve	1979	2.50	5.00	10.00
❑ Arista AL 9518	The Turn of a Friendly Card	1980	2.50	5.00	10.00
❑ Arista AL 9599	Eye in the Sky	1982	2.50	5.00	10.00
❑ Casablanca 822784-1	Tales of Mystery and Imagination - Edgar Allan Poe	1984	2.50	5.00	10.00
—Reissue of 20th Century LP					
❑ 20th Century T-508	Tales of Mystery and Imagination - Edgar Allan Poe	1976	3.75	7.50	15.00
PARTON, DOLLY					
45s					
❑ Columbia 07665	The River Unbroken/More Than I Can Say	1988	—	—	3.00
❑ Columbia 07727	I Know You by Heart/Could I Have Your Autograph	1988	—	—	3.00
—With Smokey Robinson					
❑ Columbia 07995	Make Love Mine/Two Lovers	1988	—	—	3.00
❑ Columbia 68760	Why'd You Come In Here Lookin' Like That/Wait Til I Get You Home	1989	—	—	3.00
❑ Columbia 69040	Yellow Roses/Wait Til I Get You Home	1989	—	—	3.00
❑ Goldband 1086	Puppy Love/Girl Left Alone	1959	150.00	300.00	600.00
—Originals have a red label					
❑ Mercury 71982	It's Sure Gonna Hurt/The Love You Gave	1962	75.00	150.00	300.00
❑ Monument 869	I Wasted My Tears/What Do You Think About Lovin'	1965	3.75	7.50	15.00
❑ Monument 897	Old Enough to Know Better (Too Young to Resist)/Happy, Happy Birthday Baby	1965	3.75	7.50	15.00
❑ Monument 913	Busy Signal/I Took Him for Granted	1965	3.75	7.50	15.00
❑ Monument 922	Control Yourself/Don't Drop Out	1966	3.75	7.50	15.00
❑ Monument 948	Little Things/I'll Put It Off Until Tomorrow	1966	3.75	7.50	15.00
❑ Monument 982	Dumb Blonde/The Giving and the Taking	1967	2.50	5.00	10.00
❑ Monument 1007	Something Fishy/I've Lived My Life	1967	2.50	5.00	10.00
❑ Monument 1032	Why, Why, Why/I Couldn't Wait Forever	1967	2.50	5.00	10.00
❑ Monument 1047	I'm Not Worth the Tears/Ping Pong	1968	2.00	4.00	8.00
❑ Monument 03408	Everything Is Beautiful (In Its Own Way)/Put It Off Until Tomorrow	1982	—	2.00	4.00
—A-side with Willie Nelson; B-side with Kris Kristofferson					
❑ Monument 03781	What Do You Think About Lovin'/You're Gonna Love Yourself (In the Morning)	1983	—	2.00	4.00
—A-side: Dolly Parton and Brenda Lee; B-side: Willie Nelson and Brenda Lee					
❑ RCA 5001-7-R	Do I Ever Cross Your Mind/We Had It All	1986	—	—	3.00

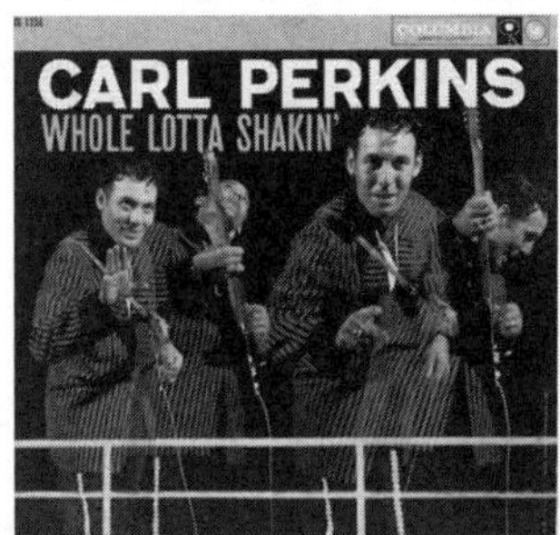

Number	Title (A Side/B Side)	Yr	VG	VG+	NM
❑ RCA PB-10935	Light of a Clear Blue Morning/There	1977	—	2.00	4.00
❑ RCA PB-11123	Here You Come Again/Me and Little Andy	1977	—	2.00	4.00
❑ RCA PB-11240	Two Doors Down/It's All Wrong, But It's All Right	1978	—	2.00	4.00
❑ RCA PB-11296	Heartbreaker/Sure Thing	1978	—	2.00	4.00
❑ RCA PB-11420	Baby I'm Burning/I Really Got the Feeling	1978	—	2.00	4.00
❑ RCA GB-11505	Here You Come Again/Two Doors Down	1979	—	—	3.00
—Gold Standard Series					
❑ RCA PB-11577	You're the Only One/Down	1979	—	2.00	4.00
❑ RCA PB-11705	Sweet Summer Lovin'/Great Balls of Fire	1979	—	2.00	4.00
❑ RCA PB-11926	Starting Over Again/Sweet Agony	1980	—	2.00	4.00
❑ RCA GB-11993	Baby I'm Burnin'/Heartbreaker	1980	—	—	3.00
—Gold Standard Series					
❑ RCA PB-12040	Old Flames Can't Hold a Candle to You/I Knew You When	1980	—	2.00	4.00
❑ RCA PB-12133	9 to 5/Sing for the Common Man	1980	—	2.00	4.00
❑ RCA PB-12200	But You Know I Love You/Poor Folks' Town	1981	—	2.00	4.00
❑ RCA PB-12282	The House of the Rising Sun/Working Girl	1981	—	2.00	4.00
❑ RCA GB-12316	9 to 5/Old Flames Can't Hold a Candle to You	1981	—	—	3.00
—Gold Standard Series					
❑ RCA PB-13057	Single Women/Barbara on Your Mind	1982	—	2.00	4.00
❑ RCA PB-13234	Heartbreak Express/Act Like a Fool	1982	—	2.00	4.00
❑ RCA PB-13260	I Will Always Love You/Do I Ever Cross Your Mind	1982	—	2.00	4.00
—A-side is the same song, but a different recording than that on APBO-0234					
❑ RCA PB-13361	Hard Candy Christmas/Me and Little Andy	1982	—	2.00	4.00
❑ RCA PB-13514	Potential New Boyfriend/One of Those Days	1983	—	—	3.00
❑ RCA PB-13619	Tennessee Homesick Blues/Butterflies	1984	—	—	3.00
❑ RCA PB-13703	Save the Last Dance for Me/Elusive Butterfly	1983	—	—	3.00
❑ RCA PB-13756	The Great Pretender/Downtown	1984	—	—	3.00
❑ RCA PB-13856	Sweet Lovin' Friends/Too Much Water	1984	—	—	—
—Unreleased					
❑ RCA PB-13883	Sweet Lovin' Friends/God Won't Get You	1984	—	—	3.00
—With Sylvester Stallone					
❑ RCA PB-13944	Medley: Winter Wonderland-Sleigh Ride/The Christmas Song	1984	—	—	3.00
—B-side by Kenny Rogers					
❑ RCA PB-13987	Don't Call It Love/We Got Too Much	1985	—	—	3.00
❑ RCA GB-14070	Tennessee Homesick Blues/Hard Candy Christmas	1985	—	—	3.00
—Gold Standard Series					
❑ RCA PB-14218	Think About Love/Come Back to Me	1985	—	—	3.00
❑ RCA PB-14297	Tie Our Love (In a Double Knot)/I Hope You're Never Happy	1986	—	—	3.00
❑ RCA GB-14346	Don't Call It Love/Real Love	1986	—	—	3.00
—Gold Standard Series					
❑ RCA Victor 47-9548	Just Because I'm a Woman/I Wish I Felt This Way at Home	1968	2.00	4.00	8.00
❑ RCA Victor 47-9657	In the Good Old Days (When Times Were Bad)/Try Being Lonely	1968	2.00	4.00	8.00
❑ RCA Victor 47-9784	Daddy Come and Get Me/Chas	1969	—	3.00	6.00
❑ RCA Victor 47-9863	Mule Skinner Blues/More Than Their Share	1970	—	3.00	6.00
❑ RCA Victor 47-9928	Joshua/I'm Doing This for Your Sake	1970	—	3.00	6.00
❑ RCA Victor 47-9971	Comin' For to Carry Me Home/Golden Streets of Glory	1971	2.50	5.00	10.00
❑ RCA Victor 47-9999	My Blue Tears/The Mystery of the Mystery	1971	—	3.00	6.00
❑ RCA Victor 74-0132	Daddy/He's a Go-Getter	1969	—	3.00	6.00
❑ RCA Victor 74-0192	In the Ghetto/Bridge	1969	—	3.00	6.00
❑ RCA Victor 74-0243	My Blue Ridge Mountain Boy/'Til Death Do Us Part	1969	—	3.00	6.00
❑ RCA Victor 74-0538	Coat of Many Colors/Here I Am	1971	—	3.00	6.00
❑ RCA Victor 74-0662	Touch Your Woman/Mission Chapel Memories	1972	—	2.50	5.00
❑ RCA Victor 74-0757	Washday Blues/Just As Good As Gone	1972	2.50	5.00	10.00
❑ RCA Victor 74-0797	Lord, Hold My Hand/When I Sing for Him	1972	—	2.50	5.00
❑ RCA Victor 74-0868	My Tennessee Mountain Home/Better Part of Life	1973	—	2.50	5.00
❑ RCA Victor 74-0950	Traveling Man/I Remember	1973	—	2.50	5.00
❑ RCA Victor APBO-0145	Jolene/Love, You're So Beautiful Tonight	1973	—	2.50	5.00
❑ RCA Victor APBO-0234	I Will Always Love You/Lonely Comin' Down	1974	—	2.50	5.00
❑ RCA Victor PB-10031	Love Is Like a Butterfly/Sacred Memories	1974	—	2.00	4.00
❑ RCA Victor PB-10164	The Bargain Store/I'll Never Forget	1975	—	2.00	4.00
❑ RCA Victor GB-10165	Jolene/My Tennessee Mountain Home	1975	—	—	3.00
—Gold Standard Series					
❑ RCA Victor PB-10310	The Seeker/Love with Feeling	1975	2.00	4.00	8.00
❑ RCA Victor PB-10396	We Used To/My Heart Started Breaking	1975	—	2.00	4.00
❑ RCA Victor GB-10504	Love Is Like a Butterfly/Sacred Memories	1975	—	—	3.00
—Gold Standard Series					

Number	Title (A Side/B Side)	Yr	VG	VG+	NM
❑ RCA Victor GB-10505	I Will Always Love You/Lovely Comin' Down	1975	—	—	3.00
—Gold Standard Series					
❑ RCA Victor PB-10564	Hey, Lucky Lady/Most of All, Why	1976	—	2.00	4.00
❑ RCA Victor GB-10676	The Bargain Store/The Seeker	1976	—	—	3.00
—Gold Standard Series					
❑ RCA Victor PB-10730	All I Can Do/Falling Out of Love with Me	1976	—	2.00	4.00
Albums					
❑ Columbia FC 40968	Rainbow	1987	2.50	5.00	10.00
❑ Columbia FC 44384	White Limozeen	1989	3.00	6.00	12.00
❑ Columbia C 46882	Eagle When She Flies	1991	5.00	10.00	20.00
—Available on vinyl only through Columbia House					
❑ Monument 7623	In the Beginning	197?	3.00	6.00	12.00
❑ Monument MLP-8085 [M]	Hello, I'm Dolly	1967	7.50	15.00	30.00
❑ Monument SLP-18085 [S]	Hello, I'm Dolly	1967	10.00	20.00	40.00
❑ Monument SLP-18136	As Long As I Love	1970	5.00	10.00	20.00
❑ Monument KZG 31913 [(2)]	The World of Dolly	1972	5.00	10.00	20.00
❑ Monument KZG 33876 [(2)]	Hello, I'm Dolly	1975	5.00	10.00	20.00
❑ Pair PDL2-1009 [(2)]	Just the Way I Am	1986	3.00	6.00	12.00
❑ Pair PDL2-1116 [(2)]	Portrait	1986	3.00	6.00	12.00
❑ RCA 5706-1-R	The Best of Dolly Parton, Vol. 3	1987	2.50	5.00	10.00
❑ RCA 6497-1-R	The Best There Is	1987	2.50	5.00	10.00
❑ RCA Camden ACL1-0307	Mine	1973	2.50	5.00	10.00
❑ RCA Camden CAS-2583	Just the Way I Am	1972	2.50	5.00	10.00
❑ RCA Victor APL1-0033	My Tennessee Mountain Home	1973	3.00	6.00	12.00
❑ RCA Victor APL1-0286	Bubbling Over	1973	3.00	6.00	12.00
❑ RCA Victor APL1-0473	Jolene	1974	3.00	6.00	12.00
❑ RCA Victor APL1-0712	Love Is Like a Butterfly	1974	3.00	6.00	12.00
❑ RCA Victor APL1-0950	The Bargain Store	1975	3.00	6.00	12.00
❑ RCA Victor APL1-1117	The Best of Dolly Parton	1975	3.00	6.00	12.00
❑ RCA Victor APL1-1221	Dolly	1975	3.00	6.00	12.00
❑ RCA Victor APL1-1665	All I Can Do	1976	3.00	6.00	12.00
❑ RCA Victor APL1-2188	New Harvest...First Gathering	1977	3.00	6.00	12.00
❑ RCA Victor AFL1-2544	Here You Come Again	1977	3.00	6.00	12.00
❑ RCA Victor AFL1-2797	Heartbreaker	1978	3.00	6.00	12.00
❑ RCA Victor AHL1-3361	Great Balls of Fire	1979	3.00	6.00	12.00
❑ RCA Victor AHL1-3546	Dolly Dolly Dolly	1980	3.00	6.00	12.00
❑ RCA Victor AYL1-3665	Heartbreaker	1980	2.00	4.00	8.00
—"Best Buy Series" reissue					
❑ RCA Victor AYL1-3764	My Tennessee Mountain Home	1980	2.00	4.00	8.00
—"Best Buy Series" reissue					
❑ RCA Victor AHL1-3852	9 to 5 and Odd Jobs	1980	3.00	6.00	12.00
❑ RCA Victor AYL1-3898	Jolene	1981	2.00	4.00	8.00
—"Best Buy Series" reissue					
❑ RCA Victor LPM-3949 [M]	Just Because I'm a Woman	1968	25.00	50.00	100.00
❑ RCA Victor LSP-3949 [S]	Just Because I'm a Woman	1968	5.00	10.00	20.00
—Orange label					
❑ RCA Victor LSP-3949 [S]	Just Because I'm a Woman	1968	7.50	15.00	30.00
—"Stereo" on black label					
❑ RCA Victor AYL1-3980	New Harvest	1981	2.00	4.00	8.00
—"Best Buy Series" reissue					
❑ RCA Victor LSP-4099	In the Good Old Days	1969	5.00	10.00	20.00
❑ RCA Victor LSP-4188	My Blue Ridge Mountain Boy	1969	5.00	10.00	20.00
❑ RCA Victor LSP-4288	The Fairest of Them All	1970	5.00	10.00	20.00
❑ RCA Victor AHL1-4289	Heartbreak Express	1982	3.00	6.00	12.00
❑ RCA Victor LSP-4387	A Real Live Dolly	1970	6.25	12.50	25.00
—Four songs feature Porter Wagoner					
❑ RCA Victor LSP-4398	Golden Streets of Glory	1971	5.00	10.00	20.00
❑ RCA Victor AHL1-4422	Greatest Hits	1982	3.00	6.00	12.00
❑ RCA Victor LSP-4449	The Best of Dolly Parton	1970	5.00	10.00	20.00
❑ RCA Victor LSP-4507	Joshua	1971	5.00	10.00	20.00
❑ RCA Victor LSP-4603	Coat of Many Colors	1971	5.00	10.00	20.00
❑ RCA Victor LSP-4686	Touch Your Woman	1972	5.00	10.00	20.00
❑ RCA Victor AHL1-4691	Burlap & Satin	1983	2.50	5.00	10.00
❑ RCA Victor LSP-4752	My Favorite Song Writer: Porter Wagoner	1972	5.00	10.00	20.00
❑ RCA Victor LSP-4762	Dolly Parton Sings	1972	3.75	7.50	15.00
❑ RCA Victor AYL1-4829	Here You Come Again	1984	2.00	4.00	8.00
—"Best Buy Series" reissue					
❑ RCA Victor AYL1-4830	9 to 5 and Odd Jobs	1984	2.00	4.00	8.00
—"Best Buy Series" reissue					
❑ RCA Victor AHL1-4940	The Great Pretender	1984	2.50	5.00	10.00
❑ RCA Victor AYL1-5146	The Best of Dolly Parton	1984	2.00	4.00	8.00
—"Best Buy Series" reissue					
❑ RCA Victor AHL1-5414	Real Love	1985	2.50	5.00	10.00
❑ RCA Victor AYL1-5437	Burlap & Satin	1985	2.00	4.00	8.00
—"Best Buy Series" reissue					
❑ RCA Victor AHL1-5471	Collector's Series	1985	2.50	5.00	10.00
❑ RCA Victor AHL1-9508	Think About Love	1986	2.50	5.00	10.00
❑ Time-Life STW-107	Country Music	1981	2.50	5.00	10.00

PARTRIDGE FAMILY, THE

45s

Number	Title (A Side/B Side)	Yr	VG	VG+	NM
❑ Bell 910	I Think I Love You/Somebody Wants to Love You	1970	—	2.50	5.00
❑ Bell 910	I Think I Love You/Somebody Wants to Love You	1970	6.25	12.50	25.00
—Artist erroneously listed on both sides as "The PATRIDGE Family"					
❑ Bell 963	Doesn't Somebody Want to Be Wanted/ You Are Always on My Mind	1971	—	2.50	5.00
❑ Bell 996	I'll Meet You Halfway/Morning Rider on the Road	1971	—	2.50	5.00

Number	Title (A Side/B Side)	Yr	VG	VG+	NM
❑ Bell 45130	I Woke Up in Love This Morning/Twenty-Four Hours a Day	1971	—	2.50	5.00
❑ Bell 45160	It's One of Those Nights (Yes Love)/One Night Stand	1971	—	2.50	5.00
❑ Bell 45200	Am I Losing You/If You Ever Go	1972	—	2.00	4.00
❑ Bell 45235	Breaking Up Is Hard to Do/I'm Here, You're Here	1972	—	2.00	4.00
❑ Bell 45301	Looking Through the Eyes of Love/Storybook Love	1972	—	2.00	4.00
❑ Bell 45336	Friend and a Lover/Something's Wrong	1973	—	2.00	4.00
❑ Bell 45414	Lookin' for a Good Time/Money Money	1973	10.00	20.00	40.00
—Extremely rare as a stock copy					
Albums					
❑ Bell 1107	The Partridge Family At Home with Their Greatest Hits	1972	5.00	10.00	20.00
❑ Bell 1111	The Partridge Family Notebook	1972	6.25	12.50	25.00
❑ Bell 1122	Crossword Puzzle	1973	7.50	15.00	30.00
❑ Bell 1137	Bulletin Board	1973	12.50	25.00	50.00
❑ Bell 1319 [(2)]	The World of the Partridge Family	1974	10.00	20.00	40.00
❑ Bell 6050	The Partridge Family Album	1970	5.00	10.00	20.00
❑ Bell 6059	Up to Date	1971	5.00	10.00	20.00
❑ Bell 6064	The Partridge Family Sound Magazine	1971	5.00	10.00	20.00
❑ Bell 6066	A Partridge Family Christmas Card	1971	6.25	12.50	25.00
—With attached Christmas card					
❑ Bell 6072	The Partridge Family Shopping Bag	1972	5.00	10.00	20.00
❑ Laurie House H-8014 [(2)]	The Partridge Family	197?	12.50	25.00	50.00
PAUL, BILLY					
45s					
❑ Gamble 232	Somewhere/Bluesette	1968	3.00	6.00	12.00
❑ Jubilee 5081	That's Why I Dream/Why Am I	1952	7.50	15.00	30.00
❑ Jubilee 5086	You Didn't Know/The Stars Are Mine	1952	7.50	15.00	30.00
❑ Neptune 30	Mrs. Robinson/Let's Fall in Love All Over	1970	2.50	5.00	10.00
❑ Philadelphia Int'l. 3120	Jesus Boy (You Only Look Like a Man)/Love Buddies	1980	—	2.50	5.00
❑ Philadelphia Int'l. 3509	Love Buddies/Magic Carpet Ride	1971	—	3.00	6.00
❑ Philadelphia Int'l. 3515	This Is Your Life/I Wish It Were Yesterday	1972	—	3.00	6.00
❑ Philadelphia Int'l. 3521	Me and Mrs. Jones/Your Song	1972	—	2.50	5.00
❑ Philadelphia Int'l. 3526	Am I Black Enough for You/I'm Gonna Make It This Time	1973	—	2.50	5.00
❑ Philadelphia Int'l. 3538	Thanks for Saving My Life/I Was Married	1974	—	2.50	5.00
❑ Philadelphia Int'l. 3551	Be Truthful to Me/I Wish It Was Yesterday	1974	—	2.50	5.00
❑ Philadelphia Int'l. 3563	Billy's Back Home/I've Got So Much to Live For	1975	—	2.50	5.00
❑ Philadelphia Int'l. 3572	When It's Your Turn to Go/July, July, July, July	1975	—	2.50	5.00
❑ Philadelphia Int'l. 3584	Let's Make a Baby/My Head's On Straight	1976	—	2.50	5.00
❑ Philadelphia Int'l. 3593	People Power/I Want Cha Baby	1976	—	2.50	5.00
❑ Philadelphia Int'l. 3613	How Good Is Your Game/I Think I'll Stay Home Today	1977	—	2.50	5.00
❑ Philadelphia Int'l. 3621	Let 'Em In/We All Got a Mission	1977	—	2.50	5.00
❑ Philadelphia Int'l. 3630	I Trust You/Love Won't Come Easy	1977	—	2.50	5.00
❑ Philadelphia Int'l. 3635	Only the Strong Survive/Where I Belong	1977	—	2.50	5.00
❑ Philadelphia Int'l. 3639	Everybody's Breakin' Up/Sooner or Later	1978	—	2.50	5.00
❑ Philadelphia Int'l. 3645	One Man's Junk/Don't Give Up on Love	1978	—	2.50	5.00
❑ Philadelphia Int'l. 3676	Bring the Family Back/It's Critical	1979	—	2.50	5.00
❑ Philadelphia Int'l. 3699	False Faces/I Gotta Put This Life Down	1979	—	2.50	5.00
❑ Philadelphia Int'l. 3736	You're My Sweetness/(B-side unknown)	1979	—	2.50	5.00
❑ Philadelphia Int'l. ZS9 3737	Jesus Boy (You Only Look Like a Man)/(B-side unknown)	1979	—	3.00	6.00
❑ Total Experience 2419	Lately/(Instrumental)	1985	—	2.50	5.00
❑ Total Experience 2434	Sexual Therapy/Hot Date	1986	—	2.50	5.00
Albums					
❑ Gamble SG-5002	Feeling Good at the Cadillac Club	1968	7.50	15.00	30.00
❑ Ichiban ICH-1025	Wide Open	198?	2.50	5.00	10.00
❑ Neptune 201	Ebony Woman	1970	5.00	10.00	20.00
❑ Philadelphia Int'l. Z 30580	Going East	1971	3.00	6.00	12.00
❑ Philadelphia Int'l. KZ 31793	360 Degrees of Billy Paul	1972	3.00	6.00	12.00
❑ Philadelphia Int'l. KZ 32118	Ebony Woman	1973	3.00	6.00	12.00
—Reissue of Neptune LP					
❑ Philadelphia Int'l. KZ 32119	Feeling Good at the Cadillac Club	1973	3.00	6.00	12.00
—Reissue of Gamble LP					
❑ Philadelphia Int'l. KZ 32409	War of the Gods	1973	2.50	5.00	10.00
❑ Philadelphia Int'l. KZ 32952	Live in Europe	1974	2.50	5.00	10.00
❑ Philadelphia Int'l. PZ 33157	Got My Head On Straight	1975	2.50	5.00	10.00
❑ Philadelphia Int'l. PZ 33843	When Love Is New	1975	2.50	5.00	10.00
❑ Philadelphia Int'l. PZ 34389	Let 'Em In	1976	2.50	5.00	10.00
❑ Philadelphia Int'l. PZ 34923	Only the Strong Survive	1977	2.50	5.00	10.00

Number	Title (A Side/B Side)	Yr	VG	VG+	NM
❑ Philadelphia Int'l. JZ 35756	First Class	1979	2.50	5.00	10.00
❑ Philadelphia Int'l. Z2 36314 [(2)]	The Best of Billy Paul	1980	3.75	7.50	15.00
❑ Total Experience TEL8-5711	Lately	1985	2.50	5.00	10.00
PAUL AND PAULA					
45s					
❑ Le Cam 99	The Beginning of Love/All I Want Is You	1963	5.00	10.00	20.00
❑ Le Cam 305	From the Top of the World/All I Want Is You	197?	—	2.00	4.00
—As "Jill and Ray"					
❑ Le Cam 315	Hey Paula ('77 Disco)/(Instrumental)	1977	—	2.00	4.00
❑ Le Cam 321	Hey Paula/Paula (My Love)	1978	—	2.00	4.00
—Reissued in 1982 with the same catalog number					
❑ Le Cam 354	Hey Paula/Elmer's Tune	198?	—	2.00	4.00
❑ Le Cam 979	Hey Paula/Bobbie Is the One	1962	12.50	25.00	50.00
—As "Jill and Ray"					
❑ Philips 40084	Hey Paula/Bobby Is the One	1962	3.75	7.50	15.00
❑ Philips 40096	Young Lovers/Ba-Hey-Be	1963	3.00	6.00	12.00
❑ Philips 40114	First Quarrel/School Is Thru	1963	3.00	6.00	12.00
❑ Philips 40130	Something Old, Something New/Flipped Over You	1963	3.00	6.00	12.00
❑ Philips 40142	First Day Back at School/A Perfect Pair	1963	3.00	6.00	12.00
❑ Philips 40158	Holiday for Teens/Holiday Hootenanny	1963	3.00	6.00	12.00
❑ Philips 40168	We'll Never Break Up for Good/Crazy Little Things	1964	2.50	5.00	10.00
❑ Philips 40209	The Young Years/Darlin'	1964	2.50	5.00	10.00
❑ Philips 40234	No Other Baby/Too Dark to See	1964	2.50	5.00	10.00
❑ Philips 40268	True Love/Any Way You Want Me	1965	2.00	4.00	8.00
❑ Philips 40296	Dear Paula/All the Love	1965	2.00	4.00	8.00
❑ Philips 40352	All I Want Is You/The Beginning of Love	1966	2.50	5.00	10.00
❑ Uni 55052	All These Things/Wedding	1968	2.00	4.00	8.00
❑ United Artists 50712	Moments Like These/Mrs. Bean	1970	—	3.00	6.00
Albums					
❑ Philips PHM 200078 [M]	Paul and Paula Sing for Young Lovers	1963	7.50	15.00	30.00
❑ Philips PHM 200089 [M]	We Go Together	1963	7.50	15.00	30.00
❑ Philips PHM 200101 [M]	Holiday for Teens	1963	7.50	15.00	30.00
❑ Philips PHS 600078 [S]	Paul and Paula Sing for Young Lovers	1963	10.00	20.00	40.00
❑ Philips PHS 600089 [S]	We Go Together	1963	10.00	20.00	40.00
❑ Philips PHS 600101 [S]	Holiday for Teens	1963	10.00	20.00	40.00
PAYNE, FREDA					
45s					
❑ ABC 12079	Shadows on the Wall/I Get Carried Away	1975	—	2.50	5.00
❑ ABC 12139	Lost in Love/You	1975	—	2.50	5.00
❑ ABC Dunhill 15018	It's Yours to Have/Run for Life	1974	—	2.50	5.00
❑ ABC-Paramount 10366	Desafinado/He Who Laughs Last	1962	5.00	10.00	20.00
❑ ABC-Paramount 10437	Pretty Baby/Grin and Bear It	1963	5.00	10.00	20.00
❑ Capitol 4383	I Can't Live on a Memory/I Get High (On Your Memory)	1976	—	2.50	5.00
❑ Capitol 4431	Baby, You've Got What It Takes/Bring Back the Joy	1977	—	2.50	5.00
❑ Capitol 4494	Love Magnet/Loving You Means So Much to Me	1977	—	2.50	5.00
❑ Capitol 4537	Feed Me Your Love/Stares and Whispers	1978	—	2.50	5.00
❑ Capitol 4631	Happy Days Are Here Again-Happy Music (Dance the Night Away)/Falling in Love	1978	—	2.50	5.00
❑ Capitol 4695	I'll Do Anything for You (Part 1)/I'll Do Anything for You (Part 2)	1979	—	2.50	5.00
❑ Capitol 4775	Red Hot/Longest Night	1979	—	2.50	5.00
❑ Capitol 4805	Can't Wait/Longest Night	1979	—	2.50	5.00
❑ Impulse! 221	It's Time/Sweet September	1963	5.00	10.00	20.00
❑ Invictus 1255	Two Wrongs Don't Make a Right/ We've Gotta Find a Way Back to Love	1973	—	3.00	6.00
❑ Invictus 1257	For No Reason/Mother Misery's Favorite Child	1973	—	3.00	6.00
❑ Invictus 9073	The Unhooked Generation/Easiest Way to Fall	1969	—	3.00	6.00
❑ Invictus 9075	Band of Gold/Easiest Way to Fall	1970	—	3.00	6.00
❑ Invictus 9080	Deeper and Deeper/The Unhooked Genration	1970	—	3.00	6.00
❑ Invictus 9085	Cherish What Is Dear to You (While It Is Near to You)/ They Don't Owe Me a Thing	1971	—	3.00	6.00
❑ Invictus 9092	Bring the Boys Home/I Shall Not Be Moved	1971	—	3.00	6.00
❑ Invictus 9100	You Brought the Joy/Suddenly It's Yesterday	1971	—	3.00	6.00
❑ Invictus 9109	I'm Not Getting Any Better/The Road We Didn't Take	1972	—	3.00	6.00
❑ Invictus 9128	She's in My Life/Through the Memory of My Mind	1972	—	3.00	6.00
❑ MGM 13509	You've Lost That Lovin' Feelin'/Sad Sad September	1966	5.00	10.00	20.00
❑ Sutra 117	In Motion/(Instrumental)	1982	—	2.50	5.00
Albums					
❑ ABC D-901	Out of Payne Comes Love	1976	3.00	6.00	12.00
❑ ABC Dunhill DSX-50176	Payne and Pleasure	1974	3.75	7.50	15.00
❑ ABC Impulse! AS-53 [S]	After the Lights Go Down Low…And Much More	1968	3.75	7.50	15.00
❑ Capitol ST-11700	Stares and Whispers	1977	3.00	6.00	12.00
❑ Capitol ST-11864	Supernatural	1978	3.00	6.00	12.00
❑ Capitol ST-12003	Hot	1979	3.00	6.00	12.00
❑ Impulse! A-53 [M]	After the Lights Go Down Low…And Much More	1964	7.50	15.00	30.00
❑ Impulse! AS-53 [S]	After the Lights Go Down Low…And Much More	1964	10.00	20.00	40.00
❑ Invictus ST-7301	Band of Gold	1970	3.75	7.50	15.00
❑ Invictus SMAS-7307	Contact	1971	3.75	7.50	15.00
❑ Invictus ST-9804	The Best of Freda Payne	1972	3.75	7.50	15.00
❑ Invictus Z 32493	Reaching Out	1973	3.75	7.50	15.00
❑ MGM GAS-128	Freda Payne (Golden Archive Series)	1970	3.75	7.50	15.00
❑ MGM E-4370 [M]	How Do You Say I Don't Love You Anymore	1966	5.00	10.00	20.00
❑ MGM SE-4370 [S]	How Do You Say I Don't Love You Anymore	1966	6.25	12.50	25.00

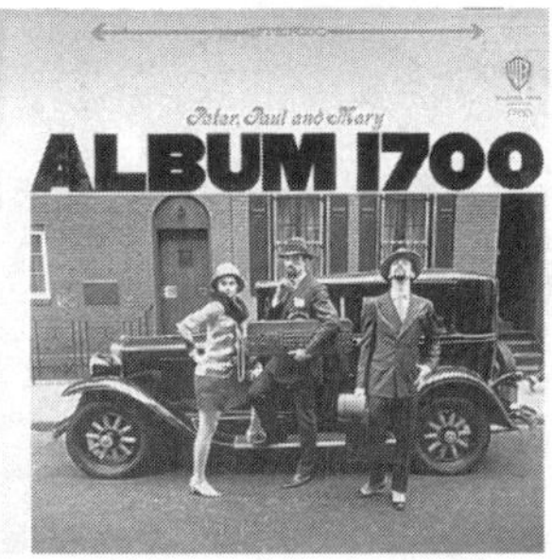

Number	Title (A Side/B Side)	Yr	VG	VG+	NM
PEACHES AND HERB					
45s					
❑ Columbia 03872	Remember/Come to Me	1983	—	2.00	4.00
❑ Columbia 04081	In My World/Keep On Smiling	1983	—	2.00	4.00
❑ Columbia 45386	The Sound of Silence/The Two of Us	1971	—	2.50	5.00
❑ Columbia 45554	God Save This World/I Can't Forget the One I Love	1972	—	2.50	5.00
❑ Date 1523	Let's Fall in Love/We're In This Thing Together	1966	2.50	5.00	10.00
❑ Date 1549	Close Your Eyes/I Will Watch Over You	1967	2.50	5.00	10.00
❑ Date 1555	Cupid-Venus/Darling, How Long	1967	3.75	7.50	15.00
❑ Date 1563	For Your Love/I Need Your Love So Desperately	1967	2.50	5.00	10.00
❑ Date 1574	Love Is Strange/It's True I Love You	1967	2.50	5.00	10.00
❑ Date 1586	Two Little Kids/We've Got to Love One Another	1967	2.00	4.00	8.00
❑ Date 1592	The Ten Commandments of Love/ What a Lovely Way (To Say Goodnight)	1968	2.00	4.00	8.00
❑ Date 1603	United/Thank You	1968	2.00	4.00	8.00
❑ Date 1623	Let's Make a Promise/Me and You	1968	2.00	4.00	8.00
❑ Date 1633	We've Got to Love One Another/So True	1968	2.50	5.00	10.00
❑ Date 1637	When He Touches Me (Nothing Else Matters)/Thank You	1969	2.00	4.00	8.00
❑ Date 1649	Let Me Be the One/I Need Your Love So Desperately	1969	2.00	4.00	8.00
❑ Date 1655	Cupid/Darling, How Long	1969	2.00	4.00	8.00
❑ Date 1669	It's Just a Game, Love/Satisfy My Hunger	1970	2.00	4.00	8.00
❑ Date 1676	Soothe Me with Your Love/We're So Much in Love	1970	2.00	4.00	8.00
❑ MCA 40701	We're Still Together/Love Is Here Beside Us	1977	—	2.50	5.00
❑ MCA 40782	It Will Never Be the Same Again/I'm Counting on You	1977	—	2.50	5.00
❑ Mercury 73350	Keep It Coming/I'm a-Hurtin' Inside	1973	—	2.50	5.00
❑ Mercury 73388	Can't It Wait/Thank Heaven for You	1973	—	2.50	5.00
❑ Polydor 2031	Roller-Skatin' Mate (Part 1)/Roller-Skatin' Mate (Part 2)	1979	—	2.00	4.00
❑ Polydor 2053	I Pledge My Love/(I Want Us) Back Together	1980	—	2.00	4.00
❑ Polydor 2115	Funtime (Part 1)/Funtime (Part 2)	1980	—	2.00	4.00
❑ Polydor 2140	One Child of Love/Hearsay	1980	—	2.00	4.00
❑ Polydor 2157	Surrender/Love Stealers	1981	—	2.00	4.00
❑ Polydor 2178	Freeway/Pickin' Up the Pieces	1981	—	2.00	4.00
❑ Polydor 2187	Bluer Than Blue/Go with the Flow	1981	—	2.00	4.00
❑ Polydor 14514	Shake Your Groove Thing/All Your Love (Get It Here)	1978	—	2.00	4.00
❑ Polydor 14547	Reunited/Easy as Pie	1979	—	2.00	4.00
❑ Polydor 14577	We've Got Love/Four's a Traffic Jam	1979	—	2.00	4.00
Albums					
❑ Columbia FC 38746	Remember	1983	2.50	5.00	10.00
❑ Date TEM 3004 [M]	Let's Fall in Love	1967	5.00	10.00	20.00
❑ Date TEM 3005 [M]	For Your Love	1967	6.25	12.50	25.00
❑ Date TEM 3007 [M]	Golden Duets	1968	7.50	15.00	30.00
❑ Date TES 4004 [S]	Let's Fall in Love	1967	6.25	12.50	25.00
❑ Date TES 4005 [S]	For Your Love	1967	5.00	10.00	20.00
❑ Date TES 4007 [S]	Golden Duets	1968	5.00	10.00	20.00
❑ Date TES 4012	Peaches and Herb's Greatest Hits	1968	5.00	10.00	20.00
❑ Epic E 36089 *—Reissue of Date material*	Love Is Strange	1979	2.50	5.00	10.00
❑ Epic JE 36099 *—Reissue of Date 4012*	Peaches and Herb's Greatest Hits	1979	2.50	5.00	10.00
❑ MCA 2261	Peaches and Herb	1977	3.00	6.00	12.00
❑ Polydor PD-1-6172	2 Hot!	1978	2.50	5.00	10.00
❑ Polydor PD-1-6239	Twice the Fire	1979	2.50	5.00	10.00
❑ Polydor PD-1-6298	Worth the Wait	1980	2.50	5.00	10.00
❑ Polydor PD-1-6332	Sayin' Something!	1981	2.50	5.00	10.00
PERKINS, CARL					
45s					
❑ Columbia 41131	Pink Pedal Pushers/Jive After Five	1958	7.50	15.00	30.00
❑ Columbia 41207	Levi Jacket/Pop, Let Me Have the Car	1958	6.25	12.50	25.00
❑ Columbia 41296	Y-O-U/This Life I Live	1958	6.25	12.50	25.00
❑ Columbia 41379	Pointed Toe Shoes/Highway of Love	1959	6.25	12.50	25.00
❑ Columbia 41449	One Ticket to Loneliness/I Don't See Me in Your Eyes Anymore	1959	6.25	12.50	25.00
❑ Columbia 41651	L-O-V-E-V-I-L-L-E/Too Much for a Man to Understand	1960	6.25	12.50	25.00
❑ Columbia 41825	Honey, 'Cause I Love You/Just for You	1960	6.25	12.50	25.00
❑ Columbia 42061	Anyway the Wind Blows/The Unhappy Girls	1961	6.25	12.50	25.00
❑ Columbia 42405	Hollywood City/The Fool I Used to Be	1962	6.25	12.50	25.00
❑ Columbia 42514	Sister Twister/Hambone	1962	6.25	12.50	25.00

Number	Title (A Side/B Side)	Yr	VG	VG+	NM
❑ Columbia 42753	I Just Got Back from There/Forget Me Next Time Around	1963	6.25	12.50	25.00
❑ Columbia 44723	Restless/1143	1968	2.00	4.00	8.00
❑ Columbia 44883	For Your Love/Four Letter Word	1969	2.00	4.00	8.00
❑ Columbia 44993	C.C. Rider/Soul Beat	1969	2.00	4.00	8.00
❑ Columbia 45107	All Mama's Children/Step Aside	1970	2.00	4.00	8.00
—With NRBQ					
❑ Columbia 45132	State of Confusion/My Son, My Son	1970	—	3.00	6.00
❑ Columbia 45253	What Every Little Boy Ought to Know/Just As Long	1970	—	2.50	5.00
❑ Columbia 45347	Me Without You/Red Headed Woman	1971	—	2.50	5.00
❑ Columbia 45466	Cotton Top/About All I Can Give You Is My Love	1971	—	2.50	5.00
❑ Columbia 45582	High on Love/Take Me Back to Memphis	1972	—	2.50	5.00
❑ Columbia 45694	Someday/The Trip	1972	—	2.50	5.00
❑ Decca 31548	Help Me Find My Baby/For a Little While	1963	3.75	7.50	15.00
❑ Decca 31591	After Sundown/I Wouldn't Have Told You	1964	3.75	7.50	15.00
❑ Decca 31709	The Monkeyshine/Let My Baby Be	1964	3.75	7.50	15.00
❑ Decca 31786	One of These Days/Mama of My Song	1965	3.75	7.50	15.00
❑ Dollie 505	Country Boy's Dream/If I Could Come Back	1966	3.00	6.00	12.00
❑ Dollie 508	Shine, Shine, Shine/Almost Love	1967	3.00	6.00	12.00
❑ Dollie 512	Without You/You Can Take the Boy Out of the Country	1967	3.00	6.00	12.00
❑ Dollie 514	My Old Home Town/Back to Tennessee	1967	3.00	6.00	12.00
❑ Dollie 516	It's You/Lake County Cotton Country	1968	3.00	6.00	12.00
❑ Flip 501	Movie Magg/Turn Around	1955	250.00	500.00	1000.
❑ Jet 5054	Blue Suede Shoes/Rock Around the World	1979	—	2.00	4.00
❑ Mercury 55009	The E.P. Express/Big Bad Blues	1977	—	2.00	4.00
❑ Mercury 73425	(Let's Get) Dixiefried/One More Loser Goin' Home	1973	—	3.00	6.00
❑ Mercury 73489	Ruby, Don't Take Your Love to Town/Sing My Song	1974	—	2.50	5.00
❑ Mercury 73653	You'll Always Be a Lady to Me/Low Class	1974	—	2.50	5.00
❑ Mercury 73690	The E.P. Express/Big Bad Blues	1975	—	2.50	5.00
❑ Mercury 73993	Help Me Dream/You Tore My Heaven All to Hell	1973	—	3.00	6.00
❑ MMI 1016	Don't Get Off Gettin' It On/Georgia Court Room	1977	—	2.00	4.00
❑ MMI 1019	Standing in the Need of Love/Georgia Court Room	1977	—	2.00	4.00
❑ Music Mill 1007	Born to Boogie/Take Me Back	1976	—	2.00	4.00
❑ Smash 884760-7	Birth of Rock and Roll/Rock and Roll (Fais-Do-Do)	1986	—	2.00	4.00
—B-side with Jerry Lee Lewis, Roy Orbison and Johnny Cash					
❑ Smash 884934-7	Sixteen Candles/Rock & Roll (Fais-Do-Do)	1986	—	2.00	4.00
—B-side with Jerry Lee Lewis, Roy Orbison and Johnny Cash; A-side by Jerry Lee Lewis					
❑ Smash 888142-7	Class of '55/We Remember the King	1987	—	2.00	4.00
—B-side with Jerry Lee Lewis, Roy Orbison and Johnny Cash					
❑ Suede 101	I Don't Want to Fall in Love Again/We Did It in '54.	1978	—	2.00	4.00
❑ Suede 102	Rock-a-Billy Fever/Till You Get Through with Me.	1978	—	2.00	4.00
❑ Suede 6777	Little Teardrops/Green Grass of Home.	1977	—	2.00	4.00
❑ Sun 224	Gone, Gone, Gone/Let the Jukebox Keep On Playing.	1955	25.00	50.00	100.00
❑ Sun 234	Blue Suede Shoes/Honey Don't.	1956	15.00	30.00	60.00
❑ Sun 243	Boppin' the Blues/All Mama's Children.	1956	10.00	20.00	40.00
❑ Sun 249	Dixie Fried/I'm Sorry, I'm Not Sorry	1956	7.50	15.00	30.00
❑ Sun 261	Matchbox/Your True Love	1957	7.50	15.00	30.00
❑ Sun 274	That's Right/Forever Yours	1957	7.50	15.00	30.00
❑ Sun 287	Glad All Over/Lend Me Your Comb	1958	7.50	15.00	30.00
❑ Universal UVL-66002	Charlene/Love Makes Dreams Come True	1989	—	2.00	4.00
❑ Universal UVL-66019	Hambone/Love Makes Dreams Come True	1989	—	2.00	4.00
Albums					
❑ Accord SN-7169	Presenting Carl Perkins	1982	2.50	5.00	10.00
❑ Album Globe 8118	Country Soul	1980	2.50	5.00	10.00
❑ Album Globe 9037	Goin' Back to Memphis	1980	2.50	5.00	10.00
❑ Allegiance AV-5001	The Heart and Soul of Carl Perkins	198?	2.50	5.00	10.00
❑ Bulldog BDL-2034	Twenty Golden Pieces	198?	2.50	5.00	10.00
❑ Columbia CL 1234 [M]	Whole Lotta Shakin'	1958	100.00	200.00	400.00
❑ Columbia CS 9833	Carl Perkins' Greatest Hits	1969	6.25	12.50	25.00
—Red "360 Sound Stereo" label					
❑ Columbia CS 9931	Carl Perkins On Top	1969	6.25	12.50	25.00
—Red "360 Sound Stereo" label					
❑ Columbia CS 9981	Boppin' the Blues	1970	6.25	12.50	25.00
—Red "360 Sound Stereo" label					
❑ Columbia FC 37961	The Survivors	1982	2.50	5.00	10.00
—With Johnny Cash and Jerry Lee Lewis					
❑ Design DLP-611 [M]	Tennessee	1963	7.50	15.00	30.00
❑ Design SDLP-611 [R]	Tennessee	1963	5.00	10.00	20.00
❑ Dollie 4001	Country Boy's Dream	1967	7.50	15.00	30.00
❑ Harmony HS 11385	Carl Perkins	1970	3.75	7.50	15.00
❑ Harmony KH 31179	Brown Eyed Handsome Man	1971	3.00	6.00	12.00
❑ Harmony KH 31792	Greatest Hits	1972	3.00	6.00	12.00
❑ Hilltop 6103	Matchbox	197?	3.00	6.00	12.00
❑ Jet JT-LA856-H	Ol' Blue Suede's Back	1978	3.75	7.50	15.00
❑ Jet JZ 35604	Ol' Blue Suede's Back	1978	2.50	5.00	10.00
❑ Koala AW 14164	Country Soul	198?	2.50	5.00	10.00
❑ MCA Dot 39035	Carl Perkins	1985	2.50	5.00	10.00
❑ Mercury SRM-1-691	My Kind of Country	1973	3.00	6.00	12.00
❑ Rhino RNLP-70221	Original Sun Greatest Hits (1955-1957)	1986	3.00	6.00	12.00
❑ Rounder SS-27	Honky Tonk Gal: Rare and Unissued Sun Masters	1989	3.00	6.00	12.00
❑ Smash 830002-1	Class of '55	1986	3.00	6.00	12.00
—With Jerry Lee Lewis, Roy Orbison and Johnny Cash					
❑ Suede 002	Live at Austin City Limits	1981	2.50	5.00	10.00
❑ Sun LP-111	Original Golden Hits	1969	3.00	6.00	12.00
❑ Sun LP-112	Blue Suede Shoes	1969	3.00	6.00	12.00
❑ Sun SLP-1225 [M]	The Dance Album of Carl Perkins	1957	300.00	600.00	1200.
❑ Sun SLP-1225 [M]	Teen Beat — The Best of Carl Perkins	1961	125.00	250.00	500.00
—Reissue with new title					

Number	Title (A Side/B Side)	Yr	VG	VG+	NM
❑ Sunnyvale 9330803	The Sun Story, Vol. 3	1977	3.00	6.00	12.00
❑ Trip TLP-8503 [(2)]	The Best of Carl Perkins	1974	3.00	6.00	12.00
❑ Universal UVL-76001	Born to Rock	1989	3.75	7.50	15.00

PETER AND GORDON

45s

Number	Title (A Side/B Side)	Yr	VG	VG+	NM
❑ Capitol 2071	Greener Days/Never Ever	1968	2.50	5.00	10.00
❑ Capitol 2214	You've Had Better Times/Sipping My Wine	1968	2.50	5.00	10.00
❑ Capitol 2544	I Can Remember (Not Too Long Ago)/Hard Time, Rainy Day	1969	2.50	5.00	10.00
❑ Capitol 5175	A World Without Love/If I Were You	1964	3.00	6.00	12.00
❑ Capitol 5211	Nobody I Know/You Don't Have to Tell Me	1964	3.00	6.00	12.00
❑ Capitol 5272	I Don't Want to See You Again/I Would Buy You Presents	1964	3.00	6.00	12.00
❑ Capitol 5335	I Go to Pieces/Love Me, Baby	1965	3.00	6.00	12.00
❑ Capitol 5406	True Love Ways/If You Wish	1965	3.00	6.00	12.00
❑ Capitol 5461	To Know You Is to Love You/I Told You So	1965	2.50	5.00	10.00
❑ Capitol 5532	Don't Pity Me/Crying in the Rain	1965	2.50	5.00	10.00
❑ Capitol 5579	Woman/Wrong from the Start	1966	2.50	5.00	10.00
—A-side composer listed as "A. Smith"					
❑ Capitol 5579	Woman/Wrong from the Start	1966	3.00	6.00	12.00
—A-side composer listed as "Bernard Webb"					
❑ Capitol 5650	There's No Living Without Your Loving/ A Stranger with a Black Dove	1966	2.50	5.00	10.00
❑ Capitol 5684	To Show I Love You/Start Trying Someone Else	1966	2.50	5.00	10.00
❑ Capitol 5740	Lady Godiva/Morning's Calling	1966	2.50	5.00	10.00
❑ Capitol 5740	Lady Godiva/The House I Live In	1966	3.75	7.50	15.00
❑ Capitol 5808	Knight in Rusty Armour/Flower Lady	1966	2.50	5.00	10.00
❑ Capitol 5864	Sunday for Tea/Hurtin' Is Lovin'	1967	2.50	5.00	10.00
❑ Capitol 5919	The Jokers/Red Cream and Velvet	1967	2.50	5.00	10.00
❑ Capitol Starline 6076	A World Without Love/Nobody I Know	1965	2.00	4.00	8.00
—Green swirl label original					
❑ Capitol Starline 6103	I Go to Pieces/Love Me Baby	1966	2.00	4.00	8.00
—Green swirl label original					
❑ Capitol Starline 6104	There's No Living Without Your Loving/Stranger with a Black Dove	1966	2.00	4.00	8.00
—Green swirl label original					
❑ Capitol Starline 6155	I Don't Want to See You Again/Woman	197?	—	3.00	6.00
—Red and white "bullseye" label original					
❑ Capitol Starline 6156	Lady Godiva/You've Had Better Times	197?	—	3.00	6.00
—Red and white "bullseye" label original					

Albums

Number	Title (A Side/B Side)	Yr	VG	VG+	NM
❑ Capitol ST 2115 [S]	A World Without Love	1964	6.25	12.50	25.00
❑ Capitol T 2115 [M]	A World Without Love	1964	5.00	10.00	20.00
❑ Capitol ST 2220 [S]	I Don't Want to See You Again	1964	6.25	12.50	25.00
❑ Capitol T 2220 [M]	I Don't Want to See You Again	1964	5.00	10.00	20.00
❑ Capitol ST 2324 [S]	I Go to Pieces	1965	6.25	12.50	25.00
❑ Capitol T 2324 [M]	I Go to Pieces	1965	5.00	10.00	20.00
❑ Capitol ST 2368 [S]	True Love Ways	1965	6.25	12.50	25.00
❑ Capitol T 2368 [M]	True Love Ways	1965	5.00	10.00	20.00
❑ Capitol ST 2430 [S]	Peter and Gordon Sing the Hits of Nashville	1966	6.25	12.50	25.00
❑ Capitol T 2430 [M]	Peter and Gordon Sing the Hits of Nashville	1966	5.00	10.00	20.00
❑ Capitol ST 2477 [P]	Woman	1966	6.25	12.50	25.00
—"Woman" is rechanneled					
❑ Capitol T 2477 [M]	Woman	1966	5.00	10.00	20.00
❑ Capitol ST 2549 [P]	The Best of Peter and Gordon	1966	4.50	9.00	18.00
—Black label with colorband; "Woman" is rechanneled					
❑ Capitol ST 2549 [P]	The Best of Peter and Gordon	1967	3.75	7.50	15.00
—"Starline" label					
❑ Capitol T 2549 [M]	The Best of Peter and Gordon	1966	3.75	7.50	15.00
—Black label with colorband					
❑ Capitol T 2549 [M]	The Best of Peter and Gordon	1967	3.00	6.00	12.00
—"Starline" label					
❑ Capitol ST 2664 [S]	Lady Godiva	1967	5.00	10.00	20.00
❑ Capitol T 2664 [M]	Lady Godiva	1967	3.75	7.50	15.00
❑ Capitol ST 2729 [S]	Knight in Rusty Armour	1967	5.00	10.00	20.00
❑ Capitol T 2729 [M]	Knight in Rusty Armour	1967	3.75	7.50	15.00
❑ Capitol ST 2747 [S]	In London for Tea	1967	5.00	10.00	20.00
❑ Capitol T 2747 [M]	In London for Tea	1967	3.75	7.50	15.00
❑ Capitol ST 2882 [S]	Hot, Cold and Custard	1968	6.25	12.50	25.00
❑ Capitol SN-16084 [S]	The Best of Peter and Gordon	1979	2.00	4.00	8.00

Number	Title (A Side/B Side)	Yr	VG	VG+	NM
PETER, PAUL AND MARY					
45s					
❑ Warner Bros. 5274	Lemon Tree/Early in the Morning	1962	2.50	5.00	10.00
❑ Warner Bros. 5296	If I Had a Hammer/Gone the Rainbow	1962	2.50	5.00	10.00
❑ Warner Bros. 5325	Big Boat/Tiny Sparrow	1962	2.50	5.00	10.00
❑ Warner Bros. 5334	Settle Down (Goin' Down That Highway)/500 Miles	1963	2.50	5.00	10.00
❑ Warner Bros. 5348	Puff/Pretty Mary	1963	3.00	6.00	12.00
—First pressings have no subtitle on A-side					
❑ Warner Bros. 5348	Puff (The Magic Dragon)/Pretty Mary	1963	2.50	5.00	10.00
—Later pressings add subtitle					
❑ Warner Bros. 5368	Blowin' in the Wind/Flora	1963	2.50	5.00	10.00
❑ Warner Bros. 5385	Don't Think Twice, It's All Right/Autumn to May	1963	2.50	5.00	10.00
❑ Warner Bros. 5399	Stewball/The Cruel War	1963	2.50	5.00	10.00
❑ Warner Bros. 5402	A-Soalin'/High-A-Bye	1963	3.00	6.00	12.00
❑ Warner Bros. 5418	Tell It on the Mountain/Old Coat	1964	2.50	5.00	10.00
❑ Warner Bros. 5442	Oh, Rock My Soul (Part 1)/Oh, Rock My Soul (Part 2)	1964	2.50	5.00	10.00
❑ Warner Bros. 5496	For Lovin' Me/Monday Morning	1965	2.00	4.00	8.00
❑ Warner Bros. 5625	When the Ship Comes In/The Times They Are a-Changin'	1965	2.00	4.00	8.00
❑ Warner Bros. 5659	Early Morning Rain/The Rising of the Moon	1965	2.00	4.00	8.00
❑ Warner Bros. 5809	The Cruel War/Mon Vrai Destin	1966	2.00	4.00	8.00
❑ Warner Bros. 5842	Hurry Sundown/Sometime Lover	1966	—	—	—
—Unreleased?					
❑ Warner Bros. 5849	The Other Side of This Life/Sometime Lover	1966	2.00	4.00	8.00
❑ Warner Bros. 5883	For Baby (For Bobbie)/Hurry Sundown	1967	2.00	4.00	8.00
❑ Warner Bros. 7067	I Dig Rock and Roll Music/The Great Mandella (The Wheel of Life)	1967	2.50	5.00	10.00
❑ Warner Bros. 7092	Too Much of Nothing/The House Song	1967	2.00	4.00	8.00
❑ Warner Bros. 7232	Yesterday's Tomorrow/Love City (Postcards to Duluth)	1968	2.00	4.00	8.00
❑ Warner Bros. 7279	Day Is Done/Make Believe Town	1969	2.00	4.00	8.00
❑ Warner Bros. 7340	Leaving on a Jet Plane/The House Song	1969	2.50	5.00	10.00
❑ Warner Bros. 7359	Christmas Dinner/The Marvelous Toy	1969	2.50	5.00	10.00
❑ Warner Bros. 8684	Like the First Time/Best of Friends	1978	—	2.00	4.00
❑ Warner Bros. 8728	Forever Young/Best of Friends	1978	—	2.00	4.00
Albums					
❑ Gold Castle D1-71301	No Easy Walk to Freedom	1988	2.50	5.00	10.00
—Reissue of 171001					
❑ Gold Castle D1-71316	A Holiday Celebration	1988	2.50	5.00	10.00
❑ Gold Castle 171001	No Easy Walk to Freedom	1987	3.00	6.00	12.00
❑ Warner Bros. W 1449 [M]	Peter, Paul and Mary	1962	5.00	10.00	20.00
❑ Warner Bros. WS 1449 [S]	Peter, Paul and Mary	1962	6.25	12.50	25.00
—Gold label					
❑ Warner Bros. W 1473 [M]	(Moving)	1963	5.00	10.00	20.00
❑ Warner Bros. WS 1473 [S]	(Moving)	1963	6.25	12.50	25.00
—Gold label					
❑ Warner Bros. W 1507 [M]	In the Wind	1963	5.00	10.00	20.00
❑ Warner Bros. WS 1507 [S]	In the Wind	1963	6.25	12.50	25.00
—Gold label					
❑ Warner Bros. 2W 1555 [(2)M]	Peter, Paul and Mary In Concert	1964	6.25	12.50	25.00
❑ Warner Bros. 2WS 1555 [(2)S]	Peter, Paul and Mary In Concert	1964	7.50	15.00	30.00
—Gold labels					
❑ Warner Bros. W 1589 [M]	A Song Will Rise	1965	5.00	10.00	20.00
❑ Warner Bros. WS 1589 [S]	A Song Will Rise	1965	6.25	12.50	25.00
—Gold label					
❑ Warner Bros. W 1615 [M]	See What Tomorrow Brings	1965	5.00	10.00	20.00
❑ Warner Bros. WS 1615 [S]	See What Tomorrow Brings	1965	6.25	12.50	25.00
—Gold label					
❑ Warner Bros. W 1648 [M]	Peter, Paul and Mary Album	1966	5.00	10.00	20.00
❑ Warner Bros. WS 1648 [S]	Peter, Paul and Mary Album	1966	6.25	12.50	25.00
—Gold label					
❑ Warner Bros. W 1700 [M]	Album 1700	1967	6.25	12.50	25.00
❑ Warner Bros. WS 1700 [S]	Album 1700	1967	6.25	12.50	25.00
—Gold label					
❑ Warner Bros. WS 1751	Late Again	1968	3.75	7.50	15.00
—Green "W7" label					
❑ Warner Bros. WS 1785	Peter, Paul and Mommy	1969	3.75	7.50	15.00
—Green "W7" label					
❑ Warner Bros. BS 2552	(Ten) Years Together — The Best of Peter, Paul and Mary	1970	3.75	7.50	15.00
—Green "WB" label					
❑ Warner Bros. BSK 3105	(Ten) Years Together — The Best of Peter, Paul and Mary	1977	2.50	5.00	10.00
—"Burbank" palm-trees label					
❑ Warner Bros. BSK 3231	Reunion	1978	2.50	5.00	10.00
PETERSEN, PAUL					
45s					
❑ Colpix 620	She Can't Find Her Keys/Very Likely	1962	3.75	7.50	15.00
❑ Colpix 631	What Did They Do Before Rock and Roll/Very Unlikely	1962	5.00	10.00	20.00
—With Shelly Fabares					
❑ Colpix 632	Keep Your Love Locked (Deep in Your Heart)/ Be Everything to Anyone You Love	1962	3.00	6.00	12.00
❑ Colpix 649	Lollipops and Roses/Please Mr. Sun	1962	3.00	6.00	12.00
❑ Colpix 663	My Dad/Little Boy Sad	1962	3.75	7.50	15.00
❑ Colpix 676	Amy/I Only Have Eyes for You	1963	3.00	6.00	12.00
❑ Colpix 676	Amy/Goody Goody	1963	3.00	6.00	12.00
❑ Colpix 697	Girls in the Summertime/Mama, Your Little Boy Fell	1963	3.00	6.00	12.00
❑ Colpix 707	The Cheer Leader/Polka Dots and Moonbeams	1963	3.00	6.00	12.00

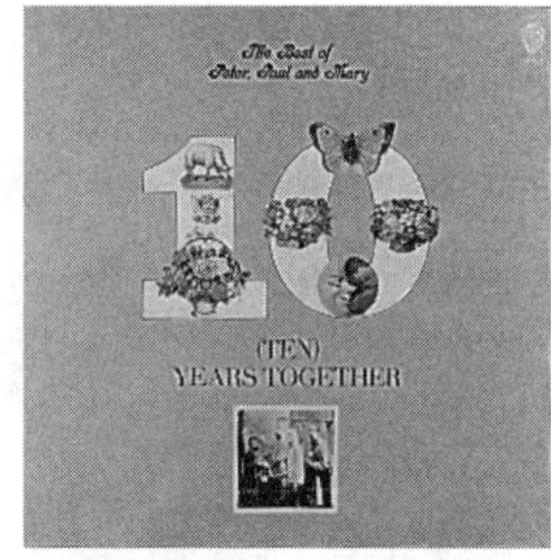

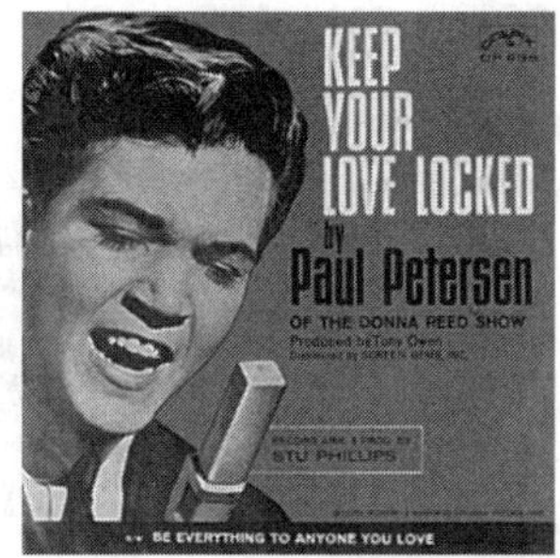

Number	Title (A Side/B Side)	Yr	VG	VG+	NM
❑ Colpix 720	She Rides with Me/Poorest Boy in Town	1964	20.00	40.00	80.00
—A-side produced by Brian Wilson					
❑ Colpix 730	Where Is She/Hey There Beautiful	1964	3.00	6.00	12.00
❑ Colpix 763	Happy/Little Dreamer	1965	3.00	6.00	12.00
❑ Colpix 785	The Ring/You Don't Need Money	1965	3.00	6.00	12.00
❑ Motown 1108	Chained/Don't Let It Happen	1967	5.00	10.00	20.00
❑ Motown 1129	A Little Bit for Sandy/Your Love's Got Me Runnin'	1968	5.00	10.00	20.00

Albums

Number	Title (A Side/B Side)	Yr	VG	VG+	NM
❑ Colpix CP-429 [M]	Lollipops and Roses	1962	12.50	25.00	50.00
❑ Colpix SCP-429 [S]	Lollipops and Roses	1962	15.00	30.00	60.00
❑ Colpix CP-442 [M]	My Dad	1963	12.50	25.00	50.00
❑ Colpix SCP-442 [S]	My Dad	1963	15.00	30.00	60.00

PETERSON, RAY

45s

Number	Title (A Side/B Side)	Yr	VG	VG+	NM
❑ Cloud 9 134	Nobody But Me/(B-side unknown)	1975	—	2.50	5.00
❑ Decca 32861	Stamp Out Loneliness/There's a Better Way	1971	—	2.50	5.00
❑ Dunes 2002	Corrina, Corinna/Be My Girl	1960	6.25	12.50	25.00
—Produced by Phil Spector					
❑ Dunes 2004	Sweet Little Kathy/You Didn't Care	1961	3.75	7.50	15.00
❑ Dunes 2006	Missing You/You Thrill Me	1961	3.75	7.50	15.00
❑ Dunes 2009	I Could Have Loved You So Well/Why Don't You Write Me	1961	5.00	10.00	20.00
—Produced by Phil Spector					
❑ Dunes 2013	You Know Me Much Too Well/You Didn't Care	1962	3.75	7.50	15.00
❑ Dunes 2018	If Only Tomorrow/You Didn't Care	1962	3.75	7.50	15.00
❑ Dunes 2019	Is It Wrong/Slowly	1963	3.75	7.50	15.00
❑ Dunes 2022	A Love to Remember/I'm Not Jimmy	1963	3.75	7.50	15.00
❑ Dunes 2024	Where Are You/Deep Are the Roots	1963	3.75	7.50	15.00
❑ Dunes 2025	Give Us Your Blessing/Without Love (There Is Nothing)	1963	3.75	7.50	15.00
❑ Dunes 2027	I Forgot What It Was Like/Be My Girl	1963	3.75	7.50	15.00
❑ Dunes 2030	Promises/Sweet Little Kathy	1963	3.75	7.50	15.00
❑ MGM 13269	If You Were Here/Oh No	1964	2.50	5.00	10.00
❑ MGM 13299	Across the Street (Is a Million Miles Away)/When I Stop Dreaming	1964	2.50	5.00	10.00
❑ MGM 13330	Unchained Melody/That's All	1965	2.00	4.00	8.00
❑ MGM 13336	A House Without WIndows/Wish I Could Say No to You	1965	2.00	4.00	8.00
❑ MGM 13388	I'm Only Human/One Lonesome Rose	1965	2.00	4.00	8.00
❑ MGM 13436	Love Hurts/Everybody	1966	2.00	4.00	8.00
❑ MGM 13508	Amanda/I'm Gonna Change Everything	1966	2.00	4.00	8.00
❑ MGM 13564	Just One Smile/The Whole World's Goin' Crazy	1966	2.00	4.00	8.00
❑ RCA GB-11758	Tell Laura I Love Her/The Wonder of You	1979	—	—	3.00
—Gold Standard Series					
❑ RCA Victor 37-7845	My Blue Angel/I'm Tired	1961	12.50	25.00	50.00
—"Compact Single 33" (small hole, plays at LP speed)					
❑ RCA Victor 47-7087	Fever/We're Old Enough to Cry	1957	6.25	12.50	25.00
❑ RCA Victor 47-7165	Let's Try Romance/Shirley Purley	1958	5.00	10.00	20.00
❑ RCA Victor 47-7255	Suddenly/Tall Light	1958	5.00	10.00	20.00
❑ RCA Victor 47-7303	Patricia/The Blue-Eyed Baby	1958	5.00	10.00	20.00
❑ RCA Victor 47-7336	Dream Way/I'll Always Want You Near	1958	5.00	10.00	20.00
❑ RCA Victor 47-7404	Richer Than I/Love Is a Woman	1958	5.00	10.00	20.00
❑ RCA Victor 47-7513	The Wonder of You/I'm Gone	1959	6.25	12.50	25.00
❑ RCA Victor 47-7578	My Blue Angel/Come and Get It	1959	5.00	10.00	20.00
❑ RCA Victor 47-7635	Goodnight My Love (Pleasant Dreams)/Till Then	1959	5.00	10.00	20.00
❑ RCA Victor 47-7703	Answer Me, My Love/What Do You Want to Make Those Eyes At Me For	1960	5.00	10.00	20.00
❑ RCA Victor 47-7745	Tell Laura I Love Her/Wedding Days	1960	6.25	12.50	25.00
❑ RCA Victor 47-7779	Teenage Heartache/I'll Always Want You Near	1960	5.00	10.00	20.00
❑ RCA Victor 47-7845	My Blue Angel/I'm Tired	1961	5.00	10.00	20.00
❑ RCA Victor 47-8333	The Wonder of You/Goodnight My Love	1964	2.50	5.00	10.00
❑ Reprise 0811	Love Rules the World/Together	1969	2.00	4.00	8.00
❑ Uni 55249	Love the Understanding Way/Oklahoma City Rimes	1970	2.00	4.00	8.00
❑ Uni 55268	Tell Laura I Love Her/To Wait for Love	1971	—	3.00	6.00
❑ Uni 55275	Fever/Changes	1971	—	3.00	6.00

Albums

Number	Title (A Side/B Side)	Yr	VG	VG+	NM
❑ Decca DL 75307	Ray Peterson Country	1971	5.00	10.00	20.00
❑ MGM E-4250 [M]	The Very Best of Ray Peterson	1964	6.25	12.50	25.00
❑ MGM SE-4250 [S]	The Very Best of Ray Peterson	1964	7.50	15.00	30.00
❑ MGM E-4277 [M]	The Other Side of Ray Peterson	1965	6.25	12.50	25.00

Number	Title (A Side/B Side)	Yr	VG	VG+	NM
❑ MGM SE-4277 [S]	The Other Side of Ray Peterson	1965	7.50	15.00	30.00
❑ RCA Camden CAL-2119 [M]	Goodnight My Love	1966	3.00	6.00	12.00
❑ RCA Camden CAS-2119 [S]	Goodnight My Love	1966	3.00	6.00	12.00
❑ RCA Victor LPM-2297 [M]	Tell Laura I Love Her	1960	25.00	50.00	100.00
❑ RCA Victor LSP-2297 [S]	Tell Laura I Love Her	1960	37.50	75.00	150.00
❑ Uni 73078	Missing You/Featuring His Greatest Hits!	1969	5.00	10.00	20.00

PETTY, TOM, AND THE HEARTBREAKERS

45s

Number	Title (A Side/B Side)	Yr	VG	VG+	NM
❑ Backstreet 41138	Don't Do Me Like That/Casa Dega	1979	—	2.00	4.00
❑ Backstreet 41169	Refugee/It's Rainin' Again	1980	—	2.00	4.00
❑ Backstreet 41227	Here Comes My Girl/Louisiana Rain	1980	—	2.00	4.00
❑ Backstreet 51100	The Waiting/Nightwatchman	1981	—	2.00	4.00
❑ Backstreet 51136	A Woman in Love (It's Not Me)/Gator on the Lawn	1981	—	2.00	4.00
❑ Backstreet 52144	You Got Lucky/Between Two Worlds	1982	—	2.00	4.00
❑ Backstreet 52181	Change of Heart/Heartbreakers Beach Party	1983	2.00	4.00	8.00
—Red vinyl in clear plastic sleeve with sticker					
❑ MCA 52496	Don't Come Around Here No More/Trailer	1985	—	2.00	4.00
—Original copies have a 4:19 version of the A-side					
❑ MCA 52605	Make It Better (Forget About Me)/Crackin' Up	1985	—	—	3.00
❑ MCA 52658	Rebels/Southern Accents	1985	—	—	3.00
❑ MCA 52772	Needles and Pins/Spike	1985	—	—	3.00
—A-side: With Stevie Nicks					
❑ MCA 53065	Jammin' Me/Make That Connection.	1987	—	—	3.00
❑ MCA 53153	All Mixed Up/Let Me Up (I've Had Enough).	1987	—	—	3.00
❑ MCA 53669	I Won't Back Down/The Apartment Song.	1989	—	2.00	4.00
❑ MCA 53682	Runnin' Down a Dream/Alright for Now	1989	—	2.00	4.00
❑ MCA 53748	Free Fallin'/Down the Line.	1989	—	2.50	5.00
❑ MCA 53781	A Face in the Crowd/A Mind with a Heart of Its Own.	1990	—	2.00	4.00
❑ Shelter 62006	Breakdown/The Wild One, Forever.	1976	—	—	—
—Unreleased?					
❑ Shelter 62007	American Girl/Luna	1977	—	3.00	6.00
❑ Shelter 62008	Breakdown/Fooled Again (I Can't Take It)	1977	—	3.00	6.00
❑ Shelter 62010	I Need to Know/No Second Thoughts	1978	—	2.50	5.00
❑ Shelter 62011	Listen to Her Heart/I Don't Know What to Say to You	1978	—	2.50	5.00

Albums

Number	Title (A Side/B Side)	Yr	VG	VG+	NM
❑ American 44285-1 [(2)]	Highway Companion	2007	6.25	12.50	25.00
—180-gram issue; CD released in 2006					
❑ Backstreet BSR-5105	Damn the Torpedoes	1979	2.50	5.00	10.00
❑ Backstreet BSR-5160	Hard Promises	1981	2.50	5.00	10.00
❑ Backstreet BSR-5360	Long After Dark	1982	2.50	5.00	10.00
❑ MCA 5486	Southern Accents	1985	2.50	5.00	10.00
❑ MCA 5836	Let Me Up (I've Had Enough)	1987	2.50	5.00	10.00
❑ MCA 6253	Full Moon Fever	1989	2.50	5.00	10.00
❑ MCA 2-8021 [(2)]	Pack Up the Plantation — Live!	1985	3.00	6.00	12.00
❑ MCA 37116	You're Gonna Get It!	1982	2.00	4.00	8.00
❑ MCA 37143	Tom Petty and the Heartbreakers	1982	2.00	4.00	8.00
❑ MCA 37239	Hard Promises	1984	2.00	4.00	8.00
❑ Shelter SRL-52006	Tom Petty and the Heartbreakers	1976	3.75	7.50	15.00
—Original copies were distributed by ABC					
❑ Shelter DA-52029	You're Gonna Get It!	1978	3.75	7.50	15.00
—Original copies were distributed by ABC					

PICKETT, BOBBY "BORIS"

45s

Number	Title (A Side/B Side)	Yr	VG	VG+	NM
❑ Anthem 205	Monster Concert/Am I	1973	—	3.00	6.00
❑ Capitol 5063	Simon the Sensible Surfer/Simon Says So What	1963	6.25	12.50	25.00
❑ Garpax P-1	Monster Mash/Monster's Mash Party	1962	7.50	15.00	30.00
—Orange label, first release of 44167?					
❑ Garpax 724	I'm Down to My Last Heartbreak/I Can't Stop	1962	6.25	12.50	25.00
❑ Garpax 44167	Monster Mash/Monster's Mash Party	1962	6.25	12.50	25.00
❑ Garpax 44171	Monster's Holiday/Monster's Motion	1962	6.25	12.50	25.00
❑ Garpax 44175	Graduation Day/The Humpty Dumpty	1963	6.25	12.50	25.00
❑ Garpax 44185	Blood Bank Blues/Me and My Mummy	1965	6.25	12.50	25.00
❑ Metromedia BMBO-0089	Me and My Mummy/It's Not the Same Without You	1973	2.50	5.00	10.00
—B-side by Pickett and Payne					
❑ Parrot 348	Monster Mash/Monster's Mash Party	1970	2.50	5.00	10.00
—Reissued in 1973 with the same number and label design					
❑ Parrot 366	Monster's Holiday/Monster Minuet	1971	2.50	5.00	10.00
❑ Pizzeria 1	Star Drek/Mangy Old Sidewinder	1977	2.00	5.00	10.00
—With Peter Ferrara; originals are autographed on the label by both					
❑ Polydor 14361	King Kong (Your Song)/Disco Kong	1976	—	2.50	5.00
—With Peter Ferrara					
❑ RCA Victor 47-8312	Smoke! Smoke! Smoke! (That Cigarette)/Gotta Leave This Town	1964	3.75	7.50	15.00
❑ RCA Victor 47-8459	The Werewolf Watusi/Monster Swim	1964	3.75	7.50	15.00
❑ White Whale 363	Monster Man Jam/Am I	1970	6.25	12.50	25.00
—B-side by Bobby and Joan Pickett					
❑ White Whale 365	Monster Concert/(B-side unknown)	1970	6.25	12.50	25.00

Albums

Number	Title (A Side/B Side)	Yr	VG	VG+	NM
❑ Garpax GPX 57001 [M]	The Original Monster Mash	1962	37.50	75.00	150.00
❑ Garpax SGP 67001 [S]	The Original Monster Mash	1962	62.50	125.00	250.00
❑ Parrot XPAS 71063 [R]	The Original Monster Mash	1973	6.25	12.50	25.00
—Reissue of Garpax LP with four tracks deleted and one added					

PICKETT, WILSON

45s

Number	Title (A Side/B Side)	Yr	VG	VG+	NM
❑ Atlantic 2233	I'm Gonna Cry/For Better or Worse	1964	3.75	7.50	15.00

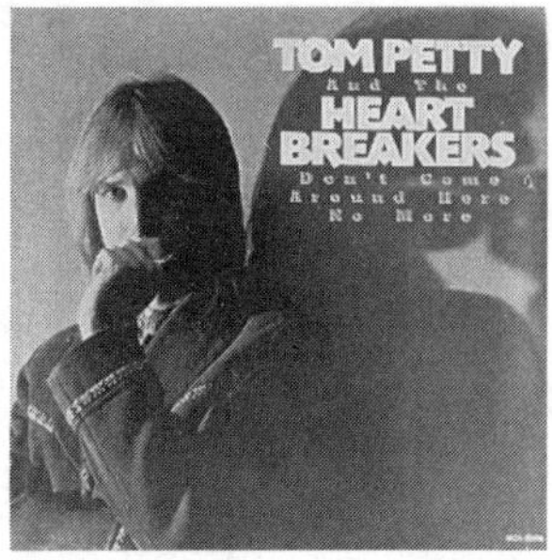

Number	Title (A Side/B Side)	Yr	VG	VG+	NM
❑ Atlantic 2271	Come Home Baby/Take a Little Love	1965	3.75	7.50	15.00
❑ Atlantic 2289	In the Midnight Hour/I'm Not Tired	1965	3.75	7.50	15.00
❑ Atlantic 2306	Don't Fight It/It's All Over	1965	3.75	7.50	15.00
❑ Atlantic 2320	634-5789 (Soulsville, U.S.A.)/That's a Man's Way	1966	3.75	7.50	15.00
❑ Atlantic 2334	Ninety-Nine and a Half (Won't Do)/Danger Zone	1966	3.75	7.50	15.00
❑ Atlantic 2348	Land of 1000 Dances/You're So Fine	1966	3.75	7.50	15.00
❑ Atlantic 2365	Mustang Sally/Three Time Loser	1966	3.75	7.50	15.00
❑ Atlantic 2381	Eveybody Needs Somebody to Love/Nothing You Can Do	1967	3.00	6.00	12.00
❑ Atlantic 2394	I Found a Love — Part I/I Found a Love — Part II	1967	3.00	6.00	12.00
❑ Atlantic 2412	Soul Dance Number Three/You Can't Stand Alone	1967	3.00	6.00	12.00
❑ Atlantic 2430	Funky Broadway/I'm Sorry About That	1967	3.00	6.00	12.00
❑ Atlantic 2448	Stag-O-Lee/I'm In Love	1967	3.00	6.00	12.00
❑ Atlantic 2484	Jealous Love/I've Come a Long Way	1968	2.50	5.00	10.00
❑ Atlantic 2504	She's Lookin' Good/We've Got to Have Love	1968	2.50	5.00	10.00
❑ Atlantic 2528	I'm a Midnight Mover/Deborah	1968	2.50	5.00	10.00
❑ Atlantic 2558	I Found a True Love/For Better or Worse	1968	2.50	5.00	10.00
❑ Atlantic 2575	A Man and a Half/People Make the World (What It Is)	1968	2.50	5.00	10.00
❑ Atlantic 2591	Hey Jude/Search Your Heart	1968	2.50	5.00	10.00
❑ Atlantic 2611	Mini-Skirt Minnie/Back in Your Arms	1969	2.00	4.00	8.00
❑ Atlantic 2631	Born to Be Wild/Toe Hold	1969	2.00	4.00	8.00
❑ Atlantic 2648	Hey Joe/Night Owl	1969	2.00	4.00	8.00
❑ Atlantic 2682	You Keep Me Hangin' On/Now You See Me, Now You Don't	1969	2.00	4.00	8.00
❑ Atlantic 2722	Sugar, Sugar/Cole, Cooke, and Redding	1970	2.00	4.00	8.00
❑ Atlantic 2753	She Said Yes/It's Still Good	1970	—	3.00	6.00
❑ Atlantic 2765	Engine Number Nine/International Playboy	1970	—	3.00	6.00
❑ Atlantic 2781	Don't Let the Green Grass Fool You/Ain't No Doubt About It	1971	—	3.00	6.00
❑ Atlantic 2797	Don't Knock My Love (Part 1)/Don't Knock My Love (Part 2)	1971	—	3.00	6.00
❑ Atlantic 2824	Call My Name, I'll Be There/Woman Let Me Down Home	1971	—	3.00	6.00
❑ Atlantic 2852	Fire and Water/Pledging My Love	1971	—	3.00	6.00
❑ Atlantic 2878	Funk Factory/One Step Away	1972	—	3.00	6.00
❑ Atlantic 2909	Mama Told Me Not to Come/Covering the Same Old Ground	1972	—	3.00	6.00
❑ Atlantic 2961	Come Right Here/International Playboy	1973	—	3.00	6.00
❑ Big Tree 16121	Who Turned You On/Dance You Down	1978	—	2.50	5.00
❑ Big Tree 16129	Groovin'/Time to Let the Sun Shine In	1978	—	2.50	5.00
❑ Correc-Tone 501	Let Me Be Your Boy/My Heart Belongs to You	1962	15.00	30.00	60.00
❑ Cub 9113	Let Me Be Your Boy/My Heart Belongs to You	1962	7.50	15.00	30.00
❑ Double L 713	If You Need Me/Baby Call on Me	1963	5.00	10.00	20.00
❑ Double L 717	It's Too Late/I'm Gonna Love You	1963	5.00	10.00	20.00
❑ Double L 724	I'm Down to My Last Heartbreak/I Can't Stop	1963	3.75	7.50	15.00
❑ EMI America 8027	I Want You/Love of My Life	1979	—	2.50	5.00
❑ EMI America 8034	Live with Me/Granny	1980	—	2.50	5.00
❑ EMI America 8070	Ain't Gonna Give You No More/ Don't Underestimate the Power of Love	1981	—	2.50	5.00
❑ EMI America 8082	Back on the Right Track/It's You	1981	—	2.50	5.00
❑ Erva 318	Love Dagger/Time to Let the Sun Shine on Me	1977	—	2.50	5.00
❑ Motown 1898	Don't Turn Away/Can't Stop Now	1987	—	2.00	4.00
❑ Motown 1916	In the Midnight Hour/Just Let Her Know	1987	—	2.00	4.00
❑ Motown 1938	Love Never Let Me Down/Just Let Her Know	1988	—	2.00	4.00
❑ Motown 53407	Love Never Let Me Down/Just Let Her Know	1988	—	2.00	4.00
❑ RCA Victor 74-0908	Mr. Magic Man/I Sho' Love You	1973	—	3.00	6.00
❑ RCA Victor APBO-0049	Take a Closer Look at the Woman You're With/ Two Woman and a Wife	1973	—	3.00	6.00
❑ RCA Victor APBO-0174	Soft Soul Boogie Woogie/Take That Pollution Out of Your Throat	1973	—	3.00	6.00
❑ RCA Victor APBO-0309	Take Your Pleasure Where You FInd It/What Good Is a Lie	1974	—	3.00	6.00
❑ RCA Victor PB-10067	I Was Too Nice/Isn't That So	1974	—	3.00	6.00
❑ Verve 10378	Let Me Be Your Boy/My Heart Belongs to You	1966	5.00	10.00	20.00
❑ Wicked 8101	The Best Part of a Man/How Will I Ever Know	1975	—	3.00	6.00
❑ Wicked 8102	Love Will Keep Us Together/It's Gonna Be Good	1976	—	3.00	6.00
Albums					
❑ Atlantic SD 2-501 [(2)]	Wilson Pickett's Greatest Hits	1973	5.00	10.00	20.00
❑ Atlantic 8114 [M]	In the Midnight Hour	1965	10.00	20.00	40.00
❑ Atlantic SD 8114 [R]	In the Midnight Hour	1965	7.50	15.00	30.00
❑ Atlantic 8129 [M]	The Exciting Wilson Pickett	1966	10.00	20.00	40.00
❑ Atlantic SD 8129 [R]	The Exciting Wilson Pickett	1966	7.50	15.00	30.00
❑ Atlantic 8136 [M]	The Wicked Pickett	1967	10.00	20.00	40.00
❑ Atlantic SD 8136 [R]	The Wicked Pickett	1967	7.50	15.00	30.00
❑ Atlantic 8145 [M]	The Sound of Wilson Pickett	1967	10.00	20.00	40.00

Number	Title (A Side/B Side)	Yr	VG	VG+	NM
❑ Atlantic SD 8145 [P]	The Sound of Wilson Pickett	1967	10.00	20.00	40.00
❑ Atlantic 8151 [M]	The Best of Wilson Pickett	1967	10.00	20.00	40.00
❑ Atlantic SD 8151 [R]	The Best of Wilson Pickett	1967	5.00	10.00	20.00
❑ Atlantic SD 8175	I'm in Love	1968	6.25	12.50	25.00
❑ Atlantic SD 8183	The Midnight Mover	1968	6.25	12.50	25.00
❑ Atlantic SD 8215	Hey Jude	1969	5.00	10.00	20.00
❑ Atlantic SD 8250	Right On	1970	5.00	10.00	20.00
❑ Atlantic SD 8270	Wilson Pickett in Philadelphia	1970	5.00	10.00	20.00
❑ Atlantic SD 8290 [S]	The Best of Wilson Pickett, Vol. II	1971	3.75	7.50	15.00
❑ Atlantic SD 8300	Don't Knock My Love	1971	3.75	7.50	15.00
❑ Atlantic 81283	The Best of Wilson Pickett	1985	2.50	5.00	10.00
❑ Big Tree SD 76011	Funky Situation	1978	3.00	6.00	12.00
❑ Double-L DL-2300 [M]	It's Too Late	1963	12.50	25.00	50.00
❑ Double-L SDL-8300 [S]	It's Too Late	1963	17.50	35.00	70.00
❑ EMI America SW-17019	I Want You	1979	3.00	6.00	12.00
❑ EMI America SW-17043	Right Track	1981	3.00	6.00	12.00
❑ Motown 6244 ML	American Soul Man	1987	2.50	5.00	10.00
❑ RCA Victor APL1-0312	Miz Lena's Boy	1973	3.75	7.50	15.00
❑ RCA Victor APL1-0495	Pickett in the Pocket	1974	3.75	7.50	15.00
❑ RCA Victor APL1-0856	Join Me and Let's Be Free	1975	3.75	7.50	15.00
❑ RCA Victor ANL1-2149	Join Me and Let's Be Free	1977	2.50	5.00	10.00
—Reissue					
❑ RCA Victor LSP-4858	Mr. Magic Man	1973	3.75	7.50	15.00
❑ Trip 8010	Wickedness	1972	2.50	5.00	10.00
❑ Wand WD-672 [M]	Great Wilson Pickett Hits	1966	7.50	15.00	30.00
❑ Wand WDS-672 [R]	Great Wilson Pickett Hits	1966	5.00	10.00	20.00
❑ Wicked 9001	Chocolate Mountain	1976	6.25	12.50	25.00
PINK FLOYD					
45s					
❑ Columbia 02165	Run Like Hell/Comfortably Numb	1981	—	—	3.00
—Reissue					
❑ Columbia 03118	Another Brick in the Wall, Part 2/One of My Turns	1982	—	—	3.00
—Reissue					
❑ Columbia 03142	When the Tigers Broke Free/Bring the Boys Back Home	1982	—	2.00	4.00
❑ Columbia X18-03176	When the Tigers Broke Free/Bring the Boys Back Home	1982	2.50	5.00	10.00
❑ Columbia 03905	Not Now John (Obscured Version)/The Heroes Return	1983	—	2.00	4.00
❑ Columbia 07363	Learning to Fly/Terminal Frost	1987	—	2.00	4.00
❑ Columbia 07660	On the Turning Away/Run Like Hell	1987	—	2.00	4.00
❑ Columbia 10248	Have a Cigar/Welcome to the Machine	1975	3.00	6.00	12.00
❑ Columbia 11187	Another Brick in the Wall (Part 2)/One of My Turns	1980	—	2.50	5.00
—Custom "wall" label					
❑ Columbia 11265	Run Like Hell/Don't Leave Me Now	1980	—	2.00	4.00
❑ Columbia 11311	Comfortably Numb/Hey You	1980	—	2.00	4.00
❑ Harvest 3240	Fearless/One of These Days	1971	5.00	10.00	20.00
❑ Harvest 3391	Stay/Free Four	1972	5.00	10.00	20.00
❑ Harvest 3609	Money/Any Colour You Like	1973	3.75	7.50	15.00
❑ Harvest 3832	Time/Us and Them	1974	5.00	10.00	20.00
❑ Tower 333	Arnold Layne/Candy and a Currant Bun	1967	50.00	100.00	200.00
❑ Tower 356	See Emily Play/Scarecrow	1967	50.00	100.00	200.00
❑ Tower 378	The Gnome/Flaming	1967	37.50	75.00	150.00
❑ Tower 426	It Would Be So Nice/Julia Dream	1968	62.50	125.00	250.00
❑ Tower 440	Let There Be More Light/Remember a Day	1968	75.00	150.00	300.00
Albums					
❑ Capitol ST-12276	Works	1983	2.50	5.00	10.00
❑ Capitol SN-16230	More	1982	2.00	4.00	8.00
—Budget-line reissue					
❑ Capitol SN-16234	Relics	1982	2.00	4.00	8.00
—Budget-line reissue					
❑ Capitol SN-16330	Obscured by Clouds	1985	2.00	4.00	8.00
—Budget-line reissue					
❑ Capitol SN-16337	Atom Heart Mother	1985	2.00	4.00	8.00
—Budget-line reissue					
❑ Columbia PC 33453	Wish You Were Here	1975	6.25	12.50	25.00
—Original copies had a blue wraparound with title/artist sticker. Most buyers threw this out upon opening the LP!					
❑ Columbia JC 34474	Animals	1977	2.50	5.00	10.00
❑ Columbia PC2 36183 [(2)]	The Wall	1979	3.75	7.50	15.00
❑ Columbia TC 37680	A Collection of Great Dance Songs	1981	2.50	5.00	10.00
❑ Columbia OC 40599	A Momentary Lapse of Reason	1987	2.50	5.00	10.00
❑ Columbia PC2 44484 [(2)]	Delicate Sound of Thunder	1988	5.00	10.00	20.00
❑ Harvest SKAO-382	Atom Heart Mother	1970	6.25	12.50	25.00
—Without title on front cover					
❑ Harvest SKBB-388 [(2)]	Ummagumma	1969	10.00	20.00	40.00
—With the soundtrack LP from "Gigi" leaning against wall on front cover					
❑ Harvest SW-759	Relics	1971	3.75	7.50	15.00
❑ Harvest SMAS-832	Meddle	1971	3.75	7.50	15.00
❑ Harvest ST-11078	Obscured by Clouds	1972	3.75	7.50	15.00
❑ Harvest SMAS-11163	The Dark Side of the Moon	1973	6.25	12.50	25.00
—With poster and two stickers					
❑ Harvest ST-11198	More	1973	3.00	6.00	12.00
—Reissue of Tower 5169					
❑ Harvest SABB-11257 [(2)]	A Nice Pair	1973	3.75	7.50	15.00
❑ Tower ST 5093 [S]	Pink Floyd (The Piper at the Gates of Dawn)	1967	20.00	40.00	80.00
—Orange label					
❑ Tower ST 5093 [S]	Pink Floyd (The Piper at the Gates of Dawn)	1968	10.00	20.00	40.00
—Multi-color striped label					
❑ Tower T 5093 [M]	Pink Floyd (The Piper at the Gates of Dawn)	1967	62.50	125.00	250.00

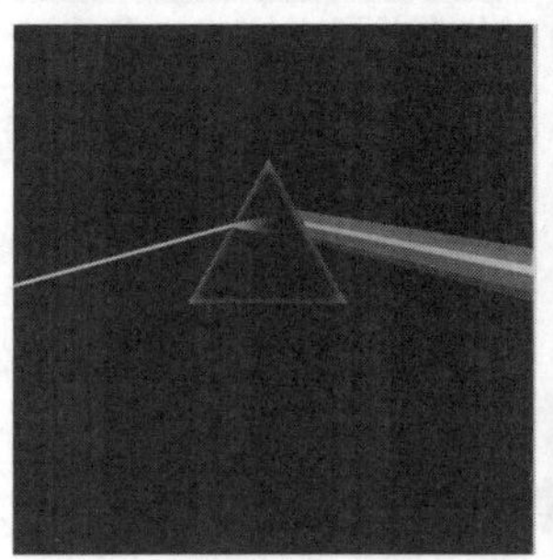

Number	Title (A Side/B Side)	Yr	VG	VG+	NM
❑ Tower ST 5131	A Saucerful of Secrets	1968	20.00	40.00	80.00
—Orange label					
❑ Tower ST 5131	A Saucerful of Secrets	1968	10.00	20.00	40.00
—Multi-color striped label					
❑ Tower ST 5169	More	1968	12.50	25.00	50.00

PITNEY, GENE

45s

Number	Title (A Side/B Side)	Yr	VG	VG+	NM
❑ Blaze 351	Going Back to My Love/Cradle of My Arms	1958	7.50	15.00	30.00
—As "Billy Bryan"					
❑ Epic 50332	Dedication AKA This Song I Want to Dedicate to You/Sandman	1977	—	2.50	5.00
❑ Epic 50461	It's Over, It's Over/Walkin' in the Sun	1977	—	2.50	5.00
❑ Festival 25002	Please Come Back/I'll Find You	1960	7.50	15.00	30.00
❑ Musicor 1002	(I Wanna) Love My Life Away/I Laughed So Hard I Cried	1960	3.75	7.50	15.00
❑ Musicor 1006	Louisiana Mama/Take Me Tonight	1961	3.75	7.50	15.00
❑ Musicor 1009	Town Without Pity/Air Mail Special Delivery	1961	3.75	7.50	15.00
❑ Musicor 1011	Every Breath I Take/Mr. Moon, Mr. Cupid and I	1961	5.00	10.00	20.00
—Produced by Phil Spector; mostly brown label					
❑ Musicor 1011	Every Breath I Take/Mr. Moon, Mr. Cupid and I	1961	7.50	15.00	30.00
—Produced by Phil Spector; mostly gunmetal gray label with color inserts					
❑ Musicor 1020	(The Man Who Shot) Liberty Valance/Take It Like a Man	1962	3.75	7.50	15.00
—Mostly brown label					
❑ Musicor 1022	Only Love Can Break a Heart/If I Didn't Have a Dime	1962	3.75	7.50	15.00
—Mostly brown label					
❑ Musicor 1026	Half Heaven-Half Heartache/Tower Tall	1962	3.75	7.50	15.00
—Mostly black label					
❑ Musicor 1026	Half Heaven-Half Heartache/Tower Tall	1962	6.25	12.50	25.00
—Mostly brown label					
❑ Musicor 1028	Mecca/Teardrop by Teardrop	1963	3.75	7.50	15.00
❑ Musicor 1032	True Love Never Runs Smooth/Donna Means Heartbreak	1963	3.75	7.50	15.00
❑ Musicor 1034	Twenty-Four Hours from Tulsa/Lonely Night Dream	1963	3.75	7.50	15.00
❑ Musicor 1036	That Girl Belongs to Yesterday/Who Needs It	1964	5.00	10.00	20.00
—A-side written by Mick Jagger and Keith Richards and produced by Andrew Oldham					
❑ Musicor 1038	Yesterday's Hero/Cornflower Blue	1964	3.75	7.50	15.00
❑ Musicor 1039	I'm Gonna Find Myself a Girl/Lips Are Redder	1964	—	—	—
—Unreleased?					
❑ Musicor 1040	It Hurts to Be in Love/Hawaii	1964	3.75	7.50	15.00
❑ Musicor 1045	I'm Gonna Be Strong/E Se Domani	1964	3.75	7.50	15.00
❑ Musicor 1045	I'm Gonna Be Strong/Aladdin's Lamp	1964	5.00	10.00	20.00
❑ Musicor 1065	Amici Miri/I Tuoi Anni Piu Belli	1965	—	—	—
—Unreleased?					
❑ Musicor 1070	I Must Be Seeing Things/Marianne	1965	3.00	6.00	12.00
❑ Musicor 1093	Last Chance to Turn Around/Save Your Love	1965	3.00	6.00	12.00
❑ Musicor 1103	Looking Through the Eyes of Love/ There's No Living Without Your Loving	1965	3.00	6.00	12.00
❑ Musicor 1130	Princess in Rags/Amore Mio	1965	3.00	6.00	12.00
❑ Musicor 1150	Me Voy Para El Compo/Hojas Muertas	1966	—	—	—
—Unreleased?					
❑ Musicor 1155	Lei Mi Aspetta/Nessuno Mi Puo' Guidcare	1966	3.75	7.50	15.00
❑ Musicor 1171	Backstage/Blue Color	1966	2.50	5.00	10.00
❑ Musicor 1200	(In the) Cold Light of Day/The Boss' Daughter	1966	2.50	5.00	10.00
❑ Musicor 1219	Just One Smile/Innamorato	1966	2.50	5.00	10.00
❑ Musicor 1233	For Me, This Is Happy/I'm Gonna Listen to Me	1967	2.50	5.00	10.00
❑ Musicor 1235	Don't Mean to Be a Preacher/ Animal Crackers (In Cellophane Boxes)	1967	2.50	5.00	10.00
❑ Musicor 1245	Tremblin'/Where Did the Magic Go	1967	2.50	5.00	10.00
❑ Musicor 1252	Somethin' Gotten Hold of My Heart/Building Up My Dream World	1967	2.50	5.00	10.00
❑ Musicor 1299	The More I Saw of Her/Won't Take Long	1968	2.00	4.00	8.00
❑ Musicor 1306	She's a Heartbreaker/Conquistador	1968	2.50	5.00	10.00
❑ Musicor 1308	Somewhere in the Country/Lonely Drifter	1968	2.00	4.00	8.00
❑ Musicor 1331	Billy, You're My Friend/She Believes in Me	1968	2.00	4.00	8.00
❑ Musicor 1331	Billy, You're My Friend/Lonely Drifter	1968	2.00	4.00	8.00
❑ Musicor 1348	Baby, You're My Kind of Woman/Hate	1969	2.00	4.00	8.00
❑ Musicor 1358	Maria Elena/The French Horn	1969	2.00	4.00	8.00
❑ Musicor 1361	Playing Games of Love/California	1969	2.00	4.00	8.00
❑ Musicor 1384	She Lets Her Hair Down (Early in the Morning)/I Remember	1969	2.00	4.00	8.00
❑ Musicor 1394	All the Young Women/I Remember	1970	—	3.00	6.00

Number	Title (A Side/B Side)	Yr	VG	VG+	NM
❑ Musicor 1405	A Street Called Hope/Think of Us	1970	—	3.00	6.00
❑ Musicor 1419	Shady Lady/Billy, You're My Friend	1970	—	3.00	6.00
❑ Musicor 1439	Higher and Higher/Beautiful Sounds	1971	—	3.00	6.00
❑ Musicor 1442	A Thousand Arms (Five Hundred Hearts)/Gene, Are You There?	1971	—	3.00	6.00
❑ Musicor 1453	I Just Can't Help Myself/Beautiful Sounds	1972	—	3.00	6.00
❑ Musicor 1461	Summertime Dreaming/A Thousand Arms (Five Hundred Hearts)	1972	—	3.00	6.00
❑ Musicor 1474	Shady Lady/Run, Run Roadrunner	1973	—	3.00	6.00
Albums					
❑ Music Disc MDS 1003	The Man Who Shot Liberty Valance	1969	3.00	6.00	12.00
❑ Music Disc MDS 1005	Town Without Pity	1969	3.00	6.00	12.00
❑ Music Disc MDS 1006	America's Greatest Country Songs	1969	3.00	6.00	12.00
❑ Music Disc MDS 1008	Twenty Four Hours from Tulsa	1969	3.00	6.00	12.00
❑ Music Disc MDS 1014	Baby, I Need Your Lovin'	1969	3.00	6.00	12.00
❑ Musicor MM-2001 [M]	The Many Sides of Gene Pitney	1962	12.50	25.00	50.00
—Brown label					
❑ Musicor MM-2003 [M]	Only Love Can Break a Heart	1962	10.00	20.00	40.00
—Brown label					
❑ Musicor MM-2004 [M]	Gene Pitney Sings Just for You	1963	7.50	15.00	30.00
❑ Musicor MM-2005 [M]	World-Wide Winners	1963	7.50	15.00	30.00
❑ Musicor MM-2006 [M]	Blue Gene	1963	7.50	15.00	30.00
❑ Musicor MM-2007 [M]	Gene Pitney Meets the Fair Young Ladies of Folkland	1964	7.50	15.00	30.00
❑ Musicor MM-2008 [M]	Gene Pitney's Big Sixteen	1964	7.50	15.00	30.00
❑ Musicor MM-2015 [M]	Gene Italiano	1964	6.25	12.50	25.00
❑ Musicor MM-2019 [M]	It Hurts to Be in Love	1964	6.25	12.50	25.00
❑ Musicor MM-2043 [M]	Gene Pitney's More Big Sixteen	1965	6.25	12.50	25.00
❑ Musicor MM-2056 [M]	I Must Be Seeing Things	1965	6.25	12.50	25.00
❑ Musicor MM-2069 [M]	Looking Through the Eyes of Love	1965	6.25	12.50	25.00
❑ Musicor MM-2072 [M]	Gene Pitney En Espanol	1965	6.25	12.50	25.00
❑ Musicor MM-2085 [M]	Big Sixteen, Vol. 3	1966	5.00	10.00	20.00
❑ Musicor MM-2095 [M]	Backstage I'm Lonely	1966	5.00	10.00	20.00
❑ Musicor MM-2100 [M]	Messumo Mi Puo Giudicare	1966	5.00	10.00	20.00
❑ Musicor MM-2101 [M]	The Gene Pitney Show	1966	5.00	10.00	20.00
❑ Musicor MM-2102 [M]	Greatest Hits of All Times	1966	5.00	10.00	20.00
❑ Musicor MM-2104 [M]	The Country Side of Gene Pitney	1967	5.00	10.00	20.00
❑ Musicor MM-2108 [M]	Young and Warm and Wonderful	1967	5.00	10.00	20.00
❑ Musicor MM-2117 [M]	Just One Smile	1967	5.00	10.00	20.00
❑ Musicor MM-2134 [M]	Golden Greats	1967	6.25	12.50	25.00
❑ Musicor MS-3001 [R]	The Many Sides of Gene Pitney	1962	7.50	15.00	30.00
—Brown label					
❑ Musicor MS-3003 [S]	Only Love Can Break a Heart	1962	12.50	25.00	50.00
—Brown label					
❑ Musicor MS-3004 [S]	Gene Pitney Sings Just for You	1963	10.00	20.00	40.00
❑ Musicor MS-3005 [P]	World-Wide Winners	1963	10.00	20.00	40.00
❑ Musicor MS-3006 [S]	Blue Gene	1963	10.00	20.00	40.00
❑ Musicor MS-3007 [S]	Gene Pitney Meets the Fair Young Ladies of Folkland	1964	10.00	20.00	40.00
❑ Musicor MS-3008 [P]	Gene Pitney's Big Sixteen	1964	10.00	20.00	40.00
❑ Musicor MS-3015 [S]	Gene Italiano	1964	7.50	15.00	30.00
❑ Musicor MS-3019 [P]	It Hurts to Be in Love	1964	7.50	15.00	30.00
❑ Musicor MS-3043 [P]	Gene Pitney's More Big Sixteen	1965	7.50	15.00	30.00
❑ Musicor MS-3056 [S]	I Must Be Seeing Things	1965	7.50	15.00	30.00
❑ Musicor MS-3069 [S]	Looking Through the Eyes of Love	1965	7.50	15.00	30.00
❑ Musicor MS-3072 [S]	Gene Pitney En Espanol	1965	7.50	15.00	30.00
❑ Musicor MS-3085 [S]	Big Sixteen, Vol. 3	1966	6.25	12.50	25.00
❑ Musicor MS-3095 [S]	Backstage I'm Lonely	1966	6.25	12.50	25.00
❑ Musicor MS-3100 [S]	Messumo Mi Puo Giudicare	1966	6.25	12.50	25.00
❑ Musicor MS-3101 [S]	The Gene Pitney Show	1966	6.25	12.50	25.00
❑ Musicor MS-3102 [P]	Greatest Hits of All Times	1966	6.25	12.50	25.00
❑ Musicor MS-3104 [S]	The Country Side of Gene Pitney	1967	6.25	12.50	25.00
❑ Musicor MS-3108 [S]	Young and Warm and Wonderful	1967	6.25	12.50	25.00
❑ Musicor MS-3117 [S]	Just One Smile	1967	6.25	12.50	25.00
❑ Musicor MS-3134 [S]	Golden Greats	1967	5.00	10.00	20.00
❑ Musicor M2-3148 [(2)M]	The Gene Pitney Story	1968	10.00	20.00	40.00
—Mono is promo only					
❑ Musicor M2S-3148 [(2)S]	The Gene Pitney Story	1968	6.25	12.50	25.00
—Add 40% if bonus photo is enclosed					
❑ Musicor MS-3161	Gene Pitney Sings Burt Bacharach	1968	5.00	10.00	20.00
❑ Musicor MS-3164	She's a Heartbreaker	1968	5.00	10.00	20.00
❑ Musicor MS-3174	The Greatest Hits of Gene Pitney	1969	5.00	10.00	20.00
❑ Musicor MS-3183	Gene Pitney Sings the Platters' Golden Platters	1970	3.75	7.50	15.00
❑ Musicor MS-3193	Gene Pitney Super Star	1971	3.75	7.50	15.00
❑ Musicor MS-3206	Ten Years After	1971	3.75	7.50	15.00
❑ Musicor MS-3233	Golden Hour	1972	3.75	7.50	15.00
❑ Musicor MUX-4600 [(2)]	The Best of Gene Pitney (Double Gold Series)	1977	3.75	7.50	15.00
❑ Rhino RNDA-1102 [(2)]	Anthology (1961-1968)	1984	3.00	6.00	12.00
❑ Springboard SPB-4057	Gene Pitney	1975	2.50	5.00	10.00

PLATTERS, THE

45s

Number	Title (A Side/B Side)	Yr	VG	VG+	NM
❑ Antler 3000/1	I Do It All the Time/Shake What Your Mama Gave You	1982	—	3.00	6.00
❑ Avalanche XW224	Sunday with You/If the World Loved	1973	2.00	4.00	8.00
—As "The Buck Ram Platters"					
❑ Entree 107	Won't You Be My Friend/Run While It's Dark	1965	2.00	4.00	8.00
—As "The Platters 1965"					
❑ Federal 12153	Give Thanks/Hey Now	1953	100.00	200.00	400.00
—As "Tony Williams and the Platters"					
❑ Federal 12164	I'll Cry When You're Gone/I Need You All the Time	1954	250.00	500.00	1000.
❑ Federal 12181	Roses of Picardy/Beer Barrel Polka	1954	75.00	150.00	300.00

Number	Title (A Side/B Side)	Yr	VG	VG+	NM
❑ Federal 12188	Tell the World/Love All Night	1954	50.00	100.00	200.00
❑ Federal 12198	Voo-Vee-Ah-Bee/Shake It Up Mambo	1954	50.00	100.00	200.00
❑ Federal 12204	Maggie Doesn't Work Here Anymore/ Take Me Back, Take Me Back	1955	50.00	100.00	200.00
❑ Federal 12244	Only You (And You Alone)/You Made Me Cry	1955	75.00	150.00	300.00
❑ Federal 12250	Tell the World/I Need You All the Time	1956	30.00	60.00	120.00
❑ Federal 12271	Give Thanks/I Need You All the Time	1956	20.00	40.00	80.00
❑ Mercury 70633	Only You (And You Alone)/Bark, Battle and Ball	1955	12.50	25.00	50.00
—Earliest pressings have pink labels					
❑ Mercury 70633	Only You (And You Alone)/Bark, Battle and Ball	1955	10.00	20.00	40.00
—Black label					
❑ Mercury 70753	The Great Pretender/I'm Just a Dancing Partner	1955	10.00	20.00	40.00
—Maroon label					
❑ Mercury 70819	(You've Got) The Magic Touch/Winner Take All	1956	10.00	20.00	40.00
—Maroon label					
❑ Mercury 70893	My Prayer/Heaven on Earth	1956	10.00	20.00	40.00
—Maroon label					
❑ Mercury 70948	You'll Never Never Know/It Isn't Right	1956	7.50	15.00	30.00
—Maroon label					
❑ Mercury 71011	One in a Million/On My Word of Honor	1956	7.50	15.00	30.00
❑ Mercury 71032	I'm Sorry/He's Mine	1957	7.50	15.00	30.00
—Maroon label					
❑ Mercury 71093	My Dream/I Wanna	1957	7.50	15.00	30.00
—Maroon label					
❑ Mercury 71184	Only Because/The Mystery of You	1957	6.25	12.50	25.00
❑ Mercury 71246	Helpless/Indifferent	1957	6.25	12.50	25.00
❑ Mercury 71289	Twilight Time/Out of My Mind	1958	6.25	12.50	25.00
❑ Mercury 71320	You're Making a Mistake/My Old Flame	1958	6.25	12.50	25.00
❑ Mercury 71353	I Wish/It's Raining Outside	1958	6.25	12.50	25.00
—Black label					
❑ Mercury 71383	Smoke Gets In Your Eyes/No Matter What You Are	1958	6.25	12.50	25.00
—Black label					
❑ Mercury 71427	Enchanted/The Sound and the Fury	1959	5.00	10.00	20.00
❑ Mercury 71467 [M]	Remember When/Love of a Lifetime	1959	5.00	10.00	20.00
❑ Mercury 71502	Where/Wish It Were Me	1959	5.00	10.00	20.00
❑ Mercury 71538	My Secret/What Does It Matter	1959	5.00	10.00	20.00
❑ Mercury 71563	Harbor Lights/Sleepy Lagoon	1960	5.00	10.00	20.00
❑ Mercury 71624	Ebb Tide/(I'll Be With You) In Apple Blossom Time	1960	5.00	10.00	20.00
❑ Mercury 71656	Red Sails in the Sunset/Sad River	1960	5.00	10.00	20.00
❑ Mercury 71697	To Each His Own/Down the River of Golden Dreams	1960	5.00	10.00	20.00
❑ Mercury 71749	If I Didn't Care/True Lover	1961	3.75	7.50	15.00
❑ Mercury 71791	Trees/Immortal Love	1961	3.75	7.50	15.00
❑ Mercury 71847	I'll Never Smile Again/You Don't Say	1961	3.75	7.50	15.00
❑ Mercury 71904	Song for the Lonely/You'll Never Know	1961	3.75	7.50	15.00
❑ Mercury 71921	It's Magic/Reaching for a Star	1962	3.75	7.50	15.00
❑ Mercury 71986	More Than You Know/Every Little Moment	1962	3.00	6.00	12.00
❑ Mercury 72060	Memories/Heartbreak	1962	3.00	6.00	12.00
❑ Mercury 72107	Once in a While/I'll See You in My Dreams	1963	2.50	5.00	10.00
❑ Mercury 72129	Strangers/Here Comes Heaven Again	1963	2.50	5.00	10.00
❑ Mercury 72194	Viva Ju Joy/Quando Caliente El Sol	1963	2.50	5.00	10.00
❑ Mercury 72242	Java Jive/Michael Row the Boat Ashore	1964	2.50	5.00	10.00
❑ Mercury 72305	Sincerely/P.S. I Love You	1964	2.50	5.00	10.00
❑ Mercury 72359	Love Me Tender/Little Things Mean a Lot	1964	2.50	5.00	10.00
❑ Mercury 76160	Platterama Medley/Red Sails in the Sunset	1982	—	3.00	6.00
❑ Musicor 1166	I Love You 1000 Times/Don't Hear, Speak, See No Evil	1966	2.00	4.00	8.00
❑ Musicor 1195	Alone in the Light (Without You)/Devri	1966	2.00	4.00	8.00
❑ Musicor 1211	I'll Be Home/(You've Got) The Magic Touch	1966	2.00	4.00	8.00
❑ Musicor 1229	With This Ring/If I Had a Love	1967	2.50	5.00	10.00
❑ Musicor 1251	Washed Ashore (On a Lonely Island in the Sea)/One in a Million	1967	2.00	4.00	8.00
❑ Musicor 1251	Washed Ashore (On a Lonely Island in the Sea)/What Name Shall I Give You, My Love	1967	2.00	4.00	8.00
❑ Musicor 1262	On Top of My Mind/Shing-a-Ling-a-Loo	1967	2.00	4.00	8.00
❑ Musicor 1275	Sweet, Sweet Lovin'/Sonata	1967	2.00	4.00	8.00
❑ Musicor 1288	Love Must Go On/How Beautiful Our Love Is	1968	2.00	4.00	8.00
❑ Musicor 1302	So Many Tears/Think Before You Walk Away	1968	2.00	4.00	8.00
❑ Musicor 1322	Hard to Get a Thing Called Love/Why	1968	2.00	4.00	8.00
❑ Musicor 1341	Fear of Loving You/Sonata	1968	2.00	4.00	8.00

Number	Title (A Side/B Side)	Yr	VG	VG+	NM
❑ Musicor 1443	Be My Love/Sweet Sweet Lovin'	1971	2.00	4.00	8.00
❑ Owl 320	Sixteen Tons/Are You Sincere	1973	2.00	4.00	8.00
❑ Power 7012	Only You/Voo Vee Ah Bee	195?	2.00	4.00	8.00
—Reissue from "S.P.C. Newark, N.J."					
❑ Ram 1002	Only You/Here Comes the Boogie Man	1977	2.00	4.00	8.00
❑ Ram 1004/5	My Ship Is Coming In/Guilty	1977	2.00	4.00	8.00
❑ Ram 4852	Personality/Who's Sorry Now	1978	2.00	4.00	8.00
Albums					
❑ Candelite Music CMI 1000 [(5)]	The 50 Golden Hits of the Platters	197?	10.00	20.00	40.00
❑ Federal 549 [M]	The Platters	1957	400.00	800.00	1600.
—Records on Federal 651 are bootlegs from the 1970s					
❑ King 651 [M]	The Platters	1959	200.00	400.00	800.00
—Records on Federal 651 are bootlegs from the 1970s					
❑ King 5002	19 Hits of the Platters	197?	3.00	6.00	12.00
❑ Mercury SRM-1-4050	Platterama	1982	2.50	5.00	10.00
❑ Mercury MG-20146 [M]	The Platters	1956	25.00	50.00	100.00
❑ Mercury MG-20216 [M]	The Platters, Volume Two	1956	25.00	50.00	100.00
❑ Mercury MG-20298 [M]	The Flying Platters	1957	25.00	50.00	100.00
❑ Mercury MG-20366 [M]	The Flying Platters Around the World	1958	7.50	15.00	30.00
❑ Mercury MG-20410 [M]	Remember When?	1959	7.50	15.00	30.00
❑ Mercury MG-20472 [M]	Encore of Golden Hits	1960	7.50	15.00	30.00
❑ Mercury MG-20481 [M]	Reflections	1960	6.25	12.50	25.00
❑ Mercury MG-20589 [M]	Life Is Just a Bowl of Cherries	1960	6.25	12.50	25.00
❑ Mercury MG-20591 [M]	More Encore of Golden Hits	1960	6.25	12.50	25.00
❑ Mercury MG-20613 [M]	Encore of Broadway Golden Hits	1961	5.00	10.00	20.00
❑ Mercury MG-20669 [M]	Song for the Lonely	1962	5.00	10.00	20.00
❑ Mercury MG-20759 [M]	Moonlight Memories	1963	5.00	10.00	20.00
❑ Mercury MG-20782 [M]	The Platters Present All-Time Movie Hits	1963	5.00	10.00	20.00
❑ Mercury MG-20808 [M]	The Platters Sing Latino	1963	5.00	10.00	20.00
❑ Mercury MG-20841 [M]	Christmas with the Platters	1963	7.50	15.00	30.00
❑ Mercury MG-20893 [M]	Encore of Golden Hits of the Groups	1964	5.00	10.00	20.00
❑ Mercury MG-20933 [M]	10th Anniversary Album	1964	5.00	10.00	20.00
❑ Mercury MG-20983 [M]	The New Soul of the Platters	1965	3.75	7.50	15.00
❑ Mercury SR-60043 [S]	The Flying Platters Around the World	1959	12.50	25.00	50.00
❑ Mercury SR-60087 [S]	Remember When?	1959	12.50	25.00	50.00
❑ Mercury SR-60160 [S]	Reflections	1960	7.50	15.00	30.00
❑ Mercury SR-60243 [P]	Encore of Golden Hits	1960	10.00	20.00	40.00
—Original: Black label, silver print; 12 songs on LP					
❑ Mercury SR-60243 [P]	Encore of Golden Hits	1965	6.25	12.50	25.00
—Second edition: Red label, "MERCURY" in white across top; may or may not have "Gold Record Award" insignia on back cover; 12 songs on LP					
❑ Mercury SR-60245 [S]	Life Is Just a Bowl of Cherries	1960	7.50	15.00	30.00
❑ Mercury SR-60252 [S]	More Encore of Golden Hits	1960	7.50	15.00	30.00
❑ Mercury SR-60613 [S]	Encore of Broadway Golden Hits	1961	6.25	12.50	25.00
❑ Mercury SR-60669 [S]	Song for the Lonely	1962	6.25	12.50	25.00
❑ Mercury SR-60759 [S]	Moonlight Memories	1963	6.25	12.50	25.00
❑ Mercury SR-60782 [S]	The Platters Present All-Time Movie Hits	1963	6.25	12.50	25.00
❑ Mercury SR-60808 [S]	The Platters Sing Latino	1963	6.25	12.50	25.00
❑ Mercury SR-60841 [S]	Christmas with the Platters	1963	10.00	20.00	40.00
—Same as above, but in stereo					
❑ Mercury SR-60893 [S]	Encore of Golden Hits of the Groups	1964	6.25	12.50	25.00
❑ Mercury SR-60933 [S]	10th Anniversary Album	1964	6.25	12.50	25.00
❑ Mercury SR-60983 [S]	The New Soul of the Platters	1965	5.00	10.00	20.00
❑ Mercury 828246-1	More Encore of Golden Hits	198?	2.00	4.00	8.00
—Reissue					
❑ Mercury 828254-1	Encore of Golden Hits	198?	2.00	4.00	8.00
—Reissue					
❑ Music Disc MDS-1002	Only You	1969	3.00	6.00	12.00
❑ Musicor MM-2091 [M]	I Love You 1,000 Times	1966	3.75	7.50	15.00
❑ Musicor MM-2111 [M]	The Platters Have the Magic Touch	1966	3.75	7.50	15.00
❑ Musicor MM-2125 [M]	Going Back to Detroit	1967	3.75	7.50	15.00
❑ Musicor MM-2141 [M]	New Golden Hits of the Platters	1967	5.00	10.00	20.00
❑ Musicor MS-3091 [S]	I Love You 1,000 Times	1966	5.00	10.00	20.00
❑ Musicor MS-3111 [S]	The Platters Have the Magic Touch	1966	5.00	10.00	20.00
❑ Musicor MS-3125 [S]	Going Back to Detroit	1967	3.75	7.50	15.00
❑ Musicor MS-3141 [S]	New Golden Hits of the Platters	1967	3.75	7.50	15.00
❑ Musicor MS-3156	Sweet, Sweet Lovin'	1968	3.75	7.50	15.00
❑ Musicor MS-3171	I Get the Sweetest Feeling	1968	3.75	7.50	15.00
❑ Musicor MS-3185	Singing the Great Hits Our Way	1969	3.75	7.50	15.00
❑ Musicor MS-3231	Golden Hour	1973	3.00	6.00	12.00
❑ Musicor MS-3254	The Golden Hits of the Platters	1973	3.00	6.00	12.00
❑ Pickwick PTP-2083 [(2)]	Only You	1973	3.00	6.00	12.00
❑ Pickwick SPC-3236	Super Hits	197?	2.50	5.00	10.00
❑ Rhino RNFP-71495 [(2)]	Anthology (1955-1967)	1986	3.00	6.00	12.00
❑ Springboard SPB-4059	The Platters	197?	2.50	5.00	10.00
❑ Wing MGW-12112 [M]	Encores!	1959	7.50	15.00	30.00
—With liner notes on back cover					
❑ Wing MGW-12112 [M]	Encores!	196?	3.75	7.50	15.00
—With photos of other Wing LPs on back cover					
❑ Wing MGW-12226 [M]	Flying Platters	1963	3.00	6.00	12.00
❑ Wing MGW-12272 [M]	Reflections	1964	3.00	6.00	12.00
❑ Wing MGW-12346 [M]	10th Anniversary Album	196?	3.00	6.00	12.00
❑ Wing SRW-16112 [R]	Encores!	196?	3.00	6.00	12.00
❑ Wing SRW-16226 [S]	Flying Platters	1963	3.00	6.00	12.00
❑ Wing SRW-16272 [S]	Reflections	1964	3.00	6.00	12.00
❑ Wing SRW-16346 [S]	10th Anniversary Album	196?	3.00	6.00	12.00

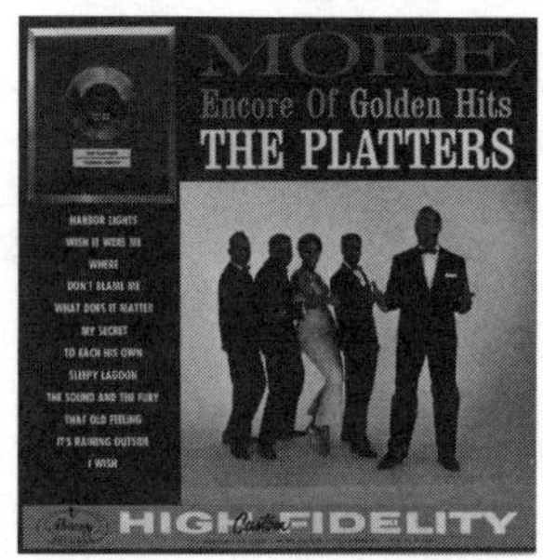

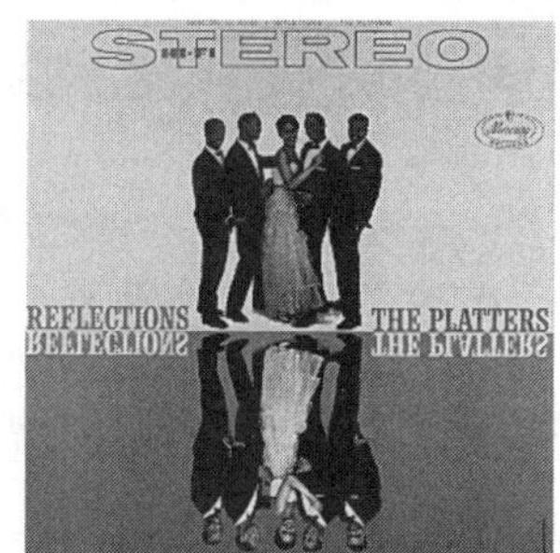

Number	Title (A Side/B Side)	Yr	VG	VG+	NM
POCO					
45s					
❑ ABC 12126	Keep On Tryin'/Georgia, Bind My Ties	1975	—	2.50	5.00
❑ ABC 12159	Makin' Love/Flyin' Solo	1976	—	2.50	5.00
❑ ABC 12204	Rose of Cimarron/Tulsa Turnaround	1976	—	2.50	5.00
❑ ABC 12295	Indian Summer/Me and You	1977	—	2.50	5.00
❑ ABC 12439	Crazy Love/Barbados	1978	—	2.50	5.00
❑ Atlantic 89629	Save a Corner of Your Heart/The Storm	1984	—	2.50	5.00
❑ Atlantic 89650	This Old Flame/The Storm	1984	—	—	3.00
❑ Atlantic 89674	Days Gone By/Daylight	1984	—	—	3.00
❑ Atlantic 89851	Break of Hearts/Love's So Cruel	1983	—	2.50	5.00
❑ Atlantic 89919	Shoot for the Moon/The Midnight Rodeo	1982	—	—	3.00
❑ Atlantic 89970	Ghostown/High Sierra	1982	—	—	3.00
❑ Epic 10501	Pickin' Up the Pieces/First Love	1969	2.50	5.00	10.00
❑ Epic 10543	My Kind of Love/Hard Luck	1969	2.50	5.00	10.00
❑ Epic 10636	You Better Think Twice/Anyway, Bye Bye	1970	2.00	4.00	8.00
❑ Epic 10714	C'Mon/I Guess You Made It	1971	2.00	4.00	8.00
❑ Epic 10804	Just for Me and You/Ol' Forgiver	1971	2.00	4.00	8.00
❑ Epic 10816	You Are the One/Railroad Days	1971	2.00	4.00	8.00
❑ Epic 10890	Good Feeling to Know/Early Times	1972	—	3.00	6.00
❑ Epic 10958	I Can See Everything/Go and Say Goodbye	1973	—	3.00	6.00
❑ Epic 11055	Here We Go Again/Fools Gold	1973	—	3.00	6.00
❑ Epic 11092	Magnolia/Blue Water	1974	—	3.00	6.00
❑ Epic 11141	Rocky Mountain Breakdown/Faith in the Families	1974	—	3.00	6.00
❑ Epic 50076	Bitter Blue/High and Dry	1975	—	3.00	6.00
❑ MCA 41023	Heart of the Night/Last Goodbye	1979	—	2.00	4.00
❑ MCA 41103	Legend/Indian Summer	1979	—	2.00	4.00
❑ MCA 41269	Under the Gun/Reputation	1980	—	2.00	4.00
❑ MCA 41326	Midnight Rain/Fool's Paradise	1980	—	2.00	4.00
❑ MCA 51034	Everlasting Kind/Friends in the Distance	1980	—	2.00	4.00
❑ MCA 51172	Down on the River Again/Widowmaker	1981	—	2.00	4.00
❑ MCA 52001	Seas of Heartbreaks/Feudin'	1982	—	2.00	4.00
❑ RCA 9038-7-R	Call It Love/Lovin' You Every Minute	1989	—	—	3.00
❑ RCA 9131-7-R	Nothin' to Hide/If It Wasn't for You	1989	—	—	3.00
Albums					
❑ ABC D-890	Head Over Heels	1975	2.50	5.00	10.00
❑ ABC D-946	Rose of Cimarron	1976	2.50	5.00	10.00
❑ ABC D-989	Indian Summer	1977	2.50	5.00	10.00
❑ ABC AA-1099	Legend	1978	3.00	6.00	12.00
❑ Atlantic 80008	Ghost Town	1982	2.50	5.00	10.00
❑ Atlantic 80148	Inamorata	1984	2.50	5.00	10.00
❑ Epic BN 26460 *—Yellow label*	Pickin' Up the Pieces	1969	3.75	7.50	15.00
❑ Epic BN 26522 *—Yellow label*	Poco	1970	3.75	7.50	15.00
❑ Epic KE 30209 *—Yellow label*	Deliverin'	1971	3.75	7.50	15.00
❑ Epic KE 30753 *—Yellow label*	From the Inside	1971	3.75	7.50	15.00
❑ Epic KE 31601 *—Yellow label*	A Good Feelin' to Know	1972	3.75	7.50	15.00
❑ Epic KE 32354 *—Orange label*	Crazy Eyes	1973	3.00	6.00	12.00
❑ Epic KE 32895 *—Orange label*	Seven	1974	3.00	6.00	12.00
❑ Epic PE 33192 *—Orange label*	Cantamos	1974	3.00	6.00	12.00
❑ Epic PE 33336 *—Orange label*	Live	1976	3.00	6.00	12.00
❑ Epic PEG 33537 [(2)] *—Orange labels*	The Very Best of Poco	1975	3.75	7.50	15.00
❑ Epic JE 36210	The Songs of Paul Cotton	1980	2.50	5.00	10.00
❑ Epic JE 36211	The Songs of Richie Furay	1980	2.50	5.00	10.00
❑ MCA AA-1099 *—Reissue of ABC 1099*	Legend	1979	2.50	5.00	10.00
❑ MCA 5132	Under the Gun	1980	2.50	5.00	10.00

Number	Title (A Side/B Side)	Yr	VG	VG+	NM
❑ MCA 5227	Blue and Gray	1981	2.50	5.00	10.00
❑ MCA 5288	Cowboys & Englishmen	1982	2.50	5.00	10.00
❑ MCA 5363	Backtracks	1983	2.50	5.00	10.00
❑ MCA 37009	Head Over Heels	1980	2.00	4.00	8.00
—Budget-line reissue					
❑ MCA 37010	Rose of Cimarron	1980	2.00	4.00	8.00
—Budget-line reissue					
❑ MCA 37011	Indian Summer	1980	2.00	4.00	8.00
—Budget-line reissue					
❑ MCA 37117	Legend	1981	2.00	4.00	8.00
—Budget-line reissue					
❑ MCA 37160	Under the Gun	198?	2.00	4.00	8.00
—Budget-line reissue					
❑ RCA 9694-1-R	Legacy	1989	2.50	5.00	10.00

POINTER SISTERS, THE

45s

Number	Title (A Side/B Side)	Yr	VG	VG+	NM
❑ Atlantic 2845	Don't Try to Take the Fifth/Tulsa County	1971	5.00	10.00	20.00
❑ Atlantic 2893	Destination No More Heartaches/Send Him Back	1972	10.00	20.00	40.00
❑ Blue Thumb 229	Yes We Can Can/Jada	1973	—	3.00	6.00
❑ Blue Thumb 243	Wang Dang Doodle/Cloudburst	1973	—	3.00	6.00
❑ Blue Thumb 248	Steam Heat/Shaky Flat Blues	1974	—	3.00	6.00
❑ Blue Thumb 254	Fairytale/Love In Them Thar Hills	1974	—	2.50	5.00
—Second pressing has a multicolor label with ABC logo					
❑ Blue Thumb 254	Fairytale/Love In Them Thar Hills	1974	2.50	5.00	10.00
—First pressing has a gray to white label and no reference to ABC					
❑ Blue Thumb 262	Live Your Life Before You Die/Shaky Flat Blues	1975	—	2.50	5.00
❑ Blue Thumb 265	How Long (Betcha' Got a Chick on the Side)/Easy Days	1975	—	2.50	5.00
❑ Blue Thumb 268	Going Down Slowly/Sleeping Alone	1975	—	2.50	5.00
❑ Blue Thumb 271	You Gotta Believe/Shaky Flat Blues	1976	—	2.50	5.00
❑ Blue Thumb 275	Having a Party/Lonely Gal	1977	—	2.50	5.00
❑ Blue Thumb 277	I Need a Man/I'll Get By Without You	1978	—	2.50	5.00
❑ Columbia 08015	Power of Persuasion/(Instrumental)	1988	—	—	3.00
❑ MCA 53120	Be There/(Instrumental)	1987	—	—	3.00
❑ Motown 902	Friends' Advice (Don't Take It)/ Friends' Advice (Don't Take It) (Dub)	1990	—	2.00	4.00
❑ Planet YB-13254	American Music/I Want to Do It with You	1982	—	2.00	4.00
❑ Planet YB-13327	I'm So Excited/Nothing But a Heartache (Live)	1982	—	2.00	4.00
❑ Planet YB-13430	If You Wanna Get Back Your Lady/I'm So Excited	1983	—	2.00	4.00
❑ Planet GB-13485	American Music/I'm So Excited	1983	—	—	3.00
—Gold Standard Series					
❑ Planet YB-13639	I Need You/If You Wanna Get Back Your Lady	1983	—	2.00	4.00
❑ Planet YB-13730	Automatic/Nightline	1984	—	2.00	4.00
❑ Planet YB-13780	Jump (For My Love)/Heart Beat	1984	—	2.00	4.00
❑ Planet GB-13795	I Need You/If You Wanna Get Back Your Lady	1984	—	—	3.00
—Gold Standard Series					
❑ Planet YB-13857	I'm So Excited/Dance Electric	1984	—	2.00	4.00
❑ Planet YB-13951	Neutron Dance/Telegraph Your Love	1984	—	2.00	4.00
❑ Planet YB-14041	Baby Come and Get It/Operator	1985	—	2.00	4.00
❑ Planet GB-14072	Jump (For My Love)/Automatic	1985	—	—	3.00
—Gold Standard Series					
❑ Planet GB-14076	Fire/He's So Shy	1985	—	—	3.00
—Gold Standard Series					
❑ Planet GB-14077	Slow Hand/Should I Do It	1985	—	—	3.00
—Gold Standard Series					
❑ Planet 45901	Fire/Love Is Like a Rolling Stone	1978	—	2.00	4.00
❑ Planet 45902	Happiness/Too Late	1979	—	2.00	4.00
❑ Planet 45906	Blind Faith/The Shape I'm In	1979	—	2.00	4.00
❑ Planet 47916	He's So Shy/Movin' On	1980	—	2.00	4.00
❑ Planet 47918	Es Tan Timido/Cosas Especiales	1980	—	3.00	6.00
❑ Planet 47920	Could I Be Dreaming/Evil	1980	—	2.00	4.00
❑ Planet 47925	Where Did the Time Go/Special Things	1981	—	2.00	4.00
❑ Planet 47929	Slow Hand/Holdin' Out for Love	1981	—	2.00	4.00
❑ Planet 47937	What a Surprise/Fall in Love Again	1981	—	2.00	4.00
❑ Planet 47945	Sweet Lover Man/Got to Find Love	1981	—	2.00	4.00
❑ Planet 47960	Should I Do It/We're Gonna Make It	1982	—	2.00	4.00
❑ RCA 5062-7-R	Goldmine/Sexual Power	1986	—	—	3.00
❑ RCA 5112-7-R	All I Know Is the Way I Feel/Translation	1987	—	—	3.00
❑ RCA 5230-7-R	Mercury Rising/Say the Word	1987	—	—	3.00
❑ RCA 6865-7-R	He Turned Me Out/Translation	1988	—	—	3.00
❑ RCA 8378-7-R	I'm in Love/Uh-Oh	1988	—	—	3.00
❑ RCA PB-14126	Dare Me/I'll Be There	1985	—	—	3.00
❑ RCA PB-14197	Twist My Arm/Easy Persuasion	1986	—	—	3.00
❑ RCA PB-14224	Freedom/Telegraph Your Love	1985	—	—	3.00
❑ RCA GB-14354	Neutron Dance/Baby Come and Get It	1986	—	—	3.00
—Gold Standard Series					

Albums

Number	Title (A Side/B Side)	Yr	VG	VG+	NM
❑ ABC Blue Thumb BT-6021	Steppin	1975	3.00	6.00	12.00
❑ ABC Blue Thumb BT-6023	Having a Party	1977	3.00	6.00	12.00
❑ ABC Blue Thumb BTSY-6026 [(2)]	The Best of the Pointer Sisters	1976	3.75	7.50	15.00
❑ Blue Thumb BTS-48	The Pointer Sisters	1973	3.00	6.00	12.00
❑ Blue Thumb BTS-6009	That's a Plenty	1974	3.00	6.00	12.00
❑ Blue Thumb BTS-8002 [(2)]	Live at the Opera House	1974	3.75	7.50	15.00
❑ MCA 3275	Retrospect	1981	2.50	5.00	10.00
—Reissue of Blue Thumb material					

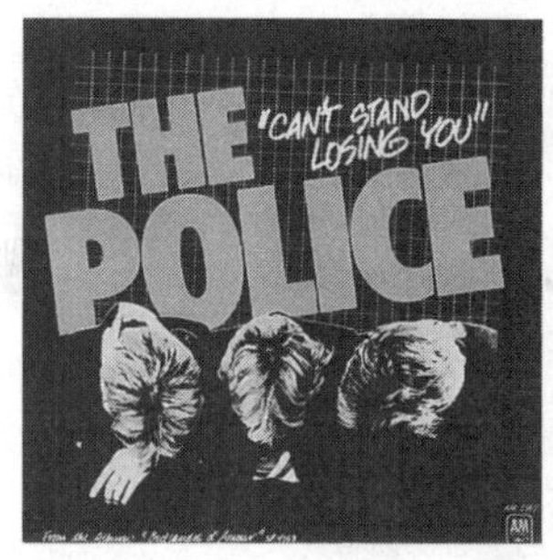

Number	Title (A Side/B Side)	Yr	VG	VG+	NM
❑ Motown 6287 ML	Right Rhythm	1990	3.00	6.00	12.00
❑ Planet P-1	Energy	1978	2.50	5.00	10.00
❑ Planet P-9	Special Things	1980	2.50	5.00	10.00
❑ Planet P-18	Black and White	1981	2.50	5.00	10.00
❑ Planet BXL1-4355	So Excited!	1982	2.50	5.00	10.00
❑ Planet BEL1-4705A	Break Out	1984	2.00	4.00	8.00
—Reissue has "I'm So Excited" plus a remix of "Jump (For My Love)"					
❑ Planet BXL1-4705	Break Out	1983	2.50	5.00	10.00
—Original does not have "I'm So Excited"					
❑ Planet P-9003	Priority	1979	2.50	5.00	10.00
❑ Planet 60203	Pointer Sisters' Greatest Hits	1982	2.50	5.00	10.00
❑ RCA 5609-1-R	Hot Together	1986	2.50	5.00	10.00
❑ RCA 6562-1-R	Serious Slammin'	1988	2.50	5.00	10.00
❑ RCA Victor AYL1-5088	Special Things	1985	2.00	4.00	8.00
—Budget-line reissue					
❑ RCA Victor AYL1-5089	Priority	1985	2.00	4.00	8.00
—Budget-line reissue					
❑ RCA Victor AYL1-5091	Energy	1985	2.00	4.00	8.00
—Budget-line reissue					
❑ RCA Victor AYL1-5092	Black and White	1985	2.00	4.00	8.00
—Budget-line reissue					
❑ RCA Victor AJL1-5487	Contact	1985	2.50	5.00	10.00

POLICE, THE

45s

Number	Title (A Side/B Side)	Yr	VG	VG+	NM
❑ A&M 2096	Roxanne/Dead End Job	1978	—	3.00	6.00
❑ A&M 2147	Can't Stand Losing You/No Time This Time	1979	—	2.50	5.00
❑ A&M 2190	Message in a Bottle/Landlord	1979	—	2.50	5.00
❑ A&M 2218	Bring On the Night/Visions of the Night	1980	—	2.50	5.00
❑ A&M 2275	De Do Do Do, De Da Da Da/Friends	1980	—	2.00	4.00
—Standard A&M late-1970s label					
❑ A&M 2301	Don't Stand So Close to Me/A Sermon	1981	—	—	3.00
❑ A&M 2371	Every Little Thing She Does Is Magic/Shambelle	1981	—	—	3.00
❑ A&M 2390	Spirits in the Material World/Flexible Strategies	1982	—	—	3.00
❑ A&M 2408	Secret Journey/Darkness	1982	—	—	3.00
❑ A&M 2542	Every Breath You Take/Murder by Numbers	1983	—	—	3.00
❑ A&M 2569	King of Pain/Someone to Talk To	1983	—	—	3.00
❑ A&M 2571	Synchronicity II/Once Upon a Daydream	1983	—	—	3.00
❑ A&M 2614	Wrapped Around Your Finger/Tea in the Sahara (Live)	1984	—	—	3.00
❑ A&M 2879	Don't Stand So Close to Me '86/Don't Stand So Close to Me (Live)	1986	—	—	3.00
❑ A&M 2908	Walking on the Moon/Message in a Bottle	1986	—	2.50	5.00
❑ A&M 8622	Roxanne/Can't Stand Losing You	198?	—	—	3.00
—Reissue					
❑ A&M 8631	De Do Do Do, De Da Da Da/Don't Stand So Close to Me	198?	—	—	3.00
—Reissue					
❑ A&M 8633	Every Little Thing She Does Is Magic/Spirits in the Material World	198?	—	—	3.00
—Reissue					
❑ A&M 8640	Every Breath You Take/Wrapped Around Your Finger	198?	—	—	3.00
—Reissue					
❑ A&M 8649	King of Pain/Synchronicity II	198?	—	—	3.00
—Reissue					
❑ A&M 25000	De Do Do Do, De Da Da Da (Japanese)/ De Do Do Do, De Da Da Da (Spanish)	1981	—	2.50	5.00
—Small center hole					

Albums

Number	Title (A Side/B Side)	Yr	VG	VG+	NM
❑ A&M SP-3311	Outlandos d'Amour	198?	2.00	4.00	8.00
—Reissue					
❑ A&M SP-3312	Reggatta de Blanc	198?	2.00	4.00	8.00
—Reissue					
❑ A&M SP-3713 [(2)10]	Reggatta de Blanc	1979	10.00	20.00	40.00
—Two 10" records with poster					
❑ A&M SP-3720	Zenyatta Mondatta	1980	2.50	5.00	10.00
❑ A&M SP-3730	Ghost in the Machine	1981	2.50	5.00	10.00
❑ A&M SP-3735	Synchronicity	1983	2.50	5.00	10.00
—With blue, yellow and red color bands; 93 versions of this cover exist, none more valuable than any other					
❑ A&M SP-3902	Every Breath You Take — The Singles	1986	2.50	5.00	10.00

Number	Title (A Side/B Side)	Yr	VG	VG+	NM
❑ A&M SP-4753	Outlandos d'Amour	1979	3.00	6.00	12.00
❑ A&M SP-4792	Reggatta de Blanc	1979	3.00	6.00	12.00
❑ A&M SP-6018 [(2)10]	Reggatta de Blanc	1980	7.50	15.00	30.00
—Reissue of SP-3713					

PONI-TAILS, THE

45s

Number	Title (A Side/B Side)	Yr	VG	VG+	NM
❑ ABC-Paramount 9846	Wild Eyes and Tender Lips/It's Just My Luck to Be Fifteen	1957	5.00	10.00	20.00
❑ ABC-Paramount 9934	Born Too Late/Come On Joey Dance With Me	1958	6.25	12.50	25.00
❑ ABC-Paramount 9969	Close Friends/Seven Minutes in Heaven	1958	5.00	10.00	20.00
❑ ABC-Paramount 9995	Early to Bed/Father Time	1959	5.00	10.00	20.00
❑ ABC-Paramount 10027	Moody/Ooh-Pah Polka	1959	5.00	10.00	20.00
❑ ABC-Paramount 10047	I'll Be Seeing You/I'll Keep Tryin'	1959	5.00	10.00	20.00
❑ ABC-Paramount 10077	Before We Say Goodnight/Come Be My Love	1960	5.00	10.00	20.00
❑ ABC-Paramount 10114	Who, When and Why/Oh My, You	1960	5.00	10.00	20.00
❑ Marc 1001	Can I Be Sure/Still in Your Teens	1957	6.25	12.50	25.00
❑ Point 8	Your Wild Heart/Que La Bozena	1957	6.25	12.50	25.00

POPPY FAMILY, THE

45s

Number	Title (A Side/B Side)	Yr	VG	VG+	NM
❑ London 128	Another Year, Another Day/You Don't Know What Love Is	1970	2.50	5.00	10.00
—Deleted quickly; a more common Margaret Whiting single was also issued as London 128					
❑ London 129	Which Way You Goin' Billy/Endless Sleep	1970	—	3.00	6.00
❑ London 139	That's When I Went Wrong/Shadows on My Wall	1970	—	2.50	5.00
❑ London 148	I Was Wondering/Where Evil Grows	1971	—	2.50	5.00
❑ London 164	No Good to Cry/I'll See You There	1971	—	2.50	5.00
❑ London 172	Good Friends/Tryin'	1972	—	2.50	5.00

Albums

Number	Title (A Side/B Side)	Yr	VG	VG+	NM
❑ London PS 574	Which Way You Goin' Billy?	1970	3.75	7.50	15.00
❑ London PS 599	Seeds	1971	3.75	7.50	15.00

PRESLEY, ELVIS

45s

Number	Title (A Side/B Side)	Yr	VG	VG+	NM
❑ RCA 8760-7-R	Heartbreak Hotel/Heartbreak Hotel	1988	—	2.50	5.00
—B-side by "David Keith & Charlie Schlatter with Zulu Time"					
❑ RCA PB-10601	Hurt/For the Heart	1976	25.00	50.00	100.00
—Second pressings (very rare) on the 1976-88 "dog near top" black label					
❑ RCA PB-10857	Moody Blue/She Thinks I Still Care	1976	—	2.50	5.00
❑ RCA PB-10998	Way Down/Pledging My Love	1977	—	2.50	5.00
❑ RCA PB-11099	Hound Dog/Don't Be Cruel	1977	—	2.00	4.00
❑ RCA PB-11100	In the Ghetto/Any Day Now	1977	—	2.00	4.00
❑ RCA PB-11101	Jailhouse Rock/Treat Me Nice	1977	—	2.00	4.00
❑ RCA PB-11102	Can't Help Falling in Love/Rock-a-Hula Baby	1977	—	2.00	4.00
❑ RCA PB-11103	Suspicious Minds/You'll Think of Me	1977	—	2.00	4.00
❑ RCA PB-11104	Are You Lonesome To-Night?/I Gotta Know	1977	—	2.00	4.00
❑ RCA PB-11105	Heartbreak Hotel/I Was the One	1977	—	2.00	4.00
❑ RCA PB-11106	All Shook Up/That's When Your Heartaches Begin	1977	—	2.00	4.00
❑ RCA PB-11107	Blue Suede Shoes/Tutti Frutti	1977	—	2.00	4.00
❑ RCA PB-11108	Love Me Tender/Any Way You Want Me (That's How I Will Be)	1977	—	2.00	4.00
❑ RCA PB-11109	(Let Me Be Your) Teddy Bear/Loving You	1977	—	2.00	4.00
❑ RCA PB-11110	It's Now or Never/A Mess of Blues	1977	—	2.00	4.00
❑ RCA PB-11111	Return to Sender/Where Do You Come From	1977	—	2.00	4.00
❑ RCA PB-11112	One Night/I Got Stung	1977	—	2.00	4.00
❑ RCA PB-11113	Crying in the Chapel/I Believe in the Man in the Sky	1977	—	2.00	4.00
❑ RCA PB-11165	My Way/America	1977	—	2.50	5.00
❑ RCA PB-11165	My Way/America the Beautiful	1977	5.00	10.00	20.00
❑ RCA PB-11212	Unchained Melody/Softly, As I Leave You	1978	—	2.50	5.00
—No credit to Sherrill Nielsen on the "Unchained Melody" side					
❑ RCA PP-11301	15 Golden Records, 30 Golden Hits	1977	15.00	30.00	60.00
—Includes 15 records (11099-11113) and outer box					
❑ RCA PB-11320	(Let Me Be Your) Teddy Bear/Puppet on a String	1978	—	2.50	5.00
❑ RCA GB-11326	Moody Blue/For the Heart	1978	—	2.00	4.00
—Gold Standard Series					
❑ RCA PP-11340	20 Golden Hits in Full Color Sleeves	1977	20.00	40.00	80.00
—Includes 10 records (11099, 11100, 11102, 11104-11109, 11111) and outer box					
❑ RCA GB-11504	Way Down/My Way	1979	—	2.00	4.00
—Gold Standard Series					
❑ RCA PB-11533	Are You Sincere/Solitaire	1979	—	2.50	5.00
❑ RCA PB-11679	There's a Honky Tonk Angel (Who Will Take Me Back In)/ I Got a Feelin' in My Body	1979	—	2.50	5.00
—Has production credits removed; only producers are listed					
❑ RCA GB-11988	Unchained Melody/Are You Sincere	1980	—	2.00	4.00
—Gold Standard Series					
❑ RCA PB-12158	Guitar Man/Faded Love	1981	—	2.50	5.00
❑ RCA PB-12205	Lovin' Arms/You Asked Me To	1981	—	3.00	6.00
—Not issued with picture sleeve (bootlegs exist)					
❑ RCA PB-13058	There Goes My Everything/You'll Never Walk Alone	1982	—	2.50	5.00
❑ RCA GB-13275	Suspicious Minds/You'll Think of Me	1982	—	2.00	4.00
—Gold Standard Series					
❑ RCA JH-13302	The Impossible Dream (The Quest)/An American Trilogy	1982	25.00	50.00	100.00
❑ RCA PB-13351	The Elvis Medley/Always on My Mind	1982	—	2.50	5.00
❑ RCA PB-13500	I Was the One/Wear My Ring Around Your Neck	1983	—	2.50	5.00
❑ RCA PB-13547	Little Sister/Paralyzed	1983	—	2.50	5.00
❑ RCA PB-13875	Baby Let's Play House/Hound Dog	1984	10.00	20.00	40.00
—Gold vinyl, custom label					
❑ RCA PB-13885	Blue Suede Shoes/Tutti Frutti	1984	—	2.00	4.00
—From box "Elvis' Greatest Hits, Golden Singles, Volume 1"; gold vinyl					

Number	Title (A Side/B Side)	Yr	VG	VG+	NM
❑ RCA PB-13886	Don't Be Cruel/Hound Dog	1984	—	2.00	4.00
—From box "Elvis' Greatest Hits, Golden Singles, Volume 1"; gold vinyl					
❑ RCA PB-13887	I Want You, I Need You, I Love You/Love Me	1984	—	2.00	4.00
—From box "Elvis' Greatest Hits, Golden Singles, Volume 1"; gold vinyl					
❑ RCA PB-13888	All Shook Up/(Let Me Be Your) Teddy Bear	1984	—	2.00	4.00
—From box "Elvis' Greatest Hits, Golden Singles, Volume 1"; gold vinyl					
❑ RCA PB-13889	It's Now or Never/Surrender	1984	—	2.00	4.00
—From box "Elvis' Greatest Hits, Golden Singles, Volume 1"; gold vinyl					
❑ RCA PB-13890	In the Ghetto/If I Can Dream	1984	—	2.00	4.00
—From box "Elvis' Greatest Hits, Golden Singles, Volume 1"; gold vinyl					
❑ RCA PB-13891	That's All Right/Blue Moon of Kentucky	1984	—	2.00	4.00
—From box "Elvis' Greatest Hits, Golden Singles, Volume 2"; gold vinyl					
❑ RCA PB-13892	Heartbreak Hotel/Jailhouse Rock	1984	—	2.00	4.00
—From box "Elvis' Greatest Hits, Golden Singles, Volume 2"; gold vinyl					
❑ RCA PB-13893	Love Me Tender/Loving You	1984	—	2.00	4.00
—From box "Elvis' Greatest Hits, Golden Singles, Volume 2"; gold vinyl					
❑ RCA PB-13894	(Marie's the Name) His Latest Flame/Little Sister	1984	—	2.00	4.00
—From box "Elvis' Greatest Hits, Golden Singles, Volume 2"; gold vinyl					
❑ RCA PB-13895	Are You Lonesome Tonight/Can't Help Falling in Love	1984	—	2.00	4.00
—From box "Elvis' Greatest Hits, Golden Singles, Volume 2"; gold vinyl					
❑ RCA PB-13896	Suspicious Minds/Burning Love	1984	—	2.00	4.00
—From box "Elvis' Greatest Hits, Golden Singles, Volume 2"; gold vinyl					
❑ RCA PB-13897	Elvis' Greatest Hits, Golden Singles, Volume 1	1984	3.75	7.50	15.00
—Box set of six 45s with sleeves (13885-13890) with box					
❑ RCA PB-13898	Elvis' Greatest Hits, Golden Singles, Volume 2	1984	3.75	7.50	15.00
—Box set of six 45s with sleeves (13891-13896) with box					
❑ RCA PB-13929	Blue Suede Shoes/Promised Land	1984	3.00	6.00	12.00
—Blue vinyl; correct label — "Blue Suede Shoes" side says "Mono" and "Promised Land" side says "Stereo"					
❑ RCA PB-14090	Always on My Mind/My Boy	1985	2.50	5.00	10.00
—Purple vinyl					
❑ RCA PB-14237	Merry Christmas Baby/Santa Claus Is Back in Town	1985	—	2.50	5.00
—Normal black RCA label					
❑ RCA Victor 47-6357	I Forgot to Remember to Forget/Mystery Train	1955	15.00	30.00	60.00
—No horizontal line on label					
❑ RCA Victor 47-6380	That's All Right/Blue Moon of Kentucky	1955	15.00	30.00	60.00
—No horizontal line on label					
❑ RCA Victor 47-6381	Good Rockin' Tonight/I Don't Care If the Sun Don't Shine	1955	15.00	30.00	60.00
—No horizontal line on label					
❑ RCA Victor 47-6382	Milkcow Blues Boogie/You're a Heartbreaker	1955	15.00	30.00	60.00
—No horizontal line on label					
❑ RCA Victor 47-6383	Baby Let's Play House/I'm Left, You're Right, She's Gone	1955	15.00	30.00	60.00
—No horizontal line on label					
❑ RCA Victor 47-6420	Heartbreak Hotel/I Was the One	1956	10.00	20.00	40.00
—No horizontal line on label					
❑ RCA Victor 47-6540	I Want You, I Need You, I Love You/My Baby Left Me	1956	10.00	20.00	40.00
—No horizontal line on label					
❑ RCA Victor 47-6604	Don't Be Cruel/Hound Dog	1956	7.50	15.00	30.00
—No horizontal line on label					
❑ RCA Victor 47-6636	Blue Suede Shoes/Tutti Frutti	1956	20.00	40.00	80.00
—No horizontal line on label					
❑ RCA Victor 47-6637	I Got a Woman/I'm Countin' On You	1956	20.00	40.00	80.00
—No horizontal line on label					
❑ RCA Victor 47-6638	I'm Gonna Sit Right Down and Cry (Over You)/ I'll Never Let You Go (Little Darlin')	1956	17.50	35.00	70.00
—No horizontal line on label					
❑ RCA Victor 47-6639	Tryin' to Get to You/I Love You Because	1956	17.50	35.00	70.00
—No horizontal line on label					
❑ RCA Victor 47-6640	Blue Moon/Just Because	1956	15.00	30.00	60.00
—No horizontal line on label					
❑ RCA Victor 47-6641	Money Honey/One-Sided Love Affair	1956	12.50	25.00	50.00
—No horizontal line on label					
❑ RCA Victor 47-6642	Lawdy Miss Clawdy/Shake, Rattle, and Roll	1956	10.00	20.00	40.00
—No horizontal line on label					
❑ RCA Victor 47-6643	Love Me Tender/Anyway You Want Me (That's How I Will Be)	1956	7.50	15.00	30.00
—No horizontal line on label					

Number	Title (A Side/B Side)	Yr	VG	VG+	NM
❑ RCA Victor 47-6800	Too Much/Playing for Keeps	1957	7.50	15.00	30.00
—No horizontal line on label					
❑ RCA Victor 47-6870	All Shook Up/That's When Your Heartaches Begin	1957	7.50	15.00	30.00
—No horizontal line on label					
❑ RCA Victor 47-7000	(Let Me Be Your) Teddy Bear/Loving You	1957	7.50	15.00	30.00
—Parentheses around "Let Me Be Your", no horizontal line on label					
❑ RCA Victor 47-7035	Jailhouse Rock/Treat Me Nice	1957	7.50	15.00	30.00
—No horizontal line on label					
❑ RCA Victor 47-7150	Don't/I Beg of You	1958	6.25	12.50	25.00
—No horizontal line on label					
❑ RCA Victor 47-7240	Wear My Ring Around Your Neck/Don'tcha Think It's Time	1958	6.25	12.50	25.00
❑ RCA Victor 47-7280	Hard Headed Woman/Don't Ask Me Why	1958	6.25	12.50	25.00
❑ RCA Victor 47-7410	One Night/I Got Stung	1958	6.25	12.50	25.00
❑ RCA Victor 47-7506	(Now and Then There's) A Fool Such As I/ I Need Your Love Tonight	1959	6.25	12.50	25.00
❑ RCA Victor 47-7600	A Big Hunk o'Love/My Wish Came True	1959	6.25	12.50	25.00
❑ RCA Victor 47-7740	Stuck on You/Fame and Fortune	1960	5.00	10.00	20.00
❑ RCA Victor 47-7777	It's Now or Never/A Mess of Blues	1960	5.00	10.00	20.00
—All other pressings with overdubbed piano					
❑ RCA Victor 47-7810	Are You Lonesome To-Night?/I Gotta Know	1960	5.00	10.00	20.00
❑ RCA Victor 47-7850	Surrender/Lonely Man	1961	5.00	10.00	20.00
❑ RCA Victor 47-7880	I Feel So Bad/Wild in the Country	1961	5.00	10.00	20.00
❑ RCA Victor 47-7908	(Marie's the Name) His Latest Flame/Little Sister	1961	5.00	10.00	20.00
—All copies of this record actually read "Marie's the Name HIS LATEST FLAME" (no parentheses)					
❑ RCA Victor 47-7968	Can't Help Falling in Love/Rock-a-Hula Baby	1961	5.00	10.00	20.00
❑ RCA Victor 47-7992	Good Luck Charm/Anything That's Part of You	1962	5.00	10.00	20.00
❑ RCA Victor 47-8041	She's Not You/Just Tell Her Jim Said Hello	1962	5.00	10.00	20.00
❑ RCA Victor 47-8100	Return to Sender/Where Do You Come From	1962	5.00	10.00	20.00
❑ RCA Victor 47-8134	One Broken Heart for Sale/They Remind Me Too Much of You	1963	3.00	6.00	12.00
❑ RCA Victor 47-8188	(You're the) Devil in Disguise/ Please Don't Drag That String Around	1963	3.00	6.00	12.00
—Second pressing with correct B-side title					
❑ RCA Victor 47-8243	Bossa Nova Baby/Witchcraft	1963	3.00	6.00	12.00
❑ RCA Victor 47-8307	Kissin' Cousins/It Hurts Me	1964	3.00	6.00	12.00
❑ RCA Victor 47-8360	Viva Las Vegas/What'd I Say	1964	3.00	6.00	12.00
❑ RCA Victor 47-8400	Such a Night/Never Ending	1964	3.00	6.00	12.00
❑ RCA Victor 47-8440	Ain't That Loving You Baby/Ask Me	1964	2.50	5.00	10.00
❑ RCA Victor 47-8500	Do the Clam/You'll Be Gone	1965	2.50	5.00	10.00
❑ RCA Victor 47-8585	(Such An) Easy Question/It Feels So Right	1965	2.50	5.00	10.00
❑ RCA Victor 47-8657	I'm Yours/(It's a) Long, Lonely Highway	1965	2.50	5.00	10.00
❑ RCA Victor 47-8740	Tell Me Why/Blue River	1965	2.50	5.00	10.00
❑ RCA Victor 47-8780	Frankie and Johnny/Please Don't Stop Loving Me	1966	2.50	5.00	10.00
❑ RCA Victor 47-8870	Love Letters/Come What May	1966	2.50	5.00	10.00
❑ RCA Victor 47-8941	Spinout/All That I Am	1966	2.50	5.00	10.00
❑ RCA Victor 47-8950	If Every Day Was Like Christmas/How Would You Like to Be	1966	5.00	10.00	20.00
❑ RCA Victor 47-9056	Indescribably Blue/Fools Fall in Love	1966	2.50	5.00	10.00
❑ RCA Victor 47-9115	Long Legged Girl (With the Short Dress On)/ That's Someone You Never Forget	1967	2.50	5.00	10.00
❑ RCA Victor 47-9287	There's Always Me/Judy	1967	2.50	5.00	10.00
❑ RCA Victor 47-9341	Big Boss Man/You Don't Know Me	1967	2.50	5.00	10.00
❑ RCA Victor 47-9425	Guitar Man/High Heel Sneakers	1968	2.50	5.00	10.00
❑ RCA Victor 47-9465	U.S. Male/Stay Away	1968	2.50	5.00	10.00
❑ RCA Victor 47-9547	Let Yourself Go/Your Time Hasn't Come Yet, Baby	1968	2.50	5.00	10.00
❑ RCA Victor 47-9600	You'll Never Walk Alone/We Call on Him	1968	3.00	6.00	12.00
❑ RCA Victor 47-9610	A Little Less Conversation/Almost in Love	1968	2.50	5.00	10.00
❑ RCA Victor 47-9670	If I Can Dream/Edge of Reality	1968	2.00	4.00	8.00
—First Elvis single on orange label					
❑ RCA Victor 47-9731	Memories/Charro	1969	2.00	4.00	8.00
❑ RCA Victor 47-9741	In the Ghetto/Any Day Now	1969	2.00	4.00	8.00
❑ RCA Victor 47-9747	Clean Up Your Own Back Yard/The Fair Is Moving On	1969	2.00	4.00	8.00
❑ RCA Victor 47-9764	Suspicious Minds/You'll Think of Me	1969	2.00	4.00	8.00
❑ RCA Victor 47-9768	Don't Cry Daddy/Rubberneckin'	1969	2.00	4.00	8.00
❑ RCA Victor 47-9791	Kentucky Rain/My Little Friend	1969	2.00	4.00	8.00
❑ RCA Victor 47-9835	The Wonder of You/Mama Liked the Roses	1970	2.00	4.00	8.00
❑ RCA Victor 47-9873	I've Lost You/The Next Step Is Love	1970	—	3.00	6.00
❑ RCA Victor 47-9916	You Don't Have to Say You Love Me/Patch It Up	1970	—	3.00	6.00
❑ RCA Victor 47-9960	I Really Don't Want to Know/There Goes My Everything	1971	—	3.00	6.00
❑ RCA Victor 47-9980	Where Did They Go, Lord/Rags to Riches	1971	—	3.00	6.00
❑ RCA Victor 47-9985	Life/Only Believe	1971	—	3.00	6.00
❑ RCA Victor 47-9998	I'm Leavin'/Heart of Rome	1971	—	3.00	6.00
❑ RCA Victor 48-1017	It's Only Love/The Sound of Your Cry	1971	—	3.00	6.00
❑ RCA Victor 74-0130	How Great Thou Art/His Hand in Mine	1969	6.25	12.50	25.00
❑ RCA Victor 74-0572	Merry Christmas Baby/O Come All Ye Faithful	1971	3.75	7.50	15.00
❑ RCA Victor 74-0619	Until It's Time for You to Go/We Can Make the Morning	1971	—	3.00	6.00
❑ RCA Victor 74-0651	He Touched Me/The Bosom of Abraham	1972	2.00	4.00	8.00
—"He Touched Me" plays correctly. A-side has "APKS-1277" stamped in trail-off wax.					
❑ RCA Victor 74-0672	An American Trilogy/The First Time Ever I Saw Your Face	1972	5.00	10.00	20.00
❑ RCA Victor 74-0769	Burning Love/It's a Matter of Time	1972	—	3.00	6.00
—Originals have orange labels					
❑ RCA Victor 74-0815	Separate Ways/Always on My Mind	1972	—	3.00	6.00
❑ RCA Victor 74-0910	Steamroller Blues/Fool	1973	—	3.00	6.00
❑ RCA Victor 447-0600	I Forgot to Remember to Forget/Mystery Train	1959	3.75	7.50	15.00
—Note: All RCA Victor releases with a "447" prefix are from the Gold Standard Series. Black label, dog on top					
❑ RCA Victor 447-0601	That's All Right/Blue Moon of Kentucky	1959	3.75	7.50	15.00
—Black label, dog on top					
❑ RCA Victor 447-0602	Good Rockin' Tonight/I Don't Care If the Sun Don't Shine	1959	3.75	7.50	15.00
—Black label, dog on top					

Number	Title (A Side/B Side)	Yr	VG	VG+	NM
❑ RCA Victor 447-0603 —*Black label, dog on top*	Milkcow Blues Boogie/You're a Heartbreaker	1959	3.75	7.50	15.00
❑ RCA Victor 447-0604 —*Black label, dog on top*	Baby Let's Play House/I'm Left, You're Right, She's Gone	1959	3.75	7.50	15.00
❑ RCA Victor 447-0605 —*Black label, dog on top*	Heartbreak Hotel/I Was the One	1959	3.75	7.50	15.00
❑ RCA Victor 447-0607 —*Black label, dog on top*	I Want You, I Need You, I Love You/My Baby Left Me	1959	3.75	7.50	15.00
❑ RCA Victor 447-0608 —*Black label, dog on top*	Hound Dog/Don't Be Cruel	1959	3.75	7.50	15.00
❑ RCA Victor 447-0609 —*Black label, dog on top*	Blue Suede Shoes/Tutti Frutti	1959	3.75	7.50	15.00
❑ RCA Victor 447-0610 —*Black label, dog on top*	I Got a Woman/I'm Countin' On You	1959	3.75	7.50	15.00
❑ RCA Victor 447-0611 —*Black label, dog on top*	I'm Gonna Sit Right Down and Cry (Over You)/ I'll Never Let You Go (Little Darlin')	1959	3.75	7.50	15.00
❑ RCA Victor 447-0612 —*Black label, dog on top*	Tryin' to Get to You/I Love You Because	1959	3.75	7.50	15.00
❑ RCA Victor 447-0613 —*Black label, dog on top*	Blue Moon/Just Because	1959	3.75	7.50	15.00
❑ RCA Victor 447-0614 —*Black label, dog on top*	Money Honey/One-Sided Love Affair	1959	3.75	7.50	15.00
❑ RCA Victor 447-0615 —*Black label, dog on top*	Lawdy Miss Clawdy/Shake, Rattle, and Roll	1959	3.75	7.50	15.00
❑ RCA Victor 447-0616 —*Black label, dog on top*	Love Me Tender/Anyway You Want Me (That's How I Will Be)	1959	3.75	7.50	15.00
❑ RCA Victor 447-0617 —*Black label, dog on top*	Too Much/Playing for Keeps	1959	3.75	7.50	15.00
❑ RCA Victor 447-0618 —*Black label, dog on top*	All Shook Up/That's When Your Heartaches Begin	1959	3.75	7.50	15.00
❑ RCA Victor 447-0619 —*Black label, dog on top*	Jailhouse Rock/Treat Me Nice	1959	3.75	7.50	15.00
❑ RCA Victor 447-0620 —*Black label, dog on top*	(Let Me Be Your) Teddy Bear/Loving You	1959	3.75	7.50	15.00
❑ RCA Victor 447-0621 —*Black label, dog on top*	Don't/I Beg of You	1961	3.00	6.00	12.00
❑ RCA Victor 447-0622 —*Black label, dog on top*	Wear My Ring Around Your Neck/Don'tcha Think It's Time	1961	3.00	6.00	12.00
❑ RCA Victor 447-0623 —*Black label, dog on top*	Hard Headed Woman/Don't Ask Me Why	1961	3.75	7.50	15.00
❑ RCA Victor 447-0624 —*Black label, dog on top*	One Night/I Got Stung	1961	3.00	6.00	12.00
❑ RCA Victor 447-0625 —*Black label, dog on top*	(Now and Then There's) A Fool Such As I/ I Need Your Love Tonight	1961	3.75	7.50	15.00
❑ RCA Victor 447-0626 —*Black label, dog on top*	A Big Hunk o'Love/My Wish Came True	1962	3.75	7.50	15.00
❑ RCA Victor 447-0627 —*Black label, dog on top*	Stuck on You/Fame and Fortune	1962	3.00	6.00	12.00
❑ RCA Victor 447-0628 —*Black label, dog on top*	It's Now or Never/A Mess of Blues	1962	3.00	6.00	12.00
❑ RCA Victor 447-0629 —*Black label, dog on top*	Are You Lonesome To-Night?/I Gotta Know	1962	3.75	7.50	15.00
❑ RCA Victor 447-0630 —*Black label, dog on top*	Surrender/Lonely Man	1962	6.25	12.50	25.00
❑ RCA Victor 447-0631 —*Black label, dog on top*	I Feel So Bad/Wild in the Country	1962	3.00	6.00	12.00
❑ RCA Victor 447-0634 —*Black label, dog on top*	(Marie's the Name) His Latest Flame/Little Sister	1962	3.00	6.00	12.00
❑ RCA Victor 447-0635 —*Black label, dog on top*	Can't Help Falling in Love/Rock-a-Hula Baby	1962	3.00	6.00	12.00
❑ RCA Victor 447-0636 —*Black label, dog on top*	Good Luck Charm/Anything That's Part of You	1962	3.00	6.00	12.00
❑ RCA Victor 447-0637 —*Black label, dog on top*	She's Not You/Just Tell Her Jim Said Hello	1963	3.00	6.00	12.00

Number	Title (A Side/B Side)	Yr	VG	VG+	NM
❑ RCA Victor 447-0638	Return to Sender/Where Do You Come From	1963	3.00	6.00	12.00
—Black label, dog on top					
❑ RCA Victor 447-0639	Kiss Me Quick/Suspicion	1964	2.50	5.00	10.00
—Black label, dog on top					
❑ RCA Victor 447-0640	One Broken Heart for Sale/They Remind Me Too Much of You	1964	6.25	12.50	25.00
—Black label, dog on top					
❑ RCA Victor 447-0641	(You're the) Devil in Disguise/Please Don't Drag That String Around	1964	6.25	12.50	25.00
—Black label, dog on top					
❑ RCA Victor 447-0642	Bossa Nova Baby/Witchcraft	1964	6.25	12.50	25.00
—Black label, dog on top					
❑ RCA Victor 447-0643	Crying in the Chapel/I Believe in the Man in the Sky	1965	2.50	5.00	10.00
—Black label, dog on left					
❑ RCA Victor 447-0644	Kissin' Cousins/It Hurts Me	1965	2.50	5.00	10.00
—Black label, dog on left					
❑ RCA Victor 447-0645	Such a Night/Never Ending	1965	10.00	20.00	40.00
—Black label, dog on top					
❑ RCA Victor 447-0646	Viva Las Vegas/What'd I Say	1965	6.25	12.50	25.00
—Black label, dog on top					
❑ RCA Victor 447-0647	Blue Christmas/Santa Claus Is Back in Town	1965	3.00	6.00	12.00
—Black label, dog on side					
❑ RCA Victor 447-0648	Do the Clam/You'll Be Gone	1965	2.50	5.00	10.00
—Black label, dog on left					
❑ RCA Victor 447-0649	Ain't That Loving You Baby/Ask Me	1965	2.50	5.00	10.00
—Black label, dog on left					
❑ RCA Victor 447-0650	Puppet on a String/Wooden Heart	1965	2.50	5.00	10.00
—Black label, dog on left					
❑ RCA Victor 447-0651	Joshua Fit the Battle/Known Only to Him	1966	3.75	7.50	15.00
—Black label, dog on left					
❑ RCA Victor 447-0652	Milky White Way/Swing Down Sweet Chariot	1966	3.75	7.50	15.00
—Black label, dog on left					
❑ RCA Victor 447-0653	(Such An) Easy Question/It Feels So Right	1966	2.50	5.00	10.00
—Black label, dog on left					
❑ RCA Victor 447-0654	I'm Yours/(It's a) Long, Lonely Highway	1966	2.50	5.00	10.00
—Black label, dog on left					
❑ RCA Victor 447-0655	Tell Me Why/Blue River	1968	2.50	5.00	10.00
—Black label, dog on left					
❑ RCA Victor 447-0656	Frankie and Johnny/Please Don't Stop Loving Me	1968	2.50	5.00	10.00
—Black label, dog on left					
❑ RCA Victor 447-0657	Love Letters/Come What May	1968	2.50	5.00	10.00
—Black label, dog on left					
❑ RCA Victor 447-0658	Spinout/All That I Am	1968	2.50	5.00	10.00
—Black label, dog on left					
❑ RCA Victor 447-0659	Indescribably Blue/Fools Fall in Love	1969	6.25	12.50	25.00
—Orange label					
❑ RCA Victor 447-0660	Long Legged Girl (With the Short Dress On)/ That's Someone You Never Forget	1970	10.00	20.00	40.00
❑ RCA Victor 447-0661	There's Always Me/Judy	1970	3.75	7.50	15.00
❑ RCA Victor 447-0662	Big Boss Man/You Don't Know Me	1970	2.50	5.00	10.00
❑ RCA Victor 447-0663	Guitar Man/High Heel Sneakers	1970	2.00	4.00	8.00
❑ RCA Victor 447-0664	U.S. Male/Stay Away	1970	2.00	4.00	8.00
❑ RCA Victor 447-0665	You'll Never Walk Alone/We Call on Him	1970	2.50	5.00	10.00
❑ RCA Victor 447-0666	Let Yourself Go/Your Time Hasn't Come Yet, Baby	1970	2.00	4.00	8.00
❑ RCA Victor 447-0667	A Little Less Conversation/Almost in Love	1970	2.00	4.00	8.00
❑ RCA Victor 447-0668	If I Can Dream/Edge of Reality	1970	2.00	4.00	8.00
❑ RCA Victor 447-0669	Memories/Charro	1970	2.00	4.00	8.00
❑ RCA Victor 447-0670	How Great Thou Art/His Hand in Mine	1970	2.50	5.00	10.00
❑ RCA Victor 447-0671	In the Ghetto/Any Day Now	1970	2.00	4.00	8.00
❑ RCA Victor 447-0672	Clean Up Your Own Back Yard/The Fair Is Moving On	1970	2.00	4.00	8.00
❑ RCA Victor 447-0673	Suspicious Minds/You'll Think of Me	1970	2.00	4.00	8.00
❑ RCA Victor 447-0674	Don't Cry Daddy/Rubberneckin'	1970	2.00	4.00	8.00
❑ RCA Victor 447-0675	Kentucky Rain/My Little Friend	1971	2.00	4.00	8.00
❑ RCA Victor 447-0676	The Wonder of You/Mama Liked the Roses	1971	2.00	4.00	8.00
❑ RCA Victor 447-0677	I've Lost You/The Next Step Is Love	1971	2.00	4.00	8.00
❑ RCA Victor 447-0678	You Don't Have to Say You Love Me/Patch It Up	1972	2.00	4.00	8.00
❑ RCA Victor 447-0679	I Really Don't Want to Know/There Goes My Everything	1972	2.00	4.00	8.00
❑ RCA Victor 447-0680	Where Did They Go, Lord/Rags to Riches	1972	2.00	4.00	8.00
❑ RCA Victor 447-0681	If Every Day Was Like Christmas/How Would You Like to Be	1972	2.00	4.00	8.00
❑ RCA Victor 447-0682	Life/Only Believe	1972	2.50	5.00	8.00
❑ RCA Victor 447-0683	I'm Leavin'/Heart of Rome	1972	2.00	4.00	8.00
❑ RCA Victor 447-0684	It's Only Love/The Sound of Your Cry	1972	2.00	4.00	8.00
❑ RCA Victor 447-0685	An American Trilogy/Until It's Time for You to Go	1973	2.00	4.00	8.00
❑ RCA Victor 447-0720	Blue Christmas/Wooden Heart	1964	3.75	7.50	15.00
❑ RCA Victor APBO-0088	Raised on Rock/For Ol' Times Sake	1973	—	3.00	6.00
❑ RCA Victor APBO-0196	Take Good Care of Her/I've Got a Thing About You, Baby	1973	—	3.00	6.00
❑ RCA Victor APBO-0280	If You Talk in Your Sleep/Help Me	1974	—	3.00	6.00
—On label, the title "If You Talk" is on one line and "In Your Sleep" is on another line					
❑ RCA Victor PB-10074	Promised Land/It's Midnight	1974	—	2.50	5.00
—Gray label (available at the same time as orange label)					
❑ RCA Victor PB-10074	Promised Land/It's Midnight	1974	—	2.50	5.00
—Orange label (available at the same time as gray label)					
❑ RCA Victor GB-10156	Burning Love/Steamroller Blues	1975	2.00	4.00	8.00
—Gold Standard Series; red label					
❑ RCA Victor GB-10157	Raised on Rock/If You Talk in Your Sleep	1975	2.00	4.00	8.00
—Gold Standard Series; red label					

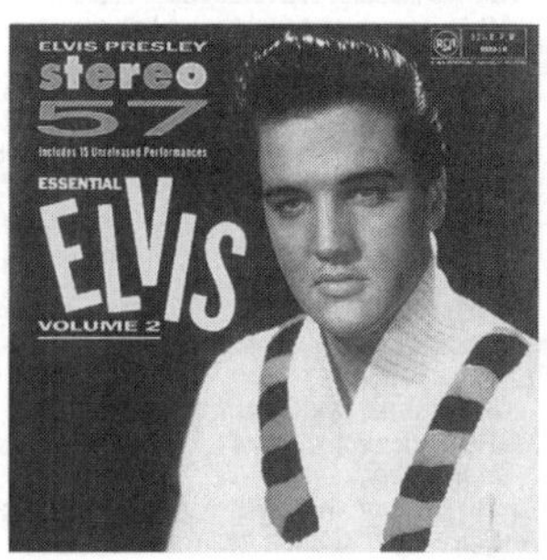

Number	Title (A Side/B Side)	Yr	VG	VG+	NM
❑ RCA Victor PB-10191	My Boy/Thinking About You	1975	—	2.50	5.00
—Orange label					
❑ RCA Victor PB-10191	My Boy/Thinking About You	1975	—	2.50	5.00
—Tan label					
❑ RCA Victor PB-10278	T-R-O-U-B-L-E/Mr. Songman	1975	2.50	5.00	10.00
—Tan label					
❑ RCA Victor PB-10278	T-R-O-U-B-L-E/Mr. Songman	1975	—	2.50	5.00
—Orange label					
❑ RCA Victor PB-10401	Bringing It Back/Pieces of My Life	1975	—	2.50	5.00
—Tan label					
❑ RCA Victor GB-10485	Take Good Care of Her/I've Got a Thing About You, Baby	1975	2.00	4.00	8.00
—Gold Standard Series; red label					
❑ RCA Victor GB-10486	Separate Ways/Always on My Mind	1975	2.00	4.00	8.00
—Gold Standard Series; red label					
❑ RCA Victor GB-10487	T-R-O-U-B-L-E/Mr. Songman	1975	2.00	4.00	8.00
—Gold Standard Series; red label					
❑ RCA Victor GB-10488	Promised Land/It's Midnight	1975	2.00	4.00	8.00
—Gold Standard Series; red label					
❑ RCA Victor GB-10489	My Boy/Thinking About You	1975	2.00	4.00	8.00
—Gold Standard Series; red label					
❑ RCA Victor PB-10601	Hurt/For the Heart	1976	—	2.50	5.00
—Originals on tan labels					
❑ Sun 209	That's All Right/Blue Moon of Kentucky	1954	2000.	4000.	6000.
—A mint copy of this has sold for over $17,000, but so far that is an aberration. VG 2000 ; VG+ 4000					
❑ Sun 210	Good Rockin' Tonight/I Don't Care If the Sun Don't Shine	1954	1500.	2500.	3500.
—VG 1500; VG+ 2500					
❑ Sun 215	Milkcow Blues Boogie/You're a Heartbreaker	1955	2000.	3500.	5000.
—VG 2000 ; VG+ 3500					
❑ Sun 217	Baby Let's Play House/I'm Left, You're Right, She's Gone	1955	1000.	2000.	3000.
—VG 1,000; VG+ 2,000					
❑ Sun 223	I Forgot to Remember to Forget/Mystery Train	1955	625.00	1250.	2500.
Albums					
❑ Boxcar (no #)	Having Fun with Elvis on Stage	1974	37.50	75.00	150.00
—All-talking record sold at Elvis concerts in 1974					
❑ Golden Editions KING-1	The First Year (Elvis, Scotty and Bill)	1979	3.75	7.50	15.00
❑ Golden Editions GEL-101	The First Year (Elvis, Scotty and Bill)	1979	5.00	10.00	20.00
❑ Great Northwest GV-2004	The King Speaks (February 1961, Memphis, Tennessee)	1977	2.50	5.00	10.00
—Label says this is on "Green Valley" while sleeve says "Great Northwest"					
❑ Great Northwest GNW-4005	The Elvis Tapes	1977	3.00	6.00	12.00
❑ Great Northwest GNW-4006	The King Speaks (February 1961, Memphis, Tennessee)	1977	2.00	4.00	8.00
—Both label and sleeve say this is on "Great Northwest"					
❑ Green Valley GV-2001	Elvis Exclusive Live Press Conference (Memphis, Tennessee, February 1961)	1977	10.00	20.00	40.00
—Issued with two slightly different covers					
❑ Green Valley GV-2001/3 [(2)]	Elvis (Speaks to You)	1978	7.50	15.00	30.00
—Elvis interviews plus tracks by the Jordanaires					
❑ Gusto SD-995	Interviews with Elvis (Canada 1957)	1978	10.00	20.00	40.00
—Reissue of Great Northwest album					
❑ HALW HALW-0001	The First Years	1978	5.00	10.00	20.00
—Without limited edition number					
❑ K-Tel NU 9900	Love Songs	1981	5.00	10.00	20.00
❑ Louisiana Hayride LH-3061	Beginning Years	1984	5.00	10.00	20.00
—With booklet and facsimile contract					
❑ Marvenco 101	Beginning (1954-1955)	1988	3.75	7.50	15.00
—Pink vinyl with booklet and facsimile contract					
❑ Music Works PB-3601	The First Live Recordings	1984	3.75	7.50	15.00
❑ Music Works PB-3602	The Hillbilly Cat	1984	3.75	7.50	15.00
❑ Oak 1003	Vintage 1955 Elvis	1990	15.00	30.00	60.00
❑ Pair PDL2-1010 [(2)]	Double Dynamite	1982	5.00	10.00	20.00
❑ Pair PDL2-1037 [(2)]	Remembering	1983	7.50	15.00	30.00
❑ Pair PDL2-1185 [(2)]	Elvis Aron Presley Forever	1988	5.00	10.00	20.00
❑ Pickwick CAS-2304	Elvis Sings Flaming Star	1976	2.50	5.00	10.00
❑ Pickwick CAS-2408	Let's Be Friends	1975	2.50	5.00	10.00

Number	Title (A Side/B Side)	Yr	VG	VG+	NM
❑ Pickwick CAS-2428 [M]	Elvis' Christmas Album	1975	3.00	6.00	12.00
—Same contents as RCA Camden LP; no Christmas trim on border; despite the "CAS" catalog number, this album is mono					
❑ Pickwick CAS-2440	Almost in Love	1975	2.50	5.00	10.00
❑ Pickwick CAL-2472	You'll Never Walk Alone	1975	2.50	5.00	10.00
❑ Pickwick CAL-2518	C'mon Everybody	1975	2.50	5.00	10.00
❑ Pickwick CAS-2533	I Got Lucky	1975	2.50	5.00	10.00
❑ Pickwick CAS-2567	Elvis Sings Hits from His Movies, Volume 1	1975	2.50	5.00	10.00
❑ Pickwick CAS-2595	Burning Love And Hits from His Movies, Vol. 2	1975	3.00	6.00	12.00
—First cover contains a notice about the upcoming "Aloha from Hawaii" show					
❑ Pickwick CAS-2611	Separate Ways	1975	2.50	5.00	10.00
❑ Pickwick DL2-5001 [(2)]	Double Dynamite	1975	6.25	12.50	25.00
❑ Pickwick ACL-7007	Frankie and Johnny	1976	2.50	5.00	10.00
❑ Pickwick ACL-7064	Mahalo from Elvis	1978	5.00	10.00	20.00
❑ Premore PL-589	Early Elvis (1954-1956 Live at the Louisiana Hayride)	1989	7.50	15.00	30.00
❑ RCA 2023-1-R	The Million Dollar Quartet	1990	3.00	6.00	12.00
—With Jerry Lee Lewis, Carl Perkins, and perhaps Johnny Cash					
❑ RCA 2227-1-R	The Great Performances	1990	10.00	20.00	40.00
❑ RCA 3114-1-R [(3)]	Collectors Gold	1991	50.00	100.00	200.00
❑ RCA 5600-1-R	Return of the Rocker	1986	5.00	10.00	20.00
❑ RCA 6221-1-R [(2)]	The Memphis Record	1987	7.50	15.00	30.00
❑ RCA 6313-1-R	Elvis Talks!	1987	7.50	15.00	30.00
❑ RCA 6382-1-R	The Number One Hits	1987	7.50	15.00	30.00
❑ RCA 6383-1-R [(2)]	The Top Ten Hits	1987	7.50	15.00	30.00
❑ RCA 6414-1-R [(2)]	The Complete Sun Sessions	1987	7.50	15.00	30.00
❑ RCA 6738-1-R	Essential Elvis: The First Movies	1988	6.25	12.50	25.00
❑ RCA 6985-1-R	The Alternate Aloha	1988	5.00	10.00	20.00
❑ RCA 8468-1-R	Elvis in Nashville (1956-1971)	1988	10.00	20.00	40.00
❑ RCA 9586-1-R	Elvis Gospel 1957-1971 (Known Only to Him)	1989	10.00	20.00	40.00
❑ RCA 9589-1-R	Essential Elvis, Vol. 2 (Stereo '57)	1989	6.25	12.50	25.00
❑ RCA Camden CAS-2304	Elvis Sings Flaming Star	1969	7.50	15.00	30.00
❑ RCA Camden CAS-2408	Let's Be Friends	1970	7.50	15.00	30.00
❑ RCA Camden CAL-2428 [M]	Elvis' Christmas Album	1970	7.50	15.00	30.00
—Blue label, non-flexible vinyl					
❑ RCA Camden CAS-2440	Almost in Love	1973	6.25	12.50	25.00
—Last song on Side 2 is "Stay Away"					
❑ RCA Camden CAL-2518	C'mon Everybody	1971	5.00	10.00	20.00
❑ RCA Camden CAL-2533	I Got Lucky	1971	6.25	12.50	25.00
❑ RCA Camden CAS-2567	Elvis Sings Hits from His Movies, Volume 1	1972	5.00	10.00	20.00
❑ RCA Camden CAS-2595	Burning Love And Hits from His Movies, Vol. 2	1972	6.25	12.50	25.00
—With star on front cover advertising a bonus photo, the presence of which doubles the value of this LP					
❑ RCA Camden CAS-2611	Separate Ways	1973	7.50	15.00	30.00
❑ RCA Victor APL1-0283	Elvis	1973	12.50	25.00	50.00
❑ RCA Victor CPL1-0341	A Legendary Performer, Volume 1	1974	6.25	12.50	25.00
—Includes booklet (deduct 40% if missing); with die-cut hole in front cover					
❑ RCA Victor APL1-0388	Raised on Rock/For Ol' Times Sake	1973	7.50	15.00	30.00
—Orange label					
❑ RCA Victor CPL1-0475	Good Times	1974	12.50	25.00	50.00
—Orange label					
❑ RCA Victor CPL1-0606	Elvis Recorded Live on Stage in Memphis	1974	6.25	12.50	25.00
—Orange label					
❑ RCA Victor CPM1-0818	Having Fun with Elvis on Stage	1974	7.50	15.00	30.00
—Commercial issue of Boxcar LP; orange label					
❑ RCA Victor APL1-0873	Promised Land	1975	5.00	10.00	20.00
—Tan label					
❑ RCA Victor ANL1-0971(e)	Pure Gold	1975	3.75	7.50	15.00
—Orange label					
❑ RCA Victor LOC-1035 [M]	Elvis' Christmas Album	1957	125.00	250.00	500.00
—Gatefold cover; title printed in gold on LP spine; includes bound-in booklet but not sticker					
❑ RCA Victor LOC-1035 [M]	Elvis' Christmas Album	1957	125.00	250.00	500.00
—Gatefold cover; title printed in silver on LP spine; includes bound-in booklet but not sticker					
❑ RCA Victor APL1-1039	Elvis Today	1975	7.50	15.00	30.00
—Tan label					
❑ RCA Victor LPM-1254 [M]	Elvis Presley	1956	100.00	200.00	400.00
—Version 2: "Long Play" on label; "Elvis" in pale pink, "Presley" in neon green on cover; neon green logo box in upper right front cover					
❑ RCA Victor LPM-1254 [M]	Elvis Presley	1956	125.00	250.00	500.00
—Version 1: "Long Play" on label; "Elvis" in pale pink, "Presley" in pale green on cover; pale green logo box in upper right front cover					
❑ RCA Victor LSP-1254(e) [R]	Elvis Presley	1962	50.00	100.00	200.00
—"Stereo Electronically Reprocessed" and silver "RCA Victor" on label					
❑ RCA Victor ANL1-1319 [S]	His Hand in Mine	1976	3.75	7.50	15.00
—Reissue with more tightly cropped photo of Elvis on front cover					
❑ RCA Victor CPL1-1349	A Legendary Performer, Volume 2	1976	7.50	15.00	30.00
—Includes booklet (deduct 40% if missing); with die-cut hole in front cover					
❑ RCA Victor LPM-1382 [M]	Elvis	1956	75.00	150.00	300.00
—Back cover has ads for other albums. At least 11 different variations of this are known, all of equal value.					
❑ RCA Victor LPM-1382 [M]	Elvis	1956	200.00	400.00	800.00
—With alternate take of "Old Shep" on side 2. Matrix number on the "Old Shep" side ends in "15S," "17S" or "19S," but should be played for positive ID. On alternate take, Elvis sings "he grew old AND his eyes were growing dim" (no AND on standard press)					
❑ RCA Victor LSP-1382(e) [R]	Elvis	1962	50.00	100.00	200.00
—"Stereo Electronically Reprocessed" and silver "RCA Victor" on label					
❑ RCA Victor APL1-1506	From Elvis Presley Boulevard, Memphis, Tennessee	1976	7.50	15.00	30.00
—Tan label					
❑ RCA Victor LPM-1515 [M]	Loving You	1957	75.00	150.00	300.00
—"Long Play" on label					

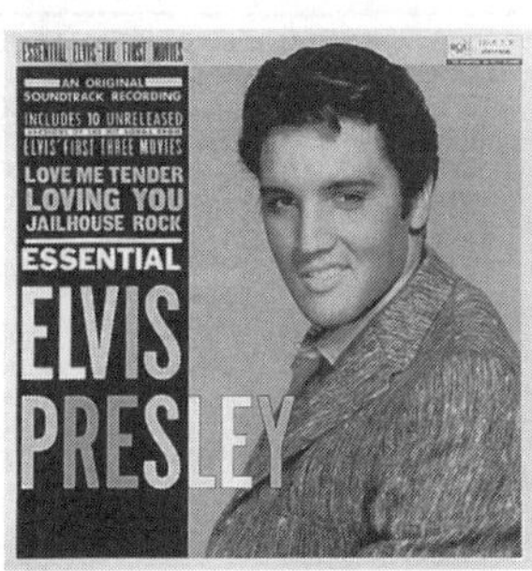

Number	Title (A Side/B Side)	Yr	VG	VG+	NM
❑ RCA Victor LSP-1515(e) [R]	Loving You	1962	37.50	75.00	150.00
—"Stereo Electronically Reprocessed" and silver "RCA Victor" on label					
❑ RCA Victor APM1-1675	The Sun Sessions	1976	5.00	10.00	20.00
—Tan label					
❑ RCA Victor LPM-1707 [M]	Elvis' Golden Records	1958	62.50	125.00	250.00
—Title on cover in light blue letters; no song titles listed on front cover					
❑ RCA Victor LSP-1707(e) [R]	Elvis' Golden Records	1962	50.00	100.00	200.00
—"Stereo Electronically Reprocessed" and silver "RCA Victor" on label					
❑ RCA Victor LPM-1884 [M]	King Creole	1958	50.00	100.00	200.00
—"Long Play" on label; contrary to some other sources, this was NOT issued with a bonus photo					
❑ RCA Victor LSP-1884(e) [R]	King Creole	1962	37.50	75.00	150.00
—"Stereo Electronically Reprocessed" and silver "RCA Victor" on label					
❑ RCA Victor ANL1-1936	Elvis Sings the Wonderful World of Christmas	1975	3.75	7.50	15.00
—New number; same contents as LSP-4579. Orange label.					
❑ RCA Victor LPM-1951 [M]	Elvis' Christmas Album	1958	37.50	75.00	150.00
—Same contents as LOC-1035, but with non-gatefold blue cover; "Long Play" at bottom of label					
❑ RCA Victor LSP-1951(e) [R]	Elvis' Christmas Album	1964	12.50	25.00	50.00
—Black label, dog on top; "Stereo Electronically Reprocessed" at bottom of label					
❑ RCA Victor LPM-1990 [M]	For LP Fans Only	1959	62.50	125.00	250.00
—"Long Play" on label					
❑ RCA Victor LSP-1990(e) [R]	For LP Fans Only	1965	12.50	25.00	50.00
—"Stereo Electronically Reprocessed" on label; normal cover with different front and back cover photos					
❑ RCA Victor LSP-1990(e) [R]	For LP Fans Only	1965	75.00	150.00	300.00
—"Stereo Electronically Reprocessed" on label; error cover with same photo on both front and back					
❑ RCA Victor LPM-2011 [M]	A Date with Elvis	1959	100.00	200.00	400.00
—"Long Play" on label; gatefold cover, no sticker on cover					
❑ RCA Victor LSP-2011(e) [R]	A Date with Elvis	1965	12.50	25.00	50.00
—Black label, "Stereo Electronically Reprocessed" on label					
❑ RCA Victor LPM-2075 [M]	Elvis' Gold Records Volume 2 — 50,000,000 Elvis Fans Can't Be Wrong	1960	50.00	100.00	200.00
—"Long Play" on label; "Magic Millions" on upper right front cover with RCA Victor logo					
❑ RCA Victor LSP-2075(e) [R]	Elvis' Gold Records Volume 2 — 50,000,000 Elvis Fans Can't Be Wrong	1962	37.50	75.00	150.00
—"Stereo Electronically Reprocessed" on label; label has words "50,000,000 Elvis Presley Fans Can't Be Wrong"					
❑ RCA Victor LPM-2231 [M]	Elvis Is Back!	1960	50.00	100.00	200.00
—With no sticker attached to front cover. Side 2, Song 4 is listed as "The Girl Next Door Went a-Walking."					
❑ RCA Victor LPM-2231 [M]	Elvis Is Back!	1960	50.00	100.00	200.00
—With no sticker attached to front cover. Side 2, Song 4 is listed as "The Girl Next Door."					
❑ RCA Victor LSP-2231 [S]	Elvis Is Back!	1960	75.00	150.00	300.00
—"Living Stereo" on label; with no sticker attached to front cover. Side 2, Song 4 is listed as "The Girl Next Door Went a-Walking."					
❑ RCA Victor LSP-2231 [S]	Elvis Is Back!	1960	75.00	150.00	300.00
—"Living Stereo" on label; with no sticker attached to front cover. Side 2, Song 4 is listed as "The Girl Next Door."					
❑ RCA Victor LPM-2256 [M]	G.I. Blues	1960	30.00	60.00	120.00
—"Long Play" on label; with no sticker on front cover					
❑ RCA Victor LSP-2256 [S]	G.I. Blues	1960	25.00	50.00	100.00
—"Living Stereo" on label; with no sticker on front cover					
❑ RCA Victor APL1-2274	Welcome to My World	1977	5.00	10.00	20.00
—Black label, dog near top					
❑ RCA Victor LPM-2328 [M]	His Hand in Mine	1960	30.00	60.00	120.00
—"Long Play" on label					
❑ RCA Victor LSP-2328 [S]	His Hand in Mine	1960	50.00	100.00	200.00
—"Living Stereo" on label					
❑ RCA Victor AHL1-2347	Greatest Hits, Volume One	1981	6.25	12.50	25.00
—With embossed cover					
❑ RCA Victor LPM-2370 [M]	Something for Everybody	1961	30.00	60.00	120.00
—"Long Play" on label; back cover advertises RCA Compact 33 singles and doubles					
❑ RCA Victor LSP-2370 [S]	Something for Everybody	1961	50.00	100.00	200.00
—"Living Stereo" on label; back cover advertises RCA Compact 33 singles and doubles					

Number	Title (A Side/B Side)	Yr	VG	VG+	NM
❑ RCA Victor LPM-2426 [M]	Blue Hawaii	1961	25.00	50.00	100.00
—"Long Play" on label; with sticker on cover advertising the presence of "Can't Help Falling in Love" and "Rock-a-Hula Baby"					
❑ RCA Victor LSP-2426 [S]	Blue Hawaii	1961	37.50	75.00	150.00
—"Living Stereo" on label and upper right front cover; with sticker on cover advertising the presence of "Can't Help Falling in Love" and "Rock-a-Hula Baby"					
❑ RCA Victor AFL1-2428	Moody Blue	1977	2.50	5.00	10.00
—Blue vinyl					
❑ RCA Victor AFL1-2428	Moody Blue	1977	50.00	100.00	200.00
—Black vinyl					
❑ RCA Victor LPM-2523 [M]	Pot Luck with Elvis	1962	25.00	50.00	100.00
—"Long Play" on label					
❑ RCA Victor LSP-2523 [S]	Pot Luck with Elvis	1962	37.50	75.00	150.00
—"Living Stereo" on label					
❑ RCA Victor APL1-2558 [S]	Harum Scarum	1977	3.00	6.00	12.00
—Black label, dog near top					
❑ RCA Victor APL1-2560 [S]	Spinout	1977	3.00	6.00	12.00
—Black label, dog near top					
❑ RCA Victor APL1-2564 [S]	Double Trouble	1977	3.00	6.00	12.00
—Black label, dog near top; includes copies with sticker wrapped around spine with new number					
❑ RCA Victor APL1-2565	Clambake	1977	3.00	6.00	12.00
❑ RCA Victor APL1-2568 [S]	It Happened at the World's Fair	1977	3.00	6.00	12.00
❑ RCA Victor APL2-2587 [(2)]	Elvis in Concert	1977	6.25	12.50	25.00
❑ RCA Victor LPM-2621 [M]	Girls! Girls! Girls!	1962	20.00	40.00	80.00
—"Long Play" on label					
❑ RCA Victor LSP-2621 [S]	Girls! Girls! Girls!	1962	37.50	75.00	150.00
—"Living Stereo" on label					
❑ RCA Victor CPD2-2642 [(2)Q]	Aloha from Hawaii Via Satellite	1975	7.50	15.00	30.00
—Orange labels					
❑ RCA Victor LPM-2697 [M]	It Happened at the World's Fair	1963	30.00	60.00	120.00
❑ RCA Victor LSP-2697 [S]	It Happened at the World's Fair	1963	50.00	100.00	200.00
—"Living Stereo" and silver "RCA Victor" on black label					
❑ RCA Victor LPM-2756 [M]	Fun in Acapulco	1963	20.00	40.00	80.00
—"Mono" on label					
❑ RCA Victor LSP-2756 [S]	Fun in Acapulco	1963	25.00	50.00	100.00
—"Stereo" and silver "RCA Victor" on black label					
❑ RCA Victor LPM-2765 [M]	Elvis' Golden Records, Volume 3	1963	25.00	50.00	100.00
—"Mono" on label					
❑ RCA Victor LSP-2765 [S]	Elvis' Golden Records, Volume 3	1963	37.50	75.00	150.00
—"Stereo" and silver "RCA Victor" on black label					
❑ RCA Victor AFL1-2772	He Walks Beside Me	1978	6.25	12.50	25.00
—Includes 20-page photo booklet					
❑ RCA Victor LPM-2894 [M]	Kissin' Cousins	1964	20.00	40.00	80.00
—"Mono" on label; front cover has a small black and white photo of six cast members in lower right					
❑ RCA Victor LSP-2894 [S]	Kissin' Cousins	1964	30.00	60.00	120.00
—"Stereo" and silver "RCA Victor" on black label; front cover has a small black and white photo of six cast members in lower right					
❑ RCA Victor CPL1-2901	Elvis Sings for Children and Grownups Too!	1978	5.00	10.00	20.00
—With two slits for removable greeting card on back cover (card should be with package)					
❑ RCA Victor LPM-2999 [M]	Roustabout	1964	25.00	50.00	100.00
—"Mono" on label					
❑ RCA Victor LSP-2999 [S]	Roustabout	1964	15.00	30.00	60.00
—"Stereo" and white "RCA Victor" on black label					
❑ RCA Victor CPL1-3078 [PD]	A Legendary Performer, Volume 3	1978	6.25	12.50	25.00
—Picture disc applied to blue vinyl LP; with booklet (deduct 40% if missing)					
❑ RCA Victor CPL1-3082	A Legendary Performer, Volume 3	1978	6.25	12.50	25.00
—Includes booklet (deduct 40% if missing); with die-cut hole in front cover					
❑ RCA Victor AQL1-3279	Our Memories of Elvis	1979	5.00	10.00	20.00
❑ RCA Victor LPM-3338 [M]	Girl Happy	1965	15.00	30.00	60.00
❑ RCA Victor LSP-3338 [S]	Girl Happy	1965	15.00	30.00	60.00
—"Stereo" on black label					
❑ RCA Victor AQL1-3448	Our Memories of Elvis, Volume 2	1979	5.00	10.00	20.00
❑ RCA Victor LPM-3450 [M]	Elvis for Everyone	1965	15.00	30.00	60.00
❑ RCA Victor LSP-3450 [P]	Elvis for Everyone	1965	15.00	30.00	60.00
—Black label, "Stereo" on label					
❑ RCA Victor LPM-3468 [M]	Harum Scarum	1965	15.00	30.00	60.00
❑ RCA Victor LSP-3468 [S]	Harum Scarum	1965	15.00	30.00	60.00
—"Stereo" on black label					
❑ RCA Victor LPM-3553 [M]	Frankie and Johnny	1966	15.00	30.00	60.00
❑ RCA Victor LSP-3553 [S]	Frankie and Johnny	1966	15.00	30.00	60.00
—"Stereo" on black label					
❑ RCA Victor LPM-3643 [M]	Paradise, Hawaiian Style	1966	15.00	30.00	60.00
❑ RCA Victor LSP-3643 [S]	Paradise, Hawaiian Style	1966	15.00	30.00	60.00
—"Stereo" on black label					
❑ RCA Victor AYL1-3683 [S]	Blue Hawaii	1980	2.50	5.00	10.00
—"Best Buy Series" reissue					
❑ RCA Victor AYL1-3684 [S]	Spinout	1980	2.00	4.00	8.00
—"Best Buy Series" reissue					
❑ RCA Victor CPL8-3699 [(8)]	Elvis Aron Presley	1980	25.00	50.00	100.00
—Box set; regular issue with booklet					
❑ RCA Victor LPM-3702 [M]	Spinout	1966	15.00	30.00	60.00
❑ RCA Victor LSP-3702 [S]	Spinout	1966	15.00	30.00	60.00
—"Stereo" on black label					
❑ RCA Victor AYL1-3732	Pure Gold	1980	2.00	4.00	8.00
—"Best Buy Series" reissue					

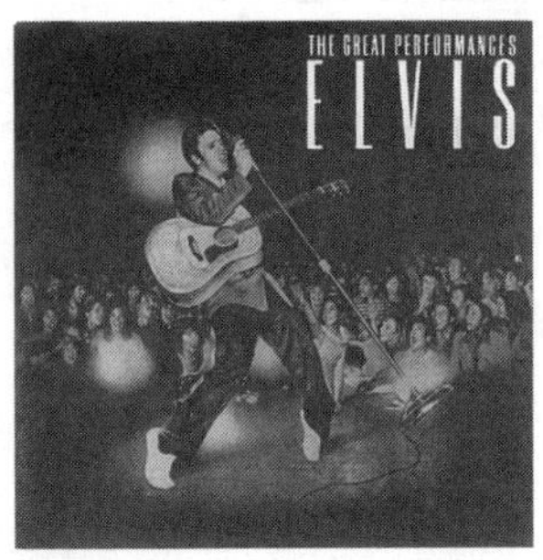

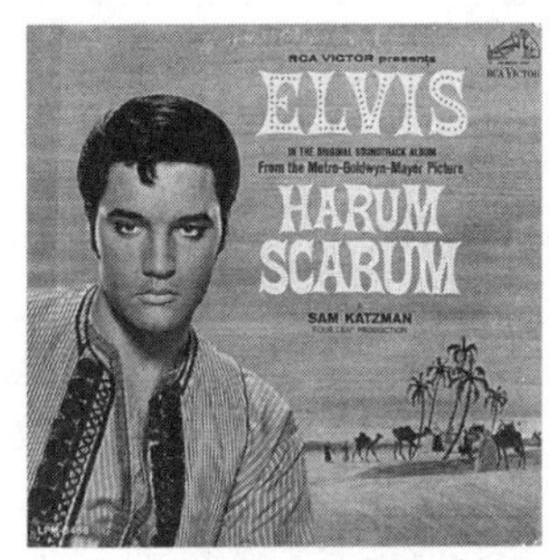

Number	Title (A Side/B Side)	Yr	VG	VG+	NM
❑ RCA Victor AYL1-3733 [R]	King Creole	1980	2.00	4.00	8.00
—"Best Buy Series" reissue; includes copies with sticker wrapped around spine with new number					
❑ RCA Victor AYL1-3734 [S]	Harum Scarum	1980	2.00	4.00	8.00
—"Best Buy Series" reissue					
❑ RCA Victor AYL1-3735 [S]	G.I. Blues	1980	2.00	4.00	8.00
—"Best Buy Series" reissue					
❑ RCA Victor LPM-3758 [M]	How Great Thou Art	1967	15.00	30.00	60.00
—"Mono Dynagroove" on label					
❑ RCA Victor LSP-3758 [S]	How Great Thou Art	1967	15.00	30.00	60.00
—"Stereo Dynagroove" on black label					
❑ RCA Victor LPM-3787 [M]	Double Trouble	1967	15.00	30.00	60.00
—With bonus photo announcement on cover					
❑ RCA Victor LSP-3787 [S]	Double Trouble	1967	15.00	30.00	60.00
—With bonus photo announcement on cover					
❑ RCA Victor AYL1-3892	Elvis in Person at the International Hotel, Las Vegas, Nevada	1981	2.00	4.00	8.00
—"Best Buy Series" reissue					
❑ RCA Victor AYM1-3893	The Sun Sessions	1981	2.00	4.00	8.00
—"Best Buy Series" reissue; includes copies with sticker wrapped around spine with new number					
❑ RCA Victor LPM-3893 [M]	Clambake	1967	62.50	125.00	250.00
❑ RCA Victor LSP-3893 [S]	Clambake	1967	15.00	30.00	60.00
❑ RCA Victor AYM1-3894	Elvis (NBC-TV Special)	1981	2.00	4.00	8.00
—"Best Buy Series" reissue					
❑ RCA Victor AAL1-3917	Guitar Man	1981	7.50	15.00	30.00
❑ RCA Victor LPM-3921 [M]	Elvis' Gold Records, Volume 4	1968	500.00	1000.	2000.
—"Monaural" on label					
❑ RCA Victor LSP-3921 [P]	Elvis' Gold Records, Volume 4	1968	12.50	25.00	50.00
—"Stereo" and white "RCA Victor" on black label					
❑ RCA Victor AYL1-3935 [S]	His Hand in Mine	1981	2.00	4.00	8.00
—"Best Buy Series" reissue; includes copies with sticker wrapped around spine with new number					
❑ RCA Victor AYL1-3956	Elvis Country ("I'm 10,000 Years Old")	1981	2.00	4.00	8.00
—"Best Buy Series" reissue					
❑ RCA Victor LPM-3989 [M]	Speedway	1968	500.00	1000.	2000.
❑ RCA Victor LSP-3989 [S]	Speedway	1968	15.00	30.00	60.00
—"Stereo" on black label					
❑ RCA Victor CPL2-4031 [(2)]	This Is Elvis	1980	3.75	7.50	15.00
❑ RCA Victor LPM-4088	Elvis (NBC-TV Special)	1968	10.00	20.00	40.00
—Orange label, non-flexible vinyl					
❑ RCA Victor AYL1-4114	That's the Way It Is	1981	2.00	4.00	8.00
—"Best Buy Series" reissue; includes copies with sticker wrapped around spine with new number					
❑ RCA Victor AYL1-4115 [S]	Kissin' Cousins	1981	2.00	4.00	8.00
—"Best Buy Series" reissue; includes copies with sticker wrapped around spine with new number					
❑ RCA Victor AYL1-4116 [S]	Something for Everybody	1981	2.00	4.00	8.00
—"Best Buy Series" reissue; includes copies with sticker wrapped around spine with new number					
❑ RCA Victor LSP-4155	From Elvis in Memphis	1969	10.00	20.00	40.00
—Orange label, non-flexible vinyl					
❑ RCA Victor AYL1-4232 [P]	Elvis for Everyone	1982	2.00	4.00	8.00
—"Best Buy Series" reissue					
❑ RCA Victor LSP-4362	On Stage February, 1970	1970	10.00	20.00	40.00
—Orange label, non-flexible vinyl					
❑ RCA Victor CPL1-4395	Memories of Christmas	1982	3.75	7.50	15.00
—With greeting card (deduct 1/3 if missing)					
❑ RCA Victor LSP-4428	Elvis in Person at the International Hotel, Las Vegas, Nevada	1970	12.50	25.00	50.00
—Orange label, non-flexible vinyl					
❑ RCA Victor LSP-4429	Back in Memphis	1970	10.00	20.00	40.00
—Orange label, non-flexible vinyl					
❑ RCA Victor LSP-4445	That's the Way It Is	1970	20.00	40.00	80.00
—Orange label, non-flexible vinyl					
❑ RCA Victor LSP-4460	Elvis Country ("I'm 10,000 Years Old")	1971	10.00	20.00	40.00
—Orange label, non-flexible vinyl					
❑ RCA Victor AHL1-4530	The Elvis Medley	1982	3.00	6.00	12.00
❑ RCA Victor LSP-4530	Love Letters from Elvis	1971	10.00	20.00	40.00
—Orange label; "Love Letters from" on one line of cover, "Elvis" on a second line					
❑ RCA Victor LSP-4530	Love Letters from Elvis	1971	7.50	15.00	30.00
—Orange label; "Love Letters" on one line of cover; "from" on a second line, "Elvis" on a third line					
❑ RCA Victor LSP-4579	Elvis Sings the Wonderful World of Christmas	1971	7.50	15.00	30.00
—Orange label. Bonus postcard is priced separately					

Number	Title (A Side/B Side)	Yr	VG	VG+	NM
❑ RCA Victor LSP-4671	Elvis Now	1972	7.50	15.00	30.00
—Orange label					
❑ RCA Victor AHL1-4678	I Was the One	1983	2.50	5.00	10.00
❑ RCA Victor LSP-4690	He Touched Me	1972	10.00	20.00	40.00
—Orange label					
❑ RCA Victor LSP-4776	Elvis As Recorded at Madison Square Garden	1972	7.50	15.00	30.00
—Orange label					
❑ RCA Victor CPL1-4848	A Legendary Performer, Volume 4	1983	7.50	15.00	30.00
—Includes booklet (deduct 40% if missing); with die-cut hole in front cover					
❑ RCA Victor AFL1-4941	Elvis' Gold Records, Volume 5	1984	2.50	5.00	10.00
❑ RCA Victor CPM6-5172 [(6)]	A Golden Celebration	1984	25.00	50.00	100.00
❑ RCA Victor AFM1-5182	Rocker	1984	5.00	10.00	20.00
❑ RCA Victor AFM1-5196 [M]	Elvis' Golden Records	1984	5.00	10.00	20.00
—50th Anniversary reissue in mono with banner					
❑ RCA Victor AFM1-5197 [M]	Elvis' Gold Records Volume 2 — 50,000,000 Elvis Fans Can't Be Wrong	1984	5.00	10.00	20.00
—50th Anniversary reissue in mono with banner					
❑ RCA Victor AFM1-5198 [M]	Elvis Presley	1984	5.00	10.00	20.00
—50th Anniversary reissue in mono with banner					
❑ RCA Victor AFM1-5199 [M]	Elvis	1984	5.00	10.00	20.00
—50th Anniversary reissue in mono with banner					
❑ RCA Victor AFL1-5353	A Valentine Gift for You	1985	5.00	10.00	20.00
—Red vinyl					
❑ RCA Victor AFL1-5418	Reconsider Baby	1985	5.00	10.00	20.00
—All copies on blue vinyl					
❑ RCA Victor AFL1-5430	Always on My Mind	1985	5.00	10.00	20.00
—All copies on purple vinyl					
❑ RCA Victor AFM1-5486 [M]	Elvis' Christmas Album	1985	5.00	10.00	20.00
—Same as LOC-1035; green vinyl with booklet					
❑ RCA Victor LSP-6020 [(2)]	From Memphis to Vegas/From Vegas to Memphis	1969	25.00	50.00	100.00
—Orange labels, non-flexible vinyl; with composers of "Words" correctly listed as Barry, Robin and Maurice Gibb					
❑ RCA Victor VPSX-6089 [(2)Q]	Aloha from Hawaii Via Satellite	1973	10.00	20.00	40.00
—Lighter orange labels, "RCA" on side					
❑ RCA Victor LPM-6401 [(4)]	Worldwide 50 Gold Award Hits, Vol. 1	1970	20.00	40.00	80.00
—Orange labels, non-flexible vinyl; with blurb for photo book on cover					
❑ RCA Victor LPM-6402 [(4)]	The Other Sides: Worldwide 50 Gold Award Hits, Vol. 2	1971	17.50	35.00	70.00
—Orange labels, flexible vinyl; with blurb for inserts on cover					
❑ RCA Victor KKL1-7065	A Canadian Tribute	1978	5.00	10.00	20.00
—Gold vinyl, embossed cover					
❑ Reader's Digest RD-10/A [(8)]	His Greatest Hits	1979	100.00	200.00	400.00
—White box					
❑ Reader's Digest RBA-072/D	Great Hits of 1956-57	1987	5.00	10.00	20.00
❑ Reader's Digest RD4A-181/D	Elvis Sings Inspirational Favorites	1983	5.00	10.00	20.00
❑ Reader's Digest RB4-191/A [(7)]	The Legend Lives On	1986	15.00	30.00	60.00
❑ Reader's Digest RDA-242/D	Elvis Sings Country Favorites	1984	15.00	30.00	60.00
❑ Show-Land LP-2001	The First of Elvis	1979	25.00	50.00	100.00
❑ Silhouette 10001/2 [(2)]	Personally Elvis	1979	7.50	15.00	30.00
—Interview records; no music					
❑ Sun 1001	The Sun Years — Interviews and Memories	1977	6.25	12.50	25.00
—With "Memphis, Tennessee" on label					
❑ Time-Life STL-106 [(2)]	Elvis Presley: 1954-1961	1986	7.50	15.00	30.00
❑ Time-Life STW-106	Country Music	1981	5.00	10.00	20.00
❑ Time-Life STL-126 [(2)]	Elvis the King: 1954-1965	1989	20.00	40.00	80.00

PRESTON, BILLY

45s

Number	Title (A Side/B Side)	Yr	VG	VG+	NM
❑ A&M 1320	Outa-Space/I Wrote a Simple Song	1972	—	2.50	5.00
❑ A&M 1340	Should Have Known Better/The Bus	1972	—	2.50	5.00
❑ A&M 1380	Slaughter/God Loves You	1972	—	2.50	5.00
❑ A&M 1411	Will It Go Round in Circles/Blackbird	1973	—	2.00	4.00
❑ A&M 1463	Space Race/We're Gonna Make It	1973	—	2.00	4.00
❑ A&M 1492	You're So Unique/How Long Has the Train Been Gone	1973	—	2.00	4.00
❑ A&M 1536	Creature Feature/My Soul Is a Witness	1974	—	2.00	4.00
❑ A&M 1544	Nothing from Nothing/My Soul Is a Witness	1974	—	2.00	4.00
❑ A&M 1644	Struttin'/You Are So Beautiful	1974	—	2.00	4.00
❑ A&M 1735	Fancy Lady/Song of Joy	1975	—	2.00	4.00
❑ A&M 1768	Do It While You Can/Song of Joy	1975	—	2.00	4.00
❑ A&M 1892	Do What You Want/I've Got the Spirit	1976	—	2.00	4.00
❑ A&M 1925	Girl/Ecstasy	1977	—	2.00	4.00
❑ A&M 1954	Wide Stride/When You Are Mine	1977	—	2.00	4.00
❑ A&M 1980	A Whole New Thing/Wide Stride	1977	—	2.00	4.00
❑ A&M 2012	I Really Miss You/Attitudes	1978	—	2.00	4.00
❑ A&M 2071	Get Back/Space Race	1978	—	2.00	4.00
❑ Apple 1808	That's the Way God Planned It/What About You	1969	2.00	4.00	8.00
❑ Apple 1814	Everything's All Right/I Want to Thank You	1969	2.00	4.00	8.00
❑ Apple 1817	All That I've Got (I'm Gonna Give It to You)/As I Get Older	1970	2.00	4.00	8.00
❑ Apple 1826	My Sweet Lord/Little Girl	1970	2.00	4.00	8.00
❑ Capitol 2309	Hey Brother (Part 1)/Hey Brother (Part 2)	1968	2.00	4.00	8.00
❑ Capitol 5611	The Girl's Got "It"/The Night	1966	2.00	4.00	8.00
❑ Capitol 5660	In the Midnight Hour/Advice	1966	2.00	4.00	8.00
❑ Capitol 5730	Sunny/Let the Music Play	1966	2.00	4.00	8.00

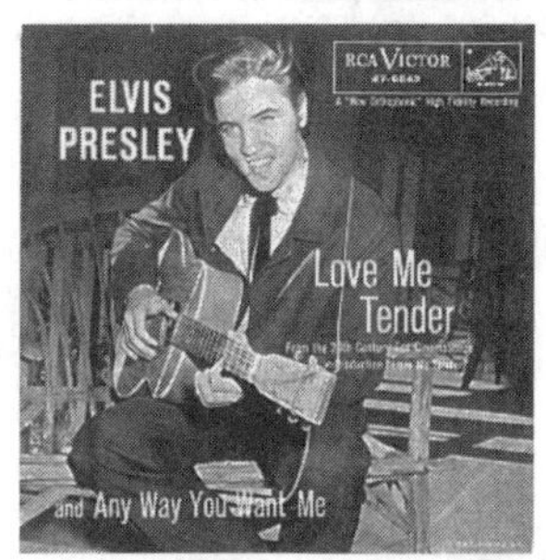

Number	Title (A Side/B Side)	Yr	VG	VG+	NM
❑ Capitol 5797	Phony Friends/Can't She Tell	1966	2.00	4.00	8.00
❑ Contract 5102	Volcano/Young Heartaches	1961	75.00	150.00	300.00
❑ Derby 1002	Greazee (Part 1)/(Part 2)	1963	6.25	12.50	25.00
❑ MGM 14001	The Split/It's Just a Love Game	1968	2.00	4.00	8.00
❑ Motown 1470	It Will Come In Time/All I Wanted Was You	1979	—	2.00	4.00
❑ Motown 1505	Sock-It Rocket/Hope	1981	—	2.00	4.00
❑ Motown 1511	A Change Is Gonna Come/You	1981	—	2.00	4.00
❑ Motown 1625	I'm Never Gonna Say Goodbye/Love You So	1982	—	2.00	4.00
❑ Myrrh 216	One with the Lord/Universal Love	1979	2.00	4.00	8.00
❑ Vee Jay 646	Don't Let the Sun Catch You Cryin'/(B-side unknown)	1965	—	—	—
—Canceled?					
❑ Vee Jay 653	Don't Let the Sun Catch You Cryin'/Billy's Bag	1965	2.50	5.00	10.00
❑ Vee Jay 692	Log Cabin/Drown in My Own Tears	1965	2.50	5.00	10.00
Albums					
❑ A&M SP-3205	The Best of Billy Preston	1982	2.50	5.00	10.00
❑ A&M SP-3507	I Wrote a Simple Song	1971	3.00	6.00	12.00
❑ A&M SP-3516	Music Is My Life	1972	3.00	6.00	12.00
❑ A&M SP-3526	Everybody Likes Some Kind of Music	1973	3.00	6.00	12.00
❑ A&M SP-3637	Live European Tour	1974	3.00	6.00	12.00
❑ A&M SP-3645	The Kids & Me	1974	3.00	6.00	12.00
❑ A&M SP-4532	It's My Pleasure	1975	3.00	6.00	12.00
❑ A&M SP-4587	Billy Preston	1976	3.00	6.00	12.00
❑ A&M SP-4657	It's a Whole New Thing	1977	3.00	6.00	12.00
❑ Apple ST-3359	That's the Way God Planned It	1969	12.50	25.00	50.00
—Cover has close-up of Billy Preston					
❑ Apple ST-3359	That's the Way God Planned It	1972	5.00	10.00	20.00
—Cover has multiple images of Billy Preston					
❑ Apple ST-3370	Encouraging Words	1970	5.00	10.00	20.00
❑ Buddah BDS-7502	Billy Preston	1969	3.75	7.50	15.00
❑ Capitol ST 2532 [S]	Wildest Organ in Town!	1966	10.00	20.00	40.00
❑ Capitol T 2532 [M]	Wildest Organ in Town!	1966	7.50	15.00	30.00
❑ Capitol DT 2607 [R]	Club Meetin'	1967	—	—	—
❑ Capitol T 2607 [M]	Club Meetin'	1967	—	—	—
—The above versions of Club Meetin' may not exist					
❑ Derby LPM-701 [M]	16 Year Old Soul	1963	62.50	125.00	250.00
❑ Exodus 304 [M]	Early Hits of 1965	1965	6.25	12.50	25.00
❑ GNP Crescendo GNPS-2071 [(2)]	Soul'd Out	1973	3.75	7.50	15.00
❑ MCA 28037	Gospel Soul	198?	2.00	4.00	8.00
—Reissue of Peacock LP					
❑ Motown M7-925	Late at Night	1980	2.50	5.00	10.00
❑ Motown M8-941	The Way I Am	1981	2.50	5.00	10.00
❑ Motown M7-958	Billy Preston & Syreeta	1981	2.50	5.00	10.00
❑ Motown 6020 ML	Pressin' On	1982	2.50	5.00	10.00
❑ Myrrh MSB-6605	Behold	1978	3.00	6.00	12.00
❑ Myrrh MSB-6607	Universal Love	1979	3.00	6.00	12.00
❑ Peacock 179	Gospel Soul	197?	3.00	6.00	12.00
❑ Pickwick SPC-3315	Organ Transplant	197?	2.50	5.00	10.00
❑ Vee Jay LP-1123 [M]	The Most Exciting Organ Ever	1965	7.50	15.00	30.00
❑ Vee Jay LPS-1123 [S]	The Most Exciting Organ Ever	1965	12.50	25.00	50.00
❑ Vee Jay LP-1142 [M]	Greatest Hits	1966	7.50	15.00	30.00
❑ Vee Jay LPS-1142 [S]	Greatest Hits	1966	12.50	25.00	50.00

PRESTON, BILLY, AND SYREETA

45s

Number	Title (A Side/B Side)	Yr	VG	VG+	NM
❑ Motown 1460	With You I'm Born Again/Go For It	1979	—	2.50	5.00
❑ Motown 1477	With You I'm Born Again/All I Wanted Was You	1979	—	2.00	4.00
❑ Motown 1520	Searchin'/Hey You	1981	—	2.00	4.00
❑ Motown 1522	Just for You (Put the Boogie in Your Body)/Hey You	1981	—	2.00	4.00
❑ Tamla 54312	Dance For Me Children/One More Time for Love	1980	—	2.00	4.00
❑ Tamla 54319	Please Stay/Signed, Sealed, Delivered (I'm Yours)	1980	—	2.00	4.00

PRESTON, JOHNNY

45s

Number	Title (A Side/B Side)	Yr	VG	VG+	NM
❑ ABC 11085	I'm Only Human/There's No One Like You	1968	2.50	5.00	10.00
❑ ABC 11187	Kick the Can/I've Just Been Wasting My Time	1969	2.50	5.00	10.00
❑ Hallway 1201	All Around the World/Just Plain Hurt	1964	3.75	7.50	15.00

Number	Title (A Side/B Side)	Yr	VG	VG+	NM
❑ Hallway 1204	Willie and the Hand Jive/I've Got My Eyes on You	1964	3.75	7.50	15.00
❑ Hallway 1927	Running Bear '65/Dedicated to the One I Love	1965	3.75	7.50	15.00
❑ Imperial 5924	This Little Bitty Tear/The Day the World Stood Still	1963	2.50	5.00	10.00
❑ Imperial 5947	I've Got My Eyes on You/I Couldn't Take It Again	1963	2.50	5.00	10.00
❑ Mercury 71474	Running Bear/My Heart Knows	1959	6.25	12.50	25.00
❑ Mercury 71598 [M]	Cradle of Love/City of Tears	1960	5.00	10.00	20.00
❑ Mercury 71651 [M]	Feel So Fine/I'm Starting to Go Steady	1960	5.00	10.00	20.00
❑ Mercury 71691	Charming Billy/Up in the Air	1960	5.00	10.00	20.00
❑ Mercury 71728	New Baby for Christmas/(I Want a) Rock and Roll Guitar	1960	5.00	10.00	20.00
❑ Mercury 71761	Leave My Kitten Alone/Token of Love	1961	5.00	10.00	20.00
❑ Mercury 71803	I Feel Good/Willy Walk	1961	5.00	10.00	20.00
❑ Mercury 71865	Let Them Talk/She Once Belonged to Me	1961	5.00	10.00	20.00
❑ Mercury 71908	Free Me/Kissin' Tree	1961	5.00	10.00	20.00
❑ Mercury 71951	Let's Leave It That Way/Broken Hearts Anonymous	1962	3.75	7.50	15.00
❑ Mercury 72049	Let the Big Boss Man (Pull You Through)/The Day After Forever	1962	3.75	7.50	15.00
❑ TCF Hall 101	Running Bear '65/Dedicated to the One I Love	1965	2.50	5.00	10.00
❑ TCF Hall 110	Sounds Like Trouble/You Can Make It If You Try	1965	3.75	7.50	15.00
❑ TCF Hall 120	I'm Askin' Forgiveness/Good Good Lovin'	1965	2.50	5.00	10.00
Albums					
❑ Mercury MG-20592 [M]	Running Bear	1960	25.00	50.00	100.00
❑ Mercury MG-20609 [M]	Come Rock with Me	1960	25.00	50.00	100.00
❑ Mercury SR-60250 [S]	Running Bear	1960	37.50	75.00	150.00
—Black label					
❑ Mercury SR-60250 [S]	Running Bear	1981	3.00	6.00	12.00
—Reissue on Chicago skyline label					
❑ Mercury SR-60609 [S]	Come Rock with Me	1960	37.50	75.00	150.00
❑ Wing MGW-12246 [M]	Running Bear	1963	5.00	10.00	20.00
❑ Wing SRW-16246 [S]	Running Bear	1963	6.25	12.50	25.00
PRETENDERS					
45s					
❑ Polydor 887816-7	Window of the World/1969	1988	—	—	3.00
❑ Sire GSRE 0448	Back on the Chain Gang/My City Was Gone	198?	—	—	3.00
—"Back to Back Hits" reissue					
❑ Sire GSRE 0474	Brass in Pocket/Middle of the Road	198?	—	—	3.00
—"Back to Back Hits" reissue					
❑ Sire GSRE 0496	Show Me/Thin Line Between Love and Hate	198?	—	—	3.00
—"Back to Back Hits" reissue					
❑ Sire 28354	Hymn to Her (She Will Always Carry On)/Tradition of Love	1987	—	—	3.00
❑ Sire 28496	My Baby/Room Full of Mirrors	1987	—	—	3.00
❑ Sire 28630	Don't Get Me Wrong/Dance!	1986	—	—	3.00
❑ Sire 29249	Thin Line Between Love and Hate/Time the Avenger	1984	—	—	3.00
❑ Sire 29317	Show Me/Fast or Slow (The Law Is The Law)	1984	—	—	3.00
❑ Sire 29444	Middle of the Road/2000 Miles	1983	—	—	3.00
❑ Sire 29840	Back on the Chain Gang/My City Was Gone	1982	—	—	3.00
❑ Sire 49181	Brass in Pocket (I'm Special)/Space Invader	1980	—	2.00	4.00
❑ Sire 49506	Stop Your Sobbing/Phone Call	1980	—	2.00	4.00
❑ Sire 49533	Kid/Tattooed Love Boys	1980	—	2.00	4.00
❑ Sire 49819	Louie Louie/In the Sticks	1981	—	2.00	4.00
❑ Sire 49861	I Go to Sleep/Waste Not Want Not	1981	—	2.00	4.00
❑ Warner Bros. 28259	If There Was a Man/Into Vienna	1987	—	—	3.00
—B-side by John Barry					
Albums					
❑ Sire MINI 3563 [EP]	Extended Play	1981	2.50	5.00	10.00
❑ Sire SRK 3572	Pretenders II	1981	2.50	5.00	10.00
❑ Sire SRK 6083	Pretenders	1980	2.50	5.00	10.00
❑ Sire 23980	Learning to Crawl	1983	2.50	5.00	10.00
❑ Sire 25488	Get Close	1986	2.50	5.00	10.00
❑ Sire 25664	The Singles	1987	2.50	5.00	10.00
❑ Sire 26219	Packed!	1990	3.00	6.00	12.00
PRICE, LLOYD					
45s					
❑ ABC 1237	Stagger Lee/Personality	1969	—	3.00	6.00
—"Golden Treasure Chest" reissue; contains the "samitized" version of "Stagger Lee" with Mr. Lee and Billy arguing over a woman					
❑ ABC 11016	Personality/Just Because	1967	2.00	4.00	8.00
❑ ABC-Paramount 9792	Just Because/Why	1957	5.00	10.00	20.00
❑ ABC-Paramount 9972 [M]	Stagger Lee/You Need Love	1958	5.00	10.00	20.00
—Most, if not all, copies contain the "raunchy" version of "Stagger Lee" with Mr. Lee and Billy playing cards					
❑ ABC-Paramount S-9972 [S]	Stagger Lee/You Need Love	1958	10.00	20.00	40.00
❑ ABC-Paramount 9997 [M]	Where Were You (On Our Wedding Day)?/Is It Really Love	1959	5.00	10.00	20.00
❑ ABC-Paramount S-9997 [S]	Where Were You (On Our Wedding Day)?/Is It Really Love	1959	10.00	20.00	40.00
❑ ABC-Paramount 10018 [M]	Personality/Have You Ever Had the Blues	1959	5.00	10.00	20.00
❑ ABC-Paramount 10018 [M]	(You've Got) Personality/Have You Ever Had the Blues	1959	5.00	10.00	20.00
—Note longer title					
❑ ABC-Paramount S-10018 [S]	Personality/Have You Ever Had the Blues	1959	12.50	25.00	50.00
❑ ABC-Paramount 10032 [M]	I'm Gonna Get Married/Three Little Pigs	1959	5.00	10.00	20.00
❑ ABC-Paramount S-10032 [S]	I'm Gonna Get Married/Three Little Pigs	1959	12.50	25.00	50.00
❑ ABC-Paramount 10062	Come Into My Heart/Won't Cha Come Home	1959	3.75	7.50	15.00
❑ ABC-Paramount S-10062 [S]	Come Into My Heart/Won't Cha Come Home	1959	12.50	25.00	50.00
❑ ABC-Paramount 10075	Lady Luck/Never Let Me Go	1960	3.75	7.50	15.00
❑ ABC-Paramount 10102	No If's — No And's/For Love	1960	3.75	7.50	15.00
❑ ABC-Paramount 10123	Question/If I Look a Little Blue	1960	3.75	7.50	15.00
❑ ABC-Paramount 10139	Just Call Me (And I'll Understand)/Who Could've Told You	1960	3.75	7.50	15.00

Number	Title (A Side/B Side)	Yr	VG	VG+	NM
❑ ABC-Paramount 10162	(You Better) Know What You're Doin'/ That's Why Tears Come and Go	1960	3.75	7.50	15.00
❑ ABC-Paramount 10177	Boo Hoo/I Made You Cry	1961	3.75	7.50	15.00
❑ ABC-Paramount 10197	One Hundred Percent/Say I'm the One	1961	3.75	7.50	15.00
❑ ABC-Paramount 10206	String of Pearls/Chantilly Lace	1961	3.75	7.50	15.00
❑ ABC-Paramount 10221	Mary and Man-O/I Ain't Givin' Up Nothin'	1961	3.75	7.50	15.00
❑ ABC-Paramount 10229	Talk to Me/I Cover the Waterfront	1961	3.75	7.50	15.00
❑ ABC-Paramount 10288	Be a Leader/'Nother Fairy Tale	1962	3.75	7.50	15.00
❑ ABC-Paramount 10299	Twistin' the Blues/Pop Eye's Irresistable You	1962	3.75	7.50	15.00
❑ ABC-Paramount 10342	Counterfeit Friends/Your Picture	1962	3.75	7.50	15.00
❑ ABC-Paramount 10372	Under Your Spell Again/Happy Birthday Mama	1962	3.75	7.50	15.00
❑ ABC-Paramount 10412	Who's Sorry Now/Hello Bill	1963	3.75	7.50	15.00
❑ Double-L 714	Pistol Packin' Mama/Tennessee Waltz	1963	2.50	5.00	10.00
❑ Double-L 722	Misty/Cry On	1963	2.50	5.00	10.00
❑ Double-L 728	Merry Christmas Mama/Auld Lang Syne	1963	3.00	6.00	12.00
❑ Double-L 729	Billie Baby/Try a Little Bit of Tenderness	1964	2.50	5.00	10.00
❑ Double-L 730	I'll Be a Fool for You/You're Nobody Till Somebody Loves You	1964	2.50	5.00	10.00
❑ Double-L 736	Go On Little Girl/You're Reading Me	1965	2.50	5.00	10.00
❑ Double-L 739	Every Night/Peeping and Hiding	1966	2.50	5.00	10.00
❑ Double-L 740	Send Me Some Loving/Somewhere Along the Way	1966	2.50	5.00	10.00
❑ GSF 6882	Sing a Song/(B-side unknown)	1972	—	3.00	6.00
❑ GSF 6894	Love Music/Just for Baby	1973	—	3.00	6.00
❑ GSF 6904	Trying to Slip (Away)/They Get Down	1973	—	3.00	6.00
❑ Hurd 82	Misty '66/Saturday Night	1966	2.00	4.00	8.00
❑ Jad 208	Luv, Luv, Luv/Take All	1968	2.00	4.00	8.00
❑ Jad 212	Don't Stop Now/The Truth	1968	2.00	4.00	8.00
❑ KRC 301	Lonely Chair/The Chicken and the Bop	1957	12.50	25.00	50.00
❑ KRC 303	Hello Little Girl/Georgianna	1957	6.25	12.50	25.00
❑ KRC 305	How Many Times/To Love and Be Loved	1957	6.25	12.50	25.00
❑ KRC 587	Just Because/Why	1957	20.00	40.00	80.00
❑ KRC 5000	No Limit to Love/Such a Mess	195?	6.25	12.50	25.00
❑ KRC 5002	Gonna Let You Come Back Home/Down by the River	195?	6.25	12.50	25.00
❑ LPG 111	What Did You Do with My Love/Love Music	1976	—	3.00	6.00
❑ Ludix 4747	Feelin' Good/Cupid's Bandwagon	197?	—	3.00	6.00
❑ Monument 856	Don't Cry/I Love You, I Just Love You	1964	2.50	5.00	10.00
❑ Monument 865	Amen/I'd Fight the World	1964	2.50	5.00	10.00
❑ Monument 877	Oh, Lady Luck/Woman	1965	2.50	5.00	10.00
❑ Monument 887	If I Had My Life to Live Over/Two for Love	1965	2.50	5.00	10.00
❑ Paramount 0168	In the Eyes of God/The Legend of Nigger Charley	1972	—	3.00	6.00
❑ Reprise 0499	I Won't Cry Anymore/The Man Who Took the Valise Off the Floor at Grand Central Station at Noon	1966	2.00	4.00	8.00
❑ Scepter 12310	Hooked on a Feeling/If You Really Love Him	1971	—	3.00	6.00
❑ Scepter 12327	Mr. and Mrs. Untrue/Natural SInner	1971	—	3.00	6.00
❑ Specialty 428 *—Red vinyl*	Lawdy Miss Clawdy/Mailman Blues	1952	375.00	750.00	1500.
❑ Specialty 428	Lawdy Miss Clawdy/Mailman Blues	1952	62.50	125.00	250.00
❑ Specialty 440	Oooh-Oooh-Oooh/Restless Heart	1952	25.00	50.00	100.00
❑ Specialty 452	Ain't It a Shame?/Tell Me Pretty Baby	1953	25.00	50.00	100.00
❑ Specialty 457	What's the Matter Now/So Long	1953	25.00	50.00	100.00
❑ Specialty 463	Where You At?/Baby Don't Turn Your Back on Me	1953	25.00	50.00	100.00
❑ Specialty 471	I Wish Your Picture Was You/Frog Legs	1953	25.00	50.00	100.00
❑ Specialty 483	Let Me Come Home, Baby/Too Late for Tears	1954	20.00	40.00	80.00
❑ Specialty 494	Walkin' the Track/Jimmie Lee	1954	20.00	40.00	80.00
❑ Specialty 535	Oo-Ee Baby/Chee-Koo Baby	1954	10.00	20.00	40.00
❑ Specialty 540	Trying to Find Someone to Love/Lord, Lord, Amen!	1955	10.00	20.00	40.00
❑ Specialty 571	Woe Ho Ho/I Yi Yi Gomen-a-Sai (I'm Sorry)	1956	10.00	20.00	40.00
❑ Specialty 578	Country Boy Rock/Rock 'N' Dance	1956	12.50	25.00	50.00
❑ Specialty 582	Forgive Me, Clawdy/I'm Glad	1956	7.50	15.00	30.00
❑ Specialty 602	Baby Please Come Home/Breaking My Heart (All Over Again)	1957	7.50	15.00	30.00
❑ Specialty 661	Lawdy Miss Clawdy/Mailman Blues	1959	5.00	10.00	20.00
❑ Turntable 501	I Understand/The Grass Will Sing (For You)	1969	2.00	4.00	8.00
❑ Turntable 502	I Heard It Through the Grapevine/It's Your Thing	1969	2.00	4.00	8.00
❑ Turntable 506	Bad Conditions/The Truth	1969	2.00	4.00	8.00
❑ Turntable 509	Lawdy Miss Clawdy/Little Volcano	1969	2.00	4.00	8.00
Albums					
❑ ABC X-763	16 Greatest Hits	1972	3.75	7.50	15.00
❑ ABC AC-30006	The ABC Collection	1976	3.75	7.50	15.00

Number	Title (A Side/B Side)	Yr	VG	VG+	NM
❑ ABC-Paramount ABC-277 [M]	The Exciting Lloyd Price	1959	10.00	20.00	40.00
❑ ABC-Paramount ABCS-277 [S]	The Exciting Lloyd Price	1959	20.00	40.00	80.00
❑ ABC-Paramount ABC-297 [M]	Mr. Personality	1959	10.00	20.00	40.00
❑ ABC-Paramount ABCS-297 [S]	Mr. Personality	1959	20.00	40.00	80.00
❑ ABC-Paramount ABC-315 [M]	Mr. Personality Sings the Blues	1960	10.00	20.00	40.00
❑ ABC-Paramount ABCS-315 [S]	Mr. Personality Sings the Blues	1960	20.00	40.00	80.00
❑ ABC-Paramount ABC-324 [M]	Mr. Personality's 15 Hits	1960	10.00	20.00	40.00
—Label calls this "Mr. Personality's Big Hits"					
❑ ABC-Paramount ABC-346 [M]	The Fantastic Lloyd Price	1960	10.00	20.00	40.00
❑ ABC-Paramount ABCS-346 [R]	The Fantastic Lloyd Price	196?	6.25	12.50	25.00
❑ ABC-Paramount ABC-366 [M]	Lloyd Price Sings the Million Sellers	1961	10.00	20.00	40.00
❑ ABC-Paramount ABCS-366 [S]	Lloyd Price Sings the Million Sellers	1961	12.50	25.00	50.00
❑ ABC-Paramount ABC-382 [M]	Cookin' with Lloyd Price	1961	10.00	20.00	40.00
❑ ABC-Paramount ABCS-382 [S]	Cookin' with Lloyd Price	1961	12.50	25.00	50.00
❑ Double-L DL-2301 [M]	The Lloyd Price Orchestra	1963	6.25	12.50	25.00
❑ Double-L DL-2303 [M]	Misty	1963	6.25	12.50	25.00
❑ Double-L SDL-8301 [S]	The Lloyd Price Orchestra	1963	10.00	20.00	40.00
❑ Double-L SDL-8303 [S]	Misty	1963	10.00	20.00	40.00
❑ Grand Prix 422 [M]	Mr. Rhythm and Blues	196?	3.00	6.00	12.00
❑ Grand Prix S-422 [R]	Mr. Rhythm and Blues	196?	2.50	5.00	10.00
❑ Guest Star G-1910 [M]	Come to Me	196?	3.00	6.00	12.00
❑ Guest Star GS-1910 [R]	Come to Me	196?	2.50	5.00	10.00
❑ Jad 1002	Lloyd Price Now	1969	6.25	12.50	25.00
❑ LPG 001	Music…Music	1976	2.50	5.00	10.00
❑ MCA 1503	Greatest Hits	1982	2.00	4.00	8.00
❑ Monument MLP-8032 [M]	Lloyd Swings for Sammy	1965	6.25	12.50	25.00
❑ Monument SLP-18032 [S]	Lloyd Swings for Sammy	1965	10.00	20.00	40.00
❑ Pickwick SPC-3518	Big Hits	197?	2.00	4.00	8.00
❑ Scepter Citation CTN-18006	The Best of Lloyd Price	1972	2.50	5.00	10.00
❑ Specialty SP-2105 [M]	Lloyd Price	1959	45.00	90.00	180.00
❑ Trip TOP 16-5	16 Greatest Hits	1976	2.50	5.00	10.00
❑ Turntable TTS-5001	Lloyd Price Now	197?	3.75	7.50	15.00
❑ Upfront UPF-126	Misty	197?	3.00	6.00	12.00

PRINCE

45s

Number	Title (A Side/B Side)	Yr	VG	VG+	NM
❑ Paisley Park GWB 0528	Purple Rain/Raspberry Beret	1986	—	—	3.00
—"Back to Back Hits" reissue					
❑ Paisley Park GWB 0529	Pop Life/America	1986	—	—	3.00
—"Back to Back Hits" reissue					
❑ Paisley Park 27745	I Wish U Heaven/Scarlet Pussy	1988	—	—	3.00
❑ Paisley Park 27806	Glam Slam/Escape	1988	—	—	3.00
❑ Paisley Park 27900	Alphabet St./Alphabet St. (Cont.)	1988	—	—	3.00
❑ Paisley Park 28288	I Could Never Take the Place of Your Man/Hot Thing	1987	—	—	3.00
❑ Paisley Park 28289	U Got the Look/Housequake	1987	—	—	3.00
❑ Paisley Park 28334	If I Was Your Girlfriend/Shockadelica	1987	—	—	3.00
❑ Paisley Park 28399	Sign "O" the Times/La, La, La, Hee, Hee, Hee	1987	—	—	3.00
❑ Paisley Park 28620	Anotherloverholenyohead/Girls and Boys	1986	—	—	3.00
❑ Paisley Park 28711	Mountains/Alexa de Paris	1986	—	—	3.00
❑ Paisley Park 28751	Kiss/Love or $	1986	—	—	3.00
❑ Paisley Park 28972	Raspberry Beret/She's Always In My Hair	1985	—	—	3.00
❑ Paisley Park 28998	Pop Life/Hello	1985	—	—	3.00
❑ Paisley Park 28999	America/Girl	1985	—	2.00	4.00
❑ Warner Bros. GWB 0392	I Wanna Be Your Lover/Why You Wanna Treat Me So Bad?	1982	—	2.00	4.00
—"Back to Back Hits" reissue					
❑ Warner Bros. GWB 0468	1999/Little Red Corvette	1984	—	—	3.00
—"Back to Back Hits" reissue					
❑ Warner Bros. GWB 0476	Delirious/Let's Pretend We're Married	1984	—	—	3.00
—"Back to Back Hits" reissue					
❑ Warner Bros. GWB 0516	When Doves Cry/Let's Go Crazy	1985	—	—	3.00
—"Back to Back Hits" reissue					
❑ Warner Bros. GWB 0517	I Would Die 4 U/Take Me With U	1985	—	—	3.00
—"Back to Back Hits" reissue					
❑ Warner Bros. 8619	Soft and Wet/So Blue	1978	7.50	15.00	30.00
—Two slightly different variations exist; one has the time of each side under the catalog number, the other has the time of each side after the titles					
❑ Warner Bros. 8713	Just As Long As We're Together/In Love	1978	7.50	15.00	30.00
❑ Warner Bros. 21938	Sign "O" the Times/U Got the Look	1988	—	—	3.00
—"Back to Back Hits" series					
❑ Warner Bros. 21980	Anotherloverholenyohead/Mountains	1987	—	—	3.00
—"Back to Back Hits" series					
❑ Warner Bros. 21981	Uptown/Controversy	1987	—	—	3.00
—"Back to Back Hits" series					

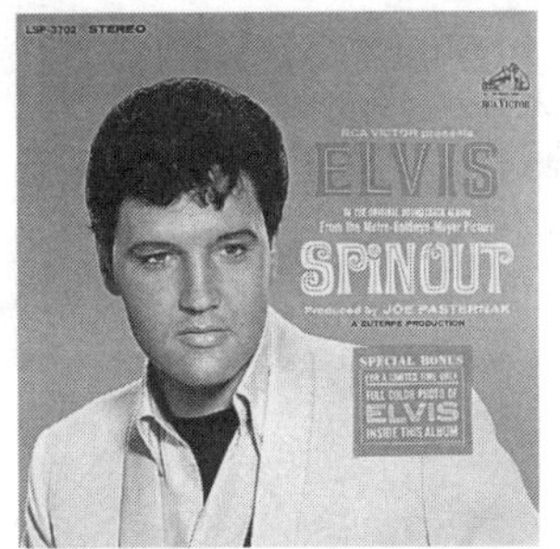

Number	Title (A Side/B Side)	Yr	VG	VG+	NM
❑ Warner Bros. 21982	Kiss/Soft and Wet	1987	—	—	3.00
—"Back to Back Hits" series					
❑ Warner Bros. 22757	The Arms of Orion/I Love U in Me	1989	—	—	3.00
❑ Warner Bros. 22814	Partyman/Feel U Up	1989	—	—	3.00
❑ Warner Bros. 22824	Scandalous/When 2 R In Love	1989	—	—	3.00
❑ Warner Bros. 22924	Batdance/200 Balloons	1989	—	—	3.00
❑ Warner Bros. 29079	Take Me With U/Baby I'm a Star	1985	—	2.00	4.00
❑ Warner Bros. 29121	I Would Die 4 U/Another Lonely Christmas	1984	—	2.00	4.00
❑ Warner Bros. 29174	Purple Rain/God	1984	—	2.00	4.00
—Purple vinyl					
❑ Warner Bros. 29216	Let's Go Crazy/Erotic City	1984	—	2.00	4.00
❑ Warner Bros. 29286	When Doves Cry/17 Days	1984	—	—	3.00
—Black vinyl					
❑ Warner Bros. 29503	Delirious/Horny Toad	1983	—	—	5.00
—Label lists correct A-side time of 2:36					
❑ Warner Bros. 29548	Let's Pretend We're Married/Irresistible Bitch	1983	—	2.50	5.00
❑ Warner Bros. 29746	Little Red Corvette/All the Critics Love U in New York	1983	—	2.50	5.00
❑ Warner Bros. 29896	1999/How Come U Don't Call Me Anymore?	1982	—	2.50	5.00
❑ Warner Bros. 29942	Do Me, Baby/Private Joy	1982	3.75	7.50	15.00
❑ Warner Bros. 49050	I Wanna Be Your Lover/My Love Is Forever	1979	2.50	5.00	10.00
❑ Warner Bros. 49178	Why You Wanna Treat Me So Bad?/Baby	1980	7.50	15.00	30.00
❑ Warner Bros. 49226	Still Waiting/Bambi	1980	3.75	7.50	15.00
❑ Warner Bros. 49559	Uptown/Crazy You	1980	3.75	7.50	15.00
❑ Warner Bros. 49638	Dirty Mind/When We're Dancing Close and Slow	1980	3.75	7.50	15.00
❑ Warner Bros. 49808	Controversy/When You Were Mine	1981	3.75	7.50	15.00
❑ Warner Bros. 50002	Let's Work/Ronnie Talk to Russia	1982	3.75	7.50	15.00

Albums

Number	Title	Yr	VG	VG+	NM
❑ Paisley Park 25286	Around the World in a Day	1985	2.50	5.00	10.00
—Original copies have a fold-over flap (deduct 25% or more if missing)					
❑ Paisley Park 25395	Parade	1986	2.00	4.00	8.00
❑ Paisley Park 25577 [(2)]	Sign "O" The Times	1987	3.75	7.50	15.00
❑ Paisley Park 25677	The Black Album	1987	500.00	1000.	2000.
—Withdrawn prior to release, though a few copies escaped. Numerous counterfeits exist on other labels and colored vinyl.					
❑ Paisley Park 25720	Lovesexy	1988	3.00	6.00	12.00
❑ Warner Bros. BSK 3150	For You	1978	5.00	10.00	20.00
—First edition on Burbank "palm trees" label					
❑ Warner Bros. BSK 3366	Prince	1979	3.00	6.00	12.00
❑ Warner Bros. BSK 3478	Dirty Mind	1980	3.00	6.00	12.00
❑ Warner Bros. BSK 3601	Controversy	1981	3.00	6.00	12.00
❑ Warner Bros. 23720 [(2)]	1999	1982	3.75	7.50	15.00
❑ Warner Bros. 25110	Purple Rain	1984	2.50	5.00	10.00
—With poster					
❑ Warner Bros. 25936	Batman (Soundtrack)	1989	2.50	5.00	10.00

PROCOL HARUM

45s

Number	Title	Yr	VG	VG+	NM
❑ A&M 885	Homburg/Good Captain Clack	1967	3.00	6.00	12.00
❑ A&M 927	In the Wee Small Hours of Sixpence/Quite Rightly So	1968	3.00	6.00	12.00
❑ A&M 1069	A Salty Dog/Long Gone Geek	1969	2.00	4.00	8.00
❑ A&M 1111	The Devil Came from Kansas/Boredom	1969	2.00	4.00	8.00
❑ A&M 1218	Whiskey Train/About to Die	1970	—	3.00	6.00
❑ A&M 1264	Power Failure/Broken Barricades	1971	—	3.00	6.00
❑ A&M 1287	Song for a Dreamer/Simple Sister	1971	—	3.00	6.00
❑ A&M 1347	Conquistador/A Salty Dog	1972	—	2.50	5.00
❑ A&M 1389	A Whiter Shade of Pale/Lime Street Blues	1972	—	2.50	5.00
❑ Chrysalis 2013	Grand Hotel/Fires	1973	—	2.50	5.00
❑ Chrysalis 2032	Nothing But the Truth/Drunk Again	1973	—	2.50	5.00
❑ Chrysalis 2109	Pandora's Box/Piper's Tune	1975	—	2.50	5.00
❑ Deram 7507	A Whiter Shade of Pale/Lime Street Blues	1967	3.75	7.50	15.00
❑ Warner Bros. CRS 2115	Wizard Man/Something Magic	1977	—	3.00	6.00
—Warner Bros. label with Chrysalis number; possible factory mispress?					

Albums

Number	Title	Yr	VG	VG+	NM
❑ A&M SP-3123	A Salty Dog	1979	2.00	4.00	8.00
—Reissue of 4179					
❑ A&M SP-3259	The Best of Procol Harum	198?	2.00	4.00	8.00
—Reissue of 4401					
❑ A&M SP-4151	Shine On Brightly	1968	6.25	12.50	25.00

Number	Title (A Side/B Side)	Yr	VG	VG+	NM
❑ A&M SP-4179	A Salty Dog	1969	3.75	7.50	15.00
❑ A&M SP-4261	Home	1970	3.00	6.00	12.00
❑ A&M SP-4294	Broken Barricades	1971	3.00	6.00	12.00
❑ A&M SP-4335	Procol Harum Live in Concert with the Edmonton Symphony Orchestra	1972	3.00	6.00	12.00
❑ A&M SP-4373	A Whiter Shade of Pale	1972	3.00	6.00	12.00
—Reissue of Deram 18008 with one more track					
❑ A&M SP-4401	The Best of Procol Harum	1973	3.00	6.00	12.00
❑ Chrysalis CHR 1037	Grand Hotel	1973	3.00	6.00	12.00
—Green label with "3300 Warner Blvd." address					
❑ Chrysalis CHR 1058	Exotic Birds and Fruit	1974	3.00	6.00	12.00
—Green label with "3300 Warner Blvd." address					
❑ Chrysalis CHR 1080	Procol's Ninth	1975	3.00	6.00	12.00
—Green label with "3300 Warner Blvd." address					
❑ Chrysalis CHR 1130	Something Magic	1977	2.50	5.00	10.00
❑ Chrysalis PV 41037	Grand Hotel	1985	2.00	4.00	8.00
❑ Chrysalis PV 41058	Exotic Birds and Fruit	1985	2.00	4.00	8.00
❑ Chrysalis PV 41080	Procol's Ninth	1985	2.00	4.00	8.00
❑ Deram DE 16008 [M]	Procol Harum	1967	20.00	40.00	80.00
❑ Deram DES 18008 [R]	Procol Harum	1967	10.00	20.00	40.00

PUCKETT, GARY, AND THE UNION GAP

45s

Number	Title (A Side/B Side)	Yr	VG	VG+	NM
❑ Columbia 44297	Woman, Woman/Don't Make Promises	1967	2.00	4.00	8.00
❑ Columbia 44450	Young Girl/I'm Losing You	1968	2.00	4.00	8.00
—As "The Union Gap Featuring Gary Puckett"					
❑ Columbia 44547	Lady Willpower/Daylight Strangers	1968	2.00	4.00	8.00
❑ Columbia 44644	Over You/If the Day Would Come	1968	—	3.00	6.00
❑ Columbia 44788	Don't Give In to Him/Could I	1969	—	3.00	6.00
❑ Columbia 44967	This Girl Is a Woman Now/His Other Woman	1969	—	3.00	6.00
❑ Columbia 45097	Let's Give Adam and Eve Another Chance/The Beggar	1970	—	3.00	6.00
❑ Columbia 45249	I Just Don't Know What to Do With Myself/All That Matters	1970	—	2.50	5.00
❑ Columbia 45303	Keep the Customer Satisfied/No One Really Knows	1971	—	2.50	5.00
❑ Columbia 45358	Life Has Its Little Ups and Downs/Shimmering Eyes	1971	—	2.50	5.00
❑ Columbia 45438	Hello Morning/Gentle Woman	1971	—	2.50	5.00
❑ Columbia 45509	Hello Morning/I Can't Hold On	1971	—	2.50	5.00
❑ Columbia 45678	Bless the Child/Leavin' in the Morning	1972	—	2.50	5.00

Albums

Number	Title (A Side/B Side)	Yr	VG	VG+	NM
❑ Columbia CS 1042	Gary Puckett and the Union Gap's Greatest Hits	1970	5.00	10.00	20.00
❑ Columbia CL 2812 [M]	Woman, Woman	1968	10.00	20.00	40.00
—As "The Union Gap Featuring Gary Puckett"					
❑ Columbia CL 2864 [M]	Young Girl	1968	12.50	25.00	50.00
—Red label stock copy with "Mono" on label; this has been confirmed to exist					
❑ Columbia CL 2915 [M]	Incredible	1968	15.00	30.00	60.00
—Red label stock copy with "Mono" on label; this has been confirmed to exist					
❑ Columbia CS 9612 [S]	Woman, Woman	1968	5.00	10.00	20.00
—As "The Union Gap Featuring Gary Puckett"					
❑ Columbia CS 9664 [S]	Young Girl	1968	5.00	10.00	20.00
❑ Columbia CS 9715 [S]	Incredible	1968	5.00	10.00	20.00
❑ Columbia CS 9935	The New Gary Puckett and the Union Gap Album	1969	5.00	10.00	20.00
❑ Columbia C 30862	The Gary Puckett Album	1971	3.75	7.50	15.00
❑ Harmony KH 31184	Lady Willpower	1972	2.50	5.00	10.00

PURE PRAIRIE LEAGUE

45s

Number	Title (A Side/B Side)	Yr	VG	VG+	NM
❑ Casablanca 2266	Let Me Love You Tonight/Janny Lou	1980	—	2.00	4.00
❑ Casablanca 2294	I'm Almost Ready/You're My True Love	1980	—	2.00	4.00
❑ Casablanca 2319	I Can't Stop the Feelin'/A Lifetime of Nightime	1980	—	2.00	4.00
❑ Casablanca 2332	Still Right Here in My Heart/Don't Keep Me Hangin'	1981	—	2.00	4.00
❑ Casablanca 2337	You're Mine Tonight.Do You Love Me Truly, Julie	1981	—	2.00	4.00
❑ RCA PB-10829	Dance/Help Yourself	1976	—	2.00	4.00
❑ RCA PB-10880	All the Way/Fade Away	1977	—	2.00	4.00
❑ RCA PB-11148	The Sun Shone Lightly/Lucille Crawfield	1977	—	2.00	4.00
❑ RCA PB-11260	Working in the Coal Mine/Bad Cream	1978	—	2.00	4.00
❑ RCA PB-11282	Love Will Grow/Slim Pickin's	1978	—	2.00	4.00
❑ RCA PB-11678	Can't Hold Back/Restless Woman	1979	—	2.00	4.00
❑ RCA Victor 48-1028	Tears/You're Between Me	1972	—	3.00	6.00
❑ RCA Victor 74-0742	Woman/She Darked the Sun	1972	—	3.00	6.00
❑ RCA Victor 74-0794	Early Morning Riser/Angel #9	1972	—	3.00	6.00
❑ RCA Victor PB-10184	Amie/Memories	1975	—	2.50	5.00
❑ RCA Victor PB-10302	Two-Lane Highway/Sister's Keeper	1975	—	2.00	4.00
❑ RCA Victor PB-10382	Just Can't Believe It/Kentucky Moonshine	1975	—	2.00	4.00
❑ RCA Victor GB-10490	Amie/Memories	1975	—	—	3.00
—Gold Standard Series					
❑ RCA Victor PB-10580	Long Cold Winter/The Sun Shone Brightly	1976	—	2.00	4.00
❑ RCA Victor PB-10679	That'll Be the Day/I Can Only Dream of You	1976	—	2.00	4.00

Albums

Number	Title (A Side/B Side)	Yr	VG	VG+	NM
❑ Casablanca NBLP-7212	Firin' Up	1980	2.50	5.00	10.00
❑ Casablanca NBLP-7255	Something in the Night	1981	2.50	5.00	10.00
❑ Pair PDL2-1034 [(2)]	Home on the Range	1986	3.00	6.00	12.00
❑ RCA Victor APL1-0933	Two Lane Highway	1975	3.00	6.00	12.00
❑ RCA Victor APL1-1247	If the Shoe Fits	1976	3.00	6.00	12.00
❑ RCA Victor APL1-1924	Dance	1976	3.00	6.00	12.00
❑ RCA Victor CPL2-2404 [(2)]	Live!! Takin' the Stage	1977	3.75	7.50	15.00
❑ RCA Victor AFL1-2590	Just Fly	1978	3.00	6.00	12.00
❑ RCA Victor AFL1-3335	Can't Hold Back	1979	3.00	6.00	12.00

Number	Title (A Side/B Side)	Yr	VG	VG+	NM
❑ RCA Victor AYL1-3669	Two Lane Highway	1980	2.00	4.00	8.00
—*"Best Buy Series" reissue*					
❑ RCA Victor AYL1-3717	If the Shoe Fits	1981	2.00	4.00	8.00
—*"Best Buy Series" reissue*					
❑ RCA Victor AYL1-3718	Just Fly	1981	2.00	4.00	8.00
—*"Best Buy Series" reissue*					
❑ RCA Victor AYL1-3719	Pure Prairie League	1981	2.00	4.00	8.00
—*"Best Buy Series" reissue*					
❑ RCA Victor AYL1-3723	Dance	1981	2.00	4.00	8.00
—*"Best Buy Series" reissue*					
❑ RCA Victor LSP-4650	Pure Prairie League	1972	3.00	6.00	12.00
❑ RCA Victor AYL1-4656	Bustin' Out	1984	2.00	4.00	8.00
—*"Best Buy Series" reissue*					
❑ RCA Victor LSP-4769	Bustin' Out	1972	3.00	6.00	12.00

PURIFY, JAMES AND BOBBY

45s

Number	Title (A Side/B Side)	Yr	VG	VG+	NM
❑ Bell 648	I'm Your Puppet/So Many Reasons	1966	3.75	7.50	15.00
❑ Bell 660	Wish You Didn't Have to Go/You Can't Keep a Good Man Down	1967	2.00	4.00	8.00
❑ Bell 669	Shake a Tail Feather/Goodness Gracious	1967	3.00	6.00	12.00
❑ Bell 680	I Take What I Want/Sixteen Tons	1967	2.00	4.00	8.00
❑ Bell 685	Let Love Come Between Us/I Don't Want to Have to Wait	1967	2.00	4.00	8.00
❑ Bell 700	Do Unto Me/Everybody Needs Somebody	1967	2.00	4.00	8.00
❑ Bell 721	I Can Remember/I Was Born to Lose Out	1968	2.00	4.00	8.00
❑ Bell 735	Help Yourself (To All of My Lovin')/Last Piece of Love	1968	2.00	4.00	8.00
❑ Bell 751	Untie Me/We're Finally Gonna Make It	1968	2.00	4.00	8.00
❑ Bell 774	I Don't Know What It Is You Got/Section C	1969	2.00	4.00	8.00
❑ Casablanca 812	Do Your Thing/Why Love	1974	—	2.50	5.00
❑ Casablanca 827	Man Can't Be a Man Without a Woman/ You and Me Together Forever	1975	—	2.50	5.00
❑ Casablanca 830	All the Love I Got/(B-side unknown)	1975	—	2.50	5.00
❑ Mercury 73767	I'm Your Puppet/Lay Me Down Easy	1976	—	2.50	5.00
❑ Mercury 73806	Morning Glory/Turning Back the Pages	1976	—	2.50	5.00
❑ Mercury 73884	I Ain't Got to Love Nobody Else/What's Better Than Love	1977	—	2.50	5.00
❑ Mercury 73893	Get Closer/What's Better Than Love	1977	—	2.50	5.00
❑ Sphere Sound 77004	I'm Your Puppet/Everybody Needs Somebody	196?	2.00	4.00	8.00

Albums

Number	Title (A Side/B Side)	Yr	VG	VG+	NM
❑ Bell 6003 [M]	James and Bobby Purify	1966	6.25	12.50	25.00
❑ Bell S-6003 [S]	James and Bobby Purify	1966	7.50	15.00	30.00
❑ Bell 6010 [M]	The Pure Sound of the Purifys	1967	6.25	12.50	25.00
❑ Bell S-6010 [S]	The Pure Sound of the Purifys	1967	7.50	15.00	30.00
❑ Mercury SRM-1-1134	The Purify Brothers	1977	3.00	6.00	12.00

PYRAMIDS, THE (1)

45s

Number	Title (A Side/B Side)	Yr	VG	VG+	NM
❑ Best 1	Pyramid's Stomp/Paul	1963	7.50	15.00	30.00
❑ Best 102	Penetration/Here Comes Marsha	1963	10.00	20.00	40.00
❑ Best 13001	Pyramid's Stomp/Paul	1963	5.00	10.00	20.00
❑ Best 13002	Penetration/Here Comes Marsha	1964	5.00	10.00	20.00
—*No mention of London Records on label*					
❑ Best 13002	Penetration/Here Comes Marsha	1964	3.75	7.50	15.00
—*With "Dist. by London" or similar wording on label*					
❑ Cedwicke 13005	Midnight Run/Custom Caravan	1964	10.00	20.00	40.00
❑ Cedwicke 13006	Contact/Pressure	1964	10.00	20.00	40.00

Albums

Number	Title (A Side/B Side)	Yr	VG	VG+	NM
❑ Best LPM-1001 [M]	The Original Penetration! And Other Favorites	1964	62.50	125.00	250.00
—*Original issue with "Walkin' the Dog"*					
❑ Best BR 16501 [M]	The Original Penetration! And Other Favorites	1964	50.00	100.00	200.00
—*Reissue with "Road Runnah"*					
❑ Best BS 36501 [R]	The Original Penetration! And Other Favorites	1964	30.00	60.00	120.00

PYRAMIDS, THE (2)

45s

Number	Title (A Side/B Side)	Yr	VG	VG+	NM
❑ Cub 9112	I'm the Playboy/Cryin'	1962	5.00	10.00	20.00
❑ Sonbert 82861	I'm the Playboy/Cryin'	1962	10.00	20.00	40.00
❑ Vee Jay 489	What Is Love/Shakin' Fit	1963	6.25	12.50	25.00

Number	Title (A Side/B Side)	Yr	VG	VG+	NM
PYRAMIDS, THE (U)					
45s					
❑ Davis 453	At Any Cost/Okay, Baby!	1956	12.50	25.00	50.00
❑ Davis 457	Why Did You Go/Before It's Too Late	1957	12.50	25.00	50.00
❑ Federal 12233	Deep in My Heart for You/And I Need You	1955	100.00	200.00	400.00
❑ Hollywood 1047	Someday/Bow Wow	1955	125.00	250.00	500.00
❑ RCA Victor 47-7556	Long Long Time/Oh No You Won't (Oh Yes You Will)	1959	3.75	7.50	15.00
❑ Shell 304	Ankle Bracelet/Hot Dog Dooly Wah	1961	6.25	12.50	25.00
—As "The Original Pyramids"					
❑ Shell 711	Ankle Bracelet/Hot Dog Dooly Wah	1958	12.50	25.00	50.00

Q

Number	Title (A Side/B Side)	Yr	VG	VG+	NM
QUARTERFLASH					
45s					
❑ Geffen GGEF 0426	Harden My Heart/Find Another Fool	1983	—	—	3.00
—"Back to Back Hits" reissue series					
❑ Geffen 28894	Walking on Ice/Come to Me	1985	—	—	3.00
❑ Geffen 28908	Talk to Me/Grace Under Fire	1985	—	—	3.00
❑ Geffen 29523	Take Another Picture/One More Round to Go	1983	—	2.00	4.00
❑ Geffen 29603	Take Me to Heart/Nowhere Left to Hide	1983	—	2.00	4.00
❑ Geffen 29882	Critical Times/Try to Make It True	1982	—	2.00	4.00
❑ Geffen 29994	Right Kind of Love/You're Holdin' Me Back	1982	—	2.00	4.00
❑ Geffen 49824	Harden My Heart/Don't Be Lonely	1981	—	2.00	4.00
❑ Geffen 50006	Find Another Fool/Cruisin' with the Deuce	1982	—	2.00	4.00
❑ Warner Bros. 29932	Night Shift/Love Should Be So Kind	1982	—	2.00	4.00
Albums					
❑ Geffen GHS 2003	Quarterflash	1981	2.00	4.00	8.00
❑ Geffen GHS 4011	Take Another Picture	1983	2.00	4.00	8.00
❑ Geffen GHS 24078	Back Into Blue	1985	2.00	4.00	8.00
QUEEN					
45s					
❑ Capitol B-5317	Radio Ga Ga/I Go Crazy	1984	—	2.00	4.00
❑ Capitol B-5350	I Want to Break Free/Machines (Or Back to Humans)	1984	—	2.00	4.00
❑ Capitol B-5372	It's a Hard Life/Is This the World We Created?	1984	—	2.50	5.00
❑ Capitol B-5424	Hammer to Fall/Tear It Up	1984	—	2.50	5.00
❑ Capitol B-5530	One Vision/Blurred Vision	1985	—	2.00	4.00
❑ Capitol B-5568	Princes of the Universe/A Dozen Red Roses for My Darling	1985	—	2.00	4.00
❑ Capitol B-5590	A Kind of Magic/Gimme the Prize (Kurgan's Theme)	1986	—	2.00	4.00
❑ Capitol B-5633	Pain Is So Close to Pleasure/Don't Lose Your Head	1986	—	2.00	4.00
❑ Capitol B-44372	I Want It All/Hang On In There	1989	—	2.50	5.00
❑ Elektra 45080	Killer Queen/Liar	1977	—	2.00	4.00
—"Spun Gold" reissue					
❑ Elektra 45083	Bohemian Rhapsody/You're My Best Friend	1977	—	2.00	4.00
—"Spun Gold" reissue					
❑ Elektra 45090	We Are the Champions/We Will Rock You	1979	—	2.00	4.00
—"Spun Gold" reissue					
❑ Elektra 45103	Crazy Little Thing Called Love/Bicycle Race	1981	—	2.00	4.00
—"Spun Gold" reissue					
❑ Elektra 45106	Another One Bites the Dust/Keep Yourself Alive	1981	—	2.00	4.00
—"Spun Gold" reissue					
❑ Elektra 45226	Killer Queen/Flick of the Wrist	1975	2.00	4.00	8.00
—Butterfly label					
❑ Elektra 45268	Keep Yourself Alive//Lily of the Valley/God Save the Queen	1975	2.00	4.00	8.00
❑ Elektra 45297	Bohemian Rhapsody/I'm in Love with My Car	1975	2.00	4.00	8.00
—Butterfly label					
❑ Elektra 45318	You're My Best Friend/'39	1976	—	3.00	6.00
—Butterfly label					
❑ Elektra 45362	Somebody to Love/White Man	1976	—	3.00	6.00
—Butterfly label					
❑ Elektra 45385	Tie Your Mother Down/Drowse	1977	—	3.00	6.00
❑ Elektra 45412	Long Away/You and I	1977	2.00	4.00	8.00
❑ Elektra 45441	We Are the Champions/We Will Rock You	1977	—	3.00	6.00
❑ Elektra 45478	It's Late/Sheer Heart Attack	1978	—	3.00	6.00
❑ Elektra 45541	Bicycle Race/Fat Bottomed Girls	1978	—	3.00	6.00
❑ Elektra 45863	Keep Yourself Alive/Son and Daughter	1973	6.25	12.50	25.00
❑ Elektra 45884	Liar/Doing All Right	1974	5.00	10.00	20.00
❑ Elektra 45891	Seven Seas of Rhye/See What a Fool I've Been	1974	5.00	10.00	20.00
❑ Elektra 46008	Don't Stop Me Now/More of That Jazz	1979	—	3.00	6.00
❑ Elektra 46039	Jealousy/Fun It	1979	—	3.00	6.00
❑ Elektra 46532	We Will Rock You (Live)/Let Me Entertain You	1979	2.00	4.00	8.00
❑ Elektra 46579	Crazy Little Thing Called Love/Spread Your Wings	1979	—	2.00	4.00
❑ Elektra 46652	Play the Game/A Human Body	1980	—	2.00	4.00
❑ Elektra 47031	Another One Bites the Dust/Don't Try Suicide	1980	—	2.00	4.00
❑ Elektra 47086	Need Your Loving Tonight/Rock It (prime jive)	1980	—	2.00	4.00
❑ Elektra 47092	Flash's Theme AKA Flash/Football Fight	1980	—	2.00	4.00
❑ Elektra 47235	Under Pressure/Soul Brother	1981	—	2.00	4.00
—A-side with David Bowie					
❑ Elektra 47452	Body Language/Life Is Real (Song for Lennon)	1982	—	2.00	4.00
—Most copies of this did not come with picture sleeves					
❑ Elektra 69941	Back Chat/Staying Power	1982	—	2.00	4.00
❑ Elektra 69981	Calling All Girls/Put Out the Fire	1982	—	2.00	4.00
Albums					
❑ Capitol ST-12322	The Works	1984	2.50	5.00	10.00
❑ Capitol SMAS-12476	A Kind of Magic	1986	2.50	5.00	10.00

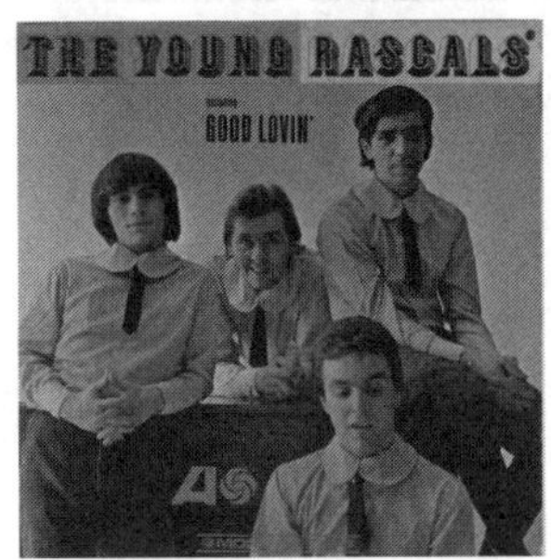

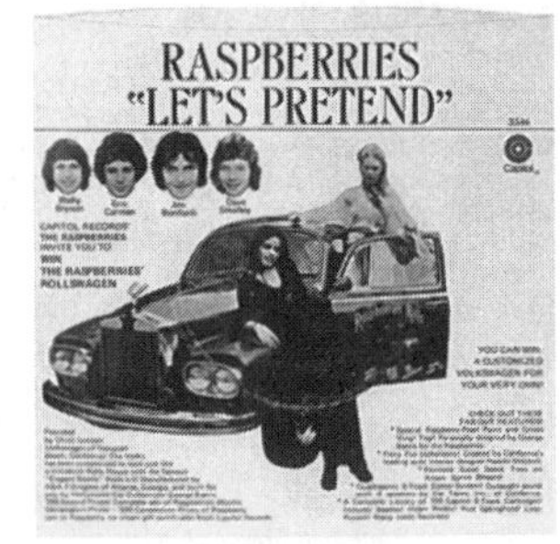

Number	Title (A Side/B Side)	Yr	VG	VG+	NM
❑ Capitol C1-92357	The Miracle	1989	3.75	7.50	15.00
❑ Elektra 6E-101	A Day at the Races	1977	2.50	5.00	10.00
—Butterfly, red, or red/black labels					
❑ Elektra 6E-112	News of the World	1977	2.50	5.00	10.00
❑ Elektra 6E-166	Jazz	1978	3.00	6.00	12.00
—With poster of the nude bicycle race					
❑ Elektra 5E-513	The Game	1980	3.75	7.50	15.00
—With shiny, mirrorlike cover; all copies have custom white labels					
❑ Elektra 5E-564	Queen's Greatest Hits	1981	3.00	6.00	12.00
❑ Elektra BB-702 [(2)]	Live Killers	1979	3.00	6.00	12.00
❑ Elektra 7E-1026	Sheer Heart Attack	1974	2.50	5.00	10.00
—Butterfly, red, or red/black labels					
❑ Elektra 7E-1053	A Night at the Opera	1975	2.50	5.00	10.00
—Butterfly, red, or red/black labels					
❑ Elektra 60128	Hot Space	1982	2.50	5.00	10.00
❑ Elektra EKS-75064	Queen	1973	7.50	15.00	30.00
—With "Queen" gold-embossed on the cover					
❑ Elektra EKS-75082	Queen II	1974	2.50	5.00	10.00
—Butterfly, red, or red/black labels					

? (QUESTION MARK) AND THE MYSTERIANS

45s

Number	Title (A Side/B Side)	Yr	VG	VG+	NM
❑ Abkco 4020	96 Tears/Can't Get Enough of You, Baby	1973	3.00	6.00	12.00
—Reissue; contains full-length version of A-side (most Cameo singles are edited)					
❑ Abkco 4033	I Need Somebody/Girl (You Captivate Me)	1973	3.00	6.00	12.00
—Reissue					
❑ Cameo 428	96 Tears/Midnight Hour	1966	7.50	15.00	30.00
—Contains the LP version of the A-side and an alternate version (different vocal and words) of the B-side; trail-off wax markings are "C 428 A-1A" and "C 428 B-1B"					
❑ Cameo 428	96 Tears/Midnight Hour	1966	5.00	10.00	20.00
—Contains an early fade of the A-side and the LP version of the B-side; trail-off wax markings are "C 428 A R" and "C 428 B R"; composer of both songs listed as "Rudy Martinez"					
❑ Cameo 428	96 Tears/Midnight Hour	1966	3.75	7.50	15.00
—Contains an early fade of the A-side and the LP version of the B-side; trail-off wax markings are "C 428 A R" and "C 428 B R"; composer of both songs listed as "The Mysterians"					
❑ Cameo 428	96 Tears/Midnight Hour	1966	3.75	7.50	15.00
—Label credit is "? and the Mysterians"; contains an early fade of the A-side (even though the time is listed as "2:53") and the LP version of the B-side; trail-off wax markings are "C 428 A" and "62831" on Side 1 and "C 428 B" and "62831-X" on Side 2; composer of both songs listed as "The Mysterians"					
❑ Cameo 441	I Need Somebody/"8" Teen	1966	3.75	7.50	15.00
❑ Cameo 467	Can't Get Enough of You, Baby/Smokes	1967	3.75	7.50	15.00
❑ Cameo 479	Girl (You Captivate Me)/Got To	1967	3.75	7.50	15.00
❑ Cameo 496	Do Something to Me/Love Me, Baby	1967	3.75	7.50	15.00
❑ Capitol 2162	Make You Mine/I Love You, Baby (Like Nobody's Business)	1968	5.00	10.00	20.00
❑ Chicory 410	Talk Is Cheap/She Goes to Church on Sunday	1968	7.50	15.00	30.00
❑ Luv 159	Funky Lady/Hot N' Groovin'	1975	3.75	7.50	15.00
❑ Pa-Go-Go 102	96 Tears/Midnight Hour	1965	175.00	350.00	700.00
❑ Super K 102	Hang In/Sha La La	1969	3.75	7.50	15.00
❑ Tangerine 989	Ain't It a Shame/Turn Around Baby (Don't Ever Look Back)	1970	3.75	7.50	15.00

Albums

Number	Title (A Side/B Side)	Yr	VG	VG+	NM
❑ Cameo C-2004 [M]	96 Tears	1966	25.00	50.00	100.00
❑ Cameo CS-2004 [P]	96 Tears	1966	20.00	40.00	80.00
—"96 Tears," "I Need Somebody," "Up Side" and "8-Teen" are rechanneled					
❑ Cameo C-2006 [M]	Action	1967	37.50	75.00	150.00
❑ Cameo CS-2006 [P]	Action	1967	25.00	50.00	100.00
—"Don't Hold It Against Me," "Like a Rose" and "Girl (You Captivate Me)" are rechanneled					

R

R.E.M.

45s

Number	Title (A Side/B Side)	Yr	VG	VG+	NM
❑ Hib-Tone HT-0001	Radio Free Europe/Sitting Still	1981	18.75	37.50	75.00
—First pressing, with no address for Hib-Tone Records on label					
❑ I.R.S. 9916	Radio Free Europe/There She Goes Again	1983	2.50	5.00	10.00
❑ I.R.S. 9927	So. Central Rain (I'm Sorry)/King of the Road	1984	—	3.00	6.00
❑ I.R.S. 9931	(Don't Go Back to) Rockville/Catapult (Live)	1984	2.50	5.00	10.00

Number	Title (A Side/B Side)	Yr	VG	VG+	NM
❑ I.R.S. 52642	Can't Get There from Here/Bandwagon	1985	—	3.00	6.00
❑ I.R.S. 52678	Driver 8/Crazy	1985	—	3.00	6.00
❑ I.R.S. 52883	Fall on Me/Rotary Ten	1986	—	2.50	5.00
❑ I.R.S. 52971	Superman/White Tornado	1986	—	2.50	5.00
❑ I.R.S. 53171	The One I Love/Maps and Legends	1987	—	—	3.00
❑ I.R.S. 53220	It's the End of the World As We Know It (And I Feel Fine)/Last Date	1987	—	—	3.00
❑ Warner Bros. 22791	Get Up/Funtime	1989	—	—	3.00
❑ Warner Bros. 27640	Pop Song 89/Pop Song 89 (Acoustic Version)	1989	—	—	3.00
❑ Warner Bros. 27688	Stand/Memphis Train Blues	1988	—	—	3.00
Albums					
❑ I.R.S. 5592	Fables of the Reconstruction	1985	3.00	6.00	12.00
❑ I.R.S. 5783	Lifes Rich Pageant	1986	3.00	6.00	12.00
❑ I.R.S. 6262	Eponymous	1988	2.50	5.00	10.00
❑ I.R.S. 42059	Document	1987	2.50	5.00	10.00
❑ I.R.S. SP-70014	Murmur	1983	3.00	6.00	12.00
—Reissue?					
❑ I.R.S. SP-70044	Reckoning	1984	3.00	6.00	12.00
❑ I.R.S. SP-70054	Dead Letter Office	1987	3.00	6.00	12.00
❑ I.R.S. SP-70502 [EP]	Chronic Town	1982	3.00	6.00	12.00
—Original pressings have a custom gargoyle label					
❑ I.R.S. SP-70604	Murmur	1983	3.75	7.50	15.00
—Original number?					
❑ Warner Bros. 25795	Green	1988	3.00	6.00	12.00
RAFFERTY, GERRY					
45s					
❑ Blue Thumb 231	Can I Have My Money Back/Sign on the Dotted Line	1973	2.00	4.00	8.00
❑ Liberty 1482	Good Intentions/Standing at the Gates	1982	—	2.00	4.00
❑ Signpost 70001	Make You, Break You/Mary Skeffington	1972	2.50	5.00	10.00
❑ United Artists XW1098	Mattie's Rag/City to City	1977	—	2.50	5.00
❑ United Artists XW1192	Baker Street/Big Change in the Weather	1978	2.00	4.00	8.00
—Mispress with the full-length album version of "Baker Street" on A-side There is no "E" in the trail-off wax.					
❑ United Artists XW1192	Baker Street/Big Change in the Weather	1978	—	2.00	4.00
—Regular press with the edited, slightly sped-up version of "Baker Street" on A-side					
❑ United Artists XW1233	Right Down the Line/Waiting for the Day	1978	—	2.00	4.00
❑ United Artists XW1266	Home and Dry/Mattie's Rag	1978	—	2.00	4.00
❑ United Artists XW1298	Days Gone Down (Still Got That Light in Your Eyes)/Why Won't You Talk to Me	1979	—	2.00	4.00
❑ United Artists 1316	Get It Right Next Time/It's Gonna Be a Long Night	1979	—	2.00	4.00
❑ United Artists 1366	The Royal Mile/In Transit	1980	—	2.00	4.00
Albums					
❑ ABC/Blue Thumb 6031	Can I Have My Money Back?	1978	3.00	6.00	12.00
❑ Blue Thumb BTS-58	Can I Have My Money Back?	1973	5.00	10.00	20.00
❑ Liberty LO-840	City to City	1981	2.00	4.00	8.00
—Reissue of United Artists 840					
❑ Liberty LOO-958	Night and Day	1981	2.00	4.00	8.00
—Reissue of United Artists 958					
❑ Liberty LOO-1039	Snakes and Ladders	1981	2.00	4.00	8.00
—Reissue of United Artists 1039					
❑ Liberty LT-51132	Sleepwalking	1982	2.50	5.00	10.00
❑ Polydor 835449-1	North and South	1988	2.50	5.00	10.00
❑ United Artists UA-LA840-H	City to City	1978	2.50	5.00	10.00
❑ United Artists UA-LA958-I	Night Owl	1979	2.50	5.00	10.00
❑ United Artists LOO-1039	Snakes and Ladders	1980	2.50	5.00	10.00
❑ Visa 7006	Gerry Rafferty	1978	2.50	5.00	10.00
—Reissue of Blue Thumb material					
RAINDROPS, THE (1)					
45s					
❑ Jubilee 5444	What a Guy/It's So Wonderful	1963	5.00	10.00	20.00
❑ Jubilee 5455	The Kind of Boy You Can't Forget/Even Though You Can't Dance	1963	6.25	12.50	25.00
❑ Jubilee 5466	That Boy John/Hanky Panky	1963	6.25	12.50	25.00
❑ Jubilee 5469	Book of Love/I Won't Cry	1964	5.00	10.00	20.00
❑ Jubilee 5475	Let;s Go Together/You Got What I Like	1964	5.00	10.00	20.00
❑ Jubilee 5487	One More Tear/Another Boy Like Mine	1964	5.00	10.00	20.00
❑ Jubilee 5497	Don't Let Go/My Mama Don't Like Him	1965	5.00	10.00	20.00
Albums					
❑ Jubilee JGM-5023 [M]	The Raindrops	1963	37.50	75.00	150.00
❑ Jubilee JGS-5023 [S]	The Raindrops	1963	75.00	150.00	300.00
RANDY AND THE RAINBOWS					
45s					
❑ Ambient Sound 02872	Debbie/Try the Impossible	1982	—	2.50	5.00
❑ B.T. Puppy 535	I'll Be Seeing You/Oh to Get Away	1967	2.50	5.00	10.00
❑ Mike 4001	Lovely Lies/I'll Forget Her Tomorrow	1966	3.00	6.00	12.00
❑ Mike 4004	Quarter to Three/He's a Fugitive	1966	3.00	6.00	12.00
❑ Mike 4008	Bonnie's Part of Town/Can It Be	1966	3.00	6.00	12.00
❑ Rust 5059	Denise/Come Back	1963	5.00	10.00	20.00
—Mostly white label					
❑ Rust 5059	Denise/Come Back	197?	2.50	5.00	10.00
—Later pressing on gold label					
❑ Rust 5073	She's My Angel/Why Do Kids Grow Up	1964	3.75	7.50	15.00
❑ Rust 5080	Happy Teenager/Dry Your Eyes	1964	3.75	7.50	15.00
❑ Rust 5091	Little Star/Sharin'	1964	3.75	7.50	15.00
❑ Rust 5101	Joy Ride/Little Hot Rod Suzie	1965	3.75	7.50	15.00
Albums					
❑ Ambient Sound ASR-601	Remember	1985	3.00	6.00	12.00

Number	Title (A Side/B Side)	Yr	VG	VG+	NM
❑ Ambient Sound FZ 37715	C'mon, Let's Go	1982	3.00	6.00	12.00

RARE EARTH

45s

Number	Title (A Side/B Side)	Yr	VG	VG+	NM
❑ Prodigal 0637	Crazy Love/Is Your Teacher Cool	1977	—	2.50	5.00
❑ Prodigal 0640	Warm Ride/Would You Like to Come Along	1978	—	2.50	5.00
❑ Prodigal 0643	I Can Feel My Love Risin'/S.O.S. (Stop Her On Sight)	1978	—	2.50	5.00
❑ Rare Earth 5010	Generation (Light of the Sky)/Magic Key	1969	3.00	6.00	12.00
❑ Rare Earth 5012	Get Ready/Magic Key	1970	—	3.00	6.00
❑ Rare Earth 5017	(I Know) I'm Losing You/When Joanie Smiles	1970	—	3.00	6.00
❑ Rare Earth 5021	Born to Wander/Here Comes the Night	1970	—	3.00	6.00
❑ Rare Earth 5031	I Just Want to Celebrate/The Seed	1971	—	3.00	6.00
❑ Rare Earth 5038	Hey Big Brother/Under God's Light	1971	—	3.00	6.00
❑ Rare Earth 5043	What'd I Say/Nice to Be with You	1972	—	3.00	6.00
❑ Rare Earth 5048	Good Time Sally/Love Shines Down	1972	—	3.00	6.00
❑ Rare Earth 5052	We're Gonna Have a Good Time/Would You Like to Come Along	1973	—	3.00	6.00
❑ Rare Earth 5053	Ma/(Instrumental)	1973	—	3.00	6.00
❑ Rare Earth 5054	Hum Along and Dance/Come with Me	1973	—	3.00	6.00
❑ Rare Earth 5056	Big John Is My Name/Ma	1974	—	3.00	6.00
❑ Rare Earth 5057	Chained/Fresh from the Can	1974	—	3.00	6.00
❑ Rare Earth 5058	It Makes You Happy (But It Ain't Gonna Last Too Long)/ Boogie with Me Children	1975	—	3.00	6.00
❑ Rare Earth 5059	Let Me Be Your Sunshine/Keep Me Out of the Storm	1976	—	3.00	6.00
❑ Rare Earth 5060	Midnight Lady/Walking Shtick	1976	—	3.00	6.00
❑ RCA PB-13076	Howzabout Some Love/Let Me Take You Out	1982	—	—	—
—Unreleased					
❑ Verve 10622	Stop-Where Did Our Love Go/Mother's Oats	1968	3.00	6.00	12.00

Albums

Number	Title (A Side/B Side)	Yr	VG	VG+	NM
❑ Motown M5-116V1	Motown Superstar Series, Vol. 16	1981	2.50	5.00	10.00
❑ Motown M5-202V1	Ecology	1981	2.00	4.00	8.00
❑ Motown 5229 ML	Get Ready	1982	2.00	4.00	8.00
❑ Prodigal P6-10019	Rare Earth	1977	2.50	5.00	10.00
❑ Prodigal P7-10025	Band Together	1978	2.50	5.00	10.00
❑ Prodigal P7-10027	Grand Slam	1979	2.50	5.00	10.00
❑ Rare Earth RS 507	Get Ready	1970	3.00	6.00	12.00
—Regular square cover					
❑ Rare Earth RS 510	Generation	1970	125.00	250.00	500.00
—At least one copy of this album has been confirmed to exist					
❑ Rare Earth RS 514	Ecology	1970	3.75	7.50	15.00
❑ Rare Earth RS 520	One World	1971	3.75	7.50	15.00
❑ Rare Earth R 534 [(2)]	Rare Earth in Concert	1971	3.75	7.50	15.00
❑ Rare Earth R 543	Willie Remembers	1972	3.00	6.00	12.00
❑ Rare Earth R6-546	Ma	1973	3.00	6.00	12.00
❑ Rare Earth R6-548	Back to Earth	1975	3.00	6.00	12.00
❑ Rare Earth R7-550	Midnight Lady	1976	3.00	6.00	12.00
❑ Verve V6-5066	Dreams/Answers	1968	12.50	25.00	50.00

RASCALS, THE

45s

Number	Title (A Side/B Side)	Yr	VG	VG+	NM
❑ Atlantic 2312	I Ain't Gonna Eat Out My Heart Anymore/Slow Down	1965	3.75	7.50	15.00
—From here through Atlantic 2463, as "The Young Rascals"					
❑ Atlantic 2321	Good Lovin'/Mustang Sally	1966	3.75	7.50	15.00
❑ Atlantic 2338	You Better Run/Love Is a Beautiful Thing	1966	2.50	5.00	10.00
❑ Atlantic 2353	Come On Up/What Is the Reason	1966	2.50	5.00	10.00
❑ Atlantic 2377	I've Been Lonely Too Long/If You Knew	1967	2.50	5.00	10.00
❑ Atlantic 2401	Groovin'/Sueno	1967	2.00	4.00	8.00
❑ Atlantic 2424	A Girl Like You/It's Love	1967	2.00	4.00	8.00
❑ Atlantic 2428	Groovin' (Spanish)/Groovin' (Italian)	1967	5.00	10.00	20.00
❑ Atlantic 2438	How Can I Be Sure/I'm So Happy Now	1967	2.00	4.00	8.00
❑ Atlantic 2463	It's Wonderful/Of Course	1967	2.00	4.00	8.00
❑ Atlantic 2493	A Beautiful Morning/Rainy Day	1968	—	3.00	6.00
—First record as "The Rascals"					
❑ Atlantic 2537	People Got to Be Free/My World	1968	—	3.00	6.00
❑ Atlantic 2584	A Ray of Hope/Any Dance'll Do	1968	—	3.00	6.00
❑ Atlantic 2599	Heaven/Baby I'm Blue	1969	—	3.00	6.00
❑ Atlantic 2634	See/Away Away	1969	—	3.00	6.00
❑ Atlantic 2664	Carry Me Back/Real Thing	1969	—	3.00	6.00

Number	Title (A Side/B Side)	Yr	VG	VG+	NM
❑ Atlantic 2695	Hold On/I Believe	1969	—	3.00	6.00
❑ Atlantic 2743	Glory Glory/You Don't Know	1970	—	3.00	6.00
❑ Atlantic 2773	Right On/Almost Home	1970	—	3.00	6.00
❑ Columbia 45400	Love Me/Happy Song	1971	—	3.00	6.00
❑ Columbia 45491	Lucky Day/Love Letter	1971	—	3.00	6.00
❑ Columbia 45568	Brother Tree/Saga of New York	1972	—	3.00	6.00
❑ Columbia 45600	Echoes/Hummin' Song	1972	—	3.00	6.00
❑ Columbia 45649	Jungle Walk/Saga of New York	1972	2.50	5.00	10.00
Albums					
❑ Atlantic SD 2-901 [(2)]	Freedom Suite	1969	5.00	10.00	20.00
❑ Atlantic 8123 [M]	The Young Rascals	1966	7.50	15.00	30.00
❑ Atlantic SD 8123 [S]	The Young Rascals	1966	10.00	20.00	40.00
—Green and blue label					
❑ Atlantic 8134 [M]	Collections	1967	6.25	12.50	25.00
❑ Atlantic SD 8134 [S]	Collections	1967	7.50	15.00	30.00
—Green and blue label					
❑ Atlantic 8148 [M]	Groovin'	1967	6.25	12.50	25.00
❑ Atlantic SD 8148 [S]	Groovin'	1967	7.50	15.00	30.00
—Green and blue label					
❑ Atlantic 8169 [M]	Once Upon a Dream	1968	10.00	20.00	40.00
❑ Atlantic SD 8169 [S]	Once Upon a Dream	1968	6.25	12.50	25.00
—Green and blue label					
❑ Atlantic SD 8190 [S]	Time Peace/The Rascals' Greatest Hits	1968	6.25	12.50	25.00
—Green and blue label					
❑ Atlantic SD 8246 [S]	See	1969	3.75	7.50	15.00
❑ Atlantic SD 8276 [S]	Search and Nearness	1970	3.75	7.50	15.00
❑ Columbia G 30462 [(2)]	Peaceful World	1971	3.75	7.50	15.00
❑ Columbia KC 31103	The Island of Real	1972	3.00	6.00	12.00
❑ Pair PDL2-1106 [(2)]	Rock and Roll Treasures	1986	3.75	7.50	15.00
❑ Rhino RNLP 70237	The Young Rascals	1988	2.50	5.00	10.00
❑ Rhino RNLP 70238	Collections	1988	2.50	5.00	10.00
❑ Rhino RNLP 70239	Groovin'	1988	2.50	5.00	10.00
❑ Rhino R1-70240	Once Upon a Dream	1988	2.50	5.00	10.00
❑ Rhino R1-70241	Freedom Suite	1988	2.50	5.00	10.00
❑ Rhino R1-70242	Searching for Ecstasy: The Rest of the Rascals 1969-1972	1988	2.50	5.00	10.00

RASPBERRIES

45s

Number	Title (A Side/B Side)	Yr	VG	VG+	NM
❑ Capitol 3280	Don't Want to Say Goodbye/Rock and Roll Mama	1972	2.00	4.00	8.00
❑ Capitol 3348	Go All the Way/With You in My Life	1972	—	3.00	6.00
❑ Capitol 3473	I Wanna Be with You/Goin' Nowhere Tonight	1972	—	3.00	6.00
❑ Capitol 3546	Let's Pretend/Every Way I Can	1973	—	3.00	6.00
❑ Capitol 3610	Tonight/Had to Get Over a Heartbreak	1973	—	3.00	6.00
❑ Capitol 3765	I'm a Rocker/Money Down	1973	—	3.00	6.00
❑ Capitol 3826	Don't Want to Say Goodbye/Ecstasy	1974	—	3.00	6.00
❑ Capitol 3885	Drivin' Around/Might As Well	1974	—	3.00	6.00
❑ Capitol 3946	Overnight Sensation (Hit Record)/Hands on You	1974	—	3.00	6.00
❑ Capitol 4001	The Party's Over/Cruisin' Music	1974	—	3.00	6.00
Albums					
❑ Capitol SK-11036	Raspberries	1972	7.50	15.00	30.00
—Originals have red labels and a "scratch 'n' sniff" cover, the smell of which fades over time					
❑ Capitol ST-11123	Fresh	1972	5.00	10.00	20.00
❑ Capitol SMAS-11220	Side 3	1973	5.00	10.00	20.00
—With cover cut in the shape of a basket of raspberries					
❑ Capitol ST-11329	Starting Over	1974	5.00	10.00	20.00
❑ Capitol ST-11524	Raspberries' Best Featuring Eric Carmen	1976	3.75	7.50	15.00
❑ Capitol SN-16095	Raspberries' Best Featuring Eric Carmen	1979	2.50	5.00	10.00

RAWLS, LOU

45s

Number	Title (A Side/B Side)	Yr	VG	VG+	NM
❑ Arista 0103	Baby You Don't Know How Good You Are/Hour Glass	1975	—	3.00	6.00
❑ Bell 45608	She's Gone/Hour Glass	1974	—	3.00	6.00
❑ Bell 45616	Who Can Tell Us Why?/Now You're Coming Back Michelle	1974	—	3.00	6.00
❑ Candix 305	In My Little Black Book/Just Thought You'd Like to Know	1960	5.00	10.00	20.00
❑ Candix 312	When We Get Old/Eighty Ways	1961	5.00	10.00	20.00
❑ Capitol 2026	Little Drummer Boy/A Child with a Toy	1967	2.00	4.00	8.00
❑ Capitol 2084	Evil Woman/My Ancestors	1968	2.00	4.00	8.00
❑ Capitol 2172	Soul Serenade/You're Good for Me	1968	2.00	4.00	8.00
❑ Capitol 2252	Down Here on the Ground/I'm Satisfied (The Duffy Theme)	1968	2.00	4.00	8.00
❑ Capitol 2348	The Split/Why Can't I Speak	1968	2.00	4.00	8.00
❑ Capitol 2408	It's You/Sweet Charity	1969	2.00	4.00	8.00
❑ Capitol 2550	Your Good Thing (Is About to End)/Season of the Witch	1969	2.00	4.00	8.00
❑ Capitol 2668	I Can't Make It Alone/Make the World Go Away	1969	2.00	4.00	8.00
❑ Capitol 2734	You've Made Me So Very Happy/Let's Burn Down the Cornfield	1970	2.00	4.00	8.00
❑ Capitol 2856	Bring It On Home/Can You Dig It-Take Me for What I Am	1970	2.00	4.00	8.00
❑ Capitol 2942	Win Your Love for Me/Coppin' a Plea	1970	2.00	4.00	8.00
❑ Capitol 4622	That Lucky Old Sun/In My Heart	1961	3.75	7.50	15.00
❑ Capitol 4669	Nine-Pound Hammer/Above My Head	1961	3.75	7.50	15.00
❑ Capitol 4695	The Wedding (The Bride)/The Biggest Lover in Town	1962	3.00	6.00	12.00
❑ Capitol 4743	Trust Me/Please Let Me Be the First to Know	1962	3.00	6.00	12.00
❑ Capitol 4761	Save Your Love for Me/Trust Me	1962	3.00	6.00	12.00
❑ Capitol 4803	Stormy Monday/Sweet Lover	1962	3.00	6.00	12.00
—With Les McCann					
❑ Capitol 5049	Tobacco Road/Blues for Four-String Guitar	1963	3.00	6.00	12.00
❑ Capitol 5160	The House Next Door/Come On In, Mr. Blues	1964	3.00	6.00	12.00
❑ Capitol 5227	Love Is Blind/I Fell in Love	1964	3.00	6.00	12.00
❑ Capitol 5424	Three O'Clock in the Morning/Nothing Really Feels the Same	1965	3.00	6.00	12.00

Number	Title (A Side/B Side)	Yr	VG	VG+	NM
❑ Capitol 5505	What'll I Do/Can I Please	1965	3.00	6.00	12.00
❑ Capitol 5655	The Shadow of Your Smile/Southside Blues	1966	2.50	5.00	10.00
❑ Capitol 5709	Love Is a Hurtin' Thing/Memory Lane	1966	2.50	5.00	10.00
❑ Capitol 5790	You Can Bring Me All Your Heartaches/ A Woman Who's a Woman	1966	2.50	5.00	10.00
❑ Capitol 5824	Trouble Down Here Below/The Life That I Lead	1967	2.50	5.00	10.00
❑ Capitol 5869	Dead End Street/Yes It Hurts, Doesn't It	1967	2.50	5.00	10.00
❑ Capitol 5941	Show Business/When Love Goes Wrong	1967	2.50	5.00	10.00
❑ Epic 02999	Now Is the Time for Love/Will You Kiss Me One More Time	1982	—	2.00	4.00
❑ Epic 03299	Together Again/Here Comes Garfield	1982	—	2.00	4.00
—Lou Rawls and Desiree Goyette					
❑ Epic 03357	Let Me Show You How/Watch Your Back	1982	—	2.00	4.00
❑ Epic 03758	Wind Beneath My Wings/Midnight Sun	1983	—	2.00	4.00
❑ Epic 03944	Couple More Years/Upside Down	1983	—	2.00	4.00
❑ Epic 04079	The One I Sing My Love Songs To/You Can't Take It With You	1983	—	2.00	4.00
❑ Epic 04550	All-Time Lover/When We Were Young	1984	—	2.00	4.00
❑ Epic 04677	Close Company/The Lady in My Life	1984	—	2.00	4.00
❑ Epic 04773	Close Company/Forever I Do	1985	—	2.00	4.00
❑ Epic 05714	Learn to Love Again/Ready or Not	1985	—	2.00	4.00
❑ Epic 05831	Are You With Me/(Instrumental)	1986	—	2.00	4.00
❑ Epic 06145	Stop Me from Starting This Feeling/Never Entered My Mind	1986	—	2.00	4.00
❑ Gamble & Huff 310	I Wish You Belonged to Me/It's a Tough Job	1987	—	2.50	5.00
❑ Gamble & Huff 316	Two Happy Hearts/Jealous Lover	1988	—	2.50	5.00
❑ MGM 14262	A Natural Man/Believe in Me	1971	—	3.00	6.00
❑ MGM 14262	A Natural Man/You Can't Hold On	1971	—	3.00	6.00
❑ MGM 14349	His Song Shall Be Sung/I'm Waiting	1972	—	3.00	6.00
❑ MGM 14428	Politician/Walk On In	1972	—	3.00	6.00
❑ MGM 14489	Man of Value/Learning Cup	1973	—	3.00	6.00
❑ MGM 14527	Star Spangled Banner/Just a Closer Walk with Thee	1973	—	3.00	6.00
❑ MGM 14574	Send for Me/Morning Comes Around	1973	—	3.00	6.00
❑ MGM 14652	Dead End Street/Love Is a Hurtin' Thing	1973	—	3.00	6.00
❑ Philadelphia Int'l. ZS9 3102	Ain't That Loving You (For More Reasons Than One)/ (B-side unknown)	1980	—	2.50	5.00
❑ Philadelphia Int'l. ZS9 3114	I Go Crazy/Be Anything (But Be Mine)	1980	—	2.50	5.00
❑ Philadelphia Int'l. ZS8 3592	You'll Never Find Another Love Like Mine/ Let's Fall in Love All Over Again	1976	—	2.50	5.00
❑ Philadelphia Int'l. ZS8 3604	Groovy People/This Song Will Last Forever	1976	—	2.50	5.00
❑ Philadelphia Int'l. ZS8 3623	See You When I Git There/Spring Again	1977	—	2.50	5.00
❑ Philadelphia Int'l. ZS8 3634	Lady Love/Not the Staying Kind	1977	—	2.50	5.00
❑ Philadelphia Int'l. ZS8 3643	One Life to Live/If I Coulda, Woulda, Shoulda	1978	—	2.50	5.00
❑ Philadelphia Int'l. ZS8 3653	There Will Be Love/Unforgettable	1978	—	2.50	5.00
❑ Philadelphia Int'l. ZS8 3672	Send In the Clowns/This Song Will Last Forever	1978	—	2.50	5.00
❑ Philadelphia Int'l. ZS8 3684	Let Me Be Good to You/Lover's Holiday	1979	—	2.50	5.00
❑ Philadelphia Int'l. ZS9 3715	What's the Matter with the World/Tomorrow	1979	—	2.50	5.00
❑ Philadelphia Int'l. ZS9 3738	Sit Down and Talk to Me/When You Get Home	1979	—	2.50	5.00
❑ Philadelphia Int'l. ZS9 3750	You're My Blessing/Heartaches	1980	—	2.50	5.00
❑ Philadelphia Int'l. ZS8 3765	See You When I Git There/Groovy People	197?	—	2.00	4.00
—Reissue					
❑ Philadelphia Int'l. ZS8 3770	You'll Never Find Another Love Like Mine/One Life to Live	197?	—	2.00	4.00
—Reissue					
❑ Philadelphia Int'l. ZS8 3775	Lady Love/Send In the Clowns	197?	—	2.00	4.00
—Reissue					
❑ Philadelphia Int'l. 70051	Hoochie Coochie Man/You've Lost That Lovin' Feelin'	1981	—	2.50	5.00
Albums					
❑ Allegiance AV-5016	Trying As Hard As I Can	198?	2.50	5.00	10.00
❑ Bell 1318	She's Gone	1974	3.00	6.00	12.00
❑ Blue Note B1-91441	Stormy Monday	1990	3.00	6.00	12.00
—Reissue of Capitol 1714					
❑ Blue Note B1-91937	At Last	1989	3.00	6.00	12.00
❑ Blue Note B1-93841	It's Supposed to Be Fun	1990	3.75	7.50	15.00
❑ Capitol ST-122	The Way It Was	1969	3.75	7.50	15.00
❑ Capitol ST-215	The Way It Was — The Way It Is	1969	3.75	7.50	15.00
❑ Capitol SWBB-261 [(2)]	Close-Up	1969	5.00	10.00	20.00
—Reissue of 1824 and 2042 in one package					
❑ Capitol ST-325	Your Good Thing	1969	3.75	7.50	15.00
❑ Capitol ST-427	You've Made Me So Very Happy	1970	3.75	7.50	15.00

Number	Title (A Side/B Side)	Yr	VG	VG+	NM
❑ Capitol ST-479	Bring It on Home	1970	3.75	7.50	15.00
❑ Capitol STBB-720 [(2)]	Down Here on the Ground/I'd Rather Drink Muddy Water	1971	5.00	10.00	20.00
❑ Capitol ST 1714 [S]	Stormy Monday	1962	6.25	12.50	25.00
❑ Capitol T 1714 [M]	Stormy Monday	1962	5.00	10.00	20.00
❑ Capitol ST 1824 [S]	Black and Blue	1963	6.25	12.50	25.00
❑ Capitol T 1824 [M]	Black and Blue	1963	5.00	10.00	20.00
❑ Capitol ST 2042 [S]	Tobacco Road	1964	6.25	12.50	25.00
❑ Capitol T 2042 [M]	Tobacco Road	1964	5.00	10.00	20.00
❑ Capitol ST 2273 [S]	Nobody But Lou	1965	6.25	12.50	25.00
❑ Capitol T 2273 [M]	Nobody But Lou	1965	5.00	10.00	20.00
❑ Capitol ST 2401 [S]	Lou Rawls and Strings	1965	6.25	12.50	25.00
❑ Capitol T 2401 [M]	Lou Rawls and Strings	1965	5.00	10.00	20.00
❑ Capitol ST 2459 [S]	Lou Rawls Live!	1966	5.00	10.00	20.00
❑ Capitol T 2459 [M]	Lou Rawls Live!	1966	3.75	7.50	15.00
❑ Capitol ST 2566 [S]	Lou Rawls Soulin'	1966	5.00	10.00	20.00
❑ Capitol T 2566 [M]	Lou Rawls Soulin'	1966	3.75	7.50	15.00
❑ Capitol ST 2632 [S]	Lou Rawls Carryin' On!	1966	5.00	10.00	20.00
❑ Capitol T 2632 [M]	Lou Rawls Carryin' On!	1966	3.75	7.50	15.00
❑ Capitol ST 2713 [S]	Too Much!	1967	3.75	7.50	15.00
❑ Capitol T 2713 [M]	Too Much!	1967	5.00	10.00	20.00
❑ Capitol ST 2756 [S]	That's Lou	1967	3.75	7.50	15.00
❑ Capitol T 2756 [M]	That's Lou	1967	5.00	10.00	20.00
❑ Capitol ST 2790 [S]	Merry Christmas, Ho, Ho, Ho	1967	3.00	6.00	12.00
❑ Capitol T 2790 [M]	Merry Christmas, Ho, Ho, Ho	1967	3.75	7.50	15.00
❑ Capitol ST 2864 [S]	Feelin' Good	1968	3.75	7.50	15.00
❑ Capitol T 2864 [M]	Feelin' Good	1968	7.50	15.00	30.00
❑ Capitol ST 2927	You're Good for Me	1968	3.75	7.50	15.00
❑ Capitol SKAO 2948	The Best of Lou Rawls	1968	3.75	7.50	15.00
❑ Capitol SKBB-11585 [(2)]	The Best from Lou Rawls	1976	3.00	6.00	12.00
❑ Capitol SN-16096	The Best of Lou Rawls	1980	2.00	4.00	8.00
—Budget-line reissue					
❑ Capitol SN-16097	Lou Rawls Live!	1980	2.00	4.00	8.00
—Budget-line reissue					
❑ Epic FE 37448	Now Is the Time	1982	2.50	5.00	10.00
❑ Epic FE 38553	When the Night Comes	1983	2.50	5.00	10.00
❑ Epic FE 39403	Close Company	1984	2.50	5.00	10.00
❑ Epic FE 40210	Love All Your Blues Away	1986	2.50	5.00	10.00
❑ MGM SE-4771	Natural Man	1971	3.00	6.00	12.00
❑ MGM SE-4809	Silk & Soul	1972	3.00	6.00	12.00
❑ MGM SE-4861	A Man of Value	1973	3.00	6.00	12.00
❑ MGM SE-4965	Live at the Century Plaza	1974	3.00	6.00	12.00
❑ Philadelphia Int'l. PZ 33957	All Things in Time	1976	2.50	5.00	10.00
—No bar code on cover					
❑ Philadelphia Int'l. PZ 34488	Unmistakably Lou	1977	2.50	5.00	10.00
❑ Philadelphia Int'l. JZ 35036	When You Hear Lou, You've Heard It All	1977	2.50	5.00	10.00
❑ Philadelphia Int'l. PZ2 35517 [(2)]	Lou Rawls Live	1978	3.00	6.00	12.00
❑ Philadelphia Int'l. JZ 36006	Let Me Be Good to You	1979	2.50	5.00	10.00
❑ Philadelphia Int'l. JZ 36304	Sit Down and Talk to Me	1979	2.50	5.00	10.00
❑ Philadelphia Int'l. JZ 36774	Shades of Blue	1980	2.50	5.00	10.00
❑ Pickwick SPC-3156	Come On In, Mr. Blues	1971	2.50	5.00	10.00
❑ Pickwick SPC-3228	Gee Baby	1972	2.50	5.00	10.00
❑ Polydor PD-1-6086	Naturally	1976	2.50	5.00	10.00

RAYS, THE

45s

Number	Title (A Side/B Side)	Yr	VG	VG+	NM
❑ Amy 900	Love Another Girl/Sad Saturday	1964	2.00	4.00	8.00
❑ Cameo 117	Silhouettes/Daddy Cool	1957	6.25	12.50	25.00
❑ Cameo 128	Rendezvous/Triangle	1958	7.50	15.00	30.00
❑ Cameo 133	Rags to Riches/The Man Above	1958	7.50	15.00	30.00
❑ Chess 1613	Tippity Top/Moo-Goo-Gai-Pan	1956	6.25	12.50	25.00
❑ Chess 1678	How Long Must I Wait/Second Fiddle	1957	6.25	12.50	25.00
❑ Unart 2001	Souvenirs of Summertime/Elevator Operator	1958	10.00	20.00	40.00
❑ XYZ 100	My Steady Girl/No One Loves You Like I Do	1957	15.00	30.00	60.00
❑ XYZ 102	Silhouettes/Daddy Cool	1957	50.00	100.00	200.00
—Gray label					
❑ XYZ 106	Souvenirs of Summertime/Elevator Operator	1958	12.50	25.00	50.00
❑ XYZ 600	Why Do You Look the Other Way/Zimbo Lula	1959	12.50	25.00	50.00
❑ XYZ 605	It's a Cryin' Shame/Mediterranean Moon	1959	10.00	20.00	40.00
❑ XYZ 607	Magic Moon/Louie Hoo Hoo	1960	10.00	20.00	40.00
—Blue label					
❑ XYZ 608	Old Devil Moon/Silver Starlight	1960	6.25	12.50	25.00

REDBONE

45s

Number	Title (A Side/B Side)	Yr	VG	VG+	NM
❑ Epic 10597	Crazy Cajun Cade Walk Band/Night Come Down	1970	—	3.00	6.00
❑ Epic 10670	Maggie/New Blue Sermonette	1970	—	3.00	6.00
❑ Epic 10712	Who Can Say/Light as a Feather	1971	—	3.00	6.00
❑ Epic 10749	The Witch Queen of New Orleans/Chant: 13th Hour	1971	—	3.00	6.00
❑ Epic 10839	When You Got Trouble/(B-side unknown)	1972	—	2.50	5.00
❑ Epic 10866	One Monkey (Don't Stop No Show)/Message from a Drum	1972	—	2.50	5.00
❑ Epic 10910	Already Here/Fais-Do	1972	—	2.50	5.00
❑ Epic 10946	Poison Ivy/Condition Your Condition	1973	—	2.50	5.00
❑ Epic 10979	We Were All Wounded at Wounded Knee/Speakeasy	1973	—	2.50	5.00
❑ Epic 11035	Come and Get Your Love/Day to Day Life	1973	—	2.50	5.00
❑ Epic 11035	Come and Get Your Love/Your Miserable Face	1973	—	2.50	5.00
❑ Epic 11131	Wovoka/Clouds in My Sunshine	1974	—	2.00	4.00
❑ Epic 50015	Suzie Girl/Interstate Highway 101	1974	—	2.00	4.00

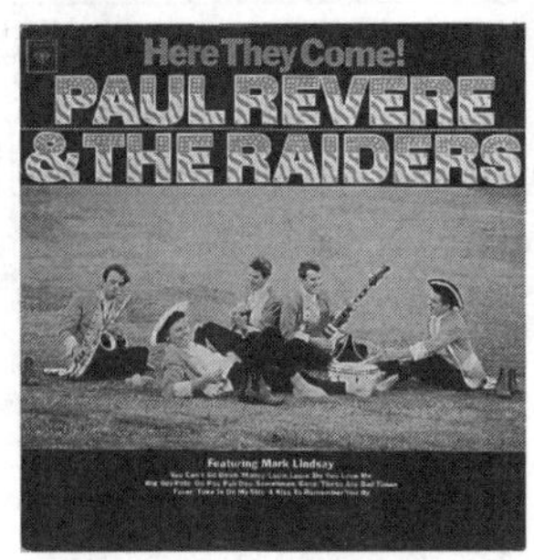

Number	Title (A Side/B Side)	Yr	VG	VG+	NM
❑ Epic 50043	One More Time/Blood, Sweat and Tears	1974	—	2.00	4.00
❑ Epic 50074	Only You and Rock and Roll/Interstate Highway 101	1975	—	2.00	4.00
❑ Epic 50107	Physical Attraction/I've Got to Find the Right Woman	1975	—	2.00	4.00
❑ RCA PB-11096	Give Our Love Another Try/Funny Silk	1977	—	2.00	4.00
❑ RCA PB-11182	Checkin' It Out/Funky Silk	1977	—	2.00	4.00
Albums					
❑ Epic EGP 501 [(2)]	Redbone	1970	5.00	10.00	20.00
❑ Epic E 30109	Potlatch	1970	3.75	7.50	15.00
❑ Epic KE 30815	Message from a Drum	1972	3.75	7.50	15.00
❑ Epic KE 31598	Already Here	1972	3.75	7.50	15.00
❑ Epic KE 32462	Wovoka	1974	3.75	7.50	15.00
❑ Epic KE 33053	Bearded Dreams Through Turquoise Eyes	1974	3.75	7.50	15.00
❑ Epic KEG 33456 [(2)]	Come & Get Your Redbone	1975	5.00	10.00	20.00
❑ RCA Victor AFL1-2352	Cycles	1977	3.00	6.00	12.00
REDDING, OTIS					
45s					
❑ Atco 6592	Hard to Handle/Amen	1968	2.50	5.00	10.00
❑ Atco 6612	I've Got Dreams to Remember/Nobody's Fault But Mine	1968	2.50	5.00	10.00
❑ Atco 6631	White Christmas/Merry Christmas, Baby	1968	2.50	5.00	10.00
❑ Atco 6636	Papa's Got a Brand New Bag/Direct Me	1968	2.50	5.00	10.00
❑ Atco 6654	A Lover's Question/You Made a Man Out of Me	1969	2.50	5.00	10.00
❑ Atco 6677	Love Man/I Can't Turn You Loose	1969	2.50	5.00	10.00
❑ Atco 6700	Free Me/Higher and Higher	1969	2.50	5.00	10.00
❑ Atco 6723	Look at the Girl/That's a Good Idea	1969	2.50	5.00	10.00
❑ Atco 6742	Demonstration/Johnny's Heartbreak	1970	2.00	4.00	8.00
❑ Atco 6766	Giving Away None of My Love/Snatch a Little Piece	1970	2.00	4.00	8.00
❑ Atco 6802	Try a Little Tenderness/I've Been Loving You Too Long (To Stop Now)	1971	—	3.00	6.00
❑ Atco 6907	My Girl/Good to Me	1972	—	2.50	5.00
❑ Atco 7069	White Christmas/Merry Christmas, Baby	1976	—	2.50	5.00
❑ Atco 7321	White Christmas/Merry Christmas, Baby	1980	—	2.00	4.00
❑ Atco 99955	White Christmas/Merry Christmas, Baby	1982	—	2.00	4.00
❑ Bethlehem 3083	Shout Bamalama/Fat Girl	1964	5.00	10.00	20.00
❑ Confederate 135	Shout Bamalama/Fat Girl	1962	12.50	25.00	50.00
❑ Finer Arts 2016	She's Alright/Tough Enuff	1961	12.50	25.00	50.00
—Originally released on Trans World by "The Shooters"					
❑ King 6149	Shout Bamalama/Fat Girl	1968	2.50	5.00	10.00
❑ Orbit 135	Shout Bamalama/Fat Girl	1961	75.00	150.00	300.00
❑ Stone 209	You Left the Water Running/The Otis Jam	1976	3.00	6.00	12.00
—B-side by the Memphis Studio Band					
❑ Volt 103	These Arms of Mine/Hey, Hey Baby	1962	5.00	10.00	20.00
❑ Volt 109	That's What My Heart Needs/Mary's Little Lamb	1963	5.00	10.00	20.00
❑ Volt 112	Pain in My Heart/Something Is Worrying Me	1963	5.00	10.00	20.00
❑ Volt 116	Come to Me/Don't Leave Me This Way	1964	3.75	7.50	15.00
❑ Volt 117	Security/I Want to Thank You	1964	3.75	7.50	15.00
❑ Volt 121	Chained and Bound/Your One and Only Man	1964	3.75	7.50	15.00
❑ Volt 124	Mr. Pitiful/That's How Strong My Love Is	1965	3.75	7.50	15.00
❑ Volt 126	I've Been Loving You Too Long (To Stop Now)/ I'm Depending on You	1965	3.75	7.50	15.00
❑ Volt 128	Respect/Ole Man Trouble	1965	3.75	7.50	15.00
❑ Volt 130	I Can't Turn You Loose/Just One More Day	1965	3.75	7.50	15.00
❑ Volt 132	Satisfaction/Any Ole Way	1966	3.75	7.50	15.00
❑ Volt 136	My Lover's Prayer/Don't Mess with Cupid	1966	3.75	7.50	15.00
❑ Volt 138	Fa-Fa-Fa-Fa-Fa (Sad Song)/Good to Me	1966	3.75	7.50	15.00
❑ Volt 141	Try a Little Tenderness/I'm Sick Y'All	1966	3.75	7.50	15.00
❑ Volt 146	I Love You More Than Words Can Say/Let Me Come On Home	1967	3.00	6.00	12.00
❑ Volt 149	Shake/You Don't Miss Your Water	1967	3.00	6.00	12.00
❑ Volt 152	Glory of Love/I'm Coming Home	1967	3.00	6.00	12.00
❑ Volt 157	(Sittin' On) The Dock of the Bay/Sweet Lorene	1968	3.00	6.00	12.00
—Black and red label					
❑ Volt 163	The Happy Song (Dum-Dum)/Open That Door	1968	2.50	5.00	10.00
Albums					
❑ Atco 33-161 [M]	Pain in My Heart	1964	62.50	125.00	250.00
❑ Atco SD 33-161 [R]	Pain in My Heart	1968	62.50	125.00	250.00
❑ Atco SD 33-252 [S]	The Immortal Otis Redding	1968	3.75	7.50	15.00

Number	Title (A Side/B Side)	Yr	VG	VG+	NM
❑ Atco SD 33-261	History of Otis Redding	1968	3.75	7.50	15.00
—Reissue of Volt 418					
❑ Atco SD 33-265	Otis Redding In Person at the Whiskey A-Go-Go	1968	3.75	7.50	15.00
❑ Atco SD 33-284	Otis Blue/Otis Redding Sings Soul	1969	3.75	7.50	15.00
—Reissue of Volt 412					
❑ Atco SD 33-285	The Soul Album	1969	3.75	7.50	15.00
—Reissue of Volt 413					
❑ Atco SD 33-286	Otis Redding Live in Europe	1969	3.75	7.50	15.00
—Reissue of Volt 416					
❑ Atco SD 33-287	Complete & Unbelievable...The Otis Redding Dictionary of Soul	1969	3.75	7.50	15.00
—Reissue of Volt 415					
❑ Atco SD 33-288	The Dock of the Bay	1969	3.75	7.50	15.00
—Reissue of Volt 419					
❑ Atco SD 33-289	Love Man	1969	3.75	7.50	15.00
❑ Atco SD 33-333	Tell the Truth	1970	3.75	7.50	15.00
❑ Atco SD 2-801 [(2)]	The Best of Otis Redding	1972	5.00	10.00	20.00
❑ Atlantic SD 19346	Recorded Live	198?	2.50	5.00	10.00
❑ Atlantic 81282	The Best of Otis Redding	1985	2.50	5.00	10.00
❑ Atlantic 81762 [(4)]	The Otis Redding Story	1987	7.50	15.00	30.00
❑ 4 Men With Beards 4M 105	The Great Otis Redding Sings Soul Ballads	2002	3.75	7.50	15.00
—Reissue on 180-gram vinyl					
❑ Pair PDL2-1062 [(2)]	The Legend of Otis Redding	1984	3.75	7.50	15.00
❑ Volt 411 [M]	The Great Otis Redding Sings Soul Ballads	1965	22.50	45.00	90.00
❑ Volt S-411 [R]	The Great Otis Redding Sings Soul Ballads	1968	27.50	55.00	110.00
❑ Volt 412 [M]	Otis Blue/Otis Redding Sings Soul	1965	10.00	20.00	40.00
❑ Volt S-412 [S]	Otis Blue/Otis Redding Sings Soul	1965	12.50	25.00	50.00
❑ Volt 413 [M]	The Soul Album	1966	10.00	20.00	40.00
❑ Volt S-413 [S]	The Soul Album	1966	12.50	25.00	50.00
❑ Volt 415 [M]	Complete & Unbelievable...The Otis Redding Dictionary of Soul	1966	10.00	20.00	40.00
❑ Volt S-415 [S]	Complete & Unbelievable...The Otis Redding Dictionary of Soul	1966	12.50	25.00	50.00
❑ Volt 416 [M]	Otis Redding Live in Europe	1967	7.50	15.00	30.00
❑ Volt S-416 [S]	Otis Redding Live in Europe	1967	10.00	20.00	40.00
❑ Volt 418 [M]	History of Otis Redding	1967	10.00	20.00	40.00
❑ Volt S-418 [S]	History of Otis Redding	1967	7.50	15.00	30.00
❑ Volt S-419	The Dock of the Bay	1968	7.50	15.00	30.00

REDDY, HELEN

45s

Number	Title (A Side/B Side)	Yr	VG	VG+	NM
❑ Capitol 3027	I Don't Know How to Love Him/I Believe in Music	1971	—	2.50	5.00
❑ Capitol 3138	Crazy Love/Best Friend	1971	—	2.50	5.00
❑ Capitol 3231	No Sad Song/More Than You Could Take	1971	—	2.50	5.00
❑ Capitol 3350	I Am Woman/More Than You Could Take	1972	—	2.50	5.00
—Red and orange "target" label					
❑ Capitol 3527	Peaceful/What Would They Say	1973	—	2.00	4.00
❑ Capitol 3645	Delta Dawn/If We Could Still Be Friends	1973	—	2.00	4.00
❑ Capitol 3768	Leave Me Alone (Ruby Red Dress)/The Old Fashioned Way	1973	—	2.00	4.00
❑ Capitol 3845	Keep On Singing/You're My Home	1974	—	2.00	4.00
❑ Capitol 3897	You and Me Against the World/Love Song for Jeffrey	1974	—	2.00	4.00
❑ Capitol 3972	Angie Baby/I Think I'll Write a Song	1974	—	2.00	4.00
❑ Capitol 4021	Emotion/I've Been Waiting for You So Long	1974	—	2.00	4.00
❑ Capitol 4098	You Don't Need a Reason/Long Time Looking	1975	—	2.00	4.00
❑ Capitol 4108	Bluebird/You Don't Need a Reason	1975	—	2.00	4.00
❑ Capitol 4128	Ain't No Way to Treat a Lady/Long Time Looking	1975	—	2.00	4.00
❑ Capitol 4192	Somewhere in the Night/Ten to Eight	1975	—	2.00	4.00
❑ Capitol 4312	I Can't Hear You No More/Music Is My Life	1976	—	2.00	4.00
❑ Capitol 4350	You Make It So Easy/Gladiola	1976	—	2.00	4.00
❑ Capitol 4418	You're My World/Thank You	1977	—	2.00	4.00
❑ Capitol 4487	The Happy Girls/Laissez Les Bontemps Rouler	1977	—	2.00	4.00
❑ Capitol 4521	Candle on the Water/Brazzle Dazzle Day	1977	—	2.00	4.00
❑ Capitol 4555	We'll Sing in the Sunshine/I'd Rather Be Alone	1978	—	2.00	4.00
❑ Capitol 4582	Ready or Not/If I Ever Had to Say Goodbye to You	1978	—	2.00	4.00
❑ Capitol 4628	Lady of the Night/Poor Little Fool	1978	—	2.00	4.00
❑ Capitol 4654	Mama/West Wind Circus	1978	—	2.00	4.00
❑ Capitol 4712	Make Love to Me/More Than You Could Take	1979	—	2.00	4.00
❑ Capitol 4786	Trying to Get to You/Let Me Be Your Woman	1979	—	2.00	4.00
❑ Capitol 4867	Love's Not the Question/Take What You Find	1980	—	2.00	4.00
❑ Capitol 4918	Way with the Ladies/Killer Barracuda	1980	—	2.00	4.00
❑ Fontana 1611	One Way Ticket/Go	1968	3.75	7.50	15.00
❑ MCA 51106	I Can't Say Goodbye to You/Let's Just Stay Home Tonight	1981	—	2.00	4.00
❑ MCA 51143	Stars Fell on California/When I Dream	1981	—	2.00	4.00
❑ MCA 51186	Theme from "Continental Divide"/When I Dream	1981	—	2.00	4.00
❑ MCA 52170	Don't Tell Me Tonight/Yesterday Can't Hurt Me	1983	—	2.00	4.00
❑ MCA 52221	Imagination/The Way I Feel	1983	—	2.00	4.00

Albums

Number	Title (A Side/B Side)	Yr	VG	VG+	NM
❑ Capitol ST-762	I Don't Know How to Love Him	1971	3.75	7.50	15.00
❑ Capitol ST-857	Helen Reddy	1971	3.75	7.50	15.00
❑ Capitol ST-11068	I Am Woman	1972	2.50	5.00	10.00
❑ Capitol SMAS-11213	Long Hard Climb	1973	2.50	5.00	10.00
❑ Capitol SO-11284	Love Song for Jeffrey	1974	2.50	5.00	10.00
❑ Capitol ST-11348	Free and Easy	1974	2.50	5.00	10.00
❑ Capitol ST-11418	No Way to Treat a Lady	1975	2.50	5.00	10.00
❑ Capitol ST-11467	Helen Reddy's Greatest Hits	1975	2.50	5.00	10.00
—Orange label					
❑ Capitol ST-11547	Music, Music	1976	2.50	5.00	10.00
❑ Capitol SO-11640	Ear Candy	1977	2.50	5.00	10.00
❑ Capitol SW-11759	We'll Sing in the Sunshine	1978	2.50	5.00	10.00
❑ Capitol SKBO-11873 [(2)]	Live	1979	3.00	6.00	12.00

Number	Title (A Side/B Side)	Yr	VG	VG+	NM
❑ Capitol SO-11949	Reddy	1979	2.50	5.00	10.00
❑ Capitol SOO-12068	Take What You Find	1980	2.50	5.00	10.00
❑ Capitol SN-16098	Helen Reddy	1980	2.00	4.00	8.00
—Budget-line reissue					
❑ Capitol SN-16099	I Am Woman	1980	2.00	4.00	8.00
—Budget-line reissue					
❑ Capitol SN-16100	I Don't Know How to Love Him	1980	2.00	4.00	8.00
—Budget-line reissue					
❑ Capitol SN-16101	Long Hard Climb	1980	2.00	4.00	8.00
—Budget-line reissue					
❑ Capitol SN-16195	Love Song for Jeffrey	198?	2.00	4.00	8.00
—Budget-line reissue					
❑ Capitol SN-16196	No Way to Treat a Lady	1980	2.00	4.00	8.00
—Budget-line reissue					
❑ Capitol SN-16199	We'll Sing in the Sunshine	1980	2.00	4.00	8.00
—Budget-line reissue					
❑ Capitol SN-16200	Reddy	1980	2.00	4.00	8.00
—Budget-line reissue					
❑ Capitol SN-16248	Take What You Find	198?	2.00	4.00	8.00
—Budget-line reissue					
❑ Capitol SN-16249	Free and Easy	198?	2.00	4.00	8.00
—Budget-line reissue					
❑ Capitol SN-16250 [(2)]	Live	198?	2.00	4.00	8.00
—Budget-line reissue					
❑ Capitol SN-16333	Helen Reddy's Greatest Hits	1984	—	3.00	6.00
—Budget-line reissue					
❑ MCA 5376	Imagination	198?	2.00	4.00	8.00
❑ Pair PDL2-1066 [(2)]	Lust for Life	1986	3.00	6.00	12.00

REED, LOU

45s

Number	Title (A Side/B Side)	Yr	VG	VG+	NM
❑ A&M 2781	September Song/Oh Heavenly Salvation	1985	—	2.00	4.00
—B-side by Mark Bingham/Johnny Adams/Aaron Neville					
❑ A&M 2883	Soul Man/Sweet Sarah	1986	—	—	3.00
—With Sam Moore					
❑ Arista 0215	I Believe in Love/Senselessly Cruel	1976	—	2.00	4.00
❑ Arista 0431	City Lights/I Want to Boogie with You	1979	—	2.00	4.00
❑ Arista 0535	Growing Up in Public/The Power of Positive Drinking	1980	—	2.00	4.00
❑ Atlantic 89468	My Love Is Chemical/People Have Got to Move	1985	—	—	3.00
—B-side by Jenny Burton					
❑ RCA PB-13841	I Love You Suzanne/My Friend George	1984	—	—	3.00
❑ RCA PB-14368	No Money Down/Don't Hurt a Woman	1986	—	—	3.00
❑ RCA Victor 74-0727	I Can't Stand It/Going Down	1972	—	3.00	6.00
❑ RCA Victor 74-0784	Walk and Talk It/Wild Child	1972	—	3.00	6.00
❑ RCA Victor 74-0887	Walk on the Wild Side/Perfect Day	1973	—	3.00	6.00
❑ RCA Victor 74-0964	Satellite of Love/Walk and Talk It	1973	—	3.00	6.00
❑ RCA Victor APBO-0054	Vicious/Good Night Ladies	1973	—	2.50	5.00
❑ RCA Victor APBO-0172	Lady Day/How Do You Think It Feels	1973	—	2.50	5.00
❑ RCA Victor APBO-0238	Sweet Jane/Lady Day	1974	7.50	15.00	30.00
—Part of U.S. numbering system, but pressed for export.					
❑ RCA Victor PB-10053	Sally Can't Dance/Vicious	1974	—	2.00	4.00
❑ RCA Victor PB-10081	Sally Can't Dance/Ennui	1974	—	2.00	4.00
❑ RCA Victor GB-10162	Walk on the Wild Side/Vicious	1975	—	—	3.00
—Gold Standard Series reissue					
❑ RCA Victor PB-10573	Charley's Girl/Nowhere At All	1976	—	2.00	4.00
❑ RCA Victor PB-10648	Crazy Feeling/Nowhere At All	1976	—	2.00	4.00
❑ Sire 22876	Romeo Had Juliette/Busload of Faith	1989	—	—	3.00

Albums

Number	Title	Yr	VG	VG+	NM
❑ Arista AL 4100	Rock and Roll Heart	1976	3.75	7.50	15.00
—Originals on light blue labels					
❑ Arista AL 4169	Street Hassle	1978	3.75	7.50	15.00
❑ Arista AL 4229	The Bells	1979	3.00	6.00	12.00
❑ Arista ALB6-8390	City Lights — Classic Performances by Lou Reed	1985	2.50	5.00	10.00
❑ Arista AL11 8434 [(2)]	Rock and Roll Diary 1967-1980	198?	4.00	8.00	16.00
—Reissue					
❑ Arista AL 8502 [(2)]	Live! Take No Prisoners	1978	4.50	9.00	18.00

Number	Title (A Side/B Side)	Yr	VG	VG+	NM
❑ Arista A2L 8603 [(2)]	Rock and Roll Diary 1967-1980	1980	4.50	9.00	18.00
❑ Arista AL 9522	Growing Up in Public	1980	3.00	6.00	12.00
❑ RCA Victor APL1-0207	Berlin	1973	3.00	6.00	12.00
❑ RCA Victor APL1-0472	Rock & Roll Animal	1974	3.00	6.00	12.00
❑ RCA Victor CPL1-0611	Sally Can't Dance	1974	5.00	10.00	20.00
❑ RCA Victor APL1-0915	Coney Island Baby	1976	4.00	8.00	16.00
❑ RCA Victor APL1-0959	Lou Reed Live	1975	3.75	7.50	15.00
❑ RCA Victor CPL2-1101 [(2)]	Metal Machine Music	1975	12.50	25.00	50.00
—Orange or brown label					
❑ RCA Victor APL1-2001	Walk on the Wild Side	1977	3.00	6.00	12.00
❑ RCA Victor ANL1-2480	Coney Island Baby	1977	2.00	4.00	8.00
—Reissue					
❑ RCA Victor AYL1-3664	Rock & Roll Animal	1980	2.00	4.00	8.00
—Best Buy Series reissue					
❑ RCA Victor AYL1-3752	Lou Reed Live	1980	2.00	4.00	8.00
—Best Buy Series reissue					
❑ RCA Victor AYL1-3753	Walk on the Wild Side	1980	2.00	4.00	8.00
—Best Buy Series reissue					
❑ RCA Victor AYL1-3806	Transformer	1980	2.00	4.00	8.00
—Best Buy Series reissue					
❑ RCA Victor AYL1-3807	Coney Island Baby	1980	2.00	4.00	8.00
—Best Buy Series reissue					
❑ RCA Victor AFL1-4221	The Blue Mask	1982	2.50	5.00	10.00
❑ RCA Victor AYL1-4388	Berlin	1983	2.00	4.00	8.00
—Best Buy Series reissue					
❑ RCA Victor AYL1-4555	Sally Can't Dance	1983	2.00	4.00	8.00
—Best Buy Series reissue					
❑ RCA Victor AFL1-4568	Legendary Hearts	1983	2.50	5.00	10.00
❑ RCA Victor LSP-4701	Lou Reed	1972	5.00	10.00	20.00
❑ RCA Victor AYL1-4780	The Blue Mask	1984	2.00	4.00	8.00
—Best Buy Series reissue					
❑ RCA Victor AFL1-4807	Transformer	1977	2.00	4.00	8.00
—Reissue					
❑ RCA Victor LSP-4807	Transformer	1972	5.00	10.00	20.00
❑ RCA Victor AFL1-4998	New Sensations	1984	2.00	4.00	8.00
❑ RCA Victor AFL1-7190	Mistrial	1986	3.00	6.00	12.00
❑ Sire 25829	New York	1989	2.50	5.00	10.00

REFLECTIONS, THE (1)

45s

Number	Title (A Side/B Side)	Yr	VG	VG+	NM
❑ ABC 10794	Like Adam and Eve/Vito's House	1966	25.00	50.00	100.00
❑ ABC 10822	You're Gonna Find Out (You Love Me)/Long Cigarette	1966	7.50	15.00	30.00
❑ Golden World 9	(Just Like) Romeo and Juliet/ Can't You Tell By the Look in His Eyes	1964	5.00	10.00	20.00
❑ Golden World 12	Like Columbus Did/Lonely Girl	1964	3.75	7.50	15.00
❑ Golden World 15	Oowee Now/Talkin' Bout My Girl	1964	3.75	7.50	15.00
❑ Golden World 16	Henpecked Guy/Don't Do That to Me	1964	3.75	7.50	15.00
❑ Golden World 19	You're My Baby/Shabby Little Hut	1964	3.75	7.50	15.00
❑ Golden World 20	Poor Man's Son/Comin' At You	1965	3.75	7.50	15.00
❑ Golden World 22	Wheelin' and Dealin'/Deborah Ann	1965	3.75	7.50	15.00
❑ Golden World 24	June Bride/Out of the Picture	1965	3.75	7.50	15.00
❑ Golden World 29	Girl in the Candy Store/Your Kind of Love	1965	3.75	7.50	15.00
❑ Lana 140	(Just Like) Romeo and Juliet/Can't You Tell by the Look in My Eyes	196?	—	3.00	6.00
—Oldies reissue					

REGENTS, THE (1)

45s

Number	Title (A Side/B Side)	Yr	VG	VG+	NM
❑ Cousins 1002	Barbara-Ann/I'm So Lonely	1961	300.00	600.00	1200.
❑ Gee 1065	Barbara-Ann/I'm So Lonely	1961	7.50	15.00	30.00
❑ Gee 1071	Runaround/Laura My Darling	1961	6.25	12.50	25.00
❑ Gee 1073	Don't Be a Fool/Liar	1961	6.25	12.50	25.00
❑ Gee 1075	Lonesome Boy/Oh Baby	1961	6.25	12.50	25.00

Albums

Number	Title (A Side/B Side)	Yr	VG	VG+	NM
❑ Gee GLP-706 [M]	Barbara Ann	1961	37.50	75.00	150.00
❑ Gee SGLP-706	Barbara Ann	197?	6.25	12.50	25.00
—Reissue by Publishers Central Bureau (clearly marked as such on cover)					
❑ Gee SGLP-706 [S]	Barbara Ann	1961	62.50	125.00	250.00

REO SPEEDWAGON

45s

Number	Title (A Side/B Side)	Yr	VG	VG+	NM
❑ Epic 19-01054	Take It on the Run/Someone Tonight	1981	—	2.00	4.00
❑ Epic 19-02127	Don't Let Him Go/I Wish You Were There	1981	—	2.00	4.00
❑ Epic 15-02153	Keep On Loving You/Time for Me to Fly	1981	—	—	3.00
—Reissue					
❑ Epic 14-02457	In Your Letter/Shakin' It Loose	1981	—	2.00	4.00
❑ Epic 14-02967	Keep the Fire Burnin'/I'll Follow You	1982	—	2.00	4.00
❑ Epic 14-03175	Sweet Time/Stillness of the Night	1982	—	2.00	4.00
❑ Epic ENR-03264	Sweet Time/(B-side blank)	1982	—	2.50	5.00
—One-sided budget release					
❑ Epic 34-03400	The Key/Let's Be-Bop	1982	—	2.00	4.00
❑ Epic 15-03846	Keep the Fire Burnin'/Take It on the Run	1983	—	—	3.00
—Reissue					
❑ Epic 15-03847	In Your Letter/Don't Let Him Go	1983	—	—	3.00
—Reissue					
❑ Epic 34-04659	I Do'Wanna Know/Rock 'N Roll Star	1984	—	—	3.00
❑ Epic 34-04713	Can't Fight This Feeling/Break His Spell	1984	—	—	3.00
❑ Epic 34-04848	One Lonely Night/Wheels Are Turnin'	1985	—	—	3.00

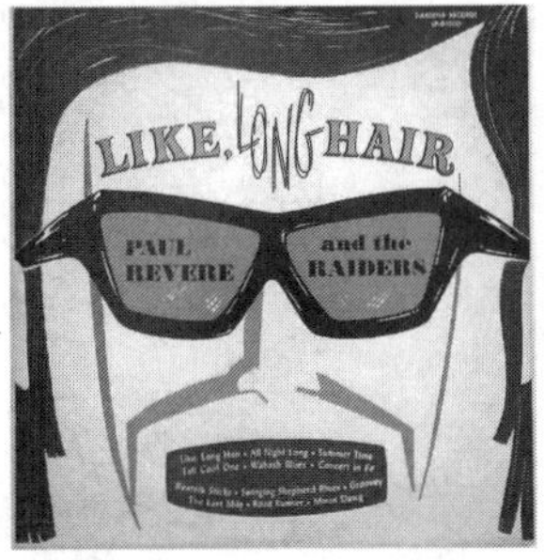

Number	Title (A Side/B Side)	Yr	VG	VG+	NM
❑ Epic 34-05412	Live Every Moment/Gotta Feel More	1985	—	—	3.00
❑ Epic 34-06656	That Ain't Love/Accidents Can Happen	1987	—	—	3.00
❑ Epic 34-07055	Variety Tonight/Tired of Gettin' Nowhere	1987	—	—	3.00
❑ Epic 34-07255	In My Dreams/Over the Edge	1987	—	—	3.00
❑ Epic 34-07901	Here with Me/Wherever You're Goin' (It's Alright)	1988	—	—	3.00
❑ Epic 34-08030	I Don't Want to Lose You/On the Road Again	1988	—	—	3.00
❑ Epic 5-10827	Sophisticated Lady/Prison Women	1972	3.75	7.50	15.00
❑ Epic 5-10847	157 Riverside Avenue/Five Men Were Killed Today	1972	3.75	7.50	15.00
❑ Epic 5-10892	Lay Me Down/Gypsy Woman's Passion	1972	3.75	7.50	15.00
❑ Epic 5-10975	Little Queenie/Golden Country	1973	3.75	7.50	15.00
❑ Epic 5-10975 [DJ]	Little Queenie (stereo/mono)	1973	2.00	4.00	8.00
❑ Epic 5-11078	Ridin' the Storm Out/Whiskey Night	1974	3.75	7.50	15.00
❑ Epic 5-11132	Open Up/Start a New Life	1974	3.00	6.00	12.00
❑ Epic 8-50059	Throw the Chains Away/Sky Blues	1975	2.00	4.00	8.00
❑ Epic 8-50120	Out of Control/Running Blind	1975	2.00	4.00	8.00
❑ Epic 8-50180	Reelin'/Headed for a Fall	1975	2.00	4.00	8.00
❑ Epic 8-50254	Keep Pushin'/Tonight	1976	2.00	4.00	8.00
❑ Epic 8-50288	Keep Pushin'/Flying Turkey Trot	1976	2.00	4.00	8.00
❑ Epic 8-50367	Ridin' the Storm Out/Being Kind	1977	2.00	4.00	8.00
❑ Epic 8-50459	Keep Pushin'/Flying Turkey Trot	1977	—	3.50	7.00
❑ Epic 8-50545	Roll with the Changes/The Unidentified Flying Tuna Trot	1978	—	3.00	6.00
❑ Epic 8-50582	Time for Me to Fly/Runnin' Blind	1978	—	3.00	6.00
❑ Epic 9-50764	Easy Money/I Need You Tonight	1979	—	3.00	6.00
❑ Epic 9-50790	Only the Strong Survive/Drop It (An Old Disguise)	1979	—	3.00	6.00
❑ Epic 9-50858	Time for Me to Fly/Lightning	1980	—	2.50	5.00
❑ Epic 19-50953	Keep On Loving You/Follow My Heart	1980	—	2.00	4.00
❑ Epic 19-51006	Take It on the Run/Someone Tonight	1981	—	—	—
—Unreleased; reassigned to 19-01054					
❑ Epic 34-73499	Live It Up/All Heaven Broke Loose	1990	—	2.00	4.00
❑ Epic 34-73540	Love Is a Rock/Go for Broke	1990	—	2.00	4.00
Albums					
❑ Epic E 31089	REO Speedwagon	1972	3.75	7.50	15.00
—Yellow label original					
❑ Epic KE 31745	R.E.O./T.W.O.	1972	3.75	7.50	15.00
—Yellow label original					
❑ Epic KE 32378	Ridin' the Storm Out	1973	3.00	6.00	12.00
—Orange label					
❑ Epic PE 32948	Lost in a Dream	1974	3.00	6.00	12.00
—Orange label					
❑ Epic PE 33338	This Time We Mean It	1975	3.00	6.00	12.00
—Orange label					
❑ Epic PE 34143	R.E.O.	1976	3.00	6.00	12.00
—Orange label					
❑ Epic PEG 34494 [(2)]	REO Speedwagon Live/You Get What You Play For	1977	3.75	7.50	15.00
—Orange labels					
❑ Epic JE 35082	You Can Tune a Piano, But You Can't Tuna Fish	1978	3.00	6.00	12.00
—Orange label; no bar code on back cover					
❑ Epic FE 35988	Nine Lives	1979	2.50	5.00	10.00
❑ Epic KE2 36444 [(2)]	A Decade of Rock and Roll 1970 to 1980	1980	3.00	6.00	12.00
❑ Epic FE 36844	Hi Infidelity	1980	2.00	4.00	8.00
❑ Epic FE 38100	Good Trouble	1982	2.50	5.00	10.00
❑ Epic QE 39593	Wheels Are Turnin'	1984	2.00	4.00	8.00
❑ Epic FE 40444	Life As We Know It	1987	2.00	4.00	8.00
❑ Epic OE 44202	The Hits	1988	2.50	5.00	10.00
❑ Epic E 45246	The Earth, a Small Man, His Dog and a Chicken	1990	3.00	6.00	12.00

REVERE, PAUL, AND THE RAIDERS

45s

Number	Title (A Side/B Side)	Yr	VG	VG+	NM
❑ Columbia 10126	Gonna Have a Good Time/Your Love (Is the Only Love)	1975	2.50	5.00	10.00
❑ Columbia 42814	Louie Louie/Night Train	1963	10.00	20.00	40.00
❑ Columbia 43008	Louie Go Home/Have Love Will Travel	1964	3.75	7.50	15.00
❑ Columbia 43114	Over You/Swim	1964	3.75	7.50	15.00
❑ Columbia 43273	Ooh Poo Pah Doo/Sometimes	1965	3.75	7.50	15.00
❑ Columbia 43375	Steppin' Out/Blue Fox	1965	2.50	5.00	10.00
❑ Columbia 43461	Just Like Me/B.F.R.D.F. Blues	1965	2.50	5.00	10.00
❑ Columbia 43556	Kicks/Shake It Up	1966	2.50	5.00	10.00
❑ Columbia 43678	Hungry/There She Goes	1966	2.50	5.00	10.00

Number	Title (A Side/B Side)	Yr	VG	VG+	NM
❑ Columbia 43810	The Great Airplane Strike/In My Community	1966	2.50	5.00	10.00
❑ Columbia 43907	Good Thing/Undecided Man	1966	2.50	5.00	10.00
❑ Columbia 44018	Ups and Downs/Leslie	1967	2.50	5.00	10.00
❑ Columbia 44094	Him or Me — What's It Gonna Be?/Legend of Paul Revere	1967	2.50	5.00	10.00
❑ Columbia 44227	I Had a Dream/Upon Your Leaving	1967	2.00	4.00	8.00
❑ Columbia 44335	Peace of Mind/Do Unto Others	1967	2.00	4.00	8.00
❑ Columbia 44444	Too Much Talk/Happening '68	1968	2.00	4.00	8.00
❑ Columbia 44553	Don't Take It Too Hard/Observation from Flight 285 (In 3/4 Time)	1968	—	3.00	6.00
❑ Columbia 44655	Cinderella Sunshine/It's Happening	1968	2.00	4.00	8.00
❑ Columbia 44744	Mr. Sun, Mr. Moon/Without You	1969	—	3.00	6.00
❑ Columbia 44854	Let Me/I Don't Know	1969	—	3.00	6.00
❑ Columbia 44970	We Gotta All Get Together/Frankfort Side Street	1969	—	3.00	6.00
❑ Columbia 45082	Just Seventeen/Sorceress with Blue Eyes	1970	—	3.00	6.00
—As "Raiders"					
❑ Columbia 45150	Gone Movin' On/Interlude (To Be Forgotten)	1970	—	3.00	6.00
—As "Raiders"					
❑ Columbia 45332	Indian Reservation (The Lament of the Cherokee Reservation Indian)/Terry's Tune	1971	2.00	4.00	8.00
—As "Raiders"; red label, black print					
❑ Columbia 45453	Birds of a Feather/The Turkey	1971	—	3.00	6.00
—As "Raiders"					
❑ Columbia 45535	Country Wine/It's So Hard Getting Up Today	1972	—	3.00	6.00
—As "The Raiders"; orange label with "COLUMBIA" background					
❑ Columbia 45601	Powder Blue Mercedes Queen/Golden Girls Sometimes	1972	2.00	4.00	8.00
—As "Raiders"					
❑ Columbia 45688	Song Seller/A Simple Song	1972	2.00	4.00	8.00
—As "Raiders"					
❑ Columbia 45759	Love Music/Goodbye, No. 9	1973	2.00	4.00	8.00
—As "Raiders"					
❑ Columbia 45898	All Over You/Seaboard Line Boogie	1973	2.00	4.00	8.00
—As "Raiders"					
❑ Drive 6248	Ain't Nothing Wrong/You're Really Saying Something	1976	—	2.50	5.00
❑ Gardena 106	Beatnick Sticks/Orbit (The Spy)	1960	7.50	15.00	30.00
❑ Gardena 115	Paul Revere's Ride/Unfinished Fifth	1960	10.00	20.00	40.00
❑ Gardena 116	Like, Long Hair/Sharon	1961	7.50	15.00	30.00
❑ Gardena 118	Like, Charleston/Midnite Ride	1961	6.25	12.50	25.00
❑ Gardena 124	All Night Long/Groovey	1962	10.00	20.00	40.00
❑ Gardena 127	Like, Bluegrass/Leatherneck	1962	10.00	20.00	40.00
❑ Gardena 131	Shake It Up (Part 1)/Shake It Up (Part 2)	1962	10.00	20.00	40.00
❑ Gardena 137	Tall Cool One/Road Runner	1963	12.50	25.00	50.00
❑ Hitbound X-2	Jingle Bell Rock/Jingle Bells	1983	3.00	6.00	12.00
—B-side by Mike Love and Dean Torrence					
❑ Jerden 807	So Fine/Blues Stay Away	1966	6.25	12.50	25.00
❑ Sande 101	Louie Louie/Night Train	1963	62.50	125.00	250.00
❑ 20th Century 2283	The British Are Coming/Surrender at Appomattox	1976	—	3.00	6.00
—B-side by Susie Allanson					
7-					
❑ Jerden LP JRLS-7004	Shake Rattle & Roll/Work with Me Annie/So Fine//Mojo Workout/ Blues Stay Away/Irresistible You	1966	12.50	25.00	50.00
—Jukebox issue; small hole, plays at 33 1/3 rpm					
❑ Jerden LP JRLS-7004 [Picture Sleeve]	In the Beginning	1966	12.50	25.00	50.00
Albums					
❑ Columbia GP 12 [(2)]	Two All Time Great Selling LPs	1969	6.25	12.50	25.00
—Combines 9395 and 9521 in one package; red labels					
❑ Columbia CL 2307 [M]	Here They Come!	1965	7.50	15.00	30.00
—"Guaranteed High Fidelity" on label					
❑ Columbia CL 2451 [M]	Just Like Us!	1966	6.25	12.50	25.00
❑ Columbia CL 2508 [M]	Midnight Ride	1966	6.25	12.50	25.00
❑ Columbia CL 2595 [M]	The Spirit of '67	1966	6.25	12.50	25.00
❑ Columbia KCL 2662 [M]	Greatest Hits	1967	7.50	15.00	30.00
—Add 20% if booklet is included; at least some copies actually are stereo with the "XSS" prefix on the label's master numbers rather than "XLP," though we don't know if all of them are					
❑ Columbia CL 2721 [M]	Revolution!	1967	7.50	15.00	30.00
❑ Columbia CL 2755 [M]	A Christmas Present…And Past	1967	15.00	30.00	60.00
❑ Columbia CL 2805 [M]	Goin' to Memphis	1968	20.00	40.00	80.00
❑ Columbia CS 9107 [S]	Here They Come!	1965	10.00	20.00	40.00
—"360 Sound Stereo" in black on label					
❑ Columbia CS 9251 [S]	Just Like Us!	1966	7.50	15.00	30.00
❑ Columbia CS 9308 [S]	Midnight Ride	1966	7.50	15.00	30.00
❑ Columbia CS 9395 [S]	The Spirit of '67	1966	7.50	15.00	30.00
❑ Columbia KCS 9462 [P]	Greatest Hits	1967	6.25	12.50	25.00
—Add 20% if booklet is included					
❑ Columbia CS 9521 [S]	Revolution!	1967	6.25	12.50	25.00
❑ Columbia CS 9555 [S]	A Christmas Present…And Past	1967	6.25	12.50	25.00
❑ Columbia CS 9605 [S]	Goin' to Memphis	1968	5.00	10.00	20.00
❑ Columbia CS 9665	Something Happening	1968	5.00	10.00	20.00
❑ Columbia CS 9753	Hard 'N' Heavy (With Marshmallow)	1969	5.00	10.00	20.00
—Black and white cover					
❑ Columbia CS 9905	Alias Pink Puzz	1969	5.00	10.00	20.00
❑ Columbia CS 9964	Collage	1970	5.00	10.00	20.00
❑ Columbia C 30386	Greatest Hits, Volume 2	1971	5.00	10.00	20.00
❑ Columbia C 30768	Indian Reservation	1971	3.75	7.50	15.00
❑ Columbia KC 31106	Country Wine	1972	3.75	7.50	15.00
❑ Columbia KG 31464 [(2)]	All-Time Greatest Hits	1972	5.00	10.00	20.00
❑ Columbia PC 35593	Greatest Hits	1978	2.50	5.00	10.00

Number	Title (A Side/B Side)	Yr	VG	VG+	NM
❑ Columbia Limited Edition LE 10170 [S]	Midnight Ride	197?	3.75	7.50	15.00
—Reissue of 9308					
❑ Gardena LP-G-1000 [M]	Like, Long Hair	1961	150.00	300.00	600.00
❑ Harmony H 30089	Paul Revere and the Raiders Featuring Mark Lindsay	1970	3.00	6.00	12.00
❑ Harmony KH 30975	Good Thing	1971	3.00	6.00	12.00
❑ Harmony KH 31183	Movin' On	1972	3.00	6.00	12.00
❑ Jerden JRL-7004 [M]	Paul Revere and the Raiders In the Beginning	1966	15.00	30.00	60.00
❑ Jerden JRS-7004 [R]	Paul Revere and the Raiders In the Beginning	1966	7.50	15.00	30.00
❑ Pickwick SPC-3176 [R]	Paul Revere and the Raiders	1969	2.50	5.00	10.00
❑ Sande S-1001 [M]	Paul Revere and the Raiders	1963	300.00	600.00	1200.
—Original version with "Sande" and no mention of "Etiquette" in trail-off area					
❑ Sande S-1001 [M]	Paul Revere and the Raiders	1979	6.25	12.50	25.00
—Legitimate reissue with "Sande" and "Etiquette" in trail-off area					
❑ Sears SPS-493	Paul Revere and the Raiders	1969	6.25	12.50	25.00

REYNOLDS, JODY

45s

Number	Title (A Side/B Side)	Yr	VG	VG+	NM
❑ Brent 7042	Raggedy Ann/The Girl from King Marie	1963	2.50	5.00	10.00
❑ Demon 1507	Endless Sleep/Tight Capris	1958	7.50	15.00	30.00
❑ Demon 1509	Fire of Love/Daisy Mae	1958	6.25	12.50	25.00
❑ Demon 1511	Closin' In/Elope with Me	1958	6.25	12.50	25.00
❑ Demon 1515	Golden Idol/Beulah Lee	1959	6.25	12.50	25.00
❑ Demon 1519	The Storm/Please Remember	1959	6.25	12.50	25.00
❑ Demon 1523	Whipping Post/I Wanna Be with You Tonight	1960	6.25	12.50	25.00
❑ Demon 1524	Stone Cold/(The Girl with) The Raven Hair	1960	6.25	12.50	25.00
❑ Indigo 127	Tarantula/Thunder	1961	12.50	25.00	50.00
❑ Pulsar 2419	Endless Sleep/My Baby's Eyes	1969	—	3.00	6.00
❑ Smash 1810	Don't Jmp/Stormy	1963	3.00	6.00	12.00
❑ Titan 1734	Devil Girl/A Tear for Hesse	1963	3.75	7.50	15.00
❑ Titan 1736	Requiem for Love/Stranger in the Mirror	1963	3.75	7.50	15.00
—With Bobbie Gentry					

Albums

Number	Title (A Side/B Side)	Yr	VG	VG+	NM
❑ Tru-Gems 1002	Endless Sleep	1978	3.00	6.00	12.00

RICH, CHARLIE

45s

Number	Title (A Side/B Side)	Yr	VG	VG+	NM
❑ Elektra 45553	I'll Wake You Up When I Get Home/Salty Dog Blues	1978	—	2.00	4.00
❑ Elektra 47047	A Man Just Doesn't Know What a Woman Goes Through/Marie	1980	—	2.00	4.00
❑ Elektra 47104	Are We Dreamin' the Same Dream/Angelina	1981	—	2.00	4.00
❑ Epic 02058	You Made It Beautiful/How Good It Used to Be	1981	—	2.00	4.00
❑ Epic 03165	Try a Little Tenderness/As Time Goes By	1982	—	2.00	4.00
❑ Epic 10287	Set Me Free/I'll Just Go Away	1968	—	3.00	6.00
❑ Epic 10358	Raggedy Ann/Nothing in the World	1968	—	3.00	6.00
❑ Epic 10492	Life's Little Ups and Downs/It Takes Time	1969	—	3.00	6.00
❑ Epic 10585	July 12, 1939/I'm Flying to Nashville Tonight	1970	—	3.00	6.00
❑ Epic 10662	Nice 'N' Easy/I Can't Even Drink It Away	1970	—	3.00	6.00
❑ Epic 10745	A Woman Left Lonely/Have a Heart	1971	—	2.50	5.00
❑ Epic 10809	A Part of Your Life/A Sunday Kind of Woman	1971	—	2.50	5.00
❑ Epic 10867	I Take It On Home/Peace on You	1972	—	2.50	5.00
❑ Epic 10950	Behind Closed Doors/A Sunday Kind of Woman	1973	—	2.50	5.00
—Originals have yellow labels					
❑ Epic 11040	The Most Beautiful Girl/I Feel Like Going Home	1973	—	2.00	4.00
❑ Epic 11091	A Very Special Love Song/I Can't Even Drink It Away	1974	—	2.00	4.00
❑ Epic 20006	I Love My Friend/Why Oh Why	1974	—	2.00	4.00
❑ Epic 50064	My Elusive Dreams/Whatever Happened	1975	—	2.00	4.00
❑ Epic 50103	Every Time You Touch Me (I Get High)/Pass On By	1975	—	2.00	4.00
❑ Epic 50142	All Over Me/You & I	1975	—	2.00	4.00
❑ Epic 50182	Since I Fell for You/She	1975	—	2.00	4.00
❑ Epic 50222	America the Beautiful (1976)/Down By the Riverside	1976	—	2.00	4.00
❑ Epic 50268	Road Song/The Grass Is Always Greener	1976	—	2.00	4.00
❑ Epic 50328	Easy Look/My Lady	1976	—	2.00	4.00
❑ Epic 50392	Rollin' with the Flow/To Sing a Love Song	1977	—	2.00	4.00
❑ Epic 50562	Beautiful Woman/Everybody Wrote That Song for Me	1978	—	2.00	4.00
❑ Epic 50616	On My Knees/Mellow Melody	1978	—	2.00	4.00
❑ Epic 50701	Spanish Eyes/I Do My Swingin' at Home	1979	—	2.00	4.00
❑ Epic 50869	Even a Fool Would Let Go/Pretty People	1980	—	2.00	4.00

Number	Title (A Side/B Side)	Yr	VG	VG+	NM
❑ Groove 58-0020	The Grass Is Always Greener/She Loved Everybody But Me	1963	3.75	7.50	15.00
❑ Groove 58-0025	Big Boss Man/Let Me Go My Merry Way	1963	3.75	7.50	15.00
❑ Groove 58-0032	Lady Love/Why, Oh Why	1964	3.75	7.50	15.00
❑ Groove 58-0035	The Ways of a Woman in Love/My Mountain Dew	1964	3.75	7.50	15.00
❑ Groove 58-0041	Nice 'N' Easy/Turn Around and Face Me	1964	3.75	7.50	15.00
❑ Hi 2116	Love Is After Me/Pass On By	1966	2.50	5.00	10.00
❑ Hi 2123	My Heart Would Know/Nobody's Lonesome for Me	1967	2.50	5.00	10.00
❑ Hi 2134	Hurry Up Freight Train/Only Me	1967	2.50	5.00	10.00
❑ Mercury 73466	I Washed My Hands in Muddy Water/No Home	1974	—	2.50	5.00
❑ Mercury 73498	A Field of Yellow Daisies/Party Girl	1974	—	2.50	5.00
❑ Mercury 73646	Something Just Came Over Me/Best Years	1974	—	2.50	5.00
❑ Phillips Int'l. 3532	Whirlwind/Philadelphia Baby	1959	6.25	12.50	25.00
❑ Phillips Int'l. 3542	Rebound/Big Man	1959	6.25	12.50	25.00
❑ Phillips Int'l. 3552	Lonely Weekends/Everything I Do Is Wrong	1960	6.25	12.50	25.00
❑ Phillips Int'l. 3560	School Days/Gonna Be Waiting	1960	6.25	12.50	25.00
❑ Phillips Int'l. 3562	On My Knees/Stay	1960	6.25	12.50	25.00
❑ Phillips Int'l. 3566	Who Will the Next Fool Be/Caught in the Middle	1961	6.25	12.50	25.00
❑ Phillips Int'l. 3572	Just a Little Sweet/It's Too Late	1962	5.00	10.00	20.00
❑ Phillips Int'l. 3576	Easy Money/Midnight Blues	1962	5.00	10.00	20.00
❑ Phillips Int'l. 3582	Sittin' and Thinkin'/Finally Found Out	1962	5.00	10.00	20.00
❑ Phillips Int'l. 3584	There's Another Place I Can't Go/I Need Your Love	1963	5.00	10.00	20.00
❑ RCA PB-10859	My Mountain Dew/Nice 'N Easy	1976	—	2.00	4.00
❑ RCA PB-10966	Nice 'N Easy/It's All Over Now	1977	—	2.00	4.00
❑ RCA Victor 47-8468	It's All Over Now/Too Many Teardrops	1964	3.75	7.50	15.00
❑ RCA Victor 47-8536	There Won't Be Anymore/Gentleman Jim	1965	5.00	10.00	20.00
❑ RCA Victor 47-8817	Nice 'N' Easy/Ol' Man River	1966	3.00	6.00	12.00
❑ RCA Victor 74-0983	Tomorrow Night/The Ways of a Woman in Love	1973	—	2.00	4.00
❑ RCA Victor APBO-0195	There Won't Be Anymore/It's All Over Now	1973	—	2.50	5.00
❑ RCA Victor APBO-0260	I Don't See Me in Your Eyes Anymore/No Room to Dance	1974	—	2.00	4.00
❑ RCA Victor PB-10062	She Called Me Baby/$10 and a Clean White Shirt	1974	—	2.00	4.00
❑ RCA Victor GB-10159	There Won't Be Anymore/Tomorrow Night	1975	—	—	3.00
—Gold Standard Series					
❑ RCA Victor PB-10256	It's All Over Now/Big Jack	1975	—	2.00	4.00
❑ RCA Victor PB-10458	Not Everybody Knows/I've Got You Under My Skin	1975	—	2.00	4.00
❑ RCA Victor GB-10512	She Called Me Baby/$10 and a Clean White Shirt	1975	—	—	3.00
—Gold Standard Series					
❑ Smash 1993	Mohair Sam/I Washed My Hands in Muddy Water	1965	5.00	10.00	20.00
❑ Smash 2012	Dance of Love/I Can't Go On	1965	3.75	7.50	15.00
❑ Smash 2022	Hawg Jaw/Something Just Came Over Me	1966	3.75	7.50	15.00
❑ Smash 2038	No Home/Tears a-Go-Go	1966	3.75	7.50	15.00
❑ Smash 2060	That's the Way/When My Baby Comes Home	1966	3.75	7.50	15.00
❑ Sun 1110	Who Will the Next Fool Be/Stay	1970	—	2.50	5.00
❑ Sun 1151	The Breakup/Be-Bop-a-Lula	1980	—	2.00	4.00
—B-side by Jerry Lee Lewis; both sides are duets with Orion					
❑ United Artists XW1193	Puttin' In Overtime at Home/Ghost of Another Man	1978	—	2.00	4.00
❑ United Artists XW1223	I Still Believe in Love/Wishful Thinking	1978	—	2.00	4.00
❑ United Artists XW1269	The Fool Strikes Again/I Loved You All the Way	1978	—	2.00	4.00
❑ United Artists XW1280	I Lost My Head/She Knows Just How to Touch Me	1979	—	2.00	4.00
❑ United Artists XW1307	Life Goes On/Standing Tall	1979	—	2.00	4.00
❑ United Artists 1325	You're Gonna Love Yourself in the Morning/Top of the Stairs	1979	—	2.00	4.00
❑ United Artists 1340	I'd Build a Bridge/All You Ever Have to Do Is Touch Me	1980	—	2.00	4.00
Albums					
❑ Buckboard 1019	The Entertainer	197?	2.50	5.00	10.00
❑ Elektra 6E-301	Once a Drifter	1981	2.50	5.00	10.00
❑ Epic BN 26376	Set Me Free	1968	5.00	10.00	20.00
❑ Epic BN 26516	The Fabulous Charlie Rich	1970	5.00	10.00	20.00
❑ Epic E 30214	Boss Man	1970	5.00	10.00	20.00
❑ Epic KE 31933	The Best of Charlie Rich	1972	3.75	7.50	15.00
—Yellow label; add 80 percent if bonus record AE7 1065 and its special sleeve are still there					
❑ Epic KE 32247	Behind Closed Doors	1973	3.00	6.00	12.00
❑ Epic PE 32531	Very Special Love Songs	1974	3.00	6.00	12.00
❑ Epic PE 33250	The Silver Fox	1974	3.00	6.00	12.00
❑ Epic PE 33455	Every Time You Touch Me (I Get High)	1975	3.00	6.00	12.00
❑ Epic PE 33545	Silver Linings	1976	2.50	5.00	10.00
❑ Epic PE 34240	Greatest Hits	1976	2.50	5.00	10.00
—Without bar code on cover					
❑ Epic PE 34444	Take Me	1977	2.50	5.00	10.00
❑ Epic PE 34891	Rollin' with the Flow	1977	2.50	5.00	10.00
❑ Epic JE 35394	Classic Rich, Vol. 1	1978	2.50	5.00	10.00
❑ Epic JE 35624	Classic Rich, Vol. 2	1978	2.50	5.00	10.00
❑ Groove GM-1000 [M]	Charlie Rich	1964	37.50	75.00	150.00
❑ Groove GS-1000 [S]	Charlie Rich	1964	75.00	150.00	300.00
❑ Harmony KH 32166	I Do My Swingin' at Home	1973	3.00	6.00	12.00
❑ Hi 8006	I'm So Lonesome I Could Cry	198?	2.00	4.00	8.00
—Reissue of Hi 32084					
❑ Hi HL 12037 [M]	Charlie Rich Sings Country and Western	1967	7.50	15.00	30.00
❑ Hi SHL 32037 [S]	Charlie Rich Sings Country and Western	1967	5.00	10.00	20.00
❑ Hi SHL 32084	Charlie Rich Sings the Songs of Hank Williams & Others	1974	3.00	6.00	12.00
—Reissue of 32037					
❑ Hilltop 6139	Lonely Weekends	197?	2.50	5.00	10.00
❑ Hilltop 6149	Songs for Beautiful Girls	1974	2.50	5.00	10.00
❑ Hilltop 6160	Entertainer of the Year	197?	2.50	5.00	10.00
❑ Mercury SRM-2-7505 [(2)]	Fully Realized	1974	3.75	7.50	15.00
❑ Phillips International PLP-1970 [M]	Lonely Weekends	1960	150.00	300.00	600.00
❑ Pickwick ACL-7001	Too Many Teardrops	1975	2.50	5.00	10.00
❑ Power Pak PO-241	There Won't Be Anymore	197?	2.50	5.00	10.00

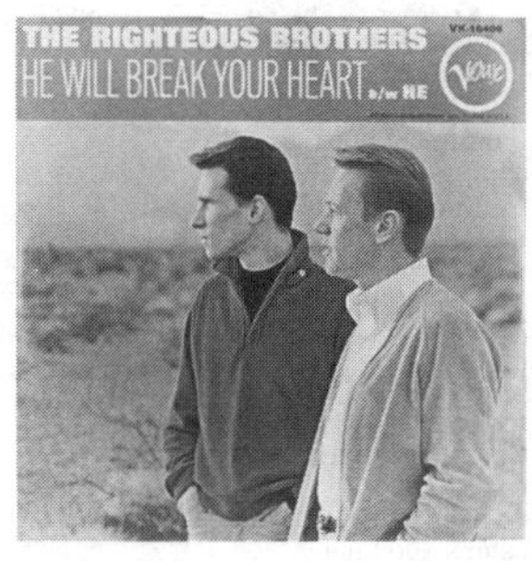

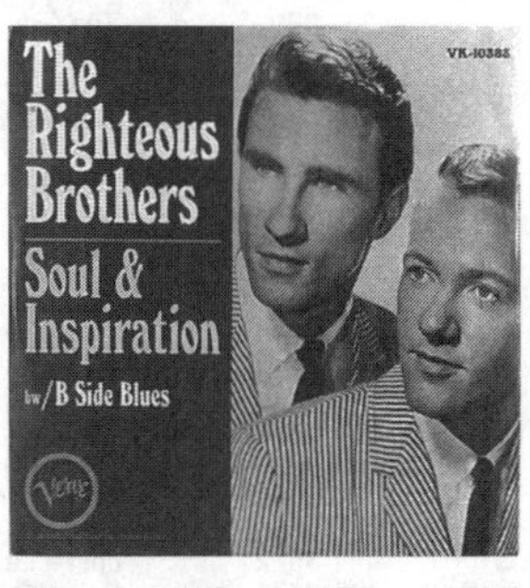

Number	Title (A Side/B Side)	Yr	VG	VG+	NM
❑ Power Pak PO-245	Arkansas Traveler	197?	2.50	5.00	10.00
❑ Power Pak PO-252	The Silver Fox	197?	2.50	5.00	10.00
❑ Quicksilver QS-1005	Midnight Blue	198?	3.00	6.00	12.00
❑ RCA Camden CAS-2417	The Versatile and Talented Charlie Rich	1970	2.50	5.00	10.00
❑ RCA Victor APL1-0258	Tomorrow Night	1973	3.00	6.00	12.00
❑ RCA Victor APL1-0433	There Won't Be Anymore	1974	3.00	6.00	12.00
❑ RCA Victor APL1-0686	She Called Me Baby	1974	3.00	6.00	12.00
❑ RCA Victor APL1-0857	Greatest Hits	1975	3.00	6.00	12.00
❑ RCA Victor APL1-1242	Now Everybody Knows	1975	3.00	6.00	12.00
❑ RCA Victor ANL1-1542	Tomorrow Night	1976	2.50	5.00	10.00
—Reissue					
❑ RCA Victor APL1-2260	Big Boss Man/My Mountain Dew	1977	3.00	6.00	12.00
❑ RCA Victor ANL1-2424	She Called Me Baby	1977	2.50	5.00	10.00
—Reissue of APL1-0686					
❑ RCA Victor LPM-3352 [M]	That's Rich	1965	10.00	20.00	40.00
❑ RCA Victor LSP-3352 [S]	That's Rich	1965	12.50	25.00	50.00
❑ RCA Victor LPM-3537 [M]	Big Boss Man	1966	10.00	20.00	40.00
❑ RCA Victor LSP-3557 [S]	Big Boss Man	1966	12.50	25.00	50.00
❑ RCA Victor AHL1-5496	Collector's Series	1985	2.00	4.00	8.00
❑ Smash MGS-27070 [M]	The Many New Sides of Charlie Rich	1965	7.50	15.00	30.00
❑ Smash MGS-27078 [M]	The Best Years	1966	7.50	15.00	30.00
❑ Smash SRS-67070 [S]	The Many New Sides of Charlie Rich	1965	10.00	20.00	40.00
❑ Smash SRS-67070 [S]	The Best Years	1966	10.00	20.00	40.00
❑ Sun LP 110	Lonely Weekend	1970	3.00	6.00	12.00
❑ Sun LP 123	A Time for Tears	1971	3.00	6.00	12.00
❑ Sun LP 132	The Early Years	1974	3.00	6.00	12.00
❑ Sun LP 133	The Memphis Sound of Charlie Rich	1974	3.00	6.00	12.00
❑ Sun LP 134	Golden Treasures	1974	3.00	6.00	12.00
❑ Sun LP 135	Sun's Best of Charlie Rich	1974	3.00	6.00	12.00
❑ Sun 1003	20 Golden Hits	1979	2.50	5.00	10.00
—Gold vinyl					
❑ Sun 1007	The Original Charlie Rich	1979	2.50	5.00	10.00
❑ Sunnyvale 9330	The Sun Story Vol. 2	1977	2.50	5.00	10.00
❑ Time-Life STW-115	Country Music	1981	2.50	5.00	10.00
❑ Trip TLP-8502 [(2)]	The Best of Charlie Rich	1974	3.00	6.00	12.00
❑ United Artists UA-LA876-H	I Still Believe in Love	1978	3.00	6.00	12.00
❑ United Artists UA-LA925-H	The Fool Strikes Again	1978	2.50	5.00	10.00
❑ Wing SRW-16375	A Lonely Weekend	1969	3.00	6.00	12.00

RICHARD, CLIFF

45s

Number	Title (A Side/B Side)	Yr	VG	VG+	NM
❑ ABC-Paramount 10042	Living Doll/Apron Strings	1959	6.25	12.50	25.00
❑ ABC-Paramount 10066	Travellin' Light/Dynamite	1959	5.00	10.00	20.00
❑ ABC-Paramount 10093	Voice in the Wilderness/Don't Be Mad at Me	1960	5.00	10.00	20.00
❑ ABC-Paramount 10109	Fall in Love with You/Choppin' 'N' Changin'	1960	5.00	10.00	20.00
❑ ABC-Paramount 10136	Please Don't Tease/Where Is My Heart	1960	5.00	10.00	20.00
❑ ABC-Paramount 10175	Catch Me, I'm Falling/"D" in Love	1961	5.00	10.00	20.00
❑ ABC-Paramount 10195	Theme for a Dream/Mumblin' Mosie	1961	10.00	20.00	40.00
❑ Big Top 3101	The Young Ones/We Say Yeah	1962	5.00	10.00	20.00
❑ Capitol F4096	Move It/High Class Baby	1958	10.00	20.00	40.00
❑ Capitol F4154	Livin' Lovin' Doll/Steady with You	1959	10.00	20.00	40.00
❑ Dot 16399	Wonderful to Be Young/Got a Funny Feeling	1962	5.00	10.00	20.00
❑ EMI America 8025	We Don't Talk Anymore/Count Me Out	1979	—	2.00	4.00
❑ EMI America 8035	Carrie/Language of Love	1980	—	2.00	4.00
❑ EMI America 8057	Dreaming/Dynamite	1980	—	2.50	5.00
—Green label					
❑ EMI America 8068	A Little in Love/Everyman	1980	—	2.00	4.00
❑ EMI America 8076	Give a Little Bit More/Keep Lookin'	1981	—	2.00	4.00
❑ EMI America 8095	Wired for Sound/Hold On	1981	—	2.00	4.00
❑ EMI America 8103	Daddy's Home/Summer Rain	1982	—	2.00	4.00
❑ EMI America 8135	The Only Way Out/Be in My Heart	1982	—	2.00	4.00
❑ EMI America 8149	Little Town/Be in My Heart	1982	—	2.00	4.00
❑ EMI America 8180	Never Say Die (Give a Little Bit More)/Front Page	1983	—	2.00	4.00
❑ EMI America 8193	Donna/Ocean Deep	1984	—	2.00	4.00
❑ Epic 9597	Lucky Lips/Next Time	1963	5.00	10.00	20.00
❑ Epic 9633	It's All in the Game/I'm Looking Out the Window	1963	5.00	10.00	20.00
❑ Epic 9670	I'm the Lonely One/I Only Have Eyes for You	1964	5.00	10.00	20.00

Number	Title (A Side/B Side)	Yr	VG	VG+	NM
❑ Epic 9691	Bachelor Boy/True, True Lovin'	1964	5.00	10.00	20.00
❑ Epic 9737	I Don't Wanna Love You/Look in My Eyes Maria	1964	3.75	7.50	15.00
❑ Epic 9757	Again/The Minute You're Gone	1965	3.75	7.50	15.00
❑ Epic 9810	I Could Easily Fall (In Love with You)/On My Word	1965	3.75	7.50	15.00
❑ Epic 9839	The Twelfth of Never/Paradise Lost	1965	3.75	7.50	15.00
❑ Epic 9866	Wind Me Up (and Let Me Go)/Eye of a Needle	1965	3.75	7.50	15.00
❑ Epic 10018	Blue Turns to Grey/I'll Walk Alone	1966	3.75	7.50	15.00
❑ Epic 10070	Visions/Quando, Quando, Quando	1966	3.75	7.50	15.00
❑ Epic 10101	Time Drags By/The La La La Song	1966	3.75	7.50	15.00
❑ Epic 10178	It's All Over/Heartbeat	1967	3.75	7.50	15.00
❑ Monument 1211	Goodbye Sam, Hello Samantha/You Never Can Tell	1970	—	3.00	6.00
❑ Monument 1229	I Ain't Got Time Anymore/Morning Comes Too Soon	1970	—	3.00	6.00
❑ Polydor 885336-7	All I Ask of You/Phantom of the Opera Overture, Act 2	1987	—	—	3.00
—With Sarah Brightman					
❑ Rocket YB-11463	Green Light/Needing a Friend	1979	—	2.00	4.00
❑ Rocket 40531	Miss You Nights/Love Enough	1976	—	2.00	4.00
❑ Rocket 40574	Devil Woman/Love On (Shine On)	1976	—	2.50	5.00
❑ Rocket 40652	Junior Cowboy/I Can't Ask for Anymore Than You	1976	—	2.00	4.00
❑ Rocket 40724	Don't Turn the Light Out/Nothing Left for Me to Say	1977	—	2.00	4.00
❑ Rocket 40771	You've Got Me Wondering/Try a Smile	1977	—	2.00	4.00
❑ Sire 703	Living in Harmony/Jesus	1973	—	2.50	5.00
❑ Sire 707	Power to All Our Friends/Come Back Billie Joe	1973	—	2.50	5.00
❑ Striped Horse 7008	My Pretty One/Love Ya	1988	—	—	3.00
❑ Striped Horse 7011	Some People/Love Ya	1988	—	—	3.00
❑ Uni 55061	All My Love/Our Story Book	1968	2.50	5.00	10.00
❑ Uni 55069	Congratulations/High 'N' Dry	1968	2.50	5.00	10.00
❑ Uni 55145	The Day I Met Marie/Sweet Little Jesus Boy	1969	3.00	6.00	12.00
❑ Warner Bros. 7344	Throw Down a Line/Reflections	1969	2.00	4.00	8.00
—A-side by Cliff and Hank (Marvin)					
Albums					
❑ ABC-Paramount 321 [M]	Cliff Sings	1960	20.00	40.00	80.00
❑ ABC-Paramount S-321 [S]	Cliff Sings	1960	25.00	50.00	100.00
❑ ABC-Paramount 391 [M]	Listen to Cliff	1961	20.00	40.00	80.00
❑ ABC-Paramount S-391 [S]	Listen to Cliff	1961	25.00	50.00	100.00
❑ EMI America SN-16220	Green Light	1981	2.00	4.00	8.00
❑ EMI America SN-16221	I'm Nearly Famous	1981	2.00	4.00	8.00
❑ EMI America SN-16253	Every Face Tells a Story	1981	2.00	4.00	8.00
❑ EMI America SW-17018	We Don't Talk Anymore	1979	2.50	5.00	10.00
❑ EMI America SW-17039	I'm No Hero	1980	2.50	5.00	10.00
❑ EMI America SW-17059	Wired for Sound	1981	2.50	5.00	10.00
❑ EMI America ST-17081	Now You See Me, Now You Don't	1982	2.50	5.00	10.00
❑ EMI America ST-17105	Give a Little Bit More	1983	2.50	5.00	10.00
❑ Epic LN 24063 [M]	Summer Holiday	1963	10.00	20.00	40.00
❑ Epic LN 24089 [M]	It's All in the Game	1964	7.50	15.00	30.00
❑ Epic LN 24115 [M]	Cliff Richard in Spain	1965	7.50	15.00	30.00
❑ Epic BN 26063 [S]	Summer Holiday	1963	12.50	25.00	50.00
❑ Epic BN 26089 [S]	It's All in the Game	1964	10.00	20.00	40.00
❑ Epic BN 26115 [S]	Cliff Richard in Spain	1965	10.00	20.00	40.00
❑ Rocket PIG-2210	I'm Nearly Famous	1976	3.00	6.00	12.00
❑ Rocket PIG-2268	Every Face Tells a Story	1977	3.00	6.00	12.00
❑ Rocket BXL1-2958	Green Light	1978	3.00	6.00	12.00
❑ Word WR-8306	Walking in the Light	1985	3.00	6.00	12.00

RIGHTEOUS BROTHERS, THE

Number	Title (A Side/B Side)	Yr	VG	VG+	NM
45s					
❑ Haven 800	Hold On to What You Got/Let Me Make the Music	1976	—	2.00	4.00
❑ Haven 7002	Rock and Roll Heaven/I Just Wanna Be Me	1974	—	2.50	5.00
❑ Haven 7004	Give It to the People/Love Is Not a Dirty Word	1974	—	2.00	4.00
❑ Haven 7006	Dream On/Dr. Rock and Roll	1974	—	2.00	4.00
❑ Haven 7011	High Blood Pressure/Never Say I Love You	1975	—	2.00	4.00
❑ Haven 7014	Young Blood/Substitute	1975	—	2.00	4.00
❑ Moonglow 215	Little Latin Lupe Lu/I'm So Lonely	1963	5.00	10.00	20.00
❑ Moonglow 221	Gotta Tell You How I Feel/If You're Lying, You'll Be Crying	1963	5.00	10.00	20.00
❑ Moonglow 223	My Babe/Fee-Fi-Fidily-I-Oh	1963	5.00	10.00	20.00
❑ Moonglow 224	Ko Ko Joe/B-Flat Blues	1963	5.00	10.00	20.00
❑ Moonglow 231	Try to Find Another Man/I Still Love You	1964	5.00	10.00	20.00
❑ Moonglow 234	Bring Your Love to Me/If You're Lying, You'll Be Crying	1964	5.00	10.00	20.00
❑ Moonglow 235	This Little Girl of Mine/If You're Lying, You'll Be Crying	1964	3.75	7.50	15.00
❑ Moonglow 238	Bring Your Love to Me/Fannie Mae	1965	3.75	7.50	15.00
❑ Moonglow 239	You Can Have Her/Love or Magic	1965	3.75	7.50	15.00
❑ Moonglow 242	Justine/In That Great Gettin' Up Morning	1965	3.75	7.50	15.00
❑ Moonglow 243	For Your Love/Gotta Tell You How I Feel	1965	3.75	7.50	15.00
❑ Moonglow 244	Georgia on My Mind/My Tears Will Go Away	1966	3.75	7.50	15.00
❑ Moonglow 245	I Need a Girl/Bring Your Love to Me	1966	3.75	7.50	15.00
❑ Philles 124	You've Lost That Lovin' Feelin'/There's a Woman	1964	3.75	7.50	15.00
❑ Philles 127	Just Once in My Life/The Blues	1965	3.75	7.50	15.00
❑ Philles 129	Unchained Melody/Hung on You	1965	3.75	7.50	15.00
—With "Producer: Phil Spector" on the "Unchained Melody" side					
❑ Philles 130	Ebb Tide/(I Love You) For Sentimental Reasons	1965	3.75	7.50	15.00
❑ Philles 132	The White Cliffs of Dover/She's Mine, All Mine	1966	5.00	10.00	20.00
❑ Verve 10383	(You're My) Soul and Inspiration/B Side Blues	1966	3.75	7.50	15.00
❑ Verve 10403	Rat Race/Green Onions	1966	3.75	7.50	15.00
❑ Verve 10406	He/He Will Break Your Heart	1966	2.50	5.00	10.00
❑ Verve 10430	Go Ahead and Cry/Things Didn't Go Your Way	1966	2.50	5.00	10.00
❑ Verve 10449	On This Side of Goodbye/A Man Without a Dream	1966	2.50	5.00	10.00
❑ Verve 10479	Along Came Jones/Jimmy's Blues	1967	2.00	4.00	8.00
❑ Verve 10507	Melancholy Music Man/Don't Give Up on Me	1967	2.00	4.00	8.00

Number	Title (A Side/B Side)	Yr	VG	VG+	NM
❑ Verve 10520	(You're My) Soul and Inspiration/Go Ahead and Cry	1967	2.50	5.00	10.00
❑ Verve 10521	Hold On, I'm Coming/He Will Break Your Heart	1967	2.50	5.00	10.00
❑ Verve 10522	Melancholy Music Man/I Believe	1967	2.50	5.00	10.00
❑ Verve 10523	I (Who Have Nothing)/Island in the Sun	1967	2.50	5.00	10.00
❑ Verve 10524	My Girl/Something You Got	1967	2.50	5.00	10.00
❑ Verve 10551	Stranded in the Middle of No Place/Been So Nice	1967	2.00	4.00	8.00
❑ Verve 10577	Here I Am/So Many Lonely Nights Ahead	1968	2.00	4.00	8.00
❑ Verve 10637	Let the Good Times Roll/You've Lost That Lovin' Feelin'	1968	2.00	4.00	8.00
❑ Verve 10648	And the Party Goes On/Woman, Man Needs Ya	1968	2.00	4.00	8.00
❑ Verve 10649	Good N' Nuff/Po' Folks	1968	2.00	4.00	8.00
❑ Verve 871882-7	Unchained Melody/Hung on You	1989	—	2.00	4.00
Albums					
❑ Haven ST-9201	Give It to the People	1974	3.75	7.50	15.00
❑ Haven ST-9203	Sons of Mrs. Righteous	1975	3.75	7.50	15.00
❑ MGM GAS-102	The Righteous Brothers (Golden Archive Series)	1970	3.75	7.50	15.00
❑ MGM SE-4885	The History of the Righteous Brothers	1973	3.75	7.50	15.00
❑ Moonglow MLP-1001 [M]	Right Now!	1963	10.00	20.00	40.00
❑ Moonglow MSP-1001 [S]	Right Now!	1963	15.00	30.00	60.00
❑ Moonglow MLP-1002 [M]	Some Blue-Eyed Soul	1964	10.00	20.00	40.00
❑ Moonglow MSP-1002 [S]	Some Blue-Eyed Soul	1964	15.00	30.00	60.00
❑ Moonglow MLP-1003 [M]	This Is New!	1965	10.00	20.00	40.00
❑ Moonglow MSP-1003 [S]	This Is New!	1965	15.00	30.00	60.00
❑ Moonglow MLP-1004 [M]	The Best of the Righteous Brothers	1966	6.25	12.50	25.00
❑ Moonglow MSP-1004 [S]	The Best of the Righteous Brothers	1966	7.50	15.00	30.00
❑ Philles PHLP-4007 [M]	You've Lost That Lovin' Feelin'	1964	6.25	12.50	25.00
❑ Philles PHLPS-4007 [S]	You've Lost That Lovin' Feelin'	1964	10.00	20.00	40.00
❑ Philles PHLP-4008 [M]	Just Once in My Life	1965	6.25	12.50	25.00
❑ Philles PHLPS-4008 [S]	Just Once in My Life	1965	10.00	20.00	40.00
❑ Philles PHLP-4009 [M]	Back to Back	1965	6.25	12.50	25.00
❑ Philles PHLPS-4009 [S]	Back to Back	1965	10.00	20.00	40.00
❑ Rhino R1-71488 [(2)]	Anthology	1989	3.75	7.50	15.00
❑ Verve V-5001 [M]	Soul and Inspiration	1966	5.00	10.00	20.00
❑ Verve V6-5001 [S]	Soul and Inspiration	1966	6.25	12.50	25.00
❑ Verve V-5004 [M]	Go Ahead and Cry	1966	5.00	10.00	20.00
❑ Verve V6-5004 [S]	Go Ahead and Cry	1966	6.25	12.50	25.00
❑ Verve V-5010 [M]	Sayin' Somethin'	1967	5.00	10.00	20.00
❑ Verve V6-5010 [S]	Sayin' Somethin'	1967	6.25	12.50	25.00
❑ Verve V-5020 [M]	Greatest Hits	1967	6.25	12.50	25.00
❑ Verve V6-5020 [S]	Greatest Hits	1967	5.00	10.00	20.00
❑ Verve V-5031 [M]	Souled Out	1967	7.50	15.00	30.00
❑ Verve V6-5031 [S]	Souled Out	1967	5.00	10.00	20.00
❑ Verve V6-5051	Standards	1968	5.00	10.00	20.00
❑ Verve V6-5058	One for the Road	1968	5.00	10.00	20.00
—Without The Blossoms credited on the back cover					
❑ Verve V6-5071	Greatest Hits, Vol. 2	1969	5.00	10.00	20.00
❑ Verve V6-5076	Re-Birth	1970	5.00	10.00	20.00
❑ Verve 823662-1	Greatest Hits	198?	2.50	5.00	10.00

RIP CHORDS, THE

45s

Number	Title (A Side/B Side)	Yr	VG	VG+	NM
❑ Columbia 42687	Here I Stand/Karen	1963	3.75	7.50	15.00
❑ Columbia 42812	Gone/She Thinks I Still Care	1963	3.75	7.50	15.00
❑ Columbia 42921	Hey, Little Cobra/The Queen	1963	5.00	10.00	20.00
❑ Columbia 43035	Three Window Coupe/Hot Rod U.S.A.	1964	3.75	7.50	15.00
❑ Columbia 43093	One Piece Topless Bathing Suit/Wah-Wahini	1964	3.75	7.50	15.00
❑ Columbia 43221	Don't Be Scared/Bunny Hill	1965	3.75	7.50	15.00
❑ Sundazed SEP 188	Sting Ray//Red Hot Roadster/Shut Down	2006	—	—	3.00
—Yellow vinyl					
❑ Sundazed SEP 188 [Picture Sleeve]	Sting Ray//Red Hot Roadster/Shut Down	2006	—	—	3.00
—Cardboard sleeve					
Albums					
❑ Columbia CL 2151 [M]	Hey Little Cobra and Other Hot Rod Hits	1964	10.00	20.00	40.00
—"Guaranteed High Fidelity" on label					
❑ Columbia CL 2151 [M]	Hey Little Cobra and Other Hot Rod Hits	1966	6.25	12.50	25.00
—"360 Sound Mono" on label					
❑ Columbia CL 2216 [M]	Three Window Coupe	1964	12.50	25.00	50.00

Number	Title (A Side/B Side)	Yr	VG	VG+	NM
❑ Columbia CS 8951 [S]	Hey Little Cobra and Other Hot Rod Hits	1964	12.50	25.00	50.00
❑ Columbia CS 9016 [S]	Three Window Coupe	1964	17.50	35.00	70.00
RIPERTON, MINNIE					
45s					
❑ Capitol 4706	Memory Lane/I'm a Woman	1979	—	2.00	4.00
❑ Capitol 4761	Lover and Friend/Return to Forever	1979	—	2.00	4.00
❑ Capitol 4902	Here We Go/Return to Forever	1980	—	2.00	4.00
❑ Capitol 4955	Give Me Time/Island in the Sun	1980	—	2.00	4.00
❑ Chess 1980	Lonely Girl/You Gave Me Soul	1966	2.50	5.00	10.00
—As "Andrea Davis"					
❑ Epic 11139	Every Time He Comes Around/Reasons	1974	—	2.50	5.00
❑ Epic 50020	Edge of a Dream/Seeing You This Way	1974	—	2.50	5.00
❑ Epic 50057	Lovin' You/Edge of a Dream	1974	—	2.50	5.00
❑ Epic 50128	Don't Let Anyone Bring You Down/Inside My Love	1975	—	2.50	5.00
❑ Epic 50155	When It Comes Down To It/Minnie's Lament	1975	—	2.50	5.00
❑ Epic 50166	Simple Things/Minnie's Lament	1975	—	2.50	5.00
❑ Epic 50190	Adventures in Paradise/When It Comes Down To It	1976	—	2.50	5.00
❑ Epic 50337	Stick Together (Part One)/Stick Together (Part Two)	1977	—	2.50	5.00
❑ Epic 50351	Young, Willing and Able/Stick Together	1977	—	2.50	5.00
❑ Epic 50394	Wouldn't Matter Where You Are	1977	—	2.50	5.00
❑ Epic 50427	How Could I Love You More/Young, Willing and Able	1977	—	2.50	5.00
❑ GRT 42	Oh! By the Way/Le Fleur	1972	—	3.00	6.00
Albums					
❑ Accord SN-7205	Wistful Memories	1981	2.50	5.00	10.00
❑ Capitol SO-11936	Minnie	1979	2.50	5.00	10.00
❑ Capitol SN-12004	Perfect Angel	1979	2.50	5.00	10.00
—Reissue of Epic 32561					
❑ Capitol SN-12005	Adventures in Paradise	1979	2.50	5.00	10.00
—Reissue of Epic 33454					
❑ Capitol SN-12006	Stay in Love	1979	2.50	5.00	10.00
—Reissue of Epic 34191					
❑ Capitol SOO-12097	Love Lives Forever	1980	2.50	5.00	10.00
❑ Capitol ST-12189	The Best of Minnie Riperton	1981	2.50	5.00	10.00
❑ Capitol SN-16145	Perfect Angel	1980	2.00	4.00	8.00
—Budget-line reissue					
❑ Capitol SN-16146	Adventures in Paradise	1980	2.00	4.00	8.00
—Budget-line reissue					
❑ Capitol SN-16147	Stay in Love	1980	2.00	4.00	8.00
—Budget-line reissue					
❑ Epic KE 32561	Perfect Angel	1974	3.00	6.00	12.00
❑ Epic PE 33454	Adventures in Paradise	1975	3.00	6.00	12.00
❑ Epic PE 34191	Stay in Love	1977	3.00	6.00	12.00
❑ GRT 30001	Come To My Garden	1970	3.75	7.50	15.00
❑ Janus 7011	Come To My Garden	1974	3.00	6.00	12.00
—Reissue of GRT LP					
RIVERS, JOHNNY					
45s					
❑ Atlantic 3011	Sitting in Limbo/Artists and Poets	1974	—	2.50	5.00
❑ Atlantic 3028	Six Days on the Road/Artists and Poets	1974	—	2.50	5.00
❑ Atlantic 3230	John Lee Hooker '74/Get It Up for Love	1974	—	2.50	5.00
❑ Big Tree 16094	Swayin' to the Music (Slow Dancin')/Outside Help	1977	—	2.00	4.00
❑ Big Tree 16106	Curious Mind (Um, Um, Um, Um, Um, Um)/Ashes and Sand	1977	—	2.00	4.00
❑ Capitol 4850	Long Black Veil/This Could Be the One	1962	3.75	7.50	15.00
❑ Capitol 4913	If You Want It, I've Got It/My Heart Is In Your Hands	1963	3.75	7.50	15.00
❑ Capitol 5232	Long Black Veil/Don't Look Now	1964	3.75	7.50	15.00
❑ Chancellor 1070	I Get So Doggone Lonesome/Knock Three Times	1961	5.00	10.00	20.00
❑ Chancellor 1108	To Be Loved/Too Good to Last	1962	5.00	10.00	20.00
❑ Coral 62425	That's My Baby/Your First and Last Love	1964	3.75	7.50	15.00
❑ Cub 9047	Everyday/Darling Talk to Me	1959	6.25	12.50	25.00
❑ Cub 9058	Answer Me My Love/The Customary Thing	1960	5.00	10.00	20.00
❑ Dee Dee 239	The White Cliffs of Dover/Your First and Last Love	1959	5.00	10.00	20.00
❑ Epic 50121	Help Me Rhonda/New Lovers and Old Friends	1975	—	2.50	5.00
—A-side features Brian Wilson on backing vocals					
❑ Epic 50150	Can I Change My Mind/John Lee Hooker	1975	—	2.00	4.00
❑ Epic 50208	Welcome Home/Outside Help	1976	—	2.00	4.00
❑ Epic 50248	Linda Lue/Outside Help	1976	—	2.00	4.00
❑ Era 3037	Call Me/Andersonville	1961	5.00	10.00	20.00
❑ Gone 5026	Baby Come Back/Long Long Walk	1958	10.00	20.00	40.00
❑ Guyden 2003	You're the One/A Hole in the Ground	1958	6.25	12.50	25.00
❑ Guyden 2110	You're the One/A Hole in the Ground	1964	3.75	7.50	15.00
❑ Imperial 66032	Memphis/It Wouldn't Happen with Me	1964	3.00	6.00	12.00
❑ Imperial 66056	Maybelline/Walk Myself On Home	1964	2.50	5.00	10.00
❑ Imperial 66075	Mountain of Love/Moody River	1964	2.50	5.00	10.00
❑ Imperial 66087	Midnight Special/Cupid	1965	2.50	5.00	10.00
❑ Imperial 66112	Seventh Son/Unsquare Dance	1965	2.50	5.00	10.00
❑ Imperial 66133	Where Have All the Flowers Gone/Love Me While You Can	1965	2.50	5.00	10.00
❑ Imperial 66144	Under Your Spell Again/Long Time Man	1965	2.50	5.00	10.00
❑ Imperial 66159	Secret Agent Man/You Dig	1966	3.00	6.00	12.00
❑ Imperial 66175	(I Washed My Hands In) Muddy Water/Roogalator	1966	2.50	5.00	10.00
❑ Imperial 66205	Poor Side of Town/A Man Can Cry	1966	3.00	6.00	12.00
❑ Imperial 66227	Baby I Need Your Lovin'/Gettin' Ready for Tomorrow	1967	2.50	5.00	10.00
❑ Imperial 66244	The Tracks of My Tears/Rewind Medley	1967	2.50	5.00	10.00
❑ Imperial 66267	Summer Rain/Memory of the Coming Good	1967	2.50	5.00	10.00
❑ Imperial 66286	Look To Your Soul/Something's Strange	1968	2.00	4.00	8.00

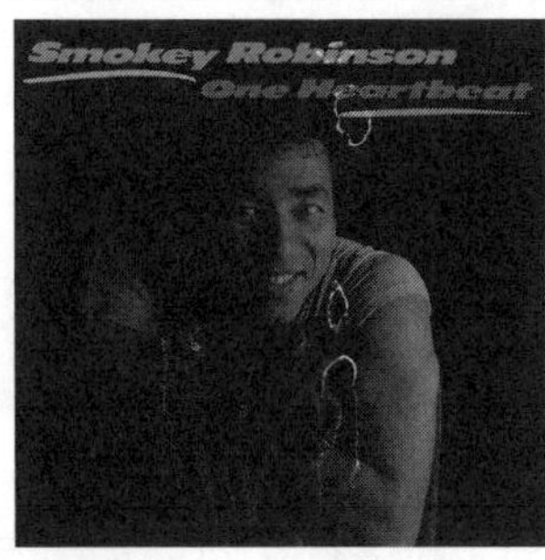

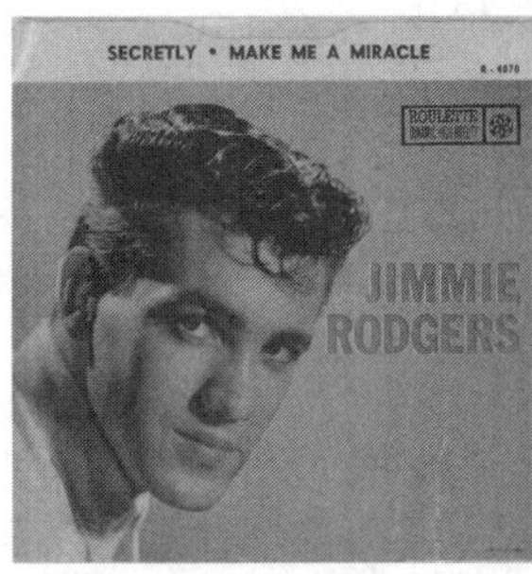

Number	Title (A Side/B Side)	Yr	VG	VG+	NM
❑ Imperial 66314	Everybody's Talkin'/The Way We Live	1968	—	—	—
—Unreleased					
❑ Imperial 66335	Right Relations/Better Life	1968	2.00	4.00	8.00
❑ Imperial 66360	These Are Not My People/Going Back to Big Sur	1969	2.00	4.00	8.00
❑ Imperial 66386	Muddy River/Resurrection	1969	2.00	4.00	8.00
❑ Imperial 66418	One Woman/Ode to John Lee	1969	2.00	4.00	8.00
❑ Imperial 66448	Into the Mystic/Jesus Is a Soul Man	1970	2.00	4.00	8.00
❑ Imperial 66453	Fire and Rain/Apple Tree	1970	2.00	4.00	8.00
❑ MCA 52502	Heartbreak Love/Why Can't We Communicate	1984	—	2.00	4.00
❑ MGM 13266	Answer Me, My Love/Customary Thing	1964	3.75	7.50	15.00
❑ Riveraire 1001	Don't Bug Me Baby/Haunting Black Eyes	1959	7.50	15.00	30.00
❑ Roulette 4565	Baby Come Back/Long Long Walk	1964	5.00	10.00	20.00
❑ RSO 1030	Romance (Give Me a Chance)/Don't Need No Other Now	1980	—	2.00	4.00
❑ RSO 1045	China/The Price	1980	—	2.00	4.00
❑ Soul City 007	Ashes and Sand/Outside Help	1977	—	2.50	5.00
❑ Soul City 008	Swayin' to the Music (Slow Dancin')/Outside Help	1977	2.00	4.00	8.00
❑ Soul City 010	Little White Lie/Be My Baby	1980	—	2.50	5.00
❑ Soul City 014	RSVP/The Price	1982	—	2.50	5.00
❑ Suede 1401	Little Girl/Two by Two	1957	25.00	50.00	100.00
—As "Johnny Ramistella"					
❑ United Artists 0101	Memphis/Secret Agent Man	1973	—	2.00	4.00
❑ United Artists 0102	Mountain of Love/Maybellene	1973	—	2.00	4.00
❑ United Artists 0103	Seventh Son/Midnight Special	1973	—	2.00	4.00
❑ United Artists 0104	Poor Side of Town/Baby I Need Your Lovin'	1973	—	2.00	4.00
❑ United Artists 0105	Summer Rain/The Tracks of My Tears	1973	—	2.00	4.00
—0101 through 0105 are "Silver Spotlight Series" reissues					
❑ United Artists XW198	Blue Suede Shoes/Stories to a Child	1973	—	2.50	5.00
❑ United Artists XW226	Searchin'-So Fine/New York City Dues	1973	—	2.50	5.00
❑ United Artists XW310	I'll Feel a Whole Lot Better/Over the Line	1973	—	2.50	5.00
❑ United Artists XW522	Rockin' Pneumonia-Boogie Woogie Flu/Blue Suede Shoes	1974	—	2.00	4.00
—Reissue					
❑ United Artists XW523	Where Have All the Flowers Gone/(I Washed My Hands in) Muddy Water	1974	—	2.00	4.00
—Reissue					
❑ United Artists 741	Oh What a Kiss/Knock Three Times	1964	3.00	6.00	12.00
❑ United Artists 769	Dream Doll/To Be Loved	1964	3.00	6.00	12.00
❑ United Artists 50778	Sea Cruise/Our Lady of the Well	1971	—	3.00	6.00
❑ United Artists 50822	Think His Name/Permanent Change	1971	—	3.00	6.00
❑ United Artists 50948	On the Borderline/Come Home America	1972	—	2.50	5.00
❑ United Artists 50960	Rockin' Pneumonia-Boogie Woogie Flu/Come Home America	1972	—	3.00	6.00
—On most pressings, the intro of the A-side lasts about 35 seconds					
Albums					
❑ Atlantic SD 7301	The Road	1974	3.00	6.00	12.00
❑ Big Tree BT 76004	Outside Help	1977	3.00	6.00	12.00
❑ Capitol ST 2161 [S]	The Sensational Johnny Rivers	1964	6.25	12.50	25.00
❑ Capitol T 2161 [M]	The Sensational Johnny Rivers	1964	5.00	10.00	20.00
❑ Columbia FE 38429	Not a Through Street	1983	2.50	5.00	10.00
❑ Epic PE 33681	New Lovers and Old Friends	1975	3.00	6.00	12.00
❑ Imperial LP-9264 [M]	Johnny Rivers at the Whiskey A-Go-Go	1964	5.00	10.00	20.00
—Black label with pink and white at left					
❑ Imperial LP-9274 [M]	Here We A-Go-Go Again!	1964	5.00	10.00	20.00
—Black label with pink and white at left					
❑ Imperial LP-9280 [M]	Johnny Rivers In Action!	1965	5.00	10.00	20.00
—Black label with pink and white at left					
❑ Imperial LP-9284 [M]	Meanwhile Back at the Whiskey a-Go-Go	1965	5.00	10.00	20.00
—Black label with pink and white at left					
❑ Imperial LP-9293 [M]	Johnny Rivers Rocks the Folk	1965	5.00	10.00	20.00
—Black label with pink and white at left					
❑ Imperial LP-9307 [M]	...And I Know You Wanna Dance	1966	5.00	10.00	20.00
—Black label with pink and white at left					
❑ Imperial LP-9324 [M]	Johnny Rivers' Golden Hits	1966	3.75	7.50	15.00
❑ Imperial LP-9334 [M]	Changes	1966	3.75	7.50	15.00
❑ Imperial LP-9341 [M]	Rewind	1967	5.00	10.00	20.00
❑ Imperial LP-9372 [M]	Realization	1968	10.00	20.00	40.00
❑ Imperial LP-12264 [S]	Johnny Rivers at the Whiskey A-Go-Go	1964	6.25	12.50	25.00
—Black label with pink and white at left					

Number	Title (A Side/B Side)	Yr	VG	VG+	NM
❑ Imperial LP-12274 [S]	Here We A-Go-Go Again!	1964	6.25	12.50	25.00
—Black label with pink and white at left					
❑ Imperial LP-12280 [S]	Johnny Rivers In Action!	1965	6.25	12.50	25.00
—Black label with pink and white at left					
❑ Imperial LP-12284 [S]	Meanwhile Back at the Whiskey a-Go-Go	1965	6.25	12.50	25.00
—Black label with pink and white at left					
❑ Imperial LP-12293 [S]	Johnny Rivers Rocks the Folk	1965	6.25	12.50	25.00
—Black label with pink and white at left					
❑ Imperial LP-12307 [S]	…And I Know You Wanna Dance	1966	6.25	12.50	25.00
—Black label with pink and white at left					
❑ Imperial LP-12324 [S]	Johnny Rivers' Golden Hits	1966	5.00	10.00	20.00
❑ Imperial LP-12341 [S]	Rewind	1967	5.00	10.00	20.00
❑ Imperial LP-12372 [S]	Realization	1968	5.00	10.00	20.00
❑ Imperial LP-12427	A Touch of Gold	1969	5.00	10.00	20.00
❑ Imperial LP-16001	Slim Slo Slider	1970	5.00	10.00	20.00
❑ Liberty LN-10120	The Best of Johnny Rivers	1981	2.00	4.00	8.00
❑ Liberty LN-10121	Changes	1981	2.00	4.00	8.00
—Budget-line reissue					
❑ Liberty LN-10154	Blue Suede Shoes	1981	2.00	4.00	8.00
—Budget-line reissue					
❑ Liberty LO-12324	Johnny Rivers' Golden Hits	198?	2.00	4.00	8.00
—Budget-line reissue					
❑ Liberty LW-12427	A Touch of Gold	198?	2.00	4.00	8.00
—Budget-line reissue					
❑ MCA 917	Greatest Hits	1985	2.50	5.00	10.00
❑ Pickwick PC-3022 [M]	Johnny Rivers	196?	3.75	7.50	15.00
❑ Pickwick SPC-3022 [R]	Johnny Rivers	196?	3.00	6.00	12.00
—First pressing covers have no "electronically enhanced for STEREO" at upper right					
❑ RSO RS-1-3082	Borrowed Time	1980	2.50	5.00	10.00
❑ Sears SPS-417	Mr. Teenage	196?	6.25	12.50	25.00
❑ Sears SPS-487	Groovin'	1968	6.25	12.50	25.00
❑ Sunset SUM-1157 [M]	Whiskey A-Go-Go Revisited	1967	3.00	6.00	12.00
❑ Sunset SUS-5157 [S]	Whiskey A-Go-Go Revisited	1967	2.50	5.00	10.00
❑ Sunset SUS-5251	The Early Years	1969	2.50	5.00	10.00
❑ Unart M-20007 [M]	The Great Johnny Rivers	1967	3.00	6.00	12.00
❑ Unart S-21007 [S]	The Great Johnny Rivers	1967	3.00	6.00	12.00
❑ United Artists UA-LA075-F	Blue Suede Shoes	1973	3.00	6.00	12.00
❑ United Artists USX-93 [(2)]	Johnny Rivers Superpak	1971	5.00	10.00	20.00
❑ United Artists UA-LA253-G	The Very Best of Johnny Rivers	1974	3.00	6.00	12.00
❑ United Artists UA-LA387-E	The Very Best of Johnny Rivers	1975	3.00	6.00	12.00
❑ United Artists UA-LA486-G	Wild Night	1976	3.00	6.00	12.00
❑ United Artists UAL-3386 [M]	Go, Johnny, Go	1964	5.00	10.00	20.00
❑ United Artists UAS-5532	Home Grown	1971	3.75	7.50	15.00
❑ United Artists UAS-5650	L.A. Reggae	1972	3.75	7.50	15.00
❑ United Artists UAS-6386 [S]	Go, Johnny, Go	1964	6.25	12.50	25.00

RIVIERAS, THE (2)

45s

Number	Title (A Side/B Side)	Yr	VG	VG+	NM
❑ Lana 136	California Sun/H.B. Goose Step	196?	2.00	4.00	8.00
—Oldies reissue					
❑ Riviera 1401	California Sun/H.B. Goose Step	1964	5.00	10.00	20.00
❑ Riviera 1401	California Sun/Played On	1964	10.00	20.00	40.00
—Possibly as few as 1,000 were pressed with this B-side					
❑ Riviera 1402	Little Donna/Let's Have a Party	1964	3.75	7.50	15.00
❑ Riviera 1403	Rockin' Robin/Battle Line	1964	3.75	7.50	15.00
❑ Riviera 1405	Whole Lotta Shakin'/Rip It Up	1965	3.75	7.50	15.00
❑ Riviera 1405	Whole Lotta Shakin'/Lakeview Lane	1965	5.00	10.00	20.00
❑ Riviera 1406	Let's Go to Hawaii/Lakeview Lane	1965	3.75	7.50	15.00
❑ Riviera 1407	Somebody Asked Me/Somebody New	1965	3.75	7.50	15.00
—Credited to the Rivieras, but actually by Bobby Whiteside					
❑ Riviera 1409	Bug Juice/Never Feel the Pain	1965	5.00	10.00	20.00

Albums

Number	Title (A Side/B Side)	Yr	VG	VG+	NM
❑ Riviera 701 [M]	Campus Party	1964	62.50	125.00	250.00
❑ U.S.A. 102 [M]	Let's Have a Party	1964	37.50	75.00	150.00

ROBBINS, MARTY

45s

Number	Title (A Side/B Side)	Yr	VG	VG+	NM
❑ Columbia 02444	Jumper Cable Man/Good Hearted Woman	1981	—	2.00	4.00
❑ Columbia 02575	Teardrops on My Heart/Honeycomb	1981	—	2.00	4.00
❑ Columbia 02854	Lover, Lover/Some Memories Just Won't Die	1982	—	2.00	4.00
❑ Columbia 03236	Tie Your Dream to Mine/That's All She Wrote	1982	—	2.00	4.00
❑ Columbia 03789	Change of Heart/Devil in a Cowboy Hat	1983	—	2.00	4.00
❑ Columbia 03927	Baby That's Love/What If I Said I Love You	1983	—	2.00	4.00
❑ Columbia 10305	El Paso City/When I'm Gone	1976	—	2.50	5.00
❑ Columbia 10396	Among My Souvenirs/She's Just a Drifter	1976	—	2.50	5.00
❑ Columbia 10472	Adios Amigo/Helen	1977	—	2.50	5.00
❑ Columbia 10536	I Don't Know Why (I Just Do)/Inspiration for a Song	1977	—	2.50	5.00
❑ Columbia 10629	Don't Let Me Touch You/Tomorrow, Tomorrow, Tomorrow	1977	—	2.50	5.00
❑ Columbia 10673	Return to Me/More Than Anything, I Miss You	1978	—	2.50	5.00
❑ Columbia 10821	Please Don't Play a Love Song/Jenny	1978	—	2.50	5.00
❑ Columbia 10905	Touch Me with Magic/Confused and Lonely	1979	—	2.50	5.00
❑ Columbia 11016	All Around Cowboy/The Dreamer	1979	—	2.50	5.00
❑ Columbia 11102	Buenos Dias Argentina/Ballad of a Small Man	1979	—	2.50	5.00
❑ Columbia 11240	She's Made of Faith/Misery in My Soul	1980	—	2.00	4.00
❑ Columbia 11291	One Man's Trash (Is Another Man's Treasure)/ I Can't Wait Until Tomorrow	1980	—	2.00	4.00
❑ Columbia 11372	An Occasional Rose/Holding On to You	1980	—	2.00	4.00

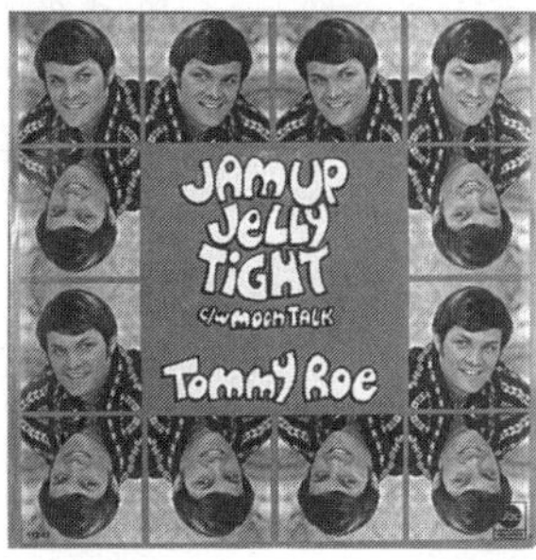

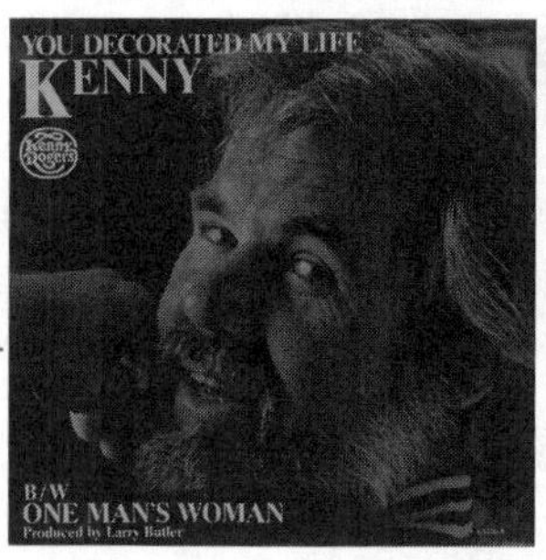

Number	Title (A Side/B Side)	Yr	VG	VG+	NM
❑ Columbia 11425	Completely Out of Love/Another Cup of Coffee	1981	—	2.00	4.00
❑ Columbia 20925	Tomorrow You'll Be Gone/Love Me or Leave Me Alone	1952	7.50	15.00	30.00
❑ Columbia 20965	Crying 'Cause I Love You/I Wish Somebody Loved Me	1952	7.50	15.00	30.00
❑ Columbia 21022	I'll Go On Alone/You're Breaking My Heart	1952	7.50	15.00	30.00
❑ Columbia 21032 —*Unreleased*	My Isle of Golden Dreams/Sweet Hawaiian Dream	1952	—	—	—
❑ Columbia 21075	I Couldn't Keep from Crying/After You Leave	1953	7.50	15.00	30.00
❑ Columbia 21111	A Castle in the Sky/A Half-Way Chance with You	1953	7.50	15.00	30.00
❑ Columbia 21145	Sing Me Something Sentimental/At the End of Long, Lonely Days	1953	7.50	15.00	30.00
❑ Columbia 21172	Blesserd Jesus Should I Fall Don't Let Me Lay/ Kneel and Let the Lord Take Your Load	1953	7.50	15.00	30.00
❑ Columbia 21176	Don't Make Me Ashamed/It's a Long, Long Ride	1953	7.50	15.00	30.00
❑ Columbia 21213	My Isle of Golden Dreams/Aloha Oe	1954	7.50	15.00	30.00
❑ Columbia 21246	Pretty Words/Your Heart's Turn to Break	1954	7.50	15.00	30.00
❑ Columbia 21291	Call Me Up (And I'll Come Calling on You)/I'm Too Big to Cry	1954	7.50	15.00	30.00
❑ Columbia 21324	Time Goes By/It's a Pity What Money Can Do	1954	7.50	15.00	30.00
❑ Columbia 21351	That's All Right/Gossip	1955	12.50	25.00	50.00
❑ Columbia 21352	God Understands/Have Thine Own Way, Lord	1955	6.25	12.50	25.00
❑ Columbia 21388	Daddy Loves You/Pray for Me, Mother of Mine	1955	6.25	12.50	25.00
❑ Columbia 21414	It Looks Like I'm Just in the Way/I'll Love You Till the Day I Die	1955	6.25	12.50	25.00
❑ Columbia 21446	Maybellene/This Broken Heart of Mine	1955	12.50	25.00	50.00
❑ Columbia 21461	Pretty Mama/Don't Let Me Hang Around	1955	12.50	25.00	50.00
❑ Columbia 21477	Tennessee Toddy/Mean Mama Blues	1955	12.50	25.00	50.00
❑ Columbia 21508	Singing the Blues/I Can't Quit (I've Gone Too Far)	1956	10.00	20.00	40.00
❑ Columbia 21525 —*With Lee Emerson*	I'll Know You're Gone/How Long Will It Be	1956	6.25	12.50	25.00
❑ Columbia 21545	Singing the Blues/I Can't Quit (I've Gone Too Far)	1956	7.50	15.00	30.00
❑ Columbia 40679	Long Tall Sally/Mr. Teardrop	1956	12.50	25.00	50.00
❑ Columbia 40706	Respectfully Miss Brooks/You Don't Owe Me a Thing	1956	12.50	25.00	50.00
❑ Columbia 40815	Knee Deep in the Blues/The Same Two Lips	1957	6.25	12.50	25.00
❑ Columbia 40864	A White Sport Coat (And a Pink Carnation)/Grown Up Tears	1957	6.25	12.50	25.00
❑ Columbia 40868 —*With Lee Emerson*	I Cried Like a Baby/Where D'Ja Go	1957	6.25	12.50	25.00
❑ Columbia 40969	Please Don't Blame Me/Teen-Age Dream	1957	6.25	12.50	25.00
❑ Columbia 41013	The Story of My Life/Once-a-Week Date	1957	6.25	12.50	25.00
❑ Columbia 41143	Just Married/Stairway of Love	1958	5.00	10.00	20.00
❑ Columbia 41208	She Was Only Seventeen (He Was One Year More)/ Sittin' in a Tree House	1958	5.00	10.00	20.00
❑ Columbia 41282	Ain't I the Lucky One/The Last Time I Saw My Heart	1958	5.00	10.00	20.00
❑ Columbia 41325	The Hanging Tree/The Blues, Country Style	1959	5.00	10.00	20.00
❑ Columbia 41408	Cap and Gown/Last Night About This Time	1959	5.00	10.00	20.00
❑ Columbia 41511 [M]	El Paso/Running Gun	1959	5.00	10.00	20.00
❑ Columbia 41589 [M]	Big Iron/Saddle Tramp	1960	3.75	7.50	15.00
❑ Columbia 41686	Is There Any Chance/I Told My Heart	1960	3.75	7.50	15.00
❑ Columbia 41766 —*Unreleased*	Don't Worry/A Time and a Place for Everything	1960	—	—	—
❑ Columbia 41771 [M]	Five Brothers/Ride, Cowboy, Ride	1960	3.75	7.50	15.00
❑ Columbia 41809 [M]	Ballad of the Alamo/A Time and a Place for Everything	1960	3.75	7.50	15.00
❑ Columbia 41922	Don't Worry/Like All the Other Times	1961	3.75	7.50	15.00
❑ Columbia 42008	Jimmy Martinez/Ghost Train	1961	3.75	7.50	15.00
❑ Columbia 42065	It's Your World/You Told Me So	1961	3.75	7.50	15.00
❑ Columbia 42246	I Told the Brook/Sometimes I'm Tempted	1961	3.75	7.50	15.00
❑ Columbia 42375	Love Can't Wait/Too Far Gone	1962	3.75	7.50	15.00
❑ Columbia 42486	Devil Woman/April Fool's Day	1962	3.75	7.50	15.00
❑ Columbia 42614	Ruby Ann/Won't You Forgive	1962	3.75	7.50	15.00
❑ Columbia 42672	Hawaii's Calling Me/Ka-Lu-A	1963	3.00	6.00	12.00
❑ Columbia 42701	Cigarettes and Coffee Blues/Teenager's Dad	1963	3.00	6.00	12.00
❑ Columbia 42781	No Sign of Loneliness Here/I'm Not Ready Yet	1963	3.00	6.00	12.00
❑ Columbia 42831	Not So Long Ago/I Hope You Learn a Lot	1963	3.00	6.00	12.00
❑ Columbia 42890	Begging to You/Over High Mountain	1963	3.00	6.00	12.00
❑ Columbia 42968	Girl from Spanish Town/Kingston Girl	1964	2.50	5.00	10.00
❑ Columbia 43049	The Cowboy in the Continental Suit/Man Walks Among Us	1964	2.50	5.00	10.00
❑ Columbia 43134	One of These Days/Up in the Air	1964	2.50	5.00	10.00
❑ Columbia 43196	I Eish-Tay-Mah-Su (I Love You)/A Whole Lot Easier	1964	2.50	5.00	10.00
❑ Columbia 43258	Ribbon of Darkness/Little Robin	1965	2.50	5.00	10.00
❑ Columbia 43377	Old Red/Matilda	1965	2.00	4.00	8.00
❑ Columbia 43428	While You're Dancing/Lonely Too Long	1965	2.00	4.00	8.00

Number	Title (A Side/B Side)	Yr	VG	VG+	NM
❑ Columbia 43500	Count Me Out/Private Wilson White	1965	2.00	4.00	8.00
❑ Columbia 43651	Ain't I Right/My Own Native Land	1966	—	—	—
—Unreleased					
❑ Columbia 43680	The Shoe Goes On the Other Foot Tonight/ It Kind of Reminds Me of You	1966	2.00	4.00	8.00
❑ Columbia 43845	No Tears Milady/Fly Butterfly Fly	1966	2.00	4.00	8.00
❑ Columbia 43870	Mr. Shorty/Tall Handsome Strangers	1966	2.00	4.00	8.00
❑ Columbia 44128	Tonight Carmen/Waiting in Reno	1967	—	3.00	6.00
❑ Columbia 44271	Gardenias in Her Hair/In the Valley of the Rio Grande	1967	—	3.00	6.00
❑ Columbia 44509	Love Is In the Air/I've Been Leaving Everyday	1968	—	3.00	6.00
❑ Columbia 44633	I Walk Alone/Lily of the Valley	1968	—	3.00	6.00
❑ Columbia 44641	It Finally Happened/Big Mouthin' Around	1968	—	3.00	6.00
—By "Marty Robbins Jr. and Sr."					
❑ Columbia 44739	It's a Sin/I Feel Another Heartache Coming On	1969	—	2.50	5.00
❑ Columbia 44895	I Can't Say Goodbye/Hello Daily News	1969	—	2.50	5.00
❑ Columbia 44968	Girl from Spanish Town/Kingston Girl	1969	2.00	4.00	8.00
❑ Columbia 45024	Camelia/Virginia	1969	—	2.50	5.00
❑ Columbia 45091	My Woman, My Woman, My Wife/Martha Ellen Jenkins	1970	—	2.50	5.00
❑ Columbia 45215	Jolie Girl/The City	1970	—	2.50	5.00
❑ Columbia 45273	Padre/At Times	1970	—	3.00	6.00
❑ Columbia 45346	Little Spot in Heaven/Wait a Little Longer Please, Jesus	1971	—	3.00	6.00
❑ Columbia 45377	The Chair/Seventeen Years	1971	—	2.50	5.00
❑ Columbia 45442	Early Morning Sunshine/Another Day Has Gone By	1971	—	2.50	5.00
❑ Columbia 45520	The Best Part of Living/Gone with the Wind	1971	—	2.50	5.00
❑ Columbia 45668	I've Got a Woman's Love/A Little Spot in Heaven	1972	—	2.50	5.00
❑ Columbia 45775	Laura (What's He Got That I Ain't Got)/ It Kind of Reminds Me of You	1973	—	2.50	5.00
❑ Decca 33006	This Much a Man/Guess I'll Stand Here Looking Dumb	1972	—	3.50	7.00
❑ MCA 40012	Franklin, Tennessee/Walking Piece of Heaven	1973	—	2.50	5.00
❑ MCA 40067	A Man and a Train/Las Vegas, Nevada	1973	—	2.50	5.00
❑ MCA 40134	Love Me/Crawling on My Knees	1973	—	2.50	5.00
❑ MCA 40172	I'm Wanting To/Twentieth Century Drifter	1973	—	2.50	5.00
❑ MCA 40236	Don't You Think/I Couldn't Believe It Was True	1974	—	2.50	5.00
❑ MCA 40296	Two-Gun Daddy/Queen of the Big Rodeo	1974	—	2.50	5.00
❑ MCA 40342	Life/It Takes Faith	1974	—	2.50	5.00
❑ MCA 40425	These Are My Souvenirs/Shotgun Rider	1975	—	2.50	5.00
❑ MCA 52197	Two Gun Daddy/Life	1983	—	2.50	5.00
❑ Warner Bros. 29847	Honkytonk Man/Shotgun Rag	1982	—	2.00	4.00
—B-side by Johnny Gimble and the Texas Swing Band					
Albums					
❑ Artco 110	The Best of Marty Robbins	1973	10.00	20.00	40.00
❑ CBS Special Products P 17730	The Great Love Songs	1984	2.50	5.00	10.00
❑ Columbia GP 15 [(2)]	Marty's Country	1969	6.25	12.50	25.00
❑ Columbia CL 976 [M]	The Song of Robbins	1957	25.00	50.00	100.00
—Red and black label with six "eye" logos					
❑ Columbia CL 1087 [M]	Song of the Islands	1957	30.00	60.00	120.00
—Red and black label with six "eye" logos					
❑ Columbia CL 1189 [M]	Marty Robbins	1958	20.00	40.00	80.00
—Red and black label with six "eye" logos					
❑ Columbia CL 1325 [M]	Marty's Greatest Hits	1959	20.00	40.00	80.00
—Red and black label with six "eye" logos					
❑ Columbia CL 1349 [M]	Gunfighter Ballads and Trail Songs	1959	7.50	15.00	30.00
—Red and black label with six "eye" logos					
❑ Columbia CL 1481 [M]	More Gunfighter Ballads and Trail Songs	1960	7.50	15.00	30.00
—Red and black label with six "eye" logos					
❑ Columbia CL 1635 [M]	More Greatest Hits	1961	6.25	12.50	25.00
—Red and black label with six "eye" logos					
❑ Columbia CL 1666 [M]	Just a Little Sentimental	1961	6.25	12.50	25.00
—Red and black label with six "eye" logos					
❑ Columbia CL 1801 [M]	Marty After Midnight	1962	12.50	25.00	50.00
—Red and black label with six "eye" logos					
❑ Columbia CL 1855 [M]	Portrait of Marty	1962	10.00	20.00	40.00
❑ Columbia CL 1918 [M]	Devil Woman	1962	6.25	12.50	25.00
—Red label with "Guaranteed High Fidelity"					
❑ Columbia CL 2040 [M]	Hawaii's Calling Me	1963	6.25	12.50	25.00
—Red label with "Guaranteed High Fidelity"					
❑ Columbia CL 2072 [M]	Return of the Gunfighter	1963	5.00	10.00	20.00
—Red label with "Guaranteed High Fidelity"					
❑ Columbia CL 2176 [M]	Island Woman	1964	7.50	15.00	30.00
—Red label with "Guaranteed High Fidelity"					
❑ Columbia CL 2220 [M]	R.F.D.	1964	5.00	10.00	20.00
—Red label with "Guaranteed High Fidelity"					
❑ Columbia CL 2304 [M]	Turn the Lights Down Low	1965	6.25	12.50	25.00
—Red label with "Guaranteed High Fidelity"					
❑ Columbia CL 2448 [M]	What God Has Done	1966	3.75	7.50	15.00
❑ Columbia CL 2527 [M]	The Drifter	1966	3.75	7.50	15.00
❑ Columbia CL 2601 [10]	Rock 'N Roll 'N Robbins	1956	250.00	500.00	1000.
❑ Columbia CL 2645 [M]	My Kind of Country	1967	6.25	12.50	25.00
❑ Columbia CL 2725 [M]	Tonight Carmen	1967	7.50	15.00	30.00
❑ Columbia CL 2735 [M]	Christmas with Marty Robbins	1967	12.50	25.00	50.00
❑ Columbia CL 2817 [M]	By the Time I Get to Phoenix	1968	15.00	30.00	60.00
❑ Columbia CS 8158 [S]	Gunfighter Ballads and Trail Songs	1959	10.00	20.00	40.00
—Red and black label with six "eye" logos					
❑ Columbia CS 8272 [S]	More Gunfighter Ballads and Trail Songs	1960	10.00	20.00	40.00
—Red and black label with six "eye" logos					
❑ Columbia CS 8435 [S]	More Greatest Hits	1961	7.50	15.00	30.00
—Red and black label with six "eye" logos					

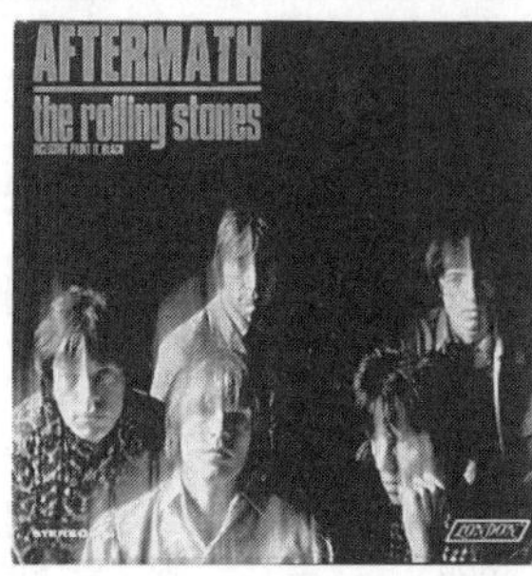

Number	Title (A Side/B Side)	Yr	VG	VG+	NM
❑ Columbia CS 8466 [S]	Just a Little Sentimental	1961	7.50	15.00	30.00
—Red and black label with six "eye" logos					
❑ Columbia CS 8601 [S]	Marty After Midnight	1962	20.00	40.00	80.00
—Red and black label with six "eye" logos					
❑ Columbia CS 8639 [P]	Marty's Greatest Hits	1962	7.50	15.00	30.00
—Red label with "360 Sound Stereo" in black					
❑ Columbia CS 8655 [S]	Portrait of Marty	1962	12.50	25.00	50.00
❑ Columbia CS 8718 [S]	Devil Woman	1962	7.50	15.00	30.00
—Red label with "360 Sound Stereo" in black					
❑ Columbia CS 8840 [S]	Hawaii's Calling Me	1963	7.50	15.00	30.00
—Red label with "360 Sound Stereo" in black					
❑ Columbia CS 8872 [S]	Return of the Gunfighter	1963	6.25	12.50	25.00
—Red label with "360 Sound Stereo" in black					
❑ Columbia CS 8976 [S]	Island Woman	1964	10.00	20.00	40.00
—Red label with "360 Sound Stereo" in black					
❑ Columbia CS 9020 [S]	R.F.D.	1964	6.25	12.50	25.00
—Red label with "360 Sound Stereo" in black					
❑ Columbia CS 9104 [S]	Turn the Lights Down Low	1965	7.50	15.00	30.00
—Red label with "360 Sound Stereo" in black					
❑ Columbia CS 9248 [S]	What God Has Done	1966	5.00	10.00	20.00
—Red "360 Sound" label					
❑ Columbia CS 9327 [S]	The Drifter	1966	5.00	10.00	20.00
—Red "360 Sound" label					
❑ Columbia CS 9421 [R]	The Song of Robbins	1967	3.75	7.50	15.00
—Red "360 Sound" label					
❑ Columbia CS 9425 [R]	Song of the Islands	1967	3.75	7.50	15.00
❑ Columbia CS 9445 [S]	My Kind of Country	1967	5.00	10.00	20.00
❑ Columbia CS 9525 [S]	Tonight Carmen	1967	5.00	10.00	20.00
—Red "360 Sound" label					
❑ Columbia CS 9535 [S]	Christmas with Marty Robbins	1967	7.50	15.00	30.00
❑ Columbia CS 9617 [S]	By the Time I Get to Phoenix	1968	5.00	10.00	20.00
❑ Columbia CS 9725	I Walk Alone	1968	5.00	10.00	20.00
—Red "360 Sound" label					
❑ Columbia CS 9811	It's a Sin	1969	5.00	10.00	20.00
—Red "360 Sound" label					
❑ Columbia CS 9978	My Woman, My Woman, My Wife	1970	5.00	10.00	20.00
—Red "360 Sound" label					
❑ Columbia PC 30316	El Paso	198?	2.00	4.00	8.00
—Reissue of Harmony 30316					
❑ Columbia C 30571	Marty Robbins' Greatest Hits Vol. III	1971	3.75	7.50	15.00
❑ Columbia C 30816	Today	1971	3.75	7.50	15.00
❑ Columbia G 30881 [(2)]	The World of Marty Robbins	1971	5.00	10.00	20.00
❑ Columbia KC 31341	Bound for Old Mexico (Great Hits from South of the Border)	1973	3.75	7.50	15.00
❑ Columbia CG 31361 [(2)]	All Time Greatest Hits	1972	4.50	9.00	18.00
❑ Columbia KC 31628	I've Got a Woman's Love	1972	3.75	7.50	15.00
❑ Columbia KC 32586	Have I Told You Lately That I Love You	1974	3.75	7.50	15.00
❑ Columbia KC 33476	No Sign of Loneliness Here	1976	3.00	6.00	12.00
❑ Columbia CG 33630 [(2)]	Gunfighter Ballads and Trail Songs/My Woman, My Woman, My Wife	1976	3.75	7.50	15.00
❑ Columbia PC 34303	El Paso City	198?	2.00	4.00	8.00
—With bar code on cover					
❑ Columbia PC 34448	Adios Amigo	1977	3.00	6.00	12.00
—No bar code on cover					
❑ Columbia KC 35040	Don't Let Me Touch You	1977	3.00	6.00	12.00
❑ Columbia JC 35446	The Performer	1979	3.00	6.00	12.00
❑ Columbia KC 35629	Greatest Hits Vol. IV	1978	3.00	6.00	12.00
❑ Columbia JC 36085	All Around Cowboy	1979	3.00	6.00	12.00
❑ Columbia JC 36507	With Love	1980	3.00	6.00	12.00
❑ Columbia JC 36860	Everything I've Always Wanted	1981	3.00	6.00	12.00
❑ Columbia FC 37353	Encore	1981	3.00	6.00	12.00
❑ Columbia FC 37541	The Legend	1982	3.00	6.00	12.00
❑ Columbia FC 37995	Come Back to Me	1982	3.00	6.00	12.00
❑ Columbia FC 38309	Biggest Hits	1982	3.00	6.00	12.00
❑ Columbia FC 38603	Some Memories Just Won't Die	1983	3.00	6.00	12.00
❑ Columbia C2 38870 [(2)]	A Lifetime of Song 1951-1982	1983	3.75	7.50	15.00
❑ Columbia KC2 39575 [(2)]	Long, Long Ago	1984	3.75	7.50	15.00
❑ Decca DL 75389	This Much a Man	1972	3.75	7.50	15.00

Number	Title (A Side/B Side)	Yr	VG	VG+	NM
❑ Harmony HS 11338	Singing the Blues	1969	3.75	7.50	15.00
❑ Harmony HS 11409	The Story of My Life	1970	3.75	7.50	15.00
❑ Harmony KH 30316	El Paso	1971	3.00	6.00	12.00
❑ Harmony KH 31257	Marty Robbins Favorites	1972	3.00	6.00	12.00
❑ Harmony H 31258	Songs of the Islands	1972	5.00	10.00	20.00
❑ Harmony KH 32286	Streets of Laredo	1973	3.00	6.00	12.00
❑ MCA 61	This Much a Man	1973	3.00	6.00	12.00
—Reissue of Decca LP					
❑ MCA 342	Marty Robbins	1973	3.75	7.50	15.00
❑ MCA 421	Good'n Country	1974	3.75	7.50	15.00
❑ MCA 27060	20th Century Drifter	1983	3.75	7.50	15.00
—Reissue of older material					
❑ Time-Life STW-109	Country Music	1981	3.00	6.00	12.00
ROBINSON, SMOKEY					
45s					
❑ Columbia 07727	I Know You by Heart/Could I Have Your Autograph	1988	—	—	3.00
—With Dolly Parton					
❑ Motown 914	(It's the) Same Old Love/(Instrumental)	1990	—	2.00	4.00
❑ Motown 1877	Just to See Her/I'm Gonna Love You Like There's No Tomorrow	1987	—	—	3.00
❑ Motown 1897	One Heartbeat/Love Will Set You Free (Theme from Solarbabies)	1987	—	—	3.00
❑ Motown 1911	What's Too Much/I've Made Love to You a Thousand Times	1987	—	—	3.00
❑ Motown 1925	Love Don't Give No Reason/Hanging On by a Thread	1988	—	—	3.00
❑ SBK 07379	Double Good Everything/Guess What I Got for You	1991	—	2.00	4.00
❑ Tamla 1601	Tell Me Tomorrow (Part 1)/Tell Me Tomorrow (Part 2)	1982	—	2.00	4.00
❑ Tamla 1615	Old Fashioned Love/Destiny	1982	—	2.00	4.00
❑ Tamla 1630	Are You Still Here/Yes It's You Lady	1982	—	2.00	4.00
❑ Tamla 1655	I've Made Love to You a Thousand Times/Into Each Rain Some Life Must Fall	1983	—	2.00	4.00
❑ Tamla 1678	Touch the Sky/All My Life's a Lie	1983	—	2.00	4.00
❑ Tamla 1684	Blame It on Love/Even Tho'	1983	—	2.00	4.00
—With Barbara Mitchell					
❑ Tamla 1700	Don't Play Another Love Song/Wouldn't You Like to Know	1983	—	2.00	4.00
❑ Tamla 1735	And I Don't Love You/Dynamite	1984	—	2.00	4.00
❑ Tamla 1756	I Can't Find/Gimme What You Want	1984	—	2.00	4.00
❑ Tamla 1786	First Time on a Ferris Wheel/Train of Thought	1985	—	2.00	4.00
❑ Tamla 1828	Hold On to Your Love/Train of Thought	1985	—	2.00	4.00
❑ Tamla 1839	Sleepless Nights/Close Encounters of the First Kind	1986	—	2.00	4.00
❑ Tamla 1855	Girl I'm Standing There/Because of You (It's the Best It's Ever Been)	1986	—	2.00	4.00
❑ Tamla 1868	Love Will Set You Free (Theme from Solarbabies) (Parts 1 & 2)	1986	—	2.00	4.00
❑ Tamla 54233	Sweet Harmony/Want to Know My Mind	1973	—	2.50	5.00
❑ Tamla 54239	Baby Come Close/A Silent Partner in a Three-Way Love Affair	1973	—	2.50	5.00
❑ Tamla 54246	It's Her Turn to Live/Just My Soul Responding	1974	—	2.50	5.00
❑ Tamla 54250	Virgin Man/Fulfill Your Need	1974	—	2.50	5.00
❑ Tamla 54251	I Am, I Am/The Family Song	1974	—	2.50	5.00
❑ Tamla 54258	Baby That's Backatcha/Just Passing Through	1975	—	2.50	5.00
❑ Tamla 54261	The Agony and the Ecstasy/Wedding Song	1975	—	2.50	5.00
❑ Tamla 54265	Quiet Storm/Asleep on My Love	1975	—	2.50	5.00
❑ Tamla 54267	Open/Coincidentally	1976	—	2.50	5.00
❑ Tamla 54269	When You Came/Coincidentally	1976	3.00	6.00	12.00
—Released only in Canada					
❑ Tamla 54272	An Old Fashioned Man/(B-side unassigned)	1976	—	—	—
—Unreleased					
❑ Tamla 54276	An Old Fashioned Man/Just Passing Through	1976	—	2.50	5.00
❑ Tamla 54279	There Will Come a Day (I'm Gonna Happen to You)/Humming Song	1977	—	2.50	5.00
❑ Tamla 54284	Vitamin U/Holly	1977	—	2.50	5.00
❑ Tamla 54288	Theme from Big Time (Part 1)/Theme from Big Time (Part 2)	1977	—	2.50	5.00
❑ Tamla 54293	Daylight and Darkness/Why You Wanna See My Bad Side	1978	—	2.50	5.00
❑ Tamla 54296	I'm Loving You Softly/Shoe Soul	1978	—	2.50	5.00
❑ Tamla 54301	Get Ready/Ever Had a Dream	1979	—	2.00	4.00
❑ Tamla 54306	Cruisin'/Ever Had a Dream	1979	—	2.00	4.00
❑ Tamla 54311	Let Me Be the Clock/Travelin' Through	1980	—	2.00	4.00
❑ Tamla 54313	Heavy on Pride/I Love the Nearness of You	1980	—	2.00	4.00
❑ Tamla 54318	I Want to Be Your Love/Wine, Women and Song	1980	—	2.00	4.00
❑ Tamla 54321	Being with You/What's In Your Life for Me	1981	—	2.00	4.00
❑ Tamla 54325	Aquicontigo/Being with You (Aquicontigo)	1981	—	2.00	4.00
❑ Tamla 54327	You Are Forever/I Hear the Children Singing	1981	—	2.00	4.00
❑ Tamla 54332	Who's Sad/Food for Thought	1981	—	2.00	4.00
Albums					
❑ Motown M5-118V1	Motown Superstar Series, Vol. 18	1981	2.50	5.00	10.00
❑ Motown M5-134V1	Smokey	1981	2.00	4.00	8.00
—Reissue of Tamla 328					
❑ Motown M5-154V1	Deep in My Soul	1981	2.00	4.00	8.00
—Reissue of Tamla 350					
❑ Motown M5-168V1	Pure Smokey	1981	2.00	4.00	8.00
—Reissue of Tamla 331					
❑ Motown M5-197V1	A Quiet Storm	1981	2.00	4.00	8.00
—Reissue of Tamla 337					
❑ Motown 5267ML	Where There;s Smoke	1982	2.00	4.00	8.00
—Reissue of Tamla 366					
❑ Motown 5349ML	Being with You	1983	2.00	4.00	8.00
—Reissue of Tamla 375					
❑ Motown MOT-6226	One Heartbeat	1987	2.50	5.00	10.00
❑ Motown MOT-6268	Love, Smokey	1990	3.00	6.00	12.00
❑ Tamla T 328	Smokey	1973	3.00	6.00	12.00
❑ Tamla T6-331	Pure Smokey	1974	3.00	6.00	12.00
❑ Tamla T6-337	A Quiet Storm	1975	3.00	6.00	12.00

Number	Title (A Side/B Side)	Yr	VG	VG+	NM
❑ Tamla T6-341	Smokey's Family Robinson	1976	3.00	6.00	12.00
❑ Tamla T6-350	Deep in My Soul	1977	3.00	6.00	12.00
❑ Tamla T7-359	Love Breeze	1978	3.00	6.00	12.00
❑ Tamla T9-363 [(2)]	Smokin'	1979	3.75	7.50	15.00
❑ Tamla T7-366	Where There's Smoke	1979	2.50	5.00	10.00
❑ Tamla T8-367	Warm Thoughts	1980	2.50	5.00	10.00
❑ Tamla T8-375	Being with You	1981	2.50	5.00	10.00
❑ Tamla 6001TL	Yes It's You Lady	1982	2.50	5.00	10.00
❑ Tamla 6030TL	Touch the Sky	1983	2.50	5.00	10.00
❑ Tamla 6064TL	Blame It on Love & All the Great Hits	1983	2.50	5.00	10.00
❑ Tamla 6098TL	Essar	1984	2.50	5.00	10.00
❑ Tamla 6156TL	Smoke Signals	1986	2.50	5.00	10.00

ROCKIN' REBELS, THE

45s

Number	Title (A Side/B Side)	Yr	VG	VG+	NM
❑ Corsican 0056	Rockin' Crickets/Shakin' and Stompin'	1959	10.00	20.00	40.00
—As "The Hot-Toddys"					
❑ Itzy 8	Wild Weekend/Wild Weekend Cha Cha	1963	5.00	10.00	20.00
❑ Lost-Nite 239	Wild Weekend/Donkey Twine	196?	—	2.50	5.00
—Reissue					
❑ Mar-Lee 0094	Wild Weekend/Wild Weekend Cha Cha	1960	25.00	50.00	100.00
—As "The Rebels"					
❑ Mar-Lee 0095	Buffalo Blues/Donkey Walk	1961	7.50	15.00	30.00
—As "The Buffalo Rebels"					
❑ Mar-Lee 0096	Theme from Rebel/Any Way You Want Me	1961	7.50	15.00	30.00
—As "The Buffalo Rebels"					
❑ Shan-Todd 0056	Rockin' Crickets/Shakin' and Stompin'	1959	20.00	40.00	80.00
—As "The Hot-Toddys"					
❑ Stork STK-3	Bongo Blue Beat/Burn Baby Burn	1964	6.25	12.50	25.00
❑ Swan 4125	Wild Weekend/Wild Weekend Cha Cha	1962	10.00	20.00	40.00
—First pressings credit "The Rebels"					
❑ Swan 4125	Wild Weekend/Wild Weekend Cha Cha	1962	7.50	15.00	30.00
—Second pressings credit "Rockin' Rebels" and do not have "Don't Drop Out" on the label					
❑ Swan 4140	Rockin' Crickets/Hully Gully Rock	1963	6.25	12.50	25.00
—A-side is the same recording as on Corsican and Shan-Todd					
❑ Swan 4150	Another Wild Weekend/Happy Popcorn	1963	6.25	12.50	25.00
❑ Swan 4161	Monday Morning/Flibbity Jibbit	1963	6.25	12.50	25.00
❑ Swan 4248	Wild Weekend/Donkey Twine	1966	5.00	10.00	20.00

Albums

Number	Title (A Side/B Side)	Yr	VG	VG+	NM
❑ Swan SLP-509 [M]	Wild Weekend	1963	50.00	100.00	200.00

RODGERS, JIMMIE (2)

45s

Number	Title (A Side/B Side)	Yr	VG	VG+	NM
❑ A&M 842	I'll Say Goodbye/Shadows	1967	—	3.00	6.00
❑ A&M 871	Child of Clay/Turnaround	1967	—	3.00	6.00
❑ A&M 898	If I Were the Man/What a Strange Town	1967	—	3.00	6.00
❑ A&M 902	I Believe It All/You Pass Me By	1968	—	3.00	6.00
❑ A&M 930	How Do You Say Goodbye/I Wanna Be Free	1968	—	3.00	6.00
❑ A&M 976	Today/The Lovers	1968	—	3.00	6.00
❑ A&M 1055	The Windmills of Your Mind/L.A. Break Down (And Take Me Back In)	1969	—	3.00	6.00
❑ A&M 1120	Father Paul/Me About You	1969	—	3.00	6.00
❑ A&M 1152	Cycles/Tomorrow My Friends	1969	—	3.00	6.00
❑ A&M 1213	Troubled Times/The Dum Dum Song	1970	—	2.50	5.00
❑ Dot 16378	No One Will Ever Know/Because	1962	2.50	5.00	10.00
❑ Dot 16407	Rainbow at Midnight/Rhumba Boogie	1962	2.50	5.00	10.00
❑ Dot 16428	I'll Never Stand in Your Way/Afraid	1963	2.50	5.00	10.00
❑ Dot 16450	Lonely Tears/A Face in the Crowd	1963	2.50	5.00	10.00
❑ Dot 16467	(I Don't Know Why) I Just Do/Load 'Em Up (And Keep a Steppin')	1963	2.50	5.00	10.00
❑ Dot 16490	Poor Little Raggedy Ann/I'm Gonna Be the Winner	1963	2.50	5.00	10.00
❑ Dot 16527	Two-Ten Six-Eighteen (Doesn't Anybody Know My Name)/ The Banana Boat Song	1963	2.50	5.00	10.00
❑ Dot 16561	Together/Mama Was a Cotton Picker	1963	2.50	5.00	10.00
❑ Dot 16595	The World I Used to Know/I Forgot More Than You'll Ever Know	1964	2.50	5.00	10.00
❑ Dot 16653	Water Boy/Someplace Green	1964	2.50	5.00	10.00
❑ Dot 16673	Two Tickets/I Forgot More Than You'll Ever Know	1964	2.50	5.00	10.00
❑ Dot 16694	(All My Friends Are Gonna Be) Strangers/Bon Soir Mademoiselle	1965	2.00	4.00	8.00
❑ Dot 16720	Careless Love/When I'm Right You Don't Remember	1965	2.00	4.00	8.00

Number	Title (A Side/B Side)	Yr	VG	VG+	NM
❑ Dot 16749	Are You Going My Way (Little Beachcomber)/Little Schoolgirl	1965	2.00	4.00	8.00
❑ Dot 16781	Bye Bye Love/Hollow Words	1965	2.00	4.00	8.00
❑ Dot 16795	The Chipmunk Song (Christmas Don't Be Late)/In the Snow	1965	2.00	4.00	8.00
❑ Dot 16826	A Falen Star/Brother, Where Are You	1966	2.00	4.00	8.00
❑ Dot 16861	It's Over/Anita, You're Dreaming	1966	2.50	5.00	10.00
❑ Dot 16916	Morning Means Tomorrow/New Ideas	1966	2.00	4.00	8.00
❑ Dot 16973	Love Me, Please Love Me/Wonderful You	1966	2.00	4.00	8.00
❑ Dot 17040	Time/Yours and Mine	1967	2.00	4.00	8.00
❑ Epic 10828	Froggy's Fable/Daylight Lights the Dawning	1972	—	2.50	5.00
❑ Epic 10857	Kick the Can/Go On By	1972	—	2.50	5.00
❑ MGM 11732	Mama, Don't Cry at My Wedding/You Don't Live Here No More	1954	6.25	12.50	25.00
❑ Roulette 4015	Honeycomb/Their Hearts Were Full of Spring	1957	5.00	10.00	20.00
❑ Roulette 4031	Kisses Sweeter Than Wine/Better Loved You'll Never Be	1957	5.00	10.00	20.00
❑ Roulette 4045	Oh-Oh, I'm Falling in Love Again/The Long Hot Summer	1958	5.00	10.00	20.00
—Red label					
❑ Roulette 4070	Secretly/Make Me a Miracle	1958	5.00	10.00	20.00
❑ Roulette 4090	Are You Really Mine/The Wizard	1958	3.75	7.50	15.00
❑ Roulette 4116	Bimbombey/You Understand Me	1958	3.75	7.50	15.00
❑ Roulette 4129	I'm Never Gonna Tell/Because You're Young	1959	3.75	7.50	15.00
❑ Roulette 4158 [M]	Ring-a-Ling-a-Lario/Wonderful You	1959	3.75	7.50	15.00
❑ Roulette SSR-4158 [S]	Ring-a-Ling-a-Lario/Wonderful You	1959	7.50	15.00	30.00
❑ Roulette 4191	Tucumcari/That Night You Became Seventeen	1959	3.75	7.50	15.00
❑ Roulette 4205	It's Christmas Once Again/Wistful Willie	1959	5.00	10.00	20.00
❑ Roulette 4218 [M]	T.L.C. Tender Love and Care/Waltzing Matilda	1960	3.00	6.00	12.00
❑ Roulette SSR-4218 [S]	T.L.C. Tender Love and Care/Waltzing Matilda	1960	7.50	15.00	30.00
❑ Roulette 4234	Just a Closer Walk with Thee/Joshua Fit the Battle of Jericho	1960	3.00	6.00	12.00
❑ Roulette 4260	The Wreck of the John B/Four Little Girls in Boston	1960	3.00	6.00	12.00
❑ Roulette 4293	Woman from Liberia/Come Along Julie	1960	3.00	6.00	12.00
❑ Roulette 4318	When Love Is Young/The Little Shepherd of Kingdom Come	1960	3.00	6.00	12.00
❑ Roulette 4349	Everytime My Heart Sings/I'm On My Way	1961	3.00	6.00	12.00
❑ Roulette 4371	John Brown's Baby/I'm Going Home	1961	3.00	6.00	12.00
❑ Roulette 4384	A Little Dog Cried/Englidh Country Garden	1961	3.00	6.00	12.00
❑ Roulette 4439	You Are Everything to Me/Wanderin' Eyes	1962	3.00	6.00	12.00
❑ ScrimShaw 1313	A Good Woman Likes to Drink with the Boys/Dancing on the Moon	1977	—	2.00	4.00
❑ ScrimShaw 1314	Everytime I Sing a Love Song/Just a Little Time	1978	—	2.00	4.00
❑ ScrimShaw 1316	When Our Love Began (Cowboys and Indians)/(B-side unknown)	1978	—	2.00	4.00
❑ ScrimShaw 1318	Secretly/Shovelin' Coal	1978	—	2.00	4.00
❑ ScrimShaw 1319/20	Easy to Love/Easy	1979	—	2.00	4.00
—With Michele					
Albums					
❑ A&M SP-130 [M]	Child of Clay	1967	6.25	12.50	25.00
❑ A&M SP-4130 [S]	Child of Clay	1967	3.75	7.50	15.00
❑ A&M SP-4187	Windmills of Your Mind	1969	3.75	7.50	15.00
❑ A&M SP-4242	Troubled Times	1970	3.75	7.50	15.00
❑ Accord SN-7198	Honeycomb & Other Hits	198?	2.50	5.00	10.00
❑ Dot DLP-3453 [M]	No One Will Ever Know	1962	3.75	7.50	15.00
❑ Dot DLP-3496 [M]	Jimmie Rodgers Folk Concert	1963	3.75	7.50	15.00
❑ Dot DLP-3502 [M]	My Favorite Hymns	1963	3.75	7.50	15.00
❑ Dot DLP-3525 [M]	Honeycomb & Kisses Sweeter Than Wine	1963	3.75	7.50	15.00
❑ Dot DLP-3556 [M]	Town and Country	1964	5.00	10.00	20.00
❑ Dot DLP-3556 [M]	The World I Used to Know	1964	3.75	7.50	15.00
—Retitled version of above					
❑ Dot DLP-3579 [M]	12 Great Hits	1964	3.75	7.50	15.00
❑ Dot DLP-3614 [M]	Deep Purple	1965	3.75	7.50	15.00
❑ Dot DLP 3657 [M]	Christmas with Jimmie	1965	3.00	6.00	12.00
❑ Dot DLP-3687 [M]	The Nashville Sound	1966	3.75	7.50	15.00
❑ Dot DLP-3710 [M]	Country Music 1966	1966	3.75	7.50	15.00
❑ Dot DLP-3717 [M]	It's Over	1966	3.75	7.50	15.00
❑ Dot DLP-3780 [M]	Love Me, Please Love Me	1967	3.75	7.50	15.00
❑ Dot DLP-3815 [M]	Golden Hits/15 Hits of Jimmie Rodgers	1967	5.00	10.00	20.00
❑ Dot DLP-25453 [S]	No One Will Ever Know	1962	5.00	10.00	20.00
❑ Dot DLP-25496 [S]	Jimmie Rodgers Folk Concert	1963	5.00	10.00	20.00
❑ Dot DLP-25502 [S]	My Favorite Hymns	1963	5.00	10.00	20.00
❑ Dot DLP-25525 [S]	Honeycomb & Kisses Sweeter Than Wine	1963	5.00	10.00	20.00
❑ Dot DLP-25556 [S]	The World I Used to Know	1964	5.00	10.00	20.00
—Retitled version of above					
❑ Dot DLP-25556 [S]	Town and Country	1964	6.25	12.50	25.00
❑ Dot DLP-25579 [S]	12 Great Hits	1964	5.00	10.00	20.00
❑ Dot DLP-25614 [S]	Deep Purple	1965	5.00	10.00	20.00
❑ Dot DLP 25657 [S]	Christmas with Jimmie	1965	3.75	7.50	15.00
❑ Dot DLP-25687 [S]	The Nashville Sound	1966	5.00	10.00	20.00
❑ Dot DLP-25710 [S]	Country Music 1966	1966	5.00	10.00	20.00
❑ Dot DLP-25717 [S]	It's Over	1966	5.00	10.00	20.00
❑ Dot DLP-25780 [S]	Love Me, Please Love Me	1967	5.00	10.00	20.00
❑ Dot DLP-25815 [S]	Golden Hits/15 Hits of Jimmie Rodgers	1967	3.75	7.50	15.00
❑ Forum F-9025 [M]	At Home with Jimmie Rodgers: An Evening of Folk Songs	196?	3.00	6.00	12.00
❑ Forum SF-9025 [S]	At Home with Jimmie Rodgers: An Evening of Folk Songs	196?	3.00	6.00	12.00
❑ Forum F-9049 [M]	Just for You	196?	3.00	6.00	12.00
❑ Forum SF-9049 [S]	Just for You	196?	3.00	6.00	12.00
❑ Forum F-9059 [M]	Jimmie Rodgers Sings Folk Songs	196?	3.00	6.00	12.00
❑ Forum SF-9059 [S]	Jimmie Rodgers Sings Folk Songs	196?	3.00	6.00	12.00
❑ Hamilton HL-114 [M]	6 Favorite Hymns and 6 Favorite Folk Ballads	1964	3.00	6.00	12.00
❑ Hamilton HL-148 [M]	12 Immortal Songs	196?	3.00	6.00	12.00
❑ Hamilton HS-12114 [S]	6 Favorite Hymns and 6 Favorite Folk Ballads	1964	3.00	6.00	12.00
❑ Hamilton HS-12148 [S]	12 Immortal Songs	196?	3.00	6.00	12.00
❑ Paramount PAS-2-1042 [(2)]	Honeycomb	1974	3.75	7.50	15.00
❑ Pickwick PC-3040 [M]	Jimmie Rodgers	196?	3.00	6.00	12.00

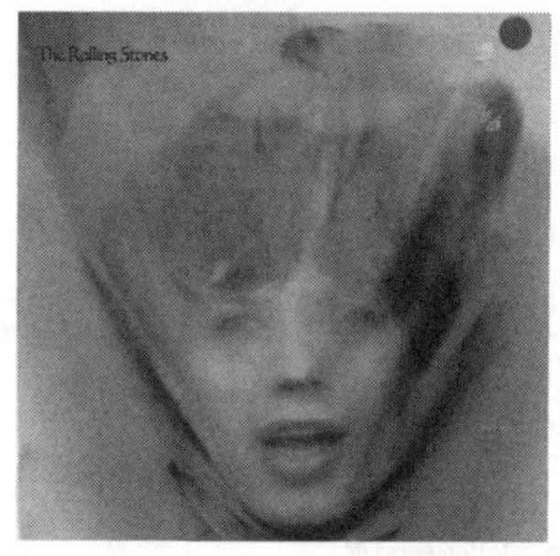

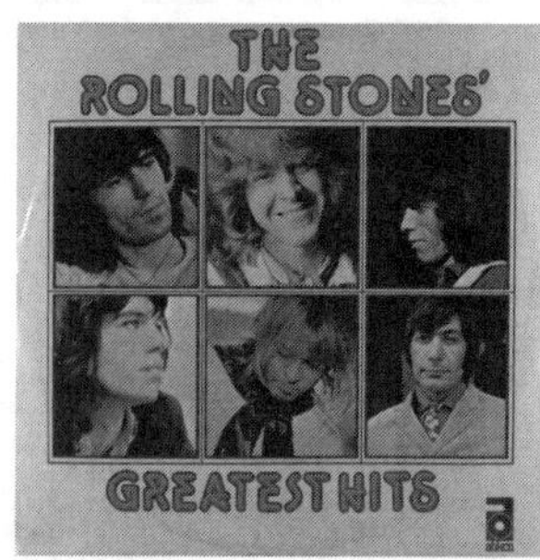

Number	Title (A Side/B Side)	Yr	VG	VG+	NM
❑ Pickwick SPC-3040 [S]	Jimmie Rodgers	196?	3.00	6.00	12.00
❑ Pickwick SPC-3599	Big Hits	197?	2.50	5.00	10.00
❑ Roulette R-25020 [M]	Jimmie Rodgers	1959	6.25	12.50	25.00
—White label with colored spokes					
❑ Roulette R-25033 [M]	Number One Ballads	1958	12.50	25.00	50.00
—Black label					
❑ Roulette R-25042 [M]	Jimmie Rodgers Sings Folk Songs	1958	12.50	25.00	50.00
—Black label					
❑ Roulette R-25057 [M]	His Golden Year	1959	6.25	12.50	25.00
❑ Roulette R-25071 [M]	TV Favorites	1959	7.50	15.00	30.00
❑ Roulette SR-25071 [S]	TV Favorites	1959	12.50	25.00	50.00
❑ Roulette R-25081 [M]	Twilight on the Trail	1959	7.50	15.00	30.00
❑ Roulette SR-25081 [S]	Twilight on the Trail	1959	12.50	25.00	50.00
❑ Roulette R 25095 [M]	It's Christmas Once Again	1959	7.50	15.00	30.00
❑ Roulette SR 25095 [S]	It's Christmas Once Again	1959	12.50	25.00	50.00
❑ Roulette R-25103 [M]	When the Spirit Moves You	1960	7.50	15.00	30.00
❑ Roulette SR-25103 [S]	When the Spirit Moves You	1960	10.00	20.00	40.00
❑ Roulette R-25128 [M]	At Home with Jimmie Rodgers: An Evening of Folk Songs	1960	7.50	15.00	30.00
❑ Roulette SR-25128 [S]	At Home with Jimmie Rodgers: An Evening of Folk Songs	1960	10.00	20.00	40.00
❑ Roulette R-25150 [M]	The Folk Song World of Jimmie Rodgers	1961	7.50	15.00	30.00
❑ Roulette SR-25150 [S]	The Folk Song World of Jimmie Rodgers	1961	10.00	20.00	40.00
❑ Roulette R-25160 [M]	The Best of Jimmie Rodgers' Folk Tunes	1961	7.50	15.00	30.00
❑ Roulette SR-25160 [S]	The Best of Jimmie Rodgers' Folk Tunes	1961	10.00	20.00	40.00
—Black vinyl					
❑ Roulette SR-25160 [S]	The Best of Jimmie Rodgers' Folk Tunes	1961	62.50	125.00	250.00
—Red vinyl					
❑ Roulette R-25179 [M]	15 Million Sellers	1962	6.25	12.50	25.00
❑ Roulette SR-25179 [P]	15 Million Sellers	1962	5.00	10.00	20.00
—Orange and yellow label					
❑ Roulette SR-25179 [P]	15 Million Sellers	1962	7.50	15.00	30.00
—White label with colored spokes					
❑ Roulette R-25199 [M]	Folk Songs	1963	5.00	10.00	20.00
❑ Roulette SR-25199 [S]	Folk Songs	1963	6.25	12.50	25.00
❑ Roulette SR-42006	Yours Truly	1968	3.75	7.50	15.00

ROE, TOMMY

45s

Number	Title (A Side/B Side)	Yr	VG	VG+	NM
❑ ABC 10762	Sweet Pea/Much More Love	1966	2.50	5.00	10.00
—Reissue; this was the common version when this song was a hit; earliest copies have "ABC Records" standing alone (not in a circle)					
❑ ABC 10852	Hooray for Hazel/Need Your Love	1966	2.50	5.00	10.00
❑ ABC 10888	It's Now Winters Day/Kick Me Charlie	1966	2.00	4.00	8.00
❑ ABC 10908	Sing Along with Me/Night Time	1967	2.00	4.00	8.00
❑ ABC 10933	Moon Talk/Sweet Sounds	1967	2.00	4.00	8.00
❑ ABC 10945	Little Miss Sunshine/You I Need	1967	2.00	4.00	8.00
❑ ABC 10989	Melancholy Mood/Paisley Dreams	1967	2.00	4.00	8.00
❑ ABC 11039	Dottie I Like It/Soft Words	1968	2.00	4.00	8.00
❑ ABC 11076	An Oldie But a Goodie/Sugar Cane	1968	2.00	4.00	8.00
❑ ABC 11140	It's Gonna Hurt Me/Gotta Keep Rolling Along	1968	2.00	4.00	8.00
❑ ABC 11164	Dizzy/The You I Need	1969	2.50	5.00	10.00
❑ ABC 11211	Heather Honey/Money Is My Pay	1969	—	3.00	6.00
❑ ABC 11229	Jack and Jill/Tip Toe Tina	1969	—	3.00	6.00
❑ ABC 11247	Jam Up Jelly Tight/Moontalk	1969	2.00	4.00	8.00
❑ ABC 11258	Stir It Up and Serve It/Fire Fly	1970	—	3.00	6.00
❑ ABC 11266	Pearl/A Dollar's Worth of Pennies	1970	—	3.00	6.00
❑ ABC 11273	We Can Make Music/Gotta Keep Rolling Along	1970	—	3.00	6.00
❑ ABC 11281	King of Fools/Brush a Little Sunshine	1970	—	3.00	6.00
❑ ABC 11287	Little Miss Goodie Two Shoes/Traffic Jam	1971	—	3.00	6.00
❑ ABC 11293	King of Fools/Pistol-Legged Mama	1971	—	3.00	6.00
❑ ABC 11307	Stagger Lee/Back Streets and Alleys	1971	—	3.00	6.00
❑ ABC-Paramount 10329	Sheila/Save Your Kisses	1962	3.75	7.50	15.00
❑ ABC-Paramount 10362	Susie Darlin'/Piddle De Pat	1962	3.00	6.00	12.00
❑ ABC-Paramount 10379	Town Crier/Rainbow	1962	3.00	6.00	12.00
❑ ABC-Paramount 10389	Don't Cry Donna/Gonna Take a Chance	1962	3.00	6.00	12.00
❑ ABC-Paramount 10423	The Folk Singer/Count on Me	1963	2.50	5.00	10.00
❑ ABC-Paramount 10454	Kiss and Run/What Makes the Blues	1963	2.50	5.00	10.00
❑ ABC-Paramount 10478	Everybody/Sorry I'm Late, Lisa	1963	3.75	7.50	15.00
❑ ABC-Paramount 10515	Come On/There Will Be Better Years	1964	2.50	5.00	10.00

Number	Title (A Side/B Side)	Yr	VG	VG+	NM
❑ ABC-Paramount 10543	Carol/Be a Good Little Girl	1964	2.50	5.00	10.00
❑ ABC-Paramount 10555	Dance with Henry/Wild Water Skiing Weekend	1964	5.00	10.00	20.00
❑ ABC-Paramount 10579	Oh So Right/I Think I Love You	1964	3.00	6.00	12.00
❑ ABC-Paramount 10604	Party Girl/Oh How I Could Love You	1964	2.50	5.00	10.00
❑ ABC-Paramount 10623	Love Me, Love Me/Diane from Manchester Square	1965	3.00	6.00	12.00
❑ ABC-Paramount 10665	Fourteen Pair of Shoes/Combo Music	1965	2.50	5.00	10.00
❑ ABC-Paramount 10696	The Gunfighter/I'm a Rambler, I'm a Gambler	1965	5.00	10.00	20.00
❑ ABC-Paramount 10706	I Keep Remembering (Things I Forgot)/Wish You Didn't Have to Go	1965	2.50	5.00	10.00
❑ ABC-Paramount 10738	Doesn't Anybody Know My Name/Everytime a Bluebird Cries	1965	2.50	5.00	10.00
❑ ABC-Paramount 10762	Sweet Pea/Much More Love	1966	6.25	12.50	25.00
❑ Awesome 104	First Things First/(B-side unknown)	1984	—	3.00	6.00
❑ Awesome 108	Sittin' on a Mood/(B-side unknown)	1984	—	3.00	6.00
❑ BGO 1003	She Do Run Run/(B-side unknown)	1982	2.50	5.00	10.00
❑ Judd 1018	Caveman/I Gotta Girl	1960	12.50	25.00	50.00
❑ Judd 1022	Sheila/Pretty Girl	1960	37.50	75.00	150.00
❑ Mark IV 001	Caveman/I Gotta Girl	1960	25.00	50.00	100.00
❑ MCA Curb 52711	Some Such Foolishness/Barbara Lou	1985	—	2.00	4.00
❑ MCA Curb 52778	Radio Romance/Barbara Lou	1986	—	2.00	4.00
❑ Mercury 888206-7	Let's Be Fools Like That Again/Barbara Lou	1986	—	—	3.00
❑ Mercury 888497-7	Back When It Really Mattered/Radio Romance	1987	—	—	3.00
❑ MGM South 7001	Mean Little Woman, Rosalie/Skyline	1972	—	2.50	5.00
❑ MGM South 7008	Sarah My Love/Chewing on Sugar Cane	1972	—	2.50	5.00
❑ MGM South 7013	Working Class Hero/Sun in My Eyes	1973	—	2.50	5.00
❑ MGM South 7025	Silver Eyes/Memphis Me	1973	—	3.00	6.00
❑ Monument 45-205	Early in the Morning/Bad News	1976	—	2.50	5.00
❑ Monument 45-228	Your Love Will See Me Through/Working Class Hero	1977	—	2.50	5.00
❑ Monument 8644	Glitter and Gleam/Bad News	1975	—	2.50	5.00
❑ Monument 8662	Snowing Me Under/Rita and Her Band	1975	—	2.50	5.00
❑ Monument 8684	Slow Dancing/Burn On Love Light	1976	—	2.50	5.00
❑ Monument 8705	Everybody/Energy	1976	—	2.50	5.00
❑ Trumpet 1401	Caveman/I Gotta Girl	1960	50.00	100.00	200.00
❑ Warner Bros. 8660	Dreamin' Again/Love the Way You Love Me Up	1978	—	2.00	4.00
❑ Warner Bros. 8720	Just Look at Me/Love the Way You Love Me Up	1978	—	2.50	5.00
❑ Warner Bros. 8800	Massachusetts/Just Look at Me	1979	—	2.50	5.00
❑ Warner Bros. 49085	You Better Move On/Just Look at Me	1979	—	2.00	4.00
❑ Warner Bros. 49235	Charlie, I Love Your Wife/There Is No Sun on Sunset Boulevard	1980	—	2.00	4.00

Albums

Number	Title (A Side/B Side)	Yr	VG	VG+	NM
❑ ABC S-467 [R]	Something for Everybody	1968	12.50	25.00	50.00
—Issued in rechanneled stereo four years after its original release					
❑ ABC 594 [M]	It's Now Winters Day	1967	5.00	10.00	20.00
❑ ABC S-594 [S]	It's Now Winters Day	1967	6.25	12.50	25.00
❑ ABC 610 [M]	Phantasy	1967	10.00	20.00	40.00
❑ ABC S-610 [S]	Phantasy	1967	10.00	20.00	40.00
❑ ABC S-683	Dizzy	1969	5.00	10.00	20.00
❑ ABC S-700	12 in a Roe/A Collection of Tommy Roe's Greatest Hits	1969	5.00	10.00	20.00
❑ ABC S-714	We Can Make Music	1970	3.75	7.50	15.00
❑ ABC S-732	Beginnings	1971	3.75	7.50	15.00
❑ ABC X-762	16 Greatest Hits	1972	3.75	7.50	15.00
❑ ABC-Paramount 432 [M]	Sheila	1962	10.00	20.00	40.00
❑ ABC-Paramount S-432 [S]	Sheila	1962	12.50	25.00	50.00
❑ ABC-Paramount 467 [M]	Something for Everybody	1964	7.50	15.00	30.00
❑ ABC-Paramount 575 [M]	Sweet Pea	1966	7.50	51.00	30.00
❑ ABC-Paramount S-575 [S]	Sweet Pea	1966	10.00	20.00	40.00
❑ Accord SN-7155	Sheila	1981	2.50	5.00	10.00
❑ MCA 1519	Collectibles — Greatest Hits	1982	2.00	4.00	8.00
❑ Monument 7604	Energy	1977	2.50	5.00	10.00
—Reissue of 34182					
❑ Monument 7614	Full Bloom	1977	2.50	5.00	10.00
❑ Monument PZ 34182	Energy	1976	3.00	6.00	12.00
❑ Pickwick SPC-3361	Dizzy	197?	2.50	5.00	10.00

ROGERS, KENNY

45s

Number	Title (A Side/B Side)	Yr	VG	VG+	NM
❑ Carlton 454	That Crazy Feeling/We'll Always Have Each Other	1958	25.00	50.00	100.00
—As "Kenny Rogers"					
❑ Carlton 454	That Crazy Feeling/We'll Always Have Each Other	1958	25.00	50.00	100.00
—As "Kenneth Rogers"					
❑ Carlton 468	For You Alone/I've Got a Lot to Learn	1958	15.00	30.00	60.00
❑ Ken-Lee 102	Jole Blon/Lonely	195?	25.00	50.00	100.00
❑ Liberty 1380	Lady/Sweet Music Man	1980	—	2.00	4.00
❑ Liberty 1391	Long Arm of the Law/You Were a Good Friend	1980	—	2.00	4.00
❑ Liberty 1415	I Don't Need You/Without You in My Life	1981	—	—	3.00
❑ Liberty 1430	Share Your Love with Me/Greybeard	1981	—	—	3.00
❑ Liberty 1438	Kentucky Homemade Christmas/Carol of the Bells	1981	—	2.50	5.00
❑ Liberty 1441	Blaze of Glory/The Good Life	1981	—	—	3.00
❑ Liberty 1444	Through the Years/So In Love with You	1981	—	—	3.00
❑ Liberty 1471	Love Will Turn You Around/I Want a Son	1982	—	—	3.00
❑ Liberty 1485	A Love Song/Fool in Me	1982	—	—	3.00
❑ Liberty 1492	We've Got Tonight/You Are So Beautiful	1983	—	2.00	4.00
—A-side with Sheena Easton					
❑ Liberty 1495	All My Life/The Farther I Go	1983	—	—	3.00
❑ Liberty 1503	Scarlet Fever/What I Learned from Loving You	1983	—	—	3.00
❑ Liberty B-1511	You Were a Good Friend/Sweet Music Man	1983	—	—	3.00
❑ Liberty 1524	A Stranger in My Place/Love Is What We Make It	1985	—	—	3.00
❑ Liberty 1525	Twentieth Century Fool/It Turns Me Inside Out	1985	—	—	3.00
❑ Liberty 1526	Abraham, Martin and John/Goodbye Marie	1985	—	—	3.00
❑ Mercury 72545	Here's That Rainy Day/Take Life in Stride	1966	6.25	12.50	25.00

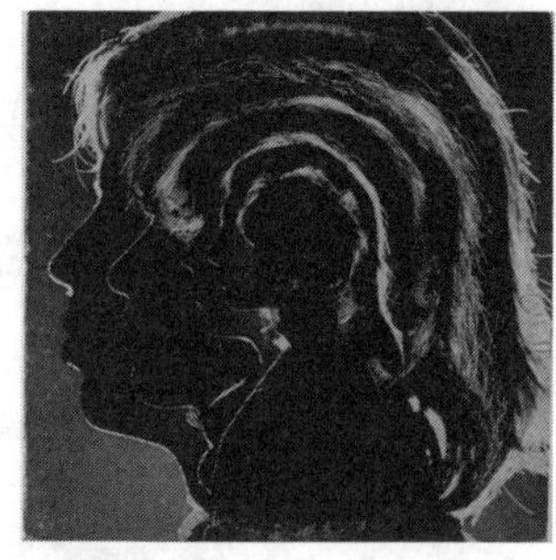

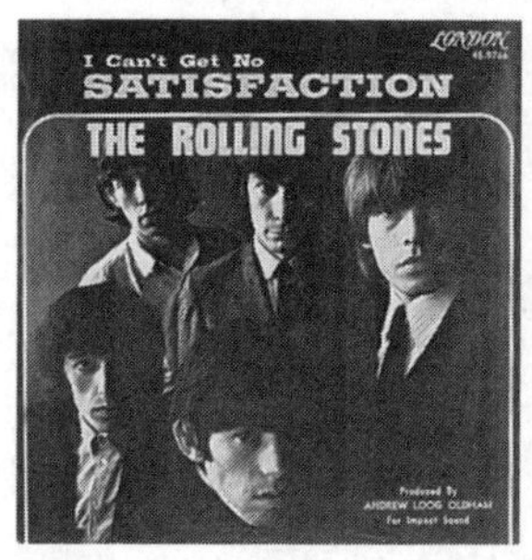

Number	Title (A Side/B Side)	Yr	VG	VG+	NM
❑ RCA 5016-7-R	They Don't Make Them Like They Used To/ Just the Thought of Losing You	1986	—	—	3.00
❑ RCA 5078-7-R	Twenty Years Ago/The Heart of the Matter	1986	—	—	3.00
❑ RCA 5209-7-R	Make No Mistake, She's Mine/You're My Love	1987	—	—	3.00
—With Ronnie Milsap					
❑ RCA 5258-7-R	I Prefer the Moonlight/We're Doin' Alright	1987	—	—	3.00
❑ RCA 6832-7-R	The Factory/One More Day	1987	—	—	3.00
❑ RCA 8381-7-R	I Prefer the Moonlight/Make No Mistake, She's Mine	1988	—	—	3.00
—Gold Standard Series; B-side with Ronnie Milsap					
❑ RCA 8390-7-R	I Don't Call Him Daddy/We're Doin' Alright	1988	—	—	3.00
❑ RCA PB-13710	This Woman/Buried Treasure	1984	—	—	3.00
❑ RCA PB-13774	Eyes That See in the Dark/Hold Me	1984	—	—	3.00
❑ RCA PB-13832	Evening Star/Midsummer Nights	1984	—	—	3.00
❑ RCA PB-13899	What About Me/The Rest of Last Night	1984	—	—	3.00
—With Kim Carnes and James Ingram					
❑ RCA PB-13944	The Christmas Song/Medley: Winter Wonderland-Sleigh Ride	1984	—	2.00	4.00
—B-side by Dolly Parton					
❑ RCA PB-13975	Crazy/The Stranger	1984	—	—	3.00
❑ RCA GB-14074	This Woman/What About Me	1985	—	—	3.00
—Gold Standard Series; B-side by Kenny Rogers, Kim Carnes and James Ingram					
❑ RCA PB-14194	Morning Desire/People in Love	1985	—	—	3.00
❑ RCA PB-14298	Tomb of the Unknown Love/Our Perfect Song	1986	—	—	3.00
❑ RCA GB-14353	Crazy/Morning Desire	1986	—	—	3.00
—Gold Standard Series					
❑ RCA PB-14384	The Pride Is Back/Didn't We?	1986	—	2.00	4.00
—A-side: With Nickie Ryder					
❑ Reprise 22750	Christmas in America/Joy to the World	1989	—	—	3.00
❑ Reprise 22828	The Vows Go Unbroken (Always True to You)/One Night	1989	—	—	3.00
❑ Reprise 22853	(Something Inside) So Strong/When You Put Your Heart In It	1989	—	—	3.00
❑ Reprise 27690	Planet Texas/When You Put Your Heart in It	1988	—	—	3.00
❑ Reprise 27812	When You Put Your Heart In It/(Instrumental)	1988	—	—	3.00
❑ United Artists XW746	Love Lifted Me/Home-Made Love	1975	—	2.00	4.00
❑ United Artists XW798	There's an Old Man in Our Town/Home-Made Love	1976	—	2.00	4.00
❑ United Artists XW812	I Would Like to See You Again/While the Feeling's Good	1976	—	2.00	4.00
❑ United Artists XW868	Laura (What's He Got That I Ain't Got)/I Wasn't Mad Enough	1976	—	2.00	4.00
❑ United Artists XW929	Lucille/Till I Get It Right	1976	—	2.00	4.00
❑ United Artists XW1027	Daytime Friends/We Don't Make Love Anymore	1977	—	2.00	4.00
❑ United Artists XW1095	Sweet Music Man/Lying Again	1977	—	2.00	4.00
❑ United Artists XW1151	Love Lifted Me/Reuben James	1978	—	2.00	4.00
❑ United Artists XW1152	Today I Started Loving You Again/Just Dropped In (To See What Condition My Condition Was In)	1978	—	2.00	4.00
❑ United Artists XW1153	Daytime Friends/But You Know I Love You	1978	—	2.00	4.00
❑ United Artists XW1154	Lucille/Something's Burning	1978	—	2.00	4.00
❑ United Artists XW1155	Sweet Music Man/Ruby, Don't Take Your Love to Town	1978	—	2.00	4.00
—B-sides of the above five singles are re-recordings of First Edition hits paired with early United Artists country hits					
❑ United Artists XW1210	Love Or Something Like It/Starting Again	1978	—	2.00	4.00
❑ United Artists XW1250	The Gambler/Momma's Waiting	1978	—	2.00	4.00
❑ United Artists XW1273	She Believes in Me/Morgana Jones	1979	—	2.00	4.00
❑ United Artists 1315	You Decorated My Life/One Man's Woman	1979	—	2.00	4.00
❑ United Artists 1327	Coward of the County/I Wanna Make You Smile	1979	—	2.00	4.00
❑ United Artists 1345	Don't Fall in Love with a Dreamer/ Intro: Goin' Home to the Rock-Gideon Tanner	1980	—	2.00	4.00
—A-side: With Kim Carnes					
❑ United Artists 1359	Love the World Away/Sayin' Goodbye-Requiem	1980	—	2.00	4.00
Albums					
❑ Liberty LO-607	Love Lifted Me	1981	2.00	4.00	8.00
—Reissue of United Artists 607					
❑ Liberty LO-689	Kenny Rogers	1981	2.00	4.00	8.00
—Reissue of United Artists 689					
❑ Liberty LO-754	Daytime Friends	1981	2.00	4.00	8.00
—Reissue of United Artists 754					
❑ Liberty LO-835	Ten Years of Gold	1981	2.00	4.00	8.00
—Reissue of United Artists 835					
❑ Liberty LO-903	Love Or Something Like It	1981	2.00	4.00	8.00
—Reissue of United Artists 903					
❑ Liberty LO-934	The Gambler	1981	2.00	4.00	8.00
—Reissue of United Artists 934					

Number	Title (A Side/B Side)	Yr	VG	VG+	NM
❑ Liberty LOO-979	Kenny	1981	2.00	4.00	8.00
—Reissue of United Artists 979					
❑ Liberty LOO-1035	Gideon	1981	2.00	4.00	8.00
—Reissue of United Artists 1035					
❑ Liberty LOO-1072	Kenny Rogers' Greatest Hits	1980	2.00	4.00	8.00
❑ Liberty LOO-1108	Share Your Love	1981	2.00	4.00	8.00
❑ Liberty LN-10207	Love Lifted Me	1984	—	3.00	6.00
—Budget-line reissue					
❑ Liberty LN-10208	Kenny Rogers	1983	—	3.00	6.00
—Budget-line reissue					
❑ Liberty LN-10240	Christmas	198?	2.00	4.00	8.00
—Reissue of LOO 51115					
❑ Liberty LN-10243	Gideon	1984	—	3.00	6.00
—Budget-line reissue					
❑ Liberty LN-10245	We've Got Tonight	1984	—	3.00	6.00
—Budget-line reissue					
❑ Liberty LN-10246	Love Will Turn You Around	1984	—	3.00	6.00
—Budget-line reissue					
❑ Liberty LN-10247	The Gambler	1984	—	3.00	6.00
—Budget-line reissue					
❑ Liberty LN-10248	Kenny	1984	—	3.00	6.00
—Budget-line reissue					
❑ Liberty LN-10249	Daytime Friends	1984	—	3.00	6.00
—Budget-line reissue					
❑ Liberty LN-10250	Love Or Something Like It	1984	—	3.00	6.00
—Budget-line reissue					
❑ Liberty LN-10254	Ten Years of Gold	1984	—	3.00	6.00
—Budget-line reissue					
❑ Liberty LOO-51115	Christmas	1981	2.50	5.00	10.00
❑ Liberty LO-51124	Love Will Turn You Around	1982	2.00	4.00	8.00
❑ Liberty LO-51143	We've Got Tonight	1983	2.00	4.00	8.00
❑ Liberty LV-51152	Twenty Greatest Hits	1983	2.00	4.00	8.00
❑ Liberty LO-51154	Duets	1984	2.00	4.00	8.00
❑ Liberty LO-51157	Love Is What We Make It	1985	2.00	4.00	8.00
❑ RCA 5833-1-R	They Don't Make Them Like They Used To	1986	2.00	4.00	8.00
❑ RCA 6484-1-R	I Prefer the Moonlight	1987	2.00	4.00	8.00
❑ RCA 8371-1-R	Greatest Hits	1988	2.00	4.00	8.00
❑ RCA Victor AFL1-4697	Eyes That See in the Dark	1983	2.00	4.00	8.00
❑ RCA Victor AJL1-5335	What About Me	1984	2.00	4.00	8.00
❑ RCA Victor AJL1-7023	The Heart of the Matter	1985	2.00	4.00	8.00
❑ Reprise 25792	Something Inside So Strong	1989	2.50	5.00	10.00
❑ Reprise 25973	Christmas in America	1989	3.00	6.00	12.00
❑ United Artists UA-LA607-G	Love Lifted Me	1976	3.75	7.50	15.00
❑ United Artists UA-LA689-G	Kenny Rogers	1976	2.50	5.00	10.00
❑ United Artists UA-LA754-G	Daytime Friends	1977	2.50	5.00	10.00
❑ United Artists UA-LA835-H	Ten Years of Gold	1978	2.50	5.00	10.00
❑ United Artists UA-LA903-H	Love Or Something Like It	1978	2.50	5.00	10.00
❑ United Artists UA-LA934-H	The Gambler	1978	2.50	5.00	10.00
❑ United Artists LWAK-979	Kenny	1979	2.50	5.00	10.00
❑ United Artists LOO-1035	Gideon	1980	2.50	5.00	10.00

ROGERS, KENNY, AND DOLLY PARTON

45s

Number	Title (A Side/B Side)	Yr	VG	VG+	NM
❑ RCA 5352-7-R	Christmas Without You/I Believe in Santa Claus	1987	—	—	3.00
—B-side by Dolly Parton					
❑ RCA 9070-7-R	Christmas Without You/Medley: Winter Wonderland-Sleigh Ride	1989	—	—	3.00
—B-side by Dolly Parton					
❑ RCA PB-13615	Islands in the Stream/I Will Always Love You	1983	—	—	3.00
❑ RCA PB-13945	The Greatest Gift of All/White Christmas	1984	—	2.00	4.00
❑ RCA PB-14058	Real Love/I Can't Be True	1985	—	—	3.00
❑ RCA GB-14073	Islands in the Stream/Eyes That See in the Dark	1985	—	—	3.00
—Gold Standard Series; B-side by Kenny Rogers					
❑ RCA PB-14261	Christmas Without You/A Christmas to Remember	1985	—	—	3.00

Albums

Number	Title (A Side/B Side)	Yr	VG	VG+	NM
❑ RCA Victor ASL1-5307	Once Upon a Christmas	1984	2.50	5.00	10.00

ROLLING STONES, THE

45s

Number	Title (A Side/B Side)	Yr	VG	VG+	NM
❑ Abkco 4701	I Don't Know Why/Try a Little Harder	1975	—	2.50	5.00
—With A-side writing credits of "Wonder, Riser, Hunter, Hardaway"					
❑ Abkco 4702	Out of Time/Jiving Sister Fanny	1975	—	3.00	6.00
❑ London 901	Paint It, Black/Stupid Girl	1966	3.75	7.50	15.00
❑ London 902	Mothers Little Helper/Lady Jane	1966	3.75	7.50	15.00
❑ London 903	Have You Seen Your Mother, Baby, Standing in the Shadow?/ Who's Driving My Plane	1966	3.75	7.50	15.00
❑ London 904	Ruby Tuesday/Let's Spend the Night Together	1967	3.75	7.50	15.00
❑ London 905	Dandelion/We Love You	1967	5.00	10.00	20.00
❑ London 906	She's a Rainbow/2000 Light Years from Home	1967	5.00	10.00	20.00
❑ London 907	In Another Land/The Lantern	1967	6.25	12.50	25.00
—A-side credited to Bill Wyman, though taken from "Their Satanic Majesties Request"					
❑ London 908	Jumpin' Jack Flash/Child of the Moon	1968	3.75	7.50	15.00
❑ London 909	Street Fighting Man/No Expectations	1968	5.00	10.00	20.00
❑ London 910	Honky Tonk Women/You Can't Always Get What You Want	1969	3.75	7.50	15.00
❑ London 9641	I Wanna Be Your Man/Stoned	1964	3000.	6000.	9000.
—VG 3000; VG+ 6000					
❑ London 9657	Not Fade Away/I Wanna Be Your Man	1964	10.00	20.00	40.00
—White, purple and blue label					

Number	Title (A Side/B Side)	Yr	VG	VG+	NM
❑ London 9682	Tell Me (You're Coming Back)/I Just Want to Make Love to You	1964	10.00	20.00	40.00
—White, purple and blue label					
❑ London 9687	It's All Over Now/Good Times, Bad Times	1964	10.00	20.00	40.00
—White, purple and blue label					
❑ London 9708	Time Is On My Side/Congratulations	1964	7.50	15.00	30.00
—White, purple and blue label					
❑ London 9725	Heart of Stone/What a Shame	1964	7.50	15.00	30.00
—White, purple and blue label					
❑ London 9741	The Last Time/Play with Fire	1965	6.25	12.50	25.00
—White, purple and blue label					
❑ London 9766	(I Can't Get No) Satisfaction/The Under Assistant West Coast Promotion Man	1965	5.00	10.00	20.00
❑ London 9792	Get Off of My Cloud/I'm Free	1965	5.00	10.00	20.00
❑ London 9808	As Tears Go By/Gotta Get Away	1965	3.75	7.50	15.00
❑ London 9823	19th Nervous Breakdown/Sad Day	1966	3.75	7.50	15.00
❑ Rolling Stones 38-05802	Harlem Shuffle/Had It with You	1986	—	—	3.00
❑ Rolling Stones 38-05906	One Hit (To the Body)/Fight	1986	—	—	3.00
❑ Rolling Stones 19100	Brown Sugar/Bitch	1971	—	2.50	5.00
❑ Rolling Stones 19101	Wild Horses/Sway	1971	—	2.50	5.00
❑ Rolling Stones 19103	Tumbling Dice/Sweet Black Angel	1972	—	2.50	5.00
❑ Rolling Stones 19104	Happy/All Down the Line	1972	—	2.50	5.00
❑ Rolling Stones 19105	Angie/Silver Train	1973	—	2.50	5.00
—With "Angie" listed as "Side One" and "Silver Train" listed as "Side Two", or with no reference at all to "Side One" and "Side Two"					
❑ Rolling Stones 19109	Doo Doo Doo Doo Doo (Heartbreaker)/Dancing with Mr. D.	1973	—	2.50	5.00
❑ Rolling Stones 19301	It's Only Rock 'N' Roll (But I Like It)/Through the Lonely Nights	1974	—	2.50	5.00
❑ Rolling Stones 19302	Ain't Too Proud to Beg/Dance Little Sister	1974	—	2.50	5.00
❑ Rolling Stones 19304	Fool to Cry/Hot Stuff	1976	—	2.00	4.00
❑ Rolling Stones 19307	Miss You/Far Away Eyes	1978	—	2.00	4.00
❑ Rolling Stones 19309	Beast of Burden/When the Whip Comes Down	1978	—	2.00	4.00
❑ Rolling Stones 19310	Shattered/Everything Is Turning to Gold	1978	—	2.00	4.00
❑ Rolling Stones 20001	Emotional Rescue/Down in the Hole	1980	—	2.00	4.00
❑ Rolling Stones 21001	She's So Cold/Send It to Me	1980	—	2.00	4.00
❑ Rolling Stones 21003	Start Me Up/No Use in Crying	1981	—	2.00	4.00
❑ Rolling Stones 21004	Waiting on a Friend/Little T & A	1981	—	2.00	4.00
❑ Rolling Stones 21300	Hang Fire/Neighbours	1982	—	2.00	4.00
❑ Rolling Stones 21301	Going to A-Go-Go/Beast of Burden	1982	—	2.00	4.00
❑ Rolling Stones 38-69008	Mixed Emotions/Fancy Man Blues	1989	—	—	3.00
❑ Rolling Stones 38-73057	Rock and a Hard Place/Cook Cook Blues	1989	—	—	3.00
❑ Rolling Stones 38-73093	Almost Hear You Sigh/Break the Spell	1989	—	—	3.00
❑ Rolling Stones 99724	Too Tough/Miss You	1984	10.00	20.00	40.00
❑ Rolling Stones 99788	She Was Hot/Think I'm Going Mad	1984	—	—	3.00
❑ Rolling Stones 99813	Undercover of the Night/All the Way Down	1983	—	—	3.00
❑ Rolling Stones 99978	Time Is On My Side (Live)/Twenty Flight Rock	1982	—	2.50	5.00
Albums					
❑ Abkco 1218-1 [(4)]	Singles Collection: The London Years	1989	12.50	25.00	50.00
❑ London NP 1 [M]	Big Hits (High Tide and Green Grass)	1966	10.00	20.00	40.00
—With five lines of type on the front cover, all in capital letters					
❑ London NPS 1 [R]	Big Hits (High Tide and Green Grass)	1966	2.50	5.00	10.00
❑ London NP 2 [M]	Their Satanic Majesties Request	1967	62.50	125.00	250.00
❑ London NPS 2 [S]	Their Satanic Majesties Request	1967	10.00	20.00	40.00
—With 3-D cover					
❑ London NPS 3 [P]	Through the Past, Darkly (Big Hits Vol. 2)	1969	2.50	5.00	10.00
—With hexagonal cover					
❑ London NPS 4 [S]	Let It Bleed	1969	3.75	7.50	15.00
—With poster					
❑ London PS 375 [R]	England's Newest Hit Makers — The Rolling Stones	1964	75.00	150.00	300.00
—Dark blue label; lower left-hand corner of cover advertises a bonus photo					
❑ London PS 402 [R]	12 x 5	1964	6.25	12.50	25.00
—Dark blue label with "London" unboxed at top					
❑ London PS 420 [R]	The Rolling Stones, Now!	1965	6.25	12.50	25.00
—Dark blue label with "London" unboxed at top. Add 20% for complete liner notes (or sticker) on back cover (both columns of type about equal in length).					
❑ London PS 429 [R]	Out of Our Heads	1965	25.00	50.00	100.00
—Dark blue label with "London/ffrr" in a box at top and "Made in England by the Decca Record Co. Ltd." at top edge					
❑ London PS 451 [P]	December's Children (and Everybody's)	1965	6.25	12.50	25.00
—Dark blue label with "London" unboxed at top					
❑ London PS 476 [S]	Aftermath	1966	2.50	5.00	10.00

Number	Title (A Side/B Side)	Yr	VG	VG+	NM
❑ London PS 493 [P]	Got Live If You Want It!	1966	2.50	5.00	10.00
—"Fortune Teller" is rechanneled (it's actually an early studio recording with overdubbed crowd noise)					
❑ London PS 499 [S]	Between the Buttons	1967	2.50	5.00	10.00
❑ London PS 509 [P]	Flowers	1967	2.50	5.00	10.00
—"Have You Seen Your Mother, Baby, Standing in the Shadow?" and "Mother's Little Helper" are rechanneled; all others are true stereo					
❑ London PS 539 [S]	Beggars Banquet	1968	2.50	5.00	10.00
—With "Rev. Wilkins: credited as composer of "Prodigal Son"					
❑ London 2PS 606/7 [(2)P]	Hot Rocks 1964-1971	1971	5.00	10.00	20.00
—With regular versions of all tracks. All of Side 1 and "Mothers Little Helper" and "19th Nervous Breakdown" on Side 2 are rechanneled. All of Side 3 and 4 are stereo.					
❑ London 2PS 626/7 [(2)P]	More Hot Rocks (Big Hits and Fazed Cookies)	1972	5.00	10.00	20.00
—All of Sides 1 and 4 are rechanneled; Side 2 and 3, except "Have You Seen Your Mother, Baby, Standing in the Shadow?" are in true stereo					
❑ London LL 3375 [M]	England's Newest Hit Makers — The Rolling Stones	1964	75.00	150.00	300.00
—Maroon label with "Full Frequency Range Recording" inside horizontal lines that go through the center hole; lower left-hand corner of cover advertises a bonus photo					
❑ London LL 3402 [M]	12 x 5	1964	15.00	30.00	60.00
—Maroon label with "London" unboxed at top					
❑ London LL 3420 [M]	The Rolling Stones, Now!	1965	15.00	30.00	60.00
—Maroon label with "London" unboxed at top and no lines on label. Add 20% for complete liner notes (or sticker) on back cover (both columns of type about equal in length).					
❑ London LL 3429 [M]	Out of Our Heads	1965	10.00	20.00	40.00
—Maroon label with "London" unboxed at top					
❑ London LL 3451 [M]	December's Children (and Everybody's)	1965	10.00	20.00	40.00
—Maroon label with "London" unboxed at top					
❑ London LL 3476 [M]	Aftermath	1966	10.00	20.00	40.00
❑ London LL 3493 [M]	Got Live If You Want It!	1966	10.00	20.00	40.00
❑ London LL 3499 [M]	Between the Buttons	1967	10.00	20.00	40.00
❑ London LL 3509 [M]	Flowers	1967	12.50	25.00	50.00
❑ London/Abkco 62671 [(2)P]	More Hot Rocks (Big Hits and Fazed Cookies)	1986	3.75	7.50	15.00
—"Digitally Remastered from Original Master Recording" on cover; red label					
❑ London/Abkco 62671 [(2)P]	Hot Rocks 1964-1971	1986	3.75	7.50	15.00
—"Digitally Remastered from Original Master Recording" on cover; red label; same stereo content as original					
❑ London/Abkco 73751 [M]	England's Newest Hit Makers — The Rolling Stones	1986	2.00	4.00	8.00
—"Digitally Remastered from Original Master Recording" on cover; red label					
❑ London/Abkco 74021 [M]	12 x 5	1986	2.00	4.00	8.00
—"Digitally Remastered from Original Master Recording" on cover; red label					
❑ London/Abkco 74201 [P]	The Rolling Stones, Now!	1986	2.00	4.00	8.00
—"Digitally Remastered from Original Master Recording" on cover; red label; four tracks are in true stereo					
❑ London/Abkco 74291 [P]	Out of Our Heads	1986	2.00	4.00	8.00
—"Digitally Remastered from Original Master Recording" on cover; red label					
❑ London/Abkco 74511 [M]	December's Children (and Everybody's)	1986	2.00	4.00	8.00
—"Digitally Remastered from Original Master Recording" on cover; red label					
❑ London/Abkco 74761 [S]	Aftermath	1986	2.00	4.00	8.00
—"Digitally Remastered from Original Master Recording" on cover; red label					
❑ London/Abkco 74931 [S]	Got Live If You Want It!	1986	2.00	4.00	8.00
—"Digitally Remastered from Original Master Recording" on cover; red label					
❑ London/Abkco 74991 [S]	Between the Buttons	1986	2.00	4.00	8.00
—"Digitally Remastered from Original Master Recording" on cover; red label					
❑ London/Abkco 75091 [S]	Flowers	1986	2.00	4.00	8.00
—"Digitally Remastered from Original Master Recording" on cover; red label					
❑ London/Abkco 75391 [S]	Beggars Banquet	1986	3.00	6.00	12.00
—"Digitally Remastered from Original Master Recording" on cover; red label; original banned "toilet cover" released for the first time on this reissue					
❑ London/Abkco 80011 [M]	Big Hits (High Tide and Green Grass)	1986	2.00	4.00	8.00
—"Digitally Remastered from Original Master Recording" on cover; red label					
❑ London/Abkco 80021 [S]	Their Satanic Majesties Request	1986	2.00	4.00	8.00
—"Digitally Remastered from Original Master Recording" on cover; red label					
❑ London/Abkco 80031 [S]	Through the Past, Darkly (Big Hits Vol. 2)	1986	2.00	4.00	8.00
—"Digitally Remastered from Original Master Recording" on cover; red label					
❑ London/Abkco 80041	Let It Bleed	1986	2.00	4.00	8.00
—"Digitally Remastered from Original Master Recording" on cover; red label					
❑ London/Abkco 80051	Get Yer Ya-Ya's Out!	1986	2.00	4.00	8.00
—"Digitally Remastered from Original Master Recording" on cover; red label					
❑ Radio Pulsebeat News 4	It's Here Luv!!	1965	45.00	90.00	180.00
—Ed Rudy interview album; this has been counterfeited, but originals can be identified thus: Charlie Watts' jacket should be completely black with no white marks; the label is very clear; the vinyl is all black					
❑ Rolling Stones COC 2-2900 [(2)]	Exile on Main St.	1972	3.75	7.50	15.00
—Original covers have Unipak design -- cover has to be opened to remove the records. Add 33% for sheet of postcards.					
❑ Rolling Stones COC 2-9001 [(2)]	Love You Live	1977	3.00	6.00	12.00
❑ Rolling Stones COC 16015	Emotional Rescue	1980	3.75	7.50	15.00
—Originally released with a large poster wrapped around the outside of the record jacket					
❑ Rolling Stones COC 16028	Sucking in the Seventies	1981	2.50	5.00	10.00
❑ Rolling Stones COC 16052	Tattoo You	1981	2.50	5.00	10.00
❑ Rolling Stones COC 39100	Jamming with Edward	1972	3.75	7.50	15.00
—Not an official Stones album, this includes Jagger, Watts and Wyman with Ry Cooder and Nicky Hopkins					
❑ Rolling Stones COC 39105	Sticky Fingers	1977	2.50	5.00	10.00
—Reissue on Atlantic with working zipper					
❑ Rolling Stones COC 39106	Goats Head Soup	1977	2.00	4.00	8.00
—Reissue on Atlantic					
❑ Rolling Stones COC 39107	Made in the Shade	1977	2.00	4.00	8.00
—Reissue on Atlantic					
❑ Rolling Stones COC 39108	Some Girls	1978	3.75	7.50	15.00
—With all women's faces visible. Nine different color schemes exist for the front cover.					
❑ Rolling Stones COC 39113	Still Life (American Concert 1981)	1982	2.50	5.00	10.00

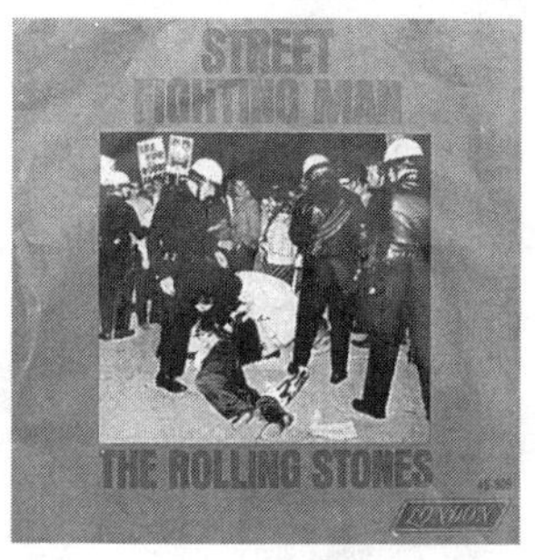

Number	Title (A Side/B Side)	Yr	VG	VG+	NM
❑ Rolling Stones OC 40250	Dirty Work	1986	2.00	4.00	8.00
—Originals came with red shrink wrap; add 50% if it is still with the package					
❑ Rolling Stones FC 40488	Sticky Fingers	1986	2.00	4.00	8.00
—Reissue on CBS with photo of zipper only					
❑ Rolling Stones CG2 40489 [(2)]	Exile on Main St.	1986	2.50	5.00	10.00
—Reissue on CBS					
❑ Rolling Stones FC 40492	Goats Head Soup	1986	2.00	4.00	8.00
—Reissue on CBS					
❑ Rolling Stones FC 40493	It's Only Rock 'n' Roll	1986	2.00	4.00	8.00
—Reissue on CBS					
❑ Rolling Stones FC 40494	Made in the Shade	1986	2.00	4.00	8.00
—Reissue on CBS					
❑ Rolling Stones FC 40495	Black and Blue	1986	2.00	4.00	8.00
—Reissue on CBS					
❑ Rolling Stones CG2 40496 [(2)]	Love You Live	1986	2.50	5.00	10.00
—Reissue on CBS					
❑ Rolling Stones FC 40499	Some Girls	1986	2.00	4.00	8.00
—Reissue on CBS					
❑ Rolling Stones FC 40500	Emotional Rescue	1986	2.00	4.00	8.00
—Reissue on CBS					
❑ Rolling Stones FC 40501	Sucking in the Seventies	1986	2.00	4.00	8.00
—Reissue on CBS					
❑ Rolling Stones FC 40502	Tattoo You	1986	2.00	4.00	8.00
—Reissue on CBS					
❑ Rolling Stones FC 40503	Still Life (American Concert 1981)	1986	2.00	4.00	8.00
—Reissue on CBS					
❑ Rolling Stones FC 40504	Undercover	1986	2.00	4.00	8.00
—Reissue on CBS has no stickers on cover					
❑ Rolling Stones FC 40505	Rewind (1971-1984)	1986	2.00	4.00	8.00
—Reissue on CBS					
❑ Rolling Stones OC 45333	Steel Wheels	1989	2.50	5.00	10.00
❑ Rolling Stones C 47456	Flashpoint	1991	5.00	10.00	20.00
❑ Rolling Stones COC 59100	Sticky Fingers	1971	3.00	6.00	12.00
—With working zipper					
❑ Rolling Stones COC 59101	Goats Head Soup	1973	3.75	7.50	15.00
—With bonus photo					
❑ Rolling Stones COC 79101	It's Only Rock 'n' Roll	1974	2.50	5.00	10.00
❑ Rolling Stones COC 79102	Made in the Shade	1975	2.50	5.00	10.00
❑ Rolling Stones COC 79104	Black and Blue	1976	2.50	5.00	10.00
❑ Rolling Stones 90120	Undercover	1983	3.00	6.00	12.00
—With stickers intact					
❑ Rolling Stones 90176	Rewind (1971-1984)	1984	6.25	12.50	25.00

RONETTES, THE

45s

Number	Title (A Side/B Side)	Yr	VG	VG+	NM
❑ A&M 1040	You Came, You Saw, You Conquered/Oh, I Love You	1969	4.00	8.00	16.00
❑ Buddah 384	Go Out and Get It/Lover, Lover	1973	5.00	10.00	20.00
—As "Ronnie Spector and the Ronettes"					
❑ Buddah 408	I Wish I Never Saw the Sunshine/I Wonder What He's Doing	1974	5.00	10.00	20.00
❑ Colpix 601	I Want a Boy/Sweet Sixteen	1961	25.00	50.00	100.00
—As "Ronnie and the Relatives"					
❑ Colpix 646	I'm Gonna Quit While I'm Ahead/I'm On the Wagon	1962	15.00	30.00	60.00
❑ Dimension 1046	He Did It/Recipe for Love	1965	12.50	25.00	50.00
❑ May 111	My Darling Angel/I'm Gonna Quit While I'm Ahead	1961	37.50	75.00	150.00
—As "Ronnie and the Relatives"					
❑ May 114	Silhouettes/You Bet I Would	1962	12.50	25.00	50.00
❑ May 138	Memory/Good Girls	1963	12.50	25.00	50.00
❑ Pavillion 03333	I Saw Mommy Kissing Santa Claus/ Rudolph the Red-Nosed Reindeer	1982	—	2.50	5.00
—B-side by The Crystals					
❑ Philles 116	Be My Baby/Tedesco and Pittman	1963	7.50	15.00	30.00
❑ Philles 118	Baby I Love You/Miss Joan and Mr. Sam	1963	7.50	15.00	30.00
❑ Philles 120	(The Best Part of) Breakin' Up/Big Red	1964	7.50	15.00	30.00
❑ Philles 121	Do I Love You?/Bebe and Susu	1964	7.50	15.00	30.00
❑ Philles 123	Walkin' in the Rain/How Does It Feel	1964	10.00	20.00	40.00

Number	Title (A Side/B Side)	Yr	VG	VG+	NM
❑ Philles 126	Born to Be Together/Blues for Baby	1965	6.25	12.50	25.00
❑ Philles 128	Is This What I Get for Loving You?/Oh, I Love You	1965	6.25	12.50	25.00
❑ Philles 133	I Can Hear Music/When I Saw You	1966	7.50	15.00	30.00
Albums					
❑ Colpix CP-486 [M]	The Ronettes Featuring Veronica	1965	50.00	100.00	200.00
—Gold label					
❑ Colpix SCP-486 [S]	The Ronettes Featuring Veronica	1965	75.00	150.00	300.00
—Gold label					
❑ Philles PHLP-4006 [M]	Presenting the Fabulous Ronettes Featuring Veronica	1964	100.00	200.00	400.00
—Yellow and red label					
❑ Philles PHLP-ST-4006 [S]	Presenting the Fabulous Ronettes Featuring Veronica	1965	150.00	300.00	600.00

RONNY AND THE DAYTONAS

45s

Number	Title (A Side/B Side)	Yr	VG	VG+	NM
❑ Mala 481	G.T.O./Hot Rod Baby	1964	6.25	12.50	25.00
❑ Mala 490	California Bound/Hey Little Girl	1964	5.00	10.00	20.00
❑ Mala 492	Bucket "T"/Little Rail Job	1964	5.00	10.00	20.00
❑ Mala 497	Little Scrambler/Teenage Years	1965	5.00	10.00	20.00
❑ Mala 503	Beach Boy/No Wheels	1965	6.25	12.50	25.00
❑ Mala 513	Sandy/(Instrumental)	1965	5.00	10.00	20.00
❑ Mala 525	Goodbye Baby/Somebody to Love Me	1966	5.00	10.00	20.00
❑ Mala 531	Antique '32 Studebaker Dictator Coupe/Then the Rains Came	1966	5.00	10.00	20.00
❑ Mala 542	I'll Think of Summer/Little Scrambler	1966	3.75	7.50	15.00
❑ RCA Victor 47-8896	All American Girl/Dianne, Dianne	1966	3.00	6.00	12.00
❑ RCA Victor 47-9022	Winter Weather/Young	1966	3.00	6.00	12.00
❑ RCA Victor 47-9107	Walk with the Sun/The Last Letter	1967	3.00	6.00	12.00
❑ RCA Victor 47-9253	Brave New World/Hold Onto Your Heart	1968	3.00	6.00	12.00
❑ RCA Victor 47-9435	The Girls and the Boys/Alfie	1968	3.00	6.00	12.00
Albums					
❑ Mala 4001 [M]	G.T.O.	1964	30.00	60.00	120.00
❑ Mala 4002 [M]	Sandy	1966	20.00	40.00	80.00
❑ Mala 4002S [S]	Sandy	1966	25.00	50.00	100.00

RONSTADT, LINDA

45s

Number	Title (A Side/B Side)	Yr	VG	VG+	NM
❑ Asylum 11026	Love Has No Pride/I Can Almost See It	1973	—	2.50	5.00
❑ Asylum 11032	Silver Threads and Golden Needles/Don't Cry Now	1974	—	2.50	5.00
❑ Asylum 11039	Desperado/Colorado	1974	—	2.50	5.00
❑ Asylum 45271	Love Is a Rose/Silver Blue	1975	—	3.00	6.00
❑ Asylum 45282	Heat Wave/Love Is a Rose	1975	—	2.00	4.00
❑ Asylum 45295	Tracks of My Tears/The Sweetest Gift	1975	—	2.00	4.00
—B-side with Emmylou Harris					
❑ Asylum 45340	That'll Be the Day/Try Me Again	1976	—	2.00	4.00
—Clouds label					
❑ Asylum 45340	That'll Be the Day/Try Me Again	1976	—	2.50	5.00
—All-blue label					
❑ Asylum 45361	Someone to Lay Down Beside Me/Crazy	1976	—	2.00	4.00
❑ Asylum 45402	Lose Again/Lo Siento Mi Vida	1977	2.00	4.00	8.00
❑ Asylum 45431	Blue Bayou/Old Paint	1977	—	2.00	4.00
❑ Asylum 45438	It's So Easy/Lo Siento Mi Vida	1977	—	2.00	4.00
❑ Asylum 45462	Poor Poor Pitiful Me/Simple Man, Simple Dream	1978	—	2.00	4.00
❑ Asylum 45464	Lago Azul/Lo Siento Mi Vida	1978	3.00	6.00	12.00
❑ Asylum 45479	Tumbling Dice/I Never Will Marry	1978	—	2.00	4.00
❑ Asylum 45519	Back in the U.S.A./White Rhythm and Blues	1978	—	2.00	4.00
❑ Asylum 45546	Ooh Baby Baby/Blowing Away	1978	—	2.00	4.00
❑ Asylum 46011	Just One Look/Love Me Tender	1979	—	2.00	4.00
❑ Asylum 46034	Alison/Mohammed's Radio	1979	—	2.00	4.00
❑ Asylum 46602	How Do I Make You/Rambler Gambler	1980	—	2.00	4.00
❑ Asylum 46624	Hurt So Bad/Justine	1980	—	2.00	4.00
❑ Asylum 46654	I Can't Let Go/Look Out for My Love	1980	—	2.00	4.00
❑ Asylum 69476	(I Love You) For Sentimental Reasons/Straighten Up and Fly Right	1987	—	2.00	4.00
❑ Asylum 69507	When You Wish Upon a Star/Little Girl Blue	1986	—	2.00	4.00
❑ Asylum 69653	When I Fall in Love/It Never Entered My Mind	1985	—	2.00	4.00
❑ Asylum 69671	Lush Life/Skylark	1985	—	2.00	4.00
❑ Asylum 69725	Someone to Watch Over Me/What'll I Do	1984	—	2.00	4.00
❑ Asylum 69752	I've Got a Crush on You/Lover Man	1984	—	2.00	4.00
❑ Asylum 69780	What's New/Crazy He Calls Me	1983	—	2.00	4.00
❑ Asylum 69838	Easy for You to Say/Mr. Radio	1983	—	2.00	4.00
❑ Asylum 69853	I Knew You When/Talk to Me of Mendocino	1982	—	2.00	4.00
❑ Asylum 69948	Get Closer/Sometimes You Just Can't Win	1982	—	2.00	4.00
❑ Capitol 2438	Dolphins/The Long Way Around	1969	3.00	6.00	12.00
❑ Capitol 2767	Lovesick Blues/Will You Love Me Tomorrow	1970	2.00	4.00	8.00
❑ Capitol 2846	Long Long Time/Nobody's	1970	2.00	4.00	8.00
❑ Capitol 3021	The Long Way Around/(She's a) Very Lovely Woman	1971	—	3.00	6.00
❑ Capitol 3210	I Fall to Pieces/Can It Be True	1971	—	3.00	6.00
❑ Capitol 3273	Rock Me on the Water/Crazy Arms	1972	—	3.00	6.00
❑ Capitol 3990	You're No Good/I Can't Help It (If I'm Still in Love with You)	1974	—	2.00	4.00
❑ Capitol 4050	When Will I Be Loved/It Doesn't Matter Anymore	1975	—	2.00	4.00
❑ Elektra 64987	All My Life/Shattered	1990	—	—	3.00
—With Aaron Neville					
❑ Elektra 69261	Don't Know Much/Cry Like a Rainstorm	1989	—	—	3.00
—With Aaron Neville					
❑ MCA 52973	Somewhere Out There/(Instrumental)	1986	—	—	3.00
—With James Ingram					
Albums					
❑ Asylum 6E-104	Simple Dreams	1977	2.50	5.00	10.00
❑ Asylum 6E-106	Greatest Hits	1977	2.50	5.00	10.00

Number	Title (A Side/B Side)	Yr	VG	VG+	NM
❑ Asylum 6E-155	Living in the U.S.A.	1978	2.50	5.00	10.00
❑ Asylum 5E-510	Mad Love	1980	2.50	5.00	10.00
❑ Asylum 5E-516	Greatest Hits, Volume 2	1980	2.50	5.00	10.00
❑ Asylum 7E-1045	Prisoner in Disguise	1975	2.50	5.00	10.00
❑ Asylum 7E-1072	Hasten Down the Wind	1976	2.50	5.00	10.00
—"Clouds" label					
❑ Asylum 7E-1092	Greatest Hits	1976	3.00	6.00	12.00
❑ Asylum SD 5064	Don't Cry Now	1973	2.50	5.00	10.00
❑ Asylum 60185	Get Closer	1982	2.50	5.00	10.00
❑ Asylum 60260	What's New	1983	2.50	5.00	10.00
❑ Asylum 60387	Lush Life	1984	2.50	5.00	10.00
❑ Asylum 60474	For Sentimental Reasons	1987	2.50	5.00	10.00
❑ Asylum 60489 [(3)]	'Round Midnight: The Nelson Riddle Sessions	1987	6.25	12.50	25.00
❑ Asylum 60765	Canciones De Mi Padre	1988	3.00	6.00	12.00
❑ Capitol ST-208	Hand Sown...Home Grown	1969	5.00	10.00	20.00
—Black label with colorband					
❑ Capitol ST-407	Silk Purse	1970	3.75	7.50	15.00
—Green label					
❑ Capitol SMAS-635	Linda Ronstadt	1972	3.00	6.00	12.00
❑ Capitol ST-11269	Different Drum	1974	3.00	6.00	12.00
—Also includes Stone Poneys tracks					
❑ Capitol ST-11358	Heart Like a Wheel	1974	3.00	6.00	12.00
❑ Capitol SKBB-11629 [(2)]	A Retrospective	1977	3.75	7.50	15.00
—Also includes Stone Poneys tracks					
❑ Capitol SN-16130	Hand Sown...Home Grown	1980	2.00	4.00	8.00
❑ Capitol SN-16131	Silk Purse	1980	2.00	4.00	8.00
❑ Capitol SN-16132	Linda Ronstadt	1980	2.00	4.00	8.00
❑ Capitol SN-16133	Beginnings	1980	2.00	4.00	8.00
❑ Capitol SN-16299	Different Drum	198?	2.00	4.00	8.00
—Budget-line reissue					
❑ Elektra 60872	Cry Like a Rainstorm, Howl Like the Wind	1989	3.00	6.00	12.00
❑ Pair PDL2-1070 [(2)]	Prime of Life	1986	3.00	6.00	12.00
❑ Pair PDL2-1125 [(2)]	Rockfile	1986	3.00	6.00	12.00

ROSE GARDEN, THE

45s

Number	Title (A Side/B Side)	Yr	VG	VG+	NM
❑ Atco 6510	Next Plane to London/Flower Town	1967	3.00	6.00	12.00
❑ Atco 6564	Here's Today/If My World Falls Through	1968	2.50	5.00	10.00

Albums

Number	Title (A Side/B Side)	Yr	VG	VG+	NM
❑ Atco 33-225 [M]	The Rose Garden	1968	15.00	30.00	60.00
❑ Atco SD 33-225 [S]	The Rose Garden	1968	6.25	12.50	25.00

ROSIE AND THE ORIGINALS

45s

Number	Title (A Side/B Side)	Yr	VG	VG+	NM
❑ Brunswick 55205	Lonely Blue Nights/We'll Have a Chance	1961	6.25	12.50	25.00
—By "Rosie, formerly with the Originals"					
❑ Brunswick 55212	My Darling Forever/The Time Is Near	1961	6.25	12.50	25.00
—By "Rosie, formerly with the Originals"					
❑ Era Back to Back Hits 038	Angel Baby/Bumble Boogie	197?	—	3.00	6.00
—B-side by B. Bumble and the Stingers					
❑ Highland 1011	Angel Baby/Give Me Love	1960	6.25	12.50	25.00
❑ Highland 1025	Why Did You Leave Me/Angel from Above	196?	5.00	10.00	20.00
❑ Highland 1032	Lonely Blue Nights/We'll Have a Chance	196?	6.25	12.50	25.00
—Actually a reissue of Brunswick 55205, but harder to find					

Albums

Number	Title (A Side/B Side)	Yr	VG	VG+	NM
❑ Brunswick BL 54102 [M]	Lonely Blue Nights with Rosie	1961	37.50	75.00	150.00
❑ Brunswick BL 754102 [S]	Lonely Blue Nights with Rosie	1961	50.00	100.00	200.00

ROSS, DIANA

45s

Number	Title (A Side/B Side)	Yr	VG	VG+	NM
❑ MCA 40947	Ease On Down the Road/Poppy Girls	1978	—	2.50	5.00
—With Michael Jackson; B-side by Quincy Jones					
❑ MCA 53448	If We Hold On Together/(Instrumental)	1988	—	—	3.00
❑ Motown 1165	Reach Out and Touch (Somebody's Hand)/Dark Side of the World	1970	—	2.50	5.00
❑ Motown 1169	Ain't No Mountain High Enough/Can't It Wait Until Tomorrow	1970	—	2.50	5.00
❑ Motown 1176	Remember Me/What About You	1971	—	2.50	5.00
❑ Motown 1184	Reach Out I'll Be There/Close to You	1971	—	2.50	5.00
❑ Motown 1188	Surrender/I'm a Winner	1971	—	2.50	5.00

Number	Title (A Side/B Side)	Yr	VG	VG+	NM
❑ Motown 1192	I'm Still Waiting/A Simple Thing Like Cry	1971	—	2.50	5.00
❑ Motown 1211	Good Morning Heartache/God Bless the Child	1972	—	2.50	5.00
❑ Motown 1239	Touch Me in the Morning/I Won't Last a Day Without You	1973	—	2.50	5.00
❑ Motown 1278	Last Time I Saw Him/Save the Children	1973	—	2.50	5.00
❑ Motown 1295	Sleepin'/You	1974	—	2.50	5.00
❑ Motown 1335	Sorry Doesn't Always Make It Right/Together	1975	—	2.50	5.00
❑ Motown 1377	Theme from Mahogany (Do You Know Where You're Going To)/ No One's Gonna Be a Fool Forever	1975	—	2.50	5.00
❑ Motown 1387	I Thought It Took a Little Time (But Today I Fell in Love)/After You	1976	—	2.50	5.00
❑ Motown 1392	Love Hangover/Kiss Me Now	1976	—	2.50	5.00
❑ Motown 1398	One Love in My Lifetime/Smile	1976	—	2.50	5.00
❑ Motown 1427	Gettin' Ready for Love/Confide in Me	1977	—	2.50	5.00
❑ Motown 1436	Your Love Is So Good for Me/Baby It's Me	1978	—	2.50	5.00
❑ Motown 1442	You Got It/Too Shy to Say	1978	—	2.50	5.00
❑ Motown 1456	What You Gave Me/Together	1979	—	2.00	4.00
❑ Motown 1462	The Boss/I'm in the World	1979	—	2.00	4.00
❑ Motown 1471	It's My House/Sparkle	1979	—	2.00	4.00
❑ Motown 1491	I'm Coming Out/Give Up	1980	—	2.00	4.00
❑ Motown 1494	Upside Down/Friend to Friend	1980	—	2.00	4.00
❑ Motown 1496	It's My Turn/Together	1980	—	2.00	4.00
❑ Motown 1508	One More Chance/After You	1981	—	2.00	4.00
❑ Motown 1513	To Love Again/Crying My Heart Out for You	1981	—	2.00	4.00
❑ Motown 1519	Endless Love/(Instrumental)	1981	—	2.00	4.00
—With Lionel Richie					
❑ Motown 1531	My Old Piano/Now That You're Gone	1981	—	2.00	4.00
❑ Motown 1626	We Can Never Light That Old Flame Again/Old Funky Rolls	1982	—	2.00	4.00
❑ Motown 1964	Workin' Overtime/(Instrumental)	1989	—	—	3.00
❑ Motown 1998	This House/Paradise	1989	—	—	3.00
❑ Motown 2003	Bottom Line/(Instrumental)	1989	—	—	3.00
❑ Motown 2139	When You Tell Me That You Love Me/You and I	1991	—	2.00	4.00
❑ RCA 5172-7-R	Dirty Looks/So Close	1987	—	—	3.00
❑ RCA 5297-7-R	Tell Me Again/I Am Me	1987	—	—	3.00
❑ RCA PB-12349	Why Do Fools Fall in Love/Think I'm in Love	1981	—	2.00	4.00
❑ RCA PB-13021	Mirror, Mirror/Sweet Nothings	1981	—	2.00	4.00
❑ RCA PB-13201	Work That Body/You Can Make It	1982	—	2.00	4.00
❑ RCA PB-13348	Muscles/I Am Me	1982	—	2.00	4.00
❑ RCA PB-13424	So Close/Fool for Your Love	1983	—	2.00	4.00
❑ RCA GB-13479	Why Do Fools Fall in Love/Mirror, Mirror	1983	—	—	3.00
—Gold Standard Series					
❑ RCA PB-13549	Pieces of Ice/Still in Love	1983	—	2.00	4.00
❑ RCA PB-13624	Up Front/Love or Loneliness	1983	—	2.00	4.00
❑ RCA PB-13671	Let's Go Up/Girls	1983	—	2.00	4.00
❑ RCA GB-13798	Muscles/Pieces of Ice	1984	—	—	3.00
—Gold Standard Series					
❑ RCA PB-13864	Swept Away/Fight for It	1984	—	—	3.00
❑ RCA PB-13966	Missing You/We Are the Children of the World	1984	—	—	3.00
❑ RCA PB-14032	Telephone/Fool for Your Love	1985	—	—	3.00
❑ RCA PB-14181	Eaten Alive/(Instrumental)	1985	—	—	3.00
❑ RCA PB-14244	Chain Reaction/More and More	1985	—	2.00	4.00
❑ RCA GB-14342	Missing You/Swept Away	1986	—	—	3.00
—Gold Standard Series					
Albums					
❑ Motown M5-135V1	Diana Ross	1981	2.00	4.00	8.00
—Reissue of 711					
❑ Motown M5-155V1	Diana!	1981	2.00	4.00	8.00
—Reissue of 719					
❑ Motown M5-163V1	Touch Me in the Morning	1981	2.00	4.00	8.00
—Reissue of 772					
❑ Motown M5-169V1	Diana Ross Live at Caesars Palace	1981	2.00	4.00	8.00
—Reissue of 801					
❑ Motown M5-198V1	The Boss	1981	2.00	4.00	8.00
—Reissue of 923					
❑ Motown M5-214V1	Duets with Diana	1981	2.50	5.00	10.00
❑ Motown MS-711	Diana Ross	1970	3.75	7.50	15.00
❑ Motown MS-719	Diana!	1971	3.75	7.50	15.00
❑ Motown MS-723	Surrender	1971	3.75	7.50	15.00
❑ Motown MS-724	Everything Is Everything	1970	3.75	7.50	15.00
❑ Motown M-758D [(2)]	Lady Sings the Blues	1972	3.75	7.50	15.00
—With booklet; all but four tracks are by Diana Ross					
❑ Motown M-772L	Touch Me in the Morning	1973	3.75	7.50	15.00
❑ Motown M6-801S1	Diana Ross Live at Caesars Palace	1974	3.00	6.00	12.00
❑ Motown M7-812V1	Last Time I Saw Him	1974	3.00	6.00	12.00
❑ Motown M6-861S1	Diana Ross	1976	3.00	6.00	12.00
❑ Motown M6-869S1	Diana Ross' Greatest Hits	1976	3.00	6.00	12.00
❑ Motown M7-877R2 [(2)]	An Evening with Diana Ross	1977	3.75	7.50	15.00
❑ Motown M7-890R1	Baby It's Me	1977	3.00	6.00	12.00
❑ Motown M7-907R1	Ross	1978	3.00	6.00	12.00
❑ Motown M8-923M1	The Boss	1979	2.50	5.00	10.00
❑ Motown M8-936	Diana	1980	2.50	5.00	10.00
❑ Motown M8-951M1	To Love Again	1981	2.50	5.00	10.00
❑ Motown M13-960C2 [(2)]	All the Great Hits	1981	3.00	6.00	12.00
❑ Motown 5294 ML	Diana Ross	1983	2.00	4.00	8.00
—Reissue of 861					
❑ Motown 6049 ML2 [(2)]	Diana Ross Anthology	1983	3.75	7.50	15.00
❑ Motown MOT-6274	Workin' Overtime	1989	2.50	5.00	10.00
❑ RCA Victor AFL1-4153	Why Do Fools Fall in Love	1981	2.50	5.00	10.00
❑ RCA Victor AFL1-4384	Silk Electric	1982	2.50	5.00	10.00

Number	Title (A Side/B Side)	Yr	VG	VG+	NM
❑ RCA Victor AFL1-4677	Ross	1983	2.00	4.00	8.00
❑ RCA Victor AFL1-5009	Swept Away	1984	2.00	4.00	8.00
❑ RCA Victor AYL1-5162	Why Do Fools Fall in Love	1985	—	3.00	6.00
—"Best Buy Series" reissue					
❑ RCA Victor AFL1-5422	Eaten Alive	1985	2.00	4.00	8.00
❑ RCA Victor 6388-1-R	Red Hot Rhythm and Blues	1987	2.00	4.00	8.00

ROSS, DIANA, AND MARVIN GAYE

45s

Number	Title (A Side/B Side)	Yr	VG	VG+	NM
❑ Motown 1269	My Mistake (Was to Love You)/Include Me in Your Life	1973	—	2.50	5.00
❑ Motown 1280	You're a Special Part of Me/I'm Falling in Love with You	1973	—	2.50	5.00
❑ Motown 1296	Don't Knock My Love/Just Say Just Say	1974	—	2.50	5.00

Albums

Number	Title (A Side/B Side)	Yr	VG	VG+	NM
❑ Motown M5-124V1	Diana & Marvin	1981	2.00	4.00	8.00
—Reissue					
❑ Motown M7-803	Diana & Marvin	1973	3.75	7.50	15.00

ROYAL, BILLY JOE

45s

Number	Title (A Side/B Side)	Yr	VG	VG+	NM
❑ All Wood 401	Wait for Me Baby/If It Wasn't for a Woman	1962	5.00	10.00	20.00
❑ Atlantic 2328	Never in a Hundred Years/We Haven't a Moment to Lose	1966	2.50	5.00	10.00
❑ Atlantic 87770	If the Jukebox Took Teardrops/How Could You	1991	—	2.00	4.00
❑ Atlantic 87867	Ring Where a Ring Used to Be/We Need to Walk	1990	—	2.00	4.00
❑ Atlantic 87933	Searchin' for Some Kind of Clue/This Too Shall Pass	1990	—	2.00	4.00
❑ Atlantic 88815	Till I Can't Take It Anymore/He Don't Know	1990	—	2.00	4.00
❑ Atlantic America 99217	Love Has No Right/Cross My Heart and Hope to Try	1989	—	—	3.00
❑ Atlantic America 99242	Tell It Like It Is/Losing You	1989	—	—	3.00
❑ Atlantic America 99295	It Keeps Right On Hurtin'/Let It Rain	1988	—	—	3.00
❑ Atlantic America 99364	Out of Sight and On My Mind/She Don't Cry Like She Used To	1988	—	—	3.00
❑ Atlantic America 99404	I'll Pin a Note on Your Pillow/A Place for a Heartache	1987	—	—	3.00
❑ Atlantic America 99485	Old Bridges Burn Slow/We've Both Got a Lot to Learn	1987	—	—	3.00
❑ Atlantic America 99519	I Miss You Already/Another Endless Night	1986	—	—	3.00
❑ Atlantic America 99555	Boardwalk Angel/Out of Sight and On My Mind	1986	—	—	3.00
❑ Atlantic America 99599	Burned Like a Rocket/Lonely Loving You	1985	—	—	3.00
❑ Columbia 43305	Down in the Boondocks/Oh, What a Night	1965	2.50	5.00	10.00
❑ Columbia 43390	I Knew You When/Steal Away	1965	2.50	5.00	10.00
❑ Columbia 43465	I've Got to Be Somebody/You Make Me Feel Like a Man	1965	2.00	4.00	8.00
❑ Columbia 43538	It's a Good Time/Don't Wait Up for Me Mama	1966	2.00	4.00	8.00
❑ Columbia 43622	Heart's Desire/Keep Inside Me	1966	2.00	4.00	8.00
❑ Columbia 43740	Campfire Girls/Should I Come Back	1966	2.00	4.00	8.00
❑ Columbia 43883	Yo-Yo/We Tried	1966	2.00	4.00	8.00
❑ Columbia 44003	Wisdom of a Fool/Everything Turned Blue	1967	2.00	4.00	8.00
❑ Columbia 44103	These Are Not My People/The Greatest Love	1967	2.00	4.00	8.00
❑ Columbia 44277	Hush/Watching from the Bandstand	1967	2.00	4.00	8.00
❑ Columbia 44468	Don't You Be Ashamed (To Call My Name)/Don't You Think It's Time	1968	2.00	4.00	8.00
❑ Columbia 44574	Storybook Children/Just Between You and Me	1968	2.00	4.00	8.00
❑ Columbia 44677	Movies in My Mind/Gabriel	1968	—	3.00	6.00
❑ Columbia 44743	Bed of Roses/The Greatest Love	1969	—	3.00	6.00
❑ Columbia 44814	Nobody Loves You But Me/Baby I'm Thinking of You	1969	—	2.50	5.00
❑ Columbia 44902	Cherry Hill Park/Helping Hand	1969	2.00	4.00	8.00
❑ Columbia 45085	Mama's Song/Me Without You	1970	—	2.50	5.00
❑ Columbia 45220	Burning a Hole/Every Night	1970	—	2.50	5.00
❑ Columbia 45289	Tulsa/Pick Up the Pieces	1970	—	2.50	5.00
❑ Columbia 45406	Poor Little Pearl/Lady Lives to Love	1971	—	2.50	5.00
❑ Columbia 45495	Colorado Rain/We Go Back	1971	—	2.50	5.00
❑ Columbia 45557	Later/The Family	1972	—	3.00	6.00
❑ Columbia 45620	Child of Mine/Natchez Trace	1972	—	3.00	6.00
❑ Fairlane 21009	Never in a Hundred Years/We Haven't a Moment to Lose	1961	7.50	15.00	30.00
❑ Fairlane 21013	Dark Glasses/Perhaps	1962	7.50	15.00	30.00
❑ Kat Family 01044	(Who is Like You) Sweet America/No Love Like a First Love	1981	—	2.00	4.00
❑ Kat Family 02074	You Really Got a Hold on Me/No Love Like a First Love	1981	—	2.00	4.00
❑ Kat Family 02297	Wasted Time/Outrun the Sun	1981	—	2.00	4.00
❑ Mercury 76069	Mr. Kool/Let's Talk It Over	1980	—	2.00	4.00
❑ MGM South 7011	This Magic Moment/Mountain Woman	1973	—	2.50	5.00
❑ MGM South 7018	Summertime Skies/Look What I Found	1973	—	2.50	5.00
❑ MGM South 7022	If This Is the Last Time/Perfect Harmony	1973	—	2.50	5.00
❑ MGM South 7032	Star Again/Sugar Blue	1974	—	2.50	5.00
❑ Player's 1	I'm Specialized/Really You	1965	5.00	10.00	20.00

Number	Title (A Side/B Side)	Yr	VG	VG+	NM
❑ Private Stock 45,192	Under the Boardwalk/Precious Time	1978	—	2.50	5.00
❑ Scepter 12419	All Night Rain/Time Don't Pass By Here	1976	—	2.00	4.00
❑ Tollie 9011	Mama Didn't Raise No Fools/Get Behind Me, Devil	1964	3.75	7.50	15.00
Albums					
❑ Atlantic America 90508	Looking Ahead	1986	2.50	5.00	10.00
❑ Atlantic America 90658	The Royal Treatment	1987	2.50	5.00	10.00
❑ Atlantic America 91064	Tell It Like It Is	1989	2.50	5.00	10.00
❑ Columbia CL 2403 [M]	Down in the Boondocks	1965	5.00	10.00	20.00
❑ Columbia CL 2781 [M]	Billy Joe Royal	1967	6.25	12.50	25.00
❑ Columbia CS 9203 [S]	Down in the Boondocks	1965	6.25	12.50	25.00
❑ Columbia CS 9581 [S]	Billy Joe Royal	1967	6.25	12.50	25.00
❑ Columbia CS 9974	Cherry Hill Park	1969	6.25	12.50	25.00
❑ Kat Family JW 37342	Billy Joe Royal	1982	2.50	5.00	10.00
❑ Mercury SRM-1-3837	Billy Joe Royal	1980	2.50	5.00	10.00
ROYAL GUARDSMEN, THE					
45s					
❑ Laurie 112	Snoopy's Christmas/The Smallest Astronaut	197?	—	2.00	4.00
—B-side by Barry Winslow; reissue					
❑ Laurie 3359	Baby Let's Wait/Leaving Me	1966	2.50	5.00	10.00
❑ Laurie 3366	Snoopy vs. the Red Baron/I Needed You	1966	3.00	6.00	12.00
—Regular red, black and white label					
❑ Laurie 3379	The Return of the Red Baron/Sweetmeats Slide	1967	2.50	5.00	10.00
❑ Laurie 3391	Airplane Song (My Airplane)/Om	1967	2.00	4.00	8.00
❑ Laurie 3397	Wednesday/So Right (To Be in Love)	1967	2.00	4.00	8.00
❑ Laurie 3416	Snoopy's Christmas/It Kinda Looks Like Christmas	1967	2.50	5.00	10.00
❑ Laurie 3428	I Say Love/I'm Not Gonna Stay	1968	2.00	4.00	8.00
❑ Laurie 3451	Snoopy for President/Down Behind the Lines	1968	2.00	4.00	8.00
❑ Laurie 3461	Baby Let's Wait/Biplane "Evermore"	1968	2.00	4.00	8.00
❑ Laurie 3461	Baby Let's Wait/So Right (To Be in Love)	1968	2.00	4.00	8.00
❑ Laurie 3494	Magic Window/Mother, Where's Your Daughter	1969	2.50	5.00	8.00
❑ Laurie 3590	Snoopy for President/Down Behind the Lines	1972	—	3.00	6.00
❑ Laurie 3646	Snoopy for President/Sweetmeats Slide	1976	—	2.50	5.00
Albums					
❑ Holiday HDY 1913	Merry Snoopy's Christmas	1980	2.50	5.00	10.00
—Reissue of Laurie 2042					
❑ Laurie LLP-2038 [M]	Snoopy vs. the Red Baron	1967	5.00	10.00	20.00
❑ Laurie SLP-2038 [S]	Snoopy vs. the Red Baron	1967	6.25	12.50	25.00
❑ Laurie LLP-2039 [M]	The Return of the Red Baron	1967	5.00	10.00	20.00
❑ Laurie SLP-2039 [S]	The Return of the Red Baron	1967	6.25	12.50	25.00
❑ Laurie LLP 2042 [M]	Snoopy and His Friends	1967	3.75	7.50	15.00
—With "Merry Snoopy's Christmas" poster missing					
❑ Laurie LLP 2042 [M]	Snoopy and His Friends	1967	6.25	12.50	25.00
—With "Merry Snoopy's Christmas" poster still attached to back cover					
❑ Laurie SLP 2042 [S]	Snoopy and His Friends	1967	7.50	15.00	30.00
—With "Merry Snoopy's Christmas" poster still attached to back cover					
❑ Laurie SLP 2042 [S]	Snoopy and His Friends	1967	5.00	10.00	20.00
—With "Merry Snoopy's Christmas" poster missing					
❑ Laurie SLP-2046	Snoopy for President	1968	6.25	12.50	25.00
ROYAL TEENS, THE					
45s					
❑ ABC-Paramount 9882	Short Shorts/Planet Rock	1958	7.50	15.00	30.00
❑ ABC-Paramount 9918	Big Name Button/Sham Rock	1958	6.25	12.50	25.00
❑ ABC-Paramount 9945	Harvey's Got a Girl Friend/Hangin' Around	1958	6.25	12.50	25.00
❑ ABC-Paramount 9955	Open the Door/My Kind of Dream	1958	6.25	12.50	25.00
❑ Allnew 1415	Short Short Twist/Royal Twist	1962	5.00	10.00	20.00
❑ Astra 1012	Mad Gass/Sittin' with My Baby	196?	3.75	7.50	15.00
❑ Capitol F4261	Believe Me/Little Cricket	1959	7.50	15.00	30.00
❑ Capitol 4335	The Moon's Not Meant for Lovers/Was It a Dream	1960	7.50	15.00	30.00
❑ Capitol 4402	With You/It's the Talk of the Town	1960	7.50	15.00	30.00
❑ Jubilee 5418	Short Short Twist/Royal Twist	1962	3.75	7.50	15.00
❑ Mighty 111	Leotards/Royal Blues	1959	6.25	12.50	25.00
❑ Mighty 112	Cave Man/Wounded Heart	1959	7.50	15.00	30.00
❑ Mighty 200	My Memories of You/Little Trixie	1961	10.00	20.00	40.00
❑ Musicor 1398	Smile a Little Smile for Me/Hey Jude	1969	2.50	5.00	10.00
❑ Power 113	Mad Gass/Sittin' with My Baby	1959	10.00	20.00	40.00
❑ Power 215	Short Shorts/Planet Rock	1957	37.50	75.00	150.00
❑ Swan 4200	I'll Love You ('Til the End of Time)/(Instrumental)	1965	25.00	50.00	100.00
❑ TCF Hall 117	Bad Girl/Do the Montoona	1965	3.75	7.50	15.00
Albums					
❑ Collectables COL-5094	Short Shorts: Golden Classics	198?	2.50	5.00	10.00
❑ Musicor MS-3186	Newies But Oldies	1970	5.00	10.00	20.00
❑ Tru-Gems 1001	Short Shorts & Others	1975	5.00	10.00	20.00
RUBY AND THE ROMANTICS					
45s					
❑ A&M 1042	Hurting Each Other/Baby, I Could Be So Good at Loving You	1969	2.00	4.00	8.00
❑ ABC 10911	Twilight Time/Una Bella Brazilian Melody	1967	2.50	5.00	10.00
❑ ABC 10941	Only Heaven Knows/This Is No Laughing Matter	1967	2.50	5.00	10.00
❑ ABC 11065	On a Clear Day You Can See Forever/More Than Yesterday, Less Than Tomorrow	1968	2.50	5.00	10.00
❑ Kapp 501	Our Day Will Come/Moonlight and Music	1963	3.75	7.50	15.00
❑ Kapp 525	My Summer Love/Sweet Love and Sweet Forgiveness	1963	3.00	6.00	12.00
❑ Kapp 544	Hey There Lonely Boy/Not a Moment Too Soon	1963	3.00	6.00	12.00
❑ Kapp 557	Young Wings Can Fly (Higher Than You Know)/Day Dreaming	1963	3.00	6.00	12.00
❑ Kapp 578	Our Everlasting Love/Much Better Off Than I've Ever Been	1964	3.00	6.00	12.00
❑ Kapp 601	Baby Come Home/Every Day's a Holiday	1964	3.00	6.00	12.00

Number	Title (A Side/B Side)	Yr	VG	VG+	NM
❑ Kapp 615	When You're Young and In Love/I Cry Alone	1964	3.00	6.00	12.00
❑ Kapp 646	Does He Really Care for Me/Nevertheless (I'm in Love with You)	1965	3.00	6.00	12.00
❑ Kapp 665	We'll Meet Again/Your Baby Doesn't Love You Anymore	1965	3.00	6.00	12.00
❑ Kapp 702	Nobody But My Baby/Imagination	1965	3.00	6.00	12.00
❑ Kapp 759	We Can Make It/Remember Me	1966	2.50	5.00	10.00
❑ Kapp 773	Hey There Lonely Boy/Think	1966	2.50	5.00	10.00
❑ Kapp 839	I Know/We'll Love Again	1967	2.50	5.00	10.00
Albums					
❑ ABC S-638	More Than Yesterday	1968	5.00	10.00	20.00
❑ Kapp KL-1323 [M]	Our Day Will Come	1963	7.50	15.00	30.00
❑ Kapp KL-1341 [M]	Till Then	1963	6.25	12.50	25.00
❑ Kapp KL-1458 [M]	The Greatest Hits Album	1966	5.00	10.00	20.00
❑ Kapp KL-1526 [M]	Ruby and the Romantics	1967	6.25	12.50	25.00
❑ Kapp KS-3323 [S]	Our Day Will Come	1963	10.00	20.00	40.00
❑ Kapp KS-3341 [S]	Till Then	1963	7.50	15.00	30.00
❑ Kapp KS-3458 [S]	The Greatest Hits Album	1966	6.25	12.50	25.00
❑ Kapp KS-3526 [S]	Ruby and the Romantics	1967	6.25	12.50	25.00
❑ MCA 541	The Greatest Hits Album	197?	2.50	5.00	10.00
❑ Pickwick SPC-3519	Makin' Out	197?	2.50	5.00	10.00
RUFFIN, DAVID					
45s					
❑ Anna 1127	I'm in Love/One of These Days	1961	15.00	30.00	60.00
❑ Check Mate 1003	You Can Get What I Got/Action Speaks Louder Than Words	1961	15.00	30.00	60.00
❑ Check Mate 1010	Mr. Bus Driver — Hurry!/Knock You Out (With Love)	1962	15.00	30.00	60.00
❑ Motown 1140	My Whole World Ended (The Moment You Left Me)/ I've Got to Find Myself a Brand New Baby	1968	—	3.00	6.00
❑ Motown 1149	I've Lost Everything I've Ever Loved/ We'll Have a Good Thing Going On	1969	—	3.00	6.00
❑ Motown 1158	I'm So Glad I Fell for You/I Pray Every Day You Won't Regret Loving Me	1969	—	3.00	6.00
❑ Motown 1178	Each Day Is a Lifetime/Don't Stop Loving Me	1971	—	3.00	6.00
❑ Motown 1187	You Can Come Right Back to Me/Dinah	1971	—	3.00	6.00
❑ Motown 1204	A Day in the Life of a Working Man/A Little More Trust	1972	—	3.00	6.00
❑ Motown 1223	Blood Donors Needed/Go On with Your Bad Self	1973	—	3.00	6.00
❑ Motown 1259	Common Man/I'm Just a Mortal Man	1973	—	3.00	6.00
❑ Motown 1327	Me and Rock and Roll (Are Here to Stay)/Smiling Faces Sometimes	1974	—	3.00	6.00
❑ Motown 1332 *—Unreleased*	Take Me Clear from Here/I Just Want to Celebrate	1975	—	—	—
❑ Motown 1336	Superstar/No Matter Where	1975	—	2.50	5.00
❑ Motown 1376	Walk Away from Love/Love Can Be Hazardous to Your Health	1975	—	2.50	5.00
❑ Motown 1388	Heavy Love/Love Can Be Hazardous To Your Health	1976	—	2.50	5.00
❑ Motown 1393	Everything's Coming Up Love/No Matter Where	1976	—	2.50	5.00
❑ Motown 1405	On and Off/Statue of a Fool	1976	—	2.50	5.00
❑ Motown 1420	Just Let Me Hold You for a Night/Rode by the Place (Where We Used to Stay)	1977	—	2.50	5.00
❑ Motown 1435	You're My Peace of Mind/Rose By the Place (Where We Used to Stay)	1978	—	2.50	5.00
❑ Warner Bros. 49030	Sexy Dancer/Break My Heart	1979	—	2.00	4.00
❑ Warner Bros. 49123	I Get Excited/Chain on the Brain	1979	—	2.00	4.00
❑ Warner Bros. 49277	Slow Dance/Don't You Go Home	1980	—	2.00	4.00
❑ Warner Bros. 49577	Still in Love with You/I Wanna Be with You	1980	—	2.00	4.00
Albums					
❑ Motown M5-146V1 *—Reissue*	My Whole World Ended	1981	2.00	4.00	8.00
❑ Motown M5-211V1 *—Reissue*	At His Best	1981	2.00	4.00	8.00
❑ Motown MS-685	My Whole World Ended	1969	5.00	10.00	20.00
❑ Motown MS-696	Feelin' Good	1969	3.75	7.50	15.00
❑ Motown M 733 *—Canceled*	David Ruffin	1971	—	—	—
❑ Motown M-762	David Ruffin	1973	3.00	6.00	12.00
❑ Motown M6-818	Me 'N' Rock 'N' Roll Are Here to Stay	1974	3.00	6.00	12.00
❑ Motown M6-849	Who I Am	1975	3.00	6.00	12.00
❑ Motown M6-866	Everything's Coming Up Love	1976	3.00	6.00	12.00
❑ Motown M6-885	In My Stride	1977	3.00	6.00	12.00

Number	Title (A Side/B Side)	Yr	VG	VG+	NM
❑ Motown M7-895	At His Best	1978	3.00	6.00	12.00
❑ Warner Bros. BSK 3306	So Soon We Change	1979	2.50	5.00	10.00
❑ Warner Bros. BSK 3416	Gentleman Ruffin	1980	2.50	5.00	10.00

RUFFIN, JIMMY

45s

Number	Title (A Side/B Side)	Yr	VG	VG+	NM
❑ Atco 6926	Tears of Joy/Goin' Home	1973	2.00	4.00	8.00
❑ Chess 2160	Tell Me What You Want/Do You Know Me	1974	—	2.50	5.00
❑ Chess 2168	What You See (Ain't Always What You Get)/Boy from Mississippi	1975	—	2.50	5.00
❑ Epic 50339	Fallin' in Love with You/Fallin' in Love with You	1977	—	2.50	5.00
❑ Epic 50384	Fallin' in Love with You/Fallin' in Love with You	1977	—	2.50	5.00
❑ Miracle 1	Don't Feel Sorry for Me/Heart	1961	50.00	100.00	200.00
❑ RSO 1021	Hold On to My Love/(Instrumental)	1980	—	2.50	5.00
❑ RSO 1042	Night of Love/Searchin'	1980	—	2.50	5.00
❑ Soul 35002	Since I've Lost You/I Want Her Love	1964	10.00	20.00	40.00
❑ Soul 35016	As Long As There Is L-O-V-E/How Can I Say I'm Sorry	1965	2.50	5.00	10.00
❑ Soul 35022	What Becomes of the Brokenhearted/Baby I've Got It	1966	3.75	7.50	15.00
❑ Soul 35027	I've Passed This Way Before/Tomorrow's Tears	1966	2.50	5.00	10.00
❑ Soul 35032	Gonna Give Her All the Love I've Got/World So Wide (Nowhere to Hide from Your Heart)	1967	2.00	4.00	8.00
❑ Soul 35035	Don't You Miss Me A Little Bit Baby/I Want Her Love	1967	2.00	4.00	8.00
❑ Soul 35043	I'll Say Forever My Love/Everybody Needs Love	1968	2.00	4.00	8.00
❑ Soul 35046	Don't Let Him Take Your Love from Me/Lonely, Lonely Man Am I	1968	2.00	4.00	8.00
❑ Soul 35053	Sad and Lonesome Feeling/Gonna Keep On Trying Till I Win Your Love	1968	2.00	4.00	8.00
❑ Soul 35060	Farewell Is a Lonely Sound/If You Will Let Me, I Know I Can	1969	2.00	4.00	8.00
❑ Soul 35077	Maria (You Were the Only One)/Living in a World I Created For Myself	1970	2.00	4.00	8.00
❑ Soul 35092	Our Favorite Melody/You Gave Me Love	1972	—	3.00	6.00

Albums

Number	Title (A Side/B Side)	Yr	VG	VG+	NM
❑ RSO RS-1-3078	Sunrise	1980	2.50	5.00	10.00
❑ Soul 704 [M] *—One-color cover*	Top Ten	1967	12.50	25.00	50.00
❑ Soul 704 [M] *—Full-color cover*	Top Ten	1967	6.25	12.50	25.00
❑ Soul S-704 [S]	Top Ten	1967	6.25	12.50	25.00
❑ Soul S-708	Ruff'n Ready	1969	6.25	12.50	25.00
❑ Soul SS-727	The Groove Governor	1970	5.00	10.00	20.00

RUFUS

45s

Number	Title (A Side/B Side)	Yr	VG	VG+	NM
❑ ABC 11356	Slip 'N Slide/I Finally Found You	1973	2.00	4.00	8.00
❑ ABC 11376	Whoever's Thrilling You (Is Killing Me)/I Finally Found You	1973	—	3.00	6.00
❑ ABC 11394	Feel Good/Keep It Coming	1973	—	3.00	6.00
❑ ABC 11427	Tell Me Something Good/Smokin' Room	1974	—	3.00	6.00
❑ ABC 12010	Tell Me Something Good/Smokin' Room	1974	—	2.50	5.00
❑ ABC 12032	You Got the Love/Rags to Rufus	1974	—	2.50	5.00
❑ ABC 12066	Once You Get Started/Rufusized	1975	—	2.50	5.00
❑ ABC 12099	Please Pardon Me (You Remind Me of a Friend)/ Somebody's Watching You	1975	—	2.50	5.00
❑ ABC 12149	Sweet Thing/Circles	1975	—	2.50	5.00
❑ ABC 12179	Dance Wit' Me/Everybody's Got an Aura	1976	—	2.50	5.00
❑ ABC 12197	Jive Talkin'/On Time	1976	—	2.50	5.00
❑ ABC 12239	At Midnight (My Love Will Lift You Up)/Better Days	1976	—	2.50	5.00
❑ ABC 12269	Holywood/Earth Song	1977	—	2.50	5.00
❑ ABC 12296	Everlasting Love/Close the Door	1977	—	2.50	5.00
❑ ABC 12349	Stay/My Ship Will Sail	1978	—	2.50	5.00
❑ ABC 12390	Blue Love/Turn	1978	—	2.50	5.00
❑ ABC 12444	Keep It Together (Declaration of Love)/Red Hot Poker	1979	—	2.50	5.00
❑ Epic 10691	Read All About It/Brand New Day	1971	3.00	6.00	12.00
❑ Epic 10726	Follow the Lamb/Fire One, Fire Two, Fire Three	1971	3.00	6.00	12.00
❑ MCA 41025	Ain't Nobody Like You/You're to Blame	1979	—	2.00	4.00
❑ MCA 41131	Do You Love What You Feel/Dancin' Mood	1979	—	2.00	4.00
❑ MCA 41191	What Am I Missing/Any Love	1980	—	2.00	4.00
❑ MCA 41230	I'm Dancing for Your Love/Walk the Rockway	1980	—	2.00	4.00
❑ MCA 51070	Tonight We Love/Afterwards	1981	—	2.00	4.00
❑ MCA 51125	Party 'Til You're Broke/Hold On to a Friend	1981	—	2.00	4.00
❑ MCA 51203	Sharing the Love/We Got the Way	1981	—	2.00	4.00
❑ MCA 52002	True Love/Better Together	1982	—	2.00	4.00
❑ Warner Bros. 29406	One Million Kisses/Stay	1983	—	2.00	4.00
❑ Warner Bros. 29555	Ain't Nobody/Sweet Thing	1983	—	2.00	4.00
❑ Warner Bros. 29675	Blinded by the Boogie/You're Really Out of Line	1983	—	2.00	4.00
❑ Warner Bros. 29790	Take It to the Hop/Distant Lover	1983	—	2.00	4.00

Albums

Number	Title (A Side/B Side)	Yr	VG	VG+	NM
❑ ABC X-783	Rufus	1973	2.50	5.00	10.00
❑ ABC X-809	Rags to Rufus	1974	2.50	5.00	10.00
❑ ABC D-837	Rufusized	1974	2.50	5.00	10.00
❑ ABC D-909	Rufus Featuring Chaka Khan	1975	2.50	5.00	10.00
❑ ABC D-975	Ask Rufus	1977	2.50	5.00	10.00
❑ ABC AA-1049	Street Player	1978	2.50	5.00	10.00
❑ ABC AA-1098	Numbers	1979	2.50	5.00	10.00
❑ MCA 642 *—Reissue of ABC 783*	Rufus	1980	—	3.00	6.00
❑ MCA 5103	Masterjam	1979	2.50	5.00	10.00
❑ MCA 5159	Party 'Til You're Broke	1981	2.50	5.00	10.00
❑ MCA 5270	Camouflage	1982	2.50	5.00	10.00
❑ MCA 5339	The Very Best of Rufus	1983	2.50	5.00	10.00
❑ MCA 37034 *—Reissue of ABC 809*	Rags to Rufus	1980	—	3.00	6.00

Number	Title (A Side/B Side)	Yr	VG	VG+	NM
❑ MCA 37035	Rufusized	1980	—	3.00	6.00
—Reissue of ABC 837					
❑ MCA 37036	Rufus Featuring Chaka Khan	1980	—	3.00	6.00
—Reissue of ABC 909					
❑ MCA 37037	Ask Rufus	1980	—	3.00	6.00
—Reissue of ABC 975					
❑ MCA 37038	Street Player	1980	—	3.00	6.00
—Reissue of ABC 1049					
❑ MCA 37039	Numbers	1980	—	3.00	6.00
—Reissue of ABC 1098					
❑ MCA 37157	Masterjam	198?	—	3.00	6.00
—Reissue of 5103					
❑ Warner Bros. 23679 [(2)]	Live: Stompin' at the Savoy	1983	3.00	6.00	12.00
❑ Warner Bros. 23753	Seal in Red	1984	2.50	5.00	10.00
RUNDGREN, TODD					
45s					
❑ Ampex 31001	We Gotta Get You a Woman/Medley	1970	2.50	5.00	10.00
—As "Runt"					
❑ Bearsville 0003	I Saw the Light/Marlene	1972	3.00	6.00	12.00
—Blue vinyl					
❑ Bearsville 0007	Couldn't I Just Tell You/Wolfman Jack	1972	—	3.00	6.00
❑ Bearsville 0009	Hello It's Me/Cold Morning Light	1973	—	3.00	6.00
❑ Bearsville 0020	A Dream Goes On Forever/Heavy Metal Kids	1974	—	3.00	6.00
❑ Bearsville 0030	We Gotta Get You a Woman/I Saw the Light	1973	—	2.00	4.00
—"Back to Back Hits" series					
❑ Bearsville 0301	Breathless/Wolfman Jack	1974	—	3.00	6.00
❑ Bearsville 0304	Real Man/Prana	1975	—	2.50	5.00
❑ Bearsville 0309	Good Vibrations/When I Pray	1976	—	2.50	5.00
❑ Bearsville 0310	Love of the Common Man/Black and White	1976	—	2.50	5.00
❑ Bearsville 0324	Can We Still Be Friends/Determination	1978	—	2.50	5.00
❑ Bearsville 0324	Can We Still Be Friends/Out of Control	1978	—	2.50	5.00
❑ Bearsville 0330	You Cried Wolf/Onomatopoeia	1978	—	2.50	5.00
❑ Bearsville 0335	It Wouldn't Have Made Any Difference/Did You Ever Learn	1979	—	2.50	5.00
❑ Bearsville 29686	Bang the Drum All Day/Chant	1983	—	3.00	6.00
❑ Bearsville 29759	Emperor of the Highway/Hideaway	1983	—	2.00	4.00
❑ Bearsville 31002	Be Nice to Me/Broke Down and Busted	1971	2.00	4.00	8.00
—As "Runt-Todd Rundgren"					
❑ Bearsville 31004	A Long Time, A Long Way to Go/Parole	1971	2.00	4.00	8.00
—As "Runt-Todd Rundgren"					
❑ Bearsville 49696	Time Heals/Tiny Demons	1981	—	2.00	4.00
❑ Bearsville 49771	Compassion/Pulse	1981	—	2.50	5.00
❑ Columbia 06151	Loving You's a Dirty Job (But Somebody's Gotta Do It)/ Before This Night Is Through	1986	—	2.00	4.00
—With Bonnie Tyler					
❑ Rhino 74426	Bang the Drum All Day/Can We Still Be Friends	1987	—	2.00	4.00
❑ Warner Bros. 22868	I Love My Life/Parallel Lines	1989	—	—	3.00
❑ Warner Bros. 28821	Something to Fall Back On/Lockjaw	1986	—	2.00	4.00
Albums					
❑ Ampex A-10105	Runt	1970	12.50	25.00	50.00
—LP jacket and label list 10 tracks and album actually has 10					
❑ Bearsville BR 2046	Runt	1972	3.75	7.50	15.00
—Another reissue, after switch from Ampex to Warner Bros. distribution					
❑ Bearsville BR 2047	The Ballad of Todd Rundgren	1972	3.75	7.50	15.00
—Reissue of 10116					
❑ Bearsville 2BX 2066 [(2)]	Something/Anything?	1972	6.25	12.50	25.00
—Regular copy with black vinyl					
❑ Bearsville BR 2133	A Wizard/A True Star	1973	3.00	6.00	12.00
❑ Bearsville BHS 3522	Healing	1981	2.50	5.00	10.00
—Add $5 if bonus 7-inch 33 1/3 single (Time Heals/Tiny Demons) is included					
❑ Bearsville 2BR 6952 [(2)]	Todd	1974	3.75	7.50	15.00
❑ Bearsville BR 6957	Initiation	1975	2.50	5.00	10.00
❑ Bearsville BR 6963	Faithful	1976	2.50	5.00	10.00
❑ Bearsville BRK 6981	Hermit of Mink Hollow	1978	2.50	5.00	10.00
❑ Bearsville 2BRX 6986 [(2)]	Back to the Bars	1978	3.00	6.00	12.00
❑ Bearsville A-10105	Runt	1971	6.25	12.50	25.00
—Reissue with new label					

Number	Title (A Side/B Side)	Yr	VG	VG+	NM
❑ Bearsville A-10116	The Ballad of Todd Rundgren	1971	20.00	40.00	80.00
❑ Bearsville 23732	The Ever Popular Tortured Artist Effect	1983	2.50	5.00	10.00
❑ Rhino RNLP 70862	Runt	1987	2.50	5.00	10.00
❑ Rhino RNLP 70863	The Ballad of Todd Rundgren	1987	2.50	5.00	10.00
❑ Rhino RNLP 70864	A Wizard/A True Star	1987	2.50	5.00	10.00
❑ Rhino RNLP 70866	Initiation	1987	2.50	5.00	10.00
❑ Rhino RNLP 70868	Faithful	1987	2.50	5.00	10.00
❑ Rhino RNLP 70871	Hermit of Mink Hollow	1988	2.50	5.00	10.00
❑ Rhino RNLP 70874	Healing	1987	2.50	5.00	10.00
❑ Rhino RNLP 70876	The Ever Popular Tortured Artist Effect	1988	2.50	5.00	10.00
❑ Rhino RNDA 71107	Something/Anything?	1987	3.00	6.00	12.00
❑ Rhino RNDA 71108	Todd	1987	3.00	6.00	12.00
❑ Rhino RNDA 71109	Back to the Bars	1987	3.00	6.00	12.00
❑ Rhino R1-71491	Anthology (1968-1985)	1989	5.00	10.00	20.00
❑ Warner Bros. 25128	A Cappella	1985	2.50	5.00	10.00
❑ Warner Bros. 25881	Nearly Human	1989	3.75	7.50	15.00
RUSH					
45s					
❑ Mercury 73623	Finding My Way/Need Some Love	1974	20.00	40.00	80.00
❑ Mercury 73647	In the Mood/What You're Doing	1974	20.00	40.00	80.00
❑ Mercury 73681	Fly by Night/Anthem	1975	20.00	40.00	80.00
❑ Mercury 73728	Return of the Prince/I Think I'm Going Bald	1975	20.00	40.00	80.00
❑ Mercury 73737	Lakeside Park/Bastille Day	1975	20.00	40.00	80.00
❑ Mercury 73803	The Twilight Zone/Lessons	1976	20.00	40.00	80.00
❑ Mercury 73873	Fly by Night-In the Mood/Something for Nothing	1976	2.50	5.00	10.00
❑ Mercury 73912	Making Memories/The Temples of Syrinx	1977	2.50	5.00	10.00
❑ Mercury 73958	Closer to the Heart/Madrigal	1977	2.50	5.00	10.00
❑ Mercury 73990	Fly by Night/Anthem	1978	2.50	5.00	10.00
❑ Mercury 74051	The Trees/Circumstances	1979	2.50	5.00	10.00
❑ Mercury 76044	The Spirit of Radio/Circumstances	1980	2.50	5.00	10.00
❑ Mercury 76060	Entre Nous/Different Strings	1980	2.50	5.00	10.00
❑ Mercury 76095	Limelight/XYZ	1981	2.50	5.00	10.00
❑ Mercury 76109	Tom Sawyer/Witch Hunt	1981	2.50	5.00	10.00
❑ Mercury 76124	Closer to the Heart/Freewill	1981	2.00	4.00	8.00
❑ Mercury 76179	New World Man/Vital Signs	1982	2.00	4.00	8.00
❑ Mercury 76196	Subdivisions/Countdown	1982	2.50	5.00	10.00
❑ Mercury 880050-7	The Body Electric/Between the Wheels	1984	2.50	5.00	10.00
❑ Mercury 884191-7	The Big Money/Red Sector A	1985	2.00	4.00	8.00
❑ Mercury 888891-7	Time Stand Still/High Water	1987	—	3.00	6.00
❑ Moon 001	Not Fade Away/You Can't Fight It	1973	125.00	250.00	500.00
—Canada-only release					
Albums					
❑ Atlantic 82040	Presto	1989	5.00	10.00	20.00
❑ Atlantic 83728	Feedback	2004	3.00	6.00	12.00
❑ Mercury SRM-1-1011	Rush	1974	2.50	5.00	10.00
—Based on the LP's release date, original copies theoretically have red labels, rather than the common "Chicago skyline" labels; those would be worth at least twice this price					
❑ Mercury SRM-1-1023	Fly by Night	1975	2.50	5.00	10.00
—"Chicago skyline" label					
❑ Mercury SRM-1-1046	Caress of Steel	1975	2.50	5.00	10.00
—"Chicago skyline" label					
❑ Mercury SRM-1-1079	2112	1976	2.50	5.00	10.00
—"Chicago skyline" label					
❑ Mercury SRM-1-1184	A Farewell to Kings	1977	2.50	5.00	10.00
—"Chicago skyline" label					
❑ Mercury SRP-1-1300 [PD]	Hemispheres	1979	10.00	20.00	40.00
❑ Mercury SRM-1-3743	Hemispheres	1978	2.50	5.00	10.00
—"Chicago skyline" label; with poster					
❑ Mercury SRM-1-4001	Permanent Waves	1980	2.50	5.00	10.00
—Custom label					
❑ Mercury SRM-1-4013	Moving Pictures	1981	2.50	5.00	10.00
—Custom label					
❑ Mercury SRM-1-4063	Signals	1982	2.50	5.00	10.00
❑ Mercury SRM-2-7001 [(2)]	Exit... Stage Left	1981	3.00	6.00	12.00
❑ Mercury SRM-2-7508 [(2)]	All the World's a Stage	1976	3.00	6.00	12.00
—"Chicago skyline" labels					
❑ Mercury SRM-3-9200 [(3)]	Archives	1978	5.00	10.00	20.00
—"Chicago skyline" labels					
❑ Mercury 818476-1	Grace Under Pressure	1984	2.50	5.00	10.00
❑ Mercury 826098-1	Power Windows	1985	2.50	5.00	10.00
❑ Mercury 832464-1	Hold Your Fire	1987	2.50	5.00	10.00
❑ Mercury 836346-1 [(2)]	A Show of Hands	1988	3.00	6.00	12.00
RUSSELL, LEON					
45s					
❑ A&M 734	Cindy/Misty	1964	5.00	10.00	20.00
❑ Dot 16771	Everybody's Talkin' 'Bout the Young/It's Alright with Me	1965	3.75	7.50	15.00
❑ Paradise 628	Good Time Charlie's Got the Blues/Ain't No Love in the City	1984	—	2.00	4.00
❑ Paradise 629	Wabash Cannonball/Tennessee Waltz	1984	—	2.00	4.00
—As "Hank Wilson"; A-side with Willie Nelson					
❑ Paradise 631	Rescue My Heart/Lost Love	1985	—	2.00	4.00
❑ Paradise 8208	Rainbow in Your Eyes/Love's Supposed to Be That Way	1976	—	2.00	4.00
—As "Leon and Mary Russell"					
❑ Paradise 8274	Satisfy You/Windsong	1976	—	2.00	4.00
—As "Leon and Mary Russell"					
❑ Paradise 8369	Love Crazy/Say You Will	1977	—	2.00	4.00
—As "Leon and Mary Russell"					

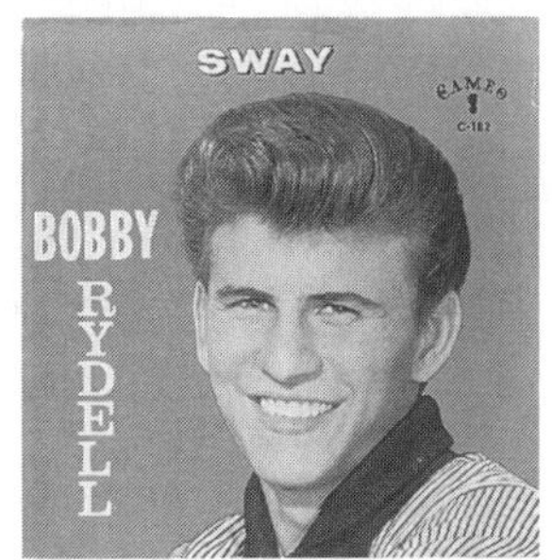

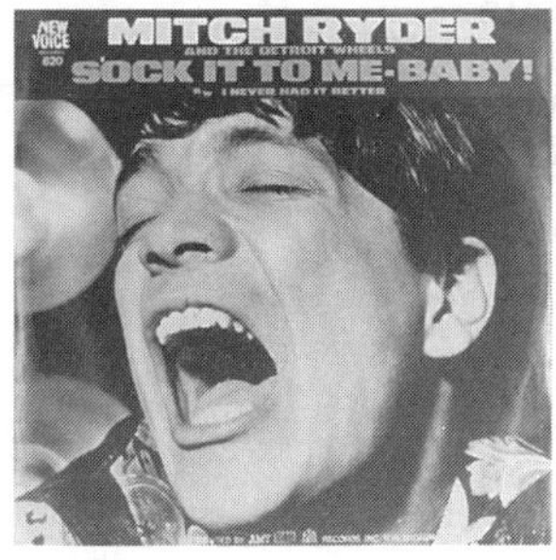

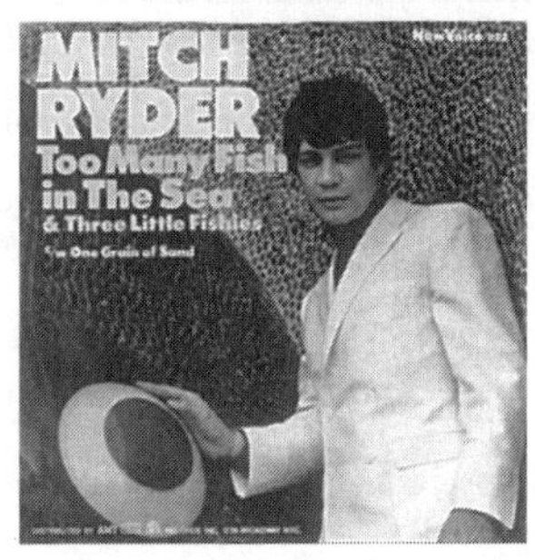

Number	Title (A Side/B Side)	Yr	VG	VG+	NM
❑ Paradise 8438	Easy Love/Hold On to This Feeling	1977	—	2.00	4.00
—As "Leon and Mary Russell"					
❑ Paradise 8667	Elvis and Marilyn/Anita Bryant	1978	—	2.50	5.00
❑ Paradise 8719	Midnight Lover/From Maine to Mexico	1978	—	2.50	5.00
❑ Paradise 49662	Over the Rainbow/I've Just Seen a Face	1981	—	2.00	4.00
❑ RCA Victor 47-6884	(I Tasted) Tears on Your Lips/A Catchy Tune	1957	7.50	15.00	30.00
—As "Lee Russell"					
❑ Roulette 4049	Honky Tonk Woman/Rainbow at Midnight	1958	6.25	12.50	25.00
—As "Lee Russell"					
❑ Shelter 301	Roll Away the Stone/Hummingbird	1970	—	3.00	6.00
❑ Shelter 7302	It Takes a Lot to Laugh, It Takes a Train to Cry/Home Sweet Oklahoma	1970	—	3.00	6.00
❑ Shelter 7305	A Hard Rain's A-Gonna Fall/Me and Baby Jane	1971	—	3.00	6.00
❑ Shelter 7316	A Song for You/A Hard Rain's A-Gonna Fall	1971	—	3.00	6.00
❑ Shelter 7325	Tight Rope/This Masquerade	1972	—	2.50	5.00
❑ Shelter 7328	Slipping Into Christmas/Christmas in Chicago	1972	—	2.50	5.00
❑ Shelter 7336	Roll in My Sweet Baby's Arms/I'm So Lonesome I Could Cry	1973	—	2.50	5.00
—As "Hank Wilson"					
❑ Shelter 7337	Queen of the Roller Derby/Roll Away the Stone	1973	—	2.50	5.00
❑ Shelter 7338	A Six Pack to Go/Uncle Pen	1973	—	2.50	5.00
—As "Hank Wilson"					
❑ Shelter 40210	If I Were a Carpenter/Wild Horses	1974	—	2.00	4.00
❑ Shelter 40277	Time for Love/Leaving Whipporwhill	1974	—	2.00	4.00
❑ Shelter 40378	Lady Blue/Laying Right Here in Heaven	1975	—	2.00	4.00
❑ Shelter 40483	Back to the Island/Little Hideaway	1975	—	2.00	4.00
❑ Shelter 62004	Bluebird/Back to the Island	1976	—	2.00	4.00
❑ Shelter 65033	Slipping Into Christmas/Christmas in Chicago	1975	—	2.50	5.00
—Reissue of 7328					
Albums					
❑ MCA 682	Leon Russell	1979	2.00	4.00	8.00
—Reissue of Shelter 52007					
❑ MCA 683	Leon Russell and the Shelter People	1979	2.00	4.00	8.00
—Reissue of Shelter 52008					
❑ MCA 685	Carney	1979	2.00	4.00	8.00
—Reissue of Shelter 52011					
❑ MCA 686	Will O' the Wisp	1979	2.00	4.00	8.00
—Reissue of Shelter 52020					
❑ MCA 37114	Best of Leon	1980	2.00	4.00	8.00
—Reissue of Shelter 52004					
❑ Paradise 0002	Hank Wilson Vol. II	1984	3.00	6.00	12.00
❑ Paradise PR 2943	Wedding Album	1976	3.00	6.00	12.00
—As "Leon and Mary Russell"					
❑ Paradise BSK 3066	Make Love to the Music	1977	3.00	6.00	12.00
—As "Leon and Mary Russell"					
❑ Paradise BSK 3172	Americana	1978	3.00	6.00	12.00
❑ Paradise BSK 3341	Life and Love	1979	3.00	6.00	12.00
❑ Paradise BSK 3532	The Live Album	1981	2.50	5.00	10.00
❑ Shelter SHE-1001	Leon Russell	1968	5.00	10.00	20.00
❑ Shelter SR 2108	Stop All That Jazz	1974	3.75	7.50	15.00
❑ Shelter SR 2118	Leon Russell	1974	3.00	6.00	12.00
—Reissue of 8901					
❑ Shelter SR 2119	Leon Russell and the Shelter People	1974	3.00	6.00	12.00
—Reissue of 8903					
❑ Shelter SR 2121	Carney	1974	3.00	6.00	12.00
—Reissue of 8911					
❑ Shelter SR 2138	Will O' the Wisp	1975	3.75	7.50	15.00
❑ Shelter SW-8901	Leon Russell	1970	3.75	7.50	15.00
—Early reissue of 1001					
❑ Shelter SW-8903	Leon Russell and the Shelter People	1971	3.75	7.50	15.00
❑ Shelter SW-8911	Carney	1972	3.75	7.50	15.00
❑ Shelter STCO-8917 [(3)]	Leon Live	1973	5.00	10.00	20.00
❑ Shelter SW-8923	Hank Wilson's Back, Vol. 1	1973	3.75	7.50	15.00
—As "Hank Wilson"					
❑ Shelter 52004	Best of Leon	1976	2.50	5.00	10.00
❑ Shelter 52007	Leon Russell	1977	2.50	5.00	10.00
—Reissue of 2118					

Number	Title (A Side/B Side)	Yr	VG	VG+	NM
❑ Shelter 52008 *—Reissue of 2119*	Leon Russell and the Shelter People	1977	2.50	5.00	10.00
❑ Shelter 52011 *—Reissue of 2121*	Carney	1977	2.50	5.00	10.00
❑ Shelter 52014 *—Reissue of 8923*	Hank Wilson's Back, Vol. 1	1977	2.50	5.00	10.00
❑ Shelter 52016 *—Reissue of 2108*	Stop All That Jazz	1977	2.50	5.00	10.00
❑ Shelter 52020 *—Reissue of 2138*	Will O' the Wisp	1977	2.50	5.00	10.00

RYDELL, BOBBY

45s

Number	Title (A Side/B Side)	Yr	VG	VG+	NM
❑ Cameo 160	Please Don't Be Mad/Makin' Time	1959	12.50	25.00	50.00
❑ Cameo 164	All I Want Is You/For You, For You	1959	5.00	10.00	20.00
❑ Cameo 167	Kissin' Time/You'll Never Tame Me	1959	3.75	7.50	15.00
❑ Cameo 169	We Got Love/I Dig Girls	1959	3.75	7.50	15.00
❑ Cameo 171	Wild One/Little Bitty Girl	1960	3.75	7.50	15.00
❑ Cameo 175	Swingin' School/Ding-a-Ling	1960	3.75	7.50	15.00
❑ Cameo 179	Volare/I'd Do It Again	1960	3.75	7.50	15.00
❑ Cameo 182	Sway/Groovy Tonight	1961	3.75	7.50	15.00
❑ Cameo 186	Good Time Baby/Cherie	1961	3.75	7.50	15.00
❑ Cameo 190	That Old Black Magic/Don't Be Afraid (To Fall in Love)	1961	3.75	7.50	15.00
❑ Cameo 192	The Fish/The Third House	1961	3.75	7.50	15.00
❑ Cameo 201	I Wanna Thank You/The Door to Paradise	1961	3.75	7.50	15.00
❑ Cameo 209	I've Got Bonnie/Lose Her	1962	3.00	6.00	12.00
❑ Cameo 217	I'll Never Dance Again/Gee It's Wonderful	1962	3.00	6.00	12.00
❑ Cameo 228	The Cha-Cha-Cha/The Best Man Cried	1962	3.75	7.50	15.00
❑ Cameo 242	Butterfly Baby/Love Is Blind	1963	3.75	7.50	15.00
❑ Cameo 252	Wildwood Days/Will You Be My Baby	1963	3.00	6.00	12.00
❑ Cameo 265	Little Queenie/The Woodpecker Song	1963	3.75	7.50	15.00
❑ Cameo 272	Let's Make Love Tonight/Childhood Sweetheart	1963	3.00	6.00	12.00
❑ Cameo 280	Forget Him/Love, Love Go Away	1963	3.00	6.00	12.00
❑ Cameo 309	Make Me Forget/Little Girl, You've Had a Busy Day	1964	3.00	6.00	12.00
❑ Cameo 320	A World Without Love/Our Faded Love	1964	3.75	7.50	15.00
❑ Cameo 361	Ciao, Ciao Bambino/Voce de la Notte	1965	3.75	7.50	15.00
❑ Capitol 5305	I Just Can't Say Goodbye/Two Is the Loneliest Number	1964	2.50	5.00	10.00
❑ Capitol 5352	Diana/Stranger in the World	1965	2.50	5.00	10.00
❑ Capitol 5436	The Joker/Side Show	1965	2.50	5.00	10.00
❑ Capitol 5513	When I See That Girl of Mine/It Takes Two	1965	2.50	5.00	10.00
❑ Capitol 5556	Roses in the Snow/A Word for Today	1965	2.50	5.00	10.00
❑ Capitol 5696	She Was the Girl/Not You	1966	2.50	5.00	10.00
❑ Capitol 5780	Open for Business As Usual/You Gotta Enjoy Joy	1966	2.50	5.00	10.00
❑ P.I.P. 6515	Sway/Feels Good	1976	—	2.50	5.00
❑ P.I.P. 6521	You're Not the Only Girl for Me/Give Me Your Answer	1976	—	2.00	4.00
❑ P.I.P. 6531	It's Getting Better/The Singles Scene	1976	—	2.00	4.00
❑ Perception 519	California Sunshine/Honey Buns	1973	—	2.50	5.00
❑ Perception 552	Everything Seemed Better (When I Was Younger)/Sunday Son	1974	—	2.50	5.00
❑ RCA Victor 47-9892	Chapel on the Hill/It Must Be Love	1970	—	3.00	6.00
❑ Reprise 0656	The Lovin' Things/That's What I Call Lovin'	1968	2.00	4.00	8.00
❑ Reprise 0684	The River Is Wide/Absence Makes the Heart Grow Fonder	1968	2.00	4.00	8.00
❑ Reprise 0751	Every Little Bit Hurts/Time and Changes	1968	2.00	4.00	8.00
❑ Veko 730/1	Dream Age/Fatty Fatty	1958	30.00	60.00	120.00
❑ Venise 201	Fatty, Fatty/Happy Happy	1961	7.50	15.00	30.00

Albums

Number	Title (A Side/B Side)	Yr	VG	VG+	NM
❑ Cameo C-1006 [M]	We Got Love	1959	15.00	30.00	60.00
❑ Cameo C-1007 [M]	Bobby Sings	1960	12.50	25.00	50.00
❑ Cameo C-1009 [M] *—Original with die-cut cover and textured inner sleeve*	Bobby's Biggest Hits	1961	20.00	40.00	80.00
❑ Cameo C-1009 [M] *—Standard cover*	Bobby's Biggest Hits	1961	6.25	12.50	25.00
❑ Cameo C-1010 [M]	Bobby Rydell Salutes "The Great Ones"	1961	6.25	12.50	25.00
❑ Cameo SC-1010 [S]	Bobby Rydell Salutes "The Great Ones"	1961	10.00	20.00	40.00
❑ Cameo C-1011 [M]	Rydell at the Copa	1961	6.25	12.50	25.00
❑ Cameo SC-1011 [S]	Rydell at the Copa	1961	10.00	20.00	40.00
❑ Cameo C-1019 [M] *—Black vinyl*	All the Hits	1962	6.25	12.50	25.00
❑ Cameo C-1019 [M] *—Red vinyl*	All the Hits	1962	37.50	75.00	150.00
❑ Cameo C-1028 [M]	Bobby Rydell's Biggest Hits, Volume 2	1962	6.25	12.50	25.00
❑ Cameo C-1040 [M]	All the Hits, Volume 2	1963	6.25	12.50	25.00
❑ Cameo SC-1040 [P]	All the Hits, Volume 2	1963	10.00	20.00	40.00
❑ Cameo C-1043 [M]	Bye Bye Birdie	1963	6.25	12.50	25.00
❑ Cameo C-1055 [M]	Wild (Wood) Days	1963	5.00	10.00	20.00
❑ Cameo SC-1055 [S]	Wild (Wood) Days	1963	7.50	15.00	30.00
❑ Cameo C-1070 [M] *—Came with bonus single, also numbered 1070*	The Top Hits of 1963	1963	5.00	10.00	20.00
❑ Cameo SC-1070 [S] *—Came with bonus single, also numbered 1070*	The Top Hits of 1963	1963	7.50	15.00	30.00
❑ Cameo C-1080 [M]	Forget Him	1964	5.00	10.00	20.00
❑ Cameo SC-1080 [R]	Forget Him	1964	5.00	10.00	20.00
❑ Cameo C-2001 [M]	16 Golden Hits	1965	5.00	10.00	20.00
❑ Cameo SC-2001 [R]	16 Golden Hits	1965	5.00	10.00	20.00
❑ Capitol ST 2281 [S]	Somebody Loves You	1965	5.00	10.00	20.00
❑ Capitol T 2281 [M]	Somebody Loves You	1965	3.75	7.50	15.00
❑ P.I.P. 6818	Born with a Smile	1976	2.50	5.00	10.00
❑ Spin-O-Rama 143 [M]	Starring Bobby Rydell	196?	3.00	6.00	12.00

Number	Title (A Side/B Side)	Yr	VG	VG+	NM
❑ Spin-O-Rama S-143 [S]	Starring Bobby Rydell	196?	3.00	6.00	12.00
❑ Strand SL-1120 [M]	Bobby Rydell Sings	196?	6.25	12.50	25.00
❑ Strand SLS-1120 [R]	Bobby Rydell Sings	196?	5.00	10.00	20.00
❑ Venise 10035 [M]	Twistin'	1962	6.25	12.50	25.00
—Also includes tracks by Barry Norman and Stephen Garrick					

RYDELL, BOBBY/CHUBBY CHECKER

45s

Number	Title (A Side/B Side)	Yr	VG	VG+	NM
❑ Cameo 205	Jingle Bell Rock/Jingle Bell Imitations	1961	3.75	7.50	15.00
❑ Cameo 214	Teach Me to Twist/Swingin' Together	1962	3.75	7.50	15.00

Albums

Number	Title (A Side/B Side)	Yr	VG	VG+	NM
❑ Cameo C 1013 [M]	Bobby Rydell/Chubby Checker	1961	7.50	15.00	30.00
❑ Cameo C-1063 [M]	Chubby Checker and Bobby Rydell	1963	5.00	10.00	20.00

RYDER, MITCH, AND THE DETROIT WHEELS

45s

Number	Title (A Side/B Side)	Yr	VG	VG+	NM
❑ New Voice 801	I Need Help/I Hope	1965	2.50	5.00	10.00
❑ New Voice 806	Jenny Takes a Ride!/Baby Jane (Mo-Mo Jane)	1965	6.25	12.50	25.00
—Note slightly different A-side title					
❑ New Voice 808	Little Latin Lupe Lu/I Hope	1966	2.50	5.00	10.00
❑ New Voice 811	Break Out/I Need Help	1966	2.50	5.00	10.00
❑ New Voice 814	Takin' All I Can Get/You Get Your Kicks	1966	2.50	5.00	10.00
❑ New Voice 817	Devil with a Blue Dress On & Good Golly Miss Molly/I Had It Made	1966	3.00	6.00	12.00
❑ New Voice 820	Sock It To Me — Baby!/I Never Had It Better	1967	2.50	5.00	10.00
—Version 2: With lyric "Hits me like a PUNCH!" with no doubt about the last word. The copies of this we've seen have a blue label, both "painted on" and not "painted on," but we can't say yet that ALL copies with that label have this version.					
❑ New Voice 822	Too Many Fish in the Sea & Three Little Fishes/One Grain of Sand	1967	2.50	5.00	10.00

Albums

Number	Title (A Side/B Side)	Yr	VG	VG+	NM
❑ Crewe CR-1335	All Mitch Ryder Hits!	1969	3.75	7.50	15.00
—Reissue of New Voice 2004					
❑ New Voice 2000 [M]	Take a Ride	1966	6.25	12.50	25.00
❑ New Voice S-2000 [S]	Take a Ride	1966	7.50	15.00	30.00
❑ New Voice 2002 [M]	Breakout...!!!	1966	5.00	10.00	20.00
—With "Devil with a Blue Dress On/Good Golly Miss Molly"					
❑ New Voice S-2002 [S]	Breakout...!!!	1966	6.25	12.50	25.00
—With "Devil with a Blue Dress On/Good Golly Miss Molly"					
❑ New Voice 2003 [M]	Sock It To Me!	1967	6.25	12.50	25.00
❑ New Voice S-2003 [S]	Sock It To Me!	1967	7.50	15.00	30.00
❑ New Voice 2004 [M]	All Mitch Ryder Hits!	1967	7.50	15.00	30.00
❑ New Voice NVS-2004 [S]	All Mitch Ryder Hits!	1967	5.00	10.00	20.00
❑ New Voice S-2005	Mitch Ryder Sings the Hits	1968	5.00	10.00	20.00
❑ Rhino R1-70941	Rev Up: The Best of Mitch Ryder and the Detroit Wheels	1989	3.00	6.00	12.00
❑ Virgo 12001	The Best of Mitch Ryder and the Detroit Wheels	1972	3.00	6.00	12.00

S

SADLER, SSGT. BARRY

45s

Number	Title (A Side/B Side)	Yr	VG	VG+	NM
❑ RCA Victor 47-8739	The Ballad of the Green Berets/Letter from Vietnam	1966	—	3.00	6.00
❑ RCA Victor 47-8804	The "A" Team/An Empty Glass	1966	—	3.00	6.00
❑ RCA Victor 47-8966	Not Just Lonely/One Day Nearer Home	1966	—	3.00	6.00
❑ RCA Victor 47-9008	I Won't Be Home This Christmas/A Woman Is a Weepin' Willow Tree	1966	2.00	4.00	8.00

Albums

Number	Title (A Side/B Side)	Yr	VG	VG+	NM
❑ RCA Victor LPM-3547 [M]	Ballads of the Green Berets	1966	3.75	7.50	15.00
❑ RCA Victor LSP-3547 [S]	Ballads of the Green Berets	1966	5.00	10.00	20.00
❑ RCA Victor LPM-3605 [M]	"A" Team, The	1966	3.75	7.50	15.00
❑ RCA Victor LSP-3605 [S]	"A" Team, The	1966	5.00	10.00	20.00
❑ RCA Victor LPM-3691 [M]	Back Home	1967	5.00	10.00	20.00
❑ RCA Victor LSP-3691 [S]	Back Home	1967	3.75	7.50	15.00

ST. GERMAIN

Albums

Number	Title (A Side/B Side)	Yr	VG	VG+	NM
❑ Blue Note 25114 [(2)]	Tourist	2000	7.50	15.00	30.00

ST. PETERS, CRISPIAN

45s

Number	Title (A Side/B Side)	Yr	VG	VG+	NM
❑ Jamie 1302	At This Moment/You'll Forget Me, Goodbye	1965	3.75	7.50	15.00
❑ Jamie 1309	At This Moment/No No No	1966	2.50	5.00	10.00

Number	Title (A Side/B Side)	Yr	VG	VG+	NM
❑ Jamie 1310	You Were On My Mind/What I'm Gonna Be	1966	2.50	5.00	10.00
❑ Jamie 1320	The Pied Piper/Sweet Dawn My True Love	1966	3.00	6.00	12.00
❑ Jamie 1324	Changes/My Little Brown Eyes	1966	2.50	5.00	10.00
❑ Jamie 1328	Your Ever Changin' Mind/But She's Untrue	1966	2.50	5.00	10.00
❑ Jamie 1334	Almost Persuaded/You Are Gone	1967	2.50	5.00	10.00
❑ Jamie 1344	Free Spirit/I'm Always Crying	1967	2.50	5.00	10.00
❑ Jamie 1359	Please Take Me Back/Look Into My Teardrops	1968	2.00	4.00	8.00
Albums					
❑ Jamie JLPM-3027 [M]	The Pied Piper	1966	12.50	25.00	50.00
❑ Jamie JLPS-3027 [R]	The Pied Piper	1966	8.75	17.50	35.00

SAM AND DAVE

45s

Number	Title (A Side/B Side)	Yr	VG	VG+	NM
❑ Alston 777	Never, Never/Lotta Lovin'	1964	5.00	10.00	20.00
❑ Atlantic 2517	You Don't Know What You Mean to Me/This Is Your World	1968	—	3.00	6.00
❑ Atlantic 2540	Can't You Find Another Way (Of Doing It)/Still Is the Night	1968	—	3.00	6.00
❑ Atlantic 2568	Everybody Got to Believe in Somebody/If I Didn't Have a Girl Like You	1968	—	3.00	6.00
❑ Atlantic 2590	Soul Sister, Brown Sugar/Come On In	1968	—	3.00	6.00
❑ Atlantic 2608	Born Again/Get It	1969	—	3.00	6.00
❑ Atlantic 2668	Holdin' On/Ooh Ooh Ooh	1969	—	3.00	6.00
❑ Atlantic 2714	I'm Not an Indian Giver/Baby-Baby Don't Stop Now	1970	—	3.00	6.00
❑ Atlantic 2728	One Part Love, Two Parts Pain/When You Steal from Me	1970	—	3.00	6.00
❑ Atlantic 2733	When You Steal from Me (You're Only Hurting Yourself)/You Easily Excite Me	1970	—	3.00	6.00
❑ Atlantic 2839	Don't Pull Your Love/Jody Ryder Got Killed	1971	—	3.00	6.00
❑ Contempo 7004	We Can Work It Out/Why Did You Do It	1977	—	2.50	5.00
❑ Marlin 6100	I Need Love/Keep a-Walkin'	1961	10.00	20.00	40.00
❑ Marlin 6104	No More Pain/My Love Belongs to You	1961	10.00	20.00	40.00
❑ Roulette 4419	I Need Love/Keep a-Walkin'	1962	3.00	6.00	12.00
❑ Roulette 4445	No More Pain/My Love Belongs to You	1962	3.00	6.00	12.00
❑ Roulette 4461	She's Alright/It Feels So Nice	1962	3.00	6.00	12.00
❑ Roulette 4480	It Was So Nice While It Lasted/You Ain't No Big Thing, Baby	1963	3.00	6.00	12.00
❑ Roulette 4508	If She'll Still Have Me/Listening for My Name	1963	3.00	6.00	12.00
❑ Roulette 4533	I Found Out/I Got a Thing Going On	1963	3.00	6.00	12.00
❑ Roulette 4671	It Feels So Nice/It Was So Nice While It Lasted	1966	2.00	4.00	8.00
❑ Stax 168	Goodnight Baby/A Place Nobody Can Find	1965	3.75	7.50	15.00
❑ Stax 175	I Take What I Want/Sweet Home	1965	3.00	6.00	12.00
❑ Stax 180	You Don't Know Like I Know/Blame Me (Don't Blame My Heart)	1965	3.00	6.00	12.00
❑ Stax 189	Hold On! I'm a-Comin'/I Got Everything I Need	1966	3.75	7.50	15.00
❑ Stax 198	Said I Wasn't Gonna Tell Nobody/If You Got the Loving	1966	2.50	5.00	10.00
❑ Stax 204	You Got Me Hummin'/Sleep Good Tonight	1967	2.50	5.00	10.00
❑ Stax 210	When Something Is Wrong with My Baby/Small Portion of Your Love	1967	2.50	5.00	10.00
❑ Stax 218	Soothe Me/I Can't Stand Up for Falling Down	1967	2.50	5.00	10.00
❑ Stax 231	Soul Man/May I Baby	1967	3.00	6.00	12.00
❑ Stax 242	I Thank You/Wrap It Up	1968	3.00	6.00	12.00
❑ United Artists XW438	A Little Bit of Good (Cures a Whole Lot of Bad)/Blinded by Love	1974	—	3.00	6.00
❑ United Artists XW531	Under the Boardwalk/Give It What You Can	1974	—	3.00	6.00
Albums					
❑ Atlantic SD 8205	I Thank You	1968	6.25	12.50	25.00
❑ Atlantic SD 8218	The Best of Sam and Dave	1969	5.00	10.00	20.00
❑ Atlantic 81279	The Best of Sam and Dave	1985	2.50	5.00	10.00
❑ Atlantic 81718	Soul Men	1987	2.50	5.00	10.00
—Reissue of Stax 725					
❑ Gusto 0045	Sweet and Funky Gold	197?	2.50	5.00	10.00
❑ Roulette R-25323 [M]	Sam and Dave	1966	7.50	15.00	30.00
❑ Roulette SR-25323 [S]	Sam and Dave	1966	10.00	20.00	40.00
❑ Stax ST-708 [M]	Hold On, I'm Comin'	1966	10.00	20.00	40.00
❑ Stax STS-708 [S]	Hold On, I'm Comin'	1966	12.50	25.00	50.00
❑ Stax ST-712 [M]	Double Dynamite	1966	7.50	15.00	30.00
❑ Stax STS-712 [S]	Double Dynamite	1966	10.00	20.00	40.00
❑ Stax ST-725 [M]	Soul Men	1967	7.50	15.00	30.00
❑ Stax STS-725 [S]	Soul Men	1967	10.00	20.00	40.00
❑ United Artists UA-LA524-G	Back At 'Cha!	1975	3.00	6.00	12.00

SAM THE SHAM AND THE PHARAOHS

45s

Number	Title (A Side/B Side)	Yr	VG	VG+	NM
❑ Atlantic 2767	Me and Bobby McGee/Key to the Highway	1970	—	2.50	5.00
—As "Sam Samudio"					
❑ Dingo 001	Haunted House/How Does a Cheating Woman Feel	1964	50.00	100.00	200.00
❑ Fretone 048	Wookie (Part 1)/Wookie (Part 2)	1977	2.50	5.00	10.00
—As "Sam the Sham"					
❑ Fretone 049	Ain't No Lie/Baby You Got It	1977	2.50	5.00	10.00
—As "Sam the Sham"					
❑ MGM 13322	Wooly Bully/Ain't Gonna Move	1965	3.75	7.50	15.00
❑ MGM 13364	Ju Ju Hand/Big City Lights	1965	3.00	6.00	12.00
❑ MGM 13397	Ring Dang Doo/Don't Try It Again	1965	3.00	6.00	12.00
❑ MGM 13452	Red Hot/Long Long Way	1966	3.00	6.00	12.00
❑ MGM 13506	Lil' Red Riding Hood/Love Me Like Before	1966	3.75	7.50	15.00
❑ MGM 13581	The Hair on My Chinny Chin Chin/(I'm In with the) Out Crowd	1966	3.00	6.00	12.00
❑ MGM 13649	How Do You Catch a Girl/Love You Left Behind	1966	3.00	6.00	12.00
❑ MGM 13713	Oh That's Good, No That's Bad/Take What You Can Get	1967	2.50	5.00	10.00
❑ MGM 13747	Black Sheep/My Day's Gonna Come	1967	2.50	5.00	10.00
❑ MGM 13803	Banned in Boston/Money's My Problem	1967	2.50	5.00	10.00
—As "The Sam the Sham Revue"					
❑ MGM 13863	Yakety Yak/Let Our Love Light Shine	1967	2.50	5.00	10.00
—As "The Sam the Sham Revue"					
❑ MGM 13920	Old Mac Donald Has a Boogaloo Farm/I Never Was No One	1968	2.50	5.00	10.00
❑ MGM 13972	I Couldn't Spell !!@!/Down Home Strut	1968	3.75	7.50	15.00

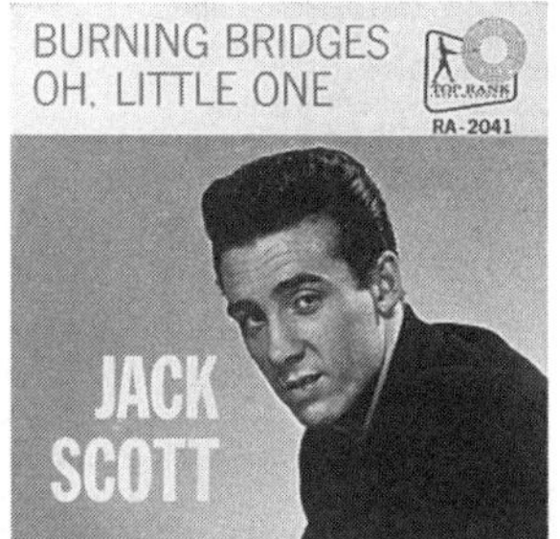

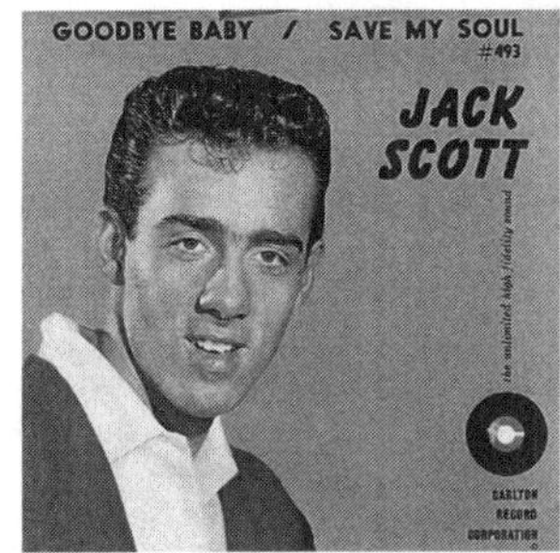

Number	Title (A Side/B Side)	Yr	VG	VG+	NM
❑ MGM 14021	Wolly Bully/Ain't Gonna Move	1968	2.50	5.00	10.00
❑ MGM 14642	Fate/Oh Lo	1973	2.50	5.00	10.00
❑ Tupelo 2982	Betty and Dupree/Manchild	1963	15.00	30.00	60.00
❑ XL 905	The Signifyin' Monkey/Juimonos	1964	12.50	25.00	50.00
❑ XL 906	Wooly Bully/Ain't Gonna Move	1965	75.00	150.00	300.00
Albums					
❑ Atlantic SD 8271	Hard and Heavy	1971	3.75	7.50	15.00
—As "Sam Samudio"					
❑ MGM E-4297 [M]	Wooly Bully	1965	7.50	15.00	30.00
❑ MGM SE-4297 [S]	Wooly Bully	1965	10.00	20.00	40.00
❑ MGM E-4317 [M]	Their Second Album	1965	6.25	12.50	25.00
❑ MGM SE-4317 [S]	Their Second Album	1965	7.50	15.00	30.00
❑ MGM E-4347 [M]	On Tour	1966	6.25	12.50	25.00
❑ MGM SE-4347 [S]	On Tour	1966	7.50	15.00	30.00
❑ MGM E-4407 [M]	Lil' Red Riding Hood	1966	6.25	12.50	25.00
❑ MGM SE-4407 [S]	Lil' Red Riding Hood	1966	7.50	15.00	30.00
❑ MGM E-4422 [M]	The Best of Sam the Sham and the Pharoahs	1967	5.00	10.00	20.00
❑ MGM SE-4422 [S]	The Best of Sam the Sham and the Pharoahs	1967	6.25	12.50	25.00
❑ MGM E-4477 [M]	Nefertiti	1967	6.25	12.50	25.00
❑ MGM SE-4477	The Sam The Sham Revue	1968	5.00	10.00	20.00
—Retitled reissue					
❑ MGM SE-4477 [S]	Nefertiti	1967	6.25	12.50	25.00
❑ MGM SE-4526	Ten of Pentacles	1968	5.00	10.00	20.00
❑ Polydor 827917-1	The Best of Sam the Sham and the Pharoahs	1985	2.50	5.00	10.00
❑ Rhino RNLP-122	Pharoahization: The Best of Sam the Sham and the Pharoahs (1965-1967)	1986	2.50	5.00	10.00

SANDS, TOMMY

45s

Number	Title (A Side/B Side)	Yr	VG	VG+	NM
❑ ABC-Paramount 10466	Connie/Young Man's Fancy	1963	2.50	5.00	10.00
❑ ABC-Paramount 10480	Cinderella/Only 'Cause I'm Lonely	1963	2.50	5.00	10.00
❑ ABC-Paramount 10539	Won't You Be My Girl/Ten Dollars and a Clean White Shirt	1964	2.50	5.00	10.00
❑ ABC-Paramount 10591	Something More/Kisses (Love Theme)	1964	2.50	5.00	10.00
❑ Capitol F3639	Teen-Age Crush/Hep Dee Hootie	1957	6.25	12.50	25.00
❑ Capitol F3690	Ring-A-Ding-A-Ding/My Love Song	1957	6.25	12.50	25.00
❑ Capitol F3723	Goin' Steady/Ring My Phone	1957	6.25	12.50	25.00
❑ Capitol F3743	Let Me Be Loved/Fantastically Foolish	1957	5.00	10.00	20.00
❑ Capitol F3810	A Swingin' Romance/Man, Like Wow!	1957	5.00	10.00	20.00
❑ Capitol F3867	Sing, Boy, Sing/Crazy 'Cause I Love You	1957	5.00	10.00	20.00
❑ Capitol F3953	Teenage Doll/Hawaiian Rock	1958	5.00	10.00	20.00
❑ Capitol F3985	Big Date/After the Senior Prom	1958	5.00	10.00	20.00
❑ Capitol F4036	Blue Ribbon Baby/I Love You Because	1958	5.00	10.00	20.00
❑ Capitol F4082	Bigger Than Texas/The Worryin' Kind	1958	5.00	10.00	20.00
❑ Capitol F4160	Is It Ever Gonna Happen/I Ain't Gittin' Rid of You	1959	3.75	7.50	15.00
❑ Capitol F4231	Sinner Man/Bring Me Your Love	1959	3.75	7.50	15.00
❑ Capitol F4259	I'll Be Seeing You/That's the Way I Am	1959	3.75	7.50	15.00
❑ Capitol 4316	You Hold the Future/I Gotta Have You	1959	3.75	7.50	15.00
❑ Capitol 4366	That's Love/Crossroads	1960	3.75	7.50	15.00
❑ Capitol 4405	The Old Oaken Bucket/These Are the Things You Are	1960	3.75	7.50	15.00
❑ Capitol 4470	Doctor Heartache/On and On	1960	3.75	7.50	15.00
❑ Capitol 4580	Love in a Goldfish Bowl/I Love My Baby	1961	3.00	6.00	12.00
❑ Capitol 4611	Rainbow/Remember Me to Jennie	1961	3.00	6.00	12.00
❑ Capitol 4660	Wrong Side of Love/Jimmy's Song	1961	3.00	6.00	12.00
❑ Imperial 66174	As Long As I'm Travelin'/It's the Only One I've Got	1966	2.00	4.00	8.00
❑ Imperial 66229	Second Star to the Left/Candy Store Prophet	1967	2.00	4.00	8.00
❑ Liberty 55807	Love's Funny/One Rose Today, One Rose Tomorrow	1965	2.00	4.00	8.00
❑ Liberty 55842	The Statue/Little Rosita	1965	2.00	4.00	8.00
❑ Liberty 55864	Waitin' in Your Welfare Line/Don't Do It Darlin'	1966	—	—	—
—Unreleased					
❑ RCA Victor 47-5435	Love Pains/Transfer	1953	7.50	15.00	30.00
❑ RCA Victor 47-5510	Roses Speak Louder Than Words/Spanish Coquita	1953	7.50	15.00	30.00
❑ RCA Victor 47-5628	A Dime and a Dollar/Life Is So Lonesome	1954	7.50	15.00	30.00
❑ RCA Victor 47-5697	Never Let Me Go/I Know About the Bees	1954	7.50	15.00	30.00
❑ RCA Victor 47-5800	Don't Drop It/A Place for Girls Like You	1954	7.50	15.00	30.00
❑ RCA Victor 47-6007	Kissin' Ain't No Fun/Something's Bound to Go Wrong	1955	7.50	15.00	30.00
❑ RCA Victor 47-6868	Don't Drop It/Love Pains	1957	5.00	10.00	20.00
❑ Superscope 007	Seasons in the Sun/Ain't No Big Thing	1969	—	3.00	6.00

Number	Title (A Side/B Side)	Yr	VG	VG+	NM
Albums					
❑ Capitol T 848 [M]	Steady Date with Tommy Sands	1957	15.00	30.00	60.00
❑ Capitol T 929 [M]	Sing Boy Sing	1958	15.00	30.00	60.00
❑ Capitol T 1081 [M]	Sands Storm	1959	12.50	25.00	50.00
❑ Capitol ST 1123 [S]	This Thing Called Love	1959	10.00	20.00	40.00
❑ Capitol T 1123 [M]	This Thing Called Love	1959	7.50	15.00	30.00
❑ Capitol ST 1239 [S]	When I'm Thinking of You	1960	10.00	20.00	40.00
❑ Capitol T 1239 [M]	When I'm Thinking of You	1960	7.50	15.00	30.00
❑ Capitol ST 1364 [S]	Sands at the Sands	1960	10.00	20.00	40.00
❑ Capitol T 1364 [M]	Sands at the Sands	1960	7.50	15.00	30.00
❑ Capitol ST 1426 [S]	Dream with Me	1961	10.00	20.00	40.00
❑ Capitol T 1426 [M]	Dream with Me	1961	7.50	15.00	30.00
SANTANA					
45s					
❑ Columbia 01050	Winning/The Brightest Star	1981	—	2.00	4.00
❑ Columbia 02178	The Sensitive Kind/American Gypsy	1981	—	2.00	4.00
❑ Columbia 02519	Searchin'/Tales of Kilimanjaro	1981	—	2.00	4.00
❑ Columbia 03160	Hold On/Oxun	1982	—	2.00	4.00
❑ Columbia 03268	Hold On	1982	—	3.00	6.00
—One-sided budget release					
❑ Columbia 03376	Nowhere to Run/Nueva York	1982	—	2.00	4.00
❑ Columbia 04034	Havana Moon/Lightnin'	1983	—	2.00	4.00
❑ Columbia 04758	Say It Again/Touchdown Raiders	1985	—	—	3.00
❑ Columbia 04912	I'm the One Who Loves You/Right Now	1985	—	—	3.00
❑ Columbia 05677	They All Went to Mexico/Slow Movin' Outlaw	1985	—	—	3.00
—A-side: Willie Nelson and Carlos Santana; B-side: Willie and Lacy J. Dalton					
❑ Columbia 06654	Vera Cruz/Manuela	1987	—	2.00	4.00
❑ Columbia 07038	Vera Cruz (Remix)/Manuela	1987	—	—	3.00
❑ Columbia 07140	Praise/Love Is You	1987	—	—	3.00
❑ Columbia 10073	Mirage/Flor de Canela	1974	—	2.50	5.00
❑ Columbia 10088	Give and Take/Love Is Anew	1975	—	2.50	5.00
❑ Columbia 10336	Let It Shine/Tell Me Are You Tired	1976	—	2.50	5.00
❑ Columbia 10353	Dance Sister Dance (Baila Mi Hermana)/Let Me	1976	—	2.50	5.00
❑ Columbia 10421	Take Me with You/Europa (Earth's Cry Heaven's Smile)	1976	—	2.50	5.00
❑ Columbia 10481	Let the Children Play/Carnival	1977	—	2.50	5.00
❑ Columbia 10524	Give Me Love/Revelations	1977	—	2.50	5.00
❑ Columbia 10616	She's Not There/Zulu	1977	—	2.50	5.00
❑ Columbia 10677	Black Magic Woman/I'll Be Waiting	1978	—	2.50	5.00
❑ Columbia 10839	Well, All Right/Jericho	1978	—	2.50	5.00
❑ Columbia 10873	Stormy/Move On	1978	—	2.50	5.00
❑ Columbia 10938	One Chain (Don't Make a Prison)/Life Is a Lady-Holiday	1979	—	2.00	4.00
❑ Columbia 11144	You Know That I Love You/Aqua Marine	1979	—	2.00	4.00
❑ Columbia 11218	All I Ever Wanted/Lightning in the Sky	1980	—	2.00	4.00
❑ Columbia 45010	Jingo/Persuasion	1969	—	3.00	6.00
❑ Columbia 45010	Jin-Go-Lo-Ba/Persuasion	1969	—	3.00	6.00
—Same song, different A-side title					
❑ Columbia 45069	Evil Ways/Waiting	1970	—	3.00	6.00
❑ Columbia 45270	Black Magic Woman/Hope You're Feeling Better	1970	—	3.00	6.00
❑ Columbia 45330	Oye Como Va/Samba Pa Ti	1971	—	2.50	5.00
❑ Columbia 45472	Everybody's Everything/Guajira	1971	—	2.50	5.00
❑ Columbia 45552	No One to Depend On/Taboo	1972	—	2.50	5.00
—Gray label					
❑ Columbia 45753	Look Up/All the Love of the Universe	1973	—	2.50	5.00
❑ Columbia 45999	When I Look Into Your Eyes/Samba De Sausalito	1974	—	2.50	5.00
❑ Columbia 46067	Incident at Neshabur/Samba Pa Ti	1974	—	2.50	5.00
Albums					
❑ Cicadelic 1004	Santana '68	1988	3.00	6.00	12.00
❑ Columbia CS 9781	Santana	1969	3.75	7.50	15.00
—"360 Sound" on label					
❑ Columbia KC 30130	Abraxas	1970	3.75	7.50	15.00
—Original copies have a poster					
❑ Columbia KC 30595	Santana	1971	3.00	6.00	12.00
—Not the same album as CS 9781; this is often called "Santana III"					
❑ Columbia KC 31610	Caravanserai	1972	3.00	6.00	12.00
❑ Columbia PC 32455	Welcome	1973	3.00	6.00	12.00
—No bar code on cover					
❑ Columbia PC 33050	Santana's Greatest Hits	1974	3.00	6.00	12.00
—No bar code on cover					
❑ Columbia PC 33135	Borboletta	1974	3.00	6.00	12.00
—No bar code on cover					
❑ Columbia PC 33576	Amigos	1976	3.00	6.00	12.00
—No bar code on cover					
❑ Columbia JC 34423	Festival	1977	3.00	6.00	12.00
❑ Columbia C2 34914 [(2)]	Moonflower	1977	3.75	7.50	15.00
❑ Columbia FC 35600	Inner Secrets	1978	3.00	6.00	12.00
❑ Columbia FC 36154	Marathon	1979	3.00	6.00	12.00
❑ Columbia C2 36590 [(2)]	Swing of Delight	1980	3.75	7.50	15.00
❑ Columbia FC 37158	Zebop!	1981	3.00	6.00	12.00
❑ Columbia FC 38122	Shango	1982	3.00	6.00	12.00
❑ Columbia FC 39527	Beyond Appearances	1985	2.50	5.00	10.00
❑ Columbia FC 40272	Freedom	1987	2.50	5.00	10.00
❑ Columbia C3X 44344 [(3)]	Viva Santana	1988	5.00	10.00	20.00
SANTO AND JOHNNY					
45s					
❑ Canadian American 103	Sleep Walk/All Night Diner	1959	6.25	12.50	25.00

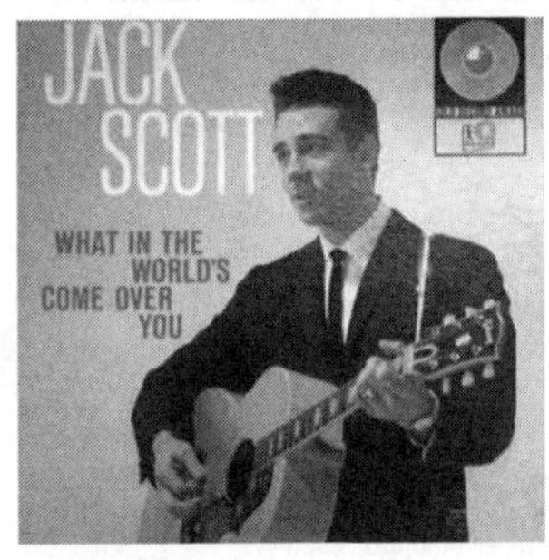

Number	Title (A Side/B Side)	Yr	VG	VG+	NM
❑ Canadian American 107	Tear Drop/The Long Walk Home	1959	3.75	7.50	15.00
❑ Canadian American 111	Caravan/Summertime	1960	3.75	7.50	15.00
❑ Canadian American 115	The Breeze and I/Lazy Day	1960	3.75	7.50	15.00
❑ Canadian American 118	Love Lost/Annie	1960	3.75	7.50	15.00
❑ Canadian American 120	Twistin' Bells/Bullseye!	1960	4.00	8.00	16.00
❑ Canadian American 124	Hop Scotch/Sea Shells	1961	3.75	7.50	15.00
❑ Canadian American 128	Theme from Come September/The Long Walk Home	1961	3.75	7.50	15.00
❑ Canadian American 131	The Mouse/Birmingham	1961	3.75	7.50	15.00
❑ Canadian American 132	Twistin' Bells/Christmas Day	1961	5.00	10.00	20.00
—B-side by Linda Scott					
❑ Canadian American 137	Spanish Harlem/Stage to Cimarron	1962	3.00	6.00	12.00
❑ Canadian American 141	Three Caballeros/Step Aside	1962	3.00	6.00	12.00
❑ Canadian American 144	Misirlou/Tokyo Twilight	1962	3.00	6.00	12.00
❑ Canadian American 148	Twistin' Bells/Manhattan	1962	3.00	6.00	12.00
❑ Canadian American 151	On Your Mark/Manhattan	1963	3.00	6.00	12.00
❑ Canadian American 155	The Wandering Sea/Manhattan Spiritual	1963	3.00	6.00	12.00
❑ Canadian American 161	Love Letters in the Sand/Lido Beach	1963	3.00	6.00	12.00
❑ Canadian American 164	I'll Remember (In the Still of the Night)/Song for Rosemary	1964	3.00	6.00	12.00
❑ Canadian American 167	A Thousand Miles Away/Road Block	1964	3.00	6.00	12.00
❑ Canadian American 174	Sugar Stroll/Rattler	1964	3.00	6.00	12.00
❑ Canadian American 177	A Hard Day's Night/And I Love Her	1964	3.75	7.50	15.00
❑ Canadian American 182	Goldfinger/Sleep Walk	1964	3.00	6.00	12.00
❑ Canadian American 189	Brazilian Summer/Off Tempo	1965	3.00	6.00	12.00
❑ Canadian American 194	Watermelon Man/Return to Naples	1965	3.00	6.00	12.00
❑ Canadian American 204	Come with Me/The Young World	1967	2.50	5.00	10.00
❑ Imperial 66269	Live for Life/See You in September	1968	2.50	5.00	10.00
❑ Imperial 66292	Sleep Walk '68/It Must Be Him	1968	2.50	5.00	10.00
❑ Pausa 703	Come Back Soldier/Flamingo	1976	—	2.50	5.00
❑ United Artists 970	Thunderball/Mister Kiss Kiss Bang Bang	1966	2.50	5.00	10.00
Albums					
❑ Canadian American CALP-1001 [M]	Santo & Johnny	1959	15.00	30.00	60.00
❑ Canadian American SCALP-1001 [S]	Santo & Johnny	1959	20.00	40.00	80.00
❑ Canadian American CALP-1002 [M]	Encore	1960	10.00	20.00	40.00
❑ Canadian American SCALP-1002 [S]	Encore	1960	12.50	25.00	50.00
❑ Canadian American CALP-1004 [M]	Hawaii	1961	10.00	20.00	40.00
❑ Canadian American SCALP-1004 [S]	Hawaii	1961	12.50	25.00	50.00
❑ Canadian American CALP-1006 [M]	Come On In	1962	7.50	15.00	30.00
❑ Canadian American SCALP-1006 [S]	Come On In	1962	10.00	20.00	40.00
❑ Canadian American CALP-1008 [M]	Around the World with Santo and Johnny	1962	7.50	15.00	30.00
❑ Canadian American SCALP-1008 [S]	Around the World with Santo and Johnny	1962	10.00	20.00	40.00
❑ Canadian American CALP-1011 [M]	Off Shore	1963	7.50	15.00	30.00
❑ Canadian American SCALP-1011 [S]	Off Shore	1963	10.00	20.00	40.00
❑ Canadian American CALP-1014 [M]	In the Still of the Night	1963	7.50	15.00	30.00
❑ Canadian American SCALP-1014 [S]	In the Still of the Night	1963	10.00	20.00	40.00
❑ Canadian American CALP-1016 [M]	Wish You Love	1964	7.50	15.00	30.00
❑ Canadian American SCALP-1016 [S]	Wish You Love	1964	10.00	20.00	40.00
❑ Canadian American CALP-1017 [M]	The Beatles' Greatest Hits	1965	10.00	20.00	40.00
❑ Canadian American SCALP-1017 [S]	The Beatles' Greatest Hits	1965	12.50	25.00	50.00
❑ Canadian American CALP-1018 [M]	Mucho	1965	7.50	15.00	30.00

Number	Title (A Side/B Side)	Yr	VG	VG+	NM
❑ Canadian American SCALP-1018 [S]	Mucho	1965	10.00	20.00	40.00
❑ Imperial LP-9363 [M]	Brilliant Guitar Sounds	1967	3.75	7.50	15.00
❑ Imperial LP-12363 [S]	Brilliant Guitar Sounds	1967	5.00	10.00	20.00
❑ Imperial LP-12366	Golden Guitars	1968	3.75	7.50	15.00
❑ Imperial LP-12418	On the Road Again	1968	3.75	7.50	15.00

SAYER, LEO

45s

Number	Title (A Side/B Side)	Yr	VG	VG+	NM
❑ Warner Bros. GWB 0336	Long Tall Glasses (I Can Dance)/The Show Must Go On	197?	—	2.00	4.00
—"Back to Back Hits" reissue					
❑ Warner Bros. GWB 0351	When I Need You/You Make Me Feel Like Dancing	197?	—	2.00	4.00
—"Back to Back Hits" reissue					
❑ Warner Bros. 7768	The Show Must Go On/Innocent Bystander	1974	2.00	4.00	8.00
❑ Warner Bros. 7824	One Man Band/Drop Back	1974	—	3.50	7.00
❑ Warner Bros. 8043	Long Tall Glasses/In My Life	1974	—	3.00	6.00
—First pressings have no A-side subtitle					
❑ Warner Bros. 8043	Long Tall Glasses (I Can Dance)/In My Life	1975	—	2.50	5.00
—Later pressings add subtitle to A-side					
❑ Warner Bros. 8097	One Man Band/Telepath	1975	—	2.50	5.00
❑ Warner Bros. 8153	Moonlighting/Streets of Your Town	1975	—	3.00	6.00
❑ Warner Bros. 8283	You Make Me Feel Like Dancing/Magdalena	1976	—	2.50	5.00
❑ Warner Bros. 8319	How Much Love/I Hear the Laughter	1977	—	2.50	5.00
❑ Warner Bros. 8332	When I Need You/I Think We Fell in Love Too Fast	1977	—	2.50	5.00
❑ Warner Bros. 8465	Thunder in My Heart/Get the Girl	1977	—	2.50	5.00
❑ Warner Bros. 8502	Easy to Love/Haunting Me	1977	—	2.50	5.00
❑ Warner Bros. 8682	Raining in My Heart/No Looking Back	1978	—	2.50	5.00
❑ Warner Bros. 8738	Don't Look Away/No Looking Back	1979	—	2.50	5.00
❑ Warner Bros. 7-29904	Paris Dies in the Morning/We've Got Ourselves in Love	1982	—	2.50	5.00
❑ Warner Bros. 7-29960	Heart (Stop Beating in Time)/The End of the Game	1982	—	3.00	6.00
❑ Warner Bros. 49134	Oh Girl/Englishman in the U.S.A.	1979	—	2.50	5.00
❑ Warner Bros. 49565	More Than I Can Say/Millionaire	1980	—	2.00	4.00
❑ Warner Bros. 49657	Living in a Fantasy/Only Foolin'	1981	—	2.00	4.00
❑ Warner Bros. 49714	Where Did We Go Wrong/She's Not Coming Back	1981	—	2.50	5.00
❑ Warner Bros. 50060	Have You Ever Been in Love/I Don't Need Dreaming Anymore	1982	—	2.50	5.00

Albums

Number	Title (A Side/B Side)	Yr	VG	VG+	NM
❑ Chrysalis PV 41087	Another Year	1985	2.00	4.00	8.00
—Reissue of Warner Bros. 2885					
❑ Chrysalis PV 41125	Endless Flight	1985	2.00	4.00	8.00
—Reissue of Warner Bros. 3101					
❑ Chrysalis PV 41154	Thunder in My Heart	1985	2.00	4.00	8.00
—Reissue of Warner Bros. 3089					
❑ Chrysalis PV 41198	Leo Sayer	1985	2.00	4.00	8.00
—Reissue of Warner Bros. 3200					
❑ Chrysalis PV 41240	Here	1985	2.00	4.00	8.00
—Reissue of Warner Bros. 3374					
❑ Warner Bros. BS 2738	Silverbird	1973	3.00	6.00	12.00
❑ Warner Bros. BS 2836	Just a Boy	1974	2.50	5.00	10.00
❑ Warner Bros. BS 2885	Another Year	1975	2.50	5.00	10.00
❑ Warner Bros. BS 2962	Endless Flight	1976	2.50	5.00	10.00
❑ Warner Bros. BSK 3089	Thunder in My Heart	1977	2.50	5.00	10.00
❑ Warner Bros. BSK 3101	Endless Flight	1977	2.00	4.00	8.00
—Reissue of 2962					
❑ Warner Bros. BSK 3200	Leo Sayer	1978	2.50	5.00	10.00
❑ Warner Bros. BSK 3374	Here	1979	2.50	5.00	10.00
❑ Warner Bros. BSK 3483	Living in a Fantasy	1980	2.50	5.00	10.00
❑ Warner Bros. 23560	World Radio	1982	2.50	5.00	10.00
❑ Warner Bros. 25073	Have You Ever Been in Love	1984	2.50	5.00	10.00

SCAGGS, BOZ

45s

Number	Title (A Side/B Side)	Yr	VG	VG+	NM
❑ Atlantic 2692	I'm Easy/I'll Be Long Gone	1969	2.50	5.00	10.00
❑ Columbia 01023	You Can Have Me Anytime/Georgia	1981	—	2.00	4.00
❑ Columbia 02423	Jojo/Miss Sun	1981	—	—	3.00
—Reissue					
❑ Columbia 02424	Breakdown Dead Ahead/Look What You've Done to Me	1981	—	—	3.00
—Reissue					
❑ Columbia 07780	Heart of Mine/You'll Never Know	1988	—	—	3.00
❑ Columbia 07981	Cool Running/You'll Never Know	1988	—	—	3.00
❑ Columbia 08068	What's Number 1/Claudia	1988	—	—	3.00
❑ Columbia 10027	Slow Dancer/Pain of Love	1974	—	3.00	6.00
❑ Columbia 10124	You Make It So Hard (To Say Goodbye)/There Is Something Else	1975	—	2.50	5.00
❑ Columbia 10319	It's Over/Harbor Lights	1976	—	2.50	5.00
❑ Columbia 10367	Lowdown/Harbor Lights	1976	—	2.50	5.00
❑ Columbia 10440	What Can I Say/We're All Alone	1976	—	2.50	5.00
❑ Columbia 10491	Lido Shuffle/We're All Alone	1977	—	2.50	5.00
❑ Columbia 10606	Hard Times/We're Waiting	1977	—	2.50	5.00
❑ Columbia 10679	Hollywood/A Clue	1978	—	2.50	5.00
❑ Columbia 11241	Breakdown Dead Ahead/Isn't It Time	1980	—	2.00	4.00
❑ Columbia 11281	Jojo/Do Like You Do in New York	1980	—	2.00	4.00
❑ Columbia 11349	Look What You've Done to Me/Simone	1980	—	2.00	4.00
❑ Columbia 11406	Miss Sun/Dinah Flo	1980	—	2.00	4.00
❑ Columbia 45353	We Were Always Sweethearts/Painted Bells	1971	—	3.00	6.00
❑ Columbia 45408	Near You/Downright Woman	1971	—	3.00	6.00
❑ Columbia 45540	Here to Stay/Runnin' Blue	1972	—	3.00	6.00
❑ Columbia 45670	Dinah Flo/He's a Fool for You	1972	—	3.00	6.00
❑ Columbia 46025	You Make It So Hard (To Say Goodbye)/There Is Someone Else	1974	—	3.00	6.00

Number	Title (A Side/B Side)	Yr	VG	VG+	NM
❑ Full Moon 49676	You Make It So Hard (To Say Goodbye)/ Something's Missing in My Life	1981	—	2.00	4.00
—B-side by Lady Sylvia					
Albums					
❑ Atlantic SD 8239	Boz Scaggs	1969	3.00	6.00	12.00
❑ Atlantic SD 19166	Boz Scaggs	1977	2.00	4.00	8.00
❑ Columbia KC 30454	Moments	1971	2.50	5.00	10.00
❑ Columbia KC 30976	Boz Scaggs & Band	1971	2.50	5.00	10.00
❑ Columbia KC 31384	My Time	1972	2.50	5.00	10.00
❑ Columbia KC 32760	Slow Dancer	1974	3.00	6.00	12.00
—Original cover has Boz Scaggs on a beach in only a bathing suit					
❑ Columbia PC 33920	Silk Degrees	1976	3.00	6.00	12.00
—Original edition with "PC" prefix and no bar code on back cover					
❑ Columbia FC 36106	Middle Man	1980	2.50	5.00	10.00
❑ Columbia FC 36841	Hits!	1980	2.50	5.00	10.00
❑ Columbia PC 37249	Down Two Then Left	198?	2.00	4.00	8.00
—Budget-line reissue					
❑ Columbia FC 40463	Other Roads	1988	2.50	5.00	10.00

SCOTT, JACK

45s

Number	Title (A Side/B Side)	Yr	VG	VG+	NM
❑ ABC 10843	Before the Bird Flies/Insane	1966	5.00	10.00	20.00
❑ ABC-Paramount 9818	Baby She's Gone/You Can Bet Your Bottom Dollar	1957	37.50	75.00	150.00
❑ ABC-Paramount 9860	Two Timin' Woman/I Need Your Love	1957	37.50	75.00	150.00
❑ Capitol 4554	A Little Feeling (Called Love)/Now That I	1961	6.25	12.50	25.00
❑ Capitol 4597	My Dream Came True/Strange Desire	1961	5.00	10.00	20.00
❑ Capitol 4637	Steps 1 and 2/One of These Days	1961	5.00	10.00	20.00
❑ Capitol 4689	Cry, Cry, Cry/Grizzly Bear	1962	5.00	10.00	20.00
❑ Capitol 4738	The Part Where I Cry/You Only See What You Wanna See	1962	5.00	10.00	20.00
❑ Capitol 4796	Sad Story/I Can't Hold Your Letters	1962	5.00	10.00	20.00
❑ Capitol 4855	If Only/Green, Green Valley	1962	5.00	10.00	20.00
❑ Capitol 4903	Strangers/Laugh and the World Laughs With You	1963	5.00	10.00	20.00
❑ Capitol 4955	All I See Is Blue/Meo Myo	1963	5.00	10.00	20.00
❑ Carlton 462	My True Love/Leroy	1958	7.50	15.00	30.00
❑ Carlton 483	With Your Love/Geraldine	1958	7.50	15.00	30.00
❑ Carlton 493	Goodbye Baby/Save My Soul	1959	7.50	15.00	30.00
❑ Carlton 504	I Never Felt Like This/Bella	1959	7.50	15.00	30.00
❑ Carlton 514	The Way I Walk/Midgie	1959	7.50	15.00	30.00
❑ Carlton 519 [M]	There Comes a Time/Baby Marie	1959	5.00	10.00	20.00
❑ Carlton ST-519 [S]	There Comes a Time/Baby Marie	1959	10.00	20.00	40.00
❑ Dot 17475	May You Never Be Alone/Face to the Wall	1973	—	2.50	5.00
❑ Dot 17504	You're Just Getting Better/Walk Through My Mind	1974	—	2.50	5.00
❑ Groove 58-0027	There's Trouble Brewin'/Jingle Bell Slide	1963	5.00	10.00	20.00
❑ Groove 58-0031	Blue Skies (Moving In on Me)/I Knew You First	1964	3.75	7.50	15.00
❑ Groove 58-0037	Wiggle On Out/What a Wonderful Night Out	1964	5.00	10.00	20.00
❑ Groove 58-0042	Thou Shalt Not Steal/I Prayed for an Angel	1964	3.75	7.50	15.00
❑ Groove 58-0049	Flakey John/Tall Tales	1964	5.00	10.00	20.00
❑ GRT 35	Billy Jack/Mary, Marry Me	1971	—	2.50	5.00
❑ Guaranteed 209	What Am I Living For/Indiana Waltz	1960	7.50	15.00	30.00
❑ Guaranteed 211	No One Will Ever Know/Go Wild Little Sadie	1960	7.50	15.00	30.00
❑ Jubilee 5606	My Special Angel/I Keep Changin' My Mind	1967	5.00	10.00	20.00
❑ Ponie 7021-10	Geraldine/Midgie	197?	—	2.00	4.00
❑ Ponie 7021-11	There's Trouble Brewin'/Jingle Bell Slide	197?	—	2.00	4.00
❑ Ponie 7021-12	Flakey John/Wiggle On Out	197?	—	2.00	4.00
❑ Ponie 5121-15	Baby She's Gone/Two Timin' Woman	197?	—	2.00	4.00
❑ Ponie 6063-20	Leroy/Go Wild Little Sadie	197?	—	2.00	4.00
❑ Ponie 6083-20	Country Witch/Blues, Stay Away from Me-Stones	197?	—	2.00	4.00
❑ Ponie 4104-30	Spirit of '76/(Instrumental)	1976	—	2.00	4.00
❑ RCA Victor 47-8505	Separation's Now Granted/I Don't Believe in Tea Leaves	1965	3.75	7.50	15.00
❑ RCA Victor 47-8685	Looking for Linda/I Hope I Think I Wish	1965	3.75	7.50	15.00
❑ RCA Victor 47-8724	Don't Hush the Laughter/Let's Learn to Live and Love Again	1965	3.75	7.50	15.00
❑ Top Rank 2028 [M]	What in the World's Come Over You/Baby Baby	1959	7.50	15.00	30.00
❑ Top Rank 2028 [S]	What in the World's Come Over You/Baby Baby	1959	10.00	20.00	40.00
❑ Top Rank 2041 [M]	Burning Bridges/Oh Little One	1960	6.25	12.50	25.00
❑ Top Rank 2041 [S]	Burning Bridges/Oh Little One	1960	15.00	30.00	60.00
❑ Top Rank 2055	It Only Happened Yesterday/Cool Water	1960	5.00	10.00	20.00
❑ Top Rank 2075	Patsy/Old Time Religion	1960	5.00	10.00	20.00

Number	Title (A Side/B Side)	Yr	VG	VG+	NM
❑ Top Rank 2093	Is There Something on Your Mind/Found a Woman	1960	5.00	10.00	20.00
Albums					
❑ Capitol ST 2035 [S]	Burning Bridges	1964	37.50	75.00	150.00
❑ Capitol T 2035 [M]	Burning Bridges	1964	20.00	40.00	80.00
❑ Carlton LP-12-107 [M]	Jack Scott	1959	37.50	75.00	150.00
❑ Carlton STLP-12-107 [S]	Jack Scott	1959	100.00	200.00	400.00
—With "Stereo" in felt letters vertically along the left of cover					
❑ Carlton STLP-12-107 [S]	Jack Scott	1959	50.00	100.00	200.00
—With "Stereo" printed across the top					
❑ Carlton STLP-12-107 [S]	Jack Scott	1959	75.00	150.00	300.00
—With "Stereo" in felt letters horizontally along the top of cover					
❑ Carlton LP-12-122 [M]	What Am I Living For	1959	30.00	60.00	120.00
❑ Carlton STLP-12-122 [S]	What Am I Living For	1959	80.00	160.00	320.00
❑ Jade J33-113	Jack Is Back	198?	3.75	7.50	15.00
❑ Jade J33-114	The Way I Rock	198?	3.75	7.50	15.00
❑ Ponie 563	Jack Scott	1974	3.75	7.50	15.00
❑ Ponie 7055	Jack Scott	1977	3.75	7.50	15.00
❑ Top Rank RM-319 [M]	I Remember Hank Williams	1960	37.50	75.00	150.00
❑ Top Rank RM-326 [M]	What in the World's Come Over You	1960	37.50	75.00	150.00
❑ Top Rank RM-348 [M]	The Spirit Moves Me	1961	37.50	75.00	150.00
❑ Top Rank SM-619 [S]	I Remember Hank Williams	1960	62.50	125.00	250.00
❑ Top Rank SM-626 [S]	What in the World's Come Over You	1960	62.50	125.00	250.00
❑ Top Rank SM-648 [S]	The Spirit Moves Me	1961	62.50	125.00	250.00

SCOTT, LINDA

45s

Number	Title (A Side/B Side)	Yr	VG	VG+	NM
❑ Canadian American 123	I've Told Every Little Star/Three Guesses	1961	5.00	10.00	20.00
❑ Canadian American 127	Don't Bet Money Honey/Starlight, Starbright	1961	5.00	10.00	20.00
❑ Canadian American 129	I Don't Know Why/It's All Because	1961	5.00	10.00	20.00
❑ Canadian American 132	Christmas Day/Twistin' Bells	1961	5.00	10.00	20.00
—B-side by Santo and Johnny					
❑ Canadian American 133	Count Every Star/Land of Stars	1962	3.75	7.50	15.00
❑ Canadian American 134	Bermuda/Lonely for You	1962	3.75	7.50	15.00
❑ Congress 101	Yessiree/Town Crier	1962	3.75	7.50	15.00
❑ Congress 103	Never in a Million Years/Through the Summer	1962	3.75	7.50	15.00
❑ Congress 106	I Left My Heart in the Balcony/Lopsided Love Affair	1962	3.75	7.50	15.00
❑ Congress 108	I'm So Afraid of Losing You/The Loneliest Girl in Town	1962	3.75	7.50	15.00
❑ Congress 110	I'm Gonna Sit Right Down and Write Myself a Letter/Ain't That Fun	1963	3.75	7.50	15.00
❑ Congress 200	Let's Fall in Love/I Know It, You Know It	1963	3.75	7.50	15.00
❑ Congress 204	Who's Been Sleeping in My Bed/My Baby	1963	3.75	7.50	15.00
❑ Congress 206	Let's Fall in Love/I Know It, You Know It	1964	3.75	7.50	15.00
❑ Congress 209	I Envy You/Everybody Stopped Laughing at Jane	1964	3.75	7.50	15.00
❑ Kapp 610	That Old Feeling/This Is My Prayer	1964	2.50	5.00	10.00
❑ Kapp 641	If I Love Again/Patch It Up	1965	2.50	5.00	10.00
❑ Kapp 677	Don't Lose Your Head/I'll See You in My Dreams	1965	2.50	5.00	10.00
❑ Kapp 713	You Baby/I Can't Get Through to You	1965	2.50	5.00	10.00
❑ Kapp 762	Toys/Take a Walk Bobby	1966	2.50	5.00	10.00
❑ RCA Victor 47-9424	They Don't Know You/Three Miles High	1967	2.50	5.00	10.00
Albums					
❑ Canadian American CALP-1005 [M]	Starlight, Starbright	1961	25.00	50.00	100.00
❑ Canadian American SCALP-1005 [S]	Starlight, Starbright	1961	37.50	75.00	150.00
❑ Canadian American CALP-1007 [M]	Great Scott!! Her Greatest Hits	1962	25.00	50.00	100.00
❑ Canadian American SCALP-1007 [S]	Great Scott!! Her Greatest Hits	1962	37.50	75.00	150.00
❑ Congress CGL-3001 [M]	Linda	1962	10.00	20.00	40.00
❑ Congress CGS-3001 [S]	Linda	1962	12.50	25.00	50.00
❑ Kapp KL-1424 [M]	Hey, Look at Me Now	1965	10.00	20.00	40.00
❑ Kapp KS-3424 [S]	Hey, Look at Me Now	1965	12.50	25.00	50.00

SEALS AND CROFTS

45s

Number	Title (A Side/B Side)	Yr	VG	VG+	NM
❑ T-A 188	In Tune/Seldom's Sister	1969	2.00	4.00	8.00
❑ T-A 191	See My Life/(B-side unknown)	1969	2.00	4.00	8.00
❑ T-A 206	See My Life/In Tune//Hollow Reed/Leave	1970	2.50	5.00	10.00
❑ T-A 208	Ridin' Thumb/Leave	1970	2.00	4.00	8.00
❑ T-A 210	Gabriel Go On Home/Robin	1971	2.00	4.00	8.00
❑ Warner Bros. 7536	When I Meet Them/Irish Linen	1971	—	3.00	6.00
❑ Warner Bros. 7565	Sudan Village/High on a Mountain	1972	—	3.00	6.00
❑ Warner Bros. 7606	Summer Breeze/East of Ginger Trees	1972	—	2.50	5.00
❑ Warner Bros. 7671	Hummingbird/Say	1972	—	2.50	5.00
❑ Warner Bros. 7697	We May Never Pass This Way (Again)/Intone My Servant	1973	—	—	—
—Unreleased?					
❑ Warner Bros. 7708	Diamond Girl/Wisdom	1973	—	2.50	5.00
❑ Warner Bros. 7740	We May Never Pass This Way (Again)/Jessica	1973	—	2.50	5.00
❑ Warner Bros. 7771	Unborn Child/Ledges	1974	—	2.00	4.00
❑ Warner Bros. 7810	King of Nothing/Follow Me	1974	—	2.00	4.00
❑ Warner Bros. 8075	I'll Play for You/Truth Is But a Woman	1975	—	2.00	4.00
❑ Warner Bros. 8130	Castles in the Sand/Golden Rainbow	1975	—	2.00	4.00
❑ Warner Bros. 8190	Get Closer/Don't Fail	1976	—	2.00	4.00
❑ Warner Bros. 8277	Baby, I'll Give It to You/Advance Guards	1976	—	2.00	4.00
❑ Warner Bros. 8405	My Fair Share/East of Ginger Trees	1977	—	2.00	4.00
❑ Warner Bros. 8551	You're the Love/Midnight Blue	1978	—	2.00	4.00
❑ Warner Bros. 8639	Magnolia Moon/Takin' It Easy	1978	—	2.00	4.00
❑ Warner Bros. 49522	First Love/Kite Dreams	1980	—	2.00	4.00

Number	Title (A Side/B Side)	Yr	VG	VG+	NM
Albums					
❑ K-Tel NU 9610	Collection: 16 of Their Greatest Hits	1979	3.00	6.00	12.00
❑ T-A 5001	Seals and Crofts	1969	6.25	12.50	25.00
❑ T-A 5004	Down Home	1970	6.25	12.50	25.00
❑ Warner Bros. BS 2568	Year of Sunday	1971	3.00	6.00	12.00
—Green "WB" label					
❑ Warner Bros. BS 2629	Summer Breeze	1972	3.00	6.00	12.00
—Green "WB" label					
❑ Warner Bros. BS 2699	Diamond Girl	1973	3.00	6.00	12.00
—"Burbank" palm-tree label					
❑ Warner Bros. BS 2761	Unborn Child	1974	3.00	6.00	12.00
❑ Warner Bros. 2WS 2809 [(2)]	Seals & Crofts I and II	1974	3.75	7.50	15.00
—Reissue of the two T-A LPs in one package					
❑ Warner Bros. BS 2848	I'll Play for You	1975	2.50	5.00	10.00
❑ Warner Bros. BS 2886	Greatest Hits	1975	2.50	5.00	10.00
❑ Warner Bros. BS 2907	Get Closer	1976	2.50	5.00	10.00
❑ Warner Bros. BS 2976	Sudan Village	1976	2.50	5.00	10.00
❑ Warner Bros. BSK 3109	Greatest Hits	1977	2.00	4.00	8.00
—Reissue; any label variation					
❑ Warner Bros. BSK 3165	Takin' It Easy	1978	2.50	5.00	10.00
❑ Warner Bros. BSK 3365	The Longest Road	1980	2.50	5.00	10.00

SEARCHERS, THE

Number	Title (A Side/B Side)	Yr	VG	VG+	NM
45s					
❑ Kapp KJB-22	Needles and Pins/Ain't That Just Like Me	1964	2.00	4.00	8.00
—Orange label "Winners Circle Series"					
❑ Kapp KJB-27	Love Potion Number Nine/Hi-Heel Sneakers	1964	2.50	5.00	10.00
—Orange label "Winners Circle Series"; no black label counterpart					
❑ Kapp KJB-29	Bumble Bee/Everything You Do	1964	2.50	5.00	10.00
—Orange label "Winners Circle Series"; no black label counterpart					
❑ Kapp KJB-49	Bumble Bee/Everything You Do	1964	3.00	6.00	12.00
—Orange label "Winners Circle Series"; no black label counterpart					
❑ Kapp KJB-49	Bumble Bee/A Tear Fell	1965	2.50	5.00	10.00
—Orange label "Winners Circle Series"; no black label counterpart					
❑ Kapp 577	Needles and Pins/Ain't That Just Like Me	1964	3.00	6.00	12.00
❑ Kapp 577	Needles and Pins/Saturday Night Out	1964	2.50	5.00	10.00
❑ Kapp 584	Ain't That Just Like Me/Ain't Gonna Kiss You	1964	2.50	5.00	10.00
❑ Kapp 593	Don't Throw Your Love Away/I Pretend I'm with You	1964	2.50	5.00	10.00
❑ Kapp 609	Someday We're Gonna Love Again/No One Else Could Love Me	1964	2.50	5.00	10.00
❑ Kapp 618	When You Walk in the Room/I'll Be Missing You	1964	2.50	5.00	10.00
❑ Kapp 644	What Have They Done to the Rain/This Feeling Inside	1965	2.50	5.00	10.00
❑ Kapp 658	Goodbye My Lover Goodbye/'Til I Met You	1965	2.50	5.00	10.00
❑ Kapp 686	He's Got No Love/So Far Away	1965	2.50	5.00	10.00
❑ Kapp 706	Don't You Know Why/You Can't Lie to a Liar	1965	2.50	5.00	10.00
❑ Kapp 729	Take Me for What I'm Worth/Too Many Miles	1966	2.50	5.00	10.00
❑ Kapp 783	Have You Ever Loved Somebody/It's Just the Way	1966	2.50	5.00	10.00
❑ Kapp 811	Lovers/Popcorn Double Feature	1966	2.50	5.00	10.00
❑ Liberty 55646	Sugar and Spice/Saints and Sinners	1963	6.25	12.50	25.00
❑ Liberty 55689	Sugar and Spice/Saints and Sinners	1964	3.75	7.50	15.00
❑ Mercury 72172	Sweets for My Sweet/It's All Been a Dream	1963	6.25	12.50	25.00
❑ Mercury 72390	(Ain't That) Just Like Me/I Can Tell	1964	3.75	7.50	15.00
❑ RCA Victor 74-0484	Desdemona/The World Is Waiting for Tomorrow	1971	—	3.00	6.00
❑ RCA Victor 74-0652	Love Is Everywhere/And the Button	1972	—	3.00	6.00
❑ Sire 49175	It's Too Late/Don't Hang On	1980	—	2.00	4.00
❑ Sire 49665	Love's Melody/Little Bit of Heaven	1981	—	2.00	4.00
❑ World Pacific 77908	Umbrella Man/Over the Weekend	1969	2.00	4.00	8.00
Albums					
❑ Kapp KL-1363 [M]	Meet the Searchers	1964	10.00	20.00	40.00
—With black and blue label					
❑ Kapp KL-1409 [M]	This Is Us	1964	6.25	12.50	25.00
—Version 1: No sticker on front cover					
❑ Kapp KL-1412 [M]	The New Searchers LP	1965	6.25	12.50	25.00
❑ Kapp KL-1449 [M]	The Searchers No. 4	1965	6.25	12.50	25.00
❑ Kapp KL-1477 [M]	Take Me for What I'm Worth	1966	6.25	12.50	25.00
❑ Kapp KS-3363 [S]	Meet the Searchers	1964	12.50	25.00	50.00
—With black and blue label					

Number	Title (A Side/B Side)	Yr	VG	VG+	NM
❑ Kapp KS-3409 [S]	This Is Us	1964	7.50	15.00	30.00
—Version 1: No sticker on front cover					
❑ Kapp KS-3412 [S]	The New Searchers LP	1965	7.50	15.00	30.00
❑ Kapp KS-3419 [S]	The Searchers No. 4	1965	7.50	15.00	30.00
❑ Kapp KS-3477 [S]	Take Me for What I'm Worth	1966	7.50	15.00	30.00
❑ Mercury MG-20914 [M]	Hear! Hear!	1964	12.50	25.00	50.00
—Version 1: With only the title on the front cover					
❑ Mercury MG-20994 [M]	The Searchers Meet the Rattles	1965	18.75	37.50	75.00
❑ Mercury SR-60914 [S]	Hear! Hear!	1964	10.00	20.00	40.00
—Version 1: With only the title on the front cover					
❑ Mercury SR-60994 [S]	The Searchers Meet the Rattles	1965	12.50	25.00	50.00
❑ Pye 501	The Searchers	197?	3.75	7.50	15.00
—Reissue of Kapp hits					
❑ Pye 508	The Searchers, Vol. 2	1976	3.75	7.50	15.00
❑ Rhino RNLP 162	Greatest Hits	1985	2.50	5.00	10.00
❑ Rhino R1-70162	Greatest Hits	1988	2.00	4.00	8.00
—Reissue of RNLP 162					
❑ Sire SRK 3523	Love's Melodies	1981	2.50	5.00	10.00
❑ Sire SRK 6082	The Searchers	1980	2.50	5.00	10.00

SEBASTIAN, JOHN

45s

Number	Title (A Side/B Side)	Yr	VG	VG+	NM
❑ Kama Sutra 254	She's a Lady/The Room Nobody Lives In	1968	2.50	5.00	10.00
❑ Kama Sutra 505	Younger Generation/Boredom	1970	2.00	4.00	8.00
❑ MGM 14122	Rainbows All Over Your Blues/You're a Big Boy Now	1970	—	3.00	6.00
❑ Reprise 0902	Fa-Fana-Fa/Magical Connection	1970	—	3.00	6.00
❑ Reprise 0918	What She Thinks About/Red-Eye Express	1970	—	3.00	6.00
❑ Reprise 1026	I Don't Want Nobody Else/Sweet Muse	1971	—	3.00	6.00
❑ Reprise 1050	We'll See/Well, Well, Well	1971	—	3.00	6.00
❑ Reprise 1074	Give Us a Break/Music for People Who Don't Speak English	1972	—	3.00	6.00
❑ Reprise 1349	Welcome Back/Warm Baby	1976	—	2.00	4.00
—Revised A-side title					
❑ Reprise 1349	Welcome Back Kotter/Warm Baby	1976	2.00	4.00	8.00
—Original A-side title					
❑ Reprise 1355	Hideaway/One Step Forward, Two Steps Back	1976	—	2.00	4.00

Albums

Number	Title (A Side/B Side)	Yr	VG	VG+	NM
❑ MGM SE-4654	John B. Sebastian	1969	3.75	7.50	15.00
❑ MGM SE-4720	John Sebastian Live	1970	3.75	7.50	15.00
❑ Reprise MS 2036	Cheapo-Cheapo Productions Presents Real Live John Sebastian	1971	3.00	6.00	12.00
❑ Reprise MS 2041	The Four of Us	1971	3.00	6.00	12.00
❑ Reprise MS 2187	Tarzana Kid	1974	3.00	6.00	12.00
❑ Reprise MS 2249	Welcome Back	1976	3.00	6.00	12.00
❑ Reprise RS 6379	John B. Sebastian	1969	5.00	10.00	20.00
—Same album as MGM 4654, but a different mix					
❑ Rhino R1-70170	The Best of John Sebastian (1969-1976)	1989	3.00	6.00	12.00

SEDAKA, NEIL

45s

Number	Title (A Side/B Side)	Yr	VG	VG+	NM
❑ Decca 30520	Laura Lee/Snowtime	1957	15.00	30.00	60.00
❑ Elektra 45406	Amarillo/The Leaving Game	1977	—	2.00	4.00
❑ Elektra 45421	Alone at Last/Sleazy Love	1977	—	2.00	4.00
❑ Elektra 45525	Candy Kisses/All You Need Is the Music	1978	—	2.00	4.00
❑ Elektra 46017	Sad, Sad Story/Tillie the Twirler	1979	—	2.00	4.00
❑ Elektra 46615	Should've Never Let You Go/You're So Good for Me	1980	—	2.00	4.00
—With Dara Sedaka					
❑ Elektra 47017	Letting Go/It's Good to Be Alive Again	1980	—	3.00	6.00
❑ Elektra 47184	My World Keeps Slipping Away/Love Is Spreading Over the World	1981	—	2.00	4.00
❑ Guyden 2004	Ring-a-Rockin'/Fly, Don't Fly on Me	1958	12.50	25.00	50.00
❑ Kirshner 63-5017	I'm a Song (Sing Me)/Silent Movies	1971	—	2.50	5.00
—As "Sedaka"					
❑ Kirshner 63-5020	Superbird/Rosemary Blue	1972	—	2.50	5.00
❑ Kirshner 63-5024	Beautiful You/Anywhere You're Gonna Be (Leba's Song)	1972	—	3.00	6.00
❑ Legion 133	Ring-a-Rockin'/Fly, Don't Fly on Me	1958	25.00	50.00	100.00
❑ MCA 60189	Laughter in the Rain/The Immigrant	197?	—	—	3.00
—Reissue					
❑ MCA Curb 52307	Your Precious Love/Searchin'	1983	—	2.00	4.00
—With Dara Sedaka					
❑ MCA Curb 52400	New Orleans/Rhythm of the Rain	1984	—	2.00	4.00
—With Gary U.S. Bonds					
❑ MGM 14564	Standing on the Inside/Let Daddy Know	1973	—	2.50	5.00
❑ MGM 14661	Alone in New York in the Rain/Suspicions	1973	—	2.50	5.00
❑ Pyramid 623	Oh Delilah/Neil's Twist	1962	7.50	15.00	30.00
—B-side is an instrumental version of the A-side credited to The Marvels					
❑ RCA Victor 47-7408	The Diary/No Vacancy	1958	5.00	10.00	20.00
❑ RCA Victor 47-7473	I Go Ape/Moon of Gold	1959	5.00	10.00	20.00
❑ RCA Victor 47-7530	You Gotta Learn Your Rhythm and Blues/Crying My Heart Out for You	1959	6.25	12.50	25.00
❑ RCA Victor 47-7595	Oh! Carol/One Way Ticket (To the Blues)	1959	5.00	10.00	20.00
❑ RCA Victor 47-7709	Stairway to Heaven/Forty Winks Away	1960	3.75	7.50	15.00
❑ RCA Victor 47-7781	You Mean Everything to Me/Run Samson Run	1960	3.75	7.50	15.00
❑ RCA Victor 47-7829	Calendar Girl/The Same Old Fool	1960	3.75	7.50	15.00
❑ RCA Victor 47-7874	Little Devil/I Must Be Dreaming	1961	3.75	7.50	15.00
❑ RCA Victor 47-7922	Sweet Little You/I Found My World in You	1961	3.75	7.50	15.00
❑ RCA Victor 47-7957	Happy Birthday Sweet Sixteen/Don't Lead Me On	1961	3.75	7.50	15.00
❑ RCA Victor 47-8007	King of Clowns/Walk with Me	1962	3.75	7.50	15.00
❑ RCA Victor 47-8046	Breaking Up Is Hard to Do/As Long As I Live	1962	3.75	7.50	15.00
❑ RCA Victor 47-8086	Next Door to An Angel/I Belong to You	1962	3.75	7.50	15.00

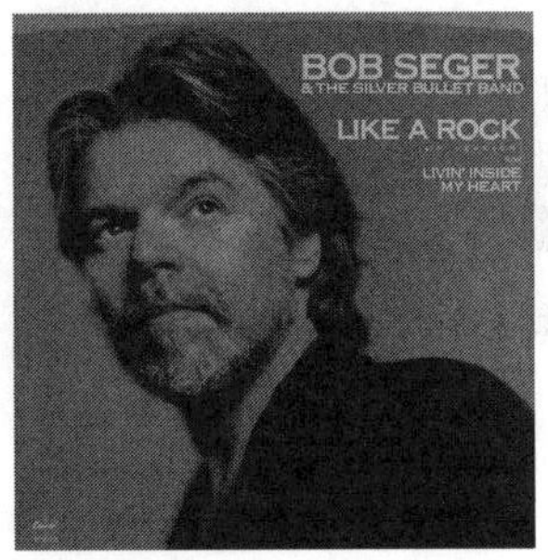

Number	Title (A Side/B Side)	Yr	VG	VG+	NM
❑ RCA Victor 47-8137	Alice in Wonderland/Circulate	1963	3.00	6.00	12.00
❑ RCA Victor 47-8169	Let's Go Steady Again/Waiting for Never	1963	3.00	6.00	12.00
❑ RCA Victor 47-8209	The Dreamer/Look Inside Your Heart	1963	3.00	6.00	12.00
❑ RCA Victor 47-8254	Bad Girl/Wait 'Til You See My Baby	1963	3.00	6.00	12.00
❑ RCA Victor 47-8341	The Closest Thing to Heaven/Without a Song	1964	2.50	5.00	10.00
❑ RCA Victor 47-8382	Sunny/She'll Never Be You	1964	2.50	5.00	10.00
❑ RCA Victor 47-8453	I Hope He Breaks Your Heart/Too Late	1964	2.50	5.00	10.00
❑ RCA Victor 47-8511	Let the People Talk/In the Chapel with You	1965	2.50	5.00	10.00
❑ RCA Victor 47-8637	The World Through a Tear/High On a Mountain	1965	2.50	5.00	10.00
❑ RCA Victor 47-8737	The Answer to My Prayer/Blue Boy	1965	2.50	5.00	10.00
❑ RCA Victor 47-8844	The Answer Lies Within/Grown-Up Games	1966	2.50	5.00	10.00
❑ RCA Victor 47-9004	We Can Make It If We Try/Too Late	1966	2.50	5.00	10.00
❑ RCA Victor 447-0575	Oh! Carol/Calendar Girl	196?	—	3.00	6.00
—Gold Standard Series; black label					
❑ RCA Victor 447-0575	Oh! Carol/Calendar Girl	197?	—	2.00	4.00
—Gold Standard Series; red label					
❑ RCA Victor 447-0597	The Diary/Happy Birthday Sweet Sixteen	196?	—	3.00	6.00
—Gold Standard Series; black label					
❑ RCA Victor 447-0597	The Diary/Happy Birthday Sweet Sixteen	197?	—	2.00	4.00
—Gold Standard Series; red label					
❑ RCA Victor 447-0701	Breaking Up Is Hard to Do/Next Door to An Angel	196?	—	3.00	6.00
—Gold Standard Series; black label					
❑ RCA Victor 447-0701	Breaking Up Is Hard to Do/Next Door to An Angel	197?	—	2.00	4.00
—Gold Standard Series; red label					
❑ RCA Victor 447-0939	Little Devil/Stairway to Heaven	196?	—	3.00	6.00
—Gold Standard Series; black label					
❑ Rocket 40313	Laughter in the Rain/Endlessly	1974	—	2.00	4.00
❑ Rocket 40370	The Immigrant/Hey Mister Sunshine	1975	—	2.00	4.00
—No mention of John Lennon on label					
❑ Rocket 40426	That's When the Music Takes Me/Standing on the Inside	1975	—	2.00	4.00
❑ Rocket 40460	Bad Blood/Your Favorite Entertainer	1975	—	2.00	4.00
❑ Rocket 40500	Breaking Up Is Hard to Do/Nana's Song	1975	—	2.00	4.00
❑ Rocket 40543	Love in the Shadows/Baby Don't Let It Mess Your Mind	1976	—	2.00	4.00
❑ Rocket 40582	Steppin' Out/I Let You Walk Away	1976	—	2.00	4.00
❑ Rocket 40614	You Gotta Make Your Own Sunshine/Perfect Strangers	1976	—	2.00	4.00
❑ SGC 005	Star-Crossed Lovers/We Had a Good Thing Going	1969	—	3.00	6.00
❑ SGC 008	Rainy Jane/Jeannine	1970	—	3.00	6.00
Albums					
❑ Accord SN-7152	Singer, Songwriter, Melody Maker	1981	2.50	5.00	10.00
❑ Elektra 6E-102	A Song	1977	2.50	5.00	10.00
❑ Elektra 6E-161	All You Need Is Music	1978	2.50	5.00	10.00
❑ Elektra 6E-259	In the Pocket	1980	2.50	5.00	10.00
❑ Elektra 6E-348	Neil Sedaka Now	1981	2.50	5.00	10.00
❑ Kirshner KES-111	Emergence	1971	3.75	7.50	15.00
❑ Kirshner KES-117	Solitaire	1972	3.75	7.50	15.00
❑ MCA 2357	Sedaka's Back	1978	2.50	5.00	10.00
—Reissue of Rocket 463					
❑ MCA 5466	Come See About Me	1984	2.50	5.00	10.00
❑ Pickwick ACL1-7006	Breaking Up Is Hard to Do	197?	2.00	4.00	8.00
❑ Polydor 831235-1	My Friend	1986	2.50	5.00	10.00
❑ RCA Camden ACL1-7006	Breaking Up Is Hard to Do	197?	2.50	5.00	10.00
❑ RCA Victor ANL1-0879	Oh! Carol	1975	2.50	5.00	10.00
❑ RCA Victor APL1-0928	Neil Sedaka Sings His Greatest Hits	1975	3.00	6.00	12.00
—Reissue of LSP-2627					
❑ RCA Victor ANL1-1314	Pure Gold	1976	2.50	5.00	10.00
❑ RCA Victor VPL1-1540	Live in Australia	1976	3.00	6.00	12.00
❑ RCA Victor APL1-1789	Emergence	1976	3.00	6.00	12.00
—Reissue of Kirshner 111					
❑ RCA Victor APL1-1790	Solitaire	1976	3.00	6.00	12.00
—Reissue of Kirshner 117					
❑ RCA Victor LPM-2035 [M]	Neil Sedaka	1959	15.00	30.00	60.00
❑ RCA Victor LSP-2035 [S]	Neil Sedaka	1959	25.00	50.00	100.00
❑ RCA Victor AFL1-2254	Sedaka — The '50s and '60s	1977	2.50	5.00	10.00
❑ RCA Victor LPM-2317 [M]	Circulate	1960	12.50	25.00	50.00
❑ RCA Victor LSP-2317 [S]	Circulate	1960	15.00	30.00	60.00
❑ RCA Victor LPM-2421 [M]	"Little Devil" and His Other Hits	1961	12.50	25.00	50.00

Number	Title (A Side/B Side)	Yr	VG	VG+	NM
❑ RCA Victor LSP-2421 [S]	"Little Devil" and His Other Hits	1961	15.00	30.00	60.00
❑ RCA Victor AFL1-2524	The Many Sides of Neil Sedaka	1978	2.50	5.00	10.00
❑ RCA Victor LPM-2627 [M]	Neil Sedaka Sings His Greatest Hits	1962	10.00	20.00	40.00
❑ RCA Victor LSP-2627 [S]	Neil Sedaka Sings His Greatest Hits	1962	12.50	25.00	50.00
—Black label, dog on top, "Living Stereo" at bottom					
❑ RCA Victor ANL1-3465	Neil Sedaka Sings His Greatest Hits	1979	2.00	4.00	8.00
—Reissue of AFL1-0928					
❑ Rocket MCA-463	Sedaka's Back	1974	3.00	6.00	12.00
❑ Rocket PIG-2157	The Hungry Years	1975	3.00	6.00	12.00
❑ Rocket PIG-2195	Steppin' Out	1976	3.00	6.00	12.00
❑ Rocket PIG-2297	Neil Sedaka's Greatest Hits	1977	3.00	6.00	12.00

SEDAKA, NEIL, AND THE TOKENS WITH THE COINS

Albums

Number	Title (A Side/B Side)	Yr	VG	VG+	NM
❑ Crown CST-366 [R]	Neil Sedaka and the Tokens and the Coins	1963	5.00	10.00	20.00
❑ Crown CLP-5366 [M]	Neil Sedaka and the Tokens and the Coins	1963	7.50	15.00	30.00

SEEKERS, THE

45s

Number	Title (A Side/B Side)	Yr	VG	VG+	NM
❑ Atmos 711	Myra/Wild Rover	1965	3.75	7.50	15.00
❑ Capitol 2013	When the Good Apples Fall/Myra (Shake Up the Party)	1967	2.50	5.00	10.00
❑ Capitol 2122	Love Is Kind, Love Is Wine/All I Can Remember	1968	2.50	5.00	10.00
❑ Capitol 5383	I'll Never Find Another You/Open Up Them Pearly Gates	1965	3.00	6.00	12.00
❑ Capitol 5430	A World of Our Own/Sinner Man	1965	3.00	6.00	12.00
❑ Capitol 5531	The Carnival Is Over/We Shall Not Be Moved	1965	2.50	5.00	10.00
❑ Capitol 5622	Some Day, One Day/Nobody Knows the Trouble I've Seen	1966	2.50	5.00	10.00
❑ Capitol 5756	Georgy Girl/When the Stars Begin to Fall	1966	3.00	6.00	12.00
❑ Capitol 5787	Morningtown Ride/Walk with Me	1967	2.50	5.00	10.00
❑ Capitol 5974	I Wish You Could Be Here/On the Other Side	1967	2.50	5.00	10.00
❑ Marvel 1060	Chilly Winds/The Light from the Lighthouse	1965	3.75	7.50	15.00

Albums

Number	Title (A Side/B Side)	Yr	VG	VG+	NM
❑ Capitol ST-135 [S]	The Seekers Live	1969	3.00	6.00	12.00
❑ Capitol ST 2319 [S]	The New Seekers	1965	3.75	7.50	15.00
❑ Capitol T 2319 [M]	The New Seekers	1965	3.00	6.00	12.00
❑ Capitol DT 2369 [R]	A World of Our Own	1965	3.00	6.00	12.00
❑ Capitol T 2369 [M]	A World of Our Own	1965	3.00	6.00	12.00
❑ Capitol ST 2431 [S]	Georgy Girl	1966	3.75	7.50	15.00
❑ Capitol T 2431 [M]	Georgy Girl	1966	3.00	6.00	12.00
❑ Capitol ST 2746 [P]	The Best of the Seekers	1967	3.00	6.00	12.00
—Red and white "target" Starline label; though the cover has an "ST" prefix, the record and trail-off wax have a "DT" prefix; "Morningtown Ride," Turn, Turn, Turn," and "We're Moving On" are in stereo					
❑ Capitol T 2746 [M]	The Best of the Seekers	1967	3.00	6.00	12.00
❑ Capitol KAO 2821 [M]	The Seekers Seen in Green	1968	10.00	20.00	40.00
❑ Capitol SKAO 2821 [S]	The Seekers Seen in Green	1968	3.75	7.50	15.00
❑ Capitol SN-16104 [P]	The Best of the Seekers	1980	2.00	4.00	8.00
❑ Marvel 2060 [M]	The Seekers	1965	3.00	6.00	12.00
❑ Marvel 3060 [R]	The Seekers	1965	2.50	5.00	10.00

SEGER, BOB

45s

Number	Title (A Side/B Side)	Yr	VG	VG+	NM
❑ Abkco 4015	East Side Story/East Side Sound	1973	—	3.00	6.00
❑ Abkco 4016	Chain Smokin'/Persecution Smith	1973	—	3.00	6.00
❑ Abkco 4017	Heavy Music - Pt. I/Heavy Music - Pt. II	1973	—	3.00	6.00
❑ Abkco 4031	Heavy Music - Pt. I/Heavy Music - Pt. II	1973	—	2.50	5.00
❑ Cameo 438	East Side Story/East Side Sound	1966	6.25	12.50	25.00
❑ Cameo 444	Sock It To Me, Santa/Florida Time	1966	7.50	15.00	30.00
❑ Cameo 465	Chain Smokin'/Persecution Smith	1967	6.25	12.50	25.00
❑ Cameo 473	Vagrant Winter/Very Few	1967	6.25	12.50	25.00
❑ Cameo 494	Heavy Music/Heavy Music (Part 2)	1967	5.00	10.00	20.00
❑ Capitol 2143	2 + 2 = ?/Death Row	1968	3.75	7.50	15.00
❑ Capitol 2297	Ramblin' Gamblin' Man/Tales of Lucy Blue	1968	3.00	6.00	12.00
❑ Capitol 2480	Ivory/The Lost Song (Love Needs to Be Loved)	1969	2.00	4.00	8.00
❑ Capitol 2576	Noah/Lennie Johnson	1969	2.00	4.00	8.00
❑ Capitol 2640	Lonely Man/Innervenus Eyes	1970	2.00	4.00	8.00
❑ Capitol 2748	Lucifer/Big River	1970	2.00	4.00	8.00
❑ Capitol 3187	Lookin' Back/Highway Child	1971	2.00	4.00	8.00
❑ Capitol 4062	Beautiful Loser/Fine Memory	1975	—	2.50	5.00
❑ Capitol 4116	Katmandu/Black Night	1975	—	2.50	5.00
❑ Capitol 4183	Nutbush City Limits/Travelin' Man	1975	—	2.50	5.00
❑ Capitol 4269	Nutbush City Limits/Lookin' Back	1976	—	2.50	5.00
❑ Capitol 4300	Beautiful Loser/Travelin' Man	1976	—	2.50	5.00
❑ Capitol 4369	Night Moves/Ship of Fools	1976	—	2.00	4.00
❑ Capitol 4422	Mainstreet/Jody Girl	1977	—	2.00	4.00
❑ Capitol 4449	Rock and Roll Never Forgets/Fire Down Below	1977	—	2.00	4.00
❑ Capitol 4581	Still the Same/Feel Like a Number	1978	—	2.00	4.00
❑ Capitol 4618	Hollywood Nights/Brave Strangers	1978	—	2.00	4.00
❑ Capitol 4653	We've Got Tonite/Ain't Got No Money	1978	—	2.00	4.00
❑ Capitol 4702	Old Time Rock and Roll/Sunspot Baby	1979	—	2.00	4.00
❑ Capitol 4836	Fire Lake/Long Twin Silver Line	1980	—	2.00	4.00
❑ Capitol 4863	Against the Wind/No Man's Land	1980	—	2.00	4.00
❑ Capitol 4904	You'll Accomp'ny Me/Betty Lou's Gettin' Out Tonight	1980	—	2.50	5.00
❑ Capitol 4951	The Horizontal Bop/Her Strut	1980	—	2.50	5.00
❑ Capitol A-5042	Tryin' to Live My Life Without You/Brave Strangers	1981	—	—	3.00
❑ Capitol A-5077	Feel Like a Number/Hollywood Nights	1981	—	2.00	4.00
❑ Capitol B-5187	Shame on the Moon/House Behind a House	1982	—	—	3.00
❑ Capitol B-5213	Even Now/Little Victories	1983	—	—	3.00
❑ Capitol B-5235	Roll Me Away/Boomtown Blues	1983	—	—	3.00
❑ Capitol B-5276	Old Time Rock and Roll/Till It Shines	1983	—	—	3.00
❑ Capitol B-5413	Understanding/East L.A.	1984	—	—	3.00

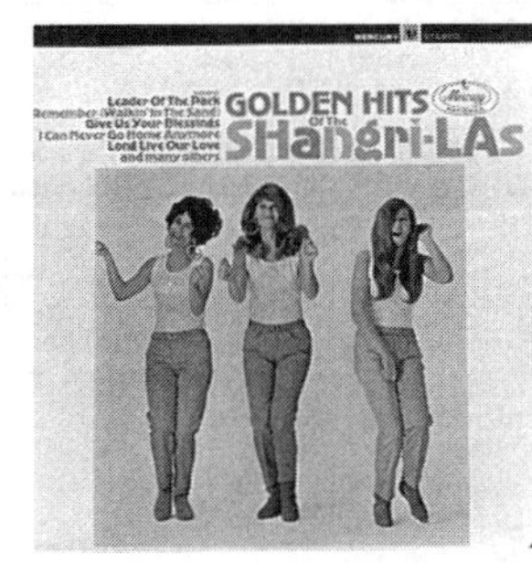

Number	Title (A Side/B Side)	Yr	VG	VG+	NM
❑ Capitol B-5532	American Storm/Fortunate Son	1986	—	—	3.00
❑ Capitol B-5592	Like a Rock/Livin' Inside My Heart	1986	—	—	3.00
❑ Capitol B-5623	It's You/The Aftermath (12" Remix)	1986	—	—	3.00
❑ Capitol B-5658	Miami/Somewhere Tonight	1986	—	—	3.00
❑ Hideout 1013	East Side Story/East Side Sound	1966	12.50	25.00	50.00
❑ Hideout 1014	Chain Smokin'/Persecution Smith	1966	12.50	25.00	50.00
❑ MCA 53094	Shakedown/The Aftermath	1987	—	—	3.00
❑ Palladium 1079	If I Were a Carpenter/Jesse James	1972	2.50	5.00	10.00
❑ Palladium 1117	Turn On Your Love Light/Who Do You Love?	1972	2.50	5.00	10.00
❑ Palladium 1143	Rosalie/Neon Sky	1972	2.50	5.00	10.00
❑ Palladium 1171	Need Ya/Seen a Lot of Floors	1973	2.50	5.00	10.00
❑ Palladium 1205	Get Out of Denver/Long Song Comin'	1974	2.50	5.00	10.00
❑ Palladium 1316	This Ole House/U.M.C.	1974	3.75	7.50	15.00
Albums					
❑ Capitol ST-172	Ramblin' Gamblin' Man	1969	7.50	15.00	30.00
—Black label with colorband					
❑ Capitol ST-236	Noah	1969	20.00	40.00	80.00
❑ Capitol SKAO-499	Mongrel	1970	6.25	12.50	25.00
❑ Capitol ST-731	Brand New Morning	1971	25.00	50.00	100.00
❑ Capitol ST-11378	Beautiful Loser	1975	2.50	5.00	10.00
—Originals have orange labels					
❑ Capitol SKBB-11523 [(2)]	Live Bullet	1976	3.75	7.50	15.00
—Originals have orange labels					
❑ Capitol ST-11557	Night Moves	1976	2.50	5.00	10.00
❑ Capitol SW-11698	Stranger in Town	1978	2.50	5.00	10.00
❑ Capitol ST-11746	Smokin' O.P.'s	1978	2.50	5.00	10.00
❑ Capitol ST-11748	Seven	1978	2.50	5.00	10.00
❑ Capitol SOO-12041	Against the Wind	1980	2.50	5.00	10.00
❑ Capitol STBK-12182 [(2)]	Nine Tonight	1981	3.75	7.50	15.00
❑ Capitol ST-12254	The Distance	1983	2.50	5.00	10.00
❑ Capitol PT-12398	Like a Rock	1986	2.50	5.00	10.00
❑ Capitol SN-16105	Ramblin' Gamblin' Man	1980	2.00	4.00	8.00
❑ Capitol SN-16106	Mongrel	1980	2.00	4.00	8.00
❑ Capitol SN-16107	Smokin' O.P.'s	1980	2.00	4.00	8.00
❑ Capitol SN-16108	Seven	1980	2.00	4.00	8.00
❑ Capitol SN-16315	Beautiful Loser	1984	2.00	4.00	8.00
❑ Capitol R124284	Ramblin' Gamblin' Man	197?	5.00	10.00	20.00
—Orange label, "Capitol"at bottom; RCA Music Service edition with B-side label error listing the title as "Ramblin' Bamblin' Man"					
❑ Palladium P-1006	Smokin' O.P.'s	1972	6.25	12.50	25.00
❑ Reprise MS 2109	Smokin' O.P.'s	1972	3.75	7.50	15.00
❑ Reprise MS 2126	Back in '72	1973	15.00	30.00	60.00
❑ Reprise MS 2184	Seven	1974	5.00	10.00	20.00
SEX PISTOLS					
45s					
❑ Warner Bros. 8516	Pretty Vacant/Sub-Mission	1978	5.00	10.00	20.00
❑ Warner Bros. 8516 [DJ]	Pretty Vacant (mono/stereo)	1978	2.50	5.00	10.00
❑ Warner Bros. 8516 [Picture Sleeve]	Pretty Vacant/Sub-Mission	1978	2.50	5.00	10.00
Albums					
❑ Restless 72255	Better Live Than Dead	1988	3.00	6.00	12.00
❑ Restless 72256 [EP]	The Mini-Album	1988	2.00	4.00	8.00
❑ Restless 72257	The Ex-Pistols: The Swindle Continues	1988	3.00	6.00	12.00
❑ Restless 72511	Live at Chelmsford Top Security Prison	1990	2.50	5.00	10.00
❑ Skyclad SEX 6	We've Cum For Your Children	1988	3.00	6.00	12.00
❑ Warner Bros. BSK 3147	Never Mind the Bollocks Here's the Sex Pistols	1978	2.50	5.00	10.00
—With white WB label					
❑ Warner Bros. BSK 3147	Never Mind the Bollocks Here's the Sex Pistols	1978	6.25	12.50	25.00
—Any other version with custom label					
❑ Warner Bros. BSK 3147	Never Mind the Bollocks Here's the Sex Pistols	1978	7.50	15.00	30.00
—With sticker "Contains Sub-Mission"					
SEX PISTOLS, THE					
45s					
❑ Warner Bros. 8516 [DJ]	Pretty Vacant (mono/stereo)	1978	2.50	5.00	10.00
SHADES OF BLUE					
45s					
❑ Impact 1007	Oh, How Happy/Little Orphan Boy	1966	5.00	10.00	20.00

Number	Title (A Side/B Side)	Yr	VG	VG+	NM
❑ Impact 1014	Lonely Summer/With This Ring	1966	5.00	10.00	20.00
❑ Impact 1015	Happiness/The Night	1966	5.00	10.00	20.00
❑ Impact 1026	All I Want Is Love/How Do You Save a Dying Love	1967	5.00	10.00	20.00
❑ Impact 1028	Penny Arcade/Funny Kind of Love	1967	5.00	10.00	20.00
Albums					
❑ Impact IM-101 [M]	Happiness Is the Shades of Blue	1966	12.50	25.00	50.00
❑ Impact IM-1001 [S]	Happiness Is the Shades of Blue	1966	15.00	30.00	60.00

SHADOWS OF KNIGHT, THE

45s

Number	Title (A Side/B Side)	Yr	VG	VG+	NM
❑ Atco 6634	Gloria '69/A Spaniard at My Door	1968	4.00	8.00	16.00
❑ Atco 6776	I Am the Hunter/Warwick County Affair	1970	4.00	8.00	16.00
❑ Dunwich 116	Gloria/Dark Side	1966	3.75	7.50	15.00
—Dark pink and yellow label; other label variations may exist					
❑ Dunwich 122	Oh Yeah/Light Bulb Blues	1966	5.00	10.00	20.00
❑ Dunwich 128	Bad Little Woman/Gospel Zone	1966	3.75	7.50	15.00
❑ Dunwich 141	I'm Gonna Make You Mine/I'll Make You Sorry	1966	6.25	12.50	25.00
❑ Dunwich 151	The Behemoth/Willie Jean	1967	5.00	10.00	20.00
❑ Dunwich 167	Someone Like Me/There for Love	1967	5.00	10.00	20.00
❑ Phonograph 1002/2001	Sweetness in Motion/Nikki-Hoki (No One Else Will Ever Do)	1986	2.00	4.00	8.00
❑ Super K 108	Taurus/My Fire Department Needs a Fireman	1969	2.50	5.00	10.00
❑ Super K 110	Run, Run, Billy Porter/My Fire Department Needs a Fireman	1969	2.50	5.00	10.00
❑ Team 520	Shake/From Way Out to Way In	1968	4.00	8.00	16.00
Albums					
❑ Dunwich 666 [M]	Gloria	1966	12.50	25.00	50.00
❑ Dunwich S-666 [S]	Gloria	1966	20.00	40.00	80.00
❑ Dunwich 667 [M]	Back Door Men	1966	12.50	25.00	50.00
❑ Dunwich S-667 [S]	Back Door Men	1966	20.00	40.00	80.00
❑ Super K SKS-6002	The Shadows of Knight	1969	12.50	25.00	50.00

SHANGRI-LAS, THE

45s

Number	Title (A Side/B Side)	Yr	VG	VG+	NM
❑ Lana 143	Leader of the Pack/What Is Love	196?	2.50	5.00	10.00
—Oldies reissue					
❑ Mercury 72645	I'll Never Learn/Sweet Sounds of Summer	1966	5.00	10.00	20.00
❑ Mercury 72670	Footsteps on the Roof/Take the Time	1967	5.00	10.00	20.00
❑ Red Bird 10-008	Remember (Walkin' in the Sand)/It's Easier to Cry	1964	6.25	12.50	25.00
❑ Red Bird 10-014	Leader of the Pack/What Is Love	1964	6.25	12.50	25.00
❑ Red Bird 10-018	Give Him a Great Big Kiss/Twist and Shout	1964	6.25	12.50	25.00
❑ Red Bird 10-019	Maybe/Shout	1964	5.00	10.00	20.00
❑ Red Bird 10-025	Out in the Streets/The Boy	1965	5.00	10.00	20.00
❑ Red Bird 10-030	Give Us Your Blessings/Heaven Only Knows	1965	5.00	10.00	20.00
❑ Red Bird 10-036	Right Now and Not Later/The Train from Kansas City	1965	5.00	10.00	20.00
❑ Red Bird 10-043	I Can Never Go Home Anymore/Bull Dog	1965	5.00	10.00	20.00
❑ Red Bird 10-043	I Can Never Go Home Anymore/Sophisticated Boom Boom	1965	7.50	15.00	30.00
❑ Red Bird 10-048	Long Live Our Love/Bull Dog	1966	5.00	10.00	20.00
❑ Red Bird 10-048	Long Live Our Love/Sophisticated Boom Boom	1966	5.00	10.00	20.00
❑ Red Bird 10-053	He Cried/Dressed in Black	1966	5.00	10.00	20.00
❑ Red Bird 10-068	Past, Present and Future/Paradise	1966	5.00	10.00	20.00
❑ Red Bird 10-068	Past, Present and Future/Love You More Than Yesterday	1966	5.00	10.00	20.00
❑ Scepter 1291	Wishing Well/Hate to Say I Told You So	1964	5.00	10.00	20.00
❑ Smash 1866	Simon Says/Simon Speaks	1963	10.00	20.00	40.00
❑ Spokane 4006	Wishing Well/Hate to Say I Told You So	1964	7.50	15.00	30.00
Albums					
❑ Collectables COL-5011	Remember…Their Greatest Hits	198?	2.50	5.00	10.00
❑ Mercury MG-21099 [M]	The Shangri-Las' Golden Hits	1966	10.00	20.00	40.00
❑ Mercury SR-61099 [S]	The Shangri-Las' Golden Hits	1966	12.50	25.00	50.00
❑ Polydor 824807-1	Golden Hits of the Shangri-Las	1985	2.50	5.00	10.00
❑ Post 4000	The Shangri-Las Sing	196?	5.00	10.00	20.00
❑ Red Bird 20101 [M]	Leader of the Pack	1965	37.50	75.00	150.00
❑ Red Bird 20104 [M]	Shangri-Las '65	1965	37.50	75.00	150.00
❑ Red Bird 20104 [M]	I Can Never Go Home Anymore	1966	25.00	50.00	100.00
—Retitled version with title song added and "Sophisticated Boom Boom" dropped					

SHANNON, DEL

45s

Number	Title (A Side/B Side)	Yr	VG	VG+	NM
❑ ABC Dunhill 4193	Sweet Mary Lou/Comin' Back to me	1969	3.75	7.50	15.00
❑ ABC Dunhill 4224	Sister Isabelle/Colorado Rain	1970	3.75	7.50	15.00
❑ Amy 897	Mary Jane/Stains on My Letter	1964	6.25	12.50	25.00
❑ Amy 905	Handy Man/Give Her Lots of Lovin'	1964	3.75	7.50	15.00
❑ Amy 911	Do You Want to Dance/This Is All I Have to Give	1964	3.75	7.50	15.00
❑ Amy 915	Keep Searchin' (We'll Follow the Sun)/Broken Promises	1964	4.00	8.00	16.00
❑ Amy 919	Stranger in Town/Over You	1965	4.00	8.00	16.00
❑ Amy 925	Why Don't You Tell Him/Break Up	1965	3.75	7.50	15.00
❑ Amy 937	Move It On Over/She Still Remembers Tony	1965	3.75	7.50	15.00
❑ Amy 947	I Can't Believe My Ears/I Wish I Wasn't Me Tonight	1966	10.00	20.00	40.00
—Withdrawn shortly after release; promos worth about half these values					
❑ Berlee 501	Sue's Gotta Be Mine/Now She's Gone	1963	3.75	7.50	15.00
❑ Berlee 502	That's the Way Love Is/Time of the Day	1964	3.75	7.50	15.00
❑ Big Top 3067	Runaway/Jody	1961	7.50	15.00	30.00
❑ Big Top 3075	Hats Off to Larry/Don't Gild the Lily, Lily	1961	6.25	12.50	25.00
❑ Big Top 3083	So Long Baby/The Answer to Everything	1961	6.25	12.50	25.00
❑ Big Top 3091	Hey! Little Girl/I Don't Care Anymore	1961	6.25	12.50	25.00
❑ Big Top 3098	Ginny in the Mirror/I Won't Be There	1962	6.25	12.50	25.00
❑ Big Top 3112	Cry Myself to Sleep/I'm Gonna Move On	1962	6.25	12.50	25.00
❑ Big Top 3117	The Swiss Maid/You Never Talked About Me	1962	6.25	12.50	25.00
❑ Big Top 3131	Little Town Flirt/The Wamboo	1962	6.25	12.50	25.00
❑ Big Top 3143	Two Kinds of Teardrops/Kelly	1963	6.25	12.50	25.00

Number	Title (A Side/B Side)	Yr	VG	VG+	NM
❑ Big Top 3152	From Me to You/Two Silhouettes	1963	15.00	30.00	60.00
—A-side is the first American version of a Beatles song					
❑ Eric 189 [S]	Runaway/Hats Off to Larry	1972	—	3.00	6.00
—Both sides of this reissue are the original recordings in true stereo!					
❑ Island 021	Tell Her No/Restless	1975	3.75	7.50	15.00
❑ Island 038	Cry Baby Cry/In My Arms Again	1975	3.75	7.50	15.00
❑ Lana 141	Runaway/Jody	196?	2.00	4.00	8.00
—Oldies reissue					
❑ Lana 142	Hats Off to Larry/Don't Gild the Lily, Lily	196?	2.00	4.00	8.00
—Oldies reissue					
❑ Liberty 55866	The Big Hurt/I Got It Bad	1966	3.00	6.00	12.00
❑ Liberty 55889	Hey Little Star/For a Little While	1966	3.00	6.00	12.00
❑ Liberty 55894	Show Me/Never Thought I Could	1966	3.00	6.00	12.00
❑ Liberty 55904	Under My Thumb/She Was Mine	1966	3.00	6.00	12.00
❑ Liberty 55939	She/What Makes You Run	1967	3.00	6.00	12.00
❑ Liberty 55961	Led Along/I Can't Be True	1967	3.00	6.00	12.00
❑ Liberty 55993	Runaway '67/He Cheated	1967	3.75	7.50	15.00
❑ Liberty 56018	Runnin' On Back/Thinkin' It Over	1968	2.50	5.00	10.00
❑ Liberty 56036	Magical Musical Box/Gemini	1968	2.50	5.00	10.00
❑ Liberty 56070	Raindrops/You Don't Love Me	1968	2.50	5.00	10.00
❑ Lost-Nite 220	Runaway/Hey Little Girl	196?	—	2.50	5.00
—Reissue					
❑ Lost-Nite 222	Hats Off to Larry/Little Town Flirt	196?	—	2.50	5.00
—Reissue					
❑ Network 47951	Sea of Love/Midnight Train	1981	—	2.50	5.00
❑ Network 48006	To Love Someone/Liar	1982	—	2.50	5.00
❑ Twirl 4001	Runaway/Hey Little Girl	196?	—	3.00	6.00
❑ Twirl 4002	Hats Off to Larry/Little Town Flirt	196?	—	3.00	6.00
❑ Warner Bros. 28853	Stranger on the Run/What You Gonna Do with That	1985	—	2.50	5.00
❑ Warner Bros. 29098	In My Arms Again/You Can't Forgive Me	1985	—	2.50	5.00
Albums					
❑ Amy 8003 [M]	Handy Man	1964	12.50	25.00	50.00
❑ Amy S-8003 [S]	Handy Man	1964	20.00	40.00	80.00
❑ Amy 8004 [M]	Del Shannon Sings Hank Williams	1965	12.50	25.00	50.00
❑ Amy S-8004 [S]	Del Shannon Sings Hank Williams	1965	20.00	40.00	80.00
❑ Amy 8006 [M]	1,661 Seconds with Del Shannon	1965	12.50	25.00	50.00
❑ Amy S-8006 [S]	1,661 Seconds with Del Shannon	1965	20.00	40.00	80.00
❑ Big Top 12-1303 [M]	Runaway	1961	75.00	150.00	300.00
❑ Big Top 12-1303 [S]	Runaway	1961	400.00	800.00	1600.
❑ Big Top 12-1308 [B]	Little Town Flirt	1963	250.00	500.00	1000.
—One side is mono, one side is stereo; should be played to identify					
❑ Big Top 12-1308 [M]	Little Town Flirt	1963	37.50	75.00	150.00
❑ Big Top 12-1308 [S]	Little Town Flirt	1963	375.00	750.00	1500.
—Stereo copies are not identified as such on either cover or label; some, but not all, copies have an "S" in the dead wax. Playing is the best way to identify.					
❑ Dot DLP 3824 [M]	The Best of Del Shannon	1967	12.50	25.00	50.00
❑ Dot DLP 25824 [R]	The Best of Del Shannon	1967	10.00	20.00	40.00
❑ Elektra 5E-568	Drop Down and Get Me	1981	2.50	5.00	10.00
❑ Liberty LRP-3453 [M]	This Is My Bag	1966	7.50	15.00	30.00
❑ Liberty LRP-3479 [M]	Total Commitment	1966	7.50	15.00	30.00
❑ Liberty LRP-3539 [M]	The Further Adventures of Charles Westover	1967	12.50	25.00	50.00
❑ Liberty LST-7453 [S]	This Is My Bag	1966	10.00	20.00	40.00
❑ Liberty LST-7479 [S]	Total Commitment	1966	10.00	20.00	40.00
❑ Liberty LST-7539 [S]	The Further Adventures of Charles Westover	1967	20.00	40.00	80.00
❑ Pickwick SPC-3595 [R]	The Best of Del Shannon	197?	2.50	5.00	10.00
❑ Post 9000 [R]	Del Shannon Sings	196?	10.00	20.00	40.00
❑ Rhino RNLP-71056 [M]	Runaway Hits	1986	2.50	5.00	10.00
❑ Sire SASH-3708 [(2)P]	The Vintage Years	1975	6.25	12.50	25.00
❑ United Artists UA-LA151-E	Del Shannon Live in England	1973	6.25	12.50	25.00

SHARP, DEE DEE

45s

Number	Title (A Side/B Side)	Yr	VG	VG+	NM
❑ Atco 6445	Bye Bye Baby/My Best Friend's Man	1966	2.50	5.00	10.00
❑ Atco 6502	Baby I Love You/What Am I Gonna Do	1967	2.00	4.00	8.00
❑ Atco 6557	We Got a Thing Goin' On/What 'Cha Gonna Do About It	1968	2.00	4.00	8.00
—With Ben E. King					
❑ Atco 6576	Woman Will Do Wrong/You're Just a Fool in Love	1968	2.00	4.00	8.00

Number	Title (A Side/B Side)	Yr	VG	VG+	NM
❑ Atco 6587	This Love Won't Run Out/Help Me Find My Glove	1968	2.00	4.00	8.00
❑ Cameo 212	Mashed Potato Time/Set My Heart at Ease	1962	5.00	10.00	20.00
❑ Cameo 219	Gravy (For My Mashed Potatoes)/Baby Cakes	1962	3.75	7.50	15.00
❑ Cameo 230	Ride!/The Night	1962	3.75	7.50	15.00
❑ Cameo 244	Do the Bird/Lover Boy	1963	3.75	7.50	15.00
❑ Cameo 260	Rock Me in the Cradle of Love/You'll Never Be Mine	1963	3.75	7.50	15.00
❑ Cameo 274	Wild!/Why Doncha Ask Me	1963	3.75	7.50	15.00
❑ Cameo 296	Where Did I Go Wrong/Willyam, Willyam	1964	3.00	6.00	12.00
❑ Cameo 329	Never Pick a Pretty Boy/He's No Ordinary Guy	1964	3.00	6.00	12.00
❑ Cameo 335	Deep Dark Secret/Good	1964	125.00	250.00	500.00
❑ Cameo 347	To Know Him Is to Love Him/There Ain't Nothin' I Wouldn't Do for You	1965	2.50	5.00	10.00
❑ Cameo 357	Let's Twine/That's What My Mama Said	1965	2.50	5.00	10.00
❑ Cameo 375	I Really Love You/Standing in the Need of Love	1965	2.50	5.00	10.00
❑ Cameo 382	It's a Funny Situation/There Ain't Nothin' I Wouldn't Do for You	1965	2.50	5.00	10.00
❑ Fairmount 1004	(It's Wonderful) The Love I Feel for You/Willyam, Wilyam	1966	2.50	5.00	10.00
❑ Gamble 219	What Kind of Lady/You're Gonna Miss Me (When I'm Gone)	1968	5.00	10.00	20.00
❑ Gamble 4005	The Bottle or Me/You're Gonna Miss Me (When I'm Gone)	1969	3.75	7.50	15.00
❑ Philadelphia Int'l. 02041	Breaking and Entering/I Love You Anyway	1981	—	2.00	4.00
❑ Philadelphia Int'l. 3512	Conquer the World Together/We Gotta Good Thing Goin'	1971	—	3.00	6.00
—With Bunny Sigler					
❑ Philadelphia Int'l. 3625	Flashback/Nobody Can Take Your Place	1977	—	2.50	5.00
❑ Philadelphia Int'l. 3636	I'd Really Love to See You Tonight/What Color Is Love	1977	—	2.50	5.00
❑ Philadelphia Int'l. 3638	I Believe in Love/Just As Long As I Know You're Mine	1978	—	2.50	5.00
❑ Philadelphia Int'l. 3644	Tryin' to Get the Feeling Again/I Wanna Be Your Woman	1978	—	2.50	5.00
❑ Philadelphia Int'l. 70058	I Love You Anyway/Easy Money	1981	—	2.00	4.00
—Philadelphia International records as "Dee Dee Sharp Gamble"					
❑ TSOP 4776	Happy 'Bout the Whole Thing/Touch My Life	1976	—	2.50	5.00
❑ TSOP 4778	I'm Not in Love/Make It Till Tomorrow	1976	—	2.50	5.00
Albums					
❑ Cameo C-1018 [M]	It's Mashed Potato Time	1962	15.00	30.00	60.00
❑ Cameo C-1022 [M]	Songs of Faith	1962	10.00	20.00	40.00
❑ Cameo SC-1022 [S]	Songs of Faith	1962	12.50	25.00	50.00
❑ Cameo C-1027 [M]	All the Hits	1962	10.00	20.00	40.00
❑ Cameo SC-1027 [S]	All the Hits	1962	12.50	25.00	50.00
❑ Cameo C-1032 [M]	All the Hits, Vol. 2	1963	10.00	20.00	40.00
❑ Cameo SC-1032 [S]	All the Hits, Vol. 2	1963	12.50	25.00	50.00
❑ Cameo C-1050 [M]	Do the Bird	1963	10.00	20.00	40.00
❑ Cameo SC-1050 [S]	Do the Bird	1963	12.50	25.00	50.00
❑ Cameo C-1062 [M]	Biggest Hits	1963	10.00	20.00	40.00
❑ Cameo C-1074 [M]	Down Memory Lane	1963	10.00	20.00	40.00
❑ Cameo C-2002 [M]	18 Golden Hits	1964	10.00	20.00	40.00
❑ Cameo SC-2002 [S]	18 Golden Hits	1964	12.50	25.00	50.00
❑ Philadelphia Int'l. PZ 33839	Happy 'Bout the Whole Thing	1976	2.50	5.00	10.00
❑ Philadelphia Int'l. PZ 34437	What Color Is Love	1977	2.50	5.00	10.00
❑ Philadelphia Int'l. JZ 36370	Dee Dee	1980	2.50	5.00	10.00

SHARP, DEE DEE, AND CHUBBY CHECKER

Albums

Number	Title (A Side/B Side)	Yr	VG	VG+	NM
❑ Cameo C-1029 [M]	Down to Earth	1962	10.00	20.00	40.00
❑ Cameo SC-1029 [S]	Down to Earth	1962	12.50	25.00	50.00

SHAW, ARTIE

Albums

Number	Title (A Side/B Side)	Yr	VG	VG+	NM
❑ RCA Victor VPM-6062 [(2)]	This Is Artie Shaw, Volume 2	1976	3.00	6.00	12.00
—Black labels, dog near top					

SHEP AND THE LIMELITES

45s

Number	Title (A Side/B Side)	Yr	VG	VG+	NM
❑ Hull 740	Daddy's Home/This I Know	1961	10.00	20.00	40.00
—Pink label					
❑ Hull 742	Ready for Your Love/You'll Be Sorry	1961	5.00	10.00	20.00
❑ Hull 747	Three Steps from the Altar/Oh What a Feeling	1961	5.00	10.00	20.00
❑ Hull 748	Our Anniversary/Who Told the Sandman	1962	5.00	10.00	20.00
❑ Hull 751	What Did Daddy Do/Teach Me, Teach Me How to Twist	1962	5.00	10.00	20.00
❑ Hull 753	Gee Baby, What About You/Everything Is Going to Be Alright	1962	5.00	10.00	20.00
❑ Hull 756	Remember Baby/The Monkey	1963	5.00	10.00	20.00
❑ Hull 757	Stick By Me (And I'll Stick By You)/It's All Over Now	1963	5.00	10.00	20.00
❑ Hull 759	Steal Away (With Your Baby)/For All My Love	1963	5.00	10.00	20.00
❑ Hull 761	Easy to Remember (When You Want to Forget)/Why, Why Won't You Believe Me	1964	5.00	10.00	20.00
❑ Hull 767	I'm All Alone/Why Did You Fall for Me	1964	5.00	10.00	20.00
❑ Hull 770	Party for Two/You Better Believe	1965	7.50	15.00	30.00
❑ Hull 772	In Case I Forget/I'm a-Hurting Inside	1965	5.00	10.00	20.00
Albums					
❑ Hull 1001 [M]	Our Anniversary	1962	300.00	600.00	1200.
❑ Roulette R-25350 [M]	Our Anniversary	1967	20.00	40.00	80.00
❑ Roulette SR-25350 [R]	Our Anniversary	1967	12.50	25.00	50.00

SHERMAN, BOBBY

45s

Number	Title (A Side/B Side)	Yr	VG	VG+	NM
❑ Cameo 403	Happiness Is/Can't Get Used to Loving You	1966	2.50	5.00	10.00
❑ Condor 1002	I'll Never Tell You/Telegram	1969	2.50	5.00	10.00
❑ Decca 31672	Man Overboard/You Make Me Happy	1964	3.75	7.50	15.00
❑ Decca 31741	It Hurts Me/Give Me Your Word	1965	3.75	7.50	15.00
❑ Decca 31779	Hey Little Girl/Well All Right	1965	3.75	7.50	15.00
❑ Dot 16566	I Want to Hear It From Her/Nobody's Sweetheart	1963	3.75	7.50	15.00
❑ Epic 10181	Cold Girl/Think of Rain	1967	2.50	5.00	10.00
❑ Janus 246	Runaway/Mr. Success	1975	—	2.00	4.00

Number	Title (A Side/B Side)	Yr	VG	VG+	NM
❑ Janus 254	Our Last Song Together/Sunshine Rose	1975	—	2.00	4.00
❑ Metromedia 68-0100	Early in the Morning/Unborn Lullaby	1973	—	2.50	5.00
❑ Metromedia 121	Little Woman/One Too Many Mornings	1969	—	2.50	5.00
❑ Metromedia 150	La La La (If I Had You)/Time	1969	—	2.50	5.00
❑ Metromedia 177	Easy Come, Easy Go/July Seventeen	1970	—	2.50	5.00
❑ Metromedia 177	Easy Come, Easy Go/Sounds Along the Way	1970	—	2.50	5.00
❑ Metromedia 188	Hey, Mister Sun/Two Blind Mice	1970	—	2.50	5.00
❑ Metromedia 194	Julie, Do Ya Love Me/Spend Some Time Lovin' Me	1970	—	2.50	5.00
❑ Metromedia 204	Goin' Home (Sing a Song of Christmas Cheer)/Love's What You're Gettin' for Christmas	1970	—	3.00	6.00
❑ Metromedia 206	Cried Like a Baby/Is Anybody There	1971	—	2.50	5.00
❑ Metromedia 217	The Drum/Free Now to Roam	1971	—	2.50	5.00
❑ Metromedia 222	Waiting at the Bus Stop/Run Away	1971	—	2.50	5.00
❑ Metromedia 227	Jennifer/Getting Together	1971	—	2.50	5.00
❑ Metromedia 240	Together Again/Picture a Little Girl	1972	—	2.50	5.00
❑ Metromedia 249	I Don't Believe in Magic/Just a Little While Longer	1972	—	2.50	5.00
❑ Parkway 967	Goody Galumshus/Anything Your Little Heart Desires	1966	2.50	5.00	10.00
❑ Starcrest 100	Judy, You'll Never Know/Telegram	1962	5.00	10.00	20.00
❑ Trophy Series MTS 1	Little Woman/La La La (If I Had You)	197?	—	2.50	5.00
—Reissue on Metromedia's short-lived "oldies" label					
❑ Trophy Series MTS 3	Easy Come, Easy Go/Hey, Mister Sun	197?	—	2.50	5.00
—Reissue on Metromedia's short-lived "oldies" label					
❑ Trophy Series MTS 4	Julie, Do Ya Love Me/Spend Some Time Lovin' Me	197?	—	2.50	5.00
—Reissue on Metromedia's short-lived "oldies" label					
Albums					
❑ Metromedia MD 1014	Bobby Sherman	1969	3.75	7.50	15.00
❑ Metromedia MD 1028	Here Comes Bobby	1970	3.75	7.50	15.00
❑ Metromedia MD 1032	With Love, Bobby	1970	3.75	7.50	15.00
❑ Metromedia MD 1038	Bobby Sherman Christmas Album	1970	3.75	7.50	15.00
❑ Metromedia MD 1040	Portrait of Bobby	1971	3.75	7.50	15.00
❑ Metromedia MD 1045	Getting Together	1971	3.75	7.50	15.00
❑ Metromedia KMD 1048	Bobby Sherman's Greatest Hits	1972	3.00	6.00	12.00
❑ Metromedia MD 1060	Just for You	1973	3.75	7.50	15.00
SHIRELLES, THE					
45s					
❑ Bell 760	A Most Unusual Boy/Look What You've Done to My Heart	1969	2.50	5.00	10.00
❑ Bell 787	Looking Glass/Playthings	1969	2.50	5.00	10.00
❑ Bell 815	Never Give You Up/Go Away and Find Yourself	1969	2.50	5.00	10.00
❑ Blue Rock 4051	Don't Mess with Cupid/Sweet Sweet Lovin'	1968	2.50	5.00	10.00
❑ Blue Rock 4066	Call Me/There's a Storm Goin' Home in My Heart	1968	2.50	5.00	10.00
❑ Decca 25506	I Met Him on a Sunday/My Love Is a Charm	196?	3.75	7.50	15.00
—Early reissue					
❑ Decca 30588	I Met Him on a Sunday/I Want You to Be My Boyfriend	1958	6.25	12.50	25.00
❑ Decca 30669	My Love Is a Charm/Slop Time	1958	10.00	20.00	40.00
❑ Decca 30761	Stop Me/I Got the Message	1958	10.00	20.00	40.00
❑ RCA Victor 47-0902	Let's Give Each Other Love/Deep in the Night	1973	2.00	4.00	8.00
❑ RCA Victor 48-1019	No Sugar Tonight/Strange, I Still Love You	1971	2.50	5.00	10.00
❑ RCA Victor 48-1032	Brother, Brother/Sunday Dreaming	1972	2.50	5.00	10.00
❑ RCA Victor APBO-0192	Touch the Wind (Eres Tu)/Do What You've a Mind To	1973	2.00	4.00	8.00
❑ Scepter 1203	Dedicated to the One I Love/Look A Here Baby	1958	5.00	10.00	20.00
—Red label					
❑ Scepter 1205	A Teardrop and a Lollipop/Doin' the Ronde	1959	5.00	10.00	20.00
—Red label					
❑ Scepter 1207	Please Be My Boyfriend/I Saw a Tear	1960	5.00	10.00	20.00
—Red label					
❑ Scepter 1208	Tonight's the Night/The Dance Is Over	1960	5.00	10.00	20.00
—Red label					
❑ Scepter 1211	Tomorrow/Boys	1960	10.00	20.00	40.00
—Original A-side title					
❑ Scepter 1211	Will You Love Me Tomorrow/Boys	1960	7.50	15.00	30.00
—Revised A-side title					
❑ Scepter 1217	Mama Said/Blue Holiday	1961	5.00	10.00	20.00
❑ Scepter 1220	A Thing of the Past/What a Sweet Thing That Was	1961	5.00	10.00	20.00
❑ Scepter 1223	Big John/Twenty-One	1961	5.00	10.00	20.00
❑ Scepter 1227	Baby It's You/Things I Want to Hear (Pretty Words)	1961	5.00	10.00	20.00
❑ Scepter 1228	Soldier Boy/Love Is a Swingin' Thing	1962	3.75	7.50	15.00

Number	Title (A Side/B Side)	Yr	VG	VG+	NM
❑ Scepter 1234	Welcome Home Baby/Mama, Here Comes the Bride	1962	3.75	7.50	15.00
❑ Scepter 1237	Stop the Music/It's Love That Really Counts	1962	3.75	7.50	15.00
❑ Scepter 1243	Everybody Loves a Lover/I Don't Think So	1962	3.75	7.50	15.00
❑ Scepter 1248	Foolish Little Girl/Not for All the Money in the World	1963	3.75	7.50	15.00
❑ Scepter 1255	Don't Say Goodnight and Mean Goodbye/I Didn't Mean to Hurt You	1963	3.00	6.00	12.00
❑ Scepter 1259	What Does a Girl Do?/Don't Let It Happen to You	1963	3.00	6.00	12.00
❑ Scepter 1260	It's a Mad, Mad, Mad, Mad World/31 Flavors	1963	3.00	6.00	12.00
❑ Scepter 1264	Tonight You're Gonna Fall in Love with Me/20th Century Rock and Roll	1963	3.00	6.00	12.00
❑ Scepter 1267	Sha-La-La/His Lips Get In the Way	1964	3.00	6.00	12.00
❑ Scepter 1278	Thank You Baby/Doomsday	1964	3.00	6.00	12.00
❑ Scepter 1284	Maybe Tonight/Lost Love	1964	3.00	6.00	12.00
❑ Scepter 1292	Are You Still My Baby/I Saw a Tear	1964	3.00	6.00	12.00
❑ Scepter 1296	Shh, I'm Watching the Movies/A Plus B	1965	3.00	6.00	12.00
❑ Scepter 12101	March (You'll Be Sorry)/Everybody's Goin' Mad	1965	2.50	5.00	10.00
❑ Scepter 12114	My Heart Belongs to You/Love That Man	1965	2.50	5.00	10.00
❑ Scepter 12123	(Mama) My Soldier Boy Is Coming Home/Soldier Boy	1965	2.50	5.00	10.00
❑ Scepter 12132	I Met Him on a Sunday — '66/Love That Man	1966	2.50	5.00	10.00
❑ Scepter 12150	Till My Baby Comes Home/Que Sera, Sera	1966	2.50	5.00	10.00
❑ Scepter 12162	Shades of Blue/After Midnight	1966	2.50	5.00	10.00
❑ Scepter 12162	Shades of Blue/Looking Around	1966	2.50	5.00	10.00
❑ Scepter 12178	Teasin' Me/Look Away	1966	2.50	5.00	10.00
❑ Scepter 12185	Don't Go Home (My Little Baby)/Nobody Baby After You	1967	2.50	5.00	10.00
❑ Scepter 12192	Too Much of a Good Thing/Bright Shiny Colors	1967	2.50	5.00	10.00
❑ Scepter 12198	Last Minute Miracle/No Doubt About It	1967	2.50	5.00	10.00
❑ Scepter 12209	Wild and Sweet/Wait Till I Give the Signal	1968	2.50	5.00	10.00
❑ Scepter 12217	Hippie Walk (Part 1)/Hippie Walk (Part 2)	1968	2.50	5.00	10.00
❑ Tiara 6112	I Met Him on a Sunday/I Want You to Be My Boyfriend	1958	200.00	400.00	800.00
—Note: Copies with any catalog number except 6112 are reproductions with little collector value					
❑ United Artists 50648	There Goes My Baby-Be My Baby/Strange, I Still Love You	1970	2.00	4.00	8.00
❑ United Artists 50693	It's Gonna Take a Miracle/Lost	1970	2.00	4.00	8.00
❑ United Artists 50740	Take Me for a Little While/Dedicated to the One I Love	1971	2.00	4.00	8.00
Albums					
❑ RCA Victor LSP-4581	Happy and In Love	1971	3.75	7.50	15.00
❑ RCA Victor LSP-4698	The Shirelles	1972	3.75	7.50	15.00
❑ Rhino RNDA-1101 [(2)]	Anthology (1959-1967)	1984	3.00	6.00	12.00
❑ Scepter S-501 [M]	Tonight's the Night	1961	50.00	100.00	200.00
—"Scepter" in scroll at top of label					
❑ Scepter SPS-501 [S]	Tonight's the Night	1965	25.00	50.00	100.00
❑ Scepter S-502 [M]	The Shirelles Sing to Trumpets and Strings	1961	50.00	100.00	200.00
—"Scepter" in scroll at top of label					
❑ Scepter SPS-502 [S]	The Shirelles Sing to Trumpets and Strings	1965	25.00	50.00	100.00
❑ Scepter SPM-504 [M]	Baby It's You	1962	25.00	50.00	100.00
❑ Scepter SPS-504 [S]	Baby It's You	1965	25.00	50.00	100.00
❑ Scepter SPM-505 [M]	A Twist Party	1962	20.00	40.00	80.00
❑ Scepter SPS-505 [S]	A Twist Party	1965	25.00	50.00	100.00
❑ Scepter SPM-507 [M]	The Shirelles' Greatest Hits	1962	10.00	20.00	40.00
❑ Scepter SPS-507 [S]	The Shirelles' Greatest Hits	1965	12.50	25.00	50.00
❑ Scepter SPM-511 [M]	Foolish Little Girl	1963	12.50	25.00	50.00
❑ Scepter SPS-511 [S]	Foolish Little Girl	1965	20.00	40.00	80.00
❑ Scepter SPM-514 [M]	It's a Mad, Mad, Mad, Mad World	1963	10.00	20.00	40.00
❑ Scepter SPS-514 [S]	It's a Mad, Mad, Mad, Mad World	1963	12.50	25.00	50.00
❑ Scepter SPM-516 [M]	The Shirelles Sing the Golden Oldies	1964	10.00	20.00	40.00
❑ Scepter SPS-516 [S]	The Shirelles Sing the Golden Oldies	1964	12.50	25.00	50.00
❑ Scepter SPM-560 [M]	The Shirelles' Greatest Hits, Volume 2	1967	5.00	10.00	20.00
❑ Scepter SPS-560 [S]	The Shirelles' Greatest Hits, Volume 2	1967	6.25	12.50	25.00
❑ Scepter SPM-562 [M]	Spontaneous Combustion	1967	10.00	20.00	40.00
❑ Scepter SPS-562 [S]	Spontaneous Combustion	1967	12.50	25.00	50.00
❑ Scepter SPS-569	Eternally Soul	1968	7.50	15.00	30.00
❑ Scepter SPS-2-599 [(2)]	Remember When	1972	5.00	10.00	20.00
❑ Springboard 4006	The Shirelles Sing Their Very Best	1973	2.00	4.00	8.00
❑ United Artists UA-LA340-E	The Very Best of the Shirelles	1974	2.50	5.00	10.00

SHOCKING BLUE, THE

45s

Number	Title (A Side/B Side)	Yr	VG	VG+	NM
❑ Buddah 258	Sleepless at Midnight/Serenade	1971	—	3.00	6.00
❑ Colossus 108	Venus/Hot Sand	1969	2.50	5.00	10.00
❑ Colossus 111	Mighty Joe/I'm a Woman	1970	2.00	4.00	8.00
❑ Colossus 116	Long and Lonesome Road/Ackaragh	1970	2.00	4.00	8.00
❑ Colossus 123	Never Love a Railroad Man/Never Marry	1970	2.00	4.00	8.00
❑ Colossus 141	Boll Weevil/Long and Lonesome Road	1971	—	3.00	6.00
❑ MGM 14481	When I Was a Girl/Eve and the Apple	1973	—	3.00	6.00
❑ MGM 14543	Oh Love/Inkpot	1973	—	3.00	6.00
❑ 21 Records 99517	Venus/Mighty Joe	1986	—	2.00	4.00
Albums					
❑ Colossus CS-1000	The Shocking Blue	1970	6.25	12.50	25.00

SILHOUETTES, THE

45s

Number	Title (A Side/B Side)	Yr	VG	VG+	NM
❑ Ace 552	I Sold My Heart to the Junkman/What Would You Do	1958	5.00	10.00	20.00
❑ Ace 562	Evelyn/Never Will Part	1959	5.00	10.00	20.00
—As "Bill Horton and the Silhouettes"					
❑ Ember 1029	Get a Job/I Am Lonely	1958	7.50	15.00	30.00
—Red label					
❑ Ember 1032	Headin' for the Poorhouse/Miss Thing	1958	5.00	10.00	20.00
❑ Ember 1037	Bing Bong/Voodoo Eyes	1958	5.00	10.00	20.00
❑ Goodway 101	Not Me Baby/Gaucho Serenade	1966	50.00	100.00	200.00
—As "The New Silhouettes"					

Number	Title (A Side/B Side)	Yr	VG	VG+	NM
❑ Grand 142	Wish I Could Be There/Move On Over	1956	50.00	100.00	200.00
❑ Imperial 5899	The Push/Which Way Did She Go	1962	3.00	6.00	12.00
❑ Junior 391	Get a Job/I Am Lonely	1957	200.00	400.00	800.00
—Brown label (first press)					
❑ Junior 396	I Sold My Heart to the Junkman/What Would You Do	1958	25.00	50.00	100.00
❑ Junior 400	Evelyn/Never Will Part	1959	50.00	100.00	200.00
❑ Junior 993	Your Love/Rent Man	1963	7.50	15.00	30.00
❑ Lost-Nite 418	Bing Bong/Voodoo Eyes	197?	—	2.50	5.00
—Reissue					
❑ United Artists 147	I Sold My Heart to the Junkman/What Would You Do	1958	—	—	—
—Canceled					
Albums					
❑ Goodway GLP-100	The Silhouettes 1958-1968/Get a Job	1968	75.00	150.00	300.00
SILKIE, THE					
45s					
❑ Fontana 1525	You've Got to Hide Your Love Away/City Winds	1965	3.75	7.50	15.00
—Light blue label; A-side was produced by John Lennon and Paul McCartney, with the two and George Harrison playing along					
❑ Fontana 1525	You've Got to Hide Your Love Away/City Wind	1965	5.00	10.00	20.00
—Dark blue label					
❑ Fontana 1536	The Keys to My Soul/Leave Me to Cry	1965	2.50	5.00	10.00
❑ Fontana 1551	Born to Be With You/I'm So Sorry	1966	2.50	5.00	10.00
Albums					
❑ Fontana MGF 27548 [M]	You've Got to Hide Your Love Away	1965	10.00	20.00	40.00
—With purplish, black and white cover					
❑ Fontana MGF 27548 [M]	You've Got to Hide Your Love Away	1965	12.50	25.00	50.00
—With full-color cover					
❑ Fontana SRF 67548 [R]	You've Got to Hide Your Love Away	1965	7.50	15.00	30.00
—With purplish, black and white cover					
❑ Fontana SRF 67548 [R]	You've Got to Hide Your Love Away	1965	10.00	20.00	40.00
—With full-color cover					
SILVER CONVENTION					
45s					
❑ Midland Int'l. MB-10212	Save Me/Save Me Again	1975	—	2.00	4.00
❑ Midland Int'l. MB-10339	Fly, Robin, Fly/Chains of Love	1975	—	2.00	4.00
—Second pressing: "Fly, Robin, Fly" is 3:05, matrix number is 10339-Z					
❑ Midland Int'l. MB-10339	Fly, Robin, Fly/Chains of Love	1975	—	3.00	6.00
—First pressing: "Fly, Robin, Fly" is 3:45, matrix number is 10339-A					
❑ Midland Int'l. MB-10571	Get Up and Boogie (That's Right)/Son of a Gun	1976	—	2.00	4.00
—Second pressing: "Get Up and Boogie" is under three minutes long					
❑ Midland Int'l. MB-10571	Get Up and Boogie (That's Right)/Son of a Gun	1976	—	3.00	6.00
—First pressing: "Get Up and Boogie" is 4:05, matrix number is 10571-A					
❑ Midland Int'l. MB-10723	No, No Joe/Another Girl	1976	—	2.00	4.00
❑ Midland Int'l. MB-10849	Thank You Mr. D.J./Dancing in the Aisles (Take Me Higher)	1976	—	2.00	4.00
❑ Midsong Int'l. GB-10939	Fly, Robin, Fly/Get Up and Boogie (That's Right)	1977	—	—	3.00
—Gold Standard Series					
❑ Midsong Int'l. MB-10972	Telegram/(B-side unknown)	1977	—	2.00	4.00
❑ Midsong Int'l. MB-11062	Save Me '77/Hotshot	1977	—	2.00	4.00
❑ Midsong Int'l. 40896	Breakfast in Bed/Spend the Night with Me	1978	—	2.00	4.00
Albums					
❑ Midland Int'l. BKL1-1129	Save Me	1975	2.50	5.00	10.00
❑ Midland Int'l. BKL1-1369	Silver Convention	1976	2.50	5.00	10.00
❑ Midland Int'l. BKL1-1824	Madhouse	1976	2.50	5.00	10.00
❑ Midsong Int'l. BKL1-2296	Golden Girls	1977	2.50	5.00	10.00
SIMON, CARLY					
45s					
❑ Arista 2083	Better Not Tell Her/Happy Birthday	1990	—	—	3.00
❑ Arista 2164	Life Is Eternal/We Just Got Here	1990	—	—	3.00
❑ Arista 9525	Coming Around Again/Itsy Bitsy Spider	1986	—	—	3.00
❑ Arista 9587	Give Me All Night/Sleight of Hand	1987	—	—	3.00
❑ Arista 9619	The Stuff That Dreams Are Made Of/As Time Goes By	1987	—	—	3.00
❑ Arista 9653	All I Want Is You/On a Hot Summer Night	1987	—	—	3.00
❑ Arista 9754	You're So Vain/Do the Walls Come Down	1988	—	—	3.00
❑ Arista 9793	Let the River Run/The Turn of the Tide	1988	—	—	3.00
❑ Elektra 45246	Attitude Dancing/Are You Ticklish	1975	—	2.50	5.00

Number	Title (A Side/B Side)	Yr	VG	VG+	NM
❑ Elektra 45248	Slave/Look Me in the Eyes	1975	—	—	—
—Unreleased?					
❑ Elektra 45263	Waterfall/After the Storm	1975	—	2.50	5.00
❑ Elektra 45278	More and More/Love Out in the Street	1975	—	2.50	5.00
❑ Elektra 45325	It Keeps You Runnin'/Look Me in the Eyes	1976	—	2.00	4.00
❑ Elektra 45341	Half a Chance/Libby	1976	—	2.00	4.00
—Butterfly label					
❑ Elektra 45413	Nobody Does It Better/After the Storm	1977	—	2.00	4.00
❑ Elektra 45477	You Belong to Me/In a Small Moment	1978	—	2.00	4.00
❑ Elektra 45506	Devoted to You/Boys in the Trees	1978	—	2.00	4.00
—A-side with James Taylor					
❑ Elektra 45544	Tranquillo (Melt My Heart)/Back Down to Earth	1978	—	2.00	4.00
❑ Elektra 45724	That's the Way I've Always Heard It Should Be/Alone	1971	—	3.00	6.00
❑ Elektra 45748	Our First Day Together/Share the Land	1971	—	—	—
—Unreleased					
❑ Elektra 45759	Anticipation/The Garden	1971	—	3.00	6.00
❑ Elektra 45774	Legend in Your Own Time/Julie Through the Glass	1972	—	3.00	6.00
❑ Elektra 45796	The Girl You Think You Are/Share the Land	1972	—	3.00	6.00
❑ Elektra 45824	You're So Vain/His Friends Are More Than Fond of Robin	1972	—	3.00	6.00
❑ Elektra 45843	The Right Thing to Do/We Have No Secrets	1973	—	2.50	5.00
❑ Elektra 45880	Mockingbird/Grownup	1974	—	2.50	5.00
—A-side with James Taylor					
❑ Elektra 45887	Haven't Got Time for the Pain/Mind on My Man	1974	—	2.50	5.00
❑ Elektra 46051	Vengeance/Love You by Heart	1979	—	2.00	4.00
❑ Elektra 46514	Spy/Pure Sin	1979	—	2.00	4.00
❑ Elektra 69953	Hidin' Away/Fight for It	1982	—	2.00	4.00
—With Jesse Colin Young					
❑ Epic 05419	Tired of Being Blonde/Black Honeymoon	1985	—	—	3.00
❑ Epic 05596	My New Boyfriend/The Wives Are in Connecticut	1985	—	—	3.00
❑ Mirage 4051	Why/Why	1982	—	2.00	4.00
—B-side by Chic					
❑ Mirage 99963	Why/(Instrumental)	1982	—	2.00	4.00
❑ Planet YB-13779	Someone Waits for You/(B-side unknown)	1984	—	2.00	4.00
❑ Warner Bros. 29428	Hello Big Man/Dawn You Get to Me	1983	—	2.00	4.00
❑ Warner Bros. 29484	You Know What to Do/Orpheus	1983	—	2.00	4.00
❑ Warner Bros. 49518	Jesse/Stardust	1980	—	2.00	4.00
❑ Warner Bros. 49630	Take Me As I Am/James	1980	—	2.00	4.00
❑ Warner Bros. 49689	Come Upstairs/Them	1981	—	2.00	4.00
❑ Warner Bros. 49880	From the Heart/Hurt	1981	—	2.00	4.00
❑ Warner Bros. 50027	Body and Soul/Get Along Without You Very Well	1982	—	2.00	4.00
Albums					
❑ Arista AL-8443	Coming Around Again	1987	2.00	4.00	8.00
❑ Arista AL-8526	Greatest Hits Live	1988	2.00	4.00	8.00
❑ Arista AL-8582	My Romance	1990	3.00	6.00	12.00
❑ Arista AL-8650	Have You Seen Me Lately?	1990	3.00	6.00	12.00
❑ Elektra 6E-109	The Best of Carly Simon	1977	2.00	4.00	8.00
—Reissue of 7E-1048					
❑ Elektra 6E-128	Boys in the Trees	1978	2.50	5.00	10.00
❑ Elektra 5E-506	Spy	1979	2.50	5.00	10.00
❑ Elektra 7E-1002	Hotcakes	1974	2.50	5.00	10.00
❑ Elektra 7E-1033	Playing Possum	1975	2.50	5.00	10.00
❑ Elektra 7E-1048	The Best of Carly Simon	1975	2.50	5.00	10.00
❑ Elektra 7E-1064	Another Passenger	1976	2.50	5.00	10.00
❑ Elektra EKS-74082	Carly Simon	1971	3.00	6.00	12.00
❑ Elektra EKS-75016	Anticipation	1971	3.00	6.00	12.00
❑ Elektra EKS-75049	No Secrets	1972	3.00	6.00	12.00
—With lyrics on innersleeve					
❑ Elektra EKS-75049	No Secrets	1973	2.50	5.00	10.00
—Without lyrics on innersleeve					
❑ Epic FE 39970	Spoiled Girl	1985	2.50	5.00	10.00
❑ Warner Bros. BSK 3443	Come Upstairs	1980	2.50	5.00	10.00
❑ Warner Bros. BSK 3592	Torch	1981	2.50	5.00	10.00
❑ Warner Bros. 23886	Hello Big Man	1983	2.50	5.00	10.00

SIMON, JOE

45s

Number	Title (A Side/B Side)	Yr	VG	VG+	NM
❑ Compleat 140	It Turns Me Inside Out/Morning, Noon and Night	1985	—	2.00	4.00
❑ Compleat 146	Mr. Right or Mr. Right Now/Let Me Have My Way with You	1985	—	2.00	4.00
❑ Dot 16570	Just Like Yesterday/Only a Dream	1964	2.00	4.00	8.00
❑ Hush 103	It's a Miracle/Land of Love	1960	3.00	6.00	12.00
❑ Hush 104	Call My Name/Everybody Needs Somebody	1961	3.00	6.00	12.00
❑ Hush 106	Pledge of Love/It's All Over	1961	3.00	6.00	12.00
❑ Hush 107	I See Your Face/Troubles	1961	3.00	6.00	12.00
❑ Hush 108	Land of Love/I Keep Remembering	1962	3.00	6.00	12.00
❑ Posse 5001	Baby, When Love Is In Your Heart (It's In Your Eyes)/ Are We Breaking Up	1980	—	2.50	5.00
❑ Posse 5005	Glad You Came My Way/I Don't Wanna Make Love	1980	—	2.50	5.00
❑ Posse 5010	Are We Breaking Up/We're Together	1981	—	2.50	5.00
❑ Posse 5014	Fallin' in Love with You/Magnolia	1981	—	2.50	5.00
❑ Posse 5018	You Give Life to Me/(Instrumental)	1982	—	2.50	5.00
—With Clare Bathe					
❑ Posse 5019	Go Sam/(Instrumental)	1982	—	2.50	5.00
❑ Posse 5021	Get Down, Get Down "82"/It Be's That Way Sometime	1982	—	2.50	5.00
❑ Posse 5038	Deeper Than Love/Step by Step	198?	—	2.50	5.00
❑ Sound Stage 7 1508	Misty Blue/That's the Way I Want Our Love	1972	—	2.50	5.00
❑ Sound Stage 7 1512	Who's Julie/The Girl's Alright with Me	1973	—	2.50	5.00
❑ Sound Stage 7 1514	Someone to Lean On/I Got a Whole Lotta Lovin'	1974	—	2.50	5.00

Number	Title (A Side/B Side)	Yr	VG	VG+	NM
❑ Sound Stage 7 1521	Funny How Time Slips Away/Message from Maria	1976	—	2.50	5.00
❑ Sound Stage 7 2564	Teenager's Prayer/Long Hot Summer	1966	2.00	4.00	8.00
❑ Sound Stage 7 2569	Too Many Teardrops/What Makes a Man Feel Good	1966	2.00	4.00	8.00
❑ Sound Stage 7 2577	My Special Prayer/Travelin' Man	1966	2.00	4.00	8.00
❑ Sound Stage 7 2583	Put Your Trust in Me (Depend on Me)/Just a Dream	1967	2.00	4.00	8.00
❑ Sound Stage 7 2589	Nine Pound Steel/The Girl's Alright with Me	1967	2.00	4.00	8.00
❑ Sound Stage 7 2602	No Sad Songs/Come On and Get It	1967	2.00	4.00	8.00
❑ Sound Stage 7 2608	(You Keep Me) Hangin' On/Long Hot Summer	1968	2.00	4.00	8.00
❑ Sound Stage 7 2617	Message from Maria/I Worry About You	1968	2.00	4.00	8.00
❑ Sound Stage 7 2622	Looking Back/Standing in the Safety Zone	1968	2.00	4.00	8.00
❑ Sound Stage 7 2628	The Chokin' Kind/Come On and Get It	1969	—	3.00	6.00
❑ Sound Stage 7 2634	Baby, Don't Be Looking in My Mind/Don't Let Me Lose the Feeling	1969	—	3.00	6.00
❑ Sound Stage 7 2637	Oon-Guela (Part 1)/Oon-Guela (Part 2)	1969	2.00	4.00	8.00
❑ Sound Stage 7 2641	It's Hard to Get Along/San Francisco Is a Lonely Town	1969	—	3.00	6.00
❑ Sound Stage 7 2651	Moon Walk Part 1/Moon Walk Part 2	1969	—	3.00	6.00
❑ Sound Stage 7 2656	Farther On Down the Road/Wounded Man	1970	—	3.00	6.00
❑ Sound Stage 7 2664	Yours Love/I Got a Whole Lotta Lovin'	1970	—	3.00	6.00
❑ Sound Stage 7 2667	That's the Way I Want Our Love/When	1970	—	3.00	6.00
❑ Spring 108	Your Time to Cry/I Love You More (Than Anything)	1970	—	2.50	5.00
❑ Spring 113	Help Me Make It Through the Night/To Lay Down Beside You	1971	—	2.50	5.00
❑ Spring 115	You're the One for Me/I Ain't Givin' Up	1971	—	2.50	5.00
❑ Spring 118	Georgia Blues/All My Hard Times	1971	—	2.50	5.00
❑ Spring 120	Drowning in the Sea of Love/Let Me Be the One	1971	—	2.50	5.00
❑ Spring 124	Pool of Bad Luck/Glad to Be Your Lover	1972	—	2.50	5.00
❑ Spring 128	Power of Love/The Mirror Don't Lie	1972	—	2.50	5.00
❑ Spring 130	Trouble in My Home/I Found My Dad	1972	—	2.50	5.00
❑ Spring 133	Step by Step/Talk Don't Bother Me	1973	—	2.50	5.00
❑ Spring 138	Theme from Cleopatra Jones/Who Is That Lady	1973	—	2.50	5.00
❑ Spring 141	River/Love Never Hurt Nobody	1973	—	2.50	5.00
❑ Spring 145	Carry Me/Do You Know What It's Like to Be Lonesome	1974	—	2.50	5.00
❑ Spring 149	The Best Time of My Life/What We Gonna Do Now	1974	—	2.50	5.00
❑ Spring 156	Get Down, Get Down (Get On the Floor)/In My Baby's Arms	1975	—	2.50	5.00
❑ Spring 159	Music in My Bones/Fire Burning	1975	—	2.50	5.00
❑ Spring 163	I Need You, You Need Me/I'll Take Care (Of You)	1975	—	2.50	5.00
❑ Spring 166	Come Get to This/Let the Good Times Roll	1976	—	2.50	5.00
❑ Spring 169	Easy to Love/Can't Stand the Pain	1976	—	2.50	5.00
❑ Spring 172	You Didn't Have to Play No Games/What's Left to Do	1977	—	2.50	5.00
❑ Spring 176	One Step at a Time/Track of Your Love	1977	—	2.50	5.00
❑ Spring 178	For Your Love, Love, Love/I've Got a Jones on You Baby	1977	—	2.50	5.00
❑ Spring 184	I.O.U./It Must Be Love	1978	—	2.50	5.00
❑ Spring 190	Love Vibration/(Instrumental)	1978	—	2.50	5.00
❑ Spring 194	Going Through These Changes/I Can't Stand a Liar	1979	—	2.50	5.00
❑ Spring 3003	I Wanna Taste Your Love/Make Every Moment Count	1979	—	2.50	5.00
❑ Spring 3006	Hooked on Disco Music/I Still Love You	1980	—	2.50	5.00
❑ Vee Jay 609	My Adorable One/Say (That My Love Is True)	1964	2.00	4.00	8.00
❑ Vee Jay 663	When You're Near/When I'm Gone	1965	2.00	4.00	8.00
❑ Vee Jay 694	Let's Do It Over/The Whoo Pee	1965	2.00	4.00	8.00
Albums					
❑ Buddah BDS-7512	Joe Simon	1969	6.25	12.50	25.00
❑ Compleat 671015-1	Mr. Right	1985	3.00	6.00	12.00
❑ Posse 10002	Glad You Came My Way	1981	3.00	6.00	12.00
❑ Posse 10003	By Popular Demand	1982	3.00	6.00	12.00
❑ Sound Stage 7 5000 [(2)]	The World of Joe Simon	197?	3.00	6.00	12.00
—Reissue of 32536					
❑ Sound Stage 7 SSM-5003 [M]	Pure Soul	1967	7.50	15.00	30.00
❑ Sound Stage 7 SSS-15003 [S]	Pure Soul	1967	10.00	20.00	40.00
❑ Sound Stage 7 SSS-15004	No Sad Songs	1968	10.00	20.00	40.00
❑ Sound Stage 7 SSS-15005	Simon Sings	1968	10.00	20.00	40.00
❑ Sound Stage 7 SSS-15006	The Chokin' Kind	1969	7.50	15.00	30.00
❑ Sound Stage 7 SSS-15008	Joe Simon...Better Than Ever	1969	7.50	15.00	30.00
❑ Sound Stage 7 SSS-15009	The Best of Joe Simon	1972	3.75	7.50	15.00
❑ Sound Stage 7 KZ 31916	Greatest Hits	1972	3.00	6.00	12.00
❑ Sound Stage 7 ZG 32536 [(2)]	The World of Joe Simon	1974	3.75	7.50	15.00
❑ Sound Stage 7 ZG 33879 [(2)]	The Chokin' Kind/Joe Simon...Better Than Ever	1975	3.75	7.50	15.00

Number	Title (A Side/B Side)	Yr	VG	VG+	NM
❑ Spring SPR-4701	The Sounds of Simon	1971	6.25	12.50	25.00
❑ Spring SPR-5702	Drowning in the Sea of Love	1972	6.25	12.50	25.00
❑ Spring SPR-5704	The Power of Joe Simon	1973	6.25	12.50	25.00
❑ Spring SPR-5705	Simon Country	1973	3.75	7.50	15.00
❑ Spring SPR-6702	Mood, Heart and Soul	1974	3.75	7.50	15.00
❑ Spring SPR-6706	Get Down	1975	3.75	7.50	15.00
❑ Spring SPR-6710	Today	1975	3.75	7.50	15.00
❑ Spring SPR-6713	Easy to Love	1976	3.75	7.50	15.00
❑ Spring SPR-6716	Bad Case of Love	1977	3.75	7.50	15.00
❑ Spring SPR-6720	Love Vibrations	1979	3.75	7.50	15.00

SIMON, PAUL

45s

Number	Title (A Side/B Side)	Yr	VG	VG+	NM
❑ Amy 875	The Lone Teen Ranger/Lisa	1962	15.00	30.00	60.00
—As "Jerry Landis"					
❑ Big 614	True or False/Teenage Fool	1958	25.00	50.00	100.00
—As "True Taylor"					
❑ Canadian American 130	I'm Lonely/I Wish I Weren't in Love	1961	25.00	50.00	100.00
—As "Jerry Landis"; the rarest of his pre-Columbia solo singles					
❑ Columbia 10197	Gone at Last/Take Me to the Mardi Gras	1975	—	2.50	5.00
—A-side with Phoebe Snow and the Jesse Dixon Singers					
❑ Columbia 10270	50 Ways to Leave Your Lover/Some Folks Lives Roll Easy	1975	—	2.50	5.00
❑ Columbia 10332	Still Crazy After All These Years/I Do It for Your Love (Live)	1976	—	2.50	5.00
❑ Columbia 10630	Slip Slidin' Away/Something So Right	1977	—	3.00	6.00
—First pressings claim the A-side came from the LP "Blatant Greatest Hits." The Oak Ridge Boys are not mentioned.					
❑ Columbia 10711	Stranded in a Limousine/Have a Good Time	1978	—	3.00	6.00
❑ Columbia 45547	Mother and Child Reunion/Paranoia Blues	1972	—	2.50	5.00
—Orange label					
❑ Columbia 45585	Me and Julio Down by the Schoolyard/Congratulations	1972	—	2.50	5.00
—Orange label					
❑ Columbia 45638	Duncan/Run That Body Down	1972	—	2.50	5.00
❑ Columbia 45859	Kodachrome/Tenderness	1973	—	3.00	6.00
—With no trademark disclaimer on label					
❑ Columbia 45900	American Tune/One Man's Ceiling Is Another Man's Floor	1973	—	2.50	5.00
❑ Columbia 45907	Loves Me Like a Rock/Learn How to Fall	1973	—	2.50	5.00
—With the Dixie Hummingbirds					
❑ Columbia 46038	The Sound of Silence/Mother and Child Reunion	1974	2.00	4.00	8.00
❑ MGM 12822	Anna Belle/Loneliness	1959	12.50	25.00	50.00
—As "Jerry Landis"					
❑ Tribute 128	Carlos Dominguez/He Was My Brother	1963	15.00	30.00	60.00
—As "Paul Kane"; authentic copies make no mention of Paul Simon on the label					
❑ Warner Bros. 27903	Graceland/Hearts and Bones	1988	—	2.50	5.00
❑ Warner Bros. 28221	Under African Skies/I Know What I Know	1987	—	—	3.00
—A-side with Linda Ronstadt					
❑ Warner Bros. 28389	Diamonds on the Soles of Her Shoes/ All Around the World Or the Myth of Fingerprints	1987	—	—	3.00
❑ Warner Bros. 28460	The Boy in the Bubble/Crazy Love, Part 2	1987	—	—	3.00
❑ Warner Bros. 28522	Graceland/Hearts and Bones	1986	—	—	3.00
❑ Warner Bros. 28667	You Can Call Me Al/Gumboots	1986	—	—	3.00
❑ Warner Bros. 29333	Think Too Much/Song About the Moon	1984	—	2.00	4.00
❑ Warner Bros. 29453	Allergies/Think Too Much (ii)	1983	—	2.00	4.00
❑ Warner Bros. 49511	Late in the Evening/How the Heart Approaches What It Yearns	1980	—	2.00	4.00
❑ Warner Bros. 49601	One-Trick Pony/Long, Long Day	1980	—	2.00	4.00
❑ Warner Bros. 49675	Oh, Marion/God Bless the Absentee	1981	—	2.00	4.00
❑ Warwick 522	Swanee/Toot, Toot, Tootsie Goodbye	1960	12.50	25.00	50.00
—As "Jerry Landis"					
❑ Warwick 552	Shy/Just a Boy	1960	12.50	25.00	50.00
—As "Jerry Landis"					
❑ Warwick 588	I'd Like to Be/Just a Boy	1960	12.50	25.00	50.00
—As "Jerry Landis"					
❑ Warwick 619	Play Me a Sad Song/It Means a Lot to Them	1961	12.50	25.00	50.00
—As "Jerry Landis"					

Albums

Number	Title (A Side/B Side)	Yr	VG	VG+	NM
❑ Columbia KC 30750	Paul Simon	1972	2.50	5.00	10.00
❑ Columbia KC 32280	There Goes Rhymin' Simon	1973	2.50	5.00	10.00
❑ Columbia PC 32280	There Goes Rhymin' Simon	1980	2.00	4.00	8.00
❑ Columbia PC 32855	Paul Simon in Concert — Live Rhymin'	1974	2.50	5.00	10.00
❑ Columbia PC 33540	Still Crazy After All These Years	1975	2.50	5.00	10.00
—Original release has no bar code on cover					
❑ Columbia JC 35032	Greatest Hits, Etc.	1977	2.50	5.00	10.00
❑ Columbia C5X 37581 [(5)]	Collected Works	1981	10.00	20.00	40.00
—Contains his first four post-S&G solo albums plus the elusive "Paul Simon Songbook," otherwise unavailable in U.S.					
❑ Warner Bros. HS 3472	One-Trick Pony	1980	2.50	5.00	10.00
❑ Warner Bros. 23942	Hearts and Bones	1983	2.50	5.00	10.00
❑ Warner Bros. 25447	Graceland	1986	2.50	5.00	10.00
❑ Warner Bros. 25588	Paul Simon	1988	3.00	6.00	12.00
❑ Warner Bros. 25589	There Goes Rhymin' Simon	1988	3.00	6.00	12.00
❑ Warner Bros. 25590	Paul Simon in Concert — Live Rhymin'	1988	3.00	6.00	12.00
❑ Warner Bros. 25591	Still Crazy After All These Years	1988	3.00	6.00	12.00
❑ Warner Bros. 25789 [(2)]	Negotiations and Love Songs	1988	3.75	7.50	15.00
❑ Warner Bros. 26098	The Rhythm of the Saints	1990	3.75	7.50	15.00

SIMON AND GARFUNKEL

45s

Number	Title (A Side/B Side)	Yr	VG	VG+	NM
❑ ABC-Paramount 10788	That's My Story/Tia-Juana Blues	1966	5.00	10.00	20.00
—Outtakes from Tom and Jerry days					
❑ Columbia 10230	My Little Town//Art Garfunkel: Rag Doll/Paul Simon: You're Kind	1975	—	2.50	5.00

Number	Title (A Side/B Side)	Yr	VG	VG+	NM
❑ Columbia 43396	The Sounds of Silence/We've Got a Groovey Thing Goin'	1965	2.50	5.00	10.00
—With the "folk-rock" hit version of the A-side					
❑ Columbia 43511	Homeward Bound/Leaves That Are Green	1966	2.50	5.00	10.00
❑ Columbia 43617	I Am a Rock/Flowers Never Bend with the Rainfall	1966	2.50	5.00	10.00
❑ Columbia 43728	The Dangling Conversation/The Big Bright Green Pleasure Machine	1966	2.50	5.00	10.00
❑ Columbia 43873	A Hazy Shade of Winter/For Emily, Wherever I May Find Her	1966	2.50	5.00	10.00
❑ Columbia 44046	At the Zoo/The 59th Street Bridge Song (Feelin' Groovy)	1967	2.50	5.00	10.00
❑ Columbia 44232	Fakin' It/You Don't Know Where Your Interest Lies	1967	2.50	5.00	10.00
—As far as we can tell, all copies have the A-side listed with a time of "2:74"					
❑ Columbia 44465	Scarborough Fair (/Canticle)/April Come She Will	1968	2.50	5.00	10.00
❑ Columbia 44511	Mrs. Robinson/Old Friends-Bookends	1968	2.50	5.00	10.00
—Label says "From the Motion Picture 'The Graduate'"					
❑ Columbia 44785	The Boxer/Baby Driver	1969	—	3.00	6.00
—B-side mix (mono) is different than stereo LP version, especially near the end of the song					
❑ Columbia 45079	Bridge Over Troubled Water/Keep the Customer Satisfied	1970	—	3.00	6.00
❑ Columbia 45133	Cecilia/The Only Living Boy in New York	1970	—	3.00	6.00
—Red label, "Columbia" in black at top					
❑ Columbia 45237	El Condor Pasa/Why Don't You Write Me	1970	—	3.00	6.00
❑ Columbia 45663	America/For Emily, Whenever I May Find Her	1972	—	3.00	6.00
❑ Warner Bros. 50053	Wake Up Little Susie/Me and Julio Down by the Schoolyard	1982	—	2.00	4.00
Albums					
❑ Columbia CL 2249 [M]	Wednesday Morning, 3 A.M.	1964	6.25	12.50	25.00
—"Guaranteed High Fidelity" on label					
❑ Columbia CL 2469 [M]	Sounds of Silence	1966	7.50	15.00	30.00
—With "Simon and Garfunkel" and "Sounds of Silence" in all capital letters on front cover with no list of songs					
❑ Columbia CL 2563 [M]	Parsley, Sage, Rosemary and Thyme	1966	5.00	10.00	20.00
❑ Columbia KCL 2729 [M]	Bookends	1968	25.00	50.00	100.00
—Red label, "Mono" at bottom					
❑ Columbia CS 9049 [S]	Wednesday Morning, 3 A.M.	1964	6.25	12.50	25.00
—"360 Sound Stereo" in black on label					
❑ Columbia CS 9269 [S]	Sounds of Silence	1966	7.50	15.00	30.00
—With "Simon and Garfunkel" and "Sounds of Silence" in all capital letters on front cover with no list of songs					
❑ Columbia CS 9363 [S]	Parsley, Sage, Rosemary and Thyme	1966	3.75	7.50	15.00
—"360 Sound Stereo" on label					
❑ Columbia KCS 9529 [S]	Bookends	1968	3.00	6.00	12.00
—"360 Sound Stereo" on label; add 25% for poster					
❑ Columbia KCS 9914	Bridge Over Troubled Water	1970	3.00	6.00	12.00
—"360 Sound Stereo" on label					
❑ Columbia KC 31350	Simon and Garfunkel's Greatest Hits	1972	3.00	6.00	12.00
—Original covers are slightly oversized					
❑ Columbia C5X 37587 [(5)]	Collected Works	1981	10.00	20.00	40.00
❑ Pickwick PC-3059 [M]	The Hit Sounds of Simon and Garfunkel	1966	15.00	30.00	60.00
❑ Pickwick SPC-3059 [R]	The Hit Sounds of Simon and Garfunkel	1966	7.50	15.00	30.00
❑ Sears SPS-435	Simon and Garfunkel	196?	7.50	15.00	30.00
❑ Tee Vee TV-2002 [(5)]	The Complete Collection	1980	12.50	25.00	50.00
—Alternate number is Columbia Special Products P5-15333; also contains solo material by both Paul Simon and Art Garfunkel, plus a rare true stereo mix of "You Don't Know Where Your Interest Lies"					
❑ Warner Bros. 2BSK 3654 [(2)]	The Concert in Central Park	1982	3.00	6.00	12.00

SINATRA, FRANK

Number	Title (A Side/B Side)	Yr	VG	VG+	NM
45s					
❑ Capitol F1699	Young at Heart/I've Got the World on a String	1955	25.00	50.00	100.00
—Early reissue					
❑ Capitol F2450	I'm Walking Behind You/Lean Baby	1953	6.25	12.50	25.00
—Add 50% for intact center					
❑ Capitol F2505	My One and Only Love/I've Got the World on a String	1953	5.00	10.00	20.00
—Add 50% for intact center					
❑ Capitol F2560	Anytime, Anywhere/From Here to Eternity	1953	5.00	10.00	20.00
❑ Capitol F2638	I Love You/South of the Border	1953	5.00	10.00	20.00
❑ Capitol F2703	Young at Heart/Take a Chance	1953	5.00	10.00	20.00
❑ Capitol F2787	Don't Worry 'Bout Me/I Could Have Told You	1954	5.00	10.00	20.00
❑ Capitol F2816	Three Coins in the Fountain/Rain	1954	5.00	10.00	20.00
❑ Capitol F2864	The Girl That Got Away/Half as Lovely	1954	5.00	10.00	20.00
❑ Capitol F2922	It Worries Me/When I Stop Loving You	1954	5.00	10.00	20.00
❑ Capitol F2954	White Christmas/The Christmas Waltz	1954	5.00	10.00	20.00
❑ Capitol F2993	You My Love/Someone to Watch Over Me	1954	5.00	10.00	20.00

Number	Title (A Side/B Side)	Yr	VG	VG+	NM
❑ Capitol F3018	Melody of Love/I'm Gonna Live Till I Die	1954	5.00	10.00	20.00
❑ Capitol F3050	Why Should I Cry Over You?/Don't Change Your Mind About Me	1954	5.00	10.00	20.00
❑ Capitol F3084	Two Hearts, Two Kisses/From the Bottom to the Top	1955	3.75	7.50	15.00
❑ Capitol F3102	Learnin' the Blues/If I Had Three Wishes	1955	3.75	7.50	15.00
❑ Capitol F3130	Not as a Stranger/How Could You Do a Thing Like That to Me?	1955	3.75	7.50	15.00
❑ Capitol F3218	Same Old Saturday Night/Fairy Tale	1955	3.75	7.50	15.00
❑ Capitol F3260	Love and Marriage/The Impatient Years	1955	5.00	10.00	20.00
❑ Capitol F3290	(Love Is) The Tender Trap/Weep They Will	1955	3.75	7.50	15.00
❑ Capitol F3350	Flowers Mean Forgiveness/You'll Get Yours	1956	3.75	7.50	15.00
❑ Capitol F3423	(How Little It Maters) How Little We Know/Five Hundred Guys	1956	3.75	7.50	15.00
❑ Capitol F3469	You're Sensational/Johnny Concho Theme (Wait for Me)	1956	3.75	7.50	15.00
❑ Capitol F3507	Well, Did You Evah?/True Love	1956	3.75	7.50	15.00
—A-side by Bing Crosby and Frank Sinatra; B-side by Bing Crosby and Grace Kelly					
❑ Capitol F3508	Who Wants to Be a Millionaire/Mind If I Make Love to You?	1956	3.75	7.50	15.00
❑ Capitol F3552	Jealous Lover/You Forgot All the Words	1956	6.25	12.50	25.00
—Original pressings contain this title					
❑ Capitol F3552	Hey! Jealous Lover/You Forgot All the Words	1956	3.75	7.50	15.00
❑ Capitol F3608	Can I Steal a Little Love/Your Love for Me	1956	3.75	7.50	15.00
❑ Capitol F3703	Crazy Love/So Long, My Love	1957	3.00	6.00	12.00
❑ Capitol F3744	You're Cheatin' Yourself (If You're Cheatin' On Me)/Something Wonderful Happens in Summer	1957	3.00	6.00	12.00
❑ Capitol F3793	All the Way/Chicago	1957	3.00	6.00	12.00
❑ Capitol F3859	Witchcraft/Tell Her You Love Her	1957	3.00	6.00	12.00
❑ Capitol F3900	Mistletoe and Holly/The Christmas Waltz	1957	3.75	7.50	15.00
—"The Christmas Waltz" here is a different version than that on Capitol 2954.					
❑ Capitol F3952	How Are Ya' Fixed for Love?/Nothin' in Common	1958	3.00	6.00	12.00
—By Frank Sinatra and Keely Smith					
❑ Capitol F4003	Same Old Song and Dance/Monique (Song from Kings Go Forth)	1958	3.00	6.00	12.00
❑ Capitol F4070	Mr. Success/Sleep Warm	1958	3.00	6.00	12.00
❑ Capitol F4103	To Love and Be Loved/No One Ever Tells You	1958	3.00	6.00	12.00
❑ Capitol F4155	French Foreign Legion/Time After Time	1959	3.00	6.00	12.00
❑ Capitol F4214	High Hopes/All My Tomorrows	1959	3.75	7.50	15.00
❑ Capitol F4284	Talk to Me/They Came to Cordura	1959	3.00	6.00	12.00
❑ Capitol 4376	River, Stay 'Way from My Door/It's Over, It's Over, It's Over	1960	3.00	6.00	12.00
❑ Capitol 4408	Nice 'N' Easy/This Was My Love	1960	3.00	6.00	12.00
❑ Capitol 4466	Ol' MacDonald/You'll Always Be the One I Love	1960	3.00	6.00	12.00
❑ Capitol 4546	My Blue Heaven/Sentimental Baby	1960	3.00	6.00	12.00
❑ Capitol 4615	American Beauty Rose/Sentimental Journey	1961	3.00	6.00	12.00
❑ Capitol 4677	The Moon Was Yellow/I've Heard That Song Before	1962	3.00	6.00	12.00
❑ Capitol 4729	Five Minutes More/I'll Remember April	1962	3.00	6.00	12.00
❑ Capitol 4815	I Love Paris/Hidden Persuasion	1962	3.00	6.00	12.00
❑ Capitol 6019	Young at Heart/Learnin' the Blues	196?	—	3.00	6.00
—Starline reissue label					
❑ Capitol 6027	All the Way/High Hopes	196?	—	3.00	6.00
—Starline reissue label					
❑ Capitol 6078	Witchcraft/Chicago	1966	—	3.00	6.00
—Starline reissue label					
❑ Capitol 6193	One for My Baby/I've Got You Under My Skin	197?	—	3.00	6.00
❑ Capitol 6195	In the Wee Small Hours of the Morning/Night and Day	197?	—	3.00	6.00
❑ Columbia 6-718	Goodnight Irene/My Blue Heaven	1950	7.50	15.00	30.00
❑ Columbia 6-888	Nevertheless/I Guess I'll Have to Dream the Rest	1950	7.50	15.00	30.00
❑ Columbia 6-924	Remember Me in Your Dreams/Let It Snow, Let It Snow, Let It Snow	1950	7.50	15.00	30.00
❑ Columbia 6-936	I Am Loved/You Don't Remind Me	1950	7.50	15.00	30.00
❑ Columbia 4-33011	Nancy/Ol' Man River	1960	2.50	5.00	10.00
❑ Columbia 33306	I've Got a Crush on You/The Birth of the Blues	1977	—	3.00	6.00
—Hall of Fame series					
❑ Columbia 33319	Among My Souvenirs/September Song	1977	—	3.00	6.00
—Hall of Fame series					
❑ Columbia 36814	If You Are But a Dream/Put Your Dreams Away	1950	5.00	10.00	20.00
—Most Columbia 45s from 36000-39000 are reissues of titles that first appeared on 78s					
❑ Columbia 36825	You'll Never Walk Alone/If I Loved You	1950	5.00	10.00	20.00
❑ Columbia 36918	You Go to My Head/I Don't Know Why	1950	5.00	10.00	20.00
❑ Columbia 36919	These Foolish Things/A Ghost of a Chance	1950	5.00	10.00	20.00
❑ Columbia 36920	Why Shouldn't I?/Try a Little Tenderness	1950	5.00	10.00	20.00
❑ Columbia 36921	Paradise/Someone to Watch Over Me	1950	5.00	10.00	20.00
—The above four comprise the box set The Voice of Frank Sinatra, B-112					
❑ Columbia 37161	Among My Souvenirs/September Song	1950	5.00	10.00	20.00
❑ Columbia 37257	That Old Black Magic/How Deep Is the Ocean?	1950	5.00	10.00	20.00
❑ Columbia 37259	She's Funny That Way/Embraceable You	1950	5.00	10.00	20.00
❑ Columbia 38151	I've Got a Crush on You/Ever Homeward	1950	5.00	10.00	20.00
❑ Columbia 38163	All of Me/I Went Down to Virginia	1950	5.00	10.00	20.00
❑ Columbia 38256	Silent Night/Adeste Fideles	1950	5.00	10.00	20.00
❑ Columbia 38257	Jingle Bells/White Christmas	1950	5.00	10.00	20.00
❑ Columbia 38258	O Little Town Of Bethlehem/It Came Upon A Midnight Clear	1950	5.00	10.00	20.00
❑ Columbia 38259	Have Yourself a Merry Little Christmas/Santa Claus Is Comin' to Town	1950	5.00	10.00	20.00
—The above four comprise the box set Christmas Songs by Sinatra, B-167					
❑ Columbia 38446	Bali Ha'i/Some Enchanted Evening	1950	5.00	10.00	20.00
❑ Columbia 38683	The Moon Was Yellow/The Music Stopped	1950	5.00	10.00	20.00
❑ Columbia 38684	Strange Music/I Love You	1950	5.00	10.00	20.00
❑ Columbia 38685	Where or When/None But the Lonely Heart	1950	5.00	10.00	20.00
❑ Columbia 38686	Always/Why Was I Born?	1950	5.00	10.00	20.00
—The above four comprise the box set Dedicated to You, B-197					
❑ Columbia 38829	Poinciana/There's No Business Like Show Business	1950	5.00	10.00	20.00
❑ Columbia 38892	Goodnight Irene/My Blue Heaven	1950	3.75	7.50	15.00
—Reissue of Columbia 6-718					
❑ Columbia 38996	Lover/When You're Smiling	1950	5.00	10.00	20.00
❑ Columbia 38997	The Continental/It's Only a Paper Moon	1950	5.00	10.00	20.00

Number	Title (A Side/B Side)	Yr	VG	VG+	NM
❑ Columbia 38998	Should I?/My Blue Heaven	1950	5.00	10.00	20.00
❑ Columbia 38999	It All Depends on You/You Do Something to Me	1950	5.00	10.00	20.00
—The above four comprise the box set Sing and Dance with Frank Sinatra, B-218					
❑ Columbia 39044	Nevertheless/I Guess I'll Have to Dream the Rest	1950	3.75	7.50	15.00
—Reissue of Columbia 6-888					
❑ Columbia 39069	Remember Me in Your Dreams/Let It Snow, Let It Snow, Let It Snow	1950	3.75	7.50	15.00
—Reissue of Columbia 6-924					
❑ Columbia 39079	I Am Loved/You Don't Remind Me	1950	3.75	7.50	15.00
—Reissue of Columbia 6-936					
❑ Columbia 39118	Take My Love/Come Back to Sorrento	1950	3.75	7.50	15.00
❑ Columbia 39141	Love Means Love/Cherry Pies Ought to Be You	1951	6.25	12.50	25.00
❑ Columbia 39213	Faithful/You're the One	1951	5.00	10.00	20.00
❑ Columbia 39294	Hello, Young Lovers/We Kissed in a Shadow	1951	3.75	7.50	15.00
❑ Columbia 39346	I Whistle a Happy Tune/Love Me	1951	3.75	7.50	15.00
❑ Columbia 39425	Mama Will Bark/I'm a Fool to Want You	1951	10.00	20.00	40.00
—"Frank Sinatra & Dagmar"; the record Ol' Blue Eyes called his worst					
❑ Columbia 39493	I Fall in Love with You Everyday/It's a Long Way from Your House	1951	5.00	10.00	20.00
❑ Columbia 39498	It Never Entered My Mind/Try a Little Tenderness	1951	3.75	7.50	15.00
❑ Columbia 39527	Castle Rock/Deep Night	1951	5.00	10.00	20.00
❑ Columbia 39592	April in Paris/London by Night	1951	3.75	7.50	15.00
❑ Columbia 39652	I Hear a Rhapsody/I Could Write a Book	1952	3.75	7.50	15.00
❑ Columbia 39687	Feet of Clay/Don't Ever Be Afraid to Go Home	1952	5.00	10.00	20.00
❑ Columbia 39726	My Girl/Walkin' in the Sunshine	1952	5.00	10.00	20.00
❑ Columbia 39787	Luna Rosa/Tennessee Newsboy	1952	5.00	10.00	20.00
❑ Columbia 39819	Azure-Te/Bim Bam Baby	1952	3.75	7.50	15.00
❑ Columbia 39882	The Birth of the Blues/Why Try to Change Me Now?	1952	3.75	7.50	15.00
❑ Columbia 40229	I'm Glad There Is You/You Can Take My Word For It Baby	1954	5.00	10.00	20.00
❑ Columbia 40522	Dream/American Beauty Rose	1955	3.75	7.50	15.00
❑ Columbia 40565	Sheila/Day by Day	1955	7.50	15.00	30.00
❑ Columbia 41133	I'm a Fool to Want You/If I Forget You	1958	3.75	7.50	15.00
❑ Columbia 50003	Among My Souvenirs/September Song	1954	2.50	5.00	10.00
—Hall of Fame series					
❑ Columbia 50028	I've Got a Crush on You/The Birth of the Blues	1954	2.50	5.00	10.00
—Hall of Fame series					
❑ Columbia 50053	Nancy/The Girl That I Marry	1955	2.50	5.00	10.00
—Hall of Fame series					
❑ Columbia 50066	You'll Never Walk Alone/If I Loved You	1955	2.50	5.00	10.00
—Hall of Fame series					
❑ Columbia 50069	Saturday Night/Five Minutes More	1955	2.50	5.00	10.00
—Hall of Fame series					
❑ Columbia 50079	Silent Night/Adeste Fideles	1955	2.50	5.00	10.00
—Hall of Fame series					
❑ Qwest 28844	The Best of Everything/Teach Me Tonight	1985	—	2.00	4.00
❑ Qwest 29139	Mack the Knife/It's All Right with Me	1984	—	2.50	5.00
❑ Qwest 29223	L.A. Is My Lady/Until the Real Thing Comes Along	1984	—	2.50	5.00
❑ RCA Victor 27-0012	Night and Day/The Lamplighter's Serenade	1948	3.75	7.50	15.00
—All RCA and 45s are reissues of material first issued on 78s. Part of WPT-5					
❑ RCA Victor 27-0076	Stardust/(B-side unknown)	1949	3.75	7.50	15.00
—From WDT 15					
❑ RCA Victor 27-0077	I'll Never Smile Again/(B-side unknown)	1949	3.75	7.50	15.00
—From WDT 15					
❑ RCA Victor 27-0095	Somewhere A Voice Is Calling/(B-side unknown)	1949	3.75	7.50	15.00
—From WDT 20					
❑ RCA Victor 27-0151	Daybreak/There Are Such Things	1948	3.75	7.50	15.00
❑ RCA Victor 447-0116	I'll Never Smile Again/I'll Be Seeing You	1950	3.00	6.00	12.00
❑ RCA Victor 447-0123	Stardust/There Are Such Things	1950	3.00	6.00	12.00
❑ RCA Victor 447-0408	Night and Day/The Lamplighter's Serenade	1952	3.00	6.00	12.00
❑ RCA Victor 447-0445	Street of Dreams/East of the Sun	1952	3.00	6.00	12.00
❑ RCA Victor 447-0928	Night and Day/The Night We Called It a Day	1972	—	3.00	6.00
❑ RCA Victor 447-0929	The Song Is You/The Lamplighter's Serenade	1972	—	3.00	6.00
❑ Reprise 0053	I'll Be Seeing You/Without a Song	1962	50.00	100.00	200.00
—Released in Great Britain as 20,053; pressed in the United States later					
❑ Reprise GRE 0113	Bad, Bad Leroy Brown/Let Me Try Again	1975	5.00	10.00	20.00
—"Back to Back Hits" series					
❑ Reprise GRE 0122	Theme from New York, New York/You and Me (We Wanted It All)	1981	—	2.00	4.00
—"Back to Back Hits" series					

Number	Title (A Side/B Side)	Yr	VG	VG+	NM
❑ Reprise 243	Have Yourself a Merry Little Christmas/How Shall I Send Thee?	1963	5.00	10.00	20.00
—B-side by Les Baxter					
❑ Reprise 0249	Stay with Me/Talk to Me Baby	1963	2.50	5.00	10.00
❑ Reprise 0279	My Kind of Town/I Like to Lead When I Dance	1964	2.50	5.00	10.00
❑ Reprise 0301	Softly, As I Leave You/Then Suddenly Love	1964	2.50	5.00	10.00
❑ Reprise 0314	I Heard the Bells on Christmas Day/The Little Drummer Boy	1964	5.00	10.00	20.00
❑ Reprise 0317	We Wish You the Merriest/Go Tell It on the Mountain	1964	10.00	20.00	40.00
—By Frank Sinatra/Bing Crosby/Fred Waring					
❑ Reprise 0332	Somewhere in Your Heart/Emily	1964	2.00	4.00	8.00
—From here through 0677, originals on dark brown & orange label					
❑ Reprise 0350	Anytime at All/Available	1964	2.00	4.00	8.00
❑ Reprise 0373	Tell Her (You Love Her Each Day)/Here's to the Losers	1965	2.00	4.00	8.00
❑ Reprise 0380	Forget Domani/I Can't Believe I'm Losing You	1965	2.00	4.00	8.00
❑ Reprise 0398	When Somebody Loves You/When I'm Not Near the Girl I Love	1965	2.00	4.00	8.00
❑ Reprise 0410	Everybody Has the Right to Be Wrong/ I'll Only Miss Her When I Think of Her	1965	2.00	4.00	8.00
❑ Reprise 0429	It Was a Very Good Year/Moment to Moment	1965	2.00	4.00	8.00
❑ Reprise 0470	Strangers in the Night/Oh, You Crazy Moon	1966	2.50	5.00	10.00
❑ Reprise 0509	Summer Wind/You Make Me Feel So Young	1966	2.50	5.00	10.00
❑ Reprise 0531	That's Life/The September of My Years	1966	2.50	5.00	10.00
❑ Reprise 0561	Somethin' Stupid/Give Her Love	1967	2.50	5.00	10.00
—A-side: Nancy Sinatra and Frank Sinatra					
❑ Reprise 0561	Somethin' Stupid/I Will Wait for You	1967	2.00	4.00	8.00
—A-side: Nancy Sinatra and Frank Sinatra					
❑ Reprise 0610	The World We Knew (Over and Over)/You Are There	1967	2.00	4.00	8.00
❑ Reprise 0631	This Town/This Is My Love	1967	2.00	4.00	8.00
❑ Reprise 0677	I Can't Believe I'm Losing You/How Old Am I?	1967	2.00	4.00	8.00
❑ Reprise 0702	My Kind of Town/That's Life	1968	—	2.50	5.00
—"Back to Back Hits" series					
❑ Reprise 0706	September of My Years/Softly, As I Leave You	1968	—	2.50	5.00
—"Back to Back Hits" series					
❑ Reprise 0710	Strangers in the Night/Summer Wind	1968	—	2.50	5.00
—"Back to Back Hits" series					
❑ Reprise 0713	It Was a Very Good Year/Stay with Me	1968	—	2.50	5.00
—"Back to Back Hits" series					
❑ Reprise 0727	Somethin' Stupid/The World We Knew (Over and Over)	1968	—	2.50	5.00
—"Back to Back Hits" series; A-side with Nancy Sinatra					
❑ Reprise 0734	My Way/Cycles	1970	—	2.50	5.00
—"Back to Back Hits" series					
❑ Reprise 0764	Cycles/My Way of Life	1968	—	3.00	6.00
—From here though 0865, orange/tan label with "W7/:r" logo					
❑ Reprise 0790	Whatever Happened to Christmas?/I Wouldn't Trade Christmas	1968	3.00	6.00	12.00
—B-side by The Sinatra Family					
❑ Reprise 0798	Rain in My Heart/Star	1968	—	3.00	6.00
❑ Reprise 0817	My Way/Blue Lace	1969	2.50	5.00	10.00
❑ Reprise 0852	Love's Been Good to Me/A Man Alone	1969	2.00	4.00	8.00
❑ Reprise 0865	Goin' Out of My Head/Forget to Remember	1969	2.00	4.00	8.00
❑ Reprise 0895	I Would Be in Love (Anyway)/Watertown	1970	2.00	4.00	8.00
—From here through 29903, orange (or tan) label with ":r" logo in square					
❑ Reprise 0920	The Train/What's Now Is Now	1969	2.00	4.00	8.00
❑ Reprise 0970	Lady Day/Song of the Sabia	1969	2.00	4.00	8.00
❑ Reprise 0980	Feelin' Kinda Sunday/Kids	1970	2.00	4.00	8.00
—A-side by Nancy Sinatra and Frank Sinatra; B-side by Nancy Sinatra					
❑ Reprise 0981	Something/Bein' Green	1970	2.00	4.00	8.00
❑ Reprise 1010	Witchcraft/Young at Heart	1971	2.00	4.00	8.00
❑ Reprise 1011	Life's a Trippy Thing/I'm Not Afraid	1971	2.00	4.00	8.00
—A-side by Nancy Sinatra and Frank Sinatra					
❑ Reprise 1181	Let Me Try Again/Send In the Clowns	1973	2.00	4.00	8.00
❑ Reprise 1190	You Will Be My Music/Winners	1973	2.00	4.00	8.00
❑ Reprise 1196	Bad, Bad Leroy Brown/I'm Gonna Make It All the Way	1974	2.00	4.00	8.00
❑ Reprise 1208	You Turned My World Around/Satisfy Me One More Time	1974	2.00	4.00	8.00
❑ Reprise 1327	Anytime (I'll Be There)/The Hurt Doesn't Go Away	1975	2.00	4.00	8.00
❑ Reprise 1335	I Believe I'm Gonna Love You/The Only Couple on the Floor	1975	2.00	4.00	8.00
❑ Reprise 1342	A Baby Just Like You/Christmas Mem'ries	1975	2.50	5.00	10.00
❑ Reprise 1343	Empty Tables/The Saddest Thing of All	1976	2.00	4.00	8.00
❑ Reprise 1347	I Sing the Songs (I Write the Songs)/Empty Tables	1976	2.50	5.00	10.00
❑ Reprise 1364	Stargazer/The Best I Ever Had	1976	2.00	4.00	8.00
❑ Reprise 1377	Dry Your Eyes/Like a Sad Song	1976	2.00	4.00	8.00
❑ Reprise 1382	I Love My Wife/Send In the Clowns	1976	2.50	5.00	10.00
❑ Reprise 1386	Night and Day/Everybody Ought to Be in Love	1977	2.00	4.00	8.00
❑ Reprise 20001	The Second Time Around/Tina	1961	6.25	12.50	25.00
—Originals on light blue label					
❑ Reprise 20010	Granada/The Curse of an Aching Heart	1961	3.75	7.50	15.00
—From here through 0317, originals on peach label					
❑ Reprise 20023	I'll Be Seeing You/The One I Love	1961	3.75	7.50	15.00
❑ Reprise 20024	Imagination/It's Always You	1961	3.75	7.50	15.00
❑ Reprise 20025	I'm Getting Sentimental Over You/East of the Sun (And West of the Moon)	1961	3.75	7.50	15.00
❑ Reprise 20026	There Are Such Things/Polkadots and Moonbeams	1961	3.75	7.50	15.00
❑ Reprise 20027	Without a Song/It Started All Over Again	1961	3.75	7.50	15.00
❑ Reprise 20028	Take Me/Daybreak	1961	3.75	7.50	15.00
❑ Reprise 20040	Pocketful of Miracles/Name It and It's Yours	1961	3.75	7.50	15.00
❑ Reprise 20059	Stardust/Come Rain or Come Shine	1962	3.75	7.50	15.00
❑ Reprise 20063	Everybody's Twistin'/Nothin' But the Best	1962	3.75	7.50	15.00
❑ Reprise 20092	Goody, Goody/Love Is Just Around the Corner	1962	3.00	6.00	12.00
❑ Reprise 20107	The Look of Love/Indiscreet	1962	12.50	25.00	50.00
❑ Reprise 20107	The Look of Love/I Left My Heart in San Francisco	1962	12.50	25.00	50.00

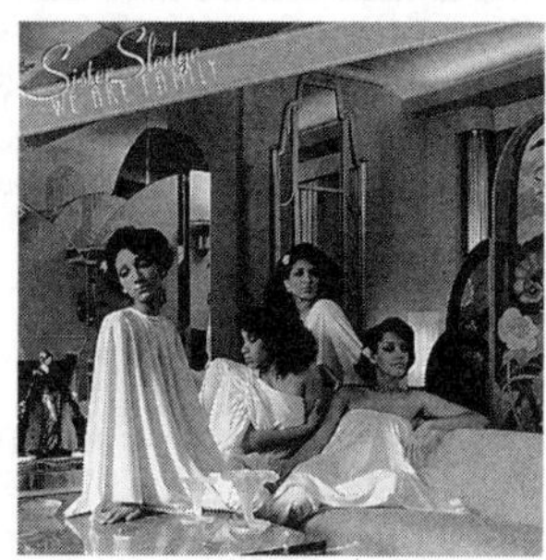

Number	Title (A Side/B Side)	Yr	VG	VG+	NM
❑ Reprise 20128	Me and My Shadow/Sam's Song	1962	3.75	7.50	15.00
—A-side by Frank Sinatra and Sammy Davis, Jr.; B-side by Sammy Davis Jr. and Dean Martin					
❑ Reprise 20151	Call Me Irresponsible/Tina	1963	2.50	5.00	10.00
—B-side changed for commercial release					
❑ Reprise 20151	Call Me Irresponsible/Come Blow Your Horn	1963	125.00	250.00	500.00
—One stock copy is known to exist!					
❑ Reprise 20184	I Have Dreamed/Come Blow Your Horn	1963	2.50	5.00	10.00
❑ Reprise 20209	Love Isn't Just for the Young/You Brought a New Kind of Love to Me	1963	3.00	6.00	12.00
❑ Reprise 20217	Fugue for Tinhorns/The Oldest Established (Permanent Floating Crap Game in New York)	1963	3.75	7.50	15.00
—By Frank Sinatra/Bing Crosby/Dean Martin					
❑ Reprise 20235	Tangerine/A New Kind of Love	1963	—	—	—
—Unreleased					
❑ Reprise 29677	Here's to the Band/It's Sunday	1983	2.00	4.00	8.00
❑ Reprise 29903	To Love a Child/That's What God Looks Like to Me	1982	2.00	4.00	8.00
❑ Reprise 49233	Theme from New York, New York/That's What God Looks Like to Me	1980	2.50	5.00	10.00
❑ Reprise 49517	You and Me (We Wanted It All)/I've Been There	1980	2.00	4.00	8.00
❑ Reprise 49827	Say Hello/Good Thing Going	1981	2.00	4.00	8.00
—B-side listed on label as "RE-1"					
Albums					
❑ Capitol DWBB-254 [(2)R]	Close-Up	1969	5.00	10.00	20.00
—Reissue in one package of "This Is Sinatra" and "This Is Sinatra, Volume Two"					
❑ Capitol DKAO-374 [R]	Frank Sinatra's Greatest Hits	1969	3.00	6.00	12.00
❑ Capitol H 488 [10]	Songs for Young Lovers	1954	15.00	30.00	60.00
❑ Capitol H 528 [10]	Swing Easy	1954	15.00	30.00	60.00
❑ Capitol STBB-529 [(2)]	What Is This Thing Called Love?/The Night We Called It a Day	1970	3.75	7.50	15.00
❑ Capitol DW 581 [R]	In the Wee Small Hours	196?	3.00	6.00	12.00
❑ Capitol H1-581 [10]	In the Wee Small Hours, Part 1	1955	25.00	50.00	100.00
❑ Capitol H2-581 [10]	In the Wee Small Hours, Part 2	1955	25.00	50.00	100.00
❑ Capitol W 581 [M]	In the Wee Small Hours	1955	10.00	20.00	40.00
—Gray label original					
❑ Capitol W 587 [M]	Swing Easy/Songs for Young Lovers	1955	10.00	20.00	40.00
—Gray label original; 12-inch version of two 10-inch LPs					
❑ Capitol DW 653 [R]	Songs for Swingin' Lovers!	196?	3.00	6.00	12.00
❑ Capitol W 653 [M]	Songs for Swingin' Lovers!	1956	10.00	20.00	40.00
—Gray label; cover has Sinatra facing toward the embracing couple					
❑ Capitol W 653 [M]	Songs for Swingin' Lovers!	1956	12.50	25.00	50.00
—Gray label; cover has Sinatra facing away from the embracing couple					
❑ Capitol STBB-724 [(2)]	My One and Only Love/Sentimental Journey	1971	3.75	7.50	15.00
❑ Capitol T 735 [M]	Frank Sinatra Conducts Tone Poems of Color	1956	15.00	30.00	60.00
—Turquoise label					
❑ Capitol DT 768 [R]	This Is Sinatra!	196?	3.00	6.00	12.00
❑ Capitol T 768 [M]	This Is Sinatra!	1956	7.50	15.00	30.00
—Turquoise label					
❑ Capitol DW 789 [R]	Close to You	196?	3.00	6.00	12.00
❑ Capitol W 789 [M]	Close to You	1957	7.50	15.00	30.00
—Gray label					
❑ Capitol DW 803 [R]	A Swingin' Affair!	196?	3.00	6.00	12.00
❑ Capitol W 803 [M]	A Swingin' Affair!	1957	7.50	15.00	30.00
—Gray label					
❑ Capitol SW 855 [S]	Where Are You?	1959	10.00	20.00	40.00
—Originals do not include "I Cover the Waterfront"					
❑ Capitol W 855 [M]	Where Are You?	1957	7.50	15.00	30.00
—Gray label					
❑ Capitol DT 894 [R]	The Sinatra Christmas Album	196?	2.50	5.00	10.00
—Rechanneled reissue of A Jolly Christmas with Frank Sinatra with same contents; some copies have this cover and "A Jolly Christmas" labels					
❑ Capitol W 894 [M]	A Jolly Christmas from Frank Sinatra	1957	10.00	20.00	40.00
—Original mono with gray label					
❑ Capitol SW 920 [S]	Come Fly with Me	1959	7.50	15.00	30.00
❑ Capitol W 920 [M]	Come Fly with Me	1958	10.00	20.00	40.00
—Gray label					
❑ Capitol DW 982 [R]	This Is Sinatra, Volume Two	196?	3.00	6.00	12.00
❑ Capitol W 982 [M]	This Is Sinatra, Volume Two	1958	10.00	20.00	40.00
—Gray label					
❑ Capitol SW 1053 [S]	Frank Sinatra Sings for Only the Lonely	1959	7.50	15.00	30.00
—Originals do not include "It's a Lonesome Old Town" and "Spring Is Here"					

Number	Title (A Side/B Side)	Yr	VG	VG+	NM
❑ Capitol W 1053 [M]	Frank Sinatra Sings for Only the Lonely	1958	10.00	20.00	40.00
—Gray label					
❑ Capitol SW 1069 [S]	Come Dance with Me!	1959	7.50	15.00	30.00
❑ Capitol W 1069 [M]	Come Dance with Me!	1959	5.00	10.00	20.00
❑ Capitol DW 1164 [R]	Look to Your Heart	196?	3.00	6.00	12.00
❑ Capitol W 1164 [M]	Look to Your Heart	1959	7.50	15.00	30.00
❑ Capitol SW 1221 [S]	No One Cares	1959	7.50	15.00	30.00
❑ Capitol W 1221 [M]	No One Cares	1959	5.00	10.00	20.00
❑ Capitol SW 1417 [S]	Nice 'N' Easy	1960	6.25	12.50	25.00
❑ Capitol W 1417 [M]	Nice 'N' Easy	1960	5.00	10.00	20.00
❑ Capitol DW 1429 [R]	Swing Easy	1960	3.00	6.00	12.00
❑ Capitol W 1429 [M]	Swing Easy	1960	5.00	10.00	20.00
❑ Capitol DW 1432 [R]	Songs for Young Lovers	1960	3.00	6.00	12.00
❑ Capitol W 1432 [M]	Songs for Young Lovers	1960	5.00	10.00	20.00
❑ Capitol SW 1491 [S]	Sinatra's Swingin' Session!!!	1961	6.25	12.50	25.00
❑ Capitol W 1491 [M]	Sinatra's Swingin' Session!!!	1961	5.00	10.00	20.00
❑ Capitol SW 1538 [S]	All the Way	1961	6.25	12.50	25.00
❑ Capitol W 1538 [M]	All the Way	1961	5.00	10.00	20.00
❑ Capitol SW 1594 [S]	Come Swing with Me!	1961	6.25	12.50	25.00
❑ Capitol W 1594 [M]	Come Swing with Me!	1961	5.00	10.00	20.00
❑ Capitol SW 1676 [S]	Point of No Return	1962	6.25	12.50	25.00
❑ Capitol W 1676 [M]	Point of No Return	1962	5.00	10.00	20.00
❑ Capitol SW 1729 [P]	Sinatra Sings...Of Love and Things	1962	5.00	10.00	20.00
❑ Capitol W 1729 [M]	Sinatra Sings...Of Love and Things	1962	5.00	10.00	20.00
❑ Capitol SWCO 1762 [(3)P]	Sinatra, The Great Years	1962	10.00	20.00	40.00
❑ Capitol WCO 1762 [(3)M]	Sinatra, The Great Years	1962	7.50	15.00	30.00
❑ Capitol DW 1825 [R]	Sinatra Sings Rodgers and Hart	1963	3.00	6.00	12.00
❑ Capitol W 1825 [M]	Sinatra Sings Rodgers and Hart	1963	5.00	10.00	20.00
❑ Capitol DT 1919 [R]	Tell Her You Love Her	1963	3.00	6.00	12.00
❑ Capitol T 1919 [M]	Tell Her You Love Her	1963	5.00	10.00	20.00
❑ Capitol DW 1994 [R]	Sinatra Sings the Select Johnny Mercer	1963	3.00	6.00	12.00
❑ Capitol W 1994 [M]	Sinatra Sings the Select Johnny Mercer	1963	5.00	10.00	20.00
❑ Capitol DT 2036 [R]	The Greatest Hits of Frank Sinatra	1964	3.00	6.00	12.00
❑ Capitol T 2036 [M]	The Greatest Hits of Frank Sinatra	1964	5.00	10.00	20.00
❑ Capitol T 2123 [M]	Sinatra Sings the Select Harold Arlen	1964	25.00	50.00	100.00
—Only released in Canada, Australia and the UK					
❑ Capitol DW 2301 [R]	Sinatra Sings the Select Cole Porter	1965	3.00	6.00	12.00
❑ Capitol W 2301 [M]	Sinatra Sings the Select Cole Porter	1965	5.00	10.00	20.00
❑ Capitol DT 2602 [R]	Forever Frank	1966	3.00	6.00	12.00
❑ Capitol T 2602 [M]	Forever Frank	1966	5.00	10.00	20.00
❑ Capitol DT 2700 [R]	The Movie Songs	1967	3.00	6.00	12.00
❑ Capitol T 2700 [M]	The Movie Songs	1967	5.00	10.00	20.00
❑ Capitol STFL 2814 [(6)P]	The Frank Sinatra Deluxe Set	1968	15.00	30.00	60.00
❑ Capitol TFL 2814 [(6)M]	The Frank Sinatra Deluxe Set	1968	25.00	50.00	100.00
❑ Capitol DKAO 2900 [R]	The Best of Frank Sinatra	1968	3.75	7.50	15.00
❑ Capitol ST-11309	One More for the Road	1973	2.50	5.00	10.00
❑ Capitol SABB-11367 [(2)P]	Round #1	1974	3.75	7.50	15.00
❑ Capitol SM-11502	A Swingin' Affair!	1976	2.50	5.00	10.00
❑ Capitol SM-11801	Come Swing with Me	1978	2.50	5.00	10.00
❑ Capitol M-11883	This Is Sinatra!	1979	2.50	5.00	10.00
❑ Capitol SN-16109	The Best of Frank Sinatra	198?	2.00	4.00	8.00
—Budget-line reissue					
❑ Capitol DN-16110	What Is This Thing Called Love	198?	2.00	4.00	8.00
—Budget-line reissue					
❑ Capitol SN-16111	The Night We Called It a Day	198?	2.00	4.00	8.00
—Budget-line reissue					
❑ Capitol N-16112	My One and Only Love	198?	2.00	4.00	8.00
—Budget-line reissue					
❑ Capitol SN-16113	Sentimental Journey	198?	2.00	4.00	8.00
—Budget-line reissue					
❑ Capitol N-16148	Look to Your Heart	198?	2.00	4.00	8.00
—Budget-line reissue					
❑ Capitol SN-16149	Sinatra Sings...Of Love and Things	198?	2.00	4.00	8.00
—Budget-line reissue					
❑ Capitol SN-16202	Frank Sinatra Sings for Only the Lonely	198?	2.00	4.00	8.00
—Budget-line reissue					
❑ Capitol SN-16203	Come Dance with Me!	198?	2.00	4.00	8.00
—Budget-line reissue					
❑ Capitol SN-16204	Nice 'N' Easy	198?	2.00	4.00	8.00
—Budget-line reissue					
❑ Capitol SN-16205	All the Way	198?	2.00	4.00	8.00
—Budget-line reissue					
❑ Capitol SN-16267	Where Are You	198?	2.00	4.00	8.00
—Budget-line reissue					
❑ Capitol DN-16268	This Is Sinatra, Volume Two	198?	2.00	4.00	8.00
—Budget-line reissue					
❑ Capitol Pickwick Series PC-3450 [M]	The Nearness of You	196?	3.00	6.00	12.00
❑ Capitol Pickwick Series SPC-3450 [R]	The Nearness of You	196?	2.50	5.00	10.00
❑ Capitol Pickwick Series PC-3452 [M]	Try a Little Tenderness	196?	3.00	6.00	12.00
❑ Capitol Pickwick Series SPC-3452 [R]	Try a Little Tenderness	196?	2.50	5.00	10.00
❑ Capitol Pickwick Series PC-3456 [M]	Nevertheless	196?	3.00	6.00	12.00

Number	Title (A Side/B Side)	Yr	VG	VG+	NM
❑ Capitol Pickwick Series SPC-3456 [R]	Nevertheless	196?	2.50	5.00	10.00
❑ Capitol Pickwick Series PC-3457 [M]	Just One of Those Things	196?	3.00	6.00	12.00
❑ Capitol Pickwick Series SPC-3457 [R]	Just One of Those Things	196?	2.50	5.00	10.00
❑ Capitol Pickwick Series PC-3458 [M]	This Love of Mine	196?	3.00	6.00	12.00
❑ Capitol Pickwick Series SPC-3458 [R]	This Love of Mine	196?	2.50	5.00	10.00
❑ Capitol Pickwick Series PC-3463 [M]	My Cole Porter	196?	3.00	6.00	12.00
❑ Capitol Pickwick Series SPC-3463 [R]	My Cole Porter	196?	2.50	5.00	10.00
❑ Columbia C2L 6 [(2)M]	The Frank Sinatra Story	1958	7.50	15.00	30.00
❑ Columbia S3L 42 [(3)M]	The Essential Frank Sinatra	1966	25.00	50.00	100.00
❑ Columbia S3S 42 [(3)R]	The Essential Frank Sinatra	1966	12.50	25.00	50.00
❑ Columbia CL 606 [M]	Frankie	1955	6.25	12.50	25.00
—Cover has Frank with Debbie Reynolds					
❑ Columbia CL 606 [M]	Frankie	1955	7.50	15.00	30.00
—Cover has drawing of Frank Sinatra wearing a hat					
❑ Columbia CL 743 [M]	The Voice	1956	6.25	12.50	25.00
❑ Columbia CL 884 [M]	Frank Sinatra Conducts Music of Alec Wilder	1956	10.00	20.00	40.00
—Reissue of Columbia Masterworks ML 4271					
❑ Columbia CL 902 [M]	That Old Feeling	1956	6.25	12.50	25.00
❑ Columbia CL 953 [M]	Adventures of the Heart	1957	6.25	12.50	25.00
❑ Columbia CL 1032 [M]	Christmas Dreaming	1957	20.00	40.00	80.00
❑ Columbia CL 1136 [M]	Put Your Dreams Away	1958	6.25	12.50	25.00
❑ Columbia CL 1241 [M]	Love Is a Kick	1958	6.25	12.50	25.00
❑ Columbia CL 1297 [M]	The Broadway Kick	1958	6.25	12.50	25.00
❑ Columbia CL 1359 [M]	Come Back to Sorrento	1959	6.25	12.50	25.00
❑ Columbia CL 1448 [M]	Reflections	1959	15.00	30.00	60.00
❑ Columbia CL 2474 [M]	Greatest Hits, The Early Years, Vol. 1	1966	3.75	7.50	15.00
❑ Columbia CL 2521 [10]	Get Happy	1955	15.00	30.00	60.00
—"House Party Series" release					
❑ Columbia CL 2539 [10]	I've Got a Crush on You	1955	15.00	30.00	60.00
—"House Party Series" release; different contents from CL 6290					
❑ Columbia CL 2542 [10]	Christmas with Sinatra	1955	15.00	30.00	60.00
—"House Party Series" release					
❑ Columbia CL 2572 [M]	Greatest Hits, The Early Years, Vol. 2	1966	3.75	7.50	15.00
❑ Columbia CL 2739 [M]	The Essential Frank Sinatra, Volume 1	1967	6.25	12.50	25.00
❑ Columbia CL 2740 [M]	The Essential Frank Sinatra, Volume 2	1967	6.25	12.50	25.00
❑ Columbia CL 2741 [M]	The Essential Frank Sinatra, Volume 3	1967	6.25	12.50	25.00
❑ Columbia CL 2913 [M]	Frank Sinatra in Hollywood	1968	20.00	40.00	80.00
❑ Columbia CL 6001 [10]	The Voice of Frank Sinatra	1949	17.50	35.00	70.00
—Original in pink paper cover					
❑ Columbia CL 6019 [10]	Christmas Songs by Sinatra	1948	25.00	50.00	100.00
—With "gingerbread man" cover					
❑ Columbia CL 6059 [10]	Frankly Sentimental	1951	15.00	30.00	60.00
❑ Columbia CL 6087 [10]	Songs by Sinatra, Volume 1	1952	15.00	30.00	60.00
❑ Columbia CL 6096 [10]	Dedicated to You	1952	25.00	50.00	100.00
—Three of the tracks on this LP are alternate takes unavailable on vinyl anywhere else					
❑ Columbia CL 6143 [10]	Sing and Dance with Frank Sinatra	1953	15.00	30.00	60.00
❑ Columbia CL 6290 [10]	I've Got a Crush on You	1954	15.00	30.00	60.00
❑ Columbia CS 9274 [R]	Greatest Hits, The Early Years, Vol. 1	1966	2.50	5.00	10.00
❑ Columbia CS 9372 [R]	Greatest Hits, The Early Years, Vol. 2	1966	2.50	5.00	10.00
❑ Columbia CS 9539 [R]	The Essential Frank Sinatra, Volume 1	1967	3.00	6.00	12.00
❑ Columbia CS 9540 [R]	The Essential Frank Sinatra, Volume 2	1967	3.00	6.00	12.00
❑ Columbia CS 9541 [R]	The Essential Frank Sinatra, Volume 3	1967	3.00	6.00	12.00
❑ Columbia CS 9713 [R]	Frank Sinatra in Hollywood	1968	3.00	6.00	12.00
❑ Columbia KG 31358 [(2)]	In the Beginning	1971	10.00	20.00	40.00
—Original edition; titles of songs at left on front cover					
❑ Columbia C6X 40343 [(6)]	The Voice: The Columbia Years 1943-1952	1986	20.00	40.00	80.00
❑ Columbia PC 40707	Christmas Dreaming	1987	7.50	15.00	30.00
—Reissue of CL 1032 with an extra track					
❑ Columbia C2X 40897 [(2)]	Hello Young Lovers	1988	7.50	15.00	30.00
❑ Columbia PC 44238 [M]	Sinatra Rarities	1989	10.00	20.00	40.00

Number	Title (A Side/B Side)	Yr	VG	VG+	NM
❑ Columbia Masterworks ML 4271 [M]	Frank Sinatra Conducts Music of Alec Wilder	1955	25.00	50.00	100.00
❑ Harmony HL 7400 [M]	Have Yourself a Merry Little Christmas	1967	7.50	15.00	30.00
❑ Harmony HL 7405 [M]	Romantic Scenes from the Early Years	1967	7.50	15.00	30.00
❑ Harmony HS 11200 [R]	Have Yourself a Merry Little Christmas	1967	5.00	10.00	20.00
—At least two different cover designs exist					
❑ Harmony HS 11205 [R]	Romantic Scenes from the Early Years	1967	3.00	6.00	12.00
❑ Harmony HS 11277 [R]	Someone to Watch Over Me	1968	3.75	7.50	15.00
❑ Harmony HS 11390 [R]	Frank Sinatra	1969	3.75	7.50	15.00
❑ Harmony KH 30318 [R]	Greatest Hits, Early Years	1971	3.75	7.50	15.00
❑ Pair PDL2-1027 [(2)]	All-Time Classics	1986	3.00	6.00	12.00
❑ Pair PDL2-1028 [(2)]	Timeless	1986	3.00	6.00	12.00
❑ Pair PDL2-1122 [(2)]	Classic Performances	1986	3.00	6.00	12.00
❑ Qwest 25145	L.A. Is My Lady	1984	3.00	6.00	12.00
❑ RCA Victor APL1-0497 [R]	What'll I Do	1974	3.00	6.00	12.00
❑ RCA Victor LPV-583 [M]	This Love of Mine	1971	10.00	20.00	40.00
❑ RCA Victor ANL1-1050 [R]	What'll I Do	1976	2.50	5.00	10.00
❑ RCA Victor LPM-1569 [M]	Frankie and Tommy	1957	15.00	30.00	60.00
—First issue of this LP					
❑ RCA Victor LPM-1569 [M]	Tommy Plays, Frankie Sings	1957	10.00	20.00	40.00
—Second issue with new title					
❑ RCA Victor LPM-1632 [M]	We Three	1958	15.00	30.00	60.00
—First issue					
❑ RCA Victor LPT-3063 [10]	Fabulous Frankie	1953	15.00	30.00	60.00
❑ RCA Victor CPL2-4334 [(2)]	The Sinatra/Dorsey Sessions, Vol. 1	1982	6.25	12.50	25.00
❑ RCA Victor CPL2-4335 [(2)]	The Sinatra/Dorsey Sessions, Vol. 2	1982	6.25	12.50	25.00
❑ RCA Victor CPL2-4336 [(2)]	The Sinatra/Dorsey Sessions, Vol. 3	1982	6.25	12.50	25.00
❑ RCA Victor AFL1-4741 [R]	Radio Years (Sinatra/Dorsey/Stordahl)	1983	3.75	7.50	15.00
❑ Reprise F 1001 [M]	Ring-a-Ding-Ding!	1961	5.00	10.00	20.00
❑ Reprise R9 1001 [S]	Ring-a-Ding-Ding!	1961	6.25	12.50	25.00
❑ Reprise F 1002 [M]	Sinatra Swings	1961	5.00	10.00	20.00
—Retitled version of "Swing Along with Me"; Capitol threatened legal action because of its "Come Swing With Me!" collection					
❑ Reprise F 1002 [M]	Swing Along with Me	1961	10.00	20.00	40.00
—Original title					
❑ Reprise R9 1002 [S]	Swing Along with Me	1961	12.50	25.00	50.00
—Original title					
❑ Reprise R9 1002 [S]	Sinatra Swings	1961	6.25	12.50	25.00
—Retitled version of "Swing Along with Me"; Capitol threatened legal action because of its "Come Swing With Me!" collection					
❑ Reprise F 1003 [M]	I Remember Tommy	1961	5.00	10.00	20.00
❑ Reprise R9 1003 [S]	I Remember Tommy	1961	6.25	12.50	25.00
❑ Reprise F 1004 [M]	Sinatra & Strings	1962	3.75	7.50	15.00
❑ Reprise R9 1004 [S]	Sinatra & Strings	1962	5.00	10.00	20.00
❑ Reprise F 1005 [M]	Sinatra and Swingin' Brass	1962	3.75	7.50	15.00
❑ Reprise R9 1005 [S]	Sinatra and Swingin' Brass	1962	5.00	10.00	20.00
❑ Reprise F 1007 [M]	All Alone	1962	3.75	7.50	15.00
❑ Reprise R9 1007 [S]	All Alone	1962	5.00	10.00	20.00
❑ Reprise F 1008 [M]	Sinatra-Basie	1963	3.75	7.50	15.00
❑ Reprise R9 1008 [S]	Sinatra-Basie	1963	5.00	10.00	20.00
❑ Reprise F 1009 [M]	The Concert Sinatra	1963	3.75	7.50	15.00
❑ Reprise R9 1009 [S]	The Concert Sinatra	1963	6.25	12.50	25.00
—Original pressings declare this was recorded in "35mm Stereo"					
❑ Reprise R-1010 [M]	Sinatra's Sinatra	1963	3.75	7.50	15.00
—Gatefold jacket; some copies have eight photos of previous Frank Sinatra Reprise LPs at the right side of the inside gatefold; we don't yet know the relative rarity of these variations, or which came first, or whether they also exist on stereo copies					
❑ Reprise R9 1010 [S]	Sinatra's Sinatra	1963	5.00	10.00	20.00
❑ Reprise F 1011 [M]	Days of Wine and Roses, Moon River, and Other Academy Award Winners	1964	3.75	7.50	15.00
❑ Reprise FS 1011 [S]	Days of Wine and Roses, Moon River, and Other Academy Award Winners	1964	5.00	10.00	20.00
❑ Reprise F 1012 [M]	It Might As Well Be Swing	1964	3.75	7.50	15.00
❑ Reprise FS 1012 [S]	It Might As Well Be Swing	1964	5.00	10.00	20.00
❑ Reprise F 1013 [M]	Softly, As I Leave You	1964	3.75	7.50	15.00
❑ Reprise FS 1013 [S]	Softly, As I Leave You	1964	5.00	10.00	20.00
❑ Reprise F 1014 [M]	September of My Years	1965	3.75	7.50	15.00
❑ Reprise FS 1014 [S]	September of My Years	1965	5.00	10.00	20.00
❑ Reprise F 1015 [M]	My Kind of Broadway	1965	3.75	7.50	15.00
❑ Reprise FS 1015 [S]	My Kind of Broadway	1965	5.00	10.00	20.00
❑ Reprise 2F 1016 [(2)M]	A Man and His Music	1965	5.00	10.00	20.00
❑ Reprise 2FS 1016 [(2)S]	A Man and His Music	1965	6.25	12.50	25.00
❑ Reprise F 1017 [M]	Strangers in the Night	1966	3.00	6.00	12.00
❑ Reprise FS 1017 [S]	Strangers in the Night	1966	3.75	7.50	15.00
❑ Reprise F 1018 [M]	Moonlight Sinatra	1966	3.75	7.50	15.00
❑ Reprise FS 1018 [S]	Moonlight Sinatra	1966	5.00	10.00	20.00
❑ Reprise 2F 1019 [(2)M]	Sinatra at the Sands	1966	5.00	10.00	20.00
❑ Reprise 2FS 1019 [(2)S]	Sinatra at the Sands	1966	6.25	12.50	25.00
❑ Reprise F 1020 [M]	That's Life	1966	3.00	6.00	12.00
❑ Reprise FS 1020 [S]	That's Life	1966	3.75	7.50	15.00
❑ Reprise F 1021 [M]	Francis Albert Sinatra & Antonio Carlos Jobim	1967	3.00	6.00	12.00
❑ Reprise FS 1021 [S]	Francis Albert Sinatra & Antonio Carlos Jobim	1967	3.75	7.50	15.00
❑ Reprise F 1022 [M]	Frank Sinatra (The World We Knew)	1967	3.75	7.50	15.00
❑ Reprise FS 1022 [S]	Frank Sinatra (The World We Knew)	1967	3.75	7.50	15.00
❑ Reprise FS 1024	Francis A. and Edward K.	1968	5.00	10.00	20.00
❑ Reprise FS 1025	Frank Sinatra's Greatest Hits	1968	3.75	7.50	15.00
❑ Reprise FS 1027	Cycles	1969	3.75	7.50	15.00
❑ Reprise FS 1029	My Way	1969	3.75	7.50	15.00
❑ Reprise FS 1030	A Man Alone & Other Songs of Rod McKuen	1969	3.75	7.50	15.00
❑ Reprise FS 1031	Watertown	1970	6.25	12.50	25.00
—With gatefold and poster					

Number	Title (A Side/B Side)	Yr	VG	VG+	NM
❑ Reprise FS 1033	Sinatra and Company	1971	3.75	7.50	15.00
❑ Reprise FS 1034	Frank Sinatra's Greatest Hits, Vol. 2	1972	3.75	7.50	15.00
❑ Reprise FS 2155	Ol' Blue Eyes Is Back	1973	3.00	6.00	12.00
❑ Reprise FS 2195	Some Nice Things I've Missed	1974	3.00	6.00	12.00
❑ Reprise FS 2207	Sinatra — The Main Event Live	1974	3.00	6.00	12.00
❑ Reprise 3FS 2300 [(3)]	Trilogy: Past, Present, Future	1980	5.00	10.00	20.00
❑ Reprise FS 2305	She Shot Me Down	1981	3.00	6.00	12.00
❑ Reprise F 6045 [M]	Sinatra Conducts Music from Pictures and Plays	1962	7.50	15.00	30.00
❑ Reprise R9 6045 [S]	Sinatra Conducts Music from Pictures and Plays	1962	10.00	2.00	40.00
❑ Reprise R 6167 [M]	Sinatra '65	1965	3.75	7.50	15.00
❑ Reprise RS 6167 [S]	Sinatra '65	1965	5.00	10.00	20.00
SINATRA, NANCY					
45s					
❑ Elektra 46659	Let's Keep It That Way/One Jump Ahead of the Storm	1979	—	2.50	5.00
❑ Private Stock 45,022	Annabel of Mobile/(B-side unknown)	1975	—	2.50	5.00
❑ Private Stock 45,075	Kinky Love/She Played the Piano and He Beat the Drum	1976	—	2.50	5.00
❑ Private Stock 45,108	Indian Summer/Holly and Hawkeye	1976	—	2.50	5.00
—With Lee Hazelwood					
❑ Private Stock 45,158	It's For My Dad/A Gentle Man Like You	1977	—	2.50	5.00
❑ RCA Victor 47-0864	It's the Love/Kind of a Woman	1973	2.00	4.00	8.00
❑ RCA Victor 74-0614	Paris Summer/Down from Dover	1971	2.00	4.00	8.00
—With Lee Hazlewood					
❑ RCA Victor APBO-0029	Ain't No Sunshine/Sugar Me	1973	—	2.50	5.00
❑ Reprise 0238	Tammy/Thanks to You	1963	5.00	10.00	20.00
❑ Reprise 0263	Where Do the Lonely Go/Just Think About the Good Times	1964	5.00	10.00	20.00
❑ Reprise 0292	This Love of Mine/There Goes the Bride	1964	5.00	10.00	20.00
❑ Reprise 0335	The Answer to Everything/True Love	1965	3.75	7.50	15.00
❑ Reprise 0407	So Long Babe/If He'd Love Me	1965	3.75	7.50	15.00
❑ Reprise 0432	These Boots Are Made for Walkin'/The City Never Sleeps at Night	1965	3.00	6.00	12.00
❑ Reprise 0461	How Does That Grab You, Darlin'?/The Last of the Secret Agents	1966	2.50	5.00	10.00
❑ Reprise 0491	Friday's Child/Hutchinson Jail	1966	2.50	5.00	10.00
❑ Reprise 0514	In Our Time/Leave My Dog Alone	1966	2.50	5.00	10.00
❑ Reprise 0527	Sugar Town/Summer Wine	1966	3.00	6.00	12.00
❑ Reprise 0559	Love Eyes/Coastin'	1967	2.50	5.00	10.00
❑ Reprise 0561	Somethin' Stupid/I Will Wait for You	1967	2.00	4.00	8.00
—A-side: Nancy Sinatra and Frank Sinatra; B-side: Frank Sinatra					
❑ Reprise 0561	Somethin' Stupid/Give Her Love	1967	2.50	5.00	10.00
—A-side: Nancy Sinatra and Frank Sinatra; B-side: Frank Sinatra					
❑ Reprise 0595	Jackson/You Only Live Twice	1967	2.50	5.00	10.00
—A-side: With Lee Hazlewood					
❑ Reprise 0620	Lightning's Girl/Until It's Time for You to Go	1967	2.50	5.00	10.00
❑ Reprise 0629	Lady Bird/Sand	1967	2.00	4.00	8.00
—With Lee Hazlewood					
❑ Reprise 0636	Tony Rome/This Town	1967	2.00	4.00	8.00
❑ Reprise 0651	Some Velvet Morning/Oh Lonesome Me	1967	2.00	4.00	8.00
—With Lee Hazlewood					
❑ Reprise 0670	100 Years/See the Little Children	1968	2.00	4.00	8.00
❑ Reprise 0701	These Boots Are Made for Walkin'/Love Eyes	1968	—	2.50	5.00
—"Back to Back Hits" series					
❑ Reprise 0721	Sugar Town/Summer Wine	1968	—	2.50	5.00
—"Back to Back Hits" series					
❑ Reprise 0726	Jackson/Summer Wine	1968	—	2.50	5.00
—With Lee Hazlewood; "Back to Back Hits" series					
❑ Reprise 0729	Lightning's Girl/One Velvet Morning	1968	—	2.50	5.00
—B-side with Lee Hazlewood; "Back to Back Hits" series					
❑ Reprise 0756	Happy/Nice 'N' Easy	1968	2.00	4.00	8.00
❑ Reprise 0789	Good Time Girl/Old Devil Moon	1968	2.00	4.00	8.00
❑ Reprise 0813	God Knows I Love You/Just Plain Old Me	1969	2.00	4.00	8.00
❑ Reprise 0821	Here We Go Again/Memories	1969	2.00	4.00	8.00
❑ Reprise 0851	Drummer Man/Home	1969	2.00	4.00	8.00
❑ Reprise 0869	Highway Song/(B-side unknown)	1969	5.00	10.00	20.00
—Released only in England					
❑ Reprise 0880	It's Such a Lonely Time of the Year/Kids	1969	2.50	5.00	10.00
❑ Reprise 0890	I Love Them All/Home	1970	2.00	4.00	8.00
❑ Reprise 0932	Hello L.A., Bye Bye Birmingham/White Tattoo	1970	2.00	4.00	8.00
❑ Reprise 0968	I'm Not a Girl Anymore/How Are Things in California	1970	2.00	4.00	8.00

Number	Title (A Side/B Side)	Yr	VG	VG+	NM
❑ Reprise 0980	Feelin' Kinda Sunday/Kids	1970	2.00	4.00	8.00
—A-side by Nancy Sinatra and Frank Sinatra					
❑ Reprise 0991	Is Anybody Goin' to San Antone/Hook and Ladder	1971	2.00	4.00	8.00
❑ Reprise 1011	Life's a Trippy Thing/I'm Not Afraid	1971	2.00	4.00	8.00
—A-side by Nancy Sinatra and Frank Sinatra; B-side by Frank Sinatra solo					
❑ Reprise 1021	Did You Ever/Back on the Road	1971	2.00	4.00	8.00
—As "Nancy and Lee" (Hazlewood)					
❑ Reprise 1034	Glory Road/Is Anybody Goin' to San Antone	1971	2.00	4.00	8.00
❑ Reprise 20017	Not Just Your Friend/Cuff Links and a Tie Clip	1961	5.00	10.00	20.00
❑ Reprise 20045	To Know Him Is to Love Him/Like I Do	1962	5.00	10.00	20.00
❑ Reprise 20097	June, July and August/Think of Me	1962	5.00	10.00	20.00
❑ Reprise 20127	Tonight You Belong to Me/You Can Have Any Boy	1962	5.00	10.00	20.00
❑ Reprise 20144	Put Your Head on My Shoulder/I See the Moon	1963	5.00	10.00	20.00
❑ Reprise 20188	The Cruel War/One Way	1963	5.00	10.00	20.00
Albums					
❑ RCA Victor LSP-4645	Nancy and Lee Again	1972	7.50	15.00	30.00
—With Lee Hazlewood					
❑ RCA Victor LSP-4774	Woman	1973	6.25	12.50	25.00
❑ RCA Victor VPS-6078 [(2)]	This Is Nancy Sinatra	1972	12.50	25.00	50.00
❑ Reprise R-6202 [M]	Boots	1966	6.25	12.50	25.00
❑ Reprise RS-6202 [S]	Boots	1966	7.50	15.00	30.00
❑ Reprise R-6207 [M]	How Does That Grab You?	1966	5.00	10.00	20.00
❑ Reprise RS-6207 [S]	How Does That Grab You?	1966	6.25	12.50	25.00
❑ Reprise R-6221 [M]	Nancy in London	1966	5.00	10.00	20.00
❑ Reprise RS-6221 [S]	Nancy in London	1966	6.25	12.50	25.00
❑ Reprise R-6239 [M]	Sugar	1967	6.25	12.50	25.00
❑ Reprise RS-6239 [S]	Sugar	1967	5.00	10.00	20.00
❑ Reprise R-6251 [M]	Country, My Way	1967	6.25	12.50	25.00
❑ Reprise RS-6251 [S]	Country, My Way	1967	5.00	10.00	20.00
❑ Reprise RS-6273	Nancy and Lee	1968	5.00	10.00	20.00
—With Lee Hazlewood					
❑ Reprise R-6277 [M]	Movin' with Nancy	1967	6.25	12.50	25.00
❑ Reprise RS-6277 [S]	Movin' with Nancy	1967	5.00	10.00	20.00
❑ Reprise RS-6333	Nancy	1969	5.00	10.00	20.00
❑ Reprise RS-6409	Nancy's Greatest Hits	1970	5.00	10.00	20.00
❑ Rhino R1-70166	Fairy Tales and Fantasies: The Best of Nancy and Lee	1989	2.50	5.00	10.00
—With Lee Hazlewood					
❑ Rhino RNLP-70227	Boots: Nancy Sinatra's All-Time Hits (1966-1970)	1987	2.50	5.00	10.00

SIR DOUGLAS QUINTET

Number	Title (A Side/B Side)	Yr	VG	VG+	NM
45s					
❑ Atlantic 2965	The Nitty Gritty/I'm Just Tired of Getting Burned	1973	2.00	4.00	8.00
❑ Atlantic 2985	Texas Tornado/Blue Horizon	1973	2.00	4.00	8.00
—As "Sir Douglas Band"					
❑ Casablanca 828	Roll With the Punches/I'm Not That Kat Anymore	1975	6.25	12.50	25.00
❑ Mercury 73257	Michoacan/Westside Blues Again	1971	—	3.00	6.00
❑ Pacemaker 280	Sugar Bee/Blue Norther	1964	5.00	10.00	20.00
❑ Philips 40676	What About Tomorrow/A Nice Song	1970	2.00	4.00	8.00
❑ Philips 40687	Pretty Flower/Catch the Man on the Fly	1970	2.00	4.00	8.00
❑ Philips 40708	Wasted Days, Wasted Nights/Me and My Destiny	1971	2.00	4.00	8.00
❑ Smash 2169	Are Inlaws Really Outlaws/Sell a Song	1968	2.00	4.00	8.00
❑ Smash 2191	Mendocino/I Wanna Be Your Mama Again	1968	2.00	4.00	8.00
❑ Smash 2222	Lawd, I'm Just a Country Boy in This Great Big Freaky City/It Didn't Even Bring Me Down	1969	2.00	4.00	8.00
❑ Smash 2233	Dynamite Woman/Too Many Dociled Minds	1969	2.00	4.00	8.00
❑ Smash 2253	At the Crossroads/Texas Me	1969	2.00	4.00	8.00
❑ Smash 2259	Nuevo Laredo/I Don't Wanna Go Home	1970	2.00	4.00	8.00
❑ Tribe 8308	She's About a Mover/We'll Take Our Last Walk Tonight	1965	3.00	6.00	12.00
—Gray label with Indian head					
❑ Tribe 8308	She's About a Mover/We'll Take Our Last Walk Tonight	1965	3.75	7.50	15.00
—White label (not marked as a promo)					
❑ Tribe 8310	The Tracker/Blue Brother	1965	2.50	5.00	10.00
—Gray label with Indian head					
❑ Tribe 8310	The Tracker/Blue Brother	1965	3.00	6.00	12.00
—White label (not marked as a promo)					
❑ Tribe 8312	In Time/The Story of John Hardy	1965	2.50	5.00	10.00
❑ Tribe 8314	The Rains Came/Bacon Fat	1966	2.50	5.00	10.00
❑ Tribe 8317	She's Gotta Be Boss/Quarter to Three	1966	2.50	5.00	10.00
❑ Tribe 8318	Beginning of the End/Love Don't Treat Me Fair	1966	2.50	5.00	10.00
❑ Tribe 8321	She Digs My Love/When I Sing the Blues	1966	2.50	5.00	10.00
❑ Tribe 8323	Hang Loose/I'm Sorry	1967	2.50	5.00	10.00
Albums					
❑ ABC Dot DO-2057	Texas Rock for Country Rollers	1976	3.75	7.50	15.00
—As "Sir Doug and the Texas Tornadoes"					
❑ Atlantic SD 7287	Texas Tornado	1974	3.75	7.50	15.00
—As "Sir Douglas Band"					
❑ Philips PHS 600344	1 + 1 + 1 = 4	1970	6.25	12.50	25.00
❑ Philips PHS 600353	The Return of Doug Saldana	1971	6.25	12.50	25.00
❑ R&M UDL-2343	The Tracker	1981	5.00	10.00	20.00
❑ Smash SRS-67108	Sir Douglas Quintet + 2 = Honkey Blues	1968	7.50	15.00	30.00
❑ Smash SRS-67115	Mendocino	1969	6.25	12.50	25.00
❑ Smash SRS-67130	Together After Five	1970	6.25	12.50	25.00
❑ Takoma TAK-7086	The Best of the Sir Douglas Quintet	1980	3.00	6.00	12.00
❑ Takoma TAK-7088	Border Wave	1981	3.00	6.00	12.00
❑ Takoma TAK-7095	Sir Douglas Quintet Live	1985	3.00	6.00	12.00
❑ Tribe TR 37001 [M]	The Best of the Sir Douglas Quintet	1966	17.50	35.00	70.00
❑ Tribe TRS 47001 [R]	The Best of the Sir Douglas Quintet	1966	12.50	25.00	50.00

Number	Title (A Side/B Side)	Yr	VG	VG+	NM
❑ Varrick 004	Quintessence	1983	3.00	6.00	12.00

SISTER SLEDGE

45s

Number	Title (A Side/B Side)	Yr	VG	VG+	NM
❑ Atco 6924	The Weatherman/Have You Met My Friend	1973	10.00	20.00	40.00
❑ Atco 6940	Mama Never Told Me/Neither One of Us (Wants to Be the First to Say Goodbye)	1973	15.00	30.00	60.00
❑ Atco 7008	Love Don't You Go Through No Changes on Me/Don't You Miss Him	1974	3.00	6.00	12.00
❑ Atco 7020	Circle of Love (Caught in the Middle)/Cross My Heart	1975	3.00	6.00	12.00
❑ Atco 7035	Love Has Found Me/Love Ain't Easy	1975	3.00	6.00	12.00
❑ Atlantic 7-89357	Here to Stay/Make a Wish	1986	—	2.00	4.00
—B-side by Joe Cruz					
❑ Atlantic 7-89466	You're Fine/(B-side unknown)	1985	—	3.00	6.00
❑ Atlantic 7-89520	Dancing on the Jagged Edge/You Need Me	1985	—	2.00	4.00
❑ Atlantic 7-89547	Frankie/Peer Pressure	1985	—	2.00	4.00
❑ Cotillion 44202	Thank You for Today/Have Love Will Travel	1976	—	2.50	5.00
❑ Cotillion 44208	Cream of the Crop/Love Ain't Easy	1976	2.00	4.00	8.00
❑ Cotillion 44220	Blockbuster Boy/Moondancer	1977	—	3.00	6.00
❑ Cotillion 44226	Baby, It's the Rain/Hold Onto This Feeling	1977	—	3.00	6.00
❑ Cotillion 44234	I've Seen Better Days/Do It to the Max	1978	—	3.00	6.00
❑ Cotillion 44245	He's the Greatest Dancer/Somebody Loves Me	1978	—	2.50	5.00
❑ Cotillion 44251	We Are Family/Easier to Love	1979	—	2.50	5.00
❑ Cotillion 45001	Lost in Music/Thinking of You	1979	—	2.50	5.00
❑ Cotillion 45007	Got to Love Somebody/Good Girl Now	1979	—	2.50	5.00
❑ Cotillion 45013	Reach Your Peak/You Fooled Around	1980	—	2.50	5.00
❑ Cotillion 45020	Let's Go on Vacation/Easy Street	1980	—	2.50	5.00
❑ Cotillion 46007	All American Girls/Happy Feeling	1981	—	2.50	5.00
❑ Cotillion 46012	Next Time You'll Know/If You Really Want Me	1981	—	2.50	5.00
❑ Cotillion 46017	He's Just a Runaway (A Tribute to Bob Marley)/(Long Version)	1981	—	2.50	5.00
❑ Cotillion 47000	My Guy/Il Macquillage Lady	1982	—	3.50	7.00
❑ Cotillion 47007	All the Man That I Need/Light Footin'	1982	—	2.50	5.00
❑ Cotillion 7-99834	Gotta Get Back to Love/Lifetime Lover	1983	—	2.50	5.00
❑ Cotillion 7-99885	B.Y.O.B. (Bring Your Own Baby)/(B-side unknown)	1983	—	2.50	5.00

Albums

Number	Title (A Side/B Side)	Yr	VG	VG+	NM
❑ Atco SD 36-105	Circle of Love	1975	5.00	10.00	20.00
❑ Atlantic 81255	When the Boys Meet the Girls	1985	2.50	5.00	10.00
❑ Cotillion SD 5209	We Are Family	1979	2.50	5.00	10.00
❑ Cotillion SD 5231	The Sisters	1982	2.50	5.00	10.00
❑ Cotillion SD 9919	Together	1976	5.00	10.00	20.00
❑ Cotillion SD 16012	Love Somebody Today	1980	2.50	5.00	10.00
❑ Cotillion SD 16027	All American Girls	1981	2.50	5.00	10.00
❑ Cotillion 90069	Bet Cha Say That to All the Girls	1983	2.50	5.00	10.00

SKYLINERS, THE

45s

Number	Title (A Side/B Side)	Yr	VG	VG+	NM
❑ Atco 6270	Since I Fell for You/I'd Die	1963	10.00	20.00	40.00
❑ Calico 103/4	Since I Don't Have You/One Night, One Night	1959	12.50	25.00	50.00
❑ Calico 106	This I Swear/Tomorrow	1959	7.50	15.00	30.00
❑ Calico 109	It Happened Today/Lonely Way	1959	7.50	15.00	30.00
❑ Calico 114	How Much/Lorraine from Spain	1960	6.25	12.50	25.00
❑ Calico 117	Pennies from Heaven/I'll Be Seeing You	1960	6.25	12.50	25.00
❑ Calico 120	Believe Me/Happy Time	1960	6.25	12.50	25.00
❑ Cameo 215	Three Coins in the Fountain/Everyone But You	1962	10.00	20.00	40.00
❑ Capitol 3979	Where Have They Gone/I Could Have Loved You So Well	1974	6.25	12.50	25.00
—As "Jimmy Beaumont and the Skyliners"					
❑ Classic Artists 123	You're My Christmas Present/Another Lonely New Year's Eve	1990	—	2.50	5.00
❑ Colpix 188	I'll Close My Eyes/The Door Is Still Open	1961	10.00	20.00	40.00
❑ Colpix 607	Ba'ion Rhythms/The End of a Story	196?	10.00	20.00	40.00
—As "Jimmy Beaumont and the Skyliners"					
❑ Colpix 613	Close Your Eyes/Our Love Will Last	1961	10.00	20.00	40.00
❑ Drive 6250	Our Day Is Here/The Day the Clown Cried	1976	2.00	4.00	8.00
❑ Jubilee 5506	The Loser/Everything Is Fine	1965	3.75	7.50	15.00
❑ Jubilee 5512	Who Do You Love/Get Yourself a Baby	1965	3.75	7.50	15.00
❑ Jubilee 5520	I Run to You/Don't Hurt Me Baby	1965	3.75	7.50	15.00
❑ Original Sound 35	Since I Don't Have You/One Night, One Night	1963	3.75	7.50	15.00
❑ Original Sound 36	Pennies from Heaven/I'll Be Seeing You	1963	3.75	7.50	15.00
❑ Original Sound 37	This I Swear/It Happened Today	1963	3.75	7.50	15.00

Number	Title (A Side/B Side)	Yr	VG	VG+	NM
❑ Tortoise Int'l. PB-11243	Oh How Happy/We've Got Love on Our Side	1978	2.00	4.00	8.00
❑ Tortoise Int'l. PB-11312	Smile On Me/Love Bug (Done Bit Me Again)	1978	2.00	4.00	8.00
❑ Viscount 104	Comes Love/Tell Me	1962	5.00	10.00	20.00
Albums					
❑ Calico LP-3000 [M]	The Skyliners	1959	200.00	400.00	600.00
—Yellow and blue label					
❑ Calico LP-3000 [M]	The Skyliners	196?	50.00	100.00	200.00
—Blue label					
❑ Kama Sutra KSBS-2026	Once Upon a Time	1971	6.25	12.50	25.00
❑ Original Sound OS-5010 [M]	Since I Don't Have You	1963	12.50	25.00	50.00
❑ Original Sound OSS-8873 [S]	Since I Don't Have You	1963	17.50	35.00	70.00
❑ Original Sound OSS-8873 [S]	Since I Don't Have You	197?	3.75	7.50	15.00
—Reissue on thinner vinyl					

SLEDGE, PERCY

45s

Number	Title (A Side/B Side)	Yr	VG	VG+	NM
❑ Atlantic 2326	When a Man Loves a Woman/Love Me Like You Mean It	1966	3.75	7.50	15.00
❑ Atlantic 2342	Warm and Tender Love/Sugar Puddin'	1966	3.00	6.00	12.00
❑ Atlantic 2358	It Tears Me Up/Heart of a Child	1966	2.50	5.00	10.00
❑ Atlantic 2383	Baby, Help Me/You Got That Something Wonderful	1967	5.00	10.00	20.00
❑ Atlantic 2396	Out of Left Field/It Can't Be Stopped	1967	3.00	6.00	12.00
❑ Atlantic 2414	Love Me Tender/What Am I Living For	1967	3.00	6.00	12.00
❑ Atlantic 2434	Just Out of Reach (Of My Two Empty Arms)/Hard to Believe	1967	3.00	6.00	12.00
❑ Atlantic 2453	Cover Me/Behind Every Great Man There Is a Woman	1967	3.00	6.00	12.00
❑ Atlantic 2490	Take Time to Know Her/It's All Wrong But It's Alright	1968	3.00	6.00	12.00
❑ Atlantic 2539	Sudden Stop/Between These Arms	1968	3.75	7.50	15.00
❑ Atlantic 2563	You're All Around Me/Self-Preservation	1968	2.50	5.00	10.00
❑ Atlantic 2594	My Special Prayer/Bless Your Little Sweet Soul	1969	3.00	6.00	12.00
❑ Atlantic 2616	Any Day Now/The Angels Listened In	1969	6.25	12.50	25.00
❑ Atlantic 2646	Woman of the Night/Kind Woman	1969	3.00	6.00	12.00
❑ Atlantic 2679	Faithful and True/True Love Travels on a Gravel Road	1969	3.75	7.50	15.00
❑ Atlantic 2719	Too Many Rivers to Cross/Push Mr. Pride Aside	1970	3.00	6.00	12.00
❑ Atlantic 2754	Help Me Make It Through the Night/Thief in the Night	1970	2.00	4.00	8.00
❑ Atlantic 2826	Stop the World Tonight/That's the Way I Want to Live My Life	1971	2.00	4.00	8.00
❑ Atlantic 2848	Rainbow Road/Standing on the Mountain	1971	3.00	6.00	12.00
❑ Atlantic 2886	Sunday Brother/Everything You'll Ever Need	1972	2.00	4.00	8.00
❑ Atlantic 2963	Sunshine/Unchanging Love	1973	2.50	5.00	10.00
❑ Atlantic 7-88802	When a Man Loves a Woman/Twentieth Century Fox	1989	2.50	5.00	10.00
—B-side by the Escape Club					
❑ Atlantic 7-89262	When a Man Loves a Woman/Cover Me	1987	—	—	3.00
❑ Atlantic Oldies Series OS 13021	When a Man Loves a Woman/Cover Me	197?	—	2.50	5.00
—Gold label					
❑ Atlantic Oldies Series OS 13021	When a Man Loves a Woman/Cover Me	198?	—	—	3.00
—Silver, black and red label					
❑ Atlantic Oldies Series OS 13022	Take Time to Know Her/Warm and Tender Love	197?	—	2.50	5.00
—Gold label					
❑ Atlantic Oldies Series OS 13022	Take Time to Know Her/Warm and Tender Love	198?	—	—	3.00
—Silver, black and red label					
❑ Capricorn 0209	I'll Be Your Everything/Blue Water	1974	2.00	4.00	8.00
❑ Capricorn 0220	If This Is the Last Time/Behind Closed Doors	1975	2.50	5.00	10.00
❑ Capricorn 0273	When She's Touching Me/When a Boy Becomes a Man	1977	2.00	4.00	8.00
❑ Eric 4014	When a Man Loves a Woman/Goodnight My Love	197?	—	2.00	4.00
—Reissue; B-side by Jesse Belvin					
❑ Monument WS4 03612	You Had to Be There/Hard Lovin' Woman	1983	2.50	5.00	10.00
❑ Monument WS4 03878	She's Too Pretty to Cry/Home Type Thing	1983	2.50	5.00	10.00
❑ Philco-Ford HP-12	When a Man Loves a Woman/Baby Help Me	1967	6.25	12.50	25.00
—4-inch plastic "Hip Pocket Record" with color sleeve					
❑ Trip 129	When a Man Loves a Woman/Any Day Now	197?	—	2.50	5.00
—Reissue; B-side by Chuck Jackson					
Albums					
❑ Atlantic 8125 [M]	When a Man Loves a Woman	1966	12.50	25.00	50.00
❑ Atlantic SD 8125 [R]	When a Man Loves a Woman	1966	7.50	15.00	30.00
❑ Atlantic 8132 [M]	Warm and Tender Soul	1966	12.50	25.00	50.00
❑ Atlantic SD 8132 [R]	Warm and Tender Soul	1966	7.50	15.00	30.00
❑ Atlantic 8146 [M]	The Percy Sledge Way	1967	12.50	25.00	50.00
❑ Atlantic SD 8146 [S]	The Percy Sledge Way	1967	12.50	25.00	50.00
❑ Atlantic SD 8180	Take Time to Know Her	1968	12.50	25.00	50.00
❑ Atlantic SD 8210	The Best of Percy Sledge	1969	6.25	12.50	25.00
❑ Atlantic 80212	The Ultimate Collection: When a Man Loves a Woman	1983	3.00	6.00	12.00
❑ Capricorn CP 0147	I'll Be Your Everything	1974	3.75	7.50	15.00
❑ Monument FW 38532	Percy!	1983	3.00	6.00	12.00

SLY AND THE FAMILY STONE

45s

Number	Title (A Side/B Side)	Yr	VG	VG+	NM
❑ Epic 10229	Higher/Underdog	1967	2.50	5.00	10.00
❑ Epic 10256	Dance to the Music/Let Me Hear It from You	1967	2.50	5.00	10.00
❑ Epic 10353	Life/M'Lady	1968	2.00	4.00	8.00
❑ Epic 10407	Everyday People/Sing a Simple Song	1968	2.50	5.00	10.00
❑ Epic 10450	Stand!/I Want to Take You Higher	1969	2.50	5.00	10.00
❑ Epic 10497	Hot Fun in the Summertime/Fun	1969	2.50	5.00	10.00
❑ Epic 10555	Thank You Falettinme Be Mice Elf Agin/Everybody Is a Star	1969	—	3.00	6.00
❑ Epic 10805	Family Affair/Luv N' Haight	1971	—	3.00	6.00
❑ Epic 10829	Runnin' Away/Brave & Strong	1972	—	3.00	6.00
❑ Epic 10850	Smilin'/Luv N' Haight	1972	—	3.00	6.00
❑ Epic 11017	If You Want Me to Stay/Babies Makin' Babies	1973	—	3.00	6.00

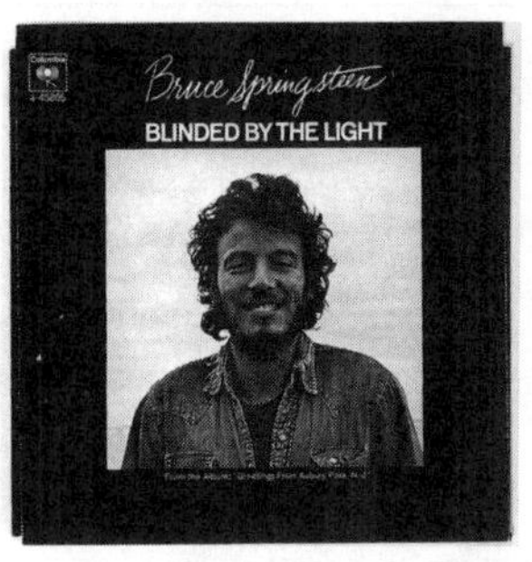

Number	Title (A Side/B Side)	Yr	VG	VG+	NM
❑ Epic 11017	If You Want Me to Stay/Thankful N' Thoughtful	1973	—	3.00	6.00
❑ Epic 11060	Frisky/If It Were Left Up to Me	1973	—	3.00	6.00
❑ Epic 11140	Time for Livin'/Small Talk	1974	—	3.00	6.00
❑ Epic 8-50033	Loose Booty/Can't Strain My Brain	1974	—	3.00	6.00
❑ Epic 50119	Hot Fun in the Summertime/Fun	1975	2.00	4.00	8.00
❑ Epic 50135	I Get High on You/That's Lovin' You	1975	—	2.50	5.00
❑ Epic 50175	Li Lo Li/Who Do You Love	1975	—	2.50	5.00
❑ Epic 50201	Greed/Crossword Puzzle	1976	—	2.50	5.00
❑ Epic 50331	Family Again/Nothing Less Than Happiness	1977	—	2.50	5.00
❑ Loadstone 3951	I Ain't Got Nobody/I Can't Turn You Loose	1967	5.00	10.00	20.00
❑ Warner Bros. 29682	High Y'All/Ha Ha He He	1983	—	2.00	4.00
❑ Warner Bros. 49062	Sheer Energy/Remember Who You Are	1979	—	2.00	4.00
❑ Warner Bros. 49132	Who's to Say/Same Thing	1979	—	2.00	4.00
Albums					
❑ Epic LN 24324 [M]	A Whole New Thing	1967	5.00	10.00	20.00
❑ Epic LN 24371 [M]	Dance to the Music	1968	10.00	20.00	40.00
❑ Epic BN 26324 [S]	A Whole New Thing	1967	5.00	10.00	20.00
❑ Epic BN 26371 [S]	Dance to the Music	1968	3.75	7.50	15.00
❑ Epic BN 26397	Life	1968	3.75	7.50	15.00
❑ Epic BN 26456	Stand!	1969	3.75	7.50	15.00
❑ Epic KE 30325	Sly and the Family Stone's Greatest Hits	1970	3.00	6.00	12.00
—Yellow label, gatefold cover					
❑ Epic E 30333	Life	1971	3.00	6.00	12.00
—Reissue of 26397					
❑ Epic E 30334	Dance to the Music	1971	3.00	6.00	12.00
—Reissue of 26371					
❑ Epic E 30335	A Whole New Thing	1971	3.00	6.00	12.00
—Reissue of 26324					
❑ Epic KE 30986	There's a Riot Goin' On	1971	3.00	6.00	12.00
—Yellow label, gatefold cover					
❑ Epic KE 32134	Fresh	1973	2.50	5.00	10.00
—Orange label					
❑ Epic PE 32930	Small Talk	1974	2.50	5.00	10.00
—Orange label					
❑ Epic PE 33835	High on You	1975	2.50	5.00	10.00
—Orange label					
❑ Epic PE 34348	Heard Ya Missed Me, Well I'm Back	1976	2.50	5.00	10.00
—Orange label					
❑ Epic JE 35974	Ten Years Too Soon	1979	2.50	5.00	10.00
❑ Epic E2 37071 [(2)]	Anthology	1981	3.75	7.50	15.00
❑ Warner Bros. BSK 3303	Back on the Right Track	1979	2.50	5.00	10.00
❑ Warner Bros. 23700	Ain't But the Right Way	1983	2.50	5.00	10.00

SMALL FACES

45s

Number	Title (A Side/B Side)	Yr	VG	VG+	NM
❑ Immediate 501	Itchykoo Park/I'm Only Dreaming	1967	3.00	6.00	12.00
❑ Immediate 1902	Here Come the Nice/Talk to You	1967	2.50	5.00	10.00
❑ Immediate 5003	Tin Soldier/I Feel Much Better	1968	2.50	5.00	10.00
❑ Immediate 5007	Lazy Sunday/Rollin' Over	1968	2.50	5.00	10.00
❑ Immediate 5009	The Universal/Donkey Rides A Penny A Glass	1968	3.75	7.50	15.00
❑ Immediate 5012	Mad John/The Journey	1969	3.75	7.50	15.00
❑ Immediate 5014	Afterglow of Your Love/Wham, Bam, Thank You Ma'am	1969	3.75	7.50	15.00
❑ Press 5007	Almost Grown/Hey Girl	1969	5.00	10.00	20.00
❑ Press 9794	What 'Cha Gonna Do About It/What's a Matter	1965	6.25	12.50	25.00
❑ Press 9826	Sha-La-La-La-Lee/Grow Your Own	1966	3.75	7.50	15.00
❑ Pride 1006	Runaway/Shake	1972	3.00	6.00	12.00
❑ RCA Victor 47-8949	Understanding/All or Nothing	1966	5.00	10.00	20.00
❑ RCA Victor 47-9055	My Mind's Eye/I Can't Dance with You	1966	5.00	10.00	20.00
Albums					
❑ Accord AN-7157	By Appointment	1982	2.50	5.00	10.00
❑ Atlantic SD 19113	Playmates	1977	2.50	5.00	10.00
❑ Atlantic SD 19171	78 in the Shade	1978	2.50	5.00	10.00
❑ Compleat 67-2004 [(2)]	Big Music	1985	3.00	6.00	12.00
❑ Compleat 67-5003	Ogden's Nut Gone Flake	1985	2.50	5.00	10.00
—Reissue					
❑ Immediate 4225	Ogden's Nut Gone Flake	1973	3.75	7.50	15.00
—Reissue has a standard square cover					

Number	Title (A Side/B Side)	Yr	VG	VG+	NM
❑ Immediate Z12 52002 [S]	There Are But Four Small Faces	1967	12.50	25.00	50.00
—Color cover (counterfeits have either black and white or black and green covers)					
❑ Immediate Z12 52008 [S]	Ogden's Nut Gone Flake	1968	12.50	25.00	50.00
—Originals have a round cover					
❑ MGM M3F-4955	Archetypes	1974	3.00	6.00	12.00
❑ Pride PRD 0001 [R]	Early Faces	1972	3.75	7.50	15.00
❑ Pride PRD 0014 [P]	The History of the Small Faces	1973	3.00	6.00	12.00
❑ Sire SASH-3709 [(2)]	The Vintage Years	1976	3.75	7.50	15.00

SMITH

45s

Number	Title (A Side/B Side)	Yr	VG	VG+	NM
❑ ABC Dunhill 4206	Baby It's You/I Don't Believe (I Believe)	1969	2.00	4.00	8.00
❑ ABC Dunhill 4228	Take a Look Around/Mojalesky Ridge	1970	—	3.00	6.00
❑ ABC Dunhill 4238	What Am I Gonna Do/Born in Boston	1970	—	3.00	6.00
❑ ABC Dunhill 4246	Comin' Back to Me (Ooh Baby)/Minus-Plus	1970	—	3.00	6.00

Albums

Number	Title (A Side/B Side)	Yr	VG	VG+	NM
❑ ABC Dunhill DS-50056	A Group Called Smith	1969	3.75	7.50	15.00
❑ ABC Dunhill DS-50081	Minus-Plus	1970	3.75	7.50	15.00

SMITH, HUEY "PIANO"

45s

Number	Title (A Side/B Side)	Yr	VG	VG+	NM
❑ Ace 521	Everybody's Wailin'/Little Liza Jane	1956	6.25	12.50	25.00
❑ Ace 530	Rockin' Pneumonia and the Boogie Woogie Flu (Part 1/Part 2)	1957	7.50	15.00	30.00
❑ Ace 538	Free, Single and Disengaged/Just a Lonely Clown	1957	6.25	12.50	25.00
❑ Ace 545	Don't You Just Know It/High Blood Pressure	1958	6.25	12.50	25.00
❑ Ace 548	Havin' a Good Time/We Like Birdland	1958	6.25	12.50	25.00
❑ Ace 553	Don't You Know Yockomo/Well, I'll Be John Brown	1958	6.25	12.50	25.00
❑ Ace 562	Would You Believe It (I Have a Cold)/Genevieve	1959	5.00	10.00	20.00
❑ Ace 571	Tu-Ber-Cu-Lucas and the Sinus Blues/Dearest Darling	1959	5.00	10.00	20.00
❑ Ace 584	Beatnik Blues/For Cryin' Out Loud	1960	3.75	7.50	15.00
❑ Ace 638	She Got Low Down/Mean, Mean, Mean	1961	3.75	7.50	15.00
❑ Ace 639	She Got Low Down/Mean, Mean, Mean//Little Liza Jane/ Rockin' Pnuemonia	1961	6.25	12.50	25.00
❑ Ace 649	Pop-Eye/Scald Dog	1962	3.75	7.50	15.00
❑ Ace 672	Every Once in a While/Somebody Told It	1962	3.00	6.00	12.00
❑ Ace 8002	Talk to Me Baby/If It Ain't One Thing, It's Another	1962	3.00	6.00	12.00
❑ Ace 8008	Let's Bring 'Em Back Again/Quiet as It's Kept	1963	3.75	7.50	15.00
❑ Constellation 102	He's Back Again/Quiet As It's Kept	1963	2.50	5.00	10.00
❑ Cotillion 44142	Rockin' Pneumonia and the Boogie Woogie Flu (Part 1/Part 2)	1971	—	3.00	6.00
❑ Imperial 5721	The Little Moron/Someone to Love	1961	3.00	6.00	12.00
❑ Imperial 5747	Behind the Wheel — Part 1/Behind the Wheel — Part 2	1961	3.00	6.00	12.00
❑ Imperial 5772	More Girls/Sassy Sara	1961	3.00	6.00	12.00
❑ Imperial 5789	Don't Knock It/Shag-a-Tooth	1961	3.00	6.00	12.00
❑ Instant 3287	I'll Never Forget/Bury Me Dead	1967	2.00	4.00	8.00
❑ Instant 3297	Two Way Pockaway (Part 1)/Two Way Pockaway (Part 2)	1969	2.00	4.00	8.00
❑ Instant 3301	Epitaph of Uncle Tom/Eight Bars of Amen	1969	2.00	4.00	8.00
❑ Instant 3303	You Got Too (Part 1)/You Got Too (Part 2)	1969	2.00	4.00	8.00
❑ Instant 3305	Ballad of a Black Man/The Whatcha Call 'Em	1970	2.00	4.00	8.00
❑ Savoy 1113	You Made Me Cry/You're Down with Me	1953	25.00	50.00	100.00
❑ Vin 1024	I Didn't Do It/They Kept On	1960	3.75	7.50	15.00

Albums

Number	Title (A Side/B Side)	Yr	VG	VG+	NM
❑ Ace LP-1004 [M]	Having a Good Time	1959	100.00	200.00	400.00
❑ Ace LP-1015 [M]	For Dancing	1961	62.50	125.00	250.00
❑ Ace LP-1027 [M]	'Twas the Night Before Christmas	1962	62.50	125.00	250.00
❑ Ace LP-1027 [M]	'Twas the Night Before Christmas	198?	3.75	7.50	15.00
—Reissue with "Dr. John Band" credited on front cover and label					
❑ Ace LP-2021	Rock 'N' Roll Revival	197?	7.50	15.00	30.00
❑ Ace 2038	Good Old Rock & Roll	198?	3.75	7.50	15.00
❑ Grand Prix K-418 [M]	Huey "Piano" Smith	196?	5.00	10.00	20.00
❑ Grand Prix KS-418 [R]	Huey "Piano" Smith	196?	3.00	6.00	12.00
❑ Rhino RNLP-70222	Serious Clownin': The History of Huey "Piano" Smith and the Clowns	1986	3.00	6.00	12.00

SMITH, HURRICANE

45s

Number	Title (A Side/B Side)	Yr	VG	VG+	NM
❑ Capitol 3148	Don't Let It Die/The Writer Sings His Song	1971	—	2.50	5.00
❑ Capitol 3383	Oh Babe, What Would You Say?/Getting to Know You	1972	—	2.00	4.00
—Orange label with "Capitol" at bottom					
❑ Capitol 3455	Who Was It?/Take Suki Home	1972	—	2.00	4.00
❑ EMI 3809	Beautiful Day-Beautiful Night/Sam	1973	—	2.00	4.00

Albums

Number	Title (A Side/B Side)	Yr	VG	VG+	NM
❑ Capitol ST-11139	Hurricane Smith	1972	2.50	5.00	10.00

SMITH, PATTI, GROUP

45s

Number	Title (A Side/B Side)	Yr	VG	VG+	NM
❑ Arista 0171	Gloria/My Generation	1976	2.50	5.00	10.00
❑ Arista 0318	Because the Night/God Speed	1978	—	2.00	4.00
—A-side co-written by Bruce Springsteen					
❑ Arista 0427	Frederick/Frederick (Live)	1979	—	2.00	4.00
❑ Arista 0453	So You Want to Be a Rock and Roll Star//5-4-3-2-1/A Fire of Unknown Origin	1979	—	2.00	4.00
❑ Arista 9173	Because the Night/So You Want to Be a Rock 'n' Roll Star	198?	—	—	3.00
—"Flashback" reissue					
❑ Arista 9689	People Have the Power/Wild Leaves	1988	—	—	3.00
❑ Arista 9762	I Was (Looking for You)/Up There Down There	1988	—	—	3.00
❑ Mer 601	Hey Joe/Piss Factory	1974	20.00	40.00	80.00
❑ Sire 1009	Hey Joe/Piss Factory	1977	2.00	4.00	8.00

Albums

Number	Title (A Side/B Side)	Yr	VG	VG+	NM
❑ Arista AL 4066	Horses	1975	3.75	7.50	15.00
—With the word "Horses" in black letters on the front cover					

Number	Title (A Side/B Side)	Yr	VG	VG+	NM
❑ Arista AL 4097	Radio Ethiopia	1977	3.00	6.00	12.00
❑ Arista AB 4171	Easter	1978	3.00	6.00	12.00
❑ Arista AB 4221	Wave	1979	2.50	5.00	10.00
❑ Arista ALB6-8349	Easter	198?	2.00	4.00	8.00
—Reissue					
❑ Arista ALB6-8362	Horses	198?	2.00	4.00	8.00
—Reissue					
❑ Arista ALB6-8379	Radio Ethiopia	198?	2.00	4.00	8.00
—Reissue					
❑ Arista AL 8453	Dreams of Life	1988	2.50	5.00	10.00
❑ Arista AL 8546	Wave	1990	2.00	4.00	8.00
—Reissue					
❑ Arista R 100469	Dreams of Life	1988	3.00	6.00	12.00
—BMG Music Service edition					
❑ Columbia C2 90330 [(2)]	Trampin'	2004	3.75	7.50	15.00

SNOW, PHOEBE

45s

Number	Title (A Side/B Side)	Yr	VG	VG+	NM
❑ Columbia 10315	Two Fisted Love/Inspired Insanity	1976	—	2.50	5.00
❑ Columbia 10351	All Over/No Regrets	1976	—	2.50	5.00
❑ Columbia 10463	Shakey Ground/Don't Sleep with Your Eyes Closed	1976	—	2.50	5.00
❑ Columbia 10504	Teach Me Tonight/Autobiography (Shine, Shine, Shine)	1977	—	2.50	5.00
❑ Columbia 10626	Never Letting Go/The Middle of the Night	1977	—	2.50	5.00
❑ Columbia 10654	Love Makes a Woman/Electra	1977	—	2.50	5.00
❑ Columbia 10856	Every Night/Random Time	1978	—	2.50	5.00
❑ Elektra 69290	Something Real/Best of My Love	1989	—	—	3.00
❑ Elektra 69305	If I Can Just Get Through the Night/Soothin'	1989	—	—	3.00
❑ Mirage 3800	Games/Down in the Basement	1981	—	2.00	4.00
❑ Mirage 3818	Mercy, Mercy, Mercy/Something Good	1981	—	2.00	4.00
❑ Mirage 3843	Rock Away/Baby Please	1981	—	2.00	4.00
❑ Shelter 40278	Harpo's Blues/Let the Good Times Roll	1974	—	2.50	5.00
❑ Shelter 40353	Poetry Man/Either or Both	1974	—	3.00	6.00
❑ Shelter 40400	Easy Street/Harpo's Blues	1975	—	2.50	5.00

Albums

Number	Title (A Side/B Side)	Yr	VG	VG+	NM
❑ Columbia PC 33952	Second Childhood	1976	2.50	5.00	10.00
—Original with no bar code					
❑ Columbia PC 34387	It Looks Like Snow	1976	2.50	5.00	10.00
—Original with no bar code					
❑ Columbia JC 34875	Never Letting Go	1977	2.50	5.00	10.00
❑ Columbia JC 35456	Against the Grain	1978	2.50	5.00	10.00
❑ Columbia JC 37091	The Best of Phoebe Snow	1981	2.50	5.00	10.00
❑ Elektra 60852	Something Real	1989	2.50	5.00	10.00
❑ MCA 37119	Phoebe Snow	198?	2.00	4.00	8.00
—Budget-line reissue of Shelter LP					
❑ Mirage SD 19297	Rock Away	1981	2.50	5.00	10.00
❑ Shelter 2109	Phoebe Snow	1974	2.50	5.00	10.00
❑ Shelter 52017	Phoebe Snow	1977	2.00	4.00	8.00
—Reissue with ABC distribution					

SOMMERS, JOANIE

45s

Number	Title (A Side/B Side)	Yr	VG	VG+	NM
❑ ABC 12323	Peppermint Choo Choo/Peppermint Engineer	1978	—	2.50	5.00
❑ Capitol 5936	Trains and Boats and Planes/Yesterday's Morning	1967	2.00	4.00	8.00
❑ Columbia 43567	You've Got Possibilities/Never Throw Your Dreams Away	1966	25.00	50.00	100.00
❑ Columbia 43731	Alfie/You Take What Comes Along	1966	2.00	4.00	8.00
❑ Columbia 43950	It Doesn't Matter Anymore/Take a Broken Heart	1966	2.00	4.00	8.00
❑ Happy Tiger 522	Step Inside Love/Little Girl from Greenwood, Ga.	1970	—	3.00	6.00
❑ Happy Tiger 537	Sunshine After the Rain/Tell Him	1970	—	3.00	6.00
❑ Warner Bros. 5157	One Boy/I'll Never Be Free	1960	3.75	7.50	15.00
❑ Warner Bros. 5177	Be My Love/Why Don't You Do Right	1960	3.75	7.50	15.00
❑ Warner Bros. 5183	Ruby Duby Du/Bob White	1960	3.75	7.50	15.00
❑ Warner Bros. 5201	I Don't Want to Walk Without You/Seems Like Long, Long Ago	1961	3.75	7.50	15.00
❑ Warner Bros. 5226	Piano Boy/Serenade of the Bells	1961	3.75	7.50	15.00
❑ Warner Bros. 5241	Makin' Whoopee/What's Wrong with Me	1961	3.75	7.50	15.00
❑ Warner Bros. 5275	Johnny Get Angry/(Theme from) A Summer Place	1962	5.00	10.00	20.00
❑ Warner Bros. 5308	When the Boys Get Together/Passing Strangers	1962	3.00	6.00	12.00
❑ Warner Bros. 5324	Goodbye Joey/Bobby's Hobbies	1962	3.00	6.00	12.00
❑ Warner Bros. 5339	Memories, Memories/Since Randy Moved Away	1963	3.00	6.00	12.00

Number	Title (A Side/B Side)	Yr	VG	VG+	NM
❑ Warner Bros. 5350	Little Bit of Everything/Henny Penny	1963	3.00	6.00	12.00
❑ Warner Bros. 5361	One Boy/June Is Bustin' Out All Over	1963	3.00	6.00	12.00
❑ Warner Bros. 5374	Little Girl Bad/Wishing Well	1963	3.00	6.00	12.00
❑ Warner Bros. 5390	Goodbye Summer/Big Man	1963	3.00	6.00	12.00
❑ Warner Bros. 5437	I'd Be So Good for You/I'm Gonna Know He's Mine	1964	2.50	5.00	10.00
❑ Warner Bros. 5454	If You Love Him/I Think I'm Gonna Cry Now	1964	2.50	5.00	10.00
❑ Warner Bros. 5507	Makin' Whoopee/What's Wrong with Me + 2	1961	6.25	12.50	25.00
—Part of Warner Bros. "+2" series, with two new songs and excerpts of two prior hits					
❑ Warner Bros. 5629	Don't Pity Me/My Block	1965	50.00	100.00	200.00
❑ Warner Bros. 7129	Johnny Get Angry/One Boy	1968	—	3.00	6.00
—"Back to Back Hits" series — originals have green labels with "W7" logo					
❑ Warner Bros. 7251	Great Divide/Talk Until Midnight	1968	2.00	4.00	8.00
Albums					
❑ Columbia CL 2495 [M]	Come Alive	1966	5.00	10.00	20.00
❑ Columbia CS 9295 [S]	Come Alive	1966	6.25	12.50	25.00
❑ Discovery DS-883	Dream	1983	3.00	6.00	12.00
—With Bob Florence					
❑ Warner Bros. W 1346 [M]	Positively the Most	1960	7.50	15.00	30.00
❑ Warner Bros. WS 1346 [S]	Positively the Most	1960	10.00	20.00	40.00
❑ Warner Bros. B 1348 [M]	Behind Closed Doors at a Recording Session	1960	37.50	75.00	150.00
—Record comes in a box with a booklet included					
❑ Warner Bros. W 1412 [M]	Joanie Sommers	1961	7.50	15.00	30.00
❑ Warner Bros. WS 1412 [S]	Joanie Sommers	1961	10.00	20.00	40.00
❑ Warner Bros. W 1436 [M]	For Those Who Think Young	1962	7.50	15.00	30.00
❑ Warner Bros. WS 1436 [S]	For Those Who Think Young	1962	10.00	20.00	40.00
❑ Warner Bros. W 1470 [M]	Johnny Get Angry	1962	10.00	20.00	40.00
❑ Warner Bros. WS 1470 [S]	Johnny Get Angry	1962	12.50	25.00	50.00
❑ Warner Bros. W 1474 [M]	Let's Talk About Love	1962	7.50	15.00	30.00
❑ Warner Bros. WS 1474 [S]	Let's Talk About Love	1962	10.00	20.00	40.00
❑ Warner Bros. W 1504 [M]	Sommers' Seasons	1963	6.25	12.50	25.00
❑ Warner Bros. WS 1504 [S]	Sommers' Seasons	1963	7.50	15.00	30.00
❑ Warner Bros. W 1575 [M]	Softly, The Brazilian Sound	1964	6.25	12.50	25.00
❑ Warner Bros. WS 1575 [S]	Softly, The Brazilian Sound	1964	7.50	15.00	30.00

SONNY

45s

Number	Title (A Side/B Side)	Yr	VG	VG+	NM
❑ Atco 6369	Laugh at Me/Tony	1965	3.00	6.00	12.00
—B-side credited to "Sonny's Group"					
❑ Atco 6386	The Revolution Kind/Georgia and John Quetzal	1965	3.00	6.00	12.00
❑ Atco 6505	Misty Roses/I Told My Girl to Go Away	1967	2.50	5.00	10.00
❑ Atco 6531	Pammie's on a Bummer/My Best Friend's Girl Is Out of Sight	1967	2.50	5.00	10.00
❑ Fidelity 3020	Wearing Black/Don't Have to Tell Me	1960	6.25	12.50	25.00
—As "Don Christy"					
❑ Go 1001	As Long As You Love Me/I'll Always Be Grateful	1960	6.25	12.50	25.00
—As "Don Christy"					
❑ Highland 1160	I'll Change/Try It Out on Me	1963	7.50	15.00	30.00
—As "Sonny Bono"					
❑ MCA 40139	Rub Your Nose/Laugh at Me	1973	—	2.00	4.00
—As "Sonny Bono"					
❑ MCA 40271	Our Last Show/Classified 1A	1974	—	2.00	4.00
—As "Sonny Bono"					
❑ Name 3	As Long As You Love Me/I'll Always Be Grateful	1960	6.25	12.50	25.00
—As "Don Christy"					
❑ Specialty 672	Wearing Black/One Little Answer	1959	6.25	12.50	25.00
—As "Don Christy"					
❑ Specialty 733	One Little Answer/Comin' Down the Chimney	1974	—	3.00	6.00
—As "Sonny Bono and Little Tootsie"					
❑ Swami 1001	Don't Shake My Tree/(Mama) Come Get Your Baby Boy	1961	6.25	12.50	25.00
—As "Ronny Sommers"					
❑ Vee Jay 710	Midnight Surf/Ride the Wild Quetzal	1966	6.25	12.50	25.00
—As "Sonny Bono"					
Albums					
❑ Atco 33-229 [M]	Inner Views	1967	5.00	10.00	20.00
❑ Atco SD 33-229 [S]	Inner Views	1967	5.00	10.00	20.00

SONNY AND CHER

45s

Number	Title (A Side/B Side)	Yr	VG	VG+	NM
❑ Atco 6345	Just You/Sing C'est La Vie	1965	2.50	5.00	10.00
❑ Atco 6359	I Got You Babe/It's Gonna Rain	1965	3.00	6.00	12.00
❑ Atco 6381	But You're Mine/Hello	1965	3.00	6.00	12.00
❑ Atco 6395	What Now My Love/I Look for You	1965	3.00	6.00	12.00
❑ Atco 6420	Have I Stayed Too Long/Leave Me Be	1966	2.50	5.00	10.00
❑ Atco 6440	Little Man/Monday	1966	2.50	5.00	10.00
❑ Atco 6449	Living for You/Love Don't Come	1966	2.50	5.00	10.00
❑ Atco 6461	The Beat Goes On/Love Don't Come	1967	3.00	6.00	12.00
❑ Atco 6480	A Beautiful Story/Podunk	1967	2.50	5.00	10.00
❑ Atco 6486	Plastic Man/It's the Little Things	1967	2.50	5.00	10.00
❑ Atco 6507	It's the Little Things/Don't Talk to Strangers	1967	2.50	5.00	10.00
❑ Atco 6541	Good Combination/You and Me	1968	2.50	5.00	10.00
❑ Atco 6555	Circus/I Would Marry You Today	1968	2.50	5.00	10.00
❑ Atco 6605	You Gotta Have a Thing of Your Own/I Got You Babe	1968	2.50	5.00	10.00
❑ Atco 6684	You're a Friend of Mine/I Would Marry You Today	1969	2.50	5.00	10.00
❑ Atco 6758	Get It Together/Hold Me Tighter	1970	2.00	4.00	8.00
❑ Kapp 2141	Real People/Somebody	1971	—	2.00	4.00
❑ Kapp 2151	All I Ever Need Is You/I Got You Babe	1971	—	2.50	5.00
❑ Kapp 2163	A Cowboy's Work Is Never Done/Somebody	1972	—	2.50	5.00
❑ Kapp 2176	When You Say Love/Crystal Clear and Muddy Waters	1972	—	2.00	4.00

Number	Title (A Side/B Side)	Yr	VG	VG+	NM
❑ MCA 40026	Mama Was a Rock and Roll Singer, Papa Used to Write All Her Songs (Parts 1 & 2)	1973	—	2.00	4.00
❑ MCA 40083	The Greatest Show on Earth/You Know Darn Well	1973	—	2.00	4.00
❑ Reprise 0308	Love Is Strange/Do You Want to Dance	1964	5.00	10.00	20.00
—As "Caesar and Cleo"					
❑ Reprise 0309	Baby Don't Go/Walkin' the Quetzal	1964	5.00	10.00	20.00
❑ Reprise 0392	Baby Don't Go/Walkin' the Quetzal	1965	3.75	7.50	15.00
❑ Reprise 0419	Love Is Strange/Let the Good Times Roll	1965	5.00	10.00	20.00
—As "Caesar and Cleo"					
❑ Reprise 0723	Baby Don't Go/Love Is Strange	1968	—	2.50	5.00
—"Back to Back Hits" series — originals have both "r:" and "W7" logos					
❑ Vault 909	The Letter/Spring Fever	1964	7.50	15.00	30.00
—As "Caesar and Cleo"					
❑ Vault 916	The Letter/Spring Fever	1965	3.00	6.00	12.00
❑ Warner Bros. 8341	You're Not Right for Me/Wrong Number	1977	—	2.50	5.00
Albums					
❑ Atco 33-177 [M]	Look At Us	1965	3.75	7.50	15.00
—With white box that says "Includes Their Big Hit 'I Got You Babe'" (second edition)					
❑ Atco 33-177 [M]	Look At Us	1965	5.00	10.00	20.00
—Without white box that says "Includes Their Big Hit 'I Got You Babe'" (original)					
❑ Atco SD 33-177 [S]	Look At Us	1965	3.75	7.50	15.00
—With white box that says "Includes Their Big Hit 'I Got You Babe'" (second edition)					
❑ Atco SD 33-177 [S]	Look At Us	1965	6.25	12.50	25.00
—Without white box that says "Includes Their Big Hit 'I Got You Babe'" (original)					
❑ Atco 33-183 [M]	The Wondrous World of Sonny and Cher	1966	3.75	7.50	15.00
❑ Atco SD 33-183 [S]	The Wondrous World of Sonny and Cher	1966	5.00	10.00	20.00
❑ Atco 33-203 [M]	In Case You're in Love	1967	3.75	7.50	15.00
❑ Atco SD 33-203 [S]	In Case You're in Love	1967	5.00	10.00	20.00
❑ Atco 33-214 [M]	Good Times	1967	3.75	7.50	15.00
❑ Atco SD 33-214 [S]	Good Times	1967	5.00	10.00	20.00
❑ Atco 33-219 [M]	The Best of Sonny and Cher	1967	3.75	7.50	15.00
❑ Atco SD 33-219 [P]	The Best of Sonny and Cher	1967	5.00	10.00	20.00
—"What Now My Love," "A Beautiful Story," "But You're Mine" and "Laugh at Me" are rechanneled					
❑ Atco SD 2-804 [(2)]	The Two of Us	1972	5.00	10.00	20.00
—Combines "Look at Us" and "In Case You're in Love"					
❑ Atco SD 11000	The Beat Goes On	1975	3.75	7.50	15.00
❑ Kapp KS-3654	Sonny & Cher Live	1971	3.75	7.50	15.00
❑ Kapp KS-3660	All I Ever Need Is You	1972	3.75	7.50	15.00
—Orange and red swirl label					
❑ MCA 2009	Sonny & Cher Live	1973	3.00	6.00	12.00
—Reissue of Kapp 3654					
❑ MCA 2021	All I Ever Need Is You	1973	3.00	6.00	12.00
—Reissue of Kapp 3660					
❑ MCA 2101	Mama Was a Rock & Roll Singer Papa Used to Write All Her Songs	1973	3.00	6.00	12.00
❑ MCA 2117	Greatest Hits	1974	3.00	6.00	12.00
❑ MCA 2-8004 [(2)]	Sonny & Cher Live in Las Vegas, Vol. 2	1973	3.75	7.50	15.00
❑ Pair PDL2-1140 [(2)]	Sonny & Cher At Their Best	1986	3.00	6.00	12.00
❑ Reprise R 6177 [M]	Baby Don't Go	1965	7.50	15.00	30.00
❑ Reprise RS 6177 [P]	Baby Don't Go	1965	7.50	15.00	30.00
—By "Sonny & Cher & Friends" (also includes The Lettermen, Bill Medley and The Blendells)					
❑ TVP TVP-1021	The Hits of Sonny & Cher	1977	3.00	6.00	12.00

SOUL, DAVID

45s

Number	Title (A Side/B Side)	Yr	VG	VG+	NM
❑ MGM 13510	The Covered Man/I Will Warm Your Heart	1966	2.50	5.00	10.00
❑ MGM 13589	Was I Ever So Wrong/Before	1966	2.50	5.00	10.00
❑ MGM 13842	No One's Gonna Cry/Quiet Kind of Hate	1967	2.50	5.00	10.00
❑ Private Stock 45,129	Don't Give Up on Us/Black Bean Soup	1976	—	2.00	4.00
❑ Private Stock 45,150	Going In with My Eyes Open/Topanga	1977	—	2.00	4.00
❑ Private Stock 45,163	Silver Lady/The Rider	1977	—	2.00	4.00
Albums					
❑ Private Stock PS-2019	David Soul	1977	2.50	5.00	10.00
❑ Private Stock PS-7001	Playing to an Audience of One	1977	2.50	5.00	10.00

SOUL, JIMMY

45s

Number	Title (A Side/B Side)	Yr	VG	VG+	NM
❑ SPQR 3221	My Little Room/Ella Is Yella	1964	2.50	5.00	10.00

Number	Title (A Side/B Side)	Yr	VG	VG+	NM
❑ SPQR 3300	Twistin' Matilda/I Can't Hold Out Any Longer	1962	3.00	6.00	12.00
❑ SPQR 3302	When Matilda Comes Back/Some Kinda Nut	1962	3.00	6.00	12.00
❑ SPQR 3304	Guess Things Happen That Way/My Baby Loves to Bowl	1963	3.00	6.00	12.00
❑ SPQR 3305	If You Wanna Be Happy/Don't Release Me	1963	3.75	7.50	15.00
❑ SPQR 3310	Treat 'Em Tough/Church Street in the Summertime	1963	3.00	6.00	12.00
❑ SPQR 3312	Go 'Way Christina/Everybody's Gone Ape	1963	3.00	6.00	12.00
❑ SPQR 3314	Change Partners/I Hate You Baby	1963	3.00	6.00	12.00
❑ SPQR 3315	My Girl-She Sure Can Cook/A Woman Is Smarter in Every Kinda Way	1964	2.50	5.00	10.00
❑ SPQR 3318	You Can't Have Your Cake/Take Me to Los Angeles	1964	2.50	5.00	10.00
❑ SPQR 3319	Twistin' Matilda/Treat 'Em Tough	1964	2.50	5.00	10.00
❑ 20th Fox 413	Respectable/I Wish I Could Dance	1963	2.50	5.00	10.00
Albums					
❑ SPQR E 16001	If You Wanna Be Happy	1963	37.50	75.00	150.00

SOUL SURVIVORS

45s

Number	Title (A Side/B Side)	Yr	VG	VG+	NM
❑ Atco 6627	Turn Out the Fire/Go Out Walking	1968	2.00	4.00	8.00
❑ Atco 6650	Tell Daddy/Mama Soul	1969	2.00	4.00	8.00
❑ Atco 6735	Still Got My Head/Tempting 'Bout to Get Me	1970	2.00	4.00	8.00
❑ Crimson 1010	Expressway to Your Heart/Hey Gyp	1967	3.00	6.00	12.00
❑ Crimson 1012	Explosion (In My Soul)/Dathon's Theme	1967	2.50	5.00	10.00
❑ Crimson 1016	Poor Man's Dream/Impossible Mission	1968	2.50	5.00	10.00
❑ Decca 32080	Devil with a Blue Dress On/Shakin' with Linda	1967	3.75	7.50	15.00
❑ Dot 16793	Look at Me/Can't Stand to Be in Love with You	1965	5.00	10.00	20.00
❑ Dot 16830	Hung Up on Losin'/Snow Man	1966	3.00	6.00	12.00
❑ Lost-Nite 331	Expressway to Your Heart/Hey Gyp	197?	—	2.50	5.00
—Reissue					
❑ Philadelphia Int'l. 3595	Happy Birthday America (Part 1)/Happy Birthday America (Part 2)	1976	—	2.50	5.00
❑ TSOP 4756	City of Brotherly Love/The Best Time Was the Last Time	1974	—	3.00	6.00
❑ TSOP 4760	What It Takes/Virgin Girl	1974	—	3.00	6.00
❑ TSOP 4768	Your Love/Lover to Me	1975	—	3.00	6.00
Albums					
❑ Atco SD 33-277	Take Another Look	1969	6.25	12.50	25.00
❑ Crimson CR-502 [M]	When the Whistle Blows Anything Goes	1967	12.50	25.00	50.00
❑ Crimson CR-502 S [S]	When the Whistle Blows Anything Goes	1967	7.50	15.00	30.00
❑ TSOP KZ 33186	The Soul Survivors	1975	3.00	6.00	12.00

SOUNDS ORCHESTRAL

45s

Number	Title (A Side/B Side)	Yr	VG	VG+	NM
❑ Janus 124	Love in the Shadows/Louie, Louie	1970	—	3.00	6.00
❑ Parkway 120	Pretty Flamingo/Sounds Like Jacques	1966	2.00	4.00	8.00
❑ Parkway 155	A Man and a Woman/West of Carnaby	1967	2.00	4.00	8.00
❑ Parkway 942	Cast Your Fate to the Wind/To Wendy With Love	1965	2.50	5.00	10.00
❑ Parkway 958	Canadian Sunset/Have Faith in Your Love	1965	2.00	4.00	8.00
❑ Parkway 968	A Boy and a Girl/Go Home Girl	1966	2.00	4.00	8.00
❑ Parkway 973	Thunderball/Mr. Kiss Kiss Bang Bang	1966	2.00	4.00	8.00
Albums					
❑ Janus JLS-3014	One More Time	197?	3.75	7.50	15.00
❑ Parkway P 7046 [M]	Cast Your Fate to the Wind	1965	3.75	7.50	15.00
❑ Parkway SP 7046 [S]	Cast Your Fate to the Wind	1965	5.00	10.00	20.00
❑ Parkway P 7047 [M]	The Soul of Sounds Orchestral	1965	3.75	7.50	15.00
❑ Parkway SP 7047 [S]	The Soul of Sounds Orchestral	1965	5.00	10.00	20.00
❑ Parkway P 7050 [M]	Impressions of James Bond	1966	5.00	10.00	20.00
❑ Parkway SP 7050 [S]	Impressions of James Bond	1966	7.50	15.00	30.00

SOUTH, JOE

45s

Number	Title (A Side/B Side)	Yr	VG	VG+	NM
❑ Allwood 402	Just Remember You're Mine/Silly Me	1962	3.00	6.00	12.00
❑ Apt 25084	Deep Inside Me/I Want to Be Somebody	1965	2.50	5.00	10.00
❑ Capitol 2060	Birds of a Feather/It Got Away	1967	2.00	4.00	8.00
❑ Capitol 2169	How Can I Unlove You/She's Almost You	1968	2.00	4.00	8.00
❑ Capitol 2248	Games People Play/Mirror of Your Mind	1968	2.00	4.00	8.00
❑ Capitol 2284	Redneck/Don't Throw Your Love to the Wind	1968	2.00	4.00	8.00
❑ Capitol 2491	Leanin' On You/Don't You Be Ashamed	1969	—	3.00	6.00
❑ Capitol 2532	Birds of a Feather/These Are Not My People	1969	—	3.00	6.00
❑ Capitol 2592	Don't It Make You Want to Go Home/Heart's Desire	1969	—	3.00	6.00
❑ Capitol 2704	Walk a Mile in My Shoes/Sheltered	1969	—	3.00	6.00
❑ Capitol 2755	Children/The Clock Up On the Wall	1970	—	2.50	5.00
❑ Capitol 2916	Why Does a Man Do What He Has to Do/Be a Believer	1970	—	2.50	5.00
❑ Capitol 3008	Rose Garden/Mirror of Your Mind	1971	—	3.00	6.00
❑ Capitol 3053	United We Stand/So the Seeds Are Growing	1971	—	2.50	5.00
❑ Capitol 3204	Fool Me/Devil May Care	1971	—	2.50	5.00
❑ Capitol 3450	One Man Band/Coming Down All Alone	1972	—	2.50	5.00
❑ Capitol 3487	I'm a Star/Misunderstanding	1972	—	2.50	5.00
❑ Capitol 3554	Real Thing/Save Your Best	1973	—	2.50	5.00
❑ Capitol 3717	Riverdog/It Hurts Me Too	1973	—	2.50	5.00
❑ Columbia 43983	Backfield in Motion/I'll Come Back to You	1967	3.00	6.00	12.00
❑ Columbia 44218	A Fool in Love/Great Day	1967	3.00	6.00	12.00
❑ Fairlane 21006	You're the Reason/Jukebox	1961	5.00	10.00	20.00
❑ Fairlane 21010	Masquerade/I'm Sorry for You	1961	3.75	7.50	15.00
❑ Fairlane 21015	Slippin' Around/Just to Be with You Again	1962	3.75	7.50	15.00
❑ Island 034	To Have, to Hold and Let Go/Midnight Rainbows	1975	—	2.00	4.00
❑ MGM 13145	Same Old Song/Standing Invitation	1963	2.50	5.00	10.00
❑ MGM 13196	Concrete Jungle/The Last One to Know	1963	2.50	5.00	10.00
❑ MGM 13276	Naughty Claudie/Little Queenie	1964	2.50	5.00	10.00
❑ NRC 002	I'm Snowed/It's Only You	1958	10.00	20.00	40.00
❑ NRC 022	Chills/What a Night	1959	3.75	7.50	15.00
❑ NRC 041	Little Bluebird/Play It Cool	1959	3.75	7.50	15.00

Number	Title (A Side/B Side)	Yr	VG	VG+	NM
❑ NRC 053	Tell the Truth/If You Only Knew Her	1960	3.75	7.50	15.00
❑ NRC 065	Let's Talk It Over/Formality	1961	3.75	7.50	15.00
❑ NRC 5000	The Purple People Eater Meets the Witch Doctor/My Fondest Memories	1958	3.75	7.50	15.00
❑ NRC 5001	One Fool to Another/Texas Ain't the Biggest Anymore	1958	3.75	7.50	15.00
Albums					
❑ Accord SN-7119	Party People	1981	2.50	5.00	10.00
❑ Capitol ST-108	Introspect	1968	5.00	10.00	20.00
❑ Capitol ST-235	Games People Play	1969	3.75	7.50	15.00
❑ Capitol ST-392	Don't It Make You Want to Go Home	1969	3.75	7.50	15.00
❑ Capitol ST-450	Joe South's Greatest Hits	1970	3.75	7.50	15.00
❑ Capitol ST-637	So the Seeds Are Growing	1971	3.00	6.00	12.00
❑ Capitol ST-845	Joe South	1972	3.00	6.00	12.00
❑ Capitol ST-11074	A Look Inside	1972	3.00	6.00	12.00
❑ Island ILPS-9328	Midnight Rainbows	1975	2.50	5.00	10.00
❑ Mine MSG-1100	Walkin' Shoes	1971	3.00	6.00	12.00
—Reissue with new title					
❑ Mine MSG-1100	The Joe South Story	1971	3.75	7.50	15.00
❑ Nashville 2092	You're the Reason	1970	3.00	6.00	12.00
❑ Pickwick SPC-3314	Games People Play	197?	2.50	5.00	10.00

SOUTHER, J.D.

Number	Title (A Side/B Side)	Yr	VG	VG+	NM
45s					
❑ Asylum 11009	How Long/The Fast One	1972	—	2.50	5.00
❑ Asylum 45332	Silver Blue/Black Rose	1976	—	2.00	4.00
—As "John David Souther"					
❑ Asylum 45364	Faithless Love/Midnight Prowl	1976	—	2.00	4.00
—As "John David Souther"					
❑ Columbia 02422	You're Only Lonely/If You Don't Want My Love	1981	—	—	3.00
—Reissue					
❑ Columbia 11079	You're Only Lonely/Songs of Love	1979	—	2.00	4.00
❑ Columbia 11196	White Rhythm and Blues/The Last in Love	1980	—	2.00	4.00
❑ Columbia 11302	'Til the Bar Burns Down/If You Don't Want My Love	1980	—	2.00	4.00
—With Johnny Duncan					
❑ Full Moon 49612	You're Only Lonely/Once in a Lifetime	1980	—	2.00	4.00
—B-side by Bonnie Raitt					
❑ Warner Bros. 29289	Go Ahead and Rain/All I Want	1984	—	—	3.00
Albums					
❑ Asylum 7E-1059	Black Rose	1976	2.50	5.00	10.00
❑ Asylum SD 5055	John David Souther	1972	3.00	6.00	12.00
❑ Columbia JC 36093	You're Only Lonely	1979	2.50	5.00	10.00
❑ Columbia PC 36093	You're Only Lonely	198?	2.00	4.00	8.00
—Budget-line reissue					
❑ Warner Bros. 25081	Home By Dawn	1985	2.50	5.00	10.00

SPANKY AND OUR GANG

Number	Title (A Side/B Side)	Yr	VG	VG+	NM
45s					
❑ Epic 50170	When I Wanna/I Won't Brand You	1975	—	2.50	5.00
❑ Epic 50206	L.A. Freeway/Standing Room Only	1976	—	2.50	5.00
❑ Mercury 72598	And Your Bird Can Sing/Sealed with a Kiss	1966	5.00	10.00	20.00
❑ Mercury 72679	Sunday Will Never Be the Same/Distance	1967	2.00	4.00	8.00
❑ Mercury 72714	Making Every Minute Count/If You Could Only Be Me	1967	2.00	4.00	8.00
❑ Mercury 72732	Lazy Day/(It Ain't Necessarily) Byrd Avenue	1967	2.00	4.00	8.00
❑ Mercury 72765	Sunday Morning/Echoes	1968	2.00	4.00	8.00
❑ Mercury 72795	Like to Get to Know You/Three Ways from Tomorrow	1968	2.00	4.00	8.00
—Orange and tan swirl label					
❑ Mercury 72831	Give a Damn/Swinging Gate	1968	2.00	4.00	8.00
❑ Mercury 72871	Yesterday's Rain/Without Rhyme or Reason	1968	2.00	4.00	8.00
❑ Mercury 72890	Anything You Choose/Mecca Flat Blues	1969	2.00	4.00	8.00
❑ Mercury 72926	And She's Mine/Leopard Skinned Phones	1969	2.00	4.00	8.00
❑ Mercury 72982	Everybody's Talkin'/(B-side unknown)	1969	2.00	4.00	8.00
Albums					
❑ Epic PE 33580	Change	1975	3.00	6.00	12.00
❑ Mercury MG-21124 [M]	Spanky and Our Gang	1967	7.50	15.00	30.00
❑ Mercury SR-61124 [S]	Spanky and Our Gang	1967	5.00	10.00	20.00
❑ Mercury SR-61161	Like to Get to Know You	1968	5.00	10.00	20.00
❑ Mercury SR-61183	Anything You Choose/Without Rhyme or Reason	1969	5.00	10.00	20.00

Number	Title (A Side/B Side)	Yr	VG	VG+	NM
❑ Mercury SR-61227	Spanky's Greatest Hit(s)	1969	5.00	10.00	20.00
❑ Mercury SR-61326	Live	1971	3.75	7.50	15.00
❑ Rhino RNLP-70131	The Best of Spanky and Our Gang (1967-1969)	1986	3.00	6.00	12.00

SPINNERS

45s

Number	Title (A Side/B Side)	Yr	VG	VG+	NM
❑ Atlantic 2904	I'll Be Around/How Could I Let You Get Away	1972	—	2.50	5.00
❑ Atlantic 2927	Could It Be I'm Falling in Love/Just You and Me Baby	1972	—	2.50	5.00
❑ Atlantic 2962	One of a Kind (Love Affair)/Don't Let the Green Grass Fool You	1973	—	2.50	5.00
❑ Atlantic 2973	Ghetto Child/We Belong Together	1973	—	2.50	5.00
❑ Atlantic 3006	Mighty Love — Pt. 1/Mighty Love — Pt. 2	1974	—	2.50	5.00
❑ Atlantic 3027	I'm Coming Home/He'll Never Love You Like I Do	1974	—	2.50	5.00
❑ Atlantic 3029	Then Came You/Just As Long As We Have Love	1974	—	3.00	6.00
—With Dionne Warwicke					
❑ Atlantic 3202	Then Came You/Just As Long As We Have Love	1974	—	2.50	5.00
—With Dionne Warwicke					
❑ Atlantic 3206	Love Don't Love Nobody (Part 1)/Love Don't Love Nobody (Part 2)	1974	—	2.50	5.00
❑ Atlantic 3252	Living a Little, Loving a Little/Smile, We Have Each Other	1975	—	2.50	5.00
❑ Atlantic 3268	Sadie/Lazy Susan	1975	—	2.50	5.00
❑ Atlantic 3284	Games People Play/I Don't Want to Lose You	1975	2.50	5.00	10.00
❑ Atlantic 3284	They Just Can't Stop it the (Games People Play)/ I Don't Want to Lose You	1975	—	2.50	5.00
—Same A-side, altered title					
❑ Atlantic 3309	Love Or Leave/You Made a Promise to Me	1975	—	2.50	5.00
❑ Atlantic 3341	Wake Up Susan/If You Can't Be in Love	1976	—	2.50	5.00
❑ Atlantic 3355	The Rubberband Man/Now That We're Together	1976	—	2.50	5.00
❑ Atlantic 3382	You're Throwing a Good Love Away/You're All I Need in Life	1977	—	2.50	5.00
❑ Atlantic 3400	Me and My Music/I'm Riding Your Shadow	1977	—	2.50	5.00
❑ Atlantic 3425	Heaven on Earth (So Fine)/I'm Tired of Giving	1977	—	2.50	5.00
❑ Atlantic 3462	Easy Come, Easy Go/Love Is One Step Away	1978	—	2.50	5.00
❑ Atlantic 3483	If You Wanna Do a Dance/One in a Life Proposal	1978	—	2.50	5.00
❑ Atlantic 3546	Are You Ready for Love/Once You Fall in Love	1978	—	2.50	5.00
❑ Atlantic 3590	Don't Let the Man Get You/I Love the Music	1979	—	2.50	5.00
❑ Atlantic 3619	Body Language/With My Eyes	1979	—	2.50	5.00
❑ Atlantic 3637	Working My Way Back to You/Disco Ride	1979	2.00	4.00	8.00
—Original pressings mention only one song on the A-side					
❑ Atlantic 3637	Working My Way Back to You-Forgive Me, Girl/Disco Ride	1979	—	2.00	4.00
❑ Atlantic 3664	Cupid-I've Loved You for a Long Time/Pipedreams	1980	—	2.00	4.00
❑ Atlantic 3757	Love Trippin'/Now That You're Mine Again	1980	—	2.00	4.00
❑ Atlantic 3765	I Just Want to Fall in Love/Heavy on the Sunshine	1980	—	2.00	4.00
❑ Atlantic 3798	Yesterday Once More-Nothing Remains the Same/Be My Love	1981	—	2.00	4.00
❑ Atlantic 3814	Long Live Soul Music/Give Your Lady What She Wants	1981	—	2.00	4.00
❑ Atlantic 3827	Winter of Our Love/The Deacon	1981	—	2.00	4.00
❑ Atlantic 3848	What You Feel Is Real/Street Talk	1981	—	2.00	4.00
—With Gino Soccio					
❑ Atlantic 3865	You Go Your Way (I'll Go Mine)/Got to Be Love	1981	—	2.00	4.00
❑ Atlantic 4007	Never Thought I'd Fall in Love/Send a Little Love	1982	—	2.00	4.00
❑ Atlantic 89226	Spaceballs/Spaceballs (Dub Version)	1987	—	—	3.00
❑ Atlantic 89648	(We Have Come Into) Our Time for All/All Your Love	1984	—	2.00	4.00
❑ Atlantic 89689	Right or Wrong/Love Is In Season	1984	—	2.00	4.00
❑ Atlantic 89862	City Full of Memories/No Other Love	1983	—	2.00	4.00
❑ Atlantic 89922	Funny How Time Slips Away/I'm Calling You Now	1982	—	2.00	4.00
❑ Atlantic 89962	Magic in the Moonlight/So Far Away	1982	—	2.00	4.00
❑ Mirage 99580	She Does/(B-side unknown)	1986	—	—	3.00
❑ Mirage 99604	Put Us Together Again/Show Us Your Magic	1985	—	—	3.00
❑ Motown 1067	Sweet Thing/How Can I	1964	3.75	7.50	15.00
❑ Motown 1078	I'll Always Love You/Tomorrow May Never Come	1965	3.75	7.50	15.00
❑ Motown 1093	Truly Yours/Where Is That Girl	1966	3.75	7.50	15.00
❑ Motown 1109	For All We Know/Cross My Heart	1967	3.75	7.50	15.00
❑ Motown 1136	I Just Can't Help But Feel the Pain/Bad, Bad Weather	1968	3.75	7.50	15.00
❑ Motown 1155	In My Diary/(She's Gonna Love Me) At Sundown	1969	375.00	750.00	1500.
❑ Motown 1235	Together We Can Make Such Sweet Music/Bad, Bad Weather	1973	2.00	4.00	8.00
❑ Tri-Phi 1001	That's What Girls Are Made For/Heebie-Jeebies	1961	6.25	12.50	25.00
❑ Tri-Phi 1004	Love (I'm So Glad I Found You)/Sudbuster	1961	6.25	12.50	25.00
❑ Tri-Phi 1007	What Did She Use/Itching for My Baby, I Know Where to Scratch	1962	6.25	12.50	25.00
❑ Tri-Phi 1010	She Loves Me So/Whistling About You	1962	6.25	12.50	25.00
❑ Tri-Phi 1013	I've Been Hurt/I Got Your Water Boiling Baby (I'm Gonna Cook Your Goose)	1962	6.25	12.50	25.00
❑ Tri-Phi 1018	She Don't Love Me/Too Young, Too Much, Too Soon	1962	7.50	15.00	30.00
❑ V.I.P. 25050	In My Diary/(She's Gonna Love Me) At Sundown	1969	6.25	12.50	25.00
❑ V.I.P. 25054	Message from a Black Man/(She's Gonna Love Me) At Sundown	1970	3.00	6.00	12.00
❑ V.I.P. 25057	It's a Shame/Together We Can Make Such Sweet Music	1970	3.00	6.00	12.00
❑ V.I.P. 25060	We'll Have It Made/My Whole World Ended (The Moment You Left Me)	1971	3.00	6.00	12.00

Albums

Number	Title	Yr	VG	VG+	NM
❑ Atlantic SD 2-910 [(2)]	Spinners Live!	1975	3.75	7.50	15.00
❑ Atlantic SD 7256	Spinners	1973	3.00	6.00	12.00
❑ Atlantic SD 7296	Mighty Love	1974	3.00	6.00	12.00
❑ Atlantic SD 16032	Labor of Love	1981	2.50	5.00	10.00
❑ Atlantic SD 18118	New and Improved	1974	3.00	6.00	12.00
❑ Atlantic SD 18141	Pick of the Litter	1975	3.00	6.00	12.00
❑ Atlantic SD 18181	Happiness is Being with the Spinners	1976	3.00	6.00	12.00
❑ Atlantic SD 19100	Yesterday, Today & Tomorrow	1977	3.00	6.00	12.00
❑ Atlantic SD 19146	Spinners/8	1977	3.00	6.00	12.00
❑ Atlantic SD 19179	The Best of the Spinners	1978	3.00	6.00	12.00
❑ Atlantic SD 19219	From Here to Eternally	1979	3.00	6.00	12.00
❑ Atlantic SD 19256	Dancin' and Lovin'	1980	2.50	5.00	10.00

Number	Title (A Side/B Side)	Yr	VG	VG+	NM
❑ Atlantic SD 19270	Love Trippin'	1980	2.50	5.00	10.00
❑ Atlantic SD 19318	Can't Shake This Feelin'	1981	2.50	5.00	10.00
❑ Atlantic 80020	Grand Slam	1982	2.50	5.00	10.00
❑ Mirage 90456	Lovin' Feelings	1985	2.50	5.00	10.00
❑ Motown M5-109V1	Motown Superstar Series, Vol. 9	1982	2.00	4.00	8.00
❑ Motown M5-132V1	The Original Spinners	1981	3.00	6.00	12.00
—Reissue of Motown 639					
❑ Motown M5-199V1	The Best of the Spinners	1981	3.00	6.00	12.00
—Reissue of Motown 769					
❑ Motown M 639 [M]	The Original Spinners	1967	6.25	12.50	25.00
❑ Motown MS 639 [P]	The Original Spinners	1967	7.50	15.00	30.00
❑ Motown M 769	The Best of the Spinners	1973	3.75	7.50	15.00
❑ V.I.P. 405	2nd Time Around	1970	10.00	20.00	40.00
❑ Volt V-3403	Down to Business	1989	3.00	6.00	12.00

SPIRAL STARECASE

45s

Number	Title (A Side/B Side)	Yr	VG	VG+	NM
❑ Columbia 44442	Makin' My Mind Up/Baby What I Mean	1968	—	3.00	6.00
❑ Columbia 44566	Inside, Outside, Upside Down/I'll Run	1968	—	3.00	6.00
❑ Columbia 44741	More Today Than Yesterday/Broken Hearted Man	1969	2.00	4.00	8.00
❑ Columbia 44924	Sweet Little Thing/No One for Me to Turn To	1969	—	2.50	5.00
❑ Columbia 45048	She's Ready/Judas to the Love We Know	1969	—	2.50	5.00

Albums

Number	Title (A Side/B Side)	Yr	VG	VG+	NM
❑ Columbia CS 9852	More Today Than Yesterday	1969	6.25	12.50	25.00
—"360 Sound" label					

SPRINGFIELD, DUSTY

45s

Number	Title (A Side/B Side)	Yr	VG	VG+	NM
❑ ABC Dunhill 4341	Who Gets Your Love/Of All the Things	1973	—	3.00	6.00
❑ ABC Dunhill 4344	Mama's Little Girl/Learn to Say Goodbye	1973	—	3.00	6.00
❑ ABC Dunhill 4357	Mama's Little Girl/Learn to Say Goodbye	1973	2.00	4.00	8.00
❑ Atlantic 2580	Son-of-a-Preacher-Man/Just a Little Lovin'	1968	2.50	5.00	10.00
❑ Atlantic 2606	Breakfast in Bed/Don't Forget About Me	1969	2.00	4.00	8.00
❑ Atlantic 2623	The Windmills of Your Mind/I Don't Want to Hear It Anymore	1969	2.00	4.00	8.00
❑ Atlantic 2647	Willie & Laura May Jones/That Old Sweet Roll	1969	—	3.00	6.00
❑ Atlantic 2673	In the Land of Make Believe/So Much Love	1969	—	3.00	6.00
❑ Atlantic 2685	A Brand New Me/Bad Case of the Blues	1969	—	3.00	6.00
❑ Atlantic 2705	Silly, Silly, Fool/Joe	1970	—	3.00	6.00
❑ Atlantic 2729	I Wanna Be a Free Girl/Let Me In Your Way	1970	—	3.00	6.00
❑ Atlantic 2739	Never Love Again/Lost	1970	—	3.00	6.00
❑ Atlantic 2771	What Good Is I Love You/What Do You Do When Love Dies	1970	—	3.00	6.00
❑ Atlantic 2825	Nothing Is Forever/Haunted	1971	—	3.00	6.00
❑ Atlantic 2841	I Believe in You/Someone Who Cared	1971	—	3.00	6.00
❑ Casablanca 2356	I Am Curious/Donnez-Moi	1981	—	2.00	4.00
❑ Enigma 75042	Nothing Has Been Proved/(Instrumental)	1989	—	2.50	5.00
❑ Philips 40162	I Only Want to Be with You/Once Upon a Time	1963	3.00	6.00	12.00
❑ Philips 40180	Stay Awhile/Something Special	1964	2.50	5.00	10.00
❑ Philips 40207	Wishin' and Hopin'/Do Re Mi (Forget About the Do and Think About Me)	1964	3.00	6.00	12.00
❑ Philips 40229	All Cried Out/I Wish I'd Never Loved You	1964	2.50	5.00	10.00
❑ Philips 40245	Guess Who/Live It Up	1964	2.50	5.00	10.00
❑ Philips 40270	Losing You/Here She Comes	1965	2.50	5.00	10.00
❑ Philips 40303	In the Middle of Nowhere/Baby, Don't You Know	1965	2.50	5.00	10.00
❑ Philips 40319	I Just Don't Know What to Do with Myself/Some of Your Lovin'	1965	2.50	5.00	10.00
❑ Philips 40371	You Don't Have to Say You Love Me/Little by Little	1966	2.50	5.00	10.00
❑ Philips 40396	All I See Is You/I'm Gonna Leave You	1966	2.50	5.00	10.00
❑ Philips 40439	I'll Try Anything/The Corrupt Ones	1967	2.50	5.00	10.00
❑ Philips 40465	The Look of Love/Give Me Time	1967	2.50	5.00	10.00
❑ Philips 40498	What's It Gonna Be/Small Town Girl	1967	2.50	5.00	10.00
❑ Philips 40547	Sweet Ride/No Stranger Am I	1968	2.50	5.00	10.00
❑ Philips 40553	La Bamba/I Close My Eyes and Count to Ten	1968	2.50	5.00	10.00
❑ 20th Century 2457	It Goes Like It Goes/I Wish That Love Would Last	1980	—	2.50	5.00
❑ United Artists XW1006	Let Me Love You Once Before You Go/I'm Your Child	1977	—	2.50	5.00
❑ United Artists XW1205	Checkmate/Sandra	1978	—	2.50	5.00
❑ United Artists XW1225	Give Me the Night/Checkmate	1978	—	2.50	5.00
❑ United Artists XW1255	Living Without Your Love/Get Yourself to Love	1978	—	2.50	5.00

Albums

Number	Title (A Side/B Side)	Yr	VG	VG+	NM
❑ ABC Dunhill DSX-50128	Cameo	1973	3.75	7.50	15.00

Number	Title (A Side/B Side)	Yr	VG	VG+	NM
❑ ABC Dunhill DSX-50186	Longings	1974	—	—	—
—Unreleased					
❑ Atlantic SD 8214	Dusty in Memphis	1969	7.50	15.00	30.00
—Originals have purple and brown labels					
❑ Atlantic SD 8249	A Brand New Me	1970	3.75	7.50	15.00
❑ Casablanca NBLP-7271	White Heat	1982	3.00	6.00	12.00
❑ 4 Men With Beards 4M 112	Dusty in Memphis	2002	3.75	7.50	15.00
—Reissue on 180-gram vinyl					
❑ Liberty LN-10024	It Begins Again	1980	2.00	4.00	8.00
—Budget-line reissue of United Artists LP of same name					
❑ Liberty LN-10026	Living Without Your Love	1980	2.00	4.00	8.00
—Budget-line reissue of United Artists LP of same name					
❑ Philips PHM-200133 [M]	Stay Awhile	1964	7.50	15.00	30.00
❑ Philips PHM-200156 [M]	Dusty	1964	7.50	15.00	30.00
❑ Philips PHM-200174 [M]	Oooooo Weeeee!	1965	10.00	20.00	40.00
❑ Philips PHM-200210 [M]	You Don't Have to Say You Love Me	1966	7.50	15.00	30.00
❑ Philips PHM-200220 [M]	Dusty Springfield's Golden Hits	1966	6.25	12.50	25.00
—With "Goin' Back"					
❑ Philips PHM-200256 [M]	The Look of Love	1967	6.25	12.50	25.00
❑ Philips PHM-200303 [M]	Everything's Coming Up Dusty	1967	6.25	12.50	25.00
❑ Philips PHS-600133 [P]	Stay Awhile	1964	10.00	20.00	40.00
❑ Philips PHS-600156 [P]	Dusty	1964	10.00	20.00	40.00
❑ Philips PHS-600174 [S]	Oooooo Weeeee!	1965	12.50	25.00	50.00
❑ Philips PHS-600210 [S]	You Don't Have to Say You Love Me	1966	10.00	20.00	40.00
❑ Philips PHS-600220 [P]	Dusty Springfield's Golden Hits	1966	8.75	17.50	35.00
—With "Goin' Back"					
❑ Philips PHS-600256 [S]	The Look of Love	1967	7.50	15.00	30.00
❑ Philips PHS-600303 [S]	Everything's Coming Up Dusty	1967	7.50	15.00	30.00
❑ Polydor 824467-1	Dusty Springfield's Golden Hits	1985	2.50	5.00	10.00
❑ United Artists UA-LA791	It Begins Again	1978	3.75	7.50	15.00
❑ United Artists UA-LA936	Living Without Your Love	1979	3.75	7.50	15.00
❑ Wing PKW-2-120 [(2)]	Something Special	196?	5.00	10.00	20.00
❑ Wing SRW-16380	Just Dusty	196?	3.00	6.00	12.00

SPRINGFIELD, RICK

45s

Number	Title (A Side/B Side)	Yr	VG	VG+	NM
❑ Capitol 3340	Speak to the Sky/Why	1972	2.00	4.00	8.00
❑ Capitol 3466	What Would the Children Think/Come On Everybody	1972	2.00	4.00	8.00
❑ Capitol 3637	I'm Your Superman/Why Are You Waiting	1973	2.00	4.00	8.00
❑ Capitol 3713	Believe in Me/The Liar	1973	3.00	6.00	12.00
❑ Chelsea 3051	Take a Hand/Archangel	1976	—	2.50	5.00
❑ Chelsea 3055	Million Dollar Face/(B-side unknown)	1976	—	2.50	5.00
❑ Chelsea 3056	Jessica/Archangel	1976	—	2.50	5.00
❑ Columbia 45935	Believe in Me/The Liar	1973	—	3.00	6.00
❑ Columbia 46032	Streakin' Across the U.S.A./Music to Streak By	1974	—	3.00	6.00
❑ Columbia 46057	American Girls/Weep No More	1974	—	2.50	5.00
❑ Mercury 880405-7	Bruce/Guenevere	1984	—	2.00	4.00
❑ RCA 6853-7-R	Rock of Life/The Language of Love	1988	—	—	3.00
❑ RCA 8391-7-R	Honeymoon in Beirut/My Father's Chair	1988	—	—	3.00
❑ RCA PB-12166	I've Done Everything for You/Red Hot and Blue Love	1981	—	2.00	4.00
❑ RCA PB-12201	Jessie's Girl/Carry Me Away	1981	—	2.00	4.00
❑ RCA PB-13008	Love Is Alright Tonite/Everybody's Girl	1981	—	2.00	4.00
❑ RCA PB-13070	Don't Talk to Strangers/Tonight	1982	—	2.00	4.00
❑ RCA PB-13245	What Kind of Fool Am I/How Do You Talk to Girls	1982	—	2.00	4.00
❑ RCA PB-13303	I Get Excited/Kristina	1982	—	2.00	4.00
❑ RCA GB-13482	Jessie's Girl/I've Done Everything for You	1983	—	—	3.00
—Gold Standard Series					
❑ RCA GB-13483	Don't Talk to Strangers/What Kind of Fool Am I	1983	—	—	3.00
—Gold Standard Series					
❑ RCA PB-13497	Affair of the Heart/Like Father, Like Son	1983	—	—	3.00
❑ RCA PB-13576	Human Touch/Alyson	1983	—	—	3.00
❑ RCA PB-13650	Souls/Souls (Live)	1983	—	—	3.00
❑ RCA PB-13738	Love Somebody/The Great Lost Art of Conversation	1984	—	—	3.00
❑ RCA GB-13794	Affair of the Heart/Human Touch	1984	—	—	3.00
—Gold Standard Series					
❑ RCA PB-13813	Don't Walk Away/S.F.O.	1984	—	—	3.00
❑ RCA PB-13861	Bop 'Til You Drop/Taxi Dancing	1984	—	—	3.00
—B-side: With Randy Crawford					
❑ RCA PB-14047	Celebrate Youth/Stranger in the House	1985	—	—	3.00
❑ RCA PB-14120	State of the Heart/The Power of Love (The Tao of Love)	1985	—	—	3.00

Albums

Number	Title (A Side/B Side)	Yr	VG	VG+	NM
❑ Capitol SMAS-11047	Beginnings	1972	5.00	10.00	20.00
❑ Capitol SMAS-11206	Comic Book Heroes	1973	10.00	20.00	40.00
—Withdrawn and reissued on Columbia					
❑ Capitol SN-16251	Beginnings	1981	2.00	4.00	8.00
—Budget-line reissue					
❑ Chelsea 515	Wait for Night	1976	3.75	7.50	15.00
❑ Columbia KC 32704	Comic Book Heroes	1973	3.75	7.50	15.00
❑ Columbia PC 32704	Comic Book Heroes	1981	2.00	4.00	8.00
—Budget-line reissue					
❑ Mercury 824107-1	Beautiful Feelings	1984	2.50	5.00	10.00
❑ RCA 6620-1-R	Rock of Life	1988	2.00	4.00	8.00
❑ RCA 9817-1-R	Rick Springfield's Greatest Hits	1989	3.00	6.00	12.00
❑ RCA Victor ARL1-3697	Working Class Dog	1981	2.50	5.00	10.00
❑ RCA Victor AFL1-4125	Success Hasn't Spoiled Me Yet	1982	2.50	5.00	10.00
❑ RCA Victor AFL1-4235	Wait for Night	1982	2.50	5.00	10.00
—Reissue of Chelsea LP					

Number	Title (A Side/B Side)	Yr	VG	VG+	NM
❑ RCA Victor AFL1-4660	Living in Oz	1983	2.50	5.00	10.00
❑ RCA Victor AYL1-4766	Working Class Dog	1983	2.00	4.00	8.00
—"Best Buy Series" reissue					
❑ RCA Victor AYL1-4767	Success Hasn't Spoiled Me Yet	1983	2.00	4.00	8.00
—"Best Buy Series" reissue					
❑ RCA Victor ABL1-4935	Hard to Hold	1984	2.50	5.00	10.00
❑ RCA Victor AJL1-5370	Tao	1985	2.50	5.00	10.00
SPRINGFIELDS, THE					
45s					
❑ Philips 40038	Silver Threads and Golden Needles/Aunt Rhody	1962	3.75	7.50	15.00
❑ Philips 40072	Dear Hearts and Gentle People/Gotta Travel On	1962	3.00	6.00	12.00
❑ Philips 40092	Little By Little/Waf-Woof	1963	3.00	6.00	12.00
❑ Philips 40099	Foggy Mountain Top/Island of Dreams	1963	3.00	6.00	12.00
❑ Philips 40121	Say I Won't Be There/Little Boat	1963	3.00	6.00	12.00
Albums					
❑ Philips PHM 200052 [M]	Silver Threads and Golden Needles	1962	7.50	15.00	30.00
❑ Philips PHM 200076 [M]	Folksongs from the Hills	1963	7.50	15.00	30.00
❑ Philips PHS 600052 [S]	Silver Threads and Golden Needles	1962	10.00	20.00	40.00
❑ Philips PHS 600076 [S]	Folksongs from the Hills	1963	10.00	20.00	40.00
SPRINGSTEEN, BRUCE					
45s					
❑ Columbia 03243	Hungry Heart/Fade Away	1983	—	2.00	4.00
—"Columbia Hall of Fame" series; red label					
❑ Columbia 04463	Dancing in the Dark/Pink Cadillac	1984	—	2.00	4.00
❑ Columbia 04561	Cover Me/Jersey Girl	1984	—	2.00	4.00
—Spoken intro to "Jersey Girl" is deleted. Dead wax has matrix number followed by "-2" and a letter.					
❑ Columbia 04680	Born in the U.S.A./Shut Out the Light	1984	—	2.00	4.00
❑ Columbia 04772	I'm on Fire/Johnny Bye Bye	1985	—	2.00	4.00
❑ Columbia 04924	Glory Days/Stand On It	1985	—	2.00	4.00
❑ Columbia 05603	I'm Goin' Down/Janey, Don't You Lose Heart	1985	—	2.00	4.00
❑ Columbia 05728	My Hometown/Santa Claus Is Coming to Town	1985	—	2.00	4.00
❑ Columbia 06432	War/Merry Christmas Baby	1986	—	2.00	4.00
❑ Columbia 06657	Fire/Incident on 57th Street	1987	—	2.50	5.00
❑ Columbia 07595	Brilliant Disguise/Lucky Man	1987	—	2.00	4.00
❑ Columbia 07663	Tunnel of Love/Two for the Road	1987	—	2.00	4.00
❑ Columbia 07726	One Step Up/Roulette	1988	—	2.00	4.00
❑ Columbia 08408	Dancing in the Dark/Pink Cadillac	1984	—	—	3.00
—Gray label reissue					
❑ Columbia 08409	Cover Me/Jersey Girl	1984	—	—	3.00
—Gray label reissue					
❑ Columbia 08410	Born in the U.S.A./Shut Out the Light	1984	—	—	3.00
—Gray label reissue					
❑ Columbia 08411	I'm on Fire/Johnny Bye Bye	1985	—	—	3.00
—Gray label reissue					
❑ Columbia 08412	Glory Days/Stand On It	1985	—	—	3.00
—Gray label reissue					
❑ Columbia 08413	I'm Goin' Down/Janey, Don't You Lose Heart	1985	—	—	3.00
—Gray label reissue					
❑ Columbia 08414	My Hometown/Santa Claus Is Coming to Town	1985	—	—	3.00
—Gray label reissue; many copies of this were issued with Columbia 05728 picture sleeves					
❑ Columbia 10209	Born to Run/Meeting Across the River	1975	5.00	10.00	20.00
❑ Columbia 10274	Tenth Avenue Freeze-Out/She's the One	1976	3.75	7.50	15.00
❑ Columbia 10763	Prove It All Night/Factory	1978	3.00	6.00	12.00
❑ Columbia 10801	Badlands/Streets of Fire	1978	3.00	6.00	12.00
❑ Columbia 11391	Hungry Heart/Held Up Without a Gun	1980	—	2.00	4.00
❑ Columbia 11431	Fade Away/Be True	1981	—	2.00	4.00
—Corrected second pressing					
❑ Columbia 33323	Born to Run/Spirit in the Night	1976	—	2.00	4.00
—"Columbia Hall of Fame" series; red label					
❑ Columbia 45805	Blinded by the Light/The Angel	1972	125.00	250.00	500.00
❑ Columbia 45864	Spirit in the Night/For You	1973	375.00	750.00	1500.
Albums					
❑ Columbia KC 31903	Greetings from Asbury Park, N.J.	1973	5.00	10.00	20.00
❑ Columbia KC 32432	The Wild, the Innocent & the E Street Shuffle	1973	5.00	10.00	20.00
❑ Columbia PC 33795	Born to Run	1975	2.50	5.00	10.00
—Jon Landau's name is correct on the back cover					

Number	Title (A Side/B Side)	Yr	VG	VG+	NM
❑ Columbia JC 35318	Darkness on the Edge of Town	1978	2.50	5.00	10.00
—Original pressings have thick paper innersleeves and small titles on back cover					
❑ Columbia PC2 36854 [(2)]	The River	1980	3.00	6.00	12.00
❑ Columbia TC 38358	Nebraska	1982	2.50	5.00	10.00
❑ Columbia QC 38653	Born in the U.S.A.	1984	2.50	5.00	10.00
❑ Columbia C5X 40558 [(5)]	Bruce Springsteen and the E Street Band: Live 1975-1985	1986	10.00	20.00	40.00
❑ Columbia OC 40999	Tunnel of Love	1987	2.50	5.00	10.00
❑ Columbia 3C 44445 [EP]	Chimes of Freedom	1988	2.50	5.00	10.00
STAFFORD, JIM					
45s					
❑ Columbia 04339	Little Bits and Pieces/Banjo Billy	1984	—	—	3.00
❑ Elektra 47013	Don't Fool Around (When There's a Fool Around)/ I Took Your Love Lightly	1980	—	2.00	4.00
❑ Elektra 47226	Isabel and Samantha/Yeller Dog Blues	1981	—	2.00	4.00
❑ MGM 14496	Swamp Witch/Nifty Fifties Blues	1973	—	2.00	4.00
❑ MGM 14648	Spiders and Snakes/Undecided	1973	—	2.00	4.00
❑ MGM 14718	My Girl Bill/L.A. Mama	1974	—	2.00	4.00
❑ MGM 14737	Wildwood Weed/The Last Chant	1974	—	2.00	4.00
❑ MGM 14775	Your Bulldog Drinks Champagne/Real Good Time	1974	—	2.00	4.00
❑ MGM 14819	I Got Stoned and I Missed It/I Ain't Workin'	1975	—	2.00	4.00
❑ Polydor 14309	Jasper/I Can't Find Nobody Home	1976	—	2.00	4.00
❑ Town House 1062	What Mama Don't Know/That's What Little Kids Do	1982	—	2.00	4.00
❑ Warner Bros. 8299	Turn Loose of My Leg/The Fight	1976	—	2.00	4.00
❑ Warner Bros. 8538	You Can Call Me Clyde/One Step Ahead of the Law	1978	—	2.00	4.00
❑ Warner Bros. 49611	Cow Patti/Texas Guitar Song	1980	—	2.00	4.00
Albums					
❑ MGM M3G-4947	Jim Stafford	1974	2.50	5.00	10.00
❑ MGM M3G-4984	Not Just Another Pretty Foot	1975	2.50	5.00	10.00
❑ Polydor PD-1-6072	Jim Stafford	1976	2.00	4.00	8.00
—Reissue of MGM 4947					
STAFFORD, TERRY					
45s					
❑ A&M 707	Heartaches on the Way/You Left Me Here to Cry	1963	3.00	6.00	12.00
❑ Atlantic CY-4006	Amarillo by Morning/Say, Has Anybody Seen My Sweet Gypsy Rose	1973	2.00	4.00	8.00
❑ Atlantic 4015	Captured/It Sure Is Bad to Love Her	1974	—	3.00	6.00
❑ Atlantic 4026	Stop If You Love Me/We've Grown Close	1974	—	3.00	6.00
❑ Casino 113	It Sure Is Bad to Love Her/(B-side unknown)	1977	—	3.00	6.00
❑ Crusader 101	Suspicion/Judy	1964	3.75	7.50	15.00
❑ Crusader 105	I'll Touch a Star/Playing with Fire	1964	3.00	6.00	12.00
❑ Crusader 109	Follow the Rainbow/Are You a Fool Like Me	1964	3.00	6.00	12.00
❑ Crusader 110	A Little Bit Better/Hoping	1964	3.00	6.00	12.00
❑ Eastland 101	Back Together/Life's Railway to Heaven	198?	—	2.50	5.00
❑ Lana 139	Suspicion/Judy	196?	2.00	4.00	8.00
—Oldies reissue					
❑ Melodyland 6009	Darling, Think It Over/I Can't Find It	1975	—	2.50	5.00
❑ Mercury 72538	Out of the Picture/Forbidden	1966	2.50	5.00	10.00
❑ MGM 14232	Mean Woman Blues-Candy Man/Chilly Chicago	1971	—	3.00	6.00
❑ MGM 14271	California Dancer/The Walk	1971	—	3.00	6.00
❑ Player 134	Lonestar Lonesome/(B-side unknown)	1989	—	3.00	6.00
❑ Sidewalk 902	Soldier Boy/When Sin Stops, Love Begins	1966	2.50	5.00	10.00
❑ Sidewalk 914	A Step or Two Behind You/The Joke's on Me	1967	2.50	5.00	10.00
❑ Warner Bros. 7286	Big in Dallas/Will a Man Ever Learn	1969	—	3.00	6.00
Albums					
❑ Atlantic SD 7282	Say, Has Anybody Seen My Sweet Gypsy Rose	1974	3.00	6.00	12.00
❑ Crusader CLP-1001 [M]	Suspicion!	1964	10.00	20.00	40.00
❑ Crusader CLP-1001S [S]	Suspicion!	1964	15.00	30.00	60.00
STAMPEDERS					
45s					
❑ Bell 45120	Sweet City Woman/Gator Road	1971	—	3.00	6.00
❑ Bell 45154	Devil You/Giant in the Streets	1971	—	2.50	5.00
❑ Bell 45188	Monday Morning Choo-Choo/Then Came the White Man	1972	—	3.00	6.00
❑ Bell 45226	Wild Eyes/Carryin' On	1972	—	3.00	6.00
❑ Bell 45331	Oh My Lady/No Destination	1973	—	3.00	6.00
❑ Capitol 3868	Goodbye Goodbye/Me and My Stone	1974	—	2.00	4.00
❑ Capitol 3964	Running Out of Time/Ramona	1974	—	2.00	4.00
❑ MGM 13970	Be a Woman/I Don't Believe	1968	3.00	6.00	12.00
❑ Polydor 14060	Carry Me/I Didn't Need You Anyhow	1970	2.50	5.00	10.00
❑ Quality 501	Hard Lovin' Woman/Hit the Road Jack	1976	—	2.00	4.00
❑ Quality 505	Sweet Love Bandit/Let It Begin	1976	—	2.00	4.00
Albums					
❑ Bell 6068	Sweet City Woman	1971	3.75	7.50	15.00
❑ Capitol ST-11288	From the Fire	1973	3.00	6.00	12.00
❑ Capitol ST-11328	New Day	1974	3.00	6.00	12.00
❑ Quality 1001	Hit the Road	1976	3.00	6.00	12.00
STANDELLS, THE					
45s					
❑ Liberty 55680	The Peppermint Beatle/The Shake	1964	6.25	12.50	25.00
❑ Liberty 55722	Help Yourself/I'll Go Crazy	1964	5.00	10.00	20.00
❑ Liberty 55743	So Fine/Linda Lou	1964	5.00	10.00	20.00
❑ MGM 13350	Someday You'll Cry/Zebra in the Kitchen	1965	7.50	15.00	30.00
❑ Sunset 61000	Ooh Poo Pah Doo/Help Yourself	1966	5.00	10.00	20.00
❑ Tower 185	Dirty Water/Rari	1966	5.00	10.00	20.00
❑ Tower 257	Sometimes Good Guys Don't Wear White/Why Did You Hurt Me	1966	3.75	7.50	15.00
❑ Tower 282	Why Pick on Me/Mr. Nobody	1966	3.75	7.50	15.00

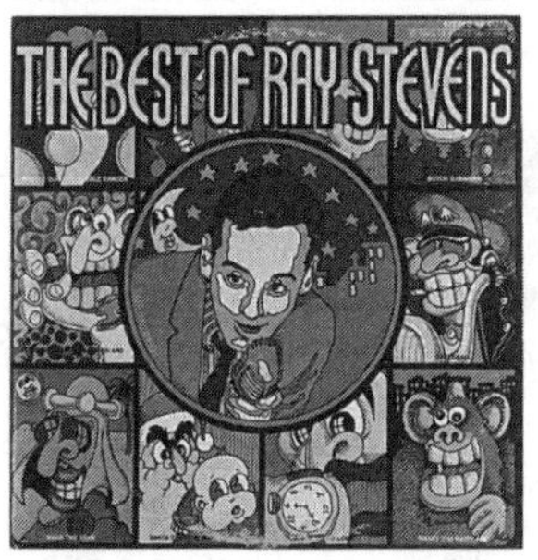

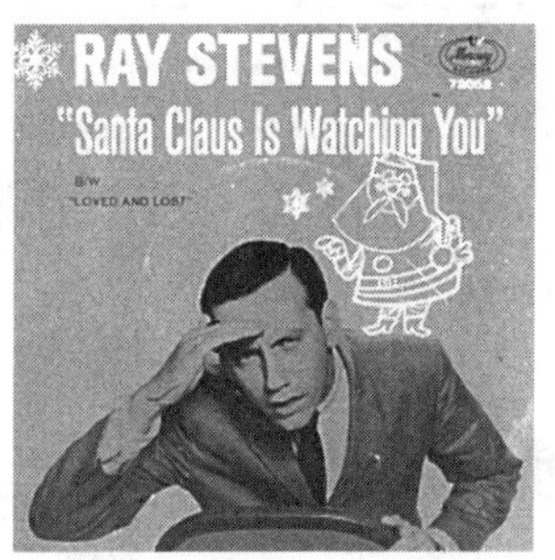

Number	Title (A Side/B Side)	Yr	VG	VG+	NM
❑ Tower 310	Try It/Poor Shell of a Man	1967	3.75	7.50	15.00
❑ Tower 312	Don't Tell Me What to Do/When I Was a Cowboy	1967	20.00	40.00	80.00
—By "The Sllednats" (Standells backwards)					
❑ Tower 314	Riot on Sunset Strip/Black Hearted Woman	1967	3.75	7.50	15.00
❑ Tower 348	Can't Help But Love You/Ninety-Nine and One Half	1967	3.75	7.50	15.00
❑ Tower 398	Animal Girl/Soul Drippin'	1968	3.75	7.50	15.00
❑ Vee Jay 643	The Boy Next Door/B.J. Quetzal	1965	5.00	10.00	20.00
❑ Vee Jay 679	Big Boss Man/Don't Say Goodbye	1965	5.00	10.00	20.00
Albums					
❑ Liberty LRP-3384 [M]	The Standells In Person at P.J.'s	1964	20.00	40.00	80.00
❑ Liberty LST-7384 [S]	The Standells In Person at P.J.'s	1964	25.00	50.00	100.00
❑ Rhino RNLP-107	The Best of the Standells	1983	2.50	5.00	10.00
❑ Rhino RNLP-115	Rarities	1983	2.50	5.00	10.00
❑ Rhino RNLP-70176	The Best of the Standells (Golden Archive Series)	1987	2.50	5.00	10.00
❑ Sunset SUM-1136 [M]	Live and Out of Sight	1966	6.25	12.50	25.00
❑ Sunset SUS-5136 [S]	Live and Out of Sight	1966	7.50	15.00	30.00
❑ Tower ST 5027 [R]	Dirty Water	1966	12.50	25.00	50.00
❑ Tower T 5027 [M]	Dirty Water	1966	15.00	30.00	60.00
❑ Tower ST 5044 [S]	Why Pick on Me	1966	15.00	30.00	60.00
❑ Tower T 5044 [M]	Why Pick on Me	1966	12.50	25.00	50.00
❑ Tower ST 5049 [S]	The Hot Ones	1966	15.00	30.00	60.00
❑ Tower T 5049 [M]	The Hot Ones	1966	12.50	25.00	50.00
❑ Tower ST 5098 [S]	Try It	1967	15.00	30.00	60.00
❑ Tower T 5098 [M]	Try It	1967	12.50	25.00	50.00

STARR, EDWIN

45s

Number	Title (A Side/B Side)	Yr	VG	VG+	NM
❑ Gordy 7066	Gonna Keep On Tryin' Til I Win Your Love/I Want My Baby Back	1967	—	3.00	6.00
❑ Gordy 7071	I Am the Man for You Baby/My Weakness Is You	1968	—	3.00	6.00
❑ Gordy 7078	Way Over There/If My Heart Could Tell the Story	1968	—	3.00	6.00
❑ Gordy 7083	Twenty-Five Miles/Love Is the Destination	1969	—	3.00	6.00
❑ Gordy 7083 [DJ]	Twenty-Five Miles (same on both sides)	1969	5.00	10.00	20.00
—Promo only on red vinyl					
❑ Gordy 7087	I'm Still a Struggling Man/Pretty Little Angel	1969	—	3.00	6.00
❑ Gordy 7090	Oh How Happy/Ooh Baby Baby	1969	—	3.00	6.00
—With Blinky					
❑ Gordy 7097	Time/Running Back and Forth	1970	—	3.00	6.00
❑ Gordy 7101	War/He Who Picks a Rose	1970	—	3.00	6.00
❑ Gordy 7104	Stop the War Now/Gonna Keep On Tryin' Til I Win Your Love	1970	—	3.00	6.00
❑ Gordy 7107	Funky Music Sho Nuff Turns Me On/Cloud Nine	1971	—	3.00	6.00
❑ Granite 522	Pain/I'll Never Forget You	1975	—	2.50	5.00
❑ Granite 528	Stay with Me/Party	1975	—	2.50	5.00
❑ Granite 532	Abyssinia Jones/Beginning	1975	—	2.50	5.00
❑ Montage 1216	Tired of It/(B-side unknown)	1982	—	2.00	4.00
❑ Motown 1276	You've Got My Soul on Fire/Love (The Lonely People's Prayer)	1973	—	2.50	5.00
❑ Motown 1284	Ain't It Hell Up in Harlem/Don't It Feel Good to Be Free	1973	—	2.50	5.00
❑ Motown 1300	Big Papa/Like We Used to Do	1974	—	2.50	5.00
❑ Motown 1326	Who's Right or Wrong/Lonely Rainy Days in San Diego	1974	—	2.50	5.00
❑ Ric-Tic 103	Agent Double-O-Soul/(Instrumental)	1965	3.75	7.50	15.00
❑ Ric-Tic 107	Back Street/(Instrumental)	1965	3.75	7.50	15.00
❑ Ric-Tic 109	Stop Her on Sight (S.O.S.)/I Have Faith in You	1966	3.75	7.50	15.00
❑ Ric-Tic 114	Headline News/Harlem	1966	3.75	7.50	15.00
❑ Ric-Tic 118	It's My Turn Now/Girls Are Getting Prettier	1967	3.75	7.50	15.00
❑ Ric-Tic 120	You're My Mellow/My Kind of Woman	1967	15.00	30.00	60.00
❑ Soul 35096	Take Me Clear from Here/Ball of Confusion	1972	—	3.00	6.00
❑ Soul 35100	Who Is the Leader of the People/Don't Tell Me I'm Crazy	1972	—	3.00	6.00
❑ Soul 35103	There You Go/(Instrumental)	1973	—	3.00	6.00
❑ 20th Century 2338	I Just Wanna Do My Thing/Mr. Davenport and Mr. James	1977	—	2.00	4.00
❑ 20th Century 2389	I'm So Into You/Don't Waste Your Time	1978	—	2.00	4.00
❑ 20th Century 2396	Contact/Don't Waste Your Time	1978	—	2.00	4.00
❑ 20th Century 2408	H.A.P.P.Y. Radio/My Friend	1979	—	2.00	4.00
❑ 20th Century 2420	It's Called the Rock/Patiently	1979	—	2.00	4.00
❑ 20th Century 2423	It's Called the Rock/H.A.P.P.Y. Radio	1979	—	2.00	4.00
❑ 20th Century 2441	It's Called the Rock/H.A.P.P.Y. Radio	1980	—	2.00	4.00
❑ 20th Century 2445	Stronger Than You Think I Am/(Instrumental)	1980	—	2.00	4.00
❑ 20th Century 2450	Tell-A-Star/Boop Boop Song	1980	—	2.00	4.00
❑ 20th Century 2455	Get Up-Whirlpool/Better and Better	1980	—	2.00	4.00

Number	Title (A Side/B Side)	Yr	VG	VG+	NM
❑ 20th Century 2477	Twenty-Five Miles/Never Turn My Back on You	1980	—	2.00	4.00
❑ 20th Century 2496	Real Live #10/Sweat	1981	—	2.00	4.00
Albums					
❑ Gordy GS-931	Soul Master	1968	6.25	12.50	25.00
❑ Gordy GS-940	25 Miles	1969	6.25	12.50	25.00
❑ Gordy GS-945	Just We Two	1969	5.00	10.00	20.00
—With Blinky					
❑ Gordy GS-948	War & Peace	1970	5.00	10.00	20.00
❑ Gordy GS-956	Involved	1971	5.00	10.00	20.00
❑ Granite 1005	Free to Be Myself	1975	3.00	6.00	12.00
❑ Motown M5-103V1	Superstar Series, Vol. 3	1981	2.50	5.00	10.00
❑ Motown M5-170V1	War & Peace	1981	2.50	5.00	10.00
❑ Pickwick SPC-3387	25 Miles	197?	2.50	5.00	10.00
❑ 20th Century T-538	Edwin Starr	1977	2.50	5.00	10.00
❑ 20th Century T-559	Clean	1978	2.50	5.00	10.00
❑ 20th Century T-591	Happy Radio	1979	2.50	5.00	10.00
❑ 20th Century T-615	Stronger Than You	1980	2.50	5.00	10.00
❑ 20th Century T-634	The Best of Edwin Starr	1981	2.50	5.00	10.00
STARR, RINGO					
45s					
❑ Apple 1831	It Don't Come Easy/Early 1970	1971	2.00	4.00	8.00
❑ Apple 1849	Back Off Boogaloo/Blindman	1972	2.00	4.00	8.00
—Green-background label					
❑ Apple 1865	Photograph/Down and Out	1973	—	3.00	6.00
—Custom star label					
❑ Apple 1870	You're Sixteen/Devil Woman	1973	—	3.00	6.00
—Custom star label					
❑ Apple 1872	Oh My My/Step Lightly	1974	—	3.00	6.00
—Custom star label					
❑ Apple 1876	Only You/Call Me	1974	—	3.00	6.00
—Custom nebula label					
❑ Apple 1880	No No Song/Snookeroo	1975	—	3.00	6.00
—Custom nebula label					
❑ Apple 1882	It's All Down to Goodnight Vienna/Oo-Wee	1975	—	3.00	6.00
—Custom nebula label					
❑ Apple 2969	Beaucoups of Blues/Coochy-Coochy	1970	2.00	4.00	8.00
—With "Mfd. by Apple" on label and no star on A-side label					
❑ Atlantic 3361	A Dose of Rock 'N' Roll/Cryin'	1976	2.50	5.00	10.00
❑ Atlantic 3371	Hey Baby/Lady Gaye	1976	7.50	15.00	30.00
❑ Atlantic 3412	Drowning in the Sea of Love/Just a Dream	1977	30.00	60.00	120.00
❑ Atlantic 3429	Wings/Just a Dream	1977	7.50	15.00	30.00
❑ Boardwalk NB7-11-130	Wrack My Brain/Drumming Is My Madness	1981	—	2.50	5.00
❑ Boardwalk NB7-11-134	Private Property/Stop and Take the Time to Smell the Roses	1982	3.00	6.00	12.00
❑ Portrait 6-70015	Lipstick Traces (On a Cigarette)/Old Time Relovin'	1978	3.75	7.50	15.00
❑ Portrait 6-70018	Heart on My Sleeve/Who Needs a Heart	1978	3.75	7.50	15.00
Albums					
❑ Apple SW-3365	Sentimental Journey	1970	5.00	10.00	20.00
❑ Apple SMAS-3368	Beaucoups of Blues	1970	5.00	10.00	20.00
❑ Apple SWAL-3413	Ringo	1973	5.00	10.00	20.00
—Standard issue with booklet; Side 1, Song 2 identified on cover as "Hold On"					
❑ Apple SW-3417	Goodnight Vienna	1974	3.00	6.00	12.00
❑ Apple SW-3422	Blast from Your Past	1975	3.75	7.50	15.00
❑ Atlantic SD 18193	Ringo's Rotogravure	1976	3.75	7.50	15.00
—Deduct 2/3 for cut-outs					
❑ Atlantic SD 19108	Ringo the 4th	1977	3.75	7.50	15.00
—Deduct 1/2 for cut-outs					
❑ Boardwalk NB1-33246	Stop and Smell the Roses	1981	2.50	5.00	10.00
—Deduct 1/2 for cut-outs					
❑ Capitol SN-16114	Ringo	198?	3.75	7.50	15.00
—Green label budget-line reissue with all errors corrected					
❑ Capitol SN-16218	Sentimental Journey	198?	6.25	12.50	25.00
—Green label budget-line reissue					
❑ Capitol SN-16219	Goodnight Vienna	198?	6.25	12.50	25.00
—Green label budget-line reissue					
❑ Capitol SN-16235	Beaucoups of Blues	198?	5.00	10.00	20.00
—Green label budget-line reissue					
❑ Capitol SN-16236	Blast from Your Past	198?	3.75	7.50	15.00
—Green label budget-line reissue					
❑ Portrait JR 35378	Bad Boy	1978	3.75	7.50	15.00
—Deduct 1/3 for cut-outs					
❑ Rykodisc RALP 0190	Ringo Starr and His All-Starr Band	1990	7.50	15.00	30.00
—With limited, numbered obi (deduct $5 if missing)					
STARSHIP					
45s					
❑ Elektra 69349	Wild Again/Laying It on the Line	1988	—	—	3.00
❑ Grunt 5109-7-R	Nothing's Gonna Stop Us Now/Layin' It on the Line	1987	—	—	3.00
❑ Grunt 5225-7-R	It's Not Over ('Til It's Over)/Babylon	1987	—	—	3.00
❑ Grunt 5308-7-R	Beat Patrol/Girls Like You	1987	—	—	3.00
❑ Grunt PB-14170	We Built This City/Private Room	1985	—	—	3.00
❑ Grunt PB-14253	Sara/Hearts of the World (Will Understand)	1985	—	—	3.00
❑ Grunt PB-14332	Tomorrow Doesn't Matter Tonight/Love Rusts	1986	—	—	3.00
❑ Grunt PB-14393	Before I Go/Cut You Down to Size	1986	—	—	3.00
❑ RCA 6964-7-R	Set the Night to Music/I Don't Know Why	1988	—	2.00	4.00
❑ RCA 8377-7-R	Nothing's Gonna Stop Us Now/Beat Patrol	1988	—	—	3.00
—Gold Standard Series					
❑ RCA 9032-7-R	It's Not Enough/Love Among the Cannibals	1989	—	—	3.00

Number	Title (A Side/B Side)	Yr	VG	VG+	NM
Albums					
❑ Grunt BXL1-5488	Knee Deep in the Hoopla	1985	2.00	4.00	8.00
❑ Grunt 6413-1-G	No Protection	1987	2.00	4.00	8.00
❑ RCA 9693-1-R	Love Among the Cannibals	1989	2.50	5.00	10.00
STATUS QUO					
45s					
❑ A&M 1425	Don't Waste My TIme/All the Reasons	1973	—	2.50	5.00
❑ A&M 1445	Paper Plane/All the Reasons	1973	—	2.50	5.00
❑ A&M 1510	Carolina/Softer Ride	1974	—	2.50	5.00
❑ Bell 45417	Gerdundula/(B-side unknown)	1973	—	2.50	5.00
❑ Cadet Concept 7001	Pictures of Matchstick Men/Gentleman Joe's Sidewalk Café	1968	2.50	5.00	10.00
❑ Cadet Concept 7006	Ice in the Sun/When My Mind Is Not Live	1968	2.00	4.00	8.00
❑ Cadet Concept 7010	Technicolor Dreams/Spicks and Specks	1969	2.00	4.00	8.00
❑ Cadet Concept 7015	Black Veils of Melancholy/To Be Free	1969	2.00	4.00	8.00
❑ Cadet Concept 7017	The Price of Love/Little Miss Nothing	1969	2.00	4.00	8.00
❑ Capitol 4039	Nightride/Down Down	1975	—	2.00	4.00
❑ Capitol 4125	Bye Bye Johnny/Down Down	1975	—	2.00	4.00
❑ Capitol 4407	Wild Side of Life/All Through the Night	1977	—	2.00	4.00
❑ Janus 127	Down the Dustpipe/Face Without a Soul	1970	—	3.00	6.00
❑ Janus 141	Gerdundula/In My Chair	1970	—	3.00	6.00
❑ Pye 65000	Good Thinking/Tuned to the Music	1971	—	3.00	6.00
❑ Pye 65017	Mean Girl/Everything	1971	—	3.00	6.00
❑ Riva 206	Living on an Island/(B-side unknown)	1980	—	2.50	5.00
Albums					
❑ A&M SP-3615	Hello!	1974	3.00	6.00	12.00
❑ A&M SP-3649	Quo	1974	3.00	6.00	12.00
❑ A&M SP-4381	Piledriver	1973	3.00	6.00	12.00
❑ Cadet Concept LPS-315	Messages from the Status Quo	1968	12.50	25.00	50.00
❑ Capitol ST-11381	On the Level	1975	2.50	5.00	10.00
❑ Capitol ST-11509	Status Quo	1976	2.50	5.00	10.00
❑ Capitol SKBB-11623 [(2)]	Status Quo Live	1977	3.00	6.00	12.00
❑ Capitol ST-11749	Rockin' All Over the World	1978	2.50	5.00	10.00
❑ Janus JLS-3018	Ma Kelly's Greasy Spoon	1970	3.75	7.50	15.00
❑ Mercury 836651-1	Status Quo	1989	3.00	6.00	12.00
❑ Pye 3301	Dog of Two Head	1971	3.75	7.50	15.00
❑ Riva 7402	Now Here This	1980	2.50	5.00	10.00
STEALERS WHEEL					
45s					
❑ A&M 1416	Stuck in the Middle with You/Jose	1973	—	2.50	5.00
❑ A&M 1450	Everyone's Agreed That Everything Will Turn Out Fine/Next to Me	1973	—	2.00	4.00
❑ A&M 1483	Star/What More Could You Want	1973	—	2.00	4.00
❑ A&M 1529	You Put Something Better Inside of Me/Wheelin'	1974	—	2.00	4.00
❑ A&M 1675	This Morning/Found My Way to You	1975	—	2.00	4.00
❑ A&M 2075	(Everyone's Agreed That) Everything Will Turn Out Fine/Who Cares	1978	—	2.50	5.00
Albums					
❑ A&M SP-4377	Stealers Wheel	1973	3.00	6.00	12.00
❑ A&M SP-4419	Ferguslie Park	1974	3.00	6.00	12.00
❑ A&M SP-4517	Right or Wrong	1974	3.00	6.00	12.00
❑ A&M SP-4708	Stuck in the Middle with You — The Best of Stealers Wheel	1978	2.50	5.00	10.00
STEAM					
45s					
❑ Fontana 1667	Na Na Hey Hey Kiss Him Goodbye/It's the Magic in You Girl	1969	2.00	4.00	8.00
❑ Mercury 30160	Na Na Hey Hey Kiss Him Goodbye/Don't Stop Lovin' Me	1976	—	2.00	4.00
—Reissue					
❑ Mercury 73020	I've Gotta Make You Love Me/One Good Woman	1970	—	3.00	6.00
❑ Mercury 73053	What I'm Saying Is True/I'm the One Who Loves You	1970	—	3.00	6.00
❑ Mercury 73117	Don't Stop Lovin' Me/Do Unto Others	1970	—	3.00	6.00
Albums					
❑ Mercury SR 61254	Steam	1969	5.00	10.00	20.00
STEELY DAN					
45s					
❑ ABC 11323	Dallas/Sail the Waterway	1972	7.50	15.00	30.00
—Neither of these songs has appeared on a U.S. Steely Dan album -- not even the "complete" CD box set!					
❑ ABC 11338	Do It Again/Fire in the Hole	1972	—	2.00	4.00

Number	Title (A Side/B Side)	Yr	VG	VG+	NM
❑ ABC 11352	Reeling In the Years/Only a Fool Would Say That	1973	—	2.50	5.00
—Original pressings have "abc" children's blocks in a white triangle					
❑ ABC 11382	Show Biz Kids/Razor Boy	1973	—	2.00	4.00
❑ ABC 11396	My Old School/Pearl of the Quarter	1973	—	2.00	4.00
❑ ABC 11439	Rikki Don't Lose That Number/Any Major Dude Will Tell You	1974	—	2.00	4.00
❑ ABC 12014	Rikki Don't Lose That Number/Any Major Dude Will Tell You	1974	—	3.00	6.00
❑ ABC 12033	Pretzel Logic/Through with Buzz	1974	—	2.00	4.00
❑ ABC 12101	Black Friday/Throw Back the Little Ones	1975	—	2.00	4.00
❑ ABC 12128	Chain Lightning/Bad Sneakers	1975	—	2.00	4.00
❑ ABC 12195	Kid Charlemagne/Green Earrings	1976	—	2.00	4.00
❑ ABC 12222	The Fez/Sign In Stranger	1976	—	2.00	4.00
❑ ABC 12320	Peg/I Got the News	1977	—	2.00	4.00
❑ ABC 12355	Deacon Blues/Home at Last	1978	—	2.00	4.00
❑ ABC 12404	Josie/Black Cow	1978	—	2.00	4.00
❑ MCA 40894	FM (No Static at All)/(Instrumental)	1978	—	2.00	4.00
❑ MCA 51036	Hey Nineteen/Bodhisattva	1980	—	2.00	4.00
❑ MCA 51082	Time Out of Mind/Bodhisattva	1981	—	2.00	4.00
Albums					
❑ ABC 758	Can't Buy a Thrill	1972	3.00	6.00	12.00
—Black label					
❑ ABC 779	Countdown to Ecstasy	1973	3.00	6.00	12.00
—Black label					
❑ ABC 806	Pretzel Logic	1974	3.00	6.00	12.00
—Black label					
❑ ABC 846	Katy Lied	1975	3.00	6.00	12.00
❑ ABC 931	The Royal Scam	1976	3.00	6.00	12.00
❑ ABC AA-1006	Aja	1977	3.00	6.00	12.00
❑ ABC AK-1107 [(2)]	Greatest Hits	1978	3.75	7.50	15.00
❑ MCA AA-1006	Aja	1980	2.50	5.00	10.00
❑ MCA 1591	Can't Buy a Thrill	1987	—	3.00	6.00
❑ MCA 1592	Countdown to Ecstasy	1987	—	3.00	6.00
❑ MCA 1593	Pretzel Logic	1987	—	3.00	6.00
❑ MCA 1594	Katy Lied	1987	—	3.00	6.00
❑ MCA 1595	The Royal Scam	1987	—	3.00	6.00
❑ MCA 1688	Aja	1987	—	3.00	6.00
❑ MCA 1693	Gaucho	1987	—	3.00	6.00
—Many in the 1500 and 1600 series have a gold stamp with the new number on the cover					
❑ MCA 5324	Gold	1982	2.50	5.00	10.00
❑ MCA 2-6008 [(2)]	Greatest Hits	1980	3.00	6.00	12.00
❑ MCA 6102	Gaucho	1980	2.50	5.00	10.00
❑ MCA 37040	Can't Buy a Thrill	1980	2.00	4.00	8.00
❑ MCA 37041	Countdown to Ecstasy	1980	2.00	4.00	8.00
❑ MCA 37042	Pretzel Logic	1980	2.00	4.00	8.00
❑ MCA 37043	Katy Lied	1980	2.00	4.00	8.00
❑ MCA 37044	The Royal Scam	1980	2.00	4.00	8.00
❑ MCA 37243	Gold	1984	2.00	4.00	8.00

STEPPENWOLF

45s

Number	Title (A Side/B Side)	Yr	VG	VG+	NM
❑ ABC 1436	The Pusher/Born to Be Wild	1970	—	2.00	4.00
—"Goldies 45" series					
❑ ABC Dunhill 4138	Born to Be Wild/Everybody's Next One	1968	2.00	4.00	8.00
❑ ABC Dunhill 4161	Magic Carpet Ride/Sookie Sookie	1968	2.00	4.00	8.00
❑ ABC Dunhill 4182	Rock Me/Jupiter Child	1969	2.00	4.00	8.00
❑ ABC Dunhill 4192	It's Never Too Late/Happy Birthday	1969	—	3.00	6.00
❑ ABC Dunhill 4205	Move Over/Power Play	1969	—	3.00	6.00
❑ ABC Dunhill 4221	Monster/Berry Rides Again	1969	—	3.00	6.00
❑ ABC Dunhill 4234	Hey Lawdy Mama/Twisted	1970	—	3.00	6.00
❑ ABC Dunhill 4248	Screaming Night Hog/Spiritual Fantasy	1970	—	3.00	6.00
❑ ABC Dunhill 4261	Who Needs Ya/Earschplittenloudenboomer	1970	—	3.00	6.00
❑ ABC Dunhill 4269	Snow Blind Friend/Hippo Stomp	1971	—	2.50	5.00
❑ ABC Dunhill 4283	Ride with Me/For Madmen Only	1971	—	2.50	5.00
❑ ABC Dunhill 4283	Ride with Me/Black Pit	1971	10.00	20.00	40.00
—This is much rarer than the version with the other flip side					
❑ ABC Dunhill 4292	For Ladies Only/Sparkle Eyes	1971	—	2.50	5.00
❑ Allegiance 3909	Hot Night in a Cold Town/Every Man for Himself	1983	—	2.00	4.00
—As "John Kay and Steppenwolf"					
❑ Dunhill 4109	The Ostrich/A Girl I Know	1967	2.50	5.00	10.00
❑ Dunhill 4123	Sookie Sookie/Take What You Need	1968	2.50	5.00	10.00
❑ Mums 6031	Straight Shootin' Woman/Justice, Don't Be Slow	1974	—	2.00	4.00
❑ Mums 6034	Get Into the Wind/Morning Blue	1974	—	2.00	4.00
❑ Mums 6036	Fool's Fantasy/Smokey Factory Blues	1975	—	2.00	4.00
❑ Mums 6040	Caroline (Are You Ready for the Outlaw)/Angel Drawers	1975	—	2.00	4.00
Albums					
❑ ABC AC-30008	The ABC Collection	1976	3.75	7.50	15.00
❑ ABC Dunhill DS-50029 [S]	Steppenwolf	1968	5.00	10.00	20.00
❑ ABC Dunhill DS-50037	The Second	1968	6.25	12.50	25.00
—With chrome border on cover					
❑ ABC Dunhill DSX-50053	At Your Birthday Party	1969	5.00	10.00	20.00
❑ ABC Dunhill DS-50060	Early Steppenwolf	1969	5.00	10.00	20.00
—Actually a 1967 concert by Sparrow (pre-Steppenwolf)					
❑ ABC Dunhill DS-50066	Monster	1969	5.00	10.00	20.00
❑ ABC Dunhill DSD-50075 [(2)]	Steppenwolf 'Live'	1970	6.25	12.50	25.00
❑ ABC Dunhill DSX-50090	Steppenwolf 7	1970	5.00	10.00	20.00
❑ ABC Dunhill DSX-50099	Steppenwolf Gold/Their Great Hits	1971	5.00	10.00	20.00
❑ ABC Dunhill DSX-50110	For Ladies Only	1971	5.00	10.00	20.00
❑ ABC Dunhill DSX-50124	Rest in Peace	1972	5.00	10.00	20.00

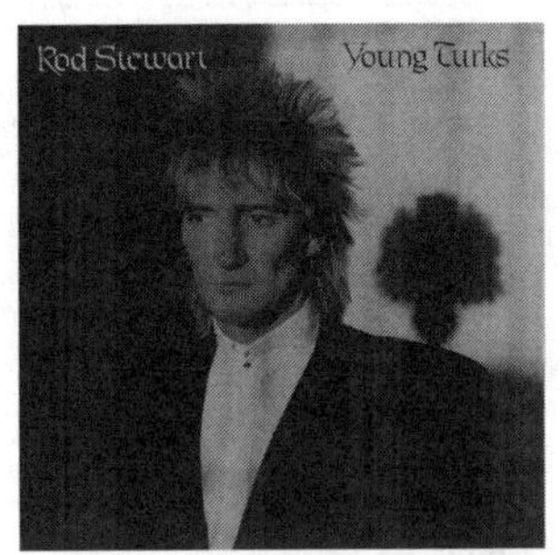

Number	Title (A Side/B Side)	Yr	VG	VG+	NM
❑ ABC Dunhill DSX-50135	16 Greatest Hits	1973	5.00	10.00	20.00
❑ Dunhill D-50029 [M]	Steppenwolf	1968	37.50	75.00	150.00
❑ Dunhill DS-50029 [S]	Steppenwolf	1968	10.00	20.00	40.00
❑ Epic PE 33583	Hour of the Wolf	1975	3.00	6.00	12.00
❑ Epic PE 34120	Skullduggery	1976	3.00	6.00	12.00
❑ Epic JE 34382	Reborn to Be Wild	1977	3.00	6.00	12.00
❑ MCA 2-6013 [(2)]	Steppenwolf 'Live'	198?	2.50	5.00	10.00
❑ MCA 37045	Steppenwolf	1979	2.00	4.00	8.00
❑ MCA 37046	The Second	1979	2.00	4.00	8.00
❑ MCA 37047	Steppenwolf 7	1979	2.00	4.00	8.00
❑ MCA 37049	16 Greatest Hits	1979	2.00	4.00	8.00
❑ MCA DSX-50099	Steppenwolf Gold/Their Great Hits	1980	3.00	6.00	12.00
—Columbia House edition on blue rainbow label, but retaining the original ABC Dunhill catalog number					
❑ Mums PZ 33093	Slow Flux	1974	3.75	7.50	15.00

STEVENS, CAT

45s

Number	Title (A Side/B Side)	Yr	VG	VG+	NM
❑ A&M 1211	Lady D'Arbanville/Time — Fill My Eyes	1970	—	2.50	5.00
❑ A&M 1231	Wild World/Miles from Nowhere	1970	—	2.50	5.00
❑ A&M 1265	Moon Shadow/I Think I See the Light	1971	—	2.00	4.00
❑ A&M 1291	Peace Train/Where Do the Children Play	1971	—	2.00	4.00
❑ A&M 1335	Morning Has Broken/I Want to Live in a Wigwam	1972	—	2.00	4.00
❑ A&M 1396	Sitting/Crab Dance	1972	—	2.00	4.00
❑ A&M 1418	The Hurt/Silent Sunlight	1973	—	2.00	4.00
❑ A&M 1503	Oh Very Young/100 I Dream	1974	—	2.00	4.00
❑ A&M 1602	Another Saturday Night/Home in the Sky	1974	—	2.00	4.00
❑ A&M 1645	Ready/I Think I See the Light	1974	—	2.00	4.00
❑ A&M 1700	Two Fine People/Bad Penny	1975	—	2.00	4.00
❑ A&M 1785	Banapple Gas/Ghost Town	1976	—	2.00	4.00
❑ A&M 1924	(I Never Wanted) To Be a Star/Land O' Freelove and Goodbye	1977	—	2.00	4.00
❑ A&M 1948	(Remember the Days of the) Old School Yard/ Land O' Freelove and Goodbye	1977	—	2.00	4.00
❑ A&M 1971	Was Dog a Doughnut/Sweet Jamaica	1977	—	2.00	4.00
❑ A&M 2109	Bad Brakes/Nascimento	1979	—	2.00	4.00
❑ A&M 2126	Randy/Nascimento	1979	—	2.00	4.00
❑ A&M 2683	If You Want to Sing Out, Sing Out/I Want to Live in a Wigwam	1984	—	2.00	4.00
❑ Deram 7501	I Love My Dog/Portobello Road	1966	2.50	5.00	10.00
❑ Deram 7505	Matthew and Son/Granny	1967	2.50	5.00	10.00
❑ Deram 7518	Kitty/The Blackness of the Night	1968	2.00	4.00	8.00
❑ Deram 85006	I'm Gonna Get Me a Gun/School Is Out	1967	2.50	5.00	10.00
❑ Deram 85015	Laughing Apple/Bad Night	1967	2.50	5.00	10.00
❑ Deram 85079	Kitty/Where Are You	1972	—	3.00	6.00

Albums

Number	Title (A Side/B Side)	Yr	VG	VG+	NM
❑ A&M SP-3160	Mona Bone Jakon	198?	2.00	4.00	8.00
—Reissue of 4260					
❑ A&M SP-3285	Footsteps in the Dark — Greatest Hits, Volume Two	1986	2.00	4.00	8.00
—Reissue of 3736					
❑ A&M SP-3623	Buddha and the Chocolate Box	1974	3.00	6.00	12.00
❑ A&M SP-3736	Footsteps in the Dark — Greatest Hits, Volume Two	1984	2.50	5.00	10.00
❑ A&M SP-4260	Mona Bone Jakon	1970	3.00	6.00	12.00
—Brown label					
❑ A&M SP-4280	Tea for the Tillerman	1971	3.00	6.00	12.00
—Brown label					
❑ A&M SP-4313	Teaser and the Firecat	1971	3.00	6.00	12.00
—Brown label					
❑ A&M SP-4365	Catch Bull at Four	1972	3.00	6.00	12.00
❑ A&M SP-4391	Foreigner	1973	3.00	6.00	12.00
❑ A&M SP-4519	Greatest Hits	1975	3.00	6.00	12.00
❑ A&M SP-4555	Numbers	1975	3.00	6.00	12.00
❑ A&M SP-4702	Izitso	1977	3.00	6.00	12.00
❑ A&M SP-4735	Back to Earth	1978	3.00	6.00	12.00
❑ Deram DE 16005 [M]	Matthew and Son	1967	5.00	10.00	20.00
❑ Deram DES 18005 [P]	Matthew and Son	1967	3.75	7.50	15.00
❑ Deram DES 18005/10 [(2)P]	Matthew and Son/New Masters	1971	3.75	7.50	15.00
❑ Deram DES 18010 [S]	New Masters	1968	3.75	7.50	15.00
❑ Deram DES 18061 [P]	Very Young and Early Songs	1972	3.00	6.00	12.00
❑ London LC-50010	Cat's Cradle	1977	3.00	6.00	12.00
❑ London 820321-1	Cat's Cradle	1985	2.00	4.00	8.00

Number	Title (A Side/B Side)	Yr	VG	VG+	NM
STEVENS, RAY					
45s					
❑ Barnaby 514	Gitarzan/Unwind	197?	—	2.00	4.00
❑ Barnaby 515	Everything Is Beautiful/Turn Your Radio On	197?	—	2.00	4.00
❑ Barnaby 516	Mr. Businessman/Sunday Morning Comin' Down	197?	—	2.00	4.00
❑ Barnaby 517	Ahab the Arab/Along Came Jones	197?	—	2.00	4.00
❑ Barnaby 518	Freddie Feelgood (And His Funky Little Five Piece Band)/ Isn't It Lonely Together	197?	—	2.00	4.00
❑ Barnaby 519	Have a Little Talk with Myself/Bridget the Midget (The Queen of the Blues)	197?	—	2.00	4.00
—Barnaby releases in the 500 series are reissues; some may be re-recordings					
❑ Barnaby 600	The Streak/You've Got the Music Inside	1974	—	2.00	4.00
—Multicolor label					
❑ Barnaby 600	The Streak/You've Got the Music Inside	1974	—	2.50	5.00
—White label (not a promo)					
❑ Barnaby 604	Moonlight Special/Just So Proud to Be Here	1974	—	2.00	4.00
❑ Barnaby 610	Everybody Needs a Rainbow/Inside	1974	—	2.00	4.00
❑ Barnaby 614	Misty/Sunshine	1975	—	2.00	4.00
❑ Barnaby 616	Indian Love Call/Piece of Paradise	1975	—	2.00	4.00
❑ Barnaby 618	Young Love/Deep Purple	1975	—	2.00	4.00
❑ Barnaby 619	Lady of Spain/Mockingbird Hill	1976	—	2.00	4.00
❑ Barnaby 2011	Everything Is Beautiful/A Brighter Day	1970	—	3.00	6.00
❑ Barnaby 2016	America, Communicate with Me/Monkey See, Monkey Do	1970	—	2.50	5.00
❑ Barnaby 2021	Sunset Strip/Islands	1970	—	2.50	5.00
❑ Barnaby 2024	Bridget the Midget (The Queen of the Blues)/Night People	1970	—	2.50	5.00
❑ Barnaby 2029	A Mama and a Papa/Melt	1971	—	2.50	5.00
❑ Barnaby 2039	All My Trials/Have a Little Talk with Myself	1971	—	2.50	5.00
❑ Barnaby 2048	Turn Your Radio On/Loving You on Paper	1971	—	2.50	5.00
❑ Barnaby 2058	Love Lifted Me/Monkey See, Monkey Do	1972	—	2.50	5.00
❑ Barnaby 2058	Love Lifted Me/Glory Special	1972	—	2.50	5.00
❑ Barnaby 2065	Losing Streak/Inside	1972	—	2.50	5.00
❑ Barnaby 5020	Golden Age/Nashville	1973	—	2.00	4.00
❑ Barnaby 5028	Love Me Longer/Float	1973	—	2.00	4.00
❑ Capitol F3967	Chickie Chickie Wah Wah/Crying Goodbye	1958	6.25	12.50	25.00
❑ Capitol F4030	Cat Pants/Love Goes On Forever	1958	7.50	15.00	30.00
❑ Capitol F4101	The School/The Clown	1958	6.25	12.50	25.00
❑ MCA 52451	Joggin'/I'm Kissin' You Goodbye	1984	—	2.00	4.00
❑ MCA 52492	Mississippi Squirrel Revival/Ned Nostril	1984	—	2.00	4.00
❑ MCA 52548	It's Me Again, Margaret/Joggin'	1985	—	—	3.00
❑ MCA 52657	The Haircut Song/Punk Country Love	1985	—	—	3.00
❑ MCA 52738	Santa Claus Is Watching You/Armchair Quarterback	1985	—	2.00	4.00
❑ MCA 52771	Vacation Bible School/The Ballad of the Blue Cyclone	1986	—	—	3.00
❑ MCA 52906	The Camping Trip/Southern Air	1986	—	—	3.00
❑ MCA 52924	People's Court/Dudley Doright (Of the Highway Patrol)	1986	—	—	3.00
❑ MCA 53007	Can He Love You Half As Much As I Do/Dudley Doright (Of the Highway Patrol)	1987	—	—	3.00
❑ MCA 53101	Would Jesus Wear a Rolex?/Cool Down Willard	1987	—	2.00	4.00
❑ MCA 53178	Three-Legged Man/Doctor, Doctor (Have Mercy on Me)	1987	—	—	3.00
❑ MCA 53232	Sex Symbols/The Ballad of Cactus Pete and Lefty	1987	—	—	3.00
❑ MCA 53372	Surfin' U.S.S.R./Language, Nudity, Violence & Sex	1988	—	—	3.00
❑ MCA 53423	The Day I Tried to Teach Charlene MacKenzie How to Drive/I Don't Need None of That	1988	—	—	3.00
❑ MCA 53661	I Saw Elvis in a U.F.O./I Used to Be Crazy	1989	2.50	5.00	10.00
❑ Mercury 71843	Jeremiah Peabody's Poly Unsaturated Quick Dissolving Fast Acting Pleasant Tasting Green and Purple Pills/Teen Years	1961	3.75	7.50	15.00
❑ Mercury 71888	Scratch My Back/When You Wish Upon a Star	1961	3.75	7.50	15.00
❑ Mercury 71966	Ahab, the Arab/It's Been So Long	1962	3.75	7.50	15.00
❑ Mercury 72039	Further More/Saturday Night at the Movies	1962	3.75	7.50	15.00
❑ Mercury 72058	Santa Claus Is Watching You/Loved and Lost	1962	3.75	7.50	15.00
❑ Mercury 72098	Funny Man/Just One of Life's Little Tragedies	1963	3.75	7.50	15.00
❑ Mercury 72125	Harry the Hairy Ape/Little Stone Statue	1963	3.75	7.50	15.00
❑ Mercury 72189	Speed Ball/It's Party Time	1963	3.75	7.50	15.00
❑ Mercury 72255	Butch Barbarian (Sure Footed Mountain Climber World Famous Yodeling Champion)/Don't Say Anything	1963	3.75	7.50	15.00
❑ Mercury 72307	Bubble Gum the Bubble Dancer/Laughing Over My Grave	1964	3.75	7.50	15.00
❑ Mercury 72382	Rockin' Teenage Mummies/It Only Hurts When I Love	1965	5.00	10.00	20.00
❑ Mercury 72430	Mr. Baker the Undertaker/Old English Surfer	1965	5.00	10.00	20.00
❑ Mercury 72816	Funny Man/Just One of Life's Little Tragedies	1968	3.00	6.00	12.00
❑ Mercury 812496-7	Pice of Paradise Called Tennessee/Mary Lou Nights	1983	—	2.00	4.00
❑ Mercury 812906-7	My Dad/Game Show Love	1983	—	2.50	5.00
❑ Mercury 814196-7	Love Will Beat Your Brains Out/Game Show Love	1983	—	2.00	4.00
❑ Mercury 818057-7	My Dad/Me	1984	—	2.00	4.00
❑ Monument 911	A-B-C/Party People	1966	2.50	5.00	10.00
❑ Monument 927	Devil-May-Care/Make a Few Memories	1966	2.50	5.00	10.00
❑ Monument 946	Freddy Feelgood (And His Funky Little Five Piece Band)/ There's One in Every Crowd	1966	2.50	5.00	10.00
❑ Monument 1001	Mary, My Secretary/Answer Me, My Love	1967	2.00	4.00	8.00
❑ Monument 1048	Unwind/For He's a Jolly Good Fellow	1968	2.00	4.00	8.00
❑ Monument 1083	Mr. Businessman/Face the Music	1968	2.00	4.00	8.00
❑ Monument 1099	Isn't It Lonely Together/The Great Escape	1968	2.00	4.00	8.00
❑ Monument 1131	Gitarzan/Bagpipes-That's My Bag	1969	2.00	4.00	8.00
❑ Monument 1150	Along Came Jones/Yakety Yak	1969	2.00	4.00	8.00
❑ Monument 1163	Sunday Mornin' Comin' Down/The Minority	1969	—	3.00	6.00
❑ Monument 1171	Have a Little Talk with Myself/Little Woman	1969	—	3.00	6.00
❑ Monument 1187	I'll Be Your Baby Tonight/Fool on the Hill	1970	—	3.00	6.00
❑ NRC 031	High School Yearbook (Deck of Cards)/Truly True	1959	6.25	12.50	25.00
❑ NRC 042	What Would I Do Without You/My Heart Cries for You	1959	6.25	12.50	25.00

Number	Title (A Side/B Side)	Yr	VG	VG+	NM
❑ NRC 057	Sergeant Preston of the Yukon/Who Do You Love	1960	6.25	12.50	25.00
❑ NRC 063	Happy Blue Year/White Christmas	1960	6.25	12.50	25.00
❑ Prep 108	Rang Tang Ding Dong (I'm the Japanese Sandman)/Silver Bracelet	1957	6.25	12.50	25.00
❑ Prep 122	Five More Steps/Tingle	1957	6.25	12.50	25.00
❑ RCA PB-11911	Shriner's Convention/You're Never Goin' to Tampa With Me	1980	—	2.00	4.00
❑ RCA PB-12069	Night Games/Let's Do It Right This Time	1980	—	2.00	4.00
❑ RCA PB-12170	One More Last Chance/I Believe You Love Me	1981	—	2.00	4.00
❑ RCA PB-12185	The Streak/Misty	1981	—	2.00	4.00
❑ RCA GB-12368	Everything Is Beautiful/Gitarzan	1981	—	—	3.00
—Gold Standard Series					
❑ RCA GB-12370	Shriner's Convention/You're Never Goin' to Tampa With Me	1981	—	—	3.00
—Gold Standard Series					
❑ RCA PB-13038	Written Down in My Heart/Country Boy, Country Club Girl	1981	—	2.00	4.00
❑ RCA PB-13207	Where the Sun Don't Shine/Why Don't We Go Somewhere and Love	1982	—	2.00	4.00
❑ Warner Bros. 8198	You Are So Beautiful/One Man Band	1976	—	2.00	4.00
❑ Warner Bros. 8237	Honky Tonk Waltz/Om	1976	—	2.00	4.00
❑ Warner Bros. 8301	In the Mood/Classical Cluck	1976	—	3.00	6.00
—As "Henhouse Five Plus Too"					
❑ Warner Bros. 8318	Get Crazy with Me/Dixie Hummingbird	1977	—	2.00	4.00
❑ Warner Bros. 8393	Dixie Hummingbird/Feel the Music	1977	—	2.00	4.00
❑ Warner Bros. 8603	Be Your Own Best Friend/With a Smile	1978	—	2.00	4.00
❑ Warner Bros. 8785	I Need Your Help Barry Manilow/Daydream Romance	1979	—	2.00	4.00
❑ Warner Bros. 8849	The Feeling's Not Right Again/Get Crazy with Me	1979	—	2.00	4.00
Albums					
❑ Barnaby 5004	Ray Stevens' Greatest Hits	1974	2.50	5.00	10.00
—Reissue of 30770					
❑ Barnaby 5005	Nashville	1974	2.50	5.00	10.00
—Reissue of 15007					
❑ Barnaby 6003	Boogity Boogity	1974	3.00	6.00	12.00
❑ Barnaby 6012	Misty	1975	3.00	6.00	12.00
❑ Barnaby 6018	The Very Best of Ray Stevens	1975	3.00	6.00	12.00
❑ Barnaby BR 15007	Nashville	1973	3.00	6.00	12.00
❑ Barnaby Z 30092	Ray Stevens...Unreal!!!	1970	3.00	6.00	12.00
❑ Barnaby Z 30770	Ray Stevens' Greatest Hits	1971	3.00	6.00	12.00
❑ Barnaby Z 30809	Turn Your Radio On	1972	3.00	6.00	12.00
❑ Barnaby KZ 32139	Losin' Streak	1972	3.00	6.00	12.00
❑ Barnaby Z12 35005	Everything Is Beautiful	1970	3.75	7.50	15.00
❑ MCA 5517	He Thinks He's Ray Stevens	1984	2.50	5.00	10.00
❑ MCA 5635	I Have Returned	1985	2.50	5.00	10.00
❑ MCA 5795	Surely You Joust	1986	2.50	5.00	10.00
❑ MCA 5918	Greatest Hits	1987	2.50	5.00	10.00
❑ MCA 42020	Crackin' Up!	1987	2.50	5.00	10.00
❑ MCA 42062	Greatest Hits, Volume 2	1987	2.50	5.00	10.00
❑ MCA 42172	I Never Made a Record I Didn't Like	1988	2.50	5.00	10.00
❑ MCA 42303	Beside Myself	1989	2.50	5.00	10.00
❑ Mercury MG-20732 [M]	1,837 Seconds of Humor	1962	10.00	20.00	40.00
❑ Mercury MG-20828 [M]	This Is Ray Stevens	1963	6.25	12.50	25.00
❑ Mercury SR-60732 [S]	1,837 Seconds of Humor	1962	12.50	25.00	50.00
❑ Mercury SR-60828 [S]	This Is Ray Stevens	1963	7.50	15.00	30.00
❑ Mercury SR-61272	The Best of Ray Stevens	1968	3.75	7.50	15.00
❑ Mercury 812780-1	Me	1984	2.50	5.00	10.00
❑ Monument SLP-18102	Even Stevens	1968	3.75	7.50	15.00
❑ Monument SLP-18115	Gitarzan	1969	3.75	7.50	15.00
❑ Monument SLP-18134	Have a Little Talk with Myself	1970	3.75	7.50	15.00
❑ Pickwick SPC-3266	Rock and Roll Show	1971	2.50	5.00	10.00
❑ Priority PU 38075	Turn Your Radio On	1982	2.50	5.00	10.00
—Reissue of Barnaby 30809					
❑ RCA Victor AHL1-3574	Shriner's Convention	1980	2.50	5.00	10.00
❑ RCA Victor AHL1-3841	One More Last Chance	1981	2.50	5.00	10.00
❑ RCA Victor AYL1-4253	Shriner's Convention	1982	2.00	4.00	8.00
—"Best Buy Series" reissue					
❑ RCA Victor AHL1-4288	Don't Laugh Now	1982	2.50	5.00	10.00
❑ RCA Victor AHL1-4727	Greatest Hits	1983	2.50	5.00	10.00
❑ RCA Victor AYL1-5153	Greatest Hits	1985	2.00	4.00	8.00
—"Best Buy Series" reissue					
❑ RCA Victor CPL1-7161	Collector's Series	1986	2.50	5.00	10.00
❑ Warner Bros. BS 2914	Just for the Record	1976	2.50	5.00	10.00

Number	Title (A Side/B Side)	Yr	VG	VG+	NM
❑ Warner Bros. BS 2997	Feel the Music	1977	2.50	5.00	10.00
❑ Warner Bros. BS 3098	There Is Something...	1977	2.50	5.00	10.00
❑ Warner Bros. BS 3195	Be Your Own Best Friend	1978	2.50	5.00	10.00
❑ Warner Bros. BSK 3332	The Feeling's Not Right Again	1979	2.50	5.00	10.00

STEWART, AL

45s

Number	Title (A Side/B Side)	Yr	VG	VG+	NM
❑ Arista 0362	Time Passages/Almost Lucy	1978	—	2.00	4.00
❑ Arista 0389	Song on the Radio/A Man for All Seasons	1979	—	2.00	4.00
❑ Arista 0552	Midnight Rocks/Constantinople	1980	—	2.00	4.00
❑ Arista 0576	Paint by Numbers/Optical Illusion	1980	—	2.00	4.00
❑ Arista 0585	Running Man/Merlin's Theme	1981	—	2.00	4.00
❑ Arista 0639	Indian Summer/Soko (Needless to Say)	1981	—	2.00	4.00
❑ Janus 243	Nostradamus/Terminal Eyes	1974	—	2.50	5.00
❑ Janus 250	Carol/Sirens of Titan	1975	—	2.50	5.00
❑ Janus 266	Year of the Cat/Broadway Hotel	1976	—	2.50	5.00
❑ Janus 267	On the Border/Flying Sorcery	1977	—	2.50	5.00

Albums

Number	Title (A Side/B Side)	Yr	VG	VG+	NM
❑ Arista AL 4190	Time Passages	1978	2.50	5.00	10.00
❑ Arista AL6-8326	Year of the Cat	198?	2.00	4.00	8.00
—Reissue of Arista 9503					
❑ Arista AL6-8342	Time Passages	198?	2.00	4.00	8.00
—Reissue of 4190					
❑ Arista AL6-8359	Past, Present and Future	198?	2.00	4.00	8.00
—Reissue of Arista 9524					
❑ Arista A2L 8607 [(2)]	Live/Indian Summer	1981	3.00	6.00	12.00
❑ Arista AL 9503	Year of the Cat	1979	2.50	5.00	10.00
—Reissue of Janus 7022					
❑ Arista AL 9520	24 Carrots	1980	2.50	5.00	10.00
❑ Arista AL 9524	Past, Present and Future	1980	2.50	5.00	10.00
—Reissue of Janus 3063					
❑ Arista AL 9525	Modern Times	1980	2.50	5.00	10.00
—Reissue of Janus 7012					
❑ Enigma D1-73316	Last Days of the Century	1988	3.00	6.00	12.00
❑ Epic BN 26564	Love Chronicles	1970	5.00	10.00	20.00
❑ Janus 3063	Past, Present and Future	1974	3.75	7.50	15.00
❑ Janus 7012	Modern Times	1975	3.00	6.00	12.00
❑ Janus 7022	Year of the Cat	1976	3.00	6.00	12.00
❑ Janus 7026 [(2)]	The Early Years	1977	3.75	7.50	15.00
❑ Passport PB-6042	Russians and Americans	1986	3.00	6.00	12.00

STEWART, BILLY

45s

Number	Title (A Side/B Side)	Yr	VG	VG+	NM
❑ Argo 5256	Billy's Blues (Part 1)/Billy's Blues (Part 2)	1956	10.00	20.00	40.00
❑ Chess 1625	Billy's Blues (Part 1)/Billy's Blues (Part 2)	1956	15.00	30.00	60.00
❑ Chess 1820	Reap What You Sow/Fat Boy	1962	3.00	6.00	12.00
❑ Chess 1835	True Fine Lovin'/Wedding Bells	1962	3.00	6.00	12.00
❑ Chess 1852	Scramble/Oh What Can the Matter Be	1963	3.00	6.00	12.00
❑ Chess 1868	Strange Feeling/Sugar and Spice	1963	3.00	6.00	12.00
❑ Chess 1888	Count Me Out/A Fat Boy Can Cry	1964	2.50	5.00	10.00
❑ Chess 1905	Tell It Like It Is/My Sweet Senorita	1964	2.50	5.00	10.00
❑ Chess 1922	I Do Love You/Keep Loving	1965	2.50	5.00	10.00
❑ Chess 1932	Sitting in the Park/Once Again	1965	2.50	5.00	10.00
❑ Chess 1941	How Nice It Is/No Girl	1965	2.50	5.00	10.00
❑ Chess 1948	Because I Love You/Mountain of Love	1965	2.50	5.00	10.00
❑ Chess 1960	Love Me/Why Am I Lonely	1966	2.50	5.00	10.00
❑ Chess 1966	Summertime/To Love, To Love	1966	3.00	6.00	12.00
—Blueish label					
❑ Chess 1978	Secret Love/Look Back and Smile	1966	2.50	5.00	10.00
❑ Chess 1991	Every Day I Have the Blues/Ol' Man River	1967	2.50	5.00	10.00
❑ Chess 2002	Cross My Heart/Why (Do I Love You So)	1967	2.50	5.00	10.00
❑ Chess 2053	Tell Me the Truth/What Have I Done	1968	2.50	5.00	10.00
❑ Chess 2063	I'm in Love (Oh Yes I Am)/Crazy 'Bout You Baby	1969	2.50	5.00	10.00
❑ Chess 2080	By the Time I Get to Phoenix/We'll Always Be Together	1969	2.50	5.00	10.00
❑ Okeh 7095	Baby, You're My Only Love/Billy's Heartache	1957	75.00	150.00	300.00
❑ United Artists 340	This Is a Fine Time/Young in Years	1961	3.75	7.50	15.00

Albums

Number	Title (A Side/B Side)	Yr	VG	VG+	NM
❑ Chess LP-1496 [M]	I Do Love You	1965	20.00	40.00	80.00
—Red cover, black "wheel"					
❑ Chess LPS-1496 [S]	I Do Love You	1965	25.00	50.00	100.00
—Red cover, black "wheel"					
❑ Chess LP-1499 [M]	Unbelievable	1966	7.50	15.00	30.00
❑ Chess LPS-1499 [S]	Unbelievable	1966	10.00	20.00	40.00
❑ Chess LP-1513 [M]	Billy Stewart Teaches Old Standards New Tricks	1967	7.50	15.00	30.00
❑ Chess LPS-1513 [S]	Billy Stewart Teaches Old Standards New Tricks	1967	10.00	20.00	40.00
❑ Chess LPS-1547	Billy Stewart Remembered	1970	6.25	12.50	25.00
❑ Chess CH-9104	The Greatest Sides	198?	2.50	5.00	10.00
❑ Chess CH-50059	Cross My Heart	1974	3.75	7.50	15.00

STEWART, JOHN

45s

Number	Title (A Side/B Side)	Yr	VG	VG+	NM
❑ Allegiance 3900	The Queen of Hollywood High/Judy in G Major	198?	—	2.00	4.00
❑ Capitol 2469	Mother Country/Shackles and Chains	1969	—	3.00	6.00
❑ Capitol 2538	July, You're a Woman/She Believes in Me	1969	—	3.00	6.00
❑ Capitol 2605	Armstrong/Anna on a Memory	1969	—	3.00	6.00
❑ Capitol 2711	Earth Rider/The Lady and the Outlaw	1969	—	3.00	6.00
❑ Capitol 2712	World of No Return/Wild Is Love	1969	2.00	4.00	8.00
—B-side by Patti Drew					

Number	Title (A Side/B Side)	Yr	VG	VG+	NM
❑ Capitol 2842	Clack Clack/Marshall Wind	1970	—	3.00	6.00
❑ RCA Victor 74-0970	Chilly Winds/Durango	1973	—	2.50	5.00
❑ RCA Victor APBO-0109	Anna on a Memory/Wheatfield	1973	—	2.50	5.00
❑ RCA Victor PB-10003	July, You're a Woman/Runaway Fool of Love	1974	—	2.50	5.00
❑ RCA Victor PB-10227	Survivors/Josie	1975	—	2.50	5.00
❑ RCA Victor PB-10268	Survivors/Josie	1975	—	2.50	5.00
❑ RSO 894	Promise the Wind/Morning Thunder	1978	—	2.00	4.00
❑ RSO 931	Gold/Comin' Out of Nowhere	1979	—	2.00	4.00
❑ RSO 1000	Midnight Wind/Somewhere Down the Line	1979	—	2.00	4.00
❑ RSO 1016	Lost Her in the Sun/Heart of the Dream	1979	—	2.00	4.00
❑ RSO 1031	(Odin) Spirit of the Water/Love Has Tied My Wings	1980	—	2.00	4.00
❑ Vita 169	Rockin' Anna/Lorraine	1958	62.50	125.00	250.00
—As "Johnny Stewart"					
❑ Warner Bros. 7525	Daydream Believer/Sweet Lizard	1971	—	2.50	5.00
❑ Warner Bros. 7552	Light Come Shine/A Little Road and a Stone to Roll	1972	—	2.50	5.00
❑ Warner Bros. 7592	An Accent of Halley's Comet/Arkansas Breakout	1972	—	2.50	5.00
Albums					
❑ Affordable Dreams AD-01	Trancas	1984	2.50	5.00	10.00
❑ Allegiance AV-431	Blondes	1982	2.50	5.00	10.00
❑ Capitol ST-203	California Bloodlines	1969	3.75	7.50	15.00
❑ Capitol ST-540	Willard	1970	3.75	7.50	15.00
❑ Capitol ST 2975	Signals Through the Glass	1968	5.00	10.00	20.00
❑ Capitol SN-16150	California Bloodlines	198?	2.00	4.00	8.00
—Budget-line reissue					
❑ Capitol SN-16151	Willard	198?	2.00	4.00	8.00
—Budget-line reissue					
❑ Cypress 661117-1	Punch the Big Guy	1987	2.50	5.00	10.00
❑ Homecoming HC-0200	Centennial	1984	2.50	5.00	10.00
❑ Homecoming HC-0300	The Last Campaign	1985	2.50	5.00	10.00
❑ Homecoming HC-0500	The Trio Years	1986	2.50	5.00	10.00
❑ RCA Victor CPL2-0265 [(2)]	The Phoenix Concerts — Live	1974	3.75	7.50	15.00
❑ RCA Victor APL1-0816	Wingless Angels	1975	3.00	6.00	12.00
❑ RCA Victor AFL1-3513	John Stewart in Concert	1980	2.50	5.00	10.00
❑ RCA Victor AYL1-3731	Cannons in the Rain	1981	2.00	4.00	8.00
—"Best Buy Series" reissue					
❑ RCA Victor LSP-4827	Cannons in the Rain	1973	3.00	6.00	12.00
❑ RSO RS-1-3027	Fire in the Wind	1977	2.50	5.00	10.00
❑ RSO RS-1-3051	Bombs Away Dream Babies	1979	2.50	5.00	10.00
❑ RSO RS-1-3074	Dream Babies Go Hollywood	1980	2.50	5.00	10.00
❑ Warner Bros. WS 1948	The Lonesome Picker Rides Again	1971	3.00	6.00	12.00
❑ Warner Bros. BS 2611	Sunstorm	1972	3.00	6.00	12.00

STEWART, ROD

45s

Number	Title (A Side/B Side)	Yr	VG	VG+	NM
❑ Geffen 28303	Twistin' the Night Away/Let's Get Small	1987	—	2.00	4.00
—B-side by Steve Martin					
❑ Mercury 73009	Handbags and Gladrags/An Old Raincoat Won't Ever Let You Down	1970	2.50	5.00	10.00
❑ Mercury 73031	Handbags and Gladrags/Man of Constant Sorrow	1970	2.00	4.00	8.00
❑ Mercury 73095	It's All Over Now/Joe's Lament	1970	2.50	5.00	10.00
❑ Mercury 73115	Only a Hero/Gasoline Alley	1970	2.50	5.00	10.00
❑ Mercury 73156	Cut Across Shorty/Gasoline Alley	1970	2.50	5.00	10.00
❑ Mercury 73175	My Way of Giving/Lady Day	1971	—	3.00	6.00
❑ Mercury 73196	Country Comfort/Gasoline Alley	1971	—	3.00	6.00
❑ Mercury 73224	Maggie May/Reason to Believe	1971	—	3.00	6.00
❑ Mercury 73244	(I Know) I'm Losing You/Mandolin Wind	1971	—	2.50	5.00
❑ Mercury 73330	You Wear It Well/True Blue	1972	—	2.50	5.00
❑ Mercury 73344	Angel/Lost Paraguayos	1972	—	2.50	5.00
❑ Mercury 73412	Twistin' the Night Away//True Blue-Lady Day	1973	—	2.50	5.00
❑ Mercury 73426	Oh No Not My Baby/Jodie	1973	—	2.50	5.00
❑ Mercury 73636	Mine for Me/Farewell	1974	—	2.50	5.00
❑ Mercury 73660	Let Me Be Your Car/Sailor	1974	—	3.00	6.00
❑ Mercury 73802	Every Picture Tells a Story/What's Made Milwaukee Famous (Has Made a Loser Out of Me)	1976	—	2.50	5.00
❑ Press 9722	Good Morning Little Schoolgirl/I'm Gonna Move to the Outskirts of Town	1965	10.00	20.00	40.00
❑ Private Stock 45,130	Shake/Bright Lights, Big City	1976	—	3.00	6.00
❑ Warner Bros. GWB 0349	Tonight's the Night (Gonna Be Alright)/The First Cut Is the Deepest	1978	—	—	3.00
—"Back to Back Hits" series					

Number	Title (A Side/B Side)	Yr	VG	VG+	NM
❑ Warner Bros. GWB 0359 *—"Back to Back Hits" series*	You're In My Heart (The Final Acclaim)/Hot Legs	1979	—	—	3.00
❑ Warner Bros. GWB 0371 *—"Back to Back Hits" series*	I Was Only Joking/The Killing of Georgie (Part 1 and 2)	1979	—	—	3.00
❑ Warner Bros. GWB 0382 *—"Back to Back Hits" series*	Da Ya Think I'm Sexy?/Ain't Love a Bitch	1980	—	—	3.00
❑ Warner Bros. GWB 0404 *—"Back to Back Hits" series*	Passion/Somebody Special	1981	—	—	3.00
❑ Warner Bros. GWB 0427 *—"Back to Back Hits" series*	Young Turks/Tonight I'm Yours (Don't Hurt Me)	1982	—	—	3.00
❑ Warner Bros. GWB 0469 *—"Back to Back Hits" series*	Baby Jane/What Am I Gonna Do (I'm So in Love with You)	1984	—	—	3.00
❑ Warner Bros. GWB 0522 *—"Back to Back Hits" series*	Infatuation/Some Guys Have All the Luck	1985	—	—	3.00
❑ Warner Bros. 8066 *—As "Rod Stewart and Faces"*	As Long As You Tell Him/You Can Make Me Dance, Sing or Anything	1975	—	2.50	5.00
❑ Warner Bros. 8102 *—As "Rod Stewart and Faces"*	As Long As You Tell Him/You Can Make Me Dance, Sing or Anything	1975	—	2.00	4.00
❑ Warner Bros. 8146	Sailing/All in the Name of Rock and Roll	1975	—	2.00	4.00
❑ Warner Bros. 8170	This Old Heart of Mine/Still Love Again	1975	—	2.50	5.00
❑ Warner Bros. 8262	Tonight's the Night (Gonna Be Alright)/Fool for You	1976	—	2.00	4.00
❑ Warner Bros. 8321	The First Cut Is the Deepest/Ball Trap	1977	—	2.00	4.00
❑ Warner Bros. 8396	The Killing of Georgie (Part 1 and 2)/Rosie	1977	—	2.00	4.00
❑ Warner Bros. 8475	You're In My Heart (The Final Acclaim)/You Got a Nerve	1977	—	2.00	4.00
❑ Warner Bros. 8535	Hot Legs/You're Insane	1978	—	2.00	4.00
❑ Warner Bros. 8568	I Was Only Joking/Born Loose	1978	—	2.00	4.00
❑ Warner Bros. 8724 *—Off-white label*	Da Ya Think I'm Sexy?/Scarred and Scared	1978	—	2.00	4.00
❑ Warner Bros. 8724 *—"Burbank" palm trees label*	Da Ya Think I'm Sexy?/Scarred and Scared	1978	2.50	5.00	10.00
❑ Warner Bros. 8810	Ain't Love a Bitch/Last Summer	1979	—	2.00	4.00
❑ Warner Bros. 21976 *—"Back to Back Hits" series*	Love Touch (Love Theme from Legal Eagles)/Hot Legs	1988	—	—	3.00
❑ Warner Bros. 22685	Downtown Train/The Killing of Georgie (Part 1 and 2)	1989	—	—	3.00
❑ Warner Bros. 27657	Crazy About Her/Dynamite	1989	—	—	3.00
❑ Warner Bros. 27729	My Heart Can't Tell You No/The Wild Horse	1988	—	—	3.00
❑ Warner Bros. 27796	Forever Young/Days of Rage	1988	—	—	3.00
❑ Warner Bros. 27927	Lost in You/Almost Illegal	1988	—	—	3.00
❑ Warner Bros. 28625	Every Beat of My Heart/Trouble	1986	—	—	3.00
❑ Warner Bros. 28631	Another Heartache/You're In My Heart (The Final Acclaim)	1986	—	—	3.00
❑ Warner Bros. 28668	Love Touch (Love Theme from Legal Eagles)/Heart Is on the Line	1986	—	—	3.00
❑ Warner Bros. 29122	All Right Now/Dancin' Alone	1984	—	2.00	4.00
❑ Warner Bros. 29215	Some Guys Have All the Luck/I Was Only Joking	1984	—	2.00	4.00
❑ Warner Bros. 29256	Infatuation/She Won't Dance with Me	1984	—	2.00	4.00
❑ Warner Bros. 29256	Infatuation/Three Time Loser	1984	—	2.00	4.00
❑ Warner Bros. 29564	What Am I Gonna Do (I'm So in Love with You)/Dancin' Alone	1983	—	2.00	4.00
❑ Warner Bros. 29608	Baby Jane/Ready Now	1983	—	2.00	4.00
❑ Warner Bros. 29874	Guess I'll Always Love You/Rock My Plimsoul	1982	—	2.00	4.00
❑ Warner Bros. 49138	I Don't Want to Talk About It/Best Days of My Life	1979	—	2.00	4.00
❑ Warner Bros. 49617	Passion/Better Off Dead	1980	—	2.00	4.00
❑ Warner Bros. 49686	Somebody Special/She Won't Dance with Me	1981	—	2.00	4.00
❑ Warner Bros. 49843	Young Turks/Sonny	1981	—	2.00	4.00
❑ Warner Bros. 49886	Tonight I'm Yours (Don't Hurt Me)/Tora, Tora, Tora	1981	—	2.00	4.00
❑ Warner Bros. 50051	How Long/Jealous	1982	—	2.00	4.00
Albums					
❑ Accord SN-7142	Rod the Mod	1981	3.00	6.00	12.00
❑ Mercury SRM-1-609 *—Original cover has an attached, perforated poster*	Every Picture Tells a Story	1971	3.75	7.50	15.00
❑ Mercury SRM-1-697 *—By "Rod Stewart/Faces"*	Rod Stewart/Faces Live: Coast to Coast Overtures and Beginners	1973	3.75	7.50	15.00
❑ Mercury SRM-1-1017 *—Chicago skyline label*	Smiler	1974	3.00	6.00	12.00
❑ Mercury SRM-2-7507 [(2)]	The Best of Rod Stewart	1976	3.75	7.50	15.00
❑ Mercury SRM-2-7509 [(2)]	The Best of Rod Stewart, Volume 2	1977	3.75	7.50	15.00
❑ Mercury SR-61237 *—Cover is yellow with no black border*	The Rod Stewart Album	1969	6.25	12.50	25.00
❑ Mercury SR-61264 *—Cover is textured, most noticeably on the pebbles*	Gasoline Alley	1970	5.00	10.00	20.00
❑ Mercury 822385-1	Every Picture Tells a Story	1984	2.00	4.00	8.00
❑ Mercury 822791-1 [(2)]	The Best of Rod Stewart, Volume 2	1985	3.00	6.00	12.00
❑ Mercury 824881-1	Gasoline Alley	1985	2.00	4.00	8.00
❑ Mercury 824882-1	Sing It Again Rod	1985	2.00	4.00	8.00
❑ Mercury 826287-1 [(2)]	The Best of Rod Stewart	1985	3.00	6.00	12.00
❑ Private Stock PS-2021	A Shot of Rhythm and Blues	1976	3.75	7.50	15.00
❑ Springboard SPB-4030	Rod Stewart and The Faces	197?	3.00	6.00	12.00
❑ Springboard SPB-4063	Rod Stewart and Steampacket	197?	3.00	6.00	12.00
❑ Trip TOP-16-31	Looking Back/16 Early Hits	1974	3.00	6.00	12.00
❑ United Distributors UDL-2391	The Day Will Come	1981	5.00	10.00	20.00
❑ Warner Bros. BS 2875	Atlantic Crossing	1975	2.50	5.00	10.00
❑ Warner Bros. BS 2938	A Night on the Town	1976	2.50	5.00	10.00
❑ Warner Bros. BSK 3092	Foot Loose and Fancy Free	1977	2.50	5.00	10.00
❑ Warner Bros. BSK 3108 *—Reissue of 2875*	Atlantic Crossing	1977	2.00	4.00	8.00
❑ Warner Bros. BSK 3116 *—Reissue of 2938*	A Night on the Town	1977	2.00	4.00	8.00
❑ Warner Bros. BSK 3261	Blondes Have More Fun	1978	2.50	5.00	10.00

Number	Title (A Side/B Side)	Yr	VG	VG+	NM
❑ Warner Bros. HS 3373	Rod Stewart Greatest Hits	1979	2.50	5.00	10.00
❑ Warner Bros. HS 3485	Foolish Behaviour	1980	2.50	5.00	10.00
❑ Warner Bros. BSK 3602	Tonight I'm Yours	1981	2.50	5.00	10.00
❑ Warner Bros. 23743 [(2)]	Absolutely Live	1982	3.00	6.00	12.00
❑ Warner Bros. 23877	Body Wishes	1983	2.00	4.00	8.00
❑ Warner Bros. 25095	Camouflage	1984	2.00	4.00	8.00
—Issued with 16 different back covers, all of equal value, that, when assembled, form a giant poster					
❑ Warner Bros. 25446	Rod Stewart	1986	2.00	4.00	8.00
❑ Warner Bros. 25884	Out of Order	1988	2.00	4.00	8.00
❑ Warner Bros. 26158	Downtown Train: Selections from the Storyteller Anthology	1990	3.00	6.00	12.00
STILLS, STEPHEN					
45s					
❑ Atlantic 2778	Love the One You're With/To a Flame	1970	—	3.00	6.00
❑ Atlantic 2790	Sit Yourself Down/We Are Not Helpless	1971	—	2.50	5.00
❑ Atlantic 2806	Change Partners/Relaxing Town	1971	—	2.50	5.00
❑ Atlantic 2820	Marianne/Nothin' to Do But Today	1971	—	2.50	5.00
❑ Atlantic 2876	It Doesn't Matter/Rock & Roll's Crazy Medley	1972	—	2.50	5.00
❑ Atlantic 2888	Rock and Roll Crazies/Colorado	1972	—	2.50	5.00
—With Manassas					
❑ Atlantic 2917	Down the Road/Guaguanco De Vero	1972	—	2.50	5.00
—With Manassas					
❑ Atlantic 2959	So Many Times/Isn't It About Time	1973	—	2.50	5.00
❑ Atlantic 89597	Only Love Can Break Your Heart/Love Again	1984	—	2.00	4.00
❑ Atlantic 89611	Can't Let Go/Grey to Green	1984	—	2.00	4.00
—With Walter Finnegan					
❑ Atlantic 89633	Stranger/No Hiding Place	1984	—	2.00	4.00
❑ Columbia 10179	Turn Back the Pages/Shuffle Just as Bad	1975	—	2.50	5.00
❑ Columbia 10369	Buyin' Time/Soldier	1976	—	2.50	5.00
❑ Columbia 10804	Lowdown/Can't Get No Booty	1978	—	2.50	5.00
❑ Columbia 10872	Thoroughfare Gap/Lowdown	1978	—	2.50	5.00
Albums					
❑ Atlantic SD 2-903 [(2)]	Manassas	1972	3.75	7.50	15.00
❑ Atlantic SD 7202	Stephen Stills	1970	3.00	6.00	12.00
❑ Atlantic SD 7206	Stephen Stills 2	1971	3.00	6.00	12.00
❑ Atlantic SD 7250	Down the Road	1973	3.00	6.00	12.00
❑ Atlantic SD 18156	Stephen Stills Live	1975	3.00	6.00	12.00
❑ Atlantic SD 18201	Still Stills — The Best of Stephen Stills	1976	2.50	5.00	10.00
❑ Atlantic 80177	Right By You	1984	2.00	4.00	8.00
❑ Columbia PC 33575	Stills	1975	2.50	5.00	10.00
—No bar code on cover					
❑ Columbia PC 34348	Illegal Stills	1976	2.50	5.00	10.00
❑ Columbia JC 35380	Thoroughfare Gap	1978	2.50	5.00	10.00
STONE PONEYS					
45s					
❑ Capitol 2004	Different Drum/I've Got to Know	1967	3.75	7.50	15.00
❑ Capitol 2110	Up to My Neck in High Muddy Water/Carnival Bear	1968	2.50	5.00	10.00
❑ Capitol 2195	Hobo (Mornin' Glory)/Some of Shelly's Blues	1968	2.50	5.00	10.00
❑ Capitol 5838	All the Beautiful Things/Sweet Summer Blue and Gold	1967	2.50	5.00	10.00
❑ Capitol 5910	One for One/Evergreen	1967	2.50	5.00	10.00
❑ Sidewalk 937	So Fine/Everyone Has Their Own Ideas	1968	50.00	100.00	200.00
Albums					
❑ Capitol ST 2666 [S]	The Stone Poneys	1967	7.50	15.00	30.00
❑ Capitol T 2666 [M]	The Stone Poneys	1967	6.25	12.50	25.00
❑ Capitol ST 2763 [S]	Evergreen, Vol. 2	1967	7.50	15.00	30.00
❑ Capitol T 2763 [M]	Evergreen, Vol. 2	1967	10.00	20.00	40.00
❑ Capitol ST 2863	Linda Ronstadt/Stone Poneys and Friends Vol. III	1968	12.50	25.00	50.00
❑ Capitol ST-11383	The Stone Poneys Featuring Linda Ronstadt	1974	2.50	5.00	10.00
❑ Pickwick SPC-3298	Stoney End	1976	3.00	6.00	12.00
STORIES					
45s					
❑ Kama Sutra 545	I'm Coming Home/You Told Me	1972	—	2.00	4.00
❑ Kama Sutra 558	Top of the City/Stepback	1972	—	2.00	4.00
❑ Kama Sutra 566	Darling/Take Cover	1972	—	2.00	4.00
❑ Kama Sutra 574	Love in Motion/Changes Have Begun	1973	—	2.00	4.00
❑ Kama Sutra 577	Brother Louie/What Comes After	1973	—	2.50	5.00

Number	Title (A Side/B Side)	Yr	VG	VG+	NM
❑ Kama Sutra 577	Brother Louie/Changes Have Begun	1973	—	3.00	6.00
❑ Kama Sutra 584	Mammy Blue/Travelling Underground	1973	—	2.00	4.00
❑ Kama Sutra 588	Circles/If It Feels Good	1974	—	2.00	4.00
❑ Kama Sutra 594	Another Love/Love Is In Motion	1974	—	2.00	4.00
Albums					
❑ Kama Sutra KSBS-2051	Stories	1972	3.00	6.00	12.00
❑ Kama Sutra KSBS-2068	About Us	1973	7.50	15.00	30.00
—Gatefold; does NOT contain "Brother Louie"					
❑ Kama Sutra KSBS-2078	Traveling Underground	1974	3.00	6.00	12.00
STRANGELOVES, THE					
45s					
❑ Bang 501	I Want Candy/It's About My Baby	1965	3.75	7.50	15.00
❑ Bang 508	Cara-Lin/(Roll On) Mississippi	1965	3.00	6.00	12.00
❑ Bang 514	Night Time/Rhythm of Love	1965	3.00	6.00	12.00
❑ Bang 524	Hand Jive/I Gotta Dance	1966	3.00	6.00	12.00
❑ Bang 544	Just the Way You Are/Quarter to Three	1967	3.00	6.00	12.00
❑ Sire 4102	I Wanna Do It/Honey Do	1968	2.50	5.00	10.00
❑ Swan 4192	Love Love (That's All I Want from You)/I'm on Fire	1964	5.00	10.00	20.00
Albums					
❑ Bang BLP-211 [M]	I Want Candy	1965	20.00	40.00	80.00
❑ Bang BLPS-211 [S]	I Want Candy	1965	25.00	50.00	100.00
STRAWBERRY ALARM CLOCK					
45s					
❑ All American 373	Incense and Peppermints/The Birdman of Alcatrash	1967	50.00	100.00	200.00
❑ Uni 55018	Incense and Peppermints/The Birdman of Alcatrash	1967	3.00	6.00	12.00
❑ Uni 55046	Tomorrow/Birds in My Tree	1967	2.50	5.00	10.00
❑ Uni 55055	Pretty Song from Psych-Out/Sit with the Guru	1968	2.50	5.00	10.00
❑ Uni 55076	Barefoot in Baltimore/Angry Young Man	1968	2.50	5.00	10.00
❑ Uni 55093	Paxton's Back Street Carnival/Sea Shell	1968	2.50	5.00	10.00
❑ Uni 55113	Stand By/Miss Attraction	1969	2.00	4.00	8.00
❑ Uni 55125	Good Morning Starshine/Me and the Township	1969	2.00	4.00	8.00
❑ Uni 55158	Desiree/Changes	1969	2.00	4.00	8.00
❑ Uni 55185	Small Package/Starting Out the Day	1969	2.00	4.00	8.00
❑ Uni 55190	I Climbed the Mountain/Three	1969	2.00	4.00	8.00
❑ Uni 55218	California Day/Three	1970	5.00	10.00	20.00
❑ Uni 55241	Girl from the City/Three	1970	5.00	10.00	20.00
Albums					
❑ Uni 3014 [M]	Incense and Peppermints	1967	12.50	25.00	50.00
❑ Uni 73014 [S]	Incense and Peppermints	1967	10.00	20.00	40.00
❑ Uni 73025	Wake Up It's Tomorrow	1968	10.00	20.00	40.00
❑ Uni 73035	The World in a Sea Shell	1968	10.00	20.00	40.00
❑ Uni 73054	Good Morning Starshine	1969	10.00	20.00	40.00
❑ Uni 73074	The Best of the Strawberry Alarm Clock	1970	10.00	20.00	40.00
❑ Vocalion VL 73915	Changes	1971	12.50	25.00	50.00
STREISAND, BARBRA					
45s					
❑ Arista 0123	How Lucky Can You Get/More Than You Know	1975	—	3.00	6.00
❑ Columbia 11-02065	Promises/Make It Like a Memory	1981	—	2.00	4.00
❑ Columbia 18-02621	Comin' In and Out of Your Life/Lost Inside of You	1981	—	2.00	4.00
❑ Columbia 18-02717	Memory/Evergreen (Love Theme from "A Star Is Born")	1982	—	2.00	4.00
❑ Columbia 38-04177	The Way He Makes Me Feel (Studio)/(Film Version)	1983	—	—	3.00
❑ Columbia 38-04357	Papa Can You Hear Me?/Will Someone Ever Look at Me That Way	1984	—	—	3.00
❑ Columbia 38-04605	Left in the Dark/Here We Are at Last	1984	—	—	3.00
❑ Columbia 38-04695	Make No Mistake, He's Mine/Clear Sailing	1984	—	—	3.00
—A-side with Kim Carnes					
❑ Columbia 38-04707	Emotion/Here We Are at Last	1984	—	—	3.00
❑ Columbia 38-05680	Somewhere/Not While I'm Around	1985	—	—	3.00
❑ Columbia 38-05837	Send In the Clowns/Being Alive	1986	—	2.00	4.00
❑ Columbia 38-08026	All I Ask of You/On My Way to You	1988	—	2.00	4.00
❑ Columbia 38-08062	Till I Loved You/Two People	1988	—	—	3.00
—A-side with Don Johnson					
❑ Columbia 10075	Love in the Afternoon/Guava Jelly	1974	—	2.50	5.00
❑ Columbia 10130	Let the Good Times Roll/Jubilation	1975	—	2.50	5.00
❑ Columbia 10198	My Father's Song/By the Way	1975	—	2.50	5.00
❑ Columbia 10272	Shake Me, Wake Me, When It's Over/Widescreen	1975	—	2.50	5.00
❑ Columbia 3-10450	Love Theme from "A Star Is Born" (Evergreen)/I Believe in Love	1976	—	2.50	5.00
❑ Columbia 3-10555	My Heart Belongs to Me/Answer Me	1977	—	2.50	5.00
❑ Columbia 3-10756	Songbird/Honey Can I Put On Your Clothes	1978	—	2.00	4.00
❑ Columbia 3-10777	Love Theme from "Eyes of Laura Mars" (Prisoner)/Laura and Nevil	1978	—	2.00	4.00
❑ Columbia 3-10931	Superman/A Man I Loved	1979	—	2.00	4.00
❑ Columbia 3-11008	The Main Event/Fight//(Instrumental)	1979	—	2.00	4.00
❑ Columbia 1-11125	No More Tears (Enough Is Enough)/Wet	1979	—	2.00	4.00
—A-side with Donna Summer					
❑ Columbia 1-11179	Kiss Me in the Rain/I Ain't Gonna Cry Tonight	1980	—	2.00	4.00
❑ Columbia 1-11364	Woman in Love/Run Wild	1980	—	2.00	4.00
❑ Columbia 11-11390	Guilty/Life Story	1980	—	2.00	4.00
—A-side with Barry Gibb					
❑ Columbia 11-11430	What Kind of Fool/The Love Inside	1981	—	2.00	4.00
—A-side with Barry Gibb					
❑ Columbia 42631	Happy Days Are Here Again/When the Sun Comes Out	1962	5.00	10.00	20.00
❑ Columbia 42648	My Coloring Book/Lover Come Back to Me	1962	3.75	7.50	15.00
❑ Columbia 42937	Gotta Move/Make Believe	1964	3.75	7.50	15.00
❑ Columbia 42965	People/I Am Woman	1964	2.50	5.00	10.00
❑ Columbia 43127	Funny Girl/Absent Minded Me	1964	2.50	5.00	10.00
❑ Columbia 43248	Why Did I Choose You/My Love	1965	2.00	4.00	8.00

Number	Title (A Side/B Side)	Yr	VG	VG+	NM
❑ Columbia 43323	My Man/Where Is the Wonder	1965	2.00	4.00	8.00
❑ Columbia 43403	He Touched Me/I Like Him	1965	2.00	4.00	8.00
❑ Columbia 43469	Second Hand Rose/The Kind of Man a Woman Needs	1965	2.00	4.00	8.00
❑ Columbia 43518	Where Am I Going?/You Wanna Bet	1966	—	3.00	6.00
❑ Columbia 43612	Sam, You Made the Pants Too Long/The Minute Waltz	1966	—	3.00	6.00
❑ Columbia 43739	La Mer/C'est Rien	1966	2.00	4.00	8.00
❑ Columbia 43808	Free Again/I've Been Here	1966	—	3.00	6.00
❑ Columbia 43896	Sleep in Heavenly Peace (Silent Night)/Gounod's Ave Maria	1966	2.50	5.00	10.00
❑ Columbia 44225	Stout-Hearted Men/Look	1967	—	3.00	6.00
❑ Columbia 44331	Lover Man (Oh, Where Can You Be)/My Funny Valentine	1967	—	3.00	6.00
❑ Columbia 44350	Jingle Bells?/White Christmas	1967	7.50	15.00	30.00
❑ Columbia 44351	Have Yourself a Merry Little Christmas/The Best Gift	1967	2.50	5.00	10.00
❑ Columbia 44352	My Favorite Things/The Christmas Song	1967	7.50	15.00	30.00
❑ Columbia 44354	I Wonder As I Wander/The Lord's Prayer	1967	7.50	15.00	30.00
❑ Columbia 44474	Our Corner of the Night/He Could Show Me	1968	—	2.50	5.00
❑ Columbia 44532	Morning After/Where Is the Wonder	1968	—	2.50	5.00
❑ Columbia 44622	Funny Girl/I'd Rather Be Blue Over You	1968	—	2.50	5.00
❑ Columbia 44704	Don't Rain on My Parade/My Man	1968	—	3.00	6.00
❑ Columbia 44775	Punky's Dilemma/Frank Mills	1969	—	2.50	5.00
❑ Columbia 44921	Honey Pie/Little Tin Soldier	1969	—	2.50	5.00
❑ Columbia 45040	What About Today/What Are You Doing the Rest of Your Life	1969	—	2.50	5.00
❑ Columbia 45072	Love Is Only Love/Before the Parade Passes By	1970	—	2.50	5.00
❑ Columbia 45147	The Best Thing You've Ever Done/Summer Me, Winter Me	1970	—	2.50	5.00
❑ Columbia 45236	Stoney End/I'll Be Home	1970	—	2.50	5.00
❑ Columbia 45341	Time and Love/No Easy Way Down	1971	—	2.50	5.00
❑ Columbia 45384	Flim Flam Man/Maybe	1971	—	2.50	5.00
❑ Columbia 45414	Where You Lead/Since I Fell for You	1971	—	2.50	5.00
❑ Columbia 45471	Mother/The Summer Knows	1971	—	2.50	5.00
❑ Columbia 45511	One Less Bell to Answer-A House Is Not a Home/Space Captain	1971	—	2.50	5.00
❑ Columbia 45626	Sweet Inspiration-Where You Lead/Didn't We	1972	—	2.50	5.00
❑ Columbia 45686	Sing a Song-Make Your Own Kind of Music/ Starting Here-Starting Now	1972	—	2.50	5.00
❑ Columbia 45739	Didn't We/On a Clear Day	1972	—	2.50	5.00
❑ Columbia 45780	If I Close My Eyes/(Instrumental)	1973	—	2.50	5.00
❑ Columbia 45944	The Way We Were/What Are You Doing the Rest of Your Life	1973	—	2.50	5.00
—A-side contains a different vocal than most of the album versions					
❑ Columbia 46024	All in Love Is Fair/My Buddy-How About Me	1974	—	2.50	5.00
❑ Columbia 68691	What Were We Thinking Of/Why Let It Go	1989	—	—	3.00
Albums					
❑ Columbia CL 2007 [M]	The Barbra Streisand Album	1963	5.00	10.00	20.00
—"Guaranteed High Fidelity" on label					
❑ Columbia CL 2054 [M]	The Second Barbra Streisand Album	1963	5.00	10.00	20.00
—"Guaranteed High Fidelity" on label					
❑ Columbia CL 2154 [M]	The Third Album	1964	5.00	10.00	20.00
—"Guaranteed High Fidelity" on label					
❑ Columbia CL 2215 [M]	People	1964	5.00	10.00	20.00
—"Guaranteed High Fidelity" on label					
❑ Columbia CL 2336 [M]	My Name Is Barbra	1965	5.00	10.00	20.00
—"Guaranteed High Fidelity" on label					
❑ Columbia CL 2409 [M]	My Name Is Barbra, Two	1965	3.75	7.50	15.00
❑ Columbia CL 2478 [M]	Color Me Barbra	1966	3.75	7.50	15.00
❑ Columbia CL 2547 [M]	Je M'Appelle Barbra	1966	3.75	7.50	15.00
❑ Columbia CL 2682 [M]	Simply Streisand	1967	7.50	15.00	30.00
❑ Columbia CL 2757 [M]	A Christmas Album	1967	6.25	12.50	25.00
❑ Columbia CS 8807 [S]	The Barbra Streisand Album	1963	6.25	12.50	25.00
—"360 Sound Stereo" in black on label					
❑ Columbia CS 8854 [S]	The Second Barbra Streisand Album	1963	6.25	12.50	25.00
—"360 Sound Stereo" in black on label					
❑ Columbia CS 8954 [S]	The Third Album	1964	6.25	12.50	25.00
—"360 Sound Stereo" in black on label					
❑ Columbia CS 9015 [S]	People	1964	6.25	12.50	25.00
—"360 Sound Stereo" in black on label					
❑ Columbia CS 9136 [S]	My Name Is Barbra	1965	6.25	12.50	25.00
—"360 Sound Stereo" in black on label					
❑ Columbia CS 9209 [S]	My Name Is Barbra, Two	1965	5.00	10.00	20.00
—Red "360 Sound Stereo" label					

Number	Title (A Side/B Side)	Yr	VG	VG+	NM
❑ Columbia CS 9278 [S]	Color Me Barbra	1966	5.00	10.00	20.00
—Red "360 Sound Stereo" label					
❑ Columbia CS 9347 [S]	Je M'Appelle Barbra	1966	5.00	10.00	20.00
—Red "360 Sound Stereo" label					
❑ Columbia CS 9482 [S]	Simply Streisand	1967	5.00	10.00	20.00
—Red "360 Sound Stereo" label					
❑ Columbia CS 9557 [S]	A Christmas Album	1967	5.00	10.00	20.00
—Red "360 Sound Stereo" label					
❑ Columbia CS 9710	A Happening in Central Park	1968	3.75	7.50	15.00
—Red "360 Sound Stereo" label					
❑ Columbia CS 9816	What About Today?	1969	3.75	7.50	15.00
—Red "360 Sound Stereo" label					
❑ Columbia KCS 9968	Barbra Streisand's Greatest Hits	1970	3.75	7.50	15.00
—Red "360 Sound Stereo" label					
❑ Columbia KC 30378	Stoney End	1971	3.75	7.50	15.00
❑ Columbia KC 30792	Barbra Joan Streisand	1971	3.75	7.50	15.00
❑ Columbia KC 31760	Live Concert at the Forum	1972	3.75	7.50	15.00
❑ Columbia KC 32655	Barbra Streisand...And Other Musical Instruments	1973	3.00	6.00	12.00
❑ Columbia PC 32801	The Way We Were	1974	3.00	6.00	12.00
—Revised version; has this title on spine, label and front cover					
❑ Columbia PC 32801	Barbra Streisand Featuring The Way We Were and All In Love Is Fair	1974	5.00	10.00	20.00
—Original version with this title on spine and label, and no title on front cover					
❑ Columbia PC 33095	Butterfly	1974	3.00	6.00	12.00
—Original with no bar code					
❑ Columbia PC 33815	Lazy Afternoon	1975	3.00	6.00	12.00
—Original with no bar code					
❑ Columbia JS 34403	A Star Is Born	1976	3.00	6.00	12.00
—With Kris Kristofferson					
❑ Columbia JC 34830	Streisand Superman	1977	3.00	6.00	12.00
❑ Columbia PC 35275	Songbird	198?	2.00	4.00	8.00
—Budget-line reissue					
❑ Columbia FC 35679	Barbra Streisand's Greatest Hits, Volume 2	1978	3.00	6.00	12.00
❑ Columbia FC 36258	Wet	1979	2.50	5.00	10.00
❑ Columbia FC 36750	Guilty	1980	2.50	5.00	10.00
❑ Columbia TC 37678	Memories	1981	2.50	5.00	10.00
❑ Columbia JS 39152	Yentl	1983	2.50	5.00	10.00
❑ Columbia QC 39480	Emotion	1984	2.50	5.00	10.00
❑ Columbia OC 40092	The Broadway Album	1985	2.50	5.00	10.00
❑ Columbia OC 40788	One Voice	1987	2.50	5.00	10.00
❑ Columbia OC 40880	Till I Loved You	1988	2.50	5.00	10.00
❑ Columbia HC 42801	The Way We Were	1982	7.50	5.00	30.00
—Half-speed mastered edition					
❑ Columbia OC 45369	A Collection: Greatest Hits.. And More	1989	3.75	7.50	15.00
❑ Columbia Masterworks M 33452	Classical Barbra	1976	3.00	6.00	12.00

STYLISTICS, THE

45s

Number	Title (A Side/B Side)	Yr	VG	VG+	NM
❑ Amherst 301	Because I Love You Girl/My Love, Come Live With Me	1985	—	2.00	4.00
❑ Avco 4581	You Are Everything/Country Living	1971	—	2.50	5.00
❑ Avco 4591	Betcha by Golly, Wow/Ebony Eyes	1972	—	2.50	5.00
❑ Avco 4595	People Make the World Go Round/Point of No Return	1972	—	2.50	5.00
❑ Avco 4603	I'm Stone in Love with You/Make It Last	1972	—	2.50	5.00
❑ Avco 4611	Break Up to Make Up/You and Me	1973	—	2.50	5.00
❑ Avco 4618	You'll Never Get to Heaven (If You Break My Heart)/ If You Don't Watch Out	1973	—	2.50	5.00
❑ Avco 4625	Rockin' Roll Baby/Pieces	1973	—	2.50	5.00
❑ Avco 4634	You Make Me Feel Brand New/Only for the Children	1974	—	2.50	5.00
❑ Avco 4640	Let's Put It All Together/I Take It Out on You	1974	—	2.50	5.00
❑ Avco 4647	Heavy Fallin' Out/Go Now	1974	—	2.50	5.00
❑ Avco 4649	Star on a TV Show/Hey Girl, Come and Get It	1975	—	2.50	5.00
❑ Avco 4652	Thank You Baby/Sing, Baby, Sing	1975	—	2.50	5.00
❑ Avco 4656	Can't Give You Anything (But My Love)/I'd Rather Be Hurt by You	1975	—	2.50	5.00
❑ Avco 4661	Funky Weekend/If You Are There	1975	—	2.50	5.00
❑ Avco 4664	You Are Beautiful/Michael and Me	1976	—	2.50	5.00
❑ Avco Embassy 4555	You're a Big Girl Now/Let the Junkie Beat the Pusher	1970	—	3.00	6.00
❑ Avco Embassy 4572	Stop, Look, Listen (To Your Heart)/If I Love You	1971	—	3.00	6.00
❑ H&L 4669	Can't Help Falling in Love/Jenny	1976	—	2.00	4.00
❑ H&L 4674	Because I Love You, Girl/You Are	1976	—	2.00	4.00
❑ H&L 4676	Only You/What Goes Around Comes Around	1976	—	2.00	4.00
❑ H&L 4678	I Got a Letter/Satin Doll	1977	—	2.00	4.00
❑ H&L 4681	Shame and Scandal in the Family/That Don't Shake Me	1977	—	2.00	4.00
❑ H&L 4686	I'm Coming Home/I Run to You	1977	—	2.00	4.00
❑ H&L 4695	Fool of the Year/Good Thing Goin'	1978	—	2.00	4.00
❑ Mercury 74005	First Impressions/Your Love's Too Good to Be Forgotten	1978	—	2.00	4.00
❑ Mercury 74022	I Can't Stop Livin'/You're the Best Thing in My Life	1978	—	2.00	4.00
❑ Mercury 74042	Love at First Sight/Broken Wing	1979	—	2.00	4.00
❑ Mercury 74057	Don't Know Where I'm Going/You Make Me Feel So Doggone Good	1979	—	2.00	4.00
❑ Philadelphia Int'l. 02901	Callin' You/Don't Come Telling Me Lies	1982	—	2.00	4.00
❑ Philadelphia Int'l. 03085	Lighten Up/We Should Be Lovers	1982	—	2.00	4.00
❑ Sebring 8370	You're a Big Girl Now/Let the Junkie Beat the Pusher	1970	7.50	15.00	30.00
❑ Streetwise 1136	Give a Little Love/Give a Little Love (Sing Along Version)	1984	—	2.00	4.00
❑ Streetwise 1137	Some Things Never Change/Row Your Love	1985	—	2.00	4.00
❑ Streetwise 1138	Special/(B-side unknown)	1985	—	2.00	4.00
❑ TSOP 02195	What's Your Name/Almost There	1981	—	2.00	4.00
❑ TSOP 02588	Mine All Mine/Closer Than Close	1981	—	2.00	4.00
❑ TSOP 02702	Habit/I've Got This Feeling	1982	—	2.00	4.00

Number	Title (A Side/B Side)	Yr	VG	VG+	NM
❑ TSOP 4789	Hurry Up This Way Again/It Started Out	1980	—	2.00	4.00
❑ TSOP 4798	And I'll See You No More/Driving Me Wild	1980	—	2.00	4.00
Albums					
❑ Amherst AMH-743	The Best of the Stylistics	1986	2.50	5.00	10.00
❑ Amherst AMH-744	All-Time Classics	1986	2.50	5.00	10.00
❑ Amherst AMH-745	The Best of the Stylistics, Vol. 2	1986	2.50	5.00	10.00
❑ Amherst AMH-746	Greatest Love Hits	1986	2.50	5.00	10.00
❑ Avco 11006	Round 2: The Stylistics	1972	5.00	10.00	20.00
❑ Avco 11010	Rockin' Roll Baby	1973	5.00	10.00	20.00
❑ Avco AV-33023	The Stylistics	1971	5.00	10.00	20.00
❑ Avco AV-69001	Let's Put It All Together	1974	3.75	7.50	15.00
❑ Avco AV-69004	Heavy	1974	3.75	7.50	15.00
❑ Avco AV-69005	The Best of the Stylistics	1975	3.75	7.50	15.00
❑ Avco 69008	Thank You Baby	1975	3.75	7.50	15.00
❑ Avco 69010	You Are Beautiful	1975	3.75	7.50	15.00
❑ H&L 69013	Fabulous	1976	3.00	6.00	12.00
❑ H&L 69032	Wonder Woman	1978	3.00	6.00	12.00
❑ Mercury SRM-1-3727	In Fashion	1978	3.00	6.00	12.00
❑ Mercury SRM-1-3753	Love Spell	1979	3.00	6.00	12.00
❑ Philadelphia Int'l. FZ 37955	1982	1982	2.50	5.00	10.00
❑ TSOP JZ 36470	Hurry Up This Way Again	1980	2.50	5.00	10.00
❑ TSOP FZ 37458	Closer Than Close	1981	2.50	5.00	10.00
STYX					
45s					
❑ A&M 1786	Lorelei/Midnight Ride	1976	—	2.00	4.00
❑ A&M 1818	Born for Adventure/Light Up	1976	—	2.50	5.00
❑ A&M 1877	Mademoiselle/Light Up	1976	—	2.50	5.00
❑ A&M 1900	Jennifer/Shooz	1976	—	2.50	5.00
❑ A&M 1931	Crystal Ball/Put Me On	1977	—	2.50	5.00
❑ A&M 1977	Come Sail Away/Put Me On	1977	—	2.00	4.00
❑ A&M 2007	Fooling Yourself (The Angry Young Man)/The Grand Finale	1978	—	2.00	4.00
❑ A&M 2087	Blue Collar Man (Long Nights)/Superstars	1978	—	2.00	4.00
❑ A&M 2110	Renegade/Sing for the Day	1979	—	2.00	4.00
❑ A&M 2110	Sing for the Day/Queen of Spades	1979	—	2.50	5.00
❑ A&M 2188	Babe/I'm O.K.	1979	—	2.00	4.00
❑ A&M 2206	Why Me/Lights	1979	—	2.00	4.00
❑ A&M 2228	Borrowed Time/Eddie	1980	—	2.00	4.00
❑ A&M 2294	The Best of Times/Lights	1980	—	—	—
—Unreleased?					
❑ A&M 2300	The Best of Times/Lights	1981	—	2.00	4.00
❑ A&M 2323	Too Much Time on My Hands/Queen of Spades	1981	—	2.00	4.00
❑ A&M 2348	Nothing Ever Goes As Planned/Never Say Never	1981	—	2.00	4.00
❑ A&M 2525	Mr. Roboto/Snowblind	1983	—	—	3.00
❑ A&M 2543	Don't Let It End/Rockin' the Paradise	1983	—	—	3.00
❑ A&M 2560	Double Life/Haven't We Been Here Before	1983	—	—	3.00
❑ A&M 2568	High Time/Double Life	1983	—	—	3.00
❑ A&M 2625	Music Time/Heavy Metal Poisoning	1984	—	—	3.00
❑ A&M 8696	Show Me the Way/Love at First Sight	1993	—	2.00	4.00
—Reissue series; both songs were unreleased on 45 until this record					
❑ Wooden Nickel BWBO-0065	You Need Love/Winner Take All	1973	—	2.50	5.00
❑ Wooden Nickel 65-0106	Best Thing/What Has Come Between	1972	—	2.50	5.00
❑ Wooden Nickel 65-0111	I'm Gonna Make You Feel It/Quick Is the Beat of My Heart	1972	—	2.50	5.00
❑ Wooden Nickel 65-0116	Lady/You Better Ask	1973	2.50	5.00	10.00
❑ Wooden Nickel BWBO-0252	Young Man/Unfinished Song	1974	—	2.50	5.00
❑ Wooden Nickel WB-10027	Lies/22 Years	1974	—	2.50	5.00
❑ Wooden Nickel WB-10102	Lady/Children of the Land	1974	—	2.50	5.00
❑ Wooden Nickel WB-10272	You Need Love/You Better Ask	1975	—	2.50	5.00
❑ Wooden Nickel WB-10329	Best Thing/Havin' a Ball	1975	—	2.50	5.00
❑ Wooden Nickel GB-10492	Lady/Children of the Land	1975	—	2.00	4.00
—Gold Standard Series					
❑ Wooden Nickel WB-11205	Winner Take All/Best Thing	1978	—	2.50	5.00
Albums					
❑ A&M SP-3217	Equinox	1984	2.00	4.00	8.00
❑ A&M SP-3218	Crystal Ball	1984	2.00	4.00	8.00
❑ A&M SP-3223	The Grand Illusion	1984	2.00	4.00	8.00
❑ A&M SP-3224	Pieces of Eight	1984	2.00	4.00	8.00

Number	Title (A Side/B Side)	Yr	VG	VG+	NM
❑ A&M SP-3239	Cornerstone	1984	2.00	4.00	8.00
❑ A&M SP-3240	Paradise Theater	1984	2.00	4.00	8.00
—3200 series LPs are reissues					
❑ A&M SP-3711	Cornerstone	1979	2.50	5.00	10.00
❑ A&M SP-3719	Paradise Theater	1981	2.50	5.00	10.00
❑ A&M SP-3734	Kilroy Was Here	1983	2.50	5.00	10.00
❑ A&M SP-4559	Equinox	1975	2.50	5.00	10.00
❑ A&M SP-4604	Crystal Ball	1976	2.50	5.00	10.00
❑ A&M SP-4637	The Grand Illusion	1977	2.50	5.00	10.00
❑ A&M SP-4724	Pieces of Eight	1978	2.50	5.00	10.00
❑ A&M 75021 5327 1	Edge of the Century	1990	5.00	10.00	20.00
❑ A&M SP-6514 [(2)]	Caught in the Act	1984	3.00	6.00	12.00
❑ RCA Victor AFL1-3593	Styx	1979	2.50	5.00	10.00
❑ RCA Victor AFL1-3594	Lady	1979	2.50	5.00	10.00
—Retitled version of "Styx II"					
❑ RCA Victor AFL1-3595	Serpent	1979	2.50	5.00	10.00
—Retitled version of "The Serpent Is Rising"					
❑ RCA Victor AFL1-3596	Miracles	1979	2.50	5.00	10.00
—Retitled version of "Man of Miracles"					
❑ RCA Victor AFL1-3597	Best of Styx	1979	2.50	5.00	10.00
❑ RCA Victor AYL1-3888	Styx	1980	2.00	4.00	8.00
❑ RCA Victor AYL1-4233	Lady	1981	2.00	4.00	8.00
—Retitled version of "Styx II"					
❑ RCA Victor AYL1-4756	Best of Styx	1982	2.00	4.00	8.00
❑ Wooden Nickel BWL1-0287	The Serpent Is Rising	1974	5.00	10.00	20.00
❑ Wooden Nickel BWL1-0638	Man of Miracles	1974	5.00	10.00	20.00
—Second version contains "Best Thing"					
❑ Wooden Nickel BWL1-0638	Man of Miracles	1974	7.50	15.00	30.00
—Original version contains "Lies"					
❑ Wooden Nickel WNS-1008	Styx	1972	5.00	10.00	20.00
❑ Wooden Nickel WNS-1012	Styx II	1973	5.00	10.00	20.00
—With die-cut cover					
❑ Wooden Nickel BWL1-2250	Best of Styx	1977	3.00	6.00	12.00

SUGARLOAF

45s

Number	Title (A Side/B Side)	Yr	VG	VG+	NM
❑ Brut 805	Round and Round/Colorado Jones	1973	—	2.50	5.00
❑ Brut 815	I Got a Song/Myra, Myra	1973	—	2.50	5.00
❑ Claridge 402	Don't Call Us, We'll Call You/Texas Two-Lane	1974	—	2.50	5.00
❑ Claridge 405	Stars in My Eyes/Myra, Myra	1975	—	2.50	5.00
❑ Claridge 408	Boogie Man/I Got a Song	1975	—	2.50	5.00
❑ Claridge 415	Have a Good Time/You Set My Dreams to Music	1976	—	2.50	5.00
❑ Claridge 422	Last Dance, Take a Chance/Satisfaction Guaranteed	1976	—	2.50	5.00
❑ Liberty 56183	Green-Eyed Lady/West of Tomorrow	1970	—	3.00	6.00
❑ Liberty 56218	Tongue in Cheek/Woman	1970	—	2.50	5.00
❑ United Artists 0062	Green-Eyed Lady/Tongue in Cheek	1973	—	2.00	4.00
—"Silver Spotlight Series" reissue					
❑ United Artists 50757	Woman/Tongue in Cheek	1971	—	—	—
—Unreleased					
❑ United Artists 50784	Chest Fever/Mother Nature's Wine	1971	—	2.50	5.00

Albums

Number	Title (A Side/B Side)	Yr	VG	VG+	NM
❑ Brut 6006	I Got a Song	1973	3.75	7.50	15.00
❑ Claridge 1000	Don't Call Us, We'll Call You	1975	3.00	6.00	12.00
❑ Liberty LST-7640	Sugarloaf	1970	5.00	10.00	20.00
❑ Liberty LST-11010	Spaceship Earth	1971	5.00	10.00	20.00

SUMMER, DONNA

45s

Number	Title (A Side/B Side)	Yr	VG	VG+	NM
❑ Atlantic 88792	Breakaway/Thinkin' Bout My Baby	1989	—	2.00	4.00
❑ Atlantic 88840	Love's About to Change My Heart (PWL 7" Mix)/ (Clivilles & Cole 7" Mix)	1989	—	—	3.00
❑ Atlantic 88899	This Time I Know It's for Real/If It Makes You Feel Good	1989	—	—	3.00
❑ Casablanca 872	Spring Affair/Come with Me	1976	—	2.50	5.00
❑ Casablanca 874	Winter Melody/Spring Affair	1977	—	2.50	5.00
❑ Casablanca 884	Can't We Just Sit Down (And Talk It Over)/I Feel Love	1977	—	3.00	6.00
—Original copies have "Can't We Just Sit Down" labeled as "Side A"					
❑ Casablanca 884	I Feel Love/Can't We Just Sit Down (And Talk It Over)	1977	—	2.50	5.00
—Second pressings have "I Feel Love" listed as "Side A"					
❑ Casablanca 907	I Love You/Once Upon a Time	1977	—	2.50	5.00
❑ Casablanca 916	Rumour Has It/Once Upon a Time	1978	—	2.50	5.00
❑ Casablanca 926	Last Dance/With Your Love	1978	—	2.00	4.00
❑ Casablanca 939	Mac Arthur Park/Once Upon a Time	1978	—	2.00	4.00
❑ Casablanca 959	Heaven Knows/Only One Love	1979	—	2.00	4.00
—A-side with Brooklyn Dreams					
❑ Casablanca 978	Hot Stuff/Journey to the Center of Your Heart	1979	—	2.00	4.00
❑ Casablanca 988	Bad Girls/On My Honor	1979	—	2.00	4.00
❑ Casablanca 2201	Dim All the Lights/There Will Always Be a You	1979	—	2.00	4.00
❑ Casablanca 2236	On the Radio/There Will Always Be a You	1980	—	2.00	4.00
❑ Casablanca 2273	Our Love/Sunset People	1980	—	2.50	5.00
❑ Casablanca 2300	Walk Away/Could It Be Magic	1980	—	2.00	4.00
❑ Geffen 27939	Fascination/All Systems Go	1988	—	2.00	4.00
❑ Geffen 28165	Only the Fool Survives/Love Shock	1987	—	2.00	4.00
—A-side with Mickey Thomas					
❑ Geffen 28418	Dinner with Gershwin/(Instrumental)	1987	—	2.00	4.00
❑ Geffen 29142	Supernatural Love/Face the Music	1984	—	2.00	4.00
❑ Geffen 29291	There Goes My Baby/Maybe It's Over	1984	—	2.00	4.00
❑ Geffen 29805	The Woman in Me/Livin' in America	1982	—	2.00	4.00

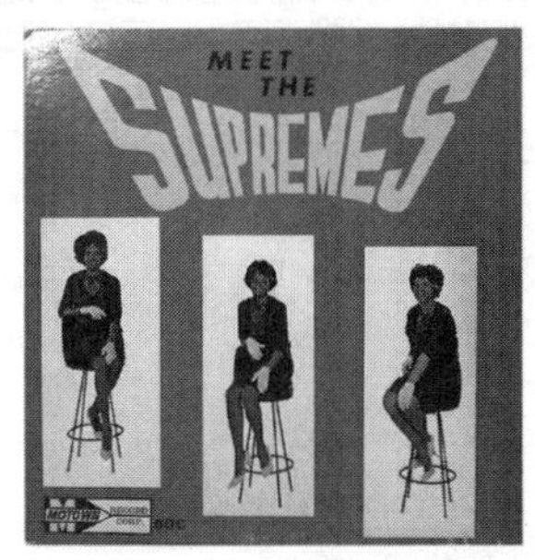

Number	Title (A Side/B Side)	Yr	VG	VG+	NM
❑ Geffen 29895	State of Independence/Love Is Just a Breath Away	1982	—	2.00	4.00
❑ Geffen 29982	Love Is In Control (Finger on the Trigger)/Sometimes Like Butterflies	1982	—	2.00	4.00
❑ Geffen 49563	The Wanderer/Stop Me	1980	—	2.00	4.00
—Second pressings have WB logo replaced by Geffen logo					
❑ Geffen 49634	Cold Love/Grand Illusion	1980	—	2.00	4.00
❑ Geffen 49664	Who Do You Think You're Foolin'/Runnin' for Cover	1981	—	2.00	4.00
❑ Mercury 812370-7	She Works Hard for the Money/I Do Believe (I'll Fall in Love)	1983	—	2.00	4.00
❑ Mercury 814088-7	Unconditional Love/Woman	1983	—	2.00	4.00
❑ Mercury 814922-7	Love Has a Mind of Its Own/Stop, Look and Listen	1983	—	2.00	4.00
—A-side with Matthew Ward					
❑ Oasis 401 AA/BB	Love to Love You Baby (4:55)/Love to Love You Baby (3:24)	1975	—	3.00	6.00
—Both sides are remixed compared to the original 45 mix					
❑ Oasis 405	Could It Be Magic/Whispering Waves	1976	—	3.00	6.00
❑ Oasis 406	Try Me, I Know We Can Make It/Wasted	1976	—	3.00	6.00
❑ Warner Bros./Geffen 49563	The Wanderer/Stop Me	1980	—	3.00	6.00
—Original pressings have a WB logo on the left side and "Geffen Records" in a box at the top of the label					
Albums					
❑ Atlantic 81987	Another Place and Time	1989	3.00	6.00	12.00
❑ Casablanca NBLP 7038	Four Seasons of Love	1976	2.50	5.00	10.00
❑ Casablanca NBLP 7056	I Remember Yesterday	1977	2.50	5.00	10.00
❑ Casablanca NBLP 7078 [(2)]	Once Upon a Time...	1977	3.00	6.00	12.00
❑ Casablanca NBLP 7119 [(2)]	Live and More	1978	3.00	6.00	12.00
❑ Casablanca NBLP 7150 [(2)]	Bad Girls	1979	3.00	6.00	12.00
❑ Casablanca NBLP 7191 [(2)]	On the Radio — Greatest Hits Vols. 1 and 2	1979	3.00	6.00	12.00
❑ Casablanca NBLP 7201	Greatest Hits, Vol. 1	1979	2.00	4.00	8.00
❑ Casablanca NBLP 7202	Greatest Hits, Vol. 2	1979	2.00	4.00	8.00
❑ Casablanca NBLP 7244	Walk Away — Collector's Edition (The Best of 1977-1980)	1980	2.50	5.00	10.00
❑ Casablanca 811123-1 [(2)]	Live and More	1985	2.50	5.00	10.00
❑ Casablanca 822557-1 [(2)]	Bad Girls	1984	2.50	5.00	10.00
❑ Casablanca 822558-1 [(2)]	On the Radio — Greatest Hits Vols. 1 and 2	1984	2.50	5.00	10.00
❑ Casablanca 822559-1	Greatest Hits, Vol. 2	1984	2.00	4.00	8.00
❑ Casablanca 822560-1	Walk Away	1984	2.00	4.00	8.00
❑ Geffen GHS 2000	The Wanderer	1980	2.50	5.00	10.00
❑ Geffen GHS 2005	Donna Summer	1982	2.50	5.00	10.00
❑ Geffen GHS 24040	Cats Without Claws	1984	2.50	5.00	10.00
❑ Geffen GHS 24102	All Systems Go	1987	2.50	5.00	10.00
❑ Mercury 812265-1	She Works Hard for the Money	1983	2.50	5.00	10.00
❑ Mercury 826144-1	The Summer Collection	1985	2.50	5.00	10.00
❑ Oasis OCLP 5003	Love to Love You Baby	1975	3.00	6.00	12.00
—Add 50% if poster is included					
❑ Oasis OCLP 5004	A Love Trilogy	1976	3.00	6.00	12.00
❑ Oasis 822792-1	Love to Love You Baby	1985	2.00	4.00	8.00
SUPERTRAMP					
45s					
❑ A&M 1305	Forever/Your Poppa Don't Mind	1971	—	3.00	6.00
❑ A&M 1660	Bloody Well Right/Dreamer	1975	—	2.50	5.00
❑ A&M 1766	Lady/You Started Laughing When I Held You in My Arms	1975	—	—	—
—Unreleased?					
❑ A&M 1793	Lady/You Started Laughing When I Held You in My Arms	1976	—	2.50	5.00
❑ A&M 1814	Sister Moonshine/Ain't Nobody But Me	1976	—	2.50	5.00
❑ A&M 1938	Give a Little Bit/Downstream	1977	—	2.00	4.00
❑ A&M 1981	Dreamer/From Now On	1977	—	2.50	5.00
❑ A&M 2128	The Logical Song/Just Another Nervous Wreck	1979	—	2.00	4.00
❑ A&M 2162	Goodbye Stranger/Even in the Quietest Moments	1979	—	2.00	4.00
❑ A&M 2193	Take the Long Way Home/Ruby	1979	—	2.00	4.00
❑ A&M 2269	Dreamer/From Now On	1980	—	2.00	4.00
❑ A&M 2292	Breakfast in America/You Started Laughing	1980	—	2.00	4.00
❑ A&M 2502	It's Raining Again/Bonnie	1982	—	2.00	4.00
❑ A&M 2517	My Kind of Lady/Know Who You Are	1983	—	2.00	4.00
❑ A&M 2731	Cannonball/Every Open Door	1985	—	—	3.00
❑ A&M 2760	Better Days/No In-Between	1985	—	—	3.00
❑ A&M 2985	I'm Beggin' You/No Inbetween	1987	—	—	3.00
❑ A&M 2996	Free as a Bird/Thing for You	1987	—	—	3.00
❑ A&M 8663	Cannonball/Better Days	198?	—	—	3.00
—"A&M Memories" reissue					
Albums					
❑ A&M SP-3129	Indelibly Stamped	198?	2.00	4.00	8.00
—Budget-line reissue					

Number	Title (A Side/B Side)	Yr	VG	VG+	NM
❑ A&M SP-3149	Supertramp	198?	2.00	4.00	8.00
—Budget-line reissue					
❑ A&M SP-3214	Crisis? What Crisis?	1982	2.00	4.00	8.00
—Budget-line reissue					
❑ A&M SP-3215	Even in the Quietest Moments	1982	2.00	4.00	8.00
—Budget-line reissue					
❑ A&M SP-3284	...Famous Last Words...	1986	2.00	4.00	8.00
—Budget-line reissue					
❑ A&M SP-3647	Crime of the Century	1974	3.00	6.00	12.00
❑ A&M SP-3708	Breakfast in America	1979	2.50	5.00	10.00
❑ A&M SP-3732	...Famous Last Words...	1982	2.50	5.00	10.00
❑ A&M SP-4274	Supertramp	1970	5.00	10.00	20.00
—First edition with brown label					
❑ A&M SP-4311	Indelibly Stamped	1971	5.00	10.00	20.00
—First edition with brown label					
❑ A&M SP-4560	Crisis? What Crisis?	1975	3.00	6.00	12.00
❑ A&M SP-4634	Even in the Quietest Moments...	1977	3.00	6.00	12.00
❑ A&M SP-4665	Supertramp	1978	3.00	6.00	12.00
—Reissue of 4274					
❑ A&M SP-5013	Brother Where You Bound	1985	2.50	5.00	10.00
❑ A&M SP-5181	Free as a Bird	1987	2.50	5.00	10.00
❑ A&M SP-6702 [(2)]	Paris	1980	3.00	6.00	12.00

SUPREMES, THE

45s

Number	Title (A Side/B Side)	Yr	VG	VG+	NM
❑ Motown 1008	I Want a Guy/Never Again	1961	75.00	150.00	300.00
❑ Motown 1027	Your Heart Belongs to Me/(He's) Seventeen	1962	6.25	12.50	25.00
❑ Motown 1034	Let Me Go the Right Way/Time Changes Things	1962	12.50	25.00	50.00
❑ Motown 1040	My Heart Can't Take It No More/You Bring Back Memories	1963	10.00	20.00	40.00
❑ Motown 1044	A Breath Taking Guy/Rock and Roll Banjo Band	1963	6.25	12.50	25.00
❑ Motown 1044	A Breath Taking, First Sight Soul Shaking, One Night Love Making, Next Day Heart Breaking Guy/Rock and Roll Banjo Band	1963	25.00	50.00	100.00
—Original pressing with long title. This does exist on stock copies as well as on promos.					
❑ Motown 1051	When the Lovelight Starts Shining Through His Eyes/ Standing at the Crossroads of Love	1963	5.00	10.00	20.00
❑ Motown 1054	Run, Run, Run/I'm Giving You Your Freedom	1964	6.25	12.50	25.00
❑ Motown 1060	Where Did Our Love Go/He Means the World to Me	1964	5.00	10.00	20.00
❑ Motown 1066	Baby Love/Ask Any Girl	1964	5.00	10.00	20.00
❑ Motown 1068	Come See About Me/Always in My Heart	1964	5.00	10.00	20.00
❑ Motown 1074	Stop! In the Name of Love/I'm in Love Again	1965	3.75	7.50	15.00
❑ Motown 1075	Back in My Arms Again/Whisper You Love Me Boy	1965	3.75	7.50	15.00
❑ Motown 1080	Nothing But Heartaches/He Holds His Own	1965	3.75	7.50	15.00
❑ Motown 1083	I Hear a Symphony/Who Could Ever Doubt My Love	1965	3.75	7.50	15.00
❑ Motown 1085	Children's Christmas Song/Twinkle, Twinkle Little Me	1965	5.00	10.00	20.00
❑ Motown 1089	My World Is Empty Without You/Everything Is Good About You	1966	3.75	7.50	15.00
❑ Motown 1094	Love Is Like an Itching in My Heart/He's All I Got	1966	3.75	7.50	15.00
❑ Motown 1097	You Can't Hurry Love/Put Yourself in My Place	1966	3.75	7.50	15.00
❑ Motown 1101	You Keep Me Hangin' On/Remove This Doubt	1966	3.75	7.50	15.00
❑ Motown 1103	Love Is Here and Now You're Gone/There's No Stopping Us Now	1967	3.00	6.00	12.00
❑ Motown 1107	The Happening/All I Know About You	1967	3.00	6.00	12.00
❑ Motown 1111	Reflections/Going Down for the Third Time	1967	2.00	4.00	8.00
—Starting here, through 1156, as "Diana Ross and the Supremes"					
❑ Motown 1116	In and Out of Love/I Guess I'll Always Love You	1967	2.00	4.00	8.00
❑ Motown 1122	Forever Came Today/Time Changes Things	1968	2.00	4.00	8.00
❑ Motown 1125	What the World Needs Now/Your Kiss of Fire	1968	—	—	—
—Unreleased					
❑ Motown 1126	Some Things You Never Get Used To/You've Been So Wonderful to Me	1968	2.00	4.00	8.00
❑ Motown 1135	Love Child/Will This Be the Day	1968	2.00	4.00	8.00
❑ Motown 1139	I'm Livin' in Shame/I'm So Glad I Got Somebody	1969	2.00	4.00	8.00
❑ Motown 1146	The Composer/The Beginning of the End	1969	2.00	4.00	8.00
❑ Motown 1148	No Matter What Sign You Are/The Young Folks	1969	2.00	4.00	8.00
❑ Motown 1156	Someday We'll Be Together/He's My Sunny Boy	1969	2.00	4.00	8.00
❑ Motown 1162	Up the Ladder to the Roof/Bill, When Are You Coming Home	1970	—	3.00	6.00
—Starting here, name reverts to "The Supremes" (unless noted)					
❑ Motown 1167	Everybody's Got the Right to Love/But I Love You More	1970	—	3.00	6.00
❑ Motown 1172	Stoned Love/Shine on Me	1970	—	3.00	6.00
❑ Motown 1182	Nathan Jones/Happy (Is a Bumpy Road)	1971	—	3.00	6.00
❑ Motown 1190	Touch/It's So Hard for Me to Say Goodbye	1971	—	3.00	6.00
❑ Motown 1195	Floy Joy/This Is the Story	1972	—	2.50	5.00
❑ Motown 1200	Automatically Sunshine/Precious Little Things	1972	—	2.50	5.00
❑ Motown 1206	Your Wonderful, Sweet Sweet Love/The Wisdom of Time	1972	—	2.50	5.00
❑ Motown 1213	I Guess I'll Miss the Man/Over and Over	1972	—	2.50	5.00
❑ Motown 1225	Bad Weather/Oh Be My Love	1973	—	2.50	5.00
❑ Motown 1350	It's All Been Said Before/(B-side unassigned)	1975	—	—	—
—Unreleased					
❑ Motown 1357	He's My Man/Give Out But Don't Give Up	1975	—	2.50	5.00
❑ Motown 1374	Where Do I Go from Here/Give Out But Don't Give Up	1975	—	2.50	5.00
❑ Motown 1391	I'm Gonna Let My Heart Do the Walking/Early Morning Love	1976	—	2.50	5.00
❑ Motown 1407	You're My Driving Wheel/You're What's Missing in My Life	1976	—	2.50	5.00
❑ Motown 1415	Let Yourself Go/You Are the Heart of Me	1977	—	2.50	5.00
❑ Motown 1488	Medley of Hits/Where Did We Go Wrong	1980	—	2.00	4.00
—As "Diana Ross and the Supremes"					
❑ Motown 1523	Medley of Hits/Where Did We Go Wrong	1981	—	2.00	4.00
—As "Diana Ross and the Supremes"					
❑ Tamla 54038	I Want a Guy/Never Again	1961	31.25	62.50	125.00
—Lines label					

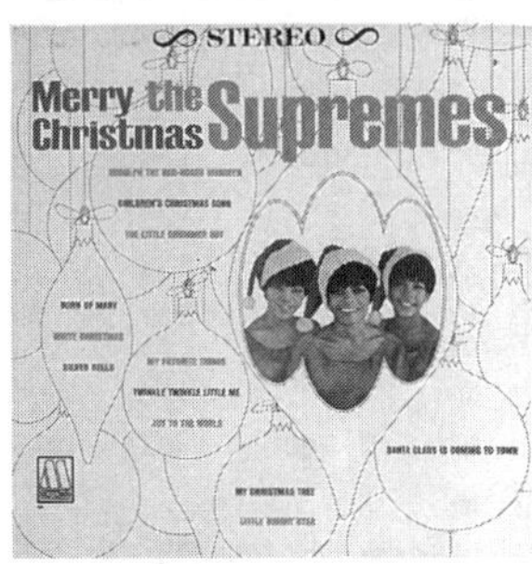

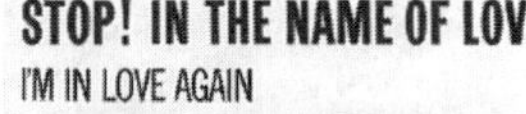

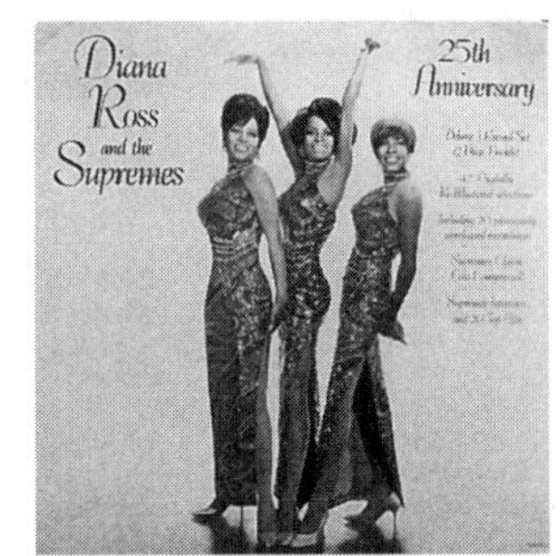

Number	Title (A Side/B Side)	Yr	VG	VG+	NM
❑ Tamla 54045	Buttered Popcorn/Who's Lovin' You	1961	15.00	30.00	60.00
—Globes label					
Albums					
❑ Motown M5-101V1	Superstar Series, Vol. 1	1981	3.00	6.00	12.00
—By "Diana Ross and the Supremes"					
❑ Motown M5-138V1	The Supremes A' Go-Go	1981	3.00	6.00	12.00
—Reissue of Motown 649					
❑ Motown M5-147V1	I Hear a Symphony	1981	3.00	6.00	12.00
—Reissue of Motown 643					
❑ Motown M5-158V1	The Supremes Sing Country Western and Pop	1981	2.00	4.00	8.00
—Reissue of Motown 625					
❑ Motown M5-162V1	The Supremes at the Copa	1981	3.00	6.00	12.00
—Reissue of Motown 636					
❑ Motown M5-182V1	The Supremes Sing Holland-Dozier-Holland	1981	3.00	6.00	12.00
—Reissue of Motown 650					
❑ Motown M5-203V1	Diana Ross and the Supremes Greatest Hits, Volume 3	1981	3.00	6.00	12.00
—Reissue of Motown 702					
❑ Motown M5-223V1	Meet the Supremes	1982	2.00	4.00	8.00
—Reissue of Motown 606					
❑ Motown M5-237V1	Greatest Hits	1982	2.50	5.00	10.00
—Reissue (unknown if it's the complete 2-record set or an edited version)					
❑ Motown M 606 [M]	Meet the Supremes	1963	225.00	450.00	900.00
—With group sitting on stools					
❑ Motown M 606 [M]	Meet the Supremes	1963	7.50	15.00	30.00
—With close-up of group's faces					
❑ Motown MS 606 [S]	Meet the Supremes	1964	10.00	20.00	40.00
—With close-up of group's faces					
❑ Motown M 621 [M]	Where Did Our Love Go	1964	7.50	15.00	30.00
❑ Motown MS 621 [S]	Where Did Our Love Go	1964	10.00	20.00	40.00
❑ Motown M 623 [M]	A Bit of Liverpool	1964	10.00	20.00	40.00
❑ Motown MS 623 [S]	A Bit of Liverpool	1964	12.50	25.00	50.00
❑ Motown MS 625 [S]	The Supremes Sing Country, Western & Pop	1965	7.50	15.00	30.00
❑ Motown MT-625 [M]	The Supremes Sing Country, Western & Pop	1965	6.25	12.50	25.00
❑ Motown M 627 [M]	More Hits by the Supremes	1965	6.25	12.50	25.00
❑ Motown MS 627 [S]	More Hits by the Supremes	1965	7.50	15.00	30.00
❑ Motown M 629 [M]	We Remember Sam Cooke	1965	6.25	12.50	25.00
❑ Motown MS 629 [S]	We Remember Sam Cooke	1965	7.50	15.00	30.00
—The above LP came out before Motown 627					
❑ Motown M 636 [M]	The Supremes at the Copa	1965	6.25	12.50	25.00
❑ Motown MS 636 [S]	The Supremes at the Copa	1965	7.50	15.00	30.00
❑ Motown MS 638 [S]	Merry Christmas	1965	10.00	20.00	40.00
—Same as above, but in stereo					
❑ Motown MT 638 [M]	Merry Christmas	1965	7.50	15.00	30.00
❑ Motown M 643 [M]	I Hear a Symphony	1966	6.25	12.50	25.00
❑ Motown MS 643 [S]	I Hear a Symphony	1966	7.50	15.00	30.00
❑ Motown M 649 [M]	The Supremes A' Go-Go	1966	6.25	12.50	25.00
❑ Motown MS 649 [S]	The Supremes A' Go-Go	1966	7.50	15.00	30.00
❑ Motown M 650 [M]	The Supremes Sing Holland-Dozier-Holland	1967	6.25	12.50	25.00
❑ Motown MS 650 [S]	The Supremes Sing Holland-Dozier-Holland	1967	7.50	15.00	30.00
❑ Motown M 659 [M]	The Supremes Sing Rodgers & Hart	1967	6.25	12.50	25.00
❑ Motown MS 659 [S]	The Supremes Sing Rodgers & Hart	1967	7.50	15.00	30.00
❑ Motown M 663 [(2)M]	Diana Ross and the Supremes Greatest Hits	1967	7.50	15.00	30.00
❑ Motown MS 663 [(2)S]	Diana Ross and the Supremes Greatest Hits	1967	10.00	20.00	40.00
❑ Motown M 665 [M]	Reflections	1968	7.50	15.00	30.00
❑ Motown MS 665 [S]	Reflections	1968	5.00	10.00	20.00
❑ Motown MS 670	Love Child	1968	5.00	10.00	20.00
❑ Motown MS 672 [S]	Funny Girl	1968	5.00	10.00	20.00
—The above LP came out before Motown 670					
❑ Motown MS 676 [S]	Live at London's Talk of the Town	1968	5.00	10.00	20.00
—The above LP came out before Motown 670 and 672					
❑ Motown MS 689	Let the Sunshine In	1969	5.00	10.00	20.00
❑ Motown MS 694	Cream of the Crop.	1969	5.00	10.00	20.00
❑ Motown MS 702	Diana Ross and the Supremes Greatest Hits, Volume 3.	1970	5.00	10.00	20.00
❑ Motown MS 705	Right On.	1970	3.75	7.50	15.00
—By "The Supremes"; the first LP after Diana Ross left					
❑ Motown MS 708 [(2)]	Farewell	1970	6.25	12.50	25.00
—By "Diana Ross and the Supremes"					

Number	Title (A Side/B Side)	Yr	VG	VG+	NM
❑ Motown MS 720	New Ways But Love Stays	1970	3.75	7.50	15.00
❑ Motown MS 737	Touch	1971	3.75	7.50	15.00
❑ Motown MS 746	Promises Kept	1972	—	—	—
—Unreleased					
❑ Motown M 751L	Floy Joy	1972	3.75	7.50	15.00
❑ Motown M 756L	The Supremes	1972	3.75	7.50	15.00
❑ Motown M9-794L3 [(3)]	Anthology (1962-1969)	1974	6.25	12.50	25.00
—By "Diana Ross and the Supremes"					
❑ Motown M6-828	The Supremes	1975	3.75	7.50	15.00
❑ Motown M6-863S1	High Energy	1976	3.75	7.50	15.00
❑ Motown M6-873S1	Mary, Scherrie and Susaye	1976	3.75	7.50	15.00
❑ Motown M7-904R1	The Supremes at Their Best	1978	3.75	7.50	15.00
❑ Motown 5245 ML	Love Child	1982	2.00	4.00	8.00
—Reissue of MS 670					
❑ Motown 5252 ML	Merry Christmas	1982	2.50	5.00	10.00
—Reissue of MS 638					
❑ Motown 5270 ML	Where Did Our Love Go	1982	2.00	4.00	8.00
—Reissue of MS 621					
❑ Motown 5278 ML	Captured Live on Stage	1982	2.00	4.00	8.00
—Reissue?					
❑ Motown 5305 ML	Let the Sunshine In	1983	2.00	4.00	8.00
—Reissue of MS 689					
❑ Motown 5313 ML	Great Songs and Performances That Inspired the Motown 25th Anniversary TV Special	1983	2.50	5.00	10.00
❑ Motown 5361 ML	Motown Legends	1985	2.50	5.00	10.00
❑ Motown 5371 ML	Diana Ross and the Supremes Sing Motown	1985	2.50	5.00	10.00
❑ Motown 5381 ML3 [(3)]	25th Anniversary	1986	5.00	10.00	20.00
—By "Diana Ross and the Supremes"					
❑ Natural Resources NR 4006T1	Where Did Our Love Go	1978	3.00	6.00	12.00
—Reissue of Motown 621					
❑ Natural Resources NR 4010	Merry Christmas	1978	3.00	6.00	12.00
—Reissue of Motown 638					
❑ Pickwick SPC-3383	Baby Love	197?	3.00	6.00	12.00
—Edited reissue of Motown 621					

SUPREMES, THE, AND THE FOUR TOPS

45s

Number	Title (A Side/B Side)	Yr	VG	VG+	NM
❑ Motown 1173	River Deep-Mountain High/Together We Can Make Such Sweet Music	1970	—	3.00	6.00
❑ Motown 1181	You Gotta Have Love in Your Heart/I'm Glad About It	1971	—	3.00	6.00

Albums

Number	Title (A Side/B Side)	Yr	VG	VG+	NM
❑ Motown M5-123V1A	The Magnificent Seven	1981	3.00	6.00	12.00
—Reissue of Motown 717					
❑ Motown MS 717	The Magnificent Seven	1970	3.75	7.50	15.00
❑ Motown MS 736	The Return of the Magnificent Seven	1971	3.75	7.50	15.00
❑ Motown MS 745	Dynamite	1971	3.75	7.50	15.00

SUPREMES, THE, DIANA ROSS AND, AND THE TEMPTATIONS

45s

Number	Title (A Side/B Side)	Yr	VG	VG+	NM
❑ Motown 1137	I'm Gonna Make You Love Me/A Place in the Sun	1968	—	3.50	7.00
❑ Motown 1142	I'll Try Something New/The Way You Do the Things You Do	1969	—	3.50	7.00
❑ Motown 1150	Stubborn Kind of Fellow/Try It Baby	1969	—	3.50	7.00
❑ Motown 1153	The Weight/For Better or Worse	1969	—	3.50	7.00

Albums

Number	Title (A Side/B Side)	Yr	VG	VG+	NM
❑ Motown M5-139V1	Diana Ross and the Supremes Join the Temptations	1981	3.00	6.00	12.00
—Reissue of Motown 679					
❑ Motown M5-171V1	TCB	1981	3.00	6.00	12.00
—Reissue of Motown 682					
❑ Motown MS 679 [S]	Diana Ross and the Supremes Join the Temptations	1968	5.00	10.00	20.00
❑ Motown MS 682	TCB	1968	5.00	10.00	20.00
❑ Motown MS 692	Together	1969	5.00	10.00	20.00
❑ Motown MS 699	On Broadway	1969	5.00	10.00	20.00

SURFARIS, THE (1)

45s

Number	Title (A Side/B Side)	Yr	VG	VG+	NM
❑ Decca 31538	Point Panic/Waikiki Run	1963	3.75	7.50	15.00
❑ Decca 31561	A Surfer's Christmas List/Santa's Speed Shop	1963	7.50	15.00	30.00
❑ Decca 31581	I Wanna Take a trip to the Islands/Scatter Shield	1964	5.00	10.00	20.00
❑ Decca 31605	Murphy the Surfie/Go Go Go For Louie's Place	1964	3.75	7.50	15.00
❑ Decca 31641	Bossa Barracuda/Dune Buggy	1964	3.75	7.50	15.00
❑ Decca 31682	Hot Rod High/Karen	1964	3.75	7.50	15.00
❑ Decca 31731	Beat '65/Black Denim	1965	5.00	10.00	20.00
❑ Decca 31784	Theme of the Battle Maiden/Somethin' Else	1965	5.00	10.00	20.00
❑ Decca 31835	Catch a Little Ride with Me/Don't Hurt My Little Sister	1965	5.00	10.00	20.00
❑ Decca 31954	Hey Joe Where Are You Going/So Get Out	1966	5.00	10.00	20.00
❑ Decca 32003	Wipe Out/I'm a Hog for You	1966	2.50	5.00	10.00
❑ DFS 11/12	Wipe Out/Surfer Joe	1963	1500.	2250.	3000.
—VG 1500; VG+ 2250					
❑ Dot 144	Wipe Out/Surfer Joe	1966	2.50	5.00	10.00
—Black label, script "Dot" in multicolor letters					
❑ Dot 16479	Wipe Out/Surfer Joe	1963	3.75	7.50	15.00
❑ Dot 16757	Surfer Joe/Can't Sit Down	1965	7.50	15.00	30.00
—B-side by the Challengers, but credited to the Surfaris					
❑ Dot 16757	Surfer Joe/Can't Sit Down	1965	12.50	25.00	50.00
—B-side by the Challengers, and credited correctly					

Number	Title (A Side/B Side)	Yr	VG	VG+	NM
❑ Dot 16966	Show Biz/Chicago Green	1966	2.50	5.00	10.00
❑ Dot 17008	Shake/The Search	1967	2.50	5.00	10.00
❑ Princess 50	Wipe Out/Surfer Joe	1963	100.00	200.00	400.00
—With long versions of both songs. No "RE-1" is in the trail-off area.					
Albums					
❑ Decca DL 4470 [M]	The Surfaris Play Wipe Out	1963	6.25	12.50	25.00
❑ Decca DL 4487 [M]	Hit City '64	1964	10.00	20.00	40.00
❑ Decca DL 4560 [M]	Fun City, U.S.A.	1964	10.00	20.00	40.00
❑ Decca DL 4614 [M]	Hit City '65	1965	10.00	20.00	40.00
❑ Decca DL 4663 [M]	It Ain't Me, Babe	1965	10.00	20.00	40.00
❑ Decca DL 74470 [S]	The Surfaris Play Wipe Out	1963	7.50	15.00	30.00
❑ Decca DL 74487 [S]	Hit City '64	1964	12.50	25.00	50.00
❑ Decca DL 74560 [S]	Fun City, U.S.A.	1964	12.50	25.00	50.00
❑ Decca DL 74614 [S]	Hit City '65	1965	12.50	25.00	50.00
❑ Decca DL 74663 [S]	It Ain't Me, Babe	1965	12.50	25.00	50.00
❑ Dot DLP-3535 [M]	Wipe Out	1963	12.50	25.00	50.00
—With back cover photo featuring five Surfaris					
❑ Dot DLP-25535 [S]	Wipe Out	1963	20.00	40.00	80.00
—With back cover photo featuring five Surfaris					

SWEET, THE (1)

45s

Number	Title (A Side/B Side)	Yr	VG	VG+	NM
❑ Bell 45106	Funny, Funny/You're Not Wrong for Loving Me	1971	2.00	4.00	8.00
❑ Bell 45126	Co-Co/You're Not Wrong for Loving Me	1971	—	3.00	6.00
❑ Bell 45184	Poppa Joe/Jeanie	1972	—	3.00	6.00
❑ Bell 45251	Little Willy/Man from Mecca	1972	—	3.00	6.00
❑ Bell 45361	Blockbuster/Need a Lot of Lovin'	1973	—	2.50	5.00
❑ Bell 45408	Wig-Wam Bam/New York Connection	1973	—	2.50	5.00
❑ Capitol 4055	Ballroom Blitz/Restless	1975	—	2.50	5.00
❑ Capitol 4157	Fox on the Run/Burn On the Flame	1975	—	2.50	5.00
❑ Capitol 4220	Action/Medussa	1976	—	2.50	5.00
❑ Capitol 4429	Fever of Love/Heartbreak Today	1977	—	2.50	5.00
❑ Capitol 4454	Funk It Up (David's Song)/Stairway to the Stars	1977	—	2.50	5.00
❑ Capitol 4549	Love Is Like Oxygen/Cover Girl	1978	—	2.50	5.00
❑ Capitol 4610	California Nights/Dream On	1978	—	2.50	5.00
❑ Capitol 4730	Mother Earth/Why Don't You	1979	—	2.00	4.00
❑ Capitol 4908	Sixties Man/Water's Edge	1980	—	2.00	4.00
❑ Paramount 0044	All You'll Ever Get from Me/The Juicer	1970	5.00	10.00	20.00
❑ 20th Century 2033	It's Lonely Out There/I'm On My Way	1973	2.50	5.00	10.00
—U.S. issue of 1968 material that was on Fontana in the U.K.					
Albums					
❑ Bell 1125	The Sweet	1973	6.25	12.50	25.00
❑ Capitol ST-11395	Desolation Boulevard	1975	3.00	6.00	12.00
❑ Capitol ST-11496	Give Us a Wink	1976	3.00	6.00	12.00
❑ Capitol STAO-11636	Off the Record	1977	3.00	6.00	12.00
❑ Capitol SKAO-11744	Level Headed	1978	3.00	6.00	12.00
❑ Capitol ST-11929	Cut Above the Rest	1979	3.00	6.00	12.00
❑ Capitol ST-12106	Sweet VI	1980	3.00	6.00	12.00
❑ Capitol SN-16115	Give Us a Wink	1980	2.00	4.00	8.00
—Budget-line reissue					
❑ Capitol SN-16116	Off the Record	1980	2.00	4.00	8.00
—Budget-line reissue					
❑ Capitol SN-16117	Level Headed	1980	2.00	4.00	8.00
—Budget-line reissue					
❑ Capitol SN-16118	Cut Above the Rest	1980	2.00	4.00	8.00
—Budget-line reissue					
❑ Capitol SN-16287	Desolation Boulevard	1981	2.00	4.00	8.00
—Budget-line reissue					
❑ Kory 3009	The Sweet	1977	2.50	5.00	10.00
—Reissue of Bell LP					

SWEET INSPIRATIONS, THE

45s

Number	Title (A Side/B Side)	Yr	VG	VG+	NM
❑ Atlantic 2410	Why (Am I Treated So Bad)/I Don't Want to Go On Without You	1967	2.00	4.00	8.00
❑ Atlantic 2418	Let It Be Me/When Something Is Wrong with My Baby	1967	2.00	4.00	8.00
❑ Atlantic 2436	I've Been Loving You Too Long (To Stop Now)/ That's How Strong My Love Is	1967	2.00	4.00	8.00

Number	Title (A Side/B Side)	Yr	VG	VG+	NM
❑ Atlantic 2449	O' What a Fool I've Been/Don't Fight It	1967	2.00	4.00	8.00
❑ Atlantic 2465	Reach Out for Me/Do Right Woman — Do Right Man	1967	2.00	4.00	8.00
❑ Atlantic 2476	Sweet Inspiration/I'm Blue	1968	2.00	4.00	8.00
❑ Atlantic 2529	To Love Somebody/Where Did It Go	1968	2.00	4.00	8.00
❑ Atlantic 2551	Unchained Melody/Am I Ever Gonna See My Baby Again	1968	2.00	4.00	8.00
❑ Atlantic 2571	What the World Needs Now Is Love/You Really Didn't Mean It	1968	2.00	4.00	8.00
❑ Atlantic 2620	Crying in the Rain/Everyday WIll Be Like a Holiday	1969	2.00	4.00	8.00
❑ Atlantic 2638	Sweets for My Sweet/Get a Little Order	1969	2.00	4.00	8.00
❑ Atlantic 2653	Don't Go/Chained	1969	2.00	4.00	8.00
❑ Atlantic 2686	(Gotta Find) A Brand New Lover — Part I/ (Gotta Find) A Brand New Lover — Part II	1969	2.00	4.00	8.00
❑ Atlantic 2720	At Last I Found a Love/That's the Way My Baby Is	1970	—	3.00	6.00
❑ Atlantic 2732	Them Boys/Flash in the Pan	1970	—	3.00	6.00
❑ Atlantic 2750	This World/A Light Sings	1970	—	3.00	6.00
❑ Atlantic 2779	Evidence/Change Me Not	1970	—	3.00	6.00
❑ Caribou 9022	Black Sunday/(Instrumental)	1977	—	2.00	4.00
❑ RSO 932	Love Is On the Way/(Instrumental)	1979	—	2.50	5.00
❑ RSO 1013	Love Is On the Way/(Instrumental)	1979	—	2.00	4.00
❑ Stax 0178	Emercury/Slipped and Tripped	1973	—	2.50	5.00
❑ Stax 0203	Try a Little Tenderness/Dirty Tricks	1974	—	2.50	5.00
Albums					
❑ Atlantic SD 8155	The Sweet Inspirations	1968	5.00	10.00	20.00
❑ Atlantic SD 8182	Songs of Faith and Inspiration	1968	5.00	10.00	20.00
❑ Atlantic SD 8201 [S]	What the World Needs Now Is Love	1969	5.00	10.00	20.00
❑ Atlantic SD 8225	Sweets for My Sweet	1969	5.00	10.00	20.00
❑ Atlantic SD 8253	Sweet, Sweet Soul	1970	5.00	10.00	20.00
❑ RSO RS-1-3058	Hot Butterfly	1979	2.50	5.00	10.00
❑ Stax STS-3017	Estelle, Myrna and Sylvia	1973	5.00	10.00	20.00

SWINGIN' MEDALLIONS

45s

Number	Title (A Side/B Side)	Yr	VG	VG+	NM
❑ Capitol 2338	Sun, Sand and Sea/Hey, Hey Baby	1968	2.00	4.00	8.00
❑ Dot 16721	Bye Bye, Silly Girl/I Want to Be Your Guy	1965	3.00	6.00	12.00
❑ 4 Sale 002	Double Shot (Of My Baby's Love)/Here It Comes Again	1966	25.00	50.00	100.00
❑ 1-2-3 1723	We're Gonna Hate Ourselves in the Morning/It's Alright	1970	2.00	4.00	8.00
❑ 1-2-3 1732	Rollin' Rovin' River/Don't Let Your Feet Touch the Ground	1971	2.00	4.00	8.00
❑ Smash 2033	Double Shot (Of My Baby's Love)/Here It Comes Again	1966	3.75	7.50	15.00
❑ Smash 2050	She Drives Me Out of My Mind/You Gotta Have Faith	1966	3.00	6.00	12.00
❑ Smash 2075	I Don't Want to Lose It for You Baby/Night Owl	1966	3.00	6.00	12.00
❑ Smash 2084	Don't Cry No More/I Found a Rainbow	1967	2.50	5.00	10.00
❑ Smash 2107	Turn On the Music/Summer's Not the Same This Year	1967	2.50	5.00	10.00
❑ Smash 2129	Bow and Arrow/Where Can I Go to Get Soul	1967	2.50	5.00	10.00
Albums					
❑ Smash MGS-27083 [M]	Double Shot (Of My Baby's Love)	1966	10.00	20.00	40.00
—First pressing contains the original 45 version of the title song					
❑ Smash SRS-67083 [S]	Double Shot (Of My Baby's Love)	1966	12.50	25.00	50.00
—First pressing contains the original 45 version of the title song					

SYLVERS, THE

45s

Number	Title (A Side/B Side)	Yr	VG	VG+	NM
❑ Capitol 4179	Boogie Fever/Free Style	1975	—	2.00	4.00
❑ Capitol 4255	Cotton Candy/I Can Be for Real	1976	—	2.00	4.00
❑ Capitol 4336	Hot Line/That's What Love Is Made Of	1976	—	2.00	4.00
❑ Capitol 4405	High School Dance/Lovin' You Is Like Lovin' the Wind	1977	—	2.00	4.00
❑ Capitol 4493	Any Way You Want Me/Lovin' Me Back	1977	—	2.00	4.00
❑ Capitol 4532	New Horizon/Charisma	1978	—	2.00	4.00
❑ Casablanca 938	Don't Stop, Get Off/Love Won't Let Me Go	1978	—	2.00	4.00
❑ Casablanca 953	Forever Yours/Diamonds Are Rare	1978	—	2.00	4.00
❑ Casablanca 992	I Feel So Good Tonight/Hoochie Coochie Dancin'	1979	—	2.00	4.00
❑ Casablanca 2207	I Feels So Good Tonight/Mahogany	1979	—	2.00	4.00
❑ Geffen 29061	Falling for Your Love/(Instrumental)	1985	—	—	3.00
❑ Geffen 29293	In One Love and Out the Other/Falling for Your Love	1984	—	—	3.00
❑ MGM 14352	You Got What It Takes/Time to Ride	1972	—	3.00	6.00
❑ MGM 14579	Stay Away from Me/I'll Never Be Ashamed	1973	—	3.00	6.00
❑ MGM 14678	Through the Love in My Heart/Cry of a Dreamer	1973	—	2.00	4.00
❑ MGM 14698	Hang On Sloopy/Na Na Hey Hey Kiss Him Goodbye	1974	—	2.00	4.00
—As "Foster, Pat & Angie Sylivers"					
❑ MGM 14721	I Aim to Please/Wish You Were Here	1974	—	2.00	4.00
❑ Pride 1001	Fool's Paradise/I'm Truly Happy	1972	—	2.50	5.00
❑ Pride 1019	Wish That I Could Talk to You/How Love Hurts	1972	—	2.50	5.00
❑ Pride 1029	Stay Away from Me/I'll Never Be Ashamed	1973	—	2.50	5.00
❑ Solar 47949	Come Back, Lover, Come Back/There's a Place	1981	—	2.00	4.00
❑ Solar 48002	Take It to the Top/I'm Getting Over	1982	—	2.00	4.00
❑ Verve 10664	Come On Give Me a Chance/I'm Just a Lonely Soul	1971	2.50	5.00	10.00
Albums					
❑ Capitol ST-11465	Showcase	1976	2.50	5.00	10.00
❑ Capitol ST-11580	Something Special	1976	2.50	5.00	10.00
❑ Capitol ST-11705	New Horizons	1977	2.50	5.00	10.00
❑ Capitol ST-11868	Best of the Sylvers	1978	2.50	5.00	10.00
❑ Casablanca NBLP 7103	Forever Yours	1978	2.50	5.00	10.00
❑ Casablanca NBLP 7151	Disco Fever	1979	2.50	5.00	10.00
❑ Geffen GHS 24039	Bizarre	1984	2.50	5.00	10.00
❑ MGM SE-4930	The Sylvers III	1974	2.50	5.00	10.00
❑ Pride 0007	The Sylvers	1972	3.00	6.00	12.00
❑ Pride 0026	The Sylvers II	1973	3.00	6.00	12.00
❑ Solar 22	Concept	1981	2.50	5.00	10.00

Number	Title (A Side/B Side)	Yr	VG	VG+	NM
SYNDICATE OF SOUND					
45s					
❑ Bell 640	Little Girl/You	1966	5.00	10.00	20.00
❑ Bell 646	Rumors/Upper Hand	1966	3.75	7.50	15.00
❑ Bell 655	Goodtime Music/Keep It Up	1966	3.75	7.50	15.00
❑ Bell 666	Mary/That Kind of Man	1967	3.75	7.50	15.00
❑ Buddah 156	Brown Paper Bag/Reverb Beat	1970	2.50	5.00	10.00
❑ Buddah 183	Mexico/First to Love You	1970	2.50	5.00	10.00
❑ Capitol 2426	You're Looking Fine/Change the World	1969	2.50	5.00	10.00
❑ Del-Fi 4304	Prepare for Love/Tell the World	1965	5.00	10.00	20.00
❑ Hush 228	Little Girl/You	1966	12.50	25.00	50.00
❑ Scarlet 503	Prepare for Love/Tell the World	1965	7.50	15.00	30.00
Albums					
❑ Bell 6001 [M]	Little Girl	1966	12.50	25.00	50.00
❑ Bell S-6001 [S]	Little Girl	1966	20.00	40.00	80.00

T

Number	Title (A Side/B Side)	Yr	VG	VG+	NM
T. REX					
45s					
❑ A&M 955	Child Star/Debora	1968	3.00	6.00	12.00
—As "Tyrannosaurus Rex"					
❑ Blue Thumb 212	By the Light of the Magical Moon/Find a Little Wood	1971	—	3.00	6.00
❑ Blue Thumb 7121	Ride a White Swan/Summertime Blues	1970	2.00	4.00	8.00
—As "Tyrannosaurus Rex"					
❑ Casablanca 810	Precious Star/(B-side unknown)	1974	—	3.00	6.00
❑ Reprise 1006	Hot Love//One Inch Rock/Seagull Woman	1971	—	3.00	6.00
❑ Reprise 1032	Bang a Gong (Get It On)/Raw Ramp	1971	2.00	4.00	8.00
❑ Reprise 1056	Jeepster/Rip Off	1971	—	3.00	6.00
❑ Reprise 1078	Telegram Sam/Cadillac	1972	—	3.00	6.00
❑ Reprise 1095	Metal Guru/Lady	1972	—	3.00	6.00
❑ Reprise 1122	The Slider/Rock On	1972	—	3.00	6.00
❑ Reprise 1150	Bang a Gong (Get It On)/Telegram Sam	1972	—	2.00	4.00
—"Back to Back Hits" series					
❑ Reprise 1151	Jeepster/Metal Guru	1972	—	2.00	4.00
—"Back to Back Hits" series					
❑ Reprise 1161	Born to Boogie/The Groover	1973	—	2.50	5.00
❑ Reprise 1170	Hot Love/Rip Off	1973	—	2.50	5.00
Albums					
❑ A&M SP-3514 [(2)]	Tyrannosaurus Rex (A Beginning)	1972	3.75	7.50	15.00
—Compilation of early LPs Prophets, Seers & Sages and My People Were Fair and Had Sky in Their Hair But Now They're Content to Wear Stars on Their Brows					
❑ Blue Thumb BTS 7	Unicorn	1969	5.00	10.00	20.00
❑ Blue Thumb BTS 18	A Beard of Stars	1970	5.00	10.00	20.00
—Add $5 for bonus single SP-6115/6, "Ride a White Swan"/"Is It Love." For reasons unknown, the single seems to be much more readily available than the LP					
❑ Casablanca NBLP 7005	Light of Love	1974	3.00	6.00	12.00
—Reissue of 9006					
❑ Casablanca NB 9006	Light of Love	1974	3.75	7.50	15.00
—Original, distributed by Warner Bros.					
❑ Reprise MS 2095	The Slider	1972	3.00	6.00	12.00
❑ Reprise MS 2132	Tanx	1973	3.00	6.00	12.00
❑ Reprise RS 6440	T. Rex	1971	3.00	6.00	12.00
❑ Reprise RS 6466	Electric Warrior	1971	3.00	6.00	12.00
❑ Warner Bros. 25333	T. Rextasy: The Best of T. Rex, 1970-1973	1985	2.50	5.00	10.00
T-BONES, THE					
45s					
❑ Liberty 55677	Draggin'/Rail-Vette	1964	5.00	10.00	20.00
❑ Liberty 55814	That's Where It's At/Pearlin'	1965	3.75	7.50	15.00
❑ Liberty 55836	No Matter What Shape (Your Stomach's In)/Feelin' Fine	1965	3.00	6.00	12.00
❑ Liberty 55867	Sippin' & Chippin'/Moment of Softness	1966	2.50	5.00	10.00
❑ Liberty 55885	Wherever You Look, Wherever You Go/Underwater	1966	2.50	5.00	10.00
❑ Liberty 55906	Let's Go Get Stoned/Farre Thee Well	1966	2.50	5.00	10.00
❑ Liberty 55925	Balboa Blues/Walkin' My Cat Named Dog	1966	2.50	5.00	10.00
❑ Liberty 55951	Tee Hee Hee (My Life Seems Different Now)/Proper Thing to Do	1967	2.50	5.00	10.00

Number	Title (A Side/B Side)	Yr	VG	VG+	NM
❑ United Artists 0068	No Matter What Shape (Your Stomach's In)/Sippin' N Chippin'	1973	—	2.50	5.00
—"Silver Spotlight Series" reissue					
Albums					
❑ Liberty LRP-3346 [M]	Boss Drag	1963	15.00	30.00	60.00
❑ Liberty LRP-3363 [M]	Boss Drag at the Beach	1964	15.00	30.00	60.00
❑ Liberty LRP-3404 [M]	Doin' the Jerk	1965	10.00	20.00	40.00
❑ Liberty LRP-3439 [M]	No Matter What Shape (Your Stomach's In)	1966	5.00	10.00	20.00
❑ Liberty LRP-3446 [M]	Sippin' and Chippin'	1966	5.00	10.00	20.00
❑ Liberty LRP-3471 [M]	Everyone's Gone to the Moon	1966	5.00	10.00	20.00
❑ Liberty LST-7346 [S]	Boss Drag	1963	25.00	50.00	100.00
❑ Liberty LST-7363 [S]	Boss Drag at the Beach	1964	25.00	50.00	100.00
❑ Liberty LST-7404 [S]	Doin' the Jerk	1965	15.00	30.00	60.00
❑ Liberty LST-7439 [S]	No Matter What Shape (Your Stomach's In)	1966	6.25	12.50	25.00
❑ Liberty LST-7446 [S]	Sippin' and Chippin'	1966	6.25	12.50	25.00
❑ Liberty LST-7471 [S]	Everyone's Gone to the Moon	1966	6.25	12.50	25.00
❑ Sunset SUM-1119 [M]	Shapin' Things Up	196?	3.00	6.00	12.00
❑ Sunset SUS-5119 [S]	Shapin' Things Up	196?	3.75	7.50	15.00

TALKING HEADS

45s

Number	Title (A Side/B Side)	Yr	VG	VG+	NM
❑ Sire GSRE 0452	Take Me to the River/Life During Wartime	198?	—	—	3.00
—"Back to Back Hits" reissue					
❑ Sire GSRE 0479	Burning Down the House/This Must Be the Place	198?	—	—	3.00
—"Back to Back Hits" reissue					
❑ Sire 737	Love Goes to Bulding on Fire/New Feeling	1977	2.00	4.00	8.00
❑ Sire 1002	Uh-Oh, Love Comes to Town/I Wish You Wouldn't Say That	1977	—	3.00	6.00
❑ Sire 1013	Psycho Killer/Psycho Killer (Acoustic)	1978	2.00	4.00	8.00
❑ Sire 1032	Take Me to the River/Thank You for Sending Me an Angel (Ver.)	1978	—	2.00	4.00
❑ Sire 21975	Wild, Wild Life/And She Was	198?	—	—	3.00
—"Back to Back Hits" reissue					
❑ Sire 27948	Blind/Still	1988	—	—	2.00
❑ Sire 27992	(Nothing But) Flowers/Ruby Dear	1988	—	—	2.00
❑ Sire 28497	Love for Sale/Hey Now	1987	—	—	2.00
❑ Sire 28629	Wild Wild Life/People Like Us (Movie Version)	1986	—	—	2.00
❑ Sire 28917	And She Was/And She Was (Dub)	1985	—	—	2.00
❑ Sire 28987	Road to Nowhere/Give Me Back My Name	1985	—	—	3.00
❑ Sire 29080	Stop Making Sense (Girlfriend Is Better)/Heaven	1985	—	—	3.00
❑ Sire 29163	Once in a Lifetime/This Must Be the Place (Naive Melody)	1984	—	—	3.00
❑ Sire 29451	This Must Be the Place (Naive Melody)/Moon Rocks	1983	—	—	3.00
❑ Sire 29565	Burning Down the House/I Get Wild-Wild Gravity	1983	—	—	3.00
❑ Sire 49075	Life During Wartime (This Ain't No Party...This Ain't No Disco...This Ain't No Foolin' Around)/Electric Guitar	1979	—	2.00	4.00
❑ Sire 49649	Once in a Lifetime/Seen and Not Seen	1981	—	2.00	4.00
❑ Sire 49734	Houses in Motion/The Overload	1981	—	2.00	4.00
Albums					
❑ Rhino Vinyl R1-70802	Remain in Light	2006	3.75	7.50	15.00
—Reissue on 180-gram vinyl					
❑ Sire 2SR 3590 [(2)]	The Name of This Band Is Talking Heads	1982	5.00	10.00	20.00
❑ Sire SR 6036	Talking Heads '77	1977	3.00	6.00	12.00
❑ Sire SR 6058	More Songs About Buildings and Food	1978	3.00	6.00	12.00
❑ Sire SRK 6076	Fear of Music	1979	2.50	5.00	10.00
❑ Sire SRK 6095	Remain in Light	1981	2.50	5.00	10.00
❑ Sire 23771	Speaking in Tongues	1983	5.00	10.00	20.00
—Clear vinyl in oversize plastic container with Robert Rauschenberg artwork					
❑ Sire 23883	Speaking in Tongues	1983	2.50	5.00	10.00
—Standard issue					
❑ Sire 25121	Stop Making Sense (Soundtrack)	1984	3.75	7.50	15.00
—First issue with booklet and black & white cover					
❑ Sire 25186	Stop Making Sense (Soundtrack)	1984	2.50	5.00	10.00
—Second issue: No booklet, color cover					
❑ Sire 25305	Little Creatures	1985	2.50	5.00	10.00
❑ Sire 25512	True Stories	1986	2.50	5.00	10.00
❑ Sire 25654	Naked	1988	2.50	5.00	10.00

TAVARES

45s

Number	Title (A Side/B Side)	Yr	VG	VG+	NM
❑ Capitol 3674	Check It Out/The Judgment Day	1973	—	2.50	5.00
❑ Capitol 3794	That's the Sound That Lonely Makes/Little Girl	1973	—	2.50	5.00
❑ Capitol 3882	Too Late/Leave It Up to the Lady	1974	—	2.50	5.00
❑ Capitol 3957	She's Gone/To Love You	1974	—	2.50	5.00
❑ Capitol 4010	Remember What I Told You to Forget/My Ship	1974	—	2.50	5.00
❑ Capitol 4111	It Only Takes a Minute/I Hope She Chooses Me	1975	—	2.50	5.00
❑ Capitol 4184	Free Ride/In the Eyes of Love	1975	—	2.50	5.00
❑ Capitol 4221	The Love I Never Had/In the City	1976	—	2.50	5.00
❑ Capitol 4270	Heaven Must Be Missing An Angel (Part 1)/Heaven Must Be Missing An Angel (Part 2)	1976	—	2.50	5.00
❑ Capitol 4348	Don't Take Away the Music/Guiding Star	1976	—	2.50	5.00
❑ Capitol 4398	Whodunit/Fool of the Year	1977	—	2.50	5.00
❑ Capitol 4453	Goodnight My Love/Watchin' the Woman's Movement	1977	—	2.50	5.00
❑ Capitol 4500	More Than a Woman/Keep in Touch	1977	—	2.00	4.00
❑ Capitol 4544	The Ghost of Love (Part 1)/The Ghost of Love (Part 2)	1978	—	2.00	4.00
❑ Capitol 4583	Timber/Feel So Good	1978	—	2.00	4.00
❑ Capitol 4658	Never Had a Love Like This Before/Positive Forces	1978	—	2.00	4.00
❑ Capitol 4703	Straight from the Heart/I'm Back for Me	1979	—	2.00	4.00
❑ Capitol 4738	One Telephone Call Away/Let Me Heal the Bruises	1979	—	2.00	4.00
❑ Capitol 4781	Hard Core Poetry/Stabilize	1979	—	2.00	4.00
❑ Capitol 4811	Bad Times/Got to Have Your Love	1979	—	2.00	4.00

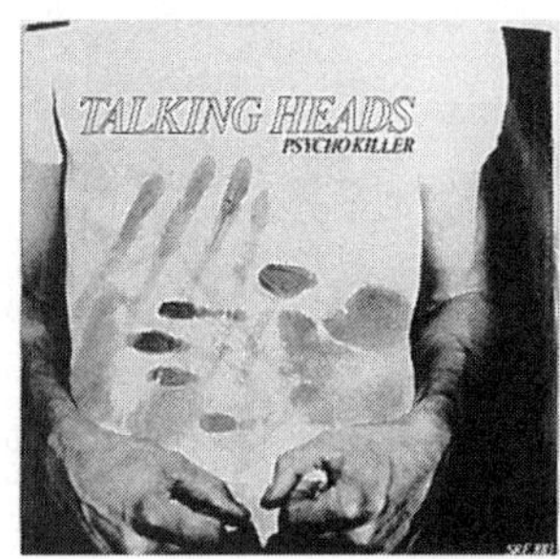

Number	Title (A Side/B Side)	Yr	VG	VG+	NM
❑ Capitol 4846	I Can't Go On Living Without You/Why Can't We Fall in Love	1980	—	2.00	4.00
❑ Capitol 4880	I Don't Want You Anymore/Paradise	1980	—	2.00	4.00
❑ Capitol 4933	Love Uprising/Not Love	1980	—	2.00	4.00
❑ Capitol 4969	Loneliness/Break Down for Love	1981	—	2.00	4.00
❑ Capitol A-5019	Turn Out the Nightlight/House of Music	1981	—	2.00	4.00
❑ Capitol A-5043	Loveline/Right On Time	1981	—	2.00	4.00
❑ RCA PB-13292	A Penny for Your Thoughts/The Skin You're In	1982	—	2.00	4.00
❑ RCA PB-13433	Got to Find My Way Back to You/I Hope You Will Be Very Unhappy Without Me	1983	—	2.00	4.00
❑ RCA PB-13530	Abra-Ca-Dabra Love You Too/Mystery Lady	1983	—	2.00	4.00
❑ RCA PB-13611	Deeper in Love/I Really Miss You Baby	1983	—	2.00	4.00
❑ RCA PB-13684	Words and Music/I'll Send Love (We Go Together)	1983	—	2.00	4.00
❑ RCA GB-13799	A Penny for Your Thoughts/Got to Find My Way Back to You	1984	—	—	3.00
—Gold Standard Series					
Albums					
❑ Capitol ST-11258	Check It Out	1973	2.50	5.00	10.00
❑ Capitol ST-11316	Hard Core Poetry	1974	2.50	5.00	10.00
❑ Capitol ST-11396	In the City	1975	2.50	5.00	10.00
❑ Capitol ST-11533	Sky-High!	1976	2.50	5.00	10.00
❑ Capitol ST-11628	Love Storm	1977	2.50	5.00	10.00
❑ Capitol ST-11701	The Best of Tavares	1977	2.50	5.00	10.00
❑ Capitol SW-11719	Future Bound	1978	2.50	5.00	10.00
❑ Capitol SW-11874	Madam Butterfly	1979	2.50	5.00	10.00
❑ Capitol ST-12026	Supercharged	1980	2.50	5.00	10.00
❑ Capitol ST-12117	Love Uprising	1981	2.50	5.00	10.00
❑ Capitol ST-12167	Loveline	1982	2.50	5.00	10.00
❑ Capitol SN-16206	Love Storm	1981	2.00	4.00	8.00
—Budget-line reissue					
❑ Capitol SN-16207	Future Bound	1981	2.00	4.00	8.00
—Budget-line reissue					
❑ RCA Victor AFL1-4357	New Directions	1982	2.50	5.00	10.00
❑ RCA Victor AFL1-4700	Words and Music	1983	2.50	5.00	10.00

TAYLOR, BOBBY, AND THE VANCOUVERS

Number	Title (A Side/B Side)	Yr	VG	VG+	NM
45s					
❑ Gordy 7069	Does Your Mama Know About Me/Fading Away	1968	5.00	10.00	20.00
❑ Gordy 7073	I Am Your Man/If You Love Her	1968	5.00	10.00	20.00
❑ Gordy 7079	Malinda/It's Growing	1968	5.00	10.00	20.00
❑ Gordy 7088	Oh I've Been Blessed/It Should Have Been Me Loving Her	1969	150.00	300.00	600.00
❑ Gordy 7092	My Girl Is Gone/It Should Have Been Me Loving Her	1969	5.00	10.00	20.00
❑ Integra 103	This Is My Woman/(B-side unknown)	1968	25.00	50.00	100.00
❑ Mowest 5006	Hey Lordy/Just a Little Bit Closer	1971	3.75	7.50	15.00
❑ Playboy 6046	Why Play Games/Don't Wonder Why	1975	—	2.50	5.00
❑ Sunflower 126	There Are Roses Somewhere in the World/It Was a Good Time	1972	6.25	12.50	25.00
❑ V.I.P. 25053	Oh I've Been Blessed/Blackmail	1969	6.25	12.50	25.00
Albums					
❑ Gordy G-930 [M]	Bobby Taylor and the Vancouvers	1968	20.00	40.00	80.00
—Mono is promo only					
❑ Gordy GS-930 [S]	Bobby Taylor and the Vancouvers	1968	15.00	30.00	60.00
❑ Gordy GS-942	Taylor Made Soul	1969	15.00	30.00	60.00

TAYLOR, JAMES

Number	Title (A Side/B Side)	Yr	VG	VG+	NM
45s					
❑ Apple 1805	Carolina in My Mind/Something's Wrong	1970	2.00	4.00	8.00
—Without star on A-side label					
❑ Columbia 02093	Hard Times/Summer's Here	1981	—	—	3.00
❑ Columbia 05681	Everyday/Limousine Driver	1985	—	—	3.00
❑ Columbia 05785	Only One/Mona	1986	—	—	3.00
❑ Columbia 05884	That's Why I'm Here/Going Around One More Time	1986	—	—	3.00
❑ Columbia 06278	Only a Dream in Rio/Turn Away	1986	—	—	3.00
❑ Columbia 07616	Never Die Young/Valentine's Day	1987	—	—	3.00
❑ Columbia 07948	Baby Boom Baby/Letter in the Mail	1988	—	—	3.00
❑ Columbia 08493	Sweet Potato Pie/First of May	1988	—	—	3.00
❑ Columbia 10557	Handy Man/Bartender's Blues	1977	—	2.00	4.00
❑ Columbia 10602	Your Smiling Face/If I Keep My Heart Out of Sight	1977	—	2.00	4.00
❑ Columbia 10676	(What a) Wonderful World/Wooden Planes	1978	—	3.00	6.00
—By Art Garfunkel with Paul Simon and James Taylor; B-side is Garfunkel solo					

Number	Title (A Side/B Side)	Yr	VG	VG+	NM
❑ Columbia 10689	Honey Don't Leave L.A./Another Grey Morning	1978	—	2.00	4.00
❑ Columbia 11005	Up on the Roof/Chanson Francaise	1979	—	2.00	4.00
❑ Columbia 60514	Her Town Too/Believe It or Not	1981	—	2.00	4.00
—A-side: James Taylor and J.D. Souther					
❑ Warner Bros. 7387	Sweet Baby James/Suite for 20G	1970	2.00	4.00	8.00
❑ Warner Bros. 7423	Fire and Rain/Anywhere Like Heaven	1970	2.00	4.00	8.00
❑ Warner Bros. 7460	Country Road/Sunny Skies	1970	—	3.00	6.00
❑ Warner Bros. 7498	You've Got a Friend/You Can Close Your Eyes	1971	—	3.00	6.00
❑ Warner Bros. 7521	Long Ago and Far Away/Let Me Ride	1971	—	2.50	5.00
❑ Warner Bros. 7655	Don't Let Me Be Lonely Tonight/Wow, Don't You Know	1972	—	2.50	5.00
❑ Warner Bros. 7682	One Man Parade/Nobody But You	1973	—	2.50	5.00
❑ Warner Bros. 7695	Hymn/Fanfare	1973	—	2.50	5.00
❑ Warner Bros. 8015	Let It All Fall Down/Daddy's Baby	1974	—	2.50	5.00
❑ Warner Bros. 8028	Walking Man/Daddy's Baby	1974	—	2.50	5.00
❑ Warner Bros. 8109	How Sweet It Is (To Be Loved By You)/Sarah Maria	1975	—	2.50	5.00
❑ Warner Bros. 8137	Mexico/Gorilla	1975	—	2.50	5.00
❑ Warner Bros. 8222	Shower the People/I Can Dream of You	1976	—	2.50	5.00
❑ Warner Bros. 8278	Woman's Gotta Have It/You Make It Easy	1976	—	2.50	5.00
Albums					
❑ Apple SKAO 3352	James Taylor	1970	5.00	10.00	20.00
—With title in orange print					
❑ Columbia JC 34811	JT	1977	2.50	5.00	10.00
❑ Columbia FC 36058	Flag	1979	2.50	5.00	10.00
❑ Columbia TC 37009	Dad Loves His Work	1981	2.50	5.00	10.00
❑ Columbia FC 40052	That's Why I'm Here	1985	2.50	5.00	10.00
❑ Columbia FC 40851	Never Die Young	1988	2.50	5.00	10.00
❑ Euphoria EST-2	James Taylor and the Original Flying Machine 1967	1971	3.00	6.00	12.00
❑ Trip TLP-9513	Rainy Day Man	197?	2.50	5.00	10.00
—Reissue of Euphoria album					
❑ Warner Bros. WS 1843	Sweet Baby James	1970	2.50	5.00	10.00
—Green "WB" label with "Contains Fire and Rain and Country Road" added to front cover					
❑ Warner Bros. BS 2561	Mud Slide Slim and the Blue Horizon	1971	2.50	5.00	10.00
—Green "WB" label					
❑ Warner Bros. BS 2660	One Man Dog	1972	2.50	5.00	10.00
—Green "WB" label					
❑ Warner Bros. BS 2794	Walking Man	1973	2.50	5.00	10.00
—"Burbank" label					
❑ Warner Bros. BS 2866	Gorilla	1975	2.50	5.00	10.00
—"Burbank" label					
❑ Warner Bros. BS 2912	In the Pocket	1976	2.50	5.00	10.00
—"Burbank" label					
❑ Warner Bros. BS 2979	Greatest Hits	1976	3.00	6.00	12.00
—This and other variations of this title have re-recorded versions of "Carolina in My Mind" and "Something in the Way She Moves."					
❑ Warner Bros. BSK 3113	Greatest Hits	1977	2.50	5.00	10.00
—"Burbank" label					

TAYLOR, JOHNNIE

45s

Number	Title (A Side/B Side)	Yr	VG	VG+	NM
❑ Beverly Glen 2003	What About My Love/Reaganomics	1982	—	2.00	4.00
❑ Beverly Glen 2004	I'm So Proud/I Need a Freak	1982	—	2.00	4.00
❑ Beverly Glen 2007	Just Ain't Good Enough/Don't Wait	1983	—	2.00	4.00
❑ Beverly Glen 2016	Seconds of Your Love/Shoot for the Stars	1983	—	2.00	4.00
❑ Columbia 10281	Disco Lady/You're the Best in the World	1976	—	2.50	5.00
❑ Columbia 10334	Somebody's Gettin' It/Please Don't Stop (That Song from Playing)	1976	—	2.50	5.00
❑ Columbia 10478	Love Is Better in the A.M. (Part 1)/Love Is Better in the A.M. (Part 2)	1977	—	2.50	5.00
❑ Columbia 10541	Your Love Is Rated X/Here I Go (Through These Chains Again)	1977	—	2.50	5.00
❑ Columbia 10610	Disco 9000/Right Now	1977	—	2.00	4.00
❑ Columbia 10709	Keep On Dancing/I Love to Make Love When It's Raining	1978	—	2.00	4.00
❑ Columbia 10776	Give Me My Baby/Ever Ready	1978	—	2.00	4.00
❑ Columbia 11084	(Ooh-Wee) She's Killing Me/Play Something Pretty	1979	—	2.00	4.00
❑ Columbia 11315	I Got This Thing for Your Love/Signing Off with Love	1980	—	2.00	4.00
❑ Columbia 11373	I Wanna Get Into You/Baby Don't Hesitate	1980	—	2.00	4.00
❑ Derby 101	Shine, Shine, Shine/Dance What You Wanna	1963	3.75	7.50	15.00
❑ Derby 1006	Baby, We've Got Love/In Love with You	1963	3.75	7.50	15.00
❑ Derby 1010	I Need Lots of Love/Getting Married Soon	1964	3.75	7.50	15.00
❑ Malaco 2107	Lady, My Whole World Is You/L-O-V-E	1984	—	—	3.00
❑ Malaco 2111	Good with My Hips/This Is Your Night	1985	—	—	3.00
❑ Malaco 2118	Still Called the Blues/She's Cheatin' on Me	1985	—	—	3.00
❑ Malaco 2125	Wall to Wall/(B-side unknown)	1986	—	—	3.00
❑ Malaco 2128	Can I Love You/There's Nothing I Wouldn't Do	1986	—	—	3.00
❑ Malaco 2132	Just Because/When She Stops Asking	1987	—	—	3.00
❑ Malaco 2135	Don't Make Me Late/Happy Time	1987	—	—	3.00
❑ Malaco 2140	If I Lose Your Love/Something Is Going Wrong	1987	—	—	3.00
❑ Malaco 2143	Everything's Out in the Open/Got to Leave This Woman	1988	—	—	3.00
❑ Malaco 2153	In Control/I Found a Love	1989	—	—	3.00
❑ Malaco 2159	Still Crazy for You/(B-side unknown)	1989	—	—	3.00
❑ RCA PB-11137	I Want You Back Again/Heaven Bless This Home	1977	—	2.50	5.00
❑ Sar 114	A Whole Lotta Woman/Why Oh Why	1961	5.00	10.00	20.00
❑ Sar 131	Never Never/Rome (Wasn't Built in a Day)	1962	10.00	20.00	40.00
❑ Sar 156	Oh, How I Love You/Run, But You Can't Hide	1964	3.75	7.50	15.00
❑ Stax 0009	Who's Making Love/I'm Trying	1968	2.00	4.00	8.00
❑ Stax 0023	Take Care of Your Homework/Hold On This Time	1969	2.00	4.00	8.00
❑ Stax 0033	Testify (I Wanna)/I Had a Fight with Love	1969	2.00	4.00	8.00
❑ Stax 0042	Just Keep On Loving Me/My Life	1969	2.00	4.00	8.00
—With Carla Thomas					
❑ Stax 0046	I Could Never Be President/It's Amazing	1969	2.00	4.00	8.00
❑ Stax 0055	Love Bones/Mr. Nobody Is Somebody	1969	2.00	4.00	8.00

Number	Title (A Side/B Side)	Yr	VG	VG+	NM
❑ Stax 0068	Steal Away/Friday Night	1970	—	3.00	6.00
❑ Stax 0078	I Am Somebody (Part 1)/I Am Somebody (Part 2)	1970	—	3.00	6.00
❑ Stax 0085	Jody's Got Your Girl and Gone/A Fool Like Me	1970	—	3.00	6.00
❑ Stax 0089	I Don't Wanna Lose You/Party Life	1971	—	3.00	6.00
❑ Stax 0096	Hijackin' Love/Love in the Streets	1971	—	3.00	6.00
❑ Stax 0114	Standing In for Jody/Shackin' Up	1972	—	3.00	6.00
❑ Stax 0122	Doing My Own Thing (Part 1)/Doing My Own Thing (Part 2)	1972	—	3.00	6.00
❑ Stax 0142	Stop Doggin' Me/Stop Teasin' Me	1972	—	3.00	6.00
❑ Stax 0155	Don't You Fool with My Soul (Part 1)/Don't You Fool with My Soul (Part 2)	1973	—	3.00	6.00
❑ Stax 0161	I Believe in You (You Believe in Me)/Love Depression	1973	—	3.00	6.00
—With A-side time listed at 4:37					
❑ Stax 0176	Cheaper to Keep Her/I Can Read Between the Lines	1973	—	3.00	6.00
❑ Stax 186	I Had a Dream/Changes	1966	2.50	5.00	10.00
❑ Stax 193	I Got to Love Somebody's Baby/Just the One I've Been Looking For	1966	2.50	5.00	10.00
❑ Stax 0193	We're Getting Careless with Our Love/Poor Make Believer	1974	—	3.00	6.00
❑ Stax 202	Little Bluebird/Toe Hold	1967	2.50	5.00	10.00
❑ Stax 0208	I've Been Born Again/At Night Time	1974	—	3.00	6.00
❑ Stax 209	Ain't That Loving You/Outside Love	1967	2.50	5.00	10.00
❑ Stax 226	If I Had It to Do Over/You Can't Get Away from It	1967	2.50	5.00	10.00
❑ Stax 0226	It's September/Just One Moment	1974	—	3.00	6.00
❑ Stax 235	Somebody's Sleeping in My Bed/Strange Thing	1967	2.50	5.00	10.00
❑ Stax 0241	Try Me Tonight/Free	1975	—	3.00	6.00
❑ Stax 247	Next Time/Sundown	1968	2.50	5.00	10.00
❑ Stax 253	I Ain't Particular/Where There's Smoke There's Fire	1968	2.50	5.00	10.00
❑ Stax 3201	It Don't Pay to Get Up in the Mornin'/Just Keep On Loving Me	1977	—	2.50	5.00
Albums					
❑ Beverly Glen 10001	Just Ain't Good Enough	1982	3.00	6.00	12.00
❑ Columbia PC 33951	Eargasm	1976	3.00	6.00	12.00
—Originals have no bar code					
❑ Columbia PC 34401	Rated Extraordinaire	1977	3.00	6.00	12.00
❑ Columbia JC 35340	Ever Ready	1978	3.00	6.00	12.00
❑ Columbia JC 36061	She's Killing Me	1979	3.00	6.00	12.00
❑ Columbia JC 36548	A New Day	1980	3.00	6.00	12.00
❑ Columbia JC 37127	The Best of Johnnie Taylor	1981	3.00	6.00	12.00
❑ Ichiban ICH-1022	Stuck in the Mud	198?	2.50	5.00	10.00
❑ Ichiban ICH-1042	Ugly Man	198?	2.50	5.00	10.00
❑ Malaco MAL-7421	This Is Your Night	198?	2.50	5.00	10.00
❑ Malaco MAL-7431	Wall to Wall	198?	2.50	5.00	10.00
❑ Malaco MAL-7440	Lover Boy	198?	2.50	5.00	10.00
❑ Malaco MAL-7446	In Control	198?	2.50	5.00	10.00
❑ Malaco MAL-7452	Crazy 'Bout You	1989	2.50	5.00	10.00
❑ Malaco MAL-7460	Just Can't Do Right	1991	2.50	5.00	10.00
❑ Malaco MAL-7463	The Best of Johnnie Taylor on Malaco, Vol. 1	1992	2.50	5.00	10.00
❑ Stax ST-715 [M]	Wanted: One Soul Singer	1967	12.50	25.00	50.00
❑ Stax STS-715 [S]	Wanted: One Soul Singer	1967	15.00	30.00	60.00
❑ Stax STS-2005	Who's Making Love	1968	10.00	20.00	40.00
❑ Stax STS-2008	Raw Blues	1969	6.25	12.50	25.00
❑ Stax STS-2012	Rare Stamps	1969	6.25	12.50	25.00
❑ Stax STS-2023	The Johnnie Taylor Philosophy Continues	1969	6.25	12.50	25.00
❑ Stax STS-2030	One Step Beyond	1971	6.25	12.50	25.00
❑ Stax STS-2032	Johnnie Taylor's Greatest Hits	1970	6.25	12.50	25.00
❑ Stax STS-3014	Taylored in Silk	1973	5.00	10.00	20.00
❑ Stax STX-4115	Who's Making Love	198?	2.50	5.00	10.00
—Reissue of 2005					
❑ Stax STS-5509	Super Taylor	1974	5.00	10.00	20.00
❑ Stax STS-5521	The Best of Johnnie Taylor	1975	5.00	10.00	20.00
❑ Stax MPS-8508	Raw Blues	1982	2.50	5.00	10.00
❑ Stax MPS-8520	Super Hits	1983	2.50	5.00	10.00
❑ Stax MPS-8537	Taylored in Silk	1987	2.50	5.00	10.00
—Reissue of 3014					
❑ Stax MPS-8558	Little Bluebird	1988	2.50	5.00	10.00
❑ Stax 88001 [(2)]	Chronicle	1977	5.00	10.00	20.00

TEDDY BEARS, THE

45s

Number	Title (A Side/B Side)	Yr	VG	VG+	NM
❑ Dore 503	To Know Him, Is to Love Him/Don't You Worry My Little Pet	1958	7.50	15.00	30.00

Number	Title (A Side/B Side)	Yr	VG	VG+	NM
❑ Dore 520	Wonderful Loveable You/Till You'll Be Mine	1959	5.00	10.00	20.00
❑ Imperial 5562	Oh Why/I Don't Need You Anymore	1959	7.50	15.00	30.00
❑ Imperial 5581	You Said Goodbye/If You Only Knew	1959	7.50	15.00	30.00
❑ Imperial 5594	Seven Lonely Days/Don't Go Away	1959	7.50	15.00	30.00
Albums					
❑ Imperial LP-9067 [M]	The Teddy Bears Sing!	1959	75.00	150.00	300.00
❑ Imperial LP-12010 [S]	The Teddy Bears Sing!	1959	300.00	600.00	1200.

TEE SET, THE

45s

Number	Title (A Side/B Side)	Yr	VG	VG+	NM
❑ Colossus 107	Ma Belle Amie/Angels Coming in the Holy Night	1969	—	2.50	5.00
❑ Colossus 114	If You Do Believe in Love/Charmaine	1970	—	2.00	4.00
❑ Colossus 139	She Likes Weeds/(B-side unknown)	1971	—	2.00	4.00
Albums					
❑ Colossus CCS-1001	Ma Belle Amie	1970	3.75	7.50	15.00

TEMPO, NINO, AND APRIL STEVENS

45s

Number	Title (A Side/B Side)	Yr	VG	VG+	NM
❑ A&M 1394	Love Story/Hoochy Coochy — Wing Dang Doo	1972	—	2.00	4.00
❑ A&M 1443	Put It Where You Want It/I Can't Get Over You Baby	1973	—	2.00	4.00
❑ A&M 1674	Never Had a Lover/You Turn Me On	1975	—	2.00	4.00
❑ Atco 6224	Sweet and Lovely/True Love	1962	2.50	5.00	10.00
❑ Atco 6248	Indian Love Call/Paradise	1962	2.50	5.00	10.00
❑ Atco 6263	(We'll Always Be) Together/Baby Weemus	1963	2.50	5.00	10.00
❑ Atco 6273	Deep Purple/I've Been Carrying a Torch for You So Long That I Burned a Great Big Hole in My Heart	1963	3.00	6.00	12.00
❑ Atco 6281	Whispering/Tweedlee Dee	1963	2.50	5.00	10.00
❑ Atco 6286	Stardust/I-45	1964	2.00	4.00	8.00
❑ Atco 6294	Tea for Two/I'm Confessin' (That I Love You)	1964	2.00	4.00	8.00
❑ Atco 6306	I Surrender Dear/Who	1964	2.00	4.00	8.00
❑ Atco 6314	Melancholy Baby/Ooh La La	1964	2.00	4.00	8.00
❑ Atco 6325	Our Love/Honeywell Rose	1964	2.00	4.00	8.00
❑ Atco 6337	These Arms of Mine/The Coldest Night of the Year	1965	2.00	4.00	8.00
❑ Atco 6350	Swing Me/Tomorrow Is Soon a Memory	1965	2.00	4.00	8.00
❑ Atco 6360	Think of You/I'm Sweet on You	1965	2.00	4.00	8.00
❑ Atco 6368	That's My Desire/King Kong	1965	2.00	4.00	8.00
❑ Atco 6375	I Love How You Love Me/Tears of Sorrow	1965	2.00	4.00	8.00
❑ Atco 6391	Hey Baby/The Poison of Your Kisses	1965	2.00	4.00	8.00
❑ Atco 6410	Bye Bye Blues/King Kong	1966	2.00	4.00	8.00
❑ Atco 6897	She's My Baby/Tomorrow Is Soon a Memory	1972	—	3.00	6.00
❑ Bell 769	Did I or Didn't I/Yesterday I Heard the Rain	1969	2.00	4.00	8.00
❑ Bell 823	Seas of Love-Dock of the Bay/Twilight	1969	2.00	4.00	8.00
❑ Chelsea 3052	What Kind of Fool Am I/(B-side unknown)	1976	—	2.00	4.00
❑ MGM 13825	Falling in Love Again/Wanting You	1967	2.00	4.00	8.00
❑ MGM 14266	How About Me/Makin' Love to Rainbow Colors	1971	—	3.00	6.00
❑ United Artists 272	Ooeah (That's What You Do to Me)/High School Sweetheart	1960	2.50	5.00	10.00
❑ White Whale 236	All Strung Out/I Can't Go On Living Baby Without You	1966	2.00	4.00	8.00
❑ White Whale 241	You'll Be Needing Me Baby/Habit of Lovin' You Baby	1966	2.00	4.00	8.00
❑ White Whale 246	Wings of Love/My Old Flame	1967	2.00	4.00	8.00
❑ White Whale 252	I Can't Go On Living Without You Baby/Little Child	1967	3.00	6.00	12.00
—Some copies have the above erroneous A-side title					
❑ White Whale 252	I Can't Go On Living Baby Without You/Little Child	1967	2.00	4.00	8.00
❑ White Whale 268	Let It Be Me/Words of Love	1968	2.00	4.00	8.00
❑ White Whale 271	Ooh Poo Pa Doo/Let It Be Me	1968	2.00	4.00	8.00
Albums					
❑ Atco 33-156 [M]	Deep Purple	1963	10.00	20.00	40.00
❑ Atco SD 33-156 [S]	Deep Purple	1963	12.50	25.00	50.00
❑ Atco 33-162 [M]	Nino and April Sing the Great Songs	1964	7.50	15.00	30.00
❑ Atco SD 33-162 [S]	Nino and April Sing the Great Songs	1964	10.00	20.00	40.00
❑ Atco 33-180 [M]	Hey Baby	1966	7.50	15.00	30.00
❑ Atco SD 33-180 [S]	Hey Baby	1966	10.00	20.00	40.00
❑ RCA Camden CAL-824 [M]	A Nino Tempo/April Stevens Program	1964	3.00	6.00	12.00
—Actually contains solo recordings by each, packaged together to capitalize on the success of "Deep Purple"					
❑ White Whale WW-113 [M]	All Strung Out	1967	5.00	10.00	20.00
❑ White Whale WWS-7113 [S]	All Strung Out	1967	6.25	12.50	25.00

TEMPTATIONS, THE

45s

Number	Title (A Side/B Side)	Yr	VG	VG+	NM
❑ Atlantic 3436	In a Lifetime/I Could Never Stop Loving You	1977	—	2.00	4.00
❑ Atlantic 3461	Think for Yourself/Let's Live in Place	1978	—	2.00	4.00
❑ Atlantic 3517	Bare Back/I See My Child	1978	—	2.00	4.00
❑ Atlantic 3538	Ever Ready Love/Touch Me Again	1978	—	2.00	4.00
❑ Atlantic 3567	Mystic Woman/I Just Don't Know How to Let You Go	1979	—	2.00	4.00
❑ Gordy 1616	Standing on the Top-Part 1/Part 2	1982	—	2.00	4.00
—With Rick James					
❑ Gordy 1631	More on the Inside/Money's Hard to Get	1982	—	2.00	4.00
❑ Gordy 1654	Silent Night/Everything for Christmas	1982	—	3.00	6.00
❑ Gordy 1666	Love on My Mind Tonight/Bring Your Body Here	1983	—	2.00	4.00
❑ Gordy 1683	Made in America/Surface Thrills	1983	—	2.00	4.00
❑ Gordy 1707	Miss Busy Body (Get Your Body Busy)/(Instrumental)	1983	—	2.00	4.00
❑ Gordy 1713	Silent Night/Everything for Christmas	1983	—	2.50	5.00
❑ Gordy 1720	Sail Away/Isn't the Night Fantastic	1984	—	2.00	4.00
❑ Gordy 1765	Treat Her Like a Lady/Isn't the Night Fantastic	1984	—	2.00	4.00
❑ Gordy 1781	My Love Is True (Truly for You)/Set Your Love Right	1985	—	2.00	4.00
❑ Gordy 1789	How Can You Say That It's Over/I'll Keep My Light in My Window	1985	—	2.00	4.00
❑ Gordy 1818	Do You Really Love Your Baby/I'll Keep My Light in My Window	1985	—	2.00	4.00
❑ Gordy 1834	Touch Me/Set Your Love Right	1986	—	2.00	4.00
❑ Gordy 1856	Lady Soul/Put Us Together Again	1986	—	2.00	4.00

Number	Title (A Side/B Side)	Yr	VG	VG+	NM
❑ Gordy 1871	To Be Continued/You're the One	1986	—	2.00	4.00
❑ Gordy 1881	Someone/Love Me Right	1987	—	2.00	4.00
❑ Gordy 7001	Dream Come True/Isn't She Pretty	1962	10.00	20.00	40.00
❑ Gordy 7010	Paradise/Slow Down Heart	1962	7.50	15.00	30.00
❑ Gordy 7015	I Want a Love I Can See/The Further You Look, The Less You See	1963	6.25	12.50	25.00
❑ Gordy 7020	May I Have This Dance?/Farewell, My Love	1963	6.25	12.50	25.00
❑ Gordy 7028	The Way You Do the Things You Do/Just Let Me Know	1964	3.75	7.50	15.00
❑ Gordy 7032	I'll Be in Trouble/The Girl's Alright with Me	1964	3.75	7.50	15.00
❑ Gordy 7035	Girl (Why You Wanna Make Me Blue)/Baby, Baby I Need You	1964	3.75	7.50	15.00
❑ Gordy 7038	My Girl/Nobody But My Baby	1965	3.75	7.50	15.00
❑ Gordy 7040	It's Growing/What Love Has Joined Together	1965	3.75	7.50	15.00
❑ Gordy 7043	Since I Lost My Baby/You've Got to Earn It	1965	3.75	7.50	15.00
❑ Gordy 7047	My Baby/Don't Look Back	1965	3.75	7.50	15.00
❑ Gordy 7049	Get Ready/Fading Away	1966	3.75	7.50	15.00
❑ Gordy 7054	Ain't Too Proud to Beg/You'll Lose a Precious Love	1966	3.75	7.50	15.00
❑ Gordy 7055	Beauty Is Only Skin Deep/You're Not an Ordinary Girl	1966	3.75	7.50	15.00
❑ Gordy 7057	(I Know) I'm Losing You/I Couldn't Cry If I Wanted To	1966	3.75	7.50	15.00
❑ Gordy 7061	All I Need/Sorry Is a Sorry Word	1967	2.50	5.00	10.00
❑ Gordy 7063	You're My Everything/I've Been Good to You	1967	2.50	5.00	10.00
—"Gordy" on left					
❑ Gordy 7065	(Loneliness Made Me Realize) It's You That I Need/ Don't Send Me Away	1967	2.50	5.00	10.00
❑ Gordy 7068	I Wish It Would Rain/I Truly, Truly Believe	1967	2.50	5.00	10.00
❑ Gordy 7072	I Could Never Love Another (After Loving You)/ Gonna Give Her All the Love I've Got	1968	2.50	5.00	10.00
❑ Gordy 7074	Please Return Your Love to Me/How Can I Forget	1968	2.50	5.00	10.00
❑ Gordy 7081	Cloud Nine/Why Did She Have to Leave Me	1968	2.00	4.00	8.00
❑ Gordy 7082	Silent Night/Rudolph, the Red-Nosed Reindeer	1968	3.00	6.00	12.00
❑ Gordy 7084	Run Away Child, Running Wild/I Need Your Love	1969	2.00	4.00	8.00
❑ Gordy 7086	Don't Let the Joneses Get You Down/Since I've Lost You	1969	2.00	4.00	8.00
❑ Gordy 7093	I Can't Get Next to You/Running Away (Ain't Gonna Help You)	1969	2.00	4.00	8.00
❑ Gordy 7096	Psychedelic Shack/That's the Way Love Is	1970	—	3.00	6.00
❑ Gordy 7099	Ball of Confusion (That's What the World Is Today)/It's Summer	1970	—	3.00	6.00
❑ Gordy 7102	Ungena Za Ulimwengu (Unite the World)/Hum Along and Dance	1970	—	3.00	6.00
❑ Gordy 7105	Just My Imagination (Running Away with Me)/You Make Your Own Heaven and Hell Right Here on Earth	1971	—	3.00	6.00
❑ Gordy 7109	It's Summer/I'm the Exception to the Rule	1971	—	3.00	6.00
❑ Gordy 7111	Superstar (Remember How You Got Where You Are)/Gonna Keep On Tryin' Till I Win Your Love	1971	—	3.00	6.00
❑ Gordy 7115	Take a Look Around/Smooth Sailing (From Now On)	1972	—	3.00	6.00
❑ Gordy 7119	Mother Nature/Funky Music Sho Nuff Turns Me On	1972	—	3.00	6.00
❑ Gordy 7121	Papa Was a Rollin' Stone/(Instrumental)	1972	—	3.00	6.00
❑ Gordy 7126	Masterpiece/(Instrumental)	1973	—	3.00	6.00
❑ Gordy 7129	Plastic Man/Hurry Tomorrow	1973	—	3.00	6.00
❑ Gordy 7131	Hey Girl (I Like Your Style)/Ma	1973	—	3.00	6.00
❑ Gordy 7133	Let Your Hair Down/Ain't No Justice	1973	—	3.00	6.00
❑ Gordy 7135	Heavenly/Zoom	1974	—	3.00	6.00
❑ Gordy 7136	You've Got My Soul on Fire/I Need You	1974	—	3.00	6.00
❑ Gordy 7138	Happy People/(Instrumental)	1974	—	3.00	6.00
❑ Gordy 7142	Shakey Ground/I'm a Bachelor	1975	—	3.00	6.00
❑ Gordy 7144	Glasshouse/The Prophet	1975	—	3.00	6.00
❑ Gordy 7146	Keep Holding On/What You Need Most (I Do Best of All)	1975	—	3.00	6.00
❑ Gordy 7150	Up the Creek (Without a Paddle)/Darling Stand By Me (Song for a Woman)	1976	—	3.00	6.00
❑ Gordy 7151	Who Are You (And What Are You Doing the Rest of Your Life)/ Darling Stand By Me (Song for a Woman)	1976	—	—	—
—Unreleased					
❑ Gordy 7152	Let Me Count the Ways (I Love You)/Who Are You (And What Are You Doing the Rest of Your Life)	1976	—	3.00	6.00
❑ Gordy 7183	Power/Power (Part 2)	1980	—	2.00	4.00
❑ Gordy 7188	Struck by Lightning Twice/I'm Coming Home	1980	—	2.00	4.00
❑ Gordy 7208	Aiming at Your Heart/Life of a Cowboy	1981	10.00	20.00	40.00
❑ Gordy 7213	Oh What a Night/Isn't the Night Fantastic	1981	—	2.00	4.00
❑ Miracle 5	Oh, Mother of Mine/Romance Without Finance	1961	25.00	50.00	100.00
❑ Miracle 12	Check Yourself/Your Wonderful Love	1961	25.00	50.00	100.00
❑ Motown 903	One Step at a Time/(Instrumental)	1990	—	2.00	4.00
❑ Motown 1501	Take Me Away/There's More Where That Came From	1980	—	2.00	4.00

Number	Title (A Side/B Side)	Yr	VG	VG+	NM
❑ Motown 1837	A Fine Mess/Wishful Thinking	1986	—	2.00	4.00
❑ Motown 1908	I Wonder Who She's Seeing Now/Girls (They Like It)	1987	—	—	3.00
❑ Motown 1920	Look What You Started/More Love, Your Love	1987	—	—	3.00
❑ Motown 1933	Do You Wanna Go with Me/Put Your Foot Down	1988	—	—	3.00
❑ Motown 1974	All I Want from You/(Instrumental)	1989	—	—	3.00
❑ Motown 2004	Special/O.A.O. Lover	1989	—	2.00	4.00
❑ Motown 2023	Soul to Soul (same on both sides?)	1990	—	2.00	4.00
❑ Motown Yesteryear Y-690F	Silent Night/Give Love at Christmas	1985	—	2.00	4.00
Albums					
❑ Atlantic SD 19143	Hear to Tempt You	1977	3.00	6.00	12.00
❑ Atlantic SD 19188	Bare Back	1978	3.00	6.00	12.00
❑ Gordy G 911 [M]	Meet the Temptations	1964	7.50	15.00	30.00
❑ Gordy GS 911 [S]	Meet the Temptations	1964	10.00	20.00	40.00
—Script "Gordy" at top of label					
❑ Gordy G 912 [M]	The Temptations Sing Smokey	1965	7.50	15.00	30.00
❑ Gordy GS 912 [S]	The Temptations Sing Smokey	1965	10.00	20.00	40.00
—Script "Gordy" at top of label					
❑ Gordy G 914 [M]	Temptin' Temptations	1965	6.25	12.50	25.00
❑ Gordy GS 914 [S]	Temptin' Temptations	1965	7.50	15.00	30.00
—Script "Gordy" at top of label					
❑ Gordy G 918 [M]	Gettin' Ready	1966	6.25	12.50	25.00
❑ Gordy GS 918 [S]	Gettin' Ready	1966	7.50	15.00	30.00
—Script "Gordy" at top of label					
❑ Gordy G 919 [M]	The Temptations' Greatest Hits	1966	6.25	12.50	25.00
❑ Gordy GS 919 [S]	The Temptations' Greatest Hits	1966	7.50	15.00	30.00
—Script "Gordy" at top of label					
❑ Gordy G 921 [M]	Temptations Live!	1967	6.25	12.50	25.00
❑ Gordy GS 921 [S]	Temptations Live!	1967	7.50	15.00	30.00
—Script "Gordy" at top of label					
❑ Gordy G 922 [M]	With a Lot o' Soul	1967	6.25	12.50	25.00
❑ Gordy GS 922 [S]	With a Lot o' Soul	1967	6.25	12.50	25.00
—Script "Gordy" at top of label					
❑ Gordy G 924 [M]	The Temptations in a Mellow Mood	1967	6.25	12.50	25.00
❑ Gordy GS 924 [S]	The Temptations in a Mellow Mood	1967	6.25	12.50	25.00
❑ Gordy GS 927 [S]	The Temptations Wish It Would Rain	1968	5.00	10.00	20.00
❑ Gordy GS 933	The Temptations Show	1969	5.00	10.00	20.00
❑ Gordy GS 938	Live at the Copa	1968	5.00	10.00	20.00
❑ Gordy GS 939	Cloud Nine	1969	5.00	10.00	20.00
❑ Gordy GS 947	Psychedelic Shack	1970	5.00	10.00	20.00
❑ Gordy GS 949	Puzzle People	1969	5.00	10.00	20.00
❑ Gordy GS 951	The Temptations' Christmas Card	1969	6.25	12.50	25.00
❑ Gordy GS 953	Live at London's Talk of the Town	1970	5.00	10.00	20.00
❑ Gordy GS 954	Temptations Greatest Hits II	1970	5.00	10.00	20.00
❑ Gordy GS 957	Sky's the Limit	1971	5.00	10.00	20.00
❑ Gordy G 961L	Solid Rock	1972	5.00	10.00	20.00
❑ Gordy G 962L	All Directions	1972	5.00	10.00	20.00
❑ Gordy G 965L	Masterpiece	1973	5.00	10.00	20.00
❑ Gordy G 966V1	1990	1973	3.75	7.50	15.00
❑ Gordy G6-969S1	A Song for You	1975	3.75	7.50	15.00
❑ Gordy G6-971S1	Wings of Love	1976	3.75	7.50	15.00
❑ Gordy G6-973S1	House Party	1975	3.75	7.50	15.00
❑ Gordy G7-975S1	The Temptations Do the Temptations	1976	3.75	7.50	15.00
❑ Gordy G8-994M1	Power	1980	3.00	6.00	12.00
❑ Gordy G8-998M1	Give Love at Christmas	1980	3.75	7.50	15.00
❑ Gordy G8-1006M1	The Temptations	1981	3.00	6.00	12.00
❑ Gordy 6008 GL	Reunion	1982	3.00	6.00	12.00
❑ Gordy 6032 GL	Surface Thrills	1983	3.00	6.00	12.00
❑ Gordy 6085 GL	Back to Basics	1984	3.00	6.00	12.00
❑ Gordy 6119 GL	Truly for You	1984	3.00	6.00	12.00
❑ Gordy 6164 GL	Touch Me	1986	3.00	6.00	12.00
❑ Gordy 6207 GL	To Be Continued	1986	3.00	6.00	12.00
❑ Motown M5-140V1	Meet the Temptations	1981	3.00	6.00	12.00
—Reissue of Gordy 911					
❑ Motown M5-144V1	Masterpiece	1981	3.00	6.00	12.00
—Reissue of Gordy 965					
❑ Motown M5-159V1	Cloud Nine	1981	3.00	6.00	12.00
—Reissue of Gordy 939					
❑ Motown M5-164V1	Psychedelic Shack	1981	3.00	6.00	12.00
—Reissue of Gordy 947					
❑ Motown M5-172V1	Puzzle People	1981	3.00	6.00	12.00
—Reissue of Gordy 949					
❑ Motown M5-205V1	The Temptations Sing Smokey	1981	3.00	6.00	12.00
—Reissue of Gordy 912					
❑ Motown M5-212V1	All the Million Sellers	1982	3.00	6.00	12.00
❑ Motown M 782 [(3)]	Anthology	1973	6.25	12.50	25.00
❑ Motown 5251 ML	The Temptations Christmas Card	1982	2.50	5.00	10.00
—Reissue of Gordy 951					
❑ Motown 5279 ML	Give Love at Christmas	1983	2.50	5.00	10.00
—Reissue of Gordy 998					
❑ Motown 5389 ML [(2)]	25th Anniversary	1986	3.75	7.50	15.00
❑ Motown 6246 ML	Together Again	1987	3.00	6.00	12.00
❑ Motown MOT-6275	Special	1989	3.00	6.00	12.00
❑ Natural Resources NR 4005T1	The Temptations in a Mellow Mood	1978	3.00	6.00	12.00
—Reissue of Gordy 924					

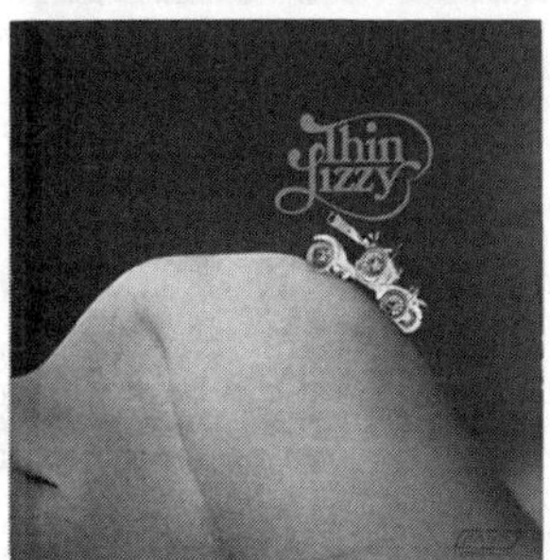

Number	Title (A Side/B Side)	Yr	VG	VG+	NM
10CC					
45s					
❑ Mercury 73678	I'm Not in Love/Channel Swimmer	1975	—	2.50	5.00
❑ Mercury 73725	Art for Art's Sake/Get It While You Can	1975	—	2.50	5.00
❑ Mercury 73779	I'm Mandy Fly Me/How Dare You	1976	—	2.50	5.00
❑ Mercury 73875	The Things We Do for Love/Hot to Trot	1976	—	2.50	5.00
❑ Mercury 73917	People in Love/Don't Squeeze Me Like Toothpaste	1977	—	2.50	5.00
❑ Mercury 73943	Good Morning Judge/I'm So Laid Back I'm Laid Out	1977	—	2.50	5.00
❑ Mercury 73980	You've Got a Cold/The Wall Street Shuffle	1977	—	2.50	5.00
❑ Polydor 14511	Dreadlock Holiday/Nothing Can Move Me	1978	—	2.50	5.00
❑ Polydor 14528	For You and I/Take These Chains	1978	—	2.50	5.00
❑ UK 49005	Donna/Hot Sun Rock	1972	—	3.00	6.00
❑ UK 49015	Ruber Bullets/Waterfall	1973	—	3.00	6.00
❑ UK 49019	Headline Hustler/Speed Kills	1973	—	3.00	6.00
❑ UK 49023	The Wall Street Shuffle/Gismo My Way	1974	—	3.00	6.00
❑ Warner Bros. 29973	Power of Love/Action Man in Motown Suit	1982	—	2.50	5.00
❑ Warner Bros. 49266	It Doesn't Matter Anymore/Strange Lover	1980	—	2.50	5.00
Albums					
❑ Mercury SRM-1-1029	The Original Soundtrack	1975	3.00	6.00	12.00
❑ Mercury SRM-1-1061	How Dare You!	1976	3.00	6.00	12.00
❑ Mercury SRM-1-3702	Deceptive Bends	1977	3.00	6.00	12.00
❑ Mercury SRM-2-8600 [(2)]	Live and Let Live	1977	3.75	7.50	15.00
❑ Polydor PD-1-6161	Bloody Tourists	1978	2.50	5.00	10.00
❑ Polydor PD-1-6244	Greatest Hits 1972-1978	1979	2.50	5.00	10.00
❑ U.K. 53105	10cc	1973	3.75	7.50	15.00
❑ U.K. AUKS 53107	Sheet Music	1974	3.75	7.50	15.00
❑ U.K. 53110	100cc	1975	3.75	7.50	15.00
❑ Warner Bros. BSK 3442	Look Hear?	1980	2.50	5.00	10.00
❑ Warner Bros. BSK 3575	Ten Out of Ten	1981	2.50	5.00	10.00
TEX, JOE					
45s					
❑ Ace 544	Cut It Out/Just for You and Me	1958	15.00	30.00	60.00
❑ Ace 550	Mother's Advice/You Little Baby Face Thing	1958	20.00	40.00	80.00
❑ Ace 559	Charlie Brown Got Expelled/Blessed Are These Tears	1959	15.00	30.00	60.00
❑ Ace 572	Don't Hold It Against Me/Yum, Yum, Yum	1959	15.00	30.00	60.00
❑ Ace 591	Boys Will Be Boys/Grannie Stole the Show	1960	10.00	20.00	40.00
❑ Ace 674	Boys Will Be Boys/Baby You're Right	1963	3.75	7.50	15.00
❑ Anna 1119	All I Could Do Was Cry (Part 1)/All I Could Do Was Cry (Part 2)	1960	10.00	20.00	40.00
❑ Anna 1124	I'll Never Break Your Heart (Part 1)/I'll Never Break Your Heart (Part 2)	1960	10.00	20.00	40.00
❑ Anna 1128	Baby, You're Right/Ain't It a Mess	1961	10.00	20.00	40.00
❑ Atlantic 2874	I'll Never Fall in Love Again (Part 1)/I'll Never Fall in Love Again (Part 2)	1972	—	3.00	6.00
❑ Checker 1104	Baby, You're Right/All I Could Do Was Cry (Part 2)	1965	3.00	6.00	12.00
❑ Dial 1001	Bad Feet/I Know Him	1971	—	3.00	6.00
❑ Dial 1003	Papa's Dream/I'm Comin' Home	1971	—	3.00	6.00
❑ Dial 1008	Give the Baby Anything the Baby Wants/Takin' a Chance	1971	—	3.00	6.00
❑ Dial 1010	I Gotcha/A Mother's Prayer	1972	—	3.00	6.00
❑ Dial 1012	You Said a Bad Word/It Ain't Gonna Work Baby	1972	—	3.00	6.00
❑ Dial 1018	Rain Go Away/King Thaddeus	1973	—	3.00	6.00
❑ Dial 1020	Woman Stealer/Cat's Got Her Tongue	1973	—	3.00	6.00
❑ Dial 1021	All the Heaven a Man Really Needs/Let's Go Somewhere and Talk	1973	—	3.00	6.00
❑ Dial 1024	Trying to Win Your Love/I've Seen Enough	1973	—	3.00	6.00
❑ Dial 1154	Sassy Sexy Wiggle/Under Your Powerful Love	1975	—	3.00	6.00
❑ Dial 1155	I'm Goin' Back Again/My Body Wants You	1975	—	3.00	6.00
❑ Dial 1156	Baby, It's Rainin'/Have You Ever	1975	—	3.00	6.00
❑ Dial 1157	Mama Red/Love Shortage	1975	—	3.00	6.00
❑ Dial 2800	Loose Caboose/Music Ain't Got No Color	1979	—	2.50	5.00
❑ Dial 2801	Who Gave Birth to the Funk/If You Don't Want the Man	1979	—	2.50	5.00
❑ Dial 2802	Discomania/Fat People	1979	—	2.50	5.00
❑ Dial 3000	What Should I Do/The Only Girl I've Ever Loved	1961	3.00	6.00	12.00
❑ Dial 3002	One Giant Step/The Rib	1961	3.00	6.00	12.00
❑ Dial 3003	Popeye Johnny/Hand Shakin', Love Makin', Girl Talkin', Son-of-a-Gun From Next Door	1962	3.00	6.00	12.00
❑ Dial 3007	Meet Me in Church/Be Your Own Judge	1962	3.00	6.00	12.00
❑ Dial 3009	I Let Her Get Away/The Peck	1963	3.00	6.00	12.00

Number	Title (A Side/B Side)	Yr	VG	VG+	NM
❑ Dial 3013	Someone to Take Your Place/I Should Have Kissed You More	1963	3.00	6.00	12.00
❑ Dial 3016	I Wanna Be Free/Blood's Thicker Than Water	1963	37.50	75.00	150.00
❑ Dial 3019	Looking for My Pig/Say Thank You	1964	3.00	6.00	12.00
❑ Dial 3020	I'd Rather Have You/Old Time Lover	1964	3.00	6.00	12.00
❑ Dial 3023	I Had a Good Thing But I Left (Part 1)/I Had a Good Thing But I Left (Part 2)	1964	3.00	6.00	12.00
❑ Dial 4001	Hold What You've Got/Fresh Out of Tears	1964	3.75	7.50	15.00
❑ Dial 4003	You Better Get It/You Got What It Takes	1965	2.50	5.00	10.00
❑ Dial 4006	A Woman Can Change a Man/Don't Let Your Left Hand Know	1965	2.50	5.00	10.00
❑ Dial 4011	One Monkey Don't Stop No Show/Build Your Love on a Solid Foundation	1965	2.50	5.00	10.00
❑ Dial 4016	I Want To (Do Everything For You)/Funny Bone	1965	2.50	5.00	10.00
❑ Dial 4022	A Sweet Woman Like You/Close the Door	1965	2.50	5.00	10.00
❑ Dial 4026	The Love You Save (May Be Your Own)/ If Sugar Was As Sweet As You	1966	2.50	5.00	10.00
❑ Dial 4028	S.Y.S.L.J.F.M. (Letter Song)/I'm a Man	1966	2.50	5.00	10.00
❑ Dial 4033	I Believe I'm Gonna Make It/Better Believe It, Baby	1966	2.50	5.00	10.00
❑ Dial 4045	I've Got to Do a Little Bit Better/What in the World	1966	2.50	5.00	10.00
❑ Dial 4051	Papa Was Too/Truest Woman in the World	1966	2.50	5.00	10.00
❑ Dial 4055	Show Me/A Woman Sees a Hard Time (When Her Man Is Gone)	1967	2.00	4.00	8.00
❑ Dial 4059	Woman Like That, Yeah/I'm Going and Get It	1967	2.00	4.00	8.00
❑ Dial 4061	A Woman's Hands/See See Rider	1967	2.00	4.00	8.00
❑ Dial 4063	Skinny Legs and All/Watch the One	1967	2.50	5.00	10.00
❑ Dial 4068	I'll Make Every Day Christmas (For My Woman)/Don't Give Up	1967	3.00	6.00	12.00
❑ Dial 4069	Men Are Gettin' Scarce/You're Gonna Thank Me, Woman	1968	2.00	4.00	8.00
❑ Dial 4076	I'll Never Do You Wrong/Wooden Spoon	1968	2.00	4.00	8.00
❑ Dial 4079	Chocolate Cherry/Betwixt and Between	1968	2.00	4.00	8.00
❑ Dial 4083	Keep the One You Got/Go Home and Do It	1968	2.00	4.00	8.00
❑ Dial 4086	You Need Me, Baby/Baby, Be Good	1968	2.00	4.00	8.00
❑ Dial 4089	That's Your Baby/Sweet, Sweet Woman	1968	2.00	4.00	8.00
❑ Dial 4090	Buying a Book/Chicken Crazy	1969	2.00	4.00	8.00
❑ Dial 4093	That's the Way/Anything You Wanna Know	1969	2.00	4.00	8.00
❑ Dial 4094	We Can't Sit Down Now/It Ain't Sanitary	1969	2.00	4.00	8.00
❑ Dial 4095	I Can't See You No More (When Johnny Comes Marching Home Again)/Sure Is Good	1969	2.00	4.00	8.00
❑ Dial 4096	Everything Happens on Time/You're Right, Ray Charles	1970	2.00	4.00	8.00
❑ Dial 4098	I'll Never Fall in Love Again/The Only Way I Know to Love You	1970	2.00	4.00	8.00
❑ Epic 50313	Ain't Gonna Bump No More (With No Big Fat Woman)/I Mess Up Everything I Get My Hands On	1976	—	2.50	5.00
❑ Epic 50426	Hungry for Your Love/I Almost Got to Heaven Once	1977	—	2.50	5.00
❑ Epic 50494	Rub Down/Be Kind to Old People	1977	—	2.50	5.00
❑ Epic 50530	Get Back, Leroy/You Can Be My Star	1978	—	2.50	5.00
❑ Handshake 02565	Don't Do Da Do/Here Comes No. 34 (Do the Earl Campbell)	1981	—	2.00	4.00
❑ King 4840	Come In This House/Davy, You Upset My Home	1955	15.00	30.00	60.00
❑ King 4884	My Biggest Mistake/Right Back to My Arms	1956	12.50	25.00	50.00
❑ King 4911	She's Mine/I Had to Come Back to You	1956	12.50	25.00	50.00
❑ King 4980	Get Way Back/Pneumonia	1956	12.50	25.00	50.00
❑ King 5064	I Want to Have a Talk with You/Ain't Nobody's Business	1957	12.50	25.00	50.00
❑ King 5981	Come In This House/I Want to Have a Talk with You	1965	2.50	5.00	10.00
Albums					
❑ Accord SN-7174	J.T.'s Funk	1982	2.50	5.00	10.00
❑ Atlantic 8106 [M]	Hold What You've Got	1965	10.00	20.00	40.00
❑ Atlantic SD 8106 [P]	Hold What You've Got	1965	12.50	25.00	50.00
❑ Atlantic 8115 [M]	The New Boss	1965	10.00	20.00	40.00
❑ Atlantic SD 8115 [S]	The New Boss	1965	12.50	25.00	50.00
❑ Atlantic 8124 [M]	The Love You Save	1966	10.00	20.00	40.00
❑ Atlantic SD 8124 [S]	The Love You Save	1966	12.50	25.00	50.00
❑ Atlantic 8133 [M]	I've Got to Do a Little Better	1966	10.00	20.00	40.00
❑ Atlantic SD 8133 [S]	I've Got to Do a Little Better	1966	12.50	25.00	50.00
❑ Atlantic 8144 [M]	The Best of Joe Tex	1967	5.00	10.00	20.00
❑ Atlantic SD 8144 [P]	The Best of Joe Tex	1967	6.25	12.50	25.00
❑ Atlantic SD 8156	Live and Lively	1968	5.00	10.00	20.00
❑ Atlantic SD 8187 [S]	Soul Country	1968	5.00	10.00	20.00
❑ Atlantic SD 8211	Happy Soul	1969	5.00	10.00	20.00
❑ Atlantic SD 8231	Buying a Book	1969	5.00	10.00	20.00
❑ Atlantic SD 8254	Joe Tex Sings with Strings and Things	1970	3.75	7.50	15.00
❑ Atlantic SD 8292	From the Roots Came the Rapper	1972	3.75	7.50	15.00
❑ Atlantic 81278	The Best of Joe Tex	1985	2.50	5.00	10.00
❑ Checker LP-2993 [M]	Hold On	1965	37.50	75.00	150.00
❑ Dial DL 6002	I Gotcha	1972	3.75	7.50	15.00
❑ Dial DL 6004	Joe Tex Spills the Beans	1973	3.75	7.50	15.00
❑ Dial DL 6100	He Who Is Without Funk Cast the First Stone	1979	2.50	5.00	10.00
❑ Epic PE 34666	Bumps and Bruises	1977	3.00	6.00	12.00
❑ King 935 [M]	The Best of Joe Tex	1965	25.00	50.00	100.00
❑ King KS-935 [R]	The Best of Joe Tex	1965	18.75	37.50	75.00
❑ London LC-50017	Super Soul	1977	2.50	5.00	10.00
❑ Parrot PA 61002 [M]	The Best of Joe Tex	1965	12.50	25.00	50.00
❑ Parrot PAS 71002 [R]	The Best of Joe Tex	1965	7.50	15.00	30.00
❑ Pride PRD-0020	The History of Joe Tex	1973	2.50	5.00	10.00
❑ Rhino RNLP-70191	I Believe I'm Gonna Make It: The Best of Joe Tex 1964-1972	1988	2.50	5.00	10.00
THIN LIZZY					
45s					
❑ London 20076	Whiskey in the Jar/Black Boys on the Corner	1972	2.00	4.00	8.00
❑ London 20078	Broken Dreams/Randolph's Tango	1973	2.00	4.00	8.00
❑ London 20082	Little Darling/The Rocket	1973	2.00	4.00	8.00
❑ Mercury 73786	The Boys Are Back in Town/Jailbreak	1976	—	2.50	5.00
❑ Mercury 73841	Cowboy Song/Angel from the Coast	1976	—	2.50	5.00

Number	Title (A Side/B Side)	Yr	VG	VG+	NM
❑ Mercury 73867	Rocky/Half-Caste	1976	—	2.50	5.00
❑ Mercury 73882	Old Flame/Johnny the Fox Meets Jimmy the Weed	1977	—	2.50	5.00
❑ Mercury 73892	Don't Believe a Word/Boogie Woogie Dance	1977	—	2.50	5.00
❑ Mercury 73945	Bad Reputation/Dancing in the Moonlight (It's Caught Me in the Spotlight)	1977	—	2.50	5.00
❑ Vertigo 202	Night Life/Showdown	1974	—	3.00	6.00
❑ Vertigo 205	Wild One/Freedom Song	1975	—	3.00	6.00
❑ Warner Bros. 8648	Cowboy Song/Johnny the Fox Meets Jimmy the Weed	1978	—	2.50	5.00
❑ Warner Bros. 49019	S & M/Do Anything You Want To	1979	—	2.50	5.00
❑ Warner Bros. 49078	Got to Give It Up/With Love	1979	—	2.50	5.00
❑ Warner Bros. 49643	Killer on the Loose/Sugar Blues	1980	—	2.00	4.00
❑ Warner Bros. 49679	We Will Be Strong/Sweetheart	1981	—	2.00	4.00
❑ Warner Bros. 50056	Hollywood/Pressure Will Blow	1982	—	2.00	4.00

Albums

Number	Title (A Side/B Side)	Yr	VG	VG+	NM
❑ London PS 594	Thin Lizzy	1971	10.00	20.00	40.00
❑ London PS 636	Vagabonds of the Western World	1973	7.50	15.00	30.00
❑ London LC-50004	The Rocker (1971-1974)	1977	3.00	6.00	12.00
❑ Mercury SRM-1-1081	Jailbreak	1976	3.00	6.00	12.00
❑ Mercury SRM-1-1107	Night Life	1976	3.00	6.00	12.00
—Reissue of Vertigo 2002					
❑ Mercury SRM-1-1108	Fighting	1976	3.00	6.00	12.00
—Reissue of Vertigo 2005					
❑ Mercury SRM-1-1119	Johnny the Fox	1976	3.00	6.00	12.00
❑ Mercury SRM-1-1186	Bad Reputation	1977	3.00	6.00	12.00
❑ Vertigo VEL-2002	Night Life	1974	3.75	7.50	15.00
❑ Vertigo VEL-2005	Fighting	1975	3.75	7.50	15.00
❑ Warner Bros. BS2 3213 [(2)]	Live and Dangerous	1978	3.00	6.00	12.00
❑ Warner Bros. BSK 3338	Black Rose/A Rock Legend	1979	2.50	5.00	10.00
❑ Warner Bros. BSK 3496	Chinatown	1980	2.50	5.00	10.00
❑ Warner Bros. BSK 3622	Renegade	1982	2.50	5.00	10.00
❑ Warner Bros. 23831	Thunder and Lightning	1983	2.50	5.00	10.00
❑ Warner Bros. 23986 [(2)]	"Life" — Live	1984	3.00	6.00	12.00

.38 SPECIAL

45s

Number	Title (A Side/B Side)	Yr	VG	VG+	NM
❑ A&M 1246	Rock and Roll Strategy/Love Strikes	1988	—	—	3.00
❑ A&M 1273	Second Chance/Comin' Down Tonight	1989	—	—	3.00
❑ A&M 1424	Comin' Down Tonight/Chauahoocie	1989	—	—	3.00
❑ A&M 1946	Long Time Gone/Four Wheels	1977	—	2.00	4.00
❑ A&M 1964	Tell Everybody/Play a Simple Song	1977	—	2.00	4.00
❑ A&M 2051	I'm a Fool for You/Travelin' Man	1978	—	2.00	4.00
❑ A&M 2205	Rockin' Into the Night/Robin Hood	1979	—	2.00	4.00
❑ A&M 2242	Stone Cold Believer/Stone Cold Believer (Part 2)	1980	—	2.00	4.00
❑ A&M 2316	Hold On Loosely/Throw Out the Line	1981	—	2.00	4.00
❑ A&M 2330	Fantasy Girl/Honky Tonk Dancer	1981	—	2.00	4.00
❑ A&M 2412	Caught Up in You/Firestarter	1982	—	2.00	4.00
❑ A&M 2431	You Keep Runnin' Away/Prisoners of Rock and Roll	1982	—	2.00	4.00
❑ A&M 2505	Chain Lightnin'/Back on the Track	1982	—	2.00	4.00
❑ A&M 2594	If I'd Been the One/Twentieth Century Fox	1983	—	—	3.00
❑ A&M 2615	Back Where You Belong/Undercover Lover	1984	—	—	3.00
❑ A&M 2633	Long Distance Affair/One Time for Old Times	1984	—	—	3.00
❑ A&M 2831	Like No Other Night/Hearts on Fire	1986	—	—	3.00
❑ A&M 2854	Somebody Like You/Against the Night	1986	—	—	3.00
❑ A&M 2873	One in a Million/Last Time	1986	—	—	3.00
❑ A&M 2955	Back to Paradise/Hold On Loosely	1987	—	—	3.00
❑ Capitol B-5405	Teacher Teacher/Twentieth Century Fox	1984	—	—	3.00

Albums

Number	Title (A Side/B Side)	Yr	VG	VG+	NM
❑ A&M SP-3164	.38 Special	198?	2.00	4.00	8.00
—Budget-line reissue of 4638					
❑ A&M SP-3165	Special Delivery	198?	2.00	4.00	8.00
—Budget-line reissue of 4684					
❑ A&M SP-3216	Rockin' Into the Night	198?	2.00	4.00	8.00
—Budget-line reissue of 4782					
❑ A&M SP-3298	Wild-Eyed Southern Boys	198?	2.00	4.00	8.00
—Budget-line reissue of 4835					
❑ A&M SP-3299	Special Forces	198?	2.00	4.00	8.00
—Budget-line reissue of 4888					

Number	Title (A Side/B Side)	Yr	VG	VG+	NM
❑ A&M SP-3310	Tour de Force	198?	2.00	4.00	8.00
—Budget-line reissue of 4971					
❑ A&M SP-3910	Flashback	1987	2.50	5.00	10.00
—Includes bonus 7-inch 33 1/3 rpm small hole single "Flashback Live EP"; deduct 40 percent if missing					
❑ A&M SP-4638	.38 Special	1977	3.00	6.00	12.00
❑ A&M SP-4684	Special Delivery	1978	3.00	6.00	12.00
❑ A&M SP-4782	Rockin' Into the Night	1979	3.00	6.00	12.00
❑ A&M SP-4835	Wild-Eyed Southern Boys	1981	2.50	5.00	10.00
❑ A&M SP-4888	Special Forces	1982	2.50	5.00	10.00
❑ A&M SP-4971	Tour de Force	1983	2.50	5.00	10.00
❑ A&M SP-5115	Strength in Numbers	1986	2.50	5.00	10.00
❑ A&M SP-5218	Rock & Roll Strategy	1988	2.50	5.00	10.00

THOMAS, B.J.

45s

Number	Title (A Side/B Side)	Yr	VG	VG+	NM
❑ ABC 12054	(Hey, Won't You Play) Another Somebody Done Somebody Wrong Song/City Blues	1974	—	2.00	4.00
❑ ABC 12121	We Are Happy Together/Help Me Make It (To My Rockin' Chair)	1975	—	2.00	4.00
❑ Bragg 103	Billy and Sue/Never Tell	1964	5.00	10.00	20.00
❑ Cleveland Int'l. 03492	Whatever Happened to Old Fashioned Love/I Just Sing	1983	—	2.00	4.00
❑ Cleveland Int'l. 04608	From This Moment On/The Girl Most Likely To	1984	—	2.00	4.00
❑ Columbia 03985	New Looks from an Old Lover/You Keep the Man in Me Happy	1983	—	2.00	4.00
❑ Columbia 04237	Two Car Garage/Beautiful World	1983	—	2.00	4.00
❑ Columbia 04431	The Whole World's in Love When You're Lonely/We're Here to Love	1984	—	—	3.00
❑ Columbia 04531	Rock and Roll Shoes/Then I'll Be Over You	1984	—	—	3.00
—Ray Charles and B.J. Thomas					
❑ Columbia 05647	A Part of Me That Needs You Most/Northern Lights	1985	—	—	3.00
❑ Columbia 05771	America Is/Broken Toys	1986	—	—	3.00
❑ Columbia 06314	Night Life/Make the World Go Away	1986	—	—	3.00
❑ Hickory 1395	Billy and Sue/Never Tell	1966	2.50	5.00	10.00
❑ Lori 9547	I've Got a Feeling/Hey Judy	1963	6.25	12.50	25.00
❑ Lori 9561	For Your Precious Love/Here I Am Again	1964	6.25	12.50	25.00
❑ MCA 40735	Don't Worry Baby/My Love	1977	—	2.00	4.00
❑ MCA 40812	Still the Lovin' Is Fun/Play Me a Little Traveling Music	1977	—	2.00	4.00
❑ MCA 40854	Everybody Loves a Rain Song/Dusty Roads	1978	—	2.00	4.00
❑ MCA 40914	Sweet Young America/Aloha	1978	—	2.00	4.00
❑ MCA 40986	We Could Have Been the Closest of Friends/In My Heart	1979	—	2.00	4.00
❑ MCA 41134	God Bless the Children/On This Christmas Night	1979	—	2.00	4.00
❑ MCA 41207	Nothin' Could Be Better/Walkin' on a Cloud	1980	—	2.00	4.00
❑ MCA 41281	Everything Always Works Out for the Best/No Limit	1980	—	2.00	4.00
❑ MCA 51087	Some Love Songs Never Die/There Ain't No Love	1981	—	2.00	4.00
❑ MCA 51151	The Lovin' Kind/I Recall a Gypsy Woman	1981	—	2.00	4.00
❑ MCA 52053	I Really Got the Feeling/But Love Me	1982	—	2.00	4.00
❑ Myrrh 166	Home Where I Belong/Hallelujah	1977	—	2.50	5.00
❑ Myrrh 176	Without a Doubt/(B-side unknown)	1977	—	2.50	5.00
❑ Myrrh 234	Uncloudy Day/(B-side unknown)	1981	—	2.50	5.00
❑ Pacemaker 227	I'm So Lonesome I Could Cry/Candy Baby	1964	5.00	10.00	20.00
❑ Pacemaker 231	Mama/Wendy	1965	3.75	7.50	15.00
❑ Pacemaker 234	Bring Back the Time/I Don't Have a Mind of My Own	1965	3.75	7.50	15.00
❑ Pacemaker 239	Tomorrow Never Comes/Your Tears Leave Me Cold	1965	3.75	7.50	15.00
❑ Pacemaker 247	Plain Jane/My Home Town	1965	3.75	7.50	15.00
❑ Pacemaker 253	I'm Not a Fool Anymore/Baby Cried	1965	3.75	7.50	15.00
❑ Pacemaker 256	I Can't Help It (If I'm Still in Love with You)/Baby Cried	1965	3.75	7.50	15.00
❑ Pacemaker 259	Pretty Country Girl/Houston Town	1965	3.75	7.50	15.00
❑ Paramount 0218	Songs/Goodbye's a Long, Long Time	1973	—	2.50	5.00
❑ Paramount 0239	Sunday Sunrise/Early Morning Rush	1973	—	2.50	5.00
❑ Paramount 0239	Sunday Sunrise/Talkin' Confidentially	1973	—	2.50	5.00
❑ Paramount 0277	Play Something Sweet (Brickyard Blues)/Talkin' Confidentially	1974	—	2.50	5.00
❑ Reprise 22837	Don't Leave Love (Out There All Alone)/One Woman	1989	—	—	3.00
❑ Scepter 12129	I'm So Lonesome I Could Cry/Candy Baby	1966	2.50	5.00	10.00
❑ Scepter 12139	Mama/Wendy	1966	2.00	4.00	8.00
❑ Scepter 12154	Bring Back the Time/I Don't Have a Mind of My Own	1966	2.00	4.00	8.00
❑ Scepter 12165	Tomorrow Never Comes/Your Tears Leave Me Cold	1966	2.00	4.00	8.00
❑ Scepter 12179	Plain Jane/My Home Town	1966	2.00	4.00	8.00
❑ Scepter 12194	I Can't Help It (If I'm Still in Love with You)/Baby Cried	1967	2.00	4.00	8.00
❑ Scepter 12200	Just the Wisdom of a Fool/Treasure of Love	1967	2.00	4.00	8.00
❑ Scepter 12201	Wisdom of a Fool/Human	1967	2.00	4.00	8.00
❑ Scepter 12205	The Girl Can't Help It/Walkin' Back	1967	2.00	4.00	8.00
❑ Scepter 12219	The Eyes of a New York Woman/I May Never Get to Heaven	1968	2.00	4.00	8.00
❑ Scepter 12230	Hooked on a Feeling/I've Been Down This Road Before	1968	2.00	4.00	8.00
❑ Scepter 12244	It's Only Love/You Don't Love Me Anymore	1969	—	3.00	6.00
❑ Scepter 12255	Pass the Apple Eve/Fairy Tale of Time	1969	—	3.00	6.00
❑ Scepter 12259	You Don't Love Me Anymore/Skip a Rope	1969	—	3.00	6.00
❑ Scepter 12265	Raindrops Keep Fallin' on My Head/Never Had It So Good	1969	—	3.50	7.00
❑ Scepter 12277	Everybody's Out of Town/Living Again	1970	—	3.00	6.00
❑ Scepter 12283	I Just Can't Help Believing/Send My Picture to Scranton, Pa.	1970	—	3.00	6.00
❑ Scepter 12299	Most of All/The Mask	1970	—	2.50	5.00
❑ Scepter 12307	No Love at All/Have a Heart	1971	—	2.50	5.00
❑ Scepter 12320	Mighty Clouds of Joy/Life	1971	—	2.50	5.00
❑ Scepter 12335	Long Ago Tomorrow/Burnin' a Hole in My Mind	1971	—	2.50	5.00
❑ Scepter 12344	Rock and Roll Lullaby/Are We Losing Touch	1972	—	3.00	6.00
❑ Scepter 12354	That's What Friends Are For/I Get Enthused	1972	—	2.50	5.00
❑ Scepter 12364	Happier Than the Morning Sun/We Have Got to Get Out Ship Together	1972	—	2.50	5.00
❑ Scepter 12379	Sweet Cherry Wine/Roads	1973	—	2.50	5.00
❑ Valerie 226	I've Got a Feeling/Hey Judy	1963	5.00	10.00	20.00
❑ Warner Bros. 5491	Billy and Sue/Never Tell	1964	5.00	10.00	20.00

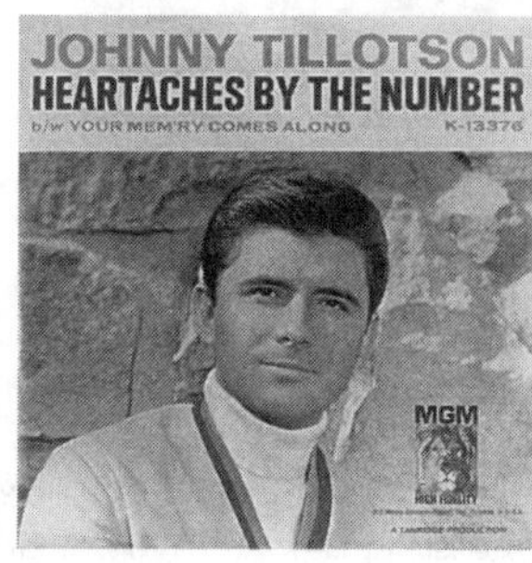

Number	Title (A Side/B Side)	Yr	VG	VG+	NM
Albums					
❑ ABC ABDP-858	Reunion	1975	2.50	5.00	10.00
❑ ABC ABCD-912	Help Me Make It to My Rockin' Chair	1976	2.50	5.00	10.00
❑ Accord SN-7106	Lovin' You	198?	2.50	5.00	10.00
❑ Buckboard 1023	B.J. Thomas Sings Hank Williams and Other Favorites	198?	2.50	5.00	10.00
❑ Cleveland Int'l. FC 38561	New Looks	1983	2.50	5.00	10.00
❑ Cleveland Int'l. FC 39111	The Great American Dream	1983	2.50	5.00	10.00
❑ Cleveland Int'l. FC 39337	Shining	1984	2.50	5.00	10.00
❑ Cleveland Int'l. FC 40157	Throwing Rocks at the Moon	1985	2.50	5.00	10.00
❑ Columbia PC 38400	Love Shines	1984	2.00	4.00	8.00
—Reissue of Priority 38400					
❑ Columbia PC 40148	All Is Calm, All Is Bright...	1985	2.50	5.00	10.00
❑ Columbia FC 40496	Night Life	1986	2.50	5.00	10.00
❑ Everest 4104	Golden Greats	1981	2.50	5.00	10.00
❑ Hickory LPM-133 [M]	The Very Best of B.J. Thomas	1966	5.00	10.00	20.00
❑ Hickory LPS-133 [S]	The Very Best of B.J. Thomas	1966	6.25	12.50	25.00
❑ MCA 746	Everybody Loves a Rain Song	1980	2.00	4.00	8.00
—Budget-line reissue					
❑ MCA 2286	B.J. Thomas	1977	2.50	5.00	10.00
❑ MCA 3035	Everybody Loves a Rain Song	1978	2.50	5.00	10.00
❑ MCA 3231	For the Best	1979	2.50	5.00	10.00
❑ MCA 5155	In Concert	1980	2.50	5.00	10.00
❑ MCA 5195	Some Love Songs Never Die	1980	2.50	5.00	10.00
❑ MCA 5296	As We Know Him	1982	2.50	5.00	10.00
❑ MCA 27032	In Concert	198?	2.00	4.00	8.00
—Reissue of MCA 5155					
❑ Myrrh MSB-6574	Home Where I Belong	1978	2.50	5.00	10.00
❑ Myrrh MSB-6593	A Happy Man	1979	2.50	5.00	10.00
❑ Myrrh MSB-6633	You Gave Me Love	1979	2.50	5.00	10.00
❑ Myrrh MSB-6653	The Best of B.J. Thomas	1980	2.50	5.00	10.00
❑ Myrrh MSB-6675	Amazing Grace	1981	2.50	5.00	10.00
❑ Myrrh MSB-6705	Miracle	1983	2.50	5.00	10.00
❑ Myrrh MSB-6710	Peace in the Valley	1983	2.50	5.00	10.00
❑ Myrrh MSB-6725	The Best of B.J. Thomas, Volume 2	1984	2.50	5.00	10.00
❑ Myrrh WR-8153	Peace in the Valley	1985	2.50	5.00	10.00
—Reissue of 6710					
❑ Myrrh WR-8200	Amazing Grace	1985	2.00	4.00	8.00
—Reissue of 6675					
❑ Pacemaker PLP-3001 [M]	B.J. Thomas and the Triumphs	1965	50.00	100.00	200.00
❑ Pair PDL2-1099 [(2)]	Greatest Hits	1986	3.00	6.00	12.00
❑ Paramount PAS 1020	Longhorns & Londonbridges	1974	3.00	6.00	12.00
❑ Paramount PAS-6052	B.J. Thomas Songs	1973	3.00	6.00	12.00
❑ Pickwick SPC-3623	The Best of B.J. Thomas	197?	2.50	5.00	10.00
❑ Priority JU 38400	Love Shines	1982	2.50	5.00	10.00
❑ Reprise 25898	Midnight Minute	1989	3.00	6.00	12.00
❑ Scepter SPS-535 [S]	I'm So Lonesome I Could Cry	1966	6.25	12.50	25.00
❑ Scepter SRM-535 [M]	I'm So Lonesome I Could Cry	1966	5.00	10.00	20.00
❑ Scepter SPS-556 [S]	Tomorrow Never Comes	1966	5.00	10.00	20.00
❑ Scepter SRM-556 [M]	Tomorrow Never Comes	1966	3.75	7.50	15.00
❑ Scepter SPS-561 [S]	For Lovers and Losers	1967	3.75	7.50	15.00
❑ Scepter SRM-561 [M]	For Lovers and Losers	1967	5.00	10.00	20.00
❑ Scepter SPS-570 [S]	On My Way	1968	3.75	7.50	15.00
❑ Scepter SPS-576	Young and In Love	1969	3.75	7.50	15.00
❑ Scepter SPS-578	Greatest Hits, Volume 1	1969	3.00	6.00	12.00
❑ Scepter SPS-580	Raindrops Keep Fallin' on My Head	1970	3.00	6.00	12.00
—Remixed version; trail-off wax number on Side 1 is "SPS-580-A-1C" or "SPS-580-A-1D" and on Side 2 is "SPS-580-B-1C"					
❑ Scepter SPS-582	Everybody's Out of Town	1970	3.00	6.00	12.00
❑ Scepter SPS-586	Most of All	1970	3.00	6.00	12.00
❑ Scepter SPS-597	Greatest Hits, Volume Two	1971	3.00	6.00	12.00
❑ Scepter 5101	Billy Joe Thomas	1972	3.00	6.00	12.00
❑ Scepter 5108	B.J. Thomas Country	1972	3.00	6.00	12.00
❑ Scepter 5112 [(2)]	Greatest All-Time Hits	1973	3.75	7.50	15.00
❑ Starday 992	The Best of B.J. Thomas	197?	2.50	5.00	10.00
❑ United Artists UA-LA389-E	The Very Best of B.J. Thomas	1974	3.00	6.00	12.00
THOMAS, CARLA					
45s					
❑ Atlantic 2086	Gee Whiz (Look at His Eyes)/For You	1960	3.75	7.50	15.00

Number	Title (A Side/B Side)	Yr	VG	VG+	NM
❑ Atlantic 2101	A Love of My Own/Promises	1961	3.00	6.00	12.00
❑ Atlantic 2113	Wish Me Good Luck/In Your Spare Time	1961	3.00	6.00	12.00
❑ Atlantic 2132	The Masquerade Is Over/I Kinda Think He Does	1962	3.00	6.00	12.00
❑ Atlantic 2163	I'll Bring It On Home to You/I Can't Take It	1962	3.00	6.00	12.00
❑ Atlantic 2189	What a Fool I've Been/The Life I Live	1963	3.00	6.00	12.00
❑ Atlantic 2212	Gee Whiz, It's Christmas/All I Want for Christmas Is You	1963	3.75	7.50	15.00
❑ Atlantic 2238	I've Got No Time to Lose/A Boy Named Tom	1964	3.00	6.00	12.00
❑ Atlantic 2258	A Woman's Love/Don't Let the Love Light Leave	1964	3.00	6.00	12.00
❑ Atlantic 2272	How Do You Quit (Someone You Love)/The Puppet	1965	3.00	6.00	12.00
❑ Gusto 816	All I Want for Christmas Is You/Gee Whiz, It's Christmas	1979	2.50	5.00	10.00
—A Canadian import ($5) from 1986 exists on King					
❑ Satellite 104	Gee Whiz (Look at His Eyes)/For You	1960	125.00	250.00	500.00
❑ Stax 0011	I've Fallen in Love/Where Do I Go	1968	2.00	4.00	8.00
❑ Stax 0024	I Like What You're Doing (To Me)/Strung Out	1969	2.00	4.00	8.00
❑ Stax 0042	Just Keep On Loving Me/My Love	1969	2.00	4.00	8.00
—With Johnnie Taylor					
❑ Stax 0044	I Can't Stop/I Need You Woman	1969	—	2.50	5.00
—With William Bell					
❑ Stax 0056	Guide Me Well/Some Other Man (Is Beating Your Time)	1970	2.00	4.00	8.00
❑ Stax 0061	The Time for Love Is Anytime/Living in the City	1970	—	3.00	6.00
❑ Stax 0067	All I Have to Do Is Dream/Leave the Girl Alone	1970	—	2.50	5.00
—With William Bell					
❑ Stax 0080	Hi De Ho (That Old Sweet Roll)/I Loved You Like I Love My Very Life	1970	—	3.00	6.00
❑ Stax 0113	You've Got a Cushion to Fall On/Love Means (You Never Have to Say You're Sorry)	1972	—	3.00	6.00
❑ Stax 0133	Sugar/You've Got a Cushion to Fall On	1972	—	3.00	6.00
❑ Stax 0149	I May Not Be All You Want/Sugar	1972	—	3.00	6.00
❑ Stax 172	Stop! Look What You're Doing/Every Ounce of Strength	1965	3.00	6.00	12.00
❑ Stax 0173	I Have a God Who Loves/Love Among People	1973	—	3.00	6.00
❑ Stax 183	Comfort Me/I'm for You	1966	3.00	6.00	12.00
❑ Stax 188	Let Me Be Good to You/Another Night Without My Man	1966	3.00	6.00	12.00
❑ Stax 195	B-A-B-Y/What Have You Got to Offer Me	1966	3.75	7.50	15.00
❑ Stax 206	All I Want for Christmas Is You/Winter Snow	1966	3.00	6.00	12.00
❑ Stax 207	Something Good (Is Going to Happen to You)/It's Starting to Grow	1967	2.50	5.00	10.00
❑ Stax 214	Unchanging Love/When Tomorrow Comes	1967	2.50	5.00	10.00
❑ Stax 222	I'll Always Have Faith in You/Stop Thief	1967	2.50	5.00	10.00
❑ Stax 239	Pick Up the Pieces/Separation	1967	2.50	5.00	10.00
❑ Stax 251	A Dime a Dozen/I Want You Back	1968	2.50	5.00	10.00
Albums					
❑ Atlantic 8057 [M]	Gee Whiz	1961	25.00	50.00	100.00
—With white "fan" logo					
❑ Atlantic SD 8057 [S]	Gee Whiz	1961	37.50	75.00	150.00
—With white "fan" logo					
❑ Atlantic SD 8232	The Best of Carla Thomas	1969	6.25	12.50	25.00
❑ Stax 706 [M]	Comfort Me	1966	8.75	17.50	35.00
❑ Stax 706 [P]	Comfort Me	1966	12.50	25.00	50.00
❑ Stax 709 [M]	Carla	1966	8.75	17.50	35.00
❑ Stax 709 [S]	Carla	1966	12.50	25.00	50.00
❑ Stax 718 [M]	The Queen Alone	1967	8.75	17.50	35.00
❑ Stax 718 [S]	The Queen Alone	1967	12.50	25.00	50.00
❑ Stax STS-2019	Memphis Queen	1969	8.75	17.50	35.00
❑ Stax STS-2044	Love Means Carla Thomas	1971	8.75	17.50	35.00
❑ Stax MPS-8538	Memphis Queen	1987	2.50	5.00	10.00
—Budget-line reissue					
THREE DOG NIGHT					
45s					
❑ ABC 12114	'Til the World Ends/Yo Te Quiero Hablo (Take You Down)	1975	—	2.00	4.00
❑ ABC 12192	Everybody Is a Masterpiece/Drive On, Ride On	1976	—	2.00	4.00
❑ ABC Dunhill 4168	Nobody/It's for You	1968	3.00	6.00	12.00
❑ ABC Dunhill 4177	Try a Little Tenderness/That No One Ever Hurt So Bad	1969	2.00	4.00	8.00
❑ ABC Dunhill 4191	One/Chest Fever	1969	2.00	4.00	8.00
❑ ABC Dunhill 4203	Easy to Be Hard/Dreaming Isn't Good for You	1969	2.00	4.00	8.00
❑ ABC Dunhill 4215	Eli's Coming/Circle for a Landing	1969	2.00	4.00	8.00
❑ ABC Dunhill 4229	Celebrate/Feeling Alright	1970	—	3.00	6.00
❑ ABC Dunhill 4239	Mama Told Me (Not to Come)/Rock and Roll Widow	1970	—	3.00	6.00
❑ ABC Dunhill 4250	Out in the Country/Good Time Living	1970	—	3.00	6.00
❑ ABC Dunhill 4262	One Man Band/It Ain't Easy	1970	—	3.00	6.00
❑ ABC Dunhill 4272	Joy to the World/I Can Hear You Calling	1971	—	2.50	5.00
❑ ABC Dunhill 4282	Liar/Can't Get Enough of It	1971	—	2.50	5.00
❑ ABC Dunhill 4294	An Old Fashioned Love Song/Jam	1971	—	2.50	5.00
❑ ABC Dunhill 4299	Never Been to Spain/Peace of Mind	1972	—	2.50	5.00
❑ ABC Dunhill 4306	The Family of Man/Going in Circles	1972	—	2.50	5.00
❑ ABC Dunhill 4317	Black and White/Freedom for the Stallion	1972	—	2.50	5.00
❑ ABC Dunhill 4331	Pieces of April/The Writings on the Wall	1972	—	2.50	5.00
❑ ABC Dunhill 4352	Shambala/Our "B" Side	1973	—	2.50	5.00
—First pressings have "Dunhill" spelled out in children's blocks					
❑ ABC Dunhill 4370	Let Me Serenade You/Storybook Feeling	1973	—	2.00	4.00
❑ ABC Dunhill 4382	The Show Must Go On/On the Way Back Home	1974	—	2.00	4.00
❑ ABC Dunhill 15001	Sure As I'm Sittin' Here/Anytime Babe	1974	—	2.00	4.00
❑ ABC Dunhill 15010	The Show Must Go On/On the Way Back Home	1974	2.00	4.00	8.00
❑ ABC Dunhill 15013	Play Something Sweet (Brickyard Blues)/I'd Be So Happy	1974	—	2.00	4.00
❑ Passport 7921	It's a Jungle Out There/Somebody's Gonna Get Hurt	1983	—	2.50	5.00
Albums					
❑ ABC 888	Coming Down Your Way	1975	2.50	5.00	10.00
❑ ABC 928	American Pastime	1976	2.50	5.00	10.00
❑ ABC Command CQD-40014 [Q]	Hard Labor	1974	5.00	10.00	20.00

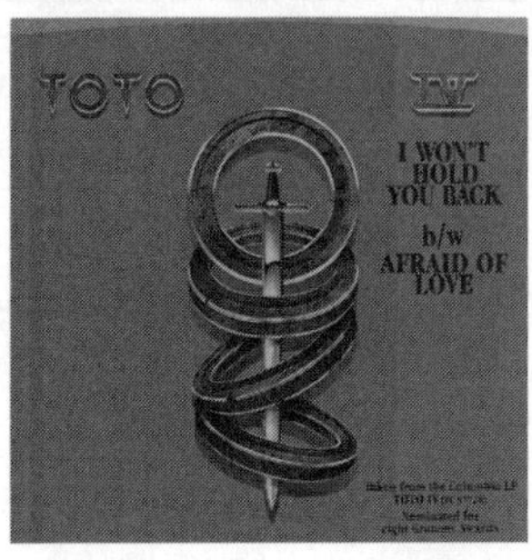

Number	Title (A Side/B Side)	Yr	VG	VG+	NM
❑ ABC Command CQD-40018 [Q]	Coming Down Your Way	1975	5.00	10.00	20.00
❑ ABC Dunhill DS-50048	Three Dog Night	1968	3.75	7.50	15.00
❑ ABC Dunhill DS-50048	Three Dog Night "One"	1969	3.00	6.00	12.00
—Same album as above, but with revised title on cover					
❑ ABC Dunhill DS-50058	Suitable for Framing	1969	3.00	6.00	12.00
❑ ABC Dunhill DS-50068	Three Dog Night Was Captured Live at the Forum	1969	3.00	6.00	12.00
❑ ABC Dunhill DS-50078	It Ain't Easy	1970	3.00	6.00	12.00
—Regular front cover with gatefold					
❑ ABC Dunhill DSX-50088	Naturally	1970	3.00	6.00	12.00
—With detachable cardboard poster intact					
❑ ABC Dunhill DSX-50098	Golden Bisquits	1971	3.00	6.00	12.00
—With detachable cardboard poster intact; interestingly, the label spells the LP title "Golden Biscuits"					
❑ ABC Dunhill DSX-50108	Harmony	1971	3.00	6.00	12.00
❑ ABC Dunhill DSD-50118	Seven Separate Fools	1972	3.00	6.00	12.00
—With seven oversize playing cards included					
❑ ABC Dunhill DSY-50138 [(2)]	Around the World with Three Dog Night	1973	3.75	7.50	15.00
❑ ABC Dunhill DSX-50158	Cyan	1973	3.00	6.00	12.00
❑ ABC Dunhill DSD-50168	Hard Labor	1974	2.50	5.00	10.00
—With huge Band-Aid as part of the LP artwork					
❑ ABC Dunhill DSD-50178	Joy to the World: Their Greatest Hits	1974	3.00	6.00	12.00
—With gatefold cover					
❑ ABC Dunhill SKAO-92057	Suitable for Framing	1969	3.75	7.50	15.00
—Capitol Record Club edition					
❑ ABC Dunhill SKAO-93211	It Ain't Easy	1970	3.75	7.50	15.00
—Capitol Record Club edition					
❑ ABC Dunhill SMAS-93422	Naturally	1970	3.75	7.50	15.00
—Capitol Record Club edition					
❑ ABC Dunhill SVAS-94772	Seven Separate Fools	1972	3.75	7.50	15.00
—Capitol Record Club edition					
❑ Columbia Special Products P 14769	Three Dog Night	1978	3.75	7.50	15.00
❑ MCA 6018 [(2)]	The Best of Three Dog Night	1982	3.00	6.00	12.00
❑ MCA 37120	Joy to the World: Their Greatest Hits	1980	2.00	4.00	8.00
❑ Passport PB 5001 [EP]	It's a Jungle	1983	2.00	4.00	8.00

TILLOTSON, JOHNNY

45s

Number	Title (A Side/B Side)	Yr	VG	VG+	NM
❑ Amos 117	Tears on My Pillow/Remember When	1969	—	3.00	6.00
❑ Amos 125	What Am I Living For/Joy to the World	1969	—	3.00	6.00
❑ Amos 128	Raining in My Heart/Today I Started Loving You Again	1969	—	3.00	6.00
❑ Amos 136	Susan/Love Waits for Me	1970	—	3.00	6.00
❑ Amos 146	I Don't Believe In It Anymore/Kansas City, Kansas	1970	—	3.00	6.00
❑ Atlantic 87978	Bim Bam Boom/(B-side unknown)	1990	—	2.00	4.00
❑ Buddah 232	Star Spangled Bus/Apple Bend	1971	—	2.50	5.00
❑ Buddah 256	Welfare Hero/The Flower Kissed the Shoes That Jesus Wore	1971	—	2.50	5.00
❑ Buddah 279	Make Me Believe/The Flower Kissed the Shoes That Jesus Wore	1972	—	2.50	5.00
❑ Buddah 311	Your Love's Been a Long Time Comin'/Apple Bend	1972	—	2.50	5.00
❑ Cadence 1353	Dreamy Eyes/Well, I'm Your Man	1958	5.00	10.00	20.00
❑ Cadence 1354	I'm Never Gonna Kiss You/Cherie, Cherie	1958	6.25	12.50	25.00
—With Genevieve					
❑ Cadence 1365	True True Happiness/Love Is Blind	1959	5.00	10.00	20.00
❑ Cadence 1372	Why Do I Love You So/Never Let Me Go	1959	5.00	10.00	20.00
❑ Cadence 1377	Earth Angel/Pledging My Love	1960	5.00	10.00	20.00
❑ Cadence 1384	Poetry in Motion/Princess, Princess	1960	5.00	10.00	20.00
❑ Cadence 1391	Jimmy's Girl/His True Love Said Godbye	1960	3.75	7.50	15.00
❑ Cadence 1404	Without You/Cutie Pie	1961	3.75	7.50	15.00
❑ Cadence 1409	Dreamy Eyes/Well, I'm Your Man	1961	3.75	7.50	15.00
❑ Cadence 1418	It Keeps Right On a-Hurtin'/She Gave Sweet Love to Me	1962	3.75	7.50	15.00
❑ Cadence 1424	Send Me the Pillow You Dream On/What'll I Do	1962	3.75	7.50	15.00
❑ Cadence 1432	I Can't Help It (If I'm Still in Love with You)/I'm So Lonesome I Could Cry	1962	3.75	7.50	15.00
❑ Cadence 1434	Out of My Mind/Empty Feelin'	1963	3.75	7.50	15.00
❑ Cadence 1437	You Can Never Stop Me Loving You/Judy, Judy, Judy	1963	3.75	7.50	15.00
❑ Cadence 1441	Funny How Time Slips Away/A Very Good Year for Girls	1963	3.75	7.50	15.00
❑ Columbia 10125	Big Ole Jean/Mississippi Lady	1975	—	2.50	5.00

Number	Title (A Side/B Side)	Yr	VG	VG+	NM
❑ Columbia 10199	Right Here in Your Arms/Willow County Request Live	1975	—	2.50	5.00
❑ Columbia 45842	Sunshine of My Life/If You Wouldn't Be My Lady	1973	—	2.50	5.00
❑ Columbia 45984	So Much of My Life/I Love How She Needs Me	1973	—	2.50	5.00
❑ Columbia 46065	Till I Can't Take It Anymore/Sunday Kind of Woman	1974	—	2.50	5.00
❑ MGM 13181	Talk Back Trembling Lips/Another You	1963	3.00	6.00	12.00
❑ MGM 13193	Worried Guy/Please Don't Go Away	1963	2.50	5.00	10.00
❑ MGM 13232	I Rise, I Fall/I'm Watching My Watch	1964	2.50	5.00	10.00
❑ MGM 13255	Worry/Sufferin' from a Heartache	1964	2.50	5.00	10.00
❑ MGM 13284	She Understands Me/Tomorrow	1964	2.50	5.00	10.00
❑ MGM 13316	Angel/Little Boy	1965	2.50	5.00	10.00
❑ MGM 13344	Then I'll Count Again/One's Yours, One's Mine	1965	2.50	5.00	10.00
❑ MGM 13376	Heartaches by the Number/Your Mem'ry Comes Along	1965	2.50	5.00	10.00
❑ MGM 13408	Our World/(Wait 'Till You See) My Gidget	1965	2.50	5.00	10.00
❑ MGM 13445	Hello Enemy/I Never Loved You Anyway	1966	2.50	5.00	10.00
❑ MGM 13499	Me, Myself and I/Country Boy, Country Boy	1966	2.50	5.00	10.00
❑ MGM 13519	No Love at All/What Am I Gonna Do	1966	2.50	5.00	10.00
❑ MGM 13598	More Than Before/Open Up Your Heart	1966	2.50	5.00	10.00
❑ MGM 13598	More Than Before/Baby's Gone	1966	2.50	5.00	10.00
❑ MGM 13633	Christmas Country Style/Christmas Is the Best of All	1966	2.50	5.00	10.00
❑ MGM 13684	Strange Things Happen/Tommy Jones	1967	2.50	5.00	10.00
❑ MGM 13738	Don't Tell Me It's Raining/Takin' It Easy	1967	2.50	5.00	10.00
❑ MGM 13829	You're the Reason/Countin' My Teardrops	1967	2.50	5.00	10.00
❑ MGM 13888	I Can Spot a Cheater/It Keeps Right On a-Hurtin'	1968	2.00	4.00	8.00
❑ MGM 13924	I Haven't Begun to Love You Yet/Why So Lonely	1968	2.00	4.00	8.00
❑ MGM 13977	Letter to Emily/Your Mem'ry Comes Along	1968	2.00	4.00	8.00
❑ Reward 03327	Baby You Do It for Me (And I'll Do It for You)/She's Not As Married As She Used to Be	1982	—	2.00	4.00
❑ Reward 03901	Crying/You're a Beautiful Place to Be	1983	—	2.00	4.00
❑ Reward 04123	Burnin'/What's Another Year	1983	—	2.00	4.00
❑ Reward 04346	Lay Back (In the Arms of Somebody)/What's Another Year	1984	—	2.00	4.00
❑ Scepter 12389	Song for Hank Williams (mono/stereo)	1973	2.00	4.00	8.00
—With John Edward Beland; may be promo-only					
❑ United Artists XW860	It Could've Been Nashville/Summertime Lovin'	1976	—	2.50	5.00
❑ United Artists XW986	Toy Hearts/Just An Ordinary Man	1977	—	2.50	5.00
Albums					
❑ Accord SN-7194	Scrapbook	1982	2.50	5.00	10.00
❑ Amos AAS 7006	Tears on My Pillow	1969	5.00	10.00	20.00
❑ Barnaby BR-4007	Johnny Tillotson's Greatest	1977	3.00	6.00	12.00
❑ Buddah BDS-5112	Johnny Tillotson	1972	3.75	7.50	15.00
❑ Cadence CLP-3052 [M]	Johnny Tillotson's Best	1961	10.00	20.00	40.00
—Maroon and silver label					
❑ Cadence CLP-3058 [M]	It Keeps Right On a-Hurtin'	1962	7.50	15.00	30.00
❑ Cadence CLP-3067 [M]	You Can Never Stop Me Loving You	1963	7.50	15.00	30.00
❑ Cadence CLP-25052 [P]	Johnny Tillotson's Best	1961	12.50	25.00	50.00
—Maroon and silver label					
❑ Cadence CLP-25052 [P]	Johnny Tillotson's Best	1962	7.50	15.00	30.00
—Red and black label					
❑ Cadence CLP-25058 [S]	It Keeps Right On a-Hurtin'	1962	10.00	20.00	40.00
❑ Cadence CLP-25067 [P]	You Can Never Stop Me Loving You	1963	10.00	20.00	40.00
❑ Everest 4113	Johnny Tillotson's Greatest Hits	1982	2.50	5.00	10.00
❑ Metro M-561 [M]	Johnny Tillotson Sings Tillotson	1967	3.75	7.50	15.00
❑ Metro MS-561 [S]	Johnny Tillotson Sings Tillotson	1967	5.00	10.00	20.00
❑ MGM E-4188 [M]	Talk Back Trembling Lips	1964	5.00	10.00	20.00
❑ MGM SE-4188 [S]	Talk Back Trembling Lips	1964	6.25	12.50	25.00
❑ MGM E-4224 [M]	The Tillotson Touch	1964	5.00	10.00	20.00
❑ MGM SE-4224 [S]	The Tillotson Touch	1964	6.25	12.50	25.00
❑ MGM E-4270 [M]	She Understands Me	1965	5.00	10.00	20.00
❑ MGM SE-4270 [S]	She Understands Me	1965	6.25	12.50	25.00
❑ MGM E-4302 [M]	That's My Style	1965	5.00	10.00	20.00
❑ MGM SE-4302 [S]	That's My Style	1965	6.25	12.50	25.00
❑ MGM E-4328 [M]	Our World	1965	5.00	10.00	20.00
❑ MGM SE-4328 [S]	Our World	1965	6.25	12.50	25.00
❑ MGM E-4395 [M]	No Love at All	1966	5.00	10.00	20.00
❑ MGM SE-4395 [S]	No Love at All	1966	6.25	12.50	25.00
❑ MGM E-4402 [M]	The Christmas Touch	1966	5.00	10.00	20.00
❑ MGM SE-4402 [S]	The Christmas Touch	1966	6.25	12.50	25.00
❑ MGM E-4452 [M]	Here I Am	1967	5.00	10.00	20.00
❑ MGM SE-4452 [S]	Here I Am	1967	6.25	12.50	25.00
❑ MGM E-4532 [M]	The Best of Johnny Tillotson	1968	7.50	15.00	30.00
—May be promo only (yellow label)					
❑ MGM SE-4532 [S]	The Best of Johnny Tillotson	1968	5.00	10.00	20.00
❑ MGM SE-4814	The Very Best of Johnny Tillotson	1971	3.00	6.00	12.00
❑ United Artists UA-LA759-G	Johnny Tillotson	1977	2.50	5.00	10.00

TIN TIN

45s

Number	Title (A Side/B Side)	Yr	VG	VG+	NM
❑ Atco 6794	Toast and Marmalade for Tea/Manhattan Woman	1971	2.00	4.00	8.00
❑ Atco 6821	Is That the Way/Swans on the Canal	1971	—	3.00	6.00
❑ Atco 6853	Set Sail for England/The Cavalry Is Coming	1971	—	3.00	6.00
❑ Polydor 15055	Talking Turkey/The Cavalry Is Coming	1972	—	3.00	6.00
❑ Sire 29750	Kiss Me/Kiss Me	1983	—	2.50	5.00
Albums					
❑ Atco SD 33-350	Tin Tin	1970	3.75	7.50	15.00
❑ Atco SD 33-370	Astral Taxi	1971	3.75	7.50	15.00

TINY TIM

45s

Number	Title (A Side/B Side)	Yr	VG	VG+	NM
❑ Blue Cat 127	April Showers/Little Girl	1966	3.00	6.00	12.00
❑ Clouds 17	Tip Toe to the Gas Pumps/The Hicky (On Your Neck)	1979	2.50	5.00	10.00

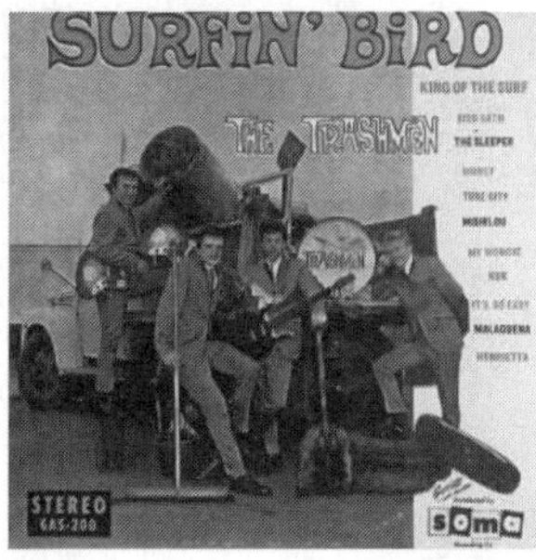

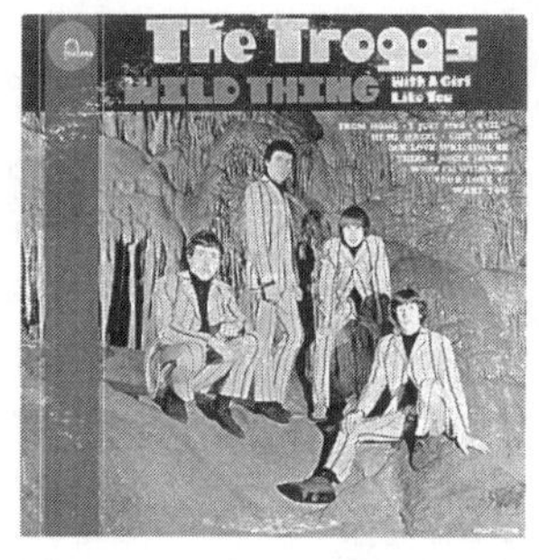

Number	Title (A Side/B Side)	Yr	VG	VG+	NM
❑ NLT 1993	Leave Me Satisfied/I Wanna' Get Crazy with You	1988	2.00	4.00	8.00
❑ Reprise 0679	Tip-Toe Thru' the Tulips with Me/Fill Your Heart	1968	2.00	4.00	8.00
❑ Reprise 0740	Tip-Toe Thru' the Tulips with Me/Don't Bite the Hand That's Feeding You	1971	—	2.00	4.00
—"Back to Back Hits" series					
❑ Reprise 0760	Bring Back Those Rock-A-Bye Baby Days/This Is All I Ask	1968	—	3.00	6.00
❑ Reprise 0760	Bring Back Those Rock-A-Bye Baby Days/Hello, Hello	1968	—	3.00	6.00
❑ Reprise 0769	Be My Love/This Is All I Ask	1968	—	3.00	6.00
❑ Reprise 0802	Great Balls of Fire/As Time Goes By	1969	—	3.00	6.00
❑ Reprise 0837	On the Good Ship Lollipop/America I Love You	1969	—	3.00	6.00
❑ Reprise 0855	Mickey the Monkey/Neighborhood Children	1969	—	3.00	6.00
❑ Reprise 0867	I'm a Lonesome Little Raindrop/What the World Needs Now Is Love	1969	—	3.00	6.00
❑ Reprise 0939	Don't Bite the Hand That's Feeding You/What Kind of American Are You	1970	—	3.00	6.00
❑ Reprise 0985	Why/Spaceship Song	1971	—	3.00	6.00
—With Miss Vicky					
❑ Reprise 20174	Bring Back Rockabye Baby Days/Just Say I Love Her	1963	3.00	6.00	12.00
—B-side by Johnny Prophet					
❑ Scepter 12351	Am I Just Another Pretty Face/The Movies	1972	—	3.00	6.00
❑ Victim 1001	Rudolph The Red-Nosed Reindeer/White Christmas	198?	3.00	6.00	12.00
Albums					
❑ Bouquet SLP-711	Love and Kisses from Tiny Tim	1968	3.00	6.00	12.00
❑ Reprise R 6292 [M]	God Bless Tiny Tim	1968	10.00	20.00	40.00
—Mono copies may all be white label promos					
❑ Reprise RS 6292 [S]	God Bless Tiny Tim	1968	3.75	7.50	15.00
❑ Reprise RS 6323	Tiny Tim's Second Album	1969	3.75	7.50	15.00
❑ Reprise RS 6351	For All My Little Friends	1969	3.75	7.50	15.00

TOKENS, THE

45s

Number	Title (A Side/B Side)	Yr	VG	VG+	NM
❑ Atco 7009	The Lord Can't Sing a Solo/Penny Whistle Band	1974	—	3.00	6.00
❑ B.T. Puppy 500	A Girl Named Arlene/Swing	1964	3.00	6.00	12.00
❑ B.T. Puppy 502	He's in Town/Oh Cathy	1964	3.00	6.00	12.00
❑ B.T. Puppy 504	You're My Girl/Havin' Fun	1964	3.00	6.00	12.00
❑ B.T. Puppy 505	Nobody But You/Mr. Cupid	1965	2.50	5.00	10.00
❑ B.T. Puppy 507	A Message to the World/Sylvie Sleepin'	1965	2.50	5.00	10.00
❑ B.T. Puppy 512	Only My Friend/Cattle Call	1965	2.50	5.00	10.00
❑ B.T. Puppy 513	The Bells of St. Mary/Just One Smile	1966	2.50	5.00	10.00
❑ B.T. Puppy 515	The Three Bells/Message to the World	1966	2.50	5.00	10.00
❑ B.T. Puppy 518	I Hear Trumpets Blow/Don't Cry, Sing Along with the Music	1966	2.50	5.00	10.00
❑ B.T. Puppy 519	Breezy/Greatest Moments of a Girl's Life	1966	2.50	5.00	10.00
❑ B.T. Puppy 525	Green Plant/Saloogy	1967	2.50	5.00	10.00
❑ B.T. Puppy 552	Please Say You Want Me/Get a Job	1969	2.50	5.00	10.00
❑ Bell 45190	You and Me/I Like to Throw My Head Back and Sing	1972	—	3.00	6.00
❑ Buddah 151	She Lets Her Hair Down (Early in the Morning)/Oh to Get Away	1970	—	3.00	6.00
❑ Buddah 159	Don't Worry Baby/If the Shoe Fits Ya Baby	1970	—	2.50	5.00
❑ Buddah 159	Don't Worry Baby/Some People Sleep	1970	—	2.50	5.00
❑ Buddah 174	Both Sides Now/I Could See Me (Dancin' with You)	1970	—	2.50	5.00
❑ Buddah 187	Listen to the Words (Listen to the Music)/Groovin' On the Sunshine	1970	—	2.50	5.00
❑ Date 2737	Oh What a Night/(Hey Hey) Juanita	1961	12.50	25.00	50.00
❑ Gary 1006	Doom-Lang/Come Dance with Me	1961	25.00	50.00	100.00
❑ Laurie 3180	I'll Always Love You/Please Write	1963	5.00	10.00	20.00
❑ Melba 104	While I Dream/I Love My Baby	1956	12.50	25.00	50.00
❑ RCA 8749-7-R	Re-Doo-Wopp/I'm Through with You	1988	—	2.00	4.00
❑ RCA 8836-7-R	Re-Doo-Wopp (Edit)/I'm Through with You	1988	—	2.00	4.00
❑ RCA Victor 37-7896	When I Go to Sleep at Night/Dry Your Eyes	1961	10.00	20.00	40.00
—"Compact Single 33" (small hole, plays at LP speed)					
❑ RCA Victor 47-7896	When I Go to Sleep at Night/Dry Your Eyes	1961	5.00	10.00	20.00
❑ RCA Victor 47-7925	Sincerely/When the Summer Is Through	1961	5.00	10.00	20.00
❑ RCA Victor 47-7954	The Lion Sleeps Tonight/Tina	1961	6.25	12.50	25.00
❑ RCA Victor 47-7991	B'wa Nina/Weeping River	1962	5.00	10.00	20.00
❑ RCA Victor 47-8018	The Riddle/Big Boat	1962	5.00	10.00	20.00
❑ RCA Victor 47-8052	La Bomba/A Token of Love	1962	5.00	10.00	20.00
❑ RCA Victor 47-8089	I'll Do My Crying Tomorrow/Dream Angel Goodnight	1962	5.00	10.00	20.00
❑ RCA Victor 47-8114	A Bird Flies Out of Sight/Wishing	1962	5.00	10.00	20.00
❑ RCA Victor 47-8148	Tonight I Met An Angel/Hindi Lullabye	1963	3.75	7.50	15.00

Number	Title (A Side/B Side)	Yr	VG	VG+	NM
❑ RCA Victor 47-8210	Hear the Bells/ABC 1-2-3	1963	3.75	7.50	15.00
❑ RCA Victor 47-8309	Two Cars/Let's Go to the Drag Strip	1963	3.75	7.50	15.00
❑ Roulette 4174	Roses Are Red/Pictures in My Wallet	1959	7.50	15.00	30.00
—As "Darrell and the Oxfords"					
❑ Roulette 4230	Can't You Tell/Your Mother Said So	1960	7.50	15.00	30.00
—As "Darrell and the Oxfords"					
❑ Rust 5094	Arlene/Rumble in the Park	1965	2.50	5.00	10.00
❑ Warner Bros. 5900	Portrait of My Love/She Comes and Goes	1967	2.00	4.00	8.00
❑ Warner Bros. 7056	It's a Happening World/How Nice	1967	—	3.00	6.00
❑ Warner Bros. 7099	Ain't That Peculiar/Bye, Bye, Bye	1967	—	3.00	6.00
❑ Warner Bros. 7118	Portrait of My Love/It's a Happening World	1968	—	2.50	5.00
—"Back to Back Hits" series — originals have green labels with "W7" logo					
❑ Warner Bros. 7169	Till/Poor Man	1968	—	3.00	6.00
❑ Warner Bros. 7183	Mister Swail/Needles of Evergreen	1968	2.50	5.00	10.00
—As "Margo, Margo, Medress and Siegel"					
❑ Warner Bros. 7202	Animal/Bathroom Wall	1968	—	3.00	6.00
❑ Warner Bros. 7233	Grandfather/The Banana Boat Song	1968	—	3.00	6.00
❑ Warner Bros. 7255	The World Is Full of Wonderful Things/Some People Sleep	1968	—	3.00	6.00
❑ Warner Bros. 7280	Go Away Little Girl-Young Girl/I Want to Make Love to You	1969	—	3.00	6.00
❑ Warner Bros. 7323	I Could Be/End of the World	1969	—	3.00	6.00
❑ Warwick 615	Tonight I Fell in Love/I'll Always Love You	1961	7.50	15.00	30.00
Albums					
❑ B.T. Puppy BTP-1000 [M]	I Hear Trumpets Blow	1966	5.00	10.00	20.00
❑ B.T. Puppy BTPS-1000 [P]	I Hear Trumpets Blow	1966	6.25	12.50	25.00
❑ B.T. Puppy BTPS-1006	Tokens of Gold	1969	6.25	12.50	25.00
❑ B.T. Puppy BTPS-1012	Greatest Moments	1970	6.25	12.50	25.00
❑ B.T. Puppy BTPS-1014	December 5th	1971	50.00	100.00	200.00
❑ B.T. Puppy BTPS-1027	Intercourse	1971	150.00	300.00	600.00
❑ Buddah BDS-5059	Both Sides Now	1971	3.75	7.50	15.00
❑ Diplomat D-2308 [M]	Kings of the Hot Rods	196?	6.25	12.50	25.00
❑ Diplomat DS-2308 [S]	Kings of the Hot Rods	196?	7.50	15.00	30.00
❑ RCA 8534-1-R	Re-Doo-Wopp	1988	2.50	5.00	10.00
❑ RCA Victor LPM-2514 [M]	The Lion Sleeps Tonight	1961	20.00	40.00	80.00
❑ RCA Victor LSP-2514 [S]	The Lion Sleeps Tonight	1961	37.50	75.00	150.00
❑ RCA Victor LPM-2631 [M]	We, The Tokens, Sing Folk	1962	10.00	20.00	40.00
❑ RCA Victor LSP-2631 [S]	We, The Tokens, Sing Folk	1962	12.50	25.00	50.00
❑ RCA Victor LPM-2886 [M]	Wheels	1964	20.00	40.00	80.00
❑ RCA Victor LSP-2886 [S]	Wheels	1964	25.00	50.00	100.00
❑ RCA Victor LPM-3685 [M]	The Tokens Again	1966	10.00	20.00	40.00
❑ RCA Victor LSP-3685 [S]	The Tokens Again	1966	12.50	25.00	50.00
❑ Warner Bros. W 1685 [M]	It's a Happening World	1967	6.25	12.50	25.00
❑ Warner Bros. WS 1685 [S]	It's a Happening World	1967	5.00	10.00	20.00

TOKENS, THE AND THE HAPPENINGS

Albums

Number	Title (A Side/B Side)	Yr	VG	VG+	NM
❑ B.T. Puppy BTP-1002 [M]	Back to Back	1967	6.00	10.00	20.00
—Half this LP is by the Tokens, the other half by the Happenings					
❑ B.T. Puppy BTPS-1002 [S]	Back to Back	1967	6.25	12.50	25.00

TORNADOES, THE (1)

45s

Number	Title (A Side/B Side)	Yr	VG	VG+	NM
❑ Date 1519	Hey Baby!/Next Stop Kansas City	1966	3.00	6.00	12.00
❑ London 9561	Telstar/Jungle Fever	1962	6.25	12.50	25.00
❑ London 9579	Globetrottin'/Like Locomotion	1963	5.00	10.00	20.00
❑ London 9581	Ridin' the Wind/The Breeze and I	1963	5.00	10.00	20.00
❑ London 9599	Life on Venus (Telstar II)/Robot	1963	5.00	10.00	20.00
❑ London 9614	Theme from "The Scales of Justice"/The Ice Cream Man	1963	5.00	10.00	20.00
❑ London 11003	Telestar/Jungle Fever	1964	5.00	10.00	20.00
—Gold label "Demand Performance" with misspelled A-side					
❑ Tower 152	Stompin' Through the Rye/Early Bird	1965	3.75	7.50	15.00
❑ Tower 171	Stingray/Aqua Marina	1965	3.75	7.50	15.00
Albums					
❑ London LL 3279 [M]	Telstar	1963	50.00	100.00	200.00
❑ London LL 3293 [M]	The Sounds of the Tornadoes	1963	50.00	100.00	200.00
—Basically the same album as above, but with a new cover, one different track and the song order shuffled.					

TOTO

45s

Number	Title (A Side/B Side)	Yr	VG	VG+	NM
❑ Columbia 11-01056	It's the Last Night/Turn Back	1981	—	3.00	6.00
❑ Columbia 18-02811	Rosanna/It's a Feeling	1982	—	2.00	4.00
❑ Columbia 18-03143	Make Believe/We Made It	1982	—	2.00	4.00
❑ Columbia CNR-03267	Make Believe/(B-side blank)	1982	—	3.00	6.00
—One-sided budget release					
❑ Columbia 38-03335	Africa/Good for You	1982	—	2.00	4.00
❑ Columbia CNR-03399	Africa/(B-side blank)	1982	—	3.00	6.00
—One-sided budget release					
❑ Columbia 38-03597	I Won't Hold You Back/Afraid of Love	1983	—	—	3.00
❑ Columbia 38-03981	Waiting for Your Love/Lovers in the Night	1983	—	—	3.00
❑ Columbia 38-04672	Stranger in Town/Change of Heart	1984	—	—	3.00
❑ Columbia 38-04752	Holyanna/Mr. Friendly	1985	—	—	3.00
❑ Columbia 38-04844	How Does It Feel/Mr. Friendly	1985	—	—	3.00
❑ Columbia 38-06280	I'll Be Over You/In a Word	1986	—	—	3.00
❑ Columbia 38-06570	Without Your Love/Can't Stand It Any Longer	1987	—	—	3.00
❑ Columbia 38-07030	Till the End/Don't Stop Me Now	1987	—	2.00	4.00
❑ Columbia 38-07715	Pamela/The Seventh One	1988	—	—	3.00
❑ Columbia 38-07945	Straight for the Heart/The Seventh One	1988	—	—	3.00
❑ Columbia 38-08010	Anna/The Seventh One	1988	2.00	4.00	8.00
—Scarce as stock copy					

Number	Title (A Side/B Side)	Yr	VG	VG+	NM
❑ Columbia 3-10830	Hold the Line/Takin' It Back	1978	—	2.50	5.00
❑ Columbia 3-10898	I'll Supply the Love/You Are the Flower	1979	—	2.50	5.00
❑ Columbia 3-10944	Georgy Porgy/Child's Anthem	1979	—	2.50	5.00
❑ Columbia 1-11173	99/Hydra	1980	—	2.00	4.00
❑ Columbia 1-11238	All Us Boys/Hydra	1980	—	2.50	5.00
❑ Columbia 11-11437	Goodbye Elenore/Turn Back	1981	—	3.00	6.00
❑ Polydor 881628-7	Dune (Desert Theme)/Theme from Dune	1985	—	2.50	5.00
Albums					
❑ Columbia JC 35317	Toto	1978	2.50	5.00	10.00
❑ Columbia FC 36229	Hydra	1979	2.50	5.00	10.00
❑ Columbia FC 36813	Turn Back	1981	2.50	5.00	10.00
❑ Columbia FC 37728	Toto IV	1982	2.50	5.00	10.00
❑ Columbia QC 38962	Isolation	1984	2.50	5.00	10.00
❑ Columbia FC 40273	Fahrenheit	1986	2.50	5.00	10.00
❑ Columbia FC 40873	The Seventh One	1988	2.50	5.00	10.00
TOWNSEND, ED					
45s					
❑ Aladdin 3373	Every Night/Love Never Dies	1957	6.25	12.50	25.00
❑ Capitol F3926	For Your Love/Over and Over Again	1958	3.75	7.50	15.00
❑ Capitol F3994	What Shall I Do/Please Never Change	1958	3.00	6.00	12.00
❑ Capitol F4048	When I Grow Too Old to Dream/You Are My Everything	1958	3.00	6.00	12.00
❑ Capitol F4104	Richer Than I/Getting By Without You	1958	3.00	6.00	12.00
❑ Capitol F4171	Don't Ever Leave Me/Lover Come Back to Me	1959	3.00	6.00	12.00
❑ Capitol F4240	This Little Love of Mine/Hold On	1959	3.00	6.00	12.00
❑ Capitol 4314	Be My Love/With No One to Love	1959	3.00	6.00	12.00
❑ Challenge 9118	Ed Townsend's Boogie Woogie (Part 1)/Ed Townsend's Boogie Woogie (Part 2)	1961	3.00	6.00	12.00
❑ Challenge 9129	And Then Came Love/Little Bitty Dave	1961	3.00	6.00	12.00
❑ Challenge 9144	You Walked In/I Love to Hear That Best	1962	3.00	6.00	12.00
❑ Dot 15596	Tall Grows the Sycamore/My Need for You	1957	5.00	10.00	20.00
❑ Liberty 55516	Tell Her/Down Home	1962	3.00	6.00	12.00
❑ Liberty 55516	Tell Her/Hard Way to Go	1962	3.00	6.00	12.00
❑ Liberty 55542	That's What I Get for Loving You/There's No End	1963	3.00	6.00	12.00
❑ Maxx 325	I Love You/I Might Like It	1964	2.50	5.00	10.00
❑ MGM 13784	Mommy's Never Comin' Back Again/Who Would Deny Me	1967	2.50	5.00	10.00
❑ Polydor 14021	No/Color Me Human	1970	—	3.00	6.00
❑ Warner Bros. 5174	Stay with Me/I Love Everything About You	1960	3.00	6.00	12.00
❑ Warner Bros. 5200	Cherrigale/Dream World	1961	3.00	6.00	12.00
Albums					
❑ Capitol ST 1140 [S]	New in Town	1959	7.50	15.00	30.00
❑ Capitol T 1140 [M]	New in Town	1959	6.25	12.50	25.00
❑ Capitol ST 1214 [S]	Glad to Be Here	1959	7.50	15.00	30.00
❑ Capitol T 1214 [M]	Glad to Be Here	1959	6.25	12.50	25.00
❑ Curtom 5006	Ed Townsend Now	1976	3.00	6.00	12.00
TOWNSHEND, PETE					
45s					
❑ Atco 7217	Let My Love Open the Door/And I Moved	1980	—	2.00	4.00
❑ Atco 7312	A Little Is Enough/Cat's in a Cupboard	1980	—	2.00	4.00
❑ Atco 7318	Rough Boys/Jools and Jim	1980	—	2.00	4.00
❑ Atco 99499	Barefootin'/Behind Blue Eyes	1986	—	—	3.00
❑ Atco 99553	Secondhand Love/White City Fighting	1986	—	—	3.00
❑ Atco 99577	Give Blood/Magic Bus	1986	—	—	3.00
❑ Atco 99590	Face the Face/Hiding Out	1985	—	—	3.00
❑ Atco 99884	Bargain/Dirty Water	1983	—	2.00	4.00
❑ Atco 99973	Slit Skirts/Uniforms	1982	—	2.00	4.00
❑ Atco 99989	Face Dances Part Two/Man Watching	1982	—	2.00	4.00
❑ Atlantic 88875	A Friend Is a Friend/Man Machines	1989	—	—	3.00
Albums					
❑ Atco SD 32-100	Empty Glass	1980	2.50	5.00	10.00
❑ Atco SD 38-149	All the Best Cowboys Have Chinese Eyes	1982	2.50	5.00	10.00
❑ Atco 90063 [(2)]	Scoop	1983	3.00	6.00	12.00
❑ Atco 90473	White City — A Novel	1985	2.50	5.00	10.00
❑ Atco 90539 [(2)]	Another Scoop	1987	3.00	6.00	12.00
❑ Atco 90553	Pete Townshend's Deep End Live!	1986	2.50	5.00	10.00
❑ Atlantic 81996	The Iron Man: The Musical by Pete Townshend	1989	2.50	5.00	10.00

—Also includes tracks by John Lee Hooker, Simon Townshend, Nina Simone, The Who

Number	Title (A Side/B Side)	Yr	VG	VG+	NM
❑ Decca 79189	Who Came First	1972	5.00	10.00	20.00
—With poster (deduct 50% if missing). Evidently a near-simultaneous release with Track 79189					
❑ MCA 2026	Who Came First	1973	3.00	6.00	12.00
—Reissue of 79189					
❑ Track 79189	Who Came First	1972	5.00	10.00	20.00
—With poster (deduct 50% if missing)					

TOYS, THE

45s

Number	Title (A Side/B Side)	Yr	VG	VG+	NM
❑ Dyno Voice 209	A Lover's Concerto/This Night	1965	3.00	6.00	12.00
❑ Dyno Voice 214	Attack/See How They Run	1965	2.50	5.00	10.00
❑ Dyno Voice 218	My My Heart Be Cast Into Stone/On Backstreet	1966	2.50	5.00	10.00
❑ Dyno Voice 219	Can't Get Enough of You Baby/Silver Spoon	1966	2.50	5.00	10.00
❑ Dyno Voice 222	Baby Toys/Happy Birthday Broken Heart	1966	2.50	5.00	10.00
❑ Dyno Vox 209	A Lover's Concerto/This Night	1965	6.25	12.50	25.00
❑ Musicor 1300	You Got It Baby/You've Got to Give Her Love	1968	2.00	4.00	8.00
❑ Musicor 1319	Sealed with a Kiss/I Got My Heart Set on You	1968	2.00	4.00	8.00
❑ Philips 40432	Ciao Baby/I Got Carried Away	1967	2.50	5.00	10.00
❑ Philips 40456	My Love Sonata/I Close My Eyes	1967	2.50	5.00	10.00

Albums

Number	Title (A Side/B Side)	Yr	VG	VG+	NM
❑ DynoVoice 9002 [M]	The Toys Sing "A Lover's Concerto" and "Attack!"	1966	10.00	20.00	40.00
❑ DynoVoice S-9002 [P]	The Toys Sing "A Lover's Concerto" and "Attack!"	1966	12.50	25.00	50.00

TRASHMEN, THE

45s

Number	Title (A Side/B Side)	Yr	VG	VG+	NM
❑ Argo 5516	Bird '65/Ubangi Stomp	1965	12.50	25.00	50.00
❑ Bear 1966	Keep Your Hands Off My Baby/Lost Angel	1965	5.00	10.00	20.00
❑ Era Back to Back Hits 016	Liar, Liar/Surfin' Bird	197?	—	2.50	5.00
—B-side by the Castaways					
❑ Eric 247	Surfin' Bird/Liar, Liar	197?	—	2.50	5.00
—B-side by the Castaways; reissue					
❑ Garrett 4002	Surfin' Bird/King of the Surf	1963	7.50	15.00	30.00
❑ Garrett 4003	Bird Dance Beat/A-Bone	1964	5.00	10.00	20.00
❑ Garrett 4005	Bad News/On the Move	1964	5.00	10.00	20.00
❑ Garrett 4010	Peppermint Man/New Generation	1964	5.00	10.00	20.00
❑ Garrett 4012	Whoa Dad/Walkin' My Baby	1964	5.00	10.00	20.00
❑ Garrett 4013	Dancing with Santa/Real Live Doll	1964	6.25	12.50	25.00
❑ Lana 136	Surfin' Bird/King of the Surf	196?	2.50	5.00	10.00
—Oldies reissue					
❑ Metrobeat 7927	Green, Green Backs of Home/Address Enclosed	1968	3.75	7.50	15.00
❑ Oldies 45 301	Surfin' Bird/King of the Surf	1965	3.00	6.00	12.00
—Early reissue					
❑ Soma 1469	Surfin' Bird/Liar, Liar	1966	3.00	6.00	12.00
—B-side by the Castaways					
❑ Terrific 5003	Surfin' Bird/Bird Dance Beat	196?	2.50	5.00	10.00
—Early reissue					
❑ Tribe 8315	Hanging On Me/Some Lies	1966	6.25	12.50	25.00

Albums

Number	Title (A Side/B Side)	Yr	VG	VG+	NM
❑ Garrett GA-200 [M]	Surfin' Bird	1964	55.00	110.00	220.00
❑ Garrett GAS-200 [R]	Surfin' Bird	1964	87.50	175.00	350.00

TRAVOLTA, JOHN

45s

Number	Title (A Side/B Side)	Yr	VG	VG+	NM
❑ Midland Int'l. MB-10623	Let Her In/Big Trouble	1976	—	2.50	5.00
❑ Midland Int'l. MB-10780	Whenever I'm Away from You/Razzamatazz	1976	—	2.50	5.00
❑ Midland Int'l. MB-10907	All Strung Out on You/Easy Evil	1977	—	2.50	5.00
❑ Midsong Int'l. 1000	Big Trouble/Can't Let You Go	1978	—	2.50	5.00
❑ Midsong Int'l. MB-10977	Slow Dancin'/Moonlight	1977	—	2.50	5.00
❑ Midsong Int'l. MB-11206	What Would They Say/Razzamatazz	1978	—	2.50	5.00
❑ Midsong Int'l. 72007	You Set My Dreams to Music/It Had to Be You	1980	—	2.50	5.00
❑ RCA GB-10945	Let Her In/Whenever I'm Away from You	1977	—	2.00	4.00
—Gold Standard Series					
❑ RSO 909	Greased Lightnin'/Rock and Roll Is Here to Stay	1978	—	2.00	4.00
—B-side by Sha Na Na					
❑ RSO 930	Sandy/Blue Moon	1979	—	2.00	4.00
—B-side by Sha Na Na					

Albums

Number	Title (A Side/B Side)	Yr	VG	VG+	NM
❑ Midland Int'l. BKL1-1563	John Travolta	1976	3.00	6.00	12.00
❑ Midland Int'l. BKL1-2211	Can't Let You Go	1977	3.00	6.00	12.00
❑ Midsong Int'l. MTF 001 [(2)]	Travolta Fever	1978	3.75	7.50	15.00
—Reissue of his two LPs in one package					

TRAVOLTA, JOHN, AND OLIVIA NEWTON-JOHN

45s

Number	Title (A Side/B Side)	Yr	VG	VG+	NM
❑ RSO 891	You're the One That I Want/Alone at a Drive-In Movie	1978	—	2.00	4.00
❑ RSO 906	Summer Nights/Rock 'N' Roll Party Queen	1978	—	2.00	4.00
—B-side by Louis St. Louis					

TREMELOES, THE

45s

Number	Title (A Side/B Side)	Yr	VG	VG+	NM
❑ DJM 1008	Hard Woman/My Friend Delaney	1976	—	2.50	5.00
❑ DJM 1016	September, November, December/(B-side unknown)	1976	—	2.50	5.00
❑ Epic 10075	Good Day Sunshine/What a State I'm In	1966	3.00	6.00	12.00
❑ Epic 10139	Here Comes My Baby/Gentlemen of Pleasure	1967	2.50	5.00	10.00
❑ Epic 10184	Silence Is Golden/Let Your Hair Hang Down	1967	2.50	5.00	10.00
❑ Epic 10233	Even the Bad Times Are Good/Jenny's All Right	1967	2.00	4.00	8.00
❑ Epic 10293	Suddenly You Love Me/Suddenly Winter	1968	2.00	4.00	8.00
❑ Epic 10328	Girl from Nowhere/Helule, Helule	1968	2.00	4.00	8.00

Number	Title (A Side/B Side)	Yr	VG	VG+	NM
❑ Epic 10376	My Little Lady/All the World to Me	1968	2.00	4.00	8.00
❑ Epic 10437	I Shall Be Released/I Miss My Baby	1969	2.00	4.00	8.00
❑ Epic 10467	Up, Down, All Around/Hello World	1969	2.00	4.00	8.00
❑ Epic 10548	(Call Me) Number One/Instant Whip	1969	2.00	4.00	8.00
❑ Epic 10621	Breakheart Motel/By the Way	1970	2.50	5.00	10.00
❑ Epic 10682	Me and My Life/Try Me	1970	2.00	4.00	8.00
❑ Epic 10807	My Woman/Hello Buddy	1971	—	3.00	6.00
❑ Epic 10996	Yodelay/Blue Suede Tie	1973	—	3.00	6.00
Albums					
❑ DJM 2	Shiner	1974	3.00	6.00	12.00
❑ Epic LN 24310 [M]	Here Comes My Baby	1967	7.50	15.00	30.00
❑ Epic LN 24326 [M]	Even the Bad Times Are Good	1967	6.25	12.50	25.00
❑ Epic LN 24363 [M]	Suddenly You Love Me	1968	7.50	15.00	30.00
❑ Epic BN 26310 [R]	Here Comes My Baby	1967	5.00	10.00	20.00
❑ Epic BN 26326 [P]	Even the Bad Times Are Good	1967	7.50	15.00	30.00
❑ Epic BN 26363 [R]	Suddenly You Love Me	1968	5.00	10.00	20.00
❑ Epic BN 26388 [S]	World Explosion '58/'68	1968	7.50	15.00	30.00
TROGGS, THE					
45s					
❑ Atco 6415	Wild Thing/I Want You	1966	5.00	10.00	20.00
❑ Atco 6415	Wild Thing/With a Girl Like You	1966	5.00	10.00	20.00
—"Wild Thing" writer is correctly credited as "Taylor."					
❑ Atco 6444	I Can't Control Myself/Gonna Make You	1966	3.75	7.50	15.00
❑ Bell 45405	Listen to the Man/Queen of Sorrow	1973	2.00	4.00	8.00
❑ Bell 45426	Strange Movies/I'm on Fire	1973	2.00	4.00	8.00
❑ Fontana 1548	Wild Thing/From Home	1966	2.50	5.00	10.00
❑ Fontana 1552	With a Girl Like You/I Want You	1966	2.50	5.00	10.00
❑ Fontana 1557	I Can't Control Myself/Gonna Make You	1966	2.50	5.00	10.00
❑ Fontana 1576	You're Lying/Give It To Me	1967	2.00	4.00	8.00
❑ Fontana 1585	6-5-4-3-2-1/Anyway That You Want Me	1967	2.00	4.00	8.00
❑ Fontana 1593	Night of the Long Grass/Girl in Black	1967	2.00	4.00	8.00
❑ Fontana 1607	Love Is All Around/When Will the Rain Come	1967	2.50	5.00	10.00
❑ Fontana 1622	You Can Cry If You Want To/There's Something About You	1968	2.00	4.00	8.00
❑ Fontana 1630	Surprise, Surprise/Cousin Jane	1968	2.00	4.00	8.00
❑ Fontana 1634	Hip Hip Hooray/Say Darlin'	1968	2.00	4.00	8.00
❑ Page One 21026	Evil Woman/Heads Or Tails	1969	—	3.00	6.00
❑ Page One 21030	Easy Lovin'/Give Me Something	1970	—	3.00	6.00
❑ Page One 21032	Come Now/Lover	1970	—	3.00	6.00
❑ Page One 21035	The Raver/You	1970	—	3.00	6.00
❑ Private Stock 45,102	Rolling Stone/(B-side unknown)	1976	—	2.50	5.00
❑ Pye 65011	Feels Like a Woman/Everything's Funny	1972	2.00	4.00	8.00
❑ Pye 71015	Good Vibrations/Push It Up to Me	1975	—	2.50	5.00
❑ Pye 71035	Summertime/Jerry Come Down	1975	—	2.50	5.00
❑ Pye 71054	Satisfaction/(B-side unknown)	1975	—	2.50	5.00
Albums					
❑ Atco 33-193 [M]	Wild Thing	1966	12.50	25.00	50.00
❑ Atco SD 33-193 [R]	Wild Thing	1966	10.00	20.00	40.00
❑ Fontana MGF 27556 [M]	Wild Thing/With a Girl Like You	1966	10.00	20.00	40.00
—Contents identical to the Atco LP; two slightly different cover variations are known; record has mono number and plays mono; number "27556" in trail-off					
❑ Fontana MGF 27556 [R]	Wild Thing/With a Girl Like You	1966	7.50	15.00	30.00
—Contents identical to the Atco LP; two slightly different cover variations are known; record has mono number but plays in rechanneled stereo; number "2/67556" in trail-off					
❑ Fontana SRF 67556 [R]	Wild Thing/With a Girl Like You	1966	7.50	15.00	30.00
—Contents identical to the Atco LP; two slightly different cover variations are known					
❑ Fontana SRF 67576 [R]	Love Is All Around	1968	7.50	15.00	30.00
❑ MKC 214	Live at Max's Kansas City	1980	3.00	6.00	12.00
❑ Private Stock PS-2008	The Troggs Tapes	1976	3.00	6.00	12.00
❑ Pye 12112	The Troggs	1975	3.00	6.00	12.00
❑ Rhino RNLP-118	The Best of the Troggs	1985	2.50	5.00	10.00
❑ Rhino R1 70118	The Best of the Troggs	1988	2.00	4.00	8.00
❑ Sire SASH-3714 [(2)]	The Vintage Years	1976	3.75	7.50	15.00
TROY, DORIS					
45s					
❑ Apple 1820	Ain't That Cute/Vaya Con Dios	1970	2.00	4.00	8.00
❑ Apple 1824	Jacob's Ladder/Get Back	1970	2.00	4.00	8.00

Number	Title (A Side/B Side)	Yr	VG	VG+	NM
❑ Atlantic 2188	Just One Look/Bossa Nova Blues	1963	5.00	10.00	20.00
❑ Atlantic 2206	Tomorrow Is Another Day/What'cha Gonna Do About It	1963	3.00	6.00	12.00
❑ Atlantic 2222	One More Chance/Please Little Angel	1964	3.00	6.00	12.00
❑ Atlantic 2269	Hurry/He Don't Belong to Me	1965	3.00	6.00	12.00
❑ Calla 114	Heartaches/I'll Do Anything	1966	5.00	10.00	20.00
❑ Capitol 2043	Face Up to the Truth/He's Qualified	1967	2.00	4.00	8.00
❑ Midland Int'l. MB-10806	Lyin' Eyes/Give God Glory	1976	—	2.50	5.00
❑ Midland Int'l. MB-11082	Can't Hold On/Another Look	1977	—	2.50	5.00
Albums					
❑ Apple ST-3371	Doris Troy	1970	6.25	12.50	25.00
❑ Atlantic 8088 [M]	Just One Look	1964	7.50	15.00	30.00
❑ Atlantic SD 8088 [P]	Just One Look	1964	12.50	25.00	50.00
—The title song is rechanneled					

TUNE WEAVERS, THE

45s

Number	Title (A Side/B Side)	Yr	VG	VG+	NM
❑ Casa Grande 101	Little Boy/Look Down That Lonesome Road	1959	10.00	20.00	40.00
❑ Casa Grande 3038	My Congratulations Baby/This Can't Be Love	1960	7.50	15.00	30.00
❑ Casa Grande 4037	Happy, Happy Birthday Baby/Ol' Man River	1957	37.50	75.00	150.00
❑ Casa Grande 4038	I Remember Dear/Pamela Jean	1957	7.50	15.00	30.00
❑ Casa Grande 4040	There Stands My Love/I'm Cold	1958	10.00	20.00	40.00
❑ Checker 872	Happy, Happy Birthday Baby/Ol' Man River	1957	6.25	12.50	25.00
❑ Checker 872	Happy, Happy Birthday Baby/Yo Yo Walk	1957	6.25	12.50	25.00
—B-side by Paul Gayten					
❑ Checker 880	Ol' Man River/Tough Enough	1957	6.25	12.50	25.00
—B-side by Paul Gayten					
❑ Checker 1007	Congratulations on Your Wedding/Your Skies of Blue	1962	6.25	12.50	25.00
❑ Classic Artists 104	Come Back to Me/I've Tried	1988	—	2.00	4.00
—As "Margo Sylvia and Tune Weavers"					
❑ Classic Artists 107	Merry, Merry Christmas Baby/What Are You Doing New Year's Eve	1988	—	2.00	4.00
—As "Margo Sylvia and Tune Weavers"					

TURNER, IKE AND TINA

45s

Number	Title (A Side/B Side)	Yr	VG	VG+	NM
❑ A&M 1118	River Deep, Mountain High/I'll Keep You Happy	1969	2.50	5.00	10.00
❑ A&M 1170	A Love Like Yours/Save the Last Dance for Me	1970	2.50	5.00	10.00
❑ Blue Thumb 101	I've Been Loving You Too Long/Grumbling	1969	—	3.00	6.00
❑ Blue Thumb 102	The Hunter/Crazy 'Bout You Baby	1969	—	3.00	6.00
❑ Blue Thumb 104	Bold Soul Sister/I Know	1969	—	3.00	6.00
❑ Blue Thumb 202	I've Been Loving You Too Long/Crazy 'Bout You Baby	1971	6.25	12.50	25.00
❑ Cenco 112	Get It-Get It/You Weren't Ready (For My Love)	1967	3.75	7.50	15.00
❑ Innis 6666	Betcha Can't Kiss Me/Don't Lie to Me	1968	2.50	5.00	10.00
❑ Innis 6667	So Fine/So Blue Over You	1968	2.50	5.00	10.00
❑ Kent 402	I Can't Believe What You Say (For Seeing What You Do)/ My Baby Now	1964	2.50	5.00	10.00
❑ Kent 409	Am I a Fool in Love/Please, Please, Please	1964	2.50	5.00	10.00
❑ Kent 418	Chicken Shack/He's the One	1965	2.50	5.00	10.00
❑ Kent 4514	Plaese, Please, Please (Part 1)/Please, Please, Please (Part 2)	1970	—	3.00	6.00
❑ Liberty 56177	I Want to Take You Higher/Contact High	1970	—	3.00	6.00
❑ Liberty 56207	Workin' Together/The Way You Love Me	1970	—	3.00	6.00
❑ Liberty 56216	Proud Mary/Funkier Than a Mosquito's Tweeter	1970	—	3.00	6.00
❑ Loma 2011	I'm Thru with Love/Tell Her I'm Not Home	1965	2.50	5.00	10.00
❑ Loma 2015	Somebody Needs You/Just to Be with You	1965	2.50	5.00	10.00
❑ Minit 32060	I'm Gonna Do All I Can (To Do Right By My Man)/ You've Got Too Many Ties That Bind	1969	—	3.00	6.00
❑ Minit 32068	I Wish It Would Rain/With a Little Help from My Friends	1969	—	3.00	6.00
❑ Minit 32077	I Wanna Jump/Treating Us Funky	1969	—	3.00	6.00
❑ Minit 32087	Come Together/Honky Tonk Women	1970	—	3.00	6.00
❑ Modern 1007	Good Bye, So Long/Hurt Is All You Gave Me	1965	2.50	5.00	10.00
❑ Modern 1012	I Don't Need/Gonna Have Fun	1965	2.50	5.00	10.00
❑ Philles 131	River Deep — Mountain High/I'll Keep You Happy	1966	5.00	10.00	20.00
❑ Philles 134	Two to Tango/A Man Is a Man Is a Man	1966	3.75	7.50	15.00
❑ Philles 135	I'll Never Need More Love Than This/The Cash Box Blues Or (Oops We Printed the Wrong Story Again)	1967	3.75	7.50	15.00
❑ Philles 136	I Idolize You/A Love Like Yours	1967	3.75	7.50	15.00
❑ Pompeii 7003	Betcha Can't Kiss Me/Cussin', Cryin', and Carryin' On	1969	2.00	4.00	8.00
❑ Pompeii 66675	It Sho' Ain't Me/We Need An Understanding	1968	2.00	4.00	8.00
❑ Pompeii 66700	Shake a Tail Feather/Cussin', Cryin', and Carryin' On	1969	2.00	4.00	8.00
❑ Sonja 2001	If I Can't Be First/I'm Going Back Home	1968	3.00	6.00	12.00
❑ Sonja 2005	You Can't Miss Nothing That You Never Had/God Gave Me You	1968	3.00	6.00	12.00
❑ Sue 135	Two Is a Couple/Tin Top House	1965	3.75	7.50	15.00
❑ Sue 138	The New Breed (Part 1)/The New Breed (Part 2)	1965	3.75	7.50	15.00
❑ Sue 139	Stagger Lee and Billy/Can't Chance a Breakup	1965	3.75	7.50	15.00
❑ Sue 146	Dear John/I Made a Promise Up Above	1966	3.00	6.00	12.00
❑ Sue 730	A Fool in Love/The Way You Love Me	1960	7.50	15.00	30.00
❑ Sue 734	You're My Baby/A Fool Too Long	1960	6.25	12.50	25.00
❑ Sue 735	I Idolize You/Letter from Tina	1960	6.25	12.50	25.00
❑ Sue 740	I'm Jealous/You're My Baby	1961	6.25	12.50	25.00
❑ Sue 749	It's Gonna Work Out Fine/Won't You Forgive Me	1961	7.50	15.00	30.00
—With correct A-side title					
❑ Sue 753	Poor Fool/You Can't Blame Me	1961	5.00	10.00	20.00
❑ Sue 757	Tra La La La La/Puppy Love	1962	3.75	7.50	15.00
❑ Sue 760	Prancing/It's Gonna Work Out Fine	1962	3.75	7.50	15.00
❑ Sue 765	You Shoulda Treated Me Right/Sleepless	1962	3.75	7.50	15.00
❑ Sue 768	Tina's Dilemma/I Idolize You	1962	3.75	7.50	15.00
❑ Sue 772	The Argument/Mind in a Whirl	1962	3.75	7.50	15.00
❑ Sue 774	Please Don't Hurt Me/Worried and Hurtin' Inside	1962	3.75	7.50	15.00

Number	Title (A Side/B Side)	Yr	VG	VG+	NM
❑ Sue 784	Don't Play Me Cheap/Wake Up	1963	3.75	7.50	15.00
❑ Tangerine 963	Beauty Is Only Skin Deep/Anything You Wasn't Born With	1966	2.50	5.00	10.00
❑ Tangerine 967	Dust My Broom/I'm Hooked	1966	2.50	5.00	10.00
❑ United Artists 0119	A Fool in Love/I Idolize You	1973	—	2.00	4.00
❑ United Artists 0120	It's Gonna Work Out Fine/Poor Fool	1973	—	2.00	4.00
❑ United Artists 0121	I Want to Take You Higher/Come Together	1973	—	2.00	4.00
❑ United Artists 0122	Proud Mary/Tra La La La La	1973	—	2.00	4.00
—0119 through 0122 are "Silver Spotlight Series" reissues					
❑ United Artists XW174	With a Little Help from My Friends/Early One Morning	1973	—	2.50	5.00
❑ United Artists XW257	Work On Me/Born Free	1973	—	2.50	5.00
❑ United Artists XW298	Nutbosh City Limits/Help Him	1973	—	3.00	6.00
❑ United Artists XW409	Get it Out of Your Mind/Sweet Rhode Island Red	1974	—	2.50	5.00
❑ United Artists XW524	Nutbush City Limits/Ooh Poo Pah Doo	1974	—	2.00	4.00
—Reissue					
❑ United Artists XW528	Sexy Ida (Part 1)/Sexy Ida (Part 2)	1974	—	2.50	5.00
❑ United Artists XW598X	Baby, Get It On/Baby, Get It On (Disco Version)	1975	—	2.50	5.00
❑ United Artists 50782	Ooh Poo Pah Doo/I Wanna Jump	1971	—	2.50	5.00
❑ United Artists 50837	I'm Yours/Doin' It	1971	—	2.50	5.00
❑ United Artists 50881	Do Wah Ditty (Got to Get Ya)/Up in Heah	1972	—	2.50	5.00
❑ United Artists 50913	Outrageous/Feel Good	1972	—	2.50	5.00
❑ United Artists 50939	Games People Play/Pick Me Up	1972	—	2.50	5.00
❑ United Artists 50955	Let Me Touch Your Mind/Chopper	1972	—	2.50	5.00
❑ Warner Bros. 5433	A Fool for a Fool/No Tears to Cry	1964	3.00	6.00	12.00
❑ Warner Bros. 5461	It's All Over/Finger Poppin'	1964	3.00	6.00	12.00
❑ Warner Bros. 5493	Ooh Poop A Doo/Merry Christmas Baby	1964	3.00	6.00	12.00
Albums					
❑ A&M SP-3179	River Deep — Mountain High	1982	2.50	5.00	10.00
—Budget-line reissue					
❑ A&M SP-4178	River Deep — Mountain High	1969	6.25	12.50	25.00
—Official release of Philles 4011					
❑ ABC 4014	16 Great Performances	1975	3.00	6.00	12.00
❑ Accord SN-7147	Hot and Sassy	1981	2.50	5.00	10.00
❑ Blue Thumb BTS 5	Outta Season	1968	3.75	7.50	15.00
❑ Blue Thumb BTS 11	The Hunter	1969	3.75	7.50	15.00
❑ Blue Thumb BTS 49	The Best of Ike & Tina Turner	1973	3.00	6.00	12.00
❑ Blue Thumb BTS-8805	Outta Season	1971	3.00	6.00	12.00
—Early reissue of Blue Thumb 5					
❑ Capitol ST-571	Her Man, His Woman	1971	3.75	7.50	15.00
❑ Collectables COL-5107	Golden Classics	198?	2.50	5.00	10.00
❑ Collectables COL-5137	It's Gonna Work Out Fine	198?	2.50	5.00	10.00
❑ EMI America ST-17212	It's Gonna Work Out Fine	1986	2.50	5.00	10.00
❑ EMI America SQ-17216	Workin' Together	1986	2.50	5.00	10.00
❑ Harmony HS 11360	Ooh Poo Pah Doo	1969	3.75	7.50	15.00
❑ Harmony H 30567	Something's Got a Hold on Me	1971	3.75	7.50	15.00
❑ Kent KST-514 [S]	The Ike and Tina Turner Revue Live	1964	10.00	20.00	40.00
❑ Kent KST-519 [S]	The Soul of Ike and Tina	1966	10.00	20.00	40.00
❑ Kent KST-538	Festival of Live Performances	1969	7.50	15.00	30.00
❑ Kent KST-550	Please Please Please	1971	7.50	15.00	30.00
❑ Kent K-5014 [M]	The Ike and Tina Turner Revue Live	1964	7.50	15.00	30.00
❑ Kent K-5019 [M]	The Soul of Ike and Tina	1966	7.50	15.00	30.00
❑ Liberty LT-917	Airwaves	1981	2.00	4.00	8.00
❑ Liberty LST-7637	Come Together	1970	3.75	7.50	15.00
❑ Liberty LST-7650	Workin' Together	1970	3.75	7.50	15.00
❑ Liberty LO-51156	Get Back!	1985	2.50	5.00	10.00
❑ Loma L 5904 [M]	Live! The Ike & Tina Turner Show Vol. 2	1966	6.25	12.50	25.00
❑ Loma LS 5904 [S]	Live! The Ike & Tina Turner Show, Vol. 2	1966	7.50	15.00	30.00
—Reissue of Warner Bros. 1579?					
❑ Minit 24018	In Person	1969	5.00	10.00	20.00
❑ Philles PHLP 4011 [M]	River Deep — Mountain High	1967	2000.	4000.	8000.
—Value is for record alone; covers were not printed					
❑ Pickwick SPC-3284	Too Hot to Hold	197?	2.50	5.00	10.00
❑ Pompeii SD 6000 [S]	So Fine	1968	6.25	12.50	25.00
❑ Pompeii SD 6004	Cussin', Cryin' and Carryin' On	1969	6.25	12.50	25.00
❑ Pompeii SD 6006	Get It Together	1969	6.25	12.50	25.00
❑ Striped Horse SHL-2001	Golden Empire	1986	2.50	5.00	10.00
❑ Sue LP 1038 [M]	The Greatest Hits of Ike and Tina Turner	1965	75.00	150.00	300.00
❑ Sue LP 2001 [M]	The Soul of Ike and Tina Turner	1961	100.00	200.00	400.00

Number	Title (A Side/B Side)	Yr	VG	VG+	NM
❑ Sue LP 2003 [M]	Ike and Tina Turner's Kings of Rhythm Dance	1962	100.00	200.00	400.00
—Despite the title, this is an all-instrumental album (Tina's vocals do not appear)					
❑ Sue LP 2004 [M]	Dynamite	1963	100.00	200.00	400.00
❑ Sue LP 2005 [M]	Don't Play Me Cheap	1963	100.00	200.00	400.00
❑ Sue LP 2007 [M]	It's Gonna Work Out Fine	1963	100.00	200.00	400.00
❑ Sunset SUS-5265	The Fantastic Ike & Tina Turner	1969	3.75	7.50	15.00
❑ Sunset SUS-5286	Ike & Tina Turner's Greatest Hits	1969	3.75	7.50	15.00
❑ Unart S 21021	Greatest Hits	197?	2.50	5.00	10.00
❑ United Artists UA-LA064-G [(2)]	The World of Ike & Tina Live	1973	3.75	7.50	15.00
❑ United Artists UA-LA180-F	Nutbush City Limits	1973	3.00	6.00	12.00
❑ United Artists UA-LA203-G	The Gospel According to Ike & Tina Turner	1974	3.00	6.00	12.00
❑ United Artists UA-LA312-G	Sweet Rhode Island Red	1974	3.00	6.00	12.00
❑ United Artists UA-LA592-G	Greatest Hits	1976	3.00	6.00	12.00
❑ United Artists UA-LA707-G	Delilah's Power	1977	3.00	6.00	12.00
❑ United Artists UA-LA917-H	Airwaves	1978	3.00	6.00	12.00
❑ United Artists UAS-5530	'Nuff Said	1971	3.00	6.00	12.00
❑ United Artists UAS-5598	Feel Good	1972	3.00	6.00	12.00
❑ United Artists UAS-5660	Let Me Touch Your Mind	1972	3.00	6.00	12.00
❑ United Artists UAS-5667	Ike & Tina Turner's Greatest Hits	1972	3.00	6.00	12.00
❑ United Artists UAS-9953 [(2)]	Live at Carnegie Hall/What You Hear Is What You Get	1971	3.75	7.50	15.00
❑ Warner Bros. W 1579 [M]	Live! The Ike & Tina Turner Show	1965	7.50	15.00	30.00
❑ Warner Bros. WS 1579 [S]	Live! The Ike & Tina Turner Show	1965	10.00	20.00	40.00
❑ Warner Bros. WS 1810	Ike & Tina Turner's Greatest Hits	1969	6.25	12.50	25.00

TURNER, TINA

45s

Number	Title (A Side/B Side)	Yr	VG	VG+	NM
❑ Capitol B-5322	Let's Stay Together/I Wrote a Letter	1984	—	—	3.00
❑ Capitol B-5354	What's Love Got to Do with It/Rock 'N' Roll Widow	1984	—	—	3.00
❑ Capitol B-5387	Better Be Good to Me/When I Was Young	1984	—	—	3.00
❑ Capitol B-5433	Private Dancer/Nutbush City Limits	1984	—	—	3.00
❑ Capitol B-5461	Show Some Respect/Let's Pretend We're Married	1985	—	—	3.00
❑ Capitol B-5491	We Don't Need Another Hero (Thunderdome)/(Instrumental)	1985	—	—	3.00
❑ Capitol B-5518	One of the Living/One of the Living (Dub)	1985	—	—	3.00
❑ Capitol B-5615	Typical Male/Don't Turn Around	1986	—	—	3.00
❑ Capitol B-5644	Two People/Havin' a Party	1986	—	—	3.00
❑ Capitol B-5668	What You Get Is What You See/What You Get Is What You See (Live)	1987	—	—	3.00
❑ Capitol B-44003	Break Every Rule/Take Me to the River	1987	—	—	3.00
❑ Capitol B-44111	Afterglow/(B-side unknown)	1987	—	2.00	4.00
❑ Capitol B-44442	The Best/Undercover Agent for the Blues	1989	—	—	3.00
❑ Capitol B-44473	Steamy Windows/The Best	1989	—	—	3.00
❑ Capitol NR-44510	Look Me in the Heart/Stronger Than the Wind	1990	—	—	3.00
❑ Fantasy 948	Lean On Me/Shame, Shame, Shame	1984	—	2.00	4.00
❑ Pompeii 66682	Too Hot to Hold/You Got What You Wanted	1968	2.50	5.00	10.00
❑ United Artists XW 724	Whole Lotta Love/Rockin' 'N' Rollin'	1975	—	3.00	6.00
❑ United Artists XW 730	Delilah's Power/That's My Power	1975	—	3.00	6.00
❑ United Artists XW 920	Come Together/I Want to Take You Higher	1977	—	3.00	6.00
❑ United Artists XW 1265	Fire Down Below/Viva La Money	1979	—	2.50	5.00

Albums

Number	Title (A Side/B Side)	Yr	VG	VG+	NM
❑ Capitol ST-12330	Private Dancer	1984	2.00	4.00	8.00
❑ Capitol PJ-12530	Break Every Rule	1986	2.00	4.00	8.00
❑ Capitol C1-90126 [(2)]	Tina Live in Europe	1988	3.00	6.00	12.00
❑ Capitol C1-91873	Foreign Affair	1989	2.00	4.00	8.00
❑ Fantasy MFP-4520 [EP]	Mini	1984	2.00	4.00	8.00
❑ Springboard SPB-4033	The Queen	1972	2.50	5.00	10.00
❑ United Artists UA-LA200-F	Tina Turns the Country On	1973	3.75	7.50	15.00
❑ United Artists UA-LA495-G	Acid Queen	1975	3.00	6.00	12.00
❑ United Artists UA-LA919-G	Rough	1978	3.00	6.00	12.00
❑ Wagner 14108	Good Hearted Woman	1979	3.00	6.00	12.00

TURTLES, THE

45s

Number	Title (A Side/B Side)	Yr	VG	VG+	NM
❑ Lost-Nite 435	Elenore/Is It Any Wonder	197?	—	2.50	5.00
❑ Lost-Nite 436	Happy Together/The Walking Song	197?	—	2.50	5.00
❑ Lost-Nite 437	It Ain't Me, Babe/Almost There	197?	—	2.50	5.00
—Reissue					
❑ Lost-Nite 438	Let Me Be/Your Maw Said You Cried	197?	—	2.50	5.00
—Reissue					
❑ Lost-Nite 439	She'd Rather Be with Me/Rugs of Woods & Flowers	197?	—	2.50	5.00
❑ Lost-Nite 440	She's My Girl/Chicken Little Was Right	197?	—	2.50	5.00
—Reissue					
❑ Lost-Nite 441	You Baby/Wanderin' Kind	197?	—	2.50	5.00
—Reissue					
❑ Lost-Nite 442	You Showed Me/Buzz Saw	197?	—	2.50	5.00
—Reissue					
❑ Rhino RNOR 4504	You Know What I Mean/She's My Girl	1984	—	2.00	4.00
❑ White Whale 222	It Ain't Me, Babe/Almost There	1965	3.00	6.00	12.00
❑ White Whale 224	Let Me Be/Your Maw Said You Cried	1965	2.50	5.00	10.00
❑ White Whale 227	You Baby/Wanderin' Kind	1966	2.50	5.00	10.00
❑ White Whale 231	Grim Reaper of Love/Come Back	1966	5.00	10.00	20.00
❑ White Whale 234	We'll Meet Again/Outside Chance	1966	3.75	7.50	15.00
❑ White Whale 237	Outside Chance/Making My Mind Up	1966	2.50	5.00	10.00
❑ White Whale 238	Can I Get to Know You Better?/Like the Seasons	1966	2.50	5.00	10.00
❑ White Whale 244	Happy Together/Like the Seasons	1967	2.00	4.00	8.00
❑ White Whale 249	She'd Rather Be with Me/The Walking Song	1967	2.00	4.00	8.00
❑ White Whale 251	Guide for the Married Man/Think I'll Run Away	1967	10.00	20.00	40.00
—Withdrawn shortly after release					

Number	Title (A Side/B Side)	Yr	VG	VG+	NM
❑ White Whale 254	You Know What I Mean/Rugs of Woods and Flowers	1967	2.00	4.00	8.00
❑ White Whale 260	She's My Girl/Chicken Little Was Right	1967	2.50	5.00	10.00
—All-blue label					
❑ White Whale 260	She's My Girl/Chicken Little Was Right	1967	2.00	4.00	8.00
—White concentric circles on mostly blue label					
❑ White Whale 264	Sound Asleep/Umbassa the Dragon	1968	2.00	4.00	8.00
❑ White Whale 273	The Story of Rock and Roll/Can't You Hear the Cows	1968	2.00	4.00	8.00
❑ White Whale 276	Elenore/Surfer Dan	1968	2.00	4.00	8.00
❑ White Whale 292	You Showed Me/Buzz Saw	1969	2.00	4.00	8.00
❑ White Whale 306	House on the Hill/Come Over	1969	5.00	10.00	20.00
❑ White Whale 308	You Don't Have to Walk in the Rain/Come Over	1969	2.00	4.00	8.00
❑ White Whale 326	Love in the City/Bachelor Mother	1969	2.00	4.00	8.00
❑ White Whale 334	Lady-O/Somewhere Friday Nite	1969	2.00	4.00	8.00
❑ White Whale 341	Who Would Ever Think That I Would Marry Margaret?/We Ain't Gonna Party No More	1970	3.75	7.50	15.00
❑ White Whale 350	Is It Any Wonder?/Wanderin' Kind	1970	2.00	4.00	8.00
❑ White Whale 355	Eve of Destruction/Wanderin' Kind	1970	2.00	4.00	8.00
❑ White Whale 364	Me About You/Think I'll Run Away	1970	2.00	4.00	8.00
Albums					
❑ Rhino RNLP 151	It Ain't Me Babe	1983	2.50	5.00	10.00
❑ Rhino RNLP 152	Happy Together	1983	2.50	5.00	10.00
❑ Rhino RNLP 153	You Baby	1983	2.50	5.00	10.00
❑ Rhino RNLP 154	Wooden Head	1983	2.50	5.00	10.00
❑ Rhino RNLP 160	Greatest Hits	1983	2.50	5.00	10.00
❑ Rhino RNDF 280 [EP]	Turtle-Sized	1984	3.00	6.00	12.00
—Green vinyl turtle-shaped EP					
❑ Rhino RNPD 900	1968	1984	2.00	4.00	8.00
❑ Rhino RNLP 70155	Chalon Road	1986	2.50	5.00	10.00
❑ Rhino RNLP 70156	The Turtles Present the Battle of the Bands	1986	2.50	5.00	10.00
❑ Rhino RNLP 70157	Turtle Soup	1986	2.50	5.00	10.00
❑ Rhino RNLP 70158	Shell Shock	1986	2.50	5.00	10.00
❑ Rhino RNLP 70159	Turtle Wax: The Best of the Turtles, Vol. 2	1988	2.50	5.00	10.00
❑ Rhino RNLP 70177	The Best of the Turtles (Golden Archives Series)	1987	2.50	5.00	10.00
❑ Sire SASH-3703 [(2)]	The Turtles' Greatest Hits/Happy Together Again	1974	5.00	10.00	20.00
❑ White Whale WW 111 [M]	It Ain't Me Babe	1965	7.50	15.00	30.00
❑ White Whale WW 112 [M]	You Baby	1966	7.50	15.00	30.00
❑ White Whale WW 114 [M]	Happy Together	1967	5.00	10.00	20.00
❑ White Whale WW 115 [M]	The Turtles! Golden Hits	1967	6.25	12.50	25.00
❑ White Whale WWS 7111 [S]	It Ain't Me Babe	1965	10.00	20.00	40.00
❑ White Whale WWS 7112 [S]	You Baby	1966	10.00	20.00	40.00
❑ White Whale WWS 7114 [S]	Happy Together	1967	6.25	12.50	25.00
❑ White Whale WWS 7115 [S]	The Turtles! Golden Hits	1967	5.00	10.00	20.00
❑ White Whale WWS 7118	The Turtles Present the Battle of the Bands	1968	6.25	12.50	25.00
❑ White Whale WW 7124	Turtle Soup	1969	6.25	12.50	25.00
❑ White Whale WW 7127	The Turtles! More Golden Hits	1970	5.00	10.00	20.00
❑ White Whale WW 7133	Wooden Head	1970	5.00	10.00	20.00

TWILLEY, DWIGHT

45s

Number	Title (A Side/B Side)	Yr	VG	VG+	NM
❑ Arista 0278	Rock and Roll 47/Twilley Don't Mind	1977	—	2.50	5.00
❑ Arista 0299	Trying to Find My Baby/Here She Comes	1977	—	2.50	5.00
❑ Arista 0311	Looking for the Magic/Invasion	1978	—	2.50	5.00
❑ Arista 0415	Out of My Hands/Nothing's Ever Gonna Change So Fast	1979	—	2.00	4.00
❑ Arista 0433	Runaway/Burnin' Sand	1979	—	2.00	4.00
❑ Arista 0478	Somebody to Love/Money (That's What I Want)	1979	—	2.00	4.00
❑ CBS Associated 06050	Sexual/Wild Dogs	1986	—	—	3.00
❑ EMI America 8109	Later That Night/Somebody to Love	1982	—	2.00	4.00
❑ EMI America 8115	I Found the Magic/I'm Back Again	1982	—	2.00	4.00
❑ EMI America 8196	Girls/To Get to You	1984	—	—	3.00
❑ EMI America 8206	Little Bit of Love/Mad Dog	1984	—	—	3.00
❑ EMI America 8235	Why You Wanna Break My Heart/Chilly D's Theme	1984	—	—	3.00
❑ Private I 04820	Keep On Working/(Instrumental)	1985	—	—	3.00
❑ Shelter 40380	I'm on Fire/Did You See What Happened	1975	—	2.50	5.00
❑ Shelter 40450	Sincerely/You Were So Warm	1975	—	2.50	5.00
❑ Shelter 62003	Could Be Love/Feeling in the Dark	1976	—	2.50	5.00
Albums					
❑ Arista AB 4140	Twilley Don't Mind	1977	2.50	5.00	10.00
❑ Arista AB 4214	Twilley	1979	2.50	5.00	10.00

Number	Title (A Side/B Side)	Yr	VG	VG+	NM
❑ Arista AB 4251	Blueprint	1980	—	—	—
—Unreleased					
❑ CBS Associated BFZ 40266	Wild Dogs	1986	2.00	4.00	8.00
❑ EMI America ST-17064	Scuba Divers	1982	2.50	5.00	10.00
❑ EMI America ST-17107	Jungle	1984	2.50	5.00	10.00
❑ MCA 688	Sincerely	1981	2.00	4.00	8.00
—Reissue of Shelter LP					
❑ Shelter SA-52001	Sincerely	1976	2.50	5.00	10.00

TYMES, THE

45s

Number	Title (A Side/B Side)	Yr	VG	VG+	NM
❑ Capitol 3440	When I Look Around Me/Smile a Tender Smile	1972	—	3.00	6.00
❑ Columbia 44630	People/For Love of Ivy	1968	2.00	4.00	8.00
❑ Columbia 44799	God Bless the Child/The Love That You're Looking For	1969	—	3.00	6.00
❑ Columbia 44917	Find My Way/If You Love Me Baby	1969	—	3.00	6.00
❑ Columbia 45078	Love Child/Most Beautiful Married Lady	1970	—	3.00	6.00
❑ Columbia 45336	She's Gone/Someone to Watch Over Me	1971	—	3.00	6.00
❑ MGM 13536	Pretend/Street Talk	1966	5.00	10.00	20.00
❑ MGM 13631	(Touch of) Baby/What Would I Do	1966	5.00	10.00	20.00
❑ Parkway 871	So Much in Love/Roscoe James McClain	1963	3.75	7.50	15.00
❑ Parkway 871	So in Love/Roscoe James McClain	1963	6.25	12.50	25.00
—Original title of A-side					
❑ Parkway 884	Wonderful! Wonderful!/Come with Me to the Sea	1963	3.75	7.50	15.00
❑ Parkway 891	Somewhere/View from My Window	1963	3.75	7.50	15.00
❑ Parkway 908	To Each His Own/Wonderland of Love	1964	3.75	7.50	15.00
❑ Parkway 919	The Magic of Our Summer Love/With All My Heart	1964	3.75	7.50	15.00
❑ Parkway 924	Here She Comes/Malibu	1964	3.75	7.50	15.00
❑ Parkway 933	The Twelfth of Never/Here She Comes	1964	3.75	7.50	15.00
❑ RCA PB-10862	Love's Illusion/Savannah Sunny Sunday	1976	—	2.00	4.00
❑ RCA PB-11136	I'll Take You There/How Am I to Know (The Things a Girl in Love Should Know)	1977	—	2.00	4.00
❑ RCA GB-12082	You Little Trustmaker/Ms. Grace	1980	—	—	—
—Unreleased?					
❑ RCA Victor PB-10022	You Little Trustmaker/The North Hills	1974	—	2.50	5.00
❑ RCA Victor PB-10128	Ms. Grace/The Crutch	1974	—	2.00	4.00
❑ RCA Victor PB-10244	Interloop/Someday, Somehow I'm Keeping You	1975	—	2.00	4.00
❑ RCA Victor PB-10422	God's Gonna Punish You/If I Can't Make You Smile	1975	—	2.00	4.00
❑ RCA Victor GB-10493	You Little Trustmaker/The North Hills	1975	—	2.00	4.00
—Gold Standard Series					
❑ RCA Victor PB-10561	Good Morning Dear Lord/It's Cool	1976	—	2.00	4.00
❑ RCA Victor PB-10713	Goin' Through the Motions/Only Your Love	1976	—	2.00	4.00
❑ Winchester 1002	These Foolish Things (Remind Me of You)/This Time It's Love	1967	2.50	5.00	10.00

Albums

Number	Title (A Side/B Side)	Yr	VG	VG+	NM
❑ Abkco 4228	The Best of Tymes	1973	3.00	6.00	12.00
❑ Columbia CS 9778	People	1969	3.75	7.50	15.00
❑ Parkway P 7032 [M]	So Much in Love	1963	10.00	20.00	40.00
—With group standing in front-cover photo					
❑ Parkway P 7038 [M]	The Sound of the Wonderful Tymes	1963	10.00	20.00	40.00
❑ Parkway SP 7038 [S]	The Sound of the Wonderful Tymes	1963	12.50	25.00	50.00
❑ Parkway P 7039 [M]	Somewhere	1964	12.50	25.00	50.00
—Includes bonus single 7039 (deduct 20 percent if missing)					
❑ Parkway P 7049 [M]	18 Greatest Hits	1964	10.00	20.00	40.00
❑ RCA Victor APL1-0727	Trustmaker	1974	3.00	6.00	12.00
❑ RCA Victor APL1-1835	Turning Point	1976	3.00	6.00	12.00
❑ RCA Victor APL1-2406	Diggin' Their Roots	1977	3.00	6.00	12.00

U

U2

45s

Number	Title (A Side/B Side)	Yr	VG	VG+	NM
❑ Island 49716	I Will Follow/Out of Control (Live)	1980	5.00	10.00	20.00
❑ Island 94961	With or Without You/In God's Country	1988	—	2.50	5.00
—Gold label "Revival of the Fittest" series					
❑ Island 94974	Gloria/Sunday Bloody Sunday	1987	—	3.00	6.00
—Gold label "Revival of the Fittest" series; only U.S. 45 release for either track; "Sunday Bloody Sunday" has a unique edit					
❑ Island 94975	New Year's Day/Two Hearts Beat As One	1987	—	3.00	6.00
—Gold label "Revival of the Fittest" series					
❑ Island 94976	I Will Follow/Pride (In the Name of Love)	1987	—	3.00	6.00
—Gold label "Revival of the Fittest" series					
❑ Island 99199	All I Want Is You/Unchained Melody.	1989	—	2.00	4.00
❑ Island 99225	When Love Comes to Town/Dancing Barefoot.	1989	—	—	3.00
—A-side with B.B. King					
❑ Island 99250	Desire/Hallelujah Here She Comes.	1988	—	—	3.00
❑ Island 99254	Angel of Harlem/A Room at the Heartbreak Hotel.	1988	—	—	3.00
❑ Island 99384	In God's Country/Bullet the Blue Sky.	1988	—	2.50	5.00
—Black label jukebox pressing; both sides play at 45 rpm					
❑ Island 99385	In God's Country//Bullet the Blue Sky/Running to Stand Still.	1988	—	2.00	4.00
—A-side plays at 45 rpm, B-side at 33 1/3 rpm					
❑ Island 99407	Where the Streets Have No Name/Silver and Gold	1987	—	3.00	6.00
—Black label jukebox pressing; both sides play at 45 rpm					
❑ Island 99408	Where the Streets Have No Name//Silver and Gold/Sweetest Thing	1987	—	—	3.00
—A-side plays at 45 rpm, B-side at 33 1/3 rpm					
❑ Island 99430	I Still Haven't Found What I'm Looking For//Spanish Eyes/ Deep in the Heart	1987	—	—	3.00
—A-side plays at 45 rpm, B-side at 33 1/3 rpm					

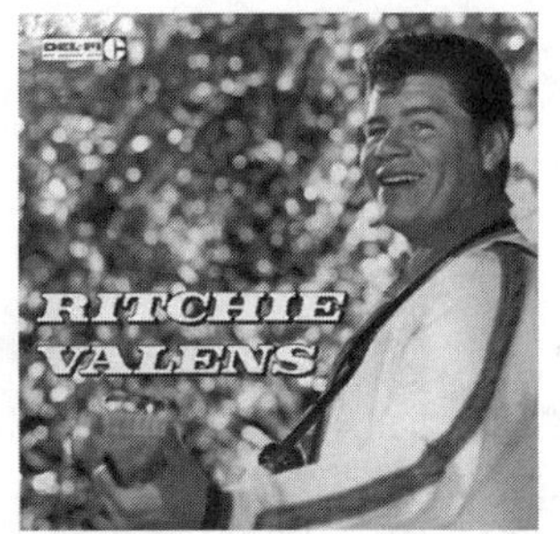

Number	Title (A Side/B Side)	Yr	VG	VG+	NM
❑ Island 99431	I Still Haven't Found What I'm Looking For/Spanish Eyes	1987	3.00	6.00	12.00
—Black label jukebox pressing; both sides play at 45 rpm					
❑ Island 99453	With or Without You/Walk on the Water	1987	5.00	10.00	20.00
—White label jukebox pressing, both sides play at 45 rpm					
❑ Island 99469	With or Without You//Luminous Times (Hold On to Love)/ Walk on the Water	1987	—	—	3.00
—A-side plays at 45 rpm, B-side at 33 1/3 rpm					
❑ Island 99704	Pride (In the Name of Love)/Boomerang II	1984	—	2.50	5.00
❑ Island 99789	I Will Follow (Live)/Two Hearts Beat as One (Live)	1983	—	3.00	6.00
❑ Island 99861	Two Hearts Beat as One/Endless Deep	1983	2.00	4.00	8.00
❑ Island 99915	New Year's Day/Treasure (Whatever Happened to Pete the Chop?)	1983	2.00	4.00	8.00
Albums					
❑ Island ILPS 9646	Boy	1980	3.75	7.50	15.00
❑ Island ILPS 9680	October	1981	3.00	6.00	12.00
—Back cover has engineering credits, etc., in upper left					
❑ Island ILPS 9680	October	1981	3.75	7.50	15.00
—Back cover is blank (no engineering credits, etc.) in upper left					
❑ Island 90040	Boy	1983	3.00	6.00	12.00
—Reissue; first pressings have dark purple labels					
❑ Island 90067	War	1983	3.00	6.00	12.00
—Original pressings have dark purple labels					
❑ Island 90092	October	1983	2.50	5.00	10.00
—Reissue; first pressings have dark purple labels					
❑ Island 90127-1-B [EP]	Under a Blood Red Sky	1983	3.75	7.50	15.00
—White labels with "Mini LP" logo; with version of "The Electric Co." in which Bono sings snippets of "A-Me-Ri-Ca" from West Side Story and "Send In The Clowns" during the instrumental break.					
❑ Island 90231	The Unforgettable Fire	1984	2.50	5.00	10.00
❑ Island 90279-1-A [EP]	Wide Awake in America	1985	2.50	5.00	10.00
❑ Island 90581	The Joshua Tree	1987	2.50	5.00	10.00
—With lyric sheet					
❑ Island 91003 [(2)]	Rattle and Hum	1988	3.75	7.50	15.00

UNDISPUTED TRUTH, THE

Number	Title (A Side/B Side)	Yr	VG	VG+	NM
45s					
❑ Gordy 7106	Save My Love for a Rainy Day/Since I've Lost You	1971	2.00	4.00	8.00
❑ Gordy 7108	Smiling Faces Sometimes/You Got the Love I Need	1971	—	3.00	6.00
❑ Gordy 7112	You Make Your Own Heaven and Hell Right Here on Earth/Ball of Confusion (That's What the World Is Today)	1971	—	3.00	6.00
❑ Gordy 7114	What It Is/California Soul	1972	—	3.00	6.00
❑ Gordy 7117	Papa Was a Rollin' Stone/Friendship Train	1972	—	3.00	6.00
❑ Gordy 7122	With a Little Help from My Friends/Girl You're Alright	1972	—	3.00	6.00
❑ Gordy 7124	Mama I Got a Brand New Thing (Don't Say No)/Gonna Keep On Tryin' Till I Win Your Love	1973	—	3.00	6.00
❑ Gordy 7130	Law of the Land/Just My Imagination (Running Away with Me)	1973	—	3.00	6.00
❑ Gordy 7134	Help Yourself/What's Going On	1974	—	3.00	6.00
❑ Gordy 7139	I'm a Fool for You/Girl's Alright with Me	1974	—	3.00	6.00
❑ Gordy 7140	Big John Is My Name/L'il Red Ridin' Hood	1974	—	3.00	6.00
❑ Gordy 7141	Earthquake Shake/Spaced Out	1975	—	—	—
—Unreleased					
❑ Gordy 7143	UFO's/Got to Get My Hands on Some Lovin'	1975	—	3.00	6.00
❑ Gordy 7145	Higher Than High/Spaced Out	1975	—	3.00	6.00
❑ Gordy 7147	Boogie Bump Boogie/I Saw Her When You Met Her	1975	—	3.00	6.00
❑ Whitfield 8231	You + Me = Love/(Instrumental)	1976	—	3.00	6.00
❑ Whitfield 8295	Let's Get Down to the Disco/Loose	1977	—	3.00	6.00
❑ Whitfield 8362	Hole in the Wall/Sunshine	1977	—	3.00	6.00
❑ Whitfield 8781	Show Time (Part 1)/(Part 2)	1979	—	3.00	6.00
❑ Whitfield 8873	I Can't Get Enough of Your Love/Misunderstood	1979	—	3.00	6.00
Albums					
❑ Gordy G 955L	The Undisputed Truth	1971	6.25	12.50	25.00
❑ Gordy G5-959	Face to Face with the Truth	1972	5.00	10.00	20.00
❑ Gordy G5-963	Law of the Land	1973	5.00	10.00	20.00
❑ Gordy G6-968	Down to Earth	1974	5.00	10.00	20.00
❑ Gordy G6-970	Cosmic Truth	1975	5.00	10.00	20.00
❑ Gordy G6-972	Higher Than High	1975	5.00	10.00	20.00
❑ Whitfield BS 2967	Method to the Madness	1977	5.00	10.00	20.00
❑ Whitfield BSK 3202	Smokin'	1979	3.75	7.50	15.00

Number	Title (A Side/B Side)	Yr	VG	VG+	NM

V

VALENS, RITCHIE

45s

Number	Title (A Side/B Side)	Yr	VG	VG+	NM
❑ Del-Fi 1287	La Bamba '87/La Bamba	1987	—	2.50	5.00
❑ Del-Fi 4106	Come On, Let's Go/Framed	1958	20.00	40.00	80.00
❑ Del-Fi 4110	Donna/La Bamba	1958	7.50	15.00	30.00
—Light blue label					
❑ Del-Fi 4111	Fast Freight/Big Baby Blues	1959	12.50	25.00	50.00
—As "Arvee Allens"					
❑ Del-Fi 4114	That's My Little Susie/In a Turkish Town	1959	10.00	20.00	40.00
❑ Del-Fi 4117	Little Girl/We Belong Together	1959	7.50	15.00	30.00
❑ Del-Fi 4128	Stay Beside Me/Big Baby Blues	1959	6.25	12.50	25.00
❑ Del-Fi 4133	The Paddiwack Song/Cry, Cry, Cry	1960	6.25	12.50	25.00
❑ Lana 153	Donna/La Bamba	196?	2.00	4.00	8.00
—Oldies reissue					

Albums

Number	Title (A Side/B Side)	Yr	VG	VG+	NM
❑ Del-Fi DFLP 1201 [M]	Ritchie Valens	1959	62.50	125.00	250.00
—Blue label with black border					
❑ Del-Fi DFLP 1206 [M]	Ritchie	1959	37.50	75.00	150.00
❑ Del-Fi DFLP 1214 [M]	In Concert at Pacoima Jr. High	1960	62.50	125.00	250.00
❑ Del-Fi DFLP 1225 [M]	His Greatest Hits	1963	87.50	175.00	350.00
—Black cover					
❑ Del-Fi DFLP 1247 [M]	His Greatest Hits, Volume 2	1965	37.50	75.00	150.00
❑ Guest Star GS-1469 [M]	The Original Ritchie Valens	1963	7.50	15.00	30.00
❑ Guest Star GSS-1469 [R]	The Original Ritchie Valens	1963	5.00	10.00	20.00
❑ Guest Star GS-1484 [M]	The Original La Bamba	1963	7.50	15.00	30.00
❑ Guest Star GSS-1484 [R]	The Original La Bamba	1963	5.00	10.00	20.00
❑ MGM GAS-117	Ritchie Valens (Golden Archive Series)	1970	7.50	15.00	30.00
❑ Rhino RNDF-200	The Best of Ritchie Valens	1981	3.00	6.00	12.00
❑ Rhino RNBC-2798 [(3)]	The History of Ritchie Valens	198?	6.25	12.50	25.00
❑ Rhino RNLP-70178	The Best of Ritchie Valens (Golden Archive Series)	1987	2.50	5.00	10.00
❑ Rhino RNLP-70231	Ritchie Valens	1987	2.50	5.00	10.00
❑ Rhino RNLP-70232	Ritchie	1987	2.50	5.00	10.00
❑ Rhino RNLP-70233	In Concert at Pacoima Jr. High	1987	2.50	5.00	10.00

VALLI, FRANKIE

45s

Number	Title (A Side/B Side)	Yr	VG	VG+	NM
❑ Atlantic 89720	American Pop/Why	1983	—	2.00	4.00
—With Manhattan Transfer					
❑ Capitol B-5115	Can't Say No to You/You Make It Beautiful	1982	—	2.00	4.00
—With Cheryl Ladd					
❑ Cindy 3012	Come Si Bella/Real (This Is Real)	1958	50.00	100.00	200.00
—As "Franke Valli and the Romans"					
❑ Corona 1234	My Mother's Eyes/The Laugh's on Me	1953	500.00	1000.	1500.
—As "Frank Valley"					
❑ Decca 30994	It May Be Wrong/Please Take a Chance	1959	50.00	100.00	200.00
—As "Frankie Vally"					
❑ MCA 41253	Doctor Dance/Where Did We Go Wrong	1980	—	2.50	5.00
—With Chris Forde					
❑ Mercury 70381	Forgive and Forget/Somebody Else Took Her Home	1954	75.00	150.00	300.00
—As "Frankie Valley"; maroon label					
❑ Motown 1279	The Scalawag Song (And I Will Love You)/Listen to Yesterday	1973	3.00	6.00	12.00
❑ Mowest 5011	Love Isn't Here/Poor Fool	1972	3.00	6.00	12.00
❑ Okeh 7103	I Go Ape/If You Care	1958	75.00	150.00	300.00
—As "Frankie Tyler"					
❑ Philips 40407	The Proud One/Ivy	1966	2.50	5.00	10.00
❑ Philips 40446	Can't Take My Eyes Off You/The Trouble with Me	1967	2.50	5.00	10.00
❑ Philips 40484	I Make a Fool of Myself/September Rain (Here Comes the Rain)	1967	2.50	5.00	10.00
❑ Philips 40510	To Give (The Reason I Live)/Watch Where You Walk	1967	2.50	5.00	10.00
❑ Philips 40622	The Girl I'll Never Know (Angels Never Fly This Low)/A Face Without a Name	1969	2.50	5.00	10.00
❑ Philips 40661	You've Got Your Troubles/A Dream of Kings	1970	3.00	6.00	12.00
❑ Philips 40680	Circles in the Sand/My Mother's Eyes	1970	2.50	5.00	10.00
❑ Private Stock 45,003	My Eyes Adored You/Watch Where You Walk	1974	—	2.50	5.00
❑ Private Stock 45,021	Swearin' to God/Why	1975	—	2.50	5.00
❑ Private Stock 45,043	Our Day Will Come/You Can Bet	1975	—	2.50	5.00
❑ Private Stock 45,074	Fallen Angel/Carrie (I Would Marry You)	1976	—	2.50	5.00
❑ Private Stock 45,098	We're All Alone/You to Me Are Everything	1976	—	2.50	5.00
❑ Private Stock 45,109	Boomerang/Look at the World, It's Changing	1976	—	2.50	5.00
❑ Private Stock 45,140	Easily/What Good Am I Without You	1977	—	2.50	5.00
❑ Private Stock 45,154	Second Thoughts/So She Says	1977	—	2.50	5.00
❑ Private Stock 45,169	I Need You/I'm Gonna Love You	1977	—	2.50	5.00
❑ Private Stock 45,180	I Could Have Loved You/Rainstorm	1978	—	2.50	5.00
❑ RSO 897	Grease/Grease (Instrumental)	1978	—	3.00	6.00
❑ Smash 1995	The Sun Ain't Gonna Shine (Anymore)/This Is Goodbye	1965	2.50	5.00	10.00
❑ Smash 2015	(You're Gonna) Hurt Yourself/Night Hawk	1965	3.75	7.50	15.00
—B-side by the Valli Boys					
❑ Smash 2037	You're Ready Now/Cry for Me	1966	2.50	5.00	10.00
❑ Warner Bros. 8670	No Love at All/Save Me, Save Me	1978	—	2.50	5.00
❑ Warner Bros. 8734	Fancy Dancer/Needing You	1979	—	2.50	5.00

Albums

Number	Title (A Side/B Side)	Yr	VG	VG+	NM
❑ MCA 743	Heaven Above Me	1982	2.00	4.00	8.00
—Reissue of 5134					
❑ MCA 756	The Very Best of Frankie Valli	1982	2.00	4.00	8.00
—Reissue of 3198					

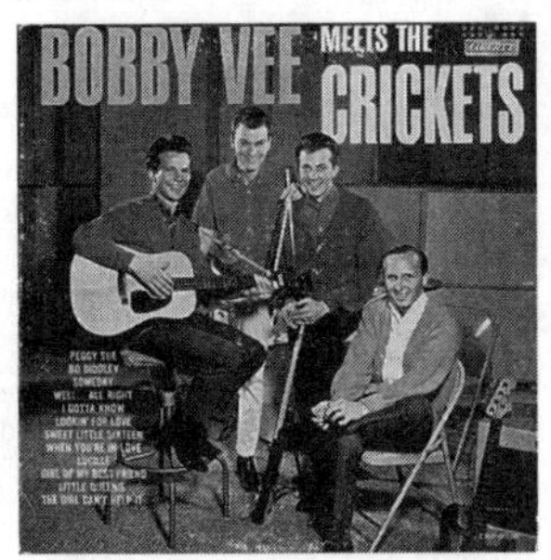

Number	Title (A Side/B Side)	Yr	VG	VG+	NM
❑ MCA 3198	The Very Best of Frankie Valli	1980	2.50	5.00	10.00
❑ MCA 5134	Heaven Above Me	1979	2.50	5.00	10.00
❑ Motown M5-104V1	Motown Superstar Series, Vol. 4	1981	2.50	5.00	10.00
❑ Motown M6-852	Inside You	1975	3.75	7.50	15.00
❑ Philips PHM 200247 [M]	Frankie Valli — Solo	1967	10.00	20.00	40.00
❑ Philips PHS 600247 [S]	Frankie Valli — Solo	1967	7.50	15.00	30.00
❑ Philips PHS 600274	Timeless	1968	6.25	12.50	25.00
❑ Private Stock PS-2000	Closeup	1975	3.00	6.00	12.00
❑ Private Stock PS-2001	Frankie Valli Gold	1975	3.00	6.00	12.00
❑ Private Stock PS-2006	Our Day Will Come	1975	3.00	6.00	12.00
❑ Private Stock PS-2017	Valli	1976	3.00	6.00	12.00
❑ Private Stock PS-7002	Lady Put the Light Out	1977	3.00	6.00	12.00
❑ Private Stock PS-7012	Hits	1978	3.00	6.00	12.00
❑ Warner Bros. BSK 3233	Frankie Valli…Is the Word	1978	2.50	5.00	10.00
VAN DYKE, EARL, AND THE SOUL BROTHERS					
45s					
❑ Renaissance 5000	September Song/(B-side unknown)	196?	18.75	37.50	75.00
❑ Soul 35006	Soul Stomp/Hot 'N' Tot	1964	5.00	10.00	20.00
❑ Soul 35009	All for You/Too Many Fish in the Sea	1965	200.00	400.00	800.00
❑ Soul 35014	I Can't Help Myself/How Sweet It Is To Be Loved By You	1965	5.00	10.00	20.00
❑ Soul 35018	The Flick (Part 1)/The Flick (Part 2)	1966	5.00	10.00	20.00
❑ Soul 35028	6 x 6/There Is No Greater Love	1967	5.00	10.00	20.00
—By Earl Van Dyke and the Motown Brass					
❑ Soul 35059	Runaway Child, Running Wild/Gonna Give Her All the Love I've Got	1969	5.00	10.00	20.00
Albums					
❑ Motown M-631 [M]	The Motown Sound	1965	10.00	20.00	40.00
❑ Motown MS-631 [S]	The Motown Sound	1965	12.50	25.00	50.00
❑ Soul SS-715	The Earl of Funk	1970	10.00	20.00	40.00
VAN HALEN					
45s					
❑ Warner Bros. 8515	You Really Got Me/Atomic Punk	1978	—	2.50	5.00
❑ Warner Bros. 8556	Runnin' with the Devil/Eruption	1978	2.50	5.00	10.00
❑ Warner Bros. 8631	Jamie's Cryin'/I'm the One	1978	2.50	5.00	10.00
❑ Warner Bros. 8707	Feel Your Love Tonight/Ain't Talkin' 'Bout Love	1978	2.50	5.00	10.00
❑ Warner Bros. 8823	Dance the Night Away/Outta Love Again	1979	—	2.00	4.00
❑ Warner Bros. 27565	Feels So Good/Sucker in a 3-Piece	1989	—	—	3.00
❑ Warner Bros. 27746	Finish What Ya Started/Sucker in a 3-Piece	1988	—	—	3.00
❑ Warner Bros. 27827	When It's Love/Cabo Wabo	1988	—	—	3.00
❑ Warner Bros. 27891	Black and Blue/Apolitical Blues	1988	—	—	3.00
❑ Warner Bros. 28505	Best of Both Worlds/Best of Both Worlds (Live)	1986	—	—	3.00
❑ Warner Bros. 28626	Love Walks In/Summer Nights	1986	—	—	3.00
❑ Warner Bros. 28702	Dreams/Inside	1986	—	—	3.00
❑ Warner Bros. 28740	Why Can't This Be Love/Get Up	1986	—	—	3.00
❑ Warner Bros. 29199	Hot for Teacher/Little Dreamer	1984	—	—	3.00
❑ Warner Bros. 29250	Panama/Drop Dead Legs	1984	—	—	3.00
❑ Warner Bros. 29307	I'll Wait/Girl Gone Bad	1984	—	—	3.00
❑ Warner Bros. 29384	Jump/House of Pain	1984	—	—	3.00
❑ Warner Bros. 29929	Secrets/Big Bad Bill	1982	—	2.50	5.00
❑ Warner Bros. 29986	Dancing in the Street/Full Bug	1982	—	2.00	4.00
❑ Warner Bros. 49035	Beautiful Girls/D.O.A.	1979	—	2.50	5.00
❑ Warner Bros. 49501	And the Cradle Will Rock.../Could This Be Magic	1980	—	2.50	5.00
❑ Warner Bros. 49751	So This Is Love/Read About It Later	1981	—	2.50	5.00
❑ Warner Bros. 50003	Pretty Woman/Happy Trails	1982	—	2.50	5.00
❑ Warner Bros. 50003	(Oh) Pretty Woman/Happy Trails	1982	—	2.00	4.00
Albums					
❑ Warner Bros. BSK 3075	Van Halen	1978	3.00	6.00	12.00
—Early pressings have "Burbank" labels					
❑ Warner Bros. HS 3312	Van Halen II	1979	2.50	5.00	10.00
❑ Warner Bros. HS 3415	Women and Children First	1980	2.50	5.00	10.00
❑ Warner Bros. HS 3540	Fair Warning	1981	2.50	5.00	10.00
❑ Warner Bros. BSK 3677	Diver Down	1982	2.50	5.00	10.00
❑ Warner Bros. 23985	1984	1984	2.50	5.00	10.00
❑ Warner Bros. 25394	5150	1986	2.50	5.00	10.00
❑ Warner Bros. 25732	OU812	1988	2.50	5.00	10.00
VANILLA FUDGE					
45s					
❑ Atco 6495	You Keep Me Hangin' On/Take Me for a Little While	1967	3.00	6.00	12.00

Number	Title (A Side/B Side)	Yr	VG	VG+	NM
❑ Atco 6554	The Look of Love/Where Is My Mind	1968	2.00	4.00	8.00
❑ Atco 6590	You Keep Me Hangin' On/Come by Day, Come by Night	1968	2.50	5.00	10.00
❑ Atco 6616	Take Me for a Little While/Thoughts	1968	2.00	4.00	8.00
❑ Atco 6632	Season of the Witch (Part 1)/Season of the Witch (Part 2)	1968	2.00	4.00	8.00
❑ Atco 6655	Good Good Lovin'/Shot Gun	1969	2.00	4.00	8.00
❑ Atco 6679	People/Some Velvet Morning	1969	2.00	4.00	8.00
❑ Atco 6703	Need Love/I Can't Make It Alone	1969	2.00	4.00	8.00
❑ Atco 6728	Windmills of Your Mind/Lord in the Country	1970	—	3.00	6.00
❑ Atco 99729	Mystery/The Stranger	1984	—	2.00	4.00
Albums					
❑ Atco 33-224 [M]	Vanilla Fudge	1967	6.25	12.50	25.00
❑ Atco SD 33-224 [S]	Vanilla Fudge	1967	5.00	10.00	20.00
—Purple and brown label					
❑ Atco 33-237 [M]	The Beat Goes On	1968	10.00	20.00	40.00
❑ Atco SD 33-237	The Beat Goes On	1968	5.00	10.00	20.00
—Purple and brown label					
❑ Atco SD 33-244	Renaissance	1968	5.00	10.00	20.00
—Purple and brown label					
❑ Atco SD 33-278	Near the Beginning	1969	3.75	7.50	15.00
❑ Atco SD 33-303	Rock 'N' Roll	1969	3.75	7.50	15.00
❑ Atco 90006	The Best of Vanilla Fudge	1982	2.50	5.00	10.00
❑ Atco 90149	Mystery	1984	3.00	6.00	12.00
VANNELLI, GINO					
45s					
❑ A&M 1449	Granny Goodbye/Hollywood Holiday	1973	—	2.50	5.00
❑ A&M 1467	Crazy Life/There's No Time	1973	—	2.50	5.00
❑ A&M 1614	People Gotta Move/Son of a New York Gun	1974	—	2.00	4.00
❑ A&M 1652	Powerful People/Lady	1974	—	2.00	4.00
❑ A&M 1732	Father and Son/Love Me Now	1975	—	2.00	4.00
❑ A&M 1760	Gettin' High/Mama Coco	1975	—	2.00	4.00
❑ A&M 1790	Keep On Walking/Love Is a Night	1976	—	2.00	4.00
❑ A&M 1861	Love of My Life/Omens of Love	1976	—	2.00	4.00
❑ A&M 1879	Summers of My Life/Omens of Love	1976	—	2.00	4.00
❑ A&M 1911	Fly Into This Night/Ugly Man	1977	—	2.00	4.00
❑ A&M 2002	Feel the Fire (Valleys of Valhalla)/Black and Blue	1977	—	2.00	4.00
❑ A&M 2025	One Night with You/Black and Blue	1978	—	2.00	4.00
❑ A&M 2072	I Just Wanna Stop/The Surest Things Can Change	1978	—	2.00	4.00
❑ A&M 2114	Wheels of Life/Mardi Gras	1979	—	2.00	4.00
❑ A&M 2133	The River Must Flow/Mardi Gras	1979	—	2.00	4.00
❑ Arista 0588	Living Inside Myself/Stay with Me	1981	—	—	3.00
❑ Arista 0613	Nightwalker/Sally She Says the Sweetest Things	1981	—	—	3.00
❑ Arista 0664	The Longer You Wait/Bandito	1982	—	—	3.00
❑ CBS Associated 05586	Hurts to Be in Love/Here She Comes	1985	—	—	3.00
❑ CBS Associated 06663	In the Name of Money/Shape Me Like a Man	1987	—	—	3.00
❑ CBS Associated 06699	Wild Horses/Shape Me Like a Man	1987	—	—	3.00
❑ HME 04889	Black Cars/Imagination	1985	—	—	3.00
Albums					
❑ A&M SP-3112	The Gist of the Gemini	1981	2.00	4.00	8.00
—Reissue of 4596					
❑ A&M SP-3120	Powerful People	1981	2.00	4.00	8.00
—Reissue of 3630					
❑ A&M SP-3139	Crazy Life	1981	2.00	4.00	8.00
—Reissue of 4395					
❑ A&M SP-3170	Brother to Brother	1981	2.00	4.00	8.00
—Reissue of 4722					
❑ A&M SP-3260	The Best of Gino Vannelli	1982	2.00	4.00	8.00
—Reissue of 3729					
❑ A&M SP-3630	Powerful People	1974	2.50	5.00	10.00
❑ A&M SP-3729	The Best of Gino Vannelli	1981	2.50	5.00	10.00
❑ A&M SP-4395	Crazy Life	1973	3.00	6.00	12.00
❑ A&M SP-4533	Storm at Sunup	1975	2.50	5.00	10.00
❑ A&M SP-4596	The Gist of the Gemini	1976	2.50	5.00	10.00
❑ A&M SP-4664	A Pauper in Paradise	1977	2.50	5.00	10.00
❑ A&M SP-4722	Brother to Brother	1978	2.50	5.00	10.00
❑ Arista AB 9539	Nightwalker	1981	2.50	5.00	10.00
❑ CBS Associated BFZ 40337	Big Dreamers Never Sleep	1987	2.50	5.00	10.00
❑ HME FZ 40077	Black Cars	1985	2.50	5.00	10.00
VEE, BOBBY					
45s					
❑ Cognito 010	Tremble On/Always Be Each Other's Best Friend	1981	—	2.50	5.00
❑ Liberty 54510	Devil or Angel/Rubber Ball	196?	—	3.00	6.00
❑ Liberty 54511	More Than I Can Say/Stayin' In	196?	—	3.00	6.00
❑ Liberty 54523	Take Good Care of My Baby/Please Don't Ask About Barbara	196?	—	3.00	6.00
❑ Liberty 54524	Run to Him/Sharing You	196?	—	3.00	6.00
❑ Liberty 54536	The Night Has a Thousand Eyes/Charms	196?	—	3.00	6.00
❑ Liberty 54559	Come Back When You Grow Up/Beautiful People	196?	—	3.00	6.00
—Records in the 54500s are from a reissue series					
❑ Liberty 55208	Suzie Baby/Flyin' High	1959	6.25	12.50	25.00
❑ Liberty 55234	What Do You Want/My Love Loves Me	1959	5.00	10.00	20.00
❑ Liberty 55251	Laurie/One Last Kiss	1960	3.75	7.50	15.00
❑ Liberty 55270	Devil or Angel/Since I Met You Baby	1960	5.00	10.00	20.00
❑ Liberty 55287	Rubber Ball/Everyday	1960	5.00	10.00	20.00
❑ Liberty 55296	More Than I Can Say/Stayin' In	1961	3.75	7.50	15.00
❑ Liberty 55325	How Many Tears/Baby Face	1961	3.75	7.50	15.00
❑ Liberty 55354	Take Good Care of My Baby/Bashful Bob	1961	3.75	7.50	15.00

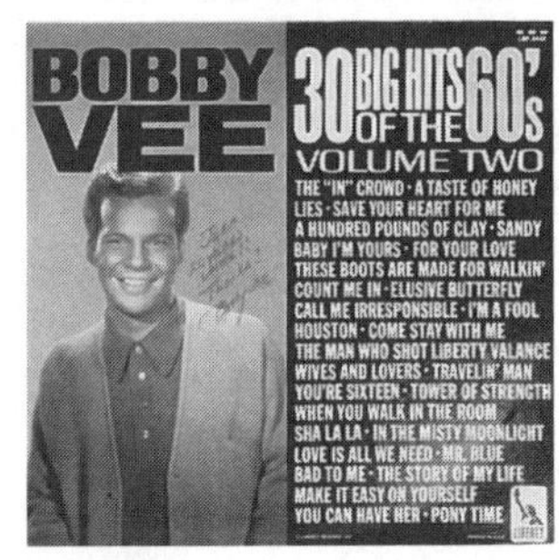

Number	Title (A Side/B Side)	Yr	VG	VG+	NM
❑ Liberty 55388	Run to Him/Walkin' with My Angel	1961	5.00	10.00	20.00
❑ Liberty 55419	Please Don't Ask About Barbara/I Can't Say Goodbye	1962	3.75	7.50	15.00
❑ Liberty 55451	Sharing You/In My Baby's Eyes	1962	3.75	7.50	15.00
❑ Liberty 55479	Punish Her/Someday (When I'm Gone from You)	1962	5.00	10.00	20.00
❑ Liberty 55517	A Not-So-Merry Christmas/Christmas Vacation	1962	7.50	15.00	30.00
—This record's existence has been questioned					
❑ Liberty 55521	The Night Has a Thousand Eyes/Anonymous Phone Call	1962	3.00	6.00	12.00
❑ Liberty 55530	Charms/Bobby Tomorrow	1963	3.00	6.00	12.00
❑ Liberty 55581	Be True to Yourself/A Letter from Betty	1963	2.50	5.00	10.00
❑ Liberty 55636	Yesterday and You (Armen's Theme)/Never Love a Robin	1963	2.50	5.00	10.00
❑ Liberty 55654	Stranger in Your Arms/1963	1963	2.50	5.00	10.00
❑ Liberty 55670	I'll Make You Mine/She's Sorry	1964	2.50	5.00	10.00
❑ Liberty 55700	Hickory, Dick and Doc/I Wish You Were Mine Again	1964	2.50	5.00	10.00
❑ Liberty 55726	Where Is She/How to Make a Farewell	1964	2.50	5.00	10.00
❑ Liberty 55751	(There'll Come a Day When) Ev'ry Little Bit Hurts/ Pretend You Don't See Her	1964	2.50	5.00	10.00
❑ Liberty 55761	Cross My Heart/This Is the End	1965	2.00	4.00	8.00
❑ Liberty 55790	Keep On Trying/You Won't Forget Me	1965	2.00	4.00	8.00
❑ Liberty 55828	Run Like the Devil/Take a Look Around Us	1965	2.00	4.00	8.00
❑ Liberty 55843	The Story of My Life/High Coin	1965	2.00	4.00	8.00
❑ Liberty 55854	A Girl I Used to Know/Gone	1965	2.00	4.00	8.00
❑ Liberty 55877	Look at Me Girl/Save a Love	1966	2.00	4.00	8.00
❑ Liberty 55921	Before You Go/Here Today	1966	2.00	4.00	8.00
❑ Liberty 55964	Come Back When You Grow Up/Swahili Serenade	1967	2.00	4.00	8.00
❑ Liberty 55964	Come Back When You Grow Up/That's All There Is to That	1967	2.00	4.00	8.00
❑ Liberty S-55964 [S]	Come Back When You Grow Up/Swahili Serenade	1967	5.00	10.00	20.00
—Small hole, plays at 33 1/3 rpm; promo "Audition Record" only					
❑ Liberty 56009	Beautiful People/I May Be Gone	1967	2.00	4.00	8.00
❑ Liberty 56014	Maybe Just Today/You're a Big Girl Now	1968	—	3.00	6.00
❑ Liberty 56033	Medley: My Girl-Hey Girl/Just Keep It Up	1968	—	3.00	6.00
❑ Liberty 56057	Do What You Gotta Do/Thank You	1968	—	3.00	6.00
❑ Liberty 56080	I'm Into Lookin' for Someone to Love Me/Thank You	1968	—	3.00	6.00
❑ Liberty 56096	Jenny Come to Me/Santa Cruz	1969	—	3.00	6.00
❑ Liberty 56124	Let's Call It a Day Girl/I'm Gonna Make It Up to You	1969	—	3.00	6.00
❑ Liberty 56149	Electric Trains and You/In and Out of Love	1969	—	3.00	6.00
❑ Liberty 56178	The Woman in My Life/No Obligations	1970	—	3.00	6.00
❑ Liberty 56208	Sweet Sweetheart/Rock and Roll Music and You	1970	—	3.00	6.00
❑ Shady Brook 45013	Saying Goodbye/(I'm) Lovin' You	1975	—	2.50	5.00
❑ Shady Brook 45026	You're Never Gonna Find Someone Like Me (Long Version)/ You're Never Gonna Find Someone Like Me (Short Version)	1976	—	2.50	5.00
❑ Shady Brook 45030	It's Good to Be Here/If I Needed You	1976	—	2.50	5.00
❑ Soma 1110	Suzie Baby/Flyin' High	1959	15.00	30.00	60.00
❑ United Artists 0020	Devil or Angel/Stayin' In	1973	—	2.00	4.00
❑ United Artists 0021	Rubber Ball/Punish Her	1973	—	2.00	4.00
❑ United Artists 0022	Take Good Care of My Baby/Please Don't Ask About Barbara	1973	—	2.00	4.00
❑ United Artists 0023	Run to Him/Sharing You	1973	—	2.00	4.00
❑ United Artists 0024	The Night Has a Thousand Eyes/Charms	1973	—	2.00	4.00
❑ United Artists 0025	Come Back When You Grow Up/Beautiful People	1973	—	2.00	4.00
—0020 through 0025 are "Silver Spotlight Series" reissues					
❑ United Artists XW199	Take Good Care of My Baby/Every Opportunity	1973	—	2.50	5.00
—As "Robert Thomas Velline"					
❑ United Artists XW1142	Well All Right/Something Has Come Between Us	1978	—	2.50	5.00
❑ United Artists 50755	Signs/Something to Say	1971	—	2.50	5.00
❑ United Artists 50875	Sweet Sweetheart/Electric Trains and You	1972	—	2.50	5.00
Albums					
❑ Liberty LRP-3165 [M]	Bobby Vee Sings Your Favorites	1960	12.50	25.00	50.00
❑ Liberty LRP-3181 [M]	Bobby Vee	1961	10.00	20.00	40.00
❑ Liberty LRP-3186 [M]	Bobby Vee With Strings and Things	1961	10.00	20.00	40.00
❑ Liberty LRP-3205 [M]	Bobby Vee Sings Hits of the Rockin' 50's	1961	10.00	20.00	40.00
❑ Liberty LRP-3211 [M]	Take Good Care of My Baby	1962	7.50	15.00	30.00
❑ Liberty LRP-3228 [M]	Bobby Vee Meets the Crickets	1962	10.00	20.00	40.00
❑ Liberty LRP-3232 [M]	A Bobby Vee Recording Session	1962	7.50	15.00	30.00
❑ Liberty LRP-3245 [M]	Bobby Vee's Golden Greats	1962	7.50	15.00	30.00
❑ Liberty LRP-3267 [M]	Merry Christmas from Bobby Vee	1962	7.50	15.00	30.00
❑ Liberty LRP-3285 [M]	The Night Has a Thousand Eyes	1963	7.50	15.00	30.00
❑ Liberty LRP-3289 [M]	Bobby Vee Meets the Ventures	1963	10.00	20.00	40.00
❑ Liberty LRP-3336 [M]	I Remember Buddy Holly	1963	10.00	20.00	40.00

Number	Title (A Side/B Side)	Yr	VG	VG+	NM
❑ Liberty LRP-3352 [M]	Bobby Vee Sings the New Sound from England!	1964	6.25	12.50	25.00
❑ Liberty LRP-3385 [M]	30 Big Hits From the 60's	1964	6.25	12.50	25.00
❑ Liberty LRP-3393 [M]	Bobby Vee Live on Tour	1965	6.25	12.50	25.00
❑ Liberty LRP-3448 [M]	30 Big Hits From the 60's, Volume 2	1966	6.25	12.50	25.00
❑ Liberty LRP-3464 [M]	Bobby Vee's Golden Greats, Volume 2	1966	5.00	10.00	20.00
❑ Liberty LRP-3480 [M]	Look at Me Girl	1966	5.00	10.00	20.00
❑ Liberty LRP-3534 [M]	Come Back When You Grow Up	1967	5.00	10.00	20.00
❑ Liberty LST-7165 [S]	Bobby Vee Sings Your Favorites	1960	20.00	40.00	80.00
❑ Liberty LST-7181 [S]	Bobby Vee	1961	12.50	25.00	50.00
❑ Liberty LST-7186 [S]	Bobby Vee With Strings and Things	1961	12.50	25.00	50.00
❑ Liberty LST-7205 [S]	Bobby Vee Sings Hits of the Rockin' 50's	1961	12.50	25.00	50.00
❑ Liberty LST-7211 [S]	Take Good Care of My Baby	1962	10.00	20.00	40.00
❑ Liberty LST-7228 [S]	Bobby Vee Meets the Crickets	1962	12.50	25.00	50.00
❑ Liberty LST-7232 [S]	A Bobby Vee Recording Session	1962	10.00	20.00	40.00
❑ Liberty LST-7245 [S]	Bobby Vee's Golden Greats	1962	10.00	20.00	40.00
❑ Liberty LST-7267 [S]	Merry Christmas from Bobby Vee	1962	10.00	20.00	40.00
❑ Liberty LST-7285 [S]	The Night Has a Thousand Eyes	1963	10.00	20.00	40.00
❑ Liberty LST-7289 [S]	Bobby Vee Meets the Ventures	1963	12.50	25.00	50.00
❑ Liberty LST-7336 [S]	I Remember Buddy Holly	1963	12.50	25.00	50.00
❑ Liberty LST-7352 [S]	Bobby Vee Sings the New Sound from England!	1964	7.50	15.00	30.00
❑ Liberty LST-7385 [S]	30 Big Hits From the 60's	1964	7.50	15.00	30.00
❑ Liberty LST-7393 [S]	Bobby Vee Live on Tour	1965	7.50	15.00	30.00
❑ Liberty LST-7448 [S]	30 Big Hits From the 60's, Volume 2	1966	7.50	15.00	30.00
❑ Liberty LST-7464 [S]	Bobby Vee's Golden Greats, Volume 2	1966	6.25	12.50	25.00
❑ Liberty LST-7480 [S]	Look at Me Girl	1966	6.25	12.50	25.00
❑ Liberty LST-7534 [S]	Come Back When You Grow Up	1967	6.25	12.50	25.00
❑ Liberty LST-7554 [S]	Just Today	1968	6.25	12.50	25.00
❑ Liberty LST-7592	Do What You Gotta Do	1968	7.50	15.00	30.00
❑ Liberty LST-7612	Gates, Grills and Railings	1969	7.50	15.00	30.00
❑ Liberty LN-10223	I Remember Buddy Holly	198?	2.00	4.00	8.00
❑ Liberty LM-51008	Bobby Vee's Golden Greats	198?	2.00	4.00	8.00
❑ Sunset SUM-1111 [M]	Bobby Vee	1966	2.50	5.00	10.00
❑ Sunset SUM-1162 [M]	A Forever Kind of Love	1967	2.50	5.00	10.00
❑ Sunset SUM-1186 [M]	The Christmas Album	1967	3.00	6.00	12.00
—Reissue of Liberty album with two fewer tracks					
❑ Sunset SUS-5111 [S]	Bobby Vee	1966	3.00	6.00	12.00
❑ Sunset SUS-5162 [S]	A Forever Kind of Love	1967	3.00	6.00	12.00
❑ Sunset SUS-5186 [S]	The Christmas Album	1967	3.00	6.00	12.00
❑ United Artists UA-LA025-G2 [(2)]	Legendary Masters Series	1973	75.00	150.00	300.00
—Withdrawn before release, but a few copies survived					
❑ United Artists UA-LA085-G	Robert Thomas Velline	1973	5.00	10.00	20.00
❑ United Artists UA-LA332-E	The Very Best of Bobby Vee	1975	3.00	6.00	12.00
❑ United Artists LT-1008	Bobby Vee's Golden Greats	1980	2.50	5.00	10.00
❑ United Artists UAS-5656	Nothin' Like a Sunny Day	1972	3.00	6.00	12.00

VELVELETTES, THE

45s

Number	Title (A Side/B Side)	Yr	VG	VG+	NM
❑ I.P.G. 1002	There He Goes/That's the Reason Why	1963	25.00	50.00	100.00
❑ Soul 35025	These Things Will Keep Me Loving You/Since You've Been Loving Me	1966	5.00	10.00	20.00
❑ V.I.P. 25007	Needle in a Haystack/Should I Tell Them	1964	6.25	12.50	25.00
❑ V.I.P. 25013	He Was Realy Sayin' Somethin'/Throw a Farewell Kiss	1965	6.25	12.50	25.00
❑ V.I.P. 25017	I'm the Exception to the Rule/Lonely, Lonely Girl Am I	1965	5.00	10.00	20.00
❑ V.I.P. 25021	A Bird in the Hand (Is Worth Two in the Bush)/(B-side unknown)	1965	200.00	400.00	800.00
❑ V.I.P. 25030	A Bird in the Hand (Is Worth Two in the Bush)/ Since You've Been Loving Me	1965	5.00	10.00	20.00
❑ V.I.P. 25034	These Things Will Keep Me Loving You/Since You've Been Loving Me	1966	7.50	15.00	30.00

VENTURES, THE

45s

Number	Title (A Side/B Side)	Yr	VG	VG+	NM
❑ Blue Horizon 100	The Real McCoy/Cookies and Coke	1960	150.00	300.00	600.00
❑ Blue Horizon 101	Walk-Don't Run/Home	1960	625.00	1250.	2500.
❑ Blue Horizon 102	Hold Me, Thrill Me, Kiss Me/No Next Time	1960	50.00	100.00	200.00
—As "Scott Douglas and the Venture Quintet"					
❑ Dolton 25	Walk — Don't Run/Home	1960	6.25	12.50	25.00
❑ Dolton 25X	Walk — Don't Run/The McCoy	1960	5.00	10.00	20.00
❑ Dolton 28	Perfidia/No Trespassing	1960	5.00	10.00	20.00
❑ Dolton 32	Ram-Bunk-Shush/Lonely Heart	1961	5.00	10.00	20.00
❑ Dolton 41	Lullaby of the Leaves/Ginchy	1961	5.00	10.00	20.00
❑ Dolton 44	(Theme from) Silver City/Bluer Than Blue	1961	5.00	10.00	20.00
❑ Dolton 47	Blue Moon/Lady of Spain	1961	5.00	10.00	20.00
❑ Dolton 50	Yellow Jacket/Genesis	1962	5.00	10.00	20.00
❑ Dolton 55	Instant Mashed/My Bonnie	1962	5.00	10.00	20.00
❑ Dolton 60	Lolita Ya-Ya/Lucille	1962	5.00	10.00	20.00
❑ Dolton 67	The 2,000 Pound Bee (Part 1)/The 2,000 Pound Bee (Part 2)	1962	5.00	10.00	20.00
❑ Dolton 68	El Cumbanchero/Skip To M'Limbo	1963	3.75	7.50	15.00
❑ Dolton 78	The Ninth Wave/Damaged Goods	1963	3.75	7.50	15.00
❑ Dolton 85	The Savage/The Chase	1963	3.75	7.50	15.00
❑ Dolton 91	Journey to the Stars/Walkin' with Pluto	1964	3.75	7.50	15.00
❑ Dolton 94	Fugitive/Scratchin'	1964	3.75	7.50	15.00
❑ Dolton 96	Walk... Don't Run '64/The Cruel Sea	1964	3.75	7.50	15.00
❑ Dolton 300	Slaughter on Tenth Avenue/Rap City	1964	3.00	6.00	12.00
❑ Dolton 303	Diamond Head/Lonely Girl	1965	3.00	6.00	12.00
❑ Dolton 306	Pedal Pusher/The Swingin' Creeper	1965	3.00	6.00	12.00
❑ Dolton 308	Ten Seconds to Heaven/Bird Rockers	1965	3.00	6.00	12.00
❑ Dolton 311	La Bomba/Gemini	1965	3.00	6.00	12.00

Number	Title (A Side/B Side)	Yr	VG	VG+	NM
❑ Dolton 312	Sleigh Ride/Snow Flakes	1965	3.75	7.50	15.00
❑ Dolton 316	Secret Agent Man/00-711	1966	3.00	6.00	12.00
❑ Dolton 320	Blue Star/Comin' Home Baby	1966	3.00	6.00	12.00
❑ Dolton 321	Arabesque/Ginza Lights	1966	3.00	6.00	12.00
❑ Dolton 323	Green Hornet Theme/Fuzzy and Wild	1966	3.00	6.00	12.00
❑ Dolton 325	Penetration/Wild Thing	1966	3.00	6.00	12.00
❑ Dolton 327	Theme from "The Wild Angels"/Kickstand	1967	3.00	6.00	12.00
❑ Liberty 54518	Walk — Don't Run/Ram-Bunk-Shush	196?	—	3.00	6.00
❑ Liberty 54519	Perfidia/Blue Moon	196?	—	3.00	6.00
❑ Liberty 54557	Wipe Out/Secret Agent Man	196?	—	3.50	7.00
—Records in the 54500s are from a reissue series					
❑ Liberty 55967	Strawberry Fields Forever/Endless Dream	1967	2.00	4.00	8.00
❑ Liberty 55977	Theme from "Endless Summer"/Strawberry Fields Forever	1967	2.00	4.00	8.00
❑ Liberty 56007	On the Road/Mirrors and Shadows	1967	2.00	4.00	8.00
❑ Liberty 56019	Flights of Fantasy/Vibrations	1968	—	3.00	6.00
❑ Liberty 56044	Walk Don't Run-Land of 1000 Dances/Too Young to Know My Mind	1968	—	3.00	6.00
❑ Liberty 56068	Hawaii Five-O/Soul Breeze	1968	2.00	4.00	8.00
❑ Liberty 56115	Theme from A Summer Place/A Summer Love	1969	—	3.00	6.00
❑ Liberty 56153	Expo Seven-O/Swan Lake	1970	—	3.00	6.00
❑ Liberty 56169	The Wanderer/The Mercenary	1970	—	3.00	6.00
❑ Liberty 56189	Storefront Lawyers (Theme)/Kern County Line	1970	—	3.00	6.00
❑ Tridex 501	Surfin' and Spyin'/Rumble at Newport	1981	—	2.50	5.00
—A-side with Charlotte Caffey and Jane Wiedlin of the Go-Go's, who did their own version on an early single					
❑ United Artists 0050	Walk—Don't Run/Ram-Bunk-Shush	1973	—	2.00	4.00
—0050, 0051 and 0052 are "Silver Spotlight Series" reissues					
❑ United Artists 0051	Perfidia/Telstar	1973	—	2.00	4.00
❑ United Artists 0052	Hawaii Five-O/Walk—Don't Run '64	1973	—	2.00	4.00
❑ United Artists XW207	Last Tango in Paris/Prima Vera	1973	—	3.00	6.00
❑ United Artists XW277	Skylab/The Little People	1973	—	3.00	6.00
❑ United Artists XW333	Also Sprach Zarathustra (2001)/The Cisco Kid	1973	—	3.00	6.00
❑ United Artists XW369	Main Theme from The Young and the Restless/Eloise	1973	—	3.00	6.00
❑ United Artists XW392	Main Theme from The Young and the Restless/Eloise	1974	—	3.00	6.00
❑ United Artists XW578	Theme from "Airport 1975"/The Man with the Golden Gun	1974	—	3.00	6.00
❑ United Artists XW687	Superstar Revue (Part 1)/Superstar Revue (Part 2)	1975	—	3.00	6.00
❑ United Artists XW784	Moonlight Serenade (Part 1)/Moonlight Serenade (Part 2)	1976	2.00	4.00	8.00
—As "The New Ventures"					
❑ United Artists XW942	Theme from "Charlie's Angels"/Theme from "Starsky and Hutch"	1977	2.00	4.00	8.00
❑ United Artists XW1100	Walk Don't Run '77/Amanda's Theme	1977	—	3.00	6.00
❑ United Artists XW1161	Wipe Out/Nadia's Theme	1978	—	2.00	4.00
—Reissue					
❑ United Artists 50800	Indian Sun/Squaw Man	1971	—	3.00	6.00
❑ United Artists 50851	Theme from "Shaft"/Tight Fit	1971	—	3.00	6.00
❑ United Artists 50872	Joy/Cherries Jubilee	1972	—	3.00	6.00
❑ United Artists 50903	Beethoven's Sonata in C# Minor/Peter and the Wolf	1972	—	3.00	6.00
❑ United Artists 50925	Honky Tonk (Part 1)/Honky Tonk (Part 2)	1972	—	3.00	6.00
❑ United Artists 50989	Last Night/Ram-Bunk-Shush	1972	—	3.00	6.00
Albums					
❑ Compleat 672013-1	The Best of the Ventures	1986	2.50	5.00	10.00
❑ Dolton BLP 2003 [M]	Walk Don't Run	1960	12.50	25.00	50.00
—Pale blue label with dolphins on top					
❑ Dolton BLP 2004 [M]	The Ventures	1961	12.50	25.00	50.00
—Pale blue label with dolphins on top					
❑ Dolton BLP 2006 [M]	Another Smash!!!	1961	12.50	25.00	50.00
—Pale blue label with dolphins on top					
❑ Dolton BLP 2008 [M]	The Colorful Ventures	1961	12.50	25.00	50.00
—Pale blue label with dolphins on top					
❑ Dolton BLP 2010 [M]	Twist with the Ventures	1962	12.50	25.00	50.00
—Pale blue label with dolphins on top					
❑ Dolton BLP 2014 [M]	The Ventures' Twist Party, Vol. 2	1962	12.50	25.00	50.00
—Pale blue label with dolphins on top					
❑ Dolton BLP 2016 [M]	Mashed Potatoes and Gravy	1962	7.50	15.00	30.00
❑ Dolton BLP 2017 [M]	Going to the Ventures Dance Party!	1962	7.50	15.00	30.00
❑ Dolton BLP 2019 [M]	The Ventures Play Telstar, The Lonely Bull	1962	7.50	15.00	30.00
❑ Dolton BLP 2022 [M]	Surfing	1963	6.25	12.50	25.00
❑ Dolton BLP 2023 [M]	The Ventures Play the Country Classics	1963	6.25	12.50	25.00
❑ Dolton BLP 2024 [M]	Let's Go!	1963	6.25	12.50	25.00
❑ Dolton BLP 2027 [M]	(The) Ventures in Space	1964	10.00	20.00	40.00
❑ Dolton BLP 2029 [M]	The Fabulous Ventures	1964	6.25	12.50	25.00

Number	Title (A Side/B Side)	Yr	VG	VG+	NM
❑ Dolton BLP 2031 [M]	Walk, Don't Run, Vol. 2	1964	6.25	12.50	25.00
❑ Dolton BLP 2033 [M]	The Ventures Knock Me Out!	1965	6.25	12.50	25.00
❑ Dolton BLP 2035 [M]	The Ventures on Stage	1965	6.25	12.50	25.00
❑ Dolton BLP 2037 [M]	The Ventures A-Go-Go	1965	6.25	12.50	25.00
❑ Dolton BLP-2038 [M]	The Ventures' Christmas Album	1965	7.50	15.00	30.00
❑ Dolton BLP 2040 [M]	Where the Action Is	1966	5.00	10.00	20.00
❑ Dolton BLP 2042 [M]	The Ventures/Batman Theme	1966	7.50	15.00	30.00
❑ Dolton BLP 2045 [M]	Go with the Ventures!	1966	5.00	10.00	20.00
❑ Dolton BLP 2047 [M]	Wild Things!	1966	5.00	10.00	20.00
❑ Dolton BLP 2050 [M]	Guitar Freakout	1967	5.00	10.00	20.00
❑ Dolton BST 8003 [S]	Walk Don't Run	1960	15.00	30.00	60.00
—Pale blue label with dolphins on top					
❑ Dolton BST 8004 [S]	The Ventures	1961	15.00	30.00	60.00
—Pale blue label with dolphins on top					
❑ Dolton BST 8006 [S]	Another Smash!!!	1961	15.00	30.00	60.00
—Pale blue label with dolphins on top					
❑ Dolton BST 8008 [S]	The Colorful Ventures	1961	15.00	30.00	60.00
—Pale blue label with dolphins on top					
❑ Dolton BST 8010 [S]	Twist with the Ventures	1962	15.00	30.00	60.00
—Pale blue label with dolphins on top					
❑ Dolton BST 8014 [S]	The Ventures' Twist Party, Vol. 2	1962	15.00	30.00	60.00
—Pale blue label with dolphins on top					
❑ Dolton BST 8016 [S]	Mashed Potatoes and Gravy	1962	10.00	20.00	40.00
❑ Dolton BST 8017 [S]	Going to the Ventures Dance Party!	1962	10.00	20.00	40.00
❑ Dolton BST 8019 [S]	The Ventures Play Telstar, The Lonely Bull	1962	10.00	20.00	40.00
❑ Dolton BST 8022 [S]	Surfing	1963	7.50	15.00	30.00
❑ Dolton BST 8023 [S]	The Ventures Play the Country Classics	1963	7.50	15.00	30.00
❑ Dolton BST 8024 [S]	Let's Go!	1963	7.50	15.00	30.00
❑ Dolton BST 8027 [S]	(The) Ventures in Space	1964	12.50	25.00	50.00
❑ Dolton BST 8029 [S]	The Fabulous Ventures	1964	7.50	15.00	30.00
❑ Dolton BST 8031 [S]	Walk, Don't Run, Vol. 2	1964	7.50	15.00	30.00
❑ Dolton BST 8033 [S]	The Ventures Knock Me Out!	1965	7.50	15.00	30.00
❑ Dolton BST 8035 [S]	The Ventures on Stage	1965	7.50	15.00	30.00
❑ Dolton BST 8037 [S]	The Ventures A-Go-Go	1965	7.50	15.00	30.00
❑ Dolton BST-8038 [S]	The Ventures' Christmas Album	1965	5.00	10.00	20.00
❑ Dolton BST 8040 [S]	Where the Action Is	1966	6.25	2.50	25.00
❑ Dolton BST 8042 [S]	The Ventures/Batman Theme	1966	10.00	20.00	40.00
❑ Dolton BST 8045 [S]	Go with the Ventures!	1966	6.25	12.50	25.00
❑ Dolton BST 8047 [S]	Wild Things!	1966	6.25	12.50	25.00
❑ Dolton BST 8050 [S]	Guitar Freakout	1967	6.25	12.50	25.00
❑ Dolton BLP 16501 [M]	Play Guitar with the Ventures	1965	6.25	12.50	25.00
❑ Dolton BLP 16502 [M]	Play Guitar with the Ventures, Vol. 2	196?	6.25	12.50	25.00
❑ Dolton BLP 16503 [M]	Play Guitar with the Ventures, Vol. 3	196?	6.25	12.50	25.00
❑ Dolton BLP 16504 [M]	Play Guitar with the Ventures, Vol. 4	196?	6.25	12.50	25.00
❑ Dolton BST 16504 [S]	Play Guitar with the Ventures, Vol. 4	196?	7.50	15.00	30.00
❑ Dolton BST 17501 [S]	Play Guitar with the Ventures	1965	7.50	15.00	30.00
❑ Dolton BST 17502 [S]	Play Guitar with the Ventures, Vol. 2	196?	7.50	15.00	30.00
❑ Dolton BST 17503 [S]	Play Guitar with the Ventures, Vol. 3	196?	7.50	15.00	30.00
❑ Liberty LST-8052 [S]	Super Psychedelics	1967	6.25	12.50	25.00
❑ Liberty LST-8052 [S]	Changing Times	1970	10.00	20.00	40.00
—Reissue of "Super Psychedelics"					
❑ Liberty LST-8053 [S]	Golden Greats by the Ventures	1967	5.00	10.00	20.00
❑ Liberty LST-8054 [S]	$1,000,000.00 Weekend	1967	5.00	10.00	20.00
❑ Liberty LST-8055 [S]	Flights of Fancy	1968	5.00	10.00	20.00
❑ Liberty LST-8057	The Horse	1968	5.00	10.00	20.00
❑ Liberty LST-8057	On the Scene	1970	3.75	7.50	15.00
—Reissue of "The Horse"					
❑ Liberty LST-8059	Underground Fire	1969	5.00	10.00	20.00
❑ Liberty LST-8060	More Golden Greats	1970	3.75	7.50	15.00
❑ Liberty LST-8061	Hawaii Five-O	1969	3.75	7.50	15.00
❑ Liberty LST-8062	Swamp Rock	1969	3.75	7.50	15.00
❑ Liberty LN-10122	The Very Best of the Ventures	1981	2.00	4.00	8.00
❑ Liberty LN-10155	The Ventures Play Telstar, The Lonely Bull	1981	2.00	4.00	8.00
❑ Liberty LN-10156	The Ventures Play the Country Classics	1981	2.00	4.00	8.00
❑ Liberty LN-10188	Walk, Don't Run, Vol. 2	1984	2.00	4.00	8.00
❑ Liberty LN-10190	(The) Ventures in Space	1984	2.00	4.00	8.00
❑ Liberty LN-10203	The Ventures	1984	2.00	4.00	8.00
❑ Liberty LN-10224	TV Themes	1984	2.00	4.00	8.00
❑ Liberty LST-35000 [(2)]	The Ventures 10th Anniversary Album	1970	5.00	10.00	20.00
❑ Sunset SUM-1160 [M]	The Guitar Genius of the Ventures	1967	3.00	6.00	12.00
❑ Sunset SUS-5160 [S]	The Guitar Genius of the Ventures	1967	3.75	7.50	15.00
❑ Sunset SUS-5270	Super Group	1969	3.00	6.00	12.00
❑ Sunset SUS-5317	A Decade with the Ventures	1970	3.00	6.00	12.00
❑ United Artists UXS-80 [(2)]	The Ventures	1971	3.75	7.50	15.00
❑ United Artists UA-LA147-G [(2)]	Only Hits	1973	3.75	7.50	15.00
❑ United Artists UA-LA217-E	The Jim Croce Songbook	1973	3.00	6.00	12.00
❑ United Artists UA-LA331-E	The Very Best of the Ventures	1974	3.00	6.00	12.00
❑ United Artists UA-LA586-F	Rocky Road	1976	3.00	6.00	12.00
❑ United Artists UA-LA717-F	TV Themes	1977	6.25	12.50	25.00
❑ United Artists UAS-5547	Theme from Shaft	1971	3.00	6.00	12.00
❑ United Artists UAS-5575	Joy/The Ventures Play the Classics	1972	3.00	6.00	12.00
❑ United Artists UAS-5649	Rock and Roll Forever	1972	3.00	6.00	12.00
❑ United Artists UAS-6796	New Testament	1971	3.00	6.00	12.00

VILLAGE PEOPLE

45s

Number	Title (A Side/B Side)	Yr	VG	VG+	NM
❑ Casablanca 896	San Francisco (You've Got Me)/Village People	1977	2.00	4.00	8.00
❑ Casablanca 922	Macho Man/Key West	1978	—	2.50	5.00

Number	Title (A Side/B Side)	Yr	VG	VG+	NM
❑ Casablanca 945	Y.M.C.A./The Women	1978	—	2.50	5.00
❑ Casablanca 973	In the Navy/Manhattan Woman	1979	—	2.50	5.00
❑ Casablanca 984	Go West/Citizens of the World	1979	—	2.50	5.00
❑ Casablanca 2213	Sleazy/Save Me (Uptempo)	1979	—	2.00	4.00
❑ Casablanca 2220	Ready for the 80's/Sleazy	1979	—	2.50	5.00
❑ Casablanca 2261	Can't Stop the Music/Milkshake	1980	—	2.00	4.00
❑ Casablanca 2291	Magic Night/I Love You to Death	1980	—	2.00	4.00
❑ RCA PB-12258	5 O'Clock in the Morning/Food Fight	1981	—	2.50	5.00
❑ RCA PB-12331	Action Man/Jungle City	1981	2.00	4.00	8.00
Albums					
❑ Casablanca NBLP-7064	Village People	1977	2.50	5.00	10.00
❑ Casablanca NBLP-7096	Macho Man	1978	2.50	5.00	10.00
❑ Casablanca NBLP-7118	Cruisin'	1978	2.50	5.00	10.00
❑ Casablanca NBLP-7144	Go West	1979	2.50	5.00	10.00
❑ Casablanca NBLP-7183 [(2)]	Live and Sleazy	1979	3.00	6.00	12.00
❑ Casablanca NBLP-7220	Can't Stop the Music (Soundtrack)	1980	2.50	5.00	10.00
—Also includes one song by the Ritchie Family and one song by David London					
❑ RCA Victor AFL1-4105	Renaissance	1981	2.50	5.00	10.00
❑ Rhino R1-70167	Greatest Hits	1988	2.50	5.00	10.00
VILLAGE STOMPERS, THE					
45s					
❑ Epic 9617	Washington Square/Turkish Delight	1963	2.00	4.00	8.00
❑ Epic 9655	Blue Grass/The La-Dee-La Song	1964	—	3.00	6.00
❑ Epic 9674	From Russia with Love/The Bridges of Budapest	1964	—	3.00	6.00
❑ Epic 9702	Haunted House/Mozambique	1964	—	3.00	6.00
❑ Epic 9718	Oh, Marie/Limehouse Blues	1964	—	3.00	6.00
❑ Epic 9740	Fiddler on the Roof/Moonlight on the Ganges	1964	—	3.00	6.00
❑ Epic 9785	Brother, Can You Spare a Dime/Magic Horn	1965	—	3.00	6.00
❑ Epic 9824	Those Magnificant Men in Their Flying Machines/Sweetwater Bay	1965	—	3.00	6.00
❑ Epic 9868	The Bride of Bleecker Street/Call Me	1965	—	3.00	6.00
❑ Epic 10017	Second Hand Rose/The Poet and the Prophet	1966	—	3.00	6.00
❑ Epic 10106	Chopsticks/Wilkommen	1966	—	3.00	6.00
❑ Epic 10142	Rose of Washington Square/When I Tell You That I Love You	1967	—	3.00	6.00
Albums					
❑ Epic LN 24078 [M]	Washington Square	1963	3.75	7.50	15.00
❑ Epic LN 24090 [M]	More Sounds of Washington Square	1964	3.75	7.50	15.00
❑ Epic LN 24109 [M]	Around the World with the Village Stompers	1964	3.00	6.00	12.00
❑ Epic LN 24129 [M]	New Beat on Broadway!	1964	3.00	6.00	12.00
❑ Epic LN 24161 [M]	Some Folk, a Bit of Country and a Whole Lot of Dixie	1965	3.00	6.00	12.00
❑ Epic LN 24180 [M]	A Taste of Honey	1965	3.00	6.00	12.00
❑ Epic LN 24235 [M]	One More Time	1966	3.00	6.00	12.00
❑ Epic LN 24318 [M]	The Village Stompers' Greatest Hits	1967	3.00	6.00	12.00
❑ Epic BN 26078 [S]	Washington Square	1963	5.00	10.00	20.00
❑ Epic BN 26090 [S]	More Sounds of Washington Square	1964	5.00	10.00	20.00
❑ Epic BN 26109 [S]	Around the World with the Village Stompers	1964	3.75	7.50	15.00
❑ Epic BN 26129 [S]	New Beat on Broadway!	1964	3.75	7.50	15.00
❑ Epic BN 26161 [S]	Some Folk, a Bit of Country and a Whole Lot of Dixie	1965	3.75	7.50	15.00
❑ Epic BN 26180 [S]	A Taste of Honey	1965	3.75	7.50	15.00
❑ Epic BN 26235 [S]	One More Time	1966	3.75	7.50	15.00
❑ Epic BN 26318 [S]	The Village Stompers' Greatest Hits	1967	3.75	7.50	15.00
VINCENT, GENE					
45s					
❑ Capitol F3450	Be-Bop-a-Lula/Woman Love	1956	12.50	25.00	50.00
—With small Capitol logo; counterfeits exist on a white label with blue vinyl					
❑ Capitol F3530	Race with the Devil/Gonna Back Up, Baby	1956	10.00	20.00	40.00
❑ Capitol F3558	Bluejean Bop/Who Slapped John	1956	10.00	20.00	40.00
❑ Capitol F3617	Crazy Legs/Important Words	1956	12.50	25.00	50.00
❑ Capitol F3678	B-I-Bickey-Bi-Bo-Bo-Go/Five Days, Five Days	1957	12.50	25.00	50.00
❑ Capitol F3763	Lotta Lovin'/Wear My Ring	1957	12.50	25.00	50.00
❑ Capitol F3839	Dance to the Bop/I Got It	1957	7.50	15.00	30.00
❑ Capitol 3871	Be-Bop-a-Lula/Lotta Lovin'	1974	3.75	7.50	15.00
❑ Capitol F3874	Walkin' Home from School/I Gotta Baby	1958	10.00	20.00	40.00
❑ Capitol F3959	Baby Blue/True to You	1958	12.50	25.00	50.00
❑ Capitol F4010	Yes I Love You Baby/Rocky Road Blues	1958	10.00	20.00	40.00
❑ Capitol F4051	Little Lover/Git It	1958	10.00	20.00	40.00
❑ Capitol F4105	Say Mama/Be-Bop Boogie Boy	1958	12.50	25.00	50.00

Number	Title (A Side/B Side)	Yr	VG	VG+	NM
❑ Capitol F4153	Over the Rainbow/Who's Pushin' Your Swing	1959	12.50	25.00	50.00
❑ Capitol F4237	The Night Is So Lonely/Right Now	1959	12.50	25.00	50.00
❑ Capitol 4313	Wild Cat/Right Here on Earth	1959	12.50	25.00	50.00
❑ Capitol 4442	Pistol Packin' Mama/Anna Annabella	1960	10.00	20.00	40.00
❑ Capitol 4525	Mister Loneliness/If You Want My Lovin'	1961	6.25	12.50	25.00
❑ Capitol 4665	Lucy Star/Baby Don't Believe Him	1961	6.25	12.50	25.00
❑ Challenge 59337	Bird Doggin'/Ain't That Too Much	1966	5.00	10.00	20.00
❑ Challenge 59347	Lonely Street/I've Got My Eyes on You	1966	5.00	10.00	20.00
❑ Challenge 59365	Born to Be a Rolling Stone/Pickin' Poppies	1967	5.00	10.00	20.00
❑ Forever 6001	Story of the Rockers/Pickin' Poppies	1969	12.50	25.00	50.00
❑ Kama Sutra 514	Sunshine/Geese	1970	3.00	6.00	12.00
❑ Kama Sutra 518	High On Life/The Day the World Turned Blue	1971	3.00	6.00	12.00
❑ Playground 100	Story of the Rockers/Pickin' Poppies	1968	50.00	100.00	200.00
Albums					
❑ Capitol DKAO-380 [R]	Gene Vincent's Greatest	1969	12.50	25.00	50.00
❑ Capitol T 764 [M]	Bluejean Bop!	1957	100.00	200.00	400.00
—Turquoise label stock copy					
❑ Capitol T 811 [M]	Gene Vincent and the Blue Caps	1957	100.00	200.00	400.00
—Turquoise label stock copy					
❑ Capitol T 970 [M]	Gene Vincent Rocks! And the Blue Caps Roll	1958	100.00	200.00	400.00
—Turquoise label stock copy					
❑ Capitol T 1059 [M]	A Gene Vincent Record Date	1958	100.00	200.00	400.00
—Turquoise label stock copy					
❑ Capitol T 1207 [M]	Sounds Like Gene Vincent	1959	75.00	150.00	300.00
—Black label with colorband, Capitol logo at left					
❑ Capitol ST 1342 [S]	Crazy Times	1960	125.00	250.00	500.00
—Black label with colorband, Capitol logo at left					
❑ Capitol T 1342 [M]	Crazy Times	1960	75.00	150.00	300.00
—Black label with colorband, Capitol logo at left					
❑ Capitol N-16208	Gene Vincent's Greatest	198?	3.00	6.00	12.00
—Budget-line reissue					
❑ Capitol N-16209	The Bop That Just Won't Stop	198?	3.00	6.00	12.00
—Budget-line reissue					
❑ Dandelion 9-102	I'm Back and I'm Proud	1970	12.50	25.00	50.00
❑ Intermedia QS-5074	Rockabilly Fever	198?	3.00	6.00	12.00
❑ Kama Sutra KSBS 2019	Gene Vincent	1970	12.50	25.00	50.00
❑ Kama Sutra KSBS 2027	The Day the World Turned Blue	1971	12.50	25.00	50.00
❑ Rollin' Rock 022	Forever	1981	3.75	7.50	15.00

VINTON, BOBBY

45s

Number	Title (A Side/B Side)	Yr	VG	VG+	NM
❑ ABC 12022	My Melody of Love/I'll Be Loving You	1974	—	2.50	5.00
—Black label					
❑ ABC 12056	Beer Barrel Polka/Dick and Jane	1974	—	2.00	4.00
❑ ABC 12100	Wooden Heart/Polka Pose	1975	—	2.00	4.00
❑ ABC 12131	My Gypsy Love/Midnight Show	1975	—	2.00	4.00
❑ ABC 12178	Moonight Serenade/Why Can't I Get Over You	1976	—	2.00	4.00
❑ ABC 12186	Save Your Kisses for Me/Love Shine	1976	—	2.00	4.00
❑ ABC 12229	Love Is the Reason/Nobody But Me	1976	—	2.00	4.00
❑ ABC 12265	Only Love Can Break a Heart/Once More with Feeling	1977	—	2.00	4.00
❑ ABC 12293	Hold Me, Thrill Me, Kiss Me/Her Name Is Love	1977	—	2.00	4.00
❑ ABC 12308	All My Todays/Strike Up the Band for Love	1977	—	2.00	4.00
❑ Alpine 50	First Impression/You'll Never Forget	1959	7.50	15.00	30.00
❑ Alpine 59	The Sheik/A Freshman and a Sophomore	1960	6.25	12.50	25.00
❑ Bobby Vinton 100	Santa Must Be Polish/Santa Claus Is Coming to Town	1987	—	—	3.00
❑ Curb 10512	The Last Rose/Sealed with a Kiss	1988	—	—	3.00
❑ Curb 10541	Please Tell Her That I Said Hello/Getting Used to Being Loved Again	1989	—	—	3.00
❑ Curb 10560	It's Been One of Those Days/(Now and Then There's) A Fool Such As I	1989	—	—	3.00
❑ Curb 76751	The Only Fire That Burns/What Did You Do with Your Old 45's	1990	—	2.00	4.00
❑ Diamond 121	I Love You the Way You Are/You're My Girl	1962	5.00	10.00	20.00
—B-side by Chuck and Johnny					
❑ Elektra 45503	My First, My Only Love/Summerlove Sensation	1978	—	2.00	4.00
❑ Epic 34-06537	Blue Velvet/Blue on Blue	1986	—	2.50	5.00
❑ Epic 9417	Posin'/Tornado	1960	3.75	7.50	15.00
❑ Epic 9440	Corrina, Corrina/Little Lonely One	1961	3.75	7.50	15.00
❑ Epic 9469	Hip-Swinging, High-Stepping, Drum Majorette/Will I Ask Ya	1961	3.75	7.50	15.00
❑ Epic 9509	Roses Are Red (My Love)/You and I	1962	3.00	6.00	12.00
❑ Epic 9532	Rain, Rain Go Away/Over and Over	1962	3.00	6.00	12.00
❑ Epic 9561	Trouble Is My Middle Name/Let's Kiss and Make Up	1962	2.50	5.00	10.00
❑ Epic 9577	Over the Mountain (Across the Sea)/Faded Pictures	1963	2.50	5.00	10.00
❑ Epic 9593	Blue on Blue/Those Little Things	1963	3.00	6.00	12.00
❑ Epic 9593 [DJ]	Blue on Blue/Those Little Things	1963	7.50	15.00	30.00
—Promo only on blue vinyl					
❑ Epic 9614	Blue Velvet/Is There a Place (Where I Can Go)	1963	3.00	6.00	12.00
❑ Epic 9638	There! I've Said It Again/The Girl with the Bow in Her Hair	1963	3.00	6.00	12.00
❑ Epic 9662	My Heart Belongs to Only You/Warm and Tender	1964	2.50	5.00	10.00
❑ Epic 9687	Tell Me Why/Remembering	1964	2.00	4.00	8.00
❑ Epic 9705	Clinging Vine/Imagination Is a Magic Dream	1964	2.00	4.00	8.00
❑ Epic 9730	Mr. Lonely/It's Better to Have Loved	1964	2.50	5.00	10.00
❑ Epic 9741	The Bell That Couldn't Jingle/Dearest Santa	1964	2.50	5.00	10.00
❑ Epic 9768	Long Lonely Nights/Satin	1965	2.00	4.00	8.00
❑ Epic 9791	L-O-N-E-L-Y/Graduation Tears	1965	2.00	4.00	8.00
❑ Epic 9814	Theme from "Harlow" (Lonely Girl)/If I Should Lose Your Love	1965	2.00	4.00	8.00
❑ Epic 9846	What Color (Is a Man)/Love or Infatuation	1965	2.00	4.00	8.00
❑ Epic 9869	Satin Pillows/Careless	1965	2.00	4.00	8.00
❑ Epic 9894	Tears/Go Away Pain	1966	—	3.00	6.00

Number	Title (A Side/B Side)	Yr	VG	VG+	NM
❑ Epic 10014	Dum-De-Da/Blue Clarinet	1966	—	3.00	6.00
❑ Epic 10048	Petticoat White (Summer Sky Blue)/All the King's Horses	1966	—	3.00	6.00
❑ Epic 10090	Coming Home Soldier/Don't Let My Mary Go Around	1966	—	3.00	6.00
❑ Epic 10136	For He's a Jolly Good Fellow/Sweet Maria	1967	—	3.00	6.00
❑ Epic 10168	Red Roses for Mom/College Town	1967	—	3.00	6.00
❑ Epic 10228	Please Love Me Forever/Miss America	1967	2.00	4.00	8.00
❑ Epic 10266	Just As Much As Ever/Another Memory	1967	—	3.00	6.00
❑ Epic 10305	Take Good Care of My Baby/Strange Sensations	1968	—	3.00	6.00
❑ Epic 10350	Halfway to Paradise/(My Little) Kristie	1968	2.50	5.00	10.00
—Note variation in B-side spelling					
❑ Epic 10350	Halfway to Paradise/(My Little) Christie	1968	—	3.00	6.00
❑ Epic 10397	I Love How You Love Me/Little Barefoot Boy	1968	—	3.00	6.00
❑ Epic 10461	To Know You Is to Love You/The Beat of My Heart	1969	—	2.50	5.00
❑ Epic 10485	The Days of Sand and Shovels/So Many Lonely Girls	1969	—	2.50	5.00
❑ Epic 10554	Where Is Love/For All We Know	1969	—	2.50	5.00
❑ Epic 10576	My Elusive Dreams/Over and Over	1970	—	2.50	5.00
❑ Epic 10629	No Arms Can Ever Hold You/I've Got That Lovin' Feelin'	1970	—	2.50	5.00
❑ Epic 10651	Why Don't They Understand/Where Is Love	1970	—	2.50	5.00
❑ Epic 10689	Christmas Eve in My Home Town/The Christmas Angel	1970	—	3.00	6.00
❑ Epic 10711	She Loves Me/I'll Make You My Baby	1971	—	2.50	5.00
❑ Epic 10736	And I Love You So/She Loves Me	1971	—	2.50	5.00
❑ Epic 10790	A Little Bit of You/God Bless America	1971	—	2.50	5.00
❑ Epic 10822	Every Day of My Life/You Can Do It to Me Anytime	1972	—	2.50	5.00
❑ Epic 10861	Sealed with a Kiss/All My Life	1972	—	2.50	5.00
❑ Epic 10936	But I Do/When You Love	1972	—	2.50	5.00
❑ Epic 10980	I Love You the Way You Are/Hurt	1973	—	2.50	5.00
❑ Epic 11038	Where Are the Children/I Can't Believe That It's All Over	1973	—	2.50	5.00
❑ Epic 50080	Clinging Vine/I Can't Believe That It's All Over	1975	—	2.50	5.00
❑ Epic 50169	Christmas Eve in My Home Town/The Christmas Angel	1975	—	2.50	5.00
❑ Larc 81019	You Are Love/Ghost of Another Man	1983	—	2.50	5.00
❑ Melody 5001/2	Always in My Heart/Harlem Nocturne	1960	6.25	12.50	25.00
❑ Tapestry 001	Disco Polka (Pennsylvania Polka)/I Could Have Danced All Night	1979	—	2.00	4.00
❑ Tapestry 002	Make Believe It's Your First Time/I Remember Loving You	1979	—	2.00	4.00
❑ Tapestry 003	He/My First and Only Love	1980	—	2.00	4.00
❑ Tapestry 005	It Was Nice to Know You John/Ain't That Lovin' You	1981	—	2.50	5.00
❑ Tapestry 006	Let Me Love You, Goodbye/You Are Love	1981	—	2.00	4.00
❑ Tapestry 007	Forever and Ever/Ain't That Lovin' You	1982	—	2.00	4.00
❑ Tapestry 008	She WIll Survive (Poland)/Love Is the Reason	1982	—	2.00	4.00
❑ Tapestry 010	It Hurts to Be in Love/Love Makes Everything Better	1985	—	2.00	4.00
❑ Tapestry 013	What Did You Do with Your Old 45s/(B-side unknown)	1986	—	2.00	4.00
❑ Tapestry 1986	Sweet Lady of Liberty (same on both sides)	1986	—	2.00	4.00
❑ Tapestry 4009	Bed of Roses/I Know a Goodbye	1984	—	2.00	4.00
Albums					
❑ ABC X-851	Melodies of Love	1974	2.50	5.00	10.00
❑ ABC D-891	Heart of Hearts	1975	2.50	5.00	10.00
❑ ABC D-924	The Bobby Vinton Show	1975	2.50	5.00	10.00
❑ ABC D-957	Serenades of Love	1976	2.50	5.00	10.00
❑ ABC AB-981	The Name Is Love	1977	2.50	5.00	10.00
❑ Columbia Limited Edition LE 10140	Blue Velvet	197?	2.50	5.00	10.00
—Reissue of Epic 26068					
❑ Epic BN 579 [S]	Dancing at the Hop	1961	12.50	25.00	50.00
❑ Epic BN 597 [S]	Young Man with a Big Band	1961	12.50	25.00	50.00
❑ Epic LN 3727 [M]	Dancing at the Hop	1961	7.50	15.00	30.00
❑ Epic LN 3780 [M]	Young Man with a Big Band	1961	7.50	15.00	30.00
❑ Epic LN 24020 [M]	Roses Are Red	1962	3.75	7.50	15.00
❑ Epic LN 24035 [M]	Bobby Vinton Sings the Big Ones	1962	3.75	7.50	15.00
❑ Epic LN 24049 [M]	The Greatest Hits of the Greatest Groups	1963	3.75	7.50	15.00
❑ Epic LN 24068 [M]	Blue Velvet	1963	3.75	7.50	15.00
—Retitled version of "Blue On Blue"					
❑ Epic LN 24068 [M]	Blue On Blue	1963	6.25	12.50	25.00
—Stock copy on black vinyl					
❑ Epic LN 24081 [M]	There! I've Said It Again	1964	3.75	7.50	15.00
❑ Epic LN 24098 [M]	Bobby Vinton's Greatest Hits	1964	3.00	6.00	12.00
—Despite lower number, this came out after "Tell Me Why"					
❑ Epic LN 24113 [M]	Tell Me Why	1964	3.00	6.00	12.00
❑ Epic LN 24122 [M]	A Very Merry Christmas	1964	3.00	6.00	12.00
❑ Epic LN 24136 [M]	Mr. Lonely	1965	3.00	6.00	12.00

Number	Title (A Side/B Side)	Yr	VG	VG+	NM
❑ Epic LN 24154 [M]	Bobby Vinton Sings for Lonely Nights	1965	3.00	6.00	12.00
❑ Epic LN 24170 [M]	Drive-In Movie Time	1965	3.00	6.00	12.00
❑ Epic LN 24182 [M]	Satin Pillows and Careless	1966	3.00	6.00	12.00
❑ Epic LN 24187 [M]	More of Bobby Vinton's Greatest Hits	1966	3.00	6.00	12.00
❑ Epic LN 24188 [M]	Country Boy	1966	3.00	6.00	12.00
❑ Epic LN 24203 [M]	Live at the Copa	1967	3.00	6.00	12.00
❑ Epic LN 24245 [M]	Bobby Vinton's Newest Hits	1967	3.00	6.00	12.00
❑ Epic LN 24341 [M]	Please Love Me Forever	1967	3.75	7.50	15.00
❑ Epic BN 26020 [S]	Roses Are Red	1962	5.00	10.00	20.00
❑ Epic BN 26035 [S]	Bobby Vinton Sings the Big Ones	1962	5.00	10.00	20.00
❑ Epic BN 26049 [S]	The Greatest Hits of the Greatest Groups	1963	5.00	10.00	20.00
❑ Epic BN 26068 [S]	Blue Velvet	1963	5.00	10.00	20.00
—Retitled version of "Blue On Blue"					
❑ Epic BN 26068 [S]	Blue On Blue	1963	7.50	15.00	30.00
❑ Epic BN 26081 [S]	There! I've Said It Again	1964	5.00	10.00	20.00
❑ Epic BN 26098 [S]	Bobby Vinton's Greatest Hits	1964	3.75	7.50	15.00
—Despite lower number, this came out after "Tell Me Why"					
❑ Epic PE 26098	Bobby Vinton's Greatest Hits	198?	2.00	4.00	8.00
—Budget-line reissue					
❑ Epic BN 26113 [S]	Tell Me Why	1964	3.75	7.50	15.00
❑ Epic BN 26122 [S]	A Very Merry Christmas	1964	3.75	7.50	15.00
❑ Epic BN 26136 [S]	Mr. Lonely	1965	3.75	7.50	15.00
❑ Epic BN 26154 [S]	Bobby Vinton Sings for Lonely Nights	1965	3.75	7.50	15.00
❑ Epic BN 26170 [S]	Drive-In Movie Time	1965	3.75	7.50	15.00
❑ Epic BN 26182 [S]	Satin Pillows and Careless	1966	3.75	7.50	15.00
❑ Epic BN 26187 [S]	More of Bobby Vinton's Greatest Hits	1966	3.75	7.50	15.00
❑ Epic BN 26188 [S]	Country Boy	1966	3.75	7.50	15.00
❑ Epic BN 26203 [S]	Live at the Copa	1967	3.75	7.50	15.00
❑ Epic BN 26245 [S]	Bobby Vinton's Newest Hits	1967	3.75	7.50	15.00
❑ Epic BN 26341 [S]	Please Love Me Forever	1967	3.75	7.50	15.00
❑ Epic BN 26382	Take Good Care of My Baby	1968	3.75	7.50	15.00
❑ Epic BN 26437	I Love How You Love Me	1968	3.75	7.50	15.00
❑ Epic BN 26471	Vinton	1969	3.75	7.50	15.00
❑ Epic BN 26517	Bobby Vinton's Greatest Hits of Love	1970	3.75	7.50	15.00
❑ Epic BN 26540	My Elusive Dreams	1970	3.75	7.50	15.00
❑ Epic KE 31286	Ev'ry Day of My Life	1972	3.00	6.00	12.00
❑ Epic KEG 31487 [(2)]	Bobby Vinton's All-Time Greatest Hits	1972	3.75	7.50	15.00
❑ Epic KE 31642	Sealed with a Kiss	1972	3.00	6.00	12.00
❑ Epic PE 32921	With Love	1974	2.50	5.00	10.00
❑ Epic KEG 33468 [(2)]	Bobby Vinton Sings the Golden Decade of Love	1975	3.00	6.00	12.00
❑ Epic KEG 33767 [(2)]	Greatest Hits/Greatest Hits of Love	1976	3.00	6.00	12.00
❑ Epic JE 35605	Autumn Memories	1979	2.50	5.00	10.00
❑ Epic JE 35998	Spring Sensations	1979	2.50	5.00	10.00
❑ Epic JE 35999	Summer Serenade	1979	2.50	5.00	10.00
❑ Harmony KH 11402	Vinton Sings Vinton	197?	2.50	5.00	10.00
❑ Pickwick SPC-3353	Melodies of Love	197?	2.00	4.00	8.00
❑ Tapestry TRS-1001 [EP]	Santa Must Be Polish	1987	2.50	5.00	10.00

VOGUES, THE

45s

Number	Title (A Side/B Side)	Yr	VG	VG+	NM
❑ ABC-Paramount 10672	Big Man/Golden Locket	1965	5.00	10.00	20.00
❑ Astra 1029	You're the One/Goodnight My Love	1973	—	2.50	5.00
❑ Astra 1030	Five O'Clock World/Land of Milk and Honey	1973	—	2.50	5.00
❑ Bell 991	Love Song/We're On Our Way	1971	—	2.50	5.00
❑ Bell 45127	Take Time to Tell Her/I'll Be with You	1971	—	2.50	5.00
❑ Bell 45158	An American Family/Gotta Have You Back	1971	—	2.50	5.00
❑ Blue Star 229	You're the One/Some Words	1965	6.25	12.50	25.00
❑ Co & Ce 229	You're the One/Some Words	1965	3.00	6.00	12.00
❑ Co & Ce 232	Five O'Clock World/Nothing to Offer You	1965	3.00	6.00	12.00
❑ Co & Ce 234	Magic Town/Humpty Dumpty	1966	2.50	5.00	10.00
❑ Co & Ce 238	The Land of Milk and Honey/True Lovers	1966	2.50	5.00	10.00
❑ Co & Ce 240	Please Mr. Sun/Don't Blame the Rain	1966	2.50	5.00	10.00
❑ Co & Ce 242	That's the Tune/Midnight Dreams	1966	2.50	5.00	10.00
❑ Co & Ce 244	Take a Chance on My Heart/Summer Afternoon	1967	2.50	5.00	10.00
❑ Co & Ce 246	Brighter Days/Lovers of the World Unite	1967	2.50	5.00	10.00
❑ Mainstream 5524	Need You/(B-side unknown)	1972	—	2.50	5.00
❑ MGM 13813	Brighter Days/Lovers of the World Unite	1967	2.00	4.00	8.00
❑ Reprise 0663	I've Got You on My Mind/Just What I've Been Looking For	1968	2.50	5.00	10.00
❑ Reprise 0686	Turn Around, Look at Me/Then	1968	2.00	4.00	8.00
❑ Reprise 0731	Turn Around, Look at Me/My Special Angel	1969	—	2.50	5.00
—"Back to Back Hits" series					
❑ Reprise 0736	No, Not Much/Earth Angel (Will You Be Mine)	1970	—	2.50	5.00
—"Back to Back Hits" series					
❑ Reprise 0741	Five O'Clock World/Magic Town	1970	—	3.00	6.00
—"Back to Back Hits" series; "Five O'Clock World" has overdubbed strings					
❑ Reprise 0766	My Special Angel/I Keep It Hid	1968	2.00	4.00	8.00
❑ Reprise 0788	Till/I Will	1968	2.00	4.00	8.00
❑ Reprise 0803	Woman Helping Man/I'll Know My Love	1969	2.00	4.00	8.00
❑ Reprise 0803	Woman Helping Man/No, Not Much	1969	—	3.00	6.00
❑ Reprise 0820	Earth Angel (Will You Be Mine)/P.S. I Love You	1969	—	3.00	6.00
❑ Reprise 0831	Moments to Remember/Once in a While	1969	—	3.00	6.00
❑ Reprise 0844	Green Fields/Easy to Say	1969	—	3.00	6.00
❑ Reprise 0856	See That Girl/If We Only Have Love	1969	—	3.00	6.00
❑ Reprise 0887	God Only Knows/Moody	1970	—	3.00	6.00
❑ Reprise 0909	Over the Rainbow/Hey, That's No Way to Say Goodbye	1970	—	3.00	6.00
❑ Reprise 0931	50's Medley/Come Into My Arms	1970	—	3.00	6.00
❑ Reprise 0969	Since I Don't Have You/I Know You as a Woman	1970	—	3.00	6.00
❑ 20th Century 2041	My Prayer/I've Got to Learn to Live Without You	1973	—	2.50	5.00

Number	Title (A Side/B Side)	Yr	VG	VG+	NM
❑ 20th Century 2060	Wonderful Summer/Guess Who	1973	—	2.50	5.00
❑ 20th Century 2085	As Time Goes By/Prisoner of Love	1974	—	2.50	5.00
Albums					
❑ Co & Ce LP-1229 [M]	Meet the Vogues	1965	12.50	25.00	50.00
❑ Co & Ce LP-1230 [M]	Five O'Clock World	1966	12.50	25.00	50.00
—Stereo pressings of these two albums are not known to exist!					
❑ Pickwick SPC-3188 [R]	Five O'Clock World	1971	2.50	5.00	10.00
❑ Pickwick SPC-3214 [R]	A Lover's Concerto	1971	2.50	5.00	10.00
❑ Reprise RS 6314	Turn Around, Look at Me	1968	3.75	7.50	15.00
—With "W7" and "r:" logos on two-tone orange label					
❑ Reprise RS 6326	Till	1969	3.75	7.50	15.00
—With "W7" and "r:" logos on two-tone orange label					
❑ Reprise RS 6347	Memories	1969	3.75	7.50	15.00
—With "W7" and "r:" logos on two-tone orange label					
❑ Reprise RS 6371	The Vogues' Greatest Hits	1969	3.75	7.50	15.00
—With "W7" and "r:" logos on two-tone orange label					
❑ Reprise RS 6395	The Vogues Sing the Good Old Songs	1970	3.00	6.00	12.00
❑ SSS International 34	The Vogues' Greatest Hits	1977	2.50	5.00	10.00

VOWS, THE

Number	Title (A Side/B Side)	Yr	VG	VG+	NM
45s					
❑ Markay 103	I Wanna Chance/Have You Heard	1962	10.00	20.00	40.00
—Black label					
❑ Markay 103	I Wanna Chance/Have You Heard	1962	100.00	200.00	400.00
—Orange label					
❑ Ran-Dee 112	Girl in Red/Born with the Rhythm	196?	15.00	30.00	60.00
❑ Sta-Set 402	Say You'll Be Mine/When a Boy Loves a Girl	1963	15.00	30.00	60.00
❑ Tamara 506	The Things You Do to Me/Dottie	1963	10.00	20.00	40.00
❑ Tamara 760	Say You'll Be Mine/When a Boy Loves a Girl	1964	6.25	12.50	25.00
❑ V.I.P. 25016	Buttered Popcorn/Tell Me	1965	10.00	20.00	40.00

W

WALKER, JR., AND THE ALL STARS

Number	Title (A Side/B Side)	Yr	VG	VG+	NM
45s					
❑ Harvey 113	Willie's Blues/Twist Lackawanna	1962	6.25	12.50	25.00
❑ Harvey 117	Cleo's Mood/Brain Washer	1963	5.00	10.00	20.00
❑ Harvey 119	Good Rockin'/Brain Washer	1963	5.00	10.00	20.00
❑ Motown 1352	Country Boy/What Does It Take (To Win Your Love)	1975	—	2.50	5.00
❑ Motown 1380	I'm So Glad/Hot Shot	1976	—	—	—
—Unreleased					
❑ Motown 1689	Blow the House Down/Ball Baby	1983	—	2.00	4.00
❑ Soul 35003	Monkey Jump/Satan's Blues	1964	3.75	7.50	15.00
❑ Soul 35008	Shotgun/Hot Cha	1965	3.75	7.50	15.00
❑ Soul 35008	Shot Gun/Hot Cha	1965	25.00	50.00	100.00
—Not only is the A-side title listed as two words, but the record is credited to "Jr. Walker and All The Stars"!					
❑ Soul 35012	Do the Boomerang/Tune Up	1965	2.50	5.00	10.00
❑ Soul 35013	Shake and Fingerpop/Cleo's Back	1965	2.50	5.00	10.00
❑ Soul 35015	(I'm a) Road Runner/Shoot Your Shot	1965	2.50	5.00	10.00
❑ Soul 35017	Cleo's Mood/Baby You Know It Ain't Right	1966	2.00	4.00	8.00
❑ Soul 35024	How Sweet It Is (To Be Loved By You)/Nothing But Soul	1966	2.00	4.00	8.00
❑ Soul 35026	Money (That's What I Want) Part I/Money (That's What I Want) Part II	1966	2.00	4.00	8.00
❑ Soul 35030	Pucker Up Buttercup/Anyway You Wanna	1967	2.00	4.00	8.00
❑ Soul 35036	Shoot Your Shot/Ain't That the Truth	1967	2.00	4.00	8.00
❑ Soul 35041	Come See About Me/Sweet Soul	1967	2.00	4.00	8.00
❑ Soul 35048	Hip City — Part 1/Hip City — Part 2	1968	2.00	4.00	8.00
❑ Soul 35055	Home Cookin'/Mutiny	1969	2.00	4.00	8.00
❑ Soul 35062	What Does It Take (To Win Your Love)/Brainwasher — Part 1	1969	2.00	4.00	8.00
❑ Soul 35067	These Eyes/Got to Find a Way to Win Maria Back	1969	—	3.00	6.00
❑ Soul 35070	Gotta Hold On to This Feeling/Clinging to the Theory That She's Coming Back	1970	—	3.00	6.00
❑ Soul 35073	Do You See My Love (For You Growing)/Groove and More	1970	—	3.00	6.00
❑ Soul 35081	Holly Holy/Carry Your Own Load	1970	—	3.00	6.00
❑ Soul 35084	Take Me Girl, I'm Ready/Right On Brothers and Sisters	1971	—	3.00	6.00
❑ Soul 35090	Way Back Home/(Instrumental)	1971	—	3.00	6.00
❑ Soul 35095	Walk in the Night/I Don't Want to Do Wrong	1972	—	3.00	6.00
❑ Soul 35097	Groove Thang/Me and My Family	1972	—	3.00	6.00

Number	Title (A Side/B Side)	Yr	VG	VG+	NM
❑ Soul 35104	Gimme That Beat (Part 1)/Gimme That Beat (Part 2)	1973	—	3.00	6.00
❑ Soul 35106	I Don't Need No Reason/Country Boy	1973	—	3.00	6.00
❑ Soul 35108	Peace and Understanding (Is Hard to Find)/Soul Clappin'	1973	—	3.00	6.00
❑ Soul 35110	Dancing Like They Do on Soul Train/I Ain't That Easy to Love	1973	—	3.00	6.00
❑ Soul 35116	I'm So Glad/Soul Clappin'	1975	—	2.50	5.00
❑ Soul 35118	Hot Shot/You're No Ordinary Woman	1976	—	2.50	5.00
❑ Soul 35122	Whopper Bopper Show Stopper/Hard Love	1977	—	2.50	5.00
❑ Whitfield 8861	Back Street Boogie/Don't Let Me Go Away	1979	—	2.00	4.00
❑ Whitfield 49052	Wishing on a Star/Hole in the Wall	1979	—	2.00	4.00
Albums					
❑ Motown M5-105V1	Motown Superstar Series, Vol. 5	1981	2.50	5.00	10.00
❑ Motown M5-141V1	Shotgun	1981	2.50	5.00	10.00
—Reissue of Soul 701					
❑ Motown M5-208V1	Greatest Hits	1981	2.50	5.00	10.00
—Reissue of Soul 718					
❑ Motown M7-786 [(2)]	Anthology	1974	5.00	10.00	20.00
❑ Motown 5297 ML	All the Great Hits of Jr. Walker and the All Stars	1984	2.50	5.00	10.00
❑ Motown 6053 ML	Blow the House Down	1983	2.50	5.00	10.00
❑ Pickwick SPC-3391	Shotgun	197?	3.00	6.00	12.00
❑ Soul 701 [M]	Shotgun	1965	15.00	30.00	60.00
—Mostly white label with vertical "Soul" at left					
❑ Soul SS-701 [S]	Shotgun	1965	7.50	15.00	30.00
❑ Soul 702 [M]	Soul Session	1966	15.00	30.00	60.00
—Mostly white label with vertical "Soul" at left					
❑ Soul SS-702 [S]	Soul Session	1966	7.50	15.00	30.00
❑ Soul 703 [M]	Road Runner	1966	5.00	10.00	20.00
❑ Soul SS-703 [S]	Road Runner	1966	7.50	15.00	30.00
❑ Soul 705 [M]	"Live"	1967	5.00	10.00	20.00
❑ Soul SS-705 [S]	"Live"	1967	7.50	15.00	30.00
❑ Soul SS-710	Home Cookin'	1969	5.00	10.00	20.00
❑ Soul SS-718	Greatest Hits	1969	5.00	10.00	20.00
❑ Soul SS-721	Gotta Hold on to This Feeling	1969	6.25	12.50	25.00
❑ Soul SS-721	What Does It Take to Win Your Love	1970	5.00	10.00	20.00
—Retitled version of above					
❑ Soul SS-726	A Gasssss	1970	3.75	7.50	15.00
❑ Soul S-732L	Rainbow Funk	1971	3.75	7.50	15.00
❑ Soul SS-733	Moody Jr.	1971	3.75	7.50	15.00
❑ Soul SS-738	Peace and Understanding Is Hard to Find	1973	3.75	7.50	15.00
❑ Soul S6-742	Jr. Walker and the All Stars	1973	—	—	—
—Canceled					
❑ Soul S6-745	Hot Shot	1976	3.75	7.50	15.00
❑ Soul S6-747	Sax Appeal	1976	3.75	7.50	15.00
❑ Soul S6-748	Whopper Bopper Show Stopper	1977	3.75	7.50	15.00
❑ Soul S7-750	Smooth	1978	3.75	7.50	15.00
❑ Whitfield WHK 3331	Back Street Boogie	1980	3.00	6.00	12.00

WALKER BROTHERS, THE

45s

Number	Title (A Side/B Side)	Yr	VG	VG+	NM
❑ Kay-Y 66785	Beautiful Brown Eyes/Ninety-Seven	1960	12.50	25.00	50.00
❑ Smash 1952	Doin' the Jerk/Pretty Girls Everywhere	1964	3.00	6.00	12.00
❑ Smash 1976	Love Her/Seventh Dawn	1965	3.00	6.00	12.00
❑ Smash 2000	Make It Easy on Yourself/But I Do	1965	3.75	7.50	15.00
❑ Smash 2009	Make It Easy on Yourself/Doin' the Jerk	1965	3.00	6.00	12.00
❑ Smash 2016	My Ship Is Comin' In/You're All Around Me	1966	3.00	6.00	12.00
❑ Smash 2032	The Sun Ain't Gonna Shine (Anymore)/After the Lights Go Out	1966	3.00	6.00	12.00
❑ Smash 2048	(Baby) You Don't Have to Tell Me/Young Man Cried	1966	3.00	6.00	12.00
❑ Smash 2063	Another Tear Falls/Saddest Night in the World	1966	3.00	6.00	12.00
❑ Tower 218	I Only Came to Dance with You/Greens	1966	3.00	6.00	12.00
Albums					
❑ Smash MGS-27076 [M]	Introducing the Walker Brothers	1965	12.50	25.00	50.00
❑ Smash MGS-27082 [M]	The Sun Ain't Gonna Shine (Anymore)	1966	10.00	20.00	40.00
❑ Smash SRS-67076 [R]	Introducing the Walker Brothers	1965	10.00	20.00	40.00
❑ Smash SRS-67082 [P]	The Sun Ain't Gonna Shine (Anymore)	1966	12.50	25.00	50.00
—"The Sun Ain't Gonna Shine (Anymore)" and "When the Lights Go Out" are rechanneled.					
❑ Tower ST 5026 [S]	I Only Came to Dance with You	1966	5.00	10.00	20.00
—As "Scott Engel and John Stewart"					
❑ Tower T 5026 [M]	I Only Came to Dance with You	1966	3.75	7.50	15.00
—As "Scott Engel and John Stewart"					

WALSH, JOE

45s

Number	Title (A Side/B Side)	Yr	VG	VG+	NM
❑ ABC 12115	Time Out/Help Me Through the Night	1975	—	2.50	5.00
❑ ABC 12187	Walk Away/Help Me Through the Night	1976	—	2.50	5.00
❑ ABC 12426	Rocky Mountain Way/Turn to Stone	1978	—	2.00	4.00
❑ ABC Dunhill 4327	I'll Tell the World About You/Mother Says	1972	—	2.50	5.00
❑ ABC Dunhill 4361	Rocky Mountain Way/Prayer	1973	—	2.50	5.00
❑ ABC Dunhill 4373	Meadows/Bookends	1973	—	2.50	5.00
❑ ABC Dunhill 15026	Turn to Stone/All Night Laundromat Blues	1974	—	2.50	5.00
❑ Asylum 45493	Life's Been Good/Theme from Boat Weirdos	1978	—	2.00	4.00
❑ Asylum 45536	At the Station/Over and Over	1978	—	2.00	4.00
❑ Asylum 47144	A Life of Illusion/Rockets	1981	—	2.00	4.00
❑ Asylum 47197	Made Your Mind Up/Things	1981	—	2.00	4.00
❑ Epic 73843	Ordinary Average Guy/Alphabetical Order	1991	—	—	3.00
❑ Full Moon 69951	Waffle Stomp/Things	1982	—	2.00	4.00
❑ Full Moon/Asylum 46639	All Night Long/Orange Blossom Special	1980	—	2.00	4.00
—B-side by Gilley's Urban Cowboy Band					
❑ Warner Bros. 28225	In My Car/How Ya Doin'?	1987	—	—	3.00

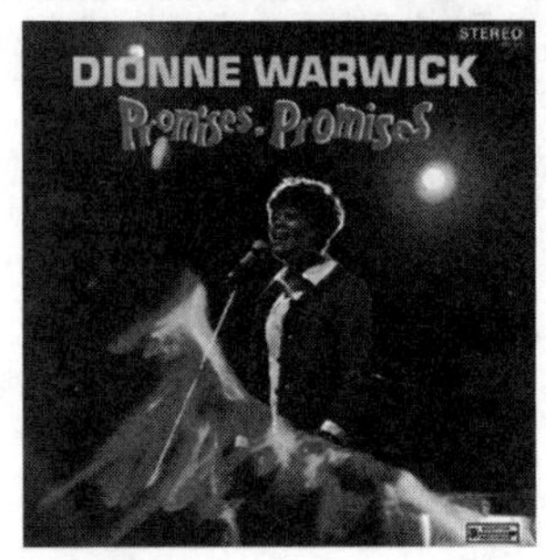

Number	Title (A Side/B Side)	Yr	VG	VG+	NM
❑ Warner Bros. 28304	The Radio Song/How Ya Doin'?	1987	—	—	3.00
❑ Warner Bros. 28910	Good Man Down/I Broke My Leg	1985	—	2.00	4.00
❑ Warner Bros. 29454	I.L.B.T.'s/Love Letters	1983	—	2.00	4.00
❑ Warner Bros. 29519	Here We Are Now/I Can Play That Rock and Roll	1983	—	2.00	4.00
❑ Warner Bros. 29611	Space Age Whiz Kids/Theme from Island Weirdos	1983	—	2.00	4.00
Albums					
❑ ABC ABCD-932	You Can't Argue with a Sick Mind	1976	2.50	5.00	10.00
❑ ABC AA-1083	The Best of Joe Walsh	1978	2.50	5.00	10.00
—Also contains two James Gang tracks					
❑ ABC Dunhill DS-50130	Barnstorm	1972	2.50	5.00	10.00
—Of the James Gang and the Eagles					
❑ ABC Dunhill DS-50140	The Smoker You Drink, the Player You Get	1973	2.50	5.00	10.00
❑ ABC Dunhill DS-51071	So What	1974	2.50	5.00	10.00
❑ Asylum 6E-141	But Seriously, Folks...	1978	2.50	5.00	10.00
❑ Asylum 5E-523	There Goes the Neighborhood	1981	2.00	4.00	8.00
❑ MCA 37051	You Can't Argue with a Sick Mind	1979	2.00	4.00	8.00
—Reissue of ABC 932					
❑ MCA 37052	The Best of Joe Walsh	1979	2.00	4.00	8.00
—Reissue of ABC 1083					
❑ MCA 37053	Barnstorm	1979	2.00	4.00	8.00
—Reissue of ABC Dunhill 50130					
❑ MCA 37054	The Smoker You Drink, the Player You Get	1979	2.00	4.00	8.00
—Reissue of ABC Dunhill 50140					
❑ MCA 37055	So What	1979	2.00	4.00	8.00
—Reissue of ABC Dunhill 50171					
❑ Warner Bros. 23884	You Bought It — You Name It	1983	2.00	4.00	8.00
❑ Warner Bros. 25281	The Confessor	1985	2.00	4.00	8.00
❑ Warner Bros. 25606	Got Any Gum?	1987	2.00	4.00	8.00
WAR					
45s					
❑ Blue Note 1009	L.A. Sunshine/Slowly We Walk Together	1977	—	2.50	5.00
❑ Coco Plum 2002	Groovin'/(Instrumental)	1985	—	2.00	4.00
❑ LAX 02120	Cinco de Mayo/Don't Let No One Get You Down	1981	—	2.50	5.00
❑ MCA 40820	Galaxy (Part 1)/Galaxy (Part 2)	1977	—	2.50	5.00
❑ MCA 40883	Hey Senorita/Sweet Fighting Lady	1978	—	2.50	5.00
❑ MCA 40995	Good, Good Feelin'/Baby Face (She Said Do Do Do Do)	1979	—	2.50	5.00
❑ MCA 41061	I'm the One Who Understands/Corns & Callouses	1979	—	2.50	5.00
❑ MCA 41158	Don't Take It Away/The Music Band 2 (We Are the Music Band)	1979	—	2.50	5.00
❑ MCA 41209	I'll Be Around/The Music Band 2 (We Are the Music Band)	1980	—	2.50	5.00
❑ RCA PB-13061	You Got the Power/Cinco de Mayo	1982	—	2.00	4.00
❑ RCA PB-13239	Outlaw/I'm About Somebody	1982	—	2.00	4.00
❑ RCA PB-13322	Just Because/The Jungle (Medley)	1982	—	2.00	4.00
❑ RCA PB-13544	Life (Is So Strange)/W.W. III	1983	—	2.00	4.00
❑ United Artists XW163	The Cisco Kid/Beetles in the Bog	1973	—	2.50	5.00
❑ United Artists XW281	Gypsy Man/Deliver the Word	1973	—	2.50	5.00
❑ United Artists XW350	Me and Baby Brother/In Your Eyes	1973	—	2.50	5.00
❑ United Artists XW432	Ballero/Slippin' Into Darkness	1974	—	2.50	5.00
❑ United Artists XW629	Why Can't We Be Friends?/In Mazatlin	1975	—	2.50	5.00
❑ United Artists XW706	Low Rider/So	1975	—	2.50	5.00
❑ United Artists XW834	Summer/All Day Music	1976	—	2.50	5.00
❑ United Artists XW1213	Youngblood/(Instrumental)	1978	—	2.50	5.00
❑ United Artists XW1247	Sing a Happy Song/This Funky Music Makes You Feel Good	1978	—	2.50	5.00
❑ United Artists 50746	Lonely Feelin'/Sun Oh Sun	1971	2.00	4.00	8.00
❑ United Artists 50815	All Day Music/Get Down	1971	2.00	4.00	8.00
❑ United Artists 50867	Slippin' Into Darkness/Happy Head	1971	—	3.00	6.00
❑ United Artists 50975	The World Is a Ghetto/Four Cornered Room	1972	—	3.00	6.00
Albums					
❑ Avenue R1 71706	Peace Sign	1994	3.75	7.50	15.00
❑ Blue Note BN-LA690-G [(2)]	Platinum Jazz	1977	3.00	6.00	12.00
❑ LAX PW 37111	All Day Music	1981	2.50	5.00	10.00
—Reissue of United Artists 5546					
❑ LAX PW 37112	The World Is a Ghetto	1981	2.50	5.00	10.00
—Reissue of United Artists 5652					
❑ LAX PW 37113	Why Can't We Be Friends?	1981	2.50	5.00	10.00
—Reissue of United Artists 441					
❑ MCA 745	Galaxy	1983	2.00	4.00	8.00
—Reissue of MCA 3030					

Number	Title (A Side/B Side)	Yr	VG	VG+	NM
❑ MCA 747	The Music Band	1983	2.00	4.00	8.00
—Reissue of MCA 3085					
❑ MCA 751	The Music Band 2	1983	2.00	4.00	8.00
—Reissue of MCA 3193					
❑ MCA 3030	Galaxy	1977	2.50	5.00	10.00
❑ MCA 3085	The Music Band	1979	2.50	5.00	10.00
❑ MCA 3193	The Music Band 2	1979	2.50	5.00	10.00
❑ MCA 5156	The Music Band Live	1980	2.50	5.00	10.00
❑ MCA 5362	Best of the Music Band	1982	2.50	5.00	10.00
❑ MCA 5411	Music Band Jazz	1983	2.50	5.00	10.00
❑ Priority SL 9467	The Best of War…And More	1987	2.50	5.00	10.00
❑ RCA Victor AFL1-4208	Outlaw	1982	2.50	5.00	10.00
❑ RCA Victor AFL1-4598	Life (Is So Strange)	1983	2.50	5.00	10.00
❑ United Artists UA-LA128-F	Deliver the Word	1973	3.00	6.00	12.00
❑ United Artists UA-LA193-J [(2)]	War Live!	1974	3.75	7.50	15.00
❑ United Artists UA-LA441-G	Why Can't We Be Friends?	1975	2.50	5.00	10.00
❑ United Artists UA-LA648-G	Greatest Hits	1976	2.50	5.00	10.00
❑ United Artists UAS-5508	War	1971	3.75	7.50	15.00
❑ United Artists UAS-5546	All Day Music	1971	3.75	7.50	15.00
❑ United Artists UAS-5652	The World Is a Ghetto	1972	3.00	6.00	12.00

WARD, BILLY, AND THE DOMINOES

45s

Number	Title (A Side/B Side)	Yr	VG	VG+	NM
❑ ABC-Paramount 10128	You're Mine/The World Is Waiting for the Sunrise	1960	5.00	10.00	20.00
❑ ABC-Paramount 10156	You/Gypsy	1960	5.00	10.00	20.00
❑ Decca 29933	St. Therese of the Roses/Home Is Where You Hang Your Hat	1956	7.50	15.00	30.00
❑ Decca 30043	Come On, Shake, Let's Crawl/Will You Remember	1956	7.50	15.00	30.00
❑ Decca 30149	Half a Love (Is Better Than None)/Evermore	1956	7.50	15.00	30.00
❑ Decca 30199	Rock, Plymouth Rock/Till Kingdom Come	1957	7.50	15.00	30.00
❑ Decca 30420	To Each His Own/I Don't Stand a Ghost of a Chance	1957	7.50	15.00	30.00
❑ Decca 30514	September Song/When the Saints Go Marching In	1957	7.50	15.00	30.00
❑ Federal 12001	Do Something For Me/Chicken Blues	1951	200.00	400.00	800.00
—Note: Federal 12010 and 12016 were issued only on 78s					
❑ Federal 12022AA	Sixty Minute Man/I Can't Escape from You	1951	125.00	250.00	500.00
❑ Federal 12022	Sixty Minute Man/I Can't Escape from You	195?	50.00	100.00	200.00
—Gold top, no "AA" on label; though this version has been counterfeited, there are legitimate copies without the "AA" on the label; the best way to confirm it is to, if possible, compare it to an "AA" pressing, as they will be exactly the same in every way except for the absence of the "AA"					
❑ Federal 12036	Heart to Heart/Looking for a Man to Satisfy My Soul	1951	125.00	250.00	500.00
—With Little Esther					
❑ Federal 12039	I Am with You/Weeping Willow Blues	1951	100.00	200.00	400.00
❑ Federal 12059	That's What You're Doing to Me/When the Swallows Come Back to Capistrano	1952	100.00	200.00	400.00
❑ Federal 12068AA	Have Mercy Baby/Deep Sea Blues	1952	62.50	125.00	250.00
❑ Federal 12072	Love, Love, Love/That's What You're Doing to Me	1952	50.00	100.00	200.00
❑ Federal 12105	I'd Be Satisfied/No Room	1952	45.00	90.00	180.00
❑ Federal 12106	I'm Lonely/Yours Forever	1952	45.00	90.00	180.00
❑ Federal 12114	The Bells/Pedal Pushin' Papa	1952	50.00	100.00	200.00
❑ Federal 12129	These Foolish Things Remind Me of You/Don't Leave Me This Way	1953	75.00	150.00	300.00
—Green label, gold top					
❑ Federal 12139	You Can't Keep a Good Man Down/Where Now Little Heart	1953	25.00	50.00	100.00
❑ Federal 12162	Until the Real Thing Comes Along/My Baby's 3 D	1954	25.00	50.00	100.00
❑ Federal 12178	Tootsie Roll/Move to the Outskirts of Town	1954	25.00	50.00	100.00
❑ Federal 12184	Handwriting on the Wall/One Moment with You	1954	50.00	100.00	200.00
❑ Federal 12193	Above Jacob's Ladder/Little Black Train	1954	12.50	25.00	50.00
❑ Federal 12209	Can't Do Sixty No More/If I Never Get to Heaven	1955	25.00	50.00	100.00
❑ Federal 12218	Love Me Now or Let Me Go/Cave Man	1955	12.50	25.00	50.00
❑ Federal 12263	Bobby Sox Baby/How Long, How Long Blues	1956	12.50	25.00	50.00
❑ Federal 12301	St. Louis Blues/One Moment with You	1957	12.50	25.00	50.00
❑ Federal 12308	Have Mercy Baby/Love, Love, Love	1957	10.00	20.00	40.00
❑ Jubliee 5163	Gimme, Gimme, Gimme/Come to Me, Baby	1954	7.50	15.00	30.00
❑ Jubliee 5213	Sweethearts on Parade/Take Me Back to Heaven	1955	7.50	15.00	30.00
❑ King 1280	Rags to Riches/Don't Ask Me	1953	12.50	25.00	50.00
❑ King 1281	Christmas in Heaven/Ringing In a Brand New Year	1953	25.00	50.00	100.00
❑ King 1342	Tenderly/Little Lie	1954	12.50	25.00	50.00
❑ King 1364	Three Coins in the Fountain/Lonesome Road	1954	12.50	25.00	50.00
❑ King 1368	Little Things Mean a Lot/I Really Don't Want to Know	1954	10.00	20.00	40.00
❑ King 1492	Learnin' the Blues/May I Never Love	1955	10.00	20.00	40.00
❑ King 1502	Over the Rainbow/Give Me You	1955	10.00	20.00	40.00
❑ King 5322	Sixty Minute Man/Have Mercy Baby	1960	5.00	10.00	20.00
❑ King 5463	Lay It on the Line/That's How You Know You're Growing Old	1961	5.00	10.00	20.00
❑ King 6002	I'm Walking Behind You/This Love of Mine	1965	5.00	10.00	20.00
❑ King 6016	O Holy Night/What Are You Doin' New Year's Eve	1965	5.00	10.00	20.00
❑ Liberty 55071	Star Dust/Lucinda	1957	6.25	12.50	25.00
❑ Liberty 55099	Deep Purple/Do It Again	1957	6.25	12.50	25.00
❑ Liberty 55111	My Proudest Possession/Someone Greater Than I	1957	6.25	12.50	25.00
❑ Liberty 55126	Solitude/You Grow Sweeter As the Years Go By	1958	6.25	12.50	25.00
❑ Liberty 55136	Jennie Lee/Music, Maestro, Please	1958	6.25	12.50	25.00
❑ Liberty 55181	Please Don't Say No/Behave, Hula Girl	1959	6.25	12.50	25.00
❑ Ro-Zan 10001	Man in the Stain Glass Window/My Fair Weather Friend	1961	5.00	10.00	20.00
❑ United Artists 0017	Stardust/These Foolish Things	1973	—	2.50	5.00
—"Silver Spotlight Series" reissue					

Albums

Number	Title (A Side/B Side)	Yr	VG	VG+	NM
❑ Decca DL 8621 [M]	Billy Ward and the Dominoes	1958	50.00	100.00	200.00
❑ Federal 295-94 [10]	Billy Ward and His Dominoes	1955	6000.	9500.	13000.
—VG value 6000; VG+ value 9500					
❑ Federal 548 [M]	Billy Ward and His Dominoes	1958	375.00	750.00	1500.

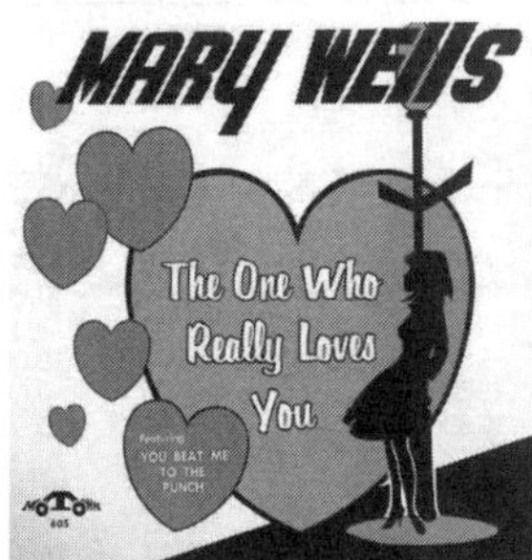

Number	Title (A Side/B Side)	Yr	VG	VG+	NM
❑ Federal 559 [M]	Clyde McPhatter with Billy Ward and His Dominoes	1958	300.00	600.00	1200.
❑ King 548 [M]	Billy Ward and His Dominoes	1958	—	—	—
—Unknown					
❑ King 559 [M]	Clyde McPhatter with Billy Ward and His Dominoes	1958	150.00	300.00	600.00
—Yellow cover					
❑ King 733 [M]	Billy Ward and His Dominoes Featuring Clyde McPhatter and Jackie Wilson	1961	150.00	300.00	600.00
❑ King 952 [M]	24 Songs	1966	12.50	25.00	50.00
❑ King 5005	14 Hits	197?	3.00	6.00	12.00
❑ King 5008	21 Hits	197?	3.00	6.00	12.00
❑ Liberty LRP-3056 [M]	Sea of Glass	1957	15.00	30.00	60.00
❑ Liberty LRP-3083 [M]	Yours Forever	1958	15.00	30.00	60.00
❑ Liberty LRP-3113 [M]	Pagan Love Song	1959	15.00	30.00	60.00
❑ Liberty LST-7113 [S]	Pagan Love Song	1959	25.00	50.00	100.00

WARWICK, DIONNE

45s

Number	Title (A Side/B Side)	Yr	VG	VG+	NM
❑ Arista 0419	I'll Never Love This Way Again/In Your Eyes	1979	—	2.00	4.00
❑ Arista 0459	Deja Vu/All the Time	1979	—	2.00	4.00
❑ Arista 0498	After You/Out of My Hands	1980	—	2.00	4.00
❑ Arista 0527	No Night So Long/Reaching for the Sky	1980	—	2.00	4.00
❑ Arista 0572	Easy Love/You Never Said Goodbye	1980	—	2.00	4.00
❑ Arista 0602	Some Changes Are For Good/This Time Is Ours	1981	—	2.00	4.00
❑ Arista 0630	There's a Long Road Ahead of Me/Medley of Hits	1981	—	2.00	4.00
❑ Arista 0673	Friends in Love/What Is This	1982	—	2.00	4.00
—A-side with Johnny Mathis					
❑ Arista 0701	For You/What Is This	1982	—	2.00	4.00
❑ Arista 1015	Heartbreaker/I Can't See Anything But You	1982	—	2.00	4.00
❑ Arista 1040	Take the Short Way Home/Just One More Night	1983	—	2.00	4.00
❑ Arista 1067	All the Love in the World/You Are My Love	1983	—	—	—
—Unreleased?					
❑ Arista 9032	All the Love in the World/You Are My Love	1983	—	2.00	4.00
❑ Arista 9073	How Many Times Can We Say Goodbye/What Can a Miracle Do	1983	—	2.00	4.00
—With Luther Vandross					
❑ Arista 9145	Got a Date/Two Ships Passing in the Night	1984	—	2.00	4.00
❑ Arista 9281	Finder of Lost Loves/It's Love	1984	—	2.00	4.00
—A-side with Glen Jones					
❑ Arista 9341	Run to Me/No Love in Sight	1985	—	—	3.00
—A-side with Barry Manilow					
❑ Arista 9460	Whisper in the Dark/Extravagant Gestures	1986	—	—	3.00
❑ Arista 9567	Love Power/In a World Such As This	1987	—	—	3.00
—A-side with Jeffrey Osborne					
❑ Arista 9638	Reservations for Two/For Everything You Are	1987	—	—	3.00
—A-side with Kashif					
❑ Arista 9652	Another Chance for Love/Cry on Me	1987	—	—	3.00
—A-side with Howard Hewett					
❑ Arista 9901	Take Good Care of You and Me/Heartbreak of Love	1989	—	—	3.00
—A-side with Jeffrey Osborne; B-side with June Pointer					
❑ Arista 9940	I Don't Need Another Love/Hertbreaker	1990	—	—	3.00
—A-side with the Spinners					
❑ Atlantic 3029	Then Came You/Just As Long As We Have Love	1974	—	3.00	6.00
—With the Spinners					
❑ Atlantic 3202	Then Came You/Just As Long As We Have Love	1974	—	2.50	5.00
—With the Spinners					
❑ Musicor 6303	If I Ruled the World/Only Love Can Break a Heart	1977	—	2.50	5.00
❑ Scepter 1239	Don't Make Me Over/I Smiled Yesterday	1962	3.00	6.00	12.00
❑ Scepter 1247	This Empty Place/Wishin' and Hopin'	1963	3.00	6.00	12.00
❑ Scepter 1253	Make the Music Play/Please Make Him Love Me	1963	3.00	6.00	12.00
❑ Scepter 1262	Anyone Who Had a Heart/The Love of a Boy	1963	3.00	6.00	12.00
❑ Scepter 1274	Walk On By/Any Old Time of Day	1964	3.00	6.00	12.00
❑ Scepter 1282	You'll Never Get to Heaven (If You Break My Heart)/A House Is Not a Home	1964	2.50	5.00	10.00
❑ Scepter 1285	Reach Out for Me/How Many Days of Sadness	1964	2.50	5.00	10.00
❑ Scepter 1294	You Can Have Him/Is There Another Way to Love Him	1965	2.50	5.00	10.00
❑ Scepter 1298	Who Can I Turn To/Don't Say I Didn't Tell You Something	1965	2.50	5.00	10.00
❑ Scepter 12104	Here I Am/They Long to Be Close to You	1965	2.50	5.00	10.00
❑ Scepter 12111	Looking with My Eyes/Only the Strong, Only the Brave	1965	2.50	5.00	10.00
❑ Scepter 12122	Are You There (With Another Girl)/If I Ever Make You Cry	1965	2.50	5.00	10.00

Number	Title (A Side/B Side)	Yr	VG	VG+	NM
❑ Scepter 12133	Message to Michael/Here Where There Is Love	1966	2.00	4.00	8.00
❑ Scepter 12153	Trains and Boats and Planes/Don't Go Breaking My Heart	1966	2.00	4.00	8.00
❑ Scepter 12167	I Just Don't Know What to Do with Myself/In Between the Heartaches	1966	2.00	4.00	8.00
❑ Scepter 12181	Another Night/Go with Love	1966	2.00	4.00	8.00
❑ Scepter 12187	Alfie/The Beginning of Loneliness	1967	2.00	4.00	8.00
❑ Scepter 12196	The Windows of the World/Walk Little Dolly	1967	2.00	4.00	8.00
❑ Scepter 12203	I Say a Little Prayer/(Theme from) Valley of the Dolls	1967	2.00	4.00	8.00
❑ Scepter 12216	Do You Know the Way to San Jose?/Let Me Be Lonely	1968	2.00	4.00	8.00
❑ Scepter 12226	Who Is Gonna Love Me?/(There's) Always Something There to Remind Me	1968	2.00	4.00	8.00
❑ Scepter 12231	Promises, Promises/Whoever You Are, I Love You	1968	—	3.50	7.00
❑ Scepter 12241	This Girl's In Love with You/Dream Sweet Dreamer	1969	—	3.50	7.00
❑ Scepter 12249	The April Fools/Slaves	1969	—	3.50	7.00
❑ Scepter 12256	Odds and Ends/As Long As There's an Apple Tree	1969	—	3.50	7.00
❑ Scepter 12262	You've Lost That Lovin' Feeling/Window Wishing	1969	—	3.50	7.00
❑ Scepter 12273	I'll Never Fall in Love Again/What the World Needs Now Is Love	1970	—	3.50	7.00
❑ Scepter 12276	Let Me Go to Him/Loneliness Remembers What Happiness Forgets	1970	—	3.00	6.00
❑ Scepter 12285	Paper Mache/The Wine Is Young	1970	—	3.00	6.00
❑ Scepter 12294	Make It Easy on Yourself/Knowing When to Leave	1970	—	3.00	6.00
❑ Scepter 12300	The Green Grass Starts to Grow/They Don't Give Medals to Yesterday's Heroes	1970	—	3.00	6.00
❑ Scepter 12309	Who Gets the Guy/Walk the Way You Talk	1971	—	3.00	6.00
❑ Scepter 12326	Amanda/He's Moving On	1971	—	3.00	6.00
❑ Scepter 12336	The Love of My Man/Hurts So Bad	1971	—	3.00	6.00
❑ Scepter 12346	Raindrops Keep Falling on My Head/Is There Another Way to Love You	1972	—	3.00	6.00
❑ Scepter 12352	I'm Your Puppet/Don't Make Me Over	1972	—	3.00	6.00
❑ Scepter 12383	Medley: Reach Out and Touch (Somebody's Hand)-All Kinds of People/The Good Life	1973	—	3.00	6.00
❑ Warner Bros. 7560	If We Only Have Love/Close to You	1972	—	2.50	5.00
❑ Warner Bros. 7669	Don't Let My Teardrops Bother TYou/I Think You Need Love	1973	—	2.50	5.00
❑ Warner Bros. 7693	(I'm) Just Being Myself/You're Gonna Need Me	1973	—	2.50	5.00
❑ Warner Bros. 8026	Sure Thing/Who Knows	1974	—	2.50	5.00
❑ Warner Bros. 8088	Take it from Me/It's Magic	1975	—	2.50	5.00
❑ Warner Bros. 8154	Once You Hit the Road/World of My Dreams	1975	—	2.50	5.00
❑ Warner Bros. 8183	His House and Me/Ronnie Lee	1976	—	2.50	5.00
❑ Warner Bros. 8280	I Didn't Mean to Love You/He's Not for You	1976	—	2.50	5.00
❑ Warner Bros. 8419	Do You Believe in Love at First Sight/Do I Have to Cry	1977	—	2.50	5.00
❑ Warner Bros. 8501	Keepin' My Head Above Water/Livin' It Up Is Startin' to Get Me Down	1977	—	2.50	5.00
❑ Warner Bros. 8530	Don't Ever Take Your Love Away/Do I Have to Cry	1978	—	2.00	4.00
Albums					
❑ Arista AB 4230	Dionne	1979	2.50	5.00	10.00
❑ Arista AL 8104	How Many Times Can We Say Goodbye	1983	2.50	5.00	10.00
❑ Arista A2L 8111 [(2)]	Hot! Live and Otherwise	1983	2.50	5.00	10.00
—Budget-line reissue					
❑ Arista AL 8262	Finder of Lost Loves	1985	2.50	5.00	10.00
❑ Arista AL 8295	Dionne	1985	2.00	4.00	8.00
—Budget-line reissue					
❑ Arista AL 8338	Heartbreaker	1985	2.00	4.00	8.00
—Budget-line reissue					
❑ Arista AL 8358	Friends in Love	1985	2.00	4.00	8.00
—Budget-line reissue					
❑ Arista AL 8398	Friends	1985	2.50	5.00	10.00
❑ Arista AL 8446	Reservations for Two	1987	2.50	5.00	10.00
❑ Arista AL 8540	Greatest Hits 1979-1990	1989	3.00	6.00	12.00
❑ Arista AL 8573	Dionne Warwick Sings Cole Porter	1990	3.00	6.00	12.00
❑ Arista A2L 8605 [(2)]	Hot! Live and Otherwise	1981	3.00	6.00	12.00
❑ Arista AL 9526	No Night So Long	1980	2.50	5.00	10.00
❑ Arista AL 9585	Friends in Love	1982	2.50	5.00	10.00
❑ Arista AL 9609	Heartbreaker	1982	2.50	5.00	10.00
❑ Everest 4103	Dionne Warwick	1981	2.50	5.00	10.00
❑ Musicor 2501	Only Love Can Break a Heart	1977	3.00	6.00	12.00
❑ Pair PDL2-1043 [(2)]	The Dynamic Dionne Warwick	1986	3.00	6.00	12.00
❑ Pair PDL2-1098 [(2)]	Masterpieces	1986	3.00	6.00	12.00
❑ Pickwick PTP-2056 [(2)]	Alfie	1973	3.00	6.00	12.00
—As "Dionne Warwicke"					
❑ Rhino RNDA-1100 [(2)]	Anthology 1962-1971	1985	3.75	7.50	15.00
❑ Scepter S-508 [M]	Presenting Dionne Warwick	1963	3.75	7.50	15.00
❑ Scepter SS-508 [S]	Presenting Dionne Warwick	1963	5.00	10.00	20.00
❑ Scepter S-517 [M]	Anyone Who Had a Heart	1964	3.75	7.50	15.00
❑ Scepter SS-517 [S]	Anyone Who Had a Heart	1964	5.00	10.00	20.00
❑ Scepter LP-523 [M]	Make Way for Dionne Warwick	1964	3.75	7.50	15.00
❑ Scepter SPS-523 [S]	Make Way for Dionne Warwick	1964	5.00	10.00	20.00
❑ Scepter LP-528 [M]	The Sensitive Sound of Dionne Warwick	1965	3.75	7.50	15.00
❑ Scepter SPS-528 [S]	The Sensitive Sound of Dionne Warwick	1965	5.00	10.00	20.00
❑ Scepter SPS-531 [S]	Here I Am	1965	5.00	10.00	20.00
❑ Scepter SRM-531 [M]	Here I Am	1965	3.75	7.50	15.00
❑ Scepter SPS-534 [S]	Dionne Warwick in Paris	1966	3.75	7.50	15.00
❑ Scepter SRM-534 [M]	Dionne Warwick in Paris	1966	3.00	6.00	12.00
❑ Scepter SPS-555 [S]	Here Where There Is Love	1966	3.75	7.50	15.00
❑ Scepter SRM-555 [M]	Here Where There Is Love	1966	3.00	6.00	12.00
❑ Scepter SPS-559 [S]	On Stage and in the Movies	1967	3.75	7.50	15.00
❑ Scepter SRM-559 [M]	On Stage and in the Movies	1967	3.00	6.00	12.00
❑ Scepter SPS-563 [S]	The Windows of the World	1967	3.75	7.50	15.00
❑ Scepter SRM-563 [M]	The Windows of the World	1967	3.00	6.00	12.00
❑ Scepter SPS-565 [S]	Dionne Warwick's Golden Hits, Part One	1967	3.75	7.50	15.00
❑ Scepter SRM-565 [M]	Dionne Warwick's Golden Hits, Part One	1967	5.00	10.00	20.00

Number	Title (A Side/B Side)	Yr	VG	VG+	NM
❑ Scepter SPS-567 [S]	The Magic of Believing	1968	5.00	10.00	20.00
❑ Scepter SRM-567 [M]	The Magic of Believing	1968	7.50	15.00	30.00
❑ Scepter SPS-568 [S]	Valley of the Dolls	1968	3.75	7.50	15.00
❑ Scepter SPS-571	Promises, Promises	1968	3.75	7.50	15.00
❑ Scepter SPS-573	Soulful	1969	3.75	7.50	15.00
❑ Scepter SPS-575	Dionne Warwick's Greatest Motion Picture Hits	1969	3.75	7.50	15.00
❑ Scepter SPS-577	Dionne Warwick's Golden Hits, Part 2	1969	3.75	7.50	15.00
❑ Scepter SPS-581	I'll Never Fall in Love Again	1970	3.75	7.50	15.00
❑ Scepter SPS-587	Very Dionne	1970	3.75	7.50	15.00
❑ Scepter SPS 2-596 [(2)] *—As "Dionne Warwicke"*	The Dionne Warwicke Story	1971	5.00	10.00	20.00
❑ Scepter SPS-598 [(2)] *—As "Dionne Warwicke"*	From Within	1972	5.00	10.00	20.00
❑ Springboard SPS-4001 *—As "Dionne Warwicke"*	The Golden Voice of Dionne Warwicke	1972	2.50	5.00	10.00
❑ Springboard SPS-4002 *—As "Dionne Warwicke"*	Dionne Warwicke Sings Her Very Best	1972	2.50	5.00	10.00
❑ Springboard SPS-4003 *—As "Dionne Warwicke"*	One Hit After Another	1972	2.50	5.00	10.00
❑ Springboard SPS-4032	Greatest Hits, Vol. 2	197?	2.50	5.00	10.00
❑ United Artists UA-LA337-G *—As "Dionne Warwicke"*	The Very Best of Dionne Warwicke	1974	3.00	6.00	12.00
❑ Warner Bros. BS 2585 *—As "Dionne Warwicke"*	Dionne	1971	3.00	6.00	12.00
❑ Warner Bros. BS 2658 *—As "Dionne Warwicke"*	Just Being Myself	1973	3.00	6.00	12.00
❑ Warner Bros. BS 2846 *—As "Dionne Warwicke"*	Then Came You	1975	3.00	6.00	12.00
❑ Warner Bros. BS 2893	Track of the Cat	1975	3.00	6.00	12.00
❑ Warner Bros. BS 3119	Love at First Sight	1976	3.00	6.00	12.00

WE FIVE

45s

Number	Title (A Side/B Side)	Yr	VG	VG+	NM
❑ A&M 770	You Were On My Mind/Small World	1965	3.00	6.00	12.00
❑ A&M 784	Let's Get Together/Cast Your Fate to the Wind	1965	2.00	4.00	8.00
❑ A&M 793	You Let a Love Burn Out/Somewhere Beyond the Sea	1966	2.00	4.00	8.00
❑ A&M 800	Somewhere/There Stands the Door	1966	2.00	4.00	8.00
❑ A&M 820	What's Goin' On/The First Time	1966	2.00	4.00	8.00
❑ A&M 894	High Flying Bird/What Do I Do	1967	—	3.00	6.00
❑ A&M 1072	Walk On By/It Really Doesn't Matter	1969	—	3.00	6.00
❑ MGM 14618	Seven Day Change/Natural Way	1973	—	2.50	5.00
❑ Vault 964	Never Goin' Back/Here Comes the Sun	1970	—	3.00	6.00
❑ Vault 969	Catch the Wind/Oh, Lonesome Me	1970	—	3.00	6.00
❑ Verve 10716	Bandstand Dancer/Rejoice	1973	—	2.50	5.00

Albums

Number	Title (A Side/B Side)	Yr	VG	VG+	NM
❑ A&M SP-111 [M]	You Were On My Mind	1965	3.75	7.50	15.00
❑ A&M SP-138 [M]	Make Someone Happy	1967	5.00	10.00	20.00
❑ A&M SP-4111 [S]	You Were On My Mind	1965	5.00	10.00	20.00
❑ A&M SP-4138 [S]	Make Someone Happy	1967	3.75	7.50	15.00
❑ A&M SP-4168	The Return of We Five	1969	3.75	7.50	15.00
❑ Vault 136	Catch the Wind	1970	3.75	7.50	15.00

WELLS, MARY

45s

Number	Title (A Side/B Side)	Yr	VG	VG+	NM
❑ Atco 6392	Dear Lover/Can't You See	1965	3.00	6.00	12.00
❑ Atco 6423	Keep Me in Suspense/Such a Sweet Thing	1966	3.00	6.00	12.00
❑ Atco 6436	Fancy Free/Me and My Baby	1966	3.00	6.00	12.00
❑ Atco 6469	Coming Home/Hey You Set My Soul on Fire	1967	3.00	6.00	12.00
❑ Epic 02664	Gigolo/I'm Changing My Ways	1982	—	2.00	4.00
❑ Epic 02855	These Arms/Spend the Night With Me	1982	—	2.00	4.00
❑ Jubilee 5621	The Doctor/Two Lovers' History	1968	3.75	7.50	15.00
❑ Jubilee 5629	Can't Get Away From Your Love/A Woman in Love	1968	3.75	7.50	15.00
❑ Jubilee 5639	Don't Look Back/500 Miles	1968	3.75	7.50	15.00
❑ Jubilee 5676	Mind Reader/Never Give a Man the World	1969	3.00	6.00	12.00
❑ Jubilee 5684	Dig the Way I Feel/Love Shooting Bandit	1969	3.00	6.00	12.00
❑ Jubilee 5695	Sweet Love/It Must Be	1970	3.00	6.00	12.00
❑ Jubilee 5718	Mr. Tough/Never Give a Man the World	1971	3.00	6.00	12.00

Number	Title (A Side/B Side)	Yr	VG	VG+	NM
❑ Motown 1003	Bye Bye Baby/Please Forgive Me	1960	12.50	25.00	50.00
❑ Motown 1011	I Don't Want to Take a Chance/I'm Sorry	1961	7.50	15.00	30.00
—Pink "lines" label					
❑ Motown 1016	Strange Love/Come to Me	1961	5.00	10.00	20.00
❑ Motown 1024	The One Who Really Loves You/I'm Gonna Stay	1962	5.00	10.00	20.00
❑ Motown 1032	You Beat Me to the Punch/Old Love (Let's Try It Again)	1962	5.00	10.00	20.00
❑ Motown 1035	Two Lovers/Operator	1962	5.00	10.00	20.00
❑ Motown 1039	Laughing Boy/Two Wrongs Don't Make a Right	1963	5.00	10.00	20.00
❑ Motown 1042	Your Old Stand By/What Love Has Joined Together	1963	5.00	10.00	20.00
❑ Motown 1048	You Lost the Sweetest Boy/What's Easy for Two Is So Hard for One	1963	5.00	10.00	20.00
❑ Motown 1056	My Guy/Oh Little Boy (What Did You Do to Me)	1964	5.00	10.00	20.00
❑ Motown 1061	When I'm Gone/Guarantee for a Lifetime	1964	150.00	300.00	600.00
❑ Motown 1065	Whisper You Love Me/I'll Be Available	1964	—	—	—
—Unreleased?					
❑ Reprise 1031	I Found What I Wanted/I See a Future in You	1971	2.50	5.00	10.00
❑ Reprise 1308	If You Can't Give Her Love (Give Her Up)/Cancel My Subscription	1974	2.50	5.00	10.00
❑ 20th Century Fox 544	Ain't It the Truth/Stop Takin' Me for Granted	1964	3.75	7.50	15.00
❑ 20th Century Fox 555	Use Your Head/Everlovin' Boy	1965	3.75	7.50	15.00
❑ 20th Century Fox 570	Never, Never Leave Me?Why Don't You Let Yourself Go	1965	3.75	7.50	15.00
❑ 20th Century Fox 590	He's a Lover/I'm Learnin'	1965	3.75	7.50	15.00
❑ 20th Century Fox 6606	Me Without You/I'm Sorry	1965	3.75	7.50	15.00
❑ 20th Century Fox 6619	I Should Have Known Better/Please Please Me	1965	5.00	10.00	20.00
Albums					
❑ Allegiance AV-444	The Old, the New, and the Best of Mary Wells	1984	2.50	5.00	10.00
❑ Atco 33-199 [M]	Two Sides of Mary Wells	1966	6.25	12.50	25.00
❑ Atco SD 33-199 [S]	Two Sides of Mary Wells	1966	7.50	15.00	30.00
❑ Epic ARE 37540	In and Out of Love	1981	3.75	7.50	15.00
❑ Jubilee JGS-8018	Servin' Up Some Soul	1968	6.25	12.50	25.00
❑ Motown M5-161V1	Bye Bye Baby/I Don't Want to Take a Chance	1981	2.50	5.00	10.00
❑ Motown M5-167V1	Mary Wells Sings My Guy	1981	2.50	5.00	10.00
❑ Motown M5-221V1	Two Lovers	1981	2.50	5.00	10.00
❑ Motown MLP-600 [M]	Bye Bye Baby/I Don't Want to Take a Chance	1961	75.00	150.00	300.00
—White label stock copy					
❑ Motown M 605 [M]	The One Who Really Loves You	1962	40.00	80.00	160.00
—With map; label address above the center hole					
❑ Motown M 607 [M]	Two Lovers and Other Great Hits	1963	30.00	60.00	120.00
—With map; label address above the center hole					
❑ Motown M 611 [M]	Recorded Live on Stage	1963	30.00	60.00	120.00
—With map; label address above the center hole					
❑ Motown M 612	Second Time Around	1963	—	—	—
—Canceled					
❑ Motown M 616 [M]	Greatest Hits	1964	10.00	20.00	40.00
❑ Motown MS 616 [S]	Greatest Hits	1964	10.00	20.00	40.00
❑ Motown M 617 [M]	Mary Wells Sings My Guy	1964	12.50	25.00	50.00
❑ Motown M 653 [M]	Vintage Stock	1967	12.50	25.00	50.00
❑ Motown MS 653 [S]	Vintage Stock	1967	12.50	25.00	50.00
❑ Motown 5233 ML	Greatest Hits	1982	2.50	5.00	10.00
❑ Movietone 71010 [M]	Ooh	1966	6.25	12.50	25.00
❑ Movietone 72010 [S]	Ooh	1966	7.50	15.00	30.00
❑ 20th Fox TFM 3171 [M]	Mary Wells	1965	10.00	20.00	40.00
❑ 20th Fox TFM 3178 [M]	Love Songs to the Beatles	1965	20.00	40.00	80.00
❑ 20th Fox TFS 4171 [S]	Mary Wells	1965	15.00	30.00	60.00
❑ 20th Fox TFS 4178 [S]	Love Songs to the Beatles	1965	25.00	50.00	100.00
WHITE, BARRY					
45s					
❑ A&M 1203	Right Night/There's a Place (Where Love Never Ends)	1988	—	—	3.00
❑ A&M 1459	Super Lover/I Wanna Do It Good to Ya	1989	—	—	3.00
❑ A&M 2943	Sho' You Right/You're What's On My Mind	1987	—	—	3.00
❑ A&M 3000	For Your Love (I'd Do Most Anything)/I'm Ready for Love	1987	—	—	3.00
❑ Faro 613	Tracy/Flame of Love	1964	3.75	7.50	15.00
—B-side by the Atlantics					
❑ 20th Century 2018	I'm Gonna Love You Just a Little More Baby/Just a Little More Baby	1973	—	2.50	5.00
❑ 20th Century 2042	I've Got So Much to Give/I've Got So Much to Give	1973	—	2.50	5.00
❑ 20th Century 2058	Never Never Gonna Give Ya Up/No, I'm Never Gonna Give Ya Up	1973	—	2.50	5.00
❑ 20th Century 2077	Honey Please Can't You See/Honey Please Can't You See	1974	—	2.50	5.00
❑ 20th Century 2120	Can't Get Enough of Your Love, Babe/Just Not Enough	1974	—	2.50	5.00
❑ 20th Century 2133	You're the First, the Last, My Everything/More Than Anything, You're My Everything	1974	—	2.50	5.00
❑ 20th Century 2177	What Am I Gonna Do with You/What Am I Gonna Do with You, Baby	1975	—	2.50	5.00
❑ 20th Century 2208	I'll Do for You Anything You Want Me To/Anything You Want Me To	1975	—	2.50	5.00
❑ 20th Century 2265	Let the Music Play/(Instrumental)	1975	—	2.50	5.00
❑ 20th Century 2277	You See the Trouble with Me/I'm So Blue When You Are Too	1976	—	2.50	5.00
❑ 20th Century 2298	Baby, We Better Try to Get It Together/If You Know, Won't You Tell Me	1976	—	2.50	5.00
❑ 20th Century 2309	Don't Make Me Wait Too Long/Can't You See It's Only You I Want	1976	—	2.50	5.00
❑ 20th Century 2328	I'm Qualified to Satisfy You/(Instrumental)	1977	—	2.50	5.00
❑ 20th Century 2350	It's Ecstasy When You Lay Down Next to Me/I Never Thought I'd Fall in Love with You	1977	—	2.50	5.00
❑ 20th Century 2361	Playing Your Game, Baby/Of All the Guys in the World	1977	—	2.50	5.00
❑ 20th Century 2365	Oh What a Night for Dancing/You're So Good You're Bad	1978	—	2.50	5.00
❑ 20th Century 2380	Your Sweetness Is My Weakness/It's Only Love Doing Its Thing	1978	—	2.50	5.00
❑ 20th Century 2395	Just the Way You Are/Now I'm Gonna Make Love to You	1979	—	2.50	5.00
❑ 20th Century 2416	I Love to Sing the Songs I Sing/Oh Me Oh My	1979	—	2.50	5.00
❑ 20th Century 2433	How Did You Know It Was Me?/Oh Me Oh My	1979	—	2.50	5.00

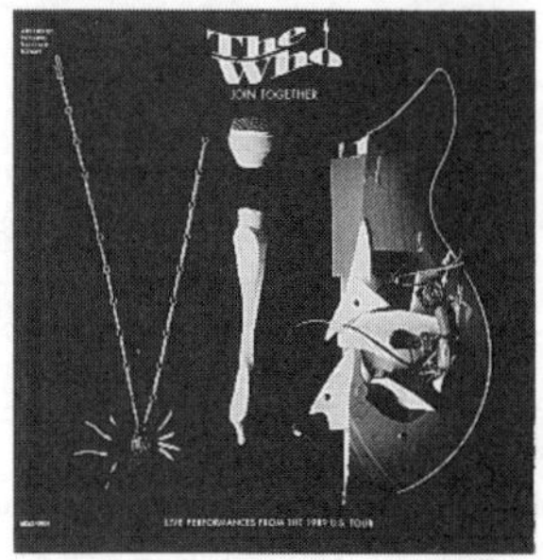

Number	Title (A Side/B Side)	Yr	VG	VG+	NM
❑ Unlimited Gold 1401	Any Fool Could See (You Were Meant for Me)/You're the One I Need	1979	—	2.00	4.00
❑ Unlimited Gold 1404	It Ain't Love, Babe (Until You Give It)/Hung Up in Your Love	1979	—	2.00	4.00
❑ Unlimited Gold 1411	Love Ain't Easy/I Found Love	1980	—	2.00	4.00
❑ Unlimited Gold 1415	Sheet Music/(Instrumental)	1980	—	2.00	4.00
❑ Unlimited Gold 1418	Love Makin' Music/Ella Es Todo Mi (She's Everything to Me)	1980	—	2.00	4.00
❑ Unlimited Gold 1420	I Believe in Love/You're the One I Need	1980	—	2.00	4.00
❑ Unlimited Gold 02425	Louie Louie/Ghetto Letto	1981	—	2.00	4.00
❑ Unlimited Gold 02580	Beware/Tell Me Who Do You Love	1981	—	2.00	4.00
❑ Unlimited Gold 02956	Change/I Like You, You Like Me	1982	—	2.00	4.00
❑ Unlimited Gold 03379	Passion/It's All About Love	1982	—	2.00	4.00
❑ Unlimited Gold 03957	America/Life	1983	—	2.00	4.00
❑ Unlimited Gold 04098	Don't Let 'Em Blow Your Mind/Dreams	1983	—	2.00	4.00
Albums					
❑ A&M SP-5154	The Right Night and Barry White	1987	2.50	5.00	10.00
❑ A&M SP-5256	The Man Is Back!	1990	2.50	5.00	10.00
❑ A&M 75021 5377 1	Put Me in Your Mix	1991	3.00	6.00	12.00
❑ Casablanca 822782-1	Barry White's Greatest Hits	1984	2.00	4.00	8.00
❑ Casablanca 822783-1	Barry White's Greatest Hits, Volume 2	1984	2.00	4.00	8.00
❑ Supremacy SUP-8002	No Limit on Love	1974	3.00	6.00	12.00
—Compilation of older material					
❑ 20th Century T-407	I've Got So Much to Give	1973	2.50	5.00	10.00
❑ 20th Century T-423	Stone Gon'	1973	2.50	5.00	10.00
❑ 20th Century T-444	Can't Get Enough	1974	2.50	5.00	10.00
❑ 20th Century T-466	Just Another Way to Say I Love You	1975	2.50	5.00	10.00
❑ 20th Century T-493	Barry White's Greatest Hits	1975	2.50	5.00	10.00
❑ 20th Century T-502	Let the Music Play	1976	2.50	5.00	10.00
❑ 20th Century T-516	Is This Whatcha Wont?	1976	2.50	5.00	10.00
❑ 20th Century T-543	Barry White Sings for Someone You Love	1977	2.50	5.00	10.00
❑ 20th Century T-571	Barry White The Man	1978	2.50	5.00	10.00
❑ 20th Century T-590	I Love to Sing the Songs I Sing	1979	2.50	5.00	10.00
❑ 20th Century T-599	Barry White's Greatest Hits, Volume 2	1981	2.50	5.00	10.00
❑ Unlimited Gold JZ 35763	The Message Is Love	1979	2.50	5.00	10.00
❑ Unlimited Gold FZ 36208	Barry White's Sheet Music	1980	2.50	5.00	10.00
❑ Unlimited Gold Z2X 36957 [(2)]	The Best of Our Love	1981	3.00	6.00	12.00
❑ Unlimited Gold FZ 37176	Beware	1982	2.50	5.00	10.00
❑ Unlimited Gold FZ 38048	Change	1982	2.50	5.00	10.00
❑ Unlimited Gold FZ 38711	Dedicated	1983	2.50	5.00	10.00

WHO, THE

45s

Number	Title (A Side/B Side)	Yr	VG	VG+	NM
❑ Atco 6409	Substitute/Waltz for a Pig	1966	12.50	25.00	50.00
❑ Atco 6509	Substitute/Waltz for a Pig	1967	5.00	10.00	20.00
❑ Decca 31725	I Can't Explain/Bald Headed Woman	1965	7.50	15.00	30.00
❑ Decca 31801	Anyway, Anyhow, Anywhere/Anytime You Want Me	1965	12.50	25.00	50.00
❑ Decca 31877	My Generation/Out in the Street (You're Going to Know Me)	1965	7.50	15.00	30.00
❑ Decca 31988	The Kids Are Alright/A Legal Matter	1966	7.50	15.00	30.00
❑ Decca 32058	I'm a Boy/In the City	1966	7.50	15.00	30.00
❑ Decca 32114	Happy Jack/Whiskey Man	1967	7.50	15.00	30.00
❑ Decca 32156	Pictures of Lily/Doctor, Doctor	1967	5.00	10.00	20.00
❑ Decca 32206	I Can See for Miles/Mary-Anne with the Shaky Hands	1967	5.00	10.00	20.00
❑ Decca 32288	Call Me Lightning/Dr. Jeckyll & Mr. Hyde	1968	6.25	12.50	25.00
❑ Decca 32362	Magic Bus/Someone's Coming	1968	3.75	7.50	15.00
❑ Decca 732465	Pinball Wizard/Dogs Part Two	1969	2.50	5.00	10.00
❑ Decca 32519	I'm Free/We're Not Gonna Take It	1969	2.50	5.00	10.00
❑ Decca 32670	The Seeker/Here for More	1970	3.00	6.00	12.00
❑ Decca 32708	Summertime Blues/Heaven and Hell	1970	3.00	6.00	12.00
❑ Decca 732729	See Me, Feel Me/Overture from Tommy	1970	3.00	6.00	12.00
—With custom gold label					
❑ Decca 32737	Young Man (Blues)/Substitute	1970	62.50	125.00	250.00
—Stock copies do exist					
❑ Decca 32846	Won't Get Fooled Again/I Don't Even Know Myself	1971	2.50	5.00	10.00
❑ Decca 32888	Behind Blue Eyes/My Wife	1971	2.50	5.00	10.00
❑ Decca 32983	Join Together/Baby, Don't You Do It	1972	2.50	5.00	10.00
❑ MCA 40475	Squeeze Box/Success Story	1975	—	2.50	5.00
❑ MCA 40603	Slip Kid/Dreaming from the Waist	1976	—	2.50	5.00
❑ MCA 40948	Who Are You/Had Enough	1978	—	2.50	5.00

Number	Title (A Side/B Side)	Yr	VG	VG+	NM
❑ MCA 40978	Trick of the Light/9:05	1978	—	2.50	5.00
❑ MCA 41053	Long Live Rock/My Wife	1979	—	2.50	5.00
❑ MCA 60106	See Me, Feel Me/Overture from Tommy	1973	—	2.50	5.00
—Reissue; black label with rainbow					
❑ MCA 60110	I Can't Explain/Bald Headed Woman	1973	—	2.50	5.00
—Reissue; black label with rainbow					
❑ MCA 60174	Pinball Wizard/Dogs Part Two	1974	—	2.50	5.00
—Reissue; black label with rainbow					
❑ Polydor 2022	5:15/I'm One	1979	—	2.00	4.00
❑ Track 32983	Join Together/Baby, Don't You Do It	1972	5.00	10.00	20.00
—Later pressing than Decca 32983, but much scarcer					
❑ Track 33041	The Relay/Waspman	1972	2.50	5.00	10.00
❑ Track 40152	Love, Reign O'er Me/Water	1973	2.00	4.00	8.00
❑ Track 40182	The Real Me/I'm One	1974	2.00	4.00	8.00
❑ Track 40330	Postcard/Put the Money Down	1974	10.00	20.00	40.00
❑ Warner Bros. 29731	It's Hard/Dangerous	1983	—	2.50	5.00
❑ Warner Bros. 29814	Eminence Front/One at a Time	1983	—	2.50	5.00
❑ Warner Bros. 29905	Athena/It's Your Turn	1982	—	2.00	4.00
❑ Warner Bros. 49698	You Better You Bet/Quiet One	1981	—	2.00	4.00
❑ Warner Bros. 49743	Don't Let Go the Coat/You	1981	—	2.00	4.00
Albums					
❑ Decca DL 4664 [M]	The Who Sing My Generation	1966	25.00	50.00	100.00
❑ Decca DL 4892 [M]	Happy Jack	1967	12.50	25.00	50.00
❑ Decca DL 4950 [M]	The Who Sell Out	1967	25.00	50.00	100.00
❑ Decca DXSW 7205 [(2)]	Tommy	1969	10.00	20.00	40.00
—With booklet					
❑ Decca DL 74664 [R]	The Who Sing My Generation	1966	15.00	30.00	60.00
❑ Decca DL 74892 [P]	Happy Jack	1967	12.50	25.00	50.00
—All stereo except that "Happy Jack" and "Don't Look Away" are rechanneled					
❑ Decca DL 74950 [S]	The Who Sell Out	1967	12.50	25.00	50.00
❑ Decca DL 75064 [P]	Magic Bus — The Who on Tour	1968	12.50	25.00	50.00
—All rechanneled except "Magic Bus" and "I Can't Reach You," which are true stereo.					
❑ Decca DL 79175	Live at Leeds	1970	10.00	20.00	40.00
—With gatefold cover and numerous inserts					
❑ Decca DL 79182	Who's Next	1971	6.25	12.50	25.00
❑ Decca DL 79184	Meaty Beaty Big and Bouncy	1971	7.50	15.00	30.00
—With poster (deduct 1/3 if missing)					
❑ MCA 1496	Who's Greatest Hits	1987	2.00	4.00	8.00
❑ MCA 1577	Live at Leeds	1988	2.00	4.00	8.00
❑ MCA 1578	Meaty Beaty Big and Bouncy	1988	2.00	4.00	8.00
❑ MCA 1579	The Who By Numbers	1988	2.00	4.00	8.00
❑ MCA 1580	Who Are You	1988	2.00	4.00	8.00
❑ MCA 2022	Live at Leeds	1973	3.00	6.00	12.00
❑ MCA 2023	Who's Next	1973	3.00	6.00	12.00
❑ MCA 2025	Meaty Beaty Big and Bouncy	1973	3.00	6.00	12.00
❑ MCA 2044 [R]	The Who Sing My Generation	1974	12.50	25.00	50.00
❑ MCA 2045 [P]	Happy Jack	1974	12.50	25.00	50.00
❑ MCA 2161	The Who By Numbers	1975	3.00	6.00	12.00
❑ MCA 3023	Live at Leeds	1977	2.50	5.00	10.00
❑ MCA 3024	Who's Next	1977	2.50	5.00	10.00
❑ MCA 3025	Meaty Beaty Big and Bouncy	1977	2.50	5.00	10.00
❑ MCA 3026	The Who By Numbers	1977	2.50	5.00	10.00
❑ MCA 3050	Who Are You	1978	2.50	5.00	10.00
❑ MCA 2-4067 [(2)P]	A Quick One/The Who Sell Out	1976	5.00	10.00	20.00
—Black labels with rainbow					
❑ MCA 2-4068 [(2)P]	Magic Bus/The Who Sing My Generation	1976	5.00	10.00	20.00
—Black labels with rainbow					
❑ MCA 5220	Who's Next	1979	2.00	4.00	8.00
❑ MCA 5408	Who's Greatest Hits	1983	2.00	4.00	8.00
❑ MCA 5641	Who's Missing	1986	2.50	5.00	10.00
❑ MCA 5712	Two's Missing	1987	2.50	5.00	10.00
❑ MCA 6895 [(2)]	Quadrophenia	1980	2.50	5.00	10.00
❑ MCA 6899 [(2)]	The Kids Are Alright	1980	2.50	5.00	10.00
—Early versions have number stamped in gold on cover with 11005 records. No difference in value.					
❑ MCA 8018 [(2)]	Who's Last	1984	2.50	5.00	10.00
❑ MCA 8031 [(2)]	Who's Better, Who's Best	1989	3.75	7.50	15.00
❑ MCA 2-10004 [(2)]	Quadrophenia	1973	3.75	7.50	15.00
—Black labels with rainbow					
❑ MCA 2-10005 [(2)]	Tommy	1973	3.75	7.50	15.00
—Black labels with rainbow					
❑ MCA 2-11005 [(2)]	The Kids Are Alright	1979	3.00	6.00	12.00
❑ MCA 2-12001 [(2)]	Hooligans	1981	2.50	5.00	10.00
❑ MCA 3-19501 [(3)]	Join Together	1990	5.00	10.00	20.00
—Box set with booklet					
❑ MCA 25986	It's Hard	1989	2.00	4.00	8.00
❑ MCA 25987	Face Dances	1989	2.00	4.00	8.00
❑ MCA 37000	Live at Leeds	1979	2.00	4.00	8.00
❑ MCA 37001	Meaty Beaty Big and Bouncy	1979	2.00	4.00	8.00
❑ MCA 37002	The Who By Numbers	1979	2.00	4.00	8.00
❑ MCA 37003	Who Are You	1979	2.00	4.00	8.00
❑ MCA 37169	Odds and Sods	1980	2.00	4.00	8.00
❑ Track 2126	Odds and Sods	1974	6.25	12.50	25.00
❑ Track 2-4067 [(2)P]	A Quick One/The Who Sell Out	1974	6.25	12.50	25.00
❑ Track 2-4068 [(2)P]	Magic Bus/The Who Sing My Generation	1974	6.25	12.50	25.00
❑ Track 2-10004 [(2)]	Quadrophenia	1973	5.00	10.00	20.00
❑ Warner Bros. HS 3516	Face Dances	1981	2.00	4.00	8.00
❑ Warner Bros. 23731	It's Hard	1982	2.00	4.00	8.00

Number	Title (A Side/B Side)	Yr	VG	VG+	NM
WILLIAMS, LARRY					
45s					
❑ Bell 813	I Could Love You Baby/Can't Find No Substitute for Love	1969	2.50	5.00	10.00
—With Johnny Watson					
❑ Chess 1736	My Baby's Got Soul/Every Day I Wonder	1959	5.00	10.00	20.00
❑ Chess 1745	Get Ready/Baby, Baby	1959	5.00	10.00	20.00
❑ Chess 1761	I Wanna Know/Like a Gentle Man	1960	5.00	10.00	20.00
❑ Chess 1764	Oh Baby/I Hear My Baby	1960	5.00	10.00	20.00
❑ Chess 1805	Lawdy Mama/Fresh Out of Tears	1961	5.00	10.00	20.00
❑ El Bam 69	Call on Me/Boss Lovin'	1965	3.00	6.00	12.00
❑ Fantasy 806	Doing the Best I Can (With What I Got)/Gimme Some	1977	—	2.50	5.00
❑ Fantasy 810	One Thing or the Other (Part 1)/One Thing or the Other (Part 2)	1977	—	2.50	5.00
❑ Fantasy 841	The Resurrection of Funk/(B-side unknown)	1978	—	2.50	5.00
❑ Mercury 72147	Woman/Can't Help Myself	1963	3.75	7.50	15.00
❑ Okeh 7259	This Old Heart (Is So Lonely)/I'd Rather Fight Than Switch	1966	2.50	5.00	10.00
❑ Okeh 7280	I Am the One/You Ask for One Good Reason	1967	2.50	5.00	10.00
❑ Okeh 7294	Just Because/Boss Lovin'	1967	2.50	5.00	10.00
❑ Smash 2035	Call on Me/Boss Lovin'	1966	3.00	6.00	12.00
❑ Specialty 597	Just Because/Let Me Tell You Baby	1957	7.50	15.00	30.00
❑ Specialty 608	Short Fat Fannie/High School Dance	1957	10.00	20.00	40.00
❑ Specialty 615	Bony Moronie/You Bug Me, Baby	1957	10.00	20.00	40.00
❑ Specialty 626	Dizzy, Miss Lizzy/Slow Down	1958	10.00	20.00	40.00
❑ Specialty 634	Hootchy-Koo/The Dummy	1958	6.25	12.50	25.00
❑ Specialty 647	I Was a Fool/Peaches and Cream	1958	6.25	12.50	25.00
❑ Specialty 658	Bad Boy/She Said "Yeah"	1959	7.50	15.00	30.00
❑ Specialty 665	Steal a Little Kiss/I Can't Stop Loving You	1959	6.25	12.50	25.00
❑ Specialty 677	Give Me Your Love/Teardrops	1959	6.25	12.50	25.00
❑ Specialty 682	Ting-a-Ling/Little Schoolgirl	1960	6.25	12.50	25.00
❑ Venture 622	Shake Your Body Girl/Love I Can't Seem to Find It	1968	2.50	5.00	10.00
❑ Venture 627	Wake Up (Nothing Comes to a Sleeper But a Dream)/Love I Can't Seem to Find It	1968	2.50	5.00	10.00
Albums					
❑ Chess LP-1457 [M]	Larry Williams	1961	50.00	100.00	200.00
❑ Okeh OKM-12123 [M]	Larry Williams' Greatest Hits	1967	7.50	15.00	30.00
❑ Okeh OKS-14123 [S]	Larry Williams' Greatest Hits	1967	10.00	20.00	40.00
❑ Specialty SP-2109 [M]	Here's Larry Williams	1959	50.00	100.00	200.00
—Original pressing on thick vinyl with no copyright information on back cover					
❑ Specialty SP-7002 [(2)]	Bad Boy	1990	5.00	10.00	20.00
WILLIS, CHUCK					
45s					
❑ Atlantic 1098	It's Too Late/Kansas City Woman	1956	6.25	12.50	25.00
❑ Atlantic 1112	Juanita/Whatcha' Gonna Do When Your Baby Leaves You	1956	6.25	12.50	25.00
❑ Atlantic 1130	C.C. Rider/Ease the Pain	1957	6.25	12.50	25.00
❑ Atlantic 1148	Love Me, Cherry/That Train Has Gone	1957	6.25	12.50	25.00
❑ Atlantic 1168	Betty and Dupree/My Crying Eyes	1958	6.25	12.50	25.00
❑ Atlantic 1179	What Am I Living For/Hang Up My Rock And Roll Shoes	1958	7.50	15.00	30.00
❑ Atlantic 1192	Thunder and Lightning/My Life	1958	5.00	10.00	20.00
❑ Atlantic 2005	You'll Be My Love/Keep a-Driving	1958	5.00	10.00	20.00
❑ Atlantic 2029	My Baby/Just One Kiss	1959	5.00	10.00	20.00
❑ Okeh 6810	I Tried/I Rule My House	1951	25.00	50.00	100.00
❑ Okeh 6841	Let's Jump Tonight/It's Too Late Baby	1951	20.00	40.00	80.00
❑ Okeh 6873	Lud Mouth Lucy/Here I Come	1952	20.00	40.00	80.00
❑ Okeh 6905	My Story/Caldonia	1952	12.50	25.00	50.00
❑ Okeh 6930	Salty Tears/Wrong Lake to Catch a Fish	1953	12.50	25.00	50.00
❑ Okeh 6952	Going to the River/Baby Has Left Me Again	1953	12.50	25.00	50.00
❑ Okeh 6985	Don't Deceive Me/I've Been Treated Wrong Too Long	1953	12.50	25.00	50.00
❑ Okeh 7004	My Baby's Coming Home/When My Day Is Over	1953	12.50	25.00	50.00
❑ Okeh 7015	You're Still My Baby/What's Your Name	1954	12.50	25.00	50.00
❑ Okeh 7029	I Feel So Bad/Need One More Chance	1954	15.00	30.00	60.00
❑ Okeh 7041	Change My Mind/My Heart's Been Broke Again	1954	10.00	20.00	40.00
❑ Okeh 7048	Give and Take/I've Been Away Too Long	1954	10.00	20.00	40.00
❑ Okeh 7051	Lawdy Miss Mary/Love-Struck	1955	10.00	20.00	40.00
❑ Okeh 7055	I Can Tell/One More Break	1955	10.00	20.00	40.00
❑ Okeh 7062	Search My Heart/Ring-Ding-Doo	1955	10.00	20.00	40.00
❑ Okeh 7067	Come On Home/It Were You	1956	10.00	20.00	40.00
❑ Okeh 7070	Two Spoons of Tears/Charged with Cheating	1956	10.00	20.00	40.00

Number	Title (A Side/B Side)	Yr	VG	VG+	NM
Albums					
❑ Atlantic 8018 [M]	The King of the Stroll	1958	75.00	150.00	300.00
—Black label					
❑ Atlantic 8079 [M]	I Remember Chuck Willis	1963	37.50	75.00	150.00
❑ Atlantic SD 8079 [P]	I Remember Chuck Willis	1963	50.00	100.00	200.00
❑ Epic LN 3425 [M]	Chuck Willis Wails the Blues	1958	125.00	250.00	500.00
❑ Epic LN 3728 [M]	A Tribute to Chuck Willis	1960	75.00	150.00	300.00

WILSON, AL

Number	Title (A Side/B Side)	Yr	VG	VG+	NM
45s					
❑ Bell 867	Mississippi Woman/Sometimes a Man Must Cry	1970	—	3.50	7.00
❑ Bell 909	You Do the Right Thing/Bachelor Man	1970	—	3.50	7.00
❑ Carousel 30051	I Hear You Knocking/Sugar Cane Girl	1971	—	3.00	6.00
❑ Carousel 30052	Falling/Bachelor Man	1971	—	3.00	6.00
❑ Playboy 6062	I've Got a Feeling (We'll Be Seeing Each Other Again)/Be Concerned	1976	—	2.50	5.00
❑ Playboy 6076	Baby I Want Your Body/Stay with Me	1976	—	2.50	5.00
❑ Playboy 6085	You Did It for Me/Differently	1976	—	2.50	5.00
❑ Roadshow PB-11583	Count the Days/Is This the End	1979	—	2.00	4.00
❑ Roadshow PB-11714	Earthquake/You Got It	1979	—	2.00	4.00
❑ Rocky Road 30060	Heavy Church/(B-side unknown)	1972	—	3.00	6.00
❑ Rocky Road 30067	Born on the Bayou/(B-side unknown)	1972	—	3.00	6.00
❑ Rocky Road 30073	Show and Tell/Listen to Me	1973	—	3.00	6.00
❑ Rocky Road 30076	Touch and Go/Settle Me Down	1974	—	3.00	6.00
❑ Rocky Road 30200	La La Peace Song/Keep On Loving You	1974	—	3.00	6.00
❑ Rocky Road 30202	I Won't Last a Day Without You-Let Me Be the One/Willoughbry Brook Road	1974	—	3.00	6.00
❑ Soul City 759	When You Love, You're Loved Too/Who Could Be Lovin' You	1967	2.50	5.00	10.00
❑ Soul City 761	Do What You Gotta Do/Now I Know What Love Is	1968	2.00	4.00	8.00
❑ Soul City 767	The Snake/Getting Ready for Tomorrow	1968	2.00	4.00	8.00
❑ Soul City 771	Poor Side of Town/The Dolphins	1969	2.00	4.00	8.00
❑ Soul City 773	I Stand Accused/Shake Me, Wake Me	1969	2.00	4.00	8.00
❑ Soul City 775	Lodi/By the Time I Get to Phoenix	1969	2.00	4.00	8.00
❑ Wand 1135	Help Me/(Instrumental)	1966	7.50	15.00	30.00
Albums					
❑ Playboy PB 410	I've Got a Feeling	1976	3.00	6.00	12.00
❑ Playboy JZ 34744	I've Got a Feeling	1977	2.50	5.00	10.00
—Reissue of 410					
❑ Rocky Road RR-3600	Weighing In	1973	3.75	7.50	15.00
❑ Rocky Road RR-3601	Show and Tell	1973	3.75	7.50	15.00
❑ Rocky Road 3700	La La Peace Song	1974	3.75	7.50	15.00
❑ Soul City SCS-92006	Searching for the Dolphins	1969	6.25	12.50	25.00

WILSON, J. FRANK, AND THE CAVALIERS

Number	Title (A Side/B Side)	Yr	VG	VG+	NM
45s					
❑ Charay 13	Last Kiss '69/Black Car	1969	—	3.00	6.00
❑ Josie 923	Last Kiss/That's How Much I Love You	1964	3.00	6.00	12.00
❑ Josie 924	Tears of Happiness/Summertime	1964	2.50	5.00	10.00
—As "The Cavaliers"					
❑ Josie 926	Hey Little One/Speak to Me	1964	2.50	5.00	10.00
❑ Josie 929	Say It Now/Six Boys	1965	2.50	5.00	10.00
❑ Josie 931	Dreams of a Fool/Open Your Eyes	1965	2.50	5.00	10.00
❑ Josie 938	Forget Me Not/A White Sport Coat (And a Pink Carnation)	1965	2.50	5.00	10.00
❑ Le Cam 722	Last Kiss/Carla	1964	7.50	15.00	30.00
❑ Solly 927	Me and My Teardrops/Unmarked and Uncovered with Sand	1966	2.50	5.00	10.00
❑ Tamara 761	Last Kiss/That's How Much I Love You	1964	6.25	12.50	25.00
❑ Virgo 506	Last Kiss/That's How Much I Love You	1973	—	3.50	7.00
Albums					
❑ Josie JM-4006 [M]	Last Kiss	1964	18.75	37.50	75.00
❑ Josie JS-4006 [S]	Last Kiss	1964	25.00	50.00	100.00

WILSON, JACKIE

Number	Title (A Side/B Side)	Yr	VG	VG+	NM
45s					
❑ Brunswick 9-55024	Reet Petite (The Finest Girl You Ever Want to Meet)/By the Light of the Silvery Moon	1957	7.50	15.00	30.00
❑ Brunswick 9-55052	To Be Loved/Come Back to Me	1958	6.25	12.50	25.00
❑ Brunswick 9-55070	As Long As I Live/I'm Wanderin'	1958	6.25	12.50	25.00
❑ Brunswick 9-55086	We Have Love/Singing a Song	1958	6.25	12.50	25.00
❑ Brunswick 9-55105	Lonely Teardrops/In the Blue of Evening	1958	7.50	15.00	30.00
❑ Brunswick 55121	That's Why (I Love You So)/Love Is All	1959	6.25	12.50	25.00
❑ Brunswick 55136	I'll Be Satisfied/Ask	1959	6.25	12.50	25.00
❑ Brunswick 55149	You Better Know It/Never Go Away	1959	5.00	10.00	20.00
❑ Brunswick 55165	Talk That Talk/Only You, Only Me	1959	5.00	10.00	20.00
❑ Brunswick 55166	Night/Doggin' Around	196?	2.50	5.00	10.00
—Black label, color-bar arrow (reissue pressing)					
❑ Brunswick 55166	Night/Doggin' Around	1960	10.00	20.00	40.00
—Maroon label (scarce original)					
❑ Brunswick 55166	Night/Doggin' Around	1960	3.75	7.50	15.00
—Orange label (standard pressing)					
❑ Brunswick 55167	(You Were Made for) All My Love/A Woman, A Lover, A Friend	1960	5.00	10.00	20.00
❑ Brunswick 55170	Alone at Last/Am I the Man	1960	5.00	10.00	20.00
❑ Brunswick 55201	My Empty Arms/The Tear of the Year	1961	3.75	7.50	15.00
❑ Brunswick 55208	Please Tell Me Why/Your One and Only Love	1961	3.75	7.50	15.00
❑ Brunswick 55216	I'm Comin' On Back to You/Lonely Life	1961	3.75	7.50	15.00
❑ Brunswick 55219	Years from Now/You Don't Know What It Means	1961	3.75	7.50	15.00
❑ Brunswick 55220	The Way I Am/My Heart Belongs to Only You	1961	3.75	7.50	15.00
❑ Brunswick 55221	The Greatest Hurt/There'll Be No Next Time	1962	3.75	7.50	15.00
❑ Brunswick 55224	I Found Love/There's Nothing Like Love	1962	3.00	6.00	12.00
—With Linda Hopkins					

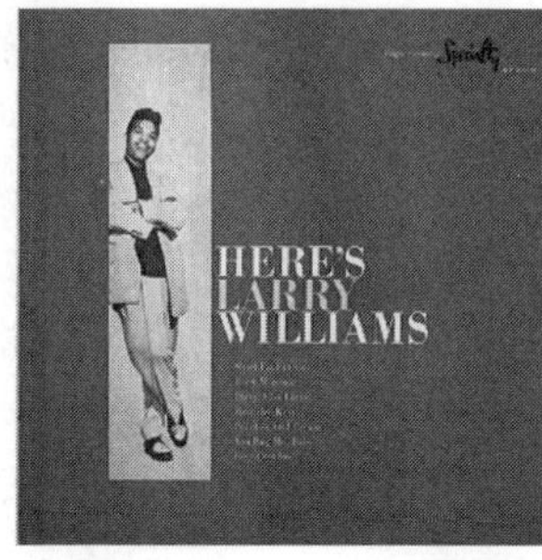

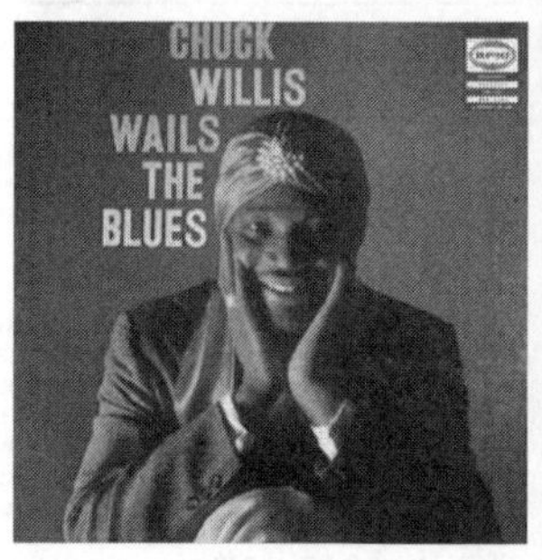

Number	Title (A Side/B Side)	Yr	VG	VG+	NM
❑ Brunswick 55225	Hearts/Sing (And Tell the Blues So Long)	1962	3.75	7.50	15.00
❑ Brunswick 55229	I Just Can't Help It/My Tale of Woe	1962	3.75	7.50	15.00
❑ Brunswick 55233	Forever and a Day/Baby That's All	1962	3.75	7.50	15.00
❑ Brunswick 55236	What Good Am I Without You/A Girl Named Tamiko	1962	3.75	7.50	15.00
❑ Brunswick 55239	Baby Workout/I'm Going Crazy	1963	5.00	10.00	20.00
❑ Brunswick 55243	Shake a Hand/Say I Do	1963	3.00	6.00	12.00
—With Linda Hopkins					
❑ Brunswick 55246	Shake! Shake! Shake!/He's a Fool	1963	3.00	6.00	12.00
❑ Brunswick 55250	Baby Get It (And Don't Quit It)/The New Breed	1963	3.00	6.00	12.00
❑ Brunswick 55254	Silent Night/Oh Holy Night	1963	3.75	7.50	15.00
❑ Brunswick 55260	Haunted House/I'm Travelin' On	1964	2.50	5.00	10.00
❑ Brunswick 55263	Call Her Up/The Kickapoo	1964	2.50	5.00	10.00
❑ Brunswick 55266	Big Boss Line/Be My Girl	1964	2.50	5.00	10.00
❑ Brunswick 55269	Squeeze Her-Tease Her (But Love Her)/Give Me Back My Heart	1964	2.50	5.00	10.00
❑ Brunswick 55273	Watch Out/She's All Right	1964	2.50	5.00	10.00
❑ Brunswick 55277	Danny Boy/Soul Time	1965	2.00	4.00	8.00
❑ Brunswick 55278	Yes Indeed/When the Saints Go Marching In	1965	2.00	4.00	8.00
—With Linda Hopkins					
❑ Brunswick 55280	No Pity (In the Naked City)/I'm So Lonely	1965	2.00	4.00	8.00
❑ Brunswick 55283	I Believe I'll Love On/Lonely Teardrops	1965	2.00	4.00	8.00
❑ Brunswick 55287	Think Twice/Please Don't Hurt Me	1965	2.00	4.00	8.00
—With LaVern Baker					
❑ Brunswick 55289	I've Got to Get Back/3 Days, 1 Hour, 30 Minutes	1966	2.00	4.00	8.00
❑ Brunswick 55290	Soul Galore/Brand New Things	1966	2.00	4.00	8.00
❑ Brunswick 55294	I Believe/Be My Love	1966	2.00	4.00	8.00
❑ Brunswick 55300	Whispers (Gettin' Louder)/The Fairest of Them All	1966	2.00	4.00	8.00
❑ Brunswick 55309	I Don't Want to Lose You/Just Be Sincere	1967	2.00	4.00	8.00
❑ Brunswick 55321	I've Lost You/Those Heartaches	1967	2.00	4.00	8.00
❑ Brunswick 55336	(Your Love Keeps Lifting Me) Higher and Higher/I'm the One to Do It	1967	2.50	5.00	10.00
❑ Brunswick 55354	Since You Showed Me How to Be Happy/The Who Who Song	1967	2.00	4.00	8.00
❑ Brunswick 55365	For Your Precious Love/Uptight	1968	2.00	4.00	8.00
❑ Brunswick 55373	Chain Gang/Funky Broadway	1968	2.00	4.00	8.00
❑ Brunswick 55381	I Get the Sweetest Feeling/Nothing But Heartaches	1968	2.00	4.00	8.00
❑ Brunswick 55392	For Once in My Life/You Brought About a Change in Me	1968	2.00	4.00	8.00
❑ Brunswick 55402	I Still Love You/Hum De Dum De Do	1969	2.00	4.00	8.00
❑ Brunswick 55418	Helpless/Do It the Right Way	1969	2.00	4.00	8.00
❑ Brunswick 55423	With These Hands/Why Don't You (Do Your Thing)	1969	2.00	4.00	8.00
❑ Brunswick 55435	Let This Be a Letter (To My Baby)/Didn't I	1970	—	3.00	6.00
❑ Brunswick 55443	(I Can Feel Those Vibrations) This Love Is Real/Love Uprising	1970	—	3.00	6.00
❑ Brunswick 55449	This Guy's in Love with You/Say You Will	1971	—	3.00	6.00
❑ Brunswick 55454	Say You Will/(B-side unknown)	1971	—	3.00	6.00
❑ Brunswick 55461	Love Is Funny That Way/Try It Again	1971	—	3.00	6.00
❑ Brunswick 55467	You Got Me Walking/The Mountain	1972	—	3.00	6.00
❑ Brunswick 55475	The Girl Turned Me On/Forever and a Day	1972	—	3.00	6.00
❑ Brunswick 55480	What a Lovely Way/You Left the Fire Burning	1972	—	3.00	6.00
❑ Brunswick 55490	Beautiful Day/What 'Cha Gonna Do About Love	1973	—	3.00	6.00
❑ Brunswick 55495	Because of You/Go Away	1973	50.00	100.00	200.00
❑ Brunswick 55499	Sing a Little Song/No More Goodbyes	1973	—	3.00	6.00
❑ Brunswick 55504	It's All Over/Shake a Leg	1973	—	3.00	6.00
❑ Brunswick 55522	Don't Burn No Bridges/(Instrumental)	1975	—	3.00	6.00
—With the Chi-Lites					
❑ Brunswick 55536	Nobody But You/I've Learned About Life	1977	—	3.00	6.00
❑ Columbia 38-07329	Reet Petite/You Better Know It	1987	—	2.50	5.00
Albums					
❑ Brunswick BL 54042 [M]	He's So Fine	1959	30.00	60.00	120.00
—All-black label					
❑ Brunswick BL 54045 [M]	Lonely Teardrops	1959	37.50	75.00	150.00
—All-black label					
❑ Brunswick BL 54050 [M]	So Much	1960	25.00	50.00	100.00
—All-black label					
❑ Brunswick BL 54055 [M]	Jackie Sings the Blues	1960	37.50	75.00	150.00
—All-black label					
❑ Brunswick BL 54058 [M]	My Golden Favorites	1960	15.00	30.00	60.00
—All-black label					
❑ Brunswick BL 54059 [M]	A Woman, a Lover, a Friend	1961	12.50	25.00	50.00
—All-black label					

Number	Title (A Side/B Side)	Yr	VG	VG+	NM
❑ Brunswick BL 54100 [M]	You Ain't Heard Nothin' Yet	1961	12.50	25.00	50.00
—All-black label					
❑ Brunswick BL 54101 [M]	By Special Request	1961	12.50	25.00	50.00
—All-black label					
❑ Brunswick BL 54105 [M]	Body and Soul	1962	12.50	25.00	50.00
—All-black label					
❑ Brunswick BL 54106 [M]	The World's Greatest Melodies	1962	12.50	25.00	50.00
—All-black label					
❑ Brunswick BL 54108 [M]	Jackie Wilson at the Copa	1962	12.50	25.00	50.00
—All-black label					
❑ Brunswick BL 54110 [M]	Baby Workout	1963	12.50	25.00	50.00
—All-black label					
❑ Brunswick BL 54112 [M]	Merry Christmas from Jackie Wilson	1963	7.50	15.00	30.00
❑ Brunswick BL 54113 [M]	Shake a Hand	1964	6.25	12.50	25.00
❑ Brunswick BL 54115 [M]	My Golden Favorites, Volume 2	1964	6.25	12.50	25.00
❑ Brunswick BL 54117 [M]	Somethin' Else	1964	6.25	12.50	25.00
❑ Brunswick BL 54118 [M]	Soul Time	1965	6.25	12.50	25.00
❑ Brunswick BL 54119 [M]	Spotlight on Jackie	1965	6.25	12.50	25.00
❑ Brunswick BL 54120 [M]	Soul Galore	1966	6.25	12.50	25.00
❑ Brunswick BL 54122 [M]	Whispers	1966	6.25	12.50	25.00
❑ Brunswick BL 54130 [M]	Higher and Higher	1967	6.25	12.50	25.00
❑ Brunswick BL 54134 [M]	Manufacturers of Soul	1968	12.50	25.00	50.00
—With Count Basie					
❑ Brunswick BL 54138 [M]	I Get the Sweetest Feeling	1968	25.00	50.00	100.00
—Yellow label promo only; "Monaural" sticker over the word "Stereo" on cover					
❑ Brunswick BL 754050 [S]	So Much	1960	37.50	75.00	150.00
—All-black label					
❑ Brunswick BL 754055 [S]	Jackie Sings the Blues	1960	50.00	100.00	200.00
—All-black label					
❑ Brunswick BL 754059 [S]	A Woman, a Lover, a Friend	1961	20.00	40.00	80.00
—All-black label					
❑ Brunswick BL 754100 [S]	You Ain't Heard Nothin' Yet	1961	20.00	40.00	80.00
—All-black label					
❑ Brunswick BL 754101 [S]	By Special Request	1961	20.00	40.00	80.00
—All-black label					
❑ Brunswick BL 754105 [S]	Body and Soul	1962	20.00	40.00	80.00
—All-black label					
❑ Brunswick BL 754106 [S]	The World's Greatest Melodies	1962	20.00	40.00	80.00
—All-black label					
❑ Brunswick BL 754108 [S]	Jackie Wilson at the Copa	1962	20.00	40.00	80.00
—All-black label					
❑ Brunswick BL 754110 [S]	Baby Workout	1963	20.00	40.00	80.00
—All-black label					
❑ Brunswick BL 754112 [S]	Merry Christmas from Jackie Wilson	1963	10.00	20.00	40.00
❑ Brunswick BL 754113 [S]	Shake a Hand	1964	7.50	15.00	30.00
❑ Brunswick BL 754115 [S]	My Golden Favorites, Volume 2	1964	7.50	15.00	30.00
❑ Brunswick BL 754117 [S]	Somethin' Else	1964	7.50	15.00	30.00
❑ Brunswick BL 754118 [S]	Soul Time	1965	7.50	15.00	30.00
❑ Brunswick BL 754119 [S]	Spotlight on Jackie	1965	7.50	15.00	30.00
❑ Brunswick BL 754120 [S]	Soul Galore	1966	7.50	15.00	30.00
❑ Brunswick BL 754122 [S]	Whispers	1966	7.50	15.00	30.00
❑ Brunswick BL 754130 [S]	Higher and Higher	1967	7.50	15.00	30.00
❑ Brunswick BL 754134 [S]	Manufacturers of Soul	1968	5.00	10.00	20.00
—With Count Basie					
❑ Brunswick BL 754138 [S]	I Get the Sweetest Feeling	1968	5.00	10.00	20.00
❑ Brunswick BL 754140	Jackie Wilson's Greatest Hits	1969	5.00	10.00	20.00
❑ Brunswick BL 754154	Do Your Thing	1969	5.00	10.00	20.00
❑ Brunswick BL 754158	It's All a Part of Love	1970	5.00	10.00	20.00
❑ Brunswick BL 754167	This Love Is Real	1971	5.00	10.00	20.00
❑ Brunswick BL 754172	You Got Me Walking	1971	5.00	10.00	20.00
❑ Brunswick BL 754185	Beautiful Day	1972	3.75	7.50	15.00
❑ Brunswick BL 754199	Nowstalgia	1974	3.75	7.50	15.00
❑ Brunswick BL 754212	Nobody But You	1977	3.75	7.50	15.00
❑ Columbia FC 40866	Reet Petite: The Best of Jackie Wilson	1987	3.00	6.00	12.00
❑ Epic EG 38623 [(2)]	The Jackie Wilson Story	1983	5.00	10.00	20.00
❑ Epic FE 39408	The Jackie Wilson Story, Vol. 2	1985	3.00	6.00	12.00
❑ Rhino RNLP-70230	Through the Years: A Collection of Rare Album Tracks and Single Sides	1987	3.00	6.00	12.00

WINTER, EDGAR

45s

Number	Title (A Side/B Side)	Yr	VG	VG+	NM
❑ Blue Sky 2758	One Day Tomorrow/Jasmine Nightdream	1975	—	2.00	4.00
❑ Blue Sky 2761	Outa Control/I Always Wanted You	1975	—	2.00	4.00
❑ Blue Sky 2762	Cool Dance/People Music	1975	—	2.00	4.00
❑ Blue Sky 2763	Diamond Eyes/Infinite Peace in Rhythm	1976	—	2.00	4.00
❑ Blue Sky 2769	Stickin' It Out/Puttin' It Back	1977	—	2.00	4.00
❑ Blue Sky 2780	Forever in Love/It's Your Life to Live	1979	—	2.00	4.00
❑ Blue Sky 2786	Above and Beyond/(Instrumental)	1980	—	2.00	4.00
❑ Blue Sky 70068	Love Is Everywhere/Everyday Man	1981	—	2.00	4.00
❑ Epic 10618	Tobacco Road/Now Is the Time	1970	2.00	4.00	8.00
❑ Epic 10740	Good Morning Music/Where Would I Be	1971	2.00	4.00	8.00
❑ Epic 10750	Where Would I Be/Feeling Like a Woman	1971	—	3.00	6.00
—B-side by Patsy Sledd					
❑ Epic 10762	Give It Everything You've Got/You Were My Light	1971	—	3.00	6.00
❑ Epic 10788	Keep Playin' That Rock 'N' Roll/Dying to Live	1971	—	3.00	6.00
❑ Epic 10855	I Can't Turn You Loose/Cool Fool	1972	—	3.00	6.00
❑ Epic 10903	Free Ride/Catchin' Up	1972	2.00	4.00	8.00

Number	Title (A Side/B Side)	Yr	VG	VG+	NM
❑ Epic 10922	Round and Round/Catchin' Up	1972	2.00	4.00	8.00
❑ Epic 10945	Frankenstein/Hangin' Around	1973	2.00	4.00	8.00
❑ Epic 10967	Frankenstein/Undercover Man	1973	—	2.00	4.00
—Orange label					
❑ Epic 11024	Free Ride/When It Comes	1973	—	2.00	4.00
❑ Epic 11069	Hangin' Around/We All Had a Real Good Time	1973	—	2.00	4.00
❑ Epic 11143	River's Risin'/Animal	1974	—	2.00	4.00
❑ Epic 50034	Easy Street/Do Like Me	1974	—	2.00	4.00
❑ Epic 50060	Miracle of Love/Someone Take My Heart Away	1975	—	2.00	4.00
Albums					
❑ Blue Sky PZ 33483	Jasmine Nightdreams	1975	3.00	6.00	12.00
❑ Blue Sky PZ 33798	The Edgar Winter Group with Rick Derringer	1975	3.00	6.00	12.00
❑ Blue Sky PZ 34858	Re-Cycled	1977	3.00	6.00	12.00
❑ Blue Sky JZ 35989	The Edger Winter Album	1979	3.00	6.00	12.00
❑ Blue Sky JZ 36494	Standing on Rock	1981	3.00	6.00	12.00
❑ Epic BN 26503	Entrance	1970	3.75	7.50	15.00
—Yellow label					
❑ Epic E 30512	Edgar Winter's White Trash	1971	3.75	7.50	15.00
—Yellow label					
❑ Epic KEG 31249 [(2)]	Roadwork	1972	5.00	10.00	20.00
—Yellow labels					
❑ Epic KE 31584	They Only Come Out at Night	1972	3.75	7.50	15.00
—Yellow label					
❑ Epic PE 32461	Shock Treatment	1974	3.75	7.50	15.00
—Orange label					
❑ Epic BG 33770 [(2)]	Entrance/White Trash	1975	3.75	7.50	15.00
—Combines 26503 and 30512 into one package					
❑ Rhino R1-70709	Mission Earth	1989	3.00	6.00	12.00
❑ Rhino R1-70895	The Edger Winter Collection	1989	2.50	5.00	10.00

WINWOOD, STEVE

45s

Number	Title (A Side/B Side)	Yr	VG	VG+	NM
❑ Island 091	Time Is Running Out/Hold On	1977	2.50	5.00	10.00
❑ Island GIS 0411	While You See a Chance/Arc of a Diver	198?	—	—	3.00
—"Back to Back Hits" reissue					
❑ Island 7-21932	The Finer Things/Back in the High Life Again	198?	—	—	3.00
—"Back to Back Hits" reissue					
❑ Island 7-21971	Higher Love/Freedom Overspill	198?	—	—	3.00
—"Back to Back Hits" reissue					
❑ Island 7-28122	Talking Back to the Night/There's a River	1988	—	2.00	4.00
❑ Island 7-28231	Valerie/Talking Back to the Night (Instrumental)	1987	—	—	3.00
❑ Island 7-28472	Back in the High Life Again/Night Train	1987	—	—	3.00
❑ Island 7-28498	The Finer Things/Night Train	1987	—	—	3.00
❑ Island 7-28595	Freedom Overspill/Help Me Angel	1986	—	—	3.00
❑ Island 7-28710	Higher Love/And I Go	1986	—	—	3.00
❑ Island 7-29879	Valerie/Slowdown Sundown	1982	—	3.50	7.00
❑ Island 7-29940	Still in the Game/Dust	1982	—	2.50	5.00
❑ Island 49656	While You See a Chance/Vacant Chair	1981	—	2.00	4.00
❑ Island 49726	Arc of a Diver/Dust	1981	—	2.00	4.00
❑ Island 49773	Night Train (Remix Edit)/(Instrumental)	1981	2.00	4.00	8.00
❑ Virgin 7-98892	One and Only Man/Always	1990	—	2.50	5.00
❑ Virgin 7-99234	Hearts On Fire (7" Remix)/(Instrumental)	1989	—	—	3.00
❑ Virgin 7-99261	Holding On/(Instrumental)	1988	—	—	3.00
❑ Virgin 7-99290	Don't You Know What the Night Can Do/(Instrumental)	1988	—	—	3.00
❑ Virgin 7-99326	Roll With It/The Morning Side	1988	—	—	3.00
Albums					
❑ Island ILPS 9387	Go	1976	3.00	6.00	12.00
—With Stomo Yamahita and Michael Shrieve					
❑ Island ILPS 9494	Steve Winwood	1977	2.50	5.00	10.00
❑ Island ILPS 9576	Arc of a Diver	1981	2.50	5.00	10.00
❑ Island ILPS 9777	Talking Back to the Night	1982	2.50	5.00	10.00
❑ Island 25448	Back in the High Life	1986	2.00	4.00	8.00
❑ Island 25660	Chronicles	1987	2.00	4.00	8.00
❑ Springboard SPB-4040	Winwood & Friends	197?	3.75	7.50	15.00
—Budget release with Winwood material on Side 1 and a collection of Jeff Beck, Yardbirds, Long John Baldry and Jack Bruce/Ginger Baker material on Side 2					
❑ United Artists UAS-9950 [(2)]	Winwood	1971	6.25	12.50	25.00
—Collection of tracks Winwood recorded with the Spencer Davis Group, Traffic and Blind Faith; with booklet					

Number	Title (A Side/B Side)	Yr	VG	VG+	NM
❑ Virgin 90946	Roll With It	1988	2.00	4.00	8.00
❑ Virgin 91405	Refugees of the Heart	1990	3.75	7.50	15.00

WONDER, STEVIE

45s

Number	Title (A Side/B Side)	Yr	VG	VG+	NM
❑ Gordy 7076	Alfie/More Than a Dream	1968	6.25	12.50	25.00
—As "Eivets Rednow" (read it backwards)					
❑ Motown 1745	I Just Called to Say I Love You/(Instrumental)	1984	—	—	3.00
❑ Motown 1769	Love Light in Flight/It's More Than You	1984	—	—	3.00
❑ Motown 1907	Skeletons/(Instrumental)	1987	—	—	3.00
❑ Motown 1919	You Will Know/(Instrumental)	1988	—	—	3.00
❑ Motown 1946	My Eyes Don't Cry/(Instrumental)	1988	—	—	3.00
❑ Motown 1953	With Each Beat of My Heart/(Instrumental)	1989	—	—	3.00
❑ Motown 1990	Keep Our Love Alive/(Instrumental)	1990	—	2.50	5.00
❑ Motown Yesteryear Y 620F	I Wish/Sir Duke	1978	—	—	3.00
—Reissue					
❑ Motown Yesteryear Y 621F	Another Star/As	1978	—	—	3.00
—Reissue					
❑ Motown Yesteryear Y 646F	Master Blaster (Jammin')/Master Blaster (Dub)	1982	—	—	3.00
—Reissue					
❑ Motown Yesteryear Y 647F	I Ain't Gonna Stand For It/Lately	1982	—	—	3.00
—Reissue					
❑ Motown Yesteryear Y 657F	That Girl/Do I Do	1983	—	—	3.00
—Reissue					
❑ Motown Yesteryear Y 684F	I Just Called to Say I Love You/Love Light in Flight	1985	—	—	3.00
—Reissue					
❑ Motown Yesteryear Y 685F	Don't Drive Drunk/(Instrumental)	1985	—	—	3.00
—First U.S. edition of this song on 45					
❑ Tamla 1602	That Girl/All I Do	1982	—	2.00	4.00
❑ Tamla 1612	Do I Do/Rocket Love	1982	—	2.00	4.00
❑ Tamla 1639	Ribbon in the Sky/Black Orchid	1982	—	2.00	4.00
❑ Tamla 1808	Part-Time Lover/(Instrumental)	1985	—	—	3.00
❑ Tamla 1817	Go Home/(Instrumental)	1985	—	—	3.00
❑ Tamla 1832	Overjoyed/(Instrumental)	1986	—	—	3.00
❑ Tamla 1846	Land of La La/(Instrumental)	1986	—	—	3.00
❑ Tamla 54061	I Call It Pretty Music But The Old People Call It the Blues (Part 1)/ I Call It Pretty Music But The Old People Call It the Blues (Part 2)	1962	7.50	15.00	30.00
❑ Tamla 54070	Little Water Boy/La La La La La	1962	6.25	12.50	25.00
❑ Tamla 54074	Contract on Love/Sunset	1963	6.25	12.50	25.00
❑ Tamla 54080	Fingertips — Pt. 2/Fingertips — Pt. 1	1963	5.00	10.00	20.00
❑ Tamla 54086	Workout Stevie, Workout/Monkey Talk	1963	3.75	7.50	15.00
❑ Tamla 54090	Castles in the Sand/Thank You (For Loving Me All the Way)	1964	3.75	7.50	15.00
—Up to and including this, as "Little Stevie Wonder"					
❑ Tamla 54096	Hey Harmonica Man/This Little Girl	1964	3.75	7.50	15.00
❑ Tamla 54103	Sad Boy/Happy Street	1964	5.00	10.00	20.00
❑ Tamla 54108	Pretty Little Angel/Tears in Vain	1964	—	—	—
—Unreleased					
❑ Tamla 54114	Kiss Me Baby/Tears in Vain	1965	3.00	6.00	12.00
❑ Tamla 54119	High Heel Sneakers/Music Talk	1965	3.00	6.00	12.00
❑ Tamla 54119	High Heel Sneakers/Funny How Time Slips Away	1965	5.00	10.00	20.00
❑ Tamla 54124	Uptight (Everything's Alright)/Purple Rain Drops	1965	3.75	7.50	15.00
❑ Tamla 54130	Nothing's Too Good for My Baby/With a Child's Heart	1966	3.00	6.00	12.00
❑ Tamla 54136	Blowin' in the Wind/Ain't That Asking for Trouble	1966	3.00	6.00	12.00
❑ Tamla 54139	A Place in the Sun/Sylvia	1966	3.00	6.00	12.00
❑ Tamla 54142	Some Day at Christmas/The Miracles of Christmas	1966	3.75	7.50	15.00
❑ Tamla 54147	Travlin' Man/Hey Love	1967	2.50	5.00	10.00
❑ Tamla 54151	I Was Made to Love Her/Hold Me	1967	2.50	5.00	10.00
❑ Tamla 54157	I'm Wondering/Every Time I See You I Go Wild	1967	2.50	5.00	10.00
❑ Tamla 54165	Shoo-Be-Doo-Be-Doo-Da-Day/Why Don't You Lead Me to Love	1968	2.00	4.00	8.00
❑ Tamla 54168	You Met Your Match/My Girl	1968	2.00	4.00	8.00
❑ Tamla 54174	For Once in My Life/Angie Girl	1968	2.00	4.00	8.00
❑ Tamla 54180	My Cherie Amour/Don't Know Why I Love You	1969	2.00	4.00	8.00
—Re-release with A and B side switched and new title on B-side					
❑ Tamla 54180	I Don't Know Why/My Cherie Amour	1969	2.50	5.00	10.00
❑ Tamla 54188	Yester-Me, Yester-You, Yesterday/I'd Be a Fool Right Now	1969	2.00	4.00	8.00
❑ Tamla 54191	Never Had a Dream Come True/Somebody Knows, Somebody Cares	1970	—	3.00	6.00
❑ Tamla 54196	Signed, Sealed, Delivered, I'm Yours/I'm More Than Happy	1970	—	3.00	6.00
❑ Tamla 54200	Heaven Help Us All/I Gotta Have a Song	1970	—	3.00	6.00
❑ Tamla 54202	We Can Work It Out/Never Dreamed You'd Leave in Summer	1971	—	3.00	6.00
❑ Tamla 54208	If You Really Love Me/Think of Me As Your Soldier	1971	—	3.00	6.00
❑ Tamla 54214	What Christmas Means to Me/Bedtime for Toys	1971	—	3.00	6.00
❑ Tamla 54216	Superwoman (Where Were You When I Needed You)/I Love Every Little Thing About You	1972	—	3.00	6.00
❑ Tamla 54223	Keep On Running/Evil	1972	—	3.00	6.00
❑ Tamla 54226	Superstition/You've Got It Bad Girl	1972	—	2.50	5.00
❑ Tamla 54232	You Are the Sunshine of My Life/Tuesday Heartbreak	1973	—	2.50	5.00
❑ Tamla 54235	Higher Ground/Too High	1973	—	2.50	5.00
❑ Tamla 54242	Living for the City/Visions	1973	—	2.50	5.00
❑ Tamla 54245	Don't You Worry 'Bout a Thing/Blame It on the Sun	1974	—	2.50	5.00
❑ Tamla 54252	You Haven't Done Nothin'/Big Brother	1974	—	2.50	5.00
❑ Tamla 54254	Boogie On Reggae Woman/Seems So Long	1974	—	2.50	5.00
—With correct spelling of A-side					
❑ Tamla 54254	Boogie On Raggae Woman/Seems So Long	1974	—	3.00	6.00
—With incorrect spelling of A-side					
❑ Tamla 54274	I Wish/You and I	1976	—	2.50	5.00
❑ Tamla 54281	Sir Duke/He's Misstra Know-It-All	1977	—	2.50	5.00
❑ Tamla 54286	Another Star/Creepin'	1977	—	2.50	5.00

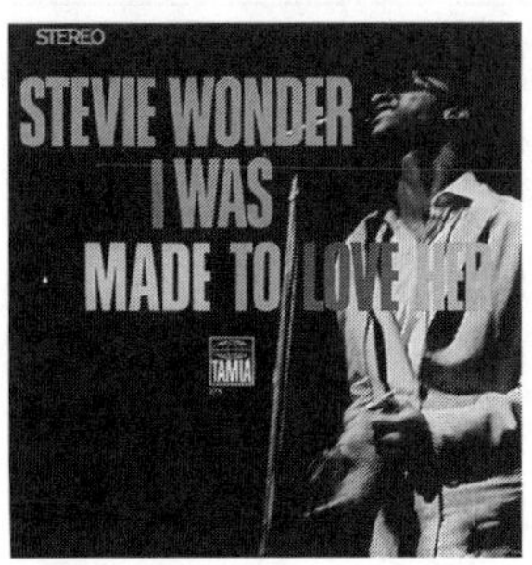

Number	Title (A Side/B Side)	Yr	VG	VG+	NM
❑ Tamla 54291	As/Contusion	1977	—	2.50	5.00
❑ Tamla 54303	Send One Your Love/(Instrumental)	1979	—	2.00	4.00
❑ Tamla 54308	Outside My Window/Same Old Story	1980	—	2.00	4.00
❑ Tamla 54317	Master Blaster (Jammin')/(Instrumental)	1980	—	2.00	4.00
❑ Tamla 54320	I Ain't Gonna Stand For It/Knocks Me Off My Feet	1980	—	2.00	4.00
❑ Tamla 54323	Lately/If It's Magic	1981	—	2.00	4.00
❑ Tamla 54328	Did I Hear You Say You Love Me/As If You Read My Mind	1981	—	2.00	4.00
Albums					
❑ Gordy GS 932	Eivets Rednow	1968	7.50	15.00	30.00
—As "Eivets Rednow"					
❑ Motown M5-131V1	Recorded Live/Little Stevie Wonder/The 12 Year Old Genius	1981	3.00	6.00	12.00
—Reissue of Tamla 240					
❑ Motown M5-150V1	With a Song in My Heart	1981	3.00	6.00	12.00
—Reissue of Tamla 250					
❑ Motown M5-166V1	Down to Earth	1981	3.00	6.00	12.00
—Reissue of Tamla 272					
❑ Motown M5-173V1	Tribute to Uncle Ray	1981	3.00	6.00	12.00
—Reissue of Tamla 232					
❑ Motown M5-176V1	Signed, Sealed and Delivered	1981	3.00	6.00	12.00
—Reissue of Tamla 304					
❑ Motown M5-179V1	My Cherie Amour	1981	3.00	6.00	12.00
—Reissue of Tamla 296					
❑ Motown M5-183V1	Up-Tight Everything's Alright.	1981	3.00	6.00	12.00
—Reissue of Tamla 268					
❑ Motown M5-219V1	The Jazz Soul of Little Stevie.	1981	3.00	6.00	12.00
—Reissue of Tamla 233					
❑ Motown M9-804A3 [(3)]	Looking Back.	1977	6.25	12.50	25.00
—Withdrawn after Stevie Wonder objected to its release					
❑ Motown 5255 ML	Someday at Christmas.	1982	2.50	5.00	10.00
—Reissue of Tamla 281					
❑ Motown 6108 ML	The Woman in Red.	1984	2.50	5.00	10.00
—With sticker at top proclaiming "New Stevie Wonder Album"					
❑ Motown 6108 ML	The Woman in Red.	1984	3.00	6.00	12.00
—With no sticker proclaiming "New Stevie Wonder Album"					
❑ Motown 6248 ML	Characters.	1987	2.50	5.00	10.00
❑ Tamla T 232 [M]	Tribute to Uncle Ray.	1962	37.50	75.00	150.00
❑ Tamla T 233 [M]	The Jazz Soul of Little Stevie.	1962	37.50	75.00	150.00
❑ Tamla T 240 [M]	Recorded Live/Little Stevie Wonder/The 12 Year Old Genius.	1963	30.00	60.00	120.00
—The above three LPs as "Little Stevie Wonder"					
❑ Tamla T 248 [M]	Workout Stevie, Workout.	1963	250.00	500.00	1000.
—Canceled; test pressings or acetates may exist					
❑ Tamla T 250 [M]	With a Song in My Heart.	1964	20.00	40.00	80.00
❑ Tamla T 255 [M]	Stevie at the Beach.	1964	20.00	40.00	80.00
❑ Tamla T 268 [M]	Up-Tight Everything's Alright.	1966	6.25	12.50	25.00
❑ Tamla TS 268 [S]	Up-Tight Everything's Alright.	1966	7.50	15.00	30.00
❑ Tamla T 272 [M]	Down to Earth.	1966	5.00	10.00	20.00
❑ Tamla TS 272 [S]	Down to Earth.	1966	6.25	12.50	25.00
❑ Tamla T 279 [M]	I Was Made to Love Her.	1967	5.00	10.00	20.00
❑ Tamla TS 279 [S]	I Was Made to Love Her.	1967	6.25	12.50	25.00
❑ Tamla T 281 [M]	Someday at Christmas.	1967	7.50	15.00	30.00
❑ Tamla TS 281 [S]	Someday at Christmas.	1967	10.00	20.00	40.00
❑ Tamla T 282 [M]	Greatest Hits.	1968	7.50	15.00	30.00
❑ Tamla TS 282 [S]	Greatest Hits.	1968	5.00	10.00	20.00
❑ Tamla TS 291	For Once in My Life.	1968	5.00	10.00	20.00
❑ Tamla TS 296	My Cherie Amour.	1969	5.00	10.00	20.00
❑ Tamla TS 298	Stevie Wonder Live.	1970	5.00	10.00	20.00
❑ Tamla TS 304	Signed Sealed and Delivered.	1970	5.00	10.00	20.00
❑ Tamla TS 308	Where I'm Coming From.	1971	5.00	10.00	20.00
❑ Tamla T 313L	Stevie Wonder's Greatest Hits Vol. 2.	1971	5.00	10.00	20.00
—Some, if not all, LP covers have the title mis-punctuated as "Stevie Wonders' Greatest Hits Vol. 2"					
❑ Tamla T 314L	Music of My Mind.	1972	5.00	10.00	20.00
❑ Tamla T 319L	Talking Book.	1972	3.75	7.50	15.00
—Original pressings have a braille note on cover					
❑ Tamla T 326L	Innervisions.	1973	3.75	7.50	15.00
❑ Tamla T6-332S1	Fulfillingness' First Finale.	1974	3.75	7.50	15.00
❑ Tamla T13-340C2 [(2)]	Songs in the Key of Life	1976	5.00	10.00	20.00
—With booklet and bonus 7-inch EP (deduct 25% if missing)					

Number	Title (A Side/B Side)	Yr	VG	VG+	NM
❑ Tamla T7-362R1	Someday at Christmas	1978	5.00	10.00	20.00
—Unusual reissue of 281					
❑ Tamla T13-371C2 [(2)]	Journey Through the Secret Life of Plants	1979	3.75	7.50	15.00
❑ Tamla T8-373S1	Hotter Than July	1980	3.00	6.00	12.00
❑ Tamla 6002 TL2 [(2)]	Stevie Wonder's Original Musiquarium I	1982	3.75	7.50	15.00
❑ Tamla 6134 TL	In Square Circle	1985	2.50	5.00	10.00

Y

YARDBIRDS, THE

45s

Number	Title (A Side/B Side)	Yr	VG	VG+	NM
❑ Epic 5-9709	I Wish You Would/A Certain Girl	1964	12.50	25.00	50.00
—With correct A-side title; also includes "Radio Station Copy" versions, some of which were used as giveaways in stores					
❑ Epic 5-9709	I Wish You Could/A Certain Girl	1964	10.00	20.00	40.00
—With typographical error on A-side					
❑ Epic 5-9790	For Your Love/Got to Hurry	1965	3.75	7.50	15.00
❑ Epic 5-9823	Heart Full of Soul/Steeled Blues	1965	3.75	7.50	15.00
❑ Epic 5-9857	I'm a Man/Still I'm Sad	1965	3.75	7.50	15.00
❑ Epic 5-9881	Shapes of Things/I'm Not Talking	1966	3.75	7.50	15.00
❑ Epic 5-10006	Shapes of Things/New York City Blues	1966	5.00	10.00	20.00
❑ Epic 5-10035	Over Under Sideways Down/Jeff's Boogie	1966	3.75	7.50	15.00
❑ Epic 5-10094	Happenings Ten Years Time Ago/The Nazz Are Blue	1966	3.75	7.50	15.00
❑ Epic 5-10156	Little Games/Puzzles	1967	5.00	10.00	20.00
❑ Epic 5-10204	Ha Ha Said the Clown/Tinker, Tailor, Soldier, Sailor	1967	5.00	10.00	20.00
❑ Epic 5-10248	Ten Little Indians/Drinking Muddy Water	1967	5.00	10.00	20.00
❑ Epic 5-10303	Goodnight Sweet Josephine/Think About It	1968	12.50	25.00	50.00

Albums

Number	Title (A Side/B Side)	Yr	VG	VG+	NM
❑ Accord SN-7143 [S]	For Your Love	1981	2.00	4.00	8.00
❑ Accord SN-7237 [R]	Having a Rave Up with the Yardbirds	1981	2.00	4.00	8.00
❑ Compleat CPL-2-2002 [(2)]	A Compleat Collection	1984	3.00	6.00	12.00
❑ Epic LN 24167 [M]	For Your Love	1965	75.00	150.00	300.00
❑ Epic LN 24177 [M]	Having a Rave Up with the Yardbirds	1965	20.00	40.00	80.00
❑ Epic LN 24210 [M]	Over Under Sideways Down	1966	15.00	30.00	60.00
❑ Epic LN 24246 [M]	The Yardbirds' Greatest Hits	1966	12.50	25.00	50.00
❑ Epic LN 24313 [M]	Little Games	1967	20.00	40.00	80.00
—Some copies with this number are stereo; look for the "XSB" prefix before the master number					
❑ Epic BN 26167 [P]	For Your Love	1965	50.00	100.00	200.00
—The album is in true stereo except for "Sweet Music"					
❑ Epic BN 26177 [R]	Having a Rave Up with the Yardbirds	1965	12.50	25.00	50.00
❑ Epic BN 26210 [P]	Over Under Sideways Down	1966	20.00	40.00	80.00
—"Over Under Sideways Down" is rechanneled					
❑ Epic BN 26246 [P]	The Yardbirds' Greatest Hits	1966	7.50	15.00	30.00
❑ Epic BN 26313 [S]	Little Games	1967	12.50	25.00	50.00
❑ Epic EG 30135 [(2)]	The Yardbirds Featuring Performances by Jeff Beck, Eric Clapton, Jimmy Page	1970	12.50	25.00	50.00
❑ Epic E 30615 [S]	Live Yardbirds Featuring Jimmy Page	1971	20.00	40.00	80.00
❑ Epic PE 34490 [P]	Yardbirds Favorites	1977	2.50	5.00	10.00
❑ Epic PE 34491 [P]	Great Hits	1977	2.50	5.00	10.00
❑ Epic FE 38455	Yardbirds (Roger the Engineer)	1982	7.50	15.00	30.00
❑ Pair PDL2-1151 [(2)]	Best of British Rock	1988	3.00	6.00	12.00
❑ Rhino RNLP 70128 [M]	Greatest Hits, Volume 1: 1964-1966	1986	2.00	4.00	8.00
❑ Rhino RNLP 70189 [M]	Five Live Yardbirds	1986	2.00	4.00	8.00
❑ Springboard SPB-4036 [R]	Eric Clapton and the Yardbirds	1972	2.50	5.00	10.00
❑ Springboard SPB-4039 [R]	Shapes of Things	1972	2.50	5.00	10.00

YES

45s

Number	Title (A Side/B Side)	Yr	VG	VG+	NM
❑ Atco 99419	Rhythm of Love/City of Love	1987	—	—	3.00
❑ Atco 99449	Love Will Find a Way/Holy Lamb	1987	—	—	3.00
❑ Atco 99745	It Can Happen/It Can Happen (Live)	1984	—	—	3.00
❑ Atco 99787	Leave It/Leave It (Acapella)	1984	—	—	3.00
❑ Atco 99817	Owner of a Lonely Heart/Our Song	1983	—	—	3.00
❑ Atlantic 2709	Every Little Thing/Sweetness	1970	—	3.00	6.00
❑ Atlantic 2819	Your Move/Clap	1971	—	2.50	5.00
❑ Atlantic 2854	Roundabout/Long Distance Runaround	1972	—	2.50	5.00
❑ Atlantic 2899	America/Total Mass Retain	1972	—	2.50	5.00
❑ Atlantic 2920	And You And I (Part 1)/And You And I (Part 2)	1972	—	2.50	5.00
❑ Atlantic 3242	Sound Chaser/Soon	1975	—	2.50	5.00
❑ Atlantic 3416	Awaken (Part 1)/Wonderful Stories	1977	—	2.50	5.00
❑ Atlantic 3534	Don't Kill the Whale/Release, Release	1978	—	2.50	5.00
❑ Atlantic 3767	Into the Lens/Does It Really Happen	1980	—	2.50	5.00
❑ Atlantic 3801	Run Through the Light/White Car	1981	—	2.50	5.00

Albums

Number	Title (A Side/B Side)	Yr	VG	VG+	NM
❑ Atco 90125	90125	1983	2.00	4.00	8.00
❑ Atco 90474	9012Live: The Solos	1985	2.00	4.00	8.00
❑ Atco 90522	Big Generator	1987	2.00	4.00	8.00
❑ Atlantic SD 3-100 [(3)]	Yessongs	1973	4.50	9.00	18.00
❑ Atlantic SD 2-510 [(2)]	Yesshows	1980	3.00	6.00	12.00
❑ Atlantic SD 2-908 [(2)]	Tales from Topographic Oceans	1974	3.75	7.50	15.00
❑ Atlantic SD 7211	Fragile	1972	3.00	6.00	12.00
❑ Atlantic SD 7244	Close to the Edge	1972	3.00	6.00	12.00
❑ Atlantic SD 8243	Yes	1969	3.00	6.00	12.00
❑ Atlantic SD 8273	Time and a Word	1970	3.00	6.00	12.00
❑ Atlantic SD 8283	The Yes Album	1971	3.00	6.00	12.00
❑ Atlantic SD 16019	Drama	1980	2.50	5.00	10.00
❑ Atlantic SD 18103	Yesterdays	1975	2.50	5.00	10.00
❑ Atlantic SD 18122	Relayer	1974	2.50	5.00	10.00
❑ Atlantic SD 19106	Going for the One	1977	2.50	5.00	10.00

Number	Title (A Side/B Side)	Yr	VG	VG+	NM
❑ Atlantic SD 19131	The Yes Album	1977	2.00	4.00	8.00
❑ Atlantic SD 19132	Fragile	1977	2.00	4.00	8.00
❑ Atlantic SD 19133	Close to the Edge	1977	2.00	4.00	8.00
❑ Atlantic SD 19134	Yesterdays	1977	2.00	4.00	8.00
❑ Atlantic SD 19135	Relayer	1977	2.00	4.00	8.00
❑ Atlantic SD 19202	Tormato	1978	2.50	5.00	10.00
❑ Atlantic SD 19320	Classic Yes	1982	3.75	7.50	15.00

—Original copies include a bonus 7-inch promo single

YOUNG, NEIL

45s

Number	Title (A Side/B Side)	Yr	VG	VG+	NM
❑ Geffen 28196	Mideast Vacation/Long Walk Home	1987	—	—	3.00
❑ Geffen 28623	Weight of the World/Pressure	1986	—	—	3.00
❑ Geffen 28753	Old Ways/Once an Angel	1986	—	—	3.00
❑ Geffen 28883	Get Back to the Country/Misfits	1985	—	—	3.00
❑ Geffen 29433	Cry, Cry, Cry/Payola Blues	1983	—	2.00	4.00
❑ Geffen 29574	Wonderin'/Payola Blues	1983	—	2.00	4.00
❑ Geffen 29707	Mr. Soul/Mr. Soul	1983	—	2.00	4.00
❑ Geffen 29887	Little Thing Called Love/We Are In Control	1982	—	2.00	4.00
❑ Reprise 0746	Only Love Can Break Your Heart/Cinnamon Girl	1971	—	—	3.00
—"Back to Back Hits" release					
❑ Reprise 0785	The Loner/Sugar Mountain	1968	30.00	60.00	120.00
❑ Reprise 0819	Everyone Knows This Is Nowhere/The Emperor of Wyoming	1969	25.00	50.00	100.00
❑ Reprise 0836	Down By the River/(When You're On the) Losing End	1969	12.50	25.00	50.00
❑ Reprise 0861	Oh, Lonesome Me/Sugar Mountain	1969	12.50	25.00	50.00
❑ Reprise 0898	I've Been Waiting for You/Oh, Lonesome Me	1970	12.50	25.00	50.00
❑ Reprise 0911	Cinnamon Girl/Sugar Mountain	1970	—	2.50	5.00
❑ Reprise 0958	Only Love Can Break Your Heart/Birds	1970	—	2.50	5.00
❑ Reprise 0992	When You Dance I Can Really Love/Sugar Mountain	1971	—	2.50	5.00
❑ Reprise 1023	Brave Belt/Rock and Roll Band	1971	—	2.50	5.00
—With Graham Nash					
❑ Reprise 1065	Heart of Gold/Sugar Mountain	1971	—	2.00	4.00
—Without reference to "Harvest" LP on label					
❑ Reprise 1084	Old Man/The Needle and the Damage Done	1972	—	2.00	4.00
❑ Reprise 1099	War Song/The Needle and the Damage Done	1972	—	2.00	4.00
—With Graham Nash					
❑ Reprise 1152	Heart of Gold/Old Man	1972	—	—	3.00
—"Back to Back Hits" release					
❑ Reprise 1184	Time Fades Away/The Last Train to Tulsa (Live)	1973	2.50	5.00	10.00
❑ Reprise 1209	Walk On/For the Turnstiles	1974	—	2.00	4.00
❑ Reprise 1344	Lookin' for a Love/Sugar Mountain	1976	—	2.00	4.00
❑ Reprise 1350	Drive Back/Stupid Girl	1976	—	2.00	4.00
❑ Reprise 1390	Hey Baby/Homegrown	1977	—	2.00	4.00
❑ Reprise 1391	Like a Hurricane/Hold Back the Tears	1978	—	2.00	4.00
❑ Reprise 1393	Sugar Mountain/The Needle and the Damage Done	1978	—	2.00	4.00
❑ Reprise 1395	Comes a Time/Motorcycle Mama	1978	—	2.00	4.00
❑ Reprise 1396	Four Strong Winds/Human Highway	1979	—	2.00	4.00
❑ Reprise 22776	Rockin' in the Free World/Rockin' in the Free World (Live)	1989	—	2.00	4.00
❑ Reprise 27848	This Note's For You (LP Version)/This Note's For You (Edited Live Version)	1988	—	2.00	4.00
❑ Reprise 27908	Ten Men Workin'/I'm Goin'	1988	—	—	3.00
❑ Reprise 49031	Rust Never Sleeps (Hey Hey, My My [Into the Black])/Rust Never Sleeps (My My, Hey Hey [Out of the Blue])	1979	—	2.00	4.00
❑ Reprise 49189	The Loner/Cinnamon Girl	1980	—	2.00	4.00
❑ Reprise 49555	Hawks and Doves/Union Man	1980	—	—	3.00
❑ Reprise 49641	Stayin' Power/Captain America	1980	—	—	3.00
❑ Reprise 49870	Southern Pacific/Motor City	1981	—	—	3.00
❑ Reprise 50014	Opera Star/Surfer Joe and Moe the Sleaze	1982	—	—	3.00

Albums

Number	Title (A Side/B Side)	Yr	VG	VG+	NM
❑ Geffen GHS 2018	Trans	1982	3.75	7.50	15.00
—First pressings have a sticker on rear cover explaining the absence of "If You've Got Love"					
❑ Geffen GHS 4013	Everybody's Rockin'	1983	2.50	5.00	10.00
❑ Geffen GHS 24068	Old Ways	1985	3.00	6.00	12.00
❑ Geffen GHS 24109	Landing on Water	1986	3.00	6.00	12.00
❑ Geffen GHS 24154	Life	1987	3.00	6.00	12.00
❑ Reprise MS 2032	Harvest	1972	3.75	7.50	15.00
—First pressings have textured cover and lyric insert					
❑ Reprise MS 2151	Time Fades Away	1973	2.50	5.00	10.00
❑ Reprise R 2180	On the Beach	1974	5.00	10.00	20.00

Number	Title (A Side/B Side)	Yr	VG	VG+	NM
❑ Reprise MS 2221	Tonight's the Night	1975	2.50	5.00	10.00
❑ Reprise MS 2242	Zuma	1975	2.50	5.00	10.00
❑ Reprise 3RS 2257 [(3)]	Decade	1977	5.00	10.00	20.00
❑ Reprise MSK 2261	American Stars 'N' Bars	1977	2.50	5.00	10.00
❑ Reprise MSK 2266	Comes A Time	1978	2.50	5.00	10.00
—With "Peace of Mind" as the last song on side 1. Covers can list either "Lotta Love" or "Peace of Mind."					
❑ Reprise MSK 2277	Harvest	1978	2.00	4.00	8.00
—Brown "Reprise" label; new number					
❑ Reprise MSK 2282	Everybody Knows This Is Nowhere	1978	2.00	4.00	8.00
—Brown "Reprise" label; new number					
❑ Reprise MSK 2283	After the Gold Rush	1978	10.00	20.00	40.00
—Contains remixed extended version of "When You Dance I Can Really Love." Title on cover in red, "RE 2" in trail-off vinyl					
❑ Reprise HS 2295	Rust Never Sleeps	1979	2.50	5.00	10.00
❑ Reprise 2RX 2296 [(2)]	Live Rust	1979	3.75	7.50	15.00
❑ Reprise HS 2297	Hawks and Doves	1980	2.50	5.00	10.00
❑ Reprise HS 2304	Re-Ac-Tor	1981	2.50	5.00	10.00
❑ Reprise RS 6317	Neil Young	1969	15.00	30.00	60.00
—Re-release: Brown and orange "Reprise/W7" label, no name on front cover, four tracks remixed ("RE 1" in trail-off wax)					
❑ Reprise RS 6349	Everybody Knows This Is Nowhere	1969	7.50	15.00	30.00
—Brown and orange "Reprise/W7" label					
❑ Reprise RS 6383	After the Gold Rush	1970	3.75	7.50	15.00
—Brown and orange label; all photos correct					
❑ Reprise 2XS 6480 [(2)]	Journey Through the Past (Soundtrack)	1972	5.00	10.00	20.00
❑ Reprise 25719	This Note's for You	1988	3.00	6.00	12.00
❑ Reprise 25899	Freedom	1989	3.75	7.50	15.00
❑ Reprise 26315	Ragged Glory	1990	5.00	10.00	20.00
❑ Reprise 48935-1 [(2)]	Greatest Hits	2005	10.00	20.00	40.00
—Distributed by Classic Records; 200-gram vinyl; with poster; also includes a bonus 7-inch single of "The Loner"/"Sugar Mountain" on either red, white or blue vinyl (not marked on packaging which color is inside; no difference in value)					
❑ Reprise 49593-1 [(2)]	Prairie Wind	2005	10.00	20.00	40.00
—Distributed by Classic Records; 200-gram vinyl					

YOUNGBLOODS, THE

45s

Number	Title (A Side/B Side)	Yr	VG	VG+	NM
❑ Mercury 72583	Sometimes/Rider	1966	5.00	10.00	20.00
—As "Jesse Colin and the Youngbloods"					
❑ Mercury 73068	Sometimes/Rider	1969	2.50	5.00	10.00
❑ RCA Victor 47-9015	Grizzly Bear/Tears Are Falling	1966	2.50	5.00	10.00
❑ RCA Victor 47-9142	Merry-Go-Round/Foolin' Around (The Waltz)	1967	2.50	5.00	10.00
❑ RCA Victor 47-9222	The Wine Song/Euphoria	1967	2.50	5.00	10.00
❑ RCA Victor 47-9264	Get Together/All My Dreams Blue	1967	3.75	7.50	15.00
❑ RCA Victor 47-9360	Fool Me/I Can Tell	1967	2.50	5.00	10.00
❑ RCA Victor 47-9422	Dreamer's Dream/Quicksand	1967	2.50	5.00	10.00
❑ RCA Victor 47-9752	Get Together/Beautiful	1969	2.00	4.00	8.00
❑ RCA Victor 74-0129	On Sir Francis Drake/Darkness, Darkness	1969	2.00	4.00	8.00
❑ RCA Victor 74-0270	Sunlight/Trillium	1969	2.00	4.00	8.00
❑ RCA Victor 74-0342	On Sir Francis Drake/Darkness, Darkness	1970	—	3.50	7.00
❑ RCA Victor 74-0380	On Sir Francis Drake/Darkness, Darkness	1970	—	3.00	6.00
❑ RCA Victor 74-0465	Reason to Believe/Sunlight	1971	—	3.00	6.00
❑ Warner Bros. 7445	Hippie from Olema/Misty Roses	1970	—	2.50	5.00
❑ Warner Bros. 7499	It's a Lovely Day/Ice Bag	1971	—	2.50	5.00
❑ Warner Bros. 7563	Will the Circle Be Unbroken/Light Shine	1972	—	2.50	5.00
❑ Warner Bros. 7639	Dreamboat/Kind Hearted Woman	1972	—	2.50	5.00
❑ Warner Bros. 7660	Running Bear/Kind Hearted Woman	1972	—	2.50	5.00

Albums

Number	Title (A Side/B Side)	Yr	VG	VG+	NM
❑ Mercury SR-61273	Two Trips	1971	5.00	10.00	20.00
—Red border on cover					
❑ Raccoon WS 1878	Rock Festival	1970	3.00	6.00	12.00
❑ Raccoon BS 2563	Ride the Wind	1971	3.00	6.00	12.00
❑ Raccoon BS 2566	Good and Dusty	1971	3.00	6.00	12.00
❑ Raccoon BS 2653	High on a Ridge Top	1972	3.00	6.00	12.00
❑ RCA Victor AYL1-3680	The Best of the Youngbloods	1980	2.00	4.00	8.00
—"Best Buy Series" reissue					
❑ RCA Victor LPM-3724 [M]	The Youngbloods	1967	10.00	20.00	40.00
❑ RCA Victor LSP-3724	Get Together	1969	3.75	7.50	15.00
—Retitled version of "The Youngbloods"					
❑ RCA Victor LSP-3724 [S]	The Youngbloods	1967	6.25	12.50	25.00
❑ RCA Victor LPM-3865 [M]	Earth Music	1968	12.50	25.00	50.00
❑ RCA Victor LSP-3865 [S]	Earth Music	1968	6.25	12.50	25.00
❑ RCA Victor LSP-4150	Elephant Mountain	1969	3.75	7.50	15.00
—Orange label					
❑ RCA Victor LSP-4399	The Best of the Youngbloods	1970	3.75	7.50	15.00
❑ RCA Victor LSP-4561	Sunlight	1971	3.00	6.00	12.00
❑ RCA Victor VPS-6051 [(2)]	This Is the Youngbloods	1972	3.75	7.50	15.00

Z

ZOMBIES, THE

45s

Number	Title (A Side/B Side)	Yr	VG	VG+	NM
❑ Columbia 44363	Care of Cell 44/Maybe After He's Gone	1967	12.50	25.00	50.00
❑ Date 2-1203	Time of the Season/Imagine the Swan	1970	—	2.50	5.00
—"Hall of Fame" series					
❑ Date 1604	Time of the Season/I'll Call You Mine	1968	5.00	10.00	20.00
❑ Date 1612	Butcher's Tale (Western Front 1914)/This Will Be Our Year	1968	2.50	5.00	10.00
❑ Date 1628	Time of the Season/Friends of Mine	1968	3.00	6.00	12.00
❑ Date 1644	Imagine the Swan/Conversation of Floral Street	1969	2.50	5.00	10.00

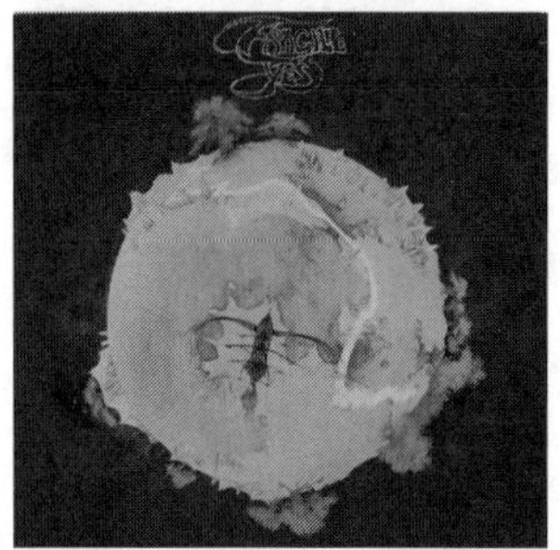

Number	Title (A Side/B Side)	Yr	VG	VG+	NM
❑ Date 1648	If It Don't Work Out/Don't Cry for Me	1969	2.50	5.00	10.00
❑ Epic 11145	Time of the Season/Imagine the Swan	1974	—	2.50	5.00
❑ Parrot 3004	Indication/How We Were Before	1966	2.50	5.00	10.00
❑ Parrot 9695	She's Not There/You Make Me Feel So Good	1964	3.75	7.50	15.00
❑ Parrot 9723	Tell Her No/Leave Me Be	1965	3.75	7.50	15.00
❑ Parrot 9747	She's Coming Home/I Must Move	1965	3.00	6.00	12.00
❑ Parrot 9769	I Want You Back Again/Once Upon a Time	1965	3.00	6.00	12.00
❑ Parrot 9786	I Love You/Whenever You're Ready	1965	3.00	6.00	12.00
❑ Parrot 9797	Just Out of Reach/Remember You	1965	3.00	6.00	12.00
❑ Parrot 9821	Don't Go Away/Is This the Dream	1966	3.00	6.00	12.00
Albums					
❑ Date TES-4013	Odessey and Oracle	1968	7.50	15.00	30.00
—With no mention of "Time of the Season" on front cover					
❑ Epic KEG 32861 [(2)B]	Time of the Zombies	1974	5.00	10.00	20.00
—Record 1 is mono; Record 2 is stereo; orange labels					
❑ London PS 557 [P]	Early Days	1969	5.00	10.00	20.00
—All tracks in true stereo except "Tell Her No"					
❑ Parrot PA 61001 [M]	The Zombies	1965	15.00	30.00	60.00
❑ Parrot PAS 71001 [R]	The Zombies	1965	10.00	20.00	40.00
❑ Rhino RNLP-120	Live on the BBC, 1965-67	1985	2.50	5.00	10.00
❑ Rhino RNLP 70186 [S]	Odessy and Oracle	1986	2.00	4.00	8.00

ZZ TOP

45s

Number	Title (A Side/B Side)	Yr	VG	VG+	NM
❑ London 45-131	Salt Lick/Miller's Farm	1970	2.50	5.00	10.00
❑ London 45-138	Neighbor, Neighbor/(Somebody Else Been) Shakin' Your Tree	1970	2.50	5.00	10.00
❑ London 45-179	Francene/Francene (Spanish)	1972	2.50	5.00	10.00
❑ London 45-203	La Grange/Just Got Paid	1973	2.00	4.00	8.00
❑ London 5N-220	Tush/Blue Jean Blues	1975	2.00	4.00	8.00
❑ London 5N-241	It's Only Love/Asleep in the Desert	1976	2.00	4.00	8.00
❑ London 5N-251	Arrested for Driving While Blind/It's Only Love	1977	—	3.50	7.00
❑ London 5N-252	Enjoy and Get It On/El Diablo	1977	2.50	5.00	10.00
❑ RCA 62812	Breakaway/Pincushion	1994	—	2.00	4.00
❑ RCA 62928	Fuzzbox Voodoo/Girl in a T-Shirt	1994	—	2.00	4.00
❑ Scat 500	Salt Lick/Miller's Farm	1969	50.00	100.00	200.00
❑ Warner Bros. 28650	Velcro Fly/Woke Up with Wood	1986	—	—	3.00
❑ Warner Bros. 28733	Rough Boy/Delirious	1986	—	—	3.00
❑ Warner Bros. 28810	Stages/Can't Stop Rockin'	1986	—	—	3.00
❑ Warner Bros. 28884	Sleeping Bag/Party on the Patio	1985	—	—	3.00
❑ Warner Bros. 29272	Legs/Bad Girl	1984	—	2.00	4.00
❑ Warner Bros. 29576	Sharp Dressed Man/I Got the Six	1983	—	2.00	4.00
❑ Warner Bros. 29693	Gimme All Your Lovin/If I Could Only Flag Her Down	1983	—	2.00	4.00
❑ Warner Bros. 49163	I Thank You/Fool for Your Stockings	1980	—	2.00	4.00
❑ Warner Bros. 49220	Cheap Sunglasses/Esther Be the One	1980	—	2.00	4.00
❑ Warner Bros. 49782	Leila/Don't Tease Me	1981	—	2.00	4.00
❑ Warner Bros. 49865	Tube Snake Boogie/Heaven, Hell or Houston	1981	—	2.50	5.00
Albums					
❑ London PS 584	ZZ Top's First Album	1971	3.00	6.00	12.00
❑ London PS 612	Rio Grande Mud	1972	3.00	6.00	12.00
❑ London XPS 631	Tres Hombres	1973	3.00	6.00	12.00
❑ London PS 656	Fandango!	1975	3.00	6.00	12.00
❑ London PS 680	Tejas	1977	3.00	6.00	12.00
❑ London PS 706	The Best of ZZ Top	1977	3.00	6.00	12.00
❑ Warner Bros. BSK 3268	ZZ Top's First Album	1979	2.00	4.00	8.00
❑ Warner Bros. BSK 3269	Rio Grande Mud	1979	2.00	4.00	8.00
❑ Warner Bros. BSK 3270	Tres Hombres	1979	2.00	4.00	8.00
❑ Warner Bros. BSK 3271	Fandango!	1979	2.00	4.00	8.00
❑ Warner Bros. BSK 3272	Tejas	1979	2.00	4.00	8.00
❑ Warner Bros. BSK 3273	The Best of ZZ Top	1979	2.00	4.00	8.00
❑ Warner Bros. HS 3361	Deguello	1979	2.50	5.00	10.00
❑ Warner Bros. BSK 3593	El Loco	1981	2.50	5.00	10.00
❑ Warner Bros. 23774	Eliminator	1983	2.00	4.00	8.00
❑ Warner Bros. 25342	Afterburner	1985	2.00	4.00	8.00
❑ Warner Bros. 26265	Recycler	1990	3.75	7.50	15.00

I Buy & Sell
the World's Rarest Records!
Blues 78's Our Specialty!
My name is John Tefteller.
I have been buying and selling rare records for the past 30 years.
I have the world's largest inventory of Blues, Rhythm & Blues and Rock & Roll 78's with over 100,000 in stock. I also have over 100,000 45's from the 1950's and early 1960's.
I have a worldwide reputation for my knowledge of rare records and I am always interested in buying more rare records!
Before you sell your records to ANYONE, you should at least talk to me. I consistently pay the highest prices for records for my collection and am more than fair when buying for resale.
To contact me:
Phone: (800) 955-1326 (U.S. Only)
Phone: (541) 476-1326
Fax: (541) 476-3523
P.O. Box 1727
Grants Pass, OR 97528-0200
John@tefteller.com
www.tefteller.com

MY BONNIE
TONY SHERIDAN
AND THE BEAT BROTHERS
5
THE BEATLES
ENGLAND'S No.1 VOCAL GROUP
H I · F I
6
THE BEATLES
SECOND ALBUM
ELECTRIFYING BIG-BEAT PERFORMANCES BY ENGLAND'S
Paul McCartney, John Lennon, George Harrison and Ringo Starr
The Beatles
Yesterday
And Today
10
JAMES BROWN
AND HIS FAMOUS FLAMES
PLEASE PLEASE PLEASE
JAMES BROWN'S
SIXTEEN BIGGEST HITS
7
8
THE BEATLES!
THE BEA
ON CAPI
ARE THE GR
Capitol
9
STEREO
MEET THE BEATLES!
The First Album by England's Phenomenal Pop Combo
11
15
Gatemouth
Moore
sings
BLUES
14
13
in the outstanding event of the
SINGER
presents
SPD-22
ELVIS
PRESLEY
18
his first TV SPECIAL!
TUES., DEC. 3rd
NBC-TV : IN COLOR
9PM EST/PST 8PM CST/MST
12
JOHN MAYALL
ALBERT KING
16
Checker
17
PROMOTIONAL
DJ COPY
19
SUN
ELVIS PRESLEY
MEMPHIS, TENNESSEE
20
JOHNNY BURNETTE
CORAL
and the
Rock'n Roll
Trio
21